The New Jersey Municipal Data Book

2009

State & Municipal Profiles Series

The New Jersey Municipal Data Book

2009

State & Municipal Profiles Series

Woodside, California

Titles from Information Publications

State & Municipal Profiles Series

Almanac of the 50 States

California Cities, Towns & Counties	*Connecticut Municipal Profiles*
Florida Cities, Towns & Counties	*Massachusetts Municipal Profiles*
The New Jersey Municipal Data Book	*North Carolina Cities, Towns & Counties*

American Profiles Series

Asian Americans: A Statistical Sourcebook and Guide to Government Data
Black Americans: A Statistical Sourcebook and Guide to Government Data
Hispanic Americans: A Statistical Sourcebook and Guide to Government Data

Essential Topics Series

Energy, Transportation & the Environment:
A Statistical Sourcebook and Guide to Government Data

ISBN 978-0-911273-46-5 Paper
ISBN 978-0-911273-47-2 CD
The New Jersey Municipal Data Book 2009

©2009 Information Publications, Inc.
Printed in the United States of America

Information Publications, Inc.
2995 Woodside Rd., Suite 400-182
Woodside, CA 94062-2446

www.informationpublications.com
info@informationpublications.com

Toll Free Phone 877.544.INFO (4636)
Toll Free Fax 877.544.4635

Direct Dial Phone 650.568.6170
Direct Dial Fax 650.568.6150

Table of Contents

Detailed Table of Contents

Municipal Profiles

Municipal Profiles (con't)

Detailed Table of Contents

Municipal Profiles (con't)

Municipal Profiles (con't)

Detailed Table of Contents

Municipal Profiles (con't)

County Profiles

New Jersey Counties

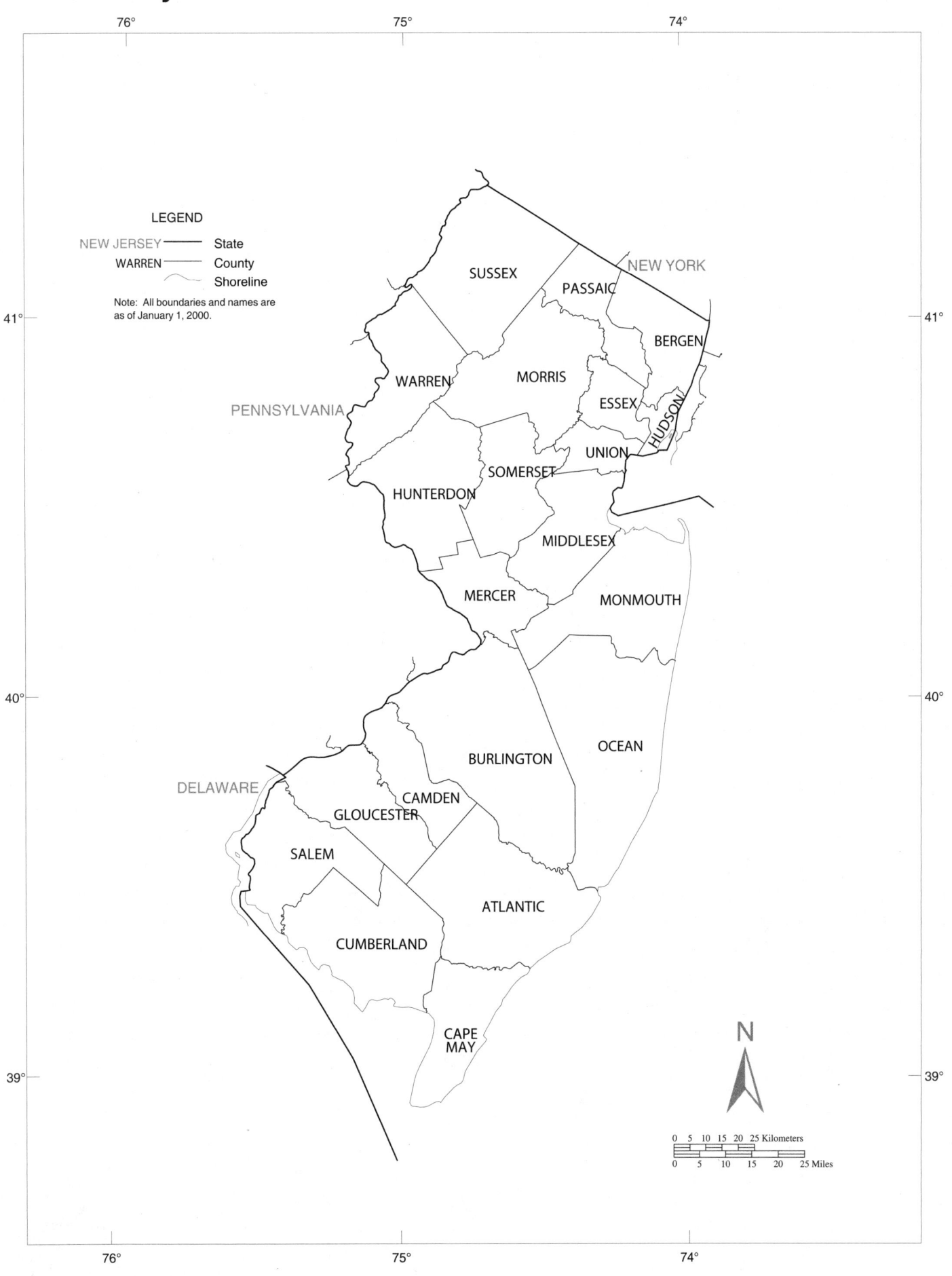

The New Jersey Municipal Data Book

2009

State & Municipal Profiles Series

The New Jersey Municipal Data Book is an annual reference book published by Information Publications since 1981. It is part of the **State & Municipal Profiles Series**, which also includes the **Almanac of the 50 States**, as well as municipal and county profile books on California, Connecticut, Florida, Massachusetts, and North Carolina.

Drawing from a variety of established sources, **The New Jersey Municipal Data Book** is designed to provide concise yet comprehensive profiles for all 566 municipalities and 21 counties in New Jersey. The book contains one page for every municipality and county in the state. (Our use of the term "municipality" in New Jersey encompasses the categories of "township," "town," "city," "borough," and "village.") Pages in the **Municipal Profiles** and **County Profiles** sections are arranged alphabetically. To aid in finding information about a specific place, as well as in making comparisons, each page has the same format, organizing the data into nine categories: **Demographics & Socioeconomic Characteristics**, **General Information**, **Government**, **Housing & Construction**, **Public Library**, **Public Safety**, **Public School District**, **Municipal Finance** or **County Finance**, and **Taxes**. Following the **Municipal Profiles** and **County Profiles**, there are seven appendices.

Some changes in municipality names should be noted. In 2005, South Belmar Borough in Monmouth County changed its name to Lake Como. In 2006, Dover Township in Ocean County changed its name to Toms River. In 2008, Washington Township in Mercer County changed its name to Robbinsville. These name changes are reflected in this edition.

Introduction to the Data

The information in this volume has been obtained from a variety of sources. To aid researchers with questions about the methodology behind the data collection or the terms used, we have identified the source for each piece of data. These questions can best be answered by the original data collectors, who are cited in the **explanation of the categories**.

Information Publications conducted mail, phone, email, and online surveys in May and June of 2009 in order to obtain the most recent names of **government officials**, **police chiefs**, **fire chiefs**, **librarians**, and **school superintendents**. Information gathered from the surveys is used to supplement other sources to provide complete and up-to-date information.

Almost all the information was originally collected by an agency of the state or federal government. Using such information assures a high level of accuracy, reliability, and comprehensiveness. However, not all the information col-

lected by government agencies has been published, nor is it necessarily readily available. Many government agencies collect information largely for their own internal use, and the data remains in the original materials used for collection. We have selected the most appropriate items from the available information.

Our goal is to provide accurate, reliable, and useful information for all 566 municipalities and 21 counties in New Jersey. Data in the profiles is the latest available for all local governing bodies as of June 1, 2009. The dates of the information are indicated in the headings or data items.

The notation "NA" stands for "not available." Although we strive to obtain all available data, there are several reasons data may not be available. Many agencies only provide data for places of a certain size or population, so data is not available for many smaller municipalities. Other times, "NA" indicates that the information was never sent to the data-collecting agency, or was not available from the agency at press time. Reporting is often voluntary, and some places have chosen not to report. Finally, sometimes the category or descriptor simply does not apply to a given place (for example, in the case of towns without police or fire chiefs).

Readers should also note that the numbers for subcategories do not always add up to the total shown. In some cases, this is due to rounding error in the original data collection. Other times, only certain subgroups of a larger category are presented.

Explanation of the Categories

Municipal Profiles Section

Demographics & Socioeconomic Characteristics

Municipal information in this category, with a few exceptions, comes from the 2000 US Census (the data shown here has been revised from the original data published by the Bureau of Census). The exceptions are the **1980** and **1990** **population** figures, which are from their respective Decennial Censuses; the **2007 population estimates**, which come from the US Census Bureau's Population Estimates division; and the **labor force** and **unemployment rate** for 2007, which come from the New Jersey Department of Labor and Workforce Development. **Population density** for 2007 was calculated by Information Publications based on the 2007 population estimates, and the **land area** figure from 2000.

Race, as used by the Bureau of the Census, is not meant to denote any scientific or biological concept of race. Terms used here match the categories used by the Census for data collection, and represent the self-categorization of respondents. It should also be noted that **Hispanic origin** is not a racial category. Persons may be of any race, and be of Hispanic origin as well.

Educational attainment applies to persons who are 25 years or older. College graduates are persons with at least a four-year degree.

Income and **poverty** information as reported in the 2000 US Census is from 1999.

A **household** includes all persons occupying a housing unit. A **family household** includes a householder and one or more other persons living in the same household who are related to the householder by birth, marriage, or adoption. The number of family households always equals the number of families in a given place. However, a family household may also include nonrelatives living with the family. A **nonfamily household** includes a householder living alone or with nonrelatives only. Not all persons live in households. For example, some are members of the armed forces, inmates of institutions, or live in group quarters. As a result, the total number of persons in a city or town can be greater than the number of persons living in all households in that town. The subgroups listed were selected for potential interest and do not represent a full breakdown of all types of households. Readers should also note that there is overlap among types of households. For example, the same household may have both members under 18 years of age and members over 65 years of age.

Total civilian labor force includes all persons at least 16 years of age who are not members of the armed forces, and are either employed or unemployed. **Self-employed workers** refers to workers who own non-incorporated businesses.

The American Community Survey (ACS), which surveys a monthly sample of the US population, is beginning to track much of the information previously only measured by the Decennial Census. Currently, the ACS provides one-year estimates for the United States, each state, and cities and counties with populations over 65,000. Beginning with the 2007 ACS, coverage has expanded to include three-year pooled estimates of all places with populations greater than 20,000 (these estimates do not appear in this volume). By 2010, the Bureau of the Census hopes to use the ACS to track all the information currently collected in the long form of the Decennial Census. The 2007 ACS provided done-year estimates for 20 of New Jersey's 566 municipalities, as well as all 21 counties. For those municipalities currently tracked by the ACS, we have provided that data in **Appendix C**. (ACS data for counties appears in the profiles in place of 2000 Census data.) You can find more information about the ACS at http://www.census.gov/acs/www.

General Information

The **address** and **telephone number** shown are for the central location of municipal business (i.e., the city hall or city administrative office), and were obtained from surveys done by Information Publications. Other information such as the **website** was also obtained from the surveys. Some municipalities do not have their own websites, but have pages on their county's website. In these cases, the notation "(county website)" is used. **Form of government** comes from the Center for Government Services at Rutgers University, supplemented by our surveys. Readers who are interested in the different forms of municipal government in New Jersey should refer to the New Jersey League of Municipalities' guide at www.njslom.com/types.html. **Year of incorporation** represents the date of a municipality's creation in its present form. Dates are taken from *The Story of New Jersey's Civil Boundaries, 1606-1968*, by John P. Snyder, with updates by the Center for Government Services at Rutgers.

Land area and **water area** are from the 2000 US Census. It should be noted that land area measurement as reported by the 2000 US Census is given in square meters. It has been converted into square miles in the profiles, using a conversion factor of 2,589,988 square meters per square mile.

Government

State legislative district comes from the Municipal and County Government section of New Jersey's official website: http://www.state.nj.us. **US congressional district** information comes from the Census Bureau's "111th Congressional Districts" summary file, and was also verified by our surveys.

All names of **local officials** are from our surveys.

Housing and Construction

Housing unit data for 2000 comes from the 2000 US Census. A **housing unit** is defined as a house, apartment, mobile home or trailer, group of rooms, or single room occupied as a separate living quarter or, if vacant, intended as a separate living quarter. Separate living quarters are those in which the occupants live and eat separately from any other persons in the building, and which have direct access from the outside of the building or through a common hall.

A **single-family unit** is defined as a housing unit which does not share the building with any other housing units, and is not attached to any other structure. In Census terminology, it is defined as a single, detached unit. **Single-family home** is equivalent to the Census term "specified owner-occupied unit," and refers to single-family houses on less than ten acres without a business or medical office on the property.

A housing unit is **owner-occupied** if the owner or co-owner lives in the unit, even if the unit is mortgaged or not fully paid for. All other housing units are considered **renter-occupied**.

Value is the Census respondent's estimate of how much the house would sell for if it were on the market. **Median value** represents the middle value of the distribution of these estimates, such that half the houses have higher values than the median and half have lower values. **Median rent** is defined in a similar fashion.

Statistics on **permits for new residential construction** for 2006 and 2007 come from the US Bureau of the Census' Manufacturing, Mining, and Construction Statistics division. Places that issue building permits are asked to report monthly to the Bureau. Readers are cautioned that estimates are updated periodically on the Census' website, so the data presented here may differ slightly from the most recent information.

Data from 2008 for **real property valuation** and **average property value & tax** comes from the New Jersey Division of Local Government Services, Department of Community Affairs.

Public Library

The name of the **library director** was obtained from our surveys. All **library statistics** come from "New Jersey Public Library Statistics, 2007." Information was obtained from the website for the New Jersey State Library, under the section for the Library Development Bureau. **Full-time staff** refers only to professionally-certified staff who work more than 35 hours per week, and does not include all employees.

The New Jersey State Library does not provide separate statistics for branches of county libraries. For municipalities whose library is a branch of a county library, the appropriate county page is listed. For municipalities whose library is the main library for the county, the county system statistics are listed.

Public Safety

Data on **number of officers, violent crimes, property crimes, domestic violence,** and **arson** come from the "Crime in the United States" reports for 2006 and 2007, published by the Uniform Crime Reports division of the Federal Bureau of Investigation and the New Jersey State Police. **Violent crime** is defined as **murder, rape, robbery,** and **aggravated assault**. **Property crime** is defined as **burglary, larceny,** and **motor vehicle theft**. **Crime rates** are defined as crimes per 1,000 residents.

Names of **police chiefs** and **fire chiefs** were obtained using our surveys.

Public School District

The municipal profiles provide information for the principal school district in each municipality. If a governing body does not maintain a school district, data is given for the system it uses. If only an elementary school system is maintained, that is the information provided. For districts that do not contain any regular public schools, the school system used by residents of that district is provided if it is available. New Jersey also has several regional public school districts. Information about these districts can be found in **Appendix D**.

The **name, address, telephone number, superintendent,** and **grade plan** of public school districts were obtained from the New Jersey School Directory, published by the New Jersey Department of Education. This information was supplemented by our surveys.

All other school information is for the school year 2006-07 except where indicated. The information comes from the "New Jersey Report Card" for 2007-08, except for **Adequate Yearly Progress (AYP), Highly-Qualified Teachers (HQT)**, and **attendance rate** for 2006-07, which come from the annual **No Child Left Behind (NCLB)** report.

Grade plan shows the range of grades available in the schools within the district. "K" denotes kindergarten, and "9-12" indicates a four-year high school. A grade plan of "K-12" means that the school district contains at least one of each of the following types of schools: an elementary school with kindergarten through sixth grade, a junior high school with seventh and eighth grades, and a four-year high school. **Number of schools** refers only to regular elementary and high schools in the district, and not vocational or special service schools.

Enrollment includes all regular day school students enrolled for all grades in the district. **Enrollment** and **grade 12 enrollment** are grouped by school districts and reflect the total enrollment of all schools within the district.

Assessment tests are a key element of New Jersey's participation in the federal **No Child Left Behind (NCLB)** program. The profiles show the percentage of students scoring at the proficient or advanced level for **math** and **language arts** on the following tests: the **New Jersey Assessment of Skills and Knowledge (NJASK)** for third and eighth graders, and the **High School Proficiency Assessment (HSPA)**. In addition, the **NCLB** program sets goals for **highly-qualified teachers** in single subjects and across all subjects. It also determines **Adequate Yearly Progress (AYP)**, an overall indicator of whether the district needs to improve to meet federal goals.

New Jersey's Department of Education does not calculate figures for **graduation rate** and **SAT results** at the district level. As a result, only districts that contain a single high school have available data for these categories.

The goals of education are complex, and standardized tests measure the degree of attainment of only a few of those goals. Standardized test scores should not be the only criterion used to evaluate an educational program. Readers must realize that only a small amount of the information that is required for a total evaluation is provided in the district profiles, and for a more in-depth look should talk with the districts directly and do extensive research of all data available from the schools, the districts, and the New Jersey Department of Education.

Municipal Finance

Information in this section is obtained from the New Jersey Department of Community Affairs. While most municipalities in New Jersey operate on calendar year budgets (January 1-December 31), approximately 50 municipalities operate on a state fiscal year (July 1-June 30). Municipalities that do so are indicated as such in their profiles.

State aid refers to funds received from the state to provide relief for property taxes, and is taken from the report "CY2009/SFY2010 State Aid." State aid information is taken from the governor's proposed budget for 2009 (or fiscal year 2010, for those municipalities using a fiscal year schedule), and figures may differ from the final budget adopted by the state legislature.

General budget information refers to property tax levies paid by residents of a municipality. Data in this section is distilled from the Abstract of Ratables and the New Jersey Property Tax Information report. **County levies** represent the municipality's share of the budget for county-administered programs (such as health departments and libraries). The **school levy** represents taxes raised to support local schools. The **municipal levy** refers to taxes that go to funding municipal government and debt service.

For a more detailed explanation, users of this data may find it helpful to contact the Department of Community Affairs, Division of Local Government Services.

Taxes

The information shown under this heading was obtained from the New Jersey Department of the Treasury, Division of Taxation's "Tables of Equalized Valuations" for 2006, 2007, and 2008, from the Abstracts of Ratables for those years. **County equalization ratio** is computed by the state for the purpose of apportioning state school aid and for equal-izing county taxes. It is computed during the final months of the year, and is used for the following year (ratios appear under the year in which they are used). Data shown for **state equalized value** is after any tax court appeals. Data for **total income** and **net charged tax** is shown in thousands of dollars.

County Profiles Section

All the information on the county pages is derived from the same sources as the municipal pages, with a few exceptions, notes, and additions.

Unlike counties in many states, New Jersey counties contain no unincorporated areas. Since the counties are essentially collections of municipalities, many agencies do not report separate county data. In these cases, the information presented here was obtained by adding the corresponding figures (where applicable) for the municipalities contained in the counties. Data obtained in this manner is marked as such in the profiles.

Demographics & Socioeconomic Characteristics

All information in this section comes from the 2007 ACS, with a few exceptions. **Population** figures for 1990, 2000, and 2008 come from the 1990 and 2000 Censuses, and the Census Bureau's Population Estimates Division, respectively. **Population density** is calculated from the 2008 estimate.

Civilian labor force projections come from the New Jersey Department of Labor's Planning & Analysis division.

General Information

The **number of municipalities** and **address** of the county (county seat) are updated annually from our own surveys. **Form of government**, **class**, and **number of freeholders** information comes from the New Jersey Association of Counties.

Government & Voters

All names of **county officials** come from our surveys.

Registered voters data is compiled from information provided by the Office of the Attorney General, New Jersey Division of Elections. Numbers do not add up to the total because not all party affiliations are shown, only Democratic, Republican, and Unaffiliated.

County School District

The **county superintendent** (a state rather than county official), **address**, and **phone number** were obtained from our own surveys and the New Jersey Department of Education.

The **number of districts** comes from the New Jersey School Directory.

Housing & Construction

Housing Unit data comes from the 2007 ACS.

Real property parcels and **valuation** are not provided separately for counties. Information on the pages is obtained by adding the corresponding figures for the municipalities contained in each county.

Public Safety

County police officers data (including officers in the sheriff's and prosecutors' departments) comes from the same "Crime in the United States" report as the rest of the crime data.

Public Library

Several counties do not have their own library (that is, one specified as a "county library"). In this case, **library statistics** shown are obtained from adding the figures for the municipalities in those counties that provide statistics. For these counties, **number of libraries** refers to the number listed in the library directory and reporting statistics.

State Income Tax

Information in this section was obtained from the New Jersey Department of Taxation's 2006 "Statistics of Income" report.

County Finance

Much of the financial data presented here is not reported separately for counties. For these data items, figures shown are the sum of the municipalities in each county. These items are marked in the profiles.

Appendices

The appendices supplement the information that appears on the individual profile pages. Information in the appendices comes from the same source as the corresponding item on the profile page unless otherwise noted below.

Appendix A is the profile for the state of New Jersey, taken from the 2009 edition of the ***Almanac of the 50 States*** (ISBN: 978-0-929960-52-4, paper; 978-0-929960-51-3, cloth), also published by Information Publications. Please refer to that volume for similar information on each of the 50 States, the District of Columbia, and the United States in summary.

Appendix B lists New Jersey's municipalities by county.

Appendix C gives ACS data for the 20 municipalities tracked in 2007.

Appendix D data for other school districts not shown in the municipal profiles.

Appendix E provides comparative tables for counties in New Jersey.

Appendix F provides comparative tables for municipalities in New Jersey.

Appendix G lists New Jersey's representatives in the US Congress and the New Jersey Legislature.

Abbreviations

Actg	Acting
Admin	Administrator
Assoc	Associates
Avg	Average
AYP	Adequate Yearly Progress
Bd Sec	Board Secretary
Chr	Chairperson
CMPTRA	Consolidated Municipal Property Tax Relief Aid
CFO	Chief Financial Officer
Coord	Coordinator
(County)	Services provided by County
DCA	Department of Community Affairs (New Jersey state agency)
Dep	Deputy
Dev	Development
Dir	Director
Dist	District
FY	Fiscal year ended in June 30
GEPA	Grade Eight Proficiency Assessment
H'holds	Households
HSPA	High School Proficiency Assessment
Int	Interim
Mgr	Manager
Muni	Municipal
NA	Not Available or Not Applicable
NJASK	New Jersey Assessment of Skills and Knowledge
(State)	Services provided by State
Superint	Superintendent
Svcs	Services
Treas	Treasurer

Disclaimer

The New Jersey Municipal Data Book contains thousands of pieces of information. Reasonable precautions and a good deal of care were taken in its preparation. Despite our efforts, it is possible that some of the information contained in this book may not be accurate. Some errors may be due to errors in the original source materials, and others may have been made by the compilers of this volume. An incorrect spelling may occur, a figure may be inverted, and similar mistakes may exist. The compilers, editors, typist, printers, and others working on this volume are all human, and in a work of this magnitude the possibility of error can never be fully eliminated. If any piece of information is believed to be inaccurate, please contact the publisher. We are eager to eliminate any errors from future editions and we will be pleased to check a piece of information. The publisher is also aware that some users may apply the data in this book to various remunerative projects. Although we have taken reasonable, responsible measures to insure accuracy, we cannot take responsibility for liability or losses suffered by users of the data. The information provided here is believed to be correct at the time of publication. No other guarantees are made or implied.

The publisher assumes no liability for losses incurred by users, and warrants only that diligence and due care were used in the production of this volume.

A Final Word

In order to continue to meet its goals, *The New Jersey Municipal Data Book* is revised and updated on an annual basis. The best suggestions for improvement in a ready-reference source such as this come from the regular users of the work. Therefore, we actively solicit your comments and ideas. If you know how this book could become more useful to you, please contact us.

The Editors
The New Jersey Municipal Data Book
Information Publications, Inc.
2995 Woodside Road, Suite 400-182
Woodside, CA 94062

www.informationpublications.com

info@informationpublications.com

Toll Free Phone: 877-544-4636
Toll Free Fax: 877-544-4635

Publisher: Eric Weiner
Lead Editor: Beth Ann Allen
Assistant Editor: Jeff Brenion

The New Jersey Municipal Data Book

2009

State & Municipal Profiles Series

Demographics & Socio-Economic Characteristics

(2000 US Census, except as noted)

Population

1980*	17,235
1990*	17,038
2000	17,454
Male	8,506
Female	8,948
2007 (estimate)*	18,478
Population density	3,335.4

Race & Hispanic Origin, 2000

Race

White	13,758
Black/African American	2,098
American Indian/Alaska Native	24
Asian	962
Native Hawaiian/Pacific Islander	1
Other race	306
Two or more races	305
Hispanic origin, total	1,225
Mexican	90
Puerto Rican	648
Cuban	96
Other Hispanic	391

Age & Nativity, 2000

Under 5 years	1,211
18 years and over	13,185
21 years and over	12,708
65 years and over	1,811
85 years and over	129
Median age	37.0
Native-born	15,392
Foreign-born	1,995

Educational Attainment, 2000

Population 25 years and over	12,263
Less than 9th grade	3.1%
High school grad or higher	87.9%
Bachelor's degree or higher	34.4%
Graduate degree	11.4%

Income & Poverty, 1999

Per capita income	$28,984
Median household income	$68,125
Median family income	$76,648
Persons in poverty	807
H'holds receiving public assistance	102
H'holds receiving social security	1,432

Households, 2000

Total households	6,421
With persons under 18	2,416
With persons over 65	1,299
Family households	4,774
Single-person households	1,300
Persons per household	2.70
Persons per family	3.14

Labor & Employment

Total civilian labor force, 2007**	10,383
Unemployment rate	3.1%
Total civilian labor force, 2000	9,742
Unemployment rate	3.5%

Employed persons 16 years and over by occupation, 2000

Managers & professionals	3,963
Service occupations	1,120
Sales & office occupations	2,712
Farming, fishing & forestry	8
Construction & maintenance	647
Production & transportation	947
Self-employed persons	396

‡ Joint library with Matawan Borough
* US Census Bureau
** New Jersey Department of Labor

General Information

Township of Aberdeen
1 Aberdeen Sq
Aberdeen, NJ 07747
732-583-4200

Website	www.aberdeennj.org
Year of incorporation	1979
Land/water area (sq. miles)	5.54/2.22
Form of government	Council-Manager

Government

Legislative Districts

US Congressional	6
State Legislative	13

Local Officials, 2009

Mayor	David Sobel
Manager	Joseph Criscuolo
Clerk	Karen Ventura
Finance Dir	Angela Morin
Tax Assessor	Holly Reycraft
Tax Collector	Marie Taylor
Attorney	Dan McCarthy
Building	John Quinn
Comm Dev/Planning	NA
Engineering	CME Associates
Public Works	James Lauro
Police Chief	John Powers
Fire/Emergency Dir	NA

Housing & Construction

Housing Units, 2000*

Total	6,558
Median rent	$817
Median SF home value	$160,800

Permits for New Residential Construction

	Units	Value
Total, 2006	16	$1,563,075
Single family	16	$1,563,075
Total, 2007	15	$1,693,577
Single family	15	$1,693,577

Real Property Valuation, 2008

	Parcels	Valuation
Total	6,796	$842,915,310
Vacant	454	14,636,030
Residential	6,136	713,846,480
Commercial	179	86,394,000
Industrial	4	11,849,700
Apartments	7	15,392,900
Farm land	12	89,500
Farm homestead	4	706,700

Average Property Value & Tax, 2008

Residential value	$116,377
Property tax	$6,121
Tax credit/rebate	$1,132

Public Library

Matawan-Aberdeen Public Library‡
165 Main St
Matawan, NJ 07747
732-583-9100

Director	Susan Pike

Library statistics, 2007

Population served	26,364
Full-time/total staff	3/6

	Total	Per capita
Holdings	104,042	3.95
Revenues	$1,085,233	$41.16
Expenditures	$822,991	$31.22
Annual visits	110,739	4.20
Internet terminals/annual users	14/15,061	

Public Safety

Number of officers, 2007	34

Crime	2006	2007
Total crimes	281	278
Violent	36	25
Murder	0	0
Rape	4	1
Robbery	12	5
Aggravated assault	20	19
Non-violent	245	253
Burglary	40	38
Larceny	191	200
Vehicle theft	14	15
Domestic violence	211	264
Arson	4	2
Total crime rate	15.3	15.1
Violent	2.0	1.4
Non-violent	13.4	13.8

Public School District

(for school year 2007-08 except as noted)

Matawan-Aberdeen Regional School District
One Crest Way
Aberdeen, NJ 07747
(732) 705-4003

Superintendent	Richard O'Malley
Number of schools	7
Grade plan	K-12
Enrollment	3,750
Attendance rate, '06-07	94.9%
Dropout rate	0.4%
Students per teacher	10.2
Per pupil expenditure	$14,513
Median faculty salary	$53,720
Median administrator salary	$119,909
Grade 12 enrollment	262
High school graduation rate	99.2%

Assessment test results

(percent scoring at proficient or advanced level)

	Language	Math
NJASK-Grade 3	90.2%	89.4%
GEPA-Grade 8	77.3%	85.8%
HSPA-High School	71.8%	87.1%

SAT Score Averages, 2006-07

Pct tested	Math	Verbal	Writing
82%	478	469	467

Teacher Qualifications

Avg. years of experience	9
Highly-qualified teachers one subject/all subjects	99.5%/99.5%

No Child Left Behind

AYP, 2006-07	Meets Standards

Municipal Finance

State Aid Programs, 2009

Total aid	$1,863,881
CMPTRA	595,775
Energy tax receipts	1,215,763
Garden State Trust	5,349

General Budget, 2008

Total tax levy	$44,388,560
County levy	5,470,890
County taxes	5,040,990
County library	0
County health	93,750
County open space	336,150
School levy	31,100,272
Muni. levy	7,817,398
Misc. revenues	7,490,256

Taxes	2006	2007	2008
General tax rate per $100	5.004	5.067	5.260
County equalization ratio	45.23	40.32	37.94
Net valuation taxable	$846,250,890	$842,941,776	$843,985,292
State equalized value	$2,099,959,424	$2,220,059,326	$7,698,068,929

See Introduction for an explanation of all data sources.

Demographics & Socio-Economic Characteristics

(2000 US Census, except as noted)

Population

1980*	6,859
1990*	7,298
2000	7,638
Male	3,660
Female	3,978
2007 (estimate)*	8,074
Population density	1,411.5

Race & Hispanic Origin, 2000

Race

White	6,363
Black/African American	459
American Indian/Alaska Native	13
Asian	570
Native Hawaiian/Pacific Islander	0
Other race	115
Two or more races	118
Hispanic origin, total	288
Mexican	30
Puerto Rican	111
Cuban	19
Other Hispanic	128

Age & Nativity, 2000

Under 5 years	460
18 years and over	5,842
21 years and over	5,672
65 years and over	1,231
85 years and over	165
Median age	40.3
Native-born	6,894
Foreign-born	799

Educational Attainment, 2000

Population 25 years and over	5,357
Less than 9th grade	3.2%
High school grad or higher	86.0%
Bachelor's degree or higher	22.4%
Graduate degree	7.3%

Income & Poverty, 1999

Per capita income	$23,615
Median household income	$55,745
Median family income	$61,563
Persons in poverty	364
H'holds receiving public assistance	30
H'holds receiving social security	836

Households, 2000

Total households	2,773
With persons under 18	996
With persons over 65	777
Family households	2,084
Single-person households	532
Persons per household	2.69
Persons per family	3.08

Labor & Employment

Total civilian labor force, 2007**	4,252
Unemployment rate	6.0%
Total civilian labor force, 2000	4,009
Unemployment rate	6.5%

Employed persons 16 years and over by occupation, 2000

Managers & professionals	1,042
Service occupations	1,097
Sales & office occupations	1,087
Farming, fishing & forestry	4
Construction & maintenance	280
Production & transportation	239
Self-employed persons	197

* US Census Bureau
** New Jersey Department of Labor

General Information

City of Absecon
Municipal Complex
500 Mill Rd
Absecon, NJ 08201
609-641-0663

Website	absecon-newjersey.org
Year of incorporation	1902
Land/water area (sq. miles)	5.72/1.21
Form of government	City

Government

Legislative Districts

US Congressional	2
State Legislative	2

Local Officials, 2009

Mayor	Peter C. Elco
Administrator	Terrence Dolan
Clerk	Carie A. Crone
Finance Dir	Jessica Thompson
Tax Assessor	Brian Conover
Tax Collector	Agnes Bambrick
Attorney	Michael Blee
Building	Michael O'Hagan
Planning	Remington & Vernick
Engineering	Remington & Vernick
Public Works	Lloyd Jones
Police Chief	Joseph Cowan
Emerg/Fire Director	Butch Stewart

Housing & Construction

Housing Units, 2000*

Total	2,902
Median rent	$792
Median SF home value	$123,000

Permits for New Residential Construction

	Units	Value
Total, 2006	68	$7,358,333
Single family	56	$6,658,333
Total, 2007	165	$14,236,542
Single family	92	$8,804,375

Real Property Valuation, 2008

	Parcels	Valuation
Total	3,757	$1,037,458,400
Vacant	351	45,629,300
Residential	3,205	813,389,900
Commercial	201	178,439,200
Industrial	0	0
Apartments	0	0
Farm land	0	0
Farm homestead	0	0

Average Property Value & Tax, 2008

Residential value	$253,788
Property tax	$4,667
Tax credit/rebate	$891

Public Library

Absecon Public Library
305 New Jersey Ave
Absecon, NJ 08201
609-646-2228

Director	Barbara Wilson

Library statistics, 2007

Population served	7,638
Full-time/total staff	0/1

	Total	Per capita
Holdings	23,790	3.11
Revenues	$300,354	$39.32
Expenditures	$208,860	$27.34
Annual visits	18,023	2.36
Internet terminals/annual users	7/10,003	

Public Safety

Number of officers, 2007 26

Crime

	2006	2007
Total crimes	319	300
Violent	35	28
Murder	1	0
Rape	3	2
Robbery	14	15
Aggravated assault	17	11
Non-violent	284	272
Burglary	41	70
Larceny	231	192
Vehicle theft	12	10
Domestic violence	70	77
Arson	2	0
Total crime rate	39.9	37.2
Violent	4.4	3.5
Non-violent	35.5	33.7

Public School District

(for school year 2007-08 except as noted)

Absecon City School District
800 Irelan Avenue
Absecon, NJ 08201
(609) 641-5375

Superintendent	James Giaquinto
Number of schools	1
Grade plan	K-8
Enrollment	822
Attendance rate, '06-07	95.6%
Dropout rate	NA
Students per teacher	10.7
Per pupil expenditure	$11,068
Median faculty salary	$54,552
Median administrator salary	$91,909
Grade 12 enrollment	NA
High school graduation rate	NA

Assessment test results

(percent scoring at proficient or advanced level)

	Language	Math
NJASK-Grade 3	87.6%	82.0%
GEPA-Grade 8	72.5%	90.1%
HSPA-High School	NA	NA

SAT Score Averages, 2006-07

Pct tested	Math	Verbal	Writing
NA	NA	NA	NA

Teacher Qualifications

Avg. years of experience	9
Highly-qualified teachers one subject/all subjects	100%/100%

No Child Left Behind

AYP, 2006-07 .... Meets Standards

Municipal Finance

State Aid Programs, 2009

Total aid	$979,843
CMPTRA	74,022
Energy tax receipts	874,393
Garden State Trust	3,443

General Budget, 2008

Total tax levy	$19,105,452
County levy	2,545,442
County taxes	2,230,937
County library	0
County health	117,082
County open space	197,422
School levy	10,015,702
Muni. levy	6,544,309
Misc. revenues	3,640,270

Taxes	2006	2007	2008
General tax rate per $100	3.778	3.817	1.839
County equalization ratio	63.39	53.87	105.42
Net valuation taxable	$452,747,300	$476,112,407	$1,038,939,327
State equalized value	$841,301,889	$969,680,928	$990,007,273

Demographics & Socio-Economic Characteristics
(2000 US Census, except as noted)

Population
1980*	2,798
1990*	3,594
2000	4,698
Male	2,353
Female	2,345
2007 (estimate)*	5,112
Population density	185.6

Race & Hispanic Origin, 2000
Race
White	4,558
Black/African American	37
American Indian/Alaska Native	5
Asian	34
Native Hawaiian/Pacific Islander	2
Other race	21
Two or more races	41
Hispanic origin, total	81
Mexican	17
Puerto Rican	30
Cuban	6
Other Hispanic	28

Age & Nativity, 2000
Under 5 years	331
18 years and over	3,378
21 years and over	3,259
65 years and over	568
85 years and over	124
Median age	40.2
Native-born	4,448
Foreign-born	250

Educational Attainment, 2000
Population 25 years and over	3,150
Less than 9th grade	3.4%
High school grad or higher	93.2%
Bachelor's degree or higher	39.7%
Graduate degree	16.0%

Income & Poverty, 1999
Per capita income	$34,622
Median household income	$92,730
Median family income	$93,619
Persons in poverty	229
H'holds receiving public assistance	8
H'holds receiving social security	319

Households, 2000
Total households	1,535
With persons under 18	679
With persons over 65	289
Family households	1,291
Single-person households	207
Persons per household	2.95
Persons per family	3.25

Labor & Employment
Total civilian labor force, 2007**	2,617
Unemployment rate	4.9%
Total civilian labor force, 2000	2,351
Unemployment rate	4.0%

Employed persons 16 years and over by occupation, 2000
Managers & professionals	1,115
Service occupations	187
Sales & office occupations	633
Farming, fishing & forestry	28
Construction & maintenance	153
Production & transportation	142
Self-employed persons	234

* US Census Bureau
** New Jersey Department of Labor

General Information
Township of Alexandria
21 Hog Hollow Rd
Pittstown, NJ 08867
908-996-7071
Website	www.alexandria-nj.us
Year of incorporation	1765
Land/water area (sq. miles)	27.54/0.10
Form of government	Township

Government
Legislative Districts
US Congressional	7
State Legislative	23

Local Officials, 2009
Mayor	Harry Fuerstenberger
Manager/Admin	NA
Clerk	Ellen Kluber
Finance Dir	William Hance
Tax Assessor	Eloise Hagaman
Tax Collector	Jack Earley
Attorney	Valerie Kimson
Building	Guenther Majewski
Comm Dev/Planning	NA
Engineering	Gerald D. Philkill
Public Works Foreman	Glenn Griffith
Police Chief	NA
Fire/Emergency Dir	NA

Housing & Construction
Housing Units, 2000*
Total	1,598
Median rent	$1,021
Median SF home value	$274,100

Permits for New Residential Construction
	Units	Value
Total, 2006	40	$9,079,396
Single family	40	$9,079,396
Total, 2007	14	$3,406,200
Single family	14	$3,406,200

Real Property Valuation, 2008
	Parcels	Valuation
Total	2,343	$815,634,158
Vacant	209	27,780,400
Residential	1,470	644,944,300
Commercial	31	21,719,788
Industrial	3	2,534,800
Apartments	1	418,900
Farm land	376	3,864,670
Farm homestead	253	114,371,300

Average Property Value & Tax, 2008
Residential value	$440,694
Property tax	$8,977
Tax credit/rebate	$1,256

Public Library
No public municipal library

Library statistics, 2007
Population served	NA
Full-time/total staff	NA/NA

	Total	Per capita
Holdings	NA	NA
Revenues	NA	NA
Expenditures	NA	NA
Annual visits	NA	NA
Internet terminals/annual users	NA/NA	

Public Safety
Number of officers, 2007	0

Crime	2006	2007
Total crimes	22	32
Violent	2	4
Murder	0	0
Rape	0	0
Robbery	0	0
Aggravated assault	2	4
Non-violent	20	28
Burglary	5	6
Larceny	15	19
Vehicle theft	0	3
Domestic violence	1	15
Arson	1	1
Total crime rate	4.4	6.3
Violent	0.4	0.8
Non-violent	4.0	5.5

Public School District
(for school year 2007-08 except as noted)

Alexandria Township School District
557 County Road 513
Pittstown, NJ 08867
(908) 996-6811
Superintendent	Matthew Jennings
Number of schools	2
Grade plan	K-8
Enrollment	628
Attendance rate, '06-07	95.9%
Dropout rate	NA
Students per teacher	9.6
Per pupil expenditure	$13,110
Median faculty salary	$61,333
Median administrator salary	$105,664
Grade 12 enrollment	NA
High school graduation rate	NA

Assessment test results
(percent scoring at proficient or advanced level)
	Language	Math
NJASK-Grade 3	93.1%	97.3%
GEPA-Grade 8	81.5%	90.0%
HSPA-High School	NA	NA

SAT Score Averages, 2006-07
Pct tested	Math	Verbal	Writing
NA	NA	NA	NA

Teacher Qualifications
Avg. years of experience	12
Highly-qualified teachers one subject/all subjects	100%/100%

No Child Left Behind
AYP, 2006-07	Meets Standards

Municipal Finance
State Aid Programs, 2009
Total aid	$436,584
CMPTRA	48,154
Energy tax receipts	358,056
Garden State Trust	12,655

General Budget, 2008
Total tax levy	$16,650,779
County levy	3,056,171
County taxes	2,557,906
County library	222,123
County health	0
County open space	276,141
School levy	11,878,060
Muni. levy	1,716,549
Misc. revenues	2,008,659

Taxes
	2006	2007	2008
General tax rate per $100	2	2.05	2.038
County equalization ratio	91.81	88.04	89.16
Net valuation taxable	$764,932,037	$787,045,773	$817,403,908
State equalized value	$849,522,252	$913,782,965	$917,800,925

See Introduction for an explanation of all data sources.

Demographics & Socio-Economic Characteristics

(2000 US Census, except as noted)

Population
1980*	2,560
1990*	3,484
2000	3,877
Male	1,800
Female	2,077
2007 (estimate)*	4,385
Population density	213.5

Race & Hispanic Origin, 2000
Race
White	3,702
Black/African American	36
American Indian/Alaska Native	2
Asian	72
Native Hawaiian/Pacific Islander	0
Other race	27
Two or more races	38
Hispanic origin, total	104
Mexican	15
Puerto Rican	28
Cuban	9
Other Hispanic	52

Age & Nativity, 2000
Under 5 years	229
18 years and over	3,142
21 years and over	3,072
65 years and over	637
85 years and over	60
Median age	44.1
Native-born	3,493
Foreign-born	384

Educational Attainment, 2000
Population 25 years and over	3,003
Less than 9th grade	1.0%
High school grad or higher	94.5%
Bachelor's degree or higher	43.8%
Graduate degree	15.2%

Income & Poverty, 1999
Per capita income	$43,552
Median household income	$70,107
Median family income	$89,653
Persons in poverty	71
H'holds receiving public assistance	42
H'holds receiving social security	420

Households, 2000
Total households	1,692
With persons under 18	423
With persons over 65	442
Family households	1,134
Single-person households	482
Persons per household	2.28
Persons per family	2.80

Labor & Employment
Total civilian labor force, 2007**	2,417
Unemployment rate	2.0%
Total civilian labor force, 2000	2,144
Unemployment rate	1.7%

Employed persons 16 years and over by occupation, 2000
Managers & professionals	1,033
Service occupations	145
Sales & office occupations	616
Farming, fishing & forestry	19
Construction & maintenance	115
Production & transportation	179
Self-employed persons	138

General Information
Township of Allamuchy
292 Alphano Rd
PO Box A
Allamuchy, NJ 07820
908-852-5132
Website	www.allamuchynj.org
Year of incorporation	1873
Land/water area (sq. miles)	20.54/0.23
Form of government	Small Municipality

Government

Legislative Districts
US Congressional	5
State Legislative	23

Local Officials, 2009
Mayor	Robert Resker
Manager	Anne Marie Tracy
Clerk	Anne Marie Tracy
Finance Dir	Jim Kozimor
Tax Assessor	Richard Motyka
Tax Collector	Betty Drake
Attorney	Edward Wacks
Building	Charles Cutler
Planning	Alfia Schemm
Engineering	Paul Sterbenz
Public Works	Edward Tracy
Police Chief	(State)
Emerg/Fire Director	Robert Quncken

Housing & Construction

Housing Units, 2000*
Total	1,774
Median rent	$1,075
Median SF home value	$192,500

Permits for New Residential Construction
	Units	Value
Total, 2006	180	$11,966,352
Single family	180	$11,966,352
Total, 2007	6	$1,299,600
Single family	6	$1,299,600

Real Property Valuation, 2008
	Parcels	Valuation
Total	2,351	$544,924,501
Vacant	191	10,786,500
Residential	1,953	492,808,800
Commercial	19	17,944,600
Industrial	1	977,300
Apartments	0	0
Farm land	118	1,333,101
Farm homestead	69	21,074,200

Average Property Value & Tax, 2008
Residential value	$254,146
Property tax	$5,596
Tax credit/rebate	$1,064

Public Library

No public municipal library

Library statistics, 2007
Population served	NA
Full-time/total staff	NA/NA

	Total	Per capita
Holdings	NA	NA
Revenues	NA	NA
Expenditures	NA	NA
Annual visits	NA	NA
Internet terminals/annual users	NA/NA	

Public Safety
Number of officers, 2007		0

Crime	2006	2007
Total crimes	40	44
Violent	3	2
Murder	0	0
Rape	0	0
Robbery	1	0
Aggravated assault	2	2
Non-violent	37	42
Burglary	11	12
Larceny	23	26
Vehicle theft	3	4
Domestic violence	0	17
Arson	4	0
Total crime rate	10.0	10.8
Violent	0.7	0.5
Non-violent	9.2	10.3

Public School District
(for school year 2007-08 except as noted)

Allamuchy Township School District
Allamuchy Township School, Box J
Allamuchy, NJ 07820
(908) 852-1894
Superintendent	Timothy Frederiks
Number of schools	1
Grade plan	K-8
Enrollment	357
Attendance rate, '06-07	95.7%
Dropout rate	NA
Students per teacher	9.8
Per pupil expenditure	$13,535
Median faculty salary	$43,350
Median administrator salary	$83,153
Grade 12 enrollment	NA
High school graduation rate	NA

Assessment test results
(percent scoring at proficient or advanced level)
	Language	Math
NJASK-Grade 3	97.3%	97.2%
GEPA-Grade 8	76.3%	92.1%
HSPA-High School	NA	NA

SAT Score Averages, 2006-07
Pct tested	Math	Verbal	Writing
NA	NA	NA	NA

Teacher Qualifications
Avg. years of experience	7
Highly-qualified teachers one subject/all subjects	96.5%/96.5%

No Child Left Behind
AYP, 2006-07	Meets Standards

Municipal Finance

State Aid Programs, 2009
Total aid	$538,337
CMPTRA	25,575
Energy tax receipts	432,310
Garden State Trust	60,375

General Budget, 2008
Total tax levy	$12,024,309
County levy	4,353,990
County taxes	3,551,175
County library	372,838
County health	0
County open space	429,977
School levy	6,550,073
Muni. levy	1,120,246
Misc. revenues	2,123,103

Taxes
	2006	2007	2008
General tax rate per $100	1.94	2.06	2.203
County equalization ratio	86.71	78.95	76.42
Net valuation taxable	$507,768,165	$522,369,304	$546,053,273
State equalized value	$644,337,810	$683,212,000	$713,262,202

* US Census Bureau
** New Jersey Department of Labor

See Introduction for an explanation of all data sources.

Demographics & Socio-Economic Characteristics

(2000 US Census, except as noted)

Population

1980*	5,901
1990*	5,900
2000	6,699
Male	3,245
Female	3,454
2007 (estimate)*	6,618
Population density	2,121.2

Race & Hispanic Origin, 2000

Race

White	6,195
Black/African American	26
American Indian/Alaska Native	4
Asian	408
Native Hawaiian/Pacific Islander	0
Other race	31
Two or more races	35
Hispanic origin, total	170
Mexican	12
Puerto Rican	41
Cuban	40
Other Hispanic	77

Age & Nativity, 2000

Under 5 years	478
18 years and over	4,663
21 years and over	4,528
65 years and over	945
85 years and over	224
Median age	39.5
Native-born	5,933
Foreign-born	766

Educational Attainment, 2000

Population 25 years and over	4,376
Less than 9th grade	2.7%
High school grad or higher	94.8%
Bachelor's degree or higher	62.5%
Graduate degree	22.6%

Income & Poverty, 1999

Per capita income	$47,772
Median household income	$105,704
Median family income	$113,390
Persons in poverty	117
H'holds receiving public assistance	11
H'holds receiving social security	484

Households, 2000

Total households	2,110
With persons under 18	1,028
With persons over 65	461
Family households	1,796
Single-person households	277
Persons per household	3.03
Persons per family	3.33

Labor & Employment

Total civilian labor force, 2007**	3,234
Unemployment rate	2.4%
Total civilian labor force, 2000	3,079
Unemployment rate	2.7%

Employed persons 16 years and over by occupation, 2000

Managers & professionals	1,583
Service occupations	216
Sales & office occupations	913
Farming, fishing & forestry	0
Construction & maintenance	138
Production & transportation	145
Self-employed persons	298

* US Census Bureau
** New Jersey Department of Labor

General Information

Borough of Allendale
500 W Crescent Ave
Allendale, NJ 07401
201-818-4400

Website	www.allendale.org
Year of incorporation	1894
Land/water area (sq. miles)	3.12/0.03
Form of government	Borough

Government

Legislative Districts

US Congressional	5
State Legislative	39

Local Officials, 2009

Mayor	Vince Barra
Borough Admin	NA
Clerk	Gwen McCarthy
Finance Dir	M. Alissa Mayer
Tax Assessor	Angela Mattiace
Tax Collector	Harold Laufeld
Attorney	David Bole
Building	John Wittekind
Comm Dev/Planning	NA
Engineering	John Yakimik
Public Works	Keith Cauwenberghs
Police Chief	Robert Herndon
Emerg/Fire Director	Dave Walters

Housing & Construction

Housing Units, 2000*

Total	2,143
Median rent	$1,778
Median SF home value	$421,800

Permits for New Residential Construction

	Units	Value
Total, 2006	1	$1,862,800
Single family	1	$1,862,800
Total, 2007	13	$3,182,316
Single family	13	$3,182,316

Real Property Valuation, 2008

	Parcels	Valuation
Total	2,236	$1,295,969,500
Vacant	64	21,320,700
Residential	2,101	1,123,463,200
Commercial	52	87,978,700
Industrial	13	61,598,800
Apartments	0	0
Farm land	5	656,200
Farm homestead	1	951,900

Average Property Value & Tax, 2008

Residential value	$534,926
Property tax	$13,609
Tax credit/rebate	$1,446

Public Library

Lee Memorial Library
500 W Crescent Ave
Allendale, NJ 07401
201-327-4338

Director	Carol Cannon

Library statistics, 2007

Population served	6,699
Full-time/total staff	1/5

	Total	Per capita
Holdings	59,934	8.95
Revenues	$643,875	$96.12
Expenditures	$555,673	$82.95
Annual visits	67,478	10.07
Internet terminals/annual users	5/16,100	

Public Safety

Number of officers, 2007	14

Crime	2006	2007
Total crimes	63	59
Violent	4	2
Murder	0	0
Rape	1	0
Robbery	2	0
Aggravated assault	1	2
Non-violent	59	57
Burglary	16	10
Larceny	41	45
Vehicle theft	2	2
Domestic violence	5	5
Arson	1	0
Total crime rate	9.3	8.8
Violent	0.6	0.3
Non-violent	8.7	8.5

Public School District

(for school year 2007-08 except as noted)

Allendale School District
100 Brookside Avenue
Allendale, NJ 07401
(201) 327-2020

Superintendent	Jerilyn Caprio
Number of schools	2
Grade plan	K-8
Enrollment	992
Attendance rate, '06-07	96.4%
Dropout rate	NA
Students per teacher	11.7
Per pupil expenditure	$13,074
Median faculty salary	$56,130
Median administrator salary	$116,780
Grade 12 enrollment	NA
High school graduation rate	NA

Assessment test results

(percent scoring at proficient or advanced level)

	Language	Math
NJASK-Grade 3	100.0%	98.0%
GEPA-Grade 8	88.3%	98.6%
HSPA-High School	NA	NA

SAT Score Averages, 2006-07

Pct tested	Math	Verbal	Writing
NA	NA	NA	NA

Teacher Qualifications

Avg. years of experience	8
Highly-qualified teachers one subject/all subjects	98.5%/98.5%

No Child Left Behind

AYP, 2006-07 .... Meets Standards

Municipal Finance

State Aid Programs, 2009

Total aid	$1,285,734
CMPTRA	0
Energy tax receipts	1,234,305
Garden State Trust	0

General Budget, 2008

Total tax levy	$33,036,039
County levy	3,419,457
County taxes	3,234,559
County library	0
County health	0
County open space	184,898
School levy	21,109,115
Muni. levy	8,507,467
Misc. revenues	3,610,857

Taxes

	2006	2007	2008
General tax rate per $100	2.36	2.45	2.546
County equalization ratio	80.51	71.56	70.29
Net valuation taxable	$1,279,103,400	$1,297,519,683	$1,298,554,732
State equalized value	$1,790,140,296	$1,844,857,600	$1,882,982,069

See Introduction for an explanation of all data sources.

Demographics & Socio-Economic Characteristics
(2000 US Census, except as noted)

Population
1980*	912
1990*	759
2000	718
Male	370
Female	348
2007 (estimate)*	703
Population density	2,703.8

Race & Hispanic Origin, 2000
Race
White	699
Black/African American	6
American Indian/Alaska Native	2
Asian	3
Native Hawaiian/Pacific Islander	0
Other race	1
Two or more races	7
Hispanic origin, total	18
Mexican	3
Puerto Rican	3
Cuban	0
Other Hispanic	12

Age & Nativity, 2000
Under 5 years	40
18 years and over	582
21 years and over	569
65 years and over	134
85 years and over	20
Median age	42.5
Native-born	700
Foreign-born	23

Educational Attainment, 2000
Population 25 years and over	556
Less than 9th grade	2.3%
High school grad or higher	96.0%
Bachelor's degree or higher	57.7%
Graduate degree	21.2%

Income & Poverty, 1999
Per capita income	$42,710
Median household income	$85,000
Median family income	$109,180
Persons in poverty	27
H'holds receiving public assistance	2
H'holds receiving social security	96

Households, 2000
Total households	285
With persons under 18	74
With persons over 65	90
Family households	189
Single-person households	71
Persons per household	2.52
Persons per family	3.08

Labor & Employment
Total civilian labor force, 2007**	395
Unemployment rate	2.5%
Total civilian labor force, 2000	370
Unemployment rate	3.5%

Employed persons 16 years and over by occupation, 2000
Managers & professionals	181
Service occupations	32
Sales & office occupations	123
Farming, fishing & forestry	0
Construction & maintenance	7
Production & transportation	14
Self-employed persons	41

General Information
Borough of Allenhurst
125 Corlies Ave
Allenhurst, NJ 07711
732-531-2757
Website	www.allenhurstnj.org
Year of incorporation	1897
Land/water area (sq. miles)	0.26/0.02
Form of government	Commission

Government
Legislative Districts
US Congressional	6
State Legislative	11

Local Officials, 2009
Mayor	David J. McLaughlin
Manager	Lori L. Osborn
Clerk	Lori L. Osborn
Finance Dir	Chris Brown
Tax Assessor	Peter Barnett
Tax Collector	Edward Mazzacco
Attorney	David Laughlin
Building	NA
Comm Dev/Planning	NA
Engineering	Peter Avakian
Public Works	Doug Caron
Police Chief	Robert Richter
Emerg/Fire Director	Frank Manfredi

Housing & Construction
Housing Units, 2000*
Total	370
Median rent	$815
Median SF home value	$359,000

Permits for New Residential Construction
	Units	Value
Total, 2006	0	$0
Single family	0	$0
Total, 2007	1	$1,275,000
Single family	1	$1,275,000

Real Property Valuation, 2008
	Parcels	Valuation
Total	335	$587,458,300
Vacant	8	7,450,200
Residential	296	539,836,900
Commercial	26	32,589,000
Industrial	1	3,666,100
Apartments	4	3,916,100
Farm land	0	0
Farm homestead	0	0

Average Property Value & Tax, 2008
Residential value	$1,823,773
Property tax	$10,561
Tax credit/rebate	$1,204

Public Library
No public municipal library

Library statistics, 2007
Population served	NA
Full-time/total staff	NA/NA

	Total	Per capita
Holdings	NA	NA
Revenues	NA	NA
Expenditures	NA	NA
Annual visits	NA	NA
Internet terminals/annual users	NA/NA	

Public Safety
Number of officers, 2007 ... 9
Crime	2006	2007
Total crimes	18	29
Violent	2	1
Murder	0	0
Rape	0	0
Robbery	1	0
Aggravated assault	1	1
Non-violent	16	28
Burglary	2	4
Larceny	13	23
Vehicle theft	1	1
Domestic violence	5	7
Arson	0	0
Total crime rate	25.5	41.4
Violent	2.8	1.4
Non-violent	22.7	39.9

Public School District
(for school year 2007-08 except as noted)

Allenhurst School District
125 Corlies Avenue
Allenhurst, NJ 07711

No schools in district

Per pupil expenditure	NA
Median faculty salary	NA
Median administrator salary	NA
Grade 12 enrollment	NA
High school graduation rate	NA

Assessment test results
(percent scoring at proficient or advanced level)
	Language	Math
NJASK-Grade 3	NA	NA
GEPA-Grade 8	NA	NA
HSPA-High School	NA	NA

SAT Score Averages, 2006-07
Pct tested	Math	Verbal	Writing
NA	NA	NA	NA

Teacher Qualifications
Avg. years of experience	NA
Highly-qualified teachers one subject/all subjects	NA/NA

No Child Left Behind
AYP, 2006-07	NA

Municipal Finance
State Aid Programs, 2009
Total aid	$212,607
CMPTRA	0
Energy tax receipts	204,103
Garden State Trust	0

General Budget, 2008
Total tax levy	$3,402,854
County levy	1,425,231
County taxes	1,264,770
County library	76,114
County health	0
County open space	84,346
School levy	24,065
Muni. levy	1,953,558
Misc. revenues	1,957,722

Taxes
	2006	2007	2008
General tax rate per $100	1.477	0.579	0.580
County equalization ratio	50.8	115.39	105.03
Net valuation taxable	$210,679,200	$589,208,759	$587,644,603
State equalized value	$510,560,989	$560,997,604	$2,199,023,854

* US Census Bureau
** New Jersey Department of Labor

See Introduction for an explanation of all data sources.

Demographics & Socio-Economic Characteristics
(2000 US Census, except as noted)

Population
1980*	1,962
1990*	1,828
2000	1,882
Male	890
Female	992
2007 (estimate)*	1,859
Population density	3,047.5

Race & Hispanic Origin, 2000
Race
White	1,706
Black/African American	121
American Indian/Alaska Native	11
Asian	12
Native Hawaiian/Pacific Islander	0
Other race	11
Two or more races	21
Hispanic origin, total	36
Mexican	2
Puerto Rican	24
Cuban	3
Other Hispanic	7

Age & Nativity, 2000
Under 5 years	136
18 years and over	1,379
21 years and over	1,327
65 years and over	184
85 years and over	22
Median age	38.5
Native-born	1,827
Foreign-born	55

Educational Attainment, 2000
Population 25 years and over	1,269
Less than 9th grade	1.7%
High school grad or higher	92.5%
Bachelor's degree or higher	41.1%
Graduate degree	15.7%

Income & Poverty, 1999
Per capita income	$29,455
Median household income	$71,193
Median family income	$79,843
Persons in poverty	44
H'holds receiving public assistance	15
H'holds receiving social security	155

Households, 2000
Total households	708
With persons under 18	271
With persons over 65	136
Family households	527
Single-person households	151
Persons per household	2.66
Persons per family	3.13

Labor & Employment
Total civilian labor force, 2007**	1,152
Unemployment rate	3.4%
Total civilian labor force, 2000	1,073
Unemployment rate	3.3%

Employed persons 16 years and over by occupation, 2000
Managers & professionals	488
Service occupations	122
Sales & office occupations	276
Farming, fishing & forestry	1
Construction & maintenance	65
Production & transportation	86
Self-employed persons	64

‡ Branch of county library
* US Census Bureau
** New Jersey Department of Labor

See Introduction for an explanation of all data sources.

General Information
Borough of Allentown
8 N Main St
PO Box 487
Allentown, NJ 08501
609-259-3151

Website	NA
Year of incorporation	1889
Land/water area (sq. miles)	0.61/0.02
Form of government	Borough

Government
Legislative Districts
US Congressional	4
State Legislative	30

Local Officials, 2009
Mayor	Stuart Fierstein
Manager/Admin	NA
Clerk	Julie Martin
Finance Dir	Robert Benick
Tax Assessor	Victoria Butchon
Tax Collector	Barbara Pater
Attorney	Donald Driggers
Building	NA
Comm Dev/Planning	NA
Engineering	Hatch Mott McDonald
Public Works	NA
Police Chief	Harvey Morrell
Emerg/Fire Director	Brad Carter

Housing & Construction
Housing Units, 2000*
Total	718
Median rent	$792
Median SF home value	$167,100

Permits for New Residential Construction
	Units	Value
Total, 2006	7	$1,294,500
Single family	7	$1,294,500
Total, 2007	0	$0
Single family	0	$0

Real Property Valuation, 2008
	Parcels	Valuation
Total	659	$101,099,600
Vacant	28	430,700
Residential	588	90,145,200
Commercial	39	8,151,000
Industrial	0	0
Apartments	2	2,368,400
Farm land	2	4,300
Farm homestead	0	0

Average Property Value & Tax, 2008
Residential value	$153,308
Property tax	$6,808
Tax credit/rebate	$1,101

Public Library
Allentown Branch Library‡
16 S Main St
Allentown, NJ 08501
609-259-7565

Branch Librarian	Nancy Stein

Library statistics, 2007
see Monmouth County profile for library system statistics

Public Safety
Number of officers, 2007	5

Crime	2006	2007
Total crimes	24	25
Violent	3	1
Murder	0	0
Rape	0	0
Robbery	0	1
Aggravated assault	3	0
Non-violent	21	24
Burglary	3	5
Larceny	17	16
Vehicle theft	1	3
Domestic violence	3	6
Arson	0	0
Total crime rate	12.9	13.5
Violent	1.6	0.5
Non-violent	11.3	13.0

Public School District
(for school year 2007-08 except as noted)

Upper Freehold Regional School District
27 High Street
Allentown, NJ 08501
(609) 259-7292

Superintendent	Richard Fitzpatrick
Number of schools	2
Grade plan	K-12
Enrollment	2,292
Attendance rate, '06-07	95.2%
Dropout rate	0.4%
Students per teacher	11.3
Per pupil expenditure	$12,560
Median faculty salary	$53,273
Median administrator salary	$106,263
Grade 12 enrollment	221
High school graduation rate	97.4%

Assessment test results
(percent scoring at proficient or advanced level)
	Language	Math
NJASK-Grade 3	91.0%	93.9%
GEPA-Grade 8	78.2%	92.4%
HSPA-High School	85.6%	90.1%

SAT Score Averages, 2006-07
Pct tested	Math	Verbal	Writing
81%	511	512	496

Teacher Qualifications
Avg. years of experience	6

Highly-qualified teachers
one subject/all subjects	96.5%/96.5%

No Child Left Behind
AYP, 2006-07	Meets Standards

Municipal Finance
State Aid Programs, 2009
Total aid	$169,667
CMPTRA	54,076
Energy tax receipts	111,349
Garden State Trust	0

General Budget, 2008
Total tax levy	$4,522,477
County levy	557,405
County taxes	486,597
County library	29,293
County health	9,046
County open space	32,468
School levy	2,821,382
Muni. levy	1,143,690
Misc. revenues	890,178

Taxes
	2006	2007	2008
General tax rate per $100	4.148	4.232	4.441
County equalization ratio	58.39	50.66	46.77
Net valuation taxable	$100,801,400	$102,316,950	$101,844,581
State equalized value	$200,091,295	$217,651,291	$549,983,495

Demographics & Socio-Economic Characteristics
(2000 US Census, except as noted)

Population
1980*	2,680
1990*	2,795
2000	2,774
Male	1,411
Female	1,363
2007 (estimate)*	3,035
Population density	92.4

Race & Hispanic Origin, 2000
Race
White	2,516
Black/African American	191
American Indian/Alaska Native	15
Asian	12
Native Hawaiian/Pacific Islander	0
Other race	11
Two or more races	29
Hispanic origin, total	66
Mexican	3
Puerto Rican	3
Cuban	1
Other Hispanic	59

Age & Nativity, 2000
Under 5 years	181
18 years and over	1,995
21 years and over	1,891
65 years and over	343
85 years and over	37
Median age	36.7
Native-born	2,726
Foreign-born	48

Educational Attainment, 2000
Population 25 years and over	1,812
Less than 9th grade	3.4%
High school grad or higher	87.4%
Bachelor's degree or higher	20.3%
Graduate degree	6.6%

Income & Poverty, 1999
Per capita income	$22,935
Median household income	$56,528
Median family income	$65,132
Persons in poverty	226
H'holds receiving public assistance	16
H'holds receiving social security	235

Households, 2000
Total households	948
With persons under 18	373
With persons over 65	239
Family households	742
Single-person households	177
Persons per household	2.80
Persons per family	3.19

Labor & Employment
Total civilian labor force, 2007**	1,434
Unemployment rate	5.4%
Total civilian labor force, 2000	1,465
Unemployment rate	9.4%

Employed persons 16 years and over by occupation, 2000
Managers & professionals	417
Service occupations	159
Sales & office occupations	311
Farming, fishing & forestry	24
Construction & maintenance	218
Production & transportation	199
Self-employed persons	112

General Information
Township of Alloway
PO Box 425
Alloway, NJ 08001
856-935-4080

Website	(county website)
Year of incorporation	1884
Land/water area (sq. miles)	32.85/0.33
Form of government	Township

Government
Legislative Districts
US Congressional	2
State Legislative	3

Local Officials, 2009
Mayor	Edwin P. Masker
Manager/Admin	NA
Clerk	Mary Lou Rutherford
Finance Dir	Marie Stout
Tax Assessor	Lisa Perella
Tax Collector	Thomas Freeman
Attorney	Adam I. Telsey
Building	Harold Underwood
Planning	Patricia Paruszewski
Engineering	Carl Gaskill
Public Works	Kenneth McKelrey
Police Chief	NA
Emerg/Fire Director	Jeffery Pompper

Housing & Construction
Housing Units, 2000*
Total	995
Median rent	$700
Median SF home value	$133,300

Permits for New Residential Construction
	Units	Value
Total, 2006	10	$2,070,000
Single family	10	$2,070,000
Total, 2007	18	$2,990,000
Single family	18	$2,990,000

Real Property Valuation, 2008
	Parcels	Valuation
Total	2,189	$197,751,000
Vacant	407	8,050,700
Residential	1,061	142,951,300
Commercial	29	8,107,900
Industrial	0	0
Apartments	0	0
Farm land	469	4,815,800
Farm homestead	223	33,825,300

Average Property Value & Tax, 2008
Residential value	$137,676
Property tax	$4,597
Tax credit/rebate	$909

Public Library
No public municipal library

Library statistics, 2007
Population served	NA
Full-time/total staff	NA/NA

	Total	Per capita
Holdings	NA	NA
Revenues	NA	NA
Expenditures	NA	NA
Annual visits	NA	NA
Internet terminals/annual users	NA/NA	

Public Safety
Number of officers, 2007 0

Crime	2006	2007
Total crimes	32	33
Violent	2	8
Murder	0	0
Rape	0	0
Robbery	0	0
Aggravated assault	2	8
Non-violent	30	25
Burglary	8	14
Larceny	19	11
Vehicle theft	3	0
Domestic violence	4	20
Arson	0	3
Total crime rate	10.7	10.8
Violent	0.7	2.6
Non-violent	10.0	8.2

Public School District
(for school year 2007-08 except as noted)

Alloway Township School District
43 Cedar Street, Box 327
Alloway, NJ 08001
(856) 935-1622

Superintendent	Robert Bazzel
Number of schools	1
Grade plan	K-8
Enrollment	476
Attendance rate, '06-07	95.7%
Dropout rate	NA
Students per teacher	12.0
Per pupil expenditure	$10,802
Median faculty salary	$49,107
Median administrator salary	$90,696
Grade 12 enrollment	NA
High school graduation rate	NA

Assessment test results
(percent scoring at proficient or advanced level)
	Language	Math
NJASK-Grade 3	87.8%	85.7%
GEPA-Grade 8	75.9%	89.7%
HSPA-High School	NA	NA

SAT Score Averages, 2006-07
Pct tested	Math	Verbal	Writing
NA	NA	NA	NA

Teacher Qualifications
Avg. years of experience	13
Highly-qualified teachers one subject/all subjects	93.5%/90.5%

No Child Left Behind
AYP, 2006-07 ....Meets Standards

Municipal Finance
State Aid Programs, 2009
Total aid	$460,316
CMPTRA	7,807
Energy tax receipts	419,904
Garden State Trust	14,261

General Budget, 2008
Total tax levy	$6,621,148
County levy	2,623,365
County taxes	2,566,764
County library	0
County health	0
County open space	56,601
School levy	3,577,080
Muni. levy	420,703
Misc. revenues	1,374,263

Taxes
	2006	2007	2008
General tax rate per $100	3.157	3.293	3.340
County equalization ratio	77.63	72.89	70.38
Net valuation taxable	$190,910,500	$197,526,284	$198,289,700
State equalized value	$262,450,918	$280,436,022	$297,908,625

* US Census Bureau
** New Jersey Department of Labor

See Introduction for an explanation of all data sources.

Demographics & Socio-Economic Characteristics

(2000 US Census, except as noted)

Population
1980*	2,644
1990*	2,530
2000	2,482
Male	1,208
Female	1,274
2007 (estimate)*	2,389
Population density	1,405.3

Race & Hispanic Origin, 2000
Race
White	2,409
Black/African American	7
American Indian/Alaska Native	1
Asian	30
Native Hawaiian/Pacific Islander	0
Other race	16
Two or more races	19
Hispanic origin, total	47
Mexican	15
Puerto Rican	12
Cuban	1
Other Hispanic	19

Age & Nativity, 2000
Under 5 years	144
18 years and over	1,876
21 years and over	1,812
65 years and over	434
85 years and over	45
Median age	37.7
Native-born	2,433
Foreign-born	49

Educational Attainment, 2000
Population 25 years and over	1,729
Less than 9th grade	6.2%
High school grad or higher	80.6%
Bachelor's degree or higher	11.9%
Graduate degree	4.4%

Income & Poverty, 1999
Per capita income	$20,104
Median household income	$42,209
Median family income	$45,435
Persons in poverty	187
H'holds receiving public assistance	26
H'holds receiving social security	375

Households, 2000
Total households	989
With persons under 18	336
With persons over 65	317
Family households	688
Single-person households	266
Persons per household	2.50
Persons per family	3.05

Labor & Employment
Total civilian labor force, 2007**	1,420
Unemployment rate	5.9%
Total civilian labor force, 2000	1,268
Unemployment rate	5.7%

Employed persons 16 years and over by occupation, 2000
Managers & professionals	255
Service occupations	212
Sales & office occupations	397
Farming, fishing & forestry	0
Construction & maintenance	144
Production & transportation	188
Self-employed persons	66

* US Census Bureau
** New Jersey Department of Labor

See Introduction for an explanation of all data sources.

General Information
Borough of Alpha
1001 East Blvd
Alpha, NJ 08865
908-454-0088
Website	www.alphaboro.org
Year of incorporation	1911
Land/water area (sq. miles)	1.70/0.04
Form of government	Borough

Government
Legislative Districts
US Congressional	5
State Legislative	23

Local Officials, 2009
Mayor	Edward Z. Hanics Jr
Manager/Admin	NA
Clerk	Laurie Barton
Finance Dir	Lorraine Rossetti
Tax Assessor	Kathy Degan
Tax Collector	Carrie Emery
Attorney	Christopher Troxell
Building	Kevin Duddy
Comm Dev/Planning	NA
Engineering	CMX
Public Works	Charles Olah
Police Chief	Paul Hager
Emerg/Fire Director	Carl Gercie Jr

Housing & Construction
Housing Units, 2000*
Total	1,034
Median rent	$710
Median SF home value	$117,200

Permits for New Residential Construction
	Units	Value
Total, 2006	3	$584,150
Single family	3	$584,150
Total, 2007	3	$456,650
Single family	3	$456,650

Real Property Valuation, 2008
	Parcels	Valuation
Total	1,032	$213,166,081
Vacant	140	11,230,200
Residential	803	145,397,400
Commercial	52	28,118,600
Industrial	15	20,844,400
Apartments	9	6,665,100
Farm land	11	218,181
Farm homestead	2	692,200

Average Property Value & Tax, 2008
Residential value	$181,478
Property tax	$5,018
Tax credit/rebate	$1,009

Public Library
W.H. Walters Free Library
1001 East Blvd
Alpha, NJ 08865
908-454-1445
Director	Myrna Minardi

Library statistics, 2007
Population served	2,482
Full-time/total staff	NA/0

	Total	Per capita
Holdings	0	NA
Revenues	$0	NA
Expenditures	$0	NA
Annual visits	NA	NA
Internet terminals/annual users	NA/NA	

Public Safety
Number of officers, 2007	0

Crime	2006	2007
Total crimes	44	46
Violent	13	18
Murder	0	0
Rape	0	0
Robbery	0	0
Aggravated assault	13	18
Non-violent	31	28
Burglary	3	2
Larceny	28	23
Vehicle theft	0	3
Domestic violence	4	15
Arson	0	0
Total crime rate	17.9	18.9
Violent	5.3	7.4
Non-violent	12.6	11.5

Public School District
(for school year 2007-08 except as noted)

Alpha School District
817 North Boulevard
Alpha, NJ 08865
(908) 454-5000
Chief School Admin	Donna Medea
Number of schools	1
Grade plan	K-8
Enrollment	266
Attendance rate, '06-07	95.7%
Dropout rate	NA
Students per teacher	8.1
Per pupil expenditure	$12,248
Median faculty salary	$47,960
Median administrator salary	$75,555
Grade 12 enrollment	NA
High school graduation rate	NA

Assessment test results
(percent scoring at proficient or advanced level)
	Language	Math
NJASK-Grade 3	80.6%	72.2%
GEPA-Grade 8	70.4%	77.8%
HSPA-High School	NA	NA

SAT Score Averages, 2006-07
Pct tested	Math	Verbal	Writing
NA	NA	NA	NA

Teacher Qualifications
Avg. years of experience	9
Highly-qualified teachers one subject/all subjects	87.5%/83.5%

No Child Left Behind
AYP, 2006-07	Meets Standards

Municipal Finance
State Aid Programs, 2009
Total aid	$277,631
CMPTRA	81,388
Energy tax receipts	192,079
Garden State Trust	0

General Budget, 2008
Total tax levy	$5,905,519
County levy	1,388,283
County taxes	1,238,467
County library	0
County health	0
County open space	149,816
School levy	2,748,105
Muni. levy	1,769,131
Misc. revenues	851,716

Taxes
	2006	2007	2008
General tax rate per $100	2.7	2.77	2.766
County equalization ratio	97.07	90.16	85.96
Net valuation taxable	$197,353,641	$207,028,137	$213,575,872
State equalized value	$219,257,802	$240,776,316	$237,103,197

Demographics & Socio-Economic Characteristics
(2000 US Census, except as noted)

Population
1980*	1,549
1990*	1,716
2000	2,183
Male	1,104
Female	1,079
2007 (estimate)*	2,451
Population density	385.4

Race & Hispanic Origin, 2000
Race
White	1,689
Black/African American	33
American Indian/Alaska Native	5
Asian	417
Native Hawaiian/Pacific Islander	1
Other race	7
Two or more races	31
Hispanic origin, total	55
Mexican	1
Puerto Rican	16
Cuban	1
Other Hispanic	37

Age & Nativity, 2000
Under 5 years	104
18 years and over	1,644
21 years and over	1,594
65 years and over	322
85 years and over	26
Median age	44.2
Native-born	1,589
Foreign-born	594

Educational Attainment, 2000
Population 25 years and over	1,530
Less than 9th grade	2.2%
High school grad or higher	93.6%
Bachelor's degree or higher	62.8%
Graduate degree	28.0%

Income & Poverty, 1999
Per capita income	$76,995
Median household income	$130,740
Median family income	$134,068
Persons in poverty	135
H'holds receiving public assistance	0
H'holds receiving social security	165

Households, 2000
Total households	708
With persons under 18	274
With persons over 65	210
Family households	623
Single-person households	70
Persons per household	3.08
Persons per family	3.24

Labor & Employment
Total civilian labor force, 2007**	1,099
Unemployment rate	2.6%
Total civilian labor force, 2000	1,037
Unemployment rate	2.6%

Employed persons 16 years and over by occupation, 2000
Managers & professionals	591
Service occupations	62
Sales & office occupations	278
Farming, fishing & forestry	0
Construction & maintenance	40
Production & transportation	39
Self-employed persons	93

General Information
Borough of Alpine
100 Church St
Alpine, NJ 07620
201-784-2900
Website	www.alpinenj07620.org
Year of incorporation	1903
Land/water area (sq. miles)	6.36/2.82
Form of government	Borough

Government
Legislative Districts
US Congressional	5
State Legislative	39

Local Officials, 2009
Mayor	Paul Tomasko
Manager/Admin	NA
Clerk	Gail Warming-Tanno
Finance Dir	Irene Kateris
Tax Assessor	Stuart Stolarz
Tax Collector	Irene Kateris
Attorney	Terry Paul Bottinelli
Building	Brian Frugis
Comm Dev/Planning	NA
Engineering	Azzolina & Feury
Public Works	Ralph Wehmann
Police Chief	Thomas Blake
Fire Chief	H. Josh Schneeweiss

Housing & Construction
Housing Units, 2000*
Total	730
Median rent	$1,844
Median SF home value	$1,000,001

Permits for New Residential Construction
	Units	Value
Total, 2006	20	$17,404,392
Single family	20	$17,404,392
Total, 2007	17	$26,659,435
Single family	17	$26,659,435

Real Property Valuation, 2008
	Parcels	Valuation
Total	738	$1,862,212,300
Vacant	73	125,001,500
Residential	646	1,642,416,500
Commercial	19	94,794,300
Industrial	0	0
Apartments	0	0
Farm land	0	0
Farm homestead	0	0

Average Property Value & Tax, 2008
Residential value	$2,542,440
Property tax	$15,809
Tax credit/rebate	$1,194

Public Library
No public municipal library

Library statistics, 2007
Population served	NA
Full-time/total staff	NA/NA

	Total	Per capita
Holdings	NA	NA
Revenues	NA	NA
Expenditures	NA	NA
Annual visits	NA	NA
Internet terminals/annual users	NA/NA	

Public Safety
Number of officers, 2007		13
Crime	**2006**	**2007**
Total crimes	9	14
Violent	4	4
Murder	0	0
Rape	0	0
Robbery	0	1
Aggravated assault	4	3
Non-violent	5	10
Burglary	2	2
Larceny	3	8
Vehicle theft	0	0
Domestic violence	5	4
Arson	1	0
Total crime rate	3.8	5.8
Violent	1.7	1.6
Non-violent	2.1	4.1

Public School District
(for school year 2007-08 except as noted)

Alpine School District
500 Hillside Avenue
Alpine, NJ 07620
(201) 768-6804
Superintendent	Kathleen Semergieff
Number of schools	1
Grade plan	K-8
Enrollment	134
Attendance rate, '06-07	96.2%
Dropout rate	NA
Students per teacher	6.4
Per pupil expenditure	$25,172
Median faculty salary	$49,691
Median administrator salary	$98,280
Grade 12 enrollment	NA
High school graduation rate	NA

Assessment test results
(percent scoring at proficient or advanced level)
	Language	Math
NJASK-Grade 3	92.8%	100.0%
GEPA-Grade 8	93.8%	93.8%
HSPA-High School	NA	NA

SAT Score Averages, 2006-07
Pct tested	Math	Verbal	Writing
NA	NA	NA	NA

Teacher Qualifications
Avg. years of experience	7
Highly-qualified teachers one subject/all subjects	100%/100%

No Child Left Behind
AYP, 2006-07 ... Meets Standards

Municipal Finance
State Aid Programs, 2009
Total aid	$448,834
CMPTRA	0
Energy tax receipts	418,940
Garden State Trust	7,829

General Budget, 2008
Total tax levy	$11,585,892
County levy	3,842,859
County taxes	3,634,556
County library	0
County health	0
County open space	208,303
School levy	4,874,481
Muni. levy	2,868,552
Misc. revenues	2,603,756

Taxes	2006	2007	2008
General tax rate per $100	0.58	0.61	0.625
County equalization ratio	115.04	97.65	89.55
Net valuation taxable	$1,774,526,700	$1,801,859,730	$1,863,234,795
State equalized value	$1,818,295,163	$2,012,002,345	$2,372,059,292

* US Census Bureau
** New Jersey Department of Labor

See Introduction for an explanation of all data sources.

Demographics & Socio-Economic Characteristics

(2000 US Census, except as noted)

Population

1980*	892
1990*	700
2000	658
Male	335
Female	323
2007 (estimate)*	639
Population density	437.7

Race & Hispanic Origin, 2000

Race

White	610
Black/African American	15
American Indian/Alaska Native	5
Asian	15
Native Hawaiian/Pacific Islander	1
Other race	8
Two or more races	4
Hispanic origin, total	17
Mexican	4
Puerto Rican	2
Cuban	0
Other Hispanic	11

Age & Nativity, 2000

Under 5 years	30
18 years and over	515
21 years and over	492
65 years and over	65
85 years and over	5
Median age	38.3
Native-born	622
Foreign-born	36

Educational Attainment, 2000

Population 25 years and over	480
Less than 9th grade	5.4%
High school grad or higher	84.2%
Bachelor's degree or higher	20.0%
Graduate degree	6.5%

Income & Poverty, 1999

Per capita income	$25,914
Median household income	$60,000
Median family income	$69,688
Persons in poverty	18
H'holds receiving public assistance	1
H'holds receiving social security	55

Households, 2000

Total households	261
With persons under 18	85
With persons over 65	50
Family households	181
Single-person households	65
Persons per household	2.52
Persons per family	2.98

Labor & Employment

Total civilian labor force, 2007**	494
Unemployment rate	5.7%
Total civilian labor force, 2000	442
Unemployment rate	4.3%

Employed persons 16 years and over by occupation, 2000

Managers & professionals	117
Service occupations	44
Sales & office occupations	127
Farming, fishing & forestry	10
Construction & maintenance	61
Production & transportation	64
Self-employed persons	14

* US Census Bureau
** New Jersey Department of Labor

See Introduction for an explanation of all data sources.

General Information

Borough of Andover
137 Main St
Andover, NJ 07821
973-786-6688

Email	andover@tellurtan.net
Year of incorporation	1904
Land/water area (sq. miles)	1.46/0.01
Form of government	Borough

Government

Legislative Districts

US Congressional	5
State Legislative	24

Local Officials, 2009

Mayor	John A. Morgan
Manager/Admin	NA
Clerk	Beth Brothman
Finance Dir	Michelle LaStarza
Tax Assessor	Joseph Ferraris
Tax Collector	Jessica M. Caruso
Attorney	Frank McGovern
Building	Brendon O'Connor
Planning	Ken Nelson
Engineering	Harold Pellow
Public Works	NA
Police Chief	NA
Emerg/Fire Director	Frank Greenhalgh

Housing & Construction

Housing Units, 2000*

Total	273
Median rent	$804
Median SF home value	$154,800

Permits for New Residential Construction

	Units	Value
Total, 2006	0	$0
Single family	0	$0
Total, 2007	0	$0
Single family	0	$0

Real Property Valuation, 2008

	Parcels	Valuation
Total	303	$45,220,300
Vacant	46	1,587,500
Residential	191	29,130,500
Commercial	47	12,518,900
Industrial	1	150,200
Apartments	2	968,100
Farm land	11	113,400
Farm homestead	5	751,700

Average Property Value & Tax, 2008

Residential value	$152,460
Property tax	$4,699
Tax credit/rebate	$963

Public Library

No public municipal library

Library statistics, 2007

Population served	NA
Full-time/total staff	NA/NA

	Total	Per capita
Holdings	NA	NA
Revenues	NA	NA
Expenditures	NA	NA
Annual visits	NA	NA
Internet terminals/annual users	NA/NA	

Public Safety

Number of officers, 2007 ... 0

Crime	2006	2007
Total crimes	12	13
Violent	1	2
Murder	0	0
Rape	0	0
Robbery	1	0
Aggravated assault	0	2
Non-violent	11	11
Burglary	5	8
Larceny	5	3
Vehicle theft	1	0
Domestic violence	0	6
Arson	0	0
Total crime rate	18.2	19.9
Violent	1.5	3.1
Non-violent	16.6	16.8

Public School District

(for school year 2007-08 except as noted)

Andover Regional School District
707 Limecrest Road
Newton, NJ 07860
(973) 383-3746

Chief School Admin	Bernard Baggs
Number of schools	2
Grade plan	K-8
Enrollment	710
Attendance rate, '06-07	95.9%
Dropout rate	NA
Students per teacher	9.8
Per pupil expenditure	$13,291
Median faculty salary	$58,997
Median administrator salary	$101,000
Grade 12 enrollment	NA
High school graduation rate	NA

Assessment test results

(percent scoring at proficient or advanced level)

	Language	Math
NJASK-Grade 3	83.5%	90.4%
GEPA-Grade 8	86.7%	95.2%
HSPA-High School	NA	NA

SAT Score Averages, 2006-07

Pct tested	Math	Verbal	Writing
NA	NA	NA	NA

Teacher Qualifications

Avg. years of experience	11
Highly-qualified teachers one subject/all subjects	100%/100%

No Child Left Behind

AYP, 2006-07 ... Meets Standards

Municipal Finance

State Aid Programs, 2009

Total aid	$164,193
CMPTRA	1,512
Energy tax receipts	158,427
Garden State Trust	61

General Budget, 2008

Total tax levy	$1,407,977
County levy	297,671
County taxes	249,806
County library	21,055
County health	7,395
County open space	19,415
School levy	910,634
Muni. levy	199,672
Misc. revenues	392,257

Taxes

	2006	2007	2008
General tax rate per $100	3.27	3.08	3.083
County equalization ratio	59.96	59.34	59.22
Net valuation taxable	$45,238,300	$45,587,731	$45,678,314
State equalized value	$76,653,224	$76,700,557	$79,061,004

Demographics & Socio-Economic Characteristics
(2000 US Census, except as noted)

Population
1980*	4,506
1990*	5,438
2000	6,033
Male	2,889
Female	3,144
2007 (estimate)*	6,520
Population density	323.1

Race & Hispanic Origin, 2000
Race
White	5,698
Black/African American	112
American Indian/Alaska Native	5
Asian	139
Native Hawaiian/Pacific Islander	2
Other race	36
Two or more races	41
Hispanic origin, total	136
Mexican	17
Puerto Rican	57
Cuban	12
Other Hispanic	50

Age & Nativity, 2000
Under 5 years	389
18 years and over	4,522
21 years and over	4,392
65 years and over	950
85 years and over	241
Median age	40.2
Native-born	5,587
Foreign-born	446

Educational Attainment, 2000
Population 25 years and over	4,298
Less than 9th grade	8.7%
High school grad or higher	84.2%
Bachelor's degree or higher	28.6%
Graduate degree	8.8%

Income & Poverty, 1999
Per capita income	$29,180
Median household income	$75,748
Median family income	$78,439
Persons in poverty	186
H'holds receiving public assistance	33
H'holds receiving social security	375

Households, 2000
Total households	1,889
With persons under 18	787
With persons over 65	331
Family households	1,500
Single-person households	304
Persons per household	2.80
Persons per family	3.16

Labor & Employment
Total civilian labor force, 2007**	3,192
Unemployment rate	2.6%
Total civilian labor force, 2000	2,879
Unemployment rate	2.2%

Employed persons 16 years and over by occupation, 2000
Managers & professionals	1,288
Service occupations	271
Sales & office occupations	804
Farming, fishing & forestry	0
Construction & maintenance	200
Production & transportation	254
Self-employed persons	176

General Information
Township of Andover
134 Newton Sparta Rd
Newton, NJ 07860
973-383-4280

Website	www.andovertwp.org
Year of incorporation	1864
Land/water area (sq. miles)	20.18/0.57
Form of government	Township

Government
Legislative Districts
US Congressional	5
State Legislative	24

Local Officials, 2009
Mayor	Bob Smith
Administrator	Jayme Alfano
Clerk	Vita Thompson
Finance Officer	Tim Day
Tax Assessor	Jack Marchione
Tax Collector	Daryn Cashin
Attorney	Fred Semrau
Building	James Cutler
Planning	Linda Paolucci
Engineering	Joseph Golden
Public Works	Darren Dickinson
Police Chief	Phillip Coleman
Emerg/Fire Director	Eric Danielson

Housing & Construction
Housing Units, 2000*
Total	1,968
Median rent	$1,033
Median SF home value	$164,600

Permits for New Residential Construction
	Units	Value
Total, 2006	37	$5,075,869
Single family	37	$5,075,869
Total, 2007	25	$4,246,043
Single family	25	$4,246,043

Real Property Valuation, 2008
	Parcels	Valuation
Total	2,571	$621,533,969
Vacant	211	13,583,100
Residential	2,013	492,553,999
Commercial	124	85,229,300
Industrial	12	6,854,400
Apartments	1	1,700,000
Farm land	157	1,218,870
Farm homestead	53	20,394,300

Average Property Value & Tax, 2008
Residential value	$248,281
Property tax	$7,453
Tax credit/rebate	$1,081

Public Library
No public municipal library

Library statistics, 2007
Population served	NA
Full-time/total staff	NA/NA

	Total	Per capita
Holdings	NA	NA
Revenues	NA	NA
Expenditures	NA	NA
Annual visits	NA	NA
Internet terminals/annual users	NA/NA	

Public Safety
Number of officers, 2007 ... 13

Crime
	2006	2007
Total crimes	57	43
Violent	3	5
Murder	0	0
Rape	0	0
Robbery	0	0
Aggravated assault	3	5
Non-violent	54	38
Burglary	9	8
Larceny	42	29
Vehicle theft	3	1
Domestic violence	36	41
Arson	0	2
Total crime rate	8.7	6.6
Violent	0.5	0.8
Non-violent	8.3	5.8

Public School District
(for school year 2007-08 except as noted)

Andover Regional School District
707 Limecrest Road
Newton, NJ 07860
(973) 383-3746

Chief School Admin	Bernard Baggs
Number of schools	1
Grade plan	K-8
Enrollment	710
Attendance rate, '06-07	95.9%
Dropout rate	NA
Students per teacher	9.8
Per pupil expenditure	$13,291
Median faculty salary	$58,997
Median administrator salary	$101,000
Grade 12 enrollment	NA
High school graduation rate	NA

Assessment test results
(percent scoring at proficient or advanced level)
	Language	Math
NJASK-Grade 3	83.5%	90.4%
GEPA-Grade 8	86.7%	95.2%
HSPA-High School	NA	NA

SAT Score Averages, 2006-07
Pct tested	Math	Verbal	Writing
NA	NA	NA	NA

Teacher Qualifications
Avg. years of experience	11
Highly-qualified teachers one subject/all subjects	100%/100%

No Child Left Behind
AYP, 2006-07 ... Meets Standards

Municipal Finance
State Aid Programs, 2009
Total aid	$619,268
CMPTRA	128,054
Energy tax receipts	419,213
Garden State Trust	49,356

General Budget, 2008
Total tax levy	$18,687,557
County levy	3,486,485
County taxes	2,925,846
County library	246,609
County health	86,614
County open space	227,416
School levy	10,354,607
Muni. levy	4,846,465
Misc. revenues	2,536,685

Taxes
	2006	2007	2008
General tax rate per $100	2.81	2.9	3.002
County equalization ratio	78.52	70.58	68.78
Net valuation taxable	$599,891,370	$617,159,865	$622,525,106
State equalized value	$851,211,838	$896,801,359	$899,941,049

* US Census Bureau
** New Jersey Department of Labor

See Introduction for an explanation of all data sources.

Demographics & Socio-Economic Characteristics

(2000 US Census, except as noted)

Population

1980*	17,015
1990*	16,799
2000	16,930
Male	7,943
Female	8,987
2007 (estimate)*	16,577
Population density	11,592.3

Race & Hispanic Origin, 2000

Race

White	4,194
Black/African American	10,515
American Indian/Alaska Native	55
Asian	119
Native Hawaiian/Pacific Islander	12
Other race	1,098
Two or more races	937
Hispanic origin, total	2,637
Mexican	956
Puerto Rican	1,021
Cuban	35
Other Hispanic	625

Age & Nativity, 2000

Under 5 years	1,539
18 years and over	11,841
21 years and over	11,132
65 years and over	1,891
85 years and over	305
Median age	30.6
Native-born	13,761
Foreign-born	3,169

Educational Attainment, 2000

Population 25 years and over	9,936
Less than 9th grade	9.9%
High school grad or higher	67.6%
Bachelor's degree or higher	11.2%
Graduate degree	3.5%

Income & Poverty, 1999

Per capita income	$13,516
Median household income	$23,081
Median family income	$26,370
Persons in poverty	5,006
H'holds receiving public assistance	707
H'holds receiving social security	1,675

Households, 2000

Total households	6,754
With persons under 18	2,490
With persons over 65	1,622
Family households	3,587
Single-person households	2,658
Persons per household	2.46
Persons per family	3.36

Labor & Employment

Total civilian labor force, 2007**	7,402
Unemployment rate	9.8%
Total civilian labor force, 2000	7,094
Unemployment rate	11.6%

Employed persons 16 years and over by occupation, 2000

Managers & professionals	1,324
Service occupations	1,554
Sales & office occupations	1,806
Farming, fishing & forestry	20
Construction & maintenance	590
Production & transportation	978
Self-employed persons	318

* US Census Bureau
** New Jersey Department of Labor

General Information

City of Asbury Park
1 Municipal Plz
Asbury Park, NJ 07712
732-775-2100

Website	www.cityofasburypark.com
Year of incorporation	1897
Land/water area (sq. miles)	1.43/0.17
Form of government	Municipal Mgr 1923

Government

Legislative Districts

US Congressional	6
State Legislative	11

Local Officials, 2009

Mayor	Kevin G. Sanders
Manager	Terence J. Reidy
Clerk	Stephen M. Kay
Finance Dir	Christine Paulin (Actg)
Tax Assessor	Mary Lou Hartman
Tax Collector	Dorothy Ruth
Attorney	Frederick C. Raffetto
Building	William Gray
Planning	Don Sammet
Engineering	Brian Grant
Public Works	Garrett L. Giberson
Police Chief	Mark Kinmon
Emerg/Fire Director	Kevin Keddy

Housing & Construction

Housing Units, 2000*

Total	7,744
Median rent	$615
Median SF home value	$92,800

Permits for New Residential Construction

	Units	Value
Total, 2006	442	$3,508,415
Single family	5	$1,277,864
Total, 2007	46	$1,247,748
Single family	8	$1,031,660

Real Property Valuation, 2008

	Parcels	Valuation
Total	4,157	$427,707,600
Vacant	670	19,585,500
Residential	2,971	263,924,200
Commercial	375	85,967,600
Industrial	3	694,100
Apartments	138	57,536,200
Farm land	0	0
Farm homestead	0	0

Average Property Value & Tax, 2008

Residential value	$88,833
Property tax	$4,275
Tax credit/rebate	$870

Public Library

Asbury Park Public Library
500 First Ave
Asbury Park, NJ 07712
732-774-4221

Director .... Robert Stewart

Library statistics, 2007

Population served	16,930
Full-time/total staff	2/8

	Total	Per capita
Holdings	129,732	7.66
Revenues	$591,034	$34.91
Expenditures	$593,421	$35.05
Annual visits	57,059	3.37
Internet terminals/annual users	12/40,716	

Public Safety

Number of officers, 2007	90

Crime	2006	2007
Total crimes	1,305	1,070
Violent	387	351
Murder	8	6
Rape	7	11
Robbery	194	184
Aggravated assault	178	150
Non-violent	918	719
Burglary	284	235
Larceny	541	412
Vehicle theft	93	72
Domestic violence	424	317
Arson	11	4
Total crime rate	78.5	64.7
Violent	23.3	21.2
Non-violent	55.2	43.5

Public School District

(for school year 2007-08 except as noted)

Asbury Park School District
603 Mattison Avenue
Asbury Park, NJ 07712
(732) 776-2606

Superintendent	James T. Parham (Actg)
Number of schools	4
Grade plan	K-12
Enrollment	2,176
Attendance rate, '06-07	90.4%
Dropout rate	4.2%
Students per teacher	6.0
Per pupil expenditure	$20,104
Median faculty salary	$57,065
Median administrator salary	$99,359
Grade 12 enrollment	66
High school graduation rate	65.6%

Assessment test results

(percent scoring at proficient or advanced level)

	Language	Math
NJASK-Grade 3	64.0%	64.6%
GEPA-Grade 8	14.9%	29.4%
HSPA-High School	14.8%	25.9%

SAT Score Averages, 2006-07

Pct tested	Math	Verbal	Writing
81%	380	361	353

Teacher Qualifications

Avg. years of experience	8
Highly-qualified teachers one subject/all subjects	100%/100%

No Child Left Behind

AYP, 2006-07	Needs Improvement

Municipal Finance

State Aid Programs, 2009

Total aid	$8,776,311
CMPTRA	6,618,963
Energy tax receipts	2,113,467
Garden State Trust	0

General Budget, 2008

Total tax levy	$20,673,499
County levy	3,520,439
County taxes	3,243,812
County library	0
County health	60,321
County open space	216,307
School levy	5,992,658
Muni. levy	11,160,401
Misc. revenues	28,303,001

Taxes	2006	2007	2008
General tax rate per $100	4.323	4.623	4.812
County equalization ratio	40.37	34.22	30.43
Net valuation taxable	$427,795,000	$423,063,224	$429,638,761
State equalized value	$1,252,320,449	$1,386,045,083	$213,183,729

See Introduction for an explanation of all data sources.

Demographics & Socio-Economic Characteristics

(2000 US Census, except as noted)

Population

1980*	40,199
1990*	37,986
2000	40,517
Male	19,852
Female	20,665
2007 (estimate)*	39,684
Population density	3,496.4

Race & Hispanic Origin, 2000

Race

White	10,809
Black/African American	17,892
American Indian/Alaska Native	193
Asian	4,213
Native Hawaiian/Pacific Islander	24
Other race	5,575
Two or more races	1,811
Hispanic origin, total	10,107
Mexican	2,199
Puerto Rican	3,635
Cuban	238
Other Hispanic	4,035

Age & Nativity, 2000

Under 5 years	3,041
18 years and over	30,090
21 years and over	28,568
65 years and over	5,734
85 years and over	744
Median age	34.7
Native-born	30,508
Foreign-born	10,009

Educational Attainment, 2000

Population 25 years and over	26,521
Less than 9th grade	11.9%
High school grad or higher	61.8%
Bachelor's degree or higher	10.4%
Graduate degree	3.2%

Income & Poverty, 1999

Per capita income	$15,402
Median household income	$26,969
Median family income	$31,997
Persons in poverty	9,427
H'holds receiving public assistance	1,208
H'holds receiving social security	4,821

Households, 2000

Total households	15,848
With persons under 18	5,260
With persons over 65	4,445
Family households	8,708
Single-person households	5,902
Persons per household	2.46
Persons per family	3.26

Labor & Employment

Total civilian labor force, 2007**	17,025
Unemployment rate	8.8%
Total civilian labor force, 2000	17,683
Unemployment rate	12.9%

Employed persons 16 years and over by occupation, 2000

Managers & professionals	2,114
Service occupations	7,477
Sales & office occupations	3,430
Farming, fishing & forestry	30
Construction & maintenance	758
Production & transportation	1,599
Self-employed persons	492

General Information

City of Atlantic
1301 Bacharach Blvd
Atlantic City, NJ 08401
609-347-5300

Website	www.cityofatlanticcity.org
Year of incorporation	1854
Land/water area (sq. miles)	11.35/6.00
Form of government	Mayor-Council

Government

Legislative Districts

US Congressional	2
State Legislative	2

Local Officials, 2009

Mayor	Lorenzo T. Langford
Manager	Michael Scott (Actg)
Clerk	Rosemary Adams
Finance Dir	JoAnne Shepherd
Tax Assessor	Novalette Hopkins
Tax Collector	Theresa Elberson
Attorney	Robert L. Tarver
Building	Wally Shields
Planning	William Crane
Engineering	John Faeirheller (Actg)
Public Works	Michael Scott
Police Chief	John Mooney
Emerg/Fire Director	Dennis Brooks

Housing & Construction

Housing Units, 2000*

Total	20,219
Median rent	$561
Median SF home value	$87,500

Permits for New Residential Construction

	Units	Value
Total, 2006	272	$16,489,593
Single family	81	$11,352,145
Total, 2007	70	$14,218,624
Single family	52	$13,762,925

Real Property Valuation, 2008

	Parcels	Valuation
Total	15,365	$20,493,575,600
Vacant	2,365	1,366,814,300
Residential	11,036	2,855,721,200
Commercial	1,771	15,968,033,100
Industrial	11	8,201,400
Apartments	182	294,805,600
Farm land	0	0
Farm homestead	0	0

Average Property Value & Tax, 2008

Residential value	$258,764
Property tax	$4,310
Tax credit/rebate	$708

Public Library

Atlantic City Public Library
1 N Tennessee Ave
Atlantic City, NJ 08401
609-345-2269

Director	Maureen Sherr Frank

Library statistics, 2007

Population served	40,517
Full-time/total staff	6/29

	Total	Per capita
Holdings	129,312	3.19
Revenues	$4,263,707	$105.23
Expenditures	$3,118,656	$76.97
Annual visits	427,749	10.56
Internet terminals/annual users	48/120,153	

Public Safety

Number of officers, 2007 366

Crime	2006	2007
Total crimes	5,357	4,745
Violent	822	886
Murder	18	7
Rape	46	28
Robbery	375	473
Aggravated assault	383	378
Non-violent	4,535	3,859
Burglary	510	548
Larceny	3,821	3,111
Vehicle theft	204	200
Domestic violence	1,618	1,711
Arson	8	16
Total crime rate	132.7	118.7
Violent	20.4	22.2
Non-violent	112.3	96.6

Public School District

(for school year 2007-08 except as noted)

Atlantic City School District
1300 Atlantic Avenue, 5th Floor
Atlantic City, NJ 08401
(609) 343-7200

Superintendent	Fredrick Nickles
Number of schools	11
Grade plan	K-12
Enrollment	6,358
Attendance rate, '06-07	92.0%
Dropout rate	7.8%
Students per teacher	8.7
Per pupil expenditure	$16,598
Median faculty salary	$62,734
Median administrator salary	$111,500
Grade 12 enrollment	453
High school graduation rate	75.6%

Assessment test results

(percent scoring at proficient or advanced level)

	Language	Math
NJASK-Grade 3	75.0%	77.2%
GEPA-Grade 8	33.9%	53.9%
HSPA-High School	48.7%	64.4%

SAT Score Averages, 2006-07

Pct tested	Math	Verbal	Writing
52%	454	432	421

Teacher Qualifications

Avg. years of experience	10
Highly-qualified teachers one subject/all subjects	100%/100%

No Child Left Behind

AYP, 2006-07 ....Needs Improvement

Municipal Finance

State Aid Programs, 2009

Total aid	$7,584,254
CMPTRA	0
Energy tax receipts	7,469,222
Garden State Trust	1,336

General Budget, 2008

Total tax levy	$341,466,813
County levy	53,212,341
County taxes	48,719,703
County library	0
County health	0
County open space	4,492,638
School levy	107,440,124
Muni. levy	180,814,349
Misc. revenues	35,045,474

Taxes	2006	2007	2008
General tax rate per $100	3.696	3.726	1.666
County equalization ratio	64.81	44.42	91.69
Net valuation taxable	$7,915,330,200	$8,155,061,595	$20,503,172,174
State equalized value	$17,825,942,534	$22,213,031,746	$20,409,333,385

* US Census Bureau
** New Jersey Department of Labor

See Introduction for an explanation of all data sources.

Demographics & Socio-Economic Characteristics
(2000 US Census, except as noted)

Population
1980*	4,950
1990*	4,629
2000	4,705
Male	2,274
Female	2,431
2007 (estimate)*	4,631
Population density	3,734.7

Race & Hispanic Origin, 2000
Race
White	4,440
Black/African American	108
American Indian/Alaska Native	3
Asian	58
Native Hawaiian/Pacific Islander	0
Other race	48
Two or more races	48
Hispanic origin, total	165
Mexican	32
Puerto Rican	45
Cuban	13
Other Hispanic	75

Age & Nativity, 2000
Under 5 years	285
18 years and over	3,700
21 years and over	3,585
65 years and over	665
85 years and over	69
Median age	40.2
Native-born	4,410
Foreign-born	295

Educational Attainment, 2000
Population 25 years and over	3,366
Less than 9th grade	4.0%
High school grad or higher	91.5%
Bachelor's degree or higher	36.7%
Graduate degree	11.6%

Income & Poverty, 1999
Per capita income	$34,798
Median household income	$64,955
Median family income	$79,044
Persons in poverty	231
H'holds receiving public assistance	10
H'holds receiving social security	518

Households, 2000
Total households	1,969
With persons under 18	567
With persons over 65	508
Family households	1,259
Single-person households	585
Persons per household	2.39
Persons per family	3.00

Labor & Employment
Total civilian labor force, 2007**	2,747
Unemployment rate	5.3%
Total civilian labor force, 2000	2,583
Unemployment rate	5.9%

Employed persons 16 years and over by occupation, 2000
Managers & professionals	1,131
Service occupations	367
Sales & office occupations	663
Farming, fishing & forestry	0
Construction & maintenance	157
Production & transportation	112
Self-employed persons	180

* US Census Bureau
** New Jersey Department of Labor

General Information
Borough of Atlantic Highlands
100 First Ave
Atlantic Highlands, NJ 07716
732-291-1444
Website	www.ahnj.com
Year of incorporation	1887
Land/water area (sq. miles)	1.24/3.27
Form of government	Borough

Government
Legislative Districts
US Congressional	6
State Legislative	11

Local Officials, 2009
Mayor	Frederick J. Rast III
Administrator	Adam Hubeny
Clerk	Dwayne M. Harris
CFO	Gerard Gagliano (Actg)
Tax Assessor	Eldo Magnani
Tax Collector	Judith Wierchinski
Attorney	Bernard Reilly
Building	Theresa Radigan (Int)
Planning	William Kuzman (Chr)
Engineering	David Marks
Public Works	Robert Dougherty
Police Chief	Jerry Vasto
Emerg/Fire Director	Beau Marios

Housing & Construction
Housing Units, 2000*
Total	2,056
Median rent	$812
Median SF home value	$187,700

Permits for New Residential Construction
	Units	Value
Total, 2006	1	$300,000
Single family	1	$300,000
Total, 2007	3	$1,199,000
Single family	3	$1,199,000

Real Property Valuation, 2008
	Parcels	Valuation
Total	1,828	$633,748,500
Vacant	97	9,634,800
Residential	1,629	552,573,700
Commercial	90	56,800,100
Industrial	4	3,077,000
Apartments	8	11,662,900
Farm land	0	0
Farm homestead	0	0

Average Property Value & Tax, 2008
Residential value	$339,210
Property tax	$7,504
Tax credit/rebate	$1,138

Public Library
Atlantic Highlands Public Library
100 First Ave
Atlantic Highlands, NJ 07716
732-291-1956
Director	Marilyn Scherfen

Library statistics, 2007
Population served	4,705
Full-time/total staff	0/1

	Total	Per capita
Holdings	21,154	4.50
Revenues	$96,067	$20.42
Expenditures	$93,540	$19.88
Annual visits	12,557	2.67
Internet terminals/annual users	2/2,274	

Public Safety
Number of officers, 2007	15

Crime	2006	2007
Total crimes	63	76
Violent	5	6
Murder	0	0
Rape	0	0
Robbery	2	0
Aggravated assault	3	6
Non-violent	58	70
Burglary	3	9
Larceny	55	61
Vehicle theft	0	0
Domestic violence	49	54
Arson	0	0
Total crime rate	13.6	16.5
Violent	1.1	1.3
Non-violent	12.5	15.2

Public School District
(for school year 2007-08 except as noted)

Atlantic Highlands School District
140 First Avenue
Atlantic Highlands, NJ 07716
(732) 291-2020
Superintendent	Christopher Rooney
Number of schools	1
Grade plan	K-6
Enrollment	293
Attendance rate, '06-07	94.7%
Dropout rate	NA
Students per teacher	9.1
Per pupil expenditure	$15,414
Median faculty salary	$53,035
Median administrator salary	$83,200
Grade 12 enrollment	NA
High school graduation rate	NA

Assessment test results
(percent scoring at proficient or advanced level)
	Language	Math
NJASK-Grade 3	93.9%	81.8%
GEPA-Grade 8	NA	NA
HSPA-High School	NA	NA

SAT Score Averages, 2006-07
Pct tested	Math	Verbal	Writing
NA	NA	NA	NA

Teacher Qualifications
Avg. years of experience	9
Highly-qualified teachers one subject/all subjects	100%/100%

No Child Left Behind
AYP, 2006-07	Meets Standards

Municipal Finance
State Aid Programs, 2009
Total aid	$419,174
CMPTRA	68,809
Energy tax receipts	339,885
Garden State Trust	0

General Budget, 2008
Total tax levy	$14,049,355
County levy	2,284,020
County taxes	1,993,976
County library	119,997
County health	37,078
County open space	132,969
School levy	7,912,491
Muni. levy	3,852,844
Misc. revenues	3,387,604

Taxes
	2006	2007	2008
General tax rate per $100	2.157	2.15	2.213
County equalization ratio	82.98	76.41	71.95
Net valuation taxable	$618,802,400	$632,709,049	$635,126,242
State equalized value	$811,643,298	$878,731,135	$1,353,725,093

See Introduction for an explanation of all data sources.

Demographics & Socio-Economic Characteristics
(2000 US Census, except as noted)

Population
1980*	9,533
1990*	9,205
2000	9,182
Male	4,391
Female	4,791
2007 (estimate)*	8,881
Population density	5,960.4

Race & Hispanic Origin, 2000
Race
White	8,938
Black/African American	48
American Indian/Alaska Native	10
Asian	82
Native Hawaiian/Pacific Islander	1
Other race	44
Two or more races	59
Hispanic origin, total	139
Mexican	21
Puerto Rican	68
Cuban	9
Other Hispanic	41

Age & Nativity, 2000
Under 5 years	507
18 years and over	6,907
21 years and over	6,613
65 years and over	1,456
85 years and over	192
Median age	38.1
Native-born	8,935
Foreign-born	247

Educational Attainment, 2000
Population 25 years and over	6,289
Less than 9th grade	4.0%
High school grad or higher	87.4%
Bachelor's degree or higher	25.1%
Graduate degree	6.3%

Income & Poverty, 1999
Per capita income	$24,942
Median household income	$49,250
Median family income	$59,115
Persons in poverty	502
H'holds receiving public assistance	50
H'holds receiving social security	1,159

Households, 2000
Total households	3,673
With persons under 18	1,207
With persons over 65	1,096
Family households	2,388
Single-person households	1,113
Persons per household	2.50
Persons per family	3.16

Labor & Employment
Total civilian labor force, 2007**	5,049
Unemployment rate	1.6%
Total civilian labor force, 2000	4,752
Unemployment rate	1.7%

Employed persons 16 years and over by occupation, 2000
Managers & professionals	1,640
Service occupations	675
Sales & office occupations	1,364
Farming, fishing & forestry	6
Construction & maintenance	494
Production & transportation	493
Self-employed persons	211

General Information
Borough of Audubon
606 W Nicholson Rd
Audubon, NJ 08106
856-547-0711
Website	www.boroughofaudubon.com
Year of incorporation	1905
Land/water area (sq. miles)	1.49/0.02
Form of government	Commission

Government
Legislative Districts
US Congressional	1
State Legislative	5

Local Officials, 2009
Mayor	Chris Tassi Jr
Administrator	David Taraschi
Clerk	Nancy Doman
Finance Dir	Jack Bruno
Tax Assessor	Douglas Kolton
Tax Collector	Dottie Samartino
Attorney	Joe Nardi
Building	Duane Wallace
Comm Dev/Planning	NA
Engineering	Michael Angelastro
Public Works	David Taraschi
Police Chief	Thomas Tassi
Emerg/Fire Director	Anthony Lepone

Housing & Construction
Housing Units, 2000*
Total	3,813
Median rent	$598
Median SF home value	$107,200

Permits for New Residential Construction
	Units	Value
Total, 2006	7	$460,086
Single family	4	$459,236
Total, 2007	2	$437,300
Single family	0	$286,300

Real Property Valuation, 2008
	Parcels	Valuation
Total	3,216	$353,426,750
Vacant	47	1,088,400
Residential	2,999	294,183,350
Commercial	154	50,105,100
Industrial	1	140,000
Apartments	15	7,909,900
Farm land	0	0
Farm homestead	0	0

Average Property Value & Tax, 2008
Residential value	$98,094
Property tax	$5,217
Tax credit/rebate	$951

Public Library
Audubon Public Library
239 Oakland Ave
Audubon, NJ 08106
856-547-8686
Admin Coord	Kathy Ostberg

Library statistics, 2007
Population served	9,182
Full-time/total staff	0/0

	Total	Per capita
Holdings	25,622	2.79
Revenues	$239,553	$26.09
Expenditures	$153,682	$16.74
Annual visits	16,850	1.84
Internet terminals/annual users		5/2,663

Public Safety
Number of officers, 2007	22

Crime	2006	2007
Total crimes	262	272
Violent	8	9
Murder	0	0
Rape	1	1
Robbery	4	4
Aggravated assault	3	4
Non-violent	254	263
Burglary	37	27
Larceny	210	226
Vehicle theft	7	10
Domestic violence	49	34
Arson	3	2
Total crime rate	29.0	30.3
Violent	0.9	1.0
Non-violent	28.1	29.3

Public School District
(for school year 2007-08 except as noted)

Audubon School District
350 Edgewood Avenue
Audubon, NJ 08106
(856) 547-1325
Superintendent	Donald Borden
Number of schools	3
Grade plan	K-12
Enrollment	1,523
Attendance rate, '06-07	94.8%
Dropout rate	1.6%
Students per teacher	10.7
Per pupil expenditure	$12,438
Median faculty salary	$56,900
Median administrator salary	$107,852
Grade 12 enrollment	172
High school graduation rate	97.2%

Assessment test results
(percent scoring at proficient or advanced level)
	Language	Math
NJASK-Grade 3	95.6%	90.1%
GEPA-Grade 8	82.8%	86.8%
HSPA-High School	76.0%	82.3%

SAT Score Averages, 2006-07
Pct tested	Math	Verbal	Writing
62%	514	489	477

Teacher Qualifications
Avg. years of experience	12
Highly-qualified teachers one subject/all subjects	100%/99.0%

No Child Left Behind
AYP, 2006-07	Meets Standards

Municipal Finance
State Aid Programs, 2009
Total aid	$1,069,881
CMPTRA	229,282
Energy tax receipts	813,852
Garden State Trust	0

General Budget, 2008
Total tax levy	$18,835,401
County levy	4,434,568
County taxes	4,285,393
County library	0
County health	0
County open space	149,175
School levy	10,088,255
Muni. levy	4,312,578
Misc. revenues	4,484,060

Taxes
	2006	2007	2008
General tax rate per $100	5.029	5.208	5.319
County equalization ratio	61.07	51.16	47.79
Net valuation taxable	$345,377,650	$353,050,643	$354,148,622
State equalized value	$675,502,642	$738,350,119	$764,887,818

* US Census Bureau
** New Jersey Department of Labor

See Introduction for an explanation of all data sources.

Demographics & Socio-Economic Characteristics

(2000 US Census, except as noted)

Population

1980*	1,274
1990*	1,150
2000	1,102
Male	492
Female	610
2007 (estimate)*	1,058
Population density	7,053.3

Race & Hispanic Origin, 2000

Race

White	1,090
Black/African American	4
American Indian/Alaska Native	1
Asian	2
Native Hawaiian/Pacific Islander	0
Other race	1
Two or more races	4
Hispanic origin, total	7
Mexican	2
Puerto Rican	0
Cuban	0
Other Hispanic	5

Age & Nativity, 2000

Under 5 years	45
18 years and over	868
21 years and over	843
65 years and over	202
85 years and over	18
Median age	41.9
Native-born	1,092
Foreign-born	10

Educational Attainment, 2000

Population 25 years and over	809
Less than 9th grade	5.4%
High school grad or higher	71.8%
Bachelor's degree or higher	3.2%
Graduate degree	0.4%

Income & Poverty, 1999

Per capita income	$16,926
Median household income	$34,643
Median family income	$41,029
Persons in poverty	97
H'holds receiving public assistance	25
H'holds receiving social security	170

Households, 2000

Total households	496
With persons under 18	128
With persons over 65	165
Family households	302
Single-person households	175
Persons per household	2.22
Persons per family	2.88

Labor & Employment

Total civilian labor force, 2007**	551
Unemployment rate	3.8%
Total civilian labor force, 2000	518
Unemployment rate	3.7%

Employed persons 16 years and over by occupation, 2000

Managers & professionals	79
Service occupations	88
Sales & office occupations	178
Farming, fishing & forestry	0
Construction & maintenance	43
Production & transportation	111
Self-employed persons	15

‡ Branch of county library
* US Census Bureau
** New Jersey Department of Labor

See Introduction for an explanation of all data sources.

General Information

Borough of Audubon Park
20 Road C, Second Floor
Audubon Park, NJ 08106
856-547-5236

Website	audubonparknj.org
Year of incorporation	1947
Land/water area (sq. miles)	0.15/0.02
Form of government	Borough

Government

Legislative Districts

US Congressional	1
State Legislative	6

Local Officials, 2009

Mayor	Lawrence E. Pennock
Manager/Admin	NA
Clerk	Dawn M. Pennock
Finance Dir	Dawn Thompson
Tax Assessor	Stephen Kessler
Tax Collector	Andrea Penny
Attorney	Stuart Platt
Building	NA
Comm Dev/Planning	NA
Engineering	Frank Seney
Public Works	Ken Whalen
Police Chief	NA
Emerg/Fire Director	Richard Pritchard

Housing & Construction

Housing Units, 2000*

Total	499
Median rent	$474
Median SF home value	$47,400

Permits for New Residential Construction

	Units	Value
Total, 2006	0	$0
Single family	0	$0
Total, 2007	0	$0
Single family	0	$0

Real Property Valuation, 2008

	Parcels	Valuation
Total	1	$9,267,500
Vacant	0	0
Residential	0	0
Commercial	0	0
Industrial	0	0
Apartments	1	9,267,500
Farm land	0	0
Farm homestead	0	0

Average Property Value & Tax, 2008

Residential value	$0
Property tax	$0
Tax credit/rebate	$641

Public Library

Audubon Park Library‡
20 Road C
Audubon Park, NJ 08106
856-547-9583

Librarian	Dorathea Zeoli

Library statistics, 2007

see Camden County profile
for library system statistics

Public Safety

Number of officers, 2007 ... 0

Crime	2006	2007
Total crimes	33	16
Violent	1	0
Murder	0	0
Rape	0	0
Robbery	0	0
Aggravated assault	1	0
Non-violent	32	16
Burglary	8	1
Larceny	21	13
Vehicle theft	3	2
Domestic violence	0	2
Arson	0	0
Total crime rate	30.6	14.9
Violent	0.9	0.0
Non-violent	29.6	14.9

Public School District

(for school year 2007-08 except as noted)

Audubon Park School District
20 Road C
Audubon Park, NJ 08106

No schools in district - sends students to
Audubon Borough schools

Per pupil expenditure	NA
Median faculty salary	NA
Median administrator salary	NA
Grade 12 enrollment	NA
High school graduation rate	NA

Assessment test results

(percent scoring at proficient or advanced level)

	Language	Math
NJASK-Grade 3	NA	NA
GEPA-Grade 8	NA	NA
HSPA-High School	NA	NA

SAT Score Averages, 2006-07

Pct tested	Math	Verbal	Writing
NA	NA	NA	NA

Teacher Qualifications

Avg. years of experience	NA
Highly-qualified teachers one subject/all subjects	NA/NA

No Child Left Behind

AYP, 2006-07 ... NA

Municipal Finance

State Aid Programs, 2009

Total aid	$123,190
CMPTRA	86,469
Energy tax receipts	36,105
Garden State Trust	0

General Budget, 2008

Total tax levy	$749,793
County levy	60,498
County taxes	54,676
County library	3,919
County health	0
County open space	1,902
School levy	209,224
Muni. levy	480,071
Misc. revenues	367,683

Taxes

	2006	2007	2008
General tax rate per $100	6.56	7.192	7.987
County equalization ratio	100	100	100.00
Net valuation taxable	$9,267,500	$9,300,056	$9,387,705
State equalized value	$9,299,122	$9,300,056	$9,387,705

Demographics & Socio-Economic Characteristics

(2000 US Census, except as noted)

Population

1980*	2,162
1990*	1,809
2000	2,143
Male	1,043
Female	1,100
2007 (estimate)*	2,103
Population density	499.5

Race & Hispanic Origin, 2000

Race
White	2,115
Black/African American	3
American Indian/Alaska Native	0
Asian	12
Native Hawaiian/Pacific Islander	1
Other race	1
Two or more races	11
Hispanic origin, total	12
Mexican	5
Puerto Rican	3
Cuban	0
Other Hispanic	4

Age & Nativity, 2000

Under 5 years	61
18 years and over	1,841
21 years and over	1,816
65 years and over	701
85 years and over	52
Median age	56.0
Native-born	2,106
Foreign-born	37

Educational Attainment, 2000

Population 25 years and over	1,780
Less than 9th grade	0.3%
High school grad or higher	93.1%
Bachelor's degree or higher	37.9%
Graduate degree	11.0%

Income & Poverty, 1999

Per capita income	$50,016
Median household income	$59,196
Median family income	$72,750
Persons in poverty	93
H'holds receiving public assistance	0
H'holds receiving social security	475

Households, 2000

Total households	1,045
With persons under 18	147
With persons over 65	479
Family households	669
Single-person households	349
Persons per household	2.05
Persons per family	2.56

Labor & Employment

Total civilian labor force, 2007**	1,064
Unemployment rate	2.7%
Total civilian labor force, 2000	884
Unemployment rate	3.3%

Employed persons 16 years and over by occupation, 2000
Managers & professionals	355
Service occupations	109
Sales & office occupations	257
Farming, fishing & forestry	5
Construction & maintenance	73
Production & transportation	56
Self-employed persons	95

* US Census Bureau
** New Jersey Department of Labor

General Information

Borough of Avalon
3100 Dune Dr
Avalon, NJ 08202
609-967-8200

Website	www.avalonboro.org
Year of incorporation	1892
Land/water area (sq. miles)	4.21/0.67
Form of government	Mayor-Council

Government

Legislative Districts

US Congressional	2
State Legislative	1

Local Officials, 2009

Mayor	Martin Pagliughi
Manager	Andrew Bednarek
Clerk	Amy Kleuskens
Finance Dir	James Craft
Tax Assessor	Jeffrey Hesley
Tax Collector	Connie DiCola
Attorney	Stephen D. Barse
Building	Salvatore DeSimone
Comm Dev/Planning	NA
Engineering	Thomas R. Thorton
Public Works	William Macomber
Police Chief	David P. Dean
Emerg/Fire Director	Ed Dean

Housing & Construction

Housing Units, 2000*

Total	5,281
Median rent	$719
Median SF home value	$443,300

Permits for New Residential Construction

	Units	Value
Total, 2006	93	$51,378,624
Single family	77	$48,085,574
Total, 2007	80	$56,534,185
Single family	68	$53,006,035

Real Property Valuation, 2008

	Parcels	Valuation
Total	5,545	$8,702,545,700
Vacant	216	289,371,000
Residential	5,183	8,227,657,900
Commercial	146	185,516,800
Industrial	0	0
Apartments	0	0
Farm land	0	0
Farm homestead	0	0

Average Property Value & Tax, 2008

Residential value	$1,587,432
Property tax	$5,815
Tax credit/rebate	$1,017

Public Library

Avalon Free Public Library
235 32nd Street
Avalon, NJ 08202
609-967-7155

Director	Norman Gluckman

Library statistics, 2007

Population served	2,143
Full-time/total staff	2/5

	Total	Per capita
Holdings	42,111	19.65
Revenues	$2,386,052	$1,113.42
Expenditures	$2,068,825	$965.39
Annual visits	33,120	15.45
Internet terminals/annual users	18/15,370	

Public Safety

Number of officers, 2007	20

Crime	2006	2007
Total crimes	311	302
Violent	6	4
Murder	0	0
Rape	1	1
Robbery	0	0
Aggravated assault	5	3
Non-violent	305	298
Burglary	45	48
Larceny	256	247
Vehicle theft	4	3
Domestic violence	2	10
Arson	1	1
Total crime rate	145.8	142.1
Violent	2.8	1.9
Non-violent	143.0	140.2

Public School District

(for school year 2007-08 except as noted)

Avalon School District
235 32nd Street
Avalon, NJ 08202
(609) 967-7544

Chief School Admin	David Rauenzahn
Number of schools	1
Grade plan	K-8
Enrollment	77
Attendance rate, '06-07	94.1%
Dropout rate	NA
Students per teacher	4.5
Per pupil expenditure	$30,171
Median faculty salary	$68,961
Median administrator salary	$55,539
Grade 12 enrollment	NA
High school graduation rate	NA

Assessment test results

(percent scoring at proficient or advanced level)

	Language	Math
NJASK-Grade 3	91.7%	91.7%
GEPA-Grade 8	NA	NA
HSPA-High School	NA	NA

SAT Score Averages, 2006-07

Pct tested	Math	Verbal	Writing
NA	NA	NA	NA

Teacher Qualifications

Avg. years of experience	20
Highly-qualified teachers one subject/all subjects	100%/100%

No Child Left Behind

AYP, 2006-07	Meets Standards

Municipal Finance

State Aid Programs, 2009

Total aid	$463,850
CMPTRA	0
Energy tax receipts	435,714
Garden State Trust	5,815

General Budget, 2008

Total tax levy	$31,882,793
County levy	14,073,374
County taxes	13,200,189
County library	0
County health	0
County open space	873,185
School levy	2,930,133
Muni. levy	14,879,287
Misc. revenues	5,707,806

Taxes

	2006	2007	2008
General tax rate per $100	0.32	0.35	0.368
County equalization ratio	126.23	104.31	99.92
Net valuation taxable	$8,508,952,600	$8,644,312,225	$8,704,028,556
State equalized value	$8,158,822,719	$8,651,232,019	$8,801,711,089

See Introduction for an explanation of all data sources.

Demographics & Socio-Economic Characteristics
(2000 US Census, except as noted)

Population
1980*	2,337
1990*	2,165
2000	2,244
Male	1,084
Female	1,160
2007 (estimate)*	2,185
Population density	5,081.4

Race & Hispanic Origin, 2000
Race
White	2,180
Black/African American	12
American Indian/Alaska Native	10
Asian	20
Native Hawaiian/Pacific Islander	0
Other race	14
Two or more races	8
Hispanic origin, total	54
Mexican	46
Puerto Rican	2
Cuban	0
Other Hispanic	6

Age & Nativity, 2000
Under 5 years	112
18 years and over	1,831
21 years and over	1,784
65 years and over	501
85 years and over	68
Median age	43.9
Native-born	2,161
Foreign-born	76

Educational Attainment, 2000
Population 25 years and over	1,746
Less than 9th grade	0.8%
High school grad or higher	92.6%
Bachelor's degree or higher	48.0%
Graduate degree	21.2%

Income & Poverty, 1999
Per capita income	$41,238
Median household income	$60,192
Median family income	$80,605
Persons in poverty	61
H'holds receiving public assistance	9
H'holds receiving social security	389

Households, 2000
Total households	1,043
With persons under 18	210
With persons over 65	376
Family households	535
Single-person households	429
Persons per household	2.15
Persons per family	3.04

Labor & Employment
Total civilian labor force, 2007**	1,280
Unemployment rate	3.8%
Total civilian labor force, 2000	1,198
Unemployment rate	3.7%

Employed persons 16 years and over by occupation, 2000
Managers & professionals	584
Service occupations	132
Sales & office occupations	306
Farming, fishing & forestry	4
Construction & maintenance	72
Production & transportation	56
Self-employed persons	112

* US Census Bureau
** New Jersey Department of Labor

General Information
Borough of Avon-by-the-Sea
301 Main St
Avon By the Sea, NJ 07717
732-502-4510

Email	avonboro@aol.com
Year of incorporation	1900
Land/water area (sq. miles)	0.43/0.12
Form of government	Commission

Government
Legislative Districts
US Congressional	6
State Legislative	11

Local Officials, 2009
Mayor	Robert Mahon
Administrator	Timothy Gallagher
Clerk	Timothy Gallagher
Finance Dir	John Antonides
Tax Assessor	Tim Anfuso
Tax Collector	Kerry McGrath
Attorney	Barry Cooke
Building	Paul Orlando
Comm Dev/Planning	NA
Engineering	Charles Rooney
Public Works	Jeff Bramhall
Police Chief	Terry Mahon
Emerg/Fire Director	Steve Kegelman

Housing & Construction
Housing Units, 2000*
Total	1,387
Median rent	$789
Median SF home value	$370,100

Permits for New Residential Construction
	Units	Value
Total, 2006	7	$3,099,500
Single family	7	$3,099,500
Total, 2007	22	$4,224,072
Single family	11	$3,399,072

Real Property Valuation, 2008
	Parcels	Valuation
Total	1,028	$976,922,400
Vacant	11	6,695,500
Residential	955	908,570,000
Commercial	52	45,193,000
Industrial	2	2,303,600
Apartments	8	14,160,300
Farm land	0	0
Farm homestead	0	0

Average Property Value & Tax, 2008
Residential value	$951,382
Property tax	$8,740
Tax credit/rebate	$1,242

Public Library
Avon Free Public Library
Garfield & Fifth Aves
Avon-by-the-Sea, NJ 07717
732-502-4525

Director	Sheila M. Watson

Library statistics, 2007
Population served	2,244
Full-time/total staff	1/1

	Total	Per capita
Holdings	24,629	10.98
Revenues	$258,675	$115.27
Expenditures	$216,887	$96.65
Annual visits	20,050	8.93
Internet terminals/annual users	7/5,000	

Public Safety
Number of officers, 2007	12

Crime	2006	2007
Total crimes	118	56
Violent	4	2
Murder	0	0
Rape	1	0
Robbery	1	1
Aggravated assault	2	1
Non-violent	114	54
Burglary	20	13
Larceny	93	41
Vehicle theft	1	0
Domestic violence	10	9
Arson	0	0
Total crime rate	53.9	25.9
Violent	1.8	0.9
Non-violent	52.1	24.9

Public School District
(for school year 2007-08 except as noted)

Avon Borough School District
Lincoln and 5th Avenues
Avon, NJ 07717
(732) 775-4328

Superintendent	Helen Payne
Number of schools	1
Grade plan	K-8
Enrollment	144
Attendance rate, '06-07	95.2%
Dropout rate	NA
Students per teacher	9.0
Per pupil expenditure	$16,307
Median faculty salary	$46,782
Median administrator salary	$97,734
Grade 12 enrollment	NA
High school graduation rate	NA

Assessment test results
(percent scoring at proficient or advanced level)
	Language	Math
NJASK-Grade 3	100.0%	100.0%
GEPA-Grade 8	73.7%	88.9%
HSPA-High School	NA	NA

SAT Score Averages, 2006-07
Pct tested	Math	Verbal	Writing
NA	NA	NA	NA

Teacher Qualifications
Avg. years of experience	5

Highly-qualified teachers
one subject/all subjects	100%/100%

No Child Left Behind
AYP, 2006-07	Meets Standards

Municipal Finance
State Aid Programs, 2009
Total aid	$193,509
CMPTRA	3,772
Energy tax receipts	183,448
Garden State Trust	0

General Budget, 2008
Total tax levy	$8,975,706
County levy	2,564,396
County taxes	2,362,892
County library	0
County health	43,939
County open space	157,565
School levy	3,189,310
Muni. levy	3,222,000
Misc. revenues	1,480,863

Taxes
	2006	2007	2008
General tax rate per $100	2.526	2.66	0.919
County equalization ratio	41.69	34	93.46
Net valuation taxable	$307,753,800	$311,136,658	$977,092,739
State equalized value	$905,226,078	$1,036,646,561	$894,107,000

See Introduction for an explanation of all data sources.

Demographics & Socio-Economic Characteristics
(2000 US Census, except as noted)

Population
1980*	619
1990*	675
2000	764
Male	389
Female	375
2007 (estimate)*	835
Population density	1,159.7

Race & Hispanic Origin, 2000
Race
White	751
Black/African American	4
American Indian/Alaska Native	0
Asian	2
Native Hawaiian/Pacific Islander	2
Other race	3
Two or more races	2
Hispanic origin, total	6
Mexican	3
Puerto Rican	1
Cuban	0
Other Hispanic	2

Age & Nativity, 2000
Under 5 years	25
18 years and over	654
21 years and over	641
65 years and over	262
85 years and over	23
Median age	54.9
Native-born	747
Foreign-born	25

Educational Attainment, 2000
Population 25 years and over	610
Less than 9th grade	2.0%
High school grad or higher	92.1%
Bachelor's degree or higher	38.9%
Graduate degree	17.4%

Income & Poverty, 1999
Per capita income	$34,599
Median household income	$52,361
Median family income	$66,406
Persons in poverty	36
H'holds receiving public assistance	3
H'holds receiving social security	202

Households, 2000
Total households	371
With persons under 18	61
With persons over 65	182
Family households	230
Single-person households	129
Persons per household	2.05
Persons per family	2.60

Labor & Employment
Total civilian labor force, 2007**	369
Unemployment rate	3.0%
Total civilian labor force, 2000	300
Unemployment rate	2.7%

Employed persons 16 years and over by occupation, 2000
Managers & professionals	119
Service occupations	38
Sales & office occupations	68
Farming, fishing & forestry	19
Construction & maintenance	33
Production & transportation	15
Self-employed persons	55

* US Census Bureau
** New Jersey Department of Labor

General Information
Borough of Barnegat Light
10 W 10th St
Barnegat Light, NJ 08006
609-494-9196

Website	www.barnlight.com
Year of incorporation	1948
Land/water area (sq. miles)	0.72/0.14
Form of government	Borough

Government
Legislative Districts
US Congressional	3
State Legislative	9

Local Officials, 2009
Mayor	Kirk Larson
Manager	Gail Wetmore
Clerk	Gail Wetmore
Finance Dir	T.C. Kay
Tax Assessor	Bernard Haney
Tax Collector	Joan Marcus
Attorney	Terry Brady
Building	Frank Zappavigna
Comm Dev/Planning	NA
Engineering	Owen, Little, et al
Public Works	Arthur Bahinger
Police Chief	Michael Bradley
Emerg/Fire Director	Keith Anderson

Housing & Construction
Housing Units, 2000*
Total	1,207
Median rent	$772
Median SF home value	$299,400

Permits for New Residential Construction
	Units	Value
Total, 2006	5	$2,318,000
Single family	5	$2,318,000
Total, 2007	7	$2,595,000
Single family	7	$2,595,000

Real Property Valuation, 2008
	Parcels	Valuation
Total	1,292	$1,071,921,000
Vacant	64	34,576,200
Residential	1,179	991,695,500
Commercial	47	44,492,500
Industrial	0	0
Apartments	2	1,156,800
Farm land	0	0
Farm homestead	0	0

Average Property Value & Tax, 2008
Residential value	$841,133
Property tax	$6,265
Tax credit/rebate	$1,052

Public Library
No public municipal library

Library statistics, 2007
Population served	NA
Full-time/total staff	NA/NA

	Total	Per capita
Holdings	NA	NA
Revenues	NA	NA
Expenditures	NA	NA
Annual visits	NA	NA
Internet terminals/annual users	NA/NA	

Public Safety
Number of officers, 2007		0
Crime	**2006**	**2007**
Total crimes	37	13
Violent	0	0
Murder	0	0
Rape	0	0
Robbery	0	0
Aggravated assault	0	0
Non-violent	37	13
Burglary	1	3
Larceny	36	9
Vehicle theft	0	1
Domestic violence	7	2
Arson	0	0
Total crime rate	**45.0**	**15.6**
Violent	0.0	0.0
Non-violent	45.0	15.6

Public School District
(for school year 2007-08 except as noted)

Long Beach Island School District
200 Barnegat Avenue
Surf City, NJ 08008
(609) 494-2341

Superintendent	Robert A. Garguilo
Number of schools	2
Grade plan	K-6
Enrollment	258
Attendance rate, '06-07	94.0%
Dropout rate	NA
Students per teacher	7.1
Per pupil expenditure	$23,574
Median faculty salary	$71,027
Median administrator salary	$95,218
Grade 12 enrollment	NA
High school graduation rate	NA

Assessment test results
(percent scoring at proficient or advanced level)
	Language	Math
NJASK-Grade 3	96.9%	90.6%
GEPA-Grade 8	NA	NA
HSPA-High School	NA	NA

SAT Score Averages, 2006-07
Pct tested	Math	Verbal	Writing
NA	NA	NA	NA

Teacher Qualifications
Avg. years of experience	19
Highly-qualified teachers one subject/all subjects	100%/100%

No Child Left Behind
AYP, 2006-07	Meets Standards

Municipal Finance
State Aid Programs, 2009
Total aid	$102,288
CMPTRA	0
Energy tax receipts	94,867
Garden State Trust	2,377

General Budget, 2008
Total tax levy	$7,985,892
County levy	3,668,023
County taxes	3,149,016
County library	370,080
County health	0
County open space	148,927
School levy	2,872,786
Muni. levy	1,445,083
Misc. revenues	1,443,986

Taxes
	2006	2007	2008
General tax rate per $100	0.706	0.725	0.745
County equalization ratio	101.86	94.11	86.59
Net valuation taxable	$1,049,534,600	$1,062,628,253	$1,072,238,936
State equalized value	$1,115,566,192	$1,227,143,276	$2,680,624,481

See Introduction for an explanation of all data sources.

Demographics & Socio-Economic Characteristics

(2000 US Census, except as noted)

Population
1980*	8,702
1990*	12,235
2000	15,270
Male	7,358
Female	7,912
2007 (estimate)*	21,867
Population density	630.7

Race & Hispanic Origin, 2000
Race
White	14,468
Black/African American	338
American Indian/Alaska Native	14
Asian	152
Native Hawaiian/Pacific Islander	0
Other race	107
Two or more races	191
Hispanic origin, total	590
Mexican	39
Puerto Rican	281
Cuban	68
Other Hispanic	202

Age & Nativity, 2000
Under 5 years	947
18 years and over	11,137
21 years and over	10,637
65 years and over	2,739
85 years and over	223
Median age	39.0
Native-born	14,656
Foreign-born	629

Educational Attainment, 2000
Population 25 years and over	10,068
Less than 9th grade	3.1%
High school grad or higher	84.8%
Bachelor's degree or higher	15.8%
Graduate degree	4.3%

Income & Poverty, 1999
Per capita income	$19,307
Median household income	$48,572
Median family income	$56,093
Persons in poverty	944
H'holds receiving public assistance	122
H'holds receiving social security	2,164

Households, 2000
Total households	5,493
With persons under 18	2,090
With persons over 65	1,879
Family households	4,192
Single-person households	1,110
Persons per household	2.76
Persons per family	3.19

Labor & Employment
Total civilian labor force, 2007**	7,818
Unemployment rate	4.0%
Total civilian labor force, 2000	6,589
Unemployment rate	4.4%

Employed persons 16 years and over by occupation, 2000
Managers & professionals	1,692
Service occupations	1,150
Sales & office occupations	1,864
Farming, fishing & forestry	0
Construction & maintenance	755
Production & transportation	841
Self-employed persons	355

‡ Branch of county library
* US Census Bureau
** New Jersey Department of Labor

See Introduction for an explanation of all data sources.

General Information
Township of Barnegat
900 W Bay Ave
Barnegat, NJ 08005
609-698-0080
Website	www.ci.barnegat.nj.us
Year of incorporation	1977
Land/water area (sq. miles)	34.67/6.16
Form of government	Township

Government

Legislative Districts
US Congressional	3
State Legislative	9

Local Officials, 2009
Mayor	Jeffrey Melchiondo
Administrator	David Breeden
Clerk	Kathleen West
Finance Dir	Kathleen Janeski
Tax Assessor	Ellen Kelleher
Tax Collector	Effie E. Pressley
Attorney	Jerry J. Dasti
Construction Official	Louis Fischer
Comm Dev/Planning	NA
Engineering	John Hess
Public Works	David Breeden
Police Chief	Arthur Drexler
Emerg/Fire Director	Mike Moore

Housing & Construction

Housing Units, 2000*
Total	6,066
Median rent	$898
Median SF home value	$119,200

Permits for New Residential Construction
	Units	Value
Total, 2006	300	$32,081,057
Single family	300	$32,081,057
Total, 2007	176	$26,861,703
Single family	176	$26,861,703

Real Property Valuation, 2008
	Parcels	Valuation
Total	11,527	$2,836,460,545
Vacant	3,585	199,511,100
Residential	7,712	2,415,733,945
Commercial	192	168,459,700
Industrial	15	7,122,700
Apartments	2	43,169,300
Farm land	12	78,500
Farm homestead	9	2,385,300

Average Property Value & Tax, 2008
Residential value	$313,187
Property tax	$5,107
Tax credit/rebate	$966

Public Library
Barnegat Branch Library‡
112 Burr St
Barnegat, NJ 08005
609-698-3331
Branch Librarian	Lydia Lloyd

Library statistics, 2007
see Ocean County profile
for library system statistics

Public Safety
Number of officers, 2007	43

Crime	2006	2007
Total crimes	239	209
Violent	30	28
Murder	0	1
Rape	1	1
Robbery	3	5
Aggravated assault	26	21
Non-violent	209	181
Burglary	51	43
Larceny	152	131
Vehicle theft	6	7
Domestic violence	207	161
Arson	5	5
Total crime rate	**11.8**	**9.9**
Violent	1.5	1.3
Non-violent	10.3	8.5

Public School District
(for school year 2007-08 except as noted)

Barnegat Township School District
550 Barnegat Blvd. North
Barnegat, NJ 08005
(609) 698-5800
Superintendent	Robert Mahon (Int)
Number of schools	5
Grade plan	K-12
Enrollment	3,272
Attendance rate, '06-07	93.3%
Dropout rate	0.2%
Students per teacher	10.8
Per pupil expenditure	$13,346
Median faculty salary	$48,186
Median administrator salary	$86,237
Grade 12 enrollment	252
High school graduation rate	99.6%

Assessment test results
(percent scoring at proficient or advanced level)
	Language	Math
NJASK-Grade 3	94.6%	87.6%
GEPA-Grade 8	73.9%	87.5%
HSPA-High School	76.3%	89.4%

SAT Score Averages, 2006-07
Pct tested	Math	Verbal	Writing
NA	NA	NA	NA

Teacher Qualifications
Avg. years of experience	7
Highly-qualified teachers one subject/all subjects	100%/100%

No Child Left Behind
AYP, 2006-07	Meets Standards

Municipal Finance

State Aid Programs, 2009
Total aid	$1,369,399
CMPTRA	247,005
Energy tax receipts	1,037,079
Garden State Trust	39,416

General Budget, 2008
Total tax levy	$46,354,894
County levy	8,219,479
County taxes	6,778,055
County library	796,548
County health	324,312
County open space	320,563
School levy	26,231,435
Muni. levy	11,903,980
Misc. revenues	7,060,562

Taxes
	2006	2007	2008
General tax rate per $100	3.672	1.594	1.631
County equalization ratio	48.33	110.49	106.22
Net valuation taxable	$984,159,400	$2,790,603,086	$2,842,692,658
State equalized value	$2,347,659,432	$2,627,539,081	$537,336,369

Demographics & Socio-Economic Characteristics

(2000 US Census, except as noted)

Population
1980*	7,418
1990*	6,774
2000	7,084
Male	3,376
Female	3,708
2007 (estimate)*	6,924
Population density	4,300.6

Race & Hispanic Origin, 2000
Race
White	6,490
Black/African American	295
American Indian/Alaska Native	17
Asian	102
Native Hawaiian/Pacific Islander	3
Other race	76
Two or more races	101
Hispanic origin, total	201
Mexican	25
Puerto Rican	122
Cuban	10
Other Hispanic	44

Age & Nativity, 2000
Under 5 years	410
18 years and over	5,588
21 years and over	5,366
65 years and over	1,250
85 years and over	133
Median age	38.2
Native-born	6,825
Foreign-born	227

Educational Attainment, 2000
Population 25 years and over	5,030
Less than 9th grade	4.7%
High school grad or higher	86.2%
Bachelor's degree or higher	25.8%
Graduate degree	5.9%

Income & Poverty, 1999
Per capita income	$24,434
Median household income	$45,148
Median family income	$59,706
Persons in poverty	134
H'holds receiving public assistance	43
H'holds receiving social security	1,001

Households, 2000
Total households	3,028
With persons under 18	842
With persons over 65	968
Family households	1,832
Single-person households	1,016
Persons per household	2.34
Persons per family	3.04

Labor & Employment
Total civilian labor force, 2007**	3,965
Unemployment rate	3.1%
Total civilian labor force, 2000	3,733
Unemployment rate	3.0%

Employed persons 16 years and over by occupation, 2000
Managers & professionals	1,432
Service occupations	450
Sales & office occupations	1,187
Farming, fishing & forestry	6
Construction & maintenance	291
Production & transportation	256
Self-employed persons	248

General Information
Borough of Barrington
229 Trenton Ave
Barrington, NJ 08007
856-547-0706
Website	www.barringtonboro.com
Year of incorporation	1917
Land/water area (sq. miles)	1.61/0.00
Form of government	Borough

Government
Legislative Districts
US Congressional	1
State Legislative	5

Local Officials, 2009
Mayor	John Rink
Manager/Admin	NA
Clerk	Terry Shannon
Finance Dir	Denise Moules
Tax Assessor	Steven Kessler
Tax Collector	Kristy Emmett
Attorney	Timothy Higgins
Building	John Szczerbinski
Comm Dev/Planning	NA
Engineering	Greg Fusco
Public Works	Mike Ciocco
Police Chief	Joseph Eisenhardt
Emerg/Fire Director	Jason Houck

Housing & Construction
Housing Units, 2000*
Total	3,164
Median rent	$607
Median SF home value	$111,200

Permits for New Residential Construction
	Units	Value
Total, 2006	2	$328,250
Single family	2	$328,250
Total, 2007	5	$902,250
Single family	5	$902,250

Real Property Valuation, 2008
	Parcels	Valuation
Total	2,169	$273,613,700
Vacant	56	1,699,000
Residential	2,020	217,466,000
Commercial	75	19,162,000
Industrial	10	18,061,400
Apartments	7	16,921,300
Farm land	0	0
Farm homestead	1	304,000

Average Property Value & Tax, 2008
Residential value	$107,754
Property tax	$6,540
Tax credit/rebate	$1,056

Public Library
No public municipal library

Library statistics, 2007
Population served	NA
Full-time/total staff	NA/NA

	Total	Per capita
Holdings	NA	NA
Revenues	NA	NA
Expenditures	NA	NA
Annual visits	NA	NA
Internet terminals/annual users	NA/NA	

Public Safety
Number of officers, 2007	15

Crime	2006	2007
Total crimes	73	93
Violent	11	13
Murder	0	0
Rape	1	2
Robbery	2	2
Aggravated assault	8	9
Non-violent	62	80
Burglary	11	12
Larceny	41	47
Vehicle theft	10	21
Domestic violence	59	41
Arson	1	0
Total crime rate	10.4	13.3
Violent	1.6	1.9
Non-violent	8.8	11.4

Public School District
(for school year 2007-08 except as noted)

Barrington Borough School District
311 Reading Avenue
Barrington, NJ 08007
(856) 547-8467
Superintendent	Anthony Arcodia (Int)
Number of schools	2
Grade plan	K-8
Enrollment	571
Attendance rate, '06-07	95.0%
Dropout rate	NA
Students per teacher	9.8
Per pupil expenditure	$14,199
Median faculty salary	$45,800
Median administrator salary	$96,631
Grade 12 enrollment	NA
High school graduation rate	NA

Assessment test results
(percent scoring at proficient or advanced level)
	Language	Math
NJASK-Grade 3	88.9%	85.2%
GEPA-Grade 8	85.0%	90.0%
HSPA-High School	NA	NA

SAT Score Averages, 2006-07
Pct tested	Math	Verbal	Writing
NA	NA	NA	NA

Teacher Qualifications
Avg. years of experience	11
Highly-qualified teachers one subject/all subjects	100%/100%

No Child Left Behind
AYP, 2006-07	Meets Standards

Municipal Finance
State Aid Programs, 2009
Total aid	$903,390
CMPTRA	292,474
Energy tax receipts	588,331
Garden State Trust	0

General Budget, 2008
Total tax levy	$16,630,775
County levy	3,499,572
County taxes	3,162,845
County library	226,686
County health	0
County open space	110,041
School levy	9,268,511
Muni. levy	3,862,692
Misc. revenues	2,005,620

Taxes	2006	2007	2008
General tax rate per $100	5.336	5.705	6.070
County equalization ratio	61.83	54.44	50.48
Net valuation taxable	$271,762,900	$271,426,258	$274,025,046
State equalized value	$499,563,406	$537,369,357	$578,998,151

* US Census Bureau
** New Jersey Department of Labor

See Introduction for an explanation of all data sources.

Demographics & Socio-Economic Characteristics
(2000 US Census, except as noted)

Population
1980*	1,334
1990*	1,580
2000	1,510
Male	768
Female	742
2007 (estimate)*	1,547
Population density	20.4

Race & Hispanic Origin, 2000
Race
White	1,493
Black/African American	1
American Indian/Alaska Native	1
Asian	2
Native Hawaiian/Pacific Islander	0
Other race	2
Two or more races	11
Hispanic origin, total	33
Mexican	0
Puerto Rican	17
Cuban	10
Other Hispanic	6

Age & Nativity, 2000
Under 5 years	66
18 years and over	1,105
21 years and over	1,048
65 years and over	161
85 years and over	9
Median age	38.1
Native-born	1,504
Foreign-born	48

Educational Attainment, 2000
Population 25 years and over	1,011
Less than 9th grade	4.5%
High school grad or higher	80.5%
Bachelor's degree or higher	17.9%
Graduate degree	4.8%

Income & Poverty, 1999
Per capita income	$20,382
Median household income	$47,469
Median family income	$51,167
Persons in poverty	81
H'holds receiving public assistance	13
H'holds receiving social security	161

Households, 2000
Total households	548
With persons under 18	215
With persons over 65	122
Family households	410
Single-person households	106
Persons per household	2.76
Persons per family	3.15

Labor & Employment
Total civilian labor force, 2007**	914
Unemployment rate	3.7%
Total civilian labor force, 2000	804
Unemployment rate	3.9%

Employed persons 16 years and over by occupation, 2000
Managers & professionals	178
Service occupations	122
Sales & office occupations	215
Farming, fishing & forestry	5
Construction & maintenance	171
Production & transportation	82
Self-employed persons	75

* US Census Bureau
** New Jersey Department of Labor

General Information
Township of Bass River
PO Box 307
New Gretna, NJ 08224
609-296-3337
Website	www.basriver-nj.org
Year of incorporation	1864
Land/water area (sq. miles)	75.88/2.37
Form of government	Commission

Government
Legislative Districts
US Congressional	3
State Legislative	9

Local Officials, 2009
Mayor	T. Richard Bethea
Manager/Admin	NA
Clerk	Amanda Somes
Finance Dir	Joseph Gross
Tax Assessor	Jay Renwick
Tax Collector	Linda Ash
Attorney	Matt McCrink
Building	John Ewert
Comm Dev/Planning	NA
Engineering	Kris Kluk
Public Works	NA
Police Chief	NA
Emerg/Fire Director	Tom Wetmore

Housing & Construction
Housing Units, 2000*
Total	602
Median rent	$650
Median SF home value	$98,800

Permits for New Residential Construction
	Units	Value
Total, 2006	8	$1,156,357
Single family	8	$1,156,357
Total, 2007	4	$474,545
Single family	4	$474,545

Real Property Valuation, 2008
	Parcels	Valuation
Total	1,088	$201,725,400
Vacant	449	12,596,000
Residential	536	149,795,300
Commercial	41	32,893,200
Industrial	0	0
Apartments	0	0
Farm land	47	525,300
Farm homestead	15	5,915,600

Average Property Value & Tax, 2008
Residential value	$282,597
Property tax	$3,776
Tax credit/rebate	$793

Public Library
Bass River Library
11 N Maple Ave
North Gretna, NJ 08224
609-296-6942
Branch Librarian	Sheila Daugherty

Library statistics, 2007
Population served	1,510
Full-time/total staff	NA/0

	Total	Per capita
Holdings	0	NA
Revenues	$0	NA
Expenditures	$0	NA
Annual visits	NA	NA
Internet terminals/annual users	NA/NA	

Public Safety
Number of officers, 2007	0

Crime	2006	2007
Total crimes	43	54
Violent	2	2
Murder	0	0
Rape	0	0
Robbery	0	1
Aggravated assault	2	1
Non-violent	41	52
Burglary	11	10
Larceny	28	36
Vehicle theft	2	6
Domestic violence	4	15
Arson	3	0
Total crime rate	27.5	34.4
Violent	1.3	1.3
Non-violent	26.2	33.1

Public School District
(for school year 2007-08 except as noted)

Bass River Township School District
11 North Maple Avenue, PO Box 304
New Gretna, NJ 08224
(609) 296-4230
Superintendent	Lawrence Mathis
Number of schools	1
Grade plan	K-6
Enrollment	115
Attendance rate, '06-07	94.6%
Dropout rate	NA
Students per teacher	7.6
Per pupil expenditure	$16,412
Median faculty salary	$47,341
Median administrator salary	$77,347
Grade 12 enrollment	NA
High school graduation rate	NA

Assessment test results
(percent scoring at proficient or advanced level)
	Language	Math
NJASK-Grade 3	85.0%	84.2%
GEPA-Grade 8	NA	NA
HSPA-High School	NA	NA

SAT Score Averages, 2006-07
Pct tested	Math	Verbal	Writing
NA	NA	NA	NA

Teacher Qualifications
Avg. years of experience	11
Highly-qualified teachers one subject/all subjects	100%/100%

No Child Left Behind
AYP, 2006-07	Meets Standards

Municipal Finance
State Aid Programs, 2009
Total aid	$394,683
CMPTRA	33,426
Energy tax receipts	154,423
Garden State Trust	241,618

General Budget, 2008
Total tax levy	$2,711,447
County levy	762,098
County taxes	625,844
County library	57,786
County health	0
County open space	78,469
School levy	1,925,369
Muni. levy	23,979
Misc. revenues	1,479,000

Taxes
	2006	2007	2008
General tax rate per $100	3.254	3.47	1.337
County equalization ratio	55.7	42.15	104.29
Net valuation taxable	$71,868,900	$73,975,271	$202,947,669
State equalized value	$171,165,987	$192,336,654	$189,486,758

See Introduction for an explanation of all data sources.

Demographics & Socio-Economic Characteristics

(2000 US Census, except as noted)

Population
1980*	1,340
1990*	1,226
2000	1,238
Male	587
Female	651
2007 (estimate)*	1,265
Population density	2,144.1

Race & Hispanic Origin, 2000
Race
White	1,213
Black/African American	2
American Indian/Alaska Native	1
Asian	7
Native Hawaiian/Pacific Islander	0
Other race	6
Two or more races	9
Hispanic origin, total	16
Mexican	0
Puerto Rican	0
Cuban	1
Other Hispanic	15

Age & Nativity, 2000
Under 5 years	39
18 years and over	1,047
21 years and over	1,024
65 years and over	312
85 years and over	32
Median age	51.5
Native-born	1,269
Foreign-born	23

Educational Attainment, 2000
Population 25 years and over	1,029
Less than 9th grade	1.3%
High school grad or higher	97.2%
Bachelor's degree or higher	52.8%
Graduate degree	19.9%

Income & Poverty, 1999
Per capita income	$49,639
Median household income	$77,790
Median family income	$93,055
Persons in poverty	39
H'holds receiving public assistance	4
H'holds receiving social security	243

Households, 2000
Total households	584
With persons under 18	103
With persons over 65	223
Family households	350
Single-person households	207
Persons per household	2.12
Persons per family	2.73

Labor & Employment
Total civilian labor force, 2007**	748
Unemployment rate	4.5%
Total civilian labor force, 2000	630
Unemployment rate	4.8%

Employed persons 16 years and over by occupation, 2000
Managers & professionals	285
Service occupations	52
Sales & office occupations	168
Farming, fishing & forestry	0
Construction & maintenance	73
Production & transportation	22
Self-employed persons	97

‡ Branch of county library
* US Census Bureau
** New Jersey Department of Labor

General Information
Borough of Bay Head
PO Box 248
Bay Head, NJ 08742
732-892-0636
Website	www.bayheadnj.org
Year of incorporation	1886
Land/water area (sq. miles)	0.59/0.11
Form of government	Borough

Government
Legislative Districts
US Congressional	4
State Legislative	10

Local Officials, 2009
Mayor	William W. Curtis
Manager/Admin	NA
Clerk	Patricia Applegate
Finance Dir	Michelle Swisher
Tax Assessor	Carey Rowe
Tax Collector	April J. Yezzi
Attorney	Jean L. Cipriani
Building	Douglas Applegate
Comm Dev/Planning	NA
Engineering	William England
Public Works	Charles Tillson
Police Chief	Charles B. Grace Jr
Emerg/Fire Director	William Boyle

Housing & Construction
Housing Units, 2000*
Total	1,053
Median rent	$817
Median SF home value	$450,700

Permits for New Residential Construction
	Units	Value
Total, 2006	8	$3,540,206
Single family	8	$3,540,206
Total, 2007	2	$612,002
Single family	2	$612,002

Real Property Valuation, 2008
	Parcels	Valuation
Total	1,051	$956,781,440
Vacant	47	14,237,040
Residential	954	892,385,400
Commercial	49	49,605,700
Industrial	0	0
Apartments	1	553,300
Farm land	0	0
Farm homestead	0	0

Average Property Value & Tax, 2008
Residential value	$935,414
Property tax	$10,167
Tax credit/rebate	$1,056

Public Library
Bay Head Reading Center‡
136 Meadow Ave
Bay Head, NJ 08742
732-892-0662
Director	Virginia Berkman

Library statistics, 2007
see Ocean County profile
for library system statistics

Public Safety
Number of officers, 2007	8

Crime	2006	2007
Total crimes	51	78
Violent	1	0
Murder	0	0
Rape	0	0
Robbery	0	0
Aggravated assault	1	0
Non-violent	50	78
Burglary	10	13
Larceny	39	65
Vehicle theft	1	0
Domestic violence	3	2
Arson	0	0
Total crime rate	40.5	61.9
Violent	0.8	0.0
Non-violent	39.7	61.9

Public School District
(for school year 2007-08 except as noted)

Bay Head School District
145 Grove Street
Bay Head, NJ 08742
(732) 892-0668
Superintendent	John Ravally
Number of schools	1
Grade plan	K-8
Enrollment	92
Attendance rate, '06-07	94.7%
Dropout rate	NA
Students per teacher	7.6
Per pupil expenditure	$18,389
Median faculty salary	$46,309
Median administrator salary	$50,000
Grade 12 enrollment	NA
High school graduation rate	NA

Assessment test results
(percent scoring at proficient or advanced level)
	Language	Math
NJASK-Grade 3	NA	NA
GEPA-Grade 8	100.0%	100.0%
HSPA-High School	NA	NA

SAT Score Averages, 2006-07
Pct tested	Math	Verbal	Writing
NA	NA	NA	NA

Teacher Qualifications
Avg. years of experience	11
Highly-qualified teachers one subject/all subjects	100%/100%

No Child Left Behind
AYP, 2006-07	Meets Standards

Municipal Finance
State Aid Programs, 2009
Total aid	$220,895
CMPTRA	0
Energy tax receipts	209,850
Garden State Trust	0

General Budget, 2008
Total tax levy	$10,401,554
County levy	5,227,213
County taxes	4,310,589
County library	506,551
County health	206,240
County open space	203,833
School levy	2,567,548
Muni. levy	2,606,793
Misc. revenues	1,559,835

Taxes	2006	2007	2008
General tax rate per $100	0.953	1.039	1.087
County equalization ratio	68.79	59.69	56.53
Net valuation taxable	$938,069,700	$948,161,485	$957,014,986
State equalized value	$1,571,835,250	$1,677,090,483	$1,172,969,725

See Introduction for an explanation of all data sources.

Demographics & Socio-Economic Characteristics
(2000 US Census, except as noted)

Population
1980*	65,047
1990*	61,444
2000	61,842
Male	29,269
Female	32,573
2007 (estimate)*	57,886
Population density	10,281.7

Race & Hispanic Origin, 2000
Race
White	48,631
Black/African American	3,416
American Indian/Alaska Native	106
Asian	2,562
Native Hawaiian/Pacific Islander	30
Other race	4,611
Two or more races	2,486
Hispanic origin, total	11,015
Mexican	631
Puerto Rican	4,244
Cuban	454
Other Hispanic	5,686

Age & Nativity, 2000
Under 5 years	3,603
18 years and over	48,170
21 years and over	46,048
65 years and over	10,237
85 years and over	1,141
Median age	38.1
Native-born	49,372
Foreign-born	12,470

Educational Attainment, 2000
Population 25 years and over	43,359
Less than 9th grade	7.8%
High school grad or higher	78.8%
Bachelor's degree or higher	20.9%
Graduate degree	6.7%

Income & Poverty, 1999
Per capita income	$21,553
Median household income	$41,566
Median family income	$52,413
Persons in poverty	6,262
H'holds receiving public assistance	855
H'holds receiving social security	8,406

Households, 2000
Total households	25,545
With persons under 18	7,795
With persons over 65	8,001
Family households	16,022
Single-person households	8,390
Persons per household	2.42
Persons per family	3.10

Labor & Employment
Total civilian labor force, 2007**	28,446
Unemployment rate	5.3%
Total civilian labor force, 2000	29,496
Unemployment rate	6.5%

Employed persons 16 years and over by occupation, 2000
Managers & professionals	8,811
Service occupations	3,896
Sales & office occupations	8,835
Farming, fishing & forestry	18
Construction & maintenance	2,144
Production & transportation	3,861
Self-employed persons	849

* US Census Bureau
** New Jersey Department of Labor
§ State Fiscal Year July 1–June 30

General Information
City of Bayonne
Municipal Building
630 Avenue C
Bayonne, NJ 07002
201-858-6000

Website	www.bayonnenj.org
Year of incorporation	1869
Land/water area (sq. miles)	5.63/5.63
Form of government	Mayor-Council

Government
Legislative Districts
US Congressional	10, 13
State Legislative	31

Local Officials, 2009
Mayor	Mark A. Smith
Manager	Peter Cresci
Clerk	Robert Sloan
Finance Dir	Terrence Malloy
Tax Assessor	Joseph Nichols
Tax Collector	Joanne Sisk
Attorney	John Coffey
Building	Michael Feurer
Planning	John Fussa
Engineering	Don Schlachter
Public Works	Gary Chmielewski
Police Chief	Robert Kubert
Emerg/Fire Director	Gregory Rogers

Housing & Construction
Housing Units, 2000*
Total	26,826
Median rent	$681
Median SF home value	$155,600

Permits for New Residential Construction
	Units	Value
Total, 2006	134	$12,621,345
Single family	50	$4,874,593
Total, 2007	251	$33,084,521
Single family	36	$3,394,851

Real Property Valuation, 2008
	Parcels	Valuation
Total	13,192	$2,379,682,614
Vacant	441	90,117,400
Residential	11,078	1,503,511,600
Commercial	1,189	340,967,314
Industrial	140	334,446,600
Apartments	344	110,639,700
Farm land	0	0
Farm homestead	0	0

Average Property Value & Tax, 2008
Residential value	$135,720
Property tax	$8,213
Tax credit/rebate	$1,059

Public Library
Bayonne Free Public Library
697 Ave C
Bayonne, NJ 07002
201-858-6973
Director	Sneh Bains

Library statistics, 2007
Population served	61,842
Full-time/total staff	7/24

	Total	Per capita
Holdings	293,814	4.75
Revenues	$2,085,020	$33.72
Expenditures	$2,097,516	$33.92
Annual visits	170,000	2.75
Internet terminals/annual users	42/32,276	

Public Safety
Number of officers, 2007	225

Crime	2006	2007
Total crimes	1,057	1,137
Violent	194	190
Murder	1	1
Rape	4	6
Robbery	87	84
Aggravated assault	102	99
Non-violent	863	947
Burglary	188	212
Larceny	575	632
Vehicle theft	100	103
Domestic violence	357	385
Arson	9	4
Total crime rate	17.6	19.3
Violent	3.2	3.2
Non-violent	14.4	16.1

Public School District
(for school year 2007-08 except as noted)

Bayonne School District
669 Avenue A
Bayonne, NJ 07002
(201) 858-5817
Superintendent	Patricia McGeehan
Number of schools	12
Grade plan	K-12
Enrollment	8,810
Attendance rate, '06-07	94.1%
Dropout rate	0.5%
Students per teacher	12.2
Per pupil expenditure	$11,553
Median faculty salary	$46,160
Median administrator salary	$117,168
Grade 12 enrollment	523
High school graduation rate	96.7%

Assessment test results
(percent scoring at proficient or advanced level)
	Language	Math
NJASK-Grade 3	92.0%	90.3%
GEPA-Grade 8	68.0%	83.2%
HSPA-High School	71.2%	82.9%

SAT Score Averages, 2006-07
Pct tested	Math	Verbal	Writing
74%	459	442	444

Teacher Qualifications
Avg. years of experience	11
Highly-qualified teachers one subject/all subjects	100%/100%

No Child Left Behind
AYP, 2006-07	Meets Standards

Municipal Finance§
State Aid Programs, 2009
Total aid	$10,859,195
CMPTRA	5,720,291
Energy tax receipts	4,976,016
Garden State Trust	0

General Budget, 2008
Total tax levy	$144,119,162
County levy	24,245,047
County taxes	23,601,093
County library	0
County health	0
County open space	643,954
School levy	64,998,081
Muni. levy	54,876,034
Misc. revenues	62,345,993

Taxes
	2006	2007	2008
General tax rate per $100	5.251	5.697	6.052
County equalization ratio	48.73	42.22	37.65
Net valuation taxable	$2,373,915,900	$2,381,422,330	$2,381,576,097
State equalized value	$5,625,098,505	$6,321,742,280	$6,535,892,972

See Introduction for an explanation of all data sources.

Demographics & Socio-Economic Characteristics
(2000 US Census, except as noted)

Population
1980*	1,714
1990*	1,475
2000	1,278
Male	595
Female	683
2007 (estimate)*	1,379
Population density	1,407.1

Race & Hispanic Origin, 2000
Race
White	1,263
Black/African American	1
American Indian/Alaska Native	0
Asian	7
Native Hawaiian/Pacific Islander	0
Other race	1
Two or more races	6
Hispanic origin, total	60
Mexican	52
Puerto Rican	2
Cuban	1
Other Hispanic	5

Age & Nativity, 2000
Under 5 years	62
18 years and over	1,059
21 years and over	1,032
65 years and over	354
85 years and over	43
Median age	48.6
Native-born	1,226
Foreign-born	54

Educational Attainment, 2000
Population 25 years and over	942
Less than 9th grade	2.8%
High school grad or higher	90.2%
Bachelor's degree or higher	35.6%
Graduate degree	14.1%

Income & Poverty, 1999
Per capita income	$30,267
Median household income	$48,355
Median family income	$68,036
Persons in poverty	47
H'holds receiving public assistance	12
H'holds receiving social security	264

Households, 2000
Total households	586
With persons under 18	119
With persons over 65	261
Family households	347
Single-person households	205
Persons per household	2.17
Persons per family	2.80

Labor & Employment
Total civilian labor force, 2007**	652
Unemployment rate	6.8%
Total civilian labor force, 2000	557
Unemployment rate	7.0%

Employed persons 16 years and over by occupation, 2000
Managers & professionals	208
Service occupations	79
Sales & office occupations	130
Farming, fishing & forestry	0
Construction & maintenance	64
Production & transportation	37
Self-employed persons	52

General Information
Borough of Beach Haven
300 Engleside Ave
Beach Haven, NJ 08008
609-492-0111
Website	www.beachhaven-nj.gov
Year of incorporation	1890
Land/water area (sq. miles)	0.98/1.34
Form of government	Commission

Government
Legislative Districts
US Congressional	3
State Legislative	9

Local Officials, 2009
Mayor	Michael J. Battista
Administrator	Richard Crane
Clerk	Sherry Hartman
Finance Dir	Diane Marshall
Tax Assessor	Tracy Hafner
Tax Collector	Sharon Voisine
Attorney	Richard Shackleton
Building	Frank Zappavigna
Comm Dev/Planning	NA
Engineering	Frank Little
Public Works	Kim England
Police Chief	Kevin Kohler
Emerg/Fire Director	Matt Letts

Housing & Construction
Housing Units, 2000*
Total	2,555
Median rent	$697
Median SF home value	$286,300

Permits for New Residential Construction
	Units	Value
Total, 2006	33	$8,630,449
Single family	33	$8,630,449
Total, 2007	27	$8,619,481
Single family	27	$8,619,481

Real Property Valuation, 2008
	Parcels	Valuation
Total	2,671	$1,631,964,792
Vacant	326	49,992,200
Residential	2,222	1,460,757,300
Commercial	111	107,327,192
Industrial	0	0
Apartments	12	13,888,100
Farm land	0	0
Farm homestead	0	0

Average Property Value & Tax, 2008
Residential value	$657,407
Property tax	$6,716
Tax credit/rebate	$1,157

Public Library
Beach Haven Public Library
Third St & Beach Ave
Beach Haven, NJ 08008
609-492-7081
Director	Virginia Donnelly

Library statistics, 2007
Population served	1,278
Full-time/total staff	0/0

	Total	Per capita
Holdings	33,330	26.08
Revenues	$192,353	$150.51
Expenditures	$146,015	$114.25
Annual visits	10,200	7.98
Internet terminals/annual users	3/3,558	

Public Safety
Number of officers, 2007 ... 10
Crime	2006	2007
Total crimes	133	120
Violent	4	5
Murder	0	0
Rape	1	0
Robbery	0	0
Aggravated assault	3	5
Non-violent	129	115
Burglary	11	8
Larceny	114	106
Vehicle theft	4	1
Domestic violence	15	7
Arson	0	0
Total crime rate	98.4	87.8
Violent	3.0	3.7
Non-violent	95.4	84.2

Public School District
(for school year 2007-08 except as noted)

Beach Haven Borough School District
Beach Avenue at Eighth Street
Beach Haven, NJ 08008
(609) 492-7411
Superintendent	Patricia P. Daggy
Number of schools	1
Grade plan	K-6
Enrollment	69
Attendance rate, '06-07	95.0%
Dropout rate	NA
Students per teacher	5.8
Per pupil expenditure	$17,087
Median faculty salary	$41,771
Median administrator salary	$111,202
Grade 12 enrollment	NA
High school graduation rate	NA

Assessment test results
(percent scoring at proficient or advanced level)
	Language	Math
NJASK-Grade 3	NA	NA
GEPA-Grade 8	NA	NA
HSPA-High School	NA	NA

SAT Score Averages, 2006-07
Pct tested	Math	Verbal	Writing
NA	NA	NA	NA

Teacher Qualifications
Avg. years of experience	11
Highly-qualified teachers one subject/all subjects	100%/100%

No Child Left Behind
AYP, 2006-07 ... Meets Standards

Municipal Finance
State Aid Programs, 2009
Total aid	$232,632
CMPTRA	0
Energy tax receipts	225,071
Garden State Trust	0

General Budget, 2008
Total tax levy	$16,677,206
County levy	5,644,218
County taxes	5,389,339
County library	0
County health	0
County open space	254,878
School levy	5,626,877
Muni. levy	5,406,112
Misc. revenues	3,433,787

Taxes
Taxes	2006	2007	2008
General tax rate per $100	0.977	1	1.022
County equalization ratio	86.85	78.97	77.10
Net valuation taxable	$1,600,295,592	$1,623,718,636	$1,632,421,658
State equalized value	$2,027,082,428	$2,105,856,006	$1,684,707,912

* US Census Bureau
** New Jersey Department of Labor

See Introduction for an explanation of all data sources.

Demographics & Socio-Economic Characteristics

(2000 US Census, except as noted)

Population

1980*	7,687
1990*	9,324
2000	10,375
Male	5,111
Female	5,264
2007 (estimate)*	10,789
Population density	3,909.1

Race & Hispanic Origin, 2000

Race

White	9,925
Black/African American	101
American Indian/Alaska Native	13
Asian	117
Native Hawaiian/Pacific Islander	6
Other race	115
Two or more races	98
Hispanic origin, total	438
Mexican	106
Puerto Rican	196
Cuban	53
Other Hispanic	83

Age & Nativity, 2000

Under 5 years	720
18 years and over	7,415
21 years and over	7,038
65 years and over	896
85 years and over	69
Median age	35.2
Native-born	9,928
Foreign-born	388

Educational Attainment, 2000

Population 25 years and over	6,636
Less than 9th grade	1.6%
High school grad or higher	87.4%
Bachelor's degree or higher	13.2%
Graduate degree	3.4%

Income & Poverty, 1999

Per capita income	$21,247
Median household income	$59,022
Median family income	$64,190
Persons in poverty	462
H'holds receiving public assistance	9
H'holds receiving social security	714

Households, 2000

Total households	3,475
With persons under 18	1,584
With persons over 65	678
Family households	2,817
Single-person households	521
Persons per household	2.98
Persons per family	3.31

Labor & Employment

Total civilian labor force, 2007**	6,579
Unemployment rate	4.6%
Total civilian labor force, 2000	5,538
Unemployment rate	4.7%

Employed persons 16 years and over by occupation, 2000

Managers & professionals	1,354
Service occupations	978
Sales & office occupations	1,518
Farming, fishing & forestry	0
Construction & maintenance	769
Production & transportation	656
Self-employed persons	245

General Information

Borough of Beachwood
1600 Pinewald Rd
Beachwood, NJ 08722
732-286-6000

Website	www.beachwoodusa.com
Year of incorporation	1917
Land/water area (sq. miles)	2.76/0.00
Form of government	Borough

Government

Legislative Districts

US Congressional	3
State Legislative	9

Local Officials, 2009

Mayor	Ronald W. Jones Jr
Manager	NA
Clerk	Elizabeth Mastropasqua
Finance Dir	John Mauder
Tax Assessor	Denise Siegal
Tax Collector	Jeanette Larrison
Attorney	William Hiering Jr
Building	Wayne Gibson
Comm Dev/Planning	NA
Engineering	James Oris
Public Works Supervisor	John Behrens
Police Chief	William Cairns
Emerg/Fire Director	Roger Hull

Housing & Construction

Housing Units, 2000*

Total	3,623
Median rent	$926
Median SF home value	$114,400

Permits for New Residential Construction

	Units	Value
Total, 2006	23	$1,878,547
Single family	23	$1,878,547
Total, 2007	21	$2,528,700
Single family	19	$2,393,200

Real Property Valuation, 2008

	Parcels	Valuation
Total	4,120	$1,016,832,200
Vacant	338	19,820,100
Residential	3,700	961,158,300
Commercial	77	33,989,500
Industrial	1	224,900
Apartments	4	1,639,400
Farm land	0	0
Farm homestead	0	0

Average Property Value & Tax, 2008

Residential value	$259,773
Property tax	$3,833
Tax credit/rebate	$753

Public Library

Beachwood Branch Library‡
126 Beachwood Blvd
Beachwood, NJ 08722
732-244-4573

Branch Librarian	NA

Library statistics, 2007

see Ocean County profile
for library system statistics

Public Safety

Number of officers, 2007	18

Crime	2006	2007
Total crimes	249	241
Violent	10	16
Murder	0	0
Rape	0	0
Robbery	4	3
Aggravated assault	6	13
Non-violent	239	225
Burglary	29	42
Larceny	204	181
Vehicle theft	6	2
Domestic violence	114	117
Arson	3	0
Total crime rate	23.2	22.4
Violent	0.9	1.5
Non-violent	22.3	20.9

Public School District

(for school year 2007-08 except as noted)

Toms River Regional School District
1144 Hooper Avenue
Toms River, NJ 08753
(732) 505-5510

Superintendent	Michael J. Ritacco
Number of schools	18
Grade plan	K-12
Enrollment	17,259
Attendance rate, '06-07	93.8%
Dropout rate	2.8%
Students per teacher	13.0
Per pupil expenditure	$10,496
Median faculty salary	$49,126
Median administrator salary	$114,200
Grade 12 enrollment	1,296
High school graduation rate	89.2%

Assessment test results

(percent scoring at proficient or advanced level)

	Language	Math
NJASK-Grade 3	93.4%	94.2%
GEPA-Grade 8	76.3%	87.3%
HSPA-High School	71.8%	83.4%

SAT Score Averages, 2006-07

Pct tested	Math	Verbal	Writing
NA	NA	NA	NA

Teacher Qualifications

Avg. years of experience	8
Highly-qualified teachers one subject/all subjects	99.5%/99.5%

No Child Left Behind

AYP, 2006-07	Meets Standards

Municipal Finance

State Aid Programs, 2009

Total aid	$857,772
CMPTRA	243,245
Energy tax receipts	592,297
Garden State Trust	0

General Budget, 2008

Total tax levy	$15,016,310
County levy	3,215,670
County taxes	2,651,740
County library	311,640
County health	126,881
County open space	125,409
School levy	6,376,040
Muni. levy	5,424,600
Misc. revenues	3,132,981

Taxes

	2006	2007	2008
General tax rate per $100	3.275	1.385	1.476
County equalization ratio	48.56	103.16	97.64
Net valuation taxable	$412,302,200	$1,009,421,076	$1,017,704,713
State equalized value	$966,649,776	$1,033,798,776	$2,156,288,824

‡ Branch of county library
* US Census Bureau
** New Jersey Department of Labor

See Introduction for an explanation of all data sources.

Demographics & Socio-Economic Characteristics
(2000 US Census, except as noted)

Population
1980* 2,469
1990* 7,086
2000 8,302
  Male 3,836
  Female 4,466
2007 (estimate)* 8,362
  Population density 315.9

Race & Hispanic Origin, 2000
Race
  White 7,476
  Black/African American 145
  American Indian/Alaska Native 9
  Asian 532
  Native Hawaiian/Pacific Islander 2
  Other race 69
  Two or more races 69
Hispanic origin, total 319
  Mexican 32
  Puerto Rican 53
  Cuban 22
  Other Hispanic 212

Age & Nativity, 2000
Under 5 years 482
18 years and over 6,822
21 years and over 6,710
65 years and over 890
85 years and over 64
Median age 39.3
Native-born 7,079
Foreign-born 1,223

Educational Attainment, 2000
Population 25 years and over. 6,508
Less than 9th grade 1.5%
High school grad or higher 96.2%
Bachelor's degree or higher 60.4%
Graduate degree 22.6%

Income & Poverty, 1999
Per capita income $53,549
Median household income $71,550
Median family income $96,890
Persons in poverty 254
H'holds receiving public assistance 15
H'holds receiving social security 733

Households, 2000
Total households 4,235
  With persons under 18 902
  With persons over 65 667
  Family households 2,100
  Single-person households 1,862
  Persons per household 1.96
  Persons per family 2.76

Labor & Employment
Total civilian labor force, 2007** 5,801
  Unemployment rate 2.4%
Total civilian labor force, 2000 5,117
  Unemployment rate 2.4%
Employed persons 16 years and over by occupation, 2000
  Managers & professionals 2,924
  Service occupations 345
  Sales & office occupations 1,369
  Farming, fishing & forestry 19
  Construction & maintenance 115
  Production & transportation 223
  Self-employed persons 320

‡ Joint library with Far Hills Borough
* US Census Bureau
** New Jersey Department of Labor

General Information
Township of Bedminster
One Miller Lane
Bedminster, NJ 07921
908-212-7000
Website .... www.bedminster.us
Year of incorporation 1749
Land/water area (sq. miles) 26.47/0.00
Form of government .... Township

Government
Legislative Districts
US Congressional 7
State Legislative 16

Local Officials, 2009
Mayor .... Robert F. Holtaway
Manager .... Judith A. Sullivan
Clerk .... Judith A. Sullivan
Finance Dir .... Debra M. Stern
Tax Assessor .... Edward Kerwin Jr
Tax Collector .... Deborah Giordano
Attorney .... John Belardo
Building .... Kenneth Rogers
Comm Dev/Planning .... NA
Engineering .... Paul Ferriero
Public Works .... John Mantz
Police Chief .... William Stephens
Emerg/Fire Director .... Adam Segal

Housing & Construction
Housing Units, 2000*
Total 4,467
Median rent $1,430
Median SF home value $228,000

Permits for New Residential Construction

	Units	Value
Total, 2006	1	$750,000
Single family	1	$750,000
Total, 2007	6	$4,431,500
Single family	6	$4,431,500

Real Property Valuation, 2008

	Parcels	Valuation
Total	4,791	$2,657,659,543
Vacant	87	14,810,200
Residential	4,049	1,558,141,100
Commercial	131	603,963,600
Industrial	1	470,000
Apartments	0	0
Farm land	310	3,364,943
Farm homestead	213	476,909,700

Average Property Value & Tax, 2008
Residential value $477,487
Property tax $5,315
Tax credit/rebate $696

Public Library
Clarence Dillon Public Library‡
2336 Lamington Rd
Bedminster, NJ 07921
908-234-2325
Director .... Nanette E. Geiger

Library statistics, 2007
Population served 9,161
Full-time/total staff 2/3

	Total	Per capita
Holdings	82,553	9.01
Revenues	$1,068,024	$116.58
Expenditures	$941,688	$102.79
Annual visits	81,135	8.86
Internet terminals/annual users	22/5,264	

Public Safety
Number of officers, 2007 17

Crime	2006	2007
Total crimes	77	62
Violent	3	2
Murder	0	0
Rape	1	0
Robbery	0	0
Aggravated assault	2	2
Non-violent	74	60
Burglary	17	14
Larceny	52	45
Vehicle theft	5	1
Domestic violence	57	58
Arson	1	1
Total crime rate	9.2	7.3
Violent	0.4	0.2
Non-violent	8.8	7.1

Public School District
(for school year 2007-08 except as noted)

Bedminster Township School District
234 Somerville Rd
Bedminster, NJ 07921
(908) 234-0768
Superintendent .... Andrew Rinko
Number of schools 1
Grade plan K-8
Enrollment 600
Attendance rate, '06-07 .... 95.7%
Dropout rate .... NA
Students per teacher 9.0
Per pupil expenditure $17,067
Median faculty salary $51,438
Median administrator salary $116,507
Grade 12 enrollment .... NA
High school graduation rate .... NA

Assessment test results
(percent scoring at proficient or advanced level)

	Language	Math
NJASK-Grade 3	92.2%	92.0%
GEPA-Grade 8	94.7%	100.0%
HSPA-High School	NA	NA

SAT Score Averages, 2006-07

Pct tested	Math	Verbal	Writing
NA	NA	NA	NA

Teacher Qualifications
Avg. years of experience 6
Highly-qualified teachers
  one subject/all subjects 100%/100%

No Child Left Behind
AYP, 2006-07 .... Meets Standards

Municipal Finance
State Aid Programs, 2009
Total aid $1,087,053
  CMPTRA 0
  Energy tax receipts 1,032,087
  Garden State Trust 606

General Budget, 2008
Total tax levy $29,666,977
  County levy 8,274,094
    County taxes 7,449,575
    County library 0
    County health 0
    County open space 824,519
  School levy 14,696,571
  Muni. levy 6,696,312
  Misc. revenues 3,946,443

Taxes

Taxes	2006	2007	2008
General tax rate per $100	1.14	1.12	1.114
County equalization ratio	98.05	97.56	97.12
Net valuation taxable	$2,435,033,000	$2,611,247,886	$2,665,189,213
State equalized value	$2,681,962,293	$2,720,607,723	$2,789,545,312

See Introduction for an explanation of all data sources.

Demographics & Socio-Economic Characteristics

(2000 US Census, except as noted)

Population

1980*	35,367
1990*	34,213
2000	35,928
Male	17,330
Female	18,598
2007 (estimate)*	34,044
Population density	10,192.8

Race & Hispanic Origin, 2000

Race

White	24,950
Black/African American	1,926
American Indian/Alaska Native	60
Asian	4,062
Native Hawaiian/Pacific Islander	26
Other race	3,532
Two or more races	1,372
Hispanic origin, total	8,507
Mexican	158
Puerto Rican	3,430
Cuban	454
Other Hispanic	4,465

Age & Nativity, 2000

Under 5 years	2,133
18 years and over	28,082
21 years and over	26,925
65 years and over	4,806
85 years and over	612
Median age	36.2
Native-born	26,290
Foreign-born	9,638

Educational Attainment, 2000

Population 25 years and over	25,114
Less than 9th grade	8.5%
High school grad or higher	78.2%
Bachelor's degree or higher	21.7%
Graduate degree	5.9%

Income & Poverty, 1999

Per capita income	$22,093
Median household income	$48,576
Median family income	$55,212
Persons in poverty	2,939
H'holds receiving public assistance	321
H'holds receiving social security	3,351

Households, 2000

Total households	13,731
With persons under 18	4,469
With persons over 65	3,543
Family households	9,091
Single-person households	3,828
Persons per household	2.60
Persons per family	3.23

Labor & Employment

Total civilian labor force, 2007**	17,987
Unemployment rate	4.9%
Total civilian labor force, 2000	18,387
Unemployment rate	6.6%

Employed persons 16 years and over by occupation, 2000

Managers & professionals	5,282
Service occupations	2,578
Sales & office occupations	5,453
Farming, fishing & forestry	0
Construction & maintenance	1,398
Production & transportation	2,467
Self-employed persons	619

* US Census Bureau
** New Jersey Department of Labor

General Information

Township of Belleville
152 Washington Ave
Belleville, NJ 07109
973-450-3302

Website	www.bellevillenj.org
Year of incorporation	1981
Land/water area (sq. miles)	3.34/0.07
Form of government	Council-Manager

Government

Legislative Districts

US Congressional	8
State Legislative	28

Local Officials, 2009

Mayor	Raymond Kimble
Manager	Victor Canning
Clerk	Kelly Cavanagh
Finance Dir	Arthur Minsky
Tax Assessor	William Merdinger
Tax Collector	NA
Attorney	Thom Murphy
Building	Frank DeLorenzo
Comm Dev/Planning	NA
Engineering	Tom Herits
Public Works	NA
Police Chief	Joseph Rotonda
Emerg/Fire Director	Robert Caruso

Housing & Construction

Housing Units, 2000*

Total	14,144
Median rent	$752
Median SF home value	$147,500

Permits for New Residential Construction

	Units	Value
Total, 2006	177	$16,791,268
Single family	37	$3,296,748
Total, 2007	99	$9,028,397
Single family	65	$5,528,417

Real Property Valuation, 2008

	Parcels	Valuation
Total	9,500	$3,397,667,700
Vacant	350	62,586,000
Residential	8,374	2,545,600,800
Commercial	506	339,804,000
Industrial	128	167,937,700
Apartments	142	281,739,200
Farm land	0	0
Farm homestead	0	0

Average Property Value & Tax, 2008

Residential value	$303,989
Property tax	$7,450
Tax credit/rebate	$1,101

Public Library

Belleville Public Public Library
221 Washington Ave
Belleville, NJ 07109
973-450-3434

Director	Joan Taub

Library statistics, 2007

Population served	35,928
Full-time/total staff	4/11

	Total	Per capita
Holdings	116,275	3.24
Revenues	$1,157,145	$32.21
Expenditures	$1,111,444	$30.94
Annual visits	64,446	1.79
Internet terminals/annual users	41/10,624	

Public Safety

Number of officers, 2007	105

Crime	2006	2007
Total crimes	1,014	897
Violent	132	118
Murder	0	1
Rape	3	1
Robbery	59	60
Aggravated assault	70	56
Non-violent	882	779
Burglary	163	150
Larceny	502	448
Vehicle theft	217	181
Domestic violence	57	101
Arson	2	2
Total crime rate	29.1	26.0
Violent	3.8	3.4
Non-violent	25.3	22.6

Public School District

(for school year 2007-08 except as noted)

Belleville School District
102 Passaic Avenue
Belleville, NJ 07109
(973) 450-3500

Superintendent	Melindo Persi (Int)
Number of schools	9
Grade plan	K-12
Enrollment	4,435
Attendance rate, '06-07	94.1%
Dropout rate	1.2%
Students per teacher	11.9
Per pupil expenditure	$11,675
Median faculty salary	$57,865
Median administrator salary	$128,767
Grade 12 enrollment	368
High school graduation rate	91.9%

Assessment test results

(percent scoring at proficient or advanced level)

	Language	Math
NJASK-Grade 3	76.4%	78.8%
GEPA-Grade 8	66.0%	86.4%
HSPA-High School	60.2%	70.2%

SAT Score Averages, 2006-07

Pct tested	Math	Verbal	Writing
61%	459	449	442

Teacher Qualifications

Avg. years of experience	9
Highly-qualified teachers one subject/all subjects	99.0%/99.0%

No Child Left Behind

AYP, 2006-07	Needs Improvement

Municipal Finance

State Aid Programs, 2009

Total aid	$7,910,990
CMPTRA	4,632,389
Energy tax receipts	3,159,936
Garden State Trust	0

General Budget, 2008

Total tax levy	$83,374,781
County levy	14,155,396
County taxes	13,607,630
County library	0
County health	0
County open space	547,765
School levy	31,691,984
Muni. levy	37,527,401
Misc. revenues	16,130,363

Taxes

	2006	2007	2008
General tax rate per $100	15.89	2.26	2.451
County equalization ratio	15.28	101.6	94.40
Net valuation taxable	$435,220,350	$3,418,293,147	$3,401,868,650
State equalized value	$3,345,910,882	$3,620,819,591	$3,682,126,583

See Introduction for an explanation of all data sources.

Demographics & Socio-Economic Characteristics

(2000 US Census, except as noted)

Population

1980*	13,721
1990*	12,603
2000	11,262
Male	5,531
Female	5,731
2007 (estimate)*	11,117
Population density	3,669.0

Race & Hispanic Origin, 2000

Race

White	10,450
Black/African American	133
American Indian/Alaska Native	7
Asian	344
Native Hawaiian/Pacific Islander	2
Other race	173
Two or more races	153
Hispanic origin, total	394
Mexican	115
Puerto Rican	202
Cuban	1
Other Hispanic	76

Age & Nativity, 2000

Under 5 years	571
18 years and over	8,922
21 years and over	8,522
65 years and over	1,969
85 years and over	127
Median age	40.1
Native-born	10,415
Foreign-born	847

Educational Attainment, 2000

Population 25 years and over	7,925
Less than 9th grade	6.0%
High school grad or higher	74.5%
Bachelor's degree or higher	10.4%
Graduate degree	2.8%

Income & Poverty, 1999

Per capita income	$19,863
Median household income	$44,653
Median family income	$53,839
Persons in poverty	446
H'holds receiving public assistance	50
H'holds receiving social security	1,690

Households, 2000

Total households	4,446
With persons under 18	1,356
With persons over 65	1,441
Family households	3,136
Single-person households	1,124
Persons per household	2.53
Persons per family	3.02

Labor & Employment

Total civilian labor force, 2007**	6,233
Unemployment rate	4.2%
Total civilian labor force, 2000	5,899
Unemployment rate	4.2%

Employed persons 16 years and over by occupation, 2000

Managers & professionals	1,322
Service occupations	761
Sales & office occupations	1,864
Farming, fishing & forestry	4
Construction & maintenance	672
Production & transportation	1,029
Self-employed persons	234

General Information

Borough of Bellmawr
21 E Browning Rd
PO Box 368
Bellmawr, NJ 08099
856-933-1313

Website	www.bellmawr.com
Year of incorporation	1926
Land/water area (sq. miles)	3.03/0.10
Form of government	Borough

Government

Legislative Districts

US Congressional	1
State Legislative	5

Local Officials, 2009

Mayor	Frank Filipek
Manager/Admin	NA
Clerk	Charles Sauter
Finance Dir	Maria Fasulo
Tax Assessor	John Dymond
Tax Collector	Margaret Sandrock
Attorney	Robert L. Messick
Building	William Glover
Comm Dev/Planning	NA
Engineering	Remington & Vernick
Public Works	Joseph Ciano Jr
Police Chief	William Walsh
Fire Chief	J. Burleigh/T. Calhoun

Housing & Construction

Housing Units, 2000*

Total	4,561
Median rent	$523
Median SF home value	$95,800

Permits for New Residential Construction

	Units	Value
Total, 2006	25	$892,550
Single family	10	$881,195
Total, 2007	22	$924,236
Single family	11	$915,910

Real Property Valuation, 2008

	Parcels	Valuation
Total	3,654	$429,550,300
Vacant	88	4,030,800
Residential	3,391	297,552,200
Commercial	111	40,861,800
Industrial	55	58,522,900
Apartments	9	28,582,600
Farm land	0	0
Farm homestead	0	0

Average Property Value & Tax, 2008

Residential value	$87,748
Property tax	$4,752
Tax credit/rebate	$913

Public Library

Bellmawr Branch Library‡
35 E Browning Rd
Bellmawr, NJ 08031
856-931-1400

Branch librarian	Deborah Stefano

Library statistics, 2007

see Camden County profile
for library system statistics

Public Safety

Number of officers, 2007	24

Crime	2006	2007
Total crimes	270	350
Violent	17	19
Murder	0	0
Rape	1	2
Robbery	4	4
Aggravated assault	12	13
Non-violent	253	331
Burglary	46	78
Larceny	182	227
Vehicle theft	25	26
Domestic violence	74	71
Arson	0	0
Total crime rate	24.2	31.3
Violent	1.5	1.7
Non-violent	22.7	29.6

Public School District

(for school year 2007-08 except as noted)

Bellmawr Borough School District
256 Anderson Avenue
Bellmawr, NJ 08031
(856) 931-3620

Superintendent	Annette Castiglione
Number of schools	3
Grade plan	K-8
Enrollment	1,051
Attendance rate, '06-07	94.7%
Dropout rate	NA
Students per teacher	12.0
Per pupil expenditure	$10,523
Median faculty salary	$56,649
Median administrator salary	$93,269
Grade 12 enrollment	NA
High school graduation rate	NA

Assessment test results

(percent scoring at proficient or advanced level)

	Language	Math
NJASK-Grade 3	76.4%	75.3%
GEPA-Grade 8	75.3%	87.5%
HSPA-High School	NA	NA

SAT Score Averages, 2006-07

Pct tested	Math	Verbal	Writing
NA	NA	NA	NA

Teacher Qualifications

Avg. years of experience	9
Highly-qualified teachers one subject/all subjects	98.5%/98.5%

No Child Left Behind

AYP, 2006-07	Meets Standards

Municipal Finance

State Aid Programs, 2009

Total aid	$1,453,211
CMPTRA	357,042
Energy tax receipts	1,088,903
Garden State Trust	0

General Budget, 2008

Total tax levy	$23,296,057
County levy	5,498,935
County taxes	4,969,095
County library	356,690
County health	0
County open space	173,149
School levy	10,878,047
Muni. levy	6,919,075
Misc. revenues	4,187,946

‡ Branch of county library
* US Census Bureau
** New Jersey Department of Labor

Taxes

	2006	2007	2008
General tax rate per $100	5.02	5.251	5.416
County equalization ratio	63.66	54.99	49.89
Net valuation taxable	$428,087,200	$429,807,409	$430,209,345
State equalized value	$779,290,022	$860,811,163	$842,419,382

See Introduction for an explanation of all data sources.

Demographics & Socio-Economic Characteristics

(2000 US Census, except as noted)

Population
1980*	6,771
1990*	5,877
2000	6,045
Male	3,020
Female	3,025
2007 (estimate)*	5,927
Population density	5,810.8

Race & Hispanic Origin, 2000
Race
White	5,533
Black/African American	209
American Indian/Alaska Native	11
Asian	62
Native Hawaiian/Pacific Islander	0
Other race	120
Two or more races	110
Hispanic origin, total	414
Mexican	198
Puerto Rican	86
Cuban	6
Other Hispanic	124

Age & Nativity, 2000
Under 5 years	293
18 years and over	5,007
21 years and over	4,850
65 years and over	952
85 years and over	113
Median age	38.5
Native-born	5,524
Foreign-born	521

Educational Attainment, 2000
Population 25 years and over	4,553
Less than 9th grade	4.7%
High school grad or higher	89.3%
Bachelor's degree or higher	34.0%
Graduate degree	11.9%

Income & Poverty, 1999
Per capita income	$29,456
Median household income	$44,896
Median family income	$61,250
Persons in poverty	520
H'holds receiving public assistance	76
H'holds receiving social security	763

Households, 2000
Total households	2,946
With persons under 18	564
With persons over 65	726
Family households	1,318
Single-person households	1,305
Persons per household	2.05
Persons per family	2.92

Labor & Employment
Total civilian labor force, 2007**	3,709
Unemployment rate	4.5%
Total civilian labor force, 2000	3,492
Unemployment rate	4.8%

Employed persons 16 years and over by occupation, 2000
Managers & professionals	1,333
Service occupations	461
Sales & office occupations	924
Farming, fishing & forestry	0
Construction & maintenance	314
Production & transportation	292
Self-employed persons	234

* US Census Bureau
** New Jersey Department of Labor

See Introduction for an explanation of all data sources.

General Information
Borough of Belmar
PO Box A
Belmar, NJ 07719
732-681-1176
Website	www.belmar.com
Year of incorporation	1890
Land/water area (sq. miles)	1.02/0.67
Form of government	Small Municipality

Government
Legislative Districts
US Congressional	6
State Legislative	11

Local Officials, 2009
Mayor	Kenneth Pringle
Manager	Robbin Kirk
Clerk	April Claudio
Finance Dir	Robbin Kirk
Tax Assessor	Edward Mullane
Tax Collector	Robbin Kirk
Attorney	Karl Kemm
Building	Ted Bianchi
Comm Dev/Planning	NA
Engineering	Birdsall Engineering
Public Works	Andy Meuerle
Police Chief	Thomas Palmisano
Emerg/Fire Director	John Rizzitello

Housing & Construction
Housing Units, 2000*
Total	3,996
Median rent	$779
Median SF home value	$186,700

Permits for New Residential Construction
	Units	Value
Total, 2006	24	$5,485,495
Single family	24	$5,485,495
Total, 2007	19	$3,265,900
Single family	19	$3,088,900

Real Property Valuation, 2008
	Parcels	Valuation
Total	2,886	$1,018,605,600
Vacant	106	22,038,100
Residential	2,589	865,626,900
Commercial	163	103,311,200
Industrial	0	0
Apartments	28	27,629,400
Farm land	0	0
Farm homestead	0	0

Average Property Value & Tax, 2008
Residential value	$334,348
Property tax	$5,988
Tax credit/rebate	$983

Public Library
Belmar Public Library
517 Tenth Ave
Belmar, NJ 07719
732-681-0775
Director	Natalie Gallagher

Library statistics, 2007
Population served	6,045
Full-time/total staff	NA/0

	Total	Per capita
Holdings	0	NA
Revenues	$0	NA
Expenditures	$0	NA
Annual visits	NA	NA
Internet terminals/annual users	NA/NA	

Public Safety
Number of officers, 2007	21

Crime	2006	2007
Total crimes	368	349
Violent	35	16
Murder	0	0
Rape	0	0
Robbery	3	2
Aggravated assault	32	14
Non-violent	333	333
Burglary	37	70
Larceny	281	254
Vehicle theft	15	9
Domestic violence	112	98
Arson	0	0
Total crime rate	61.7	58.9
Violent	5.9	2.7
Non-violent	55.9	56.2

Public School District
(for school year 2007-08 except as noted)

Belmar School District
1101 Main Street
Belmar, NJ 07719
(732) 681-2388
Superintendent	Paul S. Shappirio
Number of schools	1
Grade plan	K-8
Enrollment	521
Attendance rate, '06-07	95.1%
Dropout rate	NA
Students per teacher	8.9
Per pupil expenditure	$14,661
Median faculty salary	$53,600
Median administrator salary	$105,000
Grade 12 enrollment	NA
High school graduation rate	NA

Assessment test results
(percent scoring at proficient or advanced level)
	Language	Math
NJASK-Grade 3	91.2%	84.0%
GEPA-Grade 8	79.6%	89.8%
HSPA-High School	NA	NA

SAT Score Averages, 2006-07
Pct tested	Math	Verbal	Writing
NA	NA	NA	NA

Teacher Qualifications
Avg. years of experience	11
Highly-qualified teachers one subject/all subjects	100%/100%

No Child Left Behind
AYP, 2006-07	Meets Standards

Municipal Finance
State Aid Programs, 2009
Total aid	$560,827
CMPTRA	67,668
Energy tax receipts	474,932
Garden State Trust	0

General Budget, 2008
Total tax levy	$18,247,230
County levy	4,355,036
County taxes	4,012,825
County library	0
County health	74,622
County open space	267,590
School levy	7,222,776
Muni. levy	6,669,419
Misc. revenues	6,193,847

Taxes
	2006	2007	2008
General tax rate per $100	1.666	1.724	1.791
County equalization ratio	72.06	61.62	57.46
Net valuation taxable	$999,285,400	$1,005,169,363	$1,018,870,845
State equalized value	$1,621,990,735	$1,749,141,325	$1,043,667,882

Demographics & Socio-Economic Characteristics
(2000 US Census, except as noted)

Population
1980*	2,475
1990*	2,669
2000	2,771
Male	1,328
Female	1,443
2007 (estimate)*	2,645
Population density	2,003.8

Race & Hispanic Origin, 2000
Race
White	2,716
Black/African American	14
American Indian/Alaska Native	1
Asian	14
Native Hawaiian/Pacific Islander	0
Other race	7
Two or more races	19
Hispanic origin, total	64
Mexican	1
Puerto Rican	28
Cuban	12
Other Hispanic	23

Age & Nativity, 2000
Under 5 years	201
18 years and over	1,991
21 years and over	1,903
65 years and over	356
85 years and over	57
Median age	36.4
Native-born	2,703
Foreign-born	68

Educational Attainment, 2000
Population 25 years and over	1,823
Less than 9th grade	2.7%
High school grad or higher	84.0%
Bachelor's degree or higher	26.2%
Graduate degree	7.7%

Income & Poverty, 1999
Per capita income	$23,231
Median household income	$52,792
Median family income	$62,212
Persons in poverty	93
H'holds receiving public assistance	27
H'holds receiving social security	304

Households, 2000
Total households	1,088
With persons under 18	416
With persons over 65	266
Family households	717
Single-person households	310
Persons per household	2.54
Persons per family	3.17

Labor & Employment
Total civilian labor force, 2007**	1,633
Unemployment rate	5.1%
Total civilian labor force, 2000	1,454
Unemployment rate	4.6%

Employed persons 16 years and over by occupation, 2000
Managers & professionals	490
Service occupations	192
Sales & office occupations	369
Farming, fishing & forestry	1
Construction & maintenance	116
Production & transportation	219
Self-employed persons	107

* US Census Bureau
** New Jersey Department of Labor

General Information
Town of Belvidere
691 Water St
Belvidere, NJ 07823
908-475-5331
Website	www.belviderenj.com
Year of incorporation	1845
Land/water area (sq. miles)	1.32/0.02
Form of government	Town

Government
Legislative Districts
US Congressional	5
State Legislative	23

Local Officials, 2009
Mayor	Charles J. Liegel Sr
Manager	Teresa A. DeMont
Clerk	Teresa A. DeMont
Finance Dir	Kathleen Reinalda
Tax Assessor	David Gill
Tax Collector	Rita Kelly
Attorney	Dominic Santini
Building	Charles O'Connor
Planning	Maser Consulting
Engineering	Maser Consulting
Public Works	John Snyder
Police Chief	Kent Sweigert
Emerg/Fire Director	James Christine

Housing & Construction
Housing Units, 2000*
Total	1,165
Median rent	$575
Median SF home value	$124,200

Permits for New Residential Construction
	Units	Value
Total, 2006	1	$125,000
Single family	1	$125,000
Total, 2007	2	$361,000
Single family	2	$361,000

Real Property Valuation, 2008
	Parcels	Valuation
Total	1,030	$142,413,500
Vacant	78	2,704,900
Residential	832	100,419,700
Commercial	89	14,842,200
Industrial	12	21,362,200
Apartments	8	2,488,700
Farm land	8	38,500
Farm homestead	3	557,300

Average Property Value & Tax, 2008
Residential value	$120,931
Property tax	$5,496
Tax credit/rebate	$983

Public Library
Belvidere Public Library
301 Second St
Belvidere, NJ 07823
908-475-3941
Director	Teresa Aicher

Library statistics, 2007
Population served	2,771
Full-time/total staff	0/1

	Total	Per capita
Holdings	25,843	9.33
Revenues	$102,104	$36.85
Expenditures	$128,938	$46.53
Annual visits	13,721	4.95
Internet terminals/annual users	2/387	

Public Safety
Number of officers, 2007	6

Crime	2006	2007
Total crimes	20	13
Violent	2	0
Murder	0	0
Rape	0	0
Robbery	0	0
Aggravated assault	2	0
Non-violent	18	13
Burglary	3	1
Larceny	14	12
Vehicle theft	1	0
Domestic violence	34	31
Arson	0	0
Total crime rate	7.3	4.8
Violent	0.7	0.0
Non-violent	6.6	4.8

Public School District
(for school year 2007-08 except as noted)

Belvidere School District
809 Oxford Street
Belvidere, NJ 07823
(908) 475-6600
Superintendent	Dirk Swaneveld
Number of schools	3
Grade plan	K-12
Enrollment	933
Attendance rate, '06-07	93.9%
Dropout rate	0.9%
Students per teacher	10.7
Per pupil expenditure	$11,196
Median faculty salary	$48,450
Median administrator salary	$99,225
Grade 12 enrollment	161
High school graduation rate	94.3%

Assessment test results
(percent scoring at proficient or advanced level)
	Language	Math
NJASK-Grade 3	84.8%	78.8%
GEPA-Grade 8	65.9%	84.1%
HSPA-High School	75.7%	83.8%

SAT Score Averages, 2006-07
Pct tested	Math	Verbal	Writing
66%	477	475	467

Teacher Qualifications
Avg. years of experience	9
Highly-qualified teachers one subject/all subjects	100%/96.5%

No Child Left Behind
AYP, 2006-07	Meets Standards

Municipal Finance
State Aid Programs, 2009
Total aid	$620,411
CMPTRA	47,576
Energy tax receipts	550,966
Garden State Trust	5,724

General Budget, 2008
Total tax levy	$6,534,123
County levy	1,615,624
County taxes	1,441,289
County library	0
County health	0
County open space	174,335
School levy	3,335,000
Muni. levy	1,583,499
Misc. revenues	1,342,562

Taxes	2006	2007	2008
General tax rate per $100	4.15	4.38	4.545
County equalization ratio	64.04	55.61	49.94
Net valuation taxable	$144,076,800	$146,136,632	$143,775,045
State equalized value	$260,569,019	$291,293,290	$292,714,859

Demographics & Socio-Economic Characteristics
(2000 US Census, except as noted)

Population
1980*	25,568
1990*	24,458
2000	26,247
Male	12,534
Female	13,713
2007 (estimate)*	25,826
Population density	8,905.5

Race & Hispanic Origin, 2000
Race
White	16,510
Black/African American	1,812
American Indian/Alaska Native	63
Asian	5,357
Native Hawaiian/Pacific Islander	4
Other race	1,698
Two or more races	803
Hispanic origin, total	4,474
Mexican	220
Puerto Rican	926
Cuban	247
Other Hispanic	3,081

Age & Nativity, 2000
Under 5 years	1,779
18 years and over	19,726
21 years and over	18,881
65 years and over	3,556
85 years and over	387
Median age	37.6
Native-born	17,810
Foreign-born	8,437

Educational Attainment, 2000
Population 25 years and over	17,831
Less than 9th grade	4.9%
High school grad or higher	86.6%
Bachelor's degree or higher	32.3%
Graduate degree	9.9%

Income & Poverty, 1999
Per capita income	$24,706
Median household income	$62,172
Median family income	$71,187
Persons in poverty	919
H'holds receiving public assistance	105
H'holds receiving social security	2,593

Households, 2000
Total households	8,981
With persons under 18	3,542
With persons over 65	2,656
Family households	6,750
Single-person households	1,868
Persons per household	2.92
Persons per family	3.41

Labor & Employment
Total civilian labor force, 2007**	14,042
Unemployment rate	3.2%
Total civilian labor force, 2000	13,731
Unemployment rate	3.6%

Employed persons 16 years and over by occupation, 2000
Managers & professionals	5,040
Service occupations	1,898
Sales & office occupations	3,875
Farming, fishing & forestry	0
Construction & maintenance	933
Production & transportation	1,495
Self-employed persons	606

* US Census Bureau
** New Jersey Department of Labor
§ State Fiscal Year July 1–June 30

General Information
Borough of Bergenfield
198 N Washington Ave
Bergenfield, NJ 07621
201-387-4055

Website	www.bergenfield.com
Year of incorporation	1894
Land/water area (sq. miles)	2.90/0.00
Form of government	Borough

Government
Legislative Districts
US Congressional	5
State Legislative	37

Local Officials, 2009
Mayor	Timothy J. Driscoll
Administrator	Rick McGarill
Clerk	Carol Chamberlain-Berman (Actg)
Finance Dir	Alice Czykier
Tax Assessor	George Reggo
Tax Collector	Alice Czykier
Attorney	Durkin & Boggia
Building	Ken Pfammen
Planning	Louis Castellucci
Engineering	Boswell Engineering
Public Works	Edward Kneisler
Police Chief	Rick McGarill
Emerg/Fire Director	Robert Byrnes Jr

Housing & Construction
Housing Units, 2000*
Total	9,147
Median rent	$855
Median SF home value	$184,400

Permits for New Residential Construction
	Units	Value
Total, 2006	17	$3,601,835
Single family	17	$3,601,835
Total, 2007	11	$4,074,565
Single family	9	$3,892,365

Real Property Valuation, 2008
	Parcels	Valuation
Total	7,386	$2,419,001,755
Vacant	60	11,884,900
Residential	6,969	2,104,378,855
Commercial	257	194,740,800
Industrial	50	33,388,800
Apartments	50	74,608,400
Farm land	0	0
Farm homestead	0	0

Average Property Value & Tax, 2008
Residential value	$301,963
Property tax	$9,025
Tax credit/rebate	$1,365

Public Library
Bergenfield Public Library
50 W Clinton Ave
Bergenfield, NJ 07621
201-387-4040

Director	Mary Riskind

Library statistics, 2007
Population served	26,247
Full-time/total staff	6/18

	Total	Per capita
Holdings	168,243	6.41
Revenues	$1,573,173	$59.94
Expenditures	$1,537,833	$58.59
Annual visits	198,649	7.57
Internet terminals/annual users	14/17,643	

Public Safety
Number of officers, 2007	43

Crime	2006	2007
Total crimes	254	233
Violent	15	30
Murder	0	0
Rape	0	1
Robbery	5	11
Aggravated assault	10	18
Non-violent	239	203
Burglary	50	39
Larceny	168	154
Vehicle theft	21	10
Domestic violence	176	161
Arson	3	2
Total crime rate	9.7	8.9
Violent	0.6	1.1
Non-violent	9.2	7.7

Public School District
(for school year 2007-08 except as noted)

Bergenfield School District
100 So. Prospect Avenue
Bergenfield, NJ 07621
(201) 385-8202

Superintendent	Michael Kuchar
Number of schools	7
Grade plan	K-12
Enrollment	3,512
Attendance rate, '06-07	96.0%
Dropout rate	1.2%
Students per teacher	10.9
Per pupil expenditure	$14,526
Median faculty salary	$60,645
Median administrator salary	$137,032
Grade 12 enrollment	306
High school graduation rate	90.8%

Assessment test results
(percent scoring at proficient or advanced level)
	Language	Math
NJASK-Grade 3	95.5%	95.5%
GEPA-Grade 8	71.5%	83.6%
HSPA-High School	79.0%	85.0%

SAT Score Averages, 2006-07
Pct tested	Math	Verbal	Writing
80%	471	463	455

Teacher Qualifications
Avg. years of experience	8
Highly-qualified teachers one subject/all subjects	99.5%/99.5%

No Child Left Behind
AYP, 2006-07	Meets Standards

Municipal Finance§
State Aid Programs, 2009
Total aid	$2,437,110
CMPTRA	763,743
Energy tax receipts	1,636,810
Garden State Trust	0

General Budget, 2008
Total tax levy	$72,363,091
County levy	6,115,508
County taxes	5,783,204
County library	0
County health	0
County open space	332,304
School levy	41,765,231
Muni. levy	24,482,352
Misc. revenues	6,907,272

Taxes
	2006	2007	2008
General tax rate per $100	2.75	2.92	2.990
County equalization ratio	89.49	78.37	73.06
Net valuation taxable	$2,398,213,755	$2,393,894,036	$2,421,129,139
State equalized value	$3,061,286,059	$3,276,229,832	$3,286,137,369

See Introduction for an explanation of all data sources.

Demographics & Socio-Economic Characteristics

(2000 US Census, except as noted)

Population

1980*	12,549
1990*	11,980
2000	13,407
Male	6,389
Female	7,018
2007 (estimate)*	13,396
Population density	2,139.9

Race & Hispanic Origin, 2000

Race

White	12,019
Black/African American	149
American Indian/Alaska Native	11
Asian	1,055
Native Hawaiian/Pacific Islander	0
Other race	82
Two or more races	91
Hispanic origin, total	494
Mexican	37
Puerto Rican	93
Cuban	45
Other Hispanic	319

Age & Nativity, 2000

Under 5 years	1,070
18 years and over	9,812
21 years and over	9,560
65 years and over	2,200
85 years and over	354
Median age	39.7
Native-born	11,552
Foreign-born	1,855

Educational Attainment, 2000

Population 25 years and over	9,267
Less than 9th grade	3.5%
High school grad or higher	92.5%
Bachelor's degree or higher	52.3%
Graduate degree	23.2%

Income & Poverty, 1999

Per capita income	$43,981
Median household income	$107,716
Median family income	$118,862
Persons in poverty	278
H'holds receiving public assistance	12
H'holds receiving social security	1,282

Households, 2000

Total households	4,479
With persons under 18	1,910
With persons over 65	1,249
Family households	3,719
Single-person households	661
Persons per household	2.89
Persons per family	3.21

Labor & Employment

Total civilian labor force, 2007**	6,550
Unemployment rate	2.0%
Total civilian labor force, 2000	6,312
Unemployment rate	2.2%

Employed persons 16 years and over by occupation, 2000

Managers & professionals	3,494
Service occupations	541
Sales & office occupations	1,649
Farming, fishing & forestry	0
Construction & maintenance	297
Production & transportation	193
Self-employed persons	464

* US Census Bureau
** New Jersey Department of Labor

General Information

Township of Berkeley Heights
29 Park Ave
Berkeley Heights, NJ 07922
908-464-2700

Website	www.berkeleyheightstwp.com
Year of incorporation	1951
Land/water area (sq. miles)	6.26/0.01
Form of government	Mayor-Council-Admin

Government

Legislative Districts

US Congressional	7
State Legislative	21

Local Officials, 2009

Mayor	David A. Cohen
Administrator	Jack Conway
Clerk	Patricia Rapach
Finance Dir	Tracy Tedesco
Tax Assessor	Stan Belenky
Tax Collector	Rachele Sanfilippo
Attorney	Thomas Scrivo
Building	Robin Greenwald
Comm Dev/Planning	NA
Municipal Engineer	Jack D'Agostaro
Public Works	Jack D'Agostaro (Actg)
Police Chief	David Zager
Emerg/Fire Director	Anthony Padovano

Housing & Construction

Housing Units, 2000*

Total	4,562
Median rent	$1,248
Median SF home value	$324,900

Permits for New Residential Construction

	Units	Value
Total, 2006	27	$5,726,528
Single family	24	$5,576,528
Total, 2007	16	$4,535,968
Single family	16	$4,535,968

Real Property Valuation, 2008

	Parcels	Valuation
Total	4,669	$1,836,199,720
Vacant	136	30,119,200
Residential	4,383	1,334,493,700
Commercial	112	275,994,900
Industrial	35	189,657,000
Apartments	2	5,934,500
Farm land	1	420
Farm homestead	0	0

Average Property Value & Tax, 2008

Residential value	$304,470
Property tax	$9,447
Tax credit/rebate	$1,275

Public Library

Berkeley Heights Public Library
290 Plainfield Ave
Berkeley Heights, NJ 07922
908-464-9333

Director	Stephanie Bakos

Library statistics, 2007

Population served	13,407
Full-time/total staff	4/7

	Total	Per capita
Holdings	95,571	7.13
Revenues	$1,121,639	$83.66
Expenditures	$1,018,418	$75.96
Annual visits	145,220	10.83
Internet terminals/annual users	16/17,183	

Public Safety

Number of officers, 2007 ... 27

Crime	2006	2007
Total crimes	91	87
Violent	5	4
Murder	0	0
Rape	0	0
Robbery	1	0
Aggravated assault	4	4
Non-violent	86	83
Burglary	8	9
Larceny	76	68
Vehicle theft	2	6
Domestic violence	50	41
Arson	0	0
Total crime rate	6.7	6.4
Violent	0.4	0.3
Non-violent	6.3	6.1

Public School District

(for school year 2007-08 except as noted)

Berkeley Heights School District
345 Plainfield Avenue
Berkeley Heights, NJ 07922
(908) 464-1718

Superintendent	Judith Rattner
Number of schools	6
Grade plan	K-12
Enrollment	2,835
Attendance rate, '06-07	96.0%
Dropout rate	0.2%
Students per teacher	10.4
Per pupil expenditure	$13,991
Median faculty salary	$59,803
Median administrator salary	$117,578
Grade 12 enrollment	228
High school graduation rate	99.1%

Assessment test results

(percent scoring at proficient or advanced level)

	Language	Math
NJASK-Grade 3	97.5%	96.1%
GEPA-Grade 8	93.6%	98.1%
HSPA-High School	95.5%	95.8%

SAT Score Averages, 2006-07

Pct tested	Math	Verbal	Writing
99%	576	559	557

Teacher Qualifications

Avg. years of experience	8
Highly-qualified teachers one subject/all subjects	100%/100%

No Child Left Behind

AYP, 2006-07 ... Meets Standards

Municipal Finance

State Aid Programs, 2009

Total aid	$2,096,385
CMPTRA	676,433
Energy tax receipts	1,336,097
Garden State Trust	0

General Budget, 2008

Total tax levy	$57,008,146
County levy	12,005,217
County taxes	11,480,665
County library	0
County health	0
County open space	524,552
School levy	35,089,197
Muni. levy	9,913,733
Misc. revenues	6,447,633

Taxes

	2006	2007	2008
General tax rate per $100	2.958	3.005	3.103
County equalization ratio	57.49	55.97	53.20
Net valuation taxable	$1,821,418,020	$1,824,842,728	$1,837,382,239
State equalized value	$3,255,565,575	$3,429,114,197	$3,430,126,907

See Introduction for an explanation of all data sources.

Demographics & Socio-Economic Characteristics
(2000 US Census, except as noted)

Population
1980*	23,151
1990*	37,319
2000	39,991
Male	17,765
Female	22,226
2007 (estimate)*	42,664
Population density	994.5

Race & Hispanic Origin, 2000
Race
White	38,833
Black/African American	519
American Indian/Alaska Native	16
Asian	181
Native Hawaiian/Pacific Islander	4
Other race	173
Two or more races	265
Hispanic origin, total	932
Mexican	228
Puerto Rican	354
Cuban	78
Other Hispanic	272

Age & Nativity, 2000
Under 5 years	1,089
18 years and over	35,433
21 years and over	34,738
65 years and over	20,806
85 years and over	2,376
Median age	66.3
Native-born	37,308
Foreign-born	2,680

Educational Attainment, 2000
Population 25 years and over	34,037
Less than 9th grade	7.4%
High school grad or higher	72.4%
Bachelor's degree or higher	10.3%
Graduate degree	2.8%

Income & Poverty, 1999
Per capita income	$22,198
Median household income	$32,134
Median family income	$40,208
Persons in poverty	2,157
H'holds receiving public assistance	296
H'holds receiving social security	14,125

Households, 2000
Total households	19,828
With persons under 18	2,450
With persons over 65	13,931
Family households	12,175
Single-person households	7,110
Persons per household	1.99
Persons per family	2.52

Labor & Employment
Total civilian labor force, 2007**	12,668
Unemployment rate	5.3%
Total civilian labor force, 2000	11,892
Unemployment rate	9.6%

Employed persons 16 years and over by occupation, 2000
Managers & professionals	2,945
Service occupations	1,557
Sales & office occupations	3,571
Farming, fishing & forestry	0
Construction & maintenance	1,381
Production & transportation	1,302
Self-employed persons	607

‡ Branch of county library
* US Census Bureau
** New Jersey Department of Labor

General Information
Township of Berkeley
627 Pinewald Keswick Rd
PO Box B
Bayville, NJ 08721
732-244-7400
Website	twp.berkeley.nj.us
Year of incorporation	1875
Land/water area (sq. miles)	42.90/12.90
Form of government	Mayor-Council

Government
Legislative Districts
US Congressional	3
State Legislative	9

Local Officials, 2009
Mayor	Jason J. Varano
Manager	Leonard Roeber
Clerk	Beverly M. Carle
Finance Dir	Frederick Ebenau
Tax Assessor	Eric Zanetti
Tax Collector	Gerry Dorso
Attorney	Patrick Sheehan
Building	William I. Schultz
Planning	David Roberts
Engineering	Chris Theodos
Public Works	Steven J. Seiler
Police Chief	John Weinlein
Emerg/Fire Director	Tom Raneri

Housing & Construction
Housing Units, 2000*
Total	22,288
Median rent	$774
Median SF home value	$102,100

Permits for New Residential Construction
	Units	Value
Total, 2006	102	$14,913,168
Single family	99	$14,895,668
Total, 2007	78	$11,041,411
Single family	78	$11,041,411

Real Property Valuation, 2008
	Parcels	Valuation
Total	26,374	$2,676,632,190
Vacant	3,406	49,607,700
Residential	22,736	2,469,451,190
Commercial	199	122,003,200
Industrial	19	10,646,400
Apartments	9	24,630,200
Farm land	3	22,700
Farm homestead	2	270,800

Average Property Value & Tax, 2008
Residential value	$108,617
Property tax	$3,550
Tax credit/rebate	$1,024

Public Library
Berkeley Branch Library‡
30 Station Rd
Bayville, NJ 08721
732-269-2144
Branch Librarian........Heather Andolsen

Library statistics, 2007
see Ocean County profile
for library system statistics

Public Safety
Number of officers, 2007 74

Crime	2006	2007
Total crimes	735	866
Violent	46	56
Murder	0	2
Rape	3	4
Robbery	8	17
Aggravated assault	35	33
Non-violent	689	810
Burglary	167	135
Larceny	511	651
Vehicle theft	11	24
Domestic violence	477	411
Arson	13	4
Total crime rate	17.3	20.3
Violent	1.1	1.3
Non-violent	16.2	19.0

Public School District
(for school year 2007-08 except as noted)

Berkeley Township School District
53 Central Parkway
Bayville, NJ 08721
(732) 269-2233
Superintendent	Joseph H. Vicari
Number of schools	4
Grade plan	K-6
Enrollment	1,960
Attendance rate, '06-07	94.7%
Dropout rate	NA
Students per teacher	10.1
Per pupil expenditure	$13,751
Median faculty salary	$52,270
Median administrator salary	$103,657
Grade 12 enrollment	NA
High school graduation rate	NA

Assessment test results
(percent scoring at proficient or advanced level)
	Language	Math
NJASK-Grade 3	96.2%	95.3%
GEPA-Grade 8	NA	NA
HSPA-High School	NA	NA

SAT Score Averages, 2006-07
Pct tested	Math	Verbal	Writing
NA	NA	NA	NA

Teacher Qualifications
Avg. years of experience	7
Highly-qualified teachers	
one subject/all subjects	100%/100%

No Child Left Behind
AYP, 2006-07 ....Needs Improvement

Municipal Finance
State Aid Programs, 2009
Total aid	$5,576,090
CMPTRA	0
Energy tax receipts	5,297,140
Garden State Trust	64,778

General Budget, 2008
Total tax levy	$87,578,591
County levy	19,759,589
County taxes	16,294,362
County library	1,914,958
County health	779,656
County open space	770,614
School levy	43,258,241
Muni. levy	24,560,761
Misc. revenues	13,749,246

Taxes	2006	2007	2008
General tax rate per $100	2.958	3.117	3.268
County equalization ratio	51.2	44.55	41.81
Net valuation taxable	$2,625,562,640	$2,656,968,666	$2,679,924,665
State equalized value	$5,897,441,977	$6,350,044,809	$1,054,257,160

See Introduction for an explanation of all data sources.

Demographics & Socio-Economic Characteristics

(2000 US Census, except as noted)

Population

1980*	5,786
1990*	5,672
2000	6,149
Male	3,045
Female	3,104
2007 (estimate)*	7,870
Population density	2,198.3

Race & Hispanic Origin, 2000

Race

White	5,784
Black/African American	134
American Indian/Alaska Native	13
Asian	104
Native Hawaiian/Pacific Islander	4
Other race	30
Two or more races	80
Hispanic origin, total	130
Mexican	8
Puerto Rican	50
Cuban	21
Other Hispanic	51

Age & Nativity, 2000

Under 5 years	335
18 years and over	4,636
21 years and over	4,438
65 years and over	837
85 years and over	91
Median age	38.2
Native-born	5,896
Foreign-born	253

Educational Attainment, 2000

Population 25 years and over	4,222
Less than 9th grade	5.4%
High school grad or higher	84.2%
Bachelor's degree or higher	24.4%
Graduate degree	6.3%

Income & Poverty, 1999

Per capita income	$24,675
Median household income	$60,286
Median family income	$68,704
Persons in poverty	212
H'holds receiving public assistance	29
H'holds receiving social security	654

Households, 2000

Total households	2,205
With persons under 18	817
With persons over 65	581
Family households	1,660
Single-person households	432
Persons per household	2.76
Persons per family	3.19

Labor & Employment

Total civilian labor force, 2007**	3,657
Unemployment rate	4.0%
Total civilian labor force, 2000	3,471
Unemployment rate	4.6%

Employed persons 16 years and over by occupation, 2000

Managers & professionals	1,212
Service occupations	466
Sales & office occupations	971
Farming, fishing & forestry	0
Construction & maintenance	318
Production & transportation	343
Self-employed persons	130

General Information

Borough of Berlin
59 S White Horse Pike
Berlin, NJ 08009
856-767-7777

Website	www.berlinnj.org
Year of incorporation	1927
Land/water area (sq. miles)	3.58/0.00
Form of government	Borough

Government

Legislative Districts

US Congressional	1
State Legislative	6

Local Officials, 2009

Mayor	John J. Armano
Manager	Charleen Santora
Clerk	Charleen Santora
Finance Dir	Stephen Miller
Tax Assessor	Theresa Stagliano
Tax Collector	Lisa Eggert
Attorney	George Botcheos
Building	Michael DePalma
Planning	Valerie Tarus
Engineering	Pennoni Associates
Public Works	Mark Mauger
Police Chief	Robert Carrara
Emerg/Fire Director	Paul Miller

Housing & Construction

Housing Units, 2000*

Total	2,275
Median rent	$642
Median SF home value	$135,800

Permits for New Residential Construction

	Units	Value
Total, 2006	20	$2,114,315
Single family	20	$2,114,315
Total, 2007	17	$1,748,735
Single family	17	$1,748,735

Real Property Valuation, 2008

	Parcels	Valuation
Total	2,933	$405,976,440
Vacant	253	10,144,800
Residential	2,501	327,901,200
Commercial	151	58,052,700
Industrial	10	6,539,940
Apartments	12	3,036,300
Farm land	4	56,600
Farm homestead	2	244,900

Average Property Value & Tax, 2008

Residential value	$131,101
Property tax	$5,759
Tax credit/rebate	$1,019

Public Library

M. Fleche Memorial Library
49 S White Horse Pike
Berlin, NJ 08009
856-767-2448

Director	Mary Rencic

Library statistics, 2007

Population served	6,149
Full-time/total staff	0/0

	Total	Per capita
Holdings	29,996	4.88
Revenues	$78,725	$12.80
Expenditures	$92,104	$14.98
Annual visits	10,003	1.63
Internet terminals/annual users	3/1,999	

Public Safety

Number of officers, 2007 20

Crime	2006	2007
Total crimes	223	179
Violent	8	8
Murder	0	0
Rape	0	0
Robbery	5	3
Aggravated assault	3	5
Non-violent	215	171
Burglary	35	36
Larceny	170	128
Vehicle theft	10	7
Domestic violence	31	40
Arson	2	0
Total crime rate	28.4	22.6
Violent	1.0	1.0
Non-violent	27.4	21.6

Public School District

(for school year 2007-08 except as noted)

Berlin Borough School District
215 South Franklin Avenue
Berlin, NJ 08009
(856) 767-6785

Superintendent	James Lavender
Number of schools	1
Grade plan	K-8
Enrollment	837
Attendance rate, '06-07	95.7%
Dropout rate	NA
Students per teacher	12.0
Per pupil expenditure	$10,798
Median faculty salary	$50,575
Median administrator salary	$101,864
Grade 12 enrollment	NA
High school graduation rate	NA

Assessment test results

(percent scoring at proficient or advanced level)

	Language	Math
NJASK-Grade 3	96.6%	91.0%
GEPA-Grade 8	68.4%	88.0%
HSPA-High School	NA	NA

SAT Score Averages, 2006-07

Pct tested	Math	Verbal	Writing
NA	NA	NA	NA

Teacher Qualifications

Avg. years of experience	9
Highly-qualified teachers one subject/all subjects	100%/100%

No Child Left Behind

AYP, 2006-07	Meets Standards

Municipal Finance

State Aid Programs, 2009

Total aid	$898,255
CMPTRA	177,750
Energy tax receipts	698,048
Garden State Trust	1

General Budget, 2008

Total tax levy	$17,986,367
County levy	5,106,525
County taxes	4,613,060
County library	332,202
County health	0
County open space	161,262
School levy	9,560,050
Muni. levy	3,319,792
Misc. revenues	3,367,447

Taxes

	2006	2007	2008
General tax rate per $100	4.192	4.328	4.393
County equalization ratio	64.03	55.88	50.94
Net valuation taxable	$393,147,240	$404,749,492	$409,441,568
State equalized value	$707,038,122	$791,590,520	$839,495,688

* US Census Bureau
** New Jersey Department of Labor

Camden County — *Berlin Township*

Demographics & Socio-Economic Characteristics
(2000 US Census, except as noted)

Population
1980*	5,348
1990*	5,466
2000	5,290
Male	2,632
Female	2,658
2007 (estimate)*	5,381
Population density	1,655.7

Race & Hispanic Origin, 2000
Race
White	4,362
Black/African American	628
American Indian/Alaska Native	9
Asian	143
Native Hawaiian/Pacific Islander	4
Other race	64
Two or more races	80
Hispanic origin, total	254
Mexican	146
Puerto Rican	72
Cuban	6
Other Hispanic	30

Age & Nativity, 2000
Under 5 years	352
18 years and over	3,926
21 years and over	3,722
65 years and over	663
85 years and over	69
Median age	35.9
Native-born	5,015
Foreign-born	275

Educational Attainment, 2000
Population 25 years and over	3,495
Less than 9th grade	5.6%
High school grad or higher	76.7%
Bachelor's degree or higher	15.1%
Graduate degree	4.3%

Income & Poverty, 1999
Per capita income	$22,178
Median household income	$54,448
Median family income	$61,042
Persons in poverty	312
H'holds receiving public assistance	37
H'holds receiving social security	565

Households, 2000
Total households	1,893
With persons under 18	736
With persons over 65	510
Family households	1,368
Single-person households	427
Persons per household	2.78
Persons per family	3.28

Labor & Employment
Total civilian labor force, 2007**	2,927
Unemployment rate	2.8%
Total civilian labor force, 2000	2,774
Unemployment rate	3.6%

Employed persons 16 years and over by occupation, 2000
Managers & professionals	728
Service occupations	518
Sales & office occupations	695
Farming, fishing & forestry	0
Construction & maintenance	422
Production & transportation	310
Self-employed persons	75

‡ Branch of county library
* US Census Bureau
** New Jersey Department of Labor
§ State Fiscal Year July 1–June 30

See Introduction for an explanation of all data sources.

General Information
Township of Berlin
170 Bate Ave
West Berlin, NJ 08091
856-767-1854

Website	www.berlintwp.com
Year of incorporation	1910
Land/water area (sq. miles)	3.25/0.00
Form of government	Small Municipality

Government
Legislative Districts
US Congressional	1
State Legislative	6

Local Officials, 2009
Mayor	Phyllis Jeffries-Magazzu
Manager/Admin	NA
Clerk	Jamey Eggers
Finance Dir	Lori Campisano
Tax Assessor	Anthony Colavecchio
Tax Collector	Diane Zoppel
Attorney	Donafaye Zoll
Building	Mike DePalma
Comm Dev/Planning	NA
Engineering	Charles Riebel Jr
Public Works	Mike McGee
Police Chief	Michael Hayden
Emerg/Fire Director	Joseph Jackson

Housing & Construction
Housing Units, 2000*
Total	2,009
Median rent	$590
Median SF home value	$109,600

Permits for New Residential Construction
	Units	Value
Total, 2006	15	$934,235
Single family	15	$934,235
Total, 2007	23	$3,657,844
Single family	23	$3,657,844

Real Property Valuation, 2008
	Parcels	Valuation
Total	2,415	$341,041,300
Vacant	320	11,164,300
Residential	1,684	172,878,100
Commercial	344	119,255,400
Industrial	53	33,578,200
Apartments	3	3,955,600
Farm land	9	43,300
Farm homestead	2	166,400

Average Property Value & Tax, 2008
Residential value	$102,636
Property tax	$4,713
Tax credit/rebate	$955

Public Library
Berlin Township Library‡
201 Veteran's Ave
West Berlin, NJ 08901
856-767-0439

Director	Mary Holt

Library statistics, 2007
see Camden County profile for library system statistics

Public Safety
Number of officers, 2007	20

Crime	2006	2007
Total crimes	202	205
Violent	15	10
Murder	0	0
Rape	0	0
Robbery	3	5
Aggravated assault	12	5
Non-violent	187	195
Burglary	31	18
Larceny	144	163
Vehicle theft	12	14
Domestic violence	54	38
Arson	7	4
Total crime rate	37.4	37.9
Violent	2.8	1.9
Non-violent	34.6	36.1

Public School District
(for school year 2007-08 except as noted)

Berlin Township School District
225 Grove Avenue
West Berlin, NJ 08091
(856) 767-9480

Superintendent	Brian J. Betze
Number of schools	2
Grade plan	K-8
Enrollment	590
Attendance rate, '06-07	93.4%
Dropout rate	NA
Students per teacher	7.7
Per pupil expenditure	$14,148
Median faculty salary	$48,038
Median administrator salary	$99,060
Grade 12 enrollment	NA
High school graduation rate	NA

Assessment test results
(percent scoring at proficient or advanced level)
	Language	Math
NJASK-Grade 3	79.7%	84.4%
GEPA-Grade 8	60.3%	82.5%
HSPA-High School	NA	NA

SAT Score Averages, 2006-07
Pct tested	Math	Verbal	Writing
NA	NA	NA	NA

Teacher Qualifications
Avg. years of experience	10
Highly-qualified teachers one subject/all subjects	98.0%/98.0%

No Child Left Behind
AYP, 2006-07	Meets Standards

Municipal Finance§
State Aid Programs, 2009
Total aid	$1,554,441
CMPTRA	0
Energy tax receipts	1,515,268
Garden State Trust	0

General Budget, 2008
Total tax levy	$15,687,642
County levy	3,738,690
County taxes	3,379,102
County library	242,076
County health	0
County open space	117,512
School levy	7,870,719
Muni. levy	4,078,233
Misc. revenues	3,562,374

Taxes
	2006	2007	2008
General tax rate per $100	4.381	4.499	4.593
County equalization ratio	73.26	63.03	58.15
Net valuation taxable	$332,937,700	$339,541,019	$341,616,361
State equalized value	$528,862,022	$583,476,357	$599,313,298

Demographics & Socio-Economic Characteristics

(2000 US Census, except as noted)

Population

1980*	12,920
1990*	17,199
2000	24,575
Male	11,945
Female	12,630
2007 (estimate)*	26,590
Population density	1,107.9

Race & Hispanic Origin, 2000

Race

White	21,921
Black/African American	354
American Indian/Alaska Native	13
Asian	1,928
Native Hawaiian/Pacific Islander	3
Other race	98
Two or more races	258
Hispanic origin, total	646
Mexican	60
Puerto Rican	105
Cuban	82
Other Hispanic	399

Age & Nativity, 2000

Under 5 years	1,962
18 years and over	17,770
21 years and over	17,403
65 years and over	3,063
85 years and over	383
Median age	39.2
Native-born	21,499
Foreign-born	3,076

Educational Attainment, 2000

Population 25 years and over	16,950
Less than 9th grade	1.8%
High school grad or higher	95.8%
Bachelor's degree or higher	67.4%
Graduate degree	30.6%

Income & Poverty, 1999

Per capita income	$56,521
Median household income	$107,204
Median family income	$135,806
Persons in poverty	319
H'holds receiving public assistance	55
H'holds receiving social security	1,927

Households, 2000

Total households	9,242
With persons under 18	3,549
With persons over 65	2,004
Family households	6,484
Single-person households	2,442
Persons per household	2.58
Persons per family	3.17

Labor & Employment

Total civilian labor force, 2007**	14,133
Unemployment rate	2.2%
Total civilian labor force, 2000	12,279
Unemployment rate	2.7%

Employed persons 16 years and over by occupation, 2000

Managers & professionals	7,651
Service occupations	629
Sales & office occupations	2,835
Farming, fishing & forestry	0
Construction & maintenance	379
Production & transportation	452
Self-employed persons	713

* US Census Bureau
** New Jersey Department of Labor

General Information

Township of Bernards
1 Collyer Ln
Basking Ridge, NJ 07920
908-766-2510

Website	www.bernards.org
Year of incorporation	1760
Land/water area (sq. miles)	24.00/0.01
Form of government	Township

Government

Legislative Districts

US Congressional	11
State Legislative	16

Local Officials, 2009

Mayor	Mary Pavlini
Administrator	Bruce McArthur
Clerk	Denise Szabo
Finance Dir	Bruce McArthur
Tax Assessor	Marcia Sudano
Tax Collector	Peggy Warren
Attorney	John Belardo
Building	Dennis Bettler
Planning	Peter Messina
Engineering	Peter Messina
Public Works	Pat Monaco
Police Chief	Brian Bobowicz
Fire Chief	Brandon Watt

Housing & Construction

Housing Units, 2000*

Total	9,485
Median rent	$1,494
Median SF home value	$380,500

Permits for New Residential Construction

	Units	Value
Total, 2006	21	$9,127,000
Single family	21	$9,127,000
Total, 2007	22	$9,124,910
Single family	22	$9,124,910

Real Property Valuation, 2008

	Parcels	Valuation
Total	10,034	$7,136,948,580
Vacant	301	45,096,900
Residential	9,487	6,186,564,700
Commercial	159	864,983,780
Industrial	7	8,168,700
Apartments	2	9,339,600
Farm land	50	372,600
Farm homestead	28	22,422,300

Average Property Value & Tax, 2008

Residential value	$652,547
Property tax	$10,191
Tax credit/rebate	$1,156

Public Library

Bernards Township Library
32 S Maple Ave
Basking Ridge, NJ 07920
908-204-3031

Director	Anne Meany

Library statistics, 2007

Population served	24,575
Full-time/total staff	9/17

	Total	Per capita
Holdings	142,916	5.82
Revenues	$2,347,904	$95.54
Expenditures	$2,030,667	$82.63
Annual visits	242,645	9.87
Internet terminals/annual users	19/151,905	

Public Safety

Number of officers, 2007	39

Crime	2006	2007
Total crimes	172	160
Violent	8	1
Murder	1	0
Rape	3	0
Robbery	0	0
Aggravated assault	4	1
Non-violent	164	159
Burglary	42	14
Larceny	115	136
Vehicle theft	7	9
Domestic violence	123	112
Arson	3	0
Total crime rate	6.4	5.9
Violent	0.3	0.0
Non-violent	6.1	5.9

Public School District

(for school year 2007-08 except as noted)

Bernards Township School District
101 Peachtree Rd
Basking Ridge, NJ 07920
(908) 204-2600

Superintendent	Valerie A. Goger
Number of schools	6
Grade plan	K-12
Enrollment	5,501
Attendance rate, '06-07	96.3%
Dropout rate	0.3%
Students per teacher	11.4
Per pupil expenditure	$12,439
Median faculty salary	$56,047
Median administrator salary	$109,469
Grade 12 enrollment	381
High school graduation rate	98.4%

Assessment test results

(percent scoring at proficient or advanced level)

	Language	Math
NJASK-Grade 3	97.5%	98.0%
GEPA-Grade 8	94.2%	96.9%
HSPA-High School	94.4%	97.2%

SAT Score Averages, 2006-07

Pct tested	Math	Verbal	Writing
103%	594	570	567

Teacher Qualifications

Avg. years of experience	7
Highly-qualified teachers one subject/all subjects	99.5%/99.5%

No Child Left Behind

AYP, 2006-07	Meets Standards

Municipal Finance

State Aid Programs, 2009

Total aid	$2,410,229
CMPTRA	0
Energy tax receipts	2,289,718
Garden State Trust	0

General Budget, 2008

Total tax levy	$111,592,340
County levy	21,792,405
County taxes	19,619,862
County library	0
County health	0
County open space	2,172,542
School levy	70,934,294
Muni. levy	18,865,642
Misc. revenues	20,568,058

Taxes

Taxes	2006	2007	2008
General tax rate per $100	1.49	1.53	1.562
County equalization ratio	108.55	100.71	98.52
Net valuation taxable	$7,017,642,325	$7,145,579,652	$7,145,257,680
State equalized value	$6,964,618,232	$7,202,420,728	$7,296,859,529

See Introduction for an explanation of all data sources.

Demographics & Socio-Economic Characteristics
(2000 US Census, except as noted)

Population
1980*	6,715
1990*	6,597
2000	7,345
Male	3,599
Female	3,746
2007 (estimate)*	7,745
Population density	599.0

Race & Hispanic Origin, 2000
Race
White	6,900
Black/African American	18
American Indian/Alaska Native	11
Asian	194
Native Hawaiian/Pacific Islander	0
Other race	114
Two or more races	108
Hispanic origin, total	439
Mexican	28
Puerto Rican	21
Cuban	10
Other Hispanic	380

Age & Nativity, 2000
Under 5 years	557
18 years and over	5,430
21 years and over	5,280
65 years and over	933
85 years and over	76
Median age	40.0
Native-born	6,428
Foreign-born	917

Educational Attainment, 2000
Population 25 years and over	5,129
Less than 9th grade	2.3%
High school grad or higher	92.3%
Bachelor's degree or higher	59.6%
Graduate degree	24.3%

Income & Poverty, 1999
Per capita income	$69,854
Median household income	$104,162
Median family income	$126,601
Persons in poverty	202
H'holds receiving public assistance	21
H'holds receiving social security	732

Households, 2000
Total households	2,723
With persons under 18	1,010
With persons over 65	669
Family households	2,050
Single-person households	573
Persons per household	2.69
Persons per family	3.12

Labor & Employment
Total civilian labor force, 2007**	4,336
Unemployment rate	1.3%
Total civilian labor force, 2000	3,831
Unemployment rate	1.4%

Employed persons 16 years and over by occupation, 2000
Managers & professionals	1,999
Service occupations	477
Sales & office occupations	905
Farming, fishing & forestry	0
Construction & maintenance	190
Production & transportation	208
Self-employed persons	382

General Information
Borough of Bernardsville
166 Mine Brook Road
Bernardsville, NJ 07924
908-766-3000
Website	www.bernardsvilleboro.org
Year of incorporation	1924
Land/water area (sq. miles)	12.93/0.01
Form of government	Borough

Government
Legislative Districts
US Congressional	7
State Legislative	16

Local Officials, 2009
Mayor	Lee Honecker
Manager	Ralph Maresca Jr
Clerk	Sandra Jones
Finance Dir	Ralph Maresca Jr
Tax Assessor	Marcia Sudano
Tax Collector	Antonietta Marino
Attorney	John Pidgeon
Building	Len Perre
Planning	Michael Mondok
Engineering	Paul Ferriero
Public Works	John Macdowall
Police Chief	Kevin Valentine
Emerg/Fire Director	Jerry Negri Jr

Housing & Construction
Housing Units, 2000*
Total	2,807
Median rent	$1,039
Median SF home value	$409,700

Permits for New Residential Construction
	Units	Value
Total, 2006	10	$6,612,905
Single family	10	$6,612,905
Total, 2007	16	$11,944,800
Single family	16	$11,944,800

Real Property Valuation, 2008
	Parcels	Valuation
Total	3,016	$2,690,611,200
Vacant	141	38,477,700
Residential	2,505	2,304,141,200
Commercial	167	189,681,400
Industrial	26	22,330,100
Apartments	12	9,210,400
Farm land	104	405,500
Farm homestead	61	126,364,900

Average Property Value & Tax, 2008
Residential value	$947,196
Property tax	$13,085
Tax credit/rebate	$1,150

Public Library
Bernardsville Public Library
1 Anderson Hill Rd
Bernardsville, NJ 07924
908-766-0118
Director	Karen Brodsky

Library statistics, 2007
Population served	7,345
Full-time/total staff	4/6

	Total	Per capita
Holdings	99,248	13.51
Revenues	$1,023,771	$139.38
Expenditures	$954,247	$129.92
Annual visits	194,082	26.42
Internet terminals/annual users	39/74,418	

Public Safety
Number of officers, 2007	18

Crime
Crime	2006	2007
Total crimes	68	54
Violent	2	0
Murder	0	0
Rape	1	0
Robbery	0	0
Aggravated assault	1	0
Non-violent	66	54
Burglary	7	6
Larceny	58	48
Vehicle theft	1	0
Domestic violence	52	29
Arson	0	0
Total crime rate	8.9	7.0
Violent	0.3	0.0
Non-violent	8.7	7.0

Public School District
(for school year 2007-08 except as noted)

Somerset Hills Regional School District
25 Olcott Ave
Bernardsville, NJ 07924
(908) 630-3011
Superintendent	Peter Miller
Number of schools	3
Grade plan	K-12
Enrollment	2,049
Attendance rate, '06-07	95.9%
Dropout rate	0.1%
Students per teacher	10.5
Per pupil expenditure	$15,952
Median faculty salary	$64,173
Median administrator salary	$130,000
Grade 12 enrollment	175
High school graduation rate	98.3%

Assessment test results
(percent scoring at proficient or advanced level)
	Language	Math
NJASK-Grade 3	95.6%	90.4%
GEPA-Grade 8	87.1%	95.2%
HSPA-High School	93.7%	96.1%

SAT Score Averages, 2006-07
Pct tested	Math	Verbal	Writing
91%	575	561	558

Teacher Qualifications
Avg. years of experience	10
Highly-qualified teachers one subject/all subjects	99.5%/99.5%

No Child Left Behind
AYP, 2006-07	Meets Standards

Municipal Finance
State Aid Programs, 2009
Total aid	$901,062
CMPTRA	3,824
Energy tax receipts	861,195
Garden State Trust	0

General Budget, 2008
Total tax levy	$37,253,129
County levy	8,044,283
County taxes	7,242,661
County library	0
County health	0
County open space	801,623
School levy	20,809,022
Muni. levy	8,399,823
Misc. revenues	4,402,803

Taxes
Taxes	2006	2007	2008
General tax rate per $100	1.33	1.34	1.382
County equalization ratio	108.75	104.29	101.05
Net valuation taxable	$2,588,197,080	$2,678,361,185	$2,696,641,905
State equalized value	$2,549,311,975	$2,644,066,717	$2,660,540,571

* US Census Bureau
** New Jersey Department of Labor

See Introduction for an explanation of all data sources.

Demographics & Socio-Economic Characteristics
(2000 US Census, except as noted)

Population
1980*	3,045
1990*	3,104
2000	3,820
Male	1,921
Female	1,899
2007 (estimate)*	3,945
Population density	189.3

Race & Hispanic Origin, 2000
Race
White	3,725
Black/African American	33
American Indian/Alaska Native	4
Asian	39
Native Hawaiian/Pacific Islander	2
Other race	1
Two or more races	16
Hispanic origin, total	62
Mexican	5
Puerto Rican	25
Cuban	8
Other Hispanic	24

Age & Nativity, 2000
Under 5 years	283
18 years and over	2,693
21 years and over	2,598
65 years and over	249
85 years and over	27
Median age	38.8
Native-born	3,634
Foreign-born	186

Educational Attainment, 2000
Population 25 years and over	2,499
Less than 9th grade	3.6%
High school grad or higher	92.3%
Bachelor's degree or higher	45.3%
Graduate degree	18.6%

Income & Poverty, 1999
Per capita income	$35,298
Median household income	$88,048
Median family income	$92,768
Persons in poverty	40
H'holds receiving public assistance	7
H'holds receiving social security	221

Households, 2000
Total households	1,266
With persons under 18	575
With persons over 65	188
Family households	1,093
Single-person households	131
Persons per household	3.02
Persons per family	3.26

Labor & Employment
Total civilian labor force, 2007**	2,260
Unemployment rate	1.7%
Total civilian labor force, 2000	2,028
Unemployment rate	1.4%

Employed persons 16 years and over by occupation, 2000
Managers & professionals	958
Service occupations	172
Sales & office occupations	538
Farming, fishing & forestry	15
Construction & maintenance	236
Production & transportation	80
Self-employed persons	124

General Information
Township of Bethlehem
405 Mine Rd
Asbury, NJ 08802
908-735-4107

Website	www.bethlehemnj.org
Year of incorporation	1730
Land/water area (sq. miles)	20.84/0.00
Form of government	Township

Government

Legislative Districts
US Congressional	7
State Legislative	23

Local Officials, 2009
Mayor	John Graefe
Manager	Diane Pflugfelder
Clerk	Diane Pflugfelder
Finance Dir	Edward P. Rees
Tax Assessor	Eloise Hagaman
Tax Collector	Steve Davis
Attorney	Robert Kenny
Building	NA
Comm Dev/Planning	NA
Engineering	Robert O'Brien
Public Works	Steve Douglas
Police Chief	NA
Fire/Emergency Dir	NA

Housing & Construction

Housing Units, 2000*
Total	1,303
Median rent	$750
Median SF home value	$278,400

Permits for New Residential Construction
	Units	Value
Total, 2006	2	$321,400
Single family	2	$321,400
Total, 2007	1	$72,360
Single family	1	$72,360

Real Property Valuation, 2008
	Parcels	Valuation
Total	1,803	$528,126,828
Vacant	151	6,976,100
Residential	1,267	448,389,600
Commercial	23	20,956,200
Industrial	7	8,333,000
Apartments	0	0
Farm land	222	1,946,328
Farm homestead	133	41,525,600

Average Property Value & Tax, 2008
Residential value	$349,939
Property tax	$9,841
Tax credit/rebate	$1,294

Public Library
No public municipal library

Library statistics, 2007
Population served	NA
Full-time/total staff	NA/NA

	Total	Per capita
Holdings	NA	NA
Revenues	NA	NA
Expenditures	NA	NA
Annual visits	NA	NA
Internet terminals/annual users	NA/NA	

Public Safety
Number of officers, 2007	0

Crime	2006	2007
Total crimes	14	8
Violent	1	1
Murder	0	0
Rape	0	0
Robbery	0	0
Aggravated assault	1	1
Non-violent	13	7
Burglary	4	4
Larceny	5	3
Vehicle theft	4	0
Domestic violence	1	14
Arson	0	2
Total crime rate	3.5	2.0
Violent	0.3	0.2
Non-violent	3.3	1.7

Public School District
(for school year 2007-08 except as noted)

Bethlehem Township School District
940 Iron Bridge Road
Asbury, NJ 08802
(908) 537-4044

Superintendent	Carol Conger (Int)
Number of schools	2
Grade plan	K-8
Enrollment	601
Attendance rate, '06-07	97.2%
Dropout rate	NA
Students per teacher	9.5
Per pupil expenditure	$14,068
Median faculty salary	$47,591
Median administrator salary	$104,939
Grade 12 enrollment	NA
High school graduation rate	NA

Assessment test results
(percent scoring at proficient or advanced level)
	Language	Math
NJASK-Grade 3	100.0%	90.5%
GEPA-Grade 8	78.0%	90.2%
HSPA-High School	NA	NA

SAT Score Averages, 2006-07
Pct tested	Math	Verbal	Writing
NA	NA	NA	NA

Teacher Qualifications
Avg. years of experience	9
Highly-qualified teachers one subject/all subjects	100%/100%

No Child Left Behind
AYP, 2006-07	Meets Standards

Municipal Finance

State Aid Programs, 2009
Total aid	$347,167
CMPTRA	34,067
Energy tax receipts	288,351
Garden State Trust	9,262

General Budget, 2008
Total tax levy	$14,870,171
County levy	2,368,766
County taxes	1,982,569
County library	172,166
County health	0
County open space	214,032
School levy	10,712,015
Muni. levy	1,789,390
Misc. revenues	1,259,513

Taxes
	2006	2007	2008
General tax rate per $100	2.7	2.78	2.813
County equalization ratio	78.47	74.59	74.38
Net valuation taxable	$522,301,828	$527,063,675	$528,777,943
State equalized value	$670,498,896	$693,553,785	$670,862,826

* US Census Bureau
** New Jersey Department of Labor

See Introduction for an explanation of all data sources.

Demographics & Socio-Economic Characteristics

(2000 US Census, except as noted)

Population

1980*	2,919
1990*	2,973
2000	2,661
Male	1,251
Female	1,410
2007 (estimate)*	2,588
Population density	4,462.1

Race & Hispanic Origin, 2000

Race

White	1,721
Black/African American	765
American Indian/Alaska Native	3
Asian	24
Native Hawaiian/Pacific Islander	0
Other race	38
Two or more races	110
Hispanic origin, total	122
Mexican	6
Puerto Rican	88
Cuban	3
Other Hispanic	25

Age & Nativity, 2000

Under 5 years	172
18 years and over	1,907
21 years and over	1,784
65 years and over	314
85 years and over	33
Median age	35.0
Native-born	2,596
Foreign-born	65

Educational Attainment, 2000

Population 25 years and over	1,689
Less than 9th grade	4.5%
High school grad or higher	77.0%
Bachelor's degree or higher	11.2%
Graduate degree	4.6%

Income & Poverty, 1999

Per capita income	$17,760
Median household income	$45,054
Median family income	$49,519
Persons in poverty	302
H'holds receiving public assistance	25
H'holds receiving social security	256

Households, 2000

Total households	960
With persons under 18	381
With persons over 65	244
Family households	694
Single-person households	207
Persons per household	2.77
Persons per family	3.23

Labor & Employment

Total civilian labor force, 2007**	1,564
Unemployment rate	8.6%
Total civilian labor force, 2000	1,368
Unemployment rate	8.4%

Employed persons 16 years and over by occupation, 2000

Managers & professionals	276
Service occupations	288
Sales & office occupations	311
Farming, fishing & forestry	0
Construction & maintenance	126
Production & transportation	252
Self-employed persons	62

‡ Joint library with Edgewater Park
* US Census Bureau
** New Jersey Department of Labor

General Information

City of Beverly
446 Broad St
Beverly, NJ 08010
609-387-1881

Website	beverlycitynj.com
Year of incorporation	1857
Land/water area (sq. miles)	0.58/0.20
Form of government	City

Government

Legislative Districts

US Congressional	3
State Legislative	7

Local Officials, 2009

Mayor	Gail G. Cook
Manager	Barbara A. Sheipe
Clerk	Barbara A. Sheipe
Finance Dir	Victoria Boras
Tax Assessor	Joseph Robinson
Tax Collector	Victoria Boras
Attorney	Skip Reale
Building	Pete Carbone
Comm Dev/Planning	NA
Engineering	William Kirchner
Public Works	Daniel Schoen
Public Safety Dir	Michael Morton
Emerg/Fire Director	Ray Rodarmel

Housing & Construction

Housing Units, 2000*

Total	1,042
Median rent	$645
Median SF home value	$94,300

Permits for New Residential Construction

	Units	Value
Total, 2006	1	$62,188
Single family	1	$62,188
Total, 2007	5	$296,400
Single family	5	$296,400

Real Property Valuation, 2008

	Parcels	Valuation
Total	987	$83,731,600
Vacant	61	906,100
Residential	864	75,458,000
Commercial	44	4,436,900
Industrial	13	2,130,200
Apartments	5	800,400
Farm land	0	0
Farm homestead	0	0

Average Property Value & Tax, 2008

Residential value	$87,336
Property tax	$4,564
Tax credit/rebate	$919

Public Library

Beverly Public Library‡
441 Cooper St
Beverly, NJ 08010
609-387-1259

Director	Tracey Hall

Library statistics, 2007

Population served	2,661
Full-time/total staff	NA/0

	Total	Per capita
Holdings	0	NA
Revenues	$0	NA
Expenditures	$0	NA
Annual visits	NA	NA
Internet terminals/annual users	NA/NA	

Public Safety

Number of officers, 2007	7

Crime	2006	2007
Total crimes	82	65
Violent	15	17
Murder	0	0
Rape	5	0
Robbery	0	6
Aggravated assault	10	11
Non-violent	67	48
Burglary	18	16
Larceny	38	27
Vehicle theft	11	5
Domestic violence	48	56
Arson	1	0
Total crime rate	30.7	24.5
Violent	5.6	6.4
Non-violent	25.1	18.1

Public School District

(for school year 2007-08 except as noted)

Beverly City School District
601 Bentley Ave.
Beverly, NJ 08010
(609) 387-2200

Superintendent	Brian Gross (Int)
Number of schools	1
Grade plan	K-8
Enrollment	217
Attendance rate, '06-07	93.5%
Dropout rate	NA
Students per teacher	9.7
Per pupil expenditure	$18,678
Median faculty salary	$48,432
Median administrator salary	$94,907
Grade 12 enrollment	NA
High school graduation rate	NA

Assessment test results

(percent scoring at proficient or advanced level)

	Language	Math
NJASK-Grade 3	70.8%	78.3%
GEPA-Grade 8	33.3%	57.9%
HSPA-High School	NA	NA

SAT Score Averages, 2006-07

Pct tested	Math	Verbal	Writing
NA	NA	NA	NA

Teacher Qualifications

Avg. years of experience	11
Highly-qualified teachers one subject/all subjects	10.5%/10.5%

No Child Left Behind

AYP, 2006-07	Meets Standards

Municipal Finance

State Aid Programs, 2009

Total aid	$347,161
CMPTRA	111,399
Energy tax receipts	234,026
Garden State Trust	0

General Budget, 2008

Total tax levy	$4,380,347
County levy	587,229
County taxes	482,239
County library	44,526
County health	0
County open space	60,464
School levy	2,601,122
Muni. levy	1,191,997
Misc. revenues	1,846,057

Taxes	2006	2007	2008
General tax rate per $100	4.963	5.15	5.226
County equalization ratio	69.77	61.91	55.70
Net valuation taxable	$82,852,900	$83,395,044	$83,822,400
State equalized value	$133,931,508	$149,646,052	$154,891,318

See Introduction for an explanation of all data sources.

Demographics & Socio-Economic Characteristics
(2000 US Census, except as noted)

Population
1980*	4,360
1990*	5,331
2000	5,747
Male	2,866
Female	2,881
2007 (estimate)*	5,928
Population density	191.1

Race & Hispanic Origin, 2000
Race
White	5,642
Black/African American	15
American Indian/Alaska Native	8
Asian	32
Native Hawaiian/Pacific Islander	1
Other race	16
Two or more races	33
Hispanic origin, total	114
Mexican	6
Puerto Rican	35
Cuban	15
Other Hispanic	58

Age & Nativity, 2000
Under 5 years	335
18 years and over	4,278
21 years and over	4,110
65 years and over	713
85 years and over	79
Median age	40.4
Native-born	5,450
Foreign-born	298

Educational Attainment, 2000
Population 25 years and over	3,957
Less than 9th grade	5.1%
High school grad or higher	86.7%
Bachelor's degree or higher	29.8%
Graduate degree	12.7%

Income & Poverty, 1999
Per capita income	$27,775
Median household income	$64,809
Median family income	$71,214
Persons in poverty	261
H'holds receiving public assistance	27
H'holds receiving social security	582

Households, 2000
Total households	2,040
With persons under 18	773
With persons over 65	519
Family households	1,638
Single-person households	312
Persons per household	2.81
Persons per family	3.14

Labor & Employment
Total civilian labor force, 2007**	3,377
Unemployment rate	4.2%
Total civilian labor force, 2000	2,994
Unemployment rate	3.9%

Employed persons 16 years and over by occupation, 2000
Managers & professionals	1,274
Service occupations	208
Sales & office occupations	641
Farming, fishing & forestry	17
Construction & maintenance	387
Production & transportation	350
Self-employed persons	221

General Information
Township of Blairstown
106 Route 94
Blairstown, NJ 07825
908-362-6663
Website	www.blairstown-nj.org
Year of incorporation	1845
Land/water area (sq. miles)	31.02/0.75
Form of government	Township

Government
Legislative Districts
US Congressional	5
State Legislative	23

Local Officials, 2009
Mayor	Richard A. Mach
Manager/Admin	NA
Clerk	Phyllis E. Pizzaia
Finance Dir	Barbara Emery
Tax Assessor	Richard Motyka
Tax Collector	Rita Kelley
Attorney	Robert Benbrook
Building	Ralph Price
Comm Dev/Planning	NA
Engineering	Ted Rodman
Public Works	Robert DePuy
Police Chief	Tom Krisak
Fire Chief	Michael Sullivan

Housing & Construction
Housing Units, 2000*
Total	2,136
Median rent	$882
Median SF home value	$207,600

Permits for New Residential Construction
	Units	Value
Total, 2006	26	$5,302,139
Single family	26	$5,302,139
Total, 2007	13	$3,505,053
Single family	13	$3,505,053

Real Property Valuation, 2008
	Parcels	Valuation
Total	2,775	$911,211,525
Vacant	203	25,805,300
Residential	1,856	694,003,300
Commercial	125	79,884,700
Industrial	9	15,768,000
Apartments	0	0
Farm land	368	2,071,225
Farm homestead	214	93,679,000

Average Property Value & Tax, 2008
Residential value	$380,523
Property tax	$6,423
Tax credit/rebate	$1,093

Public Library
C.D. Hofman Library‡
4 Lambert Rd
Blairstown, NJ 07825
908-362-8335
Branch Librarian	Marilyn Grandin

Library statistics, 2007
see Warren County profile
for library system statistics

Public Safety
Number of officers, 2007 8
Crime	2006	2007
Total crimes	68	60
Violent	8	2
Murder	0	0
Rape	1	0
Robbery	1	0
Aggravated assault	6	2
Non-violent	60	58
Burglary	12	8
Larceny	46	48
Vehicle theft	2	2
Domestic violence	13	17
Arson	0	1
Total crime rate	11.4	10.0
Violent	1.3	0.3
Non-violent	10.0	9.7

Public School District
(for school year 2007-08 except as noted)

Blairstown Township School District
1 Sunset Hill Rd, PO Box E
Blairstown, NJ 07825
(908) 362-6111
Superintendent	Mark Saalfield
Number of schools	1
Grade plan	K-6
Enrollment	764
Attendance rate, '06-07	94.3%
Dropout rate	NA
Students per teacher	12.5
Per pupil expenditure	$10,551
Median faculty salary	$63,180
Median administrator salary	$97,287
Grade 12 enrollment	NA
High school graduation rate	NA

Assessment test results
(percent scoring at proficient or advanced level)
	Language	Math
NJASK-Grade 3	90.3%	90.3%
GEPA-Grade 8	NA	NA
HSPA-High School	NA	NA

SAT Score Averages, 2006-07
Pct tested	Math	Verbal	Writing
NA	NA	NA	NA

Teacher Qualifications
Avg. years of experience	18
Highly-qualified teachers one subject/all subjects	98.0%/96.0%

No Child Left Behind
AYP, 2006-07 .... Meets Standards

Municipal Finance
State Aid Programs, 2009
Total aid	$3,200,528
CMPTRA	0
Energy tax receipts	3,040,905
Garden State Trust	25,632

General Budget, 2008
Total tax levy	$15,421,406
County levy	5,826,693
County taxes	4,749,579
County library	500,226
County health	0
County open space	576,888
School levy	9,274,708
Muni. levy	320,005
Misc. revenues	4,904,850

Taxes	2006	2007	2008
General tax rate per $100	2.99	1.65	1.688
County equalization ratio	59.07	102	95.20
Net valuation taxable	$466,498,694	$909,363,531	$913,645,462
State equalized value	$876,015,592	$955,090,645	$946,988,228

‡ Branch of county library
* US Census Bureau
** New Jersey Department of Labor

Demographics & Socio-Economic Characteristics

(2000 US Census, except as noted)

Population

1980*	47,792
1990*	45,061
2000	47,683
Male	22,695
Female	24,988
2007 (estimate)*	44,398
Population density	8,345.5

Race & Hispanic Origin, 2000

Race

White	33,421
Black/African American	5,573
American Indian/Alaska Native	91
Asian	3,998
Native Hawaiian/Pacific Islander	31
Other race	3,061
Two or more races	1,508
Hispanic origin, total	6,901
Mexican	160
Puerto Rican	2,724
Cuban	377
Other Hispanic	3,640

Age & Nativity, 2000

Under 5 years	2,820
18 years and over	37,644
21 years and over	36,087
65 years and over	6,827
85 years and over	871
Median age	37.1
Native-born	36,791
Foreign-born	10,892

Educational Attainment, 2000

Population 25 years and over	33,673
Less than 9th grade	6.1%
High school grad or higher	83.5%
Bachelor's degree or higher	31.8%
Graduate degree	9.9%

Income & Poverty, 1999

Per capita income	$26,049
Median household income	$53,289
Median family income	$64,945
Persons in poverty	2,772
H'holds receiving public assistance	339
H'holds receiving social security	5,146

Households, 2000

Total households	19,017
With persons under 18	5,796
With persons over 65	5,034
Family households	12,069
Single-person households	5,789
Persons per household	2.49
Persons per family	3.16

Labor & Employment

Total civilian labor force, 2007**	25,559
Unemployment rate	4.2%
Total civilian labor force, 2000	26,092
Unemployment rate	5.1%

Employed persons 16 years and over by occupation, 2000

Managers & professionals	9,624
Service occupations	2,968
Sales & office occupations	7,522
Farming, fishing & forestry	15
Construction & maintenance	1,635
Production & transportation	3,006
Self-employed persons	840

* US Census Bureau
** New Jersey Department of Labor

General Information

Township of Bloomfield
1 Municipal Plaza
Bloomfield, NJ 07003
973-680-4000

Website	www.bloomfieldtwpnj.com
Year of incorporation	1981
Land/water area (sq. miles)	5.32/0.01
Form of government	Special Charter

Government

Legislative Districts

US Congressional	8
State Legislative	28

Local Officials, 2009

Mayor	Raymond J. McCarthy
Administrator	Louise M. Palagano
Clerk	Louise M. Palagano
Finance Dir	Robert Renna
Tax Assessor	Joseph Pisauro
Tax Collector	Cindy Prochilo
Attorney	Brian Aloia
Building	Carl Graziano
Comm Dev/Planning	Glenn Domenick
Engineering	Paul Lasek
Public Works	Gerald MacIntyre
Police Chief	Mark Leonard
Acting Chief	Joseph McCarthy

Housing & Construction

Housing Units, 2000*

Total	19,508
Median rent	$768
Median SF home value	$164,800

Permits for New Residential Construction

	Units	Value
Total, 2006	46	$7,881,632
Single family	42	$7,470,132
Total, 2007	31	$5,179,879
Single family	29	$4,974,129

Real Property Valuation, 2008

	Parcels	Valuation
Total	12,608	$2,079,299,000
Vacant	129	9,275,900
Residential	11,690	1,639,810,200
Commercial	661	286,204,100
Industrial	39	33,682,200
Apartments	89	110,326,600
Farm land	0	0
Farm homestead	0	0

Average Property Value & Tax, 2008

Residential value	$140,275
Property tax	$8,264
Tax credit/rebate	$1,197

Public Library

Bloomfield Public Library
90 Broad St
Bloomfield, NJ 07003
973-566-6200

Director	Gian Hasija

Library statistics, 2007

Population served	47,683
Full-time/total staff	8/15

	Total	Per capita
Holdings	174,482	3.66
Revenues	$1,514,730	$31.77
Expenditures	$1,480,271	$31.04
Annual visits	192,607	4.04
Internet terminals/annual users	28/59,607	

Public Safety

Number of officers, 2007	133

Crime	2006	2007
Total crimes	1,478	1,429
Violent	134	130
Murder	1	1
Rape	4	2
Robbery	86	84
Aggravated assault	43	43
Non-violent	1,344	1,299
Burglary	192	184
Larceny	895	914
Vehicle theft	257	201
Domestic violence	177	201
Arson	5	4
Total crime rate	32.0	31.5
Violent	2.9	2.9
Non-violent	29.1	28.6

Public School District

(for school year 2007-08 except as noted)

Bloomfield Township School District
155 Broad Street
Bloomfield, NJ 07003
(973) 680-8501

Superintendent	Frank DiGesere
Number of schools	11
Grade plan	K-12
Enrollment	5,914
Attendance rate, '06-07	93.9%
Dropout rate	3.2%
Students per teacher	11.1
Per pupil expenditure	$11,799
Median faculty salary	$52,500
Median administrator salary	$110,278
Grade 12 enrollment	446
High school graduation rate	93.1%

Assessment test results

(percent scoring at proficient or advanced level)

	Language	Math
NJASK-Grade 3	91.4%	86.1%
GEPA-Grade 8	57.3%	77.1%
HSPA-High School	63.8%	83.2%

SAT Score Averages, 2006-07

Pct tested	Math	Verbal	Writing
86%	456	456	448

Teacher Qualifications

Avg. years of experience	7
Highly-qualified teachers one subject/all subjects	100%/100%

No Child Left Behind

AYP, 2006-07	Meets Standards

Municipal Finance

State Aid Programs, 2009

Total aid	$7,840,357
CMPTRA	4,236,373
Energy tax receipts	3,486,379
Garden State Trust	0

General Budget, 2008

Total tax levy	$122,661,469
County levy	20,616,182
County taxes	19,820,232
County library	0
County health	0
County open space	795,950
School levy	56,883,680
Muni. levy	45,161,607
Misc. revenues	18,209,468

Taxes

	2006	2007	2008
General tax rate per $100	5.11	5.45	5.892
County equalization ratio	49.13	42.66	39.81
Net valuation taxable	$2,083,516,600	$2,082,553,700	$2,082,016,600
State equalized value	$4,887,217,357	$5,226,945,976	$5,257,453,511

See Introduction for an explanation of all data sources.

Demographics & Socio-Economic Characteristics
(2000 US Census, except as noted)

Population
1980*	7,867
1990*	7,530
2000	7,610
Male	3,763
Female	3,847
2007 (estimate)*	7,495
Population density	851.7

Race & Hispanic Origin, 2000
Race
White	7,271
Black/African American	32
American Indian/Alaska Native	9
Asian	167
Native Hawaiian/Pacific Islander	0
Other race	51
Two or more races	80
Hispanic origin, total	332
Mexican	93
Puerto Rican	100
Cuban	21
Other Hispanic	118

Age & Nativity, 2000
Under 5 years	509
18 years and over	5,914
21 years and over	5,698
65 years and over	903
85 years and over	117
Median age	37.9
Native-born	6,839
Foreign-born	771

Educational Attainment, 2000
Population 25 years and over	5,442
Less than 9th grade	3.4%
High school grad or higher	87.6%
Bachelor's degree or higher	25.7%
Graduate degree	7.7%

Income & Poverty, 1999
Per capita income	$27,736
Median household income	$67,885
Median family income	$75,433
Persons in poverty	251
H'holds receiving public assistance	46
H'holds receiving social security	604

Households, 2000
Total households	2,847
With persons under 18	974
With persons over 65	583
Family households	2,077
Single-person households	623
Persons per household	2.63
Persons per family	3.09

Labor & Employment
Total civilian labor force, 2007**	4,912
Unemployment rate	2.9%
Total civilian labor force, 2000	4,546
Unemployment rate	3.1%

Employed persons 16 years and over by occupation, 2000
Managers & professionals	1,649
Service occupations	589
Sales & office occupations	1,243
Farming, fishing & forestry	0
Construction & maintenance	325
Production & transportation	599
Self-employed persons	206

* US Census Bureau
** New Jersey Department of Labor

General Information
Borough of Bloomingdale
101 Hamburg Turpike
Bloomingdale, NJ 07403
973-838-0778
Website	www.bloomingdalenj.net
Year of incorporation	1918
Land/water area (sq. miles)	8.80/0.41
Form of government	Borough

Government
Legislative Districts
US Congressional	5, 11
State Legislative	26

Local Officials, 2009
Mayor	William Steenstra
Administrator	Ted Ehrenburg
Clerk	Jane McCarthy
Treasurer	Sherry Gallagher
Tax Assessor	Brian Townsend
Tax Collector	Cora Wright
Attorney	Joseph MacMahon
Building	Daniel Hagberg
Comm Dev/Planning	NA
Engineering	James Floystrop
Public Works	Albert Gallagher
Police Chief	Joseph Borell
Emerg/Fire Director	John D'Amato

Housing & Construction
Housing Units, 2000*
Total	2,940
Median rent	$899
Median SF home value	$177,000

Permits for New Residential Construction
	Units	Value
Total, 2006	0	$105,000
Single family	0	$105,000
Total, 2007	2	$221,300
Single family	2	$221,300

Real Property Valuation, 2008
	Parcels	Valuation
Total	2,720	$421,077,264
Vacant	131	12,745,900
Residential	2,465	363,721,500
Commercial	102	32,801,200
Industrial	1	6,000
Apartments	8	11,245,500
Farm land	10	64,264
Farm homestead	3	492,900

Average Property Value & Tax, 2008
Residential value	$147,575
Property tax	$8,380
Tax credit/rebate	$1,282

Public Library
Bloomingdale Public Library
101 Hamburg Turnpike
Bloomingdale, NJ 07403
973-838-0077
Director	Theresa J. Rubin

Library statistics, 2007
Population served	7,610
Full-time/total staff	0/2

	Total	Per capita
Holdings	31,377	4.12
Revenues	$344,505	$45.27
Expenditures	$336,350	$44.20
Annual visits	24,850	3.27
Internet terminals/annual users	4/3,189	

Public Safety
Number of officers, 2007	16

Crime	2006	2007
Total crimes	75	54
Violent	1	3
Murder	0	0
Rape	0	0
Robbery	0	0
Aggravated assault	1	3
Non-violent	74	51
Burglary	14	7
Larceny	50	43
Vehicle theft	10	1
Domestic violence	55	54
Arson	1	0
Total crime rate	9.8	7.1
Violent	0.1	0.4
Non-violent	9.7	6.7

Public School District
(for school year 2007-08 except as noted)

Bloomingdale School District
Captolene Avenue
Bloomingdale, NJ 07403
(973) 838-3282
Chief School Admin	Fredda Rosenberg
Number of schools	3
Grade plan	K-8
Enrollment	630
Attendance rate, '06-07	95.8%
Dropout rate	NA
Students per teacher	11.2
Per pupil expenditure	$15,632
Median faculty salary	$57,580
Median administrator salary	$116,416
Grade 12 enrollment	NA
High school graduation rate	NA

Assessment test results
(percent scoring at proficient or advanced level)
	Language	Math
NJASK-Grade 3	82.1%	94.0%
GEPA-Grade 8	72.0%	86.8%
HSPA-High School	NA	NA

SAT Score Averages, 2006-07
Pct tested	Math	Verbal	Writing
NA	NA	NA	NA

Teacher Qualifications
Avg. years of experience	9
Highly-qualified teachers one subject/all subjects	100%/100%

No Child Left Behind
AYP, 2006-07	Meets Standards

Municipal Finance
State Aid Programs, 2009
Total aid	$727,576
CMPTRA	182,425
Energy tax receipts	503,474
Garden State Trust	9,775

General Budget, 2008
Total tax levy	$23,927,094
County levy	5,190,280
County taxes	5,087,416
County library	0
County health	0
County open space	102,865
School levy	12,774,153
Muni. levy	5,962,661
Misc. revenues	2,692,675

Taxes
	2006	2007	2008
General tax rate per $100	4.94	5.4	5.679
County equalization ratio	48.94	43.36	41.06
Net valuation taxable	$420,693,199	$420,614,373	$421,379,064
State equalized value	$970,554,566	$1,023,968,862	$1,013,724,794

See Introduction for an explanation of all data sources.

Demographics & Socio-Economic Characteristics

(2000 US Census, except as noted)

Population

1980*	864
1990*	890
2000	886
Male	427
Female	459
2007 (estimate)*	865
Population density	950.5

Race & Hispanic Origin, 2000

Race

White	870
Black/African American	3
American Indian/Alaska Native	2
Asian	3
Native Hawaiian/Pacific Islander	0
Other race	1
Two or more races	7
Hispanic origin, total	13
Mexican	1
Puerto Rican	2
Cuban	2
Other Hispanic	8

Age & Nativity, 2000

Under 5 years	102
18 years and over	622
21 years and over	605
65 years and over	89
85 years and over	7
Median age	35.5
Native-born	861
Foreign-born	25

Educational Attainment, 2000

Population 25 years and over	581
Less than 9th grade	0.9%
High school grad or higher	93.6%
Bachelor's degree or higher	33.0%
Graduate degree	11.7%

Income & Poverty, 1999

Per capita income	$26,392
Median household income	$64,375
Median family income	$67,500
Persons in poverty	34
H'holds receiving public assistance	4
H'holds receiving social security	64

Households, 2000

Total households	322
With persons under 18	151
With persons over 65	62
Family households	252
Single-person households	51
Persons per household	2.74
Persons per family	3.11

Labor & Employment

Total civilian labor force, 2007**	537
Unemployment rate	4.8%
Total civilian labor force, 2000	472
Unemployment rate	3.2%

Employed persons 16 years and over by occupation, 2000

Managers & professionals	185
Service occupations	66
Sales & office occupations	116
Farming, fishing & forestry	0
Construction & maintenance	56
Production & transportation	34
Self-employed persons	31

* US Census Bureau
** New Jersey Department of Labor

General Information

Borough of Bloomsbury
91 Brunswick Ave
Bloomsbury, NJ 08804
908-479-4200

Website	bloomsburynewjersey.com
Year of incorporation	1905
Land/water area (sq. miles)	0.91/0.00
Form of government	Borough

Government

Legislative Districts

US Congressional	7
State Legislative	23

Local Officials, 2009

Mayor	Mark R. Peck
Administrator	Lisa A. Burd
Clerk	Lisa A. Burd
Finance Dir	Kim Francisco
Tax Assessor	Eloise Hagaman
Tax Collector	Jane Heater
Attorney	William Edleston
Building	NA
Comm Dev/Planning	NA
Engineering	Rick Roseburry
Public Works	NA
Police Chief	NA
Emerg/Fire Director	Peter Horsch

Housing & Construction

Housing Units, 2000*

Total	342
Median rent	$875
Median SF home value	$172,800

Permits for New Residential Construction

	Units	Value
Total, 2006	0	$0
Single family	0	$0
Total, 2007	0	$0
Single family	0	$0

Real Property Valuation, 2008

	Parcels	Valuation
Total	386	$121,934,500
Vacant	34	832,500
Residential	315	95,535,400
Commercial	22	18,955,700
Industrial	5	4,850,500
Apartments	3	1,203,900
Farm land	6	124,400
Farm homestead	1	432,100

Average Property Value & Tax, 2008

Residential value	$303,695
Property tax	$5,650
Tax credit/rebate	$980

Public Library

No public municipal library

Library statistics, 2007

Population served	NA
Full-time/total staff	NA/NA

	Total	Per capita
Holdings	NA	NA
Revenues	NA	NA
Expenditures	NA	NA
Annual visits	NA	NA
Internet terminals/annual users	NA/NA	

Public Safety

Number of officers, 2007	0

Crime	2006	2007
Total crimes	19	19
Violent	2	2
Murder	0	1
Rape	0	0
Robbery	0	0
Aggravated assault	2	1
Non-violent	17	17
Burglary	1	3
Larceny	14	14
Vehicle theft	2	0
Domestic violence	1	8
Arson	0	1
Total crime rate	21.4	21.6
Violent	2.3	2.3
Non-violent	19.2	19.3

Public School District

(for school year 2007-08 except as noted)

Bloomsbury School District
20 Main Street
Bloomsbury, NJ 08804
(908) 479-4414

Chief School Admin	Michael Slattery
Number of schools	1
Grade plan	K-8
Enrollment	146
Attendance rate, '06-07	96.2%
Dropout rate	NA
Students per teacher	9.1
Per pupil expenditure	$11,448
Median faculty salary	$46,618
Median administrator salary	$84,396
Grade 12 enrollment	NA
High school graduation rate	NA

Assessment test results

(percent scoring at proficient or advanced level)

	Language	Math
NJASK-Grade 3	94.1%	100.0%
GEPA-Grade 8	62.5%	81.3%
HSPA-High School	NA	NA

SAT Score Averages, 2006-07

Pct tested	Math	Verbal	Writing
NA	NA	NA	NA

Teacher Qualifications

Avg. years of experience	10
Highly-qualified teachers one subject/all subjects	100%/100%

No Child Left Behind

AYP, 2006-07	Meets Standards

Municipal Finance

State Aid Programs, 2009

Total aid	$75,309
CMPTRA	20,997
Energy tax receipts	51,708
Garden State Trust	336

General Budget, 2008

Total tax levy	$2,271,743
County levy	398,408
County taxes	333,453
County library	28,957
County health	0
County open space	35,998
School levy	1,547,229
Muni. levy	326,106
Misc. revenues	353,044

Taxes

	2006	2007	2008
General tax rate per $100	1.75	1.82	1.861
County equalization ratio	106.92	102.32	102.53
Net valuation taxable	$121,930,500	$122,071,027	$122,103,513
State equalized value	$109,765,900	$118,291,511	$116,175,578

See Introduction for an explanation of all data sources.

Demographics & Socio-Economic Characteristics
(2000 US Census, except as noted)

Population
1980*	8,344
1990*	7,824
2000	8,249
Male	3,917
Female	4,332
2007 (estimate)*	7,991
Population density	10,514.5

Race & Hispanic Origin, 2000
Race
White	6,246
Black/African American	473
American Indian/Alaska Native	12
Asian	639
Native Hawaiian/Pacific Islander	5
Other race	558
Two or more races	316
Hispanic origin, total	1,759
Mexican	83
Puerto Rican	422
Cuban	220
Other Hispanic	1,034

Age & Nativity, 2000
Under 5 years	538
18 years and over	6,161
21 years and over	5,891
65 years and over	915
85 years and over	93
Median age	36.5
Native-born	6,437
Foreign-born	1,812

Educational Attainment, 2000
Population 25 years and over	5,542
Less than 9th grade	5.0%
High school grad or higher	84.4%
Bachelor's degree or higher	28.4%
Graduate degree	9.2%

Income & Poverty, 1999
Per capita income	$25,505
Median household income	$59,813
Median family income	$69,841
Persons in poverty	331
H'holds receiving public assistance	68
H'holds receiving social security	647

Households, 2000
Total households	2,874
With persons under 18	1,129
With persons over 65	694
Family households	2,126
Single-person households	628
Persons per household	2.85
Persons per family	3.38

Labor & Employment
Total civilian labor force, 2007**	4,811
Unemployment rate	6.2%
Total civilian labor force, 2000	4,585
Unemployment rate	6.7%

Employed persons 16 years and over by occupation, 2000
Managers & professionals	1,471
Service occupations	637
Sales & office occupations	1,377
Farming, fishing & forestry	0
Construction & maintenance	372
Production & transportation	422
Self-employed persons	132

* US Census Bureau
** New Jersey Department of Labor

General Information
Borough of Bogota
375 Larch Ave
Bogota, NJ 07603
201-342-1736

Website	www.bogotaonline.org
Year of incorporation	1894
Land/water area (sq. miles)	0.76/0.06
Form of government	Borough

Government
Legislative Districts
US Congressional	9
State Legislative	37

Local Officials, 2009
Mayor	Patrick McHale
Manager	Leonard Nicolosi
Clerk	Fran Garlicki
Finance Dir	Helen Hegel
Tax Assessor	Edward Hynes
Tax Collector	Betty Wiemer
Attorney	Joseph Managhan
Building	Daniel Howell
Planning	Dan Schnipp
Engineering	TNM Associates
Public Works	Don Viviani
Police Chief	Frank Gurnari
Emerg/Fire Director	Lou Kern

Housing & Construction
Housing Units, 2000*
Total	2,915
Median rent	$819
Median SF home value	$166,700

Permits for New Residential Construction
	Units	Value
Total, 2006	7	$1,088,360
Single family	7	$1,088,360
Total, 2007	4	$666,940
Single family	4	$666,940

Real Property Valuation, 2008
	Parcels	Valuation
Total	2,204	$474,732,575
Vacant	52	2,791,700
Residential	2,022	396,497,975
Commercial	92	36,227,800
Industrial	13	14,550,200
Apartments	25	24,664,900
Farm land	0	0
Farm homestead	0	0

Average Property Value & Tax, 2008
Residential value	$196,092
Property tax	$7,889
Tax credit/rebate	$1,131

Public Library
Bogota Public Library
375 Larch Ave
Bogota, NJ 07603
201-488-7185

Director	Jonna Davis

Library statistics, 2007
Population served	8,249
Full-time/total staff	1/2

	Total	Per capita
Holdings	39,005	4.73
Revenues	$259,724	$31.49
Expenditures	$247,957	$30.06
Annual visits	35,170	4.26
Internet terminals/annual users	8/5,285	

Public Safety
Number of officers, 2007	16

Crime	2006	2007
Total crimes	91	83
Violent	5	8
Murder	0	0
Rape	0	0
Robbery	2	5
Aggravated assault	3	3
Non-violent	86	75
Burglary	14	12
Larceny	69	58
Vehicle theft	3	5
Domestic violence	25	30
Arson	0	0
Total crime rate	11.2	10.2
Violent	0.6	1.0
Non-violent	10.6	9.3

Public School District
(for school year 2007-08 except as noted)

Bogota School District
1 Henry C. Luthin Place
Bogota, NJ 07603
(201) 441-4800

Superintendent	John P. Hynes
Number of schools	3
Grade plan	K-12
Enrollment	1,246
Attendance rate, '06-07	95.9%
Dropout rate	0.5%
Students per teacher	11.4
Per pupil expenditure	$12,331
Median faculty salary	$54,012
Median administrator salary	$95,700
Grade 12 enrollment	71
High school graduation rate	97.3%

Assessment test results
(percent scoring at proficient or advanced level)
	Language	Math
NJASK-Grade 3	82.4%	83.5%
GEPA-Grade 8	60.0%	67.1%
HSPA-High School	74.0%	82.0%

SAT Score Averages, 2006-07
Pct tested	Math	Verbal	Writing
77%	447	449	458

Teacher Qualifications
Avg. years of experience	9
Highly-qualified teachers one subject/all subjects	96.5%/96.5%

No Child Left Behind
AYP, 2006-07	Meets Standards

Municipal Finance
State Aid Programs, 2009
Total aid	$873,731
CMPTRA	326,412
Energy tax receipts	525,475
Garden State Trust	0

General Budget, 2008
Total tax levy	$19,115,241
County levy	1,702,737
County taxes	1,610,562
County library	0
County health	0
County open space	92,175
School levy	12,181,576
Muni. levy	5,230,928
Misc. revenues	2,262,796

Taxes
	2006	2007	2008
General tax rate per $100	3.4	3.73	4.024
County equalization ratio	63.07	54.72	52.25
Net valuation taxable	$472,577,200	$474,040,356	$475,113,856
State equalized value	$864,064,997	$906,905,826	$954,042,541

See Introduction for an explanation of all data sources.

Demographics & Socio-Economic Characteristics
(2000 US Census, except as noted)

Population
1980*	8,620
1990*	8,343
2000	8,496
Male	4,214
Female	4,282
2007 (estimate)*	8,482
Population density	3,609.4

Race & Hispanic Origin, 2000
Race
White	7,052
Black/African American	337
American Indian/Alaska Native	18
Asian	660
Native Hawaiian/Pacific Islander	1
Other race	187
Two or more races	241
Hispanic origin, total	582
Mexican	46
Puerto Rican	140
Cuban	19
Other Hispanic	377

Age & Nativity, 2000
Under 5 years	621
18 years and over	6,633
21 years and over	6,418
65 years and over	1,147
85 years and over	158
Median age	36.9
Native-born	7,112
Foreign-born	1,384

Educational Attainment, 2000
Population 25 years and over	6,081
Less than 9th grade	6.4%
High school grad or higher	86.1%
Bachelor's degree or higher	32.9%
Graduate degree	9.4%

Income & Poverty, 1999
Per capita income	$29,919
Median household income	$65,322
Median family income	$75,147
Persons in poverty	559
H'holds receiving public assistance	94
H'holds receiving social security	865

Households, 2000
Total households	3,272
With persons under 18	1,000
With persons over 65	813
Family households	2,159
Single-person households	861
Persons per household	2.55
Persons per family	3.11

Labor & Employment
Total civilian labor force, 2007**	5,199
Unemployment rate	5.7%
Total civilian labor force, 2000	4,792
Unemployment rate	6.0%

Employed persons 16 years and over by occupation, 2000
Managers & professionals	1,845
Service occupations	515
Sales & office occupations	1,265
Farming, fishing & forestry	0
Construction & maintenance	327
Production & transportation	552
Self-employed persons	181

* US Census Bureau
** New Jersey Department of Labor

General Information
Town of Boonton
100 Washington St
Boonton, NJ 07005
973-402-9410

Website	www.boonton.org
Year of incorporation	1866
Land/water area (sq. miles)	2.35/0.12
Form of government	Town

Government
Legislative Districts
US Congressional	11
State Legislative	25

Local Officials, 2009
Mayor	Cyril Wekilsky
Manager	Terry McCue
Clerk	Cynthia Oravits
Finance Dir	Terry McCue
Tax Assessor	Paul Parsons
Tax Collector	June Roessler
Attorney	John Dorsey
Building	Russell Heiney
Comm Dev/Planning	NA
Engineering	John Miller
Superintendent	Michael Petonak
Police Chief	Michael Beltran
Emergency Director	George Westenberger

Housing & Construction
Housing Units, 2000*
Total	3,352
Median rent	$897
Median SF home value	$212,000

Permits for New Residential Construction
	Units	Value
Total, 2006	23	$3,361,789
Single family	23	$3,361,789
Total, 2007	23	$2,677,058
Single family	23	$2,677,058

Real Property Valuation, 2008
	Parcels	Valuation
Total	2,725	$1,290,722,800
Vacant	111	10,755,400
Residential	2,368	1,001,230,100
Commercial	191	182,340,200
Industrial	40	74,767,800
Apartments	13	21,214,600
Farm land	1	2,000
Farm homestead	1	412,700

Average Property Value & Tax, 2008
Residential value	$422,812
Property tax	$8,074
Tax credit/rebate	$1,141

Public Library
Boonton-Holmes Library
621 Main St
Boonton, NJ 07005
973-334-2980

Director	Lesley Karczewski

Library statistics, 2007
Population served	8,496
Full-time/total staff	2/4

	Total	Per capita
Holdings	27,351	3.22
Revenues	$443,163	$52.16
Expenditures	$394,607	$46.45
Annual visits	28,082	3.31
Internet terminals/annual users	6/17,783	

Public Safety
Number of officers, 2007	21

Crime	2006	2007
Total crimes	67	51
Violent	9	4
Murder	0	0
Rape	0	1
Robbery	0	0
Aggravated assault	9	3
Non-violent	58	47
Burglary	4	13
Larceny	46	30
Vehicle theft	8	4
Domestic violence	68	71
Arson	1	3
Total crime rate	7.8	5.9
Violent	1.1	0.5
Non-violent	6.8	5.5

Public School District
(for school year 2007-08 except as noted)

Boonton Town School District
434 Lathrop Avenue
Boonton, NJ 07005
(973) 335-3994

Superintendent	Christine Johnson
Number of schools	4
Grade plan	K-12
Enrollment	1,247
Attendance rate, '06-07	94.9%
Dropout rate	1.0%
Students per teacher	8.8
Per pupil expenditure	$15,750
Median faculty salary	$51,030
Median administrator salary	$92,956
Grade 12 enrollment	159
High school graduation rate	98.7%

Assessment test results
(percent scoring at proficient or advanced level)
	Language	Math
NJASK-Grade 3	90.1%	92.9%
GEPA-Grade 8	63.8%	83.1%
HSPA-High School	69.4%	80.8%

SAT Score Averages, 2006-07
Pct tested	Math	Verbal	Writing
75%	516	479	480

Teacher Qualifications
Avg. years of experience	8
Highly-qualified teachers one subject/all subjects	99.0%/99.0%

No Child Left Behind
AYP, 2006-07	Meets Standards

Municipal Finance
State Aid Programs, 2009
Total aid	$1,175,951
CMPTRA	439,371
Energy tax receipts	700,751
Garden State Trust	0

General Budget, 2008
Total tax levy	$24,790,227
County levy	3,140,528
County taxes	2,562,847
County library	0
County health	0
County open space	577,682
School levy	14,871,791
Muni. levy	6,777,908
Misc. revenues	3,845,340

Taxes
	2006	2007	2008
General tax rate per $100	3.71	4.02	1.910
County equalization ratio	49.92	46.22	97.47
Net valuation taxable	$563,994,900	$572,176,168	$1,298,268,870
State equalized value	$1,224,079,147	$1,320,683,084	$1,314,210,172

See Introduction for an explanation of all data sources.

Demographics & Socio-Economic Characteristics
(2000 US Census, except as noted)

Population
1980*	3,273
1990*	3,566
2000	4,287
Male	2,128
Female	2,159
2007 (estimate)*	4,400
Population density	522.6

Race & Hispanic Origin, 2000
Race
White	3,987
Black/African American	51
American Indian/Alaska Native	2
Asian	175
Native Hawaiian/Pacific Islander	0
Other race	27
Two or more races	45
Hispanic origin, total	92
Mexican	11
Puerto Rican	34
Cuban	7
Other Hispanic	40

Age & Nativity, 2000
Under 5 years	247
18 years and over	3,221
21 years and over	3,124
65 years and over	638
85 years and over	99
Median age	41.6
Native-born	3,932
Foreign-born	355

Educational Attainment, 2000
Population 25 years and over	3,047
Less than 9th grade	1.6%
High school grad or higher	93.1%
Bachelor's degree or higher	45.9%
Graduate degree	17.0%

Income & Poverty, 1999
Per capita income	$45,014
Median household income	$91,753
Median family income	$102,944
Persons in poverty	55
H'holds receiving public assistance	11
H'holds receiving social security	340

Households, 2000
Total households	1,476
With persons under 18	567
With persons over 65	383
Family households	1,157
Single-person households	258
Persons per household	2.78
Persons per family	3.18

Labor & Employment
Total civilian labor force, 2007**	2,416
Unemployment rate	3.3%
Total civilian labor force, 2000	2,198
Unemployment rate	3.0%

Employed persons 16 years and over by occupation, 2000
Managers & professionals	1,163
Service occupations	133
Sales & office occupations	615
Farming, fishing & forestry	0
Construction & maintenance	133
Production & transportation	88
Self-employed persons	204

* US Census Bureau
** New Jersey Department of Labor

General Information
Township of Boonton
155 Powerville Rd
Boonton, NJ 07005
973-402-4002
Website	www.boontontownship.com
Year of incorporation	1867
Land/water area (sq. miles)	8.42/0.16
Form of government	Township

Government
Legislative Districts
US Congressional	11
State Legislative	25

Local Officials, 2009
Mayor	Thomas Donadio
Manager	Barbara Shepard
Clerk	Barbara Shepard
Finance Dir	Norman Eckstein
Tax Assessor	Mark Burek
Tax Collector	Norman Eckstein
Attorney	John P. Jansen
Building	Edward Bucceri
Planning	William Denzler
Engineering	R. Henry Huelsebusch
Public Works	Barbara Shepard
Police Chief	John Speirs
Emerg/Fire Director	Ian Perrson

Housing & Construction
Housing Units, 2000*
Total	1,510
Median rent	$1,077
Median SF home value	$322,600

Permits for New Residential Construction
	Units	Value
Total, 2006	27	$7,463,515
Single family	27	$7,463,515
Total, 2007	47	$20,747,388
Single family	47	$20,747,388

Real Property Valuation, 2008
	Parcels	Valuation
Total	1,719	$1,139,212,900
Vacant	126	27,245,200
Residential	1,501	1,050,841,100
Commercial	11	16,901,200
Industrial	7	18,460,900
Apartments	1	571,000
Farm land	43	257,400
Farm homestead	30	24,936,100

Average Property Value & Tax, 2008
Residential value	$702,663
Property tax	$9,993
Tax credit/rebate	$1,170

Public Library
No public municipal library

Library statistics, 2007
Population served	NA
Full-time/total staff	NA/NA

	Total	Per capita
Holdings	NA	NA
Revenues	NA	NA
Expenditures	NA	NA
Annual visits	NA	NA
Internet terminals/annual users	NA/NA	

Public Safety
Number of officers, 2007	13

Crime	2006	2007
Total crimes	28	32
Violent	3	8
Murder	0	0
Rape	0	5
Robbery	0	0
Aggravated assault	3	3
Non-violent	25	24
Burglary	6	7
Larceny	17	17
Vehicle theft	2	0
Domestic violence	32	30
Arson	0	0
Total crime rate	6.4	7.3
Violent	0.7	1.8
Non-violent	5.7	5.5

Public School District
(for school year 2007-08 except as noted)

Boonton Township School District
11 Valley Road
Boonton Township, NJ 07005
(973) 334-4162
Superintendent	Roseann Humphrey
Number of schools	1
Grade plan	K-8
Enrollment	521
Attendance rate, '06-07	96.6%
Dropout rate	NA
Students per teacher	11.3
Per pupil expenditure	$13,655
Median faculty salary	$51,886
Median administrator salary	$113,804
Grade 12 enrollment	NA
High school graduation rate	NA

Assessment test results
(percent scoring at proficient or advanced level)
	Language	Math
NJASK-Grade 3	94.2%	94.1%
GEPA-Grade 8	86.0%	95.3%
HSPA-High School	NA	NA

SAT Score Averages, 2006-07
Pct tested	Math	Verbal	Writing
NA	NA	NA	NA

Teacher Qualifications
Avg. years of experience	12
Highly-qualified teachers one subject/all subjects	97.0%/97.0%

No Child Left Behind
AYP, 2006-07	Meets Standards

Municipal Finance
State Aid Programs, 2009
Total aid	$327,769
CMPTRA	56,611
Energy tax receipts	258,047
Garden State Trust	62

General Budget, 2008
Total tax levy	$16,214,872
County levy	2,554,280
County taxes	2,084,520
County library	0
County health	0
County open space	469,761
School levy	10,538,903
Muni. levy	3,121,688
Misc. revenues	1,897,468

Taxes
	2006	2007	2008
General tax rate per $100	2.87	1.39	1.423
County equalization ratio	55.72	107.17	104.00
Net valuation taxable	$522,586,895	$1,139,792,181	$1,140,172,068
State equalized value	$1,042,311,280	$1,095,989,135	$1,100,479,388

See Introduction for an explanation of all data sources.

Demographics & Socio-Economic Characteristics
(2000 US Census, except as noted)

Population
1980*	4,441
1990*	4,341
2000	3,969
Male	1,881
Female	2,088
2007 (estimate)*	3,854
Population density	4,189.1

Race & Hispanic Origin, 2000
Race
White	3,225
Black/African American	519
American Indian/Alaska Native	2
Asian	76
Native Hawaiian/Pacific Islander	1
Other race	32
Two or more races	114
Hispanic origin, total	112
Mexican	6
Puerto Rican	67
Cuban	5
Other Hispanic	34

Age & Nativity, 2000
Under 5 years	204
18 years and over	3,139
21 years and over	3,019
65 years and over	556
85 years and over	71
Median age	37.9
Native-born	3,896
Foreign-born	73

Educational Attainment, 2000
Population 25 years and over	2,837
Less than 9th grade	3.2%
High school grad or higher	85.7%
Bachelor's degree or higher	26.7%
Graduate degree	7.8%

Income & Poverty, 1999
Per capita income	$25,882
Median household income	$47,279
Median family income	$59,872
Persons in poverty	266
H'holds receiving public assistance	32
H'holds receiving social security	413

Households, 2000
Total households	1,757
With persons under 18	482
With persons over 65	420
Family households	990
Single-person households	627
Persons per household	2.23
Persons per family	2.93

Labor & Employment
Total civilian labor force, 2007**	2,672
Unemployment rate	3.8%
Total civilian labor force, 2000	2,352
Unemployment rate	3.8%

Employed persons 16 years and over by occupation, 2000
Managers & professionals	763
Service occupations	412
Sales & office occupations	677
Farming, fishing & forestry	0
Construction & maintenance	192
Production & transportation	219
Self-employed persons	169

‡ Branch of county library
* US Census Bureau
** New Jersey Department of Labor

See Introduction for an explanation of all data sources.

General Information
City of Bordentown
324 Farnsworth Ave
Bordentown, NJ 08505
609-298-0604
Email	btownch@verizon.net
Year of incorporation	1867
Land/water area (sq. miles)	0.92/0.05
Form of government	Commission

Government
Legislative Districts
US Congressional	4
State Legislative	30

Local Officials, 2009
Mayor	John W. Collom III
Manager/Admin	NA
Clerk	Patricia D. Ryan
Finance Dir	Patricia D. Ryan
Tax Assessor	William Tantum
Tax Collector	Ann Schubert
Attorney	Richard W. Hunt
Building	(State)
Comm Dev/Planning	(County)
Engineering	Michael Filmyer
Public Works	Robert E. Erickson
Police Chief	Matthew J. Simmons III
Emerg/Fire Director	Jason Peters

Housing & Construction
Housing Units, 2000*
Total	1,884
Median rent	$736
Median SF home value	$110,200

Permits for New Residential Construction
	Units	Value
Total, 2006	0	$0
Single family	0	$0
Total, 2007	1	$13,000
Single family	1	$13,000

Real Property Valuation, 2008
	Parcels	Valuation
Total	1,405	$402,091,000
Vacant	71	7,107,200
Residential	1,193	293,454,900
Commercial	114	56,856,000
Industrial	7	16,517,600
Apartments	20	28,155,300
Farm land	0	0
Farm homestead	0	0

Average Property Value & Tax, 2008
Residential value	$245,981
Property tax	$5,657
Tax credit/rebate	$996

Public Library
Bordentown Branch Library‡
18 E Union St
Bordentown, NJ 08505
609-298-0622
Branch Librarian.......... Isabelle Addis

Library statistics, 2007
see Burlington County profile
for library system statistics

Public Safety
Number of officers, 2007 13

Crime	2006	2007
Total crimes	42	63
Violent	4	3
Murder	0	0
Rape	0	0
Robbery	2	2
Aggravated assault	2	1
Non-violent	38	60
Burglary	8	7
Larceny	25	46
Vehicle theft	5	7
Domestic violence	12	19
Arson	0	0
Total crime rate	10.5	15.9
Violent	1.0	0.8
Non-violent	9.5	15.2

Public School District
(for school year 2007-08 except as noted)

Bordentown Regional School District
318 Ward Ave.
Bordentown, NJ 08505
(609) 298-0025
Superintendent	Constance Bauer
Number of schools	5
Grade plan	K-12
Enrollment	2,351
Attendance rate, '06-07	95.5%
Dropout rate	0.5%
Students per teacher	11.2
Per pupil expenditure	$13,627
Median faculty salary	$53,342
Median administrator salary	$88,622
Grade 12 enrollment	170
High school graduation rate	96.4%

Assessment test results
(percent scoring at proficient or advanced level)
	Language	Math
NJASK-Grade 3	94.3%	94.3%
GEPA-Grade 8	69.8%	83.4%
HSPA-High School	75.7%	85.6%

SAT Score Averages, 2006-07
Pct tested	Math	Verbal	Writing
76%	479	486	469

Teacher Qualifications
Avg. years of experience	8
Highly-qualified teachers one subject/all subjects	100%/100%

No Child Left Behind
AYP, 2006-07 .... Meets Standards

Municipal Finance
State Aid Programs, 2009
Total aid	$483,158
CMPTRA	126,525
Energy tax receipts	349,262
Garden State Trust	11

General Budget, 2008
Total tax levy	$9,255,783
County levy	1,445,523
County taxes	1,187,069
County library	109,603
County health	0
County open space	148,850
School levy	4,961,481
Muni. levy	2,848,779
Misc. revenues	1,806,565

Taxes
	2006	2007	2008
General tax rate per $100	4.934	5.051	2.300
County equalization ratio	62.07	55.03	108.84
Net valuation taxable	$179,400,260	$180,225,288	$402,442,264
State equalized value	$326,199,956	$363,535,908	$384,649,266

Demographics & Socio-Economic Characteristics

(2000 US Census, except as noted)

Population

1980*	7,170
1990*	7,683
2000	8,380
Male	4,081
Female	4,299
2007 (estimate)*	10,201
Population density	1,198.7

Race & Hispanic Origin, 2000

Race

White	7,486
Black/African American	421
American Indian/Alaska Native	17
Asian	278
Native Hawaiian/Pacific Islander	0
Other race	57
Two or more races	121
Hispanic origin, total	254
Mexican	15
Puerto Rican	121
Cuban	9
Other Hispanic	109

Age & Nativity, 2000

Under 5 years	556
18 years and over	6,394
21 years and over	6,166
65 years and over	980
85 years and over	73
Median age	37.6
Native-born	7,768
Foreign-born	612

Educational Attainment, 2000

Population 25 years and over	5,863
Less than 9th grade	3.7%
High school grad or higher	87.0%
Bachelor's degree or higher	23.9%
Graduate degree	7.5%

Income & Poverty, 1999

Per capita income	$26,934
Median household income	$60,131
Median family income	$71,627
Persons in poverty	234
H'holds receiving public assistance	18
H'holds receiving social security	808

Households, 2000

Total households	3,293
With persons under 18	1,138
With persons over 65	714
Family households	2,305
Single-person households	775
Persons per household	2.53
Persons per family	3.03

Labor & Employment

Total civilian labor force, 2007**	5,528
Unemployment rate	3.5%
Total civilian labor force, 2000	4,833
Unemployment rate	3.4%

Employed persons 16 years and over by occupation, 2000

Managers & professionals	1,622
Service occupations	650
Sales & office occupations	1,567
Farming, fishing & forestry	10
Construction & maintenance	405
Production & transportation	416
Self-employed persons	123

---

‡ Branch of county library
* US Census Bureau
** New Jersey Department of Labor

General Information

Township of Bordentown
1 Municipal Dr
Bordentown, NJ 08505
609-298-2800

Website	www.bordentowntownship.com
Year of incorporation	1852
Land/water area (sq. miles)	8.51/0.77
Form of government	Township

Government

Legislative Districts

US Congressional	4
State Legislative	30

Local Officials, 2009

Mayor	William J. Morolli
Manager	Leonard M. Klepner
Clerk	Colleen Eckert
Finance Dir	David Kocian
Tax Assessor	William Tantum
Tax Collector	Mary Picariello
Attorney	Gregory Sullivan
Building	Pete Carbone
Planning	Barbara Allen-Woolley-Dillon
Engineering	Fred Turek
Public Works	Dean Buhrer
Police Chief	Frank Nucera Jr
Fire/Emergency Dir	Andrew Law

Housing & Construction

Housing Units, 2000*

Total	3,436
Median rent	$698
Median SF home value	$136,000

Permits for New Residential Construction

	Units	Value
Total, 2006	1	$176,500
Single family	1	$176,500
Total, 2007	1	$23,750
Single family	1	$23,750

Real Property Valuation, 2008

	Parcels	Valuation
Total	3,943	$696,310,640
Vacant	222	34,690,400
Residential	3,477	505,312,150
Commercial	187	118,741,560
Industrial	19	20,537,830
Apartments	7	15,557,000
Farm land	23	522,400
Farm homestead	8	949,300

Average Property Value & Tax, 2008

Residential value	$145,269
Property tax	$6,042
Tax credit/rebate	$1,023

Public Library

Bordentown Branch Library‡
18 E Union St
Bordentown, NJ 08505
609-298-0622

Branch Librarian ... Isabelle Addis

Library statistics, 2007

see Burlington County profile
for library system statistics

Public Safety

Number of officers, 2007	22

Crime

Crime	2006	2007
Total crimes	189	190
Violent	18	22
Murder	0	0
Rape	1	1
Robbery	8	10
Aggravated assault	9	11
Non-violent	171	168
Burglary	32	27
Larceny	112	123
Vehicle theft	27	18
Domestic violence	37	61
Arson	0	1
Total crime rate	18.3	18.1
Violent	1.7	2.1
Non-violent	16.6	16.0

Public School District

(for school year 2007-08 except as noted)

Bordentown Regional School District
318 Ward Ave.
Bordentown, NJ 08505
(609) 298-0025

Superintendent	Constance Bauer
Number of schools	5
Grade plan	K-12
Enrollment	2,351
Attendance rate, '06-07	95.5%
Dropout rate	0.5%
Students per teacher	11.2
Per pupil expenditure	$13,627
Median faculty salary	$53,342
Median administrator salary	$88,622
Grade 12 enrollment	170
High school graduation rate	96.4%

Assessment test results

(percent scoring at proficient or advanced level)

	Language	Math
NJASK-Grade 3	94.3%	94.3%
GEPA-Grade 8	69.8%	83.4%
HSPA-High School	75.7%	85.6%

SAT Score Averages, 2006-07

Pct tested	Math	Verbal	Writing
76%	479	486	469

Teacher Qualifications

Avg. years of experience	8
Highly-qualified teachers one subject/all subjects	100%/100%

No Child Left Behind

AYP, 2006-07	Meets Standards

Municipal Finance

State Aid Programs, 2009

Total aid	$1,163,352
CMPTRA	268,697
Energy tax receipts	850,693
Garden State Trust	7,658

General Budget, 2008

Total tax levy	$29,051,009
County levy	5,368,286
County taxes	4,407,520
County library	407,036
County health	0
County open space	553,729
School levy	19,331,285
Muni. levy	4,351,438
Misc. revenues	5,175,038

Taxes

	2006	2007	2008
General tax rate per $100	3.815	4.108	4.160
County equalization ratio	58.86	52.47	49.77
Net valuation taxable	$672,799,540	$698,418,058	$698,446,486
State equalized value	$1,284,793,375	$1,400,932,234	$1,424,048,527

Demographics & Socio-Economic Characteristics

(2000 US Census, except as noted)

Population

1980*	9,710
1990*	9,487
2000	10,155
Male	5,251
Female	4,904
2007 (estimate)*	10,193
Population density	5,960.8

Race & Hispanic Origin, 2000

Race

White	8,385
Black/African American	256
American Indian/Alaska Native	31
Asian	292
Native Hawaiian/Pacific Islander	7
Other race	880
Two or more races	304
Hispanic origin, total	3,541
Mexican	706
Puerto Rican	246
Cuban	43
Other Hispanic	2,546

Age & Nativity, 2000

Under 5 years	699
18 years and over	7,950
21 years and over	7,569
65 years and over	1,268
85 years and over	120
Median age	34.2
Native-born	6,535
Foreign-born	3,656

Educational Attainment, 2000

Population 25 years and over	7,006
Less than 9th grade	13.5%
High school grad or higher	75.9%
Bachelor's degree or higher	23.9%
Graduate degree	7.5%

Income & Poverty, 1999

Per capita income	$22,395
Median household income	$46,858
Median family income	$51,346
Persons in poverty	1,109
H'holds receiving public assistance	55
H'holds receiving social security	994

Households, 2000

Total households	3,615
With persons under 18	1,257
With persons over 65	931
Family households	2,461
Single-person households	834
Persons per household	2.81
Persons per family	3.21

Labor & Employment

Total civilian labor force, 2007**	6,508
Unemployment rate	4.8%
Total civilian labor force, 2000	5,723
Unemployment rate	4.7%

Employed persons 16 years and over by occupation, 2000

Managers & professionals	1,406
Service occupations	1,028
Sales & office occupations	1,367
Farming, fishing & forestry	25
Construction & maintenance	479
Production & transportation	1,151
Self-employed persons	241

* US Census Bureau
** New Jersey Department of Labor

See Introduction for an explanation of all data sources.

General Information

Borough of Bound Brook
230 Hamilton St
Bound Brook, NJ 08805
732-356-0833

Website	www.boundbrooknj.net
Year of incorporation	1891
Land/water area (sq. miles)	1.71/0.00
Form of government	Borough

Government

Legislative Districts

US Congressional	7
State Legislative	16

Local Officials, 2009

Mayor	Carey Pilato
Manager	Randy W. Bahr
Clerk	Donna Marie Godleski
Finance Dir	Randy Bahr
Tax Assessor	Gary Toth
Tax Collector	Randy Bahr
Attorney	James O'Donahue
Building	Michael Wright
Planning	Scarlett Doyle
Engineering	Robert Keady
Public Works	Tom Miller
Deputy Chief	Michael Jannone
Emerg/Fire Director	Thomas Ruscetta

Housing & Construction

Housing Units, 2000*

Total	3,802
Median rent	$853
Median SF home value	$157,600

Permits for New Residential Construction

	Units	Value
Total, 2006	50	$5,696,850
Single family	2	$396,850
Total, 2007	86	$7,045,425
Single family	50	$3,070,427

Real Property Valuation, 2008

	Parcels	Valuation
Total	2,741	$424,036,800
Vacant	192	5,338,400
Residential	2,305	340,622,200
Commercial	218	58,997,500
Industrial	1	763,300
Apartments	25	18,315,400
Farm land	0	0
Farm homestead	0	0

Average Property Value & Tax, 2008

Residential value	$147,775
Property tax	$7,461
Tax credit/rebate	$1,215

Public Library

Bound Brook Memorial Library
402 E High St
Bound Brook, NJ 08805
732-356-0043

Director	Hannah Kerwin

Library statistics, 2007

Population served	NA
Full-time/total staff	NA/NA

	Total	Per capita
Holdings	NA	NA
Revenues	NA	NA
Expenditures	NA	NA
Annual visits	NA	NA
Internet terminals/annual users	NA/NA	

Public Safety

Number of officers, 2007	22

Crime	2006	2007
Total crimes	257	252
Violent	33	19
Murder	0	0
Rape	1	1
Robbery	19	11
Aggravated assault	13	7
Non-violent	224	233
Burglary	64	63
Larceny	148	160
Vehicle theft	12	10
Domestic violence	216	189
Arson	0	0
Total crime rate	25.3	24.6
Violent	3.2	1.9
Non-violent	22.0	22.8

Public School District

(for school year 2007-08 except as noted)

Bound Brook Borough School District
LaMonte Bldg, West 2nd St
Bound Brook NJ, NJ 08805
(732) 652-7920

Superintendent	Edward C. Hoffman
Number of schools	5
Grade plan	K-12
Enrollment	1,505
Attendance rate, '06-07	93.6%
Dropout rate	0.6%
Students per teacher	11.4
Per pupil expenditure	$13,551
Median faculty salary	$54,435
Median administrator salary	$108,918
Grade 12 enrollment	114
High school graduation rate	94.5%

Assessment test results

(percent scoring at proficient or advanced level)

	Language	Math
NJASK-Grade 3	85.3%	71.6%
GEPA-Grade 8	46.9%	62.5%
HSPA-High School	61.2%	68.1%

SAT Score Averages, 2006-07

Pct tested	Math	Verbal	Writing
64%	460	458	437

Teacher Qualifications

Avg. years of experience	7
Highly-qualified teachers one subject/all subjects	100%/100%

No Child Left Behind

AYP, 2006-07	Meets Standards

Municipal Finance

State Aid Programs, 2009

Total aid	$1,442,357
CMPTRA	608,959
Energy tax receipts	797,339
Garden State Trust	0

General Budget, 2008

Total tax levy	$21,585,405
County levy	3,212,197
County taxes	2,578,004
County library	348,857
County health	0
County open space	285,335
School levy	12,226,052
Muni. levy	6,147,157
Misc. revenues	5,078,076

Taxes	2006	2007	2008
General tax rate per $100	4.83	5.06	5.049
County equalization ratio	55.71	47.05	44.92
Net valuation taxable	$423,045,100	$426,823,567	$427,525,632
State equalized value	$903,475,366	$946,073,591	$1,008,553,539

Demographics & Socio-Economic Characteristics
(2000 US Census, except as noted)

Population
1980*	4,772
1990*	4,475
2000	4,793
Male	2,385
Female	2,408
2007 (estimate)*	4,816
Population density	8,162.7

Race & Hispanic Origin, 2000
Race
White	4,225
Black/African American	185
American Indian/Alaska Native	8
Asian	70
Native Hawaiian/Pacific Islander	1
Other race	192
Two or more races	112
Hispanic origin, total	615
Mexican	248
Puerto Rican	213
Cuban	19
Other Hispanic	135

Age & Nativity, 2000
Under 5 years	265
18 years and over	3,931
21 years and over	3,792
65 years and over	590
85 years and over	83
Median age	36.9
Native-born	4,258
Foreign-born	535

Educational Attainment, 2000
Population 25 years and over	3,544
Less than 9th grade	4.8%
High school grad or higher	81.8%
Bachelor's degree or higher	25.2%
Graduate degree	10.0%

Income & Poverty, 1999
Per capita income	$25,438
Median household income	$40,878
Median family income	$49,688
Persons in poverty	439
H'holds receiving public assistance	11
H'holds receiving social security	511

Households, 2000
Total households	2,297
With persons under 18	478
With persons over 65	450
Family households	1,086
Single-person households	977
Persons per household	2.09
Persons per family	2.91

Labor & Employment
Total civilian labor force, 2007**	2,885
Unemployment rate	5.8%
Total civilian labor force, 2000	2,714
Unemployment rate	6.5%

Employed persons 16 years and over by occupation, 2000
Managers & professionals	825
Service occupations	431
Sales & office occupations	759
Farming, fishing & forestry	0
Construction & maintenance	247
Production & transportation	275
Self-employed persons	153

General Information
Borough of Bradley Beach
701 Main St
Bradley Beach, NJ 07720
732-776-2999
Website	www.bradleybeachonline.com
Year of incorporation	1893
Land/water area (sq. miles)	0.59/0.02
Form of government	Small Municipality

Government
Legislative Districts
US Congressional	6
State Legislative	11

Local Officials, 2009
Mayor	Julie Schreck
Business Admin	Gail O'Reilly
Clerk	Mary Ann Solinski
Finance Dir	Joyce Wilkins
Tax Assessor	Ed Mullane
Tax Collector	Joyce Wilkins
Attorney	Michael DuPont
Building	Donald Clare
Comm Dev/Planning	NA
Engineering	Bruce Koch
Public Works	Richard Bianchi
Police Chief	Leonard Guida
Emerg/Fire Director	Joseph Malysko

Housing & Construction
Housing Units, 2000*
Total	3,132
Median rent	$729
Median SF home value	$161,200

Permits for New Residential Construction
	Units	Value
Total, 2006	52	$4,950,967
Single family	22	$2,989,537
Total, 2007	45	$6,086,312
Single family	20	$2,932,502

Real Property Valuation, 2008
	Parcels	Valuation
Total	2,064	$1,123,044,400
Vacant	63	11,149,200
Residential	1,859	987,993,700
Commercial	98	65,263,100
Industrial	4	1,774,900
Apartments	40	56,863,500
Farm land	0	0
Farm homestead	0	0

Average Property Value & Tax, 2008
Residential value	$531,465
Property tax	$6,283
Tax credit/rebate	$1,071

Public Library
Bradley Beach Public Library
511 Fourth Ave
Bradley Beach, NJ 07720
732-776-2995
Director	Karen J. Klapperstuck

Library statistics, 2007
Population served	4,793
Full-time/total staff	1/2

	Total	Per capita
Holdings	34,185	7.13
Revenues	$375,487	$78.34
Expenditures	$214,770	$44.81
Annual visits	15,632	3.26
Internet terminals/annual users		6/8,738

Public Safety
Number of officers, 2007 17
Crime	2006	2007
Total crimes	194	153
Violent	6	15
Murder	0	0
Rape	0	0
Robbery	3	3
Aggravated assault	3	12
Non-violent	188	138
Burglary	44	29
Larceny	140	108
Vehicle theft	4	1
Domestic violence	105	127
Arson	0	0
Total crime rate	40.6	32.0
Violent	1.3	3.1
Non-violent	39.3	28.8

Public School District
(for school year 2007-08 except as noted)

Bradley Beach School District
515 Brinley Avenue
Bradley Beach, NJ 07720
(732) 775-4413
Superintendent	Wayne W. Turner
Number of schools	1
Grade plan	K-8
Enrollment	264
Attendance rate, '06-07	95.9%
Dropout rate	NA
Students per teacher	7.7
Per pupil expenditure	$18,814
Median faculty salary	$57,555
Median administrator salary	$86,818
Grade 12 enrollment	NA
High school graduation rate	NA

Assessment test results
(percent scoring at proficient or advanced level)
	Language	Math
NJASK-Grade 3	57.1%	73.1%
GEPA-Grade 8	85.7%	82.1%
HSPA-High School	NA	NA

SAT Score Averages, 2006-07
Pct tested	Math	Verbal	Writing
NA	NA	NA	NA

Teacher Qualifications
Avg. years of experience	16
Highly-qualified teachers one subject/all subjects	100%/95.0%

No Child Left Behind
AYP, 2006-07 .... Meets Standards

Municipal Finance
State Aid Programs, 2009
Total aid	$470,500
CMPTRA	64,980
Energy tax receipts	390,228
Garden State Trust	0

General Budget, 2008
Total tax levy	$13,281,505
County levy	2,796,386
County taxes	2,576,607
County library	0
County health	47,892
County open space	171,888
School levy	5,211,586
Muni. levy	5,273,532
Misc. revenues	2,175,529

Taxes
	2006	2007	2008
General tax rate per $100	1.092	1.139	1.183
County equalization ratio	125.68	106.45	98.28
Net valuation taxable	$1,115,000,500	$1,118,702,991	$1,123,415,854
State equalized value	$1,047,805,007	$1,138,274,977	$1,779,799,836

* US Census Bureau
** New Jersey Department of Labor

See Introduction for an explanation of all data sources.

Demographics & Socio-Economic Characteristics
(2000 US Census, except as noted)

Population
1980*	7,846
1990*	10,888
2000	14,566
Male	7,148
Female	7,418
2007 (estimate)*	15,002
Population density	740.5

Race & Hispanic Origin, 2000
Race
White	13,174
Black/African American	284
American Indian/Alaska Native	15
Asian	898
Native Hawaiian/Pacific Islander	4
Other race	57
Two or more races	134
Hispanic origin, total	392
Mexican	20
Puerto Rican	137
Cuban	51
Other Hispanic	184

Age & Nativity, 2000
Under 5 years	1,269
18 years and over	10,583
21 years and over	10,303
65 years and over	1,206
85 years and over	98
Median age	37.5
Native-born	12,997
Foreign-born	1,565

Educational Attainment, 2000
Population 25 years and over	9,954
Less than 9th grade	1.8%
High school grad or higher	94.8%
Bachelor's degree or higher	53.7%
Graduate degree	23.0%

Income & Poverty, 1999
Per capita income	$41,241
Median household income	$96,864
Median family income	$110,268
Persons in poverty	282
H'holds receiving public assistance	63
H'holds receiving social security	942

Households, 2000
Total households	5,272
With persons under 18	2,148
With persons over 65	898
Family households	4,065
Single-person households	990
Persons per household	2.76
Persons per family	3.19

Labor & Employment
Total civilian labor force, 2007**	9,104
Unemployment rate	2.2%
Total civilian labor force, 2000	8,018
Unemployment rate	2.1%

Employed persons 16 years and over by occupation, 2000
Managers & professionals	4,376
Service occupations	453
Sales & office occupations	1,984
Farming, fishing & forestry	0
Construction & maintenance	521
Production & transportation	516
Self-employed persons	392

* US Census Bureau
** New Jersey Department of Labor

General Information
Township of Branchburg
1077 US Highway 202 N
Branchburg, NJ 08876
908-526-1300
Website	www.branchburg.nj.us
Year of incorporation	1845
Land/water area (sq. miles)	20.26/0.00
Form of government	Township

Government
Legislative Districts
US Congressional	7
State Legislative	16

Local Officials, 2009
Mayor	James Leonard
Administrator	Gregory Bonin
Township Clerk	Sharon Brienza
CFO	Diane Schubach
Tax Assessor	Frances Kuczynski
Tax Collector	Diane Wynn
Attorney	Mark S. Anderson
Code Enforcement	John Tamburini
Planning	James Melitski (Chr)
Township Engineer	Douglas Ball
Public Works	Thomas Manz
Police Chief	Brian Fitzgerald
Emerg/Fire Director	James McAleer

Housing & Construction
Housing Units, 2000*
Total	5,405
Median rent	$1,036
Median SF home value	$278,000

Permits for New Residential Construction
	Units	Value
Total, 2006	15	$3,399,708
Single family	15	$3,399,708
Total, 2007	31	$2,814,104
Single family	7	$2,314,104

Real Property Valuation, 2008
	Parcels	Valuation
Total	5,449	$3,099,679,250
Vacant	161	26,221,300
Residential	4,791	2,217,444,300
Commercial	146	225,302,800
Industrial	190	570,870,400
Apartments	1	27,851,200
Farm land	104	1,414,900
Farm homestead	56	30,574,350

Average Property Value & Tax, 2008
Residential value	$463,796
Property tax	$8,645
Tax credit/rebate	$1,213

Public Library
No public municipal library

Library statistics, 2007
Population served	NA
Full-time/total staff	NA/NA

	Total	Per capita
Holdings	NA	NA
Revenues	NA	NA
Expenditures	NA	NA
Annual visits	NA	NA
Internet terminals/annual users	NA/NA	

Public Safety
Number of officers, 2007	26

Crime	2006	2007
Total crimes	114	106
Violent	3	2
Murder	0	0
Rape	1	0
Robbery	1	1
Aggravated assault	1	1
Non-violent	111	104
Burglary	28	14
Larceny	78	86
Vehicle theft	5	4
Domestic violence	84	115
Arson	0	0
Total crime rate	7.6	7.0
Violent	0.2	0.1
Non-violent	7.4	6.9

Public School District
(for school year 2007-08 except as noted)

Branchburg Township School District
240 Baird Rd
Branchburg, NJ 08876
(908) 722-3265
Superintendent	Kenneth J. Knops
Number of schools	4
Grade plan	K-8
Enrollment	1,897
Attendance rate, '06-07	98.6%
Dropout rate	NA
Students per teacher	9.4
Per pupil expenditure	$15,034
Median faculty salary	$50,580
Median administrator salary	$122,962
Grade 12 enrollment	NA
High school graduation rate	NA

Assessment test results
(percent scoring at proficient or advanced level)
	Language	Math
NJASK-Grade 3	92.7%	88.7%
GEPA-Grade 8	88.6%	96.3%
HSPA-High School	NA	NA

SAT Score Averages, 2006-07
Pct tested	Math	Verbal	Writing
NA	NA	NA	NA

Teacher Qualifications
Avg. years of experience	9
Highly-qualified teachers one subject/all subjects	99.0%/99.0%

No Child Left Behind
AYP, 2006-07	Meets Standards

Municipal Finance
State Aid Programs, 2009
Total aid	$3,492,850
CMPTRA	0
Energy tax receipts	3,337,576
Garden State Trust	16,210

General Budget, 2008
Total tax levy	$57,877,852
County levy	10,911,742
County taxes	8,757,362
County library	1,185,096
County health	0
County open space	969,283
School levy	38,105,884
Muni. levy	8,860,227
Misc. revenues	8,665,530

Taxes
	2006	2007	2008
General tax rate per $100	1.82	1.81	1.865
County equalization ratio	105.88	99.91	96.21
Net valuation taxable	$2,990,720,700	$3,109,676,947	$3,104,918,263
State equalized value	$3,082,222,556	$3,198,787,059	$3,198,809,227

See Introduction for an explanation of all data sources.

Demographics & Socio-Economic Characteristics
(2000 US Census, except as noted)

Population
1980*	870
1990*	851
2000	845
Male	394
Female	451
2007 (estimate)*	822
Population density	1,393.2

Race & Hispanic Origin, 2000
Race
White	832
Black/African American	1
American Indian/Alaska Native	3
Asian	3
Native Hawaiian/Pacific Islander	0
Other race	1
Two or more races	5
Hispanic origin, total	11
Mexican	7
Puerto Rican	1
Cuban	0
Other Hispanic	3

Age & Nativity, 2000
Under 5 years	29
18 years and over	642
21 years and over	615
65 years and over	153
85 years and over	15
Median age	41.7
Native-born	829
Foreign-born	18

Educational Attainment, 2000
Population 25 years and over	613
Less than 9th grade	3.8%
High school grad or higher	85.2%
Bachelor's degree or higher	18.3%
Graduate degree	6.9%

Income & Poverty, 1999
Per capita income	$22,748
Median household income	$45,855
Median family income	$60,909
Persons in poverty	37
H'holds receiving public assistance	8
H'holds receiving social security	134

Households, 2000
Total households	354
With persons under 18	107
With persons over 65	119
Family households	225
Single-person households	114
Persons per household	2.37
Persons per family	3.03

Labor & Employment
Total civilian labor force, 2007**	483
Unemployment rate	5.8%
Total civilian labor force, 2000	435
Unemployment rate	4.4%

Employed persons 16 years and over by occupation, 2000
Managers & professionals	122
Service occupations	54
Sales & office occupations	122
Farming, fishing & forestry	2
Construction & maintenance	57
Production & transportation	59
Self-employed persons	27

* US Census Bureau
** New Jersey Department of Labor

General Information
Borough of Branchville
PO Box 840
Branchville, NJ 07826
973-948-4626
Website	(county website)
Year of incorporation	1898
Land/water area (sq. miles)	0.59/0.00
Form of government	Borough

Government

Legislative Districts
US Congressional	5
State Legislative	24

Local Officials, 2009
Mayor	Gerald Van Gorden
Manager/Admin	NA
Clerk	Kate Leissler
Finance Dir	Earl Snook
Tax Assessor	Katherine Kieb
Tax Collector	Beverly Bathgate
Attorney	M. Richard Valinti
Building	Wesley Powers
Comm Dev/Planning	NA
Engineering	Harold Pellow
Public Works	John Eldred
Police Chief	NA
Emerg/Fire Director	Brian Geimer

Housing & Construction

Housing Units, 2000*
Total	377
Median rent	$671
Median SF home value	$149,600

Permits for New Residential Construction
	Units	Value
Total, 2006	1	$290,000
Single family	1	$290,000
Total, 2007	0	$0
Single family	0	$0

Real Property Valuation, 2008
	Parcels	Valuation
Total	385	$154,263,950
Vacant	45	2,736,650
Residential	275	81,104,500
Commercial	57	68,381,100
Industrial	0	0
Apartments	4	1,567,000
Farm land	2	5,500
Farm homestead	2	469,200

Average Property Value & Tax, 2008
Residential value	$294,490
Property tax	$5,182
Tax credit/rebate	$835

Public Library
No public municipal library

Library statistics, 2007
Population served	NA
Full-time/total staff	NA/NA

	Total	Per capita
Holdings	NA	NA
Revenues	NA	NA
Expenditures	NA	NA
Annual visits	NA	NA
Internet terminals/annual users	NA/NA	

Public Safety
Number of officers, 2007	0

Crime	2006	2007
Total crimes	10	21
Violent	2	1
Murder	0	0
Rape	0	0
Robbery	0	0
Aggravated assault	2	1
Non-violent	8	20
Burglary	1	8
Larceny	6	12
Vehicle theft	1	0
Domestic violence	1	14
Arson	0	0
Total crime rate	11.8	25.0
Violent	2.4	1.2
Non-violent	9.5	23.8

Public School District
(for school year 2007-08 except as noted)

Branchville Borough School District
4 Pines Road
Branchville NJ, NJ 07826

No schools in district

Per pupil expenditure	NA
Median faculty salary	NA
Median administrator salary	NA
Grade 12 enrollment	NA
High school graduation rate	NA

Assessment test results
(percent scoring at proficient or advanced level)
	Language	Math
NJASK-Grade 3	NA	NA
GEPA-Grade 8	NA	NA
HSPA-High School	NA	NA

SAT Score Averages, 2006-07
Pct tested	Math	Verbal	Writing
NA	NA	NA	NA

Teacher Qualifications
Avg. years of experience	NA
Highly-qualified teachers one subject/all subjects	NA/NA

No Child Left Behind
AYP, 2006-07	NA

Municipal Finance

State Aid Programs, 2009
Total aid	$841,712
CMPTRA	698,964
Energy tax receipts	109,079
Garden State Trust	0

General Budget, 2008
Total tax levy	$2,718,414
County levy	637,441
County taxes	534,935
County library	45,088
County health	15,836
County open space	41,581
School levy	2,080,973
Muni. levy	0
Misc. revenues	1,254,727

Taxes
	2006	2007	2008
General tax rate per $100	1.25	1.38	1.760
County equalization ratio	117.59	105.07	94.38
Net valuation taxable	$189,094,500	$161,257,058	$154,482,893
State equalized value	$180,259,182	$171,025,405	$158,552,054

See Introduction for an explanation of all data sources.

Demographics & Socio-Economic Characteristics[†]

(2000 US Census, except as noted)

Population

1980*	53,629
1990*	66,473
2000	76,119
Male	36,155
Female	39,964
2007 (estimate)*	78,286
Population density	2,984.6

Race & Hispanic Origin, 2000

Race

White	72,932
Black/African American	751
American Indian/Alaska Native	76
Asian	904
Native Hawaiian/Pacific Islander	12
Other race	650
Two or more races	794
Hispanic origin, total	2,930
Mexican	491
Puerto Rican	1,229
Cuban	200
Other Hispanic	1,010

Age & Nativity, 2000

Under 5 years	4,721
18 years and over	57,965
21 years and over	55,790
65 years and over	12,963
85 years and over	1,671
Median age	39.4
Native-born	71,816
Foreign-born	4,303

Educational Attainment, 2000

Population 25 years and over	52,965
Less than 9th grade	3.3%
High school grad or higher	86.6%
Bachelor's degree or higher	19.4%
Graduate degree	5.6%

Income & Poverty, 1999

Per capita income	$24,462
Median household income	$52,092
Median family income	$61,446
Persons in poverty	3,411
H'holds receiving public assistance	420
H'holds receiving social security	10,004

Households, 2000

Total households	29,511
With persons under 18	9,995
With persons over 65	9,081
Family households	20,788
Single-person households	7,367
Persons per household	2.56
Persons per family	3.07

Labor & Employment

Total civilian labor force, 2007**	40,736
Unemployment rate	4.2%
Total civilian labor force, 2000	37,840
Unemployment rate	4.1%

Employed persons 16 years and over by occupation, 2000

Managers & professionals	11,269
Service occupations	5,427
Sales & office occupations	11,236
Farming, fishing & forestry	80
Construction & maintenance	4,211
Production & transportation	4,049
Self-employed persons	1,820

[†] see Appendix C for American Community Survey data
[‡] Branch of county library
* US Census Bureau
** New Jersey Department of Labor

General Information

Township of Brick
401 Chambersbridge Rd
Brick, NJ 08723
732-262-1000

Website	www.twp.brick.nj.us
Year of incorporation	1850
Land/water area (sq. miles)	26.23/6.03
Form of government	Mayor-Council

Government

Legislative Districts

US Congressional	4
State Legislative	10

Local Officials, 2009

Mayor	Stephen C. Acropolis
Manager	Scott Pezarras
Clerk	Virginia A. Lampman
Finance Dir	Scott Pezarras
Tax Assessor	Richard Kenny
Tax Collector	JoAnne Lambusta
Attorney	George Gilmore
Building	Daniel Newman Jr
Planning	Michael Fowler
Engineering	James Priolo
Public Works	Glen Campbell
Police Chief	Nils R. Bergquist
Fire/Emergency Dir	NA

Housing & Construction

Housing Units, 2000*

Total	32,689
Median rent	$820
Median SF home value	$136,800

Permits for New Residential Construction

	Units	Value
Total, 2006	111	$21,688,780
Single family	111	$21,688,780
Total, 2007	111	$22,640,983
Single family	111	$22,640,983

Real Property Valuation, 2008

	Parcels	Valuation
Total	32,633	$4,692,732,300
Vacant	1,364	77,661,100
Residential	30,509	4,091,642,300
Commercial	723	459,046,100
Industrial	22	10,405,300
Apartments	14	53,881,600
Farm land	0	0
Farm homestead	1	95,900

Average Property Value & Tax, 2008

Residential value	$134,111
Property tax	$5,096
Tax credit/rebate	$907

Public Library

Brick Branch Library[‡]
301 Chambers Bridge Rd
Brick, NJ 08723
732-477-4513

Branch Librarian	Eleanor Clark

Library statistics, 2007

see Ocean County profile
for library system statistics

Public Safety

Number of officers, 2007		129

Crime	2006	2007
Total crimes	1,545	1,461
Violent	80	97
Murder	0	0
Rape	3	3
Robbery	19	12
Aggravated assault	58	82
Non-violent	1,465	1,364
Burglary	303	249
Larceny	1,101	1,066
Vehicle theft	61	49
Domestic violence	830	720
Arson	0	3
Total crime rate	**19.8**	**18.7**
Violent	1.0	1.2
Non-violent	18.7	17.4

Public School District

(for school year 2007-08 except as noted)

Brick Township School District
101 Hendrickson Avenue
Brick, NJ 08724
(732) 785-3000

Superintendent	Walter Hrycenko
Number of schools	12
Grade plan	K-12
Enrollment	10,483
Attendance rate, '06-07	93.1%
Dropout rate	1.7%
Students per teacher	11.4
Per pupil expenditure	$11,680
Median faculty salary	$49,910
Median administrator salary	$106,815
Grade 12 enrollment	773
High school graduation rate	92.5%

Assessment test results

(percent scoring at proficient or advanced level)

	Language	Math
NJASK-Grade 3	90.2%	89.3%
GEPA-Grade 8	65.8%	87.4%
HSPA-High School	79.4%	86.0%

SAT Score Averages, 2006-07

Pct tested	Math	Verbal	Writing
NA	NA	NA	NA

Teacher Qualifications

Avg. years of experience	10
Highly-qualified teachers one subject/all subjects	99.5%/99.5%

No Child Left Behind

AYP, 2006-07 .... Meets Standards

Municipal Finance

State Aid Programs, 2009

Total aid	$6,946,593
CMPTRA	1,407,117
Energy tax receipts	5,364,805
Garden State Trust	1,140

General Budget, 2008

Total tax levy	$178,526,471
County levy	39,804,465
County taxes	32,823,542
County library	3,857,770
County health	1,570,665
County open space	1,552,489
School levy	91,348,419
Muni. levy	47,373,587
Misc. revenues	31,134,860

Taxes

	2006	2007	2008
General tax rate per $100	3.398	3.578	3.800
County equalization ratio	44.38	38.58	36.30
Net valuation taxable	$4,655,477,500	$4,682,741,915	$4,698,291,498
State equalized value	$12,073,730,213	$12,889,743,222	$6,374,709,257

See Introduction for an explanation of all data sources.

Demographics & Socio-Economic Characteristics

(2000 US Census, except as noted)

Population
1980*	18,795
1990*	18,942
2000	22,771
Male	12,899
Female	9,872
2007 (estimate)*	24,575
Population density	3,951.0

Race & Hispanic Origin, 2000
Race
White	8,854
Black/African American	9,528
American Indian/Alaska Native	271
Asian	159
Native Hawaiian/Pacific Islander	20
Other race	3,112
Two or more races	827
Hispanic origin, total	5,576
Mexican	3,264
Puerto Rican	1,558
Cuban	62
Other Hispanic	692

Age & Nativity, 2000
Under 5 years	1,658
18 years and over	16,843
21 years and over	15,857
65 years and over	2,485
85 years and over	342
Median age	31.5
Native-born	19,942
Foreign-born	2,829

Educational Attainment, 2000
Population 25 years and over	14,198
Less than 9th grade	14.6%
High school grad or higher	57.6%
Bachelor's degree or higher	7.3%
Graduate degree	2.6%

Income & Poverty, 1999
Per capita income	$10,917
Median household income	$26,923
Median family income	$30,502
Persons in poverty	4,880
H'holds receiving public assistance	515
H'holds receiving social security	1,840

Households, 2000
Total households	6,182
With persons under 18	2,665
With persons over 65	1,735
Family households	4,181
Single-person households	1,691
Persons per household	2.96
Persons per family	3.49

Labor & Employment
Total civilian labor force, 2007**	8,268
Unemployment rate	8.5%
Total civilian labor force, 2000	7,850
Unemployment rate	13.5%

Employed persons 16 years and over by occupation, 2000
Managers & professionals	1,301
Service occupations	1,607
Sales & office occupations	1,468
Farming, fishing & forestry	340
Construction & maintenance	436
Production & transportation	1,642
Self-employed persons	175

* US Census Bureau
** New Jersey Department of Labor
§ State Fiscal Year July 1–June 30

General Information
City of Bridgeton
181 E Commerce St
Bridgeton, NJ 08302
856-455-3230
Website	www.cityofbridgeton.com
Year of incorporation	1865
Land/water area (sq. miles)	6.22/0.23
Form of government	Mayor-Council

Government
Legislative Districts
US Congressional	2
State Legislative	3

Local Officials, 2009
Mayor	James Begley
Manager	Arch Liston
Clerk	Darlene Richmond
Finance Dir	Terry Delp
Tax Assessor	Kevin Maloney
Tax Collector	Mary Pierce
Attorney	Theodore Baker
Building	Robert Mixner
Planning	John Barry
Engineering	Charles Fralinger
Public Works	Dean Dellaquila
Police Chief	Mark Ott
Emerg/Fire Director	Dave Schoch

Housing & Construction
Housing Units, 2000*
Total	6,795
Median rent	$602
Median SF home value	$71,500

Permits for New Residential Construction
	Units	Value
Total, 2006	176	$17,872,408
Single family	176	$17,872,408
Total, 2007	94	$8,494,957
Single family	94	$8,494,957

Real Property Valuation, 2008
	Parcels	Valuation
Total	5,658	$354,162,000
Vacant	646	5,107,500
Residential	4,436	241,552,800
Commercial	475	69,160,600
Industrial	38	22,459,100
Apartments	54	15,657,400
Farm land	6	42,600
Farm homestead	3	182,000

Average Property Value & Tax, 2008
Residential value	$54,457
Property tax	$2,660
Tax credit/rebate	$764

Public Library
Bridgeton Public Library
150 E Commerce St
Bridgeton, NJ 08302
856-451-2620
Director	Gail S. Robinson

Library statistics, 2007
Population served	22,771
Full-time/total staff	1/6

	Total	Per capita
Holdings	60,028	2.64
Revenues	$331,513	$14.56
Expenditures	$326,292	$14.33
Annual visits	61,965	2.72
Internet terminals/annual users	8/10,987	

Public Safety
Number of officers, 2007	62

Crime	2006	2007
Total crimes	1,400	1,626
Violent	359	380
Murder	0	1
Rape	21	7
Robbery	156	171
Aggravated assault	182	201
Non-violent	1,041	1,246
Burglary	289	376
Larceny	666	798
Vehicle theft	86	72
Domestic violence	617	667
Arson	3	6
Total crime rate	58.4	66.7
Violent	15.0	15.6
Non-violent	43.4	51.1

Public School District
(for school year 2007-08 except as noted)

Bridgeton School District
Bank Street, PO Box 657
Bridgeton, NJ 08302
(856) 455-8030
Superintendent	H. Victor Gilson
Number of schools	8
Grade plan	K-12
Enrollment	4,708
Attendance rate, '06-07	91.8%
Dropout rate	6.2%
Students per teacher	8.9
Per pupil expenditure	$15,134
Median faculty salary	$49,145
Median administrator salary	$94,349
Grade 12 enrollment	212
High school graduation rate	70.3%

Assessment test results
(percent scoring at proficient or advanced level)
	Language	Math
NJASK-Grade 3	70.0%	67.6%
GEPA-Grade 8	40.5%	57.3%
HSPA-High School	41.7%	55.4%

SAT Score Averages, 2006-07
Pct tested	Math	Verbal	Writing
44%	414	421	418

Teacher Qualifications
Avg. years of experience	7
Highly-qualified teachers one subject/all subjects	100%/100%

No Child Left Behind
AYP, 2006-07	Meets Standards

Municipal Finance§
State Aid Programs, 2009
Total aid	$5,170,828
CMPTRA	3,613,725
Energy tax receipts	1,553,040
Garden State Trust	3,678

General Budget, 2008
Total tax levy	$17,460,070
County levy	5,486,780
County taxes	5,186,684
County library	0
County health	242,414
County open space	57,682
School levy	3,501,289
Muni. levy	8,472,001
Misc. revenues	13,263,144

Taxes
	2006	2007	2008
General tax rate per $100	4.272	4.487	4.888
County equalization ratio	81.85	73.09	64.40
Net valuation taxable	$352,619,600	$357,843,234	$357,397,029
State equalized value	$486,398,952	$553,670,763	$564,150,455

See Introduction for an explanation of all data sources.

Demographics & Socio-Economic Characteristics

(2000 US Census, except as noted)

Population

1980*	29,175
1990*	32,509
2000	42,940
Male	20,636
Female	22,304
2007 (estimate)*	44,408
Population density	1,368.5

Race & Hispanic Origin, 2000

Race

White	36,527
Black/African American	931
American Indian/Alaska Native	33
Asian	4,525
Native Hawaiian/Pacific Islander	5
Other race	381
Two or more races	538
Hispanic origin, total	2,056
Mexican	194
Puerto Rican	352
Cuban	143
Other Hispanic	1,367

Age & Nativity, 2000

Under 5 years	3,295
18 years and over	31,922
21 years and over	30,977
65 years and over	5,443
85 years and over	778
Median age	38.2
Native-born	36,128
Foreign-born	6,754

Educational Attainment, 2000

Population 25 years and over	29,686
Less than 9th grade	3.2%
High school grad or higher	92.0%
Bachelor's degree or higher	49.9%
Graduate degree	22.0%

Income & Poverty, 1999

Per capita income	$39,555
Median household income	$88,308
Median family income	$99,832
Persons in poverty	885
H'holds receiving public assistance	138
H'holds receiving social security	3,435

Households, 2000

Total households	15,561
With persons under 18	6,121
With persons over 65	3,523
Family households	11,890
Single-person households	3,083
Persons per household	2.71
Persons per family	3.14

Labor & Employment

Total civilian labor force, 2007**	25,150
Unemployment rate	2.7%
Total civilian labor force, 2000	23,028
Unemployment rate	2.8%

Employed persons 16 years and over by occupation, 2000

Managers & professionals	12,020
Service occupations	1,705
Sales & office occupations	5,808
Farming, fishing & forestry	18
Construction & maintenance	1,514
Production & transportation	1,323
Self-employed persons	1,045

‡ Main library for county
* US Census Bureau
** New Jersey Department of Labor

See Introduction for an explanation of all data sources.

General Information

Township of Bridgewater
700 Garretson Rd
Bridgewater, NJ 08807
908-725-6300

Website	www.bridgewaternj.gov
Year of incorporation	1749
Land/water area (sq. miles)	32.45/0.09
Form of government	Mayor-Council

Government

Legislative Districts

US Congressional	7, 11
State Legislative	16

Local Officials, 2009

Mayor	Patricia Flannery
Manager	James Naples
Clerk	Linda Doyle
CFO	Natasha Turchan
Tax Assessor	Anthony DiRado
Tax Collector	Darrow Murdock
Attorney	William Savo
Construction Official	Steve Rodzinak
Planner	Scarlett Doyle
Engineering	Robert Bogart
Public Works Dir	John Langel
Police Chief	Richard Borden
Fire Chief	(6 districts)

Housing & Construction

Housing Units, 2000*

Total	15,879
Median rent	$1,096
Median SF home value	$268,100

Permits for New Residential Construction

	Units	Value
Total, 2006	172	$27,363,680
Single family	32	$9,202,520
Total, 2007	46	$9,408,590
Single family	26	$6,169,035

Real Property Valuation, 2008

	Parcels	Valuation
Total	15,923	$9,078,442,300
Vacant	690	119,347,100
Residential	14,747	6,733,962,500
Commercial	384	1,804,513,500
Industrial	47	366,284,400
Apartments	13	48,523,200
Farm land	33	121,700
Farm homestead	9	5,689,900

Average Property Value & Tax, 2008

Residential value	$456,740
Property tax	$7,862
Tax credit/rebate	$1,143

Public Library

Somerset County Library‡
1 Vogt Dr
Bridgewater, NJ 08807
908-526-4016

Branch Director	James M. Hecht

County Library statistics, 2007

Population served	176,402
Full-time/total staff	51/128

	Total	Per capita
Holdings	813,024	4.61
Revenues	$13,913,797	$78.88
Expenditures	$14,250,980	$80.79
Annual visits	1,061,921	6.02
Internet terminals/annual users	118/244,011	

Public Safety

Number of officers, 2007	78

Crime	2006	2007
Total crimes	676	721
Violent	17	15
Murder	0	0
Rape	0	1
Robbery	8	6
Aggravated assault	9	8
Non-violent	659	706
Burglary	99	91
Larceny	531	584
Vehicle theft	29	31
Domestic violence	144	123
Arson	4	1
Total crime rate	15.2	16.1
Violent	0.4	0.3
Non-violent	14.8	15.8

Public School District

(for school year 2007-08 except as noted)

Bridgewater-Raritan Regional School Dist.
836 Newmans Ln, PO Box 6030
Bridgewater, NJ 08807
(908) 685-2777

Superintendent	Michael Schilder
Number of schools	11
Grade plan	K-12
Enrollment	9,115
Attendance rate, '06-07	96.4%
Dropout rate	0.3%
Students per teacher	10.3
Per pupil expenditure	$13,578
Median faculty salary	$53,650
Median administrator salary	$125,757
Grade 12 enrollment	648
High school graduation rate	98.8%

Assessment test results

(percent scoring at proficient or advanced level)

	Language	Math
NJASK-Grade 3	93.8%	90.6%
GEPA-Grade 8	86.4%	94.0%
HSPA-High School	88.9%	92.4%

SAT Score Averages, 2006-07

Pct tested	Math	Verbal	Writing
94%	568	529	529

Teacher Qualifications

Avg. years of experience	7
Highly-qualified teachers one subject/all subjects	100%/100%

No Child Left Behind

AYP, 2006-07	Meets Standards

Municipal Finance

State Aid Programs, 2009

Total aid	$8,184,961
CMPTRA	1,395,032
Energy tax receipts	6,456,652
Garden State Trust	6,123

General Budget, 2008

Total tax levy	$156,457,134
County levy	33,141,977
County taxes	26,594,233
County library	3,601,968
County health	0
County open space	2,945,775
School levy	100,990,342
Muni. levy	22,324,815
Misc. revenues	19,348,187

Taxes	2006	2007	2008
General tax rate per $100	1.64	1.7	1.722
County equalization ratio	97.82	91.98	93.24
Net valuation taxable	$9,058,616,300	$9,178,040,920	$9,088,763,868
State equalized value	$9,941,810,714	$9,676,888,191	$9,488,753,704

Demographics & Socio-Economic Characteristics

(2000 US Census, except as noted)

Population
1980*	4,068
1990*	4,406
2000	4,893
Male	2,336
Female	2,557
2007 (estimate)*	4,879
Population density	2,741.0

Race & Hispanic Origin, 2000
Race
White	4,553
Black/African American	172
American Indian/Alaska Native	3
Asian	33
Native Hawaiian/Pacific Islander	0
Other race	79
Two or more races	53
Hispanic origin, total	162
Mexican	88
Puerto Rican	31
Cuban	11
Other Hispanic	32

Age & Nativity, 2000
Under 5 years	348
18 years and over	3,733
21 years and over	3,631
65 years and over	868
85 years and over	77
Median age	42.9
Native-born	4,734
Foreign-born	159

Educational Attainment, 2000
Population 25 years and over	3,533
Less than 9th grade	1.8%
High school grad or higher	94.8%
Bachelor's degree or higher	44.7%
Graduate degree	14.7%

Income & Poverty, 1999
Per capita income	$35,785
Median household income	$68,368
Median family income	$82,867
Persons in poverty	193
H'holds receiving public assistance	24
H'holds receiving social security	693

Households, 2000
Total households	1,938
With persons under 18	640
With persons over 65	633
Family households	1,414
Single-person households	456
Persons per household	2.52
Persons per family	3.00

Labor & Employment
Total civilian labor force, 2007**	2,454
Unemployment rate	3.2%
Total civilian labor force, 2000	2,297
Unemployment rate	3.5%

Employed persons 16 years and over by occupation, 2000
Managers & professionals	1,241
Service occupations	225
Sales & office occupations	484
Farming, fishing & forestry	16
Construction & maintenance	107
Production & transportation	144
Self-employed persons	229

General Information

Borough of Brielle
601 Union Ln
Brielle, NJ 08730
732-528-6600

Website	www.briellenj.com
Year of incorporation	1919
Land/water area (sq. miles)	1.78/0.59
Form of government	Borough

Government

Legislative Districts
US Congressional	4
State Legislative	11

Local Officials, 2009
Mayor	Thomas B. Nicol
Manager	Thomas Nolan
Clerk	Thomas Nolan
Finance Dir	Stephen Mayer
Tax Assessor	Mary Lou Hartman
Tax Collector	Colleen Castronova
Attorney	Nicholas Montenegro
Building	Albert Ratz Jr
Comm Dev/Planning	NA
Engineering	Alan P. Hilla Jr
Public Works	William Burkhardt Jr
Police Chief	Michael Palmer
Emerg/Fire Director	Thomas B. Nicol

Housing & Construction

Housing Units, 2000*
Total	2,123
Median rent	$1,090
Median SF home value	$285,000

Permits for New Residential Construction
	Units	Value
Total, 2006	29	$7,888,791
Single family	29	$7,888,791
Total, 2007	17	$4,712,792
Single family	17	$4,712,792

Real Property Valuation, 2008
	Parcels	Valuation
Total	2,091	$1,704,467,500
Vacant	92	41,150,000
Residential	1,912	1,525,621,700
Commercial	84	123,714,000
Industrial	0	0
Apartments	3	13,981,800
Farm land	0	0
Farm homestead	0	0

Average Property Value & Tax, 2008
Residential value	$797,919
Property tax	$9,187
Tax credit/rebate	$1,125

Public Library

Brielle Public Library
610 South St
Brielle, NJ 08730
732-528-9381

Director	Kerri DiBrienza

Library statistics, 2007
Population served	4,893
Full-time/total staff	0/0

	Total	Per capita
Holdings	45,390	9.28
Revenues	$159,587	$32.62
Expenditures	$155,247	$31.73
Annual visits	26,000	5.31
Internet terminals/annual users		7/2,400

Public Safety

Number of officers, 2007 15
Crime	2006	2007
Total crimes	51	54
Violent	5	5
Murder	0	0
Rape	1	0
Robbery	1	0
Aggravated assault	3	5
Non-violent	46	49
Burglary	25	5
Larceny	20	44
Vehicle theft	1	0
Domestic violence	16	17
Arson	0	0
Total crime rate	10.5	11.1
Violent	1.0	1.0
Non-violent	9.4	10.1

Public School District

(for school year 2007-08 except as noted)

Brielle Borough School District
605 Union Lane
Brielle, NJ 08730
(732) 528-6400

Superintendent	Christine Carlson
Number of schools	1
Grade plan	K-8
Enrollment	712
Attendance rate, '06-07	95.2%
Dropout rate	NA
Students per teacher	11.5
Per pupil expenditure	$11,134
Median faculty salary	$47,795
Median administrator salary	$99,657
Grade 12 enrollment	NA
High school graduation rate	NA

Assessment test results
(percent scoring at proficient or advanced level)
	Language	Math
NJASK-Grade 3	93.9%	96.3%
GEPA-Grade 8	87.6%	94.5%
HSPA-High School	NA	NA

SAT Score Averages, 2006-07
Pct tested	Math	Verbal	Writing
NA	NA	NA	NA

Teacher Qualifications
Avg. years of experience	10
Highly-qualified teachers one subject/all subjects	100%/100%

No Child Left Behind
AYP, 2006-07 . . . . Meets Standards

Municipal Finance

State Aid Programs, 2009
Total aid	$402,810
CMPTRA	23,208
Energy tax receipts	363,490
Garden State Trust	0

General Budget, 2008
Total tax levy	$19,631,215
County levy	3,944,858
County taxes	3,500,552
County library	210,738
County health	0
County open space	233,568
School levy	10,738,297
Muni. levy	4,948,060
Misc. revenues	2,043,246

Taxes
	2006	2007	2008
General tax rate per $100	2.894	1.113	1.152
County equalization ratio	47.36	114.03	109.39
Net valuation taxable	$611,796,200	$1,703,970,532	$1,705,022,933
State equalized value	$1,485,900,588	$1,557,746,952	$1,166,080,817

* US Census Bureau
** New Jersey Department of Labor

See Introduction for an explanation of all data sources.

Demographics & Socio-Economic Characteristics

(2000 US Census, except as noted)

Population

1980*	8,318
1990*	11,354
2000	12,594
Male	6,138
Female	6,456
2007 (estimate)*	12,739
Population density	1,981.2

Race & Hispanic Origin, 2000

Race

White	10,472
Black/African American	496
American Indian/Alaska Native	23
Asian	720
Native Hawaiian/Pacific Islander	6
Other race	588
Two or more races	289
Hispanic origin, total	1,185
Mexican	171
Puerto Rican	526
Cuban	29
Other Hispanic	459

Age & Nativity, 2000

Under 5 years	701
18 years and over	9,973
21 years and over	9,689
65 years and over	2,090
85 years and over	161
Median age	40.7
Native-born	11,045
Foreign-born	1,549

Educational Attainment, 2000

Population 25 years and over	9,314
Less than 9th grade	3.0%
High school grad or higher	84.5%
Bachelor's degree or higher	23.8%
Graduate degree	8.5%

Income & Poverty, 1999

Per capita income	$23,950
Median household income	$44,639
Median family income	$51,679
Persons in poverty	1,185
H'holds receiving public assistance	113
H'holds receiving social security	1,711

Households, 2000

Total households	5,473
With persons under 18	1,449
With persons over 65	1,536
Family households	3,338
Single-person households	1,678
Persons per household	2.30
Persons per family	2.89

Labor & Employment

Total civilian labor force, 2007**	7,143
Unemployment rate	4.3%
Total civilian labor force, 2000	6,713
Unemployment rate	4.6%

Employed persons 16 years and over by occupation, 2000

Managers & professionals	1,844
Service occupations	2,159
Sales & office occupations	1,652
Farming, fishing & forestry	29
Construction & maintenance	373
Production & transportation	350
Self-employed persons	295

‡ Branch of county library
* US Census Bureau
** New Jersey Department of Labor

General Information

City of Brigantine
1417 W Brigantine Ave
Brigantine, NJ 08203
609-266-7600

Website	www.brigantinebeachnj.com
Year of incorporation	1924
Land/water area (sq. miles)	6.43/3.36
Form of government	Council-Manager

Government

Legislative Districts

US Congressional	2
State Legislative	2

Local Officials, 2009

Mayor	Philip Guenther
Manager	James Barber
Clerk	Lynn Sweeney
Finance Dir	Christian Johansen
Tax Assessor	Barbara Saccoccia
Tax Collector	Dana Wineland
Attorney	Timothy Maguire
Building	Rich Stevens
Comm Dev/Planning	NA
Engineering	Edward Stinson
Public Works	Ernie Purdy
Police Chief	James Frugoli
Fire Chief	James Frugoli

Housing & Construction

Housing Units, 2000*

Total	9,304
Median rent	$792
Median SF home value	$144,400

Permits for New Residential Construction

	Units	Value
Total, 2006	78	$22,410,120
Single family	70	$20,632,720
Total, 2007	25	$9,135,530
Single family	25	$9,135,530

Real Property Valuation, 2008

	Parcels	Valuation
Total	8,845	$4,697,910,800
Vacant	222	100,178,900
Residential	8,501	4,499,661,000
Commercial	117	94,761,900
Industrial	0	0
Apartments	5	3,309,000
Farm land	0	0
Farm homestead	0	0

Average Property Value & Tax, 2008

Residential value	$529,310
Property tax	$5,219
Tax credit/rebate	$974

Public Library

Brigantine Branch Library‡
201 15th St
Brigantine, NJ 08203
609-266-0110

Branch Librarian	Sue Wick

Library statistics, 2007

see Atlantic County profile
for library system statistics

Public Safety

Number of officers, 2007	38

Crime	2006	2007
Total crimes	234	209
Violent	8	12
Murder	0	0
Rape	0	0
Robbery	3	5
Aggravated assault	5	7
Non-violent	226	197
Burglary	51	49
Larceny	169	147
Vehicle theft	6	1
Domestic violence	158	59
Arson	2	0
Total crime rate	18.2	16.2
Violent	0.6	0.9
Non-violent	17.6	15.3

Public School District

(for school year 2007-08 except as noted)

Brigantine City School District
301 E. Evans Blvd., PO Box 947
Brigantine, NJ 08203
(609) 266-7671

Superintendent	Robert A. Previti
Number of schools	2
Grade plan	K-8
Enrollment	852
Attendance rate, '06-07	94.1%
Dropout rate	NA
Students per teacher	9.9
Per pupil expenditure	$17,602
Median faculty salary	$72,834
Median administrator salary	$118,069
Grade 12 enrollment	NA
High school graduation rate	NA

Assessment test results

(percent scoring at proficient or advanced level)

	Language	Math
NJASK-Grade 3	93.2%	88.0%
GEPA-Grade 8	64.4%	78.3%
HSPA-High School	NA	NA

SAT Score Averages, 2006-07

Pct tested	Math	Verbal	Writing
NA	NA	NA	NA

Teacher Qualifications

Avg. years of experience	16
Highly-qualified teachers one subject/all subjects	100%/100%

No Child Left Behind

AYP, 2006-07	Meets Standards

Municipal Finance

State Aid Programs, 2009

Total aid	$878,965
CMPTRA	27,679
Energy tax receipts	814,256
Garden State Trust	23,355

General Budget, 2008

Total tax levy	$46,343,936
County levy	13,097,199
County taxes	10,309,327
County library	1,328,082
County health	543,444
County open space	916,346
School levy	15,026,259
Muni. levy	18,220,479
Misc. revenues	5,512,779

Taxes

	2006	2007	2008
General tax rate per $100	0.909	0.95	0.987
County equalization ratio	139.47	109.55	102.64
Net valuation taxable	$4,716,824,700	$4,667,422,755	$4,699,840,568
State equalized value	$4,307,470,826	$4,547,420,248	$4,548,001,763

See Introduction for an explanation of all data sources.

Demographics & Socio-Economic Characteristics
(2000 US Census, except as noted)

Population
1980*	2,133
1990*	1,805
2000	2,354
Male	1,109
Female	1,245
2007 (estimate)*	2,265
Population density	4,819.1

Race & Hispanic Origin, 2000
Race
White	2,125
Black/African American	101
American Indian/Alaska Native	2
Asian	25
Native Hawaiian/Pacific Islander	0
Other race	56
Two or more races	45
Hispanic origin, total	111
Mexican	7
Puerto Rican	73
Cuban	0
Other Hispanic	31

Age & Nativity, 2000
Under 5 years	165
18 years and over	1,746
21 years and over	1,670
65 years and over	310
85 years and over	40
Median age	35.2
Native-born	2,283
Foreign-born	71

Educational Attainment, 2000
Population 25 years and over	1,525
Less than 9th grade	4.5%
High school grad or higher	80.1%
Bachelor's degree or higher	7.9%
Graduate degree	3.5%

Income & Poverty, 1999
Per capita income	$18,295
Median household income	$39,600
Median family income	$47,891
Persons in poverty	170
H'holds receiving public assistance	12
H'holds receiving social security	249

Households, 2000
Total households	961
With persons under 18	345
With persons over 65	246
Family households	601
Single-person households	297
Persons per household	2.45
Persons per family	3.09

Labor & Employment
Total civilian labor force, 2007**	1,336
Unemployment rate	3.1%
Total civilian labor force, 2000	1,263
Unemployment rate	3.2%

Employed persons 16 years and over by occupation, 2000
Managers & professionals	239
Service occupations	259
Sales & office occupations	352
Farming, fishing & forestry	5
Construction & maintenance	155
Production & transportation	212
Self-employed persons	48

General Information
Borough of Brooklawn
301 Christiana St
Brooklawn, NJ 08030
856-456-0750
Website	www.brooklawn.us
Year of incorporation	1924
Land/water area (sq. miles)	0.47/0.05
Form of government	Borough

Government
Legislative Districts
US Congressional	1
State Legislative	5

Local Officials, 2009
Mayor	John Soubasis
Manager/Admin	NA
Clerk	Barbara Lewis
Finance Dir	Barbara Lewis
Tax Assessor	Anthony Leone
Tax Collector	Maria S. Branson
Attorney	Timothy Higgins
Building	Christopher Mecca
Comm Dev/Planning	NA
Engineering	Chuck Reibel
Public Works	Donna Domico
Police Chief	Francis McKinney
Emerg/Fire Director	A. Sam Cilurso

Housing & Construction
Housing Units, 2000*
Total	1,025
Median rent	$622
Median SF home value	$79,300

Permits for New Residential Construction
	Units	Value
Total, 2006	0	$0
Single family	0	$0
Total, 2007	0	$0
Single family	0	$0

Real Property Valuation, 2008
	Parcels	Valuation
Total	800	$78,901,200
Vacant	30	466,300
Residential	689	52,830,000
Commercial	74	23,754,500
Industrial	3	819,700
Apartments	4	1,030,700
Farm land	0	0
Farm homestead	0	0

Average Property Value & Tax, 2008
Residential value	$76,676
Property tax	$3,233
Tax credit/rebate	$739

Public Library
No public municipal library

Library statistics, 2007
Population served	NA
Full-time/total staff	NA/NA

	Total	Per capita
Holdings	NA	NA
Revenues	NA	NA
Expenditures	NA	NA
Annual visits	NA	NA
Internet terminals/annual users	NA/NA	

Public Safety
Number of officers, 2007	7

Crime	2006	2007
Total crimes	248	211
Violent	6	15
Murder	1	0
Rape	1	0
Robbery	2	7
Aggravated assault	2	8
Non-violent	242	196
Burglary	30	17
Larceny	196	162
Vehicle theft	16	17
Domestic violence	21	22
Arson	0	0
Total crime rate	107.1	92.0
Violent	2.6	6.5
Non-violent	104.5	85.4

Public School District
(for school year 2007-08 except as noted)

Brooklawn School District
Haakon Road
Brooklawn, NJ 08030
(856) 456-4039
Superintendent	John Kellmayer
Number of schools	1
Grade plan	K-8
Enrollment	315
Attendance rate, '06-07	95.0%
Dropout rate	NA
Students per teacher	12.1
Per pupil expenditure	$11,063
Median faculty salary	$46,213
Median administrator salary	$68,133
Grade 12 enrollment	NA
High school graduation rate	NA

Assessment test results
(percent scoring at proficient or advanced level)
	Language	Math
NJASK-Grade 3	68.0%	80.0%
GEPA-Grade 8	70.6%	82.3%
HSPA-High School	NA	NA

SAT Score Averages, 2006-07
Pct tested	Math	Verbal	Writing
NA	NA	NA	NA

Teacher Qualifications
Avg. years of experience	9
Highly-qualified teachers one subject/all subjects	100%/100%

No Child Left Behind
AYP, 2006-07	Meets Standards

Municipal Finance
State Aid Programs, 2009
Total aid	$238,563
CMPTRA	44,783
Energy tax receipts	192,587
Garden State Trust	0

General Budget, 2008
Total tax levy	$3,334,059
County levy	890,487
County taxes	804,723
County library	57,736
County health	0
County open space	28,027
School levy	1,180,591
Muni. levy	1,262,981
Misc. revenues	1,342,703

Taxes	2006	2007	2008
General tax rate per $100	3.964	4.037	4.217
County equalization ratio	78.51	64.93	56.81
Net valuation taxable	$78,001,000	$78,842,199	$79,062,642
State equalized value	$120,339,285	$138,648,907	$151,371,101

See Introduction for an explanation of all data sources.

Demographics & Socio-Economic Characteristics

(2000 US Census, except as noted)

Population

1980*	3,642
1990*	4,441
2000	3,873
Male	1,887
Female	1,986
2007 (estimate)*	3,747
Population density	492.4

Race & Hispanic Origin, 2000

Race

White	2,993
Black/African American	296
American Indian/Alaska Native	20
Asian	17
Native Hawaiian/Pacific Islander	1
Other race	408
Two or more races	138
Hispanic origin, total	916
Mexican	175
Puerto Rican	660
Cuban	8
Other Hispanic	73

Age & Nativity, 2000

Under 5 years	245
18 years and over	2,876
21 years and over	2,715
65 years and over	613
85 years and over	59
Median age	36.2
Native-born	3,626
Foreign-born	247

Educational Attainment, 2000

Population 25 years and over	2,552
Less than 9th grade	17.4%
High school grad or higher	62.3%
Bachelor's degree or higher	8.8%
Graduate degree	2.5%

Income & Poverty, 1999

Per capita income	$16,717
Median household income	$35,679
Median family income	$44,352
Persons in poverty	725
H'holds receiving public assistance	28
H'holds receiving social security	513

Households, 2000

Total households	1,454
With persons under 18	525
With persons over 65	475
Family households	978
Single-person households	407
Persons per household	2.64
Persons per family	3.23

Labor & Employment

Total civilian labor force, 2007**	1,849
Unemployment rate	6.4%
Total civilian labor force, 2000	1,779
Unemployment rate	8.3%

Employed persons 16 years and over by occupation, 2000

Managers & professionals	353
Service occupations	296
Sales & office occupations	401
Farming, fishing & forestry	103
Construction & maintenance	190
Production & transportation	288
Self-employed persons	80

* US Census Bureau
** New Jersey Department of Labor

General Information

Borough of Buena
616 Central Ave
Minotola, NJ 08341
856-697-9393

Website	buenaboro.org
Year of incorporation	1948
Land/water area (sq. miles)	7.61/0.00
Form of government	Borough

Government

Legislative Districts

US Congressional	2
State Legislative	1

Local Officials, 2009

Mayor	Joseph Baruffi
Manager/Admin	NA
Clerk	Maryann Coraluzzo
Finance Dir	Nancy Brunini
Tax Assessor	Dennis Deklerk
Tax Collector	Mary Ann Coraluzzo
Attorney	Robert DeSanto
Building	Kevin Kirchner
Comm Dev/Planning	NA
Engineering	Remington & Vernick
Public Works	John Brunini
Police Chief	Douglas Adams
Fire/Emergency Dir	NA

Housing & Construction

Housing Units, 2000*

Total	1,553
Median rent	$639
Median SF home value	$98,100

Permits for New Residential Construction

	Units	Value
Total, 2006	8	$1,090,000
Single family	8	$1,090,000
Total, 2007	1	$136,250
Single family	1	$136,250

Real Property Valuation, 2008

	Parcels	Valuation
Total	1,822	$296,760,800
Vacant	220	10,142,300
Residential	1,229	221,428,500
Commercial	104	31,167,900
Industrial	3	5,409,800
Apartments	8	8,243,600
Farm land	160	1,721,000
Farm homestead	98	18,647,700

Average Property Value & Tax, 2008

Residential value	$180,917
Property tax	$4,213
Tax credit/rebate	$865

Public Library

No public municipal library

Library statistics, 2007

Population served	NA
Full-time/total staff	NA/NA

	Total	Per capita
Holdings	NA	NA
Revenues	NA	NA
Expenditures	NA	NA
Annual visits	NA	NA
Internet terminals/annual users	NA/NA	

Public Safety

Number of officers, 2007 ... 9

Crime	2006	2007
Total crimes	136	133
Violent	22	22
Murder	0	0
Rape	1	7
Robbery	1	1
Aggravated assault	20	14
Non-violent	114	111
Burglary	45	44
Larceny	66	62
Vehicle theft	3	5
Domestic violence	56	42
Arson	1	1
Total crime rate	35.3	35.0
Violent	5.7	5.8
Non-violent	29.6	29.2

Public School District

(for school year 2007-08 except as noted)

Buena Regional School District
Harding Highway, PO Box 309
Buena, NJ 08310
(856) 697-0800

Superintendent	Walter Whitaker
Number of schools	6
Grade plan	K-12
Enrollment	2,497
Attendance rate, '06-07	93.4%
Dropout rate	2.5%
Students per teacher	11.2
Per pupil expenditure	$13,367
Median faculty salary	$55,291
Median administrator salary	$103,694
Grade 12 enrollment	207
High school graduation rate	90.8%

Assessment test results

(percent scoring at proficient or advanced level)

	Language	Math
NJASK-Grade 3	80.7%	79.3%
GEPA-Grade 8	60.4%	75.7%
HSPA-High School	74.5%	83.3%

SAT Score Averages, 2006-07

Pct tested	Math	Verbal	Writing
46%	479	475	472

Teacher Qualifications

Avg. years of experience	11
Highly-qualified teachers one subject/all subjects	99.0%/97.5%

No Child Left Behind

AYP, 2006-07 ... Meets Standards

Municipal Finance

State Aid Programs, 2009

Total aid	$540,569
CMPTRA	153,125
Energy tax receipts	373,930
Garden State Trust	0

General Budget, 2008

Total tax levy	$6,954,365
County levy	872,327
County taxes	686,904
County library	88,332
County health	36,145
County open space	60,947
School levy	4,031,153
Muni. levy	2,050,885
Misc. revenues	1,824,466

Taxes	2006	2007	2008
General tax rate per $100	4.129	2.267	2.329
County equalization ratio	65.87	106.57	98.59
Net valuation taxable	$147,789,000	$295,454,759	$298,604,752
State equalized value	$274,762,119	$299,654,407	$315,577,750

See Introduction for an explanation of all data sources.

Demographics & Socio-Economic Characteristics

(2000 US Census, except as noted)

Population

1980*	6,959
1990*	7,655
2000	7,436
Male	3,622
Female	3,814
2007 (estimate)*	7,359
Population density	177.9

Race & Hispanic Origin, 2000

Race

White	5,751
Black/African American	1,167
American Indian/Alaska Native	16
Asian	17
Native Hawaiian/Pacific Islander	1
Other race	303
Two or more races	181
Hispanic origin, total	689
Mexican	63
Puerto Rican	513
Cuban	7
Other Hispanic	106

Age & Nativity, 2000

Under 5 years	409
18 years and over	5,598
21 years and over	5,317
65 years and over	1,138
85 years and over	120
Median age	39.0
Native-born	7,174
Foreign-born	262

Educational Attainment, 2000

Population 25 years and over	5,007
Less than 9th grade	9.7%
High school grad or higher	70.3%
Bachelor's degree or higher	12.2%
Graduate degree	3.8%

Income & Poverty, 1999

Per capita income	$18,382
Median household income	$43,770
Median family income	$50,403
Persons in poverty	890
H'holds receiving public assistance	47
H'holds receiving social security	861

Households, 2000

Total households	2,648
With persons under 18	935
With persons over 65	818
Family households	1,973
Single-person households	555
Persons per household	2.77
Persons per family	3.20

Labor & Employment

Total civilian labor force, 2007**	3,863
Unemployment rate	4.6%
Total civilian labor force, 2000	3,719
Unemployment rate	6.7%

Employed persons 16 years and over by occupation, 2000

Managers & professionals	683
Service occupations	599
Sales & office occupations	938
Farming, fishing & forestry	40
Construction & maintenance	550
Production & transportation	658
Self-employed persons	195

* US Census Bureau
** New Jersey Department of Labor

General Information

Township of Buena Vista
890 Harding Hwy
PO Box 605
Buena, NJ 08310
856-697-2100

Website	www.buenavistatownship.org
Year of incorporation	1867
Land/water area (sq. miles)	41.36/0.16
Form of government	Township

Government

Legislative Districts

US Congressional	2
State Legislative	1

Local Officials, 2009

Mayor	Chuck Chiarello
Manager	Ronald Trebing
Clerk	Linda Gonzales (Actg)
Finance Dir	Ronald Trebing
Tax Assessor	Bernadette Leonardi
Tax Collector	Terence S. Graff
Attorney	Mark Stein
Building	David S. Scheidegg
Comm Dev/Planning	NA
Engineering	David S. Scheidegg
Public Works	Richard Calareso
Police Chief	NA
Fire/Emergency Dir	NA

Housing & Construction

Housing Units, 2000*

Total	2,827
Median rent	$740
Median SF home value	$96,100

Permits for New Residential Construction

	Units	Value
Total, 2006	9	$1,224,947
Single family	9	$1,224,947
Total, 2007	19	$2,907,206
Single family	19	$2,907,206

Real Property Valuation, 2008

	Parcels	Valuation
Total	6,019	$276,945,800
Vacant	3,124	16,816,600
Residential	2,400	217,914,000
Commercial	84	21,806,800
Industrial	15	6,281,100
Apartments	0	0
Farm land	281	2,178,700
Farm homestead	115	11,948,600

Average Property Value & Tax, 2008

Residential value	$91,397
Property tax	$3,742
Tax credit/rebate	$872

Public Library

No public municipal library

Library statistics, 2007

Population served	NA
Full-time/total staff	NA/NA

	Total	Per capita
Holdings	NA	NA
Revenues	NA	NA
Expenditures	NA	NA
Annual visits	NA	NA
Internet terminals/annual users	NA/NA	

Public Safety

Number of officers, 2007 ... 0

Crime	2006	2007
Total crimes	184	163
Violent	20	17
Murder	0	1
Rape	1	0
Robbery	4	1
Aggravated assault	15	15
Non-violent	164	146
Burglary	59	60
Larceny	94	74
Vehicle theft	11	12
Domestic violence	20	57
Arson	1	1
Total crime rate	24.4	21.8
Violent	2.7	2.3
Non-violent	21.8	19.5

Public School District

(for school year 2007-08 except as noted)

Buena Regional School District
Harding Highway, PO Box 309
Buena, NJ 08310
(856) 697-0800

Superintendent	Walter Whitaker
Number of schools	6
Grade plan	K-12
Enrollment	2,497
Attendance rate, '06-07	93.4%
Dropout rate	2.5%
Students per teacher	11.2
Per pupil expenditure	$13,367
Median faculty salary	$55,291
Median administrator salary	$103,694
Grade 12 enrollment	207
High school graduation rate	90.8%

Assessment test results

(percent scoring at proficient or advanced level)

	Language	Math
NJASK-Grade 3	80.7%	79.3%
GEPA-Grade 8	60.4%	75.7%
HSPA-High School	74.5%	83.3%

SAT Score Averages, 2006-07

Pct tested	Math	Verbal	Writing
46%	479	475	472

Teacher Qualifications

Avg. years of experience	11
Highly-qualified teachers one subject/all subjects	99.0%/97.5%

No Child Left Behind

AYP, 2006-07 ... Meets Standards

Municipal Finance

State Aid Programs, 2009

Total aid	$932,747
CMPTRA	58,717
Energy tax receipts	822,703
Garden State Trust	25,578

General Budget, 2008

Total tax levy	$11,370,580
County levy	1,683,800
County taxes	1,324,549
County library	171,139
County health	70,029
County open space	118,082
School levy	7,687,133
Muni. levy	1,999,647
Misc. revenues	2,770,460

Taxes

	2006	2007	2008
General tax rate per $100	4.054	4.026	4.095
County equalization ratio	57.84	52.14	47.14
Net valuation taxable	$267,848,900	$274,598,634	$277,690,070
State equalized value	$514,538,404	$581,649,299	$679,034,253

See Introduction for an explanation of all data sources.

Demographics & Socio-Economic Characteristics
(2000 US Census, except as noted)

Population
1980*	10,246
1990*	9,835
2000	9,736
Male	4,618
Female	5,118
2007 (estimate)*	9,485
Population density	3,161.7

Race & Hispanic Origin, 2000
Race
White	6,638
Black/African American	2,592
American Indian/Alaska Native	26
Asian	125
Native Hawaiian/Pacific Islander	1
Other race	126
Two or more races	228
Hispanic origin, total	332
Mexican	32
Puerto Rican	193
Cuban	7
Other Hispanic	100

Age & Nativity, 2000
Under 5 years	618
18 years and over	7,408
21 years and over	7,072
65 years and over	1,636
85 years and over	189
Median age	38.1
Native-born	9,129
Foreign-born	607

Educational Attainment, 2000
Population 25 years and over	6,646
Less than 9th grade	6.7%
High school grad or higher	77.6%
Bachelor's degree or higher	12.1%
Graduate degree	3.7%

Income & Poverty, 1999
Per capita income	$20,208
Median household income	$43,115
Median family income	$47,969
Persons in poverty	776
H'holds receiving public assistance	156
H'holds receiving social security	1,357

Households, 2000
Total households	3,898
With persons under 18	1,270
With persons over 65	1,254
Family households	2,521
Single-person households	1,167
Persons per household	2.48
Persons per family	3.09

Labor & Employment
Total civilian labor force, 2007**	5,686
Unemployment rate	5.4%
Total civilian labor force, 2000	5,004
Unemployment rate	5.6%

Employed persons 16 years and over by occupation, 2000
Managers & professionals	1,161
Service occupations	794
Sales & office occupations	1,414
Farming, fishing & forestry	7
Construction & maintenance	459
Production & transportation	888
Self-employed persons	153

‡ Joint library with Burlington Township
* US Census Bureau
** New Jersey Department of Labor

See Introduction for an explanation of all data sources.

General Information
City of Burlington
525 High St
Burlington, NJ 08016
609-386-0200
Website	www.burlingtonnj.us
Year of incorporation	1693
Land/water area (sq. miles)	3.00/0.72
Form of government	Mayor-Council

Government
Legislative Districts
US Congressional	4
State Legislative	7

Local Officials, 2009
Mayor	James Fazzone
Manager	Eric Berry
Clerk	Cindy Crivaro
Finance Dir	Kenneth MacMillan
Tax Assessor	Dennis Bianchini
Tax Collector	Lynette Miller
Attorney	Andrew Bayer
Building	Howard Wilkins
Comm Dev/Planning	NA
Engineering	Jeffrey Taylor
Public Works	NA
Police Chief	John Lazzarotti
Emerg/Fire Director	Ron Devlin

Housing & Construction
Housing Units, 2000*
Total	4,181
Median rent	$620
Median SF home value	$97,600

Permits for New Residential Construction
	Units	Value
Total, 2006	6	$733,440
Single family	6	$733,440
Total, 2007	2	$289,835
Single family	2	$289,835

Real Property Valuation, 2008
	Parcels	Valuation
Total	3,830	$434,691,300
Vacant	246	7,898,400
Residential	3,233	307,927,000
Commercial	325	79,444,600
Industrial	9	26,080,000
Apartments	17	13,341,300
Farm land	0	0
Farm homestead	0	0

Average Property Value & Tax, 2008
Residential value	$95,245
Property tax	$3,660
Tax credit/rebate	$819

Public Library
Library Company of Burlington‡
23 W Union St
Burlington, NJ 08016
609-386-1273
Director	Sharon K. Vincz

Library statistics, 2007
Population served	9,736
Full-time/total staff	0/2

	Total	Per capita
Holdings	59,958	6.16
Revenues	$170,202	$17.48
Expenditures	$132,632	$13.62
Annual visits	23,300	2.39
Internet terminals/annual users	12/8,842	

Public Safety
Number of officers, 2007	36

Crime	2006	2007
Total crimes	234	263
Violent	55	46
Murder	2	2
Rape	5	2
Robbery	23	23
Aggravated assault	25	19
Non-violent	179	217
Burglary	46	40
Larceny	116	157
Vehicle theft	17	20
Domestic violence	109	106
Arson	1	5
Total crime rate	23.9	27.1
Violent	5.6	4.7
Non-violent	18.3	22.3

Public School District
(for school year 2007-08 except as noted)

Burlington City School District
518 Locust Avenue
Burlington, NJ 08016
(609) 387-5874
Superintendent	Diane DeGiacomo (Int)
Number of schools	5
Grade plan	K-12
Enrollment	1,806
Attendance rate, '06-07	93.5%
Dropout rate	2.5%
Students per teacher	9.0
Per pupil expenditure	$14,780
Median faculty salary	$53,873
Median administrator salary	$103,900
Grade 12 enrollment	154
High school graduation rate	92.8%

Assessment test results
(percent scoring at proficient or advanced level)
	Language	Math
NJASK-Grade 3	54.7%	54.4%
GEPA-Grade 8	47.2%	68.8%
HSPA-High School	53.2%	72.2%

SAT Score Averages, 2006-07
Pct tested	Math	Verbal	Writing
56%	456	438	424

Teacher Qualifications
Avg. years of experience	8
Highly-qualified teachers one subject/all subjects	100%/100%

No Child Left Behind
AYP, 2006-07	Meets Standards

Municipal Finance
State Aid Programs, 2009
Total aid	$5,971,008
CMPTRA	0
Energy tax receipts	5,821,733
Garden State Trust	4

General Budget, 2008
Total tax levy	$16,780,841
County levy	2,964,812
County taxes	2,434,725
County library	224,804
County health	0
County open space	305,283
School levy	8,631,339
Muni. levy	5,184,690
Misc. revenues	10,214,561

Taxes
	2006	2007	2008
General tax rate per $100	3.416	3.64	3.843
County equalization ratio	69.49	61.89	57.52
Net valuation taxable	$435,366,000	$436,665,516	$436,742,039
State equalized value	$706,093,128	$757,416,989	$802,292,455

Demographics & Socio-Economic Characteristics
(2000 US Census, except as noted)

Population
1980*	11,527
1990*	12,454
2000	20,294
Male	9,620
Female	10,674
2007 (estimate)*	21,359
Population density	1,585.7

Race & Hispanic Origin, 2000
Race
White	13,742
Black/African American	4,971
American Indian/Alaska Native	33
Asian	757
Native Hawaiian/Pacific Islander	6
Other race	296
Two or more races	489
Hispanic origin, total	814
Mexican	84
Puerto Rican	401
Cuban	28
Other Hispanic	301

Age & Nativity, 2000
Under 5 years	1,819
18 years and over	14,775
21 years and over	14,289
65 years and over	2,558
85 years and over	536
Median age	35.6
Native-born	18,695
Foreign-born	1,599

Educational Attainment, 2000
Population 25 years and over	13,724
Less than 9th grade	5.0%
High school grad or higher	85.1%
Bachelor's degree or higher	26.0%
Graduate degree	7.2%

Income & Poverty, 1999
Per capita income	$24,754
Median household income	$61,663
Median family income	$70,958
Persons in poverty	969
H'holds receiving public assistance	163
H'holds receiving social security	1,550

Households, 2000
Total households	7,112
With persons under 18	3,081
With persons over 65	1,313
Family households	5,280
Single-person households	1,521
Persons per household	2.72
Persons per family	3.18

Labor & Employment
Total civilian labor force, 2007**	11,981
Unemployment rate	3.8%
Total civilian labor force, 2000	10,552
Unemployment rate	3.9%

Employed persons 16 years and over by occupation, 2000
Managers & professionals	3,796
Service occupations	1,429
Sales & office occupations	2,857
Farming, fishing & forestry	43
Construction & maintenance	684
Production & transportation	1,336
Self-employed persons	314

‡ Joint library with Burlington City
* US Census Bureau
** New Jersey Department of Labor

General Information
Burlington Township
PO Box 340
Burlington, NJ 08016
609-386-4444
Website	www.twp.burlington.nj.us
Year of incorporation	1677
Land/water area (sq. miles)	13.47/0.50
Form of government	Mayor-Council

Government
Legislative Districts
US Congressional	3, 4
State Legislative	7

Local Officials, 2009
Mayor	Stephen M. George
Manager	Kevin J. McLernon
Clerk	Anthony J. Carnivale Jr
Finance Dir	Dawn M. Hubbard
Tax Assessor	Gil Goble
Tax Collector	Dolores Coolidge
Attorney	Kenneth S. Domzalski
Building	Henry Freck
Planning	Eileen Liss
Engineering	Robert L. Schreibel
Public Works	John Pinto
Police Chief	Walter J. Corter
Emerg/Fire Director	William Diamond

Housing & Construction
Housing Units, 2000*
Total	7,348
Median rent	$621
Median SF home value	$151,600

Permits for New Residential Construction
	Units	Value
Total, 2006	40	$4,744,231
Single family	40	$4,744,231
Total, 2007	52	$6,085,876
Single family	52	$6,085,876

Real Property Valuation, 2008
	Parcels	Valuation
Total	7,314	$2,383,337,558
Vacant	411	63,418,950
Residential	6,599	1,676,485,258
Commercial	184	383,155,900
Industrial	43	198,590,200
Apartments	7	55,090,000
Farm land	62	1,762,250
Farm homestead	8	4,835,000

Average Property Value & Tax, 2008
Residential value	$254,476
Property tax	$5,825
Tax credit/rebate	$971

Public Library
Library Company of Burlington‡
23 W Union St
Burlington, NJ 08016
609-386-1273
Director	Sharon K. Vincz

Library statistics, 2007
Population served	9,736
Full-time/total staff	0/2

	Total	Per capita
Holdings	59,958	6.16
Revenues	$170,202	$17.48
Expenditures	$132,632	$13.62
Annual visits	23,300	2.39
Internet terminals/annual users	12/8,842	

Public Safety
Number of officers, 2007	46

Crime	2006	2007
Total crimes	478	491
Violent	34	31
Murder	1	0
Rape	7	2
Robbery	14	14
Aggravated assault	12	15
Non-violent	444	460
Burglary	60	55
Larceny	357	382
Vehicle theft	27	23
Domestic violence	147	135
Arson	3	1
Total crime rate	21.8	22.5
Violent	1.6	1.4
Non-violent	20.3	21.1

Public School District
(for school year 2007-08 except as noted)

Burlington Township School District
P.O. Box 428
Burlington, NJ 08016
(609) 387-3955
Superintendent	Christopher Manno
Number of schools	4
Grade plan	K-12
Enrollment	4,164
Attendance rate, '06-07	95.6%
Dropout rate	0.0%
Students per teacher	11.9
Per pupil expenditure	$11,469
Median faculty salary	$50,780
Median administrator salary	$98,370
Grade 12 enrollment	246
High school graduation rate	97.2%

Assessment test results
(percent scoring at proficient or advanced level)
	Language	Math
NJASK-Grade 3	85.8%	85.8%
GEPA-Grade 8	72.0%	84.7%
HSPA-High School	80.9%	81.6%

SAT Score Averages, 2006-07
Pct tested	Math	Verbal	Writing
87%	473	467	464

Teacher Qualifications
Avg. years of experience	7
Highly-qualified teachers one subject/all subjects	100%/100%

No Child Left Behind
AYP, 2006-07	Meets Standards

Municipal Finance
State Aid Programs, 2009
Total aid	$5,470,151
CMPTRA	0
Energy tax receipts	5,333,397
Garden State Trust	0

General Budget, 2008
Total tax levy	$54,644,494
County levy	11,438,358
County taxes	9,392,969
County library	867,164
County health	0
County open space	1,178,225
School levy	35,227,628
Muni. levy	7,978,508
Misc. revenues	16,902,495

Taxes	2006	2007	2008
General tax rate per $100	2.02	2.23	2.289
County equalization ratio	96.67	87.88	81.12
Net valuation taxable	$2,360,497,260	$2,372,999,223	$2,387,283,167
State equalized value	$2,690,343,660	$2,924,371,920	$2,833,168,731

See Introduction for an explanation of all data sources.

Demographics & Socio-Economic Characteristics

(2000 US Census, except as noted)

Population

1980*	7,616
1990*	7,392
2000	7,420
Male	3,655
Female	3,765
2007 (estimate)*	8,090
Population density	3,889.4

Race & Hispanic Origin, 2000

Race

White	7,041
Black/African American	46
American Indian/Alaska Native	15
Asian	137
Native Hawaiian/Pacific Islander	1
Other race	110
Two or more races	70
Hispanic origin, total	379
Mexican	109
Puerto Rican	89
Cuban	38
Other Hispanic	143

Age & Nativity, 2000

Under 5 years	467
18 years and over	5,813
21 years and over	5,609
65 years and over	983
85 years and over	96
Median age	37.5
Native-born	6,690
Foreign-born	730

Educational Attainment, 2000

Population 25 years and over	5,293
Less than 9th grade	4.9%
High school grad or higher	85.8%
Bachelor's degree or higher	24.1%
Graduate degree	7.4%

Income & Poverty, 1999

Per capita income	$27,113
Median household income	$57,455
Median family income	$66,199
Persons in poverty	372
H'holds receiving public assistance	33
H'holds receiving social security	703

Households, 2000

Total households	2,868
With persons under 18	934
With persons over 65	725
Family households	2,025
Single-person households	691
Persons per household	2.58
Persons per family	3.09

Labor & Employment

Total civilian labor force, 2007**	4,525
Unemployment rate	2.8%
Total civilian labor force, 2000	4,156
Unemployment rate	3.0%

Employed persons 16 years and over by occupation, 2000

Managers & professionals	1,419
Service occupations	518
Sales & office occupations	1,233
Farming, fishing & forestry	4
Construction & maintenance	378
Production & transportation	481
Self-employed persons	179

* US Census Bureau
** New Jersey Department of Labor

General Information

Borough of Butler
1 Ace Rd
Butler, NJ 07405
973-838-7200

Website	www.butlerborough.com
Year of incorporation	1901
Land/water area (sq. miles)	2.08/0.02
Form of government	Borough

Government

Legislative Districts

US Congressional	11
State Legislative	26

Local Officials, 2009

Mayor	Joseph Heywang
Manager	James Lampmann
Clerk	Carol Ashley
Finance Dir	James Kozimor
Tax Assessor	Shawn Hopkins
Tax Collector	Cora Wright
Attorney	Martin Murphy
Building	Daniel Hagberg
Comm Dev/Planning	NA
Engineering	Paul Darmolfaski
Public Works	Ed Becker
Police Chief	Ed Card
Emerg/Fire Director	Earl Dean

Housing & Construction

Housing Units, 2000*

Total	2,923
Median rent	$796
Median SF home value	$187,500

Permits for New Residential Construction

	Units	Value
Total, 2006	58	$4,216,854
Single family	38	$3,414,460
Total, 2007	38	$3,755,350
Single family	38	$3,755,350

Real Property Valuation, 2008

	Parcels	Valuation
Total	2,623	$738,940,900
Vacant	145	16,397,800
Residential	2,314	586,831,500
Commercial	134	95,096,200
Industrial	16	21,111,700
Apartments	13	19,503,000
Farm land	1	700
Farm homestead	0	0

Average Property Value & Tax, 2008

Residential value	$253,600
Property tax	$6,840
Tax credit/rebate	$1,100

Public Library

Butler Public Library
1 Ace Rd
Butler, NJ 07405
973-838-3262

Director	Deborah Maynard

Library statistics, 2007

Population served	7,420
Full-time/total staff	1/1

	Total	Per capita
Holdings	37,255	5.02
Revenues	$360,351	$48.56
Expenditures	$324,079	$43.68
Annual visits	41,465	5.59
Internet terminals/annual users	5/4,712	

Public Safety

Number of officers, 2007	16

Crime	2006	2007
Total crimes	164	136
Violent	9	6
Murder	0	0
Rape	0	6
Robbery	0	0
Aggravated assault	9	0
Non-violent	155	130
Burglary	45	33
Larceny	95	90
Vehicle theft	15	7
Domestic violence	69	72
Arson	0	0
Total crime rate	20.3	16.8
Violent	1.1	0.7
Non-violent	19.2	16.1

Public School District

(for school year 2007-08 except as noted)

Butler School District
High School Annex Bldg, Bartholdi Ave
Butler, NJ 07405
(973) 492-2032

Superintendent	Mario Cardinale
Number of schools	3
Grade plan	K-12
Enrollment	1,220
Attendance rate, '06-07	95.5%
Dropout rate	2.6%
Students per teacher	9.7
Per pupil expenditure	$15,211
Median faculty salary	$56,010
Median administrator salary	$119,545
Grade 12 enrollment	130
High school graduation rate	91.6%

Assessment test results

(percent scoring at proficient or advanced level)

	Language	Math
NJASK-Grade 3	89.6%	92.0%
GEPA-Grade 8	84.4%	97.4%
HSPA-High School	69.6%	83.2%

SAT Score Averages, 2006-07

Pct tested	Math	Verbal	Writing
76%	487	488	487

Teacher Qualifications

Avg. years of experience	7

Highly-qualified teachers
one subject/all subjects	100%/100%

No Child Left Behind

AYP, 2006-07	Meets Standards

Municipal Finance

State Aid Programs, 2009

Total aid	$1,241,473
CMPTRA	95,333
Energy tax receipts	1,115,104
Garden State Trust	6,140

General Budget, 2008

Total tax levy	$19,945,780
County levy	2,475,930
County taxes	2,020,474
County library	0
County health	0
County open space	455,456
School levy	11,865,205
Muni. levy	5,604,645
Misc. revenues	4,569,091

Taxes

	2006	2007	2008
General tax rate per $100	2.5	2.61	2.697
County equalization ratio	78.89	69.69	70.18
Net valuation taxable	$718,235,000	$728,881,233	$739,559,878
State equalized value	$1,031,250,586	$1,038,339,621	$1,043,437,070

See Introduction for an explanation of all data sources.

Demographics & Socio-Economic Characteristics
(2000 US Census, except as noted)

Population
1980*	7,502
1990*	8,048
2000	8,254
Male	4,098
Female	4,156
2007 (estimate)*	8,506
Population density	403.7

Race & Hispanic Origin, 2000
Race
White	7,905
Black/African American	80
American Indian/Alaska Native	5
Asian	116
Native Hawaiian/Pacific Islander	5
Other race	53
Two or more races	90
Hispanic origin, total	243
Mexican	20
Puerto Rican	75
Cuban	29
Other Hispanic	119

Age & Nativity, 2000
Under 5 years	644
18 years and over	5,874
21 years and over	5,633
65 years and over	501
85 years and over	40
Median age	36.3
Native-born	7,730
Foreign-born	505

Educational Attainment, 2000
Population 25 years and over	5,364
Less than 9th grade	1.2%
High school grad or higher	94.1%
Bachelor's degree or higher	32.2%
Graduate degree	9.4%

Income & Poverty, 1999
Per capita income	$30,710
Median household income	$81,532
Median family income	$89,500
Persons in poverty	143
H'holds receiving public assistance	31
H'holds receiving social security	411

Households, 2000
Total households	2,833
With persons under 18	1,302
With persons over 65	383
Family households	2,317
Single-person households	395
Persons per household	2.91
Persons per family	3.24

Labor & Employment
Total civilian labor force, 2007**	5,197
Unemployment rate	4.3%
Total civilian labor force, 2000	4,632
Unemployment rate	3.3%

Employed persons 16 years and over by occupation, 2000
Managers & professionals	1,994
Service occupations	455
Sales & office occupations	1,271
Farming, fishing & forestry	5
Construction & maintenance	408
Production & transportation	345
Self-employed persons	184

‡ Branch of county library
* US Census Bureau
** New Jersey Department of Labor

General Information
Township of Byram
10 Mansfield Dr
Stanhope, NJ 07874
973-347-2500

Website	byramtwp.org
Year of incorporation	1798
Land/water area (sq. miles)	21.07/1.11
Form of government	Council-Manager

Government
Legislative Districts
US Congressional	11
State Legislative	24

Local Officials, 2009
Mayor	James Oscovitch
Manager	Joseph Sabatini
Clerk	Doris Flynn
Finance Dir	Theresa Vervaet
Tax Assessor	Penny Holenstein
Tax Collector	Theresa Vervaet
Attorney	Thomas Collins
Building	Richard O'Connor
Planning	Christopher Hellwig
Engineering	Cory Stoner
Public Works	Adolf Steyh
Police Chief	Raymond Rafferty
Emerg/Fire Director	Paul Conklin

Housing & Construction
Housing Units, 2000*
Total	3,078
Median rent	$953
Median SF home value	$175,300

Permits for New Residential Construction
	Units	Value
Total, 2006	16	$3,643,307
Single family	16	$3,643,307
Total, 2007	15	$4,984,334
Single family	15	$4,984,334

Real Property Valuation, 2008
	Parcels	Valuation
Total	4,017	$529,843,430
Vacant	560	12,114,800
Residential	3,172	464,612,100
Commercial	112	43,587,500
Industrial	5	1,139,000
Apartments	3	643,600
Farm land	128	284,330
Farm homestead	37	7,462,100

Average Property Value & Tax, 2008
Residential value	$147,109
Property tax	$7,205
Tax credit/rebate	$1,133

Public Library
E. Louise Child Branch Library‡
21 Sparta Rd
Stanhope, NJ 07874
973-770-1000

Branch Librarian	Victoria Larson

Library statistics, 2007
see Sussex County profile
for library system statistics

Public Safety
Number of officers, 2007	14

Crime	2006	2007
Total crimes	54	56
Violent	2	3
Murder	0	0
Rape	1	1
Robbery	0	0
Aggravated assault	1	2
Non-violent	52	53
Burglary	17	6
Larceny	34	45
Vehicle theft	1	2
Domestic violence	57	39
Arson	2	1
Total crime rate	6.2	6.5
Violent	0.2	0.3
Non-violent	6.0	6.1

Public School District
(for school year 2007-08 except as noted)

Byram Township School District
12 Mansfield Drive
Stanhope, NJ 07874
(973) 347-6663

Superintendent	Gayle Strauss
Number of schools	2
Grade plan	K-8
Enrollment	1,160
Attendance rate, '06-07	96.1%
Dropout rate	NA
Students per teacher	12.0
Per pupil expenditure	$10,496
Median faculty salary	$51,750
Median administrator salary	$100,791
Grade 12 enrollment	NA
High school graduation rate	NA

Assessment test results
(percent scoring at proficient or advanced level)
	Language	Math
NJASK-Grade 3	93.4%	93.9%
GEPA-Grade 8	81.9%	96.3%
HSPA-High School	NA	NA

SAT Score Averages, 2006-07
Pct tested	Math	Verbal	Writing
NA	NA	NA	NA

Teacher Qualifications
Avg. years of experience	9
Highly-qualified teachers one subject/all subjects	100%/100%

No Child Left Behind
AYP, 2006-07	Meets Standards

Municipal Finance
State Aid Programs, 2009
Total aid	$817,687
CMPTRA	196,222
Energy tax receipts	527,191
Garden State Trust	66,734

General Budget, 2008
Total tax levy	$25,985,294
County levy	4,635,401
County taxes	3,890,173
County library	327,875
County health	115,125
County open space	302,228
School levy	14,642,336
Muni. levy	6,707,557
Misc. revenues	2,871,125

Taxes
Taxes	2006	2007	2008
General tax rate per $100	4.56	4.74	4.899
County equalization ratio	50.56	45.88	43.92
Net valuation taxable	$525,051,030	$529,747,749	$530,524,750
State equalized value	$1,145,148,933	$1,205,287,953	$1,175,761,005

Demographics & Socio-Economic Characteristics

(2000 US Census, except as noted)

Population

1980*	7,624
1990*	7,549
2000	7,584
Male	3,423
Female	4,161
2007 (estimate)*	7,219
Population density	6,066.4

Race & Hispanic Origin, 2000

Race

White	6,918
Black/African American	172
American Indian/Alaska Native	8
Asian	308
Native Hawaiian/Pacific Islander	5
Other race	91
Two or more races	82
Hispanic origin, total	352
Mexican	29
Puerto Rican	103
Cuban	26
Other Hispanic	194

Age & Nativity, 2000

Under 5 years	379
18 years and over	6,215
21 years and over	5,885
65 years and over	1,350
85 years and over	226
Median age	39.1
Native-born	6,656
Foreign-born	928

Educational Attainment, 2000

Population 25 years and over	5,547
Less than 9th grade	2.8%
High school grad or higher	91.2%
Bachelor's degree or higher	44.0%
Graduate degree	18.2%

Income & Poverty, 1999

Per capita income	$34,630
Median household income	$61,250
Median family income	$81,989
Persons in poverty	347
H'holds receiving public assistance	64
H'holds receiving social security	1,043

Households, 2000

Total households	3,311
With persons under 18	796
With persons over 65	998
Family households	1,814
Single-person households	1,257
Persons per household	2.17
Persons per family	2.93

Labor & Employment

Total civilian labor force, 2007**	4,336
Unemployment rate	2.1%
Total civilian labor force, 2000	4,430
Unemployment rate	2.8%

Employed persons 16 years and over by occupation, 2000

Managers & professionals	2,257
Service occupations	368
Sales & office occupations	1,284
Farming, fishing & forestry	0
Construction & maintenance	201
Production & transportation	197
Self-employed persons	218

* US Census Bureau
** New Jersey Department of Labor

General Information

Borough of Caldwell
1 Provost Sq
Caldwell, NJ 07006
973-226-6100

Website	www.caldwell-nj.com
Year of incorporation	1892
Land/water area (sq. miles)	1.19/0.00
Form of government	Borough

Government

Legislative Districts

US Congressional	
State Legislative	27

Local Officials, 2009

Mayor	Susan Gartland
Manager	Maureen Ruane
Clerk	Maureen Ruane
Finance Dir	Maureen Ruane
Tax Assessor	Jack Kelly
Tax Collector	Rebecca Roth
Attorney	Stuart Koenig
Building	Paul Milani
Comm Dev/Planning	NA
Engineering	Anthony Marucci
Public Works	Mario Bifalco
Police Chief	Kurt Dombrowsi
Emerg/Fire Director	Anthony Grenci

Housing & Construction

Housing Units, 2000*

Total	3,396
Median rent	$905
Median SF home value	$228,800

Permits for New Residential Construction

	Units	Value
Total, 2006	5	$1,391,137
Single family	3	$825,573
Total, 2007	1	$54,500
Single family	1	$54,500

Real Property Valuation, 2008

	Parcels	Valuation
Total	2,142	$1,025,848,700
Vacant	28	7,095,800
Residential	1,897	819,061,100
Commercial	189	121,736,800
Industrial	0	0
Apartments	28	77,955,000
Farm land	0	0
Farm homestead	0	0

Average Property Value & Tax, 2008

Residential value	$431,767
Property tax	$9,452
Tax credit/rebate	$1,324

Public Library

Caldwell Public Library
268 Bloomfield Ave
Caldwell, NJ 07006
973-226-2837

Director	Karen Kleppe Lembo

Library statistics, 2007

Population served	7,584
Full-time/total staff	2/5

	Total	Per capita
Holdings	42,610	5.62
Revenues	$504,696	$66.55
Expenditures	$437,367	$57.67
Annual visits	68,744	9.06
Internet terminals/annual users		9/9,000

Public Safety

Number of officers, 2007	20

Crime	2006	2007
Total crimes	51	38
Violent	2	2
Murder	0	0
Rape	1	0
Robbery	0	0
Aggravated assault	1	2
Non-violent	49	36
Burglary	9	8
Larceny	37	25
Vehicle theft	3	3
Domestic violence	42	46
Arson	0	0
Total crime rate	6.8	5.2
Violent	0.3	0.3
Non-violent	6.5	4.9

Public School District

(for school year 2007-08 except as noted)

Caldwell-West Caldwell School District
Harrison Bldg. Gray St.
West Caldwell, NJ 07006
(973) 228-6979

Superintendent	Daniel Gerardi
Number of schools	6
Grade plan	K-12
Enrollment	2,630
Attendance rate, '06-07	95.2%
Dropout rate	0.5%
Students per teacher	11.5
Per pupil expenditure	$13,219
Median faculty salary	$55,270
Median administrator salary	$114,300
Grade 12 enrollment	190
High school graduation rate	97.9%

Assessment test results

(percent scoring at proficient or advanced level)

	Language	Math
NJASK-Grade 3	94.8%	95.3%
GEPA-Grade 8	79.6%	92.9%
HSPA-High School	87.2%	94.6%

SAT Score Averages, 2006-07

Pct tested	Math	Verbal	Writing
93%	541	529	535

Teacher Qualifications

Avg. years of experience	7
Highly-qualified teachers one subject/all subjects	100%/100%

No Child Left Behind

AYP, 2006-07	Meets Standards

Municipal Finance

State Aid Programs, 2009

Total aid	$885,769
CMPTRA	146,744
Energy tax receipts	716,706
Garden State Trust	4

General Budget, 2008

Total tax levy	$22,546,223
County levy	4,462,010
County taxes	4,289,586
County library	0
County health	0
County open space	172,424
School levy	11,224,299
Muni. levy	6,859,914
Misc. revenues	5,603,351

Taxes

	2006	2007	2008
General tax rate per $100	2.04	2.12	2.190
County equalization ratio	104.22	92.55	90.53
Net valuation taxable	$1,023,566,400	$1,028,111,010	$1,029,857,952
State equalized value	$1,110,981,864	$1,135,132,533	$1,150,336,998

See Introduction for an explanation of all data sources.

Demographics & Socio-Economic Characteristics
(2000 US Census, except as noted)

Population
1980*	1,023
1990*	1,073
2000	1,055
Male	504
Female	551
2007 (estimate)*	1,033
Population density	1,064.9

Race & Hispanic Origin, 2000
Race
White	1,041
Black/African American	0
American Indian/Alaska Native	0
Asian	8
Native Hawaiian/Pacific Islander	0
Other race	0
Two or more races	6
Hispanic origin, total	5
Mexican	3
Puerto Rican	1
Cuban	1
Other Hispanic	0

Age & Nativity, 2000
Under 5 years	67
18 years and over	772
21 years and over	746
65 years and over	112
85 years and over	8
Median age	39.1
Native-born	1,015
Foreign-born	40

Educational Attainment, 2000
Population 25 years and over	735
Less than 9th grade	3.3%
High school grad or higher	93.2%
Bachelor's degree or higher	42.4%
Graduate degree	14.8%

Income & Poverty, 1999
Per capita income	$31,064
Median household income	$76,657
Median family income	$85,963
Persons in poverty	45
H'holds receiving public assistance	2
H'holds receiving social security	75

Households, 2000
Total households	401
With persons under 18	151
With persons over 65	85
Family households	302
Single-person households	85
Persons per household	2.63
Persons per family	3.11

Labor & Employment
Total civilian labor force, 2007**	600
Unemployment rate	0.0%
Total civilian labor force, 2000	549
Unemployment rate	0.9%

Employed persons 16 years and over by occupation, 2000
Managers & professionals	264
Service occupations	44
Sales & office occupations	133
Farming, fishing & forestry	0
Construction & maintenance	60
Production & transportation	43
Self-employed persons	43

‡ Branch of county library
* US Census Bureau
** New Jersey Department of Labor

General Information
Borough of Califon
39 Academy St
PO Box 368
Califon, NJ 07830
908-832-7850
Website	www.califonborough-nj.org
Year of incorporation	1918
Land/water area (sq. miles)	0.97/0.01
Form of government	Borough

Government
Legislative Districts
US Congressional	7
State Legislative	24

Local Officials, 2009
Mayor	Robert Grant
Manager	Laura Eidsvaag
Clerk	Laura Eidsvaag
Finance Dir	Bonnie Holborow
Tax Assessor	Eloise Hagaman
Tax Collector	Bonnie Holbrow
Attorney	J. Peter Jost
Building	(Provided by Tewksbury Twp)
Comm Dev/Planning	NA
Engineering	Donald Scott
Public Works	NA
Police Chief	NA
Emerg/Fire Director	Richard Bergmann

Housing & Construction
Housing Units, 2000*
Total	410
Median rent	$883
Median SF home value	$220,900

Permits for New Residential Construction
	Units	Value
Total, 2006	0	$0
Single family	0	$0
Total, 2007	2	$507,300
Single family	2	$507,300

Real Property Valuation, 2008
	Parcels	Valuation
Total	504	$164,097,108
Vacant	61	3,024,300
Residential	385	141,995,300
Commercial	30	16,220,700
Industrial	1	396,100
Apartments	2	475,700
Farm land	19	27,508
Farm homestead	6	1,957,500

Average Property Value & Tax, 2008
Residential value	$368,166
Property tax	$8,569
Tax credit/rebate	$1,353

Public Library
Bunnvale Library‡
3 Bunnvale Rd
Califon, NJ 07830
908-638-8884
Branch Librarian	Marie Taluba

Library statistics, 2007
see Hunterdon County profile
for library system statistics

Public Safety
Number of officers, 2007	0

Crime	2006	2007
Total crimes	5	5
Violent	0	0
Murder	0	0
Rape	0	0
Robbery	0	0
Aggravated assault	0	0
Non-violent	5	5
Burglary	2	0
Larceny	3	5
Vehicle theft	0	0
Domestic violence	0	0
Arson	0	0
Total crime rate	4.7	4.8
Violent	0.0	0.0
Non-violent	4.7	4.8

Public School District
(for school year 2007-08 except as noted)

Califon School District
6 School Street
Califon, NJ 07830
(908) 832-2828
Chief School Admin	Kathleen Prystash
Number of schools	1
Grade plan	K-8
Enrollment	143
Attendance rate, '06-07	96.5%
Dropout rate	NA
Students per teacher	7.9
Per pupil expenditure	$14,277
Median faculty salary	$47,500
Median administrator salary	$96,536
Grade 12 enrollment	NA
High school graduation rate	NA

Assessment test results
(percent scoring at proficient or advanced level)
	Language	Math
NJASK-Grade 3	100.0%	85.7%
GEPA-Grade 8	66.7%	77.8%
HSPA-High School	NA	NA

SAT Score Averages, 2006-07
Pct tested	Math	Verbal	Writing
NA	NA	NA	NA

Teacher Qualifications
Avg. years of experience	10
Highly-qualified teachers one subject/all subjects	100%/92.5%

No Child Left Behind
AYP, 2006-07	Meets Standards

Municipal Finance
State Aid Programs, 2009
Total aid	$148,655
CMPTRA	31,033
Energy tax receipts	113,845
Garden State Trust	62

General Budget, 2008
Total tax levy	$3,850,041
County levy	548,364
County taxes	458,960
County library	39,856
County health	0
County open space	49,548
School levy	2,664,717
Muni. levy	636,961
Misc. revenues	374,384

Taxes
	2006	2007	2008
General tax rate per $100	2.3	2.29	2.328
County equalization ratio	105.74	100.13	100.71
Net valuation taxable	$161,171,008	$163,022,880	$165,411,262
State equalized value	$158,016,090	$163,688,986	$160,895,121

Demographics & Socio-Economic Characteristics†

(2000 US Census, except as noted)

Population
1980*	84,910
1990*	87,492
2000	79,904
Male	38,784
Female	41,120
2007 (estimate)*	78,675
Population density	8,920.1

Race & Hispanic Origin, 2000
Race
White	13,454
Black/African American	42,628
American Indian/Alaska Native	435
Asian	1,958
Native Hawaiian/Pacific Islander	59
Other race	18,239
Two or more races	3,131
Hispanic origin, total	31,019
Mexican	1,908
Puerto Rican	23,051
Cuban	206
Other Hispanic	5,854

Age & Nativity, 2000
Under 5 years	7,302
18 years and over	52,230
21 years and over	47,879
65 years and over	6,090
85 years and over	577
Median age	27.2
Native-born	72,804
Foreign-born	7,100

Educational Attainment, 2000
Population 25 years and over	42,746
Less than 9th grade	17.7%
High school grad or higher	51.0%
Bachelor's degree or higher	5.4%
Graduate degree	1.9%

Income & Poverty, 1999
Per capita income	$9,815
Median household income	$23,421
Median family income	$24,612
Persons in poverty	26,786
H'holds receiving public assistance	3,948
H'holds receiving social security	5,714

Households, 2000
Total households	24,177
With persons under 18	12,530
With persons over 65	4,818
Family households	17,434
Single-person households	5,439
Persons per household	3.12
Persons per family	3.62

Labor & Employment
Total civilian labor force, 2007**	26,615
Unemployment rate	9.6%
Total civilian labor force, 2000	27,304
Unemployment rate	15.9%

Employed persons 16 years and over by occupation, 2000
Managers & professionals	3,850
Service occupations	5,858
Sales & office occupations	5,763
Farming, fishing & forestry	68
Construction & maintenance	1,528
Production & transportation	5,906
Self-employed persons	637

---

† see Appendix C for American Community Survey data
* US Census Bureau
** New Jersey Department of Labor
§ State Fiscal Year July 1–June 30

General Information
City of Camden
PO Box 95120
Camden, NJ 08101
856-757-7000
Website	www.ci.camden.nj.us
Year of incorporation	1828
Land/water area (sq. miles)	8.82/1.56
Form of government	Mayor-Council

Government
Legislative Districts
US Congressional	1
State Legislative	5

Local Officials, 2009
Mayor	Gwendolyn A. Faison
Manager	Christine Jones-Tucker
Clerk	Luis Pastoriza
Finance Dir	Joseph Galdo
Tax Assessor	Frank Librizzi
Tax Collector	Sherry Garton
Attorney	Lewis Wilson
Building	Roberto Scouler
Planning	Ed William
Engineering	Remington & Vernick
Public Works	Patrick Keating
Police Chief	John Thompson
Emerg/Fire Director	Joseph Marini

Housing & Construction
Housing Units, 2000*
Total	29,769
Median rent	$522
Median SF home value	$40,700

Permits for New Residential Construction
	Units	Value
Total, 2006	173	$16,484,876
Single family	18	$2,680,626
Total, 2007	286	$26,329,290
Single family	53	$3,215,342

Real Property Valuation, 2008
	Parcels	Valuation
Total	26,277	$774,918,687
Vacant	4,651	20,000,480
Residential	20,006	533,543,360
Commercial	1,411	129,926,193
Industrial	92	60,830,900
Apartments	117	30,617,754
Farm land	0	0
Farm homestead	0	0

Average Property Value & Tax, 2008
Residential value	$26,669
Property tax	$1,236
Tax credit/rebate	$490

Public Library
Camden Free Public Library
418 Federal St
Camden, NJ 08103
856-757-7650
Director	Theresa M. Gorman

Library statistics, 2007
Population served	79,904
Full-time/total staff	6/21

	Total	Per capita
Holdings	203,987	2.55
Revenues	$1,287,992	$16.12
Expenditures	$1,247,890	$15.62
Annual visits	147,797	1.85
Internet terminals/annual users	51/79,002	

Public Safety
Number of officers, 2007	410

Crime	2006	2007
Total crimes	6,515	6,413
Violent	1,698	1,770
Murder	32	42
Rape	66	67
Robbery	775	784
Aggravated assault	825	877
Non-violent	4,817	4,643
Burglary	1,179	1,129
Larceny	2,458	2,353
Vehicle theft	1,180	1,161
Domestic violence	2,373	2,028
Arson	132	115
Total crime rate	81.4	80.9
Violent	21.2	22.3
Non-violent	60.2	58.5

Public School District
(for school year 2007-08 except as noted)

Camden City School District
201 North Front Street
Camden, NJ 08102
(856) 966-2040
Superintendent	Bessie LeFra Young
Number of schools	31
Grade plan	K-12
Enrollment	13,105
Attendance rate, '06-07	89.0%
Dropout rate	9.3%
Students per teacher	8.0
Per pupil expenditure	$15,407
Median faculty salary	$62,231
Median administrator salary	$105,373
Grade 12 enrollment	447
High school graduation rate	65.6%

Assessment test results
(percent scoring at proficient or advanced level)
	Language	Math
NJASK-Grade 3	56.3%	51.6%
GEPA-Grade 8	18.2%	36.1%
HSPA-High School	25.9%	42.5%

SAT Score Averages, 2006-07
Pct tested	Math	Verbal	Writing
NA	NA	NA	NA

Teacher Qualifications
Avg. years of experience	13
Highly-qualified teachers one subject/all subjects	84.5%/84.0%

No Child Left Behind
AYP, 2006-07	Needs Improvement

Municipal Finance§
State Aid Programs, 2009
Total aid	$54,100,801
CMPTRA	42,120,850
Energy tax receipts	11,979,653
Garden State Trust	179

General Budget, 2008
Total tax levy	$37,063,692
County levy	9,383,892
County taxes	9,067,842
County library	0
County health	0
County open space	316,051
School levy	7,274,966
Muni. levy	20,404,834
Misc. revenues	158,039,360

Taxes
	2006	2007	2008
General tax rate per $100	4.638	4.597	4.635
County equalization ratio	74.56	67.58	61.42
Net valuation taxable	$769,528,617	$794,027,569	$799,672,673
State equalized value	$1,166,062,898	$1,276,806,619	$1,319,738,423

See Introduction for an explanation of all data sources.

Demographics & Socio-Economic Characteristics
(2000 US Census, except as noted)

Population
1980*	4,853
1990*	4,668
2000	4,034
Male	1,987
Female	2,047
2007 (estimate)*	3,728
Population density	1,503.2

Race & Hispanic Origin, 2000
Race
White	3,684
Black/African American	212
American Indian/Alaska Native	8
Asian	16
Native Hawaiian/Pacific Islander	2
Other race	51
Two or more races	61
Hispanic origin, total	153
Mexican	49
Puerto Rican	61
Cuban	11
Other Hispanic	32

Age & Nativity, 2000
Under 5 years	167
18 years and over	3,375
21 years and over	3,133
65 years and over	1,148
85 years and over	143
Median age	47.4
Native-born	3,787
Foreign-born	247

Educational Attainment, 2000
Population 25 years and over	2,942
Less than 9th grade	2.6%
High school grad or higher	87.6%
Bachelor's degree or higher	30.8%
Graduate degree	11.8%

Income & Poverty, 1999
Per capita income	$29,902
Median household income	$33,462
Median family income	$46,250
Persons in poverty	336
H'holds receiving public assistance	53
H'holds receiving social security	904

Households, 2000
Total households	1,821
With persons under 18	348
With persons over 65	863
Family households	1,035
Single-person households	717
Persons per household	2.02
Persons per family	2.69

Labor & Employment
Total civilian labor force, 2007**	1,761
Unemployment rate	7.0%
Total civilian labor force, 2000	1,494
Unemployment rate	8.8%

Employed persons 16 years and over by occupation, 2000
Managers & professionals	459
Service occupations	286
Sales & office occupations	454
Farming, fishing & forestry	12
Construction & maintenance	81
Production & transportation	71
Self-employed persons	205

‡ Branch of county library
* US Census Bureau
** New Jersey Department of Labor

General Information
City of Cape May
643 Washington St
Cape May, NJ 08204
609-884-9530
Website	www.capemaycity.org
Year of incorporation	1869
Land/water area (sq. miles)	2.48/0.32
Form of government	Council-Manager

Government
Legislative Districts
US Congressional	2
State Legislative	1

Local Officials, 2009
Mayor	Edward J. Mahoney Jr
Manager	Bruce Maclead
Clerk	Diane Weldon
Finance Dir	James Penn
Tax Assessor	Michael Jones
Tax Collector	Bruce MacLeod
Attorney	Anthony Monzo
Building	William Callahan
Planning	Mary Rothwell
Engineering	Remington & Vernick
Public Works	Robert Smith
Police Chief	Diane Sorantino
Emerg/Fire Director	Jerome Inderwies Jr

Housing & Construction
Housing Units, 2000*
Total	4,064
Median rent	$564
Median SF home value	$212,900

Permits for New Residential Construction
	Units	Value
Total, 2006	6	$1,366,030
Single family	6	$1,366,030
Total, 2007	21	$7,195,915
Single family	13	$6,525,280

Real Property Valuation, 2008
	Parcels	Valuation
Total	3,878	$2,214,196,600
Vacant	163	44,015,600
Residential	3,320	1,693,490,500
Commercial	273	350,790,200
Industrial	0	0
Apartments	122	125,900,300
Farm land	0	0
Farm homestead	0	0

Average Property Value & Tax, 2008
Residential value	$510,088
Property tax	$4,233
Tax credit/rebate	$965

Public Library
Cape May Branch Library‡
110 Ocean St
Cape May, NJ 08204
609-884-9568
Branch Librarian	Linda Smith

Library statistics, 2007
see Cape May County profile
for library system statistics

Public Safety
Number of officers, 2007	23

Crime	2006	2007
Total crimes	291	206
Violent	7	4
Murder	0	0
Rape	0	0
Robbery	2	2
Aggravated assault	5	2
Non-violent	284	202
Burglary	20	29
Larceny	260	172
Vehicle theft	4	1
Domestic violence	72	37
Arson	3	0
Total crime rate	77.4	54.1
Violent	1.9	1.1
Non-violent	75.5	53.0

Public School District
(for school year 2007-08 except as noted)

Cape May City School District
921 Lafayette Street
Cape May, NJ 08204
(609) 884-8485
Chief School Admin	Victoria Zelenak
Number of schools	1
Grade plan	K-6
Enrollment	154
Attendance rate, '06-07	93.5%
Dropout rate	NA
Students per teacher	7.9
Per pupil expenditure	$17,964
Median faculty salary	$53,800
Median administrator salary	$88,993
Grade 12 enrollment	NA
High school graduation rate	NA

Assessment test results
(percent scoring at proficient or advanced level)
	Language	Math
NJASK-Grade 3	100.0%	93.8%
GEPA-Grade 8	NA	NA
HSPA-High School	NA	NA

SAT Score Averages, 2006-07
Pct tested	Math	Verbal	Writing
NA	NA	NA	NA

Teacher Qualifications
Avg. years of experience	14
Highly-qualified teachers one subject/all subjects	100%/100%

No Child Left Behind
AYP, 2006-07	Meets Standards

Municipal Finance
State Aid Programs, 2009
Total aid	$449,816
CMPTRA	0
Energy tax receipts	432,584
Garden State Trust	1,415

General Budget, 2008
Total tax levy	$18,380,445
County levy	5,121,299
County taxes	4,070,661
County library	781,373
County health	0
County open space	269,265
School levy	6,469,280
Muni. levy	6,789,866
Misc. revenues	7,319,208

Taxes	2006	2007	2008
General tax rate per $100	0.77	0.77	0.833
County equalization ratio	97.57	88.56	82.86
Net valuation taxable	$2,174,583,300	$2,204,049,457	$2,214,924,882
State equalized value	$2,456,304,828	$2,659,813,227	$2,736,668,724

See Introduction for an explanation of all data sources.

Demographics & Socio-Economic Characteristics

(2000 US Census, except as noted)

Population
1980*	255
1990*	248
2000	241
Male	118
Female	123
2007 (estimate)*	226
Population density	779.3

Race & Hispanic Origin, 2000
Race
White	229
Black/African American	5
American Indian/Alaska Native	0
Asian	1
Native Hawaiian/Pacific Islander	0
Other race	0
Two or more races	6
Hispanic origin, total	4
Mexican	3
Puerto Rican	0
Cuban	0
Other Hispanic	1

Age & Nativity, 2000
Under 5 years	5
18 years and over	225
21 years and over	224
65 years and over	115
85 years and over	18
Median age	64.2
Native-born	226
Foreign-born	12

Educational Attainment, 2000
Population 25 years and over	215
Less than 9th grade	1.9%
High school grad or higher	91.6%
Bachelor's degree or higher	54.9%
Graduate degree	17.7%

Income & Poverty, 1999
Per capita income	$52,689
Median household income	$55,313
Median family income	$69,750
Persons in poverty	4
H'holds receiving public assistance	0
H'holds receiving social security	89

Households, 2000
Total households	133
With persons under 18	11
With persons over 65	81
Family households	78
Single-person households	47
Persons per household	1.81
Persons per family	2.27

Labor & Employment
Total civilian labor force, 2007**	60
Unemployment rate	0.0%
Total civilian labor force, 2000	55
Unemployment rate	5.5%

Employed persons 16 years and over by occupation, 2000
Managers & professionals	23
Service occupations	4
Sales & office occupations	25
Farming, fishing & forestry	0
Construction & maintenance	0
Production & transportation	0
Self-employed persons	4

* US Census Bureau
** New Jersey Department of Labor

General Information
Borough of Cape May Point
215 Lighthouse Ave
PO Box 490
Cape May Point, NJ 08212
609-884-8468
Website	www.cmpnj.com
Year of incorporation	1878
Land/water area (sq. miles)	0.29/0.02
Form of government	Commission

Government

Legislative Districts
US Congressional	2
State Legislative	1

Local Officials, 2009
Mayor	Carl F. Schupp
Manager/Admin	Connie Mahon
Clerk	Connie Mahon
Finance Dir	Francine Springer
Tax Assessor	Mike Jones
Tax Collector	Susan Jackson
Attorney	George Neidig
Building	Jim James
Planning	NA
Engineering	Bruce Graham
Public Works	Bill Gibson
Police Chief	Diane Sorantino
Emerg/Fire Director	Robert Shepanski

Housing & Construction

Housing Units, 2000*
Total	501
Median rent	$850
Median SF home value	$301,400

Permits for New Residential Construction
	Units	Value
Total, 2006	5	$1,591,700
Single family	5	$1,591,700
Total, 2007	4	$1,122,800
Single family	4	$1,122,800

Real Property Valuation, 2008
	Parcels	Valuation
Total	670	$286,795,600
Vacant	66	18,369,100
Residential	603	268,016,400
Commercial	1	410,100
Industrial	0	0
Apartments	0	0
Farm land	0	0
Farm homestead	0	0

Average Property Value & Tax, 2008
Residential value	$444,472
Property tax	$3,502
Tax credit/rebate	$966

Public Library

No public municipal library

Library statistics, 2007
Population served	NA
Full-time/total staff	NA/NA

	Total	Per capita
Holdings	NA	NA
Revenues	NA	NA
Expenditures	NA	NA
Annual visits	NA	NA
Internet terminals/annual users	NA/NA	

Public Safety
Number of officers, 2007		0

Crime	2006	2007
Total crimes	29	10
Violent	0	0
Murder	0	0
Rape	0	0
Robbery	0	0
Aggravated assault	0	0
Non-violent	29	10
Burglary	4	3
Larceny	25	7
Vehicle theft	0	0
Domestic violence	0	1
Arson	0	0
Total crime rate	122.9	43.5
Violent	0.0	0.0
Non-violent	122.9	43.5

Public School District
(for school year 2007-08 except as noted)

Cape May Point School District
P.O. Box 143
Cape May Point, NJ 08212

No schools in district - sends students to
Cape May City schools

Per pupil expenditure	NA
Median faculty salary	NA
Median administrator salary	NA
Grade 12 enrollment	NA
High school graduation rate	NA

Assessment test results
(percent scoring at proficient or advanced level)
	Language	Math
NJASK-Grade 3	NA	NA
GEPA-Grade 8	NA	NA
HSPA-High School	NA	NA

SAT Score Averages, 2006-07
Pct tested	Math	Verbal	Writing
NA	NA	NA	NA

Teacher Qualifications
Avg. years of experience	NA
Highly-qualified teachers one subject/all subjects	NA/NA

No Child Left Behind
AYP, 2006-07	NA

Municipal Finance

State Aid Programs, 2009
Total aid	$33,211
CMPTRA	0
Energy tax receipts	31,654
Garden State Trust	10

General Budget, 2008
Total tax levy	$2,259,756
County levy	1,039,832
County taxes	826,510
County library	158,649
County health	0
County open space	54,673
School levy	27,620
Muni. levy	1,192,304
Misc. revenues	338,027

Taxes
	2006	2007	2008
General tax rate per $100	0.75	0.76	0.791
County equalization ratio	60.58	55.71	52.52
Net valuation taxable	$283,297,300	$284,974,513	$286,823,226
State equalized value	$508,550,336	$542,577,199	$559,847,263

See Introduction for an explanation of all data sources.

Demographics & Socio-Economic Characteristics

(2000 US Census, except as noted)

Population

1980*	6,166
1990*	5,510
2000	5,917
Male	2,869
Female	3,048
2007 (estimate)*	6,023
Population density	1,524.8

Race & Hispanic Origin, 2000

Race

White	5,260
Black/African American	81
American Indian/Alaska Native	5
Asian	366
Native Hawaiian/Pacific Islander	1
Other race	126
Two or more races	78
Hispanic origin, total	473
Mexican	27
Puerto Rican	97
Cuban	64
Other Hispanic	285

Age & Nativity, 2000

Under 5 years	303
18 years and over	4,790
21 years and over	4,621
65 years and over	904
85 years and over	86
Median age	38.9
Native-born	4,704
Foreign-born	1,213

Educational Attainment, 2000

Population 25 years and over	4,306
Less than 9th grade	7.8%
High school grad or higher	80.0%
Bachelor's degree or higher	21.0%
Graduate degree	5.7%

Income & Poverty, 1999

Per capita income	$28,713
Median household income	$55,058
Median family income	$62,040
Persons in poverty	357
H'holds receiving public assistance	60
H'holds receiving social security	688

Households, 2000

Total households	2,393
With persons under 18	670
With persons over 65	672
Family households	1,593
Single-person households	631
Persons per household	2.47
Persons per family	3.04

Labor & Employment

Total civilian labor force, 2007**	3,528
Unemployment rate	3.0%
Total civilian labor force, 2000	3,332
Unemployment rate	3.3%

Employed persons 16 years and over by occupation, 2000

Managers & professionals	1,175
Service occupations	400
Sales & office occupations	1,034
Farming, fishing & forestry	0
Construction & maintenance	259
Production & transportation	355
Self-employed persons	155

* US Census Bureau
** New Jersey Department of Labor

General Information

Borough of Carlstadt
500 Madison St
Carlstadt, NJ 07072
201-939-2850

Website	www.carlstadtnj.us
Year of incorporation	1894
Land/water area (sq. miles)	3.95/0.28
Form of government	Borough

Government

Legislative Districts

US Congressional	9
State Legislative	36

Local Officials, 2009

Mayor	William Jay Roseman
Administrator	Jane Fontana
Clerk	Claire Foy
Finance Dir	Domenick Giancaspro
Tax Assessor	Joyce Ranone
Tax Collector	Christopher Assenheimer
Attorney	Jay Fahy
Building	Mark Sadomis
Comm Dev/Planning	NA
Engineering	Paul Sarlo
Public Works	Paul Ritchie
Police Chief	Thomas Nielsen
Fire Chief	Christian Kronyak

Housing & Construction

Housing Units, 2000*

Total	2,473
Median rent	$839
Median SF home value	$201,900

Permits for New Residential Construction

	Units	Value
Total, 2006	35	$3,355,109
Single family	3	$439,866
Total, 2007	23	$2,093,289
Single family	3	$466,622

Real Property Valuation, 2008

	Parcels	Valuation
Total	2,092	$968,588,027
Vacant	97	17,591,430
Residential	1,544	242,799,307
Commercial	144	190,984,410
Industrial	292	511,520,980
Apartments	15	5,691,900
Farm land	0	0
Farm homestead	0	0

Average Property Value & Tax, 2008

Residential value	$157,253
Property tax	$5,507
Tax credit/rebate	$883

Public Library

William Dermody Public Library
420 Hackensack St
Carlstadt, NJ 07072
201-438-8866

Director .... Mary Disanza

Library statistics, 2007

Population served	5,917
Full-time/total staff	1/7

	Total	Per capita
Holdings	30,535	5.16
Revenues	$718,355	$121.41
Expenditures	$621,364	$105.01
Annual visits	17,994	3.04
Internet terminals/annual users		8/6,892

Public Safety

Number of officers, 2007 31

Crime	2006	2007
Total crimes	169	213
Violent	7	14
Murder	0	0
Rape	1	2
Robbery	2	4
Aggravated assault	4	8
Non-violent	162	199
Burglary	17	22
Larceny	111	157
Vehicle theft	34	20
Domestic violence	53	68
Arson	0	0
Total crime rate	28.1	35.3
Violent	1.2	2.3
Non-violent	26.9	33.0

Public School District

(for school year 2007-08 except as noted)

Carlstadt School District
550 Washington Street
Carlstadt, NJ 07072
(201) 672-3000

Superintendent	Stephen Kollinok
Number of schools	1
Grade plan	K-8
Enrollment	568
Attendance rate, '06-07	94.6%
Dropout rate	NA
Students per teacher	11.7
Per pupil expenditure	$15,162
Median faculty salary	$63,750
Median administrator salary	$114,950
Grade 12 enrollment	NA
High school graduation rate	NA

Assessment test results

(percent scoring at proficient or advanced level)

	Language	Math
NJASK-Grade 3	90.5%	82.5%
GEPA-Grade 8	67.4%	85.7%
HSPA-High School	NA	NA

SAT Score Averages, 2006-07

Pct tested	Math	Verbal	Writing
NA	NA	NA	NA

Teacher Qualifications

Avg. years of experience	9
Highly-qualified teachers one subject/all subjects	100%/100%

No Child Left Behind

AYP, 2006-07 .... Meets Standards

Municipal Finance

State Aid Programs, 2009

Total aid	$1,365,687
CMPTRA	53,337
Energy tax receipts	1,267,965
Garden State Trust	0

General Budget, 2008

Total tax levy	$33,993,984
County levy	4,324,485
County taxes	4,088,079
County library	0
County health	0
County open space	236,406
School levy	15,351,017
Muni. levy	14,318,481
Misc. revenues	5,386,402

Taxes

	2006	2007	2008
General tax rate per $100	3.06	3.3	3.505
County equalization ratio	54.15	46.51	41.42
Net valuation taxable	$980,697,377	$975,202,440	$970,669,128
State equalized value	$2,111,467,636	$2,351,192,723	$2,589,812,939

See Introduction for an explanation of all data sources.

Demographics & Socio-Economic Characteristics

(2000 US Census, except as noted)

Population

1980*	8,396
1990*	8,443
2000	7,684
Male	3,667
Female	4,017
2007 (estimate)*	7,923
Population density	452.7

Race & Hispanic Origin, 2000

Race

White	6,034
Black/African American	1,250
American Indian/Alaska Native	21
Asian	70
Native Hawaiian/Pacific Islander	3
Other race	161
Two or more races	145
Hispanic origin, total	306
Mexican	42
Puerto Rican	182
Cuban	6
Other Hispanic	76

Age & Nativity, 2000

Under 5 years	467
18 years and over	5,927
21 years and over	5,621
65 years and over	1,243
85 years and over	152
Median age	38.7
Native-born	7,385
Foreign-born	299

Educational Attainment, 2000

Population 25 years and over	5,240
Less than 9th grade	7.6%
High school grad or higher	77.6%
Bachelor's degree or higher	14.1%
Graduate degree	3.8%

Income & Poverty, 1999

Per capita income	$19,978
Median household income	$41,007
Median family income	$52,213
Persons in poverty	808
H'holds receiving public assistance	116
H'holds receiving social security	931

Households, 2000

Total households	3,121
With persons under 18	1,003
With persons over 65	847
Family households	2,052
Single-person households	916
Persons per household	2.42
Persons per family	2.99

Labor & Employment

Total civilian labor force, 2007**	3,736
Unemployment rate	6.9%
Total civilian labor force, 2000	3,669
Unemployment rate	8.3%

Employed persons 16 years and over by occupation, 2000

Managers & professionals	849
Service occupations	472
Sales & office occupations	902
Farming, fishing & forestry	13
Construction & maintenance	354
Production & transportation	773
Self-employed persons	130

‡ Joint library with Penns Grove
* US Census Bureau
** New Jersey Department of Labor

See Introduction for an explanation of all data sources.

General Information

Township of Carneys Point
303 Harding Hwy
Carneys Point, NJ 08069
856-299-0070

Website	NA
Year of incorporation	1977
Land/water area (sq. miles)	17.50/0.25
Form of government	Township

Government

Legislative Districts

US Congressional	2
State Legislative	3

Local Officials, 2009

Mayor	Edward K. Voyles
Manager	Marie Stout
Clerk	June Proffitt
Finance Dir	Marie Stout
Tax Assessor	Sandra Elliott
Tax Collector	Thomas Freeman
Attorney	Andrea Rhea
Building	Louis Palena
Comm Dev/Planning	NA
Engineering	Brian Mitchell
Public Works	Eugene Gilbert
Police Chief	Edmund Spinelli Jr
Emerg/Fire Director	Mike Hanna

Housing & Construction

Housing Units, 2000*

Total	3,330
Median rent	$607
Median SF home value	$89,700

Permits for New Residential Construction

	Units	Value
Total, 2006	44	$3,822,498
Single family	44	$3,822,498
Total, 2007	33	$3,040,969
Single family	28	$2,798,545

Real Property Valuation, 2008

	Parcels	Valuation
Total	3,391	$352,926,870
Vacant	496	11,406,300
Residential	2,496	208,526,550
Commercial	151	67,754,400
Industrial	10	42,911,200
Apartments	6	13,550,900
Farm land	160	1,926,820
Farm homestead	72	6,850,700

Average Property Value & Tax, 2008

Residential value	$83,870
Property tax	$3,752
Tax credit/rebate	$818

Public Library

Penns Grove-Carneys Point Library‡
222 S Broad St
Penns Grove, NJ 08069
856-299-4255

Director	Barbara Hunt

Library statistics, 2007

Population served	12,570
Full-time/total staff	NA/0

	Total	Per capita
Holdings	0	NA
Revenues	$0	NA
Expenditures	$0	NA
Annual visits	NA	NA
Internet terminals/annual users	NA/NA	

Public Safety

Number of officers, 2007	22

Crime	2006	2007
Total crimes	199	184
Violent	25	30
Murder	1	1
Rape	0	4
Robbery	9	6
Aggravated assault	15	19
Non-violent	174	154
Burglary	55	44
Larceny	108	94
Vehicle theft	11	16
Domestic violence	65	68
Arson	2	0
Total crime rate	25.0	23.1
Violent	3.1	3.8
Non-violent	21.9	19.3

Public School District

(for school year 2007-08 except as noted)

Penns Grove-Carneys Pt. Reg. School Dist.
100 Iona Avenue
Penns Grove, NJ 08069
(856) 299-4250

Superintendent	Joseph A. Massare
Number of schools	5
Grade plan	K-12
Enrollment	2,455
Attendance rate, '06-07	93.1%
Dropout rate	2.8%
Students per teacher	11.3
Per pupil expenditure	$12,499
Median faculty salary	$54,720
Median administrator salary	$96,416
Grade 12 enrollment	125
High school graduation rate	87.3%

Assessment test results

(percent scoring at proficient or advanced level)

	Language	Math
NJASK-Grade 3	77.3%	71.0%
GEPA-Grade 8	41.4%	56.9%
HSPA-High School	53.1%	71.3%

SAT Score Averages, 2006-07

Pct tested	Math	Verbal	Writing
71%	427	419	412

Teacher Qualifications

Avg. years of experience	12
Highly-qualified teachers one subject/all subjects	99.5%/99.5%

No Child Left Behind

AYP, 2006-07	Meets Standards

Municipal Finance

State Aid Programs, 2009

Total aid	$1,044,379
CMPTRA	305,643
Energy tax receipts	709,283
Garden State Trust	3,048

General Budget, 2008

Total tax levy	$15,822,603
County levy	5,822,112
County taxes	5,696,495
County library	0
County health	0
County open space	125,616
School levy	7,646,802
Muni. levy	2,353,690
Misc. revenues	6,653,490

Taxes	2006	2007	2008
General tax rate per $100	4.052	4.255	4.474
County equalization ratio	70.97	65.49	57.24
Net valuation taxable	$341,895,005	$345,609,329	$353,680,433
State equalized value	$522,905,263	$603,189,253	$267,571,737

Demographics & Socio-Economic Characteristics
(2000 US Census, except as noted)

Population
1980*	20,598
1990*	19,025
2000	20,709
Male	10,050
Female	10,659
2007 (estimate)*	22,725
Population density	5,212.2

Race & Hispanic Origin, 2000
Race
White	14,239
Black/African American	1,975
American Indian/Alaska Native	49
Asian	1,722
Native Hawaiian/Pacific Islander	7
Other race	1,918
Two or more races	799
Hispanic origin, total	4,839
Mexican	184
Puerto Rican	2,216
Cuban	244
Other Hispanic	2,195

Age & Nativity, 2000
Under 5 years	1,276
18 years and over	15,481
21 years and over	14,723
65 years and over	3,099
85 years and over	332
Median age	37.0
Native-born	15,866
Foreign-born	4,843

Educational Attainment, 2000
Population 25 years and over	13,745
Less than 9th grade	9.3%
High school grad or higher	74.9%
Bachelor's degree or higher	12.8%
Graduate degree	3.7%

Income & Poverty, 1999
Per capita income	$18,967
Median household income	$47,148
Median family income	$54,609
Persons in poverty	2,253
H'holds receiving public assistance	248
H'holds receiving social security	2,356

Households, 2000
Total households	7,039
With persons under 18	2,807
With persons over 65	2,213
Family households	5,212
Single-person households	1,544
Persons per household	2.88
Persons per family	3.38

Labor & Employment
Total civilian labor force, 2007**	10,584
Unemployment rate	7.3%
Total civilian labor force, 2000	9,972
Unemployment rate	9.4%

Employed persons 16 years and over by occupation, 2000
Managers & professionals	1,953
Service occupations	1,348
Sales & office occupations	3,016
Farming, fishing & forestry	8
Construction & maintenance	808
Production & transportation	1,903
Self-employed persons	264

* US Census Bureau
** New Jersey Department of Labor

General Information
Borough of Carteret
61 Cooke Ave
Carteret, NJ 07008
732-541-3800

Website	www.ci.carteret.nj.us
Year of incorporation	1922
Land/water area (sq. miles)	4.36/0.63
Form of government	Borough

Government
Legislative Districts
US Congressional	13
State Legislative	19

Local Officials, 2009
Mayor	Daniel J. Reiman
Manager/Admin	NA
Clerk	Kathleen Barney
Finance Dir	Patrick DeBlasio
Tax Assessor	Charles Heck
Tax Collector	NA
Attorney	Robert Bergen
Building	Anthony Neibert
Comm Dev/Planning	Kathleen Shaw
Engineering	John P. DuPont
Public Works	Ted Surick
Police Chief	John Pieczyski
Emerg/Fire Director	Brian O'Connor

Housing & Construction
Housing Units, 2000*
Total	7,320
Median rent	$741
Median SF home value	$135,500

Permits for New Residential Construction
	Units	Value
Total, 2006	228	$6,490,482
Single family	38	$5,016,535
Total, 2007	284	$16,855,618
Single family	26	$5,012,640

Real Property Valuation, 2008
	Parcels	Valuation
Total	5,640	$997,070,058
Vacant	293	25,150,284
Residential	5,086	610,980,074
Commercial	160	94,168,400
Industrial	85	243,790,100
Apartments	16	22,981,200
Farm land	0	0
Farm homestead	0	0

Average Property Value & Tax, 2008
Residential value	$120,130
Property tax	$6,097
Tax credit/rebate	$1,044

Public Library
Carteret Public Library
100 Cooke Ave
Carteret, NJ 07008
732-541-3830

Director	Cheryl A. Smith

Library statistics, 2007
Population served	20,709
Full-time/total staff	1/6

	Total	Per capita
Holdings	63,066	3.05
Revenues	$718,142	$34.68
Expenditures	$582,589	$28.13
Annual visits	144,273	6.97
Internet terminals/annual users	18/20,282	

Public Safety
Number of officers, 2007	62

Crime	2006	2007
Total crimes	418	415
Violent	58	56
Murder	3	0
Rape	3	4
Robbery	21	24
Aggravated assault	31	28
Non-violent	360	359
Burglary	61	62
Larceny	275	250
Vehicle theft	24	47
Domestic violence	285	303
Arson	0	8
Total crime rate	19.5	18.6
Violent	2.7	2.5
Non-violent	16.8	16.1

Public School District
(for school year 2007-08 except as noted)

Carteret Borough School District
599 Roosevelt Avenue
Carteret, NJ 07008
(732) 541-8960

Superintendent	Kevin W. Ahearn
Number of schools	5
Grade plan	K-12
Enrollment	3,901
Attendance rate, '06-07	93.2%
Dropout rate	3.2%
Students per teacher	12.3
Per pupil expenditure	$11,791
Median faculty salary	$54,177
Median administrator salary	$113,751
Grade 12 enrollment	236
High school graduation rate	93.8%

Assessment test results
(percent scoring at proficient or advanced level)
	Language	Math
NJASK-Grade 3	84.0%	86.5%
GEPA-Grade 8	64.6%	70.3%
HSPA-High School	67.6%	80.8%

SAT Score Averages, 2006-07
Pct tested	Math	Verbal	Writing
76%	472	441	432

Teacher Qualifications
Avg. years of experience	8
Highly-qualified teachers one subject/all subjects	96.0%/96.0%

No Child Left Behind
AYP, 2006-07	Meets Standards

Municipal Finance
State Aid Programs, 2009
Total aid	$3,296,603
CMPTRA	1,322,288
Energy tax receipts	1,924,866
Garden State Trust	0

General Budget, 2008
Total tax levy	$50,680,028
County levy	7,503,289
County taxes	6,712,222
County library	0
County health	0
County open space	791,068
School levy	24,365,928
Muni. levy	18,810,811
Misc. revenues	18,282,317

Taxes
	2006	2007	2008
General tax rate per $100	4.62	4.97	5.076
County equalization ratio	48.39	41.22	39.94
Net valuation taxable	$978,141,500	$978,370,983	$998,512,292
State equalized value	$2,374,704,570	$2,447,487,115	$2,656,755,305

See Introduction for an explanation of all data sources.

Demographics & Socio-Economic Characteristics

(2000 US Census, except as noted)

Population

1980*	12,600
1990*	12,053
2000	12,300
Male	5,722
Female	6,578
2007 (estimate)*	12,698
Population density	3,009.0

Race & Hispanic Origin, 2000

Race

White	11,076
Black/African American	368
American Indian/Alaska Native	6
Asian	667
Native Hawaiian/Pacific Islander	3
Other race	57
Two or more races	123
Hispanic origin, total	393
Mexican	23
Puerto Rican	112
Cuban	55
Other Hispanic	203

Age & Nativity, 2000

Under 5 years	666
18 years and over	9,934
21 years and over	9,667
65 years and over	2,766
85 years and over	539
Median age	44.0
Native-born	10,951
Foreign-born	1,349

Educational Attainment, 2000

Population 25 years and over	9,264
Less than 9th grade	3.7%
High school grad or higher	88.4%
Bachelor's degree or higher	41.3%
Graduate degree	14.0%

Income & Poverty, 1999

Per capita income	$36,558
Median household income	$78,863
Median family income	$94,475
Persons in poverty	230
H'holds receiving public assistance	22
H'holds receiving social security	1,529

Households, 2000

Total households	4,403
With persons under 18	1,321
With persons over 65	1,521
Family households	3,240
Single-person households	1,017
Persons per household	2.57
Persons per family	3.05

Labor & Employment

Total civilian labor force, 2007**	6,162
Unemployment rate	1.1%
Total civilian labor force, 2000	5,938
Unemployment rate	1.1%

Employed persons 16 years and over by occupation, 2000

Managers & professionals	3,036
Service occupations	530
Sales & office occupations	1,751
Farming, fishing & forestry	0
Construction & maintenance	218
Production & transportation	338
Self-employed persons	348

* US Census Bureau
** New Jersey Department of Labor

See Introduction for an explanation of all data sources.

General Information

Township of Cedar Grove
525 Pompton Ave
Cedar Grove, NJ 07009
973-239-1410

Website	www.cedargrovenj.org
Year of incorporation	1908
Land/water area (sq. miles)	4.22/0.13
Form of government	Council-Manager

Government

Legislative Districts

US Congressional	8
State Legislative	40

Local Officials, 2009

Mayor	Paul H. Lee
Manager	Thomas Tucci
Clerk	Kathleen Stutz
Finance Dir.	William Homa
Tax Assessor	Richard Hamilton
Tax Collector	NA
Attorney	Thomas Scrivo
Building	John D'Ascensio
Comm Dev/Planning	John D'Ascensio
Engineering	Alex Palumbo
Public Works	NA
Police Chief	Jeffrey Rowe
Emerg/Fire Director	Alec Spinella

Housing & Construction

Housing Units, 2000*

Total	4,470
Median rent	$973
Median SF home value	$237,600

Permits for New Residential Construction

	Units	Value
Total, 2006	54	$10,341,230
Single family	27	$7,125,277
Total, 2007	41	$7,349,160
Single family	20	$4,847,863

Real Property Valuation, 2008

	Parcels	Valuation
Total	4,235	$332,060,500
Vacant	139	8,045,000
Residential	3,892	273,563,000
Commercial	153	27,517,000
Industrial	43	15,701,900
Apartments	6	6,929,200
Farm land	1	2,400
Farm homestead	1	302,000

Average Property Value & Tax, 2008

Residential value	$70,348
Property tax	$8,063
Tax credit/rebate	$1,147

Public Library

Cedar Grove Public Library
One Municipal Plaza
Cedar Grove, NJ 07009
973-239-1447

Director............Catherine Wolverton

Library statistics, 2007

Population served	12,300
Full-time/total staff	3/5

	Total	Per capita
Holdings	50,908	4.14
Revenues	$865,477	$70.36
Expenditures	$709,686	$57.70
Annual visits	43,736	3.56
Internet terminals/annual users	6/2,688	

Public Safety

Number of officers, 2007	32

Crime	2006	2007
Total crimes	219	178
Violent	8	8
Murder	0	0
Rape	0	0
Robbery	0	1
Aggravated assault	8	7
Non-violent	211	170
Burglary	36	27
Larceny	168	137
Vehicle theft	7	6
Domestic violence	63	57
Arson	4	3
Total crime rate	17.2	13.9
Violent	0.6	0.6
Non-violent	16.6	13.2

Public School District

(for school year 2007-08 except as noted)

Cedar Grove Township School District
520 Pompton Avenue
Cedar Grove, NJ 07009
(973) 239-1550

Superintendent	Gene Polles
Number of schools	4
Grade plan	K-12
Enrollment	1,581
Attendance rate, '06-07	95.7%
Dropout rate	1.2%
Students per teacher	11.1
Per pupil expenditure	$13,993
Median faculty salary	$56,058
Median administrator salary	$122,400
Grade 12 enrollment	113
High school graduation rate	97.4%

Assessment test results

(percent scoring at proficient or advanced level)

	Language	Math
NJASK-Grade 3	89.8%	93.6%
GEPA-Grade 8	73.5%	92.9%
HSPA-High School	76.7%	86.7%

SAT Score Averages, 2006-07

Pct tested	Math	Verbal	Writing
92%	487	473	474

Teacher Qualifications

Avg. years of experience	10
Highly-qualified teachers one subject/all subjects	100%/100%

No Child Left Behind

AYP, 2006-07	Meets Standards

Municipal Finance

State Aid Programs, 2009

Total aid	$1,350,355
CMPTRA	184,897
Energy tax receipts	1,126,154
Garden State Trust	113

General Budget, 2008

Total tax levy	$38,086,794
County levy	9,514,027
County taxes	9,146,572
County library	0
County health	0
County open space	367,455
School levy	21,631,980
Muni. levy	6,940,788
Misc. revenues	5,889,402

Taxes

	2006	2007	2008
General tax rate per $100	10.96	10.86	11.462
County equalization ratio	15.13	14.45	13.70
Net valuation taxable	$325,012,300	$330,583,600	$332,290,000
State equalized value	$2,249,448,169	$2,411,597,863	$2,478,292,933

Demographics & Socio-Economic Characteristics
(2000 US Census, except as noted)

Population
1980*	8,537
1990*	8,007
2000	8,460
Male	4,037
Female	4,423
2007 (estimate)*	8,266
Population density	3,429.9

Race & Hispanic Origin, 2000
Race
White	8,104
Black/African American	12
American Indian/Alaska Native	5
Asian	238
Native Hawaiian/Pacific Islander	1
Other race	42
Two or more races	58
Hispanic origin, total	223
Mexican	22
Puerto Rican	29
Cuban	17
Other Hispanic	155

Age & Nativity, 2000
Under 5 years	871
18 years and over	6,068
21 years and over	5,924
65 years and over	1,098
85 years and over	148
Median age	36.9
Native-born	7,629
Foreign-born	831

Educational Attainment, 2000
Population 25 years and over	5,723
Less than 9th grade	1.5%
High school grad or higher	96.6%
Bachelor's degree or higher	66.7%
Graduate degree	28.3%

Income & Poverty, 1999
Per capita income	$53,027
Median household income	$101,991
Median family income	$119,635
Persons in poverty	188
H'holds receiving public assistance	7
H'holds receiving social security	747

Households, 2000
Total households	3,159
With persons under 18	1,271
With persons over 65	766
Family households	2,384
Single-person households	673
Persons per household	2.67
Persons per family	3.14

Labor & Employment
Total civilian labor force, 2007**	4,578
Unemployment rate	2.3%
Total civilian labor force, 2000	4,197
Unemployment rate	2.1%

Employed persons 16 years and over by occupation, 2000
Managers & professionals	2,567
Service occupations	298
Sales & office occupations	986
Farming, fishing & forestry	0
Construction & maintenance	102
Production & transportation	155
Self-employed persons	244

‡ Joint library with Chatham Township
* US Census Bureau
** New Jersey Department of Labor

General Information
Chatham Borough
54 Fairmount Ave
Chatham, NJ 07928
973-635-0674

Website	www.chathamborough.org
Year of incorporation	1897
Land/water area (sq. miles)	2.41/0.00
Form of government	Borough

Government
Legislative Districts
US Congressional	11
State Legislative	26

Local Officials, 2009
Mayor	V. Nelson Vaughan III
Manager	Robert J. Falzarano
Clerk	Susan Caljean
Finance Dir	Dorothy Klein
Tax Assessor	Pat Aceto
Tax Collector	Madeline Polidor-LeBoeuf
Attorney	Joseph J. Bell
Building	William Jankowski
Planning	H.H. Montague
Engineering	Vincent DeNave
Public Works	Robert Venezia
Police Chief	John Drake
Emerg/Fire Director	Peter Gloglolich

Housing & Construction
Housing Units, 2000*
Total	3,232
Median rent	$1,082
Median SF home value	$376,900

Permits for New Residential Construction
	Units	Value
Total, 2006	10	$2,484,716
Single family	10	$2,484,716
Total, 2007	10	$3,162,260
Single family	10	$3,162,260

Real Property Valuation, 2008
	Parcels	Valuation
Total	2,991	$2,051,702,100
Vacant	60	13,630,700
Residential	2,692	1,759,974,900
Commercial	194	217,232,100
Industrial	29	21,490,500
Apartments	15	39,373,700
Farm land	1	200
Farm homestead	0	0

Average Property Value & Tax, 2008
Residential value	$653,780
Property tax	$10,455
Tax credit/rebate	$1,274

Public Library
Library Of The Chathams‡
214 Main St
Chatham, NJ 07928
973-635-0603

Director	Diane R. O'Brien

Library statistics, 2007
Population served	18,546
Full-time/total staff	6/15

	Total	Per capita
Holdings	103,008	5.55
Revenues	$1,554,367	$83.81
Expenditures	$1,471,215	$79.33
Annual visits	222,749	12.01
Internet terminals/annual users	18/34,848	

Public Safety
Number of officers, 2007	24

Crime	2006	2007
Total crimes	98	60
Violent	5	1
Murder	0	0
Rape	1	0
Robbery	3	0
Aggravated assault	1	1
Non-violent	93	59
Burglary	22	9
Larceny	66	50
Vehicle theft	5	0
Domestic violence	14	11
Arson	0	1
Total crime rate	11.6	7.2
Violent	0.6	0.1
Non-violent	11.0	7.0

Public School District
(for school year 2007-08 except as noted)

School District of the Chathams
58 Meyersville Road
Chatham, NJ 07928
(973) 635-5656

Superintendent	James O'Neill
Number of schools	6
Grade plan	K-12
Enrollment	3,582
Attendance rate, '06-07	95.9%
Dropout rate	1.0%
Students per teacher	11.9
Per pupil expenditure	$13,323
Median faculty salary	$59,232
Median administrator salary	$121,200
Grade 12 enrollment	235
High school graduation rate	98.3%

Assessment test results
(percent scoring at proficient or advanced level)
	Language	Math
NJASK-Grade 3	98.5%	98.1%
GEPA-Grade 8	90.6%	96.6%
HSPA-High School	94.3%	97.2%

SAT Score Averages, 2006-07
Pct tested	Math	Verbal	Writing
94%	583	581	577

Teacher Qualifications
Avg. years of experience	8
Highly-qualified teachers one subject/all subjects	100%/100%

No Child Left Behind
AYP, 2006-07	Meets Standards

Municipal Finance
State Aid Programs, 2009
Total aid	$777,663
CMPTRA	105,849
Energy tax receipts	638,497
Garden State Trust	0

General Budget, 2008
Total tax levy	$32,836,455
County levy	5,463,263
County taxes	4,458,316
County library	0
County health	0
County open space	1,004,947
School levy	20,232,739
Muni. levy	7,140,452
Misc. revenues	7,194,024

Taxes
	2006	2007	2008
General tax rate per $100	1.5	1.52	1.600
County equalization ratio	99.75	92.06	87.80
Net valuation taxable	$2,033,203,200	$2,045,037,166	$2,053,319,615
State equalized value	$2,210,239,856	$2,328,969,406	$2,427,370,766

See Introduction for an explanation of all data sources.

Demographics & Socio-Economic Characteristics

(2000 US Census, except as noted)

Population

1980*	8,883
1990*	9,361
2000	10,086
Male	4,803
Female	5,283
2007 (estimate)*	10,151
Population density	1,088.0

Race & Hispanic Origin, 2000

Race

White	9,452
Black/African American	45
American Indian/Alaska Native	6
Asian	485
Native Hawaiian/Pacific Islander	1
Other race	15
Two or more races	82
Hispanic origin, total	197
Mexican	27
Puerto Rican	26
Cuban	22
Other Hispanic	122

Age & Nativity, 2000

Under 5 years	768
18 years and over	7,392
21 years and over	7,209
65 years and over	1,366
85 years and over	185
Median age	40.1
Native-born	8,874
Foreign-born	1,212

Educational Attainment, 2000

Population 25 years and over	7,013
Less than 9th grade	1.0%
High school grad or higher	96.6%
Bachelor's degree or higher	65.7%
Graduate degree	31.7%

Income & Poverty, 1999

Per capita income	$65,497
Median household income	$106,208
Median family income	$131,609
Persons in poverty	271
H'holds receiving public assistance	13
H'holds receiving social security	911

Households, 2000

Total households	3,920
With persons under 18	1,380
With persons over 65	922
Family households	2,772
Single-person households	1,030
Persons per household	2.54
Persons per family	3.11

Labor & Employment

Total civilian labor force, 2007**	5,439
Unemployment rate	1.3%
Total civilian labor force, 2000	4,995
Unemployment rate	1.3%

Employed persons 16 years and over by occupation, 2000

Managers & professionals	3,132
Service occupations	255
Sales & office occupations	1,296
Farming, fishing & forestry	0
Construction & maintenance	134
Production & transportation	111
Self-employed persons	361

‡ Joint library with Chatham Borough
* US Census Bureau
** New Jersey Department of Labor

General Information

Township of Chatham
58 Meyersville Rd
Chatham, NJ 07928
973-635-4600

Website	www.chathamtownship.org
Year of incorporation	1806
Land/water area (sq. miles)	9.33/0.02
Form of government	Township

Government

Legislative Districts

US Congressional	11
State Legislative	21

Local Officials, 2009

Mayor	Kevin R. Tubbs
Manager	Thomas Ciccarone
Clerk	Joy Wiley
Finance Dir	Thomas Ciccarone
Tax Assessor	Glen Sherman
Tax Collector	Mary Ellen Babyack
Attorney	Carl Woodward
Building	Greg Impink
Planning	Banisch Associates
Engineering	John Ruschke
Public Works	Joseph Barilla
Police Chief	John Paton
Fire Chief	Jim Condus

Housing & Construction

Housing Units, 2000*

Total	4,019
Median rent	$1,371
Median SF home value	$449,000

Permits for New Residential Construction

	Units	Value
Total, 2006	57	$24,294,233
Single family	57	$24,294,233
Total, 2007	29	$11,658,455
Single family	29	$11,658,455

Real Property Valuation, 2008

	Parcels	Valuation
Total	3,960	$2,860,548,500
Vacant	241	46,219,100
Residential	3,646	2,638,012,800
Commercial	30	121,926,400
Industrial	4	13,725,100
Apartments	2	26,525,000
Farm land	22	455,300
Farm homestead	15	13,684,800

Average Property Value & Tax, 2008

Residential value	$724,310
Property tax	$11,239
Tax credit/rebate	$1,186

Public Library

Library Of The Chathams‡
214 Main St
Chatham, NJ 07928
973-635-0603

Director	Diane R. O'Brien

Library statistics, 2007

Population served	18,546
Full-time/total staff	6/15

	Total	Per capita
Holdings	103,008	5.55
Revenues	$1,554,367	$83.81
Expenditures	$1,471,215	$79.33
Annual visits	222,749	12.01
Internet terminals/annual users	18/34,848	

Public Safety

Number of officers, 2007	24

Crime	2006	2007
Total crimes	46	38
Violent	0	1
Murder	0	0
Rape	0	0
Robbery	0	0
Aggravated assault	0	1
Non-violent	46	37
Burglary	15	3
Larceny	31	34
Vehicle theft	0	0
Domestic violence	29	27
Arson	0	0
Total crime rate	4.5	3.7
Violent	0.0	0.1
Non-violent	4.5	3.6

Public School District

(for school year 2007-08 except as noted)

School District of the Chathams
58 Meyersville Road
Chatham, NJ 07928
(973) 635-5656

Superintendent	James O'Neill
Number of schools	6
Grade plan	K-12
Enrollment	3,582
Attendance rate, '06-07	95.9%
Dropout rate	1.0%
Students per teacher	11.9
Per pupil expenditure	$13,323
Median faculty salary	$59,232
Median administrator salary	$121,200
Grade 12 enrollment	235
High school graduation rate	98.3%

Assessment test results

(percent scoring at proficient or advanced level)

	Language	Math
NJASK-Grade 3	98.5%	98.1%
GEPA-Grade 8	90.6%	96.6%
HSPA-High School	94.3%	97.2%

SAT Score Averages, 2006-07

Pct tested	Math	Verbal	Writing
94%	583	581	577

Teacher Qualifications

Avg. years of experience	8

Highly-qualified teachers
one subject/all subjects | 100%/100%

No Child Left Behind

AYP, 2006-07 | Meets Standards

Municipal Finance

State Aid Programs, 2009

Total aid	$1,122,306
CMPTRA	0
Energy tax receipts	1,077,398
Garden State Trust	16

General Budget, 2008

Total tax levy	$44,405,120
County levy	7,651,568
County taxes	6,244,358
County library	0
County health	0
County open space	1,407,210
School levy	27,912,430
Muni. levy	8,841,123
Misc. revenues	4,812,419

Taxes

	2006	2007	2008
General tax rate per $100	1.44	1.5	1.552
County equalization ratio	101.01	90.52	86.91
Net valuation taxable	$2,756,256,400	$2,794,861,217	$2,861,683,545
State equalized value	$3,046,142,630	$3,215,640,193	$3,201,927,817

See Introduction for an explanation of all data sources.

Demographics & Socio-Economic Characteristics†

(2000 US Census, except as noted)

Population

1980*	68,785
1990*	69,348
2000	69,965
Male	33,450
Female	36,515
2007 (estimate)*	71,095
Population density	2,931.8

Race & Hispanic Origin, 2000

Race

White	59,240
Black/African American	3,121
American Indian/Alaska Native	71
Asian	6,205
Native Hawaiian/Pacific Islander	24
Other race	491
Two or more races	813
Hispanic origin, total	1,778
Mexican	252
Puerto Rican	823
Cuban	96
Other Hispanic	607

Age & Nativity, 2000

Under 5 years	3,928
18 years and over	53,495
21 years and over	51,739
65 years and over	12,570
85 years and over	1,814
Median age	41.8
Native-born	61,245
Foreign-born	8,720

Educational Attainment, 2000

Population 25 years and over	49,401
Less than 9th grade	2.8%
High school grad or higher	91.0%
Bachelor's degree or higher	46.2%
Graduate degree	19.1%

Income & Poverty, 1999

Per capita income	$32,658
Median household income	$69,421
Median family income	$80,766
Persons in poverty	2,725
H'holds receiving public assistance	452
H'holds receiving social security	8,124

Households, 2000

Total households	26,227
With persons under 18	8,930
With persons over 65	8,218
Family households	19,399
Single-person households	5,900
Persons per household	2.61
Persons per family	3.08

Labor & Employment

Total civilian labor force, 2007**	38,046
Unemployment rate	3.0%
Total civilian labor force, 2000	35,499
Unemployment rate	3.7%

Employed persons 16 years and over by occupation, 2000

Managers & professionals	18,091
Service occupations	3,249
Sales & office occupations	9,710
Farming, fishing & forestry	23
Construction & maintenance	1,259
Production & transportation	1,865
Self-employed persons	2,383

† see Appendix C for American Community Survey data
* US Census Bureau
** New Jersey Department of Labor
§ State Fiscal Year July 1–June 30

General Information

Township of Cherry Hill
820 Mercer St
PO Box 5002
Cherry Hill, NJ 08034
856-665-6500

Website	www.cherryhill-nj.com
Year of incorporation	1961
Land/water area (sq. miles)	24.25/0.11
Form of government	Mayor-Council

Government

Legislative Districts

US Congressional	3
State Legislative	6

Local Officials, 2009

Mayor	Bernie Platt
Manager	Maris Kukainis
Clerk	Nancy L. Saffos
Finance Dir	Debra Campbell
Tax Assessor	Thomas Glock
Tax Collector	Carol Redmond
Attorney	Sherri Schweitzer
Building	Michael DePalma
Planning	David Benedetti
Engineering	Steve Musilli
Public Works	Steven Musilli
Police Chief	Clarence Jones
Emerg/Fire Director	Robert Giorgio

Housing & Construction

Housing Units, 2000*

Total	27,074
Median rent	$793
Median SF home value	$154,900

Permits for New Residential Construction

	Units	Value
Total, 2006	129	$14,840,150
Single family	129	$14,840,150
Total, 2007	27	$7,110,470
Single family	27	$7,110,470

Real Property Valuation, 2008

	Parcels	Valuation
Total	26,492	$4,599,135,300
Vacant	1,655	53,446,500
Residential	23,673	3,310,522,100
Commercial	914	1,013,510,800
Industrial	222	114,487,700
Apartments	15	104,025,800
Farm land	7	181,400
Farm homestead	6	2,961,000

Average Property Value & Tax, 2008

Residential value	$139,933
Property tax	$7,280
Tax credit/rebate	$1,183

Public Library

Cherry Hill Public Library
1100 Kings Highway N
Cherry Hill, NJ 08034
856-667-0300

Director	Manuel A. Paredes

Library statistics, 2007

Population served	69,965
Full-time/total staff	8/34

	Total	Per capita
Holdings	177,068	2.53
Revenues	$3,093,233	$44.21
Expenditures	$3,053,878	$43.65
Annual visits	421,608	6.03
Internet terminals/annual users	90/137,231	

Public Safety

Number of officers, 2007		140

Crime	2006	2007
Total crimes	2,376	2,258
Violent	107	99
Murder	1	1
Rape	4	3
Robbery	40	44
Aggravated assault	62	51
Non-violent	2,269	2,159
Burglary	266	255
Larceny	1,890	1,766
Vehicle theft	113	138
Domestic violence	460	479
Arson	5	1
Total crime rate	33.1	31.5
Violent	1.5	1.4
Non-violent	31.6	30.2

Public School District

(for school year 2007-08 except as noted)

Cherry Hill Township School District
45 Ranoldo Terrace
Cherry Hill, NJ 08034
(856) 429-5600

Superintendent	David Campbell
Number of schools	19
Grade plan	K-12
Enrollment	11,506
Attendance rate, '06-07	94.8%
Dropout rate	0.4%
Students per teacher	11.5
Per pupil expenditure	$13,645
Median faculty salary	$51,663
Median administrator salary	$122,166
Grade 12 enrollment	941
High school graduation rate	98.8%

Assessment test results

(percent scoring at proficient or advanced level)

	Language	Math
NJASK-Grade 3	94.1%	93.0%
GEPA-Grade 8	86.1%	93.5%
HSPA-High School	89.9%	94.4%

SAT Score Averages, 2006-07

Pct tested	Math	Verbal	Writing
NA	NA	NA	NA

Teacher Qualifications

Avg. years of experience	9
Highly-qualified teachers one subject/all subjects	99.5%/99.5%

No Child Left Behind

AYP, 2006-07	Meets Standards

Municipal Finance§

State Aid Programs, 2009

Total aid	$11,314,727
CMPTRA	3,487,679
Energy tax receipts	7,544,180
Garden State Trust	0

General Budget, 2008

Total tax levy	$239,702,061
County levy	59,395,618
County taxes	57,398,050
County library	0
County health	0
County open space	1,997,568
School levy	144,663,098
Muni. levy	35,643,345
Misc. revenues	26,820,262

Taxes

	2006	2007	2008
General tax rate per $100	4.88	5.008	5.203
County equalization ratio	54.38	50.1	46.33
Net valuation taxable	$4,587,684,000	$4,616,705,857	$4,607,750,312
State equalized value	$9,166,284,744	$9,954,618,292	$10,085,598,579

See Introduction for an explanation of all data sources.

Demographics & Socio-Economic Characteristics
(2000 US Census, except as noted)

Population
1980*	1,590
1990*	1,526
2000	1,520
Male	760
Female	760
2007 (estimate)*	1,874
Population density	1,089.5

Race & Hispanic Origin, 2000
Race
White	568
Black/African American	851
American Indian/Alaska Native	3
Asian	5
Native Hawaiian/Pacific Islander	0
Other race	44
Two or more races	49
Hispanic origin, total	62
Mexican	6
Puerto Rican	45
Cuban	2
Other Hispanic	9

Age & Nativity, 2000
Under 5 years	66
18 years and over	1,172
21 years and over	1,120
65 years and over	229
85 years and over	21
Median age	42.1
Native-born	1,486
Foreign-born	34

Educational Attainment, 2000
Population 25 years and over	1,060
Less than 9th grade	9.3%
High school grad or higher	65.7%
Bachelor's degree or higher	9.5%
Graduate degree	4.1%

Income & Poverty, 1999
Per capita income	$15,252
Median household income	$41,786
Median family income	$50,263
Persons in poverty	214
H'holds receiving public assistance	20
H'holds receiving social security	196

Households, 2000
Total households	493
With persons under 18	171
With persons over 65	165
Family households	345
Single-person households	124
Persons per household	2.81
Persons per family	3.32

Labor & Employment
Total civilian labor force, 2007**	688
Unemployment rate	7.5%
Total civilian labor force, 2000	651
Unemployment rate	8.6%

Employed persons 16 years and over by occupation, 2000
Managers & professionals	150
Service occupations	115
Sales & office occupations	152
Farming, fishing & forestry	4
Construction & maintenance	73
Production & transportation	101
Self-employed persons	26

General Information
Borough of Chesilhurst
201 Grant Ave
Chesilhurst, NJ 08089
856-767-4153
Website	www.chesilhurstgov.org
Year of incorporation	1887
Land/water area (sq. miles)	1.72/0.00
Form of government	Borough

Government
Legislative Districts
US Congressional	1
State Legislative	6

Local Officials, 2009
Mayor	Michael Blunt
Manager/Admin	NA
Clerk	Sylvia VanNockay
Finance Dir	Terry Henry
Tax Assessor	Theresa Stalgiano
Tax Collector	JoAnn Watson
Attorney	Harvey Johnson
Building	Dave Melichorre
Comm Dev/Planning	NA
Engineering	Steven Bach
Public Works	Reginald Brown
Police Chief	Sheldon Fortune
Emerg/Fire Director	Sheldon Fortune

Housing & Construction
Housing Units, 2000*
Total	535
Median rent	$817
Median SF home value	$93,300

Permits for New Residential Construction
	Units	Value
Total, 2006	7	$349,858
Single family	7	$349,858
Total, 2007	14	$1,341,650
Single family	14	$1,341,650

Real Property Valuation, 2008
	Parcels	Valuation
Total	806	$87,829,900
Vacant	332	7,328,200
Residential	452	74,505,300
Commercial	18	4,801,700
Industrial	2	778,500
Apartments	2	416,200
Farm land	0	0
Farm homestead	0	0

Average Property Value & Tax, 2008
Residential value	$164,835
Property tax	$3,691
Tax credit/rebate	$828

Public Library
No public municipal library

Library statistics, 2007
Population served	NA
Full-time/total staff	NA/NA

	Total	Per capita
Holdings	NA	NA
Revenues	NA	NA
Expenditures	NA	NA
Annual visits	NA	NA
Internet terminals/annual users	NA/NA	

Public Safety
Number of officers, 2007	10

Crime	2006	2007
Total crimes	56	57
Violent	2	5
Murder	0	0
Rape	0	0
Robbery	0	1
Aggravated assault	2	4
Non-violent	54	52
Burglary	21	16
Larceny	31	26
Vehicle theft	2	10
Domestic violence	7	10
Arson	0	0
Total crime rate	30.0	30.3
Violent	1.1	2.7
Non-violent	29.0	27.7

Public School District
(for school year 2007-08 except as noted)

Chesilhurst Borough School District
511 Edwards Avenue
Chesilhurst, NJ 08089
(856) 767-5451
Chief School Admin	Abdi Gass
Number of schools	1
Grade plan	K-6
Enrollment	104
Attendance rate, '06-07	95.1%
Dropout rate	NA
Students per teacher	8.5
Per pupil expenditure	$16,865
Median faculty salary	$54,206
Median administrator salary	$101,345
Grade 12 enrollment	NA
High school graduation rate	NA

Assessment test results
(percent scoring at proficient or advanced level)
	Language	Math
NJASK-Grade 3	78.5%	78.6%
GEPA-Grade 8	NA	NA
HSPA-High School	NA	NA

SAT Score Averages, 2006-07
Pct tested	Math	Verbal	Writing
NA	NA	NA	NA

Teacher Qualifications
Avg. years of experience	25
Highly-qualified teachers one subject/all subjects	100%/91.0%

No Child Left Behind
AYP, 2006-07	Meets Standards

Municipal Finance
State Aid Programs, 2009
Total aid	$804,871
CMPTRA	627,847
Energy tax receipts	176,841
Garden State Trust	0

General Budget, 2008
Total tax levy	$1,975,346
County levy	522,122
County taxes	471,858
County library	33,838
County health	0
County open space	16,426
School levy	786,163
Muni. levy	667,061
Misc. revenues	1,911,226

Taxes
	2006	2007	2008
General tax rate per $100	3.837	4.047	2.240
County equalization ratio	77.29	65.47	107.73
Net valuation taxable	$45,209,736	$46,536,124	$88,215,810
State equalized value	$69,272,242	$78,945,662	$69,396,596

---

* US Census Bureau
** New Jersey Department of Labor

See Introduction for an explanation of all data sources.

Demographics & Socio-Economic Characteristics
(2000 US Census, except as noted)

Population
1980*	1,433
1990*	1,214
2000	1,635
Male	819
Female	816
2007 (estimate)*	1,640
Population density	1,064.9

Race & Hispanic Origin, 2000
Race
White	1,548
Black/African American	13
American Indian/Alaska Native	0
Asian	28
Native Hawaiian/Pacific Islander	0
Other race	33
Two or more races	13
Hispanic origin, total	112
Mexican	59
Puerto Rican	1
Cuban	4
Other Hispanic	48

Age & Nativity, 2000
Under 5 years	120
18 years and over	1,229
21 years and over	1,192
65 years and over	223
85 years and over	34
Median age	39.1
Native-born	1,434
Foreign-born	201

Educational Attainment, 2000
Population 25 years and over	1,138
Less than 9th grade	3.5%
High school grad or higher	90.2%
Bachelor's degree or higher	48.3%
Graduate degree	19.9%

Income & Poverty, 1999
Per capita income	$42,564
Median household income	$80,398
Median family income	$106,260
Persons in poverty	84
H'holds receiving public assistance	4
H'holds receiving social security	172

Households, 2000
Total households	609
With persons under 18	218
With persons over 65	172
Family households	427
Single-person households	145
Persons per household	2.66
Persons per family	3.15

Labor & Employment
Total civilian labor force, 2007**	897
Unemployment rate	3.8%
Total civilian labor force, 2000	836
Unemployment rate	5.0%

Employed persons 16 years and over by occupation, 2000
Managers & professionals	394
Service occupations	108
Sales & office occupations	187
Farming, fishing & forestry	0
Construction & maintenance	51
Production & transportation	54
Self-employed persons	44

‡ Joint library with Chester Township
* US Census Bureau
** New Jersey Department of Labor

General Information
Borough of Chester
300 Main St
Chester, NJ 07930
908-879-5361
Website	www.chesterborough.org
Year of incorporation	1930
Land/water area (sq. miles)	1.54/0.00
Form of government	Borough

Government
Legislative Districts
US Congressional	11
State Legislative	24

Local Officials, 2009
Mayor	Dennis Verbaro
Manager	Valerie A. Egan
Clerk	Valerie A. Egan
Finance Dir	Vidya Nayak
Tax Assessor	Edward Kerwin
Tax Collector	Ana Hopler
Attorney	Brian Mason
Building	Steven Freedman
Planning	Frank Banisch
Engineering	Paul Ferriero
Public Works	Paul Kapral
Police Chief	Andre Kedraoitsch
Emerg/Fire Director	Steven Feller

Housing & Construction
Housing Units, 2000*
Total	627
Median rent	$802
Median SF home value	$313,600

Permits for New Residential Construction
	Units	Value
Total, 2006	3	$962,400
Single family	3	$962,400
Total, 2007	16	$1,452,900
Single family	7	$743,300

Real Property Valuation, 2008
	Parcels	Valuation
Total	659	$452,920,700
Vacant	40	5,466,500
Residential	463	245,143,100
Commercial	140	198,742,100
Industrial	0	0
Apartments	3	2,214,500
Farm land	9	44,500
Farm homestead	4	1,310,000

Average Property Value & Tax, 2008
Residential value	$527,737
Property tax	$9,980
Tax credit/rebate	$1,283

Public Library
Chester Library‡
250 West Main St
Chester, NJ 07930
908-879-7612
Director	Susan Persak

Library statistics, 2007
Population served	8,917
Full-time/total staff	1/1

	Total	Per capita
Holdings	62,687	7.03
Revenues	$880,372	$98.73
Expenditures	$629,660	$70.61
Annual visits	111,393	12.49
Internet terminals/annual users	11/36,928	

Public Safety
Number of officers, 2007	8

Crime	2006	2007
Total crimes	24	28
Violent	2	0
Murder	0	0
Rape	0	0
Robbery	0	0
Aggravated assault	2	0
Non-violent	22	28
Burglary	2	5
Larceny	20	23
Vehicle theft	0	0
Domestic violence	1	0
Arson	0	0
Total crime rate	14.5	17.0
Violent	1.2	0.0
Non-violent	13.3	17.0

Public School District
(for school year 2007-08 except as noted)

Chester Township School District
415 Route 24
Chester, NJ 07930
(908) 879-7383
Superintendent	Christine VanWoert
Number of schools	3
Grade plan	K-8
Enrollment	1,429
Attendance rate, '06-07	95.5%
Dropout rate	NA
Students per teacher	11.1
Per pupil expenditure	$13,848
Median faculty salary	$54,049
Median administrator salary	$115,976
Grade 12 enrollment	NA
High school graduation rate	NA

Assessment test results
(percent scoring at proficient or advanced level)
	Language	Math
NJASK-Grade 3	96.3%	94.3%
GEPA-Grade 8	90.4%	94.2%
HSPA-High School	NA	NA

SAT Score Averages, 2006-07
Pct tested	Math	Verbal	Writing
NA	NA	NA	NA

Teacher Qualifications
Avg. years of experience	11
Highly-qualified teachers one subject/all subjects	100%/100%

No Child Left Behind
AYP, 2006-07	Meets Standards

Municipal Finance
State Aid Programs, 2009
Total aid	$198,769
CMPTRA	17,104
Energy tax receipts	173,714
Garden State Trust	0

General Budget, 2008
Total tax levy	$8,611,457
County levy	1,086,826
County taxes	886,942
County library	0
County health	0
County open space	199,884
School levy	4,513,069
Muni. levy	3,011,562
Misc. revenues	1,613,021

Taxes
	2006	2007	2008
General tax rate per $100	1.81	1.86	1.892
County equalization ratio	109.16	101.23	97.75
Net valuation taxable	$419,032,500	$448,851,355	$455,353,437
State equalized value	$415,951,417	$459,134,619	$475,654,657

Demographics & Socio-Economic Characteristics
(2000 US Census, except as noted)

Population
1980*	5,198
1990*	5,958
2000	7,282
Male	3,586
Female	3,696
2007 (estimate)*	7,795
Population density	265.8

Race & Hispanic Origin, 2000
Race
White	6,927
Black/African American	84
American Indian/Alaska Native	1
Asian	174
Native Hawaiian/Pacific Islander	4
Other race	19
Two or more races	73
Hispanic origin, total	188
Mexican	12
Puerto Rican	49
Cuban	21
Other Hispanic	106

Age & Nativity, 2000
Under 5 years	532
18 years and over	5,064
21 years and over	4,919
65 years and over	664
85 years and over	77
Median age	39.6
Native-born	6,616
Foreign-born	666

Educational Attainment, 2000
Population 25 years and over	4,789
Less than 9th grade	1.4%
High school grad or higher	96.3%
Bachelor's degree or higher	63.7%
Graduate degree	30.7%

Income & Poverty, 1999
Per capita income	$55,353
Median household income	$117,298
Median family income	$133,586
Persons in poverty	163
H'holds receiving public assistance	0
H'holds receiving social security	396

Households, 2000
Total households	2,323
With persons under 18	1,111
With persons over 65	399
Family households	2,013
Single-person households	240
Persons per household	3.05
Persons per family	3.29

Labor & Employment
Total civilian labor force, 2007**	3,791
Unemployment rate	2.1%
Total civilian labor force, 2000	3,500
Unemployment rate	2.1%

Employed persons 16 years and over by occupation, 2000
Managers & professionals	2,113
Service occupations	197
Sales & office occupations	816
Farming, fishing & forestry	8
Construction & maintenance	207
Production & transportation	86
Self-employed persons	323

‡ Joint library with Chester Borough
* US Census Bureau
** New Jersey Department of Labor

See Introduction for an explanation of all data sources.

General Information
Township of Chester
1 Parker Rd
Chester, NJ 07930
908-879-5100

Website	www.chestertownship.org
Year of incorporation	1799
Land/water area (sq. miles)	29.33/0.01
Form of government	Small Municipality

Government
Legislative Districts
US Congressional	11
State Legislative	24

Local Officials, 2009
Mayor	William Cogger
Manager	Carol Isemann
Clerk	Carol Isemann
Finance Dir	Kevin Lifer
Tax Assessor	Maureen Kaman
Tax Collector	Toni Theesfeld
Attorney	John Suminski
Building	Jim Fania
Planning	Sarah Jane Noll
Engineering	Peter Turek
Public Works	Marc Cook
Police Chief	Adam Schuler
Emerg/Fire Director	Steve Feller

Housing & Construction
Housing Units, 2000*
Total	2,377
Median rent	$1,315
Median SF home value	$407,900

Permits for New Residential Construction
	Units	Value
Total, 2006	8	$2,408,200
Single family	8	$2,408,200
Total, 2007	11	$5,380,800
Single family	11	$5,380,800

Real Property Valuation, 2008
	Parcels	Valuation
Total	3,020	$2,266,951,233
Vacant	162	31,112,000
Residential	2,511	2,074,551,033
Commercial	81	50,305,200
Industrial	9	4,704,800
Apartments	1	910,000
Farm land	157	1,186,900
Farm homestead	99	104,181,300

Average Property Value & Tax, 2008
Residential value	$834,763
Property tax	$13,853
Tax credit/rebate	$1,371

Public Library
Chester Library‡
250 West Main St
Chester, NJ 07930
908-879-7612

Director	Susan Persak

Library statistics, 2007
Population served	8,917
Full-time/total staff	1/1

	Total	Per capita
Holdings	62,687	7.03
Revenues	$880,372	$98.73
Expenditures	$629,660	$70.61
Annual visits	111,393	12.49
Internet terminals/annual users	11/36,928	

Public Safety
Number of officers, 2007	16

Crime	2006	2007
Total crimes	52	44
Violent	1	2
Murder	0	0
Rape	0	0
Robbery	0	0
Aggravated assault	1	2
Non-violent	51	42
Burglary	3	9
Larceny	47	31
Vehicle theft	1	2
Domestic violence	25	28
Arson	0	3
Total crime rate	6.6	5.6
Violent	0.1	0.3
Non-violent	6.5	5.3

Public School District
(for school year 2007-08 except as noted)

Chester Township School District
415 Route 24
Chester, NJ 07930
(908) 879-7383

Superintendent	Christine VanWoert
Number of schools	3
Grade plan	K-8
Enrollment	1,429
Attendance rate, '06-07	95.5%
Dropout rate	NA
Students per teacher	11.1
Per pupil expenditure	$13,848
Median faculty salary	$54,049
Median administrator salary	$115,976
Grade 12 enrollment	NA
High school graduation rate	NA

Assessment test results
(percent scoring at proficient or advanced level)
	Language	Math
NJASK-Grade 3	96.3%	94.3%
GEPA-Grade 8	90.4%	94.2%
HSPA-High School	NA	NA

SAT Score Averages, 2006-07
Pct tested	Math	Verbal	Writing
NA	NA	NA	NA

Teacher Qualifications
Avg. years of experience	11
Highly-qualified teachers one subject/all subjects	100%/100%

No Child Left Behind
AYP, 2006-07	Meets Standards

Municipal Finance
State Aid Programs, 2009
Total aid	$1,144,994
CMPTRA	0
Energy tax receipts	1,079,251
Garden State Trust	20,708

General Budget, 2008
Total tax levy	$37,654,706
County levy	5,178,319
County taxes	4,226,030
County library	0
County health	0
County open space	952,289
School levy	24,439,562
Muni. levy	8,036,825
Misc. revenues	5,963,080

Taxes
	2006	2007	2008
General tax rate per $100	1.5	1.59	1.660
County equalization ratio	119.44	106.18	101.85
Net valuation taxable	$2,270,555,200	$2,260,529,892	$2,269,011,433
State equalized value	$2,140,667,996	$2,219,508,222	$2,211,995,112

Demographics & Socio-Economic Characteristics

(2000 US Census, except as noted)

Population

1980*	3,867
1990*	5,152
2000	5,955
Male	4,619
Female	1,336
2007 (estimate)*	6,919
Population density	323.2

Race & Hispanic Origin, 2000

Race

White	2,960
Black/African American	2,225
American Indian/Alaska Native	40
Asian	38
Native Hawaiian/Pacific Islander	5
Other race	503
Two or more races	184
Hispanic origin, total	735
Mexican	43
Puerto Rican	478
Cuban	27
Other Hispanic	187

Age & Nativity, 2000

Under 5 years	183
18 years and over	5,250
21 years and over	4,581
65 years and over	299
85 years and over	25
Median age	24.6
Native-born	5,752
Foreign-born	203

Educational Attainment, 2000

Population 25 years and over	2,790
Less than 9th grade	2.6%
High school grad or higher	78.5%
Bachelor's degree or higher	26.6%
Graduate degree	7.5%

Income & Poverty, 1999

Per capita income	$17,193
Median household income	$85,428
Median family income	$91,267
Persons in poverty	46
H'holds receiving public assistance	11
H'holds receiving social security	233

Households, 2000

Total households	899
With persons under 18	374
With persons over 65	209
Family households	744
Single-person households	115
Persons per household	2.91
Persons per family	3.19

Labor & Employment

Total civilian labor force, 2007**	1,599
Unemployment rate	3.5%
Total civilian labor force, 2000	1,396
Unemployment rate	3.5%

Employed persons 16 years and over by occupation, 2000

Managers & professionals	663
Service occupations	154
Sales & office occupations	296
Farming, fishing & forestry	17
Construction & maintenance	111
Production & transportation	106
Self-employed persons	104

* US Census Bureau
** New Jersey Department of Labor

General Information

Township of Chesterfield
300 Bordentown Chesterfield Rd
Chesterfield, NJ 08515
609-298-2311

Website	www.chesterfieldtwp.com
Year of incorporation	1688
Land/water area (sq. miles)	21.41/0.09
Form of government	Township

Government

Legislative Districts

US Congressional	4
State Legislative	30

Local Officials, 2009

Mayor	Michael J. Hlubik
Manager/Admin	NA
Clerk	Bonnie Haines
Finance Dir	Caryn Hoyer
Tax Assessor	William Tantum
Tax Collector	Caryn Hoyer
Attorney	John Gillespie
Building	Raymond Verner
Comm Dev/Planning	NA
Engineering	Nancy W. Jamanow
Public Works	Gregory Lebak
Police Chief	Kyle Wilson
Emerg/Fire Director	Kyle Asbrand

Housing & Construction

Housing Units, 2000*

Total	924
Median rent	$940
Median SF home value	$197,500

Permits for New Residential Construction

	Units	Value
Total, 2006	203	$27,643,323
Single family	191	$27,557,483
Total, 2007	179	$27,437,120
Single family	175	$27,393,052

Real Property Valuation, 2008

	Parcels	Valuation
Total	2,121	$720,697,800
Vacant	480	61,646,900
Residential	1,250	565,065,600
Commercial	46	32,209,000
Industrial	0	0
Apartments	1	336,700
Farm land	232	6,407,900
Farm homestead	112	55,031,700

Average Property Value & Tax, 2008

Residential value	$455,284
Property tax	$7,456
Tax credit/rebate	$1,173

Public Library

Crosswicks Public Library
483 Main St
Crosswicks, NJ 08515
609-298-0510

Director	Alice Bumbera

Library statistics, 2007

Population served	5,955
Full-time/total staff	NA/0

	Total	Per capita
Holdings	0	NA
Revenues	$0	NA
Expenditures	$0	NA
Annual visits	NA	NA
Internet terminals/annual users	NA/NA	

Public Safety

Number of officers, 2007	10

Crime	2006	2007
Total crimes	37	38
Violent	1	1
Murder	1	0
Rape	0	1
Robbery	0	0
Aggravated assault	0	0
Non-violent	36	37
Burglary	10	3
Larceny	23	34
Vehicle theft	3	0
Domestic violence	6	1
Arson	0	0
Total crime rate	6.0	5.9
Violent	0.2	0.2
Non-violent	5.8	5.7

Public School District

(for school year 2007-08 except as noted)

Chesterfield Township School District
295 Bordentown-Chesterfield Rd.
Chesterfield, NJ 08515
(609) 298-6900

Superintendent	Ellen McHenry
Number of schools	1
Grade plan	K-6
Enrollment	395
Attendance rate, '06-07	95.5%
Dropout rate	NA
Students per teacher	10.8
Per pupil expenditure	$12,952
Median faculty salary	$51,100
Median administrator salary	$109,870
Grade 12 enrollment	NA
High school graduation rate	NA

Assessment test results

(percent scoring at proficient or advanced level)

	Language	Math
NJASK-Grade 3	96.6%	91.2%
GEPA-Grade 8	NA	NA
HSPA-High School	NA	NA

SAT Score Averages, 2006-07

Pct tested	Math	Verbal	Writing
NA	NA	NA	NA

Teacher Qualifications

Avg. years of experience	11
Highly-qualified teachers one subject/all subjects	100%/100%

No Child Left Behind

AYP, 2006-07	Meets Standards

Municipal Finance

State Aid Programs, 2009

Total aid	$697,686
CMPTRA	26,621
Energy tax receipts	643,157
Garden State Trust	0

General Budget, 2008

Total tax levy	$11,820,406
County levy	2,504,863
County taxes	2,056,972
County library	189,918
County health	0
County open space	257,973
School levy	9,012,610
Muni. levy	302,933
Misc. revenues	5,457,057

Taxes	2006	2007	2008
General tax rate per $100	3.25	1.56	1.638
County equalization ratio	61.1	112.05	111.94
Net valuation taxable	$284,269,385	$673,598,296	$721,788,710
State equalized value	$493,032,223	$601,851,461	$671,382,763

See Introduction for an explanation of all data sources.

Demographics & Socio-Economic Characteristics
(2000 US Census, except as noted)

Population
1980*	16,072
1990*	14,583
2000	14,595
Male	7,121
Female	7,474
2007 (estimate)*	15,240
Population density	2,005.3

Race & Hispanic Origin, 2000
Race
White	13,334
Black/African American	742
American Indian/Alaska Native	24
Asian	274
Native Hawaiian/Pacific Islander	1
Other race	72
Two or more races	148
Hispanic origin, total	224
Mexican	24
Puerto Rican	126
Cuban	19
Other Hispanic	55

Age & Nativity, 2000
Under 5 years	701
18 years and over	11,012
21 years and over	10,576
65 years and over	2,794
85 years and over	219
Median age	42.0
Native-born	13,935
Foreign-born	660

Educational Attainment, 2000
Population 25 years and over	10,127
Less than 9th grade	2.7%
High school grad or higher	89.7%
Bachelor's degree or higher	28.8%
Graduate degree	9.3%

Income & Poverty, 1999
Per capita income	$27,790
Median household income	$68,474
Median family income	$75,920
Persons in poverty	353
H'holds receiving public assistance	67
H'holds receiving social security	1,825

Households, 2000
Total households	5,057
With persons under 18	1,834
With persons over 65	1,838
Family households	4,143
Single-person households	786
Persons per household	2.85
Persons per family	3.18

Labor & Employment
Total civilian labor force, 2007**	8,463
Unemployment rate	3.7%
Total civilian labor force, 2000	7,431
Unemployment rate	4.1%

Employed persons 16 years and over by occupation, 2000
Managers & professionals	2,791
Service occupations	652
Sales & office occupations	2,426
Farming, fishing & forestry	4
Construction & maintenance	521
Production & transportation	736
Self-employed persons	462

General Information
Township of Cinnaminson
PO Box 2100
Cinnaminson, NJ 08077
856-829-6000

Website	www.cinnaminsonnj.org
Year of incorporation	1860
Land/water area (sq. miles)	7.60/0.46
Form of government	Township

Government
Legislative Districts
US Congressional	3
State Legislative	7

Local Officials, 2009
Mayor	Sandra Iaquinto
Manager	Gerald Seneski
Clerk	Pamela McCartney
Finance Dir	Gerald Seneski
Tax Assessor	James Mancini
Tax Collector	Sandra Root
Attorney	John Gillespie
Building	Edward Schaefer
Comm Dev/Planning	NA
Engineering	Remington & Vernick
Public Works	W. Ben Young
Police Chief	Michael Wallace
Emerg/Fire Director	Danny Norman

Housing & Construction
Housing Units, 2000*
Total	5,147
Median rent	$916
Median SF home value	$158,900

Permits for New Residential Construction
	Units	Value
Total, 2006	70	$5,208,634
Single family	60	$4,365,040
Total, 2007	97	$6,161,200
Single family	62	$5,709,403

Real Property Valuation, 2008
	Parcels	Valuation
Total	6,021	$1,959,631,900
Vacant	301	27,748,600
Residential	5,431	1,602,469,900
Commercial	176	197,684,400
Industrial	99	129,724,100
Apartments	1	167,600
Farm land	7	96,600
Farm homestead	6	1,740,700

Average Property Value & Tax, 2008
Residential value	$295,054
Property tax	$6,143
Tax credit/rebate	$1,076

Public Library
Cinnaminson Branch Library‡
1619 Riverton Rd
Cinnaminson, NJ 08077
856-829-9340

Branch Librarian	NA

Library statistics, 2007
see Burlington County profile
for library system statistics

Public Safety
Number of officers, 2007	32

Crime	2006	2007
Total crimes	368	292
Violent	25	19
Murder	1	0
Rape	2	2
Robbery	12	8
Aggravated assault	10	9
Non-violent	343	273
Burglary	57	48
Larceny	256	212
Vehicle theft	30	13
Domestic violence	70	67
Arson	1	1
Total crime rate	24.3	18.9
Violent	1.7	1.2
Non-violent	22.6	17.7

Public School District
(for school year 2007-08 except as noted)

Cinnaminson Township School District
2195 Riverton Road, Box 224
Cinnaminson, NJ 08077
(856) 829-7600

Superintendent	Salvatore Illuzzi
Number of schools	4
Grade plan	K-12
Enrollment	2,469
Attendance rate, '06-07	94.8%
Dropout rate	0.5%
Students per teacher	10.4
Per pupil expenditure	$13,978
Median faculty salary	$57,200
Median administrator salary	$107,762
Grade 12 enrollment	208
High school graduation rate	95.9%

Assessment test results
(percent scoring at proficient or advanced level)
	Language	Math
NJASK-Grade 3	92.2%	90.4%
GEPA-Grade 8	66.8%	90.9%
HSPA-High School	83.9%	93.1%

SAT Score Averages, 2006-07
Pct tested	Math	Verbal	Writing
87%	522	503	486

Teacher Qualifications
Avg. years of experience	8

Highly-qualified teachers
one subject/all subjects	100%/100%

No Child Left Behind
AYP, 2006-07	Meets Standards

Municipal Finance
State Aid Programs, 2009
Total aid	$2,479,985
CMPTRA	196,439
Energy tax receipts	2,211,254
Garden State Trust	9,380

General Budget, 2008
Total tax levy	$40,890,985
County levy	7,315,787
County taxes	6,007,778
County library	554,713
County health	0
County open space	753,296
School levy	26,800,637
Muni. levy	6,774,560
Misc. revenues	6,148,170

Taxes	2006	2007	2008
General tax rate per $100	4.007	4.17	2.083
County equalization ratio	59.85	54.33	104.95
Net valuation taxable	$940,113,200	$948,449,306	$1,963,893,100
State equalized value	$1,732,929,062	$1,857,054,524	$1,997,174,756

‡ Branch of county library
* US Census Bureau
** New Jersey Department of Labor

See Introduction for an explanation of all data sources.

Demographics & Socio-Economic Characteristics
(2000 US Census, except as noted)

Population
1980*	16,699
1990*	14,629
2000	14,597
Male	6,934
Female	7,663
2007 (estimate)*	14,411
Population density	3,320.5

Race & Hispanic Origin, 2000
Race
White	13,956
Black/African American	44
American Indian/Alaska Native	2
Asian	402
Native Hawaiian/Pacific Islander	0
Other race	92
Two or more races	101
Hispanic origin, total	535
Mexican	21
Puerto Rican	99
Cuban	97
Other Hispanic	318

Age & Nativity, 2000
Under 5 years	759
18 years and over	11,562
21 years and over	11,209
65 years and over	3,163
85 years and over	381
Median age	42.7
Native-born	12,976
Foreign-born	1,621

Educational Attainment, 2000
Population 25 years and over	10,839
Less than 9th grade	5.3%
High school grad or higher	88.1%
Bachelor's degree or higher	28.2%
Graduate degree	8.6%

Income & Poverty, 1999
Per capita income	$29,883
Median household income	$65,019
Median family income	$77,291
Persons in poverty	248
H'holds receiving public assistance	28
H'holds receiving social security	2,069

Households, 2000
Total households	5,637
With persons under 18	1,681
With persons over 65	2,150
Family households	4,124
Single-person households	1,361
Persons per household	2.56
Persons per family	3.07

Labor & Employment
Total civilian labor force, 2007**	7,372
Unemployment rate	1.9%
Total civilian labor force, 2000	7,098
Unemployment rate	2.0%

Employed persons 16 years and over by occupation, 2000
Managers & professionals	2,572
Service occupations	749
Sales & office occupations	2,402
Farming, fishing & forestry	0
Construction & maintenance	596
Production & transportation	636
Self-employed persons	370

General Information
Township of Clark
430 Westfield Ave
Clark, NJ 07066
732-388-3600
Website	www.ourclark.com
Year of incorporation	1864
Land/water area (sq. miles)	4.34/0.14
Form of government	Mayor-Council

Government
Legislative Districts
US Congressional	7
State Legislative	22

Local Officials, 2009
Mayor	Salvatore F. Bonaccorso
Manager	John Laezza
Clerk	Edith L. Merkel
Finance Dir	Terry O'Neill
Tax Assessor	Michael Ross
Tax Collector	Tom Grady
Attorney	Joseph Triarsi
Building	Michael Khoda
Planning	Talley Associates
Engineering	Grotto Engineering
Public Works	Joseph Bonaccorso
Police Chief	Denis Connell
Emerg/Fire Director	Robert Venturella

Housing & Construction
Housing Units, 2000*
Total	5,709
Median rent	$941
Median SF home value	$217,500

Permits for New Residential Construction
	Units	Value
Total, 2006	18	$3,991,524
Single family	18	$3,991,524
Total, 2007	23	$5,865,368
Single family	23	$5,865,368

Real Property Valuation, 2008
	Parcels	Valuation
Total	5,161	$725,897,900
Vacant	121	10,410,600
Residential	4,812	574,882,600
Commercial	200	90,705,400
Industrial	22	31,597,100
Apartments	6	18,302,200
Farm land	0	0
Farm homestead	0	0

Average Property Value & Tax, 2008
Residential value	$119,469
Property tax	$8,177
Tax credit/rebate	$1,293

Public Library
Clark Public Library
303 Westfield Ave
Clark, NJ 07066
732-388-5999
Director....... Maureen Baker Wilkinson

Library statistics, 2007
Population served	14,597
Full-time/total staff	4/8

	Total	Per capita
Holdings	84,249	5.77
Revenues	$975,602	$66.84
Expenditures	$851,277	$58.32
Annual visits	146,066	10.01
Internet terminals/annual users	20/60,134	

Public Safety
Number of officers, 2007	38

Crime	2006	2007
Total crimes	215	227
Violent	11	8
Murder	0	0
Rape	0	1
Robbery	1	2
Aggravated assault	10	5
Non-violent	204	219
Burglary	15	17
Larceny	169	196
Vehicle theft	20	6
Domestic violence	34	38
Arson	1	0
Total crime rate	14.7	15.5
Violent	0.8	0.5
Non-violent	13.9	14.9

Public School District
(for school year 2007-08 except as noted)

Clark Township School District
365 Westfield Ave, 2nd Floor
Clark, NJ 07066
(732) 574-9600
Superintendent	Renae LaPrete (Int)
Number of schools	4
Grade plan	K-12
Enrollment	2,327
Attendance rate, '06-07	95.9%
Dropout rate	0.0%
Students per teacher	10.5
Per pupil expenditure	$12,676
Median faculty salary	$48,985
Median administrator salary	$104,800
Grade 12 enrollment	211
High school graduation rate	100.0%

Assessment test results
(percent scoring at proficient or advanced level)
	Language	Math
NJASK-Grade 3	85.4%	89.2%
GEPA-Grade 8	81.1%	94.9%
HSPA-High School	86.4%	92.3%

SAT Score Averages, 2006-07
Pct tested	Math	Verbal	Writing
81%	501	485	487

Teacher Qualifications
Avg. years of experience	8
Highly-qualified teachers one subject/all subjects	100%/100%

No Child Left Behind
AYP, 2006-07	Meets Standards

Municipal Finance
State Aid Programs, 2009
Total aid	$2,305,954
CMPTRA	702,691
Energy tax receipts	1,545,614
Garden State Trust	0

General Budget, 2008
Total tax levy	$49,713,153
County levy	9,734,905
County taxes	9,310,224
County library	0
County health	0
County open space	424,682
School levy	27,170,208
Muni. levy	12,808,040
Misc. revenues	6,155,934

Taxes
	2006	2007	2008
General tax rate per $100	6.559	6.655	6.845
County equalization ratio	31.39	28.83	25.91
Net valuation taxable	$711,498,000	$719,004,044	$726,295,445
State equalized value	$2,468,371,990	$2,773,813,416	$2,803,092,140

* US Census Bureau
** New Jersey Department of Labor

See Introduction for an explanation of all data sources.

Demographics & Socio-Economic Characteristics
(2000 US Census, except as noted)

Population
1980*	6,013
1990*	6,155
2000	7,139
Male	3,415
Female	3,724
2007 (estimate)*	7,511
Population density	1,046.1

Race & Hispanic Origin, 2000
Race
White	5,656
Black/African American	1,146
American Indian/Alaska Native	30
Asian	47
Native Hawaiian/Pacific Islander	2
Other race	68
Two or more races	190
Hispanic origin, total	234
Mexican	25
Puerto Rican	147
Cuban	5
Other Hispanic	57

Age & Nativity, 2000
Under 5 years	551
18 years and over	5,061
21 years and over	4,779
65 years and over	688
85 years and over	50
Median age	33.6
Native-born	6,840
Foreign-born	299

Educational Attainment, 2000
Population 25 years and over	4,430
Less than 9th grade	3.7%
High school grad or higher	83.7%
Bachelor's degree or higher	18.8%
Graduate degree	3.6%

Income & Poverty, 1999
Per capita income	$20,006
Median household income	$53,219
Median family income	$63,097
Persons in poverty	209
H'holds receiving public assistance	25
H'holds receiving social security	592

Households, 2000
Total households	2,464
With persons under 18	1,073
With persons over 65	538
Family households	1,886
Single-person households	485
Persons per household	2.89
Persons per family	3.31

Labor & Employment
Total civilian labor force, 2007**	4,502
Unemployment rate	4.8%
Total civilian labor force, 2000	3,800
Unemployment rate	4.6%

Employed persons 16 years and over by occupation, 2000
Managers & professionals	955
Service occupations	460
Sales & office occupations	1,065
Farming, fishing & forestry	8
Construction & maintenance	468
Production & transportation	671
Self-employed persons	112

‡ Branch of county library
* US Census Bureau
** New Jersey Department of Labor

General Information
Borough of Clayton
125 N Delsea Dr
Clayton, NJ 08312
856-881-2882

Website	claytonnj.com
Year of incorporation	1887
Land/water area (sq. miles)	7.18/0.17
Form of government	Borough

Government
Legislative Districts
US Congressional	2
State Legislative	3

Local Officials, 2009
Mayor	Melissa Hoffman
Manager	Sue Miller
Clerk	Christine Newcomb
Finance Dir	Donna Nestore
Tax Assessor	Greg Busa
Tax Collector	Donna Nestore
Attorney	Timothy Scaffidi
Building	Jerry Myers
Comm Dev/Planning	NA
Engineering	Mark Brunermer
Public Works	Richard Middleton
Police Chief	Dennis Marchei
Fire Chief	Samuel Teague

Housing & Construction
Housing Units, 2000*
Total	2,680
Median rent	$544
Median SF home value	$96,300

Permits for New Residential Construction
	Units	Value
Total, 2006	8	$1,099,600
Single family	8	$1,099,600
Total, 2007	19	$2,436,678
Single family	19	$2,436,678

Real Property Valuation, 2008
	Parcels	Valuation
Total	3,252	$281,403,900
Vacant	625	8,326,500
Residential	2,476	238,900,800
Commercial	79	13,844,400
Industrial	14	11,967,800
Apartments	9	6,222,700
Farm land	34	389,900
Farm homestead	15	1,751,800

Average Property Value & Tax, 2008
Residential value	$96,609
Property tax	$4,596
Tax credit/rebate	$910

Public Library
Glassboro Public Library‡
2 Center St
Glassboro, NJ 08028
856-881-0001

Director	Carol Wolf

Library statistics, 2007
see Gloucester County profile
for library system statistics

Public Safety
Number of officers, 2007	17

Crime	2006	2007
Total crimes	238	213
Violent	14	14
Murder	0	0
Rape	0	1
Robbery	4	9
Aggravated assault	10	4
Non-violent	224	199
Burglary	22	38
Larceny	197	152
Vehicle theft	5	9
Domestic violence	110	128
Arson	0	0
Total crime rate	32.0	28.5
Violent	1.9	1.9
Non-violent	30.1	26.6

Public School District
(for school year 2007-08 except as noted)

Clayton School District
300 West Chestnut Street
Clayton, NJ 08312
(856) 881-8700

Superintendent	Cleve Bryan
Number of schools	3
Grade plan	K-12
Enrollment	1,307
Attendance rate, '06-07	94.7%
Dropout rate	4.9%
Students per teacher	11.6
Per pupil expenditure	$11,025
Median faculty salary	$43,060
Median administrator salary	$85,725
Grade 12 enrollment	80
High school graduation rate	86.5%

Assessment test results
(percent scoring at proficient or advanced level)
	Language	Math
NJASK-Grade 3	76.0%	77.9%
GEPA-Grade 8	63.6%	84.3%
HSPA-High School	75.0%	84.1%

SAT Score Averages, 2006-07
Pct tested	Math	Verbal	Writing
55%	481	459	454

Teacher Qualifications
Avg. years of experience	6
Highly-qualified teachers	
one subject/all subjects	100%/100%

No Child Left Behind
AYP, 2006-07	Meets Standards

Municipal Finance
State Aid Programs, 2009
Total aid	$702,232
CMPTRA	159,461
Energy tax receipts	524,054
Garden State Trust	4,790

General Budget, 2008
Total tax levy	$13,419,032
County levy	2,979,191
County taxes	2,570,968
County library	206,749
County health	0
County open space	201,474
School levy	6,927,715
Muni. levy	3,512,126
Misc. revenues	3,411,545

Taxes	2006	2007	2008
General tax rate per $100	4.504	4.704	4.758
County equalization ratio	68.88	60.83	56.09
Net valuation taxable	$271,559,075	$276,490,876	$282,073,712
State equalized value	$447,118,911	$492,423,155	$524,504,324

See Introduction for an explanation of all data sources.

Demographics & Socio-Economic Characteristics
(2000 US Census, except as noted)

Population
1980*	5,764
1990*	5,601
2000	4,986
Male	2,407
Female	2,579
2007 (estimate)*	4,881
Population density	2,582.5

Race & Hispanic Origin, 2000
Race
White	4,100
Black/African American	577
American Indian/Alaska Native	11
Asian	46
Native Hawaiian/Pacific Islander	9
Other race	117
Two or more races	126
Hispanic origin, total	206
Mexican	31
Puerto Rican	90
Cuban	3
Other Hispanic	82

Age & Nativity, 2000
Under 5 years	361
18 years and over	3,752
21 years and over	3,563
65 years and over	554
85 years and over	60
Median age	35.3
Native-born	4,817
Foreign-born	169

Educational Attainment, 2000
Population 25 years and over	3,358
Less than 9th grade	3.4%
High school grad or higher	77.4%
Bachelor's degree or higher	11.0%
Graduate degree	2.6%

Income & Poverty, 1999
Per capita income	$18,510
Median household income	$42,207
Median family income	$50,963
Persons in poverty	570
H'holds receiving public assistance	72
H'holds receiving social security	473

Households, 2000
Total households	1,978
With persons under 18	660
With persons over 65	438
Family households	1,246
Single-person households	583
Persons per household	2.52
Persons per family	3.13

Labor & Employment
Total civilian labor force, 2007**	2,859
Unemployment rate	8.3%
Total civilian labor force, 2000	2,700
Unemployment rate	8.3%

Employed persons 16 years and over by occupation, 2000
Managers & professionals	643
Service occupations	436
Sales & office occupations	737
Farming, fishing & forestry	0
Construction & maintenance	299
Production & transportation	362
Self-employed persons	126

* US Census Bureau
** New Jersey Department of Labor

General Information
Borough of Clementon
101 Gibbsboro Rd
Clementon, NJ 08021
856-783-0284

Website	www.clementonborough.com
Year of incorporation	1925
Land/water area (sq. miles)	1.89/0.06
Form of government	Borough

Government
Legislative Districts
US Congressional	1
State Legislative	4

Local Officials, 2009
Mayor	Mark E. Armbruster
Manager/Admin	NA
Clerk	Jenai Johnson
Finance Dir	Joanne Micheo
Tax Assessor	Charles E. Warrington
Tax Collector	Joann Watson
Attorney	George Botcheos
Building	Albert O. Hallworth
Planning	Joseph Feldman
Engineering	Churchill Consulting
Public Works	Melvin Applegate
Police Chief	David Kunkel
Emerg/Fire Director	John Busch

Housing & Construction
Housing Units, 2000*
Total	2,206
Median rent	$604
Median SF home value	$85,300

Permits for New Residential Construction
	Units	Value
Total, 2006	9	$876,310
Single family	9	$876,310
Total, 2007	9	$728,924
Single family	9	$728,924

Real Property Valuation, 2008
	Parcels	Valuation
Total	1,890	$171,921,380
Vacant	167	3,178,100
Residential	1,632	135,158,580
Commercial	83	25,941,900
Industrial	0	0
Apartments	6	7,536,100
Farm land	1	3,600
Farm homestead	1	103,100

Average Property Value & Tax, 2008
Residential value	$82,830
Property tax	$4,045
Tax credit/rebate	$842

Public Library
Clementon Memorial Library
195 Gibbsboro Rd
Clementon, NJ 08021
856-783-3233

Director	Dale Swanson

Library statistics, 2007
Population served	4,986
Full-time/total staff	NA/0

	Total	Per capita
Holdings	0	NA
Revenues	$0	NA
Expenditures	$0	NA
Annual visits	NA	NA
Internet terminals/annual users	NA/NA	

Public Safety
Number of officers, 2007	16

Crime	2006	2007
Total crimes	244	169
Violent	36	31
Murder	0	0
Rape	0	0
Robbery	12	6
Aggravated assault	24	25
Non-violent	208	138
Burglary	38	27
Larceny	154	102
Vehicle theft	16	9
Domestic violence	148	150
Arson	2	2
Total crime rate	49.4	34.3
Violent	7.3	6.3
Non-violent	42.1	28.0

Public School District
(for school year 2007-08 except as noted)

Clementon Borough School District
Audubon Avenue
Clementon, NJ 08021
(856) 783-2300

Superintendent	Michael Adams
Number of schools	1
Grade plan	K-8
Enrollment	519
Attendance rate, '06-07	94.1%
Dropout rate	NA
Students per teacher	9.8
Per pupil expenditure	$11,797
Median faculty salary	$47,280
Median administrator salary	$84,598
Grade 12 enrollment	NA
High school graduation rate	NA

Assessment test results
(percent scoring at proficient or advanced level)
	Language	Math
NJASK-Grade 3	75.5%	69.9%
GEPA-Grade 8	81.6%	81.7%
HSPA-High School	NA	NA

SAT Score Averages, 2006-07
Pct tested	Math	Verbal	Writing
NA	NA	NA	NA

Teacher Qualifications
Avg. years of experience	10
Highly-qualified teachers one subject/all subjects	100%/100%

No Child Left Behind
AYP, 2006-07	Meets Standards

Municipal Finance
State Aid Programs, 2009
Total aid	$514,897
CMPTRA	166,985
Energy tax receipts	345,305
Garden State Trust	46

General Budget, 2008
Total tax levy	$8,414,080
County levy	1,814,203
County taxes	1,639,265
County library	117,769
County health	0
County open space	57,169
School levy	3,889,844
Muni. levy	2,710,033
Misc. revenues	2,075,490

Taxes
	2006	2007	2008
General tax rate per $100	4.49	4.829	4.883
County equalization ratio	78.15	65.38	60.48
Net valuation taxable	$170,981,430	$171,674,606	$172,316,498
State equalized value	$261,969,974	$283,586,307	$289,727,632

See Introduction for an explanation of all data sources.

Demographics & Socio-Economic Characteristics
(2000 US Census, except as noted)

Population
1980*	21,464
1990*	20,393
2000	23,007
Male	11,091
Female	11,916
2007 (estimate)*	22,830
Population density	23,781.3

Race & Hispanic Origin, 2000
Race
White	17,911
Black/African American	422
American Indian/Alaska Native	58
Asian	2,772
Native Hawaiian/Pacific Islander	5
Other race	1,144
Two or more races	695
Hispanic origin, total	4,177
Mexican	89
Puerto Rican	578
Cuban	565
Other Hispanic	2,945

Age & Nativity, 2000
Under 5 years	1,129
18 years and over	19,126
21 years and over	18,527
65 years and over	4,229
85 years and over	498
Median age	39.8
Native-born	13,054
Foreign-born	9,953

Educational Attainment, 2000
Population 25 years and over	17,382
Less than 9th grade	11.1%
High school grad or higher	78.7%
Bachelor's degree or higher	32.7%
Graduate degree	13.1%

Income & Poverty, 1999
Per capita income	$28,516
Median household income	$46,288
Median family income	$54,915
Persons in poverty	2,462
H'holds receiving public assistance	162
H'holds receiving social security	2,916

Households, 2000
Total households	10,027
With persons under 18	2,393
With persons over 65	3,185
Family households	6,041
Single-person households	3,390
Persons per household	2.29
Persons per family	2.95

Labor & Employment
Total civilian labor force, 2007**	12,293
Unemployment rate	4.0%
Total civilian labor force, 2000	11,674
Unemployment rate	4.5%

Employed persons 16 years and over by occupation, 2000
Managers & professionals	3,919
Service occupations	1,604
Sales & office occupations	3,323
Farming, fishing & forestry	5
Construction & maintenance	943
Production & transportation	1,354
Self-employed persons	893

General Information
Borough of Cliffside Park
525 Palisade Ave
Cliffside Park, NJ 07010
201-945-3456
Website	www.cliffsideparknj.gov
Year of incorporation	1895
Land/water area (sq. miles)	0.96/0.00
Form of government	Borough

Government
Legislative Districts
US Congressional	9
State Legislative	38

Local Officials, 2009
Mayor	Gerald A. Calabrese
Administrator	Bruce Bonaventuro
Clerk	Sercan Zoklu
Finance Dir	Frank Berado
Tax Assessor	Frank Bucino
Tax Collector	Frank Berardo
Attorney	Chris Diktas
Building	John Candelmo
Comm Dev/Planning	NA
Engineering	Stephen Boswell
Public Works	Al Martone
Police Chief	Donald Keane
Emerg/Fire Director	Al Deleone

Housing & Construction
Housing Units, 2000*
Total	10,375
Median rent	$864
Median SF home value	$227,500

Permits for New Residential Construction
	Units	Value
Total, 2006	98	$12,613,883
Single family	42	$8,305,476
Total, 2007	111	$7,611,592
Single family	27	$5,377,819

Real Property Valuation, 2008
	Parcels	Valuation
Total	6,845	$2,457,922,400
Vacant	102	7,707,000
Residential	6,337	2,105,334,300
Commercial	241	135,715,000
Industrial	7	5,502,700
Apartments	158	203,663,400
Farm land	0	0
Farm homestead	0	0

Average Property Value & Tax, 2008
Residential value	$332,229
Property tax	$7,019
Tax credit/rebate	$1,129

Public Library
Cliffside Park Public Library
505 Palisade Ave
Cliffside Park, NJ 07010
201-945-2867
Director	Ana Chelariu

Library statistics, 2007
Population served	23,007
Full-time/total staff	4/15

	Total	Per capita
Holdings	65,513	2.85
Revenues	$1,133,049	$49.25
Expenditures	$971,533	$42.23
Annual visits	102,600	4.46
Internet terminals/annual users	18/40,765	

Public Safety
Number of officers, 2007	46

Crime	2006	2007
Total crimes	230	251
Violent	15	27
Murder	0	0
Rape	0	0
Robbery	5	10
Aggravated assault	10	17
Non-violent	215	224
Burglary	55	50
Larceny	138	163
Vehicle theft	22	11
Domestic violence	89	73
Arson	0	0
Total crime rate	10.0	10.9
Violent	0.7	1.2
Non-violent	9.3	9.8

Public School District
(for school year 2007-08 except as noted)

Cliffside Park School District
525 Palisade Avenue
Cliffside Park, NJ 07010
(201) 313-2304
Superintendent	Michael J. Romagnino
Number of schools	6
Grade plan	K-12
Enrollment	2,588
Attendance rate, '06-07	94.0%
Dropout rate	0.3%
Students per teacher	11.6
Per pupil expenditure	$12,653
Median faculty salary	$61,318
Median administrator salary	$132,379
Grade 12 enrollment	220
High school graduation rate	94.2%

Assessment test results
(percent scoring at proficient or advanced level)
	Language	Math
NJASK-Grade 3	91.3%	93.1%
GEPA-Grade 8	64.6%	81.1%
HSPA-High School	67.2%	84.7%

SAT Score Averages, 2006-07
Pct tested	Math	Verbal	Writing
83%	459	447	438

Teacher Qualifications
Avg. years of experience	9
Highly-qualified teachers one subject/all subjects	100%/100%

No Child Left Behind
AYP, 2006-07	Meets Standards

Municipal Finance
State Aid Programs, 2009
Total aid	$1,453,158
CMPTRA	432,673
Energy tax receipts	984,156
Garden State Trust	0

General Budget, 2008
Total tax levy	$52,000,373
County levy	6,632,423
County taxes	6,272,650
County library	0
County health	0
County open space	359,773
School levy	24,910,724
Muni. levy	20,457,226
Misc. revenues	10,024,080

Taxes
Taxes	2006	2007	2008
General tax rate per $100	1.98	2.04	2.114
County equalization ratio	85.33	73.59	68.64
Net valuation taxable	$2,426,853,300	$2,456,887,669	$2,461,469,708
State equalized value	$3,302,324,421	$3,577,652,310	$3,562,143,515

* US Census Bureau
** New Jersey Department of Labor

See Introduction for an explanation of all data sources.

Demographics & Socio-Economic Characteristics[†]

(2000 US Census, except as noted)

Population
1980*	74,388
1990*	71,742
2000	78,672
Male	37,560
Female	41,112
2007 (estimate)*	78,573
Population density	6,953.4

Race & Hispanic Origin, 2000
Race
White	59,960
Black/African American	2,277
American Indian/Alaska Native	192
Asian	5,066
Native Hawaiian/Pacific Islander	27
Other race	7,553
Two or more races	3,597
Hispanic origin, total	15,608
Mexican	1,591
Puerto Rican	3,923
Cuban	510
Other Hispanic	9,584

Age & Nativity, 2000
Under 5 years	4,700
18 years and over	61,700
21 years and over	59,327
65 years and over	13,829
85 years and over	2,037
Median age	38.8
Native-born	55,680
Foreign-born	22,992

Educational Attainment, 2000
Population 25 years and over	55,730
Less than 9th grade	8.8%
High school grad or higher	78.6%
Bachelor's degree or higher	23.6%
Graduate degree	7.6%

Income & Poverty, 1999
Per capita income	$23,638
Median household income	$50,619
Median family income	$60,688
Persons in poverty	4,932
H'holds receiving public assistance	593
H'holds receiving social security	10,239

Households, 2000
Total households	30,244
With persons under 18	9,459
With persons over 65	10,261
Family households	20,352
Single-person households	8,448
Persons per household	2.59
Persons per family	3.20

Labor & Employment
Total civilian labor force, 2007**	40,639
Unemployment rate	4.7%
Total civilian labor force, 2000	39,232
Unemployment rate	4.9%

Employed persons 16 years and over by occupation, 2000
Managers & professionals	12,055
Service occupations	4,374
Sales & office occupations	11,520
Farming, fishing & forestry	11
Construction & maintenance	3,146
Production & transportation	6,211
Self-employed persons	1,623

---

† see Appendix C for American Community Survey data
* US Census Bureau
** New Jersey Department of Labor

General Information
City of Clifton
900 Clifton Ave
Clifton, NJ 07013
973-470-5800

Website	www.cliftonnj.org
Year of incorporation	1917
Land/water area (sq. miles)	11.30/0.10
Form of government	Municipal Mgr 1923

Government
Legislative Districts
US Congressional	8
State Legislative	34

Local Officials, 2009
Mayor	James Anzaldi
Manager	Albert Greco
Clerk	Barbara J. Nagy
CFO	Jonathan Capp
Tax Assessor	Jon Whiting
Tax Collector	Luisa Castillo
Attorney	Matthew Priore
Building	Joseph Lotorto
Planning	Jill Hartmann
Engineering	James Yellen
Public Works	Vincent Cahill
Police Chief	Robert Ferreri
Fire Chief	Joseph Verderosa (Actg)

Housing & Construction
Housing Units, 2000*
Total	31,060
Median rent	$784
Median SF home value	$181,600

Permits for New Residential Construction
	Units	Value
Total, 2006	60	$6,657,446
Single family	19	$3,841,395
Total, 2007	71	$6,638,048
Single family	19	$3,242,996

Real Property Valuation, 2008
	Parcels	Valuation
Total	23,153	$5,311,727,900
Vacant	376	54,923,000
Residential	21,135	3,745,403,300
Commercial	1,092	744,422,200
Industrial	434	634,379,500
Apartments	115	132,588,300
Farm land	1	11,600
Farm homestead	0	0

Average Property Value & Tax, 2008
Residential value	$177,213
Property tax	$7,622
Tax credit/rebate	$1,174

Public Library
Clifton Public Library
292 Piaget Ave
Clifton, NJ 07011
973-772-5500

Director	Christine R. Zembicki

Library statistics, 2007
Population served	78,672
Full-time/total staff	8/26

	Total	Per capita
Holdings	227,482	2.89
Revenues	$3,588,087	$45.61
Expenditures	$3,330,435	$42.33
Annual visits	306,953	3.90
Internet terminals/annual users	27/59,610	

Public Safety
Number of officers, 2007	158

Crime	2006	2007
Total crimes	2,131	2,138
Violent	179	223
Murder	1	0
Rape	2	5
Robbery	78	108
Aggravated assault	98	110
Non-violent	1,952	1,915
Burglary	361	389
Larceny	1,296	1,324
Vehicle theft	295	202
Domestic violence	591	592
Arson	1	2
Total crime rate	26.7	26.9
Violent	2.2	2.8
Non-violent	24.4	24.1

Public School District
(for school year 2007-08 except as noted)

Clifton School District
745 Clifton Avenue, PO Box 2209
Clifton, NJ 07015
(973) 470-2260

Chief School Admin	Richard Tardalo
Number of schools	17
Grade plan	K-12
Enrollment	10,524
Attendance rate, '06-07	95.0%
Dropout rate	5.3%
Students per teacher	11.4
Per pupil expenditure	$12,369
Median faculty salary	$57,225
Median administrator salary	$104,675
Grade 12 enrollment	819
High school graduation rate	80.9%

Assessment test results
(percent scoring at proficient or advanced level)
	Language	Math
NJASK-Grade 3	82.1%	81.9%
GEPA-Grade 8	58.1%	78.1%
HSPA-High School	65.2%	74.3%

SAT Score Averages, 2006-07
Pct tested	Math	Verbal	Writing
72%	482	460	461

Teacher Qualifications
Avg. years of experience	10
Highly-qualified teachers one subject/all subjects	97.0%/97.0%

No Child Left Behind
AYP, 2006-07	Meets Standards

Municipal Finance
State Aid Programs, 2009
Total aid	$12,961,180
CMPTRA	4,659,715
Energy tax receipts	7,977,435
Garden State Trust	0

General Budget, 2008
Total tax levy	$228,719,992
County levy	57,250,937
County taxes	56,115,755
County library	0
County health	0
County open space	1,135,182
School levy	111,747,537
Muni. levy	59,721,518
Misc. revenues	38,002,379

Taxes	2006	2007	2008
General tax rate per $100	3.95	4.19	4.301
County equalization ratio	58.23	50.71	47.44
Net valuation taxable	$5,254,875,900	$5,279,398,981	$5,318,046,789
State equalized value	$10,369,828,950	$11,121,668,444	$11,195,971,090

See Introduction for an explanation of all data sources.

Demographics & Socio-Economic Characteristics

(2000 US Census, except as noted)

Population

1980*	1,910
1990*	2,054
2000	2,632
Male	1,284
Female	1,348
2007 (estimate)*	2,564
Population density	1,871.5

Race & Hispanic Origin, 2000

Race

White	2,423
Black/African American	35
American Indian/Alaska Native	12
Asian	98
Native Hawaiian/Pacific Islander	0
Other race	36
Two or more races	28
Hispanic origin, total	108
Mexican	15
Puerto Rican	18
Cuban	6
Other Hispanic	69

Age & Nativity, 2000

Under 5 years	200
18 years and over	1,938
21 years and over	1,892
65 years and over	248
85 years and over	18
Median age	36.7
Native-born	2,349
Foreign-born	283

Educational Attainment, 2000

Population 25 years and over	1,852
Less than 9th grade	2.9%
High school grad or higher	93.6%
Bachelor's degree or higher	49.1%
Graduate degree	20.6%

Income & Poverty, 1999

Per capita income	$37,463
Median household income	$78,121
Median family income	$88,671
Persons in poverty	74
H'holds receiving public assistance	4
H'holds receiving social security	206

Households, 2000

Total households	1,068
With persons under 18	388
With persons over 65	196
Family households	724
Single-person households	281
Persons per household	2.46
Persons per family	3.00

Labor & Employment

Total civilian labor force, 2007**	1,693
Unemployment rate	2.3%
Total civilian labor force, 2000	1,526
Unemployment rate	1.8%

Employed persons 16 years and over by occupation, 2000

Managers & professionals	873
Service occupations	171
Sales & office occupations	329
Farming, fishing & forestry	4
Construction & maintenance	57
Production & transportation	65
Self-employed persons	130

‡ Branch of county library
* US Census Bureau
** New Jersey Department of Labor

See Introduction for an explanation of all data sources.

General Information

Town of Clinton
PO Box 5194
Clinton, NJ 08809
908-735-8616

Website	www.clintonnj.gov
Year of incorporation	1865
Land/water area (sq. miles)	1.37/0.04
Form of government	Town

Government

Legislative Districts

US Congressional	7
State Legislative	23

Local Officials, 2009

Mayor	Christine Schaumburg
Manager	Robert Cutter
Clerk	Cecilia Covino
Finance Dir	Kathleen Olsen
Tax Assessor	Ann Marie Obiedzinski
Tax Collector	NA
Attorney	Richard Cushing
Building	John Leonard
Comm Dev/Planning	NA
Engineering	Robert J. Clerico
Public Works	Robert A. Cutter
Police Chief	Richard Brett Matheis
Emerg/Fire Director	Scott Wintermute

Housing & Construction

Housing Units, 2000*

Total	1,095
Median rent	$862
Median SF home value	$222,100

Permits for New Residential Construction

	Units	Value
Total, 2006	0	$0
Single family	0	$0
Total, 2007	0	$4,820
Single family	0	$4,820

Real Property Valuation, 2008

	Parcels	Valuation
Total	1,028	$425,056,000
Vacant	40	4,979,800
Residential	855	318,996,900
Commercial	120	89,817,400
Industrial	0	0
Apartments	8	10,990,800
Farm land	4	59,300
Farm homestead	1	211,800

Average Property Value & Tax, 2008

Residential value	$372,907
Property tax	$8,673
Tax credit/rebate	$1,263

Public Library

North County Branch Library‡
65 Halstead St
Clinton, NJ 08809
908-730-6262

Branch Librarian ... Barbara Riesenfeld

Library statistics, 2007

see Hunterdon County profile
for library system statistics

Public Safety

Number of officers, 2007 10

Crime	2006	2007
Total crimes	20	15
Violent	2	0
Murder	0	0
Rape	0	0
Robbery	1	0
Aggravated assault	1	0
Non-violent	18	15
Burglary	1	0
Larceny	17	14
Vehicle theft	0	1
Domestic violence	3	3
Arson	0	0
Total crime rate	7.6	5.8
Violent	0.8	0.0
Non-violent	6.9	5.8

Public School District

(for school year 2007-08 except as noted)

Clinton Town School District
10 School Street
Clinton, NJ 08809
(908) 735-8512

Superintendent	John Alfieri
Number of schools	1
Grade plan	K-8
Enrollment	538
Attendance rate, '06-07	95.8%
Dropout rate	NA
Students per teacher	9.9
Per pupil expenditure	$12,329
Median faculty salary	$55,200
Median administrator salary	$116,000
Grade 12 enrollment	NA
High school graduation rate	NA

Assessment test results

(percent scoring at proficient or advanced level)

	Language	Math
NJASK-Grade 3	93.0%	87.8%
GEPA-Grade 8	87.3%	95.2%
HSPA-High School	NA	NA

SAT Score Averages, 2006-07

Pct tested	Math	Verbal	Writing
NA	NA	NA	NA

Teacher Qualifications

Avg. years of experience	15
Highly-qualified teachers one subject/all subjects	100%/100%

No Child Left Behind

AYP, 2006-07 .... Meets Standards

Municipal Finance

State Aid Programs, 2009

Total aid	$207,275
CMPTRA	47,372
Energy tax receipts	154,721
Garden State Trust	0

General Budget, 2008

Total tax levy	$9,906,290
County levy	1,475,759
County taxes	1,235,149
County library	107,257
County health	0
County open space	133,353
School levy	6,572,194
Muni. levy	1,858,337
Misc. revenues	1,757,745

Taxes

	2006	2007	2008
General tax rate per $100	2.3	2.29	2.326
County equalization ratio	102.18	92.55	96.29
Net valuation taxable	$401,556,800	$418,956,082	$425,940,156
State equalized value	$414,151,268	$435,917,385	$436,169,358

Demographics & Socio-Economic Characteristics
(2000 US Census, except as noted)

Population
1980*	7,345
1990*	10,816
2000	12,957
Male	7,023
Female	5,934
2007 (estimate)*	13,903
Population density	463.4

Race & Hispanic Origin, 2000
Race
White	11,365
Black/African American	902
American Indian/Alaska Native	26
Asian	304
Native Hawaiian/Pacific Islander	9
Other race	206
Two or more races	145
Hispanic origin, total	507
Mexican	36
Puerto Rican	253
Cuban	46
Other Hispanic	172

Age & Nativity, 2000
Under 5 years	852
18 years and over	9,559
21 years and over	9,081
65 years and over	951
85 years and over	120
Median age	36.4
Native-born	12,039
Foreign-born	918

Educational Attainment, 2000
Population 25 years and over	8,100
Less than 9th grade	1.8%
High school grad or higher	93.0%
Bachelor's degree or higher	50.5%
Graduate degree	22.1%

Income & Poverty, 1999
Per capita income	$37,264
Median household income	$96,570
Median family income	$106,448
Persons in poverty	105
H'holds receiving public assistance	10
H'holds receiving social security	658

Households, 2000
Total households	4,129
With persons under 18	1,782
With persons over 65	655
Family households	3,255
Single-person households	717
Persons per household	2.82
Persons per family	3.23

Labor & Employment
Total civilian labor force, 2007**	6,879
Unemployment rate	3.9%
Total civilian labor force, 2000	6,170
Unemployment rate	3.4%

Employed persons 16 years and over by occupation, 2000
Managers & professionals	3,542
Service occupations	411
Sales & office occupations	1,339
Farming, fishing & forestry	0
Construction & maintenance	296
Production & transportation	370
Self-employed persons	423

* US Census Bureau
** New Jersey Department of Labor

General Information
Township of Clinton
1225 Route 31 South
Lebanon, NJ 08833
908-735-8800
Website	www.township.clinton.nj.us
Year of incorporation	1841
Land/water area (sq. miles)	30.00/3.93
Form of government	Small Municipality

Government
Legislative Districts
US Congressional	7
State Legislative	23

Local Officials, 2009
Mayor	Kevin Cimei
Manager	Marvin Joss
Clerk	Donna Burham
Finance Dir	Kathleen Colognato
Tax Assessor	Jeffrey Ward
Tax Collector	Patricia Centofanti
Attorney	Kristina P. Hadinger
Building	Michael Wright
Comm Dev/Planning	NA
Engineering	Cathleen F. Marcelli
Public Works	Jay Meixsell
Police Dir	Robert Manney
Emerg/Fire Director	Marc Strauss

Housing & Construction
Housing Units, 2000*
Total	4,234
Median rent	$1,062
Median SF home value	$283,900

Permits for New Residential Construction
	Units	Value
Total, 2006	15	$3,466,454
Single family	15	$3,466,454
Total, 2007	6	$2,306,644
Single family	6	$2,306,644

Real Property Valuation, 2008
	Parcels	Valuation
Total	5,169	$2,593,290,816
Vacant	189	19,106,600
Residential	4,333	2,090,024,500
Commercial	275	228,922,200
Industrial	8	164,242,500
Apartments	4	18,005,800
Farm land	225	2,533,216
Farm homestead	135	70,456,000

Average Property Value & Tax, 2008
Residential value	$483,545
Property tax	$9,518
Tax credit/rebate	$1,253

Public Library
No public municipal library

Library statistics, 2007
Population served	NA
Full-time/total staff	NA/NA

	Total	Per capita
Holdings	NA	NA
Revenues	NA	NA
Expenditures	NA	NA
Annual visits	NA	NA
Internet terminals/annual users	NA/NA	

Public Safety
Number of officers, 2007	24

Crime	2006	2007
Total crimes	81	64
Violent	3	9
Murder	0	0
Rape	0	2
Robbery	0	1
Aggravated assault	3	6
Non-violent	78	55
Burglary	12	18
Larceny	62	36
Vehicle theft	4	1
Domestic violence	58	69
Arson	0	0
Total crime rate	5.8	4.5
Violent	0.2	0.6
Non-violent	5.6	3.9

Public School District
(for school year 2007-08 except as noted)

Clinton Township School District
P.O. Box 362
Lebanon, NJ 08833
(908) 735-8320
Superintendent	Dennis Fyffe (Int)
Number of schools	4
Grade plan	K-8
Enrollment	1,774
Attendance rate, '06-07	96.0%
Dropout rate	NA
Students per teacher	10.7
Per pupil expenditure	$13,072
Median faculty salary	$50,095
Median administrator salary	$112,936
Grade 12 enrollment	NA
High school graduation rate	NA

Assessment test results
(percent scoring at proficient or advanced level)
	Language	Math
NJASK-Grade 3	90.5%	94.9%
GEPA-Grade 8	81.8%	92.3%
HSPA-High School	NA	NA

SAT Score Averages, 2006-07
Pct tested	Math	Verbal	Writing
NA	NA	NA	NA

Teacher Qualifications
Avg. years of experience	7
Highly-qualified teachers one subject/all subjects	100%/100%

No Child Left Behind
AYP, 2006-07	Meets Standards

Municipal Finance
State Aid Programs, 2009
Total aid	$1,382,168
CMPTRA	161,056
Energy tax receipts	1,120,891
Garden State Trust	44,499

General Budget, 2008
Total tax levy	$51,333,039
County levy	8,829,042
County taxes	7,389,536
County library	641,672
County health	0
County open space	797,834
School levy	37,327,768
Muni. levy	5,176,229
Misc. revenues	6,728,995

Taxes
	2006	2007	2008
General tax rate per $100	1.9	2	1.969
County equalization ratio	98.46	92.88	98.21
Net valuation taxable	$2,568,797,400	$2,590,473,113	$2,607,903,895
State equalized value	$2,601,331,262	$2,683,123,925	$2,663,531,175

See Introduction for an explanation of all data sources.

Demographics & Socio-Economic Characteristics
(2000 US Census, except as noted)

Population
1980*	8,164
1990*	8,094
2000	8,383
Male	4,130
Female	4,253
2007 (estimate)*	8,681
Population density	2,738.5

Race & Hispanic Origin, 2000
Race
White	6,314
Black/African American	78
American Indian/Alaska Native	8
Asian	1,807
Native Hawaiian/Pacific Islander	0
Other race	68
Two or more races	108
Hispanic origin, total	343
Mexican	24
Puerto Rican	69
Cuban	55
Other Hispanic	195

Age & Nativity, 2000
Under 5 years	546
18 years and over	6,038
21 years and over	5,839
65 years and over	1,102
85 years and over	108
Median age	39.6
Native-born	6,264
Foreign-born	2,119

Educational Attainment, 2000
Population 25 years and over	5,687
Less than 9th grade	2.9%
High school grad or higher	93.1%
Bachelor's degree or higher	49.9%
Graduate degree	19.6%

Income & Poverty, 1999
Per capita income	$37,065
Median household income	$83,918
Median family income	$94,543
Persons in poverty	229
H'holds receiving public assistance	0
H'holds receiving social security	759

Households, 2000
Total households	2,789
With persons under 18	1,254
With persons over 65	763
Family households	2,321
Single-person households	391
Persons per household	2.98
Persons per family	3.30

Labor & Employment
Total civilian labor force, 2007**	4,125
Unemployment rate	1.9%
Total civilian labor force, 2000	3,918
Unemployment rate	1.8%

Employed persons 16 years and over by occupation, 2000
Managers & professionals	1,972
Service occupations	274
Sales & office occupations	1,216
Farming, fishing & forestry	0
Construction & maintenance	198
Production & transportation	186
Self-employed persons	323

* US Census Bureau
** New Jersey Department of Labor

See Introduction for an explanation of all data sources.

General Information
Borough of Closter
295 Closter Dock Rd
Closter, NJ 07624
201-784-0600
Website	www.closterboro.com
Year of incorporation	1904
Land/water area (sq. miles)	3.17/0.12
Form of government	Borough

Government
Legislative Districts
US Congressional	5
State Legislative	39

Local Officials, 2009
Mayor	Sophie Heymann
Manager	(vacant)
Clerk	Loretta Castano
Finance Dir	Joseph Luppino
Tax Assessor	Angela Mattiace
Tax Collector	Maria Passafalo
Attorney	Edward T. Rogan
Building	(vacant)
Comm Dev/Planning	NA
Engineering	Steven Boswell
Public Works	Bill Dahle (Actg)
Police Chief	David Berrian
Emerg/Fire Director	Brian Pierro

Housing & Construction
Housing Units, 2000*
Total	2,865
Median rent	$1,184
Median SF home value	$346,000

Permits for New Residential Construction
	Units	Value
Total, 2006	30	$13,766,520
Single family	30	$13,766,520
Total, 2007	20	$10,237,553
Single family	20	$10,237,553

Real Property Valuation, 2008
	Parcels	Valuation
Total	2,942	$2,369,015,700
Vacant	87	37,719,700
Residential	2,678	2,098,226,600
Commercial	160	208,793,300
Industrial	8	18,309,800
Apartments	1	1,005,700
Farm land	4	30,500
Farm homestead	4	4,930,100

Average Property Value & Tax, 2008
Residential value	$784,175
Property tax	$12,881
Tax credit/rebate	$1,517

Public Library
Closter Public Library
280 High St
Closter, NJ 07624
201-768-4197
Director	Ruth Rando

Library statistics, 2007
Population served	8,383
Full-time/total staff	2/5

	Total	Per capita
Holdings	53,459	6.38
Revenues	$794,021	$94.72
Expenditures	$690,171	$82.33
Annual visits	73,400	8.76
Internet terminals/annual users	17/50,700	

Public Safety
Number of officers, 2007	22

Crime
	2006	2007
Total crimes	73	46
Violent	1	2
Murder	0	0
Rape	0	0
Robbery	0	0
Aggravated assault	1	2
Non-violent	72	44
Burglary	18	7
Larceny	52	36
Vehicle theft	2	1
Domestic violence	40	46
Arson	0	0
Total crime rate	8.4	5.3
Violent	0.1	0.2
Non-violent	8.3	5.0

Public School District
(for school year 2007-08 except as noted)

Closter School District
340 Homans Avenue
Closter, NJ 07624
(201) 768-3001
Superintendent	Joanne Newberry
Number of schools	2
Grade plan	K-8
Enrollment	1,156
Attendance rate, '06-07	96.3%
Dropout rate	NA
Students per teacher	12.0
Per pupil expenditure	$13,010
Median faculty salary	$69,187
Median administrator salary	$114,350
Grade 12 enrollment	NA
High school graduation rate	NA

Assessment test results
(percent scoring at proficient or advanced level)
	Language	Math
NJASK-Grade 3	99.1%	96.5%
GEPA-Grade 8	86.2%	94.8%
HSPA-High School	NA	NA

SAT Score Averages, 2006-07
Pct tested	Math	Verbal	Writing
NA	NA	NA	NA

Teacher Qualifications
Avg. years of experience	10
Highly-qualified teachers one subject/all subjects	100%/100%

No Child Left Behind
AYP, 2006-07	Meets Standards

Municipal Finance
State Aid Programs, 2009
Total aid	$1,846,239
CMPTRA	0
Energy tax receipts	1,773,186
Garden State Trust	0

General Budget, 2008
Total tax levy	$39,005,204
County levy	4,211,023
County taxes	3,982,613
County library	0
County health	0
County open space	228,410
School levy	25,373,582
Muni. levy	9,420,599
Misc. revenues	4,459,703

Taxes
	2006	2007	2008
General tax rate per $100	1.49	1.57	1.643
County equalization ratio	117.92	106.66	104.23
Net valuation taxable	$2,363,028,100	$2,373,108,216	$2,374,626,044
State equalized value	$2,220,960,019	$2,277,023,699	$2,357,457,559

Demographics & Socio-Economic Characteristics

(2000 US Census, except as noted)

Population

1980*	15,838
1990*	15,289
2000	14,326
Male	6,732
Female	7,594
2007 (estimate)*	13,812
Population density	7,547.5

Race & Hispanic Origin, 2000

Race

White	12,388
Black/African American	955
American Indian/Alaska Native	48
Asian	395
Native Hawaiian/Pacific Islander	3
Other race	346
Two or more races	191
Hispanic origin, total	812
Mexican	112
Puerto Rican	450
Cuban	9
Other Hispanic	241

Age & Nativity, 2000

Under 5 years	785
18 years and over	11,209
21 years and over	10,708
65 years and over	2,066
85 years and over	357
Median age	37.1
Native-born	13,511
Foreign-born	826

Educational Attainment, 2000

Population 25 years and over	10,095
Less than 9th grade	3.0%
High school grad or higher	87.5%
Bachelor's degree or higher	30.3%
Graduate degree	10.2%

Income & Poverty, 1999

Per capita income	$24,358
Median household income	$43,175
Median family income	$57,987
Persons in poverty	866
H'holds receiving public assistance	126
H'holds receiving social security	1,710

Households, 2000

Total households	6,263
With persons under 18	1,733
With persons over 65	1,641
Family households	3,461
Single-person households	2,291
Persons per household	2.27
Persons per family	3.05

Labor & Employment

Total civilian labor force, 2007**	8,395
Unemployment rate	4.6%
Total civilian labor force, 2000	7,926
Unemployment rate	4.6%

Employed persons 16 years and over by occupation, 2000

Managers & professionals	3,207
Service occupations	803
Sales & office occupations	2,379
Farming, fishing & forestry	0
Construction & maintenance	606
Production & transportation	563
Self-employed persons	347

* US Census Bureau
** New Jersey Department of Labor

General Information

Borough of Collingswood
678 Haddon Ave
Collingswood, NJ 08108
856-854-0720

Website	www.collingswood.com
Year of incorporation	1888
Land/water area (sq. miles)	1.83/0.09
Form of government	Commission

Government

Legislative Districts

US Congressional	1
State Legislative	6

Local Officials, 2009

Mayor	M. James Maley Jr
Manager	Bradford Stokes
Clerk	Alice Marks
Finance Dir	Sandra Powell
Tax Assessor	John Dymond
Tax Collector	Keith Hastings
Attorney	Joseph Nardi III
Building	William Joseph
Comm Dev/Planning	John Kane
Engineering	Remington & Vernick
Public Works	Carl Jubb Jr
Police Chief	Thomas Garrity
Emerg/Fire Director	John Amet

Housing & Construction

Housing Units, 2000*

Total	6,866
Median rent	$688
Median SF home value	$101,200

Permits for New Residential Construction

	Units	Value
Total, 2006	0	$0
Single family	0	$0
Total, 2007	0	$0
Single family	0	$0

Real Property Valuation, 2008

	Parcels	Valuation
Total	4,390	$1,084,032,200
Vacant	144	10,780,100
Residential	3,910	908,917,800
Commercial	296	122,710,600
Industrial	0	0
Apartments	40	41,623,700
Farm land	0	0
Farm homestead	0	0

Average Property Value & Tax, 2008

Residential value	$232,460
Property tax	$5,715
Tax credit/rebate	$979

Public Library

Collingswood Public Library
771 Haddon Ave
Collingswood, NJ 08108
856-858-0649

Director	Kathleen Liu

Library statistics, 2007

Population served	14,326
Full-time/total staff	3/5

	Total	Per capita
Holdings	65,952	4.60
Revenues	$557,538	$38.92
Expenditures	$521,174	$36.38
Annual visits	59,878	4.18
Internet terminals/annual users	13/11,005	

Public Safety

Number of officers, 2007	37

Crime	2006	2007
Total crimes	433	460
Violent	23	27
Murder	0	0
Rape	1	4
Robbery	7	15
Aggravated assault	15	8
Non-violent	410	433
Burglary	66	79
Larceny	315	305
Vehicle theft	29	49
Domestic violence	157	125
Arson	0	2
Total crime rate	30.7	32.9
Violent	1.6	1.9
Non-violent	29.1	31.0

Public School District

(for school year 2007-08 except as noted)

Collingswood Borough School District
200 Lees Avenue
Collingswood, NJ 08108
(856) 962-5732

Superintendent	Scott A. Oswald
Number of schools	7
Grade plan	K-12
Enrollment	1,917
Attendance rate, '06-07	94.7%
Dropout rate	2.2%
Students per teacher	9.8
Per pupil expenditure	$15,090
Median faculty salary	$55,500
Median administrator salary	$104,507
Grade 12 enrollment	198
High school graduation rate	91.0%

Assessment test results
(percent scoring at proficient or advanced level)

	Language	Math
NJASK-Grade 3	88.7%	86.3%
GEPA-Grade 8	83.4%	89.5%
HSPA-High School	73.8%	79.1%

SAT Score Averages, 2006-07

Pct tested	Math	Verbal	Writing
61%	483	486	482

Teacher Qualifications

Avg. years of experience	10
Highly-qualified teachers one subject/all subjects	100%/100%

No Child Left Behind

AYP, 2006-07	Meets Standards

Municipal Finance

State Aid Programs, 2009

Total aid	$1,541,258
CMPTRA	560,351
Energy tax receipts	942,375
Garden State Trust	0

General Budget, 2008

Total tax levy	$26,742,501
County levy	6,506,262
County taxes	6,286,697
County library	0
County health	0
County open space	219,565
School levy	13,131,799
Muni. levy	7,104,440
Misc. revenues	11,834,837

Taxes

	2006	2007	2008
General tax rate per $100	5.081	5.335	2.459
County equalization ratio	59.55	50.18	101.29
Net valuation taxable	$478,689,900	$481,828,181	$1,087,721,362
State equalized value	$956,366,647	$1,069,383,628	$1,104,006,052

See Introduction for an explanation of all data sources.

Demographics & Socio-Economic Characteristics

(2000 US Census, except as noted)

Population

1980*	7,888
1990*	8,559
2000	12,331
Male	6,448
Female	5,883
2007 (estimate)*	10,091
Population density	321.1

Race & Hispanic Origin, 2000

Race

White	10,544
Black/African American	973
American Indian/Alaska Native	28
Asian	447
Native Hawaiian/Pacific Islander	1
Other race	179
Two or more races	159
Hispanic origin, total	520
Mexican	113
Puerto Rican	186
Cuban	15
Other Hispanic	206

Age & Nativity, 2000

Under 5 years	1,019
18 years and over	8,731
21 years and over	8,116
65 years and over	1,003
85 years and over	88
Median age	33.2
Native-born	11,271
Foreign-born	1,060

Educational Attainment, 2000

Population 25 years and over	7,254
Less than 9th grade	2.2%
High school grad or higher	95.0%
Bachelor's degree or higher	47.5%
Graduate degree	19.3%

Income & Poverty, 1999

Per capita income	$46,795
Median household income	$109,190
Median family income	$117,980
Persons in poverty	308
H'holds receiving public assistance	21
H'holds receiving social security	747

Households, 2000

Total households	3,513
With persons under 18	1,813
With persons over 65	697
Family households	3,195
Single-person households	262
Persons per household	3.17
Persons per family	3.33

Labor & Employment

Total civilian labor force, 2007**	4,950
Unemployment rate	3.4%
Total civilian labor force, 2000	4,692
Unemployment rate	3.6%

Employed persons 16 years and over by occupation, 2000

Managers & professionals	2,373
Service occupations	442
Sales & office occupations	1,183
Farming, fishing & forestry	8
Construction & maintenance	259
Production & transportation	259
Self-employed persons	375

‡ Branch of county library
* US Census Bureau
** New Jersey Department of Labor

See Introduction for an explanation of all data sources.

General Information

Township of Colts Neck
124 Cedar Dr
Colts Neck, NJ 07722
732-462-5470

Website	www.colts-neck.nj.us
Year of incorporation	1962
Land/water area (sq. miles)	31.43/0.68
Form of government	Township

Government

Legislative Districts

US Congressional	4
State Legislative	12

Local Officials, 2009

Mayor	Benjamin T. Forester
Manager	Robert Bowden
Clerk	Robert Bowden
Finance Dir	John Antonides
Tax Assessor	Eldo Magnani
Tax Collector	John Antonides
Attorney	John Bennett
Building	Henry Salerno
Planning	Timothy Anfuso
Engineering	Glenn Gerken
Public Works	Edward Thompson
Police Chief	Kevin Sauter
Emerg/Fire Director	Chris Quincannon

Housing & Construction

Housing Units, 2000*

Total	3,614
Median rent	$974
Median SF home value	$425,500

Permits for New Residential Construction

	Units	Value
Total, 2006	11	$4,994,905
Single family	11	$4,994,905
Total, 2007	13	$7,647,801
Single family	13	$7,647,801

Real Property Valuation, 2008

	Parcels	Valuation
Total	3,780	$1,441,492,800
Vacant	145	23,323,500
Residential	3,051	1,223,359,000
Commercial	68	78,003,100
Industrial	0	0
Apartments	0	0
Farm land	313	4,585,550
Farm homestead	203	112,221,650

Average Property Value & Tax, 2008

Residential value	$410,443
Property tax	$13,101
Tax credit/rebate	$1,343

Public Library

Colts Neck Branch Library‡
1 Winthrop Rd
Colts Neck, NJ 07722
732-431-5656

Branch Librarian	Virginia Lyons

Library statistics, 2007

see Monmouth County profile
for library system statistics

Public Safety

Number of officers, 2007	22

Crime	2006	2007
Total crimes	95	104
Violent	2	7
Murder	0	0
Rape	0	0
Robbery	1	2
Aggravated assault	1	5
Non-violent	93	97
Burglary	15	10
Larceny	76	83
Vehicle theft	2	4
Domestic violence	40	53
Arson	4	0
Total crime rate	8.2	9.0
Violent	0.2	0.6
Non-violent	8.0	8.4

Public School District

(for school year 2007-08 except as noted)

Colts Neck Township School District
70 Conover Road
Colts Neck, NJ 07722
(732) 946-0055

Superintendent	Ross E. Kasum
Number of schools	3
Grade plan	K-8
Enrollment	1,370
Attendance rate, '06-07	95.2%
Dropout rate	NA
Students per teacher	8.7
Per pupil expenditure	$14,846
Median faculty salary	$53,260
Median administrator salary	$113,353
Grade 12 enrollment	NA
High school graduation rate	NA

Assessment test results

(percent scoring at proficient or advanced level)

	Language	Math
NJASK-Grade 3	92.7%	92.7%
GEPA-Grade 8	91.5%	93.2%
HSPA-High School	NA	NA

SAT Score Averages, 2006-07

Pct tested	Math	Verbal	Writing
NA	NA	NA	NA

Teacher Qualifications

Avg. years of experience	8
Highly-qualified teachers one subject/all subjects	100%/100%

No Child Left Behind

AYP, 2006-07	Meets Standards

Municipal Finance

State Aid Programs, 2009

Total aid	$2,283,189
CMPTRA	0
Energy tax receipts	2,142,061
Garden State Trust	0

General Budget, 2008

Total tax levy	$46,051,837
County levy	8,803,474
County taxes	7,812,401
County library	470,125
County health	0
County open space	520,948
School levy	32,067,841
Muni. levy	5,180,523
Misc. revenues	5,911,040

Taxes	2006	2007	2008
General tax rate per $100	3.07	3.151	3.192
County equalization ratio	46.59	42.66	41.72
Net valuation taxable	$1,391,529,100	$1,414,928,678	$1,442,808,636
State equalized value	$3,263,252,356	$3,389,698,633	$1,592,474,271

Demographics & Socio-Economic Characteristics
(2000 US Census, except as noted)

Population
1980*	4,674
1990*	5,026
2000	5,259
Male	2,590
Female	2,669
2007 (estimate)*	5,411
Population density	166.7

Race & Hispanic Origin, 2000
Race
White	4,364
Black/African American	706
American Indian/Alaska Native	22
Asian	12
Native Hawaiian/Pacific Islander	1
Other race	53
Two or more races	101
Hispanic origin, total	203
Mexican	29
Puerto Rican	126
Cuban	1
Other Hispanic	47

Age & Nativity, 2000
Under 5 years	373
18 years and over	3,773
21 years and over	3,534
65 years and over	648
85 years and over	58
Median age	34.0
Native-born	5,200
Foreign-born	59

Educational Attainment, 2000
Population 25 years and over	3,281
Less than 9th grade	10.3%
High school grad or higher	63.2%
Bachelor's degree or higher	6.3%
Graduate degree	1.3%

Income & Poverty, 1999
Per capita income	$14,663
Median household income	$34,960
Median family income	$37,500
Persons in poverty	827
H'holds receiving public assistance	107
H'holds receiving social security	565

Households, 2000
Total households	1,873
With persons under 18	791
With persons over 65	490
Family households	1,368
Single-person households	400
Persons per household	2.80
Persons per family	3.22

Labor & Employment
Total civilian labor force, 2007**	2,551
Unemployment rate	6.1%
Total civilian labor force, 2000	2,362
Unemployment rate	9.1%

Employed persons 16 years and over by occupation, 2000
Managers & professionals	367
Service occupations	420
Sales & office occupations	421
Farming, fishing & forestry	58
Construction & maintenance	289
Production & transportation	593
Self-employed persons	137

General Information
Township of Commercial
Township Hall
1768 Main St
Port Norris, NJ 08349
856-785-3100
Website	(county website)
Year of incorporation	1874
Land/water area (sq. miles)	32.46/2.04
Form of government	Township

Government
Legislative Districts
US Congressional	2
State Legislative	3

Local Officials, 2009
Mayor	George W. Garrison
Manager	Judson Moore
Clerk	Hannah E. Nichols
Finance Dir	Judson Moore
Tax Assessor	Ruth Benz
Tax Collector	Grace Robinson
Attorney	Thomas E. Seeley
Building	David Dean
Comm Dev/Planning	NA
Engineering	Remington & Vernick
Public Works	John Barnes
Police Chief	NA
Fire/Emergency Dir	NA

Housing & Construction
Housing Units, 2000*
Total	2,171
Median rent	$689
Median SF home value	$66,100

Permits for New Residential Construction
	Units	Value
Total, 2006	9	$998,110
Single family	9	$998,110
Total, 2007	11	$1,229,539
Single family	11	$1,229,539

Real Property Valuation, 2008
	Parcels	Valuation
Total	4,061	$117,710,315
Vacant	1,768	9,268,175
Residential	2,135	97,090,890
Commercial	62	4,089,750
Industrial	18	5,914,700
Apartments	1	62,400
Farm land	55	546,000
Farm homestead	22	738,400

Average Property Value & Tax, 2008
Residential value	$45,354
Property tax	$1,916
Tax credit/rebate	$681

Public Library
Commercial Township Free Public Library
1628 Main St
Port Norris, NJ 08349
856-785-1900
Librarian	NA

Library statistics, 2007
Population served	NA
Full-time/total staff	NA/NA

	Total	Per capita
Holdings	NA	NA
Revenues	NA	NA
Expenditures	NA	NA
Annual visits	NA	NA
Internet terminals/annual users	NA/NA	

Public Safety
Number of officers, 2007	0

Crime	2006	2007
Total crimes	217	187
Violent	30	25
Murder	0	1
Rape	0	0
Robbery	6	4
Aggravated assault	24	20
Non-violent	187	162
Burglary	73	42
Larceny	102	108
Vehicle theft	12	12
Domestic violence	30	123
Arson	5	3
Total crime rate	40.2	34.5
Violent	5.6	4.6
Non-violent	34.6	29.9

Public School District
(for school year 2007-08 except as noted)

Commercial Township School District
1308 North Avenue, PO Box 650
Port Norris, NJ 08349
(856) 785-0840
Superintendent	Barry Ballard
Number of schools	2
Grade plan	K-8
Enrollment	671
Attendance rate, '06-07	92.7%
Dropout rate	NA
Students per teacher	11.1
Per pupil expenditure	$11,769
Median faculty salary	$49,300
Median administrator salary	$97,936
Grade 12 enrollment	NA
High school graduation rate	NA

Assessment test results
(percent scoring at proficient or advanced level)
	Language	Math
NJASK-Grade 3	95.0%	85.7%
GEPA-Grade 8	42.4%	72.9%
HSPA-High School	NA	NA

SAT Score Averages, 2006-07
Pct tested	Math	Verbal	Writing
NA	NA	NA	NA

Teacher Qualifications
Avg. years of experience	8
Highly-qualified teachers one subject/all subjects	100%/100%

No Child Left Behind
AYP, 2006-07	Meets Standards

Municipal Finance
State Aid Programs, 2009
Total aid	$703,320
CMPTRA	150,049
Energy tax receipts	408,659
Garden State Trust	114,689

General Budget, 2008
Total tax levy	$5,019,052
County levy	2,258,603
County taxes	2,135,035
County library	0
County health	99,817
County open space	23,751
School levy	1,662,641
Muni. levy	1,097,808
Misc. revenues	2,916,487

Taxes
	2006	2007	2008
General tax rate per $100	3.825	3.926	4.225
County equalization ratio	63.45	57.02	50.17
Net valuation taxable	$115,588,325	$116,782,824	$118,837,152
State equalized value	$204,051,705	$231,561,392	$245,339,109

* US Census Bureau
** New Jersey Department of Labor

Demographics & Socio-Economic Characteristics

(2000 US Census, except as noted)

Population

1980*	254
1990*	412
2000	468
Male	232
Female	236
2007 (estimate)*	520
Population density	65.9

Race & Hispanic Origin, 2000

Race

White	440
Black/African American	13
American Indian/Alaska Native	4
Asian	6
Native Hawaiian/Pacific Islander	0
Other race	3
Two or more races	2
Hispanic origin, total	14
Mexican	3
Puerto Rican	3
Cuban	5
Other Hispanic	3

Age & Nativity, 2000

Under 5 years	38
18 years and over	328
21 years and over	317
65 years and over	49
85 years and over	1
Median age	36.5
Native-born	453
Foreign-born	15

Educational Attainment, 2000

Population 25 years and over	325
Less than 9th grade	4.0%
High school grad or higher	84.6%
Bachelor's degree or higher	20.6%
Graduate degree	4.9%

Income & Poverty, 1999

Per capita income	$21,321
Median household income	$47,083
Median family income	$56,000
Persons in poverty	23
H'holds receiving public assistance	4
H'holds receiving social security	32

Households, 2000

Total households	172
With persons under 18	71
With persons over 65	37
Family households	121
Single-person households	39
Persons per household	2.72
Persons per family	3.21

Labor & Employment

Total civilian labor force, 2007**	245
Unemployment rate	4.0%
Total civilian labor force, 2000	231
Unemployment rate	3.5%

Employed persons 16 years and over by occupation, 2000

Managers & professionals	76
Service occupations	60
Sales & office occupations	31
Farming, fishing & forestry	0
Construction & maintenance	28
Production & transportation	28
Self-employed persons	20

* US Census Bureau
** New Jersey Department of Labor

See Introduction for an explanation of all data sources.

General Information

City of Corbin
316 Route 50
Corbin City, NJ 08270
609-628-2673

Email	corbincity@plexi.com
Year of incorporation	1922
Land/water area (sq. miles)	7.89/1.10
Form of government	City

Government

Legislative Districts

US Congressional	2
State Legislative	2

Local Officials, 2009

Mayor	Carol Foster
Manager	Carol Foster
Clerk	Joanne Siedlecki
Finance Dir	James Nicola
Tax Assessor	Bernadette Leonardi
Tax Collector	Beverly Totton
Attorney	Richard Russell
Building	(State)
Comm Dev/Planning	NA
Engineering	David Scheidegg
Public Works	NA
Police Chief	NA
Fire/Emergency Dir	NA

Housing & Construction

Housing Units, 2000*

Total	204
Median rent	$792
Median SF home value	$150,000

Permits for New Residential Construction

	Units	Value
Total, 2006	2	$115,993
Single family	2	$115,993
Total, 2007	3	$290,850
Single family	3	$290,850

Real Property Valuation, 2008

	Parcels	Valuation
Total	319	$30,488,900
Vacant	76	1,742,000
Residential	212	25,984,500
Commercial	15	2,398,900
Industrial	0	0
Apartments	0	0
Farm land	13	105,500
Farm homestead	3	258,000

Average Property Value & Tax, 2008

Residential value	$122,058
Property tax	$4,282
Tax credit/rebate	$853

Public Library

No public municipal library

Library statistics, 2007

Population served	NA
Full-time/total staff	NA/NA

	Total	Per capita
Holdings	NA	NA
Revenues	NA	NA
Expenditures	NA	NA
Annual visits	NA	NA
Internet terminals/annual users	NA/NA	

Public Safety

Number of officers, 2007	0

Crime	2006	2007
Total crimes	15	19
Violent	1	0
Murder	0	0
Rape	0	0
Robbery	0	0
Aggravated assault	1	0
Non-violent	14	19
Burglary	5	6
Larceny	8	13
Vehicle theft	1	0
Domestic violence	1	4
Arson	0	0
Total crime rate	28.2	35.8
Violent	1.9	0.0
Non-violent	26.4	35.8

Public School District

(for school year 2007-08 except as noted)

Corbin City School District
501 Atlantic Avenue, Suite 1
Ocean City, NJ 08226

No schools in district - sends students to
Upper Township and Ocean City schools

Per pupil expenditure	NA
Median faculty salary	NA
Median administrator salary	NA
Grade 12 enrollment	NA
High school graduation rate	NA

Assessment test results

(percent scoring at proficient or advanced level)

	Language	Math
NJASK-Grade 3	NA	NA
GEPA-Grade 8	NA	NA
HSPA-High School	NA	NA

SAT Score Averages, 2006-07

Pct tested	Math	Verbal	Writing
NA	NA	NA	NA

Teacher Qualifications

Avg. years of experience	NA
Highly-qualified teachers one subject/all subjects	NA/NA

No Child Left Behind

AYP, 2006-07	NA

Municipal Finance

State Aid Programs, 2009

Total aid	$155,320
CMPTRA	12
Energy tax receipts	71,656
Garden State Trust	70,569

General Budget, 2008

Total tax levy	$1,071,649
County levy	200,622
County taxes	158,067
County library	20,272
County health	8,295
County open space	13,987
School levy	786,464
Muni. levy	84,563
Misc. revenues	455,127

Taxes

	2006	2007	2008
General tax rate per $100	3.162	3.349	3.509
County equalization ratio	104.08	62.9	43.69
Net valuation taxable	$29,936,500	$29,499,474	$30,546,274
State equalized value	$47,707,801	$67,423,724	$53,621,850

Demographics & Socio-Economic Characteristics

(2000 US Census, except as noted)

Population

1980*	1,927
1990*	2,500
2000	3,227
Male	1,558
Female	1,669
2007 (estimate)*	3,944
Population density	294.1

Race & Hispanic Origin, 2000

Race

White	2,865
Black/African American	73
American Indian/Alaska Native	0
Asian	239
Native Hawaiian/Pacific Islander	0
Other race	7
Two or more races	43
Hispanic origin, total	55
Mexican	4
Puerto Rican	8
Cuban	6
Other Hispanic	37

Age & Nativity, 2000

Under 5 years	214
18 years and over	2,245
21 years and over	2,191
65 years and over	363
85 years and over	64
Median age	39.6
Native-born	2,857
Foreign-born	370

Educational Attainment, 2000

Population 25 years and over	2,142
Less than 9th grade	3.4%
High school grad or higher	93.5%
Bachelor's degree or higher	62.7%
Graduate degree	27.5%

Income & Poverty, 1999

Per capita income	$50,698
Median household income	$111,680
Median family income	$128,410
Persons in poverty	51
H'holds receiving public assistance	2
H'holds receiving social security	261

Households, 2000

Total households	1,091
With persons under 18	517
With persons over 65	236
Family households	877
Single-person households	178
Persons per household	2.92
Persons per family	3.31

Labor & Employment

Total civilian labor force, 2007**	1,694
Unemployment rate	1.9%
Total civilian labor force, 2000	1,551
Unemployment rate	1.8%

Employed persons 16 years and over by occupation, 2000

Managers & professionals	920
Service occupations	122
Sales & office occupations	360
Farming, fishing & forestry	0
Construction & maintenance	32
Production & transportation	89
Self-employed persons	114

* US Census Bureau
** New Jersey Department of Labor

General Information

Township of Cranbury
23A N Main St
Cranbury, NJ 08512
609-395-0900

Website	www.cranburytownship.org
Year of incorporation	1872
Land/water area (sq. miles)	13.41/0.04
Form of government	Township

Government

Legislative Districts

US Congressional	12
State Legislative	14

Local Officials, 2009

Mayor	Pari Stave
Manager	Christine Smeltzer
Clerk	Kathleen Cunningham
Finance Dir	Christine Smeltzer
Tax Assessor	Steve Benner
Tax Collector	NA
Attorney	Trishka Waterbury
Building	Greg Farrington
Comm Dev/Planning	NA
Engineering	Cathleen Marcelli
Public Works	Jerry Thorne
Police Chief	Edward L. Kahler III
Emerg/Fire Director	Sam Distasio

Housing & Construction

Housing Units, 2000*

Total	1,121
Median rent	$756
Median SF home value	$361,000

Permits for New Residential Construction

	Units	Value
Total, 2006	25	$3,525,955
Single family	25	$3,525,955
Total, 2007	0	$0
Single family	0	$0

Real Property Valuation, 2008

	Parcels	Valuation
Total	1,519	$1,848,504,800
Vacant	68	15,432,100
Residential	1,160	775,832,000
Commercial	98	253,948,400
Industrial	41	765,257,900
Apartments	1	904,000
Farm land	100	2,956,000
Farm homestead	51	34,174,400

Average Property Value & Tax, 2008

Residential value	$668,874
Property tax	$10,262
Tax credit/rebate	$1,110

Public Library

Cranbury Public Library
23 N Main St
Cranbury, NJ 08512
609-655-0555

Director.............. Marilynn Mullen

Library statistics, 2007

Population served	3,227
Full-time/total staff	2/2

	Total	Per capita
Holdings	26,552	8.23
Revenues	$577,798	$179.05
Expenditures	$424,690	$131.61
Annual visits	61,729	19.13
Internet terminals/annual users	29/21,000	

Public Safety

Number of officers, 2007 19

Crime	2006	2007
Total crimes	79	62
Violent	8	6
Murder	0	0
Rape	1	1
Robbery	2	0
Aggravated assault	5	5
Non-violent	71	56
Burglary	15	6
Larceny	51	45
Vehicle theft	5	5
Domestic violence	6	8
Arson	0	0
Total crime rate	20.0	15.9
Violent	2.0	1.5
Non-violent	18.0	14.4

Public School District

(for school year 2007-08 except as noted)

Cranbury Township School District
23 North Main Street
Cranbury, NJ 08512
(609) 395-1700

Superintendent	John Haney
Number of schools	1
Grade plan	K-8
Enrollment	632
Attendance rate, '06-07	96.5%
Dropout rate	NA
Students per teacher	9.5
Per pupil expenditure	$17,618
Median faculty salary	$56,044
Median administrator salary	$107,080
Grade 12 enrollment	NA
High school graduation rate	NA

Assessment test results

(percent scoring at proficient or advanced level)

	Language	Math
NJASK-Grade 3	96.9%	96.8%
GEPA-Grade 8	97.5%	100.0%
HSPA-High School	NA	NA

SAT Score Averages, 2006-07

Pct tested	Math	Verbal	Writing
NA	NA	NA	NA

Teacher Qualifications

Avg. years of experience	10
Highly-qualified teachers one subject/all subjects	98.0%/98.0%

No Child Left Behind

AYP, 2006-07 .... Meets Standards

Municipal Finance

State Aid Programs, 2009

Total aid	$635,798
CMPTRA	25,275
Energy tax receipts	583,118
Garden State Trust	1,834

General Budget, 2008

Total tax levy	$28,397,519
County levy	5,258,533
County taxes	4,701,864
County library	0
County health	0
County open space	556,668
School levy	15,818,070
Muni. levy	7,320,916
Misc. revenues	5,390,401

Taxes

	2006	2007	2008
General tax rate per $100	3.84	1.47	1.534
County equalization ratio	42.31	102.11	101.38
Net valuation taxable	$619,376,965	$1,856,220,613	$1,850,944,368
State equalized value	$1,751,591,280	$1,830,984,675	$1,848,544,432

See Introduction for an explanation of all data sources.

Demographics & Socio-Economic Characteristics

(2000 US Census, except as noted)

Population
1980*	24,573
1990*	22,633
2000	22,578
Male	10,724
Female	11,854
2007 (estimate)*	22,003
Population density	4,564.9

Race & Hispanic Origin, 2000
Race
White	21,156
Black/African American	583
American Indian/Alaska Native	9
Asian	485
Native Hawaiian/Pacific Islander	5
Other race	151
Two or more races	189
Hispanic origin, total	879
Mexican	47
Puerto Rican	241
Cuban	198
Other Hispanic	393

Age & Nativity, 2000
Under 5 years	1,465
18 years and over	17,316
21 years and over	16,793
65 years and over	4,048
85 years and over	615
Median age	40.4
Native-born	20,613
Foreign-born	1,965

Educational Attainment, 2000
Population 25 years and over	16,204
Less than 9th grade	2.9%
High school grad or higher	91.5%
Bachelor's degree or higher	43.0%
Graduate degree	16.0%

Income & Poverty, 1999
Per capita income	$33,283
Median household income	$76,338
Median family income	$86,624
Persons in poverty	553
H'holds receiving public assistance	54
H'holds receiving social security	2,438

Households, 2000
Total households	8,397
With persons under 18	2,902
With persons over 65	2,509
Family households	6,225
Single-person households	1,842
Persons per household	2.62
Persons per family	3.09

Labor & Employment
Total civilian labor force, 2007**	12,402
Unemployment rate	2.4%
Total civilian labor force, 2000	12,149
Unemployment rate	4.1%

Employed persons 16 years and over by occupation, 2000
Managers & professionals	5,895
Service occupations	1,065
Sales & office occupations	3,161
Farming, fishing & forestry	0
Construction & maintenance	798
Production & transportation	727
Self-employed persons	584

*   US Census Bureau
** New Jersey Department of Labor

General Information
Township of Cranford
8 Springfield Ave
Cranford, NJ 07016
908-709-7200
Website	www.cranford.com/township
Year of incorporation	1871
Land/water area (sq. miles)	4.82/0.02
Form of government	Township

Government

Legislative Districts
US Congressional	7
State Legislative	21

Local Officials, 2009
Mayor	David Robinson
Manager	Marlena Schmid
Clerk	Tara Rowley
Finance Dir	Thomas Grady
Tax Assessor	Peter Barnett
Tax Collector	Thomas Grady
Attorney	Carl Woodward III
Building	Richard Belluscio
Comm Dev/Planning	NA
Engineering	Richard Marsden
Public Works	Wayne Rozman
Police Chief	Eric G. Mason
Emerg/Fire Director	Leonard Dolan III

Housing & Construction

Housing Units, 2000*
Total	8,560
Median rent	$867
Median SF home value	$233,600

Permits for New Residential Construction
	Units	Value
Total, 2006	29	$3,294,076
Single family	29	$3,294,076
Total, 2007	28	$3,726,397
Single family	23	$3,419,897

Real Property Valuation, 2008
	Parcels	Valuation
Total	7,901	$1,649,946,400
Vacant	103	10,286,500
Residential	7,460	1,349,760,700
Commercial	286	235,664,800
Industrial	42	47,977,400
Apartments	9	6,151,800
Farm land	1	105,200
Farm homestead	0	0

Average Property Value & Tax, 2008
Residential value	$180,933
Property tax	$8,450
Tax credit/rebate	$1,206

Public Library
Cranford Public Library
224 Walnut Ave
Cranford, NJ 07016
908-709-7272
Director	John Malar

Library statistics, 2007
Population served	22,578
Full-time/total staff	5/11

	Total	Per capita
Holdings	139,057	6.16
Revenues	$1,451,199	$64.27
Expenditures	$1,402,860	$62.13
Annual visits	187,440	8.30
Internet terminals/annual users	9/17,286	

Public Safety
Number of officers, 2007 52
Crime	2006	2007
Total crimes	290	242
Violent	5	12
Murder	1	0
Rape	0	1
Robbery	3	6
Aggravated assault	1	5
Non-violent	285	230
Burglary	31	32
Larceny	247	192
Vehicle theft	7	6
Domestic violence	106	102
Arson	1	0
Total crime rate	12.9	10.8
Violent	0.2	0.5
Non-violent	12.7	10.3

Public School District
(for school year 2007-08 except as noted)

Cranford Township School District
132 Thomas Street
Cranford, NJ 07016
(908) 709-6202
Superintendent	Gayle Carrick
Number of schools	7
Grade plan	K-12
Enrollment	3,712
Attendance rate, '06-07	96.2%
Dropout rate	0.0%
Students per teacher	10.7
Per pupil expenditure	$12,939
Median faculty salary	$57,699
Median administrator salary	$115,560
Grade 12 enrollment	264
High school graduation rate	99.2%

Assessment test results
(percent scoring at proficient or advanced level)
	Language	Math
NJASK-Grade 3	92.6%	92.6%
GEPA-Grade 8	89.1%	95.4%
HSPA-High School	88.8%	94.7%

SAT Score Averages, 2006-07
Pct tested	Math	Verbal	Writing
99%	551	532	535

Teacher Qualifications
Avg. years of experience	9
Highly-qualified teachers one subject/all subjects	100%/100%

No Child Left Behind
AYP, 2006-07	Meets Standards

Municipal Finance

State Aid Programs, 2009
Total aid	$3,739,898
CMPTRA	372,413
Energy tax receipts	3,273,988
Garden State Trust	0

General Budget, 2008
Total tax levy	$77,180,659
County levy	14,453,145
County taxes	13,818,896
County library	0
County health	0
County open space	634,249
School levy	42,630,358
Muni. levy	20,097,156
Misc. revenues	9,553,597

Taxes
Taxes	2006	2007	2008
General tax rate per $100	4.191	4.458	4.671
County equalization ratio	43.85	41.48	39.24
Net valuation taxable	$1,658,492,700	$1,647,063,669	$1,652,671,044
State equalized value	$4,001,321,019	$4,193,673,827	$4,297,223,343

See Introduction for an explanation of all data sources.

Demographics & Socio-Economic Characteristics
(2000 US Census, except as noted)

Population
1980*	7,609
1990*	7,558
2000	7,746
Male	3,726
Female	4,020
2007 (estimate)*	8,553
Population density	3,996.7

Race & Hispanic Origin, 2000
Race
White	6,046
Black/African American	71
American Indian/Alaska Native	3
Asian	1,444
Native Hawaiian/Pacific Islander	0
Other race	50
Two or more races	132
Hispanic origin, total	309
Mexican	7
Puerto Rican	71
Cuban	79
Other Hispanic	152

Age & Nativity, 2000
Under 5 years	530
18 years and over	5,710
21 years and over	5,563
65 years and over	1,308
85 years and over	177
Median age	40.9
Native-born	5,848
Foreign-born	1,898

Educational Attainment, 2000
Population 25 years and over	5,408
Less than 9th grade	2.6%
High school grad or higher	92.3%
Bachelor's degree or higher	50.1%
Graduate degree	17.6%

Income & Poverty, 1999
Per capita income	$41,573
Median household income	$84,692
Median family income	$96,245
Persons in poverty	232
H'holds receiving public assistance	36
H'holds receiving social security	807

Households, 2000
Total households	2,630
With persons under 18	1,113
With persons over 65	873
Family households	2,163
Single-person households	418
Persons per household	2.91
Persons per family	3.26

Labor & Employment
Total civilian labor force, 2007**	3,943
Unemployment rate	2.2%
Total civilian labor force, 2000	3,731
Unemployment rate	2.3%

Employed persons 16 years and over by occupation, 2000
Managers & professionals	1,955
Service occupations	284
Sales & office occupations	982
Farming, fishing & forestry	0
Construction & maintenance	291
Production & transportation	132
Self-employed persons	274

* US Census Bureau
** New Jersey Department of Labor

General Information
Borough of Cresskill
67 Union Ave
Cresskill, NJ 07626
201-569-5400

Website	www.cresskillboro.com
Year of incorporation	1894
Land/water area (sq. miles)	2.14/0.00
Form of government	Borough

Government
Legislative Districts
US Congressional	5
State Legislative	39

Local Officials, 2009
Mayor	Benedict Romeo
Manager/Admin	Andrew Vaccaro
Clerk	Barbara Nasuto
Finance Dir	Harold Laufeld
Tax Assessor	James Anzevino
Tax Collector	Harold Laufeld
Attorney	Vincent Salvatore
Building	Edward Rossi
Comm Dev/Planning	NA
Engineering	Paul Azzolina
Public Works	Kevin Terhune
Police Chief	Edward Wrixon
Fire Chief	Christopher Ulshoefer

Housing & Construction
Housing Units, 2000*
Total	2,702
Median rent	$1,571
Median SF home value	$281,100

Permits for New Residential Construction
	Units	Value
Total, 2006	90	$9,366,762
Single family	14	$6,587,385
Total, 2007	51	$8,012,750
Single family	11	$4,552,750

Real Property Valuation, 2008
	Parcels	Valuation
Total	2,902	$1,792,646,400
Vacant	96	29,370,600
Residential	2,716	1,623,996,100
Commercial	83	129,953,800
Industrial	2	3,985,100
Apartments	5	5,340,800
Farm land	0	0
Farm homestead	0	0

Average Property Value & Tax, 2008
Residential value	$597,937
Property tax	$12,547
Tax credit/rebate	$1,345

Public Library
Cresskill Public Library
53 Union Ave
Cresskill, NJ 07626
201-567-3521

Director	Alice Chi

Library statistics, 2007
Population served	7,746
Full-time/total staff	2/5

	Total	Per capita
Holdings	60,226	7.78
Revenues	$795,645	$102.72
Expenditures	$708,111	$91.42
Annual visits	76,300	9.85
Internet terminals/annual users	11/15,572	

Public Safety
Number of officers, 2007 ... 22
Crime	2006	2007
Total crimes	28	67
Violent	1	0
Murder	0	0
Rape	0	0
Robbery	0	0
Aggravated assault	1	0
Non-violent	27	67
Burglary	8	6
Larceny	18	60
Vehicle theft	1	1
Domestic violence	0	5
Arson	0	1
Total crime rate	3.3	7.9
Violent	0.1	0.0
Non-violent	3.2	7.9

Public School District
(for school year 2007-08 except as noted)

Cresskill School District
One Lincoln Drive
Cresskill, NJ 07626
(201) 227-7791

Superintendent	Loretta Bellina
Number of schools	3
Grade plan	K-12
Enrollment	1,689
Attendance rate, '06-07	96.1%
Dropout rate	0.4%
Students per teacher	12.0
Per pupil expenditure	$12,964
Median faculty salary	$62,913
Median administrator salary	$119,175
Grade 12 enrollment	135
High school graduation rate	97.7%

Assessment test results
(percent scoring at proficient or advanced level)
	Language	Math
NJASK-Grade 3	96.2%	93.8%
GEPA-Grade 8	88.7%	94.6%
HSPA-High School	89.6%	96.0%

SAT Score Averages, 2006-07
Pct tested	Math	Verbal	Writing
94%	563	542	553

Teacher Qualifications
Avg. years of experience	7
Highly-qualified teachers one subject/all subjects	100%/100%

No Child Left Behind
AYP, 2006-07	Meets Standards

Municipal Finance
State Aid Programs, 2009
Total aid	$1,085,575
CMPTRA	0
Energy tax receipts	1,042,152
Garden State Trust	0

General Budget, 2008
Total tax levy	$37,629,078
County levy	4,633,840
County taxes	4,381,203
County library	0
County health	0
County open space	252,637
School levy	22,062,479
Muni. levy	10,932,759
Misc. revenues	3,911,339

Taxes
	2006	2007	2008
General tax rate per $100	1.87	1.99	2.101
County equalization ratio	87.6	77.03	71.10
Net valuation taxable	$1,773,432,200	$1,797,946,077	$1,793,285,475
State equalized value	$2,303,050,977	$2,528,486,659	$2,692,300,336

See Introduction for an explanation of all data sources.

Demographics & Socio-Economic Characteristics

(2000 US Census, except as noted)

Population

1980*	1,952
1990*	1,179
2000	1,070
Male	535
Female	535
2007 (estimate)*	1,047
Population density	858.2

Race & Hispanic Origin, 2000

Race

White	1,010
Black/African American	13
American Indian/Alaska Native	1
Asian	3
Native Hawaiian/Pacific Islander	0
Other race	29
Two or more races	14
Hispanic origin, total	54
Mexican	10
Puerto Rican	7
Cuban	2
Other Hispanic	35

Age & Nativity, 2000

Under 5 years	53
18 years and over	851
21 years and over	818
65 years and over	286
85 years and over	25
Median age	44.6
Native-born	935
Foreign-born	135

Educational Attainment, 2000

Population 25 years and over	756
Less than 9th grade	2.2%
High school grad or higher	88.6%
Bachelor's degree or higher	26.9%
Graduate degree	8.2%

Income & Poverty, 1999

Per capita income	$38,510
Median household income	$58,472
Median family income	$65,313
Persons in poverty	120
H'holds receiving public assistance	3
H'holds receiving social security	191

Households, 2000

Total households	434
With persons under 18	96
With persons over 65	194
Family households	290
Single-person households	126
Persons per household	2.46
Persons per family	3.02

Labor & Employment

Total civilian labor force, 2007**	384
Unemployment rate	2.5%
Total civilian labor force, 2000	359
Unemployment rate	3.1%

Employed persons 16 years and over by occupation, 2000

Managers & professionals	131
Service occupations	51
Sales & office occupations	139
Farming, fishing & forestry	0
Construction & maintenance	15
Production & transportation	12
Self-employed persons	35

* US Census Bureau
** New Jersey Department of Labor

See Introduction for an explanation of all data sources.

General Information

Borough of Deal
PO Box 56
Deal, NJ 07723
732-531-1454

Website	www.dealborough.com
Year of incorporation	1898
Land/water area (sq. miles)	1.22/0.08
Form of government	Commission

Government

Legislative Districts

US Congressional	6
State Legislative	11

Local Officials, 2009

Mayor	Harry Franco
Manager	James Rogers
Clerk	James Rogers
Finance Dir	Thomas Seaman
Tax Assessor	Peter Barnett
Tax Collector	Theresa Davis
Attorney	Martin Barger
Building	Joe Ciccone
Comm Dev/Planning	NA
Engineering	Leon Avakian
Public Works	Brendan Kelly
Police Chief	Stephen Carasia
Emerg/Fire Director	Richard Fronapfel

Housing & Construction

Housing Units, 2000*

Total	953
Median rent	$950
Median SF home value	$553,800

Permits for New Residential Construction

	Units	Value
Total, 2006	3	$31,500
Single family	3	$31,500
Total, 2007	6	$1,110,000
Single family	6	$1,110,000

Real Property Valuation, 2008

	Parcels	Valuation
Total	932	$1,105,594,300
Vacant	57	47,043,100
Residential	855	1,042,771,600
Commercial	16	13,309,100
Industrial	0	0
Apartments	4	2,470,500
Farm land	0	0
Farm homestead	0	0

Average Property Value & Tax, 2008

Residential value	$1,219,616
Property tax	$14,318
Tax credit/rebate	$1,323

Public Library

No public municipal library

Library statistics, 2007

Population served	NA
Full-time/total staff	NA/NA

	Total	Per capita
Holdings	NA	NA
Revenues	NA	NA
Expenditures	NA	NA
Annual visits	NA	NA
Internet terminals/annual users	NA/NA	

Public Safety

Number of officers, 2007	16

Crime	2006	2007
Total crimes	43	55
Violent	3	3
Murder	0	0
Rape	0	1
Robbery	0	0
Aggravated assault	3	2
Non-violent	40	52
Burglary	5	22
Larceny	35	29
Vehicle theft	0	1
Domestic violence	4	4
Arson	0	0
Total crime rate	41.2	52.7
Violent	2.9	2.9
Non-violent	38.4	49.8

Public School District

(for school year 2007-08 except as noted)

Deal Borough School District
201 Roseld Avenue
Deal, NJ 07723
(732) 531-0480

Superintendent	Anthony F. Moro Jr
Number of schools	1
Grade plan	K-8
Enrollment	108
Attendance rate, '06-07	94.2%
Dropout rate	NA
Students per teacher	7.8
Per pupil expenditure	$19,209
Median faculty salary	$45,360
Median administrator salary	$139,482
Grade 12 enrollment	NA
High school graduation rate	NA

Assessment test results

(percent scoring at proficient or advanced level)

	Language	Math
NJASK-Grade 3	NA	NA
GEPA-Grade 8	73.3%	100.0%
HSPA-High School	NA	NA

SAT Score Averages, 2006-07

Pct tested	Math	Verbal	Writing
NA	NA	NA	NA

Teacher Qualifications

Avg. years of experience	11
Highly-qualified teachers one subject/all subjects	100%/100%

No Child Left Behind

AYP, 2006-07 .... Meets Standards

Municipal Finance

State Aid Programs, 2009

Total aid	$479,456
CMPTRA	0
Energy tax receipts	455,483
Garden State Trust	0

General Budget, 2008

Total tax levy	$12,984,849
County levy	6,736,631
County taxes	5,978,131
County library	359,775
County health	0
County open space	398,725
School levy	1,818,628
Muni. levy	4,429,590
Misc. revenues	3,778,518

Taxes

	2006	2007	2008
General tax rate per $100	0.999	1.087	1.174
County equalization ratio	58.2	48.99	41.71
Net valuation taxable	$1,101,444,300	$1,106,427,167	$1,106,060,108
State equalized value	$2,249,013,616	$2,651,846,696	$3,445,743,076

Demographics & Socio-Economic Characteristics

(2000 US Census, except as noted)

Population
1980*	2,523
1990*	2,933
2000	2,927
Male	1,425
Female	1,502
2007 (estimate)*	3,242
Population density	192.5

Race & Hispanic Origin, 2000
Race
White	2,289
Black/African American	382
American Indian/Alaska Native	45
Asian	30
Native Hawaiian/Pacific Islander	0
Other race	89
Two or more races	92
Hispanic origin, total	174
Mexican	27
Puerto Rican	104
Cuban	1
Other Hispanic	42

Age & Nativity, 2000
Under 5 years	160
18 years and over	2,154
21 years and over	2,037
65 years and over	412
85 years and over	39
Median age	38.8
Native-born	2,841
Foreign-born	86

Educational Attainment, 2000
Population 25 years and over	1,912
Less than 9th grade	12.2%
High school grad or higher	73.4%
Bachelor's degree or higher	10.6%
Graduate degree	2.6%

Income & Poverty, 1999
Per capita income	$18,468
Median household income	$45,365
Median family income	$47,225
Persons in poverty	268
H'holds receiving public assistance	12
H'holds receiving social security	334

Households, 2000
Total households	1,013
With persons under 18	412
With persons over 65	304
Family households	785
Single-person households	178
Persons per household	2.86
Persons per family	3.22

Labor & Employment
Total civilian labor force, 2007**	1,537
Unemployment rate	4.3%
Total civilian labor force, 2000	1,402
Unemployment rate	6.1%

Employed persons 16 years and over by occupation, 2000
Managers & professionals	275
Service occupations	224
Sales & office occupations	357
Farming, fishing & forestry	11
Construction & maintenance	146
Production & transportation	303
Self-employed persons	60

* US Census Bureau
** New Jersey Department of Labor

General Information
Township of Deerfield
PO Box 350
Rosenhayn, NJ 08352
856-455-3200
Website	www.deerfieldtownship.org
Year of incorporation	1748
Land/water area (sq. miles)	16.84/0.00
Form of government	Township

Government
Legislative Districts
US Congressional	2
State Legislative	3

Local Officials, 2009
Mayor	Carol Musso
Manager	Karen Seifrit
Clerk	Karen Seifrit
Finance Dir	Ruth Moynihan
Tax Assessor	Donald Seifrit
Tax Collector	Ruth Moynihan
Attorney	Michael Testa
Building	Theodore Cooper
Comm Dev/Planning	NA
Engineering	J. Michael Fralinger
Public Works	Michael Laurella
Police Chief	NA
Fire/Emergency Dir	NA

Housing & Construction
Housing Units, 2000*
Total	1,065
Median rent	$646
Median SF home value	$99,500

Permits for New Residential Construction
	Units	Value
Total, 2006	16	$2,093,642
Single family	16	$2,093,642
Total, 2007	12	$1,441,237
Single family	12	$1,441,237

Real Property Valuation, 2008
	Parcels	Valuation
Total	1,716	$182,672,700
Vacant	287	7,483,900
Residential	938	124,748,600
Commercial	70	16,477,000
Industrial	2	8,193,600
Apartments	0	0
Farm land	255	2,702,600
Farm homestead	164	23,067,000

Average Property Value & Tax, 2008
Residential value	$134,134
Property tax	$4,319
Tax credit/rebate	$924

Public Library
No public municipal library

Library statistics, 2007
Population served	NA
Full-time/total staff	NA/NA

	Total	Per capita
Holdings	NA	NA
Revenues	NA	NA
Expenditures	NA	NA
Annual visits	NA	NA
Internet terminals/annual users	NA/NA	

Public Safety
Number of officers, 2007	0

Crime	2006	2007
Total crimes	47	81
Violent	4	5
Murder	0	0
Rape	0	0
Robbery	1	0
Aggravated assault	3	5
Non-violent	43	76
Burglary	17	27
Larceny	20	36
Vehicle theft	6	13
Domestic violence	1	18
Arson	2	3
Total crime rate	14.7	25.1
Violent	1.3	1.5
Non-violent	13.4	23.5

Public School District
(for school year 2007-08 except as noted)

Deerfield Township School District
Morton Avenue, PO Box 375
Rosenhayn, NJ 08352
(856) 451-6610
Chief School Admin	Edythe Austermuhl
Number of schools	1
Grade plan	K-8
Enrollment	352
Attendance rate, '06-07	94.7%
Dropout rate	NA
Students per teacher	10.2
Per pupil expenditure	$12,193
Median faculty salary	$59,373
Median administrator salary	$94,750
Grade 12 enrollment	NA
High school graduation rate	NA

Assessment test results
(percent scoring at proficient or advanced level)
	Language	Math
NJASK-Grade 3	87.8%	62.5%
GEPA-Grade 8	47.3%	65.8%
HSPA-High School	NA	NA

SAT Score Averages, 2006-07
Pct tested	Math	Verbal	Writing
NA	NA	NA	NA

Teacher Qualifications
Avg. years of experience	12
Highly-qualified teachers one subject/all subjects	100%/100%

No Child Left Behind
AYP, 2006-07	Meets Standards

Municipal Finance
State Aid Programs, 2009
Total aid	$398,693
CMPTRA	44,582
Energy tax receipts	340,307
Garden State Trust	759

General Budget, 2008
Total tax levy	$5,907,616
County levy	2,367,075
County taxes	2,237,734
County library	0
County health	104,480
County open space	24,861
School levy	3,521,896
Muni. levy	18,645
Misc. revenues	1,956,516

Taxes
	2006	2007	2008
General tax rate per $100	2.968	2.931	3.223
County equalization ratio	100.84	94.01	74.36
Net valuation taxable	$174,553,500	$181,724,786	$183,451,765
State equalized value	$186,636,081	$244,065,846	$225,027,408

See Introduction for an explanation of all data sources.

Demographics & Socio-Economic Characteristics

(2000 US Census, except as noted)

Population

1980*	3,730
1990*	3,316
2000	3,237
Male	1,568
Female	1,669
2007 (estimate)*	4,377
Population density	1,757.8

Race & Hispanic Origin, 2000

Race

White	3,104
Black/African American	62
American Indian/Alaska Native	8
Asian	13
Native Hawaiian/Pacific Islander	0
Other race	13
Two or more races	37
Hispanic origin, total	63
Mexican	13
Puerto Rican	42
Cuban	2
Other Hispanic	6

Age & Nativity, 2000

Under 5 years	184
18 years and over	2,430
21 years and over	2,326
65 years and over	430
85 years and over	36
Median age	37.0
Native-born	3,076
Foreign-born	161

Educational Attainment, 2000

Population 25 years and over	2,213
Less than 9th grade	4.7%
High school grad or higher	85.2%
Bachelor's degree or higher	14.8%
Graduate degree	4.7%

Income & Poverty, 1999

Per capita income	$21,096
Median household income	$50,106
Median family income	$56,985
Persons in poverty	305
H'holds receiving public assistance	36
H'holds receiving social security	268

Households, 2000

Total households	1,227
With persons under 18	444
With persons over 65	325
Family households	892
Single-person households	280
Persons per household	2.64
Persons per family	3.09

Labor & Employment

Total civilian labor force, 2007**	1,975
Unemployment rate	5.7%
Total civilian labor force, 2000	1,731
Unemployment rate	6.0%

Employed persons 16 years and over by occupation, 2000

Managers & professionals	426
Service occupations	223
Sales & office occupations	528
Farming, fishing & forestry	3
Construction & maintenance	178
Production & transportation	269
Self-employed persons	80

General Information

Township of Delanco
770 Coopertown Rd
Delanco, NJ 08075
856-461-0561

Website	www.delancotownship.com
Year of incorporation	1926
Land/water area (sq. miles)	2.49/0.90
Form of government	Township

Government

Legislative Districts

US Congressional	3
State Legislative	7

Local Officials, 2009

Mayor	Kate Fitzpatrick
Manager	Richard Schwab (Actg)
Clerk	Janice Lohr
Finance Dir	Robert Hudnell
Tax Assessor	Joseph Robinson
Tax Collector	Lynn Davis
Attorney	Doug Heinold
Building	Edward Schaefer
Comm Dev/Planning	NA
Engineering	Land Engineering
Public Works	John Fenimore
Police Chief	Edmund Parsons
Emerg/Fire Director	Keith Mohrmann

Housing & Construction

Housing Units, 2000*

Total	1,285
Median rent	$615
Median SF home value	$111,600

Permits for New Residential Construction

	Units	Value
Total, 2006	111	$10,301,535
Single family	111	$10,301,535
Total, 2007	135	$12,583,519
Single family	135	$12,583,519

Real Property Valuation, 2008

	Parcels	Valuation
Total	1,986	$469,097,700
Vacant	330	15,622,700
Residential	1,588	382,597,200
Commercial	43	27,602,300
Industrial	13	40,513,500
Apartments	4	1,730,000
Farm land	5	28,100
Farm homestead	3	1,003,900

Average Property Value & Tax, 2008

Residential value	$241,107
Property tax	$4,936
Tax credit/rebate	$956

Public Library

Delanco Public Library
1303 Burlington Ave
Delanco, NJ 08075
856-461-6850

Director	Katharina Radcliffe

Library statistics, 2007

Population served	3,237
Full-time/total staff	0/0

	Total	Per capita
Holdings	33,675	10.40
Revenues	$45,536	$14.07
Expenditures	$67,664	$20.90
Annual visits	5,345	1.65
Internet terminals/annual users	2/2,125	

Public Safety

Number of officers, 2007	10

Crime	2006	2007
Total crimes	90	95
Violent	4	6
Murder	0	0
Rape	0	1
Robbery	1	0
Aggravated assault	3	5
Non-violent	86	89
Burglary	20	31
Larceny	61	54
Vehicle theft	5	4
Domestic violence	39	64
Arson	1	0
Total crime rate	22.7	22.5
Violent	1.0	1.4
Non-violent	21.7	21.1

Public School District

(for school year 2007-08 except as noted)

Delanco Township School District
1301 Burlington Ave.
Delanco, NJ 08075
(856) 461-1905

Superintendent	Walter Bowyer (Int)
Number of schools	2
Grade plan	K-8
Enrollment	388
Attendance rate, '06-07	95.6%
Dropout rate	NA
Students per teacher	10.3
Per pupil expenditure	$12,732
Median faculty salary	$53,900
Median administrator salary	$92,404
Grade 12 enrollment	NA
High school graduation rate	NA

Assessment test results

(percent scoring at proficient or advanced level)

	Language	Math
NJASK-Grade 3	90.2%	87.8%
GEPA-Grade 8	63.6%	81.8%
HSPA-High School	NA	NA

SAT Score Averages, 2006-07

Pct tested	Math	Verbal	Writing
NA	NA	NA	NA

Teacher Qualifications

Avg. years of experience	12
Highly-qualified teachers one subject/all subjects	97.0%/97.0%

No Child Left Behind

AYP, 2006-07	Meets Standards

Municipal Finance

State Aid Programs, 2009

Total aid	$520,653
CMPTRA	147,635
Energy tax receipts	359,997
Garden State Trust	39

General Budget, 2008

Total tax levy	$9,613,879
County levy	1,745,568
County taxes	1,433,464
County library	132,331
County health	0
County open space	179,773
School levy	5,143,864
Muni. levy	2,724,446
Misc. revenues	3,445,014

Taxes

	2006	2007	2008
General tax rate per $100	3.887	1.97	2.048
County equalization ratio	64.38	114.25	105.82
Net valuation taxable	$214,307,200	$461,699,048	$469,585,913
State equalized value	$380,508,303	$436,330,855	$461,926,045

* US Census Bureau
** New Jersey Department of Labor

See Introduction for an explanation of all data sources.

Demographics & Socio-Economic Characteristics
(2000 US Census, except as noted)

Population
1980*	3,816
1990*	4,512
2000	4,478
Male	2,226
Female	2,252
2007 (estimate)*	4,688
Population density	127.6

Race & Hispanic Origin, 2000
Race
White	4,375
Black/African American	18
American Indian/Alaska Native	2
Asian	46
Native Hawaiian/Pacific Islander	1
Other race	11
Two or more races	25
Hispanic origin, total	51
Mexican	3
Puerto Rican	15
Cuban	12
Other Hispanic	21

Age & Nativity, 2000
Under 5 years	220
18 years and over	3,429
21 years and over	3,301
65 years and over	530
85 years and over	43
Median age	42.4
Native-born	4,279
Foreign-born	202

Educational Attainment, 2000
Population 25 years and over	3,163
Less than 9th grade	1.9%
High school grad or higher	91.1%
Bachelor's degree or higher	39.1%
Graduate degree	17.8%

Income & Poverty, 1999
Per capita income	$38,285
Median household income	$80,756
Median family income	$90,842
Persons in poverty	154
H'holds receiving public assistance	13
H'holds receiving social security	374

Households, 2000
Total households	1,643
With persons under 18	573
With persons over 65	367
Family households	1,303
Single-person households	243
Persons per household	2.72
Persons per family	3.06

Labor & Employment
Total civilian labor force, 2007**	2,761
Unemployment rate	1.9%
Total civilian labor force, 2000	2,482
Unemployment rate	1.8%

Employed persons 16 years and over by occupation, 2000
Managers & professionals	1,124
Service occupations	302
Sales & office occupations	587
Farming, fishing & forestry	5
Construction & maintenance	235
Production & transportation	184
Self-employed persons	291

General Information
Township of Delaware
PO Box 500
Sergeantsville, NJ 08557
609-397-3240
Website	www.delawaretwpnj.org
Year of incorporation	1838
Land/water area (sq. miles)	36.74/0.28
Form of government	Township

Government
Legislative Districts
US Congressional	12
State Legislative	23

Local Officials, 2009
Mayor	Kristin McCarthy
Manager/Admin	Erica DiGiovanni (Int)
Clerk	Judith Allen
Finance Dir	Linda Zengel
Tax Assessor	Michelle Trivigno
Tax Collector	Brigid Pfenninger
Attorney	Kristina Hadinger
Building	Phillip Izzo
Comm Dev/Planning	NA
Engineering	Richard Roseberry
Public Works	Jay Trstensky
Police Chief	Bruce Mast
Emerg/Fire Director	Ed Fleming

Housing & Construction
Housing Units, 2000*
Total	1,701
Median rent	$1,130
Median SF home value	$275,900

Permits for New Residential Construction
	Units	Value
Total, 2006	17	$4,406,569
Single family	17	$4,406,569
Total, 2007	9	$2,799,263
Single family	9	$2,799,263

Real Property Valuation, 2008
	Parcels	Valuation
Total	2,662	$896,606,420
Vacant	147	13,593,120
Residential	1,288	586,262,500
Commercial	34	18,483,500
Industrial	10	8,742,900
Apartments	2	1,065,700
Farm land	710	6,567,900
Farm homestead	471	261,890,800

Average Property Value & Tax, 2008
Residential value	$482,179
Property tax	$9,924
Tax credit/rebate	$1,281

Public Library
No public municipal library

Library statistics, 2007
Population served	NA
Full-time/total staff	NA/NA

	Total	Per capita
Holdings	NA	NA
Revenues	NA	NA
Expenditures	NA	NA
Annual visits	NA	NA
Internet terminals/annual users	NA/NA	

Public Safety
Number of officers, 2007 7
Crime	2006	2007
Total crimes	39	24
Violent	2	1
Murder	0	0
Rape	0	0
Robbery	0	0
Aggravated assault	2	1
Non-violent	37	23
Burglary	21	6
Larceny	16	12
Vehicle theft	0	5
Domestic violence	18	12
Arson	1	0
Total crime rate	8.3	5.1
Violent	0.4	0.2
Non-violent	7.8	4.9

Public School District
(for school year 2007-08 except as noted)

Delaware Township School District
501 Rosemont-Ringoes Road, PO Box 1000
Sergeantsville, NJ 08557
(609) 397-3179
Superintendent	Richard Wiener
Number of schools	1
Grade plan	K-8
Enrollment	479
Attendance rate, '06-07	95.5%
Dropout rate	NA
Students per teacher	9.2
Per pupil expenditure	$15,834
Median faculty salary	$57,749
Median administrator salary	$97,520
Grade 12 enrollment	NA
High school graduation rate	NA

Assessment test results
(percent scoring at proficient or advanced level)
	Language	Math
NJASK-Grade 3	92.6%	90.6%
GEPA-Grade 8	84.5%	87.7%
HSPA-High School	NA	NA

SAT Score Averages, 2006-07
Pct tested	Math	Verbal	Writing
NA	NA	NA	NA

Teacher Qualifications
Avg. years of experience	10
Highly-qualified teachers one subject/all subjects	97.5%/97.5%

No Child Left Behind
AYP, 2006-07 .... Meets Standards

Municipal Finance
State Aid Programs, 2009
Total aid	$476,626
CMPTRA	79,029
Energy tax receipts	366,014
Garden State Trust	44,291

General Budget, 2008
Total tax levy	$18,482,097
County levy	3,482,817
County taxes	2,914,987
County library	253,137
County health	0
County open space	314,693
School levy	12,361,155
Muni. levy	2,638,125
Misc. revenues	1,553,174

Taxes
	2006	2007	2008
General tax rate per $100	1.89	2.04	2.059
County equalization ratio	96.91	85.21	86.09
Net valuation taxable	$886,605,720	$891,383,319	$897,994,980
State equalized value	$967,603,697	$1,035,053,448	$1,031,142,115

* US Census Bureau
** New Jersey Department of Labor

See Introduction for an explanation of all data sources.

Demographics & Socio-Economic Characteristics

(2000 US Census, except as noted)

Population

1980*	14,811
1990*	13,178
2000	15,536
Male	7,646
Female	7,890
2007 (estimate)*	16,929
Population density	2,549.5

Race & Hispanic Origin, 2000

Race

White	12,875
Black/African American	1,464
American Indian/Alaska Native	27
Asian	435
Native Hawaiian/Pacific Islander	25
Other race	253
Two or more races	457
Hispanic origin, total	505
Mexican	51
Puerto Rican	253
Cuban	7
Other Hispanic	194

Age & Nativity, 2000

Under 5 years	970
18 years and over	11,722
21 years and over	11,197
65 years and over	1,672
85 years and over	132
Median age	36.7
Native-born	13,931
Foreign-born	1,605

Educational Attainment, 2000

Population 25 years and over	10,463
Less than 9th grade	3.9%
High school grad or higher	88.2%
Bachelor's degree or higher	27.3%
Graduate degree	8.1%

Income & Poverty, 1999

Per capita income	$25,312
Median household income	$58,526
Median family income	$67,895
Persons in poverty	637
H'holds receiving public assistance	140
H'holds receiving social security	1,249

Households, 2000

Total households	5,816
With persons under 18	2,175
With persons over 65	1,233
Family households	4,330
Single-person households	1,222
Persons per household	2.67
Persons per family	3.11

Labor & Employment

Total civilian labor force, 2007**	9,880
Unemployment rate	3.0%
Total civilian labor force, 2000	8,665
Unemployment rate	3.0%

Employed persons 16 years and over by occupation, 2000

Managers & professionals	3,206
Service occupations	858
Sales & office occupations	2,442
Farming, fishing & forestry	7
Construction & maintenance	738
Production & transportation	1,152
Self-employed persons	267

General Information

Township of Delran
900 S Chester Ave
Delran, NJ 08075
856-461-7734

Website	www.delrantownship.org
Year of incorporation	1880
Land/water area (sq. miles)	6.64/0.61
Form of government	Mayor-Council

Government

Legislative Districts

US Congressional	3
State Legislative	7

Local Officials, 2009

Mayor	Kenneth H. Paris
Manager	Jeffrey Hatcher
Clerk	Jamey Eggers
Treasurer	Teresa Leisse
Tax Assessor	Tom Davis
Tax Collector	Donna Ibbetson
Attorney	Douglas Long
Building	Hugh McCurley
Comm Dev/Planning	NA
Engineering	Gregory Valesi
Public Works	Ed Bart
Police Chief	Al Parente
Emerg/Fire Director	Joseph Bennett Sr

Housing & Construction

Housing Units, 2000*

Total	5,936
Median rent	$698
Median SF home value	$145,600

Permits for New Residential Construction

	Units	Value
Total, 2006	35	$6,412,980
Single family	35	$6,412,980
Total, 2007	5	$684,200
Single family	5	$684,200

Real Property Valuation, 2008

	Parcels	Valuation
Total	5,503	$1,553,748,900
Vacant	144	10,615,400
Residential	5,156	1,207,542,700
Commercial	142	174,869,700
Industrial	31	97,679,200
Apartments	2	60,038,300
Farm land	17	179,900
Farm homestead	11	2,823,700

Average Property Value & Tax, 2008

Residential value	$234,249
Property tax	$6,252
Tax credit/rebate	$1,068

Public Library

No public municipal library

Library statistics, 2007

Population served	NA
Full-time/total staff	NA/NA

	Total	Per capita
Holdings	NA	NA
Revenues	NA	NA
Expenditures	NA	NA
Annual visits	NA	NA
Internet terminals/annual users	NA/NA	

Public Safety

Number of officers, 2007	32

Crime	2006	2007
Total crimes	259	239
Violent	20	21
Murder	0	1
Rape	0	1
Robbery	8	11
Aggravated assault	12	8
Non-violent	239	218
Burglary	43	36
Larceny	183	159
Vehicle theft	13	23
Domestic violence	106	87
Arson	2	0
Total crime rate	14.9	13.8
Violent	1.1	1.2
Non-violent	13.7	12.6

Public School District

(for school year 2007-08 except as noted)

Delran Township School District
52 Hartford Road
Delran, NJ 08075
(856) 461-6800

Superintendent	George Sharp
Number of schools	4
Grade plan	K-12
Enrollment	2,850
Attendance rate, '06-07	94.9%
Dropout rate	0.0%
Students per teacher	12.0
Per pupil expenditure	$12,465
Median faculty salary	$53,500
Median administrator salary	$100,833
Grade 12 enrollment	199
High school graduation rate	98.6%

Assessment test results

(percent scoring at proficient or advanced level)

	Language	Math
NJASK-Grade 3	91.9%	91.0%
GEPA-Grade 8	68.7%	82.9%
HSPA-High School	76.8%	78.5%

SAT Score Averages, 2006-07

Pct tested	Math	Verbal	Writing
90%	483	471	461

Teacher Qualifications

Avg. years of experience	10

Highly-qualified teachers
one subject/all subjects ... 100%/100%

No Child Left Behind

AYP, 2006-07 ... Meets Standards

Municipal Finance

State Aid Programs, 2009

Total aid	$1,649,352
CMPTRA	369,572
Energy tax receipts	1,238,348
Garden State Trust	385

General Budget, 2008

Total tax levy	$41,524,892
County levy	7,213,854
County taxes	5,924,073
County library	546,979
County health	0
County open space	742,803
School levy	24,465,038
Muni. levy	9,846,000
Misc. revenues	5,452,550

Taxes

	2006	2007	2008
General tax rate per $100	2.405	2.63	2.670
County equalization ratio	98.94	88.78	84.09
Net valuation taxable	$1,530,562,200	$1,549,963,948	$1,555,805,607
State equalized value	$1,726,126,454	$1,842,850,095	$1,861,497,707

Demographics & Socio-Economic Characteristics
(2000 US Census, except as noted)

Population
1980*	4,963
1990*	4,800
2000	4,845
Male	2,376
Female	2,469
2007 (estimate)*	5,122
Population density	2,474.4

Race & Hispanic Origin, 2000
Race
White	3,744
Black/African American	24
American Indian/Alaska Native	1
Asian	981
Native Hawaiian/Pacific Islander	1
Other race	23
Two or more races	71
Hispanic origin, total	167
Mexican	14
Puerto Rican	27
Cuban	48
Other Hispanic	78

Age & Nativity, 2000
Under 5 years	297
18 years and over	3,444
21 years and over	3,320
65 years and over	698
85 years and over	67
Median age	41.1
Native-born	3,661
Foreign-born	1,184

Educational Attainment, 2000
Population 25 years and over	3,251
Less than 9th grade	2.9%
High school grad or higher	94.4%
Bachelor's degree or higher	58.9%
Graduate degree	24.1%

Income & Poverty, 1999
Per capita income	$51,939
Median household income	$103,286
Median family income	$113,144
Persons in poverty	79
H'holds receiving public assistance	14
H'holds receiving social security	448

Households, 2000
Total households	1,601
With persons under 18	752
With persons over 65	487
Family households	1,387
Single-person households	186
Persons per household	3.02
Persons per family	3.27

Labor & Employment
Total civilian labor force, 2007**	2,396
Unemployment rate	3.6%
Total civilian labor force, 2000	2,267
Unemployment rate	3.9%

Employed persons 16 years and over by occupation, 2000
Managers & professionals	1,344
Service occupations	186
Sales & office occupations	502
Farming, fishing & forestry	0
Construction & maintenance	75
Production & transportation	72
Self-employed persons	208

General Information
Borough of Demarest
118 Serpentine Rd
Demarest, NJ 07627
201-768-0167

Website	www.demarestnj.net
Year of incorporation	1903
Land/water area (sq. miles)	2.07/0.00
Form of government	Borough

Government
Legislative Districts
US Congressional	5
State Legislative	39

Local Officials, 2009
Mayor	Jim Carroll
Manager/Admin	NA
Clerk	Susan Jarsiewicz
Finance Dir	Maureen Neville
Tax Assessor	George Reggo
Tax Collector	Maureen Neville
Attorney	Gregg Paster
Building	Edward Rossi
Comm Dev/Planning	NA
Engineering	AFR Group
Public Works	John Crosman
Police Chief	James Powderly III
Emerg/Fire Director	Al Bolduc

Housing & Construction
Housing Units, 2000*
Total	1,634
Median rent	$2,001
Median SF home value	$360,300

Permits for New Residential Construction
	Units	Value
Total, 2006	33	$15,071,074
Single family	33	$15,071,074
Total, 2007	19	$11,957,201
Single family	19	$11,957,201

Real Property Valuation, 2008
	Parcels	Valuation
Total	1,685	$1,173,476,800
Vacant	64	21,534,400
Residential	1,612	1,113,563,000
Commercial	8	37,029,400
Industrial	0	0
Apartments	1	1,350,000
Farm land	0	0
Farm homestead	0	0

Average Property Value & Tax, 2008
Residential value	$690,796
Property tax	$14,507
Tax credit/rebate	$1,525

Public Library
Demarest Public Library
90 Hardenburgh Ave
Demarest, NJ 07627
201-768-8714

Director	Edna Ortega

Library statistics, 2007
Population served	4,845
Full-time/total staff	0/2

	Total	Per capita
Holdings	33,550	6.92
Revenues	$302,045	$62.34
Expenditures	$237,480	$49.02
Annual visits	12,000	2.48
Internet terminals/annual users	5/6,500	

Public Safety
Number of officers, 2007 14

Crime	2006	2007
Total crimes	46	28
Violent	0	0
Murder	0	0
Rape	0	0
Robbery	0	0
Aggravated assault	0	0
Non-violent	46	28
Burglary	3	4
Larceny	43	24
Vehicle theft	0	0
Domestic violence	6	3
Arson	0	0
Total crime rate	9.2	5.5
Violent	0.0	0.0
Non-violent	9.2	5.5

Public School District
(for school year 2007-08 except as noted)

Demarest School District
568 Piermont Road
Demarest, NJ 07627
(201) 768-6060

Superintendent	Gregg Hauser (Int)
Number of schools	3
Grade plan	K-8
Enrollment	663
Attendance rate, '06-07	96.2%
Dropout rate	NA
Students per teacher	10.0
Per pupil expenditure	$15,853
Median faculty salary	$56,994
Median administrator salary	$129,921
Grade 12 enrollment	NA
High school graduation rate	NA

Assessment test results
(percent scoring at proficient or advanced level)
	Language	Math
NJASK-Grade 3	100.0%	98.3%
GEPA-Grade 8	91.9%	95.4%
HSPA-High School	NA	NA

SAT Score Averages, 2006-07
Pct tested	Math	Verbal	Writing
NA	NA	NA	NA

Teacher Qualifications
Avg. years of experience	10
Highly-qualified teachers one subject/all subjects	98.0%/98.0%

No Child Left Behind
AYP, 2006-07	Meets Standards

Municipal Finance
State Aid Programs, 2009
Total aid	$552,253
CMPTRA	0
Energy tax receipts	530,163
Garden State Trust	0

General Budget, 2008
Total tax levy	$24,656,047
County levy	2,625,256
County taxes	2,483,195
County library	0
County health	0
County open space	142,061
School levy	17,045,280
Muni. levy	4,985,511
Misc. revenues	2,615,854

Taxes
	2006	2007	2008
General tax rate per $100	2	2.06	2.102
County equalization ratio	93.78	83	82.69
Net valuation taxable	$1,125,453,900	$1,143,304,777	$1,174,113,947
State equalized value	$1,356,579,708	$1,382,516,291	$1,430,660,057

See Introduction for an explanation of all data sources.

Demographics & Socio-Economic Characteristics
(2000 US Census, except as noted)

Population
1980*	3,989
1990*	5,574
2000	6,492
Male	3,188
Female	3,304
2007 (estimate)*	5,791
Population density	94.4

Race & Hispanic Origin, 2000
Race
White	6,325
Black/African American	62
American Indian/Alaska Native	6
Asian	28
Native Hawaiian/Pacific Islander	1
Other race	40
Two or more races	30
Hispanic origin, total	98
Mexican	45
Puerto Rican	34
Cuban	6
Other Hispanic	13

Age & Nativity, 2000
Under 5 years	429
18 years and over	4,656
21 years and over	4,442
65 years and over	798
85 years and over	162
Median age	37.4
Native-born	6,351
Foreign-born	152

Educational Attainment, 2000
Population 25 years and over	4,275
Less than 9th grade	5.2%
High school grad or higher	83.2%
Bachelor's degree or higher	20.5%
Graduate degree	5.1%

Income & Poverty, 1999
Per capita income	$21,455
Median household income	$56,595
Median family income	$61,445
Persons in poverty	346
H'holds receiving public assistance	38
H'holds receiving social security	533

Households, 2000
Total households	2,159
With persons under 18	970
With persons over 65	460
Family households	1,738
Single-person households	333
Persons per household	2.91
Persons per family	3.24

Labor & Employment
Total civilian labor force, 2007**	3,957
Unemployment rate	3.8%
Total civilian labor force, 2000	3,362
Unemployment rate	4.8%

Employed persons 16 years and over by occupation, 2000
Managers & professionals	968
Service occupations	557
Sales & office occupations	769
Farming, fishing & forestry	6
Construction & maintenance	574
Production & transportation	328
Self-employed persons	249

General Information
Township of Dennis
571 Petersburg Rd
Dennisville, NJ 08214
609-861-9700

Website	www.dennistwp.org
Year of incorporation	1827
Land/water area (sq. miles)	61.35/2.94
Form of government	Township

Government
Legislative Districts
US Congressional	2
State Legislative	1

Local Officials, 2009
Mayor	John Murphy
Manager	NA
Clerk	Jacqueline B. Justice
Finance Dir	Glenn O. Clarke
Tax Assessor	Patricia Sutton
Tax Collector	Michele T. Heim
Attorney	Jeffrey A. April
Building	James P. Cannon
Comm Dev/Planning	NA
Engineering	Andrew Previti
Public Works	Clarence F. Ryan
Police Chief	NA
Fire/Emergency Dir	NA

Housing & Construction
Housing Units, 2000*
Total	2,327
Median rent	$981
Median SF home value	$135,500

Permits for New Residential Construction
	Units	Value
Total, 2006	13	$2,390,018
Single family	13	$2,390,018
Total, 2007	13	$2,350,020
Single family	13	$2,350,020

Real Property Valuation, 2008
	Parcels	Valuation
Total	4,536	$1,041,122,800
Vacant	597	63,876,400
Residential	3,496	816,253,600
Commercial	176	142,283,700
Industrial	0	0
Apartments	0	0
Farm land	205	1,579,900
Farm homestead	62	17,129,200

Average Property Value & Tax, 2008
Residential value	$234,228
Property tax	$2,558
Tax credit/rebate	$723

Public Library
No public municipal library

Library statistics, 2007
Population served	NA
Full-time/total staff	NA/NA

	Total	Per capita
Holdings	NA	NA
Revenues	NA	NA
Expenditures	NA	NA
Annual visits	NA	NA
Internet terminals/annual users	NA/NA	

Public Safety
Number of officers, 2007 0
Crime	2006	2007
Total crimes	141	119
Violent	8	8
Murder	0	0
Rape	0	0
Robbery	2	2
Aggravated assault	6	6
Non-violent	133	111
Burglary	43	39
Larceny	86	67
Vehicle theft	4	5
Domestic violence	6	40
Arson	0	0
Total crime rate	23.2	20.1
Violent	1.3	1.4
Non-violent	21.9	18.8

Public School District
(for school year 2007-08 except as noted)

Dennis Township School District
601 Hagen Road
Cape May Court House, NJ 08210
(609) 861-0549

Superintendent	George Papp
Number of schools	2
Grade plan	K-8
Enrollment	697
Attendance rate, '06-07	84.2%
Dropout rate	NA
Students per teacher	8.7
Per pupil expenditure	$14,660
Median faculty salary	$52,991
Median administrator salary	$91,894
Grade 12 enrollment	NA
High school graduation rate	NA

Assessment test results
(percent scoring at proficient or advanced level)
	Language	Math
NJASK-Grade 3	95.4%	87.7%
GEPA-Grade 8	76.8%	89.9%
HSPA-High School	NA	NA

SAT Score Averages, 2006-07
Pct tested	Math	Verbal	Writing
NA	NA	NA	NA

Teacher Qualifications
Avg. years of experience	12
Highly-qualified teachers one subject/all subjects	100%/100%

No Child Left Behind
AYP, 2006-07 .... Meets Standards

Municipal Finance
State Aid Programs, 2009
Total aid	$1,939,277
CMPTRA	0
Energy tax receipts	1,660,860
Garden State Trust	193,198

General Budget, 2008
Total tax levy	$11,401,069
County levy	1,987,310
County taxes	1,579,588
County library	303,235
County health	0
County open space	104,486
School levy	8,102,428
Muni. levy	1,311,332
Misc. revenues	3,677,212

Taxes
	2006	2007	2008
General tax rate per $100	1.02	1.06	1.096
County equalization ratio	134.56	111.01	100.00
Net valuation taxable	$1,021,979,900	$1,028,766,249	$1,043,777,371
State equalized value	$923,078,987	$1,028,766,249	$1,057,597,118

* US Census Bureau
** New Jersey Department of Labor

See Introduction for an explanation of all data sources.

Demographics & Socio-Economic Characteristics
(2000 US Census, except as noted)

Population
1980*	14,380
1990*	13,812
2000	15,824
Male	7,617
Female	8,207
2007 (estimate)*	16,528
Population density	1,364.8

Race & Hispanic Origin, 2000
Race
White	14,659
Black/African American	181
American Indian/Alaska Native	12
Asian	734
Native Hawaiian/Pacific Islander	5
Other race	70
Two or more races	163
Hispanic origin, total	418
Mexican	30
Puerto Rican	115
Cuban	55
Other Hispanic	218

Age & Nativity, 2000
Under 5 years	1,147
18 years and over	12,047
21 years and over	11,689
65 years and over	2,376
85 years and over	487
Median age	39.7
Native-born	14,151
Foreign-born	1,673

Educational Attainment, 2000
Population 25 years and over	11,319
Less than 9th grade	2.0%
High school grad or higher	92.3%
Bachelor's degree or higher	44.0%
Graduate degree	17.0%

Income & Poverty, 1999
Per capita income	$38,607
Median household income	$76,778
Median family income	$90,651
Persons in poverty	436
H'holds receiving public assistance	49
H'holds receiving social security	1,656

Households, 2000
Total households	5,990
With persons under 18	2,074
With persons over 65	1,624
Family households	4,315
Single-person households	1,416
Persons per household	2.59
Persons per family	3.11

Labor & Employment
Total civilian labor force, 2007**	8,776
Unemployment rate	2.7%
Total civilian labor force, 2000	8,054
Unemployment rate	2.8%

Employed persons 16 years and over by occupation, 2000
Managers & professionals	3,821
Service occupations	559
Sales & office occupations	2,297
Farming, fishing & forestry	6
Construction & maintenance	599
Production & transportation	548
Self-employed persons	507

* US Census Bureau
** New Jersey Department of Labor

General Information
Township of Denville
1 Saint Marys Pl
Denville, NJ 07834
973-625-8300
Website	www.denvillenj.org
Year of incorporation	1913
Land/water area (sq. miles)	12.11/0.52
Form of government	Mayor-Council

Government
Legislative Districts
US Congressional	11
State Legislative	25

Local Officials, 2009
Mayor	Philip Ted Hussa
Manager	Marie A. Goble
Clerk	Donna Costello
Finance Dir	Marie Goble
Tax Assessor	Ginny Klein
Tax Collector	Annemarie Hopler
Attorney	John Dorsey
Building	Walter Stefanacci
Planning	Bill Denzler
Engineering	Nick Rosania
Public Works	Joe Lowell
Police Chief	Christopher Wagner
Emerg/Fire Director	Michael Leravolo

Housing & Construction
Housing Units, 2000*
Total	6,178
Median rent	$1,129
Median SF home value	$228,300

Permits for New Residential Construction
	Units	Value
Total, 2006	46	$9,745,444
Single family	36	$7,887,444
Total, 2007	31	$6,417,400
Single family	15	$3,441,400

Real Property Valuation, 2008
	Parcels	Valuation
Total	7,061	$2,268,777,700
Vacant	696	48,382,100
Residential	5,941	1,842,271,000
Commercial	354	295,343,300
Industrial	38	70,122,400
Apartments	3	7,729,600
Farm land	17	86,900
Farm homestead	12	4,842,400

Average Property Value & Tax, 2008
Residential value	$310,283
Property tax	$8,019
Tax credit/rebate	$1,079

Public Library
Denville Public Library
121 Diamond Spring Rd
Denville, NJ 07834
973-627-6555
Director	Elizabeth L. Kanouse

Library statistics, 2007
Population served	15,824
Full-time/total staff	4/8

	Total	Per capita
Holdings	61,107	3.86
Revenues	$1,171,733	$74.05
Expenditures	$994,223	$62.83
Annual visits	120,003	7.58
Internet terminals/annual users	8/25,449	

Public Safety
Number of officers, 2007	35

Crime	2006	2007
Total crimes	190	175
Violent	6	2
Murder	0	0
Rape	1	0
Robbery	1	0
Aggravated assault	4	2
Non-violent	184	173
Burglary	33	29
Larceny	140	137
Vehicle theft	11	7
Domestic violence	67	64
Arson	1	0
Total crime rate	11.5	10.5
Violent	0.4	0.1
Non-violent	11.2	10.4

Public School District
(for school year 2007-08 except as noted)

Denville Township School District
501 Openaki Road
Denville, NJ 07834
(973) 983-6500
Superintendent	Drucilla Clark
Number of schools	3
Grade plan	K-8
Enrollment	1,980
Attendance rate, '06-07	96.0%
Dropout rate	NA
Students per teacher	11.8
Per pupil expenditure	$12,833
Median faculty salary	$48,074
Median administrator salary	$106,796
Grade 12 enrollment	NA
High school graduation rate	NA

Assessment test results
(percent scoring at proficient or advanced level)
	Language	Math
NJASK-Grade 3	93.2%	91.0%
GEPA-Grade 8	76.6%	91.3%
HSPA-High School	NA	NA

SAT Score Averages, 2006-07
Pct tested	Math	Verbal	Writing
NA	NA	NA	NA

Teacher Qualifications
Avg. years of experience	8
Highly-qualified teachers one subject/all subjects	100%/100%

No Child Left Behind
AYP, 2006-07	Meets Standards

Municipal Finance
State Aid Programs, 2009
Total aid	$2,339,627
CMPTRA	21,784
Energy tax receipts	2,247,501
Garden State Trust	11,391

General Budget, 2008
Total tax levy	$58,758,237
County levy	8,204,263
County taxes	6,695,108
County library	0
County health	0
County open space	1,509,155
School levy	39,253,559
Muni. levy	11,300,415
Misc. revenues	8,550,006

Taxes
	2006	2007	2008
General tax rate per $100	2.32	2.45	2.585
County equalization ratio	74.34	67.78	64.70
Net valuation taxable	$2,210,435,200	$2,258,051,846	$2,273,457,077
State equalized value	$3,265,798,617	$3,487,392,842	$3,528,720,539

See Introduction for an explanation of all data sources.

Demographics & Socio-Economic Characteristics

(2000 US Census, except as noted)

Population

1980*	23,473
1990*	24,137
2000	26,763
Male	12,911
Female	13,852
2007 (estimate)*	30,529
Population density	1,744.5

Race & Hispanic Origin, 2000

Race

White	22,330
Black/African American	3,314
American Indian/Alaska Native	56
Asian	410
Native Hawaiian/Pacific Islander	9
Other race	266
Two or more races	378
Hispanic origin, total	766
Mexican	114
Puerto Rican	421
Cuban	25
Other Hispanic	206

Age & Nativity, 2000

Under 5 years	1,668
18 years and over	20,383
21 years and over	19,533
65 years and over	4,012
85 years and over	421
Median age	37.3
Native-born	25,646
Foreign-born	1,117

Educational Attainment, 2000

Population 25 years and over	18,448
Less than 9th grade	4.5%
High school grad or higher	80.0%
Bachelor's degree or higher	15.2%
Graduate degree	4.2%

Income & Poverty, 1999

Per capita income	$21,477
Median household income	$50,147
Median family income	$56,642
Persons in poverty	1,535
H'holds receiving public assistance	140
H'holds receiving social security	2,935

Households, 2000

Total households	10,013
With persons under 18	3,572
With persons over 65	2,648
Family households	7,083
Single-person households	2,435
Persons per household	2.62
Persons per family	3.12

Labor & Employment

Total civilian labor force, 2007**	16,125
Unemployment rate	3.3%
Total civilian labor force, 2000	13,829
Unemployment rate	5.5%

Employed persons 16 years and over by occupation, 2000

Managers & professionals	3,508
Service occupations	1,752
Sales & office occupations	3,886
Farming, fishing & forestry	5
Construction & maintenance	1,612
Production & transportation	2,305
Self-employed persons	446

* US Census Bureau
** New Jersey Department of Labor

General Information

Township of Deptford
1011 Cooper St
Deptford, NJ 08096
856-845-5300

Website	www.deptford-nj.org
Year of incorporation	1695
Land/water area (sq. miles)	17.50/0.08
Form of government	Council-Manager

Government

Legislative Districts

US Congressional	1
State Legislative	5

Local Officials, 2009

Mayor	Paul Medany
Manager	Denise Rose
Clerk	Dina Zawadski
Finance Dir	Joanne Strange
Tax Assessor	Joseph Harasta
Tax Collector	Joyce Michaels
Attorney	Harvey C. Johnson
Building	Fred Fritz
Comm Dev/Planning	NA
Engineering	Jonathon Bryson
Public Works	Michael Storms
Police Chief	Dan Murphy
Emerg/Fire Director	Steve Hubbs

Housing & Construction

Housing Units, 2000*

Total	10,647
Median rent	$664
Median SF home value	$106,000

Permits for New Residential Construction

	Units	Value
Total, 2006	99	$7,855,056
Single family	99	$7,855,056
Total, 2007	53	$7,901,491
Single family	53	$7,901,491

Real Property Valuation, 2008

	Parcels	Valuation
Total	12,080	$1,703,659,860
Vacant	1,653	42,448,900
Residential	9,851	1,117,506,900
Commercial	339	473,462,260
Industrial	28	10,001,000
Apartments	14	53,584,400
Farm land	134	419,900
Farm homestead	61	6,236,500

Average Property Value & Tax, 2008

Residential value	$113,372
Property tax	$4,290
Tax credit/rebate	$910

Public Library

Johnson Memorial Library
670 Ward Dr
Deptford, NJ 08096
856-848-9149

Director .... Arn Ellsworth Winter

Library statistics, 2007

Population served	26,763
Full-time/total staff	3/10

	Total	Per capita
Holdings	75,378	2.82
Revenues	$996,173	$37.22
Expenditures	$749,685	$28.01
Annual visits	128,752	4.81
Internet terminals/annual users	10/22,972	

Public Safety

Number of officers, 2007 71

Crime	2006	2007
Total crimes	1,549	1,453
Violent	109	151
Murder	1	1
Rape	1	0
Robbery	37	58
Aggravated assault	70	92
Non-violent	1,440	1,302
Burglary	209	166
Larceny	1,157	1,053
Vehicle theft	74	83
Domestic violence	355	342
Arson	13	17
Total crime rate	52.1	48.1
Violent	3.7	5.0
Non-violent	48.4	43.1

Public School District

(for school year 2007-08 except as noted)

Deptford Township School District
2022 Good Intent Road
Deptford, NJ 08096
(856) 232-2700

Superintendent	Joseph F. Canataro
Number of schools	9
Grade plan	K-12
Enrollment	4,322
Attendance rate, '06-07	94.6%
Dropout rate	1.2%
Students per teacher	11.7
Per pupil expenditure	$12,448
Median faculty salary	$53,950
Median administrator salary	$101,759
Grade 12 enrollment	237
High school graduation rate	91.3%

Assessment test results

(percent scoring at proficient or advanced level)

	Language	Math
NJASK-Grade 3	82.8%	85.1%
GEPA-Grade 8	65.3%	80.7%
HSPA-High School	74.8%	85.4%

SAT Score Averages, 2006-07

Pct tested	Math	Verbal	Writing
65%	479	457	451

Teacher Qualifications

Avg. years of experience	8
Highly-qualified teachers one subject/all subjects	100%/99.0%

No Child Left Behind

AYP, 2006-07 .... Meets Standards

Municipal Finance

State Aid Programs, 2009

Total aid	$2,862,224
CMPTRA	629,635
Energy tax receipts	2,159,323
Garden State Trust	1,600

General Budget, 2008

Total tax levy	$64,566,955
County levy	16,047,421
County taxes	14,881,255
County library	0
County health	0
County open space	1,166,166
School levy	33,339,035
Muni. levy	15,180,499
Misc. revenues	12,795,299

Taxes

	2006	2007	2008
General tax rate per $100	3.57	3.709	3.784
County equalization ratio	68	59.46	58.53
Net valuation taxable	$1,648,843,860	$1,681,506,598	$1,706,376,431
State equalized value	$2,775,914,850	$2,871,054,992	$3,111,017,720

See Introduction for an explanation of all data sources.

Demographics & Socio-Economic Characteristics

(2000 US Census, except as noted)

Population

1980*	14,681
1990*	15,115
2000	18,188
Male	9,377
Female	8,811
2007 (estimate)*	17,997
Population density	6,715.3

Race & Hispanic Origin, 2000

Race

White	12,631
Black/African American	1,242
American Indian/Alaska Native	62
Asian	450
Native Hawaiian/Pacific Islander	5
Other race	2,909
Two or more races	889
Hispanic origin, total	10,539
Mexican	1,557
Puerto Rican	2,413
Cuban	98
Other Hispanic	6,471

Age & Nativity, 2000

Under 5 years	1,278
18 years and over	13,976
21 years and over	13,203
65 years and over	1,922
85 years and over	310
Median age	33.7
Native-born	10,400
Foreign-born	7,788

Educational Attainment, 2000

Population 25 years and over	12,011
Less than 9th grade	16.8%
High school grad or higher	66.9%
Bachelor's degree or higher	12.5%
Graduate degree	4.4%

Income & Poverty, 1999

Per capita income	$18,056
Median household income	$53,423
Median family income	$57,141
Persons in poverty	2,381
H'holds receiving public assistance	183
H'holds receiving social security	1,446

Households, 2000

Total households	5,436
With persons under 18	2,242
With persons over 65	1,277
Family households	3,918
Single-person households	1,156
Persons per household	3.29
Persons per family	3.55

Labor & Employment

Total civilian labor force, 2007**	10,418
Unemployment rate	7.7%
Total civilian labor force, 2000	9,523
Unemployment rate	7.4%

Employed persons 16 years and over by occupation, 2000

Managers & professionals	1,713
Service occupations	1,845
Sales & office occupations	2,262
Farming, fishing & forestry	0
Construction & maintenance	789
Production & transportation	2,207
Self-employed persons	296

General Information

Town of Dover
37 N Sussex St
Dover, NJ 07801
973-366-2200

Website	www.dover.nj.us
Year of incorporation	1869
Land/water area (sq. miles)	2.68/0.03
Form of government	Town

Government

Legislative Districts

US Congressional	11
State Legislative	25

Local Officials, 2009

Mayor	James Dodd
Manager	William E. Close Jr
Clerk	Margaret Verga
Finance Dir	Kelly Toohey
Tax Assessor	Therese dePierro
Tax Collector	Silvio Esposito
Attorney	David Pennella
Building	Robert Young
Planning	Mike Hantson
Engineering	Mike Hantson
Public Works	Carl Rossi
Police Chief	Harold Valentine
Fire Chief	Paul McDougall

Housing & Construction

Housing Units, 2000*

Total	5,568
Median rent	$870
Median SF home value	$150,500

Permits for New Residential Construction

	Units	Value
Total, 2006	1	$86,530
Single family	1	$86,530
Total, 2007	5	$567,175
Single family	5	$567,175

Real Property Valuation, 2008

	Parcels	Valuation
Total	4,158	$681,374,900
Vacant	134	6,847,800
Residential	3,615	481,322,400
Commercial	326	110,579,800
Industrial	55	60,546,800
Apartments	28	22,078,100
Farm land	0	0
Farm homestead	0	0

Average Property Value & Tax, 2008

Residential value	$133,146
Property tax	$5,341
Tax credit/rebate	$975

Public Library

Dover Free Public Library
32 E Clinton St
Dover, NJ 07801
973-361-0172

Director	Robert F. Tambini

Library statistics, 2007

Population served	18,188
Full-time/total staff	2/4

	Total	Per capita
Holdings	60,517	3.33
Revenues	$636,264	$34.98
Expenditures	$626,283	$34.43
Annual visits	59,202	3.26
Internet terminals/annual users	9/40,404	

Public Safety

Number of officers, 2007	35

Crime	2006	2007
Total crimes	419	379
Violent	64	66
Murder	0	0
Rape	2	4
Robbery	30	39
Aggravated assault	32	23
Non-violent	355	313
Burglary	85	53
Larceny	240	235
Vehicle theft	30	25
Domestic violence	116	120
Arson	1	2
Total crime rate	22.7	20.6
Violent	3.5	3.6
Non-violent	19.3	17.0

Public School District

(for school year 2007-08 except as noted)

Dover Town School District
100 Grace Street
Dover, NJ 07801
(973) 989-2000

Superintendent	Robert Becker
Number of schools	5
Grade plan	K-12
Enrollment	2,924
Attendance rate, '06-07	95.1%
Dropout rate	1.9%
Students per teacher	12.7
Per pupil expenditure	$12,097
Median faculty salary	$56,412
Median administrator salary	$98,971
Grade 12 enrollment	188
High school graduation rate	91.2%

Assessment test results

(percent scoring at proficient or advanced level)

	Language	Math
NJASK-Grade 3	87.4%	87.3%
GEPA-Grade 8	49.6%	78.6%
HSPA-High School	72.3%	81.1%

SAT Score Averages, 2006-07

Pct tested	Math	Verbal	Writing
44%	461	457	460

Teacher Qualifications

Avg. years of experience	10
Highly-qualified teachers one subject/all subjects	99.5%/99.5%

No Child Left Behind

AYP, 2006-07	Meets Standards

Municipal Finance

State Aid Programs, 2009

Total aid	$1,592,159
CMPTRA	699,327
Energy tax receipts	860,971
Garden State Trust	0

General Budget, 2008

Total tax levy	$27,450,072
County levy	3,962,378
County taxes	3,233,533
County library	0
County health	0
County open space	728,845
School levy	12,907,391
Muni. levy	10,580,303
Misc. revenues	8,336,569

Taxes

	2006	2007	2008
General tax rate per $100	3.78	3.87	4.012
County equalization ratio	51.17	43.52	40.50
Net valuation taxable	$681,246,600	$685,128,983	$684,265,660
State equalized value	$1,568,401,820	$1,687,809,761	$1,620,589,953

* US Census Bureau
** New Jersey Department of Labor

See Introduction for an explanation of all data sources.

Demographics & Socio-Economic Characteristics

(2000 US Census, except as noted)

Population
1980*	1,803
1990*	1,702
2000	1,631
Male	846
Female	785
2007 (estimate)*	1,664
Population density	32.8

Race & Hispanic Origin, 2000
Race
White	1,485
Black/African American	79
American Indian/Alaska Native	24
Asian	3
Native Hawaiian/Pacific Islander	0
Other race	16
Two or more races	24
Hispanic origin, total	55
Mexican	4
Puerto Rican	49
Cuban	0
Other Hispanic	2

Age & Nativity, 2000
Under 5 years	91
18 years and over	1,247
21 years and over	1,201
65 years and over	309
85 years and over	13
Median age	42.3
Native-born	1,607
Foreign-born	24

Educational Attainment, 2000
Population 25 years and over	1,151
Less than 9th grade	9.9%
High school grad or higher	71.2%
Bachelor's degree or higher	7.8%
Graduate degree	2.2%

Income & Poverty, 1999
Per capita income	$17,366
Median household income	$34,667
Median family income	$39,375
Persons in poverty	213
H'holds receiving public assistance	23
H'holds receiving social security	255

Households, 2000
Total households	658
With persons under 18	216
With persons over 65	232
Family households	439
Single-person households	180
Persons per household	2.48
Persons per family	3.03

Labor & Employment
Total civilian labor force, 2007**	772
Unemployment rate	4.8%
Total civilian labor force, 2000	704
Unemployment rate	6.8%

Employed persons 16 years and over by occupation, 2000
Managers & professionals	110
Service occupations	117
Sales & office occupations	168
Farming, fishing & forestry	13
Construction & maintenance	84
Production & transportation	164
Self-employed persons	42

* US Census Bureau
** New Jersey Department of Labor

See Introduction for an explanation of all data sources.

General Information
Township of Downe
288 Main St
Newport, NJ 08345
856-447-3100
Website	www.downetwpnj.org
Year of incorporation	1722
Land/water area (sq. miles)	50.76/3.47
Form of government	Township

Government

Legislative Districts
US Congressional	2
State Legislative	3

Local Officials, 2009
Mayor	Renee Blizzard
Manager/Admin	NA
Municipal Clerk	Diane Patterson (Actg)
CFO	John Miller
Tax Assessor	Doris Sanza
Tax Collector	Jennafer Hernandez
Solicitor	Tom Farnoly
Construction	(State)
Comm Dev/Planning	NA
Engineering	David Battistini
Public Works Supervisor	Mike Day
Police Chief	NA
Emergency Management	Charles Lupton

Housing & Construction

Housing Units, 2000*
Total	1,134
Median rent	$581
Median SF home value	$74,500

Permits for New Residential Construction
	Units	Value
Total, 2006	3	$48,650
Single family	3	$48,650
Total, 2007	12	$812,673
Single family	12	$812,673

Real Property Valuation, 2008
	Parcels	Valuation
Total	1,778	$74,590,700
Vacant	678	6,254,500
Residential	943	58,311,500
Commercial	48	6,309,200
Industrial	0	0
Apartments	1	123,500
Farm land	54	295,900
Farm homestead	54	3,296,100

Average Property Value & Tax, 2008
Residential value	$61,793
Property tax	$2,278
Tax credit/rebate	$765

Public Library

No public municipal library

Library statistics, 2007
Population served	NA
Full-time/total staff	NA/NA

	Total	Per capita
Holdings	NA	NA
Revenues	NA	NA
Expenditures	NA	NA
Annual visits	NA	NA
Internet terminals/annual users	NA/NA	

Public Safety
Number of officers, 2007	0

Crime	2006	2007
Total crimes	35	29
Violent	4	1
Murder	0	0
Rape	0	0
Robbery	0	0
Aggravated assault	4	1
Non-violent	31	28
Burglary	13	11
Larceny	17	13
Vehicle theft	1	4
Domestic violence	5	17
Arson	3	0
Total crime rate	20.9	17.3
Violent	2.4	0.6
Non-violent	18.5	16.7

Public School District
(for school year 2007-08 except as noted)

Downe Township School District
220 Main Street
Newport, NJ 08345
(856) 447-3878
Superintendent	Dina Elliott
Number of schools	1
Grade plan	K-8
Enrollment	169
Attendance rate, '06-07	94.2%
Dropout rate	NA
Students per teacher	7.3
Per pupil expenditure	$17,113
Median faculty salary	$61,821
Median administrator salary	$78,225
Grade 12 enrollment	NA
High school graduation rate	NA

Assessment test results
(percent scoring at proficient or advanced level)
	Language	Math
NJASK-Grade 3	79.0%	84.2%
GEPA-Grade 8	86.4%	95.4%
HSPA-High School	NA	NA

SAT Score Averages, 2006-07
Pct tested	Math	Verbal	Writing
NA	NA	NA	NA

Teacher Qualifications
Avg. years of experience	21
Highly-qualified teachers one subject/all subjects	100%/100%

No Child Left Behind
AYP, 2006-07	Meets Standards

Municipal Finance

State Aid Programs, 2009
Total aid	$653,180
CMPTRA	31,900
Energy tax receipts	240,295
Garden State Trust	363,735

General Budget, 2008
Total tax levy	$2,759,890
County levy	1,519,339
County taxes	1,435,638
County library	0
County health	67,613
County open space	16,088
School levy	1,240,551
Muni. levy	0
Misc. revenues	1,218,697

Taxes
	2006	2007	2008
General tax rate per $100	3.475	3.543	3.688
County equalization ratio	57.96	52.07	46.98
Net valuation taxable	$75,872,800	$76,357,897	$74,867,354
State equalized value	$146,030,867	$162,203,349	$184,360,316

Demographics & Socio-Economic Characteristics
(2000 US Census, except as noted)

Population
1980*	18,334
1990*	17,187
2000	17,503
Male	8,416
Female	9,087
2007 (estimate)*	17,105
Population density	8,595.5

Race & Hispanic Origin, 2000
Race
White	14,663
Black/African American	261
American Indian/Alaska Native	17
Asian	1,918
Native Hawaiian/Pacific Islander	1
Other race	339
Two or more races	304
Hispanic origin, total	1,463
Mexican	59
Puerto Rican	419
Cuban	160
Other Hispanic	825

Age & Nativity, 2000
Under 5 years	1,173
18 years and over	13,239
21 years and over	12,787
65 years and over	2,702
85 years and over	309
Median age	38.4
Native-born	14,250
Foreign-born	3,253

Educational Attainment, 2000
Population 25 years and over	12,229
Less than 9th grade	3.6%
High school grad or higher	88.5%
Bachelor's degree or higher	27.4%
Graduate degree	8.2%

Income & Poverty, 1999
Per capita income	$26,489
Median household income	$65,490
Median family income	$73,880
Persons in poverty	459
H'holds receiving public assistance	119
H'holds receiving social security	2,009

Households, 2000
Total households	6,370
With persons under 18	2,345
With persons over 65	2,000
Family households	4,757
Single-person households	1,422
Persons per household	2.75
Persons per family	3.24

Labor & Employment
Total civilian labor force, 2007**	9,574
Unemployment rate	2.6%
Total civilian labor force, 2000	9,072
Unemployment rate	2.9%

Employed persons 16 years and over by occupation, 2000
Managers & professionals	3,319
Service occupations	1,154
Sales & office occupations	2,776
Farming, fishing & forestry	10
Construction & maintenance	766
Production & transportation	784
Self-employed persons	356

General Information
Borough of Dumont
50 Washington Ave
Dumont, NJ 07628
201-387-5022
Website	www.dumontboro.org
Year of incorporation	1898
Land/water area (sq. miles)	1.99/0.00
Form of government	Borough

Government
Legislative Districts
US Congressional	5
State Legislative	39

Local Officials, 2009
Mayor	Matthew McHale
Manager	John Perkins
Clerk	Susan Connelly
Finance Dir	Rosemarie Giotis
Tax Assessor	James Anzevino
Tax Collector	Barbara Kozay
Attorney	Gregg Paster
Building	Steve Cavadias
Comm Dev/Planning	NA
Engineering	T&M Associates
Public Works	William Ebenhack
Police Chief	Brian Venezio
Emerg/Fire Director	James Molinaro

Housing & Construction
Housing Units, 2000*
Total	6,465
Median rent	$882
Median SF home value	$195,000

Permits for New Residential Construction
	Units	Value
Total, 2006	6	$920,300
Single family	6	$920,300
Total, 2007	10	$2,275,280
Single family	10	$2,275,280

Real Property Valuation, 2008
	Parcels	Valuation
Total	5,173	$2,084,109,600
Vacant	15	1,141,800
Residential	4,977	1,907,992,400
Commercial	144	98,896,200
Industrial	11	6,762,200
Apartments	25	69,306,500
Farm land	1	10,500
Farm homestead	0	0

Average Property Value & Tax, 2008
Residential value	$383,362
Property tax	$8,854
Tax credit/rebate	$1,371

Public Library
Dixon Homestead Library
180 Washington Ave
Dumont, NJ 07628
201-384-2030
Director	Carolyn M. Blowers

Library statistics, 2007
Population served	17,503
Full-time/total staff	2/7

	Total	Per capita
Holdings	51,216	2.93
Revenues	$783,600	$44.77
Expenditures	$717,954	$41.02
Annual visits	90,445	5.17
Internet terminals/annual users	11/19,431	

Public Safety
Number of officers, 2007	31

Crime	2006	2007
Total crimes	181	183
Violent	10	13
Murder	0	0
Rape	2	4
Robbery	0	0
Aggravated assault	8	9
Non-violent	171	170
Burglary	17	16
Larceny	147	151
Vehicle theft	7	3
Domestic violence	157	101
Arson	1	0
Total crime rate	10.4	10.5
Violent	0.6	0.7
Non-violent	9.8	9.8

Public School District
(for school year 2007-08 except as noted)

Dumont School District
25 Depew Street
Dumont, NJ 07628
(201) 387-3082
Superintendent	Emanuele Triggiano
Number of schools	5
Grade plan	K-12
Enrollment	2,817
Attendance rate, '06-07	95.4%
Dropout rate	0.0%
Students per teacher	12.2
Per pupil expenditure	$13,261
Median faculty salary	$72,810
Median administrator salary	$124,166
Grade 12 enrollment	209
High school graduation rate	100.0%

Assessment test results
(percent scoring at proficient or advanced level)
	Language	Math
NJASK-Grade 3	94.3%	92.3%
GEPA-Grade 8	71.3%	82.9%
HSPA-High School	89.6%	91.5%

SAT Score Averages, 2006-07
Pct tested	Math	Verbal	Writing
81%	497	475	481

Teacher Qualifications
Avg. years of experience	11
Highly-qualified teachers one subject/all subjects	100%/100%

No Child Left Behind
AYP, 2006-07	Meets Standards

Municipal Finance
State Aid Programs, 2009
Total aid	$1,747,332
CMPTRA	422,061
Energy tax receipts	1,281,587
Garden State Trust	0

General Budget, 2008
Total tax levy	$48,203,899
County levy	4,220,878
County taxes	3,992,616
County library	0
County health	0
County open space	228,262
School levy	30,078,288
Muni. levy	13,904,733
Misc. revenues	4,111,685

Taxes
	2006	2007	2008
General tax rate per $100	2.12	2.23	2.311
County equalization ratio	106.18	95.16	91.55
Net valuation taxable	$2,077,344,700	$2,084,122,878	$2,087,052,772
State equalized value	$2,186,281,418	$2,276,190,963	$2,365,879,226

* US Census Bureau
** New Jersey Department of Labor

See Introduction for an explanation of all data sources.

Demographics & Socio-Economic Characteristics

(2000 US Census, except as noted)

Population

1980*	6,593
1990*	6,528
2000	6,823
Male	3,428
Female	3,395
2007 (estimate)*	6,963
Population density	6,695.2

Race & Hispanic Origin, 2000

Race

White	5,736
Black/African American	250
American Indian/Alaska Native	17
Asian	243
Native Hawaiian/Pacific Islander	1
Other race	435
Two or more races	141
Hispanic origin, total	1,010
Mexican	71
Puerto Rican	121
Cuban	29
Other Hispanic	789

Age & Nativity, 2000

Under 5 years	503
18 years and over	5,124
21 years and over	4,917
65 years and over	773
85 years and over	91
Median age	35.8
Native-born	5,715
Foreign-born	1,108

Educational Attainment, 2000

Population 25 years and over	4,715
Less than 9th grade	3.0%
High school grad or higher	86.0%
Bachelor's degree or higher	22.2%
Graduate degree	6.2%

Income & Poverty, 1999

Per capita income	$26,529
Median household income	$59,205
Median family income	$67,188
Persons in poverty	224
H'holds receiving public assistance	24
H'holds receiving social security	550

Households, 2000

Total households	2,451
With persons under 18	918
With persons over 65	559
Family households	1,711
Single-person households	575
Persons per household	2.75
Persons per family	3.30

Labor & Employment

Total civilian labor force, 2007**	4,049
Unemployment rate	6.3%
Total civilian labor force, 2000	3,779
Unemployment rate	7.8%

Employed persons 16 years and over by occupation, 2000

Managers & professionals	1,233
Service occupations	444
Sales & office occupations	909
Farming, fishing & forestry	11
Construction & maintenance	363
Production & transportation	524
Self-employed persons	220

* US Census Bureau
** New Jersey Department of Labor
§ State Fiscal Year July 1–June 30

See Introduction for an explanation of all data sources.

General Information

Borough of Dunellen
355 North Ave
Dunellen, NJ 08812
732-968-3033

Website	www.dunellen.com
Year of incorporation	1887
Land/water area (sq. miles)	1.04/0.00
Form of government	Borough

Government

Legislative Districts

US Congressional	6
State Legislative	22

Local Officials, 2009

Mayor	Robert Seader
Manager	William Robins
Clerk	William Robins
Finance Dir	Scott Olsen
Tax Assessor	Richard Gianchiglia
Tax Collector	Eileen Leonard
Attorney	John Bruder
Building	Scott Luthman
Comm Dev/Planning	NA
Engineering	CME Associates
Public Works	Jerry Schafer
Police Chief	Gerard Cappella
Emerg/Fire Director	Jonathan Scott

Housing & Construction

Housing Units, 2000*

Total	2,520
Median rent	$811
Median SF home value	$155,800

Permits for New Residential Construction

	Units	Value
Total, 2006	28	$1,947,704
Single family	8	$836,592
Total, 2007	27	$1,803,982
Single family	7	$692,870

Real Property Valuation, 2008

	Parcels	Valuation
Total	2,079	$143,472,050
Vacant	38	629,700
Residential	1,932	124,392,350
Commercial	95	13,451,500
Industrial	6	3,374,700
Apartments	8	1,623,800
Farm land	0	0
Farm homestead	0	0

Average Property Value & Tax, 2008

Residential value	$64,385
Property tax	$6,907
Tax credit/rebate	$1,058

Public Library

Dunellen Free Public Library
New Market Rd
Dunellen, NJ 08812
732-968-4585

Director.................Joan F. Henry

Library statistics, 2007

Population served	6,823
Full-time/total staff	1/2

	Total	Per capita
Holdings	41,626	6.10
Revenues	$281,265	$41.22
Expenditures	$289,740	$42.47
Annual visits	23,580	3.46
Internet terminals/annual users	9/7,233	

Public Safety

Number of officers, 2007...........18

Crime	2006	2007
Total crimes	147	164
Violent	7	8
Murder	0	0
Rape	0	0
Robbery	3	4
Aggravated assault	4	4
Non-violent	140	156
Burglary	19	17
Larceny	115	133
Vehicle theft	6	6
Domestic violence	83	114
Arson	2	5
Total crime rate	21.0	23.6
Violent	1.0	1.2
Non-violent	20.0	22.5

Public School District

(for school year 2007-08 except as noted)

Dunellen School District
High Street & Lehigh Street
Dunellen, NJ 08812
(732) 968-3226

Superintendent	Pio Pennisi
Number of schools	3
Grade plan	K-12
Enrollment	1,098
Attendance rate, '06-07	94.5%
Dropout rate	1.3%
Students per teacher	11.1
Per pupil expenditure	$11,248
Median faculty salary	$46,800
Median administrator salary	$102,105
Grade 12 enrollment	85
High school graduation rate	95.0%

Assessment test results

(percent scoring at proficient or advanced level)

	Language	Math
NJASK-Grade 3	85.1%	89.8%
GEPA-Grade 8	65.9%	85.7%
HSPA-High School	80.0%	87.2%

SAT Score Averages, 2006-07

Pct tested	Math	Verbal	Writing
68%	470	474	473

Teacher Qualifications

Avg. years of experience	8
Highly-qualified teachers one subject/all subjects	100%/98.5%

No Child Left Behind

AYP, 2006-07...........Meets Standards

Municipal Finance§

State Aid Programs, 2009

Total aid	$777,391
CMPTRA	255,721
Energy tax receipts	502,235
Garden State Trust	0

General Budget, 2008

Total tax levy	$15,454,808
County levy	2,073,854
County taxes	1,856,500
County library	0
County health	0
County open space	217,354
School levy	9,070,217
Muni. levy	4,310,737
Misc. revenues	2,612,682

Taxes

	2006	2007	2008
General tax rate per $100	9.31	10.31	10.728
County equalization ratio	25.05	22.36	20.09
Net valuation taxable	$143,133,775	$143,903,300	$144,066,125
State equalized value	$640,946,411	$713,722,855	$710,149,218

Demographics & Socio-Economic Characteristics

(2000 US Census, except as noted)

Population
1980*	1,009
1990*	1,476
2000	1,441
Male	726
Female	715
2007 (estimate)*	1,645
Population density	100.5

Race & Hispanic Origin, 2000
Race
White	1,426
Black/African American	1
American Indian/Alaska Native	4
Asian	3
Native Hawaiian/Pacific Islander	0
Other race	0
Two or more races	7
Hispanic origin, total	16
Mexican	1
Puerto Rican	8
Cuban	4
Other Hispanic	3

Age & Nativity, 2000
Under 5 years	73
18 years and over	1,085
21 years and over	1,038
65 years and over	207
85 years and over	16
Median age	39.4
Native-born	1,413
Foreign-born	28

Educational Attainment, 2000
Population 25 years and over	974
Less than 9th grade	4.4%
High school grad or higher	75.8%
Bachelor's degree or higher	10.1%
Graduate degree	2.4%

Income & Poverty, 1999
Per capita income	$20,617
Median household income	$38,625
Median family income	$49,453
Persons in poverty	51
H'holds receiving public assistance	10
H'holds receiving social security	194

Households, 2000
Total households	546
With persons under 18	190
With persons over 65	156
Family households	395
Single-person households	122
Persons per household	2.64
Persons per family	3.11

Labor & Employment
Total civilian labor force, 2007**	855
Unemployment rate	3.9%
Total civilian labor force, 2000	717
Unemployment rate	3.8%

Employed persons 16 years and over by occupation, 2000
Managers & professionals	131
Service occupations	105
Sales & office occupations	186
Farming, fishing & forestry	4
Construction & maintenance	183
Production & transportation	81
Self-employed persons	104

* US Census Bureau
** New Jersey Department of Labor

General Information
Township of Eagleswood
146 Division St
PO Box 409
West Creek, NJ 08092
609-296-3040
Email... ekennedy_eagleswood@comcast.net	
Year of incorporation	1874
Land/water area (sq. miles)	16.37/2.49
Form of government	Township

Government

Legislative Districts
US Congressional	3
State Legislative	9

Local Officials, 2009
Mayor	Debra Rivas
Administrator	Elaine B. Kennedy
Clerk	Elaine B. Kennedy
Finance Officer	Linda Picaro-Covello
Tax Assessor	Fred Millman
Tax Collector	Sandra A. Cramer
Attorney	Tom Monahan
Building	Robert Gaestel
Comm Dev/Planning	NA
Engineering	Jack Mallon
Public Works	Richard Lombardo
Police Chief	NA
Emerg/Fire Director	Anthony Cahill

Housing & Construction

Housing Units, 2000*
Total	693
Median rent	$678
Median SF home value	$115,700

Permits for New Residential Construction
	Units	Value
Total, 2006	18	$4,029,407
Single family	18	$4,029,407
Total, 2007	17	$3,706,181
Single family	17	$3,706,181

Real Property Valuation, 2008
	Parcels	Valuation
Total	1,170	$284,392,200
Vacant	371	41,450,500
Residential	688	204,913,500
Commercial	92	33,293,500
Industrial	4	3,967,600
Apartments	1	436,900
Farm land	13	48,700
Farm homestead	1	281,500

Average Property Value & Tax, 2008
Residential value	$297,816
Property tax	$4,823
Tax credit/rebate	$897

Public Library
No public municipal library

Library statistics, 2007
Population served	NA
Full-time/total staff	NA/NA

	Total	Per capita
Holdings	NA	NA
Revenues	NA	NA
Expenditures	NA	NA
Annual visits	NA	NA
Internet terminals/annual users	NA/NA	

Public Safety
Number of officers, 2007	0

Crime	2006	2007
Total crimes	29	65
Violent	4	4
Murder	0	0
Rape	0	0
Robbery	0	0
Aggravated assault	4	4
Non-violent	25	61
Burglary	3	13
Larceny	18	44
Vehicle theft	4	4
Domestic violence	1	11
Arson	0	1
Total crime rate	18.5	40.3
Violent	2.6	2.5
Non-violent	16.0	37.8

Public School District
(for school year 2007-08 except as noted)

Eagleswood Township School District
511 Route 9, Box 355
West Creek, NJ 08092
(609) 597-3663
Superintendent	Deborah Snyder
Number of schools	1
Grade plan	K-6
Enrollment	142
Attendance rate, '06-07	95.1%
Dropout rate	NA
Students per teacher	7.9
Per pupil expenditure	$13,875
Median faculty salary	$45,576
Median administrator salary	$84,125
Grade 12 enrollment	NA
High school graduation rate	NA

Assessment test results
(percent scoring at proficient or advanced level)
	Language	Math
NJASK-Grade 3	100.0%	84.6%
GEPA-Grade 8	NA	NA
HSPA-High School	NA	NA

SAT Score Averages, 2006-07
Pct tested	Math	Verbal	Writing
NA	NA	NA	NA

Teacher Qualifications
Avg. years of experience	9
Highly-qualified teachers one subject/all subjects	100%/93.0%

No Child Left Behind
AYP, 2006-07	Meets Standards

Municipal Finance

State Aid Programs, 2009
Total aid	$268,321
CMPTRA	3,077
Energy tax receipts	231,218
Garden State Trust	10,952

General Budget, 2008
Total tax levy	$4,613,935
County levy	944,253
County taxes	778,664
County library	91,505
County health	37,257
County open space	36,827
School levy	2,864,008
Muni. levy	805,674
Misc. revenues	1,157,223

Taxes
	2006	2007	2008
General tax rate per $100	1.436	1.562	1.620
County equalization ratio	118.4	94.43	92.43
Net valuation taxable	$271,355,000	$279,203,605	$284,883,694
State equalized value	$305,145,407	$302,035,914	$17,352,111,758

See Introduction for an explanation of all data sources.

Demographics & Socio-Economic Characteristics
(2000 US Census, except as noted)

Population
1980*	3,468
1990*	4,332
2000	4,455
Male	2,265
Female	2,190
2007 (estimate)*	4,483
Population density	156.3

Race & Hispanic Origin, 2000
Race
White	4,320
Black/African American	32
American Indian/Alaska Native	6
Asian	41
Native Hawaiian/Pacific Islander	1
Other race	21
Two or more races	34
Hispanic origin, total	68
Mexican	15
Puerto Rican	6
Cuban	6
Other Hispanic	41

Age & Nativity, 2000
Under 5 years	269
18 years and over	3,328
21 years and over	3,218
65 years and over	455
85 years and over	52
Median age	40.8
Native-born	4,189
Foreign-born	266

Educational Attainment, 2000
Population 25 years and over	3,135
Less than 9th grade	1.8%
High school grad or higher	92.2%
Bachelor's degree or higher	39.6%
Graduate degree	15.9%

Income & Poverty, 1999
Per capita income	$37,187
Median household income	$85,664
Median family income	$90,000
Persons in poverty	74
H'holds receiving public assistance	45
H'holds receiving social security	382

Households, 2000
Total households	1,581
With persons under 18	606
With persons over 65	336
Family households	1,306
Single-person households	210
Persons per household	2.80
Persons per family	3.07

Labor & Employment
Total civilian labor force, 2007**	2,710
Unemployment rate	2.9%
Total civilian labor force, 2000	2,426
Unemployment rate	2.5%

Employed persons 16 years and over by occupation, 2000
Managers & professionals	1,144
Service occupations	137
Sales & office occupations	534
Farming, fishing & forestry	20
Construction & maintenance	262
Production & transportation	269
Self-employed persons	248

General Information
Township of East Amwell
1070 Route 202
Ringoes, NJ 08551
908-782-8536
Website	www.eastamwelltownship.com
Year of incorporation	1846
Land/water area (sq. miles)	28.68/0.04
Form of government	Township

Government
Legislative Districts
US Congressional	12
State Legislative	23

Local Officials, 2009
Mayor	Peter Kneski
Administrator	Timothy L. Matheny
Clerk	Teresa Stahl
Finance Dir	Jane Luhrs
Tax Assessor	Marianne Busher
Tax Collector	Mary Hyland
Attorney	Richard Cushing
Building	Stewart Doddy
Planning	Frank Banisch
Engineering	Dennis O'Neal
Public Works	Bob Kadezabek
Police Chief	NA
Emerg/Fire Director	Marty Alexander

Housing & Construction
Housing Units, 2000*
Total	1,624
Median rent	$913
Median SF home value	$252,500

Permits for New Residential Construction
	Units	Value
Total, 2006	9	$3,749,578
Single family	9	$3,749,578
Total, 2007	9	$2,799,238
Single family	9	$2,799,238

Real Property Valuation, 2008
	Parcels	Valuation
Total	2,135	$790,452,818
Vacant	168	14,132,800
Residential	1,219	523,094,200
Commercial	61	103,980,461
Industrial	0	0
Apartments	5	2,188,600
Farm land	429	5,287,057
Farm homestead	253	141,769,700

Average Property Value & Tax, 2008
Residential value	$451,674
Property tax	$7,892
Tax credit/rebate	$1,221

Public Library
No public municipal library

Library statistics, 2007
Population served	NA
Full-time/total staff	NA/NA

	Total	Per capita
Holdings	NA	NA
Revenues	NA	NA
Expenditures	NA	NA
Annual visits	NA	NA
Internet terminals/annual users	NA/NA	

Public Safety
Number of officers, 2007	0

Crime	2006	2007
Total crimes	20	41
Violent	0	3
Murder	0	0
Rape	0	0
Robbery	0	1
Aggravated assault	0	2
Non-violent	20	38
Burglary	8	13
Larceny	11	23
Vehicle theft	1	2
Domestic violence	3	16
Arson	0	0
Total crime rate	4.4	9.0
Violent	0.0	0.7
Non-violent	4.4	8.3

Public School District
(for school year 2007-08 except as noted)

East Amwell Township School District
43 Wertsville Road, PO Box 680
Ringoes, NJ 08551
(908) 782-6464
Superintendent	Edward Stoloski
Number of schools	1
Grade plan	K-8
Enrollment	488
Attendance rate, '06-07	98.0%
Dropout rate	NA
Students per teacher	10.1
Per pupil expenditure	$13,281
Median faculty salary	$55,108
Median administrator salary	$84,901
Grade 12 enrollment	NA
High school graduation rate	NA

Assessment test results
(percent scoring at proficient or advanced level)
	Language	Math
NJASK-Grade 3	92.9%	96.4%
GEPA-Grade 8	92.8%	96.4%
HSPA-High School	NA	NA

SAT Score Averages, 2006-07
Pct tested	Math	Verbal	Writing
NA	NA	NA	NA

Teacher Qualifications
Avg. years of experience	9
Highly-qualified teachers one subject/all subjects	100%/100%

No Child Left Behind
AYP, 2006-07 ... Meets Standards

Municipal Finance
State Aid Programs, 2009
Total aid	$438,527
CMPTRA	78,207
Energy tax receipts	316,542
Garden State Trust	24,748

General Budget, 2008
Total tax levy	$13,833,263
County levy	2,814,598
County taxes	2,355,723
County library	204,556
County health	0
County open space	254,320
School levy	9,593,508
Muni. levy	1,425,157
Misc. revenues	2,970,959

Taxes
	2006	2007	2008
General tax rate per $100	1.78	1.76	1.748
County equalization ratio	101.14	92.59	93.84
Net valuation taxable	$783,040,722	$786,307,681	$791,724,997
State equalized value	$808,202,098	$827,017,335	$835,699,307

* US Census Bureau
** New Jersey Department of Labor

See Introduction for an explanation of all data sources.

Demographics & Socio-Economic Characteristics

(2000 US Census, except as noted)

Population
1980*	37,711
1990*	43,548
2000	46,756
Male	22,692
Female	24,064
2007 (estimate)*	47,430
Population density	2,160.8

Race & Hispanic Origin, 2000
Race
White	36,265
Black/African American	1,321
American Indian/Alaska Native	42
Asian	7,607
Native Hawaiian/Pacific Islander	5
Other race	526
Two or more races	990
Hispanic origin, total	1,957
Mexican	160
Puerto Rican	718
Cuban	189
Other Hispanic	890

Age & Nativity, 2000
Under 5 years	2,768
18 years and over	34,588
21 years and over	33,305
65 years and over	5,429
85 years and over	480
Median age	39.1
Native-born	35,774
Foreign-born	10,982

Educational Attainment, 2000
Population 25 years and over	31,652
Less than 9th grade	3.2%
High school grad or higher	92.1%
Bachelor's degree or higher	47.1%
Graduate degree	19.5%

Income & Poverty, 1999
Per capita income	$33,286
Median household income	$75,956
Median family income	$86,863
Persons in poverty	1,321
H'holds receiving public assistance	186
H'holds receiving social security	3,764

Households, 2000
Total households	16,372
With persons under 18	6,916
With persons over 65	3,836
Family households	13,074
Single-person households	2,815
Persons per household	2.84
Persons per family	3.23

Labor & Employment
Total civilian labor force, 2007**	26,640
Unemployment rate	3.1%
Total civilian labor force, 2000	25,008
Unemployment rate	3.5%

Employed persons 16 years and over by occupation, 2000
Managers & professionals	11,965
Service occupations	1,840
Sales & office occupations	7,210
Farming, fishing & forestry	0
Construction & maintenance	1,364
Production & transportation	1,757
Self-employed persons	1,276

General Information
Township of East Brunswick
PO Box 1081
East Brunswick, NJ 08816
732-390-6810

Website	www.eastbrunswick.org
Year of incorporation	1860
Land/water area (sq. miles)	21.95/0.43
Form of government	Mayor-Council

Government
Legislative Districts
US Congressional	12
State Legislative	18

Local Officials, 2009
Mayor	David Stahl
Manager	James White
Clerk	Nennette Perry
Finance Dir	L. Mason Neely
Tax Assessor	Frank Colon
Tax Collector	Michelle O'Hara
Attorney	Catherine Tamasik
Building	Edward Grobelny
Planning	Leslie McGowan
Engineering	CME Associates
Public Works	Thomas Williams
Police Chief	Barry Roberson
Fire/Emergency Dir	NA

Housing & Construction
Housing Units, 2000*
Total	16,640
Median rent	$877
Median SF home value	$212,800

Permits for New Residential Construction
	Units	Value
Total, 2006	12	$2,424,500
Single family	12	$2,424,500
Total, 2007	16	$2,873,400
Single family	16	$2,873,400

Real Property Valuation, 2008
	Parcels	Valuation
Total	16,920	$2,017,751,600
Vacant	642	17,546,800
Residential	15,470	1,525,964,300
Commercial	616	342,894,700
Industrial	108	95,344,300
Apartments	13	32,988,700
Farm land	49	259,900
Farm homestead	22	2,752,900

Average Property Value & Tax, 2008
Residential value	$98,678
Property tax	$8,179
Tax credit/rebate	$1,160

Public Library
East Brunswick Public Library
2 Jean Walling Civic Center
East Brunswick, NJ 08816
732-390-6950

Director	Carol Nersinger

Library statistics, 2007
Population served	46,756
Full-time/total staff	11/25

	Total	Per capita
Holdings	184,821	3.95
Revenues	$4,620,432	$98.82
Expenditures	$4,262,536	$91.17
Annual visits	583,244	12.47
Internet terminals/annual users	45/80,393	

Public Safety
Number of officers, 2007	93

Crime	2006	2007
Total crimes	932	881
Violent	37	43
Murder	0	1
Rape	0	9
Robbery	9	11
Aggravated assault	28	22
Non-violent	895	838
Burglary	137	92
Larceny	717	715
Vehicle theft	41	31
Domestic violence	239	207
Arson	2	13
Total crime rate	19.3	18.5
Violent	0.8	0.9
Non-violent	18.5	17.6

Public School District
(for school year 2007-08 except as noted)

East Brunswick Township School District
760 Route #18
East Brunswick, NJ 08816
(732) 613-6705

Superintendent	Jo Ann Magistro
Number of schools	11
Grade plan	K-12
Enrollment	8,837
Attendance rate, '06-07	94.6%
Dropout rate	0.4%
Students per teacher	12.3
Per pupil expenditure	$14,493
Median faculty salary	$66,319
Median administrator salary	$110,486
Grade 12 enrollment	710
High school graduation rate	98.4%

Assessment test results
(percent scoring at proficient or advanced level)
	Language	Math
NJASK-Grade 3	91.8%	91.7%
GEPA-Grade 8	78.7%	90.2%
HSPA-High School	91.1%	92.3%

SAT Score Averages, 2006-07
Pct tested	Math	Verbal	Writing
97%	581	537	544

Teacher Qualifications
Avg. years of experience	10
Highly-qualified teachers one subject/all subjects	100%/100%

No Child Left Behind
AYP, 2006-07	Meets Standards

Municipal Finance
State Aid Programs, 2009
Total aid	$5,379,575
CMPTRA	1,050,594
Energy tax receipts	4,187,114
Garden State Trust	0

General Budget, 2008
Total tax levy	$167,548,355
County levy	23,020,419
County taxes	20,615,573
County library	0
County health	0
County open space	2,404,845
School levy	113,892,934
Muni. levy	30,635,003
Misc. revenues	33,583,031

Taxes
	2006	2007	2008
General tax rate per $100	7.35	7.91	8.290
County equalization ratio	28.41	26.23	25.06
Net valuation taxable	$2,022,361,800	$2,019,089,899	$2,021,393,376
State equalized value	$7,714,221,594	$8,045,895,380	$8,246,091,122

* US Census Bureau
** New Jersey Department of Labor

See Introduction for an explanation of all data sources.

Demographics & Socio-Economic Characteristics
(2000 US Census, except as noted)

Population
1980*	4,144
1990*	5,258
2000	5,430
Male	2,591
Female	2,839
2007 (estimate)*	7,256
Population density	491.9

Race & Hispanic Origin, 2000
Race
White	5,141
Black/African American	177
American Indian/Alaska Native	7
Asian	35
Native Hawaiian/Pacific Islander	0
Other race	13
Two or more races	57
Hispanic origin, total	76
Mexican	15
Puerto Rican	40
Cuban	7
Other Hispanic	14

Age & Nativity, 2000
Under 5 years	311
18 years and over	4,070
21 years and over	3,891
65 years and over	811
85 years and over	120
Median age	40.7
Native-born	5,241
Foreign-born	189

Educational Attainment, 2000
Population 25 years and over	3,661
Less than 9th grade	3.6%
High school grad or higher	88.1%
Bachelor's degree or higher	23.9%
Graduate degree	7.0%

Income & Poverty, 1999
Per capita income	$25,345
Median household income	$65,701
Median family income	$74,455
Persons in poverty	203
H'holds receiving public assistance	11
H'holds receiving social security	558

Households, 2000
Total households	1,901
With persons under 18	732
With persons over 65	507
Family households	1,516
Single-person households	330
Persons per household	2.77
Persons per family	3.12

Labor & Employment
Total civilian labor force, 2007**	3,160
Unemployment rate	3.7%
Total civilian labor force, 2000	2,672
Unemployment rate	3.0%

Employed persons 16 years and over by occupation, 2000
Managers & professionals	1,051
Service occupations	237
Sales & office occupations	683
Farming, fishing & forestry	9
Construction & maintenance	260
Production & transportation	351
Self-employed persons	103

General Information
Township of East Greenwich
159 Democrat Rd
Mickleton, NJ 08056
856-423-0654

Website	county website)
Year of incorporation	1881
Land/water area (sq. miles)	14.75/0.22
Form of government	Township

Government
Legislative Districts
US Congressional	1
State Legislative	3

Local Officials, 2009
Mayor	Frederick J. Grant
Manager/Admin	NA
Clerk	Susan Costill
Finance Dir	Robert E. Scharle
Tax Assessor	NA
Tax Collector	Gail Capasso
Attorney	Timothy W. Chell
Building	James Sabetta
Planning	Bach Associates
Engineering	Remington & Vernick
Public Works	Joseph Schweigart
Police Chief	William Giordano
Emerg/Fire Director	Nelson Wiest

Housing & Construction
Housing Units, 2000*
Total	1,971
Median rent	$706
Median SF home value	$155,000

Permits for New Residential Construction
	Units	Value
Total, 2006	173	$29,625,267
Single family	108	$27,970,017
Total, 2007	206	$35,266,822
Single family	206	$35,266,822

Real Property Valuation, 2008
	Parcels	Valuation
Total	3,885	$519,423,300
Vacant	791	24,720,000
Residential	2,680	434,840,200
Commercial	64	27,791,300
Industrial	23	12,534,600
Apartments	7	1,799,600
Farm land	222	2,429,900
Farm homestead	98	15,307,700

Average Property Value & Tax, 2008
Residential value	$162,040
Property tax	$6,864
Tax credit/rebate	$1,076

Public Library
East Greenwich Public Library
535 Kings Highway
Mickleton, NJ 08056
856-423-3480

Director	Carol Baughman

Library statistics, 2007
Population served	5,430
Full-time/total staff	0/1

	Total	Per capita
Holdings	21,441	3.95
Revenues	$60,391	$11.12
Expenditures	$64,845	$11.94
Annual visits	14,600	2.69
Internet terminals/annual users	6/5,000	

Public Safety
Number of officers, 2007	20

Crime	2006	2007
Total crimes	109	102
Violent	5	11
Murder	0	0
Rape	2	2
Robbery	1	0
Aggravated assault	2	9
Non-violent	104	91
Burglary	31	24
Larceny	69	64
Vehicle theft	4	3
Domestic violence	26	42
Arson	1	1
Total crime rate	17.1	15.0
Violent	0.8	1.6
Non-violent	16.3	13.4

Public School District
(for school year 2007-08 except as noted)

East Greenwich Township School District
559 Kings Highway
Mickleton, NJ 08056
(856) 423-0412

Superintendent	Joseph P. Conroy
Number of schools	2
Grade plan	K-6
Enrollment	806
Attendance rate, '06-07	96.3%
Dropout rate	NA
Students per teacher	11.8
Per pupil expenditure	$11,800
Median faculty salary	$49,278
Median administrator salary	$93,467
Grade 12 enrollment	NA
High school graduation rate	NA

Assessment test results
(percent scoring at proficient or advanced level)
	Language	Math
NJASK-Grade 3	95.1%	94.1%
GEPA-Grade 8	NA	NA
HSPA-High School	NA	NA

SAT Score Averages, 2006-07
Pct tested	Math	Verbal	Writing
NA	NA	NA	NA

Teacher Qualifications
Avg. years of experience	8
Highly-qualified teachers one subject/all subjects	100%/100%

No Child Left Behind
AYP, 2006-07	Meets Standards

Municipal Finance
State Aid Programs, 2009
Total aid	$2,071,705
CMPTRA	0
Energy tax receipts	1,985,591
Garden State Trust	3,083

General Budget, 2008
Total tax levy	$22,042,510
County levy	6,092,113
County taxes	5,257,365
County library	422,759
County health	0
County open space	411,989
School levy	14,052,122
Muni. levy	1,898,275
Misc. revenues	4,904,940

Taxes
	2006	2007	2008
General tax rate per $100	4.026	4.086	4.237
County equalization ratio	62.8	55.75	50.44
Net valuation taxable	$456,088,450	$490,492,524	$520,346,815
State equalized value	$818,998,322	$971,547,882	$1,018,801,822

* US Census Bureau
** New Jersey Department of Labor

See Introduction for an explanation of all data sources.

Demographics & Socio-Economic Characteristics
(2000 US Census, except as noted)

Population
1980*	9,319
1990*	9,926
2000	11,393
Male	5,520
Female	5,873
2007 (estimate)*	11,427
Population density	1,400.4

Race & Hispanic Origin, 2000
Race
White	9,921
Black/African American	66
American Indian/Alaska Native	3
Asian	1,269
Native Hawaiian/Pacific Islander	0
Other race	27
Two or more races	107
Hispanic origin, total	312
Mexican	22
Puerto Rican	71
Cuban	53
Other Hispanic	166

Age & Nativity, 2000
Under 5 years	713
18 years and over	8,828
21 years and over	8,511
65 years and over	1,662
85 years and over	138
Median age	40.7
Native-born	9,274
Foreign-born	2,119

Educational Attainment, 2000
Population 25 years and over	8,147
Less than 9th grade	4.9%
High school grad or higher	88.1%
Bachelor's degree or higher	33.4%
Graduate degree	13.4%

Income & Poverty, 1999
Per capita income	$32,129
Median household income	$82,133
Median family income	$88,348
Persons in poverty	192
H'holds receiving public assistance	23
H'holds receiving social security	1,214

Households, 2000
Total households	3,843
With persons under 18	1,407
With persons over 65	1,163
Family households	3,214
Single-person households	521
Persons per household	2.96
Persons per family	3.26

Labor & Employment
Total civilian labor force, 2007**	6,482
Unemployment rate	3.2%
Total civilian labor force, 2000	5,952
Unemployment rate	3.1%

Employed persons 16 years and over by occupation, 2000
Managers & professionals	2,553
Service occupations	748
Sales & office occupations	1,528
Farming, fishing & forestry	0
Construction & maintenance	474
Production & transportation	462
Self-employed persons	317

* US Census Bureau
** New Jersey Department of Labor

General Information
Township of East Hanover
411 Ridgedale Ave
East Hanover, NJ 07936
973-428-3000
Website	www.easthanovertownship.com
Year of incorporation	1928
Land/water area (sq. miles)	8.16/0.00
Form of government	Small Municipality

Government
Legislative Districts
US Congressional	11
State Legislative	26

Local Officials, 2009
Mayor	Joseph Pannullo
Manager	C. Richard Paduch
Clerk	Marilyn J. Snow
Finance Dir	Smruti Amin
Tax Assessor	Kevin Esposito
Tax Collector	Carole Reardon
Attorney	Matthew O'Donnell
Building	Thomas Pershouse
Comm Dev/Planning	NA
Engineering	Lawrence Palmer
Public Works	Marc Macaluso
Police Chief	Stanley Hansen
Emerg/Fire Director	Raymond Serra

Housing & Construction
Housing Units, 2000*
Total	3,895
Median rent	$1,504
Median SF home value	$322,800

Permits for New Residential Construction
	Units	Value
Total, 2006	23	$4,299,742
Single family	23	$4,299,742
Total, 2007	16	$2,996,508
Single family	16	$2,996,508

Real Property Valuation, 2008
	Parcels	Valuation
Total	4,333	$2,499,824,800
Vacant	138	25,273,000
Residential	3,928	1,412,610,900
Commercial	177	903,419,300
Industrial	90	158,521,600
Apartments	0	0
Farm land	0	0
Farm homestead	0	0

Average Property Value & Tax, 2008
Residential value	$359,626
Property tax	$6,795
Tax credit/rebate	$1,074

Public Library
East Hanover Township Library
415 Ridgedale Ave
East Hanover, NJ 07936
973-428-3075
Director	Gayle Carlson

Library statistics, 2007
Population served	11,393
Full-time/total staff	1/6

	Total	Per capita
Holdings	77,915	6.84
Revenues	$1,206,341	$105.88
Expenditures	$908,997	$79.79
Annual visits	100,000	8.78
Internet terminals/annual users	13/10,000	

Public Safety
Number of officers, 2007	33

Crime	2006	2007
Total crimes	273	249
Violent	11	4
Murder	0	0
Rape	0	0
Robbery	3	2
Aggravated assault	8	2
Non-violent	262	245
Burglary	21	16
Larceny	219	216
Vehicle theft	22	13
Domestic violence	65	72
Arson	0	0
Total crime rate	23.5	21.4
Violent	0.9	0.3
Non-violent	22.6	21.1

Public School District
(for school year 2007-08 except as noted)

East Hanover Township School District
20 School Avenue
East Hanover, NJ 07936
(973) 887-2112
Superintendent	Larry Santos
Number of schools	3
Grade plan	K-8
Enrollment	1,127
Attendance rate, '06-07	96.3%
Dropout rate	NA
Students per teacher	10.4
Per pupil expenditure	$14,246
Median faculty salary	$54,755
Median administrator salary	$102,500
Grade 12 enrollment	NA
High school graduation rate	NA

Assessment test results
(percent scoring at proficient or advanced level)
	Language	Math
NJASK-Grade 3	93.8%	93.8%
GEPA-Grade 8	80.4%	91.5%
HSPA-High School	NA	NA

SAT Score Averages, 2006-07
Pct tested	Math	Verbal	Writing
NA	NA	NA	NA

Teacher Qualifications
Avg. years of experience	11
Highly-qualified teachers one subject/all subjects	100%/100%

No Child Left Behind
AYP, 2006-07	Meets Standards

Municipal Finance
State Aid Programs, 2009
Total aid	$3,378,458
CMPTRA	0
Energy tax receipts	3,268,457
Garden State Trust	117

General Budget, 2008
Total tax levy	$47,277,736
County levy	8,698,215
County taxes	7,098,114
County library	0
County health	0
County open space	1,600,101
School levy	25,587,020
Muni. levy	12,992,500
Misc. revenues	7,075,500

Taxes
	2006	2007	2008
General tax rate per $100	1.78	1.85	1.890
County equalization ratio	75.27	71.28	67.37
Net valuation taxable	$2,439,426,400	$2,446,386,012	$2,502,207,519
State equalized value	$3,424,519,698	$3,630,082,392	$3,720,700,137

See Introduction for an explanation of all data sources.

Demographics & Socio-Economic Characteristics

(2000 US Census, except as noted)

Population
1980*	1,923
1990*	2,157
2000	2,377
Male	1,211
Female	1,166
2007 (estimate)*	2,174
Population density	21,740.0

Race & Hispanic Origin, 2000
Race
White	1,593
Black/African American	40
American Indian/Alaska Native	12
Asian	60
Native Hawaiian/Pacific Islander	1
Other race	499
Two or more races	172
Hispanic origin, total	1,130
Mexican	48
Puerto Rican	124
Cuban	59
Other Hispanic	899

Age & Nativity, 2000
Under 5 years	161
18 years and over	1,761
21 years and over	1,657
65 years and over	181
85 years and over	23
Median age	32.3
Native-born	1,104
Foreign-born	1,273

Educational Attainment, 2000
Population 25 years and over	1,495
Less than 9th grade	22.9%
High school grad or higher	60.9%
Bachelor's degree or higher	13.2%
Graduate degree	5.0%

Income & Poverty, 1999
Per capita income	$16,415
Median household income	$44,352
Median family income	$46,375
Persons in poverty	298
H'holds receiving public assistance	18
H'holds receiving social security	152

Households, 2000
Total households	767
With persons under 18	351
With persons over 65	137
Family households	605
Single-person households	123
Persons per household	3.10
Persons per family	3.40

Labor & Employment
Total civilian labor force, 2007**	1,084
Unemployment rate	3.9%
Total civilian labor force, 2000	1,122
Unemployment rate	6.4%

Employed persons 16 years and over by occupation, 2000
Managers & professionals	163
Service occupations	184
Sales & office occupations	278
Farming, fishing & forestry	4
Construction & maintenance	150
Production & transportation	271
Self-employed persons	29

* US Census Bureau
** New Jersey Department of Labor

General Information
Borough of East Newark
34 Sherman Ave
East Newark, NJ 07029
973-481-2902
Website	www.boroughofeastnewark.com
Year of incorporation	1895
Land/water area (sq. miles)	0.10/0.02
Form of government	Borough

Government
Legislative Districts
US Congressional	13
State Legislative	32

Local Officials, 2009
Mayor	Joseph R. Smith
Manager/Admin	NA
Clerk	Carla A. Hanowitz
Finance Dir	Elizabeth Higgins
Tax Assessor	Denis McGuire
Tax Collector	Anthony Blasi
Attorney	Neil Marotta
Building	Mark Sadonis
Comm Dev/Planning	NA
Engineering	CME Associates
Public Works	NA
Police Chief	Kenneth Sheehan
Emerg/Fire Director	Robert Tomasko

Housing & Construction
Housing Units, 2000*
Total	799
Median rent	$725
Median SF home value	$126,300

Permits for New Residential Construction
	Units	Value
Total, 2006	2	$134,000
Single family	0	$0
Total, 2007	0	$0
Single family	0	$0

Real Property Valuation, 2008
	Parcels	Valuation
Total	381	$40,011,800
Vacant	7	558,400
Residential	334	25,521,800
Commercial	22	2,786,800
Industrial	6	9,650,500
Apartments	12	1,494,300
Farm land	0	0
Farm homestead	0	0

Average Property Value & Tax, 2008
Residential value	$76,413
Property tax	$6,129
Tax credit/rebate	$914

Public Library
No public municipal library

Library statistics, 2007
Population served	NA
Full-time/total staff	NA/NA

	Total	Per capita
Holdings	NA	NA
Revenues	NA	NA
Expenditures	NA	NA
Annual visits	NA	NA
Internet terminals/annual users	NA/NA	

Public Safety
Number of officers, 2007 ... 7
Crime	2006	2007
Total crimes	30	36
Violent	10	5
Murder	1	0
Rape	1	0
Robbery	1	0
Aggravated assault	7	5
Non-violent	20	31
Burglary	3	4
Larceny	11	23
Vehicle theft	6	4
Domestic violence	4	2
Arson	0	0
Total crime rate	13.3	16.2
Violent	4.4	2.3
Non-violent	8.8	14.0

Public School District
(for school year 2007-08 except as noted)

East Newark School District
501 -11 North Third Street
East Newark, NJ 07029
(973) 481-6803
Superintendent	Richard Corbett
Number of schools	1
Grade plan	K-8
Enrollment	225
Attendance rate, '06-07	95.2%
Dropout rate	NA
Students per teacher	14.3
Per pupil expenditure	$12,986
Median faculty salary	$42,464
Median administrator salary	$59,117
Grade 12 enrollment	NA
High school graduation rate	NA

Assessment test results
(percent scoring at proficient or advanced level)
	Language	Math
NJASK-Grade 3	79.3%	71.4%
GEPA-Grade 8	56.3%	56.3%
HSPA-High School	NA	NA

SAT Score Averages, 2006-07
Pct tested	Math	Verbal	Writing
NA	NA	NA	NA

Teacher Qualifications
Avg. years of experience	11
Highly-qualified teachers one subject/all subjects	85.5%/85.5%

No Child Left Behind
AYP, 2006-07 ... Meets Standards

Municipal Finance
State Aid Programs, 2009
Total aid	$704,305
CMPTRA	517,894
Energy tax receipts	182,889
Garden State Trust	0

General Budget, 2008
Total tax levy	$3,211,011
County levy	764,321
County taxes	744,240
County library	0
County health	0
County open space	20,081
School levy	1,150,756
Muni. levy	1,295,934
Misc. revenues	2,176,602

Taxes
	2006	2007	2008
General tax rate per $100	7.116	7.474	8.022
County equalization ratio	28.34	24.42	21.22
Net valuation taxable	$39,310,900	$39,714,673	$40,029,984
State equalized value	$161,003,505	$187,082,278	$177,690,475

See Introduction for an explanation of all data sources.

Demographics & Socio-Economic Characteristics†

(2000 US Census, except as noted)

Population
1980*	77,025
1990*	73,552
2000	69,824
Male	31,429
Female	38,395
2007 (estimate)*	65,952
Population density	16,781.7

Race & Hispanic Origin, 2000
Race
White	2,683
Black/African American	62,462
American Indian/Alaska Native	177
Asian	302
Native Hawaiian/Pacific Islander	51
Other race	1,496
Two or more races	2,653
Hispanic origin, total	3,284
Mexican	196
Puerto Rican	1,248
Cuban	138
Other Hispanic	1,702

Age & Nativity, 2000
Under 5 years	5,535
18 years and over	50,188
21 years and over	47,327
65 years and over	7,845
85 years and over	879
Median age	33.0
Native-born	57,145
Foreign-born	12,759

Educational Attainment, 2000
Population 25 years and over	43,509
Less than 9th grade	7.5%
High school grad or higher	72.4%
Bachelor's degree or higher	15.0%
Graduate degree	4.5%

Income & Poverty, 1999
Per capita income	$16,488
Median household income	$32,346
Median family income	$38,562
Persons in poverty	13,159
H'holds receiving public assistance	2,415
H'holds receiving social security	6,691

Households, 2000
Total households	26,024
With persons under 18	10,289
With persons over 65	6,072
Family households	16,079
Single-person households	8,584
Persons per household	2.63
Persons per family	3.37

Labor & Employment
Total civilian labor force, 2007**	29,462
Unemployment rate	7.0%
Total civilian labor force, 2000	31,605
Unemployment rate	13.3%

Employed persons 16 years and over by occupation, 2000
Managers & professionals	6,740
Service occupations	6,079
Sales & office occupations	8,823
Farming, fishing & forestry	9
Construction & maintenance	1,612
Production & transportation	4,136
Self-employed persons	821

† see Appendix C for American Community Survey data
* US Census Bureau
** New Jersey Department of Labor
§ State Fiscal Year July 1–June 30

General Information
City of East Orange
44 City Hall Plz
East Orange, NJ 07017
973-266-5100
Website	www.eastorange-nj.org
Year of incorporation	1899
Land/water area (sq. miles)	3.93/0.00
Form of government	City

Government
Legislative Districts
US Congressional	10
State Legislative	34

Local Officials, 2009
Mayor	Robert L. Bowser
Manager	Reginald Lewis
Clerk	Cynthia Brown
Finance Dir	Victoria Y. Walker
Tax Assessor	Barbara Williams
Tax Collector	Annmarie Corbitt
Attorney	Jason Holt
Building	Lloyd Abdul Raheem
Planning	Ernest Freeman
Engineering	Michael Johnson
Public Works	Michael Johnson
Police Chief	Ronald Borgo (Actg)
Emerg/Fire Director	John Straut

Housing & Construction
Housing Units, 2000*
Total	28,485
Median rent	$650
Median SF home value	$122,000

Permits for New Residential Construction
	Units	Value
Total, 2006	106	$8,659,704
Single family	12	$1,912,158
Total, 2007	131	$12,628,500
Single family	40	$5,162,150

Real Property Valuation, 2008
	Parcels	Valuation
Total	10,269	$3,511,073,150
Vacant	489	57,721,600
Residential	8,734	2,096,396,850
Commercial	680	534,042,300
Industrial	39	55,784,900
Apartments	327	767,127,500
Farm land	0	0
Farm homestead	0	0

Average Property Value & Tax, 2008
Residential value	$240,027
Property tax	$6,333
Tax credit/rebate	$1,034

Public Library
East Orange Public Library
21 S Arlington Ave
East Orange, NJ 07018
973-266-5607
Director	Carolyn Ryan Reed

Library statistics, 2007
Population served	69,824
Full-time/total staff	13/45

	Total	Per capita
Holdings	396,272	5.68
Revenues	$4,188,305	$59.98
Expenditures	$4,188,299	$59.98
Annual visits	375,213	5.37
Internet terminals/annual users	110/114,668	

Public Safety
Number of officers, 2007	277

Crime	2006	2007
Total crimes	3,181	2,350
Violent	721	529
Murder	9	8
Rape	25	32
Robbery	373	241
Aggravated assault	314	248
Non-violent	2,460	1,821
Burglary	593	446
Larceny	1,229	896
Vehicle theft	638	479
Domestic violence	564	521
Arson	50	28
Total crime rate	46.6	34.9
Violent	10.6	7.9
Non-violent	36.1	27.1

Public School District
(for school year 2007-08 except as noted)

East Orange School District
715 Park Avenue
East Orange, NJ 07017
(973) 266-5760
Superintendent	Clarence C. Hoover III
Number of schools	20
Grade plan	K-12
Enrollment	9,892
Attendance rate, '06-07	93.8%
Dropout rate	4.0%
Students per teacher	9.2
Per pupil expenditure	$17,160
Median faculty salary	$79,186
Median administrator salary	$128,762
Grade 12 enrollment	527
High school graduation rate	78.2%

Assessment test results
(percent scoring at proficient or advanced level)
	Language	Math
NJASK-Grade 3	74.9%	75.6%
GEPA-Grade 8	31.8%	55.3%
HSPA-High School	23.1%	49.7%

SAT Score Averages, 2006-07
Pct tested	Math	Verbal	Writing
NA	NA	NA	NA

Teacher Qualifications
Avg. years of experience	11
Highly-qualified teachers one subject/all subjects	98.0%/98.0%

No Child Left Behind
AYP, 2006-07	Meets Standards

Municipal Finance§
State Aid Programs, 2009
Total aid	$25,784,043
CMPTRA	19,605,395
Energy tax receipts	6,178,646
Garden State Trust	2

General Budget, 2008
Total tax levy	$92,838,496
County levy	12,404,489
County taxes	11,923,539
County library	0
County health	0
County open space	480,950
School levy	19,549,192
Muni. levy	60,884,815
Misc. revenues	72,890,655

Taxes	2006	2007	2008
General tax rate per $100	27.21	2.42	2.639
County equalization ratio	13.23	126.9	111.42
Net valuation taxable	$300,518,000	$3,519,868,772	$3,518,713,410
State equalized value	$2,740,463,385	$3,159,862,968	$3,451,894,871

Demographics & Socio-Economic Characteristics

(2000 US Census, except as noted)

Population

1980*	7,849
1990*	7,902
2000	8,716
Male	4,241
Female	4,475
2007 (estimate)*	8,798
Population density	2,309.2

Race & Hispanic Origin, 2000

Race

White	6,945
Black/African American	324
American Indian/Alaska Native	10
Asian	932
Native Hawaiian/Pacific Islander	4
Other race	280
Two or more races	221
Hispanic origin, total	928
Mexican	42
Puerto Rican	221
Cuban	91
Other Hispanic	574

Age & Nativity, 2000

Under 5 years	475
18 years and over	7,027
21 years and over	6,803
65 years and over	1,250
85 years and over	168
Median age	37.9
Native-born	6,202
Foreign-born	2,514

Educational Attainment, 2000

Population 25 years and over	6,434
Less than 9th grade	9.0%
High school grad or higher	78.5%
Bachelor's degree or higher	25.5%
Graduate degree	10.0%

Income & Poverty, 1999

Per capita income	$28,072
Median household income	$50,163
Median family income	$59,583
Persons in poverty	832
H'holds receiving public assistance	55
H'holds receiving social security	980

Households, 2000

Total households	3,644
With persons under 18	1,004
With persons over 65	952
Family households	2,156
Single-person households	1,216
Persons per household	2.35
Persons per family	3.05

Labor & Employment

Total civilian labor force, 2007**	4,924
Unemployment rate	4.7%
Total civilian labor force, 2000	4,809
Unemployment rate	5.5%

Employed persons 16 years and over by occupation, 2000

Managers & professionals	1,557
Service occupations	647
Sales & office occupations	1,402
Farming, fishing & forestry	12
Construction & maintenance	285
Production & transportation	643
Self-employed persons	188

* US Census Bureau
** New Jersey Department of Labor

See Introduction for an explanation of all data sources.

General Information

Borough of East Rutherford
1 Everett Pl
East Rutherford, NJ 07073
201-933-3444

Website	www.eastrutherfordnj.net
Year of incorporation	1894
Land/water area (sq. miles)	3.81/0.34
Form of government	Borough

Government

Legislative Districts

US Congressional	9
State Legislative	36

Local Officials, 2009

Mayor	James Cassella
Manager/Admin	NA
Clerk	Danielle Lorenc
Finance Dir	Anthony Bianchi
Tax Assessor	Dennis McGuire
Tax Collector	Linda Ramsaier
Attorney	Richard Allen
Dir of Inspections	Frank Recanati
Planning/Zoning	John Giancaspro
Engineering	Glenn Beckmeyer
Public Works	Alan DeRosa
Police Chief	Larry Minda (Dep)
Fire Chief	Harold Tilt

Housing & Construction

Housing Units, 2000*

Total	3,771
Median rent	$817
Median SF home value	$196,200

Permits for New Residential Construction

	Units	Value
Total, 2006	1	$189,500
Single family	1	$189,500
Total, 2007	622	$71,654,975
Single family	0	$489,000

Real Property Valuation, 2008

	Parcels	Valuation
Total	2,280	$932,865,631
Vacant	66	20,490,500
Residential	1,917	280,089,160
Commercial	168	294,412,871
Industrial	94	291,950,000
Apartments	35	45,923,100
Farm land	0	0
Farm homestead	0	0

Average Property Value & Tax, 2008

Residential value	$146,108
Property tax	$4,148
Tax credit/rebate	$785

Public Library

East Rutherford Mem Library
143 Boiling Springs Ave
East Rutherford, NJ 07073
201-939-3930

Director	Karen S. DiNardo

Library statistics, 2007

Population served	8,716
Full-time/total staff	1/3

	Total	Per capita
Holdings	30,934	3.55
Revenues	$700,541	$80.37
Expenditures	$398,070	$45.67
Annual visits	12,680	1.45
Internet terminals/annual users	3/3,622	

Public Safety

Number of officers, 2007	33

Crime	2006	2007
Total crimes	407	336
Violent	16	7
Murder	1	0
Rape	0	0
Robbery	3	2
Aggravated assault	12	5
Non-violent	391	329
Burglary	39	22
Larceny	292	262
Vehicle theft	60	45
Domestic violence	56	42
Arson	0	1
Total crime rate	45.4	37.6
Violent	1.8	0.8
Non-violent	43.6	36.8

Public School District

(for school year 2007-08 except as noted)

East Rutherford School District
Grove and Uhland Streets
East Rutherford, NJ 07073
(201) 804-3100

Superintendent	Daniel Swirsky
Number of schools	2
Grade plan	K-8
Enrollment	682
Attendance rate, '06-07	95.0%
Dropout rate	NA
Students per teacher	8.4
Per pupil expenditure	$13,805
Median faculty salary	$70,264
Median administrator salary	$121,323
Grade 12 enrollment	NA
High school graduation rate	NA

Assessment test results

(percent scoring at proficient or advanced level)

	Language	Math
NJASK-Grade 3	94.3%	88.6%
GEPA-Grade 8	70.2%	83.1%
HSPA-High School	NA	NA

SAT Score Averages, 2006-07

Pct tested	Math	Verbal	Writing
NA	NA	NA	NA

Teacher Qualifications

Avg. years of experience	9
Highly-qualified teachers one subject/all subjects	100%/100%

No Child Left Behind

AYP, 2006-07	Meets Standards

Municipal Finance

State Aid Programs, 2009

Total aid	$1,924,350
CMPTRA	34,611
Energy tax receipts	1,838,411
Garden State Trust	2,975

General Budget, 2008

Total tax levy	$26,543,800
County levy	3,551,741
County taxes	3,359,277
County library	0
County health	0
County open space	192,464
School levy	16,819,256
Muni. levy	6,172,803
Misc. revenues	12,730,778

Taxes	2006	2007	2008
General tax rate per $100	2.69	2.58	2.841
County equalization ratio	58.14	56.11	54.83
Net valuation taxable	$879,975,231	$929,872,429	$934,917,058
State equalized value	$1,570,443,342	$1,694,247,878	$1,976,788,156

©2009 Information Publications, Inc. All rights reserved. Photocopying prohibited. For additional copies, contact the publisher at www.informationpublications.com or (877)544-INFO (4636)

Demographics & Socio-Economic Characteristics

(2000 US Census, except as noted)

Population

1980*	21,041
1990*	22,353
2000	24,919
Male	12,153
Female	12,766
2007 (estimate)*	26,686
Population density	1,705.2

Race & Hispanic Origin, 2000

Race

White	18,545
Black/African American	2,217
American Indian/Alaska Native	49
Asian	2,380
Native Hawaiian/Pacific Islander	31
Other race	1,148
Two or more races	549
Hispanic origin, total	3,559
Mexican	282
Puerto Rican	515
Cuban	96
Other Hispanic	2,666

Age & Nativity, 2000

Under 5 years	1,915
18 years and over	18,935
21 years and over	18,221
65 years and over	2,062
85 years and over	402
Median age	35.6
Native-born	19,155
Foreign-born	5,764

Educational Attainment, 2000

Population 25 years and over	17,196
Less than 9th grade	4.0%
High school grad or higher	88.6%
Bachelor's degree or higher	42.0%
Graduate degree	15.5%

Income & Poverty, 1999

Per capita income	$28,695
Median household income	$63,616
Median family income	$73,461
Persons in poverty	1,312
H'holds receiving public assistance	67
H'holds receiving social security	1,451

Households, 2000

Total households	9,448
With persons under 18	3,451
With persons over 65	1,485
Family households	6,557
Single-person households	2,320
Persons per household	2.61
Persons per family	3.12

Labor & Employment

Total civilian labor force, 2007**	16,674
Unemployment rate	2.9%
Total civilian labor force, 2000	14,352
Unemployment rate	3.1%

Employed persons 16 years and over by occupation, 2000

Managers & professionals	6,312
Service occupations	1,332
Sales & office occupations	4,026
Farming, fishing & forestry	19
Construction & maintenance	498
Production & transportation	1,721
Self-employed persons	476

‡ Branch of county library
* US Census Bureau
** New Jersey Department of Labor

General Information

Township of East Windsor
16 Lanning Blvd
East Windsor, NJ 08520
609-443-4000

Website	www.east-windsor.nj.us
Year of incorporation	1797
Land/water area (sq. miles)	15.65/0.05
Form of government	Council-Manager

Government

Legislative Districts

US Congressional	4
State Legislative	12

Local Officials, 2009

Mayor	Janice Mironov
Manager	Alan M. Fisher
Clerk	Cindy A. Dye
Finance Dir	Margaret Gorman
Tax Assessor	H. Rick Kline
Tax Collector	Lois A. Burns
Attorney	David Orron
Building	Roman Petruniak
Planning	Richard Coppola
Engineering	Raymond Jordan
Public Works	William Askenstedt
Police Chief	William Spain
Fire/Emergency Dir	NA

Housing & Construction

Housing Units, 2000*

Total	9,880
Median rent	$791
Median SF home value	$152,600

Permits for New Residential Construction

	Units	Value
Total, 2006	66	$7,630,450
Single family	66	$7,630,450
Total, 2007	36	$4,246,765
Single family	36	$4,246,765

Real Property Valuation, 2008

	Parcels	Valuation
Total	8,415	$1,406,908,680
Vacant	413	25,868,000
Residential	7,672	1,024,066,400
Commercial	151	224,239,200
Industrial	11	52,647,300
Apartments	19	72,789,000
Farm land	115	1,457,280
Farm homestead	34	5,841,500

Average Property Value & Tax, 2008

Residential value	$133,650
Property tax	$6,906
Tax credit/rebate	$1,077

Public Library

Hickory Corner Branch Library‡
138 Hickory Corner Rd
East Windsor, NJ 08520
609-448-1330

Branch Librarian	Marilyn Fischer

Library statistics, 2007

see Mercer County profile
for library system statistics

Public Safety

Number of officers, 2007	49

Crime	2006	2007
Total crimes	397	371
Violent	41	20
Murder	1	0
Rape	3	3
Robbery	8	4
Aggravated assault	29	13
Non-violent	356	351
Burglary	73	42
Larceny	257	300
Vehicle theft	26	9
Domestic violence	194	159
Arson	7	3
Total crime rate	**14.8**	**13.8**
Violent	1.5	0.7
Non-violent	13.2	13.0

Public School District

(for school year 2007-08 except as noted)

East Windsor Regional School District
25A Leshin Lane
Hightstown, NJ 08520
(609) 443-7717

Superintendent	Ronald Bolandi
Number of schools	6
Grade plan	K-12
Enrollment	4,947
Attendance rate, '06-07	95.7%
Dropout rate	1.3%
Students per teacher	11.3
Per pupil expenditure	$14,400
Median faculty salary	$71,855
Median administrator salary	$124,738
Grade 12 enrollment	317
High school graduation rate	92.5%

Assessment test results

(percent scoring at proficient or advanced level)

	Language	Math
NJASK-Grade 3	90.0%	85.7%
GEPA-Grade 8	73.1%	84.2%
HSPA-High School	79.1%	89.2%

SAT Score Averages, 2006-07

Pct tested	Math	Verbal	Writing
86%	536	517	508

Teacher Qualifications

Avg. years of experience	15
Highly-qualified teachers one subject/all subjects	99.5%/99.5%

No Child Left Behind

AYP, 2006-07	Needs Improvement

Municipal Finance

State Aid Programs, 2009

Total aid	$4,535,285
CMPTRA	148,382
Energy tax receipts	4,273,220
Garden State Trust	414

General Budget, 2008

Total tax levy	$72,785,762
County levy	16,018,334
County taxes	13,700,936
County library	1,376,992
County health	0
County open space	940,406
School levy	48,748,006
Muni. levy	8,019,422
Misc. revenues	12,635,751

Taxes	2006	2007	2008
General tax rate per $100	4.83	5.07	5.168
County equalization ratio	51.49	45.5	45.05
Net valuation taxable	$1,393,251,480	$1,410,709,636	$1,408,570,313
State equalized value	$3,063,907,037	$3,129,455,594	$3,124,655,373

See Introduction for an explanation of all data sources.

Demographics & Socio-Economic Characteristics
(2000 US Census, except as noted)

Population
1980*	3,814
1990*	4,962
2000	6,202
Male	3,085
Female	3,117
2007 (estimate)*	6,535
Population density	1,136.5

Race & Hispanic Origin, 2000
Race
White	4,853
Black/African American	730
American Indian/Alaska Native	14
Asian	336
Native Hawaiian/Pacific Islander	0
Other race	89
Two or more races	180
Hispanic origin, total	293
Mexican	28
Puerto Rican	149
Cuban	17
Other Hispanic	99

Age & Nativity, 2000
Under 5 years	443
18 years and over	4,371
21 years and over	4,185
65 years and over	444
85 years and over	26
Median age	34.9
Native-born	5,705
Foreign-born	497

Educational Attainment, 2000
Population 25 years and over	3,945
Less than 9th grade	2.7%
High school grad or higher	90.1%
Bachelor's degree or higher	29.6%
Graduate degree	8.6%

Income & Poverty, 1999
Per capita income	$24,534
Median household income	$66,406
Median family income	$71,765
Persons in poverty	179
H'holds receiving public assistance	28
H'holds receiving social security	321

Households, 2000
Total households	2,226
With persons under 18	995
With persons over 65	338
Family households	1,639
Single-person households	478
Persons per household	2.78
Persons per family	3.29

Labor & Employment
Total civilian labor force, 2007**	3,941
Unemployment rate	2.6%
Total civilian labor force, 2000	3,453
Unemployment rate	2.5%

Employed persons 16 years and over by occupation, 2000
Managers & professionals	1,200
Service occupations	442
Sales & office occupations	1,021
Farming, fishing & forestry	8
Construction & maintenance	251
Production & transportation	446
Self-employed persons	141

* US Census Bureau
** New Jersey Department of Labor

See Introduction for an explanation of all data sources.

General Information
Township of Eastampton
12 Manorhouse Ct
Eastampton, NJ 08060
609-267-5723
Website	www.eastampton.com
Year of incorporation	1880
Land/water area (sq. miles)	5.75/0.08
Form of government	Council-Manager

Government
Legislative Districts
US Congressional	3
State Legislative	8

Local Officials, 2009
Mayor	Keith Nagler
Manager	Scott Carew
Municipal Clerk	Kim-Marie White
CFO	Gerald Mingin
Tax Assessor	Karen McMahon
Tax Collector	Doris LaVacca
Attorney	Eileen Fahey
Building	Gene Blair
Planning	Linda M. Lovins
Engineering	Nancy Jamanow
Public Works	Richard Parks
Police Chief	Gerald Mingin
Emerg/Fire Director	Phillip Polios

Housing & Construction
Housing Units, 2000*
Total	2,312
Median rent	$722
Median SF home value	$143,100

Permits for New Residential Construction
	Units	Value
Total, 2006	6	$728,970
Single family	6	$728,970
Total, 2007	27	$4,761,299
Single family	23	$4,149,913

Real Property Valuation, 2008
	Parcels	Valuation
Total	1,858	$521,954,300
Vacant	163	8,672,100
Residential	1,594	437,682,600
Commercial	37	30,941,000
Industrial	4	2,655,000
Apartments	4	36,900,000
Farm land	39	461,600
Farm homestead	17	4,642,000

Average Property Value & Tax, 2008
Residential value	$274,565
Property tax	$6,160
Tax credit/rebate	$1,113

Public Library
No public municipal library

Library statistics, 2007
Population served	NA
Full-time/total staff	NA/NA

	Total	Per capita
Holdings	NA	NA
Revenues	NA	NA
Expenditures	NA	NA
Annual visits	NA	NA
Internet terminals/annual users	NA/NA	

Public Safety
Number of officers, 2007	17

Crime	2006	2007
Total crimes	79	101
Violent	13	13
Murder	0	0
Rape	1	4
Robbery	4	3
Aggravated assault	8	6
Non-violent	66	88
Burglary	11	20
Larceny	46	62
Vehicle theft	9	6
Domestic violence	51	45
Arson	0	3
Total crime rate	11.7	15.1
Violent	1.9	1.9
Non-violent	9.8	13.1

Public School District
(for school year 2007-08 except as noted)

Eastampton Township School District
1 Student Drive
Eastampton, NJ 08060
(609) 267-9172
Superintendent	Robert Krastek
Number of schools	1
Grade plan	K-8
Enrollment	743
Attendance rate, '06-07	95.9%
Dropout rate	NA
Students per teacher	9.3
Per pupil expenditure	$11,203
Median faculty salary	$49,950
Median administrator salary	$100,775
Grade 12 enrollment	NA
High school graduation rate	NA

Assessment test results
(percent scoring at proficient or advanced level)
	Language	Math
NJASK-Grade 3	79.2%	87.0%
GEPA-Grade 8	85.6%	94.4%
HSPA-High School	NA	NA

SAT Score Averages, 2006-07
Pct tested	Math	Verbal	Writing
NA	NA	NA	NA

Teacher Qualifications
Avg. years of experience	9

Highly-qualified teachers
one subject/all subjects	98.5%/98.5%

No Child Left Behind
AYP, 2006-07	Meets Standards

Municipal Finance
State Aid Programs, 2009
Total aid	$550,464
CMPTRA	71,253
Energy tax receipts	465,450
Garden State Trust	0

General Budget, 2008
Total tax levy	$11,724,984
County levy	2,043,631
County taxes	1,678,229
County library	154,950
County health	0
County open space	210,452
School levy	6,634,107
Muni. levy	3,047,246
Misc. revenues	1,906,919

Taxes
	2006	2007	2008
General tax rate per $100	2.207	2.297	2.244
County equalization ratio	121.51	105.93	99.31
Net valuation taxable	$520,362,400	$521,083,404	$522,632,943
State equalized value	$491,879,139	$524,699,210	$532,959,186

Demographics & Socio-Economic Characteristics
(2000 US Census, except as noted)

Population
1980*	12,703
1990*	13,800
2000	14,008
Male	6,813
Female	7,195
2007 (estimate)*	14,109
Population density	2,383.3

Race & Hispanic Origin, 2000
Race
White	10,267
Black/African American	1,626
American Indian/Alaska Native	48
Asian	1,305
Native Hawaiian/Pacific Islander	5
Other race	323
Two or more races	434
Hispanic origin, total	928
Mexican	158
Puerto Rican	378
Cuban	35
Other Hispanic	357

Age & Nativity, 2000
Under 5 years	958
18 years and over	10,796
21 years and over	10,441
65 years and over	1,867
85 years and over	288
Median age	36.6
Native-born	11,691
Foreign-born	2,307

Educational Attainment, 2000
Population 25 years and over	9,877
Less than 9th grade	3.7%
High school grad or higher	89.1%
Bachelor's degree or higher	33.5%
Graduate degree	13.4%

Income & Poverty, 1999
Per capita income	$26,965
Median household income	$53,833
Median family income	$69,397
Persons in poverty	777
H'holds receiving public assistance	110
H'holds receiving social security	1,206

Households, 2000
Total households	5,780
With persons under 18	1,783
With persons over 65	1,232
Family households	3,447
Single-person households	1,951
Persons per household	2.35
Persons per family	3.08

Labor & Employment
Total civilian labor force, 2007**	7,989
Unemployment rate	3.7%
Total civilian labor force, 2000	7,511
Unemployment rate	4.4%

Employed persons 16 years and over by occupation, 2000
Managers & professionals	3,215
Service occupations	958
Sales & office occupations	2,046
Farming, fishing & forestry	0
Construction & maintenance	384
Production & transportation	579
Self-employed persons	288

General Information
Borough of Eatontown
47 Broad St
Eatontown, NJ 07724
732-389-7621
Website	www.eatontownnj.com
Year of incorporation	1926
Land/water area (sq. miles)	5.92/0.01
Form of government	Borough

Government
Legislative Districts
US Congressional	12
State Legislative	11

Local Officials, 2009
Mayor	Gerald Tarantolo
Manager/Admin	NA
Clerk	Karen Siano
Finance Dir	Lesley Connolly
Tax Assessor	John Gillooly
Tax Collector	Patricia DePonti
Attorney	Andrew Bayer
Building	Djongo Weigers
Comm Dev/Planning	NA
Engineering	Edward Broberg
Public Works	Frank Cannella
Police Chief	George Jackson
Emerg/Fire Director	William Mego

Housing & Construction
Housing Units, 2000*
Total	6,341
Median rent	$766
Median SF home value	$178,200

Permits for New Residential Construction
	Units	Value
Total, 2006	26	$4,429,828
Single family	26	$4,429,828
Total, 2007	89	$8,408,866
Single family	17	$2,347,366

Real Property Valuation, 2008
	Parcels	Valuation
Total	3,210	$2,448,534,000
Vacant	156	41,936,400
Residential	2,784	1,111,379,400
Commercial	197	907,558,600
Industrial	42	211,999,300
Apartments	23	175,227,100
Farm land	6	16,300
Farm homestead	2	416,900

Average Property Value & Tax, 2008
Residential value	$399,065
Property tax	$6,693
Tax credit/rebate	$996

Public Library
Eatontown Public Library
33 Broad St
Eatontown, NJ 07724
732-389-2665
Director	Amy Garibay

Library statistics, 2007
Population served	14,008
Full-time/total staff	NA/0

	Total	Per capita
Holdings	0	NA
Revenues	$0	NA
Expenditures	$0	NA
Annual visits	NA	NA
Internet terminals/annual users	NA/NA	

Public Safety
Number of officers, 2007	37

Crime	2006	2007
Total crimes	639	595
Violent	36	20
Murder	0	0
Rape	4	0
Robbery	16	12
Aggravated assault	16	8
Non-violent	603	575
Burglary	50	53
Larceny	536	506
Vehicle theft	17	16
Domestic violence	47	62
Arson	0	1
Total crime rate	45.4	42.4
Violent	2.6	1.4
Non-violent	42.8	41.0

Public School District
(for school year 2007-08 except as noted)

Eatontown School District
5 Grant Ave
Eatontown, NJ 07724
(732) 542-1310
Superintendent	Barbara Struble
Number of schools	4
Grade plan	K-8
Enrollment	1,134
Attendance rate, '06-07	95.6%
Dropout rate	NA
Students per teacher	8.8
Per pupil expenditure	$15,266
Median faculty salary	$60,490
Median administrator salary	$104,000
Grade 12 enrollment	NA
High school graduation rate	NA

Assessment test results
(percent scoring at proficient or advanced level)
	Language	Math
NJASK-Grade 3	89.1%	85.2%
GEPA-Grade 8	76.5%	88.2%
HSPA-High School	NA	NA

SAT Score Averages, 2006-07
Pct tested	Math	Verbal	Writing
NA	NA	NA	NA

Teacher Qualifications
Avg. years of experience	13
Highly-qualified teachers one subject/all subjects	99.0%/99.0%

No Child Left Behind
AYP, 2006-07	Meets Standards

Municipal Finance
State Aid Programs, 2009
Total aid	$1,888,335
CMPTRA	393,567
Energy tax receipts	1,447,557
Garden State Trust	2

General Budget, 2008
Total tax levy	$41,203,477
County levy	5,968,571
County taxes	5,295,744
County library	319,133
County health	0
County open space	353,693
School levy	22,633,104
Muni. levy	12,601,803
Misc. revenues	8,467,105

Taxes
	2006	2007	2008
General tax rate per $100	1.441	1.615	1.678
County equalization ratio	124.46	111.25	102.97
Net valuation taxable	$2,626,436,100	$2,490,880,992	$2,456,688,843
State equalized value	$2,368,717,720	$2,419,254,321	$2,810,822,442

* US Census Bureau
** New Jersey Department of Labor

See Introduction for an explanation of all data sources.

Demographics & Socio-Economic Characteristics

(2000 US Census, except as noted)

Population
1980*	4,628
1990*	5,001
2000	7,677
Male	3,739
Female	3,938
2007 (estimate)*	9,582
Population density	11,272.9

Race & Hispanic Origin, 2000
Race
White	5,153
Black/African American	270
American Indian/Alaska Native	16
Asian	1,775
Native Hawaiian/Pacific Islander	3
Other race	226
Two or more races	234
Hispanic origin, total	802
Mexican	71
Puerto Rican	169
Cuban	102
Other Hispanic	460

Age & Nativity, 2000
Under 5 years	430
18 years and over	6,494
21 years and over	6,362
65 years and over	687
85 years and over	67
Median age	36.3
Native-born	4,954
Foreign-born	2,723

Educational Attainment, 2000
Population 25 years and over	6,124
Less than 9th grade	2.8%
High school grad or higher	90.8%
Bachelor's degree or higher	51.4%
Graduate degree	18.6%

Income & Poverty, 1999
Per capita income	$42,650
Median household income	$63,455
Median family income	$72,692
Persons in poverty	662
H'holds receiving public assistance	51
H'holds receiving social security	551

Households, 2000
Total households	3,836
With persons under 18	800
With persons over 65	551
Family households	1,973
Single-person households	1,499
Persons per household	2.00
Persons per family	2.70

Labor & Employment
Total civilian labor force, 2007**	5,078
Unemployment rate	3.6%
Total civilian labor force, 2000	4,817
Unemployment rate	4.0%

Employed persons 16 years and over by occupation, 2000
Managers & professionals	2,494
Service occupations	342
Sales & office occupations	1,203
Farming, fishing & forestry	0
Construction & maintenance	202
Production & transportation	385
Self-employed persons	174

* US Census Bureau
** New Jersey Department of Labor
§ State Fiscal Year July 1–June 30

General Information
Borough of Edgewater
916 River Rd
Edgewater, NJ 07020
201-943-1700
Website	www.edgewaternj.org
Year of incorporation	1899
Land/water area (sq. miles)	0.85/1.57
Form of government	Borough

Government
Legislative Districts
US Congressional	9
State Legislative	38

Local Officials, 2009
Mayor	Nancy Merse
Manager	Greg Franz
Clerk	Barbara Rae
Finance Dir	Joseph Iannaconi Jr
Tax Assessor	Art Carlson
Tax Collector	Joseph Iannaconi Jr
Attorney	Philip Boggia
Building	John Candelmo
Planning	John Candelmo
Engineering	Michael Neglia
Public Works	Thomas Quinton
Police Chief	Donald Martin
Fire Chief	Joseph Chevalier

Housing & Construction
Housing Units, 2000*
Total	4,277
Median rent	$1,209
Median SF home value	$283,900

Permits for New Residential Construction
	Units	Value
Total, 2006	55	$7,359,454
Single family	1	$25,000
Total, 2007	77	$7,076,424
Single family	8	$2,183,724

Real Property Valuation, 2008
	Parcels	Valuation
Total	3,538	$3,020,532,600
Vacant	172	52,490,700
Residential	3,197	1,760,369,900
Commercial	110	613,151,200
Industrial	12	42,425,700
Apartments	47	552,095,100
Farm land	0	0
Farm homestead	0	0

Average Property Value & Tax, 2008
Residential value	$550,632
Property tax	$6,006
Tax credit/rebate	$922

Public Library
Edgewater Free Public Library
49 Hudson Ave
Edgewater, NJ 07020
201-224-6144
Director	Linda Corona

Library statistics, 2007
Population served	7,677
Full-time/total staff	2/6

	Total	Per capita
Holdings	23,159	3.02
Revenues	$658,963	$85.84
Expenditures	$568,812	$74.09
Annual visits	51,831	6.75
Internet terminals/annual users	15/43,850	

Public Safety
Number of officers, 2007	33

Crime	2006	2007
Total crimes	194	229
Violent	16	9
Murder	0	0
Rape	0	0
Robbery	5	1
Aggravated assault	11	8
Non-violent	178	220
Burglary	30	9
Larceny	135	201
Vehicle theft	13	10
Domestic violence	40	40
Arson	0	0
Total crime rate	20.1	23.8
Violent	1.7	0.9
Non-violent	18.5	22.9

Public School District
(for school year 2007-08 except as noted)

Edgewater School District
251 Undercliff Avenue
Edgewater, NJ 07020
(201) 945-4106
Superintendent	Ted I. Blumstein
Number of schools	1
Grade plan	K-6
Enrollment	443
Attendance rate, '06-07	95.4%
Dropout rate	NA
Students per teacher	11.0
Per pupil expenditure	$17,259
Median faculty salary	$50,265
Median administrator salary	$100,580
Grade 12 enrollment	NA
High school graduation rate	NA

Assessment test results
(percent scoring at proficient or advanced level)
	Language	Math
NJASK-Grade 3	96.7%	94.7%
GEPA-Grade 8	NA	NA
HSPA-High School	NA	NA

SAT Score Averages, 2006-07
Pct tested	Math	Verbal	Writing
NA	NA	NA	NA

Teacher Qualifications
Avg. years of experience	11
Highly-qualified teachers one subject/all subjects	100%/100%

No Child Left Behind
AYP, 2006-07	Meets Standards

Municipal Finance§
State Aid Programs, 2009
Total aid	$1,013,650
CMPTRA	477,181
Energy tax receipts	503,526
Garden State Trust	0

General Budget, 2008
Total tax levy	$32,959,928
County levy	5,290,629
County taxes	5,001,485
County library	0
County health	0
County open space	289,144
School levy	12,075,816
Muni. levy	15,593,483
Misc. revenues	5,908,876

Taxes
	2006	2007	2008
General tax rate per $100	2.84	2.96	1.093
County equalization ratio	55.45	42.38	108.78
Net valuation taxable	$1,095,842,800	$1,116,344,757	$3,021,624,313
State equalized value	$2,586,322,619	$2,753,039,045	$2,802,290,452

See Introduction for an explanation of all data sources.

Demographics & Socio-Economic Characteristics

(2000 US Census, except as noted)

Population

1980*	9,273
1990*	8,388
2000	7,864
Male	3,789
Female	4,075
2007 (estimate)*	7,762
Population density	2,667.4

Race & Hispanic Origin, 2000

Race

White	5,353
Black/African American	1,683
American Indian/Alaska Native	13
Asian	256
Native Hawaiian/Pacific Islander	1
Other race	252
Two or more races	306
Hispanic origin, total	519
Mexican	70
Puerto Rican	211
Cuban	4
Other Hispanic	234

Age & Nativity, 2000

Under 5 years	462
18 years and over	6,053
21 years and over	5,773
65 years and over	1,025
85 years and over	58
Median age	37.9
Native-born	7,188
Foreign-born	676

Educational Attainment, 2000

Population 25 years and over	5,527
Less than 9th grade	3.5%
High school grad or higher	85.8%
Bachelor's degree or higher	19.6%
Graduate degree	4.1%

Income & Poverty, 1999

Per capita income	$22,920
Median household income	$48,936
Median family income	$52,016
Persons in poverty	677
H'holds receiving public assistance	95
H'holds receiving social security	973

Households, 2000

Total households	3,152
With persons under 18	1,044
With persons over 65	782
Family households	2,099
Single-person households	868
Persons per household	2.49
Persons per family	3.03

Labor & Employment

Total civilian labor force, 2007**	4,945
Unemployment rate	4.8%
Total civilian labor force, 2000	4,322
Unemployment rate	4.8%

Employed persons 16 years and over by occupation, 2000

Managers & professionals	1,384
Service occupations	578
Sales & office occupations	1,105
Farming, fishing & forestry	0
Construction & maintenance	389
Production & transportation	658
Self-employed persons	192

‡ Joint library with Beverly City
* US Census Bureau
** New Jersey Department of Labor

General Information

Township of Edgewater Park
400 Delanco Rd
Edgewater Park, NJ 08010
609-877-2050

Website	www.edgewaterpark-nj.com
Year of incorporation	1924
Land/water area (sq. miles)	2.91/0.13
Form of government	Township

Government

Legislative Districts

US Congressional	3
State Legislative	7

Local Officials, 2009

Mayor	Donna Mount
Manager	Linda Dougherty
Clerk	Linda Dougherty
Finance Dir	Margaret Peak
Tax Assessor	Leo Midure
Tax Collector	Tanyika Johns
Attorney	William Kearns
Building	Jim Scott
Comm Dev/Planning	NA
Engineering	Environmental Resolutions
Public Works	Aubrey Painter
Public Safety Dir	Robert Brian
Emerg/Fire Director	(Beverly Fire Dept)

Housing & Construction

Housing Units, 2000*

Total	3,301
Median rent	$661
Median SF home value	$119,800

Permits for New Residential Construction

	Units	Value
Total, 2006	0	$260,087
Single family	0	$260,087
Total, 2007	1	$177,100
Single family	1	$177,100

Real Property Valuation, 2008

	Parcels	Valuation
Total	2,550	$310,754,200
Vacant	70	3,678,100
Residential	2,389	237,762,400
Commercial	59	34,417,300
Industrial	9	4,442,100
Apartments	9	29,717,400
Farm land	10	134,700
Farm homestead	4	602,200

Average Property Value & Tax, 2008

Residential value	$99,609
Property tax	$4,157
Tax credit/rebate	$852

Public Library

Beverly Public Library‡
441 Cooper St
Beverly, NJ 08010
609-387-1259

Director	Tracey Hall

Library statistics, 2007

Population served	2,661
Full-time/total staff	NA/0

	Total	Per capita
Holdings	0	NA
Revenues	$0	NA
Expenditures	$0	NA
Annual visits	NA	NA
Internet terminals/annual users	NA/NA	

Public Safety

Number of officers, 2007	14

Crime	2006	2007
Total crimes	224	188
Violent	23	16
Murder	0	0
Rape	5	0
Robbery	8	8
Aggravated assault	10	8
Non-violent	201	172
Burglary	52	39
Larceny	127	115
Vehicle theft	22	18
Domestic violence	105	112
Arson	1	2
Total crime rate	27.9	23.6
Violent	2.9	2.0
Non-violent	25.1	21.6

Public School District

(for school year 2007-08 except as noted)

Edgewater Park Township School District
25 Washington Avenue
Edgewater Park, NJ 08010
(609) 877-2124

Superintendent	Scott Streckenbein
Number of schools	2
Grade plan	K-8
Enrollment	827
Attendance rate, '06-07	94.9%
Dropout rate	NA
Students per teacher	10.4
Per pupil expenditure	$12,631
Median faculty salary	$58,345
Median administrator salary	$97,798
Grade 12 enrollment	NA
High school graduation rate	NA

Assessment test results

(percent scoring at proficient or advanced level)

	Language	Math
NJASK-Grade 3	85.7%	83.4%
GEPA-Grade 8	48.2%	65.5%
HSPA-High School	NA	NA

SAT Score Averages, 2006-07

Pct tested	Math	Verbal	Writing
NA	NA	NA	NA

Teacher Qualifications

Avg. years of experience	14
Highly-qualified teachers one subject/all subjects	100%/100%

No Child Left Behind

AYP, 2006-07	Meets Standards

Municipal Finance

State Aid Programs, 2009

Total aid	$871,620
CMPTRA	200,076
Energy tax receipts	649,754
Garden State Trust	0

General Budget, 2008

Total tax levy	$12,983,166
County levy	2,493,932
County taxes	2,048,037
County library	189,097
County health	0
County open space	256,798
School levy	7,404,521
Muni. levy	3,084,713
Misc. revenues	2,679,685

Taxes

	2006	2007	2008
General tax rate per $100	3.695	4.03	4.173
County equalization ratio	62.82	54.09	48.75
Net valuation taxable	$309,653,200	$310,588,619	$311,134,167
State equalized value	$572,933,783	$636,679,491	$672,135,695

See Introduction for an explanation of all data sources.

Demographics & Socio-Economic Characteristics[†]

(2000 US Census, except as noted)

Population

1980*	70,193
1990*	88,680
2000	97,687
Male	47,926
Female	49,761
2007 (estimate)*	99,884
Population density	3,316.2

Race & Hispanic Origin, 2000

Race
White	58,116
Black/African American	6,728
American Indian/Alaska Native	132
Asian	28,597
Native Hawaiian/Pacific Islander	37
Other race	1,973
Two or more races	2,104
Hispanic origin, total	6,226
Mexican	546
Puerto Rican	2,095
Cuban	590
Other Hispanic	2,995

Age & Nativity, 2000

Under 5 years	6,299
18 years and over	75,365
21 years and over	72,264
65 years and over	11,668
85 years and over	1,247
Median age	36.3
Native-born	65,336
Foreign-born	32,351

Educational Attainment, 2000

Population 25 years and over	67,649
Less than 9th grade	4.4%
High school grad or higher	87.6%
Bachelor's degree or higher	42.3%
Graduate degree	17.2%

Income & Poverty, 1999

Per capita income	$30,148
Median household income	$69,746
Median family income	$77,976
Persons in poverty	4,606
H'holds receiving public assistance	455
H'holds receiving social security	7,681

Households, 2000

Total households	35,136
With persons under 18	12,887
With persons over 65	7,991
Family households	25,881
Single-person households	7,419
Persons per household	2.72
Persons per family	3.19

Labor & Employment

Total civilian labor force, 2007**	55,440
Unemployment rate	3.1%
Total civilian labor force, 2000	52,409
Unemployment rate	4.1%

Employed persons 16 years and over by occupation, 2000
Managers & professionals	23,944
Service occupations	4,449
Sales & office occupations	14,077
Farming, fishing & forestry	13
Construction & maintenance	2,626
Production & transportation	5,144
Self-employed persons	1,684

[†] see Appendix C for American Community Survey data
* US Census Bureau
** New Jersey Department of Labor
§ State Fiscal Year July 1–June 30

See Introduction for an explanation of all data sources.

General Information

Township of Edison
100 Municipal Blvd
Edison, NJ 08817
732-248-7200

Website	www.edisonnj.org
Year of incorporation	1954
Land/water area (sq. miles)	30.12/0.57
Form of government	Mayor-Council

Government

Legislative Districts

US Congressional	6, 7
State Legislative	18

Local Officials, 2009

Mayor	Jun H. Choi
Manager	Anthony Cancro
Clerk	Reina Murphy
Finance Dir	Mark Acker
Tax Assessor	Victoria Riddle
Tax Collector	Richard Lorentzen
Attorney	Jeffrey Lehrer
Building	Edward Wheeler
Planning	Brandy Forbes
Engineering	John Medina
Public Works	Jeff Roderman
Police Chief	Ronald Gerba (Actg)
Emerg/Fire Director	Norman Jensen

Housing & Construction

Housing Units, 2000*

Total	36,018
Median rent	$913
Median SF home value	$186,900

Permits for New Residential Construction

	Units	Value
Total, 2006	338	$19,490,628
Single family	19	$15,625,996
Total, 2007	89	$17,063,831
Single family	33	$15,247,831

Real Property Valuation, 2008

	Parcels	Valuation
Total	27,560	$7,358,605,000
Vacant	1,381	168,454,100
Residential	24,921	4,359,806,200
Commercial	869	1,113,955,400
Industrial	309	1,259,429,800
Apartments	74	456,944,900
Farm land	6	14,600
Farm homestead	0	0

Average Property Value & Tax, 2008

Residential value	$174,945
Property tax	$6,900
Tax credit/rebate	$1,059

Public Library

Edison Public Library
340 Plainfield Ave
Edison, NJ 08817
732-287-2298

Director ..... Judith Mansbach

Library statistics, 2007

Population served	97,687
Full-time/total staff	1/3

	Total	Per capita
Holdings	323,208	3.31
Revenues	$5,824,691	$59.63
Expenditures	$5,668,631	$58.03
Annual visits	527,278	5.40
Internet terminals/annual users	24/56,747	

Public Safety

Number of officers, 2007 200

Crime	2006	2007
Total crimes	2,618	2,471
Violent	295	226
Murder	1	0
Rape	15	0
Robbery	86	86
Aggravated assault	193	140
Non-violent	2,323	2,245
Burglary	369	437
Larceny	1,686	1,584
Vehicle theft	268	224
Domestic violence	364	334
Arson	12	6
Total crime rate	26.1	24.8
Violent	2.9	2.3
Non-violent	23.1	22.6

Public School District

(for school year 2007-08 except as noted)

Edison Township School District
312 Pierson Avenue
Edison, NJ 08837
(732) 452-4963

Superintendent	John DiMuzio (Actg)
Number of schools	17
Grade plan	K-12
Enrollment	13,920
Attendance rate, '06-07	96.2%
Dropout rate	1.0%
Students per teacher	11.0
Per pupil expenditure	$12,871
Median faculty salary	$69,025
Median administrator salary	$111,331
Grade 12 enrollment	1,104
High school graduation rate	97.7%

Assessment test results

(percent scoring at proficient or advanced level)
	Language	Math
NJASK-Grade 3	93.3%	94.3%
GEPA-Grade 8	78.2%	91.1%
HSPA-High School	87.4%	90.9%

SAT Score Averages, 2006-07

Pct tested	Math	Verbal	Writing
NA	NA	NA	NA

Teacher Qualifications

Avg. years of experience	9
Highly-qualified teachers one subject/all subjects	100%/100%

No Child Left Behind

AYP, 2006-07 .... Meets Standards

Municipal Finance[§]

State Aid Programs, 2009

Total aid	$19,999,703
CMPTRA	0
Energy tax receipts	19,471,182
Garden State Trust	26,107

General Budget, 2008

Total tax levy	$290,628,840
County levy	44,212,113
County taxes	39,613,638
County library	0
County health	0
County open space	4,598,475
School levy	168,732,074
Muni. levy	77,684,653
Misc. revenues	40,353,957

Taxes

	2006	2007	2008
General tax rate per $100	3.59	3.72	3.945
County equalization ratio	58.05	52.93	47.67
Net valuation taxable	$7,291,812,000	$7,339,891,295	$7,368,359,893
State equalized value	$13,787,645,360	$15,385,939,240	$16,080,086,843

Demographics & Socio-Economic Characteristics

(2000 US Census, except as noted)

Population
1980*	4,618
1990*	4,583
2000	4,545
Male	2,197
Female	2,348
2007 (estimate)*	4,398
Population density	395.9

Race & Hispanic Origin, 2000
Race
White	3,036
Black/African American	645
American Indian/Alaska Native	17
Asian	57
Native Hawaiian/Pacific Islander	4
Other race	613
Two or more races	173
Hispanic origin, total	1,116
Mexican	77
Puerto Rican	880
Cuban	10
Other Hispanic	149

Age & Nativity, 2000
Under 5 years	305
18 years and over	3,261
21 years and over	3,070
65 years and over	633
85 years and over	57
Median age	34.9
Native-born	4,286
Foreign-born	259

Educational Attainment, 2000
Population 25 years and over	2,928
Less than 9th grade	8.5%
High school grad or higher	70.0%
Bachelor's degree or higher	10.2%
Graduate degree	2.5%

Income & Poverty, 1999
Per capita income	$15,151
Median household income	$32,956
Median family income	$40,040
Persons in poverty	588
H'holds receiving public assistance	33
H'holds receiving social security	534

Households, 2000
Total households	1,658
With persons under 18	645
With persons over 65	459
Family households	1,150
Single-person households	413
Persons per household	2.70
Persons per family	3.20

Labor & Employment
Total civilian labor force, 2007**	2,281
Unemployment rate	8.7%
Total civilian labor force, 2000	2,170
Unemployment rate	9.7%

Employed persons 16 years and over by occupation, 2000
Managers & professionals	297
Service occupations	455
Sales & office occupations	579
Farming, fishing & forestry	0
Construction & maintenance	242
Production & transportation	387
Self-employed persons	49

‡ Branch of county library
* US Census Bureau
** New Jersey Department of Labor

General Information
City of Egg Harbor
500 London Ave
Egg Harbor City, NJ 08215
609-965-0081
Website	www.eggharborcity.org
Year of incorporation	1858
Land/water area (sq. miles)	11.11/0.43
Form of government	City

Government
Legislative Districts
US Congressional	2
State Legislative	2

Local Officials, 2009
Mayor	Joseph A. Kuehner Jr
Manager	Thomas Henshaw
Clerk	Lillian DeBow
Finance Dir	Jodi Kahn
Tax Assessor	Bill Johnson
Tax Collector	Beverly Totten
Attorney	James Carroll
Building	Wayne Gibson
Planner	Tim Michel
Engineering	Remington & Vernick
Public Works	NA
Police Chief	John McColgan
Emerg/Fire Director	Russell Fenton

Housing & Construction
Housing Units, 2000*
Total	1,770
Median rent	$615
Median SF home value	$86,800

Permits for New Residential Construction
	Units	Value
Total, 2006	14	$1,456,544
Single family	14	$1,456,544
Total, 2007	12	$1,166,589
Single family	12	$1,166,589

Real Property Valuation, 2008
	Parcels	Valuation
Total	2,488	$297,233,500
Vacant	1,081	7,473,400
Residential	1,232	232,881,600
Commercial	148	41,998,600
Industrial	16	7,936,500
Apartments	11	6,943,400
Farm land	0	0
Farm homestead	0	0

Average Property Value & Tax, 2008
Residential value	$189,027
Property tax	$4,912
Tax credit/rebate	$935

Public Library
Egg Harbor City Branch Library‡
134 Philadelphia Ave
Egg Harbor City, NJ 08215
609-804-1063
Branch Librarian	Molly Montee

Library statistics, 2007
see Atlantic County profile
for library system statistics

Public Safety
Number of officers, 2007	14

Crime	2006	2007
Total crimes	106	120
Violent	13	21
Murder	0	1
Rape	0	1
Robbery	6	8
Aggravated assault	7	11
Non-violent	93	99
Burglary	28	36
Larceny	63	54
Vehicle theft	2	9
Domestic violence	30	40
Arson	0	1
Total crime rate	23.6	26.9
Violent	2.9	4.7
Non-violent	20.7	22.2

Public School District
(for school year 2007-08 except as noted)

Egg Harbor City School District
527 Philadelphia Avenue
Egg Harbor City, NJ 08215
(609) 965-1034
Superintendent	John Gilly III
Number of schools	2
Grade plan	K-8
Enrollment	502
Attendance rate, '06-07	93.4%
Dropout rate	NA
Students per teacher	7.8
Per pupil expenditure	$15,630
Median faculty salary	$47,248
Median administrator salary	$84,115
Grade 12 enrollment	NA
High school graduation rate	NA

Assessment test results
(percent scoring at proficient or advanced level)
	Language	Math
NJASK-Grade 3	78.8%	78.8%
GEPA-Grade 8	41.2%	71.2%
HSPA-High School	NA	NA

SAT Score Averages, 2006-07
Pct tested	Math	Verbal	Writing
NA	NA	NA	NA

Teacher Qualifications
Avg. years of experience	7
Highly-qualified teachers one subject/all subjects	100%/97.5%

No Child Left Behind
AYP, 2006-07	Meets Standards

Municipal Finance
State Aid Programs, 2009
Total aid	$553,538
CMPTRA	170,412
Energy tax receipts	383,020
Garden State Trust	142

General Budget, 2008
Total tax levy	$7,780,387
County levy	949,170
County taxes	747,266
County library	96,182
County health	39,357
County open space	66,364
School levy	3,453,884
Muni. levy	3,377,333
Misc. revenues	2,803,174

Taxes
	2006	2007	2008
General tax rate per $100	2.309	2.479	2.599
County equalization ratio	131.9	100.88	91.09
Net valuation taxable	$295,460,100	$299,694,731	$299,436,382
State equalized value	$295,187,653	$328,777,953	$322,118,392

See Introduction for an explanation of all data sources.

Demographics & Socio-Economic Characteristics
(2000 US Census, except as noted)

Population
1980*	19,381
1990*	24,544
2000	30,726
Male	14,934
Female	15,792
2007 (estimate)*	39,493
Population density	586.4

Race & Hispanic Origin, 2000
Race
White	24,404
Black/African American	3,185
American Indian/Alaska Native	66
Asian	1,552
Native Hawaiian/Pacific Islander	15
Other race	868
Two or more races	636
Hispanic origin, total	2,076
Mexican	213
Puerto Rican	1,098
Cuban	44
Other Hispanic	721

Age & Nativity, 2000
Under 5 years	2,278
18 years and over	22,142
21 years and over	21,198
65 years and over	2,815
85 years and over	274
Median age	36.0
Native-born	28,047
Foreign-born	2,572

Educational Attainment, 2000
Population 25 years and over	20,071
Less than 9th grade	5.4%
High school grad or higher	82.8%
Bachelor's degree or higher	19.0%
Graduate degree	5.5%

Income & Poverty, 1999
Per capita income	$22,328
Median household income	$52,550
Median family income	$60,032
Persons in poverty	1,637
H'holds receiving public assistance	245
H'holds receiving social security	2,411

Households, 2000
Total households	11,199
With persons under 18	4,617
With persons over 65	2,167
Family households	8,106
Single-person households	2,467
Persons per household	2.74
Persons per family	3.23

Labor & Employment
Total civilian labor force, 2007**	21,314
Unemployment rate	5.1%
Total civilian labor force, 2000	16,367
Unemployment rate	4.2%

Employed persons 16 years and over by occupation, 2000
Managers & professionals	4,188
Service occupations	4,276
Sales & office occupations	4,058
Farming, fishing & forestry	16
Construction & maintenance	1,708
Production & transportation	1,437
Self-employed persons	803

‡ Branch of county library
* US Census Bureau
** New Jersey Department of Labor

See Introduction for an explanation of all data sources.

General Information
Egg Harbor Township
3515 Bargaintown Rd
Egg Harbor Township, NJ 08234
609-926-4000

Website	www.ehtgov.org
Year of incorporation	1693
Land/water area (sq. miles)	67.35/7.61
Form of government	Township

Government
Legislative Districts
US Congressional	2
State Legislative	2

Local Officials, 2009
Mayor	James McCullough
Manager	Peter J. Miller
Clerk	Eileen M. Tedesco
Finance Dir	Charlene Canale
Tax Assessor	Maryanne Lavner
Tax Collector	Sharon D. Riley
Attorney	Marc Friedman
Building	Pat Natcchione
Planning	Theresa Wilbert
Township Engineer	James Mott
Public Works	Al Simerson
Police Chief	Blaze Catania
Emerg/Fire Director	Bill Danz Jr

Housing & Construction
Housing Units, 2000*
Total	12,067
Median rent	$700
Median SF home value	$131,300

Permits for New Residential Construction
	Units	Value
Total, 2006	616	$58,813,683
Single family	573	$58,315,183
Total, 2007	335	$34,774,721
Single family	335	$34,774,721

Real Property Valuation, 2008
	Parcels	Valuation
Total	19,545	$2,514,285,900
Vacant	4,814	137,144,000
Residential	13,730	1,911,350,500
Commercial	888	426,413,900
Industrial	20	27,295,200
Apartments	12	8,210,400
Farm land	62	508,400
Farm homestead	19	3,363,500

Average Property Value & Tax, 2008
Residential value	$139,262
Property tax	$5,186
Tax credit/rebate	$880

Public Library
Egg Harbor Township Branch Library‡
1 Swift Ave
Egg Harbor Township, NJ 08234
609-927-8664
Branch Librarian......William D. Paulin

Library statistics, 2007
see Atlantic County profile
for library system statistics

Public Safety
Number of officers, 2007	100

Crime	2006	2007
Total crimes	1,290	1,035
Violent	88	88
Murder	7	0
Rape	6	8
Robbery	35	26
Aggravated assault	40	54
Non-violent	1,202	947
Burglary	283	210
Larceny	888	684
Vehicle theft	31	53
Domestic violence	400	390
Arson	13	15
Total crime rate	33.9	26.7
Violent	2.3	2.3
Non-violent	31.6	24.4

Public School District
(for school year 2007-08 except as noted)

Egg Harbor Township School District
13 Swift Drive
Egg Harbor Township, NJ 08234
(609) 646-7911

Superintendent	Scott McCartney
Number of schools	7
Grade plan	K-12
Enrollment	7,665
Attendance rate, '06-07	94.8%
Dropout rate	2.9%
Students per teacher	10.9
Per pupil expenditure	$12,360
Median faculty salary	$48,480
Median administrator salary	$91,124
Grade 12 enrollment	510
High school graduation rate	91.9%

Assessment test results
(percent scoring at proficient or advanced level)
	Language	Math
NJASK-Grade 3	82.1%	87.7%
GEPA-Grade 8	70.3%	81.2%
HSPA-High School	69.9%	76.8%

SAT Score Averages, 2006-07
Pct tested	Math	Verbal	Writing
61%	486	477	468

Teacher Qualifications
Avg. years of experience	7

Highly-qualified teachers
one subject/all subjects......100%/100%

No Child Left Behind
AYP, 2006-07 ....Meets Standards

Municipal Finance
State Aid Programs, 2009
Total aid	$6,965,260
CMPTRA	0
Energy tax receipts	6,759,716
Garden State Trust	14,986

General Budget, 2008
Total tax levy	$93,860,442
County levy	15,217,104
County taxes	11,987,872
County library	1,538,336
County health	629,479
County open space	1,061,417
School levy	65,587,592
Muni. levy	13,055,746
Misc. revenues	21,212,983

Taxes
	2006	2007	2008
General tax rate per $100	3.359	3.579	3.724
County equalization ratio	57.29	50.97	47.61
Net valuation taxable	$2,281,667,500	$2,422,334,498	$2,520,668,104
State equalized value	$4,483,497,977	$5,080,876,657	$5,233,587,817

Demographics & Socio-Economic Characteristics†

(2000 US Census, except as noted)

Population
1980*	106,201
1990*	110,002
2000	120,568
Male	59,674
Female	60,894
2007 (estimate)*	124,862
Population density	10,217.8

Race & Hispanic Origin, 2000
Race
White	67,250
Black/African American	24,090
American Indian/Alaska Native	580
Asian	2,830
Native Hawaiian/Pacific Islander	55
Other race	18,702
Two or more races	7,061
Hispanic origin, total	59,627
Mexican	1,612
Puerto Rican	12,989
Cuban	7,069
Other Hispanic	37,957

Age & Nativity, 2000
Under 5 years	9,266
18 years and over	88,888
21 years and over	83,630
65 years and over	12,041
85 years and over	1,556
Median age	32.6
Native-born	67,593
Foreign-born	52,975

Educational Attainment, 2000
Population 25 years and over	75,912
Less than 9th grade	18.1%
High school grad or higher	61.7%
Bachelor's degree or higher	12.1%
Graduate degree	4.2%

Income & Poverty, 1999
Per capita income	$15,114
Median household income	$35,175
Median family income	$38,370
Persons in poverty	20,963
H'holds receiving public assistance	2,532
H'holds receiving social security	8,924

Households, 2000
Total households	40,482
With persons under 18	16,813
With persons over 65	9,034
Family households	28,170
Single-person households	9,944
Persons per household	2.91
Persons per family	3.45

Labor & Employment
Total civilian labor force, 2007**	55,119
Unemployment rate	6.2%
Total civilian labor force, 2000	52,403
Unemployment rate	9.0%

Employed persons 16 years and over by occupation, 2000
Managers & professionals	8,698
Service occupations	8,488
Sales & office occupations	12,356
Farming, fishing & forestry	44
Construction & maintenance	4,539
Production & transportation	13,546
Self-employed persons	1,774

† see Appendix C for American Community Survey data
* US Census Bureau
** New Jersey Department of Labor
§ State Fiscal Year July 1–June 30

General Information
City of Elizabeth
50 Winfield Scott Plz
Elizabeth, NJ 07201
908-820-4000

Website	www.elizabethnj.org
Year of incorporation	1855
Land/water area (sq. miles)	12.22/1.43
Form of government	Mayor-Council

Government
Legislative Districts
US Congressional	10, 13
State Legislative	20

Local Officials, 2009
Mayor	J. Christian Bollwage
Manager	Bridget S. Zellner
Clerk	Yolanda M. Roberts
Finance Dir	Robert Mack
Tax Assessor	Enrico Emma
Tax Collector	Robert A. Mack
Attorney	William Holzapfel
Building	Michael Mazza
Comm Dev/Planning	NA
Engineering	Ernesto Marticorena
Public Works	John F. Papetti Jr
Police Chief	Ronald Simon
Emerg/Fire Director	Edward Sisk

Housing & Construction
Housing Units, 2000*
Total	42,838
Median rent	$681
Median SF home value	$143,000

Permits for New Residential Construction
	Units	Value
Total, 2006	433	$34,406,218
Single family	16	$2,827,400
Total, 2007	337	$23,680,760
Single family	6	$406,700

Real Property Valuation, 2008
	Parcels	Valuation
Total	18,445	$902,283,400
Vacant	1,127	46,523,400
Residential	14,707	500,936,900
Commercial	1,837	177,735,100
Industrial	176	78,542,000
Apartments	598	98,546,000
Farm land	0	0
Farm homestead	0	0

Average Property Value & Tax, 2008
Residential value	$34,061
Property tax	$6,411
Tax credit/rebate	$974

Public Library
Elizabeth Free Public Library
11 South Broad St
Elizabeth, NJ 07202
908-354-6060

Director	Dorothy M. Key

Library statistics, 2007
Population served	120,568
Full-time/total staff	16/39

	Total	Per capita
Holdings	395,062	3.28
Revenues	$3,801,077	$31.53
Expenditures	$3,736,566	$30.99
Annual visits	430,066	3.57
Internet terminals/annual users	119/11,938	

Public Safety
Number of officers, 2007	349

Crime	2006	2007
Total crimes	5,772	6,275
Violent	905	945
Murder	17	16
Rape	35	25
Robbery	539	612
Aggravated assault	314	292
Non-violent	4,867	5,330
Burglary	682	786
Larceny	2,948	3,187
Vehicle theft	1,237	1,357
Domestic violence	873	807
Arson	11	14
Total crime rate	45.9	49.7
Violent	7.2	7.5
Non-violent	38.7	42.2

Public School District
(for school year 2007-08 except as noted)

Elizabeth School District
500 North Broad Street
Elizabeth, NJ 07207
(908) 436-5010

Superintendent	Pablo Munoz
Number of schools	30
Grade plan	K-12
Enrollment	21,303
Attendance rate, '06-07	93.8%
Dropout rate	6.2%
Students per teacher	8.9
Per pupil expenditure	$16,254
Median faculty salary	$56,331
Median administrator salary	$108,579
Grade 12 enrollment	959
High school graduation rate	77.1%

Assessment test results
(percent scoring at proficient or advanced level)
	Language	Math
NJASK-Grade 3	81.9%	80.1%
GEPA-Grade 8	36.9%	57.3%
HSPA-High School	45.3%	57.5%

SAT Score Averages, 2006-07
Pct tested	Math	Verbal	Writing
50%	404	395	391

Teacher Qualifications
Avg. years of experience	7
Highly-qualified teachers one subject/all subjects	99.5%/99.5%

No Child Left Behind
AYP, 2006-07	Needs Improvement

Municipal Finance§
State Aid Programs, 2009
Total aid	$34,121,201
CMPTRA	16,234,782
Energy tax receipts	17,886,418
Garden State Trust	1

General Budget, 2008
Total tax levy	$170,089,713
County levy	31,430,515
County taxes	30,027,595
County library	0
County health	0
County open space	1,402,920
School levy	40,970,810
Muni. levy	97,688,387
Misc. revenues	106,844,560

Taxes
	2006	2007	2008
General tax rate per $100	16.813	17.844	18.822
County equalization ratio	12.23	10.98	9.81
Net valuation taxable	$908,000,600	$905,207,567	$903,721,608
State equalized value	$8,271,743,551	$9,212,942,198	$9,284,189,237

See Introduction for an explanation of all data sources.

Demographics & Socio-Economic Characteristics
(2000 US Census, except as noted)

Population
1980*	3,187
1990*	3,806
2000	3,514
Male	1,722
Female	1,792
2007 (estimate)*	3,910
Population density	199.2

Race & Hispanic Origin, 2000
Race
White	2,884
Black/African American	501
American Indian/Alaska Native	20
Asian	15
Native Hawaiian/Pacific Islander	0
Other race	48
Two or more races	46
Hispanic origin, total	103
Mexican	34
Puerto Rican	57
Cuban	2
Other Hispanic	10

Age & Nativity, 2000
Under 5 years	213
18 years and over	2,558
21 years and over	2,432
65 years and over	443
85 years and over	44
Median age	38.2
Native-born	3,444
Foreign-born	70

Educational Attainment, 2000
Population 25 years and over	2,349
Less than 9th grade	6.0%
High school grad or higher	78.6%
Bachelor's degree or higher	13.8%
Graduate degree	5.2%

Income & Poverty, 1999
Per capita income	$18,621
Median household income	$51,047
Median family income	$55,472
Persons in poverty	297
H'holds receiving public assistance	8
H'holds receiving social security	393

Households, 2000
Total households	1,263
With persons under 18	489
With persons over 65	326
Family households	959
Single-person households	248
Persons per household	2.74
Persons per family	3.16

Labor & Employment
Total civilian labor force, 2007**	1,907
Unemployment rate	4.7%
Total civilian labor force, 2000	1,641
Unemployment rate	4.7%

Employed persons 16 years and over by occupation, 2000
Managers & professionals	479
Service occupations	273
Sales & office occupations	367
Farming, fishing & forestry	11
Construction & maintenance	223
Production & transportation	211
Self-employed persons	130

‡ Branch of county library
* US Census Bureau
** New Jersey Department of Labor

See Introduction for an explanation of all data sources.

General Information
Township of Elk
667 Whig Lane Rd
Monroeville, NJ 08343
856-881-6525
Website	www.elktownshipnj.gov
Year of incorporation	1891
Land/water area (sq. miles)	19.63/0.08
Form of government	Township

Government

Legislative Districts
US Congressional	2
State Legislative	3

Local Officials, 2009
Mayor	Philip A. Barbaro Jr
Manager/Admin	NA
Clerk	Debbie Pine
Finance Dir	Steve Considine
Tax Assessor	Darlene Campbell
Tax Collector	Susan DeFrancesco
Attorney	Brian J. Duffield
Building	Anthony Dariano Sr
Planning	Leah Furey
Engineering	J. Michael Fralinger
Public Works	Steven Alexander
Police Chief	Charles DeFalco
Emerg/Fire Director	Dennis Marchei

Housing & Construction

Housing Units, 2000*
Total	1,347
Median rent	$715
Median SF home value	$127,900

Permits for New Residential Construction
	Units	Value
Total, 2006	15	$1,724,898
Single family	15	$1,724,898
Total, 2007	19	$2,344,457
Single family	19	$2,344,457

Real Property Valuation, 2008
	Parcels	Valuation
Total	2,266	$384,510,000
Vacant	514	24,226,600
Residential	1,321	304,093,100
Commercial	57	25,485,800
Industrial	1	1,137,400
Apartments	0	0
Farm land	267	4,324,100
Farm homestead	106	25,243,000

Average Property Value & Tax, 2008
Residential value	$230,789
Property tax	$4,989
Tax credit/rebate	$945

Public Library
Glassboro Public Library‡
2 Center St
Glassboro, NJ 08028
856-881-0001
Director	Carol Wolf

Library statistics, 2007
see Gloucester County profile
for library system statistics

Public Safety
Number of officers, 2007	10

Crime	2006	2007
Total crimes	132	111
Violent	11	1
Murder	0	0
Rape	3	0
Robbery	3	0
Aggravated assault	5	1
Non-violent	121	110
Burglary	29	28
Larceny	86	74
Vehicle theft	6	8
Domestic violence	51	44
Arson	2	3
Total crime rate	34.8	28.7
Violent	2.9	0.3
Non-violent	31.9	28.4

Public School District
(for school year 2007-08 except as noted)

Elk Township School District
98 Unionville Rd
Glassboro, NJ 08028
(856) 881-4551
Superintendent	Frank Borelli
Number of schools	1
Grade plan	K-6
Enrollment	373
Attendance rate, '06-07	95.8%
Dropout rate	NA
Students per teacher	9.6
Per pupil expenditure	$13,058
Median faculty salary	$43,102
Median administrator salary	$74,430
Grade 12 enrollment	NA
High school graduation rate	NA

Assessment test results
(percent scoring at proficient or advanced level)
	Language	Math
NJASK-Grade 3	90.2%	86.3%
GEPA-Grade 8	NA	NA
HSPA-High School	NA	NA

SAT Score Averages, 2006-07
Pct tested	Math	Verbal	Writing
NA	NA	NA	NA

Teacher Qualifications
Avg. years of experience	10
Highly-qualified teachers one subject/all subjects	100%/100%

No Child Left Behind
AYP, 2006-07	Meets Standards

Municipal Finance

State Aid Programs, 2009
Total aid	$467,134
CMPTRA	75,123
Energy tax receipts	380,333
Garden State Trust	0

General Budget, 2008
Total tax levy	$8,483,259
County levy	2,179,894
County taxes	1,881,202
County library	151,275
County health	0
County open space	147,417
School levy	4,324,083
Muni. levy	1,979,282
Misc. revenues	2,410,073

Taxes
	2006	2007	2008
General tax rate per $100	3.643	2.046	2.199
County equalization ratio	70.95	117.17	104.82
Net valuation taxable	$195,826,000	$381,289,205	$385,820,507
State equalized value	$315,856,551	$363,807,941	$381,938,105

Demographics & Socio-Economic Characteristics
(2000 US Census, except as noted)

Population
1980*	1,569
1990*	1,571
2000	1,384
Male	671
Female	713
2007 (estimate)*	1,343
Population density	1,543.7

Race & Hispanic Origin, 2000
Race
White	1,346
Black/African American	9
American Indian/Alaska Native	0
Asian	7
Native Hawaiian/Pacific Islander	0
Other race	10
Two or more races	12
Hispanic origin, total	21
Mexican	0
Puerto Rican	15
Cuban	0
Other Hispanic	6

Age & Nativity, 2000
Under 5 years	75
18 years and over	1,046
21 years and over	982
65 years and over	214
85 years and over	24
Median age	36.7
Native-born	1,368
Foreign-born	16

Educational Attainment, 2000
Population 25 years and over	920
Less than 9th grade	3.7%
High school grad or higher	85.2%
Bachelor's degree or higher	14.8%
Graduate degree	3.8%

Income & Poverty, 1999
Per capita income	$21,356
Median household income	$46,172
Median family income	$58,438
Persons in poverty	73
H'holds receiving public assistance	12
H'holds receiving social security	150

Households, 2000
Total households	524
With persons under 18	194
With persons over 65	146
Family households	385
Single-person households	117
Persons per household	2.61
Persons per family	3.06

Labor & Employment
Total civilian labor force, 2007**	761
Unemployment rate	3.4%
Total civilian labor force, 2000	757
Unemployment rate	5.8%

Employed persons 16 years and over by occupation, 2000
Managers & professionals	181
Service occupations	91
Sales & office occupations	209
Farming, fishing & forestry	2
Construction & maintenance	80
Production & transportation	150
Self-employed persons	39

* US Census Bureau
** New Jersey Department of Labor

General Information
Borough of Elmer
120 S Main St
PO Box 882
Elmer, NJ 08318
856-358-4010
Website	www.elmerboroughnj.com
Year of incorporation	1893
Land/water area (sq. miles)	0.87/0.01
Form of government	Borough

Government

Legislative Districts
US Congressional	2
State Legislative	3

Local Officials, 2009
Mayor	Joseph P. Stemberger
Manager/Admin	NA
Clerk	Beverly S. Richards
Finance Dir	Darla J. Timberman
Tax Assessor	Ray Duffield
Tax Collector	Joanne Marone
Attorney	Charles J. Girard
Building	Pittsgrove Township
Comm Dev/Planning	NA
Engineering	John Schweppenheiser
Public Works	NA
Police Captain	Patrick Bryan
Fire Chief	Benjamin Hitzelberger Jr

Housing & Construction

Housing Units, 2000*
Total	557
Median rent	$643
Median SF home value	$103,900

Permits for New Residential Construction
	Units	Value
Total, 2006	0	$0
Single family	0	$0
Total, 2007	3	$152,001
Single family	3	$152,001

Real Property Valuation, 2008
	Parcels	Valuation
Total	631	$104,204,700
Vacant	71	1,491,600
Residential	476	79,965,200
Commercial	62	22,186,000
Industrial	0	0
Apartments	0	0
Farm land	18	91,100
Farm homestead	4	470,800

Average Property Value & Tax, 2008
Residential value	$167,575
Property tax	$4,072
Tax credit/rebate	$850

Public Library
Elmer Public Library
120 S Main St
Elmer, NJ 08318
856-358-2014
Director	Linda Fritz

Library statistics, 2007
Population served	1,384
Full-time/total staff	0/0

	Total	Per capita
Holdings	11,158	8.06
Revenues	$4,007	$2.90
Expenditures	$25,027	$18.08
Annual visits	4,922	3.56
Internet terminals/annual users	5/1,064	

Public Safety
Number of officers, 2007	1

Crime	2006	2007
Total crimes	37	39
Violent	2	1
Murder	0	0
Rape	0	1
Robbery	0	0
Aggravated assault	2	0
Non-violent	35	38
Burglary	7	7
Larceny	26	30
Vehicle theft	2	1
Domestic violence	11	10
Arson	0	1
Total crime rate	26.8	28.5
Violent	1.5	0.7
Non-violent	25.4	27.7

Public School District
(for school year 2007-08 except as noted)

Elmer Borough School District
Front Street, PO Box 596
Elmer, NJ 08318
(856) 358-6761
Chief School Admin	Stephen E. Berkowitz
Number of schools	1
Grade plan	K-6
Enrollment	76
Attendance rate, '06-07	96.5%
Dropout rate	NA
Students per teacher	8.9
Per pupil expenditure	$13,195
Median faculty salary	$38,130
Median administrator salary	$102,301
Grade 12 enrollment	NA
High school graduation rate	NA

Assessment test results
(percent scoring at proficient or advanced level)
	Language	Math
NJASK-Grade 3	100.0%	100.0%
GEPA-Grade 8	NA	NA
HSPA-High School	NA	NA

SAT Score Averages, 2006-07
Pct tested	Math	Verbal	Writing
NA	NA	NA	NA

Teacher Qualifications
Avg. years of experience	12
Highly-qualified teachers one subject/all subjects	100%/100%

No Child Left Behind
AYP, 2006-07	Meets Standards

Municipal Finance

State Aid Programs, 2009
Total aid	$163,166
CMPTRA	66,664
Energy tax receipts	92,423
Garden State Trust	36

General Budget, 2008
Total tax levy	$2,567,358
County levy	978,345
County taxes	957,237
County library	0
County health	0
County open space	21,108
School levy	1,137,441
Muni. levy	451,572
Misc. revenues	618,877

Taxes
	2006	2007	2008
General tax rate per $100	2.184	2.218	2.430
County equalization ratio	120.92	117.33	100.88
Net valuation taxable	$103,731,800	$105,518,388	$105,653,144
State equalized value	$89,789,370	$104,780,191	$665,399,269

Demographics & Socio-Economic Characteristics

(2000 US Census, except as noted)

Population

1980*	18,377
1990*	17,623
2000	18,925
Male	9,042
Female	9,883
2007 (estimate)*	18,765
Population density	7,081.1

Race & Hispanic Origin, 2000

Race
White	15,619
Black/African American	409
American Indian/Alaska Native	21
Asian	1,477
Native Hawaiian/Pacific Islander	1
Other race	841
Two or more races	557
Hispanic origin, total	2,535
Mexican	43
Puerto Rican	535
Cuban	237
Other Hispanic	1,720

Age & Nativity, 2000

Under 5 years	1,084
18 years and over	14,971
21 years and over	14,380
65 years and over	3,115
85 years and over	386
Median age	38.5
Native-born	13,217
Foreign-born	5,708

Educational Attainment, 2000

Population 25 years and over	13,537
Less than 9th grade	7.7%
High school grad or higher	80.0%
Bachelor's degree or higher	20.6%
Graduate degree	6.0%

Income & Poverty, 1999

Per capita income	$22,588
Median household income	$52,319
Median family income	$59,131
Persons in poverty	1,212
H'holds receiving public assistance	140
H'holds receiving social security	2,336

Households, 2000

Total households	7,089
With persons under 18	2,275
With persons over 65	2,311
Family households	5,077
Single-person households	1,645
Persons per household	2.66
Persons per family	3.17

Labor & Employment

Total civilian labor force, 2007**	10,474
Unemployment rate	4.4%
Total civilian labor force, 2000	9,945
Unemployment rate	4.9%

Employed persons 16 years and over by occupation, 2000
Managers & professionals	2,680
Service occupations	1,145
Sales & office occupations	3,345
Farming, fishing & forestry	0
Construction & maintenance	871
Production & transportation	1,421
Self-employed persons	496

* US Census Bureau
** New Jersey Department of Labor

General Information

Borough of Elmwood Park
182 Market St
Elmwood Park, NJ 07407
201-796-1457

Website	www.elmwoodparknj.us
Year of incorporation	1973
Land/water area (sq. miles)	2.65/0.11
Form of government	Borough

Government

Legislative Districts

US Congressional	9
State Legislative	38

Local Officials, 2009

Mayor	Richard A. Mola
Manager/Admin	NA
Clerk	Keith Kazmark
Finance Dir	Roy Riggitano
Tax Assessor	Pasquale Aceto
Tax Collector	Frank Santora
Attorney	Brian Giblin
Building	John Buonanno
Planning	Ronald Vicari
Engineering	Boswell Engineering
Public Works	Scott Karcz
Police Chief	Donald Ingrasselino
Emerg/Fire Director	Gary Ruglio

Housing & Construction

Housing Units, 2000*

Total	7,242
Median rent	$897
Median SF home value	$184,100

Permits for New Residential Construction

	Units	Value
Total, 2006	101	$2,376,643
Single family	1	$130,000
Total, 2007	17	$2,075,500
Single family	3	$612,500

Real Property Valuation, 2008

	Parcels	Valuation
Total	5,059	$2,050,239,700
Vacant	109	26,194,300
Residential	4,650	1,553,311,900
Commercial	222	290,844,300
Industrial	58	116,621,500
Apartments	20	63,267,700
Farm land	0	0
Farm homestead	0	0

Average Property Value & Tax, 2008

Residential value	$334,046
Property tax	$7,671
Tax credit/rebate	$1,095

Public Library

Elmwood Park Public Library
210 Lee St
Elmwood Park, NJ 07407
201-796-8888

Director ..... Bobbie Protono

Library statistics, 2007

Population served	18,925
Full-time/total staff	2/7

	Total	Per capita
Holdings	83,459	4.41
Revenues	$828,493	$43.78
Expenditures	$649,203	$34.30
Annual visits	39,552	2.09
Internet terminals/annual users	6/13,932	

Public Safety

Number of officers, 2007	43

Crime	2006	2007
Total crimes	399	472
Violent	32	24
Murder	0	1
Rape	0	0
Robbery	16	13
Aggravated assault	16	10
Non-violent	367	448
Burglary	59	75
Larceny	277	337
Vehicle theft	31	36
Domestic violence	231	255
Arson	0	0
Total crime rate	21.1	25.1
Violent	1.7	1.3
Non-violent	19.4	23.8

Public School District

(for school year 2007-08 except as noted)

Elmwood Park School District
60 East 53rd Street
Elmwood Park, NJ 07407
(201) 794-2979

Superintendent	Joseph Casapulla
Number of schools	5
Grade plan	K-12
Enrollment	2,234
Attendance rate, '06-07	95.0%
Dropout rate	3.1%
Students per teacher	13.4
Per pupil expenditure	$12,143
Median faculty salary	$50,747
Median administrator salary	$107,624
Grade 12 enrollment	158
High school graduation rate	92.4%

Assessment test results

(percent scoring at proficient or advanced level)
	Language	Math
NJASK-Grade 3	86.3%	88.9%
GEPA-Grade 8	63.5%	85.7%
HSPA-High School	67.1%	77.5%

SAT Score Averages, 2006-07

Pct tested	Math	Verbal	Writing
72%	468	453	470

Teacher Qualifications

Avg. years of experience	7
Highly-qualified teachers one subject/all subjects	100%/100%

No Child Left Behind

AYP, 2006-07 ..... Meets Standards

Municipal Finance

State Aid Programs, 2009

Total aid	$1,884,839
CMPTRA	579,607
Energy tax receipts	1,258,111
Garden State Trust	0

General Budget, 2008

Total tax levy	$47,200,606
County levy	4,735,525
County taxes	4,476,733
County library	0
County health	0
County open space	258,792
School levy	27,743,212
Muni. levy	14,721,869
Misc. revenues	9,321,548

Taxes

	2006	2007	2008
General tax rate per $100	2.01	2.15	2.302
County equalization ratio	90.26	83.77	80.00
Net valuation taxable	$2,039,625,500	$2,049,282,597	$2,051,913,943
State equalized value	$2,436,746,485	$2,561,114,697	$2,565,435,278

See Introduction for an explanation of all data sources.

Demographics & Socio-Economic Characteristics
(2000 US Census, except as noted)

Population
1980*	1,290
1990*	1,170
2000	1,092
Male	518
Female	574
2007 (estimate)*	1,054
Population density	85.9

Race & Hispanic Origin, 2000
Race
White	1,038
Black/African American	39
American Indian/Alaska Native	2
Asian	0
Native Hawaiian/Pacific Islander	0
Other race	3
Two or more races	10
Hispanic origin, total	7
Mexican	0
Puerto Rican	5
Cuban	0
Other Hispanic	2

Age & Nativity, 2000
Under 5 years	52
18 years and over	861
21 years and over	847
65 years and over	216
85 years and over	17
Median age	43.6
Native-born	1,085
Foreign-born	7

Educational Attainment, 2000
Population 25 years and over	814
Less than 9th grade	4.8%
High school grad or higher	83.9%
Bachelor's degree or higher	16.5%
Graduate degree	6.9%

Income & Poverty, 1999
Per capita income	$25,415
Median household income	$50,972
Median family income	$59,688
Persons in poverty	19
H'holds receiving public assistance	5
H'holds receiving social security	170

Households, 2000
Total households	468
With persons under 18	129
With persons over 65	158
Family households	325
Single-person households	123
Persons per household	2.33
Persons per family	2.80

Labor & Employment
Total civilian labor force, 2007**	568
Unemployment rate	1.5%
Total civilian labor force, 2000	559
Unemployment rate	2.9%

Employed persons 16 years and over by occupation, 2000
Managers & professionals	162
Service occupations	77
Sales & office occupations	142
Farming, fishing & forestry	5
Construction & maintenance	67
Production & transportation	90
Self-employed persons	36

General Information
Township of Elsinboro
619 Salem Fort Elfsborg Rd
Salem, NJ 08079
856-935-2200

Website	NA
Year of incorporation	1701
Land/water area (sq. miles)	12.27/1.06
Form of government	Township

Government
Legislative Districts
US Congressional	2
State Legislative	3

Local Officials, 2009
Mayor	John Elk
Manager/Admin	NA
Clerk	Betty Jean Eby
Finance Dir	John Willadsen
Tax Assessor	R. Shidner
Tax Collector	Joanne Marone
Attorney	M. Hoffman
Building	Wayne Serfass
Planning	David Faulhaber
Engineering	Albert Fralinger Jr
Public Works	NA
Police Chief	Lee Peterson
Emerg/Fire Director	Shawn Love

Housing & Construction
Housing Units, 2000*
Total	530
Median rent	$639
Median SF home value	$110,100

Permits for New Residential Construction
	Units	Value
Total, 2006	1	$209,000
Single family	1	$209,000
Total, 2007	0	$0
Single family	0	$0

Real Property Valuation, 2008
	Parcels	Valuation
Total	844	$121,966,500
Vacant	148	4,237,500
Residential	544	100,277,500
Commercial	11	4,901,100
Industrial	0	0
Apartments	0	0
Farm land	95	1,391,400
Farm homestead	46	11,159,000

Average Property Value & Tax, 2008
Residential value	$188,875
Property tax	$3,839
Tax credit/rebate	$882

Public Library
No public municipal library

Library statistics, 2007
Population served	NA
Full-time/total staff	NA/NA

	Total	Per capita
Holdings	NA	NA
Revenues	NA	NA
Expenditures	NA	NA
Annual visits	NA	NA
Internet terminals/annual users	NA/NA	

Public Safety
Number of officers, 2007 ... 0
Crime	2006	2007
Total crimes	25	27
Violent	1	2
Murder	0	0
Rape	0	0
Robbery	0	0
Aggravated assault	1	2
Non-violent	24	25
Burglary	9	15
Larceny	14	8
Vehicle theft	1	2
Domestic violence	7	2
Arson	0	0
Total crime rate	23.2	25.2
Violent	0.9	1.9
Non-violent	22.2	23.3

Public School District
(for school year 2007-08 except as noted)

Elsinboro Township School District
631 Salem-Fort Elfsborg Rd.
Salem, NJ 08079
(856) 935-3817

Chief School Admin	Frank Vogel
Number of schools	1
Grade plan	K-8
Enrollment	103
Attendance rate, '06-07	95.5%
Dropout rate	NA
Students per teacher	NA
Per pupil expenditure	$13,965
Median faculty salary	$43,125
Median administrator salary	NA
Grade 12 enrollment	NA
High school graduation rate	NA

Assessment test results
(percent scoring at proficient or advanced level)
	Language	Math
NJASK-Grade 3	100.0%	100.0%
GEPA-Grade 8	NA	NA
HSPA-High School	NA	NA

SAT Score Averages, 2006-07
Pct tested	Math	Verbal	Writing
NA	NA	NA	NA

Teacher Qualifications
Avg. years of experience	11
Highly-qualified teachers one subject/all subjects	100%/100%

No Child Left Behind
AYP, 2006-07 ... Meets Standards

Municipal Finance
State Aid Programs, 2009
Total aid	$163,627
CMPTRA	19,618
Energy tax receipts	130,502
Garden State Trust	6,496

General Budget, 2008
Total tax levy	$2,484,280
County levy	968,550
County taxes	947,652
County library	0
County health	0
County open space	20,897
School levy	1,272,781
Muni. levy	242,949
Misc. revenues	448,047

Taxes
	2006	2007	2008
General tax rate per $100	3.882	4.125	2.033
County equalization ratio	70.18	59.64	117.60
Net valuation taxable	$56,983,700	$57,848,345	$122,236,101
State equalized value	$95,718,123	$102,505,511	$108,798,501

* US Census Bureau
** New Jersey Department of Labor

See Introduction for an explanation of all data sources.

Demographics & Socio-Economic Characteristics
(2000 US Census, except as noted)

Population
1980*	7,793
1990*	6,930
2000	7,197
Male	3,432
Female	3,765
2007 (estimate)*	7,343
Population density	3,278.1

Race & Hispanic Origin, 2000
Race
White	6,450
Black/African American	61
American Indian/Alaska Native	4
Asian	568
Native Hawaiian/Pacific Islander	0
Other race	63
Two or more races	51
Hispanic origin, total	332
Mexican	22
Puerto Rican	65
Cuban	62
Other Hispanic	183

Age & Nativity, 2000
Under 5 years	500
18 years and over	5,527
21 years and over	5,357
65 years and over	1,351
85 years and over	262
Median age	41.1
Native-born	6,072
Foreign-born	1,125

Educational Attainment, 2000
Population 25 years and over	5,166
Less than 9th grade	4.3%
High school grad or higher	89.0%
Bachelor's degree or higher	40.3%
Graduate degree	12.3%

Income & Poverty, 1999
Per capita income	$31,506
Median household income	$74,556
Median family income	$80,468
Persons in poverty	166
H'holds receiving public assistance	0
H'holds receiving social security	759

Households, 2000
Total households	2,373
With persons under 18	907
With persons over 65	770
Family households	1,964
Single-person households	344
Persons per household	2.91
Persons per family	3.23

Labor & Employment
Total civilian labor force, 2007**	3,586
Unemployment rate	1.6%
Total civilian labor force, 2000	3,413
Unemployment rate	1.8%

Employed persons 16 years and over by occupation, 2000
Managers & professionals	1,598
Service occupations	395
Sales & office occupations	1,031
Farming, fishing & forestry	0
Construction & maintenance	174
Production & transportation	152
Self-employed persons	286

* US Census Bureau
** New Jersey Department of Labor

General Information
Borough of Emerson
1 Municipal Pl
Emerson, NJ 07630
201-262-6086

Website	www.emersonnj.org
Year of incorporation	1909
Land/water area (sq. miles)	2.24/0.18
Form of government	Borough

Government
Legislative Districts
US Congressional	5
State Legislative	39

Local Officials, 2009
Mayor	Louis J. Lamatina
Manager	Joseph Scarpa
Clerk	Carol Dray
CFO	Catherine Henderson
Tax Assessor	Claire Psota
Tax Collector	Catherine Henderson
Attorney	Phillip Boggia
Building	Michael Sartori
Planning	Burgis Associates
Engineering	Paul Niehoff
Public Works	Joseph Solimando
Police Chief	Michael Saudino
Emerg/Fire Director	Mark Savino

Housing & Construction
Housing Units, 2000*
Total	2,398
Median rent	$1,096
Median SF home value	$260,600

Permits for New Residential Construction
	Units	Value
Total, 2006	48	$6,108,728
Single family	10	$1,805,728
Total, 2007	27	$4,206,886
Single family	12	$2,540,218

Real Property Valuation, 2008
	Parcels	Valuation
Total	2,535	$1,379,621,300
Vacant	85	20,893,500
Residential	2,306	1,193,607,300
Commercial	132	159,952,700
Industrial	10	4,886,000
Apartments	0	0
Farm land	1	5,100
Farm homestead	1	276,700

Average Property Value & Tax, 2008
Residential value	$517,505
Property tax	$9,520
Tax credit/rebate	$1,343

Public Library
Emerson Public Library
20 Palisade Ave
Emerson, NJ 07630
201-261-5604

Director	Jodi L. Fulgione

Library statistics, 2007
Population served	7,197
Full-time/total staff	1/2

	Total	Per capita
Holdings	40,283	5.60
Revenues	$454,095	$63.10
Expenditures	$383,001	$53.22
Annual visits	42,350	5.88
Internet terminals/annual users	6/10,915	

Public Safety
Number of officers, 2007	19

Crime	2006	2007
Total crimes	48	42
Violent	4	2
Murder	0	0
Rape	0	0
Robbery	0	1
Aggravated assault	4	1
Non-violent	44	40
Burglary	7	7
Larceny	36	32
Vehicle theft	1	1
Domestic violence	34	36
Arson	1	0
Total crime rate	6.5	5.7
Violent	0.5	0.3
Non-violent	6.0	5.5

Public School District
(for school year 2007-08 except as noted)

Emerson School District
Administration Building, Main St
Emerson, NJ 07630
(201) 262-2828

Superintendent	Vincent Taffaro
Number of schools	3
Grade plan	K-12
Enrollment	1,197
Attendance rate, '06-07	95.9%
Dropout rate	0.0%
Students per teacher	12.0
Per pupil expenditure	$13,506
Median faculty salary	$54,250
Median administrator salary	$122,265
Grade 12 enrollment	60
High school graduation rate	96.8%

Assessment test results
(percent scoring at proficient or advanced level)
	Language	Math
NJASK-Grade 3	96.9%	95.0%
GEPA-Grade 8	74.4%	92.5%
HSPA-High School	87.6%	95.9%

SAT Score Averages, 2006-07
Pct tested	Math	Verbal	Writing
96%	487	501	489

Teacher Qualifications
Avg. years of experience	6
Highly-qualified teachers one subject/all subjects	100%/100%

No Child Left Behind
AYP, 2006-07	Meets Standards

Municipal Finance
State Aid Programs, 2009
Total aid	$817,434
CMPTRA	116,017
Energy tax receipts	663,247
Garden State Trust	0

General Budget, 2008
Total tax levy	$25,404,412
County levy	2,522,817
County taxes	2,386,354
County library	0
County health	0
County open space	136,463
School levy	15,634,991
Muni. levy	7,246,604
Misc. revenues	2,961,353

Taxes
	2006	2007	2008
General tax rate per $100	3.54	1.79	1.840
County equalization ratio	55.99	105.25	101.48
Net valuation taxable	$651,457,250	$1,365,915,507	$1,380,934,990
State equalized value	$1,299,592,448	$1,346,013,280	$1,392,762,303

See Introduction for an explanation of all data sources.

Demographics & Socio-Economic Characteristics
(2000 US Census, except as noted)

Population
1980*	23,701
1990*	24,850
2000	26,203
Male	12,318
Female	13,885
2007 (estimate)*	28,009
Population density	5,692.9

Race & Hispanic Origin, 2000
Race
White	11,134
Black/African American	10,215
American Indian/Alaska Native	71
Asian	1,366
Native Hawaiian/Pacific Islander	12
Other race	2,226
Two or more races	1,179
Hispanic origin, total	5,703
Mexican	251
Puerto Rican	666
Cuban	257
Other Hispanic	4,529

Age & Nativity, 2000
Under 5 years	1,814
18 years and over	19,947
21 years and over	19,112
65 years and over	3,491
85 years and over	439
Median age	37.4
Native-born	18,124
Foreign-born	8,079

Educational Attainment, 2000
Population 25 years and over	18,010
Less than 9th grade	6.8%
High school grad or higher	82.7%
Bachelor's degree or higher	36.7%
Graduate degree	16.5%

Income & Poverty, 1999
Per capita income	$35,275
Median household income	$58,379
Median family income	$67,194
Persons in poverty	2,295
H'holds receiving public assistance	289
H'holds receiving social security	2,478

Households, 2000
Total households	9,273
With persons under 18	3,342
With persons over 65	2,559
Family households	6,486
Single-person households	2,299
Persons per household	2.79
Persons per family	3.29

Labor & Employment
Total civilian labor force, 2007**	14,212
Unemployment rate	4.0%
Total civilian labor force, 2000	13,298
Unemployment rate	6.0%

Employed persons 16 years and over by occupation, 2000
Managers & professionals	4,826
Service occupations	2,005
Sales & office occupations	3,403
Farming, fishing & forestry	18
Construction & maintenance	698
Production & transportation	1,545
Self-employed persons	721

* US Census Bureau
** New Jersey Department of Labor

General Information
City of Englewood
PO Box 228
Englewood, NJ 07631
201-871-6637
Website	www.cityofenglewood.org
Year of incorporation	1899
Land/water area (sq. miles)	4.92/0.01
Form of government	Special Charter

Government
Legislative Districts
US Congressional	9
State Legislative	37

Local Officials, 2009
Mayor	Michael Wildes
Manager	Robert Casey
Clerk	Lenore Schiavelli
Finance Dir	Howard Feinstein
Tax Assessor	Claire Psota
Tax Collector	Tamara Beamer
Attorney	William Bailey
Building	Piero Abballe
Comm Dev/Planning	NA
Engineering	Kenneth Albert
Public Works	Clyde Sweatt
Police Chief	David Bowman
Emerg/Fire Director	Robert Moran

Housing & Construction
Housing Units, 2000*
Total	9,614
Median rent	$825
Median SF home value	$212,400

Permits for New Residential Construction
	Units	Value
Total, 2006	238	$32,895,182
Single family	19	$10,563,696
Total, 2007	527	$56,141,883
Single family	15	$8,721,868

Real Property Valuation, 2008
	Parcels	Valuation
Total	7,532	$5,212,694,600
Vacant	118	27,421,700
Residential	6,708	3,817,259,000
Commercial	522	768,746,400
Industrial	129	400,016,900
Apartments	55	199,250,600
Farm land	0	0
Farm homestead	0	0

Average Property Value & Tax, 2008
Residential value	$569,061
Property tax	$10,705
Tax credit/rebate	$1,110

Public Library
Englewood Public Library
31 Engle St
Englewood, NJ 07631
201-568-2215
Director	Donald Jacobsen

Library statistics, 2007
Population served	26,203
Full-time/total staff	10/25

	Total	Per capita
Holdings	116,186	4.43
Revenues	$2,481,831	$94.72
Expenditures	$2,468,088	$94.19
Annual visits	227,955	8.70
Internet terminals/annual users	9/40,151	

Public Safety
Number of officers, 2007	81

Crime	2006	2007
Total crimes	651	488
Violent	67	70
Murder	1	0
Rape	3	1
Robbery	19	38
Aggravated assault	44	31
Non-violent	584	418
Burglary	177	145
Larceny	371	246
Vehicle theft	36	27
Domestic violence	299	278
Arson	0	2
Total crime rate	24.8	17.5
Violent	2.6	2.5
Non-violent	22.3	15.0

Public School District
(for school year 2007-08 except as noted)

Englewood City School District
12 Tenafly Road
Englewood, NJ 07631
(201) 862-6245
Superintendent	Richard Segall (Int)
Number of schools	6
Grade plan	K-12
Enrollment	2,699
Attendance rate, '06-07	95.0%
Dropout rate	0.7%
Students per teacher	8.7
Per pupil expenditure	$19,598
Median faculty salary	$62,019
Median administrator salary	$106,649
Grade 12 enrollment	216
High school graduation rate	98.3%

Assessment test results
(percent scoring at proficient or advanced level)
	Language	Math
NJASK-Grade 3	79.2%	84.9%
GEPA-Grade 8	42.0%	69.1%
HSPA-High School	62.6%	77.8%

SAT Score Averages, 2006-07
Pct tested	Math	Verbal	Writing
92%	472	456	459

Teacher Qualifications
Avg. years of experience	9
Highly-qualified teachers one subject/all subjects	99.5%/99.5%

No Child Left Behind
AYP, 2006-07	Meets Standards

Municipal Finance
State Aid Programs, 2009
Total aid	$3,478,951
CMPTRA	608,881
Energy tax receipts	2,800,491
Garden State Trust	0

General Budget, 2008
Total tax levy	$99,449,636
County levy	9,880,819
County taxes	9,344,873
County library	0
County health	0
County open space	535,946
School levy	45,930,462
Muni. levy	43,638,355
Misc. revenues	13,935,478

Taxes
	2006	2007	2008
General tax rate per $100	4.16	1.84	1.906
County equalization ratio	48.68	105.85	98.05
Net valuation taxable	$2,058,940,800	$4,992,356,340	$5,222,506,856
State equalized value	$4,605,699,341	$5,091,446,856	$5,460,711,137

See Introduction for an explanation of all data sources.

Demographics & Socio-Economic Characteristics

(2000 US Census, except as noted)

Population

1980*	5,698
1990*	5,634
2000	5,322
Male	2,508
Female	2,814
2007 (estimate)*	5,775
Population density	2,763.2

Race & Hispanic Origin, 2000

Race

White	3,557
Black/African American	73
American Indian/Alaska Native	2
Asian	1,580
Native Hawaiian/Pacific Islander	0
Other race	38
Two or more races	72
Hispanic origin, total	260
Mexican	10
Puerto Rican	24
Cuban	96
Other Hispanic	130

Age & Nativity, 2000

Under 5 years	304
18 years and over	4,221
21 years and over	4,098
65 years and over	1,171
85 years and over	106
Median age	44.8
Native-born	3,261
Foreign-born	2,061

Educational Attainment, 2000

Population 25 years and over	3,921
Less than 9th grade	4.6%
High school grad or higher	92.7%
Bachelor's degree or higher	52.5%
Graduate degree	23.7%

Income & Poverty, 1999

Per capita income	$57,399
Median household income	$106,478
Median family income	$113,187
Persons in poverty	136
H'holds receiving public assistance	20
H'holds receiving social security	660

Households, 2000

Total households	1,818
With persons under 18	599
With persons over 65	775
Family households	1,560
Single-person households	228
Persons per household	2.90
Persons per family	3.16

Labor & Employment

Total civilian labor force, 2007**	2,725
Unemployment rate	3.2%
Total civilian labor force, 2000	2,577
Unemployment rate	3.4%

Employed persons 16 years and over by occupation, 2000

Managers & professionals	1,421
Service occupations	135
Sales & office occupations	760
Farming, fishing & forestry	0
Construction & maintenance	79
Production & transportation	94
Self-employed persons	269

* US Census Bureau
** New Jersey Department of Labor

General Information

Borough of Englewood Cliffs
10 Kahn Ter
Englewood Cliffs, NJ 07632
201-569-5252

Website	www.englewoodcliffsnj.net
Year of incorporation	1895
Land/water area (sq. miles)	2.09/1.29
Form of government	Borough

Government

Legislative Districts

US Congressional	9
State Legislative	37

Local Officials, 2009

Mayor	Joseph Parisi Jr
Manager	Debra L. Fehre
Clerk	Deborah L. Fehre
Finance Dir	Joseph Iannaconi Jr
Tax Assessor	George Reggo
Tax Collector	Joseph Iannaconi Jr
Attorney	Michael Kates
Building	Paul Renaud
Comm Dev/Planning	NA
Engineering	Stephen Boswell
Public Works	Rodney Bialko
Police Chief	Thomas Bauernschmidt
Emerg/Fire Director	George Drimones

Housing & Construction

Housing Units, 2000*

Total	1,889
Median rent	$2,001
Median SF home value	$507,100

Permits for New Residential Construction

	Units	Value
Total, 2006	25	$14,937,145
Single family	25	$14,937,145
Total, 2007	29	$23,524,544
Single family	29	$23,524,544

Real Property Valuation, 2008

	Parcels	Valuation
Total	2,108	$3,440,562,700
Vacant	66	62,999,000
Residential	1,915	2,386,943,400
Commercial	125	986,983,800
Industrial	1	1,886,500
Apartments	1	1,750,000
Farm land	0	0
Farm homestead	0	0

Average Property Value & Tax, 2008

Residential value	$1,246,446
Property tax	$8,973
Tax credit/rebate	$1,129

Public Library

No public municipal library

Library statistics, 2007

Population served	NA
Full-time/total staff	NA/NA

	Total	Per capita
Holdings	NA	NA
Revenues	NA	NA
Expenditures	NA	NA
Annual visits	NA	NA
Internet terminals/annual users	NA/NA	

Public Safety

Number of officers, 2007	27

Crime	2006	2007
Total crimes	101	87
Violent	3	8
Murder	0	0
Rape	0	0
Robbery	0	1
Aggravated assault	3	7
Non-violent	98	79
Burglary	22	13
Larceny	73	62
Vehicle theft	3	4
Domestic violence	18	35
Arson	0	0
Total crime rate	17.6	15.0
Violent	0.5	1.4
Non-violent	17.1	13.6

Public School District

(for school year 2007-08 except as noted)

Englewood Cliffs School District
143 Charlotte Place
Englewood Cliffs, NJ 07632
(201) 567-7292

Superintendent	Dominic Mucci
Number of schools	2
Grade plan	K-8
Enrollment	436
Attendance rate, '06-07	96.5%
Dropout rate	NA
Students per teacher	8.2
Per pupil expenditure	$22,321
Median faculty salary	$54,226
Median administrator salary	$116,849
Grade 12 enrollment	NA
High school graduation rate	NA

Assessment test results

(percent scoring at proficient or advanced level)

	Language	Math
NJASK-Grade 3	100.0%	100.0%
GEPA-Grade 8	83.0%	89.3%
HSPA-High School	NA	NA

SAT Score Averages, 2006-07

Pct tested	Math	Verbal	Writing
NA	NA	NA	NA

Teacher Qualifications

Avg. years of experience	10
Highly-qualified teachers one subject/all subjects	100%/100%

No Child Left Behind

AYP, 2006-07	Meets Standards

Municipal Finance

State Aid Programs, 2009

Total aid	$942,504
CMPTRA	100,258
Energy tax receipts	803,040
Garden State Trust	1,569

General Budget, 2008

Total tax levy	$24,781,070
County levy	6,112,596
County taxes	5,781,251
County library	0
County health	0
County open space	331,345
School levy	9,130,542
Muni. levy	9,537,932
Misc. revenues	3,635,009

Taxes	2006	2007	2008
General tax rate per $100	1.08	1.16	0.721
County equalization ratio	79.01	65.89	105.12
Net valuation taxable	$2,033,170,200	$2,047,021,897	$3,442,274,175
State equalized value	$3,086,976,346	$3,244,889,689	$3,371,508,439

See Introduction for an explanation of all data sources.

Demographics & Socio-Economic Characteristics

(2000 US Census, except as noted)

Population
1980*	976
1990*	1,268
2000	1,764
Male	843
Female	921
2007 (estimate)*	1,893
Population density	3,321.1

Race & Hispanic Origin, 2000
Race
White	1,559
Black/African American	73
American Indian/Alaska Native	2
Asian	79
Native Hawaiian/Pacific Islander	0
Other race	29
Two or more races	22
Hispanic origin, total	110
Mexican	14
Puerto Rican	49
Cuban	16
Other Hispanic	31

Age & Nativity, 2000
Under 5 years	161
18 years and over	1,251
21 years and over	1,204
65 years and over	194
85 years and over	52
Median age	34.9
Native-born	1,556
Foreign-born	208

Educational Attainment, 2000
Population 25 years and over	1,162
Less than 9th grade	7.2%
High school grad or higher	81.6%
Bachelor's degree or higher	18.8%
Graduate degree	5.9%

Income & Poverty, 1999
Per capita income	$23,438
Median household income	$57,557
Median family income	$73,750
Persons in poverty	126
H'holds receiving public assistance	13
H'holds receiving social security	177

Households, 2000
Total households	643
With persons under 18	269
With persons over 65	161
Family households	416
Single-person households	183
Persons per household	2.74
Persons per family	3.51

Labor & Employment
Total civilian labor force, 2007**	939
Unemployment rate	3.1%
Total civilian labor force, 2000	881
Unemployment rate	3.5%

Employed persons 16 years and over by occupation, 2000
Managers & professionals	266
Service occupations	133
Sales & office occupations	230
Farming, fishing & forestry	1
Construction & maintenance	113
Production & transportation	107
Self-employed persons	47

* US Census Bureau
** New Jersey Department of Labor

General Information
Borough of Englishtown
15 Main St
Englishtown, NJ 07726
732-446-9235
Website	www.englishtownnj.com
Year of incorporation	1888
Land/water area (sq. miles)	0.57/0.01
Form of government	Borough

Government
Legislative Districts
US Congressional	12
State Legislative	12

Local Officials, 2009
Mayor	Thomas E. Reynolds
Manager	Laurie Finger
Clerk	Peter Gorbatuk
Finance Dir	Laurie Finger
Tax Assessor	Sharon Hartman
Tax Collector	Janice Garcia
Attorney	Joseph Youssouff
Building	Bob Ward
Comm Dev/Planning	NA
Engineering	Thomas Herits
Public Works	NA
Police Chief	John Niziolek
Emerg/Fire Director	Ralph Kirkland

Housing & Construction
Housing Units, 2000*
Total	680
Median rent	$772
Median SF home value	$150,600

Permits for New Residential Construction
	Units	Value
Total, 2006	30	$2,938,916
Single family	30	$2,938,916
Total, 2007	14	$1,369,807
Single family	14	$1,369,807

Real Property Valuation, 2008
	Parcels	Valuation
Total	675	$256,109,400
Vacant	25	3,353,400
Residential	599	198,838,400
Commercial	45	42,425,900
Industrial	5	10,229,600
Apartments	1	1,262,100
Farm land	0	0
Farm homestead	0	0

Average Property Value & Tax, 2008
Residential value	$331,951
Property tax	$5,280
Tax credit/rebate	$1,027

Public Library
No public municipal library

Library statistics, 2007
Population served	NA
Full-time/total staff	NA/NA

	Total	Per capita
Holdings	NA	NA
Revenues	NA	NA
Expenditures	NA	NA
Annual visits	NA	NA
Internet terminals/annual users	NA/NA	

Public Safety
Number of officers, 2007	8

Crime	2006	2007
Total crimes	16	26
Violent	0	2
Murder	0	0
Rape	0	0
Robbery	0	1
Aggravated assault	0	1
Non-violent	16	24
Burglary	3	3
Larceny	11	21
Vehicle theft	2	0
Domestic violence	8	2
Arson	0	0
Total crime rate	8.9	14.1
Violent	0.0	1.1
Non-violent	8.9	13.0

Public School District
(for school year 2007-08 except as noted)

Manalapan-Englishtown Reg. School Dist.
54 Main Street
Englishtown, NJ 07726
(732) 786-2500
Superintendent	John J. Marciante Jr
Number of schools	8
Grade plan	K-8
Enrollment	5,482
Attendance rate, '06-07	95.6%
Dropout rate	NA
Students per teacher	12.0
Per pupil expenditure	$12,214
Median faculty salary	$49,993
Median administrator salary	$99,196
Grade 12 enrollment	NA
High school graduation rate	NA

Assessment test results
(percent scoring at proficient or advanced level)
	Language	Math
NJASK-Grade 3	96.2%	96.2%
GEPA-Grade 8	87.3%	94.4%
HSPA-High School	NA	NA

SAT Score Averages, 2006-07
Pct tested	Math	Verbal	Writing
NA	NA	NA	NA

Teacher Qualifications
Avg. years of experience	8
Highly-qualified teachers one subject/all subjects	99.0%/99.0%

No Child Left Behind
AYP, 2006-07	Meets Standards

Municipal Finance
State Aid Programs, 2009
Total aid	$183,347
CMPTRA	56,062
Energy tax receipts	122,702
Garden State Trust	0

General Budget, 2008
Total tax levy	$4,133,560
County levy	615,358
County taxes	537,069
County library	32,378
County health	9,987
County open space	35,924
School levy	2,667,040
Muni. levy	851,161
Misc. revenues	1,124,734

Taxes
	2006	2007	2008
General tax rate per $100	3.861	3.96	1.591
County equalization ratio	49.83	44.22	107.11
Net valuation taxable	$95,721,600	$101,845,431	$259,882,117
State equalized value	$218,018,531	$238,835,137	$2,678,894,372

See Introduction for an explanation of all data sources.

Demographics & Socio-Economic Characteristics

(2000 US Census, except as noted)

Population

1980*	2,363
1990*	2,139
2000	2,162
Male	1,064
Female	1,098
2007 (estimate)*	2,025
Population density	1,436.2

Race & Hispanic Origin, 2000

Race

White	2,096
Black/African American	10
American Indian/Alaska Native	4
Asian	22
Native Hawaiian/Pacific Islander	0
Other race	3
Two or more races	27
Hispanic origin, total	26
Mexican	1
Puerto Rican	3
Cuban	4
Other Hispanic	18

Age & Nativity, 2000

Under 5 years	198
18 years and over	1,520
21 years and over	1,484
65 years and over	318
85 years and over	27
Median age	40.3
Native-born	2,004
Foreign-born	158

Educational Attainment, 2000

Population 25 years and over	1,438
Less than 9th grade	1.2%
High school grad or higher	97.1%
Bachelor's degree or higher	72.4%
Graduate degree	32.0%

Income & Poverty, 1999

Per capita income	$77,434
Median household income	$148,173
Median family income	$175,000
Persons in poverty	23
H'holds receiving public assistance	3
H'holds receiving social security	219

Households, 2000

Total households	737
With persons under 18	304
With persons over 65	222
Family households	605
Single-person households	111
Persons per household	2.93
Persons per family	3.28

Labor & Employment

Total civilian labor force, 2007**	1,009
Unemployment rate	2.2%
Total civilian labor force, 2000	954
Unemployment rate	1.2%

Employed persons 16 years and over by occupation, 2000

Managers & professionals	617
Service occupations	43
Sales & office occupations	247
Farming, fishing & forestry	0
Construction & maintenance	23
Production & transportation	13
Self-employed persons	110

* US Census Bureau
** New Jersey Department of Labor

General Information

Borough of Essex Fells
255 Roseland Ave
Essex Fells, NJ 07021
973-226-3400

Website	www.essexfellsboro.com
Year of incorporation	1902
Land/water area (sq. miles)	1.41/0.00
Form of government	Borough

Government

Legislative Districts

US Congressional	11
State Legislative	27

Local Officials, 2009

Mayor	Edward P. Abbot
Manager	Amey Upchurch
Clerk	Francine T. Paserchia
Finance Dir	Joe DeIorio
Tax Assessor	Jack Kelly
Tax Collector	Maureen Chumacas
Attorney	Martin Murphy
Building	Robert Young
Comm Dev/Planning	NA
Engineering	Frank Ziccelli
Public Works	Roger Kerr
Police Chief	Kelly J. Reilly
Emerg/Fire Director	Chris Boeckel

Housing & Construction

Housing Units, 2000*

Total	761
Median rent	$1,656
Median SF home value	$584,100

Permits for New Residential Construction

	Units	Value
Total, 2006	2	$2,171,050
Single family	2	$2,171,050
Total, 2007	42	$10,164,295
Single family	2	$1,854,025

Real Property Valuation, 2008

	Parcels	Valuation
Total	784	$819,611,900
Vacant	31	9,116,500
Residential	747	788,448,000
Commercial	6	22,047,400
Industrial	0	0
Apartments	0	0
Farm land	0	0
Farm homestead	0	0

Average Property Value & Tax, 2008

Residential value	$1,055,486
Property tax	$17,060
Tax credit/rebate	$1,287

Public Library

No public municipal library

Library statistics, 2007

Population served	NA
Full-time/total staff	NA/NA

	Total	Per capita
Holdings	NA	NA
Revenues	NA	NA
Expenditures	NA	NA
Annual visits	NA	NA
Internet terminals/annual users	NA/NA	

Public Safety

Number of officers, 2007	13

Crime	2006	2007
Total crimes	16	14
Violent	0	0
Murder	0	0
Rape	0	0
Robbery	0	0
Aggravated assault	0	0
Non-violent	16	14
Burglary	2	3
Larceny	13	11
Vehicle theft	1	0
Domestic violence	5	1
Arson	2	0
Total crime rate	7.6	6.8
Violent	0.0	0.0
Non-violent	7.6	6.8

Public School District

(for school year 2007-08 except as noted)

Essex Fells School District
102 Hawthorne Road
Essex Fells, NJ 07021
(973) 226-0505

Superintendent	Elaine Baldwin (Int)
Number of schools	1
Grade plan	K-6
Enrollment	250
Attendance rate, '06-07	92.9%
Dropout rate	NA
Students per teacher	9.0
Per pupil expenditure	$13,529
Median faculty salary	$50,231
Median administrator salary	$94,870
Grade 12 enrollment	NA
High school graduation rate	NA

Assessment test results

(percent scoring at proficient or advanced level)

	Language	Math
NJASK-Grade 3	95.9%	95.9%
GEPA-Grade 8	NA	NA
HSPA-High School	NA	NA

SAT Score Averages, 2006-07

Pct tested	Math	Verbal	Writing
NA	NA	NA	NA

Teacher Qualifications

Avg. years of experience	6
Highly-qualified teachers one subject/all subjects	100%/100%

No Child Left Behind

AYP, 2006-07	Meets Standards

Municipal Finance

State Aid Programs, 2009

Total aid	$243,846
CMPTRA	0
Energy tax receipts	234,092
Garden State Trust	0

General Budget, 2008

Total tax levy	$13,251,317
County levy	3,581,735
County taxes	3,443,482
County library	0
County health	0
County open space	138,253
School levy	6,798,679
Muni. levy	2,870,903
Misc. revenues	1,900,037

Taxes

	2006	2007	2008
General tax rate per $100	1.47	1.49	1.617
County equalization ratio	100.15	92.56	89.62
Net valuation taxable	$811,698,850	$815,247,863	$819,859,514
State equalized value	$877,238,805	$909,637,586	$871,156,019

See Introduction for an explanation of all data sources.

Demographics & Socio-Economic Characteristics
(2000 US Census, except as noted)

Population
1980*	848
1990*	1,404
2000	1,585
Male	800
Female	785
2007 (estimate)*	1,714
Population density	32.0

Race & Hispanic Origin, 2000
Race
White	1,493
Black/African American	57
American Indian/Alaska Native	7
Asian	5
Native Hawaiian/Pacific Islander	0
Other race	2
Two or more races	21
Hispanic origin, total	15
Mexican	1
Puerto Rican	10
Cuban	0
Other Hispanic	4

Age & Nativity, 2000
Under 5 years	111
18 years and over	1,107
21 years and over	1,053
65 years and over	153
85 years and over	13
Median age	36.6
Native-born	1,522
Foreign-born	70

Educational Attainment, 2000
Population 25 years and over	1,008
Less than 9th grade	4.1%
High school grad or higher	84.8%
Bachelor's degree or higher	17.0%
Graduate degree	4.9%

Income & Poverty, 1999
Per capita income	$19,469
Median household income	$54,653
Median family income	$56,548
Persons in poverty	77
H'holds receiving public assistance	10
H'holds receiving social security	133

Households, 2000
Total households	528
With persons under 18	234
With persons over 65	116
Family households	433
Single-person households	73
Persons per household	2.95
Persons per family	3.27

Labor & Employment
Total civilian labor force, 2007**	786
Unemployment rate	6.3%
Total civilian labor force, 2000	729
Unemployment rate	5.8%

Employed persons 16 years and over by occupation, 2000
Managers & professionals	238
Service occupations	111
Sales & office occupations	155
Farming, fishing & forestry	2
Construction & maintenance	105
Production & transportation	76
Self-employed persons	46

General Information
City of Estell Manor
PO Box 102
Estell Manor, NJ 08319
609-476-2692

Website	NA
Year of incorporation	1925
Land/water area (sq. miles)	53.57/1.34
Form of government	Small Municipality

Government
Legislative Districts
US Congressional	2
State Legislative	2

Local Officials, 2009
Mayor	Joseph Venezia
Manager	NA
Clerk	Kimberly Hodson
Finance Dir	Judson Moore
Tax Assessor	James Mancini
Tax Collector	Deborah Hample
Attorney	Alfred Scerni
Building	Charles Kane
Comm Dev/Planning	NA
Engineering	J. Michael Fralinger
Public Works	Brian Johnson
Police Chief	NA
Emerg/Fire Director	Jeff Cornew

Housing & Construction
Housing Units, 2000*
Total	546
Median rent	$838
Median SF home value	$123,500

Permits for New Residential Construction
	Units	Value
Total, 2006	10	$1,061,967
Single family	10	$1,061,967
Total, 2007	7	$527,593
Single family	7	$527,593

Real Property Valuation, 2008
	Parcels	Valuation
Total	1,547	$117,384,900
Vacant	739	9,404,200
Residential	728	97,746,500
Commercial	6	3,379,300
Industrial	5	1,573,300
Apartments	1	700,000
Farm land	49	1,664,200
Farm homestead	19	2,917,400

Average Property Value & Tax, 2008
Residential value	$134,758
Property tax	$3,280
Tax credit/rebate	$803

Public Library
No public municipal library

Library statistics, 2007
Population served	NA
Full-time/total staff	NA/NA

	Total	Per capita
Holdings	NA	NA
Revenues	NA	NA
Expenditures	NA	NA
Annual visits	NA	NA
Internet terminals/annual users	NA/NA	

Public Safety
Number of officers, 2007	0

Crime	2006	2007
Total crimes	24	22
Violent	3	1
Murder	0	0
Rape	0	0
Robbery	0	0
Aggravated assault	3	1
Non-violent	21	21
Burglary	9	7
Larceny	10	13
Vehicle theft	2	1
Domestic violence	6	11
Arson	0	0
Total crime rate	13.9	12.8
Violent	1.7	0.6
Non-violent	12.2	12.2

Public School District
(for school year 2007-08 except as noted)

Estell Manor City School District
128 Cape May Avenue
Estell Manor, NJ 08319
(609) 476-2267

Superintendent	John Cressey
Number of schools	1
Grade plan	K-8
Enrollment	221
Attendance rate, '06-07	95.3%
Dropout rate	NA
Students per teacher	10.1
Per pupil expenditure	$12,765
Median faculty salary	$55,761
Median administrator salary	$92,377
Grade 12 enrollment	NA
High school graduation rate	NA

Assessment test results
(percent scoring at proficient or advanced level)
	Language	Math
NJASK-Grade 3	88.9%	88.9%
GEPA-Grade 8	62.1%	96.6%
HSPA-High School	NA	NA

SAT Score Averages, 2006-07
Pct tested	Math	Verbal	Writing
NA	NA	NA	NA

Teacher Qualifications
Avg. years of experience	14
Highly-qualified teachers one subject/all subjects	100%/100%

No Child Left Behind
AYP, 2006-07	Meets Standards

Municipal Finance
State Aid Programs, 2009
Total aid	$473,988
CMPTRA	0
Energy tax receipts	240,930
Garden State Trust	187,768

General Budget, 2008
Total tax levy	$2,866,544
County levy	620,054
County taxes	488,531
County library	62,655
County health	25,638
County open space	43,230
School levy	2,087,896
Muni. levy	158,594
Misc. revenues	1,323,098

Taxes	2006	2007	2008
General tax rate per $100	2.487	2.495	2.435
County equalization ratio	69.28	58.29	54.54
Net valuation taxable	$116,131,100	$116,367,942	$117,781,465
State equalized value	$199,663,203	$213,030,539	$223,646,660

* US Census Bureau
** New Jersey Department of Labor

See Introduction for an explanation of all data sources.

Demographics & Socio-Economic Characteristics

(2000 US Census, except as noted)

Population

1980*	21,659
1990*	35,309
2000	42,275
Male	20,498
Female	21,777
2007 (estimate)*	45,619
Population density	1,544.3

Race & Hispanic Origin, 2000

Race

White	38,579
Black/African American	1,313
American Indian/Alaska Native	31
Asian	1,721
Native Hawaiian/Pacific Islander	8
Other race	203
Two or more races	420
Hispanic origin, total	829
Mexican	136
Puerto Rican	330
Cuban	81
Other Hispanic	282

Age & Nativity, 2000

Under 5 years	3,090
18 years and over	30,790
21 years and over	29,702
65 years and over	3,750
85 years and over	368
Median age	36.0
Native-born	39,688
Foreign-born	2,740

Educational Attainment, 2000

Population 25 years and over	28,565
Less than 9th grade	1.5%
High school grad or higher	93.3%
Bachelor's degree or higher	39.7%
Graduate degree	12.3%

Income & Poverty, 1999

Per capita income	$29,494
Median household income	$67,010
Median family income	$77,245
Persons in poverty	1,174
H'holds receiving public assistance	123
H'holds receiving social security	3,011

Households, 2000

Total households	15,712
With persons under 18	6,297
With persons over 65	2,733
Family households	11,346
Single-person households	3,584
Persons per household	2.68
Persons per family	3.21

Labor & Employment

Total civilian labor force, 2007**	27,367
Unemployment rate	2.9%
Total civilian labor force, 2000	23,374
Unemployment rate	2.6%

Employed persons 16 years and over by occupation, 2000

Managers & professionals	10,930
Service occupations	2,200
Sales & office occupations	7,092
Farming, fishing & forestry	8
Construction & maintenance	1,158
Production & transportation	1,382
Self-employed persons	1,228

‡ Branch of county library
* US Census Bureau
** New Jersey Department of Labor

General Information

Township of Evesham
984 Tuckerton Rd
Marlton, NJ 08053
856-983-2900

Website	www.evesham-nj.gov
Year of incorporation	1688
Land/water area (sq. miles)	29.54/0.17
Form of government	Council-Manager

Government

Legislative Districts

US Congressional	3
State Legislative	8

Local Officials, 2009

Mayor	Randy Brown
Manager	Thomas Czerniecki
Clerk	Carmela Bonfrisco
Finance Dir	Thomas S. Shanahan
Tax Assessor	Blackwell Albertson
Tax Collector	Kathie Sanders
Attorney	Arthur R. Sypek Jr
Building	Carlos Martinez
Comm Dev/Planning	NA
Engineering	Chris Rehmann
Public Works	William Cromie
Police Chief	Joseph Cornely
Emerg/Fire Director	Ted Lowden

Housing & Construction

Housing Units, 2000*

Total	16,324
Median rent	$886
Median SF home value	$157,000

Permits for New Residential Construction

	Units	Value
Total, 2006	30	$6,516,132
Single family	30	$6,516,132
Total, 2007	26	$4,907,246
Single family	26	$4,907,246

Real Property Valuation, 2008

	Parcels	Valuation
Total	16,493	$2,825,178,400
Vacant	695	17,059,400
Residential	15,124	2,239,682,300
Commercial	499	448,607,200
Industrial	16	18,546,600
Apartments	17	93,335,700
Farm land	95	666,600
Farm homestead	47	7,280,600

Average Property Value & Tax, 2008

Residential value	$148,109
Property tax	$6,634
Tax credit/rebate	$1,066

Public Library

Evesham Branch Library‡
984 Tuckerton Rd
Marlton, NJ 08053
856-983-1444

Branch Librarian	Susan Szymanik

Library statistics, 2007

see Burlington County profile
for library system statistics

Public Safety

Number of officers, 2007	74

Crime	2006	2007
Total crimes	765	736
Violent	42	35
Murder	0	1
Rape	6	6
Robbery	8	8
Aggravated assault	28	20
Non-violent	723	701
Burglary	92	78
Larceny	607	598
Vehicle theft	24	25
Domestic violence	354	331
Arson	8	4
Total crime rate	16.3	15.8
Violent	0.9	0.7
Non-violent	15.4	15.0

Public School District

(for school year 2007-08 except as noted)

Evesham Township School District
25 South Maple Avenue
Marlton, NJ 08053
(856) 983-1800

Superintendent	Patricia Lucas
Number of schools	9
Grade plan	K-8
Enrollment	4,919
Attendance rate, '06-07	95.1%
Dropout rate	NA
Students per teacher	10.5
Per pupil expenditure	$13,414
Median faculty salary	$51,531
Median administrator salary	$102,533
Grade 12 enrollment	NA
High school graduation rate	NA

Assessment test results

(percent scoring at proficient or advanced level)

	Language	Math
NJASK-Grade 3	93.9%	94.1%
GEPA-Grade 8	85.2%	94.1%
HSPA-High School	NA	NA

SAT Score Averages, 2006-07

Pct tested	Math	Verbal	Writing
NA	NA	NA	NA

Teacher Qualifications

Avg. years of experience	10
Highly-qualified teachers one subject/all subjects	99.5%/99.5%

No Child Left Behind

AYP, 2006-07	Meets Standards

Municipal Finance

State Aid Programs, 2009

Total aid	$4,149,298
CMPTRA	703,406
Energy tax receipts	3,274,838
Garden State Trust	2,560

General Budget, 2008

Total tax levy	$126,909,860
County levy	22,862,394
County taxes	18,774,829
County library	1,733,521
County health	0
County open space	2,354,044
School levy	83,437,305
Muni. levy	20,610,161
Misc. revenues	12,335,230

Taxes	2006	2007	2008
General tax rate per $100	4.148	4.31	4.480
County equalization ratio	59.26	52.85	48.10
Net valuation taxable	$2,799,540,400	$2,823,669,826	$2,833,213,365
State equalized value	$5,305,923,983	$5,861,448,256	$5,930,840,835

See Introduction for an explanation of all data sources.

Demographics & Socio-Economic Characteristics

(2000 US Census, except as noted)

Population

1980*	34,842
1990*	34,185
2000	35,707
Male	17,203
Female	18,504
2007 (estimate)*	36,536
Population density	2,383.3

Race & Hispanic Origin, 2000

Race

White	24,645
Black/African American	8,863
American Indian/Alaska Native	55
Asian	811
Native Hawaiian/Pacific Islander	22
Other race	653
Two or more races	658
Hispanic origin, total	1,586
Mexican	97
Puerto Rican	900
Cuban	72
Other Hispanic	517

Age & Nativity, 2000

Under 5 years	1,623
18 years and over	29,263
21 years and over	25,573
65 years and over	5,631
85 years and over	761
Median age	37.0
Native-born	32,778
Foreign-born	2,929

Educational Attainment, 2000

Population 25 years and over	23,114
Less than 9th grade	4.7%
High school grad or higher	84.1%
Bachelor's degree or higher	29.1%
Graduate degree	12.0%

Income & Poverty, 1999

Per capita income	$24,268
Median household income	$57,274
Median family income	$67,618
Persons in poverty	1,964
H'holds receiving public assistance	155
H'holds receiving social security	4,007

Households, 2000

Total households	12,551
With persons under 18	3,645
With persons over 65	3,978
Family households	8,211
Single-person households	3,480
Persons per household	2.45
Persons per family	3.00

Labor & Employment

Total civilian labor force, 2007**	20,245
Unemployment rate	3.6%
Total civilian labor force, 2000	18,364
Unemployment rate	4.6%

Employed persons 16 years and over by occupation, 2000

Managers & professionals	6,765
Service occupations	2,785
Sales & office occupations	5,269
Farming, fishing & forestry	26
Construction & maintenance	1,013
Production & transportation	1,664
Self-employed persons	686

‡ Branch of county library
* US Census Bureau
** New Jersey Department of Labor
§ State Fiscal Year July 1–June 30

General Information

Township of Ewing
2 Jake Garzio Dr
Ewing, NJ 08628
609-883-2900

Website	www.ewingtwp.net
Year of incorporation	1834
Land/water area (sq. miles)	15.33/0.27
Form of government	Mayor-Council

Government

Legislative Districts

US Congressional	12
State Legislative	15

Local Officials, 2009

Mayor	Jack Ball
Manager	David Thompson
Clerk	Stephen Elliott
Finance Dir	Chris Jack
Tax Assessor	Jeff Burd
Tax Collector	Thomas Hespe
Attorney	Michael Hartsough
Building	William Erney
Planning	Richard Owen
Engineering	Robert Mannix
Public Works	Angelo Capuano
Police Chief	Robert Coulton
Fire/Emergency Dir	NA

Housing & Construction

Housing Units, 2000*

Total	12,924
Median rent	$720
Median SF home value	$133,100

Permits for New Residential Construction

	Units	Value
Total, 2006	7	$4,177,050
Single family	7	$4,177,050
Total, 2007	4	$814,100
Single family	4	$814,100

Real Property Valuation, 2008

	Parcels	Valuation
Total	11,635	$1,819,599,200
Vacant	437	16,022,300
Residential	10,562	1,306,857,100
Commercial	594	414,891,500
Industrial	19	16,415,000
Apartments	19	65,335,700
Farm land	4	77,600
Farm homestead	0	0

Average Property Value & Tax, 2008

Residential value	$123,732
Property tax	$5,552
Tax credit/rebate	$1,003

Public Library

Ewing Branch Library‡
61 Scotch Rd
West Trenton, NJ 08628
609-882-3130

Branch Librarian .... Jacquelyn Huff

Library statistics, 2007

see Mercer County profile
for library system statistics

Public Safety

Number of officers, 2007 79

Crime	2006	2007
Total crimes	894	782
Violent	114	89
Murder	0	1
Rape	8	5
Robbery	57	27
Aggravated assault	49	56
Non-violent	780	693
Burglary	173	138
Larceny	559	497
Vehicle theft	48	58
Domestic violence	218	181
Arson	13	6
Total crime rate	24.0	21.2
Violent	3.1	2.4
Non-violent	20.9	18.8

Public School District

(for school year 2007-08 except as noted)

Ewing Township School District
1331 Lower Ferry Road
Ewing, NJ 08618
(609) 538-9800

Superintendent	Raymond Broach
Number of schools	5
Grade plan	K-12
Enrollment	3,776
Attendance rate, '06-07	95.5%
Dropout rate	0.5%
Students per teacher	10.8
Per pupil expenditure	$13,300
Median faculty salary	$56,524
Median administrator salary	$114,859
Grade 12 enrollment	236
High school graduation rate	91.8%

Assessment test results

(percent scoring at proficient or advanced level)

	Language	Math
NJASK-Grade 3	76.1%	81.6%
GEPA-Grade 8	53.4%	83.7%
HSPA-High School	65.9%	79.6%

SAT Score Averages, 2006-07

Pct tested	Math	Verbal	Writing
77%	461	458	465

Teacher Qualifications

Avg. years of experience	10
Highly-qualified teachers one subject/all subjects	100%/100%

No Child Left Behind

AYP, 2006-07 .... Meets Standards

Municipal Finance§

State Aid Programs, 2009

Total aid	$12,592,402
CMPTRA	8,360,909
Energy tax receipts	3,915,987
Garden State Trust	573

General Budget, 2008

Total tax levy	$82,032,763
County levy	18,418,446
County taxes	15,753,856
County library	1,583,237
County health	0
County open space	1,081,354
School levy	47,393,052
Muni. levy	16,221,265
Misc. revenues	32,335,714

Taxes	2006	2007	2008
General tax rate per $100	4.26	4.34	4.488
County equalization ratio	60.82	58.53	51.38
Net valuation taxable	$1,789,314,800	$1,816,428,761	$1,828,178,843
State equalized value	$3,066,541,943	$3,526,171,879	$3,707,703,855

Demographics & Socio-Economic Characteristics
(2000 US Census, except as noted)

Population
1980*	5,679
1990*	5,270
2000	5,937
Male	2,877
Female	3,060
2007 (estimate)*	5,920
Population density	3,544.9

Race & Hispanic Origin, 2000
Race
White	5,573
Black/African American	243
American Indian/Alaska Native	2
Asian	58
Native Hawaiian/Pacific Islander	0
Other race	13
Two or more races	48
Hispanic origin, total	79
Mexican	10
Puerto Rican	8
Cuban	14
Other Hispanic	47

Age & Nativity, 2000
Under 5 years	537
18 years and over	3,976
21 years and over	3,858
65 years and over	614
85 years and over	65
Median age	37.4
Native-born	5,655
Foreign-born	282

Educational Attainment, 2000
Population 25 years and over	3,747
Less than 9th grade	1.4%
High school grad or higher	97.1%
Bachelor's degree or higher	61.8%
Graduate degree	26.4%

Income & Poverty, 1999
Per capita income	$44,018
Median household income	$97,220
Median family income	$109,760
Persons in poverty	139
H'holds receiving public assistance	7
H'holds receiving social security	424

Households, 2000
Total households	1,998
With persons under 18	980
With persons over 65	438
Family households	1,658
Single-person households	304
Persons per household	2.97
Persons per family	3.33

Labor & Employment
Total civilian labor force, 2007**	2,914
Unemployment rate	2.7%
Total civilian labor force, 2000	2,728
Unemployment rate	2.9%

Employed persons 16 years and over by occupation, 2000
Managers & professionals	1,474
Service occupations	183
Sales & office occupations	717
Farming, fishing & forestry	5
Construction & maintenance	164
Production & transportation	107
Self-employed persons	298

General Information
Borough of Fair Haven
748 River Rd
Fair Haven, NJ 07704
732-747-0241
Website	www.fairhavennj.net
Year of incorporation	1912
Land/water area (sq. miles)	1.67/0.01
Form of government	Borough

Government
Legislative Districts
US Congressional	12
State Legislative	12

Local Officials, 2009
Mayor	Michael Halfacre
Manager	Mary Howell
Clerk	Allyson M. Cinquegrana
Finance Dir	Denise Jawidzik
Tax Assessor	Stephen Walters
Tax Collector	Dale Connor
Attorney	Salvatore Alfieri
Building	Paul Reinhold
Comm Dev/Planning	NA
Engineering	Richard Gardella
Public Works	Richard Gardella
Police Chief	Darryl Breckenridge
Emerg/Fire Director	Shaun Foley

Housing & Construction
Housing Units, 2000*
Total	2,037
Median rent	$1,219
Median SF home value	$305,900

Permits for New Residential Construction
	Units	Value
Total, 2006	15	$4,274,410
Single family	15	$4,274,410
Total, 2007	13	$3,675,664
Single family	13	$3,675,664

Real Property Valuation, 2008
	Parcels	Valuation
Total	2,125	$1,136,391,300
Vacant	56	10,976,600
Residential	2,006	1,088,054,500
Commercial	63	37,360,200
Industrial	0	0
Apartments	0	0
Farm land	0	0
Farm homestead	0	0

Average Property Value & Tax, 2008
Residential value	$542,400
Property tax	$11,909
Tax credit/rebate	$1,327

Public Library
Fair Haven Public Library
748 River Rd
Fair Haven, NJ 07704
732-747-5031
Director	Donna Powers

Library statistics, 2007
Population served	5,937
Full-time/total staff	NA/0

	Total	Per capita
Holdings	0	NA
Revenues	$0	NA
Expenditures	$0	NA
Annual visits	NA	NA
Internet terminals/annual users	NA/NA	

Public Safety
Number of officers, 2007	13

Crime	2006	2007
Total crimes	43	57
Violent	5	0
Murder	0	0
Rape	0	0
Robbery	1	0
Aggravated assault	4	0
Non-violent	38	57
Burglary	3	0
Larceny	35	56
Vehicle theft	0	1
Domestic violence	3	0
Arson	0	1
Total crime rate	7.3	9.7
Violent	0.8	0.0
Non-violent	6.4	9.7

Public School District
(for school year 2007-08 except as noted)

Fair Haven Borough School District
224 Hance Road
Fair Haven, NJ 07704
(732) 747-2294
Superintendent	Kathleen Cronin
Number of schools	2
Grade plan	K-8
Enrollment	1,009
Attendance rate, '06-07	95.6%
Dropout rate	NA
Students per teacher	11.7
Per pupil expenditure	$10,435
Median faculty salary	$51,647
Median administrator salary	$119,731
Grade 12 enrollment	NA
High school graduation rate	NA

Assessment test results
(percent scoring at proficient or advanced level)
	Language	Math
NJASK-Grade 3	94.9%	92.3%
GEPA-Grade 8	91.3%	96.1%
HSPA-High School	NA	NA

SAT Score Averages, 2006-07
Pct tested	Math	Verbal	Writing
NA	NA	NA	NA

Teacher Qualifications
Avg. years of experience	10
Highly-qualified teachers one subject/all subjects	100%/100%

No Child Left Behind
AYP, 2006-07	Meets Standards

Municipal Finance
State Aid Programs, 2009
Total aid	$618,577
CMPTRA	57,566
Energy tax receipts	536,268
Garden State Trust	0

General Budget, 2008
Total tax levy	$24,961,497
County levy	4,055,197
County taxes	3,598,670
County library	216,557
County health	0
County open space	239,970
School levy	15,435,741
Muni. levy	5,470,559
Misc. revenues	2,839,116

Taxes
	2006	2007	2008
General tax rate per $100	2.102	2.168	2.196
County equalization ratio	84.01	74.44	71.36
Net valuation taxable	$1,113,795,300	$1,123,605,985	$1,136,856,297
State equalized value	$1,496,562,873	$1,574,377,872	$246,645,548

* US Census Bureau
** New Jersey Department of Labor

See Introduction for an explanation of all data sources.

Demographics & Socio-Economic Characteristics
(2000 US Census, except as noted)

Population
1980*	32,229
1990*	30,548
2000	31,637
Male	15,039
Female	16,598
2007 (estimate)*	30,783
Population density	5,954.2

Race & Hispanic Origin, 2000
Race
White	28,960
Black/African American	234
American Indian/Alaska Native	13
Asian	1,558
Native Hawaiian/Pacific Islander	1
Other race	434
Two or more races	437
Hispanic origin, total	1,744
Mexican	55
Puerto Rican	456
Cuban	171
Other Hispanic	1,062

Age & Nativity, 2000
Under 5 years	1,673
18 years and over	24,423
21 years and over	23,584
65 years and over	5,919
85 years and over	711
Median age	41.8
Native-born	23,161
Foreign-born	8,476

Educational Attainment, 2000
Population 25 years and over	22,452
Less than 9th grade	3.3%
High school grad or higher	89.9%
Bachelor's degree or higher	44.8%
Graduate degree	17.6%

Income & Poverty, 1999
Per capita income	$32,273
Median household income	$72,127
Median family income	$81,220
Persons in poverty	1,161
H'holds receiving public assistance	86
H'holds receiving social security	3,823

Households, 2000
Total households	11,806
With persons under 18	4,135
With persons over 65	4,163
Family households	8,906
Single-person households	2,516
Persons per household	2.67
Persons per family	3.12

Labor & Employment
Total civilian labor force, 2007**	16,563
Unemployment rate	3.5%
Total civilian labor force, 2000	16,156
Unemployment rate	2.7%

Employed persons 16 years and over by occupation, 2000
Managers & professionals	7,563
Service occupations	1,428
Sales & office occupations	4,602
Farming, fishing & forestry	0
Construction & maintenance	912
Production & transportation	1,222
Self-employed persons	1,046

*   US Census Bureau
** New Jersey Department of Labor

General Information
Borough of Fair Lawn
8-01 Fair Lawn Ave
Fair Lawn, NJ 07410
201-796-1700

Website	www.fairlawn.org
Year of incorporation	1924
Land/water area (sq. miles)	5.17/0.05
Form of government	Council-Manager

Government
Legislative Districts
US Congressional	9
State Legislative	38

Local Officials, 2009
Mayor	Steven Weinstein
Manager	Thomas Metzler
Clerk	Joanne Kwasniewski
Finance Dir	Barry Eccleston
Tax Assessor	Timothy Henderson
Tax Collector	Alice Lee
Attorney	Bruce Rosenberg
Building	Dennis Kolano
Comm Dev/Planning	NA
Engineering	Kenneth Garrison
Public Works	Roland Conte
Police Chief	Erik Rose
Emerg/Fire Director	Thomas Karney

Housing & Construction
Housing Units, 2000*
Total	12,006
Median rent	$923
Median SF home value	$218,000

Permits for New Residential Construction
	Units	Value
Total, 2006	12	$2,630,371
Single family	9	$2,049,121
Total, 2007	11	$1,882,157
Single family	11	$1,882,157

Real Property Valuation, 2008
	Parcels	Valuation
Total	10,827	$5,069,472,500
Vacant	134	30,140,600
Residential	10,203	4,174,425,200
Commercial	401	501,403,300
Industrial	76	218,628,700
Apartments	13	144,874,700
Farm land	0	0
Farm homestead	0	0

Average Property Value & Tax, 2008
Residential value	$409,137
Property tax	$8,596
Tax credit/rebate	$1,287

Public Library
Maurice M. Pine Library
10-01 Fair Lawn Ave
Fair Lawn, NJ 07410
201-796-3400

Director	Timothy H. Murphy

Library statistics, 2007
Population served	31,637
Full-time/total staff	6/17

	Total	Per capita
Holdings	185,120	5.85
Revenues	$2,299,499	$72.68
Expenditures	$2,257,660	$71.36
Annual visits	159,918	5.05
Internet terminals/annual users	10/13,457	

Public Safety
Number of officers, 2007	64

Crime	2006	2007
Total crimes	491	431
Violent	38	35
Murder	0	0
Rape	3	2
Robbery	11	7
Aggravated assault	24	26
Non-violent	453	396
Burglary	60	62
Larceny	373	319
Vehicle theft	20	15
Domestic violence	143	141
Arson	5	0
Total crime rate	15.6	13.8
Violent	1.2	1.1
Non-violent	14.4	12.7

Public School District
(for school year 2007-08 except as noted)

Fair Lawn School District
37-01 Fair Lawn Avenue
Fair Lawn, NJ 07410
(201) 794-5500

Superintendent	Bruce Watson
Number of schools	9
Grade plan	K-12
Enrollment	4,772
Attendance rate, '06-07	95.7%
Dropout rate	0.4%
Students per teacher	11.0
Per pupil expenditure	$15,010
Median faculty salary	$64,733
Median administrator salary	$134,315
Grade 12 enrollment	373
High school graduation rate	98.4%

Assessment test results
(percent scoring at proficient or advanced level)
	Language	Math
NJASK-Grade 3	95.2%	89.8%
GEPA-Grade 8	79.1%	92.8%
HSPA-High School	82.7%	93.0%

SAT Score Averages, 2006-07
Pct tested	Math	Verbal	Writing
94%	534	500	510

Teacher Qualifications
Avg. years of experience	11
Highly-qualified teachers one subject/all subjects	100%/100%

No Child Left Behind
AYP, 2006-07	Meets Standards

Municipal Finance
State Aid Programs, 2009
Total aid	$4,827,840
CMPTRA	478,033
Energy tax receipts	4,229,111
Garden State Trust	0

General Budget, 2008
Total tax levy	$106,719,275
County levy	9,924,930
County taxes	9,387,530
County library	0
County health	0
County open space	537,401
School levy	66,978,432
Muni. levy	29,815,912
Misc. revenues	14,723,390

Taxes
	2006	2007	2008
General tax rate per $100	4.26	2.03	2.103
County equalization ratio	50.67	101.25	95.16
Net valuation taxable	$2,294,112,200	$5,074,119,673	$5,079,255,301
State equalized value	$4,988,285,128	$5,331,774,972	$5,341,579,709

Demographics & Socio-Economic Characteristics
(2000 US Census, except as noted)

Population
1980*	5,693
1990*	5,699
2000	6,283
Male	3,736
Female	2,547
2007 (estimate)*	6,748
Population density	159.6

Race & Hispanic Origin, 2000
Race
White	2,602
Black/African American	2,980
American Indian/Alaska Native	319
Asian	35
Native Hawaiian/Pacific Islander	2
Other race	150
Two or more races	195
Hispanic origin, total	557
Mexican	123
Puerto Rican	149
Cuban	0
Other Hispanic	285

Age & Nativity, 2000
Under 5 years	279
18 years and over	5,037
21 years and over	4,823
65 years and over	670
85 years and over	53
Median age	36.8
Native-born	6,165
Foreign-born	118

Educational Attainment, 2000
Population 25 years and over	4,491
Less than 9th grade	8.2%
High school grad or higher	63.3%
Bachelor's degree or higher	5.1%
Graduate degree	1.5%

Income & Poverty, 1999
Per capita income	$17,547
Median household income	$37,891
Median family income	$41,326
Persons in poverty	551
H'holds receiving public assistance	67
H'holds receiving social security	591

Households, 2000
Total households	1,751
With persons under 18	660
With persons over 65	484
Family households	1,322
Single-person households	358
Persons per household	2.78
Persons per family	3.19

Labor & Employment
Total civilian labor force, 2007**	2,428
Unemployment rate	8.2%
Total civilian labor force, 2000	2,288
Unemployment rate	12.3%

Employed persons 16 years and over by occupation, 2000
Managers & professionals	398
Service occupations	460
Sales & office occupations	433
Farming, fishing & forestry	7
Construction & maintenance	176
Production & transportation	532
Self-employed persons	101

General Information
Township of Fairfield
PO Box 240
Fairton, NJ 08320
856-451-9284
Website	www.fairfieldtwp-nj.com
Year of incorporation	1697
Land/water area (sq. miles)	42.29/1.51
Form of government	Township

Government
Legislative Districts
US Congressional	2
State Legislative	3

Local Officials, 2009
Mayor	Marion Kennedy Jr
Manager	R.J. DeVillasanta
Clerk	R.J. DeVillasanta
Finance Dir	Judson Moore
Tax Assessor	Michelle Sharp
Tax Collector	Jennifer Hernandez
Attorney	John Carr
Building	Milt Truxton
Comm Dev/Planning	NA
Engineering	Fralinger Engineering
Public Works	NA
Police Chief	NA
Fire/Emergency Dir	NA

Housing & Construction
Housing Units, 2000*
Total	1,915
Median rent	$596
Median SF home value	$84,100

Permits for New Residential Construction
	Units	Value
Total, 2006	7	$994,913
Single family	7	$994,913
Total, 2007	10	$1,561,825
Single family	10	$1,561,825

Real Property Valuation, 2008
	Parcels	Valuation
Total	2,665	$168,202,800
Vacant	714	9,240,700
Residential	1,625	135,374,500
Commercial	82	13,469,800
Industrial	0	0
Apartments	1	219,400
Farm land	182	2,827,400
Farm homestead	61	7,071,000

Average Property Value & Tax, 2008
Residential value	$84,487
Property tax	$3,044
Tax credit/rebate	$745

Public Library
No public municipal library

Library statistics, 2007
Population served	NA
Full-time/total staff	NA/NA

	Total	Per capita
Holdings	NA	NA
Revenues	NA	NA
Expenditures	NA	NA
Annual visits	NA	NA
Internet terminals/annual users	NA/NA	

Public Safety
Number of officers, 2007 0
Crime	2006	2007
Total crimes	156	164
Violent	20	17
Murder	1	0
Rape	1	0
Robbery	2	5
Aggravated assault	16	12
Non-violent	136	147
Burglary	55	57
Larceny	72	68
Vehicle theft	9	22
Domestic violence	5	46
Arson	1	2
Total crime rate	23.0	24.2
Violent	3.0	2.5
Non-violent	20.1	21.7

Public School District
(for school year 2007-08 except as noted)

Fairfield Township School District
375 Gouldtown-Woodruff Road
Bridgeton, NJ 08302
(856) 453-1882
Superintendent	John Klug
Number of schools	1
Grade plan	K-8
Enrollment	609
Attendance rate, '06-07	96.2%
Dropout rate	NA
Students per teacher	10.7
Per pupil expenditure	$11,999
Median faculty salary	$46,730
Median administrator salary	$80,000
Grade 12 enrollment	NA
High school graduation rate	NA

Assessment test results
(percent scoring at proficient or advanced level)
	Language	Math
NJASK-Grade 3	51.7%	66.7%
GEPA-Grade 8	48.7%	74.4%
HSPA-High School	NA	NA

SAT Score Averages, 2006-07
Pct tested	Math	Verbal	Writing
NA	NA	NA	NA

Teacher Qualifications
Avg. years of experience	14
Highly-qualified teachers one subject/all subjects	100%/100%

No Child Left Behind
AYP, 2006-07 .... Meets Standards

Municipal Finance
State Aid Programs, 2009
Total aid	$593,483
CMPTRA	106,708
Energy tax receipts	437,793
Garden State Trust	60,868

General Budget, 2008
Total tax levy	$6,090,074
County levy	2,767,942
County taxes	2,616,691
County library	0
County health	122,179
County open space	29,072
School levy	2,442,931
Muni. levy	879,201
Misc. revenues	2,114,980

Taxes
	2006	2007	2008
General tax rate per $100	3.007	3.421	3.608
County equalization ratio	78.11	68.06	58.20
Net valuation taxable	$161,019,200	$165,821,170	$169,030,680
State equalized value	$237,567,843	$284,265,923	$319,998,278

* US Census Bureau
** New Jersey Department of Labor

See Introduction for an explanation of all data sources.

Demographics & Socio-Economic Characteristics

(2000 US Census, except as noted)

Population

1980*	7,987
1990*	7,615
2000	7,063
Male	3,454
Female	3,609
2007 (estimate)*	7,556
Population density	723.1

Race & Hispanic Origin, 2000

Race

White	6,754
Black/African American	37
American Indian/Alaska Native	7
Asian	199
Native Hawaiian/Pacific Islander	0
Other race	28
Two or more races	38
Hispanic origin, total	244
Mexican	33
Puerto Rican	68
Cuban	32
Other Hispanic	111

Age & Nativity, 2000

Under 5 years	390
18 years and over	5,506
21 years and over	5,300
65 years and over	1,065
85 years and over	118
Median age	40.7
Native-born	6,174
Foreign-born	889

Educational Attainment, 2000

Population 25 years and over	5,028
Less than 9th grade	4.9%
High school grad or higher	86.9%
Bachelor's degree or higher	34.8%
Graduate degree	11.6%

Income & Poverty, 1999

Per capita income	$32,099
Median household income	$83,120
Median family income	$90,998
Persons in poverty	195
H'holds receiving public assistance	8
H'holds receiving social security	776

Households, 2000

Total households	2,296
With persons under 18	837
With persons over 65	703
Family households	1,982
Single-person households	251
Persons per household	3.04
Persons per family	3.29

Labor & Employment

Total civilian labor force, 2007**	3,798
Unemployment rate	2.9%
Total civilian labor force, 2000	3,652
Unemployment rate	2.7%

Employed persons 16 years and over by occupation, 2000

Managers & professionals	1,500
Service occupations	341
Sales & office occupations	1,136
Farming, fishing & forestry	0
Construction & maintenance	307
Production & transportation	270
Self-employed persons	255

* US Census Bureau
** New Jersey Department of Labor

General Information

Township of Fairfield
230 Fairfield Rd
Fairfield, NJ 07004
973-882-2700

Website	www.fairfieldnj.org
Year of incorporation	1964
Land/water area (sq. miles)	10.45/0.00
Form of government	Small Municipality

Government

Legislative Districts

US Congressional	11
State Legislative	27

Local Officials, 2009

Mayor	James Gasparini
Manager	Joseph Catenaro
Clerk	Denise D. Cafone
Finance Dir	Joseph John McClusky
Tax Assessor	E. Romeo Longo
Tax Collector	Marita Shatzel
Attorney	Dennis Galvin
Building	Phil Cheff
Comm Dev/Planning	NA
Engineering	Lawrence Gonnello
Public Works	Ron Karl
Police Chief	Charles Voelker Jr
Emerg/Fire Director	Gene Iandolo

Housing & Construction

Housing Units, 2000*

Total	2,326
Median rent	$988
Median SF home value	$274,800

Permits for New Residential Construction

	Units	Value
Total, 2006	9	$3,295,308
Single family	9	$3,295,308
Total, 2007	7	$2,617,850
Single family	7	$2,617,850

Real Property Valuation, 2008

	Parcels	Valuation
Total	3,415	$1,565,707,000
Vacant	245	23,548,300
Residential	2,476	656,158,400
Commercial	396	397,923,400
Industrial	289	476,087,700
Apartments	1	11,701,000
Farm land	7	46,600
Farm homestead	1	241,600

Average Property Value & Tax, 2008

Residential value	$264,998
Property tax	$7,385
Tax credit/rebate	$1,095

Public Library

A.P. Costa Memorial Library
261 Hollywood Ave
Fairfield, NJ 07004
973-227-3575

Director	John J. Helle

Library statistics, 2007

Population served	7,063
Full-time/total staff	2/5

	Total	Per capita
Holdings	78,462	11.11
Revenues	$1,018,760	$144.24
Expenditures	$766,684	$108.55
Annual visits	36,759	5.20
Internet terminals/annual users	4/3,364	

Public Safety

Number of officers, 2007	41

Crime	2006	2007
Total crimes	386	371
Violent	13	12
Murder	0	0
Rape	0	1
Robbery	3	2
Aggravated assault	10	9
Non-violent	373	359
Burglary	44	31
Larceny	300	314
Vehicle theft	29	14
Domestic violence	73	56
Arson	0	1
Total crime rate	49.8	48.1
Violent	1.7	1.6
Non-violent	48.1	46.6

Public School District

(for school year 2007-08 except as noted)

Fairfield Township School District
15 Knoll Road
Fairfield, NJ 07004
(973) 227-5586

Superintendent	Mary Kildow
Number of schools	2
Grade plan	K-6
Enrollment	729
Attendance rate, '06-07	96.3%
Dropout rate	NA
Students per teacher	12.1
Per pupil expenditure	$13,106
Median faculty salary	$47,400
Median administrator salary	$99,000
Grade 12 enrollment	NA
High school graduation rate	NA

Assessment test results

(percent scoring at proficient or advanced level)

	Language	Math
NJASK-Grade 3	91.4%	82.9%
GEPA-Grade 8	NA	NA
HSPA-High School	NA	NA

SAT Score Averages, 2006-07

Pct tested	Math	Verbal	Writing
NA	NA	NA	NA

Teacher Qualifications

Avg. years of experience	9
Highly-qualified teachers one subject/all subjects	100%/100%

No Child Left Behind

AYP, 2006-07	Meets Standards

Municipal Finance

State Aid Programs, 2009

Total aid	$1,578,383
CMPTRA	264,937
Energy tax receipts	1,240,374
Garden State Trust	18,611

General Budget, 2008

Total tax levy	$43,788,948
County levy	11,756,822
County taxes	11,301,142
County library	0
County health	0
County open space	455,681
School levy	21,500,144
Muni. levy	10,531,982
Misc. revenues	7,109,279

Taxes

	2006	2007	2008
General tax rate per $100	2.52	2.63	2.787
County equalization ratio	60.84	54.56	52.32
Net valuation taxable	$1,561,994,800	$1,585,913,000	$1,571,324,500
State equalized value	$2,868,924,895	$3,026,369,270	$3,107,255,773

Demographics & Socio-Economic Characteristics
(2000 US Census, except as noted)

Population
1980*	10,519
1990*	10,733
2000	13,255
Male	6,844
Female	6,411
2007 (estimate)*	13,540
Population density	15,929.4

Race & Hispanic Origin, 2000
Race
White	9,605
Black/African American	226
American Indian/Alaska Native	51
Asian	659
Native Hawaiian/Pacific Islander	4
Other race	1,712
Two or more races	998
Hispanic origin, total	4,911
Mexican	149
Puerto Rican	452
Cuban	562
Other Hispanic	3,748

Age & Nativity, 2000
Under 5 years	852
18 years and over	10,456
21 years and over	9,843
65 years and over	1,824
85 years and over	191
Median age	34.5
Native-born	6,841
Foreign-born	6,414

Educational Attainment, 2000
Population 25 years and over	8,859
Less than 9th grade	19.6%
High school grad or higher	65.4%
Bachelor's degree or higher	16.5%
Graduate degree	4.0%

Income & Poverty, 1999
Per capita income	$18,835
Median household income	$40,393
Median family income	$46,365
Persons in poverty	1,557
H'holds receiving public assistance	221
H'holds receiving social security	1,364

Households, 2000
Total households	4,861
With persons under 18	1,600
With persons over 65	1,395
Family households	3,178
Single-person households	1,362
Persons per household	2.73
Persons per family	3.31

Labor & Employment
Total civilian labor force, 2007**	6,378
Unemployment rate	6.5%
Total civilian labor force, 2000	6,053
Unemployment rate	7.0%

Employed persons 16 years and over by occupation, 2000
Managers & professionals	1,345
Service occupations	894
Sales & office occupations	1,770
Farming, fishing & forestry	0
Construction & maintenance	656
Production & transportation	964
Self-employed persons	269

General Information
Borough of Fairview
59 Anderson Ave
Fairview, NJ 07022
201-943-3300

Website	NA
Year of incorporation	1894
Land/water area (sq. miles)	0.85/0.00
Form of government	Borough

Government
Legislative Districts
US Congressional	9
State Legislative	32

Local Officials, 2009
Mayor	Vincent Bellucci Jr
Manager	Diane Testa
Clerk	Diane Testa
Finance Dir	Joseph Rutch
Tax Assessor	George Reggo
Tax Collector	Eugene Pedoto
Attorney	John Schettino
Building	Thomas Leonardi
Comm Dev/Planning	NA
Engineering	Boswell Engineering
Public Works	Paul Juliano
Police Chief	John Pinzone
Emerg/Fire Director	Anthony Amato

Housing & Construction
Housing Units, 2000*
Total	4,988
Median rent	$846
Median SF home value	$179,900

Permits for New Residential Construction
	Units	Value
Total, 2006	48	$6,464,172
Single family	4	$497,424
Total, 2007	48	$7,412,352
Single family	5	$846,068

Real Property Valuation, 2008
	Parcels	Valuation
Total	2,600	$621,965,100
Vacant	69	6,654,300
Residential	2,096	393,768,000
Commercial	202	109,705,800
Industrial	110	45,055,600
Apartments	123	66,781,400
Farm land	0	0
Farm homestead	0	0

Average Property Value & Tax, 2008
Residential value	$187,866
Property tax	$7,429
Tax credit/rebate	$1,138

Public Library
Fairview Free Public Library
213 Anderson Ave
Fairview, NJ 07022
201-943-6244

Director	Roger M. Verdi

Library statistics, 2007
Population served	13,255
Full-time/total staff	1/1

	Total	Per capita
Holdings	24,241	1.83
Revenues	$463,846	$34.99
Expenditures	$343,335	$25.90
Annual visits	38,000	2.87
Internet terminals/annual users	6/7,500	

Public Safety
Number of officers, 2007		33

Crime	2006	2007
Total crimes	307	311
Violent	54	69
Murder	0	0
Rape	3	3
Robbery	25	23
Aggravated assault	26	43
Non-violent	253	242
Burglary	113	64
Larceny	119	161
Vehicle theft	21	17
Domestic violence	202	207
Arson	1	0
Total crime rate	22.6	22.8
Violent	4.0	5.1
Non-violent	18.7	17.8

Public School District
(for school year 2007-08 except as noted)

Fairview School District
130 Hamilton Avenue
Fairview, NJ 07022
(201) 943-1699

Superintendent	Louis DeLisio
Number of schools	3
Grade plan	K-8
Enrollment	1,057
Attendance rate, '06-07	93.7%
Dropout rate	NA
Students per teacher	12.1
Per pupil expenditure	$12,375
Median faculty salary	$45,894
Median administrator salary	$116,241
Grade 12 enrollment	NA
High school graduation rate	NA

Assessment test results
(percent scoring at proficient or advanced level)
	Language	Math
NJASK-Grade 3	71.1%	83.4%
GEPA-Grade 8	64.6%	78.5%
HSPA-High School	NA	NA

SAT Score Averages, 2006-07
Pct tested	Math	Verbal	Writing
NA	NA	NA	NA

Teacher Qualifications
Avg. years of experience	9
Highly-qualified teachers one subject/all subjects	100%/100%

No Child Left Behind
AYP, 2006-07	Meets Standards

Municipal Finance
State Aid Programs, 2009
Total aid	$1,280,068
CMPTRA	447,461
Energy tax receipts	800,605
Garden State Trust	0

General Budget, 2008
Total tax levy	$24,608,872
County levy	2,431,201
County taxes	2,299,305
County library	0
County health	0
County open space	131,897
School levy	11,671,293
Muni. levy	10,506,378
Misc. revenues	4,312,677

Taxes	2006	2007	2008
General tax rate per $100	3.64	3.8	3.956
County equalization ratio	56.2	49.42	47.64
Net valuation taxable	$616,266,200	$619,922,889	$622,314,478
State equalized value	$1,247,382,324	$1,300,882,604	$1,569,383,435

* US Census Bureau
** New Jersey Department of Labor

See Introduction for an explanation of all data sources.

Demographics & Socio-Economic Characteristics

(2000 US Census, except as noted)

Population

1980*	7,767
1990*	7,115
2000	7,174
Male	3,422
Female	3,752
2007 (estimate)*	7,143
Population density	5,330.6

Race & Hispanic Origin, 2000

Race

White	6,335
Black/African American	369
American Indian/Alaska Native	7
Asian	315
Native Hawaiian/Pacific Islander	2
Other race	57
Two or more races	89
Hispanic origin, total	268
Mexican	13
Puerto Rican	105
Cuban	26
Other Hispanic	124

Age & Nativity, 2000

Under 5 years	608
18 years and over	5,323
21 years and over	5,183
65 years and over	1,055
85 years and over	136
Median age	38.6
Native-born	6,316
Foreign-born	858

Educational Attainment, 2000

Population 25 years and over	4,999
Less than 9th grade	1.9%
High school grad or higher	95.0%
Bachelor's degree or higher	51.0%
Graduate degree	18.3%

Income & Poverty, 1999

Per capita income	$34,804
Median household income	$85,233
Median family income	$99,232
Persons in poverty	243
H'holds receiving public assistance	44
H'holds receiving social security	709

Households, 2000

Total households	2,574
With persons under 18	1,042
With persons over 65	727
Family households	2,053
Single-person households	463
Persons per household	2.76
Persons per family	3.13

Labor & Employment

Total civilian labor force, 2007**	3,815
Unemployment rate	2.6%
Total civilian labor force, 2000	3,756
Unemployment rate	4.7%

Employed persons 16 years and over by occupation, 2000

Managers & professionals	1,984
Service occupations	214
Sales & office occupations	1,004
Farming, fishing & forestry	0
Construction & maintenance	181
Production & transportation	195
Self-employed persons	179

* US Census Bureau
** New Jersey Department of Labor

General Information

Borough of Fanwood
75 N Martine Ave
Fanwood, NJ 07023
908-322-8236

Website	visitfanwood.com
Year of incorporation	1895
Land/water area (sq. miles)	1.34/0.00
Form of government	Borough

Government

Legislative Districts

US Congressional	7
State Legislative	22

Local Officials, 2009

Mayor	Colleen Mahr
Manager	Eleanor McGovern
Clerk	Eleanor McGovern
Finance Dir	Fred Tomkins
Tax Assessor	Michael Ross
Tax Collector	Colleen Huehn
Attorney	Dennis Estis
Building	Bruce Helmstetter
Planning	Greg Cummings
Engineering	Joseph Pryor
Public Works	Clinton Dicksen
Police Chief	Donald Domanoski
Emerg/Fire Director	David Ziegler

Housing & Construction

Housing Units, 2000*

Total	2,615
Median rent	$1,077
Median SF home value	$224,300

Permits for New Residential Construction

	Units	Value
Total, 2006	29	$5,351,821
Single family	11	$1,926,221
Total, 2007	9	$1,785,604
Single family	9	$1,785,604

Real Property Valuation, 2008

	Parcels	Valuation
Total	2,636	$226,088,500
Vacant	68	1,930,300
Residential	2,479	209,549,200
Commercial	71	12,152,500
Industrial	18	2,456,500
Apartments	0	0
Farm land	0	0
Farm homestead	0	0

Average Property Value & Tax, 2008

Residential value	$84,530
Property tax	$9,156
Tax credit/rebate	$1,317

Public Library

Fanwood Memorial Library
14 Tillotson Rd
Fanwood, NJ 07023
908-322-6400

Director .... Dan Weiss

Library statistics, 2007

Population served	7,174
Full-time/total staff	2/4

	Total	Per capita
Holdings	50,143	6.99
Revenues	$527,132	$73.48
Expenditures	$466,412	$65.01
Annual visits	55,005	7.67
Internet terminals/annual users	8/6,739	

Public Safety

Number of officers, 2007 21

Crime	2006	2007
Total crimes	64	69
Violent	2	5
Murder	0	0
Rape	0	1
Robbery	0	2
Aggravated assault	2	2
Non-violent	62	64
Burglary	12	11
Larceny	50	51
Vehicle theft	0	2
Domestic violence	14	30
Arson	0	0
Total crime rate	8.9	9.6
Violent	0.3	0.7
Non-violent	8.6	8.9

Public School District

(for school year 2007-08 except as noted)

Scotch Plains-Fanwood School District
Evergreen Avenue & Cedar Street
Scotch Plains, NJ 07076
(908) 232-6161

Superintendent	Margaret W. Hayes
Number of schools	8
Grade plan	K-12
Enrollment	5,333
Attendance rate, '06-07	96.1%
Dropout rate	0.3%
Students per teacher	11.9
Per pupil expenditure	$13,098
Median faculty salary	$56,825
Median administrator salary	$124,394
Grade 12 enrollment	369
High school graduation rate	99.7%

Assessment test results

(percent scoring at proficient or advanced level)

	Language	Math
NJASK-Grade 3	95.9%	94.4%
GEPA-Grade 8	78.2%	92.3%
HSPA-High School	90.6%	90.2%

SAT Score Averages, 2006-07

Pct tested	Math	Verbal	Writing
105%	550	522	518

Teacher Qualifications

Avg. years of experience	7
Highly-qualified teachers one subject/all subjects	99.5%/99.5%

No Child Left Behind

AYP, 2006-07 .... Meets Standards

Municipal Finance

State Aid Programs, 2009

Total aid	$973,795
CMPTRA	59,948
Energy tax receipts	889,502
Garden State Trust	0

General Budget, 2008

Total tax levy	$24,498,407
County levy	4,074,833
County taxes	3,897,249
County library	0
County health	0
County open space	177,585
School levy	15,112,019
Muni. levy	5,311,554
Misc. revenues	3,094,571

Taxes

	2006	2007	2008
General tax rate per $100	9.872	10.299	10.832
County equalization ratio	21.19	19.95	19.13
Net valuation taxable	$224,513,400	$225,534,430	$226,179,795
State equalized value	$1,125,480,420	$1,178,572,373	$1,224,176,298

See Introduction for an explanation of all data sources.

Demographics & Socio-Economic Characteristics

(2000 US Census, except as noted)

Population

1980*	677
1990*	657
2000	859
Male	404
Female	455
2007 (estimate)*	902
Population density	185.6

Race & Hispanic Origin, 2000

Race

White	825
Black/African American	7
American Indian/Alaska Native	1
Asian	18
Native Hawaiian/Pacific Islander	0
Other race	0
Two or more races	8
Hispanic origin, total	31
Mexican	6
Puerto Rican	0
Cuban	0
Other Hispanic	25

Age & Nativity, 2000

Under 5 years	52
18 years and over	701
21 years and over	688
65 years and over	142
85 years and over	12
Median age	44.6
Native-born	756
Foreign-born	100

Educational Attainment, 2000

Population 25 years and over	669
Less than 9th grade	2.1%
High school grad or higher	94.8%
Bachelor's degree or higher	58.1%
Graduate degree	23.5%

Income & Poverty, 1999

Per capita income	$81,535
Median household income	$112,817
Median family income	$149,095
Persons in poverty	21
H'holds receiving public assistance	0
H'holds receiving social security	104

Households, 2000

Total households	368
With persons under 18	91
With persons over 65	97
Family households	253
Single-person households	94
Persons per household	2.33
Persons per family	2.76

Labor & Employment

Total civilian labor force, 2007**	500
Unemployment rate	2.3%
Total civilian labor force, 2000	444
Unemployment rate	2.5%

Employed persons 16 years and over by occupation, 2000

Managers & professionals	240
Service occupations	57
Sales & office occupations	91
Farming, fishing & forestry	4
Construction & maintenance	30
Production & transportation	11
Self-employed persons	49

‡ Joint library with Bedminster Township
* US Census Bureau
** New Jersey Department of Labor

See Introduction for an explanation of all data sources.

General Information

Borough of Far Hills
PO Box 249
Far Hills, NJ 07931
908-234-0611

Email	farhillsborough@patmedia.net
Year of incorporation	1921
Land/water area (sq. miles)	4.86/0.06
Form of government	Borough

Government

Legislative Districts

US Congressional	7
State Legislative	16

Local Officials, 2009

Mayor	Carl J. Torsilieri
Manager/Admin	NA
Clerk	Robin Collins
Finance Dir	Debra Stern
Tax Assessor	Edward Kerwin
Tax Collector	Deborah Giordano
Attorney	Maryann Nergaard
Building	Joseph Alicino
Planning	David Banisch
Engineering	Paul Ferriero
Public Works	NA
Police Chief	Kenneth Hartman
Emerg/Fire Director	Adam Segai

Housing & Construction

Housing Units, 2000*

Total	386
Median rent	$1,208
Median SF home value	$393,300

Permits for New Residential Construction

	Units	Value
Total, 2006	3	$8,400,000
Single family	3	$8,400,000
Total, 2007	0	$0
Single family	0	$0

Real Property Valuation, 2008

	Parcels	Valuation
Total	460	$508,237,263
Vacant	19	9,067,900
Residential	309	346,625,700
Commercial	28	34,417,500
Industrial	0	0
Apartments	1	455,000
Farm land	57	397,563
Farm homestead	46	117,273,600

Average Property Value & Tax, 2008

Residential value	$1,306,759
Property tax	$12,050
Tax credit/rebate	$871

Public Library

Clarence Dillon Public Library‡
2336 Lamington Rd
Bedminster, NJ 07921
908-234-2325

Director	Nanette E. Geiger

Library statistics, 2007

Population served	9,161
Full-time/total staff	2/3

	Total	Per capita
Holdings	82,553	9.01
Revenues	$1,068,024	$116.58
Expenditures	$941,688	$102.79
Annual visits	81,135	8.86
Internet terminals/annual users	22/5,264	

Public Safety

Number of officers, 2007	6

Crime	2006	2007
Total crimes	13	14
Violent	2	0
Murder	0	0
Rape	0	0
Robbery	0	0
Aggravated assault	2	0
Non-violent	11	14
Burglary	2	4
Larceny	9	10
Vehicle theft	0	0
Domestic violence	6	5
Arson	0	0
Total crime rate	14.1	15.1
Violent	2.2	0.0
Non-violent	12.0	15.1

Public School District

(for school year 2007-08 except as noted)

Somerset Hills Regional School District
25 Olcott Ave
Bernardsville, NJ 07924
(908) 630-3011

Superintendent	Peter Miller
Number of schools	3
Grade plan	K-12
Enrollment	2,049
Attendance rate, '06-07	95.9%
Dropout rate	0.1%
Students per teacher	10.5
Per pupil expenditure	$15,952
Median faculty salary	$64,173
Median administrator salary	$130,000
Grade 12 enrollment	175
High school graduation rate	98.3%

Assessment test results

(percent scoring at proficient or advanced level)

	Language	Math
NJASK-Grade 3	95.6%	90.4%
GEPA-Grade 8	87.1%	95.2%
HSPA-High School	93.7%	96.1%

SAT Score Averages, 2006-07

Pct tested	Math	Verbal	Writing
91%	575	561	558

Teacher Qualifications

Avg. years of experience	10
Highly-qualified teachers one subject/all subjects	99.5%/99.5%

No Child Left Behind

AYP, 2006-07	Meets Standards

Municipal Finance

State Aid Programs, 2009

Total aid	$88,149
CMPTRA	0
Energy tax receipts	84,623
Garden State Trust	0

General Budget, 2008

Total tax levy	$4,690,064
County levy	1,499,628
County taxes	1,350,189
County library	0
County health	0
County open space	149,439
School levy	1,596,455
Muni. levy	1,593,980
Misc. revenues	622,548

Taxes

	2006	2007	2008
General tax rate per $100	0.92	0.94	0.923
County equalization ratio	106.14	104.84	102.26
Net valuation taxable	$469,017,158	$477,863,541	$508,604,897
State equalized value	$447,691,277	$485,037,139	$505,774,618

Demographics & Socio-Economic Characteristics
(2000 US Census, except as noted)

Population
1980*	1,348
1990*	1,462
2000	1,587
Male	802
Female	785
2007 (estimate)*	1,576
Population density	2,973.6

Race & Hispanic Origin, 2000
Race
White	1,486
Black/African American	18
American Indian/Alaska Native	0
Asian	37
Native Hawaiian/Pacific Islander	0
Other race	33
Two or more races	13
Hispanic origin, total	61
Mexican	12
Puerto Rican	27
Cuban	0
Other Hispanic	22

Age & Nativity, 2000
Under 5 years	102
18 years and over	1,159
21 years and over	1,117
65 years and over	143
85 years and over	7
Median age	34.7
Native-born	1,496
Foreign-born	91

Educational Attainment, 2000
Population 25 years and over	1,041
Less than 9th grade	2.2%
High school grad or higher	88.5%
Bachelor's degree or higher	19.0%
Graduate degree	6.3%

Income & Poverty, 1999
Per capita income	$21,667
Median household income	$48,889
Median family income	$59,625
Persons in poverty	90
H'holds receiving public assistance	20
H'holds receiving social security	120

Households, 2000
Total households	625
With persons under 18	244
With persons over 65	105
Family households	406
Single-person households	181
Persons per household	2.54
Persons per family	3.21

Labor & Employment
Total civilian labor force, 2007**	908
Unemployment rate	2.2%
Total civilian labor force, 2000	860
Unemployment rate	3.1%

Employed persons 16 years and over by occupation, 2000
Managers & professionals	274
Service occupations	121
Sales & office occupations	230
Farming, fishing & forestry	0
Construction & maintenance	114
Production & transportation	94
Self-employed persons	40

* US Census Bureau
** New Jersey Department of Labor

General Information
Borough of Farmingdale
11 Asbury Ave
PO Box 58
Farmingdale, NJ 07727
732-938-4077
Email	farmingdale.borough@verizon.net
Year of incorporation	1903
Land/water area (sq. miles)	0.53/0.00
Form of government	Borough

Government
Legislative Districts
US Congressional	4
State Legislative	30

Local Officials, 2009
Mayor	John P. Morgan
Borough Admin	Donna M. Phelps
Clerk	Donna M. Phelps
Finance Dir	Robbin Kirk
Tax Assessor	Thomas Glock
Tax Collector	Robbin Kirk
Attorney	John O. Bennett III
Building	Chester Phillips
Comm Dev/Planning	NA
Engineering	Matt Shafai
Public Works	NA
Police Chief	NA
Emerg/Fire Director	William Lewis

Housing & Construction
Housing Units, 2000*
Total	638
Median rent	$780
Median SF home value	$154,100

Permits for New Residential Construction
	Units	Value
Total, 2006	6	$349,000
Single family	6	$349,000
Total, 2007	2	$121,167
Single family	2	$121,167

Real Property Valuation, 2008
	Parcels	Valuation
Total	421	$149,981,400
Vacant	25	2,129,800
Residential	351	110,554,200
Commercial	36	19,871,300
Industrial	3	2,742,800
Apartments	4	13,947,400
Farm land	1	14,200
Farm homestead	1	721,700

Average Property Value & Tax, 2008
Residential value	$316,125
Property tax	$5,346
Tax credit/rebate	$1,033

Public Library
No public municipal library

Library statistics, 2007
Population served	NA
Full-time/total staff	NA/NA

	Total	Per capita
Holdings	NA	NA
Revenues	NA	NA
Expenditures	NA	NA
Annual visits	NA	NA
Internet terminals/annual users	NA/NA	

Public Safety
Number of officers, 2007	0

Crime	2006	2007
Total crimes	27	21
Violent	2	1
Murder	0	0
Rape	0	0
Robbery	1	1
Aggravated assault	1	0
Non-violent	25	20
Burglary	3	3
Larceny	17	16
Vehicle theft	5	1
Domestic violence	2	10
Arson	0	1
Total crime rate	17.2	13.4
Violent	1.3	0.6
Non-violent	15.9	12.8

Public School District
(for school year 2007-08 except as noted)

Farmingdale Borough School District
Academy Street, PO Box 706
Farmingdale, NJ 07727
(732) 938-9611
Superintendent	Cheri-Ellen Crowl
Number of schools	1
Grade plan	K-8
Enrollment	143
Attendance rate, '06-07	93.8%
Dropout rate	NA
Students per teacher	7.7
Per pupil expenditure	$15,100
Median faculty salary	$57,901
Median administrator salary	$60,635
Grade 12 enrollment	NA
High school graduation rate	NA

Assessment test results
(percent scoring at proficient or advanced level)
	Language	Math
NJASK-Grade 3	76.9%	61.5%
GEPA-Grade 8	92.8%	92.8%
HSPA-High School	NA	NA

SAT Score Averages, 2006-07
Pct tested	Math	Verbal	Writing
NA	NA	NA	NA

Teacher Qualifications
Avg. years of experience	8
Highly-qualified teachers one subject/all subjects	100%/100%

No Child Left Behind
AYP, 2006-07	Meets Standards

Municipal Finance
State Aid Programs, 2009
Total aid	$186,708
CMPTRA	75,474
Energy tax receipts	103,766
Garden State Trust	0

General Budget, 2008
Total tax levy	$2,575,916
County levy	409,125
County taxes	357,172
County library	21,494
County health	6,642
County open space	23,817
School levy	1,902,951
Muni. levy	263,840
Misc. revenues	542,400

Taxes
	2006	2007	2008
General tax rate per $100	1.76	1.716	1.692
County equalization ratio	100.29	100.19	96.99
Net valuation taxable	$148,431,800	$151,181,169	$152,312,326
State equalized value	$150,439,213	$155,811,746	$1,597,417,358

Demographics & Socio-Economic Characteristics

(2000 US Census, except as noted)

Population

1980*	597
1990*	579
2000	522
Male	245
Female	277
2007 (estimate)*	568
Population density	2,103.7

Race & Hispanic Origin, 2000

Race

White	426
Black/African American	83
American Indian/Alaska Native	1
Asian	0
Native Hawaiian/Pacific Islander	0
Other race	2
Two or more races	10
Hispanic origin, total	13
Mexican	0
Puerto Rican	5
Cuban	1
Other Hispanic	7

Age & Nativity, 2000

Under 5 years	39
18 years and over	390
21 years and over	378
65 years and over	65
85 years and over	3
Median age	35.4
Native-born	508
Foreign-born	20

Educational Attainment, 2000

Population 25 years and over	351
Less than 9th grade	1.7%
High school grad or higher	88.6%
Bachelor's degree or higher	27.6%
Graduate degree	5.4%

Income & Poverty, 1999

Per capita income	$23,908
Median household income	$58,958
Median family income	$66,607
Persons in poverty	10
H'holds receiving public assistance	0
H'holds receiving social security	34

Households, 2000

Total households	189
With persons under 18	76
With persons over 65	45
Family households	139
Single-person households	33
Persons per household	2.76
Persons per family	3.17

Labor & Employment

Total civilian labor force, 2007**	354
Unemployment rate	6.4%
Total civilian labor force, 2000	303
Unemployment rate	4.0%

Employed persons 16 years and over by occupation, 2000

Managers & professionals	84
Service occupations	39
Sales & office occupations	99
Farming, fishing & forestry	0
Construction & maintenance	18
Production & transportation	51
Self-employed persons	8

* US Census Bureau
** New Jersey Department of Labor

See Introduction for an explanation of all data sources.

General Information

Borough of Fieldsboro
204 Washington St
Fieldsboro, NJ 08505
609-298-6344

Website	www.fieldsboro.us
Year of incorporation	1850
Land/water area (sq. miles)	0.27/0.00
Form of government	Borough

Government

Legislative Districts

US Congressional	4
State Legislative	30

Local Officials, 2009

Mayor	Edward Tyler Sr
Manager/Admin	NA
Clerk	Patrice Hansell
Finance Dir	Peter Federico
Tax Assessor	Walter Kosul
Tax Collector	Lan Chen Shen
Attorney	Kenneth Domzalski
Building	NA
Comm Dev/Planning	NA
Engineering	Birdsall Engineering
Public Works	Roger Redwanski
Police Chief	Joseph Conlin
Fire/Emergency Dir	NA

Housing & Construction

Housing Units, 2000*

Total	204
Median rent	$1,050
Median SF home value	$103,900

Permits for New Residential Construction

	Units	Value
Total, 2006	2	$330,000
Single family	2	$330,000
Total, 2007	0	$0
Single family	0	$0

Real Property Valuation, 2008

	Parcels	Valuation
Total	242	$28,913,500
Vacant	34	815,900
Residential	200	18,944,300
Commercial	7	1,287,400
Industrial	1	7,865,900
Apartments	0	0
Farm land	0	0
Farm homestead	0	0

Average Property Value & Tax, 2008

Residential value	$94,722
Property tax	$4,782
Tax credit/rebate	$893

Public Library

No public municipal library

Library statistics, 2007

Population served	NA
Full-time/total staff	NA/NA

	Total	Per capita
Holdings	NA	NA
Revenues	NA	NA
Expenditures	NA	NA
Annual visits	NA	NA
Internet terminals/annual users	NA/NA	

Public Safety

Number of officers, 2007 ... 0

Crime	2006	2007
Total crimes	7	0
Violent	2	0
Murder	0	0
Rape	0	0
Robbery	1	0
Aggravated assault	1	0
Non-violent	5	0
Burglary	1	0
Larceny	4	0
Vehicle theft	0	0
Domestic violence	1	1
Arson	0	0
Total crime rate	12.0	0.0
Violent	3.4	0.0
Non-violent	8.6	0.0

Public School District

(for school year 2007-08 except as noted)

Bordentown Regional School District
318 Ward Ave.
Bordentown, NJ 08505
(609) 298-0025

Superintendent	Constance Bauer
Number of schools	0
Grade plan	K-12
Enrollment	2,351
Attendance rate, '06-07	95.5%
Dropout rate	0.5%
Students per teacher	11.2
Per pupil expenditure	$13,627
Median faculty salary	$53,342
Median administrator salary	$88,622
Grade 12 enrollment	170
High school graduation rate	96.4%

Assessment test results

(percent scoring at proficient or advanced level)

	Language	Math
NJASK-Grade 3	94.3%	94.3%
GEPA-Grade 8	69.8%	83.4%
HSPA-High School	75.7%	85.6%

SAT Score Averages, 2006-07

Pct tested	Math	Verbal	Writing
76%	479	486	469

Teacher Qualifications

Avg. years of experience	8

Highly-qualified teachers
one subject/all subjects ... 100%/100%

No Child Left Behind

AYP, 2006-07 ... Meets Standards

Municipal Finance

State Aid Programs, 2009

Total aid	$114,363
CMPTRA	56,780
Energy tax receipts	54,724
Garden State Trust	0

General Budget, 2008

Total tax levy	$1,461,045
County levy	260,012
County taxes	213,518
County library	19,715
County health	0
County open space	26,778
School levy	892,039
Muni. levy	308,995
Misc. revenues	391,738

Taxes

	2006	2007	2008
General tax rate per $100	4.334	4.92	5.049
County equalization ratio	57.55	48.62	44.91
Net valuation taxable	$28,892,800	$28,961,828	$28,938,466
State equalized value	$59,452,878	$64,459,366	$58,014,336

Demographics & Socio-Economic Characteristics

(2000 US Census, except as noted)

Population

1980*	4,132
1990*	4,047
2000	4,200
Male	2,038
Female	2,162
2007 (estimate)*	4,237
Population density	3,959.8

Race & Hispanic Origin, 2000

Race

White	3,684
Black/African American	134
American Indian/Alaska Native	13
Asian	131
Native Hawaiian/Pacific Islander	7
Other race	132
Two or more races	99
Hispanic origin, total	461
Mexican	143
Puerto Rican	40
Cuban	3
Other Hispanic	275

Age & Nativity, 2000

Under 5 years	296
18 years and over	3,267
21 years and over	3,134
65 years and over	510
85 years and over	87
Median age	34.9
Native-born	3,618
Foreign-born	582

Educational Attainment, 2000

Population 25 years and over	2,942
Less than 9th grade	5.6%
High school grad or higher	82.6%
Bachelor's degree or higher	27.4%
Graduate degree	11.2%

Income & Poverty, 1999

Per capita income	$23,769
Median household income	$39,886
Median family income	$51,582
Persons in poverty	281
H'holds receiving public assistance	72
H'holds receiving social security	496

Households, 2000

Total households	1,804
With persons under 18	518
With persons over 65	406
Family households	998
Single-person households	680
Persons per household	2.26
Persons per family	3.00

Labor & Employment

Total civilian labor force, 2007**	2,510
Unemployment rate	3.1%
Total civilian labor force, 2000	2,259
Unemployment rate	2.9%

Employed persons 16 years and over by occupation, 2000

Managers & professionals	694
Service occupations	439
Sales & office occupations	640
Farming, fishing & forestry	37
Construction & maintenance	165
Production & transportation	219
Self-employed persons	130

* US Census Bureau
** New Jersey Department of Labor

General Information

Borough of Flemington
38 Park Ave
Flemington, NJ 08822
908-782-8840

Website	www.historicflemington.com
Year of incorporation	1910
Land/water area (sq. miles)	1.07/0.00
Form of government	Borough

Government

Legislative Districts

US Congressional	7
State Legislative	23

Local Officials, 2009

Mayor	Robert B. Hauck
Manager/Admin	NA
Clerk	Diane L. Schottman
Finance Dir	William Hance
Tax Assessor	Edward Kerwin
Tax Collector	Cathrine Park
Attorney	Barry Goodman
Building	Jeffrey Klein
Comm Dev/Planning	NA
Engineering	Robert J. Clerico
Public Works	Michael Campion
Police Chief	George Becker
Emerg/Fire Director	Paul Klinski

Housing & Construction

Housing Units, 2000*

Total	1,876
Median rent	$828
Median SF home value	$163,300

Permits for New Residential Construction

	Units	Value
Total, 2006	22	$762,300
Single family	0	$0
Total, 2007	37	$1,567,083
Single family	0	$0

Real Property Valuation, 2008

	Parcels	Valuation
Total	1,135	$531,489,700
Vacant	36	5,010,500
Residential	861	258,907,500
Commercial	226	221,209,500
Industrial	2	3,365,000
Apartments	10	42,997,200
Farm land	0	0
Farm homestead	0	0

Average Property Value & Tax, 2008

Residential value	$300,706
Property tax	$6,591
Tax credit/rebate	$1,098

Public Library

Flemington Free Public Library
118 Main St
Flemington, NJ 08822
908-782-5733

Director	Shawn Armington

Library statistics, 2007

Population served	4,200
Full-time/total staff	1/3

	Total	Per capita
Holdings	50,257	11.97
Revenues	$292,530	$69.65
Expenditures	$259,526	$61.79
Annual visits	35,835	8.53
Internet terminals/annual users	11/15,843	

Public Safety

Number of officers, 2007	14

Crime	2006	2007
Total crimes	96	163
Violent	13	11
Murder	0	0
Rape	0	1
Robbery	6	3
Aggravated assault	7	7
Non-violent	83	152
Burglary	12	21
Larceny	69	126
Vehicle theft	2	5
Domestic violence	24	26
Arson	3	2
Total crime rate	23.0	38.2
Violent	3.1	2.6
Non-violent	19.9	35.6

Public School District

(for school year 2007-08 except as noted)

Flemington-Raritan Regional School Dist.
50 Court Street
Flemington, NJ 08822
(908) 284-7575

Superintendent	Jack Farr
Number of schools	6
Grade plan	K-8
Enrollment	3,558
Attendance rate, '06-07	96.2%
Dropout rate	NA
Students per teacher	10.0
Per pupil expenditure	$13,315
Median faculty salary	$53,219
Median administrator salary	$111,026
Grade 12 enrollment	NA
High school graduation rate	NA

Assessment test results

(percent scoring at proficient or advanced level)

	Language	Math
NJASK-Grade 3	98.7%	94.7%
GEPA-Grade 8	81.0%	93.2%
HSPA-High School	NA	NA

SAT Score Averages, 2006-07

Pct tested	Math	Verbal	Writing
NA	NA	NA	NA

Teacher Qualifications

Avg. years of experience	11
Highly-qualified teachers one subject/all subjects	100%/100%

No Child Left Behind

AYP, 2006-07	Meets Standards

Municipal Finance

State Aid Programs, 2009

Total aid	$474,430
CMPTRA	134,142
Energy tax receipts	328,427
Garden State Trust	0

General Budget, 2008

Total tax levy	$11,820,992
County levy	1,738,764
County taxes	1,569,368
County library	0
County health	0
County open space	169,397
School levy	7,445,241
Muni. levy	2,636,986
Misc. revenues	2,363,014

Taxes

	2006	2007	2008
General tax rate per $100	2.38	2.28	2.192
County equalization ratio	97.24	94.63	95.90
Net valuation taxable	$480,096,900	$523,552,384	$539,340,568
State equalized value	$510,237,181	$538,349,030	$520,970,872

See Introduction for an explanation of all data sources.

Demographics & Socio-Economic Characteristics

(2000 US Census, except as noted)

Population

1980*	9,084
1990*	10,266
2000	10,746
Male	5,140
Female	5,606
2007 (estimate)*	11,440
Population density	1,178.2

Race & Hispanic Origin, 2000

Race

White	9,190
Black/African American	1,047
American Indian/Alaska Native	19
Asian	253
Native Hawaiian/Pacific Islander	1
Other race	70
Two or more races	166
Hispanic origin, total	253
Mexican	23
Puerto Rican	126
Cuban	11
Other Hispanic	93

Age & Nativity, 2000

Under 5 years	660
18 years and over	8,039
21 years and over	7,680
65 years and over	1,277
85 years and over	123
Median age	36.9
Native-born	10,059
Foreign-born	687

Educational Attainment, 2000

Population 25 years and over	7,210
Less than 9th grade	5.1%
High school grad or higher	85.5%
Bachelor's degree or higher	19.9%
Graduate degree	6.8%

Income & Poverty, 1999

Per capita income	$23,529
Median household income	$56,843
Median family income	$67,412
Persons in poverty	654
H'holds receiving public assistance	86
H'holds receiving social security	1,082

Households, 2000

Total households	4,149
With persons under 18	1,501
With persons over 65	949
Family households	2,892
Single-person households	1,037
Persons per household	2.58
Persons per family	3.10

Labor & Employment

Total civilian labor force, 2007**	6,475
Unemployment rate	5.0%
Total civilian labor force, 2000	5,661
Unemployment rate	4.9%

Employed persons 16 years and over by occupation, 2000

Managers & professionals	1,770
Service occupations	684
Sales & office occupations	1,544
Farming, fishing & forestry	6
Construction & maintenance	482
Production & transportation	895
Self-employed persons	174

* US Census Bureau
** New Jersey Department of Labor

See Introduction for an explanation of all data sources.

General Information

Township of Florence
Municipal Complex
711 Broad St
Florence, NJ 08518
609-499-2525

Website	www.florence-nj.com
Year of incorporation	1872
Land/water area (sq. miles)	9.71/0.42
Form of government	Mayor-Council

Government

Legislative Districts

US Congressional	4
State Legislative	7

Local Officials, 2009

Mayor	William E. Berry
Manager	Richard A. Brook
Clerk	Joy M. Weiler
Finance Dir	Sandra A. Blacker
Tax Assessor	Dennis Bianchini
Tax Collector	Ann Schubert
Attorney	William J. Kearns Jr
Building	Thomas Layou
Planning	Nancy Erlston
Engineering	Dante Guzzi
Public Works	Richard Pendle
Police Chief	Stephen C. Fazekas
Emerg/Fire Director	Edward Kensler

Housing & Construction

Housing Units, 2000*

Total	4,391
Median rent	$680
Median SF home value	$115,900

Permits for New Residential Construction

	Units	Value
Total, 2006	46	$3,756,800
Single family	22	$2,601,800
Total, 2007	24	$3,474,109
Single family	24	$3,474,109

Real Property Valuation, 2008

	Parcels	Valuation
Total	4,948	$599,468,850
Vacant	402	24,163,300
Residential	4,288	503,065,550
Commercial	129	24,596,300
Industrial	21	35,561,500
Apartments	6	5,834,800
Farm land	68	851,000
Farm homestead	34	5,396,400

Average Property Value & Tax, 2008

Residential value	$117,645
Property tax	$4,613
Tax credit/rebate	$930

Public Library

Florence Township Public Library
1350 Hornberger Ave
Roebling, NJ 08554
609-499-0143

Director | LaVonna Lawrence

Library statistics, 2007

Population served	10,746
Full-time/total staff	0/3

	Total	Per capita
Holdings	27,841	2.59
Revenues	$117,927	$10.97
Expenditures	$115,604	$10.76
Annual visits	10,023	0.93
Internet terminals/annual users	5/3,980	

Public Safety

Number of officers, 2007 | 27

Crime	2006	2007
Total crimes	126	171
Violent	10	17
Murder	0	0
Rape	0	2
Robbery	3	5
Aggravated assault	7	10
Non-violent	116	154
Burglary	38	51
Larceny	60	92
Vehicle theft	18	11
Domestic violence	129	128
Arson	2	1
Total crime rate	11.0	14.7
Violent	0.9	1.5
Non-violent	10.1	13.2

Public School District

(for school year 2007-08 except as noted)

Florence Township School District
201 Cedar Street
Florence, NJ 08518
(609) 499-4600

Superintendent	Louis Talarico
Number of schools	3
Grade plan	K-12
Enrollment	1,611
Attendance rate, '06-07	91.5%
Dropout rate	0.8%
Students per teacher	12.8
Per pupil expenditure	$13,160
Median faculty salary	$55,786
Median administrator salary	$117,232
Grade 12 enrollment	107
High school graduation rate	92.7%

Assessment test results

(percent scoring at proficient or advanced level)

	Language	Math
NJASK-Grade 3	79.1%	83.0%
GEPA-Grade 8	63.6%	80.0%
HSPA-High School	74.3%	89.5%

SAT Score Averages, 2006-07

Pct tested	Math	Verbal	Writing
67%	505	496	479

Teacher Qualifications

Avg. years of experience	11
Highly-qualified teachers one subject/all subjects	88.0%/88.0%

No Child Left Behind

AYP, 2006-07 | Meets Standards

Municipal Finance

State Aid Programs, 2009

Total aid	$1,742,318
CMPTRA	554,350
Energy tax receipts	1,144,410
Garden State Trust	0

General Budget, 2008

Total tax levy	$23,562,536
County levy	4,662,322
County taxes	3,828,745
County library	353,515
County health	0
County open space	480,063
School levy	15,072,777
Muni. levy	3,827,437
Misc. revenues	7,107,149

Taxes

	2006	2007	2008
General tax rate per $100	3.764	3.83	3.922
County equalization ratio	62.65	54.28	50.84
Net valuation taxable	$554,961,750	$597,221,853	$600,892,468
State equalized value	$1,024,118,144	$1,173,258,263	$1,215,414,809

Demographics & Socio-Economic Characteristics

(2000 US Census, except as noted)

Population
1980*	9,359
1990*	8,521
2000	8,857
Male	4,095
Female	4,762
2007 (estimate)*	12,404
Population density	1,669.4

Race & Hispanic Origin, 2000
Race
White	8,326
Black/African American	88
American Indian/Alaska Native	1
Asian	343
Native Hawaiian/Pacific Islander	5
Other race	34
Two or more races	60
Hispanic origin, total	190
Mexican	14
Puerto Rican	30
Cuban	28
Other Hispanic	118

Age & Nativity, 2000
Under 5 years	542
18 years and over	6,935
21 years and over	6,756
65 years and over	1,806
85 years and over	261
Median age	43.8
Native-born	7,927
Foreign-born	930

Educational Attainment, 2000
Population 25 years and over	6,484
Less than 9th grade	2.9%
High school grad or higher	92.2%
Bachelor's degree or higher	57.7%
Graduate degree	24.4%

Income & Poverty, 1999
Per capita income	$42,133
Median household income	$88,706
Median family income	$102,047
Persons in poverty	507
H'holds receiving public assistance	52
H'holds receiving social security	1,044

Households, 2000
Total households	3,239
With persons under 18	1,040
With persons over 65	1,067
Family households	2,474
Single-person households	671
Persons per household	2.62
Persons per family	3.05

Labor & Employment
Total civilian labor force, 2007**	4,710
Unemployment rate	2.4%
Total civilian labor force, 2000	4,399
Unemployment rate	3.3%

Employed persons 16 years and over by occupation, 2000
Managers & professionals	2,346
Service occupations	451
Sales & office occupations	1,074
Farming, fishing & forestry	0
Construction & maintenance	213
Production & transportation	172
Self-employed persons	246

General Information
Borough of Florham Park
111 Ridgedale Ave
Florham Park, NJ 07932
973-410-5300
Website	www.florhamparkboro.net
Year of incorporation	1899
Land/water area (sq. miles)	7.43/0.02
Form of government	Borough

Government

Legislative Districts
US Congressional	11
State Legislative	26

Local Officials, 2009
Mayor	R. Scott Eveland
Manager	Nancy C. Gage
Clerk	Sheila A. Williams
CFO	Ulrich Steinberg
Tax Assessor	James Gibbs
Tax Collector	Rosemary Schumacher
Attorney	Joseph Bell
Building	Stephen Jones
Planning	Robert Michaels
Engineering	Michael Sgaramella
Public Works	Frank Esposito
Police Chief	Patrick Montuore
Emerg/Fire Director	Robert Young

Housing & Construction

Housing Units, 2000*
Total	3,342
Median rent	$917
Median SF home value	$322,400

Permits for New Residential Construction
	Units	Value
Total, 2006	25	$6,447,699
Single family	25	$6,447,699
Total, 2007	25	$8,360,931
Single family	25	$8,360,931

Real Property Valuation, 2008
	Parcels	Valuation
Total	3,363	$3,309,739,600
Vacant	90	64,246,500
Residential	3,051	1,989,080,900
Commercial	201	917,460,600
Industrial	15	178,344,300
Apartments	4	159,770,700
Farm land	1	119,800
Farm homestead	1	716,800

Average Property Value & Tax, 2008
Residential value	$651,965
Property tax	$7,754
Tax credit/rebate	$1,142

Public Library
Florham Park Public Library
107 Ridgedale Ave
Florham Park, NJ 07932
973-377-2694
Director	Barbara M. McConville

Library statistics, 2007
Population served	8,857
Full-time/total staff	2/7

	Total	Per capita
Holdings	48,182	5.44
Revenues	$737,433	$83.26
Expenditures	$700,057	$79.04
Annual visits	97,000	10.95
Internet terminals/annual users	17/19,720	

Public Safety
Number of officers, 2007	33

Crime	2006	2007
Total crimes	110	103
Violent	6	6
Murder	0	1
Rape	1	1
Robbery	1	2
Aggravated assault	4	2
Non-violent	104	97
Burglary	10	5
Larceny	88	88
Vehicle theft	6	4
Domestic violence	41	50
Arson	0	0
Total crime rate	8.7	8.2
Violent	0.5	0.5
Non-violent	8.2	7.7

Public School District
(for school year 2007-08 except as noted)

Florham Park School District
67-71 Ridgedale Avenue, PO Box 39
Florham Park, NJ 07932
(973) 822-3888
Superintendent	William Ronzitti
Number of schools	3
Grade plan	K-8
Enrollment	1,025
Attendance rate, '06-07	95.9%
Dropout rate	NA
Students per teacher	9.9
Per pupil expenditure	$14,429
Median faculty salary	$48,430
Median administrator salary	$103,990
Grade 12 enrollment	NA
High school graduation rate	NA

Assessment test results
(percent scoring at proficient or advanced level)
	Language	Math
NJASK-Grade 3	97.5%	91.5%
GEPA-Grade 8	86.5%	97.1%
HSPA-High School	NA	NA

SAT Score Averages, 2006-07
Pct tested	Math	Verbal	Writing
NA	NA	NA	NA

Teacher Qualifications
Avg. years of experience	7
Highly-qualified teachers one subject/all subjects	100%/100%

No Child Left Behind
AYP, 2006-07	Meets Standards

Municipal Finance

State Aid Programs, 2009
Total aid	$1,399,158
CMPTRA	94,707
Energy tax receipts	1,248,413
Garden State Trust	65

General Budget, 2008
Total tax levy	$39,420,793
County levy	6,970,980
County taxes	5,682,647
County library	0
County health	0
County open space	1,288,333
School levy	21,399,396
Muni. levy	11,050,417
Misc. revenues	5,403,333

Taxes
	2006	2007	2008
General tax rate per $100	1.15	1.17	1.190
County equalization ratio	111.61	106.18	101.66
Net valuation taxable	$3,297,260,500	$3,334,145,253	$3,314,427,191
State equalized value	$3,109,902,314	$3,279,776,603	$3,334,405,498

* US Census Bureau
** New Jersey Department of Labor

Demographics & Socio-Economic Characteristics
(2000 US Census, except as noted)

Population
1980*	1,892
1990*	2,181
2000	1,972
Male	967
Female	1,005
2007 (estimate)*	1,918
Population density	231.9

Race & Hispanic Origin, 2000
Race
White	1,809
Black/African American	87
American Indian/Alaska Native	3
Asian	17
Native Hawaiian/Pacific Islander	3
Other race	31
Two or more races	22
Hispanic origin, total	68
Mexican	9
Puerto Rican	50
Cuban	5
Other Hispanic	4

Age & Nativity, 2000
Under 5 years	102
18 years and over	1,481
21 years and over	1,399
65 years and over	193
85 years and over	20
Median age	37.5
Native-born	1,919
Foreign-born	53

Educational Attainment, 2000
Population 25 years and over	1,301
Less than 9th grade	4.3%
High school grad or higher	83.0%
Bachelor's degree or higher	16.4%
Graduate degree	4.5%

Income & Poverty, 1999
Per capita income	$20,617
Median household income	$56,406
Median family income	$59,231
Persons in poverty	111
H'holds receiving public assistance	26
H'holds receiving social security	151

Households, 2000
Total households	671
With persons under 18	286
With persons over 65	133
Family households	552
Single-person households	92
Persons per household	2.93
Persons per family	3.18

Labor & Employment
Total civilian labor force, 2007**	1,151
Unemployment rate	2.6%
Total civilian labor force, 2000	1,084
Unemployment rate	3.3%

Employed persons 16 years and over by occupation, 2000
Managers & professionals	251
Service occupations	153
Sales & office occupations	327
Farming, fishing & forestry	2
Construction & maintenance	147
Production & transportation	168
Self-employed persons	36

‡ Branch of county library
* US Census Bureau
** New Jersey Department of Labor

General Information
Borough of Folsom
Route 54
1700 12th St
Folsom, NJ 08037
609-561-3178

Website	NA
Year of incorporation	1906
Land/water area (sq. miles)	8.27/0.19
Form of government	Borough

Government
Legislative Districts
US Congressional	2
State Legislative	9

Local Officials, 2009
Mayor	Thomas Ballistreri
Manager/Admin	NA
Clerk	Gail Macera
Finance Dir	Dawn Stollenwerk
Tax Assessor	Joseph Ingemi
Tax Collector	Bertha Cappuccio
Attorney	Michael Fitzgerald
Building	Patrick Newton
Comm Dev/Planning	NA
Engineering	Chuck Endicott
Public Works	John LaPollo
Police Chief	NA
Emerg/Fire Director	Larry Smith

Housing & Construction
Housing Units, 2000*
Total	702
Median rent	$883
Median SF home value	$104,700

Permits for New Residential Construction
	Units	Value
Total, 2006	3	$468,000
Single family	3	$468,000
Total, 2007	3	$883,000
Single family	3	$883,000

Real Property Valuation, 2008
	Parcels	Valuation
Total	1,242	$103,661,400
Vacant	464	4,486,400
Residential	657	76,698,600
Commercial	42	10,155,900
Industrial	11	10,383,200
Apartments	0	0
Farm land	57	192,100
Farm homestead	11	1,745,200

Average Property Value & Tax, 2008
Residential value	$117,431
Property tax	$3,057
Tax credit/rebate	$648

Public Library
Hammonton Branch Library‡
451 Egg Harbor Rd
Hammonton, NJ 08037
609-561-2264

Branch Manager	David Munn

Library statistics, 2007
see Atlantic County profile
for library system statistics

Public Safety
Number of officers, 2007	0

Crime	2006	2007
Total crimes	38	27
Violent	4	4
Murder	0	0
Rape	0	0
Robbery	0	0
Aggravated assault	4	4
Non-violent	34	23
Burglary	9	5
Larceny	21	14
Vehicle theft	4	4
Domestic violence	4	14
Arson	0	0
Total crime rate	19.3	13.9
Violent	2.0	2.1
Non-violent	17.2	11.8

Public School District
(for school year 2007-08 except as noted)

Folsom School District
1357 Mays Landing Road
Folsom, NJ 08037
(609) 561-8666

Superintendent	Jean Rishel
Number of schools	1
Grade plan	K-8
Enrollment	416
Attendance rate, '06-07	95.4%
Dropout rate	NA
Students per teacher	11.4
Per pupil expenditure	$11,606
Median faculty salary	$44,579
Median administrator salary	$73,000
Grade 12 enrollment	NA
High school graduation rate	NA

Assessment test results
(percent scoring at proficient or advanced level)
	Language	Math
NJASK-Grade 3	64.5%	82.2%
GEPA-Grade 8	80.0%	98.0%
HSPA-High School	NA	NA

SAT Score Averages, 2006-07
Pct tested	Math	Verbal	Writing
NA	NA	NA	NA

Teacher Qualifications
Avg. years of experience	12
Highly-qualified teachers one subject/all subjects	100%/100%

No Child Left Behind
AYP, 2006-07	Meets Standards

Municipal Finance
State Aid Programs, 2009
Total aid	$241,530
CMPTRA	51,930
Energy tax receipts	181,989
Garden State Trust	1,349

General Budget, 2008
Total tax levy	$2,708,383
County levy	545,914
County taxes	430,117
County library	55,163
County health	22,572
County open space	38,061
School levy	1,653,118
Muni. levy	509,350
Misc. revenues	875,488

Taxes
	2006	2007	2008
General tax rate per $100	2.4	2.55	2.602
County equalization ratio	69.53	60.93	54.99
Net valuation taxable	$102,913,900	$103,743,473	$104,025,045
State equalized value	$169,334,970	$188,343,365	$199,559,264

See Introduction for an explanation of all data sources.

Demographics & Socio-Economic Characteristics

(2000 US Census, except as noted)

Population

1980*	32,449
1990*	31,997
2000	35,461
Male	16,569
Female	18,892
2007 (estimate)*	36,521
Population density	14,435.2

Race & Hispanic Origin, 2000

Race

White	22,253
Black/African American	615
American Indian/Alaska Native	25
Asian	11,146
Native Hawaiian/Pacific Islander	20
Other race	600
Two or more races	802
Hispanic origin, total	2,791
Mexican	78
Puerto Rican	562
Cuban	425
Other Hispanic	1,726

Age & Nativity, 2000

Under 5 years	1,870
18 years and over	29,261
21 years and over	28,499
65 years and over	7,151
85 years and over	901
Median age	41.6
Native-born	19,597
Foreign-born	15,864

Educational Attainment, 2000

Population 25 years and over	27,490
Less than 9th grade	4.7%
High school grad or higher	89.5%
Bachelor's degree or higher	48.2%
Graduate degree	18.5%

Income & Poverty, 1999

Per capita income	$37,899
Median household income	$58,161
Median family income	$72,140
Persons in poverty	2,807
H'holds receiving public assistance	188
H'holds receiving social security	4,843

Households, 2000

Total households	16,544
With persons under 18	3,909
With persons over 65	5,452
Family households	9,402
Single-person households	6,448
Persons per household	2.14
Persons per family	2.88

Labor & Employment

Total civilian labor force, 2007**	18,972
Unemployment rate	2.6%
Total civilian labor force, 2000	17,802
Unemployment rate	3.4%

Employed persons 16 years and over by occupation, 2000

Managers & professionals	8,870
Service occupations	1,430
Sales & office occupations	5,324
Farming, fishing & forestry	0
Construction & maintenance	561
Production & transportation	1,020
Self-employed persons	1,160

* US Census Bureau
** New Jersey Department of Labor

General Information

Borough of Fort Lee
309 Main St
Fort Lee, NJ 07024
201-592-3546

Website	www.fortleenj.org
Year of incorporation	1904
Land/water area (sq. miles)	2.53/0.35
Form of government	Borough

Government

Legislative Districts

US Congressional	9
State Legislative	38

Local Officials, 2009

Mayor	Mark J. Sokolich
Administrator	Peggy Thomas
Clerk	Neil Grant
Finance Dir	Joseph Iannaconi Jr
Tax Assessor	Kevin Hartley
Tax Collector	Joseph Iannaconi Jr
Attorney	J. Sheldon Cohen
Building	Eric Swanson
Planning	Ray Levy
Engineering	Steven Boswell
Public Works	Anthony Lione
Police Chief	Tom Ripoli
Emerg/Fire Director	Stephan Ferraro

Housing & Construction

Housing Units, 2000*

Total	17,446
Median rent	$1,101
Median SF home value	$287,000

Permits for New Residential Construction

	Units	Value
Total, 2006	33	$9,524,095
Single family	23	$7,622,095
Total, 2007	33	$9,467,950
Single family	15	$5,921,950

Real Property Valuation, 2008

	Parcels	Valuation
Total	8,232	$6,039,700,420
Vacant	104	122,770,000
Residential	7,641	3,554,620,700
Commercial	408	937,765,700
Industrial	8	10,158,200
Apartments	71	1,414,385,820
Farm land	0	0
Farm homestead	0	0

Average Property Value & Tax, 2008

Residential value	$465,204
Property tax	$8,510
Tax credit/rebate	$944

Public Library

Fort Lee Public Library
320 Main St
Fort Lee, NJ 07024
201-592-3614

Director	Rita Altomara

Library statistics, 2007

Population served	35,461
Full-time/total staff	7/23

	Total	Per capita
Holdings	148,711	4.19
Revenues	$2,092,855	$59.02
Expenditures	$1,714,013	$48.34
Annual visits	334,221	9.43
Internet terminals/annual users	10/14,671	

Public Safety

Number of officers, 2007	108

Crime	2006	2007
Total crimes	375	332
Violent	28	21
Murder	1	0
Rape	0	0
Robbery	5	8
Aggravated assault	22	13
Non-violent	347	311
Burglary	67	64
Larceny	260	240
Vehicle theft	20	7
Domestic violence	74	67
Arson	7	2
Total crime rate	10.1	9.0
Violent	0.8	0.6
Non-violent	9.3	8.4

Public School District

(for school year 2007-08 except as noted)

Fort Lee School District
255 Whiteman Street
Fort Lee, NJ 07024
(201) 585-4610

Superintendent	Raymond Bandlow
Number of schools	6
Grade plan	K-12
Enrollment	3,472
Attendance rate, '06-07	95.6%
Dropout rate	0.2%
Students per teacher	11.7
Per pupil expenditure	$13,925
Median faculty salary	$60,470
Median administrator salary	$119,400
Grade 12 enrollment	258
High school graduation rate	97.7%

Assessment test results

(percent scoring at proficient or advanced level)

	Language	Math
NJASK-Grade 3	91.2%	90.5%
GEPA-Grade 8	83.3%	90.3%
HSPA-High School	87.5%	87.3%

SAT Score Averages, 2006-07

Pct tested	Math	Verbal	Writing
93%	546	499	500

Teacher Qualifications

Avg. years of experience	11
Highly-qualified teachers one subject/all subjects	97.5%/96.0%

No Child Left Behind

AYP, 2006-07	Meets Standards

Municipal Finance

State Aid Programs, 2009

Total aid	$2,218,961
CMPTRA	375,822
Energy tax receipts	1,809,485
Garden State Trust	375

General Budget, 2008

Total tax levy	$110,642,033
County levy	11,803,979
County taxes	11,161,886
County library	0
County health	0
County open space	642,093
School levy	45,170,822
Muni. levy	53,667,232
Misc. revenues	9,898,975

Taxes	2006	2007	2008
General tax rate per $100	1.66	1.72	1.831
County equalization ratio	102.2	99.27	94.62
Net valuation taxable	$5,929,867,820	$6,013,133,358	$6,048,037,550
State equalized value	$5,982,132,760	$6,354,548,620	$6,522,953,051

See Introduction for an explanation of all data sources.

Demographics & Socio-Economic Characteristics

(2000 US Census, except as noted)

Population
1980*	4,654
1990*	5,114
2000	5,420
Male	2,664
Female	2,756
2007 (estimate)*	5,604
Population density	164.3

Race & Hispanic Origin, 2000
Race
White	5,320
Black/African American	21
American Indian/Alaska Native	3
Asian	21
Native Hawaiian/Pacific Islander	0
Other race	27
Two or more races	28
Hispanic origin, total	96
Mexican	13
Puerto Rican	41
Cuban	17
Other Hispanic	25

Age & Nativity, 2000
Under 5 years	267
18 years and over	4,067
21 years and over	3,885
65 years and over	703
85 years and over	149
Median age	40.8
Native-born	5,254
Foreign-born	165

Educational Attainment, 2000
Population 25 years and over	3,731
Less than 9th grade	3.9%
High school grad or higher	88.8%
Bachelor's degree or higher	25.2%
Graduate degree	7.8%

Income & Poverty, 1999
Per capita income	$25,051
Median household income	$64,444
Median family income	$69,449
Persons in poverty	269
H'holds receiving public assistance	46
H'holds receiving social security	498

Households, 2000
Total households	1,839
With persons under 18	727
With persons over 65	390
Family households	1,473
Single-person households	303
Persons per household	2.81
Persons per family	3.17

Labor & Employment
Total civilian labor force, 2007**	3,087
Unemployment rate	3.6%
Total civilian labor force, 2000	2,779
Unemployment rate	3.2%

Employed persons 16 years and over by occupation, 2000
Managers & professionals	1,000
Service occupations	449
Sales & office occupations	639
Farming, fishing & forestry	10
Construction & maintenance	302
Production & transportation	291
Self-employed persons	262

‡ Main library for county
* US Census Bureau
** New Jersey Department of Labor

General Information
Township of Frankford
151 State Hwy 206
Augusta, NJ 07822
973-948-5566
Website	www.frankfordtownship.com
Year of incorporation	1797
Land/water area (sq. miles)	34.11/1.31
Form of government	Township

Government

Legislative Districts
US Congressional	5
State Legislative	24

Local Officials, 2009
Mayor	Paul Sutphen
Manager	Louanne Cular
Clerk	Louanne Cular
Finance Dir	Gail Magura
Tax Assessor	John Dyksen
Tax Collector	Stephen Lance
Attorney	Kevin Benbrook
Building	Jeff Fette
Planning	NA
Engineering	Harold Pellow
Public Works	NA
Police Chief	NA
Emerg/Fire Director	Mike Seo

Housing & Construction

Housing Units, 2000*
Total	2,295
Median rent	$675
Median SF home value	$179,100

Permits for New Residential Construction
	Units	Value
Total, 2006	20	$4,467,720
Single family	20	$4,467,720
Total, 2007	19	$4,460,767
Single family	19	$4,460,767

Real Property Valuation, 2008
	Parcels	Valuation
Total	3,335	$955,523,700
Vacant	470	42,074,100
Residential	2,141	735,232,100
Commercial	100	71,902,900
Industrial	10	6,335,800
Apartments	2	1,075,900
Farm land	380	3,324,400
Farm homestead	232	95,578,500

Average Property Value & Tax, 2008
Residential value	$350,110
Property tax	$5,937
Tax credit/rebate	$1,019

Public Library
Sussex County Library‡
125 Morris Turnpike
Newton, NJ 07860
973-948-3660
Director	Stan Pollakoff

County Library statistics, 2007
Population served	126,086
Full-time/total staff	13/56

	Total	Per capita
Holdings	334,102	2.65
Revenues	$4,975,047	$39.46
Expenditures	$4,983,330	$39.52
Annual visits	507,560	4.03
Internet terminals/annual users	55/55,404	

Public Safety
Number of officers, 2007	0

Crime	2006	2007
Total crimes	84	104
Violent	8	10
Murder	0	0
Rape	1	0
Robbery	0	1
Aggravated assault	7	9
Non-violent	76	94
Burglary	13	19
Larceny	53	71
Vehicle theft	10	4
Domestic violence	9	68
Arson	0	0
Total crime rate	14.8	18.3
Violent	1.4	1.8
Non-violent	13.4	16.5

Public School District
(for school year 2007-08 except as noted)

Frankford Township School District
2 Pines Road
Branchville, NJ 07826
(973) 948-3727
Superintendent	Braden Hirsch
Number of schools	1
Grade plan	K-8
Enrollment	687
Attendance rate, '06-07	95.1%
Dropout rate	NA
Students per teacher	9.7
Per pupil expenditure	$13,170
Median faculty salary	$71,810
Median administrator salary	$110,000
Grade 12 enrollment	NA
High school graduation rate	NA

Assessment test results
(percent scoring at proficient or advanced level)
	Language	Math
NJASK-Grade 3	83.8%	80.8%
GEPA-Grade 8	67.5%	78.3%
HSPA-High School	NA	NA

SAT Score Averages, 2006-07
Pct tested	Math	Verbal	Writing
NA	NA	NA	NA

Teacher Qualifications
Avg. years of experience	17
Highly-qualified teachers one subject/all subjects	100%/100%

No Child Left Behind
AYP, 2006-07	Meets Standards

Municipal Finance

State Aid Programs, 2009
Total aid	$648,535
CMPTRA	101,719
Energy tax receipts	492,665
Garden State Trust	17,485

General Budget, 2008
Total tax levy	$16,258,970
County levy	3,522,565
County taxes	2,956,251
County library	249,164
County health	87,497
County open space	229,652
School levy	10,860,815
Muni. levy	1,875,590
Misc. revenues	1,782,317

Taxes
	2006	2007	2008
General tax rate per $100	3.44	3.58	1.696
County equalization ratio	58.66	52.99	104.77
Net valuation taxable	$430,306,126	$436,270,916	$958,726,225
State equalized value	$813,812,418	$905,648,411	$970,821,462

See Introduction for an explanation of all data sources.

Demographics & Socio-Economic Characteristics
(2000 US Census, except as noted)

Population
1980*	4,486
1990*	4,977
2000	5,160
Male	2,444
Female	2,716
2007 (estimate)*	5,126
Population density	1,141.6

Race & Hispanic Origin, 2000
Race
White	4,907
Black/African American	32
American Indian/Alaska Native	18
Asian	76
Native Hawaiian/Pacific Islander	0
Other race	63
Two or more races	64
Hispanic origin, total	228
Mexican	16
Puerto Rican	96
Cuban	12
Other Hispanic	104

Age & Nativity, 2000
Under 5 years	357
18 years and over	3,741
21 years and over	3,579
65 years and over	603
85 years and over	85
Median age	36.7
Native-born	4,805
Foreign-born	382

Educational Attainment, 2000
Population 25 years and over	3,325
Less than 9th grade	3.6%
High school grad or higher	86.8%
Bachelor's degree or higher	15.3%
Graduate degree	4.7%

Income & Poverty, 1999
Per capita income	$19,386
Median household income	$44,985
Median family income	$52,682
Persons in poverty	360
H'holds receiving public assistance	35
H'holds receiving social security	581

Households, 2000
Total households	1,898
With persons under 18	751
With persons over 65	472
Family households	1,325
Single-person households	457
Persons per household	2.69
Persons per family	3.22

Labor & Employment
Total civilian labor force, 2007**	2,871
Unemployment rate	4.9%
Total civilian labor force, 2000	2,547
Unemployment rate	3.6%

Employed persons 16 years and over by occupation, 2000
Managers & professionals	626
Service occupations	369
Sales & office occupations	703
Farming, fishing & forestry	0
Construction & maintenance	302
Production & transportation	456
Self-employed persons	156

‡ Branch of county library
* US Census Bureau
** New Jersey Department of Labor

General Information
Borough of Franklin
46 Main St
Franklin, NJ 07416
973-827-9280
Website	www.franklinboro.com
Year of incorporation	1913
Land/water area (sq. miles)	4.49/0.06
Form of government	Borough

Government
Legislative Districts
US Congressional	5
State Legislative	24

Local Officials, 2009
Mayor	Paul Crowley
Manager	Richard R. Wolak
Clerk	Patricia Leasure
Finance Dir	Grant Rome
Tax Assessor	Scott Holzhauer
Tax Collector	Terry Beshada
Attorney	John Ursin
Building	Keith Utter
Planning	Jim Kilduff
Engineering	George Unverzagt
Public Works	Mike Gunderman
Police Chief	Joseph Kistle
Emerg/Fire Director	James Carroll

Housing & Construction
Housing Units, 2000*
Total	1,997
Median rent	$771
Median SF home value	$123,000

Permits for New Residential Construction
	Units	Value
Total, 2006	14	$1,700,801
Single family	14	$1,700,801
Total, 2007	10	$1,235,912
Single family	10	$1,235,912

Real Property Valuation, 2008
	Parcels	Valuation
Total	1,739	$241,840,000
Vacant	118	5,669,800
Residential	1,447	166,086,500
Commercial	118	57,469,500
Industrial	10	6,506,000
Apartments	11	3,433,500
Farm land	20	155,700
Farm homestead	15	2,519,000

Average Property Value & Tax, 2008
Residential value	$115,325
Property tax	$5,343
Tax credit/rebate	$961

Public Library
Franklin Branch Library‡
103 Main St
Franklin, NJ 07416
973-827-6555
Branch Librarian	Carol Crowley

Library statistics, 2007
see Sussex County profile
for library system statistics

Public Safety
Number of officers, 2007		15

Crime	2006	2007
Total crimes	96	78
Violent	2	4
Murder	0	0
Rape	0	2
Robbery	1	0
Aggravated assault	1	2
Non-violent	94	74
Burglary	18	9
Larceny	74	58
Vehicle theft	2	7
Domestic violence	101	77
Arson	2	1
Total crime rate	18.3	15.0
Violent	0.4	0.8
Non-violent	18.0	14.2

Public School District
(for school year 2007-08 except as noted)

Franklin Borough School District
50 Washington Avenue
Franklin, NJ 07416
(973) 827-9775
Chief School Admin	Thomas N. Turner
Number of schools	1
Grade plan	K-8
Enrollment	487
Attendance rate, '06-07	94.8%
Dropout rate	NA
Students per teacher	8.0
Per pupil expenditure	$16,086
Median faculty salary	$48,278
Median administrator salary	$110,259
Grade 12 enrollment	NA
High school graduation rate	NA

Assessment test results
(percent scoring at proficient or advanced level)
	Language	Math
NJASK-Grade 3	89.8%	85.7%
GEPA-Grade 8	70.0%	80.0%
HSPA-High School	NA	NA

SAT Score Averages, 2006-07
Pct tested	Math	Verbal	Writing
NA	NA	NA	NA

Teacher Qualifications
Avg. years of experience	7

Highly-qualified teachers
one subject/all subjects	100%/100%

No Child Left Behind
AYP, 2006-07	Meets Standards

Municipal Finance
State Aid Programs, 2009
Total aid	$794,670
CMPTRA	75,824
Energy tax receipts	688,062
Garden State Trust	6,454

General Budget, 2008
Total tax levy	$11,286,524
County levy	2,021,180
County taxes	1,696,098
County library	142,952
County health	50,259
County open space	131,871
School levy	5,995,494
Muni. levy	3,269,850
Misc. revenues	2,598,154

Taxes
	2006	2007	2008
General tax rate per $100	4.23	4.51	4.634
County equalization ratio	55	48.94	46.34
Net valuation taxable	$240,111,400	$243,017,024	$243,599,787
State equalized value	$493,006,684	$521,630,999	$509,080,953

See Introduction for an explanation of all data sources.

Demographics & Socio-Economic Characteristics

(2000 US Census, except as noted)

Population
1980*	8,769
1990*	9,873
2000	10,422
Male	5,146
Female	5,276
2007 (estimate)*	11,576
Population density	1,225.0

Race & Hispanic Origin, 2000
Race
White	9,521
Black/African American	96
American Indian/Alaska Native	11
Asian	660
Native Hawaiian/Pacific Islander	1
Other race	43
Two or more races	90
Hispanic origin, total	286
Mexican	11
Puerto Rican	62
Cuban	60
Other Hispanic	153

Age & Nativity, 2000
Under 5 years	703
18 years and over	7,433
21 years and over	7,209
65 years and over	1,164
85 years and over	104
Median age	40.7
Native-born	9,191
Foreign-born	1,231

Educational Attainment, 2000
Population 25 years and over	6,885
Less than 9th grade	1.7%
High school grad or higher	94.7%
Bachelor's degree or higher	52.9%
Graduate degree	21.5%

Income & Poverty, 1999
Per capita income	$59,763
Median household income	$132,373
Median family income	$142,930
Persons in poverty	331
H'holds receiving public assistance	17
H'holds receiving social security	798

Households, 2000
Total households	3,322
With persons under 18	1,508
With persons over 65	803
Family households	2,960
Single-person households	287
Persons per household	3.13
Persons per family	3.34

Labor & Employment
Total civilian labor force, 2007**	5,171
Unemployment rate	2.0%
Total civilian labor force, 2000	4,900
Unemployment rate	2.3%

Employed persons 16 years and over by occupation, 2000
Managers & professionals	2,601
Service occupations	286
Sales & office occupations	1,442
Farming, fishing & forestry	0
Construction & maintenance	221
Production & transportation	235
Self-employed persons	483

General Information

Borough of Franklin Lakes
480 De Korte Dr
Franklin Lakes, NJ 07417
201-891-0048

Website	www.franklinlakes.org
Year of incorporation	1922
Land/water area (sq. miles)	9.45/0.38
Form of government	Borough

Government

Legislative Districts
US Congressional	5
State Legislative	40

Local Officials, 2009
Mayor	Maura R. DeNicola
Manager	Gregory C. Hart
Clerk	Sally T. Bleeker
CFOr	William G. Pike (Int)
Tax Assessor	Michael Leposky
Tax Collector	Philip Moore
Attorney	Douglas Doyle
Building	Frank Horesta
Planning	Frank Conte
Engineering	Boswell Engineering
Public Works	Brian Peterson
Police Chief	Irving Conklin
Emerg/Fire Director	Chuck Bohny

Housing & Construction

Housing Units, 2000*
Total	3,395
Median rent	$1,313
Median SF home value	$609,400

Permits for New Residential Construction
	Units	Value
Total, 2006	136	$32,151,640
Single family	36	$25,642,640
Total, 2007	47	$27,865,718
Single family	32	$26,889,368

Real Property Valuation, 2008
	Parcels	Valuation
Total	3,700	$4,885,722,100
Vacant	182	90,703,100
Residential	3,430	4,349,987,800
Commercial	55	384,240,500
Industrial	15	23,568,000
Apartments	2	30,856,600
Farm land	11	21,200
Farm homestead	5	6,344,900

Average Property Value & Tax, 2008
Residential value	$1,268,219
Property tax	$14,616
Tax credit/rebate	$1,335

Public Library

Franklin Lakes Public Library
470 DeKorte Dr
Franklin Lakes, NJ 07417
201-891-2224

Director	Geraldine McMahon

Library statistics, 2007
Population served	10,422
Full-time/total staff	5/11

	Total	Per capita
Holdings	98,637	9.46
Revenues	$1,610,110	$154.49
Expenditures	$1,387,169	$133.10
Annual visits	194,804	18.69
Internet terminals/annual users	34/30,175	

Public Safety

Number of officers, 2007	22

Crime	2006	2007
Total crimes	117	132
Violent	1	4
Murder	0	0
Rape	1	0
Robbery	0	2
Aggravated assault	0	2
Non-violent	116	128
Burglary	17	16
Larceny	98	107
Vehicle theft	1	5
Domestic violence	44	40
Arson	0	0
Total crime rate	10.4	11.6
Violent	0.1	0.4
Non-violent	10.3	11.3

Public School District

(for school year 2007-08 except as noted)

Franklin Lakes School District
490 Pulis Avenue
Franklin Lakes, NJ 07417
(201) 891-1856

Superintendent	Roger Bayersdorfer
Number of schools	4
Grade plan	K-8
Enrollment	1,471
Attendance rate, '06-07	95.9%
Dropout rate	NA
Students per teacher	8.4
Per pupil expenditure	$15,571
Median faculty salary	$54,220
Median administrator salary	$130,000
Grade 12 enrollment	NA
High school graduation rate	NA

Assessment test results
(percent scoring at proficient or advanced level)
	Language	Math
NJASK-Grade 3	96.9%	96.2%
GEPA-Grade 8	79.9%	94.2%
HSPA-High School	NA	NA

SAT Score Averages, 2006-07
Pct tested	Math	Verbal	Writing
NA	NA	NA	NA

Teacher Qualifications
Avg. years of experience	7
Highly-qualified teachers one subject/all subjects	100%/100%

No Child Left Behind
AYP, 2006-07	Meets Standards

Municipal Finance

State Aid Programs, 2009
Total aid	$2,043,043
CMPTRA	0
Energy tax receipts	1,935,220
Garden State Trust	0

General Budget, 2008
Total tax levy	$56,347,974
County levy	8,573,111
County taxes	8,108,091
County library	0
County health	0
County open space	465,020
School levy	39,165,821
Muni. levy	8,609,042
Misc. revenues	6,427,999

Taxes	2006	2007	2008
General tax rate per $100	2.37	1.11	1.154
County equalization ratio	54.75	109.74	105.28
Net valuation taxable	$2,199,599,502	$4,894,273,619	$4,889,138,328
State equalized value	$4,411,116,101	$4,648,883,011	$4,807,469,424

* US Census Bureau
** New Jersey Department of Labor

See Introduction for an explanation of all data sources.

Demographics & Socio-Economic Characteristics
(2000 US Census, except as noted)

Population
1980*	12,396
1990*	14,482
2000	15,466
Male	7,723
Female	7,743
2007 (estimate)*	17,143
Population density	306.1

Race & Hispanic Origin, 2000
Race
White	13,954
Black/African American	1,030
American Indian/Alaska Native	48
Asian	63
Native Hawaiian/Pacific Islander	2
Other race	193
Two or more races	176
Hispanic origin, total	543
Mexican	86
Puerto Rican	365
Cuban	13
Other Hispanic	79

Age & Nativity, 2000
Under 5 years	956
18 years and over	11,185
21 years and over	10,543
65 years and over	1,480
85 years and over	110
Median age	36.4
Native-born	15,111
Foreign-born	355

Educational Attainment, 2000
Population 25 years and over	9,811
Less than 9th grade	4.8%
High school grad or higher	81.8%
Bachelor's degree or higher	14.9%
Graduate degree	3.4%

Income & Poverty, 1999
Per capita income	$20,277
Median household income	$55,169
Median family income	$60,518
Persons in poverty	778
H'holds receiving public assistance	103
H'holds receiving social security	1,412

Households, 2000
Total households	5,225
With persons under 18	2,333
With persons over 65	1,085
Family households	4,190
Single-person households	831
Persons per household	2.94
Persons per family	3.29

Labor & Employment
Total civilian labor force, 2007**	9,241
Unemployment rate	6.4%
Total civilian labor force, 2000	7,856
Unemployment rate	6.1%

Employed persons 16 years and over by occupation, 2000
Managers & professionals	1,949
Service occupations	1,105
Sales & office occupations	1,884
Farming, fishing & forestry	41
Construction & maintenance	1,291
Production & transportation	1,105
Self-employed persons	481

* US Census Bureau
** New Jersey Department of Labor

General Information
Township of Franklin
1571 Delsea Dr
Franklinville, NJ 08322
856-694-1234

Website	www.franklintownship.com
Year of incorporation	1820
Land/water area (sq. miles)	56.01/0.42
Form of government	Township

Government
Legislative Districts
US Congressional	2
State Legislative	4

Local Officials, 2009
Mayor	Joseph Petsch
Township Admin	William Krebs
Clerk	Carolyn K. Toy
Finance Dir	Frances Carder
Tax Assessor	Diane Hesley
Tax Collector	Lawrence Nightlinger Jr
Attorney	William Ziegler
Building	Steven Rickerschauser
Planning	Patricia Knobloch
Engineering	J. Michael Fralinger
Public Works	William Nese
Police Chief	Michael DiGiorgio
Fire/Emergency Dir	NA

Housing & Construction
Housing Units, 2000*
Total	5,461
Median rent	$710
Median SF home value	$111,700

Permits for New Residential Construction
	Units	Value
Total, 2006	91	$16,095,346
Single family	91	$16,095,346
Total, 2007	59	$10,617,527
Single family	59	$10,617,527

Real Property Valuation, 2008
	Parcels	Valuation
Total	7,868	$782,842,400
Vacant	1,087	25,204,900
Residential	5,446	656,497,100
Commercial	303	59,615,100
Industrial	0	0
Apartments	8	1,957,100
Farm land	721	5,323,100
Farm homestead	303	34,245,100

Average Property Value & Tax, 2008
Residential value	$120,150
Property tax	$4,782
Tax credit/rebate	$915

Public Library
Franklin Township Free Public Library
1584 Coles Mill Rd
Franklinville, NJ 08322
856-694-2833

Director	Denise Saia

Library statistics, 2007
Population served	15,466
Full-time/total staff	2/2

	Total	Per capita
Holdings	56,571	3.66
Revenues	$533,928	$34.52
Expenditures	$460,505	$29.78
Annual visits	69,932	4.52
Internet terminals/annual users	8/8,974	

Public Safety
Number of officers, 2007	30

Crime	2006	2007
Total crimes	351	353
Violent	22	17
Murder	1	0
Rape	0	3
Robbery	4	2
Aggravated assault	17	12
Non-violent	329	336
Burglary	114	108
Larceny	200	205
Vehicle theft	15	23
Domestic violence	187	146
Arson	1	5
Total crime rate	21.1	20.9
Violent	1.3	1.0
Non-violent	19.7	19.9

Public School District
(for school year 2007-08 except as noted)

Franklin Township School District
3228 Coles Mill Rd
Franklinville, NJ 08322
(856) 629-9500

Superintendent	Michael G Kozak
Number of schools	3
Grade plan	K-6
Enrollment	1,480
Attendance rate, '06-07	95.0%
Dropout rate	NA
Students per teacher	12.7
Per pupil expenditure	$10,189
Median faculty salary	$57,000
Median administrator salary	$92,000
Grade 12 enrollment	NA
High school graduation rate	NA

Assessment test results
(percent scoring at proficient or advanced level)
	Language	Math
NJASK-Grade 3	91.9%	88.1%
GEPA-Grade 8	NA	NA
HSPA-High School	NA	NA

SAT Score Averages, 2006-07
Pct tested	Math	Verbal	Writing
NA	NA	NA	NA

Teacher Qualifications
Avg. years of experience	17
Highly-qualified teachers one subject/all subjects	100%/100%

No Child Left Behind
AYP, 2006-07	Meets Standards

Municipal Finance
State Aid Programs, 2009
Total aid	$1,879,749
CMPTRA	275,364
Energy tax receipts	1,542,557
Garden State Trust	10,449

General Budget, 2008
Total tax levy	$31,256,932
County levy	8,306,847
County taxes	7,703,158
County library	0
County health	0
County open space	603,689
School levy	16,846,497
Muni. levy	6,103,588
Misc. revenues	5,219,372

Taxes
	2006	2007	2008
General tax rate per $100	3.619	3.872	3.980
County equalization ratio	65.97	56.52	51.92
Net valuation taxable	$732,343,700	$755,794,876	$785,370,751
State equalized value	$1,298,628,506	$1,453,303,993	$1,504,816,587

Demographics & Socio-Economic Characteristics

(2000 US Census, except as noted)

Population

1980*	2,294
1990*	2,851
2000	2,990
Male	1,482
Female	1,508
2007 (estimate)*	3,119
Population density	136.3

Race & Hispanic Origin, 2000

Race

White	2,916
Black/African American	12
American Indian/Alaska Native	7
Asian	23
Native Hawaiian/Pacific Islander	0
Other race	10
Two or more races	22
Hispanic origin, total	67
Mexican	13
Puerto Rican	20
Cuban	7
Other Hispanic	27

Age & Nativity, 2000

Under 5 years	174
18 years and over	2,244
21 years and over	2,183
65 years and over	361
85 years and over	33
Median age	41.6
Native-born	2,785
Foreign-born	205

Educational Attainment, 2000

Population 25 years and over	2,112
Less than 9th grade	2.2%
High school grad or higher	93.5%
Bachelor's degree or higher	44.5%
Graduate degree	16.2%

Income & Poverty, 1999

Per capita income	$39,668
Median household income	$91,364
Median family income	$96,320
Persons in poverty	49
H'holds receiving public assistance	5
H'holds receiving social security	258

Households, 2000

Total households	1,091
With persons under 18	403
With persons over 65	260
Family households	890
Single-person households	155
Persons per household	2.74
Persons per family	3.04

Labor & Employment

Total civilian labor force, 2007**	1,864
Unemployment rate	3.5%
Total civilian labor force, 2000	1,668
Unemployment rate	3.0%

Employed persons 16 years and over by occupation, 2000

Managers & professionals	831
Service occupations	118
Sales & office occupations	374
Farming, fishing & forestry	4
Construction & maintenance	148
Production & transportation	143
Self-employed persons	194

* US Census Bureau
** New Jersey Department of Labor

General Information

Township of Franklin
202 Sidney Rd
Pittstown, NJ 08867
908-735-5215

Website	(county website)
Year of incorporation	1845
Land/water area (sq. miles)	22.88/0.04
Form of government	Township

Government

Legislative Districts

US Congressional	12
State Legislative	23

Local Officials, 2009

Mayor	Robert Shockley
Manager/Admin	NA
Clerk	Ursula Stryker
Finance Dir	Ronald Mathews
Tax Assessor	Mary Mastro
Tax Collector	Linda Swackhamer
Attorney	William J. Caldwell
Building	Mark Fornaciari
Planning	Carl Hintz
Engineering	C. Richard Roseberry
Public Works	Alan Dilley
Police Chief	Kenneth Mandoli
Emerg/Fire Director	Bradley Patkochis

Housing & Construction

Housing Units, 2000*

Total	1,125
Median rent	$892
Median SF home value	$283,500

Permits for New Residential Construction

	Units	Value
Total, 2006	9	$1,754,138
Single family	9	$1,754,138
Total, 2007	53	$7,847,295
Single family	11	$2,597,295

Real Property Valuation, 2008

	Parcels	Valuation
Total	1,631	$549,395,839
Vacant	67	6,368,400
Residential	876	377,968,800
Commercial	22	38,588,100
Industrial	4	2,308,800
Apartments	3	1,113,400
Farm land	400	4,278,739
Farm homestead	259	118,769,600

Average Property Value & Tax, 2008

Residential value	$437,655
Property tax	$9,925
Tax credit/rebate	$1,343

Public Library

No public municipal library

Library statistics, 2007

Population served	NA
Full-time/total staff	NA/NA

	Total	Per capita
Holdings	NA	NA
Revenues	NA	NA
Expenditures	NA	NA
Annual visits	NA	NA
Internet terminals/annual users	NA/NA	

Public Safety

Number of officers, 2007	6

Crime	2006	2007
Total crimes	27	41
Violent	0	1
Murder	0	0
Rape	0	0
Robbery	0	0
Aggravated assault	0	1
Non-violent	27	40
Burglary	2	3
Larceny	23	35
Vehicle theft	2	2
Domestic violence	3	12
Arson	1	1
Total crime rate	8.6	13.0
Violent	0.0	0.3
Non-violent	8.6	12.7

Public School District

(for school year 2007-08 except as noted)

Franklin Township School District
226 Quakertown Road, PO Box 368
Quakertown, NJ 08868
(908) 735-7929

Chief School Admin	James Dwyer (Int)
Number of schools	1
Grade plan	K-8
Enrollment	345
Attendance rate, '06-07	95.8%
Dropout rate	NA
Students per teacher	9.6
Per pupil expenditure	$16,463
Median faculty salary	$67,196
Median administrator salary	$86,320
Grade 12 enrollment	NA
High school graduation rate	NA

Assessment test results

(percent scoring at proficient or advanced level)

	Language	Math
NJASK-Grade 3	100.0%	100.1%
GEPA-Grade 8	88.3%	94.1%
HSPA-High School	NA	NA

SAT Score Averages, 2006-07

Pct tested	Math	Verbal	Writing
NA	NA	NA	NA

Teacher Qualifications

Avg. years of experience	18
Highly-qualified teachers one subject/all subjects	100%/100%

No Child Left Behind

AYP, 2006-07	Meets Standards

Municipal Finance

State Aid Programs, 2009

Total aid	$362,078
CMPTRA	45,630
Energy tax receipts	300,198
Garden State Trust	1,787

General Budget, 2008

Total tax levy	$12,510,521
County levy	2,205,717
County taxes	1,846,105
County library	160,313
County health	0
County open space	199,298
School levy	8,598,804
Muni. levy	1,706,000
Misc. revenues	1,731,263

Taxes

	2006	2007	2008
General tax rate per $100	2.22	2.28	2.268
County equalization ratio	85.95	80.3	83.49
Net valuation taxable	$534,932,543	$547,311,702	$551,666,397
State equalized value	$629,194,556	$666,832,630	$638,366,238

See Introduction for an explanation of all data sources.

Demographics & Socio-Economic Characteristics

(2000 US Census, except as noted)

Population

1980*	31,358
1990*	42,780
2000	50,903
Male	24,353
Female	26,550
2007 (estimate)*	59,185
Population density	1,265.4

Race & Hispanic Origin, 2000

Race

White	28,052
Black/African American	13,223
American Indian/Alaska Native	93
Asian	6,486
Native Hawaiian/Pacific Islander	21
Other race	1,811
Two or more races	1,217
Hispanic origin, total	4,127
Mexican	522
Puerto Rican	1,372
Cuban	206
Other Hispanic	2,027

Age & Nativity, 2000

Under 5 years	3,733
18 years and over	39,361
21 years and over	38,095
65 years and over	5,805
85 years and over	943
Median age	36.1
Native-born	39,092
Foreign-born	11,811

Educational Attainment, 2000

Population 25 years and over	36,111
Less than 9th grade	4.6%
High school grad or higher	88.2%
Bachelor's degree or higher	43.3%
Graduate degree	16.0%

Income & Poverty, 1999

Per capita income	$31,209
Median household income	$67,923
Median family income	$78,177
Persons in poverty	2,535
H'holds receiving public assistance	350
H'holds receiving social security	3,694

Households, 2000

Total households	19,355
With persons under 18	6,560
With persons over 65	3,699
Family households	12,989
Single-person households	4,975
Persons per household	2.58
Persons per family	3.14

Labor & Employment

Total civilian labor force, 2007**	34,583
Unemployment rate	3.6%
Total civilian labor force, 2000	27,856
Unemployment rate	3.5%

Employed persons 16 years and over by occupation, 2000

Managers & professionals	13,889
Service occupations	2,450
Sales & office occupations	6,833
Farming, fishing & forestry	18
Construction & maintenance	1,384
Production & transportation	2,312
Self-employed persons	913

*   US Census Bureau
** New Jersey Department of Labor
§   State Fiscal Year July 1–June 30

General Information

Township of Franklin
475 Demott Ln
Somerset, NJ 08873
732-873-2500

Website	www.franklintwpnj.org
Year of incorporation	1798
Land/water area (sq. miles)	46.77/0.07
Form of government	Council-Manager

Government

Legislative Districts

US Congressional	6, 12
State Legislative	17

Local Officials, 2009

Mayor	Brian D. Levine
Manager	Kenneth Daly
Clerk	Ann Marie McCarthy
Finance Dir	Vandana Khurana
Tax Assessor	Stan Belenky
Tax Collector	Carol Langone
Attorney	Leslie G. London
Building	Vincent Lupo
Planning	Mark Healy
Engineering	Thomas Zilinek
Public Works	Victor Stevens
Police Chief	Craig Novick
Emerg/Fire Director	John Hauss

Housing & Construction

Housing Units, 2000*

Total	19,789
Median rent	$897
Median SF home value	$169,700

Permits for New Residential Construction

	Units	Value
Total, 2006	344	$34,134,970
Single family	344	$34,134,970
Total, 2007	189	$19,527,942
Single family	159	$19,345,941

Real Property Valuation, 2008

	Parcels	Valuation
Total	21,385	$8,847,097,850
Vacant	1,457	135,587,850
Residential	18,910	6,724,718,300
Commercial	472	985,424,000
Industrial	166	662,629,900
Apartments	26	275,640,000
Farm land	232	2,584,500
Farm homestead	122	60,513,300

Average Property Value & Tax, 2008

Residential value	$356,517
Property tax	$6,768
Tax credit/rebate	$1,109

Public Library

Franklin Township Library
485 DeMott Lane
Somerset, NJ 08873
732-873-8700

Director	January Adams

Library statistics, 2007

Population served	50,903
Full-time/total staff	9/14

	Total	Per capita
Holdings	155,022	3.05
Revenues	$2,883,552	$56.65
Expenditures	$2,064,013	$40.55
Annual visits	136,656	2.68
Internet terminals/annual users	27/49,605	

Public Safety

Number of officers, 2007	118

Crime	2006	2007
Total crimes	950	1,025
Violent	88	65
Murder	1	4
Rape	5	8
Robbery	45	30
Aggravated assault	37	23
Non-violent	862	960
Burglary	190	215
Larceny	569	626
Vehicle theft	103	119
Domestic violence	471	422
Arson	12	7
Total crime rate	16.3	17.0
Violent	1.5	1.1
Non-violent	14.7	15.9

Public School District

(for school year 2007-08 except as noted)

Franklin Township School District
1755 Amwell Rd
Somerset, NJ 08873
(732) 873-2400

Superintendent	Edward Seto
Number of schools	9
Grade plan	K-12
Enrollment	7,540
Attendance rate, '06-07	95.0%
Dropout rate	2.2%
Students per teacher	10.8
Per pupil expenditure	$15,654
Median faculty salary	$54,740
Median administrator salary	$111,672
Grade 12 enrollment	417
High school graduation rate	95.0%

Assessment test results

(percent scoring at proficient or advanced level)

	Language	Math
NJASK-Grade 3	86.3%	84.9%
GEPA-Grade 8	59.5%	76.2%
HSPA-High School	67.3%	81.3%

SAT Score Averages, 2006-07

Pct tested	Math	Verbal	Writing
82%	487	473	470

Teacher Qualifications

Avg. years of experience	7
Highly-qualified teachers one subject/all subjects	100%/100%

No Child Left Behind

AYP, 2006-07	Meets Standards

Municipal Finance§

State Aid Programs, 2009

Total aid	$6,008,067
CMPTRA	1,067,998
Energy tax receipts	4,695,897
Garden State Trust	94,680

General Budget, 2008

Total tax levy	$168,198,220
County levy	27,353,108
County taxes	24,627,325
County library	0
County health	0
County open space	2,725,783
School levy	107,649,348
Muni. levy	33,195,765
Misc. revenues	31,083,482

Taxes

	2006	2007	2008
General tax rate per $100	1.83	1.86	1.899
County equalization ratio	106.85	102.56	97.52
Net valuation taxable	$8,527,935,840	$8,770,370,572	$8,860,335,690
State equalized value	$8,327,912,573	$8,993,072,290	$9,484,491,293

See Introduction for an explanation of all data sources.

Demographics & Socio-Economic Characteristics

(2000 US Census, except as noted)

Population

1980*	2,341
1990*	2,404
2000	2,768
Male	1,403
Female	1,365
2007 (estimate)*	3,133
Population density	130.6

Race & Hispanic Origin, 2000

Race

White	2,686
Black/African American	23
American Indian/Alaska Native	2
Asian	24
Native Hawaiian/Pacific Islander	0
Other race	3
Two or more races	30
Hispanic origin, total	55
Mexican	8
Puerto Rican	18
Cuban	3
Other Hispanic	26

Age & Nativity, 2000

Under 5 years	195
18 years and over	1,970
21 years and over	1,903
65 years and over	281
85 years and over	20
Median age	38.2
Native-born	2,666
Foreign-born	102

Educational Attainment, 2000

Population 25 years and over	1,818
Less than 9th grade	3.7%
High school grad or higher	87.0%
Bachelor's degree or higher	21.5%
Graduate degree	6.7%

Income & Poverty, 1999

Per capita income	$27,224
Median household income	$69,115
Median family income	$72,763
Persons in poverty	86
H'holds receiving public assistance	25
H'holds receiving social security	189

Households, 2000

Total households	972
With persons under 18	415
With persons over 65	211
Family households	750
Single-person households	181
Persons per household	2.84
Persons per family	3.28

Labor & Employment

Total civilian labor force, 2007**	1,642
Unemployment rate	2.9%
Total civilian labor force, 2000	1,463
Unemployment rate	2.7%

Employed persons 16 years and over by occupation, 2000

Managers & professionals	408
Service occupations	191
Sales & office occupations	385
Farming, fishing & forestry	17
Construction & maintenance	224
Production & transportation	198
Self-employed persons	82

General Information

Township of Franklin
2093 Rt 57
PO Box 547
Broadway, NJ 08808
908-689-3994

Website	www.franklintwpwarren.org
Year of incorporation	1839
Land/water area (sq. miles)	23.99/0.04
Form of government	Township

Government

Legislative Districts

US Congressional	5
State Legislative	23

Local Officials, 2009

Mayor	Bonnie Butler
Manager/Admin	NA
Clerk	Denise L. Cicerelle
Finance Dir	Dawn Stanchina
Tax Assessor	Eloise Hagaman
Tax Collector	Karin Kneafsey
Attorney	Brian Tipton
Building	Walter Van Lieu
Comm Dev/Planning	NA
Engineering	Michael Finelli
Public Works	Ronnie Read
Police Chief	NA
Emerg/Fire Director	Raymond Read

Housing & Construction

Housing Units, 2000*

Total	1,019
Median rent	$725
Median SF home value	$176,200

Permits for New Residential Construction

	Units	Value
Total, 2006	4	$2,051,400
Single family	4	$2,051,400
Total, 2007	1	$161,500
Single family	1	$161,500

Real Property Valuation, 2008

	Parcels	Valuation
Total	1,665	$417,055,725
Vacant	117	6,012,600
Residential	955	292,976,100
Commercial	46	32,985,700
Industrial	15	31,274,600
Apartments	1	306,300
Farm land	385	5,110,225
Farm homestead	146	48,390,200

Average Property Value & Tax, 2008

Residential value	$310,051
Property tax	$8,092
Tax credit/rebate	$1,179

Public Library

Franklin Branch Library‡
1502 Rte 57 West
Washington, NJ 07882
908-689-7922

Branch Librarian	Chris Reedell

Library statistics, 2007

see Warren County profile
for library system statistics

Public Safety

Number of officers, 2007	0

Crime	2006	2007
Total crimes	36	23
Violent	2	0
Murder	0	0
Rape	0	0
Robbery	0	0
Aggravated assault	2	0
Non-violent	34	23
Burglary	9	5
Larceny	24	17
Vehicle theft	1	1
Domestic violence	0	26
Arson	1	0
Total crime rate	11.3	7.2
Violent	0.6	0.0
Non-violent	10.7	7.2

Public School District

(for school year 2007-08 except as noted)

Franklin Township School District
52 Asbury Broadway Road
Washington, NJ 07882
(908) 689-2958

Chief School Admin	Paul Rinaldi
Number of schools	1
Grade plan	K-6
Enrollment	348
Attendance rate, '06-07	94.9%
Dropout rate	NA
Students per teacher	10.0
Per pupil expenditure	$11,461
Median faculty salary	$51,393
Median administrator salary	$90,000
Grade 12 enrollment	NA
High school graduation rate	NA

Assessment test results

(percent scoring at proficient or advanced level)

	Language	Math
NJASK-Grade 3	76.3%	81.6%
GEPA-Grade 8	NA	NA
HSPA-High School	NA	NA

SAT Score Averages, 2006-07

Pct tested	Math	Verbal	Writing
NA	NA	NA	NA

Teacher Qualifications

Avg. years of experience	14
Highly-qualified teachers	
one subject/all subjects	100%/100%

No Child Left Behind

AYP, 2006-07	Meets Standards

Municipal Finance

State Aid Programs, 2009

Total aid	$357,807
CMPTRA	49,070
Energy tax receipts	284,818
Garden State Trust	8,796

General Budget, 2008

Total tax levy	$10,909,969
County levy	2,934,014
County taxes	2,393,072
County library	251,221
County health	0
County open space	289,722
School levy	7,126,482
Muni. levy	849,472
Misc. revenues	1,420,019

Taxes	2006	2007	2008
General tax rate per $100	2.35	2.53	2.611
County equalization ratio	98.36	89.32	87.08
Net valuation taxable	$404,414,025	$410,536,965	$418,005,247
State equalized value	$453,823,161	$471,304,589	$468,238,850

‡ Branch of county library
* US Census Bureau
** New Jersey Department of Labor

See Introduction for an explanation of all data sources.

Demographics & Socio-Economic Characteristics
(2000 US Census, except as noted)

Population
1980*	2,281
1990*	2,763
2000	2,860
Male	1,399
Female	1,461
2007 (estimate)*	3,345
Population density	188.3

Race & Hispanic Origin, 2000
Race
White	2,779
Black/African American	15
American Indian/Alaska Native	7
Asian	24
Native Hawaiian/Pacific Islander	0
Other race	16
Two or more races	19
Hispanic origin, total	62
Mexican	9
Puerto Rican	16
Cuban	12
Other Hispanic	25

Age & Nativity, 2000
Under 5 years	197
18 years and over	2,099
21 years and over	2,017
65 years and over	266
85 years and over	27
Median age	39.3
Native-born	2,721
Foreign-born	139

Educational Attainment, 2000
Population 25 years and over	1,946
Less than 9th grade	2.8%
High school grad or higher	92.9%
Bachelor's degree or higher	34.0%
Graduate degree	10.9%

Income & Poverty, 1999
Per capita income	$31,430
Median household income	$75,710
Median family income	$84,038
Persons in poverty	62
H'holds receiving public assistance	6
H'holds receiving social security	210

Households, 2000
Total households	982
With persons under 18	401
With persons over 65	194
Family households	818
Single-person households	131
Persons per household	2.89
Persons per family	3.18

Labor & Employment
Total civilian labor force, 2007**	1,826
Unemployment rate	1.5%
Total civilian labor force, 2000	1,645
Unemployment rate	1.1%

Employed persons 16 years and over by occupation, 2000
Managers & professionals	678
Service occupations	234
Sales & office occupations	434
Farming, fishing & forestry	5
Construction & maintenance	144
Production & transportation	132
Self-employed persons	171

* US Census Bureau
** New Jersey Department of Labor

General Information
Township of Fredon
443 State Route 94 S
Newton, NJ 07860
973-383-7025
Website	www.twp.fredon.nj.us
Year of incorporation	1904
Land/water area (sq. miles)	17.76/0.19
Form of government	Township

Government
Legislative Districts
US Congressional	5
State Legislative	24

Local Officials, 2009
Mayor	Sandra Coltelli
Manager/Admin	NA
Clerk	Joanne Charner
Finance Dir	Patrick Bailey
Tax Assessor	Kathleen Kieb
Tax Collector	Gisela Boltzer
Attorney	William Hinkes
Building	John de Jager
Comm Dev/Planning	NA
Engineering	Harold Pellow
Public Works	Donald Nelson
Police Chief	NA
Emerg/Fire Director	Wayne Tenis

Housing & Construction
Housing Units, 2000*
Total	1,019
Median rent	$708
Median SF home value	$199,700

Permits for New Residential Construction
	Units	Value
Total, 2006	21	$3,930,155
Single family	21	$3,930,155
Total, 2007	10	$2,262,145
Single family	10	$2,262,145

Real Property Valuation, 2008
	Parcels	Valuation
Total	1,523	$559,881,900
Vacant	82	9,779,500
Residential	1,077	458,629,100
Commercial	37	22,934,800
Industrial	5	7,028,300
Apartments	0	0
Farm land	197	1,945,400
Farm homestead	125	59,564,800

Average Property Value & Tax, 2008
Residential value	$431,110
Property tax	$7,899
Tax credit/rebate	$1,103

Public Library
No public municipal library

Library statistics, 2007
Population served	NA
Full-time/total staff	NA/NA

	Total	Per capita
Holdings	NA	NA
Revenues	NA	NA
Expenditures	NA	NA
Annual visits	NA	NA
Internet terminals/annual users	NA/NA	

Public Safety
Number of officers, 2007 0
Crime	2006	2007
Total crimes	22	15
Violent	1	1
Murder	0	0
Rape	0	0
Robbery	0	1
Aggravated assault	1	0
Non-violent	21	14
Burglary	8	5
Larceny	13	8
Vehicle theft	0	1
Domestic violence	0	16
Arson	0	0
Total crime rate	6.6	4.5
Violent	0.3	0.3
Non-violent	6.3	4.2

Public School District
(for school year 2007-08 except as noted)

Fredon Township School District
459 Route 94
Newton, NJ 07860
(973) 383-4151
Superintendent	Salvatore Constantino
Number of schools	1
Grade plan	K-6
Enrollment	346
Attendance rate, '06-07	96.1%
Dropout rate	NA
Students per teacher	10.5
Per pupil expenditure	$12,718
Median faculty salary	$45,393
Median administrator salary	$103,500
Grade 12 enrollment	NA
High school graduation rate	NA

Assessment test results
(percent scoring at proficient or advanced level)
	Language	Math
NJASK-Grade 3	92.0%	86.0%
GEPA-Grade 8	NA	NA
HSPA-High School	NA	NA

SAT Score Averages, 2006-07
Pct tested	Math	Verbal	Writing
NA	NA	NA	NA

Teacher Qualifications
Avg. years of experience	6
Highly-qualified teachers one subject/all subjects	100%/100%

No Child Left Behind
AYP, 2006-07 .... Meets Standards

Municipal Finance
State Aid Programs, 2009
Total aid	$350,756
CMPTRA	61,391
Energy tax receipts	267,591
Garden State Trust	10,867

General Budget, 2008
Total tax levy	$10,275,584
County levy	2,146,595
County taxes	1,801,427
County library	151,834
County health	53,325
County open space	140,008
School levy	6,704,247
Muni. levy	1,424,743
Misc. revenues	996,606

Taxes
	2006	2007	2008
General tax rate per $100	3.27	3.48	1.833
County equalization ratio	57.85	54.13	100.68
Net valuation taxable	$271,876,400	$278,728,130	$560,848,097
State equalized value	$502,876,944	$551,964,804	$555,414,504

Demographics & Socio-Economic Characteristics

(2000 US Census, except as noted)

Population
1980*	10,020
1990*	10,742
2000	10,976
Male	5,656
Female	5,320
2007 (estimate)*	11,465
Population density	5,732.5

Race & Hispanic Origin, 2000
Race
White	7,795
Black/African American	1,738
American Indian/Alaska Native	60
Asian	269
Native Hawaiian/Pacific Islander	2
Other race	729
Two or more races	383
Hispanic origin, total	3,081
Mexican	1,903
Puerto Rican	627
Cuban	31
Other Hispanic	520

Age & Nativity, 2000
Under 5 years	858
18 years and over	8,258
21 years and over	7,788
65 years and over	1,171
85 years and over	169
Median age	33.0
Native-born	8,720
Foreign-born	2,256

Educational Attainment, 2000
Population 25 years and over	7,148
Less than 9th grade	10.7%
High school grad or higher	76.0%
Bachelor's degree or higher	19.7%
Graduate degree	4.6%

Income & Poverty, 1999
Per capita income	$19,910
Median household income	$48,654
Median family income	$53,374
Persons in poverty	1,314
H'holds receiving public assistance	108
H'holds receiving social security	931

Households, 2000
Total households	3,695
With persons under 18	1,436
With persons over 65	898
Family households	2,570
Single-person households	898
Persons per household	2.96
Persons per family	3.39

Labor & Employment
Total civilian labor force, 2007**	6,153
Unemployment rate	5.7%
Total civilian labor force, 2000	5,833
Unemployment rate	7.0%

Employed persons 16 years and over by occupation, 2000
Managers & professionals	1,410
Service occupations	1,374
Sales & office occupations	1,378
Farming, fishing & forestry	36
Construction & maintenance	542
Production & transportation	683
Self-employed persons	228

* US Census Bureau
** New Jersey Department of Labor

General Information

Freehold Borough
51 W Main St
Freehold, NJ 07728
732-462-1410
Website	www.freeholdboro.org
Year of incorporation	1919
Land/water area (sq. miles)	2.00/0.00
Form of government	Borough

Government

Legislative Districts
US Congressional	4
State Legislative	12

Local Officials, 2009
Mayor	Michael Wilson
Manager	Joseph Bellina
Clerk	Traci L. DiBenedetto
Finance Dir	Nancy Forman
Tax Assessor	Mitchell Elias
Tax Collector	Nancy Fonman
Attorney	Kerry Higgins
Building	Henry Stryker
Comm Dev/Planning	NA
Engineering	Jim Kovacs
Public Works	Sal DeJesus
Police Chief	Mitchell E. Roth
Emerg/Fire Director	Jack Reichman

Housing & Construction

Housing Units, 2000*
Total	3,821
Median rent	$821
Median SF home value	$137,500

Permits for New Residential Construction
	Units	Value
Total, 2006	16	$1,682,162
Single family	16	$1,682,162
Total, 2007	16	$1,216,932
Single family	11	$1,216,432

Real Property Valuation, 2008
	Parcels	Valuation
Total	3,304	$1,069,679,000
Vacant	84	11,815,100
Residential	2,944	763,101,500
Commercial	261	237,093,900
Industrial	3	34,727,100
Apartments	12	22,941,400
Farm land	0	0
Farm homestead	0	0

Average Property Value & Tax, 2008
Residential value	$259,206
Property tax	$5,513
Tax credit/rebate	$1,000

Public Library

Freehold Public Library
28 1/2 E Main St
Freehold, NJ 07728
732-462-5135
Director	Barbara Greenberg

Library statistics, 2007
Population served	10,976
Full-time/total staff	1/3

	Total	Per capita
Holdings	26,886	2.45
Revenues	$378,287	$34.46
Expenditures	$349,762	$31.87
Annual visits	22,620	2.06
Internet terminals/annual users	7/11,310	

Public Safety
Number of officers, 2007	28

Crime	2006	2007
Total crimes	309	301
Violent	49	54
Murder	0	0
Rape	1	5
Robbery	26	28
Aggravated assault	22	21
Non-violent	260	247
Burglary	35	33
Larceny	211	204
Vehicle theft	14	10
Domestic violence	211	154
Arson	3	0
Total crime rate	27.0	26.4
Violent	4.3	4.7
Non-violent	22.7	21.7

Public School District

(for school year 2007-08 except as noted)

Freehold Borough School District
280 Park Avenue
Freehold, NJ 07728
(732) 761-2102
Superintendent	Elizabeth O'Connell
Number of schools	3
Grade plan	K-8
Enrollment	1,348
Attendance rate, '06-07	95.0%
Dropout rate	NA
Students per teacher	12.1
Per pupil expenditure	$11,247
Median faculty salary	$49,980
Median administrator salary	$93,455
Grade 12 enrollment	NA
High school graduation rate	NA

Assessment test results
(percent scoring at proficient or advanced level)
	Language	Math
NJASK-Grade 3	75.4%	68.5%
GEPA-Grade 8	50.8%	74.8%
HSPA-High School	NA	NA

SAT Score Averages, 2006-07
Pct tested	Math	Verbal	Writing
NA	NA	NA	NA

Teacher Qualifications
Avg. years of experience	9
Highly-qualified teachers one subject/all subjects	94.5%/94.5%

No Child Left Behind
AYP, 2006-07	Meets Standards

Municipal Finance

State Aid Programs, 2009
Total aid	$1,612,810
CMPTRA	648,831
Energy tax receipts	923,659
Garden State Trust	0

General Budget, 2008
Total tax levy	$22,973,069
County levy	3,008,998
County taxes	2,820,868
County library	0
County health	0
County open space	188,131
School levy	12,213,716
Muni. levy	7,750,355
Misc. revenues	6,346,435

Taxes
	2006	2007	2008
General tax rate per $100	1.949	2.04	2.127
County equalization ratio	100.99	92.47	86.90
Net valuation taxable	$1,074,863,600	$1,080,991,278	$1,080,148,969
State equalized value	$1,172,895,348	$1,242,464,230	$158,529,010

See Introduction for an explanation of all data sources.

Demographics & Socio-Economic Characteristics

(2000 US Census, except as noted)

Population

1980*	19,202
1990*	24,710
2000	31,537
Male	15,588
Female	15,949
2007 (estimate)*	34,875
Population density	907.0

Race & Hispanic Origin, 2000

Race

White	27,466
Black/African American	1,616
American Indian/Alaska Native	44
Asian	1,623
Native Hawaiian/Pacific Islander	5
Other race	374
Two or more races	409
Hispanic origin, total	1,637
Mexican	328
Puerto Rican	607
Cuban	133
Other Hispanic	569

Age & Nativity, 2000

Under 5 years	2,137
18 years and over	23,564
21 years and over	22,722
65 years and over	3,781
85 years and over	613
Median age	38.3
Native-born	28,008
Foreign-born	3,529

Educational Attainment, 2000

Population 25 years and over	21,808
Less than 9th grade	3.6%
High school grad or higher	88.8%
Bachelor's degree or higher	37.5%
Graduate degree	13.1%

Income & Poverty, 1999

Per capita income	$31,505
Median household income	$77,185
Median family income	$89,845
Persons in poverty	1,155
H'holds receiving public assistance	113
H'holds receiving social security	2,726

Households, 2000

Total households	10,814
With persons under 18	4,266
With persons over 65	2,468
Family households	8,279
Single-person households	2,163
Persons per household	2.76
Persons per family	3.21

Labor & Employment

Total civilian labor force, 2007**	18,085
Unemployment rate	3.2%
Total civilian labor force, 2000	15,970
Unemployment rate	2.8%

Employed persons 16 years and over by occupation, 2000

Managers & professionals	7,117
Service occupations	1,422
Sales & office occupations	5,002
Farming, fishing & forestry	24
Construction & maintenance	1,031
Production & transportation	934
Self-employed persons	787

* US Census Bureau
** New Jersey Department of Labor

General Information

Freehold Township
1 Municipal Plz
Freehold, NJ 07728
732-294-2000

Website	www.twp.freehold.nj.us
Year of incorporation	1693
Land/water area (sq. miles)	38.45/0.08
Form of government	Township

Government

Legislative Districts

US Congressional	4, 12
State Legislative	12

Local Officials, 2009

Mayor	Raymond Kershaw
Manager	Thomas E. Antus
Clerk	Teresa Warner
Finance Dir	Debrah Defeo
Tax Assessor	William Fitzpatrick
Tax Collector	MaryLou Angelo
Attorney	Duane O. Davison
Building	Thomas Luongo
Comm Dev/Planning	NA
Engineering	Joseph Mavuro
Public Works	Tim White
Police Chief	Ernest Schriefer
Emerg/Fire Director	Tom Luongo

Housing & Construction

Housing Units, 2000*

Total	11,032
Median rent	$904
Median SF home value	$227,500

Permits for New Residential Construction

	Units	Value
Total, 2006	101	$11,373,264
Single family	16	$8,187,109
Total, 2007	27	$9,281,089
Single family	15	$9,080,569

Real Property Valuation, 2008

	Parcels	Valuation
Total	12,442	$3,055,400,900
Vacant	525	43,886,000
Residential	11,269	2,245,621,400
Commercial	361	644,466,200
Industrial	28	74,628,300
Apartments	2	30,165,900
Farm land	175	1,700,500
Farm homestead	82	14,932,600

Average Property Value & Tax, 2008

Residential value	$199,150
Property tax	$6,963
Tax credit/rebate	$1,048

Public Library

No public municipal library

Library statistics, 2007

Population served	NA
Full-time/total staff	NA/NA

	Total	Per capita
Holdings	NA	NA
Revenues	NA	NA
Expenditures	NA	NA
Annual visits	NA	NA
Internet terminals/annual users	NA/NA	

Public Safety

Number of officers, 2007 71

Crime	2006	2007
Total crimes	957	970
Violent	36	54
Murder	0	0
Rape	8	8
Robbery	11	22
Aggravated assault	17	24
Non-violent	921	916
Burglary	76	69
Larceny	831	825
Vehicle theft	14	22
Domestic violence	283	307
Arson	4	1
Total crime rate	28.3	28.6
Violent	1.1	1.6
Non-violent	27.2	27.0

Public School District

(for school year 2007-08 except as noted)

Freehold Township School District
384 West Main Street
Freehold, NJ 07728
(732) 462-8400

Superintendent	William Setaro
Number of schools	8
Grade plan	K-8
Enrollment	4,607
Attendance rate, '06-07	95.5%
Dropout rate	NA
Students per teacher	11.3
Per pupil expenditure	$13,271
Median faculty salary	$50,500
Median administrator salary	$99,090
Grade 12 enrollment	NA
High school graduation rate	NA

Assessment test results

(percent scoring at proficient or advanced level)

	Language	Math
NJASK-Grade 3	95.3%	94.1%
GEPA-Grade 8	82.9%	92.4%
HSPA-High School	NA	NA

SAT Score Averages, 2006-07

Pct tested	Math	Verbal	Writing
NA	NA	NA	NA

Teacher Qualifications

Avg. years of experience	8
Highly-qualified teachers one subject/all subjects	99.5%/99.5%

No Child Left Behind

AYP, 2006-07 .... Meets Standards

Municipal Finance

State Aid Programs, 2009

Total aid	$10,076,051
CMPTRA	822,949
Energy tax receipts	8,816,289
Garden State Trust	29,977

General Budget, 2008

Total tax levy	$107,966,096
County levy	16,133,366
County taxes	14,312,576
County library	863,258
County health	0
County open space	957,532
School levy	77,156,670
Muni. levy	14,676,060
Misc. revenues	26,275,394

Taxes	2006	2007	2008
General tax rate per $100	3.343	3.471	3.497
County equalization ratio	54.78	49.75	47.06
Net valuation taxable	$2,982,974,600	$3,044,471,360	$3,088,181,896
State equalized value	$6,037,954,660	$6,427,750,216	$1,275,015,424

Demographics & Socio-Economic Characteristics
(2000 US Census, except as noted)

Population
1980*	1,435
1990*	1,779
2000	2,083
Male	1,028
Female	1,055
2007 (estimate)*	2,207
Population density	94.2

Race & Hispanic Origin, 2000
Race
White	2,037
Black/African American	7
American Indian/Alaska Native	1
Asian	8
Native Hawaiian/Pacific Islander	4
Other race	10
Two or more races	16
Hispanic origin, total	55
Mexican	1
Puerto Rican	17
Cuban	16
Other Hispanic	21

Age & Nativity, 2000
Under 5 years	132
18 years and over	1,540
21 years and over	1,487
65 years and over	230
85 years and over	43
Median age	40.3
Native-born	1,986
Foreign-born	97

Educational Attainment, 2000
Population 25 years and over	1,438
Less than 9th grade	4.0%
High school grad or higher	89.6%
Bachelor's degree or higher	33.4%
Graduate degree	12.7%

Income & Poverty, 1999
Per capita income	$28,792
Median household income	$72,434
Median family income	$78,464
Persons in poverty	46
H'holds receiving public assistance	11
H'holds receiving social security	146

Households, 2000
Total households	722
With persons under 18	287
With persons over 65	133
Family households	578
Single-person households	105
Persons per household	2.81
Persons per family	3.13

Labor & Employment
Total civilian labor force, 2007**	1,204
Unemployment rate	3.0%
Total civilian labor force, 2000	1,082
Unemployment rate	3.3%

Employed persons 16 years and over by occupation, 2000
Managers & professionals	450
Service occupations	135
Sales & office occupations	252
Farming, fishing & forestry	4
Construction & maintenance	126
Production & transportation	79
Self-employed persons	90

* US Census Bureau
** New Jersey Department of Labor

See Introduction for an explanation of all data sources.

General Information
Township of Frelinghuysen
PO Box 417
Johnsonburg, NJ 07846
908-852-4121
Website	www.freylinghuysen-nj.us
Year of incorporation	1848
Land/water area (sq. miles)	23.43/0.12
Form of government	Township

Government
Legislative Districts
US Congressional	5
State Legislative	23

Local Officials, 2009
Mayor	Dale Durling Jr
Manager/Admin	NA
Clerk	Brenda Kleber
Finance Dir	Gene Marie McCartney
Tax Assessor	David Gill
Tax Collector	Donna Clouse
Attorney	Edward Wacks
Building	Richard O'Connor
Comm Dev/Planning	NA
Engineering	Paul Sterbenz
Public Works	NA
Police Chief	NA
Fire/Emergency Dir	NA

Housing & Construction
Housing Units, 2000*
Total	755
Median rent	$817
Median SF home value	$211,000

Permits for New Residential Construction
	Units	Value
Total, 2006	13	$3,009,524
Single family	13	$3,009,524
Total, 2007	13	$3,708,991
Single family	13	$3,708,991

Real Property Valuation, 2008
	Parcels	Valuation
Total	1,339	$276,836,378
Vacant	109	7,496,700
Residential	604	189,917,700
Commercial	25	8,212,778
Industrial	0	0
Apartments	0	0
Farm land	408	2,375,900
Farm homestead	193	68,833,300

Average Property Value & Tax, 2008
Residential value	$324,656
Property tax	$6,817
Tax credit/rebate	$1,137

Public Library
No public municipal library

Library statistics, 2007
Population served	NA
Full-time/total staff	NA/NA

	Total	Per capita
Holdings	NA	NA
Revenues	NA	NA
Expenditures	NA	NA
Annual visits	NA	NA
Internet terminals/annual users	NA/NA	

Public Safety
Number of officers, 2007	0

Crime	2006	2007
Total crimes	19	9
Violent	1	1
Murder	0	0
Rape	0	0
Robbery	0	0
Aggravated assault	1	1
Non-violent	18	8
Burglary	3	1
Larceny	13	7
Vehicle theft	2	0
Domestic violence	0	5
Arson	0	0
Total crime rate	8.7	4.1
Violent	0.5	0.5
Non-violent	8.2	3.6

Public School District
(for school year 2007-08 except as noted)

Frelinghuysen Township School District
780 Route 94, PO Box 421
Johnsonburg, NJ 07846
(908) 362-6319
Chief School Admin	Dwight Klett
Number of schools	1
Grade plan	K-6
Enrollment	197
Attendance rate, '06-07	96.1%
Dropout rate	NA
Students per teacher	9.2
Per pupil expenditure	$11,665
Median faculty salary	$47,245
Median administrator salary	$90,488
Grade 12 enrollment	NA
High school graduation rate	NA

Assessment test results
(percent scoring at proficient or advanced level)
	Language	Math
NJASK-Grade 3	100.0%	92.3%
GEPA-Grade 8	NA	NA
HSPA-High School	NA	NA

SAT Score Averages, 2006-07
Pct tested	Math	Verbal	Writing
NA	NA	NA	NA

Teacher Qualifications
Avg. years of experience	10
Highly-qualified teachers	
one subject/all subjects	100%/100%

No Child Left Behind
AYP, 2006-07	Meets Standards

Municipal Finance
State Aid Programs, 2009
Total aid	$270,820
CMPTRA	39,015
Energy tax receipts	202,489
Garden State Trust	15,378

General Budget, 2008
Total tax levy	$5,827,086
County levy	1,906,742
County taxes	1,555,336
County library	163,198
County health	0
County open space	188,209
School levy	3,527,550
Muni. levy	392,794
Misc. revenues	1,023,662

Taxes
	2006	2007	2008
General tax rate per $100	2.13	2.17	2.100
County equalization ratio	96.98	87.8	88.92
Net valuation taxable	$267,488,578	$274,503,413	$277,492,749
State equalized value	$305,380,159	$308,626,907	$311,080,657

Demographics & Socio-Economic Characteristics
(2000 US Census, except as noted)

Population
1980*	1,573
1990*	1,528
2000	1,488
Male	721
Female	767
2007 (estimate)*	1,465
Population density	1,144.5

Race & Hispanic Origin, 2000
Race
White	1,428
Black/African American	6
American Indian/Alaska Native	3
Asian	18
Native Hawaiian/Pacific Islander	0
Other race	20
Two or more races	13
Hispanic origin, total	39
Mexican	2
Puerto Rican	5
Cuban	0
Other Hispanic	32

Age & Nativity, 2000
Under 5 years	94
18 years and over	1,153
21 years and over	1,102
65 years and over	146
85 years and over	12
Median age	38.0
Native-born	1,385
Foreign-born	103

Educational Attainment, 2000
Population 25 years and over	1,051
Less than 9th grade	3.0%
High school grad or higher	85.6%
Bachelor's degree or higher	32.4%
Graduate degree	13.1%

Income & Poverty, 1999
Per capita income	$27,765
Median household income	$52,109
Median family income	$62,132
Persons in poverty	49
H'holds receiving public assistance	9
H'holds receiving social security	120

Households, 2000
Total households	613
With persons under 18	199
With persons over 65	107
Family households	376
Single-person households	177
Persons per household	2.38
Persons per family	2.99

Labor & Employment
Total civilian labor force, 2007**	959
Unemployment rate	2.7%
Total civilian labor force, 2000	862
Unemployment rate	3.2%

Employed persons 16 years and over by occupation, 2000
Managers & professionals	356
Service occupations	78
Sales & office occupations	199
Farming, fishing & forestry	0
Construction & maintenance	104
Production & transportation	97
Self-employed persons	99

* US Census Bureau
** New Jersey Department of Labor

General Information
Borough of Frenchtown
Borough Hall
29 2nd St
Frenchtown, NJ 08825
908-996-4524
Website	www.frenchtown.com/newsite
Year of incorporation	1867
Land/water area (sq. miles)	1.28/0.06
Form of government	Borough

Government
Legislative Districts
US Congressional	12
State Legislative	23

Local Officials, 2009
Mayor	Ronald Sworen
Manager/Admin	NA
Clerk	Brenda Shepherd
Finance Dir	Diane Laudenbach
Tax Assessor	David Gill
Tax Collector	Diane Laudenbach
Attorney	Douglas Cole
Building	NA
Comm Dev/Planning	NA
Engineering	Robert J. Clerico
Public Works	Michael Reino
Police Chief	Allan Kurylka
Emerg/Fire Director	Gerald Hoffman

Housing & Construction
Housing Units, 2000*
Total	630
Median rent	$755
Median SF home value	$165,900

Permits for New Residential Construction
	Units	Value
Total, 2006	1	$163,000
Single family	1	$163,000
Total, 2007	1	$106,000
Single family	1	$106,000

Real Property Valuation, 2008
	Parcels	Valuation
Total	548	$149,531,979
Vacant	45	2,554,500
Residential	418	108,094,600
Commercial	61	28,085,300
Industrial	6	3,726,350
Apartments	10	6,119,880
Farm land	6	52,749
Farm homestead	2	898,600

Average Property Value & Tax, 2008
Residential value	$259,508
Property tax	$6,619
Tax credit/rebate	$1,102

Public Library
Frenchtown Public Library
29 Second St
Frenchtown, NJ 08825
908-996-4788
Director	Sara Heil

Library statistics, 2007
Population served	1,488
Full-time/total staff	NA/0

	Total	Per capita
Holdings	0	NA
Revenues	$0	NA
Expenditures	$0	NA
Annual visits	NA	NA
Internet terminals/annual users	NA/NA	

Public Safety
Number of officers, 2007 ... 2
Crime	2006	2007
Total crimes	26	23
Violent	1	1
Murder	0	0
Rape	0	0
Robbery	0	0
Aggravated assault	1	1
Non-violent	25	22
Burglary	2	8
Larceny	23	14
Vehicle theft	0	0
Domestic violence	4	8
Arson	0	0
Total crime rate	17.3	15.4
Violent	0.7	0.7
Non-violent	16.6	14.8

Public School District
(for school year 2007-08 except as noted)

Frenchtown Borough School District
902 Harrison Street
Frenchtown, NJ 08825
(908) 996-2751
Chief School Admin	Erik Falkenstein
Number of schools	1
Grade plan	K-8
Enrollment	146
Attendance rate, '06-07	95.4%
Dropout rate	NA
Students per teacher	7.7
Per pupil expenditure	$16,302
Median faculty salary	$47,989
Median administrator salary	$74,760
Grade 12 enrollment	NA
High school graduation rate	NA

Assessment test results
(percent scoring at proficient or advanced level)
	Language	Math
NJASK-Grade 3	100.0%	100.0%
GEPA-Grade 8	53.4%	100.0%
HSPA-High School	NA	NA

SAT Score Averages, 2006-07
Pct tested	Math	Verbal	Writing
NA	NA	NA	NA

Teacher Qualifications
Avg. years of experience	10
Highly-qualified teachers one subject/all subjects	100%/100%

No Child Left Behind
AYP, 2006-07	Meets Standards

Municipal Finance
State Aid Programs, 2009
Total aid	$187,446
CMPTRA	59,604
Energy tax receipts	86,479
Garden State Trust	32,564

General Budget, 2008
Total tax levy	$3,840,714
County levy	635,115
County taxes	531,568
County library	46,161
County health	0
County open space	57,386
School levy	2,388,863
Muni. levy	816,736
Misc. revenues	783,556

Taxes
	2006	2007	2008
General tax rate per $100	2.42	2.61	2.551
County equalization ratio	90.27	82.37	79.64
Net valuation taxable	$149,618,555	$149,049,848	$150,590,982
State equalized value	$177,616,197	$189,878,132	$188,889,651

See Introduction for an explanation of all data sources.

Demographics & Socio-Economic Characteristics

(2000 US Census, except as noted)

Population
1980*	12,176
1990*	23,330
2000	31,209
Male	14,984
Female	16,225
2007 (estimate)*	36,105
Population density	399.0

Race & Hispanic Origin, 2000
Race
White	24,081
Black/African American	3,058
American Indian/Alaska Native	75
Asian	2,498
Native Hawaiian/Pacific Islander	15
Other race	807
Two or more races	675
Hispanic origin, total	1,924
Mexican	126
Puerto Rican	1,048
Cuban	69
Other Hispanic	681

Age & Nativity, 2000
Under 5 years	2,030
18 years and over	23,147
21 years and over	20,991
65 years and over	2,830
85 years and over	237
Median age	34.0
Native-born	27,665
Foreign-born	3,494

Educational Attainment, 2000
Population 25 years and over	18,733
Less than 9th grade	3.0%
High school grad or higher	87.3%
Bachelor's degree or higher	22.8%
Graduate degree	7.3%

Income & Poverty, 1999
Per capita income	$21,048
Median household income	$51,592
Median family income	$57,156
Persons in poverty	1,907
H'holds receiving public assistance	206
H'holds receiving social security	2,344

Households, 2000
Total households	10,772
With persons under 18	4,451
With persons over 65	2,106
Family households	7,681
Single-person households	2,317
Persons per household	2.70
Persons per family	3.18

Labor & Employment
Total civilian labor force, 2007**	19,068
Unemployment rate	5.4%
Total civilian labor force, 2000	16,928
Unemployment rate	10.1%

Employed persons 16 years and over by occupation, 2000
Managers & professionals	4,380
Service occupations	4,332
Sales & office occupations	4,193
Farming, fishing & forestry	0
Construction & maintenance	1,244
Production & transportation	1,067
Self-employed persons	661

‡ Branch of county library
* US Census Bureau
** New Jersey Department of Labor

General Information
Township of Galloway
300 E Jimmie Leeds Rd
Galloway, NJ 08205
609-652-3700
Website	www.gallowaytwp-nj.gov
Year of incorporation	1774
Land/water area (sq. miles)	90.49/24.31
Form of government	Council-Manager

Government
Legislative Districts
US Congressional	2
State Legislative	2

Local Officials, 2009
Mayor	Tom Bassford
Manager	Jill A. Gougher
Clerk	Lisa A. Tilton
Finance Dir	Jill A. Gougher
Tax Assessor	David Jackson
Tax Collector	Albert Stanley
Attorney	Michael Blee
Building	Richard Roesch
Planning	Pamela Alleyne
Engineering	Kevin Dixon
Public Works	Stephen Bonanni
Police Chief	Peter Romanelli
Emerg/Fire Director	Rodney Calimer

Housing & Construction
Housing Units, 2000*
Total	11,406
Median rent	$811
Median SF home value	$130,000

Permits for New Residential Construction
	Units	Value
Total, 2006	226	$23,877,809
Single family	226	$23,877,809
Total, 2007	116	$13,537,835
Single family	116	$13,537,835

Real Property Valuation, 2008
	Parcels	Valuation
Total	17,867	$1,919,162,700
Vacant	4,024	64,965,900
Residential	13,026	1,596,589,100
Commercial	429	195,138,700
Industrial	2	6,752,100
Apartments	16	39,586,300
Farm land	257	1,302,200
Farm homestead	113	14,828,400

Average Property Value & Tax, 2008
Residential value	$122,644
Property tax	$4,313
Tax credit/rebate	$870

Public Library
Galloway Township Branch Library‡
306 E Jimmie Leeds Rd
Absecon, NJ 08201
609-652-2352
Branch Librarian	Katherine Ostrum

Library statistics, 2007
see Atlantic County profile
for library system statistics

Public Safety
Number of officers, 2007	73

Crime	2006	2007
Total crimes	861	967
Violent	90	108
Murder	0	1
Rape	6	11
Robbery	26	17
Aggravated assault	58	79
Non-violent	771	859
Burglary	200	200
Larceny	535	606
Vehicle theft	36	53
Domestic violence	656	576
Arson	4	5
Total crime rate	**24.0**	**26.7**
Violent	2.5	3.0
Non-violent	21.5	23.7

Public School District
(for school year 2007-08 except as noted)

Galloway Township School District
101 S. Reeds Rd.
Galloway, NJ 08205
(609) 748-1250
Superintendent	Douglas Groff
Number of schools	7
Grade plan	K-8
Enrollment	3,683
Attendance rate, '06-07	95.2%
Dropout rate	NA
Students per teacher	10.0
Per pupil expenditure	$11,975
Median faculty salary	$49,490
Median administrator salary	$96,498
Grade 12 enrollment	NA
High school graduation rate	NA

Assessment test results
(percent scoring at proficient or advanced level)
	Language	Math
NJASK-Grade 3	83.8%	82.5%
GEPA-Grade 8	66.7%	83.6%
HSPA-High School	NA	NA

SAT Score Averages, 2006-07
Pct tested	Math	Verbal	Writing
NA	NA	NA	NA

Teacher Qualifications
Avg. years of experience	10
Highly-qualified teachers one subject/all subjects	100%/100%

No Child Left Behind
AYP, 2006-07	Meets Standards

Municipal Finance
State Aid Programs, 2009
Total aid	$3,465,784
CMPTRA	371,038
Energy tax receipts	2,855,036
Garden State Trust	12,383

General Budget, 2008
Total tax levy	$67,679,341
County levy	11,354,417
County taxes	8,942,075
County library	1,149,188
County health	470,242
County open space	792,913
School levy	43,297,332
Muni. levy	13,027,592
Misc. revenues	10,660,419

Taxes	2006	2007	2008
General tax rate per $100	3.369	3.42	3.517
County equalization ratio	61.12	52.53	48.55
Net valuation taxable	$1,826,386,100	$1,900,451,760	$1,924,396,620
State equalized value	$3,483,028,296	$3,908,699,451	$3,916,305,247

See Introduction for an explanation of all data sources.

Demographics & Socio-Economic Characteristics
(2000 US Census, except as noted)

Population
1980*	26,803
1990*	26,727
2000	29,786
Male	14,514
Female	15,272
2007 (estimate)*	29,206
Population density	13,711.7

Race & Hispanic Origin, 2000
Race
White	24,456
Black/African American	887
American Indian/Alaska Native	99
Asian	800
Native Hawaiian/Pacific Islander	2
Other race	2,414
Two or more races	1,128
Hispanic origin, total	5,989
Mexican	469
Puerto Rican	1,348
Cuban	130
Other Hispanic	4,042

Age & Nativity, 2000
Under 5 years	1,809
18 years and over	23,124
21 years and over	22,039
65 years and over	4,185
85 years and over	479
Median age	35.6
Native-born	18,150
Foreign-born	11,636

Educational Attainment, 2000
Population 25 years and over	20,271
Less than 9th grade	13.5%
High school grad or higher	70.3%
Bachelor's degree or higher	14.0%
Graduate degree	3.8%

Income & Poverty, 1999
Per capita income	$19,530
Median household income	$42,748
Median family income	$51,654
Persons in poverty	2,305
H'holds receiving public assistance	253
H'holds receiving social security	3,264

Households, 2000
Total households	11,250
With persons under 18	3,748
With persons over 65	3,242
Family households	7,426
Single-person households	3,077
Persons per household	2.64
Persons per family	3.26

Labor & Employment
Total civilian labor force, 2007**	15,698
Unemployment rate	6.0%
Total civilian labor force, 2000	15,594
Unemployment rate	7.6%

Employed persons 16 years and over by occupation, 2000
Managers & professionals	2,954
Service occupations	2,237
Sales & office occupations	4,059
Farming, fishing & forestry	69
Construction & maintenance	2,107
Production & transportation	2,986
Self-employed persons	543

* US Census Bureau
** New Jersey Department of Labor

General Information
City of Garfield
111 Outwater Ln
Garfield, NJ 07026
973-340-2001

Website	www.garfieldnj.org
Year of incorporation	1917
Land/water area (sq. miles)	2.13/0.06
Form of government	Municipal Mgr 1923

Government
Legislative Districts
US Congressional	9
State Legislative	36

Local Officials, 2009
Mayor	Frank Calandriello
Manager	Thomas J. Duch
Clerk	Andrew J. Pavlica
Finance Dir	Roy Riggitano
Tax Assessor	Kurt Hielle
Tax Collector	Rosemarie Cokinos
Attorney	Joseph Rotolo
Building	Fred Krowl
Comm Dev/Planning	NA
Engineering	Kevin J. Boswell
Public Works	Sam Garofalo
Police Chief	Robert Andrezzi
Emerg/Fire Director	Michael Marsh

Housing & Construction
Housing Units, 2000*
Total	11,698
Median rent	$777
Median SF home value	$161,500

Permits for New Residential Construction
	Units	Value
Total, 2006	13	$1,248,503
Single family	1	$141,500
Total, 2007	17	$1,478,455
Single family	7	$528,000

Real Property Valuation, 2008
	Parcels	Valuation
Total	6,257	$1,181,621,700
Vacant	134	11,001,100
Residential	5,475	892,658,600
Commercial	453	150,046,800
Industrial	79	79,632,600
Apartments	116	48,282,600
Farm land	0	0
Farm homestead	0	0

Average Property Value & Tax, 2008
Residential value	$163,043
Property tax	$6,406
Tax credit/rebate	$986

Public Library
Garfield Public Library
500 Midland Ave
Garfield, NJ 07026
973-478-3800

Director | MacArthur Nickles

Library statistics, 2007
Population served	29,786
Full-time/total staff	3/8

	Total	Per capita
Holdings	84,424	2.83
Revenues	$945,540	$31.74
Expenditures	$887,950	$29.81
Annual visits	86,532	2.91
Internet terminals/annual users	8/31,620	

Public Safety
Number of officers, 2007	57

Crime	2006	2007
Total crimes	527	459
Violent	62	57
Murder	0	1
Rape	1	2
Robbery	28	18
Aggravated assault	33	36
Non-violent	465	402
Burglary	122	128
Larceny	276	224
Vehicle theft	67	50
Domestic violence	230	215
Arson	0	0
Total crime rate	17.7	15.5
Violent	2.1	1.9
Non-violent	15.6	13.6

Public School District
(for school year 2007-08 except as noted)

Garfield School District
125 Outwater Lane
Garfield, NJ 07026
(973) 340-5000

Superintendent	Nicholas Perrapato
Number of schools	11
Grade plan	K-12
Enrollment	4,492
Attendance rate, '06-07	94.0%
Dropout rate	0.5%
Students per teacher	10.8
Per pupil expenditure	$14,774
Median faculty salary	$50,475
Median administrator salary	$125,275
Grade 12 enrollment	278
High school graduation rate	86.3%

Assessment test results
(percent scoring at proficient or advanced level)
	Language	Math
NJASK-Grade 3	85.1%	85.7%
GEPA-Grade 8	63.4%	71.7%
HSPA-High School	62.8%	70.3%

SAT Score Averages, 2006-07
Pct tested	Math	Verbal	Writing
69%	460	430	436

Teacher Qualifications
Avg. years of experience	9
Highly-qualified teachers one subject/all subjects	100%/100%

No Child Left Behind
AYP, 2006-07	Meets Standards

Municipal Finance
State Aid Programs, 2009
Total aid	$3,264,029
CMPTRA	1,656,837
Energy tax receipts	1,590,871
Garden State Trust	1

General Budget, 2008
Total tax levy	$46,453,155
County levy	5,166,199
County taxes	4,885,543
County library	0
County health	0
County open space	280,655
School levy	21,793,924
Muni. levy	19,493,032
Misc. revenues	9,301,301

Taxes
	2006	2007	2008
General tax rate per $100	3.57	3.7	3.930
County equalization ratio	53.35	46.67	42.54
Net valuation taxable	$1,186,470,900	$1,185,151,116	$1,182,305,947
State equalized value	$2,543,044,099	$2,785,014,461	$2,758,261,143

See Introduction for an explanation of all data sources.

Demographics & Socio-Economic Characteristics
(2000 US Census, except as noted)

Population
1980*	4,752
1990*	4,227
2000	4,153
Male	2,005
Female	2,148
2007 (estimate)*	4,309
Population density	6,528.8

Race & Hispanic Origin, 2000
Race
White	3,983
Black/African American	15
American Indian/Alaska Native	0
Asian	55
Native Hawaiian/Pacific Islander	0
Other race	64
Two or more races	36
Hispanic origin, total	207
Mexican	30
Puerto Rican	15
Cuban	30
Other Hispanic	132

Age & Nativity, 2000
Under 5 years	231
18 years and over	3,322
21 years and over	3,215
65 years and over	716
85 years and over	75
Median age	38.3
Native-born	3,718
Foreign-born	435

Educational Attainment, 2000
Population 25 years and over	3,090
Less than 9th grade	4.1%
High school grad or higher	86.5%
Bachelor's degree or higher	27.6%
Graduate degree	11.2%

Income & Poverty, 1999
Per capita income	$26,944
Median household income	$52,571
Median family income	$64,053
Persons in poverty	210
H'holds receiving public assistance	11
H'holds receiving social security	572

Households, 2000
Total households	1,731
With persons under 18	487
With persons over 65	527
Family households	1,125
Single-person households	496
Persons per household	2.40
Persons per family	2.96

Labor & Employment
Total civilian labor force, 2007**	2,474
Unemployment rate	2.4%
Total civilian labor force, 2000	2,382
Unemployment rate	2.6%

Employed persons 16 years and over by occupation, 2000
Managers & professionals	893
Service occupations	243
Sales & office occupations	743
Farming, fishing & forestry	0
Construction & maintenance	245
Production & transportation	196
Self-employed persons	118

* US Census Bureau
** New Jersey Department of Labor

See Introduction for an explanation of all data sources.

General Information
Borough of Garwood
403 South Ave
Garwood, NJ 07027
908-789-0710

Website	www.garwood.org
Year of incorporation	1903
Land/water area (sq. miles)	0.66/0.00
Form of government	Borough

Government
Legislative Districts
US Congressional	7
State Legislative	21

Local Officials, 2009
Mayor	Dennis McCarthy
Manager	Christina M. Ariemma
Clerk	Christina M. Ariemma
CFO/Treasurer	Sandy Bruns
Tax Assessor	Annmarie Switzer
Tax Collector	Loretta J. Glogorski
Attorney	Robert Renaud
Building	Richard Belluscio
Comm Dev/Planning	NA
Engineering	Donald Guarriello
Public Works	Fred Corbitt
Police Chief	William Legg
Fire Chief	Ed Silver

Housing & Construction
Housing Units, 2000*
Total	1,782
Median rent	$913
Median SF home value	$181,500

Permits for New Residential Construction
	Units	Value
Total, 2006	72	$8,069,145
Single family	47	$7,500,965
Total, 2007	61	$5,133,840
Single family	22	$3,679,295

Real Property Valuation, 2008
	Parcels	Valuation
Total	1,499	$184,730,600
Vacant	62	1,762,100
Residential	1,288	131,712,300
Commercial	119	42,240,600
Industrial	22	6,815,600
Apartments	8	2,200,000
Farm land	0	0
Farm homestead	0	0

Average Property Value & Tax, 2008
Residential value	$102,261
Property tax	$7,499
Tax credit/rebate	$1,125

Public Library
Garwood Public Library
411 Third Ave
Garwood, NJ 07027
908-789-1670

Director	Carol A. Lombardo

Library statistics, 2007
Population served	4,153
Full-time/total staff	1/1

	Total	Per capita
Holdings	31,155	7.50
Revenues	$203,566	$49.02
Expenditures	$138,625	$33.38
Annual visits	9,218	2.22
Internet terminals/annual users	4/1,260	

Public Safety
Number of officers, 2007	16

Crime	2006	2007
Total crimes	52	61
Violent	3	2
Murder	0	0
Rape	0	0
Robbery	1	1
Aggravated assault	2	1
Non-violent	49	59
Burglary	11	3
Larceny	37	52
Vehicle theft	1	4
Domestic violence	6	3
Arson	0	0
Total crime rate	12.5	14.4
Violent	0.7	0.5
Non-violent	11.8	13.9

Public School District
(for school year 2007-08 except as noted)

Garwood School District
500 East Street
Garwood, NJ 07027
(908) 789-0165

Superintendent	Teresa Quigley (Actg)
Number of schools	2
Grade plan	K-8
Enrollment	413
Attendance rate, '06-07	95.6%
Dropout rate	NA
Students per teacher	12.5
Per pupil expenditure	$10,770
Median faculty salary	$52,530
Median administrator salary	$80,406
Grade 12 enrollment	NA
High school graduation rate	NA

Assessment test results
(percent scoring at proficient or advanced level)
	Language	Math
NJASK-Grade 3	89.2%	83.3%
GEPA-Grade 8	71.4%	79.2%
HSPA-High School	NA	NA

SAT Score Averages, 2006-07
Pct tested	Math	Verbal	Writing
NA	NA	NA	NA

Teacher Qualifications
Avg. years of experience	11
Highly-qualified teachers one subject/all subjects	100%/100%

No Child Left Behind
AYP, 2006-07	Meets Standards

Municipal Finance
State Aid Programs, 2009
Total aid	$625,583
CMPTRA	208,617
Energy tax receipts	407,582
Garden State Trust	0

General Budget, 2008
Total tax levy	$13,553,467
County levy	2,280,483
County taxes	2,181,017
County library	0
County health	0
County open space	99,465
School levy	6,465,870
Muni. levy	4,807,114
Misc. revenues	2,029,424

Taxes
	2006	2007	2008
General tax rate per $100	6.694	6.907	7.334
County equalization ratio	29.71	30.77	28.33
Net valuation taxable	$181,754,300	$181,931,178	$184,813,503
State equalized value	$590,779,485	$641,968,335	$684,270,310

Demographics & Socio-Economic Characteristics
(2000 US Census, except as noted)

Population
1980*	2,510
1990*	2,383
2000	2,435
Male	1,211
Female	1,224
2007 (estimate)*	2,427
Population density	1,103.2

Race & Hispanic Origin, 2000
Race
White	2,289
Black/African American	68
American Indian/Alaska Native	10
Asian	26
Native Hawaiian/Pacific Islander	0
Other race	18
Two or more races	24
Hispanic origin, total	58
Mexican	17
Puerto Rican	16
Cuban	0
Other Hispanic	25

Age & Nativity, 2000
Under 5 years	140
18 years and over	1,819
21 years and over	1,732
65 years and over	330
85 years and over	20
Median age	38.6
Native-born	2,334
Foreign-born	101

Educational Attainment, 2000
Population 25 years and over	1,650
Less than 9th grade	2.7%
High school grad or higher	84.7%
Bachelor's degree or higher	23.3%
Graduate degree	6.6%

Income & Poverty, 1999
Per capita income	$26,035
Median household income	$57,326
Median family income	$63,864
Persons in poverty	101
H'holds receiving public assistance	10
H'holds receiving social security	272

Households, 2000
Total households	829
With persons under 18	333
With persons over 65	222
Family households	665
Single-person households	138
Persons per household	2.91
Persons per family	3.28

Labor & Employment
Total civilian labor force, 2007**	1,399
Unemployment rate	3.7%
Total civilian labor force, 2000	1,319
Unemployment rate	3.9%

Employed persons 16 years and over by occupation, 2000
Managers & professionals	515
Service occupations	98
Sales & office occupations	388
Farming, fishing & forestry	0
Construction & maintenance	145
Production & transportation	121
Self-employed persons	58

* US Census Bureau
** New Jersey Department of Labor

General Information
Borough of Gibbsboro
49 Kirkwood Rd
Gibbsboro, NJ 08026
856-783-6655
Website	www.gibbsborotownhall.com
Year of incorporation	1924
Land/water area (sq. miles)	2.20/0.04
Form of government	Borough

Government
Legislative Districts
US Congressional	1
State Legislative	6

Local Officials, 2009
Mayor	Edward Campbell III
Manager/Admin	NA
Clerk	Anne Levy
Finance Dir	Deborah Jackson
Tax Assessor	Thomas G. Glock
Tax Collector	Carolyn Halbert
Attorney	John Jehl
Building	Raymond A. Hallworth
Comm Dev/Planning	NA
Engineering	Greg Fusco
Public Works	Wally Pratz
Police Chief	Joseph Mingori
Emerg/Fire Director	George Haaf

Housing & Construction
Housing Units, 2000*
Total	847
Median rent	$782
Median SF home value	$117,500

Permits for New Residential Construction
	Units	Value
Total, 2006	2	$483,045
Single family	2	$483,045
Total, 2007	2	$284,450
Single family	2	$284,450

Real Property Valuation, 2008
	Parcels	Valuation
Total	1,032	$179,941,400
Vacant	120	8,599,900
Residential	800	129,686,100
Commercial	97	28,951,700
Industrial	11	12,284,600
Apartments	1	225,000
Farm land	2	24,700
Farm homestead	1	169,400

Average Property Value & Tax, 2008
Residential value	$162,117
Property tax	$6,644
Tax credit/rebate	$1,040

Public Library
Gibbsboro Public Library
49 Kirkwood Rd
Gibbsboro, NJ 08026
856-435-3656
Director	Jodie A Favat

Library statistics, 2007
Population served	2,435
Full-time/total staff	0/0

	Total	Per capita
Holdings	12,562	5.16
Revenues	$32,099	$13.18
Expenditures	$21,447	$8.81
Annual visits	7,305	3.00
Internet terminals/annual users	2/140	

Public Safety
Number of officers, 2007 7
Crime	2006	2007
Total crimes	54	39
Violent	5	1
Murder	0	0
Rape	0	1
Robbery	2	0
Aggravated assault	3	0
Non-violent	49	38
Burglary	17	12
Larceny	31	26
Vehicle theft	1	0
Domestic violence	22	6
Arson	5	1
Total crime rate	21.9	15.9
Violent	2.0	0.4
Non-violent	19.9	15.5

Public School District
(for school year 2007-08 except as noted)

Gibbsboro School District
37 Kirkwood Road
Gibbsboro, NJ 08026
(856) 783-1140
Superintendent	James Lavender
Number of schools	1
Grade plan	K-8
Enrollment	259
Attendance rate, '06-07	96.3%
Dropout rate	NA
Students per teacher	8.2
Per pupil expenditure	$14,671
Median faculty salary	$51,932
Median administrator salary	$73,325
Grade 12 enrollment	NA
High school graduation rate	NA

Assessment test results
(percent scoring at proficient or advanced level)
	Language	Math
NJASK-Grade 3	97.0%	97.0%
GEPA-Grade 8	78.6%	82.1%
HSPA-High School	NA	NA

SAT Score Averages, 2006-07
Pct tested	Math	Verbal	Writing
NA	NA	NA	NA

Teacher Qualifications
Avg. years of experience	13
Highly-qualified teachers one subject/all subjects	100%/96.0%

No Child Left Behind
AYP, 2006-07	Meets Standards

Municipal Finance
State Aid Programs, 2009
Total aid	$364,581
CMPTRA	61,916
Energy tax receipts	293,550
Garden State Trust	0

General Budget, 2008
Total tax levy	$7,394,711
County levy	1,827,544
County taxes	1,651,068
County library	118,805
County health	0
County open space	57,672
School levy	4,128,980
Muni. levy	1,438,186
Misc. revenues	1,353,594

Taxes	2006	2007	2008
General tax rate per $100	3.665	3.9	4.099
County equalization ratio	78	66.95	63.00
Net valuation taxable	$184,170,200	$180,413,454	$180,435,040
State equalized value	$275,634,801	$286,079,816	$280,645,283

See Introduction for an explanation of all data sources.

Demographics & Socio-Economic Characteristics
(2000 US Census, except as noted)

Population
1980*	14,574
1990*	15,614
2000	19,068
Male	9,126
Female	9,942
2007 (estimate)*	19,588
Population density	2,126.8

Race & Hispanic Origin, 2000
Race
White	14,212
Black/African American	3,712
American Indian/Alaska Native	32
Asian	441
Native Hawaiian/Pacific Islander	17
Other race	282
Two or more races	372
Hispanic origin, total	728
Mexican	62
Puerto Rican	468
Cuban	28
Other Hispanic	170

Age & Nativity, 2000
Under 5 years	1,216
18 years and over	14,859
21 years and over	12,445
65 years and over	1,866
85 years and over	176
Median age	27.1
Native-born	18,310
Foreign-born	758

Educational Attainment, 2000
Population 25 years and over	9,943
Less than 9th grade	5.9%
High school grad or higher	82.1%
Bachelor's degree or higher	24.0%
Graduate degree	7.8%

Income & Poverty, 1999
Per capita income	$18,113
Median household income	$44,992
Median family income	$55,246
Persons in poverty	2,525
H'holds receiving public assistance	153
H'holds receiving social security	1,508

Households, 2000
Total households	6,225
With persons under 18	2,225
With persons over 65	1,386
Family households	4,049
Single-person households	1,472
Persons per household	2.66
Persons per family	3.17

Labor & Employment
Total civilian labor force, 2007**	10,209
Unemployment rate	5.8%
Total civilian labor force, 2000	10,552
Unemployment rate	19.2%

Employed persons 16 years and over by occupation, 2000
Managers & professionals	2,903
Service occupations	1,479
Sales & office occupations	2,348
Farming, fishing & forestry	6
Construction & maintenance	675
Production & transportation	1,114
Self-employed persons	236

‡ Branch of county library
* US Census Bureau
** New Jersey Department of Labor

General Information
Borough of Glassboro
1 S Main St
Glassboro, NJ 08028
856-881-9230
Website	www.glassboroonline.com
Year of incorporation	1920
Land/water area (sq. miles)	9.21/0.01
Form of government	Borough

Government
Legislative Districts
US Congressional	1
State Legislative	4

Local Officials, 2009
Mayor	Leo McCabe
Manager	Joseph Brigandi Jr
Clerk	Patricia A. Frontino
Finance Dir	Josephine Myers
Tax Assessor	Thomas Colavecchio
Tax Collector	Rosemary A. Turner
Attorney	Timothy Scaffidi
Building	R. Angelo Martilini
Planning	R. Angelo Martilini
Engineering	Mark Brunermer
Public Works	Russell Clark
Police Chief	Alex Fanfarillo
Emerg/Fire Director	Ralph Johnson

Housing & Construction
Housing Units, 2000*
Total	6,555
Median rent	$567
Median SF home value	$114,100

Permits for New Residential Construction
	Units	Value
Total, 2006	71	$7,146,467
Single family	71	$7,146,467
Total, 2007	71	$6,734,606
Single family	67	$6,694,606

Real Property Valuation, 2008
	Parcels	Valuation
Total	6,093	$671,355,700
Vacant	1,035	22,372,600
Residential	4,717	506,459,500
Commercial	254	103,369,100
Industrial	9	8,641,200
Apartments	31	28,549,700
Farm land	34	146,500
Farm homestead	13	1,817,100

Average Property Value & Tax, 2008
Residential value	$107,458
Property tax	$5,491
Tax credit/rebate	$998

Public Library
Glassboro Public Library‡
2 Center St
Glassboro, NJ 08028
856-881-0001
Branch Librarian	Carol Wolf

Library statistics, 2007
see Gloucester County profile
for library system statistics

Public Safety
Number of officers, 2007	45

Crime	2006	2007
Total crimes	815	745
Violent	77	85
Murder	0	4
Rape	14	6
Robbery	26	37
Aggravated assault	37	38
Non-violent	738	660
Burglary	133	148
Larceny	579	475
Vehicle theft	26	37
Domestic violence	195	248
Arson	6	10
Total crime rate	42.2	38.5
Violent	4.0	4.4
Non-violent	38.3	34.1

Public School District
(for school year 2007-08 except as noted)

Glassboro School District
Beach Admin Bldg, Joseph L Bowe Blvd
Glassboro, NJ 08028
(856) 652-2700
Superintendent	Leonard Fitts (Int)
Number of schools	5
Grade plan	K-12
Enrollment	2,347
Attendance rate, '06-07	94.7%
Dropout rate	2.7%
Students per teacher	11.1
Per pupil expenditure	$13,026
Median faculty salary	$53,088
Median administrator salary	$104,797
Grade 12 enrollment	147
High school graduation rate	87.5%

Assessment test results
(percent scoring at proficient or advanced level)
	Language	Math
NJASK-Grade 3	71.5%	74.7%
GEPA-Grade 8	49.7%	70.8%
HSPA-High School	70.1%	85.2%

SAT Score Averages, 2006-07
Pct tested	Math	Verbal	Writing
68%	484	463	448

Teacher Qualifications
Avg. years of experience	11
Highly-qualified teachers one subject/all subjects	100%/100%

No Child Left Behind
AYP, 2006-07	Meets Standards

Municipal Finance
State Aid Programs, 2009
Total aid	$3,036,345
CMPTRA	1,062,483
Energy tax receipts	1,956,376
Garden State Trust	2,177

General Budget, 2008
Total tax levy	$34,504,150
County levy	6,859,945
County taxes	5,919,958
County library	476,070
County health	0
County open space	463,917
School levy	17,044,274
Muni. levy	10,599,931
Misc. revenues	9,631,939

Taxes	2006	2007	2008
General tax rate per $100	4.687	4.901	5.110
County equalization ratio	72.17	64.01	58.88
Net valuation taxable	$653,071,600	$670,666,018	$675,284,417
State equalized value	$1,024,845,459	$1,136,140,926	$1,200,854,550

See Introduction for an explanation of all data sources.

Demographics & Socio-Economic Characteristics

(2000 US Census, except as noted)

Population
1980*	834
1990*	1,665
2000	1,902
Male	929
Female	973
2007 (estimate)*	1,958
Population density	1,255.1

Race & Hispanic Origin, 2000
Race
White	1,820
Black/African American	17
American Indian/Alaska Native	2
Asian	28
Native Hawaiian/Pacific Islander	2
Other race	11
Two or more races	22
Hispanic origin, total	65
Mexican	9
Puerto Rican	23
Cuban	7
Other Hispanic	26

Age & Nativity, 2000
Under 5 years	135
18 years and over	1,421
21 years and over	1,374
65 years and over	145
85 years and over	17
Median age	35.4
Native-born	1,810
Foreign-born	92

Educational Attainment, 2000
Population 25 years and over	1,304
Less than 9th grade	3.0%
High school grad or higher	91.0%
Bachelor's degree or higher	35.3%
Graduate degree	11.5%

Income & Poverty, 1999
Per capita income	$28,647
Median household income	$59,917
Median family income	$75,369
Persons in poverty	84
H'holds receiving public assistance	11
H'holds receiving social security	148

Households, 2000
Total households	805
With persons under 18	275
With persons over 65	123
Family households	474
Single-person households	275
Persons per household	2.33
Persons per family	3.07

Labor & Employment
Total civilian labor force, 2007**	1,203
Unemployment rate	2.2%
Total civilian labor force, 2000	1,079
Unemployment rate	2.0%

Employed persons 16 years and over by occupation, 2000
Managers & professionals	486
Service occupations	134
Sales & office occupations	269
Farming, fishing & forestry	5
Construction & maintenance	112
Production & transportation	51
Self-employed persons	47

* US Census Bureau
** New Jersey Department of Labor

General Information
Borough of Glen Gardner
PO Box 307
Glen Gardner, NJ 08826
908-537-4748
Website	www.glengardnernj.org
Year of incorporation	1919
Land/water area (sq. miles)	1.56/0.00
Form of government	Borough

Government

Legislative Districts
US Congressional	7
State Legislative	23

Local Officials, 2009
Mayor	Stanley Kovach
Manager/Admin	NA
Clerk	Marilyn Hodgson
Finance Dir	Nancy Smith
Tax Assessor	Robert Vance
Tax Collector	Diane Laudenbach
Attorney	J. Peter Jost
Building	Charles Herring
Planning	Judy Bass
Engineering	Robert J. Clerico
Public Works	John Jordan
Police Chief	NA
Fire Chief	Steve Apgar

Housing & Construction

Housing Units, 2000*
Total	829
Median rent	$866
Median SF home value	$170,700

Permits for New Residential Construction
	Units	Value
Total, 2006	0	$0
Single family	0	$0
Total, 2007	1	$121,500
Single family	1	$121,500

Real Property Valuation, 2008
	Parcels	Valuation
Total	795	$139,357,941
Vacant	43	1,363,104
Residential	707	128,991,800
Commercial	16	4,748,000
Industrial	1	568,600
Apartments	4	1,205,200
Farm land	15	50,937
Farm homestead	9	2,430,300

Average Property Value & Tax, 2008
Residential value	$183,550
Property tax	$5,118
Tax credit/rebate	$877

Public Library

No public municipal library

Library statistics, 2007
Population served	NA
Full-time/total staff	NA/NA

	Total	Per capita
Holdings	NA	NA
Revenues	NA	NA
Expenditures	NA	NA
Annual visits	NA	NA
Internet terminals/annual users	NA/NA	

Public Safety
Number of officers, 2007	0

Crime	2006	2007
Total crimes	14	13
Violent	0	2
Murder	0	0
Rape	0	0
Robbery	0	0
Aggravated assault	0	2
Non-violent	14	11
Burglary	6	9
Larceny	7	2
Vehicle theft	1	0
Domestic violence	2	9
Arson	0	0
Total crime rate	7.0	6.5
Violent	0.0	1.0
Non-violent	7.0	5.5

Public School District
(for school year 2007-08 except as noted)

Glen Gardner Borough School District
P.O. Box 158
Glen Gardner, NJ 08826

No schools in district

Per pupil expenditure	NA
Median faculty salary	NA
Median administrator salary	NA
Grade 12 enrollment	NA
High school graduation rate	NA

Assessment test results
(percent scoring at proficient or advanced level)
	Language	Math
NJASK-Grade 3	NA	NA
GEPA-Grade 8	NA	NA
HSPA-High School	NA	NA

SAT Score Averages, 2006-07
Pct tested	Math	Verbal	Writing
NA	NA	NA	NA

Teacher Qualifications
Avg. years of experience	NA
Highly-qualified teachers one subject/all subjects	NA/NA

No Child Left Behind
AYP, 2006-07	NA

Municipal Finance

State Aid Programs, 2009
Total aid	$154,411
CMPTRA	34,980
Energy tax receipts	115,409
Garden State Trust	145

General Budget, 2008
Total tax levy	$3,892,811
County levy	683,201
County taxes	571,814
County library	49,656
County health	0
County open space	61,731
School levy	2,583,981
Muni. levy	625,628
Misc. revenues	528,102

Taxes	2006	2007	2008
General tax rate per $100	2.68	2.68	2.789
County equalization ratio	76.49	67.36	68.04
Net valuation taxable	$138,740,940	$139,490,475	$139,609,415
State equalized value	$188,826,566	$198,131,648	$196,557,913

See Introduction for an explanation of all data sources.

Demographics & Socio-Economic Characteristics
(2000 US Census, except as noted)

Population
1980*	7,855
1990*	7,076
2000	7,271
Male	3,540
Female	3,731
2007 (estimate)*	6,751
Population density	5,274.2

Race & Hispanic Origin, 2000
Race
White	6,484
Black/African American	362
American Indian/Alaska Native	11
Asian	243
Native Hawaiian/Pacific Islander	0
Other race	72
Two or more races	99
Hispanic origin, total	251
Mexican	22
Puerto Rican	63
Cuban	36
Other Hispanic	130

Age & Nativity, 2000
Under 5 years	679
18 years and over	5,039
21 years and over	4,885
65 years and over	757
85 years and over	102
Median age	37.8
Native-born	6,617
Foreign-born	654

Educational Attainment, 2000
Population 25 years and over	4,727
Less than 9th grade	2.2%
High school grad or higher	96.2%
Bachelor's degree or higher	65.8%
Graduate degree	31.0%

Income & Poverty, 1999
Per capita income	$48,456
Median household income	$105,638
Median family income	$120,650
Persons in poverty	219
H'holds receiving public assistance	36
H'holds receiving social security	520

Households, 2000
Total households	2,458
With persons under 18	1,170
With persons over 65	555
Family households	1,978
Single-person households	410
Persons per household	2.95
Persons per family	3.33

Labor & Employment
Total civilian labor force, 2007**	3,683
Unemployment rate	2.7%
Total civilian labor force, 2000	3,551
Unemployment rate	2.8%

Employed persons 16 years and over by occupation, 2000
Managers & professionals	2,125
Service occupations	205
Sales & office occupations	924
Farming, fishing & forestry	0
Construction & maintenance	117
Production & transportation	82
Self-employed persons	224

General Information
Borough of Glen Ridge
825 Bloomfield Ave
Glen Ridge, NJ 07028
973-748-8400
Website	www.glenridgenj.org
Year of incorporation	1895
Land/water area (sq. miles)	1.28/0.00
Form of government	Borough

Government
Legislative Districts
US Congressional	8
State Legislative	34

Local Officials, 2009
Mayor	Peter A. Hughes
Manager	Michael Rohal
Clerk	Michael J. Rohal
Finance Dir	Irene C.W. Wheat
Tax Assessor	William Merdinger
Tax Collector	Donna Altschuler
Attorney	John Malyska
Building	Ronald Young
Planning	Michael Zichelli
Engineering	Michael Rohal
Public Works	Jay Weisenbach
Police Chief	John Magnier
Emerg/Fire Director	Chris Landers

Housing & Construction
Housing Units, 2000*
Total	2,490
Median rent	$1,058
Median SF home value	$264,700

Permits for New Residential Construction
	Units	Value
Total, 2006	0	$0
Single family	0	$0
Total, 2007	2	$43,800
Single family	2	$43,800

Real Property Valuation, 2008
	Parcels	Valuation
Total	2,318	$1,442,702,600
Vacant	7	1,339,900
Residential	2,290	1,349,284,700
Commercial	18	66,372,700
Industrial	0	0
Apartments	3	25,705,300
Farm land	0	0
Farm homestead	0	0

Average Property Value & Tax, 2008
Residential value	$589,207
Property tax	$15,826
Tax credit/rebate	$1,473

Public Library
Glen Ridge Public Library
240 Ridgewood Ave
Glen Ridge, NJ 07028
973-748-5482
Director	John A. Sitnik

Library statistics, 2007
Population served	7,271
Full-time/total staff	2/9

	Total	Per capita
Holdings	42,524	5.85
Revenues	$670,940	$92.28
Expenditures	$664,436	$91.38
Annual visits	85,277	11.73
Internet terminals/annual users	9/6,842	

Public Safety
Number of officers, 2007	28

Crime	2006	2007
Total crimes	215	160
Violent	5	10
Murder	0	0
Rape	2	0
Robbery	2	7
Aggravated assault	1	3
Non-violent	210	150
Burglary	46	22
Larceny	153	116
Vehicle theft	11	12
Domestic violence	15	29
Arson	1	1
Total crime rate	30.6	23.2
Violent	0.7	1.4
Non-violent	29.9	21.7

Public School District
(for school year 2007-08 except as noted)

Glen Ridge School District
12 High Street
Glen Ridge, NJ 07028
(973) 429-8302
Superintendent	John Mucciolo
Number of schools	4
Grade plan	K-12
Enrollment	1,876
Attendance rate, '06-07	96.4%
Dropout rate	0.0%
Students per teacher	11.4
Per pupil expenditure	$12,710
Median faculty salary	$55,821
Median administrator salary	$128,467
Grade 12 enrollment	111
High school graduation rate	100.0%

Assessment test results
(percent scoring at proficient or advanced level)
	Language	Math
NJASK-Grade 3	97.3%	94.6%
GEPA-Grade 8	84.4%	93.3%
HSPA-High School	92.7%	96.8%

SAT Score Averages, 2006-07
Pct tested	Math	Verbal	Writing
95%	573	561	550

Teacher Qualifications
Avg. years of experience	8
Highly-qualified teachers one subject/all subjects	100%/100%

No Child Left Behind
AYP, 2006-07	Meets Standards

Municipal Finance
State Aid Programs, 2009
Total aid	$539,468
CMPTRA	120,332
Energy tax receipts	401,603
Garden State Trust	0

General Budget, 2008
Total tax levy	$38,765,121
County levy	6,103,628
County taxes	5,867,945
County library	0
County health	0
County open space	235,684
School levy	24,171,677
Muni. levy	8,489,816
Misc. revenues	3,736,425

Taxes
	2006	2007	2008
General tax rate per $100	15.06	15.61	2.687
County equalization ratio	18.1	16.64	92.55
Net valuation taxable	$233,908,600	$234,629,485	$1,443,195,591
State equalized value	$1,405,786,305	$1,520,173,506	$1,582,577,211

* US Census Bureau
** New Jersey Department of Labor

See Introduction for an explanation of all data sources.

Demographics & Socio-Economic Characteristics
(2000 US Census, except as noted)

Population
1980*	11,497
1990*	10,883
2000	11,546
Male	5,622
Female	5,924
2007 (estimate)*	11,232
Population density	4,129.4

Race & Hispanic Origin, 2000
Race
White	10,399
Black/African American	209
American Indian/Alaska Native	18
Asian	748
Native Hawaiian/Pacific Islander	2
Other race	71
Two or more races	99
Hispanic origin, total	314
Mexican	37
Puerto Rican	99
Cuban	57
Other Hispanic	121

Age & Nativity, 2000
Under 5 years	962
18 years and over	8,151
21 years and over	7,945
65 years and over	1,579
85 years and over	193
Median age	39.5
Native-born	10,270
Foreign-born	1,276

Educational Attainment, 2000
Population 25 years and over	7,714
Less than 9th grade	1.3%
High school grad or higher	96.0%
Bachelor's degree or higher	61.1%
Graduate degree	24.3%

Income & Poverty, 1999
Per capita income	$45,091
Median household income	$104,192
Median family income	$111,280
Persons in poverty	278
H'holds receiving public assistance	7
H'holds receiving social security	1,135

Households, 2000
Total households	3,977
With persons under 18	1,785
With persons over 65	1,121
Family households	3,322
Single-person households	586
Persons per household	2.89
Persons per family	3.22

Labor & Employment
Total civilian labor force, 2007**	6,045
Unemployment rate	2.5%
Total civilian labor force, 2000	5,757
Unemployment rate	3.0%

Employed persons 16 years and over by occupation, 2000
Managers & professionals	3,501
Service occupations	289
Sales & office occupations	1,426
Farming, fishing & forestry	0
Construction & maintenance	159
Production & transportation	208
Self-employed persons	374

* US Census Bureau
** New Jersey Department of Labor

General Information
Borough of Glen Rock
Harding Plaza
Municipal Building
Glen Rock, NJ 07452
201-670-3956

Website	glenrocknj.net
Year of incorporation	1894
Land/water area (sq. miles)	2.72/0.01
Form of government	Borough

Government
Legislative Districts
US Congressional	5
State Legislative	35

Local Officials, 2009
Mayor	John VanKeuren
Manager	Lenora Benjamin
Clerk	Jacqueline Scalia
Finance Dir	Lenora Benjamin
Tax Assessor	Steven Rubenstein
Tax Collector	Patricia McCormick
Attorney	Robert Garibaldi Jr
Building	Brian Frugis
Comm Dev/Planning	NA
Engineering	Stantec Consulting Services
Public Works	Bob Tirserio
Police Chief	Steven Cherry
Emerg/Fire Director	Pete Flannery

Housing & Construction
Housing Units, 2000*
Total	4,024
Median rent	$1,188
Median SF home value	$316,900

Permits for New Residential Construction
	Units	Value
Total, 2006	6	$1,934,380
Single family	6	$1,934,380
Total, 2007	8	$2,883,157
Single family	8	$2,883,157

Real Property Valuation, 2008
	Parcels	Valuation
Total	4,008	$2,293,325,000
Vacant	61	14,024,400
Residential	3,839	2,088,397,700
Commercial	100	162,754,700
Industrial	8	28,148,200
Apartments	0	0
Farm land	0	0
Farm homestead	0	0

Average Property Value & Tax, 2008
Residential value	$543,995
Property tax	$12,577
Tax credit/rebate	$1,506

Public Library
Glen Rock Public Library
315 Rock Rd
Glen Rock, NJ 07452
201-670-3970

Director	Roz Pelcyger

Library statistics, 2007
Population served	11,546
Full-time/total staff	3/10

	Total	Per capita
Holdings	95,036	8.23
Revenues	$1,118,195	$96.85
Expenditures	$970,890	$84.09
Annual visits	192,950	16.71
Internet terminals/annual users	11/21,000	

Public Safety
Number of officers, 2007	21

Crime	2006	2007
Total crimes	74	62
Violent	1	2
Murder	0	0
Rape	0	0
Robbery	1	1
Aggravated assault	0	1
Non-violent	73	60
Burglary	15	12
Larceny	53	47
Vehicle theft	5	1
Domestic violence	5	6
Arson	0	0
Total crime rate	6.5	5.4
Violent	0.1	0.2
Non-violent	6.4	5.3

Public School District
(for school year 2007-08 except as noted)

Glen Rock School District
620 Harristown Road
Glen Rock, NJ 07452
(201) 445-7700

Superintendent	George Connelly
Number of schools	6
Grade plan	K-12
Enrollment	2,479
Attendance rate, '06-07	95.3%
Dropout rate	0.1%
Students per teacher	10.5
Per pupil expenditure	$15,241
Median faculty salary	$59,842
Median administrator salary	$115,973
Grade 12 enrollment	170
High school graduation rate	100.0%

Assessment test results
(percent scoring at proficient or advanced level)
	Language	Math
NJASK-Grade 3	98.9%	97.2%
GEPA-Grade 8	82.3%	90.8%
HSPA-High School	91.7%	94.2%

SAT Score Averages, 2006-07
Pct tested	Math	Verbal	Writing
107%	571	532	540

Teacher Qualifications
Avg. years of experience	10
Highly-qualified teachers one subject/all subjects	100%/100%

No Child Left Behind
AYP, 2006-07	Meets Standards

Municipal Finance
State Aid Programs, 2009
Total aid	$1,345,588
CMPTRA	222,462
Energy tax receipts	1,079,395
Garden State Trust	0

General Budget, 2008
Total tax levy	$53,052,588
County levy	4,801,282
County taxes	4,541,365
County library	0
County health	0
County open space	259,917
School levy	37,021,246
Muni. levy	11,230,060
Misc. revenues	4,615,355

Taxes
	2006	2007	2008
General tax rate per $100	2.66	2.23	2.313
County equalization ratio	82.24	92.08	88.57
Net valuation taxable	$1,835,057,000	$2,282,055,921	$2,294,648,041
State equalized value	$2,454,731,801	$2,576,375,827	$2,659,326,054

See Introduction for an explanation of all data sources.

Demographics & Socio-Economic Characteristics

(2000 US Census, except as noted)

Population
1980* 13,121
1990* 12,649
2000 11,484
  Male 5,594
  Female 5,890
2007 (estimate)* 11,377
  Population density 5,171.4

Race & Hispanic Origin, 2000
Race
  White 11,155
  Black/African American 79
  American Indian/Alaska Native 21
  Asian 78
  Native Hawaiian/Pacific Islander 4
  Other race 74
  Two or more races 73
Hispanic origin, total 216
  Mexican 15
  Puerto Rican 142
  Cuban 10
  Other Hispanic 49

Age & Nativity, 2000
Under 5 years 736
18 years and over 8,435
21 years and over 7,953
65 years and over 1,582
85 years and over 136
  Median age 36.4
Native-born 11,366
Foreign-born 109

Educational Attainment, 2000
Population 25 years and over 7,438
Less than 9th grade 6.7%
High school grad or higher 72.4%
Bachelor's degree or higher 8.2%
Graduate degree 1.7%

Income & Poverty, 1999
Per capita income $16,912
Median household income $36,855
Median family income $46,038
Persons in poverty 1,155
H'holds receiving public assistance ... 148
H'holds receiving social security ... 1,458

Households, 2000
Total households 4,213
  With persons under 18 1,556
  With persons over 65 1,248
  Family households 2,840
  Single-person households 1,145
Persons per household 2.72
Persons per family 3.32

Labor & Employment
Total civilian labor force, 2007** ... 5,772
  Unemployment rate 7.9%
Total civilian labor force, 2000 ... 5,482
  Unemployment rate 8.5%
Employed persons 16 years and over by occupation, 2000
  Managers & professionals 1,010
  Service occupations 769
  Sales & office occupations 1,500
  Farming, fishing & forestry 0
  Construction & maintenance 550
  Production & transportation 1,188
Self-employed persons 203

* US Census Bureau
** New Jersey Department of Labor

General Information
City of Gloucester
512 Monmouth St
Gloucester City, NJ 08030
856-456-0205
Website .... www.cityofgloucester.org
Year of incorporation 1868
Land/water area (sq. miles) 2.20/0.63
Form of government .... Special Charter

Government
Legislative Districts
US Congressional 1
State Legislative 5

Local Officials, 2009
Mayor .... William P. James
Manager .... Paul Kain
Clerk .... Paul Kain
Finance Dir .... Frank Robertson
Tax Assessor .... John Dymond
Tax Collector .... Joanne Marone
Attorney .... John Kearney
Building .... Robert Scouler
Planning .... Regina Dunphy
Engineering .... Remington & Vernick
Public Works .... James Johnson
Police Chief .... William Crothers
Emerg/Fire Director .... Brian Hagan

Housing & Construction
Housing Units, 2000*
Total 4,604
Median rent $625
Median SF home value $79,500

Permits for New Residential Construction
	Units	Value
Total, 2006	18	$1,105,904
Single family	18	$1,105,904
Total, 2007	55	$5,748,889
Single family	55	$5,748,889

Real Property Valuation, 2008
	Parcels	Valuation
Total	4,224	$355,104,800
Vacant	251	6,845,200
Residential	3,655	262,553,900
Commercial	272	74,025,900
Industrial	27	7,026,700
Apartments	19	4,653,100
Farm land	0	0
Farm homestead	0	0

Average Property Value & Tax, 2008
Residential value $71,834
Property tax $3,209
Tax credit/rebate $752

Public Library
Gloucester City Library
50 N Railroad Ave
Gloucester City, NJ 08030
856-456-4181
Director .... Elizabeth Egan

Library statistics, 2007
Population served 11,484
Full-time/total staff 1/4

	Total	Per capita
Holdings	68,384	5.95
Revenues	$584,536	$50.90
Expenditures	$561,506	$48.89
Annual visits	86,672	7.55
Internet terminals/annual users	...38/34,236	

Public Safety
Number of officers, 2007 30
Crime	2006	2007
Total crimes	334	356
Violent	33	39
Murder	1	0
Rape	3	8
Robbery	16	15
Aggravated assault	13	16
Non-violent	301	317
Burglary	55	65
Larceny	219	219
Vehicle theft	27	33
Domestic violence	256	240
Arson	0	0
Total crime rate	28.8	31.0
Violent	2.8	3.4
Non-violent	26.0	27.6

Public School District
(for school year 2007-08 except as noted)

Gloucester City School District
520 Cumberland Street
Gloucester City, NJ 08030
(856) 456-9394
Superintendent .... Paul Spaventa
Number of schools 3
Grade plan K-12
Enrollment 2,125
Attendance rate, '06-07 .... 94.8%
Dropout rate 1.1%
Students per teacher 9.0
Per pupil expenditure $18,387
Median faculty salary $50,690
Median administrator salary $108,317
Grade 12 enrollment 142
High school graduation rate 94.0%

Assessment test results
(percent scoring at proficient or advanced level)
	Language	Math
NJASK-Grade 3	85.4%	85.4%
GEPA-Grade 8	49.7%	62.5%
HSPA-High School	78.4%	86.2%

SAT Score Averages, 2006-07
Pct tested	Math	Verbal	Writing
47%	476	461	469

Teacher Qualifications
Avg. years of experience 8
Highly-qualified teachers
  one subject/all subjects 100%/100%

No Child Left Behind
AYP, 2006-07 .... Meets Standards

Municipal Finance
State Aid Programs, 2009
Total aid $3,186,788
  CMPTRA 910,611
  Energy tax receipts 2,276,177
  Garden State Trust 0

General Budget, 2008
Total tax levy $15,993,256
  County levy 3,865,774
    County taxes 3,735,598
    County library 0
    County health 0
    County open space 130,176
  School levy 3,415,974
  Muni. levy 8,711,508
Misc. revenues 7,772,800

Taxes
	2006	2007	2008
General tax rate per $100	3.923	4.125	4.467
County equalization ratio	78.46	65.95	57.57
Net valuation taxable	$347,356,800	$352,666,849	$358,046,217
State equalized value	$530,576,891	$610,162,041	$653,078,363

See Introduction for an explanation of all data sources.

Demographics & Socio-Economic Characteristics†

(2000 US Census, except as noted)

Population
1980*	45,156
1990*	53,797
2000	64,350
Male	31,309
Female	33,041
2007 (estimate)*	65,016
Population density	2,800.0

Race & Hispanic Origin, 2000
Race
White	53,484
Black/African American	7,432
American Indian/Alaska Native	100
Asian	1,688
Native Hawaiian/Pacific Islander	16
Other race	715
Two or more races	915
Hispanic origin, total	1,962
Mexican	248
Puerto Rican	1,160
Cuban	81
Other Hispanic	473

Age & Nativity, 2000
Under 5 years	4,405
18 years and over	47,057
21 years and over	44,616
65 years and over	6,052
85 years and over	536
Median age	34.6
Native-born	61,187
Foreign-born	3,128

Educational Attainment, 2000
Population 25 years and over	41,473
Less than 9th grade	2.8%
High school grad or higher	85.8%
Bachelor's degree or higher	22.0%
Graduate degree	6.1%

Income & Poverty, 1999
Per capita income	$22,604
Median household income	$54,280
Median family income	$62,992
Persons in poverty	3,934
H'holds receiving public assistance	523
H'holds receiving social security	4,983

Households, 2000
Total households	23,150
With persons under 18	9,456
With persons over 65	4,351
Family households	16,878
Single-person households	4,948
Persons per household	2.75
Persons per family	3.24

Labor & Employment
Total civilian labor force, 2007**	36,566
Unemployment rate	2.7%
Total civilian labor force, 2000	34,739
Unemployment rate	4.9%

Employed persons 16 years and over by occupation, 2000
Managers & professionals	11,214
Service occupations	4,410
Sales & office occupations	10,334
Farming, fishing & forestry	0
Construction & maintenance	3,332
Production & transportation	3,753
Self-employed persons	1,485

General Information
Gloucester Township
1261 Chews Landing Rd
PO Box 8
Blackwood, NJ 08012
856-228-4000
Website	www.glotwp.com
Year of incorporation	1695
Land/water area (sq. miles)	23.22/0.10
Form of government	Mayor-Council

Government
Legislative Districts
US Congressional	1
State Legislative	4

Local Officials, 2009
Mayor	Cindy Rau-Hatton
Manager	Thomas Cardis
Clerk	Rosemary Di Josie
Finance Dir	Dorothea Jones
Tax Assessor	Charles G. Palumbo Jr
Tax Collector	Sandra Ferguson
Attorney	David Carlamere
Building	Bernie Shepherd
Planning	Kenneth Lechner
Engineering	Remington & Vernick
Public Works	Gabe Busa
Police Chief	Edward Smith
Fire/Emergency Dir	NA

Housing & Construction
Housing Units, 2000*
Total	24,257
Median rent	$706
Median SF home value	$116,100

Permits for New Residential Construction
	Units	Value
Total, 2006	20	$646,057
Single family	20	$646,057
Total, 2007	5	$710,600
Single family	5	$710,600

Real Property Valuation, 2008
	Parcels	Valuation
Total	21,610	$2,439,795,400
Vacant	1,264	25,716,200
Residential	19,690	2,140,088,300
Commercial	505	151,720,300
Industrial	32	32,694,200
Apartments	26	85,262,700
Farm land	65	456,400
Farm homestead	28	3,857,300

Average Property Value & Tax, 2008
Residential value	$108,730
Property tax	$5,440
Tax credit/rebate	$1,037

Public Library
Gloucester Township Branch Library‡
15 S Black Horse Pike
Blackwood, NJ 08012
856-228-0022
Branch Librarian	Ann Ackroyd

Library statistics, 2007
see Camden County profile
for library system statistics

Public Safety
Number of officers, 2007	116

Crime	2006	2007
Total crimes	1,831	1,882
Violent	178	173
Murder	0	0
Rape	24	7
Robbery	49	47
Aggravated assault	105	119
Non-violent	1,653	1,709
Burglary	362	439
Larceny	1,171	1,154
Vehicle theft	120	116
Domestic violence	585	597
Arson	21	11
Total crime rate	27.5	28.7
Violent	2.7	2.6
Non-violent	24.8	26.0

Public School District
(for school year 2007-08 except as noted)

Gloucester Township School District
17 Erial Road
Blackwood, NJ 08012
(856) 227-1400
Superintendent	Thomas D. Seddon
Number of schools	11
Grade plan	K-8
Enrollment	7,619
Attendance rate, '06-07	95.4%
Dropout rate	NA
Students per teacher	11.8
Per pupil expenditure	$10,938
Median faculty salary	$53,375
Median administrator salary	$86,685
Grade 12 enrollment	NA
High school graduation rate	NA

Assessment test results
(percent scoring at proficient or advanced level)
	Language	Math
NJASK-Grade 3	89.7%	87.9%
GEPA-Grade 8	73.7%	87.2%
HSPA-High School	NA	NA

SAT Score Averages, 2006-07
Pct tested	Math	Verbal	Writing
NA	NA	NA	NA

Teacher Qualifications
Avg. years of experience	11
Highly-qualified teachers one subject/all subjects	100%/100%

No Child Left Behind
AYP, 2006-07	Meets Standards

Municipal Finance§
State Aid Programs, 2009
Total aid	$6,429,216
CMPTRA	1,930,168
Energy tax receipts	4,370,214
Garden State Trust	255

General Budget, 2008
Total tax levy	$122,354,785
County levy	30,705,037
County taxes	27,749,495
County library	1,989,683
County health	0
County open space	965,859
School levy	64,358,767
Muni. levy	27,290,980
Misc. revenues	17,271,179

Taxes	2006	2007	2008
General tax rate per $100	4.88	5.035	5.004
County equalization ratio	60.84	54.89	50.84
Net valuation taxable	$2,387,157,200	$2,425,179,677	$2,445,316,031
State equalized value	$4,355,545,598	$4,764,364,192	$4,820,589,508

---

† see Appendix C for American Community Survey data
‡ Branch of county library
* US Census Bureau
** New Jersey Department of Labor
§ State Fiscal Year July 1–June 30

178 **The New Jersey Municipal Data Book**

See Introduction for an explanation of all data sources.

Demographics & Socio-Economic Characteristics
(2000 US Census, except as noted)

Population
1980*	4,640
1990*	4,460
2000	5,654
Male	2,704
Female	2,950
2007 (estimate)*	6,920
Population density	1,510.9

Race & Hispanic Origin, 2000
Race
White	5,000
Black/African American	95
American Indian/Alaska Native	4
Asian	452
Native Hawaiian/Pacific Islander	2
Other race	40
Two or more races	61
Hispanic origin, total	231
Mexican	7
Puerto Rican	65
Cuban	48
Other Hispanic	111

Age & Nativity, 2000
Under 5 years	371
18 years and over	4,278
21 years and over	4,160
65 years and over	884
85 years and over	157
Median age	39.9
Native-born	4,912
Foreign-born	742

Educational Attainment, 2000
Population 25 years and over	3,984
Less than 9th grade	6.9%
High school grad or higher	88.3%
Bachelor's degree or higher	39.7%
Graduate degree	14.9%

Income & Poverty, 1999
Per capita income	$37,290
Median household income	$80,644
Median family income	$87,744
Persons in poverty	130
H'holds receiving public assistance	14
H'holds receiving social security	490

Households, 2000
Total households	1,893
With persons under 18	735
With persons over 65	449
Family households	1,508
Single-person households	301
Persons per household	2.84
Persons per family	3.20

Labor & Employment
Total civilian labor force, 2007**	3,327
Unemployment rate	2.8%
Total civilian labor force, 2000	2,939
Unemployment rate	3.0%

Employed persons 16 years and over by occupation, 2000
Managers & professionals	1,326
Service occupations	220
Sales & office occupations	802
Farming, fishing & forestry	0
Construction & maintenance	242
Production & transportation	261
Self-employed persons	187

* US Census Bureau
** New Jersey Department of Labor

See Introduction for an explanation of all data sources.

General Information
Township of Green Brook
111 Greenbrook Rd
Green Brook, NJ 08812
732-968-1023
Website	www.greenbrooktwp,org
Year of incorporation	1932
Land/water area (sq. miles)	4.58/0.00
Form of government	Township

Government
Legislative Districts
US Congressional	7
State Legislative	22

Local Officials, 2009
Mayor	Melonie K. Marano
Manager	Kathryn Kitchener
Clerk	Kelly G. Cupit
Finance Dir	Raymond S. Murray
Tax Assessor	Tom Efstathiou
Tax Collector	Raymond S. Murray
Attorney	Louis Rainone
Building	George DeLucca
Comm Dev/Planning	NA
Engineering	C. Richard Roseberry
Public Works	C. Richard Roseberry
Police Chief	Martin Rasmussen
Emerg/Fire Director	Richard Connelly

Housing & Construction
Housing Units, 2000*
Total	1,916
Median rent	$1,148
Median SF home value	$242,500

Permits for New Residential Construction
	Units	Value
Total, 2006	3	$544,904
Single family	3	$544,904
Total, 2007	2	$340,000
Single family	2	$340,000

Real Property Valuation, 2008
	Parcels	Valuation
Total	2,704	$1,466,991,000
Vacant	162	23,767,700
Residential	2,351	1,213,487,100
Commercial	173	209,698,400
Industrial	9	13,671,500
Apartments	8	6,365,200
Farm land	1	1,100
Farm homestead	0	0

Average Property Value & Tax, 2008
Residential value	$516,158
Property tax	$10,508
Tax credit/rebate	$1,222

Public Library
No public municipal library

Library statistics, 2007
Population served	NA
Full-time/total staff	NA/NA

	Total	Per capita
Holdings	NA	NA
Revenues	NA	NA
Expenditures	NA	NA
Annual visits	NA	NA
Internet terminals/annual users	NA/NA	

Public Safety
Number of officers, 2007	22

Crime	2006	2007
Total crimes	156	142
Violent	10	5
Murder	0	0
Rape	3	2
Robbery	0	3
Aggravated assault	7	0
Non-violent	146	137
Burglary	35	20
Larceny	97	100
Vehicle theft	14	17
Domestic violence	67	43
Arson	0	0
Total crime rate	23.3	20.7
Violent	1.5	0.7
Non-violent	21.8	20.0

Public School District
(for school year 2007-08 except as noted)

Green Brook Township School District
132 Jefferson Ave
Green Brook, NJ 08812
(732) 968-1171
Superintendent	Stephanie Bilenker
Number of schools	2
Grade plan	K-8
Enrollment	975
Attendance rate, '06-07	96.1%
Dropout rate	NA
Students per teacher	10.2
Per pupil expenditure	$13,025
Median faculty salary	$47,314
Median administrator salary	$113,367
Grade 12 enrollment	NA
High school graduation rate	NA

Assessment test results
(percent scoring at proficient or advanced level)
	Language	Math
NJASK-Grade 3	92.8%	94.6%
GEPA-Grade 8	83.9%	92.4%
HSPA-High School	NA	NA

SAT Score Averages, 2006-07
Pct tested	Math	Verbal	Writing
NA	NA	NA	NA

Teacher Qualifications
Avg. years of experience	6
Highly-qualified teachers one subject/all subjects	100%/100%

No Child Left Behind
AYP, 2006-07	Meets Standards

Municipal Finance
State Aid Programs, 2009
Total aid	$733,353
CMPTRA	0
Energy tax receipts	714,918
Garden State Trust	94

General Budget, 2008
Total tax levy	$29,885,033
County levy	5,195,278
County taxes	4,169,453
County library	564,307
County health	0
County open space	461,518
School levy	19,206,994
Muni. levy	5,482,762
Misc. revenues	2,564,092

Taxes
	2006	2007	2008
General tax rate per $100	1.81	1.96	2.036
County equalization ratio	107.68	98.87	95.33
Net valuation taxable	$1,442,878,300	$1,455,709,427	$1,467,984,470
State equalized value	$1,460,288,372	$1,526,975,444	$1,575,187,053

Demographics & Socio-Economic Characteristics
(2000 US Census, except as noted)

Population
1980*	2,450
1990*	2,709
2000	3,220
Male	1,647
Female	1,573
2007 (estimate)*	3,539
Population density	218.7

Race & Hispanic Origin, 2000
Race
White	3,107
Black/African American	30
American Indian/Alaska Native	1
Asian	31
Native Hawaiian/Pacific Islander	0
Other race	9
Two or more races	42
Hispanic origin, total	103
Mexican	6
Puerto Rican	40
Cuban	12
Other Hispanic	45

Age & Nativity, 2000
Under 5 years	254
18 years and over	2,227
21 years and over	2,137
65 years and over	193
85 years and over	19
Median age	36.3
Native-born	2,948
Foreign-born	264

Educational Attainment, 2000
Population 25 years and over	2,079
Less than 9th grade	2.2%
High school grad or higher	93.9%
Bachelor's degree or higher	34.2%
Graduate degree	10.7%

Income & Poverty, 1999
Per capita income	$34,127
Median household income	$84,847
Median family income	$89,788
Persons in poverty	52
H'holds receiving public assistance	0
H'holds receiving social security	150

Households, 2000
Total households	1,046
With persons under 18	499
With persons over 65	144
Family households	890
Single-person households	115
Persons per household	3.07
Persons per family	3.34

Labor & Employment
Total civilian labor force, 2007**	1,935
Unemployment rate	3.6%
Total civilian labor force, 2000	1,729
Unemployment rate	2.8%

Employed persons 16 years and over by occupation, 2000
Managers & professionals	788
Service occupations	117
Sales & office occupations	480
Farming, fishing & forestry	4
Construction & maintenance	158
Production & transportation	134
Self-employed persons	57

General Information
Township of Green
PO Box 65
150 Kennedy Rd
Tranquility, NJ 07879
908-852-9333
Website	www.greentwp.com
Year of incorporation	1824
Land/water area (sq. miles)	16.18/0.13
Form of government	Township

Government
Legislative Districts
US Congressional	5
State Legislative	24

Local Officials, 2009
Mayor	Daniel Conkling
Manager	A. Denise Stagnari
Clerk	Linda Peralta
Finance Dir	Linda Padula
Tax Assessor	Penny Holenstein
Tax Collector	Karen Ferrone (Actg)
Attorney	William Hinkes
Building	Edward Vanderberg
Comm Dev/Planning	NA
Engineering	John Miller
Public Works	Watson Perigo Jr
Police Chief	NA
Emerg/Fire Director	Richard Porzilli

Housing & Construction
Housing Units, 2000*
Total	1,069
Median rent	$968
Median SF home value	$182,500

Permits for New Residential Construction
	Units	Value
Total, 2006	20	$4,898,076
Single family	20	$4,898,076
Total, 2007	32	$6,886,540
Single family	32	$6,886,540

Real Property Valuation, 2008
	Parcels	Valuation
Total	1,542	$543,848,300
Vacant	113	13,574,000
Residential	1,118	464,033,800
Commercial	24	17,347,900
Industrial	1	6,142,000
Apartments	0	0
Farm land	191	1,618,000
Farm homestead	95	41,132,600

Average Property Value & Tax, 2008
Residential value	$416,460
Property tax	$9,133
Tax credit/rebate	$1,237

Public Library
No public municipal library

Library statistics, 2007
Population served	NA
Full-time/total staff	NA/NA

	Total	Per capita
Holdings	NA	NA
Revenues	NA	NA
Expenditures	NA	NA
Annual visits	NA	NA
Internet terminals/annual users	NA/NA	

Public Safety
Number of officers, 2007	0

Crime	2006	2007
Total crimes	22	23
Violent	2	3
Murder	0	0
Rape	0	0
Robbery	0	0
Aggravated assault	2	3
Non-violent	20	20
Burglary	8	6
Larceny	11	12
Vehicle theft	1	2
Domestic violence	0	13
Arson	0	0
Total crime rate	6.2	6.5
Violent	0.6	0.8
Non-violent	5.6	5.6

Public School District
(for school year 2007-08 except as noted)

Green Township School District
P.O. Box 14
Greendell, NJ 07839
(973) 300-3800
Superintendent	Barry Worman (Int)
Number of schools	1
Grade plan	K-8
Enrollment	525
Attendance rate, '06-07	95.5%
Dropout rate	NA
Students per teacher	11.0
Per pupil expenditure	$12,958
Median faculty salary	$53,569
Median administrator salary	$79,155
Grade 12 enrollment	NA
High school graduation rate	NA

Assessment test results
(percent scoring at proficient or advanced level)
	Language	Math
NJASK-Grade 3	93.0%	91.2%
GEPA-Grade 8	83.0%	95.0%
HSPA-High School	NA	NA

SAT Score Averages, 2006-07
Pct tested	Math	Verbal	Writing
NA	NA	NA	NA

Teacher Qualifications
Avg. years of experience	6
Highly-qualified teachers one subject/all subjects	100%/97.5%

No Child Left Behind
AYP, 2006-07	Meets Standards

Municipal Finance
State Aid Programs, 2009
Total aid	$269,976
CMPTRA	68,677
Energy tax receipts	187,497
Garden State Trust	6,682

General Budget, 2008
Total tax levy	$11,945,030
County levy	2,206,206
County taxes	1,851,444
County library	156,050
County health	54,807
County open space	143,904
School levy	7,278,639
Muni. levy	2,460,185
Misc. revenues	1,151,073

Taxes
	2006	2007	2008
General tax rate per $100	2.02	2.1	2.194
County equalization ratio	108.17	100.1	95.02
Net valuation taxable	$525,549,300	$537,484,284	$544,686,028
State equalized value	$525,971,726	$565,608,983	$569,597,715

* US Census Bureau
** New Jersey Department of Labor

See Introduction for an explanation of all data sources.

Demographics & Socio-Economic Characteristics

(2000 US Census, except as noted)

Population
1980*	973
1990*	911
2000	847
Male	420
Female	427
2007 (estimate)*	886
Population density	48.8

Race & Hispanic Origin, 2000
Race
White	762
Black/African American	43
American Indian/Alaska Native	22
Asian	2
Native Hawaiian/Pacific Islander	0
Other race	1
Two or more races	17
Hispanic origin, total	13
Mexican	4
Puerto Rican	1
Cuban	0
Other Hispanic	8

Age & Nativity, 2000
Under 5 years	47
18 years and over	661
21 years and over	629
65 years and over	126
85 years and over	13
Median age	43.4
Native-born	838
Foreign-born	4

Educational Attainment, 2000
Population 25 years and over	627
Less than 9th grade	3.8%
High school grad or higher	86.3%
Bachelor's degree or higher	22.0%
Graduate degree	7.2%

Income & Poverty, 1999
Per capita income	$22,233
Median household income	$52,188
Median family income	$56,111
Persons in poverty	67
H'holds receiving public assistance	6
H'holds receiving social security	94

Households, 2000
Total households	326
With persons under 18	104
With persons over 65	92
Family households	245
Single-person households	71
Persons per household	2.60
Persons per family	3.05

Labor & Employment
Total civilian labor force, 2007**	505
Unemployment rate	2.9%
Total civilian labor force, 2000	460
Unemployment rate	4.3%

Employed persons 16 years and over by occupation, 2000
Managers & professionals	185
Service occupations	52
Sales & office occupations	98
Farming, fishing & forestry	5
Construction & maintenance	39
Production & transportation	61
Self-employed persons	61

* US Census Bureau
** New Jersey Department of Labor

See Introduction for an explanation of all data sources.

General Information
Township of Greenwich
PO Box 64
Greenwich, NJ 08323
856-455-4677
Website	(county website)
Year of incorporation	1748
Land/water area (sq. miles)	18.16/0.72
Form of government	Township

Government

Legislative Districts
US Congressional	2
State Legislative	3

Local Officials, 2009
Mayor	Theodore Kiefer
Manager/Admin	NA
Clerk	Elaine Hancock
Finance Dir	Susan Cummins
Tax Assessor	Lois Mazza
Tax Collector	Elizabeth Wallendar
Attorney	Thomas Seeley
Building	Gordon Gross
Planning	Dean Roork
Engineering	Alexander Churchill
Public Works	NA
Police Chief	NA
Emerg/Fire Director	Wade McFarland

Housing & Construction

Housing Units, 2000*
Total	361
Median rent	$742
Median SF home value	$112,000

Permits for New Residential Construction
	Units	Value
Total, 2006	4	$459,988
Single family	4	$459,988
Total, 2007	5	$493,989
Single family	5	$493,989

Real Property Valuation, 2008
	Parcels	Valuation
Total	644	$62,791,600
Vacant	119	4,132,100
Residential	302	42,603,100
Commercial	10	2,814,800
Industrial	0	0
Apartments	0	0
Farm land	152	3,199,600
Farm homestead	61	10,042,000

Average Property Value & Tax, 2008
Residential value	$145,028
Property tax	$4,719
Tax credit/rebate	$935

Public Library

No public municipal library

Library statistics, 2007
Population served	NA
Full-time/total staff	NA/NA

	Total	Per capita
Holdings	NA	NA
Revenues	NA	NA
Expenditures	NA	NA
Annual visits	NA	NA
Internet terminals/annual users	NA/NA	

Public Safety
Number of officers, 2007	0

Crime	2006	2007
Total crimes	12	5
Violent	0	0
Murder	0	0
Rape	0	0
Robbery	0	0
Aggravated assault	0	0
Non-violent	12	5
Burglary	2	1
Larceny	7	3
Vehicle theft	3	1
Domestic violence	0	3
Arson	0	0
Total crime rate	13.7	5.6
Violent	0.0	0.0
Non-violent	13.7	5.6

Public School District
(for school year 2007-08 except as noted)

Greenwich Township School District
839 Ye Greate Street
Greenwich, NJ 08323
(856) 451-5513
Superintendent	Nancy Nosta
Number of schools	1
Grade plan	K-8
Enrollment	82
Attendance rate, '06-07	94.1%
Dropout rate	NA
Students per teacher	7.5
Per pupil expenditure	$17,142
Median faculty salary	$44,868
Median administrator salary	$78,898
Grade 12 enrollment	NA
High school graduation rate	NA

Assessment test results
(percent scoring at proficient or advanced level)
	Language	Math
NJASK-Grade 3	NA	NA
GEPA-Grade 8	NA	NA
HSPA-High School	NA	NA

SAT Score Averages, 2006-07
Pct tested	Math	Verbal	Writing
NA	NA	NA	NA

Teacher Qualifications
Avg. years of experience	10

Highly-qualified teachers
one subject/all subjects	100%/100%

No Child Left Behind
AYP, 2006-07 .... Meets Standards

Municipal Finance

State Aid Programs, 2009
Total aid	$136,386
CMPTRA	29,419
Energy tax receipts	75,492
Garden State Trust	839

General Budget, 2008
Total tax levy	$2,050,100
County levy	695,486
County taxes	657,394
County library	0
County health	30,770
County open space	7,322
School levy	1,115,820
Muni. levy	238,794
Misc. revenues	387,783

Taxes
	2006	2007	2008
General tax rate per $100	3.03	3.344	3.257
County equalization ratio	106.96	91.24	86.79
Net valuation taxable	$61,565,600	$62,572,212	$63,006,214
State equalized value	$67,706,004	$72,063,366	$73,577,857

Demographics & Socio-Economic Characteristics

(2000 US Census, except as noted)

Population
1980*	5,404
1990*	5,102
2000	4,879
Male	2,382
Female	2,497
2007 (estimate)*	4,989
Population density	535.3

Race & Hispanic Origin, 2000
Race
White	4,613
Black/African American	162
American Indian/Alaska Native	5
Asian	33
Native Hawaiian/Pacific Islander	1
Other race	13
Two or more races	52
Hispanic origin, total	75
Mexican	19
Puerto Rican	21
Cuban	3
Other Hispanic	32

Age & Nativity, 2000
Under 5 years	281
18 years and over	3,767
21 years and over	3,594
65 years and over	884
85 years and over	92
Median age	40.1
Native-born	4,702
Foreign-born	177

Educational Attainment, 2000
Population 25 years and over	3,394
Less than 9th grade	5.2%
High school grad or higher	86.9%
Bachelor's degree or higher	17.4%
Graduate degree	2.9%

Income & Poverty, 1999
Per capita income	$24,791
Median household income	$53,651
Median family income	$60,565
Persons in poverty	174
H'holds receiving public assistance	21
H'holds receiving social security	700

Households, 2000
Total households	1,866
With persons under 18	640
With persons over 65	642
Family households	1,393
Single-person households	413
Persons per household	2.61
Persons per family	3.05

Labor & Employment
Total civilian labor force, 2007**	2,864
Unemployment rate	3.6%
Total civilian labor force, 2000	2,424
Unemployment rate	3.1%

Employed persons 16 years and over by occupation, 2000
Managers & professionals	666
Service occupations	264
Sales & office occupations	652
Farming, fishing & forestry	10
Construction & maintenance	312
Production & transportation	446
Self-employed persons	82

‡ Branch of county library
* US Census Bureau
** New Jersey Department of Labor

General Information
Township of Greenwich
420 Washington St
Gibbstown, NJ 08027
856-423-1038
Website	www.greenwichtwp.com
Year of incorporation	1695
Land/water area (sq. miles)	9.32/2.74
Form of government	Small Municipality

Government
Legislative Districts
US Congressional	1
State Legislative	3

Local Officials, 2009
Mayor	George Shivery Jr
Manager	Horace Spoto
Clerk	Lori Biermann
Finance Dir	Merrie Schmidt
Tax Assessor	Brian Schneider
Tax Collector	Barbara Hoffmann
Attorney	Thomas Ward
Building	Bob DeAngelo
Planning	Raymond Shivers
Engineering	James Clancy
Public Works	John Daly
Police Chief	Jeffrey Godfrey
Emerg/Fire Director	Ken Chew

Housing & Construction
Housing Units, 2000*
Total	1,944
Median rent	$778
Median SF home value	$114,400

Permits for New Residential Construction
	Units	Value
Total, 2006	9	$988,400
Single family	9	$988,400
Total, 2007	8	$879,854
Single family	8	$879,854

Real Property Valuation, 2008
	Parcels	Valuation
Total	2,161	$546,389,701
Vacant	196	8,429,087
Residential	1,827	186,019,750
Commercial	61	27,480,500
Industrial	19	322,704,264
Apartments	3	410,300
Farm land	46	491,600
Farm homestead	9	854,200

Average Property Value & Tax, 2008
Residential value	$101,783
Property tax	$3,497
Tax credit/rebate	$816

Public Library
Greenwich Branch Library‡
415 Swedesboro Rd
Gibbstown, NJ 08027
856-423-0684
Branch Librarian	Pat Woodruff

Library statistics, 2007
see Gloucester County profile
for library system statistics

Public Safety
Number of officers, 2007	18

Crime	2006	2007
Total crimes	144	150
Violent	3	7
Murder	0	0
Rape	0	1
Robbery	1	3
Aggravated assault	2	3
Non-violent	141	143
Burglary	24	29
Larceny	114	113
Vehicle theft	3	1
Domestic violence	79	106
Arson	1	0
Total crime rate	28.9	30.2
Violent	0.6	1.4
Non-violent	28.3	28.8

Public School District
(for school year 2007-08 except as noted)

Greenwich Township School District
415 Swedesboro Rd
Gibbstown, NJ 08027
(856) 224-4920
Superintendent	Robert Suessmuth (Int)
Number of schools	2
Grade plan	K-8
Enrollment	535
Attendance rate, '06-07	95.5%
Dropout rate	NA
Students per teacher	9.4
Per pupil expenditure	$16,842
Median faculty salary	$75,066
Median administrator salary	$94,169
Grade 12 enrollment	NA
High school graduation rate	NA

Assessment test results
(percent scoring at proficient or advanced level)
	Language	Math
NJASK-Grade 3	92.9%	92.8%
GEPA-Grade 8	75.5%	91.9%
HSPA-High School	NA	NA

SAT Score Averages, 2006-07
Pct tested	Math	Verbal	Writing
NA	NA	NA	NA

Teacher Qualifications
Avg. years of experience	17
Highly-qualified teachers one subject/all subjects	100%/100%

No Child Left Behind
AYP, 2006-07	Meets Standards

Municipal Finance
State Aid Programs, 2009
Total aid	$949,751
CMPTRA	298,577
Energy tax receipts	627,399
Garden State Trust	219

General Budget, 2008
Total tax levy	$22,273,367
County levy	5,813,339
County taxes	5,016,761
County library	403,439
County health	0
County open space	393,138
School levy	8,859,387
Muni. levy	7,600,642
Misc. revenues	3,983,343

Taxes
	2006	2007	2008
General tax rate per $100	3.292	3.488	3.436
County equalization ratio	69.98	62.19	63.33
Net valuation taxable	$544,612,501	$615,649,387	$648,346,517
State equalized value	$966,782,679	$931,714,968	$1,078,873,857

See Introduction for an explanation of all data sources.

Demographics & Socio-Economic Characteristics
(2000 US Census, except as noted)

Population
1980*	1,738
1990*	1,899
2000	4,365
Male	2,154
Female	2,211
2007 (estimate)*	5,130
Population density	486.3

Race & Hispanic Origin, 2000
Race
White	4,071
Black/African American	108
American Indian/Alaska Native	12
Asian	97
Native Hawaiian/Pacific Islander	3
Other race	25
Two or more races	49
Hispanic origin, total	166
Mexican	10
Puerto Rican	64
Cuban	4
Other Hispanic	88

Age & Nativity, 2000
Under 5 years	527
18 years and over	2,897
21 years and over	2,823
65 years and over	270
85 years and over	27
Median age	33.9
Native-born	4,111
Foreign-born	254

Educational Attainment, 2000
Population 25 years and over	2,763
Less than 9th grade	2.6%
High school grad or higher	91.6%
Bachelor's degree or higher	39.0%
Graduate degree	11.1%

Income & Poverty, 1999
Per capita income	$32,886
Median household income	$87,613
Median family income	$92,579
Persons in poverty	106
H'holds receiving public assistance	20
H'holds receiving social security	226

Households, 2000
Total households	1,421
With persons under 18	752
With persons over 65	197
Family households	1,224
Single-person households	162
Persons per household	3.07
Persons per family	3.34

Labor & Employment
Total civilian labor force, 2007**	2,407
Unemployment rate	2.5%
Total civilian labor force, 2000	2,132
Unemployment rate	2.3%

Employed persons 16 years and over by occupation, 2000
Managers & professionals	1,012
Service occupations	192
Sales & office occupations	570
Farming, fishing & forestry	0
Construction & maintenance	148
Production & transportation	161
Self-employed persons	84

* US Census Bureau
** New Jersey Department of Labor

See Introduction for an explanation of all data sources.

General Information
Township of Greenwich
321 Greenwich St
Stewartsville, NJ 08886
908-859-0909
Website	greenwichtownship.com
Year of incorporation	1738
Land/water area (sq. miles)	10.55/0.00
Form of government	Township

Government
Legislative Districts
US Congressional	5
State Legislative	23

Local Officials, 2009
Mayor	Elaine Emiliani
Manager	Kim Viscomi
Clerk	Kim Viscomi
Finance Dir	Grace Brennan
Tax Assessor	Eloise Hagman
Tax Collector	Gordon Kobler
Attorney	J. Peter Jost
Building	NA
Comm Dev/Planning	NA
Engineering	Michael Finelli
Public Works	John Howell
Police Chief	Richard Guzzo
Emerg/Fire Director	Joseph Mecsey III

Housing & Construction
Housing Units, 2000*
Total	1,477
Median rent	$871
Median SF home value	$233,300

Permits for New Residential Construction
	Units	Value
Total, 2006	2	$716,000
Single family	2	$716,000
Total, 2007	0	$0
Single family	0	$0

Real Property Valuation, 2008
	Parcels	Valuation
Total	2,041	$591,351,690
Vacant	70	2,631,200
Residential	1,758	473,284,390
Commercial	52	86,629,100
Industrial	5	14,947,300
Apartments	0	0
Farm land	107	2,186,100
Farm homestead	49	11,673,600

Average Property Value & Tax, 2008
Residential value	$268,377
Property tax	$6,829
Tax credit/rebate	$1,055

Public Library
uses Phillipsburg Public Library
200 Frost Ave
Phillipsburg, NJ 08865
908-454-3712
Director	Ann DeRenzis

Library statistics, 2007
Population served	15,166
Full-time/total staff	4/11

	Total	Per capita
Holdings	99,751	6.58
Revenues	$1,249,400	$82.38
Expenditures	$1,376,158	$90.74
Annual visits	132,609	8.74
Internet terminals/annual users	15/34,306	

Public Safety
Number of officers, 2007	12

Crime	2006	2007
Total crimes	133	120
Violent	7	8
Murder	0	0
Rape	1	3
Robbery	2	0
Aggravated assault	4	5
Non-violent	126	112
Burglary	12	11
Larceny	109	99
Vehicle theft	5	2
Domestic violence	53	74
Arson	0	0
Total crime rate	25.4	22.9
Violent	1.3	1.5
Non-violent	24.1	21.4

Public School District
(for school year 2007-08 except as noted)

Greenwich Township School District
642 South Main Street
Stewartsville, NJ 08886
(908) 859-2022
Superintendent	Maria Eppolite
Number of schools	2
Grade plan	K-8
Enrollment	999
Attendance rate, '06-07	95.8%
Dropout rate	NA
Students per teacher	10.9
Per pupil expenditure	$10,246
Median faculty salary	$41,960
Median administrator salary	$99,683
Grade 12 enrollment	NA
High school graduation rate	NA

Assessment test results
(percent scoring at proficient or advanced level)
	Language	Math
NJASK-Grade 3	86.4%	89.6%
GEPA-Grade 8	73.2%	88.9%
HSPA-High School	NA	NA

SAT Score Averages, 2006-07
Pct tested	Math	Verbal	Writing
NA	NA	NA	NA

Teacher Qualifications
Avg. years of experience	6
Highly-qualified teachers one subject/all subjects	95.5%/95.5%

No Child Left Behind
AYP, 2006-07	Meets Standards

Municipal Finance
State Aid Programs, 2009
Total aid	$406,892
CMPTRA	6,853
Energy tax receipts	389,675
Garden State Trust	276

General Budget, 2008
Total tax levy	$15,091,265
County levy	5,040,367
County taxes	4,111,762
County library	431,256
County health	0
County open space	497,349
School levy	7,589,797
Muni. levy	2,461,101
Misc. revenues	1,809,744

Taxes
	2006	2007	2008
General tax rate per $100	2.5	2.52	2.545
County equalization ratio	75.82	73.24	71.63
Net valuation taxable	$577,371,990	$592,987,564	$593,094,739
State equalized value	$789,966,140	$827,204,783	$830,547,099

Demographics & Socio-Economic Characteristics

(2000 US Census, except as noted)

Population
1980*	7,340
1990*	8,268
2000	10,807
Male	5,205
Female	5,602
2007 (estimate)*	10,601
Population density	55,794.7

Race & Hispanic Origin, 2000
Race
White	7,022
Black/African American	412
American Indian/Alaska Native	41
Asian	789
Native Hawaiian/Pacific Islander	1
Other race	1,775
Two or more races	767
Hispanic origin, total	5,871
Mexican	233
Puerto Rican	608
Cuban	1,203
Other Hispanic	3,827

Age & Nativity, 2000
Under 5 years	695
18 years and over	8,520
21 years and over	8,175
65 years and over	1,273
85 years and over	170
Median age	35.5
Native-born	5,434
Foreign-born	5,259

Educational Attainment, 2000
Population 25 years and over	7,566
Less than 9th grade	11.9%
High school grad or higher	75.0%
Bachelor's degree or higher	29.8%
Graduate degree	13.4%

Income & Poverty, 1999
Per capita income	$27,931
Median household income	$44,515
Median family income	$47,440
Persons in poverty	1,377
H'holds receiving public assistance	128
H'holds receiving social security	969

Households, 2000
Total households	4,493
With persons under 18	1,344
With persons over 65	964
Family households	2,620
Single-person households	1,576
Persons per household	2.38
Persons per family	3.13

Labor & Employment
Total civilian labor force, 2007**	5,396
Unemployment rate	4.0%
Total civilian labor force, 2000	5,596
Unemployment rate	6.7%

Employed persons 16 years and over by occupation, 2000
Managers & professionals	1,798
Service occupations	714
Sales & office occupations	1,548
Farming, fishing & forestry	0
Construction & maintenance	331
Production & transportation	828
Self-employed persons	276

General Information

Town of Guttenberg
6808 Park Ave
Guttenberg, NJ 07093
201-868-2315

Website	www.guttenbergnj.org
Year of incorporation	1859
Land/water area (sq. miles)	0.19/0.04
Form of government	Town

Government

Legislative Districts
US Congressional	13
State Legislative	33

Local Officials, 2009
Mayor	Gerald R. Drasheff
Manager	Linda Martin
Clerk	Albert Cabrera
CFO	Vincent Buono
Tax Assessor	James Terhune
Tax Collector	Nicholas Goldsack
Attorney	Charles Daglian
Building	Vincent Prieto
Comm Dev/Planning	NA
Engineering	Rick McGrath
Public Works	(vacant)
Police Chief	Michael Caliguiro
Emerg Mgmt Dir	James D'Amore

Housing & Construction

Housing Units, 2000*
Total	4,650
Median rent	$794
Median SF home value	$150,200

Permits for New Residential Construction
	Units	Value
Total, 2006	46	$4,551,789
Single family	8	$756,072
Total, 2007	43	$3,625,709
Single family	4	$616,929

Real Property Valuation, 2008
	Parcels	Valuation
Total	2,637	$405,216,000
Vacant	39	4,940,700
Residential	2,337	317,815,600
Commercial	128	35,146,600
Industrial	59	12,645,400
Apartments	74	34,667,700
Farm land	0	0
Farm homestead	0	0

Average Property Value & Tax, 2008
Residential value	$135,993
Property tax	$7,396
Tax credit/rebate	$989

Public Library

No public municipal library

Library statistics, 2007
Population served	NA
Full-time/total staff	NA/NA

	Total	Per capita
Holdings	NA	NA
Revenues	NA	NA
Expenditures	NA	NA
Annual visits	NA	NA
Internet terminals/annual users	NA/NA	

Public Safety

Number of officers, 2007	22

Crime	2006	2007
Total crimes	238	154
Violent	49	39
Murder	0	0
Rape	2	0
Robbery	28	23
Aggravated assault	19	16
Non-violent	189	115
Burglary	75	30
Larceny	90	74
Vehicle theft	24	11
Domestic violence	62	67
Arson	3	0
Total crime rate	21.9	14.4
Violent	4.5	3.6
Non-violent	17.4	10.7

Public School District

(for school year 2007-08 except as noted)

Guttenberg School District
301 69th Street
Guttenberg, NJ 07093
(201) 861-3100

Superintendent	Joseph Ramos
Number of schools	1
Grade plan	K-8
Enrollment	956
Attendance rate, '06-07	95.0%
Dropout rate	NA
Students per teacher	13.5
Per pupil expenditure	$9,903
Median faculty salary	$47,332
Median administrator salary	$100,055
Grade 12 enrollment	NA
High school graduation rate	NA

Assessment test results
(percent scoring at proficient or advanced level)
	Language	Math
NJASK-Grade 3	82.3%	81.5%
GEPA-Grade 8	52.7%	76.8%
HSPA-High School	NA	NA

SAT Score Averages, 2006-07
Pct tested	Math	Verbal	Writing
NA	NA	NA	NA

Teacher Qualifications
Avg. years of experience	7
Highly-qualified teachers one subject/all subjects	100%/100%

No Child Left Behind
AYP, 2006-07	Meets Standards

Municipal Finance§

State Aid Programs, 2009
Total aid	$933,167
CMPTRA	548,511
Energy tax receipts	370,659
Garden State Trust	0

General Budget, 2008
Total tax levy	$22,786,258
County levy	4,369,849
County taxes	4,255,020
County library	0
County health	0
County open space	114,828
School levy	8,772,735
Muni. levy	9,643,675
Misc. revenues	4,585,823

Taxes
	2006	2007	2008
General tax rate per $100	5.102	5.394	5.622
County equalization ratio	46.61	38.2	35.45
Net valuation taxable	$405,518,500	$407,727,414	$405,345,833
State equalized value	$1,061,731,929	$1,149,902,010	$1,138,057,381

---

* US Census Bureau
** New Jersey Department of Labor
§ State Fiscal Year July 1–June 30

See Introduction for an explanation of all data sources.

Demographics & Socio-Economic Characteristics
(2000 US Census, except as noted)

Population
1980*	36,039
1990*	37,049
2000	42,677
Male	21,199
Female	21,478
2007 (estimate)*	43,062
Population density	10,451.9

Race & Hispanic Origin, 2000
Race
White	22,451
Black/African American	10,518
American Indian/Alaska Native	191
Asian	3,181
Native Hawaiian/Pacific Islander	23
Other race	4,144
Two or more races	2,169
Hispanic origin, total	11,061
Mexican	340
Puerto Rican	1,371
Cuban	298
Other Hispanic	9,052

Age & Nativity, 2000
Under 5 years	2,465
18 years and over	34,906
21 years and over	33,607
65 years and over	5,329
85 years and over	768
Median age	36.2
Native-born	28,231
Foreign-born	14,446

Educational Attainment, 2000
Population 25 years and over	31,518
Less than 9th grade	8.5%
High school grad or higher	79.7%
Bachelor's degree or higher	29.1%
Graduate degree	10.7%

Income & Poverty, 1999
Per capita income	$26,856
Median household income	$49,316
Median family income	$56,953
Persons in poverty	3,867
H'holds receiving public assistance	417
H'holds receiving social security	4,019

Households, 2000
Total households	18,113
With persons under 18	4,503
With persons over 65	3,924
Family households	9,549
Single-person households	7,206
Persons per household	2.26
Persons per family	3.08

Labor & Employment
Total civilian labor force, 2007**	24,216
Unemployment rate	4.6%
Total civilian labor force, 2000	23,543
Unemployment rate	6.8%

Employed persons 16 years and over by occupation, 2000
Managers & professionals	7,817
Service occupations	3,262
Sales & office occupations	6,534
Farming, fishing & forestry	4
Construction & maintenance	1,344
Production & transportation	2,992
Self-employed persons	926

* US Census Bureau
** New Jersey Department of Labor

See Introduction for an explanation of all data sources.

General Information
City of Hackensack
65 Central Ave
Hackensack, NJ 07601
201-646-3980

Website	www.hackensack.org
Year of incorporation	1921
Land/water area (sq. miles)	4.12/0.19
Form of government	Municipal Mgr 1923

Government
Legislative Districts
US Congressional	9
State Legislative	37

Local Officials, 2009
Mayor	Michael R. Melfi
Manager	Stephen Lo Iacono
Clerk	Debra Heck
Finance Dir	Ross Bobal
Tax Assessor	Arthur Carlson
Tax Collector	Elisa Coccia
Attorney	Joseph C. Zisa
Building	Joseph Mellone
Comm Dev/Planning	NA
Engineering	NA
Public Works	Jesse D'Amore
Police Chief	Charles Zisa
Emerg/Fire Director	Thomas Freeman

Housing & Construction
Housing Units, 2000*
Total	18,945
Median rent	$848
Median SF home value	$187,300

Permits for New Residential Construction
	Units	Value
Total, 2006	14	$658,500
Single family	4	$164,000
Total, 2007	51	$2,613,300
Single family	3	$463,300

Real Property Valuation, 2008
	Parcels	Valuation
Total	9,937	$6,190,776,200
Vacant	231	57,457,000
Residential	8,248	2,728,447,600
Commercial	1,016	1,987,365,400
Industrial	236	337,615,700
Apartments	206	1,079,890,500
Farm land	0	0
Farm homestead	0	0

Average Property Value & Tax, 2008
Residential value	$330,801
Property tax	$6,932
Tax credit/rebate	$1,058

Public Library
Johnson Free Public Library
274 Main St
Hackensack, NJ 07601
201-343-4169

Director . . . . Sharon Castanteen

Library statistics, 2007
Population served	42,677
Full-time/total staff	7/22

	Total	Per capita
Holdings	177,442	4.16
Revenues	$2,198,120	$51.51
Expenditures	$2,203,665	$51.64
Annual visits	128,960	3.02
Internet terminals/annual users		14/25,138

Public Safety
Number of officers, 2007	110

Crime	2006	2007
Total crimes	1,237	1,216
Violent	147	124
Murder	0	2
Rape	5	0
Robbery	61	38
Aggravated assault	81	84
Non-violent	1,090	1,092
Burglary	83	113
Larceny	885	898
Vehicle theft	122	81
Domestic violence	250	351
Arson	1	3
Total crime rate	28.3	27.8
Violent	3.4	2.8
Non-violent	24.9	25.0

Public School District
(for school year 2007-08 except as noted)

Hackensack School District
355 State Street
Hackensack, NJ 07601
(201) 646-7830

Superintendent	Edward A. Kliszus
Number of schools	7
Grade plan	K-12
Enrollment	4,879
Attendance rate, '06-07	93.6%
Dropout rate	0.7%
Students per teacher	11.1
Per pupil expenditure	$14,817
Median faculty salary	$75,086
Median administrator salary	$129,282
Grade 12 enrollment	431
High school graduation rate	88.1%

Assessment test results
(percent scoring at proficient or advanced level)
	Language	Math
NJASK-Grade 3	86.5%	92.6%
GEPA-Grade 8	56.6%	72.8%
HSPA-High School	73.2%	77.7%

SAT Score Averages, 2006-07
Pct tested	Math	Verbal	Writing
77%	462	444	437

Teacher Qualifications
Avg. years of experience	9
Highly-qualified teachers one subject/all subjects	99.5%/99.5%

No Child Left Behind
AYP, 2006-07	Meets Standards

Municipal Finance
State Aid Programs, 2009
Total aid	$5,284,087
CMPTRA	1,635,643
Energy tax receipts	3,569,183
Garden State Trust	0

General Budget, 2008
Total tax levy	$130,294,126
County levy	10,880,392
County taxes	10,286,001
County library	0
County health	0
County open space	594,391
School levy	58,652,691
Muni. levy	60,761,043
Misc. revenues	18,823,510

Taxes
	2006	2007	2008
General tax rate per $100	5.01	1.99	2.097
County equalization ratio	45.7	108.12	105.79
Net valuation taxable	$2,259,646,600	$6,298,631,089	$6,217,443,533
State equalized value	$5,778,410,390	$5,955,241,382	$6,598,616,590

Demographics & Socio-Economic Characteristics
(2000 US Census, except as noted)

Population
1980*	8,850
1990*	8,120
2000	10,403
Male	5,006
Female	5,397
2007 (estimate)*	9,422
Population density	2,546.5

Race & Hispanic Origin, 2000
Race
White	9,389
Black/African American	227
American Indian/Alaska Native	13
Asian	303
Native Hawaiian/Pacific Islander	6
Other race	208
Two or more races	257
Hispanic origin, total	833
Mexican	79
Puerto Rican	188
Cuban	48
Other Hispanic	518

Age & Nativity, 2000
Under 5 years	658
18 years and over	8,043
21 years and over	7,536
65 years and over	1,270
85 years and over	208
Median age	35.4
Native-born	9,100
Foreign-born	1,303

Educational Attainment, 2000
Population 25 years and over	6,994
Less than 9th grade	3.6%
High school grad or higher	87.1%
Bachelor's degree or higher	24.5%
Graduate degree	6.8%

Income & Poverty, 1999
Per capita income	$24,742
Median household income	$51,955
Median family income	$64,383
Persons in poverty	475
H'holds receiving public assistance	86
H'holds receiving social security	1,013

Households, 2000
Total households	4,134
With persons under 18	1,327
With persons over 65	918
Family households	2,532
Single-person households	1,311
Persons per household	2.41
Persons per family	3.10

Labor & Employment
Total civilian labor force, 2007**	6,287
Unemployment rate	2.7%
Total civilian labor force, 2000	5,820
Unemployment rate	4.7%

Employed persons 16 years and over by occupation, 2000
Managers & professionals	1,855
Service occupations	813
Sales & office occupations	1,584
Farming, fishing & forestry	11
Construction & maintenance	620
Production & transportation	665
Self-employed persons	160

* US Census Bureau
** New Jersey Department of Labor

General Information
Town of Hackettstown
215 W Stiger St
Hackettstown, NJ 07840
908-852-3130
Website	www.hackettstown.net
Year of incorporation	1853
Land/water area (sq. miles)	3.70/0.00
Form of government	Special Charter

Government
Legislative Districts
US Congressional	5
State Legislative	23

Local Officials, 2009
Mayor	Michael B. Lavery
Manager	William Kuster Jr
Clerk	William Kuster Jr
Finance Dir	Danette Dyer
Tax Assessor	Bernard Murdoch
Tax Collector	Regina McKenna
Attorney	Thomas Thorp
Building	Richard O'Connor
Comm Dev/Planning	NA
Engineering	Paul Sterbenz
Public Works	Scott Armstrong
Police Chief	Leonard Kunz
Emerg/Fire Director	Michael Gibbs

Housing & Construction
Housing Units, 2000*
Total	4,347
Median rent	$719
Median SF home value	$154,000

Permits for New Residential Construction
	Units	Value
Total, 2006	62	$4,046,550
Single family	9	$1,346,544
Total, 2007	54	$6,005,510
Single family	37	$5,004,991

Real Property Valuation, 2008
	Parcels	Valuation
Total	2,775	$603,259,932
Vacant	176	20,215,400
Residential	2,266	385,594,132
Commercial	268	109,713,750
Industrial	31	56,059,750
Apartments	34	31,676,900
Farm land	0	0
Farm homestead	0	0

Average Property Value & Tax, 2008
Residential value	$170,165
Property tax	$7,070
Tax credit/rebate	$1,142

Public Library
Hackettstown Free Public Library
110 Church St
Hackettstown, NJ 07840
908-852-4936
Director	J. Rona Mosler

Library statistics, 2007
Population served	10,403
Full-time/total staff	1/4

	Total	Per capita
Holdings	39,150	3.76
Revenues	$342,881	$32.96
Expenditures	$361,483	$34.75
Annual visits	48,000	4.61
Internet terminals/annual users	4/3,698	

Public Safety
Number of officers, 2007	19

Crime	2006	2007
Total crimes	247	189
Violent	8	16
Murder	0	0
Rape	0	0
Robbery	0	0
Aggravated assault	8	16
Non-violent	239	173
Burglary	26	24
Larceny	204	146
Vehicle theft	9	3
Domestic violence	136	164
Arson	1	1
Total crime rate	26.3	19.9
Violent	0.9	1.7
Non-violent	25.5	18.3

Public School District
(for school year 2007-08 except as noted)

Hackettstown School District
315 Washington Avenue, PO Box 465
Hackettstown, NJ 07840
(908) 850-6500
Superintendent	Robert Gratz
Number of schools	4
Grade plan	K-12
Enrollment	1,885
Attendance rate, '06-07	95.1%
Dropout rate	0.0%
Students per teacher	10.7
Per pupil expenditure	$13,781
Median faculty salary	$60,350
Median administrator salary	$108,160
Grade 12 enrollment	260
High school graduation rate	98.9%

Assessment test results
(percent scoring at proficient or advanced level)
	Language	Math
NJASK-Grade 3	92.1%	90.9%
GEPA-Grade 8	72.2%	86.7%
HSPA-High School	78.5%	86.6%

SAT Score Averages, 2006-07
Pct tested	Math	Verbal	Writing
83%	492	490	488

Teacher Qualifications
Avg. years of experience	11
Highly-qualified teachers one subject/all subjects	100%/100%

No Child Left Behind
AYP, 2006-07	Meets Standards

Municipal Finance
State Aid Programs, 2009
Total aid	$936,601
CMPTRA	274,650
Energy tax receipts	631,179
Garden State Trust	6,587

General Budget, 2008
Total tax levy	$25,186,171
County levy	6,002,009
County taxes	5,354,154
County library	0
County health	0
County open space	647,855
School levy	14,008,271
Muni. levy	5,175,892
Misc. revenues	3,527,816

Taxes
Taxes	2006	2007	2008
General tax rate per $100	3.83	3.98	4.156
County equalization ratio	69.27	61.47	56.49
Net valuation taxable	$587,260,832	$601,497,001	$606,160,838
State equalized value	$958,703,599	$1,062,500,742	$1,070,617,600

See Introduction for an explanation of all data sources.

Demographics & Socio-Economic Characteristics
(2000 US Census, except as noted)

Population
1980*	8,361
1990*	7,860
2000	7,547
Male	3,554
Female	3,993
2007 (estimate)*	7,283
Population density	4,698.7

Race & Hispanic Origin, 2000
Race
White	7,394
Black/African American	30
American Indian/Alaska Native	8
Asian	49
Native Hawaiian/Pacific Islander	3
Other race	20
Two or more races	43
Hispanic origin, total	79
Mexican	17
Puerto Rican	27
Cuban	3
Other Hispanic	32

Age & Nativity, 2000
Under 5 years	464
18 years and over	5,731
21 years and over	5,541
65 years and over	1,373
85 years and over	154
Median age	40.6
Native-born	7,325
Foreign-born	222

Educational Attainment, 2000
Population 25 years and over	5,366
Less than 9th grade	2.6%
High school grad or higher	90.7%
Bachelor's degree or higher	38.1%
Graduate degree	13.4%

Income & Poverty, 1999
Per capita income	$28,198
Median household income	$58,424
Median family income	$73,460
Persons in poverty	211
H'holds receiving public assistance	7
H'holds receiving social security	1,041

Households, 2000
Total households	3,039
With persons under 18	989
With persons over 65	1,012
Family households	2,039
Single-person households	867
Persons per household	2.48
Persons per family	3.09

Labor & Employment
Total civilian labor force, 2007**	4,082
Unemployment rate	3.3%
Total civilian labor force, 2000	3,863
Unemployment rate	3.3%

Employed persons 16 years and over by occupation, 2000
Managers & professionals	1,830
Service occupations	432
Sales & office occupations	1,022
Farming, fishing & forestry	0
Construction & maintenance	242
Production & transportation	211
Self-employed persons	232

General Information
Borough of Haddon Heights
625 Station Ave
Haddon Heights, NJ 08035
856-547-7164
Website	www.haddonhts.com
Year of incorporation	1904
Land/water area (sq. miles)	1.55/0.00
Form of government	Borough

Government
Legislative Districts
US Congressional	1
State Legislative	5

Local Officials, 2009
Mayor	Scott M. Alexander
Manager	Joan Moreland
Clerk	Joan Moreland
Finance Dir	Sharon Smith
Tax Assessor	Thomas Colavecchio
Tax Collector	Andrea Penny
Attorney	Robert Gleaner
Building	John Szczerbinski
Comm Dev/Planning	NA
Engineering	Pennoni Associates
Public Works	Richard Edelen
Police Chief	Richard Kinkler
Emerg/Fire Director	Nicholas Scardino

Housing & Construction
Housing Units, 2000*
Total	3,136
Median rent	$586
Median SF home value	$139,800

Permits for New Residential Construction
	Units	Value
Total, 2006	3	$299,600
Single family	3	$299,600
Total, 2007	133	$8,946,663
Single family	70	$6,887,563

Real Property Valuation, 2008
	Parcels	Valuation
Total	2,776	$821,788,300
Vacant	80	2,398,400
Residential	2,510	728,223,300
Commercial	171	82,956,400
Industrial	2	517,600
Apartments	13	7,692,600
Farm land	0	0
Farm homestead	0	0

Average Property Value & Tax, 2008
Residential value	$290,129
Property tax	$7,552
Tax credit/rebate	$1,176

Public Library
Haddon Heights Public Library
608 Station Ave
Haddon Heights, NJ 08035
856-547-7132
Director	Robert J. Hunter

Library statistics, 2007
Population served	7,547
Full-time/total staff	1/4

	Total	Per capita
Holdings	54,544	7.23
Revenues	$335,974	$44.52
Expenditures	$320,566	$42.48
Annual visits	43,602	5.78
Internet terminals/annual users	8/13,737	

Public Safety
Number of officers, 2007	14

Crime	2006	2007
Total crimes	143	119
Violent	5	4
Murder	0	0
Rape	1	1
Robbery	2	2
Aggravated assault	2	1
Non-violent	138	115
Burglary	19	13
Larceny	117	100
Vehicle theft	2	2
Domestic violence	23	17
Arson	3	3
Total crime rate	19.3	16.2
Violent	0.7	0.5
Non-violent	18.6	15.6

Public School District
(for school year 2007-08 except as noted)

Haddon Heights School District
316 A 7th Avenue
Haddon Heights, NJ 08035
(856) 547-1412
Superintendent	Nancy Hacker
Number of schools	4
Grade plan	K-12
Enrollment	1,310
Attendance rate, '06-07	94.4%
Dropout rate	0.7%
Students per teacher	10.6
Per pupil expenditure	$14,594
Median faculty salary	$57,170
Median administrator salary	$89,772
Grade 12 enrollment	157
High school graduation rate	97.0%

Assessment test results
(percent scoring at proficient or advanced level)
	Language	Math
NJASK-Grade 3	94.1%	92.6%
GEPA-Grade 8	91.1%	91.2%
HSPA-High School	74.6%	85.3%

SAT Score Averages, 2006-07
Pct tested	Math	Verbal	Writing
80%	497	498	491

Teacher Qualifications
Avg. years of experience	14
Highly-qualified teachers one subject/all subjects	100%/100%

No Child Left Behind
AYP, 2006-07	Meets Standards

Municipal Finance
State Aid Programs, 2009
Total aid	$972,404
CMPTRA	134,775
Energy tax receipts	813,319
Garden State Trust	0

General Budget, 2008
Total tax levy	$21,413,270
County levy	4,754,851
County taxes	4,594,805
County library	0
County health	0
County open space	160,046
School levy	11,698,768
Muni. levy	4,959,652
Misc. revenues	2,100,870

Taxes
	2006	2007	2008
General tax rate per $100	5.02	2.569	2.603
County equalization ratio	60.01	108.69	103.02
Net valuation taxable	$401,025,100	$824,910,879	$822,692,919
State equalized value	$752,643,482	$800,748,238	$806,342,529

* US Census Bureau
** New Jersey Department of Labor

See Introduction for an explanation of all data sources.

Demographics & Socio-Economic Characteristics
(2000 US Census, except as noted)

Population
1980*	15,875
1990*	14,837
2000	14,651
Male	6,876
Female	7,775
2007 (estimate)*	14,354
Population density	5,336.1

Race & Hispanic Origin, 2000
Race
White	13,980
Black/African American	173
American Indian/Alaska Native	8
Asian	294
Native Hawaiian/Pacific Islander	6
Other race	82
Two or more races	108
Hispanic origin, total	226
Mexican	39
Puerto Rican	114
Cuban	19
Other Hispanic	54

Age & Nativity, 2000
Under 5 years	801
18 years and over	11,340
21 years and over	10,972
65 years and over	2,929
85 years and over	386
Median age	40.7
Native-born	14,084
Foreign-born	576

Educational Attainment, 2000
Population 25 years and over	10,348
Less than 9th grade	2.9%
High school grad or higher	89.5%
Bachelor's degree or higher	30.6%
Graduate degree	9.7%

Income & Poverty, 1999
Per capita income	$25,610
Median household income	$51,076
Median family income	$65,269
Persons in poverty	607
H'holds receiving public assistance	81
H'holds receiving social security	2,214

Households, 2000
Total households	6,207
With persons under 18	1,804
With persons over 65	2,224
Family households	3,889
Single-person households	2,048
Persons per household	2.36
Persons per family	3.05

Labor & Employment
Total civilian labor force, 2007**	7,909
Unemployment rate	3.3%
Total civilian labor force, 2000	7,474
Unemployment rate	3.5%

Employed persons 16 years and over by occupation, 2000
Managers & professionals	3,000
Service occupations	883
Sales & office occupations	2,112
Farming, fishing & forestry	0
Construction & maintenance	633
Production & transportation	586
Self-employed persons	373

‡ Branch of county library
* US Census Bureau
** New Jersey Department of Labor

General Information
Township of Haddon
135 Haddon Ave
Westmont, NJ 08108
856-854-1176
Website	www.haddontwp.com
Year of incorporation	1865
Land/water area (sq. miles)	2.69/0.11
Form of government	Commission

Government
Legislative Districts
US Congressional	1
State Legislative	6

Local Officials, 2009
Mayor	Randall W. Teague
Manager/Admin	NA
Township Clerk	Denise P. Adams
CFO	Denise P. Adams
Tax Assessor	Martin G. Blaskey III
Tax Collector	Jennifer Dellavalle
Attorney	Richard F. Klineburger III
Construction Official	Edward Toussaint
Comm Dev/Planning	NA
Engineering	Key Engineers
Public Works Mgr	Thomas Cella
Police Chief	Mark Cavallo (Actg)
Fire Chief	John Medes

Housing & Construction
Housing Units, 2000*
Total	6,423
Median rent	$690
Median SF home value	$122,200

Permits for New Residential Construction
	Units	Value
Total, 2006	24	$1,378,138
Single family	4	$490,138
Total, 2007	24	$1,395,013
Single family	4	$507,013

Real Property Valuation, 2008
	Parcels	Valuation
Total	5,160	$681,464,100
Vacant	128	2,848,700
Residential	4,727	564,026,900
Commercial	269	78,165,400
Industrial	19	4,262,200
Apartments	17	32,160,900
Farm land	0	0
Farm homestead	0	0

Average Property Value & Tax, 2008
Residential value	$119,320
Property tax	$6,299
Tax credit/rebate	$1,082

Public Library
Haddon Township Branch Library‡
15 MacArthur Blvd
Westmont, NJ 08108
856-854-2752
Branch Librarian	Nan Rosenthal

Library statistics, 2007
see Camden County profile
for library system statistics

Public Safety
Number of officers, 2007 ... 30
Crime	2006	2007
Total crimes	427	396
Violent	29	28
Murder	0	0
Rape	1	0
Robbery	19	15
Aggravated assault	9	13
Non-violent	398	368
Burglary	51	62
Larceny	332	269
Vehicle theft	15	37
Domestic violence	123	126
Arson	2	1
Total crime rate	29.3	27.3
Violent	2.0	1.9
Non-violent	27.3	25.4

Public School District
(for school year 2007-08 except as noted)

Haddon Township School District
500 Rhoads Avenue
Westmont, NJ 08108
(856) 869-7700
Superintendent	Mark Raivetz
Number of schools	7
Grade plan	K-12
Enrollment	2,144
Attendance rate, '06-07	94.4%
Dropout rate	0.8%
Students per teacher	12.3
Per pupil expenditure	$13,146
Median faculty salary	$56,582
Median administrator salary	$96,525
Grade 12 enrollment	148
High school graduation rate	98.7%

Assessment test results
(percent scoring at proficient or advanced level)
	Language	Math
NJASK-Grade 3	88.9%	86.9%
GEPA-Grade 8	71.9%	89.5%
HSPA-High School	88.3%	90.5%

SAT Score Averages, 2006-07
Pct tested	Math	Verbal	Writing
82%	504	504	489

Teacher Qualifications
Avg. years of experience	12
Highly-qualified teachers one subject/all subjects	100%/100%

No Child Left Behind
AYP, 2006-07 ... Meets Standards

Municipal Finance
State Aid Programs, 2009
Total aid	$1,627,378
CMPTRA	450,691
Energy tax receipts	1,136,002
Garden State Trust	0

General Budget, 2008
Total tax levy	$35,999,975
County levy	8,630,623
County taxes	7,799,593
County library	559,453
County health	0
County open space	271,577
School levy	19,904,187
Muni. levy	7,465,165
Misc. revenues	4,917,506

Taxes	2006	2007	2008
General tax rate per $100	4.842	5.129	5.280
County equalization ratio	62.39	54.66	50.35
Net valuation taxable	$681,710,800	$680,543,342	$681,929,961
State equalized value	$1,247,693,816	$1,351,173,731	$1,440,888,816

See Introduction for an explanation of all data sources.

Demographics & Socio-Economic Characteristics

(2000 US Census, except as noted)

Population
1980*	12,337
1990*	11,628
2000	11,659
Male	5,536
Female	6,123
2007 (estimate)*	11,411
Population density	4,032.2

Race & Hispanic Origin, 2000
Race
White	11,247
Black/African American	148
American Indian/Alaska Native	15
Asian	131
Native Hawaiian/Pacific Islander	3
Other race	37
Two or more races	78
Hispanic origin, total	170
Mexican	22
Puerto Rican	54
Cuban	24
Other Hispanic	70

Age & Nativity, 2000
Under 5 years	743
18 years and over	8,488
21 years and over	8,250
65 years and over	1,850
85 years and over	222
Median age	41.3
Native-born	11,290
Foreign-born	370

Educational Attainment, 2000
Population 25 years and over	8,091
Less than 9th grade	1.0%
High school grad or higher	95.1%
Bachelor's degree or higher	64.8%
Graduate degree	28.9%

Income & Poverty, 1999
Per capita income	$43,170
Median household income	$86,872
Median family income	$103,597
Persons in poverty	250
H'holds receiving public assistance	33
H'holds receiving social security	1,338

Households, 2000
Total households	4,496
With persons under 18	1,620
With persons over 65	1,297
Family households	3,253
Single-person households	1,085
Persons per household	2.57
Persons per family	3.09

Labor & Employment
Total civilian labor force, 2007**	6,214
Unemployment rate	2.7%
Total civilian labor force, 2000	5,872
Unemployment rate	2.8%

Employed persons 16 years and over by occupation, 2000
Managers & professionals	3,855
Service occupations	355
Sales & office occupations	1,169
Farming, fishing & forestry	5
Construction & maintenance	76
Production & transportation	245
Self-employed persons	545

General Information
Borough of Haddonfield
242 Kings Highway E
PO Box 3005
Haddonfield, NJ 08033
856-429-4700

Website	www.haddonfieldnj.org
Year of incorporation	1875
Land/water area (sq. miles)	2.83/0.03
Form of government	Commission

Government
Legislative Districts
US Congressional	1
State Legislative	6

Local Officials, 2009
Mayor	Letitia G. Colombi
Manager	Sharon McCullough
Clerk	Deanna Bennett
Finance Dir	Terry W. Henry
Tax Assessor	Thomas Colavecchio
Tax Collector	Terry W. Henry
Attorney	Mario Iavicoli
Building	Steven P. Walko
Comm Dev/Planning	NA
Engineering	Remington & Vernick
Public Works	E. Dave Watson
Police Chief	Richard W. Tsonis
Emerg/Fire Director	Joseph Riggs Jr

Housing & Construction
Housing Units, 2000*
Total	4,620
Median rent	$732
Median SF home value	$225,300

Permits for New Residential Construction
	Units	Value
Total, 2006	18	$5,457,288
Single family	18	$5,457,288
Total, 2007	14	$5,568,802
Single family	14	$5,568,802

Real Property Valuation, 2008
	Parcels	Valuation
Total	4,450	$2,255,271,200
Vacant	64	12,511,200
Residential	4,086	2,007,692,800
Commercial	288	220,959,500
Industrial	0	0
Apartments	12	14,107,700
Farm land	0	0
Farm homestead	0	0

Average Property Value & Tax, 2008
Residential value	$491,359
Property tax	$11,350
Tax credit/rebate	$1,314

Public Library
Haddonfield Public Library
60 N Haddon Ave
Haddonfield, NJ 08033
856-429-1304

Director	Susan Briant

Library statistics, 2007
Population served	11,659
Full-time/total staff	4/6

	Total	Per capita
Holdings	87,088	7.47
Revenues	$1,027,666	$88.14
Expenditures	$1,032,891	$88.59
Annual visits	115,177	9.88
Internet terminals/annual users	13/17,367	

Public Safety
Number of officers, 2007	23

Crime	2006	2007
Total crimes	280	262
Violent	12	7
Murder	0	0
Rape	2	0
Robbery	6	2
Aggravated assault	4	5
Non-violent	268	255
Burglary	40	31
Larceny	223	219
Vehicle theft	5	5
Domestic violence	21	46
Arson	11	5
Total crime rate	24.2	22.8
Violent	1.0	0.6
Non-violent	23.1	22.1

Public School District
(for school year 2007-08 except as noted)

Haddonfield Borough School District
One Lincoln Avenue
Haddonfield, NJ 08033
(856) 429-4130

Superintendent	Alan Fegley
Number of schools	5
Grade plan	K-12
Enrollment	2,388
Attendance rate, '06-07	95.8%
Dropout rate	0.5%
Students per teacher	12.1
Per pupil expenditure	$12,192
Median faculty salary	$65,200
Median administrator salary	$113,850
Grade 12 enrollment	192
High school graduation rate	100.0%

Assessment test results
(percent scoring at proficient or advanced level)
	Language	Math
NJASK-Grade 3	94.3%	97.7%
GEPA-Grade 8	92.8%	95.6%
HSPA-High School	95.0%	97.2%

SAT Score Averages, 2006-07
Pct tested	Math	Verbal	Writing
106%	562	566	556

Teacher Qualifications
Avg. years of experience	12
Highly-qualified teachers one subject/all subjects	100%/100%

No Child Left Behind
AYP, 2006-07	Meets Standards

Municipal Finance
State Aid Programs, 2009
Total aid	$1,299,140
CMPTRA	262,191
Energy tax receipts	994,726
Garden State Trust	1

General Budget, 2008
Total tax levy	$52,247,045
County levy	13,000,568
County taxes	12,563,461
County library	0
County health	0
County open space	437,107
School levy	30,595,409
Muni. levy	8,651,068
Misc. revenues	5,301,820

Taxes
	2006	2007	2008
General tax rate per $100	4.762	4.892	2.310
County equalization ratio	58.15	51.87	103.71
Net valuation taxable	$1,027,068,300	$1,038,588,443	$2,261,891,796
State equalized value	$1,983,430,626	$2,141,295,069	$2,214,640,177

* US Census Bureau
** New Jersey Department of Labor

See Introduction for an explanation of all data sources.

Demographics & Socio-Economic Characteristics

(2000 US Census, except as noted)

Population

1980*	3,236
1990*	3,249
2000	4,126
Male	2,018
Female	2,108
2007 (estimate)*	6,014
Population density	922.4

Race & Hispanic Origin, 2000

Race
White	3,882
Black/African American	110
American Indian/Alaska Native	4
Asian	70
Native Hawaiian/Pacific Islander	0
Other race	21
Two or more races	39
Hispanic origin, total	88
Mexican	9
Puerto Rican	63
Cuban	6
Other Hispanic	10

Age & Nativity, 2000

Under 5 years	321
18 years and over	3,042
21 years and over	2,936
65 years and over	485
85 years and over	41
Median age	38.4
Native-born	4,007
Foreign-born	119

Educational Attainment, 2000

Population 25 years and over	2,784
Less than 9th grade	0.9%
High school grad or higher	88.6%
Bachelor's degree or higher	24.7%
Graduate degree	7.7%

Income & Poverty, 1999

Per capita income	$28,091
Median household income	$66,417
Median family income	$72,005
Persons in poverty	121
H'holds receiving public assistance	9
H'holds receiving social security	385

Households, 2000

Total households	1,477
With persons under 18	569
With persons over 65	355
Family households	1,150
Single-person households	259
Persons per household	2.78
Persons per family	3.16

Labor & Employment

Total civilian labor force, 2007**	2,650
Unemployment rate	3.0%
Total civilian labor force, 2000	2,307
Unemployment rate	2.7%

Employed persons 16 years and over by occupation, 2000
Managers & professionals	843
Service occupations	278
Sales & office occupations	662
Farming, fishing & forestry	4
Construction & maintenance	191
Production & transportation	266
Self-employed persons	84

* US Census Bureau
** New Jersey Department of Labor

General Information

Township of Hainesport
One Hainesport Centre
PO Box 477
Hainesport, NJ 08036
609-267-2730

Website	www.hainesporttownship.com
Year of incorporation	1924
Land/water area (sq. miles)	6.52/0.20
Form of government	Township

Government

Legislative Districts

US Congressional	3
State Legislative	8

Local Officials, 2009

Mayor	Bruce MacLachlan
Manager	Paul Tuliano Jr
Clerk	Paul Tuliano Jr
Finance Dir	Dawn Robertson
Tax Assessor	Edward Burek
Tax Collector	Sharon Deviney
Attorney	Ted Costa
Building	M. Gene Blair
Planning	Paula Tiver
Engineering	Richard Alaimo & Assoc
Public Works	Jay Jones Jr
Police Chief	NA
Emerg/Fire Director	William Wiley

Housing & Construction

Housing Units, 2000*

Total	1,555
Median rent	$744
Median SF home value	$144,400

Permits for New Residential Construction

	Units	Value
Total, 2006	5	$2,396,505
Single family	5	$2,396,505
Total, 2007	2	$258,127
Single family	2	$258,127

Real Property Valuation, 2008

	Parcels	Valuation
Total	2,589	$436,644,233
Vacant	227	9,168,000
Residential	2,178	351,430,400
Commercial	88	39,889,933
Industrial	30	29,918,500
Apartments	2	247,500
Farm land	40	221,300
Farm homestead	24	5,768,600

Average Property Value & Tax, 2008

Residential value	$162,216
Property tax	$5,499
Tax credit/rebate	$942

Public Library

No public municipal library

Library statistics, 2007

Population served	NA
Full-time/total staff	NA/NA

	Total	Per capita
Holdings	NA	NA
Revenues	NA	NA
Expenditures	NA	NA
Annual visits	NA	NA
Internet terminals/annual users	NA/NA	

Public Safety

Number of officers, 2007	0

Crime	2006	2007
Total crimes	138	132
Violent	10	9
Murder	0	0
Rape	1	1
Robbery	1	1
Aggravated assault	8	7
Non-violent	128	123
Burglary	15	34
Larceny	102	85
Vehicle theft	11	4
Domestic violence	8	37
Arson	0	1
Total crime rate	22.6	21.4
Violent	1.6	1.5
Non-violent	20.9	20.0

Public School District

(for school year 2007-08 except as noted)

Hainesport Township School District
211 Broad Street, PO Box 538
Hainesport, NJ 08036
(609) 265-8050

Superintendent	Mark Silverstein
Number of schools	1
Grade plan	K-8
Enrollment	658
Attendance rate, '06-07	95.7%
Dropout rate	NA
Students per teacher	10.3
Per pupil expenditure	$12,061
Median faculty salary	$49,775
Median administrator salary	$82,891
Grade 12 enrollment	NA
High school graduation rate	NA

Assessment test results

(percent scoring at proficient or advanced level)
	Language	Math
NJASK-Grade 3	91.3%	95.1%
GEPA-Grade 8	44.8%	75.8%
HSPA-High School	NA	NA

SAT Score Averages, 2006-07

Pct tested	Math	Verbal	Writing
NA	NA	NA	NA

Teacher Qualifications

Avg. years of experience	9
Highly-qualified teachers one subject/all subjects	100%/100%

No Child Left Behind

AYP, 2006-07	Meets Standards

Municipal Finance

State Aid Programs, 2009

Total aid	$517,789
CMPTRA	55,403
Energy tax receipts	440,696
Garden State Trust	1,069

General Budget, 2008

Total tax levy	$14,830,113
County levy	3,458,116
County taxes	2,839,665
County library	262,185
County health	0
County open space	356,266
School levy	9,264,602
Muni. levy	2,107,394
Misc. revenues	2,126,071

Taxes	2006	2007	2008
General tax rate per $100	3.255	3.41	3.390
County equalization ratio	60.69	53.19	48.97
Net valuation taxable	$423,804,600	$433,693,880	$437,489,051
State equalized value	$797,777,678	$884,705,919	$927,902,638

See Introduction for an explanation of all data sources.

Demographics & Socio-Economic Characteristics

(2000 US Census, except as noted)

Population
1980*	6,607
1990*	6,951
2000	8,252
Male	3,894
Female	4,358
2007 (estimate)*	8,389
Population density	7,231.9

Race & Hispanic Origin, 2000
Race
White	6,073
Black/African American	585
American Indian/Alaska Native	14
Asian	377
Native Hawaiian/Pacific Islander	2
Other race	833
Two or more races	368
Hispanic origin, total	1,865
Mexican	66
Puerto Rican	729
Cuban	48
Other Hispanic	1,022

Age & Nativity, 2000
Under 5 years	576
18 years and over	6,144
21 years and over	5,847
65 years and over	1,163
85 years and over	191
Median age	34.6
Native-born	6,097
Foreign-born	2,155

Educational Attainment, 2000
Population 25 years and over	5,393
Less than 9th grade	12.2%
High school grad or higher	77.1%
Bachelor's degree or higher	18.5%
Graduate degree	6.1%

Income & Poverty, 1999
Per capita income	$19,099
Median household income	$45,599
Median family income	$49,014
Persons in poverty	872
H'holds receiving public assistance	78
H'holds receiving social security	725

Households, 2000
Total households	2,820
With persons under 18	1,090
With persons over 65	744
Family households	1,975
Single-person households	660
Persons per household	2.83
Persons per family	3.41

Labor & Employment
Total civilian labor force, 2007**	4,476
Unemployment rate	7.0%
Total civilian labor force, 2000	4,168
Unemployment rate	7.2%

Employed persons 16 years and over by occupation, 2000
Managers & professionals	1,083
Service occupations	567
Sales & office occupations	1,200
Farming, fishing & forestry	0
Construction & maintenance	371
Production & transportation	645
Self-employed persons	198

* US Census Bureau
** New Jersey Department of Labor

General Information
Borough of Haledon
510 Belmont Ave
Haledon, NJ 07508
973-595-7766
Website	www.haledonboronj.com
Year of incorporation	1908
Land/water area (sq. miles)	1.16/0.00
Form of government	Borough

Government
Legislative Districts
US Congressional	8
State Legislative	35

Local Officials, 2009
Mayor	Domenick Stampone
Manager	William Close
Clerk	Allan Susen
Finance Dir	Maryann Brindisi
Tax Assessor	Brian Townsend
Tax Collector	Theresa Bosland
Attorney	Andrew Oddo
Building Inspector	Jim Booth
Comm Dev/Planning	NA
Engineering	Stephen Boswell
Superintendent	Angelo Passafaro
Police Chief	Louis Mercuro
Emerg/Fire Director	Scott Wilson

Housing & Construction
Housing Units, 2000*
Total	2,906
Median rent	$826
Median SF home value	$164,100

Permits for New Residential Construction
	Units	Value
Total, 2006	57	$1,556,400
Single family	5	$910,400
Total, 2007	69	$2,220,054
Single family	7	$1,148,720

Real Property Valuation, 2008
	Parcels	Valuation
Total	1,955	$328,364,200
Vacant	133	3,850,100
Residential	1,658	265,559,200
Commercial	129	36,981,100
Industrial	27	13,454,800
Apartments	8	8,519,000
Farm land	0	0
Farm homestead	0	0

Average Property Value & Tax, 2008
Residential value	$160,168
Property tax	$8,525
Tax credit/rebate	$1,215

Public Library
Haledon Free Public Library
404 Morrissee Ave
Haledon, NJ 07508
973-790-3808
Director	Judie Erk

Library statistics, 2007
Population served	8,252
Full-time/total staff	NA/0

	Total	Per capita
Holdings	0	NA
Revenues	$0	NA
Expenditures	$0	NA
Annual visits	NA	NA
Internet terminals/annual users	NA/NA	

Public Safety
Number of officers, 2007		17

Crime	2006	2007
Total crimes	111	171
Violent	13	19
Murder	0	0
Rape	0	0
Robbery	7	4
Aggravated assault	6	15
Non-violent	98	152
Burglary	27	41
Larceny	60	81
Vehicle theft	11	30
Domestic violence	60	56
Arson	1	0
Total crime rate	13.2	20.5
Violent	1.5	2.3
Non-violent	11.7	18.2

Public School District
(for school year 2007-08 except as noted)

Haledon School District
70 Church Street
Haledon, NJ 07508
(973) 956-2582
Chief School Admin	Raymond Kwak
Number of schools	1
Grade plan	K-8
Enrollment	1,013
Attendance rate, '06-07	93.2%
Dropout rate	NA
Students per teacher	11.9
Per pupil expenditure	$11,330
Median faculty salary	$50,085
Median administrator salary	$108,367
Grade 12 enrollment	NA
High school graduation rate	NA

Assessment test results
(percent scoring at proficient or advanced level)
	Language	Math
NJASK-Grade 3	73.2%	79.2%
GEPA-Grade 8	62.0%	79.0%
HSPA-High School	NA	NA

SAT Score Averages, 2006-07
Pct tested	Math	Verbal	Writing
NA	NA	NA	NA

Teacher Qualifications
Avg. years of experience	8
Highly-qualified teachers one subject/all subjects	95.5%/95.5%

No Child Left Behind
AYP, 2006-07	Meets Standards

Municipal Finance
State Aid Programs, 2009
Total aid	$859,862
CMPTRA	246,994
Energy tax receipts	591,372
Garden State Trust	0

General Budget, 2008
Total tax levy	$17,588,494
County levy	3,675,809
County taxes	3,602,980
County library	0
County health	0
County open space	72,829
School levy	8,902,717
Muni. levy	5,009,968
Misc. revenues	7,206,406

Taxes
	2006	2007	2008
General tax rate per $100	4.82	4.99	5.323
County equalization ratio	55.93	49.79	45.41
Net valuation taxable	$322,117,200	$325,297,777	$330,471,372
State equalized value	$649,461,511	$713,660,847	$725,217,060

See Introduction for an explanation of all data sources.

Demographics & Socio-Economic Characteristics
(2000 US Census, except as noted)

Population

1980*	1,832
1990*	2,566
2000	3,105
Male	1,489
Female	1,616
2007 (estimate)*	3,482
Population density	3,001.7

Race & Hispanic Origin, 2000

Race
White	2,892
Black/African American	23
American Indian/Alaska Native	9
Asian	71
Native Hawaiian/Pacific Islander	0
Other race	52
Two or more races	58
Hispanic origin, total	131
Mexican	7
Puerto Rican	70
Cuban	6
Other Hispanic	48

Age & Nativity, 2000

Under 5 years	229
18 years and over	2,274
21 years and over	2,194
65 years and over	252
85 years and over	14
Median age	35.0
Native-born	2,925
Foreign-born	180

Educational Attainment, 2000

Population 25 years and over	2,060
Less than 9th grade	3.3%
High school grad or higher	88.8%
Bachelor's degree or higher	19.8%
Graduate degree	6.1%

Income & Poverty, 1999

Per capita income	$24,651
Median household income	$58,246
Median family income	$64,773
Persons in poverty	142
H'holds receiving public assistance	7
H'holds receiving social security	199

Households, 2000

Total households	1,173
With persons under 18	466
With persons over 65	188
Family households	844
Single-person households	273
Persons per household	2.65
Persons per family	3.14

Labor & Employment

Total civilian labor force, 2007**	1,927
Unemployment rate	4.4%
Total civilian labor force, 2000	1,726
Unemployment rate	3.9%

Employed persons 16 years and over by occupation, 2000
Managers & professionals	594
Service occupations	215
Sales & office occupations	443
Farming, fishing & forestry	4
Construction & maintenance	170
Production & transportation	233
Self-employed persons	76

* US Census Bureau
** New Jersey Department of Labor

General Information
Borough of Hamburg
16 Wallkill Ave
Hamburg, NJ 07419
973-827-9230

Website	www.hamburgnj.org
Year of incorporation	1920
Land/water area (sq. miles)	1.16/0.01
Form of government	Borough

Government

Legislative Districts
US Congressional	5
State Legislative	24

Local Officials, 2009
Mayor	Paul Marino
Manager/Admin	NA
Clerk	Doreen Schott
Finance Dir	Amy Maronpot
Tax Assessor	John Dyksen
Tax Collector	Regina Flammer
Attorney	Richard Clemack
Building	Hardyston Township
Comm Dev/Planning	NA
Engineering	John Ruschke
Public Works	NA
Police Captain	Jan Wright (Actg)
Emerg/Fire Director	John Haig

Housing & Construction

Housing Units, 2000*
Total	1,233
Median rent	$864
Median SF home value	$124,500

Permits for New Residential Construction

	Units	Value
Total, 2006	9	$613,333
Single family	9	$613,333
Total, 2007	6	$1,222,782
Single family	6	$1,222,782

Real Property Valuation, 2008

	Parcels	Valuation
Total	1,532	$208,432,450
Vacant	145	5,610,450
Residential	1,327	179,426,800
Commercial	54	19,514,500
Industrial	3	3,375,700
Apartments	1	331,500
Farm land	1	4,500
Farm homestead	1	169,000

Average Property Value & Tax, 2008
Residential value	$135,238
Property tax	$5,159
Tax credit/rebate	$916

Public Library
No public municipal library

Library statistics, 2007
Population served	NA
Full-time/total staff	NA/NA

	Total	Per capita
Holdings	NA	NA
Revenues	NA	NA
Expenditures	NA	NA
Annual visits	NA	NA
Internet terminals/annual users	NA/NA	

Public Safety
Number of officers, 2007	8

Crime	2006	2007
Total crimes	65	50
Violent	2	4
Murder	0	0
Rape	1	1
Robbery	0	0
Aggravated assault	1	3
Non-violent	63	46
Burglary	22	22
Larceny	39	23
Vehicle theft	2	1
Domestic violence	59	73
Arson	0	3
Total crime rate	18.2	14.1
Violent	0.6	1.1
Non-violent	17.7	12.9

Public School District
(for school year 2007-08 except as noted)

Hamburg Borough School District
30 Linwood Avenue
Hamburg, NJ 07419
(973) 827-7570

Chief School Admin	Steven Engravalle
Number of schools	1
Grade plan	K-8
Enrollment	292
Attendance rate, '06-07	95.0%
Dropout rate	NA
Students per teacher	8.3
Per pupil expenditure	$16,168
Median faculty salary	$52,425
Median administrator salary	$97,560
Grade 12 enrollment	NA
High school graduation rate	NA

Assessment test results
(percent scoring at proficient or advanced level)

	Language	Math
NJASK-Grade 3	65.4%	73.1%
GEPA-Grade 8	64.9%	97.3%
HSPA-High School	NA	NA

SAT Score Averages, 2006-07

Pct tested	Math	Verbal	Writing
NA	NA	NA	NA

Teacher Qualifications
Avg. years of experience	9
Highly-qualified teachers one subject/all subjects	100%/100%

No Child Left Behind
AYP, 2006-07	Meets Standards

Municipal Finance

State Aid Programs, 2009
Total aid	$291,991
CMPTRA	75,513
Energy tax receipts	208,489
Garden State Trust	568

General Budget, 2008
Total tax levy	$7,961,880
County levy	1,477,373
County taxes	1,239,821
County library	104,500
County health	36,700
County open space	96,352
School levy	4,867,087
Muni. levy	1,617,420
Misc. revenues	1,144,936

Taxes

	2006	2007	2008
General tax rate per $100	3.43	3.64	3.815
County equalization ratio	68.02	59.44	54.46
Net valuation taxable	$206,794,350	$208,795,218	$208,711,334
State equalized value	$348,276,694	$383,139,037	$382,934,382

See Introduction for an explanation of all data sources.

Demographics & Socio-Economic Characteristics

(2000 US Census, except as noted)

Population

1980*	9,499
1990*	16,012
2000	20,499
Male	10,217
Female	10,282
2007 (estimate)*	24,553
Population density	220.6

Race & Hispanic Origin, 2000

Race

White	14,646
Black/African American	3,949
American Indian/Alaska Native	60
Asian	675
Native Hawaiian/Pacific Islander	10
Other race	682
Two or more races	477
Hispanic origin, total	1,621
Mexican	91
Puerto Rican	960
Cuban	34
Other Hispanic	536

Age & Nativity, 2000

Under 5 years	1,431
18 years and over	14,946
21 years and over	14,202
65 years and over	1,683
85 years and over	182
Median age	34.5
Native-born	19,152
Foreign-born	1,347

Educational Attainment, 2000

Population 25 years and over	13,351
Less than 9th grade	4.7%
High school grad or higher	80.4%
Bachelor's degree or higher	19.3%
Graduate degree	5.0%

Income & Poverty, 1999

Per capita income	$21,309
Median household income	$50,259
Median family income	$54,899
Persons in poverty	1,280
H'holds receiving public assistance	130
H'holds receiving social security	1,318

Households, 2000

Total households	7,148
With persons under 18	2,976
With persons over 65	1,241
Family households	5,039
Single-person households	1,586
Persons per household	2.72
Persons per family	3.21

Labor & Employment

Total civilian labor force, 2007**	10,928
Unemployment rate	4.8%
Total civilian labor force, 2000	10,275
Unemployment rate	5.2%

Employed persons 16 years and over by occupation, 2000

Managers & professionals	2,918
Service occupations	2,553
Sales & office occupations	2,507
Farming, fishing & forestry	31
Construction & maintenance	904
Production & transportation	828
Self-employed persons	341

---

* US Census Bureau
** New Jersey Department of Labor

General Information

Township of Hamilton
6101 13th St
Mays Landing, NJ 08330
609-625-1511

Website	www.townshipofhamilton.com
Year of incorporation	1813
Land/water area (sq. miles)	111.28/1.71
Form of government	Township

Government

Legislative Districts

US Congressional	2
State Legislative	2

Local Officials, 2009

Mayor	Nelson Gaskill
Manager	Edward Sasdelli
Clerk	Joan Anderson
Finance Dir	Richard Tuthill
Tax Assessor	Gerard Mead
Tax Collector	Renee DeSalvo
Attorney	Randolph Lafferty
Building	Warren Dagrosa
Planning	Philip Sartorio
Engineering	Robert Smith
Public Works	Robert Morley
Police Chief	Jay McKeen
Fire/Emergency Dir	NA

Housing & Construction

Housing Units, 2000*

Total	7,567
Median rent	$806
Median SF home value	$105,700

Permits for New Residential Construction

	Units	Value
Total, 2006	192	$18,426,606
Single family	172	$17,442,406
Total, 2007	98	$13,173,447
Single family	98	$13,173,447

Real Property Valuation, 2008

	Parcels	Valuation
Total	13,964	$1,286,204,700
Vacant	5,156	69,523,200
Residential	8,345	860,675,600
Commercial	234	286,822,700
Industrial	11	15,077,100
Apartments	14	44,823,300
Farm land	155	1,964,200
Farm homestead	49	7,318,600

Average Property Value & Tax, 2008

Residential value	$103,407
Property tax	$3,926
Tax credit/rebate	$804

Public Library

No public municipal library

Library statistics, 2007

Population served	NA
Full-time/total staff	NA/NA

	Total	Per capita
Holdings	NA	NA
Revenues	NA	NA
Expenditures	NA	NA
Annual visits	NA	NA
Internet terminals/annual users	NA/NA	

Public Safety

Number of officers, 2007 69

Crime	2006	2007
Total crimes	1,171	1,217
Violent	59	73
Murder	1	1
Rape	5	1
Robbery	18	25
Aggravated assault	35	46
Non-violent	1,112	1,144
Burglary	199	179
Larceny	863	913
Vehicle theft	50	52
Domestic violence	772	788
Arson	9	5
Total crime rate	49.0	49.8
Violent	2.5	3.0
Non-violent	46.5	46.8

Public School District

(for school year 2007-08 except as noted)

Hamilton Township School District
1876 Dr. Dennis Foreman Drive
Mays Landing, NJ 08330
(609) 476-6300

Superintendent	Michelle Cappelluti
Number of schools	3
Grade plan	K-8
Enrollment	3,229
Attendance rate, '06-07	94.9%
Dropout rate	NA
Students per teacher	11.5
Per pupil expenditure	$10,610
Median faculty salary	$46,091
Median administrator salary	$86,331
Grade 12 enrollment	NA
High school graduation rate	NA

Assessment test results

(percent scoring at proficient or advanced level)

	Language	Math
NJASK-Grade 3	86.0%	78.6%
GEPA-Grade 8	63.8%	75.7%
HSPA-High School	NA	NA

SAT Score Averages, 2006-07

Pct tested	Math	Verbal	Writing
NA	NA	NA	NA

Teacher Qualifications

Avg. years of experience	10

Highly-qualified teachers
one subject/all subjects 100%/100%

No Child Left Behind

AYP, 2006-07 . . . . Needs Improvement

Municipal Finance

State Aid Programs, 2009

Total aid	$3,784,876
CMPTRA	0
Energy tax receipts	3,463,202
Garden State Trust	144,202

General Budget, 2008

Total tax levy	$48,975,109
County levy	7,913,336
County taxes	6,234,546
County library	799,739
County health	327,249
County open space	551,802
School levy	28,036,767
Muni. levy	13,025,006
Misc. revenues	10,955,066

Taxes

	2006	2007	2008
General tax rate per $100	3.593	3.738	3.797
County equalization ratio	58.28	49.16	46.82
Net valuation taxable	$1,248,435,800	$1,266,509,452	$1,289,946,779
State equalized value	$2,543,665,795	$2,700,855,719	$2,682,219,172

See Introduction for an explanation of all data sources.

Demographics & Socio-Economic Characteristics[†]

(2000 US Census, except as noted)

Population
1980*	82,801
1990*	86,553
2000	87,109
Male	41,530
Female	45,579
2007 (estimate)*	90,365
Population density	2,290.6

Race & Hispanic Origin, 2000
Race
White	74,173
Black/African American	7,112
American Indian/Alaska Native	121
Asian	2,234
Native Hawaiian/Pacific Islander	31
Other race	1,908
Two or more races	1,530
Hispanic origin, total	4,471
Mexican	221
Puerto Rican	2,409
Cuban	113
Other Hispanic	1,728

Age & Nativity, 2000
Under 5 years	5,006
18 years and over	66,909
21 years and over	64,219
65 years and over	13,623
85 years and over	1,520
Median age	39.1
Native-born	78,943
Foreign-born	8,311

Educational Attainment, 2000
Population 25 years and over	61,062
Less than 9th grade	5.1%
High school grad or higher	83.0%
Bachelor's degree or higher	22.5%
Graduate degree	7.2%

Income & Poverty, 1999
Per capita income	$25,441
Median household income	$57,110
Median family income	$66,986
Persons in poverty	3,619
H'holds receiving public assistance	686
H'holds receiving social security	9,939

Households, 2000
Total households	33,523
With persons under 18	11,338
With persons over 65	9,655
Family households	23,681
Single-person households	8,222
Persons per household	2.58
Persons per family	3.10

Labor & Employment
Total civilian labor force, 2007**	51,009
Unemployment rate	1.9%
Total civilian labor force, 2000	46,420
Unemployment rate	3.7%

Employed persons 16 years and over by occupation, 2000
Managers & professionals	16,451
Service occupations	6,001
Sales & office occupations	13,647
Farming, fishing & forestry	60
Construction & maintenance	3,744
Production & transportation	4,813
Self-employed persons	1,942

† see Appendix C for American Community Survey data
* US Census Bureau
** New Jersey Department of Labor
§ State Fiscal Year July 1–June 30

General Information

Township of Hamilton
2090 Greenwood Ave
Hamilton, NJ 08609
609-890-3500

Website	www.hamiltonnj.com
Year of incorporation	1842
Land/water area (sq. miles)	39.45/0.92
Form of government	Mayor-Council

Government

Legislative Districts
US Congressional	4
State Legislative	14

Local Officials, 2009
Mayor	John F. Bencivengo
Manager	William Guhl
Municipal Clerk	Eileen A. Gore
Finance Dir	NA
Tax Assessor	Donald Kosul
Tax Collector	Michele Rossi
Attorney	Lindsay L. Burbage
Building	Ray Lumio
Planning	Allen Schectel
Engineering	Richard Williams
Public Works	Richard Balgowan
Police Chief	James W. Collins
Fire/Emergency Dir	NA

Housing & Construction

Housing Units, 2000*
Total	34,535
Median rent	$739
Median SF home value	$136,700

Permits for New Residential Construction
	Units	Value
Total, 2006	390	$19,272,292
Single family	148	$8,596,517
Total, 2007	217	$19,125,579
Single family	207	$18,380,259

Real Property Valuation, 2008
	Parcels	Valuation
Total	31,905	$5,170,192,044
Vacant	1,406	75,950,509
Residential	28,641	3,839,193,850
Commercial	1,557	986,974,800
Industrial	60	96,760,100
Apartments	58	155,647,200
Farm land	119	1,909,085
Farm homestead	64	13,756,500

Average Property Value & Tax, 2008
Residential value	$134,226
Property tax	$5,310
Tax credit/rebate	$960

Public Library

Hamilton Township Public Library
1 Justice Samuel A. Alito Jr Way
Hamilton, NJ 08619
609-581-4060

Director	George Conwell

Library statistics, 2007
Population served	87,109
Full-time/total staff	8/27

	Total	Per capita
Holdings	275,880	3.17
Revenues	$2,685,048	$30.82
Expenditures	$3,136,177	$36.00
Annual visits	438,000	5.03
Internet terminals/annual users	19/46,206	

Public Safety

Number of officers, 2007	182

Crime	2006	2007
Total crimes	2,117	1,935
Violent	209	198
Murder	1	0
Rape	9	8
Robbery	109	103
Aggravated assault	90	87
Non-violent	1,908	1,737
Burglary	441	346
Larceny	1,282	1,223
Vehicle theft	185	168
Domestic violence	532	575
Arson	10	8
Total crime rate	23.5	21.4
Violent	2.3	2.2
Non-violent	21.2	19.2

Public School District

(for school year 2007-08 except as noted)

Hamilton Township School District
90 Park Avenue
Hamilton Square, NJ 08690
(609) 631-4100

Superintendent	Neil Bencivengo
Number of schools	23
Grade plan	K-12
Enrollment	13,015
Attendance rate, '06-07	94.0%
Dropout rate	1.1%
Students per teacher	11.7
Per pupil expenditure	$11,891
Median faculty salary	$58,122
Median administrator salary	$102,825
Grade 12 enrollment	939
High school graduation rate	94.6%

Assessment test results
(percent scoring at proficient or advanced level)
	Language	Math
NJASK-Grade 3	85.2%	86.9%
GEPA-Grade 8	59.9%	75.4%
HSPA-High School	70.3%	78.0%

SAT Score Averages, 2006-07
Pct tested	Math	Verbal	Writing
NA	NA	NA	NA

Teacher Qualifications
Avg. years of experience	9
Highly-qualified teachers one subject/all subjects	100%/100%

No Child Left Behind
AYP, 2006-07	Meets Standards

Municipal Finance[§]

State Aid Programs, 2009
Total aid	$24,712,770
CMPTRA	2,727,668
Energy tax receipts	21,366,399
Garden State Trust	587

General Budget, 2008
Total tax levy	$205,142,058
County levy	47,149,422
County taxes	44,121,268
County library	0
County health	0
County open space	3,028,155
School levy	96,536,796
Muni. levy	61,455,840
Misc. revenues	34,944,650

Taxes
	2006	2007	2008
General tax rate per $100	3.42	3.55	3.957
County equalization ratio	63.85	54.97	51.45
Net valuation taxable	$5,041,520,430	$5,128,624,286	$5,185,400,541
State equalized value	$9,189,543,234	$9,953,326,876	$10,401,291,350

See Introduction for an explanation of all data sources.

Demographics & Socio-Economic Characteristics

(2000 US Census, except as noted)

Population

1980*	12,298
1990*	12,208
2000	12,604
Male	6,105
Female	6,499
2007 (estimate)*	13,500
Population density	327.2

Race & Hispanic Origin, 2000

Race

White	11,073
Black/African American	219
American Indian/Alaska Native	18
Asian	144
Native Hawaiian/Pacific Islander	3
Other race	987
Two or more races	160
Hispanic origin, total	1,876
Mexican	685
Puerto Rican	994
Cuban	11
Other Hispanic	186

Age & Nativity, 2000

Under 5 years	754
18 years and over	9,730
21 years and over	9,292
65 years and over	2,265
85 years and over	355
Median age	38.7
Native-born	11,581
Foreign-born	1,023

Educational Attainment, 2000

Population 25 years and over	8,696
Less than 9th grade	12.1%
High school grad or higher	72.5%
Bachelor's degree or higher	16.2%
Graduate degree	4.6%

Income & Poverty, 1999

Per capita income	$19,889
Median household income	$43,137
Median family income	$52,205
Persons in poverty	1,119
H'holds receiving public assistance	103
H'holds receiving social security	1,565

Households, 2000

Total households	4,619
With persons under 18	1,564
With persons over 65	1,513
Family households	3,269
Single-person households	1,103
Persons per household	2.65
Persons per family	3.14

Labor & Employment

Total civilian labor force, 2007**	6,563
Unemployment rate	7.2%
Total civilian labor force, 2000	6,249
Unemployment rate	8.9%

Employed persons 16 years and over by occupation, 2000

Managers & professionals	1,459
Service occupations	1,069
Sales & office occupations	1,689
Farming, fishing & forestry	97
Construction & maintenance	577
Production & transportation	803
Self-employed persons	327

General Information

Town of Hammonton
100 Central Ave
Hammonton, NJ 08037
609-567-4300

Website	www.townofhammonton.org
Year of incorporation	1866
Land/water area (sq. miles)	41.26/0.21
Form of government	Town

Government

Legislative Districts

US Congressional	2
State Legislative	9

Local Officials, 2009

Mayor	John DiDonato
Manager	Susanne Oddo
Clerk	Susanne Oddo
CFO	Robert Scharle
Tax Assessor	Mary Joan Wyatt
Tax Collector	Rosemarie Jacobs
Attorney	Brian Howell
Building	Frank Domenico
Comm Dev/Planning	NA
Engineering	Adams, Rehmann & Heggan
Public Works	NA
Police Chief	Frank Ingemi
Emerg/Fire Director	Dominic DiGiovannangelo

Housing & Construction

Housing Units, 2000*

Total	4,843
Median rent	$689
Median SF home value	$125,200

Permits for New Residential Construction

	Units	Value
Total, 2006	81	$11,353,150
Single family	81	$11,353,150
Total, 2007	27	$3,782,375
Single family	27	$3,782,375

Real Property Valuation, 2008

	Parcels	Valuation
Total	6,303	$831,626,300
Vacant	736	19,334,600
Residential	4,539	607,801,900
Commercial	403	147,236,700
Industrial	27	20,633,700
Apartments	12	7,732,900
Farm land	420	5,842,900
Farm homestead	166	23,043,600

Average Property Value & Tax, 2008

Residential value	$134,080
Property tax	$4,446
Tax credit/rebate	$938

Public Library

Hammonton West Branch‡
451 S Egg Harbor Rd
Hammonton, NJ 08037
609-561-2264

Branch Librarian	Dave Munn

Library statistics, 2007

see Atlantic County profile
for library system statistics

Public Safety

Number of officers, 2007	34

Crime	2006	2007
Total crimes	228	183
Violent	34	20
Murder	2	0
Rape	2	1
Robbery	6	4
Aggravated assault	24	15
Non-violent	194	163
Burglary	35	36
Larceny	140	116
Vehicle theft	19	11
Domestic violence	276	200
Arson	2	2
Total crime rate	16.8	13.5
Violent	2.5	1.5
Non-violent	14.3	12.0

Public School District

(for school year 2007-08 except as noted)

Hammonton Town School District
566 Old Forks Road, Box 631
Hammonton, NJ 08037
(609) 567-7000

Superintendent	Mary Lou DeFrancisco
Number of schools	4
Grade plan	K-12
Enrollment	3,285
Attendance rate, '06-07	93.2%
Dropout rate	2.5%
Students per teacher	12.4
Per pupil expenditure	$10,884
Median faculty salary	$49,602
Median administrator salary	$100,501
Grade 12 enrollment	307
High school graduation rate	92.0%

Assessment test results

(percent scoring at proficient or advanced level)

	Language	Math
NJASK-Grade 3	77.2%	84.4%
GEPA-Grade 8	71.7%	81.8%
HSPA-High School	76.2%	80.2%

SAT Score Averages, 2006-07

Pct tested	Math	Verbal	Writing
56%	518	508	493

Teacher Qualifications

Avg. years of experience	8
Highly-qualified teachers one subject/all subjects	97.5%/97.5%

No Child Left Behind

AYP, 2006-07	Meets Standards

Municipal Finance

State Aid Programs, 2009

Total aid	$1,649,628
CMPTRA	428,358
Energy tax receipts	1,127,992
Garden State Trust	52,918

General Budget, 2008

Total tax levy	$27,696,425
County levy	4,326,117
County taxes	3,407,347
County library	437,682
County health	179,097
County open space	301,991
School levy	17,023,409
Muni. levy	6,346,898
Misc. revenues	5,927,448

Taxes

	2006	2007	2008
General tax rate per $100	3.328	3.307	3.317
County equalization ratio	68.71	60.28	55.68
Net valuation taxable	$783,368,300	$816,529,774	$835,232,116
State equalized value	$1,303,830,020	$1,463,460,806	$1,546,225,553

‡ Branch of county library
* US Census Bureau
** New Jersey Department of Labor

See Introduction for an explanation of all data sources.

Demographics & Socio-Economic Characteristics
(2000 US Census, except as noted)

Population
1980*	1,614
1990*	1,515
2000	1,546
Male	798
Female	748
2007 (estimate)*	1,642
Population density	1,066.2

Race & Hispanic Origin, 2000
Race
White	1,407
Black/African American	77
American Indian/Alaska Native	6
Asian	15
Native Hawaiian/Pacific Islander	0
Other race	12
Two or more races	29
Hispanic origin, total	44
Mexican	3
Puerto Rican	26
Cuban	2
Other Hispanic	13

Age & Nativity, 2000
Under 5 years	126
18 years and over	1,148
21 years and over	1,086
65 years and over	170
85 years and over	15
Median age	34.7
Native-born	1,476
Foreign-born	70

Educational Attainment, 2000
Population 25 years and over	972
Less than 9th grade	2.8%
High school grad or higher	86.9%
Bachelor's degree or higher	22.0%
Graduate degree	6.6%

Income & Poverty, 1999
Per capita income	$22,440
Median household income	$51,111
Median family income	$64,583
Persons in poverty	121
H'holds receiving public assistance	21
H'holds receiving social security	150

Households, 2000
Total households	559
With persons under 18	218
With persons over 65	138
Family households	378
Single-person households	155
Persons per household	2.58
Persons per family	3.20

Labor & Employment
Total civilian labor force, 2007**	861
Unemployment rate	4.5%
Total civilian labor force, 2000	779
Unemployment rate	4.4%

Employed persons 16 years and over by occupation, 2000
Managers & professionals	247
Service occupations	130
Sales & office occupations	185
Farming, fishing & forestry	2
Construction & maintenance	95
Production & transportation	86
Self-employed persons	38

* US Census Bureau
** New Jersey Department of Labor

General Information
Borough of Hampton
PO Box 418
Hampton, NJ 08827
908-537-2329

Website	(county website)
Year of incorporation	1909
Land/water area (sq. miles)	1.54/0.00
Form of government	Borough

Government
Legislative Districts
US Congressional	7
State Legislative	23

Local Officials, 2009
Mayor	Rob Walton
Manager/Admin	NA
Clerk	Cathy Drummond
Finance Dir	Kathleen Olsen
Tax Assessor	Robert Vance
Tax Collector	Diane Laudenbach
Attorney	Richard Cushing
Building	NA
Comm Dev/Planning	NA
Engineering	William Burr
Public Works	John Spiridigliozzi
Police Chief	NA
Emerg/Fire Director	Jeffrey Tampier

Housing & Construction
Housing Units, 2000*
Total	574
Median rent	$543
Median SF home value	$165,200

Permits for New Residential Construction
	Units	Value
Total, 2006	5	$904,778
Single family	5	$904,778
Total, 2007	0	$0
Single family	0	$0

Real Property Valuation, 2008
	Parcels	Valuation
Total	553	$150,278,035
Vacant	55	4,460,701
Residential	449	132,531,285
Commercial	18	5,839,050
Industrial	2	1,011,500
Apartments	3	2,745,800
Farm land	19	142,299
Farm homestead	7	3,547,400

Average Property Value & Tax, 2008
Residential value	$298,418
Property tax	$6,864
Tax credit/rebate	$1,126

Public Library
No public municipal library

Library statistics, 2007
Population served	NA
Full-time/total staff	NA/NA

	Total	Per capita
Holdings	NA	NA
Revenues	NA	NA
Expenditures	NA	NA
Annual visits	NA	NA
Internet terminals/annual users	NA/NA	

Public Safety
Number of officers, 2007 0

Crime	2006	2007
Total crimes	26	17
Violent	3	1
Murder	0	0
Rape	0	0
Robbery	0	0
Aggravated assault	3	1
Non-violent	23	16
Burglary	11	3
Larceny	10	10
Vehicle theft	2	3
Domestic violence	2	14
Arson	2	0
Total crime rate	16.2	10.3
Violent	1.9	0.6
Non-violent	14.3	9.7

Public School District
(for school year 2007-08 except as noted)

Hampton Borough School District
32-41 South Street
Hampton, NJ 08827
(908) 537-4101

Chief School Admin	Joanna Hughes
Number of schools	1
Grade plan	K-8
Enrollment	171
Attendance rate, '06-07	95.9%
Dropout rate	NA
Students per teacher	7.4
Per pupil expenditure	$14,510
Median faculty salary	$49,600
Median administrator salary	$100,933
Grade 12 enrollment	NA
High school graduation rate	NA

Assessment test results
(percent scoring at proficient or advanced level)
	Language	Math
NJASK-Grade 3	72.7%	68.1%
GEPA-Grade 8	57.1%	81.0%
HSPA-High School	NA	NA

SAT Score Averages, 2006-07
Pct tested	Math	Verbal	Writing
NA	NA	NA	NA

Teacher Qualifications
Avg. years of experience	15
Highly-qualified teachers one subject/all subjects	100%/100%

No Child Left Behind
AYP, 2006-07	Meets Standards

Municipal Finance
State Aid Programs, 2009
Total aid	$125,037
CMPTRA	54,025
Energy tax receipts	66,707
Garden State Trust	726

General Budget, 2008
Total tax levy	$3,479,418
County levy	511,331
County taxes	427,965
County library	37,164
County health	0
County open space	46,202
School levy	2,499,871
Muni. levy	468,216
Misc. revenues	711,751

Taxes
	2006	2007	2008
General tax rate per $100	2.22	2.27	2.301
County equalization ratio	123.53	97.59	98.63
Net valuation taxable	$143,203,760	$148,166,403	$151,276,363
State equalized value	$129,499,366	$144,902,607	$148,982,607

See Introduction for an explanation of all data sources.

Demographics & Socio-Economic Characteristics

(2000 US Census, except as noted)

Population

1980*	3,916
1990*	4,438
2000	4,943
Male	2,413
Female	2,530
2007 (estimate)*	5,135
Population density	208.6

Race & Hispanic Origin, 2000

Race

White	4,809
Black/African American	48
American Indian/Alaska Native	1
Asian	33
Native Hawaiian/Pacific Islander	1
Other race	15
Two or more races	36
Hispanic origin, total	94
Mexican	7
Puerto Rican	38
Cuban	13
Other Hispanic	36

Age & Nativity, 2000

Under 5 years	276
18 years and over	3,632
21 years and over	3,503
65 years and over	547
85 years and over	63
Median age	39.8
Native-born	4,766
Foreign-born	177

Educational Attainment, 2000

Population 25 years and over	3,373
Less than 9th grade	2.1%
High school grad or higher	91.4%
Bachelor's degree or higher	27.3%
Graduate degree	7.1%

Income & Poverty, 1999

Per capita income	$25,353
Median household income	$60,698
Median family income	$67,386
Persons in poverty	101
H'holds receiving public assistance	32
H'holds receiving social security	466

Households, 2000

Total households	1,857
With persons under 18	720
With persons over 65	400
Family households	1,413
Single-person households	384
Persons per household	2.65
Persons per family	3.10

Labor & Employment

Total civilian labor force, 2007**	2,895
Unemployment rate	3.4%
Total civilian labor force, 2000	2,596
Unemployment rate	2.6%

Employed persons 16 years and over by occupation, 2000

Managers & professionals	941
Service occupations	324
Sales & office occupations	641
Farming, fishing & forestry	13
Construction & maintenance	326
Production & transportation	283
Self-employed persons	183

General Information

Township of Hampton
1 Municipal Complex Rd
Newton, NJ 07860
973-383-5570

Email	administrator@hamptontwp-nj.org
Year of incorporation	1864
Land/water area (sq. miles)	24.62/0.69
Form of government	Township

Government

Legislative Districts

US Congressional	5
State Legislative	24

Local Officials, 2009

Mayor	Philip Yetter
Manager	Eileen Klose
Clerk	Kathleen Armstrong
Finance Dir	Jessica Caruso
Tax Assessor	John Dyksen
Tax Collector	Jessica Caruso
Attorney	Stephen Roseman
Building	John deJager
Planning	Harold Pellow
Engineering	Harold C. Pellow
Public Works	Daniel Bayles
Police Chief	NA
Emerg/Fire Director	Russell Bellis Jr

Housing & Construction

Housing Units, 2000*

Total	2,026
Median rent	$953
Median SF home value	$149,500

Permits for New Residential Construction

	Units	Value
Total, 2006	16	$3,112,528
Single family	16	$3,112,528
Total, 2007	5	$817,696
Single family	5	$817,696

Real Property Valuation, 2008

	Parcels	Valuation
Total	2,781	$388,015,675
Vacant	464	8,643,700
Residential	1,890	281,085,400
Commercial	67	67,294,100
Industrial	2	335,000
Apartments	0	0
Farm land	236	2,036,775
Farm homestead	122	28,620,700

Average Property Value & Tax, 2008

Residential value	$153,929
Property tax	$5,601
Tax credit/rebate	$988

Public Library

No public municipal library

Library statistics, 2007

Population served	NA
Full-time/total staff	NA/NA

	Total	Per capita
Holdings	NA	NA
Revenues	NA	NA
Expenditures	NA	NA
Annual visits	NA	NA
Internet terminals/annual users	NA/NA	

Public Safety

Number of officers, 2007 0

Crime

	2006	2007
Total crimes	72	92
Violent	5	2
Murder	0	0
Rape	1	0
Robbery	0	1
Aggravated assault	4	1
Non-violent	67	90
Burglary	9	7
Larceny	55	80
Vehicle theft	3	3
Domestic violence	1	34
Arson	0	0
Total crime rate	13.8	17.6
Violent	1.0	0.4
Non-violent	12.9	17.3

Public School District

(for school year 2007-08 except as noted)

Hampton Township School District
One School Road
Newton, NJ 07860
(973) 383-5300

Chief School Admin	Everett C. Burns
Number of schools	1
Grade plan	K-6
Enrollment	424
Attendance rate, '06-07	95.4%
Dropout rate	NA
Students per teacher	10.0
Per pupil expenditure	$13,000
Median faculty salary	$53,905
Median administrator salary	$116,370
Grade 12 enrollment	NA
High school graduation rate	NA

Assessment test results

(percent scoring at proficient or advanced level)

	Language	Math
NJASK-Grade 3	96.2%	98.1%
GEPA-Grade 8	NA	NA
HSPA-High School	NA	NA

SAT Score Averages, 2006-07

Pct tested	Math	Verbal	Writing
NA	NA	NA	NA

Teacher Qualifications

Avg. years of experience	10
Highly-qualified teachers one subject/all subjects	NA/NA

No Child Left Behind

AYP, 2006-07 . . . . Meets Standards

Municipal Finance

State Aid Programs, 2009

Total aid	$574,737
CMPTRA	89,472
Energy tax receipts	428,258
Garden State Trust	39,313

General Budget, 2008

Total tax levy	$14,147,061
County levy	3,022,110
County taxes	2,536,138
County library	213,763
County health	75,078
County open space	197,131
School levy	9,106,638
Muni. levy	2,018,314
Misc. revenues	1,830,731

Taxes

	2006	2007	2008
General tax rate per $100	3.43	3.54	3.639
County equalization ratio	57.4	51.59	49.53
Net valuation taxable	$372,289,805	$384,661,546	$388,825,614
State equalized value	$722,673,955	$775,737,736	$787,859,990

* US Census Bureau
** New Jersey Department of Labor

See Introduction for an explanation of all data sources.

Demographics & Socio-Economic Characteristics
(2000 US Census, except as noted)

Population
1980*	11,846
1990*	11,538
2000	12,898
Male	6,273
Female	6,625
2007 (estimate)*	13,653
Population density	1,280.8

Race & Hispanic Origin, 2000
Race
White	11,452
Black/African American	140
American Indian/Alaska Native	7
Asian	1,123
Native Hawaiian/Pacific Islander	1
Other race	76
Two or more races	99
Hispanic origin, total	452
Mexican	44
Puerto Rican	63
Cuban	56
Other Hispanic	289

Age & Nativity, 2000
Under 5 years	828
18 years and over	9,956
21 years and over	9,658
65 years and over	1,921
85 years and over	173
Median age	40.1
Native-born	10,868
Foreign-born	2,030

Educational Attainment, 2000
Population 25 years and over	9,272
Less than 9th grade	4.6%
High school grad or higher	89.5%
Bachelor's degree or higher	41.5%
Graduate degree	15.3%

Income & Poverty, 1999
Per capita income	$37,661
Median household income	$84,115
Median family income	$93,937
Persons in poverty	152
H'holds receiving public assistance	23
H'holds receiving social security	1,449

Households, 2000
Total households	4,745
With persons under 18	1,631
With persons over 65	1,363
Family households	3,619
Single-person households	930
Persons per household	2.71
Persons per family	3.13

Labor & Employment
Total civilian labor force, 2007**	7,559
Unemployment rate	1.7%
Total civilian labor force, 2000	6,941
Unemployment rate	1.5%

Employed persons 16 years and over by occupation, 2000
Managers & professionals	3,150
Service occupations	638
Sales & office occupations	2,050
Farming, fishing & forestry	0
Construction & maintenance	510
Production & transportation	486
Self-employed persons	308

* US Census Bureau
** New Jersey Department of Labor

General Information
Township of Hanover
1000 Route 10
PO Box 250
Whippany, NJ 07981
973-428-2500

Website	www.hanovertownship.com
Year of incorporation	1720
Land/water area (sq. miles)	10.66/0.03
Form of government	Township

Government
Legislative Districts
US Congressional	11
State Legislative	26

Local Officials, 2009
Mayor	Leonardo A. Fariello
Manager	Joseph Giorgio
Clerk	Joseph Giorgio
Finance Dir	Silvio Esposito
Tax Assessor	John Dyksen
Tax Collector	Michael Zambito
Attorney	John Dorsey
Building	Steven Kaplan
Planning	Kimberly B. Howard
Engineering	Gerardo Maceira
Public Works	Brian Foran
Police Chief	Stephen Gallagher
Fire Chief	J. Cortright/J. Davidson

Housing & Construction
Housing Units, 2000*
Total	4,818
Median rent	$1,098
Median SF home value	$286,100

Permits for New Residential Construction
	Units	Value
Total, 2006	52	$9,981,946
Single family	52	$9,981,946
Total, 2007	37	$7,026,750
Single family	37	$7,026,750

Real Property Valuation, 2008
	Parcels	Valuation
Total	5,488	$2,028,641,133
Vacant	357	74,908,200
Residential	4,771	1,139,038,922
Commercial	210	573,242,511
Industrial	141	212,569,800
Apartments	6	28,868,800
Farm land	1	3,800
Farm homestead	2	9,100

Average Property Value & Tax, 2008
Residential value	$238,644
Property tax	$6,057
Tax credit/rebate	$975

Public Library
Whippanong Library
1000 Route 10
Whippany, NJ 07981
973-428-2460

Director	Sulekha Das

Library statistics, 2007
Population served	12,898
Full-time/total staff	2/3

	Total	Per capita
Holdings	54,856	4.25
Revenues	$468,334	$36.31
Expenditures	$478,247	$37.08
Annual visits	78,000	6.05
Internet terminals/annual users	9/26,520	

Public Safety
Number of officers, 2007	32

Crime	2006	2007
Total crimes	184	190
Violent	10	11
Murder	0	0
Rape	0	0
Robbery	4	2
Aggravated assault	6	9
Non-violent	174	179
Burglary	20	21
Larceny	144	143
Vehicle theft	10	15
Domestic violence	60	54
Arson	3	0
Total crime rate	13.4	13.8
Violent	0.7	0.8
Non-violent	12.7	13.0

Public School District
(for school year 2007-08 except as noted)

Hanover Township School District
61 Highland Avenue
Whippany, NJ 07981
(973) 515-2404

Superintendent	Scott Pepper
Number of schools	4
Grade plan	K-8
Enrollment	1,575
Attendance rate, '06-07	96.1%
Dropout rate	NA
Students per teacher	10.8
Per pupil expenditure	$14,228
Median faculty salary	$59,905
Median administrator salary	$117,843
Grade 12 enrollment	NA
High school graduation rate	NA

Assessment test results
(percent scoring at proficient or advanced level)
	Language	Math
NJASK-Grade 3	96.8%	92.0%
GEPA-Grade 8	83.9%	96.7%
HSPA-High School	NA	NA

SAT Score Averages, 2006-07
Pct tested	Math	Verbal	Writing
NA	NA	NA	NA

Teacher Qualifications
Avg. years of experience	11
Highly-qualified teachers one subject/all subjects	100%/100%

No Child Left Behind
AYP, 2006-07	Meets Standards

Municipal Finance
State Aid Programs, 2009
Total aid	$3,037,146
CMPTRA	828,595
Energy tax receipts	2,109,561
Garden State Trust	292

General Budget, 2008
Total tax levy	$51,777,602
County levy	9,673,209
County taxes	7,895,600
County library	0
County health	0
County open space	1,777,609
School levy	29,073,233
Muni. levy	13,031,160
Misc. revenues	9,573,266

Taxes
	2006	2007	2008
General tax rate per $100	2.34	2.45	2.539
County equalization ratio	56.88	52.19	49.31
Net valuation taxable	$2,014,007,733	$2,031,454,261	$2,039,915,715
State equalized value	$3,872,058,359	$4,107,354,947	$4,120,330,958

See Introduction for an explanation of all data sources.

Demographics & Socio-Economic Characteristics

(2000 US Census, except as noted)

Population

1980*	3,236
1990*	3,640
2000	3,180
Male	1,540
Female	1,640
2007 (estimate)*	3,319
Population density	162.4

Race & Hispanic Origin, 2000

Race

White	3,091
Black/African American	13
American Indian/Alaska Native	0
Asian	34
Native Hawaiian/Pacific Islander	1
Other race	7
Two or more races	34
Hispanic origin, total	57
Mexican	3
Puerto Rican	2
Cuban	10
Other Hispanic	42

Age & Nativity, 2000

Under 5 years	199
18 years and over	2,379
21 years and over	2,321
65 years and over	521
85 years and over	56
Median age	44.5
Native-born	2,984
Foreign-born	196

Educational Attainment, 2000

Population 25 years and over	2,265
Less than 9th grade	0.7%
High school grad or higher	97.5%
Bachelor's degree or higher	66.0%
Graduate degree	31.9%

Income & Poverty, 1999

Per capita income	$72,689
Median household income	$111,297
Median family income	$128,719
Persons in poverty	36
H'holds receiving public assistance	9
H'holds receiving social security	342

Households, 2000

Total households	1,180
With persons under 18	393
With persons over 65	361
Family households	941
Single-person households	208
Persons per household	2.69
Persons per family	3.03

Labor & Employment

Total civilian labor force, 2007**	1,497
Unemployment rate	2.3%
Total civilian labor force, 2000	1,369
Unemployment rate	2.3%

Employed persons 16 years and over by occupation, 2000

Managers & professionals	821
Service occupations	109
Sales & office occupations	313
Farming, fishing & forestry	0
Construction & maintenance	72
Production & transportation	23
Self-employed persons	129

* US Census Bureau
** New Jersey Department of Labor

See Introduction for an explanation of all data sources.

General Information

Township of Harding
PO Box 666
New Vernon, NJ 07976
973-267-8000

Website	www.hardingnj.org
Year of incorporation	1922
Land/water area (sq. miles)	20.44/0.04
Form of government	Township

Government

Legislative Districts

US Congressional	11
State Legislative	21

Local Officials, 2009

Mayor	Louis J Lanzerotti
Manager	Gail McKane
Clerk	Gail W McKane
Finance Dir	Himanshu Shah
Tax Assessor	Pat Aceto
Tax Collector	Kathy Silber
Attorney	Maryann Nergaard
Building	Mary Ellen Balady
Planning	Susan Kimball
Engineering	Paul Fox
Public Works	Tracy Toribio
Police Chief	Kevin Gaffney
Emerg/Fire Director	Mike Cherello

Housing & Construction

Housing Units, 2000*

Total	1,243
Median rent	$1,125
Median SF home value	$665,400

Permits for New Residential Construction

	Units	Value
Total, 2006	10	$13,506,559
Single family	10	$13,506,559
Total, 2007	9	$16,077,000
Single family	9	$16,077,000

Real Property Valuation, 2008

	Parcels	Valuation
Total	1,884	$1,999,503,371
Vacant	197	64,900,900
Residential	1,399	1,673,994,363
Commercial	43	72,171,800
Industrial	3	9,641,900
Apartments	0	0
Farm land	153	1,818,708
Farm homestead	89	176,975,700

Average Property Value & Tax, 2008

Residential value	$1,243,931
Property tax	$12,880
Tax credit/rebate	$1,017

Public Library

Harding Township Library
21 Blue Mill Rd
New Vernon, NJ 07976
973-267-8000

Director	Anne N. Thomas

Library statistics, 2007

Population served	3,180
Full-time/total staff	0/0

	Total	Per capita
Holdings	7,404	2.33
Revenues	$88,682	$27.89
Expenditures	$91,235	$28.69
Annual visits	7,834	2.46
Internet terminals/annual users	0/0	

Public Safety

Number of officers, 2007	14

Crime	2006	2007
Total crimes	17	23
Violent	0	3
Murder	0	0
Rape	0	0
Robbery	0	0
Aggravated assault	0	3
Non-violent	17	20
Burglary	9	2
Larceny	7	18
Vehicle theft	1	0
Domestic violence	6	11
Arson	0	0
Total crime rate	5.1	6.8
Violent	0.0	0.9
Non-violent	5.1	5.9

Public School District

(for school year 2007-08 except as noted)

Harding Township School District
Lee's Hill Road, PO Box 248
New Vernon, NJ 07976
(973) 267-6398

Superintendent	Timothy Purnell
Number of schools	1
Grade plan	K-8
Enrollment	321
Attendance rate, '06-07	96.2%
Dropout rate	NA
Students per teacher	8.0
Per pupil expenditure	$19,161
Median faculty salary	$49,665
Median administrator salary	$119,000
Grade 12 enrollment	NA
High school graduation rate	NA

Assessment test results

(percent scoring at proficient or advanced level)

	Language	Math
NJASK-Grade 3	96.3%	100.0%
GEPA-Grade 8	85.0%	92.5%
HSPA-High School	NA	NA

SAT Score Averages, 2006-07

Pct tested	Math	Verbal	Writing
NA	NA	NA	NA

Teacher Qualifications

Avg. years of experience	6
Highly-qualified teachers one subject/all subjects	100%/100%

No Child Left Behind

AYP, 2006-07	Meets Standards

Municipal Finance

State Aid Programs, 2009

Total aid	$517,871
CMPTRA	0
Energy tax receipts	491,580
Garden State Trust	347

General Budget, 2008

Total tax levy	$20,716,222
County levy	6,388,730
County taxes	5,213,416
County library	0
County health	0
County open space	1,175,314
School levy	8,437,416
Muni. levy	5,890,077
Misc. revenues	3,706,970

Taxes

	2006	2007	2008
General tax rate per $100	0.94	1.04	1.036
County equalization ratio	87.05	78.32	72.89
Net valuation taxable	$1,949,507,371	$1,966,563,766	$2,000,744,088
State equalized value	$2,490,359,978	$2,697,523,596	$2,748,943,577

Demographics & Socio-Economic Characteristics
(2000 US Census, except as noted)

Population
1980*	947
1990*	1,235
2000	1,464
Male	731
Female	733
2007 (estimate)*	1,619
Population density	44.4

Race & Hispanic Origin, 2000
Race
White	1,421
Black/African American	9
American Indian/Alaska Native	1
Asian	6
Native Hawaiian/Pacific Islander	0
Other race	13
Two or more races	14
Hispanic origin, total	34
Mexican	2
Puerto Rican	11
Cuban	1
Other Hispanic	20

Age & Nativity, 2000
Under 5 years	92
18 years and over	1,075
21 years and over	1,035
65 years and over	141
85 years and over	13
Median age	39.4
Native-born	1,398
Foreign-born	65

Educational Attainment, 2000
Population 25 years and over	994
Less than 9th grade	2.0%
High school grad or higher	92.1%
Bachelor's degree or higher	29.8%
Graduate degree	9.6%

Income & Poverty, 1999
Per capita income	$30,038
Median household income	$72,167
Median family income	$76,111
Persons in poverty	38
H'holds receiving public assistance	4
H'holds receiving social security	102

Households, 2000
Total households	502
With persons under 18	206
With persons over 65	98
Family households	410
Single-person households	70
Persons per household	2.85
Persons per family	3.15

Labor & Employment
Total civilian labor force, 2007**	877
Unemployment rate	2.7%
Total civilian labor force, 2000	784
Unemployment rate	3.1%

Employed persons 16 years and over by occupation, 2000
Managers & professionals	328
Service occupations	89
Sales & office occupations	200
Farming, fishing & forestry	8
Construction & maintenance	80
Production & transportation	55
Self-employed persons	68

General Information
Township of Hardwick
40 Spring Valley Rd
Hardwick, NJ 07825
908-362-6528
Website	www.hardwick-nj.us
Year of incorporation	1750
Land/water area (sq. miles)	36.48/1.44
Form of government	Township

Government
Legislative Districts
US Congressional	5
State Legislative	23

Local Officials, 2009
Mayor	Kevin Duffy
Manager/Admin	NA
Clerk	Judith Fisher
Finance Dir	Gregory Della Pia
Tax Assessor	David Gill
Tax Collector	Donna Clouse
Attorney	Michael Lavery
Building	David Peck
Comm Dev/Planning	NA
Engineering	Ted Rodman
Public Works	Thomas Campbell
Police Chief	NA
Fire/Emergency Dir	NA

Housing & Construction
Housing Units, 2000*
Total	530
Median rent	$775
Median SF home value	$196,700

Permits for New Residential Construction
	Units	Value
Total, 2006	8	$1,518,970
Single family	8	$1,518,970
Total, 2007	7	$1,345,869
Single family	7	$1,345,869

Real Property Valuation, 2008
	Parcels	Valuation
Total	934	$155,741,400
Vacant	85	6,259,400
Residential	451	110,940,300
Commercial	3	1,506,200
Industrial	1	627,000
Apartments	0	0
Farm land	258	1,055,300
Farm homestead	136	35,353,200

Average Property Value & Tax, 2008
Residential value	$249,222
Property tax	$7,322
Tax credit/rebate	$1,228

Public Library
No public municipal library

Library statistics, 2007
Population served	NA
Full-time/total staff	NA/NA

	Total	Per capita
Holdings	NA	NA
Revenues	NA	NA
Expenditures	NA	NA
Annual visits	NA	NA
Internet terminals/annual users	NA/NA	

Public Safety
Number of officers, 2007	0

Crime	2006	2007
Total crimes	8	16
Violent	0	1
Murder	0	0
Rape	0	0
Robbery	0	0
Aggravated assault	0	1
Non-violent	8	15
Burglary	3	4
Larceny	5	8
Vehicle theft	0	3
Domestic violence	0	18
Arson	0	0
Total crime rate	5.0	9.8
Violent	0.0	0.6
Non-violent	5.0	9.2

Public School District
(for school year 2007-08 except as noted)

Hardwick Township School District
98 Mohican Rd.
Blairstown,, NJ 07825

No schools in district - sends students to Blairstown schools

Per pupil expenditure	NA
Median faculty salary	NA
Median administrator salary	NA
Grade 12 enrollment	NA
High school graduation rate	NA

Assessment test results
(percent scoring at proficient or advanced level)
	Language	Math
NJASK-Grade 3	NA	NA
GEPA-Grade 8	NA	NA
HSPA-High School	NA	NA

SAT Score Averages, 2006-07
Pct tested	Math	Verbal	Writing
NA	NA	NA	NA

Teacher Qualifications
Avg. years of experience	NA
Highly-qualified teachers one subject/all subjects	NA/NA

No Child Left Behind
AYP, 2006-07	NA

Municipal Finance
State Aid Programs, 2009
Total aid	$200,534
CMPTRA	6,415
Energy tax receipts	151,597
Garden State Trust	33,915

General Budget, 2008
Total tax levy	$4,584,416
County levy	1,546,166
County taxes	1,260,947
County library	132,460
County health	0
County open space	152,760
School levy	2,720,707
Muni. levy	317,543
Misc. revenues	718,139

Taxes	2006	2007	2008
General tax rate per $100	2.93	2.93	2.938
County equalization ratio	70.84	65.49	61.36
Net valuation taxable	$151,348,250	$154,155,426	$156,046,474
State equalized value	$231,479,311	$251,027,594	$242,402,696

* US Census Bureau
** New Jersey Department of Labor

See Introduction for an explanation of all data sources.

Demographics & Socio-Economic Characteristics

(2000 US Census, except as noted)

Population

1980*	4,553
1990*	5,275
2000	6,171
Male	3,038
Female	3,133
2007 (estimate)*	8,344
Population density	260.0

Race & Hispanic Origin, 2000

Race

White	5,897
Black/African American	52
American Indian/Alaska Native	10
Asian	97
Native Hawaiian/Pacific Islander	0
Other race	30
Two or more races	85
Hispanic origin, total	199
Mexican	10
Puerto Rican	105
Cuban	10
Other Hispanic	74

Age & Nativity, 2000

Under 5 years	424
18 years and over	4,588
21 years and over	4,436
65 years and over	630
85 years and over	54
Median age	38.4
Native-born	5,848
Foreign-born	296

Educational Attainment, 2000

Population 25 years and over	4,267
Less than 9th grade	2.8%
High school grad or higher	90.4%
Bachelor's degree or higher	26.7%
Graduate degree	10.4%

Income & Poverty, 1999

Per capita income	$28,457
Median household income	$65,511
Median family income	$72,199
Persons in poverty	285
H'holds receiving public assistance	35
H'holds receiving social security	503

Households, 2000

Total households	2,319
With persons under 18	869
With persons over 65	465
Family households	1,715
Single-person households	500
Persons per household	2.66
Persons per family	3.12

Labor & Employment

Total civilian labor force, 2007**	3,745
Unemployment rate	4.9%
Total civilian labor force, 2000	3,340
Unemployment rate	3.8%

Employed persons 16 years and over by occupation, 2000

Managers & professionals	1,160
Service occupations	409
Sales & office occupations	851
Farming, fishing & forestry	11
Construction & maintenance	404
Production & transportation	378
Self-employed persons	178

*   US Census Bureau
** New Jersey Department of Labor

See Introduction for an explanation of all data sources.

General Information

Township of Hardyston
149 Wheatsworth Rd
Hardyston, NJ 07419
973-823-7020

Website	www.hardyston.com
Year of incorporation	1762
Land/water area (sq. miles)	32.09/0.55
Form of government	Special Charter

Government

Legislative Districts

US Congressional	5
State Legislative	24

Local Officials, 2009

Mayor	Leslie G. Hamilton
Manager	Marianne Smith
Clerk	Jane Bakalarczyk
Finance Dir	Grant Rome
Tax Assessor	Scott Holzhauer
Tax Collector	Terry Beshada
Attorney	Fred Semrau
Building	Keith Utter
Planning	Anne-Marie Wilhelm
Engineering	Robert P. Guerin
Public Works	Robert F. Schultz
Police Chief	Bret Alemy
Emerg/Fire Director	William Hickerson

Housing & Construction

Housing Units, 2000*

Total	2,690
Median rent	$740
Median SF home value	$152,300

Permits for New Residential Construction

	Units	Value
Total, 2006	110	$12,540,100
Single family	99	$11,649,100
Total, 2007	12	$2,052,700
Single family	12	$2,052,700

Real Property Valuation, 2008

	Parcels	Valuation
Total	4,556	$708,462,500
Vacant	536	23,323,200
Residential	3,707	593,257,700
Commercial	121	57,547,000
Industrial	22	13,844,300
Apartments	4	9,688,000
Farm land	118	1,111,700
Farm homestead	48	9,690,600

Average Property Value & Tax, 2008

Residential value	$160,572
Property tax	$5,280
Tax credit/rebate	$991

Public Library

No public municipal library

Library statistics, 2007

Population served	NA
Full-time/total staff	NA/NA

	Total	Per capita
Holdings	NA	NA
Revenues	NA	NA
Expenditures	NA	NA
Annual visits	NA	NA
Internet terminals/annual users	NA/NA	

Public Safety

Number of officers, 2007	21

Crime	2006	2007
Total crimes	109	68
Violent	10	6
Murder	0	0
Rape	0	2
Robbery	3	0
Aggravated assault	7	4
Non-violent	99	62
Burglary	20	24
Larceny	75	33
Vehicle theft	4	5
Domestic violence	72	96
Arson	0	0
Total crime rate	13.8	8.2
Violent	1.3	0.7
Non-violent	12.5	7.5

Public School District

(for school year 2007-08 except as noted)

Hardyston Township School District
183 Wheatsworth Road
Hamburg, NJ 07419
(973) 823-7000

Chief School Admin	Anthony Norod (Int)
Number of schools	2
Grade plan	K-8
Enrollment	758
Attendance rate, '06-07	94.7%
Dropout rate	NA
Students per teacher	10.9
Per pupil expenditure	$12,097
Median faculty salary	$53,622
Median administrator salary	$101,207
Grade 12 enrollment	NA
High school graduation rate	NA

Assessment test results

(percent scoring at proficient or advanced level)

	Language	Math
NJASK-Grade 3	78.3%	89.8%
GEPA-Grade 8	81.1%	86.5%
HSPA-High School	NA	NA

SAT Score Averages, 2006-07

Pct tested	Math	Verbal	Writing
NA	NA	NA	NA

Teacher Qualifications

Avg. years of experience	13
Highly-qualified teachers one subject/all subjects	100%/100%

No Child Left Behind

AYP, 2006-07	Meets Standards

Municipal Finance

State Aid Programs, 2009

Total aid	$885,234
CMPTRA	86,184
Energy tax receipts	542,858
Garden State Trust	46,754

General Budget, 2008

Total tax levy	$23,338,356
County levy	5,364,217
County taxes	4,501,734
County library	379,417
County health	133,375
County open space	349,691
School levy	12,475,331
Muni. levy	5,498,807
Misc. revenues	3,561,923

Taxes	2006	2007	2008
General tax rate per $100	3.35	3.35	3.289
County equalization ratio	56.37	51.33	50.77
Net valuation taxable	$601,256,000	$642,411,016	$709,778,105
State equalized value	$1,172,782,482	$1,264,052,296	$1,374,304,946

Demographics & Socio-Economic Characteristics

(2000 US Census, except as noted)

Population

1980*	2,592
1990*	2,653
2000	2,729
Male	1,349
Female	1,380
2007 (estimate)*	2,815
Population density	118.2

Race & Hispanic Origin, 2000

Race

White	2,672
Black/African American	19
American Indian/Alaska Native	2
Asian	11
Native Hawaiian/Pacific Islander	0
Other race	5
Two or more races	20
Hispanic origin, total	35
Mexican	1
Puerto Rican	22
Cuban	2
Other Hispanic	10

Age & Nativity, 2000

Under 5 years	163
18 years and over	2,071
21 years and over	2,005
65 years and over	379
85 years and over	51
Median age	40.1
Native-born	2,690
Foreign-born	39

Educational Attainment, 2000

Population 25 years and over	1,936
Less than 9th grade	4.0%
High school grad or higher	84.5%
Bachelor's degree or higher	16.0%
Graduate degree	5.3%

Income & Poverty, 1999

Per capita income	$25,776
Median household income	$60,977
Median family income	$64,196
Persons in poverty	122
H'holds receiving public assistance	18
H'holds receiving social security	280

Households, 2000

Total households	1,010
With persons under 18	370
With persons over 65	263
Family households	787
Single-person households	180
Persons per household	2.68
Persons per family	3.05

Labor & Employment

Total civilian labor force, 2007**	1,630
Unemployment rate	2.2%
Total civilian labor force, 2000	1,457
Unemployment rate	2.3%

Employed persons 16 years and over by occupation, 2000

Managers & professionals	414
Service occupations	184
Sales & office occupations	419
Farming, fishing & forestry	4
Construction & maintenance	202
Production & transportation	200
Self-employed persons	102

@2009 Information Publications, Inc. All rights reserved. Photocopying prohibited. For additional copies, contact the publisher at www.informationpublications.com or (877)544-INFO (4636)

General Information

Township of Harmony
3003 Belvidere Rd
Phillipsburg, NJ 08865
908-213-1600

Website	www.harmonytwp-nj.gov
Year of incorporation	1839
Land/water area (sq. miles)	23.81/0.33
Form of government	Township

Government

Legislative Districts

US Congressional	5
State Legislative	23

Local Officials, 2009

Mayor	Brian Tipton
Manager/Admin	NA
Clerk	Kelley D. Smith
Finance Dir	Dawn Stanchina
Tax Assessor	Richard Motyka
Tax Collector	Joseph Hriczak
Attorney	Katrina Campbell
Building	NJDCA
Comm Dev/Planning	NA
Engineering	Nevitt S. Duveneck
Public Works	James Fox
Police Chief	NA
Emerg/Fire Director	Wesley Garrison

Housing & Construction

Housing Units, 2000*

Total	1,076
Median rent	$745
Median SF home value	$156,000

Permits for New Residential Construction

	Units	Value
Total, 2006	6	$630,867
Single family	6	$630,867
Total, 2007	4	$671,411
Single family	4	$671,411

Real Property Valuation, 2008

	Parcels	Valuation
Total	1,634	$491,349,600
Vacant	229	9,986,000
Residential	977	196,694,100
Commercial	37	19,910,400
Industrial	7	234,455,400
Apartments	0	0
Farm land	278	3,774,300
Farm homestead	106	26,529,400

Average Property Value & Tax, 2008

Residential value	$206,116
Property tax	$4,621
Tax credit/rebate	$922

Public Library

No public municipal library

Library statistics, 2007

Population served	NA
Full-time/total staff	NA/NA

	Total	Per capita
Holdings	NA	NA
Revenues	NA	NA
Expenditures	NA	NA
Annual visits	NA	NA
Internet terminals/annual users	NA/NA	

Public Safety

Number of officers, 2007 ... 0

Crime	2006	2007
Total crimes	20	18
Violent	0	1
Murder	0	0
Rape	0	0
Robbery	0	0
Aggravated assault	0	1
Non-violent	20	17
Burglary	12	1
Larceny	7	15
Vehicle theft	1	1
Domestic violence	0	23
Arson	0	0
Total crime rate	7.1	6.3
Violent	0.0	0.3
Non-violent	7.1	5.9

Public School District

(for school year 2007-08 except as noted)

Harmony Township School District
2551 Belvidere Road
Phillipsburg, NJ 08865
(908) 859-1001

Chief School Admin	Jason Kornegay
Number of schools	1
Grade plan	K-8
Enrollment	307
Attendance rate, '06-07	96.1%
Dropout rate	NA
Students per teacher	9.3
Per pupil expenditure	$14,362
Median faculty salary	$57,983
Median administrator salary	$76,735
Grade 12 enrollment	NA
High school graduation rate	NA

Assessment test results

(percent scoring at proficient or advanced level)

	Language	Math
NJASK-Grade 3	96.7%	93.4%
GEPA-Grade 8	54.9%	77.4%
HSPA-High School	NA	NA

SAT Score Averages, 2006-07

Pct tested	Math	Verbal	Writing
NA	NA	NA	NA

Teacher Qualifications

Avg. years of experience	14
Highly-qualified teachers one subject/all subjects	100%/100%

No Child Left Behind

AYP, 2006-07 ... Meets Standards

Municipal Finance

State Aid Programs, 2009

Total aid	$672,671
CMPTRA	75,257
Energy tax receipts	250,246
Garden State Trust	298,825

General Budget, 2008

Total tax levy	$11,031,527
County levy	4,329,673
County taxes	3,531,257
County library	370,795
County health	0
County open space	427,622
School levy	5,673,432
Muni. levy	1,028,422
Misc. revenues	1,595,748

Taxes	2006	2007	2008
General tax rate per $100	2.1	2.17	2.243
County equalization ratio	72.54	72.49	69.38
Net valuation taxable	$497,661,100	$492,525,925	$492,033,507
State equalized value	$687,170,348	$709,597,937	$666,108,609

* US Census Bureau
** New Jersey Department of Labor

See Introduction for an explanation of all data sources.

Demographics & Socio-Economic Characteristics
(2000 US Census, except as noted)

Population
1980*	4,532
1990*	4,623
2000	4,740
Male	2,305
Female	2,435
2007 (estimate)*	4,881
Population density	2,624.2

Race & Hispanic Origin, 2000
Race
White	3,959
Black/African American	32
American Indian/Alaska Native	2
Asian	695
Native Hawaiian/Pacific Islander	0
Other race	30
Two or more races	22
Hispanic origin, total	122
Mexican	6
Puerto Rican	46
Cuban	13
Other Hispanic	57

Age & Nativity, 2000
Under 5 years	344
18 years and over	3,384
21 years and over	3,279
65 years and over	606
85 years and over	41
Median age	40.2
Native-born	3,959
Foreign-born	781

Educational Attainment, 2000
Population 25 years and over	3,114
Less than 9th grade	1.3%
High school grad or higher	96.1%
Bachelor's degree or higher	58.4%
Graduate degree	21.9%

Income & Poverty, 1999
Per capita income	$39,017
Median household income	$100,302
Median family income	$105,223
Persons in poverty	138
H'holds receiving public assistance	5
H'holds receiving social security	421

Households, 2000
Total households	1,563
With persons under 18	716
With persons over 65	430
Family households	1,344
Single-person households	191
Persons per household	3.03
Persons per family	3.31

Labor & Employment
Total civilian labor force, 2007**	2,421
Unemployment rate	2.4%
Total civilian labor force, 2000	2,299
Unemployment rate	2.9%

Employed persons 16 years and over by occupation, 2000
Managers & professionals	1,217
Service occupations	112
Sales & office occupations	676
Farming, fishing & forestry	0
Construction & maintenance	100
Production & transportation	127
Self-employed persons	153

* US Census Bureau
** New Jersey Department of Labor

See Introduction for an explanation of all data sources.

General Information
Borough of Harrington Park
85 Harriot Ave
PO Box 174
Harrington Park, NJ 07640
201-768-1700

Website	www.hpboro.net
Year of incorporation	1904
Land/water area (sq. miles)	1.86/0.21
Form of government	Borough

Government
Legislative Districts
US Congressional	5
State Legislative	39

Local Officials, 2009
Mayor	Paul A. Hoelscher
Manager/Admin	NA
Borough Clerk	Susan S. Nelson
CFO	Anne E. Murphy
Tax Assessor	Raymond Damiano
Tax Collector	Anne E. Murphy
Attorney	John R. Dineen
Construction Official	Nicola Lepore
Comm Dev/Planning	NA
Engineer	Michael Neglia
Public Works Supt.	Mark Kiernan
Police Chief	David Moppert
Emerg/Fire Director	Brian J. McElroy

Housing & Construction
Housing Units, 2000*
Total	1,583
Median rent	$1,281
Median SF home value	$349,700

Permits for New Residential Construction
	Units	Value
Total, 2006	14	$4,615,883
Single family	14	$4,615,883
Total, 2007	11	$3,938,256
Single family	11	$3,938,256

Real Property Valuation, 2008
	Parcels	Valuation
Total	1,665	$1,087,329,100
Vacant	55	20,183,000
Residential	1,583	1,029,990,700
Commercial	27	37,155,400
Industrial	0	0
Apartments	0	0
Farm land	0	0
Farm homestead	0	0

Average Property Value & Tax, 2008
Residential value	$650,657
Property tax	$11,514
Tax credit/rebate	$1,495

Public Library
Harrington Park Public Library
10 Herring St
Harrington Park, NJ 07640
201-768-5675

Director	Judith Heldman

Library statistics, 2007
Population served	4,740
Full-time/total staff	1/5

	Total	Per capita
Holdings	41,959	8.85
Revenues	$377,338	$79.61
Expenditures	$307,130	$64.80
Annual visits	23,500	4.96
Internet terminals/annual users	4/15,200	

Public Safety
Number of officers, 2007	12

Crime	2006	2007
Total crimes	11	9
Violent	0	1
Murder	0	0
Rape	0	0
Robbery	0	0
Aggravated assault	0	1
Non-violent	11	8
Burglary	1	0
Larceny	10	7
Vehicle theft	0	1
Domestic violence	10	0
Arson	0	0
Total crime rate	2.2	1.8
Violent	0.0	0.2
Non-violent	2.2	1.6

Public School District
(for school year 2007-08 except as noted)

Harrington Park School District
191 Harriot Avenue
Harrington Park, NJ 07640
(201) 768-5700

Superintendent	Adam Fried
Number of schools	1
Grade plan	K-8
Enrollment	738
Attendance rate, '06-07	96.6%
Dropout rate	NA
Students per teacher	12.7
Per pupil expenditure	$12,409
Median faculty salary	$54,195
Median administrator salary	$108,825
Grade 12 enrollment	NA
High school graduation rate	NA

Assessment test results
(percent scoring at proficient or advanced level)
	Language	Math
NJASK-Grade 3	94.4%	95.5%
GEPA-Grade 8	92.8%	94.9%
HSPA-High School	NA	NA

SAT Score Averages, 2006-07
Pct tested	Math	Verbal	Writing
NA	NA	NA	NA

Teacher Qualifications
Avg. years of experience	6
Highly-qualified teachers one subject/all subjects	98.0%/98.0%

No Child Left Behind
AYP, 2006-07	Meets Standards

Municipal Finance
State Aid Programs, 2009
Total aid	$602,001
CMPTRA	32,495
Energy tax receipts	530,343
Garden State Trust	0

General Budget, 2008
Total tax levy	$19,259,288
County levy	2,081,258
County taxes	1,968,742
County library	0
County health	0
County open space	112,516
School levy	13,076,647
Muni. levy	4,101,383
Misc. revenues	2,350,538

Taxes
	2006	2007	2008
General tax rate per $100	1.65	1.69	1.771
County equalization ratio	110.83	101.58	96.78
Net valuation taxable	$1,070,895,300	$1,074,000,773	$1,088,299,797
State equalized value	$1,055,002,891	$1,109,707,811	$1,161,407,303

Demographics & Socio-Economic Characteristics

(2000 US Census, except as noted)

Population
1980*	12,242
1990*	13,425
2000	14,424
Male	7,352
Female	7,072
2007 (estimate)*	14,152
Population density	11,600.0

Race & Hispanic Origin, 2000
Race
White	9,534
Black/African American	142
American Indian/Alaska Native	57
Asian	1,715
Native Hawaiian/Pacific Islander	4
Other race	2,302
Two or more races	670
Hispanic origin, total	5,333
Mexican	139
Puerto Rican	605
Cuban	438
Other Hispanic	4,151

Age & Nativity, 2000
Under 5 years	931
18 years and over	11,320
21 years and over	10,725
65 years and over	1,481
85 years and over	132
Median age	34.1
Native-born	6,346
Foreign-born	8,078

Educational Attainment, 2000
Population 25 years and over	9,737
Less than 9th grade	17.0%
High school grad or higher	69.3%
Bachelor's degree or higher	20.9%
Graduate degree	10.1%

Income & Poverty, 1999
Per capita income	$18,490
Median household income	$41,350
Median family income	$48,489
Persons in poverty	1,791
H'holds receiving public assistance	164
H'holds receiving social security	1,148

Households, 2000
Total households	5,136
With persons under 18	1,883
With persons over 65	1,165
Family households	3,638
Single-person households	1,154
Persons per household	2.81
Persons per family	3.27

Labor & Employment
Total civilian labor force, 2007**	7,009
Unemployment rate	4.7%
Total civilian labor force, 2000	7,287
Unemployment rate	7.7%

Employed persons 16 years and over by occupation, 2000
Managers & professionals	1,578
Service occupations	1,434
Sales & office occupations	1,637
Farming, fishing & forestry	3
Construction & maintenance	680
Production & transportation	1,394
Self-employed persons	487

* US Census Bureau
** New Jersey Department of Labor

General Information

Town of Harrison
318 Harrison Ave
Harrison, NJ 07029
973-268-2425
Website	www.townofharrison.com
Year of incorporation	1869
Land/water area (sq. miles)	1.22/0.09
Form of government	Town

Government

Legislative Districts
US Congressional	13
State Legislative	32

Local Officials, 2009
Mayor	Raymond J. McDonough
Manager/Admin	NA
Clerk	Paul J. Zarbetski
Finance Dir	Elizabeth A. Higgins
Tax Assessor	Albert J. Cifelli
Tax Collector	Margaret A. Powell
Attorney	Paul J. Zarbetski
Building	Rocco Russomanno
Comm Dev/Planning	NA
Engineering	Rocco Russomanno
Public Works	Ronald F. Catrambone
Police Chief	Derek Kearns
Emerg/Fire Director	Thomas K. Dolaghan

Housing & Construction

Housing Units, 2000*
Total	5,254
Median rent	$723
Median SF home value	$135,000

Permits for New Residential Construction
	Units	Value
Total, 2006	200	$18,470,695
Single family	144	$14,175,580
Total, 2007	519	$6,837,800
Single family	21	$976,300

Real Property Valuation, 2008
	Parcels	Valuation
Total	2,461	$478,952,905
Vacant	116	20,447,435
Residential	1,952	274,372,760
Commercial	255	62,084,480
Industrial	65	104,512,030
Apartments	73	17,536,200
Farm land	0	0
Farm homestead	0	0

Average Property Value & Tax, 2008
Residential value	$140,560
Property tax	$7,585
Tax credit/rebate	$990

Public Library

Harrison Public Library
415 Harrison Ave
Harrison, NJ 07029
973-483-2366
Director	Ellen Lucas

Library statistics, 2007
Population served	14,424
Full-time/total staff	NA/0

	Total	Per capita
Holdings	0	NA
Revenues	$0	NA
Expenditures	$0	NA
Annual visits	NA	NA
Internet terminals/annual users	NA/NA	

Public Safety

Number of officers, 2007	53

Crime	2006	2007
Total crimes	406	368
Violent	47	45
Murder	1	0
Rape	3	2
Robbery	27	28
Aggravated assault	16	15
Non-violent	359	323
Burglary	60	94
Larceny	188	179
Vehicle theft	111	50
Domestic violence	71	78
Arson	0	0
Total crime rate	28.9	26.4
Violent	3.3	3.2
Non-violent	25.5	23.2

Public School District

(for school year 2007-08 except as noted)

Harrison School District
430 William Street
Harrison, NJ 07029
(973) 483-4627
Superintendent	Anthony Comprelli
Number of schools	4
Grade plan	K-12
Enrollment	1,820
Attendance rate, '06-07	95.1%
Dropout rate	0.0%
Students per teacher	10.8
Per pupil expenditure	$14,698
Median faculty salary	$76,055
Median administrator salary	$118,676
Grade 12 enrollment	167
High school graduation rate	99.4%

Assessment test results
(percent scoring at proficient or advanced level)
	Language	Math
NJASK-Grade 3	89.5%	87.8%
GEPA-Grade 8	55.1%	83.1%
HSPA-High School	50.4%	62.6%

SAT Score Averages, 2006-07
Pct tested	Math	Verbal	Writing
57%	447	438	423

Teacher Qualifications
Avg. years of experience	12
Highly-qualified teachers one subject/all subjects	99.0%/99.0%

No Child Left Behind
AYP, 2006-07	Meets Standards

Municipal Finance

State Aid Programs, 2009
Total aid	$9,831,204
CMPTRA	1,049,894
Energy tax receipts	8,633,842
Garden State Trust	0

General Budget, 2008
Total tax levy	$25,863,641
County levy	5,310,406
County taxes	5,169,577
County library	0
County health	0
County open space	140,829
School levy	8,901,904
Muni. levy	11,651,331
Misc. revenues	23,926,413

Taxes	2006	2007	2008
General tax rate per $100	4.626	5.016	5.396
County equalization ratio	46.41	39.44	35.43
Net valuation taxable	$480,878,765	$473,338,579	$479,314,683
State equalized value	$1,219,701,441	$1,335,280,219	$1,380,231,859

See Introduction for an explanation of all data sources.

Demographics & Socio-Economic Characteristics
(2000 US Census, except as noted)

Population
1980*	3,585
1990*	4,715
2000	8,788
Male	4,360
Female	4,428
2007 (estimate)*	12,241
Population density	639.9

Race & Hispanic Origin, 2000
Race
White	8,363
Black/African American	260
American Indian/Alaska Native	11
Asian	64
Native Hawaiian/Pacific Islander	0
Other race	36
Two or more races	54
Hispanic origin, total	156
Mexican	18
Puerto Rican	79
Cuban	12
Other Hispanic	47

Age & Nativity, 2000
Under 5 years	757
18 years and over	5,866
21 years and over	5,620
65 years and over	582
85 years and over	61
Median age	35.1
Native-born	8,609
Foreign-born	179

Educational Attainment, 2000
Population 25 years and over	5,469
Less than 9th grade	1.9%
High school grad or higher	91.1%
Bachelor's degree or higher	38.5%
Graduate degree	10.8%

Income & Poverty, 1999
Per capita income	$28,645
Median household income	$77,143
Median family income	$84,379
Persons in poverty	278
H'holds receiving public assistance	23
H'holds receiving social security	516

Households, 2000
Total households	2,848
With persons under 18	1,466
With persons over 65	433
Family households	2,324
Single-person households	435
Persons per household	3.06
Persons per family	3.44

Labor & Employment
Total civilian labor force, 2007**	5,150
Unemployment rate	4.0%
Total civilian labor force, 2000	4,374
Unemployment rate	3.5%

Employed persons 16 years and over by occupation, 2000
Managers & professionals	1,951
Service occupations	289
Sales & office occupations	1,206
Farming, fishing & forestry	48
Construction & maintenance	454
Production & transportation	271
Self-employed persons	193

* US Census Bureau
** New Jersey Department of Labor

See Introduction for an explanation of all data sources.

General Information
Township of Harrison
114 Bridgeton Pike
Mullica Hill, NJ 08062
856-478-4111
Website	www.harrisontwp.us
Year of incorporation	1845
Land/water area (sq. miles)	19.13/0.05
Form of government	Township

Government
Legislative Districts
US Congressional	2
State Legislative	3

Local Officials, 2009
Mayor	Louis J. Manzo
Manager	Carole Rieck
Clerk	Diane Malloy
Finance Dir	Yvonne Bullock
Tax Assessor	Brian Rosenberg
Tax Collector	Michelle Mitchell
Attorney	Brian J. Duffield
Building	Jeffrey Kier
Planning	Susanne Rhudy
Engineering	J. Michael Fralinger
Public Works	Mike Micklasavage
Police Chief	Frank Rodgers
Fire/Emergency Dir	NA

Housing & Construction
Housing Units, 2000*
Total	2,939
Median rent	$590
Median SF home value	$181,900

Permits for New Residential Construction
	Units	Value
Total, 2006	123	$34,023,922
Single family	123	$34,023,922
Total, 2007	69	$22,186,421
Single family	69	$22,186,421

Real Property Valuation, 2008
	Parcels	Valuation
Total	4,548	$801,651,800
Vacant	530	27,451,400
Residential	3,562	706,145,500
Commercial	111	41,229,100
Industrial	0	0
Apartments	3	4,531,500
Farm land	237	3,046,700
Farm homestead	105	19,247,600

Average Property Value & Tax, 2008
Residential value	$197,816
Property tax	$7,664
Tax credit/rebate	$1,109

Public Library
No public municipal library

Library statistics, 2007
Population served	NA
Full-time/total staff	NA/NA

	Total	Per capita
Holdings	NA	NA
Revenues	NA	NA
Expenditures	NA	NA
Annual visits	NA	NA
Internet terminals/annual users	NA/NA	

Public Safety
Number of officers, 2007	18

Crime	2006	2007
Total crimes	176	169
Violent	5	6
Murder	0	0
Rape	1	0
Robbery	3	1
Aggravated assault	1	5
Non-violent	171	163
Burglary	39	21
Larceny	126	139
Vehicle theft	6	3
Domestic violence	78	93
Arson	4	3
Total crime rate	15.6	14.3
Violent	0.4	0.5
Non-violent	15.1	13.8

Public School District
(for school year 2007-08 except as noted)

Harrison Township School District
120 N Main St
Mullica Hill, NJ 08062
(856) 478-2016
Superintendent	Patricia Hoey
Number of schools	2
Grade plan	K-6
Enrollment	1,510
Attendance rate, '06-07	96.2%
Dropout rate	NA
Students per teacher	12.8
Per pupil expenditure	$9,998
Median faculty salary	$47,756
Median administrator salary	$93,726
Grade 12 enrollment	NA
High school graduation rate	NA

Assessment test results
(percent scoring at proficient or advanced level)
	Language	Math
NJASK-Grade 3	83.1%	87.5%
GEPA-Grade 8	NA	NA
HSPA-High School	NA	NA

SAT Score Averages, 2006-07
Pct tested	Math	Verbal	Writing
NA	NA	NA	NA

Teacher Qualifications
Avg. years of experience	8
Highly-qualified teachers one subject/all subjects	100%/100%

No Child Left Behind
AYP, 2006-07	Meets Standards

Municipal Finance
State Aid Programs, 2009
Total aid	$738,341
CMPTRA	61,398
Energy tax receipts	647,410
Garden State Trust	0

General Budget, 2008
Total tax levy	$31,149,510
County levy	8,925,918
County taxes	7,702,848
County library	619,436
County health	0
County open space	603,633
School levy	19,152,507
Muni. levy	3,071,085
Misc. revenues	5,145,629

Taxes
	2006	2007	2008
General tax rate per $100	3.773	3.857	3.875
County equalization ratio	62.43	55.57	53.24
Net valuation taxable	$705,936,500	$765,311,619	$803,990,329
State equalized value	$1,272,895,814	$1,435,410,436	$1,499,354,029

Demographics & Socio-Economic Characteristics
(2000 US Census, except as noted)

Population
1980*	363
1990*	362
2000	359
Male	182
Female	177
2007 (estimate)*	392
Population density	712.7

Race & Hispanic Origin, 2000
Race
White	348
Black/African American	2
American Indian/Alaska Native	1
Asian	1
Native Hawaiian/Pacific Islander	0
Other race	7
Two or more races	0
Hispanic origin, total	13
Mexican	12
Puerto Rican	0
Cuban	0
Other Hispanic	1

Age & Nativity, 2000
Under 5 years	11
18 years and over	307
21 years and over	299
65 years and over	109
85 years and over	4
Median age	53.7
Native-born	339
Foreign-born	14

Educational Attainment, 2000
Population 25 years and over	308
Less than 9th grade	1.9%
High school grad or higher	95.1%
Bachelor's degree or higher	46.1%
Graduate degree	14.3%

Income & Poverty, 1999
Per capita income	$36,757
Median household income	$61,875
Median family income	$69,722
Persons in poverty	18
H'holds receiving public assistance	6
H'holds receiving social security	102

Households, 2000
Total households	167
With persons under 18	31
With persons over 65	76
Family households	112
Single-person households	49
Persons per household	2.15
Persons per family	2.61

Labor & Employment
Total civilian labor force, 2007**	167
Unemployment rate	0.0%
Total civilian labor force, 2000	134
Unemployment rate	0.0%

Employed persons 16 years and over by occupation, 2000
Managers & professionals	56
Service occupations	20
Sales & office occupations	36
Farming, fishing & forestry	0
Construction & maintenance	18
Production & transportation	4
Self-employed persons	24

General Information
Borough of Harvey Cedars
7606 Long Beach Blvd
PO Box 3185
Harvey Cedars, NJ 08008
609-361-6000

Website	www.harveycedars.org
Year of incorporation	1894
Land/water area (sq. miles)	0.55/0.65
Form of government	Commission

Government
Legislative Districts
US Congressional	3
State Legislative	9

Local Officials, 2009
Mayor	Jonathan Oldham
Manager/Admin	NA
Clerk	Daina Dale
Finance Officer	Sharon Sulecki
Tax Assessor	Bernard Haney
Tax Collector	Sharon Sulecki
Attorney	William T. Hiering Jr
Building	Frank Zappavigna
Comm Dev/Planning	NA
Engineering	Frank Little
Public Works	J. Lloyd Vosseller
Police Chief	Jerry Falkowski
Fire Chief	Sean Marti

Housing & Construction
Housing Units, 2000*
Total	1,205
Median rent	$870
Median SF home value	$456,500

Permits for New Residential Construction
	Units	Value
Total, 2006	11	$4,070,950
Single family	11	$4,070,950
Total, 2007	7	$2,690,400
Single family	7	$2,690,400

Real Property Valuation, 2008
	Parcels	Valuation
Total	1,252	$1,367,534,000
Vacant	41	26,646,700
Residential	1,187	1,326,570,400
Commercial	24	14,316,900
Industrial	0	0
Apartments	0	0
Farm land	0	0
Farm homestead	0	0

Average Property Value & Tax, 2008
Residential value	$1,117,582
Property tax	$7,928
Tax credit/rebate	$1,268

Public Library
No public municipal library

Library statistics, 2007
Population served	NA
Full-time/total staff	NA/NA

	Total	Per capita
Holdings	NA	NA
Revenues	NA	NA
Expenditures	NA	NA
Annual visits	NA	NA
Internet terminals/annual users	NA/NA	

Public Safety
Number of officers, 2007	9

Crime	2006	2007
Total crimes	19	24
Violent	0	0
Murder	0	0
Rape	0	0
Robbery	0	0
Aggravated assault	0	0
Non-violent	19	24
Burglary	0	4
Larceny	19	20
Vehicle theft	0	0
Domestic violence	6	0
Arson	0	0
Total crime rate	49.2	61.7
Violent	0.0	0.0
Non-violent	49.2	61.7

Public School District
(for school year 2007-08 except as noted)

Long Beach Island School District
200 Barnegat Avenue
Surf City, NJ 08008
(609) 494-2341

Superintendent	Robert A. Garguilo
Number of schools	2
Grade plan	K-6
Enrollment	258
Attendance rate, '06-07	94.0%
Dropout rate	NA
Students per teacher	7.1
Per pupil expenditure	$23,574
Median faculty salary	$71,027
Median administrator salary	$95,218
Grade 12 enrollment	NA
High school graduation rate	NA

Assessment test results
(percent scoring at proficient or advanced level)
	Language	Math
NJASK-Grade 3	96.9%	90.6%
GEPA-Grade 8	NA	NA
HSPA-High School	NA	NA

SAT Score Averages, 2006-07
Pct tested	Math	Verbal	Writing
NA	NA	NA	NA

Teacher Qualifications
Avg. years of experience	19
Highly-qualified teachers one subject/all subjects	100%/100%

No Child Left Behind
AYP, 2006-07	Meets Standards

Municipal Finance
State Aid Programs, 2009
Total aid	$112,557
CMPTRA	0
Energy tax receipts	106,929
Garden State Trust	0

General Budget, 2008
Total tax levy	$9,703,989
County levy	4,179,557
County taxes	3,588,170
County library	421,691
County health	0
County open space	169,696
School levy	2,890,768
Muni. levy	2,633,665
Misc. revenues	1,211,268

Taxes
	2006	2007	2008
General tax rate per $100	0.717	0.696	0.710
County equalization ratio	109.21	101.2	96.91
Net valuation taxable	$1,356,109,000	$1,362,664,038	$1,367,870,325
State equalized value	$1,340,369,101	$1,406,102,117	$307,511,034

* US Census Bureau
** New Jersey Department of Labor

See Introduction for an explanation of all data sources.

Demographics & Socio-Economic Characteristics
(2000 US Census, except as noted)

Population
1980*	12,166
1990*	11,488
2000	11,662
Male	5,605
Female	6,057
2007 (estimate)*	11,492
Population density	7,610.6

Race & Hispanic Origin, 2000
Race
White	10,247
Black/African American	200
American Indian/Alaska Native	5
Asian	776
Native Hawaiian/Pacific Islander	1
Other race	255
Two or more races	178
Hispanic origin, total	964
Mexican	28
Puerto Rican	241
Cuban	184
Other Hispanic	511

Age & Nativity, 2000
Under 5 years	671
18 years and over	9,076
21 years and over	8,752
65 years and over	1,986
85 years and over	235
Median age	40.1
Native-born	9,685
Foreign-born	1,977

Educational Attainment, 2000
Population 25 years and over	8,311
Less than 9th grade	5.4%
High school grad or higher	86.9%
Bachelor's degree or higher	29.9%
Graduate degree	8.1%

Income & Poverty, 1999
Per capita income	$29,626
Median household income	$64,529
Median family income	$75,032
Persons in poverty	492
H'holds receiving public assistance	45
H'holds receiving social security	1,438

Households, 2000
Total households	4,521
With persons under 18	1,475
With persons over 65	1,469
Family households	3,144
Single-person households	1,185
Persons per household	2.58
Persons per family	3.16

Labor & Employment
Total civilian labor force, 2007**	6,259
Unemployment rate	3.7%
Total civilian labor force, 2000	5,916
Unemployment rate	3.9%

Employed persons 16 years and over by occupation, 2000
Managers & professionals	2,456
Service occupations	595
Sales & office occupations	1,805
Farming, fishing & forestry	6
Construction & maintenance	351
Production & transportation	473
Self-employed persons	195

* US Census Bureau
** New Jersey Department of Labor

See Introduction for an explanation of all data sources.

General Information
Borough of Hasbrouck Heights
320 Boulevard
Hasbrouck Heights, NJ 07604
201-288-0195
Website	www.hasbrouck-heights.nj.us
Year of incorporation	1894
Land/water area (sq. miles)	1.51/0.00
Form of government	Borough

Government
Legislative Districts
US Congressional	9
State Legislative	38

Local Officials, 2009
Mayor	Rose Heck
Manager	Michael Kronyak
Clerk	Rose Marie Sees
Finance Dir	Michael Kronyak
Tax Assessor	George Reggo
Tax Collector	Conchita Parker
Attorney	Ralph W. Chandless Jr
Building	Nicholas Melfi
Comm Dev/Planning	NA
Engineering	Kenneth Job
Public Works	William Spindler
Police Chief	Michael Colaneri
Emerg/Fire Director	Michael Ratkowski

Housing & Construction
Housing Units, 2000*
Total	4,617
Median rent	$874
Median SF home value	$215,300

Permits for New Residential Construction
	Units	Value
Total, 2006	23	$6,053,242
Single family	23	$6,053,242
Total, 2007	11	$2,522,977
Single family	11	$2,522,977

Real Property Valuation, 2008
	Parcels	Valuation
Total	3,626	$1,855,597,600
Vacant	108	13,438,400
Residential	3,294	1,445,430,700
Commercial	188	304,384,300
Industrial	12	20,988,000
Apartments	24	71,356,200
Farm land	0	0
Farm homestead	0	0

Average Property Value & Tax, 2008
Residential value	$438,807
Property tax	$8,757
Tax credit/rebate	$1,270

Public Library
Hasbrouck Heights Public Library
320 Boulevard
Hasbrouck Heights, NJ 07604
201-288-0488
Director	Mimi Hui

Library statistics, 2007
Population served	11,662
Full-time/total staff	3/7

	Total	Per capita
Holdings	55,358	4.75
Revenues	$844,907	$72.45
Expenditures	$846,097	$72.55
Annual visits	57,129	4.90
Internet terminals/annual users	26/28,504	

Public Safety
Number of officers, 2007 32

Crime	2006	2007
Total crimes	177	130
Violent	0	2
Murder	0	0
Rape	0	0
Robbery	0	1
Aggravated assault	0	1
Non-violent	177	128
Burglary	31	22
Larceny	128	103
Vehicle theft	18	3
Domestic violence	121	114
Arson	0	0
Total crime rate	15.2	11.2
Violent	0.0	0.2
Non-violent	15.2	11.0

Public School District
(for school year 2007-08 except as noted)

Hasbrouck Heights School District
379 Boulevard
Hasbrouck Heights, NJ 07604
(201) 393-8145
Superintendent	Joseph Luongo
Number of schools	4
Grade plan	K-12
Enrollment	1,561
Attendance rate, '06-07	94.7%
Dropout rate	1.9%
Students per teacher	10.9
Per pupil expenditure	$13,650
Median faculty salary	$56,770
Median administrator salary	$112,574
Grade 12 enrollment	110
High school graduation rate	93.0%

Assessment test results
(percent scoring at proficient or advanced level)
	Language	Math
NJASK-Grade 3	95.9%	95.9%
GEPA-Grade 8	83.7%	95.3%
HSPA-High School	93.2%	93.2%

SAT Score Averages, 2006-07
Pct tested	Math	Verbal	Writing
89%	532	505	506

Teacher Qualifications
Avg. years of experience	11
Highly-qualified teachers one subject/all subjects	100%/100%

No Child Left Behind
AYP, 2006-07 . . . . Meets Standards

Municipal Finance
State Aid Programs, 2009
Total aid	$1,396,507
CMPTRA	217,480
Energy tax receipts	1,144,115
Garden State Trust	0

General Budget, 2008
Total tax levy	$37,052,938
County levy	3,504,243
County taxes	3,314,567
County library	0
County health	0
County open space	189,676
School levy	20,709,486
Muni. levy	12,839,210
Misc. revenues	4,526,549

Taxes	2006	2007	2008
General tax rate per $100	1.78	1.89	1.997
County equalization ratio	113.7	104.81	98.16
Net valuation taxable	$1,854,140,700	$1,853,773,480	$1,856,759,375
State equalized value	$1,770,175,523	$1,888,501,013	$1,928,855,106

Demographics & Socio-Economic Characteristics
(2000 US Census, except as noted)

Population
1980*	3,509
1990*	3,384
2000	3,390
Male	1,661
Female	1,729
2007 (estimate)*	3,410
Population density	1,739.8

Race & Hispanic Origin, 2000
Race
White	2,981
Black/African American	41
American Indian/Alaska Native	0
Asian	312
Native Hawaiian/Pacific Islander	0
Other race	25
Two or more races	31
Hispanic origin, total	92
Mexican	1
Puerto Rican	12
Cuban	28
Other Hispanic	51

Age & Nativity, 2000
Under 5 years	232
18 years and over	2,411
21 years and over	2,349
65 years and over	474
85 years and over	51
Median age	41.1
Native-born	2,857
Foreign-born	533

Educational Attainment, 2000
Population 25 years and over	2,259
Less than 9th grade	1.6%
High school grad or higher	93.9%
Bachelor's degree or higher	57.0%
Graduate degree	23.9%

Income & Poverty, 1999
Per capita income	$45,615
Median household income	$101,836
Median family income	$112,500
Persons in poverty	68
H'holds receiving public assistance	13
H'holds receiving social security	304

Households, 2000
Total households	1,134
With persons under 18	519
With persons over 65	336
Family households	971
Single-person households	145
Persons per household	2.98
Persons per family	3.25

Labor & Employment
Total civilian labor force, 2007**	1,711
Unemployment rate	3.4%
Total civilian labor force, 2000	1,628
Unemployment rate	3.6%

Employed persons 16 years and over by occupation, 2000
Managers & professionals	928
Service occupations	84
Sales & office occupations	443
Farming, fishing & forestry	0
Construction & maintenance	67
Production & transportation	47
Self-employed persons	141

General Information
Borough of Haworth
300 Haworth Ave
Haworth, NJ 07641
201-384-4785

Website	www.haworthnj.org
Year of incorporation	1904
Land/water area (sq. miles)	1.96/0.40
Form of government	Borough

Government
Legislative Districts
US Congressional	5
State Legislative	39

Local Officials, 2009
Mayor	John DeRienzo
Manager	Ann Fay
Clerk	Ann Fay
Finance Dir	NA
Tax Assessor	Neil Rubenstein
Tax Collector	Dawn Wheeler
Attorney	Peter Scandariato
Building	Harry Kraus
Comm Dev/Planning	NA
Engineering	Arthur Lorenz
Public Works	Martin Mahon
Police Chief	Patrick O'Dea
Emerg/Fire Director	Robert Hennion

Housing & Construction
Housing Units, 2000*
Total	1,146
Median rent	$1,625
Median SF home value	$378,400

Permits for New Residential Construction
	Units	Value
Total, 2006	11	$5,012,919
Single family	11	$5,012,919
Total, 2007	12	$5,331,922
Single family	12	$5,331,922

Real Property Valuation, 2008
	Parcels	Valuation
Total	1,217	$763,527,800
Vacant	48	16,021,200
Residential	1,125	669,141,100
Commercial	44	78,365,500
Industrial	0	0
Apartments	0	0
Farm land	0	0
Farm homestead	0	0

Average Property Value & Tax, 2008
Residential value	$594,792
Property tax	$14,195
Tax credit/rebate	$1,516

Public Library
Haworth Municipal Library
300 Haworth Ave
Haworth, NJ 07641
201-384-1020

Director ....Elizabeth Rosenberg

Library statistics, 2007
Population served	3,390
Full-time/total staff	1/3

	Total	Per capita
Holdings	26,811	7.91
Revenues	$317,718	$93.72
Expenditures	$307,349	$90.66
Annual visits	25,000	7.37
Internet terminals/annual users	6/1,500	

Public Safety
Number of officers, 2007 13
Crime	2006	2007
Total crimes	8	14
Violent	0	2
Murder	0	0
Rape	0	0
Robbery	0	0
Aggravated assault	0	2
Non-violent	8	12
Burglary	4	4
Larceny	4	7
Vehicle theft	0	1
Domestic violence	3	0
Arson	0	0
Total crime rate	2.3	4.1
Violent	0.0	0.6
Non-violent	2.3	3.5

Public School District
(for school year 2007-08 except as noted)

Haworth School District
205 Valley Road
Haworth, NJ 07641
(201) 384-5526

Superintendent	Raymond Albano (Int)
Number of schools	1
Grade plan	K-8
Enrollment	514
Attendance rate, '06-07	94.8%
Dropout rate	NA
Students per teacher	10.5
Per pupil expenditure	$13,589
Median faculty salary	$57,070
Median administrator salary	$131,000
Grade 12 enrollment	NA
High school graduation rate	NA

Assessment test results
(percent scoring at proficient or advanced level)
	Language	Math
NJASK-Grade 3	100.0%	100.0%
GEPA-Grade 8	87.3%	95.8%
HSPA-High School	NA	NA

SAT Score Averages, 2006-07
Pct tested	Math	Verbal	Writing
NA	NA	NA	NA

Teacher Qualifications
Avg. years of experience	9
Highly-qualified teachers one subject/all subjects	100%/100%

No Child Left Behind
AYP, 2006-07 ....Meets Standards

Municipal Finance
State Aid Programs, 2009
Total aid	$747,014
CMPTRA	0
Energy tax receipts	698,634
Garden State Trust	0

General Budget, 2008
Total tax levy	$18,227,680
County levy	1,822,776
County taxes	1,724,249
County library	0
County health	0
County open space	98,527
School levy	11,207,686
Muni. levy	5,197,219
Misc. revenues	1,754,981

Taxes
	2006	2007	2008
General tax rate per $100	2.16	2.29	2.388
County equalization ratio	88.31	81	77.60
Net valuation taxable	$742,422,500	$750,686,547	$763,789,658
State equalized value	$916,849,843	$967,304,448	$988,008,042

* US Census Bureau
** New Jersey Department of Labor

See Introduction for an explanation of all data sources.

Demographics & Socio-Economic Characteristics

(2000 US Census, except as noted)

Population

1980*	18,200
1990*	17,084
2000	18,218
Male	8,686
Female	9,532
2007 (estimate)*	18,106
Population density	5,325.3

Race & Hispanic Origin, 2000

Race

White	17,080
Black/African American	137
American Indian/Alaska Native	25
Asian	344
Native Hawaiian/Pacific Islander	3
Other race	287
Two or more races	342
Hispanic origin, total	1,354
Mexican	55
Puerto Rican	345
Cuban	99
Other Hispanic	855

Age & Nativity, 2000

Under 5 years	1,155
18 years and over	14,252
21 years and over	13,797
65 years and over	2,817
85 years and over	347
Median age	38.2
Native-born	15,684
Foreign-born	2,534

Educational Attainment, 2000

Population 25 years and over	13,122
Less than 9th grade	6.4%
High school grad or higher	84.3%
Bachelor's degree or higher	25.6%
Graduate degree	7.9%

Income & Poverty, 1999

Per capita income	$26,551
Median household income	$55,340
Median family income	$65,451
Persons in poverty	619
H'holds receiving public assistance	59
H'holds receiving social security	2,140

Households, 2000

Total households	7,260
With persons under 18	2,216
With persons over 65	2,095
Family households	4,933
Single-person households	1,922
Persons per household	2.50
Persons per family	3.07

Labor & Employment

Total civilian labor force, 2007**	10,723
Unemployment rate	2.7%
Total civilian labor force, 2000	9,925
Unemployment rate	2.9%

Employed persons 16 years and over by occupation, 2000

Managers & professionals	3,462
Service occupations	1,387
Sales & office occupations	3,090
Farming, fishing & forestry	13
Construction & maintenance	826
Production & transportation	858
Self-employed persons	574

* US Census Bureau
** New Jersey Department of Labor

General Information

Borough of Hawthorne
445 Lafayette Ave
Hawthorne, NJ 07506
973-427-5555

Website	www.hawthornenj.org
Year of incorporation	1898
Land/water area (sq. miles)	3.40/0.02
Form of government	Mayor-Council

Government

Legislative Districts

US Congressional	9
State Legislative	35

Local Officials, 2009

Mayor	Richard Goldberg
Manager	Eric Maurer
Clerk	Susan Witkowski
Finance Dir	Mary Jeanne Hewitt
Tax Assessor	Tim Henderson
Tax Collector	Barbara Crowley
Attorney	Michael Pasquale
Building	John Pallotta
Comm Dev/Planning	NA
Engineering	Stephen Boswell
Public Works	Joseph Clementi
Police Chief	Robert Scully (Actg)
Emerg/Fire Director	Joseph Speranza

Housing & Construction

Housing Units, 2000*

Total	7,419
Median rent	$949
Median SF home value	$198,600

Permits for New Residential Construction

	Units	Value
Total, 2006	89	$7,632,960
Single family	89	$7,632,960
Total, 2007	6	$933,650
Single family	4	$873,650

Real Property Valuation, 2008

	Parcels	Valuation
Total	5,974	$1,232,871,950
Vacant	157	9,824,500
Residential	5,416	994,885,650
Commercial	274	121,641,800
Industrial	109	83,619,800
Apartments	18	22,900,200
Farm land	0	0
Farm homestead	0	0

Average Property Value & Tax, 2008

Residential value	$183,694
Property tax	$8,241
Tax credit/rebate	$1,194

Public Library

Louis Bay 2nd Library
345 Lafayette Ave
Hawthorne, NJ 07506
973-427-5745

Director	Thomas Frawley

Library statistics, 2007

Population served	18,218
Full-time/total staff	2/11

	Total	Per capita
Holdings	98,449	5.40
Revenues	$1,180,905	$64.82
Expenditures	$930,194	$51.06
Annual visits	85,706	4.70
Internet terminals/annual users	6/18,720	

Public Safety

Number of officers, 2007	34

Crime	2006	2007
Total crimes	259	330
Violent	10	9
Murder	1	0
Rape	0	1
Robbery	3	2
Aggravated assault	6	6
Non-violent	249	321
Burglary	42	35
Larceny	191	276
Vehicle theft	16	10
Domestic violence	100	99
Arson	0	0
Total crime rate	14.2	18.2
Violent	0.5	0.5
Non-violent	13.6	17.7

Public School District

(for school year 2007-08 except as noted)

Hawthorne School District
445 Lafayette Avenue
Hawthorne, NJ 07506
(973) 423-6401

Chief School Admin	Richard Spirito
Number of schools	5
Grade plan	K-12
Enrollment	2,423
Attendance rate, '06-07	95.5%
Dropout rate	0.0%
Students per teacher	10.6
Per pupil expenditure	$12,746
Median faculty salary	$52,420
Median administrator salary	$113,097
Grade 12 enrollment	170
High school graduation rate	100.0%

Assessment test results

(percent scoring at proficient or advanced level)

	Language	Math
NJASK-Grade 3	90.4%	91.4%
GEPA-Grade 8	67.1%	80.9%
HSPA-High School	82.3%	91.2%

SAT Score Averages, 2006-07

Pct tested	Math	Verbal	Writing
86%	496	498	488

Teacher Qualifications

Avg. years of experience	8
Highly-qualified teachers one subject/all subjects	98.5%/98.5%

No Child Left Behind

AYP, 2006-07	Meets Standards

Municipal Finance

State Aid Programs, 2009

Total aid	$1,893,057
CMPTRA	379,781
Energy tax receipts	1,465,949
Garden State Trust	0

General Budget, 2008

Total tax levy	$55,343,853
County levy	13,880,232
County taxes	13,604,385
County library	0
County health	0
County open space	275,846
School levy	29,574,279
Muni. levy	11,889,342
Misc. revenues	6,085,217

Taxes	2006	2007	2008
General tax rate per $100	4.09	4.27	4.487
County equalization ratio	52.74	47.59	44.93
Net valuation taxable	$1,221,228,650	$1,224,345,290	$1,233,653,631
State equalized value	$2,566,988,859	$2,724,053,068	$2,836,273,746

See Introduction for an explanation of all data sources.

Demographics & Socio-Economic Characteristics

(2000 US Census, except as noted)

Population
1980*	23,013
1990*	21,976
2000	21,378
Male	10,217
Female	11,161
2007 (estimate)*	21,046
Population density	3,744.8

Race & Hispanic Origin, 2000
Race
White	19,918
Black/African American	235
American Indian/Alaska Native	12
Asian	725
Native Hawaiian/Pacific Islander	1
Other race	242
Two or more races	245
Hispanic origin, total	1,254
Mexican	137
Puerto Rican	564
Cuban	107
Other Hispanic	446

Age & Nativity, 2000
Under 5 years	1,400
18 years and over	15,932
21 years and over	15,259
65 years and over	2,879
85 years and over	294
Median age	38.5
Native-born	19,719
Foreign-born	1,659

Educational Attainment, 2000
Population 25 years and over	14,567
Less than 9th grade	3.7%
High school grad or higher	83.8%
Bachelor's degree or higher	19.2%
Graduate degree	6.0%

Income & Poverty, 1999
Per capita income	$25,262
Median household income	$65,697
Median family income	$71,361
Persons in poverty	727
H'holds receiving public assistance	108
H'holds receiving social security	2,274

Households, 2000
Total households	7,244
With persons under 18	2,925
With persons over 65	2,054
Family households	5,799
Single-person households	1,253
Persons per household	2.92
Persons per family	3.32

Labor & Employment
Total civilian labor force, 2007**	11,418
Unemployment rate	4.1%
Total civilian labor force, 2000	10,746
Unemployment rate	4.6%

Employed persons 16 years and over by occupation, 2000
Managers & professionals	3,424
Service occupations	1,320
Sales & office occupations	3,265
Farming, fishing & forestry	25
Construction & maintenance	1,082
Production & transportation	1,138
Self-employed persons	373

General Information
Township of Hazlet
1766 Union Avenue
PO Box 371
Hazlet, NJ 07730
732-264-1700

Website	www.hazlettwp.org
Year of incorporation	1967
Land/water area (sq. miles)	5.62/0.04
Form of government	Township

Government

Legislative Districts
US Congressional	6
State Legislative	13

Local Officials, 2009
Mayor	Kevin Lavan
Manager	Michael F. Muscillo
Clerk	Evelyn A. Grandi
Finance Dir	Catherine M. Campbell
Tax Assessor	Elizabeth Cusumano
Tax Collector	Susan Meyer
Attorney	Daniel J. McCarthy
Building	Dennis Pino
Planning	Jeffrey Tyler
Engineering	Greg Valesi
Public Works	David Rooke
Police Chief	James Broderick
Emerg/Fire Director	Christopher Roehler

Housing & Construction

Housing Units, 2000*
Total	7,406
Median rent	$510
Median SF home value	$173,700

Permits for New Residential Construction
	Units	Value
Total, 2006	22	$3,068,644
Single family	22	$3,068,644
Total, 2007	22	$3,650,952
Single family	22	$3,650,952

Real Property Valuation, 2008
	Parcels	Valuation
Total	6,804	$1,067,477,900
Vacant	203	9,559,000
Residential	6,232	847,018,600
Commercial	362	194,355,100
Industrial	6	16,540,400
Apartments	0	0
Farm land	1	4,800
Farm homestead	0	0

Average Property Value & Tax, 2008
Residential value	$135,914
Property tax	$6,330
Tax credit/rebate	$1,082

Public Library
Hazlet Township Library‡
251 Middle Rd
Hazlet, NJ 07730
732-264-7164

Branch Librarian .... Beth Henderson

Library statistics, 2007
see Monmouth County profile
for library system statistics

Public Safety
Number of officers, 2007	46

Crime	2006	2007
Total crimes	301	336
Violent	9	7
Murder	0	0
Rape	2	0
Robbery	0	5
Aggravated assault	7	2
Non-violent	292	329
Burglary	51	42
Larceny	220	269
Vehicle theft	21	18
Domestic violence	151	170
Arson	0	8
Total crime rate	14.3	16.0
Violent	0.4	0.3
Non-violent	13.9	15.7

Public School District
(for school year 2007-08 except as noted)

Hazlet Township School District
421 Middle Road
Hazlet, NJ 07730
(732) 264-8402

Superintendent	William George
Number of schools	8
Grade plan	K-12
Enrollment	3,322
Attendance rate, '06-07	95.2%
Dropout rate	0.0%
Students per teacher	11.0
Per pupil expenditure	$12,996
Median faculty salary	$52,785
Median administrator salary	$115,988
Grade 12 enrollment	270
High school graduation rate	100.0%

Assessment test results
(percent scoring at proficient or advanced level)

	Language	Math
NJASK-Grade 3	93.6%	92.0%
GEPA-Grade 8	75.2%	88.2%
HSPA-High School	88.9%	87.3%

SAT Score Averages, 2006-07
Pct tested	Math	Verbal	Writing
87%	505	483	481

Teacher Qualifications
Avg. years of experience	10
Highly-qualified teachers one subject/all subjects	100%/100%

No Child Left Behind
AYP, 2006-07	Meets Standards

Municipal Finance

State Aid Programs, 2009
Total aid	$2,429,484
CMPTRA	610,985
Energy tax receipts	1,757,762
Garden State Trust	0

General Budget, 2008
Total tax levy	$49,749,208
County levy	6,918,079
County taxes	6,039,588
County library	363,444
County health	112,310
County open space	402,737
School levy	31,227,811
Muni. levy	11,603,318
Misc. revenues	6,765,617

Taxes	2006	2007	2008
General tax rate per $100	4.373	4.537	4.658
County equalization ratio	49.49	43.46	40.04
Net valuation taxable	$1,064,593,600	$1,067,070,090	$1,068,251,449
State equalized value	$2,450,492,919	$2,663,803,542	$2,354,039,601

‡ Branch of county library
* US Census Bureau
** New Jersey Department of Labor

Demographics & Socio-Economic Characteristics

(2000 US Census, except as noted)

Population

1980*	955
1990*	1,211
2000	1,825
Male	905
Female	920
2007 (estimate)*	2,012
Population density	2,367.1

Race & Hispanic Origin, 2000

Race

White	1,700
Black/African American	44
American Indian/Alaska Native	4
Asian	44
Native Hawaiian/Pacific Islander	1
Other race	16
Two or more races	16
Hispanic origin, total	97
Mexican	4
Puerto Rican	43
Cuban	2
Other Hispanic	48

Age & Nativity, 2000

Under 5 years	124
18 years and over	1,422
21 years and over	1,358
65 years and over	113
85 years and over	12
Median age	35.8
Native-born	1,659
Foreign-born	166

Educational Attainment, 2000

Population 25 years and over	1,308
Less than 9th grade	4.2%
High school grad or higher	88.8%
Bachelor's degree or higher	18.4%
Graduate degree	3.2%

Income & Poverty, 1999

Per capita income	$26,668
Median household income	$60,125
Median family income	$64,659
Persons in poverty	61
H'holds receiving public assistance	11
H'holds receiving social security	116

Households, 2000

Total households	746
With persons under 18	256
With persons over 65	89
Family households	495
Single-person households	191
Persons per household	2.45
Persons per family	3.01

Labor & Employment

Total civilian labor force, 2007**	1,256
Unemployment rate	4.2%
Total civilian labor force, 2000	1,141
Unemployment rate	3.9%

Employed persons 16 years and over by occupation, 2000

Managers & professionals	319
Service occupations	168
Sales & office occupations	344
Farming, fishing & forestry	0
Construction & maintenance	110
Production & transportation	156
Self-employed persons	40

* US Census Bureau
** New Jersey Department of Labor

General Information

Borough of Helmetta
60 Main St
PO Box 378
Helmetta, NJ 08828
732-521-4946

Website	www.helmettaboro.com
Year of incorporation	1888
Land/water area (sq. miles)	0.85/0.05
Form of government	Borough

Government

Legislative Districts

US Congressional	12
State Legislative	18

Local Officials, 2009

Mayor	Nancy Martin
Manager	William Schmeling
Clerk	Sandra Bohinski
Finance Dir.	Lori Russo
Tax Assessor	Kenneth Pacera
Tax Collector	Denise Jawidzik
Attorney	David Clark
Building	Robert Simonelli
Comm Dev/Planning	NA
Engineering	Terence M. Vogt
Public Works	Darren Doran
Police Chief	Cully Lewis
Emerg/Fire Director	Vincent Amobile

Housing & Construction

Housing Units, 2000*

Total	769
Median rent	$1,051
Median SF home value	$148,300

Permits for New Residential Construction

	Units	Value
Total, 2006	0	$0
Single family	0	$0
Total, 2007	3	$512,000
Single family	3	$512,000

Real Property Valuation, 2008

	Parcels	Valuation
Total	927	$249,230,300
Vacant	42	2,387,500
Residential	868	237,122,000
Commercial	12	6,167,700
Industrial	5	3,553,100
Apartments	0	0
Farm land	0	0
Farm homestead	0	0

Average Property Value & Tax, 2008

Residential value	$273,182
Property tax	$5,367
Tax credit/rebate	$945

Public Library

No public municipal library

Library statistics, 2007

Population served	NA
Full-time/total staff	NA/NA

	Total	Per capita
Holdings	NA	NA
Revenues	NA	NA
Expenditures	NA	NA
Annual visits	NA	NA
Internet terminals/annual users	NA/NA	

Public Safety

Number of officers, 2007 ... 3

Crime	2006	2007
Total crimes	8	12
Violent	3	0
Murder	0	0
Rape	0	0
Robbery	0	0
Aggravated assault	3	0
Non-violent	5	12
Burglary	0	7
Larceny	5	5
Vehicle theft	0	0
Domestic violence	4	0
Arson	0	0
Total crime rate	3.9	5.9
Violent	1.5	0.0
Non-violent	2.4	5.9

Public School District

(for school year 2007-08 except as noted)

Helmetta School District
60 Main Street, PO Box 287
Helmetta, NJ 08828

No schools in district

Per pupil expenditure	NA
Median faculty salary	NA
Median administrator salary	NA
Grade 12 enrollment	NA
High school graduation rate	NA

Assessment test results

(percent scoring at proficient or advanced level)

	Language	Math
NJASK-Grade 3	NA	NA
GEPA-Grade 8	NA	NA
HSPA-High School	NA	NA

SAT Score Averages, 2006-07

Pct tested	Math	Verbal	Writing
NA	NA	NA	NA

Teacher Qualifications

Avg. years of experience	NA
Highly-qualified teachers one subject/all subjects	NA/NA

No Child Left Behind

AYP, 2006-07	NA

Municipal Finance

State Aid Programs, 2009

Total aid	$183,429
CMPTRA	64,930
Energy tax receipts	113,914
Garden State Trust	0

General Budget, 2008

Total tax levy	$4,902,508
County levy	728,919
County taxes	652,641
County library	0
County health	0
County open space	76,278
School levy	3,069,427
Muni. levy	1,104,162
Misc. revenues	837,841

Taxes

	2006	2007	2008
General tax rate per $100	7.05	1.91	1.965
County equalization ratio	29.66	101.71	99.43
Net valuation taxable	$64,824,500	$250,640,757	$249,543,139
State equalized value	$245,724,858	$252,075,852	$255,881,235

See Introduction for an explanation of all data sources.

Demographics & Socio-Economic Characteristics
(2000 US Census, except as noted)

Population
1980*	3,435
1990*	3,886
2000	3,776
Male	1,830
Female	1,946
2007 (estimate)*	3,701
Population density	1,535.7

Race & Hispanic Origin, 2000
Race
White	3,634
Black/African American	30
American Indian/Alaska Native	13
Asian	54
Native Hawaiian/Pacific Islander	1
Other race	17
Two or more races	27
Hispanic origin, total	80
Mexican	11
Puerto Rican	39
Cuban	4
Other Hispanic	26

Age & Nativity, 2000
Under 5 years	326
18 years and over	2,732
21 years and over	2,636
65 years and over	246
85 years and over	26
Median age	36.1
Native-born	3,531
Foreign-born	245

Educational Attainment, 2000
Population 25 years and over	2,530
Less than 9th grade	1.9%
High school grad or higher	92.4%
Bachelor's degree or higher	39.1%
Graduate degree	12.1%

Income & Poverty, 1999
Per capita income	$29,276
Median household income	$68,719
Median family income	$75,357
Persons in poverty	120
H'holds receiving public assistance	9
H'holds receiving social security	202

Households, 2000
Total households	1,428
With persons under 18	587
With persons over 65	187
Family households	1,051
Single-person households	298
Persons per household	2.64
Persons per family	3.10

Labor & Employment
Total civilian labor force, 2007**	2,543
Unemployment rate	3.1%
Total civilian labor force, 2000	2,273
Unemployment rate	2.7%

Employed persons 16 years and over by occupation, 2000
Managers & professionals	892
Service occupations	310
Sales & office occupations	642
Farming, fishing & forestry	0
Construction & maintenance	212
Production & transportation	156
Self-employed persons	142

* US Census Bureau
** New Jersey Department of Labor

General Information
Borough of High Bridge
71 Main St
High Bridge, NJ 08829
908-638-6455

Website	www.highbridge.org
Year of incorporation	1898
Land/water area (sq. miles)	2.41/0.02
Form of government	Borough

Government
Legislative Districts
US Congressional	7
State Legislative	23

Local Officials, 2009
Mayor	Mark Desire
Borough Admin	Douglas Walker
Clerk	Diane Seals
Finance Dir	Bonnie Fleming
Tax Assessor	Pat Spychala
Tax Collector	Bonnie Fleming
Attorney	Barry Goodman
Building	Al Hopping
Comm Dev/Planning	NA
Engineering	Rob O'Brien
Public Works	Michael Hann
Police Chief	Edward Spinks
Fire Chief	Jeff Smith

Housing & Construction
Housing Units, 2000*
Total	1,478
Median rent	$788
Median SF home value	$163,300

Permits for New Residential Construction
	Units	Value
Total, 2006	3	$473,184
Single family	3	$473,184
Total, 2007	2	$355,415
Single family	2	$355,415

Real Property Valuation, 2008
	Parcels	Valuation
Total	1,477	$383,535,700
Vacant	86	7,594,000
Residential	1,343	354,362,300
Commercial	29	11,947,400
Industrial	7	8,024,000
Apartments	1	509,600
Farm land	8	14,200
Farm homestead	3	1,084,200

Average Property Value & Tax, 2008
Residential value	$264,076
Property tax	$7,996
Tax credit/rebate	$1,153

Public Library
High Bridge Public Library
71 Main St
High Bridge, NJ 08829
908-638-8231

Director	Teresa Streets

Library statistics, 2007
Population served	3,776
Full-time/total staff	0/0

	Total	Per capita
Holdings	8,787	2.33
Revenues	$27,971	$7.41
Expenditures	$24,560	$6.50
Annual visits	6,614	1.75
Internet terminals/annual users	1/1,050	

Public Safety
Number of officers, 2007	7

Crime	2006	2007
Total crimes	42	49
Violent	4	4
Murder	0	0
Rape	0	1
Robbery	0	0
Aggravated assault	4	3
Non-violent	38	45
Burglary	4	7
Larceny	32	36
Vehicle theft	2	2
Domestic violence	52	62
Arson	0	1
Total crime rate	11.1	13.0
Violent	1.1	1.1
Non-violent	10.1	12.0

Public School District
(for school year 2007-08 except as noted)

High Bridge Borough School District
50 Thomas Street
High Bridge, NJ 08829
(908) 638-4103

Superintendent	William Caldwell (Int)
Number of schools	2
Grade plan	K-8
Enrollment	405
Attendance rate, '06-07	96.0%
Dropout rate	NA
Students per teacher	8.0
Per pupil expenditure	$14,179
Median faculty salary	$57,800
Median administrator salary	$91,724
Grade 12 enrollment	NA
High school graduation rate	NA

Assessment test results
(percent scoring at proficient or advanced level)
	Language	Math
NJASK-Grade 3	93.4%	88.7%
GEPA-Grade 8	79.5%	89.8%
HSPA-High School	NA	NA

SAT Score Averages, 2006-07
Pct tested	Math	Verbal	Writing
NA	NA	NA	NA

Teacher Qualifications
Avg. years of experience	14
Highly-qualified teachers one subject/all subjects	100%/100%

No Child Left Behind
AYP, 2006-07	Meets Standards

Municipal Finance
State Aid Programs, 2009
Total aid	$401,180
CMPTRA	162,040
Energy tax receipts	204,910
Garden State Trust	21,765

General Budget, 2008
Total tax levy	$11,644,203
County levy	1,477,145
County taxes	1,236,292
County library	107,351
County health	0
County open space	133,501
School levy	7,147,243
Muni. levy	3,019,816
Misc. revenues	2,769,653

Taxes
	2006	2007	2008
General tax rate per $100	2.59	2.99	3.028
County equalization ratio	95.83	85.71	86.84
Net valuation taxable	$378,812,600	$380,517,106	$384,581,506
State equalized value	$415,999,654	$434,422,294	$435,351,887

See Introduction for an explanation of all data sources.

Demographics & Socio-Economic Characteristics

(2000 US Census, except as noted)

Population
1980*	13,396
1990*	13,279
2000	13,999
Male	6,758
Female	7,241
2007 (estimate)*	14,202
Population density	7,718.5

Race & Hispanic Origin, 2000
Race
White	10,087
Black/African American	1,111
American Indian/Alaska Native	16
Asian	1,908
Native Hawaiian/Pacific Islander	12
Other race	503
Two or more races	362
Hispanic origin, total	1,145
Mexican	247
Puerto Rican	287
Cuban	46
Other Hispanic	565

Age & Nativity, 2000
Under 5 years	836
18 years and over	10,955
21 years and over	10,579
65 years and over	1,672
85 years and over	220
Median age	34.7
Native-born	9,914
Foreign-born	4,085

Educational Attainment, 2000
Population 25 years and over	9,801
Less than 9th grade	2.3%
High school grad or higher	91.1%
Bachelor's degree or higher	59.5%
Graduate degree	35.2%

Income & Poverty, 1999
Per capita income	$28,767
Median household income	$53,250
Median family income	$71,267
Persons in poverty	1,181
H'holds receiving public assistance	141
H'holds receiving social security	1,279

Households, 2000
Total households	5,899
With persons under 18	1,729
With persons over 65	1,266
Family households	3,412
Single-person households	1,857
Persons per household	2.37
Persons per family	3.06

Labor & Employment
Total civilian labor force, 2007**	8,575
Unemployment rate	3.7%
Total civilian labor force, 2000	7,846
Unemployment rate	3.8%

Employed persons 16 years and over by occupation, 2000
Managers & professionals	4,646
Service occupations	616
Sales & office occupations	1,502
Farming, fishing & forestry	0
Construction & maintenance	258
Production & transportation	526
Self-employed persons	318

* US Census Bureau
** New Jersey Department of Labor

See Introduction for an explanation of all data sources.

General Information
Borough of Highland Park
221 So 5th Ave
PO Box 1330
Highland Park, NJ 08904
732-572-3400

Website	www.hpboro.com
Year of incorporation	1905
Land/water area (sq. miles)	1.84/0.00
Form of government	Borough

Government
Legislative Districts
US Congressional	6
State Legislative	17

Local Officials, 2009
Mayor	Meryl Frank
Manager	Karen Waldron
Clerk	Joan Hullings
Finance Dir	Kathleen Kovach
Tax Assessor	Thomas Mancuso
Tax Collector	Kathleen Kovach
Attorney	Edwin Schmierer
Building	Scott Luthman
Comm Dev/Planning	NA
Engineering	David Samuel
Public Works	Donald Rish
Police Chief	Stephen Rizco
Emerg/Fire Director	Doug Watt

Housing & Construction
Housing Units, 2000*
Total	6,071
Median rent	$848
Median SF home value	$183,300

Permits for New Residential Construction
	Units	Value
Total, 2006	57	$7,960,086
Single family	7	$1,126,755
Total, 2007	54	$7,443,287
Single family	7	$1,019,956

Real Property Valuation, 2008
	Parcels	Valuation
Total	3,214	$531,231,200
Vacant	78	3,412,100
Residential	2,845	394,142,800
Commercial	192	48,518,800
Industrial	11	5,044,900
Apartments	88	80,112,600
Farm land	0	0
Farm homestead	0	0

Average Property Value & Tax, 2008
Residential value	$138,539
Property tax	$8,730
Tax credit/rebate	$1,214

Public Library
Highland Park Public Library
31 N Fifth Ave
Highland Park, NJ 08904
732-572-2750

Director	Jane Stanley

Library statistics, 2007
Population served	13,999
Full-time/total staff	5/9

	Total	Per capita
Holdings	71,810	5.13
Revenues	$938,953	$67.07
Expenditures	$906,033	$64.72
Annual visits	180,054	12.86
Internet terminals/annual users	13/20,826	

Public Safety
Number of officers, 2007	30

Crime	2006	2007
Total crimes	243	224
Violent	16	10
Murder	0	0
Rape	1	1
Robbery	5	4
Aggravated assault	10	5
Non-violent	227	214
Burglary	32	47
Larceny	180	157
Vehicle theft	15	10
Domestic violence	77	99
Arson	0	2
Total crime rate	17.0	15.8
Violent	1.1	0.7
Non-violent	15.9	15.1

Public School District
(for school year 2007-08 except as noted)

Highland Park School District
435 Mansfield Street
Highland Park, NJ 08904
(732) 572-6990

Superintendent	Frances Wood
Number of schools	4
Grade plan	K-12
Enrollment	1,530
Attendance rate, '06-07	95.1%
Dropout rate	0.2%
Students per teacher	9.7
Per pupil expenditure	$15,602
Median faculty salary	$51,540
Median administrator salary	$120,139
Grade 12 enrollment	108
High school graduation rate	98.2%

Assessment test results
(percent scoring at proficient or advanced level)
	Language	Math
NJASK-Grade 3	88.1%	79.9%
GEPA-Grade 8	76.2%	82.7%
HSPA-High School	88.3%	89.3%

SAT Score Averages, 2006-07
Pct tested	Math	Verbal	Writing
91%	563	554	536

Teacher Qualifications
Avg. years of experience	7
Highly-qualified teachers one subject/all subjects	100%/100%

No Child Left Behind
AYP, 2006-07	Meets Standards

Municipal Finance
State Aid Programs, 2009
Total aid	$1,265,513
CMPTRA	458,741
Energy tax receipts	775,134
Garden State Trust	0

General Budget, 2008
Total tax levy	$33,493,017
County levy	4,251,521
County taxes	3,803,500
County library	0
County health	0
County open space	448,021
School levy	20,884,199
Muni. levy	8,357,297
Misc. revenues	4,460,633

Taxes
	2006	2007	2008
General tax rate per $100	5.72	6.05	6.301
County equalization ratio	41.78	37.28	35.72
Net valuation taxable	$534,753,800	$530,719,837	$531,537,518
State equalized value	$1,434,769,489	$1,485,219,891	$1,502,232,244

Demographics & Socio-Economic Characteristics
(2000 US Census, except as noted)

Population
1980*	5,187
1990*	4,849
2000	5,097
Male	2,554
Female	2,543
2007 (estimate)*	5,310
Population density	6,986.8

Race & Hispanic Origin, 2000
Race
White	4,847
Black/African American	81
American Indian/Alaska Native	17
Asian	51
Native Hawaiian/Pacific Islander	0
Other race	30
Two or more races	71
Hispanic origin, total	207
Mexican	22
Puerto Rican	100
Cuban	21
Other Hispanic	64

Age & Nativity, 2000
Under 5 years	259
18 years and over	4,140
21 years and over	3,998
65 years and over	576
85 years and over	70
Median age	38.6
Native-born	4,789
Foreign-born	308

Educational Attainment, 2000
Population 25 years and over	3,791
Less than 9th grade	1.0%
High school grad or higher	87.9%
Bachelor's degree or higher	26.4%
Graduate degree	9.2%

Income & Poverty, 1999
Per capita income	$29,369
Median household income	$45,692
Median family income	$50,985
Persons in poverty	625
H'holds receiving public assistance	44
H'holds receiving social security	646

Households, 2000
Total households	2,450
With persons under 18	542
With persons over 65	450
Family households	1,194
Single-person households	1,021
Persons per household	2.08
Persons per family	2.90

Labor & Employment
Total civilian labor force, 2007**	3,088
Unemployment rate	5.4%
Total civilian labor force, 2000	2,905
Unemployment rate	5.7%

Employed persons 16 years and over by occupation, 2000
Managers & professionals	955
Service occupations	454
Sales & office occupations	771
Farming, fishing & forestry	23
Construction & maintenance	293
Production & transportation	242
Self-employed persons	256

* US Census Bureau
** New Jersey Department of Labor
§ State Fiscal Year July 1–June 30

General Information
Borough of Highlands
171 Bay Ave
Highlands, NJ 07732
732-872-1224

Website	www.highlandsnj.com
Year of incorporation	1900
Land/water area (sq. miles)	0.76/0.56
Form of government	Small Municipality

Government
Legislative Districts
US Congressional	6
State Legislative	11

Local Officials, 2009
Mayor	Anna C. Little
Manager/Admin	NA
Borough Clerk	Nina Light Flannery
CFO	Stephen Pfeffer
Tax Assessor	Charles Heck
Tax Collector	Patrick DeBlaso
Attorney	Scott Arnette
Building	Paul Vitale
Comm Dev/Planning	NA
Engineering	Robert Keady
Public Works	NA
Police Chief	Joseph Blewett
Fire Chief	Rebecca Kane

Housing & Construction
Housing Units, 2000*
Total	2,820
Median rent	$760
Median SF home value	$139,300

Permits for New Residential Construction
	Units	Value
Total, 2006	10	$1,502,000
Single family	10	$1,502,000
Total, 2007	1	$48,000
Single family	1	$48,000

Real Property Valuation, 2008
	Parcels	Valuation
Total	2,519	$541,796,100
Vacant	149	5,921,900
Residential	2,262	484,293,700
Commercial	99	46,798,200
Industrial	0	0
Apartments	9	4,782,300
Farm land	0	0
Farm homestead	0	0

Average Property Value & Tax, 2008
Residential value	$214,100
Property tax	$5,785
Tax credit/rebate	$1,004

Public Library
No public municipal library

Library statistics, 2007
Population served	NA
Full-time/total staff	NA/NA

	Total	Per capita
Holdings	NA	NA
Revenues	NA	NA
Expenditures	NA	NA
Annual visits	NA	NA
Internet terminals/annual users	NA/NA	

Public Safety
Number of officers, 2007	13

Crime	2006	2007
Total crimes	86	78
Violent	7	2
Murder	0	0
Rape	0	0
Robbery	0	0
Aggravated assault	7	2
Non-violent	79	76
Burglary	16	21
Larceny	60	51
Vehicle theft	3	4
Domestic violence	108	84
Arson	1	1
Total crime rate	17.2	15.6
Violent	1.4	0.4
Non-violent	15.8	15.2

Public School District
(for school year 2007-08 except as noted)

Highlands Borough School District
360 Navesink Avenue
Highlands, NJ 07732
(732) 872-1476

Superintendent	Maryann Galassetti
Number of schools	1
Grade plan	K-6
Enrollment	179
Attendance rate, '06-07	94.4%
Dropout rate	NA
Students per teacher	7.4
Per pupil expenditure	$18,693
Median faculty salary	$50,923
Median administrator salary	$90,000
Grade 12 enrollment	NA
High school graduation rate	NA

Assessment test results
(percent scoring at proficient or advanced level)
	Language	Math
NJASK-Grade 3	85.7%	85.7%
GEPA-Grade 8	NA	NA
HSPA-High School	NA	NA

SAT Score Averages, 2006-07
Pct tested	Math	Verbal	Writing
NA	NA	NA	NA

Teacher Qualifications
Avg. years of experience	9
Highly-qualified teachers one subject/all subjects	94.0%/94.0%

No Child Left Behind
AYP, 2006-07	Meets Standards

Municipal Finance§
State Aid Programs, 2009
Total aid	$458,164
CMPTRA	93,362
Energy tax receipts	352,345
Garden State Trust	610

General Budget, 2008
Total tax levy	$14,648,302
County levy	2,055,254
County taxes	1,823,872
County library	109,758
County health	0
County open space	121,624
School levy	7,314,036
Muni. levy	5,279,012
Misc. revenues	2,944,922

Taxes
	2006	2007	2008
General tax rate per $100	2.517	2.601	2.703
County equalization ratio	83.59	72.55	67.16
Net valuation taxable	$533,838,400	$536,206,909	$542,093,646
State equalized value	$736,155,437	$798,253,973	$6,734,691,283

See Introduction for an explanation of all data sources.

Demographics & Socio-Economic Characteristics
(2000 US Census, except as noted)

Population
1980*	4,581
1990*	5,126
2000	5,216
Male	2,651
Female	2,565
2007 (estimate)*	5,271
Population density	4,285.4

Race & Hispanic Origin, 2000
Race
White	3,992
Black/African American	444
American Indian/Alaska Native	19
Asian	119
Native Hawaiian/Pacific Islander	4
Other race	503
Two or more races	135
Hispanic origin, total	1,046
Mexican	69
Puerto Rican	135
Cuban	12
Other Hispanic	830

Age & Nativity, 2000
Under 5 years	379
18 years and over	4,042
21 years and over	3,873
65 years and over	562
85 years and over	141
Median age	35.5
Native-born	4,115
Foreign-born	1,101

Educational Attainment, 2000
Population 25 years and over	3,671
Less than 9th grade	8.0%
High school grad or higher	82.1%
Bachelor's degree or higher	39.5%
Graduate degree	17.4%

Income & Poverty, 1999
Per capita income	$28,605
Median household income	$64,299
Median family income	$72,092
Persons in poverty	380
H'holds receiving public assistance	25
H'holds receiving social security	426

Households, 2000
Total households	2,001
With persons under 18	658
With persons over 65	423
Family households	1,300
Single-person households	559
Persons per household	2.60
Persons per family	3.15

Labor & Employment
Total civilian labor force, 2007**	3,821
Unemployment rate	4.2%
Total civilian labor force, 2000	3,076
Unemployment rate	3.0%

Employed persons 16 years and over by occupation, 2000
Managers & professionals	1,257
Service occupations	405
Sales & office occupations	690
Farming, fishing & forestry	15
Construction & maintenance	207
Production & transportation	411
Self-employed persons	100

‡ Branch of county library
* US Census Bureau
** New Jersey Department of Labor

General Information
Borough of Hightstown
148 N Main St
Hightstown, NJ 08520
609-490-5100
Website	www.hightstownborough.com
Year of incorporation	1853
Land/water area (sq. miles)	1.23/0.02
Form of government	Borough

Government
Legislative Districts
US Congressional	4
State Legislative	12

Local Officials, 2009
Mayor	Robert Patten
Manager	Candace Gallagher
Clerk	Candace Gallagher
Chief Financial Officer	George Lang
Tax Assessor	Ken Pacera
Tax Collector	Kathryn Monzo
Attorney	Frederick C. Raffetto
Construction Official	George Chin
Comm Dev/Planning	Tamara Lee
Engineer	Carmela Roberts
Public Works	Larry Blake
Police Chief	James Eufemia
Fire/Emerg Management	John Archer

Housing & Construction
Housing Units, 2000*
Total	2,081
Median rent	$820
Median SF home value	$141,300

Permits for New Residential Construction
	Units	Value
Total, 2006	21	$2,940,875
Single family	21	$2,940,875
Total, 2007	22	$3,825,065
Single family	22	$3,825,065

Real Property Valuation, 2008
	Parcels	Valuation
Total	1,648	$214,897,100
Vacant	125	3,469,600
Residential	1,413	168,747,700
Commercial	99	33,275,800
Industrial	6	1,936,000
Apartments	5	7,468,000
Farm land	0	0
Farm homestead	0	0

Average Property Value & Tax, 2008
Residential value	$119,425
Property tax	$7,718
Tax credit/rebate	$1,164

Public Library
Hightstown Mem Library‡
114 Franklin St
Hightstown, NJ 08520
609-448-1474
Branch Librarian	Linda Chorewiak

Library statistics, 2007
see Mercer County profile
for library system statistics

Public Safety
Number of officers, 2007	14

Crime	2006	2007
Total crimes	125	101
Violent	17	12
Murder	0	0
Rape	3	0
Robbery	6	4
Aggravated assault	8	8
Non-violent	108	89
Burglary	25	14
Larceny	77	70
Vehicle theft	6	5
Domestic violence	66	57
Arson	1	1
Total crime rate	23.6	19.1
Violent	3.2	2.3
Non-violent	20.4	16.8

Public School District
(for school year 2007-08 except as noted)

East Windsor Regional School District
25A Leshin Lane
Hightstown, NJ 08520
(609) 443-7717
Superintendent	Ronald Bolandi
Number of schools	6
Grade plan	K-12
Enrollment	4,947
Attendance rate, '06-07	95.7%
Dropout rate	1.3%
Students per teacher	11.3
Per pupil expenditure	$14,400
Median faculty salary	$71,855
Median administrator salary	$124,738
Grade 12 enrollment	317
High school graduation rate	92.5%

Assessment test results
(percent scoring at proficient or advanced level)
	Language	Math
NJASK-Grade 3	90.0%	85.7%
GEPA-Grade 8	73.1%	84.2%
HSPA-High School	79.1%	89.2%

SAT Score Averages, 2006-07
Pct tested	Math	Verbal	Writing
86%	536	517	508

Teacher Qualifications
Avg. years of experience	15
Highly-qualified teachers	
one subject/all subjects	99.5%/99.5%

No Child Left Behind
AYP, 2006-07	Needs Improvement

Municipal Finance
State Aid Programs, 2009
Total aid	$649,228
CMPTRA	234,068
Energy tax receipts	398,930
Garden State Trust	0

General Budget, 2008
Total tax levy	$14,014,645
County levy	2,664,544
County taxes	2,279,065
County library	229,044
County health	0
County open space	156,435
School levy	7,891,400
Muni. levy	3,458,702
Misc. revenues	2,581,321

Taxes
	2006	2007	2008
General tax rate per $100	5.7	6.06	6.463
County equalization ratio	51.05	44.47	41.62
Net valuation taxable	$215,855,800	$218,806,857	$216,854,688
State equalized value	$487,461,972	$523,267,394	$524,440,204

See Introduction for an explanation of all data sources.

Demographics & Socio-Economic Characteristics
(2000 US Census, except as noted)

Population
1980*	19,061
1990*	28,808
2000	36,634
Male	18,091
Female	18,543
2007 (estimate)*	38,597
Population density	705.7

Race & Hispanic Origin, 2000
Race
White	31,491
Black/African American	1,379
American Indian/Alaska Native	32
Asian	2,679
Native Hawaiian/Pacific Islander	23
Other race	468
Two or more races	562
Hispanic origin, total	1,740
Mexican	203
Puerto Rican	436
Cuban	133
Other Hispanic	968

Age & Nativity, 2000
Under 5 years	2,898
18 years and over	25,963
21 years and over	24,938
65 years and over	2,508
85 years and over	257
Median age	35.7
Native-born	32,233
Foreign-born	4,421

Educational Attainment, 2000
Population 25 years and over	23,743
Less than 9th grade	2.6%
High school grad or higher	92.7%
Bachelor's degree or higher	46.6%
Graduate degree	16.2%

Income & Poverty, 1999
Per capita income	$33,091
Median household income	$83,290
Median family income	$93,933
Persons in poverty	1,140
H'holds receiving public assistance	87
H'holds receiving social security	1,867

Households, 2000
Total households	12,649
With persons under 18	5,843
With persons over 65	1,740
Family households	9,797
Single-person households	2,249
Persons per household	2.88
Persons per family	3.31

Labor & Employment
Total civilian labor force, 2007**	22,190
Unemployment rate	2.9%
Total civilian labor force, 2000	20,181
Unemployment rate	2.0%

Employed persons 16 years and over by occupation, 2000
Managers & professionals	10,534
Service occupations	1,632
Sales & office occupations	5,063
Farming, fishing & forestry	92
Construction & maintenance	1,133
Production & transportation	1,326
Self-employed persons	862

General Information
Township of Hillsborough
379 S Branch Rd
Hillsborough, NJ 08844
908-369-4313
Website	www.hillsborough-nj.org
Year of incorporation	1771
Land/water area (sq. miles)	54.69/0.10
Form of government	Township

Government
Legislative Districts
US Congressional	7
State Legislative	16

Local Officials, 2009
Mayor	Frank A. DelCore
Manager	Kevin Davis
Clerk	Kevin Davis
Finance Dir	Nancy Haberle
Tax Assessor	Debra Blaney
Tax Collector	Nancy Haberle
Attorney	Albert Cruz
Building	Ron Skobo
Planning	Robert Ringleheim
Engineering	Tom Belanger
Public Works	Buck Sixt
Police Chief	Paul Kaminsky
Fire/Emergency Dir	Chris Weniger

Housing & Construction
Housing Units, 2000*
Total	12,854
Median rent	$931
Median SF home value	$238,600

Permits for New Residential Construction
	Units	Value
Total, 2006	114	$16,577,025
Single family	37	$14,344,977
Total, 2007	186	$37,660,520
Single family	165	$33,319,860

Real Property Valuation, 2008
	Parcels	Valuation
Total	14,355	$3,729,887,400
Vacant	1,153	65,075,900
Residential	12,227	3,150,143,900
Commercial	332	274,004,000
Industrial	122	131,105,600
Apartments	25	46,315,900
Farm land	323	4,445,900
Farm homestead	173	58,796,200

Average Property Value & Tax, 2008
Residential value	$258,785
Property tax	$7,695
Tax credit/rebate	$1,117

Public Library
Hillsborough Branch Library‡
379 S Branch Rd
Hillsborough, NJ 08844
908-369-2200
Branch Librarian	Edward Hoag

Library statistics, 2007
see Somerset County profile
for library system statistics

Public Safety
Number of officers, 2007	56

Crime	2006	2007
Total crimes	368	360
Violent	21	11
Murder	0	1
Rape	5	4
Robbery	5	2
Aggravated assault	11	4
Non-violent	347	349
Burglary	80	72
Larceny	251	262
Vehicle theft	16	15
Domestic violence	341	341
Arson	2	3
Total crime rate	9.7	9.4
Violent	0.6	0.3
Non-violent	9.2	9.2

Public School District
(for school year 2007-08 except as noted)

Hillsborough Township School District
379 South Branch Rd
Hillsborough NJ, NJ 08844
(908) 369-0030
Superintendent	Edward J. Forsthoffer III
Number of schools	9
Grade plan	K-12
Enrollment	7,521
Attendance rate, '06-07	96.0%
Dropout rate	1.0%
Students per teacher	10.3
Per pupil expenditure	$12,482
Median faculty salary	$61,202
Median administrator salary	$114,553
Grade 12 enrollment	555
High school graduation rate	96.6%

Assessment test results
(percent scoring at proficient or advanced level)
	Language	Math
NJASK-Grade 3	95.6%	95.9%
GEPA-Grade 8	79.0%	93.8%
HSPA-High School	90.3%	95.0%

SAT Score Averages, 2006-07
Pct tested	Math	Verbal	Writing
92%	550	520	524

Teacher Qualifications
Avg. years of experience	11
Highly-qualified teachers one subject/all subjects	100%/100%

No Child Left Behind
AYP, 2006-07	Meets Standards

Municipal Finance
State Aid Programs, 2009
Total aid	$4,218,251
CMPTRA	449,077
Energy tax receipts	3,639,028
Garden State Trust	23,105

General Budget, 2008
Total tax levy	$111,138,624
County levy	20,725,562
County taxes	16,633,626
County library	2,250,903
County health	0
County open space	1,841,033
School levy	73,611,384
Muni. levy	16,801,678
Misc. revenues	12,705,697

Taxes	2006	2007	2008
General tax rate per $100	2.82	2.93	2.974
County equalization ratio	70.09	64.06	60.93
Net valuation taxable	$3,622,804,700	$3,693,852,115	$3,737,778,962
State equalized value	$5,664,669,359	$6,056,883,688	$6,182,179,594

‡ Branch of county library
* US Census Bureau
** New Jersey Department of Labor

See Introduction for an explanation of all data sources.

Demographics & Socio-Economic Characteristics

(2000 US Census, except as noted)

Population

1980*	10,495
1990*	9,750
2000	10,087
Male	4,915
Female	5,172
2007 (estimate)*	9,908
Population density	3,324.8

Race & Hispanic Origin, 2000

Race

White	9,321
Black/African American	86
American Indian/Alaska Native	7
Asian	512
Native Hawaiian/Pacific Islander	4
Other race	87
Two or more races	70
Hispanic origin, total	429
Mexican	76
Puerto Rican	70
Cuban	55
Other Hispanic	228

Age & Nativity, 2000

Under 5 years	736
18 years and over	7,465
21 years and over	7,235
65 years and over	1,493
85 years and over	146
Median age	39.5
Native-born	8,744
Foreign-born	1,343

Educational Attainment, 2000

Population 25 years and over	6,903
Less than 9th grade	2.4%
High school grad or higher	92.4%
Bachelor's degree or higher	45.8%
Graduate degree	17.0%

Income & Poverty, 1999

Per capita income	$34,651
Median household income	$82,904
Median family income	$90,861
Persons in poverty	334
H'holds receiving public assistance	51
H'holds receiving social security	1,021

Households, 2000

Total households	3,502
With persons under 18	1,405
With persons over 65	1,041
Family households	2,849
Single-person households	551
Persons per household	2.87
Persons per family	3.20

Labor & Employment

Total civilian labor force, 2007**	5,475
Unemployment rate	2.4%
Total civilian labor force, 2000	5,207
Unemployment rate	2.8%

Employed persons 16 years and over by occupation, 2000

Managers & professionals	2,326
Service occupations	553
Sales & office occupations	1,612
Farming, fishing & forestry	0
Construction & maintenance	382
Production & transportation	186
Self-employed persons	348

* US Census Bureau
** New Jersey Department of Labor

See Introduction for an explanation of all data sources.

General Information

Borough of Hillsdale
380 Hillsdale Ave
Hillsdale, NJ 07642
201-666-4800

Website	www.hillsdalenj.org
Year of incorporation	1923
Land/water area (sq. miles)	2.98/0.00
Form of government	Borough

Government

Legislative Districts

US Congressional	5
State Legislative	39

Local Officials, 2009

Mayor	John Sapanara
Manager	Harold Karns
Clerk	Robert Sandt
Finance Dir	Harold Karns
Tax Assessor	Richard Mohr
Tax Collector	Marilyn Feigle
Attorney	Steven Paul
Building	Keith Durie
Comm Dev/Planning	NA
Engineering	Christopher Statile
Public Works	Keith Durie
Police Chief	Elwood Stalter
Emerg/Fire Director	Christopher P. Statile

Housing & Construction

Housing Units, 2000*

Total	3,547
Median rent	$926
Median SF home value	$291,800

Permits for New Residential Construction

	Units	Value
Total, 2006	4	$1,401,150
Single family	4	$1,401,150
Total, 2007	11	$2,837,300
Single family	1	$687,300

Real Property Valuation, 2008

	Parcels	Valuation
Total	3,478	$1,956,102,000
Vacant	63	12,449,200
Residential	3,298	1,818,907,400
Commercial	99	107,676,500
Industrial	12	14,315,500
Apartments	2	1,995,300
Farm land	2	13,100
Farm homestead	2	745,000

Average Property Value & Tax, 2008

Residential value	$551,410
Property tax	$10,314
Tax credit/rebate	$1,334

Public Library

Hillsdale Public Library
509 Hillsdale Ave
Hillsdale, NJ 07642
201-358-5072

Director	David J. Franz

Library statistics, 2007

Population served	10,087
Full-time/total staff	3/4

	Total	Per capita
Holdings	68,784	6.82
Revenues	$724,384	$71.81
Expenditures	$721,525	$71.53
Annual visits	113,760	11.28
Internet terminals/annual users	18/31,000	

Public Safety

Number of officers, 2007	20

Crime	2006	2007
Total crimes	92	77
Violent	3	4
Murder	0	0
Rape	0	1
Robbery	0	1
Aggravated assault	3	2
Non-violent	89	73
Burglary	7	7
Larceny	81	66
Vehicle theft	1	0
Domestic violence	18	20
Arson	0	0
Total crime rate	9.1	7.7
Violent	0.3	0.4
Non-violent	8.8	7.3

Public School District

(for school year 2007-08 except as noted)

Hillsdale School District
32 Ruckman Road
Hillsdale, NJ 07642
(201) 664-0282

Superintendent	Anthony S. DeNorchia
Number of schools	3
Grade plan	K-8
Enrollment	1,439
Attendance rate, '06-07	96.6%
Dropout rate	NA
Students per teacher	12.2
Per pupil expenditure	$11,288
Median faculty salary	$55,131
Median administrator salary	$128,000
Grade 12 enrollment	NA
High school graduation rate	NA

Assessment test results

(percent scoring at proficient or advanced level)

	Language	Math
NJASK-Grade 3	95.9%	95.8%
GEPA-Grade 8	77.7%	96.5%
HSPA-High School	NA	NA

SAT Score Averages, 2006-07

Pct tested	Math	Verbal	Writing
NA	NA	NA	NA

Teacher Qualifications

Avg. years of experience	8
Highly-qualified teachers one subject/all subjects	100%/100%

No Child Left Behind

AYP, 2006-07	Meets Standards

Municipal Finance

State Aid Programs, 2009

Total aid	$1,523,770
CMPTRA	99,317
Energy tax receipts	1,384,114
Garden State Trust	0

General Budget, 2008

Total tax levy	$36,727,815
County levy	3,669,418
County taxes	3,470,939
County library	0
County health	0
County open space	198,479
School levy	25,183,838
Muni. levy	7,874,558
Misc. revenues	4,477,566

Taxes	2006	2007	2008
General tax rate per $100	3.8	1.79	1.873
County equalization ratio	48.6	100.7	99.16
Net valuation taxable	$846,424,800	$1,964,439,900	$1,963,564,332
State equalized value	$1,932,943,252	$1,981,023,836	$2,049,535,617

Demographics & Socio-Economic Characteristics

(2000 US Census, except as noted)

Population

1980*	21,440
1990*	21,044
2000	21,747
Male	10,199
Female	11,548
2007 (estimate)*	21,320
Population density	7,641.6

Race & Hispanic Origin, 2000

Race

White	8,705
Black/African American	10,122
American Indian/Alaska Native	50
Asian	751
Native Hawaiian/Pacific Islander	17
Other race	1,144
Two or more races	958
Hispanic origin, total	3,153
Mexican	56
Puerto Rican	832
Cuban	402
Other Hispanic	1,863

Age & Nativity, 2000

Under 5 years	1,390
18 years and over	16,185
21 years and over	15,321
65 years and over	2,410
85 years and over	253
Median age	35.7
Native-born	15,788
Foreign-born	5,959

Educational Attainment, 2000

Population 25 years and over	14,279
Less than 9th grade	10.0%
High school grad or higher	76.1%
Bachelor's degree or higher	18.5%
Graduate degree	5.6%

Income & Poverty, 1999

Per capita income	$21,724
Median household income	$59,136
Median family income	$64,635
Persons in poverty	1,147
H'holds receiving public assistance	279
H'holds receiving social security	1,849

Households, 2000

Total households	7,161
With persons under 18	3,081
With persons over 65	1,808
Family households	5,579
Single-person households	1,288
Persons per household	3.04
Persons per family	3.45

Labor & Employment

Total civilian labor force, 2007**	11,866
Unemployment rate	6.8%
Total civilian labor force, 2000	11,436
Unemployment rate	7.0%

Employed persons 16 years and over by occupation, 2000

Managers & professionals	2,935
Service occupations	1,567
Sales & office occupations	3,210
Farming, fishing & forestry	9
Construction & maintenance	969
Production & transportation	1,943
Self-employed persons	295

* US Census Bureau
** New Jersey Department of Labor
§ State Fiscal Year July 1–June 30

General Information

Township of Hillside
Liberty & Hillside Aves
Hillside, NJ 07205
973-926-3000

Website	NA
Year of incorporation	1913
Land/water area (sq. miles)	2.79/0.00
Form of government	Mayor-Council

Government

Legislative Districts

US Congressional	10
State Legislative	29

Local Officials, 2009

Mayor	Karen McCoy Oliver
Manager/Admin	NA
Clerk	Janet Vlaisavljevic
Finance Dir	Marie Pardo
Tax Assessor	Benard Murdoch
Tax Collector	Joe Skelly
Attorney	Christine Burgess
Building	Larry Ditzel
Comm Dev/Planning	NA
Engineering	Victor Vinegra
Public Works	Scott Anderson
Police Chief	Robert Quinlan
Emerg/Fire Director	Dominick Naples

Housing & Construction

Housing Units, 2000*

Total	7,388
Median rent	$797
Median SF home value	$135,200

Permits for New Residential Construction

	Units	Value
Total, 2006	25	$2,839,290
Single family	11	$1,541,000
Total, 2007	9	$997,000
Single family	5	$708,000

Real Property Valuation, 2008

	Parcels	Valuation
Total	6,291	$915,286,094
Vacant	186	7,756,600
Residential	5,650	699,587,544
Commercial	256	69,550,600
Industrial	176	126,967,050
Apartments	23	11,424,300
Farm land	0	0
Farm homestead	0	0

Average Property Value & Tax, 2008

Residential value	$123,821
Property tax	$8,035
Tax credit/rebate	$1,210

Public Library

Hillside Free Public Library
John F Kennedy Plaza
Hillside, NJ 07205
973-923-4413

Director	Miriam Bein

Library statistics, 2007

Population served	21,747
Full-time/total staff	2/6

	Total	Per capita
Holdings	100,433	4.62
Revenues	$976,902	$44.92
Expenditures	$866,002	$39.82
Annual visits	48,000	2.21
Internet terminals/annual users	30/20,000	

Public Safety

Number of officers, 2007	73

Crime	2006	2007
Total crimes	756	804
Violent	102	97
Murder	1	2
Rape	10	6
Robbery	53	67
Aggravated assault	38	22
Non-violent	654	707
Burglary	129	141
Larceny	374	425
Vehicle theft	151	141
Domestic violence	258	282
Arson	3	5
Total crime rate	34.8	37.1
Violent	4.7	4.5
Non-violent	30.1	32.6

Public School District

(for school year 2007-08 except as noted)

Hillside Township School District
195 Virginia Street
Hillside, NJ 07205
(908) 352-7664

Superintendent	Michael Roth (Int)
Number of schools	6
Grade plan	K-12
Enrollment	3,161
Attendance rate, '06-07	95.0%
Dropout rate	4.3%
Students per teacher	11.2
Per pupil expenditure	$13,389
Median faculty salary	$56,357
Median administrator salary	$111,026
Grade 12 enrollment	212
High school graduation rate	84.6%

Assessment test results

(percent scoring at proficient or advanced level)

	Language	Math
NJASK-Grade 3	83.7%	85.5%
GEPA-Grade 8	40.9%	69.7%
HSPA-High School	47.5%	72.1%

SAT Score Averages, 2006-07

Pct tested	Math	Verbal	Writing
80%	394	406	393

Teacher Qualifications

Avg. years of experience	8
Highly-qualified teachers one subject/all subjects	99.5%/99.5%

No Child Left Behind

AYP, 2006-07	Meets Standards

Municipal Finance§

State Aid Programs, 2009

Total aid	$5,306,365
CMPTRA	2,836,231
Energy tax receipts	2,390,539
Garden State Trust	0

General Budget, 2008

Total tax levy	$59,430,246
County levy	8,098,017
County taxes	7,743,646
County library	0
County health	0
County open space	354,371
School levy	24,901,109
Muni. levy	26,431,120
Misc. revenues	15,671,039

Taxes

	2006	2007	2008
General tax rate per $100	5.812	6.09	6.490
County equalization ratio	51.13	44.93	39.38
Net valuation taxable	$916,214,627	$919,869,035	$915,813,726
State equalized value	$2,039,883,506	$2,335,016,834	$2,269,456,968

See Introduction for an explanation of all data sources.

Demographics & Socio-Economic Characteristics
(2000 US Census, except as noted)

Population
1980*	1,250
1990*	1,045
2000	1,029
Male	485
Female	544
2007 (estimate)*	997
Population density	4,334.8

Race & Hispanic Origin, 2000
Race
White	731
Black/African American	198
American Indian/Alaska Native	0
Asian	32
Native Hawaiian/Pacific Islander	0
Other race	45
Two or more races	23
Hispanic origin, total	71
Mexican	12
Puerto Rican	42
Cuban	5
Other Hispanic	12

Age & Nativity, 2000
Under 5 years	78
18 years and over	772
21 years and over	735
65 years and over	141
85 years and over	11
Median age	31.8
Native-born	965
Foreign-born	68

Educational Attainment, 2000
Population 25 years and over	696
Less than 9th grade	2.4%
High school grad or higher	79.2%
Bachelor's degree or higher	13.8%
Graduate degree	3.9%

Income & Poverty, 1999
Per capita income	$19,285
Median household income	$34,948
Median family income	$38,393
Persons in poverty	126
H'holds receiving public assistance	12
H'holds receiving social security	112

Households, 2000
Total households	472
With persons under 18	142
With persons over 65	105
Family households	260
Single-person households	172
Persons per household	2.18
Persons per family	2.83

Labor & Employment
Total civilian labor force, 2007**	582
Unemployment rate	8.9%
Total civilian labor force, 2000	539
Unemployment rate	8.2%

Employed persons 16 years and over by occupation, 2000
Managers & professionals	117
Service occupations	73
Sales & office occupations	190
Farming, fishing & forestry	0
Construction & maintenance	40
Production & transportation	75
Self-employed persons	9

* US Census Bureau
** New Jersey Department of Labor

See Introduction for an explanation of all data sources.

General Information
Borough of Hi-Nella
100 Wykagyl Rd
Hi Nella, NJ 08083
856-784-6237

Website	NA
Year of incorporation	1929
Land/water area (sq. miles)	0.23/0.00
Form of government	Borough

Government

Legislative Districts
US Congressional	1
State Legislative	5

Local Officials, 2009
Mayor	Merideth Dobbs
Manager/Admin	NA
Clerk	Phyllis Twisler
Finance Dir	William Hales Jr
Tax Assessor	Richard Arrowood
Tax Collector	Janice Gattone
Attorney	Robert Messick
Building	NA
Comm Dev/Planning	NA
Engineering	Churchill Consulting
Public Works	Gary Vonder Lieth
Police Chief	Dominic Palese
Emerg/Fire Director	Brian Cunningham

Housing & Construction

Housing Units, 2000*
Total	495
Median rent	$650
Median SF home value	$96,700

Permits for New Residential Construction
	Units	Value
Total, 2006	0	$0
Single family	0	$0
Total, 2007	0	$0
Single family	0	$0

Real Property Valuation, 2008
	Parcels	Valuation
Total	145	$22,764,000
Vacant	3	34,300
Residential	126	11,718,400
Commercial	12	4,754,800
Industrial	0	0
Apartments	2	6,104,900
Farm land	1	11,600
Farm homestead	1	140,000

Average Property Value & Tax, 2008
Residential value	$93,373
Property tax	$4,877
Tax credit/rebate	$1,073

Public Library
No public municipal library

Library statistics, 2007
Population served	NA
Full-time/total staff	NA/NA

	Total	Per capita
Holdings	NA	NA
Revenues	NA	NA
Expenditures	NA	NA
Annual visits	NA	NA
Internet terminals/annual users	NA/NA	

Public Safety
Number of officers, 2007 5

Crime	2006	2007
Total crimes	23	25
Violent	9	1
Murder	0	0
Rape	0	0
Robbery	3	0
Aggravated assault	6	1
Non-violent	14	24
Burglary	5	8
Larceny	8	14
Vehicle theft	1	2
Domestic violence	2	6
Arson	0	1
Total crime rate	22.7	24.8
Violent	8.9	1.0
Non-violent	13.8	23.8

Public School District
(for school year 2007-08 except as noted)

Hi Nella School District
801 Preston Avenue
Somerdale, NJ 08083

No schools in district - sends students to Oaklyn schools

Per pupil expenditure	NA
Median faculty salary	NA
Median administrator salary	NA
Grade 12 enrollment	NA
High school graduation rate	NA

Assessment test results
(percent scoring at proficient or advanced level)
	Language	Math
NJASK-Grade 3	NA	NA
GEPA-Grade 8	NA	NA
HSPA-High School	NA	NA

SAT Score Averages, 2006-07
Pct tested	Math	Verbal	Writing
NA	NA	NA	NA

Teacher Qualifications
Avg. years of experience	NA
Highly-qualified teachers one subject/all subjects	NA/NA

No Child Left Behind
AYP, 2006-07 ....NA

Municipal Finance

State Aid Programs, 2009
Total aid	$98,939
CMPTRA	24,255
Energy tax receipts	74,189
Garden State Trust	0

General Budget, 2008
Total tax levy	$1,218,614
County levy	271,299
County taxes	245,195
County library	17,573
County health	0
County open space	8,531
School levy	608,064
Muni. levy	339,252
Misc. revenues	354,453

Taxes	2006	2007	2008
General tax rate per $100	5.841	5.72	5.344
County equalization ratio	65.03	58.42	53.59
Net valuation taxable	$23,085,000	$22,807,808	$22,806,363
State equalized value	$39,563,203	$42,521,882	$40,382,608

Demographics & Socio-Economic Characteristics

(2000 US Census, except as noted)

Population

1980*	42,460
1990*	33,397
2000	38,577
Male	19,654
Female	18,923
2007 (estimate)*	40,551
Population density	31,680.5

Race & Hispanic Origin, 2000

Race

White	31,178
Black/African American	1,644
American Indian/Alaska Native	60
Asian	1,661
Native Hawaiian/Pacific Islander	21
Other race	2,942
Two or more races	1,071
Hispanic origin, total	7,783
Mexican	359
Puerto Rican	4,660
Cuban	560
Other Hispanic	2,204

Age & Nativity, 2000

Under 5 years	1,232
18 years and over	34,543
21 years and over	33,399
65 years and over	3,483
85 years and over	392
Median age	30.4
Native-born	33,081
Foreign-born	5,588

Educational Attainment, 2000

Population 25 years and over	28,637
Less than 9th grade	8.4%
High school grad or higher	83.3%
Bachelor's degree or higher	59.4%
Graduate degree	18.7%

Income & Poverty, 1999

Per capita income	$43,195
Median household income	$62,550
Median family income	$67,500
Persons in poverty	4,124
H'holds receiving public assistance	472
H'holds receiving social security	3,118

Households, 2000

Total households	19,418
With persons under 18	2,498
With persons over 65	2,819
Family households	6,842
Single-person households	8,126
Persons per household	1.92
Persons per family	2.73

Labor & Employment

Total civilian labor force, 2007**	27,893
Unemployment rate	2.4%
Total civilian labor force, 2000	26,850
Unemployment rate	4.4%

Employed persons 16 years and over by occupation, 2000

Managers & professionals	15,655
Service occupations	1,687
Sales & office occupations	6,635
Farming, fishing & forestry	5
Construction & maintenance	495
Production & transportation	1,184
Self-employed persons	852

---

* US Census Bureau
** New Jersey Department of Labor
§ State Fiscal Year July 1–June 30

General Information

City of Hoboken
94 Washington St
Hoboken, NJ 07030
201-420-2000

Website	www.hobokennj.org
Year of incorporation	1855
Land/water area (sq. miles)	1.28/0.70
Form of government	Mayor-Council

Government

Legislative Districts

US Congressional	13
State Legislative	33

Local Officials, 2009

Mayor	David Roberts
Business Admin	Richard England
Clerk	James J. Farina
Finance Dir	George D. DeStefano
Tax Assessor	Sal Bonaccorsi
Tax Collector	Sharon Curran
Attorney	Steven Kleinman
Building	Alfred N. Arezzo
Comm Dev/Planning	Fred M. Bado
Engineering	Remington & Vernick
Environmental Svcs Dir	James Ronga
Police Chief	Carmen LaBruno
Emerg/Fire Director	Richard Blohm (Actg)

Housing & Construction

Housing Units, 2000*

Total	19,915
Median rent	$1,002
Median SF home value	$428,900

Permits for New Residential Construction

	Units	Value
Total, 2006	879	$128,772,827
Single family	0	$390,000
Total, 2007	394	$84,982,994
Single family	0	$0

Real Property Valuation, 2008

	Parcels	Valuation
Total	14,212	$2,939,286,900
Vacant	812	58,627,900
Residential	12,045	1,991,674,700
Commercial	959	493,320,000
Industrial	44	43,943,600
Apartments	352	351,720,700
Farm land	0	0
Farm homestead	0	0

Average Property Value & Tax, 2008

Residential value	$165,353
Property tax	$7,098
Tax credit/rebate	$820

Public Library

Hoboken Public Library
500 Park Ave
Hoboken, NJ 07030
201-420-2346

Director	Lina Podles

Library statistics, 2007

Population served	38,577
Full-time/total staff	4/24

	Total	Per capita
Holdings	86,046	2.23
Revenues	$1,762,138	$45.68
Expenditures	$1,726,138	$44.75
Annual visits	169,216	4.39
Internet terminals/annual users	27/19,664	

Public Safety

Number of officers, 2007	150

Crime	2006	2007
Total crimes	1,194	1,183
Violent	116	158
Murder	2	0
Rape	0	4
Robbery	46	52
Aggravated assault	68	102
Non-violent	1,078	1,025
Burglary	281	252
Larceny	681	667
Vehicle theft	116	106
Domestic violence	186	173
Arson	0	1
Total crime rate	29.9	29.7
Violent	2.9	4.0
Non-violent	27.0	25.7

Public School District

(for school year 2007-08 except as noted)

Hoboken School District
1115 Clinton Street
Hoboken, NJ 07030
(201) 356-3601

Superintendent	John Raslowsky
Number of schools	6
Grade plan	K-12
Enrollment	2,294
Attendance rate, '06-07	92.5%
Dropout rate	0.0%
Students per teacher	9.8
Per pupil expenditure	$17,156
Median faculty salary	$74,902
Median administrator salary	$128,990
Grade 12 enrollment	127
High school graduation rate	95.6%

Assessment test results

(percent scoring at proficient or advanced level)

	Language	Math
NJASK-Grade 3	81.1%	82.6%
GEPA-Grade 8	52.4%	73.4%
HSPA-High School	64.1%	78.8%

SAT Score Averages, 2006-07

Pct tested	Math	Verbal	Writing
81%	405	398	394

Teacher Qualifications

Avg. years of experience	7
Highly-qualified teachers one subject/all subjects	100%/100%

No Child Left Behind

AYP, 2006-07	Meets Standards

Municipal Finance§

State Aid Programs, 2009

Total aid	$15,122,245
CMPTRA	10,964,269
Energy tax receipts	3,553,086
Garden State Trust	0

General Budget, 2008

Total tax levy	$126,221,613
County levy	37,966,774
County taxes	36,963,658
County library	0
County health	0
County open space	1,003,115
School levy	35,586,250
Muni. levy	52,668,589
Misc. revenues	58,704,028

Taxes

	2006	2007	2008
General tax rate per $100	3.434	3.49	4.293
County equalization ratio	38.01	34.45	29.79
Net valuation taxable	$2,721,640,900	$2,818,798,604	$2,940,460,490
State equalized value	$7,901,663,779	$9,459,177,444	$10,050,017,693

See Introduction for an explanation of all data sources.

Demographics & Socio-Economic Characteristics
(2000 US Census, except as noted)

Population
1980*	4,129
1990*	3,935
2000	4,060
Male	1,944
Female	2,116
2007 (estimate)*	4,037
Population density	2,320.1

Race & Hispanic Origin, 2000
Race
White	3,762
Black/African American	24
American Indian/Alaska Native	4
Asian	212
Native Hawaiian/Pacific Islander	8
Other race	15
Two or more races	35
Hispanic origin, total	80
Mexican	5
Puerto Rican	16
Cuban	21
Other Hispanic	38

Age & Nativity, 2000
Under 5 years	343
18 years and over	2,942
21 years and over	2,877
65 years and over	618
85 years and over	58
Median age	41.1
Native-born	3,700
Foreign-born	360

Educational Attainment, 2000
Population 25 years and over	2,776
Less than 9th grade	1.3%
High school grad or higher	97.7%
Bachelor's degree or higher	68.3%
Graduate degree	22.6%

Income & Poverty, 1999
Per capita income	$63,594
Median household income	$129,900
Median family income	$144,588
Persons in poverty	83
H'holds receiving public assistance	0
H'holds receiving social security	381

Households, 2000
Total households	1,433
With persons under 18	574
With persons over 65	416
Family households	1,199
Single-person households	209
Persons per household	2.82
Persons per family	3.11

Labor & Employment
Total civilian labor force, 2007**	2,023
Unemployment rate	0.5%
Total civilian labor force, 2000	1,915
Unemployment rate	0.3%

Employed persons 16 years and over by occupation, 2000
Managers & professionals	1,175
Service occupations	81
Sales & office occupations	524
Farming, fishing & forestry	0
Construction & maintenance	62
Production & transportation	67
Self-employed persons	151

* US Census Bureau
** New Jersey Department of Labor

General Information
Borough of Ho-Ho-Kus
333 Warren Ave
Ho Ho Kus, NJ 07423
201-652-4400
Website	www.ho-ho-kusboro.com
Year of incorporation	1908
Land/water area (sq. miles)	1.74/0.01
Form of government	Borough

Government
Legislative Districts
US Congressional	5
State Legislative	39

Local Officials, 2009
Mayor	Thomas W. Randall
Manager	Catherine Henderson
Clerk	Laura Borchers
Finance Dir.	Catherine Henderson
Tax Assessor	Marie Merolla
Tax Collector	NA
Attorney	David Bole
Building	Lawrence Scorzelli
Planning	Joe Clementi
Engineering	Schwanewede/Hals Eng.
Public Works	Michael Frank
Police Chief	Gregory Kallenberg
Emerg/Fire Dir.	Christopher Raimondi

Housing & Construction
Housing Units, 2000*
Total	1,465
Median rent	$1,479
Median SF home value	$456,600

Permits for New Residential Construction
	Units	Value
Total, 2006	9	$3,209,937
Single family	9	$3,209,937
Total, 2007	6	$1,730,974
Single family	6	$1,730,974

Real Property Valuation, 2008
	Parcels	Valuation
Total	1,526	$1,361,915,100
Vacant	51	15,088,500
Residential	1,431	1,287,431,000
Commercial	43	41,253,400
Industrial	1	18,142,200
Apartments	0	0
Farm land	0	0
Farm homestead	0	0

Average Property Value & Tax, 2008
Residential value	$899,672
Property tax	$12,500
Tax credit/rebate	$1,357

Public Library
Worth-Pinkham Memorial Library
91 Warren Ave
Ho-Ho-Kus, NJ 07423
201-445-8078
Director	Sandra Witkowski

Library statistics, 2007
Population served	4,060
Full-time/total staff	0/1

	Total	Per capita
Holdings	25,152	6.20
Revenues	$444,643	$109.52
Expenditures	$311,509	$76.73
Annual visits	11,000	2.71
Internet terminals/annual users		3/500

Public Safety
Number of officers, 2007	16

Crime	2006	2007
Total crimes	14	14
Violent	0	1
Murder	0	0
Rape	0	1
Robbery	0	0
Aggravated assault	0	0
Non-violent	14	13
Burglary	3	2
Larceny	11	10
Vehicle theft	0	1
Domestic violence	3	9
Arson	0	0
Total crime rate	3.4	3.4
Violent	0.0	0.2
Non-violent	3.4	3.2

Public School District
(for school year 2007-08 except as noted)

Ho-Ho-Kus School District
70 Lloyd Road
Ho-Ho-Kus, NJ 07423
(201) 689-0175
Superintendent	Joyce Snider (Int)
Number of schools	1
Grade plan	K-8
Enrollment	660
Attendance rate, '06-07	96.1%
Dropout rate	NA
Students per teacher	11.5
Per pupil expenditure	$13,183
Median faculty salary	$67,185
Median administrator salary	$131,482
Grade 12 enrollment	NA
High school graduation rate	NA

Assessment test results
(percent scoring at proficient or advanced level)
	Language	Math
NJASK-Grade 3	95.6%	95.6%
GEPA-Grade 8	89.8%	93.7%
HSPA-High School	NA	NA

SAT Score Averages, 2006-07
Pct tested	Math	Verbal	Writing
NA	NA	NA	NA

Teacher Qualifications
Avg. years of experience	11
Highly-qualified teachers one subject/all subjects	100%/100%

No Child Left Behind
AYP, 2006-07	Meets Standards

Municipal Finance
State Aid Programs, 2009
Total aid	$397,445
CMPTRA	0
Energy tax receipts	381,547
Garden State Trust	0

General Budget, 2008
Total tax levy	$18,932,896
County levy	2,539,857
County taxes	2,402,448
County library	0
County health	0
County open space	137,409
School levy	10,785,520
Muni. levy	5,607,519
Misc. revenues	2,097,266

Taxes	2006	2007	2008
General tax rate per $100	1.27	1.34	1.391
County equalization ratio	114.1	101.4	99.35
Net valuation taxable	$1,356,486,900	$1,359,069,432	$1,362,713,779
State equalized value	$1,338,294,571	$1,367,956,293	$1,378,000,722

See Introduction for an explanation of all data sources.

Demographics & Socio-Economic Characteristics
(2000 US Census, except as noted)

Population
1980*	4,593
1990*	4,892
2000	5,124
Male	2,532
Female	2,592
2007 (estimate)*	5,244
Population density	221.3

Race & Hispanic Origin, 2000
Race
White	5,026
Black/African American	22
American Indian/Alaska Native	2
Asian	22
Native Hawaiian/Pacific Islander	0
Other race	20
Two or more races	32
Hispanic origin, total	87
Mexican	21
Puerto Rican	21
Cuban	10
Other Hispanic	35

Age & Nativity, 2000
Under 5 years	290
18 years and over	3,856
21 years and over	3,715
65 years and over	741
85 years and over	74
Median age	41.2
Native-born	4,990
Foreign-born	134

Educational Attainment, 2000
Population 25 years and over	3,557
Less than 9th grade	3.1%
High school grad or higher	90.9%
Bachelor's degree or higher	24.3%
Graduate degree	8.3%

Income & Poverty, 1999
Per capita income	$28,581
Median household income	$68,083
Median family income	$71,925
Persons in poverty	111
H'holds receiving public assistance	47
H'holds receiving social security	549

Households, 2000
Total households	1,881
With persons under 18	665
With persons over 65	501
Family households	1,523
Single-person households	291
Persons per household	2.72
Persons per family	3.06

Labor & Employment
Total civilian labor force, 2007**	2,991
Unemployment rate	3.5%
Total civilian labor force, 2000	2,677
Unemployment rate	2.9%

Employed persons 16 years and over by occupation, 2000
Managers & professionals	958
Service occupations	302
Sales & office occupations	729
Farming, fishing & forestry	9
Construction & maintenance	327
Production & transportation	274
Self-employed persons	198

* US Census Bureau
** New Jersey Department of Labor

General Information
Township of Holland
61 Church Rd
Milford, NJ 08848
908-995-4847

Website	hollandtownship.org
Year of incorporation	1874
Land/water area (sq. miles)	23.70/0.39
Form of government	Township

Government
Legislative Districts
US Congressional	7
State Legislative	23

Local Officials, 2009
Mayor	Edward J. Burdzy
Manager/Admin	NA
Clerk	Catherine M. Miller
Finance Dir	Michael Balogh
Tax Assessor	Michelle Trivigno
Tax Collector	Michael Balogh
Attorney	Richard Dieterly
Building	NA
Planning	BettyAnn Bechtold
Engineering	Hatch Mott MacDonald
Public Works	Alan Turdo
Police Chief	David Van Gilson
Emerg/Fire Director	Steve Underhill

Housing & Construction
Housing Units, 2000*
Total	1,942
Median rent	$905
Median SF home value	$199,000

Permits for New Residential Construction
	Units	Value
Total, 2006	11	$1,116,446
Single family	11	$1,116,446
Total, 2007	6	$952,075
Single family	6	$952,075

Real Property Valuation, 2008
	Parcels	Valuation
Total	2,457	$768,195,300
Vacant	156	13,910,600
Residential	1,863	644,816,900
Commercial	22	16,192,600
Industrial	8	17,716,700
Apartments	1	409,900
Farm land	239	2,619,500
Farm homestead	168	72,529,100

Average Property Value & Tax, 2008
Residential value	$353,198
Property tax	$6,541
Tax credit/rebate	$1,100

Public Library
Holland Township Library
129 Spring Mills Rd
Milford, NJ 08848
908-995-4767

Director	Donna Longcor

Library statistics, 2007
Population served	9,822
Full-time/total staff	0/0

	Total	Per capita
Holdings	28,507	2.90
Revenues	$73,399	$7.47
Expenditures	$63,704	$6.49
Annual visits	22,224	2.26
Internet terminals/annual users	2/1,431	

Public Safety
Number of officers, 2007	6

Crime	2006	2007
Total crimes	20	25
Violent	1	3
Murder	0	0
Rape	0	1
Robbery	0	0
Aggravated assault	1	2
Non-violent	19	22
Burglary	5	11
Larceny	14	8
Vehicle theft	0	3
Domestic violence	6	6
Arson	0	0
Total crime rate	3.8	4.7
Violent	0.2	0.6
Non-violent	3.6	4.1

Public School District
(for school year 2007-08 except as noted)

Holland Township School District
710 Milford-Warren Glen Road
Milford, NJ 08848
(908) 995-2401

Superintendent	George Petty (Int)
Number of schools	2
Grade plan	K-8
Enrollment	681
Attendance rate, '06-07	96.1%
Dropout rate	NA
Students per teacher	9.7
Per pupil expenditure	$13,717
Median faculty salary	$48,155
Median administrator salary	$95,611
Grade 12 enrollment	NA
High school graduation rate	NA

Assessment test results
(percent scoring at proficient or advanced level)
	Language	Math
NJASK-Grade 3	90.0%	92.6%
GEPA-Grade 8	85.7%	92.4%
HSPA-High School	NA	NA

SAT Score Averages, 2006-07
Pct tested	Math	Verbal	Writing
NA	NA	NA	NA

Teacher Qualifications
Avg. years of experience	12
Highly-qualified teachers one subject/all subjects	100%/92.5%

No Child Left Behind
AYP, 2006-07	Meets Standards

Municipal Finance
State Aid Programs, 2009
Total aid	$2,915,234
CMPTRA	0
Energy tax receipts	2,782,313
Garden State Trust	30,958

General Budget, 2008
Total tax levy	$14,262,452
County levy	2,852,583
County taxes	2,387,505
County library	207,330
County health	0
County open space	257,748
School levy	11,409,869
Muni. levy	0
Misc. revenues	5,640,415

Taxes
	2006	2007	2008
General tax rate per $100	1.8	1.83	1.852
County equalization ratio	94.24	87.57	90.12
Net valuation taxable	$759,879,300	$767,370,480	$770,110,821
State equalized value	$833,097,146	$855,366,393	$858,702,606

Demographics & Socio-Economic Characteristics

(2000 US Census, except as noted)

Population

1980*	8,447
1990*	11,532
2000	15,781
Male	7,557
Female	8,224
2007 (estimate)*	16,919
Population density	941.5

Race & Hispanic Origin, 2000

Race

White	12,657
Black/African American	102
American Indian/Alaska Native	4
Asian	2,753
Native Hawaiian/Pacific Islander	1
Other race	82
Two or more races	182
Hispanic origin, total	387
Mexican	30
Puerto Rican	105
Cuban	78
Other Hispanic	174

Age & Nativity, 2000

Under 5 years	917
18 years and over	11,279
21 years and over	10,871
65 years and over	1,926
85 years and over	378
Median age	40.8
Native-born	12,811
Foreign-born	2,970

Educational Attainment, 2000

Population 25 years and over	10,400
Less than 9th grade	3.6%
High school grad or higher	91.1%
Bachelor's degree or higher	54.8%
Graduate degree	28.1%

Income & Poverty, 1999

Per capita income	$47,898
Median household income	$112,879
Median family income	$122,785
Persons in poverty	518
H'holds receiving public assistance	42
H'holds receiving social security	972

Households, 2000

Total households	4,947
With persons under 18	2,393
With persons over 65	1,043
Family households	4,330
Single-person households	549
Persons per household	3.09
Persons per family	3.35

Labor & Employment

Total civilian labor force, 2007**	7,700
Unemployment rate	2.3%
Total civilian labor force, 2000	7,210
Unemployment rate	2.6%

Employed persons 16 years and over by occupation, 2000

Managers & professionals	4,506
Service occupations	394
Sales & office occupations	1,582
Farming, fishing & forestry	0
Construction & maintenance	279
Production & transportation	262
Self-employed persons	379

General Information

Township of Holmdel
PO Box 410
Holmdel, NJ 07733
732-946-2820

Website	www.holmdeltownship-nj.com
Year of incorporation	1857
Land/water area (sq. miles)	17.97/0.12
Form of government	Township

Government

Legislative Districts

US Congressional	12
State Legislative	13

Local Officials, 2009

Mayor	Serena DiMaso
Administrator	Christopher Schultz
Clerk	Maureen Doloughty
Finance Dir	Joseph Annecharico
Tax Assessor	Eldo Magnani
Tax Collector	Leon Bruno
Attorney	Duane Davison
Building	Dennis Pino
Comm Dev/Planning	NA
Engineering	Edward Broberg
Public Works	Jeffrey Smith
Police Chief	Raymond Wilson
Emerg/Fire Director	Tom Savage

Housing & Construction

Housing Units, 2000*

Total	5,137
Median rent	$1,512
Median SF home value	$404,200

Permits for New Residential Construction

	Units	Value
Total, 2006	21	$6,320,928
Single family	16	$6,273,528
Total, 2007	25	$16,215,320
Single family	25	$16,215,320

Real Property Valuation, 2008

	Parcels	Valuation
Total	5,908	$4,570,679,000
Vacant	162	60,436,400
Residential	5,434	4,002,513,000
Commercial	204	388,531,700
Industrial	7	89,671,500
Apartments	3	8,819,200
Farm land	66	1,056,800
Farm homestead	32	19,650,400

Average Property Value & Tax, 2008

Residential value	$735,851
Property tax	$11,443
Tax credit/rebate	$1,214

Public Library

Holmdel Public Library‡
4 Crawford's Corner Rd
Holmdel, NJ 07733
732-946-4118

Branch Librarian	Karen Nealis

Library statistics, 2007

see Monmouth County profile
for library system statistics

Public Safety

Number of officers, 2007	43

Crime	2006	2007
Total crimes	236	236
Violent	7	16
Murder	0	0
Rape	2	1
Robbery	1	2
Aggravated assault	4	13
Non-violent	229	220
Burglary	25	19
Larceny	196	193
Vehicle theft	8	8
Domestic violence	98	117
Arson	2	1
Total crime rate	13.9	14.0
Violent	0.4	1.0
Non-violent	13.5	13.1

Public School District

(for school year 2007-08 except as noted)

Holmdel Township School District
4 Crawford's Corner Road, PO Box 407
Holmdel, NJ 07733
(732) 946-1800

Superintendent	Barbara Duncan
Number of schools	4
Grade plan	K-12
Enrollment	3,385
Attendance rate, '06-07	96.1%
Dropout rate	0.1%
Students per teacher	11.5
Per pupil expenditure	$13,805
Median faculty salary	$70,052
Median administrator salary	$114,000
Grade 12 enrollment	280
High school graduation rate	99.6%

Assessment test results

(percent scoring at proficient or advanced level)

	Language	Math
NJASK-Grade 3	94.8%	95.2%
GEPA-Grade 8	90.5%	95.6%
HSPA-High School	93.9%	96.1%

SAT Score Averages, 2006-07

Pct tested	Math	Verbal	Writing
108%	607	579	576

Teacher Qualifications

Avg. years of experience	10
Highly-qualified teachers one subject/all subjects	98.0%/98.0%

No Child Left Behind

AYP, 2006-07	Meets Standards

Municipal Finance

State Aid Programs, 2009

Total aid	$2,709,120
CMPTRA	96,136
Energy tax receipts	2,471,922
Garden State Trust	641

General Budget, 2008

Total tax levy	$71,217,603
County levy	11,632,109
County taxes	10,322,275
County library	621,385
County health	0
County open space	688,450
School levy	48,965,083
Muni. levy	10,620,411
Misc. revenues	10,430,297

Taxes

	2006	2007	2008
General tax rate per $100	3.3	1.518	1.556
County equalization ratio	50.75	103.03	100.27
Net valuation taxable	$2,026,614,684	$4,621,043,569	$4,579,651,507
State equalized value	$4,461,653,247	$4,608,624,489	$2,595,518,080

‡ Branch of county library
* US Census Bureau
** New Jersey Department of Labor

See Introduction for an explanation of all data sources.

Demographics & Socio-Economic Characteristics

(2000 US Census, except as noted)

Population

1980*	15,531
1990*	15,586
2000	15,888
Male	8,022
Female	7,866
2007 (estimate)*	15,592
Population density	1,422.6

Race & Hispanic Origin, 2000

Race

White	14,792
Black/African American	310
American Indian/Alaska Native	18
Asian	286
Native Hawaiian/Pacific Islander	0
Other race	226
Two or more races	256
Hispanic origin, total	952
Mexican	45
Puerto Rican	352
Cuban	72
Other Hispanic	483

Age & Nativity, 2000

Under 5 years	1,148
18 years and over	11,687
21 years and over	11,159
65 years and over	1,073
85 years and over	102
Median age	35.7
Native-born	14,915
Foreign-born	1,036

Educational Attainment, 2000

Population 25 years and over	10,653
Less than 9th grade	2.1%
High school grad or higher	89.3%
Bachelor's degree or higher	19.4%
Graduate degree	4.5%

Income & Poverty, 1999

Per capita income	$26,698
Median household income	$65,799
Median family income	$73,277
Persons in poverty	480
H'holds receiving public assistance	123
H'holds receiving social security	972

Households, 2000

Total households	5,656
With persons under 18	2,325
With persons over 65	826
Family households	4,239
Single-person households	1,054
Persons per household	2.81
Persons per family	3.24

Labor & Employment

Total civilian labor force, 2007**	10,351
Unemployment rate	5.4%
Total civilian labor force, 2000	9,207
Unemployment rate	4.3%

Employed persons 16 years and over by occupation, 2000

Managers & professionals	2,862
Service occupations	903
Sales & office occupations	2,962
Farming, fishing & forestry	0
Construction & maintenance	972
Production & transportation	1,114
Self-employed persons	337

‡ Branch of county library
* US Census Bureau
** New Jersey Department of Labor

General Information

Borough of Hopatcong
111 River Styx Rd
Hopatcong, NJ 07843
973-770-1200

Website	www.hopatcong.org
Year of incorporation	1901
Land/water area (sq. miles)	10.96/1.38
Form of government	Borough

Government

Legislative Districts

US Congressional	11
State Legislative	24

Local Officials, 2009

Mayor	Sylvia Petillo
Manager	Joseph Moskovitz
Clerk	Lorraine Stark
Finance Dir	Kelleyanne McGann
Tax Assessor	Therese dePierro
Tax Collector	Regina Thomas
Attorney	John Ursin
Building	William O'Connor
Comm Dev/Planning	NA
Engineering	John Ruschke
Public Works	Ron Jobeless
Police Chief	John Swanson
Emerg/Fire Director	Chris Steinmetz

Housing & Construction

Housing Units, 2000*

Total	6,190
Median rent	$915
Median SF home value	$141,300

Permits for New Residential Construction

	Units	Value
Total, 2006	25	$3,919,682
Single family	25	$3,919,682
Total, 2007	18	$2,564,155
Single family	18	$2,564,155

Real Property Valuation, 2008

	Parcels	Valuation
Total	7,165	$2,056,526,250
Vacant	984	44,278,050
Residential	6,074	1,912,868,400
Commercial	80	96,350,000
Industrial	1	486,800
Apartments	0	0
Farm land	20	247,600
Farm homestead	6	2,295,400

Average Property Value & Tax, 2008

Residential value	$314,994
Property tax	$5,570
Tax credit/rebate	$961

Public Library

E. Louise Childs Branch Library‡
21 Sparta Rd
Stanhope, NJ 07874
973-770-1000

Branch Librarian	Victoria Larson

Library statistics, 2007

see Sussex County profile
for library system statistics

Public Safety

Number of officers, 2007	29

Crime	2006	2007
Total crimes	152	111
Violent	5	7
Murder	0	0
Rape	0	0
Robbery	1	0
Aggravated assault	4	7
Non-violent	147	104
Burglary	17	11
Larceny	125	88
Vehicle theft	5	5
Domestic violence	225	208
Arson	0	0
Total crime rate	9.5	7.0
Violent	0.3	0.4
Non-violent	9.2	6.5

Public School District

(for school year 2007-08 except as noted)

Hopatcong Borough School District
2 Windsor Avenue, PO Box 1029
Hopatcong, NJ 07843
(973) 398-8801

Chief School Admin	Wayne Threlkeld
Number of schools	5
Grade plan	K-12
Enrollment	2,384
Attendance rate, '06-07	93.9%
Dropout rate	2.4%
Students per teacher	10.3
Per pupil expenditure	$12,944
Median faculty salary	$62,970
Median administrator salary	$115,081
Grade 12 enrollment	174
High school graduation rate	91.1%

Assessment test results

(percent scoring at proficient or advanced level)

	Language	Math
NJASK-Grade 3	80.6%	84.0%
GEPA-Grade 8	67.4%	84.4%
HSPA-High School	74.0%	81.7%

SAT Score Averages, 2006-07

Pct tested	Math	Verbal	Writing
74%	486	461	453

Teacher Qualifications

Avg. years of experience	9
Highly-qualified teachers one subject/all subjects	100%/100%

No Child Left Behind

AYP, 2006-07	Meets Standards

Municipal Finance

State Aid Programs, 2009

Total aid	$1,229,092
CMPTRA	492,133
Energy tax receipts	706,195
Garden State Trust	34

General Budget, 2008

Total tax levy	$36,391,347
County levy	6,940,046
County taxes	5,972,950
County library	503,401
County health	0
County open space	463,694
School levy	19,769,989
Muni. levy	9,681,312
Misc. revenues	4,717,035

Taxes

	2006	2007	2008
General tax rate per $100	3.83	1.68	1.769
County equalization ratio	57.97	119.78	110.79
Net valuation taxable	$878,966,200	$2,076,503,853	$2,057,989,685
State equalized value	$1,727,633,748	$1,874,404,348	$1,934,652,239

See Introduction for an explanation of all data sources.

Demographics & Socio-Economic Characteristics
(2000 US Census, except as noted)

Population
1980*	1,468
1990*	1,719
2000	1,891
Male	947
Female	944
2007 (estimate)*	1,945
Population density	105.1

Race & Hispanic Origin, 2000
Race
White	1,858
Black/African American	8
American Indian/Alaska Native	0
Asian	8
Native Hawaiian/Pacific Islander	0
Other race	1
Two or more races	16
Hispanic origin, total	28
Mexican	2
Puerto Rican	6
Cuban	0
Other Hispanic	20

Age & Nativity, 2000
Under 5 years	122
18 years and over	1,391
21 years and over	1,342
65 years and over	208
85 years and over	20
Median age	39.5
Native-born	1,813
Foreign-born	78

Educational Attainment, 2000
Population 25 years and over	1,312
Less than 9th grade	2.2%
High school grad or higher	90.9%
Bachelor's degree or higher	26.9%
Graduate degree	8.1%

Income & Poverty, 1999
Per capita income	$27,902
Median household income	$61,319
Median family income	$68,750
Persons in poverty	36
H'holds receiving public assistance	10
H'holds receiving social security	171

Households, 2000
Total households	697
With persons under 18	267
With persons over 65	155
Family households	539
Single-person households	137
Persons per household	2.71
Persons per family	3.12

Labor & Employment
Total civilian labor force, 2007**	1,115
Unemployment rate	4.3%
Total civilian labor force, 2000	989
Unemployment rate	4.2%

Employed persons 16 years and over by occupation, 2000
Managers & professionals	342
Service occupations	113
Sales & office occupations	275
Farming, fishing & forestry	5
Construction & maintenance	108
Production & transportation	104
Self-employed persons	60

General Information
Township of Hope
PO Box 284
Hope, NJ 07844
908-459-5011
Email	townclerk@hopetwp-nj.us
Year of incorporation	1839
Land/water area (sq. miles)	18.50/0.18
Form of government	Township

Government
Legislative Districts
US Congressional	5
State Legislative	23

Local Officials, 2009
Mayor	Timothy McDonough
Manager/Admin	NA
Clerk	Mary Pat Quinn
Finance Dir	Kathleen Reinalda
Tax Assessor	Richard Motyka
Tax Collector	Stephen Lance
Attorney	Michael Selvaggi
Building	Ralph Price
Comm Dev/Planning	NA
Engineering	Ted Rodman
Public Works	Donald Whitmore
Police Chief	NA
Emerg/Fire Director	Chad Koonz

Housing & Construction
Housing Units, 2000*
Total	747
Median rent	$711
Median SF home value	$179,500

Permits for New Residential Construction
	Units	Value
Total, 2006	5	$1,201,000
Single family	5	$1,201,000
Total, 2007	7	$1,253,350
Single family	7	$1,253,350

Real Property Valuation, 2008
	Parcels	Valuation
Total	1,148	$310,241,224
Vacant	132	13,448,400
Residential	648	230,478,500
Commercial	30	16,884,900
Industrial	1	357,600
Apartments	1	523,900
Farm land	219	1,781,524
Farm homestead	117	46,766,400

Average Property Value & Tax, 2008
Residential value	$362,412
Property tax	$6,682
Tax credit/rebate	$1,088

Public Library
No public municipal library

Library statistics, 2007
Population served	NA
Full-time/total staff	NA/NA

	Total	Per capita
Holdings	NA	NA
Revenues	NA	NA
Expenditures	NA	NA
Annual visits	NA	NA
Internet terminals/annual users	NA/NA	

Public Safety
Number of officers, 2007 0
Crime	2006	2007
Total crimes	21	20
Violent	0	0
Murder	0	0
Rape	0	0
Robbery	0	0
Aggravated assault	0	0
Non-violent	21	20
Burglary	8	7
Larceny	7	12
Vehicle theft	6	1
Domestic violence	2	22
Arson	0	0
Total crime rate	10.7	10.1
Violent	0.0	0.0
Non-violent	10.7	10.1

Public School District
(for school year 2007-08 except as noted)

Hope Township School District
Hope Township School, PO Box 293
Hope, NJ 07844
(908) 459-4242
Superintendent	Alfred Annunziata
Number of schools	1
Grade plan	K-8
Enrollment	193
Attendance rate, '06-07	96.0%
Dropout rate	NA
Students per teacher	9.6
Per pupil expenditure	$12,470
Median faculty salary	$47,785
Median administrator salary	$70,380
Grade 12 enrollment	NA
High school graduation rate	NA

Assessment test results
(percent scoring at proficient or advanced level)
	Language	Math
NJASK-Grade 3	94.4%	94.1%
GEPA-Grade 8	71.4%	81.0%
HSPA-High School	NA	NA

SAT Score Averages, 2006-07
Pct tested	Math	Verbal	Writing
NA	NA	NA	NA

Teacher Qualifications
Avg. years of experience	11
Highly-qualified teachers one subject/all subjects	100%/100%

No Child Left Behind
AYP, 2006-07 . . . . Meets Standards

Municipal Finance
State Aid Programs, 2009
Total aid	$270,408
CMPTRA	22,957
Energy tax receipts	217,910
Garden State Trust	14,354

General Budget, 2008
Total tax levy	$5,745,196
County levy	1,823,370
County taxes	1,484,634
County library	157,314
County health	0
County open space	181,423
School levy	3,371,987
Muni. levy	549,839
Misc. revenues	1,049,040

Taxes
	2006	2007	2008
General tax rate per $100	3.47	1.73	1.844
County equalization ratio	56.78	111	103.42
Net valuation taxable	$140,870,300	$315,370,245	$311,579,871
State equalized value	$284,305,818	$304,984,132	$299,446,866

* US Census Bureau
** New Jersey Department of Labor

See Introduction for an explanation of all data sources.

Demographics & Socio-Economic Characteristics

(2000 US Census, except as noted)

Population

1980*	2,001
1990*	1,968
2000	2,035
Male	986
Female	1,049
2007 (estimate)*	2,000
Population density	2,898.6

Race & Hispanic Origin, 2000

Race

White	1,942
Black/African American	22
American Indian/Alaska Native	10
Asian	20
Native Hawaiian/Pacific Islander	0
Other race	25
Two or more races	16
Hispanic origin, total	47
Mexican	6
Puerto Rican	3
Cuban	0
Other Hispanic	38

Age & Nativity, 2000

Under 5 years	118
18 years and over	1,503
21 years and over	1,457
65 years and over	215
85 years and over	33
Median age	39.7
Native-born	1,878
Foreign-born	157

Educational Attainment, 2000

Population 25 years and over	1,417
Less than 9th grade	3.4%
High school grad or higher	89.6%
Bachelor's degree or higher	53.9%
Graduate degree	28.8%

Income & Poverty, 1999

Per capita income	$38,413
Median household income	$77,270
Median family income	$91,205
Persons in poverty	43
H'holds receiving public assistance	0
H'holds receiving social security	174

Households, 2000

Total households	813
With persons under 18	305
With persons over 65	167
Family households	562
Single-person households	204
Persons per household	2.50
Persons per family	3.01

Labor & Employment

Total civilian labor force, 2007**	1,522
Unemployment rate	1.2%
Total civilian labor force, 2000	1,228
Unemployment rate	1.0%

Employed persons 16 years and over by occupation, 2000

Managers & professionals	672
Service occupations	122
Sales & office occupations	243
Farming, fishing & forestry	0
Construction & maintenance	112
Production & transportation	67
Self-employed persons	95

* US Census Bureau
** New Jersey Department of Labor

General Information

Borough of Hopewell
4 Columbia Ave
PO Box 128
Hopewell, NJ 08525
609-466-2636

Website	www.hopewellboro-nj.us
Year of incorporation	1891
Land/water area (sq. miles)	0.69/0.00
Form of government	Borough

Government

Legislative Districts

US Congressional	12
State Legislative	15

Local Officials, 2009

Mayor	Paul Anzano
Manager	Michele Hovan
Clerk	Michele Hovan
Finance Dir	Judie McGrorey
Tax Assessor	Christopher Fuges
Tax Collector	Donna Griffiths
Attorney	Edmond Konin
Building	Robert Ward
Planning	Carl Lindbloom
Engineering	Dennis O'Neal
Public Works	Herbert Ruehle
Police Chief	George Meyer
Fire/Emergency Dir	NA

Housing & Construction

Housing Units, 2000*

Total	836
Median rent	$843
Median SF home value	$221,900

Permits for New Residential Construction

	Units	Value
Total, 2006	1	$45,000
Single family	1	$45,000
Total, 2007	0	$0
Single family	0	$0

Real Property Valuation, 2008

	Parcels	Valuation
Total	776	$360,251,500
Vacant	29	4,177,000
Residential	665	300,098,300
Commercial	71	50,687,800
Industrial	2	857,700
Apartments	3	2,322,900
Farm land	3	28,000
Farm homestead	3	2,079,800

Average Property Value & Tax, 2008

Residential value	$452,362
Property tax	$9,149
Tax credit/rebate	$1,295

Public Library

Hopewell Public Library
13 E Broad St
Hopewell, NJ 08525
609-466-1625

Director	Jennifer T. Spencer

Library statistics, 2007

Population served	2,035
Full-time/total staff	0/0

	Total	Per capita
Holdings	16,416	8.07
Revenues	$120,476	$59.20
Expenditures	$121,702	$59.80
Annual visits	15,837	7.78
Internet terminals/annual users	6/2,463	

Public Safety

Number of officers, 2007	0

Crime	2006	2007
Total crimes	12	29
Violent	0	3
Murder	0	0
Rape	0	0
Robbery	0	1
Aggravated assault	0	2
Non-violent	12	26
Burglary	5	11
Larceny	7	15
Vehicle theft	0	0
Domestic violence	18	12
Arson	0	0
Total crime rate	5.9	14.3
Violent	0.0	1.5
Non-violent	5.9	12.9

Public School District

(for school year 2007-08 except as noted)

Hopewell Valley Regional School District
425 South Main Street
Pennington, NJ 08534
(609) 737-4000

Chief School Admin	Thomas Butler (Int)
Number of schools	6
Grade plan	K-12
Enrollment	3,984
Attendance rate, '06-07	96.3%
Dropout rate	0.3%
Students per teacher	10.2
Per pupil expenditure	$15,378
Median faculty salary	$59,326
Median administrator salary	$109,424
Grade 12 enrollment	261
High school graduation rate	99.6%

Assessment test results

(percent scoring at proficient or advanced level)

	Language	Math
NJASK-Grade 3	94.5%	93.3%
GEPA-Grade 8	82.3%	94.1%
HSPA-High School	91.7%	94.2%

SAT Score Averages, 2006-07

Pct tested	Math	Verbal	Writing
96%	562	557	585

Teacher Qualifications

Avg. years of experience	11
Highly-qualified teachers one subject/all subjects	100%/100%

No Child Left Behind

AYP, 2006-07	Meets Standards

Municipal Finance

State Aid Programs, 2009

Total aid	$219,600
CMPTRA	53,584
Energy tax receipts	160,511
Garden State Trust	25

General Budget, 2008

Total tax levy	$7,324,629
County levy	1,634,265
County taxes	1,529,308
County library	0
County health	0
County open space	104,957
School levy	4,286,548
Muni. levy	1,403,815
Misc. revenues	1,233,928

Taxes	2006	2007	2008
General tax rate per $100	1.78	1.92	2.023
County equalization ratio	118.64	105.87	103.67
Net valuation taxable	$362,812,400	$363,186,950	$362,149,155
State equalized value	$344,339,682	$350,391,670	$334,662,758

See Introduction for an explanation of all data sources.

Demographics & Socio-Economic Characteristics

(2000 US Census, except as noted)

Population

1980*	4,365
1990*	4,215
2000	4,434
Male	2,103
Female	2,331
2007 (estimate)*	4,785
Population density	160.0

Race & Hispanic Origin, 2000

Race

White	3,862
Black/African American	306
American Indian/Alaska Native	103
Asian	25
Native Hawaiian/Pacific Islander	1
Other race	64
Two or more races	73
Hispanic origin, total	159
Mexican	55
Puerto Rican	86
Cuban	0
Other Hispanic	18

Age & Nativity, 2000

Under 5 years	210
18 years and over	3,430
21 years and over	3,290
65 years and over	906
85 years and over	129
Median age	42.4
Native-born	4,321
Foreign-born	111

Educational Attainment, 2000

Population 25 years and over	3,177
Less than 9th grade	7.1%
High school grad or higher	83.2%
Bachelor's degree or higher	18.8%
Graduate degree	7.6%

Income & Poverty, 1999

Per capita income	$22,783
Median household income	$49,767
Median family income	$59,675
Persons in poverty	279
H'holds receiving public assistance	16
H'holds receiving social security	577

Households, 2000

Total households	1,628
With persons under 18	549
With persons over 65	539
Family households	1,206
Single-person households	372
Persons per household	2.58
Persons per family	3.03

Labor & Employment

Total civilian labor force, 2007**	2,451
Unemployment rate	2.7%
Total civilian labor force, 2000	2,284
Unemployment rate	3.9%

Employed persons 16 years and over by occupation, 2000

Managers & professionals	713
Service occupations	408
Sales & office occupations	484
Farming, fishing & forestry	29
Construction & maintenance	169
Production & transportation	391
Self-employed persons	161

* US Census Bureau
** New Jersey Department of Labor

General Information

Township of Hopewell
590 Shiloh Pike
Bridgeton, NJ 08302
856-455-1230

Website	hopewelltwp-nj.com
Year of incorporation	1748
Land/water area (sq. miles)	29.90/0.88
Form of government	Township

Government

Legislative Districts

US Congressional	2
State Legislative	3

Local Officials, 2009

Mayor	Bruce Hankins Jr
Manager	Ted Ritter
Clerk	Will Daddraio
Finance Dir	Lois Butther
Tax Assessor	Lois Mazza
Tax Collector	Liz Wallender
Attorney	T. Henry Ritter
Building	Gordon Gross
Planning	Donna Hickman
Engineering	Steve Nardelli
Public Works	Ken Hildreth
Police Chief	NA
Emerg/Fire Director	D. Maxwell Dilks

Housing & Construction

Housing Units, 2000*

Total	1,683
Median rent	$495
Median SF home value	$97,000

Permits for New Residential Construction

	Units	Value
Total, 2006	18	$1,959,814
Single family	18	$1,959,814
Total, 2007	16	$1,828,385
Single family	16	$1,828,385

Real Property Valuation, 2008

	Parcels	Valuation
Total	2,385	$230,397,100
Vacant	238	5,152,000
Residential	1,435	174,858,500
Commercial	45	13,375,000
Industrial	0	0
Apartments	2	415,400
Farm land	473	6,729,900
Farm homestead	192	29,866,300

Average Property Value & Tax, 2008

Residential value	$125,830
Property tax	$4,856
Tax credit/rebate	$923

Public Library

No public municipal library

Library statistics, 2007

Population served	NA
Full-time/total staff	NA/NA

	Total	Per capita
Holdings	NA	NA
Revenues	NA	NA
Expenditures	NA	NA
Annual visits	NA	NA
Internet terminals/annual users	NA/NA	

Public Safety

Number of officers, 2007 ... 0

Crime	2006	2007
Total crimes	97	84
Violent	5	9
Murder	0	0
Rape	0	0
Robbery	0	2
Aggravated assault	5	7
Non-violent	92	75
Burglary	33	23
Larceny	42	44
Vehicle theft	17	8
Domestic violence	0	20
Arson	0	0
Total crime rate	20.5	17.7
Violent	1.1	1.9
Non-violent	19.5	15.8

Public School District

(for school year 2007-08 except as noted)

Hopewell Township School District
122 Sewall Road
Bridgeton, NJ 08302
(856) 451-9203

Chief School Admin	Terry Van Zoeren
Number of schools	1
Grade plan	K-8
Enrollment	572
Attendance rate, '06-07	95.5%
Dropout rate	NA
Students per teacher	12.2
Per pupil expenditure	$10,900
Median faculty salary	$64,447
Median administrator salary	$94,900
Grade 12 enrollment	NA
High school graduation rate	NA

Assessment test results

(percent scoring at proficient or advanced level)

	Language	Math
NJASK-Grade 3	81.4%	69.5%
GEPA-Grade 8	75.0%	83.4%
HSPA-High School	NA	NA

SAT Score Averages, 2006-07

Pct tested	Math	Verbal	Writing
NA	NA	NA	NA

Teacher Qualifications

Avg. years of experience	14
Highly-qualified teachers one subject/all subjects	97.5%/97.5%

No Child Left Behind

AYP, 2006-07 ... Meets Standards

Municipal Finance

State Aid Programs, 2009

Total aid	$408,141
CMPTRA	103,400
Energy tax receipts	282,178
Garden State Trust	8,777

General Budget, 2008

Total tax levy	$8,918,197
County levy	3,493,793
County taxes	3,302,865
County library	0
County health	154,230
County open space	36,699
School levy	4,978,241
Muni. levy	446,163
Misc. revenues	1,590,413

Taxes

	2006	2007	2008
General tax rate per $100	3.497	3.755	3.863
County equalization ratio	82.65	72.16	63.56
Net valuation taxable	$225,910,000	$229,567,880	$231,087,147
State equalized value	$313,892,520	$360,758,358	$366,515,865

See Introduction for an explanation of all data sources.

Demographics & Socio-Economic Characteristics

(2000 US Census, except as noted)

Population

1980*	10,893
1990*	11,590
2000	16,105
Male	8,208
Female	7,897
2007 (estimate)*	17,823
Population density	306.7

Race & Hispanic Origin, 2000

Race
White	14,220
Black/African American	939
American Indian/Alaska Native	20
Asian	639
Native Hawaiian/Pacific Islander	4
Other race	107
Two or more races	176
Hispanic origin, total	395
Mexican	36
Puerto Rican	152
Cuban	50
Other Hispanic	157

Age & Nativity, 2000

Under 5 years	1,076
18 years and over	11,833
21 years and over	11,413
65 years and over	1,845
85 years and over	130
Median age	39.1
Native-born	14,862
Foreign-born	1,243

Educational Attainment, 2000

Population 25 years and over	10,956
Less than 9th grade	1.2%
High school grad or higher	93.0%
Bachelor's degree or higher	55.8%
Graduate degree	27.7%

Income & Poverty, 1999

Per capita income	$43,947
Median household income	$93,640
Median family income	$101,579
Persons in poverty	173
H'holds receiving public assistance	15
H'holds receiving social security	1,334

Households, 2000

Total households	5,498
With persons under 18	2,310
With persons over 65	1,279
Family households	4,429
Single-person households	878
Persons per household	2.77
Persons per family	3.11

Labor & Employment

Total civilian labor force, 2007**	9,647
Unemployment rate	3.1%
Total civilian labor force, 2000	7,738
Unemployment rate	2.1%

Employed persons 16 years and over by occupation, 2000
Managers & professionals	4,625
Service occupations	638
Sales & office occupations	1,534
Farming, fishing & forestry	23
Construction & maintenance	422
Production & transportation	334
Self-employed persons	540

‡ Branch of county library
* US Census Bureau
** New Jersey Department of Labor

General Information

Township of Hopewell
201 Washington Crossing Rd
Titusville, NJ 08560
609-737-0605

Website	www.hopewelltwp.org
Year of incorporation	1700
Land/water area (sq. miles)	58.11/0.54
Form of government	Township

Government

Legislative Districts

US Congressional	12
State Legislative	15

Local Officials, 2009

Mayor	Vanessa Sandom
Administrator	Paul Pogorzelski
Clerk	Annette Bielawski
Finance Dir	Elaine Borges
Tax Assessor	Antoinette Sost
Tax Collector	Mary Kennedy-Nadzak
Attorney	Steven Goodell
Building	Chris Rose
Comm Dev/Planning	NA
Engineering	Paul Pogorzelski
Public Works	Victor Silvestrov
Police Chief	George Meyer
Fire/Emergency Dir	Matthew Martin

Housing & Construction

Housing Units, 2000*

Total	5,629
Median rent	$925
Median SF home value	$252,600

Permits for New Residential Construction

	Units	Value
Total, 2006	16	$2,518,530
Single family	16	$2,518,530
Total, 2007	6	$1,824,500
Single family	6	$1,824,500

Real Property Valuation, 2008

	Parcels	Valuation
Total	7,327	$4,544,452,300
Vacant	381	74,087,600
Residential	5,885	3,212,378,300
Commercial	172	581,069,700
Industrial	30	391,819,200
Apartments	6	5,231,600
Farm land	534	5,685,000
Farm homestead	319	274,180,900

Average Property Value & Tax, 2008

Residential value	$561,986
Property tax	$10,951
Tax credit/rebate	$1,300

Public Library

Hopewell Township Branch Library‡
245 Pennington/Titusville Rd
Pennington, NJ 08534
609-737-2610

Branch Librarian	Andrea Merrick

Library statistics, 2007

see Mercer County profile
for library system statistics

Public Safety

Number of officers, 2007	31

Crime	2006	2007
Total crimes	124	130
Violent	6	9
Murder	0	0
Rape	0	0
Robbery	2	1
Aggravated assault	4	8
Non-violent	118	121
Burglary	28	28
Larceny	86	87
Vehicle theft	4	6
Domestic violence	90	53
Arson	1	0
Total crime rate	7.0	7.2
Violent	0.3	0.5
Non-violent	6.7	6.7

Public School District

(for school year 2007-08 except as noted)

Hopewell Valley Regional School District
425 South Main Street
Pennington, NJ 08534
(609) 737-4000

Chief School Admin	Thomas Butler (Int)
Number of schools	6
Grade plan	K-12
Enrollment	3,984
Attendance rate, '06-07	96.3%
Dropout rate	0.3%
Students per teacher	10.2
Per pupil expenditure	$15,378
Median faculty salary	$59,326
Median administrator salary	$109,424
Grade 12 enrollment	261
High school graduation rate	99.6%

Assessment test results

(percent scoring at proficient or advanced level)
	Language	Math
NJASK-Grade 3	94.5%	93.3%
GEPA-Grade 8	82.3%	94.1%
HSPA-High School	91.7%	94.2%

SAT Score Averages, 2006-07

Pct tested	Math	Verbal	Writing
96%	562	557	585

Teacher Qualifications

Avg. years of experience	11
Highly-qualified teachers one subject/all subjects	100%/100%

No Child Left Behind

AYP, 2006-07	Meets Standards

Municipal Finance

State Aid Programs, 2009

Total aid	$2,232,370
CMPTRA	92,508
Energy tax receipts	1,999,671
Garden State Trust	48,936

General Budget, 2008

Total tax levy	$88,673,889
County levy	22,447,407
County taxes	19,200,323
County library	1,929,403
County health	0
County open space	1,317,682
School levy	53,027,985
Muni. levy	13,198,497
Misc. revenues	7,356,597

Taxes	2006	2007	2008
General tax rate per $100	1.87	1.86	1.949
County equalization ratio	112.67	108.87	104.24
Net valuation taxable	$4,588,936,100	$4,558,163,334	$4,550,576,567
State equalized value	$4,219,728,189	$4,372,990,697	$4,367,402,866

See Introduction for an explanation of all data sources.

Demographics & Socio-Economic Characteristics

(2000 US Census, except as noted)

Population
1980* 25,065
1990* 38,987
2000 48,903
  Male 23,864
  Female 25,039
2007 (estimate)* 51,353
  Population density 843.1

Race & Hispanic Origin, 2000
Race
  White 44,008
  Black/African American 1,739
  American Indian/Alaska Native 58
  Asian 1,749
  Native Hawaiian/Pacific Islander 5
  Other race 633
  Two or more races 711
Hispanic origin, total 2,610
  Mexican 229
  Puerto Rican 1,252
  Cuban 202
  Other Hispanic 927

Age & Nativity, 2000
Under 5 years 3,910
18 years and over 33,815
21 years and over 32,333
65 years and over 4,295
85 years and over 451
  Median age 35.7
Native-born 44,543
Foreign-born 4,360

Educational Attainment, 2000
Population 25 years and over 30,878
Less than 9th grade 3.3%
High school grad or higher 88.2%
Bachelor's degree or higher 29.0%
Graduate degree 8.7%

Income & Poverty, 1999
Per capita income $26,143
Median household income $68,069
Median family income $74,623
Persons in poverty 2,049
H'holds receiving public assistance 196
H'holds receiving social security 3,473

Households, 2000
Total households 16,063
  With persons under 18 7,962
  With persons over 65 3,249
  Family households 13,006
  Single-person households 2,466
  Persons per household 3.04
  Persons per family 3.42

Labor & Employment
Total civilian labor force, 2007** 26,796
  Unemployment rate 3.5%
Total civilian labor force, 2000 24,937
  Unemployment rate 4.2%
Employed persons 16 years and over
* by occupation, 2000*
  Managers & professionals 9,175
  Service occupations 3,020
  Sales & office occupations 7,350
  Farming, fishing & forestry 67
  Construction & maintenance 2,016
  Production & transportation 2,258
  Self-employed persons 1,221

‡ Branch of county library
* US Census Bureau
** New Jersey Department of Labor

See Introduction for an explanation of all data sources.

General Information
Township of Howell
251 Preventorium Rd
PO Box 580
Howell, NJ 07731
732-938-4500

Website .... www.twp.howell.nj.us
Year of incorporation 1801
Land/water area (sq. miles) 60.91/0.09
Form of government .... Council-Manager

Government

Legislative Districts
US Congressional 4
State Legislative 30

Local Officials, 2009
Mayor .... Robert F. Walsh
Manager .... Helene Schlegel
Clerk .... Bruce Davis
Finance Dir .... Jeffrey L. Fillatreault
Tax Assessor .... Greg Hutchison
Tax Collector .... Susan Davison
Attorney .... McKenna Kingdon
Building .... Paul Orlando
Planning .... Ernie Peters
Engineering .... William Nunziato
Public Works .... Jeffrey Cramer
Police Chief .... Ronald T. Carter
Emerg/Fire Director .... Robert H. Hotmar

Housing & Construction

Housing Units, 2000*
Total 16,572
Median rent $816
Median SF home value $172,400

Permits for New Residential Construction

	Units	Value
Total, 2006	88	$14,243,515
Single family	88	$14,243,515
Total, 2007	114	$17,553,664
Single family	114	$17,553,664

Real Property Valuation, 2008

	Parcels	Valuation
Total	21,541	$6,860,605,000
Vacant	4,127	264,011,700
Residential	16,228	5,707,045,800
Commercial	440	667,961,100
Industrial	66	111,543,900
Apartments	0	0
Farm land	400	2,543,100
Farm homestead	280	107,499,400

Average Property Value & Tax, 2008
Residential value $352,226
Property tax $6,767
Tax credit/rebate $1,112

Public Library
Howell Public Library‡
318 Old Tavern Rd
Howell, NJ 07731
732-938-2300

Branch Librarian .... Stephenie Acosta

Library statistics, 2007
see Monmouth County profile
for library system statistics

Public Safety
Number of officers, 2007 94

Crime	2006	2007
Total crimes	535	658
Violent	59	57
Murder	0	1
Rape	1	3
Robbery	11	15
Aggravated assault	47	38
Non-violent	476	601
Burglary	94	101
Larceny	348	467
Vehicle theft	34	33
Domestic violence	292	373
Arson	6	5
Total crime rate	10.6	13.0
Violent	1.2	1.1
Non-violent	9.4	11.9

Public School District
(for school year 2007-08 except as noted)

Howell Township School District
200 Squankum-Yellowbrook Rd., PO Box 579
Howell, NJ 07731
(732) 751-2480

Superintendent .... Enid Golden
Number of schools 13
Grade plan K-8
Enrollment 7,059
Attendance rate, '06-07 .... 95.5%
Dropout rate .... NA
Students per teacher 11.1
Per pupil expenditure $13,313
Median faculty salary $51,875
Median administrator salary $123,164
Grade 12 enrollment .... NA
High school graduation rate .... NA

Assessment test results
(percent scoring at proficient or advanced level)

	Language	Math
NJASK-Grade 3	96.3%	94.7%
GEPA-Grade 8	79.0%	90.4%
HSPA-High School	NA	NA

SAT Score Averages, 2006-07

Pct tested	Math	Verbal	Writing
NA	NA	NA	NA

Teacher Qualifications
Avg. years of experience 10
Highly-qualified teachers
  one subject/all subjects 100%/100%

No Child Left Behind
AYP, 2006-07 .... Meets Standards

Municipal Finance

State Aid Programs, 2009
Total aid $9,993,013
  CMPTRA 0
  Energy tax receipts 9,736,651
  Garden State Trust 9,201

General Budget, 2008
Total tax levy $131,985,377
  County levy 18,267,238
    County taxes 15,947,378
    County library 959,818
    County health 296,487
    County open space 1,063,555
  School levy 94,066,109
  Muni. levy 19,652,030
  Misc. revenues 25,484,264

Taxes	2006	2007	2008
General tax rate per $100	4.062	1.883	1.922
County equalization ratio	50.08	102.18	97.20
Net valuation taxable	$2,939,678,340	$6,855,681,063	$6,870,231,317
State equalized value	$6,558,866,149	$7,052,914,135	$813,927,370

Demographics & Socio-Economic Characteristics
(2000 US Census, except as noted)

Population
1980*	2,829
1990*	3,940
2000	5,603
Male	2,710
Female	2,893
2007 (estimate)*	5,681
Population density	286.3

Race & Hispanic Origin, 2000
Race
White	5,322
Black/African American	65
American Indian/Alaska Native	3
Asian	97
Native Hawaiian/Pacific Islander	0
Other race	44
Two or more races	72
Hispanic origin, total	211
Mexican	17
Puerto Rican	54
Cuban	17
Other Hispanic	123

Age & Nativity, 2000
Under 5 years	364
18 years and over	4,104
21 years and over	3,969
65 years and over	451
85 years and over	42
Median age	36.8
Native-born	5,193
Foreign-born	410

Educational Attainment, 2000
Population 25 years and over	3,811
Less than 9th grade	2.3%
High school grad or higher	91.3%
Bachelor's degree or higher	35.7%
Graduate degree	9.9%

Income & Poverty, 1999
Per capita income	$30,555
Median household income	$67,247
Median family income	$79,819
Persons in poverty	158
H'holds receiving public assistance	37
H'holds receiving social security	384

Households, 2000
Total households	2,146
With persons under 18	819
With persons over 65	354
Family households	1,490
Single-person households	525
Persons per household	2.61
Persons per family	3.18

Labor & Employment
Total civilian labor force, 2007**	3,585
Unemployment rate	1.3%
Total civilian labor force, 2000	3,191
Unemployment rate	1.2%

Employed persons 16 years and over by occupation, 2000
Managers & professionals	1,258
Service occupations	466
Sales & office occupations	834
Farming, fishing & forestry	0
Construction & maintenance	313
Production & transportation	281
Self-employed persons	150

‡ Branch of county library
* US Census Bureau
** New Jersey Department of Labor

General Information
Township of Independence
286-B Route 46
Great Meadows, NJ 07838
908-637-4133
Website	www.independencenj.com
Year of incorporation	1782
Land/water area (sq. miles)	19.84/0.05
Form of government	Township

Government
Legislative Districts
US Congressional	5
State Legislative	23

Local Officials, 2009
Mayor	Robert M. Giordano
Manager	Deborah Hrebenak
Clerk	Deborah Hrebenak
Finance Dir	Kevin Lifer
Tax Assessor	Kathleen Degan
Tax Collector	Patricia Noll
Attorney	Richard Cushing
Building	Richard O'Connor
Planning	Kathy Dossena
Engineering	Michael Finelli
Public Works	Alan Shimchook
Police Chief	Dennis Riley
Emerg/Fire Director	Cheryl Holowath

Housing & Construction
Housing Units, 2000*
Total	2,210
Median rent	$720
Median SF home value	$169,500

Permits for New Residential Construction
	Units	Value
Total, 2006	11	$2,841,283
Single family	11	$2,841,283
Total, 2007	13	$3,740,951
Single family	13	$3,740,951

Real Property Valuation, 2008
	Parcels	Valuation
Total	2,370	$690,886,593
Vacant	139	13,292,260
Residential	1,878	598,075,100
Commercial	55	30,133,000
Industrial	6	3,861,200
Apartments	9	15,564,300
Farm land	192	2,078,833
Farm homestead	91	27,881,900

Average Property Value & Tax, 2008
Residential value	$317,906
Property tax	$6,287
Tax credit/rebate	$1,032

Public Library
Northeast Branch Library‡
63 US Hwy 46
Hackettstown, NJ 07840
908-813-3858
Branch Librarian	Patricia Optiz

Library statistics, 2007
see Warren County profile
for library system statistics

Public Safety
Number of officers, 2007	8

Crime	2006	2007
Total crimes	71	47
Violent	2	3
Murder	0	0
Rape	0	0
Robbery	0	0
Aggravated assault	2	3
Non-violent	69	44
Burglary	8	10
Larceny	60	32
Vehicle theft	1	2
Domestic violence	61	64
Arson	0	0
Total crime rate	12.3	8.1
Violent	0.3	0.5
Non-violent	12.0	7.6

Public School District
(for school year 2007-08 except as noted)

Great Meadows Regional School District
PO BOX 74
Great Meadows, NJ 07838
(908) 637-6576
Superintendent	Jason Bing
Number of schools	3
Grade plan	K-8
Enrollment	956
Attendance rate, '06-07	95.5%
Dropout rate	NA
Students per teacher	10.3
Per pupil expenditure	$12,430
Median faculty salary	$54,935
Median administrator salary	$89,994
Grade 12 enrollment	NA
High school graduation rate	NA

Assessment test results
(percent scoring at proficient or advanced level)
	Language	Math
NJASK-Grade 3	92.5%	93.3%
GEPA-Grade 8	78.1%	91.3%
HSPA-High School	NA	NA

SAT Score Averages, 2006-07
Pct tested	Math	Verbal	Writing
NA	NA	NA	NA

Teacher Qualifications
Avg. years of experience	16
Highly-qualified teachers one subject/all subjects	100%/100%

No Child Left Behind
AYP, 2006-07	Meets Standards

Municipal Finance
State Aid Programs, 2009
Total aid	$411,474
CMPTRA	76,578
Energy tax receipts	312,046
Garden State Trust	6,075

General Budget, 2008
Total tax levy	$13,693,527
County levy	4,628,810
County taxes	3,775,043
County library	396,501
County health	0
County open space	457,266
School levy	7,398,483
Muni. levy	1,666,234
Misc. revenues	2,728,434

Taxes	2006	2007	2008
General tax rate per $100	1.85	1.94	1.978
County equalization ratio	104.97	94.69	91.02
Net valuation taxable	$685,510,734	$688,072,010	$692,366,725
State equalized value	$725,473,572	$755,813,516	$743,810,199

See Introduction for an explanation of all data sources.

Demographics & Socio-Economic Characteristics

(2000 US Census, except as noted)

Population
1980*	1,037
1990*	910
2000	900
Male	435
Female	465
2007 (estimate)*	884
Population density	2,525.7

Race & Hispanic Origin, 2000
Race
White	888
Black/African American	0
American Indian/Alaska Native	0
Asian	2
Native Hawaiian/Pacific Islander	1
Other race	0
Two or more races	9
Hispanic origin, total	10
Mexican	2
Puerto Rican	5
Cuban	0
Other Hispanic	3

Age & Nativity, 2000
Under 5 years	36
18 years and over	739
21 years and over	724
65 years and over	205
85 years and over	21
Median age	47.6
Native-born	861
Foreign-born	39

Educational Attainment, 2000
Population 25 years and over	705
Less than 9th grade	1.0%
High school grad or higher	97.7%
Bachelor's degree or higher	53.5%
Graduate degree	21.7%

Income & Poverty, 1999
Per capita income	$47,307
Median household income	$82,842
Median family income	$104,618
Persons in poverty	27
H'holds receiving public assistance	0
H'holds receiving social security	144

Households, 2000
Total households	386
With persons under 18	86
With persons over 65	152
Family households	261
Single-person households	106
Persons per household	2.33
Persons per family	2.86

Labor & Employment
Total civilian labor force, 2007**	501
Unemployment rate	3.9%
Total civilian labor force, 2000	465
Unemployment rate	3.0%

Employed persons 16 years and over by occupation, 2000
Managers & professionals	246
Service occupations	36
Sales & office occupations	126
Farming, fishing & forestry	0
Construction & maintenance	23
Production & transportation	20
Self-employed persons	58

* US Census Bureau
** New Jersey Department of Labor

See Introduction for an explanation of all data sources.

General Information
Borough of Interlaken
100 Grassmere Ave
Interlaken, NJ 07712
732-531-7405

Website	NA
Year of incorporation	1922
Land/water area (sq. miles)	0.35/0.04
Form of government	Borough

Government

Legislative Districts
US Congressional	6
State Legislative	11

Local Officials, 2009
Mayor	Robert Wolf
Manager	Aime Sweeney
Clerk	Aime Sweeney
Finance Dir	Aime Sweeney
Tax Assessor	Ed Mullane
Tax Collector	Eleanor Cottrell
Attorney	Dennis Crawford
Building	Paul Vitale
Planning	James Watt
Engineering	Peter Avakian
Public Works	Norman Cottrell
Police Chief	James Lanza
Fire/Emergency Dir	Thomas Collins

Housing & Construction

Housing Units, 2000*
Total	397
Median rent	$1,333
Median SF home value	$280,600

Permits for New Residential Construction
	Units	Value
Total, 2006	15	$350,000
Single family	15	$350,000
Total, 2007	0	$0
Single family	0	$0

Real Property Valuation, 2008
	Parcels	Valuation
Total	407	$198,770,600
Vacant	12	1,504,900
Residential	395	197,265,700
Commercial	0	0
Industrial	0	0
Apartments	0	0
Farm land	0	0
Farm homestead	0	0

Average Property Value & Tax, 2008
Residential value	$499,407
Property tax	$7,424
Tax credit/rebate	$1,019

Public Library
Interlaken Municipal Library
100 Grassmere Ave
Interlaken, NJ 07712
732-531-7405

Librarian	Vicki LaBella

Library statistics, 2007
Population served	NA
Full-time/total staff	NA/NA

	Total	Per capita
Holdings	NA	NA
Revenues	NA	NA
Expenditures	NA	NA
Annual visits	NA	NA
Internet terminals/annual users	NA/NA	

Public Safety
Number of officers, 2007	5

Crime	2006	2007
Total crimes	3	3
Violent	0	0
Murder	0	0
Rape	0	0
Robbery	0	0
Aggravated assault	0	0
Non-violent	3	3
Burglary	1	0
Larceny	2	3
Vehicle theft	0	0
Domestic violence	1	1
Arson	0	0
Total crime rate	3.4	3.4
Violent	0.0	0.0
Non-violent	3.4	3.4

Public School District
(for school year 2007-08 except as noted)

Interlaken Borough School District
100 Grassmere Avenue
Interlaken, NJ 07712

No schools in district - sends students to
Asbury Park schools

Per pupil expenditure	NA
Median faculty salary	NA
Median administrator salary	NA
Grade 12 enrollment	NA
High school graduation rate	NA

Assessment test results
(percent scoring at proficient or advanced level)
	Language	Math
NJASK-Grade 3	NA	NA
GEPA-Grade 8	NA	NA
HSPA-High School	NA	NA

SAT Score Averages, 2006-07
Pct tested	Math	Verbal	Writing
NA	NA	NA	NA

Teacher Qualifications
Avg. years of experience	NA
Highly-qualified teachers one subject/all subjects	NA/NA

No Child Left Behind
AYP, 2006-07	NA

Municipal Finance

State Aid Programs, 2009
Total aid	$123,563
CMPTRA	0
Energy tax receipts	118,620
Garden State Trust	0

General Budget, 2008
Total tax levy	$2,955,649
County levy	748,333
County taxes	664,087
County library	39,963
County health	0
County open space	44,283
School levy	504,034
Muni. levy	1,703,282
Misc. revenues	427,076

Taxes
	2006	2007	2008
General tax rate per $100	1.292	1.405	1.487
County equalization ratio	78.84	69.95	67.57
Net valuation taxable	$197,301,900	$198,387,185	$198,833,822
State equalized value	$282,129,903	$293,572,667	$4,643,139,596

Demographics & Socio-Economic Characteristics

(2000 US Census, except as noted)

Population

1980*	61,493
1990*	61,018
2000	60,695
Male	28,353
Female	32,342
2007 (estimate)*	56,920
Population density	19,229.7

Race & Hispanic Origin, 2000

Race

White	5,446
Black/African American	49,566
American Indian/Alaska Native	146
Asian	669
Native Hawaiian/Pacific Islander	59
Other race	2,234
Two or more races	2,575
Hispanic origin, total	5,086
Mexican	357
Puerto Rican	2,083
Cuban	105
Other Hispanic	2,541

Age & Nativity, 2000

Under 5 years	4,891
18 years and over	43,691
21 years and over	41,138
65 years and over	4,576
85 years and over	507
Median age	31.5
Native-born	45,937
Foreign-born	14,678

Educational Attainment, 2000

Population 25 years and over	37,143
Less than 9th grade	7.6%
High school grad or higher	72.0%
Bachelor's degree or higher	12.1%
Graduate degree	2.7%

Income & Poverty, 1999

Per capita income	$16,874
Median household income	$36,575
Median family income	$41,098
Persons in poverty	10,420
H'holds receiving public assistance	1,778
H'holds receiving social security	4,020

Households, 2000

Total households	22,032
With persons under 18	9,079
With persons over 65	3,679
Family households	14,403
Single-person households	6,453
Persons per household	2.74
Persons per family	3.39

Labor & Employment

Total civilian labor force, 2007**	27,637
Unemployment rate	6.6%
Total civilian labor force, 2000	29,740
Unemployment rate	12.5%

Employed persons 16 years and over by occupation, 2000

Managers & professionals	5,480
Service occupations	5,654
Sales & office occupations	8,445
Farming, fishing & forestry	4
Construction & maintenance	1,547
Production & transportation	4,878
Self-employed persons	698

* US Census Bureau
** New Jersey Department of Labor
§ State Fiscal Year July 1–June 30

General Information

Township of Irvington
1 Civic Square
Irvington, NJ 07111
973-399-8111

Website	www.irvington.net
Year of incorporation	1982
Land/water area (sq. miles)	2.96/0.00
Form of government	Mayor-Council

Government

Legislative Districts

US Congressional	10
State Legislative	28

Local Officials, 2009

Mayor	Wayne Smith
Manager	Wayne Bradley
Clerk	Harold Wiener
Finance Dir	Faheem Ra'Oof
Tax Assessor	James Gibbs
Tax Collector	Beverly Baytops
Attorney	Marvin Braker
Building	Nagy Sileem
Planning	Wayne Bradley
Engineering	John Wiggins
Public Works	Luis Mollinedo
Police Chief	Michael Chase
Emerg/Fire Director	Gary Shumlich

Housing & Construction

Housing Units, 2000*

Total	24,116
Median rent	$678
Median SF home value	$112,200

Permits for New Residential Construction

	Units	Value
Total, 2006	112	$7,776,179
Single family	11	$1,390,700
Total, 2007	48	$3,597,722
Single family	2	$300,697

Real Property Valuation, 2008

	Parcels	Valuation
Total	9,539	$3,210,441,740
Vacant	377	44,200,000
Residential	7,982	2,054,786,400
Commercial	697	497,265,600
Industrial	171	166,783,340
Apartments	312	447,406,400
Farm land	0	0
Farm homestead	0	0

Average Property Value & Tax, 2008

Residential value	$257,428
Property tax	$6,561
Tax credit/rebate	$893

Public Library

Irvington Public Library
Civic Square
Irvington, NJ 07111
973-372-6400

Director	Joan E. Whittaker

Library statistics, 2007

Population served	60,695
Full-time/total staff	8/19

	Total	Per capita
Holdings	186,724	3.08
Revenues	$1,634,490	$26.93
Expenditures	$1,639,066	$27.00
Annual visits	189,222	3.12
Internet terminals/annual users	33/51,755	

Public Safety

Number of officers, 2007	192

Crime	2006	2007
Total crimes	4,488	4,548
Violent	1,321	1,243
Murder	21	23
Rape	23	29
Robbery	681	616
Aggravated assault	596	575
Non-violent	3,167	3,305
Burglary	924	930
Larceny	1,289	1,358
Vehicle theft	954	1,017
Domestic violence	807	845
Arson	20	14
Total crime rate	76.2	78.4
Violent	22.4	21.4
Non-violent	53.8	57.0

Public School District

(for school year 2007-08 except as noted)

Irvington Township School District
1 University Place
Irvington, NJ 07111
(973) 399-6800

Superintendent	Ethel W. Davion
Number of schools	14
Grade plan	K-12
Enrollment	7,276
Attendance rate, '06-07	92.2%
Dropout rate	0.4%
Students per teacher	9.5
Per pupil expenditure	$17,179
Median faculty salary	$52,678
Median administrator salary	$110,000
Grade 12 enrollment	336
High school graduation rate	91.9%

Assessment test results

(percent scoring at proficient or advanced level)

	Language	Math
NJASK-Grade 3	67.1%	72.1%
GEPA-Grade 8	28.3%	51.9%
HSPA-High School	29.9%	60.5%

SAT Score Averages, 2006-07

Pct tested	Math	Verbal	Writing
58%	369	375	379

Teacher Qualifications

Avg. years of experience	9
Highly-qualified teachers one subject/all subjects	96.5%/96.5%

No Child Left Behind

AYP, 2006-07	Needs Improvement

Municipal Finance§

State Aid Programs, 2009

Total aid	$13,607,445
CMPTRA	9,654,013
Energy tax receipts	3,953,432
Garden State Trust	0

General Budget, 2008

Total tax levy	$82,098,069
County levy	11,329,381
County taxes	10,891,713
County library	0
County health	0
County open space	437,668
School levy	18,679,084
Muni. levy	52,089,604
Misc. revenues	34,952,444

Taxes

	2006	2007	2008
General tax rate per $100	25	2.27	2.549
County equalization ratio	12.71	133.52	111.70
Net valuation taxable	$262,646,850	$3,242,943,457	$3,221,048,260
State equalized value	$2,419,805,930	$2,904,343,383	$3,053,102,483

See Introduction for an explanation of all data sources.

Demographics & Socio-Economic Characteristics
(2000 US Census, except as noted)

Population
1980*	1,575
1990*	1,470
2000	1,751
Male	843
Female	908
2007 (estimate)*	1,875
Population density	3,125.0

Race & Hispanic Origin, 2000
Race
White	1,712
Black/African American	2
American Indian/Alaska Native	8
Asian	11
Native Hawaiian/Pacific Islander	0
Other race	1
Two or more races	17
Hispanic origin, total	24
Mexican	0
Puerto Rican	16
Cuban	4
Other Hispanic	4

Age & Nativity, 2000
Under 5 years	84
18 years and over	1,359
21 years and over	1,308
65 years and over	303
85 years and over	31
Median age	43.0
Native-born	1,663
Foreign-born	86

Educational Attainment, 2000
Population 25 years and over	1,175
Less than 9th grade	1.4%
High school grad or higher	90.8%
Bachelor's degree or higher	33.4%
Graduate degree	12.8%

Income & Poverty, 1999
Per capita income	$26,975
Median household income	$61,125
Median family income	$72,596
Persons in poverty	71
H'holds receiving public assistance	8
H'holds receiving social security	235

Households, 2000
Total households	705
With persons under 18	218
With persons over 65	212
Family households	498
Single-person households	171
Persons per household	2.48
Persons per family	2.97

Labor & Employment
Total civilian labor force, 2007**	1,010
Unemployment rate	4.4%
Total civilian labor force, 2000	856
Unemployment rate	4.7%

Employed persons 16 years and over by occupation, 2000
Managers & professionals	351
Service occupations	89
Sales & office occupations	202
Farming, fishing & forestry	0
Construction & maintenance	119
Production & transportation	55
Self-employed persons	79

‡ Branch of county library
* US Census Bureau
** New Jersey Department of Labor

General Information
Borough of Island Heights
PO Box AH
Island Heights, NJ 08732
732-270-6415
Website	www.islandheightsboro.com
Year of incorporation	1887
Land/water area (sq. miles)	0.60/0.27
Form of government	Small Municipality

Government
Legislative Districts
US Congressional	3
State Legislative	10

Local Officials, 2009
Mayor	James Biggs
Manager	Adrian Fanning
Clerk	Eleanor Rogalski
Finance Dir	Adrian Fanning
Tax Assessor	Victoria Mickiewicz
Tax Collector	Wendy Prior
Attorney	Doug Jones
Building	Ken Anderson
Comm Dev/Planning	NA
Engineering	Michael O'Donnell
Public Works	Jon Brodbeck (Int)
Police Chief	NA
Emerg/Fire Director	Robert Wilber Jr

Housing & Construction
Housing Units, 2000*
Total	807
Median rent	$830
Median SF home value	$167,400

Permits for New Residential Construction
	Units	Value
Total, 2006	10	$773,570
Single family	10	$773,570
Total, 2007	9	$696,213
Single family	9	$696,213

Real Property Valuation, 2008
	Parcels	Valuation
Total	905	$349,135,500
Vacant	67	15,209,600
Residential	807	310,714,800
Commercial	30	22,721,800
Industrial	0	0
Apartments	1	489,300
Farm land	0	0
Farm homestead	0	0

Average Property Value & Tax, 2008
Residential value	$385,025
Property tax	$5,846
Tax credit/rebate	$956

Public Library
Island Heights Branch Library‡
Summit & Central
Island Heights, NJ 08732
732-270-6266
Branch Librarian	Emily Holman

Library statistics, 2007
see Ocean County profile
for library system statistics

Public Safety
Number of officers, 2007	5

Crime	2006	2007
Total crimes	16	9
Violent	0	0
Murder	0	0
Rape	0	0
Robbery	0	0
Aggravated assault	0	0
Non-violent	16	9
Burglary	4	0
Larceny	11	9
Vehicle theft	1	0
Domestic violence	16	7
Arson	0	0
Total crime rate	8.6	4.8
Violent	0.0	0.0
Non-violent	8.6	4.8

Public School District
(for school year 2007-08 except as noted)

Island Heights School District
115 Summit Avenue, PO Box 329
Island Heights, NJ 08732
(732) 929-1222
Superintendent	John Lichtenberg
Number of schools	1
Grade plan	K-6
Enrollment	110
Attendance rate, '06-07	95.5%
Dropout rate	NA
Students per teacher	8.5
Per pupil expenditure	$15,652
Median faculty salary	$41,640
Median administrator salary	$78,984
Grade 12 enrollment	NA
High school graduation rate	NA

Assessment test results
(percent scoring at proficient or advanced level)
	Language	Math
NJASK-Grade 3	100.0%	100.0%
GEPA-Grade 8	NA	NA
HSPA-High School	NA	NA

SAT Score Averages, 2006-07
Pct tested	Math	Verbal	Writing
NA	NA	NA	NA

Teacher Qualifications
Avg. years of experience	8
Highly-qualified teachers one subject/all subjects	100%/100%

No Child Left Behind
AYP, 2006-07	Meets Standards

Municipal Finance
State Aid Programs, 2009
Total aid	$155,478
CMPTRA	21,632
Energy tax receipts	128,793
Garden State Trust	0

General Budget, 2008
Total tax levy	$5,304,044
County levy	1,293,440
County taxes	1,066,610
County library	125,351
County health	51,035
County open space	50,443
School levy	2,580,940
Muni. levy	1,429,664
Misc. revenues	1,052,401

Taxes	2006	2007	2008
General tax rate per $100	1.444	1.464	1.519
County equalization ratio	100.89	88.53	83.35
Net valuation taxable	$342,070,700	$347,331,640	$349,320,681
State equalized value	$386,587,938	$416,677,362	$1,398,346,957

See Introduction for an explanation of all data sources.

Demographics & Socio-Economic Characteristics

(2000 US Census, except as noted)

Population

1980*	25,644
1990*	33,233
2000	42,816
Male	20,911
Female	21,905
2007 (estimate)*	52,577
Population density	525.5

Race & Hispanic Origin, 2000

Race

White	39,073
Black/African American	1,670
American Indian/Alaska Native	57
Asian	882
Native Hawaiian/Pacific Islander	3
Other race	414
Two or more races	717
Hispanic origin, total	2,474
Mexican	201
Puerto Rican	1,316
Cuban	161
Other Hispanic	796

Age & Nativity, 2000

Under 5 years	3,515
18 years and over	30,114
21 years and over	28,764
65 years and over	4,009
85 years and over	456
Median age	35.2
Native-born	40,097
Foreign-born	2,713

Educational Attainment, 2000

Population 25 years and over	27,385
Less than 9th grade	3.6%
High school grad or higher	86.9%
Bachelor's degree or higher	23.1%
Graduate degree	6.0%

Income & Poverty, 1999

Per capita income	$23,981
Median household income	$65,218
Median family income	$71,045
Persons in poverty	1,573
H'holds receiving public assistance	193
H'holds receiving social security	3,181

Households, 2000

Total households	14,176
With persons under 18	6,676
With persons over 65	2,750
Family households	11,264
Single-person households	2,267
Persons per household	2.99
Persons per family	3.38

Labor & Employment

Total civilian labor force, 2007**	27,203
Unemployment rate	4.0%
Total civilian labor force, 2000	21,325
Unemployment rate	4.3%

Employed persons 16 years and over by occupation, 2000

Managers & professionals	7,163
Service occupations	2,825
Sales & office occupations	5,568
Farming, fishing & forestry	26
Construction & maintenance	2,508
Production & transportation	2,320
Self-employed persons	915

‡ Branch of county library
* US Census Bureau
** New Jersey Department of Labor

General Information

Township of Jackson
95 W Veterans Hwy
Jackson, NJ 08527
732-928-1200

Website	www.jacksontwpnj.net
Year of incorporation	1844
Land/water area (sq. miles)	100.06/0.75
Form of government	Township

Government

Legislative Districts

US Congressional	4
State Legislative	30

Local Officials, 2009

Mayor	Michael Reina
Manager	Philip Del Turco
Clerk	Ann Marie Eden
Finance Dir	Sharon Pinkava
Tax Assessor	Toni Nagle-Rowe
Tax Collector	Michael Campbell
Attorney	George Gilmore
Building	Barry Olejarz
Planning	Jeff Purpuro
Engineering	Daniel Burke
Public Works	Fred Rasiewicz
Police Chief	NA
Emerg/Fire Director	Barry Olejarz

Housing & Construction

Housing Units, 2000*

Total	14,640
Median rent	$863
Median SF home value	$156,300

Permits for New Residential Construction

	Units	Value
Total, 2006	146	$18,951,911
Single family	146	$18,951,911
Total, 2007	37	$6,095,405
Single family	37	$6,095,405

Real Property Valuation, 2008

	Parcels	Valuation
Total	19,941	$2,977,943,550
Vacant	2,405	81,777,650
Residential	17,092	2,575,062,100
Commercial	224	260,972,200
Industrial	50	17,831,100
Apartments	10	30,428,100
Farm land	96	704,800
Farm homestead	64	11,167,600

Average Property Value & Tax, 2008

Residential value	$150,748
Property tax	$5,884
Tax credit/rebate	$1,054

Public Library

Jackson Branch Library‡
2nd Jackson Rd
Jackson, NJ 08527
732-928-4400

Branch Librarian | John Glace

Library statistics, 2007

see Ocean County profile
for library system statistics

Public Safety

Number of officers, 2007 | 89

Crime	2006	2007
Total crimes	612	595
Violent	31	24
Murder	0	0
Rape	1	2
Robbery	8	3
Aggravated assault	22	19
Non-violent	581	571
Burglary	105	99
Larceny	438	441
Vehicle theft	38	31
Domestic violence	383	399
Arson	18	11
Total crime rate	11.8	11.4
Violent	0.6	0.5
Non-violent	11.2	10.9

Public School District

(for school year 2007-08 except as noted)

Jackson Township School District
151 Don Connor Blvd
Jackson, NJ 08527
(732) 833-4600

Superintendent	Thomas Gialanella
Number of schools	10
Grade plan	K-12
Enrollment	9,736
Attendance rate, '06-07	94.7%
Dropout rate	1.2%
Students per teacher	12.4
Per pupil expenditure	$12,150
Median faculty salary	$50,200
Median administrator salary	$124,069
Grade 12 enrollment	684
High school graduation rate	96.3%

Assessment test results

(percent scoring at proficient or advanced level)

	Language	Math
NJASK-Grade 3	95.1%	93.4%
GEPA-Grade 8	80.3%	91.3%
HSPA-High School	76.9%	84.7%

SAT Score Averages, 2006-07

Pct tested	Math	Verbal	Writing
73%	499	484	477

Teacher Qualifications

Avg. years of experience	9
Highly-qualified teachers one subject/all subjects	100%/100%

No Child Left Behind

AYP, 2006-07 | Meets Standards

Municipal Finance

State Aid Programs, 2009

Total aid	$4,415,616
CMPTRA	847,090
Energy tax receipts	3,366,800
Garden State Trust	86,737

General Budget, 2008

Total tax levy	$116,431,088
County levy	22,986,224
County taxes	18,955,155
County library	2,227,654
County health	906,967
County open space	896,449
School levy	68,888,054
Muni. levy	24,556,810
Misc. revenues	17,836,505

Taxes

	2006	2007	2008
General tax rate per $100	3.774	3.843	3.904
County equalization ratio	46.89	41.96	39.99
Net valuation taxable	$2,822,880,550	$2,963,469,271	$2,982,801,631
State equalized value	$6,732,766,452	$7,403,229,738	$440,568,001

See Introduction for an explanation of all data sources.

Demographics & Socio-Economic Characteristics
(2000 US Census, except as noted)

Population
1980*	4,114
1990*	5,294
2000	6,025
Male	2,935
Female	3,090
2007 (estimate)*	6,389
Population density	7,606.0

Race & Hispanic Origin, 2000
Race
White	4,990
Black/African American	532
American Indian/Alaska Native	12
Asian	134
Native Hawaiian/Pacific Islander	0
Other race	229
Two or more races	128
Hispanic origin, total	606
Mexican	119
Puerto Rican	180
Cuban	26
Other Hispanic	281

Age & Nativity, 2000
Under 5 years	457
18 years and over	4,541
21 years and over	4,364
65 years and over	646
85 years and over	117
Median age	35.4
Native-born	5,344
Foreign-born	681

Educational Attainment, 2000
Population 25 years and over	4,089
Less than 9th grade	5.5%
High school grad or higher	82.9%
Bachelor's degree or higher	20.2%
Graduate degree	5.0%

Income & Poverty, 1999
Per capita income	$23,325
Median household income	$59,461
Median family income	$67,887
Persons in poverty	206
H'holds receiving public assistance	65
H'holds receiving social security	424

Households, 2000
Total households	2,176
With persons under 18	843
With persons over 65	402
Family households	1,551
Single-person households	487
Persons per household	2.70
Persons per family	3.18

Labor & Employment
Total civilian labor force, 2007**	3,637
Unemployment rate	4.1%
Total civilian labor force, 2000	3,327
Unemployment rate	4.3%

Employed persons 16 years and over by occupation, 2000
Managers & professionals	855
Service occupations	429
Sales & office occupations	980
Farming, fishing & forestry	0
Construction & maintenance	324
Production & transportation	595
Self-employed persons	127

* US Census Bureau
** New Jersey Department of Labor

See Introduction for an explanation of all data sources.

General Information
Borough of Jamesburg
131 Perrineville Rd
Jamesburg, NJ 08831
732-521-2222

Website	www.jamesburgborough.org
Year of incorporation	1887
Land/water area (sq. miles)	0.84/0.00
Form of government	Borough

Government
Legislative Districts
US Congressional	12
State Legislative	14

Local Officials, 2009
Mayor	Anthony La Mantia
Business Admin	Denise Jawidzik
Clerk	Lauren Vande Vaarst
Finance Dir	Denise Jawidzik
Tax Assessor	Ken Pacera
Tax Collector	Kelly Taylor
Attorney	Frederick Raffetto
Building	NA
Comm Dev/Planning	NA
Engineering	Alan Dittenhofer
Public Works	Joseph Intravartola
Police Chief	Martin Horvath
Fire Chief	Dwayne Fitzpatrick

Housing & Construction
Housing Units, 2000*
Total	2,240
Median rent	$777
Median SF home value	$139,300

Permits for New Residential Construction
	Units	Value
Total, 2006	0	$6,000
Single family	0	$6,000
Total, 2007	3	$321,996
Single family	3	$321,996

Real Property Valuation, 2008
	Parcels	Valuation
Total	1,796	$239,340,300
Vacant	115	3,985,600
Residential	1,564	193,928,600
Commercial	102	32,211,000
Industrial	1	925,000
Apartments	14	8,290,100
Farm land	0	0
Farm homestead	0	0

Average Property Value & Tax, 2008
Residential value	$123,995
Property tax	$5,963
Tax credit/rebate	$1,019

Public Library
Jamesburg Public Library
229 Gatzmer Ave
Jamesburg, NJ 08831
732-521-0440

Director ... Cynthia Yasher

Library statistics, 2007
Population served	6,025
Full-time/total staff	0/1

	Total	Per capita
Holdings	28,035	4.65
Revenues	$181,118	$30.06
Expenditures	$187,131	$31.06
Annual visits	25,521	4.24
Internet terminals/annual users		2/2,280

Public Safety
Number of officers, 2007	13

Crime	2006	2007
Total crimes	72	73
Violent	12	5
Murder	0	0
Rape	3	1
Robbery	3	1
Aggravated assault	6	3
Non-violent	60	68
Burglary	20	16
Larceny	33	45
Vehicle theft	7	7
Domestic violence	39	63
Arson	0	0
Total crime rate	11.0	11.4
Violent	1.8	0.8
Non-violent	9.2	10.6

Public School District
(for school year 2007-08 except as noted)

Jamesburg School District
Augusta Street
Jamesburg, NJ 08831
(732) 521-0303

Superintendent	Gail S. Verona
Number of schools	2
Grade plan	K-8
Enrollment	630
Attendance rate, '06-07	94.8%
Dropout rate	NA
Students per teacher	10.5
Per pupil expenditure	$12,315
Median faculty salary	$46,324
Median administrator salary	$90,162
Grade 12 enrollment	NA
High school graduation rate	NA

Assessment test results
(percent scoring at proficient or advanced level)
	Language	Math
NJASK-Grade 3	86.9%	80.3%
GEPA-Grade 8	56.7%	75.7%
HSPA-High School	NA	NA

SAT Score Averages, 2006-07
Pct tested	Math	Verbal	Writing
NA	NA	NA	NA

Teacher Qualifications
Avg. years of experience	11
Highly-qualified teachers one subject/all subjects	93.5%/93.5%

No Child Left Behind
AYP, 2006-07	Meets Standards

Municipal Finance
State Aid Programs, 2009
Total aid	$533,649
CMPTRA	144,153
Energy tax receipts	376,154
Garden State Trust	0

General Budget, 2008
Total tax levy	$11,561,939
County levy	1,594,543
County taxes	1,428,080
County library	0
County health	0
County open space	166,463
School levy	6,804,193
Muni. levy	3,163,203
Misc. revenues	2,176,624

Taxes
	2006	2007	2008
General tax rate per $100	4.39	4.58	4.810
County equalization ratio	53.62	46.52	43.18
Net valuation taxable	$238,571,800	$241,151,778	$240,408,095
State equalized value	$514,239,424	$556,841,356	$565,816,025

Demographics & Socio-Economic Characteristics

(2000 US Census, except as noted)

Population

1980*	16,413
1990*	17,825
2000	19,717
Male	9,775
Female	9,942
2007 (estimate)*	21,737
Population density	535.0

Race & Hispanic Origin, 2000

Race

White	18,955
Black/African American	163
American Indian/Alaska Native	32
Asian	211
Native Hawaiian/Pacific Islander	10
Other race	122
Two or more races	224
Hispanic origin, total	672
Mexican	50
Puerto Rican	244
Cuban	53
Other Hispanic	325

Age & Nativity, 2000

Under 5 years	1,452
18 years and over	14,407
21 years and over	13,861
65 years and over	1,690
85 years and over	158
Median age	37.2
Native-born	18,474
Foreign-born	1,243

Educational Attainment, 2000

Population 25 years and over	13,398
Less than 9th grade	2.6%
High school grad or higher	89.6%
Bachelor's degree or higher	27.8%
Graduate degree	7.1%

Income & Poverty, 1999

Per capita income	$27,950
Median household income	$68,837
Median family income	$76,974
Persons in poverty	468
H'holds receiving public assistance	33
H'holds receiving social security	1,371

Households, 2000

Total households	7,131
With persons under 18	2,907
With persons over 65	1,281
Family households	5,446
Single-person households	1,316
Persons per household	2.76
Persons per family	3.17

Labor & Employment

Total civilian labor force, 2007**	12,023
Unemployment rate	3.1%
Total civilian labor force, 2000	11,023
Unemployment rate	3.1%

Employed persons 16 years and over by occupation, 2000

Managers & professionals	4,036
Service occupations	1,132
Sales & office occupations	3,210
Farming, fishing & forestry	9
Construction & maintenance	1,326
Production & transportation	968
Self-employed persons	447

* US Census Bureau
** New Jersey Department of Labor

General Information

Township of Jefferson
1033 Weldon Rd
Lake Hopatcong, NJ 07849
973-697-1500

Website	www.jeffersontownship.net
Year of incorporation	1804
Land/water area (sq. miles)	40.63/2.41
Form of government	Mayor-Council

Government

Legislative Districts

US Congressional	11
State Legislative	25

Local Officials, 2009

Mayor	Russell Felter
Manager	James Leach
Clerk	Lydia Magnotti
Finance Dir	Bill Eagen
Tax Assessor	Shawn Hopkins
Tax Collector	Elizabeth Recksiek
Attorney	Lawrence Cohen
Building	Tom Mahoney
Comm Dev/Planning	NA
Engineering	Hatch Mott McDonald
Public Works	Jeff Elam
Police Chief	John Palko
Fire Chief	Joe Williams

Housing & Construction

Housing Units, 2000*

Total	7,527
Median rent	$847
Median SF home value	$180,400

Permits for New Residential Construction

	Units	Value
Total, 2006	53	$6,121,288
Single family	48	$6,120,238
Total, 2007	41	$6,004,268
Single family	41	$6,004,268

Real Property Valuation, 2008

	Parcels	Valuation
Total	8,899	$3,237,919,900
Vacant	729	78,063,400
Residential	7,860	2,925,030,400
Commercial	213	194,892,100
Industrial	11	6,106,400
Apartments	26	24,511,500
Farm land	42	375,500
Farm homestead	18	8,940,600

Average Property Value & Tax, 2008

Residential value	$372,426
Property tax	$6,623
Tax credit/rebate	$1,081

Public Library

Jefferson Township Municipal Library
1031 Weldon Rd
Oak Ridge, NJ 07438
973-208-6115

Director	Seth Stephens

Library statistics, 2007

Population served	19,717
Full-time/total staff	1/7

	Total	Per capita
Holdings	55,366	2.81
Revenues	$1,037,146	$52.60
Expenditures	$757,848	$38.44
Annual visits	99,750	5.06
Internet terminals/annual users	15/15,978	

Public Safety

Number of officers, 2007	39

Crime	2006	2007
Total crimes	250	250
Violent	14	17
Murder	0	0
Rape	1	1
Robbery	6	3
Aggravated assault	7	13
Non-violent	236	233
Burglary	67	86
Larceny	158	142
Vehicle theft	11	5
Domestic violence	104	99
Arson	2	4
Total crime rate	11.6	11.4
Violent	0.6	0.8
Non-violent	10.9	10.6

Public School District

(for school year 2007-08 except as noted)

Jefferson Township School District
28 Bowling Green Parkway
Lake Hopatcong, NJ 07849
(973) 663-5780

Superintendent	Kathleen Fuchs
Number of schools	8
Grade plan	K-12
Enrollment	3,614
Attendance rate, '06-07	94.8%
Dropout rate	1.6%
Students per teacher	11.3
Per pupil expenditure	$13,013
Median faculty salary	$52,978
Median administrator salary	$112,774
Grade 12 enrollment	251
High school graduation rate	97.6%

Assessment test results

(percent scoring at proficient or advanced level)

	Language	Math
NJASK-Grade 3	96.0%	91.2%
GEPA-Grade 8	79.4%	90.3%
HSPA-High School	84.8%	91.6%

SAT Score Averages, 2006-07

Pct tested	Math	Verbal	Writing
69%	503	488	480

Teacher Qualifications

Avg. years of experience	9
Highly-qualified teachers one subject/all subjects	100%/100%

No Child Left Behind

AYP, 2006-07	Meets Standards

Municipal Finance

State Aid Programs, 2009

Total aid	$2,636,590
CMPTRA	23,742
Energy tax receipts	2,325,989
Garden State Trust	41,627

General Budget, 2008

Total tax levy	$57,658,650
County levy	7,477,811
County taxes	6,102,346
County library	0
County health	0
County open space	1,375,465
School levy	35,140,345
Muni. levy	15,040,494
Misc. revenues	7,400,078

Taxes

	2006	2007	2008
General tax rate per $100	1.6	1.7	1.779
County equalization ratio	118.78	106.15	101.03
Net valuation taxable	$3,203,336,300	$3,234,361,311	$3,242,448,166
State equalized value	$3,022,155,884	$3,201,431,082	$3,211,024,503

See Introduction for an explanation of all data sources.

Demographics & Socio-Economic Characteristics†

(2000 US Census, except as noted)

Population
1980*	223,532
1990*	228,537
2000	240,055
Male	117,144
Female	122,911
2007 (estimate)*	242,389
Population density	16,245.9

Race & Hispanic Origin, 2000
Race
White	81,637
Black/African American	67,994
American Indian/Alaska Native	1,071
Asian	38,881
Native Hawaiian/Pacific Islander	181
Other race	36,280
Two or more races	14,011
Hispanic origin, total	67,952
Mexican	2,495
Puerto Rican	29,777
Cuban	1,860
Other Hispanic	33,820

Age & Nativity, 2000
Under 5 years	16,631
18 years and over	180,652
21 years and over	170,621
65 years and over	23,438
85 years and over	2,805
Median age	32.4
Native-born	158,501
Foreign-born	81,554

Educational Attainment, 2000
Population 25 years and over	155,460
Less than 9th grade	10.6%
High school grad or higher	72.6%
Bachelor's degree or higher	27.5%
Graduate degree	9.3%

Income & Poverty, 1999
Per capita income	$19,410
Median household income	$37,862
Median family income	$41,639
Persons in poverty	44,075
H'holds receiving public assistance	5,977
H'holds receiving social security	17,981

Households, 2000
Total households	88,632
With persons under 18	31,837
With persons over 65	17,802
Family households	55,636
Single-person households	25,921
Persons per household	2.67
Persons per family	3.37

Labor & Employment
Total civilian labor force, 2007**	113,163
Unemployment rate	5.4%
Total civilian labor force, 2000	114,909
Unemployment rate	10.0%

Employed persons 16 years and over by occupation, 2000
Managers & professionals	34,111
Service occupations	16,436
Sales & office occupations	31,502
Farming, fishing & forestry	81
Construction & maintenance	5,313
Production & transportation	16,005
Self-employed persons	3,448

† see Appendix C for American Community Survey data
* US Census Bureau
** New Jersey Department of Labor
§ State Fiscal Year July 1–June 30

General Information
City of Jersey
280 Grove St
Jersey City, NJ 07302
201-547-5000
Website	www.cityofjerseycity.com
Year of incorporation	1820
Land/water area (sq. miles)	14.92/6.20
Form of government	Mayor-Council

Government
Legislative Districts
US Congressional	9-10, 13
State Legislative	31-33

Local Officials, 2009
Mayor	Jerramiah T. Healy
Manager	Brian O'Reilly
Clerk	Robert Byrne
Finance Dir	Paul Soyka
Tax Assessor	Eduardo Toloza
Tax Collector	Maureen Cosgrove
Attorney	William Matsikoudis
Building	Raymond Meyer
Planning	Robert Cotter
Engineering	William Goble
Public Works	John M. Yurchak
Police Chief	Thomas J. Comey
Fire Chief	William C. Sinnott

Housing & Construction
Housing Units, 2000*
Total	93,648
Median rent	$675
Median SF home value	$125,000

Permits for New Residential Construction
	Units	Value
Total, 2006	2,422	$151,232,624
Single family	5	$2,440,417
Total, 2007	1,157	$82,889,109
Single family	41	$7,789,922

Real Property Valuation, 2008
	Parcels	Valuation
Total	47,797	$5,936,514,827
Vacant	7,727	359,758,081
Residential	34,331	3,227,844,622
Commercial	3,454	1,476,859,174
Industrial	641	467,280,900
Apartments	1,644	404,772,050
Farm land	0	0
Farm homestead	0	0

Average Property Value & Tax, 2008
Residential value	$94,021
Property tax	$5,220
Tax credit/rebate	$858

Public Library
Jersey City Public Library
472 Jersey Ave
Jersey City, NJ 07302
201-547-4500
Director	Priscilla Gardner

Library statistics, 2007
Population served	240,055
Full-time/total staff	23/114

	Total	Per capita
Holdings	557,916	2.32
Revenues	$8,904,049	$37.09
Expenditures	$8,727,167	$36.35
Annual visits	265,789	1.11
Internet terminals/annual users	175/160,660	

Public Safety
Number of officers, 2007	902

Crime	2006	2007
Total crimes	10,589	9,338
Violent	2,923	2,456
Murder	22	20
Rape	60	47
Robbery	1,573	1,264
Aggravated assault	1,268	1,125
Non-violent	7,666	6,882
Burglary		1,505
Larceny	4,496	4,156
Vehicle theft	1,499	1,221
Domestic violence	1,823	1,748
Arson	97	100
Total crime rate	44.2	38.6
Violent	12.2	10.2
Non-violent	32.0	28.5

Public School District
(for school year 2007-08 except as noted)

Jersey City School District
346 Claremont Avenue
Jersey City, NJ 07305
(201) 915-6202
Superintendent	Charles T. Epps Jr
Number of schools	38
Grade plan	K-12
Enrollment	28,011
Attendance rate, '06-07	92.9%
Dropout rate	6.2%
Students per teacher	8.6
Per pupil expenditure	$16,124
Median faculty salary	$53,930
Median administrator salary	$121,882
Grade 12 enrollment	1,396
High school graduation rate	74.0%

Assessment test results
(percent scoring at proficient or advanced level)
	Language	Math
NJASK-Grade 3	71.0%	72.4%
GEPA-Grade 8	43.1%	59.9%
HSPA-High School	48.7%	64.1%

SAT Score Averages, 2006-07
Pct tested	Math	Verbal	Writing
NA	NA	NA	NA

Teacher Qualifications
Avg. years of experience	8
Highly-qualified teachers one subject/all subjects	100%/99.5%

No Child Left Behind
AYP, 2006-07	Needs Improvement

Municipal Finance§
State Aid Programs, 2009
Total aid	$79,353,755
CMPTRA	34,736,189
Energy tax receipts	42,604,435
Garden State Trust	25,966

General Budget, 2008
Total tax levy	$330,528,431
County levy	87,593,289
County taxes	85,274,972
County library	0
County health	0
County open space	2,318,317
School levy	91,735,145
Muni. levy	151,199,997
Misc. revenues	305,088,419

Taxes
	2006	2007	2008
General tax rate per $100	5.175	5.549	5.552
County equalization ratio	34.59	28.71	26.12
Net valuation taxable	$5,666,397,426	$5,716,019,239	$5,953,809,573
State equalized value	$19,758,887,061	$21,830,688,572	$23,170,628,705

See Introduction for an explanation of all data sources.

Demographics & Socio-Economic Characteristics

(2000 US Census, except as noted)

Population

1980*	10,613
1990*	11,069
2000	10,732
Male	5,237
Female	5,495
2007 (estimate)*	10,582
Population density	9,798.1

Race & Hispanic Origin, 2000

Race

White	10,014
Black/African American	229
American Indian/Alaska Native	11
Asian	132
Native Hawaiian/Pacific Islander	7
Other race	187
Two or more races	152
Hispanic origin, total	853
Mexican	61
Puerto Rican	473
Cuban	70
Other Hispanic	249

Age & Nativity, 2000

Under 5 years	755
18 years and over	7,814
21 years and over	7,407
65 years and over	1,207
85 years and over	152
Median age	34.4
Native-born	9,950
Foreign-born	782

Educational Attainment, 2000

Population 25 years and over	6,854
Less than 9th grade	6.7%
High school grad or higher	69.8%
Bachelor's degree or higher	9.5%
Graduate degree	2.8%

Income & Poverty, 1999

Per capita income	$17,417
Median household income	$36,383
Median family income	$45,438
Persons in poverty	1,874
H'holds receiving public assistance	138
H'holds receiving social security	1,052

Households, 2000

Total households	3,872
With persons under 18	1,525
With persons over 65	859
Family households	2,563
Single-person households	1,059
Persons per household	2.71
Persons per family	3.35

Labor & Employment

Total civilian labor force, 2007**	5,486
Unemployment rate	6.9%
Total civilian labor force, 2000	5,159
Unemployment rate	7.5%

Employed persons 16 years and over by occupation, 2000

Managers & professionals	1,001
Service occupations	808
Sales & office occupations	1,461
Farming, fishing & forestry	15
Construction & maintenance	678
Production & transportation	810
Self-employed persons	217

* US Census Bureau
** New Jersey Department of Labor
§ State Fiscal Year July 1–June 30

General Information

Borough of Keansburg
29 Church St
Keansburg, NJ 07734
732-787-0215

Website	keansburgboro.com
Year of incorporation	1917
Land/water area (sq. miles)	1.08/15.75
Form of government	Council-Manager

Government

Legislative Districts

US Congressional	6
State Legislative	13

Local Officials, 2009

Mayor	Arthur Boden
Manager	Terence Wall
Clerk	Thomas Cusick
Finance Dir	Pat DeBlasio
Tax Assessor	Michael Frangella
Tax Collector	Thomas Cusick
Attorney	John O. Bennett III
Building	Robert Burlew
Comm Dev/Planning	NA
Engineering	CMX Engineering
Public Works	Dennis O'Keefe
Police Chief	Raymond O'Hare
Emerg/Fire Director	James Merkel

Housing & Construction

Housing Units, 2000*

Total	4,269
Median rent	$718
Median SF home value	$99,000

Permits for New Residential Construction

	Units	Value
Total, 2006	5	$455,551
Single family	5	$455,551
Total, 2007	19	$2,238,000
Single family	19	$2,168,000

Real Property Valuation, 2008

	Parcels	Valuation
Total	3,310	$774,820,800
Vacant	97	6,036,300
Residential	3,038	669,504,500
Commercial	127	63,593,600
Industrial	3	2,850,300
Apartments	45	32,836,100
Farm land	0	0
Farm homestead	0	0

Average Property Value & Tax, 2008

Residential value	$220,377
Property tax	$4,212
Tax credit/rebate	$825

Public Library

Keansburg Public Library
55 Shore Blvd
Keansburg, NJ 07734
732-787-0636

Director	Ellen O'Brien

Library statistics, 2007

Population served	NA
Full-time/total staff	NA/NA

	Total	Per capita
Holdings	NA	NA
Revenues	NA	NA
Expenditures	NA	NA
Annual visits	NA	NA
Internet terminals/annual users	NA/NA	

Public Safety

Number of officers, 2007	35

Crime	2006	2007
Total crimes	369	315
Violent	65	46
Murder	0	0
Rape	3	4
Robbery	6	7
Aggravated assault	56	35
Non-violent	304	269
Burglary	57	42
Larceny	235	215
Vehicle theft	12	12
Domestic violence	613	758
Arson	1	2
Total crime rate	34.7	29.8
Violent	6.1	4.4
Non-violent	28.6	25.4

Public School District

(for school year 2007-08 except as noted)

Keansburg Borough School District
100 Palmer Place
Keansburg, NJ 07734
(732) 787-2007

Superintendent	Nicholas M. Eremita
Number of schools	4
Grade plan	K-12
Enrollment	1,854
Attendance rate, '06-07	92.1%
Dropout rate	1.0%
Students per teacher	6.5
Per pupil expenditure	$21,032
Median faculty salary	$48,295
Median administrator salary	$91,814
Grade 12 enrollment	92
High school graduation rate	95.8%

Assessment test results

(percent scoring at proficient or advanced level)

	Language	Math
NJASK-Grade 3	84.1%	81.7%
GEPA-Grade 8	44.1%	75.4%
HSPA-High School	65.9%	79.1%

SAT Score Averages, 2006-07

Pct tested	Math	Verbal	Writing
63%	455	432	427

Teacher Qualifications

Avg. years of experience	7
Highly-qualified teachers one subject/all subjects	99.5%/99.5%

No Child Left Behind

AYP, 2006-07	Meets Standards

Municipal Finance§

State Aid Programs, 2009

Total aid	$2,182,993
CMPTRA	1,464,782
Energy tax receipts	707,296
Garden State Trust	0

General Budget, 2008

Total tax levy	$14,818,699
County levy	2,013,808
County taxes	1,787,072
County library	107,550
County health	0
County open space	119,185
School levy	4,470,589
Muni. levy	8,334,302
Misc. revenues	5,624,494

Taxes

	2006	2007	2008
General tax rate per $100	4.747	1.764	1.912
County equalization ratio	45.49	106.32	98.20
Net valuation taxable	$277,074,590	$775,164,574	$775,263,173
State equalized value	$721,170,835	$789,365,656	$7,070,767,733

See Introduction for an explanation of all data sources.

Demographics & Socio-Economic Characteristics

(2000 US Census, except as noted)

Population

1980*	35,735
1990*	34,874
2000	40,513
Male	20,901
Female	19,612
2007 (estimate)*	37,295
Population density	4,080.4

Race & Hispanic Origin, 2000

Race
White	30,687
Black/African American	1,609
American Indian/Alaska Native	148
Asian	2,228
Native Hawaiian/Pacific Islander	27
Other race	4,068
Two or more races	1,746
Hispanic origin, total	11,075
Mexican	375
Puerto Rican	2,237
Cuban	847
Other Hispanic	7,616

Age & Nativity, 2000

Under 5 years	2,328
18 years and over	31,814
21 years and over	30,154
65 years and over	4,407
85 years and over	506
Median age	34.7
Native-born	25,038
Foreign-born	15,475

Educational Attainment, 2000

Population 25 years and over	27,690
Less than 9th grade	12.6%
High school grad or higher	70.9%
Bachelor's degree or higher	17.4%
Graduate degree	6.6%

Income & Poverty, 1999

Per capita income	$20,886
Median household income	$47,757
Median family income	$54,596
Persons in poverty	3,262
H'holds receiving public assistance	400
H'holds receiving social security	3,358

Households, 2000

Total households	13,539
With persons under 18	5,100
With persons over 65	3,276
Family households	9,809
Single-person households	2,958
Persons per household	2.81
Persons per family	3.28

Labor & Employment

Total civilian labor force, 2007**	18,019
Unemployment rate	5.1%
Total civilian labor force, 2000	19,045
Unemployment rate	6.8%

Employed persons 16 years and over by occupation, 2000
Managers & professionals	4,747
Service occupations	2,658
Sales & office occupations	5,261
Farming, fishing & forestry	15
Construction & maintenance	2,044
Production & transportation	3,016
Self-employed persons	757

* US Census Bureau
** New Jersey Department of Labor
§ State Fiscal Year July 1–June 30

See Introduction for an explanation of all data sources.

General Information

Town of Kearny
402 Kearny Ave
Kearny, NJ 07032
201-955-7400

Website	www.kearnyusa.com
Year of incorporation	1899
Land/water area (sq. miles)	9.14/1.05
Form of government	Town

Government

Legislative Districts

US Congressional	9, 13
State Legislative	32

Local Officials, 2009

Mayor	Alberto Santos
Manager	Joseph D'Arco
Clerk	Joseph D'Arco (Actg)
Finance Dir	Shuaib Firozvi
Tax Assessor	Gerard Pontrelli
Tax Collector	James Waller (Int)
Attorney	Gregory Castano
Building	Michael Martello
Comm Dev/Planning	NA
Engineering	Michael Neglia
Public Works	Gerard Kerr
Police Chief	John Dowie
Fire Chief	Steven Dyl

Housing & Construction

Housing Units, 2000*

Total	13,872
Median rent	$769
Median SF home value	$158,200

Permits for New Residential Construction

	Units	Value
Total, 2006	15	$1,392,070
Single family	1	$266,700
Total, 2007	11	$1,155,750
Single family	1	$227,000

Real Property Valuation, 2008

	Parcels	Valuation
Total	8,126	$1,068,980,500
Vacant	179	16,229,700
Residential	7,102	669,910,300
Commercial	487	104,347,400
Industrial	219	243,826,800
Apartments	139	34,666,300
Farm land	0	0
Farm homestead	0	0

Average Property Value & Tax, 2008

Residential value	$94,327
Property tax	$8,278
Tax credit/rebate	$1,160

Public Library

Kearny Public Library
318 Kearny Ave
Kearny, NJ 07032
201-998-2666

Director	Julie McCarthy

Library statistics, 2007

Population served	40,513
Full-time/total staff	4/13

	Total	Per capita
Holdings	83,584	2.06
Revenues	$1,140,518	$28.15
Expenditures	$1,132,147	$27.95
Annual visits	65,215	1.61
Internet terminals/annual users	20/31,321	

Public Safety

Number of officers, 2007	120

Crime	2006	2007
Total crimes	1,091	1,210
Violent	104	109
Murder	1	0
Rape	1	6
Robbery	44	50
Aggravated assault	58	53
Non-violent	987	1,101
Burglary	152	147
Larceny	617	762
Vehicle theft	218	192
Domestic violence	276	278
Arson	14	9
Total crime rate	28.1	31.8
Violent	2.7	2.9
Non-violent	25.5	29.0

Public School District

(for school year 2007-08 except as noted)

Kearny School District
100 Davis Avenue
Kearny, NJ 07032
(201) 955-5021

Superintendent	Robert Mooney
Number of schools	7
Grade plan	K-12
Enrollment	5,615
Attendance rate, '06-07	94.5%
Dropout rate	2.7%
Students per teacher	11.9
Per pupil expenditure	$13,014
Median faculty salary	$58,792
Median administrator salary	$120,477
Grade 12 enrollment	404
High school graduation rate	86.8%

Assessment test results

(percent scoring at proficient or advanced level)
	Language	Math
NJASK-Grade 3	89.7%	89.0%
GEPA-Grade 8	63.7%	78.3%
HSPA-High School	66.3%	77.0%

SAT Score Averages, 2006-07

Pct tested	Math	Verbal	Writing
62%	469	446	438

Teacher Qualifications

Avg. years of experience	10
Highly-qualified teachers one subject/all subjects	99.0%/98.0%

No Child Left Behind

AYP, 2006-07	Meets Standards

Municipal Finance§

State Aid Programs, 2009

Total aid	$21,622,912
CMPTRA	964,002
Energy tax receipts	20,333,543
Garden State Trust	0

General Budget, 2008

Total tax levy	$93,995,975
County levy	15,970,930
County taxes	15,551,238
County library	0
County health	0
County open space	419,692
School levy	44,220,947
Muni. levy	33,804,098
Misc. revenues	34,863,915

Taxes

	2006	2007	2008
General tax rate per $100	7.91	8.276	8.776
County equalization ratio	32.61	28.1	26.09
Net valuation taxable	$1,056,765,200	$1,066,043,901	$1,071,081,556
State equalized value	$3,763,223,911	$4,079,804,747	$4,049,736,421

Demographics & Socio-Economic Characteristics
(2000 US Census, except as noted)

Population
1980*	8,221
1990*	7,574
2000	7,675
Male	3,723
Female	3,952
2007 (estimate)*	7,647
Population density	3,573.4

Race & Hispanic Origin, 2000
Race
White	7,007
Black/African American	184
American Indian/Alaska Native	19
Asian	221
Native Hawaiian/Pacific Islander	0
Other race	138
Two or more races	106
Hispanic origin, total	663
Mexican	71
Puerto Rican	117
Cuban	93
Other Hispanic	382

Age & Nativity, 2000
Under 5 years	423
18 years and over	6,079
21 years and over	5,864
65 years and over	1,399
85 years and over	144
Median age	39.7
Native-born	6,322
Foreign-born	1,353

Educational Attainment, 2000
Population 25 years and over	5,574
Less than 9th grade	7.8%
High school grad or higher	80.0%
Bachelor's degree or higher	15.5%
Graduate degree	4.1%

Income & Poverty, 1999
Per capita income	$24,343
Median household income	$59,929
Median family income	$66,500
Persons in poverty	157
H'holds receiving public assistance	13
H'holds receiving social security	1,060

Households, 2000
Total households	2,854
With persons under 18	908
With persons over 65	1,009
Family households	2,117
Single-person households	611
Persons per household	2.69
Persons per family	3.15

Labor & Employment
Total civilian labor force, 2007**	4,145
Unemployment rate	4.4%
Total civilian labor force, 2000	3,992
Unemployment rate	4.6%

Employed persons 16 years and over by occupation, 2000
Managers & professionals	1,161
Service occupations	619
Sales & office occupations	1,194
Farming, fishing & forestry	8
Construction & maintenance	402
Production & transportation	426
Self-employed persons	198

* US Census Bureau
** New Jersey Department of Labor

General Information
Borough of Kenilworth
567 Boulevard
Kenilworth, NJ 07033
908-276-9090

Website	www.kenilworthnj.com
Year of incorporation	1907
Land/water area (sq. miles)	2.14/0.00
Form of government	Borough

Government
Legislative Districts
US Congressional	7
State Legislative	20

Local Officials, 2009
Mayor	Kathy Fiamingo
Manager/Admin	NA
Clerk	Hedy Lipke
Finance Dir	Nancy Nichols
Tax Assessor	Paul Parsons
Tax Collector	Nancy Nichols
Attorney	Harvey Fruchter
Building	Jerry Eger
Comm Dev/Planning	NA
Engineering	PMK Group
Public Works	NA
Police Chief	William Dowd
Emerg/Fire Director	Lou Giordino

Housing & Construction
Housing Units, 2000*
Total	2,926
Median rent	$967
Median SF home value	$175,900

Permits for New Residential Construction
	Units	Value
Total, 2006	24	$3,340,699
Single family	14	$2,204,249
Total, 2007	14	$1,628,652
Single family	6	$786,002

Real Property Valuation, 2008
	Parcels	Valuation
Total	2,960	$881,020,500
Vacant	121	7,644,800
Residential	2,509	440,025,800
Commercial	176	83,304,600
Industrial	154	350,045,300
Apartments	0	0
Farm land	0	0
Farm homestead	0	0

Average Property Value & Tax, 2008
Residential value	$175,379
Property tax	$6,203
Tax credit/rebate	$1,042

Public Library
Kenilworth Free Public Library
548 Boulevard
Kenilworth, NJ 07033
908-276-2451

Director	Dale Spindel

Library statistics, 2007
Population served	7,675
Full-time/total staff	1/5

	Total	Per capita
Holdings	43,993	5.73
Revenues	$622,024	$81.05
Expenditures	$523,523	$68.21
Annual visits	54,390	7.09
Internet terminals/annual users		9/9,148

Public Safety
Number of officers, 2007	30

Crime	2006	2007
Total crimes	145	138
Violent	1	1
Murder	0	0
Rape	0	0
Robbery	1	0
Aggravated assault	0	1
Non-violent	144	137
Burglary	9	7
Larceny	126	117
Vehicle theft	9	13
Domestic violence	37	32
Arson	0	0
Total crime rate	18.7	17.8
Violent	0.1	0.1
Non-violent	18.6	17.7

Public School District
(for school year 2007-08 except as noted)

Kenilworth School District
426 Boulevard
Kenilworth, NJ 07033
(908) 276-1644

Superintendent	Lloyd M. Leschuk
Number of schools	2
Grade plan	K-12
Enrollment	1,354
Attendance rate, '06-07	95.6%
Dropout rate	1.0%
Students per teacher	11.8
Per pupil expenditure	$12,968
Median faculty salary	$59,440
Median administrator salary	$114,320
Grade 12 enrollment	103
High school graduation rate	100.0%

Assessment test results
(percent scoring at proficient or advanced level)
	Language	Math
NJASK-Grade 3	89.8%	93.1%
GEPA-Grade 8	83.4%	90.0%
HSPA-High School	78.4%	89.1%

SAT Score Averages, 2006-07
Pct tested	Math	Verbal	Writing
73%	475	454	459

Teacher Qualifications
Avg. years of experience	9
Highly-qualified teachers one subject/all subjects	100%/100%

No Child Left Behind
AYP, 2006-07	Meets Standards

Municipal Finance
State Aid Programs, 2009
Total aid	$1,319,220
CMPTRA	277,282
Energy tax receipts	999,063
Garden State Trust	0

General Budget, 2008
Total tax levy	$31,181,965
County levy	6,624,392
County taxes	6,335,564
County library	0
County health	0
County open space	288,827
School levy	15,100,735
Muni. levy	9,456,838
Misc. revenues	3,793,782

Taxes
	2006	2007	2008
General tax rate per $100	3.231	3.418	3.538
County equalization ratio	51.83	48.85	46.42
Net valuation taxable	$877,740,900	$880,223,723	$881,551,373
State equalized value	$1,797,277,119	$1,895,730,588	$2,055,149,576

See Introduction for an explanation of all data sources.

Demographics & Socio-Economic Characteristics

(2000 US Census, except as noted)

Population

1980*	7,413
1990*	7,586
2000	7,568
Male	3,648
Female	3,920
2007 (estimate)*	7,502
Population density	5,320.6

Race & Hispanic Origin, 2000

Race

White	6,447
Black/African American	531
American Indian/Alaska Native	9
Asian	168
Native Hawaiian/Pacific Islander	3
Other race	224
Two or more races	186
Hispanic origin, total	839
Mexican	151
Puerto Rican	385
Cuban	29
Other Hispanic	274

Age & Nativity, 2000

Under 5 years	443
18 years and over	5,919
21 years and over	5,677
65 years and over	1,219
85 years and over	199
Median age	38.1
Native-born	6,750
Foreign-born	818

Educational Attainment, 2000

Population 25 years and over	5,345
Less than 9th grade	5.9%
High school grad or higher	82.9%
Bachelor's degree or higher	15.9%
Graduate degree	6.6%

Income & Poverty, 1999

Per capita income	$23,288
Median household income	$43,869
Median family income	$58,176
Persons in poverty	587
H'holds receiving public assistance	90
H'holds receiving social security	1,055

Households, 2000

Total households	3,264
With persons under 18	921
With persons over 65	1,013
Family households	1,797
Single-person households	1,253
Persons per household	2.31
Persons per family	3.11

Labor & Employment

Total civilian labor force, 2007**	4,252
Unemployment rate	4.6%
Total civilian labor force, 2000	3,986
Unemployment rate	4.8%

Employed persons 16 years and over by occupation, 2000

Managers & professionals	1,233
Service occupations	624
Sales & office occupations	1,176
Farming, fishing & forestry	11
Construction & maintenance	315
Production & transportation	434
Self-employed persons	156

* US Census Bureau
** New Jersey Department of Labor

General Information

Borough of Keyport
70 W Front St
Keyport, NJ 07735
732-739-3900

Website	www.keyportonline.com
Year of incorporation	1908
Land/water area (sq. miles)	1.41/0.01
Form of government	Borough

Government

Legislative Districts

US Congressional	6
State Legislative	13

Local Officials, 2009

Mayor	Robert J. Bergen
Manager	Peter R. Valesi
Clerk	Valerie T. Heilweil
Finance Dir	K. Stencel/T. Fallon
Tax Assessor	Scott Pezzaras
Tax Collector	Keri R. Stencel
Attorney	John Wisniewski
Building	Robert Burlew
Comm Dev/Planning	NA
Engineering	Donald Norbut
Public Works	George Sappah
Police Chief	Thomas Mitchell
Emerg/Fire Director	Dave Olsen

Housing & Construction

Housing Units, 2000*

Total	3,400
Median rent	$673
Median SF home value	$141,100

Permits for New Residential Construction

	Units	Value
Total, 2006	24	$2,928,391
Single family	24	$2,928,391
Total, 2007	14	$1,391,666
Single family	14	$1,391,666

Real Property Valuation, 2008

	Parcels	Valuation
Total	2,309	$327,303,150
Vacant	134	5,318,400
Residential	1,938	238,900,050
Commercial	212	62,194,500
Industrial	6	6,218,500
Apartments	19	14,671,700
Farm land	0	0
Farm homestead	0	0

Average Property Value & Tax, 2008

Residential value	$123,271
Property tax	$5,872
Tax credit/rebate	$994

Public Library

Keyport Public Library
Third St & Broad St
Keyport, NJ 07735
732-264-0543

Director .... Jacqueline LaPolla

Library statistics, 2007

Population served	7,568
Full-time/total staff	0/2

	Total	Per capita
Holdings	44,375	5.86
Revenues	$245,120	$32.39
Expenditures	$163,346	$21.58
Annual visits	22,090	2.92
Internet terminals/annual users	5/4,768	

Public Safety

Number of officers, 2007 17

Crime	2006	2007
Total crimes	172	157
Violent	11	13
Murder	0	0
Rape	1	1
Robbery	6	5
Aggravated assault	4	7
Non-violent	161	144
Burglary	24	37
Larceny	121	94
Vehicle theft	16	13
Domestic violence	59	68
Arson	8	9
Total crime rate	22.9	21.0
Violent	1.5	1.7
Non-violent	21.5	19.3

Public School District

(for school year 2007-08 except as noted)

Keyport School District
335 Broad Street
Keyport, NJ 07735
(732) 264-2840

Superintendent	C. Dan Blachford
Number of schools	2
Grade plan	K-12
Enrollment	1,178
Attendance rate, '06-07	92.0%
Dropout rate	0.0%
Students per teacher	10.1
Per pupil expenditure	$13,713
Median faculty salary	$58,310
Median administrator salary	$91,453
Grade 12 enrollment	113
High school graduation rate	94.1%

Assessment test results

(percent scoring at proficient or advanced level)

	Language	Math
NJASK-Grade 3	91.2%	75.0%
GEPA-Grade 8	50.8%	73.2%
HSPA-High School	54.0%	68.3%

SAT Score Averages, 2006-07

Pct tested	Math	Verbal	Writing
60%	423	402	420

Teacher Qualifications

Avg. years of experience	13
Highly-qualified teachers one subject/all subjects	98.5%/98.5%

No Child Left Behind

AYP, 2006-07 .... Meets Standards

Municipal Finance

State Aid Programs, 2009

Total aid	$921,173
CMPTRA	309,739
Energy tax receipts	588,405
Garden State Trust	0

General Budget, 2008

Total tax levy	$15,685,411
County levy	1,875,719
County taxes	1,758,335
County library	0
County health	0
County open space	117,384
School levy	8,528,423
Muni. levy	5,281,270
Misc. revenues	3,529,224

Taxes

	2006	2007	2008
General tax rate per $100	4.397	4.55	4.764
County equalization ratio	50.77	46.25	41.90
Net valuation taxable	$327,591,500	$331,110,697	$329,310,230
State equalized value	$710,648,220	$787,274,527	$290,961,217

See Introduction for an explanation of all data sources.

Demographics & Socio-Economic Characteristics
(2000 US Census, except as noted)

Population
1980*	2,772
1990*	3,325
2000	3,782
Male	1,910
Female	1,872
2007 (estimate)*	4,020
Population density	114.1

Race & Hispanic Origin, 2000
Race
White	3,692
Black/African American	23
American Indian/Alaska Native	3
Asian	29
Native Hawaiian/Pacific Islander	0
Other race	7
Two or more races	28
Hispanic origin, total	70
Mexican	7
Puerto Rican	22
Cuban	16
Other Hispanic	25

Age & Nativity, 2000
Under 5 years	262
18 years and over	2,750
21 years and over	2,653
65 years and over	399
85 years and over	35
Median age	38.8
Native-born	3,621
Foreign-born	161

Educational Attainment, 2000
Population 25 years and over	2,618
Less than 9th grade	4.3%
High school grad or higher	89.1%
Bachelor's degree or higher	26.5%
Graduate degree	9.5%

Income & Poverty, 1999
Per capita income	$30,219
Median household income	$71,551
Median family income	$81,642
Persons in poverty	108
H'holds receiving public assistance	19
H'holds receiving social security	346

Households, 2000
Total households	1,340
With persons under 18	550
With persons over 65	291
Family households	1,042
Single-person households	236
Persons per household	2.82
Persons per family	3.21

Labor & Employment
Total civilian labor force, 2007**	2,365
Unemployment rate	3.3%
Total civilian labor force, 2000	2,115
Unemployment rate	2.8%

Employed persons 16 years and over by occupation, 2000
Managers & professionals	749
Service occupations	383
Sales & office occupations	460
Farming, fishing & forestry	9
Construction & maintenance	326
Production & transportation	128
Self-employed persons	238

* US Census Bureau
** New Jersey Department of Labor

General Information
Township of Kingwood
PO Box 199
Baptistown, NJ 08803
908-996-4276
Website	www.kingwoodtownship.com
Year of incorporation	1749
Land/water area (sq. miles)	35.23/0.59
Form of government	Township

Government
Legislative Districts
US Congressional	12
State Legislative	23

Local Officials, 2009
Mayor	Elaine M. Niemann
Manager/Admin	NA
Clerk	Mary E. MacConnell
Finance Dir	Diane Laudenbach
Tax Assessor	David Gill
Tax Collector	Diane Laudenbach
Attorney	Judith Kopen
Building	Mark Fornaciari
Comm Dev/Planning	NA
Engineering	Thomas Decker
Public Works	Jack Search
Police Chief	NA
Fire Chief	Bob Hanley

Housing & Construction
Housing Units, 2000*
Total	1,422
Median rent	$787
Median SF home value	$231,700

Permits for New Residential Construction
	Units	Value
Total, 2006	19	$3,666,199
Single family	19	$3,666,199
Total, 2007	16	$3,186,264
Single family	16	$3,186,264

Real Property Valuation, 2008
	Parcels	Valuation
Total	2,174	$697,001,900
Vacant	164	28,977,700
Residential	1,158	490,067,000
Commercial	49	34,335,100
Industrial	4	11,539,200
Apartments	4	2,262,500
Farm land	513	5,970,400
Farm homestead	282	123,850,000

Average Property Value & Tax, 2008
Residential value	$426,331
Property tax	$7,075
Tax credit/rebate	$1,107

Public Library
No public municipal library

Library statistics, 2007
Population served	NA
Full-time/total staff	NA/NA

	Total	Per capita
Holdings	NA	NA
Revenues	NA	NA
Expenditures	NA	NA
Annual visits	NA	NA
Internet terminals/annual users	NA/NA	

Public Safety
Number of officers, 2007 0
Crime	2006	2007
Total crimes	19	21
Violent	1	5
Murder	0	0
Rape	0	0
Robbery	0	0
Aggravated assault	1	5
Non-violent	18	16
Burglary	3	3
Larceny	11	12
Vehicle theft	4	1
Domestic violence	2	22
Arson	0	0
Total crime rate	4.7	5.2
Violent	0.2	1.2
Non-violent	4.5	4.0

Public School District
(for school year 2007-08 except as noted)

Kingwood Township School District
880 County Road 519
Frenchtown, NJ 08825
(908) 996-2941
Chief School Admin	Laura Hartner
Number of schools	1
Grade plan	K-8
Enrollment	463
Attendance rate, '06-07	95.8%
Dropout rate	NA
Students per teacher	8.9
Per pupil expenditure	$13,129
Median faculty salary	$53,576
Median administrator salary	$92,000
Grade 12 enrollment	NA
High school graduation rate	NA

Assessment test results
(percent scoring at proficient or advanced level)
	Language	Math
NJASK-Grade 3	93.6%	92.0%
GEPA-Grade 8	82.0%	86.0%
HSPA-High School	NA	NA

SAT Score Averages, 2006-07
Pct tested	Math	Verbal	Writing
NA	NA	NA	NA

Teacher Qualifications
Avg. years of experience	11
Highly-qualified teachers one subject/all subjects	97.5%/97.5%

No Child Left Behind
AYP, 2006-07 .... Meets Standards

Municipal Finance
State Aid Programs, 2009
Total aid	$444,301
CMPTRA	51,070
Energy tax receipts	327,516
Garden State Trust	60,417

General Budget, 2008
Total tax levy	$11,592,447
County levy	2,345,024
County taxes	1,962,044
County library	170,590
County health	0
County open space	212,390
School levy	7,919,699
Muni. levy	1,327,725
Misc. revenues	1,550,489

Taxes
	2006	2007	2008
General tax rate per $100	3.08	1.62	1.660
County equalization ratio	57.19	97.61	97.36
Net valuation taxable	$350,903,102	$699,110,769	$698,528,149
State equalized value	$663,528,579	$708,082,819	$712,172,558

See Introduction for an explanation of all data sources.

Demographics & Socio-Economic Characteristics
(2000 US Census, except as noted)

Population
1980*	7,770
1990*	8,470
2000	9,365
Male	4,673
Female	4,692
2007 (estimate)*	9,595
Population density	536.3

Race & Hispanic Origin, 2000
Race
White	8,953
Black/African American	54
American Indian/Alaska Native	4
Asian	266
Native Hawaiian/Pacific Islander	9
Other race	22
Two or more races	57
Hispanic origin, total	218
Mexican	10
Puerto Rican	54
Cuban	49
Other Hispanic	105

Age & Nativity, 2000
Under 5 years	702
18 years and over	6,556
21 years and over	6,358
65 years and over	841
85 years and over	66
Median age	39.6
Native-born	8,465
Foreign-born	900

Educational Attainment, 2000
Population 25 years and over	6,182
Less than 9th grade	1.4%
High school grad or higher	96.4%
Bachelor's degree or higher	57.4%
Graduate degree	25.2%

Income & Poverty, 1999
Per capita income	$45,796
Median household income	$105,991
Median family income	$110,593
Persons in poverty	244
H'holds receiving public assistance	28
H'holds receiving social security	572

Households, 2000
Total households	3,062
With persons under 18	1,440
With persons over 65	586
Family households	2,685
Single-person households	287
Persons per household	3.06
Persons per family	3.27

Labor & Employment
Total civilian labor force, 2007**	5,091
Unemployment rate	2.0%
Total civilian labor force, 2000	4,664
Unemployment rate	1.8%

Employed persons 16 years and over by occupation, 2000
Managers & professionals	2,701
Service occupations	302
Sales & office occupations	1,169
Farming, fishing & forestry	0
Construction & maintenance	214
Production & transportation	192
Self-employed persons	353

General Information
Borough of Kinnelon
130 Kinnelon Rd
Kinnelon, NJ 07405
973-838-5401

Website	www.kinnelonnj.org
Year of incorporation	1922
Land/water area (sq. miles)	17.89/0.93
Form of government	Borough

Government
Legislative Districts
US Congressional	11
State Legislative	26

Local Officials, 2009
Mayor	Glenn L. Sisco
Manager	(vacant)
Clerk	Elizabeth M. Sebrowski
Finance Dir	Norman Eckstein
Tax Assessor	Robert Edgar
Tax Collector	Lisa Kimkowski
Attorney	Edward J. Buzak
Building	Dan Hegberg
Comm Dev/Planning	NA
Engineering	Paul Darmofalski
Public Works	John Whitehead
Police Chief	John Finkle
Emerg/Fire Director	Gail Bresett

Housing & Construction
Housing Units, 2000*
Total	3,123
Median rent	$1,538
Median SF home value	$354,000

Permits for New Residential Construction
	Units	Value
Total, 2006	26	$7,695,405
Single family	26	$7,695,405
Total, 2007	20	$6,286,064
Single family	20	$6,286,064

Real Property Valuation, 2008
	Parcels	Valuation
Total	3,838	$1,660,078,000
Vacant	329	41,568,100
Residential	3,399	1,535,171,700
Commercial	94	61,800,100
Industrial	0	0
Apartments	2	18,360,100
Farm land	10	21,400
Farm homestead	4	3,156,600

Average Property Value & Tax, 2008
Residential value	$452,051
Property tax	$12,040
Tax credit/rebate	$1,284

Public Library
Kinnelon Public Library
132 Kinnelon Rd
Kinnelon, NJ 07405
973-838-1321

Director	Barbara Owens

Library statistics, 2007
Population served	9,365
Full-time/total staff	3/9

	Total	Per capita
Holdings	72,049	7.69
Revenues	$931,386	$99.45
Expenditures	$820,249	$87.59
Annual visits	99,555	10.63
Internet terminals/annual users	21/15,000	

Public Safety
Number of officers, 2007	16

Crime	2006	2007
Total crimes	70	67
Violent	1	3
Murder	0	0
Rape	0	0
Robbery	0	1
Aggravated assault	1	2
Non-violent	69	64
Burglary	26	31
Larceny	38	32
Vehicle theft	5	1
Domestic violence	40	20
Arson	0	1
Total crime rate	7.3	6.9
Violent	0.1	0.3
Non-violent	7.2	6.6

Public School District
(for school year 2007-08 except as noted)

Kinnelon Borough School District
109 Kiel Avenue
Kinnelon, NJ 07405
(973) 838-1418

Superintendent	James Opiekun
Number of schools	4
Grade plan	K-12
Enrollment	2,198
Attendance rate, '06-07	96.3%
Dropout rate	0.2%
Students per teacher	11.5
Per pupil expenditure	$13,669
Median faculty salary	$64,158
Median administrator salary	$116,017
Grade 12 enrollment	158
High school graduation rate	98.4%

Assessment test results
(percent scoring at proficient or advanced level)
	Language	Math
NJASK-Grade 3	94.0%	93.3%
GEPA-Grade 8	90.9%	97.8%
HSPA-High School	89.7%	94.9%

SAT Score Averages, 2006-07
Pct tested	Math	Verbal	Writing
106%	532	519	510

Teacher Qualifications
Avg. years of experience	9
Highly-qualified teachers one subject/all subjects	99.5%/99.5%

No Child Left Behind
AYP, 2006-07	Meets Standards

Municipal Finance
State Aid Programs, 2009
Total aid	$1,116,817
CMPTRA	58,235
Energy tax receipts	670,693
Garden State Trust	286,102

General Budget, 2008
Total tax levy	$44,259,490
County levy	5,719,627
County taxes	4,667,693
County library	0
County health	0
County open space	1,051,934
School levy	30,674,498
Muni. levy	7,865,366
Misc. revenues	3,962,791

Taxes
	2006	2007	2008
General tax rate per $100	2.49	2.6	2.664
County equalization ratio	74.48	68.13	67.46
Net valuation taxable	$1,614,971,600	$1,642,274,479	$1,661,755,327
State equalized value	$2,372,089,516	$2,433,680,128	$2,461,052,142

* US Census Bureau
** New Jersey Department of Labor

See Introduction for an explanation of all data sources.

Demographics & Socio-Economic Characteristics
(2000 US Census, except as noted)

Population
1980*	2,074
1990*	2,543
2000	2,977
Male	1,502
Female	1,475
2007 (estimate)*	3,139
Population density	126.7

Race & Hispanic Origin, 2000
Race
White	2,901
Black/African American	12
American Indian/Alaska Native	2
Asian	19
Native Hawaiian/Pacific Islander	0
Other race	14
Two or more races	29
Hispanic origin, total	55
Mexican	8
Puerto Rican	24
Cuban	7
Other Hispanic	16

Age & Nativity, 2000
Under 5 years	208
18 years and over	2,154
21 years and over	2,069
65 years and over	333
85 years and over	41
Median age	38.0
Native-born	2,887
Foreign-born	129

Educational Attainment, 2000
Population 25 years and over	2,021
Less than 9th grade	4.0%
High school grad or higher	87.1%
Bachelor's degree or higher	26.8%
Graduate degree	6.5%

Income & Poverty, 1999
Per capita income	$24,631
Median household income	$63,409
Median family income	$72,130
Persons in poverty	103
H'holds receiving public assistance	8
H'holds receiving social security	240

Households, 2000
Total households	1,028
With persons under 18	432
With persons over 65	228
Family households	816
Single-person households	154
Persons per household	2.87
Persons per family	3.21

Labor & Employment
Total civilian labor force, 2007**	1,870
Unemployment rate	5.1%
Total civilian labor force, 2000	1,655
Unemployment rate	4.6%

Employed persons 16 years and over by occupation, 2000
Managers & professionals	553
Service occupations	245
Sales & office occupations	346
Farming, fishing & forestry	13
Construction & maintenance	192
Production & transportation	230
Self-employed persons	109

* US Census Bureau
** New Jersey Department of Labor

General Information
Township of Knowlton
628 Route 94
Columbia, NJ 07832
908-496-4816
Website	knowlton-nj.com
Year of incorporation	1763
Land/water area (sq. miles)	24.78/0.53
Form of government	Township

Government
Legislative Districts
US Congressional	5
State Legislative	23

Local Officials, 2009
Mayor	Frank Van Horn
Manager/Admin	NA
Clerk	Lisa Patton
Finance Dir	Gregory Della Pia
Tax Assessor	Richard Motyka
Tax Collector	Evan Howell
Attorney	Richard Cushing
Building	NA
Comm Dev/Planning	NA
Engineering	Ted Rodman
Public Works	Ramon Cowell
Police Chief	NA
Emerg/Fire Director	Tom Moritz

Housing & Construction
Housing Units, 2000*
Total	1,135
Median rent	$739
Median SF home value	$180,300

Permits for New Residential Construction
	Units	Value
Total, 2006	10	$2,581,408
Single family	10	$2,581,408
Total, 2007	10	$2,483,488
Single family	10	$2,483,488

Real Property Valuation, 2008
	Parcels	Valuation
Total	1,626	$256,398,040
Vacant	162	6,989,700
Residential	938	191,098,100
Commercial	61	21,066,700
Industrial	0	0
Apartments	3	665,700
Farm land	323	2,839,240
Farm homestead	139	33,738,600

Average Property Value & Tax, 2008
Residential value	$208,762
Property tax	$6,599
Tax credit/rebate	$1,114

Public Library
No public municipal library

Library statistics, 2007
Population served	NA
Full-time/total staff	NA/NA

	Total	Per capita
Holdings	NA	NA
Revenues	NA	NA
Expenditures	NA	NA
Annual visits	NA	NA
Internet terminals/annual users	NA/NA	

Public Safety
Number of officers, 2007 ... 0
Crime	2006	2007
Total crimes	42	31
Violent	6	5
Murder	0	0
Rape	0	0
Robbery	0	1
Aggravated assault	6	4
Non-violent	36	26
Burglary	6	6
Larceny	29	18
Vehicle theft	1	2
Domestic violence	3	25
Arson	0	1
Total crime rate	13.3	9.7
Violent	1.9	1.6
Non-violent	11.4	8.2

Public School District
(for school year 2007-08 except as noted)

Knowlton Township School District
Knowlton Township Elementary, PO Box 227
Delaware, NJ 07833
(908) 475-5118
Superintendent	Sharon Mooney
Number of schools	1
Grade plan	K-6
Enrollment	305
Attendance rate, '06-07	95.6%
Dropout rate	NA
Students per teacher	9.2
Per pupil expenditure	$12,591
Median faculty salary	$57,210
Median administrator salary	$77,305
Grade 12 enrollment	NA
High school graduation rate	NA

Assessment test results
(percent scoring at proficient or advanced level)
	Language	Math
NJASK-Grade 3	97.4%	100.0%
GEPA-Grade 8	NA	NA
HSPA-High School	NA	NA

SAT Score Averages, 2006-07
Pct tested	Math	Verbal	Writing
NA	NA	NA	NA

Teacher Qualifications
Avg. years of experience	16
Highly-qualified teachers one subject/all subjects	100%/100%

No Child Left Behind
AYP, 2006-07 ... Meets Standards

Municipal Finance
State Aid Programs, 2009
Total aid	$401,410
CMPTRA	44,270
Energy tax receipts	301,083
Garden State Trust	40,131

General Budget, 2008
Total tax levy	$8,127,866
County levy	2,523,967
County taxes	2,058,786
County library	216,036
County health	0
County open space	249,145
School levy	4,907,095
Muni. levy	696,804
Misc. revenues	1,510,890

Taxes
	2006	2007	2008
General tax rate per $100	2.97	3.08	3.162
County equalization ratio	72.37	65.06	62.12
Net valuation taxable	$246,921,740	$254,975,680	$257,119,206
State equalized value	$380,349,267	$410,014,544	$418,784,169

Demographics & Socio-Economic Characteristics
(2000 US Census, except as noted)

Population
1980*	14,161
1990*	22,141
2000	25,346
Male	12,343
Female	13,003
2007 (estimate)*	26,322
Population density	313.4

Race & Hispanic Origin, 2000
Race
White	24,800
Black/African American	91
American Indian/Alaska Native	38
Asian	139
Native Hawaiian/Pacific Islander	2
Other race	103
Two or more races	173
Hispanic origin, total	545
Mexican	78
Puerto Rican	216
Cuban	49
Other Hispanic	202

Age & Nativity, 2000
Under 5 years	1,565
18 years and over	18,863
21 years and over	18,094
65 years and over	3,854
85 years and over	360
Median age	38.9
Native-born	24,671
Foreign-born	675

Educational Attainment, 2000
Population 25 years and over	17,180
Less than 9th grade	3.5%
High school grad or higher	86.1%
Bachelor's degree or higher	19.5%
Graduate degree	6.0%

Income & Poverty, 1999
Per capita income	$23,136
Median household income	$55,938
Median family income	$61,298
Persons in poverty	1,140
H'holds receiving public assistance	107
H'holds receiving social security	2,941

Households, 2000
Total households	9,336
With persons under 18	3,480
With persons over 65	2,719
Family households	7,245
Single-person households	1,714
Persons per household	2.71
Persons per family	3.08

Labor & Employment
Total civilian labor force, 2007**	13,661
Unemployment rate	4.5%
Total civilian labor force, 2000	12,542
Unemployment rate	4.3%

Employed persons 16 years and over by occupation, 2000
Managers & professionals	3,584
Service occupations	1,975
Sales & office occupations	3,519
Farming, fishing & forestry	0
Construction & maintenance	1,719
Production & transportation	1,209
Self-employed persons	555

‡ Branch of county library
* US Census Bureau
** New Jersey Department of Labor

General Information
Township of Lacey
818 W Lacey Rd
Forked River, NJ 08731
609-693-1100
Website	www.laceytownship.org
Year of incorporation	1871
Land/water area (sq. miles)	84.00/14.52
Form of government	Township

Government
Legislative Districts
US Congressional	3
State Legislative	9

Local Officials, 2009
Mayor	John Parker
Manager	John Adams
Clerk	Veronica Laureigh
Finance Dir	Kathryn Moore
Tax Assessor	Theresa Poznanski
Tax Collector	Joe Regatts
Attorney	George Gilmore
Building	Frank Crandall
Planning	John Curtin
Engineering	James F. Stanton
Public Works	Casey Parker
Police Chief	William Nally
Fire/Emergency Dir	NA

Housing & Construction
Housing Units, 2000*
Total	10,580
Median rent	$915
Median SF home value	$131,900

Permits for New Residential Construction
	Units	Value
Total, 2006	35	$7,501,426
Single family	35	$7,501,426
Total, 2007	39	$8,104,601
Single family	39	$8,104,601

Real Property Valuation, 2008
	Parcels	Valuation
Total	15,414	$1,767,249,500
Vacant	3,794	38,150,700
Residential	11,296	1,522,697,000
Commercial	260	135,219,600
Industrial	42	66,638,700
Apartments	1	2,143,500
Farm land	14	914,300
Farm homestead	7	1,485,700

Average Property Value & Tax, 2008
Residential value	$134,848
Property tax	$4,438
Tax credit/rebate	$863

Public Library
Lacey Branch Library‡
10 E Lacey Rd
Forked River, NJ 08731
609-693-8566
Branch Librarian	Kathlyn Lanzim

Library statistics, 2007
see Ocean County profile
for library system statistics

Public Safety
Number of officers, 2007	46

Crime	2006	2007
Total crimes	641	744
Violent	18	24
Murder	1	0
Rape	0	0
Robbery	1	3
Aggravated assault	16	21
Non-violent	623	720
Burglary	94	95
Larceny	516	619
Vehicle theft	13	6
Domestic violence	302	316
Arson	1	2
Total crime rate	24.4	28.3
Violent	0.7	0.9
Non-violent	23.8	27.4

Public School District
(for school year 2007-08 except as noted)

Lacey Township School District
200 Western Blvd., PO Box 216
Lanoka Harbor, NJ 08734
(609) 971-2002
Superintendent	Richard P. Starodub
Number of schools	6
Grade plan	K-12
Enrollment	4,897
Attendance rate, '06-07	92.8%
Dropout rate	1.3%
Students per teacher	12.1
Per pupil expenditure	$11,460
Median faculty salary	$51,610
Median administrator salary	$93,500
Grade 12 enrollment	382
High school graduation rate	96.9%

Assessment test results
(percent scoring at proficient or advanced level)
	Language	Math
NJASK-Grade 3	86.7%	88.9%
GEPA-Grade 8	69.6%	83.6%
HSPA-High School	84.7%	89.7%

SAT Score Averages, 2006-07
Pct tested	Math	Verbal	Writing
61%	503	474	476

Teacher Qualifications
Avg. years of experience	11

Highly-qualified teachers
one subject/all subjects	99.5%/99.5%

No Child Left Behind
AYP, 2006-07	Meets Standards

Municipal Finance
State Aid Programs, 2009
Total aid	$12,295,373
CMPTRA	0
Energy tax receipts	11,499,077
Garden State Trust	249,602

General Budget, 2008
Total tax levy	$58,223,388
County levy	13,620,380
County taxes	11,231,792
County library	1,319,982
County health	537,418
County open space	531,188
School levy	38,440,300
Muni. levy	6,162,707
Misc. revenues	19,634,701

Taxes	2006	2007	2008
General tax rate per $100	3.123	3.315	3.292
County equalization ratio	47.49	41.69	40.01
Net valuation taxable	$1,717,585,500	$1,746,120,974	$1,769,169,433
State equalized value	$4,123,116,637	$4,359,804,907	$7,466,505,663

See Introduction for an explanation of all data sources.

Demographics & Socio-Economic Characteristics
(2000 US Census, except as noted)

Population
1980*	1,614
1990*	1,902
2000	2,300
Male	1,154
Female	1,146
2007 (estimate)*	2,477
Population density	137.5

Race & Hispanic Origin, 2000
Race
White	2,232
Black/African American	24
American Indian/Alaska Native	2
Asian	18
Native Hawaiian/Pacific Islander	0
Other race	8
Two or more races	16
Hispanic origin, total	54
Mexican	0
Puerto Rican	21
Cuban	11
Other Hispanic	22

Age & Nativity, 2000
Under 5 years	150
18 years and over	1,669
21 years and over	1,611
65 years and over	213
85 years and over	13
Median age	38.9
Native-born	2,177
Foreign-born	122

Educational Attainment, 2000
Population 25 years and over	1,509
Less than 9th grade	2.7%
High school grad or higher	91.8%
Bachelor's degree or higher	33.3%
Graduate degree	11.3%

Income & Poverty, 1999
Per capita income	$30,491
Median household income	$82,805
Median family income	$87,650
Persons in poverty	85
H'holds receiving public assistance	14
H'holds receiving social security	143

Households, 2000
Total households	771
With persons under 18	314
With persons over 65	150
Family households	648
Single-person households	93
Persons per household	2.95
Persons per family	3.20

Labor & Employment
Total civilian labor force, 2007**	1,402
Unemployment rate	5.0%
Total civilian labor force, 2000	1,270
Unemployment rate	4.4%

Employed persons 16 years and over by occupation, 2000
Managers & professionals	491
Service occupations	134
Sales & office occupations	302
Farming, fishing & forestry	16
Construction & maintenance	167
Production & transportation	104
Self-employed persons	90

General Information
Township of Lafayette
33 Morris Farm Rd
Lafayette, NJ 07848
973-383-1817

Website	(county website)
Year of incorporation	1845
Land/water area (sq. miles)	18.02/0.03
Form of government	Township

Government
Legislative Districts
US Congressional	5
State Legislative	24

Local Officials, 2009
Mayor	John D'Angeli
Manager/Admin	NA
Clerk	AnnaRose Fedish
Finance Dir	Gail Magura
Tax Assessor	Maureen Kaman
Tax Collector	Linda L. Pettenger
Attorney	Roy Kurnos
Building	Charles O'Connor
Comm Dev/Planning	NA
Engineering	Michael Finelli
Public Works	William Macko
Police Chief	NA
Emerg/Fire Director	Joel Blackford

Housing & Construction
Housing Units, 2000*
Total	799
Median rent	$815
Median SF home value	$221,100

Permits for New Residential Construction
	Units	Value
Total, 2006	3	$1,586,600
Single family	3	$1,586,600
Total, 2007	4	$1,509,000
Single family	4	$1,509,000

Real Property Valuation, 2008
	Parcels	Valuation
Total	1,373	$469,341,500
Vacant	87	11,772,000
Residential	715	302,383,600
Commercial	54	45,464,100
Industrial	18	44,689,900
Apartments	0	0
Farm land	341	2,308,700
Farm homestead	158	62,723,200

Average Property Value & Tax, 2008
Residential value	$418,221
Property tax	$7,528
Tax credit/rebate	$1,147

Public Library
No public municipal library

Library statistics, 2007
Population served	NA
Full-time/total staff	NA/NA

	Total	Per capita
Holdings	NA	NA
Revenues	NA	NA
Expenditures	NA	NA
Annual visits	NA	NA
Internet terminals/annual users	NA/NA	

Public Safety
Number of officers, 2007	0

Crime	2006	2007
Total crimes	27	22
Violent	2	2
Murder	0	0
Rape	1	0
Robbery	0	0
Aggravated assault	1	2
Non-violent	25	20
Burglary	5	4
Larceny	17	15
Vehicle theft	3	1
Domestic violence	0	27
Arson	0	0
Total crime rate	10.8	8.7
Violent	0.8	0.8
Non-violent	10.0	7.9

Public School District
(for school year 2007-08 except as noted)

Lafayette Township School District
178 Beaver Run Road
Lafayette, NJ 07848
(973) 875-3344

Chief School Admin	Keith Neuhs
Number of schools	1
Grade plan	K-8
Enrollment	310
Attendance rate, '06-07	96.2%
Dropout rate	NA
Students per teacher	9.7
Per pupil expenditure	$13,529
Median faculty salary	$49,771
Median administrator salary	$68,215
Grade 12 enrollment	NA
High school graduation rate	NA

Assessment test results
(percent scoring at proficient or advanced level)
	Language	Math
NJASK-Grade 3	97.2%	100.0%
GEPA-Grade 8	84.6%	92.3%
HSPA-High School	NA	NA

SAT Score Averages, 2006-07
Pct tested	Math	Verbal	Writing
NA	NA	NA	NA

Teacher Qualifications
Avg. years of experience	10
Highly-qualified teachers one subject/all subjects	96.0%/96.0%

No Child Left Behind
AYP, 2006-07	Meets Standards

Municipal Finance
State Aid Programs, 2009
Total aid	$260,802
CMPTRA	50,967
Energy tax receipts	189,226
Garden State Trust	7,664

General Budget, 2008
Total tax levy	$8,468,987
County levy	1,821,611
County taxes	1,528,861
County library	128,838
County health	45,227
County open space	118,685
School levy	6,006,403
Muni. levy	640,973
Misc. revenues	1,461,619

Taxes	2006	2007	2008
General tax rate per $100	1.6	1.72	1.801
County equalization ratio	121.33	102.7	99.35
Net valuation taxable	$466,370,500	$472,307,991	$470,468,740
State equalized value	$455,321,428	$475,390,307	$484,735,174

* US Census Bureau
** New Jersey Department of Labor

See Introduction for an explanation of all data sources.

Demographics & Socio-Economic Characteristics

(2000 US Census, except as noted)

Population

1980*	1,566
1990*	1,482
2000	1,806
Male	913
Female	893
2007 (estimate)*	1,782
Population density	7,128.0

Race & Hispanic Origin, 2000

Race

White	1,484
Black/African American	140
American Indian/Alaska Native	8
Asian	23
Native Hawaiian/Pacific Islander	1
Other race	106
Two or more races	44
Hispanic origin, total	183
Mexican	110
Puerto Rican	37
Cuban	1
Other Hispanic	35

Age & Nativity, 2000

Under 5 years	113
18 years and over	1,413
21 years and over	1,350
65 years and over	234
85 years and over	31
Median age	35.8
Native-born	1,666
Foreign-born	140

Educational Attainment, 2000

Population 25 years and over	1,253
Less than 9th grade	2.1%
High school grad or higher	87.5%
Bachelor's degree or higher	25.2%
Graduate degree	6.6%

Income & Poverty, 1999

Per capita income	$27,111
Median household income	$47,566
Median family income	$56,538
Persons in poverty	134
H'holds receiving public assistance	14
H'holds receiving social security	171

Households, 2000

Total households	824
With persons under 18	215
With persons over 65	191
Family households	391
Single-person households	339
Persons per household	2.19
Persons per family	3.10

Labor & Employment

Total civilian labor force, 2007**	1,130
Unemployment rate	4.3%
Total civilian labor force, 2000	1,051
Unemployment rate	4.2%

Employed persons 16 years and over by occupation, 2000

Managers & professionals	346
Service occupations	166
Sales & office occupations	241
Farming, fishing & forestry	6
Construction & maintenance	110
Production & transportation	138
Self-employed persons	49

* US Census Bureau
** New Jersey Department of Labor
§ State Fiscal Year July 1–June 30

General Information

Borough of Lake Como
1740 Main St
PO Box 569
Lake Como, NJ 07719
732-681-3232

Website	lakecomonj.org
Year of incorporation	1924
Land/water area (sq. miles)	0.25/0.01
Form of government	Borough

Government

Legislative Districts

US Congressional	6
State Legislative	11

Local Officials, 2009

Mayor	Michael Ryan
Manager	Louise Mekosh
Clerk	Louise Mekosh
Finance Dir	Louise Mekosh
Tax Assessor	Mary Lou Hartman
Tax Collector	Esther Kiss
Attorney	William Gallagher Jr
Building	John Rowe
Planning	Mark Fessler
Engineering	Birdsall Engineering
Public Works	Brendan Maas
Police Chief	Rosman Cash
Emerg/Fire Director	Steve Whille

Housing & Construction

Housing Units, 2000*

Total	1,107
Median rent	$811
Median SF home value	$124,300

Permits for New Residential Construction

	Units	Value
Total, 2006	5	$442,350
Single family	5	$442,350
Total, 2007	3	$476,899
Single family	3	$476,899

Real Property Valuation, 2008

	Parcels	Valuation
Total	983	$380,401,700
Vacant	40	9,061,000
Residential	900	345,831,700
Commercial	40	22,298,800
Industrial	2	759,200
Apartments	1	2,451,000
Farm land	0	0
Farm homestead	0	0

Average Property Value & Tax, 2008

Residential value	$384,257
Property tax	$4,861
Tax credit/rebate	$920

Public Library

No public municipal library

Library statistics, 2007

Population served	NA
Full-time/total staff	NA/NA

	Total	Per capita
Holdings	NA	NA
Revenues	NA	NA
Expenditures	NA	NA
Annual visits	NA	NA
Internet terminals/annual users	NA/NA	

Public Safety

Number of officers, 2007	9

Crime	2006	2007
Total crimes	57	40
Violent	6	4
Murder	0	0
Rape	0	0
Robbery	3	1
Aggravated assault	3	3
Non-violent	51	36
Burglary	7	8
Larceny	41	25
Vehicle theft	3	3
Domestic violence	10	13
Arson	0	0
Total crime rate	32.4	22.8
Violent	3.4	2.3
Non-violent	29.0	20.5

Public School District

(for school year 2007-08 except as noted)

Lake Como School District
Borough Hall, F. Street, PO Box 569
Belmar, NJ 07719

No schools in district - sends students to Belmar Elementary and Manasquan High School

Per pupil expenditure	NA
Median faculty salary	NA
Median administrator salary	NA
Grade 12 enrollment	NA
High school graduation rate	NA

Assessment test results

(percent scoring at proficient or advanced level)

	Language	Math
NJASK-Grade 3	NA	NA
GEPA-Grade 8	NA	NA
HSPA-High School	NA	NA

SAT Score Averages, 2006-07

Pct tested	Math	Verbal	Writing
NA	NA	NA	NA

Teacher Qualifications

Avg. years of experience	NA
Highly-qualified teachers one subject/all subjects	NA/NA

No Child Left Behind

AYP, 2006-07	NA

Municipal Finance§

State Aid Programs, 2009

Total aid	$433,358
CMPTRA	273,004
Energy tax receipts	149,520
Garden State Trust	0

General Budget, 2008

Total tax levy	$4,815,167
County levy	988,916
County taxes	863,336
County library	51,955
County health	16,052
County open space	57,574
School levy	2,422,294
Muni. levy	1,403,957
Misc. revenues	1,823,688

Taxes	2006	2007	2008
General tax rate per $100	1.204	1.291	1.268
County equalization ratio	123.98	105.45	99.59
Net valuation taxable	$369,619,400	$374,523,408	$380,603,647
State equalized value	$350,708,160	$376,064,471	$3,573,947,927

See Introduction for an explanation of all data sources.

Demographics & Socio-Economic Characteristics

(2000 US Census, except as noted)

Population

1980*	2,908
1990*	3,078
2000	2,522
Male	1,301
Female	1,221
2007 (estimate)*	2,708
Population density	2,943.5

Race & Hispanic Origin, 2000

Race

White	2,124
Black/African American	198
American Indian/Alaska Native	16
Asian	59
Native Hawaiian/Pacific Islander	2
Other race	69
Two or more races	54
Hispanic origin, total	201
Mexican	50
Puerto Rican	94
Cuban	6
Other Hispanic	51

Age & Nativity, 2000

Under 5 years	207
18 years and over	1,751
21 years and over	1,666
65 years and over	201
85 years and over	15
Median age	32.3
Native-born	2,291
Foreign-born	231

Educational Attainment, 2000

Population 25 years and over	1,558
Less than 9th grade	5.3%
High school grad or higher	73.3%
Bachelor's degree or higher	7.5%
Graduate degree	3.1%

Income & Poverty, 1999

Per capita income	$18,390
Median household income	$43,567
Median family income	$48,833
Persons in poverty	179
H'holds receiving public assistance	35
H'holds receiving social security	192

Households, 2000

Total households	870
With persons under 18	405
With persons over 65	151
Family households	662
Single-person households	172
Persons per household	2.90
Persons per family	3.33

Labor & Employment

Total civilian labor force, 2007**	1,400
Unemployment rate	6.4%
Total civilian labor force, 2000	1,173
Unemployment rate	6.1%

Employed persons 16 years and over by occupation, 2000

Managers & professionals	225
Service occupations	298
Sales & office occupations	236
Farming, fishing & forestry	5
Construction & maintenance	195
Production & transportation	142
Self-employed persons	72

‡ Branch of county library
* US Census Bureau
** New Jersey Department of Labor

General Information

Borough of Lakehurst
5 Union Ave
Lakehurst, NJ 08733
732-657-4141

Website	www.lakehurstnj.org
Year of incorporation	1921
Land/water area (sq. miles)	0.92/0.09
Form of government	Borough

Government

Legislative Districts

US Congressional	4
State Legislative	9

Local Officials, 2009

Mayor	Timothy J. Borsetti
Manager	Norbert B. MacLean Jr
Clerk	Bernadette Dugan
Finance Dir	Christine Thorne
Tax Assessor	Matcene Hopkins-Kubler
Tax Collector	Marie C. Bell
Attorney	Sean Gertner
Construction Official	William Schultz
Comm Dev/Planning	NA
Engineering	Alan Dittenhofer
Public Works	David Winton
Police Chief	Eric Higgins
Fire Chief	Edward Seaman

Housing & Construction

Housing Units, 2000*

Total	961
Median rent	$833
Median SF home value	$89,300

Permits for New Residential Construction

	Units	Value
Total, 2006	16	$1,365,000
Single family	16	$1,365,000
Total, 2007	2	$161,000
Single family	2	$161,000

Real Property Valuation, 2008

	Parcels	Valuation
Total	805	$185,628,100
Vacant	55	3,714,200
Residential	690	152,316,700
Commercial	58	29,028,200
Industrial	0	0
Apartments	2	569,000
Farm land	0	0
Farm homestead	0	0

Average Property Value & Tax, 2008

Residential value	$220,749
Property tax	$3,761
Tax credit/rebate	$755

Public Library

Manchester Branch Library‡
21 Colonial Dr
Lakehurst, NJ 08733
732-657-7600

Branch Librarian .... Louise Innella

Library statistics, 2007

see Ocean County profile
for library system statistics

Public Safety

Number of officers, 2007 9

Crime	2006	2007
Total crimes	36	47
Violent	8	8
Murder	0	0
Rape	2	1
Robbery	3	0
Aggravated assault	3	7
Non-violent	28	39
Burglary	5	8
Larceny	22	30
Vehicle theft	1	1
Domestic violence	41	33
Arson	0	0
Total crime rate	13.4	17.6
Violent	3.0	3.0
Non-violent	10.4	14.6

Public School District

(for school year 2007-08 except as noted)

Lakehurst School District
301 Union Avenue
Lakehurst, NJ 08733
(732) 657-5741

Superintendent	Kevin Carroll
Number of schools	1
Grade plan	K-8
Enrollment	446
Attendance rate, '06-07	95.0%
Dropout rate	NA
Students per teacher	10.1
Per pupil expenditure	$12,157
Median faculty salary	$49,420
Median administrator salary	$101,189
Grade 12 enrollment	NA
High school graduation rate	NA

Assessment test results

(percent scoring at proficient or advanced level)

	Language	Math
NJASK-Grade 3	97.5%	87.5%
GEPA-Grade 8	64.3%	69.0%
HSPA-High School	NA	NA

SAT Score Averages, 2006-07

Pct tested	Math	Verbal	Writing
NA	NA	NA	NA

Teacher Qualifications

Avg. years of experience	9
Highly-qualified teachers one subject/all subjects	97.0%/97.0%

No Child Left Behind

AYP, 2006-07 .... Meets Standards

Municipal Finance

State Aid Programs, 2009

Total aid	$353,270
CMPTRA	141,171
Energy tax receipts	210,333
Garden State Trust	574

General Budget, 2008

Total tax levy	$3,195,518
County levy	579,795
County taxes	478,117
County library	56,190
County health	22,877
County open space	22,611
School levy	1,036,516
Muni. levy	1,579,207
Misc. revenues	2,029,407

Taxes

Taxes	2006	2007	2008
General tax rate per $100	1.575	1.652	1.704
County equalization ratio	123.74	105.53	100.10
Net valuation taxable	$184,219,800	$186,708,124	$187,550,517
State equalized value	$176,471,589	$186,523,525	$4,396,969,672

See Introduction for an explanation of all data sources.

Demographics & Socio-Economic Characteristics[†]

(2000 US Census, except as noted)

Population

1980*	38,464
1990*	45,048
2000	60,352
Male	28,845
Female	31,507
2007 (estimate)*	69,937
Population density	2,817.8

Race & Hispanic Origin, 2000

Race

White	47,542
Black/African American	7,270
American Indian/Alaska Native	105
Asian	836
Native Hawaiian/Pacific Islander	19
Other race	2,783
Two or more races	1,797
Hispanic origin, total	8,935
Mexican	2,825
Puerto Rican	3,730
Cuban	214
Other Hispanic	2,166

Age & Nativity, 2000

Under 5 years	7,169
18 years and over	41,166
21 years and over	39,014
65 years and over	11,429
85 years and over	2,147
Median age	30.6
Native-born	52,031
Foreign-born	8,321

Educational Attainment, 2000

Population 25 years and over	35,168
Less than 9th grade	8.4%
High school grad or higher	78.6%
Bachelor's degree or higher	21.0%
Graduate degree	8.2%

Income & Poverty, 1999

Per capita income	$16,700
Median household income	$35,634
Median family income	$43,806
Persons in poverty	11,440
H'holds receiving public assistance	969
H'holds receiving social security	8,186

Households, 2000

Total households	19,876
With persons under 18	7,019
With persons over 65	7,763
Family households	13,355
Single-person households	5,674
Persons per household	2.92
Persons per family	3.64

Labor & Employment

Total civilian labor force, 2007**	24,866
Unemployment rate	4.6%
Total civilian labor force, 2000	21,234
Unemployment rate	7.5%

Employed persons 16 years and over by occupation, 2000

Managers & professionals	6,553
Service occupations	3,266
Sales & office occupations	5,137
Farming, fishing & forestry	43
Construction & maintenance	1,657
Production & transportation	2,985
Self-employed persons	974

† see Appendix C for American Community Survey data
‡ Branch of county library
* US Census Bureau
** New Jersey Department of Labor

General Information

Township of Lakewood
231 3rd St
Lakewood, NJ 08701
732-364-2500

Website	www.lakewood.nj.us
Year of incorporation	1892
Land/water area (sq. miles)	24.82/0.30
Form of government	Township

Government

Legislative Districts

US Congressional	4
State Legislative	30

Local Officials, 2009

Mayor	Robert Singer
Manager	Frank Edwards
Clerk	Mary Ann Del Mastro
Finance Dir	William Reiker
Tax Assessor	Linda Solakian
Tax Collector	Patricia Tomassini
Attorney	Lawrence E. Bathgate II
Building	Michael Saccamanno
Comm Dev/Planning	NA
Engineering	Remington & Vernick
Public Works Dir	John Franklin
Police Chief	Robert Lawson
Fire Chief	Robert Lawson

Housing & Construction

Housing Units, 2000*

Total	21,214
Median rent	$849
Median SF home value	$126,400

Permits for New Residential Construction

	Units	Value
Total, 2006	185	$22,278,056
Single family	185	$22,278,056
Total, 2007	426	$17,902,614
Single family	170	$16,790,614

Real Property Valuation, 2008

	Parcels	Valuation
Total	23,445	$7,846,594,000
Vacant	3,505	468,468,400
Residential	19,077	5,633,818,300
Commercial	556	762,189,400
Industrial	181	602,901,700
Apartments	94	374,283,300
Farm land	22	55,100
Farm homestead	10	4,877,800

Average Property Value & Tax, 2008

Residential value	$295,421
Property tax	$4,995
Tax credit/rebate	$1,075

Public Library

Lakewood Branch Library‡
301 Lexington Ave
Lakewood, NJ 08701
732-363-1435

Director	Jeff Kesper

Library statistics, 2007

see Ocean County profile
for library system statistics

Public Safety

Number of officers, 2007	131

Crime	2006	2007
Total crimes	1,887	1,633
Violent	225	183
Murder	4	3
Rape	10	1
Robbery	138	97
Aggravated assault	73	82
Non-violent	1,662	1,450
Burglary	573	462
Larceny	953	888
Vehicle theft	136	100
Domestic violence	1,077	963
Arson	8	10
Total crime rate	27.4	23.5
Violent	3.3	2.6
Non-violent	24.1	20.8

Public School District

(for school year 2007-08 except as noted)

Lakewood Township School District
655 Princeton Avenue
Lakewood, NJ 08701
(732) 905-3633

Superintendent	Eugenia Lawson (Int)
Number of schools	6
Grade plan	K-12
Enrollment	5,459
Attendance rate, '06-07	92.6%
Dropout rate	3.0%
Students per teacher	9.6
Per pupil expenditure	$17,036
Median faculty salary	$46,610
Median administrator salary	$114,002
Grade 12 enrollment	258
High school graduation rate	43.6%

Assessment test results

(percent scoring at proficient or advanced level)

	Language	Math
NJASK-Grade 3	79.6%	71.3%
GEPA-Grade 8	33.1%	49.9%
HSPA-High School	48.4%	60.9%

SAT Score Averages, 2006-07

Pct tested	Math	Verbal	Writing
38%	457	432	433

Teacher Qualifications

Avg. years of experience	6

Highly-qualified teachers
one subject/all subjects	100%/100%

No Child Left Behind

AYP, 2006-07	Needs Improvement

Municipal Finance

State Aid Programs, 2009

Total aid	$6,493,591
CMPTRA	1,829,321
Energy tax receipts	4,534,167
Garden State Trust	221

General Budget, 2008

Total tax levy	$132,922,637
County levy	24,852,071
County taxes	20,492,962
County library	2,408,866
County health	980,771
County open space	969,473
School levy	68,414,642
Muni. levy	39,655,924
Misc. revenues	34,230,621

Taxes	2006	2007	2008
General tax rate per $100	1.518	1.603	1.691
County equalization ratio	111.97	99.73	97.28
Net valuation taxable	$7,520,812,300	$7,735,617,454	$7,862,217,200
State equalized value	$7,556,744,207	$7,951,462,176	$192,329,741

See Introduction for an explanation of all data sources.

Demographics & Socio-Economic Characteristics
(2000 US Census, except as noted)

Population
1980*	4,044
1990*	3,927
2000	3,868
Male	1,882
Female	1,986
2007 (estimate)*	3,744
Population density	3,313.3

Race & Hispanic Origin, 2000
Race
White	3,661
Black/African American	75
American Indian/Alaska Native	13
Asian	41
Native Hawaiian/Pacific Islander	2
Other race	35
Two or more races	41
Hispanic origin, total	120
Mexican	69
Puerto Rican	19
Cuban	5
Other Hispanic	27

Age & Nativity, 2000
Under 5 years	145
18 years and over	3,274
21 years and over	3,156
65 years and over	589
85 years and over	62
Median age	42.8
Native-born	3,671
Foreign-born	197

Educational Attainment, 2000
Population 25 years and over	3,082
Less than 9th grade	4.1%
High school grad or higher	87.9%
Bachelor's degree or higher	37.5%
Graduate degree	18.5%

Income & Poverty, 1999
Per capita income	$36,267
Median household income	$52,647
Median family income	$80,669
Persons in poverty	230
H'holds receiving public assistance	31
H'holds receiving social security	482

Households, 2000
Total households	1,860
With persons under 18	365
With persons over 65	445
Family households	940
Single-person households	721
Persons per household	2.06
Persons per family	2.82

Labor & Employment
Total civilian labor force, 2007**	2,811
Unemployment rate	3.2%
Total civilian labor force, 2000	2,509
Unemployment rate	2.4%

Employed persons 16 years and over by occupation, 2000
Managers & professionals	1,099
Service occupations	319
Sales & office occupations	614
Farming, fishing & forestry	13
Construction & maintenance	212
Production & transportation	192
Self-employed persons	251

General Information
City of Lambertville
18 York St
Lambertville, NJ 08530
609-397-0110

Website	www.lambertvillenj.org
Year of incorporation	1872
Land/water area (sq. miles)	1.13/0.12
Form of government	Small Municipality

Government
Legislative Districts
US Congressional	12
State Legislative	23

Local Officials, 2009
Mayor	David DelVecchio
Manager/Admin	NA
Clerk	Loretta Buckelew
Finance Dir	(vacant)
Tax Assessor	Richard Carmosino
Tax Collector	Bonnie Eick
Attorney	Phillip Faherty III
Building	Ken Rogers
Comm Dev/Planning	NA
Engineering	Robert J. Clerico
Public Works	Paul Cronce
Police Dir	Bruce Cocuzza
Emerg/Fire Director	Lester Myers

Housing & Construction
Housing Units, 2000*
Total	1,961
Median rent	$811
Median SF home value	$170,500

Permits for New Residential Construction
	Units	Value
Total, 2006	1	$168,635
Single family	1	$168,635
Total, 2007	17	$3,638,744
Single family	17	$3,638,744

Real Property Valuation, 2008
	Parcels	Valuation
Total	2,047	$735,332,762
Vacant	221	8,439,598
Residential	1,584	581,642,500
Commercial	184	111,086,000
Industrial	11	10,599,600
Apartments	35	22,099,500
Farm land	10	128,264
Farm homestead	2	1,337,300

Average Property Value & Tax, 2008
Residential value	$367,579
Property tax	$5,722
Tax credit/rebate	$934

Public Library
Lambertville Public Library
6 Lilly St
Lambertville, NJ 08530
609-397-0275

Director	Harold Dunn

Library statistics, 2007
Population served	3,868
Full-time/total staff	0/0

	Total	Per capita
Holdings	22,432	5.80
Revenues	$257,818	$66.65
Expenditures	$157,539	$40.73
Annual visits	22,975	5.94
Internet terminals/annual users		8/8,100

Public Safety
Number of officers, 2007	11

Crime	2006	2007
Total crimes	68	64
Violent	10	10
Murder	0	0
Rape	0	0
Robbery	2	2
Aggravated assault	8	8
Non-violent	58	54
Burglary	16	12
Larceny	41	41
Vehicle theft	1	1
Domestic violence	27	41
Arson	0	0
Total crime rate	17.7	16.8
Violent	2.6	2.6
Non-violent	15.1	14.2

Public School District
(for school year 2007-08 except as noted)

Lambertville School District
200 North Main Street
Lambertville, NJ 08530
(609) 397-0183

Chief School Admin	Todd Fay
Number of schools	1
Grade plan	K-6
Enrollment	151
Attendance rate, '06-07	96.2%
Dropout rate	NA
Students per teacher	8.2
Per pupil expenditure	$15,942
Median faculty salary	$67,810
Median administrator salary	$79,366
Grade 12 enrollment	NA
High school graduation rate	NA

Assessment test results
(percent scoring at proficient or advanced level)
	Language	Math
NJASK-Grade 3	96.1%	96.2%
GEPA-Grade 8	NA	NA
HSPA-High School	NA	NA

SAT Score Averages, 2006-07
Pct tested	Math	Verbal	Writing
NA	NA	NA	NA

Teacher Qualifications
Avg. years of experience	20
Highly-qualified teachers one subject/all subjects	100%/100%

No Child Left Behind
AYP, 2006-07	Meets Standards

Municipal Finance
State Aid Programs, 2009
Total aid	$565,031
CMPTRA	250,431
Energy tax receipts	291,790
Garden State Trust	120

General Budget, 2008
Total tax levy	$11,467,884
County levy	2,388,866
County taxes	2,156,101
County library	0
County health	0
County open space	232,765
School levy	7,453,230
Muni. levy	1,625,787
Misc. revenues	2,574,836

Taxes
	2006	2007	2008
General tax rate per $100	1.51	1.5	1.557
County equalization ratio	96.85	96.17	95.78
Net valuation taxable	$652,181,283	$719,369,163	$736,748,465
State equalized value	$734,220,003	$768,621,386	$792,521,418

* US Census Bureau
** New Jersey Department of Labor

See Introduction for an explanation of all data sources.

Demographics & Socio-Economic Characteristics

(2000 US Census, except as noted)

Population

1980*	2,249
1990*	2,341
2000	1,970
Male	983
Female	987
2007 (estimate)*	1,902
Population density	4,046.8

Race & Hispanic Origin, 2000

Race
White	1,859
Black/African American	54
American Indian/Alaska Native	5
Asian	19
Native Hawaiian/Pacific Islander	0
Other race	14
Two or more races	19
Hispanic origin, total	32
Mexican	4
Puerto Rican	10
Cuban	2
Other Hispanic	16

Age & Nativity, 2000

Under 5 years	106
18 years and over	1,495
21 years and over	1,411
65 years and over	281
85 years and over	22
Median age	36.9
Native-born	1,929
Foreign-born	41

Educational Attainment, 2000

Population 25 years and over	1,333
Less than 9th grade	2.7%
High school grad or higher	87.0%
Bachelor's degree or higher	22.5%
Graduate degree	6.7%

Income & Poverty, 1999

Per capita income	$23,254
Median household income	$52,500
Median family income	$58,854
Persons in poverty	72
H'holds receiving public assistance	10
H'holds receiving social security	242

Households, 2000

Total households	762
With persons under 18	262
With persons over 65	204
Family households	534
Single-person households	199
Persons per household	2.59
Persons per family	3.16

Labor & Employment

Total civilian labor force, 2007**	1,124
Unemployment rate	3.7%
Total civilian labor force, 2000	1,059
Unemployment rate	4.0%

Employed persons 16 years and over by occupation, 2000
Managers & professionals	359
Service occupations	150
Sales & office occupations	288
Farming, fishing & forestry	0
Construction & maintenance	95
Production & transportation	125
Self-employed persons	43

* US Census Bureau
** New Jersey Department of Labor

General Information

Borough of Laurel Springs
135 Broadway
Laurel Springs, NJ 08021
856-784-0500

Website	www.laurelsprings-nj.com
Year of incorporation	1913
Land/water area (sq. miles)	0.47/0.00
Form of government	Borough

Government

Legislative Districts

US Congressional	1
State Legislative	4

Local Officials, 2009

Mayor	Jack Severson
Manager/Admin	NA
Clerk	Barbara M. Hawk
Finance Dir	D. Ciminera
Tax Assessor	Richard Arrowood
Tax Collector	Janice M. Gattone
Attorney	George J. Botcheos
Building	Albert Hallworth
Planning	Eric Hafer
Engineering	Remington & Vernick
Public Works	Eric P. Warner
Police Chief	Michael Wolcott
Emerg/Fire Director	Ken Cheeseman

Housing & Construction

Housing Units, 2000*

Total	806
Median rent	$605
Median SF home value	$110,200

Permits for New Residential Construction

	Units	Value
Total, 2006	2	$301,284
Single family	2	$301,284
Total, 2007	2	$317,792
Single family	2	$317,792

Real Property Valuation, 2008

	Parcels	Valuation
Total	685	$78,760,800
Vacant	15	365,000
Residential	629	68,178,400
Commercial	38	8,377,100
Industrial	0	0
Apartments	3	1,840,300
Farm land	0	0
Farm homestead	0	0

Average Property Value & Tax, 2008

Residential value	$108,392
Property tax	$6,401
Tax credit/rebate	$1,037

Public Library

No public municipal library

Library statistics, 2007

Population served	NA
Full-time/total staff	NA/NA

	Total	Per capita
Holdings	NA	NA
Revenues	NA	NA
Expenditures	NA	NA
Annual visits	NA	NA
Internet terminals/annual users	NA/NA	

Public Safety

Number of officers, 2007 7

Crime	2006	2007
Total crimes	56	38
Violent	2	10
Murder	0	0
Rape	0	1
Robbery	0	2
Aggravated assault	2	7
Non-violent	54	28
Burglary	18	8
Larceny	35	18
Vehicle theft	1	2
Domestic violence	15	15
Arson	0	0
Total crime rate	28.9	19.8
Violent	1.0	5.2
Non-violent	27.8	14.6

Public School District

(for school year 2007-08 except as noted)

Laurel Springs School District
623 Grand Avenue
Laurel Springs, NJ 08021
(856) 783-1086

Superintendent	Albert Brown
Number of schools	1
Grade plan	K-6
Enrollment	162
Attendance rate, '06-07	95.5%
Dropout rate	NA
Students per teacher	11.6
Per pupil expenditure	$11,993
Median faculty salary	$46,701
Median administrator salary	$24,490
Grade 12 enrollment	NA
High school graduation rate	NA

Assessment test results

(percent scoring at proficient or advanced level)
	Language	Math
NJASK-Grade 3	100.0%	93.6%
GEPA-Grade 8	NA	NA
HSPA-High School	NA	NA

SAT Score Averages, 2006-07

Pct tested	Math	Verbal	Writing
NA	NA	NA	NA

Teacher Qualifications

Avg. years of experience	16
Highly-qualified teachers one subject/all subjects	100%/100%

No Child Left Behind

AYP, 2006-07 ....Meets Standards

Municipal Finance

State Aid Programs, 2009

Total aid	$391,347
CMPTRA	157,023
Energy tax receipts	228,453
Garden State Trust	0

General Budget, 2008

Total tax levy	$4,869,517
County levy	959,184
County taxes	866,865
County library	62,150
County health	0
County open space	30,170
School levy	2,540,220
Muni. levy	1,370,113
Misc. revenues	1,111,887

Taxes

	2006	2007	2008
General tax rate per $100	5.076	5.591	5.906
County equalization ratio	66.83	60.07	53.64
Net valuation taxable	$79,987,300	$82,550,551	$82,452,800
State equalized value	$137,605,448	$150,398,463	$155,184,210

See Introduction for an explanation of all data sources.

Demographics & Socio-Economic Characteristics
(2000 US Census, except as noted)

Population
1980*	2,072
1990*	2,299
2000	2,665
Male	1,220
Female	1,445
2007 (estimate)*	2,757
Population density	3,446.3

Race & Hispanic Origin, 2000
Race
White	2,615
Black/African American	7
American Indian/Alaska Native	3
Asian	4
Native Hawaiian/Pacific Islander	0
Other race	17
Two or more races	19
Hispanic origin, total	43
Mexican	19
Puerto Rican	3
Cuban	10
Other Hispanic	11

Age & Nativity, 2000
Under 5 years	89
18 years and over	2,316
21 years and over	2,250
65 years and over	970
85 years and over	162
Median age	56.4
Native-born	2,578
Foreign-born	87

Educational Attainment, 2000
Population 25 years and over	2,168
Less than 9th grade	5.1%
High school grad or higher	85.1%
Bachelor's degree or higher	26.5%
Graduate degree	10.7%

Income & Poverty, 1999
Per capita income	$28,588
Median household income	$43,846
Median family income	$57,778
Persons in poverty	201
H'holds receiving public assistance	34
H'holds receiving social security	613

Households, 2000
Total households	1,208
With persons under 18	197
With persons over 65	588
Family households	742
Single-person households	417
Persons per household	2.09
Persons per family	2.66

Labor & Employment
Total civilian labor force, 2007**	1,273
Unemployment rate	2.6%
Total civilian labor force, 2000	1,062
Unemployment rate	2.7%

Employed persons 16 years and over by occupation, 2000
Managers & professionals	417
Service occupations	101
Sales & office occupations	310
Farming, fishing & forestry	0
Construction & maintenance	128
Production & transportation	77
Self-employed persons	81

‡ Branch of county library
* US Census Bureau
** New Jersey Department of Labor

General Information
Borough of Lavallette
1306 Grand Central
PO Box 67
Lavallette, NJ 08735
732-793-7477

Website	lavallette.org
Year of incorporation	1887
Land/water area (sq. miles)	0.80/0.12
Form of government	Borough

Government
Legislative Districts
US Congressional	3
State Legislative	10

Local Officials, 2009
Mayor	Walter LaCicero
Manager	Christopher Parlow
Clerk	Christopher Parlow
Finance Dir	Michele Burk
Tax Assessor	Scott Pezarras
Tax Collector	Chrissa Sierfeld
Attorney	Philip George
Building	Hans Warnebold
Comm Dev/Planning	NA
Engineering	Mike O'Donnell
Public Works	Gary Schlosser
Police Chief	Colin Grant
Emerg/Fire Director	Peter Scott

Housing & Construction
Housing Units, 2000*
Total	3,210
Median rent	$786
Median SF home value	$323,100

Permits for New Residential Construction
	Units	Value
Total, 2006	14	$2,819,208
Single family	14	$2,819,208
Total, 2007	10	$1,921,188
Single family	10	$1,921,188

Real Property Valuation, 2008
	Parcels	Valuation
Total	2,675	$1,814,247,960
Vacant	75	40,821,600
Residential	2,514	1,726,353,800
Commercial	79	42,144,860
Industrial	0	0
Apartments	7	4,927,700
Farm land	0	0
Farm homestead	0	0

Average Property Value & Tax, 2008
Residential value	$686,696
Property tax	$5,784
Tax credit/rebate	$1,069

Public Library
Upper Shores Branch Library‡
112 Jersey City Ave
Lavallette, NJ 08735
732-793-3996

Branch Librarian	June Schneider

Library statistics, 2007
see Ocean County profile
for library system statistics

Public Safety
Number of officers, 2007	12

Crime	2006	2007
Total crimes	32	71
Violent	1	0
Murder	0	0
Rape	0	0
Robbery	0	0
Aggravated assault	1	0
Non-violent	31	71
Burglary	7	19
Larceny	24	52
Vehicle theft	0	0
Domestic violence	2	3
Arson	0	0
Total crime rate	11.6	25.8
Violent	0.4	0.0
Non-violent	11.3	25.8

Public School District
(for school year 2007-08 except as noted)

Lavallette Borough School District
105 Brooklyn Avenue
Lavallette, NJ 08735
(732) 793-7722

Superintendent	Peter Morris
Number of schools	1
Grade plan	K-8
Enrollment	148
Attendance rate, '06-07	93.9%
Dropout rate	NA
Students per teacher	7.7
Per pupil expenditure	$16,480
Median faculty salary	$45,494
Median administrator salary	$111,089
Grade 12 enrollment	NA
High school graduation rate	NA

Assessment test results
(percent scoring at proficient or advanced level)
	Language	Math
NJASK-Grade 3	100.0%	100.0%
GEPA-Grade 8	100.0%	100.0%
HSPA-High School	NA	NA

SAT Score Averages, 2006-07
Pct tested	Math	Verbal	Writing
NA	NA	NA	NA

Teacher Qualifications
Avg. years of experience	11
Highly-qualified teachers one subject/all subjects	100%/100%

No Child Left Behind
AYP, 2006-07	Meets Standards

Municipal Finance
State Aid Programs, 2009
Total aid	$193,246
CMPTRA	0
Energy tax receipts	184,550
Garden State Trust	0

General Budget, 2008
Total tax levy	$15,294,760
County levy	7,449,026
County taxes	6,142,695
County library	721,907
County health	293,917
County open space	290,506
School levy	3,173,373
Muni. levy	4,672,361
Misc. revenues	1,991,419

Taxes	2006	2007	2008
General tax rate per $100	0.754	0.797	0.843
County equalization ratio	93.72	80.48	75.20
Net valuation taxable	$1,785,831,960	$1,801,656,626	$1,815,938,286
State equalized value	$2,221,296,139	$2,395,159,594	$8,249,195,078

See Introduction for an explanation of all data sources.

Demographics & Socio-Economic Characteristics
(2000 US Census, except as noted)

Population
1980*	3,042
1990*	2,841
2000	2,692
Male	1,224
Female	1,468
2007 (estimate)*	2,814
Population density	2,010.0

Race & Hispanic Origin, 2000
Race
White	47
Black/African American	2,520
American Indian/Alaska Native	27
Asian	14
Native Hawaiian/Pacific Islander	2
Other race	13
Two or more races	69
Hispanic origin, total	64
Mexican	8
Puerto Rican	40
Cuban	3
Other Hispanic	13

Age & Nativity, 2000
Under 5 years	108
18 years and over	2,065
21 years and over	1,968
65 years and over	507
85 years and over	59
Median age	42.4
Native-born	2,561
Foreign-born	163

Educational Attainment, 2000
Population 25 years and over	1,856
Less than 9th grade	6.8%
High school grad or higher	79.0%
Bachelor's degree or higher	18.8%
Graduate degree	7.0%

Income & Poverty, 1999
Per capita income	$18,831
Median household income	$45,192
Median family income	$55,197
Persons in poverty	289
H'holds receiving public assistance	48
H'holds receiving social security	419

Households, 2000
Total households	1,026
With persons under 18	331
With persons over 65	396
Family households	701
Single-person households	291
Persons per household	2.62
Persons per family	3.23

Labor & Employment
Total civilian labor force, 2007**	1,441
Unemployment rate	7.2%
Total civilian labor force, 2000	1,356
Unemployment rate	7.2%

Employed persons 16 years and over by occupation, 2000
Managers & professionals	392
Service occupations	225
Sales & office occupations	405
Farming, fishing & forestry	0
Construction & maintenance	41
Production & transportation	195
Self-employed persons	26

* US Census Bureau
** New Jersey Department of Labor
§ State Fiscal Year July 1–June 30

General Information
Borough of Lawnside
4 N Douglas Ave
Lawnside, NJ 08045
856-573-6200
Website	www.lawnsidenj.org
Year of incorporation	1926
Land/water area (sq. miles)	1.40/0.00
Form of government	Borough

Government
Legislative Districts
US Congressional	1
State Legislative	5

Local Officials, 2009
Mayor	Mark Bryant
Manager	Dwight Wilson
Clerk	Sylvia VanNockay
Finance Dir	John A. Bruno Jr
Tax Assessor	Thomas Colavecchio
Tax Collector	Jessie Harris
Attorney	Allen Zeller
Building	Mengste Thomas El
Comm Dev/Planning	NA
Engineering	SmithCo Group
Public Works	Alex Barr
Public Safety Dir	John Cunningham
Fire Chief	Michael Harper

Housing & Construction
Housing Units, 2000*
Total	1,110
Median rent	$566
Median SF home value	$99,900

Permits for New Residential Construction
	Units	Value
Total, 2006	20	$4,448,900
Single family	20	$4,448,900
Total, 2007	6	$1,218,300
Single family	6	$1,218,300

Real Property Valuation, 2008
	Parcels	Valuation
Total	1,282	$160,481,000
Vacant	219	2,924,000
Residential	994	102,282,000
Commercial	62	39,830,200
Industrial	2	12,203,200
Apartments	5	3,241,600
Farm land	0	0
Farm homestead	0	0

Average Property Value & Tax, 2008
Residential value	$102,899
Property tax	$4,613
Tax credit/rebate	$945

Public Library
No public municipal library

Library statistics, 2007
Population served	NA
Full-time/total staff	NA/NA

	Total	Per capita
Holdings	NA	NA
Revenues	NA	NA
Expenditures	NA	NA
Annual visits	NA	NA
Internet terminals/annual users	NA/NA	

Public Safety
Number of officers, 2007	7

Crime	2006	2007
Total crimes	117	120
Violent	15	23
Murder	0	0
Rape	0	2
Robbery	4	6
Aggravated assault	11	15
Non-violent	102	97
Burglary	13	9
Larceny	88	85
Vehicle theft	1	3
Domestic violence	3	4
Arson	1	0
Total crime rate	42.1	42.9
Violent	5.4	8.2
Non-violent	36.7	34.6

Public School District
(for school year 2007-08 except as noted)

Lawnside Borough School District
426 Charleston Avenue
Lawnside, NJ 08045
(856) 546-4850
Superintendent	Patricia Montgomery (Int)
Number of schools	1
Grade plan	K-8
Enrollment	297
Attendance rate, '06-07	95.1%
Dropout rate	NA
Students per teacher	9.9
Per pupil expenditure	$14,436
Median faculty salary	$56,200
Median administrator salary	$83,550
Grade 12 enrollment	NA
High school graduation rate	NA

Assessment test results
(percent scoring at proficient or advanced level)
	Language	Math
NJASK-Grade 3	75.0%	71.9%
GEPA-Grade 8	48.9%	67.4%
HSPA-High School	NA	NA

SAT Score Averages, 2006-07
Pct tested	Math	Verbal	Writing
NA	NA	NA	NA

Teacher Qualifications
Avg. years of experience	12
Highly-qualified teachers one subject/all subjects	100%/100%

No Child Left Behind
AYP, 2006-07	Meets Standards

Municipal Finance§
State Aid Programs, 2009
Total aid	$685,803
CMPTRA	0
Energy tax receipts	668,658
Garden State Trust	0

General Budget, 2008
Total tax levy	$7,205,636
County levy	1,580,511
County taxes	1,427,976
County library	102,687
County health	0
County open space	49,848
School levy	4,116,241
Muni. levy	1,508,884
Misc. revenues	2,809,000

Taxes	2006	2007	2008
General tax rate per $100	4.005	4.237	4.484
County equalization ratio	76.68	74.96	64.81
Net valuation taxable	$147,697,000	$154,372,482	$160,728,433
State equalized value	$197,228,657	$238,077,281	$256,361,381

See Introduction for an explanation of all data sources.

Demographics & Socio-Economic Characteristics
(2000 US Census, except as noted)

Population
1980*	2,166
1990*	2,433
2000	2,721
Male	1,356
Female	1,365
2007 (estimate)*	2,979
Population density	79.5

Race & Hispanic Origin, 2000
Race
White	2,228
Black/African American	283
American Indian/Alaska Native	29
Asian	7
Native Hawaiian/Pacific Islander	5
Other race	93
Two or more races	76
Hispanic origin, total	191
Mexican	77
Puerto Rican	79
Cuban	2
Other Hispanic	33

Age & Nativity, 2000
Under 5 years	168
18 years and over	1,946
21 years and over	1,854
65 years and over	287
85 years and over	21
Median age	35.7
Native-born	2,613
Foreign-born	108

Educational Attainment, 2000
Population 25 years and over	1,801
Less than 9th grade	7.9%
High school grad or higher	75.2%
Bachelor's degree or higher	11.0%
Graduate degree	2.7%

Income & Poverty, 1999
Per capita income	$17,654
Median household income	$46,083
Median family income	$48,456
Persons in poverty	242
H'holds receiving public assistance	36
H'holds receiving social security	291

Households, 2000
Total households	920
With persons under 18	402
With persons over 65	228
Family households	712
Single-person households	164
Persons per household	2.90
Persons per family	3.27

Labor & Employment
Total civilian labor force, 2007**	1,344
Unemployment rate	5.5%
Total civilian labor force, 2000	1,276
Unemployment rate	8.4%

Employed persons 16 years and over by occupation, 2000
Managers & professionals	249
Service occupations	163
Sales & office occupations	246
Farming, fishing & forestry	12
Construction & maintenance	183
Production & transportation	316
Self-employed persons	99

General Information
Township of Lawrence
357 Main St
Cedarville, NJ 08311
856-447-4554
Email	lawrencemayor@comcast.net
Year of incorporation	1885
Land/water area (sq. miles)	37.47/0.98
Form of government	Township

Government
Legislative Districts
US Congressional	2
State Legislative	3

Local Officials, 2009
Mayor	Thomas Sheppard
Manager/Admin	NA
Clerk	Ruth Dawson
Finance Dir	Teresa Delp
Tax Assessor	Donald Seifrit
Tax Collector	Ruth Dawson
Attorney	Tom Seeley
Building	David Dean
Comm Dev/Planning	NA
Engineering	Stephen Nardelli Jr
Public Works	Michael Day
Police Chief	NA
Emerg/Fire Director	Brian Scarlato

Housing & Construction
Housing Units, 2000*
Total	1,023
Median rent	$680
Median SF home value	$91,500

Permits for New Residential Construction
	Units	Value
Total, 2006	13	$1,559,500
Single family	13	$1,559,500
Total, 2007	7	$733,000
Single family	7	$733,000

Real Property Valuation, 2008
	Parcels	Valuation
Total	3,282	$116,982,600
Vacant	1,838	7,933,500
Residential	1,108	93,435,500
Commercial	32	2,982,500
Industrial	2	2,273,800
Apartments	1	80,000
Farm land	187	1,212,700
Farm homestead	114	9,064,600

Average Property Value & Tax, 2008
Residential value	$83,879
Property tax	$3,363
Tax credit/rebate	$781

Public Library
No public municipal library

Library statistics, 2007
Population served	NA
Full-time/total staff	NA/NA

	Total	Per capita
Holdings	NA	NA
Revenues	NA	NA
Expenditures	NA	NA
Annual visits	NA	NA
Internet terminals/annual users	NA/NA	

Public Safety
Number of officers, 2007 0

Crime	2006	2007
Total crimes	84	60
Violent	9	14
Murder	0	0
Rape	1	1
Robbery	0	1
Aggravated assault	8	12
Non-violent	75	46
Burglary	23	26
Larceny	46	17
Vehicle theft	6	3
Domestic violence	11	26
Arson	0	0
Total crime rate	29.2	20.4
Violent	3.1	4.8
Non-violent	26.0	15.6

Public School District
(for school year 2007-08 except as noted)

Lawrence Township School District
225 Main Street
Cedarville, NJ 08311
(856) 447-4237
Principal/Chief School Admin	Ralph Scazafabo
Number of schools	1
Grade plan	K-8
Enrollment	452
Attendance rate, '06-07	95.2%
Dropout rate	NA
Students per teacher	11.3
Per pupil expenditure	$11,547
Median faculty salary	$51,436
Median administrator salary	$76,212
Grade 12 enrollment	NA
High school graduation rate	NA

Assessment test results
(percent scoring at proficient or advanced level)
	Language	Math
NJASK-Grade 3	90.0%	82.5%
GEPA-Grade 8	57.4%	77.4%
HSPA-High School	NA	NA

SAT Score Averages, 2006-07
Pct tested	Math	Verbal	Writing
NA	NA	NA	NA

Teacher Qualifications
Avg. years of experience	10
Highly-qualified teachers one subject/all subjects	97.0%/97.0%

No Child Left Behind
AYP, 2006-07 .... Meets Standards

Municipal Finance
State Aid Programs, 2009
Total aid	$395,956
CMPTRA	64,272
Energy tax receipts	219,683
Garden State Trust	91,711

General Budget, 2008
Total tax levy	$4,722,246
County levy	2,023,202
County taxes	1,912,257
County library	0
County health	89,620
County open space	21,325
School levy	1,956,985
Muni. levy	742,060
Misc. revenues	1,392,832

Taxes
	2006	2007	2008
General tax rate per $100	3.683	3.806	4.013
County equalization ratio	74.04	63.09	55.38
Net valuation taxable	$110,364,000	$115,535,323	$117,779,054
State equalized value	$175,878,864	$207,925,634	$226,413,812

* US Census Bureau
** New Jersey Department of Labor

254   **The New Jersey Municipal Data Book**   See Introduction for an explanation of all data sources.

Demographics & Socio-Economic Characteristics

(2000 US Census, except as noted)

Population

1980*	19,724
1990*	25,787
2000	29,159
Male	13,650
Female	15,509
2007 (estimate)*	31,863
Population density	1,439.2

Race & Hispanic Origin, 2000

Race

White	23,101
Black/African American	2,707
American Indian/Alaska Native	23
Asian	2,306
Native Hawaiian/Pacific Islander	31
Other race	523
Two or more races	468
Hispanic origin, total	1,344
Mexican	180
Puerto Rican	365
Cuban	42
Other Hispanic	757

Age & Nativity, 2000

Under 5 years	1,678
18 years and over	22,836
21 years and over	20,879
65 years and over	3,953
85 years and over	524
Median age	36.7
Native-born	24,062
Foreign-born	5,097

Educational Attainment, 2000

Population 25 years and over	19,151
Less than 9th grade	3.7%
High school grad or higher	89.2%
Bachelor's degree or higher	50.5%
Graduate degree	24.0%

Income & Poverty, 1999

Per capita income	$33,120
Median household income	$67,959
Median family income	$82,704
Persons in poverty	1,311
H'holds receiving public assistance	100
H'holds receiving social security	2,771

Households, 2000

Total households	10,797
With persons under 18	3,595
With persons over 65	2,724
Family households	7,239
Single-person households	2,892
Persons per household	2.49
Persons per family	3.05

Labor & Employment

Total civilian labor force, 2007**	18,148
Unemployment rate	2.7%
Total civilian labor force, 2000	16,554
Unemployment rate	10.0%

Employed persons 16 years and over by occupation, 2000

Managers & professionals	8,020
Service occupations	1,571
Sales & office occupations	3,748
Farming, fishing & forestry	0
Construction & maintenance	673
Production & transportation	884
Self-employed persons	826

‡ Main library for county
* US Census Bureau
** New Jersey Department of Labor

General Information

Township of Lawrence
2207 Lawrenceville Rd
PO Box 6006
Lawrenceville, NJ 08648
609-844-7000

Website	www.lawrencetwp.com
Year of incorporation	1816
Land/water area (sq. miles)	22.14/0.04
Form of government	Council-Manager

Government

Legislative Districts

US Congressional	12
State Legislative	15

Local Officials, 2009

Mayor	Pamela H Mount
Manager	Richard Krawczun
Clerk	Kathleen S Norcia
Finance Dir	Richard S Krawczun
Tax Assessor	Geoffrey Acolia
Tax Collector	Alice W Fish
Attorney	Kevin P Nerwenski
Building	Anthony Cermele
Comm Dev/Planning	NA
Engineering	James Parvesse
Public Works	Greg Whitehead
Police Chief	Daniel Posluszny
Fire/Emergency Dir	NA

Housing & Construction

Housing Units, 2000*

Total	11,180
Median rent	$935
Median SF home value	$177,900

Permits for New Residential Construction

	Units	Value
Total, 2006	55	$6,471,852
Single family	55	$6,471,852
Total, 2007	19	$5,517,480
Single family	19	$5,517,480

Real Property Valuation, 2008

	Parcels	Valuation
Total	11,151	$2,688,024,423
Vacant	743	43,404,500
Residential	9,814	1,616,593,450
Commercial	407	837,686,073
Industrial	36	45,244,100
Apartments	20	128,828,700
Farm land	85	627,000
Farm homestead	46	15,640,600

Average Property Value & Tax, 2008

Residential value	$165,541
Property tax	$6,629
Tax credit/rebate	$989

Public Library

Mercer County Library‡
2751 Brunswick Pike
Lawrenceville, NJ 08648
609-689-6916

Director	Ellen Brown

County Library statistics, 2007

Population served	143,288
Full-time/total staff	47/116

	Total	Per capita
Holdings	756,413	5.28
Revenues	$11,562,328	$80.69
Expenditures	$11,562,328	$80.69
Annual visits	1,152,065	8.04
Internet terminals/annual users	123/741,103	

Public Safety

Number of officers, 2007	69

Crime	2006	2007
Total crimes	1,074	935
Violent	50	54
Murder	0	0
Rape	2	12
Robbery	27	21
Aggravated assault	21	21
Non-violent	1,024	881
Burglary	128	96
Larceny	849	733
Vehicle theft	47	52
Domestic violence	198	208
Arson	7	4
Total crime rate	34.2	29.1
Violent	1.6	1.7
Non-violent	32.6	27.5

Public School District

(for school year 2007-08 except as noted)

Lawrence Township School District
2565 Princeton Pike
Lawrenceville, NJ 08648
(609) 671-5405

Chief School Admin	Philip J. Meara
Number of schools	7
Grade plan	K-12
Enrollment	3,928
Attendance rate, '06-07	95.1%
Dropout rate	0.2%
Students per teacher	9.7
Per pupil expenditure	$16,139
Median faculty salary	$53,475
Median administrator salary	$123,161
Grade 12 enrollment	302
High school graduation rate	97.4%

Assessment test results

(percent scoring at proficient or advanced level)

	Language	Math
NJASK-Grade 3	88.4%	92.1%
GEPA-Grade 8	69.2%	86.7%
HSPA-High School	68.9%	84.5%

SAT Score Averages, 2006-07

Pct tested	Math	Verbal	Writing
90%	527	507	500

Teacher Qualifications

Avg. years of experience	10
Highly-qualified teachers one subject/all subjects	100%/100%

No Child Left Behind

AYP, 2006-07	Meets Standards

Municipal Finance

State Aid Programs, 2009

Total aid	$5,131,642
CMPTRA	487,610
Energy tax receipts	4,511,527
Garden State Trust	9,797

General Budget, 2008

Total tax levy	$107,773,918
County levy	28,833,786
County taxes	24,662,415
County library	2,478,597
County health	0
County open space	1,692,774
School levy	59,024,914
Muni. levy	19,915,218
Misc. revenues	20,735,645

Taxes	2006	2007	2008
General tax rate per $100	3.65	3.8	4.005
County equalization ratio	60.67	53.15	47.88
Net valuation taxable	$2,681,365,023	$2,695,162,162	$2,691,265,288
State equalized value	$5,048,432,000	$5,625,236,030	$5,668,202,768

See Introduction for an explanation of all data sources.

Demographics & Socio-Economic Characteristics

(2000 US Census, except as noted)

Population

1980*	.820
1990*	1,036
2000	1,065
Male	511
Female	554
2007 (estimate)*	1,896
Population density	2,179.3

Race & Hispanic Origin, 2000

Race

White	1,016
Black/African American	7
American Indian/Alaska Native	2
Asian	33
Native Hawaiian/Pacific Islander	0
Other race	4
Two or more races	3
Hispanic origin, total	22
Mexican	4
Puerto Rican	14
Cuban	1
Other Hispanic	3

Age & Nativity, 2000

Under 5 years	81
18 years and over	808
21 years and over	786
65 years and over	124
85 years and over	13
Median age	39.3
Native-born	997
Foreign-born	68

Educational Attainment, 2000

Population 25 years and over	764
Less than 9th grade	1.4%
High school grad or higher	93.2%
Bachelor's degree or higher	39.7%
Graduate degree	13.2%

Income & Poverty, 1999

Per capita income	$34,066
Median household income	$68,542
Median family income	$83,436
Persons in poverty	38
H'holds receiving public assistance	4
H'holds receiving social security	90

Households, 2000

Total households	458
With persons under 18	147
With persons over 65	96
Family households	287
Single-person households	151
Persons per household	2.33
Persons per family	2.97

Labor & Employment

Total civilian labor force, 2007**	750
Unemployment rate	5.2%
Total civilian labor force, 2000	657
Unemployment rate	3.8%

Employed persons 16 years and over by occupation, 2000

Managers & professionals	270
Service occupations	54
Sales & office occupations	206
Farming, fishing & forestry	0
Construction & maintenance	54
Production & transportation	48
Self-employed persons	42

General Information

Borough of Lebanon
6 High St
Lebanon, NJ 08833
908-236-2425

Website	www.lebanonboro.com
Year of incorporation	1926
Land/water area (sq. miles)	0.87/0.00
Form of government	Borough

Government

Legislative Districts

US Congressional	7
State Legislative	23

Local Officials, 2009

Mayor	Mark E. Paradis
Manager/Admin	NA
Clerk	Karen Romano
Finance Dir	Kay Winzenried
Tax Assessor	Curtis Schick
Tax Collector	Kay Winzenried
Attorney	Joseph Novak
Building	NA
Planning	Karen Romano
Engineering	Paul Ferriero
Public Works	NA
Police Chief	NA
Emerg/Fire Director	Albert Bross IV

Housing & Construction

Housing Units, 2000*

Total	477
Median rent	$969
Median SF home value	$168,100

Permits for New Residential Construction

	Units	Value
Total, 2006	46	$1,917,746
Single family	46	$1,917,746
Total, 2007	35	$1,447,135
Single family	35	$1,447,135

Real Property Valuation, 2008

	Parcels	Valuation
Total	671	$329,710,324
Vacant	102	22,244,800
Residential	498	182,402,100
Commercial	57	105,616,600
Industrial	6	17,298,000
Apartments	1	1,301,000
Farm land	6	5,824
Farm homestead	1	842,000

Average Property Value & Tax, 2008

Residential value	$367,223
Property tax	$5,735
Tax credit/rebate	$950

Public Library

No public municipal library

Library statistics, 2007

Population served	NA
Full-time/total staff	NA/NA

	Total	Per capita
Holdings	NA	NA
Revenues	NA	NA
Expenditures	NA	NA
Annual visits	NA	NA
Internet terminals/annual users	NA/NA	

Public Safety

Number of officers, 2007	0

Crime	2006	2007
Total crimes	21	30
Violent	1	0
Murder	0	0
Rape	0	0
Robbery	1	0
Aggravated assault	0	0
Non-violent	20	30
Burglary	3	6
Larceny	14	21
Vehicle theft	3	3
Domestic violence	2	3
Arson	0	0
Total crime rate	12.0	16.4
Violent	0.6	0.0
Non-violent	11.4	16.4

Public School District

(for school year 2007-08 except as noted)

Lebanon Borough School District
6 Maple Street
Lebanon, NJ 08833
(908) 236-2448

Superintendent	Dominic Costanzo (Int)
Number of schools	1
Grade plan	K-6
Enrollment	80
Attendance rate, '06-07	96.6%
Dropout rate	NA
Students per teacher	6.3
Per pupil expenditure	$21,123
Median faculty salary	$46,347
Median administrator salary	$60,633
Grade 12 enrollment	NA
High school graduation rate	NA

Assessment test results

(percent scoring at proficient or advanced level)

	Language	Math
NJASK-Grade 3	NA	NA
GEPA-Grade 8	NA	NA
HSPA-High School	NA	NA

SAT Score Averages, 2006-07

Pct tested	Math	Verbal	Writing
NA	NA	NA	NA

Teacher Qualifications

Avg. years of experience	7
Highly-qualified teachers one subject/all subjects	100%/100%

No Child Left Behind

AYP, 2006-07	Meets Standards

Municipal Finance

State Aid Programs, 2009

Total aid	$124,939
CMPTRA	7,205
Energy tax receipts	112,737
Garden State Trust	0

General Budget, 2008

Total tax levy	$5,170,078
County levy	1,068,344
County taxes	894,176
County library	77,642
County health	0
County open space	96,526
School levy	3,499,920
Muni. levy	601,814
Misc. revenues	1,029,954

Taxes	2006	2007	2008
General tax rate per $100	3.05	1.54	1.562
County equalization ratio	51.52	96.5	103.03
Net valuation taxable	$166,822,064	$343,851,747	$331,061,266
State equalized value	$308,114,103	$322,136,886	$326,220,707

* US Census Bureau
** New Jersey Department of Labor

Demographics & Socio-Economic Characteristics
(2000 US Census, except as noted)

Population
1980*	5,459
1990*	5,679
2000	5,816
Male	2,869
Female	2,947
2007 (estimate)*	6,209
Population density	195.9

Race & Hispanic Origin, 2000
Race
White	5,640
Black/African American	47
American Indian/Alaska Native	6
Asian	54
Native Hawaiian/Pacific Islander	1
Other race	22
Two or more races	46
Hispanic origin, total	100
Mexican	18
Puerto Rican	27
Cuban	9
Other Hispanic	46

Age & Nativity, 2000
Under 5 years	352
18 years and over	4,332
21 years and over	4,180
65 years and over	680
85 years and over	100
Median age	40.3
Native-born	5,639
Foreign-born	177

Educational Attainment, 2000
Population 25 years and over	4,028
Less than 9th grade	1.4%
High school grad or higher	94.1%
Bachelor's degree or higher	37.0%
Graduate degree	12.7%

Income & Poverty, 1999
Per capita income	$30,793
Median household income	$77,662
Median family income	$86,145
Persons in poverty	112
H'holds receiving public assistance	22
H'holds receiving social security	400

Households, 2000
Total households	1,963
With persons under 18	791
With persons over 65	354
Family households	1,556
Single-person households	305
Persons per household	2.79
Persons per family	3.15

Labor & Employment
Total civilian labor force, 2007**	3,603
Unemployment rate	5.4%
Total civilian labor force, 2000	3,213
Unemployment rate	4.5%

Employed persons 16 years and over by occupation, 2000
Managers & professionals	1,344
Service occupations	305
Sales & office occupations	788
Farming, fishing & forestry	12
Construction & maintenance	323
Production & transportation	296
Self-employed persons	222

General Information
Lebanon Township
530 W Hill Rd
Glen Gardner, NJ 08826
908-638-8523
Website	www.lebanontownship.net
Year of incorporation	1731
Land/water area (sq. miles)	31.69/0.04
Form of government	Township

Government
Legislative Districts
US Congressional	7
State Legislative	23

Local Officials, 2009
Mayor	Patricia Schriver
Manager/Admin	NA
Clerk	Karen J. Sandorse
Finance Dir	Gregory Della Pia
Tax Assessor	Mary Mastro
Tax Collector	Mary Hyland
Attorney	Eric Bernstein
Building	NA
Comm Dev/Planning	NA
Engineering	Steve Risse
Public Works	Paul R. Jones
Police Chief	Chris Mattson
Emerg/Fire Director	Warren Gadriel

Housing & Construction
Housing Units, 2000*
Total	2,020
Median rent	$871
Median SF home value	$233,400

Permits for New Residential Construction
	Units	Value
Total, 2006	9	$3,030,770
Single family	9	$3,030,770
Total, 2007	4	$658,036
Single family	4	$658,036

Real Property Valuation, 2008
	Parcels	Valuation
Total	2,810	$750,902,310
Vacant	186	11,955,500
Residential	2,036	621,807,400
Commercial	69	33,751,300
Industrial	6	4,441,300
Apartments	4	2,197,100
Farm land	295	2,020,910
Farm homestead	214	74,728,800

Average Property Value & Tax, 2008
Residential value	$309,572
Property tax	$8,249
Tax credit/rebate	$1,217

Public Library
Bunnvale Library‡
3 Bunnvale Rd
Califon, NJ 07830
908-638-8884
Branch Librarian	Maria Taluba

Library statistics, 2007
see Hunterdon County profile
for library system statistics

Public Safety
Number of officers, 2007	8

Crime	2006	2007
Total crimes	58	48
Violent	1	1
Murder	0	0
Rape	0	0
Robbery	0	0
Aggravated assault	1	1
Non-violent	57	47
Burglary	17	15
Larceny	34	31
Vehicle theft	6	1
Domestic violence	23	36
Arson	0	0
Total crime rate	9.2	7.6
Violent	0.2	0.2
Non-violent	9.0	7.5

Public School District
(for school year 2007-08 except as noted)

Lebanon Township School District
70 Bunnvale Road
Califon, NJ 07830
(908) 638-4521
Superintendent	Judith Burd
Number of schools	2
Grade plan	K-8
Enrollment	833
Attendance rate, '06-07	96.3%
Dropout rate	NA
Students per teacher	9.8
Per pupil expenditure	$15,232
Median faculty salary	$50,460
Median administrator salary	$104,587
Grade 12 enrollment	NA
High school graduation rate	NA

Assessment test results
(percent scoring at proficient or advanced level)
	Language	Math
NJASK-Grade 3	95.1%	96.3%
GEPA-Grade 8	89.6%	93.1%
HSPA-High School	NA	NA

SAT Score Averages, 2006-07
Pct tested	Math	Verbal	Writing
NA	NA	NA	NA

Teacher Qualifications
Avg. years of experience	12

Highly-qualified teachers
one subject/all subjects	100%/100%

No Child Left Behind
AYP, 2006-07	Meets Standards

Municipal Finance
State Aid Programs, 2009
Total aid	$2,919,053
CMPTRA	0
Energy tax receipts	2,774,458
Garden State Trust	25,678

General Budget, 2008
Total tax levy	$20,036,114
County levy	3,761,830
County taxes	3,148,511
County library	273,416
County health	0
County open space	339,903
School levy	15,710,948
Muni. levy	563,336
Misc. revenues	4,275,532

Taxes	2006	2007	2008
General tax rate per $100	2.64	2.67	2.665
County equalization ratio	71.15	65.5	66.57
Net valuation taxable	$739,744,421	$748,039,373	$751,918,782
State equalized value	$1,051,310,156	$1,091,515,762	$1,088,650,177

‡ Branch of county library
* US Census Bureau
** New Jersey Department of Labor

See Introduction for an explanation of all data sources.

Demographics & Socio-Economic Characteristics

(2000 US Census, except as noted)

Population
1980*	8,027
1990*	8,365
2000	8,914
Male	4,289
Female	4,625
2007 (estimate)*	8,674
Population density	5,744.4

Race & Hispanic Origin, 2000
Race
White	5,860
Black/African American	202
American Indian/Alaska Native	8
Asian	2,323
Native Hawaiian/Pacific Islander	1
Other race	285
Two or more races	235
Hispanic origin, total	1,135
Mexican	44
Puerto Rican	171
Cuban	204
Other Hispanic	716

Age & Nativity, 2000
Under 5 years	513
18 years and over	6,725
21 years and over	6,484
65 years and over	1,223
85 years and over	155
Median age	39.9
Native-born	5,719
Foreign-born	3,195

Educational Attainment, 2000
Population 25 years and over	6,221
Less than 9th grade	2.4%
High school grad or higher	92.7%
Bachelor's degree or higher	49.9%
Graduate degree	20.4%

Income & Poverty, 1999
Per capita income	$35,352
Median household income	$72,440
Median family income	$84,591
Persons in poverty	574
H'holds receiving public assistance	37
H'holds receiving social security	872

Households, 2000
Total households	3,271
With persons under 18	1,257
With persons over 65	915
Family households	2,437
Single-person households	722
Persons per household	2.72
Persons per family	3.20

Labor & Employment
Total civilian labor force, 2007**	4,967
Unemployment rate	2.5%
Total civilian labor force, 2000	4,700
Unemployment rate	2.7%

Employed persons 16 years and over by occupation, 2000
Managers & professionals	2,335
Service occupations	499
Sales & office occupations	1,209
Farming, fishing & forestry	18
Construction & maintenance	212
Production & transportation	299
Self-employed persons	413

General Information

Borough of Leonia
312 Broad Ave
Leonia, NJ 07605
201-592-5780

Website	www.leonianj.gov
Year of incorporation	1894
Land/water area (sq. miles)	1.51/0.12
Form of government	Borough

Government

Legislative Districts
US Congressional	9
State Legislative	37

Local Officials, 2009
Mayor	Mary Heveran
Manager	Jack Terhune
Clerk	Fran Lehmann
Finance Dir	Myrna Becker
Tax Assessor	Tim Henderson
Tax Collector	Mike Apicella
Attorney	Brian T. Giblin
Building	Jack Peters
Comm Dev/Planning	NA
Engineering	Katherine Elliott
Public Works	Tony Saitta
Police Chief	Jay Ziegler
Emerg/Fire Director	Ron Chace

Housing & Construction

Housing Units, 2000*
Total	3,343
Median rent	$892
Median SF home value	$282,500

Permits for New Residential Construction
	Units	Value
Total, 2006	3	$852,100
Single family	3	$852,100
Total, 2007	5	$1,399,999
Single family	5	$1,399,999

Real Property Valuation, 2008
	Parcels	Valuation
Total	2,583	$714,701,400
Vacant	48	4,481,500
Residential	2,442	623,853,900
Commercial	58	38,495,900
Industrial	5	13,685,700
Apartments	30	34,184,400
Farm land	0	0
Farm homestead	0	0

Average Property Value & Tax, 2008
Residential value	$255,468
Property tax	$10,128
Tax credit/rebate	$1,370

Public Library

Leonia Public Library
227 Fort Lee Rd
Leonia, NJ 07605
201-592-5770

Director	Deborah Bigelow

Library statistics, 2007
Population served	8,914
Full-time/total staff	3/10

	Total	Per capita
Holdings	47,917	5.38
Revenues	$841,305	$94.38
Expenditures	$854,289	$95.84
Annual visits	160,922	18.05
Internet terminals/annual users	6/24,922	

Public Safety

Number of officers, 2007	19

Crime	2006	2007
Total crimes	86	99
Violent	4	10
Murder	0	0
Rape	0	0
Robbery	2	4
Aggravated assault	2	6
Non-violent	82	89
Burglary	24	16
Larceny	54	69
Vehicle theft	4	4
Domestic violence	18	11
Arson	2	0
Total crime rate	9.7	11.3
Violent	0.5	1.1
Non-violent	9.3	10.1

Public School District

(for school year 2007-08 except as noted)

Leonia School District
570 Grand Avenue
Leonia, NJ 07605
(201) 302-5200

Superinendent	Bernard Josefsberg
Number of schools	3
Grade plan	K-12
Enrollment	1,724
Attendance rate, '06-07	95.4%
Dropout rate	0.6%
Students per teacher	8.9
Per pupil expenditure	$13,477
Median faculty salary	$48,455
Median administrator salary	$118,000
Grade 12 enrollment	162
High school graduation rate	97.5%

Assessment test results
(percent scoring at proficient or advanced level)
	Language	Math
NJASK-Grade 3	93.2%	90.9%
GEPA-Grade 8	77.1%	87.8%
HSPA-High School	75.3%	78.9%

SAT Score Averages, 2006-07
Pct tested	Math	Verbal	Writing
92%	538	508	505

Teacher Qualifications
Avg. years of experience	8
Highly-qualified teachers one subject/all subjects	100%/100%

No Child Left Behind
AYP, 2006-07	Meets Standards

Municipal Finance

State Aid Programs, 2009
Total aid	$1,327,195
CMPTRA	0
Energy tax receipts	1,294,015
Garden State Trust	0

General Budget, 2008
Total tax levy	$28,353,475
County levy	2,828,249
County taxes	2,675,072
County library	0
County health	0
County open space	153,176
School levy	16,343,007
Muni. levy	9,182,219
Misc. revenues	3,214,983

Taxes	2006	2007	2008
General tax rate per $100	3.59	3.8	3.966
County equalization ratio	54.1	47.79	46.76
Net valuation taxable	$716,961,000	$715,534,888	$715,216,769
State equalized value	$1,500,763,043	$1,529,692,786	$1,613,108,781

* US Census Bureau
** New Jersey Department of Labor

See Introduction for an explanation of all data sources.

Demographics & Socio-Economic Characteristics

(2000 US Census, except as noted)

Population

1980*	1,730
1990*	2,493
2000	2,765
Male	1,373
Female	1,392
2007 (estimate)*	2,919
Population density	247.4

Race & Hispanic Origin, 2000

Race

White	2,693
Black/African American	10
American Indian/Alaska Native	3
Asian	16
Native Hawaiian/Pacific Islander	0
Other race	15
Two or more races	28
Hispanic origin, total	74
Mexican	14
Puerto Rican	15
Cuban	13
Other Hispanic	32

Age & Nativity, 2000

Under 5 years	195
18 years and over	1,981
21 years and over	1,915
65 years and over	234
85 years and over	30
Median age	37.6
Native-born	2,556
Foreign-born	170

Educational Attainment, 2000

Population 25 years and over	1,806
Less than 9th grade	3.4%
High school grad or higher	88.3%
Bachelor's degree or higher	25.7%
Graduate degree	8.7%

Income & Poverty, 1999

Per capita income	$24,743
Median household income	$62,535
Median family income	$68,529
Persons in poverty	95
H'holds receiving public assistance	11
H'holds receiving social security	220

Households, 2000

Total households	980
With persons under 18	413
With persons over 65	171
Family households	751
Single-person households	172
Persons per household	2.79
Persons per family	3.23

Labor & Employment

Total civilian labor force, 2007**	1,599
Unemployment rate	4.5%
Total civilian labor force, 2000	1,424
Unemployment rate	4.4%

Employed persons 16 years and over by occupation, 2000

Managers & professionals	472
Service occupations	154
Sales & office occupations	300
Farming, fishing & forestry	20
Construction & maintenance	201
Production & transportation	215
Self-employed persons	78

General Information

Township of Liberty
349 Mountain Lake Rd
Great Meadows, NJ 07838
908-637-4579

Website	www.libertytownship.org
Year of incorporation	1926
Land/water area (sq. miles)	11.80/0.21
Form of government	Township

Government

Legislative Districts

US Congressional	5
State Legislative	23

Local Officials, 2009

Mayor	John Inscho
Manager	Willa Reilly
Clerk	Willa Reilly
Finance Dir	Kevin Lifer
Tax Assessor	Lydia Schmidt
Tax Collector	Patricia Noll
Attorney	Roger Skoog
Building	Ralph Price
Comm Dev/Planning	NA
Engineering	Medina Consulting
Public Works	Steve Romanowitch
Police Chief	NA
Emerg/Fire Director	Ken Lunden

Housing & Construction

Housing Units, 2000*

Total	1,088
Median rent	$686
Median SF home value	$169,600

Permits for New Residential Construction

	Units	Value
Total, 2006	11	$2,504,000
Single family	11	$2,504,000
Total, 2007	4	$411,500
Single family	4	$411,500

Real Property Valuation, 2008

	Parcels	Valuation
Total	1,567	$269,431,400
Vacant	257	6,926,400
Residential	1,016	230,138,600
Commercial	27	6,968,400
Industrial	0	0
Apartments	1	308,800
Farm land	177	722,800
Farm homestead	89	24,366,400

Average Property Value & Tax, 2008

Residential value	$230,321
Property tax	$6,576
Tax credit/rebate	$1,130

Public Library

No public municipal library

Library statistics, 2007

Population served	NA
Full-time/total staff	NA/NA

	Total	Per capita
Holdings	NA	NA
Revenues	NA	NA
Expenditures	NA	NA
Annual visits	NA	NA
Internet terminals/annual users	NA/NA	

Public Safety

Number of officers, 2007	0

Crime	2006	2007
Total crimes	24	28
Violent	2	4
Murder	0	0
Rape	0	0
Robbery	0	0
Aggravated assault	2	4
Non-violent	22	24
Burglary	8	3
Larceny	11	19
Vehicle theft	3	2
Domestic violence	3	22
Arson	0	0
Total crime rate	8.1	9.5
Violent	0.7	1.4
Non-violent	7.4	8.1

Public School District

(for school year 2007-08 except as noted)

Great Meadows Regional School District
PO BOX 74
Great Meadows, NJ 07838
(908) 637-6576

Superintendent	Jason Bing
Number of schools	3
Grade plan	K-8
Enrollment	956
Attendance rate, '06-07	95.5%
Dropout rate	NA
Students per teacher	10.3
Per pupil expenditure	$12,430
Median faculty salary	$54,935
Median administrator salary	$89,994
Grade 12 enrollment	NA
High school graduation rate	NA

Assessment test results

(percent scoring at proficient or advanced level)

	Language	Math
NJASK-Grade 3	92.5%	93.3%
GEPA-Grade 8	78.1%	91.3%
HSPA-High School	NA	NA

SAT Score Averages, 2006-07

Pct tested	Math	Verbal	Writing
NA	NA	NA	NA

Teacher Qualifications

Avg. years of experience	16
Highly-qualified teachers one subject/all subjects	100%/100%

No Child Left Behind

AYP, 2006-07	Meets Standards

Municipal Finance

State Aid Programs, 2009

Total aid	$311,190
CMPTRA	47,755
Energy tax receipts	189,332
Garden State Trust	57,894

General Budget, 2008

Total tax levy	$7,709,099
County levy	2,296,706
County taxes	1,873,453
County library	196,564
County health	0
County open space	226,688
School levy	4,516,708
Muni. levy	895,685
Misc. revenues	1,249,034

Taxes	2006	2007	2008
General tax rate per $100	2.68	2.85	2.856
County equalization ratio	83.67	77.45	71.53
Net valuation taxable	$264,298,500	$267,055,571	$270,009,757
State equalized value	$342,027,932	$373,047,554	$365,562,643

See Introduction for an explanation of all data sources.

Demographics & Socio-Economic Characteristics

(2000 US Census, except as noted)

Population

1980*	8,806
1990*	10,978
2000	10,930
Male	5,239
Female	5,691
2007 (estimate)*	10,703
Population density	1,590.3

Race & Hispanic Origin, 2000

Race

White	9,845
Black/African American	191
American Indian/Alaska Native	13
Asian	578
Native Hawaiian/Pacific Islander	1
Other race	142
Two or more races	160
Hispanic origin, total	633
Mexican	41
Puerto Rican	214
Cuban	75
Other Hispanic	303

Age & Nativity, 2000

Under 5 years	632
18 years and over	8,716
21 years and over	8,466
65 years and over	1,622
85 years and over	266
Median age	39.6
Native-born	9,449
Foreign-born	1,481

Educational Attainment, 2000

Population 25 years and over	8,139
Less than 9th grade	4.5%
High school grad or higher	86.3%
Bachelor's degree or higher	32.9%
Graduate degree	11.0%

Income & Poverty, 1999

Per capita income	$30,389
Median household income	$69,050
Median family income	$77,307
Persons in poverty	286
H'holds receiving public assistance	37
H'holds receiving social security	890

Households, 2000

Total households	4,026
With persons under 18	1,251
With persons over 65	853
Family households	2,707
Single-person households	1,072
Persons per household	2.54
Persons per family	3.14

Labor & Employment

Total civilian labor force, 2007**	6,559
Unemployment rate	3.1%
Total civilian labor force, 2000	6,021
Unemployment rate	3.2%

Employed persons 16 years and over by occupation, 2000

Managers & professionals	2,484
Service occupations	482
Sales & office occupations	1,731
Farming, fishing & forestry	11
Construction & maintenance	492
Production & transportation	629
Self-employed persons	340

General Information

Borough of Lincoln Park
34 Chapel Hill Rd
Lincoln Park, NJ 07035
973-694-6100

Website	www.linconpark.org
Year of incorporation	1922
Land/water area (sq. miles)	6.73/0.24
Form of government	Mayor-Council

Government

Legislative Districts

US Congressional	11
State Legislative	26

Local Officials, 2009

Mayor	David Runfeldt
Manager	Joseph Maiella
Clerk	Annette Maida-Smith
Finance Dir	Kerry Geisler (Int)
Tax Assessor	Tom Lenhardt
Tax Collector	Kristen Runfeldt
Attorney	Edward Buzak
Building	Salvatore Marino
Planning	Joseph Maiella
Engineering	Joseph Maiella
Public Works	Tom Piorkowski
Police Chief	Sean Cannig
Emerg/Fire Director	Sal Marino

Housing & Construction

Housing Units, 2000*

Total	4,110
Median rent	$947
Median SF home value	$194,300

Permits for New Residential Construction

	Units	Value
Total, 2006	6	$787,938
Single family	6	$787,938
Total, 2007	3	$425,415
Single family	3	$425,415

Real Property Valuation, 2008

	Parcels	Valuation
Total	3,862	$738,003,100
Vacant	133	5,160,800
Residential	3,594	618,574,400
Commercial	75	49,887,600
Industrial	26	38,154,800
Apartments	2	22,954,100
Farm land	18	318,400
Farm homestead	14	2,953,000

Average Property Value & Tax, 2008

Residential value	$172,264
Property tax	$7,161
Tax credit/rebate	$1,060

Public Library

Lincoln Park Public Library
12 Boonton Turnpike
Lincoln Park, NJ 07035
973-694-8283

Director ... Francis R. Kaiser Jr

Library statistics, 2007

Population served	10,930
Full-time/total staff	1/2

	Total	Per capita
Holdings	47,045	4.30
Revenues	$579,078	$52.98
Expenditures	$434,889	$39.79
Annual visits	51,235	4.69
Internet terminals/annual users	12/16,350	

Public Safety

Number of officers, 2007	26

Crime	2006	2007
Total crimes	87	97
Violent	8	5
Murder	0	0
Rape	2	2
Robbery	1	0
Aggravated assault	5	3
Non-violent	79	92
Burglary	13	20
Larceny	62	67
Vehicle theft	4	5
Domestic violence	42	38
Arson	0	1
Total crime rate	8.0	8.9
Violent	0.7	0.5
Non-violent	7.2	8.5

Public School District

(for school year 2007-08 except as noted)

Lincoln Park Borough School District
92 Ryerson Road
Lincoln Park, NJ 07035
(973) 696-5500

Superintendent	James W. Grube
Number of schools	2
Grade plan	K-8
Enrollment	914
Attendance rate, '06-07	96.1%
Dropout rate	NA
Students per teacher	10.3
Per pupil expenditure	$14,832
Median faculty salary	$56,700
Median administrator salary	$109,915
Grade 12 enrollment	NA
High school graduation rate	NA

Assessment test results

(percent scoring at proficient or advanced level)

	Language	Math
NJASK-Grade 3	95.4%	97.6%
GEPA-Grade 8	85.0%	92.6%
HSPA-High School	NA	NA

SAT Score Averages, 2006-07

Pct tested	Math	Verbal	Writing
NA	NA	NA	NA

Teacher Qualifications

Avg. years of experience	10
Highly-qualified teachers one subject/all subjects	100%/100%

No Child Left Behind

AYP, 2006-07	Meets Standards

Municipal Finance

State Aid Programs, 2009

Total aid	$1,195,991
CMPTRA	320,614
Energy tax receipts	785,799
Garden State Trust	51,865

General Budget, 2008

Total tax levy	$30,708,537
County levy	3,973,823
County taxes	3,242,980
County library	0
County health	0
County open space	730,843
School levy	15,936,602
Muni. levy	10,798,112
Misc. revenues	6,225,923

Taxes

	2006	2007	2008
General tax rate per $100	3.65	3.84	4.158
County equalization ratio	52.27	46.33	43.28
Net valuation taxable	$737,713,200	$738,166,918	$738,715,077
State equalized value	$1,592,990,457	$1,704,661,433	$1,694,545,119

* US Census Bureau
** New Jersey Department of Labor

See Introduction for an explanation of all data sources.

Demographics & Socio-Economic Characteristics
(2000 US Census, except as noted)

Population
1980*	37,836
1990*	36,701
2000	39,394
Male	18,703
Female	20,691
2007 (estimate)*	39,372
Population density	3,642.2

Race & Hispanic Origin, 2000
Race
White	26,031
Black/African American	8,981
American Indian/Alaska Native	56
Asian	925
Native Hawaiian/Pacific Islander	15
Other race	1,923
Two or more races	1,463
Hispanic origin, total	5,674
Mexican	153
Puerto Rican	1,512
Cuban	593
Other Hispanic	3,416

Age & Nativity, 2000
Under 5 years	2,345
18 years and over	30,548
21 years and over	29,186
65 years and over	6,426
85 years and over	881
Median age	38.0
Native-born	29,043
Foreign-born	10,351

Educational Attainment, 2000
Population 25 years and over	27,238
Less than 9th grade	8.7%
High school grad or higher	78.2%
Bachelor's degree or higher	14.1%
Graduate degree	4.5%

Income & Poverty, 1999
Per capita income	$21,314
Median household income	$46,345
Median family income	$54,903
Persons in poverty	2,490
H'holds receiving public assistance	389
H'holds receiving social security	4,896

Households, 2000
Total households	15,052
With persons under 18	4,980
With persons over 65	4,786
Family households	10,087
Single-person households	4,207
Persons per household	2.60
Persons per family	3.21

Labor & Employment
Total civilian labor force, 2007**	20,733
Unemployment rate	5.1%
Total civilian labor force, 2000	19,892
Unemployment rate	5.6%

Employed persons 16 years and over by occupation, 2000
Managers & professionals	4,311
Service occupations	2,805
Sales & office occupations	6,071
Farming, fishing & forestry	11
Construction & maintenance	1,723
Production & transportation	3,851
Self-employed persons	654

* US Census Bureau
** New Jersey Department of Labor

See Introduction for an explanation of all data sources.

General Information
City of Linden
301 N Wood Ave
Linden, NJ 07036
908-474-8452

Website	www.linden-nj.org
Year of incorporation	1925
Land/water area (sq. miles)	10.81/0.41
Form of government	City

Government
Legislative Districts
US Congressional	7, 10, 13
State Legislative	22

Local Officials, 2009
Mayor	Richard J. Gerbounka
Manager/Admin	NA
Clerk	Joseph C. Bodek
Finance Dir	Alexis Zack
Tax Assessor	Michael Frangella
Tax Collector	Stacey L. Carron
Attorney	Edward J. Kologi
Building	Thomas Caverly
Comm Dev/Planning	NA
Engineering	George Vercik
Public Works	John Mesler III
Police Chief	Michael F. Boyle
Emerg/Fire Director	Joseph Vircik

Housing & Construction
Housing Units, 2000*
Total	15,567
Median rent	$795
Median SF home value	$148,800

Permits for New Residential Construction
	Units	Value
Total, 2006	119	$5,704,938
Single family	41	$4,421,038
Total, 2007	44	$4,049,400
Single family	31	$3,507,177

Real Property Valuation, 2008
	Parcels	Valuation
Total	11,712	$2,818,604,200
Vacant	454	38,215,600
Residential	10,020	1,413,771,900
Commercial	907	448,356,300
Industrial	239	849,638,100
Apartments	92	68,622,300
Farm land	0	0
Farm homestead	0	0

Average Property Value & Tax, 2008
Residential value	$141,095
Property tax	$6,634
Tax credit/rebate	$1,036

Public Library
Linden Free Public Library
31 E Henry St
Linden, NJ 07036
908-298-3830

Director	Dennis P. Purves Jr

Library statistics, 2007
Population served	39,394
Full-time/total staff	6/18

	Total	Per capita
Holdings	84,541	2.15
Revenues	$1,985,916	$50.41
Expenditures	$1,953,919	$49.60
Annual visits	92,000	2.34
Internet terminals/annual users	14/31,233	

Public Safety
Number of officers, 2007	130

Crime	2006	2007
Total crimes	1,450	1,498
Violent	133	144
Murder	4	1
Rape	3	6
Robbery	67	86
Aggravated assault	59	51
Non-violent	1,317	1,354
Burglary	186	235
Larceny	919	908
Vehicle theft	212	211
Domestic violence	282	358
Arson	2	6
Total crime rate	36.2	37.6
Violent	3.3	3.6
Non-violent	32.9	34.0

Public School District
(for school year 2007-08 except as noted)

Linden School District
2 E. Gibbons Street
Linden, NJ 07036
(908) 486-5818

Superintendent	Joseph E. Martino
Number of schools	11
Grade plan	K-12
Enrollment	6,122
Attendance rate, '06-07	93.8%
Dropout rate	3.1%
Students per teacher	10.5
Per pupil expenditure	$15,315
Median faculty salary	$52,964
Median administrator salary	$116,315
Grade 12 enrollment	418
High school graduation rate	89.9%

Assessment test results
(percent scoring at proficient or advanced level)
	Language	Math
NJASK-Grade 3	79.8%	82.5%
GEPA-Grade 8	60.2%	71.6%
HSPA-High School	53.6%	71.7%

SAT Score Averages, 2006-07
Pct tested	Math	Verbal	Writing
59%	408	412	415

Teacher Qualifications
Avg. years of experience	8
Highly-qualified teachers one subject/all subjects	90.5%/90.5%

No Child Left Behind
AYP, 2006-07	Meets Standards

Municipal Finance
State Aid Programs, 2009
Total aid	$23,429,585
CMPTRA	0
Energy tax receipts	22,843,845
Garden State Trust	0

General Budget, 2008
Total tax levy	$132,745,604
County levy	21,048,833
County taxes	20,088,692
County library	0
County health	0
County open space	960,141
School levy	71,693,968
Muni. levy	40,002,802
Misc. revenues	52,475,399

Taxes
	2006	2007	2008
General tax rate per $100	4.029	4.399	4.703
County equalization ratio	53.95	49.47	44.95
Net valuation taxable	$2,889,715,300	$2,861,742,166	$2,823,142,942
State equalized value	$5,846,754,481	$6,360,695,672	$6,576,243,568

Demographics & Socio-Economic Characteristics
(2000 US Census, except as noted)

Population

1980*	18,196
1990*	18,734
2000	17,414
Male	8,312
Female	9,102
2007 (estimate)*	17,176
Population density	4,359.4

Race & Hispanic Origin, 2000

Race
- White 10,695
- Black/African American 4,915
- American Indian/Alaska Native 83
- Asian 614
- Native Hawaiian/Pacific Islander 10
- Other race 564
- Two or more races 533

Hispanic origin, total 1,316
- Mexican 203
- Puerto Rican 587
- Cuban 30
- Other Hispanic 496

Age & Nativity, 2000
- Under 5 years 1,258
- 18 years and over 13,299
- 21 years and over 12,619
- 65 years and over 1,539
- 85 years and over 132
- Median age 33.3
- Native-born 16,160
- Foreign-born 1,254

Educational Attainment, 2000
- Population 25 years and over 11,593
- Less than 9th grade 7.0%
- High school grad or higher 77.6%
- Bachelor's degree or higher 13.3%
- Graduate degree 3.7%

Income & Poverty, 1999
- Per capita income $18,659
- Median household income $36,080
- Median family income $40,931
- Persons in poverty 2,047
- H'holds receiving public assistance 267
- H'holds receiving social security 1,565

Households, 2000
- Total households 7,465
- With persons under 18 2,422
- With persons over 65 1,230
- Family households 4,301
- Single-person households 2,558
- Persons per household 2.32
- Persons per family 3.00

Labor & Employment
- Total civilian labor force, 2007** 10,221
- Unemployment rate 7.7%
- Total civilian labor force, 2000 9,721
- Unemployment rate 8.0%

Employed persons 16 years and over by occupation, 2000
- Managers & professionals 2,106
- Service occupations 1,783
- Sales & office occupations 2,897
- Farming, fishing & forestry 10
- Construction & maintenance 922
- Production & transportation 1,228
- Self-employed persons 235

‡ Branch of county library
* US Census Bureau
** New Jersey Department of Labor

General Information
Borough of Lindenwold
2001 Egg Harbor Rd
Lindenwold, NJ 08021
856-783-2121
- Website www.lindenwoldnj.gov
- Year of incorporation 1929
- Land/water area (sq. miles) 3.94/0.03
- Form of government Borough

Government
Legislative Districts
- US Congressional 1
- State Legislative 4

Local Officials, 2009
- Mayor Frank DeLucca Jr
- Manager Frank DeLucca Jr
- Clerk Jane Barber
- Finance Dir Dawn Thompson
- Tax Assessor Thomas Glock
- Tax Collector Margie Schieber
- Attorney John Kearney
- Building Albert Hallworth
- Comm Dev/Planning NA
- Engineering Remington & Vernick
- Public Works Robert Lodovici
- Police Chief Michael McCarthy
- Emerg/Fire Director NA

Housing & Construction
Housing Units, 2000*
- Total 8,244
- Median rent $615
- Median SF home value $84,000

Permits for New Residential Construction

	Units	Value
Total, 2006	104	$1,235,817
Single family	12	$1,234,817
Total, 2007	142	$9,096,401
Single family	10	$965,792

Real Property Valuation, 2008

	Parcels	Valuation
Total	4,620	$424,885,700
Vacant	340	5,697,300
Residential	4,111	285,719,100
Commercial	142	36,496,700
Industrial	3	1,411,100
Apartments	24	95,561,500
Farm land	0	0
Farm homestead	0	0

Average Property Value & Tax, 2008
- Residential value $69,501
- Property tax $4,222
- Tax credit/rebate $940

Public Library
Lindenwold Public Library‡
310 E Linden Ave
Lindenwold, NJ 08021
856-784-5602
Branch Librarian B. Roach/M. Cavanaugh

Library statistics, 2007
see Camden County profile for library system statistics

Public Safety
Number of officers, 2007 38

Crime	2006	2007
Total crimes	839	794
Violent	163	179
Murder	1	0
Rape	8	7
Robbery	89	96
Aggravated assault	65	76
Non-violent	676	615
Burglary	235	205
Larceny	356	329
Vehicle theft	85	81
Domestic violence	406	399
Arson	10	9
Total crime rate	48.6	46.3
Violent	9.4	10.4
Non-violent	39.2	35.8

Public School District
(for school year 2007-08 except as noted)

Lindenwold Borough School District
801 Egg Harbor Road
Lindenwold, NJ 08021
(856) 784-4071
- Superintendent Geraldine Carroll
- Number of schools 4
- Grade plan K-12
- Enrollment 2,264
- Attendance rate, '06-07 92.4%
- Dropout rate 8.3%
- Students per teacher 9.7
- Per pupil expenditure $13,402
- Median faculty salary $48,306
- Median administrator salary $95,407
- Grade 12 enrollment 124
- High school graduation rate 68.9%

Assessment test results
(percent scoring at proficient or advanced level)

	Language	Math
NJASK-Grade 3	74.9%	77.6%
GEPA-Grade 8	36.4%	58.6%
HSPA-High School	65.8%	75.9%

SAT Score Averages, 2006-07

Pct tested	Math	Verbal	Writing
52%	445	430	436

Teacher Qualifications
- Avg. years of experience 7
- Highly-qualified teachers one subject/all subjects 98.5%/98.5%

No Child Left Behind
- AYP, 2006-07 Meets Standards

Municipal Finance
State Aid Programs, 2009
- Total aid $2,469,639
- CMPTRA 1,414,597
- Energy tax receipts 1,054,943
- Garden State Trust 99

General Budget, 2008
- Total tax levy $25,852,884
- County levy 5,484,433
- County taxes 4,956,544
- County library 355,377
- County health 0
- County open space 172,512
- School levy 13,175,504
- Muni. levy 7,192,947
- Misc. revenues 5,345,062

Taxes	2006	2007	2008
General tax rate per $100	5.747	6.074	6.075
County equalization ratio	67.74	58.98	49.34
Net valuation taxable	$428,583,700	$429,742,466	$425,587,450
State equalized value	$727,555,991	$870,163,298	$804,648,202

Demographics & Socio-Economic Characteristics
(2000 US Census, except as noted)

Population
1980*	6,144
1990*	6,866
2000	7,172
Male	3,343
Female	3,829
2007 (estimate)*	7,250
Population density	1,893.0

Race & Hispanic Origin, 2000
Race
White	6,828
Black/African American	76
American Indian/Alaska Native	8
Asian	173
Native Hawaiian/Pacific Islander	0
Other race	16
Two or more races	71
Hispanic origin, total	130
Mexican	13
Puerto Rican	64
Cuban	2
Other Hispanic	51

Age & Nativity, 2000
Under 5 years	375
18 years and over	5,291
21 years and over	5,163
65 years and over	1,345
85 years and over	231
Median age	42.8
Native-born	6,877
Foreign-born	318

Educational Attainment, 2000
Population 25 years and over	5,111
Less than 9th grade	3.0%
High school grad or higher	90.5%
Bachelor's degree or higher	37.9%
Graduate degree	15.0%

Income & Poverty, 1999
Per capita income	$32,159
Median household income	$60,000
Median family income	$71,415
Persons in poverty	275
H'holds receiving public assistance	28
H'holds receiving social security	905

Households, 2000
Total households	2,647
With persons under 18	976
With persons over 65	878
Family households	1,966
Single-person households	590
Persons per household	2.65
Persons per family	3.13

Labor & Employment
Total civilian labor force, 2007**	3,504
Unemployment rate	3.7%
Total civilian labor force, 2000	3,300
Unemployment rate	4.0%

Employed persons 16 years and over by occupation, 2000
Managers & professionals	1,420
Service occupations	536
Sales & office occupations	806
Farming, fishing & forestry	0
Construction & maintenance	274
Production & transportation	133
Self-employed persons	264

General Information
City of Linwood
400 W Poplar Ave
Linwood, NJ 08221
609-927-4108
Website	www.linwoodcity.org
Year of incorporation	1931
Land/water area (sq. miles)	3.83/0.31
Form of government	City

Government

Legislative Districts
US Congressional	2
State Legislative	2

Local Officials, 2009
Mayor	Richard DePamphilis III
Manager/Admin	NA
Clerk	Leigh Ann Napoli
Finance Dir	F. Bonnie Tiemann
Tax Assessor	Arthur Amonette
Tax Collector	Carl Wentzell
Attorney	Joseph Youngblood Jr
Building	James Galentino
Comm Dev/Planning	NA
Engineering	Thomas Thornton
Public Works	Hank Kolakowski
Police Chief	James Baker
Emerg/Fire Director	Demetrios Foster

Housing & Construction

Housing Units, 2000*
Total	2,751
Median rent	$714
Median SF home value	$165,100

Permits for New Residential Construction
	Units	Value
Total, 2006	15	$3,580,413
Single family	15	$3,580,413
Total, 2007	16	$4,922,659
Single family	16	$4,922,659

Real Property Valuation, 2008
	Parcels	Valuation
Total	3,018	$777,944,500
Vacant	136	14,566,200
Residential	2,732	674,167,700
Commercial	146	88,426,600
Industrial	0	0
Apartments	0	0
Farm land	2	34,600
Farm homestead	2	749,400

Average Property Value & Tax, 2008
Residential value	$246,861
Property tax	$8,298
Tax credit/rebate	$1,162

Public Library
Linwood Public Library
301 Davis Ave
Linwood, NJ 08221
609-926-7991
Director	Maria Moss

Library statistics, 2007
Population served	7,172
Full-time/total staff	0/2

	Total	Per capita
Holdings	38,382	5.35
Revenues	$399,043	$55.64
Expenditures	$338,840	$47.24
Annual visits	20,792	2.90
Internet terminals/annual users	7/3,820	

Public Safety
Number of officers, 2007	20

Crime	2006	2007
Total crimes	94	84
Violent	9	8
Murder	0	0
Rape	1	0
Robbery	3	1
Aggravated assault	5	7
Non-violent	85	76
Burglary	30	22
Larceny	48	53
Vehicle theft	7	1
Domestic violence	87	97
Arson	4	0
Total crime rate	12.7	11.4
Violent	1.2	1.1
Non-violent	11.5	10.3

Public School District
(for school year 2007-08 except as noted)

Linwood City School District
Belhaven Middle School
Linwood, NJ 08221
(609) 926-6703
Superintendent	Thomas Baruffi
Number of schools	2
Grade plan	K-8
Enrollment	997
Attendance rate, '06-07	96.5%
Dropout rate	NA
Students per teacher	11.4
Per pupil expenditure	$12,200
Median faculty salary	$52,486
Median administrator salary	$100,848
Grade 12 enrollment	NA
High school graduation rate	NA

Assessment test results
(percent scoring at proficient or advanced level)
	Language	Math
NJASK-Grade 3	98.1%	94.3%
GEPA-Grade 8	83.9%	96.0%
HSPA-High School	NA	NA

SAT Score Averages, 2006-07
Pct tested	Math	Verbal	Writing
NA	NA	NA	NA

Teacher Qualifications
Avg. years of experience	9
Highly-qualified teachers one subject/all subjects	98.5%/98.5%

No Child Left Behind
AYP, 2006-07	Meets Standards

Municipal Finance

State Aid Programs, 2009
Total aid	$736,977
CMPTRA	98,028
Energy tax receipts	620,524
Garden State Trust	0

General Budget, 2008
Total tax levy	$26,171,665
County levy	3,227,229
County taxes	2,827,926
County library	0
County health	148,651
County open space	250,652
School levy	16,005,937
Muni. levy	6,938,498
Misc. revenues	3,858,749

Taxes
	2006	2007	2008
General tax rate per $100	3.187	3.244	3.362
County equalization ratio	74.78	66.18	62.20
Net valuation taxable	$758,330,300	$773,023,780	$778,584,511
State equalized value	$1,146,565,765	$1,242,408,683	$1,261,694,477

* US Census Bureau
** New Jersey Department of Labor

See Introduction for an explanation of all data sources.

Demographics & Socio-Economic Characteristics

(2000 US Census, except as noted)

Population

1980*	8,483
1990*	13,333
2000	15,945
Male	7,655
Female	8,290
2007 (estimate)*	20,517
Population density	417.8

Race & Hispanic Origin, 2000

Race

White	15,342
Black/African American	126
American Indian/Alaska Native	41
Asian	96
Native Hawaiian/Pacific Islander	1
Other race	156
Two or more races	183
Hispanic origin, total	520
Mexican	79
Puerto Rican	253
Cuban	19
Other Hispanic	169

Age & Nativity, 2000

Under 5 years	931
18 years and over	12,091
21 years and over	11,618
65 years and over	2,821
85 years and over	271
Median age	39.9
Native-born	15,525
Foreign-born	494

Educational Attainment, 2000

Population 25 years and over	10,971
Less than 9th grade	3.5%
High school grad or higher	81.0%
Bachelor's degree or higher	15.1%
Graduate degree	4.5%

Income & Poverty, 1999

Per capita income	$20,619
Median household income	$45,628
Median family income	$51,580
Persons in poverty	1,028
H'holds receiving public assistance	107
H'holds receiving social security	2,299

Households, 2000

Total households	6,179
With persons under 18	2,065
With persons over 65	1,916
Family households	4,442
Single-person households	1,389
Persons per household	2.55
Persons per family	2.98

Labor & Employment

Total civilian labor force, 2007**	8,916
Unemployment rate	5.0%
Total civilian labor force, 2000	7,505
Unemployment rate	5.2%

Employed persons 16 years and over by occupation, 2000

Managers & professionals	1,875
Service occupations	1,571
Sales & office occupations	1,985
Farming, fishing & forestry	26
Construction & maintenance	943
Production & transportation	711
Self-employed persons	432

‡ Branch of county library
* US Census Bureau
** New Jersey Department of Labor

General Information

Township of Little Egg Harbor
665 Radio Rd
Little Egg Harbor Twp, NJ 08087
609-296-7241

Website	www.leht.com
Year of incorporation	1740
Land/water area (sq. miles)	49.11/24.07
Form of government	Township

Government

Legislative Districts

US Congressional	3
State Legislative	9

Local Officials, 2009

Mayor	Scott Stites
Manager	Raymond Urezzio
Clerk	Diana K. McCracken
Finance Dir	Raymond Urezzio
Tax Assessor	Joseph Sorrentino
Tax Collector	Dayna Cook
Attorney	G. Gilmore & Monahan
Building	Jay Haines
Comm Dev/Planning	NA
Engineering	James Oris
Public Works	Anthony Savino
Police Chief	Mark Siino
Fire/Emergency Dir	NA

Housing & Construction

Housing Units, 2000*

Total	7,931
Median rent	$817
Median SF home value	$98,800

Permits for New Residential Construction

	Units	Value
Total, 2006	143	$16,710,523
Single family	143	$16,710,523
Total, 2007	106	$12,746,800
Single family	100	$12,206,800

Real Property Valuation, 2008

	Parcels	Valuation
Total	11,957	$3,166,581,755
Vacant	1,847	158,794,300
Residential	9,903	2,837,818,989
Commercial	182	163,633,500
Industrial	2	566,100
Apartments	2	3,060,000
Farm land	17	70,366
Farm homestead	4	2,638,500

Average Property Value & Tax, 2008

Residential value	$286,712
Property tax	$4,145
Tax credit/rebate	$882

Public Library

Little Egg Harbor Branch Library‡
290 Mathistown Rd
Little Egg Harbor, NJ 08087
609-294-1197

Branch Librarian	Kathy Erickson

Library statistics, 2007

see Ocean County profile
for library system statistics

Public Safety

Number of officers, 2007	47

Crime	2006	2007
Total crimes	491	505
Violent	31	24
Murder	0	0
Rape	2	3
Robbery	5	3
Aggravated assault	24	18
Non-violent	460	481
Burglary	83	79
Larceny	362	391
Vehicle theft	15	11
Domestic violence	287	277
Arson	4	6
Total crime rate	24.8	24.9
Violent	1.6	1.2
Non-violent	23.2	23.7

Public School District

(for school year 2007-08 except as noted)

Little Egg Harbor Township School District
307 Frog Pond Road
Little Egg Harbor, NJ 08087
(609) 296-1719

Superintendent	Frank Kasyan
Number of schools	2
Grade plan	K-6
Enrollment	1,675
Attendance rate, '06-07	93.2%
Dropout rate	NA
Students per teacher	10.7
Per pupil expenditure	$12,226
Median faculty salary	$51,370
Median administrator salary	$95,562
Grade 12 enrollment	NA
High school graduation rate	NA

Assessment test results

(percent scoring at proficient or advanced level)

	Language	Math
NJASK-Grade 3	89.4%	84.3%
GEPA-Grade 8	NA	NA
HSPA-High School	NA	NA

SAT Score Averages, 2006-07

Pct tested	Math	Verbal	Writing
NA	NA	NA	NA

Teacher Qualifications

Avg. years of experience	10

Highly-qualified teachers
one subject/all subjects	100%/100%

No Child Left Behind

AYP, 2006-07	Meets Standards

Municipal Finance

State Aid Programs, 2009

Total aid	$1,862,506
CMPTRA	211,092
Energy tax receipts	1,423,023
Garden State Trust	191,964

General Budget, 2008

Total tax levy	$45,872,403
County levy	9,487,213
County taxes	7,822,757
County library	919,737
County health	374,429
County open space	370,289
School levy	22,328,801
Muni. levy	14,056,390
Misc. revenues	5,854,179

Taxes	2006	2007	2008
General tax rate per $100	1.318	1.381	1.447
County equalization ratio	130.54	108.8	102.54
Net valuation taxable	$3,034,192,460	$3,123,347,088	$3,173,021,725
State equalized value	$2,794,768,299	$3,046,131,766	$2,415,216,946

See Introduction for an explanation of all data sources.

Demographics & Socio-Economic Characteristics

(2000 US Census, except as noted)

Population

1980*	11,496
1990*	11,294
2000	10,855
Male	5,134
Female	5,721
2007 (estimate)*	11,694
Population density	4,252.4

Race & Hispanic Origin, 2000

Race

White	10,001
Black/African American	71
American Indian/Alaska Native	7
Asian	456
Native Hawaiian/Pacific Islander	2
Other race	144
Two or more races	174
Hispanic origin, total	579
Mexican	56
Puerto Rican	166
Cuban	66
Other Hispanic	291

Age & Nativity, 2000

Under 5 years	556
18 years and over	8,888
21 years and over	8,604
65 years and over	1,938
85 years and over	213
Median age	40.6
Native-born	9,369
Foreign-born	1,486

Educational Attainment, 2000

Population 25 years and over	8,178
Less than 9th grade	6.0%
High school grad or higher	85.3%
Bachelor's degree or higher	34.7%
Graduate degree	12.3%

Income & Poverty, 1999

Per capita income	$33,242
Median household income	$58,857
Median family income	$70,223
Persons in poverty	493
H'holds receiving public assistance	61
H'holds receiving social security	1,491

Households, 2000

Total households	4,687
With persons under 18	1,139
With persons over 65	1,474
Family households	2,871
Single-person households	1,552
Persons per household	2.32
Persons per family	2.99

Labor & Employment

Total civilian labor force, 2007**	6,290
Unemployment rate	4.2%
Total civilian labor force, 2000	5,821
Unemployment rate	4.4%

Employed persons 16 years and over by occupation, 2000

Managers & professionals	2,430
Service occupations	531
Sales & office occupations	1,804
Farming, fishing & forestry	0
Construction & maintenance	349
Production & transportation	452
Self-employed persons	291

* US Census Bureau
** New Jersey Department of Labor

General Information

Township of Little Falls
225 Main St
Little Falls, NJ 07424
973-256-0170

Website	www.lfnj.com
Year of incorporation	1868
Land/water area (sq. miles)	2.75/0.07
Form of government	Mayor-Council

Government

Legislative Districts

US Congressional	8
State Legislative	40

Local Officials, 2009

Mayor	Michael DeFrancisci
Manager	William Wilk
Clerk	William Wilk
Finance Dir	Kathy Albanese
Tax Assessor	E. Romeo Longo
Tax Collector	Denise Whiteside
Attorney	Joseph Trapanese
Building	Joseph Macones
Comm Dev/Planning	NA
Engineering	Robert Schilling
Public Works	Phil Simone
Police Chief	Gerald Hunter
Emerg/Fire Director	Jack Sweezy Jr

Housing & Construction

Housing Units, 2000*

Total	4,797
Median rent	$909
Median SF home value	$212,300

Permits for New Residential Construction

	Units	Value
Total, 2006	11	$1,003,005
Single family	11	$1,003,005
Total, 2007	8	$942,250
Single family	2	$597,900

Real Property Valuation, 2008

	Parcels	Valuation
Total	4,059	$724,508,900
Vacant	172	16,872,000
Residential	3,661	542,293,100
Commercial	174	96,911,800
Industrial	43	28,454,700
Apartments	9	39,977,300
Farm land	0	0
Farm homestead	0	0

Average Property Value & Tax, 2008

Residential value	$148,127
Property tax	$7,433
Tax credit/rebate	$1,131

Public Library

Little Falls Public Library
8 Warren St
Little Falls, NJ 07424
973-256-2784

Director	Patricia A. Pelak

Library statistics, 2007

Population served	10,855
Full-time/total staff	2/5

	Total	Per capita
Holdings	56,348	5.19
Revenues	$650,899	$59.96
Expenditures	$519,833	$47.89
Annual visits	48,802	4.50
Internet terminals/annual users	10/12,810	

Public Safety

Number of officers, 2007	24

Crime	2006	2007
Total crimes	446	471
Violent	25	16
Murder	0	0
Rape	6	0
Robbery	4	4
Aggravated assault	15	12
Non-violent	421	455
Burglary	73	79
Larceny	320	362
Vehicle theft	28	14
Domestic violence	129	146
Arson	0	0
Total crime rate	37.5	39.8
Violent	2.1	1.4
Non-violent	35.4	38.5

Public School District

(for school year 2007-08 except as noted)

Little Falls Township School District
560 Main Street
Little Falls, NJ 07424
(973) 256-1034

Chief School Admin	Bruce deLyon
Number of schools	3
Grade plan	K-8
Enrollment	878
Attendance rate, '06-07	95.3%
Dropout rate	NA
Students per teacher	11.0
Per pupil expenditure	$13,815
Median faculty salary	$56,118
Median administrator salary	$101,290
Grade 12 enrollment	NA
High school graduation rate	NA

Assessment test results

(percent scoring at proficient or advanced level)

	Language	Math
NJASK-Grade 3	85.9%	85.9%
GEPA-Grade 8	73.6%	91.2%
HSPA-High School	NA	NA

SAT Score Averages, 2006-07

Pct tested	Math	Verbal	Writing
NA	NA	NA	NA

Teacher Qualifications

Avg. years of experience	8

Highly-qualified teachers
one subject/all subjects	100%/100%

No Child Left Behind

AYP, 2006-07	Meets Standards

Municipal Finance

State Aid Programs, 2009

Total aid	$1,663,629
CMPTRA	320,209
Energy tax receipts	1,291,436
Garden State Trust	7,983

General Budget, 2008

Total tax levy	$36,478,749
County levy	9,912,497
County taxes	9,715,769
County library	0
County health	0
County open space	196,728
School levy	17,083,888
Muni. levy	9,482,364
Misc. revenues	4,544,332

Taxes

	2006	2007	2008
General tax rate per $100	4.39	4.72	5.018
County equalization ratio	42.99	38.75	37.10
Net valuation taxable	$721,434,900	$726,417,800	$726,993,600
State equalized value	$1,865,145,936	$1,953,786,856	$1,971,258,885

See Introduction for an explanation of all data sources.

Demographics & Socio-Economic Characteristics
(2000 US Census, except as noted)

Population
1980*	9,399
1990*	9,989
2000	10,800
Male	5,261
Female	5,539
2007 (estimate)*	10,568
Population density	6,907.2

Race & Hispanic Origin, 2000
Race
White	7,426
Black/African American	509
American Indian/Alaska Native	16
Asian	1,847
Native Hawaiian/Pacific Islander	6
Other race	621
Two or more races	375
Hispanic origin, total	1,641
Mexican	43
Puerto Rican	344
Cuban	199
Other Hispanic	1,055

Age & Nativity, 2000
Under 5 years	687
18 years and over	8,616
21 years and over	8,314
65 years and over	1,342
85 years and over	133
Median age	37.1
Native-born	7,443
Foreign-born	3,357

Educational Attainment, 2000
Population 25 years and over	7,762
Less than 9th grade	5.7%
High school grad or higher	81.5%
Bachelor's degree or higher	24.1%
Graduate degree	8.0%

Income & Poverty, 1999
Per capita income	$24,210
Median household income	$49,958
Median family income	$59,176
Persons in poverty	677
H'holds receiving public assistance	65
H'holds receiving social security	1,017

Households, 2000
Total households	4,366
With persons under 18	1,300
With persons over 65	1,002
Family households	2,785
Single-person households	1,364
Persons per household	2.47
Persons per family	3.16

Labor & Employment
Total civilian labor force, 2007**	6,352
Unemployment rate	4.1%
Total civilian labor force, 2000	6,021
Unemployment rate	4.6%

Employed persons 16 years and over by occupation, 2000
Managers & professionals	1,979
Service occupations	676
Sales & office occupations	1,920
Farming, fishing & forestry	0
Construction & maintenance	413
Production & transportation	758
Self-employed persons	246

General Information
Borough of Little Ferry
215-217 Liberty St
Little Ferry, NJ 07643
201-641-9234
Website	www.littleferrynj.org
Year of incorporation	1894
Land/water area (sq. miles)	1.53/0.16
Form of government	Borough

Government
Legislative Districts
US Congressional	9
State Legislative	38

Local Officials, 2009
Mayor	Mauro Raguseo
Manager	Kenneth Gabbert
Clerk	Barbara Maldonado
Finance Dir	Leonard Nicolosi
Tax Assessor	George Reggo
Tax Collector	Frank Berardo
Attorney	Joseph Monaghan
Building	Richard Bolan
Planning	NA
Engineering	Kenneth Job
Public Works	William Holly
Police Chief	Ralph Verdi
Emerg/Fire Director	Paul Schwedhelm

Housing & Construction
Housing Units, 2000*
Total	4,449
Median rent	$822
Median SF home value	$192,800

Permits for New Residential Construction
	Units	Value
Total, 2006	1	$200,000
Single family	1	$200,000
Total, 2007	1	$241,000
Single family	1	$241,000

Real Property Valuation, 2008
	Parcels	Valuation
Total	2,542	$1,222,142,800
Vacant	37	9,507,700
Residential	2,240	799,636,400
Commercial	162	152,646,400
Industrial	78	150,176,700
Apartments	25	110,175,600
Farm land	0	0
Farm homestead	0	0

Average Property Value & Tax, 2008
Residential value	$356,981
Property tax	$7,731
Tax credit/rebate	$1,165

Public Library
Little Ferry Public Library
239 Liberty St
Little Ferry, NJ 07643
201-641-3721
Director	Cheryl Ashley

Library statistics, 2007
Population served	10,800
Full-time/total staff	1/4

	Total	Per capita
Holdings	30,015	2.78
Revenues	$506,852	$46.93
Expenditures	$358,682	$33.21
Annual visits	36,088	3.34
Internet terminals/annual users	7/8,767	

Public Safety
Number of officers, 2007	28

Crime	2006	2007
Total crimes	120	144
Violent	5	20
Murder	0	0
Rape	1	2
Robbery	0	3
Aggravated assault	4	15
Non-violent	115	124
Burglary	23	16
Larceny	71	92
Vehicle theft	21	16
Domestic violence	95	113
Arson	0	0
Total crime rate	11.1	13.4
Violent	0.5	1.9
Non-violent	10.7	11.6

Public School District
(for school year 2007-08 except as noted)

Little Ferry School District
130 Liberty Street
Little Ferry, NJ 07643
(201) 641-6192
Superintendent	Frank R. Scarafile
Number of schools	2
Grade plan	K-8
Enrollment	958
Attendance rate, '06-07	96.6%
Dropout rate	NA
Students per teacher	11.7
Per pupil expenditure	$11,834
Median faculty salary	$60,539
Median administrator salary	$116,485
Grade 12 enrollment	NA
High school graduation rate	NA

Assessment test results
(percent scoring at proficient or advanced level)
	Language	Math
NJASK-Grade 3	88.9%	85.6%
GEPA-Grade 8	67.4%	88.7%
HSPA-High School	NA	NA

SAT Score Averages, 2006-07
Pct tested	Math	Verbal	Writing
NA	NA	NA	NA

Teacher Qualifications
Avg. years of experience	14
Highly-qualified teachers one subject/all subjects	100%/100%

No Child Left Behind
AYP, 2006-07	Meets Standards

Municipal Finance
State Aid Programs, 2009
Total aid	$1,209,817
CMPTRA	337,624
Energy tax receipts	841,947
Garden State Trust	0

General Budget, 2008
Total tax levy	$26,599,720
County levy	2,432,959
County taxes	2,300,262
County library	0
County health	0
County open space	132,697
School levy	15,173,133
Muni. levy	8,993,628
Misc. revenues	4,700,571

Taxes
	2006	2007	2008
General tax rate per $100	1.93	2.06	2.158
County equalization ratio	113.5	101.35	92.90
Net valuation taxable	$1,224,881,300	$1,233,156,597	$1,228,310,073
State equalized value	$1,214,969,161	$1,326,896,819	$1,335,161,183

---

* US Census Bureau
** New Jersey Department of Labor

See Introduction for an explanation of all data sources.

Demographics & Socio-Economic Characteristics
(2000 US Census, except as noted)

Population
1980*	5,548
1990*	5,721
2000	6,170
Male	2,979
Female	3,191
2007 (estimate)*	6,129
Population density	2,212.6

Race & Hispanic Origin, 2000
Race
White	5,994
Black/African American	19
American Indian/Alaska Native	10
Asian	93
Native Hawaiian/Pacific Islander	1
Other race	12
Two or more races	41
Hispanic origin, total	81
Mexican	16
Puerto Rican	14
Cuban	11
Other Hispanic	40

Age & Nativity, 2000
Under 5 years	452
18 years and over	4,479
21 years and over	4,344
65 years and over	967
85 years and over	97
Median age	41.1
Native-born	5,810
Foreign-born	360

Educational Attainment, 2000
Population 25 years and over	4,199
Less than 9th grade	0.5%
High school grad or higher	96.8%
Bachelor's degree or higher	60.5%
Graduate degree	22.0%

Income & Poverty, 1999
Per capita income	$46,798
Median household income	$94,094
Median family income	$104,033
Persons in poverty	48
H'holds receiving public assistance	21
H'holds receiving social security	659

Households, 2000
Total households	2,232
With persons under 18	869
With persons over 65	666
Family households	1,810
Single-person households	375
Persons per household	2.76
Persons per family	3.13

Labor & Employment
Total civilian labor force, 2007**	3,149
Unemployment rate	2.8%
Total civilian labor force, 2000	2,934
Unemployment rate	2.7%

Employed persons 16 years and over by occupation, 2000
Managers & professionals	1,694
Service occupations	166
Sales & office occupations	810
Farming, fishing & forestry	5
Construction & maintenance	126
Production & transportation	53
Self-employed persons	288

General Information
Borough of Little Silver
480 Prospect Ave
Little Silver, NJ 07739
732-842-2400

Website	www.littlesilver.org
Year of incorporation	1923
Land/water area (sq. miles)	2.77/0.60
Form of government	Borough

Government
Legislative Districts
US Congressional	12
State Legislative	12

Local Officials, 2009
Mayor	Suzanne Castleman
Manager	Michael Biehl
Clerk	Michael Biehl
Finance Dir	Laura Geraghty
Tax Assessor	J. Stephen Walters
Tax Collector	Laura Geraghty
Attorney	John O. Bennett III
Building	Stanley Sickels
Comm Dev/Planning	NA
Engineering	Gregory Blash
Public Works	James Gannon
Police Chief	Shannon Giblin
Emerg/Fire Director	Frank Salerno

Housing & Construction
Housing Units, 2000*
Total	2,288
Median rent	$1,125
Median SF home value	$300,400

Permits for New Residential Construction
	Units	Value
Total, 2006	13	$4,150,691
Single family	13	$4,150,691
Total, 2007	14	$6,242,963
Single family	14	$6,242,963

Real Property Valuation, 2008
	Parcels	Valuation
Total	2,521	$1,252,645,900
Vacant	103	15,409,600
Residential	2,269	1,149,913,900
Commercial	144	83,930,100
Industrial	0	0
Apartments	0	0
Farm land	3	15,800
Farm homestead	2	3,376,500

Average Property Value & Tax, 2008
Residential value	$507,834
Property tax	$10,889
Tax credit/rebate	$1,304

Public Library
Little Silver Public Library
484 Prospect Ave
Little Silver, NJ 07739
732-747-9649

Director	Susan M. Edwards

Library statistics, 2007
Population served	6,170
Full-time/total staff	1/1

	Total	Per capita
Holdings	26,937	4.37
Revenues	$257,939	$41.81
Expenditures	$259,871	$42.12
Annual visits	26,922	4.36
Internet terminals/annual users	3/2,724	

Public Safety
Number of officers, 2007	16

Crime	2006	2007
Total crimes	63	111
Violent	0	5
Murder	0	0
Rape	0	0
Robbery	0	1
Aggravated assault	0	4
Non-violent	63	106
Burglary	12	38
Larceny	49	67
Vehicle theft	2	1
Domestic violence	0	5
Arson	0	0
Total crime rate	10.3	18.2
Violent	0.0	0.8
Non-violent	10.3	17.4

Public School District
(for school year 2007-08 except as noted)

Little Silver Borough School District
124 Willow Drive
Little Silver, NJ 07739
(732) 741-2188

Superintendent	Carolyn M. Kossack
Number of schools	2
Grade plan	K-8
Enrollment	809
Attendance rate, '06-07	95.9%
Dropout rate	NA
Students per teacher	9.8
Per pupil expenditure	$13,425
Median faculty salary	$46,750
Median administrator salary	$106,000
Grade 12 enrollment	NA
High school graduation rate	NA

Assessment test results
(percent scoring at proficient or advanced level)
	Language	Math
NJASK-Grade 3	97.6%	95.2%
GEPA-Grade 8	96.8%	94.7%
HSPA-High School	NA	NA

SAT Score Averages, 2006-07
Pct tested	Math	Verbal	Writing
NA	NA	NA	NA

Teacher Qualifications
Avg. years of experience	6
Highly-qualified teachers one subject/all subjects	100%/100%

No Child Left Behind
AYP, 2006-07	Meets Standards

Municipal Finance
State Aid Programs, 2009
Total aid	$796,950
CMPTRA	51,807
Energy tax receipts	713,265
Garden State Trust	0

General Budget, 2008
Total tax levy	$26,882,490
County levy	4,228,708
County taxes	3,752,625
County library	225,828
County health	0
County open space	250,255
School levy	16,364,611
Muni. levy	6,289,171
Misc. revenues	3,973,437

Taxes
	2006	2007	2008
General tax rate per $100	2.086	2.12	2.145
County equalization ratio	84.94	77.88	75.46
Net valuation taxable	$1,235,213,600	$1,246,314,064	$1,253,700,152
State equalized value	$1,586,968,655	$1,651,284,812	$825,773,434

* US Census Bureau
** New Jersey Department of Labor

See Introduction for an explanation of all data sources.

Demographics & Socio-Economic Characteristics
(2000 US Census, except as noted)

Population
1980*	28,040
1990*	26,609
2000	27,391
Male	13,322
Female	14,069
2007 (estimate)*	27,990
Population density	2,016.6

Race & Hispanic Origin, 2000
Race
White	22,637
Black/African American	328
American Indian/Alaska Native	14
Asian	3,982
Native Hawaiian/Pacific Islander	3
Other race	190
Two or more races	237
Hispanic origin, total	695
Mexican	39
Puerto Rican	128
Cuban	88
Other Hispanic	440

Age & Nativity, 2000
Under 5 years	1,917
18 years and over	20,107
21 years and over	19,495
65 years and over	4,221
85 years and over	420
Median age	40.6
Native-born	22,237
Foreign-born	5,154

Educational Attainment, 2000
Population 25 years and over	18,769
Less than 9th grade	2.2%
High school grad or higher	94.0%
Bachelor's degree or higher	57.7%
Graduate degree	26.7%

Income & Poverty, 1999
Per capita income	$47,218
Median household income	$98,869
Median family income	$108,049
Persons in poverty	480
H'holds receiving public assistance	56
H'holds receiving social security	2,779

Households, 2000
Total households	9,300
With persons under 18	4,003
With persons over 65	2,911
Family households	7,936
Single-person households	1,207
Persons per household	2.93
Persons per family	3.21

Labor & Employment
Total civilian labor force, 2007**	14,839
Unemployment rate	2.5%
Total civilian labor force, 2000	13,724
Unemployment rate	2.1%

Employed persons 16 years and over by occupation, 2000
Managers & professionals	7,514
Service occupations	988
Sales & office occupations	3,984
Farming, fishing & forestry	0
Construction & maintenance	524
Production & transportation	420
Self-employed persons	927

General Information
Township of Livingston
357 S Livingston Ave
Livingston, NJ 07039
973-992-5000
Website	www.livingstonnj.org
Year of incorporation	1813
Land/water area (sq. miles)	13.88/0.19
Form of government	Council-Manager

Government
Legislative Districts
US Congressional	8, 11
State Legislative	27

Local Officials, 2009
Mayor	Gary Schneiderman
Manager	Michele Meade
Clerk	Glenn Turtletaub
Finance Dir	William Nadolny Jr
Tax Assessor	Lidia Dumytsch
Tax Collector	Vibha Desai
Attorney	Sharon Weiner
Building	Martin Chiarolanzio
Planning	Jackie Hollis
Engineering	Robert Schaefer
Public Works	Robert Schaefer
Police Chief	Michael Erb
Emerg/Fire Director	Christopher Mullin

Housing & Construction
Housing Units, 2000*
Total	9,457
Median rent	$1,244
Median SF home value	$290,200

Permits for New Residential Construction
	Units	Value
Total, 2006	89	$47,265,513
Single family	89	$47,265,513
Total, 2007	20	$17,922,770
Single family	20	$17,922,770

Real Property Valuation, 2008
	Parcels	Valuation
Total	10,505	$959,946,400
Vacant	327	17,553,700
Residential	9,841	785,266,900
Commercial	292	141,261,400
Industrial	43	15,766,000
Apartments	0	0
Farm land	1	6,000
Farm homestead	1	92,400

Average Property Value & Tax, 2008
Residential value	$79,797
Property tax	$11,787
Tax credit/rebate	$1,258

Public Library
R.L. Rockwood Memorial Library
10 Robert H. Harp Dr
Livingston, NJ 07039
973-992-4600
Director	Barbara Jean Sikora

Library statistics, 2007
Population served	27,391
Full-time/total staff	13/26

	Total	Per capita
Holdings	180,871	6.60
Revenues	$3,060,540	$111.74
Expenditures	$2,829,389	$103.30
Annual visits	203,025	7.41
Internet terminals/annual users	29/13,111	

Public Safety
Number of officers, 2007	75

Crime	2006	2007
Total crimes	544	460
Violent	30	21
Murder	1	0
Rape	1	2
Robbery	8	8
Aggravated assault	20	11
Non-violent	514	439
Burglary	43	33
Larceny	439	382
Vehicle theft	32	24
Domestic violence	88	59
Arson	1	2
Total crime rate	19.6	16.2
Violent	1.1	0.7
Non-violent	18.5	15.5

Public School District
(for school year 2007-08 except as noted)

Livingston Township School District
11 Foxcroft Drive
Livingston, NJ 07039
(973) 535-8000
Superintendent	Brad Draeger
Number of schools	9
Grade plan	K-12
Enrollment	5,579
Attendance rate, '06-07	96.5%
Dropout rate	0.2%
Students per teacher	11.0
Per pupil expenditure	$14,756
Median faculty salary	$66,900
Median administrator salary	$117,356
Grade 12 enrollment	397
High school graduation rate	99.5%

Assessment test results
(percent scoring at proficient or advanced level)
	Language	Math
NJASK-Grade 3	94.4%	95.2%
GEPA-Grade 8	88.0%	96.0%
HSPA-High School	90.8%	96.5%

SAT Score Averages, 2006-07
Pct tested	Math	Verbal	Writing
99%	591	562	566

Teacher Qualifications
Avg. years of experience	9
Highly-qualified teachers one subject/all subjects	100%/100%

No Child Left Behind
AYP, 2006-07	Meets Standards

Municipal Finance
State Aid Programs, 2009
Total aid	$4,032,758
CMPTRA	570,198
Energy tax receipts	3,290,872
Garden State Trust	0

General Budget, 2008
Total tax levy	$142,000,065
County levy	30,661,125
County taxes	29,473,232
County library	0
County health	0
County open space	1,187,893
School levy	84,486,478
Muni. levy	26,852,463
Misc. revenues	15,304,835

Taxes
	2006	2007	2008
General tax rate per $100	12.94	14.07	14.772
County equalization ratio	14.7	12.6	12.17
Net valuation taxable	$951,511,100	$966,964,700	$961,309,400
State equalized value	$7,553,097,297	$7,936,586,971	$8,047,854,199

Demographics & Socio-Economic Characteristics

(2000 US Census, except as noted)

Population
1980*	369
1990*	380
2000	280
Male	144
Female	136
2007 (estimate)*	275
Population density	2,750.0

Race & Hispanic Origin, 2000
Race
White	266
Black/African American	6
American Indian/Alaska Native	0
Asian	2
Native Hawaiian/Pacific Islander	0
Other race	1
Two or more races	5
Hispanic origin, total	2
Mexican	0
Puerto Rican	1
Cuban	0
Other Hispanic	1

Age & Nativity, 2000
Under 5 years	18
18 years and over	231
21 years and over	225
65 years and over	44
85 years and over	6
Median age	43.0
Native-born	273
Foreign-born	2

Educational Attainment, 2000
Population 25 years and over	200
Less than 9th grade	0.0%
High school grad or higher	100.0%
Bachelor's degree or higher	50.0%
Graduate degree	20.0%

Income & Poverty, 1999
Per capita income	$34,037
Median household income	$68,542
Median family income	$74,250
Persons in poverty	13
H'holds receiving public assistance	0
H'holds receiving social security	24

Households, 2000
Total households	120
With persons under 18	28
With persons over 65	30
Family households	77
Single-person households	33
Persons per household	2.33
Persons per family	2.88

Labor & Employment
Total civilian labor force, 2007**	170
Unemployment rate	5.7%
Total civilian labor force, 2000	162
Unemployment rate	7.4%

Employed persons 16 years and over by occupation, 2000
Managers & professionals	89
Service occupations	10
Sales & office occupations	34
Farming, fishing & forestry	0
Construction & maintenance	12
Production & transportation	5
Self-employed persons	18

General Information
Village of Loch Arbour
550 Main St
Loch Arbour, NJ 07711
732-531-4740

Website	www.locharbournj.us
Year of incorporation	1957
Land/water area (sq. miles)	0.10/0.04
Form of government	Village

Government

Legislative Districts
US Congressional	6
State Legislative	11

Local Officials, 2009
Mayor	Betty McBain
Manager/Admin	NA
Clerk	Lorraine Carafa
Finance Dir	Lorraine Carafa
Tax Assessor	Eldo Magnani
Tax Collector	Lorraine Carafa
Attorney	Stephen Foley Jr
Building	Alan Decker
Comm Dev/Planning	NA
Engineering	Peter Avakian
Public Works	NA
Police Chief	Antonio Amodio
Fire/Emergency Dir	Frank Manfredi

Housing & Construction

Housing Units, 2000*
Total	156
Median rent	$755
Median SF home value	$322,400

Permits for New Residential Construction
	Units	Value
Total, 2006	0	$0
Single family	0	$0
Total, 2007	0	$0
Single family	0	$0

Real Property Valuation, 2008
	Parcels	Valuation
Total	147	$204,796,300
Vacant	5	3,823,600
Residential	135	191,110,900
Commercial	6	9,058,600
Industrial	0	0
Apartments	1	803,200
Farm land	0	0
Farm homestead	0	0

Average Property Value & Tax, 2008
Residential value	$1,415,636
Property tax	$8,804
Tax credit/rebate	$1,035

Public Library
served by Monmouth County Library
125 Symmes Dr
Manalapan, NJ 07726
732-431-7235

Director	Ken Sheinbaum

Library statistics, 2007
Population served	399,613
Full-time/total staff	38/117

	Total	Per capita
Holdings	1,414,674	3.54
Revenues	$14,201,091	$35.54
Expenditures	$12,327,753	$30.85
Annual visits	2,214,466	5.54
Internet terminals/annual users	84/255,228	

Public Safety
Number of officers, 2007	0

Crime	2006	2007
Total crimes	18	8
Violent	0	0
Murder	0	0
Rape	0	0
Robbery	0	0
Aggravated assault	0	0
Non-violent	18	8
Burglary	4	1
Larceny	14	7
Vehicle theft	0	0
Domestic violence	0	4
Arson	0	1
Total crime rate	65.5	29.2
Violent	0.0	0.0
Non-violent	65.5	29.2

Public School District
(for school year 2007-08 except as noted)

Ocean Township School District
163 Monmouth Road
Oakhurst, NJ 07755
(732) 531-5600

Superintendent	Thomas M. Pagano
Number of schools	5
Grade plan	K-12
Enrollment	4,232
Attendance rate, '06-07	95.5%
Dropout rate	0.1%
Students per teacher	10.6
Per pupil expenditure	$14,345
Median faculty salary	$55,970
Median administrator salary	$102,150
Grade 12 enrollment	348
High school graduation rate	98.6%

Assessment test results
(percent scoring at proficient or advanced level)
	Language	Math
NJASK-Grade 3	89.4%	89.4%
GEPA-Grade 8	76.2%	86.9%
HSPA-High School	83.7%	88.9%

SAT Score Averages, 2006-07
Pct tested	Math	Verbal	Writing
96%	525	502	496

Teacher Qualifications
Avg. years of experience	10
Highly-qualified teachers one subject/all subjects	99.5%/99.5%

No Child Left Behind
AYP, 2006-07	Meets Standards

Municipal Finance

State Aid Programs, 2009
Total aid	$49,456
CMPTRA	6,769
Energy tax receipts	41,080
Garden State Trust	0

General Budget, 2008
Total tax levy	$1,274,040
County levy	479,156
County taxes	425,213
County library	25,588
County health	0
County open space	28,354
School levy	300,000
Muni. levy	494,884
Misc. revenues	526,560

Taxes
	2006	2007	2008
General tax rate per $100	1.576	1.689	0.622
County equalization ratio	52.12	40.63	109.09
Net valuation taxable	$72,907,200	$73,146,872	$204,864,904
State equalized value	$179,473,339	$187,038,594	$797,784,250

* US Census Bureau
** New Jersey Department of Labor

See Introduction for an explanation of all data sources.

Demographics & Socio-Economic Characteristics
(2000 US Census, except as noted)

Population
1980*	23,956
1990*	22,355
2000	23,971
Male	11,378
Female	12,593
2007 (estimate)*	23,972
Population density	10,607.1

Race & Hispanic Origin, 2000
Race
White	18,736
Black/African American	852
American Indian/Alaska Native	40
Asian	2,124
Native Hawaiian/Pacific Islander	8
Other race	1,498
Two or more races	713
Hispanic origin, total	4,309
Mexican	212
Puerto Rican	912
Cuban	178
Other Hispanic	3,007

Age & Nativity, 2000
Under 5 years	1,533
18 years and over	18,865
21 years and over	18,157
65 years and over	3,564
85 years and over	425
Median age	36.4
Native-born	16,840
Foreign-born	7,131

Educational Attainment, 2000
Population 25 years and over	17,017
Less than 9th grade	11.7%
High school grad or higher	75.8%
Bachelor's degree or higher	18.7%
Graduate degree	5.1%

Income & Poverty, 1999
Per capita income	$21,667
Median household income	$43,421
Median family income	$51,959
Persons in poverty	1,921
H'holds receiving public assistance	227
H'holds receiving social security	2,742

Households, 2000
Total households	9,528
With persons under 18	3,002
With persons over 65	2,619
Family households	6,100
Single-person households	2,871
Persons per household	2.50
Persons per family	3.16

Labor & Employment
Total civilian labor force, 2007**	13,112
Unemployment rate	4.3%
Total civilian labor force, 2000	12,425
Unemployment rate	4.7%

Employed persons 16 years and over by occupation, 2000
Managers & professionals	3,251
Service occupations	1,501
Sales & office occupations	4,050
Farming, fishing & forestry	5
Construction & maintenance	1,083
Production & transportation	1,949
Self-employed persons	435

* US Census Bureau
** New Jersey Department of Labor
§ State Fiscal Year July 1–June 30

General Information
Borough of Lodi
1 Memorial Drive, Suite 1
Lodi, NJ 07644
973-365-4005

Website	www.lodi-nj.org
Year of incorporation	1894
Land/water area (sq. miles)	2.26/0.01
Form of government	Municipal Mgr 1923

Government

Legislative Districts
US Congressional	9
State Legislative	38

Local Officials, 2009
Mayor	Marc N. Schrieks
Manager	Tony Luna
Clerk	Debra A. Cannizzo
Finance Dir	George F. Fenn
Tax Assessor	G. Reggo/V. Hascup
Tax Collector	Gary Stramandino
Attorney	Scott G. Sproviero
Building	Joel Lavin
Planning Rep	Tony Luna
Engineering	Thomas Solfaro
Public Works	Gerald Woods
Police Chief	Vincent Caruso
Emerg/Fire Director	Robert Cassiello

Housing & Construction

Housing Units, 2000*
Total	9,908
Median rent	$811
Median SF home value	$172,600

Permits for New Residential Construction
	Units	Value
Total, 2006	17	$2,077,500
Single family	11	$1,700,000
Total, 2007	11	$1,566,750
Single family	7	$961,650

Real Property Valuation, 2008
	Parcels	Valuation
Total	5,034	$1,961,161,500
Vacant	79	7,274,700
Residential	4,440	1,416,914,100
Commercial	309	267,186,800
Industrial	114	131,949,300
Apartments	92	137,836,600
Farm land	0	0
Farm homestead	0	0

Average Property Value & Tax, 2008
Residential value	$319,125
Property tax	$8,896
Tax credit/rebate	$1,268

Public Library
Lodi Memorial Library
1 Memorial Dr
Lodi, NJ 07644
973-365-4044

Director	Anthony P. Taormina

Library statistics, 2007
Population served	23,971
Full-time/total staff	2/8

	Total	Per capita
Holdings	92,049	3.84
Revenues	$991,195	$41.35
Expenditures	$1,055,007	$44.01
Annual visits	63,454	2.65
Internet terminals/annual users	17/30,218	

Public Safety
Number of officers, 2007	43

Crime	2006	2007
Total crimes	353	375
Violent	41	29
Murder	0	0
Rape	0	0
Robbery	9	9
Aggravated assault	32	20
Non-violent	312	346
Burglary	64	90
Larceny	195	221
Vehicle theft	53	35
Domestic violence	207	144
Arson	1	1
Total crime rate	14.5	15.4
Violent	1.7	1.2
Non-violent	12.8	14.2

Public School District
(for school year 2007-08 except as noted)

Lodi School District
8 Hunter Street
Lodi, NJ 07644
(973) 778-4620

Superintendent	Frank Quatrone
Number of schools	7
Grade plan	K-12
Enrollment	3,127
Attendance rate, '06-07	94.8%
Dropout rate	3.3%
Students per teacher	11.9
Per pupil expenditure	$13,152
Median faculty salary	$52,558
Median administrator salary	$117,772
Grade 12 enrollment	210
High school graduation rate	91.9%

Assessment test results
(percent scoring at proficient or advanced level)
	Language	Math
NJASK-Grade 3	90.5%	89.3%
GEPA-Grade 8	63.1%	83.5%
HSPA-High School	75.6%	83.6%

SAT Score Averages, 2006-07
Pct tested	Math	Verbal	Writing
73%	476	445	458

Teacher Qualifications
Avg. years of experience	11
Highly-qualified teachers one subject/all subjects	99.0%/99.0%

No Child Left Behind
AYP, 2006-07	Meets Standards

Municipal Finance§

State Aid Programs, 2009
Total aid	$2,462,512
CMPTRA	1,122,380
Energy tax receipts	1,303,194
Garden State Trust	0

General Budget, 2008
Total tax levy	$54,725,661
County levy	4,509,302
County taxes	4,264,738
County library	0
County health	0
County open space	244,564
School levy	32,600,375
Muni. levy	17,615,985
Misc. revenues	7,398,555

Taxes
	2006	2007	2008
General tax rate per $100	2.58	2.74	2.790
County equalization ratio	94.05	83.79	80.78
Net valuation taxable	$1,931,641,400	$1,950,189,705	$1,963,204,181
State equalized value	$2,307,340,572	$2,413,760,901	$2,491,458,142

See Introduction for an explanation of all data sources.

Demographics & Socio-Economic Characteristics

(2000 US Census, except as noted)

Population

1980*	3,078
1990*	5,147
2000	6,032
Male	2,974
Female	3,058
2007 (estimate)*	6,195
Population density	273.9

Race & Hispanic Origin, 2000

Race

White	4,946
Black/African American	815
American Indian/Alaska Native	8
Asian	107
Native Hawaiian/Pacific Islander	1
Other race	73
Two or more races	82
Hispanic origin, total	165
Mexican	34
Puerto Rican	97
Cuban	11
Other Hispanic	23

Age & Nativity, 2000

Under 5 years	514
18 years and over	4,095
21 years and over	3,906
65 years and over	372
85 years and over	40
Median age	33.6
Native-born	5,813
Foreign-born	219

Educational Attainment, 2000

Population 25 years and over	3,740
Less than 9th grade	2.3%
High school grad or higher	89.5%
Bachelor's degree or higher	25.0%
Graduate degree	7.6%

Income & Poverty, 1999

Per capita income	$26,853
Median household income	$67,148
Median family income	$70,771
Persons in poverty	257
H'holds receiving public assistance	16
H'holds receiving social security	372

Households, 2000

Total households	2,001
With persons under 18	1,020
With persons over 65	277
Family households	1,610
Single-person households	314
Persons per household	3.00
Persons per family	3.38

Labor & Employment

Total civilian labor force, 2007**	3,700
Unemployment rate	2.1%
Total civilian labor force, 2000	3,138
Unemployment rate	1.9%

Employed persons 16 years and over by occupation, 2000

Managers & professionals	1,157
Service occupations	335
Sales & office occupations	923
Farming, fishing & forestry	20
Construction & maintenance	199
Production & transportation	443
Self-employed persons	116

‡ Branch of county library
* US Census Bureau
** New Jersey Department of Labor

See Introduction for an explanation of all data sources.

General Information

Township of Logan
125 Main St
PO Box 314
Bridgeport, NJ 08014
856-467-3424

Website	www.logan-twp.org
Year of incorporation	1878
Land/water area (sq. miles)	22.62/4.21
Form of government	Small Municipality

Government

Legislative Districts

US Congressional	1
State Legislative	3

Local Officials, 2009

Mayor	Frank W. Minor
Manager	NA
Clerk	Linda L. Oswald
Finance Dir	Robert Best
Tax Assessor	Brian Schneider
Tax Collector	Beth Walls
Attorney	Brian Duffield
Building	Charles Bastow
Comm Dev/Planning	Beth Walls
Engineering	Annina Hogan
Public Works	Dave McCormick
Police Chief	James Schmidt
Emerg/Fire Director	NA

Housing & Construction

Housing Units, 2000*

Total	2,077
Median rent	$764
Median SF home value	$114,200

Permits for New Residential Construction

	Units	Value
Total, 2006	0	$714,950
Single family	0	$714,950
Total, 2007	19	$7,111,800
Single family	19	$7,111,800

Real Property Valuation, 2008

	Parcels	Valuation
Total	2,968	$618,072,290
Vacant	515	13,990,100
Residential	2,058	215,398,700
Commercial	144	334,464,800
Industrial	15	45,871,890
Apartments	1	127,200
Farm land	186	3,208,400
Farm homestead	49	5,011,200

Average Property Value & Tax, 2008

Residential value	$104,608
Property tax	$3,530
Tax credit/rebate	$646

Public Library

Logan Township Branch Library‡
101 Beckett Rd
Swedesboro, NJ 08085
856-241-0202

Branch Librarian .... Anne Woonick

Library statistics, 2007

see Gloucester County profile
for library system statistics

Public Safety

Number of officers, 2007	22

Crime	2006	2007
Total crimes	118	128
Violent	10	5
Murder	1	0
Rape	1	1
Robbery	0	1
Aggravated assault	8	3
Non-violent	108	123
Burglary	21	20
Larceny	76	98
Vehicle theft	11	5
Domestic violence	55	40
Arson	0	0
Total crime rate	19.0	20.7
Violent	1.6	0.8
Non-violent	17.4	19.9

Public School District

(for school year 2007-08 except as noted)

Logan Township School District
110 School Lane
Logan Twp, NJ 08085
(856) 467-5133

Superintendent	John Herbst
Number of schools	2
Grade plan	K-8
Enrollment	873
Attendance rate, '06-07	96.0%
Dropout rate	NA
Students per teacher	9.9
Per pupil expenditure	$13,632
Median faculty salary	$57,117
Median administrator salary	$87,935
Grade 12 enrollment	NA
High school graduation rate	NA

Assessment test results

(percent scoring at proficient or advanced level)

	Language	Math
NJASK-Grade 3	91.5%	86.4%
GEPA-Grade 8	83.5%	89.6%
HSPA-High School	NA	NA

SAT Score Averages, 2006-07

Pct tested	Math	Verbal	Writing
NA	NA	NA	NA

Teacher Qualifications

Avg. years of experience	15
Highly-qualified teachers	
one subject/all subjects	100%/100%

No Child Left Behind

AYP, 2006-07 .... Meets Standards

Municipal Finance

State Aid Programs, 2009

Total aid	$673,043
CMPTRA	39,006
Energy tax receipts	606,990
Garden State Trust	166

General Budget, 2008

Total tax levy	$20,913,026
County levy	6,633,501
County taxes	5,724,766
County library	460,544
County health	0
County open space	448,191
School levy	12,140,124
Muni. levy	2,139,401
Misc. revenues	6,523,176

Taxes	2006	2007	2008
General tax rate per $100	2.977	3.155	3.375
County equalization ratio	75.46	63.95	56.65
Net valuation taxable	$609,237,590	$617,982,578	$619,705,061
State equalized value	$954,687,780	$1,089,528,489	$1,161,460,675

Demographics & Socio-Economic Characteristics
(2000 US Census, except as noted)

Population
1980*	3,488
1990*	3,407
2000	3,329
Male	1,579
Female	1,750
2007 (estimate)*	3,528
Population density	664.4

Race & Hispanic Origin, 2000
Race
White	3,280
Black/African American	8
American Indian/Alaska Native	1
Asian	12
Native Hawaiian/Pacific Islander	0
Other race	11
Two or more races	17
Hispanic origin, total	70
Mexican	53
Puerto Rican	14
Cuban	0
Other Hispanic	3

Age & Nativity, 2000
Under 5 years	88
18 years and over	2,940
21 years and over	2,884
65 years and over	1,214
85 years and over	111
Median age	57.3
Native-born	3,203
Foreign-born	122

Educational Attainment, 2000
Population 25 years and over	2,847
Less than 9th grade	2.0%
High school grad or higher	92.0%
Bachelor's degree or higher	36.7%
Graduate degree	12.8%

Income & Poverty, 1999
Per capita income	$33,404
Median household income	$48,697
Median family income	$59,833
Persons in poverty	171
H'holds receiving public assistance	41
H'holds receiving social security	842

Households, 2000
Total households	1,664
With persons under 18	224
With persons over 65	857
Family households	1,039
Single-person households	562
Persons per household	2.00
Persons per family	2.50

Labor & Employment
Total civilian labor force, 2007**	1,603
Unemployment rate	4.9%
Total civilian labor force, 2000	1,351
Unemployment rate	5.0%

Employed persons 16 years and over by occupation, 2000
Managers & professionals	429
Service occupations	205
Sales & office occupations	413
Farming, fishing & forestry	0
Construction & maintenance	111
Production & transportation	125
Self-employed persons	141

‡ Branch of county library
* US Census Bureau
** New Jersey Department of Labor

General Information
Township of Long Beach
6805 Long Beach Blvd
Brant Beach, NJ 08008
609-361-1000
Website	www.longbeachtownship.com
Year of incorporation	1899
Land/water area (sq. miles)	5.31/16.69
Form of government	Commission

Government
Legislative Districts
US Congressional	3
State Legislative	9

Local Officials, 2009
Mayor	Joseph H Mancini
Administrator	Bonnie Leonetti
Clerk	Bonnie Leonetti
Finance Dir	Elizabeth Jones
Tax Assessor	Tracy A. Hafner
Tax Collector	Deborah Hample
Attorney	Shackleton & Hazeltine
Building	Ron Pingaro
Comm Dev/Planning	NA
Engineering	Frank Little
Public Works	Andrew Baran
Police Chief	Michael Bradley
Fire/Emergency Dir	NA

Housing & Construction
Housing Units, 2000*
Total	9,023
Median rent	$766
Median SF home value	$334,400

Permits for New Residential Construction
	Units	Value
Total, 2006	112	$47,935,608
Single family	108	$46,835,608
Total, 2007	68	$31,478,440
Single family	68	$31,478,440

Real Property Valuation, 2008
	Parcels	Valuation
Total	9,011	$7,388,699,300
Vacant	961	206,968,200
Residential	7,882	7,015,508,900
Commercial	159	158,503,300
Industrial	0	0
Apartments	9	7,718,900
Farm land	0	0
Farm homestead	0	0

Average Property Value & Tax, 2008
Residential value	$890,067
Property tax	$7,200
Tax credit/rebate	$1,134

Public Library
Long Beach Island Branch Library‡
217 S Central Ave
Surf City, NJ 08008
609-494-2480
Branch Librarian	Linda Feaster

Library statistics, 2007
see Ocean County profile
for library system statistics

Public Safety
Number of officers, 2007	40

Crime	2006	2007
Total crimes	228	270
Violent	5	6
Murder	0	0
Rape	0	0
Robbery	0	0
Aggravated assault	5	6
Non-violent	223	264
Burglary	24	23
Larceny	199	241
Vehicle theft	0	0
Domestic violence	9	14
Arson	0	0
Total crime rate	65.9	77.2
Violent	1.4	1.7
Non-violent	64.4	75.5

Public School District
(for school year 2007-08 except as noted)

Long Beach Island School District
200 Barnegat Avenue
Surf City, NJ 08008
(609) 494-2341
Superintendent	Robert A. Garguilo
Number of schools	2
Grade plan	K-6
Enrollment	258
Attendance rate, '06-07	94.0%
Dropout rate	NA
Students per teacher	7.1
Per pupil expenditure	$23,574
Median faculty salary	$71,027
Median administrator salary	$95,218
Grade 12 enrollment	NA
High school graduation rate	NA

Assessment test results
(percent scoring at proficient or advanced level)
	Language	Math
NJASK-Grade 3	96.9%	90.6%
GEPA-Grade 8	NA	NA
HSPA-High School	NA	NA

SAT Score Averages, 2006-07
Pct tested	Math	Verbal	Writing
NA	NA	NA	NA

Teacher Qualifications
Avg. years of experience	19
Highly-qualified teachers one subject/all subjects	100%/100%

No Child Left Behind
AYP, 2006-07	Meets Standards

Municipal Finance
State Aid Programs, 2009
Total aid	$724,137
CMPTRA	0
Energy tax receipts	687,848
Garden State Trust	119

General Budget, 2008
Total tax levy	$59,788,792
County levy	25,939,232
County taxes	22,268,956
County library	2,617,110
County health	0
County open space	1,053,166
School levy	18,970,561
Muni. levy	14,879,000
Misc. revenues	7,143,000

Taxes
	2006	2007	2008
General tax rate per $100	0.798	0.819	0.809
County equalization ratio	94.83	83.41	84.41
Net valuation taxable	$7,139,888,400	$7,281,862,420	$7,390,757,456
State equalized value	$8,562,182,884	$8,626,414,887	$3,101,827,805

Demographics & Socio-Economic Characteristics

(2000 US Census, except as noted)

Population
1980*	29,819
1990*	28,658
2000	31,340
Male	15,210
Female	16,130
2007 (estimate)*	32,349
Population density	6,197.1

Race & Hispanic Origin, 2000
Race
White	21,320
Black/African American	5,847
American Indian/Alaska Native	113
Asian	513
Native Hawaiian/Pacific Islander	15
Other race	2,220
Two or more races	1,312
Hispanic origin, total	6,477
Mexican	1,448
Puerto Rican	2,778
Cuban	84
Other Hispanic	2,167

Age & Nativity, 2000
Under 5 years	2,183
18 years and over	23,890
21 years and over	22,628
65 years and over	4,036
85 years and over	495
Median age	34.7
Native-born	25,176
Foreign-born	6,164

Educational Attainment, 2000
Population 25 years and over	20,774
Less than 9th grade	8.3%
High school grad or higher	76.3%
Bachelor's degree or higher	20.2%
Graduate degree	7.2%

Income & Poverty, 1999
Per capita income	$20,532
Median household income	$38,651
Median family income	$42,825
Persons in poverty	5,208
H'holds receiving public assistance	551
H'holds receiving social security	3,119

Households, 2000
Total households	12,594
With persons under 18	3,885
With persons over 65	3,027
Family households	7,248
Single-person households	4,295
Persons per household	2.47
Persons per family	3.19

Labor & Employment
Total civilian labor force, 2007**	16,166
Unemployment rate	4.7%
Total civilian labor force, 2000	15,398
Unemployment rate	7.4%

Employed persons 16 years and over by occupation, 2000
Managers & professionals	4,077
Service occupations	2,925
Sales & office occupations	4,016
Farming, fishing & forestry	22
Construction & maintenance	1,503
Production & transportation	1,720
Self-employed persons	1,002

* US Census Bureau
** New Jersey Department of Labor

General Information

City of Long Branch
344 Broadway
Long Branch, NJ 07740
732-222-7000

Website	www.longbranch.org
Year of incorporation	1903
Land/water area (sq. miles)	5.22/0.97
Form of government	Mayor-Council

Government

Legislative Districts
US Congressional	6
State Legislative	11

Local Officials, 2009
Mayor	Adam Schneider
Manager	Howard Woolley Jr
Clerk	Irene Joline
Finance Dir	Ronald Mehlhorn Sr
Tax Assessor	John Burtow
Tax Collector	Ed Mazzacco
Attorney	James Aaron
Building	Kevin Hayes
Planning	Jacob Jones
Engineering	Richard Brown
Public Works	Fred Migliaccio
Police Chief	Anthony Tomaine
Emerg/Fire Director	Donald Pingitore

Housing & Construction

Housing Units, 2000*
Total	13,983
Median rent	$727
Median SF home value	$135,300

Permits for New Residential Construction
	Units	Value
Total, 2006	7	$1,010,100
Single family	7	$1,010,100
Total, 2007	238	$31,088,875
Single family	22	$3,763,875

Real Property Valuation, 2008
	Parcels	Valuation
Total	9,480	$5,073,751,020
Vacant	524	180,981,900
Residential	8,298	4,009,946,400
Commercial	503	519,542,420
Industrial	6	12,197,100
Apartments	147	347,584,700
Farm land	1	4,500
Farm homestead	1	3,494,000

Average Property Value & Tax, 2008
Residential value	$483,605
Property tax	$6,874
Tax credit/rebate	$975

Public Library

Long Branch Public Library
328 Broadway
Long Branch, NJ 07740
732-222-3900

Director	Ingrid Bruck

Library statistics, 2007
Population served	31,340
Full-time/total staff	3/14

	Total	Per capita
Holdings	104,564	3.34
Revenues	$1,375,287	$43.88
Expenditures	$1,273,539	$40.64
Annual visits	192,489	6.14
Internet terminals/annual users	32/26,696	

Public Safety

Number of officers, 2007	102

Crime	2006	2007
Total crimes	978	795
Violent	174	112
Murder	4	0
Rape	2	0
Robbery	76	46
Aggravated assault	92	66
Non-violent	804	683
Burglary	230	203
Larceny	538	450
Vehicle theft	36	30
Domestic violence	449	391
Arson	0	0
Total crime rate	30.5	24.6
Violent	5.4	3.5
Non-violent	25.1	21.1

Public School District

(for school year 2007-08 except as noted)

Long Branch School District
540 Broadway
Long Branch, NJ 07740
(732) 571-2868

Superintendent	Joseph M. Ferraina
Number of schools	9
Grade plan	K-12
Enrollment	4,825
Attendance rate, '06-07	91.2%
Dropout rate	0.9%
Students per teacher	8.4
Per pupil expenditure	$17,781
Median faculty salary	$50,790
Median administrator salary	$107,866
Grade 12 enrollment	260
High school graduation rate	96.3%

Assessment test results
(percent scoring at proficient or advanced level)
	Language	Math
NJASK-Grade 3	80.8%	84.1%
GEPA-Grade 8	45.6%	73.6%
HSPA-High School	50.9%	69.3%

SAT Score Averages, 2006-07
Pct tested	Math	Verbal	Writing
56%	446	429	423

Teacher Qualifications
Avg. years of experience	7
Highly-qualified teachers one subject/all subjects	99.5%/99.5%

No Child Left Behind
AYP, 2006-07	Meets Standards

Municipal Finance

State Aid Programs, 2009
Total aid	$5,528,704
CMPTRA	2,674,906
Energy tax receipts	2,715,581
Garden State Trust	0

General Budget, 2008
Total tax levy	$72,213,556
County levy	11,981,120
County taxes	11,231,857
County library	0
County health	0
County open space	749,263
School levy	30,963,790
Muni. levy	29,268,646
Misc. revenues	15,793,054

Taxes
	2006	2007	2008
General tax rate per $100	2.442	1.347	1.422
County equalization ratio	66.89	110.33	102.12
Net valuation taxable	$2,491,582,200	$5,071,576,657	$5,080,087,292
State equalized value	$4,511,755,907	$4,966,421,513	$1,690,394,643

See Introduction for an explanation of all data sources.

Demographics & Socio-Economic Characteristics
(2000 US Census, except as noted)

Population
1980*	7,275
1990*	7,826
2000	8,777
Male	4,258
Female	4,519
2007 (estimate)*	8,652
Population density	716.2

Race & Hispanic Origin, 2000
Race
White	8,141
Black/African American	34
American Indian/Alaska Native	15
Asian	420
Native Hawaiian/Pacific Islander	3
Other race	49
Two or more races	115
Hispanic origin, total	303
Mexican	26
Puerto Rican	41
Cuban	32
Other Hispanic	204

Age & Nativity, 2000
Under 5 years	680
18 years and over	6,470
21 years and over	6,292
65 years and over	1,109
85 years and over	98
Median age	39.2
Native-born	7,785
Foreign-born	992

Educational Attainment, 2000
Population 25 years and over	5,995
Less than 9th grade	1.9%
High school grad or higher	93.8%
Bachelor's degree or higher	49.3%
Graduate degree	18.9%

Income & Poverty, 1999
Per capita income	$42,613
Median household income	$84,532
Median family income	$103,037
Persons in poverty	286
H'holds receiving public assistance	14
H'holds receiving social security	801

Households, 2000
Total households	3,139
With persons under 18	1,202
With persons over 65	782
Family households	2,458
Single-person households	570
Persons per household	2.79
Persons per family	3.19

Labor & Employment
Total civilian labor force, 2007**	4,973
Unemployment rate	2.8%
Total civilian labor force, 2000	4,559
Unemployment rate	2.8%

Employed persons 16 years and over by occupation, 2000
Managers & professionals	2,143
Service occupations	529
Sales & office occupations	1,222
Farming, fishing & forestry	14
Construction & maintenance	198
Production & transportation	325
Self-employed persons	228

* US Census Bureau
** New Jersey Department of Labor

General Information
Township of Long Hill
915 Valley Rd
Gillette, NJ 07933
908-647-8000
Website	www.longhillnj.us
Year of incorporation	1993
Land/water area (sq. miles)	12.08/0.00
Form of government	Township

Government
Legislative Districts
US Congressional	11
State Legislative	21

Local Officials, 2009
Mayor	George Vitureira
Township Admin	Richard Sheola
Clerk	Christine Gatti (Actg)
Finance Dir	Richard Sheola
Tax Assessor	Brett Trout
Tax Collector	Joan Donat
Attorney	John Pidgeon
Building	John Risso
Planning	Dawn Wolfe
Engineering	Paul Ferriero
Public Works	Tom Sweeney
Police Chief	Dan Hedden
Emergency Mgmt Dir	Ken Fullagar

Housing & Construction
Housing Units, 2000*
Total	3,206
Median rent	$1,024
Median SF home value	$297,000

Permits for New Residential Construction
	Units	Value
Total, 2006	2	$475,000
Single family	2	$475,000
Total, 2007	9	$2,709,410
Single family	9	$2,709,410

Real Property Valuation, 2008
	Parcels	Valuation
Total	3,294	$1,278,890,900
Vacant	233	19,116,300
Residential	2,894	1,129,463,700
Commercial	115	103,967,400
Industrial	21	16,541,200
Apartments	7	6,691,600
Farm land	16	40,700
Farm homestead	8	3,070,000

Average Property Value & Tax, 2008
Residential value	$390,260
Property tax	$10,005
Tax credit/rebate	$1,299

Public Library
Long Hill Township Public Library
917 Valley Rd
Gillette, NJ 07980
908-647-2088
Director	Mary Martin

Library statistics, 2007
Population served	8,777
Full-time/total staff	3/4

	Total	Per capita
Holdings	59,131	6.74
Revenues	$655,834	$74.72
Expenditures	$593,228	$67.59
Annual visits	121,300	13.82
Internet terminals/annual users	20/24,990	

Public Safety
Number of officers, 2007	26

Crime	2006	2007
Total crimes	53	58
Violent	1	3
Murder	0	0
Rape	0	0
Robbery	0	0
Aggravated assault	1	3
Non-violent	52	55
Burglary	9	8
Larceny	43	47
Vehicle theft	0	0
Domestic violence	35	21
Arson	0	0
Total crime rate	6.0	6.6
Violent	0.1	0.3
Non-violent	5.9	6.3

Public School District
(for school year 2007-08 except as noted)

Long Hill Township School District
759 Valley Road
Gillette, NJ 07933
(908) 647-1200
Superintendent	Rene Rovtar
Number of schools	3
Grade plan	K-8
Enrollment	1,063
Attendance rate, '06-07	96.1%
Dropout rate	NA
Students per teacher	10.7
Per pupil expenditure	$12,134
Median faculty salary	$53,570
Median administrator salary	$96,039
Grade 12 enrollment	NA
High school graduation rate	NA

Assessment test results
(percent scoring at proficient or advanced level)
	Language	Math
NJASK-Grade 3	92.0%	94.6%
GEPA-Grade 8	70.9%	96.6%
HSPA-High School	NA	NA

SAT Score Averages, 2006-07
Pct tested	Math	Verbal	Writing
NA	NA	NA	NA

Teacher Qualifications
Avg. years of experience	9
Highly-qualified teachers one subject/all subjects	98.5%/93.5%

No Child Left Behind
AYP, 2006-07	Meets Standards

Municipal Finance
State Aid Programs, 2009
Total aid	$1,704,867
CMPTRA	0
Energy tax receipts	1,662,048
Garden State Trust	203

General Budget, 2008
Total tax levy	$32,888,386
County levy	4,395,355
County taxes	3,586,811
County library	0
County health	0
County open space	808,544
School levy	19,481,625
Muni. levy	9,011,406
Misc. revenues	5,894,161

Taxes
	2006	2007	2008
General tax rate per $100	2.4	2.5	2.564
County equalization ratio	77.01	70.65	68.13
Net valuation taxable	$1,266,429,330	$1,278,011,246	$1,282,861,911
State equalized value	$1,796,620,576	$1,873,950,682	$1,881,379,848

Demographics & Socio-Economic Characteristics

(2000 US Census, except as noted)

Population
1980*	1,249
1990*	1,224
2000	1,054
Male	489
Female	565
2007 (estimate)*	1,081
Population density	2,844.7

Race & Hispanic Origin, 2000
Race
White	1,039
Black/African American	1
American Indian/Alaska Native	0
Asian	12
Native Hawaiian/Pacific Islander	0
Other race	0
Two or more races	2
Hispanic origin, total	5
Mexican	1
Puerto Rican	3
Cuban	0
Other Hispanic	1

Age & Nativity, 2000
Under 5 years	34
18 years and over	934
21 years and over	927
65 years and over	364
85 years and over	47
Median age	56.6
Native-born	1,022
Foreign-born	32

Educational Attainment, 2000
Population 25 years and over	900
Less than 9th grade	2.8%
High school grad or higher	86.9%
Bachelor's degree or higher	39.0%
Graduate degree	15.8%

Income & Poverty, 1999
Per capita income	$50,884
Median household income	$51,324
Median family income	$68,194
Persons in poverty	39
H'holds receiving public assistance	0
H'holds receiving social security	244

Households, 2000
Total households	544
With persons under 18	65
With persons over 65	261
Family households	317
Single-person households	204
Persons per household	1.94
Persons per family	2.53

Labor & Employment
Total civilian labor force, 2007**	533
Unemployment rate	3.7%
Total civilian labor force, 2000	505
Unemployment rate	4.0%

Employed persons 16 years and over by occupation, 2000
Managers & professionals	247
Service occupations	87
Sales & office occupations	113
Farming, fishing & forestry	0
Construction & maintenance	18
Production & transportation	20
Self-employed persons	48

General Information
Borough of Longport
2305 Atlantic Ave
Longport, NJ 08403
609-823-2731

Website	NA
Year of incorporation	1898
Land/water area (sq. miles)	0.38/1.24
Form of government	Commission

Government

Legislative Districts
US Congressional	2
State Legislative	2

Local Officials, 2009
Mayor	Nicholas Russo
Manager/Admin	NA
Clerk	Thomas Hiltner
Finance Dir	Maria Mento
Tax Assessor	Jeffrey Hesley
Tax Collector	Thomas Hiltner
Attorney	Thomas Subranni
Building	James Agnesino
Comm Dev/Planning	NA
Engineering	Richard Carter
Public Works	William Trinkle
Police Chief	A. Scott Porter
Emerg/Fire Director	Levon Clayton

Housing & Construction

Housing Units, 2000*
Total	1,574
Median rent	$909
Median SF home value	$267,300

Permits for New Residential Construction
	Units	Value
Total, 2006	23	$9,586,650
Single family	23	$9,586,650
Total, 2007	28	$14,731,682
Single family	28	$14,731,682

Real Property Valuation, 2008
	Parcels	Valuation
Total	1,660	$1,561,432,800
Vacant	77	62,606,300
Residential	1,575	1,495,095,500
Commercial	8	3,731,000
Industrial	0	0
Apartments	0	0
Farm land	0	0
Farm homestead	0	0

Average Property Value & Tax, 2008
Residential value	$949,267
Property tax	$6,849
Tax credit/rebate	$1,024

Public Library
Longport Branch Library‡
2305 Atlantic Ave
Longport, NJ 08403
609-487-0272

Director	Kathy Gindin

Library statistics, 2007
see Atlantic County profile
for library system statistics

Public Safety
Number of officers, 2007		14

Crime	2006	2007
Total crimes	33	14
Violent	0	1
Murder	0	0
Rape	0	0
Robbery	0	0
Aggravated assault	0	1
Non-violent	33	13
Burglary	15	4
Larceny	17	9
Vehicle theft	1	0
Domestic violence	3	4
Arson	0	0
Total crime rate	30.3	12.9
Violent	0.0	0.9
Non-violent	30.3	11.9

Public School District
(for school year 2007-08 except as noted)

Longport School District
2305 Atlantic Avenue
Longport, NJ 08403

No schools in district

Per pupil expenditure	NA
Median faculty salary	NA
Median administrator salary	NA
Grade 12 enrollment	NA
High school graduation rate	NA

Assessment test results
(percent scoring at proficient or advanced level)
	Language	Math
NJASK-Grade 3	NA	NA
GEPA-Grade 8	NA	NA
HSPA-High School	NA	NA

SAT Score Averages, 2006-07
Pct tested	Math	Verbal	Writing
NA	NA	NA	NA

Teacher Qualifications
Avg. years of experience	NA
Highly-qualified teachers one subject/all subjects	NA/NA

No Child Left Behind
AYP, 2006-07	NA

Municipal Finance

State Aid Programs, 2009
Total aid	$135,221
CMPTRA	0
Energy tax receipts	129,812
Garden State Trust	0

General Budget, 2008
Total tax levy	$11,267,240
County levy	5,346,381
County taxes	4,212,319
County library	540,242
County health	221,064
County open space	372,755
School levy	981,343
Muni. levy	4,939,516
Misc. revenues	2,008,545

Taxes
	2006	2007	2008
General tax rate per $100	0.7	0.695	0.722
County equalization ratio	105.98	92.72	83.83
Net valuation taxable	$1,528,220,900	$1,549,659,019	$1,561,605,377
State equalized value	$1,648,403,159	$1,848,538,274	$1,999,702,350

‡ Branch of county library
* US Census Bureau
** New Jersey Department of Labor

See Introduction for an explanation of all data sources.

Demographics & Socio-Economic Characteristics
(2000 US Census, except as noted)

Population
1980*	4,998
1990*	5,052
2000	5,765
Male	2,655
Female	3,110
2007 (estimate)*	8,369
Population density	1,182.1

Race & Hispanic Origin, 2000
Race
White	5,550
Black/African American	65
American Indian/Alaska Native	4
Asian	94
Native Hawaiian/Pacific Islander	0
Other race	28
Two or more races	24
Hispanic origin, total	115
Mexican	6
Puerto Rican	50
Cuban	16
Other Hispanic	43

Age & Nativity, 2000
Under 5 years	385
18 years and over	4,351
21 years and over	4,227
65 years and over	1,279
85 years and over	269
Median age	41.3
Native-born	5,502
Foreign-born	263

Educational Attainment, 2000
Population 25 years and over	4,137
Less than 9th grade	7.0%
High school grad or higher	82.5%
Bachelor's degree or higher	22.4%
Graduate degree	7.0%

Income & Poverty, 1999
Per capita income	$24,333
Median household income	$50,918
Median family income	$65,545
Persons in poverty	350
H'holds receiving public assistance	28
H'holds receiving social security	736

Households, 2000
Total households	2,143
With persons under 18	735
With persons over 65	746
Family households	1,524
Single-person households	562
Persons per household	2.55
Persons per family	3.09

Labor & Employment
Total civilian labor force, 2007**	2,890
Unemployment rate	2.1%
Total civilian labor force, 2000	2,578
Unemployment rate	1.9%

Employed persons 16 years and over by occupation, 2000
Managers & professionals	1,086
Service occupations	331
Sales & office occupations	621
Farming, fishing & forestry	14
Construction & maintenance	242
Production & transportation	235
Self-employed persons	124

* US Census Bureau
** New Jersey Department of Labor

General Information
Township of Lopatcong
232 S 3rd St
Phillipsburg, NJ 08865
908-859-3355
Website	www.lopatcongtwp.com
Year of incorporation	1863
Land/water area (sq. miles)	7.08/0.06
Form of government	Small Municipality

Government
Legislative Districts
US Congressional	5
State Legislative	23

Local Officials, 2009
Mayor	Douglas Steinhardt
Manager	M. Beth Dilts
Clerk	M. Beth Dilts
Finance Dir	Mary Dobes
Tax Assessor	Kathleen Degan
Tax Collector	Rachel Edinger
Attorney	Michael Lavery
Building	John Fritts
Comm Dev/Planning	NA
Engineering	Paul Sterbenz
Public Works Dir	Steve Hockman
Police Chief	Scott Marinelli
Emerg/Fire Director	Tom Nigro

Housing & Construction
Housing Units, 2000*
Total	2,429
Median rent	$624
Median SF home value	$156,600

Permits for New Residential Construction
	Units	Value
Total, 2006	45	$5,348,174
Single family	43	$5,105,674
Total, 2007	29	$3,630,571
Single family	29	$3,630,571

Real Property Valuation, 2008
	Parcels	Valuation
Total	3,394	$1,026,628,049
Vacant	471	55,445,600
Residential	2,675	784,580,256
Commercial	136	137,140,971
Industrial	12	19,067,400
Apartments	2	18,230,400
Farm land	69	695,122
Farm homestead	29	11,468,300

Average Property Value & Tax, 2008
Residential value	$294,397
Property tax	$5,843
Tax credit/rebate	$1,005

Public Library
No public municipal library

Library statistics, 2007
Population served	NA
Full-time/total staff	NA/NA

	Total	Per capita
Holdings	NA	NA
Revenues	NA	NA
Expenditures	NA	NA
Annual visits	NA	NA
Internet terminals/annual users	NA/NA	

Public Safety
Number of officers, 2007	14

Crime	2006	2007
Total crimes	99	110
Violent	11	7
Murder	1	0
Rape	0	0
Robbery	4	3
Aggravated assault	6	4
Non-violent	88	103
Burglary	19	13
Larceny	67	83
Vehicle theft	2	7
Domestic violence	66	82
Arson	0	0
Total crime rate	12.0	13.0
Violent	1.3	0.8
Non-violent	10.7	12.2

Public School District
(for school year 2007-08 except as noted)

Lopatcong Township School District
263 Route 57
Phillipsburg, NJ 08865
(908) 859-0800
Superintendent	Vicki Pede
Number of schools	2
Grade plan	K-8
Enrollment	894
Attendance rate, '06-07	96.2%
Dropout rate	NA
Students per teacher	10.1
Per pupil expenditure	$10,791
Median faculty salary	$54,709
Median administrator salary	$88,299
Grade 12 enrollment	NA
High school graduation rate	NA

Assessment test results
(percent scoring at proficient or advanced level)
	Language	Math
NJASK-Grade 3	84.0%	92.9%
GEPA-Grade 8	76.7%	89.7%
HSPA-High School	NA	NA

SAT Score Averages, 2006-07
Pct tested	Math	Verbal	Writing
NA	NA	NA	NA

Teacher Qualifications
Avg. years of experience	9
Highly-qualified teachers one subject/all subjects	98.5%/98.5%

No Child Left Behind
AYP, 2006-07 .... Meets Standards

Municipal Finance
State Aid Programs, 2009
Total aid	$1,242,744
CMPTRA	0
Energy tax receipts	1,190,342
Garden State Trust	2,488

General Budget, 2008
Total tax levy	$20,410,450
County levy	6,180,195
County taxes	5,034,349
County library	532,146
County health	0
County open space	613,700
School levy	11,919,641
Muni. levy	2,310,614
Misc. revenues	4,127,050

Taxes
	2006	2007	2008
General tax rate per $100	1.88	1.95	1.985
County equalization ratio	115	104.47	100.90
Net valuation taxable	$1,009,864,216	$1,018,383,086	$1,028,376,511
State equalized value	$967,659,558	$1,009,314,254	$1,034,885,273

Demographics & Socio-Economic Characteristics

(2000 US Census, except as noted)

Population

1980*	1,547
1990*	1,858
2000	1,851
Male	894
Female	957
2007 (estimate)*	1,883
Population density	40.3

Race & Hispanic Origin, 2000

Race

White	1,784
Black/African American	40
American Indian/Alaska Native	2
Asian	12
Native Hawaiian/Pacific Islander	0
Other race	3
Two or more races	10
Hispanic origin, total	9
Mexican	1
Puerto Rican	4
Cuban	2
Other Hispanic	2

Age & Nativity, 2000

Under 5 years	121
18 years and over	1,400
21 years and over	1,338
65 years and over	258
85 years and over	30
Median age	39.5
Native-born	1,837
Foreign-born	14

Educational Attainment, 2000

Population 25 years and over	1,284
Less than 9th grade	6.2%
High school grad or higher	82.4%
Bachelor's degree or higher	11.7%
Graduate degree	2.2%

Income & Poverty, 1999

Per capita income	$21,962
Median household income	$55,078
Median family income	$59,653
Persons in poverty	135
H'holds receiving public assistance	6
H'holds receiving social security	208

Households, 2000

Total households	693
With persons under 18	246
With persons over 65	178
Family households	538
Single-person households	126
Persons per household	2.67
Persons per family	3.00

Labor & Employment

Total civilian labor force, 2007**	978
Unemployment rate	2.6%
Total civilian labor force, 2000	947
Unemployment rate	3.0%

Employed persons 16 years and over by occupation, 2000

Managers & professionals	244
Service occupations	171
Sales & office occupations	201
Farming, fishing & forestry	8
Construction & maintenance	119
Production & transportation	176
Self-employed persons	44

General Information

Township of Lower Alloways Creek
501 Locust Island Rd
PO Box 157
Hancock's Bridge, NJ 08038
856-935-1549

Website	(county website)
Year of incorporation	1767
Land/water area (sq. miles)	46.78/25.80
Form of government	Township

Government

Legislative Districts

US Congressional	2
State Legislative	3

Local Officials, 2009

Mayor	Ellen B. Pompper
Manager/Admin	NA
Clerk	Ronald L. Campbell Sr
Finance Dir	Kevin Clour
Tax Assessor	Joseph Harasta
Tax Collector	D. Michelle Mitchell
Attorney	George G. Rosenberger
Building	Wayne Serfass
Comm Dev/Planning	NA
Engineering	J. Michael Fralinger
Public Works	Jack Lynch
Police Chief	Lee Peterson
Emerg/Fire Director	David Sowers

Housing & Construction

Housing Units, 2000*

Total	730
Median rent	$640
Median SF home value	$118,000

Permits for New Residential Construction

	Units	Value
Total, 2006	2	$355,000
Single family	2	$355,000
Total, 2007	3	$594,000
Single family	3	$594,000

Real Property Valuation, 2008

	Parcels	Valuation
Total	1,267	$207,208,210
Vacant	180	2,479,700
Residential	506	60,678,500
Commercial	10	1,527,200
Industrial	1	112,994,100
Apartments	0	0
Farm land	385	4,181,210
Farm homestead	185	25,347,500

Average Property Value & Tax, 2008

Residential value	$124,495
Property tax	$1,285
Tax credit/rebate	$475

Public Library

No public municipal library

Library statistics, 2007

Population served	NA
Full-time/total staff	NA/NA

	Total	Per capita
Holdings	NA	NA
Revenues	NA	NA
Expenditures	NA	NA
Annual visits	NA	NA
Internet terminals/annual users	NA/NA	

Public Safety

Number of officers, 2007	13

Crime	2006	2007
Total crimes	16	23
Violent	1	2
Murder	0	0
Rape	0	0
Robbery	0	0
Aggravated assault	1	2
Non-violent	15	21
Burglary	3	5
Larceny	10	16
Vehicle theft	2	0
Domestic violence	22	22
Arson	0	0
Total crime rate	8.3	12.0
Violent	0.5	1.0
Non-violent	7.8	11.0

Public School District

(for school year 2007-08 except as noted)

Lower Alloways Creek Township Dist.
967 Main Street-Canton
Salem, NJ 08079
(856) 935-2707

Chief School Admin	Fred Pratta
Number of schools	1
Grade plan	K-8
Enrollment	231
Attendance rate, '06-07	98.2%
Dropout rate	NA
Students per teacher	8.5
Per pupil expenditure	$14,850
Median faculty salary	$58,650
Median administrator salary	$65,238
Grade 12 enrollment	NA
High school graduation rate	NA

Assessment test results

(percent scoring at proficient or advanced level)

	Language	Math
NJASK-Grade 3	89.6%	86.2%
GEPA-Grade 8	81.8%	95.4%
HSPA-High School	NA	NA

SAT Score Averages, 2006-07

Pct tested	Math	Verbal	Writing
NA	NA	NA	NA

Teacher Qualifications

Avg. years of experience	22

Highly-qualified teachers
one subject/all subjects 100%/100%

No Child Left Behind

AYP, 2006-07 .... Meets Standards

Municipal Finance

State Aid Programs, 2009

Total aid	$7,755,239
CMPTRA	0
Energy tax receipts	7,535,233
Garden State Trust	53,296

General Budget, 2008

Total tax levy	$2,145,098
County levy	2,145,098
County taxes	2,098,816
County library	0
County health	0
County open space	46,282
School levy	0
Muni. levy	0
Misc. revenues	10,002,409

Taxes

	2006	2007	2008
General tax rate per $100	1.072	1.127	1.033
County equalization ratio	92.84	83.83	90.52
Net valuation taxable	$204,281,210	$205,160,269	$207,832,672
State equalized value	$244,288,066	$226,589,322	$119,168,509

* US Census Bureau
** New Jersey Department of Labor

See Introduction for an explanation of all data sources.

Lower Township

Demographics & Socio-Economic Characteristics
(2000 US Census, except as noted)

Population
1980*	17,105
1990*	20,820
2000	22,945
Male	10,888
Female	12,057
2007 (estimate)*	20,346
Population density	721.0

Race & Hispanic Origin, 2000
Race
White	22,088
Black/African American	319
American Indian/Alaska Native	52
Asian	121
Native Hawaiian/Pacific Islander	5
Other race	150
Two or more races	210
Hispanic origin, total	432
Mexican	74
Puerto Rican	250
Cuban	30
Other Hispanic	78

Age & Nativity, 2000
Under 5 years	1,177
18 years and over	17,504
21 years and over	16,815
65 years and over	4,740
85 years and over	543
Median age	41.8
Native-born	22,293
Foreign-born	655

Educational Attainment, 2000
Population 25 years and over	16,099
Less than 9th grade	4.3%
High school grad or higher	77.0%
Bachelor's degree or higher	13.1%
Graduate degree	3.4%

Income & Poverty, 1999
Per capita income	$19,786
Median household income	$38,977
Median family income	$45,058
Persons in poverty	1,742
H'holds receiving public assistance	219
H'holds receiving social security	3,693

Households, 2000
Total households	9,328
With persons under 18	2,894
With persons over 65	3,361
Family households	6,379
Single-person households	2,535
Persons per household	2.43
Persons per family	2.95

Labor & Employment
Total civilian labor force, 2007**	12,387
Unemployment rate	8.0%
Total civilian labor force, 2000	10,530
Unemployment rate	9.9%

Employed persons 16 years and over by occupation, 2000
Managers & professionals	2,269
Service occupations	2,290
Sales & office occupations	2,623
Farming, fishing & forestry	137
Construction & maintenance	1,298
Production & transportation	869
Self-employed persons	669

‡ Branch of county library
* US Census Bureau
** New Jersey Department of Labor

General Information
Township of Lower
2600 Bayshore Rd
Villas, NJ 08251
609-886-2005
Website	townshipoflower.org
Year of incorporation	1723
Land/water area (sq. miles)	28.22/2.85
Form of government	Council-Manager

Government
Legislative Districts
US Congressional	2
State Legislative	1

Local Officials, 2009
Mayor	Michael Beck
Manager	Joseph Jackson
Clerk	Claudia R. Kammer
CFO/Treasurer	Lauren Read
Tax Assessor	Arthur Amonette
Tax Collector	Susan Jackson
Attorney	Anthony Monzo
Construction	Gary Playford
Planning	Jay Dillworth (Chr)
Engineering	Hatch Mott MacDonald
Public Works	Gary Douglass
Police Chief	Edward Donohue
Fire Safety	Dave Perry

Housing & Construction
Housing Units, 2000*
Total	13,924
Median rent	$687
Median SF home value	$95,900

Permits for New Residential Construction
	Units	Value
Total, 2006	68	$16,861,895
Single family	46	$7,363,768
Total, 2007	246	$27,652,387
Single family	36	$4,452,387

Real Property Valuation, 2008
	Parcels	Valuation
Total	15,241	$4,684,640,600
Vacant	826	133,431,600
Residential	13,966	4,217,537,900
Commercial	344	309,843,800
Industrial	0	0
Apartments	4	13,262,500
Farm land	81	1,092,000
Farm homestead	20	9,472,800

Average Property Value & Tax, 2008
Residential value	$302,232
Property tax	$3,197
Tax credit/rebate	$808

Public Library
Lower Cape Branch Library‡
2600 Bayshore Rd
Villas, NJ 08251
609-886-8999
Branch Librarian	Edward Carson

Library statistics, 2007
see Cape May County profile
for library system statistics

Public Safety
Number of officers, 2007	46

Crime	2006	2007
Total crimes	526	535
Violent	43	69
Murder	0	0
Rape	2	1
Robbery	6	12
Aggravated assault	35	56
Non-violent	483	466
Burglary	119	95
Larceny	348	355
Vehicle theft	16	16
Domestic violence	454	439
Arson	4	1
Total crime rate	24.5	25.7
Violent	2.0	3.3
Non-violent	22.5	22.4

Public School District
(for school year 2007-08 except as noted)

Lower Township School District
834 Seashore Road
Cape May, NJ 08204
(609) 884-9400
Superintendent	Joseph Cirrinicione
Number of schools	4
Grade plan	K-6
Enrollment	1,837
Attendance rate, '06-07	94.0%
Dropout rate	NA
Students per teacher	11.2
Per pupil expenditure	$13,497
Median faculty salary	$65,417
Median administrator salary	$110,701
Grade 12 enrollment	NA
High school graduation rate	NA

Assessment test results
(percent scoring at proficient or advanced level)
	Language	Math
NJASK-Grade 3	86.2%	82.1%
GEPA-Grade 8	NA	NA
HSPA-High School	NA	NA

SAT Score Averages, 2006-07
Pct tested	Math	Verbal	Writing
NA	NA	NA	NA

Teacher Qualifications
Avg. years of experience	14
Highly-qualified teachers one subject/all subjects	89.5%/89.5%

No Child Left Behind
AYP, 2006-07 .... Meets Standards

Municipal Finance
State Aid Programs, 2009
Total aid	$2,059,527
CMPTRA	337,959
Energy tax receipts	1,517,216
Garden State Trust	144,912

General Budget, 2008
Total tax levy	$49,622,596
County levy	8,401,097
County taxes	6,677,694
County library	1,281,674
County health	0
County open space	441,730
School levy	24,885,263
Muni. levy	16,336,236
Misc. revenues	6,861,366

Taxes
	2006	2007	2008
General tax rate per $100	2.88	1.02	1.061
County equalization ratio	43.18	114.65	106.45
Net valuation taxable	$1,518,733,200	$4,702,561,453	$4,690,984,294
State equalized value	$4,072,227,317	$4,418,014,731	$4,473,010,933

See Introduction for an explanation of all data sources.

Demographics & Socio-Economic Characteristics

(2000 US Census, except as noted)

Population
1980*	5,236
1990*	6,705
2000	10,461
Male	4,990
Female	5,471
2007 (estimate)*	12,099
Population density	940.1

Race & Hispanic Origin, 2000
Race
White	8,192
Black/African American	1,438
American Indian/Alaska Native	24
Asian	354
Native Hawaiian/Pacific Islander	2
Other race	199
Two or more races	252
Hispanic origin, total	539
Mexican	46
Puerto Rican	337
Cuban	17
Other Hispanic	139

Age & Nativity, 2000
Under 5 years	873
18 years and over	7,524
21 years and over	7,262
65 years and over	1,158
85 years and over	156
Median age	35.6
Native-born	9,665
Foreign-born	676

Educational Attainment, 2000
Population 25 years and over	6,790
Less than 9th grade	4.5%
High school grad or higher	86.2%
Bachelor's degree or higher	30.9%
Graduate degree	9.6%

Income & Poverty, 1999
Per capita income	$25,789
Median household income	$60,571
Median family income	$70,329
Persons in poverty	381
H'holds receiving public assistance	69
H'holds receiving social security	747

Households, 2000
Total households	3,930
With persons under 18	1,630
With persons over 65	784
Family households	2,730
Single-person households	988
Persons per household	2.61
Persons per family	3.17

Labor & Employment
Total civilian labor force, 2007**	5,882
Unemployment rate	3.4%
Total civilian labor force, 2000	5,175
Unemployment rate	3.7%

Employed persons 16 years and over by occupation, 2000
Managers & professionals	2,217
Service occupations	526
Sales & office occupations	1,317
Farming, fishing & forestry	0
Construction & maintenance	336
Production & transportation	587
Self-employed persons	217

* US Census Bureau
** New Jersey Department of Labor

General Information

Township of Lumberton
PO Box 1860
35 Municipal Drive
Lumberton, NJ 08048
609-267-3217

Website	www.lumbertontwp.com
Year of incorporation	1860
Land/water area (sq. miles)	12.87/0.17
Form of government	Township

Government

Legislative Districts
US Congressional	3
State Legislative	8

Local Officials, 2009
Mayor	Michael Mansdoerfer
Manager	Daniel Van Pelt
Clerk	Stephanie Yurko (Actg)
Finance Dir	Joanna Mustafa
Tax Assessor	Patty Sporer
Tax Collector	Leslie Nealon
Attorney	Michael Mouber
Building	Brad Regn
Comm Dev/Planning	NA
Engineering	Alaimo Group
Public Works	Tommy Shover
Police Chief	Marc Sano
Emerg/Fire Director	Ernest Boegly

Housing & Construction

Housing Units, 2000*
Total	4,080
Median rent	$702
Median SF home value	$163,300

Permits for New Residential Construction
	Units	Value
Total, 2006	31	$1,948,400
Single family	31	$1,948,400
Total, 2007	1	$124,000
Single family	1	$124,000

Real Property Valuation, 2008
	Parcels	Valuation
Total	4,176	$1,433,155,780
Vacant	104	11,963,500
Residential	3,747	1,191,093,800
Commercial	146	122,340,000
Industrial	10	55,956,100
Apartments	8	28,954,400
Farm land	113	1,997,980
Farm homestead	48	20,850,000

Average Property Value & Tax, 2008
Residential value	$319,353
Property tax	$6,294
Tax credit/rebate	$951

Public Library

No public municipal library

Library statistics, 2007
Population served	NA
Full-time/total staff	NA/NA

	Total	Per capita
Holdings	NA	NA
Revenues	NA	NA
Expenditures	NA	NA
Annual visits	NA	NA
Internet terminals/annual users	NA/NA	

Public Safety

Number of officers, 2007	28

Crime	2006	2007
Total crimes	359	333
Violent	29	17
Murder	0	1
Rape	1	2
Robbery	10	6
Aggravated assault	18	8
Non-violent	330	316
Burglary	47	42
Larceny	272	266
Vehicle theft	11	8
Domestic violence	158	137
Arson	14	10
Total crime rate	28.9	27.0
Violent	2.3	1.4
Non-violent	26.6	25.6

Public School District

(for school year 2007-08 except as noted)

Lumberton Township School District
33 Municipal Drive
Lumberton, NJ 08048
(609) 265-7709

Superintendent	Frank Logandro
Number of schools	4
Grade plan	K-8
Enrollment	1,727
Attendance rate, '06-07	96.3%
Dropout rate	NA
Students per teacher	11.3
Per pupil expenditure	$11,813
Median faculty salary	$53,910
Median administrator salary	$108,326
Grade 12 enrollment	NA
High school graduation rate	NA

Assessment test results
(percent scoring at proficient or advanced level)
	Language	Math
NJASK-Grade 3	95.4%	91.4%
GEPA-Grade 8	70.4%	87.2%
HSPA-High School	NA	NA

SAT Score Averages, 2006-07
Pct tested	Math	Verbal	Writing
NA	NA	NA	NA

Teacher Qualifications
Avg. years of experience	11
Highly-qualified teachers one subject/all subjects	100%/100%

No Child Left Behind
AYP, 2006-07	Meets Standards

Municipal Finance

State Aid Programs, 2009
Total aid	$1,654,401
CMPTRA	0
Energy tax receipts	1,612,876
Garden State Trust	179

General Budget, 2008
Total tax levy	$28,288,008
County levy	5,848,643
County taxes	4,802,855
County library	443,393
County health	0
County open space	602,396
School levy	18,017,770
Muni. levy	4,421,595
Misc. revenues	6,117,766

Taxes	2006	2007	2008
General tax rate per $100	3.551	1.92	1.971
County equalization ratio	58.43	110.64	95.02
Net valuation taxable	$740,300,400	$1,434,765,770	$1,435,259,193
State equalized value	$1,383,645,024	$1,509,851,020	$1,546,785,219

See Introduction for an explanation of all data sources.

Demographics & Socio-Economic Characteristics
(2000 US Census, except as noted)

Population
1980*	20,326
1990*	18,262
2000	19,383
Male	9,242
Female	10,141
2007 (estimate)*	19,468
Population density	4,186.7

Race & Hispanic Origin, 2000
Race
White	17,433
Black/African American	119
American Indian/Alaska Native	9
Asian	1,046
Native Hawaiian/Pacific Islander	1
Other race	397
Two or more races	378
Hispanic origin, total	1,744
Mexican	97
Puerto Rican	465
Cuban	273
Other Hispanic	909

Age & Nativity, 2000
Under 5 years	959
18 years and over	15,690
21 years and over	15,142
65 years and over	3,440
85 years and over	382
Median age	39.5
Native-born	15,904
Foreign-born	3,479

Educational Attainment, 2000
Population 25 years and over	14,263
Less than 9th grade	7.8%
High school grad or higher	81.4%
Bachelor's degree or higher	21.9%
Graduate degree	6.2%

Income & Poverty, 1999
Per capita income	$25,940
Median household income	$53,375
Median family income	$63,758
Persons in poverty	890
H'holds receiving public assistance	92
H'holds receiving social security	2,664

Households, 2000
Total households	7,877
With persons under 18	2,200
With persons over 65	2,564
Family households	5,205
Single-person households	2,269
Persons per household	2.46
Persons per family	3.06

Labor & Employment
Total civilian labor force, 2007**	10,892
Unemployment rate	4.7%
Total civilian labor force, 2000	10,363
Unemployment rate	5.3%

Employed persons 16 years and over by occupation, 2000
Managers & professionals	2,976
Service occupations	1,280
Sales & office occupations	3,313
Farming, fishing & forestry	0
Construction & maintenance	882
Production & transportation	1,358
Self-employed persons	429

* US Census Bureau
** New Jersey Department of Labor
§ State Fiscal Year July 1–June 30

General Information
Township of Lyndhurst
367 Valley Brook Ave
Lyndhurst, NJ 07071
201-804-2457
Website	www.lyndhurstnj.org
Year of incorporation	1917
Land/water area (sq. miles)	4.65/0.26
Form of government	Commission

Government
Legislative Districts
US Congressional	9
State Legislative	36

Local Officials, 2009
Mayor	Richard J. DiLascio
Manager/Admin	NA
Clerk	Helen Polito
Finance Dir	Deborah Ferrato
Tax Assessor	Denis McGuire
Tax Collector	Deborah Ferrato
Attorney	Gary C. Cucchiara
Building	Mark Sadonis
Comm Dev/Planning	NA
Engineering	Michael Neglia
Public Works	Matthew T. Ruzzo
Police Chief	James O'Connor
Emerg/Fire Director	Michael Wartel

Housing & Construction
Housing Units, 2000*
Total	8,103
Median rent	$805
Median SF home value	$182,800

Permits for New Residential Construction
	Units	Value
Total, 2006	20	$3,353,392
Single family	16	$2,933,892
Total, 2007	5	$1,190,055
Single family	3	$904,855

Real Property Valuation, 2008
	Parcels	Valuation
Total	5,692	$3,524,217,600
Vacant	132	171,367,000
Residential	5,084	2,100,885,000
Commercial	323	460,341,500
Industrial	102	729,566,800
Apartments	51	62,057,300
Farm land	0	0
Farm homestead	0	0

Average Property Value & Tax, 2008
Residential value	$413,235
Property tax	$6,769
Tax credit/rebate	$1,013

Public Library
Lyndhurst Public Library
355 Valley Brook Ave
Lyndhurst, NJ 07071
201-804-2478
Director	Donna M. Romeo

Library statistics, 2007
Population served	19,383
Full-time/total staff	3/10

	Total	Per capita
Holdings	50,666	2.61
Revenues	$980,277	$50.57
Expenditures	$880,676	$45.44
Annual visits	115,000	5.93
Internet terminals/annual users	10/26,000	

Public Safety
Number of officers, 2007	48

Crime	2006	2007
Total crimes	336	396
Violent	13	9
Murder	0	1
Rape	2	0
Robbery	3	4
Aggravated assault	8	4
Non-violent	323	387
Burglary	40	62
Larceny	257	283
Vehicle theft	26	42
Domestic violence	169	141
Arson	2	0
Total crime rate	17.3	20.1
Violent	0.7	0.5
Non-violent	16.6	19.6

Public School District
(for school year 2007-08 except as noted)

Lyndhurst Township School District
420 Fern Avenue
Lyndhurst, NJ 07071
(201) 438-5683
Superintendent	Joseph Abate Jr
Number of schools	7
Grade plan	K-12
Enrollment	2,224
Attendance rate, '06-07	94.4%
Dropout rate	2.0%
Students per teacher	12.2
Per pupil expenditure	$12,813
Median faculty salary	$66,365
Median administrator salary	$115,906
Grade 12 enrollment	161
High school graduation rate	90.1%

Assessment test results
(percent scoring at proficient or advanced level)
	Language	Math
NJASK-Grade 3	86.8%	89.3%
GEPA-Grade 8	78.3%	91.2%
HSPA-High School	76.0%	85.5%

SAT Score Averages, 2006-07
Pct tested	Math	Verbal	Writing
70%	512	454	464

Teacher Qualifications
Avg. years of experience	11
Highly-qualified teachers one subject/all subjects	100%/100%

No Child Left Behind
AYP, 2006-07	Meets Standards

Municipal Finance§
State Aid Programs, 2009
Total aid	$1,817,505
CMPTRA	606,236
Energy tax receipts	1,165,404
Garden State Trust	438

General Budget, 2008
Total tax levy	$57,793,851
County levy	6,312,055
County taxes	5,967,116
County library	0
County health	0
County open space	344,939
School levy	27,990,122
Muni. levy	23,491,674
Misc. revenues	7,855,747

Taxes
	2006	2007	2008
General tax rate per $100	1.45	1.6	1.639
County equalization ratio	132.34	112.3	103.11
Net valuation taxable	$3,464,760,600	$3,472,059,121	$3,528,164,401
State equalized value	$3,088,667,349	$3,367,437,409	$3,416,571,571

See Introduction for an explanation of all data sources.

Demographics & Socio-Economic Characteristics

(2000 US Census, except as noted)

Population
1980*	15,357
1990*	15,850
2000	16,530
Male	7,832
Female	8,698
2007 (estimate)*	16,046
Population density	3,820.5

Race & Hispanic Origin, 2000
Race
White	14,826
Black/African American	496
American Indian/Alaska Native	21
Asian	624
Native Hawaiian/Pacific Islander	38
Other race	256
Two or more races	269
Hispanic origin, total	987
Mexican	43
Puerto Rican	70
Cuban	30
Other Hispanic	844

Age & Nativity, 2000
Under 5 years	981
18 years and over	13,126
21 years and over	11,333
65 years and over	2,157
85 years and over	301
Median age	34.3
Native-born	14,323
Foreign-born	2,207

Educational Attainment, 2000
Population 25 years and over	10,178
Less than 9th grade	3.8%
High school grad or higher	90.8%
Bachelor's degree or higher	56.8%
Graduate degree	26.0%

Income & Poverty, 1999
Per capita income	$38,416
Median household income	$82,847
Median family income	$101,798
Persons in poverty	469
H'holds receiving public assistance	59
H'holds receiving social security	1,524

Households, 2000
Total households	5,520
With persons under 18	1,807
With persons over 65	1,501
Family households	3,785
Single-person households	1,415
Persons per household	2.53
Persons per family	3.05

Labor & Employment
Total civilian labor force, 2007**	8,052
Unemployment rate	2.1%
Total civilian labor force, 2000	9,199
Unemployment rate	12.5%

Employed persons 16 years and over by occupation, 2000
Managers & professionals	4,256
Service occupations	789
Sales & office occupations	2,219
Farming, fishing & forestry	12
Construction & maintenance	228
Production & transportation	545
Self-employed persons	468

General Information
Borough of Madison
Hartley Dodge Memorial
50 Kings Rd
Madison, NJ 07940
973-593-3042

Website	www.rosenet.org/gov
Year of incorporation	1889
Land/water area (sq. miles)	4.20/0.00
Form of government	Borough

Government
Legislative Districts
US Congressional	11
State Legislative	21

Local Officials, 2009
Mayor	Mary-Anna Holden
Manager	Raymond M. Codey
Clerk	Marilyn Schaefer
Finance Dir	Robert Kalafut
Tax Assessor	Lisa Baratto
Tax Collector	Francine DeAngelis
Attorney	Joseph Mezzacca Jr
Building	Russell Brown
Planning	Peter G. Steck
Engineering	Robert Vogel
Public Works	David Maines
Police Chief	Vincent Chirico
Emerg/Fire Director	Douglas Atchison

Housing & Construction
Housing Units, 2000*
Total	5,641
Median rent	$1,036
Median SF home value	$362,400

Permits for New Residential Construction
	Units	Value
Total, 2006	34	$14,134,501
Single family	32	$13,794,501
Total, 2007	31	$14,425,934
Single family	31	$14,425,934

Real Property Valuation, 2008
	Parcels	Valuation
Total	4,535	$2,117,510,300
Vacant	73	15,215,000
Residential	4,196	1,706,375,600
Commercial	223	343,862,800
Industrial	6	3,422,000
Apartments	37	48,634,900
Farm land	0	0
Farm homestead	0	0

Average Property Value & Tax, 2008
Residential value	$406,667
Property tax	$10,075
Tax credit/rebate	$1,151

Public Library
Madison Public Library
39 Keep St
Madison, NJ 07940
973-377-0722
Director............Nancy S. Adamczyk

Library statistics, 2007
Population served	16,530
Full-time/total staff	6/12

	Total	Per capita
Holdings	142,983	8.65
Revenues	$1,612,847	$97.57
Expenditures	$1,595,187	$96.50
Annual visits	124,803	7.55
Internet terminals/annual users	35/24,059	

Public Safety
Number of officers, 2007	36

Crime	2006	2007
Total crimes	184	152
Violent	18	9
Murder	0	0
Rape	1	2
Robbery	1	1
Aggravated assault	16	6
Non-violent	166	143
Burglary	24	20
Larceny	139	122
Vehicle theft	3	1
Domestic violence	35	31
Arson	0	0
Total crime rate	11.6	9.5
Violent	1.1	0.6
Non-violent	10.4	8.9

Public School District
(for school year 2007-08 except as noted)

Madison School District
359 Woodland Road
Madison, NJ 07940
(973) 593-3100

Superintendent	Richard Noonan
Number of schools	5
Grade plan	K-12
Enrollment	2,246
Attendance rate, '06-07	95.1%
Dropout rate	0.8%
Students per teacher	10.2
Per pupil expenditure	$14,261
Median faculty salary	$62,556
Median administrator salary	$120,350
Grade 12 enrollment	180
High school graduation rate	97.2%

Assessment test results
(percent scoring at proficient or advanced level)
	Language	Math
NJASK-Grade 3	97.5%	96.9%
GEPA-Grade 8	89.0%	93.7%
HSPA-High School	91.7%	94.2%

SAT Score Averages, 2006-07
Pct tested	Math	Verbal	Writing
91%	569	560	561

Teacher Qualifications
Avg. years of experience	8
Highly-qualified teachers one subject/all subjects	100%/100%

No Child Left Behind
AYP, 2006-07	Meets Standards

Municipal Finance
State Aid Programs, 2009
Total aid	$1,079,075
CMPTRA	309,863
Energy tax receipts	726,049
Garden State Trust	0

General Budget, 2008
Total tax levy	$52,678,318
County levy	8,508,051
County taxes	6,943,776
County library	0
County health	0
County open space	1,564,275
School levy	31,903,062
Muni. levy	12,267,205
Misc. revenues	13,316,959

Taxes	2006	2007	2008
General tax rate per $100	2.2	2.35	2.478
County equalization ratio	65.88	60.39	57.98
Net valuation taxable	$2,105,477,500	$2,131,307,423	$2,126,394,341
State equalized value	$3,497,834,419	$3,669,134,554	$3,792,179,199

* US Census Bureau
** New Jersey Department of Labor

See Introduction for an explanation of all data sources.

Demographics & Socio-Economic Characteristics
(2000 US Census, except as noted)

Population
1980*	4,881
1990*	4,861
2000	4,409
Male	2,134
Female	2,275
2007 (estimate)*	4,334
Population density	4,468.0

Race & Hispanic Origin, 2000
Race
White	3,395
Black/African American	785
American Indian/Alaska Native	10
Asian	41
Native Hawaiian/Pacific Islander	1
Other race	68
Two or more races	109
Hispanic origin, total	179
Mexican	21
Puerto Rican	104
Cuban	12
Other Hispanic	42

Age & Nativity, 2000
Under 5 years	298
18 years and over	3,318
21 years and over	3,164
65 years and over	563
85 years and over	39
Median age	36.1
Native-born	4,262
Foreign-born	141

Educational Attainment, 2000
Population 25 years and over	2,979
Less than 9th grade	5.0%
High school grad or higher	80.7%
Bachelor's degree or higher	12.2%
Graduate degree	2.7%

Income & Poverty, 1999
Per capita income	$19,032
Median household income	$43,728
Median family income	$50,791
Persons in poverty	346
H'holds receiving public assistance	30
H'holds receiving social security	444

Households, 2000
Total households	1,710
With persons under 18	599
With persons over 65	421
Family households	1,162
Single-person households	439
Persons per household	2.57
Persons per family	3.12

Labor & Employment
Total civilian labor force, 2007**	2,627
Unemployment rate	7.9%
Total civilian labor force, 2000	2,482
Unemployment rate	7.9%

Employed persons 16 years and over by occupation, 2000
Managers & professionals	626
Service occupations	365
Sales & office occupations	678
Farming, fishing & forestry	0
Construction & maintenance	302
Production & transportation	316
Self-employed persons	120

General Information
Borough of Magnolia
438 Evesham Ave W
Magnolia, NJ 08049
856-783-1520

Website	www.magnolia-nj.org
Year of incorporation	1915
Land/water area (sq. miles)	0.97/0.00
Form of government	Borough

Government
Legislative Districts
US Congressional	1
State Legislative	5

Local Officials, 2009
Mayor	BettyAnn Cowling-Carson
Manager	John D. Keenan Jr
Clerk	John D. Keenan Jr
Finance Dir	Sharon Smith
Tax Assessor	Thomas Davis
Tax Collector	Robin Sarlo
Attorney	Sal Siciliano
Construction	John Szczerbinski
Comm Dev/Planning	NA
Engineering	Steven Bach
Public Works	Steve Pacella
Police Chief	Rob Doyle
Emerg/Fire Director	Gary Riebel

Housing & Construction
Housing Units, 2000*
Total	1,836
Median rent	$599
Median SF home value	$90,900

Permits for New Residential Construction
	Units	Value
Total, 2006	6	$396,458
Single family	6	$396,458
Total, 2007	9	$765,279
Single family	9	$765,279

Real Property Valuation, 2008
	Parcels	Valuation
Total	1,626	$160,382,000
Vacant	125	3,669,300
Residential	1,424	129,499,600
Commercial	69	15,631,600
Industrial	3	4,635,600
Apartments	5	6,945,900
Farm land	0	0
Farm homestead	0	0

Average Property Value & Tax, 2008
Residential value	$90,941
Property tax	$5,002
Tax credit/rebate	$969

Public Library
No public municipal library

Library statistics, 2007
Population served	NA
Full-time/total staff	NA/NA

	Total	Per capita
Holdings	NA	NA
Revenues	NA	NA
Expenditures	NA	NA
Annual visits	NA	NA
Internet terminals/annual users	NA/NA	

Public Safety
Number of officers, 2007 11

Crime	2006	2007
Total crimes	119	135
Violent	18	24
Murder	0	0
Rape	2	0
Robbery	1	11
Aggravated assault	15	13
Non-violent	101	111
Burglary	34	25
Larceny	55	79
Vehicle theft	12	7
Domestic violence	50	51
Arson	0	0
Total crime rate	27.1	30.8
Violent	4.1	5.5
Non-violent	23.0	25.3

Public School District
(for school year 2007-08 except as noted)

Magnolia Borough School District
420 North Warwick Road
Magnolia, NJ 08049
(856) 783-6343

Superintendent	Warren Pross
Number of schools	1
Grade plan	K-8
Enrollment	460
Attendance rate, '06-07	95.2%
Dropout rate	NA
Students per teacher	10.7
Per pupil expenditure	$12,898
Median faculty salary	$49,272
Median administrator salary	$72,800
Grade 12 enrollment	NA
High school graduation rate	NA

Assessment test results
(percent scoring at proficient or advanced level)
	Language	Math
NJASK-Grade 3	94.3%	86.8%
GEPA-Grade 8	55.2%	84.5%
HSPA-High School	NA	NA

SAT Score Averages, 2006-07
Pct tested	Math	Verbal	Writing
NA	NA	NA	NA

Teacher Qualifications
Avg. years of experience	11
Highly-qualified teachers one subject/all subjects	100%/100%

No Child Left Behind
AYP, 2006-07 .... Meets Standards

Municipal Finance
State Aid Programs, 2009
Total aid	$545,642
CMPTRA	120,040
Energy tax receipts	422,874
Garden State Trust	0

General Budget, 2008
Total tax levy	$8,829,809
County levy	1,877,978
County taxes	1,697,278
County library	121,648
County health	0
County open space	59,052
School levy	4,817,027
Muni. levy	2,134,803
Misc. revenues	2,029,446

Taxes
	2006	2007	2008
General tax rate per $100	5.128	5.481	5.501
County equalization ratio	70.94	59.79	55.40
Net valuation taxable	$159,518,800	$160,050,224	$160,521,785
State equalized value	$266,956,555	$288,788,205	$293,987,348

* US Census Bureau
** New Jersey Department of Labor

See Introduction for an explanation of all data sources.

Demographics & Socio-Economic Characteristics
(2000 US Census, except as noted)

Population
1980*	12,127
1990*	17,905
2000	24,062
Male	11,435
Female	12,627
2007 (estimate)*	24,302
Population density	937.2

Race & Hispanic Origin, 2000
Race
White	21,157
Black/African American	519
American Indian/Alaska Native	169
Asian	1,518
Native Hawaiian/Pacific Islander	7
Other race	361
Two or more races	331
Hispanic origin, total	1,028
Mexican	136
Puerto Rican	264
Cuban	89
Other Hispanic	539

Age & Nativity, 2000
Under 5 years	1,672
18 years and over	18,717
21 years and over	17,492
65 years and over	2,572
85 years and over	204
Median age	37.3
Native-born	20,868
Foreign-born	3,194

Educational Attainment, 2000
Population 25 years and over	16,374
Less than 9th grade	2.3%
High school grad or higher	93.6%
Bachelor's degree or higher	49.5%
Graduate degree	17.1%

Income & Poverty, 1999
Per capita income	$44,709
Median household income	$79,500
Median family income	$94,484
Persons in poverty	458
H'holds receiving public assistance	71
H'holds receiving social security	1,984

Households, 2000
Total households	9,340
With persons under 18	2,955
With persons over 65	1,923
Family households	6,288
Single-person households	2,612
Persons per household	2.43
Persons per family	3.01

Labor & Employment
Total civilian labor force, 2007**	13,229
Unemployment rate	3.5%
Total civilian labor force, 2000	13,481
Unemployment rate	5.6%

Employed persons 16 years and over by occupation, 2000
Managers & professionals	6,323
Service occupations	1,181
Sales & office occupations	3,932
Farming, fishing & forestry	8
Construction & maintenance	533
Production & transportation	754
Self-employed persons	777

General Information
Township of Mahwah
475 Corporate Dr
Mahwah, NJ 07430
201-529-5757

Website	www.mahwahtwp.org
Year of incorporation	1944
Land/water area (sq. miles)	25.93/0.27
Form of government	Mayor-Council

Government
Legislative Districts
US Congressional	5
State Legislative	40

Local Officials, 2009
Mayor	Richard Martel
Manager	Brian Campion
Clerk	Kathrine Coletta
Finance Dir	Kenneth Sesholtz
Tax Assessor	Stuart Stolarz
Tax Collector	Elizabeth Villano
Attorney	Terry Paul Bottinelli
Building	Gary Montroy
Planning	Mara Winokur
Engineering	Kevin Boswell
Public Works	Stanley Spiech
Police Chief	James Batelli
Emerg/Fire Director	Timothy Malone

Housing & Construction
Housing Units, 2000*
Total	9,577
Median rent	$1,160
Median SF home value	$334,100

Permits for New Residential Construction
	Units	Value
Total, 2006	32	$16,865,362
Single family	32	$16,865,362
Total, 2007	23	$17,225,451
Single family	23	$17,225,451

Real Property Valuation, 2008
	Parcels	Valuation
Total	9,952	$4,123,651,200
Vacant	463	89,819,900
Residential	9,210	3,282,523,000
Commercial	157	475,560,100
Industrial	80	231,148,000
Apartments	8	31,751,800
Farm land	21	549,800
Farm homestead	13	12,298,600

Average Property Value & Tax, 2008
Residential value	$357,240
Property tax	$7,056
Tax credit/rebate	$972

Public Library
Mahwah Public Library
100 Ridge Rd
Mahwah Township, NJ 07430
201-529-2972

Director .... Kenneth W. Giaimo

Library statistics, 2007
Population served	24,062
Full-time/total staff	5/15

	Total	Per capita
Holdings	126,098	5.24
Revenues	$2,297,940	$95.50
Expenditures	$1,797,075	$74.69
Annual visits	225,596	9.38
Internet terminals/annual users	11/11,538	

Public Safety
Number of officers, 2007	55

Crime	2006	2007
Total crimes	154	145
Violent	8	10
Murder	0	0
Rape	1	2
Robbery	0	0
Aggravated assault	7	8
Non-violent	146	135
Burglary	15	5
Larceny	116	113
Vehicle theft	15	17
Domestic violence	175	135
Arson	1	0
Total crime rate	6.3	5.9
Violent	0.3	0.4
Non-violent	5.9	5.5

Public School District
(for school year 2007-08 except as noted)

Mahwah Township School District
60 Ridge Road
Mahwah, NJ 07430
(201) 529-6803

Superintendent	Charles Montesano
Number of schools	6
Grade plan	K-12
Enrollment	3,442
Attendance rate, '06-07	96.7%
Dropout rate	1.4%
Students per teacher	11.6
Per pupil expenditure	$14,964
Median faculty salary	$62,285
Median administrator salary	$113,751
Grade 12 enrollment	222
High school graduation rate	94.9%

Assessment test results
(percent scoring at proficient or advanced level)
	Language	Math
NJASK-Grade 3	90.3%	93.8%
GEPA-Grade 8	84.5%	92.7%
HSPA-High School	89.4%	93.7%

SAT Score Averages, 2006-07
Pct tested	Math	Verbal	Writing
94%	534	507	513

Teacher Qualifications
Avg. years of experience	10
Highly-qualified teachers one subject/all subjects	98.5%/98.5%

No Child Left Behind
AYP, 2006-07	Meets Standards

Municipal Finance
State Aid Programs, 2009
Total aid	$5,777,702
CMPTRA	0
Energy tax receipts	5,540,418
Garden State Trust	6,092

General Budget, 2008
Total tax levy	$81,533,621
County levy	12,522,532
County taxes	11,843,101
County library	0
County health	0
County open space	679,431
School levy	50,006,273
Muni. levy	19,004,817
Misc. revenues	15,573,619

Taxes
	2006	2007	2008
General tax rate per $100	1.79	1.9	1.976
County equalization ratio	70.42	64.07	61.04
Net valuation taxable	$4,109,598,000	$4,105,452,839	$4,128,095,435
State equalized value	$6,418,751,769	$6,722,964,227	$7,048,604,126

* US Census Bureau
** New Jersey Department of Labor

See Introduction for an explanation of all data sources.

Demographics & Socio-Economic Characteristics
(2000 US Census, except as noted)

Population
1980*	18,914
1990*	26,716
2000	33,423
Male	16,029
Female	17,394
2007 (estimate)*	38,591
Population density	1,252.1

Race & Hispanic Origin, 2000
Race
White	30,687
Black/African American	664
American Indian/Alaska Native	9
Asian	1,514
Native Hawaiian/Pacific Islander	5
Other race	177
Two or more races	367
Hispanic origin, total	1,183
Mexican	86
Puerto Rican	579
Cuban	143
Other Hispanic	375

Age & Nativity, 2000
Under 5 years	2,220
18 years and over	23,283
21 years and over	22,349
65 years and over	3,883
85 years and over	589
Median age	38.2
Native-born	29,956
Foreign-born	3,467

Educational Attainment, 2000
Population 25 years and over	21,286
Less than 9th grade	2.4%
High school grad or higher	92.5%
Bachelor's degree or higher	39.3%
Graduate degree	14.5%

Income & Poverty, 1999
Per capita income	$32,142
Median household income	$83,575
Median family income	$94,112
Persons in poverty	1,259
H'holds receiving public assistance	56
H'holds receiving social security	2,982

Households, 2000
Total households	10,781
With persons under 18	5,252
With persons over 65	2,800
Family households	9,001
Single-person households	1,607
Persons per household	3.09
Persons per family	3.45

Labor & Employment
Total civilian labor force, 2007**	18,488
Unemployment rate	3.2%
Total civilian labor force, 2000	15,892
Unemployment rate	3.4%

Employed persons 16 years and over by occupation, 2000
Managers & professionals	7,206
Service occupations	1,264
Sales & office occupations	4,897
Farming, fishing & forestry	23
Construction & maintenance	1,047
Production & transportation	922
Self-employed persons	1,041

‡ Main library for county
* US Census Bureau
** New Jersey Department of Labor

General Information
Township of Manalapan
120 Route 522
Manalapan, NJ 07726
732-446-3200

Website	www.twp.manalapan.nj.us
Year of incorporation	1848
Land/water area (sq. miles)	30.82/0.05
Form of government	Township

Government
Legislative Districts
US Congressional	6, 12
State Legislative	12

Local Officials, 2009
Mayor	Richard Klauber
Manager	Tara L. Lovrich
Clerk	Rose Ann Weeden
Finance Dir	Patricia Addario
Tax Assessor	Sharon Hartman
Tax Collector	Hope Lewis
Attorney	Ron Cucchiaro
Building	Richard Hogan
Comm Dev/Planning	NA
Engineering	Greg Valesi
Public Works	Alan Spector
Police Chief	Stuart C. Brown
Emerg/Fire Director	Richard Hogan

Housing & Construction
Housing Units, 2000*
Total	11,066
Median rent	$1,124
Median SF home value	$257,100

Permits for New Residential Construction
	Units	Value
Total, 2006	403	$51,694,461
Single family	282	$43,132,974
Total, 2007	210	$28,670,769
Single family	193	$26,507,217

Real Property Valuation, 2008
	Parcels	Valuation
Total	15,296	$6,325,770,900
Vacant	1,553	200,478,700
Residential	13,111	5,658,484,200
Commercial	337	403,109,300
Industrial	9	24,603,500
Apartments	0	0
Farm land	187	2,315,700
Farm homestead	99	36,779,500

Average Property Value & Tax, 2008
Residential value	$431,133
Property tax	$7,321
Tax credit/rebate	$1,091

Public Library
Monmouth County Library‡
125 Symmes Dr
Manalapan, NJ 07726
732-431-7220

Director	Ken Sheinbaum

County Library statistics, 2007
Population served	399,613
Full-time/total staff	38/117

	Total	Per capita
Holdings	1,414,674	3.54
Revenues	$14,201,091	$35.54
Expenditures	$12,327,753	$30.85
Annual visits	2,214,466	5.54
Internet terminals/annual users	84/255,228	

Public Safety
Number of officers, 2007	66

Crime	2006	2007
Total crimes	393	450
Violent	25	30
Murder	3	0
Rape	2	2
Robbery	7	7
Aggravated assault	13	21
Non-violent	368	420
Burglary	56	49
Larceny	296	356
Vehicle theft	16	15
Domestic violence	178	193
Arson	1	1
Total crime rate	10.7	12.1
Violent	0.7	0.8
Non-violent	10.0	11.3

Public School District
(for school year 2007-08 except as noted)

Manalapan-Englishtown Reg. School Dist.
54 Main Street
Englishtown, NJ 07726
(732) 786-2500

Superintendent	John J. Marciante Jr
Number of schools	8
Grade plan	K-8
Enrollment	5,482
Attendance rate, '06-07	95.6%
Dropout rate	NA
Students per teacher	12.0
Per pupil expenditure	$12,214
Median faculty salary	$49,993
Median administrator salary	$99,196
Grade 12 enrollment	NA
High school graduation rate	NA

Assessment test results
(percent scoring at proficient or advanced level)
	Language	Math
NJASK-Grade 3	96.2%	96.2%
GEPA-Grade 8	87.3%	94.4%
HSPA-High School	NA	NA

SAT Score Averages, 2006-07
Pct tested	Math	Verbal	Writing
NA	NA	NA	NA

Teacher Qualifications
Avg. years of experience	8
Highly-qualified teachers one subject/all subjects	99.0%/99.0%

No Child Left Behind
AYP, 2006-07	Meets Standards

Municipal Finance
State Aid Programs, 2009
Total aid	$4,993,990
CMPTRA	36,448
Energy tax receipts	4,808,240
Garden State Trust	24,670

General Budget, 2008
Total tax levy	$107,523,096
County levy	16,400,459
County taxes	14,554,080
County library	875,834
County health	0
County open space	970,545
School levy	71,880,684
Muni. levy	19,241,953
Misc. revenues	13,715,059

Taxes	2006	2007	2008
General tax rate per $100	3.607	1.645	1.699
County equalization ratio	48.39	101.64	98.24
Net valuation taxable	$2,514,266,100	$6,157,351,118	$6,332,030,561
State equalized value	$5,837,550,667	$6,267,559,710	$172,470,574

Demographics & Socio-Economic Characteristics
(2000 US Census, except as noted)

Population
1980*	5,354
1990*	5,369
2000	6,310
Male	3,106
Female	3,204
2007 (estimate)*	6,244
Population density	4,524.6

Race & Hispanic Origin, 2000
Race
White	6,177
Black/African American	26
American Indian/Alaska Native	7
Asian	28
Native Hawaiian/Pacific Islander	0
Other race	30
Two or more races	42
Hispanic origin, total	283
Mexican	174
Puerto Rican	18
Cuban	11
Other Hispanic	80

Age & Nativity, 2000
Under 5 years	391
18 years and over	4,808
21 years and over	4,623
65 years and over	942
85 years and over	113
Median age	39.0
Native-born	6,021
Foreign-born	289

Educational Attainment, 2000
Population 25 years and over	4,398
Less than 9th grade	1.8%
High school grad or higher	92.9%
Bachelor's degree or higher	40.4%
Graduate degree	13.2%

Income & Poverty, 1999
Per capita income	$32,898
Median household income	$63,079
Median family income	$73,670
Persons in poverty	195
H'holds receiving public assistance	46
H'holds receiving social security	696

Households, 2000
Total households	2,600
With persons under 18	810
With persons over 65	715
Family households	1,635
Single-person households	785
Persons per household	2.43
Persons per family	3.06

Labor & Employment
Total civilian labor force, 2007**	3,557
Unemployment rate	2.2%
Total civilian labor force, 2000	3,328
Unemployment rate	2.4%

Employed persons 16 years and over by occupation, 2000
Managers & professionals	1,289
Service occupations	455
Sales & office occupations	1,007
Farming, fishing & forestry	9
Construction & maintenance	214
Production & transportation	273
Self-employed persons	251

* US Census Bureau
** New Jersey Department of Labor

General Information
Borough of Manasquan
201 E Main St
Manasquan, NJ 08736
732-223-0544
Website	www.manasquan-nj.com
Year of incorporation	1887
Land/water area (sq. miles)	1.38/1.15
Form of government	Borough

Government
Legislative Districts
US Congressional	4
State Legislative	10

Local Officials, 2009
Mayor	George Dempsey
Manager	John Trengrove
Clerk	Colleen Scimeca
CMFO	John Trengrove
Tax Assessor	Robyn Palughi
Tax Collector	NA
Attorney	James J. Kinneally III
Building	Sandy Ratz
Comm Dev/Planning	NA
Engineering	T&M Associates
Public Works	Tom Nicastro
Police Chief	Daniel Scimeca
Emerg/Fire Director	Peter Mayer III

Housing & Construction
Housing Units, 2000*
Total	3,531
Median rent	$808
Median SF home value	$265,300

Permits for New Residential Construction
	Units	Value
Total, 2006	37	$8,845,643
Single family	37	$8,845,643
Total, 2007	32	$7,497,221
Single family	32	$7,497,221

Real Property Valuation, 2008
	Parcels	Valuation
Total	3,175	$1,577,083,400
Vacant	121	23,854,600
Residential	2,847	1,407,843,800
Commercial	186	128,542,700
Industrial	13	8,349,900
Apartments	8	8,492,400
Farm land	0	0
Farm homestead	0	0

Average Property Value & Tax, 2008
Residential value	$494,501
Property tax	$7,261
Tax credit/rebate	$1,180

Public Library
Manasquan Public Library
55 Broad St
Manasquan, NJ 08736
732-223-1503
Director	Margo Petersen

Library statistics, 2007
Population served	6,310
Full-time/total staff	0/0

	Total	Per capita
Holdings	34,707	5.50
Revenues	$155,623	$24.66
Expenditures	$137,450	$21.78
Annual visits	38,957	6.17
Internet terminals/annual users	2/2,183	

Public Safety
Number of officers, 2007	18

Crime	2006	2007
Total crimes	167	176
Violent	4	11
Murder	0	1
Rape	0	1
Robbery	1	1
Aggravated assault	3	8
Non-violent	163	165
Burglary	13	22
Larceny	150	142
Vehicle theft	0	1
Domestic violence	22	19
Arson	1	1
Total crime rate	26.9	28.4
Violent	0.6	1.8
Non-violent	26.3	26.6

Public School District
(for school year 2007-08 except as noted)

Manasquan School District
169 Broad Street
Manasquan, NJ 08736
(732) 528-8800
Superintendent	Geraldine Margin
Number of schools	2
Grade plan	K-12
Enrollment	1,694
Attendance rate, '06-07	95.5%
Dropout rate	0.2%
Students per teacher	11.9
Per pupil expenditure	$12,897
Median faculty salary	$58,000
Median administrator salary	$123,853
Grade 12 enrollment	236
High school graduation rate	97.7%

Assessment test results
(percent scoring at proficient or advanced level)
	Language	Math
NJASK-Grade 3	91.0%	93.5%
GEPA-Grade 8	84.7%	95.3%
HSPA-High School	90.7%	92.3%

SAT Score Averages, 2006-07
Pct tested	Math	Verbal	Writing
99%	515	507	510

Teacher Qualifications
Avg. years of experience	10
Highly-qualified teachers one subject/all subjects	100%/100%

No Child Left Behind
AYP, 2006-07	Meets Standards

Municipal Finance
State Aid Programs, 2009
Total aid	$543,449
CMPTRA	20,070
Energy tax receipts	498,920
Garden State Trust	4

General Budget, 2008
Total tax levy	$23,162,828
County levy	5,627,721
County taxes	4,913,078
County library	295,657
County health	91,361
County open space	327,626
School levy	12,321,458
Muni. levy	5,213,650
Misc. revenues	2,948,964

Taxes
	2006	2007	2008
General tax rate per $100	1.429	1.431	1.469
County equalization ratio	87.95	77.71	72.58
Net valuation taxable	$1,542,440,900	$1,562,791,260	$1,577,534,400
State equalized value	$1,985,380,189	$2,153,023,232	$5,377,089,972

See Introduction for an explanation of all data sources.

Demographics & Socio-Economic Characteristics
(2000 US Census, except as noted)

Population
1980*	27,987
1990*	35,976
2000	38,928
Male	16,459
Female	22,469
2007 (estimate)*	41,713
Population density	505.0

Race & Hispanic Origin, 2000
Race
White	36,724
Black/African American	1,190
American Indian/Alaska Native	45
Asian	338
Native Hawaiian/Pacific Islander	10
Other race	267
Two or more races	354
Hispanic origin, total	1,024
Mexican	62
Puerto Rican	590
Cuban	48
Other Hispanic	324

Age & Nativity, 2000
Under 5 years	1,019
18 years and over	34,744
21 years and over	34,114
65 years and over	21,210
85 years and over	3,645
Median age	67.7
Native-born	35,971
Foreign-born	2,989

Educational Attainment, 2000
Population 25 years and over	33,532
Less than 9th grade	7.2%
High school grad or higher	75.5%
Bachelor's degree or higher	12.7%
Graduate degree	4.1%

Income & Poverty, 1999
Per capita income	$22,409
Median household income	$29,525
Median family income	$43,363
Persons in poverty	2,102
H'holds receiving public assistance	396
H'holds receiving social security	15,035

Households, 2000
Total households	20,688
With persons under 18	2,242
With persons over 65	15,118
Family households	10,814
Single-person households	9,318
Persons per household	1.85
Persons per family	2.53

Labor & Employment
Total civilian labor force, 2007**	11,326
Unemployment rate	5.9%
Total civilian labor force, 2000	10,165
Unemployment rate	6.8%

Employed persons 16 years and over by occupation, 2000
Managers & professionals	2,597
Service occupations	1,683
Sales & office occupations	2,567
Farming, fishing & forestry	8
Construction & maintenance	1,155
Production & transportation	1,467
Self-employed persons	531

‡ Branch of county library
* US Census Bureau
** New Jersey Department of Labor
§ State Fiscal Year July 1–June 30

General Information
Township of Manchester
1 Colonial Dr
Manchester, NJ 08759
732-657-8121
Website	www.manchestertwp.com
Year of incorporation	1865
Land/water area (sq. miles)	82.60/0.29
Form of government	Mayor-Council

Government
Legislative Districts
US Congressional	4
State Legislative	9

Local Officials, 2009
Mayor	Michael Fressola
Manager	Constance Lauffer
Clerk	Sabina T. Skibo
Finance Dir	Diane Lapp
Tax Assessor	Martin Lynch
Tax Collector	Andrea Gaskill
Attorney	Steve Secare
Building	Michael Martin
Planning	Tom Thomas
Engineering	Charles Rooney
Public Works	Stephen Stanziano
Police Chief	William Brase
Public Safety Dir	William Brase

Housing & Construction
Housing Units, 2000*
Total	22,681
Median rent	$940
Median SF home value	$85,000

Permits for New Residential Construction
	Units	Value
Total, 2006	1	$126,493
Single family	1	$126,493
Total, 2007	2	$287,691
Single family	2	$287,691

Real Property Valuation, 2008
	Parcels	Valuation
Total	20,248	$2,149,629,381
Vacant	4,517	67,756,300
Residential	15,523	1,650,351,281
Commercial	141	147,430,600
Industrial	9	16,353,600
Apartments	31	266,168,300
Farm land	19	501,600
Farm homestead	8	1,067,700

Average Property Value & Tax, 2008
Residential value	$106,330
Property tax	$3,355
Tax credit/rebate	$927

Public Library
Manchester Branch Library‡
21 Colonial Dr
Manchester, NJ 08759
732-657-7600
Branch Librarian	Susan Scro

Library statistics, 2007
see Ocean County profile
for library system statistics

Public Safety
Number of officers, 2007	66

Crime	2006	2007
Total crimes	335	371
Violent	19	15
Murder	0	0
Rape	2	0
Robbery	6	2
Aggravated assault	11	13
Non-violent	316	356
Burglary	72	85
Larceny	233	256
Vehicle theft	11	15
Domestic violence	245	270
Arson	13	14
Total crime rate	8.0	8.9
Violent	0.5	0.4
Non-violent	7.5	8.5

Public School District
(for school year 2007-08 except as noted)

Manchester Township School District
121 Route 539, Box 4100
Whiting, NJ 08759
(732) 350-5900
Superintendent	David Trethaway
Number of schools	6
Grade plan	K-12
Enrollment	3,251
Attendance rate, '06-07	94.0%
Dropout rate	1.7%
Students per teacher	10.2
Per pupil expenditure	$12,707
Median faculty salary	$50,030
Median administrator salary	$111,919
Grade 12 enrollment	246
High school graduation rate	89.7%

Assessment test results
(percent scoring at proficient or advanced level)
	Language	Math
NJASK-Grade 3	86.1%	80.3%
GEPA-Grade 8	73.8%	80.0%
HSPA-High School	75.3%	83.3%

SAT Score Averages, 2006-07
Pct tested	Math	Verbal	Writing
57%	512	471	483

Teacher Qualifications
Avg. years of experience	12
Highly-qualified teachers one subject/all subjects	100%/100%

No Child Left Behind
AYP, 2006-07	Meets Standards

Municipal Finance§
State Aid Programs, 2009
Total aid	$4,191,101
CMPTRA	679,162
Energy tax receipts	3,165,263
Garden State Trust	237,531

General Budget, 2008
Total tax levy	$67,919,653
County levy	14,780,470
County taxes	12,188,412
County library	1,432,426
County health	583,198
County open space	576,435
School levy	35,725,387
Muni. levy	17,413,796
Misc. revenues	13,303,460

Taxes
	2006	2007	2008
General tax rate per $100	2.838	2.982	3.156
County equalization ratio	54.56	48.68	44.87
Net valuation taxable	$2,047,333,181	$2,099,812,765	$2,152,824,758
State equalized value	$4,209,480,200	$4,675,555,147	$8,686,472,002

Demographics & Socio-Economic Characteristics

(2000 US Census, except as noted)

Population

1980*	1,740
1990*	1,693
2000	1,559
Male	763
Female	796
2007 (estimate)*	1,555
Population density	44.7

Race & Hispanic Origin, 2000

Race

White	1,179
Black/African American	326
American Indian/Alaska Native	8
Asian	6
Native Hawaiian/Pacific Islander	0
Other race	27
Two or more races	13
Hispanic origin, total	52
Mexican	12
Puerto Rican	23
Cuban	0
Other Hispanic	17

Age & Nativity, 2000

Under 5 years	86
18 years and over	1,207
21 years and over	1,182
65 years and over	365
85 years and over	78
Median age	42.7
Native-born	1,534
Foreign-born	25

Educational Attainment, 2000

Population 25 years and over	1,140
Less than 9th grade	10.2%
High school grad or higher	76.1%
Bachelor's degree or higher	20.6%
Graduate degree	6.0%

Income & Poverty, 1999

Per capita income	$24,262
Median household income	$52,625
Median family income	$62,500
Persons in poverty	98
H'holds receiving public assistance	17
H'holds receiving social security	185

Households, 2000

Total households	539
With persons under 18	173
With persons over 65	184
Family households	409
Single-person households	111
Persons per household	2.63
Persons per family	3.02

Labor & Employment

Total civilian labor force, 2007**	740
Unemployment rate	3.5%
Total civilian labor force, 2000	724
Unemployment rate	4.1%

Employed persons 16 years and over by occupation, 2000

Managers & professionals	269
Service occupations	70
Sales & office occupations	185
Farming, fishing & forestry	14
Construction & maintenance	52
Production & transportation	104
Self-employed persons	42

* US Census Bureau
** New Jersey Department of Labor

General Information

Township of Mannington
491 Route 45
Mannington, NJ 08079
856-935-2359

Email	mannington@comcast.net
Year of incorporation	1701
Land/water area (sq. miles)	34.78/3.64
Form of government	Township

Government

Legislative Districts

US Congressional	2
State Legislative	3

Local Officials, 2009

Mayor	Ernest F. Tark Jr
Manager	Esther A. Mitchell
Clerk	Esther A. Mitchell
Finance Dir	Norma Hinchman
Tax Assessor	Donna Harris
Tax Collector	Lynne H. Stiles
Attorney	William L. Horner
Construction Officials	(State)
Planning	Rebecca G. Call
Engineering	Carl Gaskill
Public Works	John W. Dubois
Police Chief	NA
Emerg/Fire Director	S. Lee Butcher

Housing & Construction

Housing Units, 2000*

Total	573
Median rent	$613
Median SF home value	$115,400

Permits for New Residential Construction

	Units	Value
Total, 2006	7	$1,312,350
Single family	7	$1,312,350
Total, 2007	4	$430,660
Single family	4	$430,660

Real Property Valuation, 2008

	Parcels	Valuation
Total	1,268	$224,326,800
Vacant	206	3,472,900
Residential	403	68,289,900
Commercial	40	45,095,300
Industrial	4	52,645,400
Apartments	0	0
Farm land	434	7,583,800
Farm homestead	181	47,239,500

Average Property Value & Tax, 2008

Residential value	$197,824
Property tax	$4,142
Tax credit/rebate	$872

Public Library

No public municipal library

Library statistics, 2007

Population served	NA
Full-time/total staff	NA/NA

	Total	Per capita
Holdings	NA	NA
Revenues	NA	NA
Expenditures	NA	NA
Annual visits	NA	NA
Internet terminals/annual users	NA/NA	

Public Safety

Number of officers, 2007 0

Crime	2006	2007
Total crimes	34	25
Violent	1	5
Murder	0	0
Rape	0	0
Robbery	0	0
Aggravated assault	1	5
Non-violent	33	20
Burglary	14	11
Larceny	18	6
Vehicle theft	1	3
Domestic violence	0	8
Arson	0	1
Total crime rate	21.8	16.0
Violent	0.6	3.2
Non-violent	21.1	12.8

Public School District

(for school year 2007-08 except as noted)

Mannington Township School District
495 Rt. 45
Salem, NJ 08079
(856) 935-1078

Superintendent	Jean Rishel
Number of schools	1
Grade plan	K-8
Enrollment	171
Attendance rate, '06-07	96.0%
Dropout rate	NA
Students per teacher	10.2
Per pupil expenditure	$14,257
Median faculty salary	$56,610
Median administrator salary	$90,000
Grade 12 enrollment	NA
High school graduation rate	NA

Assessment test results

(percent scoring at proficient or advanced level)

	Language	Math
NJASK-Grade 3	87.6%	56.3%
GEPA-Grade 8	66.7%	83.4%
HSPA-High School	NA	NA

SAT Score Averages, 2006-07

Pct tested	Math	Verbal	Writing
NA	NA	NA	NA

Teacher Qualifications

Avg. years of experience	20
Highly-qualified teachers one subject/all subjects	100%/100%

No Child Left Behind

AYP, 2006-07 .... Meets Standards

Municipal Finance

State Aid Programs, 2009

Total aid	$355,975
CMPTRA	54,321
Energy tax receipts	288,505
Garden State Trust	3,967

General Budget, 2008

Total tax levy	$4,863,127
County levy	1,965,663
County taxes	1,923,255
County library	0
County health	0
County open space	42,407
School levy	2,335,576
Muni. levy	561,888
Misc. revenues	717,790

Taxes	2006	2007	2008
General tax rate per $100	2.019	2.021	2.160
County equalization ratio	118.69	118.69	108.72
Net valuation taxable	$222,106,000	$224,172,116	$225,193,172
State equalized value	$187,926,698	$206,255,965	$311,281,449

See Introduction for an explanation of all data sources.

Demographics & Socio-Economic Characteristics

(2000 US Census, except as noted)

Population
1980*	2,523
1990*	3,874
2000	5,090
Male	2,442
Female	2,648
2007 (estimate)*	7,961
Population density	366.5

Race & Hispanic Origin, 2000
Race
White	4,857
Black/African American	97
American Indian/Alaska Native	9
Asian	76
Native Hawaiian/Pacific Islander	2
Other race	11
Two or more races	38
Hispanic origin, total	93
Mexican	9
Puerto Rican	55
Cuban	4
Other Hispanic	25

Age & Nativity, 2000
Under 5 years	241
18 years and over	4,140
21 years and over	4,019
65 years and over	1,623
85 years and over	87
Median age	48.8
Native-born	4,824
Foreign-born	266

Educational Attainment, 2000
Population 25 years and over	3,816
Less than 9th grade	3.6%
High school grad or higher	85.6%
Bachelor's degree or higher	25.1%
Graduate degree	11.4%

Income & Poverty, 1999
Per capita income	$26,559
Median household income	$50,757
Median family income	$59,040
Persons in poverty	228
H'holds receiving public assistance	4
H'holds receiving social security	1,149

Households, 2000
Total households	2,077
With persons under 18	523
With persons over 65	1,067
Family households	1,561
Single-person households	469
Persons per household	2.45
Persons per family	2.86

Labor & Employment
Total civilian labor force, 2007**	2,410
Unemployment rate	4.7%
Total civilian labor force, 2000	2,105
Unemployment rate	4.4%

Employed persons 16 years and over by occupation, 2000
Managers & professionals	674
Service occupations	282
Sales & office occupations	563
Farming, fishing & forestry	14
Construction & maintenance	257
Production & transportation	222
Self-employed persons	112

* US Census Bureau
** New Jersey Department of Labor

General Information
Township of Mansfield
PO Box 249
Columbus, NJ 08022
609-298-0542
Website	www.mansfieldburlington.com
Year of incorporation	1688
Land/water area (sq. miles)	21.72/0.14
Form of government	Township

Government

Legislative Districts
US Congressional	4
State Legislative	8

Local Officials, 2009
Mayor	Arthur R. Puglia
Township Admin	Joseph Broski
Clerk	Linda Semus
Finance Dir	Joseph Monzo
Tax Assessor	Robin Bucchi
Tax Collector	Elaine Fortin
Attorney	Michael Magee
Building	Jeffrey Jones
Comm Dev/Planning	NA
Engineering	Remington & Vernick
Public Works	Jeffrey Jones
Public Safety Dir	Richard Bendel
Emerg/Fire Director	J. Douglas Goockenough

Housing & Construction

Housing Units, 2000*
Total	2,122
Median rent	$706
Median SF home value	$153,800

Permits for New Residential Construction
	Units	Value
Total, 2006	51	$7,762,494
Single family	51	$7,762,494
Total, 2007	40	$12,985,555
Single family	40	$12,985,555

Real Property Valuation, 2008
	Parcels	Valuation
Total	4,049	$1,295,144,100
Vacant	297	40,718,500
Residential	3,316	1,105,446,900
Commercial	91	89,713,300
Industrial	2	5,301,200
Apartments	5	1,898,100
Farm land	216	4,040,600
Farm homestead	122	48,025,500

Average Property Value & Tax, 2008
Residential value	$335,507
Property tax	$6,228
Tax credit/rebate	$1,130

Public Library

No public municipal library

Library statistics, 2007
Population served	NA
Full-time/total staff	NA/NA

	Total	Per capita
Holdings	NA	NA
Revenues	NA	NA
Expenditures	NA	NA
Annual visits	NA	NA
Internet terminals/annual users	NA/NA	

Public Safety
Number of officers, 2007	13

Crime	2006	2007
Total crimes	146	129
Violent	5	3
Murder	0	0
Rape	0	1
Robbery	1	1
Aggravated assault	4	1
Non-violent	141	126
Burglary	8	17
Larceny	120	92
Vehicle theft	13	17
Domestic violence	26	21
Arson	0	3
Total crime rate	18.4	16.0
Violent	0.6	0.4
Non-violent	17.8	15.7

Public School District
(for school year 2007-08 except as noted)

Mansfield Township School District
200 Mansfield Road East
Columbus, NJ 08022
(609) 298-2037
Superintendent	Diane Bacher
Number of schools	2
Grade plan	K-6
Enrollment	695
Attendance rate, '06-07	94.9%
Dropout rate	NA
Students per teacher	10.7
Per pupil expenditure	$12,000
Median faculty salary	$47,454
Median administrator salary	$108,644
Grade 12 enrollment	NA
High school graduation rate	NA

Assessment test results
(percent scoring at proficient or advanced level)
	Language	Math
NJASK-Grade 3	94.3%	90.9%
GEPA-Grade 8	NA	NA
HSPA-High School	NA	NA

SAT Score Averages, 2006-07
Pct tested	Math	Verbal	Writing
NA	NA	NA	NA

Teacher Qualifications
Avg. years of experience	8
Highly-qualified teachers one subject/all subjects	98.0%/98.0%

No Child Left Behind
AYP, 2006-07	Meets Standards

Municipal Finance

State Aid Programs, 2009
Total aid	$673,667
CMPTRA	0
Energy tax receipts	646,720
Garden State Trust	0

General Budget, 2008
Total tax levy	$24,081,354
County levy	5,100,115
County taxes	4,188,247
County library	386,700
County health	0
County open space	525,167
School levy	16,612,881
Muni. levy	2,368,358
Misc. revenues	4,734,729

Taxes
	2006	2007	2008
General tax rate per $100	3.52	1.82	1.857
County equalization ratio	60.15	104.38	98.85
Net valuation taxable	$649,514,415	$1,290,671,921	$1,297,379,493
State equalized value	$1,187,152,098	$1,305,662,095	$1,349,939,972

See Introduction for an explanation of all data sources.

Demographics & Socio-Economic Characteristics
(2000 US Census, except as noted)

Population
1980*	5,780
1990*	7,154
2000	6,653
Male	3,237
Female	3,416
2007 (estimate)*	8,127
Population density	271.6

Race & Hispanic Origin, 2000
Race
White	6,048
Black/African American	300
American Indian/Alaska Native	16
Asian	81
Native Hawaiian/Pacific Islander	0
Other race	106
Two or more races	102
Hispanic origin, total	291
Mexican	25
Puerto Rican	63
Cuban	30
Other Hispanic	173

Age & Nativity, 2000
Under 5 years	493
18 years and over	4,857
21 years and over	4,670
65 years and over	776
85 years and over	126
Median age	37.1
Native-born	6,290
Foreign-born	363

Educational Attainment, 2000
Population 25 years and over	4,457
Less than 9th grade	3.5%
High school grad or higher	88.6%
Bachelor's degree or higher	27.5%
Graduate degree	9.3%

Income & Poverty, 1999
Per capita income	$26,277
Median household income	$61,763
Median family income	$76,102
Persons in poverty	251
H'holds receiving public assistance	30
H'holds receiving social security	508

Households, 2000
Total households	2,334
With persons under 18	961
With persons over 65	457
Family households	1,750
Single-person households	441
Persons per household	2.76
Persons per family	3.18

Labor & Employment
Total civilian labor force, 2007**	3,962
Unemployment rate	3.9%
Total civilian labor force, 2000	3,536
Unemployment rate	4.0%

Employed persons 16 years and over by occupation, 2000
Managers & professionals	1,259
Service occupations	476
Sales & office occupations	882
Farming, fishing & forestry	9
Construction & maintenance	366
Production & transportation	403
Self-employed persons	363

General Information
Township of Mansfield
100 Port Murray Rd
Port Murray, NJ 07865
908-689-6151
Website	www.mansfieldtownship-nj.gov
Year of incorporation	1754
Land/water area (sq. miles)	29.92/0.02
Form of government	Township

Government
Legislative Districts
US Congressional	5
State Legislative	23

Local Officials, 2009
Mayor	Robert Jewell
Manager	Charles Lee
Clerk	Dena Hrebenak
Finance Dir	Andrew Coppola
Tax Assessor	Bernard Murdoch
Tax Collector	Rebecca Harm
Attorney	Joel Kobert
Building	Dennis Allen
Comm Dev/Planning	NA
Engineering	Douglas Mace
Public Works	Brent Sliker
Police Chief	Douglas Ort
Fire/Emergency Dir	Robert Griffith

Housing & Construction
Housing Units, 2000*
Total	2,415
Median rent	$731
Median SF home value	$177,200

Permits for New Residential Construction
	Units	Value
Total, 2006	7	$1,181,700
Single family	7	$1,181,700
Total, 2007	6	$1,445,750
Single family	6	$1,445,750

Real Property Valuation, 2008
	Parcels	Valuation
Total	2,920	$661,507,200
Vacant	560	15,458,200
Residential	1,813	431,684,500
Commercial	50	94,972,200
Industrial	13	16,094,300
Apartments	4	49,799,900
Farm land	304	2,668,700
Farm homestead	176	50,829,400

Average Property Value & Tax, 2008
Residential value	$242,591
Property tax	$6,974
Tax credit/rebate	$1,163

Public Library
No public municipal library

Library statistics, 2007
Population served	NA
Full-time/total staff	NA/NA

	Total	Per capita
Holdings	NA	NA
Revenues	NA	NA
Expenditures	NA	NA
Annual visits	NA	NA
Internet terminals/annual users	NA/NA	

Public Safety
Number of officers, 2007 15
Crime	2006	2007
Total crimes	132	138
Violent	9	4
Murder	0	0
Rape	1	0
Robbery	1	1
Aggravated assault	7	3
Non-violent	123	134
Burglary	20	24
Larceny	94	100
Vehicle theft	9	10
Domestic violence	174	170
Arson	2	1
Total crime rate	16.0	16.7
Violent	1.1	0.5
Non-violent	14.9	16.2

Public School District
(for school year 2007-08 except as noted)

Mansfield Township School District
50 Port Murray Road
Port Murray, NJ 07865
(908) 689-3212
Superintendent	Edward Kemp Jr
Number of schools	1
Grade plan	K-6
Enrollment	702
Attendance rate, '06-07	95.6%
Dropout rate	NA
Students per teacher	10.5
Per pupil expenditure	$11,421
Median faculty salary	$63,395
Median administrator salary	$96,344
Grade 12 enrollment	NA
High school graduation rate	NA

Assessment test results
(percent scoring at proficient or advanced level)
	Language	Math
NJASK-Grade 3	87.3%	84.9%
GEPA-Grade 8	NA	NA
HSPA-High School	NA	NA

SAT Score Averages, 2006-07
Pct tested	Math	Verbal	Writing
NA	NA	NA	NA

Teacher Qualifications
Avg. years of experience	11
Highly-qualified teachers one subject/all subjects	100%/100%

No Child Left Behind
AYP, 2006-07 .... Meets Standards

Municipal Finance
State Aid Programs, 2009
Total aid	$1,146,230
CMPTRA	58,508
Energy tax receipts	1,028,680
Garden State Trust	36,558

General Budget, 2008
Total tax levy	$19,054,204
County levy	5,770,873
County taxes	4,707,233
County library	493,968
County health	0
County open space	569,672
School levy	10,700,688
Muni. levy	2,582,643
Misc. revenues	3,233,749

Taxes
	2006	2007	2008
General tax rate per $100	2.76	2.78	2.875
County equalization ratio	79.75	74.67	69.94
Net valuation taxable	$643,081,600	$652,961,468	$662,811,775
State equalized value	$862,644,762	$933,029,035	$971,256,481

* US Census Bureau
** New Jersey Department of Labor

See Introduction for an explanation of all data sources.

Demographics & Socio-Economic Characteristics

(2000 US Census, except as noted)

Population

1980*	433
1990*	334
2000	423
Male	208
Female	215
2007 (estimate)*	451
Population density	1,025.0

Race & Hispanic Origin, 2000

Race

White	413
Black/African American	7
American Indian/Alaska Native	0
Asian	2
Native Hawaiian/Pacific Islander	0
Other race	1
Two or more races	0
Hispanic origin, total	3
Mexican	0
Puerto Rican	0
Cuban	0
Other Hispanic	3

Age & Nativity, 2000

Under 5 years	9
18 years and over	380
21 years and over	372
65 years and over	153
85 years and over	12
Median age	58.0
Native-born	345
Foreign-born	24

Educational Attainment, 2000

Population 25 years and over	322
Less than 9th grade	0.0%
High school grad or higher	99.1%
Bachelor's degree or higher	59.9%
Graduate degree	20.5%

Income & Poverty, 1999

Per capita income	$114,017
Median household income	$105,841
Median family income	$125,000
Persons in poverty	3
H'holds receiving public assistance	0
H'holds receiving social security	104

Households, 2000

Total households	207
With persons under 18	25
With persons over 65	111
Family households	141
Single-person households	63
Persons per household	2.02
Persons per family	2.45

Labor & Employment

Total civilian labor force, 2007**	167
Unemployment rate	0.0%
Total civilian labor force, 2000	137
Unemployment rate	0.0%

Employed persons 16 years and over by occupation, 2000

Managers & professionals	89
Service occupations	0
Sales & office occupations	39
Farming, fishing & forestry	0
Construction & maintenance	7
Production & transportation	2
Self-employed persons	25

General Information

Borough of Mantoloking
PO Box 247
Mantoloking, NJ 08738
732-899-6600

Website	www.mantoloking.org
Year of incorporation	1911
Land/water area (sq. miles)	0.44/0.22
Form of government	Borough

Government

Legislative Districts

US Congressional	4
State Legislative	10

Local Officials, 2009

Mayor	George Nebel
Manager	Irene Ryan
Clerk	Irene Ryan
Finance Dir	Michelle Swisher
Tax Assessor	James Anderson
Tax Collector	Michelle A. Swisher
Attorney	Edwin O'Malley Jr
Building	John Wardell
Planning	Russell Henshaw
Engineering	Lawrence Plevier
Public Works	William Heckman
Police Chief	Mark Wright
Emerg/Fire Director	Lawrence Gilman

Housing & Construction

Housing Units, 2000*

Total	522
Median rent	$2,001
Median SF home value	$761,000

Permits for New Residential Construction

	Units	Value
Total, 2006	1	$1,045,700
Single family	1	$1,045,700
Total, 2007	2	$1,920,000
Single family	2	$1,920,000

Real Property Valuation, 2008

	Parcels	Valuation
Total	562	$1,809,110,800
Vacant	36	57,147,700
Residential	521	1,736,830,100
Commercial	5	15,133,000
Industrial	0	0
Apartments	0	0
Farm land	0	0
Farm homestead	0	0

Average Property Value & Tax, 2008

Residential value	$3,333,647
Property tax	$14,149
Tax credit/rebate	$1,179

Public Library

No public municipal library

Library statistics, 2007

Population served	NA
Full-time/total staff	NA/NA

	Total	Per capita
Holdings	NA	NA
Revenues	NA	NA
Expenditures	NA	NA
Annual visits	NA	NA
Internet terminals/annual users	NA/NA	

Public Safety

Number of officers, 2007 7

Crime	2006	2007
Total crimes	15	17
Violent	0	0
Murder	0	0
Rape	0	0
Robbery	0	0
Aggravated assault	0	0
Non-violent	15	17
Burglary	2	2
Larceny	13	15
Vehicle theft	0	0
Domestic violence	1	0
Arson	0	0
Total crime rate	33.3	37.7
Violent	0.0	0.0
Non-violent	33.3	37.7

Public School District

(for school year 2007-08 except as noted)

Mantoloking School District
P.O. Box 881
Mantoloking, NJ 08738

No schools in district - sends students to
Point Pleasant Beach schools

Per pupil expenditure	NA
Median faculty salary	NA
Median administrator salary	NA
Grade 12 enrollment	NA
High school graduation rate	NA

Assessment test results

(percent scoring at proficient or advanced level)

	Language	Math
NJASK-Grade 3	NA	NA
GEPA-Grade 8	NA	NA
HSPA-High School	NA	NA

SAT Score Averages, 2006-07

Pct tested	Math	Verbal	Writing
NA	NA	NA	NA

Teacher Qualifications

Avg. years of experience	NA
Highly-qualified teachers one subject/all subjects	NA/NA

No Child Left Behind

AYP, 2006-07 ..... NA

Municipal Finance

State Aid Programs, 2009

Total aid	$156,520
CMPTRA	0
Energy tax receipts	148,694
Garden State Trust	0

General Budget, 2008

Total tax levy	$7,679,349
County levy	4,940,578
County taxes	4,074,153
County library	478,806
County health	194,941
County open space	192,679
School levy	88,290
Muni. levy	2,650,481
Misc. revenues	1,135,738

Taxes

	2006	2007	2008
General tax rate per $100	0.737	0.734	0.425
County equalization ratio	69.87	66.27	112.92
Net valuation taxable	$975,442,800	$982,825,086	$1,809,279,417
State equalized value	$1,472,030,176	$1,587,953,942	$4,737,019,163

* US Census Bureau
** New Jersey Department of Labor

See Introduction for an explanation of all data sources.

Demographics & Socio-Economic Characteristics
(2000 US Census, except as noted)

Population
1980*	9,193
1990*	10,074
2000	14,217
Male	6,964
Female	7,253
2007 (estimate)*	15,201
Population density	956.0

Race & Hispanic Origin, 2000
Race
White	13,622
Black/African American	294
American Indian/Alaska Native	28
Asian	122
Native Hawaiian/Pacific Islander	0
Other race	40
Two or more races	111
Hispanic origin, total	179
Mexican	19
Puerto Rican	81
Cuban	12
Other Hispanic	67

Age & Nativity, 2000
Under 5 years	1,131
18 years and over	10,423
21 years and over	9,986
65 years and over	1,582
85 years and over	101
Median age	36.3
Native-born	13,784
Foreign-born	433

Educational Attainment, 2000
Population 25 years and over	9,517
Less than 9th grade	3.0%
High school grad or higher	85.7%
Bachelor's degree or higher	23.5%
Graduate degree	6.7%

Income & Poverty, 1999
Per capita income	$24,147
Median household income	$58,256
Median family income	$63,391
Persons in poverty	510
H'holds receiving public assistance	68
H'holds receiving social security	1,326

Households, 2000
Total households	5,265
With persons under 18	2,104
With persons over 65	1,145
Family households	3,947
Single-person households	1,111
Persons per household	2.69
Persons per family	3.14

Labor & Employment
Total civilian labor force, 2007**	9,370
Unemployment rate	4.7%
Total civilian labor force, 2000	7,934
Unemployment rate	4.5%

Employed persons 16 years and over by occupation, 2000
Managers & professionals	2,679
Service occupations	954
Sales & office occupations	2,230
Farming, fishing & forestry	15
Construction & maintenance	770
Production & transportation	926
Self-employed persons	362

‡ Main library for county
* US Census Bureau
** New Jersey Department of Labor

General Information
Mantua Township
401 Main St
Mantua, NJ 08051
856-468-1500

Website	www.mantuatownship.com
Year of incorporation	1853
Land/water area (sq. miles)	15.90/0.01
Form of government	Township

Government
Legislative Districts
US Congressional	1, 2
State Legislative	3

Local Officials, 2009
Mayor	Timothy Chell
Township Admin	Michael Datz
Clerk	Shawn Menzies
Finance Dir	Gayle Tschopp
Tax Assessor	Sandra Elliot
Tax Collector	Lois Demure
Attorney	Michael Angelini
Building	James Gallagher
Planner	Timothy Kernan
Engineering	Jon Bryson
Public Works	Michael Datz
Police Chief	Graham Land
Emerg/Fire Director	Nick Lamana

Housing & Construction
Housing Units, 2000*
Total	5,411
Median rent	$656
Median SF home value	$123,200

Permits for New Residential Construction
	Units	Value
Total, 2006	33	$6,916,788
Single family	13	$5,087,788
Total, 2007	2	$1,787,415
Single family	2	$1,787,415

Real Property Valuation, 2008
	Parcels	Valuation
Total	6,180	$753,103,500
Vacant	521	17,614,100
Residential	5,222	636,102,700
Commercial	162	74,828,500
Industrial	7	7,217,800
Apartments	3	1,672,000
Farm land	176	1,236,400
Farm homestead	89	14,432,000

Average Property Value & Tax, 2008
Residential value	$122,488
Property tax	$5,737
Tax credit/rebate	$980

Public Library
Gloucester County Library‡
389 Wolfert Station Rd
Mullica Hill, NJ 08062
856-223-6000

Director .... Robert S. Wetherall

County Library statistics, 2007
Population served	93,711
Full-time/total staff	11/42

	Total	Per capita
Holdings	236,948	2.53
Revenues	$4,492,205	$47.94
Expenditures	$4,080,940	$43.55
Annual visits	497,709	5.31
Internet terminals/annual users	67/86,230	

Public Safety
Number of officers, 2007	28

Crime	2006	2007
Total crimes	324	390
Violent	31	22
Murder	0	0
Rape	6	3
Robbery	7	7
Aggravated assault	18	12
Non-violent	293	368
Burglary	60	78
Larceny	222	279
Vehicle theft	11	11
Domestic violence	196	147
Arson	6	3
Total crime rate	21.8	26.0
Violent	2.1	1.5
Non-violent	19.7	24.6

Public School District
(for school year 2007-08 except as noted)

Mantua Township School District
684 Main St
Sewell, NJ 08080
(856) 468-2225

Superintendent	Steven Crispin
Number of schools	3
Grade plan	K-6
Enrollment	1,540
Attendance rate, '06-07	96.2%
Dropout rate	NA
Students per teacher	11.7
Per pupil expenditure	$10,677
Median faculty salary	$53,660
Median administrator salary	$94,517
Grade 12 enrollment	NA
High school graduation rate	NA

Assessment test results
(percent scoring at proficient or advanced level)
	Language	Math
NJASK-Grade 3	94.4%	93.9%
GEPA-Grade 8	NA	NA
HSPA-High School	NA	NA

SAT Score Averages, 2006-07
Pct tested	Math	Verbal	Writing
NA	NA	NA	NA

Teacher Qualifications
Avg. years of experience	11
Highly-qualified teachers one subject/all subjects	100%/100%

No Child Left Behind
AYP, 2006-07	Meets Standards

Municipal Finance
State Aid Programs, 2009
Total aid	$1,569,105
CMPTRA	148,872
Energy tax receipts	1,381,006
Garden State Trust	0

General Budget, 2008
Total tax levy	$35,380,523
County levy	8,794,558
County taxes	7,589,478
County library	610,332
County health	0
County open space	594,749
School levy	19,907,241
Muni. levy	6,678,724
Misc. revenues	6,664,873

Taxes	2006	2007	2008
General tax rate per $100	4.419	4.539	4.684
County equalization ratio	61.51	55.09	50.81
Net valuation taxable	$714,706,500	$735,939,109	$755,410,658
State equalized value	$1,300,000,719	$1,446,085,487	$1,538,626,007

See Introduction for an explanation of all data sources.

Demographics & Socio-Economic Characteristics
(2000 US Census, except as noted)

Population
1980*	11,278
1990*	10,567
2000	10,343
Male	5,072
Female	5,271
2007 (estimate)*	10,839
Population density	4,370.6

Race & Hispanic Origin, 2000
Race
White	9,928
Black/African American	47
American Indian/Alaska Native	7
Asian	136
Native Hawaiian/Pacific Islander	3
Other race	118
Two or more races	104
Hispanic origin, total	559
Mexican	46
Puerto Rican	121
Cuban	7
Other Hispanic	385

Age & Nativity, 2000
Under 5 years	516
18 years and over	8,203
21 years and over	7,905
65 years and over	1,826
85 years and over	143
Median age	39.5
Native-born	8,917
Foreign-born	1,390

Educational Attainment, 2000
Population 25 years and over	7,425
Less than 9th grade	8.3%
High school grad or higher	78.2%
Bachelor's degree or higher	13.7%
Graduate degree	3.7%

Income & Poverty, 1999
Per capita income	$23,293
Median household income	$51,258
Median family income	$61,151
Persons in poverty	394
H'holds receiving public assistance	88
H'holds receiving social security	1,386

Households, 2000
Total households	4,115
With persons under 18	1,209
With persons over 65	1,375
Family households	2,758
Single-person households	1,100
Persons per household	2.51
Persons per family	3.05

Labor & Employment
Total civilian labor force, 2007**	6,268
Unemployment rate	3.3%
Total civilian labor force, 2000	5,509
Unemployment rate	3.2%

Employed persons 16 years and over by occupation, 2000
Managers & professionals	1,369
Service occupations	788
Sales & office occupations	1,639
Farming, fishing & forestry	12
Construction & maintenance	646
Production & transportation	880
Self-employed persons	246

* US Census Bureau
** New Jersey Department of Labor

General Information
Borough of Manville
325 N Main St
Manville, NJ 08835
908-725-9478
Website	www.manvillenj.org
Year of incorporation	1929
Land/water area (sq. miles)	2.48/0.00
Form of government	Borough

Government
Legislative Districts
US Congressional	7
State Legislative	16

Local Officials, 2009
Mayor	Lillian M. Zuza
Manager	Gary Garwacke
Clerk	Philip Petrone
Finance Dir	Lori Majeski
Tax Assessor	Glenn Stives
Tax Collector	Lisa Gerickont
Attorney	Francis P. Linnus
Building	John Tamburini
Comm Dev/Planning	NA
Engineering	Gary Garwacke
Public Works	Philip Petrone
Police Chief	Mark Peltack
Emerg/Fire Director	Tom Collins

Housing & Construction
Housing Units, 2000*
Total	4,296
Median rent	$789
Median SF home value	$146,200

Permits for New Residential Construction
	Units	Value
Total, 2006	8	$1,156,300
Single family	8	$1,156,300
Total, 2007	6	$720,000
Single family	3	$420,000

Real Property Valuation, 2008
	Parcels	Valuation
Total	3,546	$1,154,122,500
Vacant	113	9,078,400
Residential	3,237	983,736,600
Commercial	145	110,809,700
Industrial	31	37,093,200
Apartments	20	13,404,600
Farm land	0	0
Farm homestead	0	0

Average Property Value & Tax, 2008
Residential value	$303,904
Property tax	$6,301
Tax credit/rebate	$1,044

Public Library
Manville Public Library
100 S Tenth Ave
Manville, NJ 08835
908-722-9722
Director	Edward R. Smith

Library statistics, 2007
Population served	10,343
Full-time/total staff	1/4

	Total	Per capita
Holdings	52,957	5.12
Revenues	$381,960	$36.93
Expenditures	$418,985	$40.51
Annual visits	41,200	3.98
Internet terminals/annual users	6/13,977	

Public Safety
Number of officers, 2007	22

Crime	2006	2007
Total crimes	218	158
Violent	11	2
Murder	0	0
Rape	0	1
Robbery	2	1
Aggravated assault	9	0
Non-violent	207	156
Burglary	17	9
Larceny	164	135
Vehicle theft	26	12
Domestic violence	94	125
Arson	1	4
Total crime rate	21.0	15.1
Violent	1.1	0.2
Non-violent	19.9	14.9

Public School District
(for school year 2007-08 except as noted)

Manville Borough School District
410 Brooks Blvd
Manville, NJ 08835
(908) 231-8545
Superintendent	Donald J. Burkhardt
Number of schools	4
Grade plan	K-12
Enrollment	1,292
Attendance rate, '06-07	94.6%
Dropout rate	1.5%
Students per teacher	11.1
Per pupil expenditure	$5,416
Median faculty salary	$46,865
Median administrator salary	$111,053
Grade 12 enrollment	90
High school graduation rate	94.9%

Assessment test results
(percent scoring at proficient or advanced level)
	Language	Math
NJASK-Grade 3	94.6%	88.1%
GEPA-Grade 8	60.5%	84.3%
HSPA-High School	64.7%	84.9%

SAT Score Averages, 2006-07
Pct tested	Math	Verbal	Writing
72%	475	469	467

Teacher Qualifications
Avg. years of experience	7
Highly-qualified teachers one subject/all subjects	100%/100%

No Child Left Behind
AYP, 2006-07	Meets Standards

Municipal Finance
State Aid Programs, 2009
Total aid	$2,053,407
CMPTRA	1,210,784
Energy tax receipts	811,811
Garden State Trust	14

General Budget, 2008
Total tax levy	$23,949,938
County levy	3,534,706
County taxes	3,182,439
County library	0
County health	0
County open space	352,267
School levy	12,184,507
Muni. levy	8,230,725
Misc. revenues	5,243,565

Taxes
Taxes	2006	2007	2008
General tax rate per $100	1.77	1.9	2.074
County equalization ratio	122.37	106.57	100.54
Net valuation taxable	$1,158,783,200	$1,156,211,776	$1,155,084,576
State equalized value	$1,088,287,882	$1,150,006,934	$1,162,284,777

See Introduction for an explanation of all data sources.

Demographics & Socio-Economic Characteristics

(2000 US Census, except as noted)

Population

1980*	20,525
1990*	19,211
2000	19,079
Male	9,339
Female	9,740
2007 (estimate)*	19,195
Population density	4,985.7

Race & Hispanic Origin, 2000

Race

White	15,868
Black/African American	1,376
American Indian/Alaska Native	30
Asian	1,164
Native Hawaiian/Pacific Islander	8
Other race	323
Two or more races	310
Hispanic origin, total	850
Mexican	154
Puerto Rican	446
Cuban	19
Other Hispanic	231

Age & Nativity, 2000

Under 5 years	1,072
18 years and over	15,382
21 years and over	14,835
65 years and over	2,930
85 years and over	315
Median age	36.5
Native-born	17,349
Foreign-born	1,730

Educational Attainment, 2000

Population 25 years and over	13,711
Less than 9th grade	4.6%
High school grad or higher	82.3%
Bachelor's degree or higher	21.4%
Graduate degree	7.1%

Income & Poverty, 1999

Per capita income	$23,812
Median household income	$45,426
Median family income	$53,912
Persons in poverty	1,009
H'holds receiving public assistance	120
H'holds receiving social security	2,125

Households, 2000

Total households	8,462
With persons under 18	2,207
With persons over 65	2,103
Family households	4,718
Single-person households	3,047
Persons per household	2.22
Persons per family	2.95

Labor & Employment

Total civilian labor force, 2007**	12,232
Unemployment rate	3.5%
Total civilian labor force, 2000	10,723
Unemployment rate	3.6%

Employed persons 16 years and over by occupation, 2000

Managers & professionals	3,403
Service occupations	1,462
Sales & office occupations	2,965
Farming, fishing & forestry	5
Construction & maintenance	909
Production & transportation	1,598
Self-employed persons	454

‡ Branch of county library
* US Census Bureau
** New Jersey Department of Labor

General Information

Township of Maple Shade
200 N Stiles Ave
Maple Shade, NJ 08052
856-779-9610

Website	www.mapleshade.com
Year of incorporation	1945
Land/water area (sq. miles)	3.85/0.00
Form of government	Council-Manager

Government

Legislative Districts

US Congressional	1
State Legislative	7

Local Officials, 2009

Mayor	James Fletcher
Manager	George Haeuber
Clerk	Andrea T. DeGolia
Finance Dir	Adriane McKendry
Tax Assessor	Karen McMahon
Tax Collector	Denise Lawler
Attorney	Eileen Fahey
Building	Roger Fort
Comm Dev/Planning	Rosemary Flaherty
Engineering	Jim Rudderman
Public Works	Jim Christy
Police Chief	Edmund Vernier
Emerg/Fire Director	William Riess

Housing & Construction

Housing Units, 2000*

Total	9,009
Median rent	$767
Median SF home value	$107,900

Permits for New Residential Construction

	Units	Value
Total, 2006	77	$4,226,104
Single family	8	$794,976
Total, 2007	68	$3,863,085
Single family	10	$973,184

Real Property Valuation, 2008

	Parcels	Valuation
Total	5,094	$1,592,039,700
Vacant	105	13,583,300
Residential	4,675	953,529,500
Commercial	269	338,496,900
Industrial	28	23,405,000
Apartments	17	263,025,000
Farm land	0	0
Farm homestead	0	0

Average Property Value & Tax, 2008

Residential value	$203,964
Property tax	$4,533
Tax credit/rebate	$915

Public Library

Maple Shade Branch Library‡
200 Stiles Ave
Maple Shade, NJ 08052
856-779-9767

Director	Michael Bennett

Library statistics, 2007

see Burlington County profile
for library system statistics

Public Safety

Number of officers, 2007	36

Crime	2006	2007
Total crimes	496	441
Violent	35	42
Murder	0	0
Rape	6	6
Robbery	10	24
Aggravated assault	19	12
Non-violent	461	399
Burglary	84	76
Larceny	327	265
Vehicle theft	50	58
Domestic violence	136	166
Arson	2	1
Total crime rate	25.4	22.6
Violent	1.8	2.1
Non-violent	23.6	20.4

Public School District

(for school year 2007-08 except as noted)

Maple Shade Township School District
170 Frederick Ave.
Maple Shade, NJ 08052
(856) 779-1750

Superintendent	Michael Livengood
Number of schools	4
Grade plan	K-12
Enrollment	2,048
Attendance rate, '06-07	92.9%
Dropout rate	2.6%
Students per teacher	11.2
Per pupil expenditure	$12,717
Median faculty salary	$52,952
Median administrator salary	$103,294
Grade 12 enrollment	138
High school graduation rate	91.9%

Assessment test results

(percent scoring at proficient or advanced level)

	Language	Math
NJASK-Grade 3	82.6%	79.9%
GEPA-Grade 8	75.2%	79.0%
HSPA-High School	69.6%	81.7%

SAT Score Averages, 2006-07

Pct tested	Math	Verbal	Writing
69%	469	450	456

Teacher Qualifications

Avg. years of experience	10
Highly-qualified teachers one subject/all subjects	100%/100%

No Child Left Behind

AYP, 2006-07	Meets Standards

Municipal Finance

State Aid Programs, 2009

Total aid	$2,204,261
CMPTRA	530,799
Energy tax receipts	1,618,355
Garden State Trust	0

General Budget, 2008

Total tax levy	$35,431,081
County levy	6,251,891
County taxes	5,133,999
County library	474,034
County health	0
County open space	643,858
School levy	21,182,343
Muni. levy	7,996,847
Misc. revenues	4,834,724

Taxes

	2006	2007	2008
General tax rate per $100	2.007	2.14	2.223
County equalization ratio	124.2	107.18	99.13
Net valuation taxable	$1,603,195,500	$1,592,773,167	$1,594,185,618
State equalized value	$1,497,825,632	$1,606,733,592	$1,661,384,792

See Introduction for an explanation of all data sources.

Demographics & Socio-Economic Characteristics
(2000 US Census, except as noted)

Population
1980*	22,950
1990*	21,652
2000	23,868
Male	11,347
Female	12,521
2007 (estimate)*	22,254
Population density	5,780.3

Race & Hispanic Origin, 2000
Race
White	14,030
Black/African American	7,788
American Indian/Alaska Native	31
Asian	682
Native Hawaiian/Pacific Islander	7
Other race	373
Two or more races	957
Hispanic origin, total	1,248
Mexican	69
Puerto Rican	438
Cuban	97
Other Hispanic	644

Age & Nativity, 2000
Under 5 years	1,882
18 years and over	17,175
21 years and over	16,560
65 years and over	2,890
85 years and over	505
Median age	37.7
Native-born	19,614
Foreign-born	4,254

Educational Attainment, 2000
Population 25 years and over	15,987
Less than 9th grade	2.5%
High school grad or higher	91.9%
Bachelor's degree or higher	50.8%
Graduate degree	22.0%

Income & Poverty, 1999
Per capita income	$36,794
Median household income	$79,637
Median family income	$92,724
Persons in poverty	1,049
H'holds receiving public assistance	77
H'holds receiving social security	1,896

Households, 2000
Total households	8,452
With persons under 18	3,646
With persons over 65	2,136
Family households	6,379
Single-person households	1,720
Persons per household	2.81
Persons per family	3.27

Labor & Employment
Total civilian labor force, 2007**	13,316
Unemployment rate	3.8%
Total civilian labor force, 2000	12,848
Unemployment rate	3.9%

Employed persons 16 years and over by occupation, 2000
Managers & professionals	6,478
Service occupations	1,124
Sales & office occupations	3,263
Farming, fishing & forestry	0
Construction & maintenance	604
Production & transportation	883
Self-employed persons	823

General Information
Township of Maplewood
574 Valley St
Maplewood, NJ 07040
973-762-8120
Website	www.twp.maplewood.nj.us
Year of incorporation	1922
Land/water area (sq. miles)	3.85/0.00
Form of government	Township

Government
Legislative Districts
US Congressional	10
State Legislative	27

Local Officials, 2009
Mayor	Victor Deluca
Manager	Joseph Manning
Clerk	Elizabeth Fritzen
Finance Dir	Peter Fresulone
Tax Assessor	Edward Galante
Tax Collector	Peter Fresulone
Attorney	Roger Desiderio
Building	Robert Mittermaier
Comm Dev/Planning	NA
Engineering	Richard Calbi Jr
Public Works	Gary Lenci
Police Chief	Robert Cimino
Emerg/Fire Director	Joseph Richardella

Housing & Construction
Housing Units, 2000*
Total	8,615
Median rent	$950
Median SF home value	$222,700

Permits for New Residential Construction
	Units	Value
Total, 2006	7	$580,679
Single family	2	$197,729
Total, 2007	14	$1,244,764
Single family	2	$278,864

Real Property Valuation, 2008
	Parcels	Valuation
Total	7,264	$2,054,998,700
Vacant	43	4,408,500
Residential	6,869	1,843,762,400
Commercial	307	182,742,100
Industrial	33	13,710,500
Apartments	12	10,375,200
Farm land	0	0
Farm homestead	0	0

Average Property Value & Tax, 2008
Residential value	$268,418
Property tax	$12,027
Tax credit/rebate	$1,276

Public Library
Maplewood Memorial Library
51 Baker St
Maplewood, NJ 07040
973-762-1622
Director................ Jane E. Kennedy

Library statistics, 2007
Population served	23,868
Full-time/total staff	9/15

	Total	Per capita
Holdings	134,240	5.62
Revenues	$1,967,726	$82.44
Expenditures	$1,920,393	$80.46
Annual visits	327,791	13.73
Internet terminals/annual users	46/51,384	

Public Safety
Number of officers, 2007	64

Crime	2006	2007
Total crimes	598	457
Violent	67	57
Murder	0	1
Rape	3	0
Robbery	30	33
Aggravated assault	34	23
Non-violent	531	400
Burglary	74	42
Larceny	357	287
Vehicle theft	100	71
Domestic violence	52	81
Arson	3	2
Total crime rate	25.9	20.1
Violent	2.9	2.5
Non-violent	23.0	17.6

Public School District
(for school year 2007-08 except as noted)

South Orange-Maplewood School District
525 Academy Street
Maplewood, NJ 07040
(973) 762-5600
Superintendent	Brian G. Osborne
Number of schools	9
Grade plan	K-12
Enrollment	6,085
Attendance rate, '06-07	95.0%
Dropout rate	0.4%
Students per teacher	11.0
Per pupil expenditure	$15,373
Median faculty salary	$67,399
Median administrator salary	$117,919
Grade 12 enrollment	430
High school graduation rate	98.0%

Assessment test results
(percent scoring at proficient or advanced level)
	Language	Math
NJASK-Grade 3	89.1%	91.8%
GEPA-Grade 8	69.9%	83.0%
HSPA-High School	80.5%	86.5%

SAT Score Averages, 2006-07
Pct tested	Math	Verbal	Writing
97%	513	500	503

Teacher Qualifications
Avg. years of experience	9
Highly-qualified teachers one subject/all subjects	100%/100%

No Child Left Behind
AYP, 2006-07 .... Needs Improvement

Municipal Finance
State Aid Programs, 2009
Total aid	$2,365,476
CMPTRA	569,562
Energy tax receipts	1,736,777
Garden State Trust	0

General Budget, 2008
Total tax levy	$92,119,125
County levy	14,898,393
County taxes	14,323,407
County library	0
County health	0
County open space	574,986
School levy	52,722,618
Muni. levy	24,498,115
Misc. revenues	11,932,724

Taxes
	2006	2007	2008
General tax rate per $100	3.98	4.23	4.481
County equalization ratio	66.38	57.58	54.18
Net valuation taxable	$2,047,983,000	$2,055,054,000	$2,055,989,880
State equalized value	$3,557,974,028	$3,792,155,742	$3,898,200,928

* US Census Bureau
** New Jersey Department of Labor

Demographics & Socio-Economic Characteristics
(2000 US Census, except as noted)

Population
1980*	9,179
1990*	8,431
2000	8,193
Male	3,861
Female	4,332
2007 (estimate)*	8,537
Population density	6,054.6

Race & Hispanic Origin, 2000
Race
White	7,843
Black/African American	71
American Indian/Alaska Native	2
Asian	128
Native Hawaiian/Pacific Islander	6
Other race	75
Two or more races	68
Hispanic origin, total	222
Mexican	39
Puerto Rican	74
Cuban	13
Other Hispanic	96

Age & Nativity, 2000
Under 5 years	298
18 years and over	6,935
21 years and over	6,800
65 years and over	2,365
85 years and over	255
Median age	49.8
Native-born	7,586
Foreign-born	607

Educational Attainment, 2000
Population 25 years and over	6,668
Less than 9th grade	2.0%
High school grad or higher	88.3%
Bachelor's degree or higher	36.5%
Graduate degree	13.4%

Income & Poverty, 1999
Per capita income	$33,566
Median household income	$45,876
Median family income	$63,917
Persons in poverty	594
H'holds receiving public assistance	47
H'holds receiving social security	1,734

Households, 2000
Total households	3,984
With persons under 18	725
With persons over 65	1,707
Family households	2,303
Single-person households	1,440
Persons per household	2.06
Persons per family	2.67

Labor & Employment
Total civilian labor force, 2007**	4,234
Unemployment rate	5.1%
Total civilian labor force, 2000	3,981
Unemployment rate	5.6%

Employed persons 16 years and over by occupation, 2000
Managers & professionals	1,415
Service occupations	783
Sales & office occupations	1,198
Farming, fishing & forestry	0
Construction & maintenance	220
Production & transportation	142
Self-employed persons	361

* US Census Bureau
** New Jersey Department of Labor

General Information
City of Margate
1 S Washington Ave
Margate City, NJ 08402
609-822-2605
Website	www.margate-nj.com
Year of incorporation	1909
Land/water area (sq. miles)	1.41/0.18
Form of government	Commission

Government
Legislative Districts
US Congressional	2
State Legislative	2

Local Officials, 2009
Mayor	Michael S. Becker
Manager/Admin	NA
Clerk	Thomas Hiltner
Finance Dir	Lisa McLaughlin
Tax Assessor	Andy Bednarek
Tax Collector	Thomas D. Hiltner
Attorney	Mary Siracusa
Building	Jim Galantino
Comm Dev/Planning	NA
Engineering	Remington & Vernick
Public Works	Frank Ricciotti
Police Chief	David Wolfson
Emerg/Fire Director	John Kelley

Housing & Construction
Housing Units, 2000*
Total	7,006
Median rent	$739
Median SF home value	$189,300

Permits for New Residential Construction
	Units	Value
Total, 2006	97	$21,605,521
Single family	54	$16,540,135
Total, 2007	49	$16,579,935
Single family	31	$12,481,533

Real Property Valuation, 2008
	Parcels	Valuation
Total	6,937	$3,406,787,400
Vacant	214	50,002,800
Residential	6,526	3,258,966,500
Commercial	187	90,548,900
Industrial	0	0
Apartments	10	7,269,200
Farm land	0	0
Farm homestead	0	0

Average Property Value & Tax, 2008
Residential value	$499,382
Property tax	$6,040
Tax credit/rebate	$1,036

Public Library
Margate City Public Library
8100 Atlantic Ave
Margate, NJ 08402
609-822-4700
Director	James J. Cahill

Library statistics, 2007
Population served	8,193
Full-time/total staff	2/5

	Total	Per capita
Holdings	52,618	6.42
Revenues	$1,038,217	$126.72
Expenditures	$1,113,217	$135.87
Annual visits	112,160	13.69
Internet terminals/annual users	11/20,060	

Public Safety
Number of officers, 2007 ... 36
Crime	2006	2007
Total crimes	186	162
Violent	5	6
Murder	0	1
Rape	0	0
Robbery	0	1
Aggravated assault	5	4
Non-violent	181	156
Burglary	44	26
Larceny	133	125
Vehicle theft	4	5
Domestic violence	44	46
Arson	0	1
Total crime rate	21.5	18.8
Violent	0.6	0.7
Non-violent	20.9	18.1

Public School District
(for school year 2007-08 except as noted)

Margate City School District
8103 Winchester Avenue
Margate City, NJ 08402
(609) 822-1686
Superintendent	Dominick A. Potena
Number of schools	3
Grade plan	K-8
Enrollment	560
Attendance rate, '06-07	95.6%
Dropout rate	NA
Students per teacher	9.3
Per pupil expenditure	$17,080
Median faculty salary	$72,670
Median administrator salary	$101,796
Grade 12 enrollment	NA
High school graduation rate	NA

Assessment test results
(percent scoring at proficient or advanced level)
	Language	Math
NJASK-Grade 3	98.1%	98.2%
GEPA-Grade 8	81.4%	93.3%
HSPA-High School	NA	NA

SAT Score Averages, 2006-07
Pct tested	Math	Verbal	Writing
NA	NA	NA	NA

Teacher Qualifications
Avg. years of experience	14
Highly-qualified teachers one subject/all subjects	100%/100%

No Child Left Behind
AYP, 2006-07 ... Meets Standards

Municipal Finance
State Aid Programs, 2009
Total aid	$880,623
CMPTRA	0
Energy tax receipts	852,003
Garden State Trust	0

General Budget, 2008
Total tax levy	$41,220,006
County levy	10,415,960
County taxes	9,128,309
County library	0
County health	479,361
County open space	808,290
School levy	11,673,118
Muni. levy	19,130,928
Misc. revenues	5,109,623

Taxes	2006	2007	2008
General tax rate per $100	1.204	1.18	1.210
County equalization ratio	102.56	88.06	84.43
Net valuation taxable	$3,307,881,900	$3,361,487,250	$3,407,846,629
State equalized value	$3,757,583,765	$3,981,194,845	$4,130,498,502

See Introduction for an explanation of all data sources.

Demographics & Socio-Economic Characteristics

(2000 US Census, except as noted)

Population

1980*	17,560
1990*	27,974
2000	36,398
Male	18,048
Female	18,350
2007 (estimate)*	40,633
Population density	1,328.3

Race & Hispanic Origin, 2000

Race

White	30,487
Black/African American	752
American Indian/Alaska Native	17
Asian	4,612
Native Hawaiian/Pacific Islander	5
Other race	171
Two or more races	354
Hispanic origin, total	1,051
Mexican	123
Puerto Rican	350
Cuban	107
Other Hispanic	471

Age & Nativity, 2000

Under 5 years	2,723
18 years and over	25,409
21 years and over	24,466
65 years and over	3,207
85 years and over	248
Median age	37.6
Native-born	30,782
Foreign-born	5,621

Educational Attainment, 2000

Population 25 years and over	23,453
Less than 9th grade	2.1%
High school grad or higher	94.0%
Bachelor's degree or higher	52.3%
Graduate degree	22.6%

Income & Poverty, 1999

Per capita income	$38,635
Median household income	$101,322
Median family income	$107,894
Persons in poverty	1,256
H'holds receiving public assistance	74
H'holds receiving social security	2,313

Households, 2000

Total households	11,478
With persons under 18	5,925
With persons over 65	2,245
Family households	10,167
Single-person households	1,110
Persons per household	3.15
Persons per family	3.38

Labor & Employment

Total civilian labor force, 2007**	20,445
Unemployment rate	2.7%
Total civilian labor force, 2000	17,945
Unemployment rate	3.3%

Employed persons 16 years and over by occupation, 2000

Managers & professionals	9,569
Service occupations	1,095
Sales & office occupations	4,973
Farming, fishing & forestry	0
Construction & maintenance	724
Production & transportation	993
Self-employed persons	1,059

General Information

Township of Marlboro
1979 Township Dr
Marlboro, NJ 07746
732-536-0200

Website	www.marlboro-nj.gov
Year of incorporation	1848
Land/water area (sq. miles)	30.59/0.00
Form of government	Mayor-Council

Government

Legislative Districts

US Congressional	6, 12
State Legislative	12

Local Officials, 2009

Mayor	Jonathan L. Hornik
Manager	Alayne Shepler
Clerk	Alida Manco
Finance Dir	Ulrich Steinberg
Tax Assessor	Walter Kosul
Tax Collector	Shirley Giaquinto
Attorney	Jonathan Williams
Building	Joseph Labruzza
Comm Dev/Planning	NA
Engineering	Birdsall Engineering
Public Works	Robert DiMarco
Police Chief	Robert Holmes
Fire/Emergency Dir	NA

Housing & Construction

Housing Units, 2000*

Total	11,896
Median rent	$1,334
Median SF home value	$286,300

Permits for New Residential Construction

	Units	Value
Total, 2006	71	$18,134,600
Single family	71	$18,134,600
Total, 2007	51	$10,931,685
Single family	51	$10,931,685

Real Property Valuation, 2008

	Parcels	Valuation
Total	14,121	$3,153,852,750
Vacant	821	49,225,500
Residential	12,804	2,869,073,200
Commercial	233	176,080,600
Industrial	27	39,136,700
Apartments	3	3,343,100
Farm land	150	770,350
Farm homestead	83	16,223,300

Average Property Value & Tax, 2008

Residential value	$223,892
Property tax	$9,244
Tax credit/rebate	$1,217

Public Library

Marlboro Library‡
1 Library Ct
Marlboro, NJ 07746
732-536-9406

Branch Librarian	Jennifer King

Library statistics, 2007

see Monmouth County profile
for library system statistics

Public Safety

Number of officers, 2007	73

Crime	2006	2007
Total crimes	418	426
Violent	16	26
Murder	0	0
Rape	1	1
Robbery	8	4
Aggravated assault	7	21
Non-violent	402	400
Burglary	73	86
Larceny	315	296
Vehicle theft	14	18
Domestic violence	184	186
Arson	9	5
Total crime rate	10.5	10.7
Violent	0.4	0.7
Non-violent	10.1	10.0

Public School District

(for school year 2007-08 except as noted)

Marlboro Township School District
1980 Township Drive
Marlboro, NJ 07746
(732) 972-2015

Superintendent	David Abbott
Number of schools	8
Grade plan	K-8
Enrollment	6,072
Attendance rate, '06-07	96.3%
Dropout rate	NA
Students per teacher	12.2
Per pupil expenditure	$11,867
Median faculty salary	$52,855
Median administrator salary	$113,306
Grade 12 enrollment	NA
High school graduation rate	NA

Assessment test results

(percent scoring at proficient or advanced level)

	Language	Math
NJASK-Grade 3	95.5%	94.3%
GEPA-Grade 8	86.1%	95.3%
HSPA-High School	NA	NA

SAT Score Averages, 2006-07

Pct tested	Math	Verbal	Writing
NA	NA	NA	NA

Teacher Qualifications

Avg. years of experience	8
Highly-qualified teachers one subject/all subjects	100%/100%

No Child Left Behind

AYP, 2006-07	Meets Standards

Municipal Finance

State Aid Programs, 2009

Total aid	$3,040,010
CMPTRA	241,180
Energy tax receipts	2,722,830
Garden State Trust	0

General Budget, 2008

Total tax levy	$130,374,912
County levy	19,788,358
County taxes	17,275,374
County library	1,039,642
County health	321,228
County open space	1,152,114
School levy	92,072,391
Muni. levy	18,514,163
Misc. revenues	16,105,342

Taxes

	2006	2007	2008
General tax rate per $100	4.037	4.099	4.129
County equalization ratio	47.36	42.7	41.21
Net valuation taxable	$3,076,715,950	$3,131,514,009	$3,157,721,264
State equalized value	$7,209,924,440	$7,592,882,321	$6,480,948,402

‡ Branch of county library
* US Census Bureau
** New Jersey Department of Labor

Demographics & Socio-Economic Characteristics

(2000 US Census, except as noted)

Population
1980*	8,837
1990*	9,270
2000	8,910
Male	4,400
Female	4,510
2007 (estimate)*	8,806
Population density	3,862.3

Race & Hispanic Origin, 2000
Race
White	7,337
Black/African American	582
American Indian/Alaska Native	2
Asian	712
Native Hawaiian/Pacific Islander	2
Other race	110
Two or more races	165
Hispanic origin, total	575
Mexican	112
Puerto Rican	242
Cuban	51
Other Hispanic	170

Age & Nativity, 2000
Under 5 years	562
18 years and over	6,900
21 years and over	6,627
65 years and over	935
85 years and over	90
Median age	36.4
Native-born	7,641
Foreign-born	1,336

Educational Attainment, 2000
Population 25 years and over	6,256
Less than 9th grade	3.9%
High school grad or higher	88.4%
Bachelor's degree or higher	30.4%
Graduate degree	11.5%

Income & Poverty, 1999
Per capita income	$30,320
Median household income	$63,594
Median family income	$72,183
Persons in poverty	485
H'holds receiving public assistance	46
H'holds receiving social security	831

Households, 2000
Total households	3,531
With persons under 18	1,153
With persons over 65	715
Family households	2,375
Single-person households	904
Persons per household	2.52
Persons per family	3.07

Labor & Employment
Total civilian labor force, 2007**	5,235
Unemployment rate	4.1%
Total civilian labor force, 2000	4,928
Unemployment rate	4.8%

Employed persons 16 years and over by occupation, 2000
Managers & professionals	1,970
Service occupations	596
Sales & office occupations	1,322
Farming, fishing & forestry	0
Construction & maintenance	384
Production & transportation	418
Self-employed persons	225

‡ Joint library with Aberdeen Township
* US Census Bureau
** New Jersey Department of Labor

See Introduction for an explanation of all data sources.

General Information
Matawan Borough
201 Broad St
Matawan, NJ 07747
732-566-3898
Website	www.matawanborough.com
Year of incorporation	1895
Land/water area (sq. miles)	2.28/0.12
Form of government	Borough

Government

Legislative Districts
US Congressional	6
State Legislative	13

Local Officials, 2009
Mayor	Paul Buccellato
Business Admin	Fred Carr
Clerk	Jean Montfort
Finance Dir	Monica Antista
Tax Assessor	Eric Zanetti
Tax Collector	Peggy Warren
Attorney	Pasquale Menna
Building	John Quinn
Planning	Bill White
Engineering	Robert Keady
Public Works	Anthony Bucco
Police Chief	James M. Alston
Emerg/Fire Director	Martin LiPera

Housing & Construction

Housing Units, 2000*
Total	3,640
Median rent	$808
Median SF home value	$178,500

Permits for New Residential Construction
	Units	Value
Total, 2006	3	$720,500
Single family	3	$720,500
Total, 2007	4	$800,000
Single family	4	$800,000

Real Property Valuation, 2008
	Parcels	Valuation
Total	2,593	$1,034,213,900
Vacant	117	8,867,500
Residential	2,315	803,708,700
Commercial	136	132,252,700
Industrial	9	9,729,100
Apartments	16	79,655,900
Farm land	0	0
Farm homestead	0	0

Average Property Value & Tax, 2008
Residential value	$347,174
Property tax	$7,986
Tax credit/rebate	$1,212

Public Library
Matawan-Aberdeen Public Library‡
165 Main St
Matawan, NJ 07747
732-583-9100
Director	Susan Pike

Library statistics, 2007
Population served	26,364
Full-time/total staff	3/6

	Total	Per capita
Holdings	104,042	3.95
Revenues	$1,085,233	$41.16
Expenditures	$822,991	$31.22
Annual visits	110,739	4.20
Internet terminals/annual users	14/15,061	

Public Safety
Number of officers, 2007	23

Crime	2006	2007
Total crimes	106	102
Violent	11	6
Murder	0	0
Rape	1	1
Robbery	6	1
Aggravated assault	4	4
Non-violent	95	96
Burglary	24	14
Larceny	63	76
Vehicle theft	8	6
Domestic violence	93	63
Arson	0	0
Total crime rate	12.0	11.6
Violent	1.2	0.7
Non-violent	10.8	10.9

Public School District
(for school year 2007-08 except as noted)

Matawan-Aberdeen Regional School District
One Crest Way
Aberdeen, NJ 07747
(732) 705-4003
Superintendent	Richard. O'Malley
Number of schools	7
Grade plan	K-12
Enrollment	3,750
Attendance rate, '06-07	94.9%
Dropout rate	0.4%
Students per teacher	10.2
Per pupil expenditure	$14,513
Median faculty salary	$53,720
Median administrator salary	$119,909
Grade 12 enrollment	262
High school graduation rate	99.2%

Assessment test results
(percent scoring at proficient or advanced level)
	Language	Math
NJASK-Grade 3	90.2%	89.4%
GEPA-Grade 8	77.3%	85.8%
HSPA-High School	71.8%	87.1%

SAT Score Averages, 2006-07
Pct tested	Math	Verbal	Writing
82%	478	469	467

Teacher Qualifications
Avg. years of experience	9
Highly-qualified teachers one subject/all subjects	99.5%/99.5%

No Child Left Behind
AYP, 2006-07	Meets Standards

Municipal Finance

State Aid Programs, 2009
Total aid	$1,870,984
CMPTRA	0
Energy tax receipts	1,824,209
Garden State Trust	0

General Budget, 2008
Total tax levy	$23,829,115
County levy	2,659,631
County taxes	2,450,641
County library	0
County health	45,571
County open space	163,419
School levy	14,990,949
Muni. levy	6,178,535
Misc. revenues	3,552,488

Taxes
	2006	2007	2008
General tax rate per $100	5.013	5.28	2.301
County equalization ratio	49.18	42.73	95.57
Net valuation taxable	$429,369,234	$432,543,706	$1,035,956,127
State equalized value	$1,005,643,015	$1,077,033,003	$2,235,863,332

Demographics & Socio-Economic Characteristics

(2000 US Census, except as noted)

Population

1980*	4,577
1990*	6,648
2000	6,928
Male	5,093
Female	1,835
2007 (estimate)*	8,034
Population density	86.0

Race & Hispanic Origin, 2000

Race

White	4,062
Black/African American	2,285
American Indian/Alaska Native	54
Asian	19
Native Hawaiian/Pacific Islander	1
Other race	307
Two or more races	200
Hispanic origin, total	634
Mexican	15
Puerto Rican	404
Cuban	51
Other Hispanic	164

Age & Nativity, 2000

Under 5 years	200
18 years and over	6,036
21 years and over	5,914
65 years and over	443
85 years and over	39
Median age	36.0
Native-born	6,710
Foreign-born	218

Educational Attainment, 2000

Population 25 years and over	5,704
Less than 9th grade	7.4%
High school grad or higher	62.8%
Bachelor's degree or higher	4.7%
Graduate degree	1.1%

Income & Poverty, 1999

Per capita income	$17,141
Median household income	$43,182
Median family income	$46,987
Persons in poverty	287
H'holds receiving public assistance	26
H'holds receiving social security	394

Households, 2000

Total households	1,332
With persons under 18	483
With persons over 65	327
Family households	1,012
Single-person households	258
Persons per household	2.68
Persons per family	3.03

Labor & Employment

Total civilian labor force, 2007**	1,946
Unemployment rate	3.8%
Total civilian labor force, 2000	1,777
Unemployment rate	5.7%

Employed persons 16 years and over by occupation, 2000

Managers & professionals	385
Service occupations	345
Sales & office occupations	328
Farming, fishing & forestry	11
Construction & maintenance	228
Production & transportation	379
Self-employed persons	72

* US Census Bureau
** New Jersey Department of Labor

General Information

Township of Maurice River
590 Main St
PO Box 218
Leesburg, NJ 08327
856-785-1120

Website	www.mauricerivertwp.org
Year of incorporation	1748
Land/water area (sq. miles)	93.41/2.31
Form of government	Township

Government

Legislative Districts

US Congressional	2
State Legislative	1

Local Officials, 2009

Mayor	Andrew Sarclette
Manager/Admin	NA
Clerk	J. Roy Oliver
Finance Dir	Sharon Lloyd
Tax Assessor	Michelle Sharp
Tax Collector	J. Roy Oliver
Attorney	Edward Duffy
Building	Gordon Gross
Comm Dev/Planning	NA
Engineering	Kent Schellinger
Public Works	Barry Creamer
Police Chief	NA
Fire Official	Keith Mitchell

Housing & Construction

Housing Units, 2000*

Total	1,461
Median rent	$613
Median SF home value	$84,100

Permits for New Residential Construction

	Units	Value
Total, 2006	14	$907,484
Single family	14	$907,484
Total, 2007	11	$1,703,010
Single family	11	$1,703,010

Real Property Valuation, 2008

	Parcels	Valuation
Total	3,650	$143,991,100
Vacant	2,056	8,638,400
Residential	1,412	114,414,900
Commercial	64	7,923,100
Industrial	30	7,661,200
Apartments	2	392,300
Farm land	69	1,688,000
Farm homestead	17	3,273,200

Average Property Value & Tax, 2008

Residential value	$82,357
Property tax	$3,349
Tax credit/rebate	$796

Public Library

No public municipal library

Library statistics, 2007

Population served	NA
Full-time/total staff	NA/NA

	Total	Per capita
Holdings	NA	NA
Revenues	NA	NA
Expenditures	NA	NA
Annual visits	NA	NA
Internet terminals/annual users	NA/NA	

Public Safety

Number of officers, 2007 ... 0

Crime	2006	2007
Total crimes	51	70
Violent	6	1
Murder	0	0
Rape	0	0
Robbery	0	0
Aggravated assault	6	1
Non-violent	45	69
Burglary	11	22
Larceny	29	37
Vehicle theft	5	10
Domestic violence	14	35
Arson	1	2
Total crime rate	6.7	8.7
Violent	0.8	0.1
Non-violent	5.9	8.5

Public School District

(for school year 2007-08 except as noted)

Maurice River Township School District
3593 Route 47, Drawer D
Port Elizabeth, NJ 08348
(856) 825-7411

Superintendent	John Saporito
Number of schools	1
Grade plan	K-8
Enrollment	393
Attendance rate, '06-07	94.6%
Dropout rate	NA
Students per teacher	9.6
Per pupil expenditure	$13,138
Median faculty salary	$49,020
Median administrator salary	$102,979
Grade 12 enrollment	NA
High school graduation rate	NA

Assessment test results

(percent scoring at proficient or advanced level)

	Language	Math
NJASK-Grade 3	97.2%	80.6%
GEPA-Grade 8	71.7%	86.8%
HSPA-High School	NA	NA

SAT Score Averages, 2006-07

Pct tested	Math	Verbal	Writing
NA	NA	NA	NA

Teacher Qualifications

Avg. years of experience	11
Highly-qualified teachers one subject/all subjects	97.0%/97.0%

No Child Left Behind

AYP, 2006-07 ... Meets Standards

Municipal Finance

State Aid Programs, 2009

Total aid	$1,188,461
CMPTRA	208,386
Energy tax receipts	591,666
Garden State Trust	343,321

General Budget, 2008

Total tax levy	$5,880,045
County levy	2,811,213
County taxes	2,657,523
County library	0
County health	124,149
County open space	29,541
School levy	2,574,317
Muni. levy	494,514
Misc. revenues	3,073,480

Taxes

	2006	2007	2008
General tax rate per $100	3.633	3.886	4.068
County equalization ratio	64.19	54.75	49.31
Net valuation taxable	$140,563,800	$143,170,899	$144,603,687
State equalized value	$257,471,837	$289,689,671	$312,957,706

See Introduction for an explanation of all data sources.

Demographics & Socio-Economic Characteristics
(2000 US Census, except as noted)

Population
1980*	9,895
1990*	9,473
2000	9,523
Male	4,428
Female	5,095
2007 (estimate)*	9,230
Population density	7,100.0

Race & Hispanic Origin, 2000
Race
White	8,054
Black/African American	266
American Indian/Alaska Native	7
Asian	682
Native Hawaiian/Pacific Islander	1
Other race	315
Two or more races	198
Hispanic origin, total	1,115
Mexican	27
Puerto Rican	301
Cuban	106
Other Hispanic	681

Age & Nativity, 2000
Under 5 years	618
18 years and over	7,514
21 years and over	7,262
65 years and over	1,670
85 years and over	263
Median age	40.2
Native-born	7,728
Foreign-born	1,795

Educational Attainment, 2000
Population 25 years and over	7,053
Less than 9th grade	4.0%
High school grad or higher	87.6%
Bachelor's degree or higher	31.2%
Graduate degree	10.1%

Income & Poverty, 1999
Per capita income	$28,117
Median household income	$62,113
Median family income	$73,419
Persons in poverty	311
H'holds receiving public assistance	58
H'holds receiving social security	1,273

Households, 2000
Total households	3,710
With persons under 18	1,161
With persons over 65	1,239
Family households	2,626
Single-person households	923
Persons per household	2.56
Persons per family	3.09

Labor & Employment
Total civilian labor force, 2007**	5,386
Unemployment rate	3.2%
Total civilian labor force, 2000	5,116
Unemployment rate	3.5%

Employed persons 16 years and over by occupation, 2000
Managers & professionals	1,858
Service occupations	422
Sales & office occupations	1,864
Farming, fishing & forestry	4
Construction & maintenance	377
Production & transportation	413
Self-employed persons	253

* US Census Bureau
** New Jersey Department of Labor

General Information
Borough of Maywood
15 Park Ave
Maywood, NJ 07607
201-845-2900
Website	www.maywoodnj.org
Year of incorporation	1894
Land/water area (sq. miles)	1.30/0.00
Form of government	Borough

Government
Legislative Districts
US Congressional	9
State Legislative	37

Local Officials, 2009
Mayor	Timothy J. Eustace
Manager/Admin	Thomas H. Richards
Clerk	Jean M. Pelligra
Finance Dir	Charles Cuccia
Tax Assessor	George Reggo
Tax Collector	Joseph Iannaconi Jr
Attorney	William Rupp
Building	James Mazzer
Comm Dev/Planning	NA
Engineering	Michael Neglia
Public Works	Donald Russell
Police Chief	David Pegg
Emerg/Fire Director	Daniel Mulvaney

Housing & Construction
Housing Units, 2000*
Total	3,777
Median rent	$880
Median SF home value	$197,900

Permits for New Residential Construction
	Units	Value
Total, 2006	2	$583,250
Single family	0	$325,700
Total, 2007	1	$329,200
Single family	1	$329,200

Real Property Valuation, 2008
	Parcels	Valuation
Total	2,943	$1,431,119,900
Vacant	69	10,218,100
Residential	2,727	1,131,820,000
Commercial	104	119,258,700
Industrial	28	110,343,600
Apartments	15	59,479,500
Farm land	0	0
Farm homestead	0	0

Average Property Value & Tax, 2008
Residential value	$415,042
Property tax	$7,765
Tax credit/rebate	$1,179

Public Library
Maywood Public Library
459 Maywood Ave
Maywood, NJ 07607
201-845-2915
Director	Diane Rhodes

Library statistics, 2007
Population served	9,523
Full-time/total staff	1/1

	Total	Per capita
Holdings	60,922	6.40
Revenues	$548,344	$57.58
Expenditures	$519,441	$54.55
Annual visits	44,650	4.69
Internet terminals/annual users	24/13,500	

Public Safety
Number of officers, 2007	24

Crime	2006	2007
Total crimes	102	91
Violent	4	2
Murder	0	0
Rape	0	0
Robbery	1	0
Aggravated assault	3	2
Non-violent	98	89
Burglary	17	32
Larceny	78	56
Vehicle theft	3	1
Domestic violence	53	44
Arson	1	0
Total crime rate	10.8	9.7
Violent	0.4	0.2
Non-violent	10.4	9.5

Public School District
(for school year 2007-08 except as noted)

Maywood School District
452 Maywood Avenue
Maywood, NJ 07607
(201) 845-9114
Superintendent	Robert Otnisky
Number of schools	2
Grade plan	K-8
Enrollment	870
Attendance rate, '06-07	95.8%
Dropout rate	NA
Students per teacher	11.3
Per pupil expenditure	$14,061
Median faculty salary	$45,820
Median administrator salary	$118,000
Grade 12 enrollment	NA
High school graduation rate	NA

Assessment test results
(percent scoring at proficient or advanced level)
	Language	Math
NJASK-Grade 3	92.8%	94.9%
GEPA-Grade 8	80.7%	89.7%
HSPA-High School	NA	NA

SAT Score Averages, 2006-07
Pct tested	Math	Verbal	Writing
NA	NA	NA	NA

Teacher Qualifications
Avg. years of experience	5

Highly-qualified teachers
one subject/all subjects	100%/100%

No Child Left Behind
AYP, 2006-07	Meets Standards

Municipal Finance
State Aid Programs, 2009
Total aid	$1,300,014
CMPTRA	86,639
Energy tax receipts	1,193,875
Garden State Trust	1

General Budget, 2008
Total tax levy	$26,781,806
County levy	2,603,421
County taxes	2,461,969
County library	0
County health	0
County open space	141,451
School levy	14,334,851
Muni. levy	9,843,534
Misc. revenues	4,521,669

Taxes
	2006	2007	2008
General tax rate per $100	3.88	4.13	1.871
County equalization ratio	52.51	45.69	101.81
Net valuation taxable	$617,708,500	$616,354,245	$1,431,538,045
State equalized value	$1,352,428,946	$1,400,909,505	$1,409,833,055

See Introduction for an explanation of all data sources.

Demographics & Socio-Economic Characteristics
(2000 US Census, except as noted)

Population
1980*	4,958
1990*	4,462
2000	4,173
Male	2,043
Female	2,130
2007 (estimate)*	4,099
Population density	3,387.6

Race & Hispanic Origin, 2000
Race
White	4,103
Black/African American	18
American Indian/Alaska Native	5
Asian	20
Native Hawaiian/Pacific Islander	0
Other race	4
Two or more races	23
Hispanic origin, total	41
Mexican	2
Puerto Rican	13
Cuban	18
Other Hispanic	8

Age & Nativity, 2000
Under 5 years	261
18 years and over	3,106
21 years and over	2,988
65 years and over	516
85 years and over	31
Median age	40.3
Native-born	4,102
Foreign-born	71

Educational Attainment, 2000
Population 25 years and over	2,910
Less than 9th grade	1.2%
High school grad or higher	95.2%
Bachelor's degree or higher	50.1%
Graduate degree	14.0%

Income & Poverty, 1999
Per capita income	$31,382
Median household income	$77,536
Median family income	$83,695
Persons in poverty	89
H'holds receiving public assistance	7
H'holds receiving social security	392

Households, 2000
Total households	1,527
With persons under 18	592
With persons over 65	363
Family households	1,239
Single-person households	231
Persons per household	2.73
Persons per family	3.04

Labor & Employment
Total civilian labor force, 2007**	2,685
Unemployment rate	1.7%
Total civilian labor force, 2000	2,346
Unemployment rate	1.5%

Employed persons 16 years and over by occupation, 2000
Managers & professionals	1,124
Service occupations	218
Sales & office occupations	735
Farming, fishing & forestry	0
Construction & maintenance	96
Production & transportation	137
Self-employed persons	134

General Information
Borough of Medford Lakes
1 Cabin Circle
Medford Lakes, NJ 08055
609-654-8898

Website	www.medfordlakes.com
Year of incorporation	1939
Land/water area (sq. miles)	1.21/0.10
Form of government	Municipal Mgr 1923

Government
Legislative Districts
US Congressional	3
State Legislative	8

Local Officials, 2009
Mayor	Paul G. Weiss
Manager	Geoffrey D. Urbanik
Clerk	Mark J. McIntosh
Finance Dir	Donna A. Condo
Tax Assessor	Douglas Kolton
Tax Collector	Sharon Deviney
Attorney	Peter Lange Jr
Building	Thomas Heck
Planning	Debbie Klemas
Engineering	Jim Giordano
Public Works	(vacant)
Police Chief	Frank Martine
Emerg/Fire Director	Dennis Staples

Housing & Construction
Housing Units, 2000*
Total	1,555
Median rent	$920
Median SF home value	$161,100

Permits for New Residential Construction
	Units	Value
Total, 2006	16	$1,546,503
Single family	16	$1,546,503
Total, 2007	17	$2,214,818
Single family	17	$2,214,818

Real Property Valuation, 2008
	Parcels	Valuation
Total	1,586	$232,478,200
Vacant	32	521,000
Residential	1,538	227,566,900
Commercial	16	4,390,300
Industrial	0	0
Apartments	0	0
Farm land	0	0
Farm homestead	0	0

Average Property Value & Tax, 2008
Residential value	$147,963
Property tax	$7,731
Tax credit/rebate	$1,227

Public Library
No public municipal library

Library statistics, 2007
Population served	NA
Full-time/total staff	NA/NA

	Total	Per capita
Holdings	NA	NA
Revenues	NA	NA
Expenditures	NA	NA
Annual visits	NA	NA
Internet terminals/annual users	NA/NA	

Public Safety
Number of officers, 2007	9

Crime	2006	2007
Total crimes	35	28
Violent	1	1
Murder	0	0
Rape	0	0
Robbery	0	0
Aggravated assault	1	1
Non-violent	34	27
Burglary	5	1
Larceny	29	26
Vehicle theft	0	0
Domestic violence	22	17
Arson	1	0
Total crime rate	8.4	6.7
Violent	0.2	0.2
Non-violent	8.1	6.5

Public School District
(for school year 2007-08 except as noted)

Medford Lakes Borough School District
135 Mudjekeewis Trail
Medford Lakes, NJ 08055
(609) 654-0991

Superintendent	James Lynch
Number of schools	2
Grade plan	K-8
Enrollment	538
Attendance rate, '06-07	95.6%
Dropout rate	NA
Students per teacher	10.7
Per pupil expenditure	$12,080
Median faculty salary	$48,309
Median administrator salary	$86,144
Grade 12 enrollment	NA
High school graduation rate	NA

Assessment test results
(percent scoring at proficient or advanced level)
	Language	Math
NJASK-Grade 3	93.4%	93.6%
GEPA-Grade 8	79.6%	94.4%
HSPA-High School	NA	NA

SAT Score Averages, 2006-07
Pct tested	Math	Verbal	Writing
NA	NA	NA	NA

Teacher Qualifications
Avg. years of experience	10
Highly-qualified teachers one subject/all subjects	100%/100%

No Child Left Behind
AYP, 2006-07	Meets Standards

Municipal Finance
State Aid Programs, 2009
Total aid	$373,383
CMPTRA	84,464
Energy tax receipts	279,584
Garden State Trust	0

General Budget, 2008
Total tax levy	$12,158,271
County levy	1,876,485
County taxes	1,540,990
County library	142,283
County health	0
County open space	193,213
School levy	7,625,721
Muni. levy	2,656,065
Misc. revenues	1,731,348

Taxes
	2006	2007	2008
General tax rate per $100	4.941	5.11	5.225
County equalization ratio	56.13	51.65	48.17
Net valuation taxable	$232,083,500	$232,075,420	$232,698,890
State equalized value	$449,498,733	$481,545,250	$491,925,851

* US Census Bureau
** New Jersey Department of Labor

See Introduction for an explanation of all data sources.

Demographics & Socio-Economic Characteristics

(2000 US Census, except as noted)

Population
1980*	17,471
1990*	20,526
2000	22,253
Male	10,779
Female	11,474
2007 (estimate)*	22,838
Population density	580.8

Race & Hispanic Origin, 2000
Race
White	21,527
Black/African American	170
American Indian/Alaska Native	26
Asian	327
Native Hawaiian/Pacific Islander	9
Other race	63
Two or more races	131
Hispanic origin, total	252
Mexican	37
Puerto Rican	99
Cuban	18
Other Hispanic	98

Age & Nativity, 2000
Under 5 years	1,416
18 years and over	16,279
21 years and over	15,684
65 years and over	2,387
85 years and over	430
Median age	40.0
Native-born	21,375
Foreign-born	878

Educational Attainment, 2000
Population 25 years and over	15,045
Less than 9th grade	1.2%
High school grad or higher	94.8%
Bachelor's degree or higher	49.9%
Graduate degree	18.5%

Income & Poverty, 1999
Per capita income	$38,641
Median household income	$83,059
Median family income	$97,135
Persons in poverty	410
H'holds receiving public assistance	67
H'holds receiving social security	1,720

Households, 2000
Total households	7,946
With persons under 18	3,188
With persons over 65	1,628
Family households	6,287
Single-person households	1,383
Persons per household	2.77
Persons per family	3.16

Labor & Employment
Total civilian labor force, 2007**	13,263
Unemployment rate	2.2%
Total civilian labor force, 2000	11,619
Unemployment rate	2.2%

Employed persons 16 years and over by occupation, 2000
Managers & professionals	6,249
Service occupations	1,007
Sales & office occupations	2,992
Farming, fishing & forestry	8
Construction & maintenance	559
Production & transportation	549
Self-employed persons	770

‡ Branch of county library
* US Census Bureau
** New Jersey Department of Labor

See Introduction for an explanation of all data sources.

General Information
Township of Medford
17 N Main St
Medford, NJ 08055
609-654-2608
Website	www.medfordtownship.com
Year of incorporation	1847
Land/water area (sq. miles)	39.32/0.49
Form of government	Council-Manager

Government
Legislative Districts
US Congressional	3
State Legislative	8

Local Officials, 2009
Mayor	David J. Brown
Manager	Mike Achey
Clerk	Katherine Burger
Finance Dir	Katherine Burger
Tax Assessor	Gilbert Goble
Tax Collector	Joan Schifferdecker
Attorney	Richard Hunt
Building	Richard Uschmann
Planning	(vacant)
Engineering	Christopher Noll
Public Works	George Snyder
Police Chief	James Kehoe
Emerg/Fire Director	Thomas Thorn

Housing & Construction
Housing Units, 2000*
Total	8,147
Median rent	$947
Median SF home value	$213,600

Permits for New Residential Construction
	Units	Value
Total, 2006	10	$2,761,900
Single family	10	$2,761,900
Total, 2007	67	$5,135,338
Single family	7	$2,310,338

Real Property Valuation, 2008
	Parcels	Valuation
Total	8,939	$1,774,029,900
Vacant	668	19,490,900
Residential	7,653	1,543,120,700
Commercial	331	148,612,500
Industrial	12	9,632,700
Apartments	7	29,815,900
Farm land	170	2,371,600
Farm homestead	98	20,985,600

Average Property Value & Tax, 2008
Residential value	$201,794
Property tax	$8,629
Tax credit/rebate	$1,145

Public Library
Pinelands Branch Library‡
39 Allen Ave
Medford, NJ 08055
609-654-6113
Branch Librarian	Judy Aley

Library statistics, 2007
see Burlington County profile
for library system statistics

Public Safety
Number of officers, 2007	44

Crime	2006	2007
Total crimes	250	280
Violent	10	14
Murder	0	0
Rape	1	2
Robbery	1	2
Aggravated assault	8	10
Non-violent	240	266
Burglary	43	62
Larceny	192	199
Vehicle theft	5	5
Domestic violence	219	226
Arson	6	8
Total crime rate	10.6	12.0
Violent	0.4	0.6
Non-violent	10.2	11.4

Public School District
(for school year 2007-08 except as noted)

Medford Township School District
128 Route 70, Suite 1
Medford, NJ 08055
(609) 654-6416
Superintendent	Joesph J. Del Rossi
Number of schools	7
Grade plan	K-8
Enrollment	3,059
Attendance rate, '06-07	96.4%
Dropout rate	NA
Students per teacher	11.9
Per pupil expenditure	$13,957
Median faculty salary	$57,152
Median administrator salary	$106,200
Grade 12 enrollment	NA
High school graduation rate	NA

Assessment test results
(percent scoring at proficient or advanced level)
	Language	Math
NJASK-Grade 3	95.3%	95.0%
GEPA-Grade 8	88.2%	96.2%
HSPA-High School	NA	NA

SAT Score Averages, 2006-07
Pct tested	Math	Verbal	Writing
NA	NA	NA	NA

Teacher Qualifications
Avg. years of experience	8
Highly-qualified teachers
one subject/all subjects	100%/100%

No Child Left Behind
AYP, 2006-07	Meets Standards

Municipal Finance
State Aid Programs, 2009
Total aid	$2,637,430
CMPTRA	333,568
Energy tax receipts	2,157,059
Garden State Trust	15,599

General Budget, 2008
Total tax levy	$76,048,724
County levy	13,178,292
County taxes	10,822,150
County library	999,230
County health	0
County open space	1,356,913
School levy	53,526,499
Muni. levy	9,343,933
Misc. revenues	13,525,424

Taxes	2006	2007	2008
General tax rate per $100	4.161	4.31	4.277
County equalization ratio	61.05	55.18	52.41
Net valuation taxable	$1,761,434,200	$1,774,726,658	$1,778,342,279
State equalized value	$3,196,017,941	$3,382,269,731	$3,486,899,540

Demographics & Socio-Economic Characteristics
(2000 US Census, except as noted)

Population
1980*	4,899
1990*	4,890
2000	5,097
Male	2,410
Female	2,687
2007 (estimate)*	5,073
Population density	842.7

Race & Hispanic Origin, 2000
Race
White	4,951
Black/African American	23
American Indian/Alaska Native	1
Asian	72
Native Hawaiian/Pacific Islander	3
Other race	14
Two or more races	33
Hispanic origin, total	125
Mexican	11
Puerto Rican	23
Cuban	3
Other Hispanic	88

Age & Nativity, 2000
Under 5 years	351
18 years and over	3,730
21 years and over	3,600
65 years and over	857
85 years and over	150
Median age	41.9
Native-born	4,681
Foreign-born	416

Educational Attainment, 2000
Population 25 years and over	3,489
Less than 9th grade	0.7%
High school grad or higher	95.3%
Bachelor's degree or higher	62.2%
Graduate degree	27.8%

Income & Poverty, 1999
Per capita income	$48,629
Median household income	$110,348
Median family income	$129,812
Persons in poverty	200
H'holds receiving public assistance	0
H'holds receiving social security	514

Households, 2000
Total households	1,781
With persons under 18	666
With persons over 65	514
Family households	1,380
Single-person households	332
Persons per household	2.72
Persons per family	3.13

Labor & Employment
Total civilian labor force, 2007**	2,479
Unemployment rate	1.4%
Total civilian labor force, 2000	2,274
Unemployment rate	1.2%

Employed persons 16 years and over by occupation, 2000
Managers & professionals	1,240
Service occupations	135
Sales & office occupations	728
Farming, fishing & forestry	14
Construction & maintenance	73
Production & transportation	57
Self-employed persons	230

* US Census Bureau
** New Jersey Department of Labor

General Information
Borough of Mendham
2 W Main St
Mendham, NJ 07945
973-543-7152
Website	www.mendhamnj.org
Year of incorporation	1906
Land/water area (sq. miles)	6.02/0.02
Form of government	Borough

Government
Legislative Districts
US Congressional	11
State Legislative	16

Local Officials, 2009
Mayor	Neil Henry
Manager	Ellen Sandman
Clerk	Maureen Massey
Finance Dir	Susan Giordano
Tax Assessor	Scott Holzhauer
Tax Collector	Donna Cummins
Attorney	Fred Semrau
Building	Russell Heiney
Comm Dev/Planning	NA
Engineering	Paul Ferriero
Public Works	Ken O'Brien
Police Chief	John Taylor
Emerg/Fire Director	Ed Tencza

Housing & Construction
Housing Units, 2000*
Total	1,828
Median rent	$1,186
Median SF home value	$397,000

Permits for New Residential Construction
	Units	Value
Total, 2006	2	$1,526,667
Single family	2	$1,526,667
Total, 2007	3	$3,021,200
Single family	3	$3,021,200

Real Property Valuation, 2008
	Parcels	Valuation
Total	1,840	$1,586,610,840
Vacant	38	14,076,500
Residential	1,623	1,369,811,900
Commercial	84	117,908,800
Industrial	0	0
Apartments	4	2,475,000
Farm land	56	696,740
Farm homestead	35	81,641,900

Average Property Value & Tax, 2008
Residential value	$875,424
Property tax	$12,763
Tax credit/rebate	$1,261

Public Library
Mendham Borough Library
10 Hilltop Rd
Mendham, NJ 07945
973-543-4152
Director	Patricia Charney

Library statistics, 2007
Population served	5,097
Full-time/total staff	0/1

	Total	Per capita
Holdings	24,529	4.81
Revenues	$236,389	$46.38
Expenditures	$266,595	$52.30
Annual visits	32,032	6.28
Internet terminals/annual users		5/9,984

Public Safety
Number of officers, 2007	12

Crime	2006	2007
Total crimes	40	27
Violent	2	1
Murder	0	0
Rape	0	0
Robbery	0	0
Aggravated assault	2	1
Non-violent	38	26
Burglary	2	1
Larceny	36	23
Vehicle theft	0	2
Domestic violence	11	5
Arson	0	0
Total crime rate	7.7	5.2
Violent	0.4	0.2
Non-violent	7.3	5.0

Public School District
(for school year 2007-08 except as noted)

Mendham Borough School District
12 Hilltop Road
Mendham, NJ 07945
(973) 543-2295
Superintendent	Janie P. Edmonds
Number of schools	2
Grade plan	K-8
Enrollment	668
Attendance rate, '06-07	96.0%
Dropout rate	NA
Students per teacher	11.0
Per pupil expenditure	$12,640
Median faculty salary	$49,998
Median administrator salary	$119,830
Grade 12 enrollment	NA
High school graduation rate	NA

Assessment test results
(percent scoring at proficient or advanced level)
	Language	Math
NJASK-Grade 3	96.2%	96.1%
GEPA-Grade 8	85.9%	93.6%
HSPA-High School	NA	NA

SAT Score Averages, 2006-07
Pct tested	Math	Verbal	Writing
NA	NA	NA	NA

Teacher Qualifications
Avg. years of experience	9
Highly-qualified teachers one subject/all subjects	100%/100%

No Child Left Behind
AYP, 2006-07	Meets Standards

Municipal Finance
State Aid Programs, 2009
Total aid	$682,024
CMPTRA	3,626
Energy tax receipts	651,040
Garden State Trust	1

General Budget, 2008
Total tax levy	$23,170,306
County levy	3,498,939
County taxes	2,855,839
County library	0
County health	0
County open space	643,100
School levy	14,700,147
Muni. levy	4,971,220
Misc. revenues	1,970,452

Taxes	2006	2007	2008
General tax rate per $100	1.29	1.38	1.458
County equalization ratio	124.13	109.49	104.96
Net valuation taxable	$1,599,198,000	$1,600,887,548	$1,589,321,867
State equalized value	$1,462,863,953	$1,525,363,801	$1,572,214,282

See Introduction for an explanation of all data sources.

Demographics & Socio-Economic Characteristics

(2000 US Census, except as noted)

Population

1980*	4,488
1990*	4,537
2000	5,400
Male	2,656
Female	2,744
2007 (estimate)*	5,539
Population density	310.1

Race & Hispanic Origin, 2000

Race

White	5,179
Black/African American	50
American Indian/Alaska Native	5
Asian	109
Native Hawaiian/Pacific Islander	0
Other race	19
Two or more races	38
Hispanic origin, total	82
Mexican	10
Puerto Rican	9
Cuban	12
Other Hispanic	51

Age & Nativity, 2000

Under 5 years	423
18 years and over	3,674
21 years and over	3,569
65 years and over	582
85 years and over	44
Median age	40.3
Native-born	4,993
Foreign-born	407

Educational Attainment, 2000

Population 25 years and over	3,467
Less than 9th grade	0.9%
High school grad or higher	97.9%
Bachelor's degree or higher	71.3%
Graduate degree	34.6%

Income & Poverty, 1999

Per capita income	$61,460
Median household income	$136,174
Median family income	$146,254
Persons in poverty	96
H'holds receiving public assistance	0
H'holds receiving social security	406

Households, 2000

Total households	1,788
With persons under 18	853
With persons over 65	382
Family households	1,539
Single-person households	198
Persons per household	3.01
Persons per family	3.27

Labor & Employment

Total civilian labor force, 2007**	2,566
Unemployment rate	0.9%
Total civilian labor force, 2000	2,355
Unemployment rate	1.1%

Employed persons 16 years and over by occupation, 2000

Managers & professionals	1,405
Service occupations	134
Sales & office occupations	605
Farming, fishing & forestry	0
Construction & maintenance	110
Production & transportation	75
Self-employed persons	205

* US Census Bureau
** New Jersey Department of Labor

General Information

Township of Mendham
Township Hall
PO Box 520
Brookside, NJ 07926
973-543-4555

Website	www.mendhamtownship.org
Year of incorporation	1749
Land/water area (sq. miles)	17.86/0.12
Form of government	Township

Government

Legislative Districts

US Congressional	11
State Legislative	25

Local Officials, 2009

Mayor	Frank V. Cioppettini Jr
Administrator	Stephen Mountain
Municipal Clerk	Ann Carlson
Finance Dir	Jeffery Theriault
Tax Assessor	Scott Holzhauer
Tax Collector	Marie Kenia
Attorney	Christopher Falcon
Building	Russell Heiney
Comm Dev/Planning	NA
Engineering	Thomas Lemanowicz
Public Works	David Read Sr
Police Chief	Thomas Costanza
Emerg/Fire Dir	Thomas Montgomery

Housing & Construction

Housing Units, 2000*

Total	1,849
Median rent	$1,139
Median SF home value	$556,200

Permits for New Residential Construction

	Units	Value
Total, 2006	13	$5,305,579
Single family	13	$5,305,579
Total, 2007	3	$4,777,580
Single family	3	$4,777,580

Real Property Valuation, 2008

	Parcels	Valuation
Total	2,233	$2,158,504,050
Vacant	103	45,234,600
Residential	1,944	2,004,169,550
Commercial	7	11,198,500
Industrial	1	3,000
Apartments	0	0
Farm land	117	1,439,900
Farm homestead	61	96,458,500

Average Property Value & Tax, 2008

Residential value	$1,047,695
Property tax	$16,272
Tax credit/rebate	$1,347

Public Library

Mendham Township Library
Cherry Lane & Main St
Brookside, NJ 07926
973-543-4018

Director	Lee Tanen

Library statistics, 2007

Population served	5,400
Full-time/total staff	0/0

	Total	Per capita
Holdings	40,988	7.59
Revenues	$243,926	$45.17
Expenditures	$214,760	$39.77
Annual visits	29,200	5.41
Internet terminals/annual users	5/6,570	

Public Safety

Number of officers, 2007	15

Crime

	2006	2007
Total crimes	50	33
Violent	1	6
Murder	0	0
Rape	0	0
Robbery	0	1
Aggravated assault	1	5
Non-violent	49	27
Burglary	5	3
Larceny	44	24
Vehicle theft	0	0
Domestic violence	5	5
Arson	0	0
Total crime rate	8.9	5.9
Violent	0.2	1.1
Non-violent	8.7	4.8

Public School District

(for school year 2007-08 except as noted)

Mendham Township School District
West Main Street
Brookside, NJ 07926
(973) 543-7107

Superintendent	Kristopher Harrison
Number of schools	2
Grade plan	K-8
Enrollment	910
Attendance rate, '06-07	96.4%
Dropout rate	NA
Students per teacher	9.9
Per pupil expenditure	$15,331
Median faculty salary	$55,275
Median administrator salary	$123,011
Grade 12 enrollment	NA
High school graduation rate	NA

Assessment test results

(percent scoring at proficient or advanced level)

	Language	Math
NJASK-Grade 3	98.1%	94.2%
GEPA-Grade 8	91.4%	97.8%
HSPA-High School	NA	NA

SAT Score Averages, 2006-07

Pct tested	Math	Verbal	Writing
NA	NA	NA	NA

Teacher Qualifications

Avg. years of experience	9
Highly-qualified teachers one subject/all subjects	100%/100%

No Child Left Behind

AYP, 2006-07	Meets Standards

Municipal Finance

State Aid Programs, 2009

Total aid	$623,076
CMPTRA	0
Energy tax receipts	570,450
Garden State Trust	554

General Budget, 2008

Total tax levy	$33,556,493
County levy	5,160,268
County taxes	4,211,234
County library	0
County health	0
County open space	949,034
School levy	21,968,382
Muni. levy	6,427,844
Misc. revenues	3,206,429

Taxes

	2006	2007	2008
General tax rate per $100	1.48	1.53	1.554
County equalization ratio	107.2	99.72	97.28
Net valuation taxable	$2,121,231,650	$2,132,489,062	$2,160,521,422
State equalized value	$2,128,482,699	$2,192,059,627	$2,235,337,651

See Introduction for an explanation of all data sources.

Demographics & Socio-Economic Characteristics
(2000 US Census, except as noted)

Population
1980*	3,972
1990*	4,095
2000	3,801
Male	1,791
Female	2,010
2007 (estimate)*	3,763
Population density	6,271.7

Race & Hispanic Origin, 2000
Race
White	3,265
Black/African American	282
American Indian/Alaska Native	11
Asian	80
Native Hawaiian/Pacific Islander	0
Other race	108
Two or more races	55

Hispanic origin, total ... 208
Mexican	4
Puerto Rican	138
Cuban	7
Other Hispanic	59

Age & Nativity, 2000
Under 5 years	250
18 years and over	2,825
21 years and over	2,719
65 years and over	526
85 years and over	62
Median age	37.2
Native-born	3,651
Foreign-born	150

Educational Attainment, 2000
Population 25 years and over	2,531
Less than 9th grade	3.1%
High school grad or higher	81.8%
Bachelor's degree or higher	27.7%
Graduate degree	8.1%

Income & Poverty, 1999
Per capita income	$25,589
Median household income	$49,392
Median family income	$60,652
Persons in poverty	259
H'holds receiving public assistance	36
H'holds receiving social security	391

Households, 2000
Total households	1,524
With persons under 18	524
With persons over 65	398
Family households	946
Single-person households	488
Persons per household	2.48
Persons per family	3.19

Labor & Employment
Total civilian labor force, 2007**	2,131
Unemployment rate	2.9%
Total civilian labor force, 2000	2,026
Unemployment rate	3.3%

Employed persons 16 years and over by occupation, 2000
Managers & professionals	704
Service occupations	233
Sales & office occupations	644
Farming, fishing & forestry	0
Construction & maintenance	186
Production & transportation	193
Self-employed persons	150

‡ Branch of county library
* US Census Bureau
** New Jersey Department of Labor

General Information
Borough of Merchantville
1 W Maple Ave
Merchantville, NJ 08109
856-662-2474
Website	merchantvillenj.gov
Year of incorporation	1915
Land/water area (sq. miles)	0.60/0.00
Form of government	Borough

Government
Legislative Districts
US Congressional	1
State Legislative	7

Local Officials, 2009
Mayor	Frank North
Manager	John Fry
Clerk	Denise Brouse (Dep)
Finance Dir	Denise Moules
Tax Assessor	John Dymond
Tax Collector	Michelle McKinney
Attorney	Timothy Higgins
Building	William Joseph
Planning	Eric Schmidt
Engineering	Joe Brickley
Public Works	Daniel Beckett
Police Chief	Wayne Bauer
Emerg/Fire Director	Roy Adair

Housing & Construction
Housing Units, 2000*
Total	1,607
Median rent	$642
Median SF home value	$122,200

Permits for New Residential Construction
	Units	Value
Total, 2006	10	$887,280
Single family	10	$887,280
Total, 2007	7	$621,096
Single family	7	$621,096

Real Property Valuation, 2008
	Parcels	Valuation
Total	1,238	$157,894,000
Vacant	47	540,600
Residential	1,083	132,375,500
Commercial	83	16,162,200
Industrial	0	0
Apartments	25	8,815,700
Farm land	0	0
Farm homestead	0	0

Average Property Value & Tax, 2008
Residential value	$122,230
Property tax	$6,167
Tax credit/rebate	$1,019

Public Library
Merchantville Library‡
130 S Centre St
Merchantville, NJ 08109
856-665-3128
Branch Librarian	Mimi Cirillo

Library statistics, 2007
see Camden County profile
for library system statistics

Public Safety
Number of officers, 2007	14

Crime	2006	2007
Total crimes	122	86
Violent	4	3
Murder	0	0
Rape	0	0
Robbery	2	3
Aggravated assault	2	0
Non-violent	118	83
Burglary	16	13
Larceny	100	65
Vehicle theft	2	5
Domestic violence	13	20
Arson	1	0
Total crime rate	31.9	22.6
Violent	1.0	0.8
Non-violent	30.9	21.8

Public School District
(for school year 2007-08 except as noted)

Merchantville School District
y30 South Centre Street
Merchantville, NJ 08109
(856) 663-1091
Chief School Admin	Christian Swanson
Number of schools	1
Grade plan	K-8
Enrollment	355
Attendance rate, '06-07	93.7%
Dropout rate	NA
Students per teacher	11.2
Per pupil expenditure	$13,744
Median faculty salary	$68,017
Median administrator salary	$94,920
Grade 12 enrollment	NA
High school graduation rate	NA

Assessment test results
(percent scoring at proficient or advanced level)
	Language	Math
NJASK-Grade 3	92.9%	92.6%
GEPA-Grade 8	59.4%	84.2%
HSPA-High School	NA	NA

SAT Score Averages, 2006-07
Pct tested	Math	Verbal	Writing
NA	NA	NA	NA

Teacher Qualifications
Avg. years of experience	24
Highly-qualified teachers one subject/all subjects	100%/100%

No Child Left Behind
AYP, 2006-07	Meets Standards

Municipal Finance
State Aid Programs, 2009
Total aid	$715,691
CMPTRA	252,848
Energy tax receipts	448,529
Garden State Trust	0

General Budget, 2008
Total tax levy	$8,134,958
County levy	1,868,096
County taxes	1,688,338
County library	121,014
County health	0
County open space	58,744
School levy	4,285,682
Muni. levy	1,981,180
Misc. revenues	2,433,031

Taxes	2006	2007	2008
General tax rate per $100	4.65	4.784	5.046
County equalization ratio	70.4	57.91	54.93
Net valuation taxable	$156,852,100	$160,970,463	$161,241,144
State equalized value	$275,047,368	$290,178,514	$290,062,234

See Introduction for an explanation of all data sources.

Demographics & Socio-Economic Characteristics

(2000 US Census, except as noted)

Population

1980*	13,762
1990*	12,804
2000	12,840
Male	6,137
Female	6,703
2007 (estimate)*	13,144
Population density	4,797.1

Race & Hispanic Origin, 2000

Race

White	10,835
Black/African American	681
American Indian/Alaska Native	13
Asian	928
Native Hawaiian/Pacific Islander	0
Other race	144
Two or more races	239
Hispanic origin, total	508
Mexican	50
Puerto Rican	188
Cuban	51
Other Hispanic	219

Age & Nativity, 2000

Under 5 years	847
18 years and over	9,849
21 years and over	9,531
65 years and over	1,910
85 years and over	173
Median age	39.5
Native-born	11,020
Foreign-born	1,820

Educational Attainment, 2000

Population 25 years and over	9,254
Less than 9th grade	2.3%
High school grad or higher	92.1%
Bachelor's degree or higher	49.2%
Graduate degree	19.8%

Income & Poverty, 1999

Per capita income	$36,749
Median household income	$75,546
Median family income	$85,022
Persons in poverty	500
H'holds receiving public assistance	40
H'holds receiving social security	1,322

Households, 2000

Total households	4,992
With persons under 18	1,726
With persons over 65	1,377
Family households	3,583
Single-person households	1,150
Persons per household	2.57
Persons per family	3.05

Labor & Employment

Total civilian labor force, 2007**	7,678
Unemployment rate	4.3%
Total civilian labor force, 2000	7,058
Unemployment rate	4.4%

Employed persons 16 years and over by occupation, 2000

Managers & professionals	3,593
Service occupations	482
Sales & office occupations	1,864
Farming, fishing & forestry	0
Construction & maintenance	282
Production & transportation	523
Self-employed persons	337

* US Census Bureau
** New Jersey Department of Labor

General Information

Borough of Metuchen
500 Main St
Metuchen, NJ 08840
732-632-8540

Website	www.metuchennj.org
Year of incorporation	1900
Land/water area (sq. miles)	2.74/0.00
Form of government	Borough

Government

Legislative Districts

US Congressional	6
State Legislative	18

Local Officials, 2009

Mayor	Thomas Vahalla
Administrator	William Boerth
Clerk	Bozena Lacina
Finance Dir	Rebecca Cuthbert
Tax Assessor	Robert Sweeney
Tax Collector	Rebecca Cuthbert
Attorney	David Frizell
Building	James Gyug
Comm Dev/Planning	NA
Engineering	Katherine Elliott
Public Works Dir	Fred Hall
Police Chief	James Keane
Emerg/Fire Director	Timothy Getty

Housing & Construction

Housing Units, 2000*

Total	5,104
Median rent	$873
Median SF home value	$194,900

Permits for New Residential Construction

	Units	Value
Total, 2006	9	$1,853,500
Single family	9	$1,853,500
Total, 2007	11	$1,426,700
Single family	9	$1,227,800

Real Property Valuation, 2008

	Parcels	Valuation
Total	5,121	$967,501,000
Vacant	104	7,471,400
Residential	4,579	791,612,800
Commercial	358	113,083,100
Industrial	62	37,991,600
Apartments	18	17,342,100
Farm land	0	0
Farm homestead	0	0

Average Property Value & Tax, 2008

Residential value	$172,879
Property tax	$7,941
Tax credit/rebate	$1,116

Public Library

Metuchen Public Library
480 Middlesex Ave
Metuchen, NJ 08840
732-632-8526

Director............. Melody B. Kokola

Library statistics, 2007

Population served	12,840
Full-time/total staff	4/5

	Total	Per capita
Holdings	75,036	5.84
Revenues	$820,419	$63.90
Expenditures	$819,989	$63.86
Annual visits	120,611	9.39
Internet terminals/annual users	10/11,932	

Public Safety

Number of officers, 2007	28

Crime	2006	2007
Total crimes	265	296
Violent	11	18
Murder	0	0
Rape	0	1
Robbery	2	5
Aggravated assault	9	12
Non-violent	254	278
Burglary	40	43
Larceny	201	233
Vehicle theft	13	2
Domestic violence	110	129
Arson	1	0
Total crime rate	19.8	22.4
Violent	0.8	1.4
Non-violent	19.0	21.0

Public School District

(for school year 2007-08 except as noted)

Metuchen School District
16 Simpson Place
Metuchen, NJ 08840
(732) 321-8700

Superintendent	Theresa Pollifrone-Sinatra
Number of schools	4
Grade plan	K-12
Enrollment	2,031
Attendance rate, '06-07	94.8%
Dropout rate	0.0%
Students per teacher	10.8
Per pupil expenditure	$13,920
Median faculty salary	$66,972
Median administrator salary	$102,031
Grade 12 enrollment	153
High school graduation rate	100.0%

Assessment test results

(percent scoring at proficient or advanced level)

	Language	Math
NJASK-Grade 3	96.9%	98.0%
GEPA-Grade 8	84.2%	91.8%
HSPA-High School	86.9%	91.4%

SAT Score Averages, 2006-07

Pct tested	Math	Verbal	Writing
92%	520	518	527

Teacher Qualifications

Avg. years of experience	10
Highly-qualified teachers one subject/all subjects	100%/100%

No Child Left Behind

AYP, 2006-07 .... Meets Standards

Municipal Finance

State Aid Programs, 2009

Total aid	$1,868,143
CMPTRA	421,535
Energy tax receipts	1,399,905
Garden State Trust	0

General Budget, 2008

Total tax levy	$44,605,863
County levy	6,570,873
County taxes	5,880,712
County library	0
County health	0
County open space	690,161
School levy	29,137,825
Muni. levy	8,897,165
Misc. revenues	6,445,742

Taxes

	2006	2007	2008
General tax rate per $100	4.13	4.38	4.594
County equalization ratio	49.61	43.65	42.31
Net valuation taxable	$961,495,900	$970,679,061	$971,120,308
State equalized value	$2,207,598,007	$2,288,410,289	$1,728,042,883

See Introduction for an explanation of all data sources.

Demographics & Socio-Economic Characteristics
(2000 US Census, except as noted)

Population
1980*	11,373
1990*	14,771
2000	16,405
Male	7,908
Female	8,497
2007 (estimate)*	16,174
Population density	226.9

Race & Hispanic Origin, 2000
Race
White	13,979
Black/African American	1,781
American Indian/Alaska Native	37
Asian	236
Native Hawaiian/Pacific Islander	4
Other race	108
Two or more races	260
Hispanic origin, total	347
Mexican	27
Puerto Rican	173
Cuban	15
Other Hispanic	132

Age & Nativity, 2000
Under 5 years	933
18 years and over	12,360
21 years and over	11,823
65 years and over	2,925
85 years and over	483
Median age	39.8
Native-born	15,906
Foreign-born	499

Educational Attainment, 2000
Population 25 years and over	11,252
Less than 9th grade	6.0%
High school grad or higher	77.8%
Bachelor's degree or higher	16.5%
Graduate degree	4.5%

Income & Poverty, 1999
Per capita income	$19,805
Median household income	$41,533
Median family income	$49,030
Persons in poverty	1,580
H'holds receiving public assistance	203
H'holds receiving social security	2,081

Households, 2000
Total households	6,009
With persons under 18	2,101
With persons over 65	1,797
Family households	4,216
Single-person households	1,481
Persons per household	2.58
Persons per family	3.08

Labor & Employment
Total civilian labor force, 2007**	9,001
Unemployment rate	5.7%
Total civilian labor force, 2000	7,610
Unemployment rate	7.1%

Employed persons 16 years and over by occupation, 2000
Managers & professionals	1,916
Service occupations	1,672
Sales & office occupations	1,811
Farming, fishing & forestry	68
Construction & maintenance	976
Production & transportation	628
Self-employed persons	568

* US Census Bureau
** New Jersey Department of Labor

General Information
Township of Middle
33 Mechanic St
Cape May Court House, NJ 08210
609-465-8732
Website	www.middletownship.com
Year of incorporation	1723
Land/water area (sq. miles)	71.27/11.83
Form of government	Township

Government
Legislative Districts
US Congressional	2
State Legislative	1

Local Officials, 2009
Mayor	F. Nathan Doughty Jr
Manager	James Alexis
Municipal Clerk	Kimberly Tomkinson
CFO	Tracey DeVico Taverner
Tax Assessor	Joseph Ravitz
Tax Collector	Sandy Beasley
Attorney	James Pickering
Building	Donald Arndt
Planning	John Ludlam
Engineer	Vincent Orlando
Public Works	Richard Ceglarski
Police Chief	Joseph Evangelista
Public Safety Dir	Susan DeLanzo

Housing & Construction
Housing Units, 2000*
Total	7,510
Median rent	$677
Median SF home value	$116,200

Permits for New Residential Construction
	Units	Value
Total, 2006	120	$17,957,954
Single family	120	$17,957,954
Total, 2007	227	$27,350,142
Single family	223	$27,030,142

Real Property Valuation, 2008
	Parcels	Valuation
Total	11,900	$3,237,703,600
Vacant	3,381	232,712,100
Residential	7,851	2,352,972,200
Commercial	526	625,096,400
Industrial	3	5,362,400
Apartments	10	5,311,300
Farm land	76	1,265,500
Farm homestead	53	14,983,700

Average Property Value & Tax, 2008
Residential value	$299,590
Property tax	$3,542
Tax credit/rebate	$784

Public Library
No public municipal library

Library statistics, 2007
Population served	NA
Full-time/total staff	NA/NA

	Total	Per capita
Holdings	NA	NA
Revenues	NA	NA
Expenditures	NA	NA
Annual visits	NA	NA
Internet terminals/annual users	NA/NA	

Public Safety
Number of officers, 2007	52

Crime	2006	2007
Total crimes	859	809
Violent	100	80
Murder	1	0
Rape	4	8
Robbery	21	22
Aggravated assault	74	50
Non-violent	759	729
Burglary	154	163
Larceny	575	527
Vehicle theft	30	39
Domestic violence	235	237
Arson	9	7
Total crime rate	51.7	49.4
Violent	6.0	4.9
Non-violent	45.7	44.5

Public School District
(for school year 2007-08 except as noted)

Middle Township School District
216 South Main Street
Cape May Court House, NJ 08210
(609) 465-1800
Superintendent	Michael Kopakowski
Number of schools	4
Grade plan	K-12
Enrollment	2,894
Attendance rate, '06-07	92.9%
Dropout rate	4.0%
Students per teacher	11.1
Per pupil expenditure	$13,494
Median faculty salary	$49,749
Median administrator salary	$92,055
Grade 12 enrollment	240
High school graduation rate	87.9%

Assessment test results
(percent scoring at proficient or advanced level)
	Language	Math
NJASK-Grade 3	82.1%	76.7%
GEPA-Grade 8	62.3%	78.8%
HSPA-High School	81.4%	84.5%

SAT Score Averages, 2006-07
Pct tested	Math	Verbal	Writing
54%	511	493	479

Teacher Qualifications
Avg. years of experience	11
Highly-qualified teachers one subject/all subjects	100%/100%

No Child Left Behind
AYP, 2006-07 .... Needs Improvement

Municipal Finance
State Aid Programs, 2009
Total aid	$4,173,422
CMPTRA	0
Energy tax receipts	4,005,258
Garden State Trust	66,845

General Budget, 2008
Total tax levy	$38,364,354
County levy	5,858,563
County taxes	4,657,105
County library	893,724
County health	0
County open space	307,734
School levy	22,145,730
Muni. levy	10,360,060
Misc. revenues	11,109,804

Taxes
	2006	2007	2008
General tax rate per $100	2.91	1.15	1.185
County equalization ratio	47.13	112.66	105.11
Net valuation taxable	$1,133,207,200	$3,208,981,699	$3,244,928,431
State equalized value	$2,747,659,774	$3,053,307,958	$3,219,232,371

See Introduction for an explanation of all data sources.

Demographics & Socio-Economic Characteristics

(2000 US Census, except as noted)

Population
1980*	13,480
1990*	13,055
2000	13,717
Male	6,682
Female	7,035
2007 (estimate)*	13,695
Population density	3,912.9

Race & Hispanic Origin, 2000
Race
White	11,970
Black/African American	461
American Indian/Alaska Native	18
Asian	570
Native Hawaiian/Pacific Islander	3
Other race	440
Two or more races	255
Hispanic origin, total	1,235
Mexican	48
Puerto Rican	244
Cuban	27
Other Hispanic	916

Age & Nativity, 2000
Under 5 years	914
18 years and over	10,411
21 years and over	10,030
65 years and over	1,942
85 years and over	168
Median age	38.0
Native-born	11,973
Foreign-born	1,744

Educational Attainment, 2000
Population 25 years and over	9,538
Less than 9th grade	4.3%
High school grad or higher	85.4%
Bachelor's degree or higher	23.4%
Graduate degree	6.3%

Income & Poverty, 1999
Per capita income	$27,834
Median household income	$60,723
Median family income	$70,343
Persons in poverty	499
H'holds receiving public assistance	65
H'holds receiving social security	1,558

Households, 2000
Total households	5,048
With persons under 18	1,849
With persons over 65	1,451
Family households	3,739
Single-person households	1,097
Persons per household	2.71
Persons per family	3.17

Labor & Employment
Total civilian labor force, 2007**	7,911
Unemployment rate	2.8%
Total civilian labor force, 2000	7,259
Unemployment rate	2.9%

Employed persons 16 years and over by occupation, 2000
Managers & professionals	2,460
Service occupations	794
Sales & office occupations	2,148
Farming, fishing & forestry	0
Construction & maintenance	698
Production & transportation	947
Self-employed persons	350

* US Census Bureau
** New Jersey Department of Labor

General Information
Borough of Middlesex
1200 Mountain Ave
Middlesex, NJ 08846
732-356-7400
Website	www.middlesexboro-nj.gov
Year of incorporation	1913
Land/water area (sq. miles)	3.50/0.02
Form of government	Borough

Government
Legislative Districts
US Congressional	6
State Legislative	22

Local Officials, 2009
Mayor	John Fuhrmann
Manager	NA
Clerk	Kathleen Anello
Finance Dir	Andrea Corcoran
Tax Assessor	Frank Betts
Tax Collector	Tonya Hubosky
Attorney	Edward J. Johnson
Building	Matthew Imperato
Comm Dev/Planning	NA
Engineering	T&M Associates
Public Works	Jerry Schaefer
Police Chief	James Benson
Emerg/Fire Director	Andy Castaldo

Housing & Construction
Housing Units, 2000*
Total	5,130
Median rent	$830
Median SF home value	$164,200

Permits for New Residential Construction
	Units	Value
Total, 2006	16	$2,896,390
Single family	10	$1,528,525
Total, 2007	8	$1,781,050
Single family	8	$1,781,050

Real Property Valuation, 2008
	Parcels	Valuation
Total	4,706	$498,716,300
Vacant	173	5,059,300
Residential	4,179	386,848,000
Commercial	201	35,778,400
Industrial	148	61,185,600
Apartments	5	9,845,000
Farm land	0	0
Farm homestead	0	0

Average Property Value & Tax, 2008
Residential value	$92,570
Property tax	$6,500
Tax credit/rebate	$1,077

Public Library
Middlesex Public Library
1300 Mountain Ave
Middlesex, NJ 08846
732-356-6602
Director	May Lein Ho

Library statistics, 2007
Population served	13,717
Full-time/total staff	3/4

	Total	Per capita
Holdings	63,990	4.67
Revenues	$582,192	$42.44
Expenditures	$557,710	$40.66
Annual visits	62,330	4.54
Internet terminals/annual users	12/19,941	

Public Safety
Number of officers, 2007		30

Crime	2006	2007
Total crimes	174	144
Violent	11	10
Murder	1	0
Rape	0	0
Robbery	3	3
Aggravated assault	7	7
Non-violent	163	134
Burglary	31	23
Larceny	117	98
Vehicle theft	15	13
Domestic violence	46	50
Arson	0	1
Total crime rate	12.5	10.5
Violent	0.8	0.7
Non-violent	11.7	9.7

Public School District
(for school year 2007-08 except as noted)

Middlesex Borough School District
300 Kennedy Drive
Middlesex, NJ 08846
(732) 317-6000
Superintendent	James Baker
Number of schools	5
Grade plan	K-12
Enrollment	2,049
Attendance rate, '06-07	95.6%
Dropout rate	0.1%
Students per teacher	10.5
Per pupil expenditure	$13,408
Median faculty salary	$54,060
Median administrator salary	$100,050
Grade 12 enrollment	174
High school graduation rate	100.0%

Assessment test results
(percent scoring at proficient or advanced level)
	Language	Math
NJASK-Grade 3	90.5%	85.4%
GEPA-Grade 8	78.7%	85.8%
HSPA-High School	75.4%	84.1%

SAT Score Averages, 2006-07
Pct tested	Math	Verbal	Writing
80%	499	467	474

Teacher Qualifications
Avg. years of experience	10

Highly-qualified teachers
one subject/all subjects	97.5%/96.5%

No Child Left Behind
AYP, 2006-07	Meets Standards

Municipal Finance
State Aid Programs, 2009
Total aid	$2,294,720
CMPTRA	756,348
Energy tax receipts	1,481,004
Garden State Trust	0

General Budget, 2008
Total tax levy	$35,058,089
County levy	4,829,094
County taxes	4,322,440
County library	0
County health	0
County open space	506,654
School levy	20,082,027
Muni. levy	10,146,969
Misc. revenues	6,237,292

Taxes
	2006	2007	2008
General tax rate per $100	6.33	6.7	7.022
County equalization ratio	35.28	31.4	29.81
Net valuation taxable	$497,602,000	$499,199,384	$499,304,039
State equalized value	$1,585,290,374	$1,673,400,618	$1,082,225,616

See Introduction for an explanation of all data sources.

Demographics & Socio-Economic Characteristics†

(2000 US Census, except as noted)

Population

1980*	62,574
1990*	68,183
2000	66,327
Male	32,267
Female	34,060
2007 (estimate)*	66,538
Population density	1,618.1

Race & Hispanic Origin, 2000

Race

White	62,819
Black/African American	803
American Indian/Alaska Native	46
Asian	1,717
Native Hawaiian/Pacific Islander	17
Other race	353
Two or more races	572
Hispanic origin, total	2,265
Mexican	116
Puerto Rican	1,087
Cuban	188
Other Hispanic	874

Age & Nativity, 2000

Under 5 years	4,510
18 years and over	48,886
21 years and over	46,945
65 years and over	8,487
85 years and over	996
Median age	38.8
Native-born	62,069
Foreign-born	4,258

Educational Attainment, 2000

Population 25 years and over	44,664
Less than 9th grade	2.7%
High school grad or higher	90.7%
Bachelor's degree or higher	35.0%
Graduate degree	12.6%

Income & Poverty, 1999

Per capita income	$34,196
Median household income	$75,566
Median family income	$86,124
Persons in poverty	2,049
H'holds receiving public assistance	228
H'holds receiving social security	6,448

Households, 2000

Total households	23,236
With persons under 18	9,311
With persons over 65	6,165
Family households	18,109
Single-person households	4,397
Persons per household	2.84
Persons per family	3.27

Labor & Employment

Total civilian labor force, 2007**	35,882
Unemployment rate	3.1%
Total civilian labor force, 2000	33,728
Unemployment rate	3.4%

Employed persons 16 years and over by occupation, 2000

Managers & professionals	13,619
Service occupations	3,571
Sales & office occupations	9,952
Farming, fishing & forestry	66
Construction & maintenance	2,679
Production & transportation	2,710
Self-employed persons	1,587

† see Appendix C for American Community Survey data
* US Census Bureau
** New Jersey Department of Labor

General Information

Township of Middletown
1 Kings Highway
Middletown, NJ 07748
732-615-2000

Website	www.middletownnj.org
Year of incorporation	1693
Land/water area (sq. miles)	41.12/18.23
Form of government	Special Charter

Government

Legislative Districts

US Congressional	6, 12
State Legislative	13

Local Officials, 2009

Mayor	Pamela M. Brightbill
Township Admin	Frederick E. Jahn (Int)
Clerk	Heidi R. Abs
Finance Dir	Richard Wright
Tax Assessor	Charles Heck
Tax Collector	Robert Kapral
Attorney	Brian Nelson
Building	Joseph Kachinsky
Planning	Anthony Mercantante
Engineering	Joseph E. Maloney
Public Works	Lawrence Werger
Police Chief	Robert Oches
Fire Chief	John Kardel

Housing & Construction

Housing Units, 2000*

Total	23,841
Median rent	$836
Median SF home value	$210,700

Permits for New Residential Construction

	Units	Value
Total, 2006	232	$31,431,559
Single family	197	$27,860,211
Total, 2007	241	$30,458,196
Single family	56	$15,071,507

Real Property Valuation, 2008

	Parcels	Valuation
Total	24,092	$4,981,310,838
Vacant	1,247	47,481,660
Residential	22,017	4,232,317,778
Commercial	600	606,184,000
Industrial	2	1,052,500
Apartments	13	45,671,100
Farm land	134	466,800
Farm homestead	79	48,137,000

Average Property Value & Tax, 2008

Residential value	$193,721
Property tax	$7,336
Tax credit/rebate	$1,091

Public Library

Middletown Township Public Library
55 New Monmouth Rd
Middletown, NJ 07748
732-671-3700

Director	Susan O'Neal

Library statistics, 2007

Population served	66,327
Full-time/total staff	11/30

	Total	Per capita
Holdings	249,540	3.76
Revenues	$4,048,217	$61.03
Expenditures	$3,800,612	$57.30
Annual visits	471,330	7.11
Internet terminals/annual users	57/71,502	

Public Safety

Number of officers, 2007	102

Crime	2006	2007
Total crimes	862	892
Violent	55	56
Murder	0	0
Rape	3	8
Robbery	11	9
Aggravated assault	41	39
Non-violent	807	836
Burglary	120	120
Larceny	652	677
Vehicle theft	35	39
Domestic violence	365	335
Arson	4	0
Total crime rate	12.7	13.2
Violent	0.8	0.8
Non-violent	11.9	12.4

Public School District

(for school year 2007-08 except as noted)

Middletown Township School District
59 Tindall Road
Middletown, NJ 07748
(732) 671-3850

Superintendent	Karen L. Bilbao
Number of schools	17
Grade plan	K-12
Enrollment	10,142
Attendance rate, '06-07	94.9%
Dropout rate	0.2%
Students per teacher	11.3
Per pupil expenditure	$13,605
Median faculty salary	$62,540
Median administrator salary	$115,630
Grade 12 enrollment	714
High school graduation rate	99.6%

Assessment test results

(percent scoring at proficient or advanced level)

	Language	Math
NJASK-Grade 3	93.0%	89.7%
GEPA-Grade 8	81.8%	92.3%
HSPA-High School	84.5%	91.5%

SAT Score Averages, 2006-07

Pct tested	Math	Verbal	Writing
NA	NA	NA	NA

Teacher Qualifications

Avg. years of experience	11
Highly-qualified teachers one subject/all subjects	100%/100%

No Child Left Behind

AYP, 2006-07	Meets Standards

Municipal Finance

State Aid Programs, 2009

Total aid	$7,801,717
CMPTRA	461,694
Energy tax receipts	7,137,215
Garden State Trust	240

General Budget, 2008

Total tax levy	$188,855,358
County levy	30,307,514
County taxes	28,412,681
County library	0
County health	0
County open space	1,894,833
School levy	119,769,276
Muni. levy	38,778,568
Misc. revenues	24,484,498

Taxes

	2006	2007	2008
General tax rate per $100	3.558	3.659	3.787
County equalization ratio	47.4	42.59	39.59
Net valuation taxable	$4,911,669,538	$4,948,064,387	$4,987,274,965
State equalized value	$11,539,217,832	$12,488,402,803	$1,080,396,691

See Introduction for an explanation of all data sources.

Demographics & Socio-Economic Characteristics
(2000 US Census, except as noted)

Population
1980*	7,381
1990*	7,047
2000	6,947
Male	3,388
Female	3,559
2007 (estimate)*	6,820
Population density	4,371.8

Race & Hispanic Origin, 2000
Race
White	6,656
Black/African American	30
American Indian/Alaska Native	4
Asian	154
Native Hawaiian/Pacific Islander	1
Other race	53
Two or more races	49
Hispanic origin, total	256
Mexican	13
Puerto Rican	50
Cuban	22
Other Hispanic	171

Age & Nativity, 2000
Under 5 years	508
18 years and over	5,258
21 years and over	5,083
65 years and over	1,015
85 years and over	111
Median age	38.8
Native-born	6,381
Foreign-born	566

Educational Attainment, 2000
Population 25 years and over	4,867
Less than 9th grade	3.4%
High school grad or higher	93.1%
Bachelor's degree or higher	38.9%
Graduate degree	10.7%

Income & Poverty, 1999
Per capita income	$32,284
Median household income	$76,462
Median family income	$83,926
Persons in poverty	141
H'holds receiving public assistance	14
H'holds receiving social security	742

Households, 2000
Total households	2,613
With persons under 18	909
With persons over 65	739
Family households	1,884
Single-person households	617
Persons per household	2.65
Persons per family	3.19

Labor & Employment
Total civilian labor force, 2007**	4,010
Unemployment rate	1.4%
Total civilian labor force, 2000	3,806
Unemployment rate	1.7%

Employed persons 16 years and over by occupation, 2000
Managers & professionals	1,625
Service occupations	437
Sales & office occupations	1,081
Farming, fishing & forestry	0
Construction & maintenance	344
Production & transportation	253
Self-employed persons	205

* US Census Bureau
** New Jersey Department of Labor

General Information
Borough of Midland Park
280 Godwin Ave
Midland Park, NJ 07432
201-445-5720

Website	mpnj.com
Year of incorporation	1894
Land/water area (sq. miles)	1.56/0.00
Form of government	Borough

Government
Legislative Districts
US Congressional	5
State Legislative	40

Local Officials, 2009
Mayor	Joseph Monahan
Manager	Michelle Dugan
Clerk	Adeline Hanna
Finance Dir	Michelle Dugan
Tax Assessor	Marie Merolla
Tax Collector	Michelle Dugan
Attorney	Robert Regan
Building	John Wittekind
Comm Dev/Planning	NA
Engineering	Vollmer Associates
Public Works	Rudy Gnehm
Police Chief	John Casson
Emerg/Fire Director	Pete Hook

Housing & Construction
Housing Units, 2000*
Total	2,650
Median rent	$1,044
Median SF home value	$256,500

Permits for New Residential Construction
	Units	Value
Total, 2006	9	$1,504,600
Single family	4	$909,600
Total, 2007	3	$530,300
Single family	3	$530,300

Real Property Valuation, 2008
	Parcels	Valuation
Total	2,415	$864,972,300
Vacant	38	5,958,000
Residential	2,199	690,356,700
Commercial	134	114,694,800
Industrial	40	42,287,800
Apartments	4	11,675,000
Farm land	0	0
Farm homestead	0	0

Average Property Value & Tax, 2008
Residential value	$313,941
Property tax	$8,961
Tax credit/rebate	$1,332

Public Library
Midland Park Mem Library
250 Godwin Ave
Midland Park, NJ 07432
201-444-2390

Director	Jean M. Scott

Library statistics, 2007
Population served	6,947
Full-time/total staff	2/5

	Total	Per capita
Holdings	71,500	10.29
Revenues	$462,933	$66.64
Expenditures	$424,290	$61.08
Annual visits	52,534	7.56
Internet terminals/annual users	7/22,340	

Public Safety
Number of officers, 2007	13

Crime	2006	2007
Total crimes	43	49
Violent	3	4
Murder	0	0
Rape	0	0
Robbery	1	0
Aggravated assault	2	4
Non-violent	40	45
Burglary	4	3
Larceny	35	41
Vehicle theft	1	1
Domestic violence	22	16
Arson	0	2
Total crime rate	6.2	7.1
Violent	0.4	0.6
Non-violent	5.8	6.5

Public School District
(for school year 2007-08 except as noted)

Midland Park Borough School District
31 Highland Avenue
Midland Park, NJ 07432
(201) 444-1400

Superintendent	William B. Heebink
Number of schools	2
Grade plan	K-12
Enrollment	1,134
Attendance rate, '06-07	95.5%
Dropout rate	0.3%
Students per teacher	10.7
Per pupil expenditure	$14,789
Median faculty salary	$56,983
Median administrator salary	$124,705
Grade 12 enrollment	81
High school graduation rate	100.0%

Assessment test results
(percent scoring at proficient or advanced level)
	Language	Math
NJASK-Grade 3	94.1%	94.1%
GEPA-Grade 8	82.8%	94.3%
HSPA-High School	84.6%	85.7%

SAT Score Averages, 2006-07
Pct tested	Math	Verbal	Writing
102%	510	525	539

Teacher Qualifications
Avg. years of experience	10
Highly-qualified teachers one subject/all subjects	99.0%/99.0%

No Child Left Behind
AYP, 2006-07	Meets Standards

Municipal Finance
State Aid Programs, 2009
Total aid	$704,870
CMPTRA	142,469
Energy tax receipts	544,780
Garden State Trust	0

General Budget, 2008
Total tax levy	$24,718,729
County levy	2,469,747
County taxes	2,336,160
County library	0
County health	0
County open space	133,587
School levy	15,989,748
Muni. levy	6,259,234
Misc. revenues	2,984,643

Taxes
	2006	2007	2008
General tax rate per $100	2.67	2.79	2.855
County equalization ratio	74.28	64.06	65.45
Net valuation taxable	$858,487,100	$862,570,429	$865,993,258
State equalized value	$1,341,027,291	$1,317,397,556	$1,319,375,325

See Introduction for an explanation of all data sources.

Demographics & Socio-Economic Characteristics
(2000 US Census, except as noted)

Population
1980*	1,368
1990*	1,273
2000	1,195
Male	606
Female	589
2007 (estimate)*	1,196
Population density	1,040.0

Race & Hispanic Origin, 2000
Race
White	1,166
Black/African American	2
American Indian/Alaska Native	2
Asian	5
Native Hawaiian/Pacific Islander	4
Other race	1
Two or more races	15
Hispanic origin, total	24
Mexican	10
Puerto Rican	2
Cuban	1
Other Hispanic	11

Age & Nativity, 2000
Under 5 years	70
18 years and over	892
21 years and over	863
65 years and over	163
85 years and over	15
Median age	38.7
Native-born	1,163
Foreign-born	32

Educational Attainment, 2000
Population 25 years and over	846
Less than 9th grade	3.1%
High school grad or higher	88.5%
Bachelor's degree or higher	26.2%
Graduate degree	6.5%

Income & Poverty, 1999
Per capita income	$25,039
Median household income	$54,519
Median family income	$62,167
Persons in poverty	44
H'holds receiving public assistance	12
H'holds receiving social security	133

Households, 2000
Total households	469
With persons under 18	165
With persons over 65	122
Family households	323
Single-person households	127
Persons per household	2.55
Persons per family	3.11

Labor & Employment
Total civilian labor force, 2007**	716
Unemployment rate	5.4%
Total civilian labor force, 2000	631
Unemployment rate	3.6%

Employed persons 16 years and over by occupation, 2000
Managers & professionals	197
Service occupations	63
Sales & office occupations	178
Farming, fishing & forestry	0
Construction & maintenance	79
Production & transportation	91
Self-employed persons	61

General Information
Borough of Milford
30 Water St
Milford, NJ 08848
908-995-4323

Website	www.milfordnj.org
Year of incorporation	1911
Land/water area (sq. miles)	1.15/0.07
Form of government	Borough

Government
Legislative Districts
US Congressional	7
State Legislative	23

Local Officials, 2009
Mayor	James A. Gallos
Manager/Admin	NA
Clerk	Karen Dysart
Finance Dir	Dawn Merante
Tax Assessor	David Gill
Tax Collector	Judy Holmberg
Attorney	Todd L. Bolig
Building	NA
Comm Dev/Planning	NA
Engineering	Robert J. Clerico
Public Works	NA
Police Chief	NA
Emerg/Fire Director	John Phillips

Housing & Construction
Housing Units, 2000*
Total	484
Median rent	$794
Median SF home value	$153,800

Permits for New Residential Construction
	Units	Value
Total, 2006	0	$0
Single family	0	$0
Total, 2007	0	$0
Single family	0	$0

Real Property Valuation, 2008
	Parcels	Valuation
Total	526	$122,322,670
Vacant	50	1,505,600
Residential	416	95,519,000
Commercial	42	12,455,970
Industrial	3	8,155,400
Apartments	1	3,238,200
Farm land	10	40,000
Farm homestead	4	1,408,500

Average Property Value & Tax, 2008
Residential value	$230,780
Property tax	$6,757
Tax credit/rebate	$1,111

Public Library
Milford Public Library
40 Frenchtown-Milford Rd
Milford, NJ 08848
908-995-4072

Director	Jennifer Locke

Library statistics, 2007
Population served	1,195
Full-time/total staff	0/1

	Total	Per capita
Holdings	20,013	16.75
Revenues	$59,035	$49.40
Expenditures	$53,470	$44.74
Annual visits	6,153	5.15
Internet terminals/annual users	1/89	

Public Safety
Number of officers, 2007	0

Crime	2006	2007
Total crimes	13	12
Violent	2	2
Murder	0	0
Rape	0	0
Robbery	0	1
Aggravated assault	2	1
Non-violent	11	10
Burglary	4	3
Larceny	7	7
Vehicle theft	0	0
Domestic violence	0	9
Arson	1	0
Total crime rate	10.7	9.8
Violent	1.6	1.6
Non-violent	9.1	8.2

Public School District
(for school year 2007-08 except as noted)

Milford Borough School District
7 Hillside Avenue
Milford, NJ 08848
(908) 995-4349

Chief School Admin	Edward Stoloski
Number of schools	1
Grade plan	K-8
Enrollment	114
Attendance rate, '06-07	96.2%
Dropout rate	NA
Students per teacher	8.4
Per pupil expenditure	$15,792
Median faculty salary	$44,040
Median administrator salary	$57,200
Grade 12 enrollment	NA
High school graduation rate	NA

Assessment test results
(percent scoring at proficient or advanced level)
	Language	Math
NJASK-Grade 3	68.8%	86.7%
GEPA-Grade 8	NA	NA
HSPA-High School	NA	NA

SAT Score Averages, 2006-07
Pct tested	Math	Verbal	Writing
NA	NA	NA	NA

Teacher Qualifications
Avg. years of experience	11
Highly-qualified teachers one subject/all subjects	100%/100%

No Child Left Behind
AYP, 2006-07	Meets Standards

Municipal Finance
State Aid Programs, 2009
Total aid	$358,831
CMPTRA	141,933
Energy tax receipts	207,927
Garden State Trust	0

General Budget, 2008
Total tax levy	$3,588,655
County levy	491,724
County taxes	443,815
County library	0
County health	0
County open space	47,909
School levy	2,315,402
Muni. levy	781,530
Misc. revenues	935,449

Taxes
	2006	2007	2008
General tax rate per $100	2.62	2.87	2.929
County equalization ratio	83.87	74.68	81.27
Net valuation taxable	$120,818,070	$122,552,705	$122,559,427
State equalized value	$151,900,421	$164,641,710	$158,870,747

* US Census Bureau
** New Jersey Department of Labor

See Introduction for an explanation of all data sources.

Demographics & Socio-Economic Characteristics

(2000 US Census, except as noted)

Population

1980*	19,543
1990*	18,630
2000	19,765
Male	9,584
Female	10,181
2007 (estimate)*	18,755
Population density	1,999.5

Race & Hispanic Origin, 2000

Race

White	17,573
Black/African American	217
American Indian/Alaska Native	10
Asian	1,660
Native Hawaiian/Pacific Islander	6
Other race	85
Two or more races	214
Hispanic origin, total	404
Mexican	48
Puerto Rican	64
Cuban	35
Other Hispanic	257

Age & Nativity, 2000

Under 5 years	1,720
18 years and over	13,789
21 years and over	13,502
65 years and over	2,581
85 years and over	304
Median age	39.2
Native-born	16,866
Foreign-born	2,899

Educational Attainment, 2000

Population 25 years and over	13,190
Less than 9th grade	1.2%
High school grad or higher	96.6%
Bachelor's degree or higher	74.0%
Graduate degree	38.4%

Income & Poverty, 1999

Per capita income	$76,796
Median household income	$130,848
Median family income	$158,888
Persons in poverty	288
H'holds receiving public assistance	50
H'holds receiving social security	1,711

Households, 2000

Total households	7,015
With persons under 18	3,158
With persons over 65	1,784
Family households	5,604
Single-person households	1,224
Persons per household	2.82
Persons per family	3.19

Labor & Employment

Total civilian labor force, 2007**	9,316
Unemployment rate	1.9%
Total civilian labor force, 2000	8,956
Unemployment rate	1.8%

Employed persons 16 years and over by occupation, 2000

Managers & professionals	5,761
Service occupations	421
Sales & office occupations	2,167
Farming, fishing & forestry	0
Construction & maintenance	170
Production & transportation	280
Self-employed persons	799

* US Census Bureau
** New Jersey Department of Labor

General Information

Township of Millburn
375 Millburn Ave
Millburn, NJ 07041
973-564-7000

Website	www.twp.millburn.nj.us
Year of incorporation	1857
Land/water area (sq. miles)	9.38/0.52
Form of government	Township

Government

Legislative Districts

US Congressional	11-Oct
State Legislative	21

Local Officials, 2009

Mayor	Sandra Haimoff
Manager	Timothy Gordon
Clerk	Joanne Monarque
Finance Dir	Jason Gabloff
Tax Assessor	Lisa Baratto
Tax Collector	Gerald Viturello
Attorney	Christopher Falcon
Building	Steven Jones
Comm Dev/Planning	NA
Engineering	W. Thomas Watkinson
Public Works	Timothy Monahan
Police Chief	Paul Boegershausen
Emerg/Fire Director	J. Michael Roberts

Housing & Construction

Housing Units, 2000*

Total	7,158
Median rent	$1,114
Median SF home value	$549,000

Permits for New Residential Construction

	Units	Value
Total, 2006	26	$15,093,990
Single family	26	$15,093,990
Total, 2007	15	$11,477,078
Single family	15	$11,477,078

Real Property Valuation, 2008

	Parcels	Valuation
Total	6,543	$8,308,414,200
Vacant	88	54,678,800
Residential	6,171	6,714,958,700
Commercial	234	1,421,030,800
Industrial	30	48,538,600
Apartments	20	69,207,300
Farm land	0	0
Farm homestead	0	0

Average Property Value & Tax, 2008

Residential value	$1,088,148
Property tax	$18,159
Tax credit/rebate	$1,364

Public Library

Millburn Public Library
200 Glen Ave
Millburn, NJ 07041
973-376-1006

Director	William R. Swinson

Library statistics, 2007

Population served	19,765
Full-time/total staff	8/16

	Total	Per capita
Holdings	104,977	5.31
Revenues	$2,984,099	$150.98
Expenditures	$2,705,639	$136.89
Annual visits	191,563	9.69
Internet terminals/annual users	16/161,244	

Public Safety

Number of officers, 2007		53

Crime	2006	2007
Total crimes	781	624
Violent	17	9
Murder	0	0
Rape	1	0
Robbery	11	6
Aggravated assault	5	3
Non-violent	764	615
Burglary	66	35
Larceny	626	536
Vehicle theft	72	44
Domestic violence	92	90
Arson	1	2
Total crime rate	40.3	32.6
Violent	0.9	0.5
Non-violent	39.4	32.1

Public School District

(for school year 2007-08 except as noted)

Millburn Township School District
434 Millburn Avenue
Millburn, NJ 07041
(973) 376-3600

Superintendent	Richard Brodow
Number of schools	7
Grade plan	K-12
Enrollment	4,664
Attendance rate, '06-07	94.9%
Dropout rate	0.0%
Students per teacher	10.7
Per pupil expenditure	$15,338
Median faculty salary	$73,115
Median administrator salary	$124,694
Grade 12 enrollment	330
High school graduation rate	100.0%

Assessment test results

(percent scoring at proficient or advanced level)

	Language	Math
NJASK-Grade 3	96.9%	96.5%
GEPA-Grade 8	92.5%	95.4%
HSPA-High School	96.1%	97.0%

SAT Score Averages, 2006-07

Pct tested	Math	Verbal	Writing
99%	628	597	605

Teacher Qualifications

Avg. years of experience	9
Highly-qualified teachers one subject/all subjects	100%/100%

No Child Left Behind

AYP, 2006-07	Meets Standards

Municipal Finance

State Aid Programs, 2009

Total aid	$3,199,410
CMPTRA	0
Energy tax receipts	3,044,903
Garden State Trust	0

General Budget, 2008

Total tax levy	$138,762,246
County levy	33,268,303
County taxes	31,975,726
County library	0
County health	0
County open space	1,292,577
School levy	70,597,999
Muni. levy	34,895,945
Misc. revenues	11,363,009

Taxes

	2006	2007	2008
General tax rate per $100	2.12	1.58	1.669
County equalization ratio	78.37	102.18	96.51
Net valuation taxable	$5,918,458,000	$8,372,472,024	$8,315,067,845
State equalized value	$8,116,490,969	$8,674,996,445	$9,183,165,905

See Introduction for an explanation of all data sources.

Demographics & Socio-Economic Characteristics

(2000 US Census, except as noted)

Population

1980*	530
1990*	450
2000	410
Male	204
Female	206
2007 (estimate)*	412
Population density	549.3

Race & Hispanic Origin, 2000

Race
White	400
Black/African American	4
American Indian/Alaska Native	0
Asian	4
Native Hawaiian/Pacific Islander	0
Other race	0
Two or more races	2
Hispanic origin, total	13
Mexican	0
Puerto Rican	10
Cuban	0
Other Hispanic	3

Age & Nativity, 2000

Under 5 years	17
18 years and over	331
21 years and over	323
65 years and over	70
85 years and over	10
Median age	45.6
Native-born	398
Foreign-born	19

Educational Attainment, 2000

Population 25 years and over	305
Less than 9th grade	2.0%
High school grad or higher	91.5%
Bachelor's degree or higher	39.0%
Graduate degree	16.4%

Income & Poverty, 1999

Per capita income	$30,694
Median household income	$76,353
Median family income	$83,118
Persons in poverty	19
H'holds receiving public assistance	2
H'holds receiving social security	44

Households, 2000

Total households	169
With persons under 18	47
With persons over 65	51
Family households	127
Single-person households	32
Persons per household	2.43
Persons per family	2.79

Labor & Employment

Total civilian labor force, 2007**	272
Unemployment rate	0.0%
Total civilian labor force, 2000	245
Unemployment rate	2.0%

Employed persons 16 years and over by occupation, 2000
Managers & professionals	127
Service occupations	20
Sales & office occupations	51
Farming, fishing & forestry	0
Construction & maintenance	23
Production & transportation	19
Self-employed persons	21

General Information

Borough of Millstone
1353 Main St
Millstone, NJ 08844
908-281-6893

Website	www.millstoneboro.org
Year of incorporation	1894
Land/water area (sq. miles)	0.75/0.00
Form of government	Borough

Government

Legislative Districts

US Congressional	7
State Legislative	16

Local Officials, 2009

Mayor	Raymond Heck
Manager/Admin	NA
Clerk	Gregory Bonin
Finance Dir	Gregory Della Pia
Tax Assessor	Marcia Sudano
Tax Collector	Donna Griffiths
Attorney	Steven Offen
Building	Robert Ward
Planning	Carter Van Dyke
Engineering	James DeMuro
Public Works	NA
Police Chief	NA
Fire/Emergency Dir	NA

Housing & Construction

Housing Units, 2000*

Total	173
Median rent	$875
Median SF home value	$205,400

Permits for New Residential Construction

	Units	Value
Total, 2006	0	$0
Single family	0	$0
Total, 2007	1	$275,000
Single family	1	$275,000

Real Property Valuation, 2008

	Parcels	Valuation
Total	184	$62,370,900
Vacant	11	415,400
Residential	155	58,114,800
Commercial	9	3,745,100
Industrial	0	0
Apartments	0	0
Farm land	9	95,600
Farm homestead	0	0

Average Property Value & Tax, 2008

Residential value	$374,934
Property tax	$6,367
Tax credit/rebate	$1,069

Public Library

No public municipal library

Library statistics, 2007

Population served	NA
Full-time/total staff	NA/NA

	Total	Per capita
Holdings	NA	NA
Revenues	NA	NA
Expenditures	NA	NA
Annual visits	NA	NA
Internet terminals/annual users	NA/NA	

Public Safety

Number of officers, 2007	0

Crime	2006	2007
Total crimes	0	2
Violent	0	0
Murder	0	0
Rape	0	0
Robbery	0	0
Aggravated assault	0	0
Non-violent	0	2
Burglary	0	0
Larceny	0	1
Vehicle theft	0	1
Domestic violence	0	1
Arson	0	0
Total crime rate	0.0	4.6
Violent	0.0	0.0
Non-violent	0.0	4.6

Public School District

(for school year 2007-08 except as noted)

Millstone Borough School District
P.O. Box 854
Somerville, NJ 08876

No schools in district - sends students to Hillsborough schools

Per pupil expenditure	NA
Median faculty salary	NA
Median administrator salary	NA
Grade 12 enrollment	NA
High school graduation rate	NA

Assessment test results

(percent scoring at proficient or advanced level)
	Language	Math
NJASK-Grade 3	NA	NA
GEPA-Grade 8	NA	NA
HSPA-High School	NA	NA

SAT Score Averages, 2006-07

Pct tested	Math	Verbal	Writing
NA	NA	NA	NA

Teacher Qualifications

Avg. years of experience	NA
Highly-qualified teachers one subject/all subjects	NA/NA

No Child Left Behind

AYP, 2006-07	NA

Municipal Finance

State Aid Programs, 2009

Total aid	$84,950
CMPTRA	1,008
Energy tax receipts	81,752
Garden State Trust	55

General Budget, 2008

Total tax levy	$1,059,988
County levy	186,875
County taxes	149,980
County library	20,295
County health	0
County open space	16,600
School levy	534,826
Muni. levy	338,287
Misc. revenues	194,160

Taxes	2006	2007	2008
General tax rate per $100	1.72	1.58	1.699
County equalization ratio	112.51	121.52	113.07
Net valuation taxable	$58,070,800	$62,615,156	$62,416,755
State equalized value	$51,534,393	$55,193,293	$55,207,171

* US Census Bureau
** New Jersey Department of Labor

See Introduction for an explanation of all data sources.

Demographics & Socio-Economic Characteristics

(2000 US Census, except as noted)

Population

1980*	3,926
1990*	5,069
2000	8,970
Male	4,472
Female	4,498
2007 (estimate)*	10,212
Population density	277.8

Race & Hispanic Origin, 2000

Race
White	8,237
Black/African American	274
American Indian/Alaska Native	9
Asian	308
Native Hawaiian/Pacific Islander	3
Other race	55
Two or more races	84
Hispanic origin, total	315
Mexican	41
Puerto Rican	130
Cuban	35
Other Hispanic	109

Age & Nativity, 2000

Under 5 years	758
18 years and over	6,028
21 years and over	5,818
65 years and over	538
85 years and over	60
Median age	37.1
Native-born	8,374
Foreign-born	596

Educational Attainment, 2000

Population 25 years and over	5,624
Less than 9th grade	2.7%
High school grad or higher	92.2%
Bachelor's degree or higher	42.7%
Graduate degree	16.1%

Income & Poverty, 1999

Per capita income	$37,285
Median household income	$94,561
Median family income	$96,116
Persons in poverty	434
H'holds receiving public assistance	36
H'holds receiving social security	377

Households, 2000

Total households	2,708
With persons under 18	1,477
With persons over 65	366
Family households	2,426
Single-person households	204
Persons per household	3.28
Persons per family	3.46

Labor & Employment

Total civilian labor force, 2007**	4,606
Unemployment rate	1.7%
Total civilian labor force, 2000	4,337
Unemployment rate	2.5%

Employed persons 16 years and over by occupation, 2000
Managers & professionals	2,184
Service occupations	391
Sales & office occupations	1,138
Farming, fishing & forestry	37
Construction & maintenance	272
Production & transportation	207
Self-employed persons	356

*   US Census Bureau
** New Jersey Department of Labor

General Information

Township of Millstone
470 Stage Coach Rd
Millstone, NJ 08510
732-446-4249

Website	www.millstone.nj.us
Year of incorporation	1844
Land/water area (sq. miles)	36.76/0.42
Form of government	Township

Government

Legislative Districts

US Congressional	4
State Legislative	12

Local Officials, 2009

Mayor	Nancy A. Grbelja
Administrator	James Pickering Jr
Clerk	Maria Dellasala
Finance Dir	Annette Murphy
Tax Assessor	Thomas Davis
Tax Collector	Dawn Mitchell
Attorney	Duane Davison
Building	Henry Salerno
Planning	Pam D'Andrea
Engineering	Matt Shafai
Public Works	Ken Gann
Police Chief	NA
Fire Chief	Ed Reed

Housing & Construction

Housing Units, 2000*

Total	2,797
Median rent	$941
Median SF home value	$319,500

Permits for New Residential Construction

	Units	Value
Total, 2006	24	$7,354,500
Single family	24	$7,354,500
Total, 2007	17	$4,784,090
Single family	17	$4,784,090

Real Property Valuation, 2008

	Parcels	Valuation
Total	4,118	$1,395,439,800
Vacant	363	39,196,900
Residential	3,006	1,226,606,600
Commercial	83	49,961,900
Industrial	4	3,925,900
Apartments	0	0
Farm land	422	4,201,200
Farm homestead	240	71,547,300

Average Property Value & Tax, 2008

Residential value	$399,924
Property tax	$10,188
Tax credit/rebate	$1,268

Public Library

No public municipal library

Library statistics, 2007

Population served	NA
Full-time/total staff	NA/NA

	Total	Per capita
Holdings	NA	NA
Revenues	NA	NA
Expenditures	NA	NA
Annual visits	NA	NA
Internet terminals/annual users	NA/NA	

Public Safety

Number of officers, 2007 0

Crime	2006	2007
Total crimes	112	87
Violent	4	8
Murder	0	0
Rape	0	0
Robbery	2	1
Aggravated assault	2	7
Non-violent	108	79
Burglary	27	15
Larceny	69	58
Vehicle theft	12	6
Domestic violence	8	52
Arson	2	0
Total crime rate	11.1	8.6
Violent	0.4	0.8
Non-violent	10.7	7.8

Public School District

(for school year 2007-08 except as noted)

Millstone Township School District
5 Dawson Court
Millstone Township, NJ 08535
(732) 786-0950

Superintendent	Mary Anne Donahue
Number of schools	3
Grade plan	K-8
Enrollment	1,653
Attendance rate, '06-07	95.2%
Dropout rate	NA
Students per teacher	11.5
Per pupil expenditure	$12,145
Median faculty salary	$50,765
Median administrator salary	$106,904
Grade 12 enrollment	NA
High school graduation rate	NA

Assessment test results

(percent scoring at proficient or advanced level)
	Language	Math
NJASK-Grade 3	95.2%	94.6%
GEPA-Grade 8	82.6%	92.1%
HSPA-High School	NA	NA

SAT Score Averages, 2006-07

Pct tested	Math	Verbal	Writing
NA	NA	NA	NA

Teacher Qualifications

Avg. years of experience	8

Highly-qualified teachers
one subject/all subjects 100%/100%

No Child Left Behind

AYP, 2006-07 .... Meets Standards

Municipal Finance

State Aid Programs, 2009

Total aid	$1,094,449
CMPTRA	0
Energy tax receipts	1,027,522
Garden State Trust	34,321

General Budget, 2008

Total tax levy	$35,651,111
County levy	5,591,114
County taxes	4,881,127
County library	293,732
County health	90,767
County open space	325,489
School levy	27,850,072
Muni. levy	2,209,925
Misc. revenues	5,623,209

Taxes	2006	2007	2008
General tax rate per $100	2.331	2.549	2.548
County equalization ratio	73.55	67.28	64.72
Net valuation taxable	$1,356,254,700	$1,383,072,039	$1,399,408,258
State equalized value	$2,017,993,414	$2,135,875,556	$12,512,393,547

See Introduction for an explanation of all data sources.

Demographics & Socio-Economic Characteristics

(2000 US Census, except as noted)

Population

1980*	7,136
1990*	6,968
2000	7,000
Male	3,377
Female	3,623
2007 (estimate)*	6,999
Population density	4,458.0

Race & Hispanic Origin, 2000

Race

White	6,570
Black/African American	53
American Indian/Alaska Native	11
Asian	215
Native Hawaiian/Pacific Islander	0
Other race	81
Two or more races	70
Hispanic origin, total	261
Mexican	16
Puerto Rican	67
Cuban	25
Other Hispanic	153

Age & Nativity, 2000

Under 5 years	387
18 years and over	5,399
21 years and over	5,200
65 years and over	1,098
85 years and over	121
Median age	39.9
Native-born	6,470
Foreign-born	530

Educational Attainment, 2000

Population 25 years and over	4,918
Less than 9th grade	4.4%
High school grad or higher	86.9%
Bachelor's degree or higher	27.2%
Graduate degree	7.4%

Income & Poverty, 1999

Per capita income	$29,996
Median household income	$68,429
Median family income	$77,869
Persons in poverty	158
H'holds receiving public assistance	34
H'holds receiving social security	799

Households, 2000

Total households	2,627
With persons under 18	882
With persons over 65	794
Family households	1,945
Single-person households	561
Persons per household	2.66
Persons per family	3.12

Labor & Employment

Total civilian labor force, 2007**	4,108
Unemployment rate	3.6%
Total civilian labor force, 2000	3,754
Unemployment rate	3.7%

Employed persons 16 years and over by occupation, 2000

Managers & professionals	1,393
Service occupations	475
Sales & office occupations	1,077
Farming, fishing & forestry	0
Construction & maintenance	336
Production & transportation	334
Self-employed persons	120

* US Census Bureau
** New Jersey Department of Labor

General Information

Borough of Milltown
39 Washington Ave
Milltown, NJ 08850
732-828-2100

Website	www.milltownnj.org
Year of incorporation	1889
Land/water area (sq. miles)	1.57/0.03
Form of government	Borough

Government

Legislative Districts

US Congressional	12
State Legislative	17

Local Officials, 2009

Mayor	Gloria Bradford
Manager	Denise Biancamono
Clerk	Michael Januszka
Finance Dir	Denise Biancamono
Tax Assessor	Eldo Magnani
Tax Collector	Diane Wagner
Attorney	Thomas Buck
Building	Vincent Lupo
Planning	Marcia Shiffman
Engineering	Michael McClelland
Public Works	Rich Williams
Police Chief	Raymond Geipel
Emerg/Fire Director	Jules DeKovics

Housing & Construction

Housing Units, 2000*

Total	2,670
Median rent	$753
Median SF home value	$178,400

Permits for New Residential Construction

	Units	Value
Total, 2006	3	$369,261
Single family	3	$369,261
Total, 2007	4	$492,348
Single family	4	$492,348

Real Property Valuation, 2008

	Parcels	Valuation
Total	2,547	$467,190,900
Vacant	54	5,353,100
Residential	2,387	396,690,000
Commercial	96	54,325,400
Industrial	5	8,927,400
Apartments	5	1,895,000
Farm land	0	0
Farm homestead	0	0

Average Property Value & Tax, 2008

Residential value	$166,188
Property tax	$6,724
Tax credit/rebate	$1,108

Public Library

Milltown Public Library
20 W Church St
Milltown, NJ 08850
732-247-2270

Director ... Bonnie J. Sterling

Library statistics, 2007

Population served	7,000
Full-time/total staff	1/3

	Total	Per capita
Holdings	38,443	5.49
Revenues	$326,013	$46.57
Expenditures	$307,761	$43.97
Annual visits	62,296	8.90
Internet terminals/annual users		5/6,841

Public Safety

Number of officers, 2007 ... 15

Crime	2006	2007
Total crimes	174	123
Violent	8	3
Murder	0	0
Rape	2	1
Robbery	2	0
Aggravated assault	4	2
Non-violent	166	120
Burglary	29	15
Larceny	128	100
Vehicle theft	9	5
Domestic violence	50	30
Arson	0	0
Total crime rate	24.4	17.5
Violent	1.1	0.4
Non-violent	23.3	17.1

Public School District

(for school year 2007-08 except as noted)

Milltown School District
80 Violet Terrace
Milltown, NJ 08850
(732) 214-2365

Superintendent	Linda A. Madison
Number of schools	2
Grade plan	K-8
Enrollment	679
Attendance rate, '06-07	98.4%
Dropout rate	NA
Students per teacher	10.4
Per pupil expenditure	$13,248
Median faculty salary	$41,978
Median administrator salary	$108,071
Grade 12 enrollment	NA
High school graduation rate	NA

Assessment test results

(percent scoring at proficient or advanced level)

	Language	Math
NJASK-Grade 3	96.2%	94.8%
GEPA-Grade 8	74.6%	94.7%
HSPA-High School	NA	NA

SAT Score Averages, 2006-07

Pct tested	Math	Verbal	Writing
NA	NA	NA	NA

Teacher Qualifications

Avg. years of experience	6
Highly-qualified teachers one subject/all subjects	100%/100%

No Child Left Behind

AYP, 2006-07 ... Meets Standards

Municipal Finance

State Aid Programs, 2009

Total aid	$499,178
CMPTRA	202,183
Energy tax receipts	284,515
Garden State Trust	0

General Budget, 2008

Total tax levy	$18,913,363
County levy	2,960,652
County taxes	2,651,431
County library	0
County health	0
County open space	309,221
School levy	11,913,908
Muni. levy	4,038,804
Misc. revenues	3,953,511

Taxes

	2006	2007	2008
General tax rate per $100	3.77	3.89	4.047
County equalization ratio	54.89	48.73	45.58
Net valuation taxable	$466,606,600	$467,046,467	$467,455,191
State equalized value	$957,824,244	$1,024,353,353	$8,036,788,818

See Introduction for an explanation of all data sources.

Demographics & Socio-Economic Characteristics
(2000 US Census, except as noted)

Population
1980* 24,815
1990* 25,992
2000 26,847
  Male 12,678
  Female 14,169
2007 (estimate)* 28,459
  Population density 672.0

Race & Hispanic Origin, 2000
Race
  White 20,438
  Black/African American 4,025
  American Indian/Alaska Native 139
  Asian 216
  Native Hawaiian/Pacific Islander 8
  Other race 1,384
  Two or more races 637
Hispanic origin, total 2,998
  Mexican 168
  Puerto Rican 2,392
  Cuban 14
  Other Hispanic 424

Age & Nativity, 2000
Under 5 years 1,871
18 years and over 19,349
21 years and over 18,311
65 years and over 3,460
85 years and over 393
  Median age 35.0
Native-born 26,261
Foreign-born 586

Educational Attainment, 2000
Population 25 years and over 16,998
Less than 9th grade 7.8%
High school grad or higher 74.1%
Bachelor's degree or higher 12.2%
Graduate degree 3.2%

Income & Poverty, 1999
Per capita income $18,632
Median household income $40,378
Median family income $46,093
Persons in poverty 4,034
H'holds receiving public assistance 555
H'holds receiving social security 2,818

Households, 2000
Total households 10,043
  With persons under 18 3,978
  With persons over 65 2,559
  Family households 7,011
  Single-person households 2,519
  Persons per household 2.65
  Persons per family 3.15

Labor & Employment
Total civilian labor force, 2007** 13,850
  Unemployment rate 8.1%
Total civilian labor force, 2000 13,003
  Unemployment rate 9.3%
Employed persons 16 years and over
* by occupation, 2000*
  Managers & professionals 2,927
  Service occupations 2,345
  Sales & office occupations 2,884
  Farming, fishing & forestry 27
  Construction & maintenance 1,270
  Production & transportation 2,338
  Self-employed persons 606

* US Census Bureau
** New Jersey Department of Labor
§ State Fiscal Year July 1–June 30

General Information
City of Millville
12 S High St
PO Box 609
Millville, NJ 08332
856-825-7000

Website .... www.millvillenj.gov
Year of incorporation 1866
Land/water area (sq. miles) 42.35/2.19
Form of government .... Commission

Government
Legislative Districts
US Congressional 2
State Legislative 1

Local Officials, 2009
Mayor .... James Quinn
Manager .... Lewis Thompson
Clerk .... Lewis Thompson
Finance Dir .... Maureen Mitchell
Tax Assessor .... Brian Rosenberger
Tax Collector .... Suzanne Olah
Attorney .... Richard McCarthy
Building .... Milton Truxton
Planning .... Kim Ayres
Engineering .... John Knoop
Public Works .... W. James Parent
Police Chief .... Ed Grennon (Actg)
Emerg/Fire Director .... Kurt Hess

Housing & Construction
Housing Units, 2000*
Total 10,652
Median rent $589
Median SF home value $86,700

Permits for New Residential Construction
	Units	Value
Total, 2006	200	$19,082,794
Single family	191	$18,477,994
Total, 2007	227	$20,087,465
Single family	146	$12,989,865

Real Property Valuation, 2008
	Parcels	Valuation
Total	10,064	$1,456,092,100
Vacant	1,185	43,449,400
Residential	8,157	1,029,826,500
Commercial	413	212,121,600
Industrial	71	120,141,600
Apartments	33	39,743,000
Farm land	148	1,372,500
Farm homestead	57	9,437,500

Average Property Value & Tax, 2008
Residential value $126,523
Property tax $3,824
Tax credit/rebate $841

Public Library
Millville Public Library
210 Buck St
Millville, NJ 08332
856-825-7087

Director .... Jennifer Druce

Library statistics, 2007
Population served 26,847
Full-time/total staff 2/4

	Total	Per capita
Holdings	53,695	2.00
Revenues	$700,364	$26.09
Expenditures	$687,563	$25.61
Annual visits	152,328	5.67
Internet terminals/annual users 8/9,582		

Public Safety
Number of officers, 2007 81

Crime	2006	2007
Total crimes	1,775	1,699
Violent	240	251
Murder	8	4
Rape	8	11
Robbery	98	102
Aggravated assault	126	134
Non-violent	1,535	1,448
Burglary	398	343
Larceny	1,084	1,057
Vehicle theft	53	48
Domestic violence	1,056	899
Arson	14	11
Total crime rate	63.7	60.3
Violent	8.6	8.9
Non-violent	55.0	51.4

Public School District
(for school year 2007-08 except as noted)

Millville School District
110 North Third Street, PO Box 5010
Millville, NJ 08332
(856) 327-6001

Superintendent .... Shelly Schneider
Number of schools 10
Grade plan K-12
Enrollment 6,267
Attendance rate, '06-07 .... 92.1%
Dropout rate 4.9%
Students per teacher 10.2
Per pupil expenditure $13,401
Median faculty salary $58,565
Median administrator salary $105,252
Grade 12 enrollment 456
High school graduation rate 77.6%

Assessment test results
(percent scoring at proficient or advanced level)
	Language	Math
NJASK-Grade 3	68.3%	73.2%
GEPA-Grade 8	47.1%	61.0%
HSPA-High School	61.5%	68.6%

SAT Score Averages, 2006-07
Pct tested	Math	Verbal	Writing
28%	470	464	453

Teacher Qualifications
Avg. years of experience 10
Highly-qualified teachers
  one subject/all subjects 99.5%/99.5%

No Child Left Behind
AYP, 2006-07 .... Meets Standards

Municipal Finance§
State Aid Programs, 2009
Total aid $5,096,975
  CMPTRA 1,239,804
  Energy tax receipts 3,780,866
  Garden State Trust 47,069

General Budget, 2008
Total tax levy $44,008,853
  County levy 17,558,643
    County taxes 16,589,200
    County library 0
    County health 783,105
    County open space 186,338
  School levy 9,974,231
  Muni. levy 16,475,979
  Misc. revenues 18,632,152

Taxes
	2006	2007	2008
General tax rate per $100	2.826	2.993	3.025
County equalization ratio	102.86	86.55	79.76
Net valuation taxable	$1,368,151,800	$1,427,591,878	$1,455,993,491
State equalized value	$1,586,676,514	$1,788,491,125	$1,947,789,318

See Introduction for an explanation of all data sources.

Demographics & Socio-Economic Characteristics

(2000 US Census, except as noted)

Population

1980*	3,325
1990*	3,333
2000	3,679
Male	1,787
Female	1,892
2007 (estimate)*	3,612
Population density	1,208.0

Race & Hispanic Origin, 2000

Race
White	3,326
Black/African American	126
American Indian/Alaska Native	4
Asian	92
Native Hawaiian/Pacific Islander	3
Other race	66
Two or more races	62
Hispanic origin, total	319
Mexican	13
Puerto Rican	105
Cuban	19
Other Hispanic	182

Age & Nativity, 2000

Under 5 years	312
18 years and over	2,778
21 years and over	2,696
65 years and over	487
85 years and over	30
Median age	37.6
Native-born	3,257
Foreign-born	422

Educational Attainment, 2000

Population 25 years and over	2,626
Less than 9th grade	2.2%
High school grad or higher	90.9%
Bachelor's degree or higher	28.2%
Graduate degree	9.2%

Income & Poverty, 1999

Per capita income	$27,119
Median household income	$64,643
Median family income	$67,467
Persons in poverty	206
H'holds receiving public assistance	20
H'holds receiving social security	414

Households, 2000

Total households	1,365
With persons under 18	499
With persons over 65	349
Family households	1,041
Single-person households	264
Persons per household	2.70
Persons per family	3.08

Labor & Employment

Total civilian labor force, 2007**	2,067
Unemployment rate	3.9%
Total civilian labor force, 2000	1,885
Unemployment rate	3.4%

Employed persons 16 years and over by occupation, 2000
Managers & professionals	737
Service occupations	180
Sales & office occupations	524
Farming, fishing & forestry	7
Construction & maintenance	199
Production & transportation	173
Self-employed persons	28

* US Census Bureau
** New Jersey Department of Labor

General Information

Township of Mine Hill
10 Baker St
Mine Hill, NJ 07803
973-366-9031

Website	www.minehill.com
Year of incorporation	1923
Land/water area (sq. miles)	2.99/0.01
Form of government	Mayor-Council

Government

Legislative Districts

US Congressional	11
State Legislative	25

Local Officials, 2009

Mayor	Richard Leary
Manager	David J. Gilbride
Clerk	Patricia Korpos
Finance Dir	Charles Wood
Tax Assessor	Joseph Ferraris
Tax Collector	Jeanette Sevret
Attorney	Stephen N. Severud
Building	Steve Kaplan
Comm Dev/Planning	NA
Engineering	Paul Sterbenz
Public Works	NA
Police Chief	NA
Emerg/Fire Director	Kenneth Thompson

Housing & Construction

Housing Units, 2000*

Total	1,388
Median rent	$1,192
Median SF home value	$161,900

Permits for New Residential Construction

	Units	Value
Total, 2006	3	$329,100
Single family	3	$329,100
Total, 2007	3	$399,400
Single family	3	$399,400

Real Property Valuation, 2008

	Parcels	Valuation
Total	1,507	$523,443,200
Vacant	105	20,309,600
Residential	1,335	454,795,300
Commercial	56	28,936,700
Industrial	8	18,655,600
Apartments	1	722,300
Farm land	2	23,700
Farm homestead	0	0

Average Property Value & Tax, 2008

Residential value	$340,671
Property tax	$6,433
Tax credit/rebate	$1,093

Public Library

Mine Hill Public Library
10 Baker St
Mine Hill, NJ 07803
(973) 366-9217

Director	NA

Library statistics, 2007

Population served	NA
Full-time/total staff	NA/NA

	Total	Per capita
Holdings	NA	NA
Revenues	NA	NA
Expenditures	NA	NA
Annual visits	NA	NA
Internet terminals/annual users	NA/NA	

Public Safety

Number of officers, 2007	0

Crime	2006	2007
Total crimes	35	36
Violent	2	0
Murder	0	0
Rape	1	0
Robbery	0	0
Aggravated assault	1	0
Non-violent	33	36
Burglary	8	10
Larceny	22	25
Vehicle theft	3	1
Domestic violence	9	17
Arson	0	0
Total crime rate	9.5	9.8
Violent	0.5	0.0
Non-violent	9.0	9.8

Public School District

(for school year 2007-08 except as noted)

Mine Hill Township School District
Canfield Avenue
Mine Hill, NJ 07803
(973) 366-0590

Superintendent	Richard Bitondo
Number of schools	1
Grade plan	K-6
Enrollment	364
Attendance rate, '06-07	96.2%
Dropout rate	NA
Students per teacher	11.6
Per pupil expenditure	$12,058
Median faculty salary	$50,312
Median administrator salary	$59,250
Grade 12 enrollment	NA
High school graduation rate	NA

Assessment test results

(percent scoring at proficient or advanced level)
	Language	Math
NJASK-Grade 3	94.8%	88.0%
GEPA-Grade 8	NA	NA
HSPA-High School	NA	NA

SAT Score Averages, 2006-07

Pct tested	Math	Verbal	Writing
NA	NA	NA	NA

Teacher Qualifications

Avg. years of experience	12
Highly-qualified teachers one subject/all subjects	100%/100%

No Child Left Behind

AYP, 2006-07	Meets Standards

Municipal Finance

State Aid Programs, 2009

Total aid	$365,316
CMPTRA	83,455
Energy tax receipts	272,728
Garden State Trust	0

General Budget, 2008

Total tax levy	$9,895,407
County levy	1,244,346
County taxes	1,015,455
County library	0
County health	0
County open space	228,891
School levy	5,840,100
Muni. levy	2,810,961
Misc. revenues	1,502,208

Taxes

	2006	2007	2008
General tax rate per $100	1.71	1.78	1.889
County equalization ratio	119.1	103.37	98.61
Net valuation taxable	$535,085,600	$536,052,138	$523,991,983
State equalized value	$518,070,390	$543,602,043	$534,892,597

See Introduction for an explanation of all data sources.

Demographics & Socio-Economic Characteristics
(2000 US Census, except as noted)

Population
1980*	3,318
1990*	3,303
2000	3,595
Male	1,684
Female	1,911
2007 (estimate)*	3,582
Population density	3,347.7

Race & Hispanic Origin, 2000
Race
White	3,511
Black/African American	19
American Indian/Alaska Native	0
Asian	31
Native Hawaiian/Pacific Islander	0
Other race	12
Two or more races	22
Hispanic origin, total	68
Mexican	5
Puerto Rican	23
Cuban	10
Other Hispanic	30

Age & Nativity, 2000
Under 5 years	206
18 years and over	2,864
21 years and over	2,812
65 years and over	732
85 years and over	70
Median age	44.6
Native-born	3,382
Foreign-born	213

Educational Attainment, 2000
Population 25 years and over	2,737
Less than 9th grade	2.2%
High school grad or higher	94.3%
Bachelor's degree or higher	48.8%
Graduate degree	19.0%

Income & Poverty, 1999
Per capita income	$52,862
Median household income	$80,484
Median family income	$93,401
Persons in poverty	68
H'holds receiving public assistance	28
H'holds receiving social security	497

Households, 2000
Total households	1,633
With persons under 18	413
With persons over 65	538
Family households	976
Single-person households	574
Persons per household	2.20
Persons per family	2.89

Labor & Employment
Total civilian labor force, 2007**	2,090
Unemployment rate	3.7%
Total civilian labor force, 2000	1,952
Unemployment rate	3.8%

Employed persons 16 years and over by occupation, 2000
Managers & professionals	1,031
Service occupations	126
Sales & office occupations	507
Farming, fishing & forestry	0
Construction & maintenance	125
Production & transportation	89
Self-employed persons	182

General Information
Borough of Monmouth Beach
22 Beach Rd
Monmouth Beach, NJ 07750
732-229-2204

Website	www.monmouthbeach.us
Year of incorporation	1906
Land/water area (sq. miles)	1.07/0.85
Form of government	Commission

Government
Legislative Districts
US Congressional	6
State Legislative	11

Local Officials, 2009
Mayor	Susan Howard
Administrator	Michael Corbally
Clerk	Joyce L. Escalante
Finance Dir	James Fuller
Tax Assessor	Timothy Anfuso
Tax Collector	James Fuller
Attorney	Dennis Collins
Building	Jackie Donovan
Comm Dev/Planning	NA
Engineering	Edward Broberg
Public Works	Allen Miller
Police Chief	Richard White
Emerg/Fire Director	Richard White

Housing & Construction
Housing Units, 2000*
Total	1,969
Median rent	$1,037
Median SF home value	$342,000

Permits for New Residential Construction
	Units	Value
Total, 2006	7	$2,703,500
Single family	7	$2,703,500
Total, 2007	7	$4,415,000
Single family	7	$4,415,000

Real Property Valuation, 2008
	Parcels	Valuation
Total	2,113	$1,247,325,400
Vacant	85	15,067,300
Residential	1,994	1,201,782,600
Commercial	34	30,475,500
Industrial	0	0
Apartments	0	0
Farm land	0	0
Farm homestead	0	0

Average Property Value & Tax, 2008
Residential value	$602,699
Property tax	$7,016
Tax credit/rebate	$1,064

Public Library
Monmouth Beach Library
18 Willow Ave
Monmouth Beach, NJ 07750
732-229-1187

Director	Nancy Leporatti

Library statistics, 2007
Population served	3,595
Full-time/total staff	0/0

	Total	Per capita
Holdings	35,028	9.74
Revenues	$102,525	$28.52
Expenditures	$94,545	$26.30
Annual visits	10,000	2.78
Internet terminals/annual users	2/5,100	

Public Safety
Number of officers, 2007	10

Crime	2006	2007
Total crimes	35	61
Violent	4	3
Murder	0	0
Rape	0	1
Robbery	0	0
Aggravated assault	4	2
Non-violent	31	58
Burglary	1	3
Larceny	27	55
Vehicle theft	3	0
Domestic violence	4	2
Arson	1	0
Total crime rate	9.7	17.1
Violent	1.1	0.8
Non-violent	8.6	16.2

Public School District
(for school year 2007-08 except as noted)

Monmouth Beach School District
7 Hastings Place
Monmouth Beach, NJ 07750
(732) 222-6139

Superintendent	Neil A. Frankenfield
Number of schools	1
Grade plan	K-8
Enrollment	322
Attendance rate, '06-07	95.4%
Dropout rate	NA
Students per teacher	11.2
Per pupil expenditure	$12,842
Median faculty salary	$51,505
Median administrator salary	$87,631
Grade 12 enrollment	NA
High school graduation rate	NA

Assessment test results
(percent scoring at proficient or advanced level)
	Language	Math
NJASK-Grade 3	94.5%	94.6%
GEPA-Grade 8	77.8%	97.2%
HSPA-High School	NA	NA

SAT Score Averages, 2006-07
Pct tested	Math	Verbal	Writing
NA	NA	NA	NA

Teacher Qualifications
Avg. years of experience	9
Highly-qualified teachers one subject/all subjects	100%/100%

No Child Left Behind
AYP, 2006-07	Meets Standards

Municipal Finance
State Aid Programs, 2009
Total aid	$392,775
CMPTRA	0
Energy tax receipts	377,064
Garden State Trust	0

General Budget, 2008
Total tax levy	$14,523,776
County levy	3,688,354
County taxes	3,273,122
County library	196,968
County health	0
County open space	218,265
School levy	7,133,381
Muni. levy	3,702,040
Misc. revenues	2,737,183

Taxes
	2006	2007	2008
General tax rate per $100	1.107	1.151	1.165
County equalization ratio	101.74	88.79	86.05
Net valuation taxable	$1,230,808,300	$1,240,583,960	$1,247,666,739
State equalized value	$1,386,566,779	$1,441,646,858	$2,105,217,969

* US Census Bureau
** New Jersey Department of Labor

See Introduction for an explanation of all data sources.

Demographics & Socio-Economic Characteristics
(2000 US Census, except as noted)

Population
1980*	21,639
1990*	26,703
2000	28,967
Male	13,988
Female	14,979
2007 (estimate)*	32,607
Population density	700.5

Race & Hispanic Origin, 2000
Race
White	24,573
Black/African American	3,231
American Indian/Alaska Native	72
Asian	356
Native Hawaiian/Pacific Islander	9
Other race	286
Two or more races	440
Hispanic origin, total	785
Mexican	96
Puerto Rican	486
Cuban	24
Other Hispanic	179

Age & Nativity, 2000
Under 5 years	1,908
18 years and over	21,540
21 years and over	20,553
65 years and over	3,737
85 years and over	331
Median age	37.1
Native-born	28,131
Foreign-born	836

Educational Attainment, 2000
Population 25 years and over	19,377
Less than 9th grade	4.4%
High school grad or higher	80.2%
Bachelor's degree or higher	15.9%
Graduate degree	4.0%

Income & Poverty, 1999
Per capita income	$20,488
Median household income	$50,037
Median family income	$56,810
Persons in poverty	1,769
H'holds receiving public assistance	174
H'holds receiving social security	3,029

Households, 2000
Total households	10,521
With persons under 18	3,996
With persons over 65	2,742
Family households	7,848
Single-person households	2,214
Persons per household	2.73
Persons per family	3.18

Labor & Employment
Total civilian labor force, 2007**	17,041
Unemployment rate	5.4%
Total civilian labor force, 2000	14,596
Unemployment rate	5.1%

Employed persons 16 years and over by occupation, 2000
Managers & professionals	3,692
Service occupations	2,237
Sales & office occupations	4,399
Farming, fishing & forestry	26
Construction & maintenance	1,588
Production & transportation	1,908
Self-employed persons	710

* US Census Bureau
** New Jersey Department of Labor

General Information
Township of Monroe
125 Virginia Ave
Williamstown, NJ 08094
856-728-9800
Website	www.monroetownshipnj.org
Year of incorporation	1859
Land/water area (sq. miles)	46.55/0.38
Form of government	Mayor-Council

Government
Legislative Districts
US Congressional	1
State Legislative	4

Local Officials, 2009
Mayor	Michael Gabbianelli
Manager	Kevin Heydel
Clerk	Susan McCormick
Finance Dir	Jeff Coles
Tax Assessor	Robyn Glocker-Hammond
Tax Collector	Alma Alexander
Attorney	Charles Fiore
Building	Ed O'Neil
Planning	Carolyn Farrell
Engineering	Adams, Rehmann & Heggan
Public Works	Vincent J. Agnesino
Police Chief	Domenic Christopher
Emerg/Fire Dir	Salvatore Tomarchio

Housing & Construction
Housing Units, 2000*
Total	11,069
Median rent	$621
Median SF home value	$114,200

Permits for New Residential Construction
	Units	Value
Total, 2006	237	$31,222,272
Single family	237	$31,222,272
Total, 2007	151	$24,666,561
Single family	131	$23,444,121

Real Property Valuation, 2008
	Parcels	Valuation
Total	13,350	$2,842,526,900
Vacant	2,048	101,403,000
Residential	10,395	2,362,935,700
Commercial	406	294,745,400
Industrial	16	14,488,100
Apartments	14	36,507,600
Farm land	329	2,186,800
Farm homestead	142	30,260,300

Average Property Value & Tax, 2008
Residential value	$227,123
Property tax	$5,788
Tax credit/rebate	$1,045

Public Library
Monroe Township Public Library
306 S Main St
Williamstown, NJ 08094
856-629-1212
Director | Elizabeth L. Lillie

Library statistics, 2007
Population served	28,967
Full-time/total staff	5/12

	Total	Per capita
Holdings	92,574	3.20
Revenues	$980,384	$33.84
Expenditures	$697,785	$24.09
Annual visits	182,440	6.30
Internet terminals/annual users	14/16,233	

Public Safety
Number of officers, 2007 ... 66
Crime	2006	2007
Total crimes	824	714
Violent	48	44
Murder	0	2
Rape	2	2
Robbery	17	10
Aggravated assault	29	30
Non-violent	776	670
Burglary	186	157
Larceny	536	466
Vehicle theft	54	47
Domestic violence	372	295
Arson	10	6
Total crime rate	26.2	22.4
Violent	1.5	1.4
Non-violent	24.7	21.0

Public School District
(for school year 2007-08 except as noted)

Monroe Township School District
75 E. Academy St
Williamstown, NJ 08094
(856) 629-6400
Superintendent	Charles Earling
Number of schools	6
Grade plan	K-12
Enrollment	6,039
Attendance rate, '06-07	95.1%
Dropout rate	4.4%
Students per teacher	12.9
Per pupil expenditure	$10,674
Median faculty salary	$51,313
Median administrator salary	$109,918
Grade 12 enrollment	405
High school graduation rate	85.4%

Assessment test results
(percent scoring at proficient or advanced level)
	Language	Math
NJASK-Grade 3	91.5%	89.7%
GEPA-Grade 8	66.7%	88.1%
HSPA-High School	80.0%	87.6%

SAT Score Averages, 2006-07
Pct tested	Math	Verbal	Writing
63%	481	456	444

Teacher Qualifications
Avg. years of experience	10
Highly-qualified teachers one subject/all subjects	100%/100%

No Child Left Behind
AYP, 2006-07 ... Meets Standards

Municipal Finance
State Aid Programs, 2009
Total aid	$5,407,080
CMPTRA	511,830
Energy tax receipts	4,545,361
Garden State Trust	21,400

General Budget, 2008
Total tax levy	$72,688,130
County levy	16,008,233
County taxes	14,844,915
County library	0
County health	0
County open space	1,163,318
School levy	38,764,260
Muni. levy	17,915,637
Misc. revenues	15,084,073

Taxes
	2006	2007	2008
General tax rate per $100	4.61	4.768	2.549
County equalization ratio	62.62	54.27	98.13
Net valuation taxable	$1,369,209,660	$1,436,115,209	$2,852,405,792
State equalized value	$2,528,772,559	$2,851,700,740	$3,069,649,506

Demographics & Socio-Economic Characteristics

(2000 US Census, except as noted)

Population

1980*	15,858
1990*	22,255
2000	27,999
Male	12,845
Female	15,154
2007 (estimate)*	36,397
Population density	867.8

Race & Hispanic Origin, 2000

Race

White	26,127
Black/African American	820
American Indian/Alaska Native	16
Asian	655
Native Hawaiian/Pacific Islander	24
Other races	189
Two or more races	168
Hispanic origin, total	666
Mexican	63
Puerto Rican	295
Cuban	57
Other Hispanic	251

Age & Nativity, 2000

Under 5 years	1,109
18 years and over	23,521
21 years and over	22,893
65 years and over	12,185
85 years and over	1,380
Median age	58.9
Native-born	25,737
Foreign-born	2,262

Educational Attainment, 2000

Population 25 years and over	22,394
Less than 9th grade	2.9%
High school grad or higher	90.0%
Bachelor's degree or higher	29.5%
Graduate degree	10.1%

Income & Poverty, 1999

Per capita income	$31,772
Median household income	$53,306
Median family income	$68,479
Persons in poverty	908
H'holds receiving public assistance	66
H'holds receiving social security	7,971

Households, 2000

Total households	12,536
With persons under 18	2,148
With persons over 65	8,107
Family households	8,233
Single-person households	4,006
Persons per household	2.15
Persons per family	2.70

Labor & Employment

Total civilian labor force, 2007**	13,116
Unemployment rate	4.7%
Total civilian labor force, 2000	10,058
Unemployment rate	5.0%

Employed persons 16 years and over by occupation, 2000

Managers & professionals	3,794
Service occupations	1,006
Sales & office occupations	2,945
Farming, fishing & forestry	34
Construction & maintenance	815
Production & transportation	961
Self-employed persons	617

* US Census Bureau
** New Jersey Department of Labor

General Information

Township of Monroe
1 Municipal Plz
Monroe Township, NJ 08831
732-521-4400

Website	monroetwp.com
Year of incorporation	1838
Land/water area (sq. miles)	41.94/0.10
Form of government	Mayor-Council

Government

Legislative Districts

US Congressional	12
State Legislative	14

Local Officials, 2009

Mayor	Richard Pucci
Manager	Wayne Hamilton
Clerk	Sharon Doerfler
Finance Dir	George Lang
Tax Assessor	Mitchell Elias
Tax Collector	Luann McGraw-Russell
Attorney	Joel Shain
Building	Robert Downey
Planning	Robert Tucker
Engineering	Ernest Feist
Public Works	Wayne Horbatt
Police Chief	John Kraivec
Fire/Emergency Dir	NA

Housing & Construction

Housing Units, 2000*

Total	13,259
Median rent	$877
Median SF home value	$174,100

Permits for New Residential Construction

	Units	Value
Total, 2006	826	$95,480,576
Single family	459	$71,035,699
Total, 2007	416	$64,736,947
Single family	356	$61,194,946

Real Property Valuation, 2008

	Parcels	Valuation
Total	19,967	$3,604,836,500
Vacant	2,460	152,463,100
Residential	16,748	2,913,669,300
Commercial	189	276,162,300
Industrial	46	198,178,200
Apartments	3	29,159,300
Farm land	365	3,746,300
Farm homestead	156	31,458,000

Average Property Value & Tax, 2008

Residential value	$174,227
Property tax	$5,741
Tax credit/rebate	$1,118

Public Library

Monroe Township Library
4 Municipal Plaza
Monroe Township, NJ 08831
732-521-5000

Director	Irene Goldberg

Library statistics, 2007

Population served	27,999
Full-time/total staff	7/18

	Total	Per capita
Holdings	134,454	4.80
Revenues	$2,408,839	$86.03
Expenditures	$2,404,897	$85.89
Annual visits	408,250	14.58
Internet terminals/annual users	18/29,873	

Public Safety

Number of officers, 2007	49

Crime	2006	2007
Total crimes	300	269
Violent	19	11
Murder	0	0
Rape	1	1
Robbery	1	1
Aggravated assault	17	9
Non-violent	281	258
Burglary	52	55
Larceny	217	191
Vehicle theft	12	12
Domestic violence	13	18
Arson	0	1
Total crime rate	8.8	7.7
Violent	0.6	0.3
Non-violent	8.3	7.4

Public School District

(for school year 2007-08 except as noted)

Monroe Township School District
423 Buckelew Avenue
Monroe Township, NJ 08831
(732) 521-2111

Chief School Admin	Kenneth Hamilton
Number of schools	6
Grade plan	K-12
Enrollment	5,125
Attendance rate, '06-07	95.4%
Dropout rate	0.9%
Students per teacher	10.5
Per pupil expenditure	$14,708
Median faculty salary	$52,975
Median administrator salary	$119,067
Grade 12 enrollment	383
High school graduation rate	95.9%

Assessment test results

(percent scoring at proficient or advanced level)

	Language	Math
NJASK-Grade 3	92.5%	91.3%
GEPA-Grade 8	71.3%	91.8%
HSPA-High School	83.1%	88.6%

SAT Score Averages, 2006-07

Pct tested	Math	Verbal	Writing
79%	522	495	490

Teacher Qualifications

Avg. years of experience	6
Highly-qualified teachers one subject/all subjects	99.5%/99.5%

No Child Left Behind

AYP, 2006-07	Meets Standards

Municipal Finance

State Aid Programs, 2009

Total aid	$2,919,600
CMPTRA	240,970
Energy tax receipts	2,604,414
Garden State Trust	1,085

General Budget, 2008

Total tax levy	$118,938,424
County levy	22,224,339
County taxes	19,827,830
County library	0
County health	0
County open space	2,396,510
School levy	73,293,226
Muni. levy	23,420,859
Misc. revenues	17,931,125

Taxes

	2006	2007	2008
General tax rate per $100	2.99	3.13	3.294
County equalization ratio	56.34	48.47	46.47
Net valuation taxable	$3,370,087,500	$3,556,604,685	$3,609,458,429
State equalized value	$6,958,094,964	$7,648,192,294	$3,465,569,264

See Introduction for an explanation of all data sources.

Demographics & Socio-Economic Characteristics
(2000 US Census, except as noted)

Population
1980*	2,066
1990*	2,832
2000	3,412
Male	1,764
Female	1,648
2007 (estimate)*	3,891
Population density	88.4

Race & Hispanic Origin, 2000
Race
White	3,250
Black/African American	61
American Indian/Alaska Native	6
Asian	23
Native Hawaiian/Pacific Islander	0
Other race	37
Two or more races	35
Hispanic origin, total	112
Mexican	9
Puerto Rican	39
Cuban	12
Other Hispanic	52

Age & Nativity, 2000
Under 5 years	241
18 years and over	2,485
21 years and over	2,377
65 years and over	378
85 years and over	22
Median age	37.0
Native-born	3,278
Foreign-born	134

Educational Attainment, 2000
Population 25 years and over	2,262
Less than 9th grade	5.4%
High school grad or higher	80.2%
Bachelor's degree or higher	14.5%
Graduate degree	6.0%

Income & Poverty, 1999
Per capita income	$20,676
Median household income	$45,368
Median family income	$50,833
Persons in poverty	406
H'holds receiving public assistance	47
H'holds receiving social security	337

Households, 2000
Total households	1,286
With persons under 18	481
With persons over 65	281
Family households	911
Single-person households	298
Persons per household	2.65
Persons per family	3.14

Labor & Employment
Total civilian labor force, 2007**	1,861
Unemployment rate	7.6%
Total civilian labor force, 2000	1,638
Unemployment rate	5.7%

Employed persons 16 years and over by occupation, 2000
Managers & professionals	397
Service occupations	252
Sales & office occupations	441
Farming, fishing & forestry	0
Construction & maintenance	262
Production & transportation	193
Self-employed persons	147

©2009 Information Publications, Inc. All rights reserved. Photocopying prohibited. For additional copies, contact the publisher at www.informationpublications.com or (877)544-INFO (4636)

* US Census Bureau
** New Jersey Department of Labor

General Information
Township of Montague
277 Clove Rd
Montague, NJ 07827
973-293-7300

Website	www.montaguenj.org
Year of incorporation	1759
Land/water area (sq. miles)	44.01/1.33
Form of government	Township

Government
Legislative Districts
US Congressional	5
State Legislative	24

Local Officials, 2009
Mayor	Joe Barbagallo
Manager/Admin	NA
Clerk	Diana Francisco
CFO	Gail Magura
Tax Assessor	Melissa Rockwell
Tax Collector	Fran Multari
Attorney	Michael Garofalo
Building	Donald Stambaugh
Comm Dev/Planning	NA
Engineering	Jack O'Krepky
Public Works Foreman	Dave Berhman
Police Chief	NA
Emerg/Fire Director	David Coss

Housing & Construction
Housing Units, 2000*
Total	1,588
Median rent	$806
Median SF home value	$129,400

Permits for New Residential Construction
	Units	Value
Total, 2006	35	$3,786,356
Single family	35	$3,786,356
Total, 2007	27	$4,171,807
Single family	27	$4,171,807

Real Property Valuation, 2008
	Parcels	Valuation
Total	2,862	$225,084,900
Vacant	906	14,229,190
Residential	1,671	176,080,600
Commercial	60	22,412,400
Industrial	6	2,136,600
Apartments	2	420,000
Farm land	153	1,108,910
Farm homestead	64	8,697,200

Average Property Value & Tax, 2008
Residential value	$106,500
Property tax	$3,688
Tax credit/rebate	$846

Public Library
No public municipal library

Library statistics, 2007
Population served	NA
Full-time/total staff	NA/NA

	Total	Per capita
Holdings	NA	NA
Revenues	NA	NA
Expenditures	NA	NA
Annual visits	NA	NA
Internet terminals/annual users	NA/NA	

Public Safety
Number of officers, 2007	0

Crime	2006	2007
Total crimes	75	50
Violent	4	6
Murder	0	0
Rape	1	0
Robbery	1	1
Aggravated assault	2	5
Non-violent	71	44
Burglary	8	8
Larceny	58	35
Vehicle theft	5	1
Domestic violence	6	63
Arson	1	0
Total crime rate	19.5	12.8
Violent	1.0	1.5
Non-violent	18.5	11.3

Public School District
(for school year 2007-08 except as noted)

Montague School District
475 Route 206
Montague, NJ 07827
(973) 293-7131

Chief School Admin	Janice Hodge
Number of schools	1
Grade plan	K-6
Enrollment	285
Attendance rate, '06-07	95.7%
Dropout rate	NA
Students per teacher	7.4
Per pupil expenditure	$14,788
Median faculty salary	$52,323
Median administrator salary	$85,178
Grade 12 enrollment	NA
High school graduation rate	NA

Assessment test results
(percent scoring at proficient or advanced level)
	Language	Math
NJASK-Grade 3	90.3%	87.5%
GEPA-Grade 8	NA	NA
HSPA-High School	NA	NA

SAT Score Averages, 2006-07
Pct tested	Math	Verbal	Writing
NA	NA	NA	NA

Teacher Qualifications
Avg. years of experience	11
Highly-qualified teachers one subject/all subjects	96.5%/93.0%

No Child Left Behind
AYP, 2006-07	Meets Standards

Municipal Finance
State Aid Programs, 2009
Total aid	$537,597
CMPTRA	14,572
Energy tax receipts	316,610
Garden State Trust	177,685

General Budget, 2008
Total tax levy	$7,818,862
County levy	1,842,106
County taxes	1,545,987
County library	130,301
County health	45,753
County open space	120,065
School levy	5,071,772
Muni. levy	904,984
Misc. revenues	1,385,405

Taxes
	2006	2007	2008
General tax rate per $100	3.32	3.47	3.464
County equalization ratio	55.21	48.83	46.99
Net valuation taxable	$215,149,060	$221,170,947	$225,771,871
State equalized value	$441,378,635	$469,911,838	$478,270,039

See Introduction for an explanation of all data sources.

Demographics & Socio-Economic Characteristics

(2000 US Census, except as noted)

Population

1980*	38,321
1990*	37,729
2000	38,977
Male	18,053
Female	20,924
2007 (estimate)*	37,052
Population density	5,881.3

Race & Hispanic Origin, 2000

Race

White	23,297
Black/African American	12,497
American Indian/Alaska Native	73
Asian	1,228
Native Hawaiian/Pacific Islander	14
Other race	688
Two or more races	1,180
Hispanic origin, total	1,995
Mexican	183
Puerto Rican	584
Cuban	171
Other Hispanic	1,057

Age & Nativity, 2000

Under 5 years	2,716
18 years and over	29,013
21 years and over	27,887
65 years and over	4,665
85 years and over	786
Median age	37.5
Native-born	33,389
Foreign-born	5,679

Educational Attainment, 2000

Population 25 years and over	26,652
Less than 9th grade	3.0%
High school grad or higher	92.0%
Bachelor's degree or higher	57.4%
Graduate degree	27.1%

Income & Poverty, 1999

Per capita income	$44,870
Median household income	$74,894
Median family income	$96,252
Persons in poverty	2,149
H'holds receiving public assistance	369
H'holds receiving social security	3,197

Households, 2000

Total households	15,020
With persons under 18	5,574
With persons over 65	3,271
Family households	9,682
Single-person households	4,396
Persons per household	2.53
Persons per family	3.16

Labor & Employment

Total civilian labor force, 2007**	20,964
Unemployment rate	3.2%
Total civilian labor force, 2000	21,484
Unemployment rate	5.0%

Employed persons 16 years and over by occupation, 2000

Managers & professionals	11,898
Service occupations	2,120
Sales & office occupations	4,833
Farming, fishing & forestry	0
Construction & maintenance	561
Production & transportation	1,002
Self-employed persons	1,532

* US Census Bureau
** New Jersey Department of Labor

See Introduction for an explanation of all data sources.

General Information

Township of Montclair
205 Claremont Ave
Montclair, NJ 07042
973-744-1400

Website	www.montclairnjusa.org
Year of incorporation	1979
Land/water area (sq. miles)	6.30/0.00
Form of government	Council-Manager

Government

Legislative Districts

US Congressional	8, 10
State Legislative	34

Local Officials, 2009

Mayor	Jerry Fried
Manager	Joseph M. Hartnett
Clerk	Linda S. Wanat
Finance Dir	Gordon Stelter
Tax Assessor	Joan Kozeniesky
Tax Collector	Maureen Montesano
Attorney	Alan Trembulak
Construction Official	Robert Mcloughlin
Planning	Karen Kadus
Engineering	Kimberli Craft
Public Works	Steve Wood
Police Chief	David Sabagh
Emerg/Fire Director	Kevin Allen

Housing & Construction

Housing Units, 2000*

Total	15,531
Median rent	$866
Median SF home value	$317,500

Permits for New Residential Construction

	Units	Value
Total, 2006	277	$57,631,786
Single family	40	$8,504,947
Total, 2007	180	$18,374,075
Single family	11	$3,336,670

Real Property Valuation, 2008

	Parcels	Valuation
Total	10,506	$7,324,562,300
Vacant	142	29,798,800
Residential	9,610	6,307,313,300
Commercial	589	692,664,300
Industrial	3	5,137,000
Apartments	162	289,648,900
Farm land	0	0
Farm homestead	0	0

Average Property Value & Tax, 2008

Residential value	$656,328
Property tax	$15,101
Tax credit/rebate	$1,371

Public Library

Montclair Public Library
50 S Fullerton Ave
Montclair, NJ 07042
973-744-0500

Director..................David Hinkley

Library statistics, 2007

Population served	38,977
Full-time/total staff	15/34

	Total	Per capita
Holdings	189,418	4.86
Revenues	$4,064,962	$104.29
Expenditures	$3,963,673	$101.69
Annual visits	296,731	7.61
Internet terminals/annual users	52/51,620	

Public Safety

Number of officers, 2007 111

Crime	2006	2007
Total crimes	1,090	877
Violent	92	97
Murder	1	2
Rape	1	5
Robbery	29	50
Aggravated assault	61	40
Non-violent	998	780
Burglary	251	207
Larceny	666	496
Vehicle theft	81	77
Domestic violence	196	175
Arson	1	1
Total crime rate	28.8	23.5
Violent	2.4	2.6
Non-violent	26.4	20.9

Public School District

(for school year 2007-08 except as noted)

Montclair School District
22 Valley Road
Montclair, NJ 07042
(973) 509-4010

Superintendent	Frank R. Alvarez
Number of schools	11
Grade plan	K-12
Enrollment	6,562
Attendance rate, '06-07	95.7%
Dropout rate	0.0%
Students per teacher	10.0
Per pupil expenditure	$15,101
Median faculty salary	$61,451
Median administrator salary	$115,980
Grade 12 enrollment	526
High school graduation rate	100.0%

Assessment test results

(percent scoring at proficient or advanced level)

	Language	Math
NJASK-Grade 3	94.7%	94.3%
GEPA-Grade 8	68.9%	87.8%
HSPA-High School	77.7%	86.8%

SAT Score Averages, 2006-07

Pct tested	Math	Verbal	Writing
92%	518	526	522

Teacher Qualifications

Avg. years of experience	8
Highly-qualified teachers	
one subject/all subjects	99.0%/99.0%

No Child Left Behind

AYP, 2006-07 ....Meets Standards

Municipal Finance

State Aid Programs, 2009

Total aid	$3,929,194
CMPTRA	948,057
Energy tax receipts	2,853,438
Garden State Trust	0

General Budget, 2008

Total tax levy	$168,770,184
County levy	27,765,752
County taxes	26,690,534
County library	0
County health	0
County open space	1,075,218
School levy	97,808,259
Muni. levy	43,196,173
Misc. revenues	19,859,600

Taxes

	2006	2007	2008
General tax rate per $100	5.36	2.15	2.301
County equalization ratio	45.16	107.33	102.52
Net valuation taxable	$2,773,446,450	$7,415,062,627	$7,335,108,076
State equalized value	$6,853,658,398	$7,233,011,190	$7,391,201,056

Demographics & Socio-Economic Characteristics
(2000 US Census, except as noted)

Population
1980*	7,360
1990*	9,612
2000	17,481
Male	8,624
Female	8,857
2007 (estimate)*	23,023
Population density	705.8

Race & Hispanic Origin, 2000
Race
White	14,781
Black/African American	361
American Indian/Alaska Native	15
Asian	2,011
Native Hawaiian/Pacific Islander	2
Other race	80
Two or more races	231
Hispanic origin, total	387
Mexican	76
Puerto Rican	96
Cuban	47
Other Hispanic	168

Age & Nativity, 2000
Under 5 years	1,514
18 years and over	11,722
21 years and over	11,395
65 years and over	1,189
85 years and over	94
Median age	36.8
Native-born	14,934
Foreign-born	2,531

Educational Attainment, 2000
Population 25 years and over	11,032
Less than 9th grade	1.4%
High school grad or higher	97.3%
Bachelor's degree or higher	70.2%
Graduate degree	34.8%

Income & Poverty, 1999
Per capita income	$48,699
Median household income	$118,850
Median family income	$129,150
Persons in poverty	261
H'holds receiving public assistance	22
H'holds receiving social security	878

Households, 2000
Total households	5,803
With persons under 18	3,006
With persons over 65	839
Family households	4,783
Single-person households	823
Persons per household	2.99
Persons per family	3.33

Labor & Employment
Total civilian labor force, 2007**	9,876
Unemployment rate	2.1%
Total civilian labor force, 2000	8,711
Unemployment rate	2.1%

Employed persons 16 years and over by occupation, 2000
Managers & professionals	5,947
Service occupations	384
Sales & office occupations	1,714
Farming, fishing & forestry	21
Construction & maintenance	249
Production & transportation	217
Self-employed persons	446

‡ Branch of county library
* US Census Bureau
** New Jersey Department of Labor

General Information
Township of Montgomery
2261 Route 206
Belle Mead, NJ 08502
908-359-8211
Website	www.twp.montgomery.nj.us
Year of incorporation	1798
Land/water area (sq. miles)	32.62/0.00
Form of government	Township

Government
Legislative Districts
US Congressional	7
State Legislative	16

Local Officials, 2009
Mayor	Louise Wilson
Manager	Donato Nieman
Clerk	Donna Kukla
Finance Dir	Walter Sheppard
Tax Assessor	Eleanor Blake
Tax Collector	Randy Bahr
Attorney	Kristina Hadinger
Building	John Marold
Planning	Lori Savron
Engineering	Gail Smith
Public Works	Arthur Villano
Police Chief	Michael Beltranena
Fire/Emergency Dir	NA

Housing & Construction
Housing Units, 2000*
Total	6,130
Median rent	$1,196
Median SF home value	$348,500

Permits for New Residential Construction
	Units	Value
Total, 2006	6	$189,900
Single family	6	$189,900
Total, 2007	6	$990,000
Single family	6	$990,000

Real Property Valuation, 2008
	Parcels	Valuation
Total	7,310	$3,757,988,200
Vacant	450	46,051,500
Residential	6,340	3,234,092,100
Commercial	164	306,651,100
Industrial	1	3,112,900
Apartments	13	102,310,600
Farm land	234	2,096,700
Farm homestead	108	63,673,300

Average Property Value & Tax, 2008
Residential value	$511,440
Property tax	$12,856
Tax credit/rebate	$1,313

Public Library
served by Mary Jacobs Branch Library‡
64 Washington St
Rocky Hill, NJ 08553
609-924-7073
Branch Librarian	Helen Morris

Library statistics, 2007
see Somerset County profile
for library system statistics

Public Safety
Number of officers, 2007	31

Crime	2006	2007
Total crimes	244	216
Violent	4	4
Murder	0	0
Rape	2	0
Robbery	0	1
Aggravated assault	2	3
Non-violent	240	212
Burglary	69	61
Larceny	170	144
Vehicle theft	1	7
Domestic violence	62	71
Arson	1	0
Total crime rate	**10.7**	**9.3**
Violent	0.2	0.2
Non-violent	10.6	9.1

Public School District
(for school year 2007-08 except as noted)

Montgomery Township School District
1014 Route 601
Skillman, NJ 08558
(609) 466-7601
Superintendent	Earl Kim
Number of schools	5
Grade plan	K-12
Enrollment	5,241
Attendance rate, '06-07	96.9%
Dropout rate	0.1%
Students per teacher	11.9
Per pupil expenditure	$12,142
Median faculty salary	$53,400
Median administrator salary	$115,616
Grade 12 enrollment	411
High school graduation rate	99.5%

Assessment test results
(percent scoring at proficient or advanced level)
	Language	Math
NJASK-Grade 3	91.3%	90.9%
GEPA-Grade 8	86.4%	94.2%
HSPA-High School	96.1%	97.4%

SAT Score Averages, 2006-07
Pct tested	Math	Verbal	Writing
102%	596	579	580

Teacher Qualifications
Avg. years of experience	7
Highly-qualified teachers one subject/all subjects	100%/100%

No Child Left Behind
AYP, 2006-07	Meets Standards

Municipal Finance
State Aid Programs, 2009
Total aid	$1,891,780
CMPTRA	9,297
Energy tax receipts	1,796,766
Garden State Trust	641

General Budget, 2008
Total tax levy	$94,570,845
County levy	16,488,342
County taxes	13,232,986
County library	1,790,879
County health	0
County open space	1,464,477
School levy	65,289,894
Muni. levy	12,792,609
Misc. revenues	16,662,961

Taxes
Taxes	2006	2007	2008
General tax rate per $100	2.31	2.42	2.514
County equalization ratio	88.54	80	76.83
Net valuation taxable	$3,741,595,852	$3,734,641,139	$3,762,277,120
State equalized value	$4,681,849,888	$4,859,619,031	$5,124,163,852

See Introduction for an explanation of all data sources.

Demographics & Socio-Economic Characteristics

(2000 US Census, except as noted)

Population

1980*	7,318
1990*	6,946
2000	7,034
Male	3,466
Female	3,568
2007 (estimate)*	7,339
Population density	1,848.6

Race & Hispanic Origin, 2000

Race

White	6,527
Black/African American	31
American Indian/Alaska Native	6
Asian	377
Native Hawaiian/Pacific Islander	0
Other race	44
Two or more races	49
Hispanic origin, total	217
Mexican	36
Puerto Rican	41
Cuban	36
Other Hispanic	104

Age & Nativity, 2000

Under 5 years	490
18 years and over	5,209
21 years and over	5,043
65 years and over	884
85 years and over	75
Median age	39.7
Native-born	6,111
Foreign-born	923

Educational Attainment, 2000

Population 25 years and over	4,818
Less than 9th grade	0.9%
High school grad or higher	95.0%
Bachelor's degree or higher	55.3%
Graduate degree	20.0%

Income & Poverty, 1999

Per capita income	$45,448
Median household income	$93,031
Median family income	$104,047
Persons in poverty	62
H'holds receiving public assistance	0
H'holds receiving social security	567

Households, 2000

Total households	2,509
With persons under 18	984
With persons over 65	626
Family households	2,000
Single-person households	437
Persons per household	2.80
Persons per family	3.18

Labor & Employment

Total civilian labor force, 2007**	3,900
Unemployment rate	2.5%
Total civilian labor force, 2000	3,698
Unemployment rate	2.8%

Employed persons 16 years and over by occupation, 2000

Managers & professionals	1,989
Service occupations	300
Sales & office occupations	1,023
Farming, fishing & forestry	0
Construction & maintenance	125
Production & transportation	159
Self-employed persons	169

* US Census Bureau
** New Jersey Department of Labor

General Information

Borough of Montvale
12 Mercedes Dr
Montvale, NJ 07645
201-391-5700

Website	www.montvale.org
Year of incorporation	1894
Land/water area (sq. miles)	3.97/0.00
Form of government	Borough

Government

Legislative Districts

US Congressional	5
State Legislative	39

Local Officials, 2009

Mayor	Roger J. Fyfe
Manager	Maureen Iarossi-Alwan
Clerk	Maureen Iarossi-Alwan
Finance Dir	Carl Bello
Tax Assessor	Michael Leposky
Tax Collector	Julia Piraino
Attorney	Philip Boggia
Building	Michael Tabback
Planning	John DePinto
Engineering	Andrew Hipolit
Public Works	Robert Culvert
Police Chief	Joseph Marigliani
Emerg/Fire Director	Clinton Miller

Housing & Construction

Housing Units, 2000*

Total	2,590
Median rent	$1,116
Median SF home value	$346,400

Permits for New Residential Construction

	Units	Value
Total, 2006	54	$10,844,690
Single family	54	$10,844,690
Total, 2007	112	$16,877,950
Single family	112	$16,877,950

Real Property Valuation, 2008

	Parcels	Valuation
Total	2,832	$2,331,619,600
Vacant	189	51,808,600
Residential	2,507	1,641,992,200
Commercial	118	603,707,200
Industrial	6	13,075,000
Apartments	1	18,753,000
Farm land	8	37,600
Farm homestead	3	2,246,000

Average Property Value & Tax, 2008

Residential value	$655,075
Property tax	$9,900
Tax credit/rebate	$1,286

Public Library

Montvale Public Library
12 Mercedes Dr
Montvale, NJ 07645
201-391-5090

Director	Susan J. Ruttenber

Library statistics, 2007

Population served	7,034
Full-time/total staff	1/2

	Total	Per capita
Holdings	81,680	11.61
Revenues	$723,516	$102.86
Expenditures	$701,469	$99.73
Annual visits	79,892	11.36
Internet terminals/annual users	19/35,000	

Public Safety

Number of officers, 2007	22

Crime	2006	2007
Total crimes	63	71
Violent	2	2
Murder	0	0
Rape	1	0
Robbery	1	0
Aggravated assault	0	2
Non-violent	61	69
Burglary	3	8
Larceny	55	59
Vehicle theft	3	2
Domestic violence	9	7
Arson	0	0
Total crime rate	8.6	9.7
Violent	0.3	0.3
Non-violent	8.3	9.4

Public School District

(for school year 2007-08 except as noted)

Montvale School District
47 Spring Valley Road
Montvale, NJ 07645
(201) 391-1662

Superintendent	Lawrence Hughes (Int)
Number of schools	2
Grade plan	K-8
Enrollment	1,002
Attendance rate, '06-07	96.4%
Dropout rate	NA
Students per teacher	10.4
Per pupil expenditure	$13,115
Median faculty salary	$57,190
Median administrator salary	$128,310
Grade 12 enrollment	NA
High school graduation rate	NA

Assessment test results

(percent scoring at proficient or advanced level)

	Language	Math
NJASK-Grade 3	98.6%	97.0%
GEPA-Grade 8	87.4%	96.7%
HSPA-High School	NA	NA

SAT Score Averages, 2006-07

Pct tested	Math	Verbal	Writing
NA	NA	NA	NA

Teacher Qualifications

Avg. years of experience	8
Highly-qualified teachers one subject/all subjects	100%/100%

No Child Left Behind

AYP, 2006-07	Meets Standards

Municipal Finance

State Aid Programs, 2009

Total aid	$1,601,766
CMPTRA	0
Energy tax receipts	1,537,695
Garden State Trust	0

General Budget, 2008

Total tax levy	$35,282,441
County levy	3,964,645
County taxes	3,748,219
County library	0
County health	0
County open space	216,425
School levy	22,166,495
Muni. levy	9,151,301
Misc. revenues	6,118,021

Taxes

	2006	2007	2008
General tax rate per $100	1.4	1.45	1.514
County equalization ratio	117.18	110.29	108.35
Net valuation taxable	$2,262,446,400	$2,303,040,681	$2,334,579,166
State equalized value	$2,053,852,927	$2,125,754,113	$2,241,027,909

See Introduction for an explanation of all data sources.

Demographics & Socio-Economic Characteristics

(2000 US Census, except as noted)

Population

1980*	14,290
1990*	15,600
2000	20,839
Male	10,138
Female	10,701
2007 (estimate)*	21,150
Population density	1,120.8

Race & Hispanic Origin, 2000

Race
White	17,703
Black/African American	193
American Indian/Alaska Native	9
Asian	2,619
Native Hawaiian/Pacific Islander	4
Other race	74
Two or more races	237
Hispanic origin, total	531
Mexican	69
Puerto Rican	158
Cuban	75
Other Hispanic	229

Age & Nativity, 2000

Under 5 years	1,435
18 years and over	15,597
21 years and over	15,126
65 years and over	2,256
85 years and over	233
Median age	38.9
Native-born	17,251
Foreign-born	3,588

Educational Attainment, 2000

Population 25 years and over	14,445
Less than 9th grade	1.9%
High school grad or higher	93.5%
Bachelor's degree or higher	51.2%
Graduate degree	20.4%

Income & Poverty, 1999

Per capita income	$43,341
Median household income	$94,557
Median family income	$105,394
Persons in poverty	794
H'holds receiving public assistance	78
H'holds receiving social security	1,403

Households, 2000

Total households	7,380
With persons under 18	2,858
With persons over 65	1,542
Family households	5,869
Single-person households	1,225
Persons per household	2.80
Persons per family	3.17

Labor & Employment

Total civilian labor force, 2007**	12,431
Unemployment rate	1.8%
Total civilian labor force, 2000	11,412
Unemployment rate	2.0%

Employed persons 16 years and over by occupation, 2000
Managers & professionals	6,023
Service occupations	686
Sales & office occupations	3,205
Farming, fishing & forestry	0
Construction & maintenance	638
Production & transportation	637
Self-employed persons	783

General Information

Township of Montville
195 Changebridge Rd
Montville, NJ 07045
973-331-3300

Website	www.montvillenj.org
Year of incorporation	1867
Land/water area (sq. miles)	18.87/0.26
Form of government	Special Charter

Government

Legislative Districts

US Congressional	11
State Legislative	26

Local Officials, 2009

Mayor	Deborah Nielson
Manager	Frank Bastone
Clerk	Gertrude Atkinson
Finance Dir	Frances Vanderhoof
Tax Assessor	Thomas Lenhardt
Tax Collector	Francine Novak
Attorney	Martin Murphy
Building	Brian Laird
Planning	Linda White
Engineering	Anthony Barile Jr
Public Works	Thomas Mazzaccaro
Police Chief	Richard Cook
Fire/Emergency Dir	NA

Housing & Construction

Housing Units, 2000*

Total	7,541
Median rent	$1,186
Median SF home value	$346,600

Permits for New Residential Construction

	Units	Value
Total, 2006	37	$14,677,802
Single family	37	$14,677,802
Total, 2007	16	$7,470,550
Single family	16	$7,470,550

Real Property Valuation, 2008

	Parcels	Valuation
Total	7,776	$2,816,007,200
Vacant	367	52,196,600
Residential	6,979	2,322,318,300
Commercial	284	154,714,800
Industrial	81	235,076,800
Apartments	4	45,146,400
Farm land	40	177,800
Farm homestead	21	6,376,500

Average Property Value & Tax, 2008

Residential value	$332,671
Property tax	$10,413
Tax credit/rebate	$1,278

Public Library

Montville Township Public Library
90 Horseneck Rd
Montville, NJ 07045
973-402-0900

Director .... Patricia K. Anderson

Library statistics, 2007

Population served	20,839
Full-time/total staff	4/11

	Total	Per capita
Holdings	113,493	5.45
Revenues	$1,842,107	$88.40
Expenditures	$1,322,604	$63.47
Annual visits	160,108	7.68
Internet terminals/annual users	17/9,400	

Public Safety

Number of officers, 2007 42

Crime	2006	2007
Total crimes	239	236
Violent	8	12
Murder	1	0
Rape	0	0
Robbery	0	4
Aggravated assault	7	8
Non-violent	231	224
Burglary	41	48
Larceny	172	168
Vehicle theft	18	8
Domestic violence	91	72
Arson	2	3
Total crime rate	**11.2**	**11.0**
Violent	0.4	0.6
Non-violent	10.8	10.4

Public School District

(for school year 2007-08 except as noted)

Montville Township School District
328 Changebridge Road
Pine Brook, NJ 07058
(973) 331-7100

Superintendent	Gary Bowen
Number of schools	7
Grade plan	K-12
Enrollment	4,255
Attendance rate, '06-07	95.7%
Dropout rate	0.2%
Students per teacher	12.2
Per pupil expenditure	$14,334
Median faculty salary	$55,820
Median administrator salary	$115,186
Grade 12 enrollment	307
High school graduation rate	98.7%

Assessment test results

(percent scoring at proficient or advanced level)
	Language	Math
NJASK-Grade 3	97.1%	97.4%
GEPA-Grade 8	87.7%	95.5%
HSPA-High School	90.2%	97.3%

SAT Score Averages, 2006-07

Pct tested	Math	Verbal	Writing
94%	576	543	541

Teacher Qualifications

Avg. years of experience	10
Highly-qualified teachers one subject/all subjects	98.5%/98.5%

No Child Left Behind

AYP, 2006-07 .... Meets Standards

Municipal Finance

State Aid Programs, 2009

Total aid	$2,820,578
CMPTRA	0
Energy tax receipts	2,705,220
Garden State Trust	1,118

General Budget, 2008

Total tax levy	$88,255,602
County levy	12,640,395
County taxes	10,315,372
County library	0
County health	0
County open space	2,325,023
School levy	57,074,884
Muni. levy	18,540,323
Misc. revenues	10,160,536

Taxes

	2006	2007	2008
General tax rate per $100	2.9	3.03	3.131
County equalization ratio	59.71	54.54	51.94
Net valuation taxable	$2,793,921,300	$2,805,003,955	$2,819,459,017
State equalized value	$5,126,582,793	$5,397,182,605	$5,576,393,040

Demographics & Socio-Economic Characteristics
(2000 US Census, except as noted)

Population
1980*	2,706
1990*	2,817
2000	2,754
Male	1,355
Female	1,399
2007 (estimate)*	2,754
Population density	1,591.9

Race & Hispanic Origin, 2000
Race
White	2,359
Black/African American	26
American Indian/Alaska Native	3
Asian	183
Native Hawaiian/Pacific Islander	0
Other race	81
Two or more races	102
Hispanic origin, total	349
Mexican	22
Puerto Rican	88
Cuban	72
Other Hispanic	167

Age & Nativity, 2000
Under 5 years	131
18 years and over	2,179
21 years and over	2,090
65 years and over	422
85 years and over	35
Median age	40.4
Native-born	2,151
Foreign-born	603

Educational Attainment, 2000
Population 25 years and over	1,982
Less than 9th grade	10.0%
High school grad or higher	72.9%
Bachelor's degree or higher	13.2%
Graduate degree	3.2%

Income & Poverty, 1999
Per capita income	$24,654
Median household income	$50,571
Median family income	$62,163
Persons in poverty	104
H'holds receiving public assistance	19
H'holds receiving social security	322

Households, 2000
Total households	1,041
With persons under 18	333
With persons over 65	328
Family households	708
Single-person households	289
Persons per household	2.65
Persons per family	3.27

Labor & Employment
Total civilian labor force, 2007**	1,511
Unemployment rate	2.5%
Total civilian labor force, 2000	1,426
Unemployment rate	2.5%

Employed persons 16 years and over by occupation, 2000
Managers & professionals	312
Service occupations	176
Sales & office occupations	513
Farming, fishing & forestry	0
Construction & maintenance	134
Production & transportation	255
Self-employed persons	66

* US Census Bureau
** New Jersey Department of Labor

General Information
Borough of Moonachie
70 Moonachie Rd
Moonachie, NJ 07074
201-641-1813
Website	www.moonachie.us
Year of incorporation	1910
Land/water area (sq. miles)	1.73/0.00
Form of government	Borough

Government
Legislative Districts
US Congressional	9
State Legislative	36

Local Officials, 2009
Mayor	Frederick Dressel
Manager	Anthony Ciannamea
Clerk	Supriya Sanyal
Finance Dir	Paul Hansen
Tax Assessor	Paul Barbire
Tax Collector	Elizabeth Bassani
Attorney	Frank Migliorino
Building	Michael Sartori
Comm Dev/Planning	NA
Engineering	Kevin Boswell
Public Works	Mary Ellen Lyons
Police Chief	Michael McGahn
Emerg/Fire Director	Justin Derevyanik

Housing & Construction
Housing Units, 2000*
Total	1,074
Median rent	$851
Median SF home value	$192,900

Permits for New Residential Construction
	Units	Value
Total, 2006	5	$970,950
Single family	5	$970,950
Total, 2007	7	$1,576,510
Single family	7	$1,576,510

Real Property Valuation, 2008
	Parcels	Valuation
Total	799	$797,187,390
Vacant	21	10,872,600
Residential	598	231,640,090
Commercial	40	66,137,200
Industrial	140	488,537,500
Apartments	0	0
Farm land	0	0
Farm homestead	0	0

Average Property Value & Tax, 2008
Residential value	$387,358
Property tax	$6,352
Tax credit/rebate	$1,037

Public Library
No public municipal library

Library statistics, 2007
Population served	NA
Full-time/total staff	NA/NA

	Total	Per capita
Holdings	NA	NA
Revenues	NA	NA
Expenditures	NA	NA
Annual visits	NA	NA
Internet terminals/annual users	NA/NA	

Public Safety
Number of officers, 2007	19

Crime	2006	2007
Total crimes	91	93
Violent	2	3
Murder	0	0
Rape	0	0
Robbery	0	1
Aggravated assault	2	2
Non-violent	89	90
Burglary	10	16
Larceny	67	64
Vehicle theft	12	10
Domestic violence	26	23
Arson	0	1
Total crime rate	32.4	33.2
Violent	0.7	1.1
Non-violent	31.7	32.2

Public School District
(for school year 2007-08 except as noted)

Moonachie School District
20 West Park Street
Moonachie, NJ 07074
(201) 641-5833
Superintendent	Mark Solimo
Number of schools	1
Grade plan	K-8
Enrollment	268
Attendance rate, '06-07	95.0%
Dropout rate	NA
Students per teacher	9.5
Per pupil expenditure	$17,290
Median faculty salary	$61,603
Median administrator salary	$118,988
Grade 12 enrollment	NA
High school graduation rate	NA

Assessment test results
(percent scoring at proficient or advanced level)
	Language	Math
NJASK-Grade 3	94.5%	77.8%
GEPA-Grade 8	74.3%	88.6%
HSPA-High School	NA	NA

SAT Score Averages, 2006-07
Pct tested	Math	Verbal	Writing
NA	NA	NA	NA

Teacher Qualifications
Avg. years of experience	19
Highly-qualified teachers one subject/all subjects	100%/100%

No Child Left Behind
AYP, 2006-07	Meets Standards

Municipal Finance
State Aid Programs, 2009
Total aid	$595,894
CMPTRA	17,571
Energy tax receipts	558,956
Garden State Trust	0

General Budget, 2008
Total tax levy	$13,090,178
County levy	1,519,973
County taxes	1,436,512
County library	0
County health	0
County open space	83,461
School levy	6,311,060
Muni. levy	5,259,145
Misc. revenues	2,767,340

Taxes	2006	2007	2008
General tax rate per $100	1.43	1.52	1.641
County equalization ratio	109.71	102.21	96.74
Net valuation taxable	$803,280,460	$804,469,433	$798,306,681
State equalized value	$787,004,696	$831,541,623	$836,833,087

See Introduction for an explanation of all data sources.

Demographics & Socio-Economic Characteristics
(2000 US Census, except as noted)

Population
1980*	15,596
1990*	16,116
2000	19,017
Male	8,974
Female	10,043
2007 (estimate)*	19,624
Population density	1,328.6

Race & Hispanic Origin, 2000
Race
White	16,962
Black/African American	1,082
American Indian/Alaska Native	30
Asian	621
Native Hawaiian/Pacific Islander	1
Other race	81
Two or more races	240
Hispanic origin, total	332
Mexican	49
Puerto Rican	140
Cuban	26
Other Hispanic	117

Age & Nativity, 2000
Under 5 years	1,218
18 years and over	13,797
21 years and over	13,363
65 years and over	3,120
85 years and over	557
Median age	40.9
Native-born	17,906
Foreign-born	1,111

Educational Attainment, 2000
Population 25 years and over	12,946
Less than 9th grade	2.7%
High school grad or higher	92.5%
Bachelor's degree or higher	52.5%
Graduate degree	23.2%

Income & Poverty, 1999
Per capita income	$42,154
Median household income	$78,826
Median family income	$94,844
Persons in poverty	634
H'holds receiving public assistance	71
H'holds receiving social security	2,048

Households, 2000
Total households	6,971
With persons under 18	2,697
With persons over 65	2,005
Family households	5,273
Single-person households	1,461
Persons per household	2.68
Persons per family	3.13

Labor & Employment
Total civilian labor force, 2007**	10,246
Unemployment rate	2.9%
Total civilian labor force, 2000	8,973
Unemployment rate	3.0%

Employed persons 16 years and over by occupation, 2000
Managers & professionals	4,877
Service occupations	599
Sales & office occupations	2,279
Farming, fishing & forestry	12
Construction & maintenance	347
Production & transportation	590
Self-employed persons	711

General Information
Township of Moorestown
111 W 2nd St
Moorestown, NJ 08057
856-235-0912
Website	www.moorestown.nj.us
Year of incorporation	1922
Land/water area (sq. miles)	14.77/0.16
Form of government	Council-Manager

Government
Legislative Districts
US Congressional	3
State Legislative	8

Local Officials, 2009
Mayor	Daniel Roccato
Manager	Christopher J. Schultz
Clerk	Patricia Hunt
Finance Dir	Thomas Merchel
Tax Assessor	Dennis DeKlerk
Tax Collector	Dorothy Samartino
Attorney	Thomas J. Coleman III
Building	Steven Holmes
Community Dev	Thomas Ford (Actg)
Engineering	Alaimo Group
Public Works	Kenneth Ewers
Police Chief	Harry Johnson
Fire Chief	W. Ruggiano

Housing & Construction
Housing Units, 2000*
Total	7,211
Median rent	$843
Median SF home value	$254,900

Permits for New Residential Construction
	Units	Value
Total, 2006	57	$9,739,529
Single family	41	$9,356,715
Total, 2007	27	$5,962,400
Single family	24	$5,694,317

Real Property Valuation, 2008
	Parcels	Valuation
Total	7,367	$4,730,150,600
Vacant	348	72,511,500
Residential	6,500	3,499,299,600
Commercial	275	642,931,600
Industrial	88	380,922,900
Apartments	24	95,993,700
Farm land	96	745,700
Farm homestead	36	37,745,600

Average Property Value & Tax, 2008
Residential value	$541,164
Property tax	$9,963
Tax credit/rebate	$1,095

Public Library
Moorestown Public Library
111 W Second St
Moorestown, NJ 08057
856-234-0333
Director	Joseph Galbraith

Library statistics, 2007
Population served	19,017
Full-time/total staff	5/13

	Total	Per capita
Holdings	149,666	7.87
Revenues	$1,653,006	$86.92
Expenditures	$1,447,083	$76.09
Annual visits	115,662	6.08
Internet terminals/annual users	10/17,967	

Public Safety
Number of officers, 2007	38

Crime	2006	2007
Total crimes	462	441
Violent	21	22
Murder	0	0
Rape	4	4
Robbery	6	5
Aggravated assault	11	13
Non-violent	441	419
Burglary	53	52
Larceny	379	351
Vehicle theft	9	16
Domestic violence	64	50
Arson	1	1
Total crime rate	23.1	22.1
Violent	1.0	1.1
Non-violent	22.0	21.0

Public School District
(for school year 2007-08 except as noted)

Moorestown Township School District
803 N. Stanwick Road
Moorestown, NJ 08057
(856) 778-6600
Superintendent	John Bach
Number of schools	6
Grade plan	K-12
Enrollment	4,399
Attendance rate, '06-07	96.0%
Dropout rate	0.1%
Students per teacher	11.1
Per pupil expenditure	$13,318
Median faculty salary	$53,752
Median administrator salary	$109,309
Grade 12 enrollment	330
High school graduation rate	98.8%

Assessment test results
(percent scoring at proficient or advanced level)
	Language	Math
NJASK-Grade 3	96.2%	93.7%
GEPA-Grade 8	84.9%	90.0%
HSPA-High School	89.9%	90.3%

SAT Score Averages, 2006-07
Pct tested	Math	Verbal	Writing
109%	561	550	546

Teacher Qualifications
Avg. years of experience	10
Highly-qualified teachers one subject/all subjects	99.5%/99.5%

No Child Left Behind
AYP, 2006-07	Meets Standards

Municipal Finance
State Aid Programs, 2009
Total aid	$2,444,470
CMPTRA	569,512
Energy tax receipts	1,774,006
Garden State Trust	3,018

General Budget, 2008
Total tax levy	$87,372,425
County levy	16,007,078
County taxes	14,223,309
County library	0
County health	0
County open space	1,783,769
School levy	57,583,936
Muni. levy	13,781,411
Misc. revenues	10,757,206

Taxes
	2006	2007	2008
General tax rate per $100	4.227	4.379	1.842
County equalization ratio	52.23	47.57	106.83
Net valuation taxable	$1,923,129,200	$1,941,169,706	$4,745,713,428
State equalized value	$4,050,655,867	$4,402,499,779	$4,607,050,500

* US Census Bureau
** New Jersey Department of Labor

See Introduction for an explanation of all data sources.

Demographics & Socio-Economic Characteristics

(2000 US Census, except as noted)

Population

1980*	5,305
1990*	5,219
2000	5,236
Male	2,512
Female	2,724
2007 (estimate)*	5,534
Population density	2,136.7

Race & Hispanic Origin, 2000

Race

White	4,865
Black/African American	70
American Indian/Alaska Native	3
Asian	226
Native Hawaiian/Pacific Islander	5
Other race	21
Two or more races	46
Hispanic origin, total	141
Mexican	28
Puerto Rican	31
Cuban	13
Other Hispanic	69

Age & Nativity, 2000

Under 5 years	379
18 years and over	4,003
21 years and over	3,913
65 years and over	848
85 years and over	127
Median age	40.7
Native-born	4,730
Foreign-born	506

Educational Attainment, 2000

Population 25 years and over	3,777
Less than 9th grade	1.9%
High school grad or higher	94.3%
Bachelor's degree or higher	51.0%
Graduate degree	21.5%

Income & Poverty, 1999

Per capita income	$36,553
Median household income	$84,806
Median family income	$98,333
Persons in poverty	124
H'holds receiving public assistance	0
H'holds receiving social security	573

Households, 2000

Total households	1,955
With persons under 18	679
With persons over 65	547
Family households	1,478
Single-person households	386
Persons per household	2.63
Persons per family	3.05

Labor & Employment

Total civilian labor force, 2007**	2,996
Unemployment rate	3.4%
Total civilian labor force, 2000	2,728
Unemployment rate	3.1%

Employed persons 16 years and over by occupation, 2000

Managers & professionals	1,496
Service occupations	235
Sales & office occupations	669
Farming, fishing & forestry	0
Construction & maintenance	147
Production & transportation	96
Self-employed persons	168

* US Census Bureau
** New Jersey Department of Labor

General Information

Borough of Morris Plains
531 Speedwell Ave
Morris Plains, NJ 07950
973-538-2224

Website	www.morrisplainsboro.org
Year of incorporation	1926
Land/water area (sq. miles)	2.59/0.02
Form of government	Borough

Government

Legislative Districts

US Congressional	11
State Legislative	26

Local Officials, 2009

Mayor	Frank J. Druetzler
Manager/Admin	NA
Clerk	June Uhrin
Finance Dir	David Banks
Tax Assessor	Allan W. Adams
Tax Collector	Ana Thomas
Attorney	Gail Fraser
Building	Edward Easse
Planning	William Denzler
Municipal Engineer	Leon C. Hall
Public Works	Joseph Signorelli Jr
Police Chief	James Abbondanzo
Emerg/Fire Director	Michael Geary

Housing & Construction

Housing Units, 2000*

Total	1,994
Median rent	$1,045
Median SF home value	$282,500

Permits for New Residential Construction

	Units	Value
Total, 2006	43	$6,096,324
Single family	11	$4,540,580
Total, 2007	51	$6,103,806
Single family	9	$4,061,892

Real Property Valuation, 2008

	Parcels	Valuation
Total	2,223	$773,908,370
Vacant	186	4,603,600
Residential	1,937	456,506,370
Commercial	96	250,380,800
Industrial	3	52,005,000
Apartments	1	10,412,600
Farm land	0	0
Farm homestead	0	0

Average Property Value & Tax, 2008

Residential value	$235,677
Property tax	$7,451
Tax credit/rebate	$1,098

Public Library

Morris Plains Public Library
77 Glenbrook Rd
Morris Plains, NJ 07950
973-538-2599

Director	Camille Garretson (Int)

Library statistics, 2007

Population served	5,236
Full-time/total staff	0/0

	Total	Per capita
Holdings	24,539	4.69
Revenues	$120,019	$22.92
Expenditures	$112,362	$21.46
Annual visits	20,000	3.82
Internet terminals/annual users	4/5,000	

Public Safety

Number of officers, 2007 17

Crime	2006	2007
Total crimes	83	71
Violent	5	4
Murder	0	0
Rape	0	0
Robbery	2	4
Aggravated assault	3	0
Non-violent	78	67
Burglary	11	6
Larceny	60	58
Vehicle theft	7	3
Domestic violence	31	25
Arson	2	0
Total crime rate	14.7	12.7
Violent	0.9	0.7
Non-violent	13.9	12.0

Public School District

(for school year 2007-08 except as noted)

Morris Plains School District
500 Speedwell Avenue
Morris Plains, NJ 07950
(973) 538-1650

Superintendent	Vicki Pede
Number of schools	2
Grade plan	K-8
Enrollment	614
Attendance rate, '06-07	96.1%
Dropout rate	NA
Students per teacher	9.9
Per pupil expenditure	$16,172
Median faculty salary	$50,888
Median administrator salary	$120,181
Grade 12 enrollment	NA
High school graduation rate	NA

Assessment test results

(percent scoring at proficient or advanced level)

	Language	Math
NJASK-Grade 3	96.7%	93.5%
GEPA-Grade 8	80.9%	96.8%
HSPA-High School	NA	NA

SAT Score Averages, 2006-07

Pct tested	Math	Verbal	Writing
NA	NA	NA	NA

Teacher Qualifications

Avg. years of experience	7
Highly-qualified teachers one subject/all subjects	100%/100%

No Child Left Behind

AYP, 2006-07	Meets Standards

Municipal Finance

State Aid Programs, 2009

Total aid	$812,950
CMPTRA	136,535
Energy tax receipts	649,994
Garden State Trust	0

General Budget, 2008

Total tax levy	$24,501,976
County levy	3,528,603
County taxes	2,879,800
County library	0
County health	0
County open space	648,804
School levy	12,461,191
Muni. levy	8,512,182
Misc. revenues	3,173,577

Taxes	2006	2007	2008
General tax rate per $100	2.88	3.05	3.162
County equalization ratio	57.34	48.41	51.31
Net valuation taxable	$778,999,850	$776,136,704	$775,043,933
State equalized value	$1,610,225,277	$1,511,662,657	$1,574,439,832

See Introduction for an explanation of all data sources.

Demographics & Socio-Economic Characteristics
(2000 US Census, except as noted)

Population
1980*	18,486
1990*	19,952
2000	21,796
Male	10,287
Female	11,509
2007 (estimate)*	21,103
Population density	1,339.0

Race & Hispanic Origin, 2000
Race
White	19,317
Black/African American	1,189
American Indian/Alaska Native	33
Asian	849
Native Hawaiian/Pacific Islander	3
Other race	199
Two or more races	206
Hispanic origin, total	830
Mexican	62
Puerto Rican	157
Cuban	56
Other Hispanic	555

Age & Nativity, 2000
Under 5 years	1,563
18 years and over	16,846
21 years and over	16,247
65 years and over	3,356
85 years and over	457
Median age	40.9
Native-born	19,460
Foreign-born	2,336

Educational Attainment, 2000
Population 25 years and over	15,565
Less than 9th grade	1.9%
High school grad or higher	95.1%
Bachelor's degree or higher	63.6%
Graduate degree	29.6%

Income & Poverty, 1999
Per capita income	$54,782
Median household income	$101,902
Median family income	$116,866
Persons in poverty	802
H'holds receiving public assistance	49
H'holds receiving social security	2,075

Households, 2000
Total households	8,116
With persons under 18	2,639
With persons over 65	2,088
Family households	5,953
Single-person households	1,766
Persons per household	2.55
Persons per family	2.99

Labor & Employment
Total civilian labor force, 2007**	12,198
Unemployment rate	3.0%
Total civilian labor force, 2000	11,579
Unemployment rate	4.2%

Employed persons 16 years and over by occupation, 2000
Managers & professionals	6,956
Service occupations	736
Sales & office occupations	2,660
Farming, fishing & forestry	0
Construction & maintenance	407
Production & transportation	330
Self-employed persons	820

General Information
Township of Morris
50 Woodland Ave
PO Box 7603
Convent Station, NJ 07961
973-326-7430

Website	www.morristwp.com
Year of incorporation	1740
Land/water area (sq. miles)	15.76/0.05
Form of government	Township

Government
Legislative Districts
US Congressional	11
State Legislative	25

Local Officials, 2009
Mayor	H. Scott Rosenbush
Manager	Fred Rossi
Clerk	Cathleen Amelio
Finance Dir	Julia Hasbrouck
Tax Assessor	Sue Aceto
Tax Collector	Audrey Adams
Attorney	John Mills III
Building	Albert Mastrobatista
Comm Dev/Planning	NA
Engineering	James Slate
Public Works	James Stoia
Police Chief	Timothy Quinn
Emerg/Fire Director	Craig Goss

Housing & Construction
Housing Units, 2000*
Total	8,298
Median rent	$1,040
Median SF home value	$350,400

Permits for New Residential Construction
	Units	Value
Total, 2006	18	$7,437,057
Single family	18	$7,437,057
Total, 2007	120	$7,821,290
Single family	120	$7,821,290

Real Property Valuation, 2008
	Parcels	Valuation
Total	8,044	$3,761,317,050
Vacant	258	26,290,650
Residential	7,606	3,000,337,500
Commercial	142	551,095,200
Industrial	21	146,472,000
Apartments	4	31,165,000
Farm land	8	48,300
Farm homestead	5	5,908,400

Average Property Value & Tax, 2008
Residential value	$394,987
Property tax	$8,939
Tax credit/rebate	$1,114

Public Library
Morristown & Morris Township Library‡
1 Miller Rd
Morristown, NJ 07960
973-538-6161

Director	Susan H. Gulick

Library statistics, 2007
Population served	40,340
Full-time/total staff	13/24

	Total	Per capita
Holdings	228,853	5.67
Revenues	$3,040,677	$75.38
Expenditures	$2,946,434	$73.04
Annual visits	389,726	9.66
Internet terminals/annual users	28/43,550	

Public Safety
Number of officers, 2007	43

Crime	2006	2007
Total crimes	219	159
Violent	38	30
Murder	0	0
Rape	4	4
Robbery	3	3
Aggravated assault	31	23
Non-violent	181	129
Burglary	31	23
Larceny	135	97
Vehicle theft	15	9
Domestic violence	78	78
Arson	0	2
Total crime rate	10.2	7.4
Violent	1.8	1.4
Non-violent	8.4	6.0

Public School District
(for school year 2007-08 except as noted)

Morris School District
31 Hazel Street
Morristown, NJ 07960
(973) 292-2300

Superintendent	Thomas Ficarra
Number of schools	10
Grade plan	K-12
Enrollment	4,569
Attendance rate, '06-07	95.6%
Dropout rate	1.5%
Students per teacher	9.5
Per pupil expenditure	$18,850
Median faculty salary	$66,409
Median administrator salary	$116,277
Grade 12 enrollment	347
High school graduation rate	96.6%

Assessment test results
(percent scoring at proficient or advanced level)
	Language	Math
NJASK-Grade 3	86.5%	87.4%
GEPA-Grade 8	74.8%	84.5%
HSPA-High School	77.7%	84.3%

SAT Score Averages, 2006-07
Pct tested	Math	Verbal	Writing
88%	534	533	526

Teacher Qualifications
Avg. years of experience	9
Highly-qualified teachers one subject/all subjects	100%/100%

No Child Left Behind
AYP, 2006-07	Meets Standards

Municipal Finance
State Aid Programs, 2009
Total aid	$4,463,280
CMPTRA	1,830,906
Energy tax receipts	2,453,797
Garden State Trust	48

General Budget, 2008
Total tax levy	$85,224,650
County levy	12,760,345
County taxes	10,416,471
County library	0
County health	0
County open space	2,343,875
School levy	51,585,180
Muni. levy	20,879,124
Misc. revenues	12,987,551

Taxes
	2006	2007	2008
General tax rate per $100	2.13	2.21	2.264
County equalization ratio	75.78	68.24	67.62
Net valuation taxable	$3,817,346,850	$3,819,837,079	$3,765,860,825
State equalized value	$5,597,988,850	$5,646,899,098	$5,844,191,423

‡ Joint library with Morristown
* US Census Bureau
** New Jersey Department of Labor

See Introduction for an explanation of all data sources.

Demographics & Socio-Economic Characteristics
(2000 US Census, except as noted)

Population
1980*	16,614
1990*	16,189
2000	18,544
Male	9,302
Female	9,242
2007 (estimate)*	19,122
Population density	6,504.1

Race & Hispanic Origin, 2000
Race
White	12,452
Black/African American	3,144
American Indian/Alaska Native	41
Asian	700
Native Hawaiian/Pacific Islander	12
Other race	1,572
Two or more races	623
Hispanic origin, total	5,034
Mexican	139
Puerto Rican	286
Cuban	50
Other Hispanic	4,559

Age & Nativity, 2000
Under 5 years	1,026
18 years and over	15,140
21 years and over	14,576
65 years and over	2,292
85 years and over	406
Median age	35.0
Native-born	12,528
Foreign-born	6,016

Educational Attainment, 2000
Population 25 years and over	13,604
Less than 9th grade	7.6%
High school grad or higher	83.0%
Bachelor's degree or higher	39.3%
Graduate degree	16.0%

Income & Poverty, 1999
Per capita income	$30,086
Median household income	$57,563
Median family income	$66,419
Persons in poverty	2,069
H'holds receiving public assistance	125
H'holds receiving social security	1,565

Households, 2000
Total households	7,252
With persons under 18	1,875
With persons over 65	1,574
Family households	3,700
Single-person households	2,805
Persons per household	2.43
Persons per family	3.19

Labor & Employment
Total civilian labor force, 2007**	11,554
Unemployment rate	3.1%
Total civilian labor force, 2000	10,747
Unemployment rate	3.4%

Employed persons 16 years and over by occupation, 2000
Managers & professionals	4,303
Service occupations	2,226
Sales & office occupations	2,144
Farming, fishing & forestry	42
Construction & maintenance	722
Production & transportation	947
Self-employed persons	387

‡ Joint library with Morris Township
* US Census Bureau
** New Jersey Department of Labor

See Introduction for an explanation of all data sources.

General Information
Town of Morristown
200 South St
PO Box 914
Morristown, NJ 07963
973-292-6600

Website	www.townofmorristown.org
Year of incorporation	1865
Land/water area (sq. miles)	2.94/0.06
Form of government	Mayor-Council

Government
Legislative Districts
US Congressional	11
State Legislative	25

Local Officials, 2009
Mayor	Donald Cresitello
Manager	Michael Rogers
Clerk	Matthew Stechauner
Finance Dir	Bob Calise
Tax Assessor	Pat Aceto
Tax Collector	NA
Attorney	Jonathan Williams
Building	Fritz Reuss
Planning	Michael D'Altilio
Engineering	Jeffrey Hartke
Public Works	Rick Wise
Police Chief	Peter Demnitz
Emerg/Fire Director	Robert Taylor

Housing & Construction
Housing Units, 2000*
Total	7,615
Median rent	$914
Median SF home value	$224,400

Permits for New Residential Construction
	Units	Value
Total, 2006	307	$54,295,400
Single family	2	$253,275
Total, 2007	129	$9,677,975
Single family	5	$1,480,482

Real Property Valuation, 2008
	Parcels	Valuation
Total	4,213	$2,257,983,942
Vacant	217	49,435,100
Residential	3,382	1,195,501,242
Commercial	533	824,460,800
Industrial	10	11,665,100
Apartments	71	176,921,700
Farm land	0	0
Farm homestead	0	0

Average Property Value & Tax, 2008
Residential value	$353,489
Property tax	$8,298
Tax credit/rebate	$1,201

Public Library
Morristown & Morris Township Library‡
1 Miller Rd
Morristown, NJ 07960
973-538-6161

Director	Susan H. Gulick

Library statistics, 2007
Population served	40,340
Full-time/total staff	13/24

	Total	Per capita
Holdings	228,853	5.67
Revenues	$3,040,677	$75.38
Expenditures	$2,946,434	$73.04
Annual visits	389,726	9.66
Internet terminals/annual users	28/43,550	

Public Safety
Number of officers, 2007	61

Crime	2006	2007
Total crimes	835	623
Violent	107	122
Murder	0	0
Rape	3	1
Robbery	37	56
Aggravated assault	67	65
Non-violent	728	501
Burglary	111	73
Larceny	581	411
Vehicle theft	36	17
Domestic violence	259	231
Arson	3	4
Total crime rate	44.3	32.9
Violent	5.7	6.4
Non-violent	38.6	26.5

Public School District
(for school year 2007-08 except as noted)

Morris School District
31 Hazel Street
Morristown, NJ 07960
(973) 292-2300

Superintendent	Thomas Ficarra
Number of schools	10
Grade plan	K-12
Enrollment	4,569
Attendance rate, '06-07	95.6%
Dropout rate	1.5%
Students per teacher	9.5
Per pupil expenditure	$18,850
Median faculty salary	$66,409
Median administrator salary	$116,277
Grade 12 enrollment	347
High school graduation rate	96.6%

Assessment test results
(percent scoring at proficient or advanced level)
	Language	Math
NJASK-Grade 3	86.5%	87.4%
GEPA-Grade 8	74.8%	84.5%
HSPA-High School	77.7%	84.3%

SAT Score Averages, 2006-07
Pct tested	Math	Verbal	Writing
88%	534	533	526

Teacher Qualifications
Avg. years of experience	9
Highly-qualified teachers	
one subject/all subjects	100%/100%

No Child Left Behind
AYP, 2006-07	Meets Standards

Municipal Finance
State Aid Programs, 2009
Total aid	$3,698,495
CMPTRA	720,239
Energy tax receipts	2,885,794
Garden State Trust	0

General Budget, 2008
Total tax levy	$53,352,508
County levy	6,777,737
County taxes	5,532,548
County library	0
County health	0
County open space	1,245,189
School levy	24,953,163
Muni. levy	21,621,608
Misc. revenues	16,193,197

Taxes
	2006	2007	2008
General tax rate per $100	2.24	2.28	2.348
County equalization ratio	91.64	85.15	76.26
Net valuation taxable	$2,197,622,042	$2,213,619,563	$2,272,701,864
State equalized value	$2,597,234,591	$2,897,676,843	$3,163,050,245

Demographics & Socio-Economic Characteristics

(2000 US Census, except as noted)

Population
1980*	4,251
1990*	3,630
2000	4,663
Male	2,216
Female	2,447
2007 (estimate)*	5,698
Population density	2,700.5

Race & Hispanic Origin, 2000
Race
White	4,263
Black/African American	85
American Indian/Alaska Native	9
Asian	178
Native Hawaiian/Pacific Islander	2
Other race	59
Two or more races	67
Hispanic origin, total	212
Mexican	16
Puerto Rican	68
Cuban	15
Other Hispanic	113

Age & Nativity, 2000
Under 5 years	310
18 years and over	3,634
21 years and over	3,526
65 years and over	496
85 years and over	30
Median age	37.9
Native-born	4,207
Foreign-born	456

Educational Attainment, 2000
Population 25 years and over	3,408
Less than 9th grade	2.4%
High school grad or higher	90.4%
Bachelor's degree or higher	35.9%
Graduate degree	11.2%

Income & Poverty, 1999
Per capita income	$32,222
Median household income	$67,213
Median family income	$79,514
Persons in poverty	153
H'holds receiving public assistance	22
H'holds receiving social security	392

Households, 2000
Total households	1,918
With persons under 18	576
With persons over 65	374
Family households	1,263
Single-person households	535
Persons per household	2.42
Persons per family	2.99

Labor & Employment
Total civilian labor force, 2007**	2,984
Unemployment rate	3.1%
Total civilian labor force, 2000	2,738
Unemployment rate	3.0%

Employed persons 16 years and over by occupation, 2000
Managers & professionals	999
Service occupations	276
Sales & office occupations	870
Farming, fishing & forestry	0
Construction & maintenance	266
Production & transportation	246
Self-employed persons	188

General Information
Borough of Mount Arlington
419 Howard Blvd
Mount Arlington, NJ 07856
973-398-6832
Website	www.ci.mount-arlington.nj.us
Year of incorporation	1890
Land/water area (sq. miles)	2.11/0.72
Form of government	Borough

Government
Legislative Districts
US Congressional	11
State Legislative	25

Local Officials, 2009
Mayor	Arthur R. Ondish
Manager	JoAnne Sendler
Clerk	Linda DeSantis
CFO	Monica Goscicki
Tax Assessor	John Marchione
Tax Collector	Patricia Simari
Attorney	Scarinci & Hollenbeck
Building	Sandor Nyari
Comm Dev/Planning	NA
Engineering	Daren Phil
Public Works	Paul Nelson
Police Chief	Richard Peterson
Emerg/Fire Director	Steve Norman

Housing & Construction
Housing Units, 2000*
Total	2,039
Median rent	$831
Median SF home value	$183,700

Permits for New Residential Construction
	Units	Value
Total, 2006	94	$6,292,661
Single family	21	$2,301,115
Total, 2007	76	$4,838,477
Single family	19	$2,090,205

Real Property Valuation, 2008
	Parcels	Valuation
Total	2,261	$690,702,900
Vacant	207	17,062,800
Residential	1,991	583,095,900
Commercial	46	69,103,400
Industrial	1	234,200
Apartments	7	21,200,000
Farm land	9	6,600
Farm homestead	0	0

Average Property Value & Tax, 2008
Residential value	$292,866
Property tax	$6,240
Tax credit/rebate	$931

Public Library
Mt Arlington Public Library
333 Howard Blvd
Mount Arlington, NJ 07856
973-398-1516
Director	James Garland

Library statistics, 2007
Population served	4,256
Full-time/total staff	0/3

	Total	Per capita
Holdings	28,962	6.80
Revenues	$278,045	$65.33
Expenditures	$260,708	$61.26
Annual visits	27,000	6.34
Internet terminals/annual users	3/2,400	

Public Safety
Number of officers, 2007	13

Crime	2006	2007
Total crimes	58	59
Violent	4	3
Murder	0	0
Rape	0	0
Robbery	0	0
Aggravated assault	4	3
Non-violent	54	56
Burglary	12	13
Larceny	38	43
Vehicle theft	4	0
Domestic violence	79	63
Arson	0	0
Total crime rate	10.9	10.3
Violent	0.8	0.5
Non-violent	10.1	9.8

Public School District
(for school year 2007-08 except as noted)

Mount Arlington School District
446 Howard Boulevard
Mount Arlington, NJ 07856
(973) 398-6400
Superintendent	Jane Mullins Jameson
Number of schools	2
Grade plan	K-8
Enrollment	390
Attendance rate, '06-07	94.6%
Dropout rate	NA
Students per teacher	9.6
Per pupil expenditure	$15,556
Median faculty salary	$53,130
Median administrator salary	$93,600
Grade 12 enrollment	NA
High school graduation rate	NA

Assessment test results
(percent scoring at proficient or advanced level)
	Language	Math
NJASK-Grade 3	90.3%	96.8%
GEPA-Grade 8	78.3%	95.6%
HSPA-High School	NA	NA

SAT Score Averages, 2006-07
Pct tested	Math	Verbal	Writing
NA	NA	NA	NA

Teacher Qualifications
Avg. years of experience	6
Highly-qualified teachers one subject/all subjects	100%/100%

No Child Left Behind
AYP, 2006-07	Meets Standards

Municipal Finance
State Aid Programs, 2009
Total aid	$436,646
CMPTRA	47,159
Energy tax receipts	378,557
Garden State Trust	11

General Budget, 2008
Total tax levy	$14,732,649
County levy	1,995,165
County taxes	1,628,349
County library	0
County health	0
County open space	366,815
School levy	8,784,211
Muni. levy	3,953,274
Misc. revenues	4,413,202

Taxes
General tax rate per $100	2006	2007	2008
General tax rate per $100	1.81	1.94	2.131
County equalization ratio	91.85	82.05	80.25
Net valuation taxable	$672,017,300	$692,720,330	$691,403,688
State equalized value	$819,790,869	$863,033,329	$855,848,615

See Introduction for an explanation of all data sources.

Demographics & Socio-Economic Characteristics

(2000 US Census, except as noted)

Population

1980*	4,863
1990*	4,517
2000	4,495
Male	2,173
Female	2,322
2007 (estimate)*	4,389
Population density	4,987.5

Race & Hispanic Origin, 2000

Race

White	4,383
Black/African American	18
American Indian/Alaska Native	3
Asian	28
Native Hawaiian/Pacific Islander	1
Other race	29
Two or more races	33
Hispanic origin, total	89
Mexican	5
Puerto Rican	67
Cuban	5
Other Hispanic	12

Age & Nativity, 2000

Under 5 years	257
18 years and over	3,491
21 years and over	3,345
65 years and over	804
85 years and over	72
Median age	39.6
Native-born	4,395
Foreign-born	100

Educational Attainment, 2000

Population 25 years and over	3,184
Less than 9th grade	5.5%
High school grad or higher	78.5%
Bachelor's degree or higher	13.3%
Graduate degree	3.4%

Income & Poverty, 1999

Per capita income	$21,150
Median household income	$44,824
Median family income	$59,468
Persons in poverty	219
H'holds receiving public assistance	39
H'holds receiving social security	671

Households, 2000

Total households	1,818
With persons under 18	541
With persons over 65	620
Family households	1,175
Single-person households	556
Persons per household	2.46
Persons per family	3.13

Labor & Employment

Total civilian labor force, 2007**	2,416
Unemployment rate	5.1%
Total civilian labor force, 2000	2,286
Unemployment rate	5.5%

Employed persons 16 years and over by occupation, 2000

Managers & professionals	672
Service occupations	218
Sales & office occupations	669
Farming, fishing & forestry	0
Construction & maintenance	259
Production & transportation	342
Self-employed persons	53

‡ Branch of county library
* US Census Bureau
** New Jersey Department of Labor

General Information

Borough of Mount Ephraim
121 S Black Horse Pike
Mount Ephraim, NJ 08059
856-931-1546

Website	www.mountephraim-nj.com
Year of incorporation	1926
Land/water area (sq. miles)	0.88/0.01
Form of government	Commission

Government

Legislative Districts

US Congressional	1
State Legislative	5

Local Officials, 2009

Mayor	Joseph E. Wolk
Manager/Admin	NA
Clerk	Terry Shannon
Finance Dir	Dean Siminera
Tax Assessor	Steve Kessler
Tax Collector	Marie Darlington
Attorney	Marrazzo & Platt
Building	Stephen Beach
Comm Dev/Planning	NA
Engineering	Remington & Vernick
Public Works	Joseph Ciano
Police Chief	Edward Dobleman
Emerg/Fire Director	Mario Scullan

Housing & Construction

Housing Units, 2000*

Total	1,881
Median rent	$542
Median SF home value	$94,000

Permits for New Residential Construction

	Units	Value
Total, 2006	2	$137,292
Single family	2	$137,292
Total, 2007	1	$206,776
Single family	1	$206,776

Real Property Valuation, 2008

	Parcels	Valuation
Total	1,758	$173,696,100
Vacant	76	3,482,600
Residential	1,584	145,833,300
Commercial	87	20,295,700
Industrial	3	741,200
Apartments	8	3,343,300
Farm land	0	0
Farm homestead	0	0

Average Property Value & Tax, 2008

Residential value	$92,066
Property tax	$5,165
Tax credit/rebate	$963

Public Library

Mount Ephraim Library‡
130 Bell Rd
Mt. Ephraim, NJ 08059
856-931-6606

Director	Gloria Marsh

Library statistics, 2007

see Camden County profile
for library system statistics

Public Safety

Number of officers, 2007	13

Crime	2006	2007
Total crimes	190	201
Violent	22	12
Murder	0	0
Rape	0	1
Robbery	10	8
Aggravated assault	12	3
Non-violent	168	189
Burglary	26	37
Larceny	126	140
Vehicle theft	16	12
Domestic violence	109	72
Arson	1	0
Total crime rate	42.5	45.3
Violent	4.9	2.7
Non-violent	37.6	42.6

Public School District

(for school year 2007-08 except as noted)

Mount Ephraim Borough School District
125 South Black Horse Pike
Mount Ephraim, NJ 08059
(856) 931-1634

Superintendent	Joseph G. Rafferty Sr
Number of schools	2
Grade plan	K-8
Enrollment	447
Attendance rate, '06-07	94.7%
Dropout rate	NA
Students per teacher	9.8
Per pupil expenditure	$12,401
Median faculty salary	$48,591
Median administrator salary	$99,225
Grade 12 enrollment	NA
High school graduation rate	NA

Assessment test results

(percent scoring at proficient or advanced level)

	Language	Math
NJASK-Grade 3	92.5%	90.6%
GEPA-Grade 8	70.8%	83.0%
HSPA-High School	NA	NA

SAT Score Averages, 2006-07

Pct tested	Math	Verbal	Writing
NA	NA	NA	NA

Teacher Qualifications

Avg. years of experience	9

Highly-qualified teachers
one subject/all subjects 100%/100%

No Child Left Behind

AYP, 2006-07 .... Meets Standards

Municipal Finance

State Aid Programs, 2009

Total aid	$494,684
CMPTRA	120,635
Energy tax receipts	371,576
Garden State Trust	0

General Budget, 2008

Total tax levy	$9,759,879
County levy	1,962,910
County taxes	1,773,951
County library	127,208
County health	0
County open space	61,751
School levy	5,103,124
Muni. levy	2,693,845
Misc. revenues	2,008,155

Taxes

	2006	2007	2008
General tax rate per $100	5.008	5.372	5.610
County equalization ratio	67.94	60.83	56.49
Net valuation taxable	$172,324,600	$173,312,920	$173,985,084
State equalized value	$283,592,977	$306,573,444	$322,306,225

See Introduction for an explanation of all data sources.

Demographics & Socio-Economic Characteristics
(2000 US Census, except as noted)

Population
1980*	10,818
1990*	10,639
2000	10,728
Male	5,356
Female	5,372
2007 (estimate)*	10,335
Population density	3,613.6

Race & Hispanic Origin, 2000
Race
White	7,368
Black/African American	2,314
American Indian/Alaska Native	45
Asian	147
Native Hawaiian/Pacific Islander	7
Other race	512
Two or more races	335
Hispanic origin, total	942
Mexican	71
Puerto Rican	638
Cuban	15
Other Hispanic	218

Age & Nativity, 2000
Under 5 years	706
18 years and over	7,905
21 years and over	7,467
65 years and over	1,335
85 years and over	153
Median age	35.0
Native-born	10,127
Foreign-born	618

Educational Attainment, 2000
Population 25 years and over	6,955
Less than 9th grade	4.5%
High school grad or higher	77.9%
Bachelor's degree or higher	18.6%
Graduate degree	4.2%

Income & Poverty, 1999
Per capita income	$19,672
Median household income	$43,284
Median family income	$52,000
Persons in poverty	1,023
H'holds receiving public assistance	180
H'holds receiving social security	1,095

Households, 2000
Total households	3,903
With persons under 18	1,430
With persons over 65	982
Family households	2,585
Single-person households	1,063
Persons per household	2.64
Persons per family	3.20

Labor & Employment
Total civilian labor force, 2007**	5,823
Unemployment rate	5.8%
Total civilian labor force, 2000	5,163
Unemployment rate	6.4%

Employed persons 16 years and over by occupation, 2000
Managers & professionals	1,317
Service occupations	839
Sales & office occupations	1,349
Farming, fishing & forestry	20
Construction & maintenance	452
Production & transportation	854
Self-employed persons	238

* US Census Bureau
** New Jersey Department of Labor

General Information
Township of Mount Holly
23 Washington St
Mount Holly, NJ 08060
609-267-0170
Website	www.mountholly.info
Year of incorporation	1931
Land/water area (sq. miles)	2.86/0.02
Form of government	Council-Manager

Government
Legislative Districts
US Congressional	3
State Legislative	7

Local Officials, 2009
Mayor	Jules K. Thiessen
Manager	Kathleen D. Hoffman
Clerk	Kathleen D. Hoffman
Finance Dir	Christina Chambers
Tax Assessor	Leo Midure
Tax Collector	Sharon Deviney
Attorney	Brian Guest
Building	Thomas Casey
Planning	Patrick Perinchief
Engineering	Richard Alaimo & Assoc
Public Works	Nick Troster
Police Chief	Steve Martin
Emerg/Fire Director	Ian Bruce

Housing & Construction
Housing Units, 2000*
Total	4,248
Median rent	$719
Median SF home value	$98,200

Permits for New Residential Construction
	Units	Value
Total, 2006	2	$828,080
Single family	2	$828,080
Total, 2007	4	$674,000
Single family	4	$674,000

Real Property Valuation, 2008
	Parcels	Valuation
Total	3,491	$315,365,800
Vacant	208	6,044,900
Residential	3,020	247,721,300
Commercial	209	45,706,700
Industrial	11	4,485,300
Apartments	39	11,250,700
Farm land	3	14,200
Farm homestead	1	142,700

Average Property Value & Tax, 2008
Residential value	$82,047
Property tax	$3,999
Tax credit/rebate	$841

Public Library
Mount Holly Public Library
307 High St
Mount Holly, NJ 08060
609-267-7111
Director	T. Michael Eck

Library statistics, 2007
Population served	10,728
Full-time/total staff	0/1

	Total	Per capita
Holdings	12,141	1.13
Revenues	$35,347	$3.29
Expenditures	$76,781	$7.16
Annual visits	20,800	1.94
Internet terminals/annual users	9/4,735	

Public Safety
Number of officers, 2007	26

Crime	2006	2007
Total crimes	390	362
Violent	55	41
Murder	0	0
Rape	0	0
Robbery	24	21
Aggravated assault	31	20
Non-violent	335	321
Burglary	55	54
Larceny	256	257
Vehicle theft	24	10
Domestic violence	342	256
Arson	2	1
Total crime rate	36.6	34.1
Violent	5.2	3.9
Non-violent	31.4	30.3

Public School District
(for school year 2007-08 except as noted)

Mount Holly Township School District
331 Levis Drive
Mount Holly, NJ 08060
(609) 267-7108
Superintendent	David Gentile
Number of schools	3
Grade plan	K-8
Enrollment	986
Attendance rate, '06-07	93.6%
Dropout rate	NA
Students per teacher	8.6
Per pupil expenditure	$17,063
Median faculty salary	$60,310
Median administrator salary	$92,000
Grade 12 enrollment	NA
High school graduation rate	NA

Assessment test results
(percent scoring at proficient or advanced level)
	Language	Math
NJASK-Grade 3	79.2%	73.3%
GEPA-Grade 8	49.6%	61.0%
HSPA-High School	NA	NA

SAT Score Averages, 2006-07
Pct tested	Math	Verbal	Writing
NA	NA	NA	NA

Teacher Qualifications
Avg. years of experience	11
Highly-qualified teachers one subject/all subjects	100%/100%

No Child Left Behind
AYP, 2006-07	Needs Improvement

Municipal Finance
State Aid Programs, 2009
Total aid	$1,911,826
CMPTRA	809,959
Energy tax receipts	1,063,614
Garden State Trust	17

General Budget, 2008
Total tax levy	$15,526,278
County levy	2,755,688
County taxes	2,262,988
County library	208,948
County health	0
County open space	283,752
School levy	9,342,611
Muni. levy	3,427,979
Misc. revenues	6,424,182

Taxes
	2006	2007	2008
General tax rate per $100	4.308	4.7	4.875
County equalization ratio	58.95	49.78	45.02
Net valuation taxable	$316,642,200	$318,628,118	$318,521,829
State equalized value	$640,306,652	$703,290,644	$689,032,062

See Introduction for an explanation of all data sources.

Demographics & Socio-Economic Characteristics
(2000 US Census, except as noted)

Population
1980*	17,614
1990*	30,270
2000	40,221
Male	18,983
Female	21,238
2007 (estimate)*	39,409
Population density	1,806.9

Race & Hispanic Origin, 2000
Race
White	35,034
Black/African American	2,785
American Indian/Alaska Native	38
Asian	1,529
Native Hawaiian/Pacific Islander	12
Other race	256
Two or more races	567
Hispanic origin, total	901
Mexican	110
Puerto Rican	407
Cuban	60
Other Hispanic	324

Age & Nativity, 2000
Under 5 years	2,460
18 years and over	30,916
21 years and over	30,015
65 years and over	5,905
85 years and over	413
Median age	38.9
Native-born	37,444
Foreign-born	2,777

Educational Attainment, 2000
Population 25 years and over	28,924
Less than 9th grade	2.2%
High school grad or higher	92.1%
Bachelor's degree or higher	42.1%
Graduate degree	14.1%

Income & Poverty, 1999
Per capita income	$32,245
Median household income	$63,750
Median family income	$76,288
Persons in poverty	1,243
H'holds receiving public assistance	96
H'holds receiving social security	4,311

Households, 2000
Total households	16,570
With persons under 18	5,279
With persons over 65	4,065
Family households	11,062
Single-person households	4,630
Persons per household	2.41
Persons per family	2.98

Labor & Employment
Total civilian labor force, 2007**	1,976
Unemployment rate	0.6%
Total civilian labor force, 2000	21,688
Unemployment rate	3.0%

Employed persons 16 years and over by occupation, 2000
Managers & professionals	10,417
Service occupations	1,930
Sales & office occupations	6,352
Farming, fishing & forestry	23
Construction & maintenance	1,015
Production & transportation	1,294
Self-employed persons	739

* US Census Bureau
** New Jersey Department of Labor

General Information
Township of Mount Laurel
100 Mount Laurel Rd
Mount Laurel, NJ 08054
856-234-0001
Website	www.mountlaurel.com
Year of incorporation	1872
Land/water area (sq. miles)	21.81/0.12
Form of government	Council-Manager

Government
Legislative Districts
US Congressional	3
State Legislative	8

Local Officials, 2009
Mayor	Jim Keenan
Manager	Debra Fourre
Clerk	Patricia Halbe
Finance Dir	Linda Lewis
Tax Assessor	Terri Paglione
Tax Collector	Brenda Kuhn
Attorney	Christopher Norman
Building	Raymond Holshue Jr
Comm Dev/Planning	NA
Engineering	William Long
Public Works	Bruce Basim
Police Chief	Dennis Moffett
Fire Chief	Robert Gallos

Housing & Construction
Housing Units, 2000*
Total	17,163
Median rent	$939
Median SF home value	$161,900

Permits for New Residential Construction
	Units	Value
Total, 2006	38	$8,234,953
Single family	38	$8,234,953
Total, 2007	45	$10,140,473
Single family	45	$10,140,473

Real Property Valuation, 2008
	Parcels	Valuation
Total	17,661	$3,410,089,000
Vacant	839	51,578,600
Residential	16,276	2,295,148,200
Commercial	418	908,640,700
Industrial	47	97,272,900
Apartments	7	51,942,000
Farm land	53	485,900
Farm homestead	21	5,020,700

Average Property Value & Tax, 2008
Residential value	$141,141
Property tax	$5,317
Tax credit/rebate	$943

Public Library
Mount Laurel Public Library
100 Walt Whitman Ave
Mount Laurel, NJ 08054
856-234-7319
Director	Joan E. Bernstein

Library statistics, 2007
Population served	40,221
Full-time/total staff	8/13

	Total	Per capita
Holdings	127,007	3.16
Revenues	$2,129,609	$52.95
Expenditures	$2,004,848	$49.85
Annual visits	301,185	7.49
Internet terminals/annual users	25/113,336	

Public Safety
Number of officers, 2007	74

Crime	2006	2007
Total crimes	814	884
Violent	37	42
Murder	2	1
Rape	9	11
Robbery	15	12
Aggravated assault	11	18
Non-violent	777	842
Burglary	107	78
Larceny	648	739
Vehicle theft	22	25
Domestic violence	250	218
Arson	2	1
Total crime rate	20.0	21.9
Violent	0.9	1.0
Non-violent	19.1	20.9

Public School District
(for school year 2007-08 except as noted)

Mount Laurel Township School District
330 Moorestown-Mt. Laurel Rd.
Mount Laurel, NJ 08054
(856) 235-3387
Superintendent	Antoinette Rath
Number of schools	8
Grade plan	K-8
Enrollment	4,387
Attendance rate, '06-07	96.0%
Dropout rate	NA
Students per teacher	11.0
Per pupil expenditure	$12,498
Median faculty salary	$54,500
Median administrator salary	$95,000
Grade 12 enrollment	NA
High school graduation rate	NA

Assessment test results
(percent scoring at proficient or advanced level)
	Language	Math
NJASK-Grade 3	94.8%	92.6%
GEPA-Grade 8	76.8%	92.1%
HSPA-High School	NA	NA

SAT Score Averages, 2006-07
Pct tested	Math	Verbal	Writing
NA	NA	NA	NA

Teacher Qualifications
Avg. years of experience	10
Highly-qualified teachers one subject/all subjects	99.5%/99.5%

No Child Left Behind
AYP, 2006-07	Meets Standards

Municipal Finance
State Aid Programs, 2009
Total aid	$3,700,262
CMPTRA	218,288
Energy tax receipts	3,333,643
Garden State Trust	365

General Budget, 2008
Total tax levy	$128,720,116
County levy	24,170,300
County taxes	21,477,399
County library	0
County health	0
County open space	2,692,902
School levy	85,845,908
Muni. levy	18,703,908
Misc. revenues	20,098,166

Taxes
	2006	2007	2008
General tax rate per $100	3.532	3.694	3.768
County equalization ratio	63.24	56.21	50.75
Net valuation taxable	$3,314,576,600	$3,363,391,074	$3,416,947,945
State equalized value	$5,905,077,433	$6,620,127,628	$6,952,050,391

See Introduction for an explanation of all data sources.

Demographics & Socio-Economic Characteristics

(2000 US Census, except as noted)

Population

1980*	18,748
1990*	21,282
2000	24,193
Male	12,119
Female	12,074
2007 (estimate)*	25,934
Population density	854.5

Race & Hispanic Origin, 2000

Race
White	20,974
Black/African American	918
American Indian/Alaska Native	40
Asian	1,452
Native Hawaiian/Pacific Islander	2
Other race	369
Two or more races	438
Hispanic origin, total	1,445
Mexican	102
Puerto Rican	466
Cuban	86
Other Hispanic	791

Age & Nativity, 2000

Under 5 years	2,108
18 years and over	17,525
21 years and over	16,896
65 years and over	1,542
85 years and over	123
Median age	34.1
Native-born	21,059
Foreign-born	3,134

Educational Attainment, 2000

Population 25 years and over	15,764
Less than 9th grade	2.4%
High school grad or higher	91.9%
Bachelor's degree or higher	36.5%
Graduate degree	11.2%

Income & Poverty, 1999

Per capita income	$28,691
Median household income	$64,515
Median family income	$75,189
Persons in poverty	735
H'holds receiving public assistance	67
H'holds receiving social security	1,267

Households, 2000

Total households	9,068
With persons under 18	3,696
With persons over 65	1,219
Family households	6,372
Single-person households	2,150
Persons per household	2.66
Persons per family	3.22

Labor & Employment

Total civilian labor force, 2007**	22,995
Unemployment rate	3.2%
Total civilian labor force, 2000	13,589
Unemployment rate	3.8%

Employed persons 16 years and over by occupation, 2000
Managers & professionals	5,728
Service occupations	1,403
Sales & office occupations	3,424
Farming, fishing & forestry	25
Construction & maintenance	1,031
Production & transportation	1,463
Self-employed persons	603

General Information

Township of Mount Olive
204 Flanders-Drakestown Rd
PO Box 450
Budd Lake, NJ 07828
973-691-0900

Website	www.mountolivetownship.com
Year of incorporation	1871
Land/water area (sq. miles)	30.35/0.70
Form of government	Mayor-Council

Government

Legislative Districts

US Congressional	11
State Legislative	25

Local Officials, 2009

Mayor	David Scapicchio
Manager	Bill Sohl
Clerk	Lisa Lashway
Finance Dir	Sherry Maniscalco
Tax Assessor	John Marchione
Tax Collector	Rose Barsanti
Attorney	John Dorsey
Building	Gary Lindsay
Planning	Catherine Natafalusy
Engineering	Eugene Buczynski
Public Works	Tim Quinn
Police Chief	Mark Spitzer
Emerg/Fire Director	Fred Detoro Jr

Housing & Construction

Housing Units, 2000*

Total	9,311
Median rent	$800
Median SF home value	$197,800

Permits for New Residential Construction

	Units	Value
Total, 2006	114	$15,588,415
Single family	64	$9,412,448
Total, 2007	23	$3,934,470
Single family	19	$3,120,970

Real Property Valuation, 2008

	Parcels	Valuation
Total	7,975	$3,667,530,650
Vacant	1,172	134,976,400
Residential	6,284	2,374,738,900
Commercial	328	523,154,950
Industrial	60	368,387,300
Apartments	6	250,006,700
Farm land	92	1,371,600
Farm homestead	33	14,894,800

Average Property Value & Tax, 2008

Residential value	$378,286
Property tax	$8,568
Tax credit/rebate	$1,156

Public Library

Mount Olive Public Library
202 Flanders-Drakestown Rd
Flanders, NJ 07836
973-691-8686

Director .... Rita L. Hilbert

Library statistics, 2007

Population served	24,193
Full-time/total staff	5/9

	Total	Per capita
Holdings	83,455	3.45
Revenues	$1,319,596	$54.54
Expenditures	$1,191,433	$49.25
Annual visits	216,392	8.94
Internet terminals/annual users	34/177,945	

Public Safety

Number of officers, 2007	54

Crime	2006	2007
Total crimes	251	272
Violent	5	6
Murder	0	0
Rape	0	1
Robbery	2	0
Aggravated assault	3	5
Non-violent	246	266
Burglary	54	38
Larceny	169	217
Vehicle theft	23	11
Domestic violence	164	184
Arson	1	0
Total crime rate	9.7	10.4
Violent	0.2	0.2
Non-violent	9.5	10.2

Public School District

(for school year 2007-08 except as noted)

Mount Olive Township School District
89 Route 46
Budd Lake, NJ 07828
(973) 691-4008

Superintendent	Rosalie Lamonte
Number of schools	6
Grade plan	K-12
Enrollment	4,904
Attendance rate, '06-07	95.3%
Dropout rate	0.9%
Students per teacher	11.5
Per pupil expenditure	$13,761
Median faculty salary	$59,142
Median administrator salary	$112,680
Grade 12 enrollment	308
High school graduation rate	96.0%

Assessment test results

(percent scoring at proficient or advanced level)
	Language	Math
NJASK-Grade 3	88.6%	88.9%
GEPA-Grade 8	78.6%	92.0%
HSPA-High School	85.1%	94.2%

SAT Score Averages, 2006-07

Pct tested	Math	Verbal	Writing
82%	528	506	503

Teacher Qualifications

Avg. years of experience	8
Highly-qualified teachers one subject/all subjects	100%/100%

No Child Left Behind

AYP, 2006-07	Meets Standards

Municipal Finance

State Aid Programs, 2009

Total aid	$2,702,036
CMPTRA	458,600
Energy tax receipts	2,013,092
Garden State Trust	109,212

General Budget, 2008

Total tax levy	$83,196,425
County levy	8,888,476
County taxes	7,255,774
County library	0
County health	0
County open space	1,632,701
School levy	56,786,067
Muni. levy	17,521,883
Misc. revenues	9,922,191

Taxes

	2006	2007	2008
General tax rate per $100	3.79	4	2.265
County equalization ratio	59.7	53.81	94.45
Net valuation taxable	$2,002,686,700	$1,978,562,802	$3,673,163,443
State equalized value	$3,724,907,741	$3,859,347,246	$3,876,377,542

Demographics & Socio-Economic Characteristics

(2000 US Census, except as noted)

Population

1980*	4,153
1990*	3,847
2000	4,256
Male	2,119
Female	2,137
2007 (estimate)*	4,276
Population density	1,601.5

Race & Hispanic Origin, 2000

Race

White	3,960
Black/African American	16
American Indian/Alaska Native	0
Asian	220
Native Hawaiian/Pacific Islander	3
Other race	22
Two or more races	35
Hispanic origin, total	72
Mexican	10
Puerto Rican	18
Cuban	11
Other Hispanic	33

Age & Nativity, 2000

Under 5 years	317
18 years and over	2,738
21 years and over	2,676
65 years and over	386
85 years and over	14
Median age	39.4
Native-born	3,839
Foreign-born	417

Educational Attainment, 2000

Population 25 years and over	2,624
Less than 9th grade	0.8%
High school grad or higher	98.4%
Bachelor's degree or higher	76.1%
Graduate degree	35.2%

Income & Poverty, 1999

Per capita income	$65,086
Median household income	$141,757
Median family income	$153,227
Persons in poverty	85
H'holds receiving public assistance	0
H'holds receiving social security	242

Households, 2000

Total households	1,330
With persons under 18	724
With persons over 65	266
Family households	1,187
Single-person households	122
Persons per household	3.20
Persons per family	3.41

Labor & Employment

Total civilian labor force, 2007**	15,090
Unemployment rate	3.4%
Total civilian labor force, 2000	1,819
Unemployment rate	1.0%

Employed persons 16 years and over by occupation, 2000

Managers & professionals	1,239
Service occupations	108
Sales & office occupations	356
Farming, fishing & forestry	0
Construction & maintenance	52
Production & transportation	46
Self-employed persons	156

* US Census Bureau
** New Jersey Department of Labor

General Information

Borough of Mountain Lakes
400 Boulevard
Mountain Lakes, NJ 07046
973-334-3131

Website	www.mtnlakes.org
Year of incorporation	1924
Land/water area (sq. miles)	2.67/0.22
Form of government	Council-Manager

Government

Legislative Districts

US Congressional	11
State Legislative	24

Local Officials, 2009

Mayor	Stephen Shaw
Manager	Joseph Tempesta
Clerk	Christina Whitaker
Finance Dir	Dana Mooney
Tax Assessor	Rick DelGuercio
Tax Collector	Dana Mooney
Attorney	Martin Murphy
Building	Rita Sharp
Comm Dev/Planning	NA
Engineering	Bill Ryden
Public Works	Mark Prusina
Police Chief	Robert Tovo
Emerg/Fire Director	Steve Butera

Housing & Construction

Housing Units, 2000*

Total	1,357
Median rent	$1,804
Median SF home value	$488,900

Permits for New Residential Construction

	Units	Value
Total, 2006	8	$3,191,661
Single family	8	$3,191,661
Total, 2007	11	$3,910,034
Single family	11	$3,910,034

Real Property Valuation, 2008

	Parcels	Valuation
Total	1,472	$1,476,158,400
Vacant	37	10,037,300
Residential	1,354	1,364,323,300
Commercial	75	98,570,200
Industrial	3	3,226,100
Apartments	0	0
Farm land	3	1,500
Farm homestead	0	0

Average Property Value & Tax, 2008

Residential value	$1,007,624
Property tax	$17,798
Tax credit/rebate	$1,454

Public Library

Mountain Lakes Public Library
9 Elm Rd
Mountain Lakes, NJ 07046
973-334-5095

Director	Margaret J. Bulfer

Library statistics, 2007

Population served	4,256
Full-time/total staff	0/1

	Total	Per capita
Holdings	43,928	10.32
Revenues	$227,396	$53.43
Expenditures	$225,745	$53.04
Annual visits	27,590	6.48
Internet terminals/annual users	8/2,897	

Public Safety

Number of officers, 2007 14

Crime	2006	2007
Total crimes	86	78
Violent	2	3
Murder	0	0
Rape	1	0
Robbery	0	0
Aggravated assault	1	3
Non-violent	84	75
Burglary	22	22
Larceny	60	52
Vehicle theft	2	1
Domestic violence	1	2
Arson	1	0
Total crime rate	19.8	18.0
Violent	0.5	0.7
Non-violent	19.4	17.3

Public School District

(for school year 2007-08 except as noted)

Mountain Lakes School District
400 Boulevard
Mountain Lakes, NJ 07046
(973) 334-8280

Superintendent	John Kazmark
Number of schools	4
Grade plan	K-12
Enrollment	1,461
Attendance rate, '06-07	95.7%
Dropout rate	0.1%
Students per teacher	7.6
Per pupil expenditure	$19,574
Median faculty salary	$68,032
Median administrator salary	$125,055
Grade 12 enrollment	171
High school graduation rate	98.8%

Assessment test results

(percent scoring at proficient or advanced level)

	Language	Math
NJASK-Grade 3	99.0%	99.0%
GEPA-Grade 8	94.3%	98.1%
HSPA-High School	86.4%	90.7%

SAT Score Averages, 2006-07

Pct tested	Math	Verbal	Writing
94%	576	575	579

Teacher Qualifications

Avg. years of experience	12
Highly-qualified teachers one subject/all subjects	99.5%/99.5%

No Child Left Behind

AYP, 2006-07 . . . . Meets Standards

Municipal Finance

State Aid Programs, 2009

Total aid	$567,839
CMPTRA	20,160
Energy tax receipts	524,966
Garden State Trust	0

General Budget, 2008

Total tax levy	$26,097,921
County levy	3,274,722
County taxes	2,672,582
County library	0
County health	0
County open space	602,141
School levy	18,271,514
Muni. levy	4,551,685
Misc. revenues	2,873,707

Taxes

	2006	2007	2008
General tax rate per $100	1.62	1.7	1.767
County equalization ratio	113.16	106.77	104.83
Net valuation taxable	$1,474,084,000	$1,475,160,245	$1,477,533,321
State equalized value	$1,381,425,994	$1,407,254,762	$1,479,898,959

See Introduction for an explanation of all data sources.

Demographics & Socio-Economic Characteristics
(2000 US Census, except as noted)

Population
1980*	7,118
1990*	6,657
2000	6,602
Male	3,112
Female	3,490
2007 (estimate)*	6,559
Population density	1,631.6

Race & Hispanic Origin, 2000
Race
White	6,278
Black/African American	62
American Indian/Alaska Native	6
Asian	185
Native Hawaiian/Pacific Islander	4
Other race	18
Two or more races	49
Hispanic origin, total	199
Mexican	16
Puerto Rican	32
Cuban	48
Other Hispanic	103

Age & Nativity, 2000
Under 5 years	405
18 years and over	5,210
21 years and over	5,102
65 years and over	1,644
85 years and over	252
Median age	46.4
Native-born	5,726
Foreign-born	876

Educational Attainment, 2000
Population 25 years and over	4,931
Less than 9th grade	2.5%
High school grad or higher	92.6%
Bachelor's degree or higher	47.9%
Graduate degree	21.9%

Income & Poverty, 1999
Per capita income	$47,474
Median household income	$97,195
Median family income	$105,773
Persons in poverty	187
H'holds receiving public assistance	35
H'holds receiving social security	1,022

Households, 2000
Total households	2,434
With persons under 18	745
With persons over 65	990
Family households	1,925
Single-person households	436
Persons per household	2.60
Persons per family	2.95

Labor & Employment
Total civilian labor force, 2007**	3,056
Unemployment rate	2.3%
Total civilian labor force, 2000	2,952
Unemployment rate	2.5%

Employed persons 16 years and over by occupation, 2000
Managers & professionals	1,519
Service occupations	289
Sales & office occupations	794
Farming, fishing & forestry	0
Construction & maintenance	160
Production & transportation	116
Self-employed persons	235

General Information
Borough of Mountainside
1385 Route 22
Mountainside, NJ 07092
908-232-2400

Website	www.mountainside-nj.com
Year of incorporation	1895
Land/water area (sq. miles)	4.02/0.03
Form of government	Borough

Government
Legislative Districts
US Congressional	7
State Legislative	21

Local Officials, 2009
Mayor	Robert Viglianti
Manager	James Debbie Jr
Clerk	Martha DeJesus
Finance Dir	Jill Goode
Tax Assessor	Eldo Magnani
Tax Collector	Dale Mathews
Attorney	John Post
Building	Jerry Eger
Planning	John Tomaine
Engineering	Mike Disko
Public Works	Ronald Romak
Police Chief	James Debbie Jr
Emerg/Fire Director	Neil Williams

Housing & Construction
Housing Units, 2000*
Total	2,478
Median rent	$950
Median SF home value	$346,100

Permits for New Residential Construction
	Units	Value
Total, 2006	17	$4,333,631
Single family	17	$4,333,631
Total, 2007	17	$5,247,151
Single family	17	$5,247,151

Real Property Valuation, 2008
	Parcels	Valuation
Total	2,651	$488,655,500
Vacant	100	6,878,300
Residential	2,395	394,297,500
Commercial	103	60,710,300
Industrial	53	26,769,400
Apartments	0	0
Farm land	0	0
Farm homestead	0	0

Average Property Value & Tax, 2008
Residential value	$164,634
Property tax	$8,561
Tax credit/rebate	$1,150

Public Library
Mountainside Public Library
Constitution Plaza
Mountainside, NJ 07092
908-233-0115

Director	Michael Banick

Library statistics, 2007
Population served	6,602
Full-time/total staff	2/3

	Total	Per capita
Holdings	60,661	9.19
Revenues	$651,502	$98.68
Expenditures	$623,518	$94.44
Annual visits	57,320	8.68
Internet terminals/annual users	11/15,998	

Public Safety
Number of officers, 2007	22

Crime	2006	2007
Total crimes	73	74
Violent	3	4
Murder	0	0
Rape	0	1
Robbery	0	0
Aggravated assault	3	3
Non-violent	70	70
Burglary	14	11
Larceny	49	54
Vehicle theft	7	5
Domestic violence	8	19
Arson	0	0
Total crime rate	11.0	11.1
Violent	0.5	0.6
Non-violent	10.6	10.5

Public School District
(for school year 2007-08 except as noted)

Mountainside School District
1497 Woodacres Drive
Mountainside, NJ 07092
(908) 232-3232

Superintendent	Jeanette Baubles
Number of schools	2
Grade plan	K-8
Enrollment	740
Attendance rate, '06-07	96.2%
Dropout rate	NA
Students per teacher	10.1
Per pupil expenditure	$14,286
Median faculty salary	$50,731
Median administrator salary	$117,000
Grade 12 enrollment	NA
High school graduation rate	NA

Assessment test results
(percent scoring at proficient or advanced level)
	Language	Math
NJASK-Grade 3	98.0%	94.9%
GEPA-Grade 8	91.0%	97.5%
HSPA-High School	NA	NA

SAT Score Averages, 2006-07
Pct tested	Math	Verbal	Writing
NA	NA	NA	NA

Teacher Qualifications
Avg. years of experience	8
Highly-qualified teachers one subject/all subjects	100%/100%

No Child Left Behind
AYP, 2006-07	Meets Standards

Municipal Finance
State Aid Programs, 2009
Total aid	$1,044,524
CMPTRA	140,805
Energy tax receipts	861,938
Garden State Trust	0

General Budget, 2008
Total tax levy	$25,427,117
County levy	6,728,594
County taxes	6,434,601
County library	0
County health	0
County open space	293,993
School levy	12,145,337
Muni. levy	6,553,186
Misc. revenues	3,857,829

Taxes
	2006	2007	2008
General tax rate per $100	4.61	4.899	5.200
County equalization ratio	27.19	26.19	25.19
Net valuation taxable	$485,203,900	$486,939,472	$488,984,345
State equalized value	$1,852,968,092	$1,932,108,895	$1,951,828,446

* US Census Bureau
** New Jersey Department of Labor

See Introduction for an explanation of all data sources.

Demographics & Socio-Economic Characteristics
(2000 US Census, except as noted)

Population
1980*	5,243
1990*	5,896
2000	5,912
Male	2,975
Female	2,937
2007 (estimate)*	6,034
Population density	106.6

Race & Hispanic Origin, 2000
Race
White	4,764
Black/African American	371
American Indian/Alaska Native	16
Asian	49
Native Hawaiian/Pacific Islander	7
Other race	509
Two or more races	196
Hispanic origin, total	975
Mexican	86
Puerto Rican	766
Cuban	3
Other Hispanic	120

Age & Nativity, 2000
Under 5 years	354
18 years and over	4,318
21 years and over	4,105
65 years and over	630
85 years and over	42
Median age	37.0
Native-born	5,696
Foreign-born	216

Educational Attainment, 2000
Population 25 years and over	3,949
Less than 9th grade	9.9%
High school grad or higher	78.5%
Bachelor's degree or higher	13.4%
Graduate degree	3.7%

Income & Poverty, 1999
Per capita income	$19,764
Median household income	$50,417
Median family income	$55,143
Persons in poverty	462
H'holds receiving public assistance	27
H'holds receiving social security	557

Households, 2000
Total households	2,044
With persons under 18	842
With persons over 65	474
Family households	1,537
Single-person households	396
Persons per household	2.87
Persons per family	3.30

Labor & Employment
Total civilian labor force, 2007**	3,126
Unemployment rate	5.7%
Total civilian labor force, 2000	2,957
Unemployment rate	6.3%

Employed persons 16 years and over by occupation, 2000
Managers & professionals	603
Service occupations	679
Sales & office occupations	680
Farming, fishing & forestry	49
Construction & maintenance	478
Production & transportation	282
Self-employed persons	112

General Information
Township of Mullica
PO Box 317
Elwood, NJ 08217
609-561-0064

Website	mullicatownship.org
Year of incorporation	1838
Land/water area (sq. miles)	56.58/0.36
Form of government	Township

Government
Legislative Districts
US Congressional	2
State Legislative	2

Local Officials, 2009
Mayor	William Kennedy
Manager/Admin	NA
Clerk	Kimberly Johnson
Finance Dir	Dawn Stollenwerk
Tax Assessor	Gerard Mead
Tax Collector	Bert Cappuccio
Attorney	Cody & Cody
Building	John Holroyd
Comm Dev/Planning	NA
Engineering	Marathon Engineering
Public Works	Pete Berenato
Police Chief	Joseph Barbera
Emerg/Fire Director	Gary Franklin

Housing & Construction
Housing Units, 2000*
Total	2,176
Median rent	$733
Median SF home value	$109,000

Permits for New Residential Construction
	Units	Value
Total, 2006	29	$3,014,244
Single family	29	$3,014,244
Total, 2007	19	$3,079,100
Single family	19	$3,079,100

Real Property Valuation, 2008
	Parcels	Valuation
Total	4,249	$287,758,400
Vacant	1,753	14,486,300
Residential	2,167	246,193,900
Commercial	85	15,682,700
Industrial	3	2,473,300
Apartments	2	515,400
Farm land	183	2,257,700
Farm homestead	56	6,149,100

Average Property Value & Tax, 2008
Residential value	$113,515
Property tax	$4,193
Tax credit/rebate	$837

Public Library
No public municipal library

Library statistics, 2007
Population served	NA
Full-time/total staff	NA/NA

	Total	Per capita
Holdings	NA	NA
Revenues	NA	NA
Expenditures	NA	NA
Annual visits	NA	NA
Internet terminals/annual users	NA/NA	

Public Safety
Number of officers, 2007	14

Crime	2006	2007
Total crimes	93	121
Violent	12	13
Murder	0	0
Rape	1	0
Robbery	0	2
Aggravated assault	11	11
Non-violent	81	108
Burglary	25	36
Larceny	50	60
Vehicle theft	6	12
Domestic violence	39	47
Arson	1	0
Total crime rate	15.2	19.9
Violent	2.0	2.1
Non-violent	13.3	17.8

Public School District
(for school year 2007-08 except as noted)

Mullica Township School District
500 Elwood Road, PO Box 318
Elwood, NJ 08217
(609) 561-3868

Superintendent	Richard Goldberg
Number of schools	3
Grade plan	K-8
Enrollment	724
Attendance rate, '06-07	95.0%
Dropout rate	NA
Students per teacher	10.7
Per pupil expenditure	$12,008
Median faculty salary	$62,025
Median administrator salary	$90,000
Grade 12 enrollment	NA
High school graduation rate	NA

Assessment test results
(percent scoring at proficient or advanced level)
	Language	Math
NJASK-Grade 3	90.2%	91.5%
GEPA-Grade 8	90.5%	90.5%
HSPA-High School	NA	NA

SAT Score Averages, 2006-07
Pct tested	Math	Verbal	Writing
NA	NA	NA	NA

Teacher Qualifications
Avg. years of experience	14
Highly-qualified teachers one subject/all subjects	100%/100%

No Child Left Behind
AYP, 2006-07	Meets Standards

Municipal Finance
State Aid Programs, 2009
Total aid	$655,012
CMPTRA	132,072
Energy tax receipts	435,843
Garden State Trust	58,165

General Budget, 2008
Total tax levy	$10,664,240
County levy	1,752,063
County taxes	1,380,421
County library	177,042
County health	72,445
County open space	122,155
School levy	5,918,154
Muni. levy	2,994,022
Misc. revenues	2,338,958

Taxes	2006	2007	2008
General tax rate per $100	3.555	3.616	3.694
County equalization ratio	61.16	50.23	47.33
Net valuation taxable	$279,433,200	$283,981,376	$288,706,046
State equalized value	$557,414,107	$598,956,545	$653,461,025

* US Census Bureau
** New Jersey Department of Labor

See Introduction for an explanation of all data sources.

Demographics & Socio-Economic Characteristics
(2000 US Census, except as noted)

Population
1980*	3,552
1990*	3,413
2000	3,205
Male	1,596
Female	1,609
2007 (estimate)*	3,230
Population density	3,230.0

Race & Hispanic Origin, 2000
Race
White	3,152
Black/African American	3
American Indian/Alaska Native	8
Asian	8
Native Hawaiian/Pacific Islander	1
Other race	17
Two or more races	16
Hispanic origin, total	46
Mexican	7
Puerto Rican	29
Cuban	3
Other Hispanic	7

Age & Nativity, 2000
Under 5 years	181
18 years and over	2,360
21 years and over	2,209
65 years and over	402
85 years and over	28
Median age	36.7
Native-born	3,177
Foreign-born	28

Educational Attainment, 2000
Population 25 years and over	2,065
Less than 9th grade	4.9%
High school grad or higher	76.7%
Bachelor's degree or higher	7.0%
Graduate degree	1.2%

Income & Poverty, 1999
Per capita income	$18,048
Median household income	$48,534
Median family income	$51,535
Persons in poverty	242
H'holds receiving public assistance	19
H'holds receiving social security	315

Households, 2000
Total households	1,111
With persons under 18	472
With persons over 65	292
Family households	865
Single-person households	207
Persons per household	2.86
Persons per family	3.24

Labor & Employment
Total civilian labor force, 2007**	1,957
Unemployment rate	5.9%
Total civilian labor force, 2000	1,652
Unemployment rate	5.4%

Employed persons 16 years and over by occupation, 2000
Managers & professionals	292
Service occupations	293
Sales & office occupations	396
Farming, fishing & forestry	4
Construction & maintenance	254
Production & transportation	324
Self-employed persons	26

General Information
Borough of National Park
7 S Grove Ave
National Park, NJ 08063
856-845-3891
Website	www.nationalparkboro.com
Year of incorporation	1892
Land/water area (sq. miles)	1.00/0.44
Form of government	Borough

Government
Legislative Districts
US Congressional	1
State Legislative	3

Local Officials, 2009
Mayor	Patricia Koloski
Manager	Robert Dougherty Jr
Clerk	Victoria Holmstrom
Finance Dir	George Damminger
Tax Assessor	Roy Duffield
Tax Collector	Catherine Couch
Attorney	Kelly Conroy
Building	William Cattell
Comm Dev/Planning	NA
Engineering	Edwin Steck
Public Works	James Walker
Police Chief	Lin T. Couch
Emerg/Fire Director	Mark Gismondi

Housing & Construction
Housing Units, 2000*
Total	1,165
Median rent	$647
Median SF home value	$92,800

Permits for New Residential Construction
	Units	Value
Total, 2006	3	$266,800
Single family	3	$266,800
Total, 2007	1	$129,000
Single family	1	$129,000

Real Property Valuation, 2008
	Parcels	Valuation
Total	1,241	$97,899,200
Vacant	118	1,548,900
Residential	1,086	91,349,500
Commercial	33	4,365,000
Industrial	0	0
Apartments	4	635,800
Farm land	0	0
Farm homestead	0	0

Average Property Value & Tax, 2008
Residential value	$84,116
Property tax	$4,684
Tax credit/rebate	$885

Public Library
No public municipal library

Library statistics, 2007
Population served	NA
Full-time/total staff	NA/NA

	Total	Per capita
Holdings	NA	NA
Revenues	NA	NA
Expenditures	NA	NA
Annual visits	NA	NA
Internet terminals/annual users	NA/NA	

Public Safety
Number of officers, 2007	7

Crime	2006	2007
Total crimes	62	76
Violent	5	7
Murder	1	0
Rape	0	1
Robbery	1	0
Aggravated assault	3	6
Non-violent	57	69
Burglary	18	10
Larceny	35	56
Vehicle theft	4	3
Domestic violence	25	15
Arson	0	0
Total crime rate	19.2	23.6
Violent	1.6	2.2
Non-violent	17.7	21.5

Public School District
(for school year 2007-08 except as noted)

National Park Borough School District
516 Lakehurst Avenue
National Park, NJ 08063
(856) 845-6876
Superintendent	Ray Bider
Number of schools	1
Grade plan	K-6
Enrollment	302
Attendance rate, '06-07	94.8%
Dropout rate	NA
Students per teacher	12.1
Per pupil expenditure	$12,142
Median faculty salary	$60,000
Median administrator salary	$97,707
Grade 12 enrollment	NA
High school graduation rate	NA

Assessment test results
(percent scoring at proficient or advanced level)
	Language	Math
NJASK-Grade 3	83.6%	83.7%
GEPA-Grade 8	NA	NA
HSPA-High School	NA	NA

SAT Score Averages, 2006-07
Pct tested	Math	Verbal	Writing
NA	NA	NA	NA

Teacher Qualifications
Avg. years of experience	13
Highly-qualified teachers one subject/all subjects	100%/100%

No Child Left Behind
AYP, 2006-07	Meets Standards

Municipal Finance
State Aid Programs, 2009
Total aid	$529,680
CMPTRA	26,888
Energy tax receipts	492,199
Garden State Trust	0

General Budget, 2008
Total tax levy	$5,455,818
County levy	1,083,711
County taxes	935,218
County library	75,206
County health	0
County open space	73,287
School levy	3,171,107
Muni. levy	1,201,000
Misc. revenues	1,461,226

Taxes	2006	2007	2008
General tax rate per $100	4.791	5.122	5.569
County equalization ratio	71.53	61.37	53.46
Net valuation taxable	$97,425,400	$97,759,919	$97,983,732
State equalized value	$158,852,187	$182,786,566	$188,533,425

* US Census Bureau
** New Jersey Department of Labor

See Introduction for an explanation of all data sources.

Demographics & Socio-Economic Characteristics

(2000 US Census, except as noted)

Population

1980*	5,276
1990*	4,997
2000	5,218
Male	2,436
Female	2,782
2007 (estimate)*	5,152
Population density	5,661.5

Race & Hispanic Origin, 2000

Race

White	4,351
Black/African American	497
American Indian/Alaska Native	12
Asian	142
Native Hawaiian/Pacific Islander	0
Other race	110
Two or more races	106
Hispanic origin, total	277
Mexican	69
Puerto Rican	145
Cuban	11
Other Hispanic	52

Age & Nativity, 2000

Under 5 years	304
18 years and over	4,096
21 years and over	3,964
65 years and over	854
85 years and over	141
Median age	39.8
Native-born	4,801
Foreign-born	417

Educational Attainment, 2000

Population 25 years and over	3,771
Less than 9th grade	5.0%
High school grad or higher	82.0%
Bachelor's degree or higher	16.9%
Graduate degree	4.6%

Income & Poverty, 1999

Per capita income	$22,191
Median household income	$43,451
Median family income	$46,393
Persons in poverty	279
H'holds receiving public assistance	19
H'holds receiving social security	636

Households, 2000

Total households	2,221
With persons under 18	644
With persons over 65	582
Family households	1,331
Single-person households	743
Persons per household	2.29
Persons per family	2.96

Labor & Employment

Total civilian labor force, 2007**	2,805
Unemployment rate	3.8%
Total civilian labor force, 2000	2,640
Unemployment rate	4.1%

Employed persons 16 years and over by occupation, 2000

Managers & professionals	690
Service occupations	436
Sales & office occupations	675
Farming, fishing & forestry	7
Construction & maintenance	366
Production & transportation	359
Self-employed persons	54

* US Census Bureau
** New Jersey Department of Labor

See Introduction for an explanation of all data sources.

General Information

Borough of Neptune City
106 W Sylvania Ave
Neptune City, NJ 07753
732-776-7224

Website	www.neptunecitynj.com
Year of incorporation	1881
Land/water area (sq. miles)	0.91/0.00
Form of government	Borough

Government

Legislative Districts

US Congressional	6
State Legislative	11

Local Officials, 2009

Mayor	Thomas Arnone
Manager	Joel Popkin
Clerk	Mary Sapp
Finance Dir	W. Folk
Tax Assessor	Stephen Walters
Tax Collector	Mary Sapp
Attorney	Mark Aikins
Building	William Doolittle
Comm Dev/Planning	NA
Engineering	Matt Shafai
Public Works	Gerrit DeVos
Police Chief	William Geschke
Emerg/Fire Director	Ed Sims

Housing & Construction

Housing Units, 2000*

Total	2,342
Median rent	$705
Median SF home value	$124,100

Permits for New Residential Construction

	Units	Value
Total, 2006	1	$189,000
Single family	1	$189,000
Total, 2007	0	$0
Single family	0	$0

Real Property Valuation, 2008

	Parcels	Valuation
Total	1,672	$434,376,200
Vacant	65	4,003,400
Residential	1,487	312,758,500
Commercial	103	77,940,700
Industrial	8	10,480,800
Apartments	9	29,192,800
Farm land	0	0
Farm homestead	0	0

Average Property Value & Tax, 2008

Residential value	$210,329
Property tax	$4,838
Tax credit/rebate	$928

Public Library

Neptune City Public Library
106 W Sylvania Ave
Neptune City, NJ 07753
732-988-8866

Director	Patricia Scott

Library statistics, 2007

Population served	5,218
Full-time/total staff	NA/0

	Total	Per capita
Holdings	0	NA
Revenues	$0	NA
Expenditures	$0	NA
Annual visits	NA	NA
Internet terminals/annual users	NA/NA	

Public Safety

Number of officers, 2007	16

Crime	2006	2007
Total crimes	177	222
Violent	17	12
Murder	0	0
Rape	2	1
Robbery	3	7
Aggravated assault	12	4
Non-violent	160	210
Burglary	30	30
Larceny	122	177
Vehicle theft	8	3
Domestic violence	48	52
Arson	1	0
Total crime rate	34.2	43.1
Violent	3.3	2.3
Non-violent	30.9	40.8

Public School District

(for school year 2007-08 except as noted)

Neptune City School District
210 West Sylvania Avenue
Neptune City, NJ 07753
(732) 775-5319

Superintendent	Thomas E. Campbell
Number of schools	1
Grade plan	K-8
Enrollment	387
Attendance rate, '06-07	93.6%
Dropout rate	NA
Students per teacher	10.2
Per pupil expenditure	$13,050
Median faculty salary	$44,281
Median administrator salary	$107,500
Grade 12 enrollment	NA
High school graduation rate	NA

Assessment test results

(percent scoring at proficient or advanced level)

	Language	Math
NJASK-Grade 3	88.6%	82.9%
GEPA-Grade 8	76.0%	86.0%
HSPA-High School	NA	NA

SAT Score Averages, 2006-07

Pct tested	Math	Verbal	Writing
NA	NA	NA	NA

Teacher Qualifications

Avg. years of experience	11
Highly-qualified teachers one subject/all subjects	100%/100%

No Child Left Behind

AYP, 2006-07	Meets Standards

Municipal Finance

State Aid Programs, 2009

Total aid	$616,115
CMPTRA	110,328
Energy tax receipts	490,384
Garden State Trust	0

General Budget, 2008

Total tax levy	$9,999,789
County levy	1,524,576
County taxes	1,330,977
County library	80,095
County health	24,750
County open space	88,754
School levy	4,657,278
Muni. levy	3,817,935
Misc. revenues	2,006,493

Taxes

	2006	2007	2008
General tax rate per $100	2.169	2.26	2.301
County equalization ratio	88.66	77.86	74.19
Net valuation taxable	$430,228,300	$431,881,853	$434,729,358
State equalized value	$552,952,996	$4,110,043,516	$4,121,209,762

Demographics & Socio-Economic Characteristics

(2000 US Census, except as noted)

Population
1980*	28,366
1990*	28,148
2000	27,690
Male	12,890
Female	14,800
2007 (estimate)*	28,394
Population density	3,454.3

Race & Hispanic Origin, 2000
Race
White	15,485
Black/African American	10,567
American Indian/Alaska Native	46
Asian	325
Native Hawaiian/Pacific Islander	12
Other race	547
Two or more races	708
Hispanic origin, total	1,537
Mexican	296
Puerto Rican	791
Cuban	46
Other Hispanic	404

Age & Nativity, 2000
Under 5 years	1,657
18 years and over	21,292
21 years and over	20,477
65 years and over	4,639
85 years and over	784
Median age	39.4
Native-born	25,663
Foreign-born	2,027

Educational Attainment, 2000
Population 25 years and over	19,450
Less than 9th grade	4.8%
High school grad or higher	84.0%
Bachelor's degree or higher	23.5%
Graduate degree	8.1%

Income & Poverty, 1999
Per capita income	$22,569
Median household income	$46,250
Median family income	$57,735
Persons in poverty	3,150
H'holds receiving public assistance	409
H'holds receiving social security	3,314

Households, 2000
Total households	10,907
With persons under 18	3,422
With persons over 65	3,062
Family households	6,802
Single-person households	3,437
Persons per household	2.46
Persons per family	3.14

Labor & Employment
Total civilian labor force, 2007**	14,584
Unemployment rate	5.4%
Total civilian labor force, 2000	13,943
Unemployment rate	7.1%

Employed persons 16 years and over by occupation, 2000
Managers & professionals	4,769
Service occupations	2,086
Sales & office occupations	3,678
Farming, fishing & forestry	14
Construction & maintenance	976
Production & transportation	1,425
Self-employed persons	611

* US Census Bureau
** New Jersey Department of Labor

General Information
Township of Neptune
PO Box 1125
Neptune, NJ 07754
732-988-5200
Website	www.neptuntownship.org
Year of incorporation	1879
Land/water area (sq. miles)	8.22/0.54
Form of government	Township

Government
Legislative Districts
US Congressional	6
State Legislative	11

Local Officials, 2009
Mayor	Michael Brantley
Manager	Philip Huhn
Clerk	Richard Cuttrell
Finance Dir	Michael Bascom
Tax Assessor	Bernard Haney
Tax Collector	Michael Bascom
Attorney	Gene Anthony
Building	William Doolittle
Planning	Martin Truscott
Engineering	Leanne Hoffman
Public Works	Wayne Rode
Police Chief	Howard O'Neil
Emerg/Fire Director	Robert McDonald

Housing & Construction
Housing Units, 2000*
Total	12,217
Median rent	$658
Median SF home value	$138,100

Permits for New Residential Construction
	Units	Value
Total, 2006	455	$15,687,215
Single family	8	$14,472,744
Total, 2007	108	$4,934,327
Single family	19	$4,666,932

Real Property Valuation, 2008
	Parcels	Valuation
Total	10,569	$2,922,258,900
Vacant	377	34,046,000
Residential	9,632	2,318,015,700
Commercial	421	410,952,900
Industrial	60	67,131,700
Apartments	74	91,495,500
Farm land	3	16,100
Farm homestead	2	601,000

Average Property Value & Tax, 2008
Residential value	$240,670
Property tax	$5,187
Tax credit/rebate	$972

Public Library
Neptune Public Library
25 Neptune Blvd
Neptune, NJ 07753
732-775-8241
Director	Marian R. Bauman

Library statistics, 2007
Population served	27,690
Full-time/total staff	4/19

	Total	Per capita
Holdings	85,731	3.10
Revenues	$1,733,735	$62.61
Expenditures	$1,652,204	$59.67
Annual visits	168,495	6.09
Internet terminals/annual users	14/19,091	

Public Safety
Number of officers, 2007	74

Crime	2006	2007
Total crimes	1,540	1,534
Violent	161	166
Murder	1	3
Rape	8	3
Robbery	78	74
Aggravated assault	74	86
Non-violent	1,379	1,368
Burglary	251	261
Larceny	1,032	1,016
Vehicle theft	96	91
Domestic violence	370	430
Arson	14	9
Total crime rate	54.5	54.5
Violent	5.7	5.9
Non-violent	48.8	48.6

Public School District
(for school year 2007-08 except as noted)

Neptune Township School District
60 Neptune Boulevard
Neptune, NJ 07753
(732) 776-2000
Superintendent	David Mooij
Number of schools	8
Grade plan	K-12
Enrollment	4,432
Attendance rate, '06-07	92.8%
Dropout rate	0.0%
Students per teacher	11.4
Per pupil expenditure	$16,701
Median faculty salary	$54,690
Median administrator salary	$118,084
Grade 12 enrollment	278
High school graduation rate	100.0%

Assessment test results
(percent scoring at proficient or advanced level)
	Language	Math
NJASK-Grade 3	79.9%	73.5%
GEPA-Grade 8	49.8%	61.0%
HSPA-High School	61.8%	71.6%

SAT Score Averages, 2006-07
Pct tested	Math	Verbal	Writing
53%	444	435	436

Teacher Qualifications
Avg. years of experience	9
Highly-qualified teachers one subject/all subjects	100%/100%

No Child Left Behind
AYP, 2006-07	Needs Improvement

Municipal Finance
State Aid Programs, 2009
Total aid	$6,443,235
CMPTRA	2,444,445
Energy tax receipts	3,837,710
Garden State Trust	0

General Budget, 2008
Total tax levy	$63,081,156
County levy	10,110,612
County taxes	9,315,795
County library	0
County health	173,203
County open space	621,614
School levy	31,986,252
Muni. levy	20,984,292
Misc. revenues	15,701,997

Taxes
	2006	2007	2008
General tax rate per $100	2.013	2.089	2.156
County equalization ratio	84.26	76.04	70.83
Net valuation taxable	$2,924,692,900	$2,912,721,639	$2,927,031,276
State equalized value	$3,852,152,565	$582,008,559	$1,440,504,600

See Introduction for an explanation of all data sources.

Demographics & Socio-Economic Characteristics

(2000 US Census, except as noted)

Population

1980*	3,557
1990*	3,311
2000	2,580
Male	1,267
Female	1,313
2007 (estimate)*	3,241
Population density	3,858.3

Race & Hispanic Origin, 2000

Race
White	2,433
Black/African American	31
American Indian/Alaska Native	1
Asian	43
Native Hawaiian/Pacific Islander	0
Other race	37
Two or more races	35
Hispanic origin, total	184
Mexican	21
Puerto Rican	38
Cuban	12
Other Hispanic	113

Age & Nativity, 2000

Under 5 years	148
18 years and over	1,987
21 years and over	1,895
65 years and over	377
85 years and over	47
Median age	37.8
Native-born	2,311
Foreign-born	269

Educational Attainment, 2000

Population 25 years and over	1,817
Less than 9th grade	7.9%
High school grad or higher	84.8%
Bachelor's degree or higher	22.0%
Graduate degree	6.2%

Income & Poverty, 1999

Per capita income	$23,472
Median household income	$55,000
Median family income	$65,833
Persons in poverty	80
H'holds receiving public assistance	12
H'holds receiving social security	276

Households, 2000

Total households	1,008
With persons under 18	328
With persons over 65	283
Family households	681
Single-person households	265
Persons per household	2.56
Persons per family	3.10

Labor & Employment

Total civilian labor force, 2007**	1,552
Unemployment rate	3.0%
Total civilian labor force, 2000	1,425
Unemployment rate	2.9%

Employed persons 16 years and over by occupation, 2000
Managers & professionals	434
Service occupations	253
Sales & office occupations	370
Farming, fishing & forestry	0
Construction & maintenance	131
Production & transportation	196
Self-employed persons	96

* US Census Bureau
** New Jersey Department of Labor

See Introduction for an explanation of all data sources.

General Information

Borough of Netcong
23 Maple Ave
Netcong, NJ 07857
973-347-0252

Website	www.netcong.org
Year of incorporation	1894
Land/water area (sq. miles)	0.84/0.06
Form of government	Borough

Government

Legislative Districts

US Congressional	11
State Legislative	24

Local Officials, 2009

Mayor	Joseph Nametko
Manager	Ralph Blakeslee
Clerk	Dolores Dalessandro
Finance Dir	Jason Gabloff
Tax Assessor	Marvin Joss
Tax Collector	Dolores Dalessandro
Attorney	Anthony Bucco
Building	Sammy LaMonto
Comm Dev/Planning	NA
Engineering	Robert Guerin
Public Works	Robert Olivo
Police Chief	Robert Weisert
Fire Chief	Shawn Bates

Housing & Construction

Housing Units, 2000*

Total	1,043
Median rent	$764
Median SF home value	$147,400

Permits for New Residential Construction

	Units	Value
Total, 2006	4	$503,108
Single family	4	$503,108
Total, 2007	2	$251,554
Single family	2	$251,554

Real Property Valuation, 2008

	Parcels	Valuation
Total	946	$338,325,100
Vacant	44	6,520,600
Residential	817	240,262,300
Commercial	76	44,059,600
Industrial	6	20,396,900
Apartments	3	27,085,700
Farm land	0	0
Farm homestead	0	0

Average Property Value & Tax, 2008

Residential value	$294,079
Property tax	$6,126
Tax credit/rebate	$1,066

Public Library

No public municipal library

Library statistics, 2007

Population served	NA
Full-time/total staff	NA/NA

	Total	Per capita
Holdings	NA	NA
Revenues	NA	NA
Expenditures	NA	NA
Annual visits	NA	NA
Internet terminals/annual users	NA/NA	

Public Safety

Number of officers, 2007	9

Crime	2006	2007
Total crimes	114	84
Violent	5	5
Murder	0	0
Rape	1	1
Robbery	2	0
Aggravated assault	2	4
Non-violent	109	79
Burglary	23	20
Larceny	75	53
Vehicle theft	11	6
Domestic violence	58	64
Arson	0	0
Total crime rate	34.6	25.5
Violent	1.5	1.5
Non-violent	33.1	24.0

Public School District

(for school year 2007-08 except as noted)

Netcong School District
26 College Road
Netcong, NJ 07857
(973) 347-0020

Superintendent	Arthur DiBenedetto (Int)
Number of schools	1
Grade plan	K-8
Enrollment	296
Attendance rate, '06-07	94.8%
Dropout rate	NA
Students per teacher	9.1
Per pupil expenditure	$11,920
Median faculty salary	$62,242
Median administrator salary	$81,425
Grade 12 enrollment	NA
High school graduation rate	NA

Assessment test results

(percent scoring at proficient or advanced level)
	Language	Math
NJASK-Grade 3	79.4%	76.5%
GEPA-Grade 8	70.6%	82.3%
HSPA-High School	NA	NA

SAT Score Averages, 2006-07

Pct tested	Math	Verbal	Writing
NA	NA	NA	NA

Teacher Qualifications

Avg. years of experience	15
Highly-qualified teachers one subject/all subjects	95.5%/95.5%

No Child Left Behind

AYP, 2006-07	Meets Standards

Municipal Finance

State Aid Programs, 2009

Total aid	$517,614
CMPTRA	158,413
Energy tax receipts	346,153
Garden State Trust	63

General Budget, 2008

Total tax levy	$7,113,543
County levy	772,754
County taxes	630,607
County library	0
County health	0
County open space	142,147
School levy	4,188,712
Muni. levy	2,152,077
Misc. revenues	1,402,053

Taxes

	2006	2007	2008
General tax rate per $100	1.92	2.02	2.084
County equalization ratio	118	106.67	103.46
Net valuation taxable	$343,530,700	$346,363,131	$341,457,883
State equalized value	$325,454,829	$334,882,208	$341,086,134

Demographics & Socio-Economic Characteristics
(2000 US Census, except as noted)

Population
1980*	41,442
1990*	41,711
2000	48,573
Male	24,085
Female	24,488
2007 (estimate)*	50,534
Population density	9,662.3

Race & Hispanic Origin, 2000
Race
White	23,701
Black/African American	11,185
American Indian/Alaska Native	224
Asian	2,584
Native Hawaiian/Pacific Islander	40
Other race	8,780
Two or more races	2,059
Hispanic origin, total	18,947
Mexican	7,364
Puerto Rican	3,178
Cuban	254
Other Hispanic	8,151

Age & Nativity, 2000
Under 5 years	3,394
18 years and over	38,824
21 years and over	31,338
65 years and over	3,146
85 years and over	389
Median age	23.6
Native-born	32,358
Foreign-born	16,215

Educational Attainment, 2000
Population 25 years and over	22,088
Less than 9th grade	21.6%
High school grad or higher	62.6%
Bachelor's degree or higher	19.2%
Graduate degree	7.5%

Income & Poverty, 1999
Per capita income	$14,308
Median household income	$36,080
Median family income	$38,222
Persons in poverty	11,454
H'holds receiving public assistance	741
H'holds receiving social security	2,396

Households, 2000
Total households	13,057
With persons under 18	4,576
With persons over 65	2,429
Family households	7,202
Single-person households	3,178
Persons per household	3.23
Persons per family	3.69

Labor & Employment
Total civilian labor force, 2007**	26,975
Unemployment rate	4.2%
Total civilian labor force, 2000	26,652
Unemployment rate	10.6%

Employed persons 16 years and over by occupation, 2000
Managers & professionals	5,929
Service occupations	5,327
Sales & office occupations	6,307
Farming, fishing & forestry	108
Construction & maintenance	1,099
Production & transportation	5,062
Self-employed persons	448

General Information
City of New Brunswick
City Hall
78 Bayard St
New Brunswick, NJ 08901
732-745-5004
Website	www.cityofnewbrunswick.org
Year of incorporation	1730
Land/water area (sq. miles)	5.23/0.52
Form of government	Mayor-Council

Government
Legislative Districts
US Congressional	6
State Legislative	17

Local Officials, 2009
Mayor	James Cahill
Manager	Thomas A. Loughlin III
Clerk	Daniel A. Torrisi
Finance Dir	Douglas A. Petix
Tax Assessor	Philip Duchesneau
Tax Collector	Marilyn Chetrancola
Attorney	William J. Hamilton Jr
Building	William Schrum
Planning	Glenn Patterson
Engineer	Thomas Guldin
Public Works	Steve Zarecki
Police Chief	Anthony Caputo
Emerg/Fire Director	Robert Rawls

Housing & Construction
Housing Units, 2000*
Total	13,893
Median rent	$837
Median SF home value	$122,600

Permits for New Residential Construction
	Units	Value
Total, 2006	226	$27,153,868
Single family	19	$938,894
Total, 2007	289	$30,050,486
Single family	40	$3,191,189

Real Property Valuation, 2008
	Parcels	Valuation
Total	7,213	$1,279,213,000
Vacant	887	15,733,500
Residential	5,412	626,332,900
Commercial	643	357,479,000
Industrial	98	145,409,700
Apartments	173	134,257,900
Farm land	0	0
Farm homestead	0	0

Average Property Value & Tax, 2008
Residential value	$115,730
Property tax	$5,651
Tax credit/rebate	$913

Public Library
New Brunswick Public Library
60 Livingston Ave
New Brunswick, NJ 08901
732-745-5108
Director	Robert Belvin

Library statistics, 2007
Population served	48,573
Full-time/total staff	7/19

	Total	Per capita
Holdings	91,258	1.88
Revenues	$1,671,922	$34.42
Expenditures	$1,656,393	$34.10
Annual visits	168,953	3.48
Internet terminals/annual users	22/25,298	

Public Safety
Number of officers, 2007	142

Crime	2006	2007
Total crimes	2,276	2,168
Violent	360	283
Murder	7	2
Rape	19	25
Robbery	207	169
Aggravated assault	127	87
Non-violent	1,916	1,885
Burglary	515	448
Larceny	1,194	1,275
Vehicle theft	207	162
Domestic violence	572	592
Arson	7	7
Total crime rate	45.4	43.2
Violent	7.2	5.6
Non-violent	38.2	37.6

Public School District
(for school year 2007-08 except as noted)

New Brunswick School District
268 Baldwin Street, PO Box 2683
New Brunswick, NJ 08903
(732) 745-5300
Superintendent	Richard Kaplan
Number of schools	10
Grade plan	K-12
Enrollment	6,707
Attendance rate, '06-07	94.7%
Dropout rate	8.7%
Students per teacher	9.5
Per pupil expenditure	$15,723
Median faculty salary	$73,233
Median administrator salary	$108,641
Grade 12 enrollment	311
High school graduation rate	70.5%

Assessment test results
(percent scoring at proficient or advanced level)
	Language	Math
NJASK-Grade 3	73.6%	67.5%
GEPA-Grade 8	40.3%	58.2%
HSPA-High School	52.2%	68.4%

SAT Score Averages, 2006-07
Pct tested	Math	Verbal	Writing
68%	441	411	412

Teacher Qualifications
Avg. years of experience	9
Highly-qualified teachers one subject/all subjects	100%/100%

No Child Left Behind
AYP, 2006-07	Needs Improvement

Municipal Finance
State Aid Programs, 2009
Total aid	$15,826,350
CMPTRA	11,709,572
Energy tax receipts	4,116,714
Garden State Trust	0

General Budget, 2008
Total tax levy	$63,546,291
County levy	10,304,169
County taxes	9,226,907
County library	0
County health	0
County open space	1,077,261
School levy	27,888,477
Muni. levy	25,353,645
Misc. revenues	45,612,089

Taxes	2006	2007	2008
General tax rate per $100	4.2	4.57	4.884
County equalization ratio	45.97	40.85	36.39
Net valuation taxable	$1,280,532,100	$1,308,981,083	$1,301,409,451
State equalized value	$3,165,681,140	$3,548,101,678	$5,220,773,622

Demographics & Socio-Economic Characteristics

(2000 US Census, except as noted)

Population

1980*	14,258
1990*	9,546
2000	9,744
Male	7,802
Female	1,942
2007 (estimate)*	9,439
Population density	423.7

Race & Hispanic Origin, 2000

Race
White	6,249
Black/African American	2,816
American Indian/Alaska Native	41
Asian	143
Native Hawaiian/Pacific Islander	8
Other race	259
Two or more races	228
Hispanic origin, total	1,890
Mexican	227
Puerto Rican	928
Cuban	77
Other Hispanic	658

Age & Nativity, 2000

Under 5 years	408
18 years and over	8,331
21 years and over	7,807
65 years and over	125
85 years and over	3
Median age	32.1
Native-born	9,498
Foreign-born	336

Educational Attainment, 2000

Population 25 years and over	6,700
Less than 9th grade	6.2%
High school grad or higher	74.1%
Bachelor's degree or higher	14.6%
Graduate degree	3.3%

Income & Poverty, 1999

Per capita income	$12,140
Median household income	$44,386
Median family income	$45,511
Persons in poverty	146
H'holds receiving public assistance	5
H'holds receiving social security	48

Households, 2000

Total households	1,162
With persons under 18	723
With persons over 65	41
Family households	991
Single-person households	159
Persons per household	3.14
Persons per family	3.46

Labor & Employment

Total civilian labor force, 2007**	1,051
Unemployment rate	3.2%
Total civilian labor force, 2000	950
Unemployment rate	3.4%

Employed persons 16 years and over by occupation, 2000
Managers & professionals	356
Service occupations	197
Sales & office occupations	216
Farming, fishing & forestry	0
Construction & maintenance	70
Production & transportation	79
Self-employed persons	38

General Information

Township of New Hanover
2 Hockamick Rd
PO Box 159
Cookstown, NJ 08511
609-758-2172

Email	nhmc@comcast.net
Year of incorporation	1723
Land/water area (sq. miles)	22.28/0.10
Form of government	Township

Government

Legislative Districts

US Congressional	3
State Legislative	30

Local Officials, 2009

Mayor	Dennis Roohr
Manager	Jay Todd
Clerk	Jay Todd
Finance Dir	Dawn Robertson
Tax Assessor	Ed Burek
Tax Collector	Dawn Mitchell
Attorney	Anthony Drollas
Building	Alan Wilkins
Comm Dev/Planning	NA
Engineering	Nancy Jamanow
Public Works	NA
Police Chief	Gary Timmons
Emerg/Fire Director	Charles Wilkins

Housing & Construction

Housing Units, 2000*

Total	1,381
Median rent	$906
Median SF home value	$133,200

Permits for New Residential Construction

	Units	Value
Total, 2006	21	$1,970,935
Single family	21	$1,970,935
Total, 2007	5	$444,604
Single family	5	$444,604

Real Property Valuation, 2008

	Parcels	Valuation
Total	373	$58,733,500
Vacant	58	1,947,700
Residential	238	40,595,500
Commercial	24	12,141,500
Industrial	1	88,000
Apartments	0	0
Farm land	35	620,300
Farm homestead	17	3,340,500

Average Property Value & Tax, 2008

Residential value	$172,298
Property tax	$3,949
Tax credit/rebate	$783

Public Library

No public municipal library

Library statistics, 2007

Population served	NA
Full-time/total staff	NA/NA

	Total	Per capita
Holdings	NA	NA
Revenues	NA	NA
Expenditures	NA	NA
Annual visits	NA	NA
Internet terminals/annual users	NA/NA	

Public Safety

Number of officers, 2007 ... 2

Crime	2006	2007
Total crimes	21	7
Violent	1	0
Murder	0	0
Rape	0	0
Robbery	0	0
Aggravated assault	1	0
Non-violent	20	7
Burglary	10	2
Larceny	7	4
Vehicle theft	3	1
Domestic violence	8	2
Arson	0	0
Total crime rate	2.2	0.7
Violent	0.1	0.0
Non-violent	2.1	0.7

Public School District

(for school year 2007-08 except as noted)

New Hanover Township School District
122 Fort Dix St.
Wrightstown, NJ 08562
(609) 723-2139

Superintendent	Terri Sackett
Number of schools	1
Grade plan	K-8
Enrollment	154
Attendance rate, '06-07	94.0%
Dropout rate	NA
Students per teacher	7.3
Per pupil expenditure	$18,607
Median faculty salary	$51,898
Median administrator salary	$87,704
Grade 12 enrollment	NA
High school graduation rate	NA

Assessment test results

(percent scoring at proficient or advanced level)

	Language	Math
NJASK-Grade 3	62.5%	79.2%
GEPA-Grade 8	50.0%	93.8%
HSPA-High School	NA	NA

SAT Score Averages, 2006-07

Pct tested	Math	Verbal	Writing
NA	NA	NA	NA

Teacher Qualifications

Avg. years of experience	10
Highly-qualified teachers one subject/all subjects	100%/100%

No Child Left Behind

AYP, 2006-07 ... Meets Standards

Municipal Finance

State Aid Programs, 2009

Total aid	$1,013,321
CMPTRA	512,290
Energy tax receipts	468,098
Garden State Trust	0

General Budget, 2008

Total tax levy	$1,426,832
County levy	346,948
County taxes	284,917
County library	26,307
County health	0
County open space	35,724
School levy	1,079,884
Muni. levy	0
Misc. revenues	2,297,988

Taxes

	2006	2007	2008
General tax rate per $100	2.293	2.34	2.400
County equalization ratio	81.07	72.46	66.46
Net valuation taxable	$54,003,400	$55,903,985	$59,475,889
State equalized value	$75,392,596	$83,721,948	$91,129,431

---

* US Census Bureau
** New Jersey Department of Labor

See Introduction for an explanation of all data sources.

Demographics & Socio-Economic Characteristics
(2000 US Census, except as noted)

Population
1980*	16,876
1990*	15,990
2000	16,400
Male	7,900
Female	8,500
2007 (estimate)*	16,052
Population density	6,948.9

Race & Hispanic Origin, 2000
Race
White	12,888
Black/African American	429
American Indian/Alaska Native	19
Asian	2,420
Native Hawaiian/Pacific Islander	4
Other race	305
Two or more races	335
Hispanic origin, total	1,326
Mexican	47
Puerto Rican	328
Cuban	190
Other Hispanic	761

Age & Nativity, 2000
Under 5 years	1,050
18 years and over	12,895
21 years and over	12,512
65 years and over	2,888
85 years and over	404
Median age	39.9
Native-born	12,334
Foreign-born	4,066

Educational Attainment, 2000
Population 25 years and over	11,853
Less than 9th grade	4.6%
High school grad or higher	87.6%
Bachelor's degree or higher	32.4%
Graduate degree	11.2%

Income & Poverty, 1999
Per capita income	$29,064
Median household income	$59,118
Median family income	$77,216
Persons in poverty	543
H'holds receiving public assistance	98
H'holds receiving social security	1,870

Households, 2000
Total households	6,346
With persons under 18	1,996
With persons over 65	1,954
Family households	4,275
Single-person households	1,817
Persons per household	2.54
Persons per family	3.18

Labor & Employment
Total civilian labor force, 2007**	9,239
Unemployment rate	3.4%
Total civilian labor force, 2000	8,748
Unemployment rate	3.7%

Employed persons 16 years and over by occupation, 2000
Managers & professionals	3,509
Service occupations	830
Sales & office occupations	2,815
Farming, fishing & forestry	0
Construction & maintenance	589
Production & transportation	681
Self-employed persons	406

General Information
Borough of New Milford
930 River Rd
New Milford, NJ 07646
201-967-5044
Website	www.newmilfordboro.com
Year of incorporation	1922
Land/water area (sq. miles)	2.31/0.00
Form of government	Borough

Government
Legislative Districts
US Congressional	5, 9
State Legislative	39

Local Officials, 2009
Mayor	Frank DeBari
Manager	Christine Demiris
Borough Clerk	Christine Demiris
Finance Dir	Mark Polito
Tax Assessor	Maureen Kaman
Tax Collector	Denise Amoroso
Attorney	S. Greg Moscaritolo
Building	James Taormino
Planning	Angelo DeCarlo
Engineering	Stephen Boswell
Public Works Dir	Mike Calamari (Int)
Police Chief	Frank Papapietro
Emerg/Fire Director	John Stormer

Housing & Construction
Housing Units, 2000*
Total	6,437
Median rent	$763
Median SF home value	$223,400

Permits for New Residential Construction
	Units	Value
Total, 2006	25	$5,119,125
Single family	15	$3,912,625
Total, 2007	18	$3,677,591
Single family	13	$3,074,341

Real Property Valuation, 2008
	Parcels	Valuation
Total	4,329	$1,952,010,600
Vacant	46	6,581,400
Residential	4,192	1,729,876,000
Commercial	75	86,686,800
Industrial	2	3,736,200
Apartments	14	125,130,200
Farm land	0	0
Farm homestead	0	0

Average Property Value & Tax, 2008
Residential value	$412,661
Property tax	$8,647
Tax credit/rebate	$1,284

Public Library
New Milford Public Library
200 Dahlia Ave
New Milford, NJ 07646
201-262-1221
Director	Terrie McColl

Library statistics, 2007
Population served	16,400
Full-time/total staff	4/9

	Total	Per capita
Holdings	66,432	4.05
Revenues	$930,658	$56.75
Expenditures	$930,361	$56.73
Annual visits	163,229	9.95
Internet terminals/annual users	6/7,941	

Public Safety
Number of officers, 2007	32

Crime	2006	2007
Total crimes	133	102
Violent	3	3
Murder	0	0
Rape	0	0
Robbery	1	1
Aggravated assault	2	2
Non-violent	130	99
Burglary	18	15
Larceny	110	81
Vehicle theft	2	3
Domestic violence	104	94
Arson	2	0
Total crime rate	8.2	6.3
Violent	0.2	0.2
Non-violent	8.0	6.1

Public School District
(for school year 2007-08 except as noted)

New Milford School District
145 Madison Avenue
New Milford, NJ 07646
(201) 261-2952
Superintendent	Joseph Picardo (Int)
Number of schools	4
Grade plan	K-12
Enrollment	2,021
Attendance rate, '06-07	94.1%
Dropout rate	1.0%
Students per teacher	11.8
Per pupil expenditure	$12,767
Median faculty salary	$48,700
Median administrator salary	$111,037
Grade 12 enrollment	150
High school graduation rate	96.2%

Assessment test results
(percent scoring at proficient or advanced level)
	Language	Math
NJASK-Grade 3	89.5%	90.7%
GEPA-Grade 8	73.3%	84.9%
HSPA-High School	79.8%	91.1%

SAT Score Averages, 2006-07
Pct tested	Math	Verbal	Writing
89%	515	494	490

Teacher Qualifications
Avg. years of experience	7
Highly-qualified teachers one subject/all subjects	97.5%/97.5%

No Child Left Behind
AYP, 2006-07	Meets Standards

Municipal Finance
State Aid Programs, 2009
Total aid	$2,084,089
CMPTRA	279,645
Energy tax receipts	1,750,622
Garden State Trust	1,492

General Budget, 2008
Total tax levy	$40,922,658
County levy	3,932,518
County taxes	3,719,508
County library	0
County health	0
County open space	213,010
School levy	24,087,876
Muni. levy	12,902,264
Misc. revenues	4,385,890

Taxes
	2006	2007	2008
General tax rate per $100	1.88	2	2.096
County equalization ratio	105.69	94.9	91.85
Net valuation taxable	$1,933,795,000	$1,946,685,143	$1,953,042,767
State equalized value	$2,038,503,655	$2,119,328,186	$2,142,803,727

* US Census Bureau
** New Jersey Department of Labor

See Introduction for an explanation of all data sources.

Demographics & Socio-Economic Characteristics

(2000 US Census, except as noted)

Population

1980*	12,426
1990*	11,439
2000	11,907
Male	5,770
Female	6,137
2007 (estimate)*	11,847
Population density	3,219.3

Race & Hispanic Origin, 2000

Race
White	10,689
Black/African American	105
American Indian/Alaska Native	4
Asian	905
Native Hawaiian/Pacific Islander	3
Other race	81
Two or more races	120
Hispanic origin, total	417
Mexican	37
Puerto Rican	57
Cuban	44
Other Hispanic	279

Age & Nativity, 2000

Under 5 years	934
18 years and over	8,771
21 years and over	8,545
65 years and over	1,821
85 years and over	212
Median age	39.0
Native-born	9,774
Foreign-born	2,133

Educational Attainment, 2000

Population 25 years and over	8,319
Less than 9th grade	2.3%
High school grad or higher	95.1%
Bachelor's degree or higher	58.1%
Graduate degree	27.6%

Income & Poverty, 1999

Per capita income	$42,995
Median household income	$90,964
Median family income	$105,013
Persons in poverty	212
H'holds receiving public assistance	0
H'holds receiving social security	1,275

Households, 2000

Total households	4,404
With persons under 18	1,709
With persons over 65	1,215
Family households	3,309
Single-person households	944
Persons per household	2.67
Persons per family	3.13

Labor & Employment

Total civilian labor force, 2007**	6,403
Unemployment rate	3.0%
Total civilian labor force, 2000	6,189
Unemployment rate	3.3%

Employed persons 16 years and over by occupation, 2000
Managers & professionals	3,601
Service occupations	437
Sales & office occupations	1,440
Farming, fishing & forestry	0
Construction & maintenance	314
Production & transportation	195
Self-employed persons	368

* US Census Bureau
** New Jersey Department of Labor

General Information

Borough of New Providence
360 Elkwood Ave
New Providence, NJ 07974
908-665-1400

Website	www.newprov.org
Year of incorporation	1899
Land/water area (sq. miles)	3.68/0.00
Form of government	Borough

Government

Legislative Districts

US Congressional	7
State Legislative	21

Local Officials, 2009

Mayor	John Thoms
Manager	Douglas Marvin
Clerk	Wendi Barry
Finance Dir	Ken DeRoberts
Tax Assessor	Pat Spychala
Tax Collector	Monica Marino
Attorney	Carl Woodward
Building	Keith Lynch
Comm Dev/Planning	NA
Engineering	Andrew Hipolit
Public Works	James Johnston
Police Chief	Anthony Buccelli
Emerg/Fire Director	Ralph Parlapiano

Housing & Construction

Housing Units, 2000*

Total	4,485
Median rent	$941
Median SF home value	$317,100

Permits for New Residential Construction

	Units	Value
Total, 2006	65	$6,190,642
Single family	38	$2,337,642
Total, 2007	60	$9,607,338
Single family	25	$4,951,224

Real Property Valuation, 2008

	Parcels	Valuation
Total	3,910	$1,294,072,865
Vacant	98	13,388,000
Residential	3,655	1,036,356,200
Commercial	130	131,263,985
Industrial	12	74,811,180
Apartments	15	38,253,500
Farm land	0	0
Farm homestead	0	0

Average Property Value & Tax, 2008

Residential value	$283,545
Property tax	$10,601
Tax credit/rebate	$1,329

Public Library

New Providence Memorial Library
377 Elkwood Ave
New Providence, NJ 07974
908-665-0311

Director	James K. Keehbler

Library statistics, 2007

Population served	11,907
Full-time/total staff	3/7

	Total	Per capita
Holdings	80,023	6.72
Revenues	$859,074	$72.15
Expenditures	$845,642	$71.02
Annual visits	156,880	13.18
Internet terminals/annual users	8/12,672	

Public Safety

Number of officers, 2007	24

Crime	2006	2007
Total crimes	145	120
Violent	5	6
Murder	0	0
Rape	0	0
Robbery	0	1
Aggravated assault	5	5
Non-violent	140	114
Burglary	19	25
Larceny	120	86
Vehicle theft	1	3
Domestic violence	68	97
Arson	0	1
Total crime rate	12.2	10.1
Violent	0.4	0.5
Non-violent	11.8	9.6

Public School District

(for school year 2007-08 except as noted)

New Providence School District
356 Elkwood Avenue
New Providence, NJ 07974
(908) 464-9050

Superintendent	David M. Miceli (Int)
Number of schools	4
Grade plan	K-12
Enrollment	2,194
Attendance rate, '06-07	96.1%
Dropout rate	0.0%
Students per teacher	10.4
Per pupil expenditure	$13,364
Median faculty salary	$60,450
Median administrator salary	$122,900
Grade 12 enrollment	156
High school graduation rate	100.0%

Assessment test results

(percent scoring at proficient or advanced level)
	Language	Math
NJASK-Grade 3	97.4%	95.2%
GEPA-Grade 8	93.4%	97.6%
HSPA-High School	96.7%	97.4%

SAT Score Averages, 2006-07

Pct tested	Math	Verbal	Writing
103%	581	552	554

Teacher Qualifications

Avg. years of experience	9
Highly-qualified teachers one subject/all subjects	100%/100%

No Child Left Behind

AYP, 2006-07	Meets Standards

Municipal Finance

State Aid Programs, 2009

Total aid	$1,713,326
CMPTRA	287,840
Energy tax receipts	1,382,652
Garden State Trust	0

General Budget, 2008

Total tax levy	$48,498,389
County levy	8,576,783
County taxes	8,192,617
County library	0
County health	0
County open space	384,166
School levy	29,224,297
Muni. levy	10,697,309
Misc. revenues	5,865,255

Taxes

	2006	2007	2008
General tax rate per $100	3.395	3.582	3.739
County equalization ratio	57.04	54.06	50.81
Net valuation taxable	$1,300,153,880	$1,294,153,494	$1,297,140,632
State equalized value	$2,409,116,454	$2,543,936,986	$2,631,694,346

See Introduction for an explanation of all data sources.

Demographics & Socio-Economic Characteristics†

(2000 US Census, except as noted)

Population

1980*	329,248
1990*	275,221
2000	273,546
Male	132,701
Female	140,845
2007 (estimate)*	280,135
Population density	11,770.4

Race & Hispanic Origin, 2000

Race

White	72,537
Black/African American	146,250
American Indian/Alaska Native	1,005
Asian	3,263
Native Hawaiian/Pacific Islander	135
Other race	38,430
Two or more races	11,926
Hispanic origin, total	80,622
Mexican	2,295
Puerto Rican	39,650
Cuban	2,962
Other Hispanic	35,715

Age & Nativity, 2000

Under 5 years	21,293
18 years and over	197,127
21 years and over	183,103
65 years and over	25,306
85 years and over	2,722
Median age	30.8
Native-born	207,489
Foreign-born	66,057

Educational Attainment, 2000

Population 25 years and over	164,298
Less than 9th grade	18.1%
High school grad or higher	57.9%
Bachelor's degree or higher	9.0%
Graduate degree	3.0%

Income & Poverty, 1999

Per capita income	$13,009
Median household income	$26,913
Median family income	$30,781
Persons in poverty	74,263
H'holds receiving public assistance	11,515
H'holds receiving social security	21,956

Households, 2000

Total households	91,382
With persons under 18	39,255
With persons over 65	19,077
Family households	61,999
Single-person households	24,331
Persons per household	2.85
Persons per family	3.43

Labor & Employment

Total civilian labor force, 2007**	105,366
Unemployment rate	7.9%
Total civilian labor force, 2000	108,256
Unemployment rate	16.1%

Employed persons 16 years and over by occupation, 2000

Managers & professionals	17,168
Service occupations	19,796
Sales & office occupations	24,985
Farming, fishing & forestry	134
Construction & maintenance	9,455
Production & transportation	19,281
Self-employed persons	2,707

† see Appendix C for American Community Survey data
* US Census Bureau
** New Jersey Department of Labor

General Information

City of Newark
920 Broad St
Newark, NJ 07102
973-733-6400

Website	www.ci.newark.nj.us
Year of incorporation	1836
Land/water area (sq. miles)	23.80/2.17
Form of government	Mayor-Council

Government

Legislative Districts

US Congressional	10, 13
State Legislative	27-29

Local Officials, 2009

Mayor	Cory A. Booker
Manager	Michelle L. Thomas (Actg)
Clerk	Robert P. Marasco
Finance Dir	Linda Landolfi (Actg)
Tax Assessor	Evelyn Laccitiello
Tax Collector	Michelle Jones
Attorney	Julien Neals
Building	Neil Midtgard
Planning/Comm Dev	Toni Griffin
Engineering	Mehdi Mohammadish (Actg)
Public Works	NA
Police Chief	Anthony Campos
Emerg/Fire Director	David Giordano

Housing & Construction

Housing Units, 2000*

Total	100,141
Median rent	$586
Median SF home value	$119,000

Permits for New Residential Construction

	Units	Value
Total, 2006	2,059	$164,085,874
Single family	100	$13,068,747
Total, 2007	948	$67,797,493
Single family	29	$5,523,070

Real Property Valuation, 2008

	Parcels	Valuation
Total	41,431	$10,785,260,000
Vacant	4,668	476,884,300
Residential	29,216	5,114,917,500
Commercial	5,388	3,545,307,500
Industrial	911	897,442,500
Apartments	1,248	750,708,200
Farm land	0	0
Farm homestead	0	0

Average Property Value & Tax, 2008

Residential value	$175,072
Property tax	$4,549
Tax credit/rebate	$801

Public Library

Newark Public Library
5 Washington St
Newark, NJ 07101
973-733-7780

Director ... Wilma J. Grey

Library statistics, 2007

Population served	273,546
Full-time/total staff	52/161

	Total	Per capita
Holdings	1,691,042	6.18
Revenues	$15,980,974	$58.42
Expenditures	$15,981,004	$58.42
Annual visits	704,155	2.57
Internet terminals/annual users	294/234,969	

Public Safety

Number of officers, 2007	1,227

Crime	2006	2007
Total crimes	15,097	13,970
Violent	2,981	2,489
Murder	107	105
Rape	88	60
Robbery	1,360	1,127
Aggravated assault	1,426	1,197
Non-violent	12,116	11,481
Burglary	2,007	1,954
Larceny	4,951	5,124
Vehicle theft	5,158	4,403
Domestic violence	2,129	1,488
Arson	168	93
Total crime rate	53.8	49.6
Violent	10.6	8.8
Non-violent	43.2	40.8

Public School District

(for school year 2007-08 except as noted)

Newark School District
2 Cedar Street
Newark, NJ 07102
(973) 733-7333

State District Superintendent	Clifford Janey
Number of schools	74
Grade plan	K-12
Enrollment	39,933
Attendance rate, '06-07	90.5%
Dropout rate	3.4%
Students per teacher	9.8
Per pupil expenditure	$17,978
Median faculty salary	$76,739
Median administrator salary	$98,789
Grade 12 enrollment	2,422
High school graduation rate	90.2%

Assessment test results

(percent scoring at proficient or advanced level)

	Language	Math
NJASK-Grade 3	69.4%	68.8%
GEPA-Grade 8	37.2%	56.5%
HSPA-High School	40.4%	51.2%

SAT Score Averages, 2006-07

Pct tested	Math	Verbal	Writing
NA	NA	NA	NA

Teacher Qualifications

Avg. years of experience	11
Highly-qualified teachers one subject/all subjects	96.0%/96.0%

No Child Left Behind

AYP, 2006-07 ... Needs Improvement

Municipal Finance

State Aid Programs, 2009

Total aid	$108,332,535
CMPTRA	67,640,102
Energy tax receipts	39,067,445
Garden State Trust	0

General Budget, 2008

Total tax levy	$282,131,756
County levy	67,113,708
County taxes	64,462,391
County library	0
County health	0
County open space	2,651,316
School levy	100,277,219
Muni. levy	114,740,829
Misc. revenues	541,183,024

Taxes	2006	2007	2008
General tax rate per $100	2.49	2.49	2.599
County equalization ratio	81.43	70.68	64.36
Net valuation taxable	$10,825,543,000	$11,001,867,400	$10,858,108,700
State equalized value	$15,438,960,530	$17,051,525,430	$18,719,563,776

See Introduction for an explanation of all data sources.

Demographics & Socio-Economic Characteristics
(2000 US Census, except as noted)

Population
1980*	1,563
1990*	1,592
2000	1,616
Male	744
Female	872
2007 (estimate)*	1,670
Population density	982.4

Race & Hispanic Origin, 2000
Race
White	1,537
Black/African American	21
American Indian/Alaska Native	11
Asian	9
Native Hawaiian/Pacific Islander	0
Other race	17
Two or more races	21
Hispanic origin, total	62
Mexican	12
Puerto Rican	32
Cuban	3
Other Hispanic	15

Age & Nativity, 2000
Under 5 years	93
18 years and over	1,222
21 years and over	1,169
65 years and over	230
85 years and over	27
Median age	38.8
Native-born	1,561
Foreign-born	55

Educational Attainment, 2000
Population 25 years and over	1,115
Less than 9th grade	5.6%
High school grad or higher	83.5%
Bachelor's degree or higher	15.7%
Graduate degree	3.7%

Income & Poverty, 1999
Per capita income	$21,063
Median household income	$51,875
Median family income	$59,934
Persons in poverty	105
H'holds receiving public assistance	9
H'holds receiving social security	178

Households, 2000
Total households	596
With persons under 18	221
With persons over 65	163
Family households	471
Single-person households	105
Persons per household	2.71
Persons per family	3.04

Labor & Employment
Total civilian labor force, 2007**	1,043
Unemployment rate	4.9%
Total civilian labor force, 2000	877
Unemployment rate	4.8%

Employed persons 16 years and over by occupation, 2000
Managers & professionals	229
Service occupations	117
Sales & office occupations	248
Farming, fishing & forestry	2
Construction & maintenance	122
Production & transportation	117
Self-employed persons	47

General Information
Borough of Newfield
18 Catawba Ave
PO Box 856
Newfield, NJ 08344
856-697-1100

Website	www.newfieldboro.com
Year of incorporation	1924
Land/water area (sq. miles)	1.70/0.00
Form of government	Borough

Government
Legislative Districts
US Congressional	2
State Legislative	4

Local Officials, 2009
Mayor	Joseph Curcio III
Manager/Admin	NA
Clerk	Toni Van Camp
Finance Dir	Robert Scharle
Tax Assessor	Dianne Hesley
Tax Collector	Lawrence Nightlinger
Attorney	John Eastlack
Building	John M. Eckler
Comm Dev/Planning	NA
Engineering	Bob Vettese
Public Works	NA
Police Chief	Michael Kappre
Emerg/Fire Dir	William Mason

Housing & Construction
Housing Units, 2000*
Total	620
Median rent	$711
Median SF home value	$103,200

Permits for New Residential Construction
	Units	Value
Total, 2006	5	$558,373
Single family	5	$558,373
Total, 2007	2	$223,350
Single family	2	$223,350

Real Property Valuation, 2008
	Parcels	Valuation
Total	775	$142,084,900
Vacant	115	5,199,900
Residential	581	119,108,700
Commercial	32	8,427,600
Industrial	23	6,531,300
Apartments	2	870,200
Farm land	15	158,400
Farm homestead	7	1,788,800

Average Property Value & Tax, 2008
Residential value	$205,608
Property tax	$4,531
Tax credit/rebate	$920

Public Library
Newfield Public Library
115 Catawba Ave
Newfield, NJ 08344
856-697-0415

Manager	Susan Mounier

Library statistics, 2007
Population served	1,616
Full-time/total staff	0/1

	Total	Per capita
Holdings	22,830	14.13
Revenues	$33,041	$20.45
Expenditures	$31,180	$19.29
Annual visits	12,877	7.97
Internet terminals/annual users	3/3,017	

Public Safety
Number of officers, 2007	6

Crime	2006	2007
Total crimes	34	25
Violent	2	3
Murder	0	0
Rape	0	0
Robbery	0	0
Aggravated assault	2	3
Non-violent	32	22
Burglary	13	14
Larceny	18	8
Vehicle theft	1	0
Domestic violence	18	11
Arson	0	0
Total crime rate	20.5	15.0
Violent	1.2	1.8
Non-violent	19.3	13.2

Public School District
(for school year 2007-08 except as noted)

Newfield School District
1122 Almond Road
Pittsgrove, NJ 08318

No schools in district

Per pupil expenditure	NA
Median faculty salary	NA
Median administrator salary	NA
Grade 12 enrollment	NA
High school graduation rate	NA

Assessment test results
(percent scoring at proficient or advanced level)
	Language	Math
NJASK-Grade 3	NA	NA
GEPA-Grade 8	NA	NA
HSPA-High School	NA	NA

SAT Score Averages, 2006-07
Pct tested	Math	Verbal	Writing
NA	NA	NA	NA

Teacher Qualifications
Avg. years of experience	NA
Highly-qualified teachers one subject/all subjects	NA/NA

No Child Left Behind
AYP, 2006-07	NA

Municipal Finance
State Aid Programs, 2009
Total aid	$167,296
CMPTRA	50,005
Energy tax receipts	113,047
Garden State Trust	59

General Budget, 2008
Total tax levy	$3,134,484
County levy	782,968
County taxes	675,684
County library	54,333
County health	0
County open space	52,951
School levy	1,673,688
Muni. levy	677,828
Misc. revenues	569,857

Taxes
	2006	2007	2008
General tax rate per $100	4.646	4.744	2.204
County equalization ratio	60.95	52.39	107.90
Net valuation taxable	$60,848,300	$62,514,808	$142,246,939
State equalized value	$116,340,006	$130,136,128	$134,941,872

---

* US Census Bureau
** New Jersey Department of Labor

See Introduction for an explanation of all data sources.

Demographics & Socio-Economic Characteristics

(2000 US Census, except as noted)

Population

1980*	7,748
1990*	7,521
2000	8,244
Male	3,951
Female	4,293
2007 (estimate)*	8,167
Population density	2,634.5

Race & Hispanic Origin, 2000

Race

White	7,582
Black/African American	281
American Indian/Alaska Native	11
Asian	162
Native Hawaiian/Pacific Islander	1
Other race	96
Two or more races	111
Hispanic origin, total	313
Mexican	50
Puerto Rican	129
Cuban	20
Other Hispanic	114

Age & Nativity, 2000

Under 5 years	522
18 years and over	6,271
21 years and over	5,992
65 years and over	1,284
85 years and over	225
Median age	37.6
Native-born	7,569
Foreign-born	675

Educational Attainment, 2000

Population 25 years and over	5,690
Less than 9th grade	4.7%
High school grad or higher	83.6%
Bachelor's degree or higher	19.2%
Graduate degree	6.7%

Income & Poverty, 1999

Per capita income	$20,577
Median household income	$41,667
Median family income	$56,484
Persons in poverty	882
H'holds receiving public assistance	98
H'holds receiving social security	1,049

Households, 2000

Total households	3,258
With persons under 18	1,042
With persons over 65	892
Family households	1,942
Single-person households	1,093
Persons per household	2.39
Persons per family	3.12

Labor & Employment

Total civilian labor force, 2007**	4,597
Unemployment rate	3.7%
Total civilian labor force, 2000	4,152
Unemployment rate	3.3%

Employed persons 16 years and over by occupation, 2000

Managers & professionals	1,318
Service occupations	661
Sales & office occupations	1,202
Farming, fishing & forestry	0
Construction & maintenance	303
Production & transportation	532
Self-employed persons	184

‡ Branch of county library
* US Census Bureau
** New Jersey Department of Labor

General Information

Town of Newton
39 Trinity St
Newton, NJ 07860
973-383-3521

Website	www.newtontownhall.com
Year of incorporation	1864
Land/water area (sq. miles)	3.10/0.01
Form of government	Council-Manager

Government

Legislative Districts

US Congressional	5
State Legislative	24

Local Officials, 2009

Mayor	Joseph Ricciardo
Manager	Eileen Kithcart
Clerk	Lorraine Read
Finance Dir	Dawn Babcock
Tax Assessor	Scott Holzhauer
Tax Collector	Linda Roth
Attorney	Sanford Hollander
Construction/Code Enf	Robert Bittle
Community Dev Dir	Debra Millikin
Engineering	Harold Pellow
Public Works	Kenneth Jaekel
Police Chief	John Tomasula
Emerg/Fire Director	Jeff Schniffer

Housing & Construction

Housing Units, 2000*

Total	3,425
Median rent	$697
Median SF home value	$136,100

Permits for New Residential Construction

	Units	Value
Total, 2006	4	$276,200
Single family	0	$0
Total, 2007	2	$305,000
Single family	0	$0

Real Property Valuation, 2008

	Parcels	Valuation
Total	2,342	$823,736,000
Vacant	68	14,008,800
Residential	1,970	533,542,800
Commercial	253	206,779,300
Industrial	12	22,616,900
Apartments	29	46,204,800
Farm land	8	39,800
Farm homestead	2	543,600

Average Property Value & Tax, 2008

Residential value	$270,835
Property tax	$6,568
Tax credit/rebate	$1,074

Public Library

Dennis Mem. Branch Library‡
101 Main St
Newton, NJ 07860
973-383-4810

Branch Librarian .... Debbie Mole

Library statistics, 2007

see Sussex County profile
for library system statistics

Public Safety

Number of officers, 2007 25

Crime	2006	2007
Total crimes	146	124
Violent	8	5
Murder	0	0
Rape	0	0
Robbery	0	1
Aggravated assault	8	4
Non-violent	138	119
Burglary	9	25
Larceny	124	90
Vehicle theft	5	4
Domestic violence	112	115
Arson	0	1
Total crime rate	17.3	14.9
Violent	1.0	0.6
Non-violent	16.4	14.3

Public School District

(for school year 2007-08 except as noted)

Newton School District
57 Trinity Street
Newton, NJ 07860
(973) 383-7392

Chief School Admin	William King
Number of schools	3
Grade plan	K-12
Enrollment	1,605
Attendance rate, '06-07	93.7%
Dropout rate	0.8%
Students per teacher	10.1
Per pupil expenditure	$12,908
Median faculty salary	$55,490
Median administrator salary	$114,425
Grade 12 enrollment	187
High school graduation rate	96.9%

Assessment test results

(percent scoring at proficient or advanced level)

	Language	Math
NJASK-Grade 3	83.1%	75.9%
GEPA-Grade 8	69.7%	80.9%
HSPA-High School	85.6%	83.4%

SAT Score Averages, 2006-07

Pct tested	Math	Verbal	Writing
75%	524	506	499

Teacher Qualifications

Avg. years of experience	11
Highly-qualified teachers one subject/all subjects	100%/100%

No Child Left Behind

AYP, 2006-07 .... Meets Standards

Municipal Finance

State Aid Programs, 2009

Total aid	$1,266,699
CMPTRA	201,430
Energy tax receipts	1,031,008
Garden State Trust	14,149

General Budget, 2008

Total tax levy	$20,235,526
County levy	3,179,297
County taxes	2,668,721
County library	224,857
County health	78,808
County open space	206,911
School levy	10,712,666
Muni. levy	6,343,564
Misc. revenues	3,348,414

Taxes	2006	2007	2008
General tax rate per $100	4.58	4.84	2.426
County equalization ratio	58.28	53.04	101.03
Net valuation taxable	$379,122,400	$388,020,571	$834,437,330
State equalized value	$719,329,158	$809,415,251	$818,523,238

See Introduction for an explanation of all data sources.

Demographics & Socio-Economic Characteristics
(2000 US Census, except as noted)

Population
1980*	16,587
1990*	13,790
2000	15,181
Male	7,137
Female	8,044
2007 (estimate)*	14,837
Population density	5,750.8

Race & Hispanic Origin, 2000
Race
White	13,603
Black/African American	70
American Indian/Alaska Native	22
Asian	852
Native Hawaiian/Pacific Islander	2
Other race	348
Two or more races	284
Hispanic origin, total	1,605
Mexican	56
Puerto Rican	390
Cuban	241
Other Hispanic	918

Age & Nativity, 2000
Under 5 years	686
18 years and over	12,445
21 years and over	12,003
65 years and over	2,942
85 years and over	361
Median age	40.9
Native-born	11,880
Foreign-born	3,301

Educational Attainment, 2000
Population 25 years and over	11,252
Less than 9th grade	6.9%
High school grad or higher	82.1%
Bachelor's degree or higher	19.5%
Graduate degree	5.2%

Income & Poverty, 1999
Per capita income	$24,441
Median household income	$51,787
Median family income	$62,483
Persons in poverty	773
H'holds receiving public assistance	114
H'holds receiving social security	2,254

Households, 2000
Total households	6,392
With persons under 18	1,669
With persons over 65	2,186
Family households	4,129
Single-person households	1,977
Persons per household	2.37
Persons per family	3.00

Labor & Employment
Total civilian labor force, 2007**	8,276
Unemployment rate	3.6%
Total civilian labor force, 2000	7,851
Unemployment rate	4.0%

Employed persons 16 years and over by occupation, 2000
Managers & professionals	2,262
Service occupations	1,047
Sales & office occupations	2,654
Farming, fishing & forestry	0
Construction & maintenance	637
Production & transportation	939
Self-employed persons	301

General Information
Borough of North Arlington
214 Ridge Rd
North Arlington, NJ 07031
201-991-6060
Website	www.northarlington.org
Year of incorporation	1896
Land/water area (sq. miles)	2.58/0.04
Form of government	Borough

Government
Legislative Districts
US Congressional	9
State Legislative	36

Local Officials, 2009
Mayor	Peter Massa
Manager	Terence M. Wall
Clerk	Terence M. Wall (Actg)
Finance Dir	Joseph Iannaconi Jr
Tax Assessor	Denis McGuire
Tax Collector	Joseph Iannaconi Jr
Attorney	Anthony D'Elia
Building	Robert Kairys
Planning	Joseph Bianchi
Engineering	Neglia Engineering
Public Works	James McCabe
Police Chief	Louis Ghione
Emerg/Fire Director	Christopher Coupe

Housing & Construction
Housing Units, 2000*
Total	6,529
Median rent	$763
Median SF home value	$183,300

Permits for New Residential Construction
	Units	Value
Total, 2006	0	$202,600
Single family	0	$202,600
Total, 2007	2	$193,300
Single family	0	$0

Real Property Valuation, 2008
	Parcels	Valuation
Total	4,077	$819,316,300
Vacant	56	11,604,300
Residential	3,744	670,453,200
Commercial	185	68,429,900
Industrial	55	31,568,900
Apartments	37	37,260,000
Farm land	0	0
Farm homestead	0	0

Average Property Value & Tax, 2008
Residential value	$179,074
Property tax	$7,838
Tax credit/rebate	$1,107

Public Library
North Arlington Public Library
210 Ridge Rd
North Arlington, NJ 07031
201-955-5640
Director	Stephanie M. Burke

Library statistics, 2007
Population served	15,181
Full-time/total staff	2/7

	Total	Per capita
Holdings	97,168	6.40
Revenues	$594,885	$39.19
Expenditures	$545,840	$35.96
Annual visits	80,000	5.27
Internet terminals/annual users	9/34,750	

Public Safety
Number of officers, 2007	32

Crime	2006	2007
Total crimes	266	218
Violent	15	15
Murder	0	0
Rape	3	1
Robbery	4	2
Aggravated assault	8	12
Non-violent	251	203
Burglary	35	22
Larceny	187	154
Vehicle theft	29	27
Domestic violence	100	105
Arson	1	0
Total crime rate	17.5	14.5
Violent	1.0	1.0
Non-violent	16.5	13.5

Public School District
(for school year 2007-08 except as noted)

North Arlington School District
222 Ridge Road
North Arlington, NJ 07031
(201) 991-6800
Superintendent	Oliver Stringham
Number of schools	5
Grade plan	K-12
Enrollment	1,598
Attendance rate, '06-07	94.4%
Dropout rate	2.2%
Students per teacher	12.1
Per pupil expenditure	$13,524
Median faculty salary	$46,495
Median administrator salary	$123,447
Grade 12 enrollment	125
High school graduation rate	97.4%

Assessment test results
(percent scoring at proficient or advanced level)
	Language	Math
NJASK-Grade 3	93.6%	92.7%
GEPA-Grade 8	81.8%	88.1%
HSPA-High School	74.3%	87.5%

SAT Score Averages, 2006-07
Pct tested	Math	Verbal	Writing
71%	490	452	450

Teacher Qualifications
Avg. years of experience	8
Highly-qualified teachers one subject/all subjects	100%/100%

No Child Left Behind
AYP, 2006-07	Meets Standards

Municipal Finance
State Aid Programs, 2009
Total aid	$1,365,372
CMPTRA	175,028
Energy tax receipts	1,169,863
Garden State Trust	0

General Budget, 2008
Total tax levy	$35,891,388
County levy	3,381,091
County taxes	3,198,087
County library	0
County health	0
County open space	183,005
School levy	19,872,245
Muni. levy	12,638,052
Misc. revenues	7,054,617

Taxes
	2006	2007	2008
General tax rate per $100	3.76	4.27	4.380
County equalization ratio	52.18	47.41	44.97
Net valuation taxable	$809,453,350	$812,629,529	$819,976,328
State equalized value	$1,708,214,379	$1,806,215,942	$1,804,129,762

---

* US Census Bureau
** New Jersey Department of Labor

See Introduction for an explanation of all data sources.

Demographics & Socio-Economic Characteristics
(2000 US Census, except as noted)

Population
1980*	47,019
1990*	48,414
2000	58,092
Male	27,758
Female	30,334
2007 (estimate)*	56,146
Population density	10,797.3

Race & Hispanic Origin, 2000
Race
White	39,131
Black/African American	1,581
American Indian/Alaska Native	235
Asian	3,756
Native Hawaiian/Pacific Islander	28
Other race	9,023
Two or more races	4,338
Hispanic origin, total	33,260
Mexican	553
Puerto Rican	4,535
Cuban	7,635
Other Hispanic	20,537

Age & Nativity, 2000
Under 5 years	3,713
18 years and over	44,887
21 years and over	42,885
65 years and over	8,028
85 years and over	1,220
Median age	35.9
Native-born	30,990
Foreign-born	27,216

Educational Attainment, 2000
Population 25 years and over	39,719
Less than 9th grade	15.4%
High school grad or higher	68.7%
Bachelor's degree or higher	19.6%
Graduate degree	7.1%

Income & Poverty, 1999
Per capita income	$20,058
Median household income	$40,844
Median family income	$46,172
Persons in poverty	6,397
H'holds receiving public assistance	669
H'holds receiving social security	5,701

Households, 2000
Total households	21,236
With persons under 18	7,481
With persons over 65	5,809
Family households	14,242
Single-person households	5,890
Persons per household	2.70
Persons per family	3.33

Labor & Employment
Total civilian labor force, 2007**	26,951
Unemployment rate	5.0%
Total civilian labor force, 2000	27,526
Unemployment rate	8.1%

Employed persons 16 years and over by occupation, 2000
Managers & professionals	6,796
Service occupations	3,653
Sales & office occupations	7,958
Farming, fishing & forestry	29
Construction & maintenance	1,685
Production & transportation	5,168
Self-employed persons	1,257

* US Census Bureau
** New Jersey Department of Labor
§ State Fiscal Year July 1–June 30

General Information
Township of North Bergen
4233 Kennedy Blvd
North Bergen, NJ 07047
201-392-2000
Website	www.northbergen.org
Year of incorporation	1843
Land/water area (sq. miles)	5.20/0.42
Form of government	Commission

Government
Legislative Districts
US Congressional	9, 13
State Legislative	32

Local Officials, 2009
Mayor	Nicholas Sacco
Manager	Christopher Pianese
Clerk	Erin Barillas (Actg)
Finance Dir	Robert Pittfield
Tax Assessor	Paul Sadlon
Tax Collector	Denise Zambardino
Attorney	Herb Klitzner
Building	Brian Ribbaro
Planning	Brian Chewcaskie
Engineering	Dereck McGrath
Public Works	Frank Gargiulo
Police Chief	William Galvin
Emerg/Fire Director	Michael DeOrio

Housing & Construction
Housing Units, 2000*
Total	22,009
Median rent	$733
Median SF home value	$162,600

Permits for New Residential Construction
	Units	Value
Total, 2006	32	$3,002,270
Single family	11	$1,587,770
Total, 2007	2	$257,985
Single family	0	$0

Real Property Valuation, 2008
	Parcels	Valuation
Total	11,969	$2,486,132,000
Vacant	727	95,489,400
Residential	10,166	1,369,305,100
Commercial	701	572,756,800
Industrial	210	276,837,100
Apartments	165	171,743,600
Farm land	0	0
Farm homestead	0	0

Average Property Value & Tax, 2008
Residential value	$134,695
Property tax	$5,637
Tax credit/rebate	$915

Public Library
North Bergen Public Library
8411 Bergenline Ave
North Bergen, NJ 07047
201-869-4715
Director	Sai Rao

Library statistics, 2007
Population served	58,092
Full-time/total staff	4/10

	Total	Per capita
Holdings	187,718	3.23
Revenues	$1,404,855	$24.18
Expenditures	$1,116,578	$19.22
Annual visits	429,452	7.39
Internet terminals/annual users	45/37,406	

Public Safety
Number of officers, 2007	116

Crime	2006	2007
Total crimes	1,035	1,114
Violent	121	104
Murder	1	0
Rape	4	5
Robbery	58	55
Aggravated assault	58	44
Non-violent	914	1,010
Burglary	166	151
Larceny	562	719
Vehicle theft	186	140
Domestic violence	597	583
Arson	1	4
Total crime rate	17.9	19.5
Violent	2.1	1.8
Non-violent	15.8	17.6

Public School District
(for school year 2007-08 except as noted)

North Bergen School District
7317 Kennedy Boulevard
North Bergen, NJ 07047
(201) 295-2706
Superintendent	Robert Dandorph
Number of schools	7
Grade plan	K-12
Enrollment	7,465
Attendance rate, '06-07	93.9%
Dropout rate	1.9%
Students per teacher	12.5
Per pupil expenditure	$12,201
Median faculty salary	$62,150
Median administrator salary	$123,500
Grade 12 enrollment	474
High school graduation rate	89.1%

Assessment test results
(percent scoring at proficient or advanced level)
	Language	Math
NJASK-Grade 3	87.6%	88.5%
GEPA-Grade 8	71.3%	86.8%
HSPA-High School	81.6%	91.8%

SAT Score Averages, 2006-07
Pct tested	Math	Verbal	Writing
83%	449	434	432

Teacher Qualifications
Avg. years of experience	9
Highly-qualified teachers one subject/all subjects	99.5%/99.5%

No Child Left Behind
AYP, 2006-07	Meets Standards

Municipal Finance§
State Aid Programs, 2009
Total aid	$8,837,095
CMPTRA	4,163,415
Energy tax receipts	4,541,124
Garden State Trust	0

General Budget, 2008
Total tax levy	$108,590,583
County levy	20,915,480
County taxes	20,358,726
County library	0
County health	0
County open space	556,754
School levy	39,113,248
Muni. levy	48,561,855
Misc. revenues	27,712,724

Taxes	2006	2007	2008
General tax rate per $100	4.159	4.23	4.362
County equalization ratio	51.29	49.57	45.14
Net valuation taxable	$2,487,457,100	$2,479,379,114	$2,489,963,745
State equalized value	$5,022,333,362	$5,487,571,552	$5,988,742,674

See Introduction for an explanation of all data sources.

Demographics & Socio-Economic Characteristics
(2000 US Census, except as noted)

Population
1980*	22,220
1990*	31,287
2000	36,287
Male	18,021
Female	18,266
2007 (estimate)*	39,676
Population density	3,300.8

Race & Hispanic Origin, 2000
Race
White	22,763
Black/African American	5,542
American Indian/Alaska Native	63
Asian	5,152
Native Hawaiian/Pacific Islander	10
Other race	1,707
Two or more races	1,050
Hispanic origin, total	3,775
Mexican	522
Puerto Rican	1,316
Cuban	161
Other Hispanic	1,776

Age & Nativity, 2000
Under 5 years	2,437
18 years and over	27,934
21 years and over	26,806
65 years and over	3,615
85 years and over	328
Median age	35.4
Native-born	27,424
Foreign-born	8,863

Educational Attainment, 2000
Population 25 years and over	25,089
Less than 9th grade	4.9%
High school grad or higher	85.8%
Bachelor's degree or higher	37.0%
Graduate degree	14.3%

Income & Poverty, 1999
Per capita income	$28,431
Median household income	$61,325
Median family income	$70,812
Persons in poverty	1,661
H'holds receiving public assistance	377
H'holds receiving social security	2,932

Households, 2000
Total households	13,635
With persons under 18	4,817
With persons over 65	2,772
Family households	9,363
Single-person households	3,339
Persons per household	2.58
Persons per family	3.12

Labor & Employment
Total civilian labor force, 2007**	22,595
Unemployment rate	3.7%
Total civilian labor force, 2000	19,586
Unemployment rate	3.6%

Employed persons 16 years and over by occupation, 2000
Managers & professionals	8,736
Service occupations	1,763
Sales & office occupations	5,365
Farming, fishing & forestry	0
Construction & maintenance	990
Production & transportation	2,022
Self-employed persons	816

* US Census Bureau
** New Jersey Department of Labor
§ State Fiscal Year July 1–June 30

General Information
Township of North Brunswick
710 Hermann Rd
North Brunswick, NJ 08902
732-247-0922
Website	www.northbrunswickonline.com
Year of incorporation	1779
Land/water area (sq. miles)	12.02/0.23
Form of government	Mayor-Council-Admin

Government
Legislative Districts
US Congressional	12
State Legislative	17

Local Officials, 2009
Mayor	Francis Womack III
Manager	Robert Lombard
Clerk	Lisa Russo
Finance Dir	Kala Sriranganthan
Tax Assessor	Dianne Walker
Tax Collector	Laurie Hammarstrom
Attorney	Ronald Gordon
Building	Tom Paun
Planning	Tom Vigna
Engineering	CME Associates
Public Works	Glenn Sandor
Police Chief	Joseph Battaglia
Emerg/Fire Director	Craig Snediker

Housing & Construction
Housing Units, 2000*
Total	13,932
Median rent	$907
Median SF home value	$179,400

Permits for New Residential Construction
	Units	Value
Total, 2006	12	$1,896,476
Single family	12	$1,896,476
Total, 2007	29	$4,149,750
Single family	29	$4,149,750

Real Property Valuation, 2008
	Parcels	Valuation
Total	11,048	$2,513,287,400
Vacant	926	53,099,800
Residential	9,630	1,519,488,800
Commercial	375	384,945,700
Industrial	57	342,852,800
Apartments	36	211,278,500
Farm land	17	171,700
Farm homestead	7	1,450,100

Average Property Value & Tax, 2008
Residential value	$157,823
Property tax	$6,866
Tax credit/rebate	$1,064

Public Library
North Brunswick Public Library
880 Hermann Rd
North Brunswick, NJ 08902
732-246-3545
Director	Cheryl McBride

Library statistics, 2007
Population served	36,287
Full-time/total staff	6/15

	Total	Per capita
Holdings	94,618	2.61
Revenues	$1,502,884	$41.42
Expenditures	$1,452,412	$40.03
Annual visits	216,685	5.97
Internet terminals/annual users	20/50,807	

Public Safety
Number of officers, 2007	84

Crime	2006	2007
Total crimes	940	978
Violent	90	90
Murder	0	0
Rape	1	3
Robbery	34	39
Aggravated assault	55	48
Non-violent	850	888
Burglary	204	203
Larceny	582	588
Vehicle theft	64	97
Domestic violence	160	160
Arson	7	2
Total crime rate	23.7	24.5
Violent	2.3	2.3
Non-violent	21.4	22.3

Public School District
(for school year 2007-08 except as noted)

North Brunswick Township School District
Old Georges Road, PO Box 6016
North Brunswick, NJ 08902
(732) 289-3030
Superintendent	Brian Zychowski
Number of schools	6
Grade plan	K-12
Enrollment	5,526
Attendance rate, '06-07	94.4%
Dropout rate	1.2%
Students per teacher	11.5
Per pupil expenditure	$13,377
Median faculty salary	$55,723
Median administrator salary	$103,081
Grade 12 enrollment	438
High school graduation rate	91.3%

Assessment test results
(percent scoring at proficient or advanced level)
	Language	Math
NJASK-Grade 3	88.3%	89.6%
GEPA-Grade 8	72.6%	80.2%
HSPA-High School	80.2%	88.2%

SAT Score Averages, 2006-07
Pct tested	Math	Verbal	Writing
78%	524	495	489

Teacher Qualifications
Avg. years of experience	7
Highly-qualified teachers one subject/all subjects	99.5%/99.5%

No Child Left Behind
AYP, 2006-07	Meets Standards

Municipal Finance§
State Aid Programs, 2009
Total aid	$5,789,719
CMPTRA	1,155,149
Energy tax receipts	4,485,290
Garden State Trust	0

General Budget, 2008
Total tax levy	$109,479,257
County levy	14,999,492
County taxes	13,433,053
County library	0
County health	0
County open space	1,566,439
School levy	69,211,892
Muni. levy	25,267,873
Misc. revenues	20,856,106

Taxes	2006	2007	2008
General tax rate per $100	4.07	4.24	4.351
County equalization ratio	62.05	54.2	48.80
Net valuation taxable	$2,473,061,200	$2,510,462,561	$2,516,524,381
State equalized value	$4,566,652,231	$5,140,798,141	$7,964,419,512

See Introduction for an explanation of all data sources.

Demographics & Socio-Economic Characteristics
(2000 US Census, except as noted)

Population
1980*	5,832
1990*	6,706
2000	7,375
Male	3,999
Female	3,376
2007 (estimate)*	7,092
Population density	2,371.9

Race & Hispanic Origin, 2000
Race
White	5,873
Black/African American	1,070
American Indian/Alaska Native	2
Asian	347
Native Hawaiian/Pacific Islander	0
Other race	19
Two or more races	64
Hispanic origin, total	159
Mexican	19
Puerto Rican	21
Cuban	39
Other Hispanic	80

Age & Nativity, 2000
Under 5 years	431
18 years and over	5,673
21 years and over	5,441
65 years and over	801
85 years and over	48
Median age	37.3
Native-born	6,740
Foreign-born	635

Educational Attainment, 2000
Population 25 years and over	4,919
Less than 9th grade	0.7%
High school grad or higher	92.6%
Bachelor's degree or higher	58.2%
Graduate degree	29.1%

Income & Poverty, 1999
Per capita income	$48,249
Median household income	$117,395
Median family income	$125,465
Persons in poverty	75
H'holds receiving public assistance	0
H'holds receiving social security	507

Households, 2000
Total households	2,070
With persons under 18	904
With persons over 65	538
Family households	1,835
Single-person households	198
Persons per household	3.02
Persons per family	3.23

Labor & Employment
Total civilian labor force, 2007**	3,329
Unemployment rate	2.7%
Total civilian labor force, 2000	3,196
Unemployment rate	2.4%

Employed persons 16 years and over by occupation, 2000
Managers & professionals	1,967
Service occupations	141
Sales & office occupations	854
Farming, fishing & forestry	0
Construction & maintenance	79
Production & transportation	77
Self-employed persons	320

General Information
Borough of North Caldwell
Gould Ave
North Caldwell, NJ 07006
973-228-6410
Website	www.northcaldwell.org
Year of incorporation	1898
Land/water area (sq. miles)	2.99/0.00
Form of government	Borough

Government
Legislative Districts
US Congressional	11
State Legislative	27

Local Officials, 2009
Mayor	Melvin Levine
Manager	Joseph Kunz
Clerk	Francine Paserchia
Finance Dir	Richard Mondelli
Tax Assessor	George Librizzi
Tax Collector	Richard Mondelli
Attorney	David Paris
Building	Ronald Young
Comm Dev/Planning	NA
Engineering	Frank Zichelli
Public Works	NA
Police Chief	Joseph Clark
Emerg/Fire Director	David Hicock

Housing & Construction
Housing Units, 2000*
Total	2,108
Median rent	$1,759
Median SF home value	$399,000

Permits for New Residential Construction
	Units	Value
Total, 2006	9	$4,939,121
Single family	9	$4,939,121
Total, 2007	12	$3,227,400
Single family	12	$3,227,400

Real Property Valuation, 2008
	Parcels	Valuation
Total	2,232	$1,820,725,300
Vacant	109	60,873,600
Residential	2,106	1,723,979,600
Commercial	13	32,327,600
Industrial	2	2,916,300
Apartments	0	0
Farm land	1	4,000
Farm homestead	1	624,200

Average Property Value & Tax, 2008
Residential value	$818,512
Property tax	$13,106
Tax credit/rebate	$1,315

Public Library
No public municipal library

Library statistics, 2007
Population served	NA
Full-time/total staff	NA/NA

	Total	Per capita
Holdings	NA	NA
Revenues	NA	NA
Expenditures	NA	NA
Annual visits	NA	NA
Internet terminals/annual users	NA/NA	

Public Safety
Number of officers, 2007	17

Crime	2006	2007
Total crimes	51	49
Violent	1	4
Murder	0	0
Rape	0	1
Robbery	1	0
Aggravated assault	0	3
Non-violent	50	45
Burglary	8	14
Larceny	39	30
Vehicle theft	3	1
Domestic violence	5	6
Arson	2	1
Total crime rate	7.0	6.8
Violent	0.1	0.6
Non-violent	6.9	6.2

Public School District
(for school year 2007-08 except as noted)

North Caldwell School District
132 Gould Avenue
North Caldwell, NJ 07006
(973) 228-6439
Superintendent	Linda Freda
Number of schools	2
Grade plan	K-6
Enrollment	634
Attendance rate, '06-07	96.1%
Dropout rate	NA
Students per teacher	9.0
Per pupil expenditure	$14,757
Median faculty salary	$48,841
Median administrator salary	$98,100
Grade 12 enrollment	NA
High school graduation rate	NA

Assessment test results
(percent scoring at proficient or advanced level)
	Language	Math
NJASK-Grade 3	96.0%	97.9%
GEPA-Grade 8	NA	NA
HSPA-High School	NA	NA

SAT Score Averages, 2006-07
Pct tested	Math	Verbal	Writing
NA	NA	NA	NA

Teacher Qualifications
Avg. years of experience	7
Highly-qualified teachers one subject/all subjects	98.0%/98.0%

No Child Left Behind
AYP, 2006-07	Meets Standards

Municipal Finance
State Aid Programs, 2009
Total aid	$623,210
CMPTRA	39,361
Energy tax receipts	558,920
Garden State Trust	72

General Budget, 2008
Total tax levy	$29,164,163
County levy	6,904,385
County taxes	6,637,886
County library	0
County health	0
County open space	266,499
School levy	17,339,909
Muni. levy	4,919,869
Misc. revenues	3,029,378

Taxes
	2006	2007	2008
General tax rate per $100	7.25	7.36	1.602
County equalization ratio	23.61	22.19	103.32
Net valuation taxable	$366,184,776	$370,917,600	$1,821,438,600
State equalized value	$1,650,375,884	$1,747,406,162	$1,794,354,616

* US Census Bureau
** New Jersey Department of Labor

See Introduction for an explanation of all data sources.

Demographics & Socio-Economic Characteristics

(2000 US Census, except as noted)

Population

1980*	8,177
1990*	7,987
2000	7,920
Male	3,737
Female	4,183
2007 (estimate)*	8,940
Population density	2,598.8

Race & Hispanic Origin, 2000

Race

White	7,526
Black/African American	114
American Indian/Alaska Native	5
Asian	79
Native Hawaiian/Pacific Islander	0
Other race	75
Two or more races	121
Hispanic origin, total	308
Mexican	14
Puerto Rican	59
Cuban	36
Other Hispanic	199

Age & Nativity, 2000

Under 5 years	436
18 years and over	6,360
21 years and over	6,055
65 years and over	1,551
85 years and over	246
Median age	40.5
Native-born	6,858
Foreign-born	1,062

Educational Attainment, 2000

Population 25 years and over	5,580
Less than 9th grade	4.9%
High school grad or higher	88.1%
Bachelor's degree or higher	33.8%
Graduate degree	9.7%

Income & Poverty, 1999

Per capita income	$30,322
Median household income	$74,700
Median family income	$80,936
Persons in poverty	298
H'holds receiving public assistance	21
H'holds receiving social security	1,002

Households, 2000

Total households	2,626
With persons under 18	807
With persons over 65	977
Family households	2,076
Single-person households	465
Persons per household	2.79
Persons per family	3.18

Labor & Employment

Total civilian labor force, 2007**	4,275
Unemployment rate	2.4%
Total civilian labor force, 2000	4,383
Unemployment rate	3.5%

Employed persons 16 years and over by occupation, 2000

Managers & professionals	1,818
Service occupations	725
Sales & office occupations	996
Farming, fishing & forestry	8
Construction & maintenance	398
Production & transportation	283
Self-employed persons	241

* US Census Bureau
** New Jersey Department of Labor

General Information

Borough of North Haledon
103 Overlook Ave
North Haledon, NJ 07508
973-427-7793

Website	www.northhaledon.com
Year of incorporation	1901
Land/water area (sq. miles)	3.44/0.03
Form of government	Borough

Government

Legislative Districts

US Congressional	8
State Legislative	35

Local Officials, 2009

Mayor	Randolph George
Manager/Admin	NA
Clerk	Renate Elatab
Finance Dir	Laura Leibowitz
Tax Assessor	Michael Barker
Tax Collector	Maureen Kurzynski
Attorney	Michael DeMarco
Building	Philip Cheff
Planning	Michael Kauker
Engineering	Boswell Engineering
Public Works	William P. Graham
Police Chief	Robert Bracco
Emerg/Fire Director	A.J. Ricciardi

Housing & Construction

Housing Units, 2000*

Total	2,675
Median rent	$891
Median SF home value	$237,900

Permits for New Residential Construction

	Units	Value
Total, 2006	9	$2,671,520
Single family	9	$2,671,520
Total, 2007	7	$1,195,621
Single family	7	$1,195,621

Real Property Valuation, 2008

	Parcels	Valuation
Total	3,082	$445,181,300
Vacant	65	3,379,000
Residential	2,925	422,150,200
Commercial	84	17,270,300
Industrial	6	2,147,700
Apartments	0	0
Farm land	1	9,300
Farm homestead	1	224,800

Average Property Value & Tax, 2008

Residential value	$144,352
Property tax	$8,755
Tax credit/rebate	$1,274

Public Library

North Haledon Public Library
129 Overlook Ave
North Haledon, NJ 07508
973-427-6213

Director	Susan Serico

Library statistics, 2007

Population served	7,920
Full-time/total staff	1/2

	Total	Per capita
Holdings	29,864	3.77
Revenues	$506,454	$63.95
Expenditures	$423,774	$53.51
Annual visits	17,312	2.19
Internet terminals/annual users	8/1,780	

Public Safety

Number of officers, 2007	18

Crime	2006	2007
Total crimes	66	77
Violent	6	7
Murder	0	0
Rape	0	0
Robbery	1	0
Aggravated assault	5	7
Non-violent	60	70
Burglary	24	11
Larceny	34	57
Vehicle theft	2	2
Domestic violence	38	40
Arson	0	0
Total crime rate	7.3	8.5
Violent	0.7	0.8
Non-violent	6.6	7.7

Public School District

(for school year 2007-08 except as noted)

North Haledon School District
515 High Mountain Road
North Haledon, NJ 07508
(973) 427-1220

Chief School Admin	Donna Cardiello
Number of schools	2
Grade plan	K-8
Enrollment	687
Attendance rate, '06-07	97.2%
Dropout rate	NA
Students per teacher	12.1
Per pupil expenditure	$10,922
Median faculty salary	$52,505
Median administrator salary	$124,401
Grade 12 enrollment	NA
High school graduation rate	NA

Assessment test results

(percent scoring at proficient or advanced level)

	Language	Math
NJASK-Grade 3	94.8%	97.4%
GEPA-Grade 8	75.1%	92.2%
HSPA-High School	NA	NA

SAT Score Averages, 2006-07

Pct tested	Math	Verbal	Writing
NA	NA	NA	NA

Teacher Qualifications

Avg. years of experience	8
Highly-qualified teachers one subject/all subjects	97.5%/97.5%

No Child Left Behind

AYP, 2006-07	Meets Standards

Municipal Finance

State Aid Programs, 2009

Total aid	$776,985
CMPTRA	184,176
Energy tax receipts	568,260
Garden State Trust	3,575

General Budget, 2008

Total tax levy	$27,024,845
County levy	7,961,722
County taxes	7,804,029
County library	0
County health	0
County open space	157,693
School levy	11,367,123
Muni. levy	7,696,000
Misc. revenues	2,916,040

Taxes	2006	2007	2008
General tax rate per $100	5.66	5.8	6.066
County equalization ratio	32.08	29.69	28.28
Net valuation taxable	$437,451,400	$441,938,062	$445,574,397
State equalized value	$1,473,804,323	$1,561,719,312	$1,578,490,580

See Introduction for an explanation of all data sources.

Demographics & Socio-Economic Characteristics
(2000 US Census, except as noted)

Population
1980*	9,050
1990*	9,994
2000	7,347
Male	3,682
Female	3,665
2007 (estimate)*	7,415
Population density	427.6

Race & Hispanic Origin, 2000
Race
White	5,924
Black/African American	805
American Indian/Alaska Native	35
Asian	156
Native Hawaiian/Pacific Islander	4
Other race	160
Two or more races	263
Hispanic origin, total	423
Mexican	107
Puerto Rican	154
Cuban	21
Other Hispanic	141

Age & Nativity, 2000
Under 5 years	818
18 years and over	4,879
21 years and over	4,646
65 years and over	452
85 years and over	17
Median age	28.7
Native-born	6,967
Foreign-born	358

Educational Attainment, 2000
Population 25 years and over	4,156
Less than 9th grade	2.9%
High school grad or higher	87.0%
Bachelor's degree or higher	13.3%
Graduate degree	3.3%

Income & Poverty, 1999
Per capita income	$17,580
Median household income	$39,988
Median family income	$45,553
Persons in poverty	387
H'holds receiving public assistance	58
H'holds receiving social security	426

Households, 2000
Total households	2,498
With persons under 18	1,351
With persons over 65	350
Family households	2,020
Single-person households	388
Persons per household	2.94
Persons per family	3.29

Labor & Employment
Total civilian labor force, 2007**	3,426
Unemployment rate	4.6%
Total civilian labor force, 2000	3,000
Unemployment rate	4.8%

Employed persons 16 years and over by occupation, 2000
Managers & professionals	767
Service occupations	389
Sales & office occupations	827
Farming, fishing & forestry	27
Construction & maintenance	379
Production & transportation	467
Self-employed persons	236

General Information
Township of North Hanover
41 Schoolhouse Rd
Jacobstown, NJ 08562
609-758-2522
Website	www.northhanover.us
Year of incorporation	1905
Land/water area (sq. miles)	17.34/0.04
Form of government	Township

Government
Legislative Districts
US Congressional	3
State Legislative	30

Local Officials, 2009
Mayor	James R. Durr
Manager/Admin	NA
Clerk	Monica L. Zur
Finance Dir	Kathleen Phelan
Tax Assessor	Donald Kosul
Tax Collector	Mary Picariello
Attorney	Mark Roselli
Building	Jeffrey Jones
Comm Dev/Planning	NA
Engineering	Remington & Vernick
Public Works	Wayne Wharton
Police Chief	Mark Keubler
Emerg/Fire Director	Chris Herbert

Housing & Construction
Housing Units, 2000*
Total	2,670
Median rent	$648
Median SF home value	$175,000

Permits for New Residential Construction
	Units	Value
Total, 2006	15	$2,873,959
Single family	15	$2,873,959
Total, 2007	11	$2,019,932
Single family	11	$2,019,932

Real Property Valuation, 2008
	Parcels	Valuation
Total	1,414	$235,201,477
Vacant	114	4,701,550
Residential	959	169,389,600
Commercial	68	29,309,650
Industrial	0	0
Apartments	9	7,120,300
Farm land	165	2,691,627
Farm homestead	99	21,988,750

Average Property Value & Tax, 2008
Residential value	$180,887
Property tax	$5,303
Tax credit/rebate	$909

Public Library
No public municipal library

Library statistics, 2007
Population served	NA
Full-time/total staff	NA/NA

	Total	Per capita
Holdings	NA	NA
Revenues	NA	NA
Expenditures	NA	NA
Annual visits	NA	NA
Internet terminals/annual users	NA/NA	

Public Safety
Number of officers, 2007	9

Crime	2006	2007
Total crimes	82	68
Violent	5	1
Murder	0	0
Rape	0	0
Robbery	2	0
Aggravated assault	3	1
Non-violent	77	67
Burglary	20	14
Larceny	51	48
Vehicle theft	6	5
Domestic violence	52	59
Arson	0	1
Total crime rate	10.8	9.0
Violent	0.7	0.1
Non-violent	10.1	8.8

Public School District
(for school year 2007-08 except as noted)

North Hanover Township School District
331 Monmouth Road
Wrightstown, NJ 08562
(609) 738-2600
Superintendent	Richard J. Carson
Number of schools	5
Grade plan	K-6
Enrollment	1,157
Attendance rate, '06-07	94.6%
Dropout rate	NA
Students per teacher	8.9
Per pupil expenditure	$15,897
Median faculty salary	$55,147
Median administrator salary	$99,185
Grade 12 enrollment	NA
High school graduation rate	NA

Assessment test results
(percent scoring at proficient or advanced level)
	Language	Math
NJASK-Grade 3	81.2%	79.2%
GEPA-Grade 8	NA	NA
HSPA-High School	NA	NA

SAT Score Averages, 2006-07
Pct tested	Math	Verbal	Writing
NA	NA	NA	NA

Teacher Qualifications
Avg. years of experience	11
Highly-qualified teachers one subject/all subjects	100%/100%

No Child Left Behind
AYP, 2006-07	Meets Standards

Municipal Finance
State Aid Programs, 2009
Total aid	$1,014,011
CMPTRA	79,354
Energy tax receipts	901,702
Garden State Trust	0

General Budget, 2008
Total tax levy	$7,032,301
County levy	1,790,812
County taxes	1,470,588
County library	135,774
County health	0
County open space	184,450
School levy	4,341,348
Muni. levy	900,141
Misc. revenues	2,824,698

Taxes	2006	2007	2008
General tax rate per $100	2.808	2.929	2.984
County equalization ratio	60.96	52.44	50.99
Net valuation taxable	$222,902,650	$232,407,963	$235,709,067
State equalized value	$425,751,605	$455,320,108	$556,802,474

* US Census Bureau
** New Jersey Department of Labor

See Introduction for an explanation of all data sources.

Demographics & Socio-Economic Characteristics

(2000 US Census, except as noted)

Population

1980*	19,108
1990*	18,820
2000	21,103
Male	10,409
Female	10,694
2007 (estimate)*	21,239
Population density	7,612.5

Race & Hispanic Origin, 2000

Race

White	13,307
Black/African American	2,824
American Indian/Alaska Native	59
Asian	1,064
Native Hawaiian/Pacific Islander	17
Other race	2,887
Two or more races	945
Hispanic origin, total	6,916
Mexican	332
Puerto Rican	787
Cuban	93
Other Hispanic	5,704

Age & Nativity, 2000

Under 5 years	1,654
18 years and over	15,664
21 years and over	14,959
65 years and over	1,996
85 years and over	282
Median age	33.7
Native-born	14,123
Foreign-born	6,980

Educational Attainment, 2000

Population 25 years and over	13,863
Less than 9th grade	8.3%
High school grad or higher	80.7%
Bachelor's degree or higher	26.5%
Graduate degree	9.3%

Income & Poverty, 1999

Per capita income	$22,791
Median household income	$55,322
Median family income	$62,875
Persons in poverty	1,340
H'holds receiving public assistance	112
H'holds receiving social security	1,413

Households, 2000

Total households	7,202
With persons under 18	2,899
With persons over 65	1,410
Family households	5,086
Single-person households	1,673
Persons per household	2.90
Persons per family	3.40

Labor & Employment

Total civilian labor force, 2007**	12,969
Unemployment rate	4.2%
Total civilian labor force, 2000	11,554
Unemployment rate	5.1%

Employed persons 16 years and over by occupation, 2000

Managers & professionals	3,386
Service occupations	1,389
Sales & office occupations	2,908
Farming, fishing & forestry	29
Construction & maintenance	955
Production & transportation	2,300
Self-employed persons	561

‡ Branch of county library
* US Census Bureau
** New Jersey Department of Labor

General Information

Borough of North Plainfield
263 Somerset St
North Plainfield, NJ 07060
908-769-2900

Website	www.northplainfield.org
Year of incorporation	1885
Land/water area (sq. miles)	2.79/0.00
Form of government	Mayor-Council

Government

Legislative Districts

US Congressional	7
State Legislative	22

Local Officials, 2009

Mayor	Michael Giordano Jr
Manager	David Hollod
Clerk	Richard K. Phoenix
Finance Dir	Patrick DeBlasio
Tax Assessor	Barbara A. Flaherty
Tax Collector	Nancy Nichols
Attorney	Eric Bernstein
Building	John Elichko
Comm Dev/Planning	NA
Engineering	Daniel Swayze
Public Works	James Rodino
Police Chief	William Parenti
Emerg/Fire Director	William F. Eaton

Housing & Construction

Housing Units, 2000*

Total	7,393
Median rent	$828
Median SF home value	$150,100

Permits for New Residential Construction

	Units	Value
Total, 2006	2	$466,600
Single family	2	$466,600
Total, 2007	1	$233,300
Single family	1	$233,300

Real Property Valuation, 2008

	Parcels	Valuation
Total	5,342	$843,744,175
Vacant	86	2,770,500
Residential	4,971	654,339,350
Commercial	244	116,728,725
Industrial	3	1,505,800
Apartments	38	68,399,800
Farm land	0	0
Farm homestead	0	0

Average Property Value & Tax, 2008

Residential value	$131,631
Property tax	$7,469
Tax credit/rebate	$1,191

Public Library

North Plainfield Branch Library‡
6 Rockview Ave
North Plainfield, NJ 07060
908-755-7909

Director..................Richard Stevens

Library statistics, 2007

see Somerset County profile
for library system statistics

Public Safety

Number of officers, 2007	47

Crime	2006	2007
Total crimes	615	606
Violent	46	61
Murder	2	0
Rape	1	3
Robbery	33	36
Aggravated assault	10	22
Non-violent	569	545
Burglary	177	126
Larceny	340	349
Vehicle theft	52	70
Domestic violence	212	211
Arson	0	5
Total crime rate	28.5	27.9
Violent	2.1	2.8
Non-violent	26.3	25.1

Public School District

(for school year 2007-08 except as noted)

North Plainfield Borough School District
33 Mountain Ave
North Plainfield, NJ 07060
(908) 769-6060

Superintendent	Marilyn E. Birnbaum
Number of schools	5
Grade plan	K-12
Enrollment	3,082
Attendance rate, '06-07	94.5%
Dropout rate	0.2%
Students per teacher	9.5
Per pupil expenditure	$14,409
Median faculty salary	$52,515
Median administrator salary	$125,614
Grade 12 enrollment	222
High school graduation rate	98.2%

Assessment test results

(percent scoring at proficient or advanced level)

	Language	Math
NJASK-Grade 3	74.9%	74.8%
GEPA-Grade 8	49.0%	71.4%
HSPA-High School	52.5%	71.6%

SAT Score Averages, 2006-07

Pct tested	Math	Verbal	Writing
60%	465	449	448

Teacher Qualifications

Avg. years of experience	7
Highly-qualified teachers one subject/all subjects	100%/100%

No Child Left Behind

AYP, 2006-07	Needs Improvement

Municipal Finance

State Aid Programs, 2009

Total aid	$1,892,239
CMPTRA	594,782
Energy tax receipts	1,269,073
Garden State Trust	0

General Budget, 2008

Total tax levy	$47,906,057
County levy	6,562,160
County taxes	5,266,306
County library	712,953
County health	0
County open space	582,901
School levy	27,581,947
Muni. levy	13,761,951
Misc. revenues	5,884,988

Taxes	2006	2007	2008
General tax rate per $100	5.17	5.52	5.675
County equalization ratio	52.02	45.89	43.25
Net valuation taxable	$838,203,325	$837,790,034	$844,299,283
State equalized value	$1,827,181,828	$1,936,344,626	$1,928,231,999

See Introduction for an explanation of all data sources.

Demographics & Socio-Economic Characteristics

(2000 US Census, except as noted)

Population

1980*	4,714
1990*	5,017
2000	4,935
Male	2,369
Female	2,566
2007 (estimate)*	4,849
Population density	2,739.5

Race & Hispanic Origin, 2000

Race
White	4,768
Black/African American	40
American Indian/Alaska Native	4
Asian	28
Native Hawaiian/Pacific Islander	1
Other race	38
Two or more races	56
Hispanic origin, total	96
Mexican	3
Puerto Rican	64
Cuban	0
Other Hispanic	29

Age & Nativity, 2000

Under 5 years	195
18 years and over	4,086
21 years and over	3,956
65 years and over	1,168
85 years and over	112
Median age	47.2
Native-born	4,706
Foreign-born	229

Educational Attainment, 2000

Population 25 years and over	3,807
Less than 9th grade	5.1%
High school grad or higher	82.3%
Bachelor's degree or higher	13.4%
Graduate degree	3.8%

Income & Poverty, 1999

Per capita income	$19,656
Median household income	$32,582
Median family income	$46,250
Persons in poverty	575
H'holds receiving public assistance	67
H'holds receiving social security	991

Households, 2000

Total households	2,309
With persons under 18	476
With persons over 65	869
Family households	1,394
Single-person households	804
Persons per household	2.14
Persons per family	2.73

Labor & Employment

Total civilian labor force, 2007**	2,666
Unemployment rate	11.0%
Total civilian labor force, 2000	2,285
Unemployment rate	13.7%

Employed persons 16 years and over by occupation, 2000
Managers & professionals	561
Service occupations	466
Sales & office occupations	624
Farming, fishing & forestry	12
Construction & maintenance	200
Production & transportation	110
Self-employed persons	108

* US Census Bureau
** New Jersey Department of Labor

General Information

City of North Wildwood
901 Atlantic Ave
North Wildwood, NJ 08260
609-522-2030

Website	www.northwildwood.com
Year of incorporation	1917
Land/water area (sq. miles)	1.77/0.36
Form of government	City

Government

Legislative Districts

US Congressional	2
State Legislative	1

Local Officials, 2009

Mayor	William J. Henfey
Manager	Ray Townsend
Clerk	Janet Harkins
Finance Dir	Ross Versaggi
Tax Assessor	Louis Belasco
Tax Collector	Todd Burkey
Attorney	William Kaufmann
Building	Glenn Franzoi
Comm Dev/Planning	NA
Engineering	Ralph Petrella
Public Works	Harry Wozunk
Police Chief	Robert Matteucci
Emerg/Fire Director	Paul Evangelista

Housing & Construction

Housing Units, 2000*

Total	7,411
Median rent	$634
Median SF home value	$129,600

Permits for New Residential Construction

	Units	Value
Total, 2006	308	$43,209,450
Single family	55	$8,294,780
Total, 2007	70	$7,488,795
Single family	10	$3,359,055

Real Property Valuation, 2008

	Parcels	Valuation
Total	7,694	$3,530,659,100
Vacant	137	69,472,400
Residential	7,250	3,042,449,300
Commercial	230	354,785,300
Industrial	0	0
Apartments	77	63,952,100
Farm land	0	0
Farm homestead	0	0

Average Property Value & Tax, 2008

Residential value	$419,648
Property tax	$3,281
Tax credit/rebate	$923

Public Library

No public municipal library

Library statistics, 2007

Population served	NA
Full-time/total staff	NA/NA

	Total	Per capita
Holdings	NA	NA
Revenues	NA	NA
Expenditures	NA	NA
Annual visits	NA	NA
Internet terminals/annual users	NA/NA	

Public Safety

Number of officers, 2007	27

Crime	2006	2007
Total crimes	366	383
Violent	15	16
Murder	0	0
Rape	4	2
Robbery	3	4
Aggravated assault	8	10
Non-violent	351	367
Burglary	50	47
Larceny	295	318
Vehicle theft	6	2
Domestic violence	72	76
Arson	0	0
Total crime rate	76.6	79.7
Violent	3.1	3.3
Non-violent	73.5	76.4

Public School District

(for school year 2007-08 except as noted)

North Wildwood City School District
1201 Atlantic Avenue
North Wildwood, NJ 08260
(609) 522-6885

Superintendent	Michael Buccialia
Number of schools	1
Grade plan	K-8
Enrollment	308
Attendance rate, '06-07	92.6%
Dropout rate	NA
Students per teacher	6.7
Per pupil expenditure	$21,201
Median faculty salary	$51,560
Median administrator salary	$91,397
Grade 12 enrollment	NA
High school graduation rate	NA

Assessment test results

(percent scoring at proficient or advanced level)
	Language	Math
NJASK-Grade 3	100.0%	88.9%
GEPA-Grade 8	68.2%	68.1%
HSPA-High School	NA	NA

SAT Score Averages, 2006-07

Pct tested	Math	Verbal	Writing
NA	NA	NA	NA

Teacher Qualifications

Avg. years of experience	15
Highly-qualified teachers one subject/all subjects	91.0%/91.0%

No Child Left Behind

AYP, 2006-07	Meets Standards

Municipal Finance

State Aid Programs, 2009

Total aid	$585,363
CMPTRA	45,293
Energy tax receipts	521,046
Garden State Trust	0

General Budget, 2008

Total tax levy	$27,614,577
County levy	5,953,936
County taxes	4,732,371
County library	908,472
County health	0
County open space	313,092
School levy	6,430,568
Muni. levy	15,230,074
Misc. revenues	7,893,635

Taxes	2006	2007	2008
General tax rate per $100	0.7	0.73	0.785
County equalization ratio	162.08	122.73	112.45
Net valuation taxable	$3,392,027,250	$3,478,546,249	$3,531,455,415
State equalized value	$2,764,535,854	$3,093,498,284	$3,260,267,419

See Introduction for an explanation of all data sources.

Demographics & Socio-Economic Characteristics
(2000 US Census, except as noted)

Population
1980*	7,795
1990*	7,305
2000	7,725
Male	3,679
Female	4,046
2007 (estimate)*	7,911
Population density	2,306.4

Race & Hispanic Origin, 2000
Race
White	7,070
Black/African American	205
American Indian/Alaska Native	8
Asian	193
Native Hawaiian/Pacific Islander	6
Other race	140
Two or more races	103
Hispanic origin, total	338
Mexican	18
Puerto Rican	90
Cuban	14
Other Hispanic	216

Age & Nativity, 2000
Under 5 years	417
18 years and over	5,755
21 years and over	5,578
65 years and over	1,373
85 years and over	182
Median age	40.4
Native-born	7,284
Foreign-born	441

Educational Attainment, 2000
Population 25 years and over	5,374
Less than 9th grade	3.4%
High school grad or higher	87.5%
Bachelor's degree or higher	22.5%
Graduate degree	5.0%

Income & Poverty, 1999
Per capita income	$25,059
Median household income	$56,875
Median family income	$62,896
Persons in poverty	420
H'holds receiving public assistance	21
H'holds receiving social security	897

Households, 2000
Total households	2,824
With persons under 18	1,068
With persons over 65	879
Family households	2,110
Single-person households	597
Persons per household	2.66
Persons per family	3.11

Labor & Employment
Total civilian labor force, 2007**	4,209
Unemployment rate	3.1%
Total civilian labor force, 2000	3,947
Unemployment rate	3.3%

Employed persons 16 years and over by occupation, 2000
Managers & professionals	1,171
Service occupations	1,104
Sales & office occupations	959
Farming, fishing & forestry	0
Construction & maintenance	307
Production & transportation	277
Self-employed persons	247

* US Census Bureau
** New Jersey Department of Labor

General Information
City of Northfield
1600 Shore Rd
Northfield, NJ 08225
609-641-2832
Website	www.cityofnorthfield.org
Year of incorporation	1905
Land/water area (sq. miles)	3.43/0.02
Form of government	City

Government
Legislative Districts
US Congressional	2
State Legislative	2

Local Officials, 2009
Mayor	Vincent Mazzeo
Manager	NA
Clerk	Mary Canesi
Finance Dir	Marilyn Dolcy
Tax Assessor	Mark Sykes
Tax Collector	Cindy Ruffo
Attorney	Keith Bonchi
Building	Matt Doran
Comm Dev/Planning	NA
Engineering	Matt Doran
Public Works	James Clark
Police Chief	Robert James
Fire Chief	Henry Martinelli

Housing & Construction
Housing Units, 2000*
Total	2,922
Median rent	$783
Median SF home value	$128,100

Permits for New Residential Construction
	Units	Value
Total, 2006	26	$3,102,432
Single family	26	$3,102,432
Total, 2007	23	$2,651,060
Single family	23	$2,651,060

Real Property Valuation, 2008
	Parcels	Valuation
Total	3,572	$552,780,200
Vacant	235	15,284,000
Residential	3,119	416,990,500
Commercial	213	119,606,500
Industrial	0	0
Apartments	3	542,900
Farm land	1	3,600
Farm homestead	1	352,700

Average Property Value & Tax, 2008
Residential value	$133,764
Property tax	$5,670
Tax credit/rebate	$985

Public Library
Otto Bruyns Public Library
241 W Mill Rd
Northfield, NJ 08225
609-646-4476
Director	Margaret E. Derascavage

Library statistics, 2007
Population served	7,725
Full-time/total staff	0/1

	Total	Per capita
Holdings	32,200	4.17
Revenues	$363,485	$47.05
Expenditures	$227,248	$29.42
Annual visits	19,711	2.55
Internet terminals/annual users		3/4,100

Public Safety
Number of officers, 2007	20

Crime	2006	2007
Total crimes	107	126
Violent	6	3
Murder	0	0
Rape	1	0
Robbery	3	3
Aggravated assault	2	0
Non-violent	101	123
Burglary	29	38
Larceny	68	82
Vehicle theft	4	3
Domestic violence	49	57
Arson	2	0
Total crime rate	13.3	15.7
Violent	0.7	0.4
Non-violent	12.6	15.4

Public School District
(for school year 2007-08 except as noted)

Northfield City School District
2000 New Road
Northfield, NJ 08225
(609) 407-4000
Superintendent	Richard Stepura
Number of schools	2
Grade plan	K-8
Enrollment	1,071
Attendance rate, '06-07	94.8%
Dropout rate	NA
Students per teacher	12.3
Per pupil expenditure	$10,781
Median faculty salary	$50,352
Median administrator salary	$99,764
Grade 12 enrollment	NA
High school graduation rate	NA

Assessment test results
(percent scoring at proficient or advanced level)
	Language	Math
NJASK-Grade 3	94.7%	91.2%
GEPA-Grade 8	76.5%	87.2%
HSPA-High School	NA	NA

SAT Score Averages, 2006-07
Pct tested	Math	Verbal	Writing
NA	NA	NA	NA

Teacher Qualifications
Avg. years of experience	9
Highly-qualified teachers one subject/all subjects	100%/100%

No Child Left Behind
AYP, 2006-07	Meets Standards

Municipal Finance
State Aid Programs, 2009
Total aid	$815,392
CMPTRA	135,390
Energy tax receipts	659,564
Garden State Trust	47

General Budget, 2008
Total tax levy	$23,469,110
County levy	3,158,138
County taxes	2,767,845
County library	0
County health	145,296
County open space	244,996
School levy	13,293,413
Muni. levy	7,017,560
Misc. revenues	5,841,729

Taxes
	2006	2007	2008
General tax rate per $100	3.885	4.088	4.239
County equalization ratio	55.08	47.05	45.34
Net valuation taxable	$543,709,800	$550,805,426	$553,688,917
State equalized value	$1,156,614,725	$1,213,754,553	$1,245,348,609

See Introduction for an explanation of all data sources.

Demographics & Socio-Economic Characteristics

(2000 US Census, except as noted)

Population

1980*	5,046
1990*	4,563
2000	4,460
Male	2,222
Female	2,238
2007 (estimate)*	4,548
Population density	3,445.5

Race & Hispanic Origin, 2000

Race

White	3,698
Black/African American	34
American Indian/Alaska Native	3
Asian	627
Native Hawaiian/Pacific Islander	0
Other race	52
Two or more races	46
Hispanic origin, total	211
Mexican	3
Puerto Rican	36
Cuban	47
Other Hispanic	125

Age & Nativity, 2000

Under 5 years	256
18 years and over	3,458
21 years and over	3,328
65 years and over	713
85 years and over	70
Median age	40.2
Native-born	3,586
Foreign-born	866

Educational Attainment, 2000

Population 25 years and over	3,190
Less than 9th grade	4.3%
High school grad or higher	87.2%
Bachelor's degree or higher	29.6%
Graduate degree	10.8%

Income & Poverty, 1999

Per capita income	$28,206
Median household income	$72,500
Median family income	$81,153
Persons in poverty	171
H'holds receiving public assistance	31
H'holds receiving social security	512

Households, 2000

Total households	1,575
With persons under 18	572
With persons over 65	520
Family households	1,237
Single-person households	291
Persons per household	2.83
Persons per family	3.21

Labor & Employment

Total civilian labor force, 2007**	2,601
Unemployment rate	2.2%
Total civilian labor force, 2000	2,456
Unemployment rate	2.3%

Employed persons 16 years and over by occupation, 2000

Managers & professionals	987
Service occupations	343
Sales & office occupations	674
Farming, fishing & forestry	0
Construction & maintenance	258
Production & transportation	137
Self-employed persons	82

* US Census Bureau
** New Jersey Department of Labor

General Information

Borough of Northvale
116 Paris Ave
Northvale, NJ 07647
201-767-3330

Website	www.boroughofnorthvale.com
Year of incorporation	1916
Land/water area (sq. miles)	1.32/0.00
Form of government	Borough

Government

Legislative Districts

US Congressional	5
State Legislative	39

Local Officials, 2009

Mayor	John S. Hogan
Manager/Admin	NA
Clerk	Wanda Worner
Finance Dir	Shuaib Firozvi
Tax Assessor	John Guercio
Tax Collector	Suzanne Burroughs
Attorney	Paul Kaufman
Building	Nick Lepore
Comm Dev/Planning	NA
Engineering	Louis Raimondi
Public Works	Edward Keegan
Police Chief	Bruce Tietjen
Emerg/Fire Director	Briant Bodrato

Housing & Construction

Housing Units, 2000*

Total	1,596
Median rent	$871
Median SF home value	$246,100

Permits for New Residential Construction

	Units	Value
Total, 2006	21	$3,442,112
Single family	21	$3,442,112
Total, 2007	79	$6,540,680
Single family	79	$6,540,680

Real Property Valuation, 2008

	Parcels	Valuation
Total	1,724	$998,612,140
Vacant	125	15,525,157
Residential	1,457	698,971,683
Commercial	83	76,040,600
Industrial	59	208,074,700
Apartments	0	0
Farm land	0	0
Farm homestead	0	0

Average Property Value & Tax, 2008

Residential value	$479,733
Property tax	$8,634
Tax credit/rebate	$1,313

Public Library

Northvale Public Library
116 Paris Ave
Northvale, NJ 07647
201-768-4784

Director	Virginia Beckman

Library statistics, 2007

Population served	4,460
Full-time/total staff	0/4

	Total	Per capita
Holdings	36,805	8.25
Revenues	$285,705	$64.06
Expenditures	$285,001	$63.90
Annual visits	26,400	5.92
Internet terminals/annual users		3/8,499

Public Safety

Number of officers, 2007	15

Crime	2006	2007
Total crimes	29	38
Violent	1	2
Murder	0	0
Rape	0	0
Robbery	0	1
Aggravated assault	1	1
Non-violent	28	36
Burglary	6	5
Larceny	20	30
Vehicle theft	2	1
Domestic violence	25	10
Arson	0	0
Total crime rate	6.4	8.3
Violent	0.2	0.4
Non-violent	6.1	7.9

Public School District

(for school year 2007-08 except as noted)

Northvale School District
441 Tappan Road
Northvale, NJ 07647
(201) 768-8484

Superintendent	Sylvan Hershey
Number of schools	2
Grade plan	K-8
Enrollment	591
Attendance rate, '06-07	96.3%
Dropout rate	NA
Students per teacher	11.7
Per pupil expenditure	$13,046
Median faculty salary	$61,959
Median administrator salary	$95,000
Grade 12 enrollment	NA
High school graduation rate	NA

Assessment test results

(percent scoring at proficient or advanced level)

	Language	Math
NJASK-Grade 3	90.0%	89.9%
GEPA-Grade 8	83.3%	95.4%
HSPA-High School	NA	NA

SAT Score Averages, 2006-07

Pct tested	Math	Verbal	Writing
NA	NA	NA	NA

Teacher Qualifications

Avg. years of experience	10
Highly-qualified teachers one subject/all subjects	100%/100%

No Child Left Behind

AYP, 2006-07	Meets Standards

Municipal Finance

State Aid Programs, 2009

Total aid	$723,693
CMPTRA	163,026
Energy tax receipts	542,575
Garden State Trust	0

General Budget, 2008

Total tax levy	$17,993,603
County levy	1,894,678
County taxes	1,792,101
County library	0
County health	0
County open space	102,577
School levy	11,501,211
Muni. levy	4,597,713
Misc. revenues	3,134,150

Taxes	2006	2007	2008
General tax rate per $100	3.42	1.78	1.801
County equalization ratio	55.37	102.32	98.55
Net valuation taxable	$474,980,140	$963,926,829	$999,800,048
State equalized value	$937,266,641	$978,101,074	$1,058,144,026

See Introduction for an explanation of all data sources.

Demographics & Socio-Economic Characteristics

(2000 US Census, except as noted)

Population

1980*	4,413
1990*	4,858
2000	5,751
Male	2,704
Female	3,047
2007 (estimate)*	6,220
Population density	2,261.8

Race & Hispanic Origin, 2000

Race

White	4,478
Black/African American	48
American Indian/Alaska Native	1
Asian	1,092
Native Hawaiian/Pacific Islander	0
Other race	54
Two or more races	78
Hispanic origin, total	172
Mexican	9
Puerto Rican	26
Cuban	39
Other Hispanic	98

Age & Nativity, 2000

Under 5 years	320
18 years and over	4,269
21 years and over	4,104
65 years and over	896
85 years and over	186
Median age	40.8
Native-born	4,465
Foreign-born	1,286

Educational Attainment, 2000

Population 25 years and over	3,900
Less than 9th grade	2.8%
High school grad or higher	91.0%
Bachelor's degree or higher	42.8%
Graduate degree	14.2%

Income & Poverty, 1999

Per capita income	$40,039
Median household income	$92,447
Median family income	$100,329
Persons in poverty	271
H'holds receiving public assistance	15
H'holds receiving social security	436

Households, 2000

Total households	1,857
With persons under 18	799
With persons over 65	484
Family households	1,563
Single-person households	254
Persons per household	2.97
Persons per family	3.26

Labor & Employment

Total civilian labor force, 2007**	2,797
Unemployment rate	3.8%
Total civilian labor force, 2000	2,654
Unemployment rate	4.1%

Employed persons 16 years and over by occupation, 2000

Managers & professionals	1,288
Service occupations	291
Sales & office occupations	688
Farming, fishing & forestry	0
Construction & maintenance	161
Production & transportation	118
Self-employed persons	263

*   US Census Bureau
** New Jersey Department of Labor

General Information

Borough of Norwood
455 Broadway
Norwood, NJ 07648
201-767-7200

Website	www.norwoodboro.org
Year of incorporation	1905
Land/water area (sq. miles)	2.75/0.01
Form of government	Borough

Government

Legislative Districts

US Congressional	5
State Legislative	39

Local Officials, 2009

Mayor	James P. Barsa
Manager	Lorraine McMackin
Clerk	Lorraine McMackin
Finance Dir	Maureen Neville
Tax Assessor	John Guercio
Tax Collector	Maureen Neville
Attorney	Andrew Fede
Building	Paul Renaud
Comm Dev/Planning	NA
Engineering	Michael J. Neglia
Public Works	Camilo DiRese
Police Chief	Jeffrey Krapels
Emerg/Fire Director	Chris Mazzilli

Housing & Construction

Housing Units, 2000*

Total	1,888
Median rent	$1,086
Median SF home value	$345,100

Permits for New Residential Construction

	Units	Value
Total, 2006	15	$3,921,189
Single family	15	$3,921,189
Total, 2007	15	$5,681,890
Single family	15	$5,681,890

Real Property Valuation, 2008

	Parcels	Valuation
Total	1,954	$1,484,512,400
Vacant	64	12,893,600
Residential	1,791	1,273,609,500
Commercial	54	78,306,000
Industrial	43	102,148,800
Apartments	1	17,510,200
Farm land	1	44,300
Farm homestead	0	0

Average Property Value & Tax, 2008

Residential value	$711,116
Property tax	$11,294
Tax credit/rebate	$1,315

Public Library

Norwood Public Library
198 Summit St
Norwood, NJ 07648
201-768-9555

Director	Siobhan Koch

Library statistics, 2007

Population served	5,751
Full-time/total staff	1/3

	Total	Per capita
Holdings	36,944	6.42
Revenues	$477,720	$83.07
Expenditures	$320,312	$55.70
Annual visits	27,143	4.72
Internet terminals/annual users	3/14,100	

Public Safety

Number of officers, 2007	14

Crime	2006	2007
Total crimes	38	19
Violent	1	1
Murder	0	0
Rape	0	0
Robbery	0	0
Aggravated assault	1	1
Non-violent	37	18
Burglary	8	5
Larceny	28	13
Vehicle theft	1	0
Domestic violence	5	18
Arson	3	0
Total crime rate	6.1	3.0
Violent	0.2	0.2
Non-violent	5.9	2.9

Public School District

(for school year 2007-08 except as noted)

Norwood School District
177 Summit Street
Norwood, NJ 07648
(201) 768-6363

Superintendent	Andrew Rose
Number of schools	1
Grade plan	K-8
Enrollment	626
Attendance rate, '06-07	96.3%
Dropout rate	NA
Students per teacher	11.6
Per pupil expenditure	$12,433
Median faculty salary	$57,650
Median administrator salary	$135,315
Grade 12 enrollment	NA
High school graduation rate	NA

Assessment test results

(percent scoring at proficient or advanced level)

	Language	Math
NJASK-Grade 3	97.1%	95.3%
GEPA-Grade 8	83.5%	91.0%
HSPA-High School	NA	NA

SAT Score Averages, 2006-07

Pct tested	Math	Verbal	Writing
NA	NA	NA	NA

Teacher Qualifications

Avg. years of experience	9
Highly-qualified teachers	
one subject/all subjects	95.5%/91.0%

No Child Left Behind

AYP, 2006-07	Meets Standards

Municipal Finance

State Aid Programs, 2009

Total aid	$761,234
CMPTRA	0
Energy tax receipts	725,280
Garden State Trust	0

General Budget, 2008

Total tax levy	$23,600,489
County levy	2,845,667
County taxes	2,691,789
County library	0
County health	0
County open space	153,878
School levy	14,916,952
Muni. levy	5,837,870
Misc. revenues	2,787,697

Taxes

	2006	2007	2008
General tax rate per $100	2.87	2.99	1.590
County equalization ratio	58.33	49.11	96.83
Net valuation taxable	$734,339,600	$745,106,346	$1,485,990,160
State equalized value	$1,496,071,641	$1,512,806,085	$1,581,082,357

See Introduction for an explanation of all data sources.

Demographics & Socio-Economic Characteristics
(2000 US Census, except as noted)

Population
1980*	28,998
1990*	27,099
2000	27,362
Male	12,912
Female	14,450
2007 (estimate)*	26,415
Population density	7,838.3

Race & Hispanic Origin, 2000
Race
White	24,064
Black/African American	511
American Indian/Alaska Native	15
Asian	1,943
Native Hawaiian/Pacific Islander	10
Other race	480
Two or more races	339
Hispanic origin, total	1,830
Mexican	72
Puerto Rican	585
Cuban	178
Other Hispanic	995

Age & Nativity, 2000
Under 5 years	1,510
18 years and over	21,396
21 years and over	20,686
65 years and over	4,402
85 years and over	476
Median age	39.3
Native-born	23,350
Foreign-born	4,012

Educational Attainment, 2000
Population 25 years and over	19,689
Less than 9th grade	4.4%
High school grad or higher	86.5%
Bachelor's degree or higher	32.9%
Graduate degree	10.5%

Income & Poverty, 1999
Per capita income	$28,039
Median household income	$59,634
Median family income	$73,264
Persons in poverty	1,312
H'holds receiving public assistance	128
H'holds receiving social security	3,273

Households, 2000
Total households	10,884
With persons under 18	3,401
With persons over 65	3,261
Family households	7,371
Single-person households	3,036
Persons per household	2.51
Persons per family	3.11

Labor & Employment
Total civilian labor force, 2007**	15,056
Unemployment rate	3.6%
Total civilian labor force, 2000	14,709
Unemployment rate	3.8%

Employed persons 16 years and over by occupation, 2000
Managers & professionals	5,815
Service occupations	1,578
Sales & office occupations	4,460
Farming, fishing & forestry	0
Construction & maintenance	1,048
Production & transportation	1,254
Self-employed persons	736

©2009 Information Publications, Inc.   All rights reserved.   Photocopying prohibited.   For additional copies, contact the publisher at www.informationpublications.com or (877)544-INFO (4636)

* US Census Bureau
** New Jersey Department of Labor

General Information
Township of Nutley
1 Kennedy Dr
Nutley, NJ 07110
973-284-4951

Website	nutleynj.org
Year of incorporation	1981
Land/water area (sq. miles)	3.37/0.06
Form of government	Commission

Government
Legislative Districts
US Congressional	8
State Legislative	36

Local Officials, 2009
Mayor	Joanne Cocchiola
Manager/Admin	NA
Clerk	Evelyn Rosario
Finance Dir	Rosemary Costa
Tax Assessor	George Librizzi
Tax Collector	Jodi De Maio
Attorney	Kevin Harkins
Building	William Spiezio
Comm Dev/Planning	NA
Engineering	Pennoni Associates
Public Works	Michael Luzzi
Police Chief	John Holland
Emerg/Fire Director	Thomas Peters

Housing & Construction
Housing Units, 2000*
Total	11,118
Median rent	$814
Median SF home value	$190,500

Permits for New Residential Construction
	Units	Value
Total, 2006	21	$2,409,802
Single family	21	$2,409,802
Total, 2007	46	$5,301,850
Single family	46	$5,301,850

Real Property Valuation, 2008
	Parcels	Valuation
Total	8,887	$4,170,091,700
Vacant	105	29,946,400
Residential	8,234	3,335,628,400
Commercial	453	625,622,300
Industrial	27	22,841,600
Apartments	68	156,053,000
Farm land	0	0
Farm homestead	0	0

Average Property Value & Tax, 2008
Residential value	$405,104
Property tax	$9,252
Tax credit/rebate	$1,321

Public Library
Nutley Public Library
93 Booth Dr
Nutley, NJ 07110
973-667-0405

Director	JoAnn A. Tropiano

Library statistics, 2007
Population served	27,362
Full-time/total staff	6/11

	Total	Per capita
Holdings	98,817	3.61
Revenues	$1,478,441	$54.03
Expenditures	$1,361,581	$49.76
Annual visits	150,198	5.49
Internet terminals/annual users	19/18,720	

Public Safety
Number of officers, 2007	67

Crime	2006	2007
Total crimes	478	465
Violent	39	48
Murder	0	0
Rape	3	2
Robbery	5	16
Aggravated assault	31	30
Non-violent	439	417
Burglary	94	58
Larceny	315	317
Vehicle theft	30	42
Domestic violence	141	128
Arson	12	11
Total crime rate	17.4	17.2
Violent	1.4	1.8
Non-violent	16.0	15.4

Public School District
(for school year 2007-08 except as noted)

Nutley School District
375 Bloomfield Avenue
Nutley, NJ 07110
(973) 661-8798

Superintendent	Joseph Zarra
Number of schools	7
Grade plan	K-12
Enrollment	4,033
Attendance rate, '06-07	94.8%
Dropout rate	0.0%
Students per teacher	11.5
Per pupil expenditure	$12,341
Median faculty salary	$59,500
Median administrator salary	$109,448
Grade 12 enrollment	339
High school graduation rate	97.8%

Assessment test results
(percent scoring at proficient or advanced level)
	Language	Math
NJASK-Grade 3	94.5%	94.4%
GEPA-Grade 8	79.0%	93.4%
HSPA-High School	79.8%	88.4%

SAT Score Averages, 2006-07
Pct tested	Math	Verbal	Writing
93%	516	499	499

Teacher Qualifications
Avg. years of experience	8
Highly-qualified teachers one subject/all subjects	99.5%/99.5%

No Child Left Behind
AYP, 2006-07	Meets Standards

Municipal Finance
State Aid Programs, 2009
Total aid	$3,256,147
CMPTRA	908,517
Energy tax receipts	2,298,788
Garden State Trust	0

General Budget, 2008
Total tax levy	$95,384,879
County levy	17,283,407
County taxes	16,615,682
County library	0
County health	0
County open space	667,725
School levy	44,885,271
Muni. levy	33,216,201
Misc. revenues	11,345,079

Taxes
	2006	2007	2008
General tax rate per $100	2.05	2.18	2.284
County equalization ratio	107.89	97.93	94.95
Net valuation taxable	$4,149,415,500	$4,163,063,500	$4,176,524,000
State equalized value	$4,242,650,566	$4,384,187,028	$4,343,501,151

See Introduction for an explanation of all data sources.

Demographics & Socio-Economic Characteristics
(2000 US Census, except as noted)

Population
1980*	13,443
1990*	11,997
2000	12,466
Male	6,090
Female	6,376
2007 (estimate)*	13,400
Population density	1,558.1

Race & Hispanic Origin, 2000
Race
White	11,813
Black/African American	97
American Indian/Alaska Native	8
Asian	337
Native Hawaiian/Pacific Islander	1
Other race	87
Two or more races	123
Hispanic origin, total	483
Mexican	49
Puerto Rican	146
Cuban	62
Other Hispanic	226

Age & Nativity, 2000
Under 5 years	970
18 years and over	9,294
21 years and over	9,012
65 years and over	1,584
85 years and over	193
Median age	38.9
Native-born	11,316
Foreign-born	1,150

Educational Attainment, 2000
Population 25 years and over	8,707
Less than 9th grade	2.6%
High school grad or higher	92.5%
Bachelor's degree or higher	41.4%
Graduate degree	14.8%

Income & Poverty, 1999
Per capita income	$35,252
Median household income	$86,629
Median family income	$93,695
Persons in poverty	206
H'holds receiving public assistance	57
H'holds receiving social security	959

Households, 2000
Total households	4,255
With persons under 18	1,730
With persons over 65	992
Family households	3,567
Single-person households	545
Persons per household	2.88
Persons per family	3.15

Labor & Employment
Total civilian labor force, 2007**	7,218
Unemployment rate	2.5%
Total civilian labor force, 2000	6,847
Unemployment rate	2.9%

Employed persons 16 years and over by occupation, 2000
Managers & professionals	3,151
Service occupations	531
Sales & office occupations	1,988
Farming, fishing & forestry	0
Construction & maintenance	580
Production & transportation	399
Self-employed persons	390

* US Census Bureau
** New Jersey Department of Labor

General Information
Borough of Oakland
1 Municipal Plz
Oakland, NJ 07436
201-337-8111
Website	www.oakland-nj.org
Year of incorporation	1902
Land/water area (sq. miles)	8.60/0.15
Form of government	Borough

Government
Legislative Districts
US Congressional	5
State Legislative	40

Local Officials, 2009
Mayor	John P. Szabo Jr
Manager	Richard S. Kunze
Clerk	Lisa Duncan
Finance Dir	James A. Mangin
Tax Assessor	Scott Holzhauer
Tax Collector	Ellen Amorino
Attorney	Brian Chewcaskie
Building	Daniel Hagberg
Comm Dev/Planning	NA
Engineering	James Kelly
Public Works	Anthony Marcucilli
Police Chief	Edward Kasper
Emerg/Fire Director	Peter Sondervan

Housing & Construction
Housing Units, 2000*
Total	4,345
Median rent	$1,173
Median SF home value	$245,300

Permits for New Residential Construction
	Units	Value
Total, 2006	17	$2,079,300
Single family	17	$2,079,300
Total, 2007	11	$433,300
Single family	11	$433,300

Real Property Valuation, 2008
	Parcels	Valuation
Total	4,817	$2,532,385,000
Vacant	193	44,786,500
Residential	4,413	2,135,944,700
Commercial	140	173,664,700
Industrial	59	174,344,700
Apartments	0	0
Farm land	8	65,800
Farm homestead	4	3,578,600

Average Property Value & Tax, 2008
Residential value	$484,384
Property tax	$9,597
Tax credit/rebate	$1,305

Public Library
Oakland Public Library
2 Municipal Plaza
Oakland, NJ 07436
210-337-3742
Director	Michele Reuty

Library statistics, 2007
Population served	12,466
Full-time/total staff	3/10

	Total	Per capita
Holdings	58,538	4.70
Revenues	$843,845	$67.69
Expenditures	$706,005	$56.63
Annual visits	21,029	1.69
Internet terminals/annual users	11/4,630	

Public Safety
Number of officers, 2007	26

Crime	2006	2007
Total crimes	131	93
Violent	1	6
Murder	0	0
Rape	0	0
Robbery	1	0
Aggravated assault	0	6
Non-violent	130	87
Burglary	13	6
Larceny	116	80
Vehicle theft	1	1
Domestic violence	71	96
Arson	3	0
Total crime rate	9.6	6.9
Violent	0.1	0.4
Non-violent	9.5	6.4

Public School District
(for school year 2007-08 except as noted)

Oakland School District
315 Ramapo Valley Road
Oakland, NJ 07436
(201) 337-6156
Superintendent	Richard Heflich
Number of schools	4
Grade plan	K-8
Enrollment	1,676
Attendance rate, '06-07	96.0%
Dropout rate	NA
Students per teacher	10.6
Per pupil expenditure	$13,606
Median faculty salary	$54,691
Median administrator salary	$141,799
Grade 12 enrollment	NA
High school graduation rate	NA

Assessment test results
(percent scoring at proficient or advanced level)
	Language	Math
NJASK-Grade 3	94.7%	95.2%
GEPA-Grade 8	89.5%	97.8%
HSPA-High School	NA	NA

SAT Score Averages, 2006-07
Pct tested	Math	Verbal	Writing
NA	NA	NA	NA

Teacher Qualifications
Avg. years of experience	7

Highly-qualified teachers
one subject/all subjects	100%/100%

No Child Left Behind
AYP, 2006-07	Meets Standards

Municipal Finance
State Aid Programs, 2009
Total aid	$1,693,447
CMPTRA	218,701
Energy tax receipts	1,430,788
Garden State Trust	1,663

General Budget, 2008
Total tax levy	$50,259,547
County levy	4,929,911
County taxes	4,662,797
County library	0
County health	0
County open space	267,114
School levy	32,440,167
Muni. levy	12,889,469
Misc. revenues	4,742,749

Taxes	2006	2007	2008
General tax rate per $100	1.8	1.91	1.983
County equalization ratio	105.95	97.29	95.23
Net valuation taxable	$2,521,205,100	$2,526,995,660	$2,536,807,455
State equalized value	$2,595,141,591	$2,653,341,139	$2,762,110,574

See Introduction for an explanation of all data sources.

Demographics & Socio-Economic Characteristics

(2000 US Census, except as noted)

Population

1980*	4,223
1990*	4,430
2000	4,188
Male	2,036
Female	2,152
2007 (estimate)*	4,029
Population density	6,604.9

Race & Hispanic Origin, 2000

Race
White	4,017
Black/African American	48
American Indian/Alaska Native	9
Asian	40
Native Hawaiian/Pacific Islander	1
Other race	35
Two or more races	38
Hispanic origin, total	97
Mexican	2
Puerto Rican	75
Cuban	1
Other Hispanic	19

Age & Nativity, 2000

Under 5 years	247
18 years and over	3,233
21 years and over	3,114
65 years and over	703
85 years and over	85
Median age	38.0
Native-born	4,104
Foreign-born	64

Educational Attainment, 2000

Population 25 years and over	2,889
Less than 9th grade	4.8%
High school grad or higher	82.5%
Bachelor's degree or higher	19.3%
Graduate degree	5.5%

Income & Poverty, 1999

Per capita income	$24,157
Median household income	$44,364
Median family income	$55,434
Persons in poverty	271
H'holds receiving public assistance	29
H'holds receiving social security	563

Households, 2000

Total households	1,791
With persons under 18	516
With persons over 65	542
Family households	1,067
Single-person households	614
Persons per household	2.34
Persons per family	3.07

Labor & Employment

Total civilian labor force, 2007**	2,354
Unemployment rate	3.5%
Total civilian labor force, 2000	2,219
Unemployment rate	3.6%

Employed persons 16 years and over by occupation, 2000
Managers & professionals	696
Service occupations	251
Sales & office occupations	726
Farming, fishing & forestry	0
Construction & maintenance	271
Production & transportation	195
Self-employed persons	87

* US Census Bureau
** New Jersey Department of Labor

General Information

Borough of Oaklyn
500 White Horse Pike
Oaklyn, NJ 08107
856-858-2457

Website	www.oaklyn-nj.com
Year of incorporation	1905
Land/water area (sq. miles)	0.61/0.08
Form of government	Borough

Government

Legislative Districts

US Congressional	1
State Legislative	6

Local Officials, 2009

Mayor	Michael LaMaina
Manager/Admin	NA
Clerk	Marie Hawkins
Finance Dir	Michael Krusen
Tax Assessor	Anthony Leone
Tax Collector	Judy Pierce
Attorney	Timothy Higgins
Building	Robert Forbes
Comm Dev/Planning	NA
Engineering	Key Engineers
Public Works	Jim Rafferty
Police Chief	Jon Shelly
Emerg/Fire Director	Mark Quinter

Housing & Construction

Housing Units, 2000*

Total	1,893
Median rent	$540
Median SF home value	$98,200

Permits for New Residential Construction

	Units	Value
Total, 2006	1	$105,000
Single family	1	$105,000
Total, 2007	1	$105,000
Single family	1	$105,000

Real Property Valuation, 2008

	Parcels	Valuation
Total	1,452	$160,573,800
Vacant	18	1,086,000
Residential	1,339	135,022,000
Commercial	75	16,266,300
Industrial	1	169,000
Apartments	19	8,030,500
Farm land	0	0
Farm homestead	0	0

Average Property Value & Tax, 2008

Residential value	$100,838
Property tax	$5,362
Tax credit/rebate	$961

Public Library

Oaklyn Memorial Library
602 Newton Ave
Oaklyn, NJ 08107
856-858-8226

Director	Ann Marie Latini

Library statistics, 2007

Population served	4,188
Full-time/total staff	NA/0

	Total	Per capita
Holdings	0	NA
Revenues	$0	NA
Expenditures	$0	NA
Annual visits	NA	NA
Internet terminals/annual users	NA/NA	

Public Safety

Number of officers, 2007	12

Crime	2006	2007
Total crimes	115	132
Violent	5	9
Murder	0	0
Rape	0	0
Robbery	2	4
Aggravated assault	3	5
Non-violent	110	123
Burglary	27	38
Larceny	80	80
Vehicle theft	3	5
Domestic violence	39	38
Arson	1	1
Total crime rate	27.9	32.4
Violent	1.2	2.2
Non-violent	26.7	30.1

Public School District

(for school year 2007-08 except as noted)

Oaklyn Borough School District
Kendall Boulevard
Oaklyn, NJ 08107
(856) 858-1731

Superintendent	Tommie Stringer
Number of schools	2
Grade plan	K-9
Enrollment	450
Attendance rate, '06-07	94.9%
Dropout rate	0.0%
Students per teacher	10.8
Per pupil expenditure	$12,345
Median faculty salary	$44,379
Median administrator salary	$91,614
Grade 12 enrollment	NA
High school graduation rate	NA

Assessment test results

(percent scoring at proficient or advanced level)
	Language	Math
NJASK-Grade 3	85.0%	90.0%
GEPA-Grade 8	77.3%	84.0%
HSPA-High School	NA	NA

SAT Score Averages, 2006-07

Pct tested	Math	Verbal	Writing
NA	NA	NA	NA

Teacher Qualifications

Avg. years of experience	11
Highly-qualified teachers one subject/all subjects	97.0%/97.0%

No Child Left Behind

AYP, 2006-07	Meets Standards

Municipal Finance

State Aid Programs, 2009

Total aid	$416,290
CMPTRA	102,576
Energy tax receipts	311,633
Garden State Trust	0

General Budget, 2008

Total tax levy	$8,546,730
County levy	1,924,181
County taxes	1,738,829
County library	124,780
County health	0
County open space	60,572
School levy	3,951,826
Muni. levy	2,670,723
Misc. revenues	1,367,950

Taxes

	2006	2007	2008
General tax rate per $100	4.963	5.195	5.318
County equalization ratio	68.79	58.47	53.20
Net valuation taxable	$159,915,300	$160,378,373	$160,725,382
State equalized value	$273,678,590	$301,325,722	$314,817,073

See Introduction for an explanation of all data sources.

Demographics & Socio-Economic Characteristics

(2000 US Census, except as noted)

Population
1980*	13,949
1990*	15,512
2000	15,378
Male	7,129
Female	8,249
2007 (estimate)*	14,923
Population density	2,156.5

Race & Hispanic Origin, 2000
Race
White	14,389
Black/African American	663
American Indian/Alaska Native	18
Asian	86
Native Hawaiian/Pacific Islander	10
Other race	80
Two or more races	132
Hispanic origin, total	306
Mexican	60
Puerto Rican	140
Cuban	15
Other Hispanic	91

Age & Nativity, 2000
Under 5 years	529
18 years and over	12,862
21 years and over	12,510
65 years and over	3,989
85 years and over	580
Median age	47.8
Native-born	14,817
Foreign-born	561

Educational Attainment, 2000
Population 25 years and over	11,981
Less than 9th grade	2.6%
High school grad or higher	89.5%
Bachelor's degree or higher	33.5%
Graduate degree	10.3%

Income & Poverty, 1999
Per capita income	$33,217
Median household income	$44,158
Median family income	$61,731
Persons in poverty	1,031
H'holds receiving public assistance	80
H'holds receiving social security	2,962

Households, 2000
Total households	7,464
With persons under 18	1,370
With persons over 65	2,815
Family households	4,007
Single-person households	3,015
Persons per household	2.02
Persons per family	2.71

Labor & Employment
Total civilian labor force, 2007**	9,431
Unemployment rate	4.6%
Total civilian labor force, 2000	7,979
Unemployment rate	6.0%

Employed persons 16 years and over by occupation, 2000
Managers & professionals	2,871
Service occupations	1,427
Sales & office occupations	2,217
Farming, fishing & forestry	36
Construction & maintenance	499
Production & transportation	454
Self-employed persons	612

*   US Census Bureau
** New Jersey Department of Labor

General Information
City of Ocean
861 Asbury Ave
Ocean, NJ 08226
609-399-6111

Website	www.ocnj.us
Year of incorporation	1897
Land/water area (sq. miles)	6.92/4.16
Form of government	Mayor-Council

Government
Legislative Districts
US Congressional	2
State Legislative	1

Local Officials, 2009
Mayor	Salvatore Perillo
Business Admin	James Rutala
Clerk	Linda MacIntyre
Finance Dir	John Hansen
Tax Assessor	Joseph Elliott
Tax Collector	Gary Hink
Attorney	Keith Szendrey
Building	Patrick Newton
Planning	Randall Scheule
Engineering	Richard Carter
Public Works	Michael Rossbach
Police Chief	Robert Blevin
Emerg/Fire Director	Joseph Foglio

Housing & Construction
Housing Units, 2000*
Total	20,298
Median rent	$722
Median SF home value	$224,700

Permits for New Residential Construction
	Units	Value
Total, 2006	286	$68,961,405
Single family	81	$33,523,665
Total, 2007	153	$37,467,997
Single family	65	$21,854,889

Real Property Valuation, 2008
	Parcels	Valuation
Total	18,937	$12,734,818,847
Vacant	781	241,947,700
Residential	17,502	11,883,281,300
Commercial	598	554,733,747
Industrial	2	733,300
Apartments	54	54,122,800
Farm land	0	0
Farm homestead	0	0

Average Property Value & Tax, 2008
Residential value	$678,967
Property tax	$4,582
Tax credit/rebate	$880

Public Library
Ocean City Free Pub Library
1735 Simpson Ave
Ocean City, NJ 08226
609-399-2434

Director............Christopher Maloney

Library statistics, 2007
Population served	15,378
Full-time/total staff	4/10

	Total	Per capita
Holdings	120,593	7.84
Revenues	$3,833,703	$249.30
Expenditures	$3,208,117	$208.62
Annual visits	274,572	17.85
Internet terminals/annual users	25/2,818	

Public Safety
Number of officers, 2007	61

Crime	2006	2007
Total crimes	1,066	1,181
Violent	23	28
Murder	0	0
Rape	0	3
Robbery	4	19
Aggravated assault	19	6
Non-violent	1,043	1,153
Burglary	182	183
Larceny	853	961
Vehicle theft	8	9
Domestic violence	159	123
Arson	0	0
Total crime rate	69.5	78.1
Violent	1.5	1.9
Non-violent	68.0	76.2

Public School District
(for school year 2007-08 except as noted)

Ocean City School District
501 Atlantic Avenue, Suite 1
Ocean City, NJ 08226
(609) 399-5150

Superintendent	Kathleen W. Taylor
Number of schools	3
Grade plan	K-12
Enrollment	2,048
Attendance rate, '06-07	94.5%
Dropout rate	0.6%
Students per teacher	8.9
Per pupil expenditure	$18,119
Median faculty salary	$84,816
Median administrator salary	$120,384
Grade 12 enrollment	343
High school graduation rate	97.5%

Assessment test results
(percent scoring at proficient or advanced level)
	Language	Math
NJASK-Grade 3	89.7%	92.6%
GEPA-Grade 8	81.8%	89.8%
HSPA-High School	85.4%	91.1%

SAT Score Averages, 2006-07
Pct tested	Math	Verbal	Writing
78%	522	501	493

Teacher Qualifications
Avg. years of experience	18
Highly-qualified teachers one subject/all subjects	100%/100%

No Child Left Behind
AYP, 2006-07............Meets Standards

Municipal Finance
State Aid Programs, 2009
Total aid	$2,382,840
CMPTRA	0
Energy tax receipts	2,304,991
Garden State Trust	1,357

General Budget, 2008
Total tax levy	$85,984,431
County levy	21,855,384
County taxes	20,499,483
County library	0
County health	0
County open space	1,355,902
School levy	21,864,170
Muni. levy	42,264,877
Misc. revenues	17,832,353

Taxes
	2006	2007	2008
General tax rate per $100	0.97	1	0.676
County equalization ratio	68.55	59.04	94.30
Net valuation taxable	$8,010,568,600	$8,249,356,764	$12,740,485,933
State equalized value	$13,571,774,950	$13,365,922,948	$13,222,915,500

See Introduction for an explanation of all data sources.

Demographics & Socio-Economic Characteristics

(2000 US Census, except as noted)

Population

1980*	1,385
1990*	2,078
2000	2,076
Male	977
Female	1,099
2007 (estimate)*	2,130
Population density	4,840.9

Race & Hispanic Origin, 2000

Race

White	2,004
Black/African American	20
American Indian/Alaska Native	3
Asian	20
Native Hawaiian/Pacific Islander	0
Other race	11
Two or more races	18
Hispanic origin, total	49
Mexican	7
Puerto Rican	29
Cuban	1
Other Hispanic	12

Age & Nativity, 2000

Under 5 years	144
18 years and over	1,536
21 years and over	1,462
65 years and over	300
85 years and over	28
Median age	37.0
Native-born	2,065
Foreign-born	11

Educational Attainment, 2000

Population 25 years and over	1,393
Less than 9th grade	4.7%
High school grad or higher	81.3%
Bachelor's degree or higher	7.3%
Graduate degree	0.6%

Income & Poverty, 1999

Per capita income	$19,239
Median household income	$41,067
Median family income	$50,847
Persons in poverty	213
H'holds receiving public assistance	9
H'holds receiving social security	216

Households, 2000

Total households	832
With persons under 18	305
With persons over 65	221
Family households	547
Single-person households	234
Persons per household	2.50
Persons per family	3.06

Labor & Employment

Total civilian labor force, 2007**	1,271
Unemployment rate	4.4%
Total civilian labor force, 2000	1,071
Unemployment rate	4.3%

Employed persons 16 years and over by occupation, 2000

Managers & professionals	215
Service occupations	171
Sales & office occupations	318
Farming, fishing & forestry	0
Construction & maintenance	188
Production & transportation	133
Self-employed persons	45

* US Census Bureau
** New Jersey Department of Labor

General Information

Borough of Ocean Gate
801 Ocean Gate Ave
CN 100
Ocean Gate, NJ 08740
732-269-3166

Website	NA
Year of incorporation	1918
Land/water area (sq. miles)	0.44/0.00
Form of government	Borough

Government

Legislative Districts

US Congressional	3
State Legislative	9

Local Officials, 2009

Mayor	Paul J. Kennedy
Manager/Admin	NA
Clerk	Jodi Pellicano
Finance Dir	NA
Tax Assessor	Scott Pezarras
Tax Collector	Elizabeth V. Barger
Attorney	James Gluck
Building	Paul E. Butow Jr
Comm Dev/Planning	NA
Engineering	Alan Dittenhofer
Public Works	George Althouse
Police Chief	Reece Fisher
Emerg/Fire Director	Jack Trovato

Housing & Construction

Housing Units, 2000*

Total	1,152
Median rent	$819
Median SF home value	$101,500

Permits for New Residential Construction

	Units	Value
Total, 2006	3	$518,780
Single family	3	$518,780
Total, 2007	6	$1,328,600
Single family	6	$1,328,600

Real Property Valuation, 2008

	Parcels	Valuation
Total	1,095	$260,342,100
Vacant	38	3,351,000
Residential	1,041	251,009,000
Commercial	13	4,683,100
Industrial	0	0
Apartments	3	1,299,000
Farm land	0	0
Farm homestead	0	0

Average Property Value & Tax, 2008

Residential value	$241,123
Property tax	$4,583
Tax credit/rebate	$904

Public Library

No public municipal library

Library statistics, 2007

Population served	NA
Full-time/total staff	NA/NA

	Total	Per capita
Holdings	NA	NA
Revenues	NA	NA
Expenditures	NA	NA
Annual visits	NA	NA
Internet terminals/annual users	NA/NA	

Public Safety

Number of officers, 2007 ... 5

Crime	2006	2007
Total crimes	57	46
Violent	6	6
Murder	0	2
Rape	0	0
Robbery	0	1
Aggravated assault	6	3
Non-violent	51	40
Burglary	12	9
Larceny	37	30
Vehicle theft	2	1
Domestic violence	45	68
Arson	0	0
Total crime rate	27.0	21.6
Violent	2.8	2.8
Non-violent	24.2	18.8

Public School District

(for school year 2007-08 except as noted)

Ocean Gate School District
126 West Arverne Avenue, PO Box 478
Ocean Gate, NJ 08740
(732) 269-3023

Superintendent	Frank Vanalesti
Number of schools	1
Grade plan	K-6
Enrollment	142
Attendance rate, '06-07	93.2%
Dropout rate	NA
Students per teacher	8.8
Per pupil expenditure	$14,803
Median faculty salary	$38,700
Median administrator salary	$91,188
Grade 12 enrollment	NA
High school graduation rate	NA

Assessment test results

(percent scoring at proficient or advanced level)

	Language	Math
NJASK-Grade 3	95.7%	100.0%
GEPA-Grade 8	NA	NA
HSPA-High School	NA	NA

SAT Score Averages, 2006-07

Pct tested	Math	Verbal	Writing
NA	NA	NA	NA

Teacher Qualifications

Avg. years of experience	10
Highly-qualified teachers one subject/all subjects	100%/100%

No Child Left Behind

AYP, 2006-07 ... Meets Standards

Municipal Finance

State Aid Programs, 2009

Total aid	$185,222
CMPTRA	37,504
Energy tax receipts	143,088
Garden State Trust	0

General Budget, 2008

Total tax levy	$4,951,574
County levy	871,602
County taxes	718,746
County library	84,472
County health	34,392
County open space	33,993
School levy	2,507,130
Muni. levy	1,572,841
Misc. revenues	1,046,680

Taxes

	2006	2007	2008
General tax rate per $100	1.747	1.884	1.901
County equalization ratio	107.58	92.99	92.17
Net valuation taxable	$256,650,000	$258,216,480	$260,522,532
State equalized value	$276,167,051	$280,138,518	$1,431,087,417

See Introduction for an explanation of all data sources.

Demographics & Socio-Economic Characteristics

(2000 US Census, except as noted)

Population

1980*	23,570
1990*	25,058
2000	26,959
Male	12,983
Female	13,976
2007 (estimate)*	28,260
Population density	2,562.1

Race & Hispanic Origin, 2000

Race

White	22,738
Black/African American	1,529
American Indian/Alaska Native	40
Asian	1,689
Native Hawaiian/Pacific Islander	20
Other race	425
Two or more races	518
Hispanic origin, total	1,215
Mexican	148
Puerto Rican	335
Cuban	63
Other Hispanic	669

Age & Nativity, 2000

Under 5 years	1,698
18 years and over	20,088
21 years and over	19,285
65 years and over	3,275
85 years and over	294
Median age	38.4
Native-born	22,719
Foreign-born	4,240

Educational Attainment, 2000

Population 25 years and over	18,333
Less than 9th grade	2.4%
High school grad or higher	90.2%
Bachelor's degree or higher	39.1%
Graduate degree	16.1%

Income & Poverty, 1999

Per capita income	$30,581
Median household income	$62,058
Median family income	$74,572
Persons in poverty	1,350
H'holds receiving public assistance	118
H'holds receiving social security	2,439

Households, 2000

Total households	10,254
With persons under 18	3,822
With persons over 65	2,421
Family households	7,338
Single-person households	2,456
Persons per household	2.63
Persons per family	3.14

Labor & Employment

Total civilian labor force, 2007**	14,773
Unemployment rate	3.4%
Total civilian labor force, 2000	13,946
Unemployment rate	4.2%

Employed persons 16 years and over by occupation, 2000

Managers & professionals	5,559
Service occupations	1,696
Sales & office occupations	4,261
Farming, fishing & forestry	14
Construction & maintenance	824
Production & transportation	1,009
Self-employed persons	822

‡ Branch of county library
* US Census Bureau
** New Jersey Department of Labor

General Information

Township of Ocean
399 Monmouth Rd
Oakhurst, NJ 07755
732-531-5000

Website	www.oceantwp.org
Year of incorporation	1849
Land/water area (sq. miles)	11.03/0.09
Form of government	Council-Manager

Government

Legislative Districts

US Congressional	6
State Legislative	11

Local Officials, 2009

Mayor	William Larkin
Manager	Andrew G. Brannen
Clerk	Vincent G. Buttiglieri
Finance Dir	Stephen Gallagher
Tax Assessor	Edward Mullane
Tax Collector	Stephen Gallagher
Attorney	Martin J. Arbus
Building	Paul Vitale
Planning	Marianne Wilensky
Engineering	Leon S. Avakian
Public Works	William McMahon
Police Chief	Antonio Amodio
Fire Chief	M. Evans/S. Newman

Housing & Construction

Housing Units, 2000*

Total	10,756
Median rent	$689
Median SF home value	$198,900

Permits for New Residential Construction

	Units	Value
Total, 2006	108	$16,754,115
Single family	108	$16,754,115
Total, 2007	67	$11,579,045
Single family	67	$11,579,045

Real Property Valuation, 2008

	Parcels	Valuation
Total	9,361	$4,636,030,600
Vacant	632	108,809,100
Residential	8,320	3,701,801,300
Commercial	391	650,095,600
Industrial	0	0
Apartments	15	174,312,600
Farm land	2	3,200
Farm homestead	1	1,008,800

Average Property Value & Tax, 2008

Residential value	$444,996
Property tax	$8,001
Tax credit/rebate	$1,137

Public Library

Ocean Township Public Library‡
601 Deal Rd
Oakhurst, NJ 07755
732-531-5092

Branch Librarian	Deborah Bagchi

Library statistics, 2007

see Monmouth County profile
for library system statistics

Public Safety

Number of officers, 2007	61

Crime	2006	2007
Total crimes	800	757
Violent	43	41
Murder	0	0
Rape	5	2
Robbery	15	18
Aggravated assault	23	21
Non-violent	757	716
Burglary	102	89
Larceny	624	600
Vehicle theft	31	27
Domestic violence	175	116
Arson	3	0
Total crime rate	29.1	27.5
Violent	1.6	1.5
Non-violent	27.5	26.1

Public School District

(for school year 2007-08 except as noted)

Ocean Township School District
163 Monmouth Road
Oakhurst, NJ 07755
(732) 531-5600

Superintendent	Thomas M. Pagano
Number of schools	5
Grade plan	K-12
Enrollment	4,232
Attendance rate, '06-07	95.5%
Dropout rate	0.1%
Students per teacher	10.6
Per pupil expenditure	$14,345
Median faculty salary	$55,970
Median administrator salary	$102,150
Grade 12 enrollment	348
High school graduation rate	98.6%

Assessment test results

(percent scoring at proficient or advanced level)

	Language	Math
NJASK-Grade 3	89.4%	89.4%
GEPA-Grade 8	76.2%	86.9%
HSPA-High School	83.7%	88.9%

SAT Score Averages, 2006-07

Pct tested	Math	Verbal	Writing
96%	525	502	496

Teacher Qualifications

Avg. years of experience	10
Highly-qualified teachers one subject/all subjects	99.5%/99.5%

No Child Left Behind

AYP, 2006-07	Meets Standards

Municipal Finance

State Aid Programs, 2009

Total aid	$3,263,751
CMPTRA	394,963
Energy tax receipts	2,783,597
Garden State Trust	3,195

General Budget, 2008

Total tax levy	$83,419,581
County levy	14,947,989
County taxes	13,265,018
County library	798,303
County health	0
County open space	884,668
School levy	52,013,439
Muni. levy	16,458,153
Misc. revenues	13,745,501

Taxes	2006	2007	2008
General tax rate per $100	1.674	1.733	1.799
County equalization ratio	94.96	83.55	78.98
Net valuation taxable	$4,542,082,300	$4,598,474,695	$4,639,365,876
State equalized value	$5,440,101,338	$5,821,430,884	$5,622,766,306

See Introduction for an explanation of all data sources.

Demographics & Socio-Economic Characteristics
(2000 US Census, except as noted)

Population
1980*	3,731
1990*	5,416
2000	6,450
Male	3,201
Female	3,249
2007 (estimate)*	8,643
Population density	415.5

Race & Hispanic Origin, 2000
Race
White	6,278
Black/African American	48
American Indian/Alaska Native	10
Asian	27
Native Hawaiian/Pacific Islander	2
Other race	23
Two or more races	62
Hispanic origin, total	200
Mexican	29
Puerto Rican	77
Cuban	32
Other Hispanic	62

Age & Nativity, 2000
Under 5 years	373
18 years and over	4,807
21 years and over	4,585
65 years and over	888
85 years and over	87
Median age	37.7
Native-born	6,358
Foreign-born	92

Educational Attainment, 2000
Population 25 years and over	4,369
Less than 9th grade	2.5%
High school grad or higher	86.2%
Bachelor's degree or higher	15.7%
Graduate degree	5.0%

Income & Poverty, 1999
Per capita income	$22,830
Median household income	$46,461
Median family income	$55,379
Persons in poverty	502
H'holds receiving public assistance	23
H'holds receiving social security	767

Households, 2000
Total households	2,446
With persons under 18	885
With persons over 65	647
Family households	1,745
Single-person households	571
Persons per household	2.61
Persons per family	3.08

Labor & Employment
Total civilian labor force, 2007**	3,738
Unemployment rate	5.6%
Total civilian labor force, 2000	3,177
Unemployment rate	6.9%

Employed persons 16 years and over by occupation, 2000
Managers & professionals	745
Service occupations	568
Sales & office occupations	685
Farming, fishing & forestry	0
Construction & maintenance	645
Production & transportation	315
Self-employed persons	222

‡ Branch of county library
* US Census Bureau
** New Jersey Department of Labor

General Information
Township of Ocean
50 Railroad Ave
Waretown, NJ 08758
609-693-3302
Website	www.townshipofocean.org
Year of incorporation	1876
Land/water area (sq. miles)	20.80/11.23
Form of government	Township

Government
Legislative Districts
US Congressional	3
State Legislative	9

Local Officials, 2009
Mayor	Robert J. Kraft
Manager/Admin	Kenneth Mosca
Clerk	Diane B. Ambrosio
Finance Dir	Christine Thorne
Tax Assessor	Martin Lynch
Tax Collector	Kammie Verdolina
Attorney	Gregory McGuckin
Building	James McBrien
Comm Dev/Planning	NA
Engineering	Alaimo Group
Public Works	Kenneth Mosca
Police Chief	Kenneth Flatt
Emerg/Fire Dir	Matthew Ambrosio

Housing & Construction
Housing Units, 2000*
Total	2,981
Median rent	$833
Median SF home value	$104,800

Permits for New Residential Construction
	Units	Value
Total, 2006	201	$23,817,911
Single family	201	$23,817,911
Total, 2007	173	$49,293,890
Single family	173	$49,293,890

Real Property Valuation, 2008
	Parcels	Valuation
Total	5,017	$1,259,741,000
Vacant	879	68,887,700
Residential	3,927	1,127,016,900
Commercial	117	59,969,800
Industrial	1	574,600
Apartments	0	0
Farm land	87	389,500
Farm homestead	6	2,902,500

Average Property Value & Tax, 2008
Residential value	$287,292
Property tax	$4,291
Tax credit/rebate	$837

Public Library
Waretown Branch Library‡
112 Main St
Waretown, NJ 08758
609-693-5133
Branch Librarian . . . . Kelly Ann Pernel

Library statistics, 2007
see Ocean County profile
for library system statistics

Public Safety
Number of officers, 2007 18
Crime	2006	2007
Total crimes	106	111
Violent	4	4
Murder	0	0
Rape	0	0
Robbery	0	0
Aggravated assault	4	4
Non-violent	102	107
Burglary	10	19
Larceny	92	88
Vehicle theft	0	0
Domestic violence	41	29
Arson	0	0
Total crime rate	13.6	13.5
Violent	0.5	0.5
Non-violent	13.0	13.0

Public School District
(for school year 2007-08 except as noted)

Ocean Township School District
64 Railroad Avenue
Waretown, NJ 08758
(609) 693-3329
Superintendent	Donald Bochicchio
Number of schools	2
Grade plan	K-6
Enrollment	543
Attendance rate, '06-07	94.9%
Dropout rate	NA
Students per teacher	8.5
Per pupil expenditure	$15,896
Median faculty salary	$52,650
Median administrator salary	$91,500
Grade 12 enrollment	NA
High school graduation rate	NA

Assessment test results
(percent scoring at proficient or advanced level)
	Language	Math
NJASK-Grade 3	88.1%	86.6%
GEPA-Grade 8	NA	NA
HSPA-High School	NA	NA

SAT Score Averages, 2006-07
Pct tested	Math	Verbal	Writing
NA	NA	NA	NA

Teacher Qualifications
Avg. years of experience	14

Highly-qualified teachers
one subject/all subjects 100%/100%

No Child Left Behind
AYP, 2006-07 . . . . Meets Standards

Municipal Finance
State Aid Programs, 2009
Total aid	$793,308
CMPTRA	19,792
Energy tax receipts	730,065
Garden State Trust	16,908

General Budget, 2008
Total tax levy	$18,837,287
County levy	4,427,902
County taxes	3,651,385
County library	429,121
County health	174,712
County open space	172,685
School levy	9,258,794
Muni. levy	5,150,591
Misc. revenues	4,722,785

Taxes
	2006	2007	2008
General tax rate per $100	1.417	1.449	1.494
County equalization ratio	105.41	92.46	87.84
Net valuation taxable	$1,148,540,400	$1,221,267,417	$1,261,091,724
State equalized value	$1,243,587,870	$1,390,144,705	$1,671,248,240

See Introduction for an explanation of all data sources.

Demographics & Socio-Economic Characteristics

(2000 US Census, except as noted)

Population

1980*	5,888
1990*	6,146
2000	5,807
Male	2,875
Female	2,932
2007 (estimate)*	5,768
Population density	1,791.3

Race & Hispanic Origin, 2000

Race

White	5,558
Black/African American	114
American Indian/Alaska Native	4
Asian	46
Native Hawaiian/Pacific Islander	1
Other race	32
Two or more races	52
Hispanic origin, total	120
Mexican	24
Puerto Rican	39
Cuban	12
Other Hispanic	45

Age & Nativity, 2000

Under 5 years	347
18 years and over	4,384
21 years and over	4,104
65 years and over	827
85 years and over	82
Median age	40.5
Native-born	5,595
Foreign-born	220

Educational Attainment, 2000

Population 25 years and over	3,891
Less than 9th grade	3.1%
High school grad or higher	90.6%
Bachelor's degree or higher	35.7%
Graduate degree	10.8%

Income & Poverty, 1999

Per capita income	$33,356
Median household income	$71,458
Median family income	$85,038
Persons in poverty	149
H'holds receiving public assistance	7
H'holds receiving social security	635

Households, 2000

Total households	2,043
With persons under 18	762
With persons over 65	613
Family households	1,555
Single-person households	443
Persons per household	2.71
Persons per family	3.18

Labor & Employment

Total civilian labor force, 2007**	2,981
Unemployment rate	2.0%
Total civilian labor force, 2000	2,798
Unemployment rate	2.3%

Employed persons 16 years and over by occupation, 2000

Managers & professionals	1,221
Service occupations	223
Sales & office occupations	875
Farming, fishing & forestry	0
Construction & maintenance	221
Production & transportation	194
Self-employed persons	159

‡ Branch of county library
* US Census Bureau
** New Jersey Department of Labor

General Information

Borough of Oceanport
222 Monmouth Blvd
PO Box 370
Oceanport, NJ 07757
732-222-8221

Website	www.oceanportboro.com
Year of incorporation	1920
Land/water area (sq. miles)	3.22/0.63
Form of government	Borough

Government

Legislative Districts

US Congressional	12
State Legislative	12

Local Officials, 2009

Mayor	Michael J. Mahon
Manager/Admin	NA
Clerk	Kimberly Jungfer
Finance Dir	Gregory Mayers
Tax Assessor	Helen Ward
Tax Collector	Cynthia Cortale
Attorney	John O. Bennett
Building	Walter Joyce
Planning/Zoning	Jeanne Smith (Bd Sec)
Engineering	William White
Public Works	Demitrio Zarate
Police Chief	Harold Sutton
Fire/Emergency Dir	NA

Housing & Construction

Housing Units, 2000*

Total	2,114
Median rent	$672
Median SF home value	$231,400

Permits for New Residential Construction

	Units	Value
Total, 2006	10	$3,741,458
Single family	10	$3,741,458
Total, 2007	6	$1,996,784
Single family	6	$1,996,784

Real Property Valuation, 2008

	Parcels	Valuation
Total	2,151	$1,342,461,900
Vacant	143	31,764,900
Residential	1,975	1,154,034,200
Commercial	30	155,484,500
Industrial	0	0
Apartments	1	669,800
Farm land	1	9,000
Farm homestead	1	499,500

Average Property Value & Tax, 2008

Residential value	$584,278
Property tax	$8,244
Tax credit/rebate	$1,138

Public Library

Oceanport Library‡
Monmouth Blvd & Myrtle Ave
Oceanport, NJ 07757
732-229-2626

Branch Librarian	Michele Blake

Library statistics, 2007

see Monmouth County profile
for library system statistics

Public Safety

Number of officers, 2007	16

Crime	2006	2007
Total crimes	41	60
Violent	1	1
Murder	0	0
Rape	1	0
Robbery	0	0
Aggravated assault	0	1
Non-violent	40	59
Burglary	9	3
Larceny	27	54
Vehicle theft	4	2
Domestic violence	10	13
Arson	3	1
Total crime rate	7.1	10.4
Violent	0.2	0.2
Non-violent	6.9	10.3

Public School District

(for school year 2007-08 except as noted)

Oceanport Borough School District
29 Wolf Hill Avenue
Oceanport, NJ 07757
(732) 544-8588

Superintendent	Andrew Orefice
Number of schools	2
Grade plan	K-8
Enrollment	719
Attendance rate, '06-07	94.9%
Dropout rate	NA
Students per teacher	10.9
Per pupil expenditure	$10,464
Median faculty salary	$46,010
Median administrator salary	$108,560
Grade 12 enrollment	NA
High school graduation rate	NA

Assessment test results

(percent scoring at proficient or advanced level)

	Language	Math
NJASK-Grade 3	92.0%	89.4%
GEPA-Grade 8	94.2%	98.8%
HSPA-High School	NA	NA

SAT Score Averages, 2006-07

Pct tested	Math	Verbal	Writing
NA	NA	NA	NA

Teacher Qualifications

Avg. years of experience	9
Highly-qualified teachers	
one subject/all subjects	100%/100%

No Child Left Behind

AYP, 2006-07	Meets Standards

Municipal Finance

State Aid Programs, 2009

Total aid	$699,896
CMPTRA	74,004
Energy tax receipts	608,395
Garden State Trust	0

General Budget, 2008

Total tax levy	$18,952,667
County levy	3,371,925
County taxes	2,943,729
County library	177,149
County health	54,742
County open space	196,305
School levy	10,748,717
Muni. levy	4,832,025
Misc. revenues	1,961,079

Taxes	2006	2007	2008
General tax rate per $100	1.306	1.346	1.411
County equalization ratio	121.39	108.17	103.35
Net valuation taxable	$1,331,283,400	$1,336,274,205	$1,343,248,986
State equalized value	$1,231,436,704	$1,292,983,314	$1,306,302,889

See Introduction for an explanation of all data sources.

Demographics & Socio-Economic Characteristics
(2000 US Census, except as noted)

Population
1980*	2,737
1990*	2,722
2000	2,638
Male	1,335
Female	1,303
2007 (estimate)*	2,568
Population density	1,126.3

Race & Hispanic Origin, 2000
Race
White	2,573
Black/African American	4
American Indian/Alaska Native	1
Asian	19
Native Hawaiian/Pacific Islander	0
Other race	7
Two or more races	34
Hispanic origin, total	110
Mexican	33
Puerto Rican	38
Cuban	5
Other Hispanic	34

Age & Nativity, 2000
Under 5 years	185
18 years and over	1,860
21 years and over	1,760
65 years and over	212
85 years and over	16
Median age	35.0
Native-born	2,480
Foreign-born	158

Educational Attainment, 2000
Population 25 years and over	1,668
Less than 9th grade	2.7%
High school grad or higher	89.3%
Bachelor's degree or higher	20.0%
Graduate degree	5.9%

Income & Poverty, 1999
Per capita income	$24,305
Median household income	$60,313
Median family income	$70,521
Persons in poverty	150
H'holds receiving public assistance	5
H'holds receiving social security	187

Households, 2000
Total households	881
With persons under 18	400
With persons over 65	162
Family households	705
Single-person households	146
Persons per household	2.99
Persons per family	3.38

Labor & Employment
Total civilian labor force, 2007**	1,588
Unemployment rate	3.5%
Total civilian labor force, 2000	1,418
Unemployment rate	2.6%

Employed persons 16 years and over by occupation, 2000
Managers & professionals	465
Service occupations	152
Sales & office occupations	406
Farming, fishing & forestry	0
Construction & maintenance	141
Production & transportation	217
Self-employed persons	43

* US Census Bureau
** New Jersey Department of Labor

General Information
Borough of Ogdensburg
14 Highland Ave
Ogdensburg, NJ 07439
973-827-3444
Website	(county website)
Year of incorporation	1914
Land/water area (sq. miles)	2.28/0.02
Form of government	Borough

Government
Legislative Districts
US Congressional	5
State Legislative	24

Local Officials, 2009
Mayor	James Sekelsky
Manager/Admin	NA
Clerk	Phyllis Drouin
Finance Dir	Monica Goscicki
Tax Assessor	Kathleen Keib
Tax Collector	Linda Pettenger
Attorney	John Ursin
Building	Jan Opt'Hof
Comm Dev/Planning	NA
Engineering	Eugene Buczynski
Public Works	Ken Smith
Police Chief	George Lott
Emerg/Fire Director	Eric Slater

Housing & Construction
Housing Units, 2000*
Total	903
Median rent	$775
Median SF home value	$141,600

Permits for New Residential Construction
	Units	Value
Total, 2006	7	$1,279,250
Single family	7	$1,279,250
Total, 2007	3	$548,250
Single family	3	$548,250

Real Property Valuation, 2008
	Parcels	Valuation
Total	892	$116,250,750
Vacant	47	2,992,800
Residential	804	103,189,750
Commercial	28	7,241,600
Industrial	3	1,446,200
Apartments	3	734,700
Farm land	4	21,100
Farm homestead	3	624,600

Average Property Value & Tax, 2008
Residential value	$128,642
Property tax	$6,268
Tax credit/rebate	$1,078

Public Library
No public municipal library

Library statistics, 2007
Population served	NA
Full-time/total staff	NA/NA

	Total	Per capita
Holdings	NA	NA
Revenues	NA	NA
Expenditures	NA	NA
Annual visits	NA	NA
Internet terminals/annual users	NA/NA	

Public Safety
Number of officers, 2007 7
Crime	2006	2007
Total crimes	7	15
Violent	0	1
Murder	0	0
Rape	0	0
Robbery	0	0
Aggravated assault	0	1
Non-violent	7	14
Burglary	2	4
Larceny	5	9
Vehicle theft	0	1
Domestic violence	24	38
Arson	0	0
Total crime rate	2.7	5.7
Violent	0.0	0.4
Non-violent	2.7	5.3

Public School District
(for school year 2007-08 except as noted)

Ogdensburg Borough School District
100 Main Street
Ogdensburg, NJ 07439
(973) 827-7126
Chief School Admin	John Petrelli
Number of schools	1
Grade plan	K-8
Enrollment	312
Attendance rate, '06-07	96.1%
Dropout rate	NA
Students per teacher	8.9
Per pupil expenditure	$13,130
Median faculty salary	$47,485
Median administrator salary	$79,870
Grade 12 enrollment	NA
High school graduation rate	NA

Assessment test results
(percent scoring at proficient or advanced level)
	Language	Math
NJASK-Grade 3	98.0%	89.6%
GEPA-Grade 8	74.3%	82.9%
HSPA-High School	NA	NA

SAT Score Averages, 2006-07
Pct tested	Math	Verbal	Writing
NA	NA	NA	NA

Teacher Qualifications
Avg. years of experience	14

Highly-qualified teachers
one subject/all subjects 96.0%/96.0%

No Child Left Behind
AYP, 2006-07 . . . . Meets Standards

Municipal Finance
State Aid Programs, 2009
Total aid	$247,691
CMPTRA	122,218
Energy tax receipts	108,282
Garden State Trust	12,132

General Budget, 2008
Total tax levy	$5,673,077
County levy	942,321
County taxes	790,837
County library	66,652
County health	23,423
County open space	61,408
School levy	2,910,866
Muni. levy	1,819,890
Misc. revenues	1,233,906

Taxes
	2006	2007	2008
General tax rate per $100	4.5	4.73	4.873
County equalization ratio	59.25	51.19	47.83
Net valuation taxable	$115,293,750	$117,122,064	$116,440,565
State equalized value	$225,496,501	$244,634,084	$245,548,089

See Introduction for an explanation of all data sources.

Demographics & Socio-Economic Characteristics[†]

(2000 US Census, except as noted)

Population

1980*	51,515
1990*	56,475
2000	60,456
Male	29,549
Female	30,907
2007 (estimate)*	66,044
Population density	1,733.9

Race & Hispanic Origin, 2000

Race
White	48,049
Black/African American	3,207
American Indian/Alaska Native	94
Asian	6,544
Native Hawaiian/Pacific Islander	27
Other race	1,133
Two or more races	1,402
Hispanic origin, total	4,578
Mexican	439
Puerto Rican	2,002
Cuban	377
Other Hispanic	1,760

Age & Nativity, 2000

Under 5 years	4,252
18 years and over	44,822
21 years and over	43,002
65 years and over	6,370
85 years and over	695
Median age	36.5
Native-born	49,341
Foreign-born	11,115

Educational Attainment, 2000

Population 25 years and over	40,677
Less than 9th grade	3.5%
High school grad or higher	88.4%
Bachelor's degree or higher	29.5%
Graduate degree	8.9%

Income & Poverty, 1999

Per capita income	$26,814
Median household income	$64,707
Median family income	$74,045
Persons in poverty	2,547
H'holds receiving public assistance	253
H'holds receiving social security	4,765

Households, 2000

Total households	21,438
With persons under 18	8,643
With persons over 65	4,524
Family households	15,959
Single-person households	4,527
Persons per household	2.80
Persons per family	3.30

Labor & Employment

Total civilian labor force, 2007**	35,330
Unemployment rate	2.8%
Total civilian labor force, 2000	31,618
Unemployment rate	4.7%

Employed persons 16 years and over by occupation, 2000
Managers & professionals	11,218
Service occupations	3,373
Sales & office occupations	9,469
Farming, fishing & forestry	21
Construction & maintenance	2,794
Production & transportation	3,265
Self-employed persons	1,097

† see Appendix C for American Community Survey data
* US Census Bureau
** New Jersey Department of Labor
§ State Fiscal Year July 1–June 30

General Information

Township of Old Bridge
1 Old Bridge Plaza
Old Bridge, NJ 08857
732-721-5600

Website	www.oldbridge.com
Year of incorporation	1976
Land/water area (sq. miles)	38.09/2.57
Form of government	Mayor-Council

Government

Legislative Districts

US Congressional	6, 12
State Legislative	13

Local Officials, 2009

Mayor	James T. Phillips
Manager	Michael Jacobs
Clerk	Rose-Marie Saracino
Finance Dir	Himanshu Shah
Tax Assessor	Brian Enright
Tax Collector	Kathleen Silber
Attorney	Jerome J. Convery
Building	Alex Tucciarone
Planning	Ellen Ritchie
Engineering	James E. Cleary
Public Works	Rocco Donatelli
Police Chief	Thomas Collow
Public Safety Dir	Michael Jacobs

Housing & Construction

Housing Units, 2000*

Total	21,896
Median rent	$770
Median SF home value	$162,800

Permits for New Residential Construction

	Units	Value
Total, 2006	270	$36,015,061
Single family	236	$33,566,570
Total, 2007	39	$5,841,106
Single family	29	$5,832,906

Real Property Valuation, 2008

	Parcels	Valuation
Total	19,759	$3,371,138,200
Vacant	1,025	66,363,800
Residential	18,026	2,741,268,300
Commercial	458	334,211,800
Industrial	58	50,693,700
Apartments	25	168,378,200
Farm land	131	4,178,000
Farm homestead	36	6,044,400

Average Property Value & Tax, 2008

Residential value	$152,105
Property tax	$6,146
Tax credit/rebate	$1,037

Public Library

Old Bridge Public Library
1 Old Bridge Plaza
Old Bridge, NJ 08857
732-721-5600

Director	Margery Kirby Cyr

Library statistics, 2007

Population served	60,456
Full-time/total staff	8/17

	Total	Per capita
Holdings	172,945	2.86
Revenues	$2,500,787	$41.37
Expenditures	$2,353,714	$38.93
Annual visits	343,456	5.68
Internet terminals/annual users	16/58,000	

Public Safety

Number of officers, 2007	105

Crime	2006	2007
Total crimes	1,000	948
Violent	54	42
Murder	0	0
Rape	5	0
Robbery	18	15
Aggravated assault	31	27
Non-violent	946	906
Burglary	239	145
Larceny	625	685
Vehicle theft	82	76
Domestic violence	447	453
Arson	9	5
Total crime rate	15.4	14.4
Violent	0.8	0.6
Non-violent	14.6	13.8

Public School District

(for school year 2007-08 except as noted)

Old Bridge Township School District
4207 Route 516
Matawan, NJ 07747
(732) 290-3976

Superintendent	Simon M. Bosco
Number of schools	15
Grade plan	K-12
Enrollment	9,648
Attendance rate, '06-07	95.2%
Dropout rate	0.7%
Students per teacher	12.3
Per pupil expenditure	$12,462
Median faculty salary	$58,237
Median administrator salary	$113,879
Grade 12 enrollment	784
High school graduation rate	96.9%

Assessment test results

(percent scoring at proficient or advanced level)
	Language	Math
NJASK-Grade 3	89.7%	90.8%
GEPA-Grade 8	69.7%	86.2%
HSPA-High School	78.1%	89.4%

SAT Score Averages, 2006-07

Pct tested	Math	Verbal	Writing
78%	502	483	489

Teacher Qualifications

Avg. years of experience	9
Highly-qualified teachers one subject/all subjects	99.0%/99.0%

No Child Left Behind

AYP, 2006-07	Meets Standards

Municipal Finance[§]

State Aid Programs, 2009

Total aid	$8,090,179
CMPTRA	2,876,117
Energy tax receipts	4,993,642
Garden State Trust	17,593

General Budget, 2008

Total tax levy	$136,378,595
County levy	22,818,205
County taxes	20,423,827
County library	0
County health	0
County open space	2,394,378
School levy	85,883,492
Muni. levy	27,676,899
Misc. revenues	29,614,299

Taxes

	2006	2007	2008
General tax rate per $100	3.82	3.99	4.041
County equalization ratio	51.55	45.47	42.58
Net valuation taxable	$3,304,444,000	$3,339,763,515	$3,375,373,060
State equalized value	$7,272,220,920	$7,837,444,066	$2,377,854,891

See Introduction for an explanation of all data sources.

Demographics & Socio-Economic Characteristics
(2000 US Census, except as noted)

Population
1980*	4,168
1990*	4,254
2000	5,482
Male	2,632
Female	2,850
2007 (estimate)*	6,027
Population density	1,865.9

Race & Hispanic Origin, 2000
Race
White	4,533
Black/African American	33
American Indian/Alaska Native	3
Asian	857
Native Hawaiian/Pacific Islander	0
Other race	24
Two or more races	32
Hispanic origin, total	151
Mexican	14
Puerto Rican	28
Cuban	36
Other Hispanic	73

Age & Nativity, 2000
Under 5 years	346
18 years and over	4,004
21 years and over	3,844
65 years and over	798
85 years and over	110
Median age	41.0
Native-born	4,562
Foreign-born	920

Educational Attainment, 2000
Population 25 years and over	3,708
Less than 9th grade	1.8%
High school grad or higher	93.5%
Bachelor's degree or higher	49.4%
Graduate degree	18.3%

Income & Poverty, 1999
Per capita income	$48,367
Median household income	$102,127
Median family income	$106,772
Persons in poverty	94
H'holds receiving public assistance	16
H'holds receiving social security	519

Households, 2000
Total households	1,778
With persons under 18	780
With persons over 65	478
Family households	1,542
Single-person households	215
Persons per household	3.02
Persons per family	3.28

Labor & Employment
Total civilian labor force, 2007**	2,758
Unemployment rate	2.8%
Total civilian labor force, 2000	2,607
Unemployment rate	3.0%

Employed persons 16 years and over by occupation, 2000
Managers & professionals	1,389
Service occupations	188
Sales & office occupations	775
Farming, fishing & forestry	0
Construction & maintenance	86
Production & transportation	92
Self-employed persons	197

* US Census Bureau
** New Jersey Department of Labor

General Information
Borough of Old Tappan
227 Old Tappan Rd
Old Tappan, NJ 07675
201-664-1849
Website	www.oldtappan.net
Year of incorporation	1894
Land/water area (sq. miles)	3.23/0.85
Form of government	Borough

Government
Legislative Districts
US Congressional	5
State Legislative	39

Local Officials, 2009
Mayor	Victor Polce
Manager	Patrick O'Brien
Clerk	Jean M. Quinn
Finance Dir	Rebecca Overgaard
Tax Assessor	Irwin Sabin
Tax Collector	Rebecca Overgaard
Attorney	Allen Bell
Building	Peiro Abballe
Planning	Rea Epstein
Engineering	Thomas W. Skrable
Public Works	Arthur Lake
Police Chief	Joseph Fasulo
Emerg/Fire Director	Nicola Lepore

Housing & Construction
Housing Units, 2000*
Total	1,804
Median rent	$940
Median SF home value	$436,900

Permits for New Residential Construction
	Units	Value
Total, 2006	35	$17,373,625
Single family	35	$17,373,625
Total, 2007	18	$7,981,372
Single family	18	$7,981,372

Real Property Valuation, 2008
	Parcels	Valuation
Total	2,051	$1,283,179,700
Vacant	72	34,314,800
Residential	1,925	1,186,252,900
Commercial	50	61,889,900
Industrial	0	0
Apartments	1	331,800
Farm land	1	9,900
Farm homestead	2	380,400

Average Property Value & Tax, 2008
Residential value	$615,793
Property tax	$12,717
Tax credit/rebate	$1,383

Public Library
Old Tappan Public Library
56 Russell Ave
Old Tappan, NJ 07675
201-664-3499
Director	Susan Meeske

Library statistics, 2007
Population served	5,482
Full-time/total staff	1/2

	Total	Per capita
Holdings	51,624	9.42
Revenues	$625,536	$114.11
Expenditures	$474,982	$86.64
Annual visits	32,940	6.01
Internet terminals/annual users	3/4,392	

Public Safety
Number of officers, 2007	13

Crime	2006	2007
Total crimes	34	21
Violent	4	1
Murder	0	0
Rape	0	0
Robbery	0	0
Aggravated assault	4	1
Non-violent	30	20
Burglary	3	2
Larceny	27	18
Vehicle theft	0	0
Domestic violence	6	5
Arson	0	0
Total crime rate	5.8	3.5
Violent	0.7	0.2
Non-violent	5.1	3.3

Public School District
(for school year 2007-08 except as noted)

Old Tappan School District
T. Baldwin Demarest School, School Street
Old Tappan, NJ 07675
(201) 664-7231
Superintendent	William Ward
Number of schools	2
Grade plan	K-8
Enrollment	872
Attendance rate, '06-07	96.3%
Dropout rate	NA
Students per teacher	12.3
Per pupil expenditure	$13,628
Median faculty salary	$64,945
Median administrator salary	$122,597
Grade 12 enrollment	NA
High school graduation rate	NA

Assessment test results
(percent scoring at proficient or advanced level)
	Language	Math
NJASK-Grade 3	97.8%	100.0%
GEPA-Grade 8	86.2%	96.3%
HSPA-High School	NA	NA

SAT Score Averages, 2006-07
Pct tested	Math	Verbal	Writing
NA	NA	NA	NA

Teacher Qualifications
Avg. years of experience	9
Highly-qualified teachers one subject/all subjects	88.0%/88.0%

No Child Left Behind
AYP, 2006-07	Meets Standards

Municipal Finance
State Aid Programs, 2009
Total aid	$1,674,571
CMPTRA	0
Energy tax receipts	1,554,229
Garden State Trust	0

General Budget, 2008
Total tax levy	$26,521,163
County levy	3,575,018
County taxes	3,381,814
County library	0
County health	0
County open space	193,204
School levy	18,985,795
Muni. levy	3,960,350
Misc. revenues	5,383,464

Taxes
	2006	2007	2008
General tax rate per $100	1.93	1.98	2.067
County equalization ratio	76.23	67.69	66.55
Net valuation taxable	$1,241,755,700	$1,265,537,977	$1,284,193,076
State equalized value	$1,835,443,517	$1,901,179,807	$1,951,134,501

Demographics & Socio-Economic Characteristics
(2000 US Census, except as noted)

Population
1980*	1,847
1990*	1,683
2000	1,798
Male	909
Female	889
2007 (estimate)*	1,804
Population density	90.3

Race & Hispanic Origin, 2000
Race
White	1,561
Black/African American	173
American Indian/Alaska Native	5
Asian	3
Native Hawaiian/Pacific Islander	0
Other race	36
Two or more races	20
Hispanic origin, total	75
Mexican	27
Puerto Rican	29
Cuban	0
Other Hispanic	19

Age & Nativity, 2000
Under 5 years	98
18 years and over	1,355
21 years and over	1,292
65 years and over	213
85 years and over	22
Median age	39.1
Native-born	1,755
Foreign-born	43

Educational Attainment, 2000
Population 25 years and over	1,236
Less than 9th grade	5.6%
High school grad or higher	81.9%
Bachelor's degree or higher	10.9%
Graduate degree	3.2%

Income & Poverty, 1999
Per capita income	$22,495
Median household income	$57,589
Median family income	$64,091
Persons in poverty	146
H'holds receiving public assistance	7
H'holds receiving social security	179

Households, 2000
Total households	654
With persons under 18	235
With persons over 65	152
Family households	517
Single-person households	111
Persons per household	2.74
Persons per family	3.07

Labor & Employment
Total civilian labor force, 2007**	975
Unemployment rate	4.4%
Total civilian labor force, 2000	950
Unemployment rate	5.9%

Employed persons 16 years and over by occupation, 2000
Managers & professionals	230
Service occupations	96
Sales & office occupations	250
Farming, fishing & forestry	5
Construction & maintenance	111
Production & transportation	202
Self-employed persons	60

* US Census Bureau
** New Jersey Department of Labor

General Information
Township of Oldmans
PO Box 416
Pedricktown, NJ 08067
856-299-0780
Website	oldmanstownship.com
Year of incorporation	1881
Land/water area (sq. miles)	19.97/0.33
Form of government	Township

Government
Legislative Districts
US Congressional	2
State Legislative	3

Local Officials, 2009
Mayor	Harry A. Moore
Manager/Admin	NA
Clerk	Susan Miller
Finance Dir	James Hackett
Tax Assessor	Michael Raio
Tax Collector	Margie L. Schieber
Attorney	John Hoffman
Building	Jeryl Goff
Comm Dev/Planning	NA
Engineering	John Bickel
Public Works	NA
Police Chief	NA
Emerg/Fire Director	Gary Moore

Housing & Construction
Housing Units, 2000*
Total	694
Median rent	$714
Median SF home value	$104,300

Permits for New Residential Construction
	Units	Value
Total, 2006	5	$612,100
Single family	5	$612,100
Total, 2007	2	$125,000
Single family	2	$125,000

Real Property Valuation, 2008
	Parcels	Valuation
Total	1,221	$114,554,750
Vacant	228	4,577,310
Residential	581	54,299,400
Commercial	38	6,695,000
Industrial	14	35,137,370
Apartments	0	0
Farm land	257	3,032,070
Farm homestead	103	10,813,600

Average Property Value & Tax, 2008
Residential value	$95,194
Property tax	$4,035
Tax credit/rebate	$863

Public Library
No public municipal library

Library statistics, 2007
Population served	NA
Full-time/total staff	NA/NA

	Total	Per capita
Holdings	NA	NA
Revenues	NA	NA
Expenditures	NA	NA
Annual visits	NA	NA
Internet terminals/annual users	NA/NA	

Public Safety
Number of officers, 2007	0

Crime	2006	2007
Total crimes	52	52
Violent	3	3
Murder	0	0
Rape	0	0
Robbery	2	0
Aggravated assault	1	3
Non-violent	49	49
Burglary	16	9
Larceny	32	39
Vehicle theft	1	1
Domestic violence	3	14
Arson	0	1
Total crime rate	28.4	28.5
Violent	1.6	1.6
Non-violent	26.7	26.8

Public School District
(for school year 2007-08 except as noted)

Oldmans Township School District
10 Freed Road
Pedricktown, NJ 08067
(856) 299-4240

Chief School Admin	Stephen Combs
Number of schools	1
Grade plan	K-8
Enrollment	213
Attendance rate, '06-07	95.1%
Dropout rate	NA
Students per teacher	9.0
Per pupil expenditure	$14,856
Median faculty salary	$68,536
Median administrator salary	$64,500
Grade 12 enrollment	NA
High school graduation rate	NA

Assessment test results
(percent scoring at proficient or advanced level)
	Language	Math
NJASK-Grade 3	92.0%	84.0%
GEPA-Grade 8	75.0%	87.5%
HSPA-High School	NA	NA

SAT Score Averages, 2006-07
Pct tested	Math	Verbal	Writing
NA	NA	NA	NA

Teacher Qualifications
Avg. years of experience	21
Highly-qualified teachers one subject/all subjects	100%/100%

No Child Left Behind
AYP, 2006-07	Meets Standards

Municipal Finance
State Aid Programs, 2009
Total aid	$314,422
CMPTRA	31,265
Energy tax receipts	269,989
Garden State Trust	618

General Budget, 2008
Total tax levy	$4,870,157
County levy	1,817,669
County taxes	1,778,451
County library	0
County health	0
County open space	39,218
School levy	2,792,251
Muni. levy	260,238
Misc. revenues	1,141,165

Taxes
	2006	2007	2008
General tax rate per $100	4.003	4.076	4.239
County equalization ratio	67.89	67.07	59.07
Net valuation taxable	$111,370,740	$111,962,987	$114,894,357
State equalized value	$166,409,453	$189,291,266	$217,168,368

See Introduction for an explanation of all data sources.

Demographics & Socio-Economic Characteristics
(2000 US Census, except as noted)

Population
1980*	8,658
1990*	8,024
2000	8,047
Male	3,849
Female	4,198
2007 (estimate)*	7,847
Population density	3,242.6

Race & Hispanic Origin, 2000
Race
White	7,248
Black/African American	39
American Indian/Alaska Native	3
Asian	651
Native Hawaiian/Pacific Islander	1
Other race	26
Two or more races	79
Hispanic origin, total	249
Mexican	12
Puerto Rican	72
Cuban	64
Other Hispanic	101

Age & Nativity, 2000
Under 5 years	509
18 years and over	6,020
21 years and over	5,852
65 years and over	1,337
85 years and over	182
Median age	41.5
Native-born	6,976
Foreign-born	1,071

Educational Attainment, 2000
Population 25 years and over	5,617
Less than 9th grade	1.8%
High school grad or higher	94.9%
Bachelor's degree or higher	51.8%
Graduate degree	21.4%

Income & Poverty, 1999
Per capita income	$39,520
Median household income	$91,014
Median family income	$102,842
Persons in poverty	193
H'holds receiving public assistance	17
H'holds receiving social security	784

Households, 2000
Total households	2,789
With persons under 18	1,097
With persons over 65	858
Family households	2,300
Single-person households	438
Persons per household	2.83
Persons per family	3.17

Labor & Employment
Total civilian labor force, 2007**	4,196
Unemployment rate	2.5%
Total civilian labor force, 2000	3,980
Unemployment rate	2.9%

Employed persons 16 years and over by occupation, 2000
Managers & professionals	2,189
Service occupations	234
Sales & office occupations	1,124
Farming, fishing & forestry	0
Construction & maintenance	124
Production & transportation	194
Self-employed persons	270

* US Census Bureau
** New Jersey Department of Labor

General Information
Borough of Oradell
355 Kinderkamack Rd
Oradell, NJ 07649
201-261-8200
Website	www.oradell.org
Year of incorporation	1922
Land/water area (sq. miles)	2.42/0.13
Form of government	Borough

Government
Legislative Districts
US Congressional	5
State Legislative	39

Local Officials, 2009
Mayor	Dianne Camelo Didio
Administrator	Wolfgang Albrecht Jr
Clerk	Laura J. Graham
Finance Dir	Ronald Amorino
Tax Assessor	James Anzevino
Tax Collector	Stephanie Stokes
Attorney	Andrew P. Oddo
Building	Stephen A. Depken
Comm Dev/Planning	NA
Engineering	Boswell McClave
Public Works	Robert Stauffer
Police Chief	Rhynie Emanuel
Emerg/Fire Director	Kevin Burns

Housing & Construction
Housing Units, 2000*
Total	2,833
Median rent	$957
Median SF home value	$330,900

Permits for New Residential Construction
	Units	Value
Total, 2006	5	$2,180,954
Single family	5	$2,180,954
Total, 2007	6	$3,095,955
Single family	6	$3,095,955

Real Property Valuation, 2008
	Parcels	Valuation
Total	2,765	$840,249,700
Vacant	25	2,479,300
Residential	2,641	739,384,400
Commercial	93	94,623,000
Industrial	1	187,100
Apartments	5	3,575,900
Farm land	0	0
Farm homestead	0	0

Average Property Value & Tax, 2008
Residential value	$279,964
Property tax	$11,317
Tax credit/rebate	$1,435

Public Library
Oradell Public Library
375 Kinderkamack Rd
Oradell, NJ 07649
201-262-2613
Director	Beth Zeigler

Library statistics, 2007
Population served	8,047
Full-time/total staff	3/6

	Total	Per capita
Holdings	73,865	9.18
Revenues	$853,605	$106.08
Expenditures	$768,646	$95.52
Annual visits	92,910	11.55
Internet terminals/annual users	7/3,440	

Public Safety
Number of officers, 2007		22

Crime	2006	2007
Total crimes	74	46
Violent	4	4
Murder	0	0
Rape	0	1
Robbery	0	1
Aggravated assault	4	2
Non-violent	70	42
Burglary	16	6
Larceny	54	36
Vehicle theft	0	0
Domestic violence	24	11
Arson	1	0
Total crime rate	9.2	5.8
Violent	0.5	0.5
Non-violent	8.7	5.3

Public School District
(for school year 2007-08 except as noted)

Oradell School District
350 Prospect Avenue
Oradell, NJ 07649
(201) 261-1153
Superintendent	Jeffrey S. Mohre
Number of schools	1
Grade plan	K-6
Enrollment	794
Attendance rate, '06-07	95.7%
Dropout rate	NA
Students per teacher	11.9
Per pupil expenditure	$11,841
Median faculty salary	$46,618
Median administrator salary	$107,792
Grade 12 enrollment	NA
High school graduation rate	NA

Assessment test results
(percent scoring at proficient or advanced level)
	Language	Math
NJASK-Grade 3	96.1%	96.2%
GEPA-Grade 8	NA	NA
HSPA-High School	NA	NA

SAT Score Averages, 2006-07
Pct tested	Math	Verbal	Writing
NA	NA	NA	NA

Teacher Qualifications
Avg. years of experience	8
Highly-qualified teachers one subject/all subjects	93.0%/93.0%

No Child Left Behind
AYP, 2006-07	Meets Standards

Municipal Finance
State Aid Programs, 2009
Total aid	$1,056,656
CMPTRA	0
Energy tax receipts	1,016,492
Garden State Trust	0

General Budget, 2008
Total tax levy	$33,999,956
County levy	3,392,247
County taxes	3,208,829
County library	0
County health	0
County open space	183,419
School levy	22,041,833
Muni. levy	8,565,876
Misc. revenues	4,547,152

Taxes
	2006	2007	2008
General tax rate per $100	3.78	3.99	4.043
County equalization ratio	49.38	45.93	45.92
Net valuation taxable	$839,991,400	$840,814,283	$841,088,101
State equalized value	$1,829,554,273	$1,830,048,422	$1,809,772,093

See Introduction for an explanation of all data sources.

Demographics & Socio-Economic Characteristics

(2000 US Census, except as noted)

Population

1980*	31,136
1990*	29,925
2000	32,868
Male	15,199
Female	17,669
2007 (estimate)*	31,290
Population density	14,158.4

Race & Hispanic Origin, 2000

Race

White	4,337
Black/African American	24,685
American Indian/Alaska Native	113
Asian	415
Native Hawaiian/Pacific Islander	33
Other race	1,712
Two or more races	1,573
Hispanic origin, total	4,097
Mexican	387
Puerto Rican	538
Cuban	38
Other Hispanic	3,134

Age & Nativity, 2000

Under 5 years	2,810
18 years and over	23,760
21 years and over	22,469
65 years and over	3,562
85 years and over	504
Median age	32.5
Native-born	22,575
Foreign-born	10,293

Educational Attainment, 2000

Population 25 years and over	20,628
Less than 9th grade	10.0%
High school grad or higher	72.2%
Bachelor's degree or higher	16.7%
Graduate degree	6.3%

Income & Poverty, 1999

Per capita income	$16,861
Median household income	$35,759
Median family income	$40,852
Persons in poverty	6,078
H'holds receiving public assistance	885
H'holds receiving social security	2,699

Households, 2000

Total households	11,885
With persons under 18	4,783
With persons over 65	2,693
Family households	7,647
Single-person households	3,589
Persons per household	2.73
Persons per family	3.38

Labor & Employment

Total civilian labor force, 2007**	14,718
Unemployment rate	6.2%
Total civilian labor force, 2000	15,403
Unemployment rate	11.0%

Employed persons 16 years and over by occupation, 2000

Managers & professionals	3,513
Service occupations	3,170
Sales & office occupations	3,975
Farming, fishing & forestry	23
Construction & maintenance	1,061
Production & transportation	1,968
Self-employed persons	491

* US Census Bureau
** New Jersey Department of Labor
§ State Fiscal Year July 1–June 30

General Information

City of Orange Township
29 N Day St
Orange, NJ 07050
973-266-4005

Website	www.ci.orange.nj.us
Year of incorporation	1981
Land/water area (sq. miles)	2.21/0.00
Form of government	Mayor-Council

Government

Legislative Districts

US Congressional	10
State Legislative	27

Local Officials, 2009

Mayor	Elridge Hawkins Jr
Manager	Jewel V. Thompson
Clerk	Dwight Mitchell
Finance Dir	Jack Kelly
Tax Assessor	Brigida Caruso
Tax Collector	Carl Smith
Attorney	Marvin Braker
Building	James Fonzino
Planning	Larry Samuels
Engineering	Amelia A. Kemp (Actg)
Public Works	Amelia A. Kemp (Actg)
Police Chief	Aric D. Webster
Emerg/Fire Director	Marty De Marzo

Housing & Construction

Housing Units, 2000*

Total	12,665
Median rent	$687
Median SF home value	$131,400

Permits for New Residential Construction

	Units	Value
Total, 2006	72	$5,417,378
Single family	25	$2,511,985
Total, 2007	69	$4,984,136
Single family	18	$1,617,512

Real Property Valuation, 2008

	Parcels	Valuation
Total	5,139	$1,610,600,800
Vacant	302	19,702,700
Residential	4,107	1,006,023,100
Commercial	508	275,715,000
Industrial	53	48,352,400
Apartments	169	260,807,600
Farm land	0	0
Farm homestead	0	0

Average Property Value & Tax, 2008

Residential value	$244,953
Property tax	$7,228
Tax credit/rebate	$1,193

Public Library

Orange Public Library
348 Main St
Orange, NJ 07050
973-673-0153

Director	Doris T. Walker

Library statistics, 2007

Population served	32,868
Full-time/total staff	4/13

	Total	Per capita
Holdings	221,951	6.75
Revenues	$997,968	$30.36
Expenditures	$950,757	$28.93
Annual visits	97,012	2.95
Internet terminals/annual users	16/48,066	

Public Safety

Number of officers, 2007	107

Crime	2006	2007
Total crimes	1,846	1,863
Violent	424	391
Murder	5	5
Rape	10	9
Robbery	266	220
Aggravated assault	143	157
Non-violent	1,422	1,472
Burglary	359	448
Larceny	630	621
Vehicle theft	433	403
Domestic violence	422	361
Arson	5	5
Total crime rate	57.5	58.5
Violent	13.2	12.3
Non-violent	44.3	46.2

Public School District

(for school year 2007-08 except as noted)

City Of Orange Township School District
451 Lincoln Avenue
Orange, NJ 07050
(973) 677-4000

Superintendent	Judith Kronin (Int)
Number of schools	10
Grade plan	K-12
Enrollment	4,569
Attendance rate, '06-07	95.6%
Dropout rate	0.0%
Students per teacher	8.6
Per pupil expenditure	$14,376
Median faculty salary	$51,292
Median administrator salary	$91,319
Grade 12 enrollment	236
High school graduation rate	91.5%

Assessment test results

(percent scoring at proficient or advanced level)

	Language	Math
NJASK-Grade 3	79.5%	76.2%
GEPA-Grade 8	24.3%	50.8%
HSPA-High School	27.2%	53.5%

SAT Score Averages, 2006-07

Pct tested	Math	Verbal	Writing
82%	366	358	364

Teacher Qualifications

Avg. years of experience	6
Highly-qualified teachers one subject/all subjects	99.0%/99.0%

No Child Left Behind

AYP, 2006-07	Needs Improvement

Municipal Finance§

State Aid Programs, 2009

Total aid	$9,787,021
CMPTRA	6,469,179
Energy tax receipts	3,317,842
Garden State Trust	0

General Budget, 2008

Total tax levy	$47,568,699
County levy	6,929,524
County taxes	6,660,965
County library	0
County health	0
County open space	268,560
School levy	9,958,528
Muni. levy	30,680,647
Misc. revenues	22,645,650

Taxes

	2006	2007	2008
General tax rate per $100	2.78	2.91	2.951
County equalization ratio	125.33	103.04	91.37
Net valuation taxable	$1,638,734,300	$1,617,154,414	$1,612,092,114
State equalized value	$1,644,606,337	$1,769,745,433	$1,837,561,537

See Introduction for an explanation of all data sources.

Demographics & Socio-Economic Characteristics

(2000 US Census, except as noted)

Population

1980*	1,659
1990*	1,790
2000	2,307
Male	1,137
Female	1,170
2007 (estimate)*	2,575
Population density	433.5

Race & Hispanic Origin, 2000

Race

White	2,228
Black/African American	28
American Indian/Alaska Native	5
Asian	12
Native Hawaiian/Pacific Islander	0
Other race	15
Two or more races	19
Hispanic origin, total	80
Mexican	2
Puerto Rican	38
Cuban	4
Other Hispanic	36

Age & Nativity, 2000

Under 5 years	163
18 years and over	1,673
21 years and over	1,621
65 years and over	261
85 years and over	32
Median age	36.4
Native-born	2,223
Foreign-born	84

Educational Attainment, 2000

Population 25 years and over	1,568
Less than 9th grade	6.1%
High school grad or higher	82.1%
Bachelor's degree or higher	19.8%
Graduate degree	5.0%

Income & Poverty, 1999

Per capita income	$23,515
Median household income	$53,359
Median family income	$63,750
Persons in poverty	92
H'holds receiving public assistance	22
H'holds receiving social security	214

Households, 2000

Total households	886
With persons under 18	340
With persons over 65	209
Family households	618
Single-person households	233
Persons per household	2.60
Persons per family	3.18

Labor & Employment

Total civilian labor force, 2007**	1,376
Unemployment rate	6.9%
Total civilian labor force, 2000	1,219
Unemployment rate	6.8%

Employed persons 16 years and over by occupation, 2000

Managers & professionals	346
Service occupations	194
Sales & office occupations	281
Farming, fishing & forestry	4
Construction & maintenance	139
Production & transportation	172
Self-employed persons	63

General Information

Township of Oxford
11 Green St
PO Box 119
Oxford, NJ 07863
908-453-3098

Website	oxfordnj.org
Year of incorporation	1874
Land/water area (sq. miles)	5.94/0.08
Form of government	Township

Government

Legislative Districts

US Congressional	5
State Legislative	23

Local Officials, 2009

Mayor	Nicol Angelo Accetturo
Manager/Admin	NA
Clerk	Sheila L. Oberly
Finance Dir	Dawn Stanchina
Tax Assessor	Richard Motyka
Tax Collector	Karen Lance
Attorney	Michael Lavery
Building	NA
Planning	Peggy Housman
Engineering	Michael Finelli
Public Works	Lou Accetturo
Police Chief	Charles Lilly
Emerg/Fire Director	Richard Calabrese

Housing & Construction

Housing Units, 2000*

Total	938
Median rent	$665
Median SF home value	$125,200

Permits for New Residential Construction

	Units	Value
Total, 2006	4	$166,500
Single family	4	$166,500
Total, 2007	5	$235,000
Single family	5	$235,000

Real Property Valuation, 2008

	Parcels	Valuation
Total	1,152	$241,712,660
Vacant	196	5,571,800
Residential	855	214,059,400
Commercial	26	9,614,200
Industrial	4	5,849,500
Apartments	0	0
Farm land	52	239,860
Farm homestead	19	6,377,900

Average Property Value & Tax, 2008

Residential value	$252,217
Property tax	$5,635
Tax credit/rebate	$986

Public Library

Oxford Public Library
42 Washington Ave
Oxford, NJ 07863
908-453-2625

Librarian	Jean Docker

Library statistics, 2007

Population served	2,307
Full-time/total staff	NA/0

	Total	Per capita
Holdings	0	NA
Revenues	$0	NA
Expenditures	$0	NA
Annual visits	NA	NA
Internet terminals/annual users	NA/NA	

Public Safety

Number of officers, 2007 4

Crime	2006	2007
Total crimes	15	30
Violent	1	1
Murder	0	0
Rape	0	0
Robbery	0	0
Aggravated assault	1	1
Non-violent	14	29
Burglary	3	4
Larceny	10	23
Vehicle theft	1	2
Domestic violence	24	9
Arson	0	1
Total crime rate	5.7	11.4
Violent	0.4	0.4
Non-violent	5.3	11.1

Public School District

(for school year 2007-08 except as noted)

Oxford Township School District
17 Kent Street
Oxford, NJ 07863
(908) 453-4101

Chief School Admin	Robert Magnuson
Number of schools	1
Grade plan	K-8
Enrollment	300
Attendance rate, '06-07	95.4%
Dropout rate	NA
Students per teacher	9.3
Per pupil expenditure	$12,830
Median faculty salary	$47,775
Median administrator salary	$98,740
Grade 12 enrollment	NA
High school graduation rate	NA

Assessment test results

(percent scoring at proficient or advanced level)

	Language	Math
NJASK-Grade 3	93.4%	86.7%
GEPA-Grade 8	72.5%	87.5%
HSPA-High School	NA	NA

SAT Score Averages, 2006-07

Pct tested	Math	Verbal	Writing
NA	NA	NA	NA

Teacher Qualifications

Avg. years of experience	8
Highly-qualified teachers one subject/all subjects	100%/96.0%

No Child Left Behind

AYP, 2006-07	Meets Standards

Municipal Finance

State Aid Programs, 2009

Total aid	$246,436
CMPTRA	45,694
Energy tax receipts	187,484
Garden State Trust	2,381

General Budget, 2008

Total tax levy	$5,424,123
County levy	1,455,329
County taxes	1,187,164
County library	124,539
County health	0
County open space	143,626
School levy	3,523,986
Muni. levy	444,808
Misc. revenues	1,937,066

Taxes

	2006	2007	2008
General tax rate per $100	3.95	2.25	2.235
County equalization ratio	57.5	106	102.08
Net valuation taxable	$117,911,708	$243,353,138	$242,763,883
State equalized value	$226,616,169	$238,414,200	$241,465,645

* US Census Bureau
** New Jersey Department of Labor

See Introduction for an explanation of all data sources.

Demographics & Socio-Economic Characteristics
(2000 US Census, except as noted)

Population
1980*	13,732
1990*	14,536
2000	17,073
Male	8,497
Female	8,576
2007 (estimate)*	19,352
Population density	15,993.4

Race & Hispanic Origin, 2000
Race
White	8,241
Black/African American	235
American Indian/Alaska Native	32
Asian	7,016
Native Hawaiian/Pacific Islander	5
Other race	991
Two or more races	553
Hispanic origin, total	2,813
Mexican	86
Puerto Rican	293
Cuban	279
Other Hispanic	2,155

Age & Nativity, 2000
Under 5 years	1,152
18 years and over	13,761
21 years and over	13,182
65 years and over	2,061
85 years and over	222
Median age	35.6
Native-born	7,348
Foreign-born	9,725

Educational Attainment, 2000
Population 25 years and over	12,173
Less than 9th grade	11.4%
High school grad or higher	79.3%
Bachelor's degree or higher	30.6%
Graduate degree	7.5%

Income & Poverty, 1999
Per capita income	$22,607
Median household income	$48,015
Median family income	$54,503
Persons in poverty	1,659
H'holds receiving public assistance	137
H'holds receiving social security	1,373

Households, 2000
Total households	6,247
With persons under 18	2,083
With persons over 65	1,537
Family households	4,445
Single-person households	1,429
Persons per household	2.73
Persons per family	3.20

Labor & Employment
Total civilian labor force, 2007**	9,360
Unemployment rate	4.0%
Total civilian labor force, 2000	8,874
Unemployment rate	4.3%

Employed persons 16 years and over by occupation, 2000
Managers & professionals	2,809
Service occupations	1,405
Sales & office occupations	2,498
Farming, fishing & forestry	0
Construction & maintenance	674
Production & transportation	1,107
Self-employed persons	482

General Information
Borough of Palisades Park
275 Broad Ave
Palisades Park, NJ 07650
201-585-4100

Website	NA
Year of incorporation	1899
Land/water area (sq. miles)	1.21/0.06
Form of government	Borough

Government
Legislative Districts
US Congressional	9
State Legislative	37

Local Officials, 2009
Mayor	James Rotundo
Manager/Admin	David Lorenzo
Clerk	Martin A. Gobbo
Finance Dir	Roy Riggitano
Tax Assessor	Jim Anzevino
Tax Collector	Michael Apicella
Attorney	Joseph Mariniello
Building	Anthony Pollotta
Comm Dev/Planning	NA
Engineering	Steven Collazuol
Public Works	Mark Pasquali
Police Chief	Michael Vietri
Emerg/Fire Director	Steven Killion

Housing & Construction
Housing Units, 2000*
Total	6,386
Median rent	$903
Median SF home value	$231,700

Permits for New Residential Construction
	Units	Value
Total, 2006	132	$21,959,450
Single family	44	$7,087,800
Total, 2007	76	$12,262,100
Single family	10	$2,117,500

Real Property Valuation, 2008
	Parcels	Valuation
Total	3,917	$2,538,642,300
Vacant	84	22,059,200
Residential	3,477	1,932,932,700
Commercial	238	304,180,100
Industrial	36	96,438,300
Apartments	82	183,032,000
Farm land	0	0
Farm homestead	0	0

Average Property Value & Tax, 2008
Residential value	$555,920
Property tax	$7,851
Tax credit/rebate	$1,143

Public Library
Palisades Park Public Library
257 Second St
Palisades Park, NJ 07650
201-585-4150

Director	Megan Doyle

Library statistics, 2007
Population served	17,073
Full-time/total staff	2/7

	Total	Per capita
Holdings	50,743	2.97
Revenues	$728,413	$42.66
Expenditures	$681,375	$39.91
Annual visits	75,192	4.40
Internet terminals/annual users	13/16,042	

Public Safety
Number of officers, 2007	31

Crime	2006	2007
Total crimes	180	164
Violent	16	24
Murder	0	1
Rape	0	1
Robbery	8	11
Aggravated assault	8	11
Non-violent	164	140
Burglary	48	40
Larceny	106	83
Vehicle theft	10	17
Domestic violence	75	48
Arson	1	0
Total crime rate	9.5	8.5
Violent	0.8	1.2
Non-violent	8.7	7.3

Public School District
(for school year 2007-08 except as noted)

Palisades Park School District
270 First Street
Palisades Park, NJ 07650
(201) 947-3560

Superintendent	Mark Hayes
Number of schools	3
Grade plan	K-12
Enrollment	1,439
Attendance rate, '06-07	94.9%
Dropout rate	1.7%
Students per teacher	10.4
Per pupil expenditure	$13,707
Median faculty salary	$44,750
Median administrator salary	$84,875
Grade 12 enrollment	99
High school graduation rate	96.9%

Assessment test results
(percent scoring at proficient or advanced level)
	Language	Math
NJASK-Grade 3	89.5%	86.1%
GEPA-Grade 8	62.3%	77.3%
HSPA-High School	79.7%	84.3%

SAT Score Averages, 2006-07
Pct tested	Math	Verbal	Writing
75%	502	459	455

Teacher Qualifications
Avg. years of experience	6
Highly-qualified teachers one subject/all subjects	100%/100%

No Child Left Behind
AYP, 2006-07	Meets Standards

Municipal Finance
State Aid Programs, 2009
Total aid	$1,223,537
CMPTRA	316,762
Energy tax receipts	876,186
Garden State Trust	0

General Budget, 2008
Total tax levy	$35,863,699
County levy	4,781,190
County taxes	4,521,120
County library	0
County health	0
County open space	260,069
School levy	18,471,482
Muni. levy	12,611,027
Misc. revenues	6,280,349

Taxes
	2006	2007	2008
General tax rate per $100	2.96	3.02	1.414
County equalization ratio	50.18	46.75	98.03
Net valuation taxable	$1,044,893,750	$1,112,429,021	$2,539,387,939
State equalized value	$2,235,399,181	$2,589,024,470	$2,667,106,630

* US Census Bureau
** New Jersey Department of Labor

See Introduction for an explanation of all data sources.

Demographics & Socio-Economic Characteristics
(2000 US Census, except as noted)

Population
1980*	7,085
1990*	7,056
2000	7,091
Male	3,421
Female	3,670
2007 (estimate)*	7,419
Population density	3,747.0

Race & Hispanic Origin, 2000
Race
White	5,743
Black/African American	1,017
American Indian/Alaska Native	21
Asian	99
Native Hawaiian/Pacific Islander	3
Other race	100
Two or more races	108
Hispanic origin, total	229
Mexican	19
Puerto Rican	146
Cuban	13
Other Hispanic	51

Age & Nativity, 2000
Under 5 years	413
18 years and over	5,508
21 years and over	5,296
65 years and over	960
85 years and over	86
Median age	38.0
Native-born	6,798
Foreign-born	293

Educational Attainment, 2000
Population 25 years and over	5,068
Less than 9th grade	3.2%
High school grad or higher	85.1%
Bachelor's degree or higher	21.8%
Graduate degree	6.1%

Income & Poverty, 1999
Per capita income	$23,454
Median household income	$51,150
Median family income	$57,192
Persons in poverty	295
H'holds receiving public assistance	45
H'holds receiving social security	705

Households, 2000
Total households	3,004
With persons under 18	894
With persons over 65	733
Family households	1,852
Single-person households	962
Persons per household	2.36
Persons per family	3.02

Labor & Employment
Total civilian labor force, 2007**	4,636
Unemployment rate	4.6%
Total civilian labor force, 2000	4,053
Unemployment rate	4.7%

Employed persons 16 years and over by occupation, 2000
Managers & professionals	1,258
Service occupations	485
Sales & office occupations	1,248
Farming, fishing & forestry	5
Construction & maintenance	394
Production & transportation	473
Self-employed persons	204

‡ Joint county branch with Riverton Borough
* US Census Bureau
** New Jersey Department of Labor

General Information
Borough of Palmyra
20 W Broad St
Palmyra, NJ 08065
856-829-6100
Website	www.boroughofpalmyra.com
Year of incorporation	1923
Land/water area (sq. miles)	1.98/0.44
Form of government	Borough

Government
Legislative Districts
US Congressional	1
State Legislative	7

Local Officials, 2009
Mayor	John J. Gural
Manager	Marianne Hulme
Clerk	Karen A. Gift
Finance Dir	Marianne Hulme
Tax Assessor	Karen Davis
Tax Collector	Marianne Hulme
Attorney	Ted Rosenburg
Building	Tracy Kilmer
Planning	Tracy Kilmer
Engineering	Land Engineering
Public Works	Brian McCleary
Police Chief	Richard K. Dreby
Emerg/Fire Director	Alan Zimmerman

Housing & Construction
Housing Units, 2000*
Total	3,219
Median rent	$818
Median SF home value	$110,500

Permits for New Residential Construction
	Units	Value
Total, 2006	10	$738,947
Single family	10	$738,947
Total, 2007	10	$908,080
Single family	10	$908,080

Real Property Valuation, 2008
	Parcels	Valuation
Total	3,108	$313,745,970
Vacant	142	3,957,700
Residential	2,776	271,022,270
Commercial	115	19,224,800
Industrial	25	6,250,400
Apartments	44	13,160,400
Farm land	6	130,400
Farm homestead	0	0

Average Property Value & Tax, 2008
Residential value	$97,631
Property tax	$4,347
Tax credit/rebate	$841

Public Library
Riverton Free Library‡
306 Main St
Riverton, NJ 08077
856-829-2476
Director	Michael Robinson

Library statistics, 2007
see Burlington County profile
for library system statistics

Public Safety
Number of officers, 2007	16

Crime	2006	2007
Total crimes	195	178
Violent	20	26
Murder	0	0
Rape	0	1
Robbery	9	5
Aggravated assault	11	20
Non-violent	175	152
Burglary	26	36
Larceny	131	105
Vehicle theft	18	11
Domestic violence	86	84
Arson	1	1
Total crime rate	25.5	23.4
Violent	2.6	3.4
Non-violent	22.9	20.0

Public School District
(for school year 2007-08 except as noted)

Palmyra Borough School District
301 Delaware Avenue
Palmyra, NJ 08065
(856) 786-2963
Superintendent	Richard Perry
Number of schools	3
Grade plan	K-12
Enrollment	947
Attendance rate, '06-07	95.1%
Dropout rate	1.4%
Students per teacher	10.0
Per pupil expenditure	$12,323
Median faculty salary	$49,590
Median administrator salary	$97,000
Grade 12 enrollment	91
High school graduation rate	96.8%

Assessment test results
(percent scoring at proficient or advanced level)
	Language	Math
NJASK-Grade 3	97.4%	94.6%
GEPA-Grade 8	55.6%	82.5%
HSPA-High School	66.6%	82.8%

SAT Score Averages, 2006-07
Pct tested	Math	Verbal	Writing
69%	493	500	487

Teacher Qualifications
Avg. years of experience	12
Highly-qualified teachers one subject/all subjects	93.0%/90.5%

No Child Left Behind
AYP, 2006-07	Meets Standards

Municipal Finance
State Aid Programs, 2009
Total aid	$686,561
CMPTRA	154,555
Energy tax receipts	521,708
Garden State Trust	0

General Budget, 2008
Total tax levy	$13,984,028
County levy	2,266,960
County taxes	1,861,654
County library	171,891
County health	0
County open space	233,416
School levy	7,161,179
Muni. levy	4,555,889
Misc. revenues	3,663,071

Taxes	2006	2007	2008
General tax rate per $100	4.002	4.33	4.453
County equalization ratio	64.8	56.77	53.99
Net valuation taxable	$313,275,570	$313,815,715	$314,070,989
State equalized value	$552,200,487	$580,965,140	$606,714,602

Demographics & Socio-Economic Characteristics

(2000 US Census, except as noted)

Population
1980*	26,474
1990*	25,067
2000	25,737
Male	12,497
Female	13,240
2007 (estimate)*	26,278
Population density	2,509.8

Race & Hispanic Origin, 2000
Race
White	20,380
Black/African American	291
American Indian/Alaska Native	12
Asian	4,434
Native Hawaiian/Pacific Islander	3
Other race	229
Two or more races	388
Hispanic origin, total	1,253
Mexican	60
Puerto Rican	211
Cuban	285
Other Hispanic	697

Age & Nativity, 2000
Under 5 years	1,331
18 years and over	19,755
21 years and over	19,117
65 years and over	5,531
85 years and over	824
Median age	42.9
Native-born	19,275
Foreign-born	6,462

Educational Attainment, 2000
Population 25 years and over	18,264
Less than 9th grade	5.8%
High school grad or higher	86.2%
Bachelor's degree or higher	38.7%
Graduate degree	14.3%

Income & Poverty, 1999
Per capita income	$29,295
Median household income	$76,918
Median family income	$84,406
Persons in poverty	803
H'holds receiving public assistance	21
H'holds receiving social security	2,809

Households, 2000
Total households	8,082
With persons under 18	3,182
With persons over 65	2,989
Family households	6,779
Single-person households	1,164
Persons per household	3.00
Persons per family	3.32

Labor & Employment
Total civilian labor force, 2007**	12,902
Unemployment rate	3.0%
Total civilian labor force, 2000	12,069
Unemployment rate	2.3%

Employed persons 16 years and over by occupation, 2000
Managers & professionals	5,206
Service occupations	1,073
Sales & office occupations	3,932
Farming, fishing & forestry	0
Construction & maintenance	736
Production & transportation	846
Self-employed persons	806

General Information
Borough of Paramus
1 Jockish Sq
Paramus, NJ 07652
201-265-2100

Website	www.paramusborough.org
Year of incorporation	1922
Land/water area (sq. miles)	10.47/0.00
Form of government	Borough

Government

Legislative Districts
US Congressional	5
State Legislative	38

Local Officials, 2009
Mayor	James Tedesco III
Manager/Admin	NA
Clerk	Ian Shore
Finance Dir	Joseph Citro
Tax Assessor	James Anzevino
Tax Collector	Emil Hrabel
Attorney	John Ten Hove
Building	NA
Planning	Gary Pucci
Engineering	Boswell Engineering
Public Works	Brian Koenig
Police Chief	NA
Emerg/Fire Director	Tony Capone

Housing & Construction

Housing Units, 2000*
Total	8,209
Median rent	$1,483
Median SF home value	$284,800

Permits for New Residential Construction
	Units	Value
Total, 2006	40	$18,503,171
Single family	40	$18,503,171
Total, 2007	25	$10,274,000
Single family	25	$10,274,000

Real Property Valuation, 2008
	Parcels	Valuation
Total	8,691	$7,977,782,700
Vacant	124	154,005,400
Residential	8,118	4,052,386,800
Commercial	414	3,625,769,000
Industrial	26	125,476,500
Apartments	1	18,642,800
Farm land	4	22,400
Farm homestead	4	1,479,800

Average Property Value & Tax, 2008
Residential value	$499,122
Property tax	$7,384
Tax credit/rebate	$1,135

Public Library
Paramus Public Library
116 E Century Rd
Paramus, NJ 07652
201-599-1300

Director	Leonard LoPinto

Library statistics, 2007
Population served	25,737
Full-time/total staff	10/27

	Total	Per capita
Holdings	114,307	4.44
Revenues	$3,113,814	$120.99
Expenditures	$2,884,382	$112.07
Annual visits	296,613	11.52
Internet terminals/annual users	34/97,000	

Public Safety
Number of officers, 2007	93

Crime	2006	2007
Total crimes	1,757	1,637
Violent	77	54
Murder	0	0
Rape	0	1
Robbery	34	25
Aggravated assault	43	28
Non-violent	1,680	1,583
Burglary	87	68
Larceny	1,487	1,471
Vehicle theft	106	44
Domestic violence	137	130
Arson	7	9
Total crime rate	66.2	61.7
Violent	2.9	2.0
Non-violent	63.3	59.6

Public School District
(for school year 2007-08 except as noted)

Paramus School District
145 Spring Valley Road
Paramus, NJ 07652
(201) 261-7800

Superintendent	James Montesano
Number of schools	8
Grade plan	K-12
Enrollment	4,328
Attendance rate, '06-07	97.4%
Dropout rate	0.6%
Students per teacher	10.8
Per pupil expenditure	$15,641
Median faculty salary	$51,260
Median administrator salary	$122,863
Grade 12 enrollment	355
High school graduation rate	98.4%

Assessment test results
(percent scoring at proficient or advanced level)
	Language	Math
NJASK-Grade 3	95.2%	96.5%
GEPA-Grade 8	82.2%	93.5%
HSPA-High School	86.8%	94.3%

SAT Score Averages, 2006-07
Pct tested	Math	Verbal	Writing
97%	542	513	520

Teacher Qualifications
Avg. years of experience	8
Highly-qualified teachers one subject/all subjects	99.5%/99.5%

No Child Left Behind
AYP, 2006-07	Meets Standards

Municipal Finance

State Aid Programs, 2009
Total aid	$5,371,643
CMPTRA	1,326,675
Energy tax receipts	3,870,390
Garden State Trust	0

General Budget, 2008
Total tax levy	$118,128,025
County levy	16,677,151
County taxes	15,739,696
County library	0
County health	0
County open space	937,455
School levy	64,239,930
Muni. levy	37,210,944
Misc. revenues	15,976,098

Taxes
	2006	2007	2008
General tax rate per $100	1.55	1.61	1.482
County equalization ratio	83.28	77.6	86.09
Net valuation taxable	$6,837,927,200	$6,893,670,571	$7,984,604,363
State equalized value	$8,816,538,442	$9,210,730,155	$9,154,605,977

* US Census Bureau
** New Jersey Department of Labor

See Introduction for an explanation of all data sources.

Demographics & Socio-Economic Characteristics
(2000 US Census, except as noted)

Population
1980*	8,515
1990*	8,102
2000	8,708
Male	4,178
Female	4,530
2007 (estimate)*	8,940
Population density	3,438.5

Race & Hispanic Origin, 2000
Race
White	8,140
Black/African American	75
American Indian/Alaska Native	12
Asian	336
Native Hawaiian/Pacific Islander	2
Other race	64
Two or more races	79
Hispanic origin, total	463
Mexican	233
Puerto Rican	52
Cuban	38
Other Hispanic	140

Age & Nativity, 2000
Under 5 years	599
18 years and over	6,664
21 years and over	6,470
65 years and over	1,408
85 years and over	253
Median age	40.9
Native-born	7,510
Foreign-born	1,198

Educational Attainment, 2000
Population 25 years and over	6,293
Less than 9th grade	2.5%
High school grad or higher	91.4%
Bachelor's degree or higher	45.0%
Graduate degree	17.3%

Income & Poverty, 1999
Per capita income	$40,351
Median household income	$86,632
Median family income	$97,294
Persons in poverty	260
H'holds receiving public assistance	33
H'holds receiving social security	863

Households, 2000
Total households	3,161
With persons under 18	1,110
With persons over 65	839
Family households	2,389
Single-person households	673
Persons per household	2.67
Persons per family	3.12

Labor & Employment
Total civilian labor force, 2007**	4,730
Unemployment rate	1.4%
Total civilian labor force, 2000	4,480
Unemployment rate	1.5%

Employed persons 16 years and over by occupation, 2000
Managers & professionals	2,082
Service occupations	493
Sales & office occupations	1,365
Farming, fishing & forestry	0
Construction & maintenance	272
Production & transportation	200
Self-employed persons	295

General Information
Borough of Park Ridge
53 Park Ave
Park Ridge, NJ 07656
201-573-1800
Website	www.parkridgeboro.com
Year of incorporation	1894
Land/water area (sq. miles)	2.60/0.04
Form of government	Borough

Government
Legislative Districts
US Congressional	5
State Legislative	39

Local Officials, 2009
Mayor	Donald Ruschman
Manager	Gene Vinci
Borough Clerk	Kelley R. O'Donnell
Finance Dir	Colleen Ennis
Tax Assessor	Robert Campora
Tax Collector	Colleen Ennis
Attorney	Robert J. Mancinelli
Building	Nick Saluzzi
Planning	Dave Mesiano
Engineering	Azzolina & Feury
Public Works	William Beattie
Police Chief	NA
Fire Chief	Robert Ludwig

Housing & Construction
Housing Units, 2000*
Total	3,258
Median rent	$996
Median SF home value	$307,000

Permits for New Residential Construction
	Units	Value
Total, 2006	51	$8,370,252
Single family	14	$5,053,920
Total, 2007	22	$5,396,861
Single family	12	$4,492,003

Real Property Valuation, 2008
	Parcels	Valuation
Total	3,073	$1,726,175,500
Vacant	64	12,580,100
Residential	2,899	1,496,844,100
Commercial	97	196,708,000
Industrial	3	3,379,800
Apartments	10	16,663,500
Farm land	0	0
Farm homestead	0	0

Average Property Value & Tax, 2008
Residential value	$516,331
Property tax	$9,586
Tax credit/rebate	$1,255

Public Library
Park Ridge Library
51 Park Ave
Park Ridge, NJ 07656
201-391-5151
Director: Christina E. Doto

Library statistics, 2007
Population served	8,708
Full-time/total staff	1/3

	Total	Per capita
Holdings	64,431	7.40
Revenues	$711,838	$81.75
Expenditures	$639,531	$73.44
Annual visits	124,688	14.32
Internet terminals/annual users	14/7,965	

Public Safety
Number of officers, 2007: 18
Crime	2006	2007
Total crimes	51	44
Violent	3	1
Murder	0	0
Rape	0	1
Robbery	1	0
Aggravated assault	2	0
Non-violent	48	43
Burglary	3	3
Larceny	42	40
Vehicle theft	3	0
Domestic violence	6	10
Arson	1	0
Total crime rate	5.7	4.9
Violent	0.3	0.1
Non-violent	5.4	4.8

Public School District
(for school year 2007-08 except as noted)

Park Ridge School District
2 Park Avenue
Park Ridge, NJ 07656
(201) 573-6000
Superintendent	Patricia Johnson
Number of schools	3
Grade plan	K-12
Enrollment	1,370
Attendance rate, '06-07	95.9%
Dropout rate	1.1%
Students per teacher	10.6
Per pupil expenditure	$14,841
Median faculty salary	$59,315
Median administrator salary	$121,547
Grade 12 enrollment	108
High school graduation rate	98.2%

Assessment test results
(percent scoring at proficient or advanced level)
	Language	Math
NJASK-Grade 3	95.5%	90.1%
GEPA-Grade 8	72.2%	86.9%
HSPA-High School	94.3%	97.7%

SAT Score Averages, 2006-07
Pct tested	Math	Verbal	Writing
93%	550	538	539

Teacher Qualifications
Avg. years of experience	11
Highly-qualified teachers one subject/all subjects	100%/100%

No Child Left Behind
AYP, 2006-07: Meets Standards

Municipal Finance
State Aid Programs, 2009
Total aid	$508,260
CMPTRA	112,788
Energy tax receipts	377,408
Garden State Trust	0

General Budget, 2008
Total tax levy	$32,076,806
County levy	3,740,131
County taxes	3,537,861
County library	0
County health	0
County open space	202,270
School levy	20,583,527
Muni. levy	7,753,148
Misc. revenues	3,789,988

Taxes	2006	2007	2008
General tax rate per $100	1.69	1.8	1.857
County equalization ratio	95.25	85.5	85.64
Net valuation taxable	$1,704,534,500	$1,719,004,988	$1,727,777,833
State equalized value	$1,995,026,966	$2,007,028,357	$1,988,223,924

Demographics & Socio-Economic Characteristics
(2000 US Census, except as noted)

Population
1980*	49,868
1990*	48,478
2000	50,649
Male	25,039
Female	25,610
2007 (estimate)*	51,144
Population density	2,136.3

Race & Hispanic Origin, 2000
Race
White	37,620
Black/African American	1,574
American Indian/Alaska Native	61
Asian	9,145
Native Hawaiian/Pacific Islander	28
Other race	963
Two or more races	1,258
Hispanic origin, total	3,535
Mexican	221
Puerto Rican	709
Cuban	228
Other Hispanic	2,377

Age & Nativity, 2000
Under 5 years	3,065
18 years and over	40,034
21 years and over	38,731
65 years and over	5,691
85 years and over	572
Median age	37.6
Native-born	37,064
Foreign-born	13,585

Educational Attainment, 2000
Population 25 years and over	36,644
Less than 9th grade	3.5%
High school grad or higher	89.9%
Bachelor's degree or higher	43.0%
Graduate degree	15.4%

Income & Poverty, 1999
Per capita income	$32,220
Median household income	$68,133
Median family income	$81,041
Persons in poverty	1,918
H'holds receiving public assistance	256
H'holds receiving social security	3,992

Households, 2000
Total households	19,624
With persons under 18	6,184
With persons over 65	4,141
Family households	13,160
Single-person households	5,321
Persons per household	2.53
Persons per family	3.13

Labor & Employment
Total civilian labor force, 2007**	30,891
Unemployment rate	2.7%
Total civilian labor force, 2000	29,230
Unemployment rate	2.9%

Employed persons 16 years and over by occupation, 2000
Managers & professionals	13,363
Service occupations	2,548
Sales & office occupations	8,115
Farming, fishing & forestry	18
Construction & maintenance	1,722
Production & transportation	2,623
Self-employed persons	1,304

* US Census Bureau
** New Jersey Department of Labor

General Information
Township of Parsippany-Troy Hills
1001 Parsippany Blvd
Parsippany, NJ 07054
973-263-4350

Website	www.parsippany.net
Year of incorporation	1928
Land/water area (sq. miles)	23.94/1.48
Form of government	Mayor-Council

Government
Legislative Districts
US Congressional	11
State Legislative	26

Local Officials, 2009
Mayor	Michael M. Luther
Manager	Jasmine Lim
Clerk	Judith Silver
Finance Dir.	Ruby Malcolm
Tax Assessor	Daniel Cassese
Tax Collector	Terence Whalen
Attorney	Alfred C. DeCotiis
Building	Ed Corcoran
Comm Dev/Planning	NA
Engineering	Justin M. Lizza
Public Works	Greg Schneider
Police Chief	Michael Peckerman
Fire/Emergency Dir.	NA

Housing & Construction
Housing Units, 2000*
Total	20,066
Median rent	$823
Median SF home value	$234,100

Permits for New Residential Construction
	Units	Value
Total, 2006	68	$12,131,554
Single family	68	$12,131,554
Total, 2007	19	$3,530,871
Single family	19	$3,530,871

Real Property Valuation, 2008
	Parcels	Valuation
Total	15,396	$7,535,638,200
Vacant	499	103,134,600
Residential	14,202	4,365,430,400
Commercial	601	2,362,622,800
Industrial	60	314,532,200
Apartments	32	389,588,700
Farm land	1	3,100
Farm homestead	1	326,400

Average Property Value & Tax, 2008
Residential value	$307,383
Property tax	$6,845
Tax credit/rebate	$1,070

Public Library
Parsippany-Troy Hills Public Library
449 Halsey Rd
Parsippany, NJ 07054
973-887-8907

Director	Jayne Beline

Library statistics, 2007
Population served	50,649
Full-time/total staff	12/43

	Total	Per capita
Holdings	192,746	3.81
Revenues	$3,256,424	$64.29
Expenditures	$3,236,516	$63.90
Annual visits	394,102	7.78
Internet terminals/annual users	64/309,728	

Public Safety
Number of officers, 2007	102

Crime	2006	2007
Total crimes	933	919
Violent	36	41
Murder	0	0
Rape	3	5
Robbery	9	13
Aggravated assault	24	23
Non-violent	897	878
Burglary	246	185
Larceny	575	646
Vehicle theft	76	47
Domestic violence	255	201
Arson	2	3
Total crime rate	18.1	17.7
Violent	0.7	0.8
Non-violent	17.4	16.9

Public School District
(for school year 2007-08 except as noted)

Parsippany-Troy Hills Township District
292 Parsippany Road
Parsippany, NJ 07054
(973) 263-7250

Superintendent	LeRoy Seitz
Number of schools	14
Grade plan	K-12
Enrollment	6,849
Attendance rate, '06-07	96.1%
Dropout rate	0.3%
Students per teacher	10.0
Per pupil expenditure	$15,508
Median faculty salary	$63,210
Median administrator salary	$109,269
Grade 12 enrollment	561
High school graduation rate	97.6%

Assessment test results
(percent scoring at proficient or advanced level)
	Language	Math
NJASK-Grade 3	93.7%	92.6%
GEPA-Grade 8	79.6%	87.9%
HSPA-High School	85.3%	91.8%

SAT Score Averages, 2006-07
Pct tested	Math	Verbal	Writing
NA	NA	NA	NA

Teacher Qualifications
Avg. years of experience	9
Highly-qualified teachers one subject/all subjects	99.5%/99.5%

No Child Left Behind
AYP, 2006-07	Meets Standards

Municipal Finance
State Aid Programs, 2009
Total aid	$5,851,790
CMPTRA	1,768,830
Energy tax receipts	3,881,733
Garden State Trust	1,066

General Budget, 2008
Total tax levy	$168,044,505
County levy	22,496,306
County taxes	18,358,225
County library	0
County health	0
County open space	4,138,081
School levy	106,919,999
Muni. levy	38,628,200
Misc. revenues	22,197,324

Taxes
	2006	2007	2008
General tax rate per $100	2.03	2.14	2.227
County equalization ratio	89.92	81.59	78.27
Net valuation taxable	$7,665,305,500	$7,588,282,376	$7,546,086,291
State equalized value	$9,405,568,902	$9,692,069,591	$9,885,481,769

See Introduction for an explanation of all data sources.

Demographics & Socio-Economic Characteristics†

(2000 US Census, except as noted)

Population

1980*	52,463
1990*	58,041
2000	67,861
Male	33,852
Female	34,009
2007 (estimate)*	67,103
Population density	21,576.5

Race & Hispanic Origin, 2000

Race

White	24,044
Black/African American	9,385
American Indian/Alaska Native	531
Asian	3,740
Native Hawaiian/Pacific Islander	29
Other race	26,709
Two or more races	3,423
Hispanic origin, total	42,387
Mexican	13,346
Puerto Rican	9,122
Cuban	654
Other Hispanic	19,265

Age & Nativity, 2000

Under 5 years	6,525
18 years and over	46,962
21 years and over	43,331
65 years and over	5,513
85 years and over	757
Median age	28.6
Native-born	36,760
Foreign-born	31,101

Educational Attainment, 2000

Population 25 years and over	38,437
Less than 9th grade	23.2%
High school grad or higher	55.5%
Bachelor's degree or higher	13.7%
Graduate degree	5.1%

Income & Poverty, 1999

Per capita income	$12,874
Median household income	$33,594
Median family income	$34,935
Persons in poverty	14,249
H'holds receiving public assistance	1,238
H'holds receiving social security	4,274

Households, 2000

Total households	19,458
With persons under 18	9,532
With persons over 65	4,228
Family households	14,456
Single-person households	3,945
Persons per household	3.46
Persons per family	3.93

Labor & Employment

Total civilian labor force, 2007**	28,309
Unemployment rate	7.0%
Total civilian labor force, 2000	28,589
Unemployment rate	10.3%

Employed persons 16 years and over by occupation, 2000

Managers & professionals	4,608
Service occupations	4,452
Sales & office occupations	6,038
Farming, fishing & forestry	82
Construction & maintenance	1,857
Production & transportation	8,601
Self-employed persons	762

---

† see Appendix C for American Community Survey data
* US Census Bureau
** New Jersey Department of Labor
§ State Fiscal Year July 1–June 30

General Information

City of Passaic
330 Passaic St
Passaic, NJ 07055
973-365-5500

Website	www.cityofpassaic.com
Year of incorporation	1873
Land/water area (sq. miles)	3.11/0.10
Form of government	Mayor-Council

Government

Legislative Districts

US Congressional	8
State Legislative	36

Local Officials, 2009

Mayor	Alex D. Blanco
Business Admin	Greg Hill
Clerk	Amada D. Curling
Finance Dir	Jose L. Agosto
Tax Assessor	Thomas Poalillo
Tax Collector	Carrie Malak
Attorney	Donald Scarinci
Building	Vincent Capuana
Planning/Dev	Ronald Van Rensalier
Engineering	Jorge L. Torres
Public Works	Theodore Evans
Police Chief	Daniel Paton
Emerg/Fire Director	Patrick Trentacost

Housing & Construction

Housing Units, 2000*

Total	20,194
Median rent	$677
Median SF home value	$153,000

Permits for New Residential Construction

	Units	Value
Total, 2006	45	$3,056,782
Single family	9	$882,092
Total, 2007	75	$3,411,238
Single family	18	$1,956,040

Real Property Valuation, 2008

	Parcels	Valuation
Total	8,179	$1,367,209,200
Vacant	248	8,267,000
Residential	6,257	818,038,000
Commercial	1,148	298,389,400
Industrial	119	90,357,100
Apartments	407	152,157,700
Farm land	0	0
Farm homestead	0	0

Average Property Value & Tax, 2008

Residential value	$130,740
Property tax	$7,929
Tax credit/rebate	$1,090

Public Library

Passaic Public Library
195 Gregory Ave
Passaic, NJ 07055
973-779-0474

Director .... Kathleen Mollica (Int)

Library statistics, 2007

Population served	67,861
Full-time/total staff	5/15

	Total	Per capita
Holdings	115,982	1.71
Revenues	$1,450,767	$21.38
Expenditures	$1,620,334	$23.88
Annual visits	121,620	1.79
Internet terminals/annual users	30/57,512	

Public Safety

Number of officers, 2007 189

Crime	2006	2007
Total crimes	2,325	2,282
Violent	647	695
Murder	5	3
Rape	3	3
Robbery	273	313
Aggravated assault	366	376
Non-violent	1,678	1,587
Burglary	394	395
Larceny	919	952
Vehicle theft	365	240
Domestic violence	698	653
Arson	8	4
Total crime rate	34.0	33.6
Violent	9.5	10.2
Non-violent	24.6	23.3

Public School District

(for school year 2007-08 except as noted)

Passaic City School District
101 Passaic Avenue
Passaic, NJ 07055
(973) 470-5201

Chief School Admin	Robert Holster
Number of schools	18
Grade plan	K-12
Enrollment	12,398
Attendance rate, '06-07	92.6%
Dropout rate	8.9%
Students per teacher	11.4
Per pupil expenditure	$16,295
Median faculty salary	$56,634
Median administrator salary	$103,227
Grade 12 enrollment	504
High school graduation rate	74.2%

Assessment test results

(percent scoring at proficient or advanced level)

	Language	Math
NJASK-Grade 3	65.9%	64.8%
GEPA-Grade 8	35.0%	51.9%
HSPA-High School	41.8%	58.7%

SAT Score Averages, 2006-07

Pct tested	Math	Verbal	Writing
54%	408	395	383

Teacher Qualifications

Avg. years of experience	9
Highly-qualified teachers one subject/all subjects	98.0%/98.0%

No Child Left Behind

AYP, 2006-07 ....Needs Improvement

Municipal Finance§

State Aid Programs, 2009

Total aid	$14,664,502
CMPTRA	10,518,522
Energy tax receipts	4,145,980
Garden State Trust	0

General Budget, 2008

Total tax levy	$83,215,897
County levy	18,955,751
County taxes	18,580,225
County library	0
County health	0
County open space	375,526
School levy	14,529,634
Muni. levy	49,730,512
Misc. revenues	30,119,037

Taxes

	2006	2007	2008
General tax rate per $100	5.25	5.6	6.067
County equalization ratio	50.11	41.71	37.43
Net valuation taxable	$1,349,349,000	$1,362,112,700	$1,372,139,800
State equalized value	$3,240,818,124	$3,630,949,879	$3,791,164,884

See Introduction for an explanation of all data sources.

Demographics & Socio-Economic Characteristics†

(2000 US Census, except as noted)

Population

1980*	137,970
1990*	140,891
2000	149,222
Male	72,473
Female	76,749
2007 (estimate)*	146,545
Population density	17,363.2

Race & Hispanic Origin, 2000

Race

White	45,913
Black/African American	49,095
American Indian/Alaska Native	901
Asian	2,831
Native Hawaiian/Pacific Islander	84
Other race	41,184
Two or more races	9,214
Hispanic origin, total	74,774
Mexican	5,004
Puerto Rican	24,013
Cuban	858
Other Hispanic	44,899

Age & Nativity, 2000

Under 5 years	12,578
18 years and over	104,785
21 years and over	97,577
65 years and over	12,399
85 years and over	1,356
Median age	30.5
Native-born	100,298
Foreign-born	48,924

Educational Attainment, 2000

Population 25 years and over	88,077
Less than 9th grade	18.1%
High school grad or higher	58.5%
Bachelor's degree or higher	8.2%
Graduate degree	2.8%

Income & Poverty, 1999

Per capita income	$13,257
Median household income	$32,778
Median family income	$35,420
Persons in poverty	32,474
H'holds receiving public assistance	3,874
H'holds receiving social security	10,102

Households, 2000

Total households	44,710
With persons under 18	21,997
With persons over 65	9,801
Family households	33,351
Single-person households	9,143
Persons per household	3.25
Persons per family	3.71

Labor & Employment

Total civilian labor force, 2007**	58,570
Unemployment rate	8.3%
Total civilian labor force, 2000	60,463
Unemployment rate	13.1%

Employed persons 16 years and over by occupation, 2000

Managers & professionals	8,774
Service occupations	10,640
Sales & office occupations	14,529
Farming, fishing & forestry	84
Construction & maintenance	4,114
Production & transportation	14,404
Self-employed persons	1,390

† see Appendix C for American Community Survey data
* US Census Bureau
** New Jersey Department of Labor
§ State Fiscal Year July 1–June 30

General Information

City of Paterson
155 Market St
Paterson, NJ 07505
973-321-1500

Website	www.patcity.com
Year of incorporation	1851
Land/water area (sq. miles)	8.44/0.29
Form of government	Mayor-Council

Government

Legislative Districts

US Congressional	8
State Legislative	35

Local Officials, 2009

Mayor	Joey Torres
Manager	Eli Burgos
Clerk	Jane Williams-Warren
Finance Dir	Anthony Zambrano
Tax Assessor	J. Krieger
Tax Collector	Kathleen Gibson
Attorney	Susan Champion
Building	Salvatore Ianelli
Planning	Anthony DeFranco
Engineering	Frederick Margron
Public Works	Manny Ojeda
Police Chief	James Wittig
Emerg/Fire Director	Michael Postorino

Housing & Construction

Housing Units, 2000*

Total	47,169
Median rent	$696
Median SF home value	$137,500

Permits for New Residential Construction

	Units	Value
Total, 2006	0	$0
Single family	0	$0
Total, 2007	19	$1,370,600
Single family	9	$768,300

Real Property Valuation, 2008

	Parcels	Valuation
Total	23,434	$9,318,217,950
Vacant	1,521	188,322,400
Residential	17,500	6,301,093,300
Commercial	3,403	1,713,639,200
Industrial	517	629,668,600
Apartments	493	485,494,450
Farm land	0	0
Farm homestead	0	0

Average Property Value & Tax, 2008

Residential value	$360,062
Property tax	$6,665
Tax credit/rebate	$964

Public Library

Paterson Free Public Library
250 Broadway
Paterson, NJ 07501
973-321-1223

Director	Cynthia Czesak

Library statistics, 2007

Population served	149,222
Full-time/total staff	7/45

	Total	Per capita
Holdings	189,425	1.27
Revenues	$2,930,392	$19.64
Expenditures	$2,720,571	$18.23
Annual visits	173,389	1.16
Internet terminals/annual users	53/78,224	

Public Safety

Number of officers, 2007		494

Crime	2006	2007
Total crimes	6,037	5,858
Violent	1,672	1,479
Murder	15	14
Rape	37	26
Robbery	808	695
Aggravated assault	812	744
Non-violent	4,365	4,379
Burglary	1,361	1,460
Larceny	1,999	2,007
Vehicle theft	1,005	912
Domestic violence	1,577	1,744
Arson	17	19
Total crime rate	40.3	39.4
Violent	11.2	9.9
Non-violent	29.1	29.4

Public School District

(for school year 2007-08 except as noted)

Paterson School District
33-35 Church Street
Paterson, NJ 07505
(973) 321-0980

State District Superintendent Dennis Clancy (Int)

Number of schools	39
Grade plan	K-12
Enrollment	24,087
Attendance rate, '06-07	91.9%
Dropout rate	6.5%
Students per teacher	9.0
Per pupil expenditure	$17,501
Median faculty salary	$55,065
Median administrator salary	$105,919
Grade 12 enrollment	1,080
High school graduation rate	80.3%

Assessment test results

(percent scoring at proficient or advanced level)

	Language	Math
NJASK-Grade 3	70.2%	68.0%
GEPA-Grade 8	40.9%	56.7%
HSPA-High School	34.4%	49.4%

SAT Score Averages, 2006-07

Pct tested	Math	Verbal	Writing
NA	NA	NA	NA

Teacher Qualifications

Avg. years of experience	9
Highly-qualified teachers one subject/all subjects	95.5%/95.5%

No Child Left Behind

AYP, 2006-07	Needs Improvement

Municipal Finance§

State Aid Programs, 2009

Total aid	$38,568,127
CMPTRA	28,455,898
Energy tax receipts	10,101,029
Garden State Trust	10,001

General Budget, 2008

Total tax levy	$172,750,983
County levy	42,638,509
County taxes	41,786,826
County library	0
County health	0
County open space	851,683
School levy	37,087,707
Muni. levy	93,024,768
Misc. revenues	116,924,623

Taxes

	2006	2007	2008
General tax rate per $100	26.3	1.75	1.853
County equalization ratio	9.52	129.64	111.14
Net valuation taxable	$572,833,674	$9,388,617,332	$9,331,884,808
State equalized value	$7,188,708,575	$8,449,017,781	$8,887,315,034

See Introduction for an explanation of all data sources.

Demographics & Socio-Economic Characteristics
(2000 US Census, except as noted)

Population

1980*	6,944
1990*	6,577
2000	6,160
Male	2,885
Female	3,275
2007 (estimate)*	6,080
Population density	3,102.0

Race & Hispanic Origin, 2000

Race

White	3,915
Black/African American	1,949
American Indian/Alaska Native	15
Asian	20
Native Hawaiian/Pacific Islander	6
Other race	81
Two or more races	174
Hispanic origin, total	268
Mexican	36
Puerto Rican	159
Cuban	4
Other Hispanic	69

Age & Nativity, 2000

Under 5 years	463
18 years and over	4,387
21 years and over	4,138
65 years and over	854
85 years and over	86
Median age	34.3
Native-born	5,921
Foreign-born	239

Educational Attainment, 2000

Population 25 years and over	3,813
Less than 9th grade	7.2%
High school grad or higher	75.4%
Bachelor's degree or higher	6.0%
Graduate degree	1.9%

Income & Poverty, 1999

Per capita income	$16,368
Median household income	$35,569
Median family income	$41,359
Persons in poverty	1,084
H'holds receiving public assistance	77
H'holds receiving social security	714

Households, 2000

Total households	2,353
With persons under 18	908
With persons over 65	658
Family households	1,615
Single-person households	633
Persons per household	2.61
Persons per family	3.15

Labor & Employment

Total civilian labor force, 2007**	3,433
Unemployment rate	12.3%
Total civilian labor force, 2000	2,874
Unemployment rate	11.1%

Employed persons 16 years and over by occupation, 2000

Managers & professionals	395
Service occupations	488
Sales & office occupations	799
Farming, fishing & forestry	12
Construction & maintenance	281
Production & transportation	579
Self-employed persons	62

General Information
Borough of Paulsboro
1211 N Delaware St
Paulsboro, NJ 08066
856-423-1500

Website	www.paulsboronj.org
Year of incorporation	1904
Land/water area (sq. miles)	1.96/0.66
Form of government	Borough

Government

Legislative Districts

US Congressional	1
State Legislative	3

Local Officials, 2009

Mayor	John J. Burzichelli
Manager	John Salvatore
Clerk	Kathy A. VanScoy
Finance Dir	John S. Salvatore
Tax Assessor	Robyn Hammond
Tax Collector	Barbara A. Sockwell
Attorney	Michael A. Angelini
Building	Phil Zimm
Comm Dev/Planning	NA
Engineering	Edward Vernick
Public Works	NA
Police Chief	Kenneth Ridinger
Emerg/Fire Dir	Michael Licciardello

Housing & Construction

Housing Units, 2000*

Total	2,628
Median rent	$570
Median SF home value	$78,600

Permits for New Residential Construction

	Units	Value
Total, 2006	3	$740,800
Single family	3	$740,800
Total, 2007	3	$270,000
Single family	3	$270,000

Real Property Valuation, 2008

	Parcels	Valuation
Total	2,343	$247,979,100
Vacant	208	2,953,400
Residential	1,980	141,034,600
Commercial	135	58,006,000
Industrial	6	39,098,600
Apartments	13	6,867,500
Farm land	1	19,000
Farm homestead	0	0

Average Property Value & Tax, 2008

Residential value	$71,230
Property tax	$3,384
Tax credit/rebate	$749

Public Library
Gill Memorial Library
145 E Broad St
Paulsboro, NJ 08066
856-432-5155

Librarian .... Violet J. Valentin

Library statistics, 2007

Population served	6,160
Full-time/total staff	0/0

	Total	Per capita
Holdings	27,387	4.45
Revenues	$177,208	$28.77
Expenditures	$120,097	$19.50
Annual visits	9,920	1.61
Internet terminals/annual users	5/6,206	

Public Safety

Number of officers, 2007 19

Crime	2006	2007
Total crimes	283	288
Violent	52	27
Murder	0	0
Rape	1	0
Robbery	21	4
Aggravated assault	30	23
Non-violent	231	261
Burglary	54	40
Larceny	163	199
Vehicle theft	14	22
Domestic violence	130	155
Arson	2	1
Total crime rate	46.4	47.5
Violent	8.5	4.5
Non-violent	37.9	43.1

Public School District
(for school year 2007-08 except as noted)

Paulsboro School District
662 N Delaware St
Paulsboro, NJ 08066
(856) 423-5515

Superintendent	Frank Scambia
Number of schools	3
Grade plan	K-12
Enrollment	1,400
Attendance rate, '06-07	91.5%
Dropout rate	3.8%
Students per teacher	10.8
Per pupil expenditure	$13,830
Median faculty salary	$69,724
Median administrator salary	$101,794
Grade 12 enrollment	106
High school graduation rate	91.3%

Assessment test results
(percent scoring at proficient or advanced level)

	Language	Math
NJASK-Grade 3	81.3%	82.5%
GEPA-Grade 8	48.0%	51.6%
HSPA-High School	64.5%	72.4%

SAT Score Averages, 2006-07

Pct tested	Math	Verbal	Writing
61%	458	419	411

Teacher Qualifications

Avg. years of experience	14
Highly-qualified teachers one subject/all subjects	100%/100%

No Child Left Behind

AYP, 2006-07 .... Meets Standards

Municipal Finance

State Aid Programs, 2009

Total aid	$668,426
CMPTRA	339,936
Energy tax receipts	328,490
Garden State Trust	0

General Budget, 2008

Total tax levy	$11,844,829
County levy	2,476,843
County taxes	2,296,850
County library	0
County health	0
County open space	179,992
School levy	4,724,987
Muni. levy	4,643,000
Misc. revenues	3,206,741

Taxes

	2006	2007	2008
General tax rate per $100	3.733	4.045	4.752
County equalization ratio	82.62	68.41	55.81
Net valuation taxable	$268,806,500	$271,118,225	$249,302,957
State equalized value	$394,777,246	$484,538,585	$452,605,204

* US Census Bureau
** New Jersey Department of Labor

See Introduction for an explanation of all data sources.

Demographics & Socio-Economic Characteristics

(2000 US Census, except as noted)

Population

1980*	2,038
1990*	2,111
2000	2,433
Male	1,203
Female	1,230
2007 (estimate)*	2,552
Population density	440.0

Race & Hispanic Origin, 2000

Race
White	2,298
Black/African American	76
American Indian/Alaska Native	2
Asian	30
Native Hawaiian/Pacific Islander	0
Other race	17
Two or more races	10
Hispanic origin, total	92
Mexican	18
Puerto Rican	8
Cuban	3
Other Hispanic	63

Age & Nativity, 2000

Under 5 years	183
18 years and over	1,801
21 years and over	1,740
65 years and over	296
85 years and over	38
Median age	39.5
Native-born	2,138
Foreign-born	295

Educational Attainment, 2000

Population 25 years and over	1,694
Less than 9th grade	3.3%
High school grad or higher	92.9%
Bachelor's degree or higher	56.9%
Graduate degree	19.2%

Income & Poverty, 1999

Per capita income	$56,542
Median household income	$99,499
Median family income	$118,770
Persons in poverty	101
H'holds receiving public assistance	0
H'holds receiving social security	224

Households, 2000

Total households	840
With persons under 18	325
With persons over 65	202
Family households	647
Single-person households	152
Persons per household	2.71
Persons per family	3.11

Labor & Employment

Total civilian labor force, 2007**	1,351
Unemployment rate	2.6%
Total civilian labor force, 2000	1,318
Unemployment rate	5.0%

Employed persons 16 years and over by occupation, 2000
Managers & professionals	648
Service occupations	160
Sales & office occupations	331
Farming, fishing & forestry	9
Construction & maintenance	56
Production & transportation	48
Self-employed persons	94

‡ Branch of county library
* US Census Bureau
** New Jersey Department of Labor

General Information

Borough of Peapack & Gladstone
1 School St
PO Box 218
Peapack, NJ 07977
908-234-2250

Website	www.peapack-gladstone-nj.gov
Year of incorporation	1912
Land/water area (sq. miles)	5.80/0.00
Form of government	Borough

Government

Legislative Districts

US Congressional	7
State Legislative	16

Local Officials, 2009

Mayor	William H. Horton
Manager	Margaret Gould
Clerk	Margaret Gould
Finance Dir	Mary Robinson
Tax Assessor	Edward Kerwin
Tax Collector	Mary Robinson
Attorney	Sharon Moore
Building	Jim Fania
Comm Dev/Planning	NA
Engineering	William Ryden
Public Works	Rodney McCathern
Police Chief	Gregory Skinner
Emerg/Fire Director	David Hill

Housing & Construction

Housing Units, 2000*

Total	871
Median rent	$1,132
Median SF home value	$461,500

Permits for New Residential Construction

	Units	Value
Total, 2006	2	$1,173,150
Single family	2	$1,173,150
Total, 2007	6	$5,519,800
Single family	6	$5,519,800

Real Property Valuation, 2008

	Parcels	Valuation
Total	953	$825,605,804
Vacant	38	14,202,500
Residential	724	545,422,500
Commercial	41	174,061,100
Industrial	1	8,035,000
Apartments	10	6,866,900
Farm land	102	495,904
Farm homestead	37	76,521,900

Average Property Value & Tax, 2008

Residential value	$817,273
Property tax	$13,243
Tax credit/rebate	$1,324

Public Library

Peapack Gladstone Branch‡
School St
Peapack, NJ 07977
908-234-0598

Branch Librarian	Karen Pifher

Library statistics, 2007

see Somerset County profile
for library system statistics

Public Safety

Number of officers, 2007	9

Crime	2006	2007
Total crimes	14	21
Violent	1	0
Murder	0	0
Rape	0	0
Robbery	0	0
Aggravated assault	1	0
Non-violent	13	21
Burglary	4	8
Larceny	9	13
Vehicle theft	0	0
Domestic violence	2	4
Arson	0	0
Total crime rate	5.7	8.5
Violent	0.4	0.0
Non-violent	5.3	8.5

Public School District

(for school year 2007-08 except as noted)

Somerset Hills Regional School District
25 Olcott Ave
Bernardsville, NJ 07924
(908) 630-3011

Superintendent	Peter Miller
Number of schools	3
Grade plan	K-12
Enrollment	2,049
Attendance rate, '06-07	95.9%
Dropout rate	0.1%
Students per teacher	10.5
Per pupil expenditure	$15,952
Median faculty salary	$64,173
Median administrator salary	$130,000
Grade 12 enrollment	175
High school graduation rate	98.3%

Assessment test results

(percent scoring at proficient or advanced level)
	Language	Math
NJASK-Grade 3	95.6%	90.4%
GEPA-Grade 8	87.1%	95.2%
HSPA-High School	93.7%	96.1%

SAT Score Averages, 2006-07

Pct tested	Math	Verbal	Writing
91%	575	561	558

Teacher Qualifications

Avg. years of experience	10

Highly-qualified teachers
one subject/all subjects	99.5%/99.5%

No Child Left Behind

AYP, 2006-07	Meets Standards

Municipal Finance

State Aid Programs, 2009

Total aid	$317,916
CMPTRA	0
Energy tax receipts	305,144
Garden State Trust	58

General Budget, 2008

Total tax levy	$13,393,324
County levy	3,089,481
County taxes	2,479,514
County library	335,536
County health	0
County open space	274,431
School levy	6,421,733
Muni. levy	3,882,109
Misc. revenues	2,691,232

Taxes

	2006	2007	2008
General tax rate per $100	1.66	1.59	1.621
County equalization ratio	99.46	93.27	90.46
Net valuation taxable	$818,012,069	$846,611,057	$826,529,097
State equalized value	$906,492,977	$909,974,352	$856,030,288

See Introduction for an explanation of all data sources.

Demographics & Socio-Economic Characteristics
(2000 US Census, except as noted)

Population
1980*	1,198
1990*	1,367
2000	1,210
Male	614
Female	596
2007 (estimate)*	1,472
Population density	2,494.9

Race & Hispanic Origin, 2000
Race
White	949
Black/African American	154
American Indian/Alaska Native	8
Asian	29
Native Hawaiian/Pacific Islander	0
Other race	33
Two or more races	37
Hispanic origin, total	104
Mexican	15
Puerto Rican	60
Cuban	2
Other Hispanic	27

Age & Nativity, 2000
Under 5 years	83
18 years and over	886
21 years and over	832
65 years and over	108
85 years and over	8
Median age	33.9
Native-born	1,130
Foreign-born	80

Educational Attainment, 2000
Population 25 years and over	767
Less than 9th grade	4.2%
High school grad or higher	83.7%
Bachelor's degree or higher	15.5%
Graduate degree	4.3%

Income & Poverty, 1999
Per capita income	$18,909
Median household income	$44,063
Median family income	$48,500
Persons in poverty	94
H'holds receiving public assistance	23
H'holds receiving social security	93

Households, 2000
Total households	470
With persons under 18	189
With persons over 65	82
Family households	317
Single-person households	124
Persons per household	2.56
Persons per family	3.06

Labor & Employment
Total civilian labor force, 2007**	742
Unemployment rate	4.6%
Total civilian labor force, 2000	648
Unemployment rate	4.3%

Employed persons 16 years and over by occupation, 2000
Managers & professionals	146
Service occupations	137
Sales & office occupations	163
Farming, fishing & forestry	0
Construction & maintenance	76
Production & transportation	98
Self-employed persons	49

General Information
Borough of Pemberton
50 Egbert St
Pemberton, NJ 08068
609-894-8222

Website	www.pembertonborough.us
Year of incorporation	1826
Land/water area (sq. miles)	0.59/0.02
Form of government	Borough

Government
Legislative Districts
US Congressional	3
State Legislative	8

Local Officials, 2009
Mayor	F. Lyman Simpkins
Manager/Admin	NA
Clerk	Donna Mull
Finance Dir	Donna Mull
Tax Assessor	Douglas Kolton
Tax Collector	Harold Griffin
Attorney	Peter Emmons
Building	Harry Wetterskog
Comm Dev/Planning	NA
Engineering	Martin Miller
Public Works	Raymond Downs
Police Chief	Joseph Conlin
Emerg/Fire Director	Chas Bozoski

Housing & Construction
Housing Units, 2000*
Total	513
Median rent	$641
Median SF home value	$113,300

Permits for New Residential Construction
	Units	Value
Total, 2006	56	$6,370,243
Single family	56	$6,370,243
Total, 2007	37	$4,242,729
Single family	37	$4,242,729

Real Property Valuation, 2008
	Parcels	Valuation
Total	594	$59,143,500
Vacant	98	1,501,000
Residential	434	47,456,200
Commercial	46	7,293,000
Industrial	0	0
Apartments	10	2,753,800
Farm land	5	10,800
Farm homestead	1	128,700

Average Property Value & Tax, 2008
Residential value	$109,391
Property tax	$3,281
Tax credit/rebate	$862

Public Library
Pemberton Library‡
18 Broadway
Browns Mills, NJ 08015
609-893-8262

Branch Librarian	NA

Library statistics, 2007
see Burlington County profile
for library system statistics

Public Safety
Number of officers, 2007	6

Crime	2006	2007
Total crimes	40	21
Violent	6	5
Murder	0	0
Rape	3	1
Robbery	1	1
Aggravated assault	2	3
Non-violent	34	16
Burglary	9	4
Larceny	25	11
Vehicle theft	0	1
Domestic violence	33	22
Arson	0	0
Total crime rate	30.2	15.2
Violent	4.5	3.6
Non-violent	25.7	11.6

Public School District
(for school year 2007-08 except as noted)

Pemberton Borough School District
50 Egbert Street
Pemberton, NJ 08068
(609) 894-2261

Superintendent	Charles Smith
Number of schools	0
Grade plan	K-6
Enrollment	NA
Attendance rate, '06-07	93.8%
Dropout rate	NA
Students per teacher	NA
Per pupil expenditure	NA
Median faculty salary	NA
Median administrator salary	NA
Grade 12 enrollment	NA
High school graduation rate	NA

Assessment test results
(percent scoring at proficient or advanced level)
	Language	Math
NJASK-Grade 3	NA	NA
GEPA-Grade 8	NA	NA
HSPA-High School	NA	NA

SAT Score Averages, 2006-07
Pct tested	Math	Verbal	Writing
NA	NA	NA	NA

Teacher Qualifications
Avg. years of experience	NA
Highly-qualified teachers one subject/all subjects	NA/NA

No Child Left Behind
AYP, 2006-07	Meets Standards

Municipal Finance
State Aid Programs, 2009
Total aid	$126,758
CMPTRA	59,905
Energy tax receipts	61,093
Garden State Trust	3,911

General Budget, 2008
Total tax levy	$1,790,615
County levy	442,607
County taxes	363,474
County library	33,560
County health	0
County open space	45,573
School levy	1,003,940
Muni. levy	344,068
Misc. revenues	903,329

Taxes	2006	2007	2008
General tax rate per $100	3.911	3.29	3.000
County equalization ratio	62.54	52.38	52.44
Net valuation taxable	$46,281,700	$54,110,992	$59,694,816
State equalized value	$89,015,943	$102,675,520	$118,791,020

Demographics & Socio-Economic Characteristics

(2000 US Census, except as noted)

Population

1980*	29,720
1990*	31,342
2000	28,691
Male	14,148
Female	14,543
2007 (estimate)*	28,158
Population density	456.5

Race & Hispanic Origin, 2000

Race

White	18,946
Black/African American	6,632
American Indian/Alaska Native	132
Asian	913
Native Hawaiian/Pacific Islander	23
Other race	828
Two or more races	1,217
Hispanic origin, total	2,477
Mexican	225
Puerto Rican	1,560
Cuban	44
Other Hispanic	648

Age & Nativity, 2000

Under 5 years	1,925
18 years and over	20,770
21 years and over	19,594
65 years and over	2,793
85 years and over	189
Median age	34.4
Native-born	26,607
Foreign-born	2,043

Educational Attainment, 2000

Population 25 years and over	18,049
Less than 9th grade	4.5%
High school grad or higher	80.0%
Bachelor's degree or higher	9.4%
Graduate degree	2.5%

Income & Poverty, 1999

Per capita income	$19,238
Median household income	$47,394
Median family income	$52,860
Persons in poverty	2,612
H'holds receiving public assistance	418
H'holds receiving social security	2,164

Households, 2000

Total households	10,050
With persons under 18	4,277
With persons over 65	2,009
Family households	7,484
Single-person households	2,048
Persons per household	2.80
Persons per family	3.22

Labor & Employment

Total civilian labor force, 2007**	14,697
Unemployment rate	5.5%
Total civilian labor force, 2000	13,931
Unemployment rate	6.1%

Employed persons 16 years and over by occupation, 2000

Managers & professionals	2,806
Service occupations	3,013
Sales & office occupations	3,769
Farming, fishing & forestry	51
Construction & maintenance	1,319
Production & transportation	2,129
Self-employed persons	566

‡ Branch of county library
* US Census Bureau
** New Jersey Department of Labor

General Information

Township of Pemberton
500 Pemberton Browns Mills Rd
Pemberton, NJ 08068
609-894-8201

Website	www.pemberton-twp.com
Year of incorporation	1846
Land/water area (sq. miles)	61.68/0.82
Form of government	Mayor-Council

Government

Legislative Districts

US Congressional	3
State Legislative	8

Local Officials, 2009

Mayor	David A. Patriarca
Manager	Christopher Vaz
Clerk	Mary Ann Young
Finance Dir	Linda Eden
Tax Assessor	Maureen Francis
Tax Collector	Michelle Adams
Attorney	Andrew Bayer
Building	Robert Benasch
Comm Dev/Planning	NA
Engineering	Adams, Rehmann & Heggan
Public Works	Phil Sager
Police Chief	Robert Lewandowski
Fire/Emergency Dir	NA

Housing & Construction

Housing Units, 2000*

Total	10,778
Median rent	$670
Median SF home value	$98,300

Permits for New Residential Construction

	Units	Value
Total, 2006	26	$2,344,288
Single family	26	$2,344,288
Total, 2007	31	$3,229,229
Single family	31	$3,229,229

Real Property Valuation, 2008

	Parcels	Valuation
Total	11,534	$876,757,935
Vacant	3,008	18,748,150
Residential	7,981	760,916,850
Commercial	146	56,224,435
Industrial	5	4,323,800
Apartments	14	18,876,300
Farm land	254	3,003,400
Farm homestead	126	14,665,000

Average Property Value & Tax, 2008

Residential value	$95,668
Property tax	$3,296
Tax credit/rebate	$758

Public Library

Pemberton Library‡
18 Broadway
Browns Mills, NJ 08015
609-893-8262

Branch Librarian	NA

Library statistics, 2007

see Burlington County profile
for library system statistics

Public Safety

Number of officers, 2007	59

Crime	2006	2007
Total crimes	774	636
Violent	75	76
Murder	2	1
Rape	4	3
Robbery	26	30
Aggravated assault	43	42
Non-violent	699	560
Burglary	250	182
Larceny	402	342
Vehicle theft	47	36
Domestic violence	570	525
Arson	11	5
Total crime rate	26.8	22.1
Violent	2.6	2.6
Non-violent	24.2	19.4

Public School District

(for school year 2007-08 except as noted)

Pemberton Township School District
1 Eggbert St, PO Box 228
Pemberton, NJ 08068
(609) 893-8141

Superintendent	Michael Gorman
Number of schools	11
Grade plan	K-12
Enrollment	5,008
Attendance rate, '06-07	93.0%
Dropout rate	1.8%
Students per teacher	8.6
Per pupil expenditure	$18,818
Median faculty salary	$64,162
Median administrator salary	$110,000
Grade 12 enrollment	281
High school graduation rate	88.0%

Assessment test results

(percent scoring at proficient or advanced level)

	Language	Math
NJASK-Grade 3	86.5%	85.9%
GEPA-Grade 8	46.4%	71.1%
HSPA-High School	63.9%	82.1%

SAT Score Averages, 2006-07

Pct tested	Math	Verbal	Writing
54%	470	467	459

Teacher Qualifications

Avg. years of experience	13
Highly-qualified teachers one subject/all subjects	99.5%/99.5%

No Child Left Behind

AYP, 2006-07	Meets Standards

Municipal Finance

State Aid Programs, 2009

Total aid	$3,605,825
CMPTRA	1,312,173
Energy tax receipts	2,245,776
Garden State Trust	42,739

General Budget, 2008

Total tax levy	$30,276,389
County levy	6,563,005
County taxes	5,389,575
County library	497,599
County health	0
County open space	675,830
School levy	11,458,950
Muni. levy	12,254,435
Misc. revenues	10,978,300

Taxes

Taxes	2006	2007	2008
General tax rate per $100	3.319	3.41	3.445
County equalization ratio	66.29	57.08	51.72
Net valuation taxable	$852,595,236	$876,162,692	$878,895,819
State equalized value	$1,496,215,906	$1,691,899,999	$1,733,492,416

See Introduction for an explanation of all data sources.

Demographics & Socio-Economic Characteristics
(2000 US Census, except as noted)

Population
1980*	2,109
1990*	2,537
2000	2,696
Male	1,293
Female	1,403
2007 (estimate)*	2,668
Population density	2,779.2

Race & Hispanic Origin, 2000
Race
White	2,560
Black/African American	71
American Indian/Alaska Native	0
Asian	27
Native Hawaiian/Pacific Islander	0
Other race	11
Two or more races	27
Hispanic origin, total	32
Mexican	4
Puerto Rican	4
Cuban	2
Other Hispanic	22

Age & Nativity, 2000
Under 5 years	173
18 years and over	1,922
21 years and over	1,859
65 years and over	405
85 years and over	51
Median age	41.3
Native-born	2,539
Foreign-born	157

Educational Attainment, 2000
Population 25 years and over	1,781
Less than 9th grade	0.4%
High school grad or higher	97.1%
Bachelor's degree or higher	69.5%
Graduate degree	33.0%

Income & Poverty, 1999
Per capita income	$45,843
Median household income	$90,366
Median family income	$107,089
Persons in poverty	64
H'holds receiving public assistance	0
H'holds receiving social security	269

Households, 2000
Total households	1,013
With persons under 18	417
With persons over 65	293
Family households	762
Single-person households	223
Persons per household	2.66
Persons per family	3.14

Labor & Employment
Total civilian labor force, 2007**	1,686
Unemployment rate	4.2%
Total civilian labor force, 2000	1,338
Unemployment rate	2.6%

Employed persons 16 years and over by occupation, 2000
Managers & professionals	837
Service occupations	60
Sales & office occupations	315
Farming, fishing & forestry	0
Construction & maintenance	43
Production & transportation	48
Self-employed persons	120

General Information
Borough of Pennington
30 N Main St
Pennington, NJ 08534
609-737-0276

Website	www.penningtonboro.org
Year of incorporation	1890
Land/water area (sq. miles)	0.96/0.00
Form of government	Borough

Government
Legislative Districts
US Congressional	12
State Legislative	15

Local Officials, 2009
Mayor	Anthony J. Persichilli
Manager	Eugene Dunworth Jr
Clerk	Betty Sterling
Finance Dir	Sandra Webb
Tax Assessor	Antoinette Sost
Tax Collector	Irene Billings
Attorney	Walter Bliss
Building	John Hall
Planning	Mary Mistretta
Engineering	Donald Fetzer
Public Works	William J. Wittkop
Police Chief	NA
Emerg/Fire Director	William Meytrott

Housing & Construction
Housing Units, 2000*
Total	1,040
Median rent	$881
Median SF home value	$283,800

Permits for New Residential Construction
	Units	Value
Total, 2006	7	$1,177,082
Single family	7	$1,177,082
Total, 2007	1	$274,750
Single family	1	$274,750

Real Property Valuation, 2008
	Parcels	Valuation
Total	980	$521,107,600
Vacant	55	2,416,800
Residential	863	455,363,500
Commercial	57	54,101,600
Industrial	2	7,594,900
Apartments	3	1,630,800
Farm land	0	0
Farm homestead	0	0

Average Property Value & Tax, 2008
Residential value	$527,652
Property tax	$10,728
Tax credit/rebate	$1,378

Public Library
Pennington Public Library
30 N Main St
Pennington, NJ 08534
609-737-0404

Director	Kathleen M. Doyle

Library statistics, 2007
Population served	2,696
Full-time/total staff	1/1

	Total	Per capita
Holdings	27,412	10.17
Revenues	$194,888	$72.29
Expenditures	$173,202	$64.24
Annual visits	27,447	10.18
Internet terminals/annual users	4/4,000	

Public Safety
Number of officers, 2007	6

Crime	2006	2007
Total crimes	23	14
Violent	1	1
Murder	0	0
Rape	1	0
Robbery	0	0
Aggravated assault	0	1
Non-violent	22	13
Burglary	3	5
Larceny	19	8
Vehicle theft	0	0
Domestic violence	0	3
Arson	1	0
Total crime rate	8.5	5.2
Violent	0.4	0.4
Non-violent	8.2	4.8

Public School District
(for school year 2007-08 except as noted)

Hopewell Valley Regional School District
425 South Main Street
Pennington, NJ 08534
(609) 737-4000

Chief School Admin	Thomas Butler (Int)
Number of schools	6
Grade plan	K-12
Enrollment	3,984
Attendance rate, '06-07	96.3%
Dropout rate	0.3%
Students per teacher	10.2
Per pupil expenditure	$15,378
Median faculty salary	$59,326
Median administrator salary	$109,424
Grade 12 enrollment	261
High school graduation rate	99.6%

Assessment test results
(percent scoring at proficient or advanced level)
	Language	Math
NJASK-Grade 3	94.5%	93.3%
GEPA-Grade 8	82.3%	94.1%
HSPA-High School	91.7%	94.2%

SAT Score Averages, 2006-07
Pct tested	Math	Verbal	Writing
96%	562	557	585

Teacher Qualifications
Avg. years of experience	11
Highly-qualified teachers one subject/all subjects	100%/100%

No Child Left Behind
AYP, 2006-07	Meets Standards

Municipal Finance
State Aid Programs, 2009
Total aid	$248,407
CMPTRA	32,091
Energy tax receipts	208,243
Garden State Trust	0

General Budget, 2008
Total tax levy	$10,643,175
County levy	2,358,034
County taxes	2,206,608
County library	0
County health	0
County open space	151,426
School levy	6,054,510
Muni. levy	2,230,631
Misc. revenues	1,155,656

Taxes
	2006	2007	2008
General tax rate per $100	1.88	1.95	2.034
County equalization ratio	118.19	107.89	103.54
Net valuation taxable	$516,087,400	$518,248,052	$523,462,225
State equalized value	$480,436,224	$500,587,856	$517,028,798

* US Census Bureau
** New Jersey Department of Labor

See Introduction for an explanation of all data sources.

Demographics & Socio-Economic Characteristics

(2000 US Census, except as noted)

Population

1980*	5,760
1990*	5,228
2000	4,886
Male	2,252
Female	2,634
2007 (estimate)*	4,704
Population density	5,058.1

Race & Hispanic Origin, 2000

Race

White	2,387
Black/African American	1,942
American Indian/Alaska Native	18
Asian	14
Native Hawaiian/Pacific Islander	8
Other race	397
Two or more races	120
Hispanic origin, total	845
Mexican	147
Puerto Rican	580
Cuban	15
Other Hispanic	103

Age & Nativity, 2000

Under 5 years	412
18 years and over	3,275
21 years and over	3,062
65 years and over	576
85 years and over	57
Median age	30.9
Native-born	4,704
Foreign-born	176

Educational Attainment, 2000

Population 25 years and over	2,803
Less than 9th grade	14.4%
High school grad or higher	65.6%
Bachelor's degree or higher	7.5%
Graduate degree	1.6%

Income & Poverty, 1999

Per capita income	$13,330
Median household income	$26,227
Median family income	$34,076
Persons in poverty	1,020
H'holds receiving public assistance	118
H'holds receiving social security	606

Households, 2000

Total households	1,827
With persons under 18	799
With persons over 65	471
Family households	1,232
Single-person households	513
Persons per household	2.67
Persons per family	3.26

Labor & Employment

Total civilian labor force, 2007**	2,167
Unemployment rate	13.0%
Total civilian labor force, 2000	2,140
Unemployment rate	15.3%

Employed persons 16 years and over by occupation, 2000

Managers & professionals	349
Service occupations	368
Sales & office occupations	431
Farming, fishing & forestry	24
Construction & maintenance	150
Production & transportation	490
Self-employed persons	73

‡ Joint library with Carneys Point
* US Census Bureau
** New Jersey Department of Labor

General Information

Borough of Penns Grove
PO Box 527
Penns Grove, NJ 08069
856-299-0098

Email	pgclerk1@verizon.net
Year of incorporation	1894
Land/water area (sq. miles)	0.93/0.00
Form of government	Borough

Government

Legislative Districts

US Congressional	2
State Legislative	3

Local Officials, 2009

Mayor	John A. Washington
Manager/Admin	NA
Clerk	Sharon R. Williams
Finance Dir	Stephen Labb
Tax Assessor	Marie Proccaci
Tax Collector	Tom Freeman
Attorney	Adam Telsey
Building	Jeryl Goff
Planning	Armondo Verdecchio
Engineering	Mark Brunermer
Public Works	Vass Wiggins
Police Chief	Gary Doubledee
Emerg/Fire Director	Joseph Grasso

Housing & Construction

Housing Units, 2000*

Total	2,075
Median rent	$526
Median SF home value	$72,900

Permits for New Residential Construction

	Units	Value
Total, 2006	1	$160,000
Single family	1	$160,000
Total, 2007	0	$0
Single family	0	$0

Real Property Valuation, 2008

	Parcels	Valuation
Total	1,677	$90,746,800
Vacant	331	2,494,200
Residential	1,226	71,006,200
Commercial	108	15,073,100
Industrial	0	0
Apartments	12	2,173,300
Farm land	0	0
Farm homestead	0	0

Average Property Value & Tax, 2008

Residential value	$57,917
Property tax	$3,584
Tax credit/rebate	$848

Public Library

Penns Grove-Carneys Point Library‡
222 S Broad St
Penns Grove, NJ 08069
856-299-4255

Director..................Barbara Hunt

Library statistics, 2007

Population served	12,570
Full-time/total staff	NA/0

	Total	Per capita
Holdings	0	NA
Revenues	$0	NA
Expenditures	$0	NA
Annual visits	NA	NA
Internet terminals/annual users	NA/NA	

Public Safety

Number of officers, 2007	16

Crime	2006	2007
Total crimes	279	208
Violent	46	35
Murder	0	1
Rape	0	1
Robbery	21	4
Aggravated assault	25	29
Non-violent	233	173
Burglary	59	56
Larceny	156	110
Vehicle theft	18	7
Domestic violence	105	56
Arson	1	4
Total crime rate	57.8	43.4
Violent	9.5	7.3
Non-violent	48.3	36.1

Public School District

(for school year 2007-08 except as noted)

Penns Grove-Carneys Pt. Reg. School Dist.
100 Iona Avenue
Penns Grove, NJ 08069
(856) 299-4250

Superintendent	Joseph A. Massare
Number of schools	5
Grade plan	K-12
Enrollment	2,455
Attendance rate, '06-07	93.1%
Dropout rate	2.8%
Students per teacher	11.3
Per pupil expenditure	$12,499
Median faculty salary	$54,720
Median administrator salary	$96,416
Grade 12 enrollment	125
High school graduation rate	87.3%

Assessment test results

(percent scoring at proficient or advanced level)

	Language	Math
NJASK-Grade 3	77.3%	71.0%
GEPA-Grade 8	41.4%	56.9%
HSPA-High School	53.1%	71.3%

SAT Score Averages, 2006-07

Pct tested	Math	Verbal	Writing
71%	427	419	412

Teacher Qualifications

Avg. years of experience	12
Highly-qualified teachers one subject/all subjects	99.5%/99.5%

No Child Left Behind

AYP, 2006-07	Meets Standards

Municipal Finance

State Aid Programs, 2009

Total aid	$1,455,119
CMPTRA	1,033,446
Energy tax receipts	421,673
Garden State Trust	0

General Budget, 2008

Total tax levy	$5,680,273
County levy	1,586,786
County taxes	1,552,550
County library	0
County health	0
County open space	34,236
School levy	2,145,369
Muni. levy	1,948,118
Misc. revenues	4,138,713

Taxes	2006	2007	2008
General tax rate per $100	5.39	5.716	6.190
County equalization ratio	67.82	60.71	54.00
Net valuation taxable	$88,691,000	$91,510,515	$91,779,679
State equalized value	$147,338,062	$168,495,434	$196,898,890

See Introduction for an explanation of all data sources.

Demographics & Socio-Economic Characteristics
(2000 US Census, except as noted)

Population
1980*	33,775
1990*	34,738
2000	35,737
Male	17,116
Female	18,621
2007 (estimate)*	35,116
Population density	3,334.9

Race & Hispanic Origin, 2000
Race
White	21,479
Black/African American	8,641
American Indian/Alaska Native	124
Asian	1,636
Native Hawaiian/Pacific Islander	7
Other race	2,954
Two or more races	896
Hispanic origin, total	5,126
Mexican	218
Puerto Rican	3,629
Cuban	32
Other Hispanic	1,247

Age & Nativity, 2000
Under 5 years	2,212
18 years and over	25,925
21 years and over	24,634
65 years and over	5,065
85 years and over	608
Median age	36.1
Native-born	32,881
Foreign-born	2,822

Educational Attainment, 2000
Population 25 years and over	22,983
Less than 9th grade	6.2%
High school grad or higher	77.2%
Bachelor's degree or higher	15.4%
Graduate degree	4.8%

Income & Poverty, 1999
Per capita income	$19,004
Median household income	$47,538
Median family income	$52,760
Persons in poverty	2,807
H'holds receiving public assistance	331
H'holds receiving social security	3,651

Households, 2000
Total households	12,389
With persons under 18	5,120
With persons over 65	3,436
Family households	9,097
Single-person households	2,865
Persons per household	2.83
Persons per family	3.34

Labor & Employment
Total civilian labor force, 2007**	17,666
Unemployment rate	5.5%
Total civilian labor force, 2000	16,881
Unemployment rate	5.4%

Employed persons 16 years and over by occupation, 2000
Managers & professionals	4,447
Service occupations	2,553
Sales & office occupations	4,967
Farming, fishing & forestry	5
Construction & maintenance	1,292
Production & transportation	2,699
Self-employed persons	542

General Information
Township of Pennsauken
5605 N Crescent Blvd
Pennsauken, NJ 08110
856-665-1000
Website	www.twp.pennsauken.nj.us
Year of incorporation	1892
Land/water area (sq. miles)	10.53/1.65
Form of government	Township

Government
Legislative Districts
US Congressional	1
State Legislative	7

Local Officials, 2009
Mayor	Bill Orth
Manager	Bob Cummings
Clerk	Gene Padalino
Finance Dir	Ronald Crane
Tax Assessor	John Dymond
Tax Collector	Daniel O'Brien
Attorney	Dave Luthman
Building	Gary Burgin
Planning	John Adams
Engineering	Dennis O'Rourke
Public Works	John Figueroa
Police Chief	John Coffey
Emerg/Fire Director	Jack Mattera

Housing & Construction
Housing Units, 2000*
Total	12,945
Median rent	$584
Median SF home value	$95,300

Permits for New Residential Construction
	Units	Value
Total, 2006	38	$2,164,925
Single family	12	$1,068,450
Total, 2007	19	$1,788,930
Single family	19	$1,788,930

Real Property Valuation, 2008
	Parcels	Valuation
Total	12,187	$1,607,539,400
Vacant	317	16,499,500
Residential	10,990	989,074,800
Commercial	780	459,986,200
Industrial	52	119,667,000
Apartments	48	22,311,900
Farm land	0	0
Farm homestead	0	0

Average Property Value & Tax, 2008
Residential value	$89,998
Property tax	$4,005
Tax credit/rebate	$843

Public Library
Pennsauken Free Public Library
5605 Crescent Blvd
Pennsauken, NJ 08110
856-665-5959
Director	John Patane

Library statistics, 2007
Population served	35,737
Full-time/total staff	3/8

	Total	Per capita
Holdings	113,432	3.17
Revenues	$961,923	$26.92
Expenditures	$889,913	$24.90
Annual visits	158,343	4.43
Internet terminals/annual users	9/43,000	

Public Safety
Number of officers, 2007	94

Crime	2006	2007
Total crimes	1,507	1,680
Violent	138	159
Murder	1	0
Rape	13	5
Robbery	49	78
Aggravated assault	75	76
Non-violent	1,369	1,521
Burglary	323	362
Larceny	911	948
Vehicle theft	135	211
Domestic violence	404	399
Arson	9	7
Total crime rate	42.4	47.4
Violent	3.9	4.5
Non-violent	38.5	42.9

Public School District
(for school year 2007-08 except as noted)

Pennsauken Township School District
1695 Hylton Road
Pennsauken, NJ 08110
(856) 662-8505
Superintendent	James Chapman
Number of schools	11
Grade plan	K-12
Enrollment	5,568
Attendance rate, '06-07	94.0%
Dropout rate	5.7%
Students per teacher	11.3
Per pupil expenditure	$13,276
Median faculty salary	$62,275
Median administrator salary	$104,656
Grade 12 enrollment	426
High school graduation rate	84.8%

Assessment test results
(percent scoring at proficient or advanced level)
	Language	Math
NJASK-Grade 3	78.8%	79.6%
GEPA-Grade 8	62.7%	64.2%
HSPA-High School	56.6%	66.3%

SAT Score Averages, 2006-07
Pct tested	Math	Verbal	Writing
68%	434	422	419

Teacher Qualifications
Avg. years of experience	9
Highly-qualified teachers one subject/all subjects	98.0%/97.5%

No Child Left Behind
AYP, 2006-07	Needs Improvement

Municipal Finance
State Aid Programs, 2009
Total aid	$7,090,369
CMPTRA	1,585,006
Energy tax receipts	5,327,817
Garden State Trust	98

General Budget, 2008
Total tax levy	$71,670,314
County levy	16,813,907
County taxes	16,247,997
County library	0
County health	0
County open space	565,910
School levy	36,471,407
Muni. levy	18,385,000
Misc. revenues	16,545,000

Taxes
	2006	2007	2008
General tax rate per $100	4.032	4.271	4.451
County equalization ratio	75.2	66.84	58.02
Net valuation taxable	$1,616,967,900	$1,616,545,946	$1,610,507,618
State equalized value	$2,422,602,983	$2,783,862,650	$2,958,547,185

* US Census Bureau
** New Jersey Department of Labor

388   **The New Jersey Municipal Data Book**   See Introduction for an explanation of all data sources.

Demographics & Socio-Economic Characteristics

(2000 US Census, except as noted)

Population

1980*	13,848
1990*	13,794
2000	13,194
Male	6,337
Female	6,857
2007 (estimate)*	13,363
Population density	578.5

Race & Hispanic Origin, 2000

Race

White	12,756
Black/African American	127
American Indian/Alaska Native	21
Asian	127
Native Hawaiian/Pacific Islander	2
Other race	51
Two or more races	110
Hispanic origin, total	211
Mexican	45
Puerto Rican	102
Cuban	6
Other Hispanic	58

Age & Nativity, 2000

Under 5 years	758
18 years and over	10,134
21 years and over	9,689
65 years and over	2,047
85 years and over	189
Median age	39.3
Native-born	12,817
Foreign-born	428

Educational Attainment, 2000

Population 25 years and over	9,260
Less than 9th grade	4.4%
High school grad or higher	82.0%
Bachelor's degree or higher	13.6%
Graduate degree	2.6%

Income & Poverty, 1999

Per capita income	$22,717
Median household income	$47,250
Median family income	$57,340
Persons in poverty	653
H'holds receiving public assistance	131
H'holds receiving social security	1,789

Households, 2000

Total households	5,317
With persons under 18	1,730
With persons over 65	1,499
Family households	3,712
Single-person households	1,380
Persons per household	2.47
Persons per family	2.98

Labor & Employment

Total civilian labor force, 2007**	6,981
Unemployment rate	3.4%
Total civilian labor force, 2000	6,821
Unemployment rate	4.5%

Employed persons 16 years and over by occupation, 2000

Managers & professionals	1,843
Service occupations	936
Sales & office occupations	1,794
Farming, fishing & forestry	23
Construction & maintenance	754
Production & transportation	1,163
Self-employed persons	224

* US Census Bureau
** New Jersey Department of Labor

General Information

Township of Pennsville
90 N Broadway
Pennsville, NJ 08070
856-678-3089

Website	www.pennsville.org
Year of incorporation	1965
Land/water area (sq. miles)	23.10/1.71
Form of government	Township

Government

Legislative Districts

US Congressional	2
State Legislative	3

Local Officials, 2009

Mayor	Richard Barnhart
Manager	Jack Lynch
Clerk	Angela Foote
Finance Dir	John Willadsen
Tax Assessor	Randal Shidner
Tax Collector	Nancy McCarthy
Attorney	Walter Ray
Building	Tony Dariano
Comm Dev/Planning	NA
Engineering	Mark Brunermer
Public Works	Jack Lynch
Police Chief	Patrick McCaffery
Fire Chief	M. Ayares

Housing & Construction

Housing Units, 2000*

Total	5,623
Median rent	$640
Median SF home value	$103,700

Permits for New Residential Construction

	Units	Value
Total, 2006	129	$12,625,005
Single family	28	$3,014,105
Total, 2007	12	$1,318,800
Single family	12	$1,318,800

Real Property Valuation, 2008

	Parcels	Valuation
Total	5,914	$748,563,300
Vacant	791	13,341,700
Residential	4,635	478,664,200
Commercial	199	79,972,000
Industrial	3	150,160,900
Apartments	14	17,513,000
Farm land	219	2,082,600
Farm homestead	53	6,828,900

Average Property Value & Tax, 2008

Residential value	$103,561
Property tax	$4,526
Tax credit/rebate	$886

Public Library

Pennsville Public Library
190 S Broadway
Pennsville, NJ 08070
856-678-5473

Director ... Nancy Whitesell

Library statistics, 2007

Population served	13,194
Full-time/total staff	1/3

	Total	Per capita
Holdings	33,439	2.53
Revenues	$252,602	$19.15
Expenditures	$252,602	$19.15
Annual visits	17,220	1.31
Internet terminals/annual users		4/2,662

Public Safety

Number of officers, 2007 ... 24

Crime	2006	2007
Total crimes	396	401
Violent	14	9
Murder	0	0
Rape	0	0
Robbery	4	1
Aggravated assault	10	8
Non-violent	382	392
Burglary	86	49
Larceny	285	333
Vehicle theft	11	10
Domestic violence	240	244
Arson	4	1
Total crime rate	29.7	30.1
Violent	1.1	0.7
Non-violent	28.7	29.4

Public School District

(for school year 2007-08 except as noted)

Pennsville Township School District
30 Church Street
Pennsville, NJ 08070
(856) 540-6210

Superintendent	Mark Jones
Number of schools	5
Grade plan	K-12
Enrollment	2,050
Attendance rate, '06-07	94.6%
Dropout rate	3.6%
Students per teacher	10.6
Per pupil expenditure	$12,709
Median faculty salary	$52,733
Median administrator salary	$90,687
Grade 12 enrollment	132
High school graduation rate	91.9%

Assessment test results

(percent scoring at proficient or advanced level)

	Language	Math
NJASK-Grade 3	88.9%	85.3%
GEPA-Grade 8	75.6%	85.3%
HSPA-High School	71.5%	82.2%

SAT Score Averages, 2006-07

Pct tested	Math	Verbal	Writing
77%	460	472	461

Teacher Qualifications

Avg. years of experience	11
Highly-qualified teachers one subject/all subjects	100%/100%

No Child Left Behind

AYP, 2006-07 ... Meets Standards

Municipal Finance

State Aid Programs, 2009

Total aid	$6,827,309
CMPTRA	1,269,379
Energy tax receipts	5,386,978
Garden State Trust	253

General Budget, 2008

Total tax levy	$32,783,024
County levy	11,494,711
County taxes	11,246,705
County library	0
County health	0
County open space	248,006
School levy	17,499,327
Muni. levy	3,788,985
Misc. revenues	10,720,443

Taxes

	2006	2007	2008
General tax rate per $100	3.869	4.123	4.370
County equalization ratio	83.23	71.74	63.91
Net valuation taxable	$738,555,300	$748,761,463	$750,198,582
State equalized value	$1,031,435,868	$1,170,611,549	$179,598,011

See Introduction for an explanation of all data sources.

Demographics & Socio-Economic Characteristics
(2000 US Census, except as noted)

Population
1980*	13,776
1990*	12,844
2000	13,888
Male	6,688
Female	7,200
2007 (estimate)*	16,769
Population density	2,371.9

Race & Hispanic Origin, 2000
Race
White	13,416
Black/African American	41
American Indian/Alaska Native	17
Asian	265
Native Hawaiian/Pacific Islander	0
Other race	69
Two or more races	80
Hispanic origin, total	408
Mexican	29
Puerto Rican	144
Cuban	42
Other Hispanic	193

Age & Nativity, 2000
Under 5 years	947
18 years and over	10,293
21 years and over	9,912
65 years and over	1,956
85 years and over	206
Median age	38.9
Native-born	12,904
Foreign-born	984

Educational Attainment, 2000
Population 25 years and over	9,495
Less than 9th grade	2.4%
High school grad or higher	92.8%
Bachelor's degree or higher	37.5%
Graduate degree	11.4%

Income & Poverty, 1999
Per capita income	$31,892
Median household income	$72,729
Median family income	$84,487
Persons in poverty	414
H'holds receiving public assistance	43
H'holds receiving social security	1,460

Households, 2000
Total households	5,026
With persons under 18	1,849
With persons over 65	1,414
Family households	3,828
Single-person households	1,052
Persons per household	2.76
Persons per family	3.23

Labor & Employment
Total civilian labor force, 2007**	7,905
Unemployment rate	3.6%
Total civilian labor force, 2000	7,243
Unemployment rate	3.7%

Employed persons 16 years and over by occupation, 2000
Managers & professionals	3,057
Service occupations	701
Sales & office occupations	2,263
Farming, fishing & forestry	7
Construction & maintenance	466
Production & transportation	484
Self-employed persons	358

* US Census Bureau
** New Jersey Department of Labor

General Information
Township of Pequannock
530 Newark Pompton Tpke
Pompton Plains, NJ 07444
973-835-5700
Website	www.pequannocktownship.org
Year of incorporation	1720
Land/water area (sq. miles)	7.07/0.14
Form of government	Council-Manager

Government
Legislative Districts
US Congressional	11
State Legislative	26

Local Officials, 2009
Mayor	Joseph L. Jorgensen
Manager	Kevin Boyle
Clerk	Dolores Sweeney
Finance Dir	Janice A. Congleton
Tax Assessor	Tracy Clarke
Tax Collector	Lori Tarnogursky
Attorney	Michael Hubner
Building	Frederick R. Hermann
Planning	Eileen Banyra
Engineering	Frederick R. Hermann
Public Works	Bill Pereira
Police Chief	Brian Spring
Emerg/Fire Director	David Hollberg

Housing & Construction
Housing Units, 2000*
Total	5,097
Median rent	$787
Median SF home value	$246,100

Permits for New Residential Construction
	Units	Value
Total, 2006	286	$25,260,550
Single family	10	$2,660,550
Total, 2007	5	$685,900
Single family	5	$685,900

Real Property Valuation, 2008
	Parcels	Valuation
Total	5,182	$2,882,211,800
Vacant	127	20,321,100
Residential	4,763	2,234,174,600
Commercial	215	236,163,700
Industrial	30	45,112,800
Apartments	3	333,506,000
Farm land	26	108,400
Farm homestead	18	12,825,200

Average Property Value & Tax, 2008
Residential value	$469,985
Property tax	$7,610
Tax credit/rebate	$1,165

Public Library
Pequannock Township Public Library
477 Newark Pompton Tpke
Pompton Plains, NJ 07444
973-825-7460
Director	Rosemary Garwood

Library statistics, 2007
Population served	13,888
Full-time/total staff	3/10

	Total	Per capita
Holdings	88,597	6.38
Revenues	$988,731	$71.19
Expenditures	$980,922	$70.63
Annual visits	139,106	10.02
Internet terminals/annual users	11/18,183	

Public Safety
Number of officers, 2007	31

Crime	2006	2007
Total crimes	154	186
Violent	0	7
Murder	0	0
Rape	0	0
Robbery	0	0
Aggravated assault	0	7
Non-violent	154	179
Burglary	31	41
Larceny	110	125
Vehicle theft	13	13
Domestic violence	73	82
Arson	0	0
Total crime rate	9.9	11.4
Violent	0.0	0.4
Non-violent	9.9	11.0

Public School District
(for school year 2007-08 except as noted)

Pequannock Township School District
538 Newark-Pompton Turnpike
Pompton Plains, NJ 07444
(973) 616-6040
Superintendent	William H. Trusheim
Number of schools	5
Grade plan	K-12
Enrollment	2,437
Attendance rate, '06-07	95.6%
Dropout rate	0.1%
Students per teacher	11.0
Per pupil expenditure	$12,963
Median faculty salary	$52,575
Median administrator salary	$110,000
Grade 12 enrollment	203
High school graduation rate	100.0%

Assessment test results
(percent scoring at proficient or advanced level)
	Language	Math
NJASK-Grade 3	97.1%	96.5%
GEPA-Grade 8	85.9%	92.3%
HSPA-High School	90.0%	94.5%

SAT Score Averages, 2006-07
Pct tested	Math	Verbal	Writing
95%	500	485	490

Teacher Qualifications
Avg. years of experience	9
Highly-qualified teachers one subject/all subjects	100%/100%

No Child Left Behind
AYP, 2006-07	Meets Standards

Municipal Finance
State Aid Programs, 2009
Total aid	$1,565,697
CMPTRA	287,747
Energy tax receipts	1,238,806
Garden State Trust	8

General Budget, 2008
Total tax levy	$46,703,074
County levy	6,754,800
County taxes	5,512,236
County library	0
County health	0
County open space	1,242,564
School levy	29,577,128
Muni. levy	10,371,146
Misc. revenues	5,710,418

Taxes
	2006	2007	2008
General tax rate per $100	1.51	1.59	1.620
County equalization ratio	116.22	102.19	99.71
Net valuation taxable	$2,755,178,700	$2,805,171,755	$2,884,392,155
State equalized value	$2,698,184,679	$2,813,324,285	$2,851,623,558

See Introduction for an explanation of all data sources.

Demographics & Socio-Economic Characteristics

(2000 US Census, except as noted)

Population

1980*	38,951
1990*	41,967
2000	47,303
Male	23,441
Female	23,862
2007 (estimate)*	48,868
Population density	10,223.4

Race & Hispanic Origin, 2000

Race

White	21,951
Black/African American	4,749
American Indian/Alaska Native	330
Asian	723
Native Hawaiian/Pacific Islander	60
Other race	16,834
Two or more races	2,656
Hispanic origin, total	33,033
Mexican	3,056
Puerto Rican	13,145
Cuban	918
Other Hispanic	15,914

Age & Nativity, 2000

Under 5 years	3,805
18 years and over	33,831
21 years and over	31,558
65 years and over	4,820
85 years and over	599
Median age	31.2
Native-born	30,408
Foreign-born	16,895

Educational Attainment, 2000

Population 25 years and over	28,309
Less than 9th grade	23.7%
High school grad or higher	55.7%
Bachelor's degree or higher	9.7%
Graduate degree	3.4%

Income & Poverty, 1999

Per capita income	$14,989
Median household income	$37,608
Median family income	$40,740
Persons in poverty	8,190
H'holds receiving public assistance	760
H'holds receiving social security	3,694

Households, 2000

Total households	14,562
With persons under 18	6,727
With persons over 65	3,493
Family households	10,768
Single-person households	2,993
Persons per household	3.20
Persons per family	3.63

Labor & Employment

Total civilian labor force, 2007**	21,952
Unemployment rate	8.2%
Total civilian labor force, 2000	20,970
Unemployment rate	10.8%

Employed persons 16 years and over by occupation, 2000

Managers & professionals	3,267
Service occupations	3,252
Sales & office occupations	4,667
Farming, fishing & forestry	15
Construction & maintenance	1,636
Production & transportation	5,861
Self-employed persons	528

---

* US Census Bureau
** New Jersey Department of Labor
§ State Fiscal Year July 1–June 30

See Introduction for an explanation of all data sources.

General Information

City of Perth Amboy
260 High St
Perth Amboy, NJ 08861
732-826-0290

Website	www.ci.perthamboy.nj.us
Year of incorporation	1718
Land/water area (sq. miles)	4.78/1.20
Form of government	Mayor-Council

Government

Legislative Districts

US Congressional	13
State Legislative	19

Local Officials, 2009

Mayor	Wilda Diaz
Manager	Dianne Roman
Clerk	Elaine M. Jasko
Finance Dir	Jill Goldy
Tax Assessor	JoAnn Jimenez
Tax Collector	Nancy Martin
Attorney	Mark J. Blunda
Building	Edward Scala
Planning	Michael Carr
Engineering	Ernest Feist
Public Works	Paul Wnek
Police Chief	Michael Kohut
Emerg/Fire Director	David Yolk

Housing & Construction

Housing Units, 2000*

Total	15,236
Median rent	$732
Median SF home value	$126,200

Permits for New Residential Construction

	Units	Value
Total, 2006	201	$10,530,901
Single family	43	$3,021,600
Total, 2007	46	$3,617,139
Single family	31	$2,097,139

Real Property Valuation, 2008

	Parcels	Valuation
Total	9,098	$3,601,477,000
Vacant	393	125,408,300
Residential	7,531	2,111,910,000
Commercial	885	521,939,300
Industrial	123	559,878,100
Apartments	166	282,341,300
Farm land	0	0
Farm homestead	0	0

Average Property Value & Tax, 2008

Residential value	$280,429
Property tax	$6,103
Tax credit/rebate	$881

Public Library

Perth Amboy Public Library
196 Jefferson St
Perth Amboy, NJ 08861
732-826-2600

Director	Patricia Gandy

Library statistics, 2007

Population served	47,303
Full-time/total staff	3/11

	Total	Per capita
Holdings	163,449	3.46
Revenues	$1,289,453	$27.26
Expenditures	$1,195,620	$25.28
Annual visits	139,316	2.95
Internet terminals/annual users	11/89,502	

Public Safety

Number of officers, 2007	124

Crime	2006	2007
Total crimes	1,373	1,327
Violent	207	216
Murder	4	3
Rape	2	1
Robbery	95	116
Aggravated assault	106	96
Non-violent	1,166	1,111
Burglary	269	187
Larceny	737	775
Vehicle theft	160	149
Domestic violence	289	263
Arson	5	3
Total crime rate	28.1	27.3
Violent	4.2	4.4
Non-violent	23.9	22.9

Public School District

(for school year 2007-08 except as noted)

Perth Amboy School District
178 Barracks Street
Perth Amboy, NJ 08861
(732) 376-6279

Superintendent	John M. Rodecker
Number of schools	10
Grade plan	K-12
Enrollment	9,462
Attendance rate, '06-07	93.3%
Dropout rate	0.4%
Students per teacher	10.7
Per pupil expenditure	$15,696
Median faculty salary	$52,500
Median administrator salary	$114,765
Grade 12 enrollment	503
High school graduation rate	95.1%

Assessment test results

(percent scoring at proficient or advanced level)

	Language	Math
NJASK-Grade 3	82.9%	83.0%
GEPA-Grade 8	41.3%	59.3%
HSPA-High School	48.4%	60.0%

SAT Score Averages, 2006-07

Pct tested	Math	Verbal	Writing
57%	434	399	399

Teacher Qualifications

Avg. years of experience	7
Highly-qualified teachers one subject/all subjects	100%/100%

No Child Left Behind

AYP, 2006-07	Needs Improvement

Municipal Finance§

State Aid Programs, 2009

Total aid	$11,045,557
CMPTRA	7,846,581
Energy tax receipts	3,143,745
Garden State Trust	12

General Budget, 2008

Total tax levy	$78,486,868
County levy	10,968,297
County taxes	9,812,237
County library	0
County health	0
County open space	1,156,060
School levy	19,563,434
Muni. levy	47,955,137
Misc. revenues	34,135,058

Taxes

	2006	2007	2008
General tax rate per $100	1.62	2.08	2.177
County equalization ratio	128.16	106.6	95.98
Net valuation taxable	$3,576,828,200	$3,580,511,749	$3,606,231,134
State equalized value	$3,360,708,703	$3,730,246,923	$3,897,821,910

Demographics & Socio-Economic Characteristics
(2000 US Census, except as noted)

Population
1980*	16,647
1990*	15,757
2000	15,166
Male	7,226
Female	7,940
2007 (estimate)*	14,542
Population density	4,516.1

Race & Hispanic Origin, 2000
Race
White	13,928
Black/African American	527
American Indian/Alaska Native	18
Asian	126
Native Hawaiian/Pacific Islander	2
Other race	306
Two or more races	259
Hispanic origin, total	816
Mexican	120
Puerto Rican	374
Cuban	30
Other Hispanic	292

Age & Nativity, 2000
Under 5 years	1,090
18 years and over	11,128
21 years and over	10,553
65 years and over	2,311
85 years and over	271
Median age	36.0
Native-born	14,537
Foreign-born	629

Educational Attainment, 2000
Population 25 years and over	9,913
Less than 9th grade	7.9%
High school grad or higher	71.3%
Bachelor's degree or higher	9.2%
Graduate degree	2.3%

Income & Poverty, 1999
Per capita income	$18,452
Median household income	$37,368
Median family income	$46,925
Persons in poverty	2,009
H'holds receiving public assistance	306
H'holds receiving social security	2,014

Households, 2000
Total households	6,044
With persons under 18	2,120
With persons over 65	1,751
Family households	3,945
Single-person households	1,793
Persons per household	2.49
Persons per family	3.08

Labor & Employment
Total civilian labor force, 2007**	8,238
Unemployment rate	6.1%
Total civilian labor force, 2000	7,320
Unemployment rate	5.9%

Employed persons 16 years and over by occupation, 2000
Managers & professionals	1,382
Service occupations	1,304
Sales & office occupations	2,032
Farming, fishing & forestry	9
Construction & maintenance	597
Production & transportation	1,566
Self-employed persons	238

* US Census Bureau
** New Jersey Department of Labor

General Information
Town of Phillipsburg
675 Corliss Ave
Phillipsburg, NJ 08865
908-454-5500
Website	www.phillipsburgnj.org
Year of incorporation	1861
Land/water area (sq. miles)	3.22/0.11
Form of government	Mayor-Council

Government
Legislative Districts
US Congressional	5
State Legislative	23

Local Officials, 2009
Mayor	Harry Wyant
Business Admin	Michele Broubalow
Clerk	Michele Broubalow
Finance Dir	Joseph Hriczak
Tax Assessor	Lydia Schmidt
Tax Collector	Joseph Hriczak
Attorney	Joel Kobert
Building	Kevin Duddy
Comm Dev/Planning	NA
Engineering	Stanley Schrek
Public Works	Dennis Viscomi
Police Chief	Edward Mirenda
Emerg/Fire Director	Richard Hay

Housing & Construction
Housing Units, 2000*
Total	6,651
Median rent	$600
Median SF home value	$90,000

Permits for New Residential Construction
	Units	Value
Total, 2006	21	$2,453,496
Single family	21	$2,453,496
Total, 2007	25	$3,048,018
Single family	25	$3,048,018

Real Property Valuation, 2008
	Parcels	Valuation
Total	5,063	$555,140,745
Vacant	178	6,779,400
Residential	4,485	401,783,134
Commercial	323	84,752,985
Industrial	39	43,011,250
Apartments	37	18,770,000
Farm land	1	43,976
Farm homestead	0	0

Average Property Value & Tax, 2008
Residential value	$89,584
Property tax	$3,577
Tax credit/rebate	$788

Public Library
Phillipsburg Public Library
200 Frost Ave
Phillipsburg, NJ 08865
908-454-3712
Director	Ann DeRenzis

Library statistics, 2007
Population served	15,166
Full-time/total staff	4/11

	Total	Per capita
Holdings	99,751	6.58
Revenues	$1,249,400	$82.38
Expenditures	$1,376,158	$90.74
Annual visits	132,609	8.74
Internet terminals/annual users	15/34,306	

Public Safety
Number of officers, 2007 36
Crime	2006	2007
Total crimes	402	329
Violent	38	24
Murder	1	2
Rape	2	2
Robbery	21	4
Aggravated assault	14	16
Non-violent	364	305
Burglary	102	71
Larceny	227	213
Vehicle theft	35	21
Domestic violence	509	461
Arson	1	4
Total crime rate	26.9	22.2
Violent	2.5	1.6
Non-violent	24.4	20.6

Public School District
(for school year 2007-08 except as noted)

Phillipsburg School District
445 Marshall Street
Phillipsburg, NJ 08865
(908) 454-3400
Superintendent	Mark Miller
Number of schools	7
Grade plan	K-12
Enrollment	3,645
Attendance rate, '06-07	92.9%
Dropout rate	2.8%
Students per teacher	8.8
Per pupil expenditure	$14,659
Median faculty salary	$59,648
Median administrator salary	$99,577
Grade 12 enrollment	384
High school graduation rate	87.9%

Assessment test results
(percent scoring at proficient or advanced level)
	Language	Math
NJASK-Grade 3	86.1%	77.6%
GEPA-Grade 8	50.2%	70.2%
HSPA-High School	79.4%	86.9%

SAT Score Averages, 2006-07
Pct tested	Math	Verbal	Writing
59%	525	505	495

Teacher Qualifications
Avg. years of experience	10
Highly-qualified teachers one subject/all subjects	100%/100%

No Child Left Behind
AYP, 2006-07 .... Needs Improvement

Municipal Finance
State Aid Programs, 2009
Total aid	$2,399,427
CMPTRA	1,244,110
Energy tax receipts	1,141,853
Garden State Trust	1,270

General Budget, 2008
Total tax levy	$22,253,464
County levy	5,922,893
County taxes	5,283,594
County library	0
County health	0
County open space	639,298
School levy	7,123,585
Muni. levy	9,206,986
Misc. revenues	6,542,613

Taxes
	2006	2007	2008
General tax rate per $100	3.45	3.74	3.994
County equalization ratio	65.21	55.53	53.38
Net valuation taxable	$555,462,650	$556,129,342	$557,308,293
State equalized value	$1,002,997,093	$1,039,925,069	$1,073,867,828

See Introduction for an explanation of all data sources.

Demographics & Socio-Economic Characteristics

(2000 US Census, except as noted)

Population

1980*	2,810
1990*	3,250
2000	3,923
Male	2,029
Female	1,894
2007 (estimate)*	4,515
Population density	129.3

Race & Hispanic Origin, 2000

Race

White	3,320
Black/African American	478
American Indian/Alaska Native	11
Asian	36
Native Hawaiian/Pacific Islander	2
Other race	42
Two or more races	34
Hispanic origin, total	117
Mexican	24
Puerto Rican	51
Cuban	0
Other Hispanic	42

Age & Nativity, 2000

Under 5 years	168
18 years and over	2,989
21 years and over	2,811
65 years and over	566
85 years and over	112
Median age	40.0
Native-born	3,864
Foreign-born	65

Educational Attainment, 2000

Population 25 years and over	2,709
Less than 9th grade	3.0%
High school grad or higher	87.7%
Bachelor's degree or higher	22.8%
Graduate degree	6.7%

Income & Poverty, 1999

Per capita income	$27,400
Median household income	$66,042
Median family income	$71,629
Persons in poverty	120
H'holds receiving public assistance	5
H'holds receiving social security	315

Households, 2000

Total households	1,216
With persons under 18	473
With persons over 65	317
Family households	995
Single-person households	181
Persons per household	2.91
Persons per family	3.24

Labor & Employment

Total civilian labor force, 2007**	1,951
Unemployment rate	3.9%
Total civilian labor force, 2000	1,895
Unemployment rate	4.2%

Employed persons 16 years and over by occupation, 2000

Managers & professionals	691
Service occupations	237
Sales & office occupations	396
Farming, fishing & forestry	24
Construction & maintenance	201
Production & transportation	266
Self-employed persons	228

‡ Joint library with Woodstown
* US Census Bureau
** New Jersey Department of Labor

General Information

Township of Pilesgrove
1180 Route 40
Pilesgrove, NJ 08098
856-769-3222

Website	www.pilesgrovenj.org
Year of incorporation	1701
Land/water area (sq. miles)	34.91/0.14
Form of government	Township

Government

Legislative Districts

US Congressional	2
State Legislative	3

Local Officials, 2009

Mayor	William Miller
Manager	Maureen R. Abdill
Clerk	Maureen R. Abdill
Finance Dir	Ruth A. Moynihan
Tax Assessor	Randall Shidner
Tax Collector	Ruth A. Moynihan
Attorney	William L. Horner
Building	John Holroyd
Comm Dev/Planning	NA
Engineering	James McKelvie
Public Works	NA
Police Chief	NA
Emerg/Fire Dir	Carlo Castagliuolo Jr

Housing & Construction

Housing Units, 2000*

Total	1,261
Median rent	$590
Median SF home value	$158,400

Permits for New Residential Construction

	Units	Value
Total, 2006	22	$4,168,357
Single family	22	$4,168,357
Total, 2007	17	$3,439,127
Single family	17	$3,439,127

Real Property Valuation, 2008

	Parcels	Valuation
Total	2,128	$484,395,800
Vacant	199	10,341,800
Residential	1,189	342,802,300
Commercial	66	48,251,500
Industrial	0	0
Apartments	4	7,466,300
Farm land	440	9,538,700
Farm homestead	230	65,995,200

Average Property Value & Tax, 2008

Residential value	$288,088
Property tax	$6,140
Tax credit/rebate	$1,046

Public Library

Woodstown-Pilesgrove Library‡
14 School Ln
Woodstown, NJ 08098
856-769-0098

Librarian	Betty Lou Wiest

Library statistics, 2007

Population served	7,059
Full-time/total staff	NA/0

	Total	Per capita
Holdings	0	NA
Revenues	$0	NA
Expenditures	$0	NA
Annual visits	NA	NA
Internet terminals/annual users	NA/NA	

Public Safety

Number of officers, 2007	0

Crime	2006	2007
Total crimes	102	76
Violent	9	11
Murder	0	0
Rape	0	0
Robbery	1	3
Aggravated assault	8	8
Non-violent	93	65
Burglary	24	9
Larceny	62	52
Vehicle theft	7	4
Domestic violence	10	23
Arson	2	1
Total crime rate	23.1	16.8
Violent	2.0	2.4
Non-violent	21.1	14.3

Public School District

(for school year 2007-08 except as noted)

Woodstown-Pilesgrove Reg. School District
135 East Avenue
Woodstown, NJ 08098
(856) 769-1664

Superintendent	James Kerfoot (Int)
Number of schools	3
Grade plan	K-12
Enrollment	1,647
Attendance rate, '06-07	95.1%
Dropout rate	0.7%
Students per teacher	11.0
Per pupil expenditure	$12,127
Median faculty salary	$51,850
Median administrator salary	$98,358
Grade 12 enrollment	136
High school graduation rate	97.8%

Assessment test results

(percent scoring at proficient or advanced level)

	Language	Math
NJASK-Grade 3	90.6%	94.7%
GEPA-Grade 8	69.2%	81.8%
HSPA-High School	85.3%	89.2%

SAT Score Averages, 2006-07

Pct tested	Math	Verbal	Writing
81%	493	494	484

Teacher Qualifications

Avg. years of experience	10
Highly-qualified teachers one subject/all subjects	100%/100%

No Child Left Behind

AYP, 2006-07	Meets Standards

Municipal Finance

State Aid Programs, 2009

Total aid	$604,408
CMPTRA	33,571
Energy tax receipts	526,912
Garden State Trust	20,014

General Budget, 2008

Total tax levy	$10,356,341
County levy	4,434,521
County taxes	4,338,840
County library	0
County health	0
County open space	95,680
School levy	5,434,804
Muni. levy	487,017
Misc. revenues	2,218,717

Taxes

	2006	2007	2008
General tax rate per $100	3.609	2.128	2.132
County equalization ratio	65.03	101.23	101.69
Net valuation taxable	$268,269,000	$484,909,771	$485,903,245
State equalized value	$465,506,072	$476,874,556	$1,280,137,929

See Introduction for an explanation of all data sources.

Demographics & Socio-Economic Characteristics
(2000 US Census, except as noted)

Population
1980*	1,796
1990*	1,954
2000	1,950
Male	940
Female	1,010
2007 (estimate)*	2,062
Population density	3,325.8

Race & Hispanic Origin, 2000
Race
White	1,919
Black/African American	5
American Indian/Alaska Native	1
Asian	12
Native Hawaiian/Pacific Islander	0
Other race	4
Two or more races	9
Hispanic origin, total	46
Mexican	2
Puerto Rican	21
Cuban	11
Other Hispanic	12

Age & Nativity, 2000
Under 5 years	101
18 years and over	1,507
21 years and over	1,454
65 years and over	337
85 years and over	38
Median age	41.6
Native-born	1,899
Foreign-born	51

Educational Attainment, 2000
Population 25 years and over	1,398
Less than 9th grade	1.7%
High school grad or higher	90.7%
Bachelor's degree or higher	32.6%
Graduate degree	11.5%

Income & Poverty, 1999
Per capita income	$26,487
Median household income	$57,366
Median family income	$67,404
Persons in poverty	68
H'holds receiving public assistance	2
H'holds receiving social security	259

Households, 2000
Total households	767
With persons under 18	254
With persons over 65	247
Family households	558
Single-person households	172
Persons per household	2.54
Persons per family	3.01

Labor & Employment
Total civilian labor force, 2007**	1,212
Unemployment rate	3.7%
Total civilian labor force, 2000	1,015
Unemployment rate	3.8%

Employed persons 16 years and over by occupation, 2000
Managers & professionals	381
Service occupations	136
Sales & office occupations	268
Farming, fishing & forestry	0
Construction & maintenance	125
Production & transportation	66
Self-employed persons	54

General Information
Borough of Pine Beach
599 Pennsylvania Ave
PO Box 425
Pine Beach, NJ 08741
732-349-6425
Website	www.pinebeachborough.us
Year of incorporation	1925
Land/water area (sq. miles)	0.62/0.01
Form of government	Borough

Government
Legislative Districts
US Congressional	3
State Legislative	9

Local Officials, 2009
Mayor	Christopher J. Boyle
Manager/Admin	NA
Clerk	Charlene Carney
Finance Dir	Mary Jane Steib
Tax Assessor	Richard Kenny
Tax Collector	Christine Dehnz
Attorney	Steven Secare
Building	Anthony Avello
Comm Dev/Planning	NA
Engineering	John Mallon
Public Works	Steve Bortko
Police Chief	John Sgro
Emerg/Fire Director	Thomas Haskell

Housing & Construction
Housing Units, 2000*
Total	872
Median rent	$858
Median SF home value	$149,100

Permits for New Residential Construction
	Units	Value
Total, 2006	16	$2,609,200
Single family	16	$2,609,200
Total, 2007	9	$1,485,875
Single family	9	$1,485,875

Real Property Valuation, 2008
	Parcels	Valuation
Total	932	$298,288,600
Vacant	35	5,920,000
Residential	879	285,233,800
Commercial	18	7,134,800
Industrial	0	0
Apartments	0	0
Farm land	0	0
Farm homestead	0	0

Average Property Value & Tax, 2008
Residential value	$324,498
Property tax	$4,684
Tax credit/rebate	$875

Public Library
No public municipal library

Library statistics, 2007
Population served	NA
Full-time/total staff	NA/NA

	Total	Per capita
Holdings	NA	NA
Revenues	NA	NA
Expenditures	NA	NA
Annual visits	NA	NA
Internet terminals/annual users	NA/NA	

Public Safety
Number of officers, 2007	6

Crime	2006	2007
Total crimes	27	33
Violent	0	1
Murder	0	0
Rape	0	0
Robbery	0	1
Aggravated assault	0	0
Non-violent	27	32
Burglary	4	5
Larceny	22	26
Vehicle theft	1	1
Domestic violence	23	9
Arson	0	0
Total crime rate	13.3	16.2
Violent	0.0	0.5
Non-violent	13.3	15.7

Public School District
(for school year 2007-08 except as noted)

Toms River Regional School District
1144 Hooper Avenue
Toms River, NJ 08753
(732) 505-5510
Superintendent	Michael J. Ritacco
Number of schools	18
Grade plan	K-12
Enrollment	17,259
Attendance rate, '06-07	93.8%
Dropout rate	2.8%
Students per teacher	13.0
Per pupil expenditure	$10,496
Median faculty salary	$49,126
Median administrator salary	$114,200
Grade 12 enrollment	1,296
High school graduation rate	89.2%

Assessment test results
(percent scoring at proficient or advanced level)
	Language	Math
NJASK-Grade 3	93.4%	94.2%
GEPA-Grade 8	76.3%	87.3%
HSPA-High School	71.8%	83.4%

SAT Score Averages, 2006-07
Pct tested	Math	Verbal	Writing
NA	NA	NA	NA

Teacher Qualifications
Avg. years of experience	8
Highly-qualified teachers one subject/all subjects	99.5%/99.5%

No Child Left Behind
AYP, 2006-07	Meets Standards

Municipal Finance
State Aid Programs, 2009
Total aid	$267,109
CMPTRA	12,880
Energy tax receipts	247,551
Garden State Trust	0

General Budget, 2008
Total tax levy	$4,307,911
County levy	991,956
County taxes	817,997
County library	96,133
County health	39,140
County open space	38,686
School levy	1,944,016
Muni. levy	1,371,939
Misc. revenues	943,850

Taxes	2006	2007	2008
General tax rate per $100	1.355	1.404	1.444
County equalization ratio	110.61	95.59	92.82
Net valuation taxable	$288,886,400	$292,578,881	$298,450,972
State equalized value	$302,357,987	$315,198,921	$285,862,534

---

* US Census Bureau
** New Jersey Department of Labor

See Introduction for an explanation of all data sources.

Demographics & Socio-Economic Characteristics

(2000 US Census, except as noted)

Population

1980*	8,684
1990*	9,854
2000	10,880
Male	5,161
Female	5,719
2007 (estimate)*	11,231
Population density	2,857.8

Race & Hispanic Origin, 2000

Race

White	8,355
Black/African American	1,996
American Indian/Alaska Native	30
Asian	153
Native Hawaiian/Pacific Islander	2
Other race	132
Two or more races	212
Hispanic origin, total	396
Mexican	47
Puerto Rican	252
Cuban	16
Other Hispanic	81

Age & Nativity, 2000

Under 5 years	811
18 years and over	7,917
21 years and over	7,499
65 years and over	923
85 years and over	74
Median age	33.3
Native-born	10,530
Foreign-born	389

Educational Attainment, 2000

Population 25 years and over	6,959
Less than 9th grade	4.1%
High school grad or higher	80.7%
Bachelor's degree or higher	13.8%
Graduate degree	3.8%

Income & Poverty, 1999

Per capita income	$18,613
Median household income	$42,035
Median family income	$50,040
Persons in poverty	768
H'holds receiving public assistance	93
H'holds receiving social security	892

Households, 2000

Total households	4,214
With persons under 18	1,687
With persons over 65	743
Family households	2,742
Single-person households	1,172
Persons per household	2.58
Persons per family	3.18

Labor & Employment

Total civilian labor force, 2007**	6,188
Unemployment rate	5.9%
Total civilian labor force, 2000	5,844
Unemployment rate	5.9%

Employed persons 16 years and over by occupation, 2000

Managers & professionals	1,423
Service occupations	966
Sales & office occupations	1,732
Farming, fishing & forestry	4
Construction & maintenance	719
Production & transportation	653
Self-employed persons	237

General Information

Borough of Pine Hill
45 W 7th Ave
Pine Hill, NJ 08021
856-783-7400

Website	www.pinehillboronj.com
Year of incorporation	1929
Land/water area (sq. miles)	3.93/0.03
Form of government	Borough

Government

Legislative Districts

US Congressional	1
State Legislative	6

Local Officials, 2009

Mayor	Fred Costantino
Manager/Admin	NA
Clerk	Loretta Buchanan
Finance Dir	Thomas Cardis
Tax Assessor	Michael Raio
Tax Collector	Diane May
Attorney	John Kearney
Building	Raymond Hallworth
Comm Dev/Planning	NA
Engineering	Robert Malissa
Public Works	William Buchanan
Police Chief	Kenneth Cheeseman
Emerg/Fire Director	Richard Wright Sr

Housing & Construction

Housing Units, 2000*

Total	4,444
Median rent	$627
Median SF home value	$88,500

Permits for New Residential Construction

	Units	Value
Total, 2006	36	$2,790,888
Single family	36	$2,790,888
Total, 2007	27	$2,256,752
Single family	27	$2,256,752

Real Property Valuation, 2008

	Parcels	Valuation
Total	3,367	$275,640,600
Vacant	275	8,189,500
Residential	3,018	244,839,400
Commercial	48	7,667,600
Industrial	2	694,700
Apartments	6	13,288,900
Farm land	12	37,800
Farm homestead	6	922,700

Average Property Value & Tax, 2008

Residential value	$81,271
Property tax	$4,941
Tax credit/rebate	$969

Public Library

No public municipal library

Library statistics, 2007

Population served	NA
Full-time/total staff	NA/NA

	Total	Per capita
Holdings	NA	NA
Revenues	NA	NA
Expenditures	NA	NA
Annual visits	NA	NA
Internet terminals/annual users	NA/NA	

Public Safety

Number of officers, 2007	22

Crime	2006	2007
Total crimes	325	290
Violent	40	43
Murder	0	0
Rape	1	1
Robbery	13	11
Aggravated assault	26	31
Non-violent	285	247
Burglary	82	53
Larceny	183	175
Vehicle theft	20	19
Domestic violence	238	234
Arson	11	19
Total crime rate	28.7	25.7
Violent	3.5	3.8
Non-violent	25.2	21.9

Public School District

(for school year 2007-08 except as noted)

Pine Hill Borough School District
1003 Turnerville Road
Pine Hill, NJ 08021
(856) 783-6900

Superintendent	Kenneth Koczur
Number of schools	4
Grade plan	K-12
Enrollment	2,182
Attendance rate, '06-07	93.2%
Dropout rate	4.0%
Students per teacher	10.4
Per pupil expenditure	$13,499
Median faculty salary	$58,471
Median administrator salary	$97,593
Grade 12 enrollment	233
High school graduation rate	82.7%

Assessment test results

(percent scoring at proficient or advanced level)

	Language	Math
NJASK-Grade 3	89.6%	79.8%
GEPA-Grade 8	65.7%	79.1%
HSPA-High School	68.9%	75.6%

SAT Score Averages, 2006-07

Pct tested	Math	Verbal	Writing
55%	473	468	448

Teacher Qualifications

Avg. years of experience	13

Highly-qualified teachers
| one subject/all subjects | 99.5%/99.5% |

No Child Left Behind

AYP, 2006-07	Meets Standards

Municipal Finance

State Aid Programs, 2009

Total aid	$1,114,057
CMPTRA	337,316
Energy tax receipts	754,460
Garden State Trust	0

General Budget, 2008

Total tax levy	$16,783,039
County levy	3,478,413
County taxes	3,143,636
County library	225,374
County health	0
County open space	109,404
School levy	9,697,669
Muni. levy	3,606,957
Misc. revenues	3,740,824

Taxes

	2006	2007	2008
General tax rate per $100	5.763	5.905	6.080
County equalization ratio	64.35	55.08	50.47
Net valuation taxable	$274,276,720	$276,080,556	$276,075,443
State equalized value	$498,461,189	$546,578,930	$556,161,859

* US Census Bureau
** New Jersey Department of Labor

See Introduction for an explanation of all data sources.

Demographics & Socio-Economic Characteristics
(2000 US Census, except as noted)

Population
1980* 23
1990* 19
2000 20
  Male 12
  Female 8
2007 (estimate)* 23
  Population density 24.2

Race & Hispanic Origin, 2000
Race
White 20
Black/African American 0
American Indian/Alaska Native 0
Asian 0
Native Hawaiian/Pacific Islander 0
Other race 0
Two or more races 0
Hispanic origin, total 0
  Mexican 0
  Puerto Rican 0
  Cuban 0
  Other Hispanic 0

Age & Nativity, 2000
Under 5 years 0
18 years and over 15
21 years and over 15
65 years and over 8
85 years and over 0
  Median age 58.5
Native-born 16
Foreign-born 0

Educational Attainment, 2000
Population 25 years and over 12
Less than 9th grade 0.0%
High school grad or higher 83.3%
Bachelor's degree or higher 0.0%
Graduate degree 0.0%

Income & Poverty, 1999
Per capita income $23,981
Median household income $31,875
Median family income $65,625
Persons in poverty 0
H'holds receiving public assistance 2
H'holds receiving social security 6

Households, 2000
Total households 8
  With persons under 18 2
  With persons over 65 5
  Family households 7
  Single-person households 1
Persons per household 2.50
Persons per family 2.71

Labor & Employment
Total civilian labor force, 2007** 0
  Unemployment rate 0.0%
Total civilian labor force, 2000 5
  Unemployment rate 0.0%
Employed persons 16 years and over
  by occupation, 2000
  Managers & professionals 2
  Service occupations 0
  Sales & office occupations 2
  Farming, fishing & forestry 0
  Construction & maintenance 0
  Production & transportation 1
Self-employed persons 0

General Information
Borough of Pine Valley
1 Club Rd
Pine Valley, NJ 08021
856-783-7078
Website ....NA
Year of incorporation 1929
Land/water area (sq. miles) 0.95/0.01
Form of government ....Commission

Government
Legislative Districts
US Congressional 1
State Legislative 6

Local Officials, 2009
Mayor ....William Carson Jr
Manager/Admin ....NA
Clerk ....Patricia M. Porter
Finance Dir ....Patricia McCunney
Tax Assessor ....Sandra Elliott
Tax Collector ....Patricia McCunney
Attorney ....Joseph Betley
Building ....Richard Wright
Comm Dev/Planning ....NA
Engineering ....William Underwood
Public Works ....NA
Police Chief ....John Elder Jr
Fire/Emergency Dir ....Richard Wright

Housing & Construction
Housing Units, 2000*
Total 21
Median rent ....NA
Median SF home value $325,000

Permits for New Residential Construction
	Units	Value
Total, 2006	0	$0
Single family	0	$0
Total, 2007	1	$456,100
Single family	1	$456,100

Real Property Valuation, 2008
	Parcels	Valuation
Total	45	$38,752,800
Vacant	6	4,326,700
Residential	23	9,340,400
Commercial	16	25,085,700
Industrial	0	0
Apartments	0	0
Farm land	0	0
Farm homestead	0	0

Average Property Value & Tax, 2008
Residential value $406,104
Property tax $5,605
Tax credit/rebate $1,125

Public Library
No public municipal library

Library statistics, 2007
Population served ....NA
Full-time/total staff ....NA/NA

	Total	Per capita
Holdings	NA	NA
Revenues	NA	NA
Expenditures	NA	NA
Annual visits	NA	NA
Internet terminals/annual users	NA/NA	

Public Safety
Number of officers, 2007 4

Crime	2006	2007
Total crimes	0	1
Violent	0	0
Murder	0	0
Rape	0	0
Robbery	0	0
Aggravated assault	0	0
Non-violent	0	1
Burglary	0	0
Larceny	0	1
Vehicle theft	0	0
Domestic violence	0	0
Arson	0	0
Total crime rate	NA	43.5
Violent	NA	0.0
Non-violent	NA	43.5

Public School District
(for school year 2007-08 except as noted)

Pine Valley School District
Pine Valley Golf Club, PO Box B
Clementon, NJ 08021

No schools in district

Per pupil expenditure ....NA
Median faculty salary ....NA
Median administrator salary ....NA
Grade 12 enrollment ....NA
High school graduation rate ....NA

Assessment test results
(percent scoring at proficient or advanced level)

	Language	Math
NJASK-Grade 3	NA	NA
GEPA-Grade 8	NA	NA
HSPA-High School	NA	NA

SAT Score Averages, 2006-07
Pct tested	Math	Verbal	Writing
NA	NA	NA	NA

Teacher Qualifications
Avg. years of experience ....NA
Highly-qualified teachers
  one subject/all subjects ....NA/NA

No Child Left Behind
AYP, 2006-07 ....NA

Municipal Finance
State Aid Programs, 2009
Total aid $2,586
  CMPTRA 0
  Energy tax receipts 2,521
  Garden State Trust 0

General Budget, 2008
Total tax levy $535,712
  County levy 247,306
    County taxes 223,510
    County library 16,019
    County health 0
    County open space 7,776
  School levy 0
  Muni. levy 288,406
  Misc. revenues 110,913

Taxes	2006	2007	2008
General tax rate per $100	1.496	1.458	1.381
County equalization ratio	100	100	100.00
Net valuation taxable	$36,902,200	$38,003,952	$38,816,431
State equalized value	$36,583,356	$37,292,838	$38,300,237

* US Census Bureau
** New Jersey Department of Labor

See Introduction for an explanation of all data sources.

Demographics & Socio-Economic Characteristics

(2000 US Census, except as noted)

Population

1980*	42,223
1990*	47,089
2000	50,482
Male	24,979
Female	25,503
2007 (estimate)*	52,565
Population density	2,799.0

Race & Hispanic Origin, 2000

Race

White	24,642
Black/African American	10,254
American Indian/Alaska Native	104
Asian	12,519
Native Hawaiian/Pacific Islander	13
Other race	1,553
Two or more races	1,397
Hispanic origin, total	4,002
Mexican	185
Puerto Rican	1,060
Cuban	202
Other Hispanic	2,555

Age & Nativity, 2000

Under 5 years	3,127
18 years and over	39,430
21 years and over	35,541
65 years and over	4,374
85 years and over	361
Median age	33.3
Native-born	35,430
Foreign-born	15,052

Educational Attainment, 2000

Population 25 years and over	32,118
Less than 9th grade	4.0%
High school grad or higher	88.5%
Bachelor's degree or higher	40.5%
Graduate degree	16.6%

Income & Poverty, 1999

Per capita income	$26,321
Median household income	$68,721
Median family income	$75,218
Persons in poverty	1,769
H'holds receiving public assistance	259
H'holds receiving social security	3,136

Households, 2000

Total households	16,500
With persons under 18	6,264
With persons over 65	3,288
Family households	12,325
Single-person households	3,219
Persons per household	2.84
Persons per family	3.29

Labor & Employment

Total civilian labor force, 2007**	29,978
Unemployment rate	3.7%
Total civilian labor force, 2000	27,973
Unemployment rate	5.7%

Employed persons 16 years and over by occupation, 2000

Managers & professionals	12,068
Service occupations	2,310
Sales & office occupations	7,223
Farming, fishing & forestry	12
Construction & maintenance	1,545
Production & transportation	3,230
Self-employed persons	701

* US Census Bureau
** New Jersey Department of Labor
§ State Fiscal Year July 1–June 30

General Information

Township of Piscataway
Municipal Complex
455 Hoes Lane
Piscataway, NJ 08854
732-562-2300

Website	www.piscatawaynj.org
Year of incorporation	1693
Land/water area (sq. miles)	18.78/0.20
Form of government	Mayor-Council

Government

Legislative Districts

US Congressional	6
State Legislative	17

Local Officials, 2009

Mayor	Brian C. Wahler
Administrator	Lyn Evers
Clerk	Ann Gordon
Finance Dir	Daniel Lamptey
Tax Assessor	Lisa Stephens
Tax Collector	NA
Attorney	James L. Clarkin III
Building	Joseph Hoff
Planning	John Donnelly
Engineering	Charles Carley
Public Works	Henry Zanetti Jr
Police Chief	Kevin Harris
Emerg/Fire Director	Robert Gorr

Housing & Construction

Housing Units, 2000*

Total	16,946
Median rent	$829
Median SF home value	$170,800

Permits for New Residential Construction

	Units	Value
Total, 2006	63	$7,487,249
Single family	31	$6,242,249
Total, 2007	17	$3,098,185
Single family	17	$3,098,185

Real Property Valuation, 2008

	Parcels	Valuation
Total	13,898	$2,226,727,900
Vacant	422	31,227,300
Residential	13,008	1,441,450,200
Commercial	224	165,284,100
Industrial	196	488,495,900
Apartments	20	96,492,600
Farm land	14	202,600
Farm homestead	14	3,575,200

Average Property Value & Tax, 2008

Residential value	$110,968
Property tax	$6,267
Tax credit/rebate	$1,003

Public Library

Piscataway Township Libraries
500 Hoes Lane
Piscataway, NJ 08854
732-463-1633

Director	Anne Roman

Library statistics, 2007

Population served	50,482
Full-time/total staff	10/25

	Total	Per capita
Holdings	195,551	3.87
Revenues	$3,019,190	$59.81
Expenditures	$3,003,090	$59.49
Annual visits	421,158	8.34
Internet terminals/annual users	18/76,675	

Public Safety

Number of officers, 2007	92

Crime	2006	2007
Total crimes	894	930
Violent	75	85
Murder	0	1
Rape	4	2
Robbery	26	29
Aggravated assault	45	53
Non-violent	819	845
Burglary	180	158
Larceny	582	626
Vehicle theft	57	61
Domestic violence	323	330
Arson	13	7
Total crime rate	17.0	17.7
Violent	1.4	1.6
Non-violent	15.5	16.0

Public School District

(for school year 2007-08 except as noted)

Piscataway Township School District
1515 Stelton Road, PO Box 1332
Piscataway, NJ 08855
(732) 572-2289

Superintendent	Robert L. Copeland
Number of schools	10
Grade plan	K-12
Enrollment	6,979
Attendance rate, '06-07	94.3%
Dropout rate	0.4%
Students per teacher	11.6
Per pupil expenditure	$13,879
Median faculty salary	$64,449
Median administrator salary	$117,125
Grade 12 enrollment	502
High school graduation rate	98.9%

Assessment test results

(percent scoring at proficient or advanced level)

	Language	Math
NJASK-Grade 3	91.1%	88.7%
GEPA-Grade 8	73.8%	83.1%
HSPA-High School	84.6%	84.7%

SAT Score Averages, 2006-07

Pct tested	Math	Verbal	Writing
95%	500	473	473

Teacher Qualifications

Avg. years of experience	7
Highly-qualified teachers one subject/all subjects	100%/100%

No Child Left Behind

AYP, 2006-07	Meets Standards

Municipal Finance§

State Aid Programs, 2009

Total aid	$7,553,488
CMPTRA	1,999,400
Energy tax receipts	5,365,250
Garden State Trust	0

General Budget, 2008

Total tax levy	$126,179,851
County levy	19,428,981
County taxes	17,400,459
County library	0
County health	0
County open space	2,028,522
School levy	78,217,642
Muni. levy	28,533,228
Misc. revenues	19,145,696

Taxes	2006	2007	2008
General tax rate per $100	5.02	5.54	5.648
County equalization ratio	38.97	34.23	32.67
Net valuation taxable	$2,248,168,700	$2,236,016,835	$2,234,380,041
State equalized value	$6,575,747,444	$6,828,903,829	$6,957,489,532

See Introduction for an explanation of all data sources.

Demographics & Socio-Economic Characteristics

(2000 US Census, except as noted)

Population

1980*	9,744
1990*	9,365
2000	9,331
Male	4,338
Female	4,993
2007 (estimate)*	9,219
Population density	4,025.8

Race & Hispanic Origin, 2000

Race

White	9,066
Black/African American	85
American Indian/Alaska Native	11
Asian	58
Native Hawaiian/Pacific Islander	1
Other race	21
Two or more races	89
Hispanic origin, total	132
Mexican	36
Puerto Rican	49
Cuban	8
Other Hispanic	39

Age & Nativity, 2000

Under 5 years	542
18 years and over	6,977
21 years and over	6,628
65 years and over	1,404
85 years and over	248
Median age	38.1
Native-born	9,125
Foreign-born	206

Educational Attainment, 2000

Population 25 years and over	6,219
Less than 9th grade	3.4%
High school grad or higher	87.9%
Bachelor's degree or higher	31.7%
Graduate degree	10.3%

Income & Poverty, 1999

Per capita income	$22,133
Median household income	$49,743
Median family income	$59,419
Persons in poverty	526
H'holds receiving public assistance	32
H'holds receiving social security	955

Households, 2000

Total households	3,473
With persons under 18	1,263
With persons over 65	898
Family households	2,431
Single-person households	903
Persons per household	2.60
Persons per family	3.15

Labor & Employment

Total civilian labor force, 2007**	5,490
Unemployment rate	5.8%
Total civilian labor force, 2000	4,892
Unemployment rate	9.6%

Employed persons 16 years and over by occupation, 2000

Managers & professionals	1,891
Service occupations	494
Sales & office occupations	1,074
Farming, fishing & forestry	4
Construction & maintenance	452
Production & transportation	507
Self-employed persons	278

* US Census Bureau
** New Jersey Department of Labor

General Information

Borough of Pitman
110 S Broadway
Pitman, NJ 08071
856-589-3522

Website	www.pitman.org
Year of incorporation	1905
Land/water area (sq. miles)	2.29/0.03
Form of government	Borough

Government

Legislative Districts

US Congressional	2
State Legislative	4

Local Officials, 2009

Mayor	Micahael Batten
Manager	DawnMarie Human
Clerk	Judith O'Donnell (Actg)
Finance Dir	Stephen Considine
Tax Assessor	Ronald Fijalkowski
Tax Collector	Beth A. Walls
Attorney	Brian Duffield
Building	Jeffrey Kier
Planning	Henry Ryder
Engineering	Fralinger Engineering
Public Works	Thomas Brown
Police Chief	Scott Campbell
Emerg/Fire Director	D. Clark Pierpont

Housing & Construction

Housing Units, 2000*

Total	3,653
Median rent	$654
Median SF home value	$118,500

Permits for New Residential Construction

	Units	Value
Total, 2006	1	$100,000
Single family	1	$100,000
Total, 2007	0	$0
Single family	0	$0

Real Property Valuation, 2008

	Parcels	Valuation
Total	3,204	$382,314,000
Vacant	56	1,920,000
Residential	2,994	325,903,100
Commercial	136	24,051,100
Industrial	4	22,074,500
Apartments	10	8,165,500
Farm land	3	10,100
Farm homestead	1	189,700

Average Property Value & Tax, 2008

Residential value	$108,879
Property tax	$5,522
Tax credit/rebate	$971

Public Library

McCowan Memorial Library
15 Pitman Ave
Pitman, NJ 08071
856-589-1656

Director	Sharon Furgason

Library statistics, 2007

Population served	9,331
Full-time/total staff	1/5

	Total	Per capita
Holdings	41,542	4.45
Revenues	$358,818	$38.45
Expenditures	$338,348	$36.26
Annual visits	98,117	10.52
Internet terminals/annual users	6/9,650	

Public Safety

Number of officers, 2007	14

Crime	2006	2007
Total crimes	152	129
Violent	3	4
Murder	1	0
Rape	0	0
Robbery	1	0
Aggravated assault	1	4
Non-violent	149	125
Burglary	10	7
Larceny	132	110
Vehicle theft	7	8
Domestic violence	103	92
Arson	1	2
Total crime rate	16.4	14.0
Violent	0.3	0.4
Non-violent	16.1	13.6

Public School District

(for school year 2007-08 except as noted)

Pitman School District
420 Hudson Ave
Pitman, NJ 08071
(856) 589-2145

Superintendent	Thomas Shulte'
Number of schools	5
Grade plan	K-12
Enrollment	1,605
Attendance rate, '06-07	93.9%
Dropout rate	2.1%
Students per teacher	10.5
Per pupil expenditure	$13,320
Median faculty salary	$54,870
Median administrator salary	$101,689
Grade 12 enrollment	126
High school graduation rate	94.0%

Assessment test results

(percent scoring at proficient or advanced level)

	Language	Math
NJASK-Grade 3	92.9%	92.9%
GEPA-Grade 8	73.0%	85.6%
HSPA-High School	93.6%	90.4%

SAT Score Averages, 2006-07

Pct tested	Math	Verbal	Writing
79%	528	504	492

Teacher Qualifications

Avg. years of experience	10
Highly-qualified teachers one subject/all subjects	100%/100%

No Child Left Behind

AYP, 2006-07	Meets Standards

Municipal Finance

State Aid Programs, 2009

Total aid	$823,152
CMPTRA	318,030
Energy tax receipts	484,543
Garden State Trust	0

General Budget, 2008

Total tax levy	$19,408,571
County levy	4,052,796
County taxes	3,758,279
County library	0
County health	0
County open space	294,517
School levy	10,743,183
Muni. levy	4,612,593
Misc. revenues	2,708,055

Taxes	2006	2007	2008
General tax rate per $100	4.549	4.862	5.073
County equalization ratio	65.59	57.59	52.22
Net valuation taxable	$380,347,900	$381,311,418	$382,657,357
State equalized value	$660,838,571	$729,872,740	$757,400,783

See Introduction for an explanation of all data sources.

Demographics & Socio-Economic Characteristics

(2000 US Census, except as noted)

Population

1980*	6,954
1990*	8,121
2000	8,893
Male	4,403
Female	4,490
2007 (estimate)*	9,434
Population density	208.8

Race & Hispanic Origin, 2000

Race
White	7,838
Black/African American	715
American Indian/Alaska Native	34
Asian	52
Native Hawaiian/Pacific Islander	4
Other race	115
Two or more races	135
Hispanic origin, total	303
Mexican	25
Puerto Rican	188
Cuban	1
Other Hispanic	89

Age & Nativity, 2000

Under 5 years	472
18 years and over	6,523
21 years and over	6,140
65 years and over	1,014
85 years and over	108
Median age	38.1
Native-born	8,719
Foreign-born	174

Educational Attainment, 2000

Population 25 years and over	5,827
Less than 9th grade	8.4%
High school grad or higher	78.8%
Bachelor's degree or higher	16.4%
Graduate degree	4.4%

Income & Poverty, 1999

Per capita income	$21,624
Median household income	$56,687
Median family income	$63,266
Persons in poverty	434
H'holds receiving public assistance	46
H'holds receiving social security	746

Households, 2000

Total households	3,020
With persons under 18	1,288
With persons over 65	667
Family households	2,421
Single-person households	490
Persons per household	2.90
Persons per family	3.23

Labor & Employment

Total civilian labor force, 2007**	4,731
Unemployment rate	4.3%
Total civilian labor force, 2000	4,656
Unemployment rate	6.3%

Employed persons 16 years and over by occupation, 2000
Managers & professionals	1,240
Service occupations	637
Sales & office occupations	983
Farming, fishing & forestry	24
Construction & maintenance	618
Production & transportation	863
Self-employed persons	275

* US Census Bureau
** New Jersey Department of Labor

General Information

Township of Pittsgrove
989 Centerton Rd
Pittsgrove, NJ 08318
856-358-2300

Website	www.pittsgrovetownship.com
Year of incorporation	1769
Land/water area (sq. miles)	45.19/0.74
Form of government	Township

Government

Legislative Districts

US Congressional	2
State Legislative	3

Local Officials, 2009

Mayor	Peter Voros
Manager	Deborah Turner-Fox
Clerk	Constance Garton
Finance Dir	Donna Jacobs
Tax Assessor	Lisa Perella
Tax Collector	Jennafer Hernandez
Attorney	Adam I. Telsey
Building	James Grasso
Planning	Nancy Huster
Engineering	Mark Brunermer
Public Works	Harry E. Snyder
Public Safety Dir	Harry E. Snyder
Fire/Emergency Dir	NA

Housing & Construction

Housing Units, 2000*

Total	3,155
Median rent	$728
Median SF home value	$125,600

Permits for New Residential Construction

	Units	Value
Total, 2006	30	$3,577,717
Single family	30	$3,577,717
Total, 2007	13	$2,293,860
Single family	13	$2,293,860

Real Property Valuation, 2008

	Parcels	Valuation
Total	3,999	$598,822,500
Vacant	453	16,892,800
Residential	2,552	471,670,200
Commercial	82	51,371,500
Industrial	0	0
Apartments	0	0
Farm land	625	5,236,200
Farm homestead	287	53,651,800

Average Property Value & Tax, 2008

Residential value	$185,038
Property tax	$5,344
Tax credit/rebate	$998

Public Library

No public municipal library

Library statistics, 2007

Population served	NA
Full-time/total staff	NA/NA

	Total	Per capita
Holdings	NA	NA
Revenues	NA	NA
Expenditures	NA	NA
Annual visits	NA	NA
Internet terminals/annual users	NA/NA	

Public Safety

Number of officers, 2007		0

Crime	2006	2007
Total crimes	164	164
Violent	8	13
Murder	0	0
Rape	1	0
Robbery	0	2
Aggravated assault	7	11
Non-violent	156	151
Burglary	51	57
Larceny	93	79
Vehicle theft	12	15
Domestic violence	3	44
Arson	2	3
Total crime rate	17.3	17.2
Violent	0.8	1.4
Non-violent	16.5	15.8

Public School District

(for school year 2007-08 except as noted)

Pittsgrove Township School District
1076 Almond Road
Pittsgrove, NJ 08318
(856) 358-3094

Superintendent	Henry Bermann
Number of schools	4
Grade plan	K-12
Enrollment	1,876
Attendance rate, '06-07	94.5%
Dropout rate	1.9%
Students per teacher	12.1
Per pupil expenditure	$11,505
Median faculty salary	$53,980
Median administrator salary	$78,820
Grade 12 enrollment	159
High school graduation rate	92.9%

Assessment test results

(percent scoring at proficient or advanced level)
	Language	Math
NJASK-Grade 3	69.5%	77.6%
GEPA-Grade 8	65.3%	83.0%
HSPA-High School	79.8%	82.4%

SAT Score Averages, 2006-07

Pct tested	Math	Verbal	Writing
78%	453	452	443

Teacher Qualifications

Avg. years of experience	13
Highly-qualified teachers one subject/all subjects	100%/99.0%

No Child Left Behind

AYP, 2006-07	Meets Standards

Municipal Finance

State Aid Programs, 2009

Total aid	$908,068
CMPTRA	152,964
Energy tax receipts	706,698
Garden State Trust	15,900

General Budget, 2008

Total tax levy	$17,341,401
County levy	6,913,510
County taxes	6,764,346
County library	0
County health	0
County open space	149,164
School levy	8,813,214
Muni. levy	1,614,677
Misc. revenues	2,440,390

Taxes

	2006	2007	2008
General tax rate per $100	2.75	2.822	2.889
County equalization ratio	97.72	87.44	80.78
Net valuation taxable	$582,260,600	$594,170,863	$600,450,594
State equalized value	$667,712,610	$735,143,635	$479,828,567

See Introduction for an explanation of all data sources.

Demographics & Socio-Economic Characteristics
(2000 US Census, except as noted)

Population
1980*	45,555
1990*	46,567
2000	47,829
Male	23,393
Female	24,436
2007 (estimate)*	46,486
Population density	7,696.4

Race & Hispanic Origin, 2000
Race
White	10,258
Black/African American	29,550
American Indian/Alaska Native	195
Asian	447
Native Hawaiian/Pacific Islander	46
Other race	5,156
Two or more races	2,177
Hispanic origin, total	12,033
Mexican	807
Puerto Rican	1,782
Cuban	145
Other Hispanic	9,299

Age & Nativity, 2000
Under 5 years	3,770
18 years and over	34,662
21 years and over	32,669
65 years and over	4,402
85 years and over	566
Median age	32.8
Native-born	36,502
Foreign-born	11,327

Educational Attainment, 2000
Population 25 years and over	29,821
Less than 9th grade	12.3%
High school grad or higher	70.6%
Bachelor's degree or higher	18.5%
Graduate degree	6.2%

Income & Poverty, 1999
Per capita income	$19,052
Median household income	$46,683
Median family income	$50,774
Persons in poverty	7,476
H'holds receiving public assistance	892
H'holds receiving social security	3,573

Households, 2000
Total households	15,137
With persons under 18	6,748
With persons over 65	3,195
Family households	10,898
Single-person households	3,194
Persons per household	3.10
Persons per family	3.49

Labor & Employment
Total civilian labor force, 2007**	25,098
Unemployment rate	6.0%
Total civilian labor force, 2000	24,966
Unemployment rate	7.9%

Employed persons 16 years and over by occupation, 2000
Managers & professionals	5,518
Service occupations	4,059
Sales & office occupations	6,272
Farming, fishing & forestry	33
Construction & maintenance	1,935
Production & transportation	5,180
Self-employed persons	639

* US Census Bureau
** New Jersey Department of Labor
§ State Fiscal Year July 1–June 30

General Information
City of Plainfield
515 Watchung Ave
Plainfield, NJ 07060
908-753-3000

Website	www.plainfield.com
Year of incorporation	1869
Land/water area (sq. miles)	6.04/0.00
Form of government	Special Charter

Government
Legislative Districts
US Congressional	6
State Legislative	22

Local Officials, 2009
Mayor	Sharon Robinson-Briggs
Manager	Marc Dashield
Clerk	Laddie Wyatt
Finance Dir	(vacant)
Tax Assessor	Tracy Bennett
Tax Collector	Maria Glavan
Attorney	Daniel Williamson
Building	Oscar L. Turk
Planning	Bill Nierstedt
Engineering	Robert Bucco
Public Works	Jennifer Wenson-Maier
Police Chief	NA
Emerg/Fire Director	Cecil Allen

Housing & Construction
Housing Units, 2000*
Total	16,180
Median rent	$726
Median SF home value	$137,500

Permits for New Residential Construction
	Units	Value
Total, 2006	25	$2,650,902
Single family	18	$2,587,827
Total, 2007	7	$444,500
Single family	2	$89,500

Real Property Valuation, 2008
	Parcels	Valuation
Total	10,316	$1,264,861,671
Vacant	379	8,043,450
Residential	9,130	1,032,202,621
Commercial	632	137,000,400
Industrial	62	24,600,300
Apartments	113	63,014,900
Farm land	0	0
Farm homestead	0	0

Average Property Value & Tax, 2008
Residential value	$113,056
Property tax	$6,759
Tax credit/rebate	$1,091

Public Library
Plainfield Public Library
800 Park Ave
Plainfield, NJ 07060
908-757-1111

Director	Joseph Hugh Da Rold

Library statistics, 2007
Population served	47,829
Full-time/total staff	7/20

	Total	Per capita
Holdings	180,450	3.77
Revenues	$2,221,095	$46.44
Expenditures	$2,308,002	$48.26
Annual visits	210,065	4.39
Internet terminals/annual users	31/34,128	

Public Safety
Number of officers, 2007	150

Crime	2006	2007
Total crimes	2,189	1,856
Violent	571	485
Murder	10	4
Rape	12	9
Robbery	260	240
Aggravated assault	289	232
Non-violent	1,618	1,371
Burglary	495	229
Larceny	948	952
Vehicle theft	175	190
Domestic violence	692	754
Arson	18	10
Total crime rate	45.9	39.2
Violent	12.0	10.2
Non-violent	34.0	29.0

Public School District
(for school year 2007-08 except as noted)

Plainfield School District
1200 Myrtle Avenue
Plainfield, NJ 07060
(908) 731-4335

Superintendent	Steve Gallon III
Number of schools	13
Grade plan	K-12
Enrollment	6,462
Attendance rate, '06-07	93.2%
Dropout rate	3.5%
Students per teacher	8.9
Per pupil expenditure	$15,346
Median faculty salary	$66,826
Median administrator salary	$107,295
Grade 12 enrollment	364
High school graduation rate	90.5%

Assessment test results
(percent scoring at proficient or advanced level)
	Language	Math
NJASK-Grade 3	65.3%	62.9%
GEPA-Grade 8	29.2%	48.7%
HSPA-High School	40.5%	59.1%

SAT Score Averages, 2006-07
Pct tested	Math	Verbal	Writing
57%	390	381	375

Teacher Qualifications
Avg. years of experience	10
Highly-qualified teachers one subject/all subjects	93.5%/93.5%

No Child Left Behind
AYP, 2006-07	Needs Improvement

Municipal Finance§
State Aid Programs, 2009
Total aid	$9,300,517
CMPTRA	5,411,843
Energy tax receipts	3,842,171
Garden State Trust	0

General Budget, 2008
Total tax levy	$75,898,384
County levy	12,043,615
County taxes	11,517,292
County library	0
County health	0
County open space	526,323
School levy	18,516,338
Muni. levy	45,338,431
Misc. revenues	26,851,601

Taxes
Taxes	2006	2007	2008
General tax rate per $100	5.407	5.668	5.979
County equalization ratio	44.98	40.03	36.48
Net valuation taxable	$1,270,415,621	$1,272,717,301	$1,269,528,809
State equalized value	$3,179,979,557	$3,480,060,844	$3,620,623,888

Demographics & Socio-Economic Characteristics

(2000 US Census, except as noted)

Population
1980*	5,605
1990*	14,213
2000	20,215
Male	10,229
Female	9,986
2007 (estimate)*	21,196
Population density	1,790.2

Race & Hispanic Origin, 2000
Race
White	11,765
Black/African American	1,533
American Indian/Alaska Native	20
Asian	6,168
Native Hawaiian/Pacific Islander	2
Other race	275
Two or more races	452
Hispanic origin, total	937
Mexican	79
Puerto Rican	284
Cuban	77
Other Hispanic	497

Age & Nativity, 2000
Under 5 years	1,428
18 years and over	15,239
21 years and over	14,873
65 years and over	853
85 years and over	83
Median age	32.9
Native-born	13,244
Foreign-born	6,971

Educational Attainment, 2000
Population 25 years and over	13,947
Less than 9th grade	0.9%
High school grad or higher	97.3%
Bachelor's degree or higher	70.3%
Graduate degree	31.7%

Income & Poverty, 1999
Per capita income	$38,982
Median household income	$72,097
Median family income	$88,783
Persons in poverty	601
H'holds receiving public assistance	57
H'holds receiving social security	589

Households, 2000
Total households	8,742
With persons under 18	2,991
With persons over 65	644
Family households	5,123
Single-person households	2,966
Persons per household	2.30
Persons per family	3.06

Labor & Employment
Total civilian labor force, 2007**	13,563
Unemployment rate	2.2%
Total civilian labor force, 2000	12,412
Unemployment rate	2.3%

Employed persons 16 years and over by occupation, 2000
Managers & professionals	8,389
Service occupations	619
Sales & office occupations	2,479
Farming, fishing & forestry	0
Construction & maintenance	252
Production & transportation	389
Self-employed persons	316

* US Census Bureau
** New Jersey Department of Labor

General Information
Township of Plainsboro
641 Plainsboro Rd
Plainsboro, NJ 08536
609-799-0909
Website	www.plainsboronj.com
Year of incorporation	1919
Land/water area (sq. miles)	11.84/0.41
Form of government	Township

Government
Legislative Districts
US Congressional	12
State Legislative	14

Local Officials, 2009
Mayor	Peter Cantu
Manager	Robert Sheehan
Clerk	Carol J. Torres
Finance Dir	Gregory Mayers
Tax Assessor	Thomas Mancuso
Tax Collector	Mary Testori
Attorney	Michael Herbert
Code Enforcement	Tom Boyd
Planning	Lester Varga
Engineering	Davids Samuels
Public Works	Neil Blitz
Police Chief	Elizabeth Bondurant
Emerg/Fire Director	Brian Stultz

Housing & Construction
Housing Units, 2000*
Total	9,133
Median rent	$942
Median SF home value	$257,100

Permits for New Residential Construction
	Units	Value
Total, 2006	35	$4,068,700
Single family	35	$4,068,700
Total, 2007	11	$1,349,700
Single family	11	$1,349,700

Real Property Valuation, 2008
	Parcels	Valuation
Total	5,842	$3,674,769,100
Vacant	385	51,891,900
Residential	5,260	2,088,361,900
Commercial	94	1,156,238,100
Industrial	4	60,501,400
Apartments	17	306,136,000
Farm land	64	833,800
Farm homestead	18	10,806,000

Average Property Value & Tax, 2008
Residential value	$397,720
Property tax	$7,868
Tax credit/rebate	$1,111

Public Library
Plainsboro Free Public Library
641 Plainsboro Rd
Plainsboro, NJ 08536
609-275-2897
Director	Jinny Baeckler

Library statistics, 2007
Population served	20,215
Full-time/total staff	4/9

	Total	Per capita
Holdings	103,462	5.12
Revenues	$1,425,729	$70.53
Expenditures	$1,312,481	$64.93
Annual visits	203,619	10.07
Internet terminals/annual users	8/59,326	

Public Safety
Number of officers, 2007	34

Crime	2006	2007
Total crimes	225	199
Violent	13	10
Murder	0	0
Rape	3	2
Robbery	1	4
Aggravated assault	9	4
Non-violent	212	189
Burglary	35	21
Larceny	163	161
Vehicle theft	14	7
Domestic violence	60	69
Arson	10	1
Total crime rate	10.5	9.4
Violent	0.6	0.5
Non-violent	9.9	8.9

Public School District
(for school year 2007-08 except as noted)

West Windsor-Plainsboro Reg. School Dist.
505 Village Road West, PO Box 505
Princeton Junction, NJ 08550
(609) 716-5000
Chief School Admin	Victoria Kniewel
Number of schools	10
Grade plan	K-12
Enrollment	9,669
Attendance rate, '06-07	96.5%
Dropout rate	0.1%
Students per teacher	11.4
Per pupil expenditure	$14,421
Median faculty salary	$74,700
Median administrator salary	$119,185
Grade 12 enrollment	714
High school graduation rate	99.0%

Assessment test results
(percent scoring at proficient or advanced level)
	Language	Math
NJASK-Grade 3	94.5%	95.8%
GEPA-Grade 8	91.3%	95.4%
HSPA-High School	91.4%	94.4%

SAT Score Averages, 2006-07
Pct tested	Math	Verbal	Writing
NA	NA	NA	NA

Teacher Qualifications
Avg. years of experience	13
Highly-qualified teachers one subject/all subjects	100%/100%

No Child Left Behind
AYP, 2006-07	Meets Standards

Municipal Finance
State Aid Programs, 2009
Total aid	$2,120,638
CMPTRA	33,347
Energy tax receipts	2,034,212
Garden State Trust	52

General Budget, 2008
Total tax levy	$72,835,426
County levy	10,951,915
County taxes	9,794,740
County library	0
County health	0
County open space	1,157,175
School levy	49,855,627
Muni. levy	12,027,885
Misc. revenues	9,137,108

Taxes
	2006	2007	2008
General tax rate per $100	2	2.06	1.979
County equalization ratio	98.68	92.63	97.29
Net valuation taxable	$3,649,446,500	$3,681,065,681	$3,681,690,898
State equalized value	$4,482,555,383	$3,783,419,991	$3,759,749,719

Demographics & Socio-Economic Characteristics
(2000 US Census, except as noted)

Population
1980*	13,435
1990*	16,027
2000	19,012
Male	8,925
Female	10,087
2007 (estimate)*	18,814
Population density	3,255.0

Race & Hispanic Origin, 2000
Race
White	4,755
Black/African American	10,969
American Indian/Alaska Native	54
Asian	371
Native Hawaiian/Pacific Islander	5
Other race	2,084
Two or more races	774
Hispanic origin, total	4,158
Mexican	451
Puerto Rican	2,085
Cuban	61
Other Hispanic	1,561

Age & Nativity, 2000
Under 5 years	1,481
18 years and over	13,234
21 years and over	12,481
65 years and over	2,124
85 years and over	373
Median age	32.7
Native-born	16,639
Foreign-born	2,457

Educational Attainment, 2000
Population 25 years and over	11,583
Less than 9th grade	7.5%
High school grad or higher	70.1%
Bachelor's degree or higher	10.2%
Graduate degree	3.1%

Income & Poverty, 1999
Per capita income	$17,668
Median household income	$36,913
Median family income	$40,016
Persons in poverty	2,939
H'holds receiving public assistance	286
H'holds receiving social security	1,705

Households, 2000
Total households	6,402
With persons under 18	2,838
With persons over 65	1,421
Family households	4,365
Single-person households	1,568
Persons per household	2.90
Persons per family	3.44

Labor & Employment
Total civilian labor force, 2007**	8,873
Unemployment rate	8.0%
Total civilian labor force, 2000	8,500
Unemployment rate	10.2%

Employed persons 16 years and over by occupation, 2000
Managers & professionals	1,347
Service occupations	2,979
Sales & office occupations	1,979
Farming, fishing & forestry	33
Construction & maintenance	466
Production & transportation	833
Self-employed persons	140

‡ Branch of county library
* US Census Bureau
** New Jersey Department of Labor

General Information
City of Pleasantville
18 N 1st St
Pleasantville, NJ 08232
609-484-3600
Website	www.pleasantville-nj.org
Year of incorporation	1914
Land/water area (sq. miles)	5.78/1.55
Form of government	City

Government
Legislative Districts
US Congressional	2
State Legislative	2

Local Officials, 2009
Mayor	Jesse Tweedle Sr
Manager	Marvin D. Hopkins
Clerk	Gloria V. Griffin
Finance Dir	Ted Freedman
Tax Assessor	Brian Vigue
Tax Collector	Flor Roman
Attorney	Alfred Scerni Jr
Building	Kevin Cain
Comm Dev/Planning	NA
Engineering	Remington & Vernick
Public Works	Robert Oglesby
Police Chief	Duane Comeaux
Emerg/Fire Director	Leroy Borden

Housing & Construction
Housing Units, 2000*
Total	7,042
Median rent	$715
Median SF home value	$86,500

Permits for New Residential Construction
	Units	Value
Total, 2006	80	$7,210,448
Single family	54	$5,588,998
Total, 2007	94	$8,654,186
Single family	94	$8,654,186

Real Property Valuation, 2008
	Parcels	Valuation
Total	5,996	$554,987,300
Vacant	465	13,849,800
Residential	5,072	362,853,000
Commercial	354	99,747,900
Industrial	82	51,727,400
Apartments	23	26,809,200
Farm land	0	0
Farm homestead	0	0

Average Property Value & Tax, 2008
Residential value	$71,540
Property tax	$3,310
Tax credit/rebate	$759

Public Library
Pleasantville Branch Library‡
132 W Washington Ave
Pleasantville, NJ 08232
609-641-1778
Branch Librarian | Pamela Saunders

Library statistics, 2007
see Atlantic County profile
for library system statistics

Public Safety
Number of officers, 2007	64

Crime	2006	2007
Total crimes	795	822
Violent	180	181
Murder	1	3
Rape	7	3
Robbery	75	81
Aggravated assault	97	94
Non-violent	615	641
Burglary	196	208
Larceny	365	380
Vehicle theft	54	53
Domestic violence	488	440
Arson	9	2
Total crime rate	41.8	43.3
Violent	9.5	9.5
Non-violent	32.3	33.8

Public School District
(for school year 2007-08 except as noted)

Pleasantville School District
900 W. Leeds Avenue, PO Box 960
Pleasantville, NJ 08232
(609) 383-6800
Superintendent	Clarence Alston
Number of schools	6
Grade plan	K-12
Enrollment	3,478
Attendance rate, '06-07	94.5%
Dropout rate	2.2%
Students per teacher	7.5
Per pupil expenditure	$15,606
Median faculty salary	$46,376
Median administrator salary	$100,000
Grade 12 enrollment	220
High school graduation rate	88.2%

Assessment test results
(percent scoring at proficient or advanced level)
	Language	Math
NJASK-Grade 3	79.5%	78.3%
GEPA-Grade 8	38.0%	52.8%
HSPA-High School	29.9%	54.4%

SAT Score Averages, 2006-07
Pct tested	Math	Verbal	Writing
69%	376	349	359

Teacher Qualifications
Avg. years of experience	6
Highly-qualified teachers one subject/all subjects	97.5%/97.5%

No Child Left Behind
AYP, 2006-07 | Needs Improvement

Municipal Finance
State Aid Programs, 2009
Total aid	$2,491,707
CMPTRA	929,111
Energy tax receipts	1,562,345
Garden State Trust	144

General Budget, 2008
Total tax levy	$26,062,798
County levy	3,482,061
County taxes	2,741,431
County library	352,820
County health	144,372
County open space	243,438
School levy	7,798,057
Muni. levy	14,782,680
Misc. revenues	10,689,260

Taxes	2006	2007	2008
General tax rate per $100	4.262	4.466	4.629
County equalization ratio	64.95	54.49	46.41
Net valuation taxable	$540,682,600	$556,480,599	$563,238,853
State equalized value	$1,003,172,440	$1,188,199,311	$1,282,327,081

Demographics & Socio-Economic Characteristics

(2000 US Census, except as noted)

Population

1980*	4,674
1990*	6,005
2000	7,275
Male	3,620
Female	3,655
2007 (estimate)*	8,177
Population density	204.3

Race & Hispanic Origin, 2000

Race

White	6,831
Black/African American	167
American Indian/Alaska Native	10
Asian	53
Native Hawaiian/Pacific Islander	1
Other race	99
Two or more races	114
Hispanic origin, total	280
Mexican	103
Puerto Rican	132
Cuban	17
Other Hispanic	28

Age & Nativity, 2000

Under 5 years	501
18 years and over	5,204
21 years and over	4,960
65 years and over	621
85 years and over	49
Median age	36.0
Native-born	6,940
Foreign-born	335

Educational Attainment, 2000

Population 25 years and over	4,720
Less than 9th grade	5.5%
High school grad or higher	84.2%
Bachelor's degree or higher	17.4%
Graduate degree	4.2%

Income & Poverty, 1999

Per capita income	$22,433
Median household income	$61,357
Median family income	$62,255
Persons in poverty	367
H'holds receiving public assistance	73
H'holds receiving social security	539

Households, 2000

Total households	2,510
With persons under 18	1,116
With persons over 65	465
Family households	2,002
Single-person households	400
Persons per household	2.90
Persons per family	3.22

Labor & Employment

Total civilian labor force, 2007**	4,601
Unemployment rate	2.9%
Total civilian labor force, 2000	3,871
Unemployment rate	3.2%

Employed persons 16 years and over by occupation, 2000

Managers & professionals	1,133
Service occupations	475
Sales & office occupations	1,028
Farming, fishing & forestry	43
Construction & maintenance	504
Production & transportation	563
Self-employed persons	182

‡ Branch of county library
* US Census Bureau
** New Jersey Department of Labor

General Information

Township of Plumsted
121 Evergreen Rd
New Egypt, NJ 08533
609-758-2241

Website	www.plumsted.org
Year of incorporation	1845
Land/water area (sq. miles)	40.02/0.20
Form of government	Township

Government

Legislative Districts

US Congressional	4
State Legislative	30

Local Officials, 2009

Mayor	Ronald S. Dancer
Manager	Richard Kachmar
Clerk	Dorothy Hendrickson
Finance Dir	June Madden
Tax Assessor	Maureen Francis
Tax Collector	Danielle Peacock
Attorney	Gilmore & Monahan
Building	Glenn Riccardi
Comm Dev/Planning	NA
Engineering	John J. Mallon
Public Works	NA
Police Chief	Michael Lynch
Emerg/Fire Director	William Allen

Housing & Construction

Housing Units, 2000*

Total	2,628
Median rent	$697
Median SF home value	$150,800

Permits for New Residential Construction

	Units	Value
Total, 2006	30	$3,391,799
Single family	30	$3,391,799
Total, 2007	21	$3,094,442
Single family	19	$3,053,442

Real Property Valuation, 2008

	Parcels	Valuation
Total	3,092	$1,080,809,200
Vacant	333	34,911,200
Residential	2,391	917,640,700
Commercial	93	60,424,600
Industrial	8	9,030,500
Apartments	8	4,079,600
Farm land	149	2,275,400
Farm homestead	110	52,447,200

Average Property Value & Tax, 2008

Residential value	$387,880
Property tax	$5,209
Tax credit/rebate	$903

Public Library

Plumsted Branch Library‡
119 Evergreen Rd
New Egypt, NJ 08533
609-758-7888

Branch Librarian	Gigi Hayes

Library statistics, 2007

see Ocean County profile
for library system statistics

Public Safety

Number of officers, 2007 13

Crime	2006	2007
Total crimes	71	91
Violent	5	4
Murder	0	0
Rape	2	0
Robbery	0	1
Aggravated assault	3	3
Non-violent	66	87
Burglary	15	19
Larceny	36	60
Vehicle theft	15	8
Domestic violence	11	11
Arson	2	0
Total crime rate	8.8	11.2
Violent	0.6	0.5
Non-violent	8.2	10.7

Public School District

(for school year 2007-08 except as noted)

Plumsted Township School District
117 Evergreen Road
New Egypt, NJ 08533
(609) 758-6800

Superintendent	Mark DeMareo
Number of schools	4
Grade plan	K-12
Enrollment	1,830
Attendance rate, '06-07	94.5%
Dropout rate	2.9%
Students per teacher	10.7
Per pupil expenditure	$10,962
Median faculty salary	$46,702
Median administrator salary	$91,100
Grade 12 enrollment	126
High school graduation rate	89.7%

Assessment test results

(percent scoring at proficient or advanced level)

	Language	Math
NJASK-Grade 3	91.6%	86.0%
GEPA-Grade 8	83.0%	89.7%
HSPA-High School	72.6%	82.1%

SAT Score Averages, 2006-07

Pct tested	Math	Verbal	Writing
58%	522	512	510

Teacher Qualifications

Avg. years of experience	5
Highly-qualified teachers one subject/all subjects	99.0%/99.0%

No Child Left Behind

AYP, 2006-07 . . . . Meets Standards

Municipal Finance

State Aid Programs, 2009

Total aid	$617,617
CMPTRA	49,417
Energy tax receipts	534,806
Garden State Trust	8,673

General Budget, 2008

Total tax levy	$14,555,246
County levy	2,962,292
County taxes	2,442,804
County library	287,076
County health	116,882
County open space	115,530
School levy	10,401,215
Muni. levy	1,191,739
Misc. revenues	2,718,521

Taxes	2006	2007	2008
General tax rate per $100	3.08	1.32	1.345
County equalization ratio	51.74	121.83	112.54
Net valuation taxable	$411,827,100	$1,094,895,051	$1,083,749,972
State equalized value	$890,763,784	$973,220,759	$325,876,065

See Introduction for an explanation of all data sources.

Demographics & Socio-Economic Characteristics

(2000 US Census, except as noted)

Population

1980*	3,856
1990*	3,591
2000	3,416
Male	1,693
Female	1,723
2007 (estimate)*	3,343
Population density	250.8

Race & Hispanic Origin, 2000

Race

White	3,348
Black/African American	15
American Indian/Alaska Native	1
Asian	10
Native Hawaiian/Pacific Islander	0
Other race	22
Two or more races	20
Hispanic origin, total	69
Mexican	5
Puerto Rican	20
Cuban	5
Other Hispanic	39

Age & Nativity, 2000

Under 5 years	221
18 years and over	2,621
21 years and over	2,538
65 years and over	546
85 years and over	48
Median age	39.8
Native-born	3,346
Foreign-born	70

Educational Attainment, 2000

Population 25 years and over	2,428
Less than 9th grade	3.5%
High school grad or higher	86.1%
Bachelor's degree or higher	17.4%
Graduate degree	5.8%

Income & Poverty, 1999

Per capita income	$24,754
Median household income	$52,188
Median family income	$60,208
Persons in poverty	148
H'holds receiving public assistance	5
H'holds receiving social security	365

Households, 2000

Total households	1,341
With persons under 18	434
With persons over 65	399
Family households	990
Single-person households	295
Persons per household	2.54
Persons per family	2.99

Labor & Employment

Total civilian labor force, 2007**	2,082
Unemployment rate	3.4%
Total civilian labor force, 2000	1,851
Unemployment rate	2.9%

Employed persons 16 years and over by occupation, 2000

Managers & professionals	629
Service occupations	236
Sales & office occupations	506
Farming, fishing & forestry	6
Construction & maintenance	243
Production & transportation	177
Self-employed persons	146

* US Census Bureau
** New Jersey Department of Labor

General Information

Township of Pohatcong
50 Municipal Dr
Phillipsburg, NJ 08865
908-454-6121

Website	www.pohatcong.com
Year of incorporation	1882
Land/water area (sq. miles)	13.33/0.28
Form of government	Small Municipality

Government

Legislative Districts

US Congressional	5
State Legislative	23

Local Officials, 2009

Mayor	Stephen Babinsky
Manager/Admin	NA
Clerk	Wanda Kutzman
Finance Dir	Andrew Coppola
Tax Assessor	Edward Kerwin
Tax Collector	Carrie Rochelle
Attorney	Kevin Benbrook
Building	Wayne Degan
Comm Dev/Planning	NA
Engineering	Gwen Steckel
Public Works	NA
Police Chief	Paul Hager
Emerg/Fire Director	Don Freeman

Housing & Construction

Housing Units, 2000*

Total	1,411
Median rent	$717
Median SF home value	$135,100

Permits for New Residential Construction

	Units	Value
Total, 2006	9	$1,448,763
Single family	9	$1,448,763
Total, 2007	8	$1,474,208
Single family	8	$1,474,208

Real Property Valuation, 2008

	Parcels	Valuation
Total	1,729	$337,993,000
Vacant	126	6,272,800
Residential	1,231	204,453,600
Commercial	54	91,432,000
Industrial	5	5,636,800
Apartments	2	399,300
Farm land	201	2,548,200
Farm homestead	110	27,250,300

Average Property Value & Tax, 2008

Residential value	$172,784
Property tax	$5,961
Tax credit/rebate	$1,057

Public Library

No public municipal library

Library statistics, 2007

Population served	NA
Full-time/total staff	NA/NA

	Total	Per capita
Holdings	NA	NA
Revenues	NA	NA
Expenditures	NA	NA
Annual visits	NA	NA
Internet terminals/annual users	NA/NA	

Public Safety

Number of officers, 2007	15

Crime	2006	2007
Total crimes	158	131
Violent	26	23
Murder	0	0
Rape	0	0
Robbery	1	2
Aggravated assault	25	21
Non-violent	132	108
Burglary	8	10
Larceny	114	94
Vehicle theft	10	4
Domestic violence	14	16
Arson	0	0
Total crime rate	46.3	38.4
Violent	7.6	6.7
Non-violent	38.7	31.7

Public School District

(for school year 2007-08 except as noted)

Pohatcong Township School District
240 Route 519
Phillipsburg, NJ 08865
(908) 859-8155

Chief School Admin	Diane Mandry
Number of schools	1
Grade plan	K-8
Enrollment	364
Attendance rate, '06-07	96.2%
Dropout rate	NA
Students per teacher	10.7
Per pupil expenditure	$13,268
Median faculty salary	$48,631
Median administrator salary	$83,600
Grade 12 enrollment	NA
High school graduation rate	NA

Assessment test results

(percent scoring at proficient or advanced level)

	Language	Math
NJASK-Grade 3	87.3%	89.3%
GEPA-Grade 8	76.4%	92.7%
HSPA-High School	NA	NA

SAT Score Averages, 2006-07

Pct tested	Math	Verbal	Writing
NA	NA	NA	NA

Teacher Qualifications

Avg. years of experience	10
Highly-qualified teachers one subject/all subjects	100%/100%

No Child Left Behind

AYP, 2006-07	Meets Standards

Municipal Finance

State Aid Programs, 2009

Total aid	$461,160
CMPTRA	81,631
Energy tax receipts	354,434
Garden State Trust	8,376

General Budget, 2008

Total tax levy	$11,682,238
County levy	2,998,640
County taxes	2,445,489
County library	256,890
County health	0
County open space	296,260
School levy	5,397,766
Muni. levy	3,285,832
Misc. revenues	2,313,901

Taxes	2006	2007	2008
General tax rate per $100	3.11	3.29	3.450
County equalization ratio	83.29	73.65	68.86
Net valuation taxable	$338,776,270	$337,979,667	$338,637,267
State equalized value	$460,625,450	$490,528,368	$459,936,290

See Introduction for an explanation of all data sources.

Demographics & Socio-Economic Characteristics

(2000 US Census, except as noted)

Population
1980*	5,415
1990*	5,112
2000	5,314
Male	2,678
Female	2,636
2007 (estimate)*	5,411
Population density	3,757.6

Race & Hispanic Origin, 2000
Race
White	5,098
Black/African American	28
American Indian/Alaska Native	18
Asian	54
Native Hawaiian/Pacific Islander	1
Other race	78
Two or more races	37
Hispanic origin, total	234
Mexican	120
Puerto Rican	33
Cuban	8
Other Hispanic	73

Age & Nativity, 2000
Under 5 years	234
18 years and over	4,292
21 years and over	4,150
65 years and over	1,012
85 years and over	141
Median age	42.6
Native-born	5,008
Foreign-born	306

Educational Attainment, 2000
Population 25 years and over	3,926
Less than 9th grade	3.8%
High school grad or higher	87.1%
Bachelor's degree or higher	34.1%
Graduate degree	11.6%

Income & Poverty, 1999
Per capita income	$27,853
Median household income	$51,105
Median family income	$61,250
Persons in poverty	325
H'holds receiving public assistance	46
H'holds receiving social security	802

Households, 2000
Total households	2,317
With persons under 18	570
With persons over 65	742
Family households	1,317
Single-person households	841
Persons per household	2.25
Persons per family	2.96

Labor & Employment
Total civilian labor force, 2007**	3,055
Unemployment rate	3.3%
Total civilian labor force, 2000	2,617
Unemployment rate	5.2%

Employed persons 16 years and over by occupation, 2000
Managers & professionals	918
Service occupations	396
Sales & office occupations	742
Farming, fishing & forestry	65
Construction & maintenance	206
Production & transportation	153
Self-employed persons	108

‡ Branch of county library
* US Census Bureau
** New Jersey Department of Labor

General Information
Borough of Point Pleasant Beach
416 New Jersey Ave
Point Pleasant Beach, NJ 08742
732-892-1118
Website	www.pointpleasantbeach.org
Year of incorporation	1886
Land/water area (sq. miles)	1.44/0.28
Form of government	Borough

Government
Legislative Districts
US Congressional	4
State Legislative	10

Local Officials, 2009
Mayor	Vincent R. Barrella
Manager	Christine Riehl
Clerk	Maryann Ellsworth
Chief Financial Officer	Christine Riehl
Tax Assessor	Howard Carpenter
Tax Collector	Christine Riehl
Attorney	Sean Gertner
Building	Michael Gardner
Comm Dev/Planning	NA
Engineering	Raymond Savacool
Public Works	John Trout
Police Chief	Daniel DePolo
Emerg/Fire Director	Vincent Storino

Housing & Construction
Housing Units, 2000*
Total	3,558
Median rent	$777
Median SF home value	$223,600

Permits for New Residential Construction
	Units	Value
Total, 2006	19	$3,032,392
Single family	19	$3,032,392
Total, 2007	13	$3,123,800
Single family	10	$3,114,000

Real Property Valuation, 2008
	Parcels	Valuation
Total	3,260	$2,554,888,200
Vacant	224	95,929,700
Residential	2,762	1,939,485,200
Commercial	268	503,915,800
Industrial	0	0
Apartments	6	15,557,500
Farm land	0	0
Farm homestead	0	0

Average Property Value & Tax, 2008
Residential value	$702,203
Property tax	$6,354
Tax credit/rebate	$995

Public Library
Point Pleasant Beach Branch‡
710 McLean Ave
Point Pleasant Beach, NJ 08742
732-892-4575
Branch Librarian	Kathy Finnan

Library statistics, 2007
see Ocean County profile
for library system statistics

Public Safety
Number of officers, 2007	25

Crime	2006	2007
Total crimes	212	274
Violent	13	9
Murder	0	0
Rape	3	2
Robbery	1	6
Aggravated assault	9	1
Non-violent	199	265
Burglary	23	35
Larceny	172	220
Vehicle theft	4	10
Domestic violence	102	111
Arson	0	1
Total crime rate	39.3	50.8
Violent	2.4	1.7
Non-violent	36.9	49.1

Public School District
(for school year 2007-08 except as noted)

Point Pleasant Beach School District
Cook's Lane and Niblick Street
Point Pleasant Beach, NJ 08742
(732) 899-8840
Superintendent	John A. Ravally
Number of schools	2
Grade plan	K-12
Enrollment	836
Attendance rate, '06-07	93.8%
Dropout rate	0.8%
Students per teacher	9.5
Per pupil expenditure	$13,727
Median faculty salary	$54,312
Median administrator salary	$122,754
Grade 12 enrollment	90
High school graduation rate	97.9%

Assessment test results
(percent scoring at proficient or advanced level)
	Language	Math
NJASK-Grade 3	84.7%	97.4%
GEPA-Grade 8	96.6%	94.9%
HSPA-High School	88.5%	92.7%

SAT Score Averages, 2006-07
Pct tested	Math	Verbal	Writing
87%	530	500	514

Teacher Qualifications
Avg. years of experience	13
Highly-qualified teachers one subject/all subjects	100%/100%

No Child Left Behind
AYP, 2006-07	Meets Standards

Municipal Finance
State Aid Programs, 2009
Total aid	$778,829
CMPTRA	7,606
Energy tax receipts	736,163
Garden State Trust	21

General Budget, 2008
Total tax levy	$23,123,162
County levy	7,212,663
County taxes	5,947,806
County library	698,972
County health	284,586
County open space	281,299
School levy	10,258,605
Muni. levy	5,651,894
Misc. revenues	17,836,505

Taxes	2006	2007	2008
General tax rate per $100	3.022	0.828	0.905
County equalization ratio	35.99	119.05	109.15
Net valuation taxable	$670,946,300	$2,559,173,953	$2,555,531,777
State equalized value	$2,126,827,335	$2,344,690,735	$3,780,517,899

See Introduction for an explanation of all data sources.

Demographics & Socio-Economic Characteristics
(2000 US Census, except as noted)

Population
1980*	17,747
1990*	18,177
2000	19,306
Male	9,279
Female	10,027
2007 (estimate)*	19,961
Population density	5,654.7

Race & Hispanic Origin, 2000
Race
White	18,887
Black/African American	56
American Indian/Alaska Native	27
Asian	105
Native Hawaiian/Pacific Islander	2
Other race	96
Two or more races	133
Hispanic origin, total	465
Mexican	171
Puerto Rican	117
Cuban	35
Other Hispanic	142

Age & Nativity, 2000
Under 5 years	1,150
18 years and over	14,729
21 years and over	14,193
65 years and over	2,883
85 years and over	412
Median age	39.4
Native-born	18,713
Foreign-born	593

Educational Attainment, 2000
Population 25 years and over	13,447
Less than 9th grade	2.6%
High school grad or higher	88.5%
Bachelor's degree or higher	27.8%
Graduate degree	7.7%

Income & Poverty, 1999
Per capita income	$25,715
Median household income	$55,987
Median family income	$64,798
Persons in poverty	616
H'holds receiving public assistance	86
H'holds receiving social security	2,079

Households, 2000
Total households	7,560
With persons under 18	2,566
With persons over 65	1,982
Family households	5,228
Single-person households	1,941
Persons per household	2.52
Persons per family	3.06

Labor & Employment
Total civilian labor force, 2007**	12,005
Unemployment rate	3.4%
Total civilian labor force, 2000	10,105
Unemployment rate	3.7%

Employed persons 16 years and over by occupation, 2000
Managers & professionals	3,511
Service occupations	1,532
Sales & office occupations	2,806
Farming, fishing & forestry	18
Construction & maintenance	1,017
Production & transportation	846
Self-employed persons	619

‡ Branch of county library
* US Census Bureau
** New Jersey Department of Labor

General Information
Borough of Point Pleasant
2233 Bridge Ave
PO Box 25
Point Pleasant, NJ 08742
732-892-3434

Website	www.ptboro.com
Year of incorporation	1920
Land/water area (sq. miles)	3.53/0.63
Form of government	Borough

Government
Legislative Districts
US Congressional	4
State Legislative	10

Local Officials, 2009
Mayor	Martin Konkus
Manager	David Maffei
Clerk	David Maffei
Finance Dir	Judith Block
Tax Assessor	Robyn Palughi
Tax Collector	Bernadine Pierce
Attorney	Jerry Dasti
Building	Michael Gardner
Planning	Robert Forsyth
Engineering	Robert Forsyth
Public Works	Dennis Sears
Police Chief	Raymond Hilling
Emerg/Fire Director	Jeff Smith

Housing & Construction
Housing Units, 2000*
Total	8,350
Median rent	$859
Median SF home value	$160,100

Permits for New Residential Construction
	Units	Value
Total, 2006	54	$5,960,971
Single family	38	$5,860,970
Total, 2007	93	$28,930,642
Single family	33	$5,265,595

Real Property Valuation, 2008
	Parcels	Valuation
Total	8,194	$1,387,631,100
Vacant	309	25,484,700
Residential	7,564	1,242,328,500
Commercial	307	108,023,200
Industrial	0	0
Apartments	14	11,794,700
Farm land	0	0
Farm homestead	0	0

Average Property Value & Tax, 2008
Residential value	$164,242
Property tax	$6,014
Tax credit/rebate	$973

Public Library
Point Pleasant Branch Library‡
834 Beaver Dam Rd
Point Pleasant, NJ 08742
732-295-1555

Branch Librarian	Barbara Kaden

Library statistics, 2007
see Ocean County profile
for library system statistics

Public Safety
Number of officers, 2007	33

Crime	2006	2007
Total crimes	346	360
Violent	16	18
Murder	0	0
Rape	0	1
Robbery	2	3
Aggravated assault	14	14
Non-violent	330	342
Burglary	51	33
Larceny	269	305
Vehicle theft	10	4
Domestic violence	145	131
Arson	0	0
Total crime rate	17.4	18.1
Violent	0.8	0.9
Non-violent	16.6	17.2

Public School District
(for school year 2007-08 except as noted)

Point Pleasant Borough School District
2100 Panther Path
Point Pleasant, NJ 08742
(732) 701-1900

Superintendent	Vincent Smith
Number of schools	4
Grade plan	K-12
Enrollment	3,158
Attendance rate, '06-07	94.4%
Dropout rate	1.9%
Students per teacher	12.2
Per pupil expenditure	$10,432
Median faculty salary	$49,540
Median administrator salary	$110,239
Grade 12 enrollment	262
High school graduation rate	95.8%

Assessment test results
(percent scoring at proficient or advanced level)
	Language	Math
NJASK-Grade 3	96.2%	90.0%
GEPA-Grade 8	80.4%	92.2%
HSPA-High School	85.2%	90.9%

SAT Score Averages, 2006-07
Pct tested	Math	Verbal	Writing
77%	490	491	478

Teacher Qualifications
Avg. years of experience	9
Highly-qualified teachers one subject/all subjects	100%/100%

No Child Left Behind
AYP, 2006-07	Meets Standards

Municipal Finance
State Aid Programs, 2009
Total aid	$1,582,718
CMPTRA	256,900
Energy tax receipts	1,286,250
Garden State Trust	0

General Budget, 2008
Total tax levy	$50,863,613
County levy	11,607,441
County taxes	9,571,840
County library	1,124,917
County health	457,998
County open space	452,685
School levy	27,888,675
Muni. levy	11,367,497
Misc. revenues	5,791,032

Taxes	2006	2007	2008
General tax rate per $100	3.4	3.566	3.662
County equalization ratio	44.6	38.92	36.92
Net valuation taxable	$1,361,017,000	$1,376,424,076	$1,389,197,202
State equalized value	$3,499,062,668	$3,724,942,024	$994,326,940

See Introduction for an explanation of all data sources.

Demographics & Socio-Economic Characteristics

(2000 US Census, except as noted)

Population

1980*	10,660
1990*	10,539
2000	10,640
Male	5,119
Female	5,521
2007 (estimate)*	11,095
Population density	3,735.7

Race & Hispanic Origin, 2000

Race
White	9,896
Black/African American	129
American Indian/Alaska Native	20
Asian	322
Native Hawaiian/Pacific Islander	1
Other race	167
Two or more races	105
Hispanic origin, total	611
Mexican	180
Puerto Rican	148
Cuban	62
Other Hispanic	221

Age & Nativity, 2000

Under 5 years	738
18 years and over	8,061
21 years and over	7,754
65 years and over	1,425
85 years and over	146
Median age	37.2
Native-born	9,542
Foreign-born	1,098

Educational Attainment, 2000

Population 25 years and over	7,297
Less than 9th grade	5.0%
High school grad or higher	88.8%
Bachelor's degree or higher	28.4%
Graduate degree	7.9%

Income & Poverty, 1999

Per capita income	$26,802
Median household income	$65,648
Median family income	$74,701
Persons in poverty	343
H'holds receiving public assistance	34
H'holds receiving social security	1,159

Households, 2000

Total households	3,949
With persons under 18	1,424
With persons over 65	1,081
Family households	2,805
Single-person households	939
Persons per household	2.69
Persons per family	3.24

Labor & Employment

Total civilian labor force, 2007**	6,401
Unemployment rate	3.6%
Total civilian labor force, 2000	5,932
Unemployment rate	4.0%

Employed persons 16 years and over by occupation, 2000
Managers & professionals	2,225
Service occupations	648
Sales & office occupations	1,559
Farming, fishing & forestry	0
Construction & maintenance	604
Production & transportation	660
Self-employed persons	196

* US Census Bureau
** New Jersey Department of Labor

General Information

Borough of Pompton Lakes
25 Lenox Ave
Pompton Lakes, NJ 07442
973-835-0143

Website	www.pomptonlakesgov.com
Year of incorporation	1895
Land/water area (sq. miles)	2.97/0.19
Form of government	Borough

Government

Legislative Districts

US Congressional	8
State Legislative	26

Local Officials, 2009

Mayor	Kathleen M. Cole
Manager	Lawrence Pollex
Clerk	Elizabeth Brandsness
Finance Dir	Vito Gadaleta
Tax Assessor	Michael Barker
Tax Collector	Gail Bado
Attorney	Joseph Ragno Jr
Building	Ron Van Dine
Comm Dev/Planning	NA
Engineering	H2M Associates
Public Works	Ben Steltzer
Police Chief	William Smith (Actg)
Emerg/Fire Director	Dennis Mangin

Housing & Construction

Housing Units, 2000*

Total	4,024
Median rent	$933
Median SF home value	$180,100

Permits for New Residential Construction

	Units	Value
Total, 2006	5	$1,111,000
Single family	5	$1,111,000
Total, 2007	7	$1,348,100
Single family	7	$1,348,100

Real Property Valuation, 2008

	Parcels	Valuation
Total	3,945	$640,723,200
Vacant	54	3,080,300
Residential	3,713	550,794,900
Commercial	164	56,518,100
Industrial	7	18,436,500
Apartments	7	11,893,400
Farm land	0	0
Farm homestead	0	0

Average Property Value & Tax, 2008

Residential value	$148,342
Property tax	$8,338
Tax credit/rebate	$1,265

Public Library

Emanuel Einstein Public Library
333 Wanaque Ave
Pompton Lakes, NJ 07442
973-835-0482

Director	Margaret M. Freathy

Library statistics, 2007

Population served	10,640
Full-time/total staff	2/4

	Total	Per capita
Holdings	40,988	3.85
Revenues	$504,049	$47.37
Expenditures	$439,832	$41.34
Annual visits	43,732	4.11
Internet terminals/annual users		3/3,848

Public Safety

Number of officers, 2007	26

Crime	2006	2007
Total crimes	108	106
Violent	6	7
Murder	0	0
Rape	0	2
Robbery	1	1
Aggravated assault	5	4
Non-violent	102	99
Burglary	24	10
Larceny	66	88
Vehicle theft	12	1
Domestic violence	59	48
Arson	0	0
Total crime rate	9.5	9.4
Violent	0.5	0.6
Non-violent	9.0	8.8

Public School District

(for school year 2007-08 except as noted)

Pompton Lakes School District
237 Van Avenue
Pompton Lakes, NJ 07442
(973) 835-4334

Chief School Admin	Terrance Brennan
Number of schools	4
Grade plan	K-12
Enrollment	1,812
Attendance rate, '06-07	95.7%
Dropout rate	0.6%
Students per teacher	10.9
Per pupil expenditure	$14,761
Median faculty salary	$55,486
Median administrator salary	$124,441
Grade 12 enrollment	181
High school graduation rate	96.2%

Assessment test results

(percent scoring at proficient or advanced level)
	Language	Math
NJASK-Grade 3	89.7%	86.3%
GEPA-Grade 8	66.4%	89.9%
HSPA-High School	85.2%	91.0%

SAT Score Averages, 2006-07

Pct tested	Math	Verbal	Writing
75%	503	481	475

Teacher Qualifications

Avg. years of experience	10
Highly-qualified teachers one subject/all subjects	100%/100%

No Child Left Behind

AYP, 2006-07	Meets Standards

Municipal Finance

State Aid Programs, 2009

Total aid	$1,361,987
CMPTRA	425,527
Energy tax receipts	861,475
Garden State Trust	34,799

General Budget, 2008

Total tax levy	$36,037,940
County levy	7,723,114
County taxes	7,570,037
County library	0
County health	0
County open space	153,077
School levy	20,276,736
Muni. levy	8,038,090
Misc. revenues	3,897,797

Taxes

	2006	2007	2008
General tax rate per $100	5.05	5.32	5.622
County equalization ratio	49.47	44.58	42.18
Net valuation taxable	$640,743,500	$642,114,136	$641,153,234
State equalized value	$1,437,771,057	$1,521,711,647	$1,562,026,914

See Introduction for an explanation of all data sources.

Demographics & Socio-Economic Characteristics
(2000 US Census, except as noted)

Population
1980*	837
1990*	992
2000	1,037
Male	510
Female	527
2007 (estimate)*	1,220
Population density	160.1

Race & Hispanic Origin, 2000
Race
White	986
Black/African American	17
American Indian/Alaska Native	4
Asian	6
Native Hawaiian/Pacific Islander	0
Other race	7
Two or more races	17
Hispanic origin, total	11
Mexican	0
Puerto Rican	7
Cuban	0
Other Hispanic	4

Age & Nativity, 2000
Under 5 years	58
18 years and over	788
21 years and over	746
65 years and over	124
85 years and over	17
Median age	41.3
Native-born	985
Foreign-born	47

Educational Attainment, 2000
Population 25 years and over	707
Less than 9th grade	3.4%
High school grad or higher	90.5%
Bachelor's degree or higher	27.7%
Graduate degree	7.5%

Income & Poverty, 1999
Per capita income	$24,369
Median household income	$65,833
Median family income	$70,714
Persons in poverty	36
H'holds receiving public assistance	3
H'holds receiving social security	85

Households, 2000
Total households	365
With persons under 18	146
With persons over 65	92
Family households	289
Single-person households	61
Persons per household	2.82
Persons per family	3.17

Labor & Employment
Total civilian labor force, 2007**	607
Unemployment rate	3.3%
Total civilian labor force, 2000	578
Unemployment rate	4.2%

Employed persons 16 years and over by occupation, 2000
Managers & professionals	161
Service occupations	89
Sales & office occupations	153
Farming, fishing & forestry	7
Construction & maintenance	79
Production & transportation	65
Self-employed persons	64

* US Census Bureau
** New Jersey Department of Labor

General Information
City of Port Republic
143 Main St
Port Republic, NJ 08241
609-652-1501
Email	portrepublic.cityclerk@comcast.net
Year of incorporation	1905
Land/water area (sq. miles)	7.62/1.05
Form of government	City

Government
Legislative Districts
US Congressional	2
State Legislative	2

Local Officials, 2009
Mayor	Gary Giberson
Manager/Admin	NA
Clerk	Lucy Samuelsen
Finance Dir	Karen Thomas
Tax Assessor	Brian Vigue
Tax Collector	NA
Attorney	Sal Perillo
Building	Jay Haines
Comm Dev/Planning	NA
Engineering	Matthew Doran
Public Works	James Milton
Police Chief	NA
Emerg/Fire Director	John Yochim

Housing & Construction
Housing Units, 2000*
Total	389
Median rent	$790
Median SF home value	$155,700

Permits for New Residential Construction
	Units	Value
Total, 2006	4	$1,800,000
Single family	4	$1,800,000
Total, 2007	3	$1,700,000
Single family	3	$1,700,000

Real Property Valuation, 2008
	Parcels	Valuation
Total	582	$75,248,500
Vacant	104	2,329,800
Residential	454	69,453,100
Commercial	11	2,290,800
Industrial	0	0
Apartments	0	0
Farm land	7	76,100
Farm homestead	6	1,098,700

Average Property Value & Tax, 2008
Residential value	$153,373
Property tax	$4,788
Tax credit/rebate	$886

Public Library
No public municipal library

Library statistics, 2007
Population served	NA
Full-time/total staff	NA/NA

	Total	Per capita
Holdings	NA	NA
Revenues	NA	NA
Expenditures	NA	NA
Annual visits	NA	NA
Internet terminals/annual users	NA/NA	

Public Safety
Number of officers, 2007	0

Crime	2006	2007
Total crimes	20	15
Violent	0	1
Murder	0	0
Rape	0	0
Robbery	0	0
Aggravated assault	0	1
Non-violent	20	14
Burglary	3	8
Larceny	17	6
Vehicle theft	0	0
Domestic violence	0	4
Arson	0	1
Total crime rate	16.8	12.2
Violent	0.0	0.8
Non-violent	16.8	11.3

Public School District
(for school year 2007-08 except as noted)

Port Republic School District
137 Pomona Avenue
Port Republic, NJ 08241
(609) 652-7377
Chief School Admin	Janet Wilbraham
Number of schools	1
Grade plan	K-8
Enrollment	108
Attendance rate, '06-07	95.0%
Dropout rate	NA
Students per teacher	7.6
Per pupil expenditure	$13,766
Median faculty salary	$44,467
Median administrator salary	$61,498
Grade 12 enrollment	NA
High school graduation rate	NA

Assessment test results
(percent scoring at proficient or advanced level)
	Language	Math
NJASK-Grade 3	92.9%	92.9%
GEPA-Grade 8	NA	NA
HSPA-High School	NA	NA

SAT Score Averages, 2006-07
Pct tested	Math	Verbal	Writing
NA	NA	NA	NA

Teacher Qualifications
Avg. years of experience	13
Highly-qualified teachers one subject/all subjects	100%/100%

No Child Left Behind
AYP, 2006-07	Meets Standards

Municipal Finance
State Aid Programs, 2009
Total aid	$220,602
CMPTRA	0
Energy tax receipts	212,756
Garden State Trust	1,917

General Budget, 2008
Total tax levy	$2,358,863
County levy	446,934
County taxes	352,228
County library	45,116
County health	18,461
County open space	31,129
School levy	1,419,966
Muni. levy	491,963
Misc. revenues	795,216

Taxes
	2006	2007	2008
General tax rate per $100	2.969	3.075	3.122
County equalization ratio	57.6	51.64	48.56
Net valuation taxable	$70,376,700	$73,058,758	$75,557,356
State equalized value	$136,629,846	$150,116,005	$159,835,038

See Introduction for an explanation of all data sources.

Demographics & Socio-Economic Characteristics

(2000 US Census, except as noted)

Population

1980*	12,035
1990*	12,016
2000	14,203
Male	7,380
Female	6,823
2007 (estimate)*	13,517
Population density	7,306.5

Race & Hispanic Origin, 2000

Race

White	11,399
Black/African American	908
American Indian/Alaska Native	40
Asian	1,060
Native Hawaiian/Pacific Islander	20
Other race	355
Two or more races	421
Hispanic origin, total	1,009
Mexican	340
Puerto Rican	113
Cuban	30
Other Hispanic	526

Age & Nativity, 2000

Under 5 years	446
18 years and over	12,774
21 years and over	9,644
65 years and over	1,321
85 years and over	264
Median age	24.7
Native-born	12,191
Foreign-born	2,012

Educational Attainment, 2000

Population 25 years and over	7,148
Less than 9th grade	4.8%
High school grad or higher	89.4%
Bachelor's degree or higher	60.1%
Graduate degree	39.6%

Income & Poverty, 1999

Per capita income	$27,292
Median household income	$67,346
Median family income	$102,957
Persons in poverty	656
H'holds receiving public assistance	16
H'holds receiving social security	811

Households, 2000

Total households	3,326
With persons under 18	780
With persons over 65	819
Family households	1,693
Single-person households	1,334
Persons per household	2.20
Persons per family	2.92

Labor & Employment

Total civilian labor force, 2007**	4,848
Unemployment rate	4.4%
Total civilian labor force, 2000	9,999
Unemployment rate	42.3%

Employed persons 16 years and over by occupation, 2000

Managers & professionals	3,620
Service occupations	1,076
Sales & office occupations	801
Farming, fishing & forestry	12
Construction & maintenance	133
Production & transportation	126
Self-employed persons	232

‡ Joint library with Princeton Township
* US Census Bureau
** New Jersey Department of Labor

General Information

Borough of Princeton
PO Box 390
Princeton, NJ 08542
609-924-3118

Website	www.princetonboro.org
Year of incorporation	1813
Land/water area (sq. miles)	1.85/0.00
Form of government	Borough

Government

Legislative Districts

US Congressional	12
State Legislative	15

Local Officials, 2009

Mayor	Mildred T. Trotman
Manager	Robert W. Bruschi
Clerk	Andrea L. Quinty
Finance Dir	Sandra L. Webb
Tax Assessor	Neal Snyder
Tax Collector	Carol Coe
Attorney	Karen Cayci
Building	Martin Vogt
Comm Dev/Planning	NA
Engineering	Christopher M. Budzinski
Public Works	Wayne Carr
Police Chief	Anthony V. Federico
Emerg/Fire Director	Daniel Tomalin

Housing & Construction

Housing Units, 2000*

Total	3,495
Median rent	$920
Median SF home value	$343,500

Permits for New Residential Construction

	Units	Value
Total, 2006	18	$5,935,977
Single family	14	$5,311,477
Total, 2007	14	$4,407,798
Single family	10	$3,783,298

Real Property Valuation, 2008

	Parcels	Valuation
Total	2,466	$1,003,940,600
Vacant	143	16,469,000
Residential	2,080	727,901,400
Commercial	201	210,978,700
Industrial	0	0
Apartments	42	48,591,500
Farm land	0	0
Farm homestead	0	0

Average Property Value & Tax, 2008

Residential value	$349,953
Property tax	$14,562
Tax credit/rebate	$1,324

Public Library

Princeton Public Library‡
65 Witherspoon St
Princeton, NJ 08542
609-924-8822

Director................... Leslie Burger

Library statistics, 2007

Population served	30,230
Full-time/total staff	17/35

	Total	Per capita
Holdings	180,900	5.98
Revenues	$4,529,035	$149.82
Expenditures	$4,517,314	$149.43
Annual visits	820,509	27.14
Internet terminals/annual users	102/242,086	

Public Safety

Number of officers, 2007	34

Crime	2006	2007
Total crimes	450	347
Violent	23	15
Murder	0	0
Rape	2	0
Robbery	11	3
Aggravated assault	10	12
Non-violent	427	332
Burglary	77	70
Larceny	339	261
Vehicle theft	11	1
Domestic violence	41	31
Arson	0	3
Total crime rate	33.3	25.4
Violent	1.7	1.1
Non-violent	31.6	24.3

Public School District

(for school year 2007-08 except as noted)

Princeton Regional School District
25 Valley Road
Princeton, NJ 08540
(609) 806-4220

Superintendent	Judith A. Wilson
Number of schools	6
Grade plan	K-12
Enrollment	3,326
Attendance rate, '06-07	96.6%
Dropout rate	0.8%
Students per teacher	10.0
Per pupil expenditure	$18,110
Median faculty salary	$65,349
Median administrator salary	$126,859
Grade 12 enrollment	319
High school graduation rate	97.3%

Assessment test results

(percent scoring at proficient or advanced level)

	Language	Math
NJASK-Grade 3	95.8%	95.2%
GEPA-Grade 8	86.0%	92.8%
HSPA-High School	93.1%	91.4%

SAT Score Averages, 2006-07

Pct tested	Math	Verbal	Writing
98%	619	601	604

Teacher Qualifications

Avg. years of experience	9
Highly-qualified teachers one subject/all subjects	100%/100%

No Child Left Behind

AYP, 2006-07	Meets Standards

Municipal Finance

State Aid Programs, 2009

Total aid	$1,309,646
CMPTRA	196,620
Energy tax receipts	1,070,459
Garden State Trust	5

General Budget, 2008

Total tax levy	$41,891,965
County levy	11,693,971
County taxes	10,942,859
County library	0
County health	0
County open space	751,112
School levy	19,726,775
Muni. levy	10,471,219
Misc. revenues	14,893,666

Taxes

	2006	2007	2008
General tax rate per $100	3.69	3.92	4.162
County equalization ratio	51.13	44.33	40.30
Net valuation taxable	$999,240,700	$999,506,688	$1,006,718,313
State equalized value	$2,257,511,679	$2,476,273,886	$2,542,470,604

See Introduction for an explanation of all data sources.

Demographics & Socio-Economic Characteristics

(2000 US Census, except as noted)

Population

1980*	13,683
1990*	13,198
2000	16,027
Male	7,750
Female	8,277
2007 (estimate)*	17,490
Population density	1,067.8

Race & Hispanic Origin, 2000

Race
White	12,807
Black/African American	852
American Indian/Alaska Native	20
Asian	1,599
Native Hawaiian/Pacific Islander	8
Other race	338
Two or more races	403
Hispanic origin, total	847
Mexican	309
Puerto Rican	70
Cuban	23
Other Hispanic	445

Age & Nativity, 2000

Under 5 years	821
18 years and over	12,121
21 years and over	11,804
65 years and over	2,463
85 years and over	228
Median age	40.8
Native-born	11,962
Foreign-born	4,065

Educational Attainment, 2000

Population 25 years and over	11,355
Less than 9th grade	2.6%
High school grad or higher	94.2%
Bachelor's degree or higher	75.9%
Graduate degree	48.2%

Income & Poverty, 1999

Per capita income	$56,360
Median household income	$94,580
Median family income	$123,098
Persons in poverty	897
H'holds receiving public assistance	45
H'holds receiving social security	1,482

Households, 2000

Total households	6,044
With persons under 18	2,121
With persons over 65	1,658
Family households	4,358
Single-person households	1,243
Persons per household	2.57
Persons per family	2.98

Labor & Employment

Total civilian labor force, 2007**	9,620
Unemployment rate	0.9%
Total civilian labor force, 2000	7,990
Unemployment rate	0.8%

Employed persons 16 years and over by occupation, 2000
Managers & professionals	5,629
Service occupations	676
Sales & office occupations	1,252
Farming, fishing & forestry	12
Construction & maintenance	113
Production & transportation	243
Self-employed persons	940

‡ Joint library with Princeton Borough
* US Census Bureau
** New Jersey Department of Labor

General Information

Township of Princeton
400 Witherspoon St
Princeton, NJ 08540
609-924-5176
Website	www.princetontwp.org
Year of incorporation	1838
Land/water area (sq. miles)	16.38/0.23
Form of government	Township

Government

Legislative Districts

US Congressional	12
State Legislative	15

Local Officials, 2009

Mayor	Bernard P. Miller
Manager	James Pascale
Clerk	Linda McDermott
Finance Dir	Kathryn Monzo
Tax Assessor	Neal Snyder
Tax Collector	Kathryn Monzo
Attorney	Edwin Schmierer
Building	John Pettenati
Planning	Lee Solow
Engineering	Robert V. Kiser
Public Works	Donald Hansen
Police Chief	Mark V. Emann
Emerg/Fire Director	Rick McKee

Housing & Construction

Housing Units, 2000*

Total	6,224
Median rent	$748
Median SF home value	$417,000

Permits for New Residential Construction

	Units	Value
Total, 2006	23	$11,066,520
Single family	23	$11,066,520
Total, 2007	11	$7,040,600
Single family	11	$7,040,600

Real Property Valuation, 2008

	Parcels	Valuation
Total	5,451	$2,424,581,410
Vacant	376	47,186,600
Residential	4,899	2,102,060,600
Commercial	113	173,643,300
Industrial	2	5,180,100
Apartments	7	78,435,100
Farm land	37	323,010
Farm homestead	17	17,752,700

Average Property Value & Tax, 2008

Residential value	$431,207
Property tax	$15,374
Tax credit/rebate	$1,255

Public Library

Princeton Public Library‡
65 Witherspoon St
Princeton, NJ 08542
609-924-8822
Director	Leslie Burger

Library statistics, 2007

Population served	30,230
Full-time/total staff	17/35

	Total	Per capita
Holdings	180,900	5.98
Revenues	$4,529,035	$149.82
Expenditures	$4,517,314	$149.43
Annual visits	820,509	27.14
Internet terminals/annual users	102/242,086	

Public Safety

Number of officers, 2007	31

Crime	2006	2007
Total crimes	183	157
Violent	16	9
Murder	0	0
Rape	4	0
Robbery	5	0
Aggravated assault	7	9
Non-violent	167	148
Burglary	35	28
Larceny	126	113
Vehicle theft	6	7
Domestic violence	45	46
Arson	0	1
Total crime rate	10.6	9.0
Violent	0.9	0.5
Non-violent	9.7	8.5

Public School District

(for school year 2007-08 except as noted)

Princeton Regional School District
25 Valley Road
Princeton, NJ 08540
(609) 806-4220
Superintendent	Judith A. Wilson
Number of schools	6
Grade plan	K-12
Enrollment	3,326
Attendance rate, '06-07	96.6%
Dropout rate	0.8%
Students per teacher	10.0
Per pupil expenditure	$18,110
Median faculty salary	$65,349
Median administrator salary	$126,859
Grade 12 enrollment	319
High school graduation rate	97.3%

Assessment test results

(percent scoring at proficient or advanced level)
	Language	Math
NJASK-Grade 3	95.8%	95.2%
GEPA-Grade 8	86.0%	92.8%
HSPA-High School	93.1%	91.4%

SAT Score Averages, 2006-07

Pct tested	Math	Verbal	Writing
98%	619	601	604

Teacher Qualifications

Avg. years of experience	9
Highly-qualified teachers one subject/all subjects	100%/100%

No Child Left Behind

AYP, 2006-07	Meets Standards

Municipal Finance

State Aid Programs, 2009

Total aid	$1,997,373
CMPTRA	112,782
Energy tax receipts	1,798,996
Garden State Trust	8,034

General Budget, 2008

Total tax levy	$86,501,910
County levy	23,909,239
County taxes	22,373,509
County library	0
County health	0
County open space	1,535,730
School levy	41,211,019
Muni. levy	21,381,653
Misc. revenues	13,630,725

Taxes

	2006	2007	2008
General tax rate per $100	3.34	3.48	3.566
County equalization ratio	53.42	49.88	47.45
Net valuation taxable	$2,397,049,510	$2,410,599,981	$2,426,146,656
State equalized value	$4,807,315,240	$5,078,540,899	$5,092,015,403

See Introduction for an explanation of all data sources.

Demographics & Socio-Economic Characteristics

(2000 US Census, except as noted)

Population

1980*	5,142
1990*	5,053
2000	5,779
Male	2,750
Female	3,029
2007 (estimate)*	5,633
Population density	11,735.4

Race & Hispanic Origin, 2000

Race

White	3,535
Black/African American	789
American Indian/Alaska Native	24
Asian	182
Native Hawaiian/Pacific Islander	4
Other race	792
Two or more races	453
Hispanic origin, total	2,211
Mexican	41
Puerto Rican	706
Cuban	43
Other Hispanic	1,421

Age & Nativity, 2000

Under 5 years	443
18 years and over	4,070
21 years and over	3,831
65 years and over	510
85 years and over	54
Median age	30.9
Native-born	3,955
Foreign-born	1,824

Educational Attainment, 2000

Population 25 years and over	3,433
Less than 9th grade	14.9%
High school grad or higher	68.3%
Bachelor's degree or higher	12.4%
Graduate degree	3.2%

Income & Poverty, 1999

Per capita income	$16,410
Median household income	$46,434
Median family income	$49,405
Persons in poverty	575
H'holds receiving public assistance	30
H'holds receiving social security	440

Households, 2000

Total households	1,822
With persons under 18	904
With persons over 65	380
Family households	1,432
Single-person households	309
Persons per household	3.17
Persons per family	3.56

Labor & Employment

Total civilian labor force, 2007**	2,925
Unemployment rate	5.9%
Total civilian labor force, 2000	2,712
Unemployment rate	6.1%

Employed persons 16 years and over by occupation, 2000

Managers & professionals	564
Service occupations	445
Sales & office occupations	818
Farming, fishing & forestry	0
Construction & maintenance	227
Production & transportation	492
Self-employed persons	34

General Information

Borough of Prospect Park
106 Brown Ave
Prospect Park, NJ 07508
973-790-7902

Website	www.prospectpark.net
Year of incorporation	1901
Land/water area (sq. miles)	0.48/0.00
Form of government	Borough

Government

Legislative Districts

US Congressional	8
State Legislative	35

Local Officials, 2009

Mayor	Mohamed T. Khairullah
Manager/Admin	NA
Clerk	Yancy Wazirmas
Finance Dir	Stephen Sanzari
Tax Assessor	Rose Farrell
Tax Collector	Stephen Sanzari
Attorney	Schwartz, Simon et al
Building	David Heerema
Comm Dev/Planning	NA
Engineering	Boswell Engineering
Public Works	Ken Valt
Police Chief	Frank Franco
Emerg/Fire Director	R.J. Dansen

Housing & Construction

Housing Units, 2000*

Total	1,889
Median rent	$852
Median SF home value	$137,600

Permits for New Residential Construction

	Units	Value
Total, 2006	0	$0
Single family	0	$0
Total, 2007	0	$0
Single family	0	$0

Real Property Valuation, 2008

	Parcels	Valuation
Total	1,171	$181,421,550
Vacant	26	3,115,200
Residential	1,085	160,822,300
Commercial	58	14,728,350
Industrial	2	2,755,700
Apartments	0	0
Farm land	0	0
Farm homestead	0	0

Average Property Value & Tax, 2008

Residential value	$148,223
Property tax	$8,479
Tax credit/rebate	$1,085

Public Library

No public municipal library

Library statistics, 2007

Population served	NA
Full-time/total staff	NA/NA

	Total	Per capita
Holdings	NA	NA
Revenues	NA	NA
Expenditures	NA	NA
Annual visits	NA	NA
Internet terminals/annual users	NA/NA	

Public Safety

Number of officers, 2007	15

Crime	2006	2007
Total crimes	107	142
Violent	10	13
Murder	1	0
Rape	0	0
Robbery	2	2
Aggravated assault	7	11
Non-violent	97	129
Burglary	14	39
Larceny	72	74
Vehicle theft	11	16
Domestic violence	42	36
Arson	0	0
Total crime rate	18.6	24.8
Violent	1.7	2.3
Non-violent	16.8	22.6

Public School District

(for school year 2007-08 except as noted)

Prospect Park School District
290 North 8th Street
Prospect Park, NJ 07508
(973) 720-1982

Chief School Admin	James F. Barriale
Number of schools	1
Grade plan	K-8
Enrollment	837
Attendance rate, '06-07	95.8%
Dropout rate	NA
Students per teacher	11.8
Per pupil expenditure	$11,450
Median faculty salary	$52,250
Median administrator salary	$100,253
Grade 12 enrollment	NA
High school graduation rate	NA

Assessment test results

(percent scoring at proficient or advanced level)

	Language	Math
NJASK-Grade 3	73.8%	76.0%
GEPA-Grade 8	60.7%	84.5%
HSPA-High School	NA	NA

SAT Score Averages, 2006-07

Pct tested	Math	Verbal	Writing
NA	NA	NA	NA

Teacher Qualifications

Avg. years of experience	7
Highly-qualified teachers one subject/all subjects	96.0%/96.0%

No Child Left Behind

AYP, 2006-07	Meets Standards

Municipal Finance

State Aid Programs, 2009

Total aid	$406,995
CMPTRA	172,416
Energy tax receipts	228,474
Garden State Trust	0

General Budget, 2008

Total tax levy	$10,391,023
County levy	2,211,066
County taxes	2,167,277
County library	0
County health	0
County open space	43,789
School levy	5,296,675
Muni. levy	2,883,281
Misc. revenues	4,205,034

Taxes

	2006	2007	2008
General tax rate per $100	4.92	5.22	5.721
County equalization ratio	52.85	46.08	41.66
Net valuation taxable	$180,738,450	$181,097,450	$181,639,550
State equalized value	$392,465,739	$434,389,606	$435,073,105

* US Census Bureau
** New Jersey Department of Labor

See Introduction for an explanation of all data sources.

Demographics & Socio-Economic Characteristics
(2000 US Census, except as noted)

Population
1980*	2,887
1990*	2,511
2000	2,786
Male	1,391
Female	1,395
2007 (estimate)*	2,838
Population density	117.4

Race & Hispanic Origin, 2000
Race
White	2,286
Black/African American	403
American Indian/Alaska Native	30
Asian	9
Native Hawaiian/Pacific Islander	0
Other race	20
Two or more races	38
Hispanic origin, total	42
Mexican	7
Puerto Rican	14
Cuban	1
Other Hispanic	20

Age & Nativity, 2000
Under 5 years	161
18 years and over	2,128
21 years and over	2,034
65 years and over	441
85 years and over	50
Median age	39.0
Native-born	2,737
Foreign-born	49

Educational Attainment, 2000
Population 25 years and over	1,931
Less than 9th grade	10.9%
High school grad or higher	72.1%
Bachelor's degree or higher	10.3%
Graduate degree	2.2%

Income & Poverty, 1999
Per capita income	$18,921
Median household income	$41,193
Median family income	$48,272
Persons in poverty	258
H'holds receiving public assistance	34
H'holds receiving social security	365

Households, 2000
Total households	1,074
With persons under 18	357
With persons over 65	324
Family households	779
Single-person households	244
Persons per household	2.56
Persons per family	3.02

Labor & Employment
Total civilian labor force, 2007**	1,301
Unemployment rate	5.3%
Total civilian labor force, 2000	1,294
Unemployment rate	8.8%

Employed persons 16 years and over by occupation, 2000
Managers & professionals	291
Service occupations	188
Sales & office occupations	267
Farming, fishing & forestry	17
Construction & maintenance	158
Production & transportation	259
Self-employed persons	63

* US Census Bureau
** New Jersey Department of Labor

General Information
Township of Quinton
885 Route 49
PO Box 65
Quinton, NJ 08072
856-935-2325

Website	(county website)
Year of incorporation	1873
Land/water area (sq. miles)	24.17/0.37
Form of government	Township

Government
Legislative Districts
US Congressional	2
State Legislative	3

Local Officials, 2009
Mayor	Joseph Donelson
Manager/Admin	NA
Clerk	Marty Uzdanovics
Finance Dir	Diane Bowman
Tax Assessor	Joseph Harasta
Tax Collector	Alice Howell
Attorney	Gary Salber
Building	Wayne Serfass
Comm Dev/Planning	NA
Engineering	T&M Associates
Public Works	NA
Police Chief	NA
Fire Chief	Patrick Foster

Housing & Construction
Housing Units, 2000*
Total	1,133
Median rent	$668
Median SF home value	$101,300

Permits for New Residential Construction
	Units	Value
Total, 2006	13	$1,678,000
Single family	13	$1,678,000
Total, 2007	6	$793,000
Single family	6	$793,000

Real Property Valuation, 2008
	Parcels	Valuation
Total	1,731	$186,044,300
Vacant	319	6,329,800
Residential	840	132,041,900
Commercial	57	16,367,400
Industrial	0	0
Apartments	1	519,000
Farm land	364	4,998,700
Farm homestead	150	25,787,500

Average Property Value & Tax, 2008
Residential value	$159,424
Property tax	$3,379
Tax credit/rebate	$872

Public Library
No public municipal library

Library statistics, 2007
Population served	NA
Full-time/total staff	NA/NA

	Total	Per capita
Holdings	NA	NA
Revenues	NA	NA
Expenditures	NA	NA
Annual visits	NA	NA
Internet terminals/annual users	NA/NA	

Public Safety
Number of officers, 2007	0

Crime	2006	2007
Total crimes	45	28
Violent	3	3
Murder	0	0
Rape	0	0
Robbery	0	1
Aggravated assault	3	2
Non-violent	42	25
Burglary	16	7
Larceny	20	16
Vehicle theft	6	2
Domestic violence	9	25
Arson	0	3
Total crime rate	15.7	9.8
Violent	1.0	1.0
Non-violent	14.7	8.7

Public School District
(for school year 2007-08 except as noted)

Quinton Township School District
Robinson Street, PO Box 365
Quinton, NJ 08072
(856) 935-2379

Chief School Admin	Donna Agnew
Number of schools	1
Grade plan	K-8
Enrollment	343
Attendance rate, '06-07	95.2%
Dropout rate	NA
Students per teacher	10.0
Per pupil expenditure	$12,453
Median faculty salary	$57,987
Median administrator salary	$73,500
Grade 12 enrollment	NA
High school graduation rate	NA

Assessment test results
(percent scoring at proficient or advanced level)
	Language	Math
NJASK-Grade 3	97.7%	88.4%
GEPA-Grade 8	47.2%	94.4%
HSPA-High School	NA	NA

SAT Score Averages, 2006-07
Pct tested	Math	Verbal	Writing
NA	NA	NA	NA

Teacher Qualifications
Avg. years of experience	16
Highly-qualified teachers one subject/all subjects	100%/100%

No Child Left Behind
AYP, 2006-07	Meets Standards

Municipal Finance
State Aid Programs, 2009
Total aid	$428,329
CMPTRA	34,506
Energy tax receipts	361,522
Garden State Trust	15,840

General Budget, 2008
Total tax levy	$3,962,531
County levy	1,386,024
County taxes	1,356,119
County library	0
County health	0
County open space	29,904
School levy	2,234,109
Muni. levy	342,399
Misc. revenues	1,195,661

Taxes
	2006	2007	2008
General tax rate per $100	3.379	3.477	2.120
County equalization ratio	79.56	73.75	126.38
Net valuation taxable	$120,065,300	$121,695,748	$186,944,783
State equalized value	$163,455,029	$147,448,365	$719,468,540

See Introduction for an explanation of all data sources.

Demographics & Socio-Economic Characteristics

(2000 US Census, except as noted)

Population

1980*	26,723
1990*	25,325
2000	26,500
Male	12,639
Female	13,861
2007 (estimate)*	28,189
Population density	7,064.9

Race & Hispanic Origin, 2000

Race

White	15,950
Black/African American	7,173
American Indian/Alaska Native	42
Asian	950
Native Hawaiian/Pacific Islander	14
Other race	1,489
Two or more races	882
Hispanic origin, total	3,675
Mexican	424
Puerto Rican	887
Cuban	216
Other Hispanic	2,148

Age & Nativity, 2000

Under 5 years	1,660
18 years and over	20,170
21 years and over	19,300
65 years and over	3,836
85 years and over	430
Median age	37.1
Native-born	21,947
Foreign-born	4,553

Educational Attainment, 2000

Population 25 years and over	18,140
Less than 9th grade	6.7%
High school grad or higher	81.5%
Bachelor's degree or higher	18.6%
Graduate degree	5.5%

Income & Poverty, 1999

Per capita income	$22,481
Median household income	$50,729
Median family income	$61,931
Persons in poverty	1,864
H'holds receiving public assistance	342
H'holds receiving social security	3,019

Households, 2000

Total households	10,028
With persons under 18	3,448
With persons over 65	2,883
Family households	6,727
Single-person households	2,806
Persons per household	2.63
Persons per family	3.24

Labor & Employment

Total civilian labor force, 2007**	14,405
Unemployment rate	4.8%
Total civilian labor force, 2000	13,495
Unemployment rate	6.6%

Employed persons 16 years and over by occupation, 2000

Managers & professionals	3,862
Service occupations	1,683
Sales & office occupations	3,924
Farming, fishing & forestry	0
Construction & maintenance	1,206
Production & transportation	1,930
Self-employed persons	427

* US Census Bureau
** New Jersey Department of Labor
§ State Fiscal Year July 1–June 30

See Introduction for an explanation of all data sources.

General Information

City of Rahway
1 City Hall Plz
Rahway, NJ 07065
732-827-2000

Website	www.cityofrahway.com
Year of incorporation	1858
Land/water area (sq. miles)	3.99/0.05
Form of government	Mayor-Council

Government

Legislative Districts

US Congressional	10
State Legislative	22

Local Officials, 2009

Mayor	James Kennedy
Manager	Peter A. Pelissier
Clerk	Jean Kuc
Finance Dir	F. Ruggiero
Tax Assessor	Richard Kulman
Tax Collector	Sally DiRini
Attorney	Louis N. Rainone
Building	Richard Watkins
Planner	Lenore Slothower
Engineering	James Housten
Public Works	Frank Mazzarella
Police Chief	John Rodger
Emerg/Fire Director	William Young

Housing & Construction

Housing Units, 2000*

Total	10,381
Median rent	$732
Median SF home value	$142,600

Permits for New Residential Construction

	Units	Value
Total, 2006	368	$16,171,533
Single family	61	$6,381,602
Total, 2007	273	$22,724,538
Single family	35	$3,284,726

Real Property Valuation, 2008

	Parcels	Valuation
Total	8,131	$1,517,697,100
Vacant	497	12,511,400
Residential	7,099	958,307,700
Commercial	372	129,044,100
Industrial	89	373,443,800
Apartments	74	44,390,100
Farm land	0	0
Farm homestead	0	0

Average Property Value & Tax, 2008

Residential value	$134,992
Property tax	$6,420
Tax credit/rebate	$1,067

Public Library

Rahway Public Library
2 City Hall Plaza
Rahway, NJ 07065
732-340-1551

Director	Gail Miller

Library statistics, 2007

Population served	26,500
Full-time/total staff	6/17

	Total	Per capita
Holdings	102,440	3.87
Revenues	$1,677,859	$63.32
Expenditures	$1,759,880	$66.41
Annual visits	127,112	4.80
Internet terminals/annual users	43/12,922	

Public Safety

Number of officers, 2007	80

Crime	2006	2007
Total crimes	711	744
Violent	79	86
Murder	1	0
Rape	3	1
Robbery	48	59
Aggravated assault	27	26
Non-violent	632	658
Burglary	117	125
Larceny	433	463
Vehicle theft	82	70
Domestic violence	612	396
Arson	5	0
Total crime rate	25.8	26.7
Violent	2.9	3.1
Non-violent	22.9	23.6

Public School District

(for school year 2007-08 except as noted)

Rahway School District
Rahway Middle School, Kline Place
Rahway, NJ 07065
(732) 396-1020

Superintendent	Frank R. Buglione
Number of schools	6
Grade plan	K-12
Enrollment	3,872
Attendance rate, '06-07	93.6%
Dropout rate	3.1%
Students per teacher	11.4
Per pupil expenditure	$12,115
Median faculty salary	$54,441
Median administrator salary	$109,016
Grade 12 enrollment	242
High school graduation rate	87.3%

Assessment test results

(percent scoring at proficient or advanced level)

	Language	Math
NJASK-Grade 3	74.4%	77.7%
GEPA-Grade 8	67.7%	69.6%
HSPA-High School	58.7%	73.9%

SAT Score Averages, 2006-07

Pct tested	Math	Verbal	Writing
78%	440	443	440

Teacher Qualifications

Avg. years of experience	7
Highly-qualified teachers one subject/all subjects	99.5%/99.5%

No Child Left Behind

AYP, 2006-07	Meets Standards

Municipal Finance§

State Aid Programs, 2009

Total aid	$4,930,374
CMPTRA	2,540,818
Energy tax receipts	2,315,600
Garden State Trust	0

General Budget, 2008

Total tax levy	$72,351,760
County levy	12,328,787
County taxes	11,790,948
County library	0
County health	0
County open space	537,839
School levy	33,242,739
Muni. levy	26,780,234
Misc. revenues	18,396,082

Taxes	2006	2007	2008
General tax rate per $100	4.354	4.585	4.756
County equalization ratio	51.62	47.35	42.83
Net valuation taxable	$1,502,865,300	$1,517,592,096	$1,521,392,355
State equalized value	$3,178,630,541	$3,538,069,996	$3,716,261,547

Demographics & Socio-Economic Characteristics

(2000 US Census, except as noted)

Population

1980*	12,899
1990*	13,228
2000	14,351
Male	6,928
Female	7,423
2007 (estimate)*	14,647
Population density	2,634.4

Race & Hispanic Origin, 2000

Race

White	13,148
Black/African American	112
American Indian/Alaska Native	14
Asian	840
Native Hawaiian/Pacific Islander	1
Other race	78
Two or more races	158
Hispanic origin, total	420
Mexican	82
Puerto Rican	81
Cuban	36
Other Hispanic	221

Age & Nativity, 2000

Under 5 years	1,088
18 years and over	10,474
21 years and over	10,173
65 years and over	1,614
85 years and over	171
Median age	38.6
Native-born	12,641
Foreign-born	1,710

Educational Attainment, 2000

Population 25 years and over	9,729
Less than 9th grade	2.0%
High school grad or higher	95.5%
Bachelor's degree or higher	54.5%
Graduate degree	19.9%

Income & Poverty, 1999

Per capita income	$41,964
Median household income	$88,187
Median family income	$104,036
Persons in poverty	276
H'holds receiving public assistance	62
H'holds receiving social security	1,193

Households, 2000

Total households	5,313
With persons under 18	2,054
With persons over 65	1,185
Family households	3,945
Single-person households	1,200
Persons per household	2.68
Persons per family	3.18

Labor & Employment

Total civilian labor force, 2007**	7,895
Unemployment rate	2.4%
Total civilian labor force, 2000	7,510
Unemployment rate	3.0%

Employed persons 16 years and over by occupation, 2000

Managers & professionals	3,917
Service occupations	505
Sales & office occupations	2,139
Farming, fishing & forestry	6
Construction & maintenance	411
Production & transportation	310
Self-employed persons	383

* US Census Bureau
** New Jersey Department of Labor

General Information

Borough of Ramsey
33 N Central Ave
Ramsey, NJ 07446
201-825-3400

Website	www.ramseynj.com
Year of incorporation	1908
Land/water area (sq. miles)	5.56/0.05
Form of government	Borough

Government

Legislative Districts

US Congressional	5
State Legislative	39

Local Officials, 2009

Mayor	Christopher Botta
Manager	Nicholas Saros
Clerk	Meredith Bendian
Finance Dir	Richard Mathieson
Tax Assessor	Angela Mattiace
Tax Collector	Linda Canavan
Attorney	Peter Scandariato
Building	Robert Connell
Comm Dev/Planning	NA
Engineering	Harold Reed
Public Works	William Horton
Police Chief	Bryan Gurney
Emerg/Fire Director	Frank Agatielli

Housing & Construction

Housing Units, 2000*

Total	5,400
Median rent	$1,120
Median SF home value	$329,700

Permits for New Residential Construction

	Units	Value
Total, 2006	36	$8,101,646
Single family	36	$8,101,646
Total, 2007	29	$7,060,402
Single family	29	$7,060,402

Real Property Valuation, 2008

	Parcels	Valuation
Total	5,491	$2,786,314,600
Vacant	184	46,368,500
Residential	5,059	2,174,431,500
Commercial	215	434,209,900
Industrial	27	116,661,200
Apartments	6	14,643,500
Farm land	0	0
Farm homestead	0	0

Average Property Value & Tax, 2008

Residential value	$429,814
Property tax	$10,010
Tax credit/rebate	$1,280

Public Library

Ramsey Free Public Library
30 Wyckoff Ave
Ramsey, NJ 07446
201-327-1445

Director	Wendy B. Bloom

Library statistics, 2007

Population served	14,351
Full-time/total staff	3/7

	Total	Per capita
Holdings	88,242	6.15
Revenues	$1,243,391	$86.64
Expenditures	$983,162	$68.51
Annual visits	139,607	9.73
Internet terminals/annual users		11/21,690

Public Safety

Number of officers, 2007	33

Crime	2006	2007
Total crimes	182	210
Violent	15	16
Murder	1	0
Rape	0	0
Robbery	3	5
Aggravated assault	11	11
Non-violent	167	194
Burglary	19	25
Larceny	139	167
Vehicle theft	9	2
Domestic violence	69	59
Arson	1	0
Total crime rate	12.5	14.2
Violent	1.0	1.1
Non-violent	11.5	13.1

Public School District

(for school year 2007-08 except as noted)

Ramsey School District
266 East Main Street
Ramsey, NJ 07446
(201) 785-2300

Superintendent	Roy Montesano
Number of schools	5
Grade plan	K-12
Enrollment	3,132
Attendance rate, '06-07	96.1%
Dropout rate	0.2%
Students per teacher	10.8
Per pupil expenditure	$14,338
Median faculty salary	$55,114
Median administrator salary	$124,858
Grade 12 enrollment	243
High school graduation rate	100.0%

Assessment test results

(percent scoring at proficient or advanced level)

	Language	Math
NJASK-Grade 3	96.8%	98.6%
GEPA-Grade 8	88.6%	97.7%
HSPA-High School	95.8%	98.6%

SAT Score Averages, 2006-07

Pct tested	Math	Verbal	Writing
97%	582	559	548

Teacher Qualifications

Avg. years of experience	9
Highly-qualified teachers one subject/all subjects	100%/100%

No Child Left Behind

AYP, 2006-07	Meets Standards

Municipal Finance

State Aid Programs, 2009

Total aid	$1,990,857
CMPTRA	87,071
Energy tax receipts	1,839,083
Garden State Trust	0

General Budget, 2008

Total tax levy	$65,067,790
County levy	7,126,833
County taxes	6,740,029
County library	0
County health	0
County open space	386,804
School levy	43,462,518
Muni. levy	14,478,439
Misc. revenues	6,435,222

Taxes

	2006	2007	2008
General tax rate per $100	2.14	2.25	2.331
County equalization ratio	84.78	76.99	72.43
Net valuation taxable	$2,741,214,900	$2,770,445,552	$2,794,052,123
State equalized value	$3,568,621,487	$3,821,936,347	$3,775,573,358

See Introduction for an explanation of all data sources.

Demographics & Socio-Economic Characteristics

(2000 US Census, except as noted)

Population

1980*	17,828
1990*	19,974
2000	24,847
Male	12,317
Female	12,530
2007 (estimate)*	25,346
Population density	1,209.3

Race & Hispanic Origin, 2000

Race

White	21,293
Black/African American	572
American Indian/Alaska Native	15
Asian	2,272
Native Hawaiian/Pacific Islander	5
Other race	326
Two or more races	364
Hispanic origin, total	1,208
Mexican	130
Puerto Rican	257
Cuban	81
Other Hispanic	740

Age & Nativity, 2000

Under 5 years	1,885
18 years and over	17,469
21 years and over	16,902
65 years and over	1,817
85 years and over	172
Median age	36.5
Native-born	20,849
Foreign-born	3,998

Educational Attainment, 2000

Population 25 years and over	16,253
Less than 9th grade	1.3%
High school grad or higher	95.7%
Bachelor's degree or higher	59.4%
Graduate degree	25.7%

Income & Poverty, 1999

Per capita income	$43,072
Median household income	$97,589
Median family income	$115,722
Persons in poverty	356
H'holds receiving public assistance	49
H'holds receiving social security	1,398

Households, 2000

Total households	8,679
With persons under 18	3,929
With persons over 65	1,341
Family households	6,806
Single-person households	1,562
Persons per household	2.86
Persons per family	3.28

Labor & Employment

Total civilian labor force, 2007**	14,164
Unemployment rate	2.7%
Total civilian labor force, 2000	13,155
Unemployment rate	2.2%

Employed persons 16 years and over by occupation, 2000

Managers & professionals	7,575
Service occupations	957
Sales & office occupations	3,019
Farming, fishing & forestry	0
Construction & maintenance	584
Production & transportation	731
Self-employed persons	1,013

General Information

Township of Randolph
502 Millbrook Ave
Randolph, NJ 07869
973-989-7100

Website	www.randolfnj.org
Year of incorporation	1806
Land/water area (sq. miles)	20.96/0.12
Form of government	Council-Manager

Government

Legislative Districts

US Congressional	11
State Legislative	25

Local Officials, 2009

Mayor	Edward Metz
Manager	John Lovell
Clerk	Donna M. Luciani
Finance Dir	Michael Soccio
Tax Assessor	Barbara Gothie
Tax Collector	Lisa Combes
Attorney	Ed Buzak
Building	Frank Howard
Planning	Darren Carney
Engineering	Paul Ferriero
Public Works	Bill Kerwick
Police Chief	Dean Kazaba
Emerg/Fire Director	William Wagner

Housing & Construction

Housing Units, 2000*

Total	8,903
Median rent	$875
Median SF home value	$329,800

Permits for New Residential Construction

	Units	Value
Total, 2006	10	$3,200,800
Single family	10	$3,200,800
Total, 2007	6	$1,457,000
Single family	4	$1,333,000

Real Property Valuation, 2008

	Parcels	Valuation
Total	7,916	$2,906,072,500
Vacant	331	34,523,800
Residential	7,191	2,409,164,000
Commercial	257	239,003,200
Industrial	57	116,292,300
Apartments	17	101,600,500
Farm land	42	196,500
Farm homestead	21	5,292,200

Average Property Value & Tax, 2008

Residential value	$334,783
Property tax	$10,181
Tax credit/rebate	$1,184

Public Library

Randolph Township Public Library
28 Calais Rd
Randolph, NJ 07869
973-895-3556

Director	Anita S. Freeman

Library statistics, 2007

Population served	24,847
Full-time/total staff	4/9

	Total	Per capita
Holdings	105,922	4.26
Revenues	$1,709,846	$68.81
Expenditures	$1,530,362	$61.59
Annual visits	154,695	6.23
Internet terminals/annual users	23/66,400	

Public Safety

Number of officers, 2007	42

Crime	2006	2007
Total crimes	212	216
Violent	8	4
Murder	0	0
Rape	0	0
Robbery	6	1
Aggravated assault	2	3
Non-violent	204	212
Burglary	24	20
Larceny	170	184
Vehicle theft	10	8
Domestic violence	213	184
Arson	1	2
Total crime rate	8.2	8.4
Violent	0.3	0.2
Non-violent	7.9	8.2

Public School District

(for school year 2007-08 except as noted)

Randolph Township School District
25 School House Road
Randolph, NJ 07869
(973) 361-0808

Superintendent	James Sheeran (Int)
Number of schools	6
Grade plan	K-12
Enrollment	5,570
Attendance rate, '06-07	95.5%
Dropout rate	0.1%
Students per teacher	11.4
Per pupil expenditure	$12,298
Median faculty salary	$57,330
Median administrator salary	$111,014
Grade 12 enrollment	430
High school graduation rate	98.6%

Assessment test results

(percent scoring at proficient or advanced level)

	Language	Math
NJASK-Grade 3	96.4%	96.6%
GEPA-Grade 8	81.7%	93.2%
HSPA-High School	90.5%	93.0%

SAT Score Averages, 2006-07

Pct tested	Math	Verbal	Writing
98%	554	534	533

Teacher Qualifications

Avg. years of experience	9

Highly-qualified teachers
one subject/all subjects...... 100%/100%

No Child Left Behind

AYP, 2006-07	Meets Standards

Municipal Finance

State Aid Programs, 2009

Total aid	$2,421,921
CMPTRA	424,823
Energy tax receipts	1,920,419
Garden State Trust	0

General Budget, 2008

Total tax levy	$88,504,283
County levy	11,600,679
County taxes	9,467,146
County library	0
County health	0
County open space	2,133,533
School levy	59,732,815
Muni. levy	17,170,789
Misc. revenues	18,181,986

Taxes

	2006	2007	2008
General tax rate per $100	2.83	2.94	3.042
County equalization ratio	66.19	59.85	58.32
Net valuation taxable	$2,878,129,200	$2,904,754,223	$2,910,303,249
State equalized value	$4,813,718,699	$4,978,028,627	$4,923,940,415

* US Census Bureau
** New Jersey Department of Labor

See Introduction for an explanation of all data sources.

Demographics & Socio-Economic Characteristics

(2000 US Census, except as noted)

Population

1980*	6,128
1990*	5,798
2000	6,338
Male	3,042
Female	3,296
2007 (estimate)*	6,970
Population density	3,416.7

Race & Hispanic Origin, 2000

Race

White	5,561
Black/African American	59
American Indian/Alaska Native	5
Asian	518
Native Hawaiian/Pacific Islander	10
Other race	104
Two or more races	81
Hispanic origin, total	533
Mexican	43
Puerto Rican	63
Cuban	13
Other Hispanic	414

Age & Nativity, 2000

Under 5 years	460
18 years and over	4,922
21 years and over	4,757
65 years and over	1,026
85 years and over	128
Median age	37.6
Native-born	4,858
Foreign-born	1,480

Educational Attainment, 2000

Population 25 years and over	4,557
Less than 9th grade	10.0%
High school grad or higher	77.3%
Bachelor's degree or higher	27.0%
Graduate degree	9.1%

Income & Poverty, 1999

Per capita income	$26,420
Median household income	$51,122
Median family income	$59,962
Persons in poverty	406
H'holds receiving public assistance	47
H'holds receiving social security	715

Households, 2000

Total households	2,556
With persons under 18	817
With persons over 65	758
Family households	1,671
Single-person households	740
Persons per household	2.48
Persons per family	3.08

Labor & Employment

Total civilian labor force, 2007**	3,657
Unemployment rate	4.4%
Total civilian labor force, 2000	3,217
Unemployment rate	4.3%

Employed persons 16 years and over by occupation, 2000

Managers & professionals	1,132
Service occupations	457
Sales & office occupations	837
Farming, fishing & forestry	0
Construction & maintenance	271
Production & transportation	382
Self-employed persons	116

* US Census Bureau
** New Jersey Department of Labor

General Information

Borough of Raritan
22 1st St
Raritan, NJ 08869
908-231-1300

Website	www.raritanboro.org
Year of incorporation	1948
Land/water area (sq. miles)	2.04/0.00
Form of government	Borough

Government

Legislative Districts

US Congressional	11
State Legislative	16

Local Officials, 2009

Mayor	Jo-Ann Liptak
Manager	Daniel Jaxel
Clerk	Pamela Huefner
Finance Dir	Carolyn Gara
Tax Assessor	Glen Stives
Tax Collector	Karin Kneafsey
Attorney	Paul Rizzo
Building	Louis Gara
Comm Dev/Planning	NA
Engineering	Stanley Schrek
Public Works	Danny Laverde
Police Chief	(vacant)
Emerg/Fire Director	Carl Memoli

Housing & Construction

Housing Units, 2000*

Total	2,644
Median rent	$801
Median SF home value	$182,500

Permits for New Residential Construction

	Units	Value
Total, 2006	133	$13,526,319
Single family	6	$886,819
Total, 2007	151	$15,217,685
Single family	5	$738,685

Real Property Valuation, 2008

	Parcels	Valuation
Total	2,143	$1,151,098,375
Vacant	43	10,612,600
Residential	1,907	608,953,934
Commercial	176	251,226,741
Industrial	13	278,406,500
Apartments	4	1,898,600
Farm land	0	0
Farm homestead	0	0

Average Property Value & Tax, 2008

Residential value	$319,326
Property tax	$6,519
Tax credit/rebate	$1,038

Public Library

Raritan Public Library
54 E Somerset St
Raritan, NJ 08869
908-725-0413

Director	Jacqueline Widows

Library statistics, 2007

Population served	6,338
Full-time/total staff	0/2

	Total	Per capita
Holdings	53,630	8.46
Revenues	$463,795	$73.18
Expenditures	$304,483	$48.04
Annual visits	8,400	1.33
Internet terminals/annual users	4/4,468	

Public Safety

Number of officers, 2007	19

Crime	2006	2007
Total crimes	125	126
Violent	9	8
Murder	0	0
Rape	1	0
Robbery	4	2
Aggravated assault	4	6
Non-violent	116	118
Burglary	29	21
Larceny	83	96
Vehicle theft	4	1
Domestic violence	96	104
Arson	0	0
Total crime rate	19.6	19.6
Violent	1.4	1.2
Non-violent	18.2	18.4

Public School District

(for school year 2007-08 except as noted)

Bridgewater-Raritan Regional School Dist.
836 Newmans Ln, PO Box 6030
Bridgewater, NJ 08807
(908) 685-2777

Superintendent	Michael Schilder
Number of schools	0
Grade plan	K-12
Enrollment	9,115
Attendance rate, '06-07	96.4%
Dropout rate	0.3%
Students per teacher	10.3
Per pupil expenditure	$13,578
Median faculty salary	$53,650
Median administrator salary	$125,757
Grade 12 enrollment	648
High school graduation rate	98.8%

Assessment test results

(percent scoring at proficient or advanced level)

	Language	Math
NJASK-Grade 3	93.8%	90.6%
GEPA-Grade 8	86.4%	94.0%
HSPA-High School	88.9%	92.4%

SAT Score Averages, 2006-07

Pct tested	Math	Verbal	Writing
94%	568	529	529

Teacher Qualifications

Avg. years of experience	7
Highly-qualified teachers one subject/all subjects	100%/100%

No Child Left Behind

AYP, 2006-07	Meets Standards

Municipal Finance

State Aid Programs, 2009

Total aid	$854,081
CMPTRA	223,254
Energy tax receipts	609,475
Garden State Trust	0

General Budget, 2008

Total tax levy	$23,524,596
County levy	3,856,495
County taxes	3,472,194
County library	0
County health	0
County open space	384,301
School levy	13,009,276
Muni. levy	6,658,826
Misc. revenues	2,821,069

Taxes

	2006	2007	2008
General tax rate per $100	1.83	2.01	2.042
County equalization ratio	97.64	90.69	90.90
Net valuation taxable	$1,148,334,789	$1,141,321,495	$1,152,275,941
State equalized value	$1,267,910,270	$1,255,461,316	$1,335,629,659

See Introduction for an explanation of all data sources.

Demographics & Socio-Economic Characteristics

(2000 US Census, except as noted)

Population

1980*	8,292
1990*	15,616
2000	19,809
Male	9,606
Female	10,203
2007 (estimate)*	22,471
Population density	593.8

Race & Hispanic Origin, 2000

Race

White	18,466
Black/African American	244
American Indian/Alaska Native	17
Asian	693
Native Hawaiian/Pacific Islander	2
Other race	135
Two or more races	252
Hispanic origin, total	552
Mexican	86
Puerto Rican	173
Cuban	80
Other Hispanic	213

Age & Nativity, 2000

Under 5 years	1,431
18 years and over	14,010
21 years and over	13,570
65 years and over	1,770
85 years and over	251
Median age	37.4
Native-born	18,188
Foreign-born	1,621

Educational Attainment, 2000

Population 25 years and over	13,086
Less than 9th grade	1.8%
High school grad or higher	94.3%
Bachelor's degree or higher	48.3%
Graduate degree	17.7%

Income & Poverty, 1999

Per capita income	$38,919
Median household income	$85,996
Median family income	$96,336
Persons in poverty	399
H'holds receiving public assistance	69
H'holds receiving social security	1,169

Households, 2000

Total households	6,939
With persons under 18	3,083
With persons over 65	1,167
Family households	5,389
Single-person households	1,263
Persons per household	2.81
Persons per family	3.24

Labor & Employment

Total civilian labor force, 2007**	11,842
Unemployment rate	1.5%
Total civilian labor force, 2000	10,655
Unemployment rate	1.4%

Employed persons 16 years and over by occupation, 2000

Managers & professionals	5,508
Service occupations	945
Sales & office occupations	2,628
Farming, fishing & forestry	17
Construction & maintenance	686
Production & transportation	717
Self-employed persons	811

‡ Main library for county
* US Census Bureau
** New Jersey Department of Labor

General Information

Township of Raritan
1 Municipal Dr
Flemington, NJ 08822
908-806-6100

Website	www.raritan-township.com
Year of incorporation	1838
Land/water area (sq. miles)	37.84/0.07
Form of government	Township

Government

Legislative Districts

US Congressional	7
State Legislative	23

Local Officials, 2009

Mayor	Richard O'Malley
Manager	Allan Pietrefesa
Clerk	Rosary Sollena
Finance Dir	Allan Pietrefesa
Tax Assessor	Marianne Busher
Tax Collector	Betty Kopp
Attorney	Albert Cruz
Building	Peter Ball
Planning	James Humphries
Engineering	Frederick Coppola
Public Works	Dirk Struening
Police Chief	Glenn S. Tabasko
Emerg/Fire Director	Mark Bishop

Housing & Construction

Housing Units, 2000*

Total	7,094
Median rent	$971
Median SF home value	$248,300

Permits for New Residential Construction

	Units	Value
Total, 2006	49	$10,562,338
Single family	45	$10,207,538
Total, 2007	18	$4,138,604
Single family	18	$4,138,604

Real Property Valuation, 2008

	Parcels	Valuation
Total	9,125	$4,301,623,875
Vacant	623	96,565,800
Residential	7,735	3,484,001,475
Commercial	290	514,729,300
Industrial	29	115,852,600
Apartments	5	12,686,700
Farm land	286	3,076,100
Farm homestead	157	74,711,900

Average Property Value & Tax, 2008

Residential value	$450,927
Property tax	$8,959
Tax credit/rebate	$1,115

Public Library

Hunterdon County Library‡
314 State Highway 12, Bldg #3
Flemington, NJ 08822
908-788-1444

Director	Mark Titus

County Library statistics, 2007

Population served	112,726
Full-time/total staff	19/54

	Total	Per capita
Holdings	436,046	3.87
Revenues	$7,243,246	$64.26
Expenditures	$6,774,289	$60.10
Annual visits	606,702	5.38
Internet terminals/annual users	27/45,073	

Public Safety

Number of officers, 2007	35

Crime	2006	2007
Total crimes	202	224
Violent	8	5
Murder	0	0
Rape	2	0
Robbery	3	0
Aggravated assault	3	5
Non-violent	194	219
Burglary	19	28
Larceny	164	185
Vehicle theft	11	6
Domestic violence	165	171
Arson	0	1
Total crime rate	8.9	9.9
Violent	0.4	0.2
Non-violent	8.6	9.6

Public School District

(for school year 2007-08 except as noted)

Flemington-Raritan Regional School Dist.
50 Court Street
Flemington, NJ 08822
(908) 284-7575

Superintendent	Jack Farr
Number of schools	6
Grade plan	K-8
Enrollment	3,558
Attendance rate, '06-07	96.2%
Dropout rate	NA
Students per teacher	10.0
Per pupil expenditure	$13,315
Median faculty salary	$53,219
Median administrator salary	$111,026
Grade 12 enrollment	NA
High school graduation rate	NA

Assessment test results

(percent scoring at proficient or advanced level)

	Language	Math
NJASK-Grade 3	98.7%	94.7%
GEPA-Grade 8	81.0%	93.2%
HSPA-High School	NA	NA

SAT Score Averages, 2006-07

Pct tested	Math	Verbal	Writing
NA	NA	NA	NA

Teacher Qualifications

Avg. years of experience	11
Highly-qualified teachers one subject/all subjects	100%/100%

No Child Left Behind

AYP, 2006-07	Meets Standards

Municipal Finance

State Aid Programs, 2009

Total aid	$2,815,827
CMPTRA	93,741
Energy tax receipts	2,604,679
Garden State Trust	4,208

General Budget, 2008

Total tax levy	$85,595,032
County levy	14,963,868
County taxes	12,524,374
County library	1,087,481
County health	0
County open space	1,352,012
School levy	60,156,107
Muni. levy	10,475,056
Misc. revenues	7,275,471

Taxes	2006	2007	2008
General tax rate per $100	3.44	1.96	1.987
County equalization ratio	53.98	93.08	95.81
Net valuation taxable	$2,250,637,500	$4,289,462,305	$4,308,108,823
State equalized value	$4,156,262,795	$4,336,655,644	$4,355,513,231

See Introduction for an explanation of all data sources.

Demographics & Socio-Economic Characteristics
(2000 US Census, except as noted)

Population
1980*	10,855
1990*	13,400
2000	15,803
Male	7,782
Female	8,021
2007 (estimate)*	16,052
Population density	336.6

Race & Hispanic Origin, 2000
Race
White	15,035
Black/African American	120
American Indian/Alaska Native	10
Asian	405
Native Hawaiian/Pacific Islander	0
Other race	84
Two or more races	149
Hispanic origin, total	324
Mexican	34
Puerto Rican	103
Cuban	35
Other Hispanic	152

Age & Nativity, 2000
Under 5 years	1,171
18 years and over	11,618
21 years and over	11,279
65 years and over	1,542
85 years and over	147
Median age	39.0
Native-born	14,684
Foreign-born	1,119

Educational Attainment, 2000
Population 25 years and over	10,767
Less than 9th grade	1.4%
High school grad or higher	94.6%
Bachelor's degree or higher	48.2%
Graduate degree	18.8%

Income & Poverty, 1999
Per capita income	$41,000
Median household income	$95,356
Median family income	$106,343
Persons in poverty	255
H'holds receiving public assistance	72
H'holds receiving social security	1,174

Households, 2000
Total households	5,676
With persons under 18	2,221
With persons over 65	1,137
Family households	4,413
Single-person households	1,032
Persons per household	2.77
Persons per family	3.18

Labor & Employment
Total civilian labor force, 2007**	9,730
Unemployment rate	2.5%
Total civilian labor force, 2000	8,784
Unemployment rate	2.3%

Employed persons 16 years and over by occupation, 2000
Managers & professionals	4,476
Service occupations	565
Sales & office occupations	2,320
Farming, fishing & forestry	17
Construction & maintenance	532
Production & transportation	676
Self-employed persons	517

‡ Branch of county library
* US Census Bureau
** New Jersey Department of Labor

General Information
Township of Readington
509 County Road 523
Whitehouse Station, NJ 08889
908-534-4051
Website	www.readingtontwp.org
Year of incorporation	1730
Land/water area (sq. miles)	47.69/0.12
Form of government	Township

Government
Legislative Districts
US Congressional	7
State Legislative	23

Local Officials, 2009
Mayor	Julia C. Allen
Manager	Vita Mekovetz
Clerk	Vita Mekovetz
Finance Dir	Thomas Carro
Tax Assessor	Mary Mastro
Tax Collector	Bonnie Holborow
Attorney	Sharon Dragan
Building	Michael Kovonuk
Comm Dev/Planning	NA
Engineering	Clay McEldowney
Public Works	Scott Jesseman
Police Chief	James Paganessi
Fire/Emergency Dir	NA

Housing & Construction
Housing Units, 2000*
Total	5,794
Median rent	$937
Median SF home value	$289,700

Permits for New Residential Construction
	Units	Value
Total, 2006	14	$12,720,328
Single family	14	$12,720,328
Total, 2007	40	$7,557,090
Single family	14	$5,409,090

Real Property Valuation, 2008
	Parcels	Valuation
Total	7,090	$2,833,325,160
Vacant	467	34,914,260
Residential	5,528	2,151,444,900
Commercial	233	452,457,800
Industrial	39	50,137,700
Apartments	2	1,281,400
Farm land	490	4,627,500
Farm homestead	331	138,461,600

Average Property Value & Tax, 2008
Residential value	$390,836
Property tax	$9,851
Tax credit/rebate	$1,278

Public Library
Readington Township Library‡
105 Route 523
Whitehouse Station, NJ 08889
908-534-4421
Branch Librarian .... Karen Konn

Library statistics, 2007
see Hunterdon County profile for library system statistics

Public Safety
Number of officers, 2007 23
Crime	2006	2007
Total crimes	167	131
Violent	14	13
Murder	0	0
Rape	3	4
Robbery	1	1
Aggravated assault	10	8
Non-violent	153	118
Burglary	35	25
Larceny	116	92
Vehicle theft	2	1
Domestic violence	64	86
Arson	4	0
Total crime rate	10.2	8.0
Violent	0.9	0.8
Non-violent	9.4	7.2

Public School District
(for school year 2007-08 except as noted)

Readington Township School District
P.O. Box 807
Whitehouse Station, NJ, NJ 08889
(908) 534-2195
Superintendent	Jorden Schiff
Number of schools	4
Grade plan	K-8
Enrollment	2,187
Attendance rate, '06-07	96.1%
Dropout rate	NA
Students per teacher	10.1
Per pupil expenditure	$13,350
Median faculty salary	$51,020
Median administrator salary	$98,514
Grade 12 enrollment	NA
High school graduation rate	NA

Assessment test results
(percent scoring at proficient or advanced level)
	Language	Math
NJASK-Grade 3	98.4%	98.8%
GEPA-Grade 8	84.0%	89.5%
HSPA-High School	NA	NA

SAT Score Averages, 2006-07
Pct tested	Math	Verbal	Writing
NA	NA	NA	NA

Teacher Qualifications
Avg. years of experience 9
Highly-qualified teachers
one subject/all subjects ... 100%/100%

No Child Left Behind
AYP, 2006-07 .... Meets Standards

Municipal Finance
State Aid Programs, 2009
Total aid	$1,888,774
CMPTRA	77,710
Energy tax receipts	1,743,828
Garden State Trust	6,033

General Budget, 2008
Total tax levy	$71,534,835
County levy	12,659,399
County taxes	10,595,595
County library	920,031
County health	0
County open space	1,143,773
School levy	47,431,416
Muni. levy	11,444,019
Misc. revenues	7,269,914

Taxes	2006	2007	2008
General tax rate per $100	2.38	2.49	2.521
County equalization ratio	79.62	72.37	74.65
Net valuation taxable	$2,813,339,275	$2,820,911,243	$2,838,252,322
State equalized value	$3,619,595,137	$3,831,917,130	$3,895,254,170

See Introduction for an explanation of all data sources.

Demographics & Socio-Economic Characteristics

(2000 US Census, except as noted)

Population

1980*	12,031
1990*	10,636
2000	11,844
Male	5,670
Female	6,174
2007 (estimate)*	11,890
Population density	6,679.8

Race & Hispanic Origin, 2000

Race

White	8,077
Black/African American	2,375
American Indian/Alaska Native	41
Asian	259
Native Hawaiian/Pacific Islander	10
Other race	797
Two or more races	285
Hispanic origin, total	2,027
Mexican	1,171
Puerto Rican	296
Cuban	24
Other Hispanic	536

Age & Nativity, 2000

Under 5 years	682
18 years and over	9,770
21 years and over	9,376
65 years and over	2,173
85 years and over	479
Median age	37.5
Native-born	10,073
Foreign-born	1,771

Educational Attainment, 2000

Population 25 years and over	8,737
Less than 9th grade	8.7%
High school grad or higher	81.6%
Bachelor's degree or higher	31.9%
Graduate degree	10.6%

Income & Poverty, 1999

Per capita income	$26,265
Median household income	$47,282
Median family income	$63,333
Persons in poverty	1,363
H'holds receiving public assistance	89
H'holds receiving social security	1,582

Households, 2000

Total households	5,201
With persons under 18	1,126
With persons over 65	1,478
Family households	2,504
Single-person households	2,233
Persons per household	2.20
Persons per family	2.99

Labor & Employment

Total civilian labor force, 2007**	6,753
Unemployment rate	5.1%
Total civilian labor force, 2000	6,354
Unemployment rate	5.7%

Employed persons 16 years and over by occupation, 2000

Managers & professionals	2,194
Service occupations	1,166
Sales & office occupations	1,788
Farming, fishing & forestry	10
Construction & maintenance	388
Production & transportation	444
Self-employed persons	333

See Introduction for an explanation of all data sources.

General Information

Borough of Red Bank
90 Monmouth St
Red Bank, NJ 07701
732-530-2740

Website	www.redbanknj.org
Year of incorporation	1908
Land/water area (sq. miles)	1.78/0.37
Form of government	Borough

Government

Legislative Districts

US Congressional	6
State Legislative	12

Local Officials, 2009

Mayor	Pasquale Menna
Manager	Stanley Sickels
Deputy Clerk	Pam Borghi
CFO	Frank Mason
Tax Assessor	Mitchell Ellias
Tax Collector	Dale Connor
Attorney	Kenneth Pringle
Building	James Williams
Planning	Donna Barr
Engineering	Christine Ballard
Public Works	Gary Watson
Police Chief	Mark Fitzgerald
Fire Chief	Joseph Forgione (Vol)

Housing & Construction

Housing Units, 2000*

Total	5,450
Median rent	$813
Median SF home value	$178,900

Permits for New Residential Construction

	Units	Value
Total, 2006	53	$9,568,206
Single family	8	$1,114,667
Total, 2007	32	$5,556,043
Single family	7	$859,633

Real Property Valuation, 2008

	Parcels	Valuation
Total	4,030	$2,262,729,800
Vacant	87	20,991,400
Residential	3,328	1,353,253,700
Commercial	536	685,713,600
Industrial	51	54,293,500
Apartments	28	148,477,600
Farm land	0	0
Farm homestead	0	0

Average Property Value & Tax, 2008

Residential value	$406,627
Property tax	$6,480
Tax credit/rebate	$1,076

Public Library

Red Bank Public Library
84 W Front St
Red Bank, NJ 07701
732-842-0690

Director .... Deborah Griffin-Sadel

Library statistics, 2007

Population served	11,844
Full-time/total staff	3/8

	Total	Per capita
Holdings	49,047	4.14
Revenues	$879,211	$74.23
Expenditures	$626,858	$52.93
Annual visits	4,859	0.41
Internet terminals/annual users	0/0	

Public Safety

Number of officers, 2007		41

Crime	2006	2007
Total crimes	377	328
Violent	50	40
Murder	0	0
Rape	5	4
Robbery	27	19
Aggravated assault	18	17
Non-violent	327	288
Burglary	36	61
Larceny	279	216
Vehicle theft	12	11
Domestic violence	143	198
Arson	0	3
Total crime rate	31.7	27.7
Violent	4.2	3.4
Non-violent	27.5	24.3

Public School District

(for school year 2007-08 except as noted)

Red Bank School District
76 Branch Avenue
Red Bank, NJ 07701
(732) 758-1507

Superintendent	Laura C. Morana
Number of schools	2
Grade plan	K-8
Enrollment	842
Attendance rate, '06-07	95.3%
Dropout rate	NA
Students per teacher	9.6
Per pupil expenditure	$14,143
Median faculty salary	$48,460
Median administrator salary	$93,005
Grade 12 enrollment	NA
High school graduation rate	NA

Assessment test results

(percent scoring at proficient or advanced level)

	Language	Math
NJASK-Grade 3	84.5%	74.3%
GEPA-Grade 8	49.2%	75.5%
HSPA-High School	NA	NA

SAT Score Averages, 2006-07

Pct tested	Math	Verbal	Writing
NA	NA	NA	NA

Teacher Qualifications

Avg. years of experience	7
Highly-qualified teachers one subject/all subjects	100%/100%

No Child Left Behind

AYP, 2006-07 .... Meets Standards

Municipal Finance

State Aid Programs, 2009

Total aid	$2,593,666
CMPTRA	171,308
Energy tax receipts	2,357,517
Garden State Trust	0

General Budget, 2008

Total tax levy	$36,200,779
County levy	5,599,219
County taxes	5,249,161
County library	0
County health	0
County open space	350,058
School levy	20,494,268
Muni. levy	10,107,292
Misc. revenues	9,064,684

Taxes

	2006	2007	2008
General tax rate per $100	3.428	1.541	1.594
County equalization ratio	50.44	102.35	98.41
Net valuation taxable	$968,840,300	$2,238,531,929	$2,271,728,671
State equalized value	$2,145,416,879	$2,274,537,024	$98,331,033

Demographics & Socio-Economic Characteristics
(2000 US Census, except as noted)

Population
1980*	10,294
1990*	9,996
2000	10,830
Male	5,240
Female	5,590
2007 (estimate)*	10,894
Population density	4,173.9

Race & Hispanic Origin, 2000
Race
White	8,217
Black/African American	83
American Indian/Alaska Native	9
Asian	1,887
Native Hawaiian/Pacific Islander	4
Other race	379
Two or more races	251
Hispanic origin, total	1,494
Mexican	30
Puerto Rican	244
Cuban	361
Other Hispanic	859

Age & Nativity, 2000
Under 5 years	567
18 years and over	8,465
21 years and over	8,192
65 years and over	1,853
85 years and over	230
Median age	39.5
Native-born	7,184
Foreign-born	3,646

Educational Attainment, 2000
Population 25 years and over	7,737
Less than 9th grade	7.3%
High school grad or higher	78.8%
Bachelor's degree or higher	26.0%
Graduate degree	6.7%

Income & Poverty, 1999
Per capita income	$25,558
Median household income	$54,081
Median family income	$66,330
Persons in poverty	709
H'holds receiving public assistance	88
H'holds receiving social security	1,356

Households, 2000
Total households	4,020
With persons under 18	1,385
With persons over 65	1,367
Family households	2,967
Single-person households	925
Persons per household	2.69
Persons per family	3.19

Labor & Employment
Total civilian labor force, 2007**	5,449
Unemployment rate	3.3%
Total civilian labor force, 2000	5,162
Unemployment rate	3.6%

Employed persons 16 years and over by occupation, 2000
Managers & professionals	1,787
Service occupations	770
Sales & office occupations	1,353
Farming, fishing & forestry	0
Construction & maintenance	480
Production & transportation	585
Self-employed persons	308

* US Census Bureau
** New Jersey Department of Labor
§ State Fiscal Year July 1–June 30

General Information
Borough of Ridgefield
604 Broad Ave
Ridgefield, NJ 07657
201-943-5215
Website	ridgefieldboro.com
Year of incorporation	1892
Land/water area (sq. miles)	2.61/0.26
Form of government	Borough

Government
Legislative Districts
US Congressional	9
State Legislative	38

Local Officials, 2009
Mayor	Anthony Suarez
Borough Admin	Roberta Stern
Clerk	Linda Prina
Finance Dir	Joseph Luppino
Tax Assessor	George Reggo
Tax Collector	Frank Berardo
Attorney	Douglas Doyle
Construction Official	Armand Marini III
Comm Dev/Planning	NA
Borough Engineer	Carl A. Jenne
Public Works	Nick Gambardella
Police Chief	Richard Stoltenborg
Emerg/Fire Director	Joe Greco

Housing & Construction
Housing Units, 2000*
Total	4,120
Median rent	$903
Median SF home value	$239,100

Permits for New Residential Construction
	Units	Value
Total, 2006	28	$4,932,273
Single family	18	$3,380,104
Total, 2007	23	$5,079,582
Single family	19	$4,458,714

Real Property Valuation, 2008
	Parcels	Valuation
Total	2,925	$1,851,573,000
Vacant	100	66,440,200
Residential	2,499	1,252,327,000
Commercial	225	242,269,400
Industrial	87	228,205,600
Apartments	14	62,330,800
Farm land	0	0
Farm homestead	0	0

Average Property Value & Tax, 2008
Residential value	$501,131
Property tax	$7,465
Tax credit/rebate	$1,048

Public Library
Ridgefield Public Library
527 Morse Avenue
Ridgefield, NJ 07657
201-941-0192
Director	Jane Forte

Library statistics, 2007
Population served	10,830
Full-time/total staff	2/8

	Total	Per capita
Holdings	60,027	5.54
Revenues	$618,484	$57.11
Expenditures	$624,224	$57.64
Annual visits	25,670	2.37
Internet terminals/annual users	17/7,500	

Public Safety
Number of officers, 2007	28

Crime	2006	2007
Total crimes	120	113
Violent	12	5
Murder	0	0
Rape	0	2
Robbery	4	1
Aggravated assault	8	2
Non-violent	108	108
Burglary	28	28
Larceny	64	63
Vehicle theft	16	17
Domestic violence	10	8
Arson	0	1
Total crime rate	10.9	10.3
Violent	1.1	0.5
Non-violent	9.8	9.8

Public School District
(for school year 2007-08 except as noted)

Ridgefield School District
555 Chestnut Street
Ridgefield, NJ 07657
(201) 945-7747
Superintendent	Richard Brockel
Number of schools	4
Grade plan	K-12
Enrollment	1,830
Attendance rate, '06-07	94.4%
Dropout rate	0.1%
Students per teacher	10.2
Per pupil expenditure	$14,837
Median faculty salary	$54,133
Median administrator salary	$93,162
Grade 12 enrollment	150
High school graduation rate	99.4%

Assessment test results
(percent scoring at proficient or advanced level)
	Language	Math
NJASK-Grade 3	92.8%	93.7%
GEPA-Grade 8	78.5%	86.2%
HSPA-High School	83.7%	79.6%

SAT Score Averages, 2006-07
Pct tested	Math	Verbal	Writing
87%	506	460	469

Teacher Qualifications
Avg. years of experience	9
Highly-qualified teachers one subject/all subjects	98.5%/98.5%

No Child Left Behind
AYP, 2006-07	Meets Standards

Municipal Finance§
State Aid Programs, 2009
Total aid	$5,925,121
CMPTRA	0
Energy tax receipts	5,776,993
Garden State Trust	0

General Budget, 2008
Total tax levy	$27,600,443
County levy	3,839,353
County taxes	3,631,124
County library	0
County health	0
County open space	208,229
School levy	15,288,924
Muni. levy	8,472,166
Misc. revenues	10,473,332

Taxes
Taxes	2006	2007	2008
General tax rate per $100	1.19	1.37	1.491
County equalization ratio	108.53	98.39	89.67
Net valuation taxable	$1,849,861,600	$1,853,343,069	$1,852,804,740
State equalized value	$1,881,416,081	$2,066,699,202	$2,189,335,025

See Introduction for an explanation of all data sources.

Demographics & Socio-Economic Characteristics
(2000 US Census, except as noted)

Population
1980*	12,738
1990*	12,454
2000	12,873
Male	6,150
Female	6,723
2007 (estimate)*	12,483
Population density	7,215.6

Race & Hispanic Origin, 2000
Race
White	10,067
Black/African American	528
American Indian/Alaska Native	28
Asian	1,011
Native Hawaiian/Pacific Islander	4
Other race	837
Two or more races	398
Hispanic origin, total	2,863
Mexican	64
Puerto Rican	491
Cuban	513
Other Hispanic	1,795

Age & Nativity, 2000
Under 5 years	755
18 years and over	9,995
21 years and over	9,615
65 years and over	1,655
85 years and over	163
Median age	37.2
Native-born	9,792
Foreign-born	3,081

Educational Attainment, 2000
Population 25 years and over	9,024
Less than 9th grade	5.1%
High school grad or higher	85.1%
Bachelor's degree or higher	26.1%
Graduate degree	8.3%

Income & Poverty, 1999
Per capita income	$24,290
Median household income	$51,825
Median family income	$62,414
Persons in poverty	865
H'holds receiving public assistance	83
H'holds receiving social security	1,280

Households, 2000
Total households	5,012
With persons under 18	1,588
With persons over 65	1,263
Family households	3,243
Single-person households	1,484
Persons per household	2.56
Persons per family	3.24

Labor & Employment
Total civilian labor force, 2007**	7,209
Unemployment rate	3.7%
Total civilian labor force, 2000	6,852
Unemployment rate	4.1%

Employed persons 16 years and over by occupation, 2000
Managers & professionals	2,115
Service occupations	848
Sales & office occupations	2,290
Farming, fishing & forestry	0
Construction & maintenance	517
Production & transportation	801
Self-employed persons	253

* US Census Bureau
** New Jersey Department of Labor

General Information
Village of Ridgefield Park
234 Main St
Ridgefield Park, NJ 07660
201-641-4950

Website	www.ridgefieldpark.org
Year of incorporation	1892
Land/water area (sq. miles)	1.73/0.19
Form of government	Commission

Government
Legislative Districts
US Congressional	9
State Legislative	37

Local Officials, 2009
Mayor	George Fosdick
Manager/Admin	NA
Clerk	Barbara Pettit
Finance Dir	Paul Hansen
Tax Assessor	Arthur Carlson
Tax Collector	Barbara Pettit
Attorney	Martin Durkin
Building	Michael Landolfi
Planning	Fredrick Rosen
Engineering	Boswell Engineering
Public Works	Alan O'Grady
Police Chief	Robert Lee
Emerg/Fire Director	John Antola

Housing & Construction
Housing Units, 2000*
Total	5,134
Median rent	$848
Median SF home value	$171,300

Permits for New Residential Construction
	Units	Value
Total, 2006	4	$617,000
Single family	2	$337,000
Total, 2007	6	$680,400
Single family	6	$680,400

Real Property Valuation, 2008
	Parcels	Valuation
Total	3,159	$1,566,597,800
Vacant	41	26,709,200
Residential	2,869	1,046,356,100
Commercial	169	321,408,400
Industrial	38	55,895,900
Apartments	42	116,228,200
Farm land	0	0
Farm homestead	0	0

Average Property Value & Tax, 2008
Residential value	$364,711
Property tax	$8,610
Tax credit/rebate	$1,238

Public Library
Ridgefield Park Public Library
107 Cedar St
Ridgefield Park, NJ 07660
201-641-0689
Director .... Eileen Mackesy-Karpoff

Library statistics, 2007
Population served	12,873
Full-time/total staff	1/5

	Total	Per capita
Holdings	47,718	3.71
Revenues	$696,760	$54.13
Expenditures	$644,236	$50.05
Annual visits	72,800	5.66
Internet terminals/annual users	8/14,478	

Public Safety
Number of officers, 2007	30

Crime	2006	2007
Total crimes	205	219
Violent	14	18
Murder	0	0
Rape	1	2
Robbery	3	7
Aggravated assault	10	9
Non-violent	191	201
Burglary	20	32
Larceny	152	161
Vehicle theft	19	8
Domestic violence	47	35
Arson	0	1
Total crime rate	16.1	17.3
Violent	1.1	1.4
Non-violent	15.0	15.9

Public School District
(for school year 2007-08 except as noted)

Ridgefield Park School District
712 Lincoln Avenue
Ridgefield Park, NJ 07660
(201) 807-2638
Superintendent	John Richardson
Number of schools	4
Grade plan	K-12
Enrollment	2,085
Attendance rate, '06-07	95.0%
Dropout rate	1.3%
Students per teacher	10.8
Per pupil expenditure	$13,264
Median faculty salary	$58,746
Median administrator salary	$115,000
Grade 12 enrollment	181
High school graduation rate	92.2%

Assessment test results
(percent scoring at proficient or advanced level)
	Language	Math
NJASK-Grade 3	97.6%	99.2%
GEPA-Grade 8	79.2%	92.3%
HSPA-High School	78.6%	90.3%

SAT Score Averages, 2006-07
Pct tested	Math	Verbal	Writing
79%	464	433	442

Teacher Qualifications
Avg. years of experience	9
Highly-qualified teachers one subject/all subjects	100%/100%

No Child Left Behind
AYP, 2006-07	Meets Standards

Municipal Finance
State Aid Programs, 2009
Total aid	$1,496,248
CMPTRA	443,781
Energy tax receipts	1,030,023
Garden State Trust	0

General Budget, 2008
Total tax levy	$37,000,905
County levy	3,043,688
County taxes	2,878,161
County library	0
County health	0
County open space	165,526
School levy	20,690,000
Muni. levy	13,267,217
Misc. revenues	5,723,073

Taxes	2006	2007	2008
General tax rate per $100	3.86	4.09	2.362
County equalization ratio	61.91	56.66	95.21
Net valuation taxable	$875,107,290	$872,909,861	$1,567,306,234
State equalized value	$1,545,284,583	$1,642,628,848	$1,556,107,362

See Introduction for an explanation of all data sources.

Demographics & Socio-Economic Characteristics
(2000 US Census, except as noted)

Population
1980*	25,208
1990*	24,152
2000	24,936
Male	12,002
Female	12,934
2007 (estimate)*	24,339
Population density	4,203.6

Race & Hispanic Origin, 2000
Race
White	21,899
Black/African American	409
American Indian/Alaska Native	11
Asian	2,162
Native Hawaiian/Pacific Islander	0
Other race	148
Two or more races	307
Hispanic origin, total	942
Mexican	110
Puerto Rican	173
Cuban	134
Other Hispanic	525

Age & Nativity, 2000
Under 5 years	1,938
18 years and over	17,461
21 years and over	16,918
65 years and over	3,031
85 years and over	418
Median age	38.6
Native-born	20,931
Foreign-born	4,005

Educational Attainment, 2000
Population 25 years and over	16,407
Less than 9th grade	1.8%
High school grad or higher	95.9%
Bachelor's degree or higher	66.7%
Graduate degree	29.0%

Income & Poverty, 1999
Per capita income	$51,658
Median household income	$104,286
Median family income	$121,848
Persons in poverty	741
H'holds receiving public assistance	112
H'holds receiving social security	2,091

Households, 2000
Total households	8,603
With persons under 18	3,910
With persons over 65	2,101
Family households	6,777
Single-person households	1,592
Persons per household	2.87
Persons per family	3.30

Labor & Employment
Total civilian labor force, 2007**	11,889
Unemployment rate	2.3%
Total civilian labor force, 2000	11,791
Unemployment rate	3.1%

Employed persons 16 years and over by occupation, 2000
Managers & professionals	7,029
Service occupations	755
Sales & office occupations	2,973
Farming, fishing & forestry	0
Construction & maintenance	379
Production & transportation	290
Self-employed persons	965

* US Census Bureau
** New Jersey Department of Labor

General Information
Village of Ridgewood
131 N Maple Ave
Ridgewood, NJ 07450
201-670-5500
Website	ridgewoodnj.net
Year of incorporation	1894
Land/water area (sq. miles)	5.79/0.05
Form of government	Council-Manager

Government
Legislative Districts
US Congressional	5
State Legislative	40

Local Officials, 2009
Mayor	David Pfund
Manager	James Ten Hoeve
Clerk	Heather Mailander
Finance Dir	Dorothy Stikna
Tax Assessor	Michael Barker
Tax Collector	Mary Jo Gilmour
Attorney	Matthew Rogers
Building	Anthony Merlino
Comm Dev/Planning	NA
Engineering	Christopher Rutishauser
Public Works	Christopher Rutishauser
Police Chief	William Corcoran
Fire Chief	James Bombace

Housing & Construction
Housing Units, 2000*
Total	8,802
Median rent	$1,220
Median SF home value	$387,200

Permits for New Residential Construction
	Units	Value
Total, 2006	34	$6,904,895
Single family	34	$6,904,895
Total, 2007	21	$5,666,355
Single family	19	$5,597,355

Real Property Valuation, 2008
	Parcels	Valuation
Total	7,898	$6,727,847,000
Vacant	92	19,347,800
Residential	7,445	5,972,283,900
Commercial	335	619,430,500
Industrial	0	0
Apartments	26	116,784,800
Farm land	0	0
Farm homestead	0	0

Average Property Value & Tax, 2008
Residential value	$802,187
Property tax	$13,805
Tax credit/rebate	$1,386

Public Library
Ridgewood Public Library
125 N Maple Ave
Ridgewood, NJ 07450
201-670-5600
Director	Nancy K. Greene

Library statistics, 2007
Population served	24,936
Full-time/total staff	9/20

	Total	Per capita
Holdings	178,960	7.18
Revenues	$2,520,814	$101.09
Expenditures	$2,459,775	$98.64
Annual visits	312,652	12.54
Internet terminals/annual users	34/116,296	

Public Safety
Number of officers, 2007	43

Crime	2006	2007
Total crimes	248	253
Violent	10	9
Murder	0	0
Rape	0	0
Robbery	2	4
Aggravated assault	8	5
Non-violent	238	244
Burglary	42	25
Larceny	193	215
Vehicle theft	3	4
Domestic violence	89	72
Arson	2	1
Total crime rate	10.0	10.3
Violent	0.4	0.4
Non-violent	9.6	9.9

Public School District
(for school year 2007-08 except as noted)

Ridgewood Village School District
49 Cottage Place
Ridgewood, NJ 07451
(201) 670-2700
Superintendent	Daniel Fishbein
Number of schools	10
Grade plan	K-12
Enrollment	5,544
Attendance rate, '06-07	97.0%
Dropout rate	0.4%
Students per teacher	11.5
Per pupil expenditure	$13,860
Median faculty salary	$68,450
Median administrator salary	$129,766
Grade 12 enrollment	387
High school graduation rate	98.2%

Assessment test results
(percent scoring at proficient or advanced level)
	Language	Math
NJASK-Grade 3	97.6%	96.9%
GEPA-Grade 8	87.9%	94.8%
HSPA-High School	95.5%	97.4%

SAT Score Averages, 2006-07
Pct tested	Math	Verbal	Writing
99%	605	581	585

Teacher Qualifications
Avg. years of experience	9
Highly-qualified teachers one subject/all subjects	100%/100%

No Child Left Behind
AYP, 2006-07	Meets Standards

Municipal Finance
State Aid Programs, 2009
Total aid	$2,540,999
CMPTRA	376,997
Energy tax receipts	2,062,353
Garden State Trust	10

General Budget, 2008
Total tax levy	$115,875,101
County levy	12,669,201
County taxes	11,984,312
County library	0
County health	0
County open space	684,889
School levy	75,238,284
Muni. levy	27,967,617
Misc. revenues	12,396,535

Taxes
	2006	2007	2008
General tax rate per $100	2.67	2.8	1.723
County equalization ratio	67.73	60.79	98.53
Net valuation taxable	$3,920,887,200	$3,953,480,368	$6,733,457,668
State equalized value	$6,454,891,621	$6,729,967,166	$6,834,525,609

Demographics & Socio-Economic Characteristics

(2000 US Census, except as noted)

Population

1980*	12,625
1990*	12,623
2000	12,396
Male	6,201
Female	6,195
2007 (estimate)*	12,704
Population density	503.1

Race & Hispanic Origin, 2000

Race

White	11,636
Black/African American	199
American Indian/Alaska Native	179
Asian	148
Native Hawaiian/Pacific Islander	1
Other race	83
Two or more races	150
Hispanic origin, total	527
Mexican	40
Puerto Rican	195
Cuban	61
Other Hispanic	231

Age & Nativity, 2000

Under 5 years	935
18 years and over	8,978
21 years and over	8,638
65 years and over	982
85 years and over	98
Median age	37.4
Native-born	11,322
Foreign-born	1,074

Educational Attainment, 2000

Population 25 years and over	8,192
Less than 9th grade	1.1%
High school grad or higher	91.5%
Bachelor's degree or higher	39.2%
Graduate degree	11.7%

Income & Poverty, 1999

Per capita income	$31,341
Median household income	$81,636
Median family income	$85,108
Persons in poverty	342
H'holds receiving public assistance	23
H'holds receiving social security	759

Households, 2000

Total households	4,108
With persons under 18	1,832
With persons over 65	691
Family households	3,446
Single-person households	496
Persons per household	3.00
Persons per family	3.28

Labor & Employment

Total civilian labor force, 2007**	7,418
Unemployment rate	3.5%
Total civilian labor force, 2000	6,877
Unemployment rate	3.8%

Employed persons 16 years and over by occupation, 2000

Managers & professionals	2,950
Service occupations	544
Sales & office occupations	1,878
Farming, fishing & forestry	0
Construction & maintenance	715
Production & transportation	531
Self-employed persons	500

* US Census Bureau
** New Jersey Department of Labor

General Information

Borough of Ringwood
60 Margaret King Ave
Ringwood, NJ 07456
973-962-7037

Website	www.ringwoodnj.net
Year of incorporation	1918
Land/water area (sq. miles)	25.25/2.78
Form of government	Council-Manager

Government

Legislative Districts

US Congressional	5
State Legislative	40

Local Officials, 2009

Mayor	Walter Davison
Manager	Kelly A. Rohde (Actg)
Clerk	Kelley A. Rohde
Finance Dir	Gail Bado
Tax Assessor	Richard Motyka
Tax Collector	NA
Attorney	Richard Clemack
Building	Michael Hafner
Comm Dev/Planning	NA
Engineering	Jeffrey Yuhas
Public Works	Scott Heck
Police Chief	Bernard Lombardo
Fire/Emergency Dir	NA

Housing & Construction

Housing Units, 2000*

Total	4,221
Median rent	$1,137
Median SF home value	$193,400

Permits for New Residential Construction

	Units	Value
Total, 2006	25	$5,490,445
Single family	25	$5,490,445
Total, 2007	19	$4,256,232
Single family	19	$4,256,232

Real Property Valuation, 2008

	Parcels	Valuation
Total	4,713	$869,291,190
Vacant	270	34,544,900
Residential	4,313	787,768,560
Commercial	49	26,299,900
Industrial	25	17,824,100
Apartments	0	0
Farm land	44	133,330
Farm homestead	12	2,720,400

Average Property Value & Tax, 2008

Residential value	$182,772
Property tax	$8,994
Tax credit/rebate	$1,259

Public Library

Ringwood Public Library
30 Cannici Dr
Ringwood, NJ 07456
973-962-6256

Director	Andrea R. Cahoon

Library statistics, 2007

Population served	12,396
Full-time/total staff	1/2

	Total	Per capita
Holdings	77,666	6.27
Revenues	$664,944	$53.64
Expenditures	$648,195	$52.29
Annual visits	89,813	7.25
Internet terminals/annual users	37/16,740	

Public Safety

Number of officers, 2007	23

Crime	2006	2007
Total crimes	70	90
Violent	7	7
Murder	0	0
Rape	2	2
Robbery	1	0
Aggravated assault	4	5
Non-violent	63	83
Burglary	14	13
Larceny	48	70
Vehicle theft	1	0
Domestic violence	79	43
Arson	1	0
Total crime rate	5.5	7.0
Violent	0.5	0.5
Non-violent	4.9	6.5

Public School District

(for school year 2007-08 except as noted)

Ringwood School District
121 Carletondale Road
Ringwood, NJ 07456
(973) 962-7028

Chief School Admin	Patrick W. Martin
Number of schools	4
Grade plan	K-8
Enrollment	1,378
Attendance rate, '06-07	96.1%
Dropout rate	NA
Students per teacher	11.5
Per pupil expenditure	$14,263
Median faculty salary	$66,000
Median administrator salary	$109,139
Grade 12 enrollment	NA
High school graduation rate	NA

Assessment test results

(percent scoring at proficient or advanced level)

	Language	Math
NJASK-Grade 3	96.1%	94.0%
GEPA-Grade 8	77.4%	88.4%
HSPA-High School	NA	NA

SAT Score Averages, 2006-07

Pct tested	Math	Verbal	Writing
NA	NA	NA	NA

Teacher Qualifications

Avg. years of experience	13
Highly-qualified teachers one subject/all subjects	99.0%/99.0%

No Child Left Behind

AYP, 2006-07	Meets Standards

Municipal Finance

State Aid Programs, 2009

Total aid	$2,151,159
CMPTRA	40,266
Energy tax receipts	1,971,687
Garden State Trust	67,038

General Budget, 2008

Total tax levy	$42,828,580
County levy	10,021,195
County taxes	9,822,572
County library	0
County health	0
County open space	198,623
School levy	23,899,300
Muni. levy	8,908,085
Misc. revenues	5,592,873

Taxes	2006	2007	2008
General tax rate per $100	4.51	4.66	4.923
County equalization ratio	51.32	47.16	43.81
Net valuation taxable	$861,318,490	$867,317,663	$870,375,673
State equalized value	$1,827,554,813	$1,978,276,677	$1,956,305,333

See Introduction for an explanation of all data sources.

Demographics & Socio-Economic Characteristics

(2000 US Census, except as noted)

Population

1980*	11,111
1990*	10,603
2000	10,946
Male	5,211
Female	5,735
2007 (estimate)*	10,721
Population density	5,672.5

Race & Hispanic Origin, 2000

Race

White	9,208
Black/African American	116
American Indian/Alaska Native	9
Asian	1,379
Native Hawaiian/Pacific Islander	1
Other race	89
Two or more races	144
Hispanic origin, total	581
Mexican	32
Puerto Rican	141
Cuban	113
Other Hispanic	295

Age & Nativity, 2000

Under 5 years	781
18 years and over	8,312
21 years and over	8,075
65 years and over	1,859
85 years and over	265
Median age	40.0
Native-born	8,602
Foreign-born	2,344

Educational Attainment, 2000

Population 25 years and over	7,807
Less than 9th grade	2.3%
High school grad or higher	93.6%
Bachelor's degree or higher	45.4%
Graduate degree	16.4%

Income & Poverty, 1999

Per capita income	$33,188
Median household income	$71,792
Median family income	$80,422
Persons in poverty	338
H'holds receiving public assistance	65
H'holds receiving social security	1,321

Households, 2000

Total households	4,165
With persons under 18	1,501
With persons over 65	1,331
Family households	3,105
Single-person households	947
Persons per household	2.62
Persons per family	3.11

Labor & Employment

Total civilian labor force, 2007**	5,812
Unemployment rate	2.6%
Total civilian labor force, 2000	5,498
Unemployment rate	2.9%

Employed persons 16 years and over by occupation, 2000

Managers & professionals	2,722
Service occupations	467
Sales & office occupations	1,600
Farming, fishing & forestry	0
Construction & maintenance	271
Production & transportation	281
Self-employed persons	298

* US Census Bureau
** New Jersey Department of Labor

General Information

Borough of River Edge
705 Kinderkamack Rd
River Edge, NJ 07661
201-599-6300

Website	www.riveredgenj.org
Year of incorporation	1930
Land/water area (sq. miles)	1.89/0.02
Form of government	Borough

Government

Legislative Districts

US Congressional	5
State Legislative	39

Local Officials, 2009

Mayor	Margaret Watkins
Manager	Alan Negreann
Clerk	Denise A. Dondiego
Finance Dir	Alan Negreann
Tax Assessor	James Anzevino
Tax Collector	Zenab Bachok
Attorney	William Lindsley
Building	Robert Byrnes
Comm Dev/Planning	NA
Engineering	Robert Costa
Public Works	John Lynch
Police Chief	Thomas Cariddi
Emerg/Fire Director	Chris Weismann

Housing & Construction

Housing Units, 2000*

Total	4,210
Median rent	$969
Median SF home value	$252,700

Permits for New Residential Construction

	Units	Value
Total, 2006	13	$3,655,372
Single family	8	$1,475,472
Total, 2007	22	$4,438,304
Single family	17	$2,258,404

Real Property Valuation, 2008

	Parcels	Valuation
Total	3,391	$1,616,501,400
Vacant	32	6,331,700
Residential	3,221	1,414,404,500
Commercial	119	113,153,700
Industrial	4	12,088,000
Apartments	15	70,523,500
Farm land	0	0
Farm homestead	0	0

Average Property Value & Tax, 2008

Residential value	$439,120
Property tax	$10,165
Tax credit/rebate	$1,437

Public Library

River Edge Free Public Library
Elm & Tenney Aves
River Edge, NJ 07661
201-261-1663

Director	Daragh O'Connor

Library statistics, 2007

Population served	10,946
Full-time/total staff	4/8

	Total	Per capita
Holdings	85,021	7.77
Revenues	$780,253	$71.28
Expenditures	$802,821	$73.34
Annual visits	119,007	10.87
Internet terminals/annual users		5/8,479

Public Safety

Number of officers, 2007	21

Crime	2006	2007
Total crimes	130	61
Violent	7	5
Murder	0	0
Rape	1	0
Robbery	2	0
Aggravated assault	4	5
Non-violent	123	56
Burglary	22	10
Larceny	97	45
Vehicle theft	4	1
Domestic violence	56	67
Arson	0	0
Total crime rate	11.9	5.6
Violent	0.6	0.5
Non-violent	11.3	5.2

Public School District

(for school year 2007-08 except as noted)

River Edge School District
410 Bogert Road
River Edge, NJ 07661
(201) 261-3404

Superintendent	Erika Steinbauer
Number of schools	2
Grade plan	K-6
Enrollment	1,126
Attendance rate, '06-07	96.6%
Dropout rate	NA
Students per teacher	11.5
Per pupil expenditure	$11,077
Median faculty salary	$52,680
Median administrator salary	$125,910
Grade 12 enrollment	NA
High school graduation rate	NA

Assessment test results

(percent scoring at proficient or advanced level)

	Language	Math
NJASK-Grade 3	91.7%	96.5%
GEPA-Grade 8	NA	NA
HSPA-High School	NA	NA

SAT Score Averages, 2006-07

Pct tested	Math	Verbal	Writing
NA	NA	NA	NA

Teacher Qualifications

Avg. years of experience	9
Highly-qualified teachers one subject/all subjects	97.5%/97.5%

No Child Left Behind

AYP, 2006-07	Meets Standards

Municipal Finance

State Aid Programs, 2009

Total aid	$1,388,989
CMPTRA	191,800
Energy tax receipts	1,136,915
Garden State Trust	23,393

General Budget, 2008

Total tax levy	$37,576,246
County levy	3,504,388
County taxes	3,314,699
County library	0
County health	0
County open space	189,689
School levy	25,165,715
Muni. levy	8,906,143
Misc. revenues	5,955,829

Taxes

	2006	2007	2008
General tax rate per $100	2.09	2.22	2.316
County equalization ratio	99.95	90.22	85.71
Net valuation taxable	$1,610,415,500	$1,619,895,547	$1,623,241,906
State equalized value	$1,792,032,609	$1,888,795,084	$1,912,093,406

Demographics & Socio-Economic Characteristics

(2000 US Census, except as noted)

Population

1980*	9,489
1990*	9,410
2000	9,449
Male	4,560
Female	4,889
2007 (estimate)*	9,667
Population density	2,369.4

Race & Hispanic Origin, 2000

Race

White	8,724
Black/African American	55
American Indian/Alaska Native	0
Asian	557
Native Hawaiian/Pacific Islander	2
Other race	41
Two or more races	70
Hispanic origin, total	304
Mexican	14
Puerto Rican	56
Cuban	74
Other Hispanic	160

Age & Nativity, 2000

Under 5 years	654
18 years and over	6,876
21 years and over	6,657
65 years and over	1,263
85 years and over	123
Median age	40.3
Native-born	8,361
Foreign-born	1,088

Educational Attainment, 2000

Population 25 years and over	6,454
Less than 9th grade	1.4%
High school grad or higher	94.3%
Bachelor's degree or higher	48.5%
Graduate degree	18.5%

Income & Poverty, 1999

Per capita income	$40,709
Median household income	$95,129
Median family income	$105,919
Persons in poverty	261
H'holds receiving public assistance	19
H'holds receiving social security	815

Households, 2000

Total households	3,275
With persons under 18	1,372
With persons over 65	866
Family households	2,677
Single-person households	503
Persons per household	2.87
Persons per family	3.22

Labor & Employment

Total civilian labor force, 2007**	4,727
Unemployment rate	2.0%
Total civilian labor force, 2000	4,468
Unemployment rate	2.3%

Employed persons 16 years and over by occupation, 2000

Managers & professionals	2,295
Service occupations	306
Sales & office occupations	1,282
Farming, fishing & forestry	0
Construction & maintenance	190
Production & transportation	293
Self-employed persons	357

* US Census Bureau
** New Jersey Department of Labor

General Information

Township of River Vale
406 Rivervale Rd
River Vale, NJ 07675
201-664-2346

Website	www.rivervalenj.org
Year of incorporation	1906
Land/water area (sq. miles)	4.08/0.23
Form of government	Mayor-Council

Government

Legislative Districts

US Congressional	5
State Legislative	39

Local Officials, 2009

Mayor	Joseph Blundo
Business Admin	Robert Gallione
Clerk	Karen Padva
Finance Dir	Gennaro Rotella
Tax Assessor	Denis McGuire
Tax Collector	Lauren Roehrer
Attorney	Holly Schepisi
Building	Mike Sartori
Comm Dev/Planning	NA
Engineering	Dennis Harrington
Public Works	Rich Campanelli
Police Chief	Aaron Back
Emerg/Fire Director	James Miles

Housing & Construction

Housing Units, 2000*

Total	3,312
Median rent	$1,119
Median SF home value	$350,300

Permits for New Residential Construction

	Units	Value
Total, 2006	22	$3,981,678
Single family	22	$3,981,678
Total, 2007	13	$14,302,951
Single family	13	$14,302,951

Real Property Valuation, 2008

	Parcels	Valuation
Total	3,399	$2,103,996,900
Vacant	63	27,018,600
Residential	3,292	1,958,207,600
Commercial	39	103,944,500
Industrial	0	0
Apartments	4	13,034,700
Farm land	0	0
Farm homestead	1	1,791,500

Average Property Value & Tax, 2008

Residential value	$595,202
Property tax	$11,240
Tax credit/rebate	$1,386

Public Library

River Vale Public Library
412 Rivervale Rd
River Vale, NJ 07675
201-391-2323

Director	Holly Deni

Library statistics, 2007

Population served	9,449
Full-time/total staff	2/5

	Total	Per capita
Holdings	60,158	6.37
Revenues	$748,011	$79.16
Expenditures	$636,991	$67.41
Annual visits	97,798	10.35
Internet terminals/annual users	7/26,000	

Public Safety

Number of officers, 2007	21

Crime	2006	2007
Total crimes	43	54
Violent	4	4
Murder	0	0
Rape	0	0
Robbery	1	0
Aggravated assault	3	4
Non-violent	39	50
Burglary	1	2
Larceny	37	48
Vehicle theft	1	0
Domestic violence	27	19
Arson	0	1
Total crime rate	4.4	5.5
Violent	0.4	0.4
Non-violent	4.0	5.1

Public School District

(for school year 2007-08 except as noted)

River Vale School District
609 Westwood Avenue
River Vale, NJ 07675
(201) 358-4020

Superintendent	David Verducci
Number of schools	3
Grade plan	K-8
Enrollment	1,391
Attendance rate, '06-07	96.6%
Dropout rate	NA
Students per teacher	11.6
Per pupil expenditure	$12,624
Median faculty salary	$56,875
Median administrator salary	$144,679
Grade 12 enrollment	NA
High school graduation rate	NA

Assessment test results

(percent scoring at proficient or advanced level)

	Language	Math
NJASK-Grade 3	97.4%	95.4%
GEPA-Grade 8	89.2%	93.8%
HSPA-High School	NA	NA

SAT Score Averages, 2006-07

Pct tested	Math	Verbal	Writing
NA	NA	NA	NA

Teacher Qualifications

Avg. years of experience	9

Highly-qualified teachers
one subject/all subjects 99.0%/99.0%

No Child Left Behind

AYP, 2006-07	Meets Standards

Municipal Finance

State Aid Programs, 2009

Total aid	$1,008,487
CMPTRA	64,249
Energy tax receipts	896,251
Garden State Trust	0

General Budget, 2008

Total tax levy	$39,757,914
County levy	4,359,039
County taxes	4,123,260
County library	0
County health	0
County open space	235,779
School levy	27,252,979
Muni. levy	8,145,895
Misc. revenues	3,587,303

Taxes

	2006	2007	2008
General tax rate per $100	3.55	3.85	1.891
County equalization ratio	51.63	46.8	89.42
Net valuation taxable	$1,002,087,367	$1,002,449,208	$2,105,406,678
State equalized value	$2,141,790,854	$2,239,507,902	$2,227,625,946

See Introduction for an explanation of all data sources.

Demographics & Socio-Economic Characteristics
(2000 US Census, except as noted)

Population
1980*	2,530
1990*	2,370
2000	2,498
Male	1,211
Female	1,287
2007 (estimate)*	2,870
Population density	1,393.2

Race & Hispanic Origin, 2000
Race
White	2,333
Black/African American	27
American Indian/Alaska Native	1
Asian	68
Native Hawaiian/Pacific Islander	0
Other race	40
Two or more races	29
Hispanic origin, total	110
Mexican	15
Puerto Rican	39
Cuban	7
Other Hispanic	49

Age & Nativity, 2000
Under 5 years	152
18 years and over	1,911
21 years and over	1,827
65 years and over	302
85 years and over	21
Median age	37.2
Native-born	2,270
Foreign-born	228

Educational Attainment, 2000
Population 25 years and over	1,724
Less than 9th grade	2.1%
High school grad or higher	89.2%
Bachelor's degree or higher	30.9%
Graduate degree	8.4%

Income & Poverty, 1999
Per capita income	$31,187
Median household income	$71,083
Median family income	$79,557
Persons in poverty	132
H'holds receiving public assistance	7
H'holds receiving social security	241

Households, 2000
Total households	919
With persons under 18	313
With persons over 65	228
Family households	672
Single-person households	194
Persons per household	2.68
Persons per family	3.14

Labor & Employment
Total civilian labor force, 2007**	1,586
Unemployment rate	4.3%
Total civilian labor force, 2000	1,464
Unemployment rate	4.4%

Employed persons 16 years and over by occupation, 2000
Managers & professionals	506
Service occupations	120
Sales & office occupations	475
Farming, fishing & forestry	0
Construction & maintenance	157
Production & transportation	142
Self-employed persons	71

General Information
Borough of Riverdale
91 Newark-Pompton Turnpike
PO Box 6
Riverdale, NJ 07457
973-835-4060

Website	www.riverdalenj.com
Year of incorporation	1923
Land/water area (sq. miles)	2.06/0.01
Form of government	Borough

Government
Legislative Districts
US Congressional	11
State Legislative	26

Local Officials, 2009
Mayor	William Budesheim
Manager/Admin	NA
Clerk	Carol Talerico
Finance Dir	Kenneth Sesholtz
Tax Assessor	Joseph De Stefano
Tax Collector	Maryann Murphy
Attorney	Robert Oostdyk
Building	Joseph Montemarano
Comm Dev/Planning	NA
Engineering	Paul Darmofalski
Public Works	Walter Mahon
Police Chief	Thomas Soules
Emerg/Fire Director	Michael Norton

Housing & Construction
Housing Units, 2000*
Total	940
Median rent	$951
Median SF home value	$210,200

Permits for New Residential Construction
	Units	Value
Total, 2006	91	$7,220,600
Single family	12	$1,420,200
Total, 2007	6	$436,000
Single family	2	$36,000

Real Property Valuation, 2008
	Parcels	Valuation
Total	1,874	$834,683,800
Vacant	259	44,919,300
Residential	1,484	532,729,300
Commercial	99	211,390,000
Industrial	25	43,368,700
Apartments	4	1,646,700
Farm land	2	5,600
Farm homestead	1	624,200

Average Property Value & Tax, 2008
Residential value	$359,161
Property tax	$5,161
Tax credit/rebate	$921

Public Library
Riverdale Public Library
93 Newark Pompton Tpke
Riverdale, NJ 07457
973-835-5044

Director	Abigail Sanner

Library statistics, 2007
Population served	2,498
Full-time/total staff	1/2

	Total	Per capita
Holdings	24,732	9.90
Revenues	$255,053	$102.10
Expenditures	$237,411	$95.04
Annual visits	18,271	7.31
Internet terminals/annual users	14/14,691	

Public Safety
Number of officers, 2007	17

Crime	2006	2007
Total crimes	79	92
Violent	0	3
Murder	0	0
Rape	0	0
Robbery	0	0
Aggravated assault	0	3
Non-violent	79	89
Burglary	18	15
Larceny	53	68
Vehicle theft	8	6
Domestic violence	23	14
Arson	0	0
Total crime rate	30.0	34.4
Violent	0.0	1.1
Non-violent	30.0	33.3

Public School District
(for school year 2007-08 except as noted)

Riverdale School District
52 Newark-Pompton Turnpike
Riverdale, NJ 07457
(973) 839-1304

Superintendent	Betty Ann Wyks
Number of schools	1
Grade plan	K-8
Enrollment	282
Attendance rate, '06-07	96.1%
Dropout rate	NA
Students per teacher	8.1
Per pupil expenditure	$14,785
Median faculty salary	$46,770
Median administrator salary	$122,102
Grade 12 enrollment	NA
High school graduation rate	NA

Assessment test results
(percent scoring at proficient or advanced level)
	Language	Math
NJASK-Grade 3	96.3%	88.9%
GEPA-Grade 8	85.0%	92.5%
HSPA-High School	NA	NA

SAT Score Averages, 2006-07
Pct tested	Math	Verbal	Writing
NA	NA	NA	NA

Teacher Qualifications
Avg. years of experience	6
Highly-qualified teachers one subject/all subjects	96.0%/96.0%

No Child Left Behind
AYP, 2006-07	Meets Standards

Municipal Finance
State Aid Programs, 2009
Total aid	$582,036
CMPTRA	80,360
Energy tax receipts	482,760
Garden State Trust	0

General Budget, 2008
Total tax levy	$12,092,263
County levy	2,071,140
County taxes	1,690,169
County library	0
County health	0
County open space	380,971
School levy	5,906,073
Muni. levy	4,115,050
Misc. revenues	2,672,720

Taxes
	2006	2007	2008
General tax rate per $100	1.3	1.42	1.438
County equalization ratio	106.11	96.09	95.10
Net valuation taxable	$684,623,850	$782,494,435	$841,435,797
State equalized value	$720,293,341	$822,463,946	$880,583,446

* US Census Bureau
** New Jersey Department of Labor

See Introduction for an explanation of all data sources.

Demographics & Socio-Economic Characteristics
(2000 US Census, except as noted)

Population
1980*	7,941
1990*	7,974
2000	7,911
Male	3,936
Female	3,975
2007 (estimate)*	7,765
Population density	5,108.6

Race & Hispanic Origin, 2000
Race
White	7,137
Black/African American	351
American Indian/Alaska Native	11
Asian	33
Native Hawaiian/Pacific Islander	1
Other race	180
Two or more races	198
Hispanic origin, total	325
Mexican	37
Puerto Rican	150
Cuban	2
Other Hispanic	136

Age & Nativity, 2000
Under 5 years	515
18 years and over	5,931
21 years and over	5,638
65 years and over	1,089
85 years and over	126
Median age	35.6
Native-born	7,105
Foreign-born	806

Educational Attainment, 2000
Population 25 years and over	5,234
Less than 9th grade	9.8%
High school grad or higher	75.6%
Bachelor's degree or higher	11.5%
Graduate degree	3.0%

Income & Poverty, 1999
Per capita income	$18,758
Median household income	$43,358
Median family income	$52,479
Persons in poverty	642
H'holds receiving public assistance	59
H'holds receiving social security	867

Households, 2000
Total households	2,978
With persons under 18	1,091
With persons over 65	806
Family households	1,992
Single-person households	814
Persons per household	2.64
Persons per family	3.21

Labor & Employment
Total civilian labor force, 2007**	4,797
Unemployment rate	4.0%
Total civilian labor force, 2000	4,199
Unemployment rate	3.9%

Employed persons 16 years and over by occupation, 2000
Managers & professionals	804
Service occupations	570
Sales & office occupations	1,240
Farming, fishing & forestry	14
Construction & maintenance	651
Production & transportation	756
Self-employed persons	188

General Information
Township of Riverside
PO Box 188
Riverside, NJ 08075
856-461-1460

Website	riversidetwp.org
Year of incorporation	1895
Land/water area (sq. miles)	1.52/0.10
Form of government	Township

Government
Legislative Districts
US Congressional	3
State Legislative	7

Local Officials, 2009
Mayor	George Conard Sr
Manager	Meghan Jack
Clerk	Susan M. Dydek
Finance Dir	Deborah Crowe
Tax Assessor	Carl Cicali
Tax Collector	Nancy Elmeaze
Attorney	George Saponaro
Building	Thomas Mahoney
Planning	Taylor Design Group
Engineering	Hugh Dougherty
Public Works	Eric March
Police Chief	Paul Tursi
Fire Chief	Lawrence Winkelspecht

Housing & Construction
Housing Units, 2000*
Total	3,118
Median rent	$670
Median SF home value	$100,400

Permits for New Residential Construction
	Units	Value
Total, 2006	11	$948,728
Single family	11	$948,728
Total, 2007	3	$256,362
Single family	3	$256,362

Real Property Valuation, 2008
	Parcels	Valuation
Total	2,751	$451,501,550
Vacant	100	5,469,800
Residential	2,449	376,888,550
Commercial	161	42,337,800
Industrial	14	13,145,500
Apartments	27	13,659,900
Farm land	0	0
Farm homestead	0	0

Average Property Value & Tax, 2008
Residential value	$153,895
Property tax	$4,322
Tax credit/rebate	$883

Public Library
Riverside Public Library
10 Zurbrugg Way
Riverside, NJ 08075
856-461-6922

Director	Jean Bowker

Library statistics, 2007
Population served	7,911
Full-time/total staff	0/0

	Total	Per capita
Holdings	37,307	4.72
Revenues	$66,612	8.42
Expenditures	$61,465	7.77
Annual visits	12,009	1.52
Internet terminals/annual users		6/2,872

Public Safety
Number of officers, 2007	16

Crime	2006	2007
Total crimes	143	108
Violent	24	19
Murder	0	0
Rape	4	1
Robbery	4	9
Aggravated assault	16	9
Non-violent	119	89
Burglary	24	23
Larceny	89	58
Vehicle theft	6	8
Domestic violence	176	149
Arson	1	0
Total crime rate	17.9	13.6
Violent	3.0	2.4
Non-violent	14.9	11.2

Public School District
(for school year 2007-08 except as noted)

Riverside Township School District
112 E Washington Street
Riverside, NJ 08075
(856) 461-1255

Superintendent	Robert Goldschmidt
Number of schools	3
Grade plan	K-12
Enrollment	1,435
Attendance rate, '06-07	93.5%
Dropout rate	3.9%
Students per teacher	11.4
Per pupil expenditure	$12,399
Median faculty salary	$56,841
Median administrator salary	$99,072
Grade 12 enrollment	117
High school graduation rate	86.2%

Assessment test results
(percent scoring at proficient or advanced level)
	Language	Math
NJASK-Grade 3	89.3%	88.3%
GEPA-Grade 8	58.4%	70.4%
HSPA-High School	62.0%	65.9%

SAT Score Averages, 2006-07
Pct tested	Math	Verbal	Writing
64%	451	440	428

Teacher Qualifications
Avg. years of experience	9
Highly-qualified teachers one subject/all subjects	94.5%/93.5%

No Child Left Behind
AYP, 2006-07	Meets Standards

Municipal Finance
State Aid Programs, 2009
Total aid	$993,179
CMPTRA	246,173
Energy tax receipts	727,143
Garden State Trust	0

General Budget, 2008
Total tax levy	$12,734,425
County levy	2,057,917
County taxes	1,689,977
County library	156,038
County health	0
County open space	211,901
School levy	7,299,845
Muni. levy	3,376,663
Misc. revenues	3,019,896

Taxes	2006	2007	2008
General tax rate per $100	2.551	2.72	2.809
County equalization ratio	107.59	93.85	86.62
Net valuation taxable	$450,217,050	$452,606,662	$453,411,651
State equalized value	$482,020,345	$522,175,178	$556,716,626

* US Census Bureau
** New Jersey Department of Labor

See Introduction for an explanation of all data sources.

Demographics & Socio-Economic Characteristics
(2000 US Census, except as noted)

Population
1980*	3,068
1990*	2,775
2000	2,759
Male	1,309
Female	1,450
2007 (estimate)*	2,652
Population density	4,018.2

Race & Hispanic Origin, 2000
Race
White	2,644
Black/African American	49
American Indian/Alaska Native	3
Asian	23
Native Hawaiian/Pacific Islander	0
Other race	8
Two or more races	32
Hispanic origin, total	30
Mexican	4
Puerto Rican	8
Cuban	2
Other Hispanic	16

Age & Nativity, 2000
Under 5 years	165
18 years and over	2,158
21 years and over	2,100
65 years and over	532
85 years and over	105
Median age	41.8
Native-born	2,687
Foreign-born	72

Educational Attainment, 2000
Population 25 years and over	2,036
Less than 9th grade	2.4%
High school grad or higher	89.8%
Bachelor's degree or higher	36.2%
Graduate degree	12.6%

Income & Poverty, 1999
Per capita income	$30,223
Median household income	$58,977
Median family income	$68,125
Persons in poverty	82
H'holds receiving public assistance	9
H'holds receiving social security	309

Households, 2000
Total households	1,066
With persons under 18	344
With persons over 65	293
Family households	746
Single-person households	270
Persons per household	2.48
Persons per family	3.00

Labor & Employment
Total civilian labor force, 2007**	1,576
Unemployment rate	2.1%
Total civilian labor force, 2000	1,382
Unemployment rate	2.2%

Employed persons 16 years and over by occupation, 2000
Managers & professionals	642
Service occupations	84
Sales & office occupations	381
Farming, fishing & forestry	0
Construction & maintenance	110
Production & transportation	135
Self-employed persons	121

‡ Joint county branch with Palmyra Borough
* US Census Bureau
** New Jersey Department of Labor

General Information
Borough of Riverton
505A Howard St
Riverton, NJ 08077
856-829-0120
Website	www.riverton-nj.com
Year of incorporation	1893
Land/water area (sq. miles)	0.66/0.29
Form of government	Borough

Government
Legislative Districts
US Congressional	1
State Legislative	7

Local Officials, 2009
Mayor	Robert Martin
Manager/Admin	NA
Clerk	Mary Longbottom
Finance Dir	Marianne E. Hulme
Tax Assessor	Tom Davis
Tax Collector	Marianne E. Hulme
Attorney	Bruce Gunn
Building	Ed Schaefer
Comm Dev/Planning	NA
Engineering	Richard Arango
Public Works	Scott Reed
Police Chief	Robert Norcross
Emerg/Fire Director	Scott Reed

Housing & Construction
Housing Units, 2000*
Total	1,113
Median rent	$695
Median SF home value	$153,600

Permits for New Residential Construction
	Units	Value
Total, 2006	6	$795,000
Single family	6	$795,000
Total, 2007	7	$1,132,400
Single family	7	$1,132,400

Real Property Valuation, 2008
	Parcels	Valuation
Total	963	$132,871,900
Vacant	27	1,460,700
Residential	877	119,219,500
Commercial	46	7,885,900
Industrial	1	932,000
Apartments	12	3,373,800
Farm land	0	0
Farm homestead	0	0

Average Property Value & Tax, 2008
Residential value	$135,940
Property tax	$7,103
Tax credit/rebate	$1,112

Public Library
Riverton Free Library‡
306 Main St
Riverton, NJ 08077
856-829-2476
Director	Michael Robinson

Library statistics, 2007
see Burlington County profile
for library system statistics

Public Safety
Number of officers, 2007	6

Crime	2006	2007
Total crimes	37	59
Violent	0	4
Murder	0	0
Rape	0	0
Robbery	0	2
Aggravated assault	0	2
Non-violent	37	55
Burglary	6	9
Larceny	31	44
Vehicle theft	0	2
Domestic violence	9	2
Arson	2	0
Total crime rate	13.5	21.7
Violent	0.0	1.5
Non-violent	13.5	20.3

Public School District
(for school year 2007-08 except as noted)

Riverton Borough School District
600 Fifth Street
Riverton, NJ 08077
(856) 829-0087
Superintendent	Mary Ellen Eck
Number of schools	1
Grade plan	K-8
Enrollment	254
Attendance rate, '06-07	96.3%
Dropout rate	NA
Students per teacher	9.5
Per pupil expenditure	$13,704
Median faculty salary	$58,762
Median administrator salary	$88,128
Grade 12 enrollment	NA
High school graduation rate	NA

Assessment test results
(percent scoring at proficient or advanced level)
	Language	Math
NJASK-Grade 3	88.2%	100.0%
GEPA-Grade 8	81.8%	95.4%
HSPA-High School	NA	NA

SAT Score Averages, 2006-07
Pct tested	Math	Verbal	Writing
NA	NA	NA	NA

Teacher Qualifications
Avg. years of experience	18
Highly-qualified teachers one subject/all subjects	100%/100%

No Child Left Behind
AYP, 2006-07	Meets Standards

Municipal Finance
State Aid Programs, 2009
Total aid	$297,283
CMPTRA	57,244
Energy tax receipts	232,607
Garden State Trust	0

General Budget, 2008
Total tax levy	$6,948,472
County levy	1,068,691
County taxes	877,621
County library	81,033
County health	0
County open space	110,037
School levy	4,091,354
Muni. levy	1,788,427
Misc. revenues	1,149,963

Taxes	2006	2007	2008
General tax rate per $100	5.019	5.19	5.226
County equalization ratio	56.34	51.97	48.42
Net valuation taxable	$131,330,500	$131,439,091	$132,982,136
State equalized value	$252,813,082	$271,341,159	$276,007,038

See Introduction for an explanation of all data sources.

Demographics & Socio-Economic Characteristics

(2000 US Census, except as noted)

Population
1980*	3,487
1990*	5,815
2000	10,275
Male	4,908
Female	5,367
2007 (estimate)*	11,979
Population density	584.9

Race & Hispanic Origin, 2000
Race
White	9,350
Black/African American	297
American Indian/Alaska Native	14
Asian	443
Native Hawaiian/Pacific Islander	0
Other race	57
Two or more races	114
Hispanic origin, total	279
Mexican	29
Puerto Rican	95
Cuban	34
Other Hispanic	121

Age & Nativity, 2000
Under 5 years	945
18 years and over	7,590
21 years and over	7,450
65 years and over	995
85 years and over	61
Median age	37.3
Native-born	9,382
Foreign-born	893

Educational Attainment, 2000
Population 25 years and over	7,241
Less than 9th grade	3.0%
High school grad or higher	92.3%
Bachelor's degree or higher	46.9%
Graduate degree	15.3%

Income & Poverty, 1999
Per capita income	$35,529
Median household income	$71,377
Median family income	$90,878
Persons in poverty	381
H'holds receiving public assistance	26
H'holds receiving social security	863

Households, 2000
Total households	4,074
With persons under 18	1,519
With persons over 65	765
Family households	2,815
Single-person households	1,074
Persons per household	2.52
Persons per family	3.09

Labor & Employment
Total civilian labor force, 2007**	6,975
Unemployment rate	3.3%
Total civilian labor force, 2000	5,605
Unemployment rate	2.3%

Employed persons 16 years and over by occupation, 2000
Managers & professionals	3,144
Service occupations	344
Sales & office occupations	1,437
Farming, fishing & forestry	0
Construction & maintenance	254
Production & transportation	296
Self-employed persons	204

General Information
Robbinsville Township
(formerly Washington Township)
1 Washington Blvd, Suite 6
Robbinsville, NJ 08691
609-918-0002
Website	www.robbinsville-twp.org
Year of incorporation	1860
Land/water area (sq. miles)	20.48/0.02
Form of government	Township

Government

Legislative Districts
US Congressional	4
State Legislative	30

Local Officials, 2009
Mayor	David Fried
Administrator	Mary Caffrey
Clerk	Michele Auletta
Finance Dir	Deborah Bauer
Tax Assessor	Gregory Busa
Tax Collector	Janice Garcia
Attorney	Mark Roselli
Building	Robert Corby
Planning	Jack West
Engineering	Jack West
Public Works	Dino Colarocco
Police Chief	Martin Masseroni
Emerg/Fire Director	David Fried

Housing & Construction

Housing Units, 2000*
Total	4,163
Median rent	$788
Median SF home value	$216,500

Permits for New Residential Construction
	Units	Value
Total, 2006	84	$12,610,500
Single family	61	$8,610,500
Total, 2007	71	$14,141,500
Single family	71	$14,141,500

Real Property Valuation, 2008
	Parcels	Valuation
Total	5,591	$2,628,168,712
Vacant	551	115,300,300
Residential	4,570	1,849,050,100
Commercial	164	277,549,000
Industrial	18	342,196,500
Apartments	1	9,849,500
Farm land	216	2,220,612
Farm homestead	71	32,002,700

Average Property Value & Tax, 2008
Residential value	$405,312
Property tax	$8,422
Tax credit/rebate	$1,176

Public Library
Robbinsville Township Branch Library‡
42 Allentown Robbinsville Rd
Robbinsville, NJ 08691
609-259-2150
Branch Librarian	Ann Marie Ehrenberg

Library statistics, 2007
see Mercer County profile
for library system statistics

Public Safety
Number of officers, 2007	27

Crime	2006	2007
Total crimes	130	102
Violent	8	9
Murder	0	0
Rape	1	0
Robbery	2	2
Aggravated assault	5	7
Non-violent	122	93
Burglary	18	18
Larceny	95	73
Vehicle theft	9	2
Domestic violence	97	94
Arson	0	1
Total crime rate	11.2	8.6
Violent	0.7	0.8
Non-violent	10.5	7.8

Public School District
(for school year 2007-08 except as noted)

Robbinsville Township School District
155 Robbinsville-Edinburg Road
Robbinsville, NJ 08691
(609) 632-0910
Superintendent	John Szabo
Number of schools	3
Grade plan	K-12
Enrollment	2,603
Attendance rate, '06-07	96.5%
Dropout rate	0.0%
Students per teacher	13.3
Per pupil expenditure	$11,184
Median faculty salary	$49,896
Median administrator salary	$104,529
Grade 12 enrollment	139
High school graduation rate	100.0%

Assessment test results
(percent scoring at proficient or advanced level)
	Language	Math
NJASK-Grade 3	94.4%	94.5%
GEPA-Grade 8	85.2%	97.0%
HSPA-High School	86.1%	90.4%

SAT Score Averages, 2006-07
Pct tested	Math	Verbal	Writing
NA	NA	NA	NA

Teacher Qualifications
Avg. years of experience	8
Highly-qualified teachers one subject/all subjects	97.5%/97.5%

No Child Left Behind
AYP, 2006-07	Meets Standards

Municipal Finance

State Aid Programs, 2009
Total aid	$1,686,907
CMPTRA	0
Energy tax receipts	1,640,701
Garden State Trust	9,581

General Budget, 2008
Total tax levy	$54,693,290
County levy	12,289,634
County taxes	10,510,198
County library	1,059,449
County health	0
County open space	719,987
School levy	31,596,063
Muni. levy	10,807,593
Misc. revenues	7,591,937

Taxes	2006	2007	2008
General tax rate per $100	4.51	2	2.078
County equalization ratio	52.16	116.41	108.03
Net valuation taxable	$961,625,705	$2,581,417,305	$2,632,063,401
State equalized value	$2,113,939,477	$2,389,812,149	$2,550,569,798

‡ Branch of county library
* US Census Bureau
** New Jersey Department of Labor

See Introduction for an explanation of all data sources.

Demographics & Socio-Economic Characteristics
(2000 US Census, except as noted)

Population
1980*	5,603
1990*	5,587
2000	5,528
Male	2,525
Female	3,003
2007 (estimate)*	6,114
Population density	5,822.9

Race & Hispanic Origin, 2000
Race
White	4,980
Black/African American	25
American Indian/Alaska Native	2
Asian	333
Native Hawaiian/Pacific Islander	0
Other race	112
Two or more races	76
Hispanic origin, total	474
Mexican	20
Puerto Rican	105
Cuban	68
Other Hispanic	281

Age & Nativity, 2000
Under 5 years	312
18 years and over	4,497
21 years and over	4,359
65 years and over	1,319
85 years and over	320
Median age	43.2
Native-born	4,640
Foreign-born	888

Educational Attainment, 2000
Population 25 years and over	4,197
Less than 9th grade	5.1%
High school grad or higher	85.3%
Bachelor's degree or higher	23.7%
Graduate degree	7.6%

Income & Poverty, 1999
Per capita income	$25,054
Median household income	$60,818
Median family income	$74,016
Persons in poverty	153
H'holds receiving public assistance	41
H'holds receiving social security	785

Households, 2000
Total households	2,061
With persons under 18	577
With persons over 65	775
Family households	1,394
Single-person households	563
Persons per household	2.52
Persons per family	3.12

Labor & Employment
Total civilian labor force, 2007**	2,944
Unemployment rate	3.9%
Total civilian labor force, 2000	2,784
Unemployment rate	4.1%

Employed persons 16 years and over by occupation, 2000
Managers & professionals	1,002
Service occupations	357
Sales & office occupations	851
Farming, fishing & forestry	0
Construction & maintenance	152
Production & transportation	307
Self-employed persons	126

* US Census Bureau
** New Jersey Department of Labor

General Information
Township of Rochelle Park
151 W Passaic St
Rochelle Park, NJ 07662
201-587-7730
Website	rochelleparknj.gov
Year of incorporation	1929
Land/water area (sq. miles)	1.05/0.00
Form of government	Township

Government
Legislative Districts
US Congressional	5
State Legislative	37

Local Officials, 2009
Mayor	Frank Valenzuela
Manager	Michael Mariniello Jr
Clerk	Virginia De Maria
Finance Dir	Michael Mariniello Jr
Tax Assessor	James Tighe
Tax Collector	Roy Riggitano
Attorney	Joseph Rotolo
Building	Richard Bolan
Comm Dev/Planning	NA
Engineering	Kenneth Job
Public Works	Brian Koenig
Police Chief	Richard Zavinsky
Emerg/Fire Director	Ted Reighard

Housing & Construction
Housing Units, 2000*
Total	2,111
Median rent	$842
Median SF home value	$190,600

Permits for New Residential Construction
	Units	Value
Total, 2006	74	$2,526,327
Single family	4	$519,588
Total, 2007	8	$118,520
Single family	1	$32,100

Real Property Valuation, 2008
	Parcels	Valuation
Total	2,018	$685,367,301
Vacant	62	8,761,001
Residential	1,801	416,907,900
Commercial	127	211,950,500
Industrial	23	23,848,800
Apartments	5	23,899,100
Farm land	0	0
Farm homestead	0	0

Average Property Value & Tax, 2008
Residential value	$231,487
Property tax	$6,000
Tax credit/rebate	$1,033

Public Library
Rochelle Park Public Library
151 W Passaic St
Rochelle Park, NJ 07662
201-587-7730
Director	Judith Sands

Library statistics, 2007
Population served	5,528
Full-time/total staff	0/1

	Total	Per capita
Holdings	18,319	3.31
Revenues	$201,119	$36.38
Expenditures	$242,940	$43.95
Annual visits	33,591	6.08
Internet terminals/annual users	3/4,679	

Public Safety
Number of officers, 2007	21

Crime	2006	2007
Total crimes	113	120
Violent	6	6
Murder	0	0
Rape	0	0
Robbery	0	0
Aggravated assault	6	6
Non-violent	107	114
Burglary	18	24
Larceny	83	83
Vehicle theft	6	7
Domestic violence	18	18
Arson	0	1
Total crime rate	19.3	19.9
Violent	1.0	1.0
Non-violent	18.3	18.9

Public School District
(for school year 2007-08 except as noted)

Rochelle Park School District
300 Rochelle Avenue
Rochelle Park, NJ 07662
(201) 843-3120
Superintendent	C. Lauren Schoen
Number of schools	1
Grade plan	K-8
Enrollment	499
Attendance rate, '06-07	95.6%
Dropout rate	NA
Students per teacher	10.2
Per pupil expenditure	$14,283
Median faculty salary	$61,071
Median administrator salary	$107,655
Grade 12 enrollment	NA
High school graduation rate	NA

Assessment test results
(percent scoring at proficient or advanced level)
	Language	Math
NJASK-Grade 3	91.8%	91.8%
GEPA-Grade 8	65.3%	91.8%
HSPA-High School	NA	NA

SAT Score Averages, 2006-07
Pct tested	Math	Verbal	Writing
NA	NA	NA	NA

Teacher Qualifications
Avg. years of experience	11
Highly-qualified teachers one subject/all subjects	100%/100%

No Child Left Behind
AYP, 2006-07	Meets Standards

Municipal Finance
State Aid Programs, 2009
Total aid	$900,600
CMPTRA	311,605
Energy tax receipts	566,480
Garden State Trust	0

General Budget, 2008
Total tax levy	$18,218,112
County levy	2,099,729
County taxes	1,985,736
County library	0
County health	0
County open space	113,994
School levy	8,914,313
Muni. levy	7,204,070
Misc. revenues	3,452,724

Taxes
	2006	2007	2008
General tax rate per $100	2.38	2.49	2.593
County equalization ratio	77.99	67.92	61.37
Net valuation taxable	$672,743,300	$706,878,653	$702,927,880
State equalized value	$1,010,816,656	$1,140,633,000	$1,330,524,757

See Introduction for an explanation of all data sources.

Demographics & Socio-Economic Characteristics
(2000 US Census, except as noted)

Population
1980*	6,852
1990*	6,243
2000	6,473
Male	3,148
Female	3,325
2007 (estimate)*	6,313
Population density	3,020.6

Race & Hispanic Origin, 2000
Race
White	5,680
Black/African American	91
American Indian/Alaska Native	13
Asian	412
Native Hawaiian/Pacific Islander	2
Other race	193
Two or more races	82
Hispanic origin, total	608
Mexican	57
Puerto Rican	158
Cuban	16
Other Hispanic	377

Age & Nativity, 2000
Under 5 years	435
18 years and over	4,968
21 years and over	4,783
65 years and over	770
85 years and over	63
Median age	37.8
Native-born	5,476
Foreign-born	997

Educational Attainment, 2000
Population 25 years and over	4,552
Less than 9th grade	3.4%
High school grad or higher	89.7%
Bachelor's degree or higher	28.7%
Graduate degree	7.6%

Income & Poverty, 1999
Per capita income	$26,500
Median household income	$61,002
Median family income	$66,997
Persons in poverty	322
H'holds receiving public assistance	39
H'holds receiving social security	476

Households, 2000
Total households	2,445
With persons under 18	881
With persons over 65	585
Family households	1,709
Single-person households	582
Persons per household	2.64
Persons per family	3.16

Labor & Employment
Total civilian labor force, 2007**	4,048
Unemployment rate	4.8%
Total civilian labor force, 2000	3,714
Unemployment rate	4.6%

Employed persons 16 years and over by occupation, 2000
Managers & professionals	1,278
Service occupations	386
Sales & office occupations	1,149
Farming, fishing & forestry	13
Construction & maintenance	254
Production & transportation	463
Self-employed persons	156

* US Census Bureau
** New Jersey Department of Labor

General Information
Borough of Rockaway
1 E Main St
Rockaway, NJ 07866
973-627-2000

Website	www.rockawayborough.com
Year of incorporation	1894
Land/water area (sq. miles)	2.09/0.02
Form of government	Borough

Government
Legislative Districts
US Congressional	11
State Legislative	25

Local Officials, 2009
Mayor	Kathyann Snyder
Manager/Admin	NA
Clerk	Sheila Seifert
Finance Dir	John Doherty
Tax Assessor	Bernard Murdoch
Tax Collector	Donna Browne
Attorney	Edward Wacks
Building	Sam LoManto
Comm Dev/Planning	NA
Engineering	Michael Spillane
Public Works	Joseph Rossi
Police Chief	Douglas Scheer
Emerg/Fire Director	Joseph Giordano

Housing & Construction
Housing Units, 2000*
Total	2,491
Median rent	$875
Median SF home value	$187,200

Permits for New Residential Construction
	Units	Value
Total, 2006	0	$0
Single family	0	$0
Total, 2007	0	$0
Single family	0	$0

Real Property Valuation, 2008
	Parcels	Valuation
Total	2,205	$770,181,400
Vacant	83	10,291,900
Residential	1,894	563,247,300
Commercial	189	143,341,900
Industrial	16	31,007,900
Apartments	23	22,292,400
Farm land	0	0
Farm homestead	0	0

Average Property Value & Tax, 2008
Residential value	$297,385
Property tax	$6,699
Tax credit/rebate	$1,067

Public Library
Rockaway Borough Library
82 E Main St
Rockaway, NJ 07866
973-627-5709

Director	Edna Puleo

Library statistics, 2007
Population served	6,473
Full-time/total staff	1/1

	Total	Per capita
Holdings	37,448	5.79
Revenues	$300,094	$46.36
Expenditures	$295,288	$45.62
Annual visits	24,100	3.72
Internet terminals/annual users	2/8,175	

Public Safety
Number of officers, 2007	15

Crime	2006	2007
Total crimes	80	60
Violent	4	4
Murder	0	0
Rape	0	0
Robbery	0	2
Aggravated assault	4	2
Non-violent	76	56
Burglary	10	9
Larceny	59	46
Vehicle theft	7	1
Domestic violence	31	33
Arson	0	0
Total crime rate	12.5	9.4
Violent	0.6	0.6
Non-violent	11.8	8.7

Public School District
(for school year 2007-08 except as noted)

Rockaway Borough School District
103 East Main Street
Rockaway, NJ 07866
(973) 625-8601

Superintendent	Emil Suarez
Number of schools	2
Grade plan	K-8
Enrollment	640
Attendance rate, '06-07	95.2%
Dropout rate	NA
Students per teacher	12.4
Per pupil expenditure	$10,925
Median faculty salary	$53,530
Median administrator salary	$89,784
Grade 12 enrollment	NA
High school graduation rate	NA

Assessment test results
(percent scoring at proficient or advanced level)
	Language	Math
NJASK-Grade 3	84.4%	74.0%
GEPA-Grade 8	71.0%	87.0%
HSPA-High School	NA	NA

SAT Score Averages, 2006-07
Pct tested	Math	Verbal	Writing
NA	NA	NA	NA

Teacher Qualifications
Avg. years of experience	10
Highly-qualified teachers one subject/all subjects	100%/97.5%

No Child Left Behind
AYP, 2006-07	Meets Standards

Municipal Finance
State Aid Programs, 2009
Total aid	$705,243
CMPTRA	222,130
Energy tax receipts	465,482
Garden State Trust	0

General Budget, 2008
Total tax levy	$17,372,699
County levy	2,217,105
County taxes	1,809,255
County library	0
County health	0
County open space	407,850
School levy	10,950,796
Muni. levy	4,204,798
Misc. revenues	2,044,940

Taxes
	2006	2007	2008
General tax rate per $100	2.02	2.12	2.253
County equalization ratio	96.36	88.01	81.85
Net valuation taxable	$762,223,300	$766,256,440	$771,256,001
State equalized value	$866,918,580	$935,998,588	$919,378,405

See Introduction for an explanation of all data sources.

Demographics & Socio-Economic Characteristics
(2000 US Census, except as noted)

Population
1980*	19,850
1990*	19,572
2000	22,930
Male	11,329
Female	11,601
2007 (estimate)*	25,411
Population density	593.4

Race & Hispanic Origin, 2000
Race
White	20,375
Black/African American	565
American Indian/Alaska Native	23
Asian	1,295
Native Hawaiian/Pacific Islander	4
Other race	367
Two or more races	301
Hispanic origin, total	1,440
Mexican	127
Puerto Rican	455
Cuban	109
Other Hispanic	749

Age & Nativity, 2000
Under 5 years	1,771
18 years and over	16,715
21 years and over	16,164
65 years and over	2,162
85 years and over	162
Median age	37.0
Native-born	19,892
Foreign-born	3,038

Educational Attainment, 2000
Population 25 years and over	15,488
Less than 9th grade	2.2%
High school grad or higher	93.0%
Bachelor's degree or higher	41.4%
Graduate degree	12.4%

Income & Poverty, 1999
Per capita income	$33,184
Median household income	$80,939
Median family income	$89,281
Persons in poverty	551
H'holds receiving public assistance	51
H'holds receiving social security	1,722

Households, 2000
Total households	8,108
With persons under 18	3,392
With persons over 65	1,586
Family households	6,381
Single-person households	1,376
Persons per household	2.82
Persons per family	3.21

Labor & Employment
Total civilian labor force, 2007**	14,629
Unemployment rate	2.3%
Total civilian labor force, 2000	12,706
Unemployment rate	3.3%

Employed persons 16 years and over by occupation, 2000
Managers & professionals	5,842
Service occupations	1,209
Sales & office occupations	3,469
Farming, fishing & forestry	0
Construction & maintenance	763
Production & transportation	1,004
Self-employed persons	603

General Information
Township of Rockaway
65 Mount Hope Rd
Rockaway, NJ 07866
973-627-7200

Website	www.rockawaytownship.org
Year of incorporation	1844
Land/water area (sq. miles)	42.82/3.17
Form of government	Mayor-Council

Government
Legislative Districts
US Congressional	11
State Legislative	25

Local Officials, 2009
Mayor	Louis Sceusi
Manager	Gergory Poff II
Clerk	Mary Cilurso
Finance Dir	Lisa Palmieri
Tax Assessor	Mark Burek
Tax Collector	Lorraine Benderoth
Attorney	Edward Buzak
Building	Andy Sanfilippo
Planning	Phyllis Hantman
Engineering	Jim Lutz
Public Works	Ed Hollenbeck
Police Chief	Walter Kimble
Emerg/Fire Director	Joe Mason

Housing & Construction
Housing Units, 2000*
Total	8,506
Median rent	$948
Median SF home value	$206,200

Permits for New Residential Construction
	Units	Value
Total, 2006	42	$7,663,771
Single family	23	$6,109,882
Total, 2007	117	$14,873,128
Single family	21	$4,243,228

Real Property Valuation, 2008
	Parcels	Valuation
Total	9,831	$2,901,100,800
Vacant	1,166	73,980,100
Residential	8,407	2,175,843,900
Commercial	160	440,184,300
Industrial	48	166,746,900
Apartments	9	40,661,200
Farm land	31	157,600
Farm homestead	10	3,526,800

Average Property Value & Tax, 2008
Residential value	$258,925
Property tax	$8,488
Tax credit/rebate	$1,202

Public Library
Rockaway Township Library
61 Mount Hope Rd
Rockaway, NJ 07866
973-627-2344

Director	Joy Kaufman

Library statistics, 2007
Population served	22,930
Full-time/total staff	4/4

	Total	Per capita
Holdings	125,016	5.45
Revenues	$1,568,820	$68.42
Expenditures	$1,340,561	$58.46
Annual visits	107,000	4.67
Internet terminals/annual users	21/62,275	

Public Safety
Number of officers, 2007	58

Crime	2006	2007
Total crimes	498	573
Violent	16	21
Murder	0	0
Rape	3	1
Robbery	6	7
Aggravated assault	7	13
Non-violent	482	552
Burglary	38	39
Larceny	424	499
Vehicle theft	20	14
Domestic violence	132	129
Arson	2	1
Total crime rate	19.5	22.2
Violent	0.6	0.8
Non-violent	18.9	21.4

Public School District
(for school year 2007-08 except as noted)

Rockaway Township School District
16 School Road, PO Box 500
Hibernia, NJ 07842
(973) 627-8200

Superintendent	Gary J. Vitta
Number of schools	6
Grade plan	K-8
Enrollment	2,744
Attendance rate, '06-07	96.0%
Dropout rate	NA
Students per teacher	8.9
Per pupil expenditure	$15,384
Median faculty salary	$53,757
Median administrator salary	$114,018
Grade 12 enrollment	NA
High school graduation rate	NA

Assessment test results
(percent scoring at proficient or advanced level)
	Language	Math
NJASK-Grade 3	96.9%	91.1%
GEPA-Grade 8	81.9%	90.7%
HSPA-High School	NA	NA

SAT Score Averages, 2006-07
Pct tested	Math	Verbal	Writing
NA	NA	NA	NA

Teacher Qualifications
Avg. years of experience	8
Highly-qualified teachers one subject/all subjects	99.5%/99.5%

No Child Left Behind
AYP, 2006-07	Meets Standards

Municipal Finance
State Aid Programs, 2009
Total aid	$2,241,653
CMPTRA	541,018
Energy tax receipts	1,361,778
Garden State Trust	124,365

General Budget, 2008
Total tax levy	$95,212,177
County levy	10,422,574
County taxes	8,505,690
County library	0
County health	0
County open space	1,916,884
School levy	62,156,689
Muni. levy	22,632,914
Misc. revenues	10,434,848

Taxes
	2006	2007	2008
General tax rate per $100	3.02	3.15	3.279
County equalization ratio	70.2	65.71	64.90
Net valuation taxable	$2,921,491,000	$2,902,847,641	$2,904,270,852
State equalized value	$4,448,507,434	$4,471,197,469	$4,589,890,684

See Introduction for an explanation of all data sources.

Demographics & Socio-Economic Characteristics
(2000 US Census, except as noted)

Population
1980*	192
1990*	270
2000	391
Male	191
Female	200
2007 (estimate)*	390
Population density	402.1

Race & Hispanic Origin, 2000
Race
White	351
Black/African American	13
American Indian/Alaska Native	1
Asian	15
Native Hawaiian/Pacific Islander	0
Other race	4
Two or more races	7
Hispanic origin, total	19
Mexican	3
Puerto Rican	2
Cuban	6
Other Hispanic	8

Age & Nativity, 2000
Under 5 years	18
18 years and over	288
21 years and over	280
65 years and over	125
85 years and over	60
Median age	49.1
Native-born	319
Foreign-born	80

Educational Attainment, 2000
Population 25 years and over	277
Less than 9th grade	13.4%
High school grad or higher	78.7%
Bachelor's degree or higher	28.9%
Graduate degree	12.6%

Income & Poverty, 1999
Per capita income	$48,935
Median household income	$152,262
Median family income	$157,816
Persons in poverty	68
H'holds receiving public assistance	3
H'holds receiving social security	15

Households, 2000
Total households	74
With persons under 18	29
With persons over 65	20
Family households	58
Single-person households	8
Persons per household	3.04
Persons per family	3.40

Labor & Employment
Total civilian labor force, 2007**	95
Unemployment rate	0.0%
Total civilian labor force, 2000	114
Unemployment rate	0.0%

Employed persons 16 years and over by occupation, 2000
Managers & professionals	68
Service occupations	9
Sales & office occupations	30
Farming, fishing & forestry	2
Construction & maintenance	3
Production & transportation	2
Self-employed persons	6

General Information
Borough of Rockleigh
26 Rockleigh Rd
Rockleigh, NJ 07647
201-768-4217
Website	www.rockleighnj.org
Year of incorporation	1923
Land/water area (sq. miles)	0.97/0.00
Form of government	Borough

Government
Legislative Districts
US Congressional	5
State Legislative	39

Local Officials, 2009
Mayor	Nicholas Langella
Manager	William J. McGuire
Clerk	Marcella Giampiccolo
Finance Dir	Anne Murphy
Tax Assessor	Raymond Damiano
Tax Collector	Anne Murphy
Attorney	John Hall
Building	William McGuire
Comm Dev/Planning	NA
Engineering	Neglia Engineering
Public Works	NA
Police Chief	Bruce Tietjen
Emerg/Fire Director	Mike Malhame

Housing & Construction
Housing Units, 2000*
Total	80
Median rent	$2,001
Median SF home value	$937,500

Permits for New Residential Construction
	Units	Value
Total, 2006	0	$0
Single family	0	$0
Total, 2007	0	$0
Single family	0	$0

Real Property Valuation, 2008
	Parcels	Valuation
Total	101	$271,930,856
Vacant	11	10,274,956
Residential	73	148,789,000
Commercial	17	112,866,900
Industrial	0	0
Apartments	0	0
Farm land	0	0
Farm homestead	0	0

Average Property Value & Tax, 2008
Residential value	$2,038,205
Property tax	$13,157
Tax credit/rebate	$1,353

Public Library
No public municipal library

Library statistics, 2007
Population served	NA
Full-time/total staff	NA/NA

	Total	Per capita
Holdings	NA	NA
Revenues	NA	NA
Expenditures	NA	NA
Annual visits	NA	NA
Internet terminals/annual users	NA/NA	

Public Safety
Number of officers, 2007	0

Crime	2006	2007
Total crimes	11	10
Violent	2	5
Murder	0	0
Rape	0	0
Robbery	0	0
Aggravated assault	2	5
Non-violent	9	5
Burglary	2	1
Larceny	7	4
Vehicle theft	0	0
Domestic violence	0	2
Arson	0	0
Total crime rate	27.8	25.4
Violent	5.1	12.7
Non-violent	22.8	12.7

Public School District
(for school year 2007-08 except as noted)

Rockleigh Board of Education
31 Highland Avenue
Midland Park, NJ 07432

No schools in district - sends students to Northvale and Northern Valley Regional schools (see Appendix D)

Per pupil expenditure	NA
Median faculty salary	NA
Median administrator salary	NA
Grade 12 enrollment	NA
High school graduation rate	NA

Assessment test results
(percent scoring at proficient or advanced level)
	Language	Math
NJASK-Grade 3	NA	NA
GEPA-Grade 8	NA	NA
HSPA-High School	NA	NA

SAT Score Averages, 2006-07
Pct tested	Math	Verbal	Writing
NA	NA	NA	NA

Teacher Qualifications
Avg. years of experience	NA
Highly-qualified teachers one subject/all subjects	NA/NA

No Child Left Behind
AYP, 2006-07	NA

Municipal Finance
State Aid Programs, 2009
Total aid	$122,473
CMPTRA	12,040
Energy tax receipts	105,534
Garden State Trust	0

General Budget, 2008
Total tax levy	$1,757,203
County levy	409,492
County taxes	387,335
County library	0
County health	0
County open space	22,157
School levy	406,335
Muni. levy	941,376
Misc. revenues	671,698

Taxes
	2006	2007	2008
General tax rate per $100	0.58	0.6	0.647
County equalization ratio	137.23	137.23	125.59
Net valuation taxable	$274,233,300	$266,820,621	$272,213,099
State equalized value	$200,102,433	$212,508,478	$232,642,199

* US Census Bureau
** New Jersey Department of Labor

See Introduction for an explanation of all data sources.

Demographics & Socio-Economic Characteristics
(2000 US Census, except as noted)

Population
1980*	717
1990*	693
2000	662
Male	328
Female	334
2007 (estimate)*	678
Population density	1,011.9

Race & Hispanic Origin, 2000
Race
White	630
Black/African American	9
American Indian/Alaska Native	0
Asian	3
Native Hawaiian/Pacific Islander	4
Other race	6
Two or more races	10
Hispanic origin, total	26
Mexican	3
Puerto Rican	13
Cuban	3
Other Hispanic	7

Age & Nativity, 2000
Under 5 years	38
18 years and over	528
21 years and over	521
65 years and over	114
85 years and over	15
Median age	43.8
Native-born	585
Foreign-born	73

Educational Attainment, 2000
Population 25 years and over	523
Less than 9th grade	2.1%
High school grad or higher	96.0%
Bachelor's degree or higher	59.7%
Graduate degree	29.1%

Income & Poverty, 1999
Per capita income	$48,357
Median household income	$79,469
Median family income	$100,314
Persons in poverty	18
H'holds receiving public assistance	3
H'holds receiving social security	84

Households, 2000
Total households	284
With persons under 18	71
With persons over 65	89
Family households	190
Single-person households	79
Persons per household	2.33
Persons per family	2.82

Labor & Employment
Total civilian labor force, 2007**	431
Unemployment rate	2.7%
Total civilian labor force, 2000	386
Unemployment rate	2.6%

Employed persons 16 years and over by occupation, 2000
Managers & professionals	230
Service occupations	30
Sales & office occupations	70
Farming, fishing & forestry	0
Construction & maintenance	25
Production & transportation	21
Self-employed persons	40

General Information
Borough of Rocky Hill
PO Box 188
Rocky Hill, NJ 08553
609-924-7445
Website	www.rockyhill-nj.gov
Year of incorporation	1889
Land/water area (sq. miles)	0.67/0.00
Form of government	Borough

Government
Legislative Districts
US Congressional	7
State Legislative	16

Local Officials, 2009
Mayor	Edward P. Zimmerman
Manager/Admin	NA
Clerk	Donna M. Griffiths
Finance Dir	G. Ross Bobal
Tax Assessor	George Sopko
Tax Collector	Donna Griffiths
Attorney	Albert Cruz
Building	NA
Comm Dev/Planning	NA
Engineering	William C. Tanner
Public Works	NA
Police Chief	NA
Emerg/Fire Director	Todd Harris

Housing & Construction
Housing Units, 2000*
Total	295
Median rent	$914
Median SF home value	$271,400

Permits for New Residential Construction
	Units	Value
Total, 2006	0	$0
Single family	0	$0
Total, 2007	0	$0
Single family	0	$0

Real Property Valuation, 2008
	Parcels	Valuation
Total	284	$62,411,300
Vacant	9	272,300
Residential	256	54,606,200
Commercial	13	3,538,500
Industrial	1	3,404,000
Apartments	2	569,400
Farm land	3	20,900
Farm homestead	0	0

Average Property Value & Tax, 2008
Residential value	$213,305
Property tax	$7,326
Tax credit/rebate	$1,031

Public Library
Mary Jacobs Branch Library‡
64 Washington St
Rocky Hill, NJ 08553
609-924-7073
Branch Librarian	Helen Morris

Library statistics, 2007
see Somerset County profile
for library system statistics

Public Safety
Number of officers, 2007	0

Crime	2006	2007
Total crimes	3	3
Violent	0	0
Murder	0	0
Rape	0	0
Robbery	0	0
Aggravated assault	0	0
Non-violent	3	3
Burglary	1	1
Larceny	2	2
Vehicle theft	0	0
Domestic violence	1	4
Arson	0	0
Total crime rate	4.4	4.4
Violent	0.0	0.0
Non-violent	4.4	4.4

Public School District
(for school year 2007-08 except as noted)

Rocky Hill Borough School District
P.O. Box 270
Rocky Hill, NJ 08853

No schools in district

Per pupil expenditure	NA
Median faculty salary	NA
Median administrator salary	NA
Grade 12 enrollment	NA
High school graduation rate	NA

Assessment test results
(percent scoring at proficient or advanced level)
	Language	Math
NJASK-Grade 3	NA	NA
GEPA-Grade 8	NA	NA
HSPA-High School	NA	NA

SAT Score Averages, 2006-07
Pct tested	Math	Verbal	Writing
NA	NA	NA	NA

Teacher Qualifications
Avg. years of experience	NA
Highly-qualified teachers one subject/all subjects	NA/NA

No Child Left Behind
AYP, 2006-07	NA

Municipal Finance
State Aid Programs, 2009
Total aid	$100,691
CMPTRA	21,204
Energy tax receipts	76,970
Garden State Trust	0

General Budget, 2008
Total tax levy	$2,146,878
County levy	462,680
County taxes	371,333
County library	50,248
County health	0
County open space	41,099
School levy	1,240,283
Muni. levy	443,915
Misc. revenues	784,724

Taxes	2006	2007	2008
General tax rate per $100	2.78	3.04	3.435
County equalization ratio	51.22	47.21	46.20
Net valuation taxable	$62,039,800	$62,303,496	$62,506,662
State equalized value	$131,506,346	$134,752,765	$139,003,219

‡ Branch of county library
* US Census Bureau
** New Jersey Department of Labor

434   **The New Jersey Municipal Data Book**   See Introduction for an explanation of all data sources.

Demographics & Socio-Economic Characteristics

(2000 US Census, except as noted)

Population

1980*	835
1990*	884
2000	933
Male	449
Female	484
2007 (estimate)*	914
Population density	466.3

Race & Hispanic Origin, 2000

Race

White	830
Black/African American	24
American Indian/Alaska Native	0
Asian	19
Native Hawaiian/Pacific Islander	1
Other race	21
Two or more races	38
Hispanic origin, total	42
Mexican	4
Puerto Rican	19
Cuban	0
Other Hispanic	19

Age & Nativity, 2000

Under 5 years	49
18 years and over	674
21 years and over	641
65 years and over	113
85 years and over	14
Median age	40.4
Native-born	848
Foreign-born	80

Educational Attainment, 2000

Population 25 years and over	584
Less than 9th grade	3.8%
High school grad or higher	93.0%
Bachelor's degree or higher	44.2%
Graduate degree	17.8%

Income & Poverty, 1999

Per capita income	$24,892
Median household income	$61,979
Median family income	$67,019
Persons in poverty	40
H'holds receiving public assistance	2
H'holds receiving social security	80

Households, 2000

Total households	337
With persons under 18	138
With persons over 65	86
Family households	258
Single-person households	63
Persons per household	2.77
Persons per family	3.17

Labor & Employment

Total civilian labor force, 2007**	533
Unemployment rate	3.7%
Total civilian labor force, 2000	496
Unemployment rate	4.4%

Employed persons 16 years and over by occupation, 2000

Managers & professionals	221
Service occupations	45
Sales & office occupations	97
Farming, fishing & forestry	0
Construction & maintenance	66
Production & transportation	45
Self-employed persons	27

* US Census Bureau
** New Jersey Department of Labor

See Introduction for an explanation of all data sources.

General Information

Borough of Roosevelt
33 N Rochdale Ave
PO Box 128
Roosevelt, NJ 08555
609-448-0539

Website	NA
Year of incorporation	1945
Land/water area (sq. miles)	1.96/0.00
Form of government	Borough

Government

Legislative Districts

US Congressional	4
State Legislative	30

Local Officials, 2009

Mayor	Beth Battel
Manager	William Schmeling
Clerk	Krystyna Bieracka-Olejnik
Treasurer	A. Debevec
Tax Assessor	Michael L. Ticktin
Tax Collector	Salvatore Cannizzaro
Attorney	Richard J. Shaklee
Building	Rick Bordeur
Comm Dev/Planning	NA
Engineering	Carmela Robert
Public Works	NA
Police Chief	NA
Emerg/Fire Director	Kim Dexheimer

Housing & Construction

Housing Units, 2000*

Total	351
Median rent	$809
Median SF home value	$134,100

Permits for New Residential Construction

	Units	Value
Total, 2006	1	$220,000
Single family	1	$220,000
Total, 2007	0	$0
Single family	0	$0

Real Property Valuation, 2008

	Parcels	Valuation
Total	336	$96,270,800
Vacant	3	718,200
Residential	308	85,676,300
Commercial	3	1,183,700
Industrial	3	1,638,700
Apartments	1	2,101,400
Farm land	9	220,000
Farm homestead	9	4,732,500

Average Property Value & Tax, 2008

Residential value	$285,201
Property tax	$6,110
Tax credit/rebate	$919

Public Library

No public municipal library

Library statistics, 2007

Population served	NA
Full-time/total staff	NA/NA

	Total	Per capita
Holdings	NA	NA
Revenues	NA	NA
Expenditures	NA	NA
Annual visits	NA	NA
Internet terminals/annual users	NA/NA	

Public Safety

Number of officers, 2007 0

Crime	2006	2007
Total crimes	4	4
Violent	1	1
Murder	0	0
Rape	0	0
Robbery	0	0
Aggravated assault	1	1
Non-violent	3	3
Burglary	1	0
Larceny	2	3
Vehicle theft	0	0
Domestic violence	0	6
Arson	0	0
Total crime rate	4.4	4.4
Violent	1.1	1.1
Non-violent	3.3	3.3

Public School District

(for school year 2007-08 except as noted)

Roosevelt Borough School District
School Lane, PO Box 160
Roosevelt, NJ 08555
(609) 448-2798

Principal	Shari Payson
Number of schools	1
Grade plan	K-6
Enrollment	90
Attendance rate, '06-07	95.2%
Dropout rate	NA
Students per teacher	10.0
Per pupil expenditure	$15,893
Median faculty salary	$42,185
Median administrator salary	$73,047
Grade 12 enrollment	NA
High school graduation rate	NA

Assessment test results

(percent scoring at proficient or advanced level)

	Language	Math
NJASK-Grade 3	NA	NA
GEPA-Grade 8	NA	NA
HSPA-High School	NA	NA

SAT Score Averages, 2006-07

Pct tested	Math	Verbal	Writing
NA	NA	NA	NA

Teacher Qualifications

Avg. years of experience	10
Highly-qualified teachers one subject/all subjects	100%/100%

No Child Left Behind

AYP, 2006-07 .... Meets Standards

Municipal Finance

State Aid Programs, 2009

Total aid	$106,906
CMPTRA	23,003
Energy tax receipts	79,887
Garden State Trust	1,230

General Budget, 2008

Total tax levy	$2,064,818
County levy	232,712
County taxes	203,161
County library	12,226
County health	3,778
County open space	13,547
School levy	1,321,316
Muni. levy	510,791
Misc. revenues	484,551

Taxes

	2006	2007	2008
General tax rate per $100	4.78	2.023	2.143
County equalization ratio	47.22	107.33	107.33
Net valuation taxable	$36,308,910	$95,936,697	$96,376,346
State equalized value	$89,169,546	$89,391,635	$3,698,079,152

Demographics & Socio-Economic Characteristics

(2000 US Census, except as noted)

Population

1980*	5,330
1990*	4,847
2000	5,298
Male	2,448
Female	2,850
2007 (estimate)*	5,357
Population density	1,479.8

Race & Hispanic Origin, 2000

Race

White	4,950
Black/African American	38
American Indian/Alaska Native	2
Asian	250
Native Hawaiian/Pacific Islander	0
Other race	23
Two or more races	35
Hispanic origin, total	121
Mexican	11
Puerto Rican	23
Cuban	12
Other Hispanic	75

Age & Nativity, 2000

Under 5 years	314
18 years and over	4,207
21 years and over	4,107
65 years and over	1,044
85 years and over	92
Median age	44.0
Native-born	4,694
Foreign-born	604

Educational Attainment, 2000

Population 25 years and over	3,988
Less than 9th grade	2.4%
High school grad or higher	92.2%
Bachelor's degree or higher	46.5%
Graduate degree	18.8%

Income & Poverty, 1999

Per capita income	$41,415
Median household income	$82,499
Median family income	$93,957
Persons in poverty	88
H'holds receiving public assistance	9
H'holds receiving social security	794

Households, 2000

Total households	2,142
With persons under 18	587
With persons over 65	768
Family households	1,525
Single-person households	550
Persons per household	2.47
Persons per family	2.99

Labor & Employment

Total civilian labor force, 2007**	2,882
Unemployment rate	3.1%
Total civilian labor force, 2000	2,760
Unemployment rate	2.7%

Employed persons 16 years and over by occupation, 2000

Managers & professionals	1,416
Service occupations	193
Sales & office occupations	840
Farming, fishing & forestry	0
Construction & maintenance	161
Production & transportation	75
Self-employed persons	169

General Information

Borough of Roseland
19 Harrison Ave
Roseland, NJ 07068
973-226-8080

Website	www.roselandnj.org
Year of incorporation	1908
Land/water area (sq. miles)	3.62/0.00
Form of government	Borough

Government

Legislative Districts

US Congressional	11
State Legislative	27

Local Officials, 2009

Mayor	John Arvanites
Manager	Thomas Kaczynski
Clerk	Thomas Kaczynski
Finance Dir	Maureen Chumacas
Tax Assessor	Kevin Dillon
Tax Collector	Maureen Chumacas
Attorney	Paul Jemas
Building	Leonard Mendola
Comm Dev/Planning	NA
Engineering	Ralph Tango
Public Works	Gail Tynam
Police Chief	Richard McDonough
Emerg/Fire Director	Michael Piltzecker

Housing & Construction

Housing Units, 2000*

Total	2,187
Median rent	$1,266
Median SF home value	$292,700

Permits for New Residential Construction

	Units	Value
Total, 2006	36	$6,233,089
Single family	36	$6,233,089
Total, 2007	27	$4,965,018
Single family	21	$4,170,018

Real Property Valuation, 2008

	Parcels	Valuation
Total	2,206	$239,421,841
Vacant	60	1,670,300
Residential	2,057	130,740,741
Commercial	63	87,252,700
Industrial	24	12,437,700
Apartments	1	7,316,900
Farm land	1	3,500
Farm homestead	0	0

Average Property Value & Tax, 2008

Residential value	$63,559
Property tax	$7,680
Tax credit/rebate	$1,050

Public Library

Roseland Free Public Library
20 Roseland Ave
Roseland, NJ 07068
973-226-8636

Director	Judith Lind

Library statistics, 2007

Population served	5,298
Full-time/total staff	3/5

	Total	Per capita
Holdings	50,756	9.58
Revenues	$698,675	$131.88
Expenditures	$631,180	$119.14
Annual visits	62,750	11.84
Internet terminals/annual users	4/22,000	

Public Safety

Number of officers, 2007	28

Crime	2006	2007
Total crimes	44	29
Violent	1	2
Murder	0	0
Rape	0	0
Robbery	0	1
Aggravated assault	1	1
Non-violent	43	27
Burglary	7	1
Larceny	32	25
Vehicle theft	4	1
Domestic violence	30	20
Arson	0	1
Total crime rate	8.1	5.4
Violent	0.2	0.4
Non-violent	8.0	5.0

Public School District

(for school year 2007-08 except as noted)

Roseland School District
Noecker School, Passaic Ave
Roseland, NJ 07068
(973) 226-1296

Superintendent	ard M. Sierchio
Number of schools	1
Grade plan	K-6
Enrollment	485
Attendance rate, '06-07	96.4%
Dropout rate	NA
Students per teacher	12.8
Per pupil expenditure	$12,593
Median faculty salary	$61,500
Median administrator salary	$100,054
Grade 12 enrollment	NA
High school graduation rate	NA

Assessment test results

(percent scoring at proficient or advanced level)

	Language	Math
NJASK-Grade 3	90.7%	96.0%
GEPA-Grade 8	NA	NA
HSPA-High School	NA	NA

SAT Score Averages, 2006-07

Pct tested	Math	Verbal	Writing
NA	NA	NA	NA

Teacher Qualifications

Avg. years of experience	10
Highly-qualified teachers one subject/all subjects	100%/100%

No Child Left Behind

AYP, 2006-07	Meets Standards

Municipal Finance

State Aid Programs, 2009

Total aid	$1,131,119
CMPTRA	23,152
Energy tax receipts	1,071,206
Garden State Trust	0

General Budget, 2008

Total tax levy	$28,956,157
County levy	7,236,562
County taxes	6,957,278
County library	0
County health	0
County open space	279,284
School levy	14,028,968
Muni. levy	7,690,628
Misc. revenues	5,561,717

Taxes

	2006	2007	2008
General tax rate per $100	10.41	11.43	12.083
County equalization ratio	14.66	13.15	13.03
Net valuation taxable	$254,991,241	$259,897,546	$239,650,017
State equalized value	$1,939,345,014	$1,993,115,140	$2,024,081,439

* US Census Bureau
** New Jersey Department of Labor

See Introduction for an explanation of all data sources.

Demographics & Socio-Economic Characteristics

(2000 US Census, except as noted)

Population

1980*	20,641
1990*	20,314
2000	21,274
Male	9,950
Female	11,324
2007 (estimate)*	20,747
Population density	7,858.7

Race & Hispanic Origin, 2000

Race

White	7,570
Black/African American	10,917
American Indian/Alaska Native	67
Asian	577
Native Hawaiian/Pacific Islander	15
Other race	1,291
Two or more races	837
Hispanic origin, total	3,641
Mexican	597
Puerto Rican	876
Cuban	230
Other Hispanic	1,938

Age & Nativity, 2000

Under 5 years	1,410
18 years and over	15,841
21 years and over	14,948
65 years and over	2,562
85 years and over	268
Median age	35.3
Native-born	16,396
Foreign-born	4,878

Educational Attainment, 2000

Population 25 years and over	14,017
Less than 9th grade	6.2%
High school grad or higher	77.6%
Bachelor's degree or higher	17.3%
Graduate degree	4.8%

Income & Poverty, 1999

Per capita income	$21,269
Median household income	$51,254
Median family income	$58,841
Persons in poverty	1,582
H'holds receiving public assistance	258
H'holds receiving social security	2,024

Households, 2000

Total households	7,520
With persons under 18	2,916
With persons over 65	1,984
Family households	5,223
Single-person households	1,895
Persons per household	2.82
Persons per family	3.41

Labor & Employment

Total civilian labor force, 2007**	11,379
Unemployment rate	6.4%
Total civilian labor force, 2000	10,970
Unemployment rate	6.6%

Employed persons 16 years and over by occupation, 2000

Managers & professionals	2,567
Service occupations	1,608
Sales & office occupations	3,456
Farming, fishing & forestry	5
Construction & maintenance	686
Production & transportation	1,925
Self-employed persons	369

* US Census Bureau
** New Jersey Department of Labor
§ State Fiscal Year July 1–June 30

General Information

Borough of Roselle
210 Chestnut St
Roselle, NJ 07203
908-245-5600

Website	www.boroughofroselle.com
Year of incorporation	1894
Land/water area (sq. miles)	2.64/0.01
Form of government	Borough

Government

Legislative Districts

US Congressional	10
State Legislative	20

Local Officials, 2009

Mayor	Garrett B. Smith
Administrator	Cheryl Fuller
Clerk	Rhona C. Bluestein
Finance Dir.	Adrien Mapp
Tax Assessor	Pamela Steele
Tax Collector	Mary Testori
Attorney	Wilfredo Benitez
Building	Jeff Guy
Comm Dev/Planning	NA
Engineering	Bill England
Public Works	Louis Williams
Police Chief	(vacant)
Fire Chief	Paul Mucha

Housing & Construction

Housing Units, 2000*

Total	7,870
Median rent	$700
Median SF home value	$129,200

Permits for New Residential Construction

	Units	Value
Total, 2006	4	$493,710
Single family	4	$493,710
Total, 2007	8	$688,956
Single family	3	$465,756

Real Property Valuation, 2008

	Parcels	Valuation
Total	5,602	$780,781,200
Vacant	57	2,955,300
Residential	5,178	616,569,100
Commercial	231	78,215,100
Industrial	87	36,721,300
Apartments	49	46,320,400
Farm land	0	0
Farm homestead	0	0

Average Property Value & Tax, 2008

Residential value	$119,075
Property tax	$8,384
Tax credit/rebate	$1,341

Public Library

Roselle Free Public Library
104 W Fourth Ave
Roselle, NJ 07203
908-245-5809

Director	W. Keith McCoy

Library statistics, 2007

Population served	21,274
Full-time/total staff	2/7

	Total	Per capita
Holdings	55,925	2.63
Revenues	$776,734	$36.51
Expenditures	$719,280	$33.81
Annual visits	88,933	4.18
Internet terminals/annual users	4/22,528	

Public Safety

Number of officers, 2007	59

Crime	2006	2007
Total crimes	501	468
Violent	87	84
Murder	1	0
Rape	4	0
Robbery	54	67
Aggravated assault	28	17
Non-violent	414	384
Burglary	109	98
Larceny	242	230
Vehicle theft	63	56
Domestic violence	163	174
Arson	0	3
Total crime rate	23.6	22.1
Violent	4.1	4.0
Non-violent	19.5	18.1

Public School District

(for school year 2007-08 except as noted)

Roselle Borough School District
710 Locust Street
Roselle, NJ 07203
(908) 298-2040

Superintendent	Elnardo Webster
Number of schools	6
Grade plan	K-12
Enrollment	2,818
Attendance rate, '06-07	93.7%
Dropout rate	0.5%
Students per teacher	10.8
Per pupil expenditure	$15,678
Median faculty salary	$49,561
Median administrator salary	$92,873
Grade 12 enrollment	163
High school graduation rate	96.9%

Assessment test results

(percent scoring at proficient or advanced level)

	Language	Math
NJASK-Grade 3	92.2%	88.6%
GEPA-Grade 8	31.3%	62.2%
HSPA-High School	47.7%	60.7%

SAT Score Averages, 2006-07

Pct tested	Math	Verbal	Writing
59%	383	391	404

Teacher Qualifications

Avg. years of experience	6
Highly-qualified teachers one subject/all subjects	98.5%/98.5%

No Child Left Behind

AYP, 2006-07	Needs Improvement

Municipal Finance§

State Aid Programs, 2009

Total aid	$3,003,232
CMPTRA	1,280,887
Energy tax receipts	1,677,297
Garden State Trust	0

General Budget, 2008

Total tax levy	$55,152,415
County levy	6,141,480
County taxes	5,868,844
County library	0
County health	0
County open space	272,636
School levy	22,988,538
Muni. levy	26,022,398
Misc. revenues	11,020,463

Taxes

	2006	2007	2008
General tax rate per $100	6.423	6.448	7.041
County equalization ratio	50.25	46.34	43.19
Net valuation taxable	$787,791,000	$786,884,003	$783,307,290
State equalized value	$1,703,355,665	$1,818,456,399	$1,847,472,215

See Introduction for an explanation of all data sources.

Demographics & Socio-Economic Characteristics
(2000 US Census, except as noted)

Population
1980*	13,377
1990*	12,805
2000	13,281
Male	6,469
Female	6,812
2007 (estimate)*	12,879
Population density	10,556.6

Race & Hispanic Origin, 2000
Race
White	10,740
Black/African American	322
American Indian/Alaska Native	14
Asian	1,214
Native Hawaiian/Pacific Islander	2
Other race	650
Two or more races	339
Hispanic origin, total	2,170
Mexican	242
Puerto Rican	423
Cuban	275
Other Hispanic	1,230

Age & Nativity, 2000
Under 5 years	781
18 years and over	10,328
21 years and over	9,904
65 years and over	1,680
85 years and over	209
Median age	36.7
Native-born	9,993
Foreign-born	3,288

Educational Attainment, 2000
Population 25 years and over	9,095
Less than 9th grade	5.5%
High school grad or higher	82.9%
Bachelor's degree or higher	25.6%
Graduate degree	7.7%

Income & Poverty, 1999
Per capita income	$24,101
Median household income	$53,717
Median family income	$63,403
Persons in poverty	571
H'holds receiving public assistance	96
H'holds receiving social security	1,265

Households, 2000
Total households	5,137
With persons under 18	1,665
With persons over 65	1,260
Family households	3,415
Single-person households	1,448
Persons per household	2.58
Persons per family	3.22

Labor & Employment
Total civilian labor force, 2007**	7,781
Unemployment rate	4.4%
Total civilian labor force, 2000	7,488
Unemployment rate	4.6%

Employed persons 16 years and over by occupation, 2000
Managers & professionals	2,480
Service occupations	1,036
Sales & office occupations	2,190
Farming, fishing & forestry	0
Construction & maintenance	530
Production & transportation	908
Self-employed persons	224

General Information
Borough of Roselle Park
110 E Westfield Ave
Roselle Park, NJ 07204
908-245-6222

Website	www.rosellepark.net
Year of incorporation	1901
Land/water area (sq. miles)	1.22/0.00
Form of government	Borough

Government
Legislative Districts
US Congressional	7
State Legislative	21

Local Officials, 2009
Mayor	Joseph DeIorio
Manager/Admin	Doreen Cali
Clerk	Doreen Cali
Finance Dir	Kenneth Blum
Tax Assessor	Paul Endler
Tax Collector	NA
Attorney	Blake Johnstone
Building	Jerry Eger
Comm Dev/Planning	NA
Engineering	Neglia Engineering
Public Works	Ben Cosentino
Police Chief	Paul Morrison
Emerg/Fire Director	Joseph Signorello

Housing & Construction
Housing Units, 2000*
Total	5,258
Median rent	$785
Median SF home value	$157,700

Permits for New Residential Construction
	Units	Value
Total, 2006	10	$848,370
Single family	10	$848,370
Total, 2007	13	$1,531,557
Single family	9	$762,957

Real Property Valuation, 2008
	Parcels	Valuation
Total	3,577	$290,032,500
Vacant	29	422,000
Residential	3,314	234,621,600
Commercial	175	25,555,900
Industrial	24	5,797,800
Apartments	35	23,635,200
Farm land	0	0
Farm homestead	0	0

Average Property Value & Tax, 2008
Residential value	$70,797
Property tax	$7,745
Tax credit/rebate	$1,201

Public Library
Veteran's Memorial Library
404 Chestnut St
Roselle Park, NJ 07204
908-245-2456

Director ... Susan Calantone

Library statistics, 2007
Population served	13,281
Full-time/total staff	2/5

	Total	Per capita
Holdings	78,289	5.89
Revenues	$616,652	$46.43
Expenditures	$474,985	$35.76
Annual visits	46,000	3.46
Internet terminals/annual users	10/17,000	

Public Safety
Number of officers, 2007 ... 34

Crime	2006	2007
Total crimes	231	278
Violent	8	29
Murder	0	0
Rape	0	1
Robbery	1	17
Aggravated assault	7	11
Non-violent	223	249
Burglary	35	47
Larceny	169	185
Vehicle theft	19	17
Domestic violence	77	83
Arson	0	0
Total crime rate	17.5	21.2
Violent	0.6	2.2
Non-violent	16.9	19.0

Public School District
(for school year 2007-08 except as noted)

Roselle Park School District
510 Chestnut Street
Roselle Park, NJ 07204
(908) 245-1197

Superintendent	Patrick Spagnoletti
Number of schools	5
Grade plan	K-12
Enrollment	2,013
Attendance rate, '06-07	95.1%
Dropout rate	1.2%
Students per teacher	10.2
Per pupil expenditure	$12,829
Median faculty salary	$53,286
Median administrator salary	$105,400
Grade 12 enrollment	152
High school graduation rate	98.1%

Assessment test results
(percent scoring at proficient or advanced level)
	Language	Math
NJASK-Grade 3	91.6%	93.7%
GEPA-Grade 8	61.1%	84.9%
HSPA-High School	72.1%	81.8%

SAT Score Averages, 2006-07
Pct tested	Math	Verbal	Writing
85%	469	457	456

Teacher Qualifications
Avg. years of experience	8
Highly-qualified teachers one subject/all subjects	100%/100%

No Child Left Behind
AYP, 2006-07 ... Meets Standards

Municipal Finance
State Aid Programs, 2009
Total aid	$1,333,246
CMPTRA	454,929
Energy tax receipts	858,318
Garden State Trust	0

General Budget, 2008
Total tax levy	$31,743,035
County levy	4,631,640
County taxes	4,428,281
County library	0
County health	0
County open space	203,359
School levy	17,417,654
Muni. levy	9,693,740
Misc. revenues	3,851,152

Taxes
	2006	2007	2008
General tax rate per $100	9.725	10.394	10.940
County equalization ratio	25.85	23.48	21.47
Net valuation taxable	$290,974,200	$290,832,123	$290,171,089
State equalized value	$1,239,408,724	$1,354,065,045	$1,369,508,277

* US Census Bureau
** New Jersey Department of Labor

See Introduction for an explanation of all data sources.

Demographics & Socio-Economic Characteristics

(2000 US Census, except as noted)

Population

1980*	18,878
1990*	20,429
2000	23,883
Male	11,674
Female	12,209
2007 (estimate)*	23,360
Population density	1,093.1

Race & Hispanic Origin, 2000

Race

White	22,110
Black/African American	456
American Indian/Alaska Native	35
Asian	855
Native Hawaiian/Pacific Islander	17
Other race	162
Two or more races	248
Hispanic origin, total	1,154
Mexican	77
Puerto Rican	393
Cuban	103
Other Hispanic	581

Age & Nativity, 2000

Under 5 years	1,705
18 years and over	17,438
21 years and over	16,751
65 years and over	2,363
85 years and over	253
Median age	37.5
Native-born	21,470
Foreign-born	2,413

Educational Attainment, 2000

Population 25 years and over	16,150
Less than 9th grade	3.3%
High school grad or higher	90.0%
Bachelor's degree or higher	33.9%
Graduate degree	10.0%

Income & Poverty, 1999

Per capita income	$30,174
Median household income	$72,982
Median family income	$83,409
Persons in poverty	642
H'holds receiving public assistance	107
H'holds receiving social security	1,908

Households, 2000

Total households	8,364
With persons under 18	3,524
With persons over 65	1,711
Family households	6,534
Single-person households	1,501
Persons per household	2.84
Persons per family	3.25

Labor & Employment

Total civilian labor force, 2007**	14,187
Unemployment rate	2.9%
Total civilian labor force, 2000	13,018
Unemployment rate	3.0%

Employed persons 16 years and over by occupation, 2000

Managers & professionals	5,430
Service occupations	1,319
Sales & office occupations	3,772
Farming, fishing & forestry	9
Construction & maintenance	1,121
Production & transportation	974
Self-employed persons	701

General Information

Roxbury Township
1715 US Highway 46
Ledgewood, NJ 07852
973-448-2000

Website	www.roxburynj.us
Year of incorporation	1740
Land/water area (sq. miles)	21.37/0.53
Form of government	Council-Manager

Government

Legislative Districts

US Congressional	11
State Legislative	25

Local Officials, 2009

Mayor	Kathy DeFillippo
Manager	Christopher Raths
Clerk	Betty Lou DeCroce
Finance Dir	Lisa A. Spring
Tax Assessor	Joseph McKeon
Tax Collector	Maryann Albrecht
Attorney	Tony Bucco Jr
Building	Rod Schmidt
Planning	Russell Stern
Engineering	Michael Kobylarz
Public Works	Rick Blood
Police Chief	Mark Noll
Fire Chief	Adam Alberti

Housing & Construction

Housing Units, 2000*

Total	8,550
Median rent	$759
Median SF home value	$207,400

Permits for New Residential Construction

	Units	Value
Total, 2006	37	$4,119,796
Single family	29	$4,014,394
Total, 2007	41	$4,082,986
Single family	31	$4,047,586

Real Property Valuation, 2008

	Parcels	Valuation
Total	8,772	$2,041,426,200
Vacant	468	33,008,400
Residential	7,804	1,623,484,500
Commercial	403	306,868,700
Industrial	44	64,422,300
Apartments	13	9,584,900
Farm land	28	228,000
Farm homestead	12	3,829,400

Average Property Value & Tax, 2008

Residential value	$208,203
Property tax	$7,574
Tax credit/rebate	$1,135

Public Library

Roxbury Public Library
103 Main St
Succasunna, NJ 07876
973-584-2400

Director	Mary C. Romance

Library statistics, 2007

Population served	23,883
Full-time/total staff	4/10

	Total	Per capita
Holdings	90,980	3.81
Revenues	$1,317,310	$55.16
Expenditures	$1,319,287	$55.24
Annual visits	243,222	10.18
Internet terminals/annual users	24/102,079	

Public Safety

Number of officers, 2007	48

Crime	2006	2007
Total crimes	344	360
Violent	21	18
Murder	0	0
Rape	2	0
Robbery	9	5
Aggravated assault	10	13
Non-violent	323	342
Burglary	66	57
Larceny	232	273
Vehicle theft	25	12
Domestic violence	120	83
Arson	0	0
Total crime rate	14.4	15.1
Violent	0.9	0.8
Non-violent	13.5	14.4

Public School District

(for school year 2007-08 except as noted)

Roxbury Township School District
42 N. Hillside Avenue
Succasunna, NJ 07876
(973) 584-6867

Superintendent	Michael Rossi
Number of schools	7
Grade plan	K-12
Enrollment	4,415
Attendance rate, '06-07	95.9%
Dropout rate	0.9%
Students per teacher	11.3
Per pupil expenditure	$13,442
Median faculty salary	$56,295
Median administrator salary	$104,645
Grade 12 enrollment	343
High school graduation rate	97.5%

Assessment test results

(percent scoring at proficient or advanced level)

	Language	Math
NJASK-Grade 3	93.5%	90.2%
GEPA-Grade 8	76.9%	90.1%
HSPA-High School	78.7%	86.5%

SAT Score Averages, 2006-07

Pct tested	Math	Verbal	Writing
85%	531	518	512

Teacher Qualifications

Avg. years of experience	11
Highly-qualified teachers one subject/all subjects	100%/100%

No Child Left Behind

AYP, 2006-07	Meets Standards

Municipal Finance

State Aid Programs, 2009

Total aid	$2,762,774
CMPTRA	648,748
Energy tax receipts	1,991,624
Garden State Trust	17,577

General Budget, 2008

Total tax levy	$74,477,307
County levy	9,335,227
County taxes	7,618,674
County library	0
County health	0
County open space	1,716,553
School levy	46,035,574
Muni. levy	19,106,507
Misc. revenues	7,365,530

Taxes

	2006	2007	2008
General tax rate per $100	3.35	3.49	3.638
County equalization ratio	58.24	54.2	50.91
Net valuation taxable	$2,042,677,000	$2,044,763,921	$2,047,302,642
State equalized value	$3,774,462,641	$4,011,289,265	$3,895,789,171

* US Census Bureau
** New Jersey Department of Labor

See Introduction for an explanation of all data sources.

Demographics & Socio-Economic Characteristics

(2000 US Census, except as noted)

Population
1980*	7,623
1990*	6,701
2000	7,137
Male	3,457
Female	3,680
2007 (estimate)*	7,226
Population density	1,384.3

Race & Hispanic Origin, 2000
Race
White	6,978
Black/African American	17
American Indian/Alaska Native	4
Asian	76
Native Hawaiian/Pacific Islander	0
Other race	26
Two or more races	36
Hispanic origin, total	99
Mexican	25
Puerto Rican	19
Cuban	20
Other Hispanic	35

Age & Nativity, 2000
Under 5 years	528
18 years and over	4,862
21 years and over	4,729
65 years and over	914
85 years and over	92
Median age	39.2
Native-born	6,845
Foreign-born	292

Educational Attainment, 2000
Population 25 years and over	4,630
Less than 9th grade	0.3%
High school grad or higher	97.1%
Bachelor's degree or higher	63.9%
Graduate degree	24.9%

Income & Poverty, 1999
Per capita income	$73,692
Median household income	$120,865
Median family income	$140,668
Persons in poverty	228
H'holds receiving public assistance	12
H'holds receiving social security	642

Households, 2000
Total households	2,452
With persons under 18	1,116
With persons over 65	651
Family households	1,989
Single-person households	412
Persons per household	2.91
Persons per family	3.29

Labor & Employment
Total civilian labor force, 2007**	3,257
Unemployment rate	2.4%
Total civilian labor force, 2000	3,047
Unemployment rate	2.6%

Employed persons 16 years and over by occupation, 2000
Managers & professionals	1,763
Service occupations	154
Sales & office occupations	844
Farming, fishing & forestry	0
Construction & maintenance	134
Production & transportation	74
Self-employed persons	204

General Information
Borough of Rumson
80 E River Rd
Rumson, NJ 07760
732-842-3300
Website	rumsonboro.com
Year of incorporation	1907
Land/water area (sq. miles)	5.22/2.01
Form of government	Borough

Government
Legislative Districts
US Congressional	12
State Legislative	11

Local Officials, 2009
Mayor	John E. Ekdahl
Administrator	Thomas S. Rogers
Clerk	Thomas S. Rogers
Chief Financial Officer	Helen L. Graves
Tax Assessor	Peter Barnett
Tax Collector	Helen L. Graves
Attorney	Martin M. Barger
Building	Paul Reinhold Jr
Planning	Frederick Andre
Engineering Firm	T & M Associates
Public Works	Mark T. Wellner
Police Chief	Rick Tobias
Fire Chief	Michael Trivett

Housing & Construction
Housing Units, 2000*
Total	2,610
Median rent	$1,187
Median SF home value	$455,300

Permits for New Residential Construction
	Units	Value
Total, 2006	44	$21,377,575
Single family	44	$21,377,575
Total, 2007	36	$16,476,490
Single family	36	$16,476,490

Real Property Valuation, 2008
	Parcels	Valuation
Total	2,586	$2,904,897,300
Vacant	94	45,975,700
Residential	2,414	2,747,446,100
Commercial	69	101,724,700
Industrial	0	0
Apartments	4	3,668,100
Farm land	4	31,000
Farm homestead	1	6,051,700

Average Property Value & Tax, 2008
Residential value	$1,140,165
Property tax	$16,160
Tax credit/rebate	$1,207

Public Library
Oceanic Free Library
109 Ave of Two Rivers
Rumson, NJ 07760
732-842-2692
Director	Ann Wissel

Library statistics, 2007
Population served	7,137
Full-time/total staff	1/1

	Total	Per capita
Holdings	20,165	2.83
Revenues	$195,343	$27.37
Expenditures	$183,878	$25.76
Annual visits	10,465	1.47
Internet terminals/annual users	6/2,167	

Public Safety
Number of officers, 2007	17

Crime	2006	2007
Total crimes	89	59
Violent	2	1
Murder	0	0
Rape	0	0
Robbery	0	0
Aggravated assault	2	1
Non-violent	87	58
Burglary	23	10
Larceny	60	48
Vehicle theft	4	0
Domestic violence	22	14
Arson	2	1
Total crime rate	12.3	8.2
Violent	0.3	0.1
Non-violent	12.0	8.1

Public School District
(for school year 2007-08 except as noted)

Rumson Borough School District
Forrest Avenue
Rumson, NJ 07760
(732) 842-4747
Superintendent	Roger A. Caruba
Number of schools	2
Grade plan	K-8
Enrollment	976
Attendance rate, '06-07	95.5%
Dropout rate	NA
Students per teacher	11.6
Per pupil expenditure	$12,739
Median faculty salary	$58,520
Median administrator salary	$104,000
Grade 12 enrollment	NA
High school graduation rate	NA

Assessment test results
(percent scoring at proficient or advanced level)
	Language	Math
NJASK-Grade 3	94.6%	95.4%
GEPA-Grade 8	86.0%	98.4%
HSPA-High School	NA	NA

SAT Score Averages, 2006-07
Pct tested	Math	Verbal	Writing
NA	NA	NA	NA

Teacher Qualifications
Avg. years of experience	8
Highly-qualified teachers one subject/all subjects	100%/100%

No Child Left Behind
AYP, 2006-07	Meets Standards

Municipal Finance
State Aid Programs, 2009
Total aid	$861,828
CMPTRA	0
Energy tax receipts	827,230
Garden State Trust	130

General Budget, 2008
Total tax levy	$41,192,248
County levy	9,245,734
County taxes	8,204,831
County library	493,762
County health	0
County open space	547,141
School levy	23,171,571
Muni. levy	8,774,944
Misc. revenues	5,689,139

Taxes
	2006	2007	2008
General tax rate per $100	1.358	1.389	1.418
County equalization ratio	90.19	81.15	79.92
Net valuation taxable	$2,824,225,500	$2,870,060,583	$2,906,237,714
State equalized value	$3,481,455,773	$3,590,848,112	$824,894,672

* US Census Bureau
** New Jersey Department of Labor

See Introduction for an explanation of all data sources.

Demographics & Socio-Economic Characteristics

(2000 US Census, except as noted)

Population

1980*	9,461
1990*	9,042
2000	8,533
Male	4,103
Female	4,430
2007 (estimate)*	8,389
Population density	4,013.9

Race & Hispanic Origin, 2000

Race

White	7,831
Black/African American	321
American Indian/Alaska Native	9
Asian	132
Native Hawaiian/Pacific Islander	1
Other race	104
Two or more races	135
Hispanic origin, total	306
Mexican	81
Puerto Rican	170
Cuban	4
Other Hispanic	51

Age & Nativity, 2000

Under 5 years	489
18 years and over	6,557
21 years and over	6,243
65 years and over	1,332
85 years and over	118
Median age	37.8
Native-born	8,182
Foreign-born	351

Educational Attainment, 2000

Population 25 years and over	5,803
Less than 9th grade	5.5%
High school grad or higher	78.6%
Bachelor's degree or higher	12.6%
Graduate degree	3.4%

Income & Poverty, 1999

Per capita income	$19,143
Median household income	$41,126
Median family income	$50,127
Persons in poverty	474
H'holds receiving public assistance	17
H'holds receiving social security	1,138

Households, 2000

Total households	3,376
With persons under 18	1,145
With persons over 65	1,001
Family households	2,274
Single-person households	938
Persons per household	2.52
Persons per family	3.08

Labor & Employment

Total civilian labor force, 2007**	4,673
Unemployment rate	6.0%
Total civilian labor force, 2000	4,434
Unemployment rate	6.1%

Employed persons 16 years and over by occupation, 2000

Managers & professionals	1,071
Service occupations	662
Sales & office occupations	1,376
Farming, fishing & forestry	0
Construction & maintenance	406
Production & transportation	648
Self-employed persons	149

General Information

Borough of Runnemede
24 N Black Horse Pike
Runnemede, NJ 08078
856-939-5161

Website	www.runnemedenj.org
Year of incorporation	1926
Land/water area (sq. miles)	2.09/0.03
Form of government	Borough

Government

Legislative Districts

US Congressional	1
State Legislative	5

Local Officials, 2009

Mayor	Virginia Betteridge
Manager/Admin	NA
Clerk	Joyce Pinto
Finance Dir	Christie Melfi
Tax Assessor	Brian Schneider
Tax Collector	Joyce Pinto
Attorney	John S. Kennedy
Building	Chris Mecca
Comm Dev/Planning	NA
Engineering	Steven Bach
Public Works	Richard Batot
Police Chief	Mark Diano
Emerg/Fire Director	Patrick Moriarty

Housing & Construction

Housing Units, 2000*

Total	3,510
Median rent	$598
Median SF home value	$97,800

Permits for New Residential Construction

	Units	Value
Total, 2006	13	$1,447,213
Single family	13	$1,447,213
Total, 2007	7	$725,074
Single family	7	$725,074

Real Property Valuation, 2008

	Parcels	Valuation
Total	2,872	$336,818,700
Vacant	88	2,952,100
Residential	2,599	257,174,700
Commercial	151	45,644,500
Industrial	13	12,749,700
Apartments	21	18,297,700
Farm land	0	0
Farm homestead	0	0

Average Property Value & Tax, 2008

Residential value	$98,951
Property tax	$4,925
Tax credit/rebate	$970

Public Library

Runnemede Public Library
Broadway & Black Horse Pike
Runnemede, NJ 08078
856-939-4688

Director	Kathleen Vasinda

Library statistics, 2007

Population served	8,533
Full-time/total staff	NA/0

	Total	Per capita
Holdings	0	NA
Revenues	$0	NA
Expenditures	$0	NA
Annual visits	NA	NA
Internet terminals/annual users	NA/NA	

Public Safety

Number of officers, 2007	20

Crime	2006	2007
Total crimes	344	368
Violent	29	32
Murder	0	0
Rape	1	1
Robbery	6	8
Aggravated assault	22	23
Non-violent	315	336
Burglary	47	42
Larceny	250	278
Vehicle theft	18	16
Domestic violence	43	61
Arson	1	3
Total crime rate	40.4	43.5
Violent	3.4	3.8
Non-violent	37.0	39.7

Public School District

(for school year 2007-08 except as noted)

Runnemede Borough School District
505 West Third Avenue
Runnemede, NJ 08078
(856) 931-5365

Superintendent	Nancy Ward
Number of schools	3
Grade plan	K-8
Enrollment	789
Attendance rate, '06-07	94.9%
Dropout rate	NA
Students per teacher	10.2
Per pupil expenditure	$13,496
Median faculty salary	$49,050
Median administrator salary	$104,500
Grade 12 enrollment	NA
High school graduation rate	NA

Assessment test results

(percent scoring at proficient or advanced level)

	Language	Math
NJASK-Grade 3	86.5%	87.3%
GEPA-Grade 8	84.2%	92.7%
HSPA-High School	NA	NA

SAT Score Averages, 2006-07

Pct tested	Math	Verbal	Writing
NA	NA	NA	NA

Teacher Qualifications

Avg. years of experience	10
Highly-qualified teachers one subject/all subjects	100%/100%

No Child Left Behind

AYP, 2006-07	Meets Standards

Municipal Finance

State Aid Programs, 2009

Total aid	$1,077,078
CMPTRA	240,190
Energy tax receipts	815,347
Garden State Trust	0

General Budget, 2008

Total tax levy	$16,815,647
County levy	3,515,772
County taxes	3,397,543
County library	0
County health	0
County open space	118,228
School levy	9,079,965
Muni. levy	4,219,911
Misc. revenues	2,942,653

Taxes

	2006	2007	2008
General tax rate per $100	4.742	4.87	4.978
County equalization ratio	70.84	63.11	57.30
Net valuation taxable	$333,496,300	$336,731,321	$337,867,063
State equalized value	$529,666,038	$586,828,053	$611,780,367

* US Census Bureau
** New Jersey Department of Labor

See Introduction for an explanation of all data sources.

Demographics & Socio-Economic Characteristics

(2000 US Census, except as noted)

Population
1980*	19,068
1990*	17,790
2000	18,110
Male	8,699
Female	9,411
2007 (estimate)*	17,620
Population density	6,270.5

Race & Hispanic Origin, 2000
Race
White	14,849
Black/African American	489
American Indian/Alaska Native	8
Asian	2,054
Native Hawaiian/Pacific Islander	5
Other race	337
Two or more races	368
Hispanic origin, total	1,555
Mexican	88
Puerto Rican	348
Cuban	280
Other Hispanic	839

Age & Nativity, 2000
Under 5 years	946
18 years and over	14,349
21 years and over	13,818
65 years and over	2,637
85 years and over	328
Median age	38.8
Native-born	14,466
Foreign-born	3,644

Educational Attainment, 2000
Population 25 years and over	12,997
Less than 9th grade	3.7%
High school grad or higher	88.3%
Bachelor's degree or higher	40.3%
Graduate degree	14.0%

Income & Poverty, 1999
Per capita income	$30,495
Median household income	$63,820
Median family income	$78,120
Persons in poverty	668
H'holds receiving public assistance	111
H'holds receiving social security	1,970

Households, 2000
Total households	7,055
With persons under 18	2,165
With persons over 65	1,976
Family households	4,672
Single-person households	1,998
Persons per household	2.52
Persons per family	3.16

Labor & Employment
Total civilian labor force, 2007**	10,165
Unemployment rate	3.7%
Total civilian labor force, 2000	9,815
Unemployment rate	4.6%

Employed persons 16 years and over by occupation, 2000
Managers & professionals	4,191
Service occupations	984
Sales & office occupations	2,834
Farming, fishing & forestry	0
Construction & maintenance	603
Production & transportation	751
Self-employed persons	484

* US Census Bureau
** New Jersey Department of Labor

General Information
Borough of Rutherford
176 Park Ave
Rutherford, NJ 07070
201-460-3000
Website	www.rutherford-nj.com
Year of incorporation	1881
Land/water area (sq. miles)	2.81/0.12
Form of government	Borough

Government

Legislative Districts
US Congressional	9
State Legislative	36

Local Officials, 2009
Mayor	John F. Hipp
Manager	(vacant)
Clerk	Mary Kriston
Finance Dir	Ed Cortright
Tax Assessor	Joseph Nichols
Tax Collector	Caryn Miller
Attorney	William T Smith
Building	John Uhl
Comm Dev/Planning	NA
Engineering	Berge Tombalakian
Public Works	Christopher Seidler
Police Chief	(vacant)
Fire Chief	Sean Walker

Housing & Construction

Housing Units, 2000*
Total	7,214
Median rent	$832
Median SF home value	$218,300

Permits for New Residential Construction
	Units	Value
Total, 2006	14	$3,330,600
Single family	10	$2,274,800
Total, 2007	1	$295,000
Single family	1	$295,000

Real Property Valuation, 2008
	Parcels	Valuation
Total	5,403	$2,848,418,700
Vacant	79	45,949,700
Residential	5,011	2,251,611,300
Commercial	251	344,226,000
Industrial	25	95,127,200
Apartments	37	111,504,500
Farm land	0	0
Farm homestead	0	0

Average Property Value & Tax, 2008
Residential value	$449,334
Property tax	$9,165
Tax credit/rebate	$1,245

Public Library
Rutherford Public Library
150 Park Ave
Rutherford, NJ 07070
201-939-8600
Director	Jane Fisher

Library statistics, 2007
Population served	18,110
Full-time/total staff	5/13

	Total	Per capita
Holdings	99,939	5.52
Revenues	$1,391,997	$76.86
Expenditures	$1,400,519	$77.33
Annual visits	224,499	12.40
Internet terminals/annual users	19/35,653	

Public Safety
Number of officers, 2007	39

Crime	2006	2007
Total crimes	275	311
Violent	12	15
Murder	0	0
Rape	0	0
Robbery	2	5
Aggravated assault	10	10
Non-violent	263	296
Burglary	47	41
Larceny	189	231
Vehicle theft	27	24
Domestic violence	67	83
Arson	1	3
Total crime rate	15.3	17.4
Violent	0.7	0.8
Non-violent	14.6	16.6

Public School District
(for school year 2007-08 except as noted)

Rutherford School District
176 Park Avenue
Rutherford, NJ 07070
(201) 939-1717
Superintendent	Leslie O'Keefe
Number of schools	5
Grade plan	K-12
Enrollment	2,447
Attendance rate, '06-07	95.8%
Dropout rate	0.2%
Students per teacher	10.9
Per pupil expenditure	$13,920
Median faculty salary	$63,182
Median administrator salary	$119,722
Grade 12 enrollment	201
High school graduation rate	98.5%

Assessment test results
(percent scoring at proficient or advanced level)
	Language	Math
NJASK-Grade 3	90.8%	90.8%
GEPA-Grade 8	76.3%	89.9%
HSPA-High School	87.9%	95.3%

SAT Score Averages, 2006-07
Pct tested	Math	Verbal	Writing
93%	529	507	493

Teacher Qualifications
Avg. years of experience	10
Highly-qualified teachers one subject/all subjects	100%/99.5%

No Child Left Behind
AYP, 2006-07	Meets Standards

Municipal Finance

State Aid Programs, 2009
Total aid	$1,785,156
CMPTRA	410,982
Energy tax receipts	1,329,545
Garden State Trust	0

General Budget, 2008
Total tax levy	$58,359,566
County levy	5,493,834
County taxes	5,194,961
County library	0
County health	0
County open space	298,873
School levy	33,633,818
Muni. levy	19,231,914
Misc. revenues	6,598,059

Taxes
	2006	2007	2008
General tax rate per $100	1.77	1.96	2.041
County equalization ratio	115.44	102.15	96.01
Net valuation taxable	$2,866,225,500	$2,881,009,587	$2,861,354,770
State equalized value	$2,819,199,566	$3,000,168,591	$3,063,288,073

See Introduction for an explanation of all data sources.

Demographics & Socio-Economic Characteristics
(2000 US Census, except as noted)

Population
1980*	14,084
1990*	13,296
2000	13,155
Male	6,210
Female	6,945
2007 (estimate)*	13,594
Population density	4,997.8

Race & Hispanic Origin, 2000
Race
White	11,936
Black/African American	183
American Indian/Alaska Native	5
Asian	623
Native Hawaiian/Pacific Islander	0
Other race	223
Two or more races	185
Hispanic origin, total	825
Mexican	19
Puerto Rican	198
Cuban	87
Other Hispanic	521

Age & Nativity, 2000
Under 5 years	744
18 years and over	10,499
21 years and over	10,124
65 years and over	2,368
85 years and over	266
Median age	40.3
Native-born	11,043
Foreign-born	2,112

Educational Attainment, 2000
Population 25 years and over	9,703
Less than 9th grade	4.6%
High school grad or higher	85.3%
Bachelor's degree or higher	25.2%
Graduate degree	6.1%

Income & Poverty, 1999
Per capita income	$27,561
Median household income	$63,545
Median family income	$73,205
Persons in poverty	434
H'holds receiving public assistance	34
H'holds receiving social security	1,605

Households, 2000
Total households	5,062
With persons under 18	1,518
With persons over 65	1,645
Family households	3,579
Single-person households	1,263
Persons per household	2.58
Persons per family	3.11

Labor & Employment
Total civilian labor force, 2007**	7,317
Unemployment rate	4.7%
Total civilian labor force, 2000	6,953
Unemployment rate	5.2%

Employed persons 16 years and over by occupation, 2000
Managers & professionals	2,335
Service occupations	714
Sales & office occupations	2,187
Farming, fishing & forestry	0
Construction & maintenance	604
Production & transportation	752
Self-employed persons	272

General Information
Township of Saddle Brook
93 Market St
Saddle Brook, NJ 07663
201-843-7100
Website	www.saddlebrooknj.gov
Year of incorporation	1955
Land/water area (sq. miles)	2.72/0.01
Form of government	Mayor-Council

Government
Legislative Districts
US Congressional	9
State Legislative	38

Local Officials, 2009
Mayor	Louis D'Arminio
Manager	Robert Elia
Clerk	Peter Lo Dico
Chief Financial Officer	Durene M. Ayer
Tax Assessor	Arthur Carlson
Tax Collector	Michele Sanzari
Attorney	Anthony Suarez
Building	Anthony Ambrogio
Comm Dev/Planning	NA
Engineering	Richard Moody
Public Works	Charles Cerone Sr
Police Chief	Robert Kugler
Fire Chief	Charles Cerone Jr (Vol)

Housing & Construction
Housing Units, 2000*
Total	5,161
Median rent	$887
Median SF home value	$198,600

Permits for New Residential Construction
	Units	Value
Total, 2006	73	$4,351,364
Single family	38	$3,452,245
Total, 2007	189	$19,837,503
Single family	22	$2,666,029

Real Property Valuation, 2008
	Parcels	Valuation
Total	4,418	$1,187,791,854
Vacant	65	9,870,800
Residential	4,143	779,770,600
Commercial	124	207,328,400
Industrial	79	161,843,754
Apartments	7	28,978,300
Farm land	0	0
Farm homestead	0	0

Average Property Value & Tax, 2008
Residential value	$188,214
Property tax	$6,632
Tax credit/rebate	$1,044

Public Library
Saddle Brook Public Library
340 Mayhill St
Saddle Brook, NJ 07663
201-843-3287
Director	Alma J. Henderson

Library statistics, 2007
Population served	13,155
Full-time/total staff	2/2

	Total	Per capita
Holdings	65,248	4.96
Revenues	$806,154	$61.28
Expenditures	$692,482	$52.64
Annual visits	63,180	4.80
Internet terminals/annual users	11/18,096	

Public Safety
Number of officers, 2007	33

Crime	2006	2007
Total crimes	317	391
Violent	7	6
Murder	0	0
Rape	1	0
Robbery	3	3
Aggravated assault	3	3
Non-violent	310	385
Burglary	45	35
Larceny	238	328
Vehicle theft	27	22
Domestic violence	61	43
Arson	1	0
Total crime rate	23.8	28.7
Violent	0.5	0.4
Non-violent	23.2	28.3

Public School District
(for school year 2007-08 except as noted)

Saddle Brook Township School District
355 Mayhill Street
Saddle Brook, NJ 07663
(201) 843-2133
Superintendent	Harry A. Groveman
Number of schools	5
Grade plan	K-12
Enrollment	1,732
Attendance rate, '06-07	94.4%
Dropout rate	1.4%
Students per teacher	11.7
Per pupil expenditure	$13,026
Median faculty salary	$54,275
Median administrator salary	$112,915
Grade 12 enrollment	136
High school graduation rate	95.8%

Assessment test results
(percent scoring at proficient or advanced level)
	Language	Math
NJASK-Grade 3	87.1%	88.8%
GEPA-Grade 8	72.4%	84.8%
HSPA-High School	79.8%	87.2%

SAT Score Averages, 2006-07
Pct tested	Math	Verbal	Writing
113%	479	454	453

Teacher Qualifications
Avg. years of experience	9
Highly-qualified teachers one subject/all subjects	97.5%/97.5%

No Child Left Behind
AYP, 2006-07	Meets Standards

Municipal Finance
State Aid Programs, 2009
Total aid	$1,856,813
CMPTRA	327,989
Energy tax receipts	1,482,404
Garden State Trust	0

General Budget, 2008
Total tax levy	$41,882,758
County levy	4,567,715
County taxes	4,320,480
County library	0
County health	0
County open space	247,235
School levy	23,857,489
Muni. levy	13,457,554
Misc. revenues	4,876,603

Taxes	2006	2007	2008
General tax rate per $100	3.12	3.3	3.525
County equalization ratio	55.69	51.11	48.48
Net valuation taxable	$1,167,242,754	$1,186,063,206	$1,188,560,803
State equalized value	$2,285,237,323	$2,444,957,120	$2,434,768,650

* US Census Bureau
** New Jersey Department of Labor

See Introduction for an explanation of all data sources.

Demographics & Socio-Economic Characteristics
(2000 US Census, except as noted)

Population
1980*	2,763
1990*	2,950
2000	3,201
Male	1,541
Female	1,660
2007 (estimate)*	3,784
Population density	759.8

Race & Hispanic Origin, 2000
Race
White	2,876
Black/African American	24
American Indian/Alaska Native	0
Asian	229
Native Hawaiian/Pacific Islander	1
Other race	26
Two or more races	45
Hispanic origin, total	82
Mexican	12
Puerto Rican	18
Cuban	22
Other Hispanic	30

Age & Nativity, 2000
Under 5 years	165
18 years and over	2,482
21 years and over	2,400
65 years and over	653
85 years and over	127
Median age	46.9
Native-born	2,638
Foreign-born	563

Educational Attainment, 2000
Population 25 years and over	2,335
Less than 9th grade	2.8%
High school grad or higher	93.7%
Bachelor's degree or higher	60.6%
Graduate degree	31.9%

Income & Poverty, 1999
Per capita income	$85,934
Median household income	$134,289
Median family income	$152,169
Persons in poverty	111
H'holds receiving public assistance	0
H'holds receiving social security	340

Households, 2000
Total households	1,118
With persons under 18	368
With persons over 65	378
Family households	927
Single-person households	159
Persons per household	2.77
Persons per family	3.05

Labor & Employment
Total civilian labor force, 2007**	1,416
Unemployment rate	2.7%
Total civilian labor force, 2000	1,344
Unemployment rate	3.2%

Employed persons 16 years and over by occupation, 2000
Managers & professionals	843
Service occupations	69
Sales & office occupations	304
Farming, fishing & forestry	0
Construction & maintenance	32
Production & transportation	53
Self-employed persons	182

* US Census Bureau
** New Jersey Department of Labor

General Information
Borough of Saddle River
100 E Allendale Rd
Saddle River, NJ 07458
201-327-2609
Website	www.saddleriver.org
Year of incorporation	1894
Land/water area (sq. miles)	4.98/0.00
Form of government	Borough

Government
Legislative Districts
US Congressional	5
State Legislative	39

Local Officials, 2009
Mayor	Saddle S. Raia
Manager	Charles Cuccia
Clerk	Marie Macari
Finance Dir	Charles Cuccia
Tax Assessor	Stuart Stolarz
Tax Collector	Linda Canavan
Attorney	Russell Huntington
Building	John Scialla
Planning	Joseph Pera
Engineering	Martin Spence
Public Works	Bruce Mauty
Police Chief	Timothy McWilliams
Emerg/Fire Director	Brian Yates

Housing & Construction
Housing Units, 2000*
Total	1,183
Median rent	$1,451
Median SF home value	$970,100

Permits for New Residential Construction
	Units	Value
Total, 2006	21	$21,395,629
Single family	21	$21,395,629
Total, 2007	16	$11,890,608
Single family	16	$11,890,608

Real Property Valuation, 2008
	Parcels	Valuation
Total	1,354	$2,142,316,600
Vacant	101	66,353,600
Residential	1,220	2,009,672,700
Commercial	18	57,162,400
Industrial	0	0
Apartments	0	0
Farm land	10	102,400
Farm homestead	5	9,025,500

Average Property Value & Tax, 2008
Residential value	$1,647,917
Property tax	$14,520
Tax credit/rebate	$1,149

Public Library
No public municipal library

Library statistics, 2007
Population served	NA
Full-time/total staff	NA/NA

	Total	Per capita
Holdings	NA	NA
Revenues	NA	NA
Expenditures	NA	NA
Annual visits	NA	NA
Internet terminals/annual users	NA/NA	

Public Safety
Number of officers, 2007	18

Crime	2006	2007
Total crimes	25	19
Violent	1	0
Murder	0	0
Rape	0	0
Robbery	0	0
Aggravated assault	1	0
Non-violent	24	19
Burglary	8	6
Larceny	16	13
Vehicle theft	0	0
Domestic violence	12	2
Arson	0	0
Total crime rate	6.6	5.0
Violent	0.3	0.0
Non-violent	6.4	5.0

Public School District
(for school year 2007-08 except as noted)

Saddle River School District
97 East Allendale Road
Saddle River, NJ 07458
(201) 327-0727
Superintendent	David Goldblatt
Number of schools	1
Grade plan	K-5
Enrollment	230
Attendance rate, '06-07	94.4%
Dropout rate	NA
Students per teacher	9.7
Per pupil expenditure	$17,477
Median faculty salary	$59,045
Median administrator salary	$124,718
Grade 12 enrollment	NA
High school graduation rate	NA

Assessment test results
(percent scoring at proficient or advanced level)
	Language	Math
NJASK-Grade 3	100.0%	96.9%
GEPA-Grade 8	NA	NA
HSPA-High School	NA	NA

SAT Score Averages, 2006-07
Pct tested	Math	Verbal	Writing
NA	NA	NA	NA

Teacher Qualifications
Avg. years of experience	9
Highly-qualified teachers one subject/all subjects	100%/100%

No Child Left Behind
AYP, 2006-07	Meets Standards

Municipal Finance
State Aid Programs, 2009
Total aid	$494,819
CMPTRA	0
Energy tax receipts	475,026
Garden State Trust	0

General Budget, 2008
Total tax levy	$18,884,701
County levy	4,764,537
County taxes	4,506,643
County library	0
County health	0
County open space	257,895
School levy	6,469,194
Muni. levy	7,650,970
Misc. revenues	2,840,664

Taxes
	2006	2007	2008
General tax rate per $100	0.8	0.84	0.883
County equalization ratio	91.74	87.3	83.12
Net valuation taxable	$2,066,134,900	$2,131,618,846	$2,143,209,753
State equalized value	$2,367,477,230	$2,564,324,365	$2,681,804,929

See Introduction for an explanation of all data sources.

Demographics & Socio-Economic Characteristics

(2000 US Census, except as noted)

Population

1980*	6,959
1990*	6,883
2000	5,857
Male	2,615
Female	3,242
2007 (estimate)*	5,678
Population density	2,175.5

Race & Hispanic Origin, 2000

Race

White	2,194
Black/African American	3,325
American Indian/Alaska Native	35
Asian	14
Native Hawaiian/Pacific Islander	0
Other race	81
Two or more races	208
Hispanic origin, total	286
Mexican	25
Puerto Rican	191
Cuban	8
Other Hispanic	62

Age & Nativity, 2000

Under 5 years	518
18 years and over	4,044
21 years and over	3,801
65 years and over	821
85 years and over	83
Median age	33.5
Native-born	5,761
Foreign-born	45

Educational Attainment, 2000

Population 25 years and over	3,385
Less than 9th grade	12.1%
High school grad or higher	67.8%
Bachelor's degree or higher	7.9%
Graduate degree	1.8%

Income & Poverty, 1999

Per capita income	$13,559
Median household income	$25,846
Median family income	$29,699
Persons in poverty	1,531
H'holds receiving public assistance	182
H'holds receiving social security	791

Households, 2000

Total households	2,383
With persons under 18	901
With persons over 65	647
Family households	1,464
Single-person households	813
Persons per household	2.43
Persons per family	3.10

Labor & Employment

Total civilian labor force, 2007**	2,209
Unemployment rate	8.1%
Total civilian labor force, 2000	2,209
Unemployment rate	10.3%

Employed persons 16 years and over by occupation, 2000

Managers & professionals	403
Service occupations	425
Sales & office occupations	449
Farming, fishing & forestry	0
Construction & maintenance	201
Production & transportation	503
Self-employed persons	44

*   US Census Bureau
** New Jersey Department of Labor

General Information

City of Salem
17 New Market St
Salem, NJ 08079
856-935-0372

Website	www.salemcitynj.com
Year of incorporation	1858
Land/water area (sq. miles)	2.61/0.19
Form of government	City

Government

Legislative Districts

US Congressional	2
State Legislative	3

Local Officials, 2009

Mayor	Earl Gage
Manager	Barbara Wright
Clerk	Barbara Wright
Finance Dir	David Crescenzi
Tax Assessor	Marie Procacci
Tax Collector	David Crescenzi
Attorney	David Puma
Building	Wayne Serfass
Comm Dev/Planning	NA
Engineering	Remington & Vernick
Public Works	Fred Mucci III
Police Chief	John Pelura III
Emerg/Fire Director	John Ayars

Housing & Construction

Housing Units, 2000*

Total	2,863
Median rent	$444
Median SF home value	$74,300

Permits for New Residential Construction

	Units	Value
Total, 2006	3	$122,742
Single family	3	$122,742
Total, 2007	1	$40,914
Single family	1	$40,914

Real Property Valuation, 2008

	Parcels	Valuation
Total	1,979	$251,130,086
Vacant	266	5,180,600
Residential	1,547	155,078,300
Commercial	125	48,814,990
Industrial	16	22,945,396
Apartments	12	18,410,100
Farm land	9	165,800
Farm homestead	4	534,900

Average Property Value & Tax, 2008

Residential value	$100,331
Property tax	$3,349
Tax credit/rebate	$790

Public Library

Salem Free Public Library
112 W Broadway
Salem, NJ 08079
856-935-0526

Director	Jeffrey Dilks

Library statistics, 2007

Population served	5,857
Full-time/total staff	0/5

	Total	Per capita
Holdings	55,727	9.51
Revenues	$111,771	$19.08
Expenditures	$155,346	$26.52
Annual visits	12,365	2.11
Internet terminals/annual users		6/5,200

Public Safety

Number of officers, 2007	23

Crime	2006	2007
Total crimes	362	434
Violent	86	78
Murder	1	1
Rape	0	8
Robbery	28	22
Aggravated assault	57	47
Non-violent	276	356
Burglary	80	121
Larceny	185	214
Vehicle theft	11	21
Domestic violence	138	139
Arson	10	3
Total crime rate	62.3	75.0
Violent	14.8	13.5
Non-violent	47.5	61.5

Public School District

(for school year 2007-08 except as noted)

Salem City School District
205 Walnut Street
Salem, NJ 08079
(856) 935-3800

Superintendent	Amiot Michel
Number of schools	3
Grade plan	K-12
Enrollment	1,425
Attendance rate, '06-07	91.3%
Dropout rate	5.2%
Students per teacher	8.2
Per pupil expenditure	$16,452
Median faculty salary	$49,748
Median administrator salary	$79,320
Grade 12 enrollment	106
High school graduation rate	79.9%

Assessment test results

(percent scoring at proficient or advanced level)

	Language	Math
NJASK-Grade 3	53.7%	58.0%
GEPA-Grade 8	30.7%	54.5%
HSPA-High School	59.2%	73.4%

SAT Score Averages, 2006-07

Pct tested	Math	Verbal	Writing
55%	433	432	422

Teacher Qualifications

Avg. years of experience	6
Highly-qualified teachers one subject/all subjects	100%/100%

No Child Left Behind

AYP, 2006-07	Meets Standards

Municipal Finance

State Aid Programs, 2009

Total aid	$1,660,844
CMPTRA	952,010
Energy tax receipts	708,834
Garden State Trust	0

General Budget, 2008

Total tax levy	$8,474,461
County levy	2,376,497
County taxes	2,325,239
County library	0
County health	0
County open space	51,258
School levy	2,466,425
Muni. levy	3,631,538
Misc. revenues	4,246,499

Taxes

	2006	2007	2008
General tax rate per $100	5.57	2.885	3.339
County equalization ratio	72.19	125.75	100.36
Net valuation taxable	$114,542,875	$256,190,568	$253,852,544
State equalized value	$203,147,079	$255,281,149	$149,048,516

See Introduction for an explanation of all data sources.

Demographics & Socio-Economic Characteristics
(2000 US Census, except as noted)

Population
1980*	1,485
1990*	1,732
2000	1,825
Male	919
Female	906
2007 (estimate)*	1,893
Population density	44.4

Race & Hispanic Origin, 2000
Race
White	1,786
Black/African American	7
American Indian/Alaska Native	3
Asian	8
Native Hawaiian/Pacific Islander	2
Other race	1
Two or more races	18
Hispanic origin, total	24
Mexican	0
Puerto Rican	10
Cuban	5
Other Hispanic	9

Age & Nativity, 2000
Under 5 years	101
18 years and over	1,365
21 years and over	1,312
65 years and over	244
85 years and over	33
Median age	40.4
Native-born	1,761
Foreign-born	68

Educational Attainment, 2000
Population 25 years and over	1,249
Less than 9th grade	2.6%
High school grad or higher	87.4%
Bachelor's degree or higher	24.7%
Graduate degree	7.6%

Income & Poverty, 1999
Per capita income	$23,854
Median household income	$55,667
Median family income	$65,774
Persons in poverty	99
H'holds receiving public assistance	8
H'holds receiving social security	201

Households, 2000
Total households	693
With persons under 18	257
With persons over 65	183
Family households	504
Single-person households	158
Persons per household	2.63
Persons per family	3.12

Labor & Employment
Total civilian labor force, 2007**	1,063
Unemployment rate	4.0%
Total civilian labor force, 2000	954
Unemployment rate	3.2%

Employed persons 16 years and over by occupation, 2000
Managers & professionals	314
Service occupations	128
Sales & office occupations	240
Farming, fishing & forestry	2
Construction & maintenance	118
Production & transportation	121
Self-employed persons	84

General Information
Township of Sandyston
133 County Road 645
Sandyston, NJ 07826
973-948-3520
Website	www.sandystontownship.com
Year of incorporation	1762
Land/water area (sq. miles)	42.61/0.70
Form of government	Township

Government
Legislative Districts
US Congressional	5
State Legislative	24

Local Officials, 2009
Mayor	George B. Harper Jr
Manager/Admin	NA
Clerk	Amanda F. Lobban
Finance Dir	Jessica Caruso
Tax Assessor	Robert W. Pastor
Tax Collector	Jessica Caruso
Attorney	Christopher Quinn
Building	John deJager
Planning	Sharon Yarosz
Engineering	Harold Pellow
Public Works	Alan Delea
Police Chief	NA
Emerg/Fire Director	Scott House

Housing & Construction
Housing Units, 2000*
Total	907
Median rent	$860
Median SF home value	$144,800

Permits for New Residential Construction
	Units	Value
Total, 2006	6	$1,078,600
Single family	6	$1,078,600
Total, 2007	4	$1,172,700
Single family	4	$1,172,700

Real Property Valuation, 2008
	Parcels	Valuation
Total	1,322	$271,793,100
Vacant	166	14,650,800
Residential	809	202,755,300
Commercial	53	20,093,100
Industrial	5	2,373,100
Apartments	0	0
Farm land	191	1,138,400
Farm homestead	98	30,782,400

Average Property Value & Tax, 2008
Residential value	$257,484
Property tax	$4,402
Tax credit/rebate	$847

Public Library
No public municipal library

Library statistics, 2007
Population served	NA
Full-time/total staff	NA/NA

	Total	Per capita
Holdings	NA	NA
Revenues	NA	NA
Expenditures	NA	NA
Annual visits	NA	NA
Internet terminals/annual users	NA/NA	

Public Safety
Number of officers, 2007	0

Crime	2006	2007
Total crimes	17	8
Violent	1	0
Murder	0	0
Rape	0	0
Robbery	1	0
Aggravated assault	0	0
Non-violent	16	8
Burglary	6	3
Larceny	9	4
Vehicle theft	1	1
Domestic violence	0	15
Arson	0	0
Total crime rate	8.9	4.2
Violent	0.5	0.0
Non-violent	8.3	4.2

Public School District
(for school year 2007-08 except as noted)

Sandyston-Walpack Township School Dist.
PO Box 128, 100 Route 560
Layton, NJ 07851
(973) 948-4450
Chief School Admin	Glenn Sumpman
Number of schools	1
Grade plan	K-6
Enrollment	176
Attendance rate, '06-07	95.4%
Dropout rate	NA
Students per teacher	9.5
Per pupil expenditure	$14,400
Median faculty salary	$57,273
Median administrator salary	$110,000
Grade 12 enrollment	NA
High school graduation rate	NA

Assessment test results
(percent scoring at proficient or advanced level)
	Language	Math
NJASK-Grade 3	100.0%	100.0%
GEPA-Grade 8	NA	NA
HSPA-High School	NA	NA

SAT Score Averages, 2006-07
Pct tested	Math	Verbal	Writing
NA	NA	NA	NA

Teacher Qualifications
Avg. years of experience	11
Highly-qualified teachers one subject/all subjects	100%/100%

No Child Left Behind
AYP, 2006-07	Meets Standards

Municipal Finance
State Aid Programs, 2009
Total aid	$378,025
CMPTRA	17,303
Energy tax receipts	205,347
Garden State Trust	133,327

General Budget, 2008
Total tax levy	$4,657,677
County levy	1,111,466
County taxes	932,760
County library	78,615
County health	27,608
County open space	72,483
School levy	3,094,612
Muni. levy	451,599
Misc. revenues	1,100,161

Taxes	2006	2007	2008
General tax rate per $100	3.03	1.62	1.710
County equalization ratio	59.92	104.08	94.37
Net valuation taxable	$134,212,400	$270,554,483	$272,454,526
State equalized value	$255,981,040	$286,655,454	$303,900,408

* US Census Bureau
** New Jersey Department of Labor

See Introduction for an explanation of all data sources.

Demographics & Socio-Economic Characteristics
(2000 US Census, except as noted)

Population
1980*	29,969
1990*	34,986
2000	40,377
Male	19,803
Female	20,574
2007 (estimate)*	42,351
Population density	2,663.6

Race & Hispanic Origin, 2000
Race
White	30,875
Black/African American	3,481
American Indian/Alaska Native	53
Asian	4,265
Native Hawaiian/Pacific Islander	8
Other race	855
Two or more races	840
Hispanic origin, total	2,942
Mexican	105
Puerto Rican	1,365
Cuban	194
Other Hispanic	1,278

Age & Nativity, 2000
Under 5 years	2,712
18 years and over	30,863
21 years and over	29,654
65 years and over	5,004
85 years and over	488
Median age	36.5
Native-born	32,279
Foreign-born	8,098

Educational Attainment, 2000
Population 25 years and over	27,872
Less than 9th grade	4.7%
High school grad or higher	85.6%
Bachelor's degree or higher	24.9%
Graduate degree	7.4%

Income & Poverty, 1999
Per capita income	$24,736
Median household income	$58,919
Median family income	$66,266
Persons in poverty	1,905
H'holds receiving public assistance	220
H'holds receiving social security	3,906

Households, 2000
Total households	14,955
With persons under 18	5,505
With persons over 65	3,639
Family households	10,923
Single-person households	3,342
Persons per household	2.68
Persons per family	3.17

Labor & Employment
Total civilian labor force, 2007**	22,883
Unemployment rate	3.7%
Total civilian labor force, 2000	20,837
Unemployment rate	4.4%

Employed persons 16 years and over by occupation, 2000
Managers & professionals	7,066
Service occupations	2,360
Sales & office occupations	6,232
Farming, fishing & forestry	21
Construction & maintenance	1,847
Production & transportation	2,397
Self-employed persons	656

* US Census Bureau
** New Jersey Department of Labor

General Information
Borough of Sayreville
167 Main St
Sayreville, NJ 08872
732-390-7000
Website	www.sayreville.com
Year of incorporation	1919
Land/water area (sq. miles)	15.90/2.85
Form of government	Borough

Government
Legislative Districts
US Congressional	6
State Legislative	19

Local Officials, 2009
Mayor	Kennedy O'Brien
Manager	Jeffry Bertrand
Clerk	Theresa Farbaniec
Finance Dir	Wayne Kronowski
Tax Assessor	Joseph Kupsch Jr
Tax Collector	Donna Brodzinski
Attorney	Decotiis, Fitzpatrick et al
Building	Kirk Miick
Planning	John Misiewicz
Engineering	CME Associates
Public Works	Bernard Bailey
Police Chief	Edward Szkodny
Fire Chief	Anthony Jackowski

Housing & Construction
Housing Units, 2000*
Total	15,235
Median rent	$795
Median SF home value	$153,400

Permits for New Residential Construction
	Units	Value
Total, 2006	23	$3,218,639
Single family	23	$3,218,639
Total, 2007	22	$2,491,669
Single family	22	$2,491,669

Real Property Valuation, 2008
	Parcels	Valuation
Total	13,016	$2,275,473,300
Vacant	590	60,388,200
Residential	11,941	1,712,742,000
Commercial	415	181,383,700
Industrial	45	162,969,600
Apartments	22	157,837,200
Farm land	2	8,700
Farm homestead	1	143,900

Average Property Value & Tax, 2008
Residential value	$143,434
Property tax	$5,725
Tax credit/rebate	$963

Public Library
Sayreville Public Library
1050 Washington Rd
Parlin, NJ 08859
732-727-0212
Director	Susan Kaplan

Library statistics, 2007
Population served	40,377
Full-time/total staff	5/13

	Total	Per capita
Holdings	97,213	2.41
Revenues	$1,710,395	$42.36
Expenditures	$1,531,890	$37.94
Annual visits	76,000	1.88
Internet terminals/annual users	10/68,183	

Public Safety
Number of officers, 2007	90

Crime	2006	2007
Total crimes	893	778
Violent	70	62
Murder	0	1
Rape	5	5
Robbery	13	20
Aggravated assault	52	36
Non-violent	823	716
Burglary	129	165
Larceny	603	497
Vehicle theft	91	54
Domestic violence	179	195
Arson	5	4
Total crime rate	20.8	18.3
Violent	1.6	1.5
Non-violent	19.1	16.8

Public School District
(for school year 2007-08 except as noted)

Sayreville School District
Lincoln Street, PO Box 997
Sayreville, NJ 08872
(732) 525-5224
Superintendent	Frank Alfano
Number of schools	8
Grade plan	K-12
Enrollment	5,764
Attendance rate, '06-07	95.0%
Dropout rate	0.2%
Students per teacher	11.8
Per pupil expenditure	$11,809
Median faculty salary	$50,963
Median administrator salary	$112,480
Grade 12 enrollment	391
High school graduation rate	95.0%

Assessment test results
(percent scoring at proficient or advanced level)
	Language	Math
NJASK-Grade 3	94.6%	91.4%
GEPA-Grade 8	72.7%	83.3%
HSPA-High School	77.5%	88.3%

SAT Score Averages, 2006-07
Pct tested	Math	Verbal	Writing
77%	493	477	474

Teacher Qualifications
Avg. years of experience	8
Highly-qualified teachers one subject/all subjects	100%/100%

No Child Left Behind
AYP, 2006-07	Meets Standards

Municipal Finance
State Aid Programs, 2009
Total aid	$11,857,041
CMPTRA	0
Energy tax receipts	11,551,799
Garden State Trust	9,070

General Budget, 2008
Total tax levy	$90,947,888
County levy	15,699,046
County taxes	14,056,047
County library	0
County health	0
County open space	1,642,999
School levy	52,488,179
Muni. levy	22,760,663
Misc. revenues	27,613,130

Taxes
	2006	2007	2008
General tax rate per $100	3.6	3.81	3.992
County equalization ratio	52.52	45.86	42.16
Net valuation taxable	$2,247,165,500	$2,267,587,707	$2,278,625,866
State equalized value	$4,904,035,443	$5,373,620,401	$5,469,098,518

See Introduction for an explanation of all data sources.

Demographics & Socio-Economic Characteristics

(2000 US Census, except as noted)

Population

1980*	20,774
1990*	21,160
2000	22,732
Male	10,890
Female	11,842
2007 (estimate)*	22,979
Population density	2,530.7

Race & Hispanic Origin, 2000

Race

White	17,931
Black/African American	2,568
American Indian/Alaska Native	21
Asian	1,648
Native Hawaiian/Pacific Islander	3
Other race	216
Two or more races	345
Hispanic origin, total	895
Mexican	53
Puerto Rican	229
Cuban	106
Other Hispanic	507

Age & Nativity, 2000

Under 5 years	1,777
18 years and over	16,967
21 years and over	16,528
65 years and over	3,214
85 years and over	344
Median age	38.6
Native-born	19,155
Foreign-born	3,577

Educational Attainment, 2000

Population 25 years and over	15,911
Less than 9th grade	2.8%
High school grad or higher	92.0%
Bachelor's degree or higher	49.7%
Graduate degree	19.9%

Income & Poverty, 1999

Per capita income	$39,913
Median household income	$81,599
Median family income	$96,238
Persons in poverty	674
H'holds receiving public assistance	131
H'holds receiving social security	2,125

Households, 2000

Total households	8,349
With persons under 18	3,179
With persons over 65	2,262
Family households	6,291
Single-person households	1,737
Persons per household	2.71
Persons per family	3.16

Labor & Employment

Total civilian labor force, 2007**	12,256
Unemployment rate	2.5%
Total civilian labor force, 2000	11,822
Unemployment rate	2.6%

Employed persons 16 years and over by occupation, 2000

Managers & professionals	6,381
Service occupations	811
Sales & office occupations	3,139
Farming, fishing & forestry	0
Construction & maintenance	533
Production & transportation	656
Self-employed persons	567

General Information

Township of Scotch Plains
430 Park Ave
Scotch Plains, NJ 07076
908-322-6700

Website	www.scotchplainsnj.com
Year of incorporation	1917
Land/water area (sq. miles)	9.08/0.01
Form of government	Council-Manager

Government

Legislative Districts

US Congressional	7
State Legislative	22

Local Officials, 2009

Mayor	Nancy Malool
Manager	Thomas Atkins
Clerk	Barbara Riepe
Finance Dir	Lori Majeski
Tax Assessor	Michael Ross
Tax Collector	Lori Majeski
Attorney	Brian Levine
Building	Robert LaCosta
Comm Dev/Planning	NA
Engineering	Edward Gottko
Public Works	Kevin Ward
Police Chief	Brian Mahoney
Emerg/Fire Director	Jonathan Ellis

Housing & Construction

Housing Units, 2000*

Total	8,479
Median rent	$985
Median SF home value	$258,800

Permits for New Residential Construction

	Units	Value
Total, 2006	70	$13,363,937
Single family	70	$13,363,937
Total, 2007	33	$8,071,090
Single family	33	$8,071,090

Real Property Valuation, 2008

	Parcels	Valuation
Total	7,853	$994,357,900
Vacant	272	7,323,800
Residential	7,298	892,649,700
Commercial	241	62,877,700
Industrial	26	6,537,800
Apartments	8	23,855,500
Farm land	4	14,500
Farm homestead	4	1,098,900

Average Property Value & Tax, 2008

Residential value	$122,398
Property tax	$10,371
Tax credit/rebate	$1,277

Public Library

Scotch Plains Public Library
1927 Bartle Ave
Scotch Plains, NJ 07076
908-322-5007

Director .... Margaret B. Kolaya

Library statistics, 2007

Population served	22,732
Full-time/total staff	6/12

	Total	Per capita
Holdings	83,452	3.67
Revenues	$1,421,877	$62.55
Expenditures	$1,419,496	$62.44
Annual visits	153,709	6.76
Internet terminals/annual users	17/25,441	

Public Safety

Number of officers, 2007	45

Crime	2006	2007
Total crimes	314	264
Violent	24	28
Murder	0	0
Rape	2	3
Robbery	10	6
Aggravated assault	12	19
Non-violent	290	236
Burglary	48	43
Larceny	224	186
Vehicle theft	18	7
Domestic violence	100	98
Arson	1	2
Total crime rate	13.5	11.4
Violent	1.0	1.2
Non-violent	12.5	10.2

Public School District

(for school year 2007-08 except as noted)

Scotch Plains-Fanwood School District
Evergreen Avenue & Cedar Street
Scotch Plains, NJ 07076
(908) 232-6161

Superintendent	Margaret W. Hayes
Number of schools	8
Grade plan	K-12
Enrollment	5,333
Attendance rate, '06-07	96.1%
Dropout rate	0.3%
Students per teacher	11.9
Per pupil expenditure	$13,098
Median faculty salary	$56,825
Median administrator salary	$124,394
Grade 12 enrollment	369
High school graduation rate	99.7%

Assessment test results
(percent scoring at proficient or advanced level)

	Language	Math
NJASK-Grade 3	95.9%	94.4%
GEPA-Grade 8	78.2%	92.3%
HSPA-High School	90.6%	90.2%

SAT Score Averages, 2006-07

Pct tested	Math	Verbal	Writing
105%	550	522	518

Teacher Qualifications

Avg. years of experience	7
Highly-qualified teachers one subject/all subjects	99.5%/99.5%

No Child Left Behind

AYP, 2006-07	Meets Standards

Municipal Finance

State Aid Programs, 2009

Total aid	$2,927,233
CMPTRA	526,491
Energy tax receipts	2,327,561
Garden State Trust	0

General Budget, 2008

Total tax levy	$84,312,016
County levy	14,795,375
County taxes	14,150,513
County library	0
County health	0
County open space	644,862
School levy	54,184,144
Muni. levy	15,332,497
Misc. revenues	9,505,318

Taxes	2006	2007	2008
General tax rate per $100	7.775	8.131	8.474
County equalization ratio	25.91	24.23	23.17
Net valuation taxable	$985,947,500	$994,137,196	$995,054,489
State equalized value	$4,069,906,196	$4,288,278,656	$4,277,504,761

* US Census Bureau
** New Jersey Department of Labor

See Introduction for an explanation of all data sources.

Demographics & Socio-Economic Characteristics
(2000 US Census, except as noted)

Population
1980*	1,812
1990*	1,693
2000	1,818
Male	951
Female	867
2007 (estimate)*	1,813
Population density	2,832.8

Race & Hispanic Origin, 2000
Race
White	1,716
Black/African American	32
American Indian/Alaska Native	0
Asian	41
Native Hawaiian/Pacific Islander	0
Other race	16
Two or more races	13
Hispanic origin, total	82
Mexican	37
Puerto Rican	16
Cuban	5
Other Hispanic	24

Age & Nativity, 2000
Under 5 years	59
18 years and over	1,615
21 years and over	1,592
65 years and over	196
85 years and over	32
Median age	40.2
Native-born	1,608
Foreign-born	217

Educational Attainment, 2000
Population 25 years and over	1,488
Less than 9th grade	2.8%
High school grad or higher	91.4%
Bachelor's degree or higher	47.0%
Graduate degree	18.5%

Income & Poverty, 1999
Per capita income	$45,066
Median household income	$65,563
Median family income	$72,031
Persons in poverty	138
H'holds receiving public assistance	21
H'holds receiving social security	164

Households, 2000
Total households	1,003
With persons under 18	127
With persons over 65	159
Family households	402
Single-person households	455
Persons per household	1.81
Persons per family	2.51

Labor & Employment
Total civilian labor force, 2007**	1,289
Unemployment rate	4.5%
Total civilian labor force, 2000	1,208
Unemployment rate	5.1%

Employed persons 16 years and over by occupation, 2000
Managers & professionals	538
Service occupations	114
Sales & office occupations	341
Farming, fishing & forestry	12
Construction & maintenance	63
Production & transportation	78
Self-employed persons	56

* US Census Bureau
** New Jersey Department of Labor

General Information
Borough of Sea Bright
1167 Ocean Ave
Sea Bright, NJ 07760
732-842-0099

Website	seabrightnj.org
Year of incorporation	1889
Land/water area (sq. miles)	0.64/0.49
Form of government	Borough

Government
Legislative Districts
US Congressional	6
State Legislative	11

Local Officials, 2009
Mayor	Maria D. Fernandes
Manager/Admin	NA
Clerk	Maryann M. Smeltzer
Finance Dir	Michael Bascom
Tax Assessor	Timothy Anfuso
Tax Collector	Patricia Spahr
Attorney	Joseph W. Oxley
Building	Edward Wheeler
Comm Dev/Planning	NA
Engineering	David Hoder
Public Works	David Bahrle
Police Chief	William Moore
Emerg/Fire Director	Joseph Eskridge

Housing & Construction
Housing Units, 2000*
Total	1,202
Median rent	$906
Median SF home value	$227,600

Permits for New Residential Construction
	Units	Value
Total, 2006	8	$2,893,774
Single family	6	$2,293,774
Total, 2007	3	$1,438,796
Single family	3	$1,438,796

Real Property Valuation, 2008
	Parcels	Valuation
Total	1,283	$523,769,800
Vacant	176	10,017,400
Residential	1,030	419,722,500
Commercial	71	88,474,800
Industrial	0	0
Apartments	6	5,555,100
Farm land	0	0
Farm homestead	0	0

Average Property Value & Tax, 2008
Residential value	$407,498
Property tax	$6,759
Tax credit/rebate	$946

Public Library
J.W. Ross/Sea Bright Library
1097 Ocean Ave
Sea Bright, NJ 07760
732-758-9554

Director	Joan Walsh

Library statistics, 2007
Population served	1,818
Full-time/total staff	NA/0

	Total	Per capita
Holdings	0	NA
Revenues	$0	NA
Expenditures	$0	NA
Annual visits	NA	NA
Internet terminals/annual users	NA/NA	

Public Safety
Number of officers, 2007	11

Crime	2006	2007
Total crimes	17	66
Violent	1	2
Murder	0	0
Rape	0	0
Robbery	0	0
Aggravated assault	1	2
Non-violent	16	64
Burglary	0	3
Larceny	16	60
Vehicle theft	0	1
Domestic violence	2	2
Arson	0	0
Total crime rate	9.5	36.7
Violent	0.6	1.1
Non-violent	8.9	35.6

Public School District
(for school year 2007-08 except as noted)

Sea Bright School District
P.O. Box 3125
Sea Bright, NJ 07760

No schools in district - sends students to Oceanport Borough and Shore Regional schools (see Appendix D)

Per pupil expenditure	NA
Median faculty salary	NA
Median administrator salary	NA
Grade 12 enrollment	NA
High school graduation rate	NA

Assessment test results
(percent scoring at proficient or advanced level)
	Language	Math
NJASK-Grade 3	NA	NA
GEPA-Grade 8	NA	NA
HSPA-High School	NA	NA

SAT Score Averages, 2006-07
Pct tested	Math	Verbal	Writing
NA	NA	NA	NA

Teacher Qualifications
Avg. years of experience	NA
Highly-qualified teachers one subject/all subjects	NA/NA

No Child Left Behind
AYP, 2006-07	NA

Municipal Finance
State Aid Programs, 2009
Total aid	$218,851
CMPTRA	15,076
Energy tax receipts	195,018
Garden State Trust	9

General Budget, 2008
Total tax levy	$8,693,276
County levy	2,213,311
County taxes	1,964,140
County library	118,196
County health	0
County open space	130,975
School levy	3,085,318
Muni. levy	3,394,647
Misc. revenues	1,396,733

Taxes
	2006	2007	2008
General tax rate per $100	1.424	1.593	1.659
County equalization ratio	79.7	58.11	60.47
Net valuation taxable	$513,096,300	$520,090,525	$524,089,850
State equalized value	$883,277,234	$859,888,235	$1,985,349,205

See Introduction for an explanation of all data sources.

Demographics & Socio-Economic Characteristics
(2000 US Census, except as noted)

Population
1980*	2,650
1990*	2,099
2000	2,148
Male	1,001
Female	1,147
2007 (estimate)*	2,051
Population density	1,934.9

Race & Hispanic Origin, 2000
Race
White	2,129
Black/African American	2
American Indian/Alaska Native	0
Asian	6
Native Hawaiian/Pacific Islander	0
Other race	1
Two or more races	10
Hispanic origin, total	30
Mexican	3
Puerto Rican	7
Cuban	1
Other Hispanic	19

Age & Nativity, 2000
Under 5 years	96
18 years and over	1,716
21 years and over	1,678
65 years and over	591
85 years and over	87
Median age	50.3
Native-born	2,083
Foreign-born	65

Educational Attainment, 2000
Population 25 years and over	1,622
Less than 9th grade	1.0%
High school grad or higher	96.5%
Bachelor's degree or higher	58.6%
Graduate degree	23.3%

Income & Poverty, 1999
Per capita income	$63,871
Median household income	$86,104
Median family income	$102,680
Persons in poverty	75
H'holds receiving public assistance	4
H'holds receiving social security	400

Households, 2000
Total households	942
With persons under 18	199
With persons over 65	412
Family households	637
Single-person households	279
Persons per household	2.28
Persons per family	2.83

Labor & Employment
Total civilian labor force, 2007**	1,004
Unemployment rate	1.9%
Total civilian labor force, 2000	940
Unemployment rate	2.9%

Employed persons 16 years and over by occupation, 2000
Managers & professionals	520
Service occupations	76
Sales & office occupations	285
Farming, fishing & forestry	0
Construction & maintenance	14
Production & transportation	18
Self-employed persons	89

General Information
Borough of Sea Girt
4th Ave & Baltimore Blvd
Sea Girt, NJ 08750
732-449-9433
Website	www.seagirtboro.com
Year of incorporation	1917
Land/water area (sq. miles)	1.06/0.39
Form of government	Borough

Government
Legislative Districts
US Congressional	4
State Legislative	11

Local Officials, 2009
Mayor	Mark E. Clemmensen
Manager/Admin	NA
Clerk	Lauren Mayer
Finance Dir	Lorraine Carafou
Tax Assessor	Mary Lou Hartman
Tax Collector	Karen Brisben
Attorney	Joseph Brennan
Building	NA
Comm Dev/Planning	NA
Engineering	Peter Avakian
Public Works	Kevin Thompson
Police Chief	Edward J. Sidley
Emerg/Fire Director	Tim Harmon

Housing & Construction
Housing Units, 2000*
Total	1,285
Median rent	$1,095
Median SF home value	$549,300

Permits for New Residential Construction
	Units	Value
Total, 2006	27	$13,566,390
Single family	27	$13,566,390
Total, 2007	22	$11,420,554
Single family	22	$11,420,554

Real Property Valuation, 2008
	Parcels	Valuation
Total	1,307	$1,947,892,700
Vacant	50	66,055,700
Residential	1,216	1,845,020,100
Commercial	41	36,816,900
Industrial	0	0
Apartments	0	0
Farm land	0	0
Farm homestead	0	0

Average Property Value & Tax, 2008
Residential value	$1,517,286
Property tax	$10,631
Tax credit/rebate	$1,296

Public Library
Sea Girt Library
The Plaza
Sea Girt, NJ 08750
732-449-1099
Librarian	Anne Ryan

Library statistics, 2007
Population served	2,148
Full-time/total staff	NA/0

	Total	Per capita
Holdings	0	NA
Revenues	$0	NA
Expenditures	$0	NA
Annual visits	NA	NA
Internet terminals/annual users	NA/NA	

Public Safety
Number of officers, 2007	12

Crime	2006	2007
Total crimes	40	45
Violent	6	2
Murder	0	0
Rape	0	1
Robbery	0	0
Aggravated assault	6	1
Non-violent	34	43
Burglary	5	8
Larceny	28	32
Vehicle theft	1	3
Domestic violence	12	7
Arson	0	0
Total crime rate	19.3	22.0
Violent	2.9	1.0
Non-violent	16.4	21.0

Public School District
(for school year 2007-08 except as noted)

Sea Girt Borough School District
Bell Place
Sea Girt, NJ 08750
(732) 449-3422
Superintendent	Stephen LaValva
Number of schools	1
Grade plan	K-8
Enrollment	164
Attendance rate, '06-07	95.4%
Dropout rate	NA
Students per teacher	8.0
Per pupil expenditure	$16,625
Median faculty salary	$58,590
Median administrator salary	$108,126
Grade 12 enrollment	NA
High school graduation rate	NA

Assessment test results
(percent scoring at proficient or advanced level)
	Language	Math
NJASK-Grade 3	85.7%	85.7%
GEPA-Grade 8	94.8%	100.0%
HSPA-High School	NA	NA

SAT Score Averages, 2006-07
Pct tested	Math	Verbal	Writing
NA	NA	NA	NA

Teacher Qualifications
Avg. years of experience	10
Highly-qualified teachers one subject/all subjects	100%/100%

No Child Left Behind
AYP, 2006-07	Meets Standards

Municipal Finance
State Aid Programs, 2009
Total aid	$273,914
CMPTRA	29,360
Energy tax receipts	233,598
Garden State Trust	0

General Budget, 2008
Total tax levy	$13,650,603
County levy	4,921,017
County taxes	4,367,014
County library	262,794
County health	0
County open space	291,208
School levy	4,022,289
Muni. levy	4,707,297
Misc. revenues	1,320,586

Taxes	2006	2007	2008
General tax rate per $100	0.669	0.692	0.701
County equalization ratio	112.5	101.75	100.74
Net valuation taxable	$1,916,022,600	$1,927,456,756	$1,948,229,473
State equalized value	$1,883,361,440	$1,913,300,566	$1,251,361,981

* US Census Bureau
** New Jersey Department of Labor

See Introduction for an explanation of all data sources.

Demographics & Socio-Economic Characteristics

(2000 US Census, except as noted)

Population

1980*	2,644
1990*	2,692
2000	2,835
Male	1,354
Female	1,481
2007 (estimate)*	2,929
Population density	1,331.4

Race & Hispanic Origin, 2000

Race
White	2,775
Black/African American	8
American Indian/Alaska Native	11
Asian	10
Native Hawaiian/Pacific Islander	1
Other race	2
Two or more races	28
Hispanic origin, total	30
Mexican	15
Puerto Rican	10
Cuban	2
Other Hispanic	3

Age & Nativity, 2000

Under 5 years	94
18 years and over	2,391
21 years and over	2,340
65 years and over	768
85 years and over	78
Median age	51.3
Native-born	2,730
Foreign-born	94

Educational Attainment, 2000

Population 25 years and over	2,176
Less than 9th grade	3.4%
High school grad or higher	85.2%
Bachelor's degree or higher	28.3%
Graduate degree	9.8%

Income & Poverty, 1999

Per capita income	$28,754
Median household income	$45,708
Median family income	$62,847
Persons in poverty	214
H'holds receiving public assistance	0
H'holds receiving social security	584

Households, 2000

Total households	1,370
With persons under 18	235
With persons over 65	552
Family households	795
Single-person households	512
Persons per household	2.07
Persons per family	2.71

Labor & Employment

Total civilian labor force, 2007**	1,627
Unemployment rate	5.2%
Total civilian labor force, 2000	1,372
Unemployment rate	6.5%

Employed persons 16 years and over by occupation, 2000
Managers & professionals	445
Service occupations	247
Sales & office occupations	373
Farming, fishing & forestry	0
Construction & maintenance	141
Production & transportation	77
Self-employed persons	89

General Information

City of Sea Isle
4416 Landis Ave
Sea Isle City, NJ 08243
609-263-4461

Website	sea-isle-city.nj.us
Year of incorporation	1907
Land/water area (sq. miles)	2.20/0.35
Form of government	Commission

Government

Legislative Districts

US Congressional	2
State Legislative	1

Local Officials, 2009

Mayor	Leonard Desiderio
Manager/Admin	George Savastano
Clerk	Cindy Griffith
Finance Dir	James Terruso
Tax Assessor	Joseph Berrodin Jr
Tax Collector	Paula Doll
Attorney	Paul Baldini
Building	Robert Bowman
Comm Dev/Planning	NA
Engineering	Andrew Previti
Public Works	John Manganaro
Police Chief	Michael Cook (Actg)
Emerg/Fire Director	John Mazurie

Housing & Construction

Housing Units, 2000*

Total	6,622
Median rent	$717
Median SF home value	$280,100

Permits for New Residential Construction

	Units	Value
Total, 2006	149	$27,760,716
Single family	149	$27,760,716
Total, 2007	88	$15,886,443
Single family	86	$15,584,643

Real Property Valuation, 2008

	Parcels	Valuation
Total	6,743	$4,780,813,300
Vacant	448	121,580,200
Residential	6,141	4,527,597,100
Commercial	154	131,636,000
Industrial	0	0
Apartments	0	0
Farm land	0	0
Farm homestead	0	0

Average Property Value & Tax, 2008

Residential value	$737,274
Property tax	$3,808
Tax credit/rebate	$848

Public Library

Sea Isle City Branch Library‡
125 JF Kennedy Blvd
Sea Isle City, NJ 08243
609-263-8485

Branch Librarian .... Elizabeth Morris

Library statistics, 2007

see Cape May County profile
for library system statistics

Public Safety

Number of officers, 2007	22

Crime	2006	2007
Total crimes	315	308
Violent	18	14
Murder	0	0
Rape	0	0
Robbery	0	0
Aggravated assault	18	14
Non-violent	297	294
Burglary	16	28
Larceny	276	264
Vehicle theft	5	2
Domestic violence	23	14
Arson	0	0
Total crime rate	106.1	104.4
Violent	6.1	4.7
Non-violent	100.1	99.7

Public School District

(for school year 2007-08 except as noted)

Sea isle City School District
4501 Park Road
Sea Isle City, NJ 08243
(609) 263-8461

Superintendent	Michael Schreiner
Number of schools	1
Grade plan	K-8
Enrollment	80
Attendance rate, '06-07	94.0%
Dropout rate	NA
Students per teacher	NA
Per pupil expenditure	$28,015
Median faculty salary	$60,029
Median administrator salary	NA
Grade 12 enrollment	NA
High school graduation rate	NA

Assessment test results

(percent scoring at proficient or advanced level)
	Language	Math
NJASK-Grade 3	NA	NA
GEPA-Grade 8	71.5%	85.7%
HSPA-High School	NA	NA

SAT Score Averages, 2006-07

Pct tested	Math	Verbal	Writing
NA	NA	NA	NA

Teacher Qualifications

Avg. years of experience	21
Highly-qualified teachers one subject/all subjects	100%/100%

No Child Left Behind

AYP, 2006-07	Meets Standards

Municipal Finance

State Aid Programs, 2009

Total aid	$303,893
CMPTRA	0
Energy tax receipts	293,009
Garden State Trust	857

General Budget, 2008

Total tax levy	$24,698,599
County levy	9,367,862
County taxes	7,445,976
County library	1,429,314
County health	0
County open space	492,571
School levy	3,196,187
Muni. levy	12,134,550
Misc. revenues	5,278,791

Taxes	2006	2007	2008
General tax rate per $100	0.61	0.64	0.518
County equalization ratio	83.07	74.46	97.36
Net valuation taxable	$3,552,214,800	$3,618,844,327	$4,782,264,692
State equalized value	$4,771,968,109	$4,866,234,292	$4,832,019,544

‡ Branch of county library
* US Census Bureau
** New Jersey Department of Labor

See Introduction for an explanation of all data sources.

Demographics & Socio-Economic Characteristics
(2000 US Census, except as noted)

Population
1980*	1,802
1990*	2,366
2000	3,155
Male	1,627
Female	1,528
2007 (estimate)*	3,319
Population density	5,441.0

Race & Hispanic Origin, 2000
Race
White	2,838
Black/African American	127
American Indian/Alaska Native	20
Asian	27
Native Hawaiian/Pacific Islander	0
Other race	37
Two or more races	106
Hispanic origin, total	306
Mexican	102
Puerto Rican	113
Cuban	5
Other Hispanic	86

Age & Nativity, 2000
Under 5 years	238
18 years and over	2,419
21 years and over	2,293
65 years and over	348
85 years and over	33
Median age	33.3
Native-born	2,917
Foreign-born	238

Educational Attainment, 2000
Population 25 years and over	2,052
Less than 9th grade	5.0%
High school grad or higher	76.3%
Bachelor's degree or higher	15.6%
Graduate degree	3.6%

Income & Poverty, 1999
Per capita income	$18,665
Median household income	$25,963
Median family income	$27,197
Persons in poverty	753
H'holds receiving public assistance	87
H'holds receiving social security	359

Households, 2000
Total households	1,408
With persons under 18	400
With persons over 65	260
Family households	692
Single-person households	564
Persons per household	2.17
Persons per family	2.93

Labor & Employment
Total civilian labor force, 2007**	1,827
Unemployment rate	6.1%
Total civilian labor force, 2000	1,590
Unemployment rate	7.5%

Employed persons 16 years and over by occupation, 2000
Managers & professionals	325
Service occupations	412
Sales & office occupations	374
Farming, fishing & forestry	10
Construction & maintenance	165
Production & transportation	184
Self-employed persons	61

General Information
Borough of Seaside Heights
PO Box 38
Seaside Heights, NJ 08751
732-793-9100
Website	www.seaside-heightsnj.org
Year of incorporation	1913
Land/water area (sq. miles)	0.61/0.15
Form of government	Borough

Government
Legislative Districts
US Congressional	3
State Legislative	10

Local Officials, 2009
Mayor	P. Kenneth Hershey
Manager	John Camera
Clerk	Diane B. Stabley
Finance Dir	Barbara Risley
Tax Assessor	Carey Rowe
Tax Collector	Christine Sierfeld
Attorney	George Gilmore
Building	Charles Lasky
Comm Dev/Planning	NA
Engineering	O'Donnell & Stanton
Public Works	Louis DiGuilio
Police Chief	Thomas Boyd
Emerg/Fire Director	William Rumbolo

Housing & Construction
Housing Units, 2000*
Total	2,840
Median rent	$635
Median SF home value	$124,400

Permits for New Residential Construction
	Units	Value
Total, 2006	79	$12,675,000
Single family	74	$9,925,000
Total, 2007	27	$5,851,150
Single family	15	$2,159,150

Real Property Valuation, 2008
	Parcels	Valuation
Total	2,014	$874,060,600
Vacant	113	43,217,800
Residential	1,682	521,942,000
Commercial	160	268,433,200
Industrial	0	0
Apartments	59	40,467,600
Farm land	0	0
Farm homestead	0	0

Average Property Value & Tax, 2008
Residential value	$310,310
Property tax	$3,755
Tax credit/rebate	$752

Public Library
No public municipal library

Library statistics, 2007
Population served	NA
Full-time/total staff	NA/NA

	Total	Per capita
Holdings	NA	NA
Revenues	NA	NA
Expenditures	NA	NA
Annual visits	NA	NA
Internet terminals/annual users	NA/NA	

Public Safety
Number of officers, 2007 ... 25
Crime	2006	2007
Total crimes	348	250
Violent	93	61
Murder	0	0
Rape	3	3
Robbery	16	10
Aggravated assault	74	48
Non-violent	255	189
Burglary	54	23
Larceny	183	152
Vehicle theft	18	14
Domestic violence	355	296
Arson	0	0
Total crime rate	108.1	77.1
Violent	28.9	18.8
Non-violent	79.2	58.3

Public School District
(for school year 2007-08 except as noted)

Seaside Heights Borough School District
1200 Bay Boulevard
Seaside Heights, NJ 08751
(732) 793-8485
Superintendent	Michael Ritacco
Number of schools	1
Grade plan	K-6
Enrollment	207
Attendance rate, '06-07	92.3%
Dropout rate	NA
Students per teacher	9.3
Per pupil expenditure	$16,250
Median faculty salary	$54,000
Median administrator salary	$1
Grade 12 enrollment	NA
High school graduation rate	NA

Assessment test results
(percent scoring at proficient or advanced level)
	Language	Math
NJASK-Grade 3	82.2%	82.1%
GEPA-Grade 8	NA	NA
HSPA-High School	NA	NA

SAT Score Averages, 2006-07
Pct tested	Math	Verbal	Writing
NA	NA	NA	NA

Teacher Qualifications
Avg. years of experience	15
Highly-qualified teachers one subject/all subjects	100%/100%

No Child Left Behind
AYP, 2006-07 ... Meets Standards

Municipal Finance
State Aid Programs, 2009
Total aid	$207,040
CMPTRA	13,617
Energy tax receipts	188,247
Garden State Trust	0

General Budget, 2008
Total tax levy	$10,580,394
County levy	2,628,979
County taxes	2,167,964
County library	254,746
County health	103,727
County open space	102,542
School levy	4,825,514
Muni. levy	3,125,901
Misc. revenues	7,494,377

Taxes
Taxes	2006	2007	2008
General tax rate per $100	3.792	1.037	1.210
County equalization ratio	35.86	121.49	101.08
Net valuation taxable	$230,871,000	$958,158,516	$874,436,890
State equalized value	$780,093,949	$873,307,749	$2,417,985,047

* US Census Bureau
** New Jersey Department of Labor

See Introduction for an explanation of all data sources.

Demographics & Socio-Economic Characteristics

(2000 US Census, except as noted)

Population
1980*	1,795
1990*	1,871
2000	2,263
Male	1,106
Female	1,157
2007 (estimate)*	2,306
Population density	3,547.7

Race & Hispanic Origin, 2000
Race
White	2,213
Black/African American	6
American Indian/Alaska Native	8
Asian	14
Native Hawaiian/Pacific Islander	2
Other race	4
Two or more races	16
Hispanic origin, total	52
Mexican	7
Puerto Rican	18
Cuban	2
Other Hispanic	25

Age & Nativity, 2000
Under 5 years	107
18 years and over	1,938
21 years and over	1,889
65 years and over	568
85 years and over	79
Median age	46.8
Native-born	2,176
Foreign-born	90

Educational Attainment, 2000
Population 25 years and over	1,819
Less than 9th grade	4.5%
High school grad or higher	88.0%
Bachelor's degree or higher	33.8%
Graduate degree	11.8%

Income & Poverty, 1999
Per capita income	$30,090
Median household income	$45,380
Median family income	$58,636
Persons in poverty	195
H'holds receiving public assistance	20
H'holds receiving social security	490

Households, 2000
Total households	1,127
With persons under 18	197
With persons over 65	404
Family households	606
Single-person households	437
Persons per household	2.01
Persons per family	2.61

Labor & Employment
Total civilian labor force, 2007**	1,365
Unemployment rate	5.7%
Total civilian labor force, 2000	1,140
Unemployment rate	5.7%

Employed persons 16 years and over by occupation, 2000
Managers & professionals	382
Service occupations	149
Sales & office occupations	336
Farming, fishing & forestry	0
Construction & maintenance	121
Production & transportation	87
Self-employed persons	120

* US Census Bureau
** New Jersey Department of Labor

General Information
Borough of Seaside Park
1701 N Ocean Ave
PO Box B
Seaside Park, NJ 08752
732-793-3700

Website	www.seasideparknj.org
Year of incorporation	1898
Land/water area (sq. miles)	0.65/0.11
Form of government	Borough

Government

Legislative Districts
US Congressional	3
State Legislative	10

Local Officials, 2009
Mayor	Thomas E. Connors
Administrator	Julie Horner-Keizer
Clerk	Julie Horner-Keizer
Finance Dir	Ella Rice
Tax Assessor	Dennis Raftery
Tax Collector	Wendy Prior (Int)
Attorney	Steven Secare
Building	NA
Planning	John Vanna (Chr)
Engineering	CME Associates
Public Works	Joseph Dolci
Police Chief	Edward Dickson
Fire Chief	John Lippincott

Housing & Construction

Housing Units, 2000*
Total	2,811
Median rent	$718
Median SF home value	$215,100

Permits for New Residential Construction
	Units	Value
Total, 2006	13	$3,741,951
Single family	13	$3,741,951
Total, 2007	16	$3,835,177
Single family	14	$3,298,777

Real Property Valuation, 2008
	Parcels	Valuation
Total	2,031	$681,426,200
Vacant	61	14,841,300
Residential	1,903	622,537,400
Commercial	53	38,525,500
Industrial	0	0
Apartments	14	5,522,000
Farm land	0	0
Farm homestead	0	0

Average Property Value & Tax, 2008
Residential value	$327,135
Property tax	$6,745
Tax credit/rebate	$1,176

Public Library
No public municipal library

Library statistics, 2007
Population served	NA
Full-time/total staff	NA/NA

	Total	Per capita
Holdings	NA	NA
Revenues	NA	NA
Expenditures	NA	NA
Annual visits	NA	NA
Internet terminals/annual users	NA/NA	

Public Safety
Number of officers, 2007	15

Crime	2006	2007
Total crimes	87	67
Violent	1	0
Murder	0	0
Rape	1	0
Robbery	0	0
Aggravated assault	0	0
Non-violent	86	67
Burglary	10	12
Larceny	74	52
Vehicle theft	2	3
Domestic violence	18	18
Arson	0	0
Total crime rate	37.8	29.1
Violent	0.4	0.0
Non-violent	37.4	29.1

Public School District
(for school year 2007-08 except as noted)

Seaside Park Borough School District
Central & Fourth Avenues
Seaside Park, NJ 08752
(732) 793-0177

Superintendent	Theresa Hamilton (Int)
Number of schools	1
Grade plan	K-6
Enrollment	78
Attendance rate, '06-07	94.5%
Dropout rate	NA
Students per teacher	5.9
Per pupil expenditure	$19,156
Median faculty salary	$44,739
Median administrator salary	$79,759
Grade 12 enrollment	NA
High school graduation rate	NA

Assessment test results
(percent scoring at proficient or advanced level)
	Language	Math
NJASK-Grade 3	NA	NA
GEPA-Grade 8	NA	NA
HSPA-High School	NA	NA

SAT Score Averages, 2006-07
Pct tested	Math	Verbal	Writing
NA	NA	NA	NA

Teacher Qualifications
Avg. years of experience	21
Highly-qualified teachers one subject/all subjects	100%/100%

No Child Left Behind
AYP, 2006-07	Meets Standards

Municipal Finance

State Aid Programs, 2009
Total aid	$250,080
CMPTRA	0
Energy tax receipts	241,952
Garden State Trust	0

General Budget, 2008
Total tax levy	$14,053,981
County levy	4,240,706
County taxes	3,497,011
County library	410,983
County health	167,327
County open space	165,386
School levy	4,987,614
Muni. levy	4,825,660
Misc. revenues	3,769,453

Taxes
	2006	2007	2008
General tax rate per $100	1.832	1.979	2.062
County equalization ratio	62.93	53.46	49.61
Net valuation taxable	$683,337,500	$675,104,221	$681,663,476
State equalized value	$1,278,496,767	$1,360,578,355	$872,344,167

See Introduction for an explanation of all data sources.

Demographics & Socio-Economic Characteristics
(2000 US Census, except as noted)

Population
1980*	13,719
1990*	14,061
2000	15,931
Male	7,879
Female	8,052
2007 (estimate)*	15,385
Population density	2,612.1

Race & Hispanic Origin, 2000
Race
White	12,512
Black/African American	709
American Indian/Alaska Native	18
Asian	1,880
Native Hawaiian/Pacific Islander	7
Other race	445
Two or more races	360
Hispanic origin, total	1,953
Mexican	47
Puerto Rican	521
Cuban	376
Other Hispanic	1,009

Age & Nativity, 2000
Under 5 years	825
18 years and over	12,866
21 years and over	12,430
65 years and over	2,571
85 years and over	311
Median age	39.5
Native-born	12,593
Foreign-born	3,246

Educational Attainment, 2000
Population 25 years and over	11,780
Less than 9th grade	6.2%
High school grad or higher	82.2%
Bachelor's degree or higher	29.1%
Graduate degree	10.5%

Income & Poverty, 1999
Per capita income	$31,684
Median household income	$59,800
Median family income	$72,568
Persons in poverty	1,149
H'holds receiving public assistance	81
H'holds receiving social security	1,934

Households, 2000
Total households	6,214
With persons under 18	1,718
With persons over 65	1,876
Family households	3,948
Single-person households	1,962
Persons per household	2.41
Persons per family	3.08

Labor & Employment
Total civilian labor force, 2007**	7,523
Unemployment rate	2.0%
Total civilian labor force, 2000	7,889
Unemployment rate	5.7%

Employed persons 16 years and over by occupation, 2000
Managers & professionals	3,032
Service occupations	673
Sales & office occupations	2,436
Farming, fishing & forestry	6
Construction & maintenance	550
Production & transportation	744
Self-employed persons	393

* US Census Bureau
** New Jersey Department of Labor

General Information
Town of Secaucus
1203 Paterson Plank Rd
Secaucus, NJ 07094
201-330-2000
Website	www.seacaucusnj.org
Year of incorporation	1917
Land/water area (sq. miles)	5.89/0.63
Form of government	Town

Government
Legislative Districts
US Congressional	9
State Legislative	32

Local Officials, 2009
Mayor	Dennis Elwell
Manager	David Drumeler
Clerk	Michael Marra
Finance Dir	Margaret Barkala
Tax Assessor	Michael Jaeger
Tax Collector	Alan Bartolozzi
Attorney	Frank Leanza
Building	Vincent Prieto
Comm Dev/Planning	NA
Engineering	Gerald Perricone
Public Works	Glenn Beckmeyer
Police Chief	Dennis Corcoran
Emerg/Fire Director	George Schoenrock

Housing & Construction
Housing Units, 2000*
Total	6,385
Median rent	$850
Median SF home value	$209,400

Permits for New Residential Construction
	Units	Value
Total, 2006	55	$5,771,677
Single family	53	$5,557,435
Total, 2007	101	$12,050,834
Single family	48	$7,062,235

Real Property Valuation, 2008
	Parcels	Valuation
Total	5,223	$2,522,418,075
Vacant	149	71,412,400
Residential	4,669	788,258,000
Commercial	238	741,522,475
Industrial	156	904,364,000
Apartments	11	16,861,200
Farm land	0	0
Farm homestead	0	0

Average Property Value & Tax, 2008
Residential value	$168,828
Property tax	$5,453
Tax credit/rebate	$862

Public Library
Secaucus Public Library
1379 Paterson Plank Rd
Secaucus, NJ 07094
201-330-2084
Director ... Katherine Steffens

Library statistics, 2007
Population served	15,931
Full-time/total staff	2/12

	Total	Per capita
Holdings	79,695	5.00
Revenues	$1,606,329	$100.83
Expenditures	$1,605,171	$100.76
Annual visits	192,625	12.09
Internet terminals/annual users	50/56,664	

Public Safety
Number of officers, 2007	62

Crime	2006	2007
Total crimes	732	680
Violent	21	25
Murder	0	0
Rape	0	0
Robbery	12	7
Aggravated assault	9	18
Non-violent	711	655
Burglary	37	22
Larceny	587	571
Vehicle theft	87	62
Domestic violence	223	205
Arson	3	0
Total crime rate	46.9	43.7
Violent	1.3	1.6
Non-violent	45.5	42.1

Public School District
(for school year 2007-08 except as noted)

Secaucus School District
20 Centre Avenue, PO Box 1496
Secaucus, NJ 07096
(201) 974-2004
Superintendent	Cynthia Randino
Number of schools	4
Grade plan	K-12
Enrollment	2,077
Attendance rate, '06-07	94.9%
Dropout rate	0.0%
Students per teacher	12.9
Per pupil expenditure	$15,104
Median faculty salary	$59,518
Median administrator salary	$138,716
Grade 12 enrollment	149
High school graduation rate	98.7%

Assessment test results
(percent scoring at proficient or advanced level)
	Language	Math
NJASK-Grade 3	97.3%	95.8%
GEPA-Grade 8	72.8%	84.0%
HSPA-High School	80.6%	93.0%

SAT Score Averages, 2006-07
Pct tested	Math	Verbal	Writing
92%	479	462	456

Teacher Qualifications
Avg. years of experience	12
Highly-qualified teachers one subject/all subjects	100%/100%

No Child Left Behind
AYP, 2006-07	Meets Standards

Municipal Finance
State Aid Programs, 2009
Total aid	$2,406,563
CMPTRA	449,304
Energy tax receipts	1,879,017
Garden State Trust	30

General Budget, 2008
Total tax levy	$81,573,021
County levy	21,209,857
County taxes	20,649,724
County library	0
County health	0
County open space	560,132
School levy	30,135,239
Muni. levy	30,227,926
Misc. revenues	12,768,293

Taxes
	2006	2007	2008
General tax rate per $100	2.834	3.001	3.230
County equalization ratio	63.47	54.37	45.38
Net valuation taxable	$2,521,402,875	$2,544,000,998	$2,525,676,396
State equalized value	$5,250,670,234	$5,601,437,675	$5,676,713,281

See Introduction for an explanation of all data sources.

Demographics & Socio-Economic Characteristics

(2000 US Census, except as noted)

Population

1980*	4,537
1990*	5,765
2000	6,462
Male	3,239
Female	3,223
2007 (estimate)*	6,738
Population density	150.4

Race & Hispanic Origin, 2000

Race
White	6,284
Black/African American	53
American Indian/Alaska Native	7
Asian	43
Native Hawaiian/Pacific Islander	0
Other race	20
Two or more races	55
Hispanic origin, total	68
Mexican	17
Puerto Rican	23
Cuban	9
Other Hispanic	19

Age & Nativity, 2000

Under 5 years	442
18 years and over	4,564
21 years and over	4,339
65 years and over	386
85 years and over	24
Median age	37.3
Native-born	6,330
Foreign-born	132

Educational Attainment, 2000

Population 25 years and over	4,134
Less than 9th grade	1.4%
High school grad or higher	92.3%
Bachelor's degree or higher	37.1%
Graduate degree	10.9%

Income & Poverty, 1999

Per capita income	$30,934
Median household income	$77,457
Median family income	$82,534
Persons in poverty	168
H'holds receiving public assistance	14
H'holds receiving social security	388

Households, 2000

Total households	2,132
With persons under 18	1,002
With persons over 65	292
Family households	1,821
Single-person households	243
Persons per household	3.03
Persons per family	3.29

Labor & Employment

Total civilian labor force, 2007**	4,101
Unemployment rate	2.7%
Total civilian labor force, 2000	3,586
Unemployment rate	2.7%

Employed persons 16 years and over by occupation, 2000
Managers & professionals	1,470
Service occupations	448
Sales & office occupations	1,014
Farming, fishing & forestry	5
Construction & maintenance	296
Production & transportation	256
Self-employed persons	245

* US Census Bureau
** New Jersey Department of Labor

General Information

Township of Shamong
105 Willow Grove Rd
Shamong, NJ 08088
609-268-2377

Website	www.shamong.net
Year of incorporation	1852
Land/water area (sq. miles)	44.81/0.25
Form of government	Township

Government

Legislative Districts

US Congressional	2, 3
State Legislative	8

Local Officials, 2009

Mayor	Sean Gray
Manager	Susan Onorato
Clerk	Susan Onorato
Finance Dir	Kathleen Phelan
Tax Assessor	James Renwick
Tax Collector	Kathryn Taylor
Attorney	Douglas L. Heinold
Building	Frank R. Pern
Comm Dev/Planning	NA
Engineering	Richard Arango
Public Works	Norman Welsh
Police Chief	NA
Emerg/Fire Director	Michael Durham

Housing & Construction

Housing Units, 2000*

Total	2,175
Median rent	$764
Median SF home value	$191,900

Permits for New Residential Construction

	Units	Value
Total, 2006	15	$2,924,532
Single family	15	$2,924,532
Total, 2007	13	$2,551,098
Single family	13	$2,551,098

Real Property Valuation, 2008

	Parcels	Valuation
Total	2,494	$405,525,100
Vacant	221	5,112,250
Residential	1,955	374,996,100
Commercial	40	7,994,900
Industrial	7	1,370,200
Apartments	0	0
Farm land	181	1,531,950
Farm homestead	90	14,519,700

Average Property Value & Tax, 2008

Residential value	$190,472
Property tax	$7,319
Tax credit/rebate	$1,065

Public Library

No public municipal library

Library statistics, 2007

Population served	NA
Full-time/total staff	NA/NA

	Total	Per capita
Holdings	NA	NA
Revenues	NA	NA
Expenditures	NA	NA
Annual visits	NA	NA
Internet terminals/annual users	NA/NA	

Public Safety

Number of officers, 2007	0

Crime	2006	2007
Total crimes	38	31
Violent	2	8
Murder	0	0
Rape	0	0
Robbery	0	0
Aggravated assault	2	8
Non-violent	36	23
Burglary	9	7
Larceny	22	14
Vehicle theft	5	2
Domestic violence	1	29
Arson	0	0
Total crime rate	5.5	4.5
Violent	0.3	1.2
Non-violent	5.2	3.3

Public School District

(for school year 2007-08 except as noted)

Shamong Township School District
295 Indian Mills Road
Shamong, NJ 08088
(609) 268-0120

Superintendent	Thomas Christensen
Number of schools	2
Grade plan	K-8
Enrollment	934
Attendance rate, '06-07	96.1%
Dropout rate	NA
Students per teacher	11.5
Per pupil expenditure	$12,785
Median faculty salary	$69,806
Median administrator salary	$97,797
Grade 12 enrollment	NA
High school graduation rate	NA

Assessment test results

(percent scoring at proficient or advanced level)
	Language	Math
NJASK-Grade 3	99.2%	93.0%
GEPA-Grade 8	92.2%	91.2%
HSPA-High School	NA	NA

SAT Score Averages, 2006-07

Pct tested	Math	Verbal	Writing
NA	NA	NA	NA

Teacher Qualifications

Avg. years of experience	13
Highly-qualified teachers one subject/all subjects	100%/100%

No Child Left Behind

AYP, 2006-07	Meets Standards

Municipal Finance

State Aid Programs, 2009

Total aid	$811,017
CMPTRA	89,237
Energy tax receipts	525,589
Garden State Trust	168,213

General Budget, 2008

Total tax levy	$15,622,850
County levy	3,117,386
County taxes	2,560,028
County library	236,371
County health	0
County open space	320,987
School levy	12,183,696
Muni. levy	321,768
Misc. revenues	2,528,991

Taxes

	2006	2007	2008
General tax rate per $100	3.566	3.729	3.843
County equalization ratio	60.64	53.97	50.62
Net valuation taxable	$401,057,300	$404,819,378	$406,565,721
State equalized value	$744,293,991	$798,663,118	$818,796,419

See Introduction for an explanation of all data sources.

Demographics & Socio-Economic Characteristics

(2000 US Census, except as noted)

Population
1980*	604
1990*	408
2000	534
Male	251
Female	283
2007 (estimate)*	660
Population density	550.0

Race & Hispanic Origin, 2000
Race
White	508
Black/African American	14
American Indian/Alaska Native	3
Asian	0
Native Hawaiian/Pacific Islander	0
Other race	0
Two or more races	9
Hispanic origin, total	16
Mexican	7
Puerto Rican	9
Cuban	0
Other Hispanic	0

Age & Nativity, 2000
Under 5 years	34
18 years and over	403
21 years and over	390
65 years and over	84
85 years and over	7
Median age	39.8
Native-born	528
Foreign-born	8

Educational Attainment, 2000
Population 25 years and over	341
Less than 9th grade	4.4%
High school grad or higher	76.8%
Bachelor's degree or higher	14.1%
Graduate degree	3.5%

Income & Poverty, 1999
Per capita income	$16,880
Median household income	$49,191
Median family income	$54,219
Persons in poverty	31
H'holds receiving public assistance	0
H'holds receiving social security	49

Households, 2000
Total households	194
With persons under 18	72
With persons over 65	59
Family households	152
Single-person households	35
Persons per household	2.75
Persons per family	3.09

Labor & Employment
Total civilian labor force, 2007**	327
Unemployment rate	4.5%
Total civilian labor force, 2000	293
Unemployment rate	5.1%

Employed persons 16 years and over by occupation, 2000
Managers & professionals	71
Service occupations	27
Sales & office occupations	61
Farming, fishing & forestry	8
Construction & maintenance	45
Production & transportation	66
Self-employed persons	7

* US Census Bureau
** New Jersey Department of Labor

General Information

Borough of Shiloh
PO Box 349
900 Main St.
Shiloh, NJ 08353
856-455-3054

Email	shilohclerk@verizon.net
Year of incorporation	1929
Land/water area (sq. miles)	1.20/0.00
Form of government	Borough

Government

Legislative Districts
US Congressional	2
State Legislative	3

Local Officials, 2009
Mayor	Harold Davis Jr
Manager/Admin	NA
Clerk	Ronald Campbell Sr
Finance Dir	Teresa Wilford
Tax Assessor	Lois Mazza
Tax Collector	Elizabeth Wallender
Attorney	Richard McCarthy
Building	Andrew Jepson
Comm Dev/Planning	NA
Engineering	J. Michael Fralinger
Public Works	NA
Police Chief	NA
Emerg/Fire Director	Ronald Dubois

Housing & Construction

Housing Units, 2000*
Total	204
Median rent	$558
Median SF home value	$97,600

Permits for New Residential Construction
	Units	Value
Total, 2006	4	$407,214
Single family	4	$407,214
Total, 2007	2	$203,608
Single family	2	$203,608

Real Property Valuation, 2008
	Parcels	Valuation
Total	241	$19,298,400
Vacant	7	171,800
Residential	186	16,419,100
Commercial	13	1,077,400
Industrial	0	0
Apartments	0	0
Farm land	25	334,400
Farm homestead	10	1,295,700

Average Property Value & Tax, 2008
Residential value	$90,382
Property tax	$3,318
Tax credit/rebate	$858

Public Library

No public municipal library

Library statistics, 2007
Population served	NA
Full-time/total staff	NA/NA

	Total	Per capita
Holdings	NA	NA
Revenues	NA	NA
Expenditures	NA	NA
Annual visits	NA	NA
Internet terminals/annual users	NA/NA	

Public Safety

Number of officers, 2007 ... 0

Crime	2006	2007
Total crimes	8	9
Violent	2	0
Murder	0	0
Rape	0	0
Robbery	0	0
Aggravated assault	2	0
Non-violent	6	9
Burglary	2	5
Larceny	4	3
Vehicle theft	0	1
Domestic violence	0	3
Arson	0	0
Total crime rate	12.5	13.8
Violent	3.1	0.0
Non-violent	9.4	13.8

Public School District

(for school year 2007-08 except as noted)

Shiloh School District
Main Street, PO Box 189
Shiloh, NJ 08353
(856) 451-5424

Consulting Superintendent	David Hitchner
Number of schools	0
Grade plan	K-8
Enrollment	NA
Attendance rate, '06-07	96.0%
Dropout rate	NA
Students per teacher	NA
Per pupil expenditure	NA
Median faculty salary	NA
Median administrator salary	$26,000
Grade 12 enrollment	NA
High school graduation rate	NA

Assessment test results
(percent scoring at proficient or advanced level)
	Language	Math
NJASK-Grade 3	NA	NA
GEPA-Grade 8	NA	NA
HSPA-High School	NA	NA

SAT Score Averages, 2006-07
Pct tested	Math	Verbal	Writing
NA	NA	NA	NA

Teacher Qualifications
Avg. years of experience	NA
Highly-qualified teachers one subject/all subjects	NA/NA

No Child Left Behind
AYP, 2006-07 ... Meets Standards

Municipal Finance

State Aid Programs, 2009
Total aid	$41,910
CMPTRA	11,064
Energy tax receipts	30,008
Garden State Trust	0

General Budget, 2008
Total tax levy	$712,578
County levy	303,252
County taxes	286,666
County library	0
County health	13,398
County open space	3,188
School levy	307,764
Muni. levy	101,563
Misc. revenues	160,780

Taxes

	2006	2007	2008
General tax rate per $100	4.05	3.667	3.674
County equalization ratio	75.87	63.72	61.13
Net valuation taxable	$19,225,800	$19,430,642	$19,412,258
State equalized value	$30,304,108	$31,713,511	$37,931,612

Demographics & Socio-Economic Characteristics

(2000 US Census, except as noted)

Population

1980*	1,427
1990*	1,352
2000	1,384
Male	666
Female	718
2007 (estimate)*	1,439
Population density	2,055.7

Race & Hispanic Origin, 2000

Race

White	1,333
Black/African American	4
American Indian/Alaska Native	10
Asian	12
Native Hawaiian/Pacific Islander	0
Other race	15
Two or more races	10
Hispanic origin, total	80
Mexican	52
Puerto Rican	5
Cuban	3
Other Hispanic	20

Age & Nativity, 2000

Under 5 years	47
18 years and over	1,179
21 years and over	1,146
65 years and over	372
85 years and over	45
Median age	50.5
Native-born	1,318
Foreign-born	77

Educational Attainment, 2000

Population 25 years and over	1,079
Less than 9th grade	2.4%
High school grad or higher	89.0%
Bachelor's degree or higher	25.4%
Graduate degree	9.4%

Income & Poverty, 1999

Per capita income	$27,870
Median household income	$42,098
Median family income	$60,417
Persons in poverty	114
H'holds receiving public assistance	3
H'holds receiving social security	291

Households, 2000

Total households	664
With persons under 18	111
With persons over 65	268
Family households	396
Single-person households	238
Persons per household	2.08
Persons per family	2.65

Labor & Employment

Total civilian labor force, 2007**	830
Unemployment rate	6.7%
Total civilian labor force, 2000	696
Unemployment rate	6.6%

Employed persons 16 years and over by occupation, 2000

Managers & professionals	219
Service occupations	128
Sales & office occupations	173
Farming, fishing & forestry	3
Construction & maintenance	77
Production & transportation	50
Self-employed persons	92

General Information

Borough of Ship Bottom
1621 Long Beach Blvd
Ship Bottom, NJ 08008
609-494-2171

Website	shipbottom.org
Year of incorporation	1947
Land/water area (sq. miles)	0.70/0.30
Form of government	Borough

Government

Legislative Districts

US Congressional	3
State Legislative	9

Local Officials, 2009

Mayor	William Huelsenbeck
Manager	T. Richard Bethea
Clerk	Kathleen Wells
Finance Dir	T. Richard Bethea
Tax Assessor	William Procacci
Tax Collector	T. Richard Bethea
Attorney	Christopher Conners
Building	Susan DeLuca
Comm Dev/Planning	NA
Engineering	Frank Little
Public Works	NA
Police Chief	Paul Sharkey
Fire Chief	Frederick Traut

Housing & Construction

Housing Units, 2000*

Total	2,218
Median rent	$783
Median SF home value	$236,000

Permits for New Residential Construction

	Units	Value
Total, 2006	26	$5,151,671
Single family	24	$5,099,571
Total, 2007	20	$5,592,182
Single family	18	$5,426,682

Real Property Valuation, 2008

	Parcels	Valuation
Total	2,036	$1,089,674,800
Vacant	64	23,365,200
Residential	1,820	943,318,000
Commercial	149	120,331,700
Industrial	0	0
Apartments	3	2,659,900
Farm land	0	0
Farm homestead	0	0

Average Property Value & Tax, 2008

Residential value	$518,307
Property tax	$4,880
Tax credit/rebate	$992

Public Library

No public municipal library

Library statistics, 2007

Population served	NA
Full-time/total staff	NA/NA

	Total	Per capita
Holdings	NA	NA
Revenues	NA	NA
Expenditures	NA	NA
Annual visits	NA	NA
Internet terminals/annual users	NA/NA	

Public Safety

Number of officers, 2007	11

Crime	2006	2007
Total crimes	93	81
Violent	7	4
Murder	0	0
Rape	0	0
Robbery	0	0
Aggravated assault	7	4
Non-violent	86	77
Burglary	25	11
Larceny	61	66
Vehicle theft	0	0
Domestic violence	6	7
Arson	1	1
Total crime rate	65.6	56.8
Violent	4.9	2.8
Non-violent	60.6	54.0

Public School District

(for school year 2007-08 except as noted)

Long Beach Island School District
200 Barnegat Avenue
Surf City, NJ 08008
(609) 494-2341

Superintendent	Robert A. Garguilo
Number of schools	2
Grade plan	K-6
Enrollment	258
Attendance rate, '06-07	94.0%
Dropout rate	NA
Students per teacher	7.1
Per pupil expenditure	$23,574
Median faculty salary	$71,027
Median administrator salary	$95,218
Grade 12 enrollment	NA
High school graduation rate	NA

Assessment test results

(percent scoring at proficient or advanced level)

	Language	Math
NJASK-Grade 3	96.9%	90.6%
GEPA-Grade 8	NA	NA
HSPA-High School	NA	NA

SAT Score Averages, 2006-07

Pct tested	Math	Verbal	Writing
NA	NA	NA	NA

Teacher Qualifications

Avg. years of experience	19
Highly-qualified teachers one subject/all subjects	100%/100%

No Child Left Behind

AYP, 2006-07	Meets Standards

Municipal Finance

State Aid Programs, 2009

Total aid	$269,692
CMPTRA	0
Energy tax receipts	257,556
Garden State Trust	0

General Budget, 2008

Total tax levy	$10,262,932
County levy	4,012,306
County taxes	3,444,585
County library	404,815
County health	0
County open space	162,905
School levy	3,045,626
Muni. levy	3,205,000
Misc. revenues	2,528,053

Taxes

	2006	2007	2008
General tax rate per $100	0.901	0.935	0.942
County equalization ratio	91.19	81.45	80.58
Net valuation taxable	$1,046,285,000	$1,068,359,499	$1,089,948,485
State equalized value	$1,284,870,972	$1,325,772,467	$1,336,629,118

* US Census Bureau
** New Jersey Department of Labor

See Introduction for an explanation of all data sources.

Demographics & Socio-Economic Characteristics

(2000 US Census, except as noted)

Population

1980*	2,962
1990*	3,096
2000	3,590
Male	1,781
Female	1,809
2007 (estimate)*	3,759
Population density	1,700.9

Race & Hispanic Origin, 2000

Race

White	3,468
Black/African American	19
American Indian/Alaska Native	0
Asian	60
Native Hawaiian/Pacific Islander	0
Other race	13
Two or more races	30
Hispanic origin, total	69
Mexican	16
Puerto Rican	13
Cuban	8
Other Hispanic	32

Age & Nativity, 2000

Under 5 years	310
18 years and over	2,485
21 years and over	2,412
65 years and over	431
85 years and over	43
Median age	38.4
Native-born	3,325
Foreign-born	265

Educational Attainment, 2000

Population 25 years and over	2,367
Less than 9th grade	2.7%
High school grad or higher	91.0%
Bachelor's degree or higher	48.7%
Graduate degree	19.6%

Income & Poverty, 1999

Per capita income	$38,218
Median household income	$86,911
Median family income	$92,719
Persons in poverty	37
H'holds receiving public assistance	13
H'holds receiving social security	290

Households, 2000

Total households	1,207
With persons under 18	567
With persons over 65	301
Family households	1,016
Single-person households	156
Persons per household	2.96
Persons per family	3.27

Labor & Employment

Total civilian labor force, 2007**	1,775
Unemployment rate	1.1%
Total civilian labor force, 2000	1,686
Unemployment rate	2.7%

Employed persons 16 years and over by occupation, 2000

Managers & professionals	832
Service occupations	137
Sales & office occupations	516
Farming, fishing & forestry	0
Construction & maintenance	83
Production & transportation	72
Self-employed persons	152

‡ Branch of county library
* US Census Bureau
** New Jersey Department of Labor

General Information

Borough of Shrewsbury
419 Sycamore Ave
Shrewsbury, NJ 07702
732-741-4200

Website	www.shrewsburyboro.com
Year of incorporation	1926
Land/water area (sq. miles)	2.21/0.02
Form of government	Borough

Government

Legislative Districts

US Congressional	12
State Legislative	12

Local Officials, 2009

Mayor	Terel Cooperhouse
Manager	Tom Seaman
Clerk/Registrar	Lynn Spillane
Finance Dir	Thomas Seaman
Tax Assessor	Stephen Walters
Tax Collector	Thomas Seaman
Attorney	Martin M. Barger
Building	Cary Costa
Comm Dev/Planning	NA
Engineering	David Cranmer
Public Works	Robert Wentway
Police Chief	John Wilson III
Fire Chief	Peter Gibson

Housing & Construction

Housing Units, 2000*

Total	1,223
Median rent	$898
Median SF home value	$258,300

Permits for New Residential Construction

	Units	Value
Total, 2006	18	$4,063,791
Single family	18	$4,063,791
Total, 2007	17	$3,647,907
Single family	17	$3,647,907

Real Property Valuation, 2008

	Parcels	Valuation
Total	1,497	$810,700,900
Vacant	26	5,154,200
Residential	1,298	517,858,900
Commercial	171	286,898,200
Industrial	0	0
Apartments	0	0
Farm land	1	10,900
Farm homestead	1	778,700

Average Property Value & Tax, 2008

Residential value	$399,259
Property tax	$9,837
Tax credit/rebate	$1,255

Public Library

Eastern Branch Library‡
1001 Rte 35
Shrewsbury, NJ 07702
732-842-5995

Branch Librarian	Janet Kranis

Library statistics, 2007

see Monmouth County profile
for library system statistics

Public Safety

Number of officers, 2007	16

Crime	2006	2007
Total crimes	79	78
Violent	9	5
Murder	0	0
Rape	1	0
Robbery	4	0
Aggravated assault	4	5
Non-violent	70	73
Burglary	16	8
Larceny	48	65
Vehicle theft	6	0
Domestic violence	6	10
Arson	0	0
Total crime rate	21.1	21.0
Violent	2.4	1.3
Non-violent	18.7	19.6

Public School District

(for school year 2007-08 except as noted)

Shrewsbury Borough School District
20 Obre Place
Shrewsbury, NJ 07702
(732) 747-0882

Superintendent	Brent A. MacConnell
Number of schools	1
Grade plan	K-8
Enrollment	499
Attendance rate, '06-07	95.8%
Dropout rate	NA
Students per teacher	10.2
Per pupil expenditure	$12,605
Median faculty salary	$56,315
Median administrator salary	$105,000
Grade 12 enrollment	NA
High school graduation rate	NA

Assessment test results

(percent scoring at proficient or advanced level)

	Language	Math
NJASK-Grade 3	100.0%	96.0%
GEPA-Grade 8	84.6%	92.3%
HSPA-High School	NA	NA

SAT Score Averages, 2006-07

Pct tested	Math	Verbal	Writing
NA	NA	NA	NA

Teacher Qualifications

Avg. years of experience	11
Highly-qualified teachers one subject/all subjects	95.0%/92.5%

No Child Left Behind

AYP, 2006-07	Meets Standards

Municipal Finance

State Aid Programs, 2009

Total aid	$515,298
CMPTRA	12,991
Energy tax receipts	485,560
Garden State Trust	0

General Budget, 2008

Total tax levy	$20,009,947
County levy	2,945,169
County taxes	2,613,595
County library	157,284
County health	0
County open space	174,290
School levy	10,930,592
Muni. levy	6,134,187
Misc. revenues	2,418,991

Taxes

	2006	2007	2008
General tax rate per $100	2.267	2.356	2.464
County equalization ratio	81.96	73.03	70.35
Net valuation taxable	$794,670,600	$807,423,411	$812,138,583
State equalized value	$1,089,726,481	$1,147,105,317	$79,268,812

Demographics & Socio-Economic Characteristics

(2000 US Census, except as noted)

Population
1980*	995
1990*	1,098
2000	1,098
Male	530
Female	568
2007 (estimate)*	1,076
Population density	11,955.6

Race & Hispanic Origin, 2000
Race
White	733
Black/African American	183
American Indian/Alaska Native	0
Asian	110
Native Hawaiian/Pacific Islander	0
Other race	31
Two or more races	41
Hispanic origin, total	73
Mexican	22
Puerto Rican	19
Cuban	0
Other Hispanic	32

Age & Nativity, 2000
Under 5 years	82
18 years and over	872
21 years and over	838
65 years and over	119
85 years and over	16
Median age	34.9
Native-born	905
Foreign-born	193

Educational Attainment, 2000
Population 25 years and over	770
Less than 9th grade	6.9%
High school grad or higher	82.5%
Bachelor's degree or higher	20.4%
Graduate degree	5.7%

Income & Poverty, 1999
Per capita income	$23,574
Median household income	$36,875
Median family income	$42,500
Persons in poverty	96
H'holds receiving public assistance	10
H'holds receiving social security	90

Households, 2000
Total households	521
With persons under 18	143
With persons over 65	102
Family households	255
Single-person households	206
Persons per household	2.10
Persons per family	2.89

Labor & Employment
Total civilian labor force, 2007**	745
Unemployment rate	6.6%
Total civilian labor force, 2000	689
Unemployment rate	7.0%

Employed persons 16 years and over by occupation, 2000
Managers & professionals	192
Service occupations	79
Sales & office occupations	232
Farming, fishing & forestry	0
Construction & maintenance	48
Production & transportation	90
Self-employed persons	20

General Information

Shrewsbury Township
1979 Crawford St
Shrewsbury Twp, NJ 07724
732-542-0675

Website	NA
Year of incorporation	1693
Land/water area (sq. miles)	0.09/0.00
Form of government	Township

Government

Legislative Districts
US Congressional	12
State Legislative	12

Local Officials, 2009
Mayor	Edward Nolan
Manager/Admin	NA
Clerk	Jan Delonardo
Finance Dir	Adeline Schmidt
Tax Assessor	Stephen Walters
Tax Collector	Adeline Schmidt
Attorney	Gene Anthony
Code Enforcement	(State)
Comm Dev/Planning	NA
Engineering	Richard Maser
Public Works	M. Willemsen/L. Delonardo
Police Chief	(State)
Fire Svcs	(Eatontown Fire Dept)

Housing & Construction

Housing Units, 2000*
Total	546
Median rent	$825
Median SF home value	$61,100

Permits for New Residential Construction
	Units	Value
Total, 2006	0	$0
Single family	0	$0
Total, 2007	0	$0
Single family	0	$0

Real Property Valuation, 2008
	Parcels	Valuation
Total	391	$72,576,200
Vacant	0	0
Residential	122	24,964,700
Commercial	0	0
Industrial	0	0
Apartments	269	47,611,500
Farm land	0	0
Farm homestead	0	0

Average Property Value & Tax, 2008
Residential value	$204,629
Property tax	$4,452
Tax credit/rebate	$720

Public Library

Eastern Branch Library‡
1001 Rte 35
Shrewsbury, NJ 07702
732-842-5995

Branch Librarian	Janet Kranis

Library statistics, 2007
see Monmouth County profile
for library system statistics

Public Safety

Number of officers, 2007	0

Crime	2006	2007
Total crimes	6	12
Violent	1	3
Murder	0	0
Rape	0	0
Robbery	0	0
Aggravated assault	1	3
Non-violent	5	9
Burglary	2	1
Larceny	3	7
Vehicle theft	0	1
Domestic violence	1	10
Arson	0	0
Total crime rate	5.6	11.2
Violent	0.9	2.8
Non-violent	4.6	8.4

Public School District

(for school year 2007-08 except as noted)

Tinton Falls School District
658 Tinton Avenue
Tinton Falls, NJ 07724
(732) 460-2404

Superintendent	John P. Russo
Number of schools	3
Grade plan	K-8
Enrollment	1,583
Attendance rate, '06-07	95.3%
Dropout rate	NA
Students per teacher	10.4
Per pupil expenditure	$16,108
Median faculty salary	$55,425
Median administrator salary	$103,794
Grade 12 enrollment	NA
High school graduation rate	NA

Assessment test results
(percent scoring at proficient or advanced level)
	Language	Math
NJASK-Grade 3	90.7%	84.2%
GEPA-Grade 8	82.9%	88.7%
HSPA-High School	NA	NA

SAT Score Averages, 2006-07
Pct tested	Math	Verbal	Writing
NA	NA	NA	NA

Teacher Qualifications
Avg. years of experience	12

Highly-qualified teachers
one subject/all subjects	100%/100%

No Child Left Behind
AYP, 2006-07	Meets Standards

Municipal Finance

State Aid Programs, 2009
Total aid	$102,718
CMPTRA	41,000
Energy tax receipts	61,204
Garden State Trust	0

General Budget, 2008
Total tax levy	$1,581,890
County levy	203,004
County taxes	180,150
County library	10,841
County health	0
County open space	12,013
School levy	754,449
Muni. levy	624,437
Misc. revenues	241,137

Taxes	2006	2007	2008
General tax rate per $100	5.095	5.535	2.176
County equalization ratio	43.26	36.21	91.13
Net valuation taxable	$27,238,100	$27,278,537	$72,717,014
State equalized value	$75,269,951	$79,684,004	$378,673,442

‡ Branch of county library
* US Census Bureau
** New Jersey Department of Labor

See Introduction for an explanation of all data sources.

Demographics & Socio-Economic Characteristics

(2000 US Census, except as noted)

Population

1980*	5,900
1990*	5,440
2000	5,192
Male	2,541
Female	2,651
2007 (estimate)*	5,079
Population density	3,707.3

Race & Hispanic Origin, 2000

Race

White	3,912
Black/African American	917
American Indian/Alaska Native	11
Asian	168
Native Hawaiian/Pacific Islander	1
Other race	56
Two or more races	127
Hispanic origin, total	202
Mexican	14
Puerto Rican	105
Cuban	5
Other Hispanic	78

Age & Nativity, 2000

Under 5 years	274
18 years and over	4,033
21 years and over	3,868
65 years and over	801
85 years and over	64
Median age	39.0
Native-born	4,850
Foreign-born	348

Educational Attainment, 2000

Population 25 years and over	3,722
Less than 9th grade	2.8%
High school grad or higher	84.5%
Bachelor's degree or higher	16.7%
Graduate degree	6.9%

Income & Poverty, 1999

Per capita income	$21,259
Median household income	$46,898
Median family income	$54,200
Persons in poverty	283
H'holds receiving public assistance	64
H'holds receiving social security	659

Households, 2000

Total households	2,068
With persons under 18	661
With persons over 65	599
Family households	1,380
Single-person households	613
Persons per household	2.51
Persons per family	3.11

Labor & Employment

Total civilian labor force, 2007**	2,904
Unemployment rate	4.6%
Total civilian labor force, 2000	2,743
Unemployment rate	4.7%

Employed persons 16 years and over by occupation, 2000

Managers & professionals	802
Service occupations	367
Sales & office occupations	765
Farming, fishing & forestry	0
Construction & maintenance	261
Production & transportation	418
Self-employed persons	92

General Information

Borough of Somerdale
105 Kennedy Blvd
Somerdale, NJ 08083
856-783-6320

Website	www.somerdale-nj.com
Year of incorporation	1929
Land/water area (sq. miles)	1.37/0.00
Form of government	Borough

Government

Legislative Districts

US Congressional	1
State Legislative	5

Local Officials, 2009

Mayor	Gary Passanante
Administrator	Victor Cantillo
Clerk	Regina J. White
Finance Dir	Victor Cantillo
Tax Assessor	Thomas Davis
Tax Collector	Virginia Knecht
Attorney	John Kearney
Building	Mike DePalma
Comm Dev/Planning	NA
Engineering	Charles Riebel Jr
Public Works	Donald Wharton
Police Chief	Anthony Campbell
Emerg/Fire Director	NA

Housing & Construction

Housing Units, 2000*

Total	2,168
Median rent	$544
Median SF home value	$97,700

Permits for New Residential Construction

	Units	Value
Total, 2006	7	$819,300
Single family	7	$819,300
Total, 2007	1	$150,900
Single family	1	$150,900

Real Property Valuation, 2008

	Parcels	Valuation
Total	1,939	$192,690,100
Vacant	95	1,852,800
Residential	1,686	148,046,400
Commercial	122	27,557,800
Industrial	29	8,351,300
Apartments	7	6,881,800
Farm land	0	0
Farm homestead	0	0

Average Property Value & Tax, 2008

Residential value	$87,809
Property tax	$4,817
Tax credit/rebate	$973

Public Library

No public municipal library

Library statistics, 2007

Population served	NA
Full-time/total staff	NA/NA

	Total	Per capita
Holdings	NA	NA
Revenues	NA	NA
Expenditures	NA	NA
Annual visits	NA	NA
Internet terminals/annual users	NA/NA	

Public Safety

Number of officers, 2007	14

Crime	2006	2007
Total crimes	171	128
Violent	23	14
Murder	0	0
Rape	3	1
Robbery	11	5
Aggravated assault	9	8
Non-violent	148	114
Burglary	32	24
Larceny	104	82
Vehicle theft	12	8
Domestic violence	28	41
Arson	1	0
Total crime rate	33.2	25.0
Violent	4.5	2.7
Non-violent	28.7	22.3

Public School District

(for school year 2007-08 except as noted)

Somerdale Borough School District
301 Grace Street
Somerdale, NJ 08083
(856) 783-2933

Superintendent	Debra L. Bruner
Number of schools	1
Grade plan	K-8
Enrollment	476
Attendance rate, '06-07	92.7%
Dropout rate	NA
Students per teacher	10.4
Per pupil expenditure	$13,033
Median faculty salary	$49,828
Median administrator salary	$75,000
Grade 12 enrollment	NA
High school graduation rate	NA

Assessment test results

(percent scoring at proficient or advanced level)

	Language	Math
NJASK-Grade 3	89.5%	92.1%
GEPA-Grade 8	67.3%	94.5%
HSPA-High School	NA	NA

SAT Score Averages, 2006-07

Pct tested	Math	Verbal	Writing
NA	NA	NA	NA

Teacher Qualifications

Avg. years of experience	12
Highly-qualified teachers one subject/all subjects	100%/100%

No Child Left Behind

AYP, 2006-07	Meets Standards

Municipal Finance

State Aid Programs, 2009

Total aid	$623,550
CMPTRA	129,226
Energy tax receipts	491,206
Garden State Trust	0

General Budget, 2008

Total tax levy	$10,585,161
County levy	2,171,431
County taxes	1,962,497
County library	140,655
County health	0
County open space	68,279
School levy	5,693,377
Muni. levy	2,720,353
Misc. revenues	2,415,677

Taxes	2006	2007	2008
General tax rate per $100	5.196	5.447	5.486
County equalization ratio	72.76	61.49	56.69
Net valuation taxable	$191,399,000	$192,194,865	$192,957,861
State equalized value	$311,686,371	$338,803,684	$341,735,243

See Introduction for an explanation of all data sources.

Demographics & Socio-Economic Characteristics

(2000 US Census, except as noted)

Population
1980*	10,330
1990*	11,216
2000	11,614
Male	5,460
Female	6,154
2007 (estimate)*	11,420
Population density	2,833.7

Race & Hispanic Origin, 2000
Race
White	9,948
Black/African American	814
American Indian/Alaska Native	29
Asian	368
Native Hawaiian/Pacific Islander	4
Other race	261
Two or more races	190
Hispanic origin, total	696
Mexican	132
Puerto Rican	332
Cuban	10
Other Hispanic	222

Age & Nativity, 2000
Under 5 years	699
18 years and over	8,899
21 years and over	8,571
65 years and over	1,748
85 years and over	245
Median age	38.4
Native-born	10,667
Foreign-born	947

Educational Attainment, 2000
Population 25 years and over	8,090
Less than 9th grade	3.8%
High school grad or higher	84.2%
Bachelor's degree or higher	19.8%
Graduate degree	5.1%

Income & Poverty, 1999
Per capita income	$22,229
Median household income	$42,222
Median family income	$51,868
Persons in poverty	799
H'holds receiving public assistance	97
H'holds receiving social security	1,391

Households, 2000
Total households	4,920
With persons under 18	1,564
With persons over 65	1,248
Family households	2,952
Single-person households	1,621
Persons per household	2.32
Persons per family	2.97

Labor & Employment
Total civilian labor force, 2007**	6,488
Unemployment rate	5.3%
Total civilian labor force, 2000	6,124
Unemployment rate	6.0%

Employed persons 16 years and over by occupation, 2000
Managers & professionals	1,569
Service occupations	1,691
Sales & office occupations	1,452
Farming, fishing & forestry	40
Construction & maintenance	573
Production & transportation	433
Self-employed persons	308

‡ Branch of county library
* US Census Bureau
** New Jersey Department of Labor

General Information
City of Somers Point
1 W New Jersey Ave
Somers Point, NJ 08244
609-927-9088
Website	www.somerspoint-nj.com
Year of incorporation	1902
Land/water area (sq. miles)	4.03/1.14
Form of government	City

Government
Legislative Districts
US Congressional	2
State Legislative	1

Local Officials, 2009
Mayor	John L. Glasser Jr
Manager	W.E. Swain
Clerk	Carol Degrassi
Finance Dir	John Hanson
Tax Assessor	Diane Hesley
Tax Collector	Lynn MacEwan
Attorney	Damon Tyner
Building	Burton Federman
Comm Dev/Planning	NA
Engineering	James Mott
Public Works	Guy Martin
Police Chief	Salvatore Armenia
Emerg/Fire Director	Frank Denan

Housing & Construction
Housing Units, 2000*
Total	5,402
Median rent	$639
Median SF home value	$122,000

Permits for New Residential Construction
	Units	Value
Total, 2006	35	$3,926,539
Single family	21	$1,802,039
Total, 2007	19	$1,768,768
Single family	17	$1,465,268

Real Property Valuation, 2008
	Parcels	Valuation
Total	4,218	$696,426,100
Vacant	187	12,735,000
Residential	3,740	469,806,200
Commercial	277	172,679,800
Industrial	0	0
Apartments	14	41,205,100
Farm land	0	0
Farm homestead	0	0

Average Property Value & Tax, 2008
Residential value	$125,617
Property tax	$4,905
Tax credit/rebate	$913

Public Library
Somers Point Branch Library‡
747 Shore Rd
Somers Point, NJ 08244
609-927-7113
Branch Librarian	Mary Jane Bolden

Library statistics, 2007
see Atlantic County profile
for library system statistics

Public Safety
Number of officers, 2007	27

Crime	2006	2007
Total crimes	357	344
Violent	41	40
Murder	0	1
Rape	0	1
Robbery	18	5
Aggravated assault	23	33
Non-violent	316	304
Burglary	72	81
Larceny	237	221
Vehicle theft	7	2
Domestic violence	251	262
Arson	4	4
Total crime rate	**30.5**	**29.7**
Violent	3.5	3.5
Non-violent	27.0	26.3

Public School District
(for school year 2007-08 except as noted)

Somers Point School District
121 W. New York Avenue
Somers Point, NJ 08244
(609) 927-2053
Superintendent	Gerald Toscano
Number of schools	3
Grade plan	K-8
Enrollment	1,115
Attendance rate, '06-07	94.3%
Dropout rate	NA
Students per teacher	9.9
Per pupil expenditure	$11,336
Median faculty salary	$46,900
Median administrator salary	$101,905
Grade 12 enrollment	NA
High school graduation rate	NA

Assessment test results
(percent scoring at proficient or advanced level)
	Language	Math
NJASK-Grade 3	76.8%	73.3%
GEPA-Grade 8	59.3%	84.6%
HSPA-High School	NA	NA

SAT Score Averages, 2006-07
Pct tested	Math	Verbal	Writing
NA	NA	NA	NA

Teacher Qualifications
Avg. years of experience	8
Highly-qualified teachers one subject/all subjects	100%/100%

No Child Left Behind
AYP, 2006-07	Meets Standards

Municipal Finance
State Aid Programs, 2009
Total aid	$1,246,884
CMPTRA	370,006
Energy tax receipts	845,702
Garden State Trust	4

General Budget, 2008
Total tax levy	$27,266,562
County levy	4,527,832
County taxes	3,563,465
County library	459,403
County health	187,985
County open space	316,978
School levy	14,580,347
Muni. levy	8,158,383
Misc. revenues	4,281,782

Taxes
	2006	2007	2008
General tax rate per $100	3.686	3.841	3.906
County equalization ratio	52.7	46.59	44.12
Net valuation taxable	$678,596,100	$687,720,915	$698,239,910
State equalized value	$1,458,570,467	$1,556,398,566	$1,570,694,414

See Introduction for an explanation of all data sources.

Demographics & Socio-Economic Characteristics

(2000 US Census, except as noted)

Population

1980*	11,973
1990*	11,632
2000	12,423
Male	6,249
Female	6,174
2007 (estimate)*	12,682
Population density	5,373.7

Race & Hispanic Origin, 2000

Race

White	8,847
Black/African American	1,606
American Indian/Alaska Native	23
Asian	913
Native Hawaiian/Pacific Islander	3
Other race	634
Two or more races	397
Hispanic origin, total	2,112
Mexican	278
Puerto Rican	402
Cuban	46
Other Hispanic	1,386

Age & Nativity, 2000

Under 5 years	869
18 years and over	9,698
21 years and over	9,285
65 years and over	1,738
85 years and over	229
Median age	35.6
Native-born	9,674
Foreign-born	2,807

Educational Attainment, 2000

Population 25 years and over	8,603
Less than 9th grade	6.6%
High school grad or higher	81.9%
Bachelor's degree or higher	31.5%
Graduate degree	10.6%

Income & Poverty, 1999

Per capita income	$23,310
Median household income	$51,237
Median family income	$60,422
Persons in poverty	926
H'holds receiving public assistance	153
H'holds receiving social security	1,430

Households, 2000

Total households	4,743
With persons under 18	1,472
With persons over 65	1,210
Family households	2,891
Single-person households	1,489
Persons per household	2.49
Persons per family	3.15

Labor & Employment

Total civilian labor force, 2007**	7,258
Unemployment rate	4.6%
Total civilian labor force, 2000	6,495
Unemployment rate	5.0%

Employed persons 16 years and over by occupation, 2000

Managers & professionals	2,313
Service occupations	1,015
Sales & office occupations	1,601
Farming, fishing & forestry	0
Construction & maintenance	535
Production & transportation	705
Self-employed persons	281

---

* US Census Bureau
** New Jersey Department of Labor

General Information

Borough of Somerville
25 W End Ave
Somerville, NJ 08876
908-725-2300

Website	www.somervillenj.org
Year of incorporation	1909
Land/water area (sq. miles)	2.36/0.00
Form of government	Borough

Government

Legislative Districts

US Congressional	11
State Legislative	16

Local Officials, 2009

Mayor	Brian Gallagher
Administrator	Kevin Sluka
Clerk	Kevin Sluka
Finance Dir	Janet Kelk
Tax Assessor	Frank Betts
Tax Collector	Janet Kelk
Attorney	Jermy Solomon
Building	Frank Vuosa
Planning	Michael Cole
Engineering	NA
Public Works	Peter Hendershot
Police Chief	Dennis Manning
Emerg/Fire Director	Scott Becker

Housing & Construction

Housing Units, 2000*

Total	4,882
Median rent	$822
Median SF home value	$156,700

Permits for New Residential Construction

	Units	Value
Total, 2006	5	$764,735
Single family	5	$764,735
Total, 2007	12	$1,824,849
Single family	12	$1,824,849

Real Property Valuation, 2008

	Parcels	Valuation
Total	3,179	$652,678,250
Vacant	68	4,189,400
Residential	2,654	395,145,400
Commercial	411	200,311,950
Industrial	14	11,187,900
Apartments	32	41,843,600
Farm land	0	0
Farm homestead	0	0

Average Property Value & Tax, 2008

Residential value	$148,887
Property tax	$7,525
Tax credit/rebate	$1,154

Public Library

Somerville Mem. Public Library
35 West End Ave
Somerville, NJ 08876
908-725-1336

Director	Melissa A. Banks

Library statistics, 2007

Population served	12,423
Full-time/total staff	3/5

	Total	Per capita
Holdings	58,500	4.71
Revenues	$756,194	$60.87
Expenditures	$652,644	$52.54
Annual visits	62,936	5.07
Internet terminals/annual users	10/10,855	

Taxes

	2006	2007	2008
General tax rate per $100	4.52	4.83	5.055
County equalization ratio	59.68	51.73	46.01
Net valuation taxable	$652,299,900	$658,992,455	$658,258,364
State equalized value	$1,267,721,925	$1,426,107,217	$1,442,564,372

Public Safety

Number of officers, 2007	32

Crime	2006	2007
Total crimes	279	316
Violent	28	20
Murder	0	0
Rape	0	0
Robbery	20	13
Aggravated assault	8	7
Non-violent	251	296
Burglary	34	42
Larceny	199	237
Vehicle theft	18	17
Domestic violence	134	128
Arson	0	0
Total crime rate	22.4	25.2
Violent	2.2	1.6
Non-violent	20.1	23.6

Public School District

(for school year 2007-08 except as noted)

Somerville Borough School District
51 West Cliff St
Somerville, NJ 08876
(908) 218-4101

Superintendent	Carolyn F. Leary
Number of schools	3
Grade plan	K-12
Enrollment	2,260
Attendance rate, '06-07	96.4%
Dropout rate	0.0%
Students per teacher	10.9
Per pupil expenditure	$14,605
Median faculty salary	$59,295
Median administrator salary	$104,000
Grade 12 enrollment	254
High school graduation rate	98.8%

Assessment test results

(percent scoring at proficient or advanced level)

	Language	Math
NJASK-Grade 3	81.6%	80.7%
GEPA-Grade 8	62.6%	86.2%
HSPA-High School	89.8%	92.2%

SAT Score Averages, 2006-07

Pct tested	Math	Verbal	Writing
90%	549	525	527

Teacher Qualifications

Avg. years of experience	9
Highly-qualified teachers one subject/all subjects	99.5%/99.5%

No Child Left Behind

AYP, 2006-07	Meets Standards

Municipal Finance

State Aid Programs, 2009

Total aid	$1,811,585
CMPTRA	349,468
Energy tax receipts	1,415,824
Garden State Trust	620

General Budget, 2008

Total tax levy	$33,271,252
County levy	4,313,950
County taxes	3,884,063
County library	0
County health	0
County open space	429,887
School levy	19,768,235
Muni. levy	9,189,067
Misc. revenues	7,316,888

Demographics & Socio-Economic Characteristics
(2000 US Census, except as noted)

Population
1980*	8,322
1990*	7,863
2000	7,913
Male	3,865
Female	4,048
2007 (estimate)*	7,819
Population density	5,044.5

Race & Hispanic Origin, 2000
Race
White	7,456
Black/African American	68
American Indian/Alaska Native	15
Asian	109
Native Hawaiian/Pacific Islander	2
Other race	135
Two or more races	128
Hispanic origin, total	534
Mexican	28
Puerto Rican	236
Cuban	21
Other Hispanic	249

Age & Nativity, 2000
Under 5 years	474
18 years and over	5,990
21 years and over	5,741
65 years and over	1,073
85 years and over	124
Median age	36.7
Native-born	7,204
Foreign-born	709

Educational Attainment, 2000
Population 25 years and over	5,393
Less than 9th grade	5.4%
High school grad or higher	81.1%
Bachelor's degree or higher	12.5%
Graduate degree	3.2%

Income & Poverty, 1999
Per capita income	$23,598
Median household income	$50,529
Median family income	$62,029
Persons in poverty	582
H'holds receiving public assistance	86
H'holds receiving social security	1,058

Households, 2000
Total households	2,967
With persons under 18	1,045
With persons over 65	839
Family households	2,042
Single-person households	768
Persons per household	2.65
Persons per family	3.22

Labor & Employment
Total civilian labor force, 2007**	4,238
Unemployment rate	4.0%
Total civilian labor force, 2000	3,893
Unemployment rate	4.2%

Employed persons 16 years and over by occupation, 2000
Managers & professionals	847
Service occupations	593
Sales & office occupations	1,258
Farming, fishing & forestry	0
Construction & maintenance	422
Production & transportation	610
Self-employed persons	108

* US Census Bureau
** New Jersey Department of Labor
§ State Fiscal Year July 1–June 30

See Introduction for an explanation of all data sources.

General Information
City of South Amboy
140 N Broadway
South Amboy, NJ 08879
732-727-4600
Website	www.southamboynj.com
Year of incorporation	1908
Land/water area (sq. miles)	1.55/1.15
Form of government	Mayor-Council

Government
Legislative Districts
US Congressional	6
State Legislative	19

Local Officials, 2009
Mayor	John O'Leary Jr
Business Admin	Camille Tooker
Clerk	Kathleen Vigilante
Finance Dir	Terance O'Neill
Tax Assessor	Brian Enright
Tax Collector	Joanne Katko
Attorney	John Lanza
Building	Thomas Kelly
Comm Dev/Planning	NA
Engineering	James E. Cleary
Public Works	Gerald Garnett
Police Chief	James Wallis
Emerg/Fire Director	James Larkin

Housing & Construction
Housing Units, 2000*
Total	3,110
Median rent	$767
Median SF home value	$138,500

Permits for New Residential Construction
	Units	Value
Total, 2006	4	$467,936
Single family	4	$467,936
Total, 2007	2	$233,968
Single family	2	$233,968

Real Property Valuation, 2008
	Parcels	Valuation
Total	2,958	$878,548,200
Vacant	143	27,783,800
Residential	2,647	743,403,500
Commercial	149	75,585,900
Industrial	11	25,962,200
Apartments	8	5,812,800
Farm land	0	0
Farm homestead	0	0

Average Property Value & Tax, 2008
Residential value	$280,848
Property tax	$5,082
Tax credit/rebate	$897

Public Library
Dowdell Public Library
100 Harold G Hoffman Plaza
South Amboy, NJ 08879
732-721-6060
Director	Elaine R. Gaber

Library statistics, 2007
Population served	7,913
Full-time/total staff	1/2

	Total	Per capita
Holdings	72,052	9.11
Revenues	$322,972	$40.82
Expenditures	$317,903	$40.17
Annual visits	40,951	5.18
Internet terminals/annual users	17/6,657	

Public Safety
Number of officers, 2007	30

Crime	2006	2007
Total crimes	147	127
Violent	13	15
Murder	2	1
Rape	0	0
Robbery	1	0
Aggravated assault	10	14
Non-violent	134	112
Burglary	32	31
Larceny	86	69
Vehicle theft	16	12
Domestic violence	72	71
Arson	1	2
Total crime rate	**18.4**	**16.1**
Violent	1.6	1.9
Non-violent	16.8	14.2

Public School District
(for school year 2007-08 except as noted)

South Amboy School District
240 John Street
South Amboy, NJ 08879
(732) 525-2100
Superintendent	Robert Sheedy
Number of schools	2
Grade plan	K-12
Enrollment	1,118
Attendance rate, '06-07	93.8%
Dropout rate	0.0%
Students per teacher	9.9
Per pupil expenditure	$12,712
Median faculty salary	$56,541
Median administrator salary	$112,091
Grade 12 enrollment	77
High school graduation rate	87.4%

Assessment test results
(percent scoring at proficient or advanced level)
	Language	Math
NJASK-Grade 3	93.5%	78.3%
GEPA-Grade 8	45.6%	68.5%
HSPA-High School	61.1%	86.2%

SAT Score Averages, 2006-07
Pct tested	Math	Verbal	Writing
74%	483	467	445

Teacher Qualifications
Avg. years of experience	12
Highly-qualified teachers one subject/all subjects	100%/100%

No Child Left Behind
AYP, 2006-07	Meets Standards

Municipal Finance§
State Aid Programs, 2009
Total aid	$4,445,465
CMPTRA	0
Energy tax receipts	4,334,328
Garden State Trust	0

General Budget, 2008
Total tax levy	$15,911,487
County levy	3,009,486
County taxes	2,691,836
County library	0
County health	0
County open space	317,650
School levy	7,863,309
Muni. levy	5,038,692
Misc. revenues	9,471,939

Taxes
	2006	2007	2008
General tax rate per $100	1.66	1.72	1.810
County equalization ratio	96.59	88.16	83.64
Net valuation taxable	$839,830,400	$861,510,236	$879,354,301
State equalized value	$953,454,509	$1,029,863,829	$1,044,832,482

Demographics & Socio-Economic Characteristics

(2000 US Census, except as noted)

Population

1980*	4,331
1990*	4,185
2000	4,492
Male	2,303
Female	2,189
2007 (estimate)*	4,850
Population density	6,217.9

Race & Hispanic Origin, 2000

Race

White	3,504
Black/African American	349
American Indian/Alaska Native	12
Asian	184
Native Hawaiian/Pacific Islander	2
Other race	295
Two or more races	146
Hispanic origin, total	1,028
Mexican	276
Puerto Rican	173
Cuban	3
Other Hispanic	576

Age & Nativity, 2000

Under 5 years	285
18 years and over	3,437
21 years and over	3,274
65 years and over	472
85 years and over	64
Median age	35.1
Native-born	3,495
Foreign-born	997

Educational Attainment, 2000

Population 25 years and over	3,061
Less than 9th grade	7.2%
High school grad or higher	78.5%
Bachelor's degree or higher	17.8%
Graduate degree	6.6%

Income & Poverty, 1999

Per capita income	$21,131
Median household income	$48,984
Median family income	$58,214
Persons in poverty	299
H'holds receiving public assistance	56
H'holds receiving social security	438

Households, 2000

Total households	1,632
With persons under 18	575
With persons over 65	364
Family households	1,104
Single-person households	409
Persons per household	2.75
Persons per family	3.31

Labor & Employment

Total civilian labor force, 2007**	2,760
Unemployment rate	5.5%
Total civilian labor force, 2000	2,426
Unemployment rate	5.3%

Employed persons 16 years and over by occupation, 2000

Managers & professionals	544
Service occupations	382
Sales & office occupations	688
Farming, fishing & forestry	17
Construction & maintenance	212
Production & transportation	454
Self-employed persons	49

* US Census Bureau
** New Jersey Department of Labor

General Information

Borough of South Bound Brook
12 Main St
South Bound Brook, NJ 08880
732-356-0258

Website	www.southboundbrook.com
Year of incorporation	1907
Land/water area (sq. miles)	0.78/0.00
Form of government	Borough

Government

Legislative Districts

US Congressional	7
State Legislative	16

Local Officials, 2009

Mayor	Terry G. Warrelmann
Administrator	Donald Kazar
Clerk	Donald Kazar
Finance Dir	Randy Bahr
Tax Assessor	Barbara Flaherty
Tax Collector	Randy Bahr
Attorney	William T. Cooper III
Building	William Boyle
Comm Dev/Planning	NA
Engineering	Maser Consulting
Public Works	Ken Pine
Police Chief	William King
Emerg/Fire Director	Matthew Tomaro

Housing & Construction

Housing Units, 2000*

Total	1,676
Median rent	$818
Median SF home value	$132,800

Permits for New Residential Construction

	Units	Value
Total, 2006	115	$10,022,847
Single family	80	$8,081,774
Total, 2007	108	$8,605,582
Single family	57	$5,769,912

Real Property Valuation, 2008

	Parcels	Valuation
Total	1,298	$165,667,336
Vacant	109	2,598,300
Residential	1,140	143,115,654
Commercial	39	11,506,700
Industrial	1	201,300
Apartments	9	8,245,382
Farm land	0	0
Farm homestead	0	0

Average Property Value & Tax, 2008

Residential value	$125,540
Property tax	$6,961
Tax credit/rebate	$1,165

Public Library

contracts with Bound Brook Library
402 E High St
Bound Brook, NJ 08805
732-356-0043

Director	Hannah Kerwin

Library statistics, 2007

Population served	NA
Full-time/total staff	NA/NA

	Total	Per capita
Holdings	NA	NA
Revenues	NA	NA
Expenditures	NA	NA
Annual visits	NA	NA
Internet terminals/annual users	NA/NA	

Public Safety

Number of officers, 2007	13

Crime	2006	2007
Total crimes	4	29
Violent	0	1
Murder	0	0
Rape	0	0
Robbery	0	1
Aggravated assault	0	0
Non-violent	4	28
Burglary	2	3
Larceny	0	22
Vehicle theft	2	3
Domestic violence	0	48
Arson	0	0
Total crime rate	0.9	6.4
Violent	0.0	0.2
Non-violent	0.9	6.2

Public School District

(for school year 2007-08 except as noted)

South Bound Brook Borough School Dist.
122 Elizabeth St
South Bound Brook, NJ 08880
(732) 356-0018

Superintendent	Carol Rosevear
Number of schools	1
Grade plan	K-8
Enrollment	455
Attendance rate, '06-07	95.1%
Dropout rate	NA
Students per teacher	10.0
Per pupil expenditure	$13,697
Median faculty salary	$52,965
Median administrator salary	$110,401
Grade 12 enrollment	NA
High school graduation rate	NA

Assessment test results

(percent scoring at proficient or advanced level)

	Language	Math
NJASK-Grade 3	87.2%	87.3%
GEPA-Grade 8	56.3%	83.4%
HSPA-High School	NA	NA

SAT Score Averages, 2006-07

Pct tested	Math	Verbal	Writing
NA	NA	NA	NA

Teacher Qualifications

Avg. years of experience	11
Highly-qualified teachers one subject/all subjects	100%/97.0%

No Child Left Behind

AYP, 2006-07	Meets Standards

Municipal Finance

State Aid Programs, 2009

Total aid	$528,049
CMPTRA	161,422
Energy tax receipts	355,905
Garden State Trust	139

General Budget, 2008

Total tax levy	$9,210,378
County levy	1,238,795
County taxes	994,133
County library	134,597
County health	0
County open space	110,064
School levy	5,421,469
Muni. levy	2,550,115
Misc. revenues	2,700,688

Taxes

	2006	2007	2008
General tax rate per $100	5.15	5.43	5.546
County equalization ratio	55.87	48.82	45.34
Net valuation taxable	$165,320,667	$164,688,605	$166,098,176
State equalized value	$339,015,650	$362,823,109	$372,215,705

See Introduction for an explanation of all data sources.

Demographics & Socio-Economic Characteristics
(2000 US Census, except as noted)

Population
1980*	17,127
1990*	25,792
2000	37,734
Male	18,281
Female	19,453
2007 (estimate)*	40,755
Population density	997.4

Race & Hispanic Origin, 2000
Race
White	26,600
Black/African American	2,975
American Indian/Alaska Native	48
Asian	6,808
Native Hawaiian/Pacific Islander	14
Other race	518
Two or more races	771
Hispanic origin, total	1,918
Mexican	190
Puerto Rican	700
Cuban	141
Other Hispanic	887

Age & Nativity, 2000
Under 5 years	3,042
18 years and over	27,005
21 years and over	26,084
65 years and over	2,761
85 years and over	252
Median age	35.0
Native-born	29,578
Foreign-born	8,156

Educational Attainment, 2000
Population 25 years and over	24,872
Less than 9th grade	1.9%
High school grad or higher	93.3%
Bachelor's degree or higher	49.0%
Graduate degree	20.0%

Income & Poverty, 1999
Per capita income	$32,104
Median household income	$78,737
Median family income	$86,891
Persons in poverty	1,156
H'holds receiving public assistance	85
H'holds receiving social security	1,876

Households, 2000
Total households	13,428
With persons under 18	6,002
With persons over 65	2,031
Family households	10,083
Single-person households	2,627
Persons per household	2.80
Persons per family	3.27

Labor & Employment
Total civilian labor force, 2007**	23,324
Unemployment rate	2.8%
Total civilian labor force, 2000	20,797
Unemployment rate	3.4%

Employed persons 16 years and over by occupation, 2000
Managers & professionals	10,822
Service occupations	1,608
Sales & office occupations	5,268
Farming, fishing & forestry	0
Construction & maintenance	1,090
Production & transportation	1,305
Self-employed persons	757

* US Census Bureau
** New Jersey Department of Labor

General Information
Township of South Brunswick
540 Ridge Road
PO Box 190
Monmouth Junction, NJ 08852
732-329-4000

Website	www.sbtnj.net
Year of incorporation	1779
Land/water area (sq. miles)	40.86/0.24
Form of government	Council-Manager

Government
Legislative Districts
US Congressional	12
State Legislative	14

Local Officials, 2009
Mayor	Frank Gambatese
Manager	Matthew U. Watkins
Clerk	Barbara Nyitrai
Finance Dir	Joseph Monzo
Tax Assessor	Keith Fasanella
Tax Collector	Wendy Bukowski
Attorney	Donald Sears
Building	Jim Dowgin
Planning	Craig Marshall
Engineering	Jay Cornell
Public Works	Raymond Olsen
Police Chief	Raymond Hayducka
Emerg/Fire Director	Alan Laird

Housing & Construction
Housing Units, 2000*
Total	13,862
Median rent	$969
Median SF home value	$202,000

Permits for New Residential Construction
	Units	Value
Total, 2006	145	$16,746,363
Single family	145	$16,746,363
Total, 2007	184	$25,906,318
Single family	184	$25,906,318

Real Property Valuation, 2008
	Parcels	Valuation
Total	13,965	$3,912,108,400
Vacant	1,205	150,909,900
Residential	11,889	2,309,240,500
Commercial	328	307,432,400
Industrial	188	1,029,656,100
Apartments	17	94,573,900
Farm land	254	4,683,900
Farm homestead	84	15,611,700

Average Property Value & Tax, 2008
Residential value	$194,175
Property tax	$7,541
Tax credit/rebate	$1,062

Public Library
South Brunswick Pub Library
110 Kingston Lane
Monmouth Junction, NJ 08852
732-329-4000
Director	Chris Carbone

Library statistics, 2007
Population served	37,734
Full-time/total staff	11/23

	Total	Per capita
Holdings	158,735	4.21
Revenues	$2,789,283	$73.92
Expenditures	$2,690,436	$71.30
Annual visits	285,708	7.57
Internet terminals/annual users	42/96,075	

Public Safety
Number of officers, 2007	82

Crime	2006	2007
Total crimes	630	478
Violent	31	21
Murder	0	0
Rape	2	2
Robbery	12	4
Aggravated assault	17	15
Non-violent	599	457
Burglary	142	47
Larceny	418	377
Vehicle theft	39	33
Domestic violence	175	166
Arson	1	3
Total crime rate	15.5	11.8
Violent	0.8	0.5
Non-violent	14.8	11.3

Public School District
(for school year 2007-08 except as noted)

South Brunswick Township School District
231 Black Horse Lane, PO Box 181
Monmouth Junction, NJ 08852
(732) 297-7800
Superintendent	Gary P. McCartney
Number of schools	10
Grade plan	K-12
Enrollment	8,822
Attendance rate, '06-07	95.7%
Dropout rate	0.5%
Students per teacher	11.4
Per pupil expenditure	$13,233
Median faculty salary	$55,445
Median administrator salary	$96,780
Grade 12 enrollment	612
High school graduation rate	97.3%

Assessment test results
(percent scoring at proficient or advanced level)
	Language	Math
NJASK-Grade 3	92.6%	90.2%
GEPA-Grade 8	81.2%	94.4%
HSPA-High School	86.8%	93.6%

SAT Score Averages, 2006-07
Pct tested	Math	Verbal	Writing
91%	550	517	527

Teacher Qualifications
Avg. years of experience	7
Highly-qualified teachers one subject/all subjects	100%/100%

No Child Left Behind
AYP, 2006-07	Meets Standards

Municipal Finance
State Aid Programs, 2009
Total aid	$6,473,452
CMPTRA	0
Energy tax receipts	6,270,561
Garden State Trust	37,324

General Budget, 2008
Total tax levy	$152,243,306
County levy	24,025,067
County taxes	21,481,049
County library	0
County health	0
County open space	2,544,018
School levy	102,133,717
Muni. levy	26,084,522
Misc. revenues	24,963,991

Taxes
	2006	2007	2008
General tax rate per $100	3.57	3.82	3.884
County equalization ratio	57.64	48.53	47.04
Net valuation taxable	$3,844,711,200	$3,930,649,851	$3,920,160,305
State equalized value	$7,931,601,455	$8,347,286,542	$8,292,906,628

See Introduction for an explanation of all data sources.

Demographics & Socio-Economic Characteristics

(2000 US Census, except as noted)

Population

1980*	2,229
1990*	2,106
2000	2,249
Male	1,082
Female	1,167
2007 (estimate)*	2,281
Population density	3,212.7

Race & Hispanic Origin, 2000

Race

White	1,865
Black/African American	49
American Indian/Alaska Native	5
Asian	129
Native Hawaiian/Pacific Islander	7
Other race	142
Two or more races	52
Hispanic origin, total	339
Mexican	13
Puerto Rican	53
Cuban	22
Other Hispanic	251

Age & Nativity, 2000

Under 5 years	128
18 years and over	1,807
21 years and over	1,730
65 years and over	372
85 years and over	32
Median age	37.7
Native-born	1,640
Foreign-born	612

Educational Attainment, 2000

Population 25 years and over	1,664
Less than 9th grade	9.9%
High school grad or higher	75.9%
Bachelor's degree or higher	13.7%
Graduate degree	4.4%

Income & Poverty, 1999

Per capita income	$27,128
Median household income	$57,917
Median family income	$66,071
Persons in poverty	159
H'holds receiving public assistance	3
H'holds receiving social security	276

Households, 2000

Total households	811
With persons under 18	258
With persons over 65	268
Family households	594
Single-person households	187
Persons per household	2.77
Persons per family	3.27

Labor & Employment

Total civilian labor force, 2007**	1,244
Unemployment rate	4.6%
Total civilian labor force, 2000	1,178
Unemployment rate	4.9%

Employed persons 16 years and over by occupation, 2000

Managers & professionals	305
Service occupations	102
Sales & office occupations	421
Farming, fishing & forestry	0
Construction & maintenance	143
Production & transportation	149
Self-employed persons	51

* US Census Bureau
** New Jersey Department of Labor

General Information

Township of South Hackensack
227 Phillips Ave
South Hackensack, NJ 07606
201-440-1815

Website	www.southhackensacknj.org
Year of incorporation	1935
Land/water area (sq. miles)	0.71/0.02
Form of government	Township

Government

Legislative Districts

US Congressional	9
State Legislative	38

Local Officials, 2009

Mayor	Rosina Romano
Manager/Admin	NA
Clerk	Linda LoPiccolo
Finance Dir	L. D'Ambrosio
Tax Assessor	George Reggo
Tax Collector	Rosemarie Giotis
Attorney	John Carbone
Building	James Riley
Comm Dev/Planning	NA
Engineering	Boswell McClave
Public Works	Larry Paladino
Police Chief	Mike Frew
Emerg/Fire Director	Walter Peterson

Housing & Construction

Housing Units, 2000*

Total	830
Median rent	$984
Median SF home value	$183,640

Permits for New Residential Construction

	Units	Value
Total, 2006	1	$200,000
Single family	1	$200,000
Total, 2007	0	$0
Single family	0	$0

Real Property Valuation, 2008

	Parcels	Valuation
Total	796	$380,234,100
Vacant	58	5,227,400
Residential	516	118,039,900
Commercial	55	44,447,700
Industrial	167	212,519,100
Apartments	0	0
Farm land	0	0
Farm homestead	0	0

Average Property Value & Tax, 2008

Residential value	$228,759
Property tax	$7,326
Tax credit/rebate	$1,097

Public Library

No public municipal library

Library statistics, 2007

Population served	NA
Full-time/total staff	NA/NA

	Total	Per capita
Holdings	NA	NA
Revenues	NA	NA
Expenditures	NA	NA
Annual visits	NA	NA
Internet terminals/annual users	NA/NA	

Public Safety

Number of officers, 2007	17

Crime	2006	2007
Total crimes	78	78
Violent	11	9
Murder	0	0
Rape	3	1
Robbery	2	4
Aggravated assault	6	4
Non-violent	67	69
Burglary	15	8
Larceny	38	56
Vehicle theft	14	5
Domestic violence	8	12
Arson	0	3
Total crime rate	33.6	33.7
Violent	4.7	3.9
Non-violent	28.9	29.8

Public School District

(for school year 2007-08 except as noted)

South Hackensack School District
Dyer Avenue
South Hackensack, NJ 07606
(201) 440-2783

Superintendent	William DeFabiis
Number of schools	1
Grade plan	K-8
Enrollment	221
Attendance rate, '06-07	96.0%
Dropout rate	NA
Students per teacher	9.2
Per pupil expenditure	$17,236
Median faculty salary	$50,650
Median administrator salary	$116,396
Grade 12 enrollment	NA
High school graduation rate	NA

Assessment test results

(percent scoring at proficient or advanced level)

	Language	Math
NJASK-Grade 3	80.0%	75.0%
GEPA-Grade 8	66.7%	92.6%
HSPA-High School	NA	NA

SAT Score Averages, 2006-07

Pct tested	Math	Verbal	Writing
NA	NA	NA	NA

Teacher Qualifications

Avg. years of experience	8
Highly-qualified teachers one subject/all subjects	100%/100%

No Child Left Behind

AYP, 2006-07	Meets Standards

Municipal Finance

State Aid Programs, 2009

Total aid	$610,259
CMPTRA	146,776
Energy tax receipts	451,278
Garden State Trust	0

General Budget, 2008

Total tax levy	$12,483,335
County levy	1,241,200
County taxes	1,173,301
County library	0
County health	0
County open space	67,898
School levy	5,943,746
Muni. levy	5,298,390
Misc. revenues	2,975,442

Taxes	2006	2007	2008
General tax rate per $100	2.95	3.12	3.282
County equalization ratio	76.71	67.71	57.21
Net valuation taxable	$380,740,900	$382,057,348	$380,512,120
State equalized value	$562,668,193	$667,580,710	$729,953,898

Demographics & Socio-Economic Characteristics

(2000 US Census, except as noted)

Population
1980*	1,486
1990*	1,919
2000	2,417
Male	1,223
Female	1,194
2007 (estimate)*	3,065
Population density	194.0

Race & Hispanic Origin, 2000
Race
White	2,250
Black/African American	91
American Indian/Alaska Native	1
Asian	7
Native Hawaiian/Pacific Islander	1
Other race	53
Two or more races	14
Hispanic origin, total	83
Mexican	42
Puerto Rican	29
Cuban	2
Other Hispanic	10

Age & Nativity, 2000
Under 5 years	155
18 years and over	1,767
21 years and over	1,684
65 years and over	226
85 years and over	20
Median age	38.4
Native-born	2,307
Foreign-born	110

Educational Attainment, 2000
Population 25 years and over	1,604
Less than 9th grade	4.4%
High school grad or higher	86.3%
Bachelor's degree or higher	27.2%
Graduate degree	9.5%

Income & Poverty, 1999
Per capita income	$25,968
Median household income	$68,491
Median family income	$76,390
Persons in poverty	193
H'holds receiving public assistance	11
H'holds receiving social security	202

Households, 2000
Total households	800
With persons under 18	350
With persons over 65	166
Family households	663
Single-person households	107
Persons per household	2.94
Persons per family	3.25

Labor & Employment
Total civilian labor force, 2007**	1,408
Unemployment rate	3.6%
Total civilian labor force, 2000	1,246
Unemployment rate	4.3%

Employed persons 16 years and over by occupation, 2000
Managers & professionals	477
Service occupations	97
Sales & office occupations	298
Farming, fishing & forestry	11
Construction & maintenance	171
Production & transportation	139
Self-employed persons	100

General Information

Township of South Harrison
664 Harrisonville Rd
PO Box 113
Harrisonville, NJ 08039
856-769-3737

Website	www.southharrison-nj.org
Year of incorporation	1883
Land/water area (sq. miles)	15.80/0.02
Form of government	Township

Government

Legislative Districts
US Congressional	2
State Legislative	3

Local Officials, 2009
Mayor	Robert S. Campbell
Manager/Admin	Colleen Bianco
Clerk	Nancy Kearns
Finance Dir	Christie Melfi
Tax Assessor	Thomas Colavecchio
Tax Collector	Maria Berkett
Attorney	John C. Eastlack Jr
Building	Andy Hoglen
Comm Dev/Planning	NA
Engineering	Steven Bach
Public Works	Michael Micklasavage
Police Chief	Warren Mabey
Emerg/Fire Director	Rob Bowen

Housing & Construction

Housing Units, 2000*
Total	829
Median rent	$656
Median SF home value	$188,900

Permits for New Residential Construction
	Units	Value
Total, 2006	37	$7,940,499
Single family	37	$7,940,499
Total, 2007	26	$4,024,565
Single family	26	$4,024,565

Real Property Valuation, 2008
	Parcels	Valuation
Total	1,422	$222,442,300
Vacant	193	6,872,100
Residential	859	177,738,000
Commercial	16	7,976,300
Industrial	0	0
Apartments	0	0
Farm land	217	2,798,800
Farm homestead	137	27,057,100

Average Property Value & Tax, 2008
Residential value	$205,618
Property tax	$7,324
Tax credit/rebate	$1,077

Public Library

No public municipal library

Library statistics, 2007
Population served	NA
Full-time/total staff	NA/NA

	Total	Per capita
Holdings	NA	NA
Revenues	NA	NA
Expenditures	NA	NA
Annual visits	NA	NA
Internet terminals/annual users	NA/NA	

Public Safety

Number of officers, 2007 6
Crime	2006	2007
Total crimes	33	28
Violent	3	5
Murder	0	0
Rape	0	0
Robbery	0	0
Aggravated assault	3	5
Non-violent	30	23
Burglary	6	5
Larceny	23	17
Vehicle theft	1	1
Domestic violence	2	3
Arson	1	1
Total crime rate	11.4	9.5
Violent	1.0	1.7
Non-violent	10.4	7.8

Public School District

(for school year 2007-08 except as noted)

South Harrison Township School District
904 Mullica Hill Rd, PO Box 112
Harrisonville, NJ 08039
(856) 769-0855

Chief School Admin	David Datz
Number of schools	1
Grade plan	K-6
Enrollment	328
Attendance rate, '06-07	95.6%
Dropout rate	NA
Students per teacher	11.6
Per pupil expenditure	$12,429
Median faculty salary	$44,902
Median administrator salary	$78,005
Grade 12 enrollment	NA
High school graduation rate	NA

Assessment test results
(percent scoring at proficient or advanced level)
	Language	Math
NJASK-Grade 3	94.0%	86.0%
GEPA-Grade 8	NA	NA
HSPA-High School	NA	NA

SAT Score Averages, 2006-07
Pct tested	Math	Verbal	Writing
NA	NA	NA	NA

Teacher Qualifications
Avg. years of experience	8
Highly-qualified teachers one subject/all subjects	96.0%/96.0%

No Child Left Behind
AYP, 2006-07 .... Meets Standards

Municipal Finance

State Aid Programs, 2009
Total aid	$176,910
CMPTRA	46,740
Energy tax receipts	123,030
Garden State Trust	8

General Budget, 2008
Total tax levy	$7,941,481
County levy	2,213,808
County taxes	1,910,460
County library	153,636
County health	0
County open space	149,713
School levy	5,329,248
Muni. levy	398,424
Misc. revenues	1,699,004

Taxes
	2006	2007	2008
General tax rate per $100	3.318	3.623	3.562
County equalization ratio	69.83	61.26	59.82
Net valuation taxable	$197,900,700	$211,512,085	$222,960,583
State equalized value	$323,568,586	$353,254,457	$371,131,912

* US Census Bureau
** New Jersey Department of Labor

See Introduction for an explanation of all data sources.

Demographics & Socio-Economic Characteristics
(2000 US Census, except as noted)

Population
1980*	15,864
1990*	16,390
2000	16,964
Male	8,142
Female	8,822
2007 (estimate)*	16,061
Population density	5,635.4

Race & Hispanic Origin, 2000
Race
White	10,248
Black/African American	5,309
American Indian/Alaska Native	16
Asian	660
Native Hawaiian/Pacific Islander	5
Other race	266
Two or more races	460
Hispanic origin, total	837
Mexican	92
Puerto Rican	266
Cuban	60
Other Hispanic	419

Age & Nativity, 2000
Under 5 years	988
18 years and over	13,187
21 years and over	11,413
65 years and over	2,024
85 years and over	289
Median age	34.7
Native-born	14,095
Foreign-born	2,869

Educational Attainment, 2000
Population 25 years and over	10,351
Less than 9th grade	2.4%
High school grad or higher	93.4%
Bachelor's degree or higher	57.4%
Graduate degree	29.2%

Income & Poverty, 1999
Per capita income	$41,035
Median household income	$83,611
Median family income	$107,641
Persons in poverty	791
H'holds receiving public assistance	89
H'holds receiving social security	1,474

Households, 2000
Total households	5,522
With persons under 18	2,010
With persons over 65	1,464
Family households	3,768
Single-person households	1,393
Persons per household	2.69
Persons per family	3.26

Labor & Employment
Total civilian labor force, 2007**	8,549
Unemployment rate	4.0%
Total civilian labor force, 2000	9,422
Unemployment rate	4.2%

Employed persons 16 years and over by occupation, 2000
Managers & professionals	4,791
Service occupations	1,135
Sales & office occupations	2,411
Farming, fishing & forestry	0
Construction & maintenance	231
Production & transportation	462
Self-employed persons	704

General Information
Township of South Orange Village
Village Hall
101 S Orange Ave
South Orange, NJ 07079
973-378-7715
Website	www.southorange.org
Year of incorporation	1977
Land/water area (sq. miles)	2.85/0.00
Form of government	Special Charter

Government

Legislative Districts
US Congressional	8, 10
State Legislative	27

Local Officials, 2009
Village President	Douglas Newman
Manager	John Gross
Clerk	Lynn Cucciniello
Finance Dir	John Gross
Tax Assessor	Ellen Foye Malgieri
Tax Collector	Aderonke Zaccheus
Attorney	Steven Rother
Building	Anthony Grenci
Comm Dev/Planning	NA
Engineering	Salvatore Renda
Public Works	Mario Luciani
Police Chief	James Chelel
Emerg/Fire Director	Jeffrey Markey

Housing & Construction

Housing Units, 2000*
Total	5,671
Median rent	$879
Median SF home value	$274,600

Permits for New Residential Construction
	Units	Value
Total, 2006	14	$2,554,550
Single family	0	$2,409,550
Total, 2007	3	$1,860,230
Single family	0	$928,230

Real Property Valuation, 2008
	Parcels	Valuation
Total	4,626	$2,860,304,700
Vacant	55	29,170,800
Residential	4,361	2,560,908,700
Commercial	178	193,548,500
Industrial	6	3,135,000
Apartments	26	73,541,700
Farm land	0	0
Farm homestead	0	0

Average Property Value & Tax, 2008
Residential value	$587,230
Property tax	$14,354
Tax credit/rebate	$1,438

Public Library
South Orange Public Library
65 Scotland Rd
South Orange, NJ 07079
973-762-0230
Director	Melissa Kopecky

Library statistics, 2007
Population served	16,964
Full-time/total staff	5/12

	Total	Per capita
Holdings	113,999	6.72
Revenues	$1,269,166	$74.82
Expenditures	$1,263,446	$74.48
Annual visits	101,880	6.01
Internet terminals/annual users	20/18,607	

Public Safety
Number of officers, 2007	57

Crime	2006	2007
Total crimes	480	449
Violent	52	56
Murder	1	0
Rape	1	0
Robbery	23	31
Aggravated assault	27	25
Non-violent	428	393
Burglary	74	69
Larceny	260	241
Vehicle theft	94	83
Domestic violence	49	81
Arson	0	0
Total crime rate	28.9	27.4
Violent	3.1	3.4
Non-violent	25.8	24.0

Public School District
(for school year 2007-08 except as noted)

South Orange-Maplewood School District
525 Academy Street
Maplewood, NJ 07040
(973) 762-5600
Superintendent	Brian G. Osborne
Number of schools	9
Grade plan	K-12
Enrollment	6,085
Attendance rate, '06-07	95.0%
Dropout rate	0.4%
Students per teacher	11.0
Per pupil expenditure	$15,373
Median faculty salary	$67,399
Median administrator salary	$117,919
Grade 12 enrollment	430
High school graduation rate	98.0%

Assessment test results
(percent scoring at proficient or advanced level)
	Language	Math
NJASK-Grade 3	89.1%	91.8%
GEPA-Grade 8	69.9%	83.0%
HSPA-High School	80.5%	86.5%

SAT Score Averages, 2006-07
Pct tested	Math	Verbal	Writing
97%	513	500	503

Teacher Qualifications
Avg. years of experience	9
Highly-qualified teachers one subject/all subjects	100%/100%

No Child Left Behind
AYP, 2006-07	Needs Improvement

Municipal Finance

State Aid Programs, 2009
Total aid	$1,929,276
CMPTRA	232,886
Energy tax receipts	1,633,688
Garden State Trust	0

General Budget, 2008
Total tax levy	$70,068,207
County levy	11,074,080
County taxes	10,646,354
County library	0
County health	0
County open space	427,726
School levy	39,189,480
Muni. levy	19,804,647
Misc. revenues	14,025,856

Taxes
	2006	2007	2008
General tax rate per $100	6.17	6.51	2.445
County equalization ratio	42.92	38.28	101.27
Net valuation taxable	$1,008,034,800	$1,016,298,304	$2,866,442,315
State equalized value	$2,635,875,327	$2,818,563,060	$2,843,460,004

* US Census Bureau
** New Jersey Department of Labor

Demographics & Socio-Economic Characteristics
(2000 US Census, except as noted)

Population
1980* 20,521
1990* 20,489
2000 21,810
  Male 10,690
  Female 11,120
2007 (estimate)* 22,696
  Population density 2,714.8

Race & Hispanic Origin, 2000
Race
  White 16,956
  Black/African American 1,866
  American Indian/Alaska Native 49
  Asian 1,652
  Native Hawaiian/Pacific Islander 1
  Other race 759
  Two or more races 527
Hispanic origin, total 1,888
  Mexican 131
  Puerto Rican 517
  Cuban 99
  Other Hispanic 1,141

Age & Nativity, 2000
Under 5 years 1,344
18 years and over 16,325
21 years and over 15,649
65 years and over 3,071
85 years and over 281
  Median age 38.0
Native-born 18,589
Foreign-born 3,221

Educational Attainment, 2000
Population 25 years and over 14,940
Less than 9th grade 5.4%
High school grad or higher 84.3%
Bachelor's degree or higher 24.0%
Graduate degree 6.7%

Income & Poverty, 1999
Per capita income $25,270
Median household income $67,466
Median family income $72,745
Persons in poverty 727
H'holds receiving public assistance 105
H'holds receiving social security 2,030

Households, 2000
Total households 7,151
  With persons under 18 2,948
  With persons over 65 2,049
  Family households 5,858
  Single-person households 1,094
  Persons per household 3.01
  Persons per family 3.35

Labor & Employment
Total civilian labor force, 2007** 12,325
  Unemployment rate 3.0%
Total civilian labor force, 2000 11,348
  Unemployment rate 3.1%
Employed persons 16 years and over by occupation, 2000
  Managers & professionals 4,126
  Service occupations 1,178
  Sales & office occupations 3,065
  Farming, fishing & forestry 5
  Construction & maintenance 946
  Production & transportation 1,671
  Self-employed persons 465

* US Census Bureau
** New Jersey Department of Labor
§ State Fiscal Year July 1–June 30

General Information
Borough of South Plainfield
2480 Plainfield Ave
South Plainfield, NJ 07080
908-754-9000

Website .... www.southplainfieldnj.com
Year of incorporation 1926
Land/water area (sq. miles) 8.36/0.04
Form of government .... Borough

Government

Legislative Districts
US Congressional 7
State Legislative 18

Local Officials, 2009
Mayor .... Charles F. Butrico Jr
Manager .... Glenn Cullen
Clerk .... Joann Graf
Finance Dir .... Glenn Cullen
Tax Assessor .... Gary Toth
Tax Collector .... Kimberly Clifford
Attorney .... Patrick Bradshaw
Building .... John Pabst
Comm Dev/Planning .... NA
Engineering .... David Samuel
Public Works .... Joseph Glowacki
Police Chief .... John Ferraro
Fire Chief .... L. DelNegro

Housing & Construction

Housing Units, 2000*
Total 7,307
Median rent $976
Median SF home value $165,800

Permits for New Residential Construction
	Units	Value
Total, 2006	19	$3,506,589
Single family	17	$3,327,489
Total, 2007	15	$2,253,943
Single family	13	$2,074,843

Real Property Valuation, 2008
	Parcels	Valuation
Total	8,076	$1,425,654,900
Vacant	360	23,492,800
Residential	7,156	867,210,700
Commercial	221	175,644,400
Industrial	324	337,224,500
Apartments	2	22,000,000
Farm land	13	82,500
Farm homestead	0	0

Average Property Value & Tax, 2008
Residential value $121,187
Property tax $5,656
Tax credit/rebate $962

Public Library
South Plainfield Public Library
2484 Plainfield Ave
South Plainfield, NJ 07080
908-754-7885
Director .... Sundra L. Randolph

Library statistics, 2007
Population served 21,810
Full-time/total staff 4/7

	Total	Per capita
Holdings	63,290	2.90
Revenues	$1,502,981	$68.91
Expenditures	$927,018	$42.50
Annual visits	76,444	3.50
Internet terminals/annual users	...11/25,928	

Public Safety
Number of officers, 2007 56

Crime	2006	2007
Total crimes	518	463
Violent	27	34
Murder	0	0
Rape	0	0
Robbery	13	15
Aggravated assault	14	19
Non-violent	491	429
Burglary	84	76
Larceny	365	321
Vehicle theft	42	32
Domestic violence	144	168
Arson	6	0
Total crime rate	22.5	20.3
Violent	1.2	1.5
Non-violent	21.3	18.8

Public School District
(for school year 2007-08 except as noted)

South Plainfield School District
125 Jackson Avenue
South Plainfield, NJ 07080
(908) 754-4620

Superintendent .... Jose Negron
Number of schools 8
Grade plan K-12
Enrollment 3,710
Attendance rate, '06-07 .... 95.4%
Dropout rate 0.8%
Students per teacher 10.8
Per pupil expenditure $13,048
Median faculty salary $62,591
Median administrator salary $104,917
Grade 12 enrollment 296
High school graduation rate 96.6%

Assessment test results
(percent scoring at proficient or advanced level)

	Language	Math
NJASK-Grade 3	89.8%	92.0%
GEPA-Grade 8	75.2%	85.9%
HSPA-High School	78.9%	87.8%

SAT Score Averages, 2006-07
Pct tested	Math	Verbal	Writing
82%	491	472	475

Teacher Qualifications
Avg. years of experience 9
Highly-qualified teachers
  one subject/all subjects 100%/100%

No Child Left Behind
AYP, 2006-07 .... Meets Standards

Municipal Finance§

State Aid Programs, 2009
Total aid $3,500,835
  CMPTRA 846,054
  Energy tax receipts 2,567,260
  Garden State Trust 0

General Budget, 2008
Total tax levy $66,656,969
  County levy 11,030,495
    County taxes 9,875,707
    County library 0
    County health 0
    County open space 1,154,789
  School levy 40,715,905
  Muni. levy 14,910,568
  Misc. revenues 10,609,710

Taxes
	2006	2007	2008
General tax rate per $100	4.31	4.39	4.688
County equalization ratio	44.61	40.71	37.10
Net valuation taxable	$1,415,809,500	$1,435,804,761	$1,428,215,294
State equalized value	$3,480,753,789	$3,865,483,242	$3,935,401,497

See Introduction for an explanation of all data sources.

Demographics & Socio-Economic Characteristics
(2000 US Census, except as noted)

Population
1980*	14,361
1990*	13,692
2000	15,322
Male	7,574
Female	7,748
2007 (estimate)*	15,738
Population density	5,600.7

Race & Hispanic Origin, 2000
Race
White	12,801
Black/African American	929
American Indian/Alaska Native	18
Asian	542
Native Hawaiian/Pacific Islander	8
Other race	587
Two or more races	437
Hispanic origin, total	1,480
Mexican	248
Puerto Rican	435
Cuban	53
Other Hispanic	744

Age & Nativity, 2000
Under 5 years	1,008
18 years and over	11,793
21 years and over	11,266
65 years and over	2,231
85 years and over	260
Median age	36.4
Native-born	11,290
Foreign-born	4,032

Educational Attainment, 2000
Population 25 years and over	10,547
Less than 9th grade	11.6%
High school grad or higher	76.5%
Bachelor's degree or higher	20.9%
Graduate degree	6.4%

Income & Poverty, 1999
Per capita income	$23,684
Median household income	$52,324
Median family income	$62,869
Persons in poverty	744
H'holds receiving public assistance	80
H'holds receiving social security	1,615

Households, 2000
Total households	5,606
With persons under 18	1,976
With persons over 65	1,624
Family households	3,985
Single-person households	1,306
Persons per household	2.72
Persons per family	3.23

Labor & Employment
Total civilian labor force, 2007**	8,635
Unemployment rate	5.8%
Total civilian labor force, 2000	7,920
Unemployment rate	6.1%

Employed persons 16 years and over by occupation, 2000
Managers & professionals	2,037
Service occupations	889
Sales & office occupations	2,141
Farming, fishing & forestry	0
Construction & maintenance	1,223
Production & transportation	1,148
Self-employed persons	341

* US Census Bureau
** New Jersey Department of Labor

General Information
Borough of South River
48 Washington St
South River, NJ 08882
732-257-1999
Website	www.southrivernj.org
Year of incorporation	1898
Land/water area (sq. miles)	2.81/0.13
Form of government	Borough

Government
Legislative Districts
US Congressional	12
State Legislative	18

Local Officials, 2009
Mayor	Raymond Eppinger
Manager	Andrew J. Salerno
Clerk	Patricia O'Connor
Finance Dir	Kanthiah Sivananthan
Tax Assessor	Michael Frangella
Tax Collector	Regina Baca
Attorney	Gary Schwartz
Building	NA
Planning	Thomas Sheehan
Engineering	David Samuel
Public Works	George Lyons
Police Chief	Wesley Bomba
Emerg/Fire Director	Julie Hughes

Housing & Construction
Housing Units, 2000*
Total	5,769
Median rent	$745
Median SF home value	$149,600

Permits for New Residential Construction
	Units	Value
Total, 2006	11	$1,028,411
Single family	6	$676,744
Total, 2007	12	$1,541,443
Single family	12	$1,541,443

Real Property Valuation, 2008
	Parcels	Valuation
Total	4,926	$426,344,400
Vacant	277	3,482,800
Residential	4,409	368,031,400
Commercial	195	25,641,000
Industrial	28	19,514,000
Apartments	17	9,675,200
Farm land	0	0
Farm homestead	0	0

Average Property Value & Tax, 2008
Residential value	$83,473
Property tax	$5,205
Tax credit/rebate	$943

Public Library
South River Public Library
55 Appleby Ave
South River, NJ 08882
732-254-2488
Director............Andrea Londensky

Library statistics, 2007
Population served	15,322
Full-time/total staff	2/5

	Total	Per capita
Holdings	42,518	2.77
Revenues	$663,222	$43.29
Expenditures	$534,705	$34.90
Annual visits	56,774	3.71
Internet terminals/annual users		7/8,800

Public Safety
Number of officers, 2007 30
Crime	2006	2007
Total crimes	231	188
Violent	20	25
Murder	0	0
Rape	1	0
Robbery	4	5
Aggravated assault	15	20
Non-violent	211	163
Burglary	43	38
Larceny	159	113
Vehicle theft	9	12
Domestic violence	238	218
Arson	0	7
Total crime rate	14.4	11.9
Violent	1.2	1.6
Non-violent	13.1	10.3

Public School District
(for school year 2007-08 except as noted)

South River School District
15 Montgomery Street
South River, NJ 08882
(732) 613-4000
Superintendent	Ronald Grygo
Number of schools	4
Grade plan	K-12
Enrollment	2,203
Attendance rate, '06-07	93.7%
Dropout rate	2.6%
Students per teacher	12.0
Per pupil expenditure	$10,306
Median faculty salary	$47,000
Median administrator salary	$103,953
Grade 12 enrollment	153
High school graduation rate	93.5%

Assessment test results
(percent scoring at proficient or advanced level)
	Language	Math
NJASK-Grade 3	74.7%	81.3%
GEPA-Grade 8	61.9%	75.4%
HSPA-High School	67.7%	85.4%

SAT Score Averages, 2006-07
Pct tested	Math	Verbal	Writing
70%	487	474	469

Teacher Qualifications
Avg. years of experience	6
Highly-qualified teachers one subject/all subjects	100%/100%

No Child Left Behind
AYP, 2006-07 ....Meets Standards

Municipal Finance
State Aid Programs, 2009
Total aid	$1,064,050
CMPTRA	523,625
Energy tax receipts	513,824
Garden State Trust	0

General Budget, 2008
Total tax levy	$26,603,757
County levy	4,921,847
County taxes	4,407,499
County library	0
County health	0
County open space	514,349
School levy	13,384,037
Muni. levy	8,297,873
Misc. revenues	6,354,119

Taxes
	2006	2007	2008
General tax rate per $100	5.53	5.85	6.237
County equalization ratio	30.89	26.72	24.91
Net valuation taxable	$425,531,400	$426,314,982	$426,628,526
State equalized value	$1,592,887,531	$1,710,536,658	$1,674,849,719

See Introduction for an explanation of all data sources.

Demographics & Socio-Economic Characteristics

(2000 US Census, except as noted)

Population
1980*	3,954
1990*	3,869
2000	3,634
Male	1,752
Female	1,882
2007 (estimate)*	3,713
Population density	3,200.9

Race & Hispanic Origin, 2000
Race
White	2,637
Black/African American	769
American Indian/Alaska Native	5
Asian	25
Native Hawaiian/Pacific Islander	0
Other race	91
Two or more races	107
Hispanic origin, total	337
Mexican	39
Puerto Rican	238
Cuban	5
Other Hispanic	55

Age & Nativity, 2000
Under 5 years	253
18 years and over	2,467
21 years and over	2,306
65 years and over	328
85 years and over	22
Median age	31.9
Native-born	3,513
Foreign-born	95

Educational Attainment, 2000
Population 25 years and over	2,201
Less than 9th grade	5.9%
High school grad or higher	74.0%
Bachelor's degree or higher	5.6%
Graduate degree	1.4%

Income & Poverty, 1999
Per capita income	$16,292
Median household income	$43,468
Median family income	$45,375
Persons in poverty	452
H'holds receiving public assistance	18
H'holds receiving social security	294

Households, 2000
Total households	1,073
With persons under 18	545
With persons over 65	252
Family households	902
Single-person households	134
Persons per household	3.39
Persons per family	3.63

Labor & Employment
Total civilian labor force, 2007**	2,098
Unemployment rate	7.4%
Total civilian labor force, 2000	1,773
Unemployment rate	8.0%

Employed persons 16 years and over by occupation, 2000
Managers & professionals	274
Service occupations	365
Sales & office occupations	511
Farming, fishing & forestry	9
Construction & maintenance	236
Production & transportation	237
Self-employed persons	54

General Information
Borough of South Toms River
144 Mill St
South Toms River, NJ 08757
732-349-0403

Website	NA
Year of incorporation	1927
Land/water area (sq. miles)	1.16/0.06
Form of government	Borough

Government
Legislative Districts
US Congressional	3
State Legislative	10

Local Officials, 2009
Mayor	Michael P. Keene
Manager/Admin	NA
Clerk	Elizabeth Silvestri
Finance Dir	Steve Gallagher
Tax Assessor	Ellen Kelleher
Tax Collector	Barbara Herr
Attorney	Guy Ryan
Building	Wayne M. Gibson
Comm Dev/Planning	NA
Engineering	Michael O'Donnell
Public Works	NA
Police Chief	Andrew Izatt
OEM Coordinator	Kevin McCormack

Housing & Construction
Housing Units, 2000*
Total	1,123
Median rent	$756
Median SF home value	$85,600

Permits for New Residential Construction
	Units	Value
Total, 2006	5	$435,770
Single family	5	$435,770
Total, 2007	2	$174,308
Single family	2	$174,308

Real Property Valuation, 2008
	Parcels	Valuation
Total	1,236	$281,424,600
Vacant	80	6,178,800
Residential	1,098	236,376,800
Commercial	57	38,503,800
Industrial	1	365,200
Apartments	0	0
Farm land	0	0
Farm homestead	0	0

Average Property Value & Tax, 2008
Residential value	$215,279
Property tax	$3,592
Tax credit/rebate	$739

Public Library
No public municipal library

Library statistics, 2007
Population served	NA
Full-time/total staff	NA/NA

	Total	Per capita
Holdings	NA	NA
Revenues	NA	NA
Expenditures	NA	NA
Annual visits	NA	NA
Internet terminals/annual users	NA/NA	

Public Safety
Number of officers, 2007 12

Crime	2006	2007
Total crimes	95	110
Violent	7	10
Murder	0	0
Rape	1	0
Robbery	1	5
Aggravated assault	5	5
Non-violent	88	100
Burglary	21	15
Larceny	56	76
Vehicle theft	11	9
Domestic violence	66	70
Arson	0	1
Total crime rate	25.7	29.6
Violent	1.9	2.7
Non-violent	23.8	26.9

Public School District
(for school year 2007-08 except as noted)

Toms River Regional School District
1144 Hooper Avenue
Toms River, NJ 08753
(732) 505-5510

Superintendent	Michael J. Ritacco
Number of schools	18
Grade plan	K-12
Enrollment	17,259
Attendance rate, '06-07	93.8%
Dropout rate	2.8%
Students per teacher	13.0
Per pupil expenditure	$10,496
Median faculty salary	$49,126
Median administrator salary	$114,200
Grade 12 enrollment	1,296
High school graduation rate	89.2%

Assessment test results
(percent scoring at proficient or advanced level)
	Language	Math
NJASK-Grade 3	93.4%	94.2%
GEPA-Grade 8	76.3%	87.3%
HSPA-High School	71.8%	83.4%

SAT Score Averages, 2006-07
Pct tested	Math	Verbal	Writing
NA	NA	NA	NA

Teacher Qualifications
Avg. years of experience	8
Highly-qualified teachers one subject/all subjects	99.5%/99.5%

No Child Left Behind
AYP, 2006-07 . . . . Meets Standards

Municipal Finance
State Aid Programs, 2009
Total aid	$395,786
CMPTRA	118,864
Energy tax receipts	274,943
Garden State Trust	0

General Budget, 2008
Total tax levy	$4,702,877
County levy	891,744
County taxes	735,360
County library	86,421
County health	35,186
County open space	34,777
School levy	1,697,689
Muni. levy	2,113,444
Misc. revenues	1,240,633

Taxes
	2006	2007	2008
General tax rate per $100	1.4	1.526	1.669
County equalization ratio	129.95	106.26	97.79
Net valuation taxable	$279,254,100	$281,002,203	$281,869,428
State equalized value	$263,225,713	$287,342,926	$1,389,987,752

* US Census Bureau
** New Jersey Department of Labor

See Introduction for an explanation of all data sources.

Demographics & Socio-Economic Characteristics
(2000 US Census, except as noted)

Population
1980*	8,008
1990*	10,202
2000	10,388
Male	4,856
Female	5,532
2007 (estimate)*	10,885
Population density	247.2

Race & Hispanic Origin, 2000
Race
White	10,086
Black/African American	125
American Indian/Alaska Native	29
Asian	65
Native Hawaiian/Pacific Islander	0
Other race	31
Two or more races	52
Hispanic origin, total	134
Mexican	34
Puerto Rican	63
Cuban	5
Other Hispanic	32

Age & Nativity, 2000
Under 5 years	411
18 years and over	8,534
21 years and over	8,285
65 years and over	3,295
85 years and over	426
Median age	49.7
Native-born	9,977
Foreign-born	356

Educational Attainment, 2000
Population 25 years and over	7,951
Less than 9th grade	3.9%
High school grad or higher	83.7%
Bachelor's degree or higher	18.0%
Graduate degree	6.1%

Income & Poverty, 1999
Per capita income	$26,977
Median household income	$44,419
Median family income	$57,419
Persons in poverty	399
H'holds receiving public assistance	51
H'holds receiving social security	2,303

Households, 2000
Total households	4,574
With persons under 18	1,001
With persons over 65	2,284
Family households	3,047
Single-person households	1,369
Persons per household	2.26
Persons per family	2.79

Labor & Employment
Total civilian labor force, 2007**	5,196
Unemployment rate	4.8%
Total civilian labor force, 2000	4,546
Unemployment rate	4.9%

Employed persons 16 years and over by occupation, 2000
Managers & professionals	1,382
Service occupations	616
Sales & office occupations	1,187
Farming, fishing & forestry	14
Construction & maintenance	494
Production & transportation	628
Self-employed persons	324

General Information
Township of Southampton
5 Retreat Rd
Southampton, NJ 08088
609-859-2736
Website	www.southamptonnj.org
Year of incorporation	1845
Land/water area (sq. miles)	44.03/0.24
Form of government	Township

Government
Legislative Districts
US Congressional	3
State Legislative	8

Local Officials, 2009
Mayor	James Young
Manager	Michael E. McFadden
Clerk	Michael E. McFadden
Finance Dir	Nancy Gower
Tax Assessor	Dennis DeKlerk
Tax Collector	Gwen Jobes
Attorney	George M. Morris
Building	Jody Mazeall
Comm Dev/Planning	NA
Engineering	Richard Alaimo
Public Works	Charles Oatman
Police Chief	NA
Fire/Emergency Dir	NA

Housing & Construction
Housing Units, 2000*
Total	4,751
Median rent	$724
Median SF home value	$113,200

Permits for New Residential Construction
	Units	Value
Total, 2006	68	$13,776,355
Single family	68	$13,776,355
Total, 2007	29	$5,572,939
Single family	29	$5,572,939

Real Property Valuation, 2008
	Parcels	Valuation
Total	5,640	$757,585,100
Vacant	476	12,746,200
Residential	4,430	640,443,000
Commercial	151	50,742,900
Industrial	22	6,445,600
Apartments	0	0
Farm land	362	6,080,900
Farm homestead	199	41,126,500

Average Property Value & Tax, 2008
Residential value	$147,239
Property tax	$4,814
Tax credit/rebate	$1,071

Public Library
Keen Memorial Library
94 Main St
Vincentown, NJ 08088
609-859-3598
Director	Lynn French

Library statistics, 2007
Population served	10,388
Full-time/total staff	0/0

	Total	Per capita
Holdings	24,476	2.36
Revenues	$0	NA
Expenditures	$0	NA
Annual visits	11,036	1.06
Internet terminals/annual users	5/515	

Public Safety
Number of officers, 2007	0

Crime	2006	2007
Total crimes	157	127
Violent	7	9
Murder	0	0
Rape	0	0
Robbery	0	0
Aggravated assault	7	9
Non-violent	150	118
Burglary	30	27
Larceny	98	74
Vehicle theft	22	17
Domestic violence	13	61
Arson	2	2
Total crime rate	14.4	11.5
Violent	0.6	0.8
Non-violent	13.7	10.7

Public School District
(for school year 2007-08 except as noted)

Southampton Township School District
177 Main Street
Southampton, NJ 08088
(609) 859-2256
Superintendent	Michael Harris
Number of schools	3
Grade plan	K-8
Enrollment	796
Attendance rate, '06-07	93.3%
Dropout rate	NA
Students per teacher	9.8
Per pupil expenditure	$14,148
Median faculty salary	$68,413
Median administrator salary	$102,778
Grade 12 enrollment	NA
High school graduation rate	NA

Assessment test results
(percent scoring at proficient or advanced level)
	Language	Math
NJASK-Grade 3	93.3%	88.9%
GEPA-Grade 8	71.6%	87.3%
HSPA-High School	NA	NA

SAT Score Averages, 2006-07
Pct tested	Math	Verbal	Writing
NA	NA	NA	NA

Teacher Qualifications
Avg. years of experience	19

Highly-qualified teachers
one subject/all subjects	100%/100%

No Child Left Behind
AYP, 2006-07	Meets Standards

Municipal Finance
State Aid Programs, 2009
Total aid	$1,618,089
CMPTRA	25,073
Energy tax receipts	1,412,405
Garden State Trust	6,345

General Budget, 2008
Total tax levy	$24,836,094
County levy	5,162,864
County taxes	4,239,787
County library	391,464
County health	0
County open space	531,614
School levy	16,855,642
Muni. levy	2,817,588
Misc. revenues	4,537,988

Taxes	2006	2007	2008
General tax rate per $100	3.189	3.239	3.270
County equalization ratio	66.15	59.88	57.15
Net valuation taxable	$723,094,700	$748,341,530	$759,599,706
State equalized value	$1,209,777,711	$1,307,869,107	$1,369,249,943

* US Census Bureau
** New Jersey Department of Labor

See Introduction for an explanation of all data sources.

Demographics & Socio-Economic Characteristics
(2000 US Census, except as noted)

Population
1980*	13,333
1990*	15,157
2000	18,080
Male	8,915
Female	9,165
2007 (estimate)*	19,198
Population density	513.5

Race & Hispanic Origin, 2000
Race
White	17,481
Black/African American	52
American Indian/Alaska Native	12
Asian	252
Native Hawaiian/Pacific Islander	5
Other race	81
Two or more races	197
Hispanic origin, total	459
Mexican	81
Puerto Rican	106
Cuban	55
Other Hispanic	217

Age & Nativity, 2000
Under 5 years	1,381
18 years and over	12,544
21 years and over	12,108
65 years and over	1,491
85 years and over	179
Median age	37.8
Native-born	16,841
Foreign-born	1,266

Educational Attainment, 2000
Population 25 years and over	11,764
Less than 9th grade	1.7%
High school grad or higher	94.8%
Bachelor's degree or higher	50.2%
Graduate degree	17.6%

Income & Poverty, 1999
Per capita income	$36,910
Median household income	$89,835
Median family income	$100,658
Persons in poverty	279
H'holds receiving public assistance	29
H'holds receiving social security	1,226

Households, 2000
Total households	6,225
With persons under 18	2,851
With persons over 65	1,120
Family households	5,032
Single-person households	1,005
Persons per household	2.90
Persons per family	3.28

Labor & Employment
Total civilian labor force, 2007**	10,314
Unemployment rate	2.7%
Total civilian labor force, 2000	9,248
Unemployment rate	2.2%

Employed persons 16 years and over by occupation, 2000
Managers & professionals	4,520
Service occupations	760
Sales & office occupations	2,541
Farming, fishing & forestry	0
Construction & maintenance	539
Production & transportation	681
Self-employed persons	543

* US Census Bureau
** New Jersey Department of Labor

See Introduction for an explanation of all data sources.

General Information
Township of Sparta
65 Main St
Sparta, NJ 07871
973-729-4493

Website	spartanj.net
Year of incorporation	1845
Land/water area (sq. miles)	37.39/1.83
Form of government	Council-Manager

Government
Legislative Districts
US Congressional	5, 11
State Legislative	24

Local Officials, 2009
Mayor	Brian Brady
Manager	Henry Underhill
Clerk	Mary J. Coe
Finance Dir	Michael Guerino
Tax Assessor	Joseph Ferraris
Tax Collector	Lorraine Markey
Attorney	Clark Laddey
Building	Jan Opt'Hof
Comm Dev/Planning	NA
Engineering	Charles Ryan
Public Works	NA
Police Chief	Ernest Reigstad
Emerg/Fire Director	John Thieka

Housing & Construction
Housing Units, 2000*
Total	6,590
Median rent	$777
Median SF home value	$222,700

Permits for New Residential Construction
	Units	Value
Total, 2006	105	$25,272,693
Single family	71	$18,656,693
Total, 2007	71	$14,215,841
Single family	52	$12,279,841

Real Property Valuation, 2008
	Parcels	Valuation
Total	8,372	$2,421,704,200
Vacant	976	69,057,500
Residential	6,859	2,132,373,400
Commercial	270	162,124,600
Industrial	45	34,483,600
Apartments	3	4,700,400
Farm land	171	929,100
Farm homestead	48	18,035,600

Average Property Value & Tax, 2008
Residential value	$311,338
Property tax	$9,290
Tax credit/rebate	$1,144

Public Library
Sparta Public Library
22 Woodport Rd
Sparta, NJ 07871
973-729-3101

Director................Carol Boutilier

Library statistics, 2007
Population served	18,080
Full-time/total staff	2/9

	Total	Per capita
Holdings	73,987	4.09
Revenues	$1,219,740	$67.46
Expenditures	$1,059,745	$58.61
Annual visits	213,412	11.80
Internet terminals/annual users	11/20,587	

Public Safety
Number of officers, 2007	40

Crime	2006	2007
Total crimes	111	101
Violent	2	5
Murder	1	0
Rape	0	0
Robbery	1	0
Aggravated assault	0	5
Non-violent	109	96
Burglary	15	9
Larceny	93	85
Vehicle theft	1	2
Domestic violence	74	64
Arson	0	0
Total crime rate	5.7	5.2
Violent	0.1	0.3
Non-violent	5.6	5.0

Public School District
(for school year 2007-08 except as noted)

Sparta Township School District
18 Mohawk Avenue
Sparta, NJ 07871
(973) 729-7886

Chief School Admin	J. Thomas Morton
Number of schools	5
Grade plan	K-12
Enrollment	4,046
Attendance rate, '06-07	94.9%
Dropout rate	0.4%
Students per teacher	12.1
Per pupil expenditure	$12,279
Median faculty salary	$61,570
Median administrator salary	$110,352
Grade 12 enrollment	272
High school graduation rate	99.3%

Assessment test results
(percent scoring at proficient or advanced level)
	Language	Math
NJASK-Grade 3	96.8%	94.3%
GEPA-Grade 8	83.2%	94.1%
HSPA-High School	93.2%	95.7%

SAT Score Averages, 2006-07
Pct tested	Math	Verbal	Writing
101%	540	535	526

Teacher Qualifications
Avg. years of experience	8
Highly-qualified teachers one subject/all subjects	100%/100%

No Child Left Behind
AYP, 2006-07	Meets Standards

Municipal Finance
State Aid Programs, 2009
Total aid	$1,663,829
CMPTRA	347,800
Energy tax receipts	1,205,212
Garden State Trust	38,643

General Budget, 2008
Total tax levy	$72,411,626
County levy	13,229,663
County taxes	11,946,600
County library	0
County health	354,077
County open space	928,986
School levy	44,845,153
Muni. levy	14,336,810
Misc. revenues	9,615,649

Taxes	2006	2007	2008
General tax rate per $100	2.78	2.87	2.984
County equalization ratio	75.31	68.29	65.45
Net valuation taxable	$2,355,745,200	$2,387,667,824	$2,426,757,347
State equalized value	$3,455,443,872	$3,645,359,933	$3,729,605,900

Demographics & Socio-Economic Characteristics

(2000 US Census, except as noted)

Population

1980*	7,840
1990*	7,983
2000	7,880
Male	3,810
Female	4,070
2007 (estimate)*	8,153
Population density	3,514.2

Race & Hispanic Origin, 2000

Race
White	7,391
Black/African American	122
American Indian/Alaska Native	6
Asian	230
Native Hawaiian/Pacific Islander	1
Other race	58
Two or more races	72
Hispanic origin, total	345
Mexican	13
Puerto Rican	138
Cuban	55
Other Hispanic	139

Age & Nativity, 2000

Under 5 years	472
18 years and over	6,117
21 years and over	5,876
65 years and over	1,369
85 years and over	117
Median age	39.7
Native-born	7,259
Foreign-born	621

Educational Attainment, 2000

Population 25 years and over	5,650
Less than 9th grade	4.7%
High school grad or higher	83.2%
Bachelor's degree or higher	18.1%
Graduate degree	4.0%

Income & Poverty, 1999

Per capita income	$25,247
Median household income	$55,833
Median family income	$73,062
Persons in poverty	336
H'holds receiving public assistance	44
H'holds receiving social security	1,091

Households, 2000

Total households	3,099
With persons under 18	985
With persons over 65	1,047
Family households	2,163
Single-person households	821
Persons per household	2.54
Persons per family	3.10

Labor & Employment

Total civilian labor force, 2007**	4,523
Unemployment rate	3.5%
Total civilian labor force, 2000	4,146
Unemployment rate	3.6%

Employed persons 16 years and over by occupation, 2000
Managers & professionals	1,112
Service occupations	452
Sales & office occupations	1,246
Farming, fishing & forestry	0
Construction & maintenance	530
Production & transportation	656
Self-employed persons	147

General Information

Borough of Spotswood
77 Summerhill Rd
Spotswood, NJ 08884
732-251-0700

Website	www.spotswoodboro.com
Year of incorporation	1908
Land/water area (sq. miles)	2.32/0.17
Form of government	Mayor-Council

Government

Legislative Districts

US Congressional	12
State Legislative	18

Local Officials, 2009

Mayor	Thomas W. Barlow
Manager	Ronald Fasanello
Clerk	Patricia DeStefano
Finance Dir	Barbara Petren
Tax Assessor	Patricia Williams
Tax Collector	Sandra Conover
Attorney	Patrick J. Diegnan Jr
Building	Bob Simonelli
Comm Dev/Planning	NA
Engineering	CME Associates
Public Works	Jean Paul Mayer
Police Chief	Karl Martin
Fire Chief	Kevin Meade

Housing & Construction

Housing Units, 2000*

Total	3,158
Median rent	$704
Median SF home value	$155,100

Permits for New Residential Construction

	Units	Value
Total, 2006	14	$2,273,026
Single family	14	$2,273,026
Total, 2007	16	$2,544,064
Single family	16	$2,544,064

Real Property Valuation, 2008

	Parcels	Valuation
Total	2,844	$749,537,600
Vacant	254	8,591,300
Residential	2,525	639,963,800
Commercial	57	63,240,900
Industrial	5	30,471,100
Apartments	3	7,270,500
Farm land	0	0
Farm homestead	0	0

Average Property Value & Tax, 2008

Residential value	$253,451
Property tax	$6,562
Tax credit/rebate	$1,090

Public Library

Spotswood Public Library
548 Main St
Spotswood, NJ 08884
732-251-1515

Director	Mary Faith Chmiel

Library statistics, 2007

Population served	7,880
Full-time/total staff	1/2

	Total	Per capita
Holdings	33,393	4.24
Revenues	$307,365	$39.01
Expenditures	$267,453	$33.94
Annual visits	35,095	4.45
Internet terminals/annual users	4/3,765	

Public Safety

Number of officers, 2007	19

Crime	2006	2007
Total crimes	115	106
Violent	5	6
Murder	0	0
Rape	0	0
Robbery	0	0
Aggravated assault	5	6
Non-violent	110	100
Burglary	19	14
Larceny	85	82
Vehicle theft	6	4
Domestic violence	65	42
Arson	1	1
Total crime rate	14.0	13.0
Violent	0.6	0.7
Non-violent	13.4	12.2

Public School District

(for school year 2007-08 except as noted)

Spotswood School District
105 Summerhill Road
Spotswood, NJ 08884
(732) 723-2236

Superintendent	John Krewer
Number of schools	4
Grade plan	K-12
Enrollment	1,763
Attendance rate, '06-07	94.6%
Dropout rate	1.2%
Students per teacher	10.6
Per pupil expenditure	$12,713
Median faculty salary	$49,857
Median administrator salary	$102,878
Grade 12 enrollment	187
High school graduation rate	92.4%

Assessment test results

(percent scoring at proficient or advanced level)
	Language	Math
NJASK-Grade 3	88.4%	86.9%
GEPA-Grade 8	74.2%	89.4%
HSPA-High School	87.2%	90.0%

SAT Score Averages, 2006-07

Pct tested	Math	Verbal	Writing
75%	525	486	485

Teacher Qualifications

Avg. years of experience	8
Highly-qualified teachers one subject/all subjects	99.0%/99.0%

No Child Left Behind

AYP, 2006-07	Meets Standards

Municipal Finance

State Aid Programs, 2009

Total aid	$922,693
CMPTRA	314,785
Energy tax receipts	584,840
Garden State Trust	0

General Budget, 2008

Total tax levy	$19,463,736
County levy	2,678,970
County taxes	2,398,133
County library	0
County health	0
County open space	280,837
School levy	11,219,716
Muni. levy	5,565,050
Misc. revenues	4,147,547

Taxes

	2006	2007	2008
General tax rate per $100	2.29	2.46	2.590
County equalization ratio	98.4	86.22	81.32
Net valuation taxable	$736,841,700	$746,290,022	$751,746,603
State equalized value	$857,431,451	$917,135,643	$947,878,445

* US Census Bureau
** New Jersey Department of Labor

See Introduction for an explanation of all data sources.

Demographics & Socio-Economic Characteristics

(2000 US Census, except as noted)

Population
1980*	4,215
1990*	3,499
2000	3,567
Male	1,650
Female	1,917
2007 (estimate)*	3,509
Population density	2,678.6

Race & Hispanic Origin, 2000
Race
White	3,523
Black/African American	12
American Indian/Alaska Native	0
Asian	10
Native Hawaiian/Pacific Islander	0
Other race	4
Two or more races	18
Hispanic origin, total	26
Mexican	5
Puerto Rican	11
Cuban	4
Other Hispanic	6

Age & Nativity, 2000
Under 5 years	205
18 years and over	2,790
21 years and over	2,725
65 years and over	897
85 years and over	133
Median age	47.7
Native-born	3,499
Foreign-born	68

Educational Attainment, 2000
Population 25 years and over	2,600
Less than 9th grade	0.5%
High school grad or higher	96.5%
Bachelor's degree or higher	59.5%
Graduate degree	26.6%

Income & Poverty, 1999
Per capita income	$59,445
Median household income	$89,885
Median family income	$103,405
Persons in poverty	91
H'holds receiving public assistance	4
H'holds receiving social security	602

Households, 2000
Total households	1,463
With persons under 18	359
With persons over 65	627
Family households	983
Single-person households	431
Persons per household	2.43
Persons per family	3.03

Labor & Employment
Total civilian labor force, 2007**	1,588
Unemployment rate	4.3%
Total civilian labor force, 2000	1,488
Unemployment rate	4.5%

Employed persons 16 years and over by occupation, 2000
Managers & professionals	757
Service occupations	142
Sales & office occupations	421
Farming, fishing & forestry	0
Construction & maintenance	67
Production & transportation	34
Self-employed persons	122

* US Census Bureau
** New Jersey Department of Labor

See Introduction for an explanation of all data sources.

General Information
Borough of Spring Lake
423 Warren Ave
Spring Lake, NJ 07762
732-449-0800

Website	springlakeboro.org
Year of incorporation	1892
Land/water area (sq. miles)	1.31/0.40
Form of government	Borough

Government
Legislative Districts
US Congressional	4
State Legislative	11

Local Officials, 2009
Mayor	Jennifer Naughton
Manager	Barry R. Lewis Jr
Clerk	Jane L. Gillespie
Finance Dir	Susan Schreck
Tax Assessor	Brian Enright
Tax Collector	Susan Schreck
Attorney	Joseph J. Colao Jr
Building	Sandy Ratz
Planning	Birdsall Svcs Group
Engineering	Leon S. Avakian Inc
Public Works	Frank Phillips
Police Chief	Robert Dawson Jr
Emerg/Fire Director	Edward Megill

Housing & Construction
Housing Units, 2000*
Total	1,930
Median rent	$1,420
Median SF home value	$638,200

Permits for New Residential Construction
	Units	Value
Total, 2006	25	$11,862,886
Single family	25	$11,862,886
Total, 2007	22	$9,902,261
Single family	22	$9,902,261

Real Property Valuation, 2008
	Parcels	Valuation
Total	2,042	$3,356,476,700
Vacant	63	68,458,600
Residential	1,876	3,135,610,200
Commercial	101	149,299,200
Industrial	1	599,100
Apartments	1	2,509,600
Farm land	0	0
Farm homestead	0	0

Average Property Value & Tax, 2008
Residential value	$1,671,434
Property tax	$10,783
Tax credit/rebate	$1,315

Public Library
Spring Lake Public Library
1501 3rd Ave
Spring Lake, NJ 07762
732-449-6654

Director	Kateri Quinn

Library statistics, 2007
Population served	3,567
Full-time/total staff	NA/0

	Total	Per capita
Holdings	0	NA
Revenues	$0	NA
Expenditures	$0	NA
Annual visits	NA	NA
Internet terminals/annual users	NA/NA	

Public Safety
Number of officers, 2007	14

Crime	2006	2007
Total crimes	80	83
Violent	0	3
Murder	0	0
Rape	0	1
Robbery	0	0
Aggravated assault	0	2
Non-violent	80	80
Burglary	5	9
Larceny	68	71
Vehicle theft	7	0
Domestic violence	7	1
Arson	0	0
Total crime rate	22.8	23.9
Violent	0.0	0.9
Non-violent	22.8	23.0

Public School District
(for school year 2007-08 except as noted)

Spring Lake School District
411 Tuttle Avenue
Spring Lake, NJ 07762
(732) 449-6380

Superintendent	Patricia Wright
Number of schools	1
Grade plan	K-8
Enrollment	254
Attendance rate, '06-07	94.5%
Dropout rate	NA
Students per teacher	9.9
Per pupil expenditure	$21,372
Median faculty salary	$51,330
Median administrator salary	$104,453
Grade 12 enrollment	NA
High school graduation rate	NA

Assessment test results
(percent scoring at proficient or advanced level)
	Language	Math
NJASK-Grade 3	100.0%	97.0%
GEPA-Grade 8	100.0%	100.0%
HSPA-High School	NA	NA

SAT Score Averages, 2006-07
Pct tested	Math	Verbal	Writing
NA	NA	NA	NA

Teacher Qualifications
Avg. years of experience	11
Highly-qualified teachers one subject/all subjects	100%/100%

No Child Left Behind
AYP, 2006-07	Meets Standards

Municipal Finance
State Aid Programs, 2009
Total aid	$349,217
CMPTRA	0
Energy tax receipts	331,756
Garden State Trust	0

General Budget, 2008
Total tax levy	$21,682,091
County levy	8,481,463
County taxes	7,951,219
County library	0
County health	0
County open space	530,245
School levy	6,471,773
Muni. levy	6,728,855
Misc. revenues	3,371,122

Taxes
	2006	2007	2008
General tax rate per $100	0.622	0.644	0.646
County equalization ratio	106.67	101.02	95.42
Net valuation taxable	$3,313,985,400	$3,336,991,589	$3,360,843,961
State equalized value	$3,284,457,843	$3,496,974,483	$1,158,427,429

Demographics & Socio-Economic Characteristics
(2000 US Census, except as noted)

Population
1980*	5,424
1990*	5,341
2000	5,227
Male	2,346
Female	2,881
2007 (estimate)*	5,136
Population density	3,890.9

Race & Hispanic Origin, 2000
Race
White	5,085
Black/African American	58
American Indian/Alaska Native	1
Asian	19
Native Hawaiian/Pacific Islander	1
Other race	35
Two or more races	28
Hispanic origin, total	111
Mexican	15
Puerto Rican	29
Cuban	16
Other Hispanic	51

Age & Nativity, 2000
Under 5 years	215
18 years and over	4,347
21 years and over	4,239
65 years and over	1,545
85 years and over	210
Median age	48.3
Native-born	5,021
Foreign-born	206

Educational Attainment, 2000
Population 25 years and over	4,079
Less than 9th grade	4.1%
High school grad or higher	89.4%
Bachelor's degree or higher	38.5%
Graduate degree	12.0%

Income & Poverty, 1999
Per capita income	$35,093
Median household income	$51,330
Median family income	$64,345
Persons in poverty	392
H'holds receiving public assistance	19
H'holds receiving social security	1,088

Households, 2000
Total households	2,511
With persons under 18	472
With persons over 65	1,115
Family households	1,359
Single-person households	1,048
Persons per household	2.04
Persons per family	2.82

Labor & Employment
Total civilian labor force, 2007**	2,391
Unemployment rate	2.9%
Total civilian labor force, 2000	2,337
Unemployment rate	7.2%

Employed persons 16 years and over by occupation, 2000
Managers & professionals	977
Service occupations	341
Sales & office occupations	631
Farming, fishing & forestry	0
Construction & maintenance	101
Production & transportation	119
Self-employed persons	213

General Information
Borough of Spring Lake Heights
555 Brighton Ave
Spring Lake Heights, NJ 07762
732-449-3500

Website	www.springlakehts.com
Year of incorporation	1927
Land/water area (sq. miles)	1.32/0.02
Form of government	Borough

Government

Legislative Districts
US Congressional	4
State Legislative	11

Local Officials, 2009
Mayor	H. Frances Enright
Manager	Theresa Casagrande
Clerk	Theresa Casagrande
Finance Dir	Colleen Lapp
Tax Assessor	Mitchell Elias
Tax Collector	Mary Grace Neuhaus
Attorney	Fred Raffetto
Building	Sandy Ratz
Comm Dev/Planning	NA
Engineering	Peter Avakian
Public Works	Art Herner
Police Chief	Mark Steets
Emerg/Fire Director	Eric Bennett

Housing & Construction

Housing Units, 2000*
Total	2,950
Median rent	$877
Median SF home value	$218,600

Permits for New Residential Construction
	Units	Value
Total, 2006	23	$3,648,647
Single family	23	$3,648,647
Total, 2007	20	$6,904,481
Single family	20	$6,904,481

Real Property Valuation, 2008
	Parcels	Valuation
Total	2,262	$1,158,175,200
Vacant	43	9,799,200
Residential	2,129	968,851,300
Commercial	81	118,763,100
Industrial	0	0
Apartments	9	60,761,600
Farm land	0	0
Farm homestead	0	0

Average Property Value & Tax, 2008
Residential value	$455,073
Property tax	$5,357
Tax credit/rebate	$1,010

Public Library
No public municipal library

Library statistics, 2007
Population served	NA
Full-time/total staff	NA/NA

	Total	Per capita
Holdings	NA	NA
Revenues	NA	NA
Expenditures	NA	NA
Annual visits	NA	NA
Internet terminals/annual users	NA/NA	

Public Safety
Number of officers, 2007	12

Crime	2006	2007
Total crimes	34	20
Violent	2	2
Murder	0	0
Rape	0	0
Robbery	0	0
Aggravated assault	2	2
Non-violent	32	18
Burglary	5	1
Larceny	26	17
Vehicle theft	1	0
Domestic violence	11	7
Arson	0	0
Total crime rate	6.6	3.9
Violent	0.4	0.4
Non-violent	6.2	3.5

Public School District
(for school year 2007-08 except as noted)

Spring Lake Heights Borough School Dist.
1110 Highway #71
Spring Lake Heights, NJ 07762
(732) 449-6149

Superintendent	Ruth Ziznewski
Number of schools	1
Grade plan	K-8
Enrollment	335
Attendance rate, '06-07	95.2%
Dropout rate	NA
Students per teacher	9.5
Per pupil expenditure	$12,924
Median faculty salary	$51,377
Median administrator salary	$84,500
Grade 12 enrollment	NA
High school graduation rate	NA

Assessment test results
(percent scoring at proficient or advanced level)
	Language	Math
NJASK-Grade 3	97.2%	89.2%
GEPA-Grade 8	88.0%	90.0%
HSPA-High School	NA	NA

SAT Score Averages, 2006-07
Pct tested	Math	Verbal	Writing
NA	NA	NA	NA

Teacher Qualifications
Avg. years of experience	10
Highly-qualified teachers one subject/all subjects	100%/100%

No Child Left Behind
AYP, 2006-07	Meets Standards

Municipal Finance

State Aid Programs, 2009
Total aid	$514,851
CMPTRA	27,986
Energy tax receipts	473,994
Garden State Trust	0

General Budget, 2008
Total tax levy	$13,640,194
County levy	3,085,445
County taxes	2,738,089
County library	164,771
County health	0
County open space	182,585
School levy	7,033,141
Muni. levy	3,521,608
Misc. revenues	1,889,008

Taxes	2006	2007	2008
General tax rate per $100	1.739	1.815	1.178
County equalization ratio	68.07	62.32	95.69
Net valuation taxable	$720,269,200	$726,508,381	$1,158,659,018
State equalized value	$1,156,071,713	$1,204,831,962	$3,139,819,093

* US Census Bureau
** New Jersey Department of Labor

See Introduction for an explanation of all data sources.

Demographics & Socio-Economic Characteristics

(2000 US Census, except as noted)

Population

1980*	1,691
1990*	3,028
2000	3,227
Male	1,614
Female	1,613
2007 (estimate)*	3,492
Population density	116.3

Race & Hispanic Origin, 2000

Race

White	2,967
Black/African American	104
American Indian/Alaska Native	10
Asian	85
Native Hawaiian/Pacific Islander	0
Other race	7
Two or more races	54
Hispanic origin, total	57
Mexican	5
Puerto Rican	28
Cuban	4
Other Hispanic	20

Age & Nativity, 2000

Under 5 years	180
18 years and over	2,394
21 years and over	2,310
65 years and over	346
85 years and over	28
Median age	39.3
Native-born	3,015
Foreign-born	212

Educational Attainment, 2000

Population 25 years and over	2,206
Less than 9th grade	3.4%
High school grad or higher	87.3%
Bachelor's degree or higher	26.4%
Graduate degree	8.3%

Income & Poverty, 1999

Per capita income	$29,322
Median household income	$69,268
Median family income	$72,292
Persons in poverty	116
H'holds receiving public assistance	5
H'holds receiving social security	283

Households, 2000

Total households	1,098
With persons under 18	439
With persons over 65	244
Family households	907
Single-person households	146
Persons per household	2.93
Persons per family	3.22

Labor & Employment

Total civilian labor force, 2007**	1,942
Unemployment rate	3.5%
Total civilian labor force, 2000	1,710
Unemployment rate	3.8%

Employed persons 16 years and over by occupation, 2000

Managers & professionals	600
Service occupations	180
Sales & office occupations	530
Farming, fishing & forestry	15
Construction & maintenance	153
Production & transportation	167
Self-employed persons	151

* US Census Bureau
** New Jersey Department of Labor

General Information

Township of Springfield
2159 Jacksonville-Jobstown Rd
PO Box 119
Jobstown, NJ 08041
609-723-2464

Website	www.springfieldtownship.org
Year of incorporation	1688
Land/water area (sq. miles)	30.03/0.01
Form of government	Council-Manager

Government

Legislative Districts

US Congressional	4
State Legislative	8

Local Officials, 2009

Mayor	Denis McDaniel
Manager	J. Paul Keller
Clerk	Patricia Clayton
Finance Dir	Judith Schetler
Tax Assessor	Dennis Bianchini
Tax Collector	Caryn M. Hoyer
Attorney	Dennis McInerney
Building	Tom Casey
Planning	Carl Hintz
Engineering	Jeffrey Richter
Public Works	NA
Police Chief	(vacant)
Fire/Emergency Dir	NA

Housing & Construction

Housing Units, 2000*

Total	1,138
Median rent	$541
Median SF home value	$185,400

Permits for New Residential Construction

	Units	Value
Total, 2006	5	$1,318,246
Single family	5	$1,318,246
Total, 2007	2	$2,124,500
Single family	2	$2,124,500

Real Property Valuation, 2008

	Parcels	Valuation
Total	1,690	$440,123,649
Vacant	106	7,097,900
Residential	1,012	322,260,900
Commercial	80	47,352,780
Industrial	0	0
Apartments	0	0
Farm land	328	9,176,159
Farm homestead	164	54,235,910

Average Property Value & Tax, 2008

Residential value	$320,150
Property tax	$7,096
Tax credit/rebate	$1,156

Public Library

No public municipal library

Library statistics, 2007

Population served	NA
Full-time/total staff	NA/NA

	Total	Per capita
Holdings	NA	NA
Revenues	NA	NA
Expenditures	NA	NA
Annual visits	NA	NA
Internet terminals/annual users	NA/NA	

Public Safety

Number of officers, 2007 ... 9

Crime	2006	2007
Total crimes	76	35
Violent	4	3
Murder	0	0
Rape	0	0
Robbery	2	1
Aggravated assault	2	2
Non-violent	72	32
Burglary	24	6
Larceny	32	19
Vehicle theft	16	7
Domestic violence	10	6
Arson	1	0
Total crime rate	21.4	9.8
Violent	1.1	0.8
Non-violent	20.2	9.0

Public School District

(for school year 2007-08 except as noted)

Springfield Township School District
2146 Jacksonville Road
Jobstown, NJ 08041
(609) 723-2479

Superintendent	Beth Godett
Number of schools	1
Grade plan	K-6
Enrollment	305
Attendance rate, '06-07	95.7%
Dropout rate	NA
Students per teacher	11.2
Per pupil expenditure	$13,631
Median faculty salary	$51,759
Median administrator salary	$82,044
Grade 12 enrollment	NA
High school graduation rate	NA

Assessment test results

(percent scoring at proficient or advanced level)

	Language	Math
NJASK-Grade 3	93.0%	97.6%
GEPA-Grade 8	NA	NA
HSPA-High School	NA	NA

SAT Score Averages, 2006-07

Pct tested	Math	Verbal	Writing
NA	NA	NA	NA

Teacher Qualifications

Avg. years of experience	16
Highly-qualified teachers one subject/all subjects	100%/96.0%

No Child Left Behind

AYP, 2006-07 ... Meets Standards

Municipal Finance

State Aid Programs, 2009

Total aid	$550,259
CMPTRA	28,295
Energy tax receipts	507,980
Garden State Trust	234

General Budget, 2008

Total tax levy	$9,779,782
County levy	1,903,061
County taxes	1,562,788
County library	144,289
County health	0
County open space	195,985
School levy	6,260,298
Muni. levy	1,616,423
Misc. revenues	1,785,978

Taxes

	2006	2007	2008
General tax rate per $100	2.163	2.28	2.217
County equalization ratio	102.34	90.55	90.19
Net valuation taxable	$429,413,029	$434,707,402	$441,218,730
State equalized value	$475,337,530	$481,877,710	$499,028,839

See Introduction for an explanation of all data sources.

Demographics & Socio-Economic Characteristics
(2000 US Census, except as noted)

Population
1980* 13,955
1990* 13,420
2000 14,429
 Male 6,805
 Female 7,624
2007 (estimate)* 14,735
 Population density 2,861.2

Race & Hispanic Origin, 2000
Race
 White 12,946
 Black/African American 537
 American Indian/Alaska Native 3
 Asian 676
 Native Hawaiian/Pacific Islander ... 0
 Other race 139
 Two or more races 128
Hispanic origin, total 597
 Mexican 20
 Puerto Rican 78
 Cuban 48
 Other Hispanic 451

Age & Nativity, 2000
Under 5 years 893
18 years and over 11,463
21 years and over 11,164
65 years and over 2,972
85 years and over 390
 Median age 42.1
Native-born 11,492
Foreign-born 2,937

Educational Attainment, 2000
Population 25 years and over 10,991
Less than 9th grade 3.9%
High school grad or higher 90.3%
Bachelor's degree or higher 46.7%
Graduate degree 16.8%

Income & Poverty, 1999
Per capita income $36,754
Median household income $73,790
Median family income $85,725
Persons in poverty 453
H'holds receiving public assistance . 30
H'holds receiving social security . 1,981

Households, 2000
Total households 6,001
 With persons under 18 1,707
 With persons over 65 2,153
 Family households 4,015
 Single-person households 1,724
 Persons per household 2.40
 Persons per family 2.98

Labor & Employment
Total civilian labor force, 2007** .. 8,007
 Unemployment rate 1.5%
Total civilian labor force, 2000 ... 7,706
 Unemployment rate 1.5%
Employed persons 16 years and over
by occupation, 2000
 Managers & professionals 3,771
 Service occupations 749
 Sales & office occupations 2,095
 Farming, fishing & forestry 8
 Construction & maintenance 438
 Production & transportation 526
Self-employed persons 630

* US Census Bureau
** New Jersey Department of Labor

General Information
Township of Springfield
100 Mountain Ave
Springfield, NJ 07081
973-912-2200

Website .... www.springfield-nj.com
Year of incorporation 1794
Land/water area (sq. miles) 5.15/0.00
Form of government .... Township

Government
Legislative Districts
US Congressional 7
State Legislative 21

Local Officials, 2009
Mayor .... Bart Fraenkel
Manager .... Edward J. Fanning
Clerk .... Kathleen Wisniewski
Treasurer .... Michael Quick
Tax Assessor .... Ed Galente
Tax Collector .... Mary Jo Walsh
Attorney .... Bruce Bergen
Building .... John Risso
Planning .... Bob Michaels
Engineering .... Todd Hay
Public Works .... Ken Homlish
Police Chief .... William Chisholm
Emerg/Fire Director .... James Sanford

Housing & Construction
Housing Units, 2000*
Total 6,204
Median rent $1,018
Median SF home value $250,500

Permits for New Residential Construction
	Units	Value
Total, 2006	136	$6,503,176
Single family	8	$1,655,926
Total, 2007	93	$4,651,075
Single family	7	$1,394,329

Real Property Valuation, 2008
	Parcels	Valuation
Total	5,198	$1,090,452,800
Vacant	81	6,980,600
Residential	4,787	764,113,000
Commercial	244	213,444,900
Industrial	67	50,735,200
Apartments	17	55,145,900
Farm land	2	33,200
Farm homestead	0	0

Average Property Value & Tax, 2008
Residential value $159,623
Property tax $8,763
Tax credit/rebate $1,262

Public Library
Springfield Public Library
66 Mountain Ave
Springfield, NJ 07081
973-376-4930
Director .... Susan Permahos

Library statistics, 2007
Population served 14,429
Full-time/total staff 5/7

	Total	Per capita
Holdings	91,314	6.33
Revenues	$1,107,889	$76.78
Expenditures	$1,026,735	$71.16
Annual visits	107,548	7.45
Internet terminals/annual users	...25/34,372	

Public Safety
Number of officers, 2007 41
Crime	2006	2007
Total crimes	244	251
Violent	17	13
Murder	0	0
Rape	0	2
Robbery	9	6
Aggravated assault	8	5
Non-violent	227	238
Burglary	26	31
Larceny	172	190
Vehicle theft	29	17
Domestic violence	121	102
Arson	10	0
Total crime rate	16.6	17.1
Violent	1.2	0.9
Non-violent	15.4	16.2

Public School District
(for school year 2007-08 except as noted)

Springfield School District
Springfield Public Schools, PO Box 210
Springfield, NJ 07081
(973) 376-1025
Superintendent .... Michael A. Davino
Number of schools 5
Grade plan K-12
Enrollment 2,049
Attendance rate, '06-07 .... 95.0%
Dropout rate 0.4%
Students per teacher 11.4
Per pupil expenditure $14,690
Median faculty salary $55,874
Median administrator salary ... $111,388
Grade 12 enrollment 132
High school graduation rate 99.2%

Assessment test results
(percent scoring at proficient or advanced level)
	Language	Math
NJASK-Grade 3	92.6%	90.5%
GEPA-Grade 8	82.6%	90.9%
HSPA-High School	80.6%	83.7%

SAT Score Averages, 2006-07
Pct tested	Math	Verbal	Writing
93%	528	507	498

Teacher Qualifications
Avg. years of experience 8
Highly-qualified teachers
 one subject/all subjects 100%/100%

No Child Left Behind
AYP, 2006-07 .... Meets Standards

Municipal Finance
State Aid Programs, 2009
Total aid $2,260,610
 CMPTRA 516,683
 Energy tax receipts 1,687,412
 Garden State Trust 0

General Budget, 2008
Total tax levy $59,904,950
 County levy 10,367,560
 County taxes 9,915,274
 County library 0
 County health 0
 County open space 452,286
 School levy 30,968,488
 Muni. levy 18,568,902
 Misc. revenues 7,423,585

Taxes
	2006	2007	2008
General tax rate per $100	5.076	5.236	5.490
County equalization ratio	40.05	39.11	36.44
Net valuation taxable	$1,087,255,800	$1,091,066,500	$1,091,228,331
State equalized value	$2,780,859,175	$2,992,752,222	$3,034,023,932

See Introduction for an explanation of all data sources.

Demographics & Socio-Economic Characteristics
(2000 US Census, except as noted)

Population
1980*	10,385
1990*	13,325
2000	22,532
Male	10,924
Female	11,608
2007 (estimate)*	26,282
Population density	564.8

Race & Hispanic Origin, 2000
Race
White	21,808
Black/African American	166
American Indian/Alaska Native	21
Asian	217
Native Hawaiian/Pacific Islander	7
Other race	114
Two or more races	199
Hispanic origin, total	542
Mexican	88
Puerto Rican	202
Cuban	55
Other Hispanic	197

Age & Nativity, 2000
Under 5 years	1,466
18 years and over	17,180
21 years and over	16,554
65 years and over	4,244
85 years and over	485
Median age	40.3
Native-born	21,533
Foreign-born	984

Educational Attainment, 2000
Population 25 years and over	16,012
Less than 9th grade	2.7%
High school grad or higher	84.9%
Bachelor's degree or higher	18.7%
Graduate degree	4.5%

Income & Poverty, 1999
Per capita income	$25,397
Median household income	$52,269
Median family income	$59,072
Persons in poverty	899
H'holds receiving public assistance	69
H'holds receiving social security	3,156

Households, 2000
Total households	8,535
With persons under 18	2,885
With persons over 65	2,756
Family households	6,433
Single-person households	1,755
Persons per household	2.61
Persons per family	3.01

Labor & Employment
Total civilian labor force, 2007**	12,584
Unemployment rate	3.9%
Total civilian labor force, 2000	10,559
Unemployment rate	4.6%

Employed persons 16 years and over by occupation, 2000
Managers & professionals	3,154
Service occupations	1,613
Sales & office occupations	2,913
Farming, fishing & forestry	35
Construction & maintenance	1,411
Production & transportation	948
Self-employed persons	772

‡ Branch of county library
* US Census Bureau
** New Jersey Department of Labor

General Information
Township of Stafford
260 E Bay Ave
Manahawkin, NJ 08050
609-597-1000
Website	www.twp.stafford.nj.us
Year of incorporation	1750
Land/water area (sq. miles)	46.53/8.29
Form of government	Small Municipality

Government
Legislative Districts
US Congressional	3
State Legislative	9

Local Officials, 2009
Mayor	Carl W. Block
Manager	Paul Shives
Clerk	Bernadette Park
Finance Dir	Douglas Gannon
Tax Assessor	James Mancini
Tax Collector	Margaret Bevilacqua
Attorney	George Gilmore
Building	Robert Gaestel
Planning	Bonnie Flynn
Engineering	John Walsh
Public Works	Ronald Cop
Police Chief	Thomas Conroy
Emerg/Fire Director	Dean Clelland

Housing & Construction
Housing Units, 2000*
Total	11,522
Median rent	$848
Median SF home value	$139,100

Permits for New Residential Construction
	Units	Value
Total, 2006	115	$18,378,006
Single family	115	$18,378,006
Total, 2007	141	$15,109,461
Single family	141	$15,109,461

Real Property Valuation, 2008
	Parcels	Valuation
Total	14,830	$4,284,164,700
Vacant	2,008	158,577,700
Residential	12,377	3,703,660,100
Commercial	420	414,723,900
Industrial	1	1,116,400
Apartments	4	4,965,400
Farm land	16	60,200
Farm homestead	4	1,061,000

Average Property Value & Tax, 2008
Residential value	$299,226
Property tax	$5,275
Tax credit/rebate	$965

Public Library
Stafford Branch Library‡
129 N Main St
Manahawkin, NJ 08050
609-597-3381
Branch Librarian	Sharon Osborn

Library statistics, 2007
see Ocean County profile
for library system statistics

Public Safety
Number of officers, 2007	59

Crime	2006	2007
Total crimes	508	515
Violent	21	22
Murder	4	1
Rape	0	0
Robbery	1	3
Aggravated assault	16	18
Non-violent	487	493
Burglary	42	51
Larceny	420	429
Vehicle theft	25	13
Domestic violence	155	132
Arson	6	0
Total crime rate	19.9	19.9
Violent	0.8	0.9
Non-violent	19.1	19.1

Public School District
(for school year 2007-08 except as noted)

Stafford Township School District
775 E. Bay Avenue
Manahawkin, NJ 08050
(609) 978-5700
Superintendent	Ronald L. Meinders
Number of schools	5
Grade plan	K-6
Enrollment	2,459
Attendance rate, '06-07	95.3%
Dropout rate	NA
Students per teacher	11.1
Per pupil expenditure	$12,829
Median faculty salary	$46,256
Median administrator salary	$82,599
Grade 12 enrollment	NA
High school graduation rate	NA

Assessment test results
(percent scoring at proficient or advanced level)
	Language	Math
NJASK-Grade 3	92.4%	92.1%
GEPA-Grade 8	NA	NA
HSPA-High School	NA	NA

SAT Score Averages, 2006-07
Pct tested	Math	Verbal	Writing
NA	NA	NA	NA

Teacher Qualifications
Avg. years of experience	10
Highly-qualified teachers one subject/all subjects	100%/100%

No Child Left Behind
AYP, 2006-07 .... Meets Standards

Municipal Finance
State Aid Programs, 2009
Total aid	$3,405,915
CMPTRA	0
Energy tax receipts	3,034,524
Garden State Trust	56,100

General Budget, 2008
Total tax levy	$75,628,080
County levy	15,726,126
County taxes	12,968,248
County library	1,524,065
County health	620,506
County open space	613,307
School levy	33,332,992
Muni. levy	26,568,961
Misc. revenues	10,083,997

Taxes	2006	2007	2008
General tax rate per $100	1.625	1.709	1.763
County equalization ratio	98.42	87.04	84.12
Net valuation taxable	$4,195,433,600	$4,250,899,637	$4,289,940,043
State equalized value	$4,826,313,291	$5,052,309,775	$290,543,375

See Introduction for an explanation of all data sources.

Demographics & Socio-Economic Characteristics
(2000 US Census, except as noted)

Population
1980*	3,638
1990*	3,393
2000	3,584
Male	1,700
Female	1,884
2007 (estimate)*	3,592
Population density	1,920.9

Race & Hispanic Origin, 2000
Race
White	3,353
Black/African American	48
American Indian/Alaska Native	2
Asian	55
Native Hawaiian/Pacific Islander	3
Other race	50
Two or more races	73
Hispanic origin, total	145
Mexican	9
Puerto Rican	52
Cuban	5
Other Hispanic	79

Age & Nativity, 2000
Under 5 years	249
18 years and over	2,686
21 years and over	2,588
65 years and over	268
85 years and over	23
Median age	36.8
Native-born	3,338
Foreign-born	183

Educational Attainment, 2000
Population 25 years and over	2,433
Less than 9th grade	0.9%
High school grad or higher	91.8%
Bachelor's degree or higher	32.3%
Graduate degree	7.5%

Income & Poverty, 1999
Per capita income	$27,535
Median household income	$63,059
Median family income	$73,203
Persons in poverty	77
H'holds receiving public assistance	4
H'holds receiving social security	239

Households, 2000
Total households	1,384
With persons under 18	501
With persons over 65	198
Family households	979
Single-person households	317
Persons per household	2.58
Persons per family	3.10

Labor & Employment
Total civilian labor force, 2007**	2,304
Unemployment rate	3.7%
Total civilian labor force, 2000	2,066
Unemployment rate	3.2%

Employed persons 16 years and over by occupation, 2000
Managers & professionals	813
Service occupations	173
Sales & office occupations	693
Farming, fishing & forestry	0
Construction & maintenance	125
Production & transportation	196
Self-employed persons	63

General Information
Borough of Stanhope
77 Main St
Stanhope, NJ 07874
973-347-0159

Email	stanhope@nac.net
Year of incorporation	1904
Land/water area (sq. miles)	1.87/0.34
Form of government	Borough

Government
Legislative Districts
US Congressional	11
State Legislative	24

Local Officials, 2009
Mayor	Diana Kuncken
Manager	Richard Stewart
Clerk	Ellen Horak
Finance Dir	Dana Mooney
Tax Assessor	Maureen Kaman
Tax Collector	Dana Mooney
Attorney	Richard Stein
Building	Thomas Pershouse
Comm Dev/Planning	NA
Engineering	Omland Engineering
Public Works	William Storms
Police Chief	Steven Pittigher
Emerg/Fire Dir	Michael Donahue Sr

Housing & Construction
Housing Units, 2000*
Total	1,419
Median rent	$965
Median SF home value	$151,100

Permits for New Residential Construction
	Units	Value
Total, 2006	3	$770,000
Single family	3	$770,000
Total, 2007	1	$228,500
Single family	1	$228,500

Real Property Valuation, 2008
	Parcels	Valuation
Total	1,598	$431,550,100
Vacant	157	4,543,000
Residential	1,360	395,609,500
Commercial	57	22,010,700
Industrial	4	5,624,300
Apartments	9	3,744,200
Farm land	11	18,400
Farm homestead	0	0

Average Property Value & Tax, 2008
Residential value	$290,889
Property tax	$6,860
Tax credit/rebate	$1,098

Public Library
E. Louise Childs Branch Library‡
21 Sparta Rd
Stanhope, NJ 07874
973-770-1000

Branch Librarian	Victoria Larson

Library statistics, 2007
see Sussex County profile
for library system statistics

Public Safety
Number of officers, 2007	8

Crime	2006	2007
Total crimes	70	52
Violent	4	1
Murder	0	0
Rape	1	1
Robbery	1	0
Aggravated assault	2	0
Non-violent	66	51
Burglary	15	12
Larceny	49	38
Vehicle theft	2	1
Domestic violence	23	34
Arson	0	3
Total crime rate	18.9	14.2
Violent	1.1	0.3
Non-violent	17.8	13.9

Public School District
(for school year 2007-08 except as noted)

Stanhope Borough School District
24 Valley Road
Stanhope, NJ 07874
(973) 347-0008

Superintendent	Art DiBenedetto
Number of schools	1
Grade plan	K-8
Enrollment	396
Attendance rate, '06-07	95.5%
Dropout rate	NA
Students per teacher	10.6
Per pupil expenditure	$11,907
Median faculty salary	$48,460
Median administrator salary	$83,200
Grade 12 enrollment	NA
High school graduation rate	NA

Assessment test results
(percent scoring at proficient or advanced level)
	Language	Math
NJASK-Grade 3	95.2%	92.7%
GEPA-Grade 8	79.7%	86.0%
HSPA-High School	NA	NA

SAT Score Averages, 2006-07
Pct tested	Math	Verbal	Writing
NA	NA	NA	NA

Teacher Qualifications
Avg. years of experience	7
Highly-qualified teachers one subject/all subjects	96.5%/96.5%

No Child Left Behind
AYP, 2006-07	Meets Standards

Municipal Finance
State Aid Programs, 2009
Total aid	$279,878
CMPTRA	102,954
Energy tax receipts	169,305
Garden State Trust	7,231

General Budget, 2008
Total tax levy	$10,188,554
County levy	1,669,804
County taxes	1,401,289
County library	118,108
County health	41,500
County open space	108,906
School levy	5,553,877
Muni. levy	2,964,874
Misc. revenues	1,175,476

Taxes	2006	2007	2008
General tax rate per $100	2.11	2.25	2.359
County equalization ratio	119.68	106.19	100.17
Net valuation taxable	$432,246,200	$432,571,360	$432,035,928
State equalized value	$407,530,051	$431,838,046	$438,074,654

‡ Branch of county library
* US Census Bureau
** New Jersey Department of Labor

See Introduction for an explanation of all data sources.

Demographics & Socio-Economic Characteristics

(2000 US Census, except as noted)

Population

1980*	3,887
1990*	4,253
2000	4,267
Male	2,105
Female	2,162
2007 (estimate)*	4,312
Population density	159.0

Race & Hispanic Origin, 2000

Race

White	4,180
Black/African American	7
American Indian/Alaska Native	9
Asian	20
Native Hawaiian/Pacific Islander	0
Other race	10
Two or more races	41
Hispanic origin, total	89
Mexican	4
Puerto Rican	31
Cuban	7
Other Hispanic	47

Age & Nativity, 2000

Under 5 years	265
18 years and over	3,072
21 years and over	2,909
65 years and over	360
85 years and over	32
Median age	37.2
Native-born	4,127
Foreign-born	140

Educational Attainment, 2000

Population 25 years and over	2,797
Less than 9th grade	2.5%
High school grad or higher	92.2%
Bachelor's degree or higher	27.1%
Graduate degree	8.4%

Income & Poverty, 1999

Per capita income	$24,933
Median household income	$63,750
Median family income	$71,563
Persons in poverty	120
H'holds receiving public assistance	0
H'holds receiving social security	324

Households, 2000

Total households	1,494
With persons under 18	653
With persons over 65	272
Family households	1,155
Single-person households	258
Persons per household	2.85
Persons per family	3.27

Labor & Employment

Total civilian labor force, 2007**	2,650
Unemployment rate	1.6%
Total civilian labor force, 2000	2,373
Unemployment rate	1.3%

Employed persons 16 years and over by occupation, 2000

Managers & professionals	793
Service occupations	236
Sales & office occupations	632
Farming, fishing & forestry	0
Construction & maintenance	387
Production & transportation	294
Self-employed persons	185

* US Census Bureau
** New Jersey Department of Labor

General Information

Stillwater Township
964 Stillwater Rd
Newton, NJ 07860
973-383-9484

Website	www.stillwaternj.us
Year of incorporation	1824
Land/water area (sq. miles)	27.12/1.26
Form of government	Township

Government

Legislative Districts

US Congressional	5
State Legislative	24

Local Officials, 2009

Mayor	William Morrison
Manager	NA
Clerk	Judith Fisher
Finance Dir	Beth Barile
Tax Assessor	Penny Holenstein
Tax Collector	Donna Clouse
Attorney	Lawrence Cohen
Building	Charles O'Connor
Comm Dev/Planning	NA
Engineering	Michael G. Vreeland
Public Works	Keith Whitehead
Police Chief	Anthony Kozlowski
Fire/Emergency Dir	NA

Housing & Construction

Housing Units, 2000*

Total	2,030
Median rent	$760
Median SF home value	$152,400

Permits for New Residential Construction

	Units	Value
Total, 2006	14	$2,596,489
Single family	14	$2,596,489
Total, 2007	12	$1,718,179
Single family	12	$1,718,179

Real Property Valuation, 2008

	Parcels	Valuation
Total	2,485	$248,610,300
Vacant	349	5,767,600
Residential	1,675	205,545,300
Commercial	46	8,930,700
Industrial	1	408,900
Apartments	0	0
Farm land	267	1,351,100
Farm homestead	147	26,606,700

Average Property Value & Tax, 2008

Residential value	$127,416
Property tax	$5,511
Tax credit/rebate	$989

Public Library

No public municipal library

Library statistics, 2007

Population served	NA
Full-time/total staff	NA/NA

	Total	Per capita
Holdings	NA	NA
Revenues	NA	NA
Expenditures	NA	NA
Annual visits	NA	NA
Internet terminals/annual users	NA/NA	

Public Safety

Number of officers, 2007 6

Crime	2006	2007
Total crimes	30	23
Violent	1	3
Murder	0	0
Rape	0	0
Robbery	0	0
Aggravated assault	1	3
Non-violent	29	20
Burglary	2	8
Larceny	24	10
Vehicle theft	3	2
Domestic violence	3	18
Arson	0	0
Total crime rate	6.8	5.2
Violent	0.2	0.7
Non-violent	6.6	4.6

Public School District

(for school year 2007-08 except as noted)

Stillwater Township School District
904 Stillwater Rd, PO Box 12
Stillwater, NJ 07875
(973) 383-6171

Chief School Admin	S. William Shelton
Number of schools	1
Grade plan	K-6
Enrollment	407
Attendance rate, '06-07	95.3%
Dropout rate	NA
Students per teacher	9.7
Per pupil expenditure	$14,492
Median faculty salary	$69,680
Median administrator salary	$102,490
Grade 12 enrollment	NA
High school graduation rate	NA

Assessment test results

(percent scoring at proficient or advanced level)

	Language	Math
NJASK-Grade 3	98.3%	94.9%
GEPA-Grade 8	NA	NA
HSPA-High School	NA	NA

SAT Score Averages, 2006-07

Pct tested	Math	Verbal	Writing
NA	NA	NA	NA

Teacher Qualifications

Avg. years of experience	18
Highly-qualified teachers one subject/all subjects	96.5%/96.5%

No Child Left Behind

AYP, 2006-07 . . . . .Meets Standards

Municipal Finance

State Aid Programs, 2009

Total aid	$445,514
CMPTRA	58,729
Energy tax receipts	290,399
Garden State Trust	106,321

General Budget, 2008

Total tax levy	$10,767,980
County levy	2,230,953
County taxes	1,872,188
County library	157,801
County health	55,425
County open space	145,538
School levy	6,584,105
Muni. levy	1,952,922
Misc. revenues	1,958,838

Taxes

	2006	2007	2008
General tax rate per $100	3.98	4.14	4.326
County equalization ratio	50.13	45.16	42.93
Net valuation taxable	$245,048,300	$247,402,880	$248,950,991
State equalized value	$543,065,869	$575,779,778	$594,107,827

See Introduction for an explanation of all data sources.

Demographics & Socio-Economic Characteristics

(2000 US Census, except as noted)

Population
1980*	643
1990*	629
2000	560
Male	262
Female	298
2007 (estimate)*	551
Population density	1,001.8

Race & Hispanic Origin, 2000
Race
White	552
Black/African American	0
American Indian/Alaska Native	0
Asian	5
Native Hawaiian/Pacific Islander	0
Other race	0
Two or more races	3
Hispanic origin, total	3
Mexican	0
Puerto Rican	0
Cuban	1
Other Hispanic	2

Age & Nativity, 2000
Under 5 years	38
18 years and over	441
21 years and over	432
65 years and over	83
85 years and over	8
Median age	40.6
Native-born	549
Foreign-born	8

Educational Attainment, 2000
Population 25 years and over	415
Less than 9th grade	4.3%
High school grad or higher	86.7%
Bachelor's degree or higher	31.1%
Graduate degree	12.3%

Income & Poverty, 1999
Per capita income	$25,712
Median household income	$51,406
Median family income	$65,000
Persons in poverty	11
H'holds receiving public assistance	5
H'holds receiving social security	77

Households, 2000
Total households	246
With persons under 18	71
With persons over 65	62
Family households	148
Single-person households	75
Persons per household	2.28
Persons per family	2.94

Labor & Employment
Total civilian labor force, 2007**	355
Unemployment rate	0.0%
Total civilian labor force, 2000	318
Unemployment rate	1.3%

Employed persons 16 years and over by occupation, 2000
Managers & professionals	125
Service occupations	30
Sales & office occupations	81
Farming, fishing & forestry	0
Construction & maintenance	29
Production & transportation	49
Self-employed persons	26

* US Census Bureau
** New Jersey Department of Labor

General Information
Borough of Stockton
2 S Main St
PO Box M
Stockton, NJ 08559
609-397-0070
Email	stocktonclerk@aol.com
Year of incorporation	1898
Land/water area (sq. miles)	0.55/0.06
Form of government	Borough

Government
Legislative Districts
US Congressional	12
State Legislative	23

Local Officials, 2009
Mayor	Stephen Giocondo
Manager/Admin	NA
Clerk	Michele Hovan
CFO	Judie A. McGrorey
Tax Assessor	Michelle Trivieno
Tax Collector	Carol Hettman
Attorney	John Bennett
Building	Edward Noval
Comm Dev/Planning	NA
Engineering	Dennis O'Neal
Public Works	NA
Police Chief	NA
Emerg/Fire Director	Paul Steffanelli

Housing & Construction
Housing Units, 2000*
Total	258
Median rent	$850
Median SF home value	$188,500

Permits for New Residential Construction
	Units	Value
Total, 2006	3	$479,037
Single family	3	$479,037
Total, 2007	2	$319,358
Single family	2	$319,358

Real Property Valuation, 2008
	Parcels	Valuation
Total	263	$97,288,800
Vacant	20	3,297,400
Residential	206	77,769,800
Commercial	26	13,969,300
Industrial	1	364,000
Apartments	2	1,018,600
Farm land	6	24,600
Farm homestead	2	845,100

Average Property Value & Tax, 2008
Residential value	$377,956
Property tax	$6,058
Tax credit/rebate	$993

Public Library
No public municipal library

Library statistics, 2007
Population served	NA
Full-time/total staff	NA/NA

	Total	Per capita
Holdings	NA	NA
Revenues	NA	NA
Expenditures	NA	NA
Annual visits	NA	NA
Internet terminals/annual users	NA/NA	

Public Safety
Number of officers, 2007	0

Crime	2006	2007
Total crimes	4	7
Violent	0	0
Murder	0	0
Rape	0	0
Robbery	0	0
Aggravated assault	0	0
Non-violent	4	7
Burglary	2	1
Larceny	2	6
Vehicle theft	0	0
Domestic violence	0	2
Arson	0	0
Total crime rate	7.1	12.6
Violent	0.0	0.0
Non-violent	7.1	12.6

Public School District
(for school year 2007-08 except as noted)

Stockton Borough School District
19 South Main Street
Stockton, NJ 08559
(609) 397-2012
Chief School Admin	Suzanne Ivans
Number of schools	1
Grade plan	K-6
Enrollment	36
Attendance rate, '06-07	94.9%
Dropout rate	NA
Students per teacher	6.4
Per pupil expenditure	$12,077
Median faculty salary	$22,350
Median administrator salary	$57,222
Grade 12 enrollment	NA
High school graduation rate	NA

Assessment test results
(percent scoring at proficient or advanced level)
	Language	Math
NJASK-Grade 3	NA	NA
GEPA-Grade 8	NA	NA
HSPA-High School	NA	NA

SAT Score Averages, 2006-07
Pct tested	Math	Verbal	Writing
NA	NA	NA	NA

Teacher Qualifications
Avg. years of experience	9
Highly-qualified teachers one subject/all subjects	100%/100%

No Child Left Behind
AYP, 2006-07	Meets Standards

Municipal Finance
State Aid Programs, 2009
Total aid	$70,013
CMPTRA	10,281
Energy tax receipts	47,005
Garden State Trust	10,248

General Budget, 2008
Total tax levy	$1,561,820
County levy	301,146
County taxes	252,048
County library	21,888
County health	0
County open space	27,210
School levy	988,225
Muni. levy	272,450
Misc. revenues	291,941

Taxes
	2006	2007	2008
General tax rate per $100	3.31	1.51	1.603
County equalization ratio	48.11	106.44	107.94
Net valuation taxable	$42,319,500	$97,479,529	$97,448,486
State equalized value	$87,730,081	$89,697,921	$91,433,539

See Introduction for an explanation of all data sources.

Demographics & Socio-Economic Characteristics

(2000 US Census, except as noted)

Population

1980*	1,187
1990*	1,025
2000	1,128
Male	518
Female	610
2007 (estimate)*	1,021
Population density	719.0

Race & Hispanic Origin, 2000

Race

White	1,114
Black/African American	9
American Indian/Alaska Native	0
Asian	0
Native Hawaiian/Pacific Islander	0
Other race	2
Two or more races	3
Hispanic origin, total	5
Mexican	0
Puerto Rican	2
Cuban	0
Other Hispanic	3

Age & Nativity, 2000

Under 5 years	27
18 years and over	989
21 years and over	973
65 years and over	437
85 years and over	44
Median age	57.5
Native-born	1,104
Foreign-born	24

Educational Attainment, 2000

Population 25 years and over	954
Less than 9th grade	1.6%
High school grad or higher	93.9%
Bachelor's degree or higher	43.8%
Graduate degree	18.7%

Income & Poverty, 1999

Per capita income	$46,427
Median household income	$51,471
Median family income	$67,250
Persons in poverty	39
H'holds receiving public assistance	5
H'holds receiving social security	291

Households, 2000

Total households	596
With persons under 18	75
With persons over 65	317
Family households	331
Single-person households	240
Persons per household	1.89
Persons per family	2.50

Labor & Employment

Total civilian labor force, 2007**	582
Unemployment rate	4.9%
Total civilian labor force, 2000	486
Unemployment rate	4.9%

Employed persons 16 years and over by occupation, 2000

Managers & professionals	203
Service occupations	61
Sales & office occupations	146
Farming, fishing & forestry	3
Construction & maintenance	27
Production & transportation	22
Self-employed persons	49

General Information

Borough of Stone Harbor
9508 2nd Ave
Stone Harbor, NJ 08247
609-368-5102

Website	www.stone-harbor.nj.us
Year of incorporation	1914
Land/water area (sq. miles)	1.42/0.57
Form of government	Borough

Government

Legislative Districts

US Congressional	2
State Legislative	1

Local Officials, 2009

Mayor	Suzanne Walters
Manager	Kenneth Hawk
Clerk	Suzanne Stanford
Finance Dir	James Nicola
Tax Assessor	Margaret Slavin
Tax Collector	Kathryn McClure
Attorney	Michael Donohue
Building	Michael Koochembere
Comm Dev/Planning	NA
Engineering	Marc DeBlasio
Public Works	Greg Sheeran
Police Chief	William Toland
Emerg/Fire Director	Roger Stanford

Housing & Construction

Housing Units, 2000*

Total	3,428
Median rent	$669
Median SF home value	$445,300

Permits for New Residential Construction

	Units	Value
Total, 2006	32	$15,008,231
Single family	32	$15,008,231
Total, 2007	34	$16,916,872
Single family	34	$16,916,872

Real Property Valuation, 2008

	Parcels	Valuation
Total	3,154	$3,625,851,200
Vacant	71	82,584,700
Residential	2,883	3,421,936,200
Commercial	198	117,897,600
Industrial	0	0
Apartments	2	3,432,700
Farm land	0	0
Farm homestead	0	0

Average Property Value & Tax, 2008

Residential value	$1,186,936
Property tax	$6,248
Tax credit/rebate	$1,076

Public Library

Stone Harbor Branch Library‡
95th & Second Ave
Stone Harbor, NJ 08247
609-368-6809

Branch Librarian .. Geraldine M. Fridmann

Library statistics, 2007

see Cape May County profile
for library system statistics

Public Safety

Number of officers, 2007	16

Crime	2006	2007
Total crimes	48	67
Violent	5	4
Murder	0	0
Rape	1	3
Robbery	0	0
Aggravated assault	4	1
Non-violent	43	63
Burglary	7	25
Larceny	35	35
Vehicle theft	1	3
Domestic violence	4	5
Arson	0	0
Total crime rate	45.2	64.5
Violent	4.7	3.8
Non-violent	40.5	60.6

Public School District

(for school year 2007-08 except as noted)

Stone Harbor School District
275 93rd St.
Stone Harbor, NJ 08247
(609) 368-4413

Principal	David Rauenzahn
Number of schools	1
Grade plan	K-8
Enrollment	84
Attendance rate, '06-07	94.2%
Dropout rate	NA
Students per teacher	6.3
Per pupil expenditure	$18,699
Median faculty salary	$64,472
Median administrator salary	$55,539
Grade 12 enrollment	NA
High school graduation rate	NA

Assessment test results

(percent scoring at proficient or advanced level)

	Language	Math
NJASK-Grade 3	NA	NA
GEPA-Grade 8	NA	NA
HSPA-High School	NA	NA

SAT Score Averages, 2006-07

Pct tested	Math	Verbal	Writing
NA	NA	NA	NA

Teacher Qualifications

Avg. years of experience	19
Highly-qualified teachers one subject/all subjects	100%/100%

No Child Left Behind

AYP, 2006-07	Meets Standards

Municipal Finance

State Aid Programs, 2009

Total aid	$224,416
CMPTRA	0
Energy tax receipts	214,317
Garden State Trust	0

General Budget, 2008

Total tax levy	$19,088,199
County levy	9,146,851
County taxes	7,270,307
County library	1,395,594
County health	0
County open space	480,951
School levy	2,047,988
Muni. levy	7,893,360
Misc. revenues	3,497,515

‡ Branch of county library
* US Census Bureau
** New Jersey Department of Labor

Taxes	2006	2007	2008
General tax rate per $100	0.48	0.51	0.529
County equalization ratio	92.52	77.73	75.63
Net valuation taxable	$3,584,070,000	$3,607,791,890	$3,626,262,310
State equalized value	$4,611,398,898	$4,770,187,175	$4,830,371,414

See Introduction for an explanation of all data sources.

Demographics & Socio-Economic Characteristics
(2000 US Census, except as noted)

Population
1980* 1,365
1990* 1,437
2000 1,429
  Male 703
  Female 726
2007 (estimate)* 1,528
  Population density 82.8

Race & Hispanic Origin, 2000
Race
White 1,335
Black/African American 50
American Indian/Alaska Native 23
Asian 3
Native Hawaiian/Pacific Islander 0
Other race 12
Two or more races 6
Hispanic origin, total 24
  Mexican 2
  Puerto Rican 12
  Cuban 0
  Other Hispanic 10

Age & Nativity, 2000
Under 5 years 74
18 years and over 1,093
21 years and over 1,044
65 years and over 207
85 years and over 12
  Median age 40.7
Native-born 1,405
Foreign-born 29

Educational Attainment, 2000
Population 25 years and over 975
Less than 9th grade 5.9%
High school grad or higher 83.1%
Bachelor's degree or higher 18.9%
Graduate degree 5.8%

Income & Poverty, 1999
Per capita income $20,925
Median household income $52,500
Median family income $58,583
Persons in poverty 96
H'holds receiving public assistance 9
H'holds receiving social security 149

Households, 2000
Total households 536
  With persons under 18 182
  With persons over 65 143
  Family households 425
  Single-person households 96
Persons per household 2.67
Persons per family 3.01

Labor & Employment
Total civilian labor force, 2007** 821
  Unemployment rate 3.6%
Total civilian labor force, 2000 746
  Unemployment rate 4.4%
Employed persons 16 years and over
by occupation, 2000
  Managers & professionals 231
  Service occupations 94
  Sales & office occupations 150
  Farming, fishing & forestry 13
  Construction & maintenance 98
  Production & transportation 127
Self-employed persons 44

General Information
Township of Stow Creek
474 Macanippuck Rd
Bridgeton, NJ 08302
856-451-8822

Website .... (county website)
Year of incorporation 1748
Land/water area (sq. miles) 18.45/0.42
Form of government .... Township

Government

Legislative Districts
US Congressional 2
State Legislative 3

Local Officials, 2009
Mayor .... Dale Cruzan Sr
Manager/Admin .... NA
Clerk .... Bruce Porter
Finance Dir .... Ron Campbell
Tax Assessor .... Donna Harris
Tax Collector .... Roberta DiGiuseppi
Attorney .... Thomas Farnoly
Building .... Robert Young
Comm Dev/Planning .... NA
Engineering .... J. Michael Fralinger
Public Works .... NA
Police Chief .... NA
Emerg/Fire Director .... Max Dilks

Housing & Construction

Housing Units, 2000*
Total 560
Median rent $620
Median SF home value $114,400

Permits for New Residential Construction
	Units	Value
Total, 2006	3	$605,000
Single family	3	$605,000
Total, 2007	0	$0
Single family	0	$0

Real Property Valuation, 2008
	Parcels	Valuation
Total	963	$79,308,200
Vacant	58	1,271,800
Residential	369	45,836,900
Commercial	16	3,212,900
Industrial	0	0
Apartments	0	0
Farm land	344	3,443,100
Farm homestead	176	25,543,500

Average Property Value & Tax, 2008
Residential value $130,973
Property tax $3,660
Tax credit/rebate $860

Public Library
No public municipal library

Library statistics, 2007
Population served .... NA
Full-time/total staff .... NA/NA

	Total	Per capita
Holdings	NA	NA
Revenues	NA	NA
Expenditures	NA	NA
Annual visits	NA	NA
Internet terminals/annual users	NA/NA	

Public Safety
Number of officers, 2007 0

Crime	2006	2007
Total crimes	19	13
Violent	1	1
Murder	0	0
Rape	0	0
Robbery	0	0
Aggravated assault	1	1
Non-violent	18	12
Burglary	11	7
Larceny	7	4
Vehicle theft	0	1
Domestic violence	1	4
Arson	0	0
Total crime rate	12.4	8.5
Violent	0.7	0.7
Non-violent	11.8	7.8

Public School District
(for school year 2007-08 except as noted)

Stow Creek Township School District
11 Gum Tree Corner Road
Bridgeton, NJ 08302
(856) 455-1717

Chief School Admin .... Donna Levick
Number of schools 1
Grade plan K-8
Enrollment 138
Attendance rate, '06-07 .... 95.0%
Dropout rate .... NA
Students per teacher 9.1
Per pupil expenditure $12,440
Median faculty salary $41,718
Median administrator salary $84,977
Grade 12 enrollment .... NA
High school graduation rate .... NA

Assessment test results
(percent scoring at proficient or advanced level)

	Language	Math
NJASK-Grade 3	84.2%	78.9%
GEPA-Grade 8	87.5%	81.3%
HSPA-High School	NA	NA

SAT Score Averages, 2006-07
Pct tested	Math	Verbal	Writing
NA	NA	NA	NA

Teacher Qualifications
Avg. years of experience 8
Highly-qualified teachers
  one subject/all subjects 93.5%/93.5%

No Child Left Behind
AYP, 2006-07 .... Meets Standards

Municipal Finance

State Aid Programs, 2009
Total aid $194,005
  CMPTRA 35,273
  Energy tax receipts 129,244
  Garden State Trust 18,111

General Budget, 2008
Total tax levy $2,231,464
  County levy 836,959
    County taxes 791,217
    County library 0
    County health 36,949
    County open space 8,792
  School levy 1,253,071
  Muni. levy 141,434
  Misc. revenues 661,703

Taxes
Taxes	2006	2007	2008
General tax rate per $100	3.077	3.072	2.798
County equalization ratio	89.28	83.25	91.61
Net valuation taxable	$76,229,100	$78,598,259	$79,845,215
State equalized value	$92,040,413	$85,754,880	$125,668,287

* US Census Bureau
** New Jersey Department of Labor

See Introduction for an explanation of all data sources.

Demographics & Socio-Economic Characteristics

(2000 US Census, except as noted)

Population
1980*	8,005
1990*	7,614
2000	7,271
Male	3,544
Female	3,727
2007 (estimate)*	7,044
Population density	4,458.2

Race & Hispanic Origin, 2000
Race
White	6,439
Black/African American	480
American Indian/Alaska Native	9
Asian	173
Native Hawaiian/Pacific Islander	1
Other race	63
Two or more races	106
Hispanic origin, total	277
Mexican	105
Puerto Rican	92
Cuban	7
Other Hispanic	73

Age & Nativity, 2000
Under 5 years	447
18 years and over	5,476
21 years and over	5,222
65 years and over	1,150
85 years and over	116
Median age	37.7
Native-born	6,885
Foreign-born	386

Educational Attainment, 2000
Population 25 years and over	4,910
Less than 9th grade	4.5%
High school grad or higher	86.3%
Bachelor's degree or higher	20.0%
Graduate degree	4.5%

Income & Poverty, 1999
Per capita income	$21,748
Median household income	$50,977
Median family income	$57,500
Persons in poverty	327
H'holds receiving public assistance	52
H'holds receiving social security	802

Households, 2000
Total households	2,736
With persons under 18	953
With persons over 65	747
Family households	1,907
Single-person households	705
Persons per household	2.61
Persons per family	3.18

Labor & Employment
Total civilian labor force, 2007**	3,859
Unemployment rate	3.8%
Total civilian labor force, 2000	3,660
Unemployment rate	3.7%

Employed persons 16 years and over by occupation, 2000
Managers & professionals	1,288
Service occupations	483
Sales & office occupations	1,181
Farming, fishing & forestry	13
Construction & maintenance	271
Production & transportation	289
Self-employed persons	133

* US Census Bureau
** New Jersey Department of Labor

General Information
Borough of Stratford
307 Union Ave
Stratford, NJ 08084
856-783-0600
Website	www.stratfordnj.org
Year of incorporation	1925
Land/water area (sq. miles)	1.58/0.00
Form of government	Borough

Government
Legislative Districts
US Congressional	1
State Legislative	5

Local Officials, 2009
Mayor	John Gentless
Manager	John Keenan Jr
Clerk	John Keenan Jr
Finance Dir	John Fabritiis
Tax Assessor	Richard Arrowood
Tax Collector	John Fabritiis
Attorney	Jeffrey Baron
Building	Chris Mecca
Planning	John Keenan Jr
Engineering	Joseph Schiavo
Public Works	Andrew Marano
Police Chief	Ronald Morello
Emerg/Fire Director	Stephen Gagliardi

Housing & Construction
Housing Units, 2000*
Total	2,849
Median rent	$594
Median SF home value	$114,000

Permits for New Residential Construction
	Units	Value
Total, 2006	2	$173,900
Single family	2	$173,900
Total, 2007	0	$0
Single family	0	$0

Real Property Valuation, 2008
	Parcels	Valuation
Total	2,268	$286,328,600
Vacant	34	1,102,000
Residential	2,118	223,214,100
Commercial	105	50,293,300
Industrial	0	0
Apartments	11	11,719,200
Farm land	0	0
Farm homestead	0	0

Average Property Value & Tax, 2008
Residential value	$105,389
Property tax	$5,676
Tax credit/rebate	$1,022

Public Library
Stratford Public Library
303 Union Ave
Stratford, NJ 08084
856-783-0602
Director	Ruth C. Roderick

Library statistics, 2007
Population served	7,271
Full-time/total staff	0/0

	Total	Per capita
Holdings	44,296	6.09
Revenues	$178,248	$24.51
Expenditures	$140,892	$19.38
Annual visits	17,259	2.37
Internet terminals/annual users		5/1,094

Public Safety
Number of officers, 2007	15

Crime	2006	2007
Total crimes	223	196
Violent	15	19
Murder	0	0
Rape	1	0
Robbery	7	9
Aggravated assault	7	10
Non-violent	208	177
Burglary	29	28
Larceny	169	137
Vehicle theft	10	12
Domestic violence	82	85
Arson	1	1
Total crime rate	31.0	27.5
Violent	2.1	2.7
Non-violent	29.0	24.9

Public School District
(for school year 2007-08 except as noted)

Stratford Borough School District
111 Warwick Road
Stratford, NJ 08084
(856) 783-2555
Superintendent	Albert K. Brown
Number of schools	2
Grade plan	K-8
Enrollment	828
Attendance rate, '06-07	97.6%
Dropout rate	NA
Students per teacher	11.0
Per pupil expenditure	$12,432
Median faculty salary	$50,485
Median administrator salary	$90,442
Grade 12 enrollment	NA
High school graduation rate	NA

Assessment test results
(percent scoring at proficient or advanced level)
	Language	Math
NJASK-Grade 3	82.5%	85.1%
GEPA-Grade 8	68.5%	84.5%
HSPA-High School	NA	NA

SAT Score Averages, 2006-07
Pct tested	Math	Verbal	Writing
NA	NA	NA	NA

Teacher Qualifications
Avg. years of experience	9
Highly-qualified teachers one subject/all subjects	100%/100%

No Child Left Behind
AYP, 2006-07	Meets Standards

Municipal Finance
State Aid Programs, 2009
Total aid	$907,265
CMPTRA	166,817
Energy tax receipts	722,303
Garden State Trust	0

General Budget, 2008
Total tax levy	$15,449,848
County levy	2,942,200
County taxes	2,842,213
County library	0
County health	0
County open space	99,986
School levy	9,171,589
Muni. levy	3,336,059
Misc. revenues	2,726,851

Taxes
	2006	2007	2008
General tax rate per $100	4.991	5.225	5.386
County equalization ratio	71.02	63.7	57.54
Net valuation taxable	$286,652,500	$286,151,557	$286,862,521
State equalized value	$450,631,471	$496,890,779	$509,020,158

See Introduction for an explanation of all data sources.

Demographics & Socio-Economic Characteristics

(2000 US Census, except as noted)

Population
1980*	21,071
1990*	19,757
2000	21,131
Male	10,225
Female	10,906
2007 (estimate)*	20,700
Population density	3,421.5

Race & Hispanic Origin, 2000
Race
White	18,546
Black/African American	914
American Indian/Alaska Native	19
Asian	941
Native Hawaiian/Pacific Islander	3
Other race	360
Two or more races	348
Hispanic origin, total	2,150
Mexican	162
Puerto Rican	207
Cuban	159
Other Hispanic	1,622

Age & Nativity, 2000
Under 5 years	1,815
18 years and over	15,434
21 years and over	15,071
65 years and over	2,769
85 years and over	349
Median age	37.3
Native-born	17,262
Foreign-born	3,869

Educational Attainment, 2000
Population 25 years and over	14,517
Less than 9th grade	2.8%
High school grad or higher	92.4%
Bachelor's degree or higher	61.6%
Graduate degree	30.0%

Income & Poverty, 1999
Per capita income	$62,598
Median household income	$92,964
Median family income	$117,053
Persons in poverty	895
H'holds receiving public assistance	74
H'holds receiving social security	1,985

Households, 2000
Total households	7,897
With persons under 18	2,908
With persons over 65	2,054
Family households	5,610
Single-person households	1,887
Persons per household	2.67
Persons per family	3.18

Labor & Employment
Total civilian labor force, 2007**	10,885
Unemployment rate	2.3%
Total civilian labor force, 2000	10,473
Unemployment rate	2.5%

Employed persons 16 years and over by occupation, 2000
Managers & professionals	5,983
Service occupations	1,079
Sales & office occupations	2,287
Farming, fishing & forestry	11
Construction & maintenance	358
Production & transportation	498
Self-employed persons	761

* US Census Bureau
** New Jersey Department of Labor

General Information
City of Summit
512 Springfield Ave
Summit, NJ 07901
908-273-6400
Website	www.cityofsummit.org
Year of incorporation	1899
Land/water area (sq. miles)	6.05/0.02
Form of government	City

Government
Legislative Districts
US Congressional	7
State Legislative	21

Local Officials, 2009
Mayor	Jordan Glatt
Manager	Christopher Cotter
Clerk	David Hughes
Finance Dir	Ronald Angelo
Tax Assessor	(vacant)
Tax Collector	(vacant)
Attorney	Barry Osmun
Building	Tony Doyle
Comm Dev/Planning	NA
Engineering	Andy Hipolit
Public Works	Paul Cascais
Police Chief	Robert Lucid
Emerg/Fire Director	Joe Houck

Housing & Construction
Housing Units, 2000*
Total	8,146
Median rent	$1,078
Median SF home value	$469,200

Permits for New Residential Construction
	Units	Value
Total, 2006	9	$2,062,155
Single family	9	$2,062,155
Total, 2007	12	$5,141,850
Single family	12	$5,141,850

Real Property Valuation, 2008
	Parcels	Valuation
Total	6,679	$3,140,283,475
Vacant	102	12,135,200
Residential	6,143	2,513,876,375
Commercial	380	312,300,700
Industrial	9	238,271,000
Apartments	45	63,700,200
Farm land	0	0
Farm homestead	0	0

Average Property Value & Tax, 2008
Residential value	$409,226
Property tax	$14,054
Tax credit/rebate	$1,203

Public Library
Summit Free Public Library
75 Maple St
Summit, NJ 07901
908-273-0350
Director	Glenn E. Devitt

Library statistics, 2007
Population served	21,131
Full-time/total staff	8/18

	Total	Per capita
Holdings	124,203	5.88
Revenues	$2,471,453	$116.96
Expenditures	$2,411,878	$114.14
Annual visits	230,700	10.92
Internet terminals/annual users		39/31,492

Public Safety
Number of officers, 2007		48
Crime	**2006**	**2007**
Total crimes	253	296
Violent	8	10
Murder	0	0
Rape	2	0
Robbery	2	4
Aggravated assault	4	6
Non-violent	245	286
Burglary	18	14
Larceny	215	260
Vehicle theft	12	12
Domestic violence	173	145
Arson	0	0
Total crime rate	11.9	14.0
Violent	0.4	0.5
Non-violent	11.6	13.6

Public School District
(for school year 2007-08 except as noted)

Summit City School District
14 Beekman Terrace
Summit, NJ 07901
(908) 918-2100
Superintendent	Nathan Parker
Number of schools	7
Grade plan	K-12
Enrollment	3,800
Attendance rate, '06-07	95.8%
Dropout rate	0.8%
Students per teacher	10.5
Per pupil expenditure	$14,248
Median faculty salary	$61,948
Median administrator salary	$127,298
Grade 12 enrollment	243
High school graduation rate	98.8%

Assessment test results
(percent scoring at proficient or advanced level)
	Language	Math
NJASK-Grade 3	95.7%	94.6%
GEPA-Grade 8	87.7%	93.9%
HSPA-High School	91.5%	94.6%

SAT Score Averages, 2006-07
Pct tested	Math	Verbal	Writing
96%	588	573	579

Teacher Qualifications
Avg. years of experience	9
Highly-qualified teachers one subject/all subjects	100%/100%

No Child Left Behind
AYP, 2006-07	Meets Standards

Municipal Finance
State Aid Programs, 2009
Total aid	$3,900,507
CMPTRA	0
Energy tax receipts	3,744,487
Garden State Trust	0

General Budget, 2008
Total tax levy	$107,946,163
County levy	24,846,419
County taxes	23,740,722
County library	0
County health	0
County open space	1,105,697
School levy	56,965,534
Muni. levy	26,134,210
Misc. revenues	15,671,701

Taxes
Taxes	2006	2007	2008
General tax rate per $100	3.102	3.306	3.435
County equalization ratio	46.81	44.02	42.79
Net valuation taxable	$3,089,282,100	$3,123,755,824	$3,143,273,737
State equalized value	$7,021,561,142	$7,296,213,486	$8,096,504,373

See Introduction for an explanation of all data sources.

Demographics & Socio-Economic Characteristics
(2000 US Census, except as noted)

Population
1980*	1,571
1990*	1,375
2000	1,442
Male	685
Female	757
2007 (estimate)*	1,549
Population density	2,151.4

Race & Hispanic Origin, 2000
Race
White	1,414
Black/African American	2
American Indian/Alaska Native	3
Asian	5
Native Hawaiian/Pacific Islander	6
Other race	8
Two or more races	4
Hispanic origin, total	28
Mexican	15
Puerto Rican	1
Cuban	1
Other Hispanic	11

Age & Nativity, 2000
Under 5 years	39
18 years and over	1,263
21 years and over	1,230
65 years and over	492
85 years and over	58
Median age	53.4
Native-born	1,385
Foreign-born	46

Educational Attainment, 2000
Population 25 years and over	1,202
Less than 9th grade	3.2%
High school grad or higher	87.5%
Bachelor's degree or higher	26.0%
Graduate degree	6.4%

Income & Poverty, 1999
Per capita income	$26,632
Median household income	$38,190
Median family income	$50,268
Persons in poverty	107
H'holds receiving public assistance	2
H'holds receiving social security	352

Households, 2000
Total households	706
With persons under 18	102
With persons over 65	343
Family households	421
Single-person households	246
Persons per household	2.04
Persons per family	2.61

Labor & Employment
Total civilian labor force, 2007**	736
Unemployment rate	4.5%
Total civilian labor force, 2000	615
Unemployment rate	4.2%

Employed persons 16 years and over by occupation, 2000
Managers & professionals	191
Service occupations	91
Sales & office occupations	209
Farming, fishing & forestry	5
Construction & maintenance	45
Production & transportation	48
Self-employed persons	77

‡ Branch of county library
* US Census Bureau
** New Jersey Department of Labor

General Information
Borough of Surf City
813 Long Beach Blvd
Surf City, NJ 08008
609-494-3064

Website	NA
Year of incorporation	1899
Land/water area (sq. miles)	0.72/0.20
Form of government	Borough

Government
Legislative Districts
US Congressional	3
State Legislative	9

Local Officials, 2009
Mayor	Leonard Connors Jr
Manager	Mary Madonna
Clerk	Mary Madonna
Finance Dir	David Pawlishak
Tax Assessor	William Procacci
Tax Collector	Grace T. DeGennaro
Attorney	Christopher Connors
Building	Frank Zappavigna
Comm Dev/Planning	NA
Engineering	Frank Little
Public Works	Edward Berg
Police Chief	William Collins
Emerg/Fire Director	B. Stasik

Housing & Construction
Housing Units, 2000*
Total	2,621
Median rent	$738
Median SF home value	$230,200

Permits for New Residential Construction
	Units	Value
Total, 2006	19	$7,188,530
Single family	19	$7,188,530
Total, 2007	21	$7,462,775
Single family	21	$7,462,775

Real Property Valuation, 2008
	Parcels	Valuation
Total	2,247	$1,506,164,800
Vacant	32	13,625,900
Residential	2,121	1,410,648,800
Commercial	94	81,890,100
Industrial	0	0
Apartments	0	0
Farm land	0	0
Farm homestead	0	0

Average Property Value & Tax, 2008
Residential value	$665,087
Property tax	$5,825
Tax credit/rebate	$1,104

Public Library
Long Beach Island Branch Library‡
217 S Central Ave
Surf City, NJ 08008
609-494-2480

Branch Librarian	Linda Feaster

Library statistics, 2007
see Ocean County profile
for library system statistics

Public Safety
Number of officers, 2007		11
Crime	**2006**	**2007**
Total crimes	42	50
Violent	1	1
Murder	0	0
Rape	0	1
Robbery	1	0
Aggravated assault	0	0
Non-violent	41	49
Burglary	3	8
Larceny	37	39
Vehicle theft	1	2
Domestic violence	3	1
Arson	0	0
Total crime rate	27.5	32.4
Violent	0.7	0.6
Non-violent	26.9	31.8

Public School District
(for school year 2007-08 except as noted)

Long Beach Island School District
200 Barnegat Avenue
Surf City, NJ 08008
(609) 494-2341

Superintendent	Robert A. Garguilo
Number of schools	2
Grade plan	K-6
Enrollment	258
Attendance rate, '06-07	94.0%
Dropout rate	NA
Students per teacher	7.1
Per pupil expenditure	$23,574
Median faculty salary	$71,027
Median administrator salary	$95,218
Grade 12 enrollment	NA
High school graduation rate	NA

Assessment test results
(percent scoring at proficient or advanced level)
	Language	Math
NJASK-Grade 3	96.9%	90.6%
GEPA-Grade 8	NA	NA
HSPA-High School	NA	NA

SAT Score Averages, 2006-07
Pct tested	Math	Verbal	Writing
NA	NA	NA	NA

Teacher Qualifications
Avg. years of experience	19
Highly-qualified teachers one subject/all subjects	100%/100%

No Child Left Behind
AYP, 2006-07	Meets Standards

Municipal Finance
State Aid Programs, 2009
Total aid	$181,006
CMPTRA	0
Energy tax receipts	172,861
Garden State Trust	0

General Budget, 2008
Total tax levy	$13,202,468
County levy	5,347,872
County taxes	4,591,175
County library	539,566
County health	0
County open space	217,131
School levy	4,378,596
Muni. levy	3,476,000
Misc. revenues	2,240,000

Taxes
	2006	2007	2008
General tax rate per $100	0.812	0.871	0.876
County equalization ratio	96.09	85.1	83.49
Net valuation taxable	$1,470,594,800	$1,491,669,073	$1,507,459,378
State equalized value	$1,729,514,169	$1,786,391,438	$5,105,364,321

See Introduction for an explanation of all data sources.

Demographics & Socio-Economic Characteristics
(2000 US Census, except as noted)

Population
1980*	2,418
1990*	2,201
2000	2,145
Male	1,025
Female	1,120
2007 (estimate)*	2,144
Population density	3,573.3

Race & Hispanic Origin, 2000
Race
White	2,066
Black/African American	24
American Indian/Alaska Native	2
Asian	26
Native Hawaiian/Pacific Islander	0
Other race	8
Two or more races	19
Hispanic origin, total	55
Mexican	6
Puerto Rican	28
Cuban	2
Other Hispanic	19

Age & Nativity, 2000
Under 5 years	133
18 years and over	1,632
21 years and over	1,552
65 years and over	273
85 years and over	27
Median age	36.1
Native-born	2,111
Foreign-born	34

Educational Attainment, 2000
Population 25 years and over	1,446
Less than 9th grade	4.2%
High school grad or higher	75.0%
Bachelor's degree or higher	10.7%
Graduate degree	2.5%

Income & Poverty, 1999
Per capita income	$18,866
Median household income	$36,172
Median family income	$45,250
Persons in poverty	235
H'holds receiving public assistance	45
H'holds receiving social security	250

Households, 2000
Total households	903
With persons under 18	287
With persons over 65	219
Family households	513
Single-person households	317
Persons per household	2.36
Persons per family	3.12

Labor & Employment
Total civilian labor force, 2007**	1,210
Unemployment rate	4.6%
Total civilian labor force, 2000	1,093
Unemployment rate	3.3%

Employed persons 16 years and over by occupation, 2000
Managers & professionals	184
Service occupations	238
Sales & office occupations	279
Farming, fishing & forestry	8
Construction & maintenance	111
Production & transportation	237
Self-employed persons	34

‡ Branch of county library
* US Census Bureau
** New Jersey Department of Labor

General Information
Borough of Sussex
2 Main St
Sussex, NJ 07461
973-875-4831

Website	(county website)
Year of incorporation	1902
Land/water area (sq. miles)	0.60/0.02
Form of government	Borough

Government
Legislative Districts
US Congressional	5
State Legislative	24

Local Officials, 2009
Mayor	Christian Parrott
Manager/Admin	NA
Clerk	Catherine Gleason
Finance Dir	Grant Rome
Tax Assessor	Melissa Rockwell
Tax Collector	Terry Beshada
Attorney	John Ursin
Building	Ed Vandenberg
Planning	Thomas Heath
Engineering	Mike Simone
Public Works	Jeffrey Card
Police Chief	NA
Emerg/Fire Director	Rich Kroll

Housing & Construction
Housing Units, 2000*
Total	961
Median rent	$667
Median SF home value	$122,500

Permits for New Residential Construction
	Units	Value
Total, 2006	11	$2,403,598
Single family	8	$1,229,118
Total, 2007	7	$1,075,480
Single family	7	$1,075,480

Real Property Valuation, 2008
	Parcels	Valuation
Total	587	$78,375,300
Vacant	48	1,021,300
Residential	460	53,019,900
Commercial	67	16,578,200
Industrial	2	464,900
Apartments	5	6,896,000
Farm land	4	21,100
Farm homestead	1	373,900

Average Property Value & Tax, 2008
Residential value	$115,822
Property tax	$4,731
Tax credit/rebate	$904

Public Library
Sussex-Wantage Branch Library‡
69 Route 639
Wantage, NJ 07461
973-875-3940

Branch Librarian	Nancy Helmer

Library statistics, 2007
see Sussex County profile
for library system statistics

Public Safety
Number of officers, 2007	0

Crime	2006	2007
Total crimes	47	57
Violent	10	9
Murder	0	0
Rape	0	0
Robbery	1	0
Aggravated assault	9	9
Non-violent	37	48
Burglary	8	14
Larceny	25	29
Vehicle theft	4	5
Domestic violence	14	75
Arson	0	1
Total crime rate	21.5	26.3
Violent	4.6	4.1
Non-violent	16.9	22.1

Public School District
(for school year 2007-08 except as noted)

Sussex-Wantage Regional School District
27 Bank Street
Sussex, NJ 07461
(973) 875-3175

Superintendent	Edward Izbicki
Number of schools	3
Grade plan	K-8
Enrollment	1,632
Attendance rate, '06-07	94.7%
Dropout rate	NA
Students per teacher	10.5
Per pupil expenditure	$13,468
Median faculty salary	$60,515
Median administrator salary	$102,581
Grade 12 enrollment	NA
High school graduation rate	NA

Assessment test results
(percent scoring at proficient or advanced level)
	Language	Math
NJASK-Grade 3	89.4%	84.5%
GEPA-Grade 8	75.1%	86.6%
HSPA-High School	NA	NA

SAT Score Averages, 2006-07
Pct tested	Math	Verbal	Writing
NA	NA	NA	NA

Teacher Qualifications
Avg. years of experience	12
Highly-qualified teachers one subject/all subjects	100%/100%

No Child Left Behind
AYP, 2006-07	Meets Standards

Municipal Finance
State Aid Programs, 2009
Total aid	$236,027
CMPTRA	85,108
Energy tax receipts	146,198
Garden State Trust	0

General Budget, 2008
Total tax levy	$3,254,329
County levy	585,242
County taxes	491,131
County library	41,396
County health	14,539
County open space	38,176
School levy	2,068,633
Muni. levy	600,454
Misc. revenues	1,217,713

Taxes	2006	2007	2008
General tax rate per $100	3.84	3.98	4.085
County equalization ratio	62.28	57.41	52.47
Net valuation taxable	$78,082,000	$79,881,585	$79,675,912
State equalized value	$137,430,730	$151,091,073	$147,169,400

See Introduction for an explanation of all data sources.

Demographics & Socio-Economic Characteristics

(2000 US Census, except as noted)

Population

1980*	2,031
1990*	2,024
2000	2,055
Male	1,009
Female	1,046
2007 (estimate)*	2,073
Population density	2,839.7

Race & Hispanic Origin, 2000

Race
White	1,581
Black/African American	339
American Indian/Alaska Native	1
Asian	7
Native Hawaiian/Pacific Islander	0
Other race	69
Two or more races	58
Hispanic origin, total	175
Mexican	10
Puerto Rican	126
Cuban	1
Other Hispanic	38

Age & Nativity, 2000

Under 5 years	153
18 years and over	1,492
21 years and over	1,406
65 years and over	258
85 years and over	38
Median age	35.9
Native-born	1,992
Foreign-born	63

Educational Attainment, 2000

Population 25 years and over	1,355
Less than 9th grade	8.8%
High school grad or higher	81.1%
Bachelor's degree or higher	14.2%
Graduate degree	4.9%

Income & Poverty, 1999

Per capita income	$20,857
Median household income	$49,286
Median family income	$58,721
Persons in poverty	198
H'holds receiving public assistance	28
H'holds receiving social security	220

Households, 2000

Total households	771
With persons under 18	300
With persons over 65	209
Family households	529
Single-person households	200
Persons per household	2.66
Persons per family	3.22

Labor & Employment

Total civilian labor force, 2007**	1,185
Unemployment rate	5.4%
Total civilian labor force, 2000	1,006
Unemployment rate	5.1%

Employed persons 16 years and over by occupation, 2000
Managers & professionals	281
Service occupations	108
Sales & office occupations	295
Farming, fishing & forestry	9
Construction & maintenance	98
Production & transportation	164
Self-employed persons	26

‡ Joint library with Woolwich Township
* US Census Bureau
** New Jersey Department of Labor

General Information

Borough of Swedesboro
PO Box 56
Swedesboro, NJ 08085
856-467-0202

Website	NA
Year of incorporation	1902
Land/water area (sq. miles)	0.73/0.03
Form of government	Borough

Government

Legislative Districts

US Congressional	2
State Legislative	3

Local Officials, 2009

Mayor	Thomas W. Fromm
Manager/Admin	NA
Clerk	Dolores Connors
Finance Dir	Jeff Coles
Tax Assessor	Horace Spoto
Tax Collector	Louis DeMore
Attorney	Timothy W. Chell
Building	Jim Sabetta
Comm Dev/Planning	NA
Engineering	Federici & Akin
Public Works	NA
Police Chief	William Dupper Jr
Emerg/Fire Director	Ed Barber

Housing & Construction

Housing Units, 2000*

Total	860
Median rent	$642
Median SF home value	$98,400

Permits for New Residential Construction

	Units	Value
Total, 2006	11	$2,029,097
Single family	11	$2,029,097
Total, 2007	77	$8,050,890
Single family	77	$8,050,890

Real Property Valuation, 2008

	Parcels	Valuation
Total	968	$79,511,200
Vacant	224	3,807,000
Residential	654	59,875,100
Commercial	78	13,925,600
Industrial	4	902,800
Apartments	8	1,000,700
Farm land	0	0
Farm homestead	0	0

Average Property Value & Tax, 2008

Residential value	$91,552
Property tax	$5,039
Tax credit/rebate	$906

Public Library

Swedesboro Public Library‡
1442 Kings Hwy
Swedesboro, NJ 08085
856-467-0111
Director............. Marge Dombrosky

Library statistics, 2007

Population served	NA
Full-time/total staff	NA/NA

	Total	Per capita
Holdings	NA	NA
Revenues	NA	NA
Expenditures	NA	NA
Annual visits	NA	NA
Internet terminals/annual users	NA/NA	

Public Safety

Number of officers, 2007	9

Crime	2006	2007
Total crimes	47	56
Violent	6	5
Murder	0	0
Rape	1	0
Robbery	3	0
Aggravated assault	2	5
Non-violent	41	51
Burglary	13	15
Larceny	27	32
Vehicle theft	1	4
Domestic violence	19	40
Arson	0	0
Total crime rate	22.9	27.4
Violent	2.9	2.4
Non-violent	20.0	25.0

Public School District

(for school year 2007-08 except as noted)

Swedesboro-Woolwich School District
15 Fredrick Blvd
Woolwich Twp, NJ 08085
(856) 241-1136
Superintendent	Richard Fisher
Number of schools	3
Grade plan	K-6
Enrollment	1,519
Attendance rate, '06-07	95.6%
Dropout rate	NA
Students per teacher	11.7
Per pupil expenditure	$9,691
Median faculty salary	$44,900
Median administrator salary	$84,407
Grade 12 enrollment	NA
High school graduation rate	NA

Assessment test results
(percent scoring at proficient or advanced level)

	Language	Math
NJASK-Grade 3	94.4%	90.7%
GEPA-Grade 8	NA	NA
HSPA-High School	NA	NA

SAT Score Averages, 2006-07

Pct tested	Math	Verbal	Writing
NA	NA	NA	NA

Teacher Qualifications
Avg. years of experience	5
Highly-qualified teachers one subject/all subjects	100%/100%

No Child Left Behind
AYP, 2006-07	Meets Standards

Municipal Finance

State Aid Programs, 2009

Total aid	$322,247
CMPTRA	146,049
Energy tax receipts	168,129
Garden State Trust	14

General Budget, 2008

Total tax levy	$4,451,682
County levy	964,791
County taxes	832,589
County library	66,955
County health	0
County open space	65,246
School levy	2,337,807
Muni. levy	1,149,085
Misc. revenues	1,128,948

Taxes	2006	2007	2008
General tax rate per $100	4.542	4.838	5.505
County equalization ratio	69.63	55.53	50.16
Net valuation taxable	$72,739,800	$77,005,620	$80,880,251
State equalized value	$132,782,909	$152,054,664	$168,094,151

See Introduction for an explanation of all data sources.

Demographics & Socio-Economic Characteristics
(2000 US Census, except as noted)

Population
1980*	6,236
1990*	7,360
2000	7,170
Male	3,632
Female	3,538
2007 (estimate)*	7,182
Population density	145.2

Race & Hispanic Origin, 2000
Race
White	6,904
Black/African American	150
American Indian/Alaska Native	7
Asian	52
Native Hawaiian/Pacific Islander	0
Other race	22
Two or more races	35
Hispanic origin, total	106
Mexican	10
Puerto Rican	61
Cuban	8
Other Hispanic	27

Age & Nativity, 2000
Under 5 years	384
18 years and over	5,166
21 years and over	4,897
65 years and over	502
85 years and over	47
Median age	38.1
Native-born	7,012
Foreign-born	158

Educational Attainment, 2000
Population 25 years and over	4,651
Less than 9th grade	1.7%
High school grad or higher	92.7%
Bachelor's degree or higher	30.6%
Graduate degree	10.0%

Income & Poverty, 1999
Per capita income	$27,874
Median household income	$76,432
Median family income	$86,729
Persons in poverty	144
H'holds receiving public assistance	28
H'holds receiving social security	510

Households, 2000
Total households	2,346
With persons under 18	1,040
With persons over 65	389
Family households	2,011
Single-person households	268
Persons per household	3.03
Persons per family	3.28

Labor & Employment
Total civilian labor force, 2007**	4,547
Unemployment rate	2.0%
Total civilian labor force, 2000	3,994
Unemployment rate	2.0%

Employed persons 16 years and over by occupation, 2000
Managers & professionals	1,630
Service occupations	357
Sales & office occupations	1,147
Farming, fishing & forestry	12
Construction & maintenance	398
Production & transportation	369
Self-employed persons	233

General Information
Township of Tabernacle
163 Carranza Rd
Tabernacle, NJ 08088
609-268-1220
Website	www.townshipoftabernacle-nj.gov
Year of incorporation	1901
Land/water area (sq. miles)	49.46/0.06
Form of government	Township

Government
Legislative Districts
US Congressional	3
State Legislative	8

Local Officials, 2009
Mayor	Richard J. Franzen
Administrator	Douglas Cramer
Clerk	LaShawn R. Barber
Finance Dir	Terry Henry
Tax Assessor	Dennis DeKlerk
Tax Collector	Susan Costales
Attorney	Peter C. Lange
Building	Frank Robert Perri
Comm Dev/Planning	NA
Engineering	Ray Worrell
Public Works	Douglas A. Cramer
Police Chief	NA
Emerg/Fire Director	Al Freeman

Housing & Construction
Housing Units, 2000*
Total	2,385
Median rent	$761
Median SF home value	$171,700

Permits for New Residential Construction
	Units	Value
Total, 2006	11	$2,215,900
Single family	11	$2,215,900
Total, 2007	14	$3,707,948
Single family	14	$3,707,948

Real Property Valuation, 2008
	Parcels	Valuation
Total	2,862	$732,189,500
Vacant	262	10,979,800
Residential	2,276	680,403,900
Commercial	55	19,451,500
Industrial	3	779,100
Apartments	0	0
Farm land	190	2,739,800
Farm homestead	76	17,835,400

Average Property Value & Tax, 2008
Residential value	$296,870
Property tax	$6,751
Tax credit/rebate	$1,093

Public Library
No public municipal library

Library statistics, 2007
Population served	NA
Full-time/total staff	NA/NA

	Total	Per capita
Holdings	NA	NA
Revenues	NA	NA
Expenditures	NA	NA
Annual visits	NA	NA
Internet terminals/annual users	NA/NA	

Public Safety
Number of officers, 2007 0
Crime	2006	2007
Total crimes	73	63
Violent	4	2
Murder	0	0
Rape	0	0
Robbery	0	0
Aggravated assault	4	2
Non-violent	69	61
Burglary	20	10
Larceny	44	45
Vehicle theft	5	6
Domestic violence	9	22
Arson	0	24
Total crime rate	9.9	8.6
Violent	0.5	0.3
Non-violent	9.4	8.3

Public School District
(for school year 2007-08 except as noted)

Tabernacle Township School District
132 New Road
Tabernacle, NJ 08088
(609) 268-0153
Superintendent	Berenice Blum-Bart
Number of schools	2
Grade plan	K-8
Enrollment	878
Attendance rate, '06-07	95.9%
Dropout rate	NA
Students per teacher	10.7
Per pupil expenditure	$14,215
Median faculty salary	$63,165
Median administrator salary	$97,755
Grade 12 enrollment	NA
High school graduation rate	NA

Assessment test results
(percent scoring at proficient or advanced level)
	Language	Math
NJASK-Grade 3	91.6%	94.1%
GEPA-Grade 8	83.0%	92.9%
HSPA-High School	NA	NA

SAT Score Averages, 2006-07
Pct tested	Math	Verbal	Writing
NA	NA	NA	NA

Teacher Qualifications
Avg. years of experience	18
Highly-qualified teachers one subject/all subjects	100%/100%

No Child Left Behind
AYP, 2006-07 . . . . Meets Standards

Municipal Finance
State Aid Programs, 2009
Total aid	$868,915
CMPTRA	57,260
Energy tax receipts	648,455
Garden State Trust	132,462

General Budget, 2008
Total tax levy	$16,673,221
County levy	3,275,959
County taxes	2,690,244
County library	248,394
County health	0
County open space	337,321
School levy	11,645,526
Muni. levy	1,751,736
Misc. revenues	1,921,148

Taxes	2006	2007	2008
General tax rate per $100	2.11	2.24	2.274
County equalization ratio	106.72	93.37	86.96
Net valuation taxable	$722,019,900	$728,499,644	$733,232,250
State equalized value	$774,352,395	$837,584,103	$854,908,056

* US Census Bureau
** New Jersey Department of Labor

Demographics & Socio-Economic Characteristics

(2000 US Census, except as noted)

Population
1980*	9
1990*	35
2000	24
Male	12
Female	12
2007 (estimate)*	28
Population density	112.0

Race & Hispanic Origin, 2000
Race
White	22
Black/African American	2
American Indian/Alaska Native	0
Asian	0
Native Hawaiian/Pacific Islander	0
Other race	0
Two or more races	0
Hispanic origin, total	0
Mexican	0
Puerto Rican	0
Cuban	0
Other Hispanic	0

Age & Nativity, 2000
Under 5 years	1
18 years and over	15
21 years and over	13
65 years and over	2
85 years and over	0
Median age	38.5
Native-born	22
Foreign-born	1

Educational Attainment, 2000
Population 25 years and over	9
Less than 9th grade	0.0%
High school grad or higher	88.9%
Bachelor's degree or higher	33.3%
Graduate degree	22.2%

Income & Poverty, 1999
Per capita income	$14,600
Median household income	$58,750
Median family income	$36,875
Persons in poverty	5
H'holds receiving public assistance	1
H'holds receiving social security	1

Households, 2000
Total households	7
With persons under 18	4
With persons over 65	2
Family households	7
Single-person households	0
Persons per household	3.43
Persons per family	3.43

Labor & Employment
Total civilian labor force, 2007**	11
Unemployment rate	0.0%
Total civilian labor force, 2000	9
Unemployment rate	0.0%

Employed persons 16 years and over by occupation, 2000
Managers & professionals	4
Service occupations	2
Sales & office occupations	0
Farming, fishing & forestry	0
Construction & maintenance	1
Production & transportation	2
Self-employed persons	4

* US Census Bureau
** New Jersey Department of Labor

See Introduction for an explanation of all data sources.

General Information
Borough of Tavistock
PO Box 8988
Turnersville, NJ 08012
856-429-0039
Website	www.tavistocknj.org
Year of incorporation	1921
Land/water area (sq. miles)	0.25/0.00
Form of government	Commission

Government

Legislative Districts
US Congressional	1
State Legislative	6

Local Officials, 2009
Mayor	George Buff III
Manager	Theresa Lappe
Clerk	Theresa Lappe
CFO	Denise M. Moules
Tax Assessor	Stephen J. Kessler
Tax Collector	Patricia A. McCunney
Attorney	Thomas T. Booth Jr
Building	NA
Planning	Larry Waetzman
Engineering	Edward J. Vernick
Public Works	NA
Police Chief	NA
Fire/Emergency Dir.	NA

Housing & Construction

Housing Units, 2000*
Total	7
Median rent	$675
Median SF home value	$137,500

Permits for New Residential Construction
	Units	Value
Total, 2006	NA	NA
Single family	NA	NA
Total, 2007	NA	NA
Single family	NA	NA

Real Property Valuation, 2008
	Parcels	Valuation
Total	5	$16,555,200
Vacant	0	0
Residential	3	4,550,000
Commercial	2	12,005,200
Industrial	0	0
Apartments	0	0
Farm land	0	0
Farm homestead	0	0

Average Property Value & Tax, 2008
Residential value	$1,516,667
Property tax	$19,225
Tax credit/rebate	$0

Public Library
No public municipal library

Library statistics, 2007
Population served	NA
Full-time/total staff	NA/NA

	Total	Per capita
Holdings	NA	NA
Revenues	NA	NA
Expenditures	NA	NA
Annual visits	NA	NA
Internet terminals/annual users	NA/NA	

Public Safety
Number of officers, 2007	0

Crime	2006	2007
Total crimes	0	1
Violent	0	0
Murder	0	0
Rape	0	0
Robbery	0	0
Aggravated assault	0	0
Non-violent	0	1
Burglary	0	0
Larceny	0	1
Vehicle theft	0	0
Domestic violence	0	0
Arson	0	0
Total crime rate	NA	38.5
Violent	NA	0.0
Non-violent	NA	38.5

Public School District
(for school year 2007-08 except as noted)

Tavistock Borough School District
P.O. Box 8988
Turnersville, NJ 08012

No schools in district - sends students to Haddonfield Borough schools

Per pupil expenditure	NA
Median faculty salary	NA
Median administrator salary	NA
Grade 12 enrollment	NA
High school graduation rate	NA

Assessment test results
(percent scoring at proficient or advanced level)
	Language	Math
NJASK-Grade 3	NA	NA
GEPA-Grade 8	NA	NA
HSPA-High School	NA	NA

SAT Score Averages, 2006-07
Pct tested	Math	Verbal	Writing
NA	NA	NA	NA

Teacher Qualifications
Avg. years of experience	NA
Highly-qualified teachers one subject/all subjects	NA/NA

No Child Left Behind
AYP, 2006-07	NA

Municipal Finance

State Aid Programs, 2009
Total aid	$3,246
CMPTRA	1,657
Energy tax receipts	1,459
Garden State Trust	0

General Budget, 2008
Total tax levy	$209,878
County levy	106,420
County taxes	96,180
County library	6,893
County health	0
County open space	3,346
School levy	12,496
Muni. levy	90,962
Misc. revenues	29,438

Taxes
	2006	2007	2008
General tax rate per $100	1.435	1.332	1.268
County equalization ratio	100	100	100.00
Net valuation taxable	$16,555,200	$16,557,398	$16,557,493
State equalized value	$13,380,078	$14,969,380	$15,763,146

Demographics & Socio-Economic Characteristics
(2000 US Census, except as noted)

Population
1980*	39,007
1990*	37,825
2000	39,260
Male	18,584
Female	20,676
2007 (estimate)*	39,019
Population density	6,449.4

Race & Hispanic Origin, 2000
Race
White	22,082
Black/African American	11,298
American Indian/Alaska Native	59
Asian	2,798
Native Hawaiian/Pacific Islander	11
Other race	1,633
Two or more races	1,379
Hispanic origin, total	4,103
Mexican	151
Puerto Rican	1,132
Cuban	329
Other Hispanic	2,491

Age & Nativity, 2000
Under 5 years	2,521
18 years and over	29,139
21 years and over	27,538
65 years and over	5,584
85 years and over	826
Median age	38.4
Native-born	29,825
Foreign-born	9,435

Educational Attainment, 2000
Population 25 years and over	26,054
Less than 9th grade	3.6%
High school grad or higher	89.7%
Bachelor's degree or higher	47.9%
Graduate degree	23.0%

Income & Poverty, 1999
Per capita income	$32,212
Median household income	$74,903
Median family income	$84,791
Persons in poverty	1,596
H'holds receiving public assistance	302
H'holds receiving social security	4,020

Households, 2000
Total households	13,418
With persons under 18	5,202
With persons over 65	4,075
Family households	10,071
Single-person households	2,838
Persons per household	2.86
Persons per family	3.34

Labor & Employment
Total civilian labor force, 2007**	20,525
Unemployment rate	3.2%
Total civilian labor force, 2000	20,106
Unemployment rate	4.7%

Employed persons 16 years and over by occupation, 2000
Managers & professionals	10,185
Service occupations	1,794
Sales & office occupations	5,137
Farming, fishing & forestry	0
Construction & maintenance	805
Production & transportation	1,230
Self-employed persons	1,268

* US Census Bureau
** New Jersey Department of Labor

General Information
Township of Teaneck
818 Teaneck Rd
Teaneck, NJ 07666
201-837-4811
Website	www.teanecknjgov.org
Year of incorporation	1895
Land/water area (sq. miles)	6.05/0.20
Form of government	Council-Manager

Government
Legislative Districts
US Congressional	9
State Legislative	37

Local Officials, 2009
Mayor	Elie Y. Katz
Manager	Helene Fall
Clerk	Lissette Aportela-Hernandez (Actg)
Finance Dir	Anthony Bianchi
Tax Assessor	James Tighe
Tax Collector	Milene Quijano
Attorney	Stanley Turitz
Construction Code Official	Steven Gluck
Comm Dev/Planning	NA
Engineering	Charles McKearnin
Public Works	Charles McKearnin
Police Chief	Fred Ahearn
Fire Chief	Robert Montgomery

Housing & Construction
Housing Units, 2000*
Total	13,719
Median rent	$873
Median SF home value	$208,800

Permits for New Residential Construction
	Units	Value
Total, 2006	9	$1,812,500
Single family	9	$1,812,500
Total, 2007	3	$2,225,000
Single family	3	$2,225,000

Real Property Valuation, 2008
	Parcels	Valuation
Total	11,881	$6,088,683,400
Vacant	149	29,911,100
Residential	11,272	5,239,172,100
Commercial	386	575,765,100
Industrial	16	45,394,000
Apartments	58	198,441,100
Farm land	0	0
Farm homestead	0	0

Average Property Value & Tax, 2008
Residential value	$464,795
Property tax	$10,205
Tax credit/rebate	$1,355

Public Library
Teaneck Public Library
840 Teaneck Rd
Teaneck, NJ 07666
201-837-4171
Director	Michael McCue

Library statistics, 2007
Population served	39,260
Full-time/total staff	7/23

	Total	Per capita
Holdings	133,046	3.39
Revenues	$2,644,095	$67.35
Expenditures	$2,372,610	$60.43
Annual visits	375,000	9.55
Internet terminals/annual users	4/35,750	

Public Safety
Number of officers, 2007	104

Crime	2006	2007
Total crimes	688	613
Violent	65	63
Murder	1	0
Rape	0	1
Robbery	27	31
Aggravated assault	37	31
Non-violent	623	550
Burglary	127	132
Larceny	451	373
Vehicle theft	45	45
Domestic violence	262	165
Arson	9	11
Total crime rate	17.4	15.5
Violent	1.6	1.6
Non-violent	15.7	13.9

Public School District
(for school year 2007-08 except as noted)

Teaneck School District
1 Merrison Street
Teaneck, NJ 07666
(201) 833-5510
Superintendent	A. Spencer Denham (Actg)
Number of schools	7
Grade plan	K-12
Enrollment	3,988
Attendance rate, '06-07	94.9%
Dropout rate	0.6%
Students per teacher	9.3
Per pupil expenditure	$18,131
Median faculty salary	$70,700
Median administrator salary	$128,245
Grade 12 enrollment	356
High school graduation rate	96.9%

Assessment test results
(percent scoring at proficient or advanced level)
	Language	Math
NJASK-Grade 3	92.3%	90.5%
GEPA-Grade 8	59.4%	82.3%
HSPA-High School	67.7%	85.6%

SAT Score Averages, 2006-07
Pct tested	Math	Verbal	Writing
80%	480	468	470

Teacher Qualifications
Avg. years of experience	10
Highly-qualified teachers one subject/all subjects	100%/100%

No Child Left Behind
AYP, 2006-07	Meets Standards

Municipal Finance
State Aid Programs, 2009
Total aid	$4,155,975
CMPTRA	845,640
Energy tax receipts	3,247,995
Garden State Trust	0

General Budget, 2008
Total tax levy	$133,791,137
County levy	11,414,276
County taxes	10,796,641
County library	0
County health	0
County open space	617,634
School levy	76,196,072
Muni. levy	46,180,789
Misc. revenues	16,032,081

Taxes	2006	2007	2008
General tax rate per $100	4.64	2.15	2.197
County equalization ratio	52.37	106.17	99.00
Net valuation taxable	$2,651,670,200	$6,080,678,681	$6,093,801,694
State equalized value	$5,690,561,461	$6,142,047,166	$6,357,422,311

Demographics & Socio-Economic Characteristics

(2000 US Census, except as noted)

Population

1980*	13,552
1990*	13,326
2000	13,806
Male	6,649
Female	7,157
2007 (estimate)*	14,302
Population density	3,102.4

Race & Hispanic Origin, 2000

Race
White	10,601
Black/African American	132
American Indian/Alaska Native	13
Asian	2,634
Native Hawaiian/Pacific Islander	3
Other race	193
Two or more races	230
Hispanic origin, total	642
Mexican	42
Puerto Rican	99
Cuban	98
Other Hispanic	403

Age & Nativity, 2000

Under 5 years	904
18 years and over	9,900
21 years and over	9,561
65 years and over	2,092
85 years and over	294
Median age	40.9
Native-born	9,862
Foreign-born	3,944

Educational Attainment, 2000

Population 25 years and over	9,173
Less than 9th grade	2.5%
High school grad or higher	93.5%
Bachelor's degree or higher	62.1%
Graduate degree	33.4%

Income & Poverty, 1999

Per capita income	$53,170
Median household income	$90,931
Median family income	$111,029
Persons in poverty	718
H'holds receiving public assistance	50
H'holds receiving social security	1,340

Households, 2000

Total households	4,774
With persons under 18	2,154
With persons over 65	1,399
Family households	3,868
Single-person households	801
Persons per household	2.86
Persons per family	3.21

Labor & Employment

Total civilian labor force, 2007**	6,906
Unemployment rate	3.3%
Total civilian labor force, 2000	6,559
Unemployment rate	3.6%

Employed persons 16 years and over by occupation, 2000
Managers & professionals	3,690
Service occupations	487
Sales & office occupations	1,650
Farming, fishing & forestry	8
Construction & maintenance	172
Production & transportation	314
Self-employed persons	621

* US Census Bureau
** New Jersey Department of Labor

General Information

Borough of Tenafly
100 Riveredge Rd
Tenafly, NJ 07670
201-568-6100

Website	www.tenaflynj.org
Year of incorporation	1894
Land/water area (sq. miles)	4.61/0.58
Form of government	Special Charter

Government

Legislative Districts

US Congressional	5
State Legislative	37

Local Officials, 2009

Mayor	Peter S. Rustin
Manager	Joseph Di Giacomo
Clerk	Nancy Hatten
Finance Dir	Karen Palermo
Tax Assessor	Carol Byrne
Tax Collector	Lily Tom
Attorney	William McClure
Building	Robert Byrnes Sr
Comm Dev/Planning	NA
Engineering	David Hals
Public Works	J. Robert Beutel
Police Chief	Michael Bruno
Emerg/Fire Director	Richard Philpott

Housing & Construction

Housing Units, 2000*

Total	4,897
Median rent	$1,186
Median SF home value	$403,600

Permits for New Residential Construction

	Units	Value
Total, 2006	51	$17,698,550
Single family	29	$12,534,550
Total, 2007	185	$27,630,217
Single family	27	$11,893,383

Real Property Valuation, 2008

	Parcels	Valuation
Total	4,640	$3,005,374,500
Vacant	159	26,820,700
Residential	4,286	2,764,805,400
Commercial	177	177,302,800
Industrial	11	8,610,300
Apartments	7	27,835,300
Farm land	0	0
Farm homestead	0	0

Average Property Value & Tax, 2008

Residential value	$645,078
Property tax	$16,669
Tax credit/rebate	$1,434

Public Library

Tenafly Public Library
100 Riveredge Rd
Tenafly, NJ 07670
201-568-8680

Director	Stephen R. Wechtler

Library statistics, 2007

Population served	13,806
Full-time/total staff	5/10

	Total	Per capita
Holdings	88,145	6.38
Revenues	$1,271,633	$92.11
Expenditures	$1,270,704	$92.04
Annual visits	87,300	6.32
Internet terminals/annual users	9/24,700	

Public Safety

Number of officers, 2007	37

Crime	2006	2007
Total crimes	107	98
Violent	1	1
Murder	0	0
Rape	0	1
Robbery	1	0
Aggravated assault	0	0
Non-violent	106	97
Burglary	22	23
Larceny	78	70
Vehicle theft	6	4
Domestic violence	31	11
Arson	2	1
Total crime rate	7.5	6.8
Violent	0.1	0.1
Non-violent	7.4	6.7

Public School District

(for school year 2007-08 except as noted)

Tenafly School District
500 Tenafly Road
Tenafly, NJ 07670
(201) 816-4501

Superintendent	Eugene Westlake (Int)
Number of schools	6
Grade plan	K-12
Enrollment	3,463
Attendance rate, '06-07	97.0%
Dropout rate	0.1%
Students per teacher	10.4
Per pupil expenditure	$14,315
Median faculty salary	$60,125
Median administrator salary	$133,400
Grade 12 enrollment	276
High school graduation rate	99.6%

Assessment test results

(percent scoring at proficient or advanced level)
	Language	Math
NJASK-Grade 3	95.8%	98.3%
GEPA-Grade 8	86.7%	94.8%
HSPA-High School	93.1%	95.3%

SAT Score Averages, 2006-07

Pct tested	Math	Verbal	Writing
106%	619	572	570

Teacher Qualifications

Avg. years of experience	8
Highly-qualified teachers one subject/all subjects	99.5%/99.5%

No Child Left Behind

AYP, 2006-07	Meets Standards

Municipal Finance

State Aid Programs, 2009

Total aid	$1,524,269
CMPTRA	92,049
Energy tax receipts	1,370,787
Garden State Trust	482

General Budget, 2008

Total tax levy	$77,689,996
County levy	7,770,682
County taxes	7,350,287
County library	0
County health	0
County open space	420,395
School levy	50,563,455
Muni. levy	19,355,860
Misc. revenues	5,566,617

Taxes

	2006	2007	2008
General tax rate per $100	2.3	2.43	2.585
County equalization ratio	83.24	73.27	71.65
Net valuation taxable	$2,907,003,900	$2,961,681,275	$3,006,577,770
State equalized value	$3,968,812,048	$4,133,076,963	$4,296,436,227

See Introduction for an explanation of all data sources.

Demographics & Socio-Economic Characteristics

(2000 US Census, except as noted)

Population
1980*	19
1990*	22
2000	18
Male	9
Female	9
2007 (estimate)*	18
Population density	16.2

Race & Hispanic Origin, 2000
Race
White	15
Black/African American	0
American Indian/Alaska Native	0
Asian	0
Native Hawaiian/Pacific Islander	0
Other race	0
Two or more races	3
Hispanic origin, total	0
Mexican	0
Puerto Rican	0
Cuban	0
Other Hispanic	0

Age & Nativity, 2000
Under 5 years	3
18 years and over	12
21 years and over	11
65 years and over	1
85 years and over	0
Median age	33.0
Native-born	16
Foreign-born	0

Educational Attainment, 2000
Population 25 years and over	10
Less than 9th grade	0.0%
High school grad or higher	100.0%
Bachelor's degree or higher	50.0%
Graduate degree	0.0%

Income & Poverty, 1999
Per capita income	$72,613
Median household income	$44,167
Median family income	$43,750
Persons in poverty	0
H'holds receiving public assistance	0
H'holds receiving social security	3

Households, 2000
Total households	7
With persons under 18	3
With persons over 65	1
Family households	5
Single-person households	1
Persons per household	2.57
Persons per family	3.00

Labor & Employment
Total civilian labor force, 2007**	21
Unemployment rate	0.0%
Total civilian labor force, 2000	13
Unemployment rate	0.0%

Employed persons 16 years and over by occupation, 2000
Managers & professionals	3
Service occupations	0
Sales & office occupations	6
Farming, fishing & forestry	0
Construction & maintenance	4
Production & transportation	0
Self-employed persons	0

General Information
Borough of Teterboro
510 Route 46 W
Municipal Building
Teterboro, NJ 07608
201-288-1200
Website	NA
Year of incorporation	1917
Land/water area (sq. miles)	1.11/0.00
Form of government	Municipal Mgr 1923

Government

Legislative Districts
US Congressional	9
State Legislative	38

Local Officials, 2009
Mayor	John Watt
Manager	Paul Busch
Clerk	Nadine Conn
Finance Dir	Rosemary McClave
Tax Assessor	James Hall
Tax Collector	Marion Semken
Attorney	David Bole
Building	Joseph Marra
Comm Dev/Planning	NA
Engineering	Boswell McClave
Public Works	John Fantacone
Police Chief	NA
Fire/Emergency Dir	NA

Housing & Construction

Housing Units, 2000*
Total	8
Median rent	$738
Median SF home value	NA

Permits for New Residential Construction
	Units	Value
Total, 2006	0	$0
Single family	0	$0
Total, 2007	0	$0
Single family	0	$0

Real Property Valuation, 2008
	Parcels	Valuation
Total	84	$418,553,400
Vacant	9	1,473,000
Residential	7	1,095,200
Commercial	9	6,344,300
Industrial	58	408,444,600
Apartments	1	1,196,300
Farm land	0	0
Farm homestead	0	0

Average Property Value & Tax, 2008
Residential value	$156,457
Property tax	$1,475
Tax credit/rebate	$0

Public Library
No public municipal library

Library statistics, 2007
Population served	NA
Full-time/total staff	NA/NA

	Total	Per capita
Holdings	NA	NA
Revenues	NA	NA
Expenditures	NA	NA
Annual visits	NA	NA
Internet terminals/annual users	NA/NA	

Public Safety
Number of officers, 2007 0
Crime	2006	2007
Total crimes	31	40
Violent	4	2
Murder	0	0
Rape	0	0
Robbery	0	2
Aggravated assault	4	0
Non-violent	27	38
Burglary	1	4
Larceny	24	27
Vehicle theft	2	7
Domestic violence	3	4
Arson	0	0
Total crime rate	NA	NA
Violent	NA	NA
Non-violent	NA	NA

Public School District
(for school year 2007-08 except as noted)

Teterboro School District
Municipal Building, Route 46
Teterboro, NJ 07608

No schools in district

Per pupil expenditure	NA
Median faculty salary	NA
Median administrator salary	NA
Grade 12 enrollment	NA
High school graduation rate	NA

Assessment test results
(percent scoring at proficient or advanced level)
	Language	Math
NJASK-Grade 3	NA	NA
GEPA-Grade 8	NA	NA
HSPA-High School	NA	NA

SAT Score Averages, 2006-07
Pct tested	Math	Verbal	Writing
NA	NA	NA	NA

Teacher Qualifications
Avg. years of experience	NA
Highly-qualified teachers one subject/all subjects	NA/NA

No Child Left Behind
AYP, 2006-07 .... NA

Municipal Finance

State Aid Programs, 2009
Total aid	$206,507
CMPTRA	67,403
Energy tax receipts	132,392
Garden State Trust	0

General Budget, 2008
Total tax levy	$3,956,425
County levy	840,450
County taxes	791,453
County library	0
County health	0
County open space	48,997
School levy	179,941
Muni. levy	2,936,034
Misc. revenues	1,792,063

Taxes
	2006	2007	2008
General tax rate per $100	1.01	1.08	0.944
County equalization ratio	93.29	80.53	88.98
Net valuation taxable	$314,313,226	$328,200,779	$419,591,956
State equalized value	$495,505,736	$470,997,272	$478,566,679

* US Census Bureau
** New Jersey Department of Labor

See Introduction for an explanation of all data sources.

Demographics & Socio-Economic Characteristics
(2000 US Census, except as noted)

Population
1980*	4,094
1990*	4,803
2000	5,541
Male	2,729
Female	2,812
2007 (estimate)*	6,048
Population density	191.2

Race & Hispanic Origin, 2000
Race
White	5,365
Black/African American	29
American Indian/Alaska Native	0
Asian	104
Native Hawaiian/Pacific Islander	0
Other race	15
Two or more races	28
Hispanic origin, total	85
Mexican	8
Puerto Rican	16
Cuban	15
Other Hispanic	46

Age & Nativity, 2000
Under 5 years	373
18 years and over	4,091
21 years and over	3,989
65 years and over	623
85 years and over	43
Median age	42.6
Native-born	5,268
Foreign-born	273

Educational Attainment, 2000
Population 25 years and over	3,886
Less than 9th grade	1.7%
High school grad or higher	95.7%
Bachelor's degree or higher	58.9%
Graduate degree	25.6%

Income & Poverty, 1999
Per capita income	$65,470
Median household income	$135,649
Median family income	$150,189
Persons in poverty	152
H'holds receiving public assistance	0
H'holds receiving social security	441

Households, 2000
Total households	1,986
With persons under 18	747
With persons over 65	441
Family households	1,663
Single-person households	249
Persons per household	2.79
Persons per family	3.05

Labor & Employment
Total civilian labor force, 2007**	3,130
Unemployment rate	2.1%
Total civilian labor force, 2000	2,814
Unemployment rate	1.8%

Employed persons 16 years and over by occupation, 2000
Managers & professionals	1,814
Service occupations	193
Sales & office occupations	559
Farming, fishing & forestry	28
Construction & maintenance	98
Production & transportation	71
Self-employed persons	382

* US Census Bureau
** New Jersey Department of Labor

See Introduction for an explanation of all data sources.

General Information
Township of Tewksbury
169 Old Turnpike Rd
Califon, NJ 07830
908-439-0022
Website	www.tewksburytwp.net
Year of incorporation	1755
Land/water area (sq. miles)	31.63/0.02
Form of government	Township

Government
Legislative Districts
US Congressional	7
State Legislative	24

Local Officials, 2009
Mayor	Louis DiMare
Manager	Jesse W. Landon
Clerk	Roberta A. Brassard
Finance Dir	Judie A. McGrorey
Tax Assessor	Ann Marie Obiedzinski
Tax Collector	Kay Winzenried
Attorney	Michael S. Selvaggi
Building	Charles Rogers
Comm Dev/Planning	NA
Engineering	Andrew Holt
Public Works	Hayden Hull
Police Chief	Russel O'Dell
Emerg/Fire Director	John Melick

Housing & Construction
Housing Units, 2000*
Total	2,052
Median rent	$1,388
Median SF home value	$461,200

Permits for New Residential Construction
	Units	Value
Total, 2006	26	$6,003,313
Single family	7	$5,749,850
Total, 2007	13	$9,483,550
Single family	13	$9,483,550

Real Property Valuation, 2008
	Parcels	Valuation
Total	3,032	$1,354,071,700
Vacant	161	14,265,900
Residential	1,923	1,049,742,100
Commercial	40	58,491,300
Industrial	1	5,304,000
Apartments	0	0
Farm land	565	3,611,000
Farm homestead	342	222,657,400

Average Property Value & Tax, 2008
Residential value	$561,766
Property tax	$12,284
Tax credit/rebate	$1,331

Public Library
Tewksbury Township Library
31 Old Turnpike Rd
Oldwick, NJ 08858
908-439-3761
Director	Judie Garey

Library statistics, 2007
Population served	5,541
Full-time/total staff	NA/0

	Total	Per capita
Holdings	0	NA
Revenues	$0	NA
Expenditures	$0	NA
Annual visits	NA	NA
Internet terminals/annual users	NA/NA	

Public Safety
Number of officers, 2007	11

Crime	2006	2007
Total crimes	37	26
Violent	3	4
Murder	0	0
Rape	1	2
Robbery	0	0
Aggravated assault	2	2
Non-violent	34	22
Burglary	11	12
Larceny	21	10
Vehicle theft	2	0
Domestic violence	8	4
Arson	0	0
Total crime rate	6.1	4.3
Violent	0.5	0.7
Non-violent	5.6	3.6

Public School District
(for school year 2007-08 except as noted)

Tewksbury Township School District
173 Old Turnpike Road
Califon, NJ 07830
(908) 439-2010
Superintendent	William Petrick (Int)
Number of schools	2
Grade plan	K-8
Enrollment	775
Attendance rate, '06-07	96.0%
Dropout rate	NA
Students per teacher	10.3
Per pupil expenditure	$14,917
Median faculty salary	$53,895
Median administrator salary	$117,771
Grade 12 enrollment	NA
High school graduation rate	NA

Assessment test results
(percent scoring at proficient or advanced level)
	Language	Math
NJASK-Grade 3	97.0%	96.0%
GEPA-Grade 8	90.4%	95.9%
HSPA-High School	NA	NA

SAT Score Averages, 2006-07
Pct tested	Math	Verbal	Writing
NA	NA	NA	NA

Teacher Qualifications
Avg. years of experience	12
Highly-qualified teachers one subject/all subjects	100%/100%

No Child Left Behind
AYP, 2006-07	Meets Standards

Municipal Finance
State Aid Programs, 2009
Total aid	$710,786
CMPTRA	34,094
Energy tax receipts	640,746
Garden State Trust	430

General Budget, 2008
Total tax levy	$29,648,793
County levy	6,450,543
County taxes	5,398,844
County library	468,836
County health	0
County open space	582,863
School levy	18,300,560
Muni. levy	4,897,691
Misc. revenues	6,152,567

Taxes
	2006	2007	2008
General tax rate per $100	2.22	2.24	2.187
County equalization ratio	73.48	67.93	70.04
Net valuation taxable	$1,320,803,900	$1,343,168,486	$1,355,876,883
State equalized value	$1,811,217,692	$1,872,287,627	$1,925,475,733

Demographics & Socio-Economic Characteristics

(2000 US Census, except as noted)

Population
1980*	7,740
1990*	12,361
2000	15,053
Male	7,157
Female	7,896
2007 (estimate)*	19,158
Population density	1,228.9

Race & Hispanic Origin, 2000
Race
White	11,862
Black/African American	1,963
American Indian/Alaska Native	36
Asian	747
Native Hawaiian/Pacific Islander	2
Other race	157
Two or more races	286
Hispanic origin, total	707
Mexican	122
Puerto Rican	305
Cuban	49
Other Hispanic	231

Age & Nativity, 2000
Under 5 years	1,184
18 years and over	11,215
21 years and over	10,908
65 years and over	1,633
85 years and over	203
Median age	36.8
Native-born	13,557
Foreign-born	1,498

Educational Attainment, 2000
Population 25 years and over	10,457
Less than 9th grade	1.9%
High school grad or higher	92.7%
Bachelor's degree or higher	42.3%
Graduate degree	14.5%

Income & Poverty, 1999
Per capita income	$31,520
Median household income	$68,697
Median family income	$79,773
Persons in poverty	577
H'holds receiving public assistance	61
H'holds receiving social security	1,173

Households, 2000
Total households	5,883
With persons under 18	2,145
With persons over 65	1,122
Family households	3,977
Single-person households	1,602
Persons per household	2.51
Persons per family	3.11

Labor & Employment
Total civilian labor force, 2007**	8,617
Unemployment rate	3.7%
Total civilian labor force, 2000	8,088
Unemployment rate	4.1%

Employed persons 16 years and over by occupation, 2000
Managers & professionals	3,570
Service occupations	869
Sales & office occupations	2,396
Farming, fishing & forestry	22
Construction & maintenance	376
Production & transportation	524
Self-employed persons	386

General Information
Borough of Tinton Falls
556 Tinton Ave
Tinton Falls, NJ 07724
732-542-3400

Website	www.tintonfalls.com
Year of incorporation	1976
Land/water area (sq. miles)	15.59/0.03
Form of government	Mayor-Council

Government
Legislative Districts
US Congressional	12
State Legislative	12

Local Officials, 2009
Mayor	Peter Maclearie
Manager	W. Bryan Dempsey
Clerk	Karen Mount-Taylor
Finance Dir	Stephen Pfeffer
Tax Assessor	Scott Imbriaco
Tax Collector	Carol Hussey
Attorney	James E. Berube Jr
Building	Robert Corby
Planning	W. Bryan Dempsey
Engineering	Birdsall Engineering
Public Works	John Bucciero
Police Chief	Gerald M. Turning Sr
Fire/Emergency Dir	NA

Housing & Construction
Housing Units, 2000*
Total	6,211
Median rent	$1,198
Median SF home value	$187,900

Permits for New Residential Construction
	Units	Value
Total, 2006	154	$14,021,805
Single family	58	$8,408,963
Total, 2007	283	$23,178,339
Single family	59	$9,910,074

Real Property Valuation, 2008
	Parcels	Valuation
Total	7,061	$2,918,765,100
Vacant	732	119,373,500
Residential	6,102	2,097,157,300
Commercial	155	439,797,200
Industrial	16	36,222,500
Apartments	3	219,667,600
Farm land	36	239,200
Farm homestead	17	6,307,800

Average Property Value & Tax, 2008
Residential value	$343,760
Property tax	$5,770
Tax credit/rebate	$980

Public Library
Tinton Falls Public Library
664 Tinton Ave
Tinton Falls, NJ 07724
732-542-3110

Director............Rosemary Tunnicliffe

Library statistics, 2007
Population served	15,053
Full-time/total staff	0/1

	Total	Per capita
Holdings	46,847	3.11
Revenues	$151,803	$10.08
Expenditures	$161,995	$10.76
Annual visits	42,634	2.83
Internet terminals/annual users	2/1,418	

Public Safety
Number of officers, 2007	40

Crime	2006	2007
Total crimes	334	325
Violent	17	14
Murder	0	1
Rape	3	4
Robbery	7	4
Aggravated assault	7	5
Non-violent	317	311
Burglary	49	43
Larceny	252	250
Vehicle theft	16	18
Domestic violence	162	133
Arson	0	2
Total crime rate	19.3	19.0
Violent	1.0	0.8
Non-violent	18.4	18.2

Public School District
(for school year 2007-08 except as noted)

Tinton Falls School District
658 Tinton Avenue
Tinton Falls, NJ 07724
(732) 460-2404

Superintendent	John P. Russo
Number of schools	3
Grade plan	K-8
Enrollment	1,583
Attendance rate, '06-07	95.3%
Dropout rate	NA
Students per teacher	10.4
Per pupil expenditure	$16,108
Median faculty salary	$55,425
Median administrator salary	$103,794
Grade 12 enrollment	NA
High school graduation rate	NA

Assessment test results
(percent scoring at proficient or advanced level)
	Language	Math
NJASK-Grade 3	90.7%	84.2%
GEPA-Grade 8	82.9%	88.7%
HSPA-High School	NA	NA

SAT Score Averages, 2006-07
Pct tested	Math	Verbal	Writing
NA	NA	NA	NA

Teacher Qualifications
Avg. years of experience	12
Highly-qualified teachers one subject/all subjects	100%/100%

No Child Left Behind
AYP, 2006-07	Meets Standards

Municipal Finance
State Aid Programs, 2009
Total aid	$1,921,872
CMPTRA	148,321
Energy tax receipts	1,725,292
Garden State Trust	218

General Budget, 2008
Total tax levy	$49,053,708
County levy	8,259,424
County taxes	7,329,133
County library	441,247
County health	0
County open space	489,043
School levy	29,599,898
Muni. levy	11,194,386
Misc. revenues	10,628,053

Taxes	2006	2007	2008
General tax rate per $100	3.59	3.683	1.679
County equalization ratio	49.74	43.01	89.46
Net valuation taxable	$1,259,348,700	$1,280,603,288	$2,922,487,599
State equalized value	$2,929,583,421	$3,226,755,881	$582,783,032

* US Census Bureau
** New Jersey Department of Labor

See Introduction for an explanation of all data sources.

Demographics & Socio-Economic Characteristics[†]

(2000 US Census, except as noted)

Population
1980*	64,455
1990*	76,371
2000	89,706
Male	43,160
Female	46,546
2007 (estimate)*	95,148
Population density	2,322.4

Race & Hispanic Origin, 2000
Race
White	83,939
Black/African American	1,568
American Indian/Alaska Native	117
Asian	2,207
Native Hawaiian/Pacific Islander	21
Other race	850
Two or more races	1,004
Hispanic origin, total	4,070
Mexican	720
Puerto Rican	1,764
Cuban	326
Other Hispanic	1,260

Age & Nativity, 2000
Under 5 years	4,956
18 years and over	68,815
21 years and over	65,852
65 years and over	15,464
85 years and over	1,708
Median age	40.2
Native-born	83,513
Foreign-born	6,254

Educational Attainment, 2000
Population 25 years and over	62,453
Less than 9th grade	3.2%
High school grad or higher	86.2%
Bachelor's degree or higher	23.8%
Graduate degree	8.0%

Income & Poverty, 1999
Per capita income	$25,010
Median household income	$54,776
Median family income	$62,561
Persons in poverty	4,988
H'holds receiving public assistance	608
H'holds receiving social security	11,254

Households, 2000
Total households	33,510
With persons under 18	11,247
With persons over 65	10,409
Family households	24,427
Single-person households	7,619
Persons per household	2.62
Persons per family	3.09

Labor & Employment
Total civilian labor force, 2007**	48,469
Unemployment rate	5.1%
Total civilian labor force, 2000	43,541
Unemployment rate	4.6%

Employed persons 16 years and over by occupation, 2000
Managers & professionals	14,278
Service occupations	6,463
Sales & office occupations	12,729
Farming, fishing & forestry	39
Construction & maintenance	4,206
Production & transportation	3,831
Self-employed persons	2,373

[†] see Appendix C for American Community Survey data
[‡] Branch of county library
[*] US Census Bureau
[**] New Jersey Department of Labor
[§] State Fiscal Year July 1–June 30

See Introduction for an explanation of all data sources.

General Information
Township of Toms River
(formerly Dover Township)
33 Washington St
Toms River, NJ 08753
732-341-1000
Website	www.townshipofdover.com
Year of incorporation	1768
Land/water area (sq. miles)	40.97/11.96
Form of government	Mayor-Council

Government
Legislative Districts
US Congressional	3
State Legislative	10

Local Officials, 2009
Mayor	Thomas Kelaher
Business Admin	Robert Chankalian
Clerk	J. Mark Mutter
Finance Dir	Christine Manolio
Tax Assessor	Glenn Seelhorst
Tax Collector	Kathleen Adams
Attorney	Kenneth Fitzsimmons
Building	Ken Anderson
Comm Dev/Planning	NA
Engineering	Frank Sadeghi
Public Works	Louis Amoruso
Police Chief	Michael Mastronardy
Emerg/Fire Director	John Lightbody

Housing & Construction
Housing Units, 2000*
Total	41,116
Median rent	$789
Median SF home value	$149,900

Permits for New Residential Construction
	Units	Value
Total, 2006	244	$39,748,316
Single family	244	$39,748,316
Total, 2007	450	$37,181,506
Single family	184	$24,063,756

Real Property Valuation, 2008
	Parcels	Valuation
Total	41,366	$6,442,566,500
Vacant	1,762	118,897,800
Residential	37,949	5,267,210,200
Commercial	1,541	932,927,400
Industrial	41	33,112,500
Apartments	36	87,789,600
Farm land	22	100,700
Farm homestead	15	2,528,300

Average Property Value & Tax, 2008
Residential value	$138,809
Property tax	$4,548
Tax credit/rebate	$882

Public Library
Toms River Branch Library[‡]
101 Washington St
Toms River, NJ 08753
732-349-6300
Branch Librarian	Diane Tralka

Library statistics, 2007
see Ocean County profile
for library system statistics

Public Safety
Number of officers, 2007	160

Crime	2006	2007
Total crimes	2,075	2,167
Violent	112	125
Murder	0	0
Rape	12	14
Robbery	44	46
Aggravated assault	56	65
Non-violent	1,963	2,042
Burglary	312	327
Larceny	1,552	1,640
Vehicle theft	99	75
Domestic violence	698	649
Arson	17	12
Total crime rate	21.9	22.8
Violent	1.2	1.3
Non-violent	20.7	21.5

Public School District
(for school year 2007-08 except as noted)

Toms River Regional School District
1144 Hooper Avenue
Toms River, NJ 08753
(732) 505-5510
Superintendent	Michael J. Ritacco
Number of schools	18
Grade plan	K-12
Enrollment	17,259
Attendance rate, '06-07	93.8%
Dropout rate	2.8%
Students per teacher	13.0
Per pupil expenditure	$10,496
Median faculty salary	$49,126
Median administrator salary	$114,200
Grade 12 enrollment	1,296
High school graduation rate	89.2%

Assessment test results
(percent scoring at proficient or advanced level)
	Language	Math
NJASK-Grade 3	93.4%	94.2%
GEPA-Grade 8	76.3%	87.3%
HSPA-High School	71.8%	83.4%

SAT Score Averages, 2006-07
Pct tested	Math	Verbal	Writing
NA	NA	NA	NA

Teacher Qualifications
Avg. years of experience	8
Highly-qualified teachers one subject/all subjects	99.5%/99.5%

No Child Left Behind
AYP, 2006-07	Meets Standards

Municipal Finance[§]
State Aid Programs, 2009
Total aid	$10,951,379
CMPTRA	1,266,101
Energy tax receipts	9,409,961
Garden State Trust	1,449

General Budget, 2008
Total tax levy	$211,556,830
County levy	53,235,299
County taxes	43,898,889
County library	5,159,449
County health	2,100,614
County open space	2,076,347
School levy	105,608,331
Muni. levy	52,713,200
Misc. revenues	42,480,635

Taxes
	2006	2007	2008
General tax rate per $100	3.052	3.061	3.277
County equalization ratio	44.23	38.71	37.40
Net valuation taxable	$6,345,008,300	$6,413,452,768	$6,457,308,775
State equalized value	$16,407,971,572	$17,123,129,561	$12,926,077,645

Demographics & Socio-Economic Characteristics
(2000 US Census, except as noted)

Population
1980*	11,448
1990*	10,177
2000	9,892
Male	4,672
Female	5,220
2007 (estimate)*	10,602
Population density	2,650.5

Race & Hispanic Origin, 2000
Race
White	9,239
Black/African American	111
American Indian/Alaska Native	2
Asian	224
Native Hawaiian/Pacific Islander	0
Other race	195
Two or more races	121
Hispanic origin, total	630
Mexican	5
Puerto Rican	253
Cuban	30
Other Hispanic	342

Age & Nativity, 2000
Under 5 years	444
18 years and over	8,085
21 years and over	7,808
65 years and over	2,113
85 years and over	257
Median age	42.7
Native-born	8,533
Foreign-born	1,313

Educational Attainment, 2000
Population 25 years and over	7,402
Less than 9th grade	11.9%
High school grad or higher	74.7%
Bachelor's degree or higher	17.8%
Graduate degree	4.1%

Income & Poverty, 1999
Per capita income	$26,561
Median household income	$60,408
Median family income	$69,354
Persons in poverty	398
H'holds receiving public assistance	0
H'holds receiving social security	1,369

Households, 2000
Total households	3,539
With persons under 18	1,028
With persons over 65	1,385
Family households	2,645
Single-person households	770
Persons per household	2.63
Persons per family	3.09

Labor & Employment
Total civilian labor force, 2007**	5,225
Unemployment rate	2.9%
Total civilian labor force, 2000	5,129
Unemployment rate	3.5%

Employed persons 16 years and over by occupation, 2000
Managers & professionals	1,330
Service occupations	702
Sales & office occupations	1,544
Farming, fishing & forestry	0
Construction & maintenance	539
Production & transportation	832
Self-employed persons	188

* US Census Bureau
** New Jersey Department of Labor

General Information
Borough of Totowa
537 Totowa Rd
Totowa, NJ 07512
973-956-1000
Website	www.totowanj.org
Year of incorporation	1898
Land/water area (sq. miles)	4.00/0.05
Form of government	Borough

Government

Legislative Districts
US Congressional	8
State Legislative	35

Local Officials, 2009
Mayor	John Coiro
Manager/Admin	NA
Clerk	Joseph Wassel
Finance Dir	J. Iandiorio
Tax Assessor	Curt Masklee
Tax Collector	Elaine Raddin
Attorney	Kristin M. Corrado
Building	Allan Burghardt
Comm Dev/Planning	NA
Engineering	Alaimo Group
Public Works	Doug Wright
Police Chief	Robert Coyle
Emerg/Fire Director	Larry Sperling

Housing & Construction

Housing Units, 2000*
Total	3,630
Median rent	$935
Median SF home value	$197,500

Permits for New Residential Construction
	Units	Value
Total, 2006	47	$8,214,455
Single family	47	$8,214,455
Total, 2007	34	$6,310,224
Single family	34	$6,310,224

Real Property Valuation, 2008
	Parcels	Valuation
Total	3,806	$1,170,342,100
Vacant	95	13,260,200
Residential	3,423	658,512,500
Commercial	223	320,241,600
Industrial	63	177,776,500
Apartments	0	0
Farm land	1	500
Farm homestead	1	550,800

Average Property Value & Tax, 2008
Residential value	$192,483
Property tax	$6,807
Tax credit/rebate	$1,062

Public Library
Dwight D. Eisenhower Library
537 Totowa Rd
Totowa, NJ 07512
973-790-3265
Director	Joan A. Krautheim

Library statistics, 2007
Population served	9,892
Full-time/total staff	2/5

	Total	Per capita
Holdings	55,522	5.61
Revenues	$836,215	$84.53
Expenditures	$656,652	$66.38
Annual visits	63,351	6.40
Internet terminals/annual users	14/10,446	

Public Safety
Number of officers, 2007	28

Crime	2006	2007
Total crimes	337	285
Violent	9	12
Murder	0	0
Rape	0	3
Robbery	6	1
Aggravated assault	3	8
Non-violent	328	273
Burglary	53	29
Larceny	235	223
Vehicle theft	40	21
Domestic violence	17	20
Arson	0	0
Total crime rate	31.8	26.8
Violent	0.8	1.1
Non-violent	31.0	25.7

Public School District
(for school year 2007-08 except as noted)

Totowa School District
10 Crews Street
Totowa, NJ 07512
(973) 956-0010
Chief School Admin	Vincent Varcadipane
Number of schools	2
Grade plan	K-8
Enrollment	982
Attendance rate, '06-07	95.5%
Dropout rate	NA
Students per teacher	10.1
Per pupil expenditure	$12,974
Median faculty salary	$60,100
Median administrator salary	$113,951
Grade 12 enrollment	NA
High school graduation rate	NA

Assessment test results
(percent scoring at proficient or advanced level)
	Language	Math
NJASK-Grade 3	93.5%	83.7%
GEPA-Grade 8	76.7%	89.3%
HSPA-High School	NA	NA

SAT Score Averages, 2006-07
Pct tested	Math	Verbal	Writing
NA	NA	NA	NA

Teacher Qualifications
Avg. years of experience	7
Highly-qualified teachers one subject/all subjects	100%/100%

No Child Left Behind
AYP, 2006-07	Meets Standards

Municipal Finance

State Aid Programs, 2009
Total aid	$1,727,129
CMPTRA	220,685
Energy tax receipts	1,450,312
Garden State Trust	0

General Budget, 2008
Total tax levy	$41,437,237
County levy	11,670,351
County taxes	11,436,819
County library	0
County health	0
County open space	233,532
School levy	19,712,477
Muni. levy	10,054,409
Misc. revenues	5,716,926

Taxes
	2006	2007	2008
General tax rate per $100	3.21	3.4	3.539
County equalization ratio	56.04	50.95	50.49
Net valuation taxable	$1,188,302,800	$1,173,139,182	$1,171,789,259
State equalized value	$2,333,856,557	$2,322,112,624	$2,511,295,111

See Introduction for an explanation of all data sources.

Demographics & Socio-Economic Characteristics†

(2000 US Census, except as noted)

Population

1980*	92,124
1990*	88,675
2000	85,403
Male	42,180
Female	43,223
2007 (estimate)*	82,804
Population density	10,809.9

Race & Hispanic Origin, 2000

Race

White	27,802
Black/African American	44,465
American Indian/Alaska Native	300
Asian	716
Native Hawaiian/Pacific Islander	199
Other race	9,190
Two or more races	2,731
Hispanic origin, total	18,391
Mexican	925
Puerto Rican	8,952
Cuban	200
Other Hispanic	8,314

Age & Nativity, 2000

Under 5 years	6,468
18 years and over	61,757
21 years and over	58,165
65 years and over	9,716
85 years and over	1,201
Median age	32.2
Native-born	73,234
Foreign-born	12,024

Educational Attainment, 2000

Population 25 years and over	53,021
Less than 9th grade	12.2%
High school grad or higher	62.4%
Bachelor's degree or higher	9.2%
Graduate degree	3.5%

Income & Poverty, 1999

Per capita income	$14,621
Median household income	$31,074
Median family income	$36,681
Persons in poverty	17,222
H'holds receiving public assistance	2,255
H'holds receiving social security	7,836

Households, 2000

Total households	29,437
With persons under 18	11,659
With persons over 65	7,490
Family households	18,695
Single-person households	8,756
Persons per household	2.75
Persons per family	3.38

Labor & Employment

Total civilian labor force, 2007**	38,156
Unemployment rate	9.9%
Total civilian labor force, 2000	36,283
Unemployment rate	10.5%

Employed persons 16 years and over by occupation, 2000

Managers & professionals	6,980
Service occupations	8,390
Sales & office occupations	8,973
Farming, fishing & forestry	99
Construction & maintenance	2,731
Production & transportation	5,297
Self-employed persons	936

† see Appendix C for American Community Survey data
* US Census Bureau
** New Jersey Department of Labor
§ State Fiscal Year July 1–June 30

General Information

City of Trenton
319 E State St
Trenton, NJ 08608
609-989-3185

Website	www.trentonnj.org
Year of incorporation	1792
Land/water area (sq. miles)	7.66/0.49
Form of government	Mayor-Council

Government

Legislative Districts

US Congressional	4, 12
State Legislative	15

Local Officials, 2009

Mayor	Douglas H. Palmer
Manager	Jane Feigenbaum
Clerk	Juanita M. Joyner (Actg)
Finance Dir	Ronald Zilinski
Tax Assessor	Patricia Hice
Tax Collector	Ed Kirkendall
Attorney	R. Denise Lyles
Building	Leonard Pucciatti
Planning	Andrew Carten
Engineering	Sean Semple
Public Works	Eric Jackson
Police Chief	Joseph Santiago
Emerg/Fire Director	Richard Laird (Actg)

Housing & Construction

Housing Units, 2000*

Total	33,843
Median rent	$604
Median SF home value	$65,500

Permits for New Residential Construction

	Units	Value
Total, 2006	5	$546,600
Single family	5	$546,600
Total, 2007	237	$25,752,860
Single family	17	$4,376,700

Real Property Valuation, 2008

	Parcels	Valuation
Total	24,637	$1,955,839,810
Vacant	1,132	18,073,280
Residential	21,137	1,319,790,070
Commercial	2,122	530,895,060
Industrial	88	43,337,200
Apartments	158	43,744,200
Farm land	0	0
Farm homestead	0	0

Average Property Value & Tax, 2008

Residential value	$62,440
Property tax	$2,736
Tax credit/rebate	$743

Public Library

Trenton Public Library
120 Academy St
Trenton, NJ 08608
609-392-7188

Director	Larry Kroah (Asst)

Library statistics, 2007

Population served	85,403
Full-time/total staff	18/49

	Total	Per capita
Holdings	460,503	5.39
Revenues	$3,523,479	$41.26
Expenditures	$3,861,901	$45.22
Annual visits	505,205	5.92
Internet terminals/annual users	98/120,112	

Public Safety

Number of officers, 2007	360

Crime	2006	2007
Total crimes	3,895	3,931
Violent	1,281	1,176
Murder	18	25
Rape	33	15
Robbery	633	597
Aggravated assault	597	539
Non-violent	2,614	2,755
Burglary	810	856
Larceny	1,340	1,512
Vehicle theft	464	387
Domestic violence	1,580	1,608
Arson	23	21
Total crime rate	46.0	46.8
Violent	15.1	14.0
Non-violent	30.9	32.8

Public School District

(for school year 2007-08 except as noted)

Trenton School District
108 North Clinton Avenue
Trenton, NJ 08609
(609) 656-4900

Superintendent	Rodney Lofton
Number of schools	21
Grade plan	K-12
Enrollment	11,447
Attendance rate, '06-07	90.3%
Dropout rate	9.8%
Students per teacher	10.1
Per pupil expenditure	$16,120
Median faculty salary	$74,151
Median administrator salary	$118,229
Grade 12 enrollment	541
High school graduation rate	82.3%

Assessment test results

(percent scoring at proficient or advanced level)

	Language	Math
NJASK-Grade 3	62.4%	66.9%
GEPA-Grade 8	22.7%	43.8%
HSPA-High School	21.4%	44.1%

SAT Score Averages, 2006-07

Pct tested	Math	Verbal	Writing
NA	NA	NA	NA

Teacher Qualifications

Avg. years of experience	15
Highly-qualified teachers one subject/all subjects	95.5%/95.0%

No Child Left Behind

AYP, 2006-07	Needs Improvement

Municipal Finance§

State Aid Programs, 2009

Total aid	$51,556,909
CMPTRA	41,485,412
Energy tax receipts	10,067,896
Garden State Trust	2,797

General Budget, 2008

Total tax levy	$86,192,236
County levy	15,232,583
County taxes	14,254,291
County library	0
County health	0
County open space	978,292
School levy	22,019,437
Muni. levy	48,940,216
Misc. revenues	147,977,163

Taxes

	2006	2007	2008
General tax rate per $100	4.1	4.19	4.383
County equalization ratio	82.25	68.32	62.25
Net valuation taxable	$1,939,226,395	$1,963,159,141	$1,967,081,328
State equalized value	$2,853,742,822	$3,145,808,409	$3,197,686,305

See Introduction for an explanation of all data sources.

Demographics & Socio-Economic Characteristics

(2000 US Census, except as noted)

Population

1980*	2,472
1990*	3,048
2000	3,517
Male	1,749
Female	1,768
2007 (estimate)*	3,846
Population density	1,050.8

Race & Hispanic Origin, 2000

Race

White	3,408
Black/African American	14
American Indian/Alaska Native	10
Asian	19
Native Hawaiian/Pacific Islander	0
Other race	19
Two or more races	47
Hispanic origin, total	109
Mexican	55
Puerto Rican	32
Cuban	4
Other Hispanic	18

Age & Nativity, 2000

Under 5 years	209
18 years and over	2,708
21 years and over	2,579
65 years and over	591
85 years and over	62
Median age	39.2
Native-born	3,349
Foreign-born	94

Educational Attainment, 2000

Population 25 years and over	2,408
Less than 9th grade	4.4%
High school grad or higher	84.6%
Bachelor's degree or higher	13.5%
Graduate degree	4.3%

Income & Poverty, 1999

Per capita income	$20,118
Median household income	$40,042
Median family income	$49,528
Persons in poverty	273
H'holds receiving public assistance	30
H'holds receiving social security	569

Households, 2000

Total households	1,477
With persons under 18	441
With persons over 65	452
Family households	921
Single-person households	467
Persons per household	2.38
Persons per family	3.02

Labor & Employment

Total civilian labor force, 2007**	1,945
Unemployment rate	6.3%
Total civilian labor force, 2000	1,634
Unemployment rate	6.3%

Employed persons 16 years and over by occupation, 2000

Managers & professionals	435
Service occupations	256
Sales & office occupations	420
Farming, fishing & forestry	15
Construction & maintenance	236
Production & transportation	169
Self-employed persons	83

‡ Branch of county library
* US Census Bureau
** New Jersey Department of Labor

General Information

Borough of Tuckerton
140 E Main St
Tuckerton, NJ 08087
609-296-2701

Website	tuckertonborough.com
Year of incorporation	1901
Land/water area (sq. miles)	3.66/0.12
Form of government	Borough

Government

Legislative Districts

US Congressional	3
State Legislative	9

Local Officials, 2009

Mayor	Lewis Eggert
Manager/Admin	NA
Clerk	Grace Di Elmo
Finance Dir	Laura Giovene
Tax Assessor	Irene Raftery
Tax Collector	E.J. Mary King
Attorney	Terry F. Brady
Building	Phil Read
Comm Dev/Planning	NA
Engineering	Frank Little
Public Works	Carl R. Hewitt Jr
Police Chief	Charles Robinson
Emerg/Fire Director	Fred Leister

Housing & Construction

Housing Units, 2000*

Total	1,971
Median rent	$747
Median SF home value	$105,900

Permits for New Residential Construction

	Units	Value
Total, 2006	16	$2,298,853
Single family	11	$2,013,138
Total, 2007	21	$3,304,524
Single family	16	$3,018,809

Real Property Valuation, 2008

	Parcels	Valuation
Total	1,877	$428,212,400
Vacant	222	24,278,600
Residential	1,556	343,774,100
Commercial	96	39,042,000
Industrial	0	0
Apartments	3	21,117,700
Farm land	0	0
Farm homestead	0	0

Average Property Value & Tax, 2008

Residential value	$220,935
Property tax	$4,422
Tax credit/rebate	$848

Public Library

Tuckerton Branch Library‡
380 Bay Ave
Tuckerton, NJ 08087
609-296-1470

Branch Librarian	Rita Oakes

Library statistics, 2007

see Ocean County profile
for library system statistics

Public Safety

Number of officers, 2007	10

Crime	2006	2007
Total crimes	73	49
Violent	4	4
Murder	0	0
Rape	0	0
Robbery	0	0
Aggravated assault	4	4
Non-violent	69	45
Burglary	16	3
Larceny	48	40
Vehicle theft	5	2
Domestic violence	42	11
Arson	0	0
Total crime rate	19.3	12.8
Violent	1.1	1.0
Non-violent	18.3	11.8

Public School District

(for school year 2007-08 except as noted)

Tuckerton Borough School District
Marine Street, PO Box 217
Tuckerton, NJ 08087
(609) 296-2858

Consulting Superintendent	Robert M. Gray Jr
Number of schools	1
Grade plan	K-6
Enrollment	287
Attendance rate, '06-07	93.9%
Dropout rate	NA
Students per teacher	8.4
Per pupil expenditure	$13,254
Median faculty salary	$40,530
Median administrator salary	$60,749
Grade 12 enrollment	NA
High school graduation rate	NA

Assessment test results

(percent scoring at proficient or advanced level)

	Language	Math
NJASK-Grade 3	94.0%	100.0%
GEPA-Grade 8	NA	NA
HSPA-High School	NA	NA

SAT Score Averages, 2006-07

Pct tested	Math	Verbal	Writing
NA	NA	NA	NA

Teacher Qualifications

Avg. years of experience	6
Highly-qualified teachers one subject/all subjects	100%/100%

No Child Left Behind

AYP, 2006-07	Meets Standards

Municipal Finance

State Aid Programs, 2009

Total aid	$418,684
CMPTRA	30,074
Energy tax receipts	377,986
Garden State Trust	162

General Budget, 2008

Total tax levy	$8,582,925
County levy	1,656,759
County taxes	1,366,221
County library	160,560
County health	65,369
County open space	64,610
School levy	4,649,684
Muni. levy	2,276,482
Misc. revenues	1,558,092

Taxes	2006	2007	2008
General tax rate per $100	1.805	1.871	2.002
County equalization ratio	96.49	85.61	79.97
Net valuation taxable	$420,024,500	$424,597,874	$428,807,230
State equalized value	$491,320,935	$530,791,238	$1,792,002,936

See Introduction for an explanation of all data sources.

Demographics & Socio-Economic Characteristics

(2000 US Census, except as noted)

Population

1980*	6,354
1990*	6,156
2000	6,649
Male	3,358
Female	3,291
2007 (estimate)*	6,666
Population density	3,545.7

Race & Hispanic Origin, 2000

Race

White	6,280
Black/African American	58
American Indian/Alaska Native	13
Asian	82
Native Hawaiian/Pacific Islander	0
Other race	90
Two or more races	126
Hispanic origin, total	538
Mexican	77
Puerto Rican	318
Cuban	49
Other Hispanic	94

Age & Nativity, 2000

Under 5 years	483
18 years and over	4,713
21 years and over	4,454
65 years and over	498
85 years and over	32
Median age	34.4
Native-born	6,310
Foreign-born	339

Educational Attainment, 2000

Population 25 years and over	4,167
Less than 9th grade	4.8%
High school grad or higher	79.0%
Bachelor's degree or higher	8.5%
Graduate degree	2.0%

Income & Poverty, 1999

Per capita income	$20,973
Median household income	$59,946
Median family income	$65,179
Persons in poverty	319
H'holds receiving public assistance	24
H'holds receiving social security	552

Households, 2000

Total households	2,143
With persons under 18	1,038
With persons over 65	388
Family households	1,722
Single-person households	332
Persons per household	3.09
Persons per family	3.44

Labor & Employment

Total civilian labor force, 2007**	3,643
Unemployment rate	5.1%
Total civilian labor force, 2000	3,418
Unemployment rate	5.5%

Employed persons 16 years and over by occupation, 2000

Managers & professionals	737
Service occupations	458
Sales & office occupations	948
Farming, fishing & forestry	0
Construction & maintenance	530
Production & transportation	557
Self-employed persons	89

---

* US Census Bureau
** New Jersey Department of Labor
§ State Fiscal Year July 1–June 30

See Introduction for an explanation of all data sources.

General Information

Borough of Union Beach
650 Poole Ave
Union Beach, NJ 07735
732-264-2277

Website	www.unionbeach.net
Year of incorporation	1925
Land/water area (sq. miles)	1.88/0.06
Form of government	Borough

Government

Legislative Districts

US Congressional	6
State Legislative	13

Local Officials, 2009

Mayor	Paul J. Smith Jr
Manager/Admin	NA
Clerk	Mary Sabik
Finance Dir	Joseph Faccone
Tax Assessor	George Lockwood
Tax Collector	NA
Attorney	John T. Lane Jr
Building	Robert Burlew
Comm Dev/Planning	NA
Engineering	Edward Broberg
Public Works	NA
Police Chief	Michael Kelly
Emerg/Fire Director	Paul Sweeney

Housing & Construction

Housing Units, 2000*

Total	2,229
Median rent	$1,002
Median SF home value	$132,800

Permits for New Residential Construction

	Units	Value
Total, 2006	10	$842,777
Single family	10	$842,777
Total, 2007	6	$504,287
Single family	6	$504,287

Real Property Valuation, 2008

	Parcels	Valuation
Total	2,318	$449,552,300
Vacant	117	7,182,800
Residential	2,137	383,651,000
Commercial	58	14,099,100
Industrial	5	44,428,600
Apartments	1	190,800
Farm land	0	0
Farm homestead	0	0

Average Property Value & Tax, 2008

Residential value	$179,528
Property tax	$5,216
Tax credit/rebate	$940

Public Library

Union Beach Mem. Library
810 Union Ave
Union Beach, NJ 07735
732-264-3792

Director	NA

Library statistics, 2007

Population served	6,649
Full-time/total staff	NA/0

	Total	Per capita
Holdings	0	NA
Revenues	$0	NA
Expenditures	$0	NA
Annual visits	NA	NA
Internet terminals/annual users	NA/NA	

Public Safety

Number of officers, 2007		16

Crime	2006	2007
Total crimes	47	100
Violent	6	12
Murder	0	0
Rape	0	0
Robbery	0	3
Aggravated assault	6	9
Non-violent	41	88
Burglary	13	17
Larceny	27	68
Vehicle theft	1	3
Domestic violence	61	58
Arson	0	0
Total crime rate	7.1	15.1
Violent	0.9	1.8
Non-violent	6.2	13.3

Public School District

(for school year 2007-08 except as noted)

Union Beach Borough School District
1207 Florance Avenue
Union Beach, NJ 07735
(732) 264-5405

Superintendent	Arthur J. Waltz
Number of schools	1
Grade plan	K-8
Enrollment	800
Attendance rate, '06-07	94.9%
Dropout rate	NA
Students per teacher	10.7
Per pupil expenditure	$12,461
Median faculty salary	$49,675
Median administrator salary	$91,818
Grade 12 enrollment	NA
High school graduation rate	NA

Assessment test results

(percent scoring at proficient or advanced level)

	Language	Math
NJASK-Grade 3	92.9%	84.3%
GEPA-Grade 8	73.8%	88.1%
HSPA-High School	NA	NA

SAT Score Averages, 2006-07

Pct tested	Math	Verbal	Writing
NA	NA	NA	NA

Teacher Qualifications

Avg. years of experience	12
Highly-qualified teachers one subject/all subjects	98.5%/98.5%

No Child Left Behind

AYP, 2006-07	Meets Standards

Municipal Finance§

State Aid Programs, 2009

Total aid	$819,618
CMPTRA	144,706
Energy tax receipts	662,618
Garden State Trust	0

General Budget, 2008

Total tax levy	$13,071,845
County levy	1,782,290
County taxes	1,555,966
County library	93,634
County health	28,934
County open space	103,757
School levy	6,263,424
Muni. levy	5,026,131
Misc. revenues	2,521,654

Taxes	2006	2007	2008
General tax rate per $100	2.627	2.847	2.909
County equalization ratio	79.67	69.38	65.66
Net valuation taxable	$444,668,600	$447,508,698	$449,916,563
State equalized value	$641,307,897	$681,371,734	$688,489,627

Demographics & Socio-Economic Characteristics[†]

(2000 US Census, except as noted)

Population

1980*	55,593
1990*	58,012
2000	67,088
Male	33,639
Female	33,449
2007 (estimate)*	62,715
Population density	49,381.9

Race & Hispanic Origin, 2000

Race

White	39,167
Black/African American	2,442
American Indian/Alaska Native	467
Asian	1,441
Native Hawaiian/Pacific Islander	54
Other race	18,911
Two or more races	4,606
Hispanic origin, total	55,226
Mexican	2,752
Puerto Rican	7,388
Cuban	10,296
Other Hispanic	34,790

Age & Nativity, 2000

Under 5 years	4,945
18 years and over	50,117
21 years and over	47,197
65 years and over	6,694
85 years and over	739
Median age	32.5
Native-born	27,710
Foreign-born	39,378

Educational Attainment, 2000

Population 25 years and over	42,677
Less than 9th grade	24.9%
High school grad or higher	54.4%
Bachelor's degree or higher	12.5%
Graduate degree	5.4%

Income & Poverty, 1999

Per capita income	$13,997
Median household income	$30,642
Median family income	$32,246
Persons in poverty	14,244
H'holds receiving public assistance	1,495
H'holds receiving social security	4,894

Households, 2000

Total households	22,872
With persons under 18	9,473
With persons over 65	5,097
Family households	16,067
Single-person households	5,259
Persons per household	2.92
Persons per family	3.40

Labor & Employment

Total civilian labor force, 2007**	27,070
Unemployment rate	6.4%
Total civilian labor force, 2000	29,551
Unemployment rate	12.4%

Employed persons 16 years and over by occupation, 2000

Managers & professionals	4,436
Service occupations	4,969
Sales & office occupations	6,315
Farming, fishing & forestry	35
Construction & maintenance	2,038
Production & transportation	8,081
Self-employed persons	1,029

[†] see Appendix C for American Community Survey data
* US Census Bureau
** New Jersey Department of Labor
§ State Fiscal Year July 1–June 30

General Information

City of Union
3715 Palisade Ave
Union City, NJ 07087
201-348-5700

Website	www.ucnj.com
Year of incorporation	1925
Land/water area (sq. miles)	1.27/0.00
Form of government	Commission

Government

Legislative Districts

US Congressional	13
State Legislative	33

Local Officials, 2009

Mayor	Brian P. Stack
Manager/Admin	NA
Clerk	William Senande
Finance Dir	Douglas Gutch
Tax Assessor	Salvatore Bonaccorsi
Tax Collector	Sonia Schulman
Attorney	Donald Scarinci
Building	Martin Martinetti
Comm Dev/Planning	NA
Engineering	NA
Public Works	NA
Police Chief	Charles Everett
Emerg/Fire Svcs	North Hudson Regional

Housing & Construction

Housing Units, 2000*

Total	23,741
Median rent	$658
Median SF home value	$141,000

Permits for New Residential Construction

	Units	Value
Total, 2006	47	$4,543,460
Single family	0	$0
Total, 2007	196	$11,221,453
Single family	1	$45,825

Real Property Valuation, 2008

	Parcels	Valuation
Total	8,308	$1,440,481,800
Vacant	380	26,332,800
Residential	5,725	695,066,600
Commercial	1,393	424,954,400
Industrial	97	34,108,700
Apartments	713	260,019,300
Farm land	0	0
Farm homestead	0	0

Average Property Value & Tax, 2008

Residential value	$121,409
Property tax	$6,227
Tax credit/rebate	$918

Public Library

Union City Public Library
324 43rd St
Union City, NJ 07087
201-866-7500

Director ... Rita Mann

Library statistics, 2007

Population served	67,088
Full-time/total staff	2/11

	Total	Per capita
Holdings	84,385	1.26
Revenues	$1,065,374	$15.88
Expenditures	$825,630	$12.31
Annual visits	92,000	1.37
Internet terminals/annual users	87/78,587	

Public Safety

Number of officers, 2007 ... 167

Crime	2006	2007
Total crimes	1,983	1,829
Violent	407	407
Murder	1	1
Rape	4	4
Robbery	214	182
Aggravated assault	188	220
Non-violent	1,576	1,422
Burglary	405	332
Larceny	931	917
Vehicle theft	240	173
Domestic violence	650	525
Arson	6	6
Total crime rate	30.4	28.6
Violent	6.2	6.4
Non-violent	24.2	22.2

Public School District

(for school year 2007-08 except as noted)

Union City School District
3912 Bergen Turnpike
Union City, NJ 07087
(201) 348-5851

Superintendent	Stanley Sanger
Number of schools	13
Grade plan	K-12
Enrollment	9,730
Attendance rate, '06-07	95.1%
Dropout rate	2.2%
Students per teacher	11.2
Per pupil expenditure	$16,280
Median faculty salary	$54,948
Median administrator salary	$124,993
Grade 12 enrollment	613
High school graduation rate	85.6%

Assessment test results

(percent scoring at proficient or advanced level)

	Language	Math
NJASK-Grade 3	87.4%	82.2%
GEPA-Grade 8	70.2%	75.7%
HSPA-High School	59.1%	69.7%

SAT Score Averages, 2006-07

Pct tested	Math	Verbal	Writing
NA	NA	NA	NA

Teacher Qualifications

Avg. years of experience	8
Highly-qualified teachers one subject/all subjects	100%/100%

No Child Left Behind

AYP, 2006-07 ... Meets Standards

Municipal Finance[§]

State Aid Programs, 2009

Total aid	$18,059,803
CMPTRA	14,232,494
Energy tax receipts	3,827,309
Garden State Trust	0

General Budget, 2008

Total tax levy	$79,202,621
County levy	14,365,430
County taxes	13,986,451
County library	0
County health	0
County open space	378,979
School levy	16,127,632
Muni. levy	48,709,559
Misc. revenues	49,770,696

Taxes

	2006	2007	2008
General tax rate per $100	4.796	5.107	5.474
County equalization ratio	49.69	42.02	38.63
Net valuation taxable	$1,415,124,500	$1,430,722,422	$1,447,116,081
State equalized value	$3,375,701,896	$3,692,454,277	$3,809,384,545

See Introduction for an explanation of all data sources.

Demographics & Socio-Economic Characteristics

(2000 US Census, except as noted)

Population

1980*	3,971
1990*	5,078
2000	6,160
Male	2,557
Female	3,603
2007 (estimate)*	6,272
Population density	330.6

Race & Hispanic Origin, 2000

Race

White	5,041
Black/African American	823
American Indian/Alaska Native	11
Asian	98
Native Hawaiian/Pacific Islander	1
Other race	98
Two or more races	88
Hispanic origin, total	316
Mexican	15
Puerto Rican	159
Cuban	38
Other Hispanic	104

Age & Nativity, 2000

Under 5 years	278
18 years and over	4,980
21 years and over	4,842
65 years and over	404
85 years and over	25
Median age	37.6
Native-born	5,818
Foreign-born	342

Educational Attainment, 2000

Population 25 years and over	4,591
Less than 9th grade	9.8%
High school grad or higher	77.1%
Bachelor's degree or higher	31.9%
Graduate degree	11.6%

Income & Poverty, 1999

Per capita income	$29,535
Median household income	$81,089
Median family income	$102,146
Persons in poverty	69
H'holds receiving public assistance	9
H'holds receiving social security	287

Households, 2000

Total households	1,666
With persons under 18	621
With persons over 65	275
Family households	1,163
Single-person households	405
Persons per household	2.61
Persons per family	3.18

Labor & Employment

Total civilian labor force, 2007**	2,643
Unemployment rate	2.9%
Total civilian labor force, 2000	2,386
Unemployment rate	3.0%

Employed persons 16 years and over by occupation, 2000

Managers & professionals	1,272
Service occupations	157
Sales & office occupations	565
Farming, fishing & forestry	9
Construction & maintenance	174
Production & transportation	138
Self-employed persons	190

* US Census Bureau
** New Jersey Department of Labor

See Introduction for an explanation of all data sources.

General Information

Township of Union
140 Perryville Rd
Hampton, NJ 08827
908-735-8027

Website	www.uniontwp-hcnj.org
Year of incorporation	1853
Land/water area (sq. miles)	18.97/1.62
Form of government	Township

Government

Legislative Districts

US Congressional	7
State Legislative	23

Local Officials, 2009

Mayor	Patricia Dzivbek
Manager/Admin	NA
Clerk	Ella M. Ruta
Finance Dir	Grace Brennan
Tax Assessor	Robert Vance
Tax Collector	John Earley
Attorney	J. Peter Jost
Building	John W. Leonard
Comm Dev/Planning	NA
Engineering	Kevin Smith
Public Works	NA
Police Chief	NA
Emerg/Fire Director	Dan VanFossen

Housing & Construction

Housing Units, 2000*

Total	1,725
Median rent	$973
Median SF home value	$285,200

Permits for New Residential Construction

	Units	Value
Total, 2006	32	$6,171,968
Single family	32	$6,171,968
Total, 2007	21	$4,004,016
Single family	21	$4,004,016

Real Property Valuation, 2008

	Parcels	Valuation
Total	2,159	$677,338,118
Vacant	127	17,071,053
Residential	1,713	519,230,400
Commercial	64	93,292,800
Industrial	6	14,192,100
Apartments	1	230,900
Farm land	154	1,073,165
Farm homestead	94	32,247,700

Average Property Value & Tax, 2008

Residential value	$305,190
Property tax	$8,188
Tax credit/rebate	$1,067

Public Library

No public municipal library

Library statistics, 2007

Population served	NA
Full-time/total staff	NA/NA

	Total	Per capita
Holdings	NA	NA
Revenues	NA	NA
Expenditures	NA	NA
Annual visits	NA	NA
Internet terminals/annual users	NA/NA	

Public Safety

Number of officers, 2007	0

Crime	2006	2007
Total crimes	41	49
Violent	3	3
Murder	0	0
Rape	0	0
Robbery	0	1
Aggravated assault	3	2
Non-violent	38	46
Burglary	6	6
Larceny	30	36
Vehicle theft	2	4
Domestic violence	0	29
Arson	0	0
Total crime rate	6.5	7.7
Violent	0.5	0.5
Non-violent	6.0	7.2

Public School District

(for school year 2007-08 except as noted)

Union Township School District
165 Perryville Road
Hampton, NJ 08827
(908) 238-6013

Superintendent	Jeffrey Bender
Number of schools	2
Grade plan	K-8
Enrollment	605
Attendance rate, '06-07	95.8%
Dropout rate	NA
Students per teacher	10.9
Per pupil expenditure	$13,479
Median faculty salary	$56,324
Median administrator salary	$92,400
Grade 12 enrollment	NA
High school graduation rate	NA

Assessment test results

(percent scoring at proficient or advanced level)

	Language	Math
NJASK-Grade 3	96.5%	98.3%
GEPA-Grade 8	84.7%	93.6%
HSPA-High School	NA	NA

SAT Score Averages, 2006-07

Pct tested	Math	Verbal	Writing
NA	NA	NA	NA

Teacher Qualifications

Avg. years of experience	10
Highly-qualified teachers one subject/all subjects	97.5%/97.5%

No Child Left Behind

AYP, 2006-07	Meets Standards

Municipal Finance

State Aid Programs, 2009

Total aid	$539,503
CMPTRA	72,442
Energy tax receipts	417,300
Garden State Trust	26,939

General Budget, 2008

Total tax levy	$18,339,260
County levy	3,460,000
County taxes	2,895,891
County library	251,478
County health	0
County open space	312,631
School levy	13,610,023
Muni. levy	1,269,236
Misc. revenues	2,316,871

Taxes	2006	2007	2008
General tax rate per $100	2.49	2.61	2.683
County equalization ratio	69.87	64.55	65.69
Net valuation taxable	$662,190,668	$674,912,841	$683,551,423
State equalized value	$920,236,400	$961,095,512	$987,436,134

Demographics & Socio-Economic Characteristics
(2000 US Census, except as noted)

Population
1980*	50,184
1990*	50,024
2000	54,405
Male	25,446
Female	28,959
2007 (estimate)*	54,062
Population density	5,927.9

Race & Hispanic Origin, 2000
Race
White	36,809
Black/African American	10,752
American Indian/Alaska Native	80
Asian	4,201
Native Hawaiian/Pacific Islander	13
Other race	1,329
Two or more races	1,221
Hispanic origin, total	4,861
Mexican	113
Puerto Rican	1,398
Cuban	666
Other Hispanic	2,684

Age & Nativity, 2000
Under 5 years	2,994
18 years and over	42,286
21 years and over	39,998
65 years and over	9,427
85 years and over	1,391
Median age	38.7
Native-born	41,045
Foreign-born	13,360

Educational Attainment, 2000
Population 25 years and over	37,595
Less than 9th grade	8.0%
High school grad or higher	80.9%
Bachelor's degree or higher	26.5%
Graduate degree	8.4%

Income & Poverty, 1999
Per capita income	$24,768
Median household income	$59,173
Median family income	$68,707
Persons in poverty	2,212
H'holds receiving public assistance	439
H'holds receiving social security	6,707

Households, 2000
Total households	19,534
With persons under 18	6,824
With persons over 65	6,827
Family households	14,164
Single-person households	4,656
Persons per household	2.71
Persons per family	3.25

Labor & Employment
Total civilian labor force, 2007**	28,566
Unemployment rate	4.1%
Total civilian labor force, 2000	27,371
Unemployment rate	4.5%

Employed persons 16 years and over by occupation, 2000
Managers & professionals	9,906
Service occupations	3,150
Sales & office occupations	8,130
Farming, fishing & forestry	0
Construction & maintenance	2,071
Production & transportation	2,878
Self-employed persons	1,089

* US Census Bureau
** New Jersey Department of Labor

General Information
Township of Union
1976 Morris Ave
Union, NJ 07083
908-688-2800
Website	uniontownship.com
Year of incorporation	1808
Land/water area (sq. miles)	9.12/0.00
Form of government	Township

Government
Legislative Districts
US Congressional	7, 10
State Legislative	20

Local Officials, 2009
Mayor	Anthony Terrezza Jr
Manager	Frank Bradley
Clerk	Eileen Birch
Finance Dir	Debra Cyburt
Tax Assessor	Paul Parsons
Tax Collector	Terri Malanda
Attorney	Daniel Antonelli
Building	Richard Malanda
Planning	Phil Haderer
Engineering	Philip Haderer Jr
Public Works	Sergio Panunzio
Police Chief	Thomas Kraemer
Emerg/Fire Director	Frederic Fretz

Housing & Construction
Housing Units, 2000*
Total	20,001
Median rent	$844
Median SF home value	$172,900

Permits for New Residential Construction
	Units	Value
Total, 2006	32	$5,687,421
Single family	22	$4,772,421
Total, 2007	12	$1,665,349
Single family	12	$1,665,349

Real Property Valuation, 2008
	Parcels	Valuation
Total	17,278	$1,060,801,900
Vacant	183	7,689,100
Residential	16,121	741,040,200
Commercial	715	190,999,300
Industrial	210	100,159,600
Apartments	49	20,913,700
Farm land	0	0
Farm homestead	0	0

Average Property Value & Tax, 2008
Residential value	$45,967
Property tax	$6,884
Tax credit/rebate	$1,125

Public Library
Union Free Public Library
1980 Morris Ave
Union, NJ 07083
908-851-5450
Director	Laurie D. Sansone

Library statistics, 2007
Population served	54,405
Full-time/total staff	8/21

	Total	Per capita
Holdings	228,113	4.19
Revenues	$2,489,586	$45.76
Expenditures	$2,433,952	$44.74
Annual visits	311,236	5.72
Internet terminals/annual users	31/55,892	

Public Safety
Number of officers, 2007	139

Crime	2006	2007
Total crimes	1,744	1,488
Violent	154	146
Murder	2	0
Rape	2	1
Robbery	69	69
Aggravated assault	81	76
Non-violent	1,590	1,342
Burglary	233	205
Larceny	1,147	946
Vehicle theft	210	191
Domestic violence	292	225
Arson	0	1
Total crime rate	31.5	27.0
Violent	2.8	2.7
Non-violent	28.7	24.4

Public School District
(for school year 2007-08 except as noted)

Union Township School District
2369 Morris Avenue
Union, NJ 07083
(908) 851-6420
Superintendent	Theodore Jakubowski
Number of schools	10
Grade plan	K-12
Enrollment	7,816
Attendance rate, '06-07	94.4%
Dropout rate	0.2%
Students per teacher	12.1
Per pupil expenditure	$13,275
Median faculty salary	$59,350
Median administrator salary	$108,725
Grade 12 enrollment	658
High school graduation rate	98.4%

Assessment test results
(percent scoring at proficient or advanced level)
	Language	Math
NJASK-Grade 3	87.9%	87.9%
GEPA-Grade 8	53.3%	76.4%
HSPA-High School	63.3%	79.2%

SAT Score Averages, 2006-07
Pct tested	Math	Verbal	Writing
74%	466	444	443

Teacher Qualifications
Avg. years of experience	9
Highly-qualified teachers one subject/all subjects	99.5%/99.5%

No Child Left Behind
AYP, 2006-07	Meets Standards

Municipal Finance
State Aid Programs, 2009
Total aid	$7,548,562
CMPTRA	2,092,123
Energy tax receipts	5,343,210
Garden State Trust	0

General Budget, 2008
Total tax levy	$159,087,842
County levy	26,720,855
County taxes	25,555,234
County library	0
County health	0
County open space	1,165,620
School levy	74,490,593
Muni. levy	57,876,394
Misc. revenues	23,294,651

Taxes
	2006	2007	2008
General tax rate per $100	13.925	14.448	14.976
County equalization ratio	15.2	14.98	13.77
Net valuation taxable	$1,063,091,600	$1,063,084,867	$1,062,297,870
State equalized value	$7,098,646,343	$7,710,370,833	$7,744,575,532

See Introduction for an explanation of all data sources.

Demographics & Socio-Economic Characteristics

(2000 US Census, except as noted)

Population

1980*	6,810
1990*	6,927
2000	7,556
Male	3,663
Female	3,893
2007 (estimate)*	8,068
Population density	259.4

Race & Hispanic Origin, 2000

Race

White	5,725
Black/African American	1,240
American Indian/Alaska Native	61
Asian	231
Native Hawaiian/Pacific Islander	1
Other race	138
Two or more races	160
Hispanic origin, total	343
Mexican	25
Puerto Rican	267
Cuban	6
Other Hispanic	45

Age & Nativity, 2000

Under 5 years	519
18 years and over	5,455
21 years and over	5,179
65 years and over	1,074
85 years and over	117
Median age	37.5
Native-born	7,314
Foreign-born	242

Educational Attainment, 2000

Population 25 years and over	4,910
Less than 9th grade	5.3%
High school grad or higher	81.1%
Bachelor's degree or higher	15.6%
Graduate degree	4.3%

Income & Poverty, 1999

Per capita income	$18,884
Median household income	$47,861
Median family income	$51,472
Persons in poverty	1,032
H'holds receiving public assistance	193
H'holds receiving social security	930

Households, 2000

Total households	2,757
With persons under 18	1,088
With persons over 65	783
Family households	2,126
Single-person households	551
Persons per household	2.73
Persons per family	3.12

Labor & Employment

Total civilian labor force, 2007**	3,877
Unemployment rate	4.6%
Total civilian labor force, 2000	3,576
Unemployment rate	7.3%

Employed persons 16 years and over by occupation, 2000

Managers & professionals	982
Service occupations	508
Sales & office occupations	938
Farming, fishing & forestry	36
Construction & maintenance	229
Production & transportation	622
Self-employed persons	255

* US Census Bureau
** New Jersey Department of Labor

General Information

Township of Upper Deerfield
1325 State Highway 77
PO Box 5098
Seabrook, NJ 08302
856-451-3811

Website	www.upperdeerfield.org
Year of incorporation	1922
Land/water area (sq. miles)	31.10/0.14
Form of government	Township

Government

Legislative Districts

US Congressional	2
State Legislative	3

Local Officials, 2009

Mayor	Bruce T. Peterson
Manager	Roy Spoltore
Clerk	Roy Spoltore
Finance Dir	Ruth Moynihan
Tax Assessor	Darlene Campbell
Tax Collector	Andrea Penny
Attorney	Theodore Baker
Building	Fred Froelich
Planning	Vicki Vagnarelli
Engineering	Brian Murphy
Public Works	(vacant)
Police Chief	NA
Fire/Emergency Dir	David Smith

Housing & Construction

Housing Units, 2000*

Total	2,881
Median rent	$535
Median SF home value	$116,000

Permits for New Residential Construction

	Units	Value
Total, 2006	57	$10,895,161
Single family	40	$8,618,161
Total, 2007	58	$10,028,228
Single family	38	$7,552,154

Real Property Valuation, 2008

	Parcels	Valuation
Total	3,617	$431,955,100
Vacant	347	9,431,400
Residential	2,487	294,139,800
Commercial	126	72,276,000
Industrial	2	10,543,800
Apartments	4	7,649,600
Farm land	441	7,029,000
Farm homestead	210	30,885,500

Average Property Value & Tax, 2008

Residential value	$120,514
Property tax	$4,556
Tax credit/rebate	$898

Public Library

No public municipal library

Library statistics, 2007

Population served	NA
Full-time/total staff	NA/NA

	Total	Per capita
Holdings	NA	NA
Revenues	NA	NA
Expenditures	NA	NA
Annual visits	NA	NA
Internet terminals/annual users	NA/NA	

Public Safety

Number of officers, 2007	0

Crime	2006	2007
Total crimes	262	254
Violent	22	19
Murder	0	0
Rape	0	0
Robbery	4	2
Aggravated assault	18	17
Non-violent	240	235
Burglary	67	37
Larceny	165	186
Vehicle theft	8	12
Domestic violence	6	66
Arson	0	0
Total crime rate	33.2	31.8
Violent	2.8	2.4
Non-violent	30.4	29.4

Public School District

(for school year 2007-08 except as noted)

Upper Deerfield Township School District
1369 Highway #77
Seabrook, NJ 08302
(856) 455-2267

Superintendent	Philip Exley
Number of schools	3
Grade plan	K-8
Enrollment	896
Attendance rate, '06-07	94.4%
Dropout rate	NA
Students per teacher	9.8
Per pupil expenditure	$13,853
Median faculty salary	$52,461
Median administrator salary	$97,011
Grade 12 enrollment	NA
High school graduation rate	NA

Assessment test results

(percent scoring at proficient or advanced level)

	Language	Math
NJASK-Grade 3	73.2%	70.4%
GEPA-Grade 8	68.2%	78.0%
HSPA-High School	NA	NA

SAT Score Averages, 2006-07

Pct tested	Math	Verbal	Writing
NA	NA	NA	NA

Teacher Qualifications

Avg. years of experience	10
Highly-qualified teachers one subject/all subjects	100%/100%

No Child Left Behind

AYP, 2006-07 .... Meets Standards

Municipal Finance

State Aid Programs, 2009

Total aid	$1,785,052
CMPTRA	0
Energy tax receipts	1,713,456
Garden State Trust	202

General Budget, 2008

Total tax levy	$16,373,177
County levy	6,930,538
County taxes	6,551,386
County library	0
County health	306,275
County open space	72,877
School levy	9,442,640
Muni. levy	0
Misc. revenues	4,909,011

Taxes

	2006	2007	2008
General tax rate per $100	3.425	3.532	3.783
County equalization ratio	79.56	73.2	60.58
Net valuation taxable	$412,746,700	$421,881,678	$433,113,262
State equalized value	$565,189,395	$695,576,745	$734,777,557

See Introduction for an explanation of all data sources.

Demographics & Socio-Economic Characteristics
(2000 US Census, except as noted)

Population

1980*	2,750
1990*	3,277
2000	4,282
Male	2,159
Female	2,123
2007 (estimate)*	6,833
Population density	145.8

Race & Hispanic Origin, 2000

Race
White	4,055
Black/African American	45
American Indian/Alaska Native	6
Asian	60
Native Hawaiian/Pacific Islander	0
Other race	36
Two or more races	80
Hispanic origin, total	151
Mexican	57
Puerto Rican	54
Cuban	3
Other Hispanic	37

Age & Nativity, 2000

Under 5 years	342
18 years and over	3,091
21 years and over	2,990
65 years and over	404
85 years and over	40
Median age	38.4
Native-born	4,051
Foreign-born	231

Educational Attainment, 2000

Population 25 years and over	2,829
Less than 9th grade	3.1%
High school grad or higher	88.8%
Bachelor's degree or higher	36.3%
Graduate degree	9.6%

Income & Poverty, 1999

Per capita income	$29,387
Median household income	$71,250
Median family income	$78,334
Persons in poverty	173
H'holds receiving public assistance	5
H'holds receiving social security	309

Households, 2000

Total households	1,437
With persons under 18	642
With persons over 65	287
Family households	1,199
Single-person households	168
Persons per household	2.96
Persons per family	3.24

Labor & Employment

Total civilian labor force, 2007**	2,426
Unemployment rate	1.6%
Total civilian labor force, 2000	2,285
Unemployment rate	2.7%

Employed persons 16 years and over by occupation, 2000
Managers & professionals	915
Service occupations	326
Sales & office occupations	538
Farming, fishing & forestry	69
Construction & maintenance	196
Production & transportation	179
Self-employed persons	169

General Information
Township of Upper Freehold
314 Route 539
PO Box 89
Cream Ridge, NJ 08514
609-758-7738

Website	www.uftnj.com
Year of incorporation	1731
Land/water area (sq. miles)	46.86/0.27
Form of government	Township

Government

Legislative Districts
US Congressional	4
State Legislative	30

Local Officials, 2009
Mayor	Stephen J. Alexander
Manager	Barbara Bascom
Clerk	Barbara Bascom
Finance Dir	Dianne Kelly
Tax Assessor	Steve Walters
Tax Collector	Barbara Pater
Attorney	Granville D. Magee
Building	Ron Gafgen
Planning	Charles P. Newcomb
Engineering	Glenn Gerken
Public Works	Wayne Golden
Police Chief	(State)
Fire/Emergency Dir	Brad Carter

Housing & Construction

Housing Units, 2000*
Total	1,501
Median rent	$743
Median SF home value	$255,500

Permits for New Residential Construction

	Units	Value
Total, 2006	59	$14,769,119
Single family	59	$14,769,119
Total, 2007	33	$11,650,887
Single family	33	$11,650,887

Real Property Valuation, 2008

	Parcels	Valuation
Total	3,350	$1,347,276,900
Vacant	239	30,601,700
Residential	2,047	1,069,197,500
Commercial	57	46,857,000
Industrial	16	14,671,100
Apartments	1	427,900
Farm land	672	9,774,100
Farm homestead	318	175,747,600

Average Property Value & Tax, 2008
Residential value	$526,404
Property tax	$8,730
Tax credit/rebate	$1,224

Public Library
No public municipal library

Library statistics, 2007
Population served	NA
Full-time/total staff	NA/NA

	Total	Per capita
Holdings	NA	NA
Revenues	NA	NA
Expenditures	NA	NA
Annual visits	NA	NA
Internet terminals/annual users	NA/NA	

Public Safety
Number of officers, 2007 0

Crime	2006	2007
Total crimes	66	62
Violent	4	6
Murder	0	0
Rape	0	0
Robbery	0	0
Aggravated assault	4	6
Non-violent	62	56
Burglary	10	15
Larceny	49	40
Vehicle theft	3	1
Domestic violence	7	25
Arson	1	0
Total crime rate	9.9	9.4
Violent	0.6	0.9
Non-violent	9.3	8.5

Public School District
(for school year 2007-08 except as noted)

Upper Freehold Regional School District
27 High Street
Allentown, NJ 08501
(609) 259-7292

Superintendent	Richard Fitzpatrick
Number of schools	2
Grade plan	K-12
Enrollment	2,292
Attendance rate, '06-07	95.2%
Dropout rate	0.4%
Students per teacher	11.3
Per pupil expenditure	$12,560
Median faculty salary	$53,273
Median administrator salary	$106,263
Grade 12 enrollment	221
High school graduation rate	97.4%

Assessment test results
(percent scoring at proficient or advanced level)

	Language	Math
NJASK-Grade 3	91.0%	93.9%
GEPA-Grade 8	78.2%	92.4%
HSPA-High School	85.6%	90.1%

SAT Score Averages, 2006-07

Pct tested	Math	Verbal	Writing
81%	511	512	496

Teacher Qualifications
Avg. years of experience	6
Highly-qualified teachers one subject/all subjects	96.5%/96.5%

No Child Left Behind
AYP, 2006-07	Meets Standards

Municipal Finance

State Aid Programs, 2009
Total aid	$706,900
CMPTRA	21,637
Energy tax receipts	646,412
Garden State Trust	10,968

General Budget, 2008
Total tax levy	$22,389,106
County levy	3,349,322
County taxes	2,972,217
County library	178,875
County health	0
County open space	198,230
School levy	16,686,349
Muni. levy	2,353,435
Misc. revenues	4,717,543

Taxes	2006	2007	2008
General tax rate per $100	1.596	1.632	1.659
County equalization ratio	118.47	106.73	102.59
Net valuation taxable	$1,278,462,600	$1,320,518,129	$1,349,984,787
State equalized value	$1,200,225,734	$1,287,243,526	$1,334,009,172

* US Census Bureau
** New Jersey Department of Labor

See Introduction for an explanation of all data sources.

Demographics & Socio-Economic Characteristics

(2000 US Census, except as noted)

Population

1980*	3,139
1990*	3,140
2000	3,468
Male	1,728
Female	1,740
2007 (estimate)*	3,566
Population density	88.3

Race & Hispanic Origin, 2000

Race

White	3,289
Black/African American	75
American Indian/Alaska Native	18
Asian	11
Native Hawaiian/Pacific Islander	0
Other race	45
Two or more races	30
Hispanic origin, total	109
Mexican	41
Puerto Rican	32
Cuban	0
Other Hispanic	36

Age & Nativity, 2000

Under 5 years	190
18 years and over	2,591
21 years and over	2,462
65 years and over	477
85 years and over	67
Median age	38.9
Native-born	3,342
Foreign-born	126

Educational Attainment, 2000

Population 25 years and over	2,299
Less than 9th grade	6.7%
High school grad or higher	81.9%
Bachelor's degree or higher	19.1%
Graduate degree	5.8%

Income & Poverty, 1999

Per capita income	$21,732
Median household income	$53,813
Median family income	$56,768
Persons in poverty	288
H'holds receiving public assistance	18
H'holds receiving social security	294

Households, 2000

Total households	1,207
With persons under 18	452
With persons over 65	299
Family households	960
Single-person households	204
Persons per household	2.80
Persons per family	3.13

Labor & Employment

Total civilian labor force, 2007**	1,764
Unemployment rate	1.9%
Total civilian labor force, 2000	1,728
Unemployment rate	3.2%

Employed persons 16 years and over by occupation, 2000

Managers & professionals	528
Service occupations	244
Sales & office occupations	410
Farming, fishing & forestry	36
Construction & maintenance	178
Production & transportation	277
Self-employed persons	136

General Information

Township of Upper Pittsgrove
431 Route 77
Elmer, NJ 08318
856-358-8500

Website	NA
Year of incorporation	1846
Land/water area (sq. miles)	40.39/0.07
Form of government	Township

Government

Legislative Districts

US Congressional	2
State Legislative	3

Local Officials, 2009

Mayor	Jack Cimprich
Manager/Admin	NA
Clerk	Alan Newkirk
Finance Dir	Alan Newkirk
Tax Assessor	Edwin F. Kay
Tax Collector	Susan DeFrancesco
Attorney	John G. Hoffman
Building	(State)
Planning	Linda S. Buzby
Engineering	J. Michael Fralinger
Public Works	Barry Foote
Police Chief	NA
Fire/Emergency Dir	NA

Housing & Construction

Housing Units, 2000*

Total	1,250
Median rent	$646
Median SF home value	$127,000

Permits for New Residential Construction

	Units	Value
Total, 2006	6	$599,580
Single family	6	$599,580
Total, 2007	12	$1,609,850
Single family	12	$1,609,850

Real Property Valuation, 2008

	Parcels	Valuation
Total	2,093	$343,118,400
Vacant	163	13,508,900
Residential	897	212,145,600
Commercial	45	21,650,000
Industrial	0	0
Apartments	0	0
Farm land	681	10,849,900
Farm homestead	307	84,964,000

Average Property Value & Tax, 2008

Residential value	$246,769
Property tax	$4,931
Tax credit/rebate	$899

Public Library

No public municipal library

Library statistics, 2007

Population served	NA
Full-time/total staff	NA/NA

	Total	Per capita
Holdings	NA	NA
Revenues	NA	NA
Expenditures	NA	NA
Annual visits	NA	NA
Internet terminals/annual users	NA/NA	

Public Safety

Number of officers, 2007	0

Crime	2006	2007
Total crimes	62	62
Violent	3	8
Murder	0	0
Rape	0	0
Robbery	1	2
Aggravated assault	2	6
Non-violent	59	54
Burglary	21	14
Larceny	30	39
Vehicle theft	8	1
Domestic violence	5	18
Arson	1	1
Total crime rate	17.1	17.1
Violent	0.8	2.2
Non-violent	16.3	14.9

Public School District

(for school year 2007-08 except as noted)

Upper Pittsgrove Township School Dist.
235 Pine Tavern Road
Monroeville, NJ 08343
(856) 358-8163

Superintendent	Robert Bazzel
Number of schools	1
Grade plan	K-8
Enrollment	376
Attendance rate, '06-07	95.7%
Dropout rate	NA
Students per teacher	10.6
Per pupil expenditure	$11,723
Median faculty salary	$52,285
Median administrator salary	$97,178
Grade 12 enrollment	NA
High school graduation rate	NA

Assessment test results

(percent scoring at proficient or advanced level)

	Language	Math
NJASK-Grade 3	88.9%	84.4%
GEPA-Grade 8	65.9%	79.5%
HSPA-High School	NA	NA

SAT Score Averages, 2006-07

Pct tested	Math	Verbal	Writing
NA	NA	NA	NA

Teacher Qualifications

Avg. years of experience	15
Highly-qualified teachers one subject/all subjects	97.0%/97.0%

No Child Left Behind

AYP, 2006-07	Meets Standards

Municipal Finance

State Aid Programs, 2009

Total aid	$605,232
CMPTRA	32,181
Energy tax receipts	548,842
Garden State Trust	94

General Budget, 2008

Total tax levy	$6,887,124
County levy	3,040,923
County taxes	2,975,317
County library	0
County health	0
County open space	65,607
School levy	3,555,966
Muni. levy	290,235
Misc. revenues	1,500,038

Taxes

	2006	2007	2008
General tax rate per $100	1.783	1.922	1.999
County equalization ratio	125.94	108.9	105.64
Net valuation taxable	$338,706,250	$341,962,941	$344,683,314
State equalized value	$312,006,005	$323,796,912	$357,238,595

* US Census Bureau
** New Jersey Department of Labor

See Introduction for an explanation of all data sources.

Demographics & Socio-Economic Characteristics

(2000 US Census, except as noted)

Population

1980*	7,958
1990*	7,198
2000	7,741
Male	3,813
Female	3,928
2007 (estimate)*	8,483
Population density	1,603.6

Race & Hispanic Origin, 2000

Race
White	7,063
Black/African American	72
American Indian/Alaska Native	2
Asian	486
Native Hawaiian/Pacific Islander	1
Other race	40
Two or more races	77
Hispanic origin, total	169
Mexican	15
Puerto Rican	33
Cuban	37
Other Hispanic	84

Age & Nativity, 2000

Under 5 years	594
18 years and over	5,368
21 years and over	5,233
65 years and over	882
85 years and over	50
Median age	40.1
Native-born	6,801
Foreign-born	940

Educational Attainment, 2000

Population 25 years and over	5,147
Less than 9th grade	1.3%
High school grad or higher	96.6%
Bachelor's degree or higher	59.9%
Graduate degree	25.5%

Income & Poverty, 1999

Per capita income	$57,239
Median household income	$127,635
Median family income	$132,401
Persons in poverty	52
H'holds receiving public assistance	0
H'holds receiving social security	585

Households, 2000

Total households	2,497
With persons under 18	1,203
With persons over 65	609
Family households	2,242
Single-person households	210
Persons per household	3.09
Persons per family	3.27

Labor & Employment

Total civilian labor force, 2007**	3,725
Unemployment rate	3.9%
Total civilian labor force, 2000	3,523
Unemployment rate	4.2%

Employed persons 16 years and over by occupation, 2000
Managers & professionals	2,057
Service occupations	123
Sales & office occupations	986
Farming, fishing & forestry	0
Construction & maintenance	127
Production & transportation	83
Self-employed persons	319

General Information

Borough of Upper Saddle River
376 W Saddle River Rd
Upper Saddle River, NJ 07458
201-327-2196

Website	www.usrtoday.org
Year of incorporation	1894
Land/water area (sq. miles)	5.29/0.00
Form of government	Borough

Government

Legislative Districts

US Congressional	5
State Legislative	39

Local Officials, 2009

Mayor	Kenneth Gabbert
Administrator	Theodore F. Preusch
Clerk	Rose Vido
CFO	Gene Leporiere
Tax Assessor	Marie Merolla
Tax Collector	Gene Leporiere
Attorney	Robert Regan
Building	James Dougherty
Comm Dev/Planning	NA
Engineering	Christopher Statile
Public Works	NA
Police Chief	Michael Fanning
Fire Chief	Erik Vierheilig

Housing & Construction

Housing Units, 2000*

Total	2,560
Median rent	$1,929
Median SF home value	$603,900

Permits for New Residential Construction

	Units	Value
Total, 2006	27	$15,316,330
Single family	27	$15,316,330
Total, 2007	15	$10,617,661
Single family	15	$10,617,661

Real Property Valuation, 2008

	Parcels	Valuation
Total	2,762	$2,173,960,500
Vacant	75	18,827,700
Residential	2,612	1,935,156,800
Commercial	69	195,207,300
Industrial	4	6,217,700
Apartments	2	18,551,000
Farm land	0	0
Farm homestead	0	0

Average Property Value & Tax, 2008

Residential value	$740,872
Property tax	$14,538
Tax credit/rebate	$1,478

Public Library

Upper Saddle River Public Library
245 Lake St
Upper Saddle River, NJ 07458
201-327-2583

Director ... Barbara Kruger

Library statistics, 2007

Population served	7,741
Full-time/total staff	3/4

	Total	Per capita
Holdings	65,842	8.51
Revenues	$1,093,068	$141.21
Expenditures	$921,295	$119.01
Annual visits	111,117	14.35
Internet terminals/annual users	16/22,773	

Public Safety

Number of officers, 2007 ... 18

Crime	2006	2007
Total crimes	42	44
Violent	5	2
Murder	0	0
Rape	0	0
Robbery	0	0
Aggravated assault	5	2
Non-violent	37	42
Burglary	10	8
Larceny	23	32
Vehicle theft	4	2
Domestic violence	39	33
Arson	2	0
Total crime rate	4.9	5.2
Violent	0.6	0.2
Non-violent	4.3	4.9

Public School District

(for school year 2007-08 except as noted)

Upper Saddle River School District
395 West Saddle River Road
Upper Saddle River, NJ 07458
(201) 961-6502

Superintendent	Monica M. Browne
Number of schools	3
Grade plan	K-8
Enrollment	1,377
Attendance rate, '06-07	96.1%
Dropout rate	NA
Students per teacher	11.1
Per pupil expenditure	$14,106
Median faculty salary	$57,216
Median administrator salary	$108,043
Grade 12 enrollment	NA
High school graduation rate	NA

Assessment test results

(percent scoring at proficient or advanced level)
	Language	Math
NJASK-Grade 3	97.6%	96.3%
GEPA-Grade 8	92.2%	95.8%
HSPA-High School	NA	NA

SAT Score Averages, 2006-07

Pct tested	Math	Verbal	Writing
NA	NA	NA	NA

Teacher Qualifications

Avg. years of experience	10
Highly-qualified teachers one subject/all subjects	100%/100%

No Child Left Behind

AYP, 2006-07 ... Meets Standards

Municipal Finance

State Aid Programs, 2009

Total aid	$1,168,432
CMPTRA	10,324
Energy tax receipts	1,099,686
Garden State Trust	0

General Budget, 2008

Total tax levy	$42,690,384
County levy	5,807,731
County taxes	5,492,190
County library	0
County health	0
County open space	315,540
School levy	29,424,620
Muni. levy	7,458,034
Misc. revenues	4,439,286

Taxes

	2006	2007	2008
General tax rate per $100	1.83	1.92	1.965
County equalization ratio	79.19	71.35	69.08
Net valuation taxable	$2,097,873,100	$2,127,845,708	$2,175,559,669
State equalized value	$2,941,549,845	$3,079,565,233	$3,170,637,799

* US Census Bureau
** New Jersey Department of Labor

See Introduction for an explanation of all data sources.

Demographics & Socio-Economic Characteristics
(2000 US Census, except as noted)

Population
1980*	6,713
1990*	10,681
2000	12,115
Male	5,837
Female	6,278
2007 (estimate)*	11,110
Population density	175.9

Race & Hispanic Origin, 2000
Race
White	11,823
Black/African American	83
American Indian/Alaska Native	15
Asian	74
Native Hawaiian/Pacific Islander	7
Other race	23
Two or more races	90
Hispanic origin, total	155
Mexican	40
Puerto Rican	66
Cuban	2
Other Hispanic	47

Age & Nativity, 2000
Under 5 years	736
18 years and over	8,648
21 years and over	8,294
65 years and over	1,472
85 years and over	130
Median age	38.4
Native-born	11,800
Foreign-born	315

Educational Attainment, 2000
Population 25 years and over	7,928
Less than 9th grade	2.0%
High school grad or higher	91.2%
Bachelor's degree or higher	32.4%
Graduate degree	8.8%

Income & Poverty, 1999
Per capita income	$27,498
Median household income	$60,942
Median family income	$68,824
Persons in poverty	417
H'holds receiving public assistance	9
H'holds receiving social security	1,133

Households, 2000
Total households	4,266
With persons under 18	1,775
With persons over 65	1,053
Family households	3,365
Single-person households	744
Persons per household	2.84
Persons per family	3.23

Labor & Employment
Total civilian labor force, 2007**	7,367
Unemployment rate	1.9%
Total civilian labor force, 2000	6,149
Unemployment rate	2.5%

Employed persons 16 years and over by occupation, 2000
Managers & professionals	2,506
Service occupations	1,038
Sales & office occupations	1,415
Farming, fishing & forestry	43
Construction & maintenance	627
Production & transportation	368
Self-employed persons	546

‡ Branch of county library
* US Census Bureau
** New Jersey Department of Labor

See Introduction for an explanation of all data sources.

General Information
Upper Township
PO Box 205
Tuckahoe, NJ 08250
609-628-2011
Website	www.uppertownship.com
Year of incorporation	1723
Land/water area (sq. miles)	63.15/5.32
Form of government	Township

Government
Legislative Districts
US Congressional	2
State Legislative	1

Local Officials, 2009
Mayor	Richard Palombo
Manager/Admin	NA
Clerk	Wanda Gaglione
Finance Dir	Barbara Spiegal (Actg)
Tax Assessor	Megan McAfee
Tax Collector	Susan Peifer
Attorney	Daniel J. Young
Building	Edward Kenney
Comm Dev/Planning	NA
Engineering	Paul E. Dietrich
Public Works	NA
Police Chief	NA
Fire/Emergency Dir	NA

Housing & Construction
Housing Units, 2000*
Total	5,472
Median rent	$827
Median SF home value	$161,700

Permits for New Residential Construction
	Units	Value
Total, 2006	22	$5,180,790
Single family	22	$5,180,790
Total, 2007	14	$3,435,851
Single family	14	$3,435,851

Real Property Valuation, 2008
	Parcels	Valuation
Total	7,293	$2,259,223,600
Vacant	1,304	106,083,800
Residential	5,575	1,916,690,500
Commercial	291	194,482,400
Industrial	1	25,986,700
Apartments	5	1,246,700
Farm land	82	531,400
Farm homestead	35	14,202,100

Average Property Value & Tax, 2008
Residential value	$344,188
Property tax	$3,977
Tax credit/rebate	$770

Public Library
Upper Cape Branch Library‡
2050 Rte 631
Petersburg, NJ 08270
609-628-2607
Branch Librarian	Beth Dusman

Library statistics, 2007
see Cape May County profile
for library system statistics

Public Safety
Number of officers, 2007	0

Crime	2006	2007
Total crimes	198	160
Violent	5	7
Murder	0	0
Rape	1	0
Robbery	0	0
Aggravated assault	4	7
Non-violent	193	153
Burglary	52	27
Larceny	135	119
Vehicle theft	6	7
Domestic violence	13	72
Arson	1	1
Total crime rate	16.9	14.1
Violent	0.4	0.6
Non-violent	16.5	13.5

Public School District
(for school year 2007-08 except as noted)

Upper Township School District
525 Perry Rd.
Petersburg, NJ 08270
(609) 628-3513
Superintendent	Vincent Palmieri Jr
Number of schools	3
Grade plan	K-8
Enrollment	1,568
Attendance rate, '06-07	94.6%
Dropout rate	NA
Students per teacher	11.4
Per pupil expenditure	$13,424
Median faculty salary	$63,628
Median administrator salary	$105,680
Grade 12 enrollment	NA
High school graduation rate	NA

Assessment test results
(percent scoring at proficient or advanced level)
	Language	Math
NJASK-Grade 3	95.0%	91.6%
GEPA-Grade 8	79.0%	87.0%
HSPA-High School	NA	NA

SAT Score Averages, 2006-07
Pct tested	Math	Verbal	Writing
NA	NA	NA	NA

Teacher Qualifications
Avg. years of experience	16
Highly-qualified teachers one subject/all subjects	100%/98.0%

No Child Left Behind
AYP, 2006-07	Meets Standards

Municipal Finance
State Aid Programs, 2009
Total aid	$6,771,173
CMPTRA	0
Energy tax receipts	6,403,875
Garden State Trust	89,994

General Budget, 2008
Total tax levy	$26,187,364
County levy	4,176,300
County taxes	3,319,545
County library	637,237
County health	0
County open space	219,518
School levy	22,011,064
Muni. levy	0
Misc. revenues	11,781,854

Taxes
	2006	2007	2008
General tax rate per $100	1.05	1.12	1.158
County equalization ratio	132.85	110.55	103.15
Net valuation taxable	$2,271,486,800	$2,248,016,808	$2,266,209,129
State equalized value	$2,061,564,657	$2,179,578,824	$2,238,758,324

Demographics & Socio-Economic Characteristics

(2000 US Census, except as noted)

Population
1980*	11,704
1990*	11,005
2000	12,910
Male	6,152
Female	6,758
2007 (estimate)*	12,316
Population density	5,755.1

Race & Hispanic Origin, 2000
Race
White	9,953
Black/African American	379
American Indian/Alaska Native	24
Asian	962
Native Hawaiian/Pacific Islander	4
Other race	1,210
Two or more races	378
Hispanic origin, total	2,213
Mexican	365
Puerto Rican	629
Cuban	44
Other Hispanic	1,175

Age & Nativity, 2000
Under 5 years	721
18 years and over	10,328
21 years and over	9,996
65 years and over	2,550
85 years and over	309
Median age	40.6
Native-born	9,938
Foreign-born	2,972

Educational Attainment, 2000
Population 25 years and over	9,470
Less than 9th grade	6.7%
High school grad or higher	80.3%
Bachelor's degree or higher	21.4%
Graduate degree	7.7%

Income & Poverty, 1999
Per capita income	$22,631
Median household income	$42,478
Median family income	$52,701
Persons in poverty	894
H'holds receiving public assistance	107
H'holds receiving social security	1,910

Households, 2000
Total households	5,480
With persons under 18	1,403
With persons over 65	1,915
Family households	3,256
Single-person households	1,837
Persons per household	2.35
Persons per family	3.02

Labor & Employment
Total civilian labor force, 2007**	6,943
Unemployment rate	5.7%
Total civilian labor force, 2000	6,530
Unemployment rate	6.1%

Employed persons 16 years and over by occupation, 2000
Managers & professionals	1,659
Service occupations	2,329
Sales & office occupations	1,452
Farming, fishing & forestry	23
Construction & maintenance	320
Production & transportation	347
Self-employed persons	330

‡ Branch of county library
* US Census Bureau
** New Jersey Department of Labor

General Information
City of Ventnor
6201 Atlantic Ave
Ventnor, NJ 08406
609-823-7900
Website	www.ventnorcity.org
Year of incorporation	1903
Land/water area (sq. miles)	2.14/1.40
Form of government	Commission

Government
Legislative Districts
US Congressional	2
State Legislative	2

Local Officials, 2009
Mayor	Theresa Kelly
Administrator	Andrew McCrosson Jr
Clerk	Sandra M. Biagi
Finance Dir	Toro Aboderin
Tax Assessor	William Johnson
Tax Collector	Julie Harron
Attorney	Timothy Maguire
Building	Jimmie Agnesino
Comm Dev/Planning	NA
Engineering	Richard Carter
Public Works	David Smith
Police Chief	Wayne Arnold
Emerg/Fire Director	Bert Sabo

Housing & Construction
Housing Units, 2000*
Total	8,009
Median rent	$729
Median SF home value	$129,700

Permits for New Residential Construction
	Units	Value
Total, 2006	2	$6,464,290
Single family	2	$6,464,290
Total, 2007	1	$2,834,100
Single family	1	$2,834,100

Real Property Valuation, 2008
	Parcels	Valuation
Total	6,588	$2,674,232,800
Vacant	147	54,747,300
Residential	6,277	2,507,263,200
Commercial	131	94,454,500
Industrial	2	1,604,100
Apartments	31	16,163,700
Farm land	0	0
Farm homestead	0	0

Average Property Value & Tax, 2008
Residential value	$399,437
Property tax	$6,453
Tax credit/rebate	$972

Public Library
Ventnor Community Library‡
6500 Atlantic Ave
Ventnor City, NJ 08406
609-823-4614
Branch Librarian	Ellen Eisen

Library statistics, 2007
see Atlantic County profile
for library system statistics

Public Safety
Number of officers, 2007	40

Crime	2006	2007
Total crimes	335	430
Violent	18	25
Murder	0	0
Rape	2	1
Robbery	8	14
Aggravated assault	8	10
Non-violent	317	405
Burglary	103	141
Larceny	201	253
Vehicle theft	13	11
Domestic violence	346	323
Arson	0	5
Total crime rate	26.3	34.2
Violent	1.4	2.0
Non-violent	24.9	32.2

Public School District
(for school year 2007-08 except as noted)

Ventnor City School District
400 N. Lafayette Avenue
Ventnor, NJ 08406
(609) 487-7918
Superintendent	Carmine Bonanni
Number of schools	2
Grade plan	K-8
Enrollment	943
Attendance rate, '06-07	94.8%
Dropout rate	NA
Students per teacher	9.6
Per pupil expenditure	$14,150
Median faculty salary	$65,318
Median administrator salary	$87,991
Grade 12 enrollment	NA
High school graduation rate	NA

Assessment test results
(percent scoring at proficient or advanced level)
	Language	Math
NJASK-Grade 3	89.3%	91.7%
GEPA-Grade 8	65.3%	82.3%
HSPA-High School	NA	NA

SAT Score Averages, 2006-07
Pct tested	Math	Verbal	Writing
NA	NA	NA	NA

Teacher Qualifications
Avg. years of experience	8
Highly-qualified teachers one subject/all subjects	99.0%/99.0%

No Child Left Behind
AYP, 2006-07	Meets Standards

Municipal Finance
State Aid Programs, 2009
Total aid	$790,119
CMPTRA	68,997
Energy tax receipts	695,443
Garden State Trust	0

General Budget, 2008
Total tax levy	$43,244,846
County levy	8,281,013
County taxes	6,515,584
County library	841,012
County health	344,138
County open space	580,279
School levy	17,191,174
Muni. levy	17,772,659
Misc. revenues	5,350,526

Taxes	2006	2007	2008
General tax rate per $100	1.421	1.59	1.616
County equalization ratio	128.29	102.52	92.38
Net valuation taxable	$2,760,704,700	$2,674,012,188	$2,676,771,501
State equalized value	$2,695,478,584	$2,894,359,113	$2,979,863,128

See Introduction for an explanation of all data sources.

Demographics & Socio-Economic Characteristics

(2000 US Census, except as noted)

Population

1980*	16,302
1990*	21,211
2000	24,686
Male	12,505
Female	12,181
2007 (estimate)*	25,011
Population density	365.7

Race & Hispanic Origin, 2000

Race

White	23,837
Black/African American	188
American Indian/Alaska Native	22
Asian	173
Native Hawaiian/Pacific Islander	7
Other race	195
Two or more races	264
Hispanic origin, total	889
Mexican	62
Puerto Rican	352
Cuban	85
Other Hispanic	390

Age & Nativity, 2000

Under 5 years	1,643
18 years and over	17,126
21 years and over	16,349
65 years and over	1,566
85 years and over	144
Median age	35.4
Native-born	23,431
Foreign-born	1,255

Educational Attainment, 2000

Population 25 years and over	15,485
Less than 9th grade	2.0%
High school grad or higher	92.8%
Bachelor's degree or higher	25.3%
Graduate degree	7.7%

Income & Poverty, 1999

Per capita income	$25,250
Median household income	$67,566
Median family income	$72,609
Persons in poverty	717
H'holds receiving public assistance	130
H'holds receiving social security	1,384

Households, 2000

Total households	8,368
With persons under 18	3,932
With persons over 65	1,168
Family households	6,607
Single-person households	1,359
Persons per household	2.95
Persons per family	3.35

Labor & Employment

Total civilian labor force, 2007**	13,840
Unemployment rate	3.3%
Total civilian labor force, 2000	13,184
Unemployment rate	4.8%

Employed persons 16 years and over by occupation, 2000

Managers & professionals	4,313
Service occupations	1,559
Sales & office occupations	3,554
Farming, fishing & forestry	22
Construction & maintenance	1,587
Production & transportation	1,511
Self-employed persons	788

‡ Branch of county library
* US Census Bureau
** New Jersey Department of Labor

General Information

Township of Vernon
21 Church St
Vernon, NJ 07462
973-764-4055

Website	www.vernontwp.com
Year of incorporation	1731
Land/water area (sq. miles)	68.39/2.14
Form of government	Council-Manager

Government

Legislative Districts

US Congressional	5
State Legislative	24

Local Officials, 2009

Mayor	Austin Carew
Manager	Melinda Carlton
Township Clerk	Robin R. Kline (Actg)
Chief Financial Officer	Robert Benecke
Tax Assessor	Lynne Schweighardt
Tax Collector	Ann Izzo
Township Attorney	Michael Witt
Construction Official	Thomas Pinand
Planning	Lou Kneip
Engineering	Louis Kneip
Director of Public Works	Dave Pullis
Police Chief	Roy Wherry
Fire Chief	Tom Davis

Housing & Construction

Housing Units, 2000*

Total	9,994
Median rent	$930
Median SF home value	$150,800

Permits for New Residential Construction

	Units	Value
Total, 2006	46	$8,368,495
Single family	46	$8,368,495
Total, 2007	28	$4,079,123
Single family	28	$4,079,123

Real Property Valuation, 2008

	Parcels	Valuation
Total	13,652	$1,527,955,106
Vacant	2,322	48,061,526
Residential	10,665	1,337,443,700
Commercial	319	108,671,820
Industrial	22	9,085,600
Apartments	4	1,416,500
Farm land	200	1,640,860
Farm homestead	120	21,635,100

Average Property Value & Tax, 2008

Residential value	$126,016
Property tax	$5,327
Tax credit/rebate	$979

Public Library

Dorothy Henry Branch Library‡
66 Rte 94
Vernon, NJ 07462
973-827-8095

Branch Librarian	Jacqueline Oregero

Library statistics, 2007

see Sussex County profile
for library system statistics

Public Safety

Number of officers, 2007	34

Crime	2006	2007
Total crimes	502	410
Violent	10	11
Murder	1	0
Rape	0	0
Robbery	2	1
Aggravated assault	7	10
Non-violent	492	399
Burglary	43	51
Larceny	447	340
Vehicle theft	2	8
Domestic violence	163	154
Arson	3	4
Total crime rate	**19.7**	**16.1**
Violent	0.4	0.4
Non-violent	19.3	15.7

Public School District

(for school year 2007-08 except as noted)

Vernon Township School District
539 Route 515, PO Box 99
Vernon, NJ 07462
(973) 764-2900

Chief School Admin	Anthony J. Macerino
Number of schools	6
Grade plan	K-12
Enrollment	4,648
Attendance rate, '06-07	92.7%
Dropout rate	0.8%
Students per teacher	10.8
Per pupil expenditure	$13,333
Median faculty salary	$72,629
Median administrator salary	$104,532
Grade 12 enrollment	386
High school graduation rate	95.3%

Assessment test results

(percent scoring at proficient or advanced level)

	Language	Math
NJASK-Grade 3	88.3%	91.6%
GEPA-Grade 8	72.9%	88.9%
HSPA-High School	83.8%	89.4%

SAT Score Averages, 2006-07

Pct tested	Math	Verbal	Writing
78%	491	494	485

Teacher Qualifications

Avg. years of experience	16
Highly-qualified teachers one subject/all subjects	100%/100%

No Child Left Behind

AYP, 2006-07	Meets Standards

Municipal Finance

State Aid Programs, 2009

Total aid	$2,845,891
CMPTRA	208,447
Energy tax receipts	2,132,531
Garden State Trust	164,928

General Budget, 2008

Total tax levy	$64,807,976
County levy	12,293,625
County taxes	10,579,877
County library	891,700
County health	0
County open space	822,048
School levy	38,582,294
Muni. levy	13,932,057
Misc. revenues	7,253,062

Taxes	2006	2007	2008
General tax rate per $100	3.92	4.12	4.228
County equalization ratio	56.16	49.55	46.65
Net valuation taxable	$1,475,740,560	$1,512,438,082	$1,532,971,856
State equalized value	$2,984,765,717	$3,235,840,167	$3,310,847,789

See Introduction for an explanation of all data sources.

Demographics & Socio-Economic Characteristics
(2000 US Census, except as noted)

Population
1980*	14,166
1990*	13,597
2000	13,533
Male	6,376
Female	7,157
2007 (estimate)*	12,651
Population density	4,600.4

Race & Hispanic Origin, 2000
Race
White	12,585
Black/African American	207
American Indian/Alaska Native	3
Asian	462
Native Hawaiian/Pacific Islander	8
Other race	96
Two or more races	172
Hispanic origin, total	467
Mexican	38
Puerto Rican	127
Cuban	72
Other Hispanic	230

Age & Nativity, 2000
Under 5 years	888
18 years and over	10,490
21 years and over	10,236
65 years and over	2,614
85 years and over	385
Median age	41.4
Native-born	12,223
Foreign-born	1,310

Educational Attainment, 2000
Population 25 years and over	9,980
Less than 9th grade	2.6%
High school grad or higher	92.4%
Bachelor's degree or higher	49.5%
Graduate degree	18.4%

Income & Poverty, 1999
Per capita income	$41,202
Median household income	$74,619
Median family income	$97,673
Persons in poverty	441
H'holds receiving public assistance	38
H'holds receiving social security	1,921

Households, 2000
Total households	5,585
With persons under 18	1,694
With persons over 65	1,954
Family households	3,695
Single-person households	1,678
Persons per household	2.42
Persons per family	3.06

Labor & Employment
Total civilian labor force, 2007**	7,238
Unemployment rate	2.2%
Total civilian labor force, 2000	6,975
Unemployment rate	2.0%

Employed persons 16 years and over by occupation, 2000
Managers & professionals	3,514
Service occupations	676
Sales & office occupations	2,020
Farming, fishing & forestry	0
Construction & maintenance	271
Production & transportation	352
Self-employed persons	572

* US Census Bureau
** New Jersey Department of Labor

General Information
Township of Verona
600 Bloomfield Ave
Verona, NJ 07044
973-239-3220

Website	veronanj.org
Year of incorporation	1981
Land/water area (sq. miles)	2.75/0.02
Form of government	Council-Manager

Government
Legislative Districts
US Congressional	8
State Legislative	40

Local Officials, 2009
Mayor	Kenneth McKenna
Manager	Joseph A. Martin
Clerk	Jean McEnroe
Finance Dir	Dee Trimmer
Tax Assessor	Romeo Longo
Tax Collector	Dee Trimmer
Attorney	Paul J. Giblin
Building	Tom Jacobson
Comm Dev/Planning	NA
Engineering	James Helb
Public Works	James Helb
Police Chief	Douglas Huber
Emerg/Fire Director	Charles Magatti

Housing & Construction
Housing Units, 2000*
Total	5,719
Median rent	$867
Median SF home value	$237,900

Permits for New Residential Construction
	Units	Value
Total, 2006	6	$1,743,750
Single family	6	$1,743,750
Total, 2007	9	$2,185,000
Single family	9	$2,185,000

Real Property Valuation, 2008
	Parcels	Valuation
Total	5,106	$504,390,200
Vacant	80	4,462,900
Residential	4,824	442,316,900
Commercial	184	47,898,700
Industrial	6	2,098,100
Apartments	12	7,613,600
Farm land	0	0
Farm homestead	0	0

Average Property Value & Tax, 2008
Residential value	$91,691
Property tax	$8,809
Tax credit/rebate	$1,250

Public Library
Verona Public Library
17 Gould St
Verona, NJ 07044
973-857-4848

Director	James A. Thomas

Library statistics, 2007
Population served	13,533
Full-time/total staff	4/6

	Total	Per capita
Holdings	66,481	4.91
Revenues	$896,252	$66.23
Expenditures	$892,642	$65.96
Annual visits	40,020	2.96
Internet terminals/annual users	7/7,286	

Public Safety
Number of officers, 2007	31

Crime	2006	2007
Total crimes	215	126
Violent	9	8
Murder	0	0
Rape	1	1
Robbery	0	0
Aggravated assault	8	7
Non-violent	206	118
Burglary	38	28
Larceny	146	82
Vehicle theft	22	8
Domestic violence	11	9
Arson	1	0
Total crime rate	16.4	9.7
Violent	0.7	0.6
Non-violent	15.7	9.1

Public School District
(for school year 2007-08 except as noted)

Verona Township School District
121 Fairview Avenue
Verona, NJ 07044
(973) 239-2100

Superintendent	Charles Sampson
Number of schools	6
Grade plan	K-12
Enrollment	2,034
Attendance rate, '06-07	94.5%
Dropout rate	0.3%
Students per teacher	11.0
Per pupil expenditure	$12,343
Median faculty salary	$57,807
Median administrator salary	$108,382
Grade 12 enrollment	150
High school graduation rate	98.7%

Assessment test results
(percent scoring at proficient or advanced level)
	Language	Math
NJASK-Grade 3	95.6%	96.2%
GEPA-Grade 8	75.0%	93.3%
HSPA-High School	86.8%	92.7%

SAT Score Averages, 2006-07
Pct tested	Math	Verbal	Writing
98%	542	524	519

Teacher Qualifications
Avg. years of experience	8
Highly-qualified teachers one subject/all subjects	98.5%/96.5%

No Child Left Behind
AYP, 2006-07	Meets Standards

Municipal Finance
State Aid Programs, 2009
Total aid	$1,495,104
CMPTRA	386,136
Energy tax receipts	1,071,591
Garden State Trust	0

General Budget, 2008
Total tax levy	$48,483,578
County levy	10,087,366
County taxes	9,698,013
County library	0
County health	0
County open space	389,353
School levy	26,188,298
Muni. levy	12,207,914
Misc. revenues	6,565,196

Taxes	2006	2007	2008
General tax rate per $100	8.77	9.09	9.608
County equalization ratio	23.71	20.94	19.64
Net valuation taxable	$503,160,200	$502,798,900	$504,648,900
State equalized value	$2,403,165,485	$2,558,991,169	$2,563,217,033

See Introduction for an explanation of all data sources.

Demographics & Socio-Economic Characteristics
(2000 US Census, except as noted)

Population
1980*	1,043
1990*	1,314
2000	1,546
Male	743
Female	803
2007 (estimate)*	1,499
Population density	9,993.3

Race & Hispanic Origin, 2000
Race
White	794
Black/African American	331
American Indian/Alaska Native	1
Asian	84
Native Hawaiian/Pacific Islander	0
Other race	236
Two or more races	100
Hispanic origin, total	783
Mexican	32
Puerto Rican	213
Cuban	2
Other Hispanic	536

Age & Nativity, 2000
Under 5 years	117
18 years and over	1,137
21 years and over	1,079
65 years and over	84
85 years and over	3
Median age	31.9
Native-born	979
Foreign-born	567

Educational Attainment, 2000
Population 25 years and over	984
Less than 9th grade	8.7%
High school grad or higher	70.1%
Bachelor's degree or higher	10.2%
Graduate degree	1.2%

Income & Poverty, 1999
Per capita income	$20,616
Median household income	$44,375
Median family income	$43,594
Persons in poverty	130
H'holds receiving public assistance	27
H'holds receiving social security	87

Households, 2000
Total households	564
With persons under 18	251
With persons over 65	65
Family households	382
Single-person households	142
Persons per household	2.74
Persons per family	3.21

Labor & Employment
Total civilian labor force, 2007**	908
Unemployment rate	3.8%
Total civilian labor force, 2000	827
Unemployment rate	3.3%

Employed persons 16 years and over by occupation, 2000
Managers & professionals	108
Service occupations	193
Sales & office occupations	241
Farming, fishing & forestry	0
Construction & maintenance	70
Production & transportation	188
Self-employed persons	14

General Information
Borough of Victory Gardens
337 S Salem St
Victory Gardens, NJ 07801
973-366-5312

Website	NA
Year of incorporation	1951
Land/water area (sq. miles)	0.15/0.00
Form of government	Borough

Government
Legislative Districts
US Congressional	11
State Legislative	25

Local Officials, 2009
Mayor	Betty Simmons
Manager	Deborah Evans
Clerk	Deborah Evans
Finance Dir	Charles Wood
Tax Assessor	Mark Burec
Tax Collector	Lorraine Benderoth
Attorney	Philip Feintuch
Building	Philip Tobayqo
Planning	Gail Frazer
Engineering	Leon Hall
Public Works	Eduardo Martinez
Police Chief	NA
Emerg/Fire Director	Chris Barrella

Housing & Construction
Housing Units, 2000*
Total	588
Median rent	$834
Median SF home value	$117,100

Permits for New Residential Construction
	Units	Value
Total, 2006	0	$0
Single family	0	$0
Total, 2007	0	$0
Single family	0	$0

Real Property Valuation, 2008
	Parcels	Valuation
Total	328	$97,568,800
Vacant	6	104,800
Residential	295	76,642,700
Commercial	25	12,308,900
Industrial	0	0
Apartments	2	8,512,400
Farm land	0	0
Farm homestead	0	0

Average Property Value & Tax, 2008
Residential value	$259,806
Property tax	$4,296
Tax credit/rebate	$885

Public Library
No public municipal library

Library statistics, 2007
Population served	NA
Full-time/total staff	NA/NA

	Total	Per capita
Holdings	NA	NA
Revenues	NA	NA
Expenditures	NA	NA
Annual visits	NA	NA
Internet terminals/annual users	NA/NA	

Public Safety
Number of officers, 2007	0

Crime	2006	2007
Total crimes	22	24
Violent	8	4
Murder	0	0
Rape	1	0
Robbery	3	0
Aggravated assault	4	4
Non-violent	14	20
Burglary	5	6
Larceny	7	14
Vehicle theft	2	0
Domestic violence	4	31
Arson	0	0
Total crime rate	14.4	15.8
Violent	5.2	2.6
Non-violent	9.2	13.1

Public School District
(for school year 2007-08 except as noted)

Victory Gardens School District
337 South Salem Street
Victory Gardens, Dover, NJ 07801

No schools in district - sends students to
Dover Town schools

Per pupil expenditure	NA
Median faculty salary	NA
Median administrator salary	NA
Grade 12 enrollment	NA
High school graduation rate	NA

Assessment test results
(percent scoring at proficient or advanced level)
	Language	Math
NJASK-Grade 3	NA	NA
GEPA-Grade 8	NA	NA
HSPA-High School	NA	NA

SAT Score Averages, 2006-07
Pct tested	Math	Verbal	Writing
NA	NA	NA	NA

Teacher Qualifications
Avg. years of experience	NA
Highly-qualified teachers one subject/all subjects	NA/NA

No Child Left Behind
AYP, 2006-07	NA

Municipal Finance
State Aid Programs, 2009
Total aid	$90,647
CMPTRA	46,147
Energy tax receipts	43,140
Garden State Trust	0

General Budget, 2008
Total tax levy	$1,614,743
County levy	233,487
County taxes	190,538
County library	0
County health	0
County open space	42,949
School levy	824,828
Muni. levy	556,428
Misc. revenues	858,048

Taxes
	2006	2007	2008
General tax rate per $100	1.83	1.7	1.654
County equalization ratio	99.39	98.66	97.63
Net valuation taxable	$97,678,800	$97,474,423	$97,662,398
State equalized value	$99,073,534	$99,838,959	$97,496,813

* US Census Bureau
** New Jersey Department of Labor

See Introduction for an explanation of all data sources.

Demographics & Socio-Economic Characteristics
(2000 US Census, except as noted)

Population
1980*	53,753
1990*	54,780
2000	56,271
Male	26,967
Female	29,304
2007 (estimate)*	58,505
Population density	851.7

Race & Hispanic Origin, 2000
Race
White	37,964
Black/African American	7,664
American Indian/Alaska Native	304
Asian	655
Native Hawaiian/Pacific Islander	43
Other race	7,881
Two or more races	1,760
Hispanic origin, total	16,880
Mexican	1,365
Puerto Rican	13,284
Cuban	232
Other Hispanic	1,999

Age & Nativity, 2000
Under 5 years	3,477
18 years and over	41,808
21 years and over	39,639
65 years and over	7,976
85 years and over	1,080
Median age	36.5
Native-born	51,686
Foreign-born	4,585

Educational Attainment, 2000
Population 25 years and over	37,333
Less than 9th grade	14.2%
High school grad or higher	67.8%
Bachelor's degree or higher	14.3%
Graduate degree	4.8%

Income & Poverty, 1999
Per capita income	$18,797
Median household income	$40,076
Median family income	$47,909
Persons in poverty	7,560
H'holds receiving public assistance	1,040
H'holds receiving social security	5,807

Households, 2000
Total households	19,930
With persons under 18	7,694
With persons over 65	5,488
Family households	14,201
Single-person households	4,731
Persons per household	2.70
Persons per family	3.17

Labor & Employment
Total civilian labor force, 2007**	27,967
Unemployment rate	6.2%
Total civilian labor force, 2000	27,593
Unemployment rate	10.7%

Employed persons 16 years and over by occupation, 2000
Managers & professionals	6,467
Service occupations	4,437
Sales & office occupations	6,045
Farming, fishing & forestry	488
Construction & maintenance	2,378
Production & transportation	4,818
Self-employed persons	1,211

General Information
City of Vineland
PO Box 1508
Vineland, NJ 08362
856-794-4000

Website	www.vinelandcity.org
Year of incorporation	1952
Land/water area (sq. miles)	68.69/0.29
Form of government	Mayor-Council

Government
Legislative Districts
US Congressional	2
State Legislative	1

Local Officials, 2009
Mayor	Robert Romano
Manager	Paul Trivellini
Clerk	Keith Petrosky
Finance Dir	Roxann Tosto
Tax Assessor	Donald Seifrit
Tax Collector	Carmen DiGiorgio
Attorney	Alfred J. Verderose
Building	Kevin Kirchner
Planning	Katheen Hicks
Engineering	Brian Myers
Public Works	Mark Guglielmi
Police Chief	Timothy Codispoti
Emerg/Fire Director	Robert Pagnini

Housing & Construction
Housing Units, 2000*
Total	20,958
Median rent	$638
Median SF home value	$97,200

Permits for New Residential Construction
	Units	Value
Total, 2006	213	$26,354,186
Single family	195	$23,374,186
Total, 2007	218	$29,943,530
Single family	208	$28,068,630

Real Property Valuation, 2008
	Parcels	Valuation
Total	19,290	$2,031,731,800
Vacant	1,595	33,968,600
Residential	15,161	1,423,693,800
Commercial	1,292	361,783,400
Industrial	149	122,757,400
Apartments	64	50,558,400
Farm land	629	4,089,800
Farm homestead	400	34,880,400

Average Property Value & Tax, 2008
Residential value	$93,733
Property tax	$3,771
Tax credit/rebate	$836

Public Library
Vineland Public Library
1058 E Landis Ave
Vineland, NJ 08360
856-794-4244

Director	Gloria G. Urban

Library statistics, 2007
Population served	56,271
Full-time/total staff	7/19

	Total	Per capita
Holdings	82,319	1.46
Revenues	$1,908,213	$33.91
Expenditures	$1,646,284	$29.26
Annual visits	221,499	3.94
Internet terminals/annual users	48/70,335	

Public Safety
Number of officers, 2007	155

Crime	2006	2007
Total crimes	3,278	2,913
Violent	541	335
Murder	6	5
Rape	19	13
Robbery	167	147
Aggravated assault	349	170
Non-violent	2,737	2,578
Burglary	539	589
Larceny	2,068	1,898
Vehicle theft	130	91
Domestic violence	1,607	1,382
Arson	15	15
Total crime rate	56.4	50.0
Violent	9.3	5.7
Non-violent	47.1	44.2

Public School District
(for school year 2007-08 except as noted)

Vineland City School District
625 Plum Street
Vineland, NJ 08360
(856) 794-6700

Superintendent	Charles Ottinger
Number of schools	20
Grade plan	K-12
Enrollment	9,768
Attendance rate, '06-07	92.6%
Dropout rate	3.0%
Students per teacher	9.2
Per pupil expenditure	$16,746
Median faculty salary	$51,264
Median administrator salary	$103,617
Grade 12 enrollment	641
High school graduation rate	87.2%

Assessment test results
(percent scoring at proficient or advanced level)
	Language	Math
NJASK-Grade 3	81.0%	75.8%
GEPA-Grade 8	48.7%	65.6%
HSPA-High School	58.7%	61.2%

SAT Score Averages, 2006-07
Pct tested	Math	Verbal	Writing
45%	485	470	465

Teacher Qualifications
Avg. years of experience	9
Highly-qualified teachers one subject/all subjects	98.5%/98.5%

No Child Left Behind
AYP, 2006-07	Meets Standards

Municipal Finance§
State Aid Programs, 2009
Total aid	$7,803,219
CMPTRA	2,926,412
Energy tax receipts	4,698,411
Garden State Trust	17,911

General Budget, 2008
Total tax levy	$82,045,184
County levy	38,354,922
County taxes	37,931,713
County library	0
County health	0
County open space	423,210
School levy	21,143,997
Muni. levy	22,546,265
Misc. revenues	38,431,828

Taxes
	2006	2007	2008
General tax rate per $100	3.839	3.832	4.025
County equalization ratio	64.04	56.12	48.86
Net valuation taxable	$1,914,625,600	$2,008,948,291	$2,039,141,028
State equalized value	$3,420,685,806	$4,103,206,337	$4,158,884,095

---

* US Census Bureau
** New Jersey Department of Labor
§ State Fiscal Year July 1–June 30

See Introduction for an explanation of all data sources.

Demographics & Socio-Economic Characteristics

(2000 US Census, except as noted)

Population
1980*	12,919
1990*	24,559
2000	28,126
Male	13,505
Female	14,621
2007 (estimate)*	29,258
Population density	2,522.2

Race & Hispanic Origin, 2000
Race
White	22,011
Black/African American	2,249
American Indian/Alaska Native	38
Asian	3,217
Native Hawaiian/Pacific Islander	8
Other race	156
Two or more races	447
Hispanic origin, total	694
Mexican	102
Puerto Rican	301
Cuban	52
Other Hispanic	239

Age & Nativity, 2000
Under 5 years	1,767
18 years and over	20,699
21 years and over	19,960
65 years and over	3,075
85 years and over	628
Median age	37.2
Native-born	24,364
Foreign-born	3,762

Educational Attainment, 2000
Population 25 years and over	18,961
Less than 9th grade	2.8%
High school grad or higher	91.2%
Bachelor's degree or higher	46.2%
Graduate degree	20.0%

Income & Poverty, 1999
Per capita income	$33,635
Median household income	$68,402
Median family income	$86,873
Persons in poverty	1,551
H'holds receiving public assistance	102
H'holds receiving social security	1,897

Households, 2000
Total households	10,489
With persons under 18	4,047
With persons over 65	1,969
Family households	7,072
Single-person households	2,826
Persons per household	2.60
Persons per family	3.23

Labor & Employment
Total civilian labor force, 2007**	16,412
Unemployment rate	2.9%
Total civilian labor force, 2000	14,938
Unemployment rate	3.2%

Employed persons 16 years and over by occupation, 2000
Managers & professionals	7,809
Service occupations	1,477
Sales & office occupations	3,902
Farming, fishing & forestry	29
Construction & maintenance	492
Production & transportation	745
Self-employed persons	870

‡ Main library for county
* US Census Bureau
** New Jersey Department of Labor

See Introduction for an explanation of all data sources.

General Information
Township of Voorhees
620 Berlin Rd
Voorhees, NJ 08043
856-429-7757

Website	www.voorhees-nj.com
Year of incorporation	1899
Land/water area (sq. miles)	11.60/0.03
Form of government	Township

Government
Legislative Districts
US Congressional	1
State Legislative	6

Local Officials, 2009
Mayor	Michael R. Mignogna
Administrator	Lawrence Spellman
Township Clerk	Jeanette Schelberg
CFO	Dean Ciminera
Tax Assessor	Michael Kane
Tax Collector	Jennifer Dukelow
Attorney	Howard Long
Building	Steve Murray
Comm Dev/Planning	NA
Engineering	Environmental Resolutions
Public Works	John Maurer
Police Chief	Keith Hummel
Emerg/Fire Director	James Pacifico

Housing & Construction
Housing Units, 2000*
Total	11,084
Median rent	$864
Median SF home value	$179,500

Permits for New Residential Construction
	Units	Value
Total, 2006	74	$9,281,747
Single family	74	$9,281,747
Total, 2007	158	$10,885,376
Single family	80	$8,925,076

Real Property Valuation, 2008
	Parcels	Valuation
Total	9,567	$3,873,678,143
Vacant	447	100,398,023
Residential	8,575	2,920,933,820
Commercial	481	683,226,500
Industrial	28	38,674,400
Apartments	17	128,030,300
Farm land	12	78,500
Farm homestead	7	2,336,600

Average Property Value & Tax, 2008
Residential value	$340,628
Property tax	$8,363
Tax credit/rebate	$1,195

Public Library
Camden County Library‡
203 Laurel Rd
Voorhees, NJ 08043
856-772-1636

Director................... Linda Devlin

County Library statistics, 2007
Population served	242,830
Full-time/total staff	33/82

	Total	Per capita
Holdings	437,576	1.80
Revenues	$9,512,902	$39.18
Expenditures	$8,262,212	$34.02
Annual visits	806,593	3.32
Internet terminals/annual users	149/299,895	

Public Safety
Number of officers, 2007	51

Crime	2006	2007
Total crimes	886	836
Violent	59	52
Murder	0	1
Rape	6	5
Robbery	16	13
Aggravated assault	37	33
Non-violent	827	784
Burglary	124	115
Larceny	687	645
Vehicle theft	16	24
Domestic violence	237	182
Arson	6	19
Total crime rate	30.6	28.4
Violent	2.0	1.8
Non-violent	28.6	26.7

Public School District
(for school year 2007-08 except as noted)

Voorhees Township School District
329 Route 73
Voorhees, NJ 08043
(856) 751-8446

Superintendent	Raymond J. Brosel Jr
Number of schools	5
Grade plan	K-8
Enrollment	3,321
Attendance rate, '06-07	96.1%
Dropout rate	NA
Students per teacher	11.4
Per pupil expenditure	$13,692
Median faculty salary	$78,575
Median administrator salary	$126,712
Grade 12 enrollment	NA
High school graduation rate	NA

Assessment test results
(percent scoring at proficient or advanced level)
	Language	Math
NJASK-Grade 3	95.0%	95.3%
GEPA-Grade 8	85.0%	93.8%
HSPA-High School	NA	NA

SAT Score Averages, 2006-07
Pct tested	Math	Verbal	Writing
NA	NA	NA	NA

Teacher Qualifications
Avg. years of experience	19
Highly-qualified teachers one subject/all subjects	99.5%/98.5%

No Child Left Behind
AYP, 2006-07	Meets Standards

Municipal Finance
State Aid Programs, 2009
Total aid	$2,881,434
CMPTRA	457,206
Energy tax receipts	2,347,499
Garden State Trust	3,857

General Budget, 2008
Total tax levy	$95,241,412
County levy	25,176,992
County taxes	22,743,985
County library	1,637,911
County health	0
County open space	795,097
School levy	54,735,666
Muni. levy	15,328,754
Misc. revenues	9,129,417

Taxes
	2006	2007	2008
General tax rate per $100	2.31	2.375	2.456
County equalization ratio	123.18	110.3	97.72
Net valuation taxable	$3,872,245,800	$3,848,807,299	$3,879,358,570
State equalized value	$3,516,320,046	$3,938,476,294	$3,941,545,234

Demographics & Socio-Economic Characteristics
(2000 US Census, except as noted)

Population
1980*	10,802
1990*	9,757
2000	9,622
Male	4,683
Female	4,939
2007 (estimate)*	9,506
Population density	4,570.2

Race & Hispanic Origin, 2000
Race
White	8,918
Black/African American	57
American Indian/Alaska Native	4
Asian	435
Native Hawaiian/Pacific Islander	0
Other race	126
Two or more races	82
Hispanic origin, total	511
Mexican	36
Puerto Rican	105
Cuban	27
Other Hispanic	343

Age & Nativity, 2000
Under 5 years	734
18 years and over	7,170
21 years and over	6,963
65 years and over	1,459
85 years and over	114
Median age	38.1
Native-born	8,434
Foreign-born	1,188

Educational Attainment, 2000
Population 25 years and over	6,676
Less than 9th grade	2.2%
High school grad or higher	92.2%
Bachelor's degree or higher	36.7%
Graduate degree	9.8%

Income & Poverty, 1999
Per capita income	$30,733
Median household income	$75,532
Median family income	$82,208
Persons in poverty	199
H'holds receiving public assistance	59
H'holds receiving social security	1,018

Households, 2000
Total households	3,428
With persons under 18	1,316
With persons over 65	1,041
Family households	2,678
Single-person households	641
Persons per household	2.81
Persons per family	3.22

Labor & Employment
Total civilian labor force, 2007**	5,373
Unemployment rate	1.8%
Total civilian labor force, 2000	5,085
Unemployment rate	1.9%

Employed persons 16 years and over by occupation, 2000
Managers & professionals	2,153
Service occupations	623
Sales & office occupations	1,522
Farming, fishing & forestry	0
Construction & maintenance	384
Production & transportation	304
Self-employed persons	315

* US Census Bureau
** New Jersey Department of Labor

General Information
Borough of Waldwick
63 Franklin Turnpike
Waldwick, NJ 07463
201-652-5300
Website	www.waldwickpd.org
Year of incorporation	1919
Land/water area (sq. miles)	2.08/0.01
Form of government	Borough

Government
Legislative Districts
US Congressional	5
State Legislative	39

Local Officials, 2009
Mayor	Russell Litchult
Manager	Gary Kratz
Clerk	Paula Jaegge
Finance Dir	MaryAnn Viviani
Tax Assessor	Angela Mattiace
Tax Collector	MaryAnn Viviani
Attorney	Craig Bossong
Building	Joseph Mysliwiec
Comm Dev/Planning	NA
Engineering	Dennis O'Brien
Public Works	Joseph Agugliaro
Police Chief	Mark Messner
Emerg/Fire Director	Walter Riker

Housing & Construction
Housing Units, 2000*
Total	3,495
Median rent	$1,127
Median SF home value	$229,400

Permits for New Residential Construction
	Units	Value
Total, 2006	13	$1,963,934
Single family	11	$1,613,934
Total, 2007	39	$5,831,841
Single family	28	$4,143,121

Real Property Valuation, 2008
	Parcels	Valuation
Total	3,616	$1,561,111,100
Vacant	147	15,491,500
Residential	3,324	1,397,629,300
Commercial	125	118,400,700
Industrial	20	29,589,600
Apartments	0	0
Farm land	0	0
Farm homestead	0	0

Average Property Value & Tax, 2008
Residential value	$420,466
Property tax	$9,069
Tax credit/rebate	$1,351

Public Library
Waldwick Public Library
19 E Prospect St
Waldwick, NJ 07463
201-652-5104
Director	Patricia Boyd

Library statistics, 2007
Population served	9,622
Full-time/total staff	2/4

	Total	Per capita
Holdings	50,186	5.22
Revenues	$722,576	$75.10
Expenditures	$655,229	$68.10
Annual visits	112,028	11.64
Internet terminals/annual users	6/28,111	

Public Safety
Number of officers, 2007	19

Crime	2006	2007
Total crimes	91	78
Violent	4	6
Murder	0	0
Rape	0	0
Robbery	2	1
Aggravated assault	2	5
Non-violent	87	72
Burglary	9	4
Larceny	78	68
Vehicle theft	0	0
Domestic violence	53	52
Arson	2	0
Total crime rate	9.4	8.1
Violent	0.4	0.6
Non-violent	9.0	7.5

Public School District
(for school year 2007-08 except as noted)

Waldwick School District
155 Summit Avenue
Waldwick, NJ 07463
(201) 445-3131
Superintendent	Robert F. Penna
Number of schools	4
Grade plan	K-12
Enrollment	1,584
Attendance rate, '06-07	95.9%
Dropout rate	0.2%
Students per teacher	10.6
Per pupil expenditure	$15,038
Median faculty salary	$53,200
Median administrator salary	$122,000
Grade 12 enrollment	104
High school graduation rate	98.1%

Assessment test results
(percent scoring at proficient or advanced level)
	Language	Math
NJASK-Grade 3	97.7%	96.0%
GEPA-Grade 8	78.4%	96.3%
HSPA-High School	86.8%	92.1%

SAT Score Averages, 2006-07
Pct tested	Math	Verbal	Writing
91%	525	488	492

Teacher Qualifications
Avg. years of experience	8
Highly-qualified teachers one subject/all subjects	100%/100%

No Child Left Behind
AYP, 2006-07	Meets Standards

Municipal Finance
State Aid Programs, 2009
Total aid	$2,993,739
CMPTRA	0
Energy tax receipts	2,918,886
Garden State Trust	10

General Budget, 2008
Total tax levy	$33,698,069
County levy	3,174,209
County taxes	3,002,598
County library	0
County health	0
County open space	171,611
School levy	22,736,618
Muni. levy	7,787,242
Misc. revenues	5,262,989

Taxes
	2006	2007	2008
General tax rate per $100	1.96	2.09	2.158
County equalization ratio	103.07	93.01	91.27
Net valuation taxable	$1,537,323,400	$1,550,532,976	$1,562,264,903
State equalized value	$1,653,590,994	$1,698,739,748	$1,774,942,123

See Introduction for an explanation of all data sources.

Demographics & Socio-Economic Characteristics
(2000 US Census, except as noted)

Population
1980*	18,952
1990*	20,244
2000	25,261
Male	12,155
Female	13,106
2007 (estimate)*	26,274
Population density	858.1

Race & Hispanic Origin, 2000
Race
White	24,526
Black/African American	155
American Indian/Alaska Native	26
Asian	319
Native Hawaiian/Pacific Islander	9
Other race	80
Two or more races	146
Hispanic origin, total	391
Mexican	60
Puerto Rican	128
Cuban	43
Other Hispanic	160

Age & Nativity, 2000
Under 5 years	1,671
18 years and over	18,887
21 years and over	18,255
65 years and over	3,641
85 years and over	450
Median age	40.3
Native-born	24,243
Foreign-born	1,018

Educational Attainment, 2000
Population 25 years and over	17,618
Less than 9th grade	2.1%
High school grad or higher	91.6%
Bachelor's degree or higher	38.9%
Graduate degree	13.9%

Income & Poverty, 1999
Per capita income	$32,954
Median household income	$73,989
Median family income	$83,795
Persons in poverty	569
H'holds receiving public assistance	91
H'holds receiving social security	2,575

Households, 2000
Total households	9,437
With persons under 18	3,361
With persons over 65	2,508
Family households	6,931
Single-person households	2,140
Persons per household	2.64
Persons per family	3.14

Labor & Employment
Total civilian labor force, 2007**	13,622
Unemployment rate	2.7%
Total civilian labor force, 2000	12,820
Unemployment rate	4.0%

Employed persons 16 years and over by occupation, 2000
Managers & professionals	5,470
Service occupations	1,190
Sales & office occupations	3,395
Farming, fishing & forestry	56
Construction & maintenance	1,238
Production & transportation	954
Self-employed persons	955

‡ Branch of county library
* US Census Bureau
** New Jersey Department of Labor

See Introduction for an explanation of all data sources.

General Information
Township of Wall
2700 Allaire Rd
Wall Township, NJ 07719
732-449-8444

Website	www.wallnj.com
Year of incorporation	1851
Land/water area (sq. miles)	30.62/0.80
Form of government	Township

Government
Legislative Districts
US Congressional	4
State Legislative	11

Local Officials, 2009
Mayor	Michael J. Clayton
Manager	Joseph Verruni
Clerk	Lorraine Kubacz
Finance Dir	Stephen Mayer
Tax Assessor	Denise Siegel
Tax Collector	Theresa Vola
Attorney	Joseph Oxley
Building	Paul Rabenda
Planning	John Hoffmann
Engineering	Matt Zahorsky
Public Works	Ken Critchlow
Police Chief	David Morris
Fire/Emergency Dir	NA

Housing & Construction
Housing Units, 2000*
Total	9,957
Median rent	$818
Median SF home value	$234,700

Permits for New Residential Construction
	Units	Value
Total, 2006	45	$5,148,319
Single family	45	$5,148,319
Total, 2007	31	$8,083,200
Single family	31	$8,083,200

Real Property Valuation, 2008
	Parcels	Valuation
Total	10,707	$3,855,759,800
Vacant	623	101,487,000
Residential	9,228	2,916,601,400
Commercial	611	656,360,100
Industrial	84	124,595,000
Apartments	9	23,878,700
Farm land	89	974,400
Farm homestead	63	31,863,200

Average Property Value & Tax, 2008
Residential value	$317,346
Property tax	$7,655
Tax credit/rebate	$1,086

Public Library
Wall Public Library‡
2700 Allaire Rd
Wall, NJ 07719
732-449-8877

Branch Librarian	Pamela Sawall

Library statistics, 2007
see Monmouth County profile
for library system statistics

Public Safety
Number of officers, 2007	71

Crime	2006	2007
Total crimes	522	419
Violent	27	29
Murder	0	0
Rape	0	0
Robbery	7	1
Aggravated assault	20	28
Non-violent	495	390
Burglary	121	85
Larceny	355	288
Vehicle theft	19	17
Domestic violence	163	183
Arson	2	0
Total crime rate	20.1	16.1
Violent	1.0	1.1
Non-violent	19.0	15.0

Public School District
(for school year 2007-08 except as noted)

Wall Township School District
18th Avenue, PO Box 1199
Wall, NJ 07719
(732) 556-2101

Superintendent	James F. Habel
Number of schools	7
Grade plan	K-12
Enrollment	4,204
Attendance rate, '06-07	92.7%
Dropout rate	.0.0%
Students per teacher	10.6
Per pupil expenditure	$13,162
Median faculty salary	$48,155
Median administrator salary	$123,951
Grade 12 enrollment	327
High school graduation rate	97.5%

Assessment test results
(percent scoring at proficient or advanced level)
	Language	Math
NJASK-Grade 3	96.0%	91.3%
GEPA-Grade 8	80.8%	88.7%
HSPA-High School	85.8%	89.0%

SAT Score Averages, 2006-07
Pct tested	Math	Verbal	Writing
87%	514	498	498

Teacher Qualifications
Avg. years of experience	8
Highly-qualified teachers one subject/all subjects	100%/100%

No Child Left Behind
AYP, 2006-07	Meets Standards

Municipal Finance
State Aid Programs, 2009
Total aid	$4,375,636
CMPTRA	0
Energy tax receipts	4,203,407
Garden State Trust	19,620

General Budget, 2008
Total tax levy	$93,113,778
County levy	17,686,837
County taxes	15,440,741
County library	929,222
County health	287,137
County open space	1,029,737
School levy	53,507,088
Muni. levy	21,919,853
Misc. revenues	11,596,596

Taxes	2006	2007	2008
General tax rate per $100	2.194	2.284	2.413
County equalization ratio	69.14	62.14	56.46
Net valuation taxable	$3,776,393,800	$3,828,389,614	$3,860,266,268
State equalized value	$6,082,284,612	$6,777,064,627	$6,613,625,083

Demographics & Socio-Economic Characteristics

(2000 US Census, except as noted)

Population
1980*	10,741
1990*	10,828
2000	11,583
Male	5,582
Female	6,001
2007 (estimate)*	11,349
Population density	11,349.0

Race & Hispanic Origin, 2000
Race
White	10,147
Black/African American	309
American Indian/Alaska Native	11
Asian	577
Native Hawaiian/Pacific Islander	2
Other race	269
Two or more races	268
Hispanic origin, total	776
Mexican	37
Puerto Rican	252
Cuban	66
Other Hispanic	421

Age & Nativity, 2000
Under 5 years	611
18 years and over	9,451
21 years and over	9,083
65 years and over	1,757
85 years and over	220
Median age	38.2
Native-born	6,849
Foreign-born	4,734

Educational Attainment, 2000
Population 25 years and over	8,434
Less than 9th grade	11.9%
High school grad or higher	72.4%
Bachelor's degree or higher	17.0%
Graduate degree	6.4%

Income & Poverty, 1999
Per capita income	$24,431
Median household income	$45,656
Median family income	$55,291
Persons in poverty	729
H'holds receiving public assistance	82
H'holds receiving social security	1,381

Households, 2000
Total households	4,752
With persons under 18	1,307
With persons over 65	1,342
Family households	3,043
Single-person households	1,415
Persons per household	2.44
Persons per family	3.05

Labor & Employment
Total civilian labor force, 2007**	6,596
Unemployment rate	5.4%
Total civilian labor force, 2000	6,269
Unemployment rate	5.9%

Employed persons 16 years and over by occupation, 2000
Managers & professionals	1,548
Service occupations	782
Sales & office occupations	1,711
Farming, fishing & forestry	0
Construction & maintenance	740
Production & transportation	1,118
Self-employed persons	272

General Information

Borough of Wallington
24 Union Blvd
Wallington, NJ 07057
973-777-0318

Website	www.wallingtonnj.org
Year of incorporation	1895
Land/water area (sq. miles)	1.00/0.04
Form of government	Borough

Government

Legislative Districts
US Congressional	9
State Legislative	36

Local Officials, 2009
Mayor	Walter Wargacki
Manager	Witold Baginski
Clerk	Witold Baginski
Finance Dir	Dorothy Siek
Tax Assessor	Stuart Stolarz
Tax Collector	Dorothy Siek
Attorney	Richard Cedzidlo
Building	Nick Melfi
Comm Dev/Planning	NA
Engineering	Kenneth Job
Public Works	Walter Bednarz
Police Chief	Anthony Benevento
Emerg/Fire Director	Raymond Dynes

Housing & Construction

Housing Units, 2000*
Total	4,906
Median rent	$756
Median SF home value	$201,800

Permits for New Residential Construction
	Units	Value
Total, 2006	43	$3,857,500
Single family	43	$3,857,500
Total, 2007	23	$2,191,139
Single family	23	$2,191,139

Real Property Valuation, 2008
	Parcels	Valuation
Total	2,439	$1,200,247,400
Vacant	49	8,502,900
Residential	2,156	888,727,800
Commercial	165	145,055,200
Industrial	38	59,260,700
Apartments	31	98,700,800
Farm land	0	0
Farm homestead	0	0

Average Property Value & Tax, 2008
Residential value	$412,211
Property tax	$6,964
Tax credit/rebate	$1,059

Public Library

JFK Memorial Library
92 Hathaway St
Wallington, NJ 07057
973-471-1692

Director	Marianne R. Willms

Library statistics, 2007
Population served	11,583
Full-time/total staff	1/2

	Total	Per capita
Holdings	32,810	2.83
Revenues	$377,715	$32.61
Expenditures	$307,364	$26.54
Annual visits	12,455	1.08
Internet terminals/annual users	19/5,060	

Public Safety

Number of officers, 2007	22

Crime	2006	2007
Total crimes	170	178
Violent	11	11
Murder	0	0
Rape	0	0
Robbery	8	8
Aggravated assault	3	3
Non-violent	159	167
Burglary	33	35
Larceny	103	112
Vehicle theft	23	20
Domestic violence	20	35
Arson	0	0
Total crime rate	**14.8**	**15.6**
Violent	1.0	1.0
Non-violent	13.8	14.6

Public School District

(for school year 2007-08 except as noted)

Wallington School District
Jefferson School, Pine St
Wallington, NJ 07057
(973) 777-4421

Superintendent	Frank A. Cocchiola Jr
Number of schools	3
Grade plan	K-12
Enrollment	1,152
Attendance rate, '06-07	94.1%
Dropout rate	1.1%
Students per teacher	11.3
Per pupil expenditure	$12,658
Median faculty salary	$52,034
Median administrator salary	$102,625
Grade 12 enrollment	96
High school graduation rate	91.3%

Assessment test results
(percent scoring at proficient or advanced level)
	Language	Math
NJASK-Grade 3	97.3%	93.3%
GEPA-Grade 8	71.5%	85.4%
HSPA-High School	85.5%	87.4%

SAT Score Averages, 2006-07
Pct tested	Math	Verbal	Writing
59%	486	452	461

Teacher Qualifications
Avg. years of experience	11
Highly-qualified teachers one subject/all subjects	100%/100%

No Child Left Behind
AYP, 2006-07	Meets Standards

Municipal Finance

State Aid Programs, 2009
Total aid	$868,287
CMPTRA	287,603
Energy tax receipts	558,977
Garden State Trust	0

General Budget, 2008
Total tax levy	$20,290,911
County levy	2,241,111
County taxes	2,119,974
County library	0
County health	0
County open space	121,137
School levy	11,517,206
Muni. levy	6,532,594
Misc. revenues	3,836,086

Taxes
	2006	2007	2008
General tax rate per $100	3.37	3.6	1.691
County equalization ratio	55.35	48.44	99.71
Net valuation taxable	$527,209,300	$531,127,045	$1,200,977,432
State equalized value	$1,088,761,381	$1,200,127,559	$1,221,361,986

* US Census Bureau
** New Jersey Department of Labor

See Introduction for an explanation of all data sources.

Demographics & Socio-Economic Characteristics
(2000 US Census, except as noted)

Population
1980*	150
1990*	67
2000	41
Male	20
Female	21
2007 (estimate)*	39
Population density	1.6

Race & Hispanic Origin, 2000
Race
White	41
Black/African American	0
American Indian/Alaska Native	0
Asian	0
Native Hawaiian/Pacific Islander	0
Other race	0
Two or more races	0
Hispanic origin, total	0
Mexican	0
Puerto Rican	0
Cuban	0
Other Hispanic	0

Age & Nativity, 2000
Under 5 years	0
18 years and over	33
21 years and over	33
65 years and over	11
85 years and over	1
Median age	49.3
Native-born	37
Foreign-born	0

Educational Attainment, 2000
Population 25 years and over	37
Less than 9th grade	0.0%
High school grad or higher	62.2%
Bachelor's degree or higher	0.0%
Graduate degree	0.0%

Income & Poverty, 1999
Per capita income	$17,624
Median household income	$22,250
Median family income	$22,250
Persons in poverty	0
H'holds receiving public assistance	0
H'holds receiving social security	14

Households, 2000
Total households	20
With persons under 18	4
With persons over 65	7
Family households	12
Single-person households	8
Persons per household	2.05
Persons per family	2.75

Labor & Employment
Total civilian labor force, 2007**	22
Unemployment rate	0.0%
Total civilian labor force, 2000	18
Unemployment rate	0.0%

Employed persons 16 years and over by occupation, 2000
Managers & professionals	0
Service occupations	10
Sales & office occupations	0
Farming, fishing & forestry	0
Construction & maintenance	8
Production & transportation	0
Self-employed persons	0

* US Census Bureau
** New Jersey Department of Labor

General Information
Township of Walpack
Walpack Center
PO Box 94
Walpack, NJ 07881
908-841-9576

Website	(county website)
Year of incorporation	1731
Land/water area (sq. miles)	24.07/0.65
Form of government	Township

Government
Legislative Districts
US Congressional	5
State Legislative	24

Local Officials, 2009
Mayor	Raymond Fuller
Manager/Admin	NA
Clerk	Betsy Cuneo
Finance Dir	Michelle Lastarza
Tax Assessor	John Dykson
Tax Collector	Terry Beshada
Attorney	Michael Garofalo
Building	Greg Chontow
Comm Dev/Planning	NA
Engineering	NA
Public Works	NA
Police Chief	NA
Fire/Emergency Dir	NA

Housing & Construction
Housing Units, 2000*
Total	34
Median rent	$400
Median SF home value	$275,000

Permits for New Residential Construction
	Units	Value
Total, 2006	0	$0
Single family	0	$0
Total, 2007	0	$0
Single family	0	$0

Real Property Valuation, 2008
	Parcels	Valuation
Total	30	$2,331,700
Vacant	7	85,100
Residential	8	645,250
Commercial	2	1,077,400
Industrial	0	0
Apartments	0	0
Farm land	9	101,950
Farm homestead	4	422,000

Average Property Value & Tax, 2008
Residential value	$88,938
Property tax	$676
Tax credit/rebate	$584

Public Library
No public municipal library

Library statistics, 2007
Population served	NA
Full-time/total staff	NA/NA

	Total	Per capita
Holdings	NA	NA
Revenues	NA	NA
Expenditures	NA	NA
Annual visits	NA	NA
Internet terminals/annual users	NA/NA	

Public Safety
Number of officers, 2007 0
Crime	2006	2007
Total crimes	3	0
Violent	1	0
Murder	0	0
Rape	0	0
Robbery	1	0
Aggravated assault	0	0
Non-violent	2	0
Burglary	2	0
Larceny	0	0
Vehicle theft	0	0
Domestic violence	0	0
Arson	0	0
Total crime rate	NA	0.0
Violent	NA	0.0
Non-violent	NA	0.0

Public School District
(for school year 2007-08 except as noted)

Sandyston-Walpack Township School Dist.
PO Box 128, 100 Route 560
Layton, NJ 07851
(973) 948-4450

Chief School Admin	Glenn Sumpman
Number of schools	1
Grade plan	K-6
Enrollment	176
Attendance rate, '06-07	95.4%
Dropout rate	NA
Students per teacher	9.5
Per pupil expenditure	$14,400
Median faculty salary	$57,273
Median administrator salary	$110,000
Grade 12 enrollment	NA
High school graduation rate	NA

Assessment test results
(percent scoring at proficient or advanced level)
	Language	Math
NJASK-Grade 3	100.0%	100.0%
GEPA-Grade 8	NA	NA
HSPA-High School	NA	NA

SAT Score Averages, 2006-07
Pct tested	Math	Verbal	Writing
NA	NA	NA	NA

Teacher Qualifications
Avg. years of experience	11
Highly-qualified teachers one subject/all subjects	100%/100%

No Child Left Behind
AYP, 2006-07 .... Meets Standards

Municipal Finance
State Aid Programs, 2009
Total aid	$43,068
CMPTRA	0
Energy tax receipts	39,228
Garden State Trust	2,150

General Budget, 2008
Total tax levy	$18,208
County levy	9,569
County taxes	9,308
County library	785
County health	276
County open space	724
School levy	8,639
Muni. levy	0
Misc. revenues	136,590

Taxes	2006	2007	2008
General tax rate per $100	1.01	0.79	0.760
County equalization ratio	95.42	95.42	95.42
Net valuation taxable	$2,331,700	$2,397,527	$2,397,086
State equalized value	$2,510,431	$2,509,445	$2,509,004

See Introduction for an explanation of all data sources.

Demographics & Socio-Economic Characteristics

(2000 US Census, except as noted)

Population

1980*	10,025
1990*	9,711
2000	10,266
Male	4,956
Female	5,310
2007 (estimate)*	11,649
Population density	1,459.8

Race & Hispanic Origin, 2000

Race

White	9,308
Black/African American	155
American Indian/Alaska Native	35
Asian	372
Native Hawaiian/Pacific Islander	3
Other race	211
Two or more races	182
Hispanic origin, total	554
Mexican	69
Puerto Rican	179
Cuban	44
Other Hispanic	262

Age & Nativity, 2000

Under 5 years	689
18 years and over	7,765
21 years and over	7,470
65 years and over	1,233
85 years and over	247
Median age	37.6
Native-born	8,973
Foreign-born	1,293

Educational Attainment, 2000

Population 25 years and over	7,162
Less than 9th grade	6.2%
High school grad or higher	84.2%
Bachelor's degree or higher	22.3%
Graduate degree	7.7%

Income & Poverty, 1999

Per capita income	$25,403
Median household income	$66,113
Median family income	$71,127
Persons in poverty	330
H'holds receiving public assistance	64
H'holds receiving social security	841

Households, 2000

Total households	3,444
With persons under 18	1,401
With persons over 65	687
Family households	2,689
Single-person households	575
Persons per household	2.86
Persons per family	3.23

Labor & Employment

Total civilian labor force, 2007**	6,132
Unemployment rate	3.3%
Total civilian labor force, 2000	5,675
Unemployment rate	3.6%

Employed persons 16 years and over by occupation, 2000

Managers & professionals	1,712
Service occupations	871
Sales & office occupations	1,763
Farming, fishing & forestry	0
Construction & maintenance	473
Production & transportation	650
Self-employed persons	210

* US Census Bureau
** New Jersey Department of Labor

General Information

Borough of Wanaque
579 Ringwood Ave
Wanaque, NJ 07465
973-839-3000

Website	www.wanaqueborough.com
Year of incorporation	1918
Land/water area (sq. miles)	7.98/1.23
Form of government	Borough

Government

Legislative Districts

US Congressional	5
State Legislative	40

Local Officials, 2009

Mayor	Daniel Mahler
Manager	Thomas Carroll
Clerk	Katherine Falone
Finance Dir	Mary Ann Brindisi
Tax Assessor	Brian Townsend
Tax Collector	Lynn Gordon
Attorney	Tony Fiorello
Building	Jeff Brusco
Planning	Richard Alaimo
Engineering	Mike Cristaldi
Public Works	Rick Crescente
Police Chief	Jack Reno
Emerg/Fire Director	Lee Smith

Housing & Construction

Housing Units, 2000*

Total	3,500
Median rent	$946
Median SF home value	$172,100

Permits for New Residential Construction

	Units	Value
Total, 2006	231	$16,871,777
Single family	3	$331,250
Total, 2007	226	$19,586,620
Single family	4	$568,000

Real Property Valuation, 2008

	Parcels	Valuation
Total	4,233	$576,343,584
Vacant	389	24,025,200
Residential	3,727	498,917,774
Commercial	94	40,972,420
Industrial	19	10,828,090
Apartments	4	1,600,100
Farm land	0	0
Farm homestead	0	0

Average Property Value & Tax, 2008

Residential value	$133,866
Property tax	$7,612
Tax credit/rebate	$1,189

Public Library

Wanaque Public Library
616 Ringwood Ave
Wanaque, NJ 07465
973-839-4434

Director . . . . Richard L. Mariconda

Library statistics, 2007

Population served	10,266
Full-time/total staff	1/5

	Total	Per capita
Holdings	42,175	4.11
Revenues	$466,893	$45.48
Expenditures	$392,010	$38.19
Annual visits	18,000	1.75
Internet terminals/annual users	9/8,255	

Public Safety

Number of officers, 2007	23

Crime	2006	2007
Total crimes	142	161
Violent	5	6
Murder	0	0
Rape	0	0
Robbery	0	2
Aggravated assault	5	4
Non-violent	137	155
Burglary	27	19
Larceny	101	131
Vehicle theft	9	5
Domestic violence	96	107
Arson	1	0
Total crime rate	13.4	14.4
Violent	0.5	0.5
Non-violent	12.9	13.9

Public School District

(for school year 2007-08 except as noted)

Wanaque School District
973 A Ringwood Avenue
Haskell, NJ 07420
(973) 835-8202

Chief School Admin	Richard B. Weisenfeld
Number of schools	2
Grade plan	K-8
Enrollment	972
Attendance rate, '06-07	96.5%
Dropout rate	NA
Students per teacher	10.8
Per pupil expenditure	$13,308
Median faculty salary	$66,795
Median administrator salary	$108,025
Grade 12 enrollment	NA
High school graduation rate	NA

Assessment test results

(percent scoring at proficient or advanced level)

	Language	Math
NJASK-Grade 3	88.0%	87.0%
GEPA-Grade 8	75.0%	88.6%
HSPA-High School	NA	NA

SAT Score Averages, 2006-07

Pct tested	Math	Verbal	Writing
NA	NA	NA	NA

Teacher Qualifications

Avg. years of experience	11
Highly-qualified teachers one subject/all subjects	98.5%/97.0%

No Child Left Behind

AYP, 2006-07	Meets Standards

Municipal Finance

State Aid Programs, 2009

Total aid	$1,172,534
CMPTRA	337,397
Energy tax receipts	796,932
Garden State Trust	7,056

General Budget, 2008

Total tax levy	$32,809,926
County levy	7,195,603
County taxes	7,053,050
County library	0
County health	0
County open space	142,553
School levy	17,847,173
Muni. levy	7,767,150
Misc. revenues	3,609,660

Taxes	2006	2007	2008
General tax rate per $100	5.26	5.52	5.687
County equalization ratio	46.45	41.9	40.59
Net valuation taxable	$518,907,284	$563,578,695	$577,020,732
State equalized value	$1,239,128,676	$1,387,533,751	$1,397,873,715

See Introduction for an explanation of all data sources.

Demographics & Socio-Economic Characteristics
(2000 US Census, except as noted)

Population
1980*	7,268
1990*	9,487
2000	10,387
Male	5,113
Female	5,274
2007 (estimate)*	11,532
Population density	171.8

Race & Hispanic Origin, 2000
Race
White	10,086
Black/African American	67
American Indian/Alaska Native	6
Asian	70
Native Hawaiian/Pacific Islander	1
Other race	43
Two or more races	114
Hispanic origin, total	300
Mexican	23
Puerto Rican	130
Cuban	34
Other Hispanic	113

Age & Nativity, 2000
Under 5 years	701
18 years and over	7,337
21 years and over	6,975
65 years and over	916
85 years and over	97
Median age	36.3
Native-born	9,895
Foreign-born	492

Educational Attainment, 2000
Population 25 years and over	6,565
Less than 9th grade	4.0%
High school grad or higher	84.6%
Bachelor's degree or higher	19.5%
Graduate degree	7.7%

Income & Poverty, 1999
Per capita income	$22,488
Median household income	$58,440
Median family income	$65,339
Persons in poverty	508
H'holds receiving public assistance	102
H'holds receiving social security	826

Households, 2000
Total households	3,441
With persons under 18	1,592
With persons over 65	667
Family households	2,857
Single-person households	467
Persons per household	3.02
Persons per family	3.33

Labor & Employment
Total civilian labor force, 2007**	5,906
Unemployment rate	5.5%
Total civilian labor force, 2000	5,261
Unemployment rate	4.4%

Employed persons 16 years and over by occupation, 2000
Managers & professionals	1,597
Service occupations	759
Sales & office occupations	1,353
Farming, fishing & forestry	51
Construction & maintenance	658
Production & transportation	610
Self-employed persons	384

‡ Branch of county library
* US Census Bureau
** New Jersey Department of Labor

See Introduction for an explanation of all data sources.

General Information
Township of Wantage
888 Route 23
Wantage, NJ 07461
973-875-7192

Website	www.wantagetwp.com
Year of incorporation	1754
Land/water area (sq. miles)	67.12/0.42
Form of government	Township

Government

Legislative Districts
US Congressional	5
State Legislative	24

Local Officials, 2009
Mayor	Parker Space
Administrator	Jim Doherty
Clerk	Jim Doherty
Finance Dir	Michelle Lastarza
Tax Assessor	Melissa Rockwell
Tax Collector	Marcia Snyder
Attorney	Mike Garofalo
Construction Official	Ed Vanderberg
Comm Dev/Planning	NA
Engineer	Harold Pellow
Public Works Supervisor	Claude Wagner
Police Chief	NA
Fire Chief	Leo Kinney

Housing & Construction

Housing Units, 2000*
Total	3,663
Median rent	$768
Median SF home value	$154,200

Permits for New Residential Construction
	Units	Value
Total, 2006	80	$14,234,975
Single family	80	$14,234,975
Total, 2007	48	$7,138,933
Single family	33	$7,063,933

Real Property Valuation, 2008
	Parcels	Valuation
Total	5,321	$1,445,405,618
Vacant	487	60,436,760
Residential	3,509	1,110,616,200
Commercial	148	113,178,362
Industrial	2	1,157,200
Apartments	3	5,822,300
Farm land	761	7,487,196
Farm homestead	411	146,707,600

Average Property Value & Tax, 2008
Residential value	$320,746
Property tax	$6,098
Tax credit/rebate	$1,029

Public Library
Sussex-Wantage Branch Library‡
69 Route 639
Wantage, NJ 07461
973-875-3940

Branch Librarian	Nancy Helmer

Library statistics, 2007
see Sussex County profile
for library system statistics

Public Safety
Number of officers, 2007	0

Crime	2006	2007
Total crimes	112	112
Violent	12	8
Murder	0	1
Rape	0	0
Robbery	0	0
Aggravated assault	12	7
Non-violent	100	104
Burglary	26	30
Larceny	66	66
Vehicle theft	8	8
Domestic violence	9	86
Arson	7	0
Total crime rate	9.8	9.7
Violent	1.0	0.7
Non-violent	8.7	9.0

Public School District
(for school year 2007-08 except as noted)

Sussex-Wantage Regional School District
27 Bank Street
Sussex, NJ 07461
(973) 875-3175

Superintendent	Edward Izbicki
Number of schools	3
Grade plan	K-8
Enrollment	1,632
Attendance rate, '06-07	94.7%
Dropout rate	NA
Students per teacher	10.5
Per pupil expenditure	$13,468
Median faculty salary	$60,515
Median administrator salary	$102,581
Grade 12 enrollment	NA
High school graduation rate	NA

Assessment test results
(percent scoring at proficient or advanced level)
	Language	Math
NJASK-Grade 3	89.4%	84.5%
GEPA-Grade 8	75.1%	86.6%
HSPA-High School	NA	NA

SAT Score Averages, 2006-07
Pct tested	Math	Verbal	Writing
NA	NA	NA	NA

Teacher Qualifications
Avg. years of experience	12
Highly-qualified teachers one subject/all subjects	100%/100%

No Child Left Behind
AYP, 2006-07	Meets Standards

Municipal Finance

State Aid Programs, 2009
Total aid	$1,075,498
CMPTRA	311,306
Energy tax receipts	674,540
Garden State Trust	42,030

General Budget, 2008
Total tax levy	$27,540,025
County levy	5,440,900
County taxes	4,566,533
County library	384,857
County health	135,080
County open space	354,431
School levy	19,274,144
Muni. levy	2,824,981
Misc. revenues	3,571,905

Taxes	2006	2007	2008
General tax rate per $100	1.74	1.86	1.902
County equalization ratio	126.42	110.28	102.23
Net valuation taxable	$1,422,032,104	$1,427,233,181	$1,448,518,793
State equalized value	$1,292,836,509	$1,396,169,750	$1,533,614,676

Demographics & Socio-Economic Characteristics

(2000 US Census, except as noted)

Population

1980*	9,805
1990*	10,830
2000	14,259
Male	7,099
Female	7,160
2007 (estimate)*	15,895
Population density	808.1

Race & Hispanic Origin, 2000

Race
White	12,303
Black/African American	180
American Indian/Alaska Native	5
Asian	1,521
Native Hawaiian/Pacific Islander	8
Other race	59
Two or more races	183
Hispanic origin, total	455
Mexican	33
Puerto Rican	66
Cuban	76
Other Hispanic	280

Age & Nativity, 2000

Under 5 years	1,019
18 years and over	10,027
21 years and over	9,708
65 years and over	1,598
85 years and over	151
Median age	39.4
Native-born	12,018
Foreign-born	2,241

Educational Attainment, 2000

Population 25 years and over	9,396
Less than 9th grade	2.4%
High school grad or higher	93.4%
Bachelor's degree or higher	58.2%
Graduate degree	28.4%

Income & Poverty, 1999

Per capita income	$49,475
Median household income	$103,677
Median family income	$121,264
Persons in poverty	299
H'holds receiving public assistance	17
H'holds receiving social security	1,046

Households, 2000

Total households	4,629
With persons under 18	2,147
With persons over 65	1,079
Family households	3,937
Single-person households	565
Persons per household	3.05
Persons per family	3.33

Labor & Employment

Total civilian labor force, 2007**	7,866
Unemployment rate	1.8%
Total civilian labor force, 2000	6,936
Unemployment rate	1.6%

Employed persons 16 years and over by occupation, 2000
Managers & professionals	3,947
Service occupations	554
Sales & office occupations	1,598
Farming, fishing & forestry	5
Construction & maintenance	345
Production & transportation	374
Self-employed persons	585

General Information

Township of Warren
46 Mountain Blvd
Warren, NJ 07059
908-753-8000

Website	www.warrennj.org
Year of incorporation	1806
Land/water area (sq. miles)	19.67/0.00
Form of government	Township

Government

Legislative Districts

US Congressional	7
State Legislative	21

Local Officials, 2009

Mayor	Gary DiNardo
Manager	Mark Krane
Clerk	Patricia DiRocco
Finance Dir	Shaw Boswell
Tax Assessor	Edward Kerwin Jr
Tax Collector	Loree Saums
Attorney	Jeffrey Lehrer
Building	Jeffrey Heiss
Planning	John Chadwick
Engineering	Christian Kastrud
Public Works	Douglas Buro
Police Chief	Russell Leffert
Emerg/Fire Director	Timothy McGowan

Housing & Construction

Housing Units, 2000*

Total	4,718
Median rent	$1,135
Median SF home value	$427,200

Permits for New Residential Construction

	Units	Value
Total, 2006	32	$5,090,982
Single family	32	$5,090,982
Total, 2007	40	$8,466,926
Single family	40	$8,466,926

Real Property Valuation, 2008

	Parcels	Valuation
Total	5,911	$4,478,921,010
Vacant	604	116,300,200
Residential	4,969	3,549,805,200
Commercial	201	736,177,000
Industrial	11	46,560,400
Apartments	0	0
Farm land	82	230,910
Farm homestead	44	29,847,300

Average Property Value & Tax, 2008

Residential value	$714,074
Property tax	$12,161
Tax credit/rebate	$1,275

Public Library

Warren Township Branch Library‡
42 Mountain Blvd
Warren, NJ 07059
908-754-5554

Branch Director .... Elaine Whiting

Library statistics, 2007

see Somerset County profile
for library system statistics

Public Safety

Number of officers, 2007 28

Crime	2006	2007
Total crimes	107	138
Violent	3	5
Murder	0	1
Rape	0	1
Robbery	2	0
Aggravated assault	1	3
Non-violent	104	133
Burglary	13	25
Larceny	89	102
Vehicle theft	2	6
Domestic violence	3	10
Arson	1	0
Total crime rate	6.8	8.7
Violent	0.2	0.3
Non-violent	6.7	8.4

Public School District

(for school year 2007-08 except as noted)

Warren Township School District
213 Mt. Horeb Rd
Warren, NJ 07059
(732) 753-5300

Superintendent	James Crisfield
Number of schools	5
Grade plan	K-8
Enrollment	2,189
Attendance rate, '06-07	96.1%
Dropout rate	NA
Students per teacher	8.7
Per pupil expenditure	$15,375
Median faculty salary	$60,348
Median administrator salary	$122,217
Grade 12 enrollment	NA
High school graduation rate	NA

Assessment test results

(percent scoring at proficient or advanced level)
	Language	Math
NJASK-Grade 3	95.9%	95.1%
GEPA-Grade 8	87.3%	94.7%
HSPA-High School	NA	NA

SAT Score Averages, 2006-07

Pct tested	Math	Verbal	Writing
NA	NA	NA	NA

Teacher Qualifications

Avg. years of experience	10
Highly-qualified teachers one subject/all subjects	100%/100%

No Child Left Behind

AYP, 2006-07 .... Meets Standards

Municipal Finance

State Aid Programs, 2009

Total aid	$1,671,298
CMPTRA	0
Energy tax receipts	1,587,684
Garden State Trust	52

General Budget, 2008

Total tax levy	$76,381,008
County levy	16,778,451
County taxes	13,465,873
County library	1,822,184
County health	0
County open space	1,490,394
School levy	49,544,786
Muni. levy	10,057,771
Misc. revenues	6,448,555

Taxes	2006	2007	2008
General tax rate per $100	1.63	1.65	1.703
County equalization ratio	96.53	91.45	90.39
Net valuation taxable	$4,196,000,263	$4,465,230,057	$4,485,141,180
State equalized value	$4,838,847,433	$4,917,070,906	$4,937,866,294

‡ Branch of county library
* US Census Bureau
** New Jersey Department of Labor

See Introduction for an explanation of all data sources.

Demographics & Socio-Economic Characteristics
(2000 US Census, except as noted)

Population
1980*	6,429
1990*	6,474
2000	6,712
Male	3,340
Female	3,372
2007 (estimate)*	6,695
Population density	3,415.8

Race & Hispanic Origin, 2000
Race
White	6,138
Black/African American	261
American Indian/Alaska Native	8
Asian	97
Native Hawaiian/Pacific Islander	1
Other race	108
Two or more races	99
Hispanic origin, total	280
Mexican	27
Puerto Rican	130
Cuban	18
Other Hispanic	105

Age & Nativity, 2000
Under 5 years	444
18 years and over	4,932
21 years and over	4,716
65 years and over	715
85 years and over	97
Median age	35.2
Native-born	6,120
Foreign-born	592

Educational Attainment, 2000
Population 25 years and over	4,414
Less than 9th grade	4.3%
High school grad or higher	83.4%
Bachelor's degree or higher	22.7%
Graduate degree	7.9%

Income & Poverty, 1999
Per capita income	$23,166
Median household income	$47,000
Median family income	$61,379
Persons in poverty	375
H'holds receiving public assistance	31
H'holds receiving social security	654

Households, 2000
Total households	2,724
With persons under 18	975
With persons over 65	578
Family households	1,685
Single-person households	862
Persons per household	2.46
Persons per family	3.15

Labor & Employment
Total civilian labor force, 2007**	4,085
Unemployment rate	3.5%
Total civilian labor force, 2000	3,629
Unemployment rate	3.3%

Employed persons 16 years and over by occupation, 2000
Managers & professionals	1,176
Service occupations	494
Sales & office occupations	906
Farming, fishing & forestry	0
Construction & maintenance	399
Production & transportation	534
Self-employed persons	180

General Information
Borough of Washington
100 Belvidere Ave
Washington, NJ 07882
908-689-3600

Website	www.washingtonboro-nj.org
Year of incorporation	1868
Land/water area (sq. miles)	1.96/0.00
Form of government	Council-Manager

Government
Legislative Districts
US Congressional	5
State Legislative	23

Local Officials, 2009
Mayor	Scott McDonald
Manager	John Corica
Clerk	Kristine Blanchard
Finance Dir	NA
Tax Assessor	Athan Efstathiou
Tax Collector	Kay Stasyshan
Attorney	Richard Cushing
Building	Chuck Herring
Comm Dev/Planning	NA
Engineering	Robert Miller
Public Works	NA
Police Chief	George Cortellesi
Emerg/Fire Director	Kurt Klausfelder

Housing & Construction
Housing Units, 2000*
Total	2,876
Median rent	$697
Median SF home value	$119,000

Permits for New Residential Construction
	Units	Value
Total, 2006	3	$135,300
Single family	3	$135,300
Total, 2007	12	$1,550,000
Single family	12	$1,550,000

Real Property Valuation, 2008
	Parcels	Valuation
Total	2,354	$381,317,760
Vacant	229	9,560,900
Residential	1,918	283,120,160
Commercial	170	48,586,900
Industrial	14	16,823,900
Apartments	18	22,783,000
Farm land	4	5,300
Farm homestead	1	437,600

Average Property Value & Tax, 2008
Residential value	$147,763
Property tax	$5,950
Tax credit/rebate	$1,049

Public Library
Washington Public Library
20 W Carlton Ave
Washington, NJ 07882
908-689-0201

Director	Barbara A. Rose

Library statistics, 2007
Population served	6,712
Full-time/total staff	0/4

	Total	Per capita
Holdings	50,722	7.56
Revenues	$326,959	$48.71
Expenditures	$297,267	$44.29
Annual visits	25,608	3.82
Internet terminals/annual users	9/5,166	

Public Safety
Number of officers, 2007		13

Crime	2006	2007
Total crimes	184	203
Violent	9	8
Murder	1	1
Rape	0	0
Robbery	1	4
Aggravated assault	7	3
Non-violent	175	195
Burglary	37	37
Larceny	128	151
Vehicle theft	10	7
Domestic violence	126	138
Arson	6	4
Total crime rate	26.8	29.7
Violent	1.3	1.2
Non-violent	25.5	28.5

Public School District
(for school year 2007-08 except as noted)

Washington Borough School District
300 West Stewart Street
Washington, NJ 07882
(908) 689-0241

Superintendent	Lance Rozsa
Number of schools	2
Grade plan	K-6
Enrollment	494
Attendance rate, '06-07	94.7%
Dropout rate	NA
Students per teacher	9.0
Per pupil expenditure	$13,381
Median faculty salary	$54,697
Median administrator salary	$83,500
Grade 12 enrollment	NA
High school graduation rate	NA

Assessment test results
(percent scoring at proficient or advanced level)
	Language	Math
NJASK-Grade 3	88.8%	83.9%
GEPA-Grade 8	NA	NA
HSPA-High School	NA	NA

SAT Score Averages, 2006-07
Pct tested	Math	Verbal	Writing
NA	NA	NA	NA

Teacher Qualifications
Avg. years of experience	13
Highly-qualified teachers one subject/all subjects	100%/100%

No Child Left Behind
AYP, 2006-07	Meets Standards

Municipal Finance
State Aid Programs, 2009
Total aid	$737,239
CMPTRA	193,222
Energy tax receipts	525,586
Garden State Trust	0

General Budget, 2008
Total tax levy	$15,437,468
County levy	3,307,117
County taxes	2,949,883
County library	0
County health	0
County open space	357,234
School levy	8,087,880
Muni. levy	4,042,471
Misc. revenues	2,655,744

Taxes
	2006	2007	2008
General tax rate per $100	3.72	3.97	4.027
County equalization ratio	74.01	66.26	64.77
Net valuation taxable	$373,195,160	$379,341,707	$383,362,790
State equalized value	$565,961,191	$584,553,362	$594,153,353

* US Census Bureau
** New Jersey Department of Labor

See Introduction for an explanation of all data sources.

Demographics & Socio-Economic Characteristics
(2000 US Census, except as noted)

Population
1980*	9,550
1990*	9,245
2000	8,938
Male	4,291
Female	4,647
2007 (estimate)*	9,581
Population density	3,292.4

Race & Hispanic Origin, 2000
Race
White	8,229
Black/African American	88
American Indian/Alaska Native	4
Asian	498
Native Hawaiian/Pacific Islander	0
Other race	39
Two or more races	80
Hispanic origin, total	299
Mexican	21
Puerto Rican	85
Cuban	83
Other Hispanic	110

Age & Nativity, 2000
Under 5 years	606
18 years and over	6,905
21 years and over	6,730
65 years and over	1,512
85 years and over	92
Median age	41.8
Native-born	7,672
Foreign-born	1,266

Educational Attainment, 2000
Population 25 years and over	6,489
Less than 9th grade	2.3%
High school grad or higher	94.0%
Bachelor's degree or higher	44.8%
Graduate degree	16.6%

Income & Poverty, 1999
Per capita income	$39,248
Median household income	$83,694
Median family income	$88,017
Persons in poverty	216
H'holds receiving public assistance	19
H'holds receiving social security	994

Households, 2000
Total households	3,219
With persons under 18	1,147
With persons over 65	1,069
Family households	2,688
Single-person households	468
Persons per household	2.77
Persons per family	3.07

Labor & Employment
Total civilian labor force, 2007**	5,036
Unemployment rate	3.4%
Total civilian labor force, 2000	4,772
Unemployment rate	3.8%

Employed persons 16 years and over by occupation, 2000
Managers & professionals	2,341
Service occupations	388
Sales & office occupations	1,447
Farming, fishing & forestry	0
Construction & maintenance	260
Production & transportation	153
Self-employed persons	240

* US Census Bureau
** New Jersey Department of Labor

General Information
Township of Washington
350 Hudson Ave
Washington Township, NJ 07676
201-664-4404
Website	www.twpofwashington.us
Year of incorporation	1840
Land/water area (sq. miles)	2.91/0.05
Form of government	Mayor-Council

Government
Legislative Districts
US Congressional	5
State Legislative	39

Local Officials, 2009
Mayor	Rudolph J. Wenzel
Manager	Agnes Smith
Clerk	Mary Ann Ozment
Finance Dir	Jacqueline Do
Tax Assessor	Raymond Damiano
Tax Collector	Joyce Campbell
Attorney	Kenneth Poller
Building	John Scialla
Comm Dev/Planning	NA
Engineering	Azzolina & Feury
Public Works	Robert Hamilton
Police Chief	William Cicchetti
Emerg/Fire Director	Jason Gugger

Housing & Construction
Housing Units, 2000*
Total	3,245
Median rent	$1,909
Median SF home value	$287,800

Permits for New Residential Construction
	Units	Value
Total, 2006	21	$5,377,387
Single family	9	$5,371,665
Total, 2007	19	$3,417,042
Single family	13	$3,414,180

Real Property Valuation, 2008
	Parcels	Valuation
Total	3,460	$1,912,528,800
Vacant	64	12,257,900
Residential	3,374	1,849,271,300
Commercial	22	50,999,600
Industrial	0	0
Apartments	0	0
Farm land	0	0
Farm homestead	0	0

Average Property Value & Tax, 2008
Residential value	$548,095
Property tax	$9,304
Tax credit/rebate	$1,305

Public Library
Washington Township Public Library
144 Woodfield Rd
Township of Washington, NJ 07676
201-664-4586
Director	Juliette L. Sobon

Library statistics, 2007
Population served	8,938
Full-time/total staff	2/4

	Total	Per capita
Holdings	43,570	4.87
Revenues	$722,778	$80.87
Expenditures	$694,660	$77.72
Annual visits	49,836	5.58
Internet terminals/annual users	8/4,050	

Public Safety
Number of officers, 2007	22

Crime	2006	2007
Total crimes	37	26
Violent	5	0
Murder	2	0
Rape	0	0
Robbery	1	0
Aggravated assault	2	0
Non-violent	32	26
Burglary	1	4
Larceny	29	22
Vehicle theft	2	0
Domestic violence	11	11
Arson	0	0
Total crime rate	3.8	2.7
Violent	0.5	0.0
Non-violent	3.3	2.7

Public School District
(for school year 2007-08 except as noted)

Westwood Regional School District
701 Ridgewood Road
Township of Washington, NJ 07676
(201) 664-2765
Superintendent	Geoffrey Zoeller
Number of schools	6
Grade plan	K-12
Enrollment	2,617
Attendance rate, '06-07	96.2%
Dropout rate	0.1%
Students per teacher	10.3
Per pupil expenditure	$14,691
Median faculty salary	$55,793
Median administrator salary	$112,104
Grade 12 enrollment	165
High school graduation rate	98.7%

Assessment test results
(percent scoring at proficient or advanced level)
	Language	Math
NJASK-Grade 3	95.6%	95.6%
GEPA-Grade 8	76.9%	91.3%
HSPA-High School	83.1%	89.9%

SAT Score Averages, 2006-07
Pct tested	Math	Verbal	Writing
92%	534	492	494

Teacher Qualifications
Avg. years of experience	8
Highly-qualified teachers one subject/all subjects	99.5%/99.5%

No Child Left Behind
AYP, 2006-07	Meets Standards

Municipal Finance
State Aid Programs, 2009
Total aid	$919,950
CMPTRA	43,009
Energy tax receipts	853,942
Garden State Trust	0

General Budget, 2008
Total tax levy	$32,482,338
County levy	3,689,176
County taxes	3,489,221
County library	0
County health	0
County open space	199,955
School levy	20,315,713
Muni. levy	8,477,449
Misc. revenues	3,184,649

Taxes
	2006	2007	2008
General tax rate per $100	1.49	1.62	1.700
County equalization ratio	111.06	98.55	95.77
Net valuation taxable	$1,909,368,500	$1,908,102,301	$1,913,535,975
State equalized value	$1,938,150,537	$1,992,348,341	$1,985,369,906

See Introduction for an explanation of all data sources.

Demographics & Socio-Economic Characteristics

(2000 US Census, except as noted)

Population

1980*	808
1990*	805
2000	621
Male	298
Female	323
2007 (estimate)*	643
Population density	6.4

Race & Hispanic Origin, 2000

Race

White	519
Black/African American	18
American Indian/Alaska Native	0
Asian	2
Native Hawaiian/Pacific Islander	0
Other race	75
Two or more races	7
Hispanic origin, total	106
Mexican	3
Puerto Rican	96
Cuban	0
Other Hispanic	7

Age & Nativity, 2000

Under 5 years	29
18 years and over	439
21 years and over	420
65 years and over	151
85 years and over	58
Median age	40.8
Native-born	572
Foreign-born	7

Educational Attainment, 2000

Population 25 years and over	384
Less than 9th grade	21.1%
High school grad or higher	55.7%
Bachelor's degree or higher	12.2%
Graduate degree	2.9%

Income & Poverty, 1999

Per capita income	$13,977
Median household income	$41,250
Median family income	$42,188
Persons in poverty	68
H'holds receiving public assistance	11
H'holds receiving social security	46

Households, 2000

Total households	160
With persons under 18	63
With persons over 65	48
Family households	113
Single-person households	39
Persons per household	2.76
Persons per family	3.27

Labor & Employment

Total civilian labor force, 2007**	194
Unemployment rate	5.8%
Total civilian labor force, 2000	174
Unemployment rate	2.9%

Employed persons 16 years and over by occupation, 2000

Managers & professionals	34
Service occupations	26
Sales & office occupations	27
Farming, fishing & forestry	30
Construction & maintenance	9
Production & transportation	43
Self-employed persons	10

* US Census Bureau
** New Jersey Department of Labor

See Introduction for an explanation of all data sources.

General Information

Washington Township
1018 River Rd
Egg Harbor City, NJ 08215
609-965-3242

Website	NA
Year of incorporation	1802
Land/water area (sq. miles)	100.14/2.72
Form of government	Township

Government

Legislative Districts

US Congressional	2
State Legislative	9

Local Officials, 2009

Mayor	Daniel James
Manager/Admin	NA
Clerk	Paul Kain
Finance Dir	John Cicalese
Tax Assessor	Jay Renwick
Tax Collector	Victoria Boras
Attorney	Daniel Kehler
Building	NA
Comm Dev/Planning	NA
Engineering	Kris Kluk
Public Works	NA
Police Chief	NA
Fire Chief	W. Homiller

Housing & Construction

Housing Units, 2000*

Total	171
Median rent	$500
Median SF home value	$95,000

Permits for New Residential Construction

	Units	Value
Total, 2006	2	$97,446
Single family	2	$97,446
Total, 2007	3	$284,239
Single family	3	$284,239

Real Property Valuation, 2008

	Parcels	Valuation
Total	498	$124,895,800
Vacant	129	4,741,300
Residential	308	91,802,600
Commercial	16	15,103,400
Industrial	3	2,399,900
Apartments	0	0
Farm land	22	1,654,300
Farm homestead	20	9,194,300

Average Property Value & Tax, 2008

Residential value	$307,917
Property tax	$3,538
Tax credit/rebate	$744

Public Library

No public municipal library

Library statistics, 2007

Population served	NA
Full-time/total staff	NA/NA

	Total	Per capita
Holdings	NA	NA
Revenues	NA	NA
Expenditures	NA	NA
Annual visits	NA	NA
Internet terminals/annual users	NA/NA	

Public Safety

Number of officers, 2007 0

Crime	2006	2007
Total crimes	17	20
Violent	0	0
Murder	0	0
Rape	0	0
Robbery	0	0
Aggravated assault	0	0
Non-violent	17	20
Burglary	3	5
Larceny	12	12
Vehicle theft	2	3
Domestic violence	0	5
Arson	2	1
Total crime rate	26.4	30.7
Violent	0.0	0.0
Non-violent	26.4	30.7

Public School District

(for school year 2007-08 except as noted)

Washington Township School District
2436 Route 563
Egg Harbor, NJ 08215

Superintendent	NA
Number of schools	1
Grade plan	K-8
Enrollment	69
Attendance rate, '06-07	94.7%
Dropout rate	NA
Students per teacher	NA
Per pupil expenditure	$20,062
Median faculty salary	$49,421
Median administrator salary	NA
Grade 12 enrollment	NA
High school graduation rate	NA

Assessment test results

(percent scoring at proficient or advanced level)

	Language	Math
NJASK-Grade 3	NA	NA
GEPA-Grade 8	NA	NA
HSPA-High School	NA	NA

SAT Score Averages, 2006-07

Pct tested	Math	Verbal	Writing
NA	NA	NA	NA

Teacher Qualifications

Avg. years of experience	15
Highly-qualified teachers one subject/all subjects	100%/100%

No Child Left Behind

AYP, 2006-07 .... Meets Standards

Municipal Finance

State Aid Programs, 2009

Total aid	$1,267,597
CMPTRA	25,970
Energy tax receipts	86,045
Garden State Trust	1,097,135

General Budget, 2008

Total tax levy	$1,440,068
County levy	522,991
County taxes	429,484
County library	39,655
County health	0
County open space	53,853
School levy	917,077
Muni. levy	0
Misc. revenues	1,693,332

Taxes

	2006	2007	2008
General tax rate per $100	2.873	1.12	1.150
County equalization ratio	51.07	113.23	94.29
Net valuation taxable	$46,469,150	$124,783,709	$125,331,590
State equalized value	$109,966,440	$132,316,228	$124,772,077

Demographics & Socio-Economic Characteristics

(2000 US Census, except as noted)

Population

1980*	27,878
1990*	41,960
2000	47,114
Male	22,834
Female	24,280
2007 (estimate)*	51,995
Population density	2,433.1

Race & Hispanic Origin, 2000

Race
White	42,497
Black/African American	2,286
American Indian/Alaska Native	39
Asian	1,558
Native Hawaiian/Pacific Islander	6
Other race	252
Two or more races	476
Hispanic origin, total	955
Mexican	138
Puerto Rican	464
Cuban	53
Other Hispanic	300

Age & Nativity, 2000

Under 5 years	2,901
18 years and over	33,571
21 years and over	31,831
65 years and over	4,233
85 years and over	491
Median age	36.0
Native-born	44,834
Foreign-born	2,280

Educational Attainment, 2000

Population 25 years and over	29,876
Less than 9th grade	2.0%
High school grad or higher	89.9%
Bachelor's degree or higher	30.4%
Graduate degree	8.8%

Income & Poverty, 1999

Per capita income	$25,705
Median household income	$66,546
Median family income	$74,661
Persons in poverty	1,518
H'holds receiving public assistance	145
H'holds receiving social security	3,435

Households, 2000

Total households	15,609
With persons under 18	7,198
With persons over 65	3,016
Family households	12,659
Single-person households	2,405
Persons per household	3.00
Persons per family	3.38

Labor & Employment

Total civilian labor force, 2007**	28,627
Unemployment rate	1.6%
Total civilian labor force, 2000	25,153
Unemployment rate	3.6%

Employed persons 16 years and over by occupation, 2000
Managers & professionals	9,895
Service occupations	3,025
Sales & office occupations	7,523
Farming, fishing & forestry	9
Construction & maintenance	1,713
Production & transportation	2,075
Self-employed persons	1,050

General Information

Washington Township
523 Egg Harbor Rd
Sewell, NJ 08080
856-589-0520

Website	www.twp.washington.nj.us
Year of incorporation	1836
Land/water area (sq. miles)	21.37/0.12
Form of government	Mayor-Council

Government

Legislative Districts

US Congressional	1
State Legislative	4

Local Officials, 2009

Mayor	Matthew Lyons
Manager	Jack Lipsett
Clerk	Jennica N. Bileci
Finance Dir	Mary Breslin
Tax Assessor	Leo Midure
Tax Collector	Penny Carre Morris
Attorney	Timothy Chell
Building	John DiStefano
Planning	Tom Krwawecz
Engineering	Remington & Vernick
Public Works	Nicholas Pileggi
Police Chief	Rafael Muniz
Emerg/Fire Director	Frank Gurcsik

Housing & Construction

Housing Units, 2000*

Total	16,020
Median rent	$833
Median SF home value	$140,700

Permits for New Residential Construction

	Units	Value
Total, 2006	4	$1,509,925
Single family	4	$1,509,925
Total, 2007	18	$2,726,481
Single family	4	$1,605,481

Real Property Valuation, 2008

	Parcels	Valuation
Total	17,503	$2,569,536,500
Vacant	492	33,660,800
Residential	16,108	2,093,518,500
Commercial	776	392,870,100
Industrial	12	6,167,100
Apartments	9	38,105,200
Farm land	75	613,600
Farm homestead	31	4,601,200

Average Property Value & Tax, 2008

Residential value	$130,003
Property tax	$6,144
Tax credit/rebate	$1,006

Public Library

Margaret E. Heggan Public Library
208 E Holly Ave
Hurffville, NJ 08080
856-589-3334

Director ... Linda H. Snyder

Library statistics, 2007

Population served	47,114
Full-time/total staff	5/11

	Total	Per capita
Holdings	80,258	1.70
Revenues	$1,764,752	$37.46
Expenditures	$1,240,940	$26.34
Annual visits	159,569	3.39
Internet terminals/annual users	12/16,577	

Public Safety

Number of officers, 2007	85

Crime	2006	2007
Total crimes	1,104	1,184
Violent	81	79
Murder	1	0
Rape	10	3
Robbery	27	19
Aggravated assault	43	57
Non-violent	1,023	1,105
Burglary	221	227
Larceny	734	791
Vehicle theft	68	87
Domestic violence	410	420
Arson	12	15
Total crime rate	21.7	22.8
Violent	1.6	1.5
Non-violent	20.1	21.3

Public School District

(for school year 2007-08 except as noted)

Washington Township School District
206 East Holly Ave
Sewell, NJ 08080
(856) 589-6644

Superintendent	Cheryl Simone
Number of schools	11
Grade plan	K-12
Enrollment	8,932
Attendance rate, '06-07	95.6%
Dropout rate	1.6%
Students per teacher	10.5
Per pupil expenditure	$13,491
Median faculty salary	$51,813
Median administrator salary	$110,453
Grade 12 enrollment	759
High school graduation rate	96.0%

Assessment test results

(percent scoring at proficient or advanced level)
	Language	Math
NJASK-Grade 3	94.7%	92.0%
GEPA-Grade 8	76.8%	92.7%
HSPA-High School	83.9%	91.0%

SAT Score Averages, 2006-07

Pct tested	Math	Verbal	Writing
80%	501	496	485

Teacher Qualifications

Avg. years of experience	13
Highly-qualified teachers one subject/all subjects	100%/100%

No Child Left Behind

AYP, 2006-07	Meets Standards

Municipal Finance

State Aid Programs, 2009

Total aid	$4,127,615
CMPTRA	1,080,578
Energy tax receipts	2,943,846
Garden State Trust	0

General Budget, 2008

Total tax levy	$121,618,310
County levy	28,262,563
County taxes	26,208,692
County library	0
County health	0
County open space	2,053,872
School levy	69,003,900
Muni. levy	24,351,848
Misc. revenues	12,451,395

Taxes	2006	2007	2008
General tax rate per $100	4.186	4.382	4.726
County equalization ratio	59.57	53.11	50.18
Net valuation taxable	$2,539,298,200	$2,567,559,483	$2,573,553,965
State equalized value	$4,785,694,009	$5,112,611,006	$5,308,593,229

Demographics & Socio-Economic Characteristics

(2000 US Census, except as noted)

Population

1980*	11,402
1990*	15,592
2000	17,592
Male	8,593
Female	8,999
2007 (estimate)*	18,469
Population density	411.7

Race & Hispanic Origin, 2000

Race

White	16,917
Black/African American	146
American Indian/Alaska Native	15
Asian	329
Native Hawaiian/Pacific Islander	9
Other race	62
Two or more races	114
Hispanic origin, total	389
Mexican	47
Puerto Rican	127
Cuban	62
Other Hispanic	153

Age & Nativity, 2000

Under 5 years	1,213
18 years and over	12,281
21 years and over	11,797
65 years and over	1,449
85 years and over	337
Median age	38.3
Native-born	16,537
Foreign-born	1,055

Educational Attainment, 2000

Population 25 years and over	11,313
Less than 9th grade	1.8%
High school grad or higher	96.3%
Bachelor's degree or higher	53.2%
Graduate degree	20.0%

Income & Poverty, 1999

Per capita income	$37,489
Median household income	$97,763
Median family income	$104,926
Persons in poverty	397
H'holds receiving public assistance	30
H'holds receiving social security	999

Households, 2000

Total households	5,755
With persons under 18	2,780
With persons over 65	960
Family households	4,874
Single-person households	701
Persons per household	3.02
Persons per family	3.31

Labor & Employment

Total civilian labor force, 2007**	9,858
Unemployment rate	2.9%
Total civilian labor force, 2000	9,048
Unemployment rate	2.7%

Employed persons 16 years and over by occupation, 2000

Managers & professionals	4,827
Service occupations	849
Sales & office occupations	2,178
Farming, fishing & forestry	18
Construction & maintenance	523
Production & transportation	406
Self-employed persons	634

* US Census Bureau
** New Jersey Department of Labor

General Information

Washington Township
43 Schooleys Mountain Rd
Long Valley, NJ 07853
908-876-3315

Website	www.wtmorris.org
Year of incorporation	1798
Land/water area (sq. miles)	44.86/0.00
Form of government	Township

Government

Legislative Districts

US Congressional	11
State Legislative	24

Local Officials, 2009

Mayor	Kenneth W. Short
Administrator	Dianne S. Gallets
Clerk	Dianne S. Gallets
Finance Dir	Kevin Lifer
Tax Assessor	Dolores Pecorari
Tax Collector	Amy Monahan
Attorney	John Jansen
Building	Neil Ruggiero
Comm Dev/Planning	NA
Engineering	Leon C. Hall
Public Works	Scott Frech
Police Chief	Michael Bailey
Fire/Emergency Dir	Mike Cuccaro

Housing & Construction

Housing Units, 2000*

Total	5,890
Median rent	$1,052
Median SF home value	$279,300

Permits for New Residential Construction

	Units	Value
Total, 2006	25	$7,489,504
Single family	25	$7,489,504
Total, 2007	15	$3,801,090
Single family	15	$3,801,090

Real Property Valuation, 2008

	Parcels	Valuation
Total	6,971	$3,216,849,200
Vacant	464	61,154,900
Residential	5,630	2,824,089,600
Commercial	174	113,518,400
Industrial	20	38,803,500
Apartments	5	43,258,300
Farm land	450	4,264,200
Farm homestead	228	131,760,300

Average Property Value & Tax, 2008

Residential value	$504,583
Property tax	$9,870
Tax credit/rebate	$1,201

Public Library

Washington Township Public Library
37 E Springtown Rd
Long Valley, NJ 07853
908-876-3596

Director	Virginia Scarlatelli

Library statistics, 2007

Population served	17,592
Full-time/total staff	4/7

	Total	Per capita
Holdings	87,693	4.98
Revenues	$1,118,278	$63.57
Expenditures	$1,015,051	$57.70
Annual visits	65,798	3.74
Internet terminals/annual users	20/29,330	

Public Safety

Number of officers, 2007	33

Crime	2006	2007
Total crimes	138	132
Violent	8	10
Murder	0	0
Rape	0	1
Robbery	0	1
Aggravated assault	8	8
Non-violent	130	122
Burglary	18	17
Larceny	102	104
Vehicle theft	10	1
Domestic violence	83	76
Arson	0	0
Total crime rate	7.4	7.1
Violent	0.4	0.5
Non-violent	7.0	6.5

Public School District

(for school year 2007-08 except as noted)

Washington Township School District
53 West Mill Road
Long Valley, NJ 07853
(908) 876-4172

Superintendent	John Sakala (Int)
Number of schools	4
Grade plan	K-8
Enrollment	2,863
Attendance rate, '06-07	96.1%
Dropout rate	NA
Students per teacher	11.8
Per pupil expenditure	$13,543
Median faculty salary	$56,225
Median administrator salary	$118,551
Grade 12 enrollment	NA
High school graduation rate	NA

Assessment test results

(percent scoring at proficient or advanced level)

	Language	Math
NJASK-Grade 3	95.9%	95.7%
GEPA-Grade 8	84.0%	95.0%
HSPA-High School	NA	NA

SAT Score Averages, 2006-07

Pct tested	Math	Verbal	Writing
NA	NA	NA	NA

Teacher Qualifications

Avg. years of experience	9
Highly-qualified teachers one subject/all subjects	100%/100%

No Child Left Behind

AYP, 2006-07	Meets Standards

Municipal Finance

State Aid Programs, 2009

Total aid	$1,836,961
CMPTRA	348,341
Energy tax receipts	1,424,581
Garden State Trust	22,063

General Budget, 2008

Total tax levy	$63,014,877
County levy	7,848,283
County taxes	6,404,515
County library	0
County health	0
County open space	1,443,768
School levy	44,758,595
Muni. levy	10,407,999
Misc. revenues	6,235,295

Taxes	2006	2007	2008
General tax rate per $100	3.39	3.5	1.957
County equalization ratio	58.33	52.84	95.68
Net valuation taxable	$1,690,287,800	$1,721,404,116	$3,221,552,577
State equalized value	$3,201,622,943	$3,327,277,751	$3,347,231,640

See Introduction for an explanation of all data sources.

Demographics & Socio-Economic Characteristics

(2000 US Census, except as noted)

Population

1980*	4,243
1990*	5,367
2000	6,248
Male	3,053
Female	3,195
2007 (estimate)*	6,855
Population density	389.9

Race & Hispanic Origin, 2000

Race

White	5,997
Black/African American	107
American Indian/Alaska Native	4
Asian	59
Native Hawaiian/Pacific Islander	0
Other race	31
Two or more races	50
Hispanic origin, total	135
Mexican	7
Puerto Rican	44
Cuban	21
Other Hispanic	63

Age & Nativity, 2000

Under 5 years	435
18 years and over	4,373
21 years and over	4,177
65 years and over	609
85 years and over	57
Median age	37.6
Native-born	5,994
Foreign-born	254

Educational Attainment, 2000

Population 25 years and over	4,049
Less than 9th grade	2.7%
High school grad or higher	90.8%
Bachelor's degree or higher	32.0%
Graduate degree	8.8%

Income & Poverty, 1999

Per capita income	$29,141
Median household income	$77,458
Median family income	$84,348
Persons in poverty	189
H'holds receiving public assistance	36
H'holds receiving social security	497

Households, 2000

Total households	2,099
With persons under 18	955
With persons over 65	442
Family households	1,740
Single-person households	297
Persons per household	2.95
Persons per family	3.26

Labor & Employment

Total civilian labor force, 2007**	3,694
Unemployment rate	4.8%
Total civilian labor force, 2000	3,271
Unemployment rate	4.5%

Employed persons 16 years and over by occupation, 2000

Managers & professionals	1,168
Service occupations	396
Sales & office occupations	949
Farming, fishing & forestry	15
Construction & maintenance	375
Production & transportation	220
Self-employed persons	142

* US Census Bureau
** New Jersey Department of Labor

General Information

Washington Township
350 Route 57 W
Washington, NJ 07882
908-689-7200

Website	www.washington-twp-warren.org
Year of incorporation	1849
Land/water area (sq. miles)	17.58/0.02
Form of government	Township

Government

Legislative Districts

US Congressional	5
State Legislative	23

Local Officials, 2009

Mayor	Samir Elbassiouny
Manager/Admin	NA
Clerk	Mary Ann O'Neil
Certified Finance Officer	Barbara Emery
Tax Assessor	Lydia Schmidt
Tax Collector	Evan Howell
Attorney	Michael B. Lavery
Building	Christopher Rose
Comm Dev/Planning	NA
Engineering	Michael Finelli
Public Works	Peter Henry de Boer Jr.
Police Chief	James McDonald
Emerg Dir	Thomas Cicerelle

Housing & Construction

Housing Units, 2000*

Total	2,174
Median rent	$822
Median SF home value	$185,400

Permits for New Residential Construction

	Units	Value
Total, 2006	6	$1,142,950
Single family	6	$1,142,950
Total, 2007	12	$1,192,411
Single family	12	$1,192,411

Real Property Valuation, 2008

	Parcels	Valuation
Total	2,941	$666,494,524
Vacant	264	12,393,800
Residential	2,276	555,261,299
Commercial	91	67,642,300
Industrial	6	3,501,200
Apartments	3	1,880,300
Farm land	200	2,416,625
Farm homestead	101	23,399,000

Average Property Value & Tax, 2008

Residential value	$243,441
Property tax	$7,091
Tax credit/rebate	$1,155

Public Library

No public municipal library

Library statistics, 2007

Population served	NA
Full-time/total staff	NA/NA

	Total	Per capita
Holdings	NA	NA
Revenues	NA	NA
Expenditures	NA	NA
Annual visits	NA	NA
Internet terminals/annual users	NA/NA	

Public Safety

Number of officers, 2007	13

Crime	2006	2007
Total crimes	66	59
Violent	4	1
Murder	0	0
Rape	0	0
Robbery	0	0
Aggravated assault	4	1
Non-violent	62	58
Burglary	10	3
Larceny	52	53
Vehicle theft	0	2
Domestic violence	73	91
Arson	0	0
Total crime rate	9.5	8.5
Violent	0.6	0.1
Non-violent	8.9	8.3

Public School District

(for school year 2007-08 except as noted)

Washington Township School District
16 Castle Street
Washington, NJ 07882
(908) 689-1119

Superintendent	Roger Jinks
Number of schools	2
Grade plan	K-6
Enrollment	647
Attendance rate, '06-07	95.7%
Dropout rate	NA
Students per teacher	10.9
Per pupil expenditure	$12,018
Median faculty salary	$62,548
Median administrator salary	$97,811
Grade 12 enrollment	NA
High school graduation rate	NA

Assessment test results

(percent scoring at proficient or advanced level)

	Language	Math
NJASK-Grade 3	93.7%	90.6%
GEPA-Grade 8	NA	NA
HSPA-High School	NA	NA

SAT Score Averages, 2006-07

Pct tested	Math	Verbal	Writing
NA	NA	NA	NA

Teacher Qualifications

Avg. years of experience	15
Highly-qualified teachers one subject/all subjects	100%/100%

No Child Left Behind

AYP, 2006-07	Meets Standards

Municipal Finance

State Aid Programs, 2009

Total aid	$699,003
CMPTRA	92,822
Energy tax receipts	586,339
Garden State Trust	2,232

General Budget, 2008

Total tax levy	$19,455,433
County levy	5,570,518
County taxes	4,543,622
County library	476,904
County health	0
County open space	549,992
School levy	10,861,642
Muni. levy	3,023,273
Misc. revenues	2,764,860

Taxes

	2006	2007	2008
General tax rate per $100	2.78	2.93	2.913
County equalization ratio	83.89	76.25	73.05
Net valuation taxable	$646,633,449	$660,917,555	$667,946,347
State equalized value	$849,627,389	$904,153,138	$920,501,084

Demographics & Socio-Economic Characteristics

(2000 US Census, except as noted)

Population
1980*	5,290
1990*	5,110
2000	5,613
Male	2,741
Female	2,872
2007 (estimate)*	6,508
Population density	1,081.1

Race & Hispanic Origin, 2000
Race
White	4,732
Black/African American	189
American Indian/Alaska Native	5
Asian	553
Native Hawaiian/Pacific Islander	5
Other race	40
Two or more races	89
Hispanic origin, total	168
Mexican	10
Puerto Rican	31
Cuban	27
Other Hispanic	100

Age & Nativity, 2000
Under 5 years	334
18 years and over	4,386
21 years and over	4,276
65 years and over	914
85 years and over	87
Median age	43.0
Native-born	4,754
Foreign-born	859

Educational Attainment, 2000
Population 25 years and over	4,144
Less than 9th grade	2.1%
High school grad or higher	93.9%
Bachelor's degree or higher	57.0%
Graduate degree	31.5%

Income & Poverty, 1999
Per capita income	$58,653
Median household income	$101,944
Median family income	$120,764
Persons in poverty	121
H'holds receiving public assistance	0
H'holds receiving social security	645

Households, 2000
Total households	2,098
With persons under 18	676
With persons over 65	558
Family households	1,618
Single-person households	399
Persons per household	2.62
Persons per family	3.00

Labor & Employment
Total civilian labor force, 2007**	3,020
Unemployment rate	2.7%
Total civilian labor force, 2000	2,699
Unemployment rate	3.7%

Employed persons 16 years and over by occupation, 2000
Managers & professionals	1,528
Service occupations	192
Sales & office occupations	570
Farming, fishing & forestry	0
Construction & maintenance	152
Production & transportation	157
Self-employed persons	288

‡ Branch of county library
* US Census Bureau
** New Jersey Department of Labor

See Introduction for an explanation of all data sources.

General Information
Borough of Watchung
15 Mountain Blvd
Watchung, NJ 07069
908-756-0080
Website	watchungnj.com
Year of incorporation	1926
Land/water area (sq. miles)	6.02/0.02
Form of government	Borough

Government
Legislative Districts
US Congressional	7
State Legislative	21

Local Officials, 2009
Mayor	Albert Ellis
Manager	Laureen Fellin
Clerk	Laureen Fellin
Finance Dir	William Hance
Tax Assessor	Edward Kerwin
Tax Collector	Catherine Park
Attorney	Albert E. Cruz
Building	Edward Bennett
Planning	Heyer & Gruel
Engineering	Maser Consulting
Public Works	C. Gunther
Police Chief	Sean Whalen
Emerg/Fire Director	Robert "Skip" Bell

Housing & Construction
Housing Units, 2000*
Total	2,155
Median rent	$854
Median SF home value	$429,400

Permits for New Residential Construction
	Units	Value
Total, 2006	22	$4,650,055
Single family	14	$4,050,055
Total, 2007	9	$3,833,391
Single family	9	$3,833,391

Real Property Valuation, 2008
	Parcels	Valuation
Total	2,211	$1,816,538,500
Vacant	199	41,366,100
Residential	1,918	1,373,917,500
Commercial	86	333,359,400
Industrial	7	7,295,500
Apartments	1	60,600,000
Farm land	0	0
Farm homestead	0	0

Average Property Value & Tax, 2008
Residential value	$716,328
Property tax	$12,029
Tax credit/rebate	$1,318

Public Library
Watchung Branch Library‡
12 Stirling Rd
Watchung, NJ 07060
908-561-0117
Branch Librarian	Douglas Poswencyk

Library statistics, 2007
see Somerset County profile
for library system statistics

Public Safety
Number of officers, 2007	29

Crime	2006	2007
Total crimes	317	293
Violent	6	5
Murder	0	0
Rape	0	1
Robbery	6	2
Aggravated assault	0	2
Non-violent	311	288
Burglary	13	15
Larceny	284	266
Vehicle theft	14	7
Domestic violence	37	51
Arson	0	1
Total crime rate	51.4	46.6
Violent	1.0	0.8
Non-violent	50.4	45.8

Public School District
(for school year 2007-08 except as noted)

Watchung Borough School District
ONE PARENTY WAY
Watchung, NJ 07069
(908) 755-8121
Superintendent	Mary Louise Malyska
Number of schools	2
Grade plan	K-8
Enrollment	686
Attendance rate, '06-07	95.7%
Dropout rate	NA
Students per teacher	10.5
Per pupil expenditure	$14,540
Median faculty salary	$52,010
Median administrator salary	$117,527
Grade 12 enrollment	NA
High school graduation rate	NA

Assessment test results
(percent scoring at proficient or advanced level)
	Language	Math
NJASK-Grade 3	96.6%	95.5%
GEPA-Grade 8	91.1%	96.4%
HSPA-High School	NA	NA

SAT Score Averages, 2006-07
Pct tested	Math	Verbal	Writing
NA	NA	NA	NA

Teacher Qualifications
Avg. years of experience	6
Highly-qualified teachers one subject/all subjects	100%/100%

No Child Left Behind
AYP, 2006-07	Meets Standards

Municipal Finance
State Aid Programs, 2009
Total aid	$952,663
CMPTRA	93,350
Energy tax receipts	821,206
Garden State Trust	0

General Budget, 2008
Total tax levy	$30,531,496
County levy	6,626,394
County taxes	5,318,102
County library	719,685
County health	0
County open space	588,607
School levy	16,237,197
Muni. levy	7,667,904
Misc. revenues	5,542,954

Taxes
Taxes	2006	2007	2008
General tax rate per $100	1.63	1.61	1.680
County equalization ratio	95.24	90.84	93.29
Net valuation taxable	$1,769,386,700	$1,846,325,175	$1,818,101,284
State equalized value	$2,020,094,241	$1,936,090,680	$1,887,895,598

Demographics & Socio-Economic Characteristics

(2000 US Census, except as noted)

Population
1980*	8,126
1990*	10,940
2000	10,494
Male	5,255
Female	5,239
2007 (estimate)*	10,636
Population density	293.9

Race & Hispanic Origin, 2000
Race
White	9,733
Black/African American	439
American Indian/Alaska Native	22
Asian	94
Native Hawaiian/Pacific Islander	1
Other race	70
Two or more races	135
Hispanic origin, total	217
Mexican	24
Puerto Rican	127
Cuban	6
Other Hispanic	60

Age & Nativity, 2000
Under 5 years	635
18 years and over	7,793
21 years and over	7,407
65 years and over	854
85 years and over	72
Median age	36.1
Native-born	10,161
Foreign-born	324

Educational Attainment, 2000
Population 25 years and over	6,979
Less than 9th grade	4.3%
High school grad or higher	82.9%
Bachelor's degree or higher	12.8%
Graduate degree	3.5%

Income & Poverty, 1999
Per capita income	$21,676
Median household income	$59,075
Median family income	$63,693
Persons in poverty	590
H'holds receiving public assistance	44
H'holds receiving social security	779

Households, 2000
Total households	3,542
With persons under 18	1,491
With persons over 65	610
Family households	2,790
Single-person households	591
Persons per household	2.90
Persons per family	3.27

Labor & Employment
Total civilian labor force, 2007**	6,200
Unemployment rate	4.7%
Total civilian labor force, 2000	6,043
Unemployment rate	7.5%

Employed persons 16 years and over by occupation, 2000
Managers & professionals	1,585
Service occupations	822
Sales & office occupations	1,560
Farming, fishing & forestry	6
Construction & maintenance	894
Production & transportation	725
Self-employed persons	337

General Information
Township of Waterford
2131 Auburn Ave
Atco, NJ 08004
856-768-2300

Website	www.waterfordtwp.org
Year of incorporation	1695
Land/water area (sq. miles)	36.19/0.07
Form of government	Township

Government
Legislative Districts
US Congressional	2
State Legislative	6

Local Officials, 2009
Mayor	NA
Township Coord	Lawrence C. Ruocco
Clerk	Virginia Chandler
Finance Dir	Stephen A. Miller
Tax Assessor	Marie-Louise Procacci
Tax Collector	Anita Wilson
Attorney	John P. Maroccia
Construction	John Holroyd
Planning	Wendy M. Parducci (Chr)
Engineering	Christopher J. Noll
Public Works	Victor E. Pangia
Police Chief	John Knoll
Emerg/Fire Director	David Cilona

Housing & Construction
Housing Units, 2000*
Total	3,671
Median rent	$725
Median SF home value	$116,500

Permits for New Residential Construction
	Units	Value
Total, 2006	18	$2,982,244
Single family	18	$2,982,244
Total, 2007	24	$3,687,948
Single family	24	$3,687,948

Real Property Valuation, 2008
	Parcels	Valuation
Total	4,469	$470,813,600
Vacant	509	11,286,600
Residential	3,540	405,205,800
Commercial	122	37,079,900
Industrial	5	1,225,400
Apartments	5	2,394,900
Farm land	205	1,528,400
Farm homestead	83	12,092,600

Average Property Value & Tax, 2008
Residential value	$115,180
Property tax	$5,495
Tax credit/rebate	$977

Public Library
Waterford Township Public Library
2204 Atco Ave
Atco, NJ 08004
856-767-7727

Director	Eva K. Lynch

Library statistics, 2007
Population served	10,494
Full-time/total staff	1/2

	Total	Per capita
Holdings	32,791	3.12
Revenues	$358,298	$34.14
Expenditures	$330,315	$31.48
Annual visits	12,000	1.14
Internet terminals/annual users	4/9,500	

Public Safety
Number of officers, 2007	24

Crime	2006	2007
Total crimes	189	210
Violent	15	13
Murder	0	0
Rape	1	0
Robbery	5	3
Aggravated assault	9	10
Non-violent	174	197
Burglary	29	49
Larceny	134	134
Vehicle theft	11	14
Domestic violence	62	60
Arson	4	6
Total crime rate	17.6	19.6
Violent	1.4	1.2
Non-violent	16.2	18.4

Public School District
(for school year 2007-08 except as noted)

Waterford Township School District
1106 Old White Horse Pike
Waterford, NJ 08089
(856) 767-0331

Superintendent	Gary L. Dentino
Number of schools	3
Grade plan	K-6
Enrollment	913
Attendance rate, '06-07	94.6%
Dropout rate	NA
Students per teacher	10.3
Per pupil expenditure	$13,223
Median faculty salary	$69,563
Median administrator salary	$102,712
Grade 12 enrollment	NA
High school graduation rate	NA

Assessment test results
(percent scoring at proficient or advanced level)
	Language	Math
NJASK-Grade 3	75.9%	75.2%
GEPA-Grade 8	NA	NA
HSPA-High School	NA	NA

SAT Score Averages, 2006-07
Pct tested	Math	Verbal	Writing
NA	NA	NA	NA

Teacher Qualifications
Avg. years of experience	19
Highly-qualified teachers one subject/all subjects	100%/100%

No Child Left Behind
AYP, 2006-07	Meets Standards

Municipal Finance
State Aid Programs, 2009
Total aid	$1,732,261
CMPTRA	272,524
Energy tax receipts	1,131,550
Garden State Trust	281,602

General Budget, 2008
Total tax levy	$22,506,948
County levy	5,256,375
County taxes	5,079,439
County library	0
County health	0
County open space	176,936
School levy	11,564,300
Muni. levy	5,686,273
Misc. revenues	4,053,419

Taxes	2006	2007	2008
General tax rate per $100	4.484	4.76	4.771
County equalization ratio	66.81	58.11	53.34
Net valuation taxable	$458,920,200	$467,672,601	$471,791,645
State equalized value	$790,891,193	$875,882,169	$930,337,698

See Introduction for an explanation of all data sources.

Demographics & Socio-Economic Characteristics
(2000 US Census, except as noted)

Population
1980*	46,474
1990*	47,025
2000	54,069
Male	25,699
Female	28,370
2007 (estimate)*	54,180
Population density	2,274.6

Race & Hispanic Origin, 2000
Race
White	48,687
Black/African American	895
American Indian/Alaska Native	54
Asian	3,066
Native Hawaiian/Pacific Islander	11
Other race	631
Two or more races	725
Hispanic origin, total	2,754
Mexican	164
Puerto Rican	726
Cuban	320
Other Hispanic	1,544

Age & Nativity, 2000
Under 5 years	3,313
18 years and over	41,543
21 years and over	39,201
65 years and over	8,765
85 years and over	1,236
Median age	40.0
Native-born	45,291
Foreign-born	8,824

Educational Attainment, 2000
Population 25 years and over	37,298
Less than 9th grade	4.4%
High school grad or higher	89.2%
Bachelor's degree or higher	41.5%
Graduate degree	15.4%

Income & Poverty, 1999
Per capita income	$35,349
Median household income	$83,651
Median family income	$95,114
Persons in poverty	1,443
H'holds receiving public assistance	155
H'holds receiving social security	5,528

Households, 2000
Total households	18,755
With persons under 18	6,801
With persons over 65	5,650
Family households	14,370
Single-person households	3,797
Persons per household	2.74
Persons per family	3.19

Labor & Employment
Total civilian labor force, 2007**	29,016
Unemployment rate	3.1%
Total civilian labor force, 2000	28,103
Unemployment rate	3.9%

Employed persons 16 years and over by occupation, 2000
Managers & professionals	12,791
Service occupations	2,614
Sales & office occupations	7,897
Farming, fishing & forestry	21
Construction & maintenance	1,627
Production & transportation	2,070
Self-employed persons	1,629

* US Census Bureau
** New Jersey Department of Labor

General Information
Township of Wayne
475 Valley Rd
Wayne, NJ 07470
973-694-1800
Website	www.waynetownship.com
Year of incorporation	1847
Land/water area (sq. miles)	23.82/1.37
Form of government	Mayor-Council

Government
Legislative Districts
US Congressional	8
State Legislative	40

Local Officials, 2009
Mayor	Christopher Vergano
Manager	Neal Bellet
Clerk	(vacant)
Finance Dir	Robert Miller
Tax Assessor	Dorothy Kreitz
Tax Collector	Zenab Bachok
Attorney	Mark Semeraro
Building	Joseph Albanese
Planning	John Szabo
Engineering	Fernando Zapata
Public Works	George Holzapfel
Police Chief	Donald Stouthamer
Emerg/Fire Director	Richard Boonstra

Housing & Construction
Housing Units, 2000*
Total	19,218
Median rent	$943
Median SF home value	$284,800

Permits for New Residential Construction
	Units	Value
Total, 2006	26	$5,722,745
Single family	26	$5,722,745
Total, 2007	17	$5,257,200
Single family	17	$5,257,200

Real Property Valuation, 2008
	Parcels	Valuation
Total	17,848	$5,334,551,500
Vacant	468	68,260,300
Residential	16,705	3,838,488,400
Commercial	566	1,127,402,400
Industrial	85	206,519,700
Apartments	9	92,400,400
Farm land	9	75,100
Farm homestead	6	1,405,200

Average Property Value & Tax, 2008
Residential value	$229,782
Property tax	$9,593
Tax credit/rebate	$1,300

Public Library
Wayne Public Library
461 Valley Rd
Wayne, NJ 07470
973-694-4272
Director	Jody C. Treadway

Library statistics, 2007
Population served	54,069
Full-time/total staff	15/35

	Total	Per capita
Holdings	238,120	4.40
Revenues	$3,785,452	$70.01
Expenditures	$3,785,452	$70.01
Annual visits	294,451	5.45
Internet terminals/annual users	59/87,005	

Public Safety
Number of officers, 2007	119

Crime	2006	2007
Total crimes	1,296	1,457
Violent	40	40
Murder	0	0
Rape	2	0
Robbery	21	18
Aggravated assault	17	22
Non-violent	1,256	1,417
Burglary	174	185
Larceny	1,004	1,179
Vehicle theft	78	53
Domestic violence	296	249
Arson	3	1
Total crime rate	23.5	26.6
Violent	0.7	0.7
Non-violent	22.8	25.8

Public School District
(for school year 2007-08 except as noted)

Wayne Township School District
50 Nellis Drive
Wayne, NJ 07470
(973) 633-3032
Chief School Admin	John Sico
Number of schools	14
Grade plan	K-12
Enrollment	8,778
Attendance rate, '06-07	95.5%
Dropout rate	0.7%
Students per teacher	11.1
Per pupil expenditure	$13,723
Median faculty salary	$60,623
Median administrator salary	$117,030
Grade 12 enrollment	705
High school graduation rate	97.4%

Assessment test results
(percent scoring at proficient or advanced level)
	Language	Math
NJASK-Grade 3	93.1%	93.2%
GEPA-Grade 8	81.2%	91.0%
HSPA-High School	90.2%	92.0%

SAT Score Averages, 2006-07
Pct tested	Math	Verbal	Writing
NA	NA	NA	NA

Teacher Qualifications
Avg. years of experience	9
Highly-qualified teachers one subject/all subjects	99.5%/99.5%

No Child Left Behind
AYP, 2006-07	Meets Standards

Municipal Finance
State Aid Programs, 2009
Total aid	$5,626,410
CMPTRA	848,319
Energy tax receipts	4,582,823
Garden State Trust	27,961

General Budget, 2008
Total tax levy	$223,038,511
County levy	56,366,233
County taxes	55,240,307
County library	0
County health	0
County open space	1,125,926
School levy	116,107,823
Muni. levy	50,564,455
Misc. revenues	22,994,517

Taxes
Taxes	2006	2007	2008
General tax rate per $100	3.77	3.98	4.175
County equalization ratio	55.06	48.89	47.60
Net valuation taxable	$5,354,726,500	$5,343,989,098	$5,342,427,118
State equalized value	$10,961,230,873	$11,218,260,495	$11,627,460,676

See Introduction for an explanation of all data sources.

Demographics & Socio-Economic Characteristics

(2000 US Census, except as noted)

Population

1980*	13,168
1990*	12,385
2000	13,501
Male	6,582
Female	6,919
2007 (estimate)*	12,441
Population density	14,636.5

Race & Hispanic Origin, 2000

Race
White	9,862
Black/African American	483
American Indian/Alaska Native	27
Asian	630
Native Hawaiian/Pacific Islander	14
Other race	1,882
Two or more races	603
Hispanic origin, total	5,487
Mexican	177
Puerto Rican	822
Cuban	1,182
Other Hispanic	3,306

Age & Nativity, 2000

Under 5 years	643
18 years and over	11,265
21 years and over	10,900
65 years and over	1,650
85 years and over	192
Median age	35.0
Native-born	8,272
Foreign-born	5,229

Educational Attainment, 2000

Population 25 years and over	10,010
Less than 9th grade	12.7%
High school grad or higher	76.0%
Bachelor's degree or higher	37.5%
Graduate degree	13.0%

Income & Poverty, 1999

Per capita income	$29,269
Median household income	$50,196
Median family income	$52,613
Persons in poverty	1,535
H'holds receiving public assistance	161
H'holds receiving social security	1,336

Households, 2000

Total households	5,975
With persons under 18	1,323
With persons over 65	1,250
Family households	3,061
Single-person households	2,126
Persons per household	2.26
Persons per family	3.02

Labor & Employment

Total civilian labor force, 2007**	7,614
Unemployment rate	3.6%
Total civilian labor force, 2000	7,854
Unemployment rate	5.8%

Employed persons 16 years and over by occupation, 2000
Managers & professionals	3,121
Service occupations	983
Sales & office occupations	2,152
Farming, fishing & forestry	5
Construction & maintenance	319
Production & transportation	818
Self-employed persons	458

* US Census Bureau
** New Jersey Department of Labor
§ State Fiscal Year July 1–June 30

General Information

Township of Weehawken
400 Park Ave
Weehawken, NJ 07086
201-319-6022

Website	www.weehawken-nj.us
Year of incorporation	1859
Land/water area (sq. miles)	0.85/0.66
Form of government	Council-Manager

Government

Legislative Districts

US Congressional	13
State Legislative	33

Local Officials, 2009

Mayor	Richard F. Turner
Manager	James V. Marchetti
Clerk	Rola Dahboul
Finance Dir	Lisa Toscano
Tax Assessor	Paul Sadlon
Tax Collector	Joseph Fredericks
Attorney	Richard P. Venino
Building	Frank Tattoli
Comm Dev/Planning	NA
Engineering	Mayo, Lynch
Public Works	Robert Barsa
Police Chief	Thomas McGorty
Emerg/Fire Director	Jeffrey Welz

Housing & Construction

Housing Units, 2000*

Total	6,159
Median rent	$781
Median SF home value	$231,200

Permits for New Residential Construction

	Units	Value
Total, 2006	30	$5,429,100
Single family	5	$2,182,800
Total, 2007	68	$10,802,936
Single family	9	$3,516,936

Real Property Valuation, 2008

	Parcels	Valuation
Total	3,120	$1,145,241,240
Vacant	260	160,959,350
Residential	2,656	643,054,740
Commercial	63	234,201,700
Industrial	23	49,504,000
Apartments	118	57,521,450
Farm land	0	0
Farm homestead	0	0

Average Property Value & Tax, 2008

Residential value	$242,114
Property tax	$8,158
Tax credit/rebate	$926

Public Library

Weehawken Public Library
49 Hauxhurst Ave
Weehawken, NJ 07086
201-863-7823

Director	Phillip R. Greco

Library statistics, 2007

Population served	13,501
Full-time/total staff	1/12

	Total	Per capita
Holdings	46,465	3.44
Revenues	$753,862	$55.84
Expenditures	$762,608	$56.49
Annual visits	50,500	3.74
Internet terminals/annual users	18/11,750	

Public Safety

Number of officers, 2007 58

Crime	2006	2007
Total crimes	374	342
Violent	43	30
Murder	1	0
Rape	1	0
Robbery	18	20
Aggravated assault	23	10
Non-violent	331	312
Burglary	76	51
Larceny	220	213
Vehicle theft	35	48
Domestic violence	48	34
Arson	0	0
Total crime rate	28.9	27.0
Violent	3.3	2.4
Non-violent	25.6	24.7

Public School District

(for school year 2007-08 except as noted)

Weehawken Township School District
53 Liberty Place
Weehawken, NJ 07086
(201) 422-6126

Superintendent	Kevin McLellan
Number of schools	3
Grade plan	K-12
Enrollment	1,164
Attendance rate, '06-07	95.1%
Dropout rate	0.0%
Students per teacher	10.0
Per pupil expenditure	$15,498
Median faculty salary	$55,205
Median administrator salary	$123,263
Grade 12 enrollment	91
High school graduation rate	97.8%

Assessment test results

(percent scoring at proficient or advanced level)
	Language	Math
NJASK-Grade 3	88.0%	82.7%
GEPA-Grade 8	75.9%	92.4%
HSPA-High School	73.9%	85.5%

SAT Score Averages, 2006-07

Pct tested	Math	Verbal	Writing
89%	459	463	457

Teacher Qualifications

Avg. years of experience	13
Highly-qualified teachers one subject/all subjects	100%/100%

No Child Left Behind

AYP, 2006-07 . . . . .Meets Standards

Municipal Finance§

State Aid Programs, 2009

Total aid	$2,930,037
CMPTRA	1,929,926
Energy tax receipts	926,172
Garden State Trust	0

General Budget, 2008

Total tax levy	$40,165,827
County levy	9,007,459
County taxes	8,770,043
County library	0
County health	0
County open space	237,417
School levy	15,399,368
Muni. levy	15,759,000
Misc. revenues	18,428,832

Taxes

	2006	2007	2008
General tax rate per $100	3.286	3.497	3.504
County equalization ratio	53.8	48.86	48.87
Net valuation taxable	$1,037,375,723	$1,092,067,867	$1,146,458,936
State equalized value	$2,124,464,493	$2,233,404,282	$2,322,809,506

Demographics & Socio-Economic Characteristics
(2000 US Census, except as noted)

Population
1980*	2,303
1990*	2,331
2000	2,317
Male	1,128
Female	1,189
2007 (estimate)*	2,341
Population density	2,413.4

Race & Hispanic Origin, 2000
Race
White	2,260
Black/African American	25
American Indian/Alaska Native	2
Asian	15
Native Hawaiian/Pacific Islander	0
Other race	0
Two or more races	15
Hispanic origin, total	17
Mexican	8
Puerto Rican	4
Cuban	1
Other Hispanic	4

Age & Nativity, 2000
Under 5 years	148
18 years and over	1,716
21 years and over	1,657
65 years and over	320
85 years and over	33
Median age	41.2
Native-born	2,281
Foreign-born	36

Educational Attainment, 2000
Population 25 years and over	1,584
Less than 9th grade	0.3%
High school grad or higher	97.2%
Bachelor's degree or higher	42.2%
Graduate degree	15.8%

Income & Poverty, 1999
Per capita income	$34,116
Median household income	$71,625
Median family income	$82,505
Persons in poverty	57
H'holds receiving public assistance	2
H'holds receiving social security	233

Households, 2000
Total households	844
With persons under 18	316
With persons over 65	211
Family households	652
Single-person households	166
Persons per household	2.70
Persons per family	3.13

Labor & Employment
Total civilian labor force, 2007**	1,410
Unemployment rate	4.6%
Total civilian labor force, 2000	1,233
Unemployment rate	7.4%

Employed persons 16 years and over by occupation, 2000
Managers & professionals	618
Service occupations	91
Sales & office occupations	266
Farming, fishing & forestry	4
Construction & maintenance	86
Production & transportation	77
Self-employed persons	82

* US Census Bureau
** New Jersey Department of Labor

General Information
Borough of Wenonah
1 S West Ave
PO Box 66
Wenonah, NJ 08090
856-468-5228

Website	www.wenonahnj.us
Year of incorporation	1883
Land/water area (sq. miles)	0.97/0.00
Form of government	Borough

Government
Legislative Districts
US Congressional	1
State Legislative	3

Local Officials, 2009
Mayor	Thomas J. Capaldi
Manager/Admin	NA
Clerk	Karen L. Sweeney
CFO	Robert E. Scharle
Tax Assessor	Roy Duffield
Tax Collector	Lorraine Roberts
Attorney	Brian J. Duffield
Building	Bob Kunkle
Comm Dev/Planning	NA
Engineering	Kreck, Wood & Hallowell
Public Works	Ken Trovarelli
Police Chief	Glenn Scheetz
Emerg/Fire Director	Andrew Sole III

Housing & Construction
Housing Units, 2000*
Total	860
Median rent	$665
Median SF home value	$161,600

Permits for New Residential Construction
	Units	Value
Total, 2006	6	$870,653
Single family	6	$870,653
Total, 2007	7	$1,143,148
Single family	7	$1,143,148

Real Property Valuation, 2008
	Parcels	Valuation
Total	862	$300,074,000
Vacant	29	2,545,000
Residential	819	292,122,000
Commercial	14	5,407,000
Industrial	0	0
Apartments	0	0
Farm land	0	0
Farm homestead	0	0

Average Property Value & Tax, 2008
Residential value	$356,681
Property tax	$8,461
Tax credit/rebate	$1,215

Public Library
Wenonah Public Library
101 E Mantua Ave
Wenonah, NJ 08090
856-468-6323

Director	Anne Zuber

Library statistics, 2007
Population served	2,317
Full-time/total staff	0/0

	Total	Per capita
Holdings	14,312	6.18
Revenues	$86,398	$37.29
Expenditures	$77,537	$33.46
Annual visits	3,360	1.45
Internet terminals/annual users	4/1,356	

Public Safety
Number of officers, 2007		7

Crime	2006	2007
Total crimes	19	20
Violent	2	1
Murder	0	0
Rape	0	0
Robbery	0	1
Aggravated assault	2	0
Non-violent	17	19
Burglary	6	8
Larceny	11	11
Vehicle theft	0	0
Domestic violence	8	2
Arson	0	0
Total crime rate	8.1	8.6
Violent	0.9	0.4
Non-violent	7.3	8.1

Public School District
(for school year 2007-08 except as noted)

Wenonah School District
200 N Clinton Ave
Wenonah, NJ 08090
(856) 468-6000

Chief School Admin	Frank Vogel
Number of schools	1
Grade plan	K-6
Enrollment	247
Attendance rate, '06-07	96.4%
Dropout rate	NA
Students per teacher	11.0
Per pupil expenditure	$10,459
Median faculty salary	$50,730
Median administrator salary	$92,500
Grade 12 enrollment	NA
High school graduation rate	NA

Assessment test results
(percent scoring at proficient or advanced level)
	Language	Math
NJASK-Grade 3	89.4%	92.1%
GEPA-Grade 8	NA	NA
HSPA-High School	NA	NA

SAT Score Averages, 2006-07
Pct tested	Math	Verbal	Writing
NA	NA	NA	NA

Teacher Qualifications
Avg. years of experience	13
Highly-qualified teachers one subject/all subjects	100%/100%

No Child Left Behind
AYP, 2006-07	Meets Standards

Municipal Finance
State Aid Programs, 2009
Total aid	$206,228
CMPTRA	54,771
Energy tax receipts	146,301
Garden State Trust	0

General Budget, 2008
Total tax levy	$7,124,593
County levy	1,511,036
County taxes	1,401,229
County library	0
County health	0
County open space	109,807
School levy	3,973,694
Muni. levy	1,639,863
Misc. revenues	1,137,349

Taxes
	2006	2007	2008
General tax rate per $100	4.744	5.034	2.373
County equalization ratio	61.93	53.7	109.48
Net valuation taxable	$136,380,400	$137,030,600	$300,354,585
State equalized value	$254,129,682	$272,231,352	$284,872,770

See Introduction for an explanation of all data sources.

Demographics & Socio-Economic Characteristics
(2000 US Census, except as noted)

Population
1980*	2,299
1990*	2,251
2000	2,383
Male	1,193
Female	1,190
2007 (estimate)*	2,930
Population density	134.9

Race & Hispanic Origin, 2000
Race
White	2,337
Black/African American	15
American Indian/Alaska Native	2
Asian	17
Native Hawaiian/Pacific Islander	0
Other race	1
Two or more races	11
Hispanic origin, total	17
Mexican	1
Puerto Rican	3
Cuban	1
Other Hispanic	12

Age & Nativity, 2000
Under 5 years	116
18 years and over	1,879
21 years and over	1,826
65 years and over	330
85 years and over	37
Median age	42.9
Native-born	2,274
Foreign-born	109

Educational Attainment, 2000
Population 25 years and over	1,782
Less than 9th grade	3.8%
High school grad or higher	89.6%
Bachelor's degree or higher	37.0%
Graduate degree	12.6%

Income & Poverty, 1999
Per capita income	$33,877
Median household income	$73,380
Median family income	$79,605
Persons in poverty	39
H'holds receiving public assistance	8
H'holds receiving social security	280

Households, 2000
Total households	949
With persons under 18	288
With persons over 65	245
Family households	697
Single-person households	202
Persons per household	2.51
Persons per family	2.93

Labor & Employment
Total civilian labor force, 2007**	1,571
Unemployment rate	2.5%
Total civilian labor force, 2000	1,411
Unemployment rate	2.2%

Employed persons 16 years and over by occupation, 2000
Managers & professionals	581
Service occupations	145
Sales & office occupations	353
Farming, fishing & forestry	19
Construction & maintenance	147
Production & transportation	135
Self-employed persons	154

General Information
Township of West Amwell
Township of West Amwell Municipal Offices
150 Rocktown-Lambertville Rd
Lambertville, NJ 08530
609-397-2054
Website	www.westamwelltwp.org
Year of incorporation	1846
Land/water area (sq. miles)	21.72/0.18
Form of government	Township

Government
Legislative Districts
US Congressional	12
State Legislative	23

Local Officials, 2009
Mayor	William J. Corboy
Manager/Admin	NA
Clerk	Lora L. Olsen
Finance Dir	Jane Luhrs
Tax Assessor	David Gill
Tax Collector	Catherine L. Park
Attorney	Phillip J. Faherty III
Building	Christopher Rose
Comm Dev/Planning	NA
Engineering	Robert J. Clerico
Public Works	Randy Hoagland
Police Chief	Stephen J. Bartzak
Emerg/Fire Director	Jeff Ent

Housing & Construction
Housing Units, 2000*
Total	984
Median rent	$865
Median SF home value	$198,800

Permits for New Residential Construction
	Units	Value
Total, 2006	17	$3,081,611
Single family	17	$3,081,611
Total, 2007	9	$1,719,096
Single family	9	$1,719,096

Real Property Valuation, 2008
	Parcels	Valuation
Total	1,592	$534,237,469
Vacant	186	12,194,200
Residential	921	393,294,500
Commercial	41	25,084,069
Industrial	7	11,864,400
Apartments	3	1,476,900
Farm land	287	2,417,000
Farm homestead	147	87,906,400

Average Property Value & Tax, 2008
Residential value	$450,563
Property tax	$8,249
Tax credit/rebate	$1,122

Public Library
No public municipal library

Library statistics, 2007
Population served	NA
Full-time/total staff	NA/NA

	Total	Per capita
Holdings	NA	NA
Revenues	NA	NA
Expenditures	NA	NA
Annual visits	NA	NA
Internet terminals/annual users	NA/NA	

Public Safety
Number of officers, 2007 ... 6

Crime	2006	2007
Total crimes	29	31
Violent	5	4
Murder	0	0
Rape	1	0
Robbery	0	0
Aggravated assault	4	4
Non-violent	24	27
Burglary	4	10
Larceny	19	17
Vehicle theft	1	0
Domestic violence	20	20
Arson	0	0
Total crime rate	9.9	10.5
Violent	1.7	1.4
Non-violent	8.2	9.2

Public School District
(for school year 2007-08 except as noted)

West Amwell Township School District
1417 Route 179
Lambertville, NJ 08530
(609) 397-0819
Superintendent	Todd Fay
Number of schools	1
Grade plan	K-6
Enrollment	262
Attendance rate, '06-07	96.3%
Dropout rate	NA
Students per teacher	12.2
Per pupil expenditure	$14,046
Median faculty salary	$54,226
Median administrator salary	$79,366
Grade 12 enrollment	NA
High school graduation rate	NA

Assessment test results
(percent scoring at proficient or advanced level)
	Language	Math
NJASK-Grade 3	94.3%	88.6%
GEPA-Grade 8	NA	NA
HSPA-High School	NA	NA

SAT Score Averages, 2006-07
Pct tested	Math	Verbal	Writing
NA	NA	NA	NA

Teacher Qualifications
Avg. years of experience	12
Highly-qualified teachers one subject/all subjects	100%/100%

No Child Left Behind
AYP, 2006-07 ... Meets Standards

Municipal Finance
State Aid Programs, 2009
Total aid	$1,316,824
CMPTRA	842,105
Energy tax receipts	342,910
Garden State Trust	61,994

General Budget, 2008
Total tax levy	$9,795,992
County levy	2,067,826
County taxes	1,730,701
County library	150,290
County health	0
County open space	186,835
School levy	6,556,358
Muni. levy	1,171,809
Misc. revenues	2,614,484

Taxes	2006	2007	2008
General tax rate per $100	1.71	1.79	1.831
County equalization ratio	89.27	87.07	86.25
Net valuation taxable	$512,718,599	$525,595,942	$535,053,320
State equalized value	$555,930,162	$583,650,217	$596,000,197

* US Census Bureau
** New Jersey Department of Labor

See Introduction for an explanation of all data sources.

Demographics & Socio-Economic Characteristics

(2000 US Census, except as noted)

Population

1980*	11,407
1990*	10,422
2000	11,233
Male	5,330
Female	5,903
2007 (estimate)*	10,566
Population density	2,092.3

Race & Hispanic Origin, 2000

Race

White	10,541
Black/African American	100
American Indian/Alaska Native	4
Asian	432
Native Hawaiian/Pacific Islander	4
Other race	68
Two or more races	84
Hispanic origin, total	314
Mexican	23
Puerto Rican	85
Cuban	68
Other Hispanic	138

Age & Nativity, 2000

Under 5 years	813
18 years and over	8,463
21 years and over	8,241
65 years and over	2,142
85 years and over	376
Median age	41.0
Native-born	10,262
Foreign-born	971

Educational Attainment, 2000

Population 25 years and over	7,982
Less than 9th grade	1.7%
High school grad or higher	93.4%
Bachelor's degree or higher	48.1%
Graduate degree	18.2%

Income & Poverty, 1999

Per capita income	$38,345
Median household income	$83,396
Median family income	$94,379
Persons in poverty	227
H'holds receiving public assistance	48
H'holds receiving social security	1,353

Households, 2000

Total households	3,990
With persons under 18	1,469
With persons over 65	1,351
Family households	3,114
Single-person households	767
Persons per household	2.75
Persons per family	3.17

Labor & Employment

Total civilian labor force, 2007**	6,056
Unemployment rate	2.9%
Total civilian labor force, 2000	5,819
Unemployment rate	2.7%

Employed persons 16 years and over by occupation, 2000

Managers & professionals	2,819
Service occupations	596
Sales & office occupations	1,699
Farming, fishing & forestry	0
Construction & maintenance	325
Production & transportation	221
Self-employed persons	356

* US Census Bureau
** New Jersey Department of Labor

General Information

Township of West Caldwell
30 Clinton Rd
West Caldwell, NJ 07006
973-226-2300

Website	www.westcaldwell.com
Year of incorporation	1904
Land/water area (sq. miles)	5.05/0.00
Form of government	Borough

Government

Legislative Districts

US Congressional	11
State Legislative	27

Local Officials, 2009

Mayor	Joseph Tempesta Jr
Administrator	Andy Katz
Clerk	Jock Watkins
Finance Dir	Lou Garbaccio
Tax Assessor	Richard Hamilton Jr
Tax Collector	Kathleen Bruchac
Attorney	Joseph Maddaloni
Building	Jock Watkins
Planning	Joe Dunn
Engineering	Benedict Martorana
Public Works	William Frint
Police Chief	Charles Tubbs
Fire Chief	Charles Holden

Housing & Construction

Housing Units, 2000*

Total	4,044
Median rent	$1,193
Median SF home value	$265,900

Permits for New Residential Construction

	Units	Value
Total, 2006	5	$1,221,623
Single family	5	$1,221,623
Total, 2007	8	$1,769,762
Single family	8	$1,769,762

Real Property Valuation, 2008

	Parcels	Valuation
Total	3,810	$1,138,522,900
Vacant	81	7,707,200
Residential	3,497	777,413,400
Commercial	154	162,519,000
Industrial	66	182,895,200
Apartments	6	7,906,700
Farm land	6	81,400
Farm homestead	0	0

Average Property Value & Tax, 2008

Residential value	$222,309
Property tax	$8,452
Tax credit/rebate	$1,202

Public Library

West Caldwell Public Library
30 Clinton Rd
West Caldwell, NJ 07006
973-226-5441

Director	April L. Judge

Library statistics, 2007

Population served	11,233
Full-time/total staff	5/9

	Total	Per capita
Holdings	67,278	5.99
Revenues	$1,205,140	$107.29
Expenditures	$1,117,436	$99.48
Annual visits	140,394	12.50
Internet terminals/annual users	14/13,491	

Public Safety

Number of officers, 2007	29

Crime	2006	2007
Total crimes	116	96
Violent	4	6
Murder	0	0
Rape	0	0
Robbery	1	0
Aggravated assault	3	6
Non-violent	112	90
Burglary	10	6
Larceny	94	81
Vehicle theft	8	3
Domestic violence	44	32
Arson	1	1
Total crime rate	10.6	8.9
Violent	0.4	0.6
Non-violent	10.2	8.3

Public School District

(for school year 2007-08 except as noted)

Caldwell-West Caldwell School District
Harrison Bldg. Gray St.
West Caldwell, NJ 07006
(973) 228-6979

Superintendent	Daniel Gerardi
Number of schools	0
Grade plan	K-12
Enrollment	2,630
Attendance rate, '06-07	95.2%
Dropout rate	0.5%
Students per teacher	11.5
Per pupil expenditure	$13,219
Median faculty salary	$55,270
Median administrator salary	$114,300
Grade 12 enrollment	190
High school graduation rate	97.9%

Assessment test results

(percent scoring at proficient or advanced level)

	Language	Math
NJASK-Grade 3	94.8%	95.3%
GEPA-Grade 8	79.6%	92.9%
HSPA-High School	87.2%	94.6%

SAT Score Averages, 2006-07

Pct tested	Math	Verbal	Writing
93%	541	529	535

Teacher Qualifications

Avg. years of experience	7
Highly-qualified teachers one subject/all subjects	100%/100%

No Child Left Behind

AYP, 2006-07	Meets Standards

Municipal Finance

State Aid Programs, 2009

Total aid	$1,735,364
CMPTRA	225,071
Energy tax receipts	1,453,894
Garden State Trust	0

General Budget, 2008

Total tax levy	$43,309,366
County levy	9,334,627
County taxes	8,974,376
County library	0
County health	0
County open space	360,252
School levy	23,040,822
Muni. levy	10,933,917
Misc. revenues	7,096,364

Taxes

	2006	2007	2008
General tax rate per $100	3.5	3.63	3.802
County equalization ratio	56.79	50.53	48.03
Net valuation taxable	$1,125,525,100	$1,133,389,100	$1,139,197,700
State equalized value	$2,228,162,743	$2,359,032,570	$2,553,416,728

See Introduction for an explanation of all data sources.

Demographics & Socio-Economic Characteristics
(2000 US Census, except as noted)

Population
1980*	1,091
1990*	1,026
2000	1,095
Male	527
Female	568
2007 (estimate)*	987
Population density	829.4

Race & Hispanic Origin, 2000
Race
White	921
Black/African American	159
American Indian/Alaska Native	4
Asian	0
Native Hawaiian/Pacific Islander	0
Other race	6
Two or more races	5
Hispanic origin, total	20
Mexican	7
Puerto Rican	7
Cuban	0
Other Hispanic	6

Age & Nativity, 2000
Under 5 years	37
18 years and over	880
21 years and over	862
65 years and over	267
85 years and over	33
Median age	46.3
Native-born	1,043
Foreign-born	52

Educational Attainment, 2000
Population 25 years and over	870
Less than 9th grade	4.7%
High school grad or higher	83.1%
Bachelor's degree or higher	31.8%
Graduate degree	9.9%

Income & Poverty, 1999
Per capita income	$25,663
Median household income	$37,500
Median family income	$47,031
Persons in poverty	81
H'holds receiving public assistance	12
H'holds receiving social security	213

Households, 2000
Total households	507
With persons under 18	121
With persons over 65	202
Family households	302
Single-person households	178
Persons per household	2.16
Persons per family	2.80

Labor & Employment
Total civilian labor force, 2007**	637
Unemployment rate	7.4%
Total civilian labor force, 2000	536
Unemployment rate	9.0%

Employed persons 16 years and over by occupation, 2000
Managers & professionals	197
Service occupations	81
Sales & office occupations	127
Farming, fishing & forestry	8
Construction & maintenance	56
Production & transportation	19
Self-employed persons	61

General Information
Borough of West Cape May
732 Broadway
West Cape May, NJ 08204
609-884-1005
Website	westcapemay.us
Year of incorporation	1884
Land/water area (sq. miles)	1.19/0.00
Form of government	Commission

Government
Legislative Districts
US Congressional	2
State Legislative	1

Local Officials, 2009
Mayor	Pamela Kaithern
Manager/Admin	NA
Clerk	Elaine Wallace
Finance Dir	John Hansen
Tax Assessor	Arthur Amonette
Tax Collector	Todd Burkey
Attorney	Frank Corrado
Building	Bill Callahan
Planning	Gary Novak
Engineering	Ray Roberts
Public Works	Rob Flynn
Police Chief	Diane Sorantino
Emerg/Fire Director	Charles McPherson

Housing & Construction
Housing Units, 2000*
Total	1,004
Median rent	$703
Median SF home value	$174,100

Permits for New Residential Construction
	Units	Value
Total, 2006	7	$2,105,757
Single family	7	$2,105,757
Total, 2007	13	$3,590,411
Single family	13	$3,590,411

Real Property Valuation, 2008
	Parcels	Valuation
Total	1,046	$510,874,500
Vacant	135	33,282,200
Residential	867	433,366,600
Commercial	34	40,370,900
Industrial	0	0
Apartments	2	1,189,500
Farm land	5	73,700
Farm homestead	3	2,591,600

Average Property Value & Tax, 2008
Residential value	$501,101
Property tax	$4,728
Tax credit/rebate	$940

Public Library
No public municipal library

Library statistics, 2007
Population served	NA
Full-time/total staff	NA/NA

	Total	Per capita
Holdings	NA	NA
Revenues	NA	NA
Expenditures	NA	NA
Annual visits	NA	NA
Internet terminals/annual users	NA/NA	

Public Safety
Number of officers, 2007 0
Crime	2006	2007
Total crimes	38	39
Violent	0	1
Murder	0	0
Rape	0	0
Robbery	0	0
Aggravated assault	0	1
Non-violent	38	38
Burglary	6	7
Larceny	31	31
Vehicle theft	1	0
Domestic violence	0	3
Arson	0	0
Total crime rate	36.6	38.7
Violent	0.0	1.0
Non-violent	36.6	37.7

Public School District
(for school year 2007-08 except as noted)

West Cape May School District
301 Moore Street
West Cape May, NJ 08204
(609) 884-4614
Chief School Admin	William Flynn
Number of schools	1
Grade plan	K-6
Enrollment	52
Attendance rate, '06-07	93.8%
Dropout rate	NA
Students per teacher	6.2
Per pupil expenditure	$26,372
Median faculty salary	$44,522
Median administrator salary	$16,356
Grade 12 enrollment	NA
High school graduation rate	NA

Assessment test results
(percent scoring at proficient or advanced level)
	Language	Math
NJASK-Grade 3	NA	NA
GEPA-Grade 8	NA	NA
HSPA-High School	NA	NA

SAT Score Averages, 2006-07
Pct tested	Math	Verbal	Writing
NA	NA	NA	NA

Teacher Qualifications
Avg. years of experience	10
Highly-qualified teachers one subject/all subjects	100%/100%

No Child Left Behind
AYP, 2006-07 .... Meets Standards

Municipal Finance
State Aid Programs, 2009
Total aid	$119,044
CMPTRA	1,198
Energy tax receipts	113,220
Garden State Trust	720

General Budget, 2008
Total tax levy	$4,822,743
County levy	936,919
County taxes	744,708
County library	142,951
County health	0
County open space	49,260
School levy	2,460,591
Muni. levy	1,425,234
Misc. revenues	711,765

Taxes	2006	2007	2008
General tax rate per $100	1.32	0.9	0.945
County equalization ratio	77.87	109.16	103.96
Net valuation taxable	$309,783,400	$507,539,041	$511,131,781
State equalized value	$458,928,006	$488,215,593	$499,987,791

* US Census Bureau
** New Jersey Department of Labor

See Introduction for an explanation of all data sources.

Demographics & Socio-Economic Characteristics
(2000 US Census, except as noted)

Population
1980*	18,002
1990*	19,380
2000	19,368
Male	9,354
Female	10,014
2007 (estimate)*	22,007
Population density	1,384.1

Race & Hispanic Origin, 2000
Race
White	17,875
Black/African American	984
American Indian/Alaska Native	45
Asian	219
Native Hawaiian/Pacific Islander	4
Other race	82
Two or more races	159
Hispanic origin, total	341
Mexican	29
Puerto Rican	172
Cuban	9
Other Hispanic	131

Age & Nativity, 2000
Under 5 years	1,137
18 years and over	14,807
21 years and over	14,147
65 years and over	2,357
85 years and over	168
Median age	37.5
Native-born	18,995
Foreign-born	373

Educational Attainment, 2000
Population 25 years and over	13,226
Less than 9th grade	2.7%
High school grad or higher	85.7%
Bachelor's degree or higher	21.7%
Graduate degree	6.8%

Income & Poverty, 1999
Per capita income	$24,219
Median household income	$50,583
Median family income	$64,477
Persons in poverty	1,015
H'holds receiving public assistance	74
H'holds receiving social security	1,954

Households, 2000
Total households	7,719
With persons under 18	2,583
With persons over 65	1,700
Family households	5,129
Single-person households	2,115
Persons per household	2.49
Persons per family	3.07

Labor & Employment
Total civilian labor force, 2007**	12,851
Unemployment rate	4.5%
Total civilian labor force, 2000	10,862
Unemployment rate	4.2%

Employed persons 16 years and over by occupation, 2000
Managers & professionals	3,324
Service occupations	1,173
Sales & office occupations	3,158
Farming, fishing & forestry	25
Construction & maintenance	941
Production & transportation	1,789
Self-employed persons	331

General Information
Township of West Deptford
400 Crown Point Rd
West Deptford, NJ 08086
856-845-4004
Website	www.westdeptford.com
Year of incorporation	1871
Land/water area (sq. miles)	15.90/1.86
Form of government	Township

Government
Legislative Districts
US Congressional	1
State Legislative	3

Local Officials, 2009
Mayor	Anna Docimo
Township Admin	Eric M. Campo
Clerk	Raymond Sherman
Finance Dir	Richard Giuliani
Tax Assessor	Alicia Melson
Tax Collector	George Damminger
Attorney	Michael Angelini
Building	Philip Zimm
Planning	Sandra Rost
Engineering	T&A Associates
Public Works	Edward J. Phelps
Police Chief	Craig Mangano
Fire Chief	J. Trautner

Housing & Construction
Housing Units, 2000*
Total	7,999
Median rent	$687
Median SF home value	$120,100

Permits for New Residential Construction
	Units	Value
Total, 2006	83	$6,728,350
Single family	48	$4,574,850
Total, 2007	13	$2,068,415
Single family	13	$2,068,415

Real Property Valuation, 2008
	Parcels	Valuation
Total	7,558	$1,415,609,700
Vacant	524	30,039,700
Residential	6,670	784,534,500
Commercial	289	301,334,000
Industrial	14	258,576,000
Apartments	11	39,499,100
Farm land	40	354,200
Farm homestead	10	1,272,200

Average Property Value & Tax, 2008
Residential value	$117,636
Property tax	$4,804
Tax credit/rebate	$858

Public Library
West Deptford Public Library
420 Crown Point Rd
Thorofare, NJ 08086
856-845-5593
Director	Marie Downes McDonald

Library statistics, 2007
Population served	19,368
Full-time/total staff	4/10

	Total	Per capita
Holdings	86,639	4.47
Revenues	$1,102,799	$56.94
Expenditures	$1,065,628	$55.02
Annual visits	241,908	12.49
Internet terminals/annual users	22/31,027	

Public Safety
Number of officers, 2007	40

Crime	2006	2007
Total crimes	582	485
Violent	42	32
Murder	1	2
Rape	11	1
Robbery	5	13
Aggravated assault	25	16
Non-violent	540	453
Burglary	93	86
Larceny	399	331
Vehicle theft	48	36
Domestic violence	291	329
Arson	8	3
Total crime rate	27.8	22.3
Violent	2.0	1.5
Non-violent	25.8	20.8

Public School District
(for school year 2007-08 except as noted)

West Deptford Township School District
675 Grove Road, Suite 804
West Deptford, NJ 08066
(856) 848-4300
Superintendent	Edward Wasilewski Jr
Number of schools	5
Grade plan	K-12
Enrollment	3,266
Attendance rate, '06-07	92.8%
Dropout rate	2.2%
Students per teacher	13.0
Per pupil expenditure	$11,631
Median faculty salary	$59,338
Median administrator salary	$110,050
Grade 12 enrollment	283
High school graduation rate	91.1%

Assessment test results
(percent scoring at proficient or advanced level)
	Language	Math
NJASK-Grade 3	88.9%	93.1%
GEPA-Grade 8	74.6%	88.9%
HSPA-High School	79.9%	90.8%

SAT Score Averages, 2006-07
Pct tested	Math	Verbal	Writing
70%	498	478	473

Teacher Qualifications
Avg. years of experience	9
Highly-qualified teachers one subject/all subjects	100%/100%

No Child Left Behind
AYP, 2006-07	Meets Standards

Municipal Finance
State Aid Programs, 2009
Total aid	$2,590,680
CMPTRA	664,682
Energy tax receipts	1,861,076
Garden State Trust	85

General Budget, 2008
Total tax levy	$59,037,039
County levy	14,460,939
County taxes	13,410,062
County library	0
County health	0
County open space	1,050,877
School levy	27,212,586
Muni. levy	17,363,514
Misc. revenues	13,657,330

Taxes
	2006	2007	2008
General tax rate per $100	3.618	3.84	4.084
County equalization ratio	65.55	59.66	54.84
Net valuation taxable	$1,380,539,500	$1,447,494,592	$1,445,754,732
State equalized value	$2,351,621,764	$2,610,796,511	$2,810,211,214

* US Census Bureau
** New Jersey Department of Labor

See Introduction for an explanation of all data sources.

Demographics & Socio-Economic Characteristics
(2000 US Census, except as noted)

Population
1980*	7,380
1990*	7,690
2000	8,258
Male	3,857
Female	4,401
2007 (estimate)*	8,383
Population density	2,900.7

Race & Hispanic Origin, 2000
Race
White	7,781
Black/African American	184
American Indian/Alaska Native	6
Asian	100
Native Hawaiian/Pacific Islander	3
Other race	41
Two or more races	143
Hispanic origin, total	241
Mexican	29
Puerto Rican	63
Cuban	20
Other Hispanic	129

Age & Nativity, 2000
Under 5 years	409
18 years and over	6,458
21 years and over	5,165
65 years and over	1,206
85 years and over	129
Median age	33.8
Native-born	7,676
Foreign-born	582

Educational Attainment, 2000
Population 25 years and over	4,722
Less than 9th grade	4.7%
High school grad or higher	87.1%
Bachelor's degree or higher	34.9%
Graduate degree	14.3%

Income & Poverty, 1999
Per capita income	$27,651
Median household income	$71,852
Median family income	$80,127
Persons in poverty	303
H'holds receiving public assistance	26
H'holds receiving social security	838

Households, 2000
Total households	2,448
With persons under 18	915
With persons over 65	889
Family households	1,860
Single-person households	522
Persons per household	2.77
Persons per family	3.25

Labor & Employment
Total civilian labor force, 2007**	3,401
Unemployment rate	4.0%
Total civilian labor force, 2000	4,169
Unemployment rate	14.7%

Employed persons 16 years and over by occupation, 2000
Managers & professionals	1,391
Service occupations	532
Sales & office occupations	1,120
Farming, fishing & forestry	0
Construction & maintenance	357
Production & transportation	156
Self-employed persons	244

General Information
Borough of West Long Branch
965 Broadway
West Long Branch, NJ 07764
732-229-1756

Website	www.westlongbranch.org
Year of incorporation	1908
Land/water area (sq. miles)	2.89/0.02
Form of government	Borough

Government
Legislative Districts
US Congressional	6
State Legislative	11

Local Officials, 2009
Mayor	Janet W. Tucci
Manager/Admin	NA
Clerk	Lori Cole
Chief Financial Officer	Gail M. Watkins
Tax Assessor	Helen J. Ward
Tax Collector	Charlotte C. Rolly
Attorney	Gregory S. Baxter
Building	Michael Martin
Comm Dev/Planning	NA
Engineering	T&M Associates
Public Works	Earl S. Reed Jr
Police Chief	Arthur N. Cosentino
Emerg/Fire Director	Dennis O'Rorke

Housing & Construction
Housing Units, 2000*
Total	2,535
Median rent	$639
Median SF home value	$203,300

Permits for New Residential Construction
	Units	Value
Total, 2006	6	$1,068,431
Single family	6	$1,068,431
Total, 2007	8	$632,178
Single family	3	$632,078

Real Property Valuation, 2008
	Parcels	Valuation
Total	2,517	$1,354,827,500
Vacant	77	11,834,400
Residential	2,270	1,081,943,400
Commercial	159	254,243,700
Industrial	2	3,254,900
Apartments	2	1,907,600
Farm land	4	17,600
Farm homestead	3	1,625,900

Average Property Value & Tax, 2008
Residential value	$476,713
Property tax	$8,234
Tax credit/rebate	$1,202

Public Library
West Long Branch Public Library
95 Poplar Ave
West Long Branch, NJ 07764
732-222-5993

Director	David M. Lisa

Library statistics, 2007
Population served	8,258
Full-time/total staff	1/3

	Total	Per capita
Holdings	42,956	5.20
Revenues	$487,194	$59.00
Expenditures	$360,623	$43.67
Annual visits	30,966	3.75
Internet terminals/annual users	7/9,778	

Public Safety
Number of officers, 2007 20
Crime	2006	2007
Total crimes	278	255
Violent	10	13
Murder	0	0
Rape	2	2
Robbery	2	3
Aggravated assault	6	8
Non-violent	268	242
Burglary	31	32
Larceny	231	205
Vehicle theft	6	5
Domestic violence	35	60
Arson	1	2
Total crime rate	33.6	30.7
Violent	1.2	1.6
Non-violent	32.3	29.1

Public School District
(for school year 2007-08 except as noted)

West Long Branch School District
135 Locust Avenue
West Long Branch, NJ 07764
(732) 222-5900

Superintendent	Karen M. Wood
Number of schools	2
Grade plan	K-8
Enrollment	666
Attendance rate, '06-07	95.4%
Dropout rate	NA
Students per teacher	10.2
Per pupil expenditure	$13,023
Median faculty salary	$52,120
Median administrator salary	$112,310
Grade 12 enrollment	NA
High school graduation rate	NA

Assessment test results
(percent scoring at proficient or advanced level)
	Language	Math
NJASK-Grade 3	86.4%	89.3%
GEPA-Grade 8	83.5%	90.5%
HSPA-High School	NA	NA

SAT Score Averages, 2006-07
Pct tested	Math	Verbal	Writing
NA	NA	NA	NA

Teacher Qualifications
Avg. years of experience	11
Highly-qualified teachers one subject/all subjects	100%/100%

No Child Left Behind
AYP, 2006-07 . . . . Meets Standards

Municipal Finance
State Aid Programs, 2009
Total aid	$1,026,504
CMPTRA	150,271
Energy tax receipts	850,570
Garden State Trust	0

General Budget, 2008
Total tax levy	$23,420,558
County levy	3,727,327
County taxes	3,307,672
County library	199,053
County health	0
County open space	220,602
School levy	14,216,409
Muni. levy	5,476,822
Misc. revenues	3,517,534

Taxes	2006	2007	2008
General tax rate per $100	1.594	1.681	1.728
County equalization ratio	111.04	95.39	92.88
Net valuation taxable	$1,357,047,700	$1,358,981,572	$1,355,949,450
State equalized value	$1,423,756,655	$1,463,073,787	$1,431,169,976

* US Census Bureau
** New Jersey Department of Labor

See Introduction for an explanation of all data sources.

Demographics & Socio-Economic Characteristics

(2000 US Census, except as noted)

Population

1980*	22,750
1990*	25,430
2000	26,410
Male	13,224
Female	13,186
2007 (estimate)*	27,839
Population density	369.0

Race & Hispanic Origin, 2000

Race

White	25,110
Black/African American	326
American Indian/Alaska Native	159
Asian	269
Native Hawaiian/Pacific Islander	4
Other race	160
Two or more races	382
Hispanic origin, total	893
Mexican	97
Puerto Rican	305
Cuban	97
Other Hispanic	394

Age & Nativity, 2000

Under 5 years	1,863
18 years and over	19,222
21 years and over	18,480
65 years and over	2,212
85 years and over	251
Median age	37.0
Native-born	24,882
Foreign-born	1,528

Educational Attainment, 2000

Population 25 years and over	17,657
Less than 9th grade	2.6%
High school grad or higher	89.3%
Bachelor's degree or higher	27.2%
Graduate degree	8.0%

Income & Poverty, 1999

Per capita income	$28,612
Median household income	$74,124
Median family income	$80,264
Persons in poverty	1,085
H'holds receiving public assistance	132
H'holds receiving social security	1,702

Households, 2000

Total households	9,190
With persons under 18	3,863
With persons over 65	1,592
Family households	7,186
Single-person households	1,536
Persons per household	2.84
Persons per family	3.23

Labor & Employment

Total civilian labor force, 2007**	16,181
Unemployment rate	4.2%
Total civilian labor force, 2000	14,817
Unemployment rate	4.3%

Employed persons 16 years and over by occupation, 2000

Managers & professionals	5,003
Service occupations	1,533
Sales & office occupations	4,182
Farming, fishing & forestry	19
Construction & maintenance	1,868
Production & transportation	1,575
Self-employed persons	913

* US Census Bureau
** New Jersey Department of Labor

See Introduction for an explanation of all data sources.

General Information

Township of West Milford
1480 Union Valley Rd
West Milford, NJ 07480
973-728-7000

Website	www.westmilford.org
Year of incorporation	1834
Land/water area (sq. miles)	75.44/4.97
Form of government	Mayor-Council-Admin

Government

Legislative Districts

US Congressional	5
State Legislative	26

Local Officials, 2009

Mayor	Bettina Bieri
Manager	Richard Kunze
Clerk	Antoinette Battaglia
Finance Dir	Arthur Magnotti
Tax Assessor	Brian Townsend
Tax Collector	Rita DeNivo
Attorney	Fred Semrau
Building	Kurt Wagner
Planning	William Drew
Engineering	Richard S. McFadden
Public Works	Gerald Storms
Police Chief	Paul Costello
Emerg/Fire Director	Ed Steines

Housing & Construction

Housing Units, 2000*

Total	9,909
Median rent	$835
Median SF home value	$171,200

Permits for New Residential Construction

	Units	Value
Total, 2006	36	$8,580,288
Single family	36	$8,580,288
Total, 2007	26	$6,516,790
Single family	26	$6,516,790

Real Property Valuation, 2008

	Parcels	Valuation
Total	11,820	$1,511,426,900
Vacant	1,255	50,439,100
Residential	9,885	1,332,623,200
Commercial	279	89,833,700
Industrial	28	9,544,700
Apartments	1	550,000
Farm land	252	649,500
Farm homestead	120	27,786,700

Average Property Value & Tax, 2008

Residential value	$135,973
Property tax	$7,677
Tax credit/rebate	$1,190

Public Library

West Milford Township Library
1490 Union Valley Rd
West Milford, NJ 07480
973-728-2820

Director .... Patricia Ann Hannon

Library statistics, 2007

Population served	26,410
Full-time/total staff	4/9

	Total	Per capita
Holdings	56,181	2.13
Revenues	$1,344,497	$50.91
Expenditures	$960,227	$36.36
Annual visits	91,026	3.45
Internet terminals/annual users		5/1,774

Public Safety

Number of officers, 2007 49

Crime	2006	2007
Total crimes	467	384
Violent	24	29
Murder	0	0
Rape	7	6
Robbery	3	1
Aggravated assault	14	22
Non-violent	443	355
Burglary	106	88
Larceny	327	251
Vehicle theft	10	16
Domestic violence	195	188
Arson	5	1
Total crime rate	16.6	13.6
Violent	0.9	1.0
Non-violent	15.7	12.6

Public School District

(for school year 2007-08 except as noted)

West Milford Township School District
46 Highlander Drive
West Milford, NJ 07480
(973) 697-1700

Chief School Admin	Bernice Colefield
Number of schools	8
Grade plan	K-12
Enrollment	4,309
Attendance rate, '06-07	95.0%
Dropout rate	0.0%
Students per teacher	11.3
Per pupil expenditure	$14,109
Median faculty salary	$65,450
Median administrator salary	$116,241
Grade 12 enrollment	359
High school graduation rate	96.2%

Assessment test results

(percent scoring at proficient or advanced level)

	Language	Math
NJASK-Grade 3	93.8%	90.1%
GEPA-Grade 8	71.4%	87.6%
HSPA-High School	76.2%	82.7%

SAT Score Averages, 2006-07

Pct tested	Math	Verbal	Writing
67%	501	481	483

Teacher Qualifications

Avg. years of experience	11
Highly-qualified teachers one subject/all subjects	100%/100%

No Child Left Behind

AYP, 2006-07 .... Meets Standards

Municipal Finance

State Aid Programs, 2009

Total aid	$3,885,476
CMPTRA	462,262
Energy tax receipts	2,457,837
Garden State Trust	130,054

General Budget, 2008

Total tax levy	$85,571,906
County levy	19,155,136
County taxes	18,774,319
County library	0
County health	0
County open space	380,817
School levy	46,230,729
Muni. levy	20,186,041
Misc. revenues	11,759,078

Taxes	2006	2007	2008
General tax rate per $100	5.19	5.44	5.647
County equalization ratio	46.58	41.91	39.79
Net valuation taxable	$1,504,617,300	$1,515,840,182	$1,515,553,271
State equalized value	$3,595,021,475	$3,803,218,990	$3,849,018,002

Demographics & Socio-Economic Characteristics

(2000 US Census, except as noted)

Population

1980*	39,194
1990*	38,125
2000	45,768
Male	22,470
Female	23,298
2007 (estimate)*	46,425
Population density	45,514.7

Race & Hispanic Origin, 2000

Race

White	27,503
Black/African American	1,626
American Indian/Alaska Native	305
Asian	1,339
Native Hawaiian/Pacific Islander	15
Other race	11,515
Two or more races	3,465
Hispanic origin, total	36,038
Mexican	2,982
Puerto Rican	2,791
Cuban	8,991
Other Hispanic	21,274

Age & Nativity, 2000

Under 5 years	3,049
18 years and over	35,562
21 years and over	33,621
65 years and over	5,828
85 years and over	614
Median age	34.0
Native-born	15,937
Foreign-born	29,831

Educational Attainment, 2000

Population 25 years and over	30,669
Less than 9th grade	25.7%
High school grad or higher	54.4%
Bachelor's degree or higher	16.4%
Graduate degree	7.3%

Income & Poverty, 1999

Per capita income	$16,719
Median household income	$31,980
Median family income	$34,083
Persons in poverty	8,635
H'holds receiving public assistance	759
H'holds receiving social security	4,149

Households, 2000

Total households	16,719
With persons under 18	5,867
With persons over 65	4,613
Family households	11,042
Single-person households	4,593
Persons per household	2.74
Persons per family	3.30

Labor & Employment

Total civilian labor force, 2007**	20,231
Unemployment rate	5.5%
Total civilian labor force, 2000	20,406
Unemployment rate	10.0%

Employed persons 16 years and over by occupation, 2000

Managers & professionals	3,626
Service occupations	3,686
Sales & office occupations	4,828
Farming, fishing & forestry	34
Construction & maintenance	1,316
Production & transportation	4,868
Self-employed persons	858

* US Census Bureau
** New Jersey Department of Labor
§ State Fiscal Year July 1–June 30

General Information

Town of West New York
428 60th St
West New York, NJ 07093
201-295-5200

Website	www.westnewyorknj.org
Year of incorporation	1898
Land/water area (sq. miles)	1.02/0.31
Form of government	Commission

Government

Legislative Districts

US Congressional	13
State Legislative	33

Local Officials, 2009

Mayor	Silverio A. Vega
Manager	Nicholas Goldsack
Clerk	Carmela Riccie
Finance Dir	Darren Maloney
Tax Assessor	Salvatore Bonaccorsi
Tax Collector	Kerri Campen
Attorney	Daniel Horgan
Building	Franco Zanardelli
Comm Dev/Planning	NA
Engineering	PMK Group
Public Works	William Parkinson
Police Chief	Oscar Fernandez
Emerg/Fire Director	Brion McEldowney

Housing & Construction

Housing Units, 2000*

Total	17,360
Median rent	$681
Median SF home value	$218,400

Permits for New Residential Construction

	Units	Value
Total, 2006	413	$114,449,160
Single family	0	$0
Total, 2007	339	$55,371,242
Single family	0	$0

Real Property Valuation, 2008

	Parcels	Valuation
Total	6,576	$960,182,000
Vacant	1,122	41,592,100
Residential	4,177	450,363,300
Commercial	745	238,616,700
Industrial	132	37,545,700
Apartments	400	192,064,200
Farm land	0	0
Farm homestead	0	0

Average Property Value & Tax, 2008

Residential value	$107,820
Property tax	$5,684
Tax credit/rebate	$872

Public Library

West New York Public Library
425 60th St
West New York, NJ 07093
201-295-5135

Director......Weiliang Lai

Library statistics, 2007

Population served	45,768
Full-time/total staff	2/15

	Total	Per capita
Holdings	69,712	1.52
Revenues	$819,679	$17.91
Expenditures	$819,679	$17.91
Annual visits	58,500	1.28
Internet terminals/annual users	42/52,610	

Public Safety

Number of officers, 2007	119

Crime	2006	2007
Total crimes	1,021	1,034
Violent	186	197
Murder	3	4
Rape	5	4
Robbery	85	97
Aggravated assault	93	92
Non-violent	835	837
Burglary	215	192
Larceny	464	543
Vehicle theft	156	102
Domestic violence	272	263
Arson	1	4
Total crime rate	21.9	22.3
Violent	4.0	4.2
Non-violent	17.9	18.0

Public School District

(for school year 2007-08 except as noted)

West New york School District
6028 Broadway
West New York, NJ 07093
(201) 553-4000

Superintendent	Robert VanZanten
Number of schools	9
Grade plan	K-12
Enrollment	7,054
Attendance rate, '06-07	94.8%
Dropout rate	0.5%
Students per teacher	11.5
Per pupil expenditure	$15,451
Median faculty salary	$61,600
Median administrator salary	$122,276
Grade 12 enrollment	318
High school graduation rate	96.7%

Assessment test results

(percent scoring at proficient or advanced level)

	Language	Math
NJASK-Grade 3	81.8%	78.6%
GEPA-Grade 8	70.3%	79.0%
HSPA-High School	59.6%	71.8%

SAT Score Averages, 2006-07

Pct tested	Math	Verbal	Writing
77%	419	405	400

Teacher Qualifications

Avg. years of experience	10
Highly-qualified teachers one subject/all subjects	100%/100%

No Child Left Behind

AYP, 2006-07......Meets Standards

Municipal Finance§

State Aid Programs, 2009

Total aid	$8,143,488
CMPTRA	5,800,432
Energy tax receipts	2,302,339
Garden State Trust	0

General Budget, 2008

Total tax levy	$53,982,106
County levy	10,522,319
County taxes	10,245,292
County library	0
County health	0
County open space	277,027
School levy	13,934,512
Muni. levy	29,525,276
Misc. revenues	37,671,715

Taxes

	2006	2007	2008
General tax rate per $100	4.826	4.962	5.620
County equalization ratio	47.08	39.66	35.29
Net valuation taxable	$941,704,400	$950,480,860	$960,679,425
State equalized value	$2,375,063,610	$2,692,352,855	$2,777,194,938

See Introduction for an explanation of all data sources.

Demographics & Socio-Economic Characteristics

(2000 US Census, except as noted)

Population

1980*	39,510
1990*	39,103
2000	44,943
Male	21,110
Female	23,833
2007 (estimate)*	42,906
Population density	3,540.1

Race & Hispanic Origin, 2000

Race

White	30,359
Black/African American	7,848
American Indian/Alaska Native	63
Asian	3,635
Native Hawaiian/Pacific Islander	17
Other race	1,584
Two or more races	1,437
Hispanic origin, total	4,514
Mexican	277
Puerto Rican	672
Cuban	214
Other Hispanic	3,351

Age & Nativity, 2000

Under 5 years	2,988
18 years and over	34,477
21 years and over	33,258
65 years and over	7,818
85 years and over	1,523
Median age	39.4
Native-born	33,369
Foreign-born	11,483

Educational Attainment, 2000

Population 25 years and over	31,694
Less than 9th grade	4.7%
High school grad or higher	86.3%
Bachelor's degree or higher	43.1%
Graduate degree	19.0%

Income & Poverty, 1999

Per capita income	$34,412
Median household income	$69,254
Median family income	$83,375
Persons in poverty	2,461
H'holds receiving public assistance	228
H'holds receiving social security	4,630

Households, 2000

Total households	16,480
With persons under 18	5,699
With persons over 65	5,053
Family households	11,682
Single-person households	4,050
Persons per household	2.66
Persons per family	3.19

Labor & Employment

Total civilian labor force, 2007**	22,842
Unemployment rate	3.5%
Total civilian labor force, 2000	22,909
Unemployment rate	4.4%

Employed persons 16 years and over by occupation, 2000

Managers & professionals	10,344
Service occupations	2,417
Sales & office occupations	6,116
Farming, fishing & forestry	22
Construction & maintenance	1,263
Production & transportation	1,738
Self-employed persons	1,514

* US Census Bureau
** New Jersey Department of Labor

General Information

Township of West Orange
66 Main St
West Orange, NJ 07052
973-325-4155

Website	www.westorange.org
Year of incorporation	1979
Land/water area (sq. miles)	12.12/0.11
Form of government	Mayor-Council

Government

Legislative Districts

US Congressional	8, 10
State Legislative	27

Local Officials, 2009

Mayor	John F. McKeon
Administrator	John Sayers
Clerk	Karen Carnevale
Finance Dir	Edward J. Coleman Jr
Tax Assessor	Kevin Dillon
Tax Collector	Joseph Antonucci
Attorney	Richard Trenk
Building	Tom Tracy
Planning	Susan Borg
Engineering	Leonard Lepore
Public Works	Leonard Lepore
Police Chief	James Abbott
Fire Chief	Peter Smeraldo

Housing & Construction

Housing Units, 2000*

Total	16,901
Median rent	$857
Median SF home value	$209,200

Permits for New Residential Construction

	Units	Value
Total, 2006	152	$25,316,440
Single family	152	$25,316,440
Total, 2007	101	$29,292,225
Single family	101	$29,292,225

Real Property Valuation, 2008

	Parcels	Valuation
Total	14,094	$1,544,393,100
Vacant	593	24,871,000
Residential	12,991	1,230,142,100
Commercial	429	239,154,000
Industrial	39	9,370,900
Apartments	42	40,855,100
Farm land	0	0
Farm homestead	0	0

Average Property Value & Tax, 2008

Residential value	$94,692
Property tax	$11,482
Tax credit/rebate	$1,400

Public Library

West Orange Public Library
46 Mt Pleasant Ave
West Orange, NJ 07052
973-736-0198

Director	Cynthia Chamberlin

Library statistics, 2007

Population served	44,943
Full-time/total staff	11/21

	Total	Per capita
Holdings	172,108	3.83
Revenues	$2,666,050	$59.32
Expenditures	$2,498,904	$55.60
Annual visits	280,134	6.23
Internet terminals/annual users	21/75,378	

Public Safety

Number of officers, 2007	119

Crime	2006	2007
Total crimes	1,159	884
Violent	83	89
Murder	0	2
Rape	0	2
Robbery	52	48
Aggravated assault	31	37
Non-violent	1,076	795
Burglary	197	162
Larceny	697	501
Vehicle theft	182	132
Domestic violence	183	163
Arson	1	0
Total crime rate	26.2	20.3
Violent	1.9	2.0
Non-violent	24.3	18.3

Public School District

(for school year 2007-08 except as noted)

West Orange School District
179 Eagle Rock Ave.
West Orange, NJ 07052
(973) 669-5400

Superintendent	Jerry Tarnoff
Number of schools	11
Grade plan	K-12
Enrollment	6,359
Attendance rate, '06-07	95.5%
Dropout rate	3.0%
Students per teacher	9.0
Per pupil expenditure	$17,196
Median faculty salary	$60,472
Median administrator salary	$114,711
Grade 12 enrollment	408
High school graduation rate	94.9%

Assessment test results

(percent scoring at proficient or advanced level)

	Language	Math
NJASK-Grade 3	85.5%	89.2%
GEPA-Grade 8	61.1%	85.5%
HSPA-High School	66.9%	82.1%

SAT Score Averages, 2006-07

Pct tested	Math	Verbal	Writing
94%	486	472	468

Teacher Qualifications

Avg. years of experience	7
Highly-qualified teachers one subject/all subjects	100%/100%

No Child Left Behind

AYP, 2006-07	Needs Improvement

Municipal Finance

State Aid Programs, 2009

Total aid	$5,774,786
CMPTRA	781,622
Energy tax receipts	4,901,300
Garden State Trust	104

General Budget, 2008

Total tax levy	$187,602,793
County levy	27,218,954
County taxes	26,167,559
County library	0
County health	0
County open space	1,051,395
School levy	109,906,822
Muni. levy	50,477,018
Misc. revenues	18,964,441

Taxes

	2006	2007	2008
General tax rate per $100	10.6	11.39	12.126
County equalization ratio	26.25	23.58	22.26
Net valuation taxable	$1,529,967,300	$1,541,054,566	$1,547,180,594
State equalized value	$6,491,170,661	$6,914,081,906	$7,080,666,046

See Introduction for an explanation of all data sources.

Demographics & Socio-Economic Characteristics

(2000 US Census, except as noted)

Population
1980*	11,293
1990*	10,982
2000	10,987
Male	5,288
Female	5,699
2007 (estimate)*	11,568
Population density	3,908.1

Race & Hispanic Origin, 2000
Race
White	9,507
Black/African American	347
American Indian/Alaska Native	9
Asian	421
Native Hawaiian/Pacific Islander	4
Other race	348
Two or more races	351
Hispanic origin, total	1,105
Mexican	38
Puerto Rican	355
Cuban	60
Other Hispanic	652

Age & Nativity, 2000
Under 5 years	669
18 years and over	8,834
21 years and over	8,527
65 years and over	1,680
85 years and over	144
Median age	38.1
Native-born	8,675
Foreign-born	2,312

Educational Attainment, 2000
Population 25 years and over	8,001
Less than 9th grade	9.3%
High school grad or higher	81.8%
Bachelor's degree or higher	25.2%
Graduate degree	8.2%

Income & Poverty, 1999
Per capita income	$29,758
Median household income	$60,273
Median family income	$67,292
Persons in poverty	368
H'holds receiving public assistance	79
H'holds receiving social security	1,289

Households, 2000
Total households	4,397
With persons under 18	1,286
With persons over 65	1,219
Family households	3,025
Single-person households	1,121
Persons per household	2.49
Persons per family	3.01

Labor & Employment
Total civilian labor force, 2007**	6,501
Unemployment rate	3.1%
Total civilian labor force, 2000	6,036
Unemployment rate	3.4%

Employed persons 16 years and over by occupation, 2000
Managers & professionals	2,305
Service occupations	705
Sales & office occupations	1,668
Farming, fishing & forestry	0
Construction & maintenance	423
Production & transportation	730
Self-employed persons	334

General Information
Borough of West Paterson
5 Brophy Ln
West Paterson, NJ 07424
973-345-8100

Website	www.westpaterson.com
Year of incorporation	1914
Land/water area (sq. miles)	2.96/0.14
Form of government	Small Municipality

Government
Legislative Districts
US Congressional	8
State Legislative	34

Local Officials, 2009
Mayor	Pat Lepore
Manager	Kevin Galland
Clerk	Kevin Galland
Finance Dir	Frederick J. Tomkins
Tax Assessor	Tim Henderson
Tax Collector	Ida Renne
Attorney	Albert Buglione
Building	Felix Esposito
Comm Dev/Planning	NA
Engineering	Vincent DeNave
Public Works	George Galbraith
Police Chief	Robert Reda
Emerg/Fire Director	Paul Salomone Jr

Housing & Construction
Housing Units, 2000*
Total	4,497
Median rent	$854
Median SF home value	$195,100

Permits for New Residential Construction
	Units	Value
Total, 2006	209	$26,085,129
Single family	91	$11,968,751
Total, 2007	174	$22,612,022
Single family	90	$12,848,321

Real Property Valuation, 2008
	Parcels	Valuation
Total	3,739	$826,977,277
Vacant	412	30,631,513
Residential	3,088	584,381,724
Commercial	199	143,528,760
Industrial	32	34,306,600
Apartments	7	34,127,000
Farm land	1	1,680
Farm homestead	0	0

Average Property Value & Tax, 2008
Residential value	$189,243
Property tax	$8,054
Tax credit/rebate	$1,204

Public Library
Alfred H. Baumann Library
7 Brophy Lane
West Paterson, NJ 07424
973-345-8120

Director	Robert Lindsley

Library statistics, 2007
Population served	10,987
Full-time/total staff	1/4

	Total	Per capita
Holdings	42,431	3.86
Revenues	$574,535	$52.29
Expenditures	$488,485	$44.46
Annual visits	35,000	3.19
Internet terminals/annual users	11/11,262	

Public Safety
Number of officers, 2007	26

Crime	2006	2007
Total crimes	272	341
Violent	12	9
Murder	0	0
Rape	0	0
Robbery	6	5
Aggravated assault	6	4
Non-violent	260	332
Burglary	53	70
Larceny	188	244
Vehicle theft	19	18
Domestic violence	73	79
Arson	1	1
Total crime rate	24.2	30.4
Violent	1.1	0.8
Non-violent	23.1	29.6

Public School District
(for school year 2007-08 except as noted)

West Paterson School District
853 McBride Avenue
Woodland Park, NJ 07424
(973) 317-7700

Chief School Admin	Scott E. Rixtord
Number of schools	3
Grade plan	K-8
Enrollment	1,013
Attendance rate, '06-07	95.8%
Dropout rate	NA
Students per teacher	11.0
Per pupil expenditure	$12,784
Median faculty salary	$61,330
Median administrator salary	$112,075
Grade 12 enrollment	NA
High school graduation rate	NA

Assessment test results
(percent scoring at proficient or advanced level)
	Language	Math
NJASK-Grade 3	94.2%	84.3%
GEPA-Grade 8	67.2%	87.1%
HSPA-High School	NA	NA

SAT Score Averages, 2006-07
Pct tested	Math	Verbal	Writing
NA	NA	NA	NA

Teacher Qualifications
Avg. years of experience	8
Highly-qualified teachers one subject/all subjects	100%/100%

No Child Left Behind
AYP, 2006-07	Meets Standards

Municipal Finance
State Aid Programs, 2009
Total aid	$1,064,519
CMPTRA	334,569
Energy tax receipts	696,829
Garden State Trust	0

General Budget, 2008
Total tax levy	$35,218,617
County levy	9,160,633
County taxes	8,978,251
County library	0
County health	0
County open space	182,381
School levy	17,325,170
Muni. levy	8,732,814
Misc. revenues	4,591,178

Taxes
	2006	2007	2008
General tax rate per $100	3.84	4.12	4.257
County equalization ratio	54.05	48.44	45.63
Net valuation taxable	$804,892,162	$812,232,705	$827,550,839
State equalized value	$1,662,228,359	$1,779,377,152	$1,888,649,537

* US Census Bureau
** New Jersey Department of Labor

See Introduction for an explanation of all data sources.

Demographics & Socio-Economic Characteristics

(2000 US Census, except as noted)

Population
1980*	360
1990*	453
2000	448
Male	217
Female	231
2007 (estimate)*	406
Population density	1,561.5

Race & Hispanic Origin, 2000
Race
White	429
Black/African American	0
American Indian/Alaska Native	0
Asian	1
Native Hawaiian/Pacific Islander	0
Other race	10
Two or more races	8
Hispanic origin, total	17
Mexican	1
Puerto Rican	15
Cuban	0
Other Hispanic	1

Age & Nativity, 2000
Under 5 years	22
18 years and over	364
21 years and over	352
65 years and over	87
85 years and over	6
Median age	47.3
Native-born	449
Foreign-born	0

Educational Attainment, 2000
Population 25 years and over	348
Less than 9th grade	4.0%
High school grad or higher	69.0%
Bachelor's degree or higher	5.2%
Graduate degree	1.4%

Income & Poverty, 1999
Per capita income	$17,839
Median household income	$33,393
Median family income	$50,625
Persons in poverty	29
H'holds receiving public assistance	9
H'holds receiving social security	95

Households, 2000
Total households	202
With persons under 18	45
With persons over 65	70
Family households	118
Single-person households	74
Persons per household	2.22
Persons per family	2.92

Labor & Employment
Total civilian labor force, 2007**	281
Unemployment rate	10.1%
Total civilian labor force, 2000	234
Unemployment rate	12.0%

Employed persons 16 years and over by occupation, 2000
Managers & professionals	34
Service occupations	47
Sales & office occupations	73
Farming, fishing & forestry	0
Construction & maintenance	31
Production & transportation	21
Self-employed persons	2

* US Census Bureau
** New Jersey Department of Labor

See Introduction for an explanation of all data sources.

General Information
Borough of West Wildwood
701 W Glenwood Ave
West Wildwood, NJ 08260
609-522-4845
Website	www.westwildwoodnj.com
Year of incorporation	1920
Land/water area (sq. miles)	0.26/0.09
Form of government	Commission

Government
Legislative Districts
US Congressional	2
State Legislative	1

Local Officials, 2009
Mayor	Herbert C. Frederick
Manager/Admin	NA
Clerk	Dorothy Tomlin
Finance Dir	Judson Moore
Tax Assessor	Joseph Gallagher
Tax Collector	Dorothy Tomlin
Attorney	Paul Baldini
Building	Glenn Franzoi
Comm Dev/Planning	NA
Engineering	John Feairheller Jr
Public Works	Francis Pellegrino
Police Chief	Alan Fox
Emerg/Fire Director	William Cripps

Housing & Construction
Housing Units, 2000*
Total	775
Median rent	$765
Median SF home value	$87,600

Permits for New Residential Construction
	Units	Value
Total, 2006	18	$3,371,000
Single family	16	$2,955,000
Total, 2007	2	$552,160
Single family	2	$552,160

Real Property Valuation, 2008
	Parcels	Valuation
Total	945	$219,374,400
Vacant	170	25,796,200
Residential	762	186,625,800
Commercial	10	5,943,900
Industrial	0	0
Apartments	3	1,008,500
Farm land	0	0
Farm homestead	0	0

Average Property Value & Tax, 2008
Residential value	$244,916
Property tax	$3,550
Tax credit/rebate	$944

Public Library
No public municipal library

Library statistics, 2007
Population served	NA
Full-time/total staff	NA/NA

	Total	Per capita
Holdings	NA	NA
Revenues	NA	NA
Expenditures	NA	NA
Annual visits	NA	NA
Internet terminals/annual users	NA/NA	

Public Safety
Number of officers, 2007	7

Crime	2006	2007
Total crimes	20	25
Violent	0	4
Murder	0	0
Rape	0	1
Robbery	0	0
Aggravated assault	0	3
Non-violent	20	21
Burglary	6	8
Larceny	14	13
Vehicle theft	0	0
Domestic violence	7	11
Arson	0	0
Total crime rate	48.4	61.3
Violent	0.0	9.8
Non-violent	48.4	51.5

Public School District
(for school year 2007-08 except as noted)

West Wildwood School District
701 W. Glenwood Avenue
West Wildwood, NJ 08260

No schools in district - sends students to
North Wildwood schools

Per pupil expenditure	NA
Median faculty salary	NA
Median administrator salary	NA
Grade 12 enrollment	NA
High school graduation rate	NA

Assessment test results
(percent scoring at proficient or advanced level)
	Language	Math
NJASK-Grade 3	NA	NA
GEPA-Grade 8	NA	NA
HSPA-High School	NA	NA

SAT Score Averages, 2006-07
Pct tested	Math	Verbal	Writing
NA	NA	NA	NA

Teacher Qualifications
Avg. years of experience	NA
Highly-qualified teachers one subject/all subjects	NA/NA

No Child Left Behind
AYP, 2006-07	NA

Municipal Finance
State Aid Programs, 2009
Total aid	$53,674
CMPTRA	565
Energy tax receipts	51,364
Garden State Trust	0

General Budget, 2008
Total tax levy	$3,180,375
County levy	589,267
County taxes	468,383
County library	89,906
County health	0
County open space	30,978
School levy	1,066,688
Muni. levy	1,524,420
Misc. revenues	746,964

Taxes
	2006	2007	2008
General tax rate per $100	1.44	1.44	1.452
County equalization ratio	89.03	73.98	70.53
Net valuation taxable	$206,370,300	$214,772,552	$219,431,624
State equalized value	$279,015,384	$304,489,962	$320,592,583

Demographics & Socio-Economic Characteristics

(2000 US Census, except as noted)

Population

1980*	8,542
1990*	16,021
2000	21,907
Male	10,858
Female	11,049
2007 (estimate)*	26,447
Population density	1,016.8

Race & Hispanic Origin, 2000

Race

White	15,670
Black/African American	605
American Indian/Alaska Native	17
Asian	4,986
Native Hawaiian/Pacific Islander	2
Other race	236
Two or more races	391
Hispanic origin, total	892
Mexican	177
Puerto Rican	152
Cuban	63
Other Hispanic	500

Age & Nativity, 2000

Under 5 years	1,541
18 years and over	14,939
21 years and over	14,470
65 years and over	1,349
85 years and over	110
Median age	37.0
Native-born	17,001
Foreign-born	4,906

Educational Attainment, 2000

Population 25 years and over	14,026
Less than 9th grade	1.5%
High school grad or higher	96.9%
Bachelor's degree or higher	73.9%
Graduate degree	39.0%

Income & Poverty, 1999

Per capita income	$48,511
Median household income	$116,335
Median family income	$127,877
Persons in poverty	548
H'holds receiving public assistance	63
H'holds receiving social security	961

Households, 2000

Total households	7,282
With persons under 18	3,730
With persons over 65	993
Family households	5,986
Single-person households	1,061
Persons per household	3.01
Persons per family	3.36

Labor & Employment

Total civilian labor force, 2007**	14,334
Unemployment rate	1.9%
Total civilian labor force, 2000	11,228
Unemployment rate	3.0%

Employed persons 16 years and over by occupation, 2000

Managers & professionals	7,731
Service occupations	487
Sales & office occupations	2,230
Farming, fishing & forestry	0
Construction & maintenance	175
Production & transportation	264
Self-employed persons	526

General Information

Township of West Windsor
271 Clarksville Rd
PO Box 38
West Windsor, NJ 08550
609-799-2400

Website	www.westwindsornj.org
Year of incorporation	1797
Land/water area (sq. miles)	26.01/0.32
Form of government	Mayor-Council

Government

Legislative Districts

US Congressional	12
State Legislative	14

Local Officials, 2009

Mayor	Shing-Fu Hsueh
Manager	Christopher R. Marion
Clerk	Sharon Young
Finance Dir	Joanne R. Louth
Tax Assessor	Steven Benner
Tax Collector	Rita Carr
Attorney	Michael Herbert
Building	Joseph Valeri
Planning	M. Patricia Ward
Engineering	Francis Guzik
Public Works	Alex Drummond
Police Chief	Joseph Pica
Emerg/Fire Director	Jim Yates

Housing & Construction

Housing Units, 2000*

Total	7,450
Median rent	$1,198
Median SF home value	$333,800

Permits for New Residential Construction

	Units	Value
Total, 2006	154	$11,451,838
Single family	154	$11,451,838
Total, 2007	62	$11,014,117
Single family	62	$11,014,117

Real Property Valuation, 2008

	Parcels	Valuation
Total	8,720	$6,223,235,653
Vacant	549	79,902,710
Residential	7,773	4,329,353,700
Commercial	253	1,551,438,394
Industrial	10	77,666,900
Apartments	5	151,373,800
Farm land	98	1,683,349
Farm homestead	32	31,816,800

Average Property Value & Tax, 2008

Residential value	$558,766
Property tax	$11,741
Tax credit/rebate	$1,290

Public Library

West Windsor Branch Library‡
333 N Post Rd
Princeton Jnc, NJ 08550
609-799-0462

Branch Librarian	Kaija Greenberg

Library statistics, 2007

see Mercer County profile
for library system statistics

Public Safety

Number of officers, 2007	47

Crime	2006	2007
Total crimes	563	555
Violent	17	15
Murder	1	0
Rape	1	0
Robbery	7	3
Aggravated assault	8	12
Non-violent	546	540
Burglary	53	55
Larceny	474	457
Vehicle theft	19	28
Domestic violence	57	57
Arson	1	1
Total crime rate	21.7	21.1
Violent	0.7	0.6
Non-violent	21.0	20.5

Public School District

(for school year 2007-08 except as noted)

West Windsor-Plainsboro Reg. School Dist.
505 Village Road West, PO Box 505
Princeton Junction, NJ 08550
(609) 716-5000

Chief School Admin	Victoria Kniewel
Number of schools	10
Grade plan	K-12
Enrollment	9,669
Attendance rate, '06-07	96.5%
Dropout rate	0.1%
Students per teacher	11.4
Per pupil expenditure	$14,421
Median faculty salary	$74,700
Median administrator salary	$119,185
Grade 12 enrollment	714
High school graduation rate	99.0%

Assessment test results

(percent scoring at proficient or advanced level)

	Language	Math
NJASK-Grade 3	94.5%	95.8%
GEPA-Grade 8	91.3%	95.4%
HSPA-High School	91.4%	94.4%

SAT Score Averages, 2006-07

Pct tested	Math	Verbal	Writing
NA	NA	NA	NA

Teacher Qualifications

Avg. years of experience	13
Highly-qualified teachers one subject/all subjects	100%/100%

No Child Left Behind

AYP, 2006-07	Meets Standards

Municipal Finance

State Aid Programs, 2009

Total aid	$2,929,041
CMPTRA	0
Energy tax receipts	2,806,961
Garden State Trust	4,402

General Budget, 2008

Total tax levy	$131,100,089
County levy	31,507,049
County taxes	26,948,947
County library	2,708,353
County health	0
County open space	1,849,750
School levy	78,132,959
Muni. levy	21,460,081
Misc. revenues	15,841,732

Taxes	2006	2007	2008
General tax rate per $100	1.91	1.99	2.102
County equalization ratio	123.05	108.25	101.34
Net valuation taxable	$6,289,299,663	$6,303,495,043	$6,239,377,281
State equalized value	$6,048,380,187	$6,220,359,254	$6,210,264,902

‡ Branch of county library
* US Census Bureau
** New Jersey Department of Labor

See Introduction for an explanation of all data sources.

Demographics & Socio-Economic Characteristics
(2000 US Census, except as noted)

Population
1980*	3,383
1990*	6,004
2000	7,217
Male	3,418
Female	3,799
2007 (estimate)*	8,618
Population density	780.6

Race & Hispanic Origin, 2000
Race
White	5,110
Black/African American	1,535
American Indian/Alaska Native	20
Asian	219
Native Hawaiian/Pacific Islander	3
Other race	132
Two or more races	198
Hispanic origin, total	448
Mexican	24
Puerto Rican	296
Cuban	8
Other Hispanic	120

Age & Nativity, 2000
Under 5 years	525
18 years and over	5,104
21 years and over	4,888
65 years and over	659
85 years and over	39
Median age	35.8
Native-born	6,730
Foreign-born	470

Educational Attainment, 2000
Population 25 years and over	4,729
Less than 9th grade	2.0%
High school grad or higher	90.9%
Bachelor's degree or higher	26.2%
Graduate degree	6.9%

Income & Poverty, 1999
Per capita income	$26,594
Median household income	$63,973
Median family income	$69,656
Persons in poverty	180
H'holds receiving public assistance	12
H'holds receiving social security	518

Households, 2000
Total households	2,525
With persons under 18	1,158
With persons over 65	467
Family households	1,966
Single-person households	456
Persons per household	2.83
Persons per family	3.24

Labor & Employment
Total civilian labor force, 2007**	4,249
Unemployment rate	3.2%
Total civilian labor force, 2000	3,724
Unemployment rate	3.2%

Employed persons 16 years and over by occupation, 2000
Managers & professionals	1,301
Service occupations	521
Sales & office occupations	1,208
Farming, fishing & forestry	0
Construction & maintenance	170
Production & transportation	404
Self-employed persons	108

* US Census Bureau
** New Jersey Department of Labor

General Information
Township of Westampton
710 Rancocas Rd
Westampton, NJ 08060
609-267-1891
Website	www.westampton.com
Year of incorporation	1850
Land/water area (sq. miles)	11.04/0.12
Form of government	Township

Government
Legislative Districts
US Congressional	3
State Legislative	7

Local Officials, 2009
Mayor	Sidney Camp
Manager	Donna Ryan
Clerk	Donna Ryan
Finance Dir	Robert Hudnell
Tax Assessor	Marie Procacci
Tax Collector	Carol Brown-Layou
Attorney	Richard Rybak
Building	Gene Blair
Comm Dev/Planning	NA
Engineering	David Denton
Public Works	NA
Police Chief	Steven VanSciver
Emerg/Fire Director	Wylie Johnson

Housing & Construction
Housing Units, 2000*
Total	2,581
Median rent	$1,112
Median SF home value	$127,300

Permits for New Residential Construction
	Units	Value
Total, 2006	25	$6,597,876
Single family	25	$6,597,876
Total, 2007	31	$7,827,650
Single family	31	$7,827,650

Real Property Valuation, 2008
	Parcels	Valuation
Total	3,480	$689,893,550
Vacant	168	10,919,600
Residential	3,112	463,505,000
Commercial	112	199,197,200
Industrial	2	11,261,400
Apartments	0	0
Farm land	65	996,650
Farm homestead	21	4,013,700

Average Property Value & Tax, 2008
Residential value	$149,224
Property tax	$4,631
Tax credit/rebate	$828

Public Library
No public municipal library

Library statistics, 2007
Population served	NA
Full-time/total staff	NA/NA

	Total	Per capita
Holdings	NA	NA
Revenues	NA	NA
Expenditures	NA	NA
Annual visits	NA	NA
Internet terminals/annual users	NA/NA	

Public Safety
Number of officers, 2007	23

Crime	2006	2007
Total crimes	250	207
Violent	20	17
Murder	0	0
Rape	3	0
Robbery	3	6
Aggravated assault	14	11
Non-violent	230	190
Burglary	24	21
Larceny	182	156
Vehicle theft	24	13
Domestic violence	108	115
Arson	0	4
Total crime rate	28.9	23.6
Violent	2.3	1.9
Non-violent	26.6	21.7

Public School District
(for school year 2007-08 except as noted)

Westampton Township School District
710 Rancocas Road
Westampton, NJ 08060
(609) 267-2053
Superintendent	Walter Keiss (Int)
Number of schools	2
Grade plan	K-8
Enrollment	930
Attendance rate, '06-07	95.5%
Dropout rate	NA
Students per teacher	10.7
Per pupil expenditure	$10,901
Median faculty salary	$48,459
Median administrator salary	$90,000
Grade 12 enrollment	NA
High school graduation rate	NA

Assessment test results
(percent scoring at proficient or advanced level)
	Language	Math
NJASK-Grade 3	86.9%	86.9%
GEPA-Grade 8	75.4%	86.0%
HSPA-High School	NA	NA

SAT Score Averages, 2006-07
Pct tested	Math	Verbal	Writing
NA	NA	NA	NA

Teacher Qualifications
Avg. years of experience	7
Highly-qualified teachers one subject/all subjects	95.5%/95.5%

No Child Left Behind
AYP, 2006-07 ... Meets Standards

Municipal Finance
State Aid Programs, 2009
Total aid	$843,724
CMPTRA	60,984
Energy tax receipts	760,370
Garden State Trust	1,453

General Budget, 2008
Total tax levy	$21,452,044
County levy	4,797,919
County taxes	3,940,100
County library	363,798
County health	0
County open space	494,021
School levy	12,355,482
Muni. levy	4,298,644
Misc. revenues	4,104,845

Taxes
	2006	2007	2008
General tax rate per $100	3.034	3.09	3.104
County equalization ratio	65.98	59.78	56.02
Net valuation taxable	$656,227,150	$673,846,216	$691,206,702
State equalized value	$1,099,184,157	$1,201,813,201	$1,247,058,096

See Introduction for an explanation of all data sources.

Demographics & Socio-Economic Characteristics
(2000 US Census, except as noted)

Population
1980*	30,447
1990*	28,870
2000	29,644
Male	14,209
Female	15,435
2007 (estimate)*	29,556
Population density	4,391.7

Race & Hispanic Origin, 2000
Race
White	26,675
Black/African American	1,151
American Indian/Alaska Native	27
Asian	1,208
Native Hawaiian/Pacific Islander	3
Other race	185
Two or more races	395
Hispanic origin, total	836
Mexican	104
Puerto Rican	176
Cuban	103
Other Hispanic	453

Age & Nativity, 2000
Under 5 years	2,369
18 years and over	21,235
21 years and over	20,704
65 years and over	4,015
85 years and over	528
Median age	38.6
Native-born	26,940
Foreign-born	2,704

Educational Attainment, 2000
Population 25 years and over	20,052
Less than 9th grade	1.8%
High school grad or higher	95.4%
Bachelor's degree or higher	62.5%
Graduate degree	29.8%

Income & Poverty, 1999
Per capita income	$47,187
Median household income	$98,390
Median family income	$112,145
Persons in poverty	791
H'holds receiving public assistance	93
H'holds receiving social security	2,626

Households, 2000
Total households	10,622
With persons under 18	4,454
With persons over 65	2,716
Family households	8,181
Single-person households	2,052
Persons per household	2.77
Persons per family	3.20

Labor & Employment
Total civilian labor force, 2007**	15,624
Unemployment rate	2.4%
Total civilian labor force, 2000	14,907
Unemployment rate	2.2%

Employed persons 16 years and over by occupation, 2000
Managers & professionals	8,811
Service occupations	1,102
Sales & office occupations	3,510
Farming, fishing & forestry	8
Construction & maintenance	484
Production & transportation	660
Self-employed persons	942

General Information
Town of Westfield
425 E Broad St
Westfield, NJ 07090
908-789-4033

Website	www.westfieldnj.gov
Year of incorporation	1903
Land/water area (sq. miles)	6.73/0.02
Form of government	Special Charter

Government
Legislative Districts
US Congressional	7
State Legislative	21

Local Officials, 2009
Mayor	Andrew Skibitsky
Manager	James Gildea
Clerk	Claire Gray
Finance Dir	Liy-Huei Tsai
Tax Assessor	Ann Switzer
Tax Collector	Susan Noon
Attorney	Robert Cockren
Building	Steve Freedman
Planning	(private firm)
Engineering	Kris McAloon
Public Works	Claude Shafter
Police Chief	John Parizeau
Emerg/Fire Director	Daniel Kelly

Housing & Construction
Housing Units, 2000*
Total	10,819
Median rent	$1,048
Median SF home value	$346,000

Permits for New Residential Construction
	Units	Value
Total, 2006	81	$20,798,335
Single family	81	$20,798,335
Total, 2007	54	$17,778,603
Single family	54	$17,778,603

Real Property Valuation, 2008
	Parcels	Valuation
Total	9,792	$1,882,187,000
Vacant	243	11,548,700
Residential	9,107	1,670,669,600
Commercial	425	176,297,300
Industrial	4	1,988,100
Apartments	12	21,679,100
Farm land	1	4,200
Farm homestead	0	0

Average Property Value & Tax, 2008
Residential value	$183,449
Property tax	$12,233
Tax credit/rebate	$1,319

Public Library
Westfield Memorial Library
550 E Broad St
Westfield, NJ 07090
908-789-4090

Director	Philip Israel

Library statistics, 2007
Population served	29,644
Full-time/total staff	8/14

	Total	Per capita
Holdings	166,862	5.63
Revenues	$2,431,139	$82.01
Expenditures	$2,189,487	$73.86
Annual visits	145,081	4.89
Internet terminals/annual users	26/24,584	

Public Safety
Number of officers, 2007	59

Crime	2006	2007
Total crimes	351	371
Violent	15	19
Murder	0	0
Rape	2	2
Robbery	6	2
Aggravated assault	7	15
Non-violent	336	352
Burglary	65	40
Larceny	259	300
Vehicle theft	12	12
Domestic violence	118	84
Arson	3	1
Total crime rate	11.7	12.4
Violent	0.5	0.6
Non-violent	11.2	11.8

Public School District
(for school year 2007-08 except as noted)

Westfield School District
302 Elm Street
Westfield, NJ 07090
(908) 789-4420

Superintendent	Margaret Dolan
Number of schools	9
Grade plan	K-12
Enrollment	6,150
Attendance rate, '06-07	95.4%
Dropout rate	0.4%
Students per teacher	11.6
Per pupil expenditure	$12,866
Median faculty salary	$60,299
Median administrator salary	$114,572
Grade 12 enrollment	442
High school graduation rate	98.5%

Assessment test results
(percent scoring at proficient or advanced level)
	Language	Math
NJASK-Grade 3	97.9%	95.0%
GEPA-Grade 8	87.1%	91.5%
HSPA-High School	91.9%	95.5%

SAT Score Averages, 2006-07
Pct tested	Math	Verbal	Writing
103%	578	565	570

Teacher Qualifications
Avg. years of experience	9
Highly-qualified teachers one subject/all subjects	100%/100%

No Child Left Behind
AYP, 2006-07	Meets Standards

Municipal Finance
State Aid Programs, 2009
Total aid	$4,182,079
CMPTRA	1,161,069
Energy tax receipts	2,853,727
Garden State Trust	0

General Budget, 2008
Total tax levy	$125,663,056
County levy	26,270,731
County taxes	25,125,241
County library	0
County health	0
County open space	1,145,490
School levy	77,318,188
Muni. levy	22,074,137
Misc. revenues	15,802,851

Taxes
Taxes	2006	2007	2008
General tax rate per $100	6.083	6.328	6.669
County equalization ratio	28.11	26.37	24.72
Net valuation taxable	$1,849,664,900	$1,864,139,453	$1,884,462,778
State equalized value	$7,016,292,401	$7,535,727,649	$7,716,156,926

* US Census Bureau
** New Jersey Department of Labor

See Introduction for an explanation of all data sources.

Demographics & Socio-Economic Characteristics

(2000 US Census, except as noted)

Population

1980*	4,786
1990*	4,573
2000	4,500
Male	2,183
Female	2,317
2007 (estimate)*	4,474
Population density	4,660.4

Race & Hispanic Origin, 2000

Race
White	4,206
Black/African American	122
American Indian/Alaska Native	6
Asian	45
Native Hawaiian/Pacific Islander	1
Other race	58
Two or more races	62
Hispanic origin, total	133
Mexican	21
Puerto Rican	59
Cuban	2
Other Hispanic	51

Age & Nativity, 2000

Under 5 years	253
18 years and over	3,396
21 years and over	3,236
65 years and over	633
85 years and over	63
Median age	36.6
Native-born	4,398
Foreign-born	102

Educational Attainment, 2000

Population 25 years and over	3,033
Less than 9th grade	4.5%
High school grad or higher	75.5%
Bachelor's degree or higher	8.9%
Graduate degree	1.2%

Income & Poverty, 1999

Per capita income	$18,747
Median household income	$39,570
Median family income	$49,005
Persons in poverty	389
H'holds receiving public assistance	41
H'holds receiving social security	535

Households, 2000

Total households	1,812
With persons under 18	590
With persons over 65	471
Family households	1,126
Single-person households	577
Persons per household	2.48
Persons per family	3.15

Labor & Employment

Total civilian labor force, 2007**	2,833
Unemployment rate	5.4%
Total civilian labor force, 2000	2,388
Unemployment rate	5.0%

Employed persons 16 years and over by occupation, 2000
Managers & professionals	466
Service occupations	350
Sales & office occupations	707
Farming, fishing & forestry	0
Construction & maintenance	339
Production & transportation	406
Self-employed persons	108

* US Census Bureau
** New Jersey Department of Labor

General Information

Borough of Westville
1035 Broadway
Westville, NJ 08093
856-456-0030

Website	www.westville-nj.com
Year of incorporation	1914
Land/water area (sq. miles)	0.96/0.39
Form of government	Borough

Government

Legislative Districts

US Congressional	1
State Legislative	5

Local Officials, 2009

Mayor	Russell W. Welsh Jr
Administrator	William J. Bittner Jr
Clerk	Christine A. Helder
Finance Dir	John A. Bruno Jr
Tax Assessor	Roy A. Duffield
Tax Collector	Christine A. Helder
Attorney	John Alice
Building	Robert Kunkle
Land Use Official	Michael Sautter (Chr)
Engineering	Norman Rodgers
Public Works	Donna M. Domico
Police Chief	Frederick Lederer III
Emerg/Fire Director	Chuck Murtaugh

Housing & Construction

Housing Units, 2000*

Total	1,938
Median rent	$569
Median SF home value	$91,500

Permits for New Residential Construction

	Units	Value
Total, 2006	6	$659,666
Single family	6	$659,666
Total, 2007	1	$92,304
Single family	1	$92,304

Real Property Valuation, 2008

	Parcels	Valuation
Total	1,605	$161,177,100
Vacant	67	1,366,600
Residential	1,395	121,349,500
Commercial	99	16,897,500
Industrial	34	15,245,800
Apartments	10	6,317,700
Farm land	0	0
Farm homestead	0	0

Average Property Value & Tax, 2008

Residential value	$86,989
Property tax	$4,594
Tax credit/rebate	$868

Public Library

Westville Public Library
1035 Broadway
Westville, NJ 08093
856-456-0357

Director	Gwen Carotenuto

Library statistics, 2007

Population served	4,500
Full-time/total staff	0/0

	Total	Per capita
Holdings	27,811	6.18
Revenues	$110,162	$24.48
Expenditures	$95,660	$21.26
Annual visits	10,114	2.25
Internet terminals/annual users		3/4,224

Public Safety

Number of officers, 2007	10

Crime	2006	2007
Total crimes	127	155
Violent	10	23
Murder	0	0
Rape	0	0
Robbery	2	8
Aggravated assault	8	15
Non-violent	117	132
Burglary	30	34
Larceny	72	78
Vehicle theft	15	20
Domestic violence	52	49
Arson	2	0
Total crime rate	28.4	34.8
Violent	2.2	5.2
Non-violent	26.2	29.6

Public School District

(for school year 2007-08 except as noted)

Westville School District
101 Birch Street
Westville, NJ 08093
(856) 456-0235

Superintendent	Shannon M. Whalen
Number of schools	1
Grade plan	K-6
Enrollment	353
Attendance rate, '06-07	95.4%
Dropout rate	NA
Students per teacher	9.5
Per pupil expenditure	$12,014
Median faculty salary	$53,545
Median administrator salary	$98,700
Grade 12 enrollment	NA
High school graduation rate	NA

Assessment test results

(percent scoring at proficient or advanced level)
	Language	Math
NJASK-Grade 3	96.5%	82.1%
GEPA-Grade 8	NA	NA
HSPA-High School	NA	NA

SAT Score Averages, 2006-07

Pct tested	Math	Verbal	Writing
NA	NA	NA	NA

Teacher Qualifications

Avg. years of experience	12
Highly-qualified teachers one subject/all subjects	100%/100%

No Child Left Behind

AYP, 2006-07	Meets Standards

Municipal Finance

State Aid Programs, 2009

Total aid	$481,165
CMPTRA	117,615
Energy tax receipts	361,144
Garden State Trust	0

General Budget, 2008

Total tax levy	$8,524,571
County levy	1,576,261
County taxes	1,461,714
County library	0
County health	0
County open space	114,547
School levy	4,466,764
Muni. levy	2,481,547
Misc. revenues	2,037,453

Taxes	2006	2007	2008
General tax rate per $100	4.516	4.979	5.282
County equalization ratio	73.04	61.88	56.62
Net valuation taxable	$160,791,900	$161,473,863	$161,406,296
State equalized value	$260,129,048	$285,002,895	$288,148,274

See Introduction for an explanation of all data sources.

Demographics & Socio-Economic Characteristics

(2000 US Census, except as noted)

Population
1980*	10,714
1990*	10,446
2000	10,999
Male	5,218
Female	5,781
2007 (estimate)*	10,780
Population density	4,646.6

Race & Hispanic Origin, 2000
Race
White	9,525
Black/African American	629
American Indian/Alaska Native	15
Asian	483
Native Hawaiian/Pacific Islander	1
Other race	184
Two or more races	162
Hispanic origin, total	660
Mexican	135
Puerto Rican	113
Cuban	60
Other Hispanic	352

Age & Nativity, 2000
Under 5 years	762
18 years and over	8,631
21 years and over	8,392
65 years and over	1,752
85 years and over	320
Median age	38.6
Native-born	9,317
Foreign-born	1,682

Educational Attainment, 2000
Population 25 years and over	8,052
Less than 9th grade	4.8%
High school grad or higher	88.1%
Bachelor's degree or higher	37.4%
Graduate degree	11.7%

Income & Poverty, 1999
Per capita income	$32,083
Median household income	$59,868
Median family income	$77,105
Persons in poverty	474
H'holds receiving public assistance	58
H'holds receiving social security	1,315

Households, 2000
Total households	4,485
With persons under 18	1,348
With persons over 65	1,279
Family households	2,878
Single-person households	1,395
Persons per household	2.42
Persons per family	3.08

Labor & Employment
Total civilian labor force, 2007**	6,218
Unemployment rate	2.0%
Total civilian labor force, 2000	5,874
Unemployment rate	2.1%

Employed persons 16 years and over by occupation, 2000
Managers & professionals	2,444
Service occupations	839
Sales & office occupations	1,678
Farming, fishing & forestry	0
Construction & maintenance	372
Production & transportation	417
Self-employed persons	311

General Information
Borough of Westwood
101 Washington Ave
Westwood, NJ 07675
201-664-7100
Website	www.westwoodnj.gov
Year of incorporation	1894
Land/water area (sq. miles)	2.32/0.00
Form of government	Borough

Government

Legislative Districts
US Congressional	5
State Legislative	39

Local Officials, 2009
Mayor	John Birkner Jr
Administrator	Robert S. Hoffmann
Clerk	Karen Hughes
Finance Dir	Raymond Herr
Tax Assessor	Barbara Potash
Tax Collector	Stephanie Stokes
Attorney	Russell Huntington
Building	Armand Marini
Planning	Jaymee Hodges
Engineering	Stephen Boswell
Public Works	Rick Woods
Police Chief	Frank Regino
Emerg/Fire Director	Marc Fedorchak

Housing & Construction

Housing Units, 2000*
Total	4,610
Median rent	$996
Median SF home value	$239,300

Permits for New Residential Construction
	Units	Value
Total, 2006	6	$1,027,800
Single family	6	$1,027,800
Total, 2007	7	$1,673,182
Single family	7	$1,673,182

Real Property Valuation, 2008
	Parcels	Valuation
Total	3,491	$1,630,044,978
Vacant	97	11,385,500
Residential	3,095	1,224,665,600
Commercial	238	247,613,678
Industrial	34	39,287,500
Apartments	27	107,092,700
Farm land	0	0
Farm homestead	0	0

Average Property Value & Tax, 2008
Residential value	$395,692
Property tax	$8,274
Tax credit/rebate	$1,266

Public Library
Westwood Public Library
49 Park Ave
Westwood, NJ 07675
201-664-0583
Director	Martha Urbiel

Library statistics, 2007
Population served	10,999
Full-time/total staff	3/6

	Total	Per capita
Holdings	51,916	4.72
Revenues	$747,595	$67.97
Expenditures	$753,033	$68.46
Annual visits	109,886	9.99
Internet terminals/annual users	11/15,000	

Public Safety
Number of officers, 2007	25

Crime	2006	2007
Total crimes	145	119
Violent	3	11
Murder	0	0
Rape	0	0
Robbery	1	2
Aggravated assault	2	9
Non-violent	142	108
Burglary	17	18
Larceny	118	84
Vehicle theft	7	6
Domestic violence	35	29
Arson	0	0
Total crime rate	**13.2**	**10.9**
Violent	0.3	1.0
Non-violent	12.9	9.9

Public School District
(for school year 2007-08 except as noted)

Westwood Regional School District
701 Ridgewood Road
Township of Washington, NJ 07676
(201) 664-2765
Superintendent	Geoffrey Zoeller
Number of schools	6
Grade plan	K-12
Enrollment	2,617
Attendance rate, '06-07	96.2%
Dropout rate	0.1%
Students per teacher	10.3
Per pupil expenditure	$14,691
Median faculty salary	$55,793
Median administrator salary	$112,104
Grade 12 enrollment	165
High school graduation rate	98.7%

Assessment test results
(percent scoring at proficient or advanced level)
	Language	Math
NJASK-Grade 3	95.6%	95.6%
GEPA-Grade 8	76.9%	91.3%
HSPA-High School	83.1%	89.9%

SAT Score Averages, 2006-07
Pct tested	Math	Verbal	Writing
92%	534	492	494

Teacher Qualifications
Avg. years of experience	8
Highly-qualified teachers one subject/all subjects	99.5%/99.5%

No Child Left Behind
AYP, 2006-07	Meets Standards

Municipal Finance

State Aid Programs, 2009
Total aid	$1,314,289
CMPTRA	175,871
Energy tax receipts	1,104,873
Garden State Trust	0

General Budget, 2008
Total tax levy	$34,119,796
County levy	3,634,747
County taxes	3,438,104
County library	0
County health	0
County open space	196,643
School levy	19,584,138
Muni. levy	10,900,911
Misc. revenues	4,491,460

Taxes
	2006	2007	2008
General tax rate per $100	1.97	2.03	2.093
County equalization ratio	93.12	87.06	83.39
Net valuation taxable	$1,609,472,600	$1,616,567,615	$1,631,694,098
State equalized value	$1,850,565,613	$1,938,277,082	$1,999,742,989

* US Census Bureau
** New Jersey Department of Labor

See Introduction for an explanation of all data sources.

Demographics & Socio-Economic Characteristics
(2000 US Census, except as noted)

Population
1980*	1,260
1990*	1,957
2000	2,257
Male	1,085
Female	1,172
2007 (estimate)*	2,257
Population density	185.0

Race & Hispanic Origin, 2000
Race
White	2,076
Black/African American	108
American Indian/Alaska Native	9
Asian	18
Native Hawaiian/Pacific Islander	0
Other race	23
Two or more races	23
Hispanic origin, total	86
Mexican	24
Puerto Rican	42
Cuban	2
Other Hispanic	18

Age & Nativity, 2000
Under 5 years	141
18 years and over	1,694
21 years and over	1,628
65 years and over	387
85 years and over	29
Median age	39.4
Native-born	2,191
Foreign-born	59

Educational Attainment, 2000
Population 25 years and over	1,530
Less than 9th grade	5.6%
High school grad or higher	79.5%
Bachelor's degree or higher	14.2%
Graduate degree	4.4%

Income & Poverty, 1999
Per capita income	$18,987
Median household income	$45,882
Median family income	$49,800
Persons in poverty	115
H'holds receiving public assistance	29
H'holds receiving social security	297

Households, 2000
Total households	851
With persons under 18	283
With persons over 65	276
Family households	624
Single-person households	183
Persons per household	2.65
Persons per family	3.06

Labor & Employment
Total civilian labor force, 2007**	1,172
Unemployment rate	3.4%
Total civilian labor force, 2000	1,098
Unemployment rate	3.8%

Employed persons 16 years and over by occupation, 2000
Managers & professionals	255
Service occupations	228
Sales & office occupations	310
Farming, fishing & forestry	0
Construction & maintenance	139
Production & transportation	124
Self-employed persons	46

* US Census Bureau
** New Jersey Department of Labor

See Introduction for an explanation of all data sources.

General Information
Township of Weymouth
45 S Jersey Ave
Dorothy, NJ 08317
609-476-2633

Website	www.weymouthnj.org
Year of incorporation	1798
Land/water area (sq. miles)	12.20/0.37
Form of government	Township

Government
Legislative Districts
US Congressional	2
State Legislative	2

Local Officials, 2009
Mayor	Frank C. Craig
Manager	Bonnie Yearsley
Clerk	Bonnie Yearsley
Finance Dir	Dawn Gorman
Tax Assessor	Bernadette Leonardi
Tax Collector	Debra D'Amore
Attorney	James J. Carroll
Building	NA
Comm Dev/Planning	NA
Engineering	Fralinger Engineering
Public Works	Ronald Carroll
Police Chief	NA
Emerg/Fire Director	Robert Gibney

Housing & Construction
Housing Units, 2000*
Total	909
Median rent	$725
Median SF home value	$119,000

Permits for New Residential Construction
	Units	Value
Total, 2006	3	$174,492
Single family	3	$174,492
Total, 2007	3	$322,160
Single family	3	$322,160

Real Property Valuation, 2008
	Parcels	Valuation
Total	1,018	$95,787,800
Vacant	319	5,468,900
Residential	654	78,687,800
Commercial	33	9,525,000
Industrial	1	206,700
Apartments	2	1,439,900
Farm land	5	28,200
Farm homestead	4	431,300

Average Property Value & Tax, 2008
Residential value	$120,242
Property tax	$3,400
Tax credit/rebate	$677

Public Library
No public municipal library

Library statistics, 2007
Population served	NA
Full-time/total staff	NA/NA

	Total	Per capita
Holdings	NA	NA
Revenues	NA	NA
Expenditures	NA	NA
Annual visits	NA	NA
Internet terminals/annual users	NA/NA	

Public Safety
Number of officers, 2007 0

Crime	2006	2007
Total crimes	29	20
Violent	1	3
Murder	0	0
Rape	0	0
Robbery	0	0
Aggravated assault	1	3
Non-violent	28	17
Burglary	10	6
Larceny	17	10
Vehicle theft	1	1
Domestic violence	4	16
Arson	0	0
Total crime rate	12.5	8.7
Violent	0.4	1.3
Non-violent	12.0	7.4

Public School District
(for school year 2007-08 except as noted)

Weymouth Township School District
1202 Eleventh Avenue
Dorothy, NJ 08317
(609) 476-2412

Administrative Principal	Donna Van Horn
Number of schools	1
Grade plan	K-8
Enrollment	256
Attendance rate, '06-07	95.7%
Dropout rate	NA
Students per teacher	10.3
Per pupil expenditure	$11,718
Median faculty salary	$45,141
Median administrator salary	$67,092
Grade 12 enrollment	NA
High school graduation rate	NA

Assessment test results
(percent scoring at proficient or advanced level)
	Language	Math
NJASK-Grade 3	85.7%	76.2%
GEPA-Grade 8	51.8%	77.8%
HSPA-High School	NA	NA

SAT Score Averages, 2006-07
Pct tested	Math	Verbal	Writing
NA	NA	NA	NA

Teacher Qualifications
Avg. years of experience	13
Highly-qualified teachers one subject/all subjects	100%/100%

No Child Left Behind
AYP, 2006-07 .... Meets Standards

Municipal Finance
State Aid Programs, 2009
Total aid	$367,172
CMPTRA	3,938
Energy tax receipts	345,206
Garden State Trust	7,626

General Budget, 2008
Total tax levy	$2,722,317
County levy	392,880
County taxes	309,501
County library	39,720
County health	16,253
County open space	27,406
School levy	1,727,797
Muni. levy	601,640
Misc. revenues	816,920

Taxes	2006	2007	2008
General tax rate per $100	2.695	2.756	2.828
County equalization ratio	79.46	79.59	70.35
Net valuation taxable	$91,904,500	$94,354,890	$96,270,290
State equalized value	$115,957,351	$133,907,442	$187,094,218

Demographics & Socio-Economic Characteristics
(2000 US Census, except as noted)

Population
1980*	5,485
1990*	5,405
2000	6,298
Male	3,043
Female	3,255
2007 (estimate)*	6,127
Population density	2,797.7

Race & Hispanic Origin, 2000
Race
White	5,170
Black/African American	277
American Indian/Alaska Native	28
Asian	198
Native Hawaiian/Pacific Islander	0
Other race	454
Two or more races	171
Hispanic origin, total	1,462
Mexican	147
Puerto Rican	391
Cuban	18
Other Hispanic	906

Age & Nativity, 2000
Under 5 years	464
18 years and over	4,660
21 years and over	4,479
65 years and over	711
85 years and over	91
Median age	35.7
Native-born	5,430
Foreign-born	868

Educational Attainment, 2000
Population 25 years and over	4,218
Less than 9th grade	5.1%
High school grad or higher	80.9%
Bachelor's degree or higher	22.7%
Graduate degree	7.9%

Income & Poverty, 1999
Per capita income	$25,168
Median household income	$56,580
Median family income	$64,957
Persons in poverty	517
H'holds receiving public assistance	45
H'holds receiving social security	607

Households, 2000
Total households	2,328
With persons under 18	871
With persons over 65	558
Family households	1,599
Single-person households	616
Persons per household	2.70
Persons per family	3.28

Labor & Employment
Total civilian labor force, 2007**	3,690
Unemployment rate	6.8%
Total civilian labor force, 2000	3,369
Unemployment rate	6.7%

Employed persons 16 years and over by occupation, 2000
Managers & professionals	1,079
Service occupations	379
Sales & office occupations	990
Farming, fishing & forestry	9
Construction & maintenance	267
Production & transportation	420
Self-employed persons	94

* US Census Bureau
** New Jersey Department of Labor

General Information
Borough of Wharton
10 Robert St
Wharton, NJ 07885
973-361-8444

Website	www.whartonnj.com
Year of incorporation	1902
Land/water area (sq. miles)	2.19/0.03
Form of government	Borough

Government
Legislative Districts
US Congressional	11
State Legislative	25

Local Officials, 2009
Mayor	William Chegwidden
Manager	Jon Rheinhardt
Clerk	Gabrielle Voight-Cherna
CFO	Jon Rheinhardt
Tax Assessor	Glen Sherman
Tax Collector	Susan Megletti
Attorney	George Johnson
Building	Rita Sharp
Comm Dev/Planning	NA
Engineering	CMX
Public Works	Walter Van Kirk
Police Chief	Anthony Fernandez
Fire Chief	Jen O'Malley Dorr

Housing & Construction
Housing Units, 2000*
Total	2,394
Median rent	$867
Median SF home value	$165,300

Permits for New Residential Construction
	Units	Value
Total, 2006	4	$658,200
Single family	4	$658,200
Total, 2007	5	$899,600
Single family	5	$899,600

Real Property Valuation, 2008
	Parcels	Valuation
Total	1,861	$843,116,300
Vacant	61	17,248,900
Residential	1,692	567,671,400
Commercial	80	102,222,100
Industrial	11	126,740,600
Apartments	13	28,526,200
Farm land	2	4,000
Farm homestead	2	703,100

Average Property Value & Tax, 2008
Residential value	$335,522
Property tax	$6,632
Tax credit/rebate	$1,062

Public Library
Wharton Public Library
15 S Main St
Wharton, NJ 07885
973-361-1333

Director	Nancy Kaminetsky

Library statistics, 2007
Population served	6,298
Full-time/total staff	2/2

	Total	Per capita
Holdings	27,262	4.33
Revenues	$298,451	$47.39
Expenditures	$194,583	$30.90
Annual visits	43,197	6.86
Internet terminals/annual users	10/11,356	

Public Safety
Number of officers, 2007	21

Crime	2006	2007
Total crimes	122	102
Violent	2	7
Murder	0	0
Rape	0	1
Robbery	0	2
Aggravated assault	2	4
Non-violent	120	95
Burglary	20	21
Larceny	96	67
Vehicle theft	4	7
Domestic violence	30	75
Arson	0	0
Total crime rate	19.6	16.4
Violent	0.3	1.1
Non-violent	19.3	15.3

Public School District
(for school year 2007-08 except as noted)

Wharton Borough School District
137 East Central Avenue
Wharton, NJ 07885
(973) 361-2592

Superintendent	Richard Bitondo
Number of schools	2
Grade plan	K-8
Enrollment	791
Attendance rate, '06-07	95.3%
Dropout rate	NA
Students per teacher	10.1
Per pupil expenditure	$13,716
Median faculty salary	$53,864
Median administrator salary	$95,505
Grade 12 enrollment	NA
High school graduation rate	NA

Assessment test results
(percent scoring at proficient or advanced level)
	Language	Math
NJASK-Grade 3	86.7%	86.3%
GEPA-Grade 8	81.6%	81.4%
HSPA-High School	NA	NA

SAT Score Averages, 2006-07
Pct tested	Math	Verbal	Writing
NA	NA	NA	NA

Teacher Qualifications
Avg. years of experience	10
Highly-qualified teachers one subject/all subjects	100%/100%

No Child Left Behind
AYP, 2006-07	Meets Standards

Municipal Finance
State Aid Programs, 2009
Total aid	$708,743
CMPTRA	132,260
Energy tax receipts	558,765
Garden State Trust	0

General Budget, 2008
Total tax levy	$16,688,769
County levy	2,039,584
County taxes	1,664,392
County library	0
County health	0
County open space	375,192
School levy	11,798,079
Muni. levy	2,851,106
Misc. revenues	4,230,347

Taxes	2006	2007	2008
General tax rate per $100	4.12	4.41	1.977
County equalization ratio	50.03	43.7	97.06
Net valuation taxable	$347,496,300	$352,012,836	$844,280,775
State equalized value	$795,611,309	$868,595,068	$858,425,583

See Introduction for an explanation of all data sources.

Demographics & Socio-Economic Characteristics

(2000 US Census, except as noted)

Population
1980*	2,748
1990*	3,603
2000	4,245
Male	2,124
Female	2,121
2007 (estimate)*	5,874
Population density	214.6

Race & Hispanic Origin, 2000
Race
White	4,090
Black/African American	51
American Indian/Alaska Native	8
Asian	26
Native Hawaiian/Pacific Islander	2
Other race	14
Two or more races	54
Hispanic origin, total	90
Mexican	6
Puerto Rican	29
Cuban	11
Other Hispanic	44

Age & Nativity, 2000
Under 5 years	236
18 years and over	3,299
21 years and over	3,160
65 years and over	772
85 years and over	55
Median age	41.5
Native-born	4,029
Foreign-born	216

Educational Attainment, 2000
Population 25 years and over	3,086
Less than 9th grade	4.3%
High school grad or higher	81.4%
Bachelor's degree or higher	22.4%
Graduate degree	5.4%

Income & Poverty, 1999
Per capita income	$24,783
Median household income	$54,732
Median family income	$66,127
Persons in poverty	201
H'holds receiving public assistance	47
H'holds receiving social security	610

Households, 2000
Total households	1,668
With persons under 18	502
With persons over 65	562
Family households	1,179
Single-person households	420
Persons per household	2.47
Persons per family	2.98

Labor & Employment
Total civilian labor force, 2007**	2,249
Unemployment rate	2.6%
Total civilian labor force, 2000	2,006
Unemployment rate	2.8%

Employed persons 16 years and over by occupation, 2000
Managers & professionals	642
Service occupations	282
Sales & office occupations	514
Farming, fishing & forestry	7
Construction & maintenance	233
Production & transportation	272
Self-employed persons	151

* US Census Bureau
** New Jersey Department of Labor

See Introduction for an explanation of all data sources.

General Information
Township of White
555 County Road 519
Belvidere, NJ 07823
908-475-2093

Email	clerk@whitetwp-nj.com
Year of incorporation	1913
Land/water area (sq. miles)	27.37/0.38
Form of government	Township

Government
Legislative Districts
US Congressional	5
State Legislative	23

Local Officials, 2009
Mayor	James Ashe
Manager/Admin	NA
Clerk	Kathleen Reinalda
Finance Dir	Kathleen Reinalda
Tax Assessor	Michelle Trivigno
Tax Collector	Susan Luthringer
Attorney	Brian Tipton
Building	Ralph Price
Planning	Maser Consulting
Engineering	Paul Sterbenz
Public Works	Paul Sterbenz
Police Chief	NA
Fire/Emergency Dir	NA

Housing & Construction
Housing Units, 2000*
Total	1,770
Median rent	$531
Median SF home value	$163,700

Permits for New Residential Construction
	Units	Value
Total, 2006	75	$6,183,030
Single family	70	$5,922,207
Total, 2007	24	$2,796,898
Single family	24	$2,796,898

Real Property Valuation, 2008
	Parcels	Valuation
Total	2,331	$629,874,948
Vacant	218	15,523,627
Residential	1,546	413,127,700
Commercial	86	41,482,200
Industrial	9	109,569,800
Apartments	5	5,478,400
Farm land	321	3,401,421
Farm homestead	146	41,291,800

Average Property Value & Tax, 2008
Residential value	$268,569
Property tax	$5,006
Tax credit/rebate	$936

Public Library
No public municipal library

Library statistics, 2007
Population served	NA
Full-time/total staff	NA/NA

	Total	Per capita
Holdings	NA	NA
Revenues	NA	NA
Expenditures	NA	NA
Annual visits	NA	NA
Internet terminals/annual users	NA/NA	

Public Safety
Number of officers, 2007	0

Crime	2006	2007
Total crimes	49	29
Violent	4	1
Murder	0	0
Rape	0	0
Robbery	0	1
Aggravated assault	4	0
Non-violent	45	28
Burglary	13	2
Larceny	28	24
Vehicle theft	4	2
Domestic violence	0	29
Arson	0	0
Total crime rate	8.7	5.0
Violent	0.7	0.2
Non-violent	8.0	4.8

Public School District
(for school year 2007-08 except as noted)

White Township School District
565 County Route 519
Belvidere, NJ 07823
(908) 475-4773

Chief School Admin	Linda Heilman
Number of schools	1
Grade plan	K-8
Enrollment	420
Attendance rate, '06-07	95.4%
Dropout rate	NA
Students per teacher	10.5
Per pupil expenditure	$12,541
Median faculty salary	$58,779
Median administrator salary	$73,866
Grade 12 enrollment	NA
High school graduation rate	NA

Assessment test results
(percent scoring at proficient or advanced level)
	Language	Math
NJASK-Grade 3	94.9%	94.7%
GEPA-Grade 8	77.8%	93.7%
HSPA-High School	NA	NA

SAT Score Averages, 2006-07
Pct tested	Math	Verbal	Writing
NA	NA	NA	NA

Teacher Qualifications
Avg. years of experience	15
Highly-qualified teachers one subject/all subjects	97.0%/97.0%

No Child Left Behind
AYP, 2006-07	Meets Standards

Municipal Finance
State Aid Programs, 2009
Total aid	$426,409
CMPTRA	71,325
Energy tax receipts	298,742
Garden State Trust	20,144

General Budget, 2008
Total tax levy	$11,762,482
County levy	4,808,005
County taxes	3,921,708
County library	411,608
County health	0
County open space	474,689
School levy	6,454,802
Muni. levy	499,675
Misc. revenues	2,587,547

Taxes
	2006	2007	2008
General tax rate per $100	1.64	1.68	1.864
County equalization ratio	94.84	83.37	80.21
Net valuation taxable	$618,065,082	$622,668,773	$631,042,288
State equalized value	$742,916,728	$775,982,745	$787,233,667

Demographics & Socio-Economic Characteristics
(2000 US Census, except as noted)

Population
1980*	4,913
1990*	4,484
2000	5,436
Male	2,657
Female	2,779
2007 (estimate)*	5,291
Population density	4,101.6

Race & Hispanic Origin, 2000
Race
White	3,835
Black/African American	905
American Indian/Alaska Native	21
Asian	26
Native Hawaiian/Pacific Islander	8
Other race	481
Two or more races	160
Hispanic origin, total	958
Mexican	163
Puerto Rican	668
Cuban	9
Other Hispanic	118

Age & Nativity, 2000
Under 5 years	412
18 years and over	4,038
21 years and over	3,802
65 years and over	770
85 years and over	83
Median age	35.5
Native-born	5,294
Foreign-born	251

Educational Attainment, 2000
Population 25 years and over	3,531
Less than 9th grade	8.2%
High school grad or higher	66.3%
Bachelor's degree or higher	6.8%
Graduate degree	1.8%

Income & Poverty, 1999
Per capita income	$13,682
Median household income	$23,981
Median family income	$28,288
Persons in poverty	1,448
H'holds receiving public assistance	201
H'holds receiving social security	821

Households, 2000
Total households	2,333
With persons under 18	694
With persons over 65	625
Family households	1,273
Single-person households	891
Persons per household	2.30
Persons per family	3.06

Labor & Employment
Total civilian labor force, 2007**	2,986
Unemployment rate	16.5%
Total civilian labor force, 2000	2,644
Unemployment rate	21.4%

Employed persons 16 years and over by occupation, 2000
Managers & professionals	383
Service occupations	533
Sales & office occupations	599
Farming, fishing & forestry	33
Construction & maintenance	209
Production & transportation	322
Self-employed persons	169

* US Census Bureau
** New Jersey Department of Labor

General Information
City of Wildwood
4400 New Jersey Ave
Wildwood, NJ 08260
609-522-2444

Website	www.wildwoodnj.org
Year of incorporation	1912
Land/water area (sq. miles)	1.29/0.09
Form of government	Commission

Government
Legislative Districts
US Congressional	2
State Legislative	1

Local Officials, 2009
Mayor	Ernest Troiano Jr
Manager/Admin	NA
Clerk	Christopher Wood
Finance Dir	Jeanette Powers
Tax Assessor	Joseph Gallagher
Tax Collector	Faith Wilson
Attorney	Marcus Karavan
Building	Glenn Franzoi
Comm Dev/Planning	NA
Engineering	Mark DeBlasio
Public Works	Kevin Verity
Police Chief	Steve Long
Emerg/Fire Director	Conrad Johnson

Housing & Construction
Housing Units, 2000*
Total	6,488
Median rent	$526
Median SF home value	$84,000

Permits for New Residential Construction
	Units	Value
Total, 2006	175	$23,873,580
Single family	61	$7,151,580
Total, 2007	97	$17,367,582
Single family	25	$6,046,452

Real Property Valuation, 2008
	Parcels	Valuation
Total	5,286	$1,835,536,500
Vacant	290	67,647,700
Residential	4,170	1,104,334,100
Commercial	569	469,532,400
Industrial	6	5,766,900
Apartments	251	188,255,400
Farm land	0	0
Farm homestead	0	0

Average Property Value & Tax, 2008
Residential value	$264,828
Property tax	$4,381
Tax credit/rebate	$919

Public Library
No public municipal library

Library statistics, 2007
Population served	NA
Full-time/total staff	NA/NA

	Total	Per capita
Holdings	NA	NA
Revenues	NA	NA
Expenditures	NA	NA
Annual visits	NA	NA
Internet terminals/annual users	NA/NA	

Public Safety
Number of officers, 2007	46

Crime	2006	2007
Total crimes	531	777
Violent	78	84
Murder	0	0
Rape	4	4
Robbery	35	41
Aggravated assault	39	39
Non-violent	453	693
Burglary	110	180
Larceny	317	480
Vehicle theft	26	33
Domestic violence	49	21
Arson	2	0
Total crime rate	100.4	146.4
Violent	14.7	15.8
Non-violent	85.6	130.5

Public School District
(for school year 2007-08 except as noted)

Wildwood City School District
4300 Pacific Avenue
Wildwood, NJ 08260
(609) 522-4157

Superintendent	Dennis Anderson
Number of schools	3
Grade plan	K-12
Enrollment	879
Attendance rate, '06-07	92.7%
Dropout rate	3.3%
Students per teacher	7.4
Per pupil expenditure	$21,043
Median faculty salary	$65,103
Median administrator salary	$92,538
Grade 12 enrollment	73
High school graduation rate	79.3%

Assessment test results
(percent scoring at proficient or advanced level)
	Language	Math
NJASK-Grade 3	83.1%	72.7%
GEPA-Grade 8	39.6%	55.6%
HSPA-High School	67.8%	68.4%

SAT Score Averages, 2006-07
Pct tested	Math	Verbal	Writing
58%	456	448	428

Teacher Qualifications
Avg. years of experience	13
Highly-qualified teachers one subject/all subjects	100%/100%

No Child Left Behind
AYP, 2006-07	Meets Standards

Municipal Finance
State Aid Programs, 2009
Total aid	$1,236,687
CMPTRA	35,176
Energy tax receipts	1,182,960
Garden State Trust	0

General Budget, 2008
Total tax levy	$30,410,695
County levy	3,941,651
County taxes	3,132,712
County library	601,627
County health	0
County open space	207,312
School levy	9,415,982
Muni. levy	17,053,062
Misc. revenues	10,252,454

Taxes
	2006	2007	2008
General tax rate per $100	1.51	1.55	1.657
County equalization ratio	102.98	89.55	89.30
Net valuation taxable	$1,762,292,800	$1,861,748,849	$1,838,284,332
State equalized value	$1,970,999,716	$2,084,499,640	$2,025,600,488

See Introduction for an explanation of all data sources.

Demographics & Socio-Economic Characteristics
(2000 US Census, except as noted)

Population
1980*	4,149
1990*	3,631
2000	3,980
Male	1,854
Female	2,126
2007 (estimate)*	4,053
Population density	3,524.3

Race & Hispanic Origin, 2000
Race
White	3,776
Black/African American	49
American Indian/Alaska Native	4
Asian	19
Native Hawaiian/Pacific Islander	0
Other race	88
Two or more races	44
Hispanic origin, total	168
Mexican	44
Puerto Rican	89
Cuban	1
Other Hispanic	34

Age & Nativity, 2000
Under 5 years	171
18 years and over	3,255
21 years and over	3,167
65 years and over	1,013
85 years and over	132
Median age	46.7
Native-born	3,746
Foreign-born	124

Educational Attainment, 2000
Population 25 years and over	2,955
Less than 9th grade	3.5%
High school grad or higher	79.5%
Bachelor's degree or higher	26.4%
Graduate degree	8.9%

Income & Poverty, 1999
Per capita income	$23,741
Median household income	$36,579
Median family income	$47,462
Persons in poverty	231
H'holds receiving public assistance	51
H'holds receiving social security	783

Households, 2000
Total households	1,833
With persons under 18	417
With persons over 65	755
Family households	1,114
Single-person households	634
Persons per household	2.17
Persons per family	2.76

Labor & Employment
Total civilian labor force, 2007**	2,223
Unemployment rate	12.8%
Total civilian labor force, 2000	1,908
Unemployment rate	15.4%

Employed persons 16 years and over by occupation, 2000
Managers & professionals	634
Service occupations	295
Sales & office occupations	475
Farming, fishing & forestry	5
Construction & maintenance	114
Production & transportation	91
Self-employed persons	160

‡ Privately owned
* US Census Bureau
** New Jersey Department of Labor

General Information
Borough of Wildwood Crest
6101 Pacific Ave
Wildwood Crest, NJ 08260
609-522-3843
Website	www.wildwoodcrest.org
Year of incorporation	1910
Land/water area (sq. miles)	1.15/0.15
Form of government	Commission

Government
Legislative Districts
US Congressional	2
State Legislative	1

Local Officials, 2009
Mayor	Carl H. Groon
Manager	Kevin Yecco
Clerk	Kevin Yecco
Finance Dir	Stephen Ritchie
Tax Assessor	Jason Hesley
Tax Collector	Carolyn Hennessey
Attorney	Doreen Corino
Building	COWCO
Planning	Linda Adams
Engineering	Ralph Petrella
Public Works	Donald Twist
Police Chief	Thomas DePaul
Emerg/Fire Director	Albert Beers

Housing & Construction
Housing Units, 2000*
Total	4,862
Median rent	$610
Median SF home value	$147,600

Permits for New Residential Construction
	Units	Value
Total, 2006	260	$31,525,403
Single family	66	$9,015,350
Total, 2007	9	$1,564,135
Single family	9	$1,522,145

Real Property Valuation, 2008
	Parcels	Valuation
Total	5,166	$1,524,455,400
Vacant	124	31,194,800
Residential	4,865	1,281,346,200
Commercial	144	201,323,900
Industrial	0	0
Apartments	33	10,590,500
Farm land	0	0
Farm homestead	0	0

Average Property Value & Tax, 2008
Residential value	$263,381
Property tax	$3,611
Tax credit/rebate	$912

Public Library
Wildwood Crest Library‡
6301 Ocean Ave
Wildwood Crest, NJ 08260
609-522-0564
Director	William Smith

Library statistics, 2007
Population served	NA
Full-time/total staff	NA/NA

	Total	Per capita
Holdings	NA	NA
Revenues	NA	NA
Expenditures	NA	NA
Annual visits	NA	NA
Internet terminals/annual users	NA/NA	

Public Safety
Number of officers, 2007	21

Crime	2006	2007
Total crimes	204	174
Violent	5	14
Murder	0	0
Rape	0	0
Robbery	1	0
Aggravated assault	4	14
Non-violent	199	160
Burglary	56	42
Larceny	137	118
Vehicle theft	6	0
Domestic violence	76	63
Arson	0	0
Total crime rate	52.7	43.7
Violent	1.3	3.5
Non-violent	51.4	40.2

Public School District
(for school year 2007-08 except as noted)

Wildwood Crest School District
9100 Pacific Ave
Wildwood Crest, NJ 08260
(609) 729-3760
Superintendent	Dennis Anderson
Number of schools	1
Grade plan	K-8
Enrollment	278
Attendance rate, '06-07	95.9%
Dropout rate	NA
Students per teacher	7.4
Per pupil expenditure	$18,942
Median faculty salary	$74,100
Median administrator salary	$69,796
Grade 12 enrollment	NA
High school graduation rate	NA

Assessment test results
(percent scoring at proficient or advanced level)
	Language	Math
NJASK-Grade 3	100.0%	100.0%
GEPA-Grade 8	76.9%	88.5%
HSPA-High School	NA	NA

SAT Score Averages, 2006-07
Pct tested	Math	Verbal	Writing
NA	NA	NA	NA

Teacher Qualifications
Avg. years of experience	22
Highly-qualified teachers one subject/all subjects	100%/100%

No Child Left Behind
AYP, 2006-07	Meets Standards

Municipal Finance
State Aid Programs, 2009
Total aid	$504,606
CMPTRA	30,123
Energy tax receipts	458,083
Garden State Trust	0

General Budget, 2008
Total tax levy	$20,903,542
County levy	4,877,893
County taxes	3,877,202
County library	744,232
County health	0
County open space	256,458
School levy	5,661,552
Muni. levy	10,364,097
Misc. revenues	7,932,347

Taxes	2006	2007	2008
General tax rate per $100	1.27	1.32	1.373
County equalization ratio	70.93	62.31	59.85
Net valuation taxable	$1,361,032,500	$1,461,561,623	$1,524,774,685
State equalized value	$2,184,635,099	$2,441,832,762	$2,371,905,159

See Introduction for an explanation of all data sources.

Demographics & Socio-Economic Characteristics
(2000 US Census, except as noted)

Population
1980*	39,912
1990*	36,291
2000	33,008
Male	15,633
Female	17,375
2007 (estimate)*	36,865
Population density	4,793.9

Race & Hispanic Origin, 2000
Race
White	8,144
Black/African American	22,021
American Indian/Alaska Native	99
Asian	562
Native Hawaiian/Pacific Islander	12
Other race	866
Two or more races	1,304
Hispanic origin, total	1,998
Mexican	103
Puerto Rican	1,273
Cuban	46
Other Hispanic	576

Age & Nativity, 2000
Under 5 years	2,024
18 years and over	23,939
21 years and over	22,672
65 years and over	4,246
85 years and over	239
Median age	37.9
Native-born	30,299
Foreign-born	2,709

Educational Attainment, 2000
Population 25 years and over	21,431
Less than 9th grade	2.7%
High school grad or higher	87.2%
Bachelor's degree or higher	18.9%
Graduate degree	5.9%

Income & Poverty, 1999
Per capita income	$21,799
Median household income	$60,869
Median family income	$64,338
Persons in poverty	1,934
H'holds receiving public assistance	342
H'holds receiving social security	3,260

Households, 2000
Total households	10,713
With persons under 18	4,617
With persons over 65	3,086
Family households	8,780
Single-person households	1,607
Persons per household	3.07
Persons per family	3.36

Labor & Employment
Total civilian labor force, 2007**	16,774
Unemployment rate	5.7%
Total civilian labor force, 2000	16,077
Unemployment rate	7.0%

Employed persons 16 years and over by occupation, 2000
Managers & professionals	4,869
Service occupations	2,348
Sales & office occupations	4,574
Farming, fishing & forestry	31
Construction & maintenance	929
Production & transportation	2,207
Self-employed persons	505

* US Census Bureau
** New Jersey Department of Labor

General Information
Township of Willingboro
1 Salem Rd
Willingboro, NJ 08046
609-877-2200
Website	www.willingboro.org/twpindex.htm
Year of incorporation	1963
Land/water area (sq. miles)	7.69/0.33
Form of government	Council-Manager

Government
Legislative Districts
US Congressional	3
State Legislative	7

Local Officials, 2009
Mayor	Jacqueline Jennings
Manager	Joanne Diggs
Clerk	Marie Annese
Finance Dir	Joanne Diggs
Tax Assessor	William Tantum
Tax Collector	NA
Attorney	Michael Armstrong
Building	Duane Wallace
Comm Dev/Planning	NA
Engineering	Remington & Vernick
Public Works	Richard Brevogel
Police Chief	(county)
Emerg/Fire Director	Tony Burnett

Housing & Construction
Housing Units, 2000*
Total	11,124
Median rent	$1,100
Median SF home value	$96,700

Permits for New Residential Construction
	Units	Value
Total, 2006	1,657	$1,856,650
Single family	0	$2,500
Total, 2007	1	$484,490
Single family	1	$484,490

Real Property Valuation, 2008
	Parcels	Valuation
Total	11,200	$1,116,987,950
Vacant	109	6,304,800
Residential	10,923	1,040,595,950
Commercial	155	61,427,800
Industrial	10	6,759,000
Apartments	1	1,752,400
Farm land	1	2,000
Farm homestead	1	146,000

Average Property Value & Tax, 2008
Residential value	$95,271
Property tax	$5,027
Tax credit/rebate	$1,009

Public Library
Willingboro Public Library
220 Willingboro Parkway
Willingboro, NJ 08046
609-877-6668
Director	Christine H. King

Library statistics, 2007
Population served	33,008
Full-time/total staff	7/19

	Total	Per capita
Holdings	96,931	2.94
Revenues	$1,728,501	$52.37
Expenditures	$1,553,119	$47.05
Annual visits	156,314	4.74
Internet terminals/annual users	20/67,883	

Public Safety
Number of officers, 2007	73

Crime	2006	2007
Total crimes	768	737
Violent	130	107
Murder	3	0
Rape	12	14
Robbery	56	51
Aggravated assault	59	42
Non-violent	638	630
Burglary	133	143
Larceny	434	433
Vehicle theft	71	54
Domestic violence	272	244
Arson	7	5
Total crime rate	23.2	22.3
Violent	3.9	3.2
Non-violent	19.3	19.1

Public School District
(for school year 2007-08 except as noted)

Willingboro Township School District
440 Beverly-Rancocas Road
Willingboro, NJ 08046
(609) 835-8665
Superintendent	Thomas McMahon
Number of schools	8
Grade plan	K-12
Enrollment	4,674
Attendance rate, '06-07	91.5%
Dropout rate	2.2%
Students per teacher	10.8
Per pupil expenditure	$13,892
Median faculty salary	$50,204
Median administrator salary	$91,318
Grade 12 enrollment	238
High school graduation rate	90.8%

Assessment test results
(percent scoring at proficient or advanced level)
	Language	Math
NJASK-Grade 3	79.6%	80.7%
GEPA-Grade 8	28.7%	58.4%
HSPA-High School	41.6%	67.1%

SAT Score Averages, 2006-07
Pct tested	Math	Verbal	Writing
77%	420	413	403

Teacher Qualifications
Avg. years of experience	7
Highly-qualified teachers one subject/all subjects	99.5%/99.5%

No Child Left Behind
AYP, 2006-07	Meets Standards

Municipal Finance
State Aid Programs, 2009
Total aid	$4,405,460
CMPTRA	1,843,765
Energy tax receipts	2,539,668
Garden State Trust	0

General Budget, 2008
Total tax levy	$59,071,645
County levy	7,734,576
County taxes	6,872,810
County library	0
County health	0
County open space	861,766
School levy	28,299,652
Muni. levy	23,037,417
Misc. revenues	13,525,763

Taxes
	2006	2007	2008
General tax rate per $100	5.18	5.18	5.277
County equalization ratio	62.17	56.03	52.00
Net valuation taxable	$1,095,908,800	$1,113,114,323	$1,119,616,538
State equalized value	$1,959,228,610	$2,137,833,646	$2,161,059,409

Demographics & Socio-Economic Characteristics
(2000 US Census, except as noted)

Population
1980*	1,785
1990*	1,576
2000	1,514
Male	691
Female	823
2007 (estimate)*	1,456
Population density	8,088.9

Race & Hispanic Origin, 2000
Race
White	1,468
Black/African American	5
American Indian/Alaska Native	3
Asian	2
Native Hawaiian/Pacific Islander	1
Other race	10
Two or more races	25
Hispanic origin, total	37
Mexican	3
Puerto Rican	16
Cuban	8
Other Hispanic	10

Age & Nativity, 2000
Under 5 years	76
18 years and over	1,198
21 years and over	1,156
65 years and over	241
85 years and over	35
Median age	38.9
Native-born	1,472
Foreign-born	42

Educational Attainment, 2000
Population 25 years and over	1,112
Less than 9th grade	3.7%
High school grad or higher	79.2%
Bachelor's degree or higher	8.0%
Graduate degree	1.9%

Income & Poverty, 1999
Per capita income	$21,565
Median household income	$37,000
Median family income	$47,167
Persons in poverty	113
H'holds receiving public assistance	12
H'holds receiving social security	233

Households, 2000
Total households	694
With persons under 18	191
With persons over 65	199
Family households	395
Single-person households	266
Persons per household	2.18
Persons per family	2.92

Labor & Employment
Total civilian labor force, 2007**	841
Unemployment rate	7.2%
Total civilian labor force, 2000	807
Unemployment rate	7.4%

Employed persons 16 years and over by occupation, 2000
Managers & professionals	140
Service occupations	142
Sales & office occupations	241
Farming, fishing & forestry	4
Construction & maintenance	90
Production & transportation	130
Self-employed persons	19

* US Census Bureau
** New Jersey Department of Labor

See Introduction for an explanation of all data sources.

General Information
Township of Winfield
12 Gulfstream Ave
Winfield, NJ 07036
908-925-3850
Website	www.winfield-nj.org
Year of incorporation	1941
Land/water area (sq. miles)	0.18/0.00
Form of government	Township

Government
Legislative Districts
US Congressional	7
State Legislative	22

Local Officials, 2009
Mayor	David P. Wright Sr
Manager/Admin	NA
Municipal Clerk / Registrar	Laura Reinertsen
Chief Finance Officer	Sue Wright
Tax Assessor	Gary Toth
Tax Collector	Kimberley Allorto
Attorney	Frank G Capece
Building	Gary Junkroft
Comm Dev/Planning	NA
Engineering	George Vircik
Public Works	NA
Police Chief	Walter L. Berg
Emerg/Fire Director	Debra Daly

Housing & Construction
Housing Units, 2000*
Total	697
Median rent	$463
Median SF home value	$74,000

Permits for New Residential Construction
	Units	Value
Total, 2006	0	$0
Single family	0	$0
Total, 2007	0	$0
Single family	0	$0

Real Property Valuation, 2008
	Parcels	Valuation
Total	691	$1,382,200
Vacant	1	220,200
Residential	689	1,072,000
Commercial	1	90,000
Industrial	0	0
Apartments	0	0
Farm land	0	0
Farm homestead	0	0

Average Property Value & Tax, 2008
Residential value	$1,556
Property tax	$3,001
Tax credit/rebate	$829

Public Library
No public municipal library

Library statistics, 2007
Population served	NA
Full-time/total staff	NA/NA

	Total	Per capita
Holdings	NA	NA
Revenues	NA	NA
Expenditures	NA	NA
Annual visits	NA	NA
Internet terminals/annual users	NA/NA	

Public Safety
Number of officers, 2007	9

Crime	2006	2007
Total crimes	8	11
Violent	0	1
Murder	0	0
Rape	0	0
Robbery	0	0
Aggravated assault	0	1
Non-violent	8	10
Burglary	1	5
Larceny	6	5
Vehicle theft	1	0
Domestic violence	12	14
Arson	0	0
Total crime rate	5.3	7.4
Violent	0.0	0.7
Non-violent	5.3	6.7

Public School District
(for school year 2007-08 except as noted)

Winfield Township School District
7 1/2 Gulfstream Avenue
Winfield, NJ 07036
(908) 486-7410
Superintendent	Alice D'Ambola
Number of schools	1
Grade plan	K-8
Enrollment	119
Attendance rate, '06-07	95.0%
Dropout rate	NA
Students per teacher	7.0
Per pupil expenditure	$16,928
Median faculty salary	$48,634
Median administrator salary	$91,510
Grade 12 enrollment	NA
High school graduation rate	NA

Assessment test results
(percent scoring at proficient or advanced level)
	Language	Math
NJASK-Grade 3	100.0%	80.0%
GEPA-Grade 8	73.4%	93.3%
HSPA-High School	NA	NA

SAT Score Averages, 2006-07
Pct tested	Math	Verbal	Writing
NA	NA	NA	NA

Teacher Qualifications
Avg. years of experience	10
Highly-qualified teachers one subject/all subjects	100%/100%

No Child Left Behind
AYP, 2006-07	Meets Standards

Municipal Finance
State Aid Programs, 2009
Total aid	$228,972
CMPTRA	153,846
Energy tax receipts	73,981
Garden State Trust	0

General Budget, 2008
Total tax levy	$2,672,895
County levy	57,031
County taxes	54,546
County library	0
County health	0
County open space	2,485
School levy	1,460,633
Muni. levy	1,155,231
Misc. revenues	337,247

Taxes
	2006	2007	2008
General tax rate per $100	171.21	175.129	192.889
County equalization ratio	7.75	8.36	8.36
Net valuation taxable	$1,382,200	$1,385,485	$1,385,722
State equalized value	$16,537,013	$16,536,778	$16,537,015

Demographics & Socio-Economic Characteristics

(2000 US Census, except as noted)

Population
1980*	20,034
1990*	30,087
2000	34,611
Male	17,039
Female	17,572
2007 (estimate)*	39,173
Population density	678.9

Race & Hispanic Origin, 2000
Race
White	22,670
Black/African American	10,154
American Indian/Alaska Native	104
Asian	449
Native Hawaiian/Pacific Islander	10
Other race	547
Two or more races	677
Hispanic origin, total	1,492
Mexican	217
Puerto Rican	958
Cuban	38
Other Hispanic	279

Age & Nativity, 2000
Under 5 years	2,838
18 years and over	24,646
21 years and over	23,558
65 years and over	2,939
85 years and over	401
Median age	34.4
Native-born	33,353
Foreign-born	1,306

Educational Attainment, 2000
Population 25 years and over	22,366
Less than 9th grade	6.3%
High school grad or higher	82.2%
Bachelor's degree or higher	18.6%
Graduate degree	4.3%

Income & Poverty, 1999
Per capita income	$21,254
Median household income	$55,990
Median family income	$62,045
Persons in poverty	2,007
H'holds receiving public assistance	239
H'holds receiving social security	2,544

Households, 2000
Total households	11,661
With persons under 18	5,354
With persons over 65	2,193
Family households	9,002
Single-person households	2,187
Persons per household	2.87
Persons per family	3.28

Labor & Employment
Total civilian labor force, 2007**	20,721
Unemployment rate	5.8%
Total civilian labor force, 2000	17,665
Unemployment rate	6.1%

Employed persons 16 years and over by occupation, 2000
Managers & professionals	5,187
Service occupations	2,484
Sales & office occupations	4,699
Farming, fishing & forestry	78
Construction & maintenance	2,003
Production & transportation	2,138
Self-employed persons	811

‡ Branch of county library
* US Census Bureau
** New Jersey Department of Labor

General Information
Township of Winslow
125 S Route 73
Braddock, NJ 08037
609-567-0700
Website	www.winslowtownship.com
Year of incorporation	1845
Land/water area (sq. miles)	57.70/0.40
Form of government	Township

Government
Legislative Districts
US Congressional	1
State Legislative	6

Local Officials, 2009
Mayor	Sue Ann Metzner
Manager	Joseph Gallagher
Clerk	Deborah Puchakjian
Finance Dir	Steven Dringus
Tax Assessor	Stephen Kessler
Tax Collector	Constance Hegyi
Attorney	Stuart A. Platt
Building	Herb Leary
Comm Dev/Planning	NA
Engineering	Gary A. White
Public Works	Edward McGlinchey
Police Chief	Anthony Bello
Emerg/Fire Director	Michael Scardino

Housing & Construction
Housing Units, 2000*
Total	12,413
Median rent	$738
Median SF home value	$112,800

Permits for New Residential Construction
	Units	Value
Total, 2006	377	$39,458,623
Single family	377	$39,458,623
Total, 2007	148	$15,159,996
Single family	148	$15,159,996

Real Property Valuation, 2008
	Parcels	Valuation
Total	15,480	$1,534,872,470
Vacant	1,848	36,846,200
Residential	12,566	1,328,369,500
Commercial	311	92,319,950
Industrial	15	19,973,900
Apartments	26	31,575,100
Farm land	504	4,238,600
Farm homestead	210	21,549,220

Average Property Value & Tax, 2008
Residential value	$105,661
Property tax	$4,953
Tax credit/rebate	$946

Public Library
South County Regional Library‡
35 Coopers Folly Rd
Atco, NJ 08004
856-753-2537
Branch Librarian . . . . Nancy Bennett

Library statistics, 2007
see Camden County profile
for library system statistics

Public Safety
Number of officers, 2007	85

Crime	2006	2007
Total crimes	1,017	906
Violent	186	162
Murder	1	1
Rape	8	11
Robbery	52	34
Aggravated assault	125	116
Non-violent	831	744
Burglary	246	252
Larceny	536	435
Vehicle theft	49	57
Domestic violence	584	447
Arson	14	14
Total crime rate	27.1	23.5
Violent	5.0	4.2
Non-violent	22.2	19.3

Public School District
(for school year 2007-08 except as noted)

Winslow Township School District
30 Cooper Folly Road
Atco, NJ 08004
(856) 767-2850
Superintendent	H. Major Poteat
Number of schools	9
Grade plan	K-12
Enrollment	6,014
Attendance rate, '06-07	94.3%
Dropout rate	0.4%
Students per teacher	9.9
Per pupil expenditure	$13,571
Median faculty salary	$70,100
Median administrator salary	$95,918
Grade 12 enrollment	377
High school graduation rate	90.0%

Assessment test results
(percent scoring at proficient or advanced level)
	Language	Math
NJASK-Grade 3	79.1%	83.3%
GEPA-Grade 8	38.2%	67.8%
HSPA-High School	55.3%	75.8%

SAT Score Averages, 2006-07
Pct tested	Math	Verbal	Writing
64%	447	448	444

Teacher Qualifications
Avg. years of experience	10
Highly-qualified teachers	
one subject/all subjects	98.5%/98.5%

No Child Left Behind
AYP, 2006-07	Meets Standards

Municipal Finance
State Aid Programs, 2009
Total aid	$7,849,598
CMPTRA	0
Energy tax receipts	7,552,813
Garden State Trust	63,664

General Budget, 2008
Total tax levy	$72,113,455
County levy	19,184,262
County taxes	17,335,620
County library	1,244,513
County health	0
County open space	604,128
School levy	41,114,104
Muni. levy	11,815,090
Misc. revenues	17,622,610

Taxes	2006	2007	2008
General tax rate per $100	4.445	4.549	4.688
County equalization ratio	65.17	56.18	51.08
Net valuation taxable	$1,426,640,470	$1,495,634,432	$1,538,441,594
State equalized value	$2,543,493,582	$2,924,416,077	$3,112,486,422

See Introduction for an explanation of all data sources.

Demographics & Socio-Economic Characteristics

(2000 US Census, except as noted)

Population
1980*	2,809
1990*	2,678
2000	2,716
Male	1,596
Female	1,120
2007 (estimate)*	2,485
Population density	310.6

Race & Hispanic Origin, 2000
Race
White	1,450
Black/African American	880
American Indian/Alaska Native	6
Asian	3
Native Hawaiian/Pacific Islander	0
Other race	299
Two or more races	78
Hispanic origin, total	577
Mexican	19
Puerto Rican	478
Cuban	5
Other Hispanic	75

Age & Nativity, 2000
Under 5 years	249
18 years and over	1,993
21 years and over	1,895
65 years and over	283
85 years and over	26
Median age	36.4
Native-born	2,680
Foreign-born	36

Educational Attainment, 2000
Population 25 years and over	1,765
Less than 9th grade	24.2%
High school grad or higher	58.1%
Bachelor's degree or higher	4.5%
Graduate degree	1.1%

Income & Poverty, 1999
Per capita income	$13,335
Median household income	$30,298
Median family income	$31,786
Persons in poverty	383
H'holds receiving public assistance	82
H'holds receiving social security	209

Households, 2000
Total households	773
With persons under 18	370
With persons over 65	181
Family households	558
Single-person households	178
Persons per household	2.77
Persons per family	3.21

Labor & Employment
Total civilian labor force, 2007**	1,123
Unemployment rate	6.8%
Total civilian labor force, 2000	954
Unemployment rate	9.0%

Employed persons 16 years and over by occupation, 2000
Managers & professionals	182
Service occupations	290
Sales & office occupations	176
Farming, fishing & forestry	10
Construction & maintenance	82
Production & transportation	128
Self-employed persons	56

‡ Branch of county library
* US Census Bureau
** New Jersey Department of Labor

See Introduction for an explanation of all data sources.

General Information
Borough of Woodbine
501 Washington Ave
Woodbine, NJ 08270
609-861-2153
Website	www.boroughofwoodbine.net
Year of incorporation	1903
Land/water area (sq. miles)	8.00/0.00
Form of government	Borough

Government

Legislative Districts
US Congressional	2
State Legislative	1

Local Officials, 2009
Mayor	William Pikolycky
Manager/Admin	NA
Clerk	Lisa Garrison
Finance Dir	John Miller
Tax Assessor	John Miller
Tax Collector	Lisa Garrison
Attorney	Paul Baldini
Building	NA
Planning	Mike Zumpino
Engineering	Vincent Orlando
Public Works	James Gurdgiel
Police Chief	NA
Emerg/Fire Director	Manuel Gonzalez

Housing & Construction

Housing Units, 2000*
Total	1,080
Median rent	$463
Median SF home value	$80,600

Permits for New Residential Construction
	Units	Value
Total, 2006	18	$280,093
Single family	18	$280,093
Total, 2007	10	$548,062
Single family	10	$548,062

Real Property Valuation, 2008
	Parcels	Valuation
Total	1,365	$177,802,200
Vacant	168	8,754,000
Residential	1,079	130,920,600
Commercial	61	23,302,300
Industrial	6	4,763,000
Apartments	2	5,061,400
Farm land	31	140,100
Farm homestead	18	4,860,800

Average Property Value & Tax, 2008
Residential value	$123,775
Property tax	$1,357
Tax credit/rebate	$584

Public Library
Upper Cape Branch‡
801 Webster Ave
Woodbine, NJ 08270
609-463-6350
Librarian	Deborah Poillon

Library statistics, 2007
see Cape May County profile
for library system statistics

Public Safety
Number of officers, 2007	0

Crime	2006	2007
Total crimes	100	109
Violent	20	13
Murder	0	1
Rape	1	0
Robbery	5	3
Aggravated assault	14	9
Non-violent	80	96
Burglary	18	21
Larceny	54	65
Vehicle theft	8	10
Domestic violence	13	48
Arson	0	2
Total crime rate	38.9	43.5
Violent	7.8	5.2
Non-violent	31.1	38.3

Public School District
(for school year 2007-08 except as noted)

Woodbine School District
801 Webster Ave
Woodbine, NJ 08270
(609) 861-5174
Superintendent	Lynda Anderson-Towns
Number of schools	1
Grade plan	K-8
Enrollment	211
Attendance rate, '06-07	92.3%
Dropout rate	NA
Students per teacher	9.6
Per pupil expenditure	$12,985
Median faculty salary	$68,582
Median administrator salary	$83,485
Grade 12 enrollment	NA
High school graduation rate	NA

Assessment test results
(percent scoring at proficient or advanced level)
	Language	Math
NJASK-Grade 3	71.5%	85.8%
GEPA-Grade 8	66.7%	82.6%
HSPA-High School	NA	NA

SAT Score Averages, 2006-07
Pct tested	Math	Verbal	Writing
NA	NA	NA	NA

Teacher Qualifications
Avg. years of experience	20
Highly-qualified teachers one subject/all subjects	100%/100%

No Child Left Behind
AYP, 2006-07	Meets Standards

Municipal Finance

State Aid Programs, 2009
Total aid	$377,890
CMPTRA	204,050
Energy tax receipts	166,914
Garden State Trust	836

General Budget, 2008
Total tax levy	$1,963,677
County levy	322,791
County taxes	256,567
County library	49,251
County health	0
County open space	16,973
School levy	1,215,375
Muni. levy	425,511
Misc. revenues	2,288,268

Taxes
	2006	2007	2008
General tax rate per $100	2.51	1	1.099
County equalization ratio	50.68	127.06	106.91
Net valuation taxable	$59,070,200	$178,440,561	$179,062,422
State equalized value	$138,100,042	$166,991,045	$178,037,116

Demographics & Socio-Economic Characteristics†

(2000 US Census, except as noted)

Population

1980*	90,074
1990*	93,086
2000	97,203
Male	48,640
Female	48,563
2007 (estimate)*	98,450
Population density	4,278.6

Race & Hispanic Origin, 2000

Race

White	68,848
Black/African American	8,507
American Indian/Alaska Native	167
Asian	14,054
Native Hawaiian/Pacific Islander	24
Other race	3,212
Two or more races	2,391
Hispanic origin, total	8,956
Mexican	390
Puerto Rican	3,838
Cuban	680
Other Hispanic	4,048

Age & Nativity, 2000

Under 5 years	6,161
18 years and over	75,460
21 years and over	72,777
65 years and over	13,005
85 years and over	1,042
Median age	37.1
Native-born	76,332
Foreign-born	20,871

Educational Attainment, 2000

Population 25 years and over	68,845
Less than 9th grade	5.2%
High school grad or higher	84.0%
Bachelor's degree or higher	26.8%
Graduate degree	8.9%

Income & Poverty, 1999

Per capita income	$25,087
Median household income	$60,683
Median family income	$68,492
Persons in poverty	4,565
H'holds receiving public assistance	643
H'holds receiving social security	9,953

Households, 2000

Total households	34,562
With persons under 18	12,405
With persons over 65	9,529
Family households	25,423
Single-person households	7,484
Persons per household	2.71
Persons per family	3.19

Labor & Employment

Total civilian labor force, 2007**	52,635
Unemployment rate	3.6%
Total civilian labor force, 2000	49,753
Unemployment rate	4.8%

Employed persons 16 years and over by occupation, 2000

Managers & professionals	17,681
Service occupations	4,982
Sales & office occupations	14,186
Farming, fishing & forestry	85
Construction & maintenance	4,000
Production & transportation	6,429
Self-employed persons	1,604

† see Appendix C for American Community Survey data
* US Census Bureau
** New Jersey Department of Labor
§ State Fiscal Year July 1–June 30

General Information

Township of Woodbridge
1 Main St
Woodbridge, NJ 07095
732-634-4500

Website	www.twp.woodbridge.nj.us
Year of incorporation	1669
Land/water area (sq. miles)	23.01/1.21
Form of government	Mayor-Council

Government

Legislative Districts

US Congressional	7, 13
State Legislative	19

Local Officials, 2009

Mayor	John E. McCormac
Manager	Robert M. Landolfi
Clerk	John M. Mitch
Finance Dir.	Richard A. Cahill
Tax Assessor	Richard Duda
Tax Collector	Richard Lorentzen
Attorney	James Nolan Jr
Building	Lawrence Esoldo
Planning	Marta Lefsky
Engineering	Scott Thompson
Public Works	Dennis Henry
Police Chief	William Trenery
Fire/Emergency Dir.	NA

Housing & Construction

Housing Units, 2000*

Total	35,298
Median rent	$879
Median SF home value	$158,100

Permits for New Residential Construction

	Units	Value
Total, 2006	2	$376,200
Single family	2	$376,200
Total, 2007	0	$0
Single family	0	$0

Real Property Valuation, 2008

	Parcels	Valuation
Total	28,739	$3,174,620,152
Vacant	1,000	57,533,452
Residential	26,424	1,986,963,200
Commercial	1,064	688,079,000
Industrial	166	276,846,400
Apartments	85	165,198,100
Farm land	0	0
Farm homestead	0	0

Average Property Value & Tax, 2008

Residential value	$75,195
Property tax	$5,510
Tax credit/rebate	$1,007

Public Library

Woodbridge Public Library
George Frederick Plaza
Woodbridge, NJ 07095
732-634-4450

Director . . . . John Hurley

Library statistics, 2007

Population served	97,203
Full-time/total staff	23/71

	Total	Per capita
Holdings	459,291	4.73
Revenues	$6,020,319	$61.94
Expenditures	$6,020,319	$61.94
Annual visits	538,097	5.54
Internet terminals/annual users	21/52,359	

Public Safety

Number of officers, 2007	205

Crime	2006	2007
Total crimes	3,117	3,155
Violent	267	242
Murder	0	1
Rape	17	14
Robbery	80	105
Aggravated assault	170	122
Non-violent	2,850	2,913
Burglary	415	439
Larceny	2,152	2,212
Vehicle theft	283	262
Domestic violence	986	800
Arson	15	23
Total crime rate	31.0	31.8
Violent	2.7	2.4
Non-violent	28.3	29.4

Public School District

(for school year 2007-08 except as noted)

Woodbridge Township School District
School Street, PO Box 428
Woodbridge, NJ 07095
(732) 602-8550

Superintendent	John A. Crowe
Number of schools	24
Grade plan	K-12
Enrollment	13,359
Attendance rate, '06-07	94.7%
Dropout rate	0.5%
Students per teacher	11.6
Per pupil expenditure	$12,335
Median faculty salary	$62,346
Median administrator salary	$108,823
Grade 12 enrollment	1,118
High school graduation rate	96.9%

Assessment test results

(percent scoring at proficient or advanced level)

	Language	Math
NJASK-Grade 3	93.8%	89.4%
GEPA-Grade 8	75.4%	85.3%
HSPA-High School	85.1%	89.9%

SAT Score Averages, 2006-07

Pct tested	Math	Verbal	Writing
NA	NA	NA	NA

Teacher Qualifications

Avg. years of experience	11
Highly-qualified teachers one subject/all subjects	100%/100%

No Child Left Behind

AYP, 2006-07	Meets Standards

Municipal Finance§

State Aid Programs, 2009

Total aid	$29,955,792
CMPTRA	5,042,839
Energy tax receipts	24,164,036
Garden State Trust	12

General Budget, 2008

Total tax levy	$233,880,940
County levy	38,157,398
County taxes	34,155,077
County library	0
County health	0
County open space	4,002,321
School levy	145,662,372
Muni. levy	50,061,170
Misc. revenues	51,469,767

Taxes

	2006	2007	2008
General tax rate per $100	6.73	7.09	7.328
County equalization ratio	30.32	26.51	23.82
Net valuation taxable	$3,213,780,952	$3,214,172,952	$3,191,810,407
State equalized value	$12,129,433,277	$13,464,599,563	$13,849,957,802

See Introduction for an explanation of all data sources.

Demographics & Socio-Economic Characteristics

(2000 US Census, except as noted)

Population

1980*	10,353
1990*	10,904
2000	10,307
Male	4,815
Female	5,492
2007 (estimate)*	10,457
Population density	5,027.4

Race & Hispanic Origin, 2000

Race

White	7,467
Black/African American	2,353
American Indian/Alaska Native	23
Asian	102
Native Hawaiian/Pacific Islander	14
Other race	132
Two or more races	216
Hispanic origin, total	406
Mexican	28
Puerto Rican	235
Cuban	17
Other Hispanic	126

Age & Nativity, 2000

Under 5 years	669
18 years and over	7,754
21 years and over	7,385
65 years and over	1,702
85 years and over	264
Median age	37.0
Native-born	10,030
Foreign-born	277

Educational Attainment, 2000

Population 25 years and over	6,842
Less than 9th grade	6.4%
High school grad or higher	80.3%
Bachelor's degree or higher	21.9%
Graduate degree	6.9%

Income & Poverty, 1999

Per capita income	$21,592
Median household income	$41,827
Median family income	$53,630
Persons in poverty	1,324
H'holds receiving public assistance	138
H'holds receiving social security	1,305

Households, 2000

Total households	4,051
With persons under 18	1,428
With persons over 65	1,199
Family households	2,588
Single-person households	1,283
Persons per household	2.43
Persons per family	3.08

Labor & Employment

Total civilian labor force, 2007**	5,537
Unemployment rate	5.8%
Total civilian labor force, 2000	4,670
Unemployment rate	5.4%

*Employed persons 16 years and over
by occupation, 2000*

Managers & professionals	1,592
Service occupations	713
Sales & office occupations	1,134
Farming, fishing & forestry	12
Construction & maintenance	335
Production & transportation	634
Self-employed persons	209

General Information

City of Woodbury
33 Delaware St
Woodbury, NJ 08096
856-845-1300

Website	www.woodbury.nj.us
Year of incorporation	1871
Land/water area (sq. miles)	2.08/0.04
Form of government	City

Government

Legislative Districts

US Congressional	1
State Legislative	5

Local Officials, 2009

Mayor	Robert A. Curtis
Manager	Thomas Bowe
Clerk	Thomas Bowe
Finance Dir	Robert Law
Tax Assessor	Roy Duffield
Tax Collector	Lorraine Roberts
Attorney	James Pierson
Building	Robert Kunkle
Planning	Brian Bosworth
Engineering	Ted Wilkinson
Public Works	Michael Walsh
Police Chief	Reed Merinuk
Emerg/Fire Director	William J. Volk Jr

Housing & Construction

Housing Units, 2000*

Total	4,310
Median rent	$523
Median SF home value	$97,100

Permits for New Residential Construction

	Units	Value
Total, 2006	12	$1,180,665
Single family	12	$1,180,665
Total, 2007	5	$774,881
Single family	5	$774,881

Real Property Valuation, 2008

	Parcels	Valuation
Total	3,396	$373,965,600
Vacant	157	4,519,500
Residential	2,919	267,656,300
Commercial	296	87,780,900
Industrial	3	2,017,800
Apartments	21	11,991,100
Farm land	0	0
Farm homestead	0	0

Average Property Value & Tax, 2008

Residential value	$91,695
Property tax	$5,732
Tax credit/rebate	$1,014

Public Library

Woodbury Public Library
33 Delaware St
Woodbury, NJ 08096
856-845-2611

Director..................Jean A. Wipf

Library statistics, 2007

Population served	10,307
Full-time/total staff	1/3

	Total	Per capita
Holdings	63,067	6.12
Revenues	$361,193	$35.04
Expenditures	$371,570	$36.05
Annual visits	58,165	5.64
Internet terminals/annual users	18/12,962	

Public Safety

Number of officers, 2007 27

Crime	2006	2007
Total crimes	712	553
Violent	55	45
Murder	0	0
Rape	5	2
Robbery	24	15
Aggravated assault	26	28
Non-violent	657	508
Burglary	100	68
Larceny	534	392
Vehicle theft	23	48
Domestic violence	200	187
Arson	3	2
Total crime rate	68.2	53.1
Violent	5.3	4.3
Non-violent	63.0	48.8

Public School District

(for school year 2007-08 except as noted)

Woodbury School District
25 North Broad Street
Woodbury, NJ 08096
(856) 853-0123

Superintendent	Joseph Jones III
Number of schools	4
Grade plan	K-12
Enrollment	1,599
Attendance rate, '06-07	93.6%
Dropout rate	3.0%
Students per teacher	10.3
Per pupil expenditure	$14,776
Median faculty salary	$54,392
Median administrator salary	$101,491
Grade 12 enrollment	83
High school graduation rate	85.9%

Assessment test results

(percent scoring at proficient or advanced level)

	Language	Math
NJASK-Grade 3	80.5%	74.0%
GEPA-Grade 8	58.7%	70.9%
HSPA-High School	64.2%	71.7%

SAT Score Averages, 2006-07

Pct tested	Math	Verbal	Writing
80%	427	419	427

Teacher Qualifications

Avg. years of experience	9
Highly-qualified teachers one subject/all subjects	100%/100%

No Child Left Behind

AYP, 2006-07 ....Meets Standards

Municipal Finance

State Aid Programs, 2009

Total aid	$1,712,548
CMPTRA	617,724
Energy tax receipts	1,086,261
Garden State Trust	0

General Budget, 2008

Total tax levy	$23,552,332
County levy	3,929,712
County taxes	3,644,140
County library	0
County health	0
County open space	285,572
School levy	11,701,790
Muni. levy	7,920,829
Misc. revenues	4,275,651

Taxes	2006	2007	2008
General tax rate per $100	5.767	6.047	6.251
County equalization ratio	67.51	59.63	52.91
Net valuation taxable	$371,682,200	$375,017,643	$376,788,880
State equalized value	$626,736,897	$706,059,097	$735,227,510

* US Census Bureau
** New Jersey Department of Labor

See Introduction for an explanation of all data sources.

Demographics & Socio-Economic Characteristics
(2000 US Census, except as noted)

Population
1980*	3,460
1990*	3,392
2000	2,988
Male	1,437
Female	1,551
2007 (estimate)*	3,042
Population density	2,473.2

Race & Hispanic Origin, 2000
Race
White	2,879
Black/African American	46
American Indian/Alaska Native	8
Asian	30
Native Hawaiian/Pacific Islander	0
Other race	14
Two or more races	11
Hispanic origin, total	37
Mexican	2
Puerto Rican	23
Cuban	1
Other Hispanic	11

Age & Nativity, 2000
Under 5 years	179
18 years and over	2,207
21 years and over	2,113
65 years and over	396
85 years and over	29
Median age	38.3
Native-born	2,896
Foreign-born	92

Educational Attainment, 2000
Population 25 years and over	2,012
Less than 9th grade	4.1%
High school grad or higher	86.5%
Bachelor's degree or higher	22.9%
Graduate degree	7.8%

Income & Poverty, 1999
Per capita income	$24,001
Median household income	$63,266
Median family income	$70,167
Persons in poverty	121
H'holds receiving public assistance	14
H'holds receiving social security	284

Households, 2000
Total households	1,027
With persons under 18	421
With persons over 65	286
Family households	826
Single-person households	171
Persons per household	2.89
Persons per family	3.24

Labor & Employment
Total civilian labor force, 2007**	1,799
Unemployment rate	3.6%
Total civilian labor force, 2000	1,537
Unemployment rate	4.0%

Employed persons 16 years and over by occupation, 2000
Managers & professionals	439
Service occupations	162
Sales & office occupations	473
Farming, fishing & forestry	6
Construction & maintenance	175
Production & transportation	221
Self-employed persons	69

* US Census Bureau
** New Jersey Department of Labor

General Information
Borough of Woodbury Heights
500 Elm Ave
Woodbury Heights, NJ 08097
856-848-2832
Email	janetpz@bwhnj.com
Year of incorporation	1915
Land/water area (sq. miles)	1.23/0.00
Form of government	Borough

Government
Legislative Districts
US Congressional	1
State Legislative	5

Local Officials, 2009
Mayor	Harry W. Elton Jr
Manager/Admin	NA
Clerk	Janet Pizzi
Finance Dir	Sandra Kraus
Tax Assessor	Brian Schneider
Tax Collector	Sandra Kraus
Attorney	Barry Lozuke
Building	Robert Kunkle
Comm Dev/Planning	NA
Engineering	Mark Brunermer
Public Works	David Baresich
Police Chief	Leo Selb
Emerg/Fire Director	Robbie Conley

Housing & Construction
Housing Units, 2000*
Total	1,045
Median rent	$742
Median SF home value	$124,300

Permits for New Residential Construction
	Units	Value
Total, 2006	9	$794,894
Single family	9	$794,894
Total, 2007	5	$373,582
Single family	5	$373,582

Real Property Valuation, 2008
	Parcels	Valuation
Total	1,290	$194,226,900
Vacant	118	2,826,400
Residential	1,074	153,152,000
Commercial	84	28,829,500
Industrial	11	8,911,800
Apartments	3	507,200
Farm land	0	0
Farm homestead	0	0

Average Property Value & Tax, 2008
Residential value	$142,600
Property tax	$6,072
Tax credit/rebate	$1,041

Public Library
No public municipal library

Library statistics, 2007
Population served	NA
Full-time/total staff	NA/NA

	Total	Per capita
Holdings	NA	NA
Revenues	NA	NA
Expenditures	NA	NA
Annual visits	NA	NA
Internet terminals/annual users	NA/NA	

Public Safety
Number of officers, 2007	7

Crime	2006	2007
Total crimes	109	72
Violent	10	1
Murder	0	0
Rape	0	0
Robbery	4	1
Aggravated assault	6	0
Non-violent	99	71
Burglary	23	16
Larceny	71	50
Vehicle theft	5	5
Domestic violence	32	22
Arson	0	0
Total crime rate	36.1	23.8
Violent	3.3	0.3
Non-violent	32.8	23.4

Public School District
(for school year 2007-08 except as noted)

Woodbury Heights School District
100 Academy Avenue
Woodbury Heights, NJ 08097
(856) 848-2610
Chief School Admin	Janie Haines
Number of schools	1
Grade plan	K-6
Enrollment	224
Attendance rate, '06-07	96.2%
Dropout rate	NA
Students per teacher	8.8
Per pupil expenditure	$11,917
Median faculty salary	$46,726
Median administrator salary	$109,200
Grade 12 enrollment	NA
High school graduation rate	NA

Assessment test results
(percent scoring at proficient or advanced level)
	Language	Math
NJASK-Grade 3	86.5%	83.4%
GEPA-Grade 8	NA	NA
HSPA-High School	NA	NA

SAT Score Averages, 2006-07
Pct tested	Math	Verbal	Writing
NA	NA	NA	NA

Teacher Qualifications
Avg. years of experience	10
Highly-qualified teachers one subject/all subjects	100%/100%

No Child Left Behind
AYP, 2006-07	Meets Standards

Municipal Finance
State Aid Programs, 2009
Total aid	$372,846
CMPTRA	79,359
Energy tax receipts	284,166
Garden State Trust	0

General Budget, 2008
Total tax levy	$8,283,594
County levy	1,724,750
County taxes	1,488,415
County library	119,696
County health	0
County open space	116,639
School levy	4,467,166
Muni. levy	2,091,679
Misc. revenues	1,189,844

Taxes
	2006	2007	2008
General tax rate per $100	3.804	4	4.259
County equalization ratio	83.64	72.96	67.01
Net valuation taxable	$193,492,500	$194,574,145	$194,539,949
State equalized value	$265,547,467	$290,205,415	$307,100,128

See Introduction for an explanation of all data sources.

Demographics & Socio-Economic Characteristics
(2000 US Census, except as noted)

Population

1980*	5,644
1990*	5,303
2000	5,745
Male	2,757
Female	2,988
2007 (estimate)*	5,939
Population density	1,783.5

Race & Hispanic Origin, 2000

Race

White	5,391
Black/African American	50
American Indian/Alaska Native	2
Asian	257
Native Hawaiian/Pacific Islander	0
Other race	11
Two or more races	34
Hispanic origin, total	134
Mexican	16
Puerto Rican	30
Cuban	28
Other Hispanic	60

Age & Nativity, 2000

Under 5 years	406
18 years and over	4,027
21 years and over	3,901
65 years and over	768
85 years and over	133
Median age	40.7
Native-born	5,162
Foreign-born	583

Educational Attainment, 2000

Population 25 years and over	3,791
Less than 9th grade	1.0%
High school grad or higher	96.1%
Bachelor's degree or higher	58.3%
Graduate degree	27.0%

Income & Poverty, 1999

Per capita income	$53,461
Median household income	$123,022
Median family income	$133,925
Persons in poverty	86
H'holds receiving public assistance	7
H'holds receiving social security	454

Households, 2000

Total households	1,824
With persons under 18	892
With persons over 65	451
Family households	1,605
Single-person households	193
Persons per household	3.08
Persons per family	3.31

Labor & Employment

Total civilian labor force, 2007**	2,846
Unemployment rate	1.3%
Total civilian labor force, 2000	2,692
Unemployment rate	1.4%

Employed persons 16 years and over by occupation, 2000

Managers & professionals	1,526
Service occupations	138
Sales & office occupations	810
Farming, fishing & forestry	0
Construction & maintenance	96
Production & transportation	83
Self-employed persons	271

* US Census Bureau
** New Jersey Department of Labor

See Introduction for an explanation of all data sources.

General Information
Borough of Woodcliff Lake
188 Pascack Rd
Woodcliff Lake, NJ 07677
201-391-4977

Website	www.wclnj.com
Year of incorporation	1910
Land/water area (sq. miles)	3.33/0.21
Form of government	Borough

Government

Legislative Districts

US Congressional	5
State Legislative	39

Local Officials, 2009

Mayor	Joseph T. La Paglia
Administrator	Edward Sandve
Clerk	Lorinda Sciara
CFO	Harold Laufeld III
Tax Assessor	Barbara Potash
Tax Collector	Lois Frezza
Attorney	Mark Madaio
Building	Nick Saluzzi
Planning	George Fry (Chr)
Engineering	Elliot Sachs
Public Works	Ed Barboni
Police Chief	Anthony Jannicelli
Fire Chief	George Fusco Jr

Housing & Construction

Housing Units, 2000*

Total	1,842
Median rent	$1,258
Median SF home value	$450,700

Permits for New Residential Construction

	Units	Value
Total, 2006	25	$8,702,913
Single family	25	$8,702,913
Total, 2007	18	$7,387,258
Single family	18	$7,387,258

Real Property Valuation, 2008

	Parcels	Valuation
Total	2,006	$1,651,042,100
Vacant	79	16,806,600
Residential	1,871	1,218,110,700
Commercial	50	415,187,600
Industrial	0	0
Apartments	0	0
Farm land	3	6,400
Farm homestead	3	930,800

Average Property Value & Tax, 2008

Residential value	$650,502
Property tax	$13,316
Tax credit/rebate	$1,377

Public Library
No public municipal library

Library statistics, 2007

Population served	NA
Full-time/total staff	NA/NA

	Total	Per capita
Holdings	NA	NA
Revenues	NA	NA
Expenditures	NA	NA
Annual visits	NA	NA
Internet terminals/annual users	NA/NA	

Public Safety

Number of officers, 2007	18

Crime	2006	2007
Total crimes	33	59
Violent	1	3
Murder	0	0
Rape	0	0
Robbery	0	0
Aggravated assault	1	3
Non-violent	32	56
Burglary	0	4
Larceny	31	49
Vehicle theft	1	3
Domestic violence	7	12
Arson	0	0
Total crime rate	5.6	9.9
Violent	0.2	0.5
Non-violent	5.4	9.4

Public School District
(for school year 2007-08 except as noted)

Woodcliff Lake School District
134 Woodcliff Avenue
Woodcliff Lake, NJ 07677
(201) 391-6570

Superintendent	Peter Lisi
Number of schools	2
Grade plan	K-8
Enrollment	830
Attendance rate, '06-07	96.4%
Dropout rate	NA
Students per teacher	9.7
Per pupil expenditure	$14,872
Median faculty salary	$55,885
Median administrator salary	$115,420
Grade 12 enrollment	NA
High school graduation rate	NA

Assessment test results
(percent scoring at proficient or advanced level)

	Language	Math
NJASK-Grade 3	94.6%	96.7%
GEPA-Grade 8	93.1%	98.0%
HSPA-High School	NA	NA

SAT Score Averages, 2006-07

Pct tested	Math	Verbal	Writing
NA	NA	NA	NA

Teacher Qualifications

Avg. years of experience	8
Highly-qualified teachers one subject/all subjects	100%/100%

No Child Left Behind

AYP, 2006-07	Meets Standards

Municipal Finance

State Aid Programs, 2009

Total aid	$695,671
CMPTRA	0
Energy tax receipts	657,106
Garden State Trust	0

General Budget, 2008

Total tax levy	$33,828,850
County levy	4,099,394
County taxes	3,874,888
County library	0
County health	0
County open space	224,507
School levy	22,276,108
Muni. levy	7,453,347
Misc. revenues	3,575,083

Taxes	2006	2007	2008
General tax rate per $100	1.87	1.98	2.049
County equalization ratio	87.18	73.96	73.70
Net valuation taxable	$1,554,952,500	$1,603,445,695	$1,652,626,979
State equalized value	$2,104,218,231	$2,175,154,381	$2,196,244,058

Demographics & Socio-Economic Characteristics
(2000 US Census, except as noted)

Population
1980*	2,285
1990*	2,063
2000	1,170
Male	582
Female	588
2007 (estimate)*	1,344
Population density	14.0

Race & Hispanic Origin, 2000
Race
White	1,147
Black/African American	7
American Indian/Alaska Native	1
Asian	4
Native Hawaiian/Pacific Islander	0
Other race	2
Two or more races	9
Hispanic origin, total	14
Mexican	2
Puerto Rican	6
Cuban	0
Other Hispanic	6

Age & Nativity, 2000
Under 5 years	57
18 years and over	868
21 years and over	824
65 years and over	90
85 years and over	7
Median age	38.4
Native-born	1,125
Foreign-born	35

Educational Attainment, 2000
Population 25 years and over	781
Less than 9th grade	4.5%
High school grad or higher	83.0%
Bachelor's degree or higher	18.4%
Graduate degree	6.1%

Income & Poverty, 1999
Per capita income	$26,126
Median household income	$59,271
Median family income	$65,972
Persons in poverty	33
H'holds receiving public assistance	8
H'holds receiving social security	76

Households, 2000
Total households	425
With persons under 18	164
With persons over 65	69
Family households	323
Single-person households	81
Persons per household	2.75
Persons per family	3.15

Labor & Employment
Total civilian labor force, 2007**	765
Unemployment rate	4.4%
Total civilian labor force, 2000	662
Unemployment rate	3.6%

Employed persons 16 years and over by occupation, 2000
Managers & professionals	181
Service occupations	91
Sales & office occupations	147
Farming, fishing & forestry	8
Construction & maintenance	118
Production & transportation	93
Self-employed persons	41

* US Census Bureau
** New Jersey Department of Labor

General Information
Township of Woodland
PO Box 388
Chatsworth, NJ 08019
609-726-1700

Website	NA
Year of incorporation	1866
Land/water area (sq. miles)	95.94/0.45
Form of government	Township

Government
Legislative Districts
US Congressional	3
State Legislative	8

Local Officials, 2009
Mayor	Robert DePetris
Manager	Maryalice Brown
Clerk	Maryalice Brown
Finance Dir	John Cicalese
Tax Assessor	Dennis DeKlerk
Tax Collector	Michele Adams
Attorney	Anthony Drollas
Building	Dan McGonigle
Comm Dev/Planning	NA
Engineering	Robert Callaway
Public Works	Matthew Henrich
Police Chief	(State)
Emergency Mgmt Dir	Stan Fayer

Housing & Construction
Housing Units, 2000*
Total	448
Median rent	$579
Median SF home value	$129,300

Permits for New Residential Construction
	Units	Value
Total, 2006	5	$657,629
Single family	5	$657,629
Total, 2007	8	$1,165,000
Single family	8	$1,165,000

Real Property Valuation, 2008
	Parcels	Valuation
Total	3,715	$169,124,160
Vacant	3,050	9,941,760
Residential	460	125,743,700
Commercial	20	5,692,000
Industrial	8	9,322,000
Apartments	0	0
Farm land	130	945,300
Farm homestead	47	17,479,400

Average Property Value & Tax, 2008
Residential value	$282,491
Property tax	$4,665
Tax credit/rebate	$883

Public Library
No public municipal library

Library statistics, 2007
Population served	NA
Full-time/total staff	NA/NA

	Total	Per capita
Holdings	NA	NA
Revenues	NA	NA
Expenditures	NA	NA
Annual visits	NA	NA
Internet terminals/annual users	NA/NA	

Public Safety
Number of officers, 2007	0

Crime	2006	2007
Total crimes	64	57
Violent	18	6
Murder	1	0
Rape	0	0
Robbery	0	0
Aggravated assault	17	6
Non-violent	46	51
Burglary	20	15
Larceny	25	30
Vehicle theft	1	6
Domestic violence	0	17
Arson	1	0
Total crime rate	46.7	41.5
Violent	13.1	4.4
Non-violent	33.6	37.1

Public School District
(for school year 2007-08 except as noted)

Woodland Township School District
2 Giles Ave, PO Box 477
Chatsworth, NJ 08019
(609) 726-1230
Superintendent	William Randazzo
Number of schools	1
Grade plan	K-8
Enrollment	159
Attendance rate, '06-07	94.1%
Dropout rate	NA
Students per teacher	10.8
Per pupil expenditure	$15,556
Median faculty salary	$59,500
Median administrator salary	$76,694
Grade 12 enrollment	NA
High school graduation rate	NA

Assessment test results
(percent scoring at proficient or advanced level)
	Language	Math
NJASK-Grade 3	75.0%	75.0%
GEPA-Grade 8	74.1%	81.5%
HSPA-High School	NA	NA

SAT Score Averages, 2006-07
Pct tested	Math	Verbal	Writing
NA	NA	NA	NA

Teacher Qualifications
Avg. years of experience	20
Highly-qualified teachers one subject/all subjects	100%/100%

No Child Left Behind
AYP, 2006-07	Meets Standards

Municipal Finance
State Aid Programs, 2009
Total aid	$1,376,813
CMPTRA	47,937
Energy tax receipts	137,099
Garden State Trust	731,138

General Budget, 2008
Total tax levy	$2,804,125
County levy	670,684
County taxes	550,860
County library	50,803
County health	0
County open space	69,021
School levy	2,133,442
Muni. levy	0
Misc. revenues	2,278,461

Taxes	2006	2007	2008
General tax rate per $100	2.989	1.65	1.652
County equalization ratio	63.78	101.89	98.08
Net valuation taxable	$95,777,305	$169,497,841	$169,818,319
State equalized value	$164,121,129	$172,803,195	$173,959,357

See Introduction for an explanation of all data sources.

Demographics & Socio-Economic Characteristics

(2000 US Census, except as noted)

Population
1980*	2,578
1990*	2,547
2000	2,796
Male	1,362
Female	1,434
2007 (estimate)*	2,687
Population density	12,213.6

Race & Hispanic Origin, 2000
Race
White	1,354
Black/African American	635
American Indian/Alaska Native	16
Asian	343
Native Hawaiian/Pacific Islander	0
Other race	324
Two or more races	124
Hispanic origin, total	576
Mexican	29
Puerto Rican	456
Cuban	5
Other Hispanic	86

Age & Nativity, 2000
Under 5 years	219
18 years and over	1,889
21 years and over	1,773
65 years and over	244
85 years and over	27
Median age	30.8
Native-born	2,401
Foreign-born	395

Educational Attainment, 2000
Population 25 years and over	1,679
Less than 9th grade	11.0%
High school grad or higher	69.3%
Bachelor's degree or higher	8.0%
Graduate degree	1.7%

Income & Poverty, 1999
Per capita income	$14,757
Median household income	$39,138
Median family income	$39,669
Persons in poverty	388
H'holds receiving public assistance	83
H'holds receiving social security	228

Households, 2000
Total households	912
With persons under 18	445
With persons over 65	197
Family households	684
Single-person households	189
Persons per household	3.07
Persons per family	3.52

Labor & Employment
Total civilian labor force, 2007**	1,409
Unemployment rate	5.9%
Total civilian labor force, 2000	1,321
Unemployment rate	5.4%

Employed persons 16 years and over by occupation, 2000
Managers & professionals	268
Service occupations	226
Sales & office occupations	353
Farming, fishing & forestry	0
Construction & maintenance	71
Production & transportation	332
Self-employed persons	29

‡ Branch of county library
* US Census Bureau
** New Jersey Department of Labor

General Information
Borough of Woodlynne
200 Cooper Ave
Woodlynne, NJ 08107
856-962-8300
Website	www.woodlynnenj.com
Year of incorporation	1901
Land/water area (sq. miles)	0.22/0.02
Form of government	Borough

Government
Legislative Districts
US Congressional	1
State Legislative	5

Local Officials, 2009
Mayor	Jeraldo Fuentes
Manager	Jeraldo Fuentes
Clerk	Lavern Davis
Finance Dir	Adriane McKendry
Tax Assessor	Bruce Coyle
Tax Collector	Paula Etschman
Attorney	Michael McKenna
Building	William Joseph
Planning	Cheryl Linthicum
Engineering	Steven Bach
Public Works	Robert Kenny
Police Chief	NA
Emerg/Fire Director	Kenneth Steward

Housing & Construction
Housing Units, 2000*
Total	1,012
Median rent	$635
Median SF home value	$56,800

Permits for New Residential Construction
	Units	Value
Total, 2006	1	$80,300
Single family	1	$80,300
Total, 2007	0	$0
Single family	0	$0

Real Property Valuation, 2008
	Parcels	Valuation
Total	931	$50,391,650
Vacant	18	298,800
Residential	876	45,579,400
Commercial	30	3,782,550
Industrial	0	0
Apartments	7	730,900
Farm land	0	0
Farm homestead	0	0

Average Property Value & Tax, 2008
Residential value	$52,031
Property tax	$3,980
Tax credit/rebate	$831

Public Library
Woodlynne Public Library‡
200 Cooper Ave
Woodlynne, NJ 08107
856-962-7172
Director	Ann Vennell

Library statistics, 2007
see Camden County profile
for library system statistics

Public Safety
Number of officers, 2007 0
Crime	2006	2007
Total crimes	127	158
Violent	18	24
Murder	0	0
Rape	0	2
Robbery	4	13
Aggravated assault	14	9
Non-violent	109	134
Burglary	20	37
Larceny	69	74
Vehicle theft	20	23
Domestic violence	36	39
Arson	0	2
Total crime rate	46.3	58.1
Violent	6.6	8.8
Non-violent	39.7	49.3

Public School District
(for school year 2007-08 except as noted)

Woodlynne Borough School District
131 Elm Avenue
Woodlynne, NJ 08107
(856) 962-8822
Superintendent	Patricia T. Doloughty
Number of schools	1
Grade plan	K-8
Enrollment	459
Attendance rate, '06-07	94.7%
Dropout rate	NA
Students per teacher	12.9
Per pupil expenditure	$10,986
Median faculty salary	$45,993
Median administrator salary	$96,273
Grade 12 enrollment	NA
High school graduation rate	NA

Assessment test results
(percent scoring at proficient or advanced level)
	Language	Math
NJASK-Grade 3	55.0%	65.0%
GEPA-Grade 8	28.3%	68.3%
HSPA-High School	NA	NA

SAT Score Averages, 2006-07
Pct tested	Math	Verbal	Writing
NA	NA	NA	NA

Teacher Qualifications
Avg. years of experience	6
Highly-qualified teachers one subject/all subjects	100%/100%

No Child Left Behind
AYP, 2006-07 ....Meets Standards

Municipal Finance
State Aid Programs, 2009
Total aid	$219,711
CMPTRA	84,290
Energy tax receipts	135,421
Garden State Trust	0

General Budget, 2008
Total tax levy	$3,857,308
County levy	639,003
County taxes	577,509
County library	41,398
County health	0
County open space	20,096
School levy	1,767,260
Muni. levy	1,451,044
Misc. revenues	1,273,378

Taxes	2006	2007	2008
General tax rate per $100	6.924	7.125	7.650
County equalization ratio	68.71	58.18	50.28
Net valuation taxable	$50,288,450	$50,438,045	$50,423,754
State equalized value	$86,471,169	$100,283,977	$106,861,975

See Introduction for an explanation of all data sources.

Demographics & Socio-Economic Characteristics
(2000 US Census, except as noted)

Population
1980*	7,929
1990*	7,506
2000	7,644
Male	3,632
Female	4,012
2007 (estimate)*	7,505
Population density	6,822.7

Race & Hispanic Origin, 2000
Race
White	6,957
Black/African American	64
American Indian/Alaska Native	6
Asian	384
Native Hawaiian/Pacific Islander	1
Other race	135
Two or more races	97
Hispanic origin, total	556
Mexican	11
Puerto Rican	138
Cuban	87
Other Hispanic	320

Age & Nativity, 2000
Under 5 years	467
18 years and over	6,021
21 years and over	5,876
65 years and over	1,297
85 years and over	153
Median age	40.3
Native-born	6,481
Foreign-born	1,162

Educational Attainment, 2000
Population 25 years and over..... 5,590
Less than 9th grade	5.6%
High school grad or higher	84.4%
Bachelor's degree or higher	27.7%
Graduate degree	6.2%

Income & Poverty, 1999
Per capita income	$29,865
Median household income	$60,949
Median family income	$72,500
Persons in poverty	119
H'holds receiving public assistance	37
H'holds receiving social security	979

Households, 2000
Total households	3,024
With persons under 18	926
With persons over 65	952
Family households	2,138
Single-person households	781
Persons per household	2.53
Persons per family	3.07

Labor & Employment
Total civilian labor force, 2007**	4,321
Unemployment rate	2.9%
Total civilian labor force, 2000	4,086
Unemployment rate	3.3%

Employed persons 16 years and over by occupation, 2000
Managers & professionals	1,563
Service occupations	376
Sales & office occupations	1,227
Farming, fishing & forestry	0
Construction & maintenance	334
Production & transportation	452
Self-employed persons	219

* US Census Bureau
** New Jersey Department of Labor

General Information
Borough of Wood-Ridge
85 Humboldt St
Wood Ridge, NJ 07075
201-939-0202
Website	njwoodridge.org
Year of incorporation	1894
Land/water area (sq. miles)	1.10/0.00
Form of government	Borough

Government
Legislative Districts
US Congressional	9
State Legislative	36

Local Officials, 2009
Mayor	Paul Sarlo
Manager	Christopher W. Eilert
Clerk	Diane Thornley
Finance Dir.	Nicholas Fargo
Tax Assessor	Stuart Stolarz
Tax Collector	Jacqueline Sharkey
Attorney	Paul Barbire
Building	Gary Ippolito
Comm Dev/Planning	NA
Engineering	Michael Neglia
Public Works	Richard Gennarelli
Police Chief	Joseph Rutigliano
Emerg/Fire Director	Tony Gentile

Housing & Construction
Housing Units, 2000*
Total	3,087
Median rent	$966
Median SF home value	$196,800

Permits for New Residential Construction
	Units	Value
Total, 2006	13	$3,720,988
Single family	13	$3,720,988
Total, 2007	8	$1,939,100
Single family	8	$1,939,100

Real Property Valuation, 2008
	Parcels	Valuation
Total	2,629	$781,909,800
Vacant	46	56,865,200
Residential	2,481	580,594,200
Commercial	66	38,213,700
Industrial	23	87,080,400
Apartments	13	19,156,300
Farm land	0	0
Farm homestead	0	0

Average Property Value & Tax, 2008
Residential value	$234,016
Property tax	$7,101
Tax credit/rebate	$1,088

Public Library
Wood-Ridge Memorial Library
231 Hackensack St
Wood-Ridge, NJ 07075
201-438-2455
Director....................John J. Trause

Library statistics, 2007
Population served	7,644
Full-time/total staff	2/4

	Total	Per capita
Holdings	36,053	4.72
Revenues	$441,833	$57.80
Expenditures	$399,930	$52.32
Annual visits	82,955	10.85
Internet terminals/annual users		7/7,183

Public Safety
Number of officers, 2007 22
Crime	2006	2007
Total crimes	62	100
Violent	7	3
Murder	0	0
Rape	0	0
Robbery	2	1
Aggravated assault	5	2
Non-violent	55	97
Burglary	7	30
Larceny	43	63
Vehicle theft	5	4
Domestic violence	26	34
Arson	0	0
Total crime rate	8.1	13.2
Violent	0.9	0.4
Non-violent	7.2	12.8

Public School District
(for school year 2007-08 except as noted)

Wood-Ridge School District
89 Hackensack Street
Wood-Ridge, NJ 07075
(201) 933-6778
Superintendent	Elaine Giugliano
Number of schools	3
Grade plan	K-12
Enrollment	1,150
Attendance rate, '06-07	95.3%
Dropout rate	0.8%
Students per teacher	12.5
Per pupil expenditure	$12,638
Median faculty salary	$50,026
Median administrator salary	$109,024
Grade 12 enrollment	98
High school graduation rate	96.2%

Assessment test results
(percent scoring at proficient or advanced level)
	Language	Math
NJASK-Grade 3	91.3%	93.8%
GEPA-Grade 8	67.4%	91.0%
HSPA-High School	78.8%	87.6%

SAT Score Averages, 2006-07
Pct tested	Math	Verbal	Writing
95%	513	491	486

Teacher Qualifications
Avg. years of experience	5
Highly-qualified teachers one subject/all subjects	97.0%/97.0%

No Child Left Behind
AYP, 2006-07 ....Meets Standards

Municipal Finance
State Aid Programs, 2009
Total aid	$1,011,745
CMPTRA	337,024
Energy tax receipts	649,428
Garden State Trust	0

General Budget, 2008
Total tax levy	$23,742,056
County levy	2,492,335
County taxes	2,357,457
County library	0
County health	0
County open space	134,878
School levy	12,328,415
Muni. levy	8,921,306
Misc. revenues	3,027,329

Taxes
	2006	2007	2008
General tax rate per $100	2.67	2.86	3.037
County equalization ratio	71.02	63.91	58.96
Net valuation taxable	$766,971,400	$781,729,040	$782,444,574
State equalized value	$1,200,694,298	$1,325,471,731	$1,342,869,195

See Introduction for an explanation of all data sources.

Demographics & Socio-Economic Characteristics

(2000 US Census, except as noted)

Population

1980*	3,250
1990*	3,154
2000	3,136
Male	1,459
Female	1,677
2007 (estimate)*	3,321
Population density	2,088.7

Race & Hispanic Origin, 2000

Race

White	2,667
Black/African American	405
American Indian/Alaska Native	6
Asian	23
Native Hawaiian/Pacific Islander	0
Other race	8
Two or more races	27
Hispanic origin, total	49
Mexican	12
Puerto Rican	14
Cuban	2
Other Hispanic	21

Age & Nativity, 2000

Under 5 years	183
18 years and over	2,360
21 years and over	2,270
65 years and over	517
85 years and over	66
Median age	37.9
Native-born	3,031
Foreign-born	105

Educational Attainment, 2000

Population 25 years and over	2,129
Less than 9th grade	2.8%
High school grad or higher	92.8%
Bachelor's degree or higher	31.6%
Graduate degree	9.8%

Income & Poverty, 1999

Per capita income	$24,182
Median household income	$44,533
Median family income	$56,328
Persons in poverty	171
H'holds receiving public assistance	10
H'holds receiving social security	434

Households, 2000

Total households	1,304
With persons under 18	435
With persons over 65	380
Family households	840
Single-person households	401
Persons per household	2.38
Persons per family	3.00

Labor & Employment

Total civilian labor force, 2007**	1,627
Unemployment rate	2.6%
Total civilian labor force, 2000	1,617
Unemployment rate	3.1%

Employed persons 16 years and over by occupation, 2000

Managers & professionals	634
Service occupations	227
Sales & office occupations	345
Farming, fishing & forestry	4
Construction & maintenance	87
Production & transportation	270
Self-employed persons	83

‡ Joint Library with Pilesgrove
* US Census Bureau
** New Jersey Department of Labor

General Information

Borough of Woodstown
PO Box 286
Woodstown, NJ 08098
856-769-2200

Website	www.historicwoodstown.org
Year of incorporation	1882
Land/water area (sq. miles)	1.59/0.04
Form of government	Borough

Government

Legislative Districts

US Congressional	2
State Legislative	3

Local Officials, 2009

Mayor	Richard S. Pfeffer
Manager/Admin	NA
Clerk	Cynthia Dalessio
Finance Dir	James Hackett
Tax Assessor	Marie Procacci
Tax Collector	Elaine Urion
Attorney	George G. Rosenberger
Building	Joe Wille
Planning	Leah Furey
Engineering	Thomas Cundey
Public Works	Frank Mitchell
Police Chief	George Lacy
Emerg/Fire Director	Brian Facemayer

Housing & Construction

Housing Units, 2000*

Total	1,389
Median rent	$644
Median SF home value	$118,800

Permits for New Residential Construction

	Units	Value
Total, 2006	25	$2,102,975
Single family	25	$2,102,975
Total, 2007	24	$2,017,525
Single family	24	$2,017,525

Real Property Valuation, 2008

	Parcels	Valuation
Total	1,280	$298,882,800
Vacant	76	4,298,000
Residential	1,094	243,424,100
Commercial	86	39,192,400
Industrial	0	0
Apartments	11	11,715,400
Farm land	12	103,400
Farm homestead	1	149,500

Average Property Value & Tax, 2008

Residential value	$222,442
Property tax	$5,270
Tax credit/rebate	$947

Public Library

Woodstown-Pilesgrove Library‡
14 School Ln
Woodstown, NJ 08098
856-769-0098

Director .... Ruth Fritz

Library statistics, 2007

Population served	7,059
Full-time/total staff	NA/0

	Total	Per capita
Holdings	0	NA
Revenues	$0	NA
Expenditures	$0	NA
Annual visits	NA	NA
Internet terminals/annual users	NA/NA	

Public Safety

Number of officers, 2007 9

Crime	2006	2007
Total crimes	67	72
Violent	4	11
Murder	0	0
Rape	0	1
Robbery	2	0
Aggravated assault	2	10
Non-violent	63	61
Burglary	14	13
Larceny	48	42
Vehicle theft	1	6
Domestic violence	41	74
Arson	0	0
Total crime rate	20.2	21.6
Violent	1.2	3.3
Non-violent	19.0	18.3

Public School District

(for school year 2007-08 except as noted)

Woodstown-Pilesgrove Reg. School District
135 East Avenue
Woodstown, NJ 08098
(856) 769-1664

Superintendent	James Kerfoot (Int)
Number of schools	3
Grade plan	K-12
Enrollment	1,647
Attendance rate, '06-07	95.1%
Dropout rate	0.7%
Students per teacher	11.0
Per pupil expenditure	$12,127
Median faculty salary	$51,850
Median administrator salary	$98,358
Grade 12 enrollment	136
High school graduation rate	97.8%

Assessment test results

(percent scoring at proficient or advanced level)

	Language	Math
NJASK-Grade 3	90.6%	94.7%
GEPA-Grade 8	69.2%	81.8%
HSPA-High School	85.3%	89.2%

SAT Score Averages, 2006-07

Pct tested	Math	Verbal	Writing
81%	493	494	484

Teacher Qualifications

Avg. years of experience	10
Highly-qualified teachers one subject/all subjects	100%/100%

No Child Left Behind

AYP, 2006-07 .... Meets Standards

Municipal Finance

State Aid Programs, 2009

Total aid	$321,117
CMPTRA	118,860
Energy tax receipts	194,229
Garden State Trust	0

General Budget, 2008

Total tax levy	$7,106,419
County levy	2,586,080
County taxes	2,530,284
County library	0
County health	0
County open space	55,797
School levy	3,168,359
Muni. levy	1,351,980
Misc. revenues	1,863,873

Taxes

	2006	2007	2008
General tax rate per $100	4.215	4.363	2.370
County equalization ratio	68.42	58.11	108.01
Net valuation taxable	$147,001,000	$152,863,474	$299,963,174
State equalized value	$254,211,007	$278,006,300	$302,312,787

See Introduction for an explanation of all data sources.

Demographics & Socio-Economic Characteristics
(2000 US Census, except as noted)

Population
1980*	1,129
1990*	1,459
2000	3,032
Male	1,505
Female	1,527
2007 (estimate)*	8,930
Population density	426.5

Race & Hispanic Origin, 2000
Race
White	2,763
Black/African American	138
American Indian/Alaska Native	0
Asian	34
Native Hawaiian/Pacific Islander	0
Other race	59
Two or more races	38
Hispanic origin, total	118
Mexican	26
Puerto Rican	65
Cuban	0
Other Hispanic	27

Age & Nativity, 2000
Under 5 years	309
18 years and over	2,081
21 years and over	2,001
65 years and over	206
85 years and over	21
Median age	33.8
Native-born	2,959
Foreign-born	73

Educational Attainment, 2000
Population 25 years and over	1,918
Less than 9th grade	4.0%
High school grad or higher	88.1%
Bachelor's degree or higher	29.2%
Graduate degree	11.6%

Income & Poverty, 1999
Per capita income	$29,503
Median household income	$83,790
Median family income	$87,111
Persons in poverty	88
H'holds receiving public assistance	8
H'holds receiving social security	151

Households, 2000
Total households	959
With persons under 18	496
With persons over 65	152
Family households	838
Single-person households	82
Persons per household	3.13
Persons per family	3.35

Labor & Employment
Total civilian labor force, 2007**	1,787
Unemployment rate	3.6%
Total civilian labor force, 2000	1,531
Unemployment rate	2.8%

Employed persons 16 years and over by occupation, 2000
Managers & professionals	664
Service occupations	123
Sales & office occupations	395
Farming, fishing & forestry	36
Construction & maintenance	127
Production & transportation	143
Self-employed persons	92

‡ Joint library with Swedesboro Borough
* US Census Bureau
** New Jersey Department of Labor

General Information
Township of Woolwich
121 Woodstown Rd
Woolwich Township, NJ 08085
856-467-2666
Website	www.woolwichtwp.org
Year of incorporation	1767
Land/water area (sq. miles)	20.94/0.24
Form of government	Township

Government
Legislative Districts
US Congressional	2
State Legislative	3

Local Officials, 2009
Mayor	Joe Chila
Administrator	Jane DiBella
Clerk	Jane DiBella
Finance Dir	Merrie Schmidt
Tax Assessor	Bruce Komito
Tax Collector	Mary Folker
Attorney	Timothy Scaffidi
Building	James Sabetta
Comm Dev/Planning	NA
Engineering	Stan Bitgood
Public Works	Anthony Bertino
Police Chief	Russell Marino
Emerg/Fire Director	Ed Barber

Housing & Construction
Housing Units, 2000*
Total	1,026
Median rent	$763
Median SF home value	$194,800

Permits for New Residential Construction
	Units	Value
Total, 2006	102	$14,458,449
Single family	102	$14,458,449
Total, 2007	86	$13,308,708
Single family	86	$13,308,708

Real Property Valuation, 2008
	Parcels	Valuation
Total	3,876	$598,218,500
Vacant	732	25,487,400
Residential	2,713	497,155,600
Commercial	67	42,973,100
Industrial	0	0
Apartments	1	12,611,300
Farm land	254	4,972,000
Farm homestead	109	15,019,100

Average Property Value & Tax, 2008
Residential value	$181,494
Property tax	$8,356
Tax credit/rebate	$1,115

Public Library
Swedesboro Public Library‡
1442 Kings Hwy
Swedesboro, NJ 08085
856-467-0111
Director	Marge Dombrosky

Library statistics, 2007
Population served	NA
Full-time/total staff	NA/NA

	Total	Per capita
Holdings	NA	NA
Revenues	NA	NA
Expenditures	NA	NA
Annual visits	NA	NA
Internet terminals/annual users	NA/NA	

Public Safety
Number of officers, 2007	19

Crime	2006	2007
Total crimes	84	55
Violent	4	7
Murder	0	0
Rape	0	0
Robbery	1	2
Aggravated assault	3	5
Non-violent	80	48
Burglary	8	11
Larceny	70	34
Vehicle theft	2	3
Domestic violence	16	32
Arson	0	0
Total crime rate	11.1	6.4
Violent	0.5	0.8
Non-violent	10.6	5.6

Public School District
(for school year 2007-08 except as noted)

Swedesboro-Woolwich School District
15 Fredrick Blvd
Woolwich Twp, NJ 08085
(856) 241-1136
Superintendent	Richard Fisher
Number of schools	3
Grade plan	K-6
Enrollment	1,519
Attendance rate, '06-07	95.6%
Dropout rate	NA
Students per teacher	11.7
Per pupil expenditure	$9,691
Median faculty salary	$44,900
Median administrator salary	$84,407
Grade 12 enrollment	NA
High school graduation rate	NA

Assessment test results
(percent scoring at proficient or advanced level)
	Language	Math
NJASK-Grade 3	94.4%	90.7%
GEPA-Grade 8	NA	NA
HSPA-High School	NA	NA

SAT Score Averages, 2006-07
Pct tested	Math	Verbal	Writing
NA	NA	NA	NA

Teacher Qualifications
Avg. years of experience	5
Highly-qualified teachers one subject/all subjects	100%/100%

No Child Left Behind
AYP, 2006-07	Meets Standards

Municipal Finance
State Aid Programs, 2009
Total aid	$535,667
CMPTRA	0
Energy tax receipts	521,444
Garden State Trust	10,046

General Budget, 2008
Total tax levy	$27,602,056
County levy	7,050,020
County taxes	6,083,995
County library	489,256
County health	0
County open space	476,770
School levy	16,587,071
Muni. levy	3,964,965
Misc. revenues	4,463,347

Taxes
	2006	2007	2008
General tax rate per $100	3.96	4.181	4.605
County equalization ratio	59.96	53.86	50.33
Net valuation taxable	$509,172,600	$564,546,727	$599,495,229
State equalized value	$946,674,886	$1,120,424,885	$1,204,935,683

See Introduction for an explanation of all data sources.

Demographics & Socio-Economic Characteristics

(2000 US Census, except as noted)

Population

1980*	3,031
1990*	3,843
2000	748
Male	364
Female	384
2007 (estimate)*	733
Population density	416.5

Race & Hispanic Origin, 2000

Race
White	373
Black/African American	226
American Indian/Alaska Native	4
Asian	54
Native Hawaiian/Pacific Islander	0
Other race	54
Two or more races	37
Hispanic origin, total	84
Mexican	27
Puerto Rican	27
Cuban	1
Other Hispanic	29

Age & Nativity, 2000

Under 5 years	58
18 years and over	526
21 years and over	496
65 years and over	64
85 years and over	5
Median age	31.2
Native-born	632
Foreign-born	115

Educational Attainment, 2000

Population 25 years and over	434
Less than 9th grade	4.1%
High school grad or higher	80.4%
Bachelor's degree or higher	7.8%
Graduate degree	1.4%

Income & Poverty, 1999

Per capita income	$14,489
Median household income	$27,500
Median family income	$29,375
Persons in poverty	179
H'holds receiving public assistance	11
H'holds receiving social security	46

Households, 2000

Total households	312
With persons under 18	118
With persons over 65	51
Family households	182
Single-person households	108
Persons per household	2.37
Persons per family	3.09

Labor & Employment

Total civilian labor force, 2007**	411
Unemployment rate	5.5%
Total civilian labor force, 2000	364
Unemployment rate	6.9%

Employed persons 16 years and over by occupation, 2000
Managers & professionals	46
Service occupations	117
Sales & office occupations	94
Farming, fishing & forestry	0
Construction & maintenance	21
Production & transportation	61
Self-employed persons	7

* US Census Bureau
** New Jersey Department of Labor

General Information

Borough of Wrightstown
21 Saylors Pond Rd
Wrightstown, NJ 08562
609-723-4450
Email	wrightstownclerk@comcast.net
Year of incorporation	1918
Land/water area (sq. miles)	1.76/0.00
Form of government	Borough

Government

Legislative Districts

US Congressional	3
State Legislative	8

Local Officials, 2009

Mayor	Thomas Harper
Manager/Admin	NA
Clerk	Ellen Thorne
Finance Dir	Ron Ghrist
Tax Assessor	Douglas Kolton
Tax Collector	Lynn Davis
Attorney	Nicholas Costa
Building	Harry Case
Planning	Ragan Design Group
Engineering	Kluk Consultants
N/A	NA
Police Chief	NA
Emerg Management	Costic M. Borsavage

Housing & Construction

Housing Units, 2000*

Total	339
Median rent	$623
Median SF home value	$98,900

Permits for New Residential Construction

	Units	Value
Total, 2006	5	$702,250
Single family	5	$702,250
Total, 2007	5	$551,100
Single family	5	$551,100

Real Property Valuation, 2008

	Parcels	Valuation
Total	201	$26,587,550
Vacant	29	839,450
Residential	125	12,862,500
Commercial	37	9,390,700
Industrial	2	252,500
Apartments	6	3,229,950
Farm land	2	12,450
Farm homestead	0	0

Average Property Value & Tax, 2008

Residential value	$102,900
Property tax	$1,945
Tax credit/rebate	$542

Public Library

No public municipal library

Library statistics, 2007

Population served	NA
Full-time/total staff	NA/NA

	Total	Per capita
Holdings	NA	NA
Revenues	NA	NA
Expenditures	NA	NA
Annual visits	NA	NA
Internet terminals/annual users	NA/NA	

Public Safety

Number of officers, 2007 0

Crime	2006	2007
Total crimes	30	26
Violent	8	3
Murder	0	0
Rape	0	0
Robbery	1	1
Aggravated assault	7	2
Non-violent	22	23
Burglary	4	2
Larceny	15	19
Vehicle theft	3	2
Domestic violence	5	10
Arson	0	1
Total crime rate	40.2	35.1
Violent	10.7	4.0
Non-violent	29.5	31.0

Public School District

(for school year 2007-08 except as noted)

New Hanover Township School District
122 Fort Dix St.
Wrightstown, NJ 08562
(609) 723-2139
Superintendent	Terri Sackett
Number of schools	1
Grade plan	K-8
Enrollment	154
Attendance rate, '06-07	94.0%
Dropout rate	NA
Students per teacher	7.3
Per pupil expenditure	$18,607
Median faculty salary	$51,898
Median administrator salary	$87,704
Grade 12 enrollment	NA
High school graduation rate	NA

Assessment test results

(percent scoring at proficient or advanced level)
	Language	Math
NJASK-Grade 3	62.5%	79.2%
GEPA-Grade 8	50.0%	93.8%
HSPA-High School	NA	NA

SAT Score Averages, 2006-07

Pct tested	Math	Verbal	Writing
NA	NA	NA	NA

Teacher Qualifications

Avg. years of experience	10
Highly-qualified teachers one subject/all subjects	100%/100%

No Child Left Behind

AYP, 2006-07 . . . . Meets Standards

Municipal Finance

State Aid Programs, 2009

Total aid	$489,060
CMPTRA	341,953
Energy tax receipts	134,880
Garden State Trust	0

General Budget, 2008

Total tax levy	$576,151
County levy	139,451
County taxes	114,517
County library	10,574
County health	0
County open space	14,359
School levy	436,701
Muni. levy	0
Misc. revenues	1,251,611

Taxes

	2006	2007	2008
General tax rate per $100	1.989	2.14	2.088
County equalization ratio	100.55	68.54	79.00
Net valuation taxable	$24,774,400	$26,657,912	$27,604,716
State equalized value	$37,652,426	$33,472,665	$48,300,733

See Introduction for an explanation of all data sources.

Demographics & Socio-Economic Characteristics
(2000 US Census, except as noted)

Population
1980*	15,500
1990*	15,372
2000	16,508
Male	7,880
Female	8,628
2007 (estimate)*	16,980
Population density	2,592.4

Race & Hispanic Origin, 2000
Race
White	15,607
Black/African American	77
American Indian/Alaska Native	25
Asian	611
Native Hawaiian/Pacific Islander	2
Other race	74
Two or more races	112
Hispanic origin, total	376
Mexican	19
Puerto Rican	94
Cuban	62
Other Hispanic	201

Age & Nativity, 2000
Under 5 years	1,185
18 years and over	11,837
21 years and over	11,512
65 years and over	2,603
85 years and over	481
Median age	40.9
Native-born	14,978
Foreign-born	1,530

Educational Attainment, 2000
Population 25 years and over	11,122
Less than 9th grade	2.5%
High school grad or higher	93.8%
Bachelor's degree or higher	56.6%
Graduate degree	23.0%

Income & Poverty, 1999
Per capita income	$49,375
Median household income	$103,614
Median family income	$117,864
Persons in poverty	290
H'holds receiving public assistance	39
H'holds receiving social security	1,607

Households, 2000
Total households	5,541
With persons under 18	2,410
With persons over 65	1,573
Family households	4,634
Single-person households	819
Persons per household	2.89
Persons per family	3.22

Labor & Employment
Total civilian labor force, 2007**	8,000
Unemployment rate	2.5%
Total civilian labor force, 2000	7,574
Unemployment rate	2.8%

Employed persons 16 years and over by occupation, 2000
Managers & professionals	4,139
Service occupations	453
Sales & office occupations	2,109
Farming, fishing & forestry	5
Construction & maintenance	289
Production & transportation	364
Self-employed persons	691

General Information
Township of Wyckoff
340 Franklin Ave
Scott Plaza
Wyckoff, NJ 07481
201-891-7000

Website	www.wyckoff-nj.com
Year of incorporation	1926
Land/water area (sq. miles)	6.55/0.02
Form of government	Township

Government
Legislative Districts
US Congressional	5
State Legislative	40

Local Officials, 2009
Mayor	Joseph B. Fiorenzo
Manager	Robert Shannon Jr
Clerk	Joyce Santimauro
Finance Dir	Diana McLeod
Tax Assessor	Pamela Steele
Tax Collector	Diana McLeod
Attorney	Robert Landel
Building	Thomas Gensheimer
Planning	J. Gordon Stanley
Engineering	Mark A. DiGennaro
Public Works	Scott Fisher
Police Chief	John W. Ydo
Emerg/Fire Director	David Murphy

Housing & Construction
Housing Units, 2000*
Total	5,638
Median rent	$1,114
Median SF home value	$417,500

Permits for New Residential Construction
	Units	Value
Total, 2006	24	$12,134,960
Single family	24	$12,134,960
Total, 2007	23	$12,879,654
Single family	23	$12,879,654

Real Property Valuation, 2008
	Parcels	Valuation
Total	5,792	$4,651,208,690
Vacant	94	36,084,500
Residential	5,533	4,357,830,290
Commercial	140	212,141,000
Industrial	18	40,155,000
Apartments	2	1,565,600
Farm land	2	27,000
Farm homestead	3	3,405,300

Average Property Value & Tax, 2008
Residential value	$787,795
Property tax	$10,949
Tax credit/rebate	$1,327

Public Library
Wyckoff Public Library
200 Woodland Ave
Wyckoff, NJ 07481
201-891-4866

Director	Judy Schmitt

Library statistics, 2007
Population served	16,508
Full-time/total staff	4/8

	Total	Per capita
Holdings	82,301	4.99
Revenues	$1,677,820	$101.64
Expenditures	$944,589	$57.22
Annual visits	150,443	9.11
Internet terminals/annual users	6/46,788	

Public Safety
Number of officers, 2007	25

Crime	2006	2007
Total crimes	115	126
Violent	4	13
Murder	0	0
Rape	0	0
Robbery	1	1
Aggravated assault	3	12
Non-violent	111	113
Burglary	18	20
Larceny	92	92
Vehicle theft	1	1
Domestic violence	49	62
Arson	0	0
Total crime rate	6.7	7.3
Violent	0.2	0.8
Non-violent	6.5	6.6

Public School District
(for school year 2007-08 except as noted)

Wyckoff Township School District
241 Morse Avenue
Wyckoff, NJ 07481
(201) 848-5700

Superintendent	Janet Razze
Number of schools	5
Grade plan	K-8
Enrollment	2,355
Attendance rate, '06-07	95.4%
Dropout rate	NA
Students per teacher	11.6
Per pupil expenditure	$13,011
Median faculty salary	$62,055
Median administrator salary	$135,586
Grade 12 enrollment	NA
High school graduation rate	NA

Assessment test results
(percent scoring at proficient or advanced level)
	Language	Math
NJASK-Grade 3	98.2%	96.0%
GEPA-Grade 8	92.2%	96.7%
HSPA-High School	NA	NA

SAT Score Averages, 2006-07
Pct tested	Math	Verbal	Writing
NA	NA	NA	NA

Teacher Qualifications
Avg. years of experience	11
Highly-qualified teachers one subject/all subjects	100%/100%

No Child Left Behind
AYP, 2006-07	Meets Standards

Municipal Finance
State Aid Programs, 2009
Total aid	$1,543,825
CMPTRA	181,197
Energy tax receipts	1,285,437
Garden State Trust	0

General Budget, 2008
Total tax levy	$64,729,298
County levy	8,557,210
County taxes	8,093,820
County library	0
County health	0
County open space	463,389
School levy	45,841,043
Muni. levy	10,331,045
Misc. revenues	6,339,092

Taxes
	2006	2007	2008
General tax rate per $100	1.26	1.34	1.391
County equalization ratio	114.6	104.59	100.65
Net valuation taxable	$4,607,255,600	$4,626,761,443	$4,657,429,627
State equalized value	$4,410,683,587	$4,596,921,479	$4,679,393,538

* US Census Bureau
** New Jersey Department of Labor

The New Jersey
Municipal Data Book

2009

State & Municipal Profiles Series

Demographics & Socio-Economic Characteristics

(2007 American Community Survey, except as noted)

Population
1990*	224,327
2000*	252,552
2007	270,644
Male	131,427
Female	139,217
2008 (estimate)*	270,681
Population density	482.4

Race & Hispanic Origin, 2007
Race
White	177,910
Black/African American	45,431
American Indian/Alaska Native	275
Asian	17,758
Native Hawaiian/Pacific Islander	48
Two or more races	5,010
Hispanic origin, total	38,894
Mexican	5,917
Puerto Rican	17,915
Cuban	991
Other Hispanic	14,071

Age & Nativity, 2007
Under 5 years	17,632
18 years and over	205,597
21 years and over	194,792
65 years and over	37,411
85 years and over	5,326
Median age	38.3
Native-born	231,237
Foreign-born	39,407

Educational Attainment, 2007
Population 25 years and over	181,602
Less than 9th grade	6.4%
High school grad or higher	84.2%
Bachelor's degree or higher	22.0%
Graduate degree	6.2%

Households, 2007
Total households	103,197
With persons under 18	37,113
With persons over 65	25,325
Family households	70,082
Single-person households	27,989
Persons per household	2.47
Persons per family	3.01

Income & Poverty, 2007
Per capita income	$26,743
Median household income	$55,767
Median family income	$67,251
Persons in poverty	12.8%
H'holds receiving public assistance	3,159
H'holds receiving social security	28,117

Labor & Employment, 2007***
Total civilian labor force	136,114
Unemployment rate	5.8%

Employed persons 16 years and over by occupation, 2007
Managers & professionals	37,139
Service occupations	38,821
Sales & office occupations	32,239
Farming, fishing & forestry	1,339
Construction & maintenance	10,440
Production & transportation	9,015
Self-employed persons	5,832

Civilian Labor Force Projections***
2009	140,900
2014	148,000
2020	156,400
2025	164,300

*US Census Bureau
**2007 American Community Survey
*** New Jersey Department of Labor
† sum of all municipalities in county

See Introduction for an explanation of all data sources.

General Information

Atlantic County
1333 Atlantic Ave
Atlantic City, NJ 08401
609-345-6700

Website	www.aclink.org
Year of formation	1837
Land/water area (sq. miles)	561.1/110.4
Class	Fifth
Government form	County Executive Plan
Number of Freeholders	9
Number of municipalities	23

Government & Voters

Legislative Districts
US Congressional	2
State Legislative	1-2, 9

Registered Voters, October 2008
Total	176,349
Democratic	52,126
Republican	42,076
Unaffiliated	82,091

County Officials, 2009
County Executive	Dennis Levinson
Administrator	Gerald DelRosso
Clerk	Edward P. McGettigan
Treasurer	Jane Lugo
Tax Administrator	Lois Finifter
Surrogate	James Carney
Prosecutor	Theodor Housel
Public Works Dir	Harry Tillett
Planning/Dev Dir	Joseph Maher
Sheriff	Frank Balles
Fire Marshal	Harold Swartz

County School District

6260 Old Harding Hwy
Mays Landing, NJ 08330
609-625-0004

Superintendent	Thomas Dowd (Actg)
Number of districts	23

Housing & Construction

Housing Units, 2007**
Total	126,388
Single family units	72,350
Multiple family units	50,820
Owner-occupied units	72,038
Renter-occupied units	31,159
Vacant units	23,191
Median rent	$915
Median SF home value	$271,900

Permits for New Residential Construction
	Units	Value
Total, 2006	1,893	$224,611,774
Single family	1,536	$206,702,890
Total, 2007	1,136	$166,014,212
Single family	1,025	$155,724,444

Real Property Valuation, 2008†
	Parcels	Valuation
Total	136,921	$44,586,085,500
Vacant	27,009	2,099,731,500
Residential	101,156	23,597,320,300
Farm land	1,652	17,879,400
Farm homestead	662	92,852,200
Non-residential	6,442	18,778,302,100
Commercial	5,887	18,104,447,300
Industrial	209	165,554,900
Apartments	346	508,299,900

Public Safety

Police Officers, 2007
County officers	174
Sheriff's department	102
Prosecutors	72
Municipal police	964

Crime
Crime	2006	2007
Total crimes	12,012	11,278
Violent	1,471	1,561
Murder	30	16
Rape	82	64
Robbery	595	682
Aggravated assault	764	799
Non-violent	10,541	9,717
Burglary	2,001	2,020
Larceny	8,062	7,198
Vehicle theft	478	499
Domestic violence	5,378	5,265
Arson	62	59
Total crime rate	44.3	41.5
Violent	5.4	5.7
Non-violent	38.9	35.8

Public Library

Atlantic County Library
40 Farragut Avenue
Mays Landing, NJ 08330
(609) 625-2776

Director.............William D. Paullin

Library statistics, 2007
Population served 181,307
	Total	Per capita
Revenues	$8,697,867	$47.97
Expenditures	$8,187,736	$45.16
Holdings	572,406	3.16
Circulation	831,057	4.58
Annual visits	957,056	5.28
Registered borrowers	61,087	
Reference transactions	23,819	
Hours open weekly	64	
Full-time/total staff	30/98	
Interlibrary loans		
Provided/received	10,272/8,912	
Internet terminals	72	
Annual users	130,473	

State Income Tax, 2006
Number of returns	118,874
Increase from previous year	0.7%
Total income	$6,091,033
Per capita	$25,180
Increase from previous year	4.3%
Net charged tax	$165,367
Per capita	$684
Average taxable income	$45,355
Average income tax	$1,391

County Finance

State Aid Programs, 2009†
Total aid	$36,546,011
CMPTRA	3,072,835
Energy tax receipts	31,797,243
Garden State Trust	605,932

General Budget, 2008†
Total tax levy	$892,327,071
County levy	153,568,334
County taxes	129,466,270
County library	8,202,126
County health	4,246,659
County open space	11,653,279
School levy	396,716,138
Muni. levy	342,042,598
Misc. revenues	144,097,559

Taxes†
	2006	2007	2008
Net valuation taxable	$30,744,680,100	$31,428,365,455	$44,640,789,066
State equalized value	$49,966,321,696	57,370,738,179	$56,589,757,221

Demographics & Socio-Economic Characteristics

(2007 American Community Survey, except as noted)

Population

1990*	825,380
2000*	884,118
2007	895,744
Male	435,175
Female	460,569
2008 (estimate)*	894,840
Population density	3820.8

Race & Hispanic Origin, 2007

Race

White	654,060
Black/African American	50,766
American Indian/Alaska Native	824
Asian	127,885
Native Hawaiian/Pacific Islander	0
Two or more races	13,189
Hispanic origin, total	129,833
Mexican	8,429
Puerto Rican	24,999
Cuban	14,501
Other Hispanic	81,904

Age & Nativity, 2007

Under 5 years	48,983
18 years and over	698,246
21 years and over	667,969
65 years and over	132,263
85 years and over	20,257
Median age	41.1
Native-born	636,875
Foreign-born	258,869

Educational Attainment, 2007

Population 25 years and over	626,148
Less than 9th grade	3.9%
High school grad or higher	91.2%
Bachelor's degree or higher	44.7%
Graduate degree	17.1%

Households, 2007

Total households	331,529
With persons under 18	116,019
With persons over 65	92,537
Family households	235,208
Single-person households	83,671
Persons per household	2.66
Persons per family	3.22

Income & Poverty, 2007

Per capita income	$41,472
Median household income	$80,482
Median family income	$98,618
Persons in poverty	5.9%
H'holds receiving public assistance	3,121
H'holds receiving social security	95,942

Labor & Employment, 2007***

Total civilian labor force	474,081
Unemployment rate	3.4%

Employed persons 16 years and over by occupation, 2007

Managers & professionals	203,449
Service occupations	58,171
Sales & office occupations	132,764
Farming, fishing & forestry	52
Construction & maintenance	29,622
Production & transportation	32,575
Self-employed persons	29,831

Civilian Labor Force Projections***

2009	471,700
2014	480,000
2020	496,400
2025	507,400

*US Census Bureau
**2007 American Community Survey
*** New Jersey Department of Labor
† sum of all municipalities in county

General Information

Bergen County
1 Bergen County Plz
Hackensack, NJ 07601
201-336-6000

Website	www.co.bergen.nj.us
Year of formation	1683
Land/water area (sq. miles)	234.2/12.6
Class	First
Government form	County Executive Plan
Number of Freeholders	7
Number of municipalities	70

Government & Voters

Legislative Districts

US Congressional	5,9
State Legislative	32, 35-40

Registered Voters, October 2008

Total	544,374
Democratic	171,379
Republican	111,872
Unaffiliated	260,887

County Officials, 2009

County Executive	Dennis McNerney
Administrator	Robert E. Laux
Clerk	Kathleen Donovan
Finance Dir	Alfred Dispoto
Tax Administrator	Robert Layton
Surrogate	Michael Dressler
Prosecutor	John Molinelli
Public Works Dir	Tom Connolly (Actg)
Planning/Dev Dir	Farouk Ahmad
Sheriff	Leo McGuire
Fire Marshal	Bryan Hennig

County School District

1 Bergen County Plaza, 3rd Floor, Room 350
Hackensack, NJ 07601
201-336-6875

Superintendent	Aaron R. Graham
Number of districts	70

Housing & Construction

Housing Units, 2007**

Total	349,534
Single family units	190,478
Multiple family units	158,284
Owner-occupied units	229,885
Renter-occupied units	101,644
Vacant units	18,005
Median rent	$1,215
Median SF home value	$492,200

Permits for New Residential Construction

	Units	Value
Total, 2006	2,164	$469,835,747
Single family	1,096	$372,519,155
Total, 2007	2,952	$553,051,634
Single family	981	$352,309,161

Real Property Valuation, 2008†

	Parcels	Valuation
Total	269,671	$154,608,441,017
Vacant	6,351	2,147,702,144
Residential	247,222	118,619,593,460
Farm land	82	1,602,200
Farm homestead	51	48,385,100
Non-residential	15,965	33,791,158,113
Commercial	11,490	21,190,278,159
Industrial	2,806	6,596,012,634
Apartments	1,669	6,004,867,320

Public Safety

Police Officers, 2007

County officers	716
Sheriff's department	456
Prosecutors	170
Municipal police	2,179

Crime	2006	2007
Total crimes	13,683	13,183
Violent	952	955
Murder	7	6
Rape	34	33
Robbery	321	323
Aggravated assault	590	593
Non-violent	12,731	12,228
Burglary	2,006	1,872
Larceny	9,700	9,595
Vehicle theft	1,025	761
Domestic violence	4,664	4,381
Arson	67	47
Total crime rate	15.2	14.6
Violent	1.1	1.1
Non-violent	14.1	13.5

Public Library

No County Library
(Library statistics are the sum of all
municipal libraries in the county)

Library statistics, 2007†

Population served ... 862,255

	Total	Per capita
Revenues	$60,789,042	$70.50
Expenditures	$54,647,470	$63.38
Holdings	4,386,582	5.09
Circulation	8,250,039	9.57
Annual visits	6,312,282	7.32

Registered borrowers	487,281
Reference transactions	686,656
Hours open weekly	NA
Number of libraries	62
Full-time/total staff	177/488
Interlibrary loans	
Provided/received	525,083/455,808
Internet terminals	691
Annual users	1,324,953

State Income Tax, 2006

Number of returns	388,245
Increase from previous year	1.4%
Total income	$39,349,076
Per capita	$48,870
Increase from previous year	8.3%
Net charged tax	$1,284,582
Per capita	$1,595
Average taxable income	$93,568
Average income tax	$3,309

County Finance

State Aid Programs, 2009†

Total aid	$117,871,021
CMPTRA	18,399,286
Energy tax receipts	96,039,698
Garden State Trust	46,330

General Budget, 2008†

Total tax levy	$3,025,867,088
County levy	336,174,051
County taxes	317,897,300
County library	0
County health	0
County open space	18,276,751
School levy	1,748,846,182
Muni. levy	940,846,855
Misc. revenues	414,447,412

Taxes†	2006	2007	2008
Net valuation taxable	$121,664,581,572	$141,301,209,895	$154,829,319,580
State equalized value	$170,543,198,365	180,207,616,315	$185,928,683,637

See Introduction for an explanation of all data sources.

Demographics & Socio-Economic Characteristics

(2007 American Community Survey, except as noted)

Population
1990* 395,066
2000* 423,394
2007 446,817
   Male 221,301
   Female 225,516
2008 (estimate)* 445,475
   Population density 553.7

Race & Hispanic Origin, 2007
Race
   White 335,121
   Black/African American 71,809
   American Indian/Alaska Native 1,348
   Asian 18,437
   Native Hawaiian/Pacific Islander 0
   Two or more races 9,945
Hispanic origin, total 23,981
   Mexican 4,553
   Puerto Rican 10,154
   Cuban 441
   Other Hispanic 8,833

Age & Nativity, 2007
Under 5 years 26,669
18 years and over 343,160
21 years and over 324,957
65 years and over 58,090
85 years and over 6,417
   Median age 38.6
Native-born 405,422
Foreign-born 41,395

Educational Attainment, 2007
Population 25 years and over 304,787
Less than 9th grade 2.8%
High school grad or higher 90.8%
Bachelor's degree or higher 33.8%
Graduate degree 12.1%

Households, 2007
Total households 166,164
   With persons under 18 58,076
   With persons over 65 40,805
   Family households 116,499
   Single-person households 42,150
Persons per household 2.62
Persons per family 3.17

Income & Poverty, 2007
Per capita income $34,020
Median household income $73,566
Median family income $87,270
Persons in poverty 4.7%
H'holds receiving public assistance . . . 2,514
H'holds receiving social security 44,626

Labor & Employment, 2007***
Total civilian labor force 240,531
   Unemployment rate 3.8%

Employed persons 16 years and over by occupation, 2007
Managers & professionals 90,924
Service occupations 29,289
Sales & office occupations 62,861
Farming, fishing & forestry 555
Construction & maintenance 17,921
Production & transportation 22,996
Self-employed persons 9,005

Civilian Labor Force Projections***
2009 248,900
2014 260,200
2020 275,700
2025 286,100

*US Census Bureau
**2007 American Community Survey
*** New Jersey Department of Labor
† sum of all municipalities in county

General Information
Burlington County
49 Rancocas Rd
County Office Bldg
Mount Holly, NJ 08060
609-265-5000

Website . . . . www.co.burlington.nj.us
Year of formation 1694
Land/water area (sq. miles) 804.6/14.9
Class . . . . Second
Government form . . . . . . Freeholder Board
Number of Freeholders 5
Number of municipalities 40

Government & Voters

Legislative Districts
US Congressional 1-4
State Legislative 7-9, 30

Registered Voters, October 2008
Total 275,904
   Democratic 91,746
   Republican 65,518
   Unaffiliated 118,527

County Officials, 2009
County Executive . . . . NA
Administrator . . . . Augustus Mosca
Clerk . . . . Timothy Tyler
Finance Dir . . . . Kurt Brock
Tax Administrator . . . . Margaret Nuzzo
Surrogate . . . . George Kotch
Prosecutor . . . . Robert Bernardi
Public Works Dir . . . . Frank Somen
Planning/Dev Dir . . . . Mark Remson
Sheriff . . . . Jean Stanfield
Fire Marshal . . . . Robert Rose

County School District
PO Box 6000
Mt. Holly, NJ 08060
609-265-5060
Superintendent . . . . Lester W. Ritchens
Number of districts 40

Housing & Construction

Housing Units, 2007**
Total 174,782
   Single family units 113,935
   Multiple family units 57,521
   Owner-occupied units 128,970
   Renter-occupied units 37,194
   Vacant units 8,618
   Median rent $998
   Median SF home value $276,600

Permits for New Residential Construction

	Units	Value
Total, 2006	2,784	$153,664,629
Single family	996	$145,912,103
Total, 2007	1,040	$145,229,295
Single family	876	$138,139,060

Real Property Valuation, 2008†

	Parcels	Valuation
Total	167,758	$35,001,298,552
Vacant	15,004	628,689,310
Residential	142,140	27,155,704,578
Farm land	3,042	51,109,666
Farm homestead	1,476	427,433,660
Non-residential	6,096	6,738,361,338
Commercial	5,148	4,579,234,958
Industrial	616	1,271,067,730
Apartments	332	888,058,650

Public Safety

Police Officers, 2007
County officers 158
   Sheriff's department 72
   Prosecutors 86
Municipal police 827

Crime	2006	2007
Total crimes	8,878	8,396
Violent	795	726
Murder	13	7
Rape	80	69
Robbery	264	277
Aggravated assault	438	373
Non-violent	8,083	7,670
Burglary	1,528	1,383
Larceny	5,968	5,791
Vehicle theft	587	496
Domestic violence	3,795	3,708
Arson	79	88
Total crime rate	19.7	18.6
Violent	1.8	1.6
Non-violent	17.9	17.0

Public Library
Burlington County Library
5 Pioneer Blvd, Box 6000
Westampton, NJ 08060
(609) 267-9660

Director . . . . Kim Ruth

Library statistics, 2007
Population served 331,148

	Total	Per capita
Revenues	$13,082,088	$39.51
Expenditures	$10,999,319	$33.22
Holdings	1,044,542	3.15
Circulation	1,995,428	6.03
Annual visits	1,355,845	4.09

Registered borrowers 107,272
Reference transactions 305,412
Hours open weekly 68
Full-time/total staff 38/121
Interlibrary loans
   Provided/received 6,784/6,088
Internet terminals 193
   Annual users 227,346

State Income Tax, 2006
Number of returns 189,183
   Increase from previous year 0.9%
Total income $13,458,574
   Per capita $34,124
   Increase from previous year 6.6%
Net charged tax $398,737
   Per capita $1,011
Average taxable income $64,127
Average income tax $2,108

County Finance

State Aid Programs, 2009†
Total aid $62,690,613
   CMPTRA 10,410,339
   Energy tax receipts 47,622,638
   Garden State Trust 2,465,532

General Budget, 2008†
Total tax levy $1,046,221,086
   County levy 194,177,108
    County taxes 162,686,033
    County library 11,089,980
    County health 0
    County open space 20,401,095
   School levy 658,067,405
   Muni. levy 193,976,573
   Misc. revenues 211,162,205

Taxes†

	2006	2007	2008
Net valuation taxable	$28,215,475,850	$30,683,525,297	$35,084,541,129
State equalized value	$46,154,712,994	50,495,888,961	$52,139,640,688

See Introduction for an explanation of all data sources.

Demographics & Socio-Economic Characteristics

(2007 American Community Survey, except as noted)

Population

1990*	502,824
2000*	508,932
2007	513,769
Male	249,507
Female	264,262
2008 (estimate)*	517,234
Population density	2326.7

Race & Hispanic Origin, 2007

Race

White	341,175
Black/African American	94,933
American Indian/Alaska Native	321
Asian	22,781
Native Hawaiian/Pacific Islander	0
Two or more races	12,535
Hispanic origin, total	61,479
Mexican	9,421
Puerto Rican	38,409
Cuban	1,239
Other Hispanic	12,410

Age & Nativity, 2007

Under 5 years	34,646
18 years and over	385,220
21 years and over	365,100
65 years and over	62,927
85 years and over	8,001
Median age	37.3
Native-born	469,468
Foreign-born	44,301

Educational Attainment, 2007

Population 25 years and over	338,088
Less than 9th grade	5.7%
High school grad or higher	84.2%
Bachelor's degree or higher	25.7%
Graduate degree	9.3%

Households, 2007

Total households	194,073
With persons under 18	70,922
With persons over 65	44,825
Family households	133,388
Single-person households	49,598
Persons per household	2.59
Persons per family	3.14

Income & Poverty, 2007

Per capita income	$27,257
Median household income	$59,288
Median family income	$70,087
Persons in poverty	10.7%
H'holds receiving public assistance	6,475
H'holds receiving social security	51,545

Labor & Employment, 2007***

Total civilian labor force	265,108
Unemployment rate	4.7%

Employed persons 16 years and over by occupation, 2007

Managers & professionals	89,231
Service occupations	39,192
Sales & office occupations	68,523
Farming, fishing & forestry	570
Construction & maintenance	18,554
Production & transportation	28,925
Self-employed persons	10,878

Civilian Labor Force Projections***

2009	273,000
2014	279,200
2020	287,700
2025	293,400

*US Census Bureau
**2007 American Community Survey
*** New Jersey Department of Labor
† sum of all municipalities in county

General Information

Camden County
520 Market St
Camden, NJ 08102
856-225-5431

Website	www.co.camden.nj.us
Year of formation	1844
Land/water area (sq. miles)	222.3/5.3
Class	Second
Government form	Freeholder Board
Number of Freeholders	7
Number of municipalities	37

Government & Voters

Legislative Districts

US Congressional	1-3
State Legislative	4-7

Registered Voters, October 2008

Total	341,132
Democratic	139,147
Republican	43,669
Unaffiliated	158,165

County Officials, 2009

County Executive	NA
Administrator	Ross Angilella
Clerk	Albert Mungioli (Actg)
Finance Dir	David McPeak
Tax Administrator	Kelly Hette
Surrogate	Patricia Jones
Prosecutor	Joshua M. Ottenberg (Actg)
Public Works Dir	Frank Moran
Planning/Dev Dir	Ron Jernegan
Sheriff	Charles H. Billingham
Fire Marshal	Paul Hartstein

County School District

Jefferson Hall, PO Box 200, College Drive
Blackwood, NJ 08012
856-401-2400

Superintendent	Peggy Nicolosi
Number of districts	37

Housing & Construction

Housing Units, 2007**

Total	205,341
Single family units	115,662
Multiple family units	88,518
Owner-occupied units	134,491
Renter-occupied units	59,582
Vacant units	11,268
Median rent	$827
Median SF home value	$223,400

Permits for New Residential Construction

	Units	Value
Total, 2006	1,183	$113,361,833
Single family	872	$97,559,903
Total, 2007	1,191	$113,276,836
Single family	652	$76,965,553

Real Property Valuation, 2008†

	Parcels	Valuation
Total	180,231	$25,366,498,520
Vacant	14,130	383,797,903
Residential	155,709	19,744,685,910
Farm land	822	6,660,900
Farm homestead	348	44,847,220
Non-residential	9,222	5,186,506,587
Commercial	7,969	3,847,325,693
Industrial	695	571,041,040
Apartments	558	768,139,854

Public Safety

Police Officers, 2007

County officers	334
Sheriff's department	149
Prosecutors	165
Municipal police	1,377

Crime	2006	2007
Total crimes	20,374	20,042
Violent	2,955	3,037
Murder	38	45
Rape	150	133
Robbery	1,222	1,260
Aggravated assault	1,545	1,599
Non-violent	17,419	17,005
Burglary	3,618	3,622
Larceny	11,796	11,225
Vehicle theft	2,005	2,158
Domestic violence	6,814	6,225
Arson	255	229
Total crime rate	39.3	38.8
Violent	5.7	5.9
Non-violent	33.6	32.9

Public Library

Camden County Library
203 Laurel Road, Echelon Urban Ctr
Voorhees, NJ 08043
(856) 772-1636

Director .... Linda Devlin

Library statistics, 2007

Population served 242,830

	Total	Per capita
Revenues	$9,512,902	$39.18
Expenditures	$8,262,212	$34.02
Holdings	437,576	1.80
Circulation	1,490,672	6.14
Annual visits	806,593	3.32
Registered borrowers	65,521	
Reference transactions	69,623	
Hours open weekly	67	
Full-time/total staff	33/82	
Interlibrary loans		
Provided/received	5,308/5,039	
Internet terminals	149	
Annual users	299,895	

State Income Tax, 2006

Number of returns	212,551
Increase from previous year	1.3%
Total income	$12,441,419
Per capita	$28,077
Increase from previous year	7.0%
Net charged tax	$317,650
Per capita	$717
Average taxable income	$52,339
Average income tax	$1,494

County Finance

State Aid Programs, 2009†

Total aid	$117,716,182
CMPTRA	57,368,071
Energy tax receipts	58,668,686
Garden State Trust	349,802

General Budget, 2008†

Total tax levy	$1,066,007,564
County levy	259,096,441
County taxes	242,271,733
County library	8,384,057
County health	0
County open space	8,440,651
School levy	570,808,872
Muni. levy	236,102,251
Misc. revenues	336,765,939

Taxes†

	2006	2007	2008
Net valuation taxable	$22,831,471,813	$23,468,795,316	$25,451,588,342
State equalized value	$37,486,792,605	41,409,021,714	$42,470,813,906

See Introduction for an explanation of all data sources.

Demographics & Socio-Economic Characteristics

(2007 American Community Survey, except as noted)

Population
1990*	95,089
2000*	102,326
2007	96,422
Male	46,466
Female	49,956
2008 (estimate)*	95,838
Population density	375.5

Race & Hispanic Origin, 2007
Race
White	88,470
Black/African American	4,817
American Indian/Alaska Native	442
Asian	442
Native Hawaiian/Pacific Islander	0
Two or more races	1,418
Hispanic origin, total	4,121
Mexican	NA
Puerto Rican	NA
Cuban	NA
Other Hispanic	NA

Age & Nativity, 2007
Under 5 years	4,595
18 years and over	76,993
21 years and over	75,067
65 years and over	19,742
85 years and over	2,212
Median age	43.9
Native-born	93,847
Foreign-born	2,575

Educational Attainment, 2007
Population 25 years and over	70,072
Less than 9th grade	2.9%
High school grad or higher	85.8%
Bachelor's degree or higher	26.9%
Graduate degree	9.2%

Households, 2007
Total households	46,717
With persons under 18	16,366
With persons over 65	14,376
Family households	31,404
Single-person households	11,280
Persons per household	1.99
Persons per family	2.31

Income & Poverty, 2007
Per capita income	$31,899
Median household income	$51,995
Median family income	$63,754
Persons in poverty	8.6%
H'holds receiving public assistance	1,755
H'holds receiving social security	17,659

Labor & Employment, 2007***
Total civilian labor force	57,135
Unemployment rate	6.5%

Employed persons 16 years and over by occupation, 2007
Managers & professionals	14,371
Service occupations	9,762
Sales & office occupations	11,971
Farming, fishing & forestry	161
Construction & maintenance	5,865
Production & transportation	3,112
Self-employed persons	3,056

Civilian Labor Force Projections***
2009	55,300
2014	55,800
2020	56,900
2025	57,900

*US Census Bureau
**2007 American Community Survey
*** New Jersey Department of Labor
† sum of all municipalities in county

General Information

Cape May County
4 Moore Rd
Cape May Court House, NJ 08210
609-465-1000

Website	www.capemaycountygov.net
Year of formation	1692
Land/water area (sq. miles)	255.2/365.1
Class	Sixth
Government form	Freeholder Board
Number of Freeholders	5
Number of municipalities	16

Government & Voters

Legislative Districts
US Congressional	2
State Legislative	1

Registered Voters, October 2008
Total	69,340
Democratic	14,405
Republican	27,638
Unaffiliated	27,261

County Officials, 2009
Freeholder Director	Daniel Beyel
Administrator	Stephen O'Connor
Clerk	Rita Marie Fulginiti
Finance Dir	Edmund J. Grant Jr
Tax Administrator	George R. Brown III
Surrogate	W. Robert Hentges
Prosecutor	Robert L. Taylor
Public Works Dir	Dale Foster
Planning Dept Dir	James Smith
Sheriff	Gary G. Schaffer
Fire/Emerg Dir	Frank McCall

County School District

4 Moore Rd
Cape May Court House, NJ 08210
609-465-1283

Superintendent	Terrence J. Crowley
Number of districts	16

Housing & Construction

Housing Units, 2007**
Total	101,212
Single family units	51,730
Multiple family units	46,493
Owner-occupied units	33,841
Renter-occupied units	12,876
Vacant units	54,495
Median rent	$1,052
Median SF home value	$340,000

Permits for New Residential Construction
	Units	Value
Total, 2006	1,580	$312,822,646
Single family	774	$190,031,006
Total, 2007	1,081	$227,023,757
Single family	625	$167,897,204

Real Property Valuation, 2008†
	Parcels	Valuation
Total	99,399	$51,366,413,947
Vacant	8,877	1,570,119,500
Residential	85,513	45,504,476,200
Farm land	480	4,682,600
Farm homestead	191	63,240,200
Non-residential	4,338	4,223,895,447
Commercial	3,755	3,707,949,447
Industrial	18	42,612,300
Apartments	565	473,333,700

Taxes†
	2006	2007	2008
Net valuation taxable	$39,149,670,150	$45,500,264,260	$51,404,829,083
State equalized value	$51,679,564,676	54,115,161,908	$54,628,522,836

Public Safety

Police Officers, 2007
County officers	159
Sheriff's department	126
Prosecutors	33
Municipal police	341

Crime	2006	2007
Total crimes	5,043	5,204
Violent	333	350
Murder	1	1
Rape	18	23
Robbery	79	105
Aggravated assault	235	221
Non-violent	4,710	4,854
Burglary	888	945
Larceny	3,697	3,779
Vehicle theft	125	130
Domestic violence	1,185	1,200
Arson	20	12
Total crime rate	50.8	53.3
Violent	3.4	3.6
Non-violent	47.4	49.7

Public Library

Cape May County Library
30 Mechanic Street
Cape May Court House, NJ 08210
(609) 463-6350

Director	Deborah Poillon

Library statistics, 2007
Population served	86,948

	Total	Per capita
Revenues	$9,621,329	$110.66
Expenditures	$6,265,205	$72.06
Holdings	388,128	4.46
Circulation	444,759	5.12
Annual visits	570,000	6.56

Registered borrowers	57,814
Reference transactions	49,500
Hours open weekly	74
Full-time/total staff	18/61
Interlibrary loans Provided/received	2,552/1,743
Internet terminals	65
Annual users	67,915

State Income Tax, 2006
Number of returns	40,897
Increase from previous year	-0.3%
Total income	$2,320,744
Per capita	$29,155
Increase from previous year	-3.7%
Net charged tax	$69,985
Per capita	$879
Average taxable income	$50,754
Average income tax	$1,711

County Finance

State Aid Programs, 2009†
Total aid	$21,678,689
CMPTRA	654,365
Energy tax receipts	19,793,064
Garden State Trust	505,959

General Budget, 2008†
Total tax levy	$396,765,215
County levy	97,650,330
County taxes	82,759,002
County library	9,417,239
County health	0
County open space	5,474,089
School levy	139,930,619
Muni. levy	159,184,267
Misc. revenues	103,229,371

See Introduction for an explanation of all data sources.

Demographics & Socio-Economic Characteristics

(2007 American Community Survey, except as noted)

Population

1990*	138,053
2000*	146,438
2007	155,544
Male	81,166
Female	74,378
2008 (estimate)*	156,830
Population density	320.5

Race & Hispanic Origin, 2007

Race

White	103,421
Black/African American	31,326
American Indian/Alaska Native	1,895
Asian	1,873
Native Hawaiian/Pacific Islander	96
Two or more races	3,859
Hispanic origin, total	36,243
Mexican	9,700
Puerto Rican	22,223
Cuban	134
Other Hispanic	4,186

Age & Nativity, 2007

Under 5 years	11,532
18 years and over	117,565
21 years and over	111,561
65 years and over	19,452
85 years and over	2,332
Median age	35.6
Native-born	141,319
Foreign-born	14,225

Educational Attainment, 2007

Population 25 years and over	103,986
Less than 9th grade	8.6%
High school grad or higher	73.0%
Bachelor's degree or higher	12.3%
Graduate degree	4.2%

Households, 2007

Total households	50,885
With persons under 18	18,702
With persons over 65	13,514
Family households	35,271
Single-person households	13,546
Persons per household	2.85
Persons per family	3.42

Income & Poverty, 2007

Per capita income	$21,317
Median household income	$47,883
Median family income	$55,771
Persons in poverty	18.5%
H'holds receiving public assistance	2,826
H'holds receiving social security	15,216

Labor & Employment, 2007***

Total civilian labor force	68,594
Unemployment rate	6.5%

Employed persons 16 years and over by occupation, 2007

Managers & professionals	16,562
Service occupations	14,720
Sales & office occupations	15,454
Farming, fishing & forestry	1,253
Construction & maintenance	7,041
Production & transportation	10,888
Self-employed persons	2,351

Civilian Labor Force Projections***

2009	71,700
2014	73,800
2020	76,900
2025	79,000

*US Census Bureau
**2007 American Community Survey
*** New Jersey Department of Labor
† sum of all municipalities in county

General Information

Cumberland County
790 E Commerce St
Administration Bldg
Bridgeton, NJ 08302
856-453-2138

Website	www.co.cumberland.nj.us
Year of formation	1748
Land/water area (sq. miles)	489.3/187.3
Class	Third
Government form	Freeholder Board
Number of Freeholders	7
Number of municipalities	14

Government & Voters

Legislative Districts

US Congressional	2
State Legislative	13

Registered Voters, October 2008

Total	90,287
Democratic	25,684
Republican	15,472
Unaffiliated	49,079

County Officials, 2009

County Executive	NA
Administrator	Ken Mecouch
Clerk	Gloria Noto
Finance Dir	Marcella D. Shepard
Tax Administrator	Patricia A. Belmont
Surrogate	Arthur J. Marchand
Prosecutor	Ronald Casella
Public Works Dir	Dan Orr
Planning/Dev Dir	Robert Brewer
Sheriff	Robert Austino
Fire Marshal	Robert Hoffman Jr

County School District

19 Landis Ave
Bridgeton, NJ 08302
856-451-0211

Superintendent	Michael Elwell
Number of districts	14

Housing & Construction

Housing Units, 2007**

Total	55,303
Single family units	37,429
Multiple family units	14,328
Owner-occupied units	35,370
Renter-occupied units	15,515
Vacant units	4,418
Median rent	$817
Median SF home value	$173,600

Permits for New Residential Construction

	Units	Value
Total, 2006	737	$84,238,864
Single family	693	$78,377,064
Total, 2007	683	$78,561,446
Single family	572	$67,112,872

Real Property Valuation, 2008†

	Parcels	Valuation
Total	60,014	$5,469,886,515
Vacant	11,536	151,503,775
Residential	40,694	3,892,306,390
Farm land	3,020	35,513,500
Farm homestead	1,541	188,643,200
Non-residential	3,223	1,201,919,650
Commercial	2,748	787,073,050
Industrial	312	299,945,200
Apartments	163	114,901,400

Public Safety

Police Officers, 2007

County officers	84
Sheriff's department	51
Prosecutors	33
Municipal police	298

Crime	2006	2007
Total crimes	7,441	7,194
Violent	1,243	1,058
Murder	15	11
Rape	50	32
Robbery	434	434
Aggravated assault	744	581
Non-violent	6,198	6,136
Burglary	1,533	1,566
Larceny	4,329	4,272
Vehicle theft	336	298
Domestic violence	3,353	3,309
Arson	44	42
Total crime rate	48.6	46.5
Violent	8.1	6.8
Non-violent	40.4	39.6

Public Library

Cumberland County Library
800 E. Commerce Street
Bridgeton, NJ 08302
(856) 453-2210

Director ... Nancy J. Forester

Library statistics, 2007

Population served ... 67,396

	Total	Per capita
Revenues	$1,387,967	$20.59
Expenditures	$1,370,048	$20.33
Holdings	99,851	1.48
Circulation	78,919	1.17
Annual visits	79,000	1.17
Registered borrowers	16,029	
Reference transactions	9,000	
Hours open weekly	60	
Full-time/total staff	6/12	
Interlibrary loans		
Provided/received	668/183	
Internet terminals	28	
Annual users	28,000	

State Income Tax, 2006

Number of returns	58,593
Increase from previous year	1.8%
Total income	$2,570,694
Per capita	$20,348
Increase from previous year	5.5%
Net charged tax	$60,714
Per capita	$481
Average taxable income	$38,779
Average income tax	$1,036

County Finance

State Aid Programs, 2009†

Total aid	$24,569,609
CMPTRA	8,564,995
Energy tax receipts	14,501,097
Garden State Trust	1,071,670

General Budget, 2008†

Total tax levy	$204,178,547
County levy	87,407,746
County taxes	84,292,000
County library	0
County health	2,175,000
County open space	940,746
School levy	65,116,373
Muni. levy	51,654,428
Misc. revenues	90,709,806

Taxes†

	2006	2007	2008
Net valuation taxable	$5,209,035,825	$5,405,826,973	$5,487,565,336
State equalized value	$7,770,530,909	9,110,946,900	$9,523,391,675

See Introduction for an explanation of all data sources.

Demographics & Socio-Economic Characteristics
(2007 American Community Survey, except as noted)

Population
1990*	778,206
2000*	793,633
2007	776,087
Male	372,787
Female	403,300
2008 (estimate)*	770,675
Population density	6101.9

Race & Hispanic Origin, 2007
Race
White	315,177
Black/African American	315,740
American Indian/Alaska Native	2,887
Asian	34,374
Native Hawaiian/Pacific Islander	0
Two or more races	13,592
Hispanic origin, total	142,744
Mexican	6,966
Puerto Rican	56,034
Cuban	5,091
Other Hispanic	74,653

Age & Nativity, 2007
Under 5 years	57,093
18 years and over	577,620
21 years and over	546,553
65 years and over	90,355
85 years and over	12,003
Median age	36.3
Native-born	597,362
Foreign-born	178,725

Educational Attainment, 2007
Population 25 years and over	504,432
Less than 9th grade	9.4%
High school grad or higher	80.5%
Bachelor's degree or higher	32.6%
Graduate degree	13.4%

Households, 2007
Total households	274,095
With persons under 18	106,542
With persons over 65	64,069
Family households	181,156
Single-person households	80,851
Persons per household	2.74
Persons per family	3.42

Income & Poverty, 2007
Per capita income	$31,260
Median household income	$53,499
Median family income	$65,806
Persons in poverty	13.3%
H'holds receiving public assistance	8,877
H'holds receiving social security	67,076

Labor & Employment, 2007***
Total civilian labor force	364,028
Unemployment rate	5.3%

Employed persons 16 years and over by occupation, 2007
Managers & professionals	134,509
Service occupations	64,290
Sales & office occupations	88,948
Farming, fishing & forestry	347
Construction & maintenance	28,303
Production & transportation	39,663
Self-employed persons	17,897

Civilian Labor Force Projections***
2009	373,200
2014	382,700
2020	393,800
2025	404,300

*US Census Bureau
**2007 American Community Survey
*** New Jersey Department of Labor
† sum of all municipalities in county

See Introduction for an explanation of all data sources.

General Information
Essex County
465 Dr Martin Luther King Jr Blvd
Newark, NJ 07102
973-621-5100
Website	www.essexcountynj.org
Year of formation	1683
Land/water area (sq. miles)	126.3/3.3
Class	First
Government form	County Executive Plan
Number of Freeholders	9
Number of municipalities	22

Government & Voters

Legislative Districts
US Congressional	8-11, 13
State Legislative	21, 27-28, 34, 36, 40

Registered Voters, October 2008
Total	446,258
Democratic	209,583
Republican	45,790
Unaffiliated	190,743

County Officials, 2009
County Exec	Joseph DeVincenzo Jr
County Admin	Joyce Wilson Harley
Clerk	Christopher Durkin
Treasurer	Paul Hopkins II
Tax Administrator	Joan Codey Durkin
Surrogate	Joseph Brennan
Prosecutor	Paula Dow
Public Works Dir	Philip LiVecchi
Planning/Dev Dir	Philip LiVecchi
Sheriff	Armando Fontoura
Fire/Emerg Mgmt Dir	NA

County School District
7 Glenwood Ave, Suite 404
East Orange, NJ 07019
973-395-4677
Superintendent. Lawrence S. Feinsod (Actg)
Number of districts.................22

Housing & Construction

Housing Units, 2007**
Total	311,180
Single family units	103,684
Multiple family units	207,068
Owner-occupied units	131,375
Renter-occupied units	142,720
Vacant units	37,085
Median rent	$932
Median SF home value	$422,800

Permits for New Residential Construction
	Units	Value
Total, 2006	3,284	$392,801,103
Single family	654	$158,403,232
Total, 2007	1,854	$221,065,904
Single family	460	$112,413,880

Real Property Valuation, 2008†
	Parcels	Valuation
Total	177,159	$60,706,044,431
Vacant	8,448	984,658,000
Residential	151,966	44,196,481,191
Farm land	17	143,900
Farm homestead	4	1,260,200
Non-residential	16,724	15,523,501,140
Commercial	12,098	9,939,957,200
Industrial	1,952	2,180,619,540
Apartments	2,674	3,402,924,400

Public Safety

Police Officers, 2007
County officers	737
Sheriff's department	432
Prosecutors	305
Municipal police	2,826

Crime	2006	2007
Total crimes	33,547	30,334
Violent	6,136	5,329
Murder	146	148
Rape	167	147
Robbery	2,990	2,551
Aggravated assault	2,833	2,483
Non-violent	27,411	25,005
Burglary	5,237	4,858
Larceny	13,838	12,942
Vehicle theft	8,336	7,205
Domestic violence	5,245	4,550
Arson	280	172
Total crime rate	42.4	38.6
Violent	7.8	6.8
Non-violent	34.7	31.8

Public Library
No County Library
(Library statistics are the sum of all
municipal libraries in the county)

Library statistics, 2007†
Population served 784,096
	Total	Per capita
Revenues	$48,824,536	$62.27
Expenditures	$47,113,297	$60.09
Holdings	4,180,195	5.33
Circulation	3,108,383	3.96
Annual visits	3,651,657	4.66
Registered borrowers	389,266	
Reference transactions	636,094	
Hours open weekly	NA	
Number of libraries	20	
Full-time/total staff	177/443	
Interlibrary loans		
Provided/received	70,986/67,921	
Internet terminals	778	
Annual users	974,424	

State Income Tax, 2006
Number of returns	309,331
Increase from previous year	1.1%
Total income	$24,155,845
Per capita	$38,265
Increase from previous year	7.5%
Net charged tax	$743,525
Per capita	$1,178
Average taxable income	$71,961
Average income tax	$2,404

County Finance

State Aid Programs, 2009†
Total aid	$207,332,056
CMPTRA	117,638,923
Energy tax receipts	86,797,986
Garden State Trust	18,906

General Budget, 2008†
Total tax levy	$1,911,732,437
County levy	363,699,855
County taxes	349,575,243
County library	0
County health	0
County open space	14,124,612
School levy	902,561,387
Muni. levy	645,471,194
Misc. revenues	855,298,297

Taxes†
	2006	2007	2008
Net valuation taxable	$40,131,037,517	$56,674,138,715	$60,852,932,618
State equalized value	$86,661,310,831	93,148,280,922	$96,914,440,800

Gloucester County

Demographics & Socio-Economic Characteristics

(2007 American Community Survey, except as noted)

Population
1990*	230,082
2000*	254,673
2007	285,753
Male	139,600
Female	146,153
2008 (estimate)*	287,860
Population density	886.5

Race & Hispanic Origin, 2007
Race
White	241,504
Black/African American	27,779
American Indian/Alaska Native	309
Asian	6,986
Native Hawaiian/Pacific Islander	0
Two or more races	5,186
Hispanic origin, total	10,379
Mexican	2,281
Puerto Rican	5,340
Cuban	686
Other Hispanic	2,072

Age & Nativity, 2007
Under 5 years	16,860
18 years and over	218,614
21 years and over	205,083
65 years and over	32,792
85 years and over	3,419
Median age	37.5
Native-born	273,979
Foreign-born	11,774

Educational Attainment, 2007
Population 25 years and over	188,358
Less than 9th grade	3.5%
High school grad or higher	87.9%
Bachelor's degree or higher	25.1%
Graduate degree	7.0%

Households, 2007
Total households	100,042
With persons under 18	37,843
With persons over 65	21,233
Family households	71,959
Single-person households	23,031
Persons per household	2.78
Persons per family	3.30

Income & Poverty, 2007
Per capita income	$29,735
Median household income	$70,881
Median family income	$81,944
Persons in poverty	8.1%
H'holds receiving public assistance	1,975
H'holds receiving social security	25,482

Labor & Employment, 2007***
Total civilian labor force	152,531
Unemployment rate	4.3%

Employed persons 16 years and over by occupation, 2007
Managers & professionals	55,141
Service occupations	18,373
Sales & office occupations	43,683
Farming, fishing & forestry	1,268
Construction & maintenance	11,423
Production & transportation	14,741
Self-employed persons	7,376

Civilian Labor Force Projections***
2009	154,100
2014	161,200
2020	172,800
2025	181,100

*US Census Bureau
**2007 American Community Survey
*** New Jersey Department of Labor
† sum of all municipalities in county

General Information
Gloucester County
PO Box 337
Woodbury, NJ 08096
856-853-3200
Website	www.co.gloucester.nj.us
Year of formation	1686
Land/water area (sq. miles)	324.7/12.2
Class	Third
Government form	Freeholder Board
Number of Freeholders	7
Number of municipalities	24

Government & Voters

Legislative Districts
US Congressional	1-2
State Legislative	3-5

Registered Voters, October 2008
Total	192,449
Democratic	71,782
Republican	35,397
Unaffiliated	85,167

County Officials, 2009
Freeholder Director	Stephen Sweeney
County Administrator	Chad M. Bruner
County Clerk	James Hogan
CFO/Treasurer	Gary Schwarz
Tax Administrator	Edward J. Burek
Surrogate	Helene Reed
Prosecutor	Sean Dalton
Public Works Dir	Larry Haynes Sr
Planning Dir	Chuck Romich
Sheriff	Carmel Morina
Fire Marshal	Edward Johnson

County School District
1492 Tanyard Rd
Sewell, NJ 08080
856-468-6500
Superintendent	H. Mark Stanwood
Number of districts	24

Housing & Construction

Housing Units, 2007**
Total	106,689
Single family units	76,798
Multiple family units	27,510
Owner-occupied units	80,363
Renter-occupied units	19,679
Vacant units	6,647
Median rent	$905
Median SF home value	$235,300

Permits for New Residential Construction
	Units	Value
Total, 2006	1,141	$175,251,137
Single family	1,021	$169,613,387
Total, 2007	920	$155,118,956
Single family	882	$152,735,516

Real Property Valuation, 2008†
	Parcels	Valuation
Total	110,694	$16,689,978,351
Vacant	12,548	438,933,887
Residential	89,407	12,489,397,350
Farm land	2,991	32,129,400
Farm homestead	1,285	204,334,600
Non-residential	4,463	3,525,183,114
Commercial	4,035	2,469,159,960
Industrial	243	794,089,754
Apartments	185	261,933,400

Public Safety

Police Officers, 2007
County officers	111
Sheriff's department	76
Prosecutors	35
Municipal police	601

Crime	2006	2007
Total crimes	8,128	7,654
Violent	610	602
Murder	7	9
Rape	58	26
Robbery	192	191
Aggravated assault	353	376
Non-violent	7,518	7,052
Burglary	1,463	1,358
Larceny	5,651	5,227
Vehicle theft	404	467
Domestic violence	3,010	2,988
Arson	73	72
Total crime rate	29.4	27.1
Violent	2.2	2.1
Non-violent	27.1	25.0

Public Library
Gloucester County Library
389 Wolfert Station Road
Mullica Hill, NJ 08062
(856) 223-6000
Director	Robert S. Wetherall

Library statistics, 2007
Population served		93,711

	Total	Per capita
Revenues	$4,492,205	$47.94
Expenditures	$4,080,940	$43.55
Holdings	236,948	2.53
Circulation	561,011	5.99
Annual visits	497,709	5.31

Registered borrowers	50,637
Reference transactions	22,521
Hours open weekly	69
Full-time/total staff	11/42
Interlibrary loans	
Provided/received	19,982/27,682
Internet terminals	67
Annual users	86,230

State Income Tax, 2006
Number of returns	118,575
Increase from previous year	1.9%
Total income	$7,235,836
Per capita	$28,291
Increase from previous year	7.5%
Net charged tax	$165,306
Per capita	$646
Average taxable income	$54,422
Average income tax	$1,394

County Finance

State Aid Programs, 2009†
Total aid	$33,071,169
CMPTRA	6,804,125
Energy tax receipts	25,270,077
Garden State Trust	54,096

General Budget, 2008†
Total tax levy	$664,656,755
County levy	158,731,159
County taxes	143,200,000
County library	4,309,686
County health	0
County open space	11,221,473
School levy	356,750,232
Muni. levy	149,175,364
Misc. revenues	125,760,464

Taxes†
	2006	2007	2008
Net valuation taxable	$14,270,861,336	$14,976,157,127	$16,863,056,445
State equalized value	$24,982,195,408	27,472,693,310	$29,101,693,337

See Introduction for an explanation of all data sources.

Demographics & Socio-Economic Characteristics

(2007 American Community Survey, except as noted)

Population

1990*	553,099
2000*	608,975
2007	598,160
Male	297,014
Female	301,146
2008 (estimate)*	595,419
Population density	12749.9

Race & Hispanic Origin, 2007

Race

White	348,229
Black/African American	83,733
American Indian/Alaska Native	2,367
Asian	66,966
Native Hawaiian/Pacific Islander	460
Two or more races	11,108
Hispanic origin, total	242,414
Mexican	19,245
Puerto Rican	47,773
Cuban	31,198
Other Hispanic	144,198

Age & Nativity, 2007

Under 5 years	39,851
18 years and over	467,296
21 years and over	445,358
65 years and over	64,953
85 years and over	8,760
Median age	36.0
Native-born	356,602
Foreign-born	241,558

Educational Attainment, 2007

Population 25 years and over	412,225
Less than 9th grade	10.8%
High school grad or higher	79.5%
Bachelor's degree or higher	32.7%
Graduate degree	10.7%

Households, 2007

Total households	228,826
With persons under 18	72,969
With persons over 65	46,804
Family households	139,745
Single-person households	73,289
Persons per household	2.59
Persons per family	3.32

Income & Poverty, 2007

Per capita income	$29,940
Median household income	$51,656
Median family income	$53,528
Persons in poverty	13.7%
H'holds receiving public assistance	5,383
H'holds receiving social security	48,235

Labor & Employment, 2007*

Total civilian labor force	290,405
Unemployment rate	5.0%

Employed persons 16 years and over by occupation, 2007

Managers & professionals	103,693
Service occupations	58,122
Sales & office occupations	82,315
Farming, fishing & forestry	109
Construction & maintenance	22,993
Production & transportation	40,265
Self-employed persons	13,555

Civilian Labor Force Projections*

2009	294,100
2014	295,100
2020	301,800
2025	302,400

*US Census Bureau
**2007 American Community Survey
*** New Jersey Department of Labor
† sum of all municipalities in county

See Introduction for an explanation of all data sources.

General Information

Hudson County
583 Newark Ave
Brennan Court House Building
Jersey City, NJ 07306
201-795-6000

Website	www.hudsoncountynj.org
Year of formation	1840
Land/water area (sq. miles)	46.7/15.7
Class	First
Government form	County Executive Plan
Number of Freeholders	9
Number of municipalities	12

Government & Voters

Legislative Districts

US Congressional	9-10, 13
State Legislative	31-33

Registered Voters, October 2008

Total	344,119
Democratic	173,890
Republican	27,230
Unaffiliated	142,827

County Officials, 2009

County Executive	Thomas DeGise
Manager	Abraham Antun
Clerk	Barbara A. Netchert
Finance Dir	Wade Frazee
Tax Administrator	Donald Kenny
Surrogate	Donald DeLeo
Prosecutor	Edward DeFazio
Public Works Dir	NA
Planning/Dev Dir	Stephen Marks
Sheriff	Juan Perez
Emerg Mgmt Dir	Frank Pizzuta

County School District

595 Newark Ave
Jersey City, NJ 07306
201-319-3850

Superintendent	Timothy Brennan (Actg)
Number of districts	12

Housing & Construction

Housing Units, 2007**

Total	254,780
Single family units	24,694
Multiple family units	229,600
Owner-occupied units	80,109
Renter-occupied units	148,717
Vacant units	25,954
Median rent	$990
Median SF home value	$419,400

Permits for New Residential Construction

	Units	Value
Total, 2006	4,275	$450,371,017
Single family	277	$32,231,367
Total, 2007	3,081	$302,280,333
Single family	161	$23,629,998

Real Property Valuation, 2008†

	Parcels	Valuation
Total	124,002	$21,803,100,661
Vacant	11,959	946,465,666
Residential	96,572	11,956,699,122
Farm land	0	0
Farm homestead	0	0
Non-residential	15,471	8,899,935,873
Commercial	9,634	4,727,563,843
Industrial	1,792	2,518,665,330
Apartments	4,045	1,653,706,700

Public Safety

Police Officers, 2007

County officers	278
Sheriff's department	179
Prosecutors	99
Municipal police	2,001

Crime	2006	2007
Total crimes	19,750	18,425
Violent	4,221	3,765
Murder	34	26
Rape	85	78
Robbery	2,193	1,862
Aggravated assault	1,909	1,799
Non-violent	15,529	14,660
Burglary	3,329	2,992
Larceny	9,422	9,456
Vehicle theft	2,778	2,212
Domestic violence	4,569	4,341
Arson	134	128
Total crime rate	32.7	30.6
Violent	7.0	6.3
Non-violent	25.7	24.4

Public Library

No County Library
(Library statistics are the sum of all municipal libraries in the county)

Library statistics, 2007†

Population served	533,949

	Total	Per capita
Revenues	$17,456,804	$32.69
Expenditures	$16,715,118	$31.30
Holdings	1,195,521	2.24
Circulation	675,692	1.27
Annual visits	1,323,297	2.48

Registered borrowers	262,238
Reference transactions	663,183
Hours open weekly	NA
Number of libraries	9
Full-time/total staff	42/211
Interlibrary loans	
Provided/received	28,022/41,248
Internet terminals	464
Annual users	448,662

State Income Tax, 2006

Number of returns	252,753
Increase from previous year	0.4%
Total income	$12,598,528
Per capita	$26,974
Increase from previous year	5.8%
Net charged tax	$232,607
Per capita	$498
Average taxable income	$45,840
Average income tax	$920

County Finance

State Aid Programs, 2009†

Total aid	$178,803,769
CMPTRA	81,076,622
Energy tax receipts	94,130,430
Garden State Trust	25,996

General Budget, 2008†

Total tax levy	$1,110,240,250
County levy	252,241,160
County taxes	245,570,034
County library	0
County health	0
County open space	6,671,126
School levy	370,075,815
Muni. levy	487,923,274
Misc. revenues	638,043,454

Taxes†

	2006	2007	2008
Net valuation taxable	$21,147,492,189	$21,399,716,001	$21,841,512,799
State equalized value	$57,639,543,726	64,070,898,191	$67,077,100,450

Demographics & Socio-Economic Characteristics

(2007 American Community Survey, except as noted)

Population
1990*	107,776
2000*	121,989
2007	129,348
Male	63,531
Female	65,817
2008 (estimate)*	129,031
Population density	300.1

Race & Hispanic Origin, 2007
Race
White	117,479
Black/African American	3,572
American Indian/Alaska Native	87
Asian	4,183
Native Hawaiian/Pacific Islander	0
Two or more races	1,551
Hispanic origin, total	5,563
Mexican	1,005
Puerto Rican	1,642
Cuban	706
Other Hispanic	2,210

Age & Nativity, 2007
Under 5 years	6,558
18 years and over	99,862
21 years and over	95,569
65 years and over	14,434
85 years and over	1,630
Median age	42.1
Native-born	119,010
Foreign-born	10,338

Educational Attainment, 2007
Population 25 years and over	89,911
Less than 9th grade	2.3%
High school grad or higher	93.0%
Bachelor's degree or higher	47.2%
Graduate degree	19.2%

Households, 2007
Total households	47,446
With persons under 18	17,913
With persons over 65	10,760
Family households	35,019
Single-person households	10,336
Persons per household	2.55
Persons per family	3.01

Income & Poverty, 2007
Per capita income	$50,043
Median household income	$100,327
Median family income	$117,001
Persons in poverty	4.1%
H'holds receiving public assistance	155
H'holds receiving social security	11,475

Labor & Employment, 2007***
Total civilian labor force	72,445
Unemployment rate	2.9%

Employed persons 16 years and over by occupation, 2007
Managers & professionals	34,888
Service occupations	7,455
Sales & office occupations	17,718
Farming, fishing & forestry	103
Construction & maintenance	5,306
Production & transportation	3,439
Self-employed persons	5,746

Civilian Labor Force Projections***
2009	74,500
2014	78,000
2020	83,100
2025	86,400

*US Census Bureau
**2007 American Community Survey
*** New Jersey Department of Labor
† sum of all municipalities in county

General Information

Hunterdon County
PO Box 2900
71 Main St
Flemington, NJ 08822
908-788-1102

Website	www.co.hunterdon.nj.us
Year of formation	1714
Land/water area (sq. miles)	429.9/7.8
Class	Third
Government form	Freeholder Board
Number of Freeholders	5
Number of municipalities	26

Government & Voters

Legislative Districts
US Congressional	7, 12
State Legislative	23-24

Registered Voters, October 2008
Total	87,413
Democratic	17,712
Republican	32,935
Unaffiliated	36,706

County Officials, 2009
County Executive	NA
County Administrator	Cynthia J. Yard
Clerk	Mary Melfi
County Treasurer	Margaret Pasqua
Tax Administrator	Athan Efstathiou
Surrogate	Susan Hoffman
Prosecutor	J. Patrick Barnes
Roads, Bridges & Eng	John P. Glynn
Planning Dir	Sue Dziamara
Sheriff	Deborah Trout
Fire Marshal	George F. Wagner

County School District

10 Court St, PO Box 2900
Flemington, NJ 08822
908-788-1414

Superintendent	Christine Harttraft (Int)
Number of districts	26

Housing & Construction

Housing Units, 2007**
Total	48,753
Single family units	36,875
Multiple family units	11,736
Owner-occupied units	41,622
Renter-occupied units	5,824
Vacant units	1,307
Median rent	$1,116
Median SF home value	$472,800

Permits for New Residential Construction
	Units	Value
Total, 2006	350	$73,999,188
Single family	305	$72,628,625
Total, 2007	316	$58,997,086
Single family	211	$50,032,003

Real Property Valuation, 2008†
	Parcels	Valuation
Total	56,115	$21,440,138,230
Vacant	3,794	383,119,236
Residential	41,367	16,501,837,060
Farm land	5,300	50,563,566
Farm homestead	3,277	1,590,870,700
Non-residential	2,377	2,913,747,668
Commercial	2,085	2,300,935,438
Industrial	177	475,569,050
Apartments	115	137,243,180

Taxes†
	2006	2007	2008
Net valuation taxable	$18,428,098,995	$21,326,236,051	$21,503,544,052
State equalized value	$23,523,607,658	24,628,614,688	24,749,646,790

Public Safety

Police Officers, 2007
County officers	49
Sheriff's department	26
Prosecutors	23
Municipal police	170

Crime	2006	2007
Total crimes	1,130	1,182
Violent	82	90
Murder	0	1
Rape	7	11
Robbery	14	10
Aggravated assault	61	68
Non-violent	1,048	1,092
Burglary	216	233
Larceny	780	815
Vehicle theft	52	44
Domestic violence	489	697
Arson	13	9
Total crime rate	8.7	9.0
Violent	0.6	0.7
Non-violent	8.0	8.3

Public Library

Hunterdon County Library
314 State Highway 12, Bldg 3
Flemington, NJ 08822
(908) 788-1444

Director	Mark Titus

Library statistics, 2007
Population served	112,726

	Total	Per capita
Revenues	$7,243,246	$64.26
Expenditures	$6,774,289	$60.10
Holdings	436,046	3.87
Circulation	1,213,820	10.77
Annual visits	606,702	5.38
Registered borrowers	66,916	
Reference transactions	33,727	
Hours open weekly	75	
Full-time/total staff	19/54	
Interlibrary loans		
Provided/received	1,146/2,753	
Internet terminals	27	
Annual users	45,073	

State Income Tax, 2006
Number of returns	54,310
Increase from previous year	1.4%
Total income	$5,994,107
Per capita	$50,209
Increase from previous year	9.2%
Net charged tax	$228,503
Per capita	$1,914
Average taxable income	$100,872
Average income tax	$4,207

County Finance

State Aid Programs, 2009†
Total aid	$19,886,009
CMPTRA	2,571,345
Energy tax receipts	16,165,470
Garden State Trust	419,865

General Budget, 2008†
Total tax levy	$460,979,443
County levy	83,036,351
County taxes	69,801,000
County library	5,699,351
County health	0
County open space	7,536,000
School levy	318,672,404
Muni. levy	59,270,688
Misc. revenues	67,821,735

See Introduction for an explanation of all data sources.

Demographics & Socio-Economic Characteristics

(2007 American Community Survey, except as noted)

Population
1990*	325,824
2000*	350,761
2007	365,449
Male	179,645
Female	185,804
2008 (estimate)*	364,883
Population density	1615.2

Race & Hispanic Origin, 2007
Race
White	239,084
Black/African American	73,113
American Indian/Alaska Native	714
Asian	28,706
Native Hawaiian/Pacific Islander	65
Two or more races	5,748
Hispanic origin, total	46,642
Mexican	6,679
Puerto Rican	11,985
Cuban	2,138
Other Hispanic	25,840

Age & Nativity, 2007
Under 5 years	22,754
18 years and over	281,285
21 years and over	261,857
65 years and over	43,781
85 years and over	5,947
Median age	37.0
Native-born	297,603
Foreign-born	67,846

Educational Attainment, 2007
Population 25 years and over	240,790
Less than 9th grade	5.4%
High school grad or higher	87.3%
Bachelor's degree or higher	37.8%
Graduate degree	17.8%

Households, 2007
Total households	128,026
With persons under 18	48,156
With persons over 65	30,248
Family households	87,400
Single-person households	33,783
Persons per household	2.76
Persons per family	3.35

Income & Poverty, 2007
Per capita income	$34,892
Median household income	$70,258
Median family income	$88,789
Persons in poverty	9.3%
H'holds receiving public assistance	2,989
H'holds receiving social security	34,670

Labor & Employment, 2007***
Total civilian labor force	196,345
Unemployment rate	3.8%

Employed persons 16 years and over by occupation, 2007
Managers & professionals	76,166
Service occupations	29,807
Sales & office occupations	48,349
Farming, fishing & forestry	653
Construction & maintenance	11,916
Production & transportation	14,570
Self-employed persons	7,315

Civilian Labor Force Projections***
2009	195,300
2014	201,600
2020	208,500
2025	213,100

*US Census Bureau
**2007 American Community Survey
*** New Jersey Department of Labor
† sum of all municipalities in county

See Introduction for an explanation of all data sources.

General Information

Mercer County
PO Box 8068
640 S Broad St
Trenton, NJ 08650
609-989-6518

Website	www.mercercounty.org
Year of formation	1838
Land/water area (sq. miles)	225.9/2.9
Class	Second
Government form	County Executive Plan
Number of Freeholders	7
Number of municipalities	13

Government & Voters

Legislative Districts
US Congressional	4, 12
State Legislative	12, 14-15, 30

Registered Voters, October 2008
Total	222,154
Democratic	83,372
Republican	32,390
Unaffiliated	106,253

County Officials, 2009
County Executive	Brian Hughes
Manager	Andrew A. Mair
Clerk	Paula Sollami-Covello
Finance Dir	David Miller
Tax Administrator	Martin Guhl
Surrogate	Diane Gerofsky
Prosecutor	Joseph L. Bocchini
Public Works Dir	NA
Planning/Dev Dir	NA
Sheriff	Kevin Larkin
Fire Marshal	George Lenhardt

County School District

1075 Old Trenton Rd
Trenton, NJ 08690
609-588-5884

Superintendent	Samuel Stewart (Actg)
Number of districts	13

Housing & Construction

Housing Units, 2007**
Total	140,428
Single family units	68,584
Multiple family units	71,316
Owner-occupied units	89,546
Renter-occupied units	38,480
Vacant units	12,402
Median rent	$979
Median SF home value	$322,400

Permits for New Residential Construction
	Units	Value
Total, 2006	847	$85,844,566
Single family	578	$70,544,291
Total, 2007	700	$97,985,114
Single family	466	$75,239,134

Real Property Valuation, 2008†
	Parcels	Valuation
Total	120,702	$30,961,199,032
Vacant	6,340	522,328,199
Residential	105,974	22,251,454,470
Farm land	1,211	14,010,936
Farm homestead	586	393,071,500
Non-residential	6,591	7,780,333,927
Commercial	5,961	5,927,430,927
Industrial	284	1,081,655,000
Apartments	346	771,248,000

Public Safety

Police Officers, 2007
County officers	245
Sheriff's department	140
Prosecutors	105
Municipal police	929

Crime	2006	2007
Total crimes	9,987	9,389
Violent	1,783	1,610
Murder	21	26
Rape	67	43
Robbery	867	766
Aggravated assault	828	775
Non-violent	8,204	7,779
Burglary	1,869	1,707
Larceny	5,510	5,349
Vehicle theft	825	723
Domestic violence	3,136	3,084
Arson	64	49
Total crime rate	27.3	25.5
Violent	4.9	4.4
Non-violent	22.4	21.2

Public Library

Mercer County Library
2751 Brunswick Pike
Lawrenceville, NJ 08648
(609) 689-6916

Director	Richard J. Cavallo

Library statistics, 2007
Population served	143,288

	Total	Per capita
Revenues	$11,562,328	$80.69
Expenditures	$11,562,328	$80.69
Holdings	756,413	5.28
Circulation	1,718,749	12.00
Annual visits	1,152,065	8.04

Registered borrowers	62,143
Reference transactions	129,943
Hours open weekly	66
Full-time/total staff	47/116
Interlibrary loans	
Provided/received	7,026/2,500
Internet terminals	123
Annual users	741,103

State Income Tax, 2006
Number of returns	146,358
Increase from previous year	0.7%
Total income	$12,519,385
Per capita	$41,653
Increase from previous year	8.0%
Net charged tax	$436,929
Per capita	$1,454
Average taxable income	$78,708
Average income tax	$2,985

County Finance

State Aid Programs, 2009†
Total aid	$109,801,580
CMPTRA	53,931,634
Energy tax receipts	54,219,501
Garden State Trust	85,151

General Budget, 2008†
Total tax levy	$988,770,329
County levy	234,156,714
County taxes	208,483,580
County library	11,365,074
County health	0
County open space	14,308,060
School levy	515,649,463
Muni. levy	238,964,152
Misc. revenues	312,914,485

Taxes†
	2006	2007	2008
Net valuation taxable	$29,175,585,406	$30,967,508,196	$31,037,844,599
State equalized value	$43,981,279,686	47,292,222,593	$48,238,394,984

Demographics & Socio-Economic Characteristics

(2007 American Community Survey, except as noted)

Population

1990*	671,780
2000*	750,162
2007	788,629
Male	390,037
Female	398,592
2008 (estimate)*	789,102
Population density	2548.0

Race & Hispanic Origin, 2007

Race

White	502,255
Black/African American	77,836
American Indian/Alaska Native	920
Asian	144,547
Native Hawaiian/Pacific Islander	94
Two or more races	13,288
Hispanic origin, total	135,023
Mexican	25,438
Puerto Rican	40,549
Cuban	3,823
Other Hispanic	65,213

Age & Nativity, 2007

Under 5 years	50,534
18 years and over	607,321
21 years and over	572,596
65 years and over	94,818
85 years and over	13,481
Median age	37.2
Native-born	565,106
Foreign-born	223,523

Educational Attainment, 2007

Population 25 years and over	529,801
Less than 9th grade	5.6%
High school grad or higher	88.2%
Bachelor's degree or higher	37.1%
Graduate degree	15.1%

Households, 2007

Total households	271,942
With persons under 18	106,018
With persons over 65	61,666
Family households	196,487
Single-person households	62,108
Persons per household	2.80
Persons per family	3.31

Income & Poverty, 2007

Per capita income	$32,019
Median household income	$75,393
Median family income	$87,929
Persons in poverty	6.7%
H'holds receiving public assistance	1,991
H'holds receiving social security	64,791

Labor & Employment, 2007***

Total civilian labor force	423,579
Unemployment rate	3.8%

Employed persons 16 years and over by occupation, 2007

Managers & professionals	158,830
Service occupations	51,293
Sales & office occupations	109,910
Farming, fishing & forestry	228
Construction & maintenance	28,466
Production & transportation	45,720
Self-employed persons	14,693

Civilian Labor Force Projections***

2009	423,900
2014	432,600
2020	447,600
2025	460,600

*US Census Bureau
**2007 American Community Survey
*** New Jersey Department of Labor
† sum of all municipalities in county

General Information

Middlesex County
PO Box 1110
75 Bayard St
New Brunswick, NJ 08901
732-745-3000

Website	www.co.middlesex.nj.us
Year of formation	1683
Land/water area (sq. miles)	309.7/12.8
Class	Second
Government form	Freeholder Board
Number of Freeholders	7
Number of municipalities	25

Government & Voters

Legislative Districts

US Congressional	6-7, 12-13
State Legislative	13-14, 17-19, 22

Registered Voters, October 2008

Total	461,823
Democratic	171,985
Republican	56,962
Unaffiliated	232,671

County Officials, 2009

County Executive	NA
Administrator	John Pulomena
Clerk	Elaine Flynn
Finance Dir	Albert P. Kuchinskas
Tax Administrator	Irving Verosloff
Surrogate	Kevin J. Hoagland
Prosecutor	Bruce Kaplan
Public Works Dir	David Campion
Planning/Dev Dir	George Ververides
Sheriff	Joseph C. Spicuzzo
Fire Marshal	Michael Gallagher

County School District

1460 Livingston Ave, Bldg 400, 2nd Floor
North Brunswick, NJ 08902
732-249-2900

Superintendent	Patrick Piegari
Number of districts	25

Housing & Construction

Housing Units, 2007**

Total	287,541
Single family units	150,987
Multiple family units	134,039
Owner-occupied units	182,242
Renter-occupied units	89,700
Vacant units	15,599
Median rent	$1,130
Median SF home value	$370,700

Permits for New Residential Construction

	Units	Value
Total, 2006	2,567	$257,214,501
Single family	1,177	$180,170,204
Total, 2007	1,597	$198,388,930
Single family	878	$144,888,011

Real Property Valuation, 2008†

	Parcels	Valuation
Total	233,378	$48,432,349,560
Vacant	13,315	1,083,251,936
Residential	207,597	31,867,355,624
Farm land	1,015	17,138,000
Farm homestead	389	106,016,600
Non-residential	11,062	15,358,587,400
Commercial	8,096	6,821,770,400
Industrial	2,130	6,213,478,100
Apartments	836	2,323,338,900

Public Safety

Police Officers, 2007

County officers	268
Sheriff's department	187
Prosecutors	81
Municipal police	1,653

Crime	2006	2007
Total crimes	17,789	16,979
Violent	1,717	1,527
Murder	18	10
Rape	85	73
Robbery	641	660
Aggravated assault	973	784
Non-violent	16,072	15,452
Burglary	3,111	2,792
Larceny	11,476	11,337
Vehicle theft	1,485	1,323
Domestic violence	5,026	4,882
Arson	97	101
Total crime rate	22.5	21.6
Violent	2.2	1.9
Non-violent	20.4	19.6

Public Library

No County Library
(Library statistics are the sum of all municipal libraries in the county)

Library statistics, 2007†

Population served ... 740,424

	Total	Per capita
Revenues	$41,683,392	$56.30
Expenditures	$39,357,238	$53.16
Holdings	2,726,764	3.68
Circulation	5,627,762	7.60
Annual visits	4,760,471	6.43

Registered borrowers	353,146
Reference transactions	953,974
Hours open weekly	NA
Number of libraries	23
Full-time/total staff	120/295
Interlibrary loans Provided/received	149,990/114,277
Internet terminals	375
Annual users	892,066

State Income Tax, 2006

Number of returns	335,028
Increase from previous year	1.5%
Total income	$21,893,423
Per capita	$31,054
Increase from previous year	7.0%
Net charged tax	$548,478
Per capita	$778
Average taxable income	$58,775
Average income tax	$1,637

County Finance

State Aid Programs, 2009†

Total aid	$148,298,561
CMPTRA	37,290,208
Energy tax receipts	107,829,055
Garden State Trust	93,089

General Budget, 2008†

Total tax levy	$2,012,797,124
County levy	314,221,516
County taxes	281,223,000
County library	0
County health	0
County open space	32,998,516
School levy	1,201,151,824
Muni. levy	497,423,784
Misc. revenues	435,395,715

Taxes†

	2006	2007	2008
Net valuation taxable	$46,444,919,492	$48,392,649,994	$48,544,253,040
State equalized value	$101,445,813,851	108,929,963,424	$111,571,217,282

See Introduction for an explanation of all data sources.

Demographics & Socio-Economic Characteristics

(2007 American Community Survey, except as noted)

Population

1990*	553,124
2000*	615,301
2007	642,030
Male	314,060
Female	327,970
2008 (estimate)*	642,448
Population density	1361.4

Race & Hispanic Origin, 2007

Race

White	528,649
Black/African American	50,409
American Indian/Alaska Native	937
Asian	32,346
Native Hawaiian/Pacific Islander	58
Two or more races	8,894
Hispanic origin, total	54,232
Mexican	18,588
Puerto Rican	16,612
Cuban	3,123
Other Hispanic	15,909

Age & Nativity, 2007

Under 5 years	37,962
18 years and over	487,332
21 years and over	461,495
65 years and over	82,597
85 years and over	12,117
Median age	40.2
Native-born	556,756
Foreign-born	85,274

Educational Attainment, 2007

Population 25 years and over	431,022
Less than 9th grade	3.6%
High school grad or higher	90.7%
Bachelor's degree or higher	37.5%
Graduate degree	14.2%

Households, 2007

Total households	232,730
With persons under 18	86,102
With persons over 65	58,350
Family households	165,328
Single-person households	57,020
Persons per household	2.74
Persons per family	3.29

Income & Poverty, 2007

Per capita income	$39,602
Median household income	$78,247
Median family income	$94,301
Persons in poverty	6.1%
H'holds receiving public assistance	3,054
H'holds receiving social security	64,856

Labor & Employment, 2007***

Total civilian labor force	330,899
Unemployment rate	3.7%

Employed persons 16 years and over by occupation, 2007

Managers & professionals	133,046
Service occupations	46,018
Sales & office occupations	89,672
Farming, fishing & forestry	996
Construction & maintenance	28,291
Production & transportation	20,965
Self-employed persons	19,153

Civilian Labor Force Projections***

2009	339,000
2014	352,200
2020	368,000
2025	382,100

*US Census Bureau
**2007 American Community Survey
*** New Jersey Department of Labor
† sum of all municipalities in county

See Introduction for an explanation of all data sources.

General Information

Monmouth County
1 E Main St
Hall of Records
Freehold, NJ 07728
732-431-7310

Website	www.visitmonmouth.com
Year of formation	1683
Land/water area (sq. miles)	471.9/193.2
Class	Fifth
Government form	Freeholder Board
Number of Freeholders	5
Number of municipalities	53

Government & Voters

Legislative Districts

US Congressional	4, 12
State Legislative	10-13, 30

Registered Voters, October 2008

Total	427,561
Democratic	107,140
Republican	94,699
Unaffiliated	225,528

County Officials, 2009

County Executive	NA
County Administrator	Robert Czech
Clerk	M. Claire French
Finance Dir	Craig Marshall
Tax Administrator	Matthew Clark
Surrogate	Rosemarie Peters
Prosecutor	Luis Valentin
Public Works Dir	John W. Tobia
Planning/Dev Dir	NA
Sheriff	Kim Guadagno
Fire Marshal	Tim Smith

County School District

PO Box 1264
Freehold, NJ 07728
732-431-7816

Superintendent	Carole K. Morris
Number of districts	53

Housing & Construction

Housing Units, 2007**

Total	255,256
Single family units	165,054
Multiple family units	86,838
Owner-occupied units	174,955
Renter-occupied units	57,775
Vacant units	22,526
Median rent	$1,080
Median SF home value	$445,000

Permits for New Residential Construction

	Units	Value
Total, 2006	2,820	$352,945,169
Single family	1,517	$317,505,946
Total, 2007	2,054	$340,904,606
Single family	1,130	$267,092,777

Real Property Valuation, 2008†

	Parcels	Valuation
Total	235,610	$91,441,995,368
Vacant	16,012	1,939,743,990
Residential	204,936	75,608,544,008
Farm land	2,694	29,084,900
Farm homestead	1,524	664,923,650
Non-residential	10,444	13,199,698,820
Commercial	8,957	10,347,047,120
Industrial	505	1,041,586,900
Apartments	982	1,811,064,800

Public Safety

Police Officers, 2007

County officers	567
Sheriff's department	488
Prosecutors	79
Municipal police	1,522

Crime	2006	2007
Total crimes	13,993	13,579
Violent	1,431	1,318
Murder	16	12
Rape	71	67
Robbery	554	496
Aggravated assault	790	743
Non-violent	12,562	12,261
Burglary	2,192	2,098
Larceny	9,748	9,617
Vehicle theft	622	546
Domestic violence	5,403	5,650
Arson	89	62
Total crime rate	22.0	21.4
Violent	2.3	2.1
Non-violent	19.8	19.3

Public Library

Monmouth County Library
125 Symmes Drive
Manalapan, NJ 07726
(732) 431-7235

Director............. Kenneth Sheinbaum

Library statistics, 2007

Population served 399,613

	Total	Per capita
Revenues	$14,201,091	$35.54
Expenditures	$12,327,753	$30.85
Holdings	1,414,674	3.54
Circulation	3,628,379	9.08
Annual visits	2,214,466	5.54
Registered borrowers		174,740
Reference transactions		491,320
Hours open weekly		68
Full-time/total staff		38/117
Interlibrary loans		
Provided/received		8,620/5,553
Internet terminals		84
Annual users		255,228

State Income Tax, 2006

Number of returns	271,372
Increase from previous year	1.7%
Total income	$25,966,034
Per capita	$44,892
Increase from previous year	9.8%
Net charged tax	$872,603
Per capita	$1,509
Average taxable income	$87,734
Average income tax	$3,216

County Finance

State Aid Programs, 2009†

Total aid	$101,171,887
CMPTRA	19,701,981
Energy tax receipts	78,547,046
Garden State Trust	140,385

General Budget, 2008†

Total tax levy	$1,875,406,434
County levy	319,588,347
County taxes	286,504,000
County library	12,043,433
County health	1,929,595
County open space	19,111,319
School levy	1,128,217,089
Muni. levy	427,600,998
Misc. revenues	347,968,763

Taxes†

	2006	2007	2008
Net valuation taxable	$70,829,766,536	$87,315,329,030	$91,600,065,288
State equalized value	$117,866,660,069	126,074,912,133	$127,813,573,023

Demographics & Socio-Economic Characteristics

(2007 American Community Survey, except as noted)

Population
1990*	421,353
2000*	470,212
2007	488,475
Male	241,387
Female	247,088
2008 (estimate)*	487,548
Population density	1039.5

Race & Hispanic Origin, 2007
Race
White	407,498
Black/African American	15,664
American Indian/Alaska Native	1,336
Asian	40,560
Native Hawaiian/Pacific Islander	102
Two or more races	6,237
Hispanic origin, total	51,792
Mexican	6,163
Puerto Rican	10,286
Cuban	2,316
Other Hispanic	33,027

Age & Nativity, 2007
Under 5 years	29,440
18 years and over	371,750
21 years and over	351,664
65 years and over	61,204
85 years and over	8,022
Median age	40.4
Native-born	392,478
Foreign-born	95,997

Educational Attainment, 2007
Population 25 years and over	332,824
Less than 9th grade	3.1%
High school grad or higher	92.9%
Bachelor's degree or higher	48.4%
Graduate degree	18.3%

Households, 2007
Total households	175,099
With persons under 18	64,009
With persons over 65	41,398
Family households	125,735
Single-person households	41,845
Persons per household	2.74
Persons per family	3.28

Income & Poverty, 2007
Per capita income	$45,516
Median household income	$94,684
Median family income	$111,464
Persons in poverty	3.9%
H'holds receiving public assistance	1,159
H'holds receiving social security	42,678

Labor & Employment, 2007***
Total civilian labor force	272,718
Unemployment rate	3.0%

Employed persons 16 years and over by occupation, 2007
Managers & professionals	122,669
Service occupations	31,762
Sales & office occupations	64,760
Farming, fishing & forestry	363
Construction & maintenance	16,286
Production & transportation	19,812
Self-employed persons	13,768

Civilian Labor Force Projections***
2009	275,400
2014	287,300
2020	301,500
2025	312,400

*US Census Bureau
**2007 American Community Survey
*** New Jersey Department of Labor
† sum of all municipalities in county

General Information

Morris County
PO Box 900
Morristown, NJ 07963
973-285-6000

Website	www.co.morris.nj.us
Year of formation	1739
Land/water area (sq. miles)	469.0/12.3
Class	Second
Government form	Freeholder Board
Number of Freeholders	7
Number of municipalities	39

Government & Voters

Legislative Districts
US Congressional	11
State Legislative	26, 34-36, 40

Registered Voters, October 2008
Total	322,515
Democratic	70,886
Republican	111,135
Unaffiliated	140,335

County Officials, 2009
County Executive	NA
County Administrator	John Bonanni
Clerk	Joan Bramhall
Finance Dir	Glenn Roe
Tax Administrator	Ralph Meloro IV
Surrogate	John Pecoraro
Prosecutor	Robert A. Bianchi
Public Works Dir	Stephen Hammond
Planning, Dev & Tech Dir	Frank Pinto
Sheriff	Edward Rochford
Fire Marshal	Scott DiGiralomo

County School District

Court House, PO Box 900
Morristown, NJ 07963
973-285-8332

Superintendent. Kathleen C. Serafino (Actg)
Number of districts ... 39

Housing & Construction

Housing Units, 2007**
Total	184,637
Single family units	127,624
Multiple family units	55,822
Owner-occupied units	133,747
Renter-occupied units	41,352
Vacant units	9,538
Median rent	$1,164
Median SF home value	$504,500

Permits for New Residential Construction
	Units	Value
Total, 2006	1,670	$301,462,308
Single family	791	$202,635,791
Total, 2007	1,052	$202,103,977
Single family	688	$173,427,898

Real Property Valuation, 2008†
	Parcels	Valuation
Total	169,238	$76,700,603,539
Vacant	10,192	1,373,940,350
Residential	148,757	58,547,857,080
Farm land	1,401	13,465,748
Farm homestead	745	709,356,800
Non-residential	8,143	16,055,983,561
Commercial	6,742	11,350,378,461
Industrial	1,016	2,711,381,200
Apartments	385	1,994,223,900

Public Safety

Police Officers, 2007
County officers	372
Sheriff's department	270
Prosecutors	69
Municipal police	1,094

Crime	2006	2007
Total crimes	6,908	6,474
Violent	450	462
Murder	1	1
Rape	28	37
Robbery	129	149
Aggravated assault	292	275
Non-violent	6,458	6,012
Burglary	1,210	1,037
Larceny	4,820	4,719
Vehicle theft	428	256
Domestic violence	2,599	2,473
Arson	22	30
Total crime rate	14.1	13.1
Violent	0.9	0.9
Non-violent	13.2	12.2

Public Library

Morris County Library
30 East Hanover Avenue
Whippany, NJ 07981
(973) 285-6930

Director ... Jo Ann Weinstein

Library statistics, 2007
Population served ... 470,212

	Total	Per capita
Revenues	$8,222,688	$17.49
Expenditures	$7,987,561	$16.99
Holdings	269,628	0.57
Circulation	486,123	1.03
Annual visits	260,372	0.55
Registered borrowers	1,119	
Reference transactions	80,890	
Hours open weekly	69	
Full-time/total staff	27/78	
Interlibrary loans		
Provided/received	86,695/72,286	
Internet terminals	77	
Annual users	180,147	

State Income Tax, 2006
Number of returns	214,686
Increase from previous year	1.6%
Total income	$23,724,989
Per capita	$51,527
Increase from previous year	5.2%
Net charged tax	$884,850
Per capita	$1,922
Average taxable income	$101,858
Average income tax	$4,122

County Finance

State Aid Programs, 2009†
Total aid	$62,444,003
CMPTRA	11,030,633
Energy tax receipts	48,260,701
Garden State Trust	695,021

General Budget, 2008†
Total tax levy	$1,680,874,836
County levy	237,084,090
County taxes	193,480,382
County library	0
County health	0
County open space	43,603,708
School levy	1,039,441,970
Muni. levy	404,348,776
Misc. revenues	257,076,555

Taxes†
	2006	2007	2008
Net valuation taxable	$70,984,491,271	$72,078,275,433	$76,843,562,901
State equalized value	$97,240,364,598	101,650,110,068	$103,192,518,259

See Introduction for an explanation of all data sources.

Demographics & Socio-Economic Characteristics

(2007 American Community Survey, except as noted)

Population

1990*	433,203
2000*	510,916
2007	565,493
Male	271,087
Female	294,406
2008 (estimate)*	569,111
Population density	894.4

Race & Hispanic Origin, 2007

Race

White	514,159
Black/African American	19,995
American Indian/Alaska Native	612
Asian	9,574
Native Hawaiian/Pacific Islander	0
Two or more races	6,514
Hispanic origin, total	38,534
Mexican	11,596
Puerto Rican	14,427
Cuban	1,098
Other Hispanic	11,413

Age & Nativity, 2007

Under 5 years	38,351
18 years and over	434,357
21 years and over	416,038
65 years and over	117,563
85 years and over	20,536
Median age	41.1
Native-born	524,258
Foreign-born	41,235

Educational Attainment, 2007

Population 25 years and over	393,238
Less than 9th grade	3.5%
High school grad or higher	88.1%
Bachelor's degree or higher	24.6%
Graduate degree	8.0%

Households, 2007

Total households	222,473
With persons under 18	70,871
With persons over 65	81,606
Family households	153,553
Single-person households	59,591
Persons per household	2.51
Persons per family	3.06

Income & Poverty, 2007

Per capita income	$29,105
Median household income	$56,281
Median family income	$71,149
Persons in poverty	8.7%
H'holds receiving public assistance	4,560
H'holds receiving social security	90,905

Labor & Employment, 2007***

Total civilian labor force	257,602
Unemployment rate	4.5%

Employed persons 16 years and over by occupation, 2007

Managers & professionals	84,642
Service occupations	38,366
Sales & office occupations	68,886
Farming, fishing & forestry	185
Construction & maintenance	29,547
Production & transportation	21,883
Self-employed persons	16,466

Civilian Labor Force Projections***

2009	272,400
2014	292,900
2020	307,200
2025	329,100

*US Census Bureau
**2007 American Community Survey
*** New Jersey Department of Labor
† sum of all municipalities in county

See Introduction for an explanation of all data sources.

General Information

Ocean County
PO Box 2191
Toms River, NJ 08754
732-244-2121

Website	www.co.ocean.nj.us
Year of formation	1850
Land/water area (sq. miles)	636.3/279.6
Class	Fifth
Government form	Freeholder Board
Number of Freeholders	5
Number of municipalities	33

Government & Voters

Legislative Districts

US Congressional	3-4
State Legislative	9-10, 30

Registered Voters, October 2008

Total	380,740
Democratic	79,872
Republican	101,122
Unaffiliated	199,597

County Officials, 2009

County Executive	NA
Manager	Alan W. Avery Jr
Clerk	Carl W. Block
Finance Dir	Julie N. Tarrant
Tax Admin	Lawrence Ozzie Vituscka
Surrogate	Jeffrey W. Moran
Prosecutor	Marlene Lynch Ford
Public Works Dir	William Santos
Planning/Dev Dir	David J. McKeon
Sheriff	William Polhemus
Fire Marshal	Daniel Mulligan

County School District

212 Washington St
Toms River, NJ 08753
732-929-2078

Superintendent	Bruce Greenfield
Number of districts	33

Housing & Construction

Housing Units, 2007**

Total	273,054
Single family units	203,581
Multiple family units	61,647
Owner-occupied units	184,003
Renter-occupied units	38,470
Vacant units	50,581
Median rent	$1,151
Median SF home value	$310,100

Permits for New Residential Construction

	Units	Value
Total, 2006	2,114	$341,607,209
Single family	2,079	$337,301,893
Total, 2007	2,160	$328,378,145
Single family	1,544	$285,077,433

Real Property Valuation, 2008†

	Parcels	Valuation
Total	276,280	$68,419,465,313
Vacant	32,964	2,289,778,690
Residential	235,262	58,787,961,305
Farm land	470	5,221,866
Farm homestead	241	83,209,800
Non-residential	7,343	7,253,293,652
Commercial	6,594	5,448,039,652
Industrial	397	780,857,300
Apartments	352	1,024,396,700

Public Safety

Police Officers, 2007

County officers	213
Sheriff's department	136
Prosecutors	77
Municipal police	1,146

Crime	2006	2007
Total crimes	11,470	11,543
Violent	803	759
Murder	9	9
Rape	47	36
Robbery	261	221
Aggravated assault	486	493
Non-violent	10,667	10,784
Burglary	2,142	1,952
Larceny	8,024	8,438
Vehicle theft	501	394
Domestic violence	5,733	5,256
Arson	91	71
Total crime rate	20.5	20.5
Violent	1.4	1.3
Non-violent	19.1	19.2

Public Library

Ocean County Library
101 Washington Street
Toms River, NJ 08753
(732) 349-6200

Director	Harry T. Applegate Jr

Library statistics, 2007

Population served	509,638

	Total	Per capita
Revenues	$32,265,878	$63.31
Expenditures	$29,891,322	$58.65
Holdings	1,423,075	2.79
Circulation	4,563,123	8.95
Annual visits	3,184,935	6.25
Registered borrowers		344,976
Reference transactions		1,740,901
Hours open weekly		68
Full-time/total staff		104/283
Interlibrary loans		
Provided/received		8,875/5,343
Internet terminals		210
Annual users		156,000

State Income Tax, 2006

Number of returns	238,354
Increase from previous year	1.6%
Total income	$13,285,780
Per capita	$26,725
Increase from previous year	6.3%
Net charged tax	$349,566
Per capita	$703
Average taxable income	$48,791
Average income tax	$1,467

County Finance

State Aid Programs, 2009†

Total aid	$66,831,770
CMPTRA	7,442,666
Energy tax receipts	56,143,758
Garden State Trust	968,724

General Budget, 2008†

Total tax levy	$1,354,699,754
County levy	332,404,543
County taxes	276,305,117
County library	31,840,066
County health	11,191,000
County open space	13,068,360
School levy	668,467,466
Muni. levy	353,827,744
Misc. revenues	272,549,790

Taxes†

	2006	2007	2008
Net valuation taxable	$60,271,799,283	$67,050,661,857	$68,505,902,121
State equalized value	$101,281,498,360	107,636,225,899	$109,024,821,004

Demographics & Socio-Economic Characteristics

(2007 American Community Survey, except as noted)

Population
1990*	453,060
2000*	489,049
2007	492,115
Male	240,323
Female	251,792
2008 (estimate)*	490,948
Population density	2649.5

Race & Hispanic Origin, 2007
Race
White	282,964
Black/African American	60,551
American Indian/Alaska Native	795
Asian	22,028
Native Hawaiian/Pacific Islander	385
Two or more races	10,374
Hispanic origin, total	170,409
Mexican	26,880
Puerto Rican	38,284
Cuban	3,476
Other Hispanic	101,769

Age & Nativity, 2007
Under 5 years	34,952
18 years and over	364,971
21 years and over	341,203
65 years and over	59,633
85 years and over	8,871
Median age	36.4
Native-born	354,146
Foreign-born	137,969

Educational Attainment, 2007
Population 25 years and over	317,919
Less than 9th grade	8.9%
High school grad or higher	82.7%
Bachelor's degree or higher	22.5%
Graduate degree	6.7%

Households, 2007
Total households	158,192
With persons under 18	57,459
With persons over 65	38,483
Family households	111,544
Single-person households	39,916
Persons per household	3.03
Persons per family	3.68

Income & Poverty, 2007
Per capita income	$24,888
Median household income	$54,551
Median family income	$67,345
Persons in poverty	13.7%
H'holds receiving public assistance	3,286
H'holds receiving social security	40,438

Labor & Employment, 2007*
Total civilian labor force	237,995
Unemployment rate	5.3%

Employed persons 16 years and over by occupation, 2007
Managers & professionals	69,135
Service occupations	38,397
Sales & office occupations	67,473
Farming, fishing & forestry	149
Construction & maintenance	17,527
Production & transportation	35,074
Self-employed persons	10,145

Civilian Labor Force Projections*
2009	241,100
2014	246,400
2020	252,000
2025	259,300

*US Census Bureau
**2007 American Community Survey
*** New Jersey Department of Labor
† sum of all municipalities in county

General Information
Passaic County
401 Grand St
Administration Bldg
Paterson, NJ 07505
973-881-4000

Website	www.passaiccountynj.org
Year of formation	1837
Land/water area (sq. miles)	185.3/11.8
Class	Second
Government form	Freeholder Board
Number of Freeholders	7
Number of municipalities	16

Government & Voters

Legislative Districts
US Congressional	5, 8-9, 11
State Legislative	26, 34-36, 40

Registered Voters, October 2008
Total	271,377
Democratic	82,759
Republican	48,686
Unaffiliated	139,890

County Officials, 2009
County Executive	NA
Manager	Anthony DeNova
Clerk	Karen Brown
Finance Dir	Daniel Gonzalez
Tax Administrator	James Murner Jr
Surrogate	Willam Bate
Prosecutor	James Avigliano
Public Works Dir	Steven J. Edmond
Planning/Dev Dir	Michael La Place
Sheriff	Jerry Speziale
Emerg Mgmt Dir	Robert Lyons

County School District
501 River St
Paterson, NJ 07524
973-569-2110
Superintendent	Robert Gilmartin (Actg)
Number of districts	16

Housing & Construction

Housing Units, 2007**
Total	171,935
Single family units	71,120
Multiple family units	100,335
Owner-occupied units	88,013
Renter-occupied units	70,179
Vacant units	13,743
Median rent	$1,029
Median SF home value	$398,800

Permits for New Residential Construction
	Units	Value
Total, 2006	850	$94,758,952
Single family	375	$58,465,306
Total, 2007	760	$82,819,949
Single family	265	$47,109,394

Real Property Valuation, 2008†
	Parcels	Valuation
Total	123,831	$30,260,235,965
Vacant	5,772	525,540,613
Residential	106,956	21,865,453,608
Farm land	319	945,274
Farm homestead	143	33,180,800
Non-residential	10,641	7,835,115,670
Commercial	8,038	4,881,582,230
Industrial	1,517	1,960,080,090
Apartments	1,086	993,453,350

Public Safety

Police Officers, 2007
County officers	746
Sheriff's department	653
Prosecutors	93
Municipal police	1,259

Crime	2006	2007
Total crimes	14,249	14,347
Violent	2,666	2,574
Murder	23	17
Rape	59	48
Robbery	1,214	1,156
Aggravated assault	1,370	1,353
Non-violent	11,583	11,773
Burglary	2,761	2,870
Larceny	6,910	7,362
Vehicle theft	1,912	1,541
Domestic violence	4,105	4,154
Arson	39	28
Total crime rate	28.6	28.9
Violent	5.3	5.2
Non-violent	23.2	23.7

Public Library
No County Library
(Library statistics are the sum of all municipal libraries in the county)

Library statistics, 2007†
Population served 483,270
	Total	Per capita
Revenues	$18,828,594	$38.96
Expenditures	$17,252,344	$35.70
Holdings	1,302,010	2.69
Circulation	1,729,274	3.58
Annual visits	1,414,005	2.93
Registered borrowers	207,211	
Reference transactions	295,764	
Hours open weekly	NA	
Number of libraries	15	
Full-time/total staff	51/170	
Interlibrary loans Provided/received	33,979/56,007	
Internet terminals	276	
Annual users	371,175	

State Income Tax, 2006
Number of returns	209,426
Increase from previous year	2.1%
Total income	$11,207,362
Per capita	$25,601
Increase from previous year	4.3%
Net charged tax	$282,667
Per capita	$646
Average taxable income	$47,330
Average income tax	$1,350

County Finance

State Aid Programs, 2009†
Total aid	$89,511,127
CMPTRA	47,789,162
Energy tax receipts	39,691,303
Garden State Trust	298,242

General Budget, 2008†
Total tax levy	$1,152,383,645
County levy	282,969,067
County taxes	277,340,015
County library	0
County health	0
County open space	5,629,052
School levy	509,763,121
Muni. levy	359,651,458
Misc. revenues	270,857,771

Taxes†
	2006	2007	2008
Net valuation taxable	$21,354,230,409	$30,268,051,426	$30,307,653,137
State equalized value	$51,774,568,393	55,623,705,991	$57,227,118,466

See Introduction for an explanation of all data sources.

Demographics & Socio-Economic Characteristics

(2007 American Community Survey, except as noted)

Population

1990*	65,294
2000*	64,285
2007	66,016
Male	32,793
Female	33,223
2008 (estimate)*	66,141
Population density	195.7

Race & Hispanic Origin, 2007

Race

White	53,048
Black/African American	10,184
American Indian/Alaska Native	243
Asian	335
Native Hawaiian/Pacific Islander	0
Two or more races	1,309
Hispanic origin, total	3,381
Mexican	NA
Puerto Rican	NA
Cuban	NA
Other Hispanic	NA

Age & Nativity, 2007

Under 5 years	4,106
18 years and over	50,977
21 years and over	47,885
65 years and over	9,177
85 years and over	1,222
Median age	39.7
Native-born	64,273
Foreign-born	1,743

Educational Attainment, 2007

Population 25 years and over	45,054
Less than 9th grade	5.7%
High school grad or higher	83.8%
Bachelor's degree or higher	17.5%
Graduate degree	6.2%

Households, 2007

Total households	25,525
With persons under 18	7,859
With persons over 65	6,518
Family households	17,584
Single-person households	6,654
Persons per household	2.53
Persons per family	3.10

Income & Poverty, 2007

Per capita income	$26,979
Median household income	$54,992
Median family income	$69,414
Persons in poverty	10.9%
H'holds receiving public assistance	681
H'holds receiving social security	7,725

Labor & Employment, 2007*

Total civilian labor force	31,886
Unemployment rate	4.9%

Employed persons 16 years and over by occupation, 2007

Managers & professionals	9,527
Service occupations	4,831
Sales & office occupations	7,319
Farming, fishing & forestry	56
Construction & maintenance	4,722
Production & transportation	6,034
Self-employed persons	2,186

Civilian Labor Force Projections*

2009	32,800
2014	33,900
2020	35,100
2025	36,000

*US Census Bureau
**2007 American Community Survey
*** New Jersey Department of Labor
† sum of all municipalities in county

See Introduction for an explanation of all data sources.

General Information

Salem County
94 Market St
Administration Bldg
Salem, NJ 08079
856-935-7510

Website	www.salemco.org
Year of formation	1694
Land/water area (sq. miles)	337.9/34.7
Class	Third
Government form	Freeholder Board
Number of Freeholders	7
Number of municipalities	15

Government & Voters

Legislative Districts

US Congressional	2
State Legislative	3

Registered Voters, October 2008

Total	44,282
Democratic	13,629
Republican	9,056
Unaffiliated	21,581

County Officials, 2009

County Executive	NA
Manager	Earl Gage
Clerk	Gilda Gill
Finance Dir	Douglas Wright
Tax Administrator	Linda Stewart
Surrogate	Nicki Burke
Prosecutor	John Lenahan
Public Works Dir	Jeffrey Ridgeway Sr
Economic Dev Dir	James Waddington
Sheriff	Charles Miller III
Fire Marshal	John Turner Jr

County School District

164 Route 45
Salem, NJ 08079
856-339-8611

Superintendent	Robert Bumpus
Number of districts	15

Housing & Construction

Housing Units, 2007**

Total	27,531
Single family units	21,187
Multiple family units	5,249
Owner-occupied units	19,888
Renter-occupied units	5,637
Vacant units	2,006
Median rent	$821
Median SF home value	$188,800

Permits for New Residential Construction

	Units	Value
Total, 2006	298	$33,415,324
Single family	197	$23,804,424
Total, 2007	148	$18,845,706
Single family	143	$18,603,282

Real Property Valuation, 2008†

	Parcels	Valuation
Total	31,612	$4,324,642,816
Vacant	4,334	108,103,810
Residential	20,047	2,821,821,150
Farm land	4,168	55,997,500
Farm homestead	1,846	373,618,200
Non-residential	1,217	965,102,156
Commercial	1,109	476,959,790
Industrial	48	416,794,366
Apartments	60	71,348,000

Public Safety

Police Officers, 2007

County officers	172
Sheriff's department	155
Prosecutors	17
Municipal police	108

Crime	2006	2007
Total crimes	1,872	1,828
Violent	208	219
Murder	2	3
Rape	1	15
Robbery	68	41
Aggravated assault	137	160
Non-violent	1,664	1,609
Burglary	463	431
Larceny	1,106	1,089
Vehicle theft	95	89
Domestic violence	663	767
Arson	22	22
Total crime rate	28.2	27.4
Violent	3.1	3.3
Non-violent	25.1	24.2

Public Library

No County Library
(Library statistics are the sum of all municipal libraries in the county)

Library statistics, 2007†

Population served ... 40,064

	Total	Per capita
Revenues	$368,380	$9.19
Expenditures	$432,975	$10.81
Holdings	100,324	2.50
Circulation	51,101	1.28
Annual visits	34,507	0.86

Registered borrowers	7,145
Reference transactions	5,459
Hours open weekly	NA
Number of libraries	5
Full-time/total staff	1/8
Interlibrary loans	
Provided/received	454/1,167
Internet terminals	15
Annual users	8,926

State Income Tax, 2006

Number of returns	26,405
Increase from previous year	1.8%
Total income	$1,446,236
Per capita	$25,781
Increase from previous year	7.8%
Net charged tax	$33,810
Per capita	$603
Average taxable income	$48,879
Average income tax	$1,280

County Finance

State Aid Programs, 2009†

Total aid	$23,067,550
CMPTRA	4,112,236
Energy tax receipts	18,301,526
Garden State Trust	133,823

General Budget, 2008†

Total tax levy	$131,965,346
County levy	50,139,854
County taxes	49,058,072
County library	0
County health	0
County open space	1,081,782
School levy	64,079,504
Muni. levy	17,745,988
Misc. revenues	49,280,375

Taxes†

	2006	2007	2008
Net valuation taxable	$3,629,370,280	$4,039,863,061	$4,341,555,494
State equalized value	$4,814,299,623	5,268,705,430	$5,651,828,293

Demographics & Socio-Economic Characteristics

(2007 American Community Survey, except as noted)

Population
1990*	240,279
2000*	297,490
2007	323,552
Male	160,887
Female	162,665
2008 (estimate)*	324,563
Population density	1065.2

Race & Hispanic Origin, 2007
Race
White	241,204
Black/African American	28,248
American Indian/Alaska Native	398
Asian	40,052
Native Hawaiian/Pacific Islander	0
Two or more races	3,451
Hispanic origin, total	39,294
Mexican	11,769
Puerto Rican	5,432
Cuban	1,834
Other Hispanic	20,259

Age & Nativity, 2007
Under 5 years	21,031
18 years and over	242,659
21 years and over	231,353
65 years and over	37,444
85 years and over	4,418
Median age	39.2
Native-born	250,950
Foreign-born	72,602

Educational Attainment, 2007
Population 25 years and over	218,529
Less than 9th grade	2.4%
High school grad or higher	93.4%
Bachelor's degree or higher	49.9%
Graduate degree	21.1%

Households, 2007
Total households	112,733
With persons under 18	43,591
With persons over 65	26,348
Family households	82,980
Single-person households	24,838
Persons per household	2.84
Persons per family	3.37

Income & Poverty, 2007
Per capita income	$47,646
Median household income	$97,658
Median family income	$111,809
Persons in poverty	2.6%
H'holds receiving public assistance	1,080
H'holds receiving social security	27,660

Labor & Employment, 2007***
Total civilian labor force	181,315
Unemployment rate	3.1%

Employed persons 16 years and over by occupation, 2007
Managers & professionals	84,857
Service occupations	18,229
Sales & office occupations	40,107
Farming, fishing & forestry	97
Construction & maintenance	11,706
Production & transportation	12,809
Self-employed persons	7,840

Civilian Labor Force Projections***
2009	179,200
2014	188,200
2020	197,700
2025	206,400

*US Census Bureau
**2007 American Community Survey
*** New Jersey Department of Labor
† sum of all municipalities in county

General Information

Somerset County
20 Grove Street
PO Box 3000
Somerville, NJ 08876
908-231-7000

Website	www.co.somerset.nj.us
Year of formation	1688
Land/water area (sq. miles)	304.7/0.4
Class	Second
Government form	Freeholder Board
Number of Freeholders	5
Number of municipalities	21

Government & Voters

Legislative Districts
US Congressional	6-7, 11-12
State Legislative	16-17, 21-22

Registered Voters, October 2008
Total	189,128
Democratic	50,005
Republican	48,874
Unaffiliated	90,147

County Officials, 2009
Freeholder Director	Rick Fontana
County Admin	Richard E. Williams
Clerk	Brett A. Radi
Finance Dir	Brian Newman
Tax Administrator	William Linville
Surrogate	Frank G. Bruno
Prosecutor	Wayne J. Forrest
Public Works Dir	Michael J. Amorosa
Planning Dir	Robert P. Bzik
Sheriff	Frank J. Provenzano
OEM Director	LeRoy Gunzelman III

County School District

27 Warren St, PO Box 3000
Somerville, NJ 08876
908-541-5700

Superintendent	Trudy Doyle
Number of districts	21

Housing & Construction

Housing Units, 2007**
Total	121,430
Single family units	73,262
Multiple family units	47,966
Owner-occupied units	90,834
Renter-occupied units	21,899
Vacant units	8,697
Median rent	$1,241
Median SF home value	$469,600

Permits for New Residential Construction
	Units	Value
Total, 2006	1,058	$149,647,930
Single family	623	$108,774,149
Total, 2007	924	$147,984,324
Single family	593	$118,132,440

Real Property Valuation, 2008†
	Parcels	Valuation
Total	113,219	$54,610,737,536
Vacant	6,093	730,648,150
Residential	99,952	42,377,100,238
Farm land	1,644	16,048,720
Farm homestead	897	1,068,586,750
Non-residential	4,633	10,418,353,678
Commercial	3,739	7,499,102,496
Industrial	652	2,173,096,400
Apartments	242	746,154,782

Public Safety

Police Officers, 2007
County officers	235
Sheriff's department	185
Prosecutors	50
Municipal police	632

Crime	2006	2007
Total crimes	4,777	4,804
Violent	295	226
Murder	4	6
Rape	24	22
Robbery	145	109
Aggravated assault	122	89
Non-violent	4,482	4,578
Burglary	923	824
Larceny	3,248	3,424
Vehicle theft	311	330
Domestic violence	2,202	2,194
Arson	25	22
Total crime rate	14.9	14.8
Violent	0.9	0.7
Non-violent	14.0	14.1

Public Library

Somerset County Library
1 Vogt Drive
Bridgewater, NJ 08807
(908) 526-4016

Director	James M. Hecht

Library statistics, 2007
Population served 176,402
	Total	Per capita
Revenues	$13,913,797	$78.88
Expenditures	$14,250,980	$80.79
Holdings	813,024	4.61
Circulation	2,592,882	14.70
Annual visits	1,061,921	6.02
Registered borrowers	95,485	
Reference transactions	122,416	
Hours open weekly	69	
Full-time/total staff	51/128	
Interlibrary loans		
Provided/received	7,983/4,358	
Internet terminals	118	
Annual users	244,011	

State Income Tax, 2006
Number of returns	139,389
Increase from previous year	1.3%
Total income	$16,153,854
Per capita	$53,719
Increase from previous year	8.6%
Net charged tax	$638,226
Per capita	$2,122
Average taxable income	$107,363
Average income tax	$4,579

County Finance

State Aid Programs, 2009†
Total aid	$40,724,991
CMPTRA	6,189,458
Energy tax receipts	33,040,644
Garden State Trust	142,397

General Budget, 2008†
Total tax levy	$1,084,290,537
County levy	203,288,602
County taxes	170,839,214
County library	13,537,509
County health	0
County open space	18,911,879
School levy	677,060,497
Muni. levy	203,941,439
Misc. revenues	165,276,701

Taxes†
	2006	2007	2008
Net valuation taxable	$53,183,937,868	$54,524,256,257	$54,695,989,018
State equalized value	$60,444,405,550	62,394,256,799	$63,431,787,374

See Introduction for an explanation of all data sources.

Demographics & Socio-Economic Characteristics

(2007 American Community Survey, except as noted)

Population
1990*	130,943
2000*	144,166
2007	151,478
Male	75,602
Female	75,876
2008 (estimate)*	150,909
Population density	289.5

Race & Hispanic Origin, 2007
Race
White	141,021
Black/African American	2,797
American Indian/Alaska Native	479
Asian	2,482
Native Hawaiian/Pacific Islander	0
Two or more races	1,187
Hispanic origin, total	8,598
Mexican	1,137
Puerto Rican	3,925
Cuban	735
Other Hispanic	2,801

Age & Nativity, 2007
Under 5 years	8,298
18 years and over	115,080
21 years and over	107,387
65 years and over	15,522
85 years and over	1,815
Median age	40.0
Native-born	140,970
Foreign-born	10,508

Educational Attainment, 2007
Population 25 years and over	101,744
Less than 9th grade	1.8%
High school grad or higher	93.3%
Bachelor's degree or higher	31.1%
Graduate degree	9.6%

Households, 2007
Total households	54,524
With persons under 18	20,262
With persons over 65	11,411
Family households	40,580
Single-person households	12,200
Persons per household	2.75
Persons per family	3.26

Income & Poverty, 2007
Per capita income	$34,296
Median household income	$78,558
Median family income	$88,686
Persons in poverty	4.6%
H'holds receiving public assistance	382
H'holds receiving social security	13,128

Labor & Employment, 2007***
Total civilian labor force	84,657
Unemployment rate	3.9%

Employed persons 16 years and over by occupation, 2007
Managers & professionals	27,762
Service occupations	13,455
Sales & office occupations	20,607
Farming, fishing & forestry	189
Construction & maintenance	10,233
Production & transportation	8,157
Self-employed persons	6,394

Civilian Labor Force Projections***
2009	87,600
2014	91,200
2020	96,600
2025	99,900

*US Census Bureau
**2007 American Community Survey
*** New Jersey Department of Labor
† sum of all municipalities in county

General Information
Sussex County
One Spring St
Administration Center
Newton, NJ 07860
973-579-0210

Website	www.sussex.nj.us
Year of formation	1753
Land/water area (sq. miles)	521.3/14.7
Class	Third
Government form	Freeholder Board
Number of Freeholders	5
Number of municipalities	24

Government & Voters

Legislative Districts
US Congressional	5, 11
State Legislative	24

Registered Voters, October 2008
Total	96,749
Democratic	16,317
Republican	36,798
Unaffiliated	43,556

County Officials, 2009
County Executive	NA
County Administrator	John H. Eskilson
Clerk	Emma Gormley
Finance Dir	Bernard A. Re
Tax Administrator	Carol Dennis
Surrogate	Nancy Fitzgibbons
Prosecutor	David Weaver
Public Works Dir	NA
Planning/Dev Dir	Eric Snyder
Sheriff	Robert Untig
Fire Marshal	NA

County School District
262 White Lake Rd
Sparta, NJ 07871
973-579-6996
Superintendent	Frank Dragotta (Int)
Number of districts	24

Housing & Construction

Housing Units, 2007**
Total	60,581
Single family units	48,663
Multiple family units	11,234
Owner-occupied units	46,162
Renter-occupied units	8,362
Vacant units	6,057
Median rent	$1,098
Median SF home value	$341,300

Permits for New Residential Construction
	Units	Value
Total, 2006	603	$105,844,827
Single family	551	$96,887,147
Total, 2007	359	$66,895,887
Single family	323	$64,579,887

Real Property Valuation, 2008†
	Parcels	Valuation
Total	72,285	$15,075,530,998
Vacant	9,394	429,601,226
Residential	54,937	12,411,226,199
Farm land	3,581	28,232,791
Farm homestead	1,797	585,799,800
Non-residential	2,576	1,620,670,982
Commercial	2,298	1,354,639,782
Industrial	192	176,684,700
Apartments	86	89,346,500

Taxes†
	2006	2007	2008
Net valuation taxable	$12,207,798,955	$13,720,392,885	$15,117,256,883
State equalized value	$19,481,397,769	20,916,597,014	$21,484,887,501

Public Safety

Police Officers, 2007
County officers	155
Sheriff's department	122
Prosecutors	33
Municipal police	220

Crime	2006	2007
Total crimes	1,902	1,648
Violent	98	99
Murder	2	1
Rape	7	7
Robbery	14	6
Aggravated assault	75	85
Non-violent	1,804	1,549
Burglary	288	301
Larceny	1,449	1,183
Vehicle theft	67	65
Domestic violence	989	1,374
Arson	15	16
Total crime rate	12.4	10.7
Violent	0.6	0.6
Non-violent	11.8	10.1

Public Library
Sussex County Library
125 Morris Turnpike
Newton, NJ 07860
(973) 948-3660

Director	Stanley Pollakoff

Library statistics, 2007
Population served	126,086

	Total	Per capita
Revenues	$4,975,047	$39.46
Expenditures	$4,983,330	$39.52
Holdings	334,102	2.65
Circulation	804,869	6.38
Annual visits	507,560	4.03

Registered borrowers	65,160
Reference transactions	8,661
Hours open weekly	65
Full-time/total staff	13/56
Interlibrary loans	
Provided/received	498/3,122
Internet terminals	55
Annual users	55,404

State Income Tax, 2006
Number of returns	62,277
Increase from previous year	0.7%
Total income	$4,639,636
Per capita	$33,825
Increase from previous year	5.4%
Net charged tax	$134,026
Per capita	$977
Average taxable income	$66,496
Average income tax	$2,152

County Finance

State Aid Programs, 2009†
Total aid	$16,768,370
CMPTRA	3,596,500
Energy tax receipts	11,243,410
Garden State Trust	950,568

General Budget, 2008†
Total tax levy	$416,246,821
County levy	80,113,847
County taxes	68,490,715
County library	4,765,620
County health	1,537,729
County open space	5,321,306
School levy	249,759,952
Muni. levy	86,373,023
Misc. revenues	58,296,307

See Introduction for an explanation of all data sources.

Demographics & Socio-Economic Characteristics

(2007 American Community Survey, except as noted)

Population

1990*	493,819
2000*	522,541
2007	524,658
Male	255,314
Female	269,344
2008 (estimate)*	523,249
Population density	5065.3

Race & Hispanic Origin, 2007

Race

White	303,621
Black/African American	113,592
American Indian/Alaska Native	740
Asian	23,526
Native Hawaiian/Pacific Islander	369
Two or more races	6,190
Hispanic origin, total	131,554
Mexican	5,854
Puerto Rican	26,850
Cuban	11,864
Other Hispanic	86,986

Age & Nativity, 2007

Under 5 years	36,629
18 years and over	393,998
21 years and over	373,815
65 years and over	66,513
85 years and over	9,351
Median age	38.4
Native-born	381,572
Foreign-born	143,086

Educational Attainment, 2007

Population 25 years and over	346,383
Less than 9th grade	7.2%
High school grad or higher	85.5%
Bachelor's degree or higher	29.4%
Graduate degree	10.9%

Households, 2007

Total households	182,933
With persons under 18	67,674
With persons over 65	45,805
Family households	124,074
Single-person households	52,359
Persons per household	2.84
Persons per family	3.54

Income & Poverty, 2007

Per capita income	$31,715
Median household income	$61,553
Median family income	$76,220
Persons in poverty	7.8%
H'holds receiving public assistance	3,265
H'holds receiving social security	44,617

Labor & Employment, 2007***

Total civilian labor force	268,736
Unemployment rate	4.5%

Employed persons 16 years and over by occupation, 2007

Managers & professionals	86,399
Service occupations	40,411
Sales & office occupations	68,449
Farming, fishing & forestry	48
Construction & maintenance	21,298
Production & transportation	36,233
Self-employed persons	14,817

Civilian Labor Force Projections***

2009	273,600
2014	282,100
2020	291,100
2025	296,300

*US Census Bureau
**2007 American Community Survey
*** New Jersey Department of Labor
† sum of all municipalities in county

General Information

Union County
10 Elizabethtown Plz
Administration Bldg
Elizabeth, NJ 07207
908-527-4000

Website	www.unioncountynj.org
Year of formation	1857
Land/water area (sq. miles)	103.3/2.2
Class	Second
Government form	County Manager Plan
Number of Freeholders	9
Number of municipalities	21

Government & Voters

Legislative Districts

US Congressional	6-7, 10
State Legislative	20-22, 29

Registered Voters, October 2008

Total	299,795
Democratic	124,349
Republican	44,909
Unaffiliated	130,442

County Officials, 2009

County Executive	NA
Manager	George Devanney
Clerk	Joanne Rajoppi
Finance Dir	Lawrence Caroselli
Tax Administrator	Christopher Duryee
Surrogate	James LaCorte
Prosecutor	Theodore Romankow
Public Works Dir	Joseph Graziano
Parks/Comm Renewal	Alfred Faella
Sheriff	Ralph Froehlich
Emerg Serv Dir	Ben Laganga

County School District

300 North Ave E
Westfield, NJ 07090
908-654-9860

Superintendent	Carmen Centuolo
Number of districts	21

Housing & Construction

Housing Units, 2007**

Total	196,958
Single family units	98,228
Multiple family units	98,208
Owner-occupied units	109,362
Renter-occupied units	73,571
Vacant units	14,025
Median rent	$1,021
Median SF home value	$422,700

Permits for New Residential Construction

	Units	Value
Total, 2006	1,593	$151,828,051
Single family	549	$92,918,557
Total, 2007	1,123	$128,954,996
Single family	350	$73,546,546

Real Property Valuation, 2008†

	Parcels	Valuation
Total	142,952	$23,945,623,425
Vacant	4,420	244,745,150
Residential	128,224	17,510,496,240
Farm land	9	157,520
Farm homestead	4	1,098,900
Non-residential	10,295	6,189,125,615
Commercial	7,613	2,953,504,485
Industrial	1,527	2,623,531,530
Apartments	1,155	612,089,600

Public Safety

Police Officers, 2007

County officers	566
Sheriff's department	169
Prosecutors	78
Municipal police	1,446

Crime	2006	2007
Total crimes	15,599	15,622
Violent	2,138	2,129
Murder	37	23
Rape	75	60
Robbery	1,125	1,247
Aggravated assault	901	799
Non-violent	13,461	13,493
Burglary	2,263	2,114
Larceny	8,930	9,053
Vehicle theft	2,268	2,326
Domestic violence	4,096	3,884
Arson	55	43
Total crime rate	29.4	29.4
Violent	4.0	4.0
Non-violent	25.3	25.4

Public Library

No County Library
(Library statistics are the sum of all municipal libraries in the county)

Library statistics, 2007†

Population served ... 521,027

	Total	Per capita
Revenues	$28,389,917	$54.49
Expenditures	$27,170,457	$52.15
Holdings	2,275,936	4.37
Circulation	2,437,232	4.68
Annual visits	2,801,989	5.38

Registered borrowers	291,077
Reference transactions	321,061
Hours open weekly	NA
Number of libraries	20
Full-time/total staff	98/230
Interlibrary loans	
Provided/received	17,891/17,269
Internet terminals	474
Annual users	461,950

State Income Tax, 2006

Number of returns	226,837
Increase from previous year	1.4%
Total income	$17,327,034
Per capita	$37,189
Increase from previous year	8.7%
Net charged tax	$517,263
Per capita	$1,110
Average taxable income	$69,656
Average income tax	$2,280

County Finance

State Aid Programs, 2009†

Total aid	$116,291,168
CMPTRA	35,935,731
Energy tax receipts	78,541,002
Garden State Trust	1

General Budget, 2008†

Total tax levy	$1,464,059,381
County levy	263,259,210
County taxes	251,657,663
County library	0
County health	0
County open space	11,601,547
School levy	708,056,755
Muni. levy	492,743,416
Misc. revenues	347,943,673

Taxes†

	2006	2007	2008
Net valuation taxable	$23,903,375,848	$23,952,106,354	$23,979,799,122
State equalized value	$70,964,438,449	76,528,105,229	$78,646,619,605

See Introduction for an explanation of all data sources.

Demographics & Socio-Economic Characteristics

(2007 American Community Survey, except as noted)

Population
1990*	91,607
2000*	102,437
2007	109,737
Male	52,883
Female	56,854
2008 (estimate)*	109,876
Population density	307.0

Race & Hispanic Origin, 2007
Race
White	101,531
Black/African American	3,534
American Indian/Alaska Native	93
Asian	2,643
Native Hawaiian/Pacific Islander	0
Two or more races	913
Hispanic origin, total	6,919
Mexican	NA
Puerto Rican	NA
Cuban	NA
Other Hispanic	NA

Age & Nativity, 2007
Under 5 years	7,073
18 years and over	83,249
21 years and over	78,477
65 years and over	14,020
85 years and over	1,731
Median age	39.5
Native-born	101,485
Foreign-born	8,252

Educational Attainment, 2007
Population 25 years and over	74,013
Less than 9th grade	2.7%
High school grad or higher	90.1%
Bachelor's degree or higher	29.8%
Graduate degree	9.8%

Households, 2007
Total households	42,759
With persons under 18	15,506
With persons over 65	10,361
Family households	30,328
Single-person households	10,409
Persons per household	2.50
Persons per family	2.98

Income & Poverty, 2007
Per capita income	$30,436
Median household income	$65,930
Median family income	$80,889
Persons in poverty	6.3%
H'holds receiving public assistance	1,179
H'holds receiving social security	12,712

Labor & Employment, 2007***
Total civilian labor force	59,568
Unemployment rate	3.7%

Employed persons 16 years and over by occupation, 2007
Managers & professionals	20,852
Service occupations	9,503
Sales & office occupations	12,854
Farming, fishing & forestry	240
Construction & maintenance	4,797
Production & transportation	6,031
Self-employed persons	3,458

Civilian Labor Force Projections***
2009	61,400
2014	65,100
2020	69,200
2025	72,300

*US Census Bureau
**2007 American Community Survey
*** New Jersey Department of Labor
† sum of all municipalities in county

See Introduction for an explanation of all data sources.

General Information

Warren County
165 County Route 519 South
Belvidere, NJ 07823
908-475-6500

Website	www.co.warren.nj.us
Year of formation	1824
Land/water area (sq. miles)	357.9/4.9
Class	Third
Government form	Freeholder Board
Number of Freeholders	3
Number of municipalities	22

Government & Voters

Legislative Districts
US Congressional	5, 13
State Legislative	23

Registered Voters, October 2008
Total	67,920
Democratic	14,788
Republican	23,175
Unaffiliated	29,914

County Officials, 2009
Freeholder Director	Richard D. Gardner
Admin/Freeholder Clerk	Steve Marvin
Clerk	Patricia J. Kolb
CFO	Charles L. Houck
Tax Administrator	Melissa Pritchett
Surrogate	Susan Dickey
Prosecutor	Thomas S. Ferguson
Supervisor of Roads	Thomas Kitchen
Planning Dir	David K. Dech
Sheriff	Sal Simonetti
Fire Marshal	Joseph Lake

County School District

1501 Route 57
Washington, NJ 07782
908-689-0464

Superintendent	Kevin Brennan
Number of districts	22

Housing & Construction

Housing Units, 2007**
Total	45,473
Single family units	30,351
Multiple family units	14,640
Owner-occupied units	32,182
Renter-occupied units	10,577
Vacant units	2,714
Median rent	$904
Median SF home value	$320,900

Permits for New Residential Construction
	Units	Value
Total, 2006	512	$57,138,556
Single family	452	$53,935,227
Total, 2007	258	$40,777,729
Single family	241	$39,777,210

Real Property Valuation, 2008†
	Parcels	Valuation
Total	46,171	$10,374,936,475
Vacant	4,330	270,791,087
Residential	33,734	7,619,896,271
Farm land	4,004	37,604,433
Farm homestead	1,936	600,590,000
Non-residential	2,167	1,846,054,684
Commercial	1,825	1,050,424,784
Industrial	205	620,088,900
Apartments	137	175,541,000

Public Safety

Police Officers, 2007
County officers	34
Sheriff's department	16
Prosecutors	18
Municipal police	163

Crime	2006	2007
Total crimes	1,898	1,693
Violent	156	130
Murder	3	3
Rape	5	5
Robbery	32	16
Aggravated assault	116	106
Non-violent	1,742	1,563
Burglary	336	259
Larceny	1,300	1,223
Vehicle theft	106	81
Domestic violence	1,295	1,519
Arson	15	13
Total crime rate	17.2	15.3
Violent	1.4	1.2
Non-violent	15.8	14.1

Public Library

Warren County Library
199 Hardwick Street
Belvidere, NJ 07823
(908) 475-6322

Director	Richard Moore

Library statistics, 2007
Population served	64,903

	Total	Per capita
Revenues	$5,727,680	$88.25
Expenditures	$3,214,041	$49.52
Holdings	265,201	4.09
Circulation	562,295	8.66
Annual visits	332,000	5.12
Registered borrowers		40,555
Reference transactions		51,335
Hours open weekly		60
Full-time/total staff		7/37
Interlibrary loans		
Provided/received		269/4,834
Internet terminals		25
Annual users		30,028

State Income Tax, 2006

Number of returns	44,761
Increase from previous year	1.0%
Total income	$2,857,364
Per capita	$29,700
Increase from previous year	5.7%
Net charged tax	$74,394
Per capita	$773
Average taxable income	$56,371
Average income tax	$1,662

County Finance

State Aid Programs, 2009†
Total aid	$16,235,362
CMPTRA	2,584,669
Energy tax receipts	12,460,097
Garden State Trust	647,411

General Budget, 2008†
Total tax levy	$273,271,342
County levy	82,229,985
County taxes	68,451,996
County library	5,484,463
County health	0
County open space	8,293,526
School levy	146,818,388
Muni. levy	44,222,969
Misc. revenues	52,017,287

Taxes†	2006	2007	2008
Net valuation taxable	$9,441,833,484	$10,308,312,140	$10,403,207,919
State equalized value	$12,837,907,870	13,620,394,720	$13,689,967,495

The New Jersey
Municipal Data Book

2009

State & Municipal Profiles Series

Note to the reader:

These pages are extracted from the 2009 edition of the *Almanac of the 50 States*, also published by Information Publications. Please refer to that volume for similar information on each of the 50 States, the District of Columbia, and the United States in general (ISBN: 978-0-929960-52-4, paper; 978-0-929960-53-1, hardcover).

New Jersey   1

State Summary

Capital city . . . . Trenton
Governor. . . . . .Jon Corzine

The State House
PO Box 001
Trenton, NJ 08625
(609) 292-6000

Admitted as a state 1787
Area (square miles) .8,721
Population, 2008 (estimate). 8,682,661
Largest city . . . . Newark
Population, 2007 280,135
Personal income per capita, 2007
(in current dollars) $49,194
Gross domestic product, 2007 ($ mil) . . . $465,484

Leading industries by payroll, 2006

Professional/Scientific/Technical, Health care/
Social assistance, Wholesale trade

Leading agricultural commodities by receipts, 2007

Greenhouse/nursery, Horses/mules, Blueberries,
Peaches, Chicken eggs

Geography & Environment

Total area (square miles). 8,721
land 7,417
water 1,304
Highest point . . . . High Point
elevation (feet) 1,803
Lowest point . . . . .Atlantic Ocean
elevation (feet) . . . . sea level
General coastline (miles) 130
Tidal shoreline (miles) 1,792
Capital city . . . . Trenton
Population 2000 85,403
Population 2007 82,804
Largest city . . . . Newark
Population 2000 273,546
Population 2007 280,135

Number of cities with over 100,000 population

1990 4
2000 4
2007 4

State park and recreation areas, 2006

Area (x 1,000 acres) 423
Number of visitors (x 1,000) 16,042
Revenues ($1,000) 9,843
percent of operating expenditures. 25.3%

National Park Service Areas, 2007

Total area (x 1,000 acres) 99.1
Federal land 38.5
Nonfederal land. 60.6
Recreation visits (x 1,000) 5,502.4

National forest system land, 2008

Acres 0

Demographics & Population Characteristics

Population

1980 7,364,823
1990 7,730,188
2000 8,414,360
2007 8,685,920
Male. 4,248,866
Female. 4,437,054
Living in group quarters, 2007 196,261
percent of total. 2.3%
2008 (estimate). 8,682,661
persons per square mile of land 1,170.6
2020 (projected). 9,461,635
2030 (projected). 9,802,440

Population of Core-Based Statistical Areas (formerly Metropolitan Areas), x 1,000

	CBSA	Non-CBSA
1990	7,730	0
2000	8,414	0
2007	8,686	0

Change in population, 2000-2008

Number 268,301
percent. 3.2%
Natural increase (births minus deaths) 343,965
Net internal migration . . . .-438,617
Net international migration 384,687

Persons by age, 2007

Under 5 years 556,673
5 to 17 years 1,507,116
18 years and over 6,622,131
65 years and over 1,134,636
85 years and over 169,186
Median age 38.4

Race, 2007

One Race
White. 6,623,779
Black or African American 1,260,339
Asian 651,787
American Indian/Alaska Native. 28,455
Hawaiian Native/Pacific Islander. 7,146
Two or more races. 114,414

Persons of Asian origin, 2007

Total Asian 648,484
Asian Indian. 242,402
Chinese 128,073
Filipino 116,903
Japanese 13,954
Korean. 91,378
Vietnamese. 19,947

Persons of Hispanic origin, 2007

Total Hispanic or Latino 1,382,029
Mexican. 182,805
Puerto Rican 401,230
Cuban 85,754

Note to the reader:

These pages are extracted from the 2009 edition of the *Almanac of the 50 States*, also published by Information Publications. Please refer to that volume for similar information on each of the 50 States, the District of Columbia, and the United States in general (ISBN: 978-0-929960-52-4, paper; 978-0-929960-53-1, hardcover).

---

2   New Jersey

Marital status, 2007

Population 15 years & over	6,992,064
Never married	2,224,590
Married	3,565,496
Separated	155,722
Widowed	475,274
Divorced	570,982

Language spoken at home, 2007

Population 5 years and older	8,130,371
English only	5,868,363
Spanish	1,132,951
French	90,785
German	36,518
Chinese	106,104

Households & families, 2007

Households	3,149,910
with persons under 18 years	1,139,972
with persons over 65 years	786,442
persons per household	2.70
Families	2,185,324
persons per family	3.27
Married couples	1,633,264
Unmarried couples	153,255
Same-sex	20,567
Male couple	10,541
Female couple	10,026
Female householder, no husband present	403,180
One-person households	816,464
Grandparents living with grandkids	180,415
Financially responsible for children	49,732
Not financially responsible	130,683

Nativity, 2007

Number of residents born in state	4,548,687
percent of population	52.4%

Immigration & naturalization, 2007

Legal permanent residents admitted	55,834
Persons naturalized	35,235
Non-immigrant admissions	883,395

Vital Statistics and Health

Marriages

2005	49,305
2006	47,727
2007	45,435

Divorces

2005	25,343
2006	25,794
2007	25,687

Physicians, 2006

Total	27,091
rate per 100,000 persons	311

Health care expenditures, 2004

Total expenditures ($ mil)	$50,384
per capita	$5,807

Births, 2006

Total	115,020
Birth rate (per 1,000)	13.2
Teen birth rate (per 1,000)	24.9
White, non-Hispanic	56,974
Black, non-Hispanic	17,459
Hispanic	29,210
Asian/Pacific Islander	11,263
American Indian/Alaska Native	193
Low birth weight (2,500g or less)	8.6%
Cesarian births	37.4%
Preterm births	12.9%
To unmarried mothers	33.0%
2007 (provisional)	115,294

Deaths, 2005

All causes	71,963
rate per 100,000	745.9
Heart disease	20,655
rate per 100,000	208.9
Malignant neoplasms	17,171
rate per 100,000	182.1
Cerebrovascular disease	3,614
rate per 100,000	36.7
Chronic lower respiratory disease	3,148
rate per 100,000	32.9
Diabetes	2,540
rate per 100,000	26.7
2006 (preliminary)	70,336
rate per 100,000	736.4
2007 (provisional)	69,172

Infant deaths

2004	651
rate per 1,000	5.7
2005	595
rate per 1,000	5.23

HIV and AIDS, 2006

HIV (non-AIDS) cases	1,477
estimated living with HIV	16,212
AIDS cases	1,065
estimated living with AIDS	17,226

Abortions, 2005

Total performed in state	31,230
rate per 1,000 women age 15-44	17
% obtained by out-of-state residents	5.5%

Health risks for adults, 2007

Cigarette smokers	17.1%
Binge drinkers	13.6%
Overweight (BMI > 25)	62.3%
Obese (BMI > 30)	24.1%
No exercise	26.1%
Recommended level of exercise	48.1%
Eat 5 fruit & vegetable servings per day	27.5%

Disability status of population, 2007

5 to 15 years	5.1%
16 to 64 years	8.9%
65 years and over	35.4%

Note to the reader:

These pages are extracted from the 2009 edition of the *Almanac of the 50 States*, also published by Information Publications. Please refer to that volume for similar information on each of the 50 States, the District of Columbia, and the United States in general (ISBN: 978-0-929960-52-4, paper; 978-0-929960-53-1, hardcover).

New Jersey 3

Education

Educational attainment, 2007
Population over 25 years 5,850,926
Less than 9th grade......................5.5%
High school graduate or more 87.0%
College graduate or more..............33.9%
Graduate or professional degree.......12.7%

Public school enrollment, 2006-07
Total..............................1,388,850
Pre-kindergarten through grade 8.... 921,055
Grades 9 through 12................ 408,143

Graduates and dropouts, 2005-06
Graduation rate........................84.8%
Dropout rate...........................1.6%

SAT scores, 2008
Average critical reading score............. 495
Average writing score...................... 496
Average math score........................ 513
Percent of graduates taking test...........76%

Public school teachers, 2008-09 (estimate)
Total (x 1,000) 115.6
Elementary............................76.3
Secondary.............................39.3
Average salary $63,018

State receipts & expenditures for public schools, 2008-09 (estimate)
Total receipts ($ mil).................. $23,100
Revenue receipts $23,098
Total expenditures ($ mil) $23,120
for public day schools............... $22,392
per capita $2,579
per pupil $15,983

NAEP proficiency scores, 2007

	Reading		Math	
	Basic	Proficient	Basic	Proficient
Grade 4	77.2%	43.1%	89.6%	51.8%
Grade 8	81.1%	39.0%	77.5%	40.4%

Higher education enrollment, fall 2006
Total.............................. 385,656
Full-time men 108,827
Full-time women................... 125,028
Part-time men 59,165
Part-time women.................... 92,636

Minority enrollment in institutions of higher education, 2006
Black, non-Hispanic................... 54,650
Hispanic 53,089
Asian/Pacific Islander 33,272
American Indian/Alaska Native..........1,217

Institutions of higher education, 2006-07
Total................................... 59
Public................................. 33
Private................................ 26

Earned degrees conferred, 2005-06
Associate's........................... 15,338
Bachelor's 32,251
Master's.............................. 12,607
First-professional......................1,696
Doctor's...............................1,203

Public Libraries, FY 2006
Number of libraries...................... 304
Number of outlets 465
Annual visits per capita 5.5
Circulation per capita.....................6.5
Print holdings per capita 3.7

State & local financial support for higher education, FY 2007
Full-time equivalent enrollment (x 1,000)....226.1
Appropriations per FTE................$7,275

Social Insurance & Welfare Programs

Social Security benefits & beneficiaries, 2007
Beneficiaries (x 1,000) 1,381
Retired & dependents..................1,016
Survivors............................. 165
Disabled & dependents................. 201
Annual benefit payments ($ mil) $17,267
Retired & dependents.............. $12,277
Survivors..........................$2,619
Disabled & dependents.............. $2,371
Median monthly benefit
Retired & dependents.............. $1,171.50
Disabled & dependents............. $992.00
Widowed.........................$1,098.50

Medicare, 2007
Enrollment (x 1,000)....................1,257
Payment per enrollee $9,520

Medicaid, 2005
Beneficiaries (x 1,000)..................... 966
Payments ($ mil) $7,010

State Children's Health Insurance Program, 2007
Enrollment (x 1,000)....................150.3
Expenditures ($ mil) $280.0

Federal and state public aid
State unemployment insurance, 2007
Recipients, first payments (x 1,000) 312
Total payments ($ mil) $1,925
Average weekly benefit $359
Temporary Assistance for Needy Families, 2007
Recipients (x 1,000).....................995.1
Families (x 1,000) 419.9
Supplemental Security Income, 2007
Recipients (x 1,000)..................... 154.5
Payments ($ mil) $799.6
Supplemental Nutritional Asst. Program, 2007
Avg monthly participants (x 1,000) 414.5
Total benefits ($ mil).................. $483.4

Note to the reader:

These pages are extracted from the 2009 edition of the *Almanac of the 50 States*, also published by Information Publications. Please refer to that volume for similar information on each of the 50 States, the District of Columbia, and the United States in general (ISBN: 978-0-929960-52-4, paper; 978-0-929960-53-1, hardcover).

4   New Jersey

Persons without health insurance, 2007
Number (x 1,000)....................... 1,348
    percent............................. 15.8%
Number of children (x 1,000) 270
    percent of children 12.9%

Type of health insurance coverage, 2007
Some coverage 84.2%
    Private............................. 71.3%
    Government....................... 21.6%
        Medicaid.......................... 8.4%
        Medicare......................... 13.9%

Housing & Construction

Housing units
Total 2006 (estimate) 3,472,740
Total 2007 (estimate) 3,499,406
    Single-family home................1,882,276
    Multifamily dwelling 1,579,172
    Mobile home or trailer.............. 36,227
Seasonal or recreational use, 2007...... 121,385
Owner-occupied, 2007...............2,118,998
    Median home value............... $372,300
    Homeowner vacancy rate.............. 1.6%
Renter-occupied, 2007 1,030,912
    Median rent $1,026
    Rental vacancy rate.................... 6.8%
Home ownership rate, 2006.............. 69.0%
Home ownership rate, 2007.............. 68.3%

New privately-owned housing units
Number authorized, 2007 (x 1,000)........25.4
    Value ($ mil)......................$3,674.7
Started 2005 (x 1,000, estimate)...........26.5
Started 2006 (x 1,000, estimate)...........26.1

Existing home sales
2006 (x 1,000)...........................154.1
2007 (x 1,000)...........................137.4

Government & Elections

State officials 2009
Governor.........................Jon Corzine
        Democratic, term expires 1/10
Lieutenant Governor. . (no Lieutenant Governor)
Secretary of State.................. Nina Wells
Attorney General............... Anne Milgram
Chief Justice ....Stuart Rabner

Governorship
Minimum age............................ 30
Length of term .... 4 years
Consecutive terms permitted 2
Who succeeds............. President of Senate

State government employment, 2007
Full-time equivalent employees 155,685
Payroll ($ mil) $811.7

Local government employment, 2007
Full-time equivalent employees 357,426
Payroll ($ mil) $1,696.0

State legislature
Name .... Legislature
Upper chamber ....Senate
    Number of members.................... 40
    Length of term.................... 4 years
    Party in majority, 2009 ....Democratic
Lower chamber.............. General Assembly
    Number of members.................... 80
    Length of term.................... 2 years
    Party in majority, 2009 ....Democratic

Federal representation, 2009 (111ᵗʰ Congress)

Senator.................... Robert Menendez
    Party ....Democratic
    Year term expires 2013
Senator.................... Frank Lautenberg
    Party ....Democratic
    Year term expires 2015
Representatives, total 13
    Democrats........................... 8
    Republicans 5

Presidential election, 2008
Total popular vote.................3,868,237
    Barack Obama..................2,215,422
    John McCain 1,613,207
Total electoral votes 15

Votes cast for US Senators
2002
Total vote (x 1,000) 2,113
Leading party....................Democratic
Percent for leading party 53.9%
2006
Total vote (x 1,000) 102
Leading party....................Democratic
Percent for leading party 57.2%

Votes cast for US Representatives
2004
Total vote (x 1,000) 3,285
    Democratic.......................1,721
    Republican 1,515
Leading party....................Democratic
Percent for leading party 52.4%

2006
Total vote (x 1,000) 2,137
    Democratic....................... 1,208
    Republican 903
Leading party....................Democratic
Percent for leading party 56.5%

Voters in November 2006 election (estimate)
Total...........................2,406,132
    Male...........................1,121,355
    Female........................1,284,777
    White.........................2,036,979
    Black 266,563
    Hispanic 83,157
    Asian 96,283

Note to the reader:

These pages are extracted from the 2009 edition of the *Almanac of the 50 States*, also published by Information Publications. Please refer to that volume for similar information on each of the 50 States, the District of Columbia, and the United States in general (ISBN: 978-0-929960-52-4, paper; 978-0-929960-53-1, hardcover).

New Jersey   5

Local governments by type, 2007

Total	1,383
County	21
Municipal	324
Township	242
School District	247
Special District	549

Women holding public office, 2009

US Congress	0
Statewide elected office	0
State legislature	35

Black public officials, 2002

Total	269
US and state legislatures	18
City/county/regional offices	162
Judicial/law enforcement	0
Education/school boards	89

Hispanic public officials, 2007

Total	103
State executives & legislators	8
City/county/regional offices	56
Judicial/law enforcement	0
Education/school boards	39

Governmental Finance

State government revenues, 2007

Total revenue (x $1,000)	$65,495,222
per capita	$7,540.39
General revenue (x $1,000)	$49,746,594
per capita, total	$5,727.27
Intergovernmental	1,319.68
Taxes	3,351.03
Sales taxes	1,374.90
General sales tax	960.82
Selective sales taxes	414.08
Individual income tax	1,328.57
Corporate income tax	331.18
License fees	174.13
Current charges	565.19
Miscellaneous	491.37

State government expenditure, 2007

Total expenditure (x $1,000)	$56,076,165
per capita	$6,455.98
General expenditure (x $1,000)	$44,920,677
per capita, total	$5,171.67
Education	1,711.25
Public welfare	1,369.54
Health	150.95
Hospitals	225.34
Highways	301.13
Police protection	60.55
Corrections	171.54
Natural resources	61.91
Parks & recreation	47.79
Governmental administration	204.27
Interest on general debt	222.32

State debt & cash, 2007 ($ per capita)

Debt	$5,915.87
Cash/security holdings	$12,876.49

Federal government grants to state & local government, 2007 (x $1,000)

Total	$12,325,796
by Federal agency	
Defense	50,830
Education	882,354
Energy	32,649
Environmental Protection Agency	92,784
Health & Human Services	7,137,196
Homeland Security	78,514
Housing & Urban Development	926,652
Justice	29,709
Labor	217,971
Transportation	2,271,727

Crime & Law Enforcement

Crime, 2007 (rates per 100,000 residents)

Property crimes	192,226
Burglary	37,482
Larceny	132,791
Motor vehicle theft	21,953
Property crime rate	2,213.1
Violent crimes	28,601
Murder	380
Forcible rape	1,050
Robbery	12,549
Aggravated assault	14,622
Violent crime rate	329.3
Hate crimes	773

Child abuse and neglect cases, 2006

Number of reports	28,134
Children subject of investigation	47,172
Number of child victims	11,680

Law enforcement agencies, 2007

Total agencies	529
Total employees	41,672
Officers	32,407
Civilians	9,265

Prisoners, probation, and parole, 2007

Total prisoners, 12/31/2007	26,827
percent change from 2006	-2.0%
in private facilities	10.0%
in local jails	5.5%
Sentenced to more than one year	26,827
rate per 100,000 residents	308
Male	597
Female	32
Adults on probation	126,390
Adults on parole	15,043

Prisoner demographics, June 30, 2005 (rate per 100,000 residents)

White	190
Black	2,352
Hispanic	630

Note to the reader:

These pages are extracted from the 2009 edition of the *Almanac of the 50 States*, also published by Information Publications. Please refer to that volume for similar information on each of the 50 States, the District of Columbia, and the United States in general (ISBN: 978-0-929960-52-4, paper; 978-0-929960-53-1, hardcover).

6   New Jersey

Arrests, 2007
Total	383,797
Persons under 18 years of age	55,824

Persons under sentence of death, 1/1/08
Total	0
White	0
Black	0
Hispanic	0

Fraud and identity theft, 2007
Fraud complaints	14,542
rate per 100,000 residents	167.4
Identity theft complaints	6,864
rate per 100,000 residents	79.0

State's highest court
Name	Supreme Court
Number of members	7
Length of term	7 years
Intermediate appeals court?	yes

Labor & Income

Civilian labor force, 2007 (x 1,000)
Total	4,516
Men	2,443
Women	2,073
Persons 16-19 years	160
White	3,477
Black	573
Hispanic	765

Civilian labor force as a percent of civilian non-institutional population, 2007
Total	66.3%
Men	74.5%
Women	58.6%
Persons 16-19 years	32.3%
White	66.3%
Black	63.0%
Hispanic	70.9%

Employment, 2007 (x 1,000)
Total	4,325
Men	2,333
Women	1,992
Persons 16-19 years	139
White	3,343
Black	528
Hispanic	720

Unemployment rate, 2007
Total	4.2%
Men	4.5%
Women	3.9%
Persons 16-19 years	13.5%
White	3.8%
Black	8.0%
Hispanic	5.9%

Hourly wages, 2007
Mean hourly wage	$22.64
Median hourly wage	$17.77

Average annual and weekly wages, 2007
Average annual wages	$53,853
increase from 2006	4.3%
Average weekly wage	$1,036

Experienced civilian labor force by private industry, 2007
Total	3,349,749
Natural resources & mining	11,979
Construction	171,086
Manufacturing	311,409
Trade, transportation & utilities	868,098
Information	96,983
Finance	263,677
Professional & business	608,185
Education & health	535,743
Leisure & hospitality	337,643
Other	126,479

Experienced civilian labor force by occupation, May 2007
Management	189,300
Business & financial	202,670
Legal	32,740
Sales	431,970
Office & admin. support	756,330
Computers & math	125,620
Architecture & engineering	58,660
Arts & entertainment	43,890
Education	274,500
Social services	56,570
Health care practitioner & technical	199,640
Health care support	109,660
Maintenance & repair	148,200
Construction	138,930
Transportation & moving	312,770
Production	221,200
Farming, fishing & forestry	4,250

Income and poverty, 2007
Median household income	$67,035
Median family income	$81,823
Personal income, per capita (current $)	$49,194
in constant (2000) dollars	$41,835
Disposable income (current $)	$42,070
in constant (2000) dollars	$35,777
Persons below poverty level	8.6%

Labor unions, 2007
Members of unions (x 1,000)	748
percent of employed	19.2%
Represented by unions (x 1,000)	802
percent of employed	20.6%

Federal individual income tax returns, 2006
Returns filed	4,229,622
Adjusted gross income ($1,000)	$302,073,205
Total tax liability ($1,000)	$45,462,675
Charitable contributions (x 1,000)	1,685.7
Total amount ($1,000)	$5,833,372

Note to the reader:

These pages are extracted from the 2009 edition of the *Almanac of the 50 States*, also published by Information Publications. Please refer to that volume for similar information on each of the 50 States, the District of Columbia, and the United States in general (ISBN: 978-0-929960-52-4, paper; 978-0-929960-53-1, hardcover).

New Jersey 7

Economy, Business, Industry & Agriculture

Bankruptcy cases filed, FY 2007.........18,702
  Business 802
  Non-business........................17,900
Patents awarded, 2008 3,172
Trademarks awarded, 2008.............. 4,029

Business firm ownership, 2002
Women-owned......................185,197
  Sales ($ mil) $35,573
Black-owned......................... 36,280
  Sales ($ mil) $3,202
Hispanic-owned...................... 49,841
  Sales ($ mil) $7,245
Asian-owned 51,957
  Sales ($ mil) $18,495
Amer. Indian/Alaska Native-owned 2,645
  Sales ($ mil) $284
Hawaiian/Pacific Islander-owned 448
  Sales ($ mil) $37

Gross domestic product, 2007 ($ mil)
Total gross domestic product $465,484
  Agriculture, forestry, fishing and
    hunting 736
  Mining.............................. 393
  Utilities 9,293
  Construction 16,126
  Manufacturing, durable goods....... 13,689
  Manufacturing, non-durable goods 27,119
  Wholesale trade.................... 36,449
  Retail trade........................ 29,363
  Transportation & warehousing 14,066
  Information 24,103
  Finance & insurance.................38,514
  Real estate, rental & leasing 77,471
  Professional and technical services.....41,967
  Educational services................. 4,064
  Health care and social assistance.......33,561
  Accommodation/food services........11,718
  Other services, except government 9,530
  Government.......................47,782

Establishments, payroll, employees & receipts, by major industry group, 2006

Total.............................. 243,055
  Annual payroll ($1,000)........$175,501,555
  Paid employees 3,645,381
Forestry, fishing & agriculture.............. 232
  Annual payroll ($1,000)............ $28,711
  Paid employees 1,143
Mining.................................. 112
  Annual payroll ($1,000)............$147,869
  Paid employees 2,384
  Receipts, 2002 ($1,000) $379,558

Utilities 338
  Annual payroll ($1,000)...........$1,629,224
  Paid employees 18,000
  Receipts, 2002 ($1,000) ....NA
Construction......................... 25,486
  Annual payroll ($1,000)...........$9,887,851
  Paid employees 181,404
  Receipts, 2002 ($1,000) $37,867,759
Manufacturing........................ 9,346
  Annual payroll ($1,000).........$15,590,977
  Paid employees 297,021
  Receipts, 2002 ($1,000) $96,599,807
Wholesale trade 16,012
  Annual payroll ($1,000).........$17,776,046
  Paid employees 271,190
  Receipts, 2002 ($1,000) $256,925,492
Retail trade 34,925
  Annual payroll ($1,000).........$11,840,330
  Paid employees 461,645
  Receipts, 2002 ($1,000) $102,153,833
Transportation & warehousing............7,266
  Annual payroll ($1,000)......... $6,920,582
  Paid employees 170,735
  Receipts, 2002 ($1,000) $16,421,043
Information............................4,118
  Annual payroll ($1,000)......... $8,022,667
  Paid employees 113,331
  Receipts, 2002 ($1,000) ....NA
Finance & insurance 13,467
  Annual payroll ($1,000).........$18,393,147
  Paid employees 227,612
  Receipts, 2002 ($1,000) ....NA
Professional, scientific & technical 31,674
  Annual payroll ($1,000).........$20,759,533
  Paid employees 295,055
  Receipts, 2002 ($1,000) $36,005,523
Education 3,128
  Annual payroll ($1,000)........... $2,872,882
  Paid employees 90,631
  Receipts, 2002 ($1,000) $1,662,096
Health care & social assistance 25,292
  Annual payroll ($1,000)......... $20,462,346
  Paid employees 494,382
  Receipts, 2002 ($1,000) $38,708,974
Arts and entertainment 3,575
  Annual payroll ($1,000)...........$1,243,557
  Paid employees 47,151
  Receipts, 2002 ($1,000) $3,303,069
Real estate 9,671
  Annual payroll ($1,000).......... $2,863,080
  Paid employees 62,474
  Receipts, 2002 ($1,000) $12,262,786
Accommodation & food service 18,881
  Annual payroll ($1,000)...........$5,386,628
  Paid employees 284,905
  Receipts, 2002 ($1,000) $15,715,595

Note to the reader:

These pages are extracted from the 2009 edition of the *Almanac of the 50 States*, also published by Information Publications. Please refer to that volume for similar information on each of the 50 States, the District of Columbia, and the United States in general (ISBN: 978-0-929960-52-4, paper; 978-0-929960-53-1, hardcover).

8   New Jersey

Exports, 2007
Value of exported goods ($ mil) $30,463
   Manufactured $22,336
   Non-manufactured $2,631

Foreign direct investment in US affiliates, 2005
Property, plants & equipment ($ mil) . . . $35,759
Employment (x 1,000) 214.0

Agriculture, 2007
Number of farms 9,800
Farm acreage (x 1,000) 790
   Acres per farm 81
Farm marketings and income ($ mil)
Total $945.9
   Crops $768.9
   Livestock $177.0
Net farm income $312.4

Principal agricultural commodities, in order by marketing receipts, 2007
Greenhouse/nursery, Horses/mules, Blueberries, Peaches, Chicken eggs

Federal economic activity in state
Expenditures, 2007 ($ mil)
   Total $63,972
      Per capita $7,365.02
   Defense $8,345
   Non-defense $55,627
Defense department, 2006 ($ mil)
   Payroll $2,004
   Contract awards $6,151
   Grants $77
Homeland security grants ($1,000)
   2007 . . . .$61,109
   2008 . . . . $64,605

FDIC-insured financial institutions, 2007
Number of institutions 127
   Assets ($ billion) $147.7
Number of offices 3,351
   Deposits ($ billion) $222.5

Communication, Energy & Transportation

Communication
Households with internet access, 2007 . . . .68.4%
   using broadband 57.1%
   using dialup 57.1%
High-speed internet providers, 12/2007 51
Total high-speed internet lines 4,923,248
   Residential 2,562,919
   Business 2,360,329
   Cable modem .1,538,490
   DSL 734,903
Wireless phone customers, 12/2007 7,654,173

FCC-licensed stations (as of January 1, 2009)
TV stations 15
FM radio stations 66
AM radio stations 27

Energy
Energy consumption, 2006
   Total (trillion Btu) 2,604.8
   Per capita (million Btu) 300.6
By source of production (trillion Btu)
   Coal 116.1
   Natural gas 568.0
   Petroleum 1,299.2
   Nuclear electric power 339.8
   Hydroelectric power .0.4
By end-use sector (trillion Btu)
   Residential 570.3
   Commercial 600.6
   Industrial 452.6
   Transportation 981.3
Energy spending, 2006 ($ mil) $35,994
   per capita $4,153
   price per million Btu $18.91
Electric energy, 2006
   Primary source of electricity . . . . Nuclear
   Net generation (billion kWh) 60.7
      percent from renewable sources 1.6%
   Net summer capability (million kW) 19.0
   Retail sales (billion kWh) 79.7
      per capita (MWh) 9.2
      price per kWh .11.88¢
Natural gas utilities, 2006
   Customers (x 1,000) 2,754
   Sales (trillion Btu) 305
   Revenues ($ mil) $4,110
Nuclear power plants, 2008 1
CO_2 *emitted, 2005* (mil. metric tons) 133.4

Transportation, 2007
Public road & street mileage 38,752
   Urban 31,455
   Rural 7,297
   Interstate 431
Vehicle miles of travel (millions) 76,152
   per capita 8,801
Total motor vehicle registrations 6,247,130
   Automobiles 3,827,017
   Trucks 2,396,824
   Motorcycles 164,024
Licensed drivers .5,782,155
   19 years & under 250,323
Deaths from motor vehicle accidents 724
   involving alcohol 35%
   driver with blood alcohol level over .08 . . .27%
Gasoline consumed (x 1,000 gallons) . . . 4,373,864
   per capita 505.5

Commuting Statistics, 2007
Average commute time (min) 29.8
   Drove to work alone 71.8%
   Carpooled 9.2%
   Public transit 10.4%
   Walk to work 3.2%
   Work from home 3.3%

Atlantic County

Absecon City
Atlantic City
Brigantine City
Buena Borough
Buena Vista Township
Corbin City
Egg Harbor City
Egg Harbor Township
Estell Manor City
Folsom Borough
Galloway Township
Hamilton Township
Hammonton Town
Linwood City
Longport Borough
Margate City
Mullica Township
Northfield City
Pleasantville City
Port Republic City
Somers Point City
Ventnor City
Weymouth Township

Bergen County

Allendale Borough
Alpine Borough
Bergenfield Borough
Bogota Borough
Carlstadt Borough
Cliffside Park Borough
Closter Borough
Cresskill Borough
Demarest Borough
Dumont Borough
East Rutherford Borough
Edgewater Borough
Elmwood Park Borough
Emerson Borough
Englewood City
Englewood Cliffs Borough
Fair Lawn Borough
Fairview Borough
Fort Lee Borough
Franklin Lakes Borough
Garfield City
Glen Rock Borough
Hackensack City
Harrington Park Borough
Hasbrouck Heights Borough
Haworth Borough
Hillsdale Borough
Ho-Ho-Kus Borough

Bergen County, cont

Leonia Borough
Little Ferry Borough
Lodi Borough
Lyndhurst Township
Mahwah Township
Maywood Borough
Midland Park Borough
Montvale Borough
Moonachie Borough
New Milford Borough
North Arlington Borough
Northvale Borough
Norwood Borough
Oakland Borough
Old Tappan Borough
Oradell Borough
Palisades Park Borough
Paramus Borough
Park Ridge Borough
Ramsey Borough
Ridgefield Borough
Ridgefield Park Village
Ridgewood Village
River Edge Borough
River Vale Township
Rochelle Park Township
Rockleigh Borough
Rutherford Borough
Saddle Brook Township
Saddle River Borough
South Hackensack
   Township
Teaneck Township
Tenafly Borough
Teterboro Borough
Upper Saddle River
   Borough
Waldwick Borough
Wallington Borough
Washington Township
Westwood Borough
Woodcliff Lake Borough
Wood-Ridge Borough
Wyckoff Township

Burlington County

Bass River Township
Beverly City
Bordentown City
Bordentown Township
Burlington City
Burlington Township
Chesterfield Township

Burlington County, cont

Cinnaminson Township
Delanco Township
Delran Township
Eastampton Township
Edgewater Park Township
Evesham Township
Fieldsboro Borough
Florence Township
Hainesport Township
Lumberton Township
Mansfield Township
Maple Shade Township
Medford Township
Medford Lakes Borough
Moorestown Township
Mount Holly Township
Mount Laurel Township
New Hanover Township
North Hanover Township
Palmyra Borough
Pemberton Borough
Pemberton Township
Riverside Township
Riverton Borough
Shamong Township
Southampton Township
Springfield Township
Tabernacle Township
Washington Township
Westampton Township
Willingboro Township
Woodland Township
Wrightstown Borough

Camden County

Audubon Borough
Audubon Park Borough
Barrington Borough
Bellmawr Borough
Berlin Borough
Berlin Township
Brooklawn Borough
Camden City
Cherry Hill Township
Chesilhurst Borough
Clementon Borough
Collingswood Borough
Gibbsboro Borough
Gloucester City
Gloucester Township
Haddon Township
Haddon Heights Borough
Haddonfield Borough

Camden County, cont

Hi-Nella Borough
Laurel Springs Borough
Lawnside Borough
Lindenwold Borough
Magnolia Borough
Merchantville Borough
Mount Ephraim Borough
Oaklyn Borough
Pennsauken Township
Pine Hill Borough
Pine Valley Borough
Runnemede Borough
Somerdale Borough
Stratford Borough
Tavistock Borough
Voorhees Township
Waterford Township
Winslow Township
Woodlynne Borough

Cape May County

Avalon Borough
Cape May City
Cape May Point Borough
Dennis Township
Lower Township
Middle Township
North Wildwood City
Ocean City
Sea Isle City
Stone Harbor Borough
Upper Township
West Cape May Borough
West Wildwood Borough
Wildwood City
Wildwood Crest Borough
Woodbine Borough

Cumberland County

Bridgeton City
Commercial Township
Deerfield Township
Downe Township
Fairfield Township
Greenwich Township
Hopewell Township
Lawrence Township
Maurice River Township
Millville City
Shiloh Borough
Stow Creek Township
Upper Deerfield Township
Vineland City

Essex County

Belleville Township
Bloomfield Township
Caldwell Borough
Cedar Grove Township
East Orange City
Essex Fells Borough
Fairfield Township
Glen Ridge Borough
Irvington Township
Livingston Township
Maplewood Township
Millburn Township
Montclair Township
Newark City
North Caldwell Borough
Nutley Township
City of Orange Township
Roseland Borough
South Orange Village
   Township
Verona Township
West Caldwell Township
West Orange Township

Gloucester County

Clayton Borough
Deptford Township
East Greenwich Township
Elk Township
Franklin Township
Glassboro Borough
Greenwich Township
Harrison Township
Logan Township
Mantua Township
Monroe Township
National Park Borough
Newfield Borough
Paulsboro Borough
Pitman Borough
South Harrison Township
Swedesboro Borough
Washington Township
Wenonah Borough
West Deptford Township
Westville Borough
Woodbury City
Woodbury Heights Borough
Woolwich Township

Hudson County

Bayonne City
East Newark Borough
Guttenberg Town
Harrison Town
Hoboken City
Jersey City
Kearny Town
North Bergen Township
Secaucus Town
Union City
Weehawken Township
West New York Town

Hunterdon County

Alexandria Township
Bethlehem Township
Bloomsbury Borough
Califon Borough
Clinton Town
Clinton Township
Delaware Township
East Amwell Township
Flemington Borough
Franklin Township
Frenchtown Borough
Glen Gardner Borough
Hampton Borough
High Bridge Borough
Holland Township
Kingwood Township
Lambertville City
Lebanon Borough
Lebanon Township
Milford Borough
Raritan Township
Readington Township
Stockton Borough
Tewksbury Township
Union Township
West Amwell Township

Mercer County

East Windsor Township
Ewing Township
Hamilton Township
Hightstown Borough
Hopewell Borough
Hopewell Township
Lawrence Township

Mercer County, cont

Pennington Borough
Princeton Borough
Princeton Township
Robbinsville Township
   (formerly Washington)
Trenton City
West Windsor Township

Middlesex County

Carteret Borough
Cranbury Township
Dunellen Borough
East Brunswick Township
Edison Township
Helmetta Borough
Highland Park Borough
Jamesburg Borough
Metuchen Borough
Middlesex Borough
Milltown Borough
Monroe Township
New Brunswick City
North Brunswick Township
Old Bridge Township
Perth Amboy City
Piscataway Township
Plainsboro Township
Sayreville Borough
South Amboy City
South Brunswick Township
South Plainfield Borough
South River Borough
Spotswood Borough
Woodbridge Township

Monmouth County

Aberdeen Township
Allenhurst Borough
Allentown Borough
Asbury Park City
Atlantic Highlands Borough
Avon-by-the-Sea Borough
Belmar Borough
Bradley Beach Borough
Brielle Borough
Colts Neck Township
Deal Borough
Eatontown Borough
Englishtown Borough

Monmouth County, cont

Fair Haven Borough
Farmingdale Borough
Freehold Borough
Freehold Township
Hazlet Township
Highlands Borough
Holmdel Township
Howell Township
Interlaken Borough
Keansburg Borough
Keyport Borough
Lake Como Borough
Little Silver Borough
Loch Arbour Village
Long Branch City
Manalapan Township
Manasquan Borough
Marlboro Township
Matawan Borough
Middletown Township
Millstone Township
Monmouth Beach Borough
Neptune Township
Neptune City Borough
Ocean Township
Oceanport Borough
Red Bank Borough
Roosevelt Borough
Rumson Borough
Sea Bright Borough
Sea Girt Borough
Shrewsbury Borough
Shrewsbury Township
Spring Lake Borough
Spring Lake Heights Borough
Tinton Falls Borough
Union Beach Borough
Upper Freehold Township
Wall Township
West Long Branch Borough

Morris County

Boonton Town
Boonton Township
Butler Borough
Chatham Borough
Chatham Township
Chester Borough
Chester Township
Denville Township
Dover Town
East Hanover Township
Florham Park Borough
Hanover Township
Harding Township
Jefferson Township
Kinnelon Borough
Lincoln Park Borough
Long Hill Township
Madison Borough
Mendham Borough
Mendham Township
Mine Hill Township
Montville Township
Morris Township
Morris Plains Borough
Morristown Town
Mount Arlington Borough
Mount Olive Township
Mountain Lakes Borough
Netcong Borough
Parsippany-Troy Hills Township
Pequannock Township
Randolph Township
Riverdale Borough
Rockaway Borough
Rockaway Township
Roxbury Township
Victory Gardens Borough
Washington Township
Wharton Borough

Ocean County

Barnegat Township
Barnegat Light Borough
Bay Head Borough
Beach Haven Borough
Beachwood Borough
Berkeley Township
Brick Township
Eagleswood Township
Harvey Cedars Borough
Island Heights Borough

Ocean County, cont

Jackson Township
Lacey Township
Lakehurst Borough
Lakewood Township
Lavallette Borough
Little Egg Harbor Township
Long Beach Township
Manchester Township
Mantoloking Borough
Ocean Township
Ocean Gate Borough
Pine Beach Borough
Plumsted Township
Point Pleasant Borough
Point Pleasant Beach Borough
Seaside Heights Borough
Seaside Park Borough
Ship Bottom Borough
South Toms River Borough
Stafford Township
Surf City Borough
Toms River
Tuckerton Borough

Passaic County

Bloomingdale Borough
Clifton City
Haledon Borough
Hawthorne Borough
Little Falls Township
North Haledon Borough
Passaic City
Paterson City
Pompton Lakes Borough
Prospect Park Borough
Ringwood Borough
Totowa Borough
Wanaque Borough
Wayne Township
West Milford Township
West Paterson Borough

Salem County

Alloway Township
Carneys Point Township
Elmer Borough
Elsinboro Township
Lower Alloways Creek
   Township
Mannington Township
Oldmans Township
Penns Grove Borough

Salem County, cont

Pennsville Township
Pilesgrove Township
Pittsgrove Township
Quinton Township
Salem City
Upper Pittsgrove Township
Woodstown Borough

Somerset County

Bedminster Township
Bernards Township
Bernardsville Borough
Bound Brook Borough
Branchburg Township
Bridgewater Township
Far Hills Borough
Franklin Township
Green Brook Township
Hillsborough Township
Manville Borough
Millstone Borough
Montgomery Township
North Plainfield Borough
Peapack & Gladstone
   Borough
Raritan Borough
Rocky Hill Borough
Somerville Borough
South Bound Brook Borough
Warren Township
Watchung Borough

Sussex County

Andover Borough
Andover Township
Branchville Borough
Byram Township
Frankford Township
Franklin Borough
Fredon Township
Green Township
Hamburg Borough
Hampton Township
Hardyston Township
Hopatcong Borough
Lafayette Township
Montague Township
Newton Town
Ogdensburg Borough
Sandyston Township
Sparta Township
Stanhope Borough

Sussex County, cont

Stillwater Township
Sussex Borough
Vernon Township
Walpack Township
Wantage Township

Union County

Berkeley Heights Township
Clark Township
Cranford Township
Elizabeth City
Fanwood Borough
Garwood Borough
Hillside Township
Kenilworth Borough
Linden City
Mountainside Borough
New Providence Borough
Plainfield City
Rahway City
Roselle Borough
Roselle Park Borough
Scotch Plains Township
Springfield Township
Summit City
Union Township
Westfield Town
Winfield Township

Warren County

Allamuchy Township
Alpha Borough
Belvidere Town
Blairstown Township
Franklin Township
Frelinghuysen Township
Greenwich Township
Hackettstown Town
Hardwick Township
Harmony Township
Hope Township
Independence Township
Knowlton Township
Liberty Township
Lopatcong Township
Mansfield Township
Oxford Township
Phillipsburg Town
Pohatcong Township
Washington Borough
Washington Township
White Township

Note: The 2007 American Community Survey (ACS) produced one-year estimates of demographic data for cities and counties with populations of at least 65,000: in New Jersey's case, 20 out of 566 municipalities. For those municipalities, the ACS data appears here as a supplement to the 2000 Census data in the profiles.

Brick Township
Ocean County

Population

Total	72,355
Male	34,385
Female	37,970

Race & Hispanic Origin

Race
White	NA
Black/African American	NA
Amer. Indian/Alaskan Native	NA
Asian	NA
Pacific Islander	NA
Other Race	NA
Two or more races	NA
Hispanic origin, total	NA
Mexican	419
Puerto Rican	1,146
Cuban	348
Other Hispanic	3,825

Age & Nativity

Under 5 years	3,142
18 years and over	57,698
21 years and over	55,195
65 years and over	12,532
85 years and over	2,572
Median age	43.0
Native-born	66,891
Foreign-born	5,464

Educational Attainment

Population 25 years and over	52,525
Less than 9th grade	3.2%
High School grad or higher	26.6%
Bachelor's degree or higher	8.8%
Graduate degree	89.5%

Households

Total households	30,148
With persons under 18	9,068
With persons over 65	9,097
Family households	20,168
Single person households	8,892
Persons per household	2.38
Persons per family	2.97

Income & Poverty

Per capita income	$31,797
Median household income	$63,521
Median family income	$78,772
Persons in poverty	3.2%
H'holds receiving public assistance	181
H'holds receiving social security	10,599

Labor & Employment

Total civilian labor force	38,878
Unemployment rate	4.4%

Employed persons 16 years and over by occupation,

Managers & professionals	12,870
Service occupations	5,988
Sales & office occupations	10,568
Farming, fishing & forestry	0
Construction & maintenance	4,279
Production & transportation	3,459
Self-employed persons	2,663

Housing Units

Total	33,613
Single family units	26,119
Multiple family units	7,259
Mobile home units	235
Owner-occupied units	26,210
Renter-occupied units	3,938
Vacant units	3,465
Median SF home value	$319,900
Median rent	$1,098

Camden City
Camden County

Population

Total	74,507
Male	34,547
Female	39,960

Race & Hispanic Origin

Race
White	9,617
Black/African American	38,418
Amer. Indian/Alaskan Native	0
Asian	2,053
Pacific Islander	0
Other Race	24,129
Two or more races	290
Hispanic origin, total	NA
Mexican	3,655
Puerto Rican	20,400
Cuban	0
Other Hispanic	5,301

Age & Nativity

Under 5 years	6,759
18 years and over	51,012
21 years and over	46,940
65 years and over	5,687
85 years and over	500
Median age	28.2
Native-born	65,929
Foreign-born	8,578

Educational Attainment

Population 25 years and over	41,513
Less than 9th grade	17.2%
High School grad or higher	5.9%
Bachelor's degree or higher	1.9%
Graduate degree	56.4%

Households

Total households	24,860
With persons under 18	11,815
With persons over 65	4,782
Family households	18,238
Single person households	5,054
Persons per household	2.88
Persons per family	3.29

Income & Poverty

Per capita income	$11,239
Median household income	$25,389
Median family income	$26,111
Persons in poverty	38.2%
H'holds receiving public assistance	3,175
H'holds receiving social security	5,524

Labor & Employment

Total civilian labor force	28,460
Unemployment rate	16.3%

Employed persons 16 years and over by occupation,

Managers & professionals	3,786
Service occupations	7,240
Sales & office occupations	4,690
Farming, fishing & forestry	201
Construction & maintenance	1,474
Production & transportation	6,440
Self-employed persons	610

Housing Units

Total	29,081
Single family units	4,164
Multiple family units	24,599
Mobile home units	318
Owner-occupied units	10,687
Renter-occupied units	14,173
Vacant units	4,221
Median SF home value	$77,600
Median rent	$754

Cherry Hill Township
Camden County

Population

Total	70,560
Male	34,134
Female	36,426

Race & Hispanic Origin

Race
White	57,995
Black/African American	1,986
Amer. Indian/Alaskan Native	112
Asian	6,948
Pacific Islander	0
Other Race	1,540
Two or more races	1,979
Hispanic origin, total	2,866
Mexican	NA
Puerto Rican	NA
Cuban	NA
Other Hispanic	NA

Age & Nativity

Under 5 years	4,233
18 years and over	55,391
21 years and over	53,014
65 years and over	12,667
85 years and over	1,996
Median age	43.9
Native-born	60,132
Foreign-born	10,428

Educational Attainment

Population 25 years and over	50,104
Less than 9th grade	3.7%
High School grad or higher	48.7%
Bachelor's degree or higher	21.9%
Graduate degree	92.9%

Households

Total households	27,334
With persons under 18	8,657
With persons over 65	8,524
Family households	20,362
Single person households	5,984
Persons per household	2.54
Persons per family	2.98

Income & Poverty

Per capita income	$36,808
Median household income	$86,352
Median family income	$94,932
Persons in poverty	2.4%
H'holds receiving public assistance	252
H'holds receiving social security	8,954

Labor & Employment

Total civilian labor force	37,801
Unemployment rate	4.6%

Employed persons 16 years and over by occupation,

Managers & professionals	19,720
Service occupations	3,535
Sales & office occupations	9,536
Farming, fishing & forestry	0
Construction & maintenance	1,491
Production & transportation	1,792
Self-employed persons	1,942

Housing Units

Total	28,194
Single family units	19,239
Multiple family units	8,831
Mobile home units	124
Owner-occupied units	22,227
Renter-occupied units	5,107
Vacant units	860
Median SF home value	$304,600
Median rent	$948

Note: The 2007 American Community Survey (ACS) produced one-year estimates of demographic data for cities and counties with populations of at least 65,000: in New Jersey's case, 20 out of 566 municipalities. For those municipalities, the ACS data appears here as a supplement to the 2000 Census data in the profiles.

Clifton City
Passaic County

Population

Total	83,207
Male	41,163
Female	42,044

Race & Hispanic Origin

Race
White	56,793
Black/African American	3,123
Amer. Indian/Alaskan Native	0
Asian	7,604
Pacific Islander	0
Other Race	14,274
Two or more races	1,413
Hispanic origin, total	21,525
Mexican	2,215
Puerto Rican	2,977
Cuban	273
Other Hispanic	16,060

Age & Nativity

Under 5 years	4,484
18 years and over	65,576
21 years and over	62,034
65 years and over	12,828
85 years and over	2,148
Median age	38.3
Native-born	56,814
Foreign-born	26,393

Educational Attainment

Population 25 years and over	57,733
Less than 9th grade	6.8%
High School grad or higher	25.9%
Bachelor's degree or higher	8.1%
Graduate degree	83.0%

Households

Total households	30,559
With persons under 18	9,276
With persons over 65	8,763
Family households	19,956
Single person households	8,913
Persons per household	2.69
Persons per family	3.42

Income & Poverty

Per capita income	$28,545
Median household income	$56,478
Median family income	$71,743
Persons in poverty	7.3%
H'holds receiving public assistance	205
H'holds receiving social security	8,832

Labor & Employment

Total civilian labor force	43,730
Unemployment rate	5.4%

Employed persons 16 years and over by occupation,

Managers & professionals	13,115
Service occupations	6,083
Sales & office occupations	12,564
Farming, fishing & forestry	75
Construction & maintenance	3,076
Production & transportation	6,442
Self-employed persons	1,615

Housing Units

Total	32,539
Single family units	14,159
Multiple family units	18,380
Mobile home units	0
Owner-occupied units	19,245
Renter-occupied units	11,314
Vacant units	1,980
Median SF home value	$389,200
Median rent	$1,043

East Orange City
Essex County

Population

Total	60,575
Male	29,371
Female	31,204

Race & Hispanic Origin

Race
White	3,184
Black/African American	51,771
Amer. Indian/Alaskan Native	29
Asian	1,410
Pacific Islander	0
Other Race	3,802
Two or more races	379
Hispanic origin, total	NA
Mexican	NA
Puerto Rican	NA
Cuban	NA
Other Hispanic	NA

Age & Nativity

Under 5 years	4,109
18 years and over	46,206
21 years and over	43,209
65 years and over	8,513
85 years and over	1,155
Median age	38.2
Native-born	46,812
Foreign-born	13,763

Educational Attainment

Population 25 years and over	40,114
Less than 9th grade	9.2%
High School grad or higher	18.4%
Bachelor's degree or higher	3.4%
Graduate degree	75.1%

Households

Total households	23,267
With persons under 18	7,390
With persons over 65	6,688
Family households	12,955
Single person households	9,263
Persons per household	2.57
Persons per family	3.50

Income & Poverty

Per capita income	$21,676
Median household income	$40,151
Median family income	$48,365
Persons in poverty	22.4%
H'holds receiving public assistance	1,617
H'holds receiving social security	6,617

Labor & Employment

Total civilian labor force	29,316
Unemployment rate	15.6%

Employed persons 16 years and over by occupation,

Managers & professionals	NA
Service occupations	NA
Sales & office occupations	NA
Farming, fishing & forestry	NA
Construction & maintenance	NA
Production & transportation	NA
Self-employed persons	669

Housing Units

Total	28,823
Single family units	5,154
Multiple family units	23,578
Mobile home units	47
Owner-occupied units	6,227
Renter-occupied units	17,040
Vacant units	5,556
Median SF home value	$272,600
Median rent	$827

Edison Township
Middlesex County

Population

Total	101,833
Male	52,067
Female	49,766

Race & Hispanic Origin

Race
White	52,936
Black/African American	9,501
Amer. Indian/Alaskan Native	175
Asian	34,456
Pacific Islander	45
Other Race	3,221
Two or more races	1,499
Hispanic origin, total	6,339
Mexican	1,321
Puerto Rican	2,186
Cuban	133
Other Hispanic	2,699

Age & Nativity

Under 5 years	6,519
18 years and over	80,706
21 years and over	76,412
65 years and over	15,349
85 years and over	2,698
Median age	39.4
Native-born	64,928
Foreign-born	36,905

Educational Attainment

Population 25 years and over	71,857
Less than 9th grade	4.3%
High School grad or higher	46.3%
Bachelor's degree or higher	20.1%
Graduate degree	90.0%

Households

Total households	34,461
With persons under 18	13,675
With persons over 65	7,976
Family households	26,212
Single person households	6,760
Persons per household	2.75
Persons per family	3.15

Income & Poverty

Per capita income	$33,075
Median household income	$80,026
Median family income	$90,686
Persons in poverty	5.9%
H'holds receiving public assistance	47
H'holds receiving social security	8,548

Labor & Employment

Total civilian labor force	52,347
Unemployment rate	4.5%

Employed persons 16 years and over by occupation,

Managers & professionals	23,142
Service occupations	4,690
Sales & office occupations	13,732
Farming, fishing & forestry	0
Construction & maintenance	3,177
Production & transportation	5,257
Self-employed persons	1,444

Housing Units

Total	35,997
Single family units	17,230
Multiple family units	18,586
Mobile home units	181
Owner-occupied units	21,268
Renter-occupied units	13,193
Vacant units	1,536
Median SF home value	$397,400
Median rent	$1,287

Note: The 2007 American Community Survey (ACS) produced one-year estimates of demographic data for cities and counties with populations of at least 65,000: in New Jersey's case, 20 out of 566 municipalities. For those municipalities, the ACS data appears here as a supplement to the 2000 Census data in the profiles.

Elizabeth City
Union County

Population

Total	130,159
Male	63,564
Female	66,595

Race & Hispanic Origin

Race
White	51,908
Black/African American	26,629
Amer. Indian/Alaskan Native	294
Asian	2,771
Pacific Islander	0
Other Race	46,686
Two or more races	1,871
Hispanic origin, total	74,521
Mexican	2,908
Puerto Rican	14,155
Cuban	5,601
Other Hispanic	51,857

Age & Nativity

Under 5 years	12,151
18 years and over	93,749
21 years and over	88,829
65 years and over	11,999
85 years and over	1,215
Median age	32.8
Native-born	72,182
Foreign-born	57,977

Educational Attainment

Population 25 years and over	81,292
Less than 9th grade	12.7%
High School grad or higher	10.9%
Bachelor's degree or higher	2.3%
Graduate degree	74.9%

Households

Total households	41,527
With persons under 18	18,218
With persons over 65	8,690
Family households	29,199
Single person households	10,443
Persons per household	3.09
Persons per family	3.68

Income & Poverty

Per capita income	$19,030
Median household income	$42,587
Median family income	$51,694
Persons in poverty	16.6%
H'holds receiving public assistance	986
H'holds receiving social security	7,235

Labor & Employment

Total civilian labor force	65,275
Unemployment rate	6.3%

Employed persons 16 years and over by occupation,

Managers & professionals	11,095
Service occupations	12,328
Sales & office occupations	15,431
Farming, fishing & forestry	0
Construction & maintenance	6,585
Production & transportation	15,715
Self-employed persons	2,415

Housing Units

Total	45,629
Single family units	5,620
Multiple family units	40,009
Mobile home units	0
Owner-occupied units	10,291
Renter-occupied units	31,236
Vacant units	4,102
Median SF home value	$437,200
Median rent	$920

Gloucester Township
Camden County

Population

Total	63,167
Male	31,052
Female	32,115

Race & Hispanic Origin

Race
White	48,838
Black/African American	9,912
Amer. Indian/Alaskan Native	0
Asian	1,912
Pacific Islander	0
Other Race	815
Two or more races	1,690
Hispanic origin, total	2,796
Mexican	NA
Puerto Rican	NA
Cuban	NA
Other Hispanic	NA

Age & Nativity

Under 5 years	4,661
18 years and over	46,121
21 years and over	43,235
65 years and over	5,258
85 years and over	414
Median age	35.5
Native-born	60,589
Foreign-born	2,578

Educational Attainment

Population 25 years and over	40,130
Less than 9th grade	3.5%
High School grad or higher	21.3%
Bachelor's degree or higher	7.0%
Graduate degree	89.6%

Households

Total households	22,608
With persons under 18	9,521
With persons over 65	3,796
Family households	16,131
Single person households	4,858
Persons per household	2.78
Persons per family	3.34

Income & Poverty

Per capita income	$27,514
Median household income	$69,396
Median family income	$82,874
Persons in poverty	4.6%
H'holds receiving public assistance	174
H'holds receiving social security	4,845

Labor & Employment

Total civilian labor force	35,035
Unemployment rate	5.7%

Employed persons 16 years and over by occupation,

Managers & professionals	10,236
Service occupations	6,167
Sales & office occupations	11,010
Farming, fishing & forestry	0
Construction & maintenance	2,617
Production & transportation	3,016
Self-employed persons	1,082

Housing Units

Total	24,483
Single family units	15,473
Multiple family units	8,783
Mobile home units	227
Owner-occupied units	17,477
Renter-occupied units	5,131
Vacant units	1,875
Median SF home value	$232,100
Median rent	$903

Hamilton Township
Mercer County

Population

Total	91,205
Male	43,402
Female	47,803

Race & Hispanic Origin

Race
White	75,032
Black/African American	9,676
Amer. Indian/Alaskan Native	219
Asian	3,232
Pacific Islander	0
Other Race	2,263
Two or more races	783
Hispanic origin, total	7,321
Mexican	1,622
Puerto Rican	2,441
Cuban	121
Other Hispanic	3,137

Age & Nativity

Under 5 years	4,675
18 years and over	72,042
21 years and over	67,623
65 years and over	13,804
85 years and over	2,375
Median age	40.0
Native-born	79,845
Foreign-born	11,360

Educational Attainment

Population 25 years and over	63,350
Less than 9th grade	3.7%
High School grad or higher	24.5%
Bachelor's degree or higher	7.2%
Graduate degree	89.7%

Households

Total households	33,555
With persons under 18	11,075
With persons over 65	9,381
Family households	22,806
Single person households	9,349
Persons per household	2.69
Persons per family	3.34

Income & Poverty

Per capita income	$31,565
Median household income	$69,736
Median family income	$84,202
Persons in poverty	3.4%
H'holds receiving public assistance	475
H'holds receiving social security	10,957

Labor & Employment

Total civilian labor force	50,254
Unemployment rate	4.6%

Employed persons 16 years and over by occupation,

Managers & professionals	15,754
Service occupations	7,649
Sales & office occupations	16,108
Farming, fishing & forestry	0
Construction & maintenance	4,405
Production & transportation	4,027
Self-employed persons	1,744

Housing Units

Total	35,310
Single family units	22,481
Multiple family units	12,829
Mobile home units	0
Owner-occupied units	25,956
Renter-occupied units	7,599
Vacant units	1,755
Median SF home value	$276,600
Median rent	$946

Note: The 2007 American Community Survey (ACS) produced one-year estimates of demographic data for cities and counties with populations of at least 65,000: in New Jersey's case, 20 out of 566 municipalities. For those municipalities, the ACS data appears here as a supplement to the 2000 Census data in the profiles.

Jersey City
Hudson County

Population

Total	222,653
Male	109,156
Female	113,497

Race & Hispanic Origin

Race

White	73,176
Black/African American	63,306
Amer. Indian/Alaskan Native	1,470
Asian	44,179
Pacific Islander	362
Other Race	35,452
Two or more races	4,708
Hispanic origin, total	62,876
Mexican	2,669
Puerto Rican	23,575
Cuban	1,353
Other Hispanic	35,279

Age & Nativity

Under 5 years	13,575
18 years and over	173,208
21 years and over	165,648
65 years and over	22,087
85 years and over	3,635
Median age	35.7
Native-born	140,804
Foreign-born	81,849

Educational Attainment

Population 25 years and over	152,423
Less than 9th grade	8.3%
High School grad or higher	37.2%
Bachelor's degree or higher	12.8%
Graduate degree	82.6%

Households

Total households	85,550
With persons under 18	27,943
With persons over 65	15,690
Family households	51,579
Single person households	28,418
Persons per household	2.58
Persons per family	3.34

Income & Poverty

Per capita income	$30,678
Median household income	$51,830
Median family income	$56,012
Persons in poverty	14.9%
H'holds receiving public assistance	2,571
H'holds receiving social security	16,654

Labor & Employment

Total civilian labor force	122,782
Unemployment rate	8.2%

Employed persons 16 years and over by occupation,

Managers & professionals	44,340
Service occupations	20,474
Sales & office occupations	29,494
Farming, fishing & forestry	61
Construction & maintenance	6,288
Production & transportation	11,998
Self-employed persons	5,224

Housing Units

Total	100,927
Single family units	7,302
Multiple family units	93,513
Mobile home units	112
Owner-occupied units	29,014
Renter-occupied units	56,536
Vacant units	15,377
Median SF home value	$393,400
Median rent	$985

Lakewood Township
Ocean County

Population

Total	86,770
Male	42,496
Female	44,274

Race & Hispanic Origin

Race

White	69,582
Black/African American	9,642
Amer. Indian/Alaskan Native	322
Asian	1,041
Pacific Islander	0
Other Race	5,008
Two or more races	1,175
Hispanic origin, total	NA
Mexican	NA
Puerto Rican	NA
Cuban	NA
Other Hispanic	NA

Age & Nativity

Under 5 years	14,020
18 years and over	53,412
21 years and over	50,001
65 years and over	12,877
85 years and over	1,893
Median age	26.2
Native-born	76,846
Foreign-born	9,924

Educational Attainment

Population 25 years and over	44,968
Less than 9th grade	6.2%
High School grad or higher	21.7%
Bachelor's degree or higher	8.6%
Graduate degree	83.2%

Households

Total households	26,238
With persons under 18	11,504
With persons over 65	8,167
Family households	18,783
Single person households	6,145
Persons per household	3.20
Persons per family	3.91

Income & Poverty

Per capita income	$16,539
Median household income	$40,084
Median family income	$42,079
Persons in poverty	26.2%
H'holds receiving public assistance	1,412
H'holds receiving social security	9,007

Labor & Employment

Total civilian labor force	27,888
Unemployment rate	7.2%

Employed persons 16 years and over by occupation,

Managers & professionals	9,291
Service occupations	4,775
Sales & office occupations	6,738
Farming, fishing & forestry	0
Construction & maintenance	2,237
Production & transportation	2,828
Self-employed persons	2,180

Housing Units

Total	28,435
Single family units	11,860
Multiple family units	16,575
Mobile home units	0
Owner-occupied units	14,045
Renter-occupied units	12,193
Vacant units	2,197
Median SF home value	$301,300
Median rent	$1,180

Middletown Township
Monmouth County

Population

Total	68,016
Male	33,353
Female	34,663

Race & Hispanic Origin

Race

White	61,931
Black/African American	3,159
Amer. Indian/Alaskan Native	0
Asian	834
Pacific Islander	0
Other Race	275
Two or more races	1,817
Hispanic origin, total	2,490
Mexican	708
Puerto Rican	1,216
Cuban	158
Other Hispanic	408

Age & Nativity

Under 5 years	3,759
18 years and over	52,190
21 years and over	48,966
65 years and over	8,674
85 years and over	793
Median age	41.1
Native-born	64,013
Foreign-born	4,003

Educational Attainment

Population 25 years and over	44,715
Less than 9th grade	2.5%
High School grad or higher	35.5%
Bachelor's degree or higher	12.0%
Graduate degree	93.0%

Households

Total households	23,546
With persons under 18	8,947
With persons over 65	6,183
Family households	18,052
Single person households	4,949
Persons per household	2.88
Persons per family	3.37

Income & Poverty

Per capita income	$39,212
Median household income	$85,049
Median family income	$99,862
Persons in poverty	4.8%
H'holds receiving public assistance	141
H'holds receiving social security	6,760

Labor & Employment

Total civilian labor force	36,351
Unemployment rate	7.3%

Employed persons 16 years and over by occupation,

Managers & professionals	13,625
Service occupations	3,924
Sales & office occupations	10,821
Farming, fishing & forestry	288
Construction & maintenance	2,840
Production & transportation	2,199
Self-employed persons	1,358

Housing Units

Total	24,002
Single family units	18,123
Multiple family units	5,879
Mobile home units	0
Owner-occupied units	19,619
Renter-occupied units	3,927
Vacant units	456
Median SF home value	$445,500
Median rent	$1,047

Note: The 2007 American Community Survey (ACS) produced one-year estimates of demographic data for cities and counties with populations of at least 65,000: in New Jersey's case, 20 out of 566 municipalities. For those municipalities, the ACS data appears here as a supplement to the 2000 Census data in the profiles.

Newark City
Essex County

Population
Total............................270,007
    Male.........................130,609
    Female.......................139,398

Race & Hispanic Origin
Race
    White.........................55,876
    Black/African American........145,294
    Amer. Indian/Alaskan Native....1,133
    Asian..........................3,975
    Pacific Islander...................0
    Other Race....................57,105
    Two or more races..............6,624
Hispanic origin, total...........82,540
    Mexican........................3,180
    Puerto Rican..................37,084
    Cuban..........................2,413
    Other Hispanic................39,863

Age & Nativity
Under 5 years.....................22,281
18 years and over................199,380
21 years and over................186,818
65 years and over.................26,278
85 years and over..................2,092
    Median age.......................33.0
Native-born......................198,040
Foreign-born......................71,967

Educational Attainment
Population 25 years and over......168,440
    Less than 9th grade.............18.5%
    High School grad or higher......11.6%
    Bachelor's degree or higher......3.7%
    Graduate degree.................64.1%

Households
Total households..................90,180
    With persons under 18..........36,280
    With persons over 65...........18,718
    Family households..............58,882
    Single person households.......27,528
Persons per household...............2.81
Persons per family..................3.48

Income & Poverty
Per capita income................$16,782
Median household income..........$34,452
Median family income.............$41,058
Persons in poverty.................23.9%
H'holds receiving public assistance...5,568
H'holds receiving social security....21,369

Labor & Employment
Total civilian labor force........123,428
    Unemployment rate..............11.5%

Employed persons 16 years and over by occupation,
    Managers & professionals.......22,490
    Service occupations............27,824
    Sales & office occupations.....26,434
    Farming, fishing & forestry........44
    Construction & maintenance.....14,668
    Production & transportation....17,713
Self-employed persons..............3,711

Housing Units
Total............................107,629
    Single family units...........12,294
    Multiple family units.........94,998
    Mobile home units................138
    Owner-occupied units..........25,875
    Renter-occupied units.........64,305
    Vacant units..................17,449
Median SF home value............$317,400
Median rent.........................$845

Old Bridge Township
Middlesex County

Population
Total.............................64,888
    Male..........................31,433
    Female........................33,455

Race & Hispanic Origin
Race
    White.........................47,652
    Black/African American.........5,643
    Amer. Indian/Alaskan Native........0
    Asian..........................9,605
    Pacific Islander...................0
    Other Race.....................1,029
    Two or more races................959
Hispanic origin, total............5,524
    Mexican..........................478
    Puerto Rican...................1,983
    Cuban............................757
    Other Hispanic.................2,306

Age & Nativity
Under 5 years......................2,958
18 years and over.................48,619
21 years and over.................46,520
65 years and over..................6,998
85 years and over....................853
    Median age.......................38.9
Native-born.......................51,954
Foreign-born......................12,934

Educational Attainment
Population 25 years and over.......43,331
    Less than 9th grade..............3.5%
    High School grad or higher......31.3%
    Bachelor's degree or higher.....10.3%
    Graduate degree.................90.5%

Households
Total households..................22,498
    With persons under 18..........9,361
    With persons over 65...........4,787
    Family households..............16,927
    Single person households.......4,815
Persons per household...............2.85
Persons per family..................3.33

Income & Poverty
Per capita income................$33,793
Median household income..........$80,641
Median family income............$100,711
Persons in poverty..................4.4%
H'holds receiving public assistance......99
H'holds receiving social security.....5,090

Labor & Employment
Total civilian labor force.........34,818
    Unemployment rate...............4.4%

Employed persons 16 years and over by occupation,
    Managers & professionals.......12,569
    Service occupations............4,690
    Sales & office occupations.....9,475
    Farming, fishing & forestry........0
    Construction & maintenance.....3,296
    Production & transportation....3,259
Self-employed persons..............1,744

Housing Units
Total.............................24,043
    Single family units...........15,208
    Multiple family units..........8,788
    Mobile home units.................47
    Owner-occupied units..........16,514
    Renter-occupied units..........5,984
    Vacant units...................1,545
Median SF home value............$373,400
Median rent.........................$963

Passaic City
Passaic County

Population
Total.............................70,059
    Male..........................35,936
    Female........................34,123

Race & Hispanic Origin
Race
    White.........................24,168
    Black/African American.........6,527
    Amer. Indian/Alaskan Native.......86
    Asian..........................2,940
    Pacific Islander...................0
    Other Race....................34,272
    Two or more races..............2,066
Hispanic origin, total...............NA
    Mexican.......................15,268
    Puerto Rican...................8,485
    Cuban............................331
    Other Hispanic................23,418

Age & Nativity
Under 5 years......................7,750
18 years and over.................47,315
21 years and over.................44,408
65 years and over..................5,569
85 years and over....................994
    Median age.......................30.2
Native-born.......................39,135
Foreign-born......................30,924

Educational Attainment
Population 25 years and over.......40,065
    Less than 9th grade.............17.3%
    High School grad or higher......12.9%
    Bachelor's degree or higher......3.8%
    Graduate degree.................73.9%

Households
Total households..................19,432
    With persons under 18..........8,936
    With persons over 65...........3,707
    Family households..............13,341
    Single person households.......5,255
Persons per household...............3.56
Persons per family..................4.50

Income & Poverty
Per capita income................$13,933
Median household income..........$27,691
Median family income.............$34,436
Persons in poverty.................30.9%
H'holds receiving public assistance.....404
H'holds receiving social security.....3,970

Labor & Employment
Total civilian labor force.........28,498
    Unemployment rate...............7.2%

Employed persons 16 years and over by occupation,
    Managers & professionals..........NA
    Service occupations...............NA
    Sales & office occupations........NA
    Farming, fishing & forestry.......NA
    Construction & maintenance........NA
    Production & transportation.......NA
Self-employed persons................848

Housing Units
Total.............................20,619
    Single family units............2,888
    Multiple family units.........17,731
    Mobile home units..................0
    Owner-occupied units...........5,461
    Renter-occupied units.........13,971
    Vacant units...................1,187
Median SF home value............$366,600
Median rent.........................$959

Note: The 2007 American Community Survey (ACS) produced one-year estimates of demographic data for cities and counties with populations of at least 65,000: in New Jersey's case, 20 out of 566 municipalities. For those municipalities, the ACS data appears here as a supplement to the 2000 Census data in the profiles.

Paterson City
Passaic County

Population

Total	135,831
Male	63,908
Female	71,923

Race & Hispanic Origin

Race

White	28,726
Black/African American	39,966
Amer. Indian/Alaskan Native	341
Asian	2,716
Pacific Islander	212
Other Race	61,335
Two or more races	2,535
Hispanic origin, total	80,169
Mexican	8,119
Puerto Rican	19,323
Cuban	1,324
Other Hispanic	51,403

Age & Nativity

Under 5 years	10,642
18 years and over	96,658
21 years and over	90,216
65 years and over	11,540
85 years and over	1,397
Median age	31.4
Native-born	87,232
Foreign-born	48,599

Educational Attainment

Population 25 years and over	83,244
Less than 9th grade	14.1%
High School grad or higher	8.0%
Bachelor's degree or higher	1.0%
Graduate degree	74.6%

Households

Total households	41,890
With persons under 18	16,941
With persons over 65	8,351
Family households	28,491
Single person households	11,537
Persons per household	3.18
Persons per family	3.90

Income & Poverty

Per capita income	$15,528
Median household income	$34,067
Median family income	$37,366
Persons in poverty	23.7%
H'holds receiving public assistance	2,250
H'holds receiving social security	8,374

Labor & Employment

Total civilian labor force	59,273
Unemployment rate	6.4%

Employed persons 16 years and over by occupation,

Managers & professionals	9,981
Service occupations	13,630
Sales & office occupations	13,866
Farming, fishing & forestry	0
Construction & maintenance	4,332
Production & transportation	13,681
Self-employed persons	1,182

Housing Units

Total	48,220
Single family units	7,938
Multiple family units	40,133
Mobile home units	149
Owner-occupied units	11,900
Renter-occupied units	29,990
Vacant units	6,330
Median SF home value	$345,600
Median rent	$986

Toms River Township
Ocean County

Population

Total	81,949
Male	38,155
Female	43,794

Race & Hispanic Origin

Race

White	76,389
Black/African American	937
Amer. Indian/Alaskan Native	0
Asian	1,140
Pacific Islander	0
Other Race	1,814
Two or more races	1,669
Hispanic origin, total	5,858
Mexican	NA
Puerto Rican	NA
Cuban	NA
Other Hispanic	NA

Age & Nativity

Under 5 years	4,979
18 years and over	64,271
21 years and over	62,096
65 years and over	15,318
85 years and over	2,812
Median age	41.5
Native-born	76,092
Foreign-born	5,857

Educational Attainment

Population 25 years and over	58,802
Less than 9th grade	3.4%
High School grad or higher	30.4%
Bachelor's degree or higher	9.0%
Graduate degree	89.0%

Households

Total households	32,696
With persons under 18	10,684
With persons over 65	10,503
Family households	22,139
Single person households	8,948
Persons per household	2.45
Persons per family	3.01

Income & Poverty

Per capita income	$33,408
Median household income	$64,852
Median family income	$87,156
Persons in poverty	3.9%
H'holds receiving public assistance	614
H'holds receiving social security	11,876

Labor & Employment

Total civilian labor force	41,915
Unemployment rate	5.7%

Employed persons 16 years and over by occupation,

Managers & professionals	16,498
Service occupations	6,077
Sales & office occupations	10,847
Farming, fishing & forestry	0
Construction & maintenance	3,497
Production & transportation	2,591
Self-employed persons	1,764

Housing Units

Total	41,443
Single family units	32,437
Multiple family units	7,742
Mobile home units	1,264
Owner-occupied units	27,245
Renter-occupied units	5,451
Vacant units	8,747
Median SF home value	$347,600
Median rent	$1,075

Trenton City
Mercer County

Population

Total	78,242
Male	41,561
Female	36,681

Race & Hispanic Origin

Race

White	24,393
Black/African American	42,963
Amer. Indian/Alaskan Native	458
Asian	814
Pacific Islander	0
Other Race	8,930
Two or more races	684
Hispanic origin, total	22,589
Mexican	2,461
Puerto Rican	7,267
Cuban	141
Other Hispanic	12,720

Age & Nativity

Under 5 years	6,012
18 years and over	58,322
21 years and over	55,064
65 years and over	8,208
85 years and over	920
Median age	32.4
Native-born	61,414
Foreign-born	16,828

Educational Attainment

Population 25 years and over	50,144
Less than 9th grade	13.9%
High School grad or higher	10.2%
Bachelor's degree or higher	3.8%
Graduate degree	68.9%

Households

Total households	25,620
With persons under 18	10,192
With persons over 65	5,792
Family households	16,442
Single person households	7,401
Persons per household	2.99
Persons per family	3.58

Income & Poverty

Per capita income	$17,389
Median household income	$36,293
Median family income	$43,712
Persons in poverty	21.4%
H'holds receiving public assistance	1,887
H'holds receiving social security	8,260

Labor & Employment

Total civilian labor force	37,733
Unemployment rate	12.7%

Employed persons 16 years and over by occupation,

Managers & professionals	5,616
Service occupations	11,312
Sales & office occupations	6,727
Farming, fishing & forestry	310
Construction & maintenance	3,743
Production & transportation	5,235
Self-employed persons	657

Housing Units

Total	32,335
Single family units	4,016
Multiple family units	28,319
Mobile home units	0
Owner-occupied units	12,283
Renter-occupied units	13,337
Vacant units	6,715
Median SF home value	$128,500
Median rent	$847

Note: The 2007 American Community Survey (ACS) produced one-year estimates of demographic data for cities and counties with populations of at least 65,000: in New Jersey's case, 20 out of 566 municipalities. For those municipalities, the ACS data appears here as a supplement to the 2000 Census data in the profiles.

Union City
Hudson County

Population

Total 67,909
  Male 35,564
  Female 32,345

Race & Hispanic Origin

Race
  White 46,624
  Black/African American 5,312
  Amer. Indian/Alaskan Native 435
  Asian 1,254
  Pacific Islander 0
  Other Race 12,558
  Two or more races 1,726
Hispanic origin, total . . . . .NA
  Mexican 6,531
  Puerto Rican 4,919
  Cuban 7,821
  Other Hispanic 30,855

Age & Nativity

Under 5 years 6,613
18 years and over 49,930
21 years and over 47,793
65 years and over 5,766
85 years and over .901
  Median age 32.6
Native-born 29,583
Foreign-born 38,326

Educational Attainment

Population 25 years and over 43,637
  Less than 9th grade 21.2%
  High School grad or higher 18.1%
  Bachelor's degree or higher 5.5%
  Graduate degree 64.7%

Households

Total households 22,170
  With persons under 18 8,578
  With persons over 65 4,200
  Family households 15,301
  Single person households 5,009
Persons per household 3.04
Persons per family 3.55

Income & Poverty

Per capita income $17,712
Median household income $38,164
Median family income $38,505
Persons in poverty 18.6%
H'holds receiving public assistance 513
H'holds receiving social security 4,162

Labor & Employment

Total civilian labor force . . . . .NA
  Unemployment rate . . . . .NA

Employed persons 16 years and over
  by occupation,
  Managers & professionals 5,477
  Service occupations 8,503
  Sales & office occupations 8,283
  Farming, fishing & forestry 0
  Construction & maintenance 3,426
  Production & transportation 8,443
Self-employed persons 1,947

Housing Units

Total 24,440
  Single family units 1,146
  Multiple family units 23,294
  Mobile home units 0
  Owner-occupied units 4,857
  Renter-occupied units 17,313
  Vacant units 2,270
Median SF home value $448,300
Median rent $893

Woodbridge Township
Middlesex County

Population

Total 99,324
  Male 51,412
  Female 47,912

Race & Hispanic Origin

Race
  White 67,965
  Black/African American 7,907
  Amer. Indian/Alaskan Native 0
  Asian 18,123
  Pacific Islander 0
  Other Race 3,651
  Two or more races 1,678
Hispanic origin, total 17,519
  Mexican 2,119
  Puerto Rican 3,860
  Cuban 541
  Other Hispanic 10,999

Age & Nativity

Under 5 years 6,626
18 years and over 78,048
21 years and over 74,986
65 years and over 10,689
85 years and over 1,425
  Median age 37.6
Native-born 69,779
Foreign-born 29,545

Educational Attainment

Population 25 years and over 69,470
  Less than 9th grade 7.1%
  High School grad or higher 30.0%
  Bachelor's degree or higher 9.9%
  Graduate degree 84.6%

Households

Total households 34,701
  With persons under 18 12,932
  With persons over 65 7,694
  Family households 25,792
  Single person households 8,012
Persons per household 2.79
Persons per family 3.32

Income & Poverty

Per capita income $30,723
Median household income $73,544
Median family income $77,945
Persons in poverty 3.6%
H'holds receiving public assistance 270
H'holds receiving social security 7,891

Labor & Employment

Total civilian labor force 55,355
  Unemployment rate 5.0%

Employed persons 16 years and over
  by occupation,
  Managers & professionals 18,531
  Service occupations 6,387
  Sales & office occupations 16,850
  Farming, fishing & forestry 63
  Construction & maintenance 4,727
  Production & transportation 6,053
Self-employed persons 1,819

Housing Units

Total 35,752
  Single family units 22,315
  Multiple family units 12,971
  Mobile home units 466
  Owner-occupied units 24,422
  Renter-occupied units 10,279
  Vacant units 1,051
Median SF home value $361,100
Median rent $1,219

Additional Public School District Data
(for school year 2007-08 except where noted)

Black Horse Pike Regional High School District
District Administration Office, 580 Erial Road
Blackwood, NJ 08012
Camden County
(856)227-4106
http://www.bhprsd.org
Superintendent. . . . . Ralph E. Ross
Number of schools. 3
Grade plan. 9-12
Enrollment 4,275
Attendance rate, '06-07 . . . . 93.8%
Dropout rate. 1.1%
Students per teacher 13.2
Per pupil expenditure. $13,608
Median faculty salary. $48,662
Median administrator salary. $98,988
Grade 12 enrollment. 971
High school graduation rate 90.7%

Assessment test results
(percent scoring at proficient or advanced level)

	Language	Math
NJASK-Gr 3	NA	NA
NJASK-Gr 8	NA	NA
HSPA-High Schl	85.6%	71.5%

SAT score averages, 2006-07

Pct tested	Math	Verbal	Writing
NA	NA	NA	NA

Teacher Qualifications
Avg years of experience 9
Highly-qualified teachers
    one subject/all subjects. 99.5%/99.5%

No Child Left Behind
AYP, 2006-07 . . . . .Needs Improvement

Carlstadt-East Rutherford Regional High School District
120 Paterson Avenue
East Rutherford, NJ 07073
Bergen County
(201)935-4155
http://www.bectonhs.org
Superintendent. . . . . James J. Jencarelli
Number of schools. 1
Grade plan. 9-12
Enrollment 523
Attendance rate, '06-07 . . . . .93.6%
Dropout rate. 0.3%
Students per teacher 10.8
Per pupil expenditure. $18,336
Median faculty salary. $66,689
Median administrator salary. $107,353
Grade 12 enrollment. 127
High school graduation rate 99.2%

Assessment test results
(percent scoring at proficient or advanced level)

	Language	Math
NJASK-Gr 3	NA	NA
NJASK-Gr 8	NA	NA
HSPA-High Schl	88.8%	83.0%

SAT score averages, 2006-07

Pct tested	Math	Verbal	Writing
75%	499	454	467

Teacher Qualifications
Avg years of experience 10
Highly-qualified teachers
    one subject/all subjects. 100%/100%

No Child Left Behind
AYP, 2006-07 . . . . .Meets Standards

Central Regional School District
Forest Hills Parkway
Bayville, NJ 08721
Ocean County
(732)269-1100
http://www.centralreg.k12.nj.us
Superintendent. . .Triantafillos Parlapanides
Number of schools. .2
Grade plan. 7-12
Enrollment 2,073
Attendance rate, '06-07 . . . . 92.4%
Dropout rate. 2.2%
Students per teacher 11.4
Per pupil expenditure. $13,829
Median faculty salary. $55,300
Median administrator salary. $103,480
Grade 12 enrollment. 312
High school graduation rate 84.5%

Assessment test results
(percent scoring at proficient or advanced level)

	Language	Math
NJASK-Gr 3	NA	NA
NJASK-Gr 8	85.3%	68.2%
HSPA-High Schl	86.2%	74.9%

SAT score averages, 2006-07

Pct tested	Math	Verbal	Writing
69%	469	461	453

Teacher Qualifications
Avg years of experience 9
Highly-qualified teachers
    one subject/all subjects. 100%/100%

No Child Left Behind
AYP, 2006-07 . . . . .Needs Improvement

Clearview Regional High School District
420 Cedar Rd
Mullica Hill, NJ 08062
Gloucester County
(856)223-2765
http://www.clearviewregional.edu
Superintendent. . . . . John Horchak III
Number of schools. .2
Grade plan. 7-12
Enrollment 2,405
Attendance rate, '06-07 . . . . .95.4%
Dropout rate. 1.3%
Students per teacher 12.4
Per pupil expenditure. $11,091
Median faculty salary. $49,500
Median administrator salary. $95,580
Grade 12 enrollment. 367
High school graduation rate 97.6%

Assessment test results
(percent scoring at proficient or advanced level)

	Language	Math
NJASK-Gr 3	NA	NA
NJASK-Gr 8	91.7%	80.1%
HSPA-High Schl	92.4%	88.9%

SAT score averages, 2006-07

Pct tested	Math	Verbal	Writing
78%	512	504	498

Teacher Qualifications
Avg years of experience 8
Highly-qualified teachers
    one subject/all subjects. 100%/100%

No Child Left Behind
AYP, 2006-07 . . . . .Meets Standards

Cumberland Regional High School District
Love Lane, PO Box 5115
Seabrook, NJ 08302
Cumberland County
(856)451-9400
http://www.crhsd.org
Superintendent. . . . . William Stonis
Number of schools. .1
Grade plan. 9-12
Enrollment 1,326
Attendance rate, '06-07 . . . . 93.0%
Dropout rate. 1.5%
Students per teacher 12.1
Per pupil expenditure. $13,125
Median faculty salary. $60,621
Median administrator salary. $104,036
Grade 12 enrollment. 299
High school graduation rate 86.5%

Assessment test results
(percent scoring at proficient or advanced level)

	Language	Math
NJASK-Gr 3	NA	NA
NJASK-Gr 8	NA	NA
HSPA-High Schl	79.0%	66.3%

SAT score averages, 2006-07

Pct tested	Math	Verbal	Writing
49%	489	463	467

Teacher Qualifications
Avg years of experience 13
Highly-qualified teachers
    one subject/all subjects. 100%/100%

No Child Left Behind
AYP, 2006-07 . . . . .Needs Improvement

Delaware Valley Regional High School
19 Senator Stout Road
Frenchtown, NJ 08825
Hunterdon County
(908)996-2131
http://www.dvrhs.k12.nj.us
Superintendent. . . . . .Elizabeth Nastus
Number of schools. .1
Grade plan. 9-12
Enrollment 977
Attendance rate, '06-07 . . . . 94.8%
Dropout rate. 1.0%
Students per teacher 11.0
Per pupil expenditure. $15,949
Median faculty salary. $53,180
Median administrator salary. $110,240
Grade 12 enrollment. 212
High school graduation rate 99.1%

Assessment test results
(percent scoring at proficient or advanced level)

	Language	Math
NJASK-Gr 3	NA	NA
NJASK-Gr 8	NA	NA
HSPA-High Schl	89.8%	87.3%

SAT score averages, 2006-07

Pct tested	Math	Verbal	Writing
83%	534	533	526

Teacher Qualifications
Avg years of experience 10
Highly-qualified teachers
    one subject/all subjects. 100%/100%

No Child Left Behind
AYP, 2006-07 . . . . .Meets Standards

Additional Public School District Data
(for school year 2007-08 except where noted)

Eastern Camden County Regional School District
Laurel Oak Road, Box 2500
Voorhees, NJ 08043
Camden County
(856)346-6740
http://www.eastern.k12.nj.us
Superintendent.........Harold Melleby Jr
Number of schools.........................2
Grade plan.........................9-12
Enrollment.......................2,126
Attendance rate, '06-07............94.0%
Dropout rate.......................0.3%
Students per teacher.................12.1
Per pupil expenditure............$14,123
Median faculty salary............$58,060
Median administrator salary......$115,131
Grade 12 enrollment..................529
High school graduation rate........98.3%

Assessment test results
(percent scoring at proficient or advanced level)

	Language	Math
NJASK-Gr 3	NA	NA
NJASK-Gr 8	NA	NA
HSPA-High Schl	91.0%	88.4%

SAT score averages, 2006-07

Pct tested	Math	Verbal	Writing
88%	550	541	538

Teacher Qualifications
Avg years of experience.................10
Highly-qualified teachers
  one subject/all subjects......100%/100%

No Child Left Behind
AYP, 2006-07............Meets Standards

Freehold Regional High School District
11 Pine Street
Englishtown, NJ 07726
Monmouth County
(732)792-7300
http://www.frhsd.com
Superintendent.............James Wasser
Number of schools.........................6
Grade plan.........................9-12
Enrollment.......................11,703
Attendance rate, '06-07............94.3%
Dropout rate.......................1.2%
Students per teacher.................13.6
Per pupil expenditure............$13,250
Median faculty salary............$64,120
Median administrator salary......$102,556
Grade 12 enrollment................2,897
High school graduation rate........98.7%

Assessment test results
(percent scoring at proficient or advanced level)

	Language	Math
NJASK-Gr 3	NA	NA
NJASK-Gr 8	NA	NA
HSPA-High Schl	93.7%	88.3%

SAT score averages, 2006-07

Pct tested	Math	Verbal	Writing
NA	NA	NA	NA

Teacher Qualifications
Avg years of experience.................9
Highly-qualified teachers
  one subject/all subjects.....99.5%/99.5%

No Child Left Behind
AYP, 2006-07............Meets Standards

Gateway Regional School District
775 Tanyard Rd
Woodbury Heights, NJ 08096
Gloucester County
(856)848-8172
http://www.gatewayhs.com
Superintendent.............Joyce Stumpo
Number of schools.........................1
Grade plan.........................7-12
Enrollment..........................971
Attendance rate, '06-07............94.4%
Dropout rate.......................1.2%
Students per teacher..................9.4
Per pupil expenditure............$15,614
Median faculty salary............$51,655
Median administrator salary.......$91,205
Grade 12 enrollment..................156
High school graduation rate........92.7%

Assessment test results
(percent scoring at proficient or advanced level)

	Language	Math
NJASK-Gr 3	NA	NA
NJASK-Gr 8	76.3%	67.5%
HSPA-High Schl	85.2%	84.1%

SAT score averages, 2006-07

Pct tested	Math	Verbal	Writing
68%	503	478	462

Teacher Qualifications
Avg years of experience.................8
Highly-qualified teachers
  one subject/all subjects......100%/98.5%

No Child Left Behind
AYP, 2006-07............Meets Standards

Greater Egg Harbor Regional High School District
1824 Dr. Dennis Foreman Drive
Mays Landing, NJ 08330
Atlantic County
(609)625-1456
http://www.gehrhsd.net
Superintendent.............Adam Pfeffer
Number of schools.........................2
Grade plan.........................9-12
Enrollment.......................3,877
Attendance rate, '06-07............93.5%
Dropout rate.......................0.9%
Students per teacher.................12.4
Per pupil expenditure............$13,385
Median faculty salary............$52,250
Median administrator salary.......$97,149
Grade 12 enrollment..................851
High school graduation rate........91.2%

Assessment test results
(percent scoring at proficient or advanced level)

	Language	Math
NJASK-Gr 3	NA	NA
NJASK-Gr 8	NA	NA
HSPA-High Schl	86.4%	77.2%

SAT score averages, 2006-07

Pct tested	Math	Verbal	Writing
NA	NA	NA	NA

Teacher Qualifications
Avg years of experience.................8
Highly-qualified teachers
  one subject/all subjects......100%/100%

No Child Left Behind
AYP, 2006-07........Needs Improvement

Hanover Park Regional High School District
75 Mt. Pleasant Avenue
East Hanover, NJ 07936
Morris County
(973)887-0320
(no website)
Superintendent.......Edward Franko (Int)
Number of schools.........................2
Grade plan.........................9-12
Enrollment.......................1,500
Attendance rate, '06-07............96.9%
Dropout rate.......................2.2%
Students per teacher.................10.2
Per pupil expenditure............$17,561
Median faculty salary............$60,584
Median administrator salary......$132,378
Grade 12 enrollment..................386
High school graduation rate........97.0%

Assessment test results
(percent scoring at proficient or advanced level)

	Language	Math
NJASK-Gr 3	NA	NA
NJASK-Gr 8	NA	NA
HSPA-High Schl	92.2%	86.0%

SAT score averages, 2006-07

Pct tested	Math	Verbal	Writing
NA	NA	NA	NA

Teacher Qualifications
Avg years of experience.................8
Highly-qualified teachers
  one subject/all subjects......100%/100%

No Child Left Behind
AYP, 2006-07............Meets Standards

Henry Hudson Regional School
1 Grand Tour
Highlands, NJ 07732
Monmouth County
(732)872-0900
http://www.henryhudsonreg.k12.nj.us
Superintendent.........Kathryn A. Fedina
Number of schools.........................1
Grade plan.........................7-12
Enrollment..........................444
Attendance rate, '06-07............92.8%
Dropout rate.......................0.3%
Students per teacher..................9.1
Per pupil expenditure............$17,838
Median faculty salary............$52,185
Median administrator salary.......$99,553
Grade 12 enrollment...................69
High school graduation rate........97.4%

Assessment test results
(percent scoring at proficient or advanced level)

	Language	Math
NJASK-Gr 3	NA	NA
NJASK-Gr 8	80.9%	63.9%
HSPA-High Schl	85.7%	81.0%

SAT score averages, 2006-07

Pct tested	Math	Verbal	Writing
65%	470	487	464

Teacher Qualifications
Avg years of experience.................7
Highly-qualified teachers
  one subject/all subjects......97.0%/97.0%

No Child Left Behind
AYP, 2006-07............Meets Standards

Additional Public School District Data
(for school year 2007-08 except where noted)

High Point Regional School District
299 Pigeon Hill Road
Sussex, NJ 07461
Sussex County
(973)875-7204
http://www.hpregional.org

Chief School Admin . . . . . John W. Hannum
Number of schools. 1
Grade plan. 9-12
Enrollment 1,298
Attendance rate, '06-07 . . . . 95.3%
Dropout rate. 1.1%
Students per teacher 10.3
Per pupil expenditure $15,571
Median faculty salary $69,323
Median administrator salary. $95,745
Grade 12 enrollment. 328
High school graduation rate 90.8%

Assessment test results
(percent scoring at proficient or advanced level)

	Language	Math
NJASK-Gr 3	NA	NA
NJASK-Gr 8	NA	NA
HSPA-High Schl	90.6%	86.0%

SAT score averages, 2006-07

Pct tested	Math	Verbal	Writing
72%	525	503	493

Teacher Qualifications
Avg years of experience 10
Highly-qualified teachers
   one subject/all subjects. 100%/100%

No Child Left Behind
AYP, 2006-07 . . . . Meets Standards

Hopewell Valley Regional High School District
425 South Main Street
Pennington, NJ 08534
Mercer County
(609)737-4000
http://www.hvrsd.k12.nj.us

Chief School Admin . . . Thomas Butler (Int)
Number of schools. 6
Grade plan. K-12
Enrollment 3,984
Attendance rate, '06-07 . . . . 96.3%
Dropout rate. 4.0%
Students per teacher 10.2
Per pupil expenditure $15,378
Median faculty salary $59,326
Median administrator salary. $109,424
Grade 12 enrollment. 261
High school graduation rate 99.6%

Assessment test results
(percent scoring at proficient or advanced level)

	Language	Math
NJASK-Gr 3	93.3%	94.5%
NJASK-Gr 8	94.1%	82.3%
HSPA-High Schl	94.2%	91.7%

SAT score averages, 2006-07

Pct tested	Math	Verbal	Writing
96%	585	557	562

Teacher Qualifications
Avg years of experience 11
Highly-qualified teachers
   one subject/all subjects. 100%/100%

No Child Left Behind
AYP, 2006-07 . . . . Meets Standards

Hunterdon Central Regional High School
84 Route 31
Flemington, NJ 08822
Hunterdon County
(908)782-5727
http://www.hcrhs.k12.nj.us

Superintendent. . . . . Lisa Brady
Number of schools. 1
Grade plan. 9-12
Enrollment 3,002
Attendance rate, '06-07 . . . . 96.8%
Dropout rate. 1.4%
Students per teacher 10.6
Per pupil expenditure $18,173
Median faculty salary $58,413
Median administrator salary. $119,604
Grade 12 enrollment. 702
High school graduation rate 96.7%

Assessment test results
(percent scoring at proficient or advanced level)

	Language	Math
NJASK-Gr 3	NA	NA
NJASK-Gr 8	NA	NA
HSPA-High Schl	93.9%	89.5%

SAT score averages, 2006-07

Pct tested	Math	Verbal	Writing
95%	553	544	546

Teacher Qualifications
Avg years of experience 8
Highly-qualified teachers
   one subject/all subjects. 100%/100%

No Child Left Behind
AYP, 2006-07 . . . . Meets Standards

Kingsway Regional School District
Administrative Offices, 213 Kings Highway
Woolwich Twp, NJ 08085
Gloucester County
(856)467-4600
http://www.kingsway.k12.nj.us

Superintendent. . . . . Ave Altersitz
Number of schools. 2
Grade plan. 7-12
Enrollment 2,046
Attendance rate, '06-07 . . . . 93.8%
Dropout rate. 0.5%
Students per teacher 11.7
Per pupil expenditure $12,578
Median faculty salary $47,878
Median administrator salary. $99,512
Grade 12 enrollment. 338
High school graduation rate 97.1%

Assessment test results
(percent scoring at proficient or advanced level)

	Language	Math
NJASK-Gr 3	NA	NA
NJASK-Gr 8	88.8%	76.8%
HSPA-High Schl	87.6%	84.3%

SAT score averages, 2006-07

Pct tested	Math	Verbal	Writing
74%	517	499	488

Teacher Qualifications
Avg years of experience 7
Highly-qualified teachers
   one subject/all subjects. 100%/100%

No Child Left Behind
AYP, 2006-07 . . . . Meets Standards

Kittatinny Regional High School
77 Halsey Road
Newton, NJ 07860
Sussex County
(973)383-1800
http://www.krhs.net

Chief School Admin . . . . . . Craig Hutcheson
Number of schools. 1
Grade plan. 7-12
Enrollment 1,185
Attendance rate, '06-07 . . . . 96.4%
Dropout rate. 1.0%
Students per teacher 10.2
Per pupil expenditure $15,321
Median faculty salary $67,290
Median administrator salary. $101,603
Grade 12 enrollment. 216
High school graduation rate 96.3%

Assessment test results
(percent scoring at proficient or advanced level)

	Language	Math
NJASK-Gr 3	NA	NA
NJASK-Gr 8	90.2%	75.9%
HSPA-High Schl	93.6%	92.4%

SAT score averages, 2006-07

Pct tested	Math	Verbal	Writing
82%	511	500	485

Teacher Qualifications
Avg years of experience 10
Highly-qualified teachers
   one subject/all subjects. 99.0%/99.0%

No Child Left Behind
AYP, 2006-07 . . . . Meets Standards

Lakeland Regional High School
205 Conklintown Road
Wanaque, NJ 07465
Passaic County
(973)835-1900
http://www.lakeland.k12.nj.us

Chief School Admin . . . . Albert Guazzo
Number of schools. 1
Grade plan. 9-12
Enrollment 1,169
Attendance rate, '06-07 . . . . 93.2%
Dropout rate. 0.7%
Students per teacher 10.5
Per pupil expenditure $17,346
Median faculty salary $58,300
Median administrator salary. $112,750
Grade 12 enrollment. 304
High school graduation rate 94.6%

Assessment test results
(percent scoring at proficient or advanced level)

	Language	Math
NJASK-Gr 3	NA	NA
NJASK-Gr 8	NA	NA
HSPA-High Schl	85.4%	78.9%

SAT score averages, 2006-07

Pct tested	Math	Verbal	Writing
79%	493	503	504

Teacher Qualifications
Avg years of experience 9
Highly-qualified teachers
   one subject/all subjects. 100%/100%

No Child Left Behind
AYP, 2006-07 . . . . Meets Standards

Additional Public School District Data
(for school year 2007-08 except where noted)

Lenape Regional High School District
93 Willow Grove Road
Shamong, NJ 08088
Burlington County
(609)268-2000
http://www.lr.k12.nj.us

Superintendent	Emily Capella
Number of schools	4
Grade plan	9-12
Enrollment	7,474
Attendance rate, '06-07	93.9%
Dropout rate	0.9%
Students per teacher	10.8
Per pupil expenditure	$16,115
Median faculty salary	$60,512
Median administrator salary	$123,192
Grade 12 enrollment	1,800
High school graduation rate	98.2%

Assessment test results
(percent scoring at proficient or advanced level)

	Language	Math
NJASK-Gr 3	NA	NA
NJASK-Gr 8	NA	NA
HSPA-High Schl	92.0%	87.3%

SAT score averages, 2006-07

Pct tested	Math	Verbal	Writing
NA	NA	NA	NA

Teacher Qualifications

Avg years of experience	9
Highly-qualified teachers one subject/all subjects	100%/100%

No Child Left Behind

AYP, 2006-07	Meets Standards

Lenape Valley Regional High School District
PO Box 578, 28 Sparta Road
Stanhope, NJ 07874
Sussex County
(973)347-7600
http://www.lvhs.org

Chief School Admin	Paul A Jr Palek
Number of schools	1
Grade plan	9-12
Enrollment	872
Attendance rate, '06-07	94.4%
Dropout rate	1.0%
Students per teacher	11.4
Per pupil expenditure	$13,783
Median faculty salary	$67,100
Median administrator salary	$109,917
Grade 12 enrollment	209
High school graduation rate	91.2%

Assessment test results
(percent scoring at proficient or advanced level)

	Language	Math
NJASK-Gr 3	NA	NA
NJASK-Gr 8	NA	NA
HSPA-High Schl	91.9%	82.8%

SAT score averages, 2006-07

Pct tested	Math	Verbal	Writing
85%	501	491	500

Teacher Qualifications

Avg years of experience	15
Highly-qualified teachers one subject/all subjects	100%/100%

No Child Left Behind

AYP, 2006-07	Meets Standards

Lower Cape May Regional School District
687 Route 9
Cape May, NJ 08204
Cape May County
(609)884-3475
http://www.lcmrschools.com

Superintendent	Jack Pfizenmayer
Number of schools	2
Grade plan	7-12
Enrollment	1,740
Attendance rate, '06-07	92.6%
Dropout rate	0.2%
Students per teacher	10.4
Per pupil expenditure	$14,604
Median faculty salary	$63,509
Median administrator salary	$95,700
Grade 12 enrollment	271
High school graduation rate	85.7%

Assessment test results
(percent scoring at proficient or advanced level)

	Language	Math
NJASK-Gr 3	NA	NA
NJASK-Gr 8	82.1%	69.5%
HSPA-High Schl	87.7%	81.1%

SAT score averages, 2006-07

Pct tested	Math	Verbal	Writing
56%	500	481	472

Teacher Qualifications

Avg years of experience	13
Highly-qualified teachers one subject/all subjects	100%/100%

No Child Left Behind

AYP, 2006-07	Meets Standards

Mainland Regional High School
1301 Oak Avenue
Linwood, NJ 08221
Atlantic County
(609)927-2461
http://mainlandregional.net

Superintendent	Russell Dever
Number of schools	1
Grade plan	9-12
Enrollment	1,591
Attendance rate, '06-07	92.7%
Dropout rate	0.0%
Students per teacher	11.1
Per pupil expenditure	$13,371
Median faculty salary	$68,300
Median administrator salary	$108,030
Grade 12 enrollment	367
High school graduation rate	94.3%

Assessment test results
(percent scoring at proficient or advanced level)

	Language	Math
NJASK-Gr 3	NA	NA
NJASK-Gr 8	NA	NA
HSPA-High Schl	90.0%	83.0%

SAT score averages, 2006-07

Pct tested	Math	Verbal	Writing
82%	521	509	507

Teacher Qualifications

Avg years of experience	11
Highly-qualified teachers one subject/all subjects	100%/100%

No Child Left Behind

AYP, 2006-07	Meets Standards

Monmouth Regional High School District
One Norman J. Field Way
Tinton Falls, NJ 07724
Monmouth County
(732)542-1170
http://www.monreghs.k12.nj.us

Superintendent	James W. Cleary
Number of schools	1
Grade plan	9-12
Enrollment	1,141
Attendance rate, '06-07	95.3%
Dropout rate	0.2%
Students per teacher	8.8
Per pupil expenditure	$20,652
Median faculty salary	$59,850
Median administrator salary	$99,000
Grade 12 enrollment	277
High school graduation rate	98.0%

Assessment test results
(percent scoring at proficient or advanced level)

	Language	Math
NJASK-Gr 3	NA	NA
NJASK-Gr 8	NA	NA
HSPA-High Schl	89.0%	80.7%

SAT score averages, 2006-07

Pct tested	Math	Verbal	Writing
84%	504	488	482

Teacher Qualifications

Avg years of experience	12
Highly-qualified teachers one subject/all subjects	100%/100%

No Child Left Behind

AYP, 2006-07	Needs Improvement

Morris Hills Regional School District
48 Knoll Drive
Rockaway, NJ 07866
Morris County
(973)664-2291
http://www.mhrd.k12.nj.us

Superintendent	Ernest Palestis
Number of schools	2
Grade plan	9-12
Enrollment	2,709
Attendance rate, '06-07	96.7%
Dropout rate	5.3%
Students per teacher	9.9
Per pupil expenditure	$18,410
Median faculty salary	$63,150
Median administrator salary	$129,353
Grade 12 enrollment	663
High school graduation rate	97.1%

Assessment test results
(percent scoring at proficient or advanced level)

	Language	Math
NJASK-Gr 3	NA	NA
NJASK-Gr 8	NA	NA
HSPA-High Schl	91.8%	87.2%

SAT score averages, 2006-07

Pct tested	Math	Verbal	Writing
NA	NA	NA	NA

Teacher Qualifications

Avg years of experience	9
Highly-qualified teachers one subject/all subjects	100%/100%

No Child Left Behind

AYP, 2006-07	Needs Improvement

Additional Public School District Data
(for school year 2007-08 except where noted)

North Hunterdon/Voorhees Regional High School District
1445 State Route 31
Annandale, NJ 08801
Hunterdon County
(908)735-2846
http://www.nhvweb.net

Superintendent	Charles M. Shaddow
Number of schools	2
Grade plan	9-12
Enrollment	2,957
Attendance rate, '06-07	98.7%
Dropout rate	1.0%
Students per teacher	10.5
Per pupil expenditure	$17,407
Median faculty salary	$58,015
Median administrator salary	$112,200
Grade 12 enrollment	701
High school graduation rate	96.8%

Assessment test results
(percent scoring at proficient or advanced level)

	Language	Math
NJASK-Gr 3	NA	NA
NJASK-Gr 8	NA	NA
HSPA-High Schl	94.9%	91.9%

SAT score averages, 2006-07

Pct tested	Math	Verbal	Writing
NA	NA	NA	NA

Teacher Qualifications

Avg years of experience	10
Highly-qualified teachers one subject/all subjects	100%/100%

No Child Left Behind

AYP, 2006-07 . . . . Meets Standards

North Warren Regional School District
10 Noe Rd, PO Box 410
Blairstown, NJ 07825
Warren County
(908)362-9342
http://www.northwarren.org

Superintendent	Brian Fogelson
Number of schools	1
Grade plan	7-12
Enrollment	1,102
Attendance rate, '06-07	93.0%
Dropout rate	4.3%
Students per teacher	11.1
Per pupil expenditure	$13,589
Median faculty salary	$49,745
Median administrator salary	$107,150
Grade 12 enrollment	174
High school graduation rate	95.1%

Assessment test results
(percent scoring at proficient or advanced level)

	Language	Math
NJASK-Gr 3	NA	NA
NJASK-Gr 8	81.4%	72.3%
HSPA-High Schl	93.1%	80.3%

SAT score averages, 2006-07

Pct tested	Math	Verbal	Writing
77%	491	493	478

Teacher Qualifications

Avg years of experience	9
Highly-qualified teachers one subject/all subjects	100%/98.5%

No Child Left Behind

AYP, 2006-07 . . . . Meets Standards

Northern Burlington County Regional High School District
160 Mansfield Road, East
Columbus, NJ 08022
Burlington County
(609)298-3900
http://www.nburlington.com

Superintendent	James Sarruda
Number of schools	2
Grade plan	7-12
Enrollment	1,821
Attendance rate, '06-07	94.3%
Dropout rate	0.3%
Students per teacher	10.0
Per pupil expenditure	$15,199
Median faculty salary	$53,887
Median administrator salary	$94,581
Grade 12 enrollment	308
High school graduation rate	96.5%

Assessment test results
(percent scoring at proficient or advanced level)

	Language	Math
NJASK-Gr 3	NA	NA
NJASK-Gr 8	91.0%	78.0%
HSPA-High Schl	88.5%	78.5%

SAT score averages, 2006-07

Pct tested	Math	Verbal	Writing
80%	509	503	505

Teacher Qualifications

Avg years of experience	8
Highly-qualified teachers one subject/all subjects	99.0%/99.0%

No Child Left Behind

AYP, 2006-07 . . . . Meets Standards

Northern Highlands Regional High School
298 Hillside Avenue
Allendale, NJ 07401
Bergen County
(201)327-8700
http://www.northernhighlands.org

Superintendent	Robert McGuire
Number of schools	1
Grade plan	9-12
Enrollment	1,274
Attendance rate, '06-07	95.3%
Dropout rate	1.3%
Students per teacher	10.1
Per pupil expenditure	$16,705
Median faculty salary	$66,692
Median administrator salary	$126,230
Grade 12 enrollment	315
High school graduation rate	99.0%

Assessment test results
(percent scoring at proficient or advanced level)

	Language	Math
NJASK-Gr 3	NA	NA
NJASK-Gr 8	NA	NA
HSPA-High Schl	97.0%	94.8%

SAT score averages, 2006-07

Pct tested	Math	Verbal	Writing
NA	578	556	572

Teacher Qualifications

Avg years of experience	10
Highly-qualified teachers one subject/all subjects	100%/100%

No Child Left Behind

AYP, 2006-07 . . . . Meets Standards

Northern Valley Regional High School District
162 Knickerbocker Rd.
Demarest, NJ 07627
Bergen County
(201)768-2200
http://www.nvnet.org

Superintendent	Jan Furman
Number of schools	2
Grade plan	9-12
Enrollment	2,526
Attendance rate, '06-07	95.8%
Dropout rate	0.4%
Students per teacher	8.9
Per pupil expenditure	$15,477
Median faculty salary	$76,653
Median administrator salary	$139,860
Grade 12 enrollment	648
High school graduation rate	100.0%

Assessment test results
(percent scoring at proficient or advanced level)

	Language	Math
NJASK-Gr 3	NA	NA
NJASK-Gr 8	NA	NA
HSPA-High Schl	96.8%	94.8%

SAT score averages, 2006-07

Pct tested	Math	Verbal	Writing
NA	NA	NA	NA

Teacher Qualifications

Avg years of experience	9
Highly-qualified teachers one subject/all subjects	100%/99.5%

No Child Left Behind

AYP, 2006-07 . . . . Needs Improvement

Pascack Valley Regional High School District
46 Akers Avenue
Montvale, NJ 07645
Bergen County
(201)358-7005
http://www.pascack.k12.nj.us

Superintendent	Benedict Tantillo
Number of schools	2
Grade plan	9-12
Enrollment	1,900
Attendance rate, '06-07	94.6%
Dropout rate	1.3%
Students per teacher	10.8
Per pupil expenditure	$19,498
Median faculty salary	$76,570
Median administrator salary	$133,744
Grade 12 enrollment	445
High school graduation rate	99.5%

Assessment test results
(percent scoring at proficient or advanced level)

	Language	Math
NJASK-Gr 3	NA	NA
NJASK-Gr 8	NA	NA
HSPA-High Schl	95.4%	91.0%

SAT score averages, 2006-07

Pct tested	Math	Verbal	Writing
NA	NA	NA	NA

Teacher Qualifications

Avg years of experience	8
Highly-qualified teachers one subject/all subjects	100%/100%

No Child Left Behind

AYP, 2006-07 . . . . Meets Standards

Additional Public School District Data
(for school year 2007-08 except where noted)

Passaic County Manchester Regional High School
70 Church Street
Haledon, NJ 07508
Passaic County
(973)389-2820
http://www.mrhs.net

Chief School Admin . . . . . .Raymond Kwak
Number of schools. 1
Grade plan. 9-12
Enrollment 775
Attendance rate, '06-07 . . . . 99.2%
Dropout rate 1.9%
Students per teacher 11.0
Per pupil expenditure $17,908
Median faculty salary. $55,370
Median administrator salary. $105,738
Grade 12 enrollment. 190
High school graduation rate 85.6%

Assessment test results
(percent scoring at proficient or advanced level)

	Language	Math
NJASK-Gr 3	NA	NA
NJASK-Gr 8	NA	NA
HSPA-High Schl	80.6%	75.0%

SAT score averages, 2006-07

Pct tested	Math	Verbal	Writing
52%	461	445	441

Teacher Qualifications
Avg years of experience 7
Highly-qualified teachers
    one subject/all subjects. 100%/100%

No Child Left Behind
AYP, 2006-07 . . . . .Meets Standards

Passaic Valley Regional High School District
East Main Street
Little Falls, NJ 07424
Passaic County
(973)890-2560
http://www.pvhs.k12.nj.us

Chief School Admin . . . . . .Viktor Joganow
Number of schools. 1
Grade plan. 9-12
Enrollment 1,304
Attendance rate, '06-07 . . . . .93.7%
Dropout rate 2.5%
Students per teacher 12.0
Per pupil expenditure $14,485
Median faculty salary. $57,456
Median administrator salary. $103,823
Grade 12 enrollment. 337
High school graduation rate 96.6%

Assessment test results
(percent scoring at proficient or advanced level)

	Language	Math
NJASK-Gr 3	NA	NA
NJASK-Gr 8	NA	NA
HSPA-High Schl	87.2%	78.2%

SAT score averages, 2006-07

Pct tested	Math	Verbal	Writing
78%	494	469	477

Teacher Qualifications
Avg years of experience 9
Highly-qualified teachers
    one subject/all subjects. 100%/100%

No Child Left Behind
AYP, 2006-07 . . . . .Meets Standards

Pinelands Regional School District
520 Nugentown Road, PO Box 248
Tuckerton, NJ 08087
Ocean County
(609)296-3106
http://www.pinelandsregional.org

Superintendent. . . . . Detlef Kern
Number of schools. 2
Grade plan. 7-12
Enrollment 1,820
Attendance rate, '06-07 . . . . .91.2%
Dropout rate 0.6%
Students per teacher 8.7
Per pupil expenditure $14,698
Median faculty salary. $46,200
Median administrator salary. $99,443
Grade 12 enrollment. 261
High school graduation rate 86.7%

Assessment test results
(percent scoring at proficient or advanced level)

	Language	Math
NJASK-Gr 3	NA	NA
NJASK-Gr 8	78.5%	59.5%
HSPA-High Schl	75.2%	76.1%

SAT score averages, 2006-07

Pct tested	Math	Verbal	Writing
54%	495	489	464

Teacher Qualifications
Avg years of experience 8
Highly-qualified teachers
    one subject/all subjects. 100%/99.5%

No Child Left Behind
AYP, 2006-07 . . . . .Meets Standards

Ramapo Indian Hills Regional High School District
131 Yawpo Avenue
Oakland, NJ 07436
Bergen County
(201)416-8100
http://www.rih.org

Superintendent. . . . . Paul Saxton
Number of schools. 2
Grade plan. 9-12
Enrollment 2,327
Attendance rate, '06-07 . . . . 94.5%
Dropout rate 2.3%
Students per teacher 11.3
Per pupil expenditure $17,748
Median faculty salary. $56,936
Median administrator salary. $120,273
Grade 12 enrollment. 531
High school graduation rate 98.9%

Assessment test results
(percent scoring at proficient or advanced level)

	Language	Math
NJASK-Gr 3	NA	NA
NJASK-Gr 8	NA	NA
HSPA-High Schl	95.4%	90.2%

SAT score averages, 2006-07

Pct tested	Math	Verbal	Writing
NA	NA	NA	NA

Teacher Qualifications
Avg years of experience 7
Highly-qualified teachers
    one subject/all subjects. 100%/100%

No Child Left Behind
AYP, 2006-07 . . . . .Meets Standards

Rancocas Valley Regional High School
520 Jacksonville Road
Mount Holly, NJ 08060
Burlington County
(609)267-0830
http://www.rancocasvalley.k12.nj.us

Superintendent. . . . . . . .Michael Moskalski
Number of schools. 2
Grade plan. 9-12
Enrollment 2,341
Attendance rate, '06-07 . . . . 94.2%
Dropout rate 0.1%
Students per teacher 15.1
Per pupil expenditure $12,614
Median faculty salary. $52,050
Median administrator salary. $89,643
Grade 12 enrollment. 549
High school graduation rate 96.1%

Assessment test results
(percent scoring at proficient or advanced level)

	Language	Math
NJASK-Gr 3	NA	NA
NJASK-Gr 8	NA	NA
HSPA-High Schl	81.9%	74.0%

SAT score averages, 2006-07

Pct tested	Math	Verbal	Writing
73%	492	487	475

Teacher Qualifications
Avg years of experience 7
Highly-qualified teachers
    one subject/all subjects. 100%/100%

No Child Left Behind
AYP, 2006-07 . . . . .Needs Improvement

Red Bank Regional High School District
101 Ridge Road
Little Silver, NJ 07739
Monmouth County
(732)842-8000
http://www.redbankregional.k12.nj.us

Superintendent. . . . . . Edward D. Westervelt
Number of schools. 1
Grade plan. 9-12
Enrollment 1,116
Attendance rate, '06-07 . . . . 94.2%
Dropout rate 2.8%
Students per teacher 9.0
Per pupil expenditure $19,630
Median faculty salary. $56,050
Median administrator salary. $99,400
Grade 12 enrollment. 257
High school graduation rate 98.5%

Assessment test results
(percent scoring at proficient or advanced level)

	Language	Math
NJASK-Gr 3	NA	NA
NJASK-Gr 8	NA	NA
HSPA-High Schl	84.9%	80.4%

SAT score averages, 2006-07

Pct tested	Math	Verbal	Writing
80%	498	500	504

Teacher Qualifications
Avg years of experience 9
Highly-qualified teachers
    one subject/all subjects. 100%/100%

No Child Left Behind
AYP, 2006-07 . . . . .Needs Improvement

Additional Public School District Data
(for school year 2007-08 except where noted)

River Dell Regional High School District
230 Woodland Avenue
River Edge, NJ 07661
Bergen County
(201)599-7206
http://www.riverdell.k12.nj.us
Superintendent. . . . . .Patrick Fletcher
Number of schools. 2
Grade plan. 7-12
Enrollment 1,526
Attendance rate, '06-07 . . . . .95.4%
Dropout rate. 0.3%
Students per teacher 11.2
Per pupil expenditure. $15,714
Median faculty salary. $67,445
Median administrator salary. $125,050
Grade 12 enrollment. 252
High school graduation rate 98.0%

Assessment test results
(percent scoring at proficient or advanced level)

	Language	Math
NJASK-Gr 3	NA	NA
NJASK-Gr 8	93.2%	85.7%
HSPA-High Schl	92.5%	88.8%

SAT score averages, 2006-07

Pct tested	Math	Verbal	Writing
97%	556	529	525

Teacher Qualifications
Avg years of experience 9
Highly-qualified teachers
   one subject/all subjects. 99.0%/99.0%

No Child Left Behind
AYP, 2006-07 . . . . .Meets Standards

Rumson-Fair Haven Regional High School District
74 Ridge Road
Rumson, NJ 07760
Monmouth County
(732)842-1597
http://www.rfh.k12.nj.us
Superintendent. . . . . .Peter Righi
Number of schools. 1
Grade plan. 9-12
Enrollment .991
Attendance rate, '06-07 . . . . 94.6%
Dropout rate. 0.7%
Students per teacher 11.1
Per pupil expenditure. $15,168
Median faculty salary. $59,840
Median administrator salary. $103,926
Grade 12 enrollment. 254
High school graduation rate 97.6%

Assessment test results
(percent scoring at proficient or advanced level)

	Language	Math
NJASK-Gr 3	NA	NA
NJASK-Gr 8	NA	NA
HSPA-High Schl	96.8%	93.8%

SAT score averages, 2006-07

Pct tested	Math	Verbal	Writing
NA	553	543	545

Teacher Qualifications
Avg years of experience 7
Highly-qualified teachers
   one subject/all subjects. 100%/100%

No Child Left Behind
AYP, 2006-07 . . . . .Meets Standards

Shore Regional High School District
Monmouth Park Highway
West Long Branch, NJ 07764
Monmouth County
(732)222-9300
http://shoreregional.org
Superintendent. . . . . Leonard G. Schnappauf
Number of schools. 1
Grade plan. 9-12
Enrollment .720
Attendance rate, '06-07 . . . . 94.8%
Dropout rate. 0.3%
Students per teacher 11.9
Per pupil expenditure. $17,168
Median faculty salary. $61,625
Median administrator salary. $110,220
Grade 12 enrollment. 173
High school graduation rate 99.4%

Assessment test results
(percent scoring at proficient or advanced level)

	Language	Math
NJASK-Gr 3	NA	NA
NJASK-Gr 8	NA	NA
HSPA-High Schl	90.1%	83.8%

SAT score averages, 2006-07

Pct tested	Math	Verbal	Writing
96%	506	499	505

Teacher Qualifications
Avg years of experience 11
Highly-qualified teachers
   one subject/all subjects. 100%/100%

No Child Left Behind
AYP, 2006-07 . . . . .Meets Standards

South Hunterdon Regional High School
301 Mt. Airy-Harbourton Road
Lambertville, NJ 08530
Hunterdon County
(609)397-2060
http://www.shrhs.org
Superintendent. . . . . Nancy Gartenberg
Number of schools. 1
Grade plan. 7-12
Enrollment .345
Attendance rate, '06-07 . . . . 98.8%
Dropout rate. 0.8%
Students per teacher 6.6
Per pupil expenditure. $24,196
Median faculty salary. $58,253
Median administrator salary. $93,600
Grade 12 enrollment. 48
High school graduation rate 92.3%

Assessment test results
(percent scoring at proficient or advanced level)

	Language	Math
NJASK-Gr 3	NA	NA
NJASK-Gr 8	88.5%	69.3%
HSPA-High Schl	88.6%	79.3%

SAT score averages, 2006-07

Pct tested	Math	Verbal	Writing
84%	517	519	518

Teacher Qualifications
Avg years of experience 9
Highly-qualified teachers
   one subject/all subjects. 100%/100%

No Child Left Behind
AYP, 2006-07 . . . . .Meets Standards

Delsea Regional High School District
PO Box 405, Fries Mill Road
Franklinville, NJ 08322
Gloucester County
(856)694-0100
http://www.delsea.k12.nj.us
Superintendent. . . . . Frank Borelli
Number of schools. 2
Grade plan. 7-12
Enrollment 1,783
Attendance rate, '06-07 . . . . 93.8%
Dropout rate. 1.0%
Students per teacher 11.4
Per pupil expenditure. $13,888
Median faculty salary. $51,720
Median administrator salary. $97,232
Grade 12 enrollment. 275
High school graduation rate 91.4%

Assessment test results
(percent scoring at proficient or advanced level)

	Language	Math
NJASK-Gr 3	NA	NA
NJASK-Gr 8	82.9%	71.1%
HSPA-High Schl	89.3%	83.5%

SAT score averages, 2006-07

Pct tested	Math	Verbal	Writing
68%	502	475	477

Teacher Qualifications
Avg years of experience 11
Highly-qualified teachers
   one subject/all subjects. 100%/100%

No Child Left Behind
AYP, 2006-07 . . . . .Meets Standards

Southern Regional School District
105 Cedar Bridge Road
Manahawkin, NJ 08050
Ocean County
(609)597-9481
http://www.srsd.org
Superintendent. . . . . .Craig Henry
Number of schools. 2
Grade plan. 7-12
Enrollment 3,038
Attendance rate, '06-07 . . . . 94.2%
Dropout rate. 1.5%
Students per teacher 11.5
Per pupil expenditure. $15,553
Median faculty salary. $59,718
Median administrator salary. $116,671
Grade 12 enrollment. 443
High school graduation rate 93.6%

Assessment test results
(percent scoring at proficient or advanced level)

	Language	Math
NJASK-Gr 3	NA	NA
NJASK-Gr 8	84.7%	73.5%
HSPA-High Schl	90.0%	84.5%

SAT score averages, 2006-07

Pct tested	Math	Verbal	Writing
71%	502	483	479

Teacher Qualifications
Avg years of experience 13
Highly-qualified teachers
   one subject/all subjects. 100%/100%

No Child Left Behind
AYP, 2006-07 . . . . .Meets Standards

Additional Public School District Data
(for school year 2007-08 except where noted)

Sterling High School District
501 South Warwick Road
Somerdale, NJ 08083
Camden County
(856)784-1287
http://www.sterling.k12.nj.us

Superintendent..........Jack L. McCulley
Number of schools.......................1
Grade plan..........................9-12
Enrollment.......................1,047
Attendance rate, '06-07............97.1%
Dropout rate.........................1.6%
Students per teacher.............11.6
Per pupil expenditure............$14,160
Median faculty salary............$53,900
Median administrator salary......$85,000
Grade 12 enrollment.................242
High school graduation rate........93.3%

Assessment test results
(percent scoring at proficient or advanced level)

	Language	Math
NJASK-Gr 3	NA	NA
NJASK-Gr 8	NA	NA
HSPA-High Schl	88.6%	71.6%

SAT score averages, 2006-07

Pct tested	Math	Verbal	Writing
73%	496	487	486

Teacher Qualifications
Avg years of experience.................8
Highly-qualified teachers
  one subject/all subjects..... 98.5%/97.0%

No Child Left Behind
AYP, 2006-07...........Meets Standards

Wallkill Valley Regional High School
10 Grumm Road
Hamburg, NJ 07419
Sussex County
(973)827-4100
http://wallkill.k12.nj.us

Superintendent........ Joseph DiPasquale
Number of schools.......................1
Grade plan..........................9-12
Enrollment........................867
Attendance rate, '06-07........... 95.0%
Dropout rate.........................3.5%
Students per teacher.................12.1
Per pupil expenditure............$15,632
Median faculty salary............$78,190
Median administrator salary......$111,710
Grade 12 enrollment.................196
High school graduation rate........90.8%

Assessment test results
(percent scoring at proficient or advanced level)

	Language	Math
NJASK-Gr 3	NA	NA
NJASK-Gr 8	NA	NA
HSPA-High Schl	89.4%	80.1%

SAT score averages, 2006-07

Pct tested	Math	Verbal	Writing
67%	516	504	498

Teacher Qualifications
Avg years of experience...............12
Highly-qualified teachers
  one subject/all subjects...... 100%/100%

No Child Left Behind
AYP, 2006-07...........Meets Standards

Warren Hills Regional School District
89 Bowerstown Road
Washington, NJ 07882
Warren County
(908)689-3143
http://www.warrenhills.org

Superintendent............Peter Merluzzi
Number of schools.......................2
Grade plan..........................7-12
Enrollment.......................2,039
Attendance rate, '06-07............93.3%
Dropout rate.........................3.7%
Students per teacher.................11.3
Per pupil expenditure............$14,351
Median faculty salary............$56,023
Median administrator salary......$107,850
Grade 12 enrollment.................293
High school graduation rate........87.4%

Assessment test results
(percent scoring at proficient or advanced level)

	Language	Math
NJASK-Gr 3	NA	NA
NJASK-Gr 8	84.2%	62.1%
HSPA-High Schl	83.5%	81.4%

SAT score averages, 2006-07

Pct tested	Math	Verbal	Writing
72%	511	504	493

Teacher Qualifications
Avg years of experience...............11
Highly-qualified teachers
  one subject/all subjects..... 99.0%/99.0%

No Child Left Behind
AYP, 2006-07........Needs Improvement

Watchung Hills Regional High School
108 Stirling Rd
Warren, NJ 07059
Somerset County
(908)647-4800
http://www.whrhs.org

Superintendent..... Frances C. Stromsland
Number of schools.......................1
Grade plan..........................9-12
Enrollment.......................2,061
Attendance rate, '06-07............93.6%
Dropout rate.........................0.3%
Students per teacher.................10.7
Per pupil expenditure............$14,661
Median faculty salary............$61,370
Median administrator salary......$112,057
Grade 12 enrollment.................472
High school graduation rate........99.6%

Assessment test results
(percent scoring at proficient or advanced level)

	Language	Math
NJASK-Gr 3	NA	NA
NJASK-Gr 8	NA	NA
HSPA-High Schl	95.2%	91.4%

SAT score averages, 2006-07

Pct tested	Math	Verbal	Writing
98%	551	536	534

Teacher Qualifications
Avg years of experience.................8
Highly-qualified teachers
  one subject/all subjects..... 99.0%/99.0%

No Child Left Behind
AYP, 2006-07...........Meets Standards

West Essex Regional School District
West Greenbrook Road
North Caldwell, NJ 07006
Essex County
(973)228-1200
http://www.westex.org

Superintendent......... Janice Dime (Int)
Number of schools.......................2
Grade plan..........................7-12
Enrollment.......................1,573
Attendance rate, '06-07............95.7%
Dropout rate.........................0.5%
Students per teacher.................9.9
Per pupil expenditure............$17,341
Median faculty salary............$65,694
Median administrator salary......$97,000
Grade 12 enrollment.................256
High school graduation rate........98.9%

Assessment test results
(percent scoring at proficient or advanced level)

	Language	Math
NJASK-Gr 3	NA	NA
NJASK-Gr 8	94.6%	80.6%
HSPA-High Schl	92.4%	84.6%

SAT score averages, 2006-07

Pct tested	Math	Verbal	Writing
89%	554	516	532

Teacher Qualifications
Avg years of experience.................8
Highly-qualified teachers
  one subject/all subjects...... 100%/100%

No Child Left Behind
AYP, 2006-07...........Meets Standards

West Morris Regional High School District
10 South Four Bridges Road
Chester, NJ 07930
Morris County
(908)879-6404
http://www.wmchs.org

Superintendent.........Anthony diBattista
Number of schools.......................2
Grade plan..........................9-12
Enrollment.......................2,621
Attendance rate, '06-07............95.5%
Dropout rate.........................0.4%
Students per teacher.................10.9
Per pupil expenditure............$16,870
Median faculty salary............$64,530
Median administrator salary......$130,800
Grade 12 enrollment.................623
High school graduation rate........98.3%

Assessment test results
(percent scoring at proficient or advanced level)

	Language	Math
NJASK-Gr 3	NA	NA
NJASK-Gr 8	NA	NA
HSPA-High Schl	96.6%	93.6%

SAT score averages, 2006-07

Pct tested	Math	Verbal	Writing
NA	NA	NA	NA

Teacher Qualifications
Avg years of experience...............10
Highly-qualified teachers
  one subject/all subjects...... 100%/99.5%

No Child Left Behind
AYP, 2006-07...........Meets Standards

Population 2008

1.	Bergen County	894,840
2.	Middlesex County	789,102
3.	Essex County	770,675
4.	Monmouth County	642,448
5.	Hudson County	595,419
6.	Ocean County	569,111
7.	Union County	523,249
8.	Camden County	517,234
9.	Passaic County	490,948
10.	Morris County	487,548
11.	Burlington County	445,475
12.	Mercer County	364,883
13.	Somerset County	324,563
14.	Gloucester County	287,860
15.	Atlantic County	270,681
16.	Cumberland County	156,830
17.	Sussex County	150,909
18.	Hunterdon County	129,031
19.	Warren County	109,876
20.	Cape May County	95,838
21.	Salem County	66,141

(estimate)

Land Area

1.	Burlington County	804.6
2.	Ocean County	636.3
3.	Atlantic County	561.1
4.	Sussex County	521.3
5.	Cumberland County	489.3
6.	Monmouth County	471.9
7.	Morris County	469.0
8.	Hunterdon County	429.9
9.	Warren County	357.9
10.	Salem County	337.9
11.	Gloucester County	324.7
12.	Middlesex County	309.7
13.	Somerset County	304.7
14.	Cape May County	255.2
15.	Bergen County	234.2
16.	Mercer County	225.9
17.	Camden County	222.3
18.	Passaic County	185.3
19.	Essex County	126.3
20.	Union County	103.3
21.	Hudson County	46.7

(square miles)

Unemployment Rate 2007

1.	Cape May County	6.5%
2.	Cumberland County	6.5
3.	Atlantic County	5.8
4.	Essex County	5.3
5.	Passaic County	5.3
6.	Hudson County	5.0
7.	Salem County	4.9
8.	Camden County	4.7
9.	Ocean County	4.5
10.	Union County	4.5
11.	Gloucester County	4.3
12.	Sussex County	3.9
13.	Burlington County	3.8
14.	Mercer County	3.8
15.	Middlesex County	3.8
16.	Monmouth County	3.7
17.	Warren County	3.7
18.	Bergen County	3.4
19.	Somerset County	3.1
20.	Morris County	3.0
21.	Hunterdon County	2.9

Income per capita 2007

1.	Hunterdon County	$50,043
2.	Somerset County	47,646
3.	Morris County	45,516
4.	Bergen County	41,472
5.	Monmouth County	39,602
6.	Mercer County	34,892
7.	Sussex County	34,296
8.	Burlington County	34,020
9.	Middlesex County	32,019
10.	Cape May County	31,899
11.	Union County	31,715
12.	Essex County	31,260
13.	Warren County	30,436
14.	Hudson County	29,940
15.	Gloucester County	29,735
16.	Ocean County	29,105
17.	Camden County	27,257
18.	Salem County	26,979
19.	Atlantic County	26,743
20.	Passaic County	24,888
21.	Cumberland County	21,317

Median Home Value 2007

1.	Morris County	$504,500
2.	Bergen County	492,200
3.	Hunterdon County	472,800
4.	Somerset County	469,600
5.	Monmouth County	445,000
6.	Essex County	422,800
7.	Union County	422,700
8.	Hudson County	419,400
9.	Passaic County	398,800
10.	Middlesex County	370,700
11.	Sussex County	341,300
12.	Cape May County	340,000
13.	Mercer County	322,400
14.	Warren County	320,900
15.	Ocean County	310,100
16.	Burlington County	276,600
17.	Atlantic County	271,900
18.	Gloucester County	235,300
19.	Camden County	223,400
20.	Salem County	188,800
21.	Cumberland County	173,600

(specified owner-occupied homes)

Crime Rate 2007

1.	Cape May County	53.3
2.	Cumberland County	46.5
3.	Atlantic County	41.5
4.	Camden County	38.8
5.	Essex County	38.6
6.	Hudson County	30.6
7.	Union County	29.4
8.	Passaic County	28.9
9.	Salem County	27.4
10.	Gloucester County	27.1
11.	Mercer County	25.5
12.	Middlesex County	21.6
13.	Monmouth County	21.4
14.	Ocean County	20.5
15.	Burlington County	18.6
16.	Warren County	15.3
17.	Somerset County	14.8
18.	Bergen County	14.6
19.	Morris County	13.1
20.	Sussex County	10.7
21.	Hunterdon County	9.0

(rate per 1,000 residents)

Population, 2007 (estimate)

	Municipality	County	Population		Municipality	County	Population
1.	Newark City	Essex	280,135	61.	Ewing Township	Mercer	36,536
2.	Jersey City	Hudson	242,389	62.	Fort Lee Borough	Bergen	36,521
3.	Paterson City	Passaic	146,545	63.	Monroe Township	Middlesex	36,397
4.	Elizabeth City	Union	124,862	64.	Galloway Township	Atlantic	36,105
5.	Edison Township	Middlesex	99,884	65.	Pennsauken Township	Camden	35,116
6.	Woodbridge Township	Middlesex	98,450	66.	Freehold Township	Monmouth	34,875
7.	Toms River Township	Ocean	95,148	67.	Belleville Township	Essex	34,044
8.	Hamilton Township	Mercer	90,365	68.	Monroe Township	Gloucester	32,607
9.	Trenton City	Mercer	82,804	69.	Long Branch City	Monmouth	32,349
10.	Camden City	Camden	78,675	70.	Lawrence Township	Mercer	31,863
11.	Clifton City	Passaic	78,573	71.	Orange City Township	Essex	31,290
12.	Brick Township	Ocean	78,286	72.	Fair Lawn Borough	Bergen	30,783
13.	Cherry Hill Township	Camden	71,095	73.	Deptford Township	Gloucester	30,529
14.	Lakewood Township	Ocean	69,937	74.	Westfield Town	Union	29,556
15.	Passaic City	Passaic	67,103	75.	Voorhees Township	Camden	29,258
16.	Middletown Township	Monmouth	66,538	76.	Garfield City	Bergen	29,206
17.	Old Bridge Township	Middlesex	66,044	77.	Millville City	Cumberland	28,459
18.	East Orange City	Essex	65,952	78.	Neptune Township	Monmouth	28,394
19.	Gloucester Township	Camden	65,016	79.	Ocean Township	Monmouth	28,260
20.	Union City	Hudson	62,715	80.	Rahway City	Union	28,189
21.	Franklin Township	Somerset	59,185	81.	Pemberton Township	Burlington	28,158
22.	Vineland City	Cumberland	58,505	82.	Englewood City	Bergen	28,009
23.	Bayonne City	Hudson	57,886	83.	Livingston Township	Essex	27,990
24.	Irvington Township	Essex	56,920	84.	West Milford Township	Passaic	27,839
25.	North Bergen Township	Hudson	56,146	85.	East Windsor Township	Mercer	26,686
26.	Wayne Township	Passaic	54,180	86.	Bernards Township	Somerset	26,590
27.	Union Township	Union	54,062	87.	West Windsor Township	Mercer	26,447
28.	Jackson Township	Ocean	52,577	88.	Nutley Township	Essex	26,415
29.	Piscataway Township	Middlesex	52,565	89.	Lacey Township	Ocean	26,322
30.	Washington Township	Gloucester	51,995	90.	Stafford Township	Ocean	26,282
31.	Howell Township	Monmouth	51,353	91.	Paramus Borough	Bergen	26,278
32.	Parsippany-Troy Hills Township	Morris	51,144	92.	Wall Township	Monmouth	26,274
33.	New Brunswick City	Middlesex	50,534	93.	Mount Olive Township	Morris	25,934
34.	Perth Amboy City	Middlesex	48,868	94.	Bergenfield Borough	Bergen	25,826
35.	East Brunswick Township	Middlesex	47,430	95.	Rockaway Township	Morris	25,411
36.	Plainfield City	Union	46,486	96.	Randolph Township	Morris	25,346
37.	West New York Town	Hudson	46,425	97.	Vernon Township	Sussex	25,011
38.	Evesham Township	Burlington	45,619	98.	Bridgeton City	Cumberland	24,575
39.	Bridgewater Township	Somerset	44,408	99.	Hamilton Township	Atlantic	24,553
40.	Bloomfield Township	Essex	44,398	100.	Ridgewood Village	Bergen	24,339
41.	Hackensack City	Bergen	43,062	101.	Mahwah Township	Bergen	24,302
42.	West Orange Township	Essex	42,906	102.	Lodi Borough	Bergen	23,972
43.	Berkeley Township	Ocean	42,664	103.	Roxbury Township	Morris	23,360
44.	Sayreville Borough	Middlesex	42,351	104.	Montgomery Township	Somerset	23,023
45.	Manchester Township	Ocean	41,713	105.	Scotch Plains Township	Union	22,979
46.	South Brunswick Township	Middlesex	40,755	106.	Medford Township	Burlington	22,838
47.	Marlboro Township	Monmouth	40,633	107.	Cliffside Park Borough	Bergen	22,830
48.	Hoboken City	Hudson	40,551	108.	Carteret Borough	Middlesex	22,725
49.	Atlantic City	Atlantic	39,684	109.	South Plainfield Borough	Middlesex	22,696
50.	North Brunswick Township	Middlesex	39,676	110.	Raritan Township	Hunterdon	22,471
51.	Egg Harbor Township	Atlantic	39,493	111.	Maplewood Township	Essex	22,254
52.	Mount Laurel Township	Burlington	39,409	112.	West Deptford Township	Gloucester	22,007
53.	Linden City	Union	39,372	113.	Cranford Township	Union	22,003
54.	Winslow Township	Camden	39,173	114.	Barnegat Township	Ocean	21,867
55.	Teaneck Township	Bergen	39,019	115.	Jefferson Township	Morris	21,737
56.	Hillsborough Township	Somerset	38,597	116.	Burlington Township	Burlington	21,359
57.	Manalapan Township	Monmouth	38,591	117.	Hillside Township	Union	21,320
58.	Kearny Town	Hudson	37,295	118.	North Plainfield Borough	Somerset	21,239
59.	Montclair Township	Essex	37,052	119.	Plainsboro Township	Middlesex	21,196
60.	Willingboro Township	Burlington	36,865	120.	Montville Township	Morris	21,150

Population, 2007 (estimate)

Municipality	County	Population	Municipality	County	Population
121. Morris Township	Morris	21,103	181. Hanover Township	Morris	13,653
122. Hazlet Township	Monmouth	21,046	182. Saddle Brook Township	Bergen	13,594
123. Roselle Borough	Union	20,747	183. Fairview Borough	Bergen	13,540
124. Summit City	Union	20,700	184. Princeton Borough	Mercer	13,517
125. Little Egg Harbor Township	Ocean	20,517	185. Hammonton Town	Atlantic	13,500
126. Lower Township	Cape May	20,346	186. Oakland Borough	Bergen	13,400
127. Point Pleasant Borough	Ocean	19,961	187. Berkeley Heights Township	Union	13,396
128. Moorestown Township	Burlington	19,624	188. Pennsville Township	Salem	13,363
129. Glassboro Borough	Gloucester	19,588	189. Metuchen Borough	Middlesex	13,144
130. Lyndhurst Township	Bergen	19,468	190. Roselle Park Borough	Union	12,879
131. Palisades Park Borough	Bergen	19,352	191. Brigantine City	Atlantic	12,739
132. Sparta Township	Sussex	19,198	192. Ringwood Borough	Passaic	12,704
133. Maple Shade Township	Burlington	19,195	193. Cedar Grove Township	Essex	12,698
134. Tinton Falls Borough	Monmouth	19,158	194. Somerville Borough	Somerset	12,682
135. Morristown Town	Morris	19,122	195. Verona Township	Essex	12,651
136. Pleasantville City	Atlantic	18,814	196. Ridgefield Park Village	Bergen	12,483
137. Elmwood Park Borough	Bergen	18,765	197. Weehawken Township	Hudson	12,441
138. Millburn Township	Essex	18,755	198. Florham Park Borough	Morris	12,404
139. Aberdeen Township	Monmouth	18,478	199. Ventnor City	Atlantic	12,316
140. Washington Township	Morris	18,469	200. Harrison Township	Gloucester	12,241
141. Hawthorne Borough	Passaic	18,106	201. Lumberton Township	Burlington	12,099
142. Dover Town	Morris	17,997	202. Robbinsville Township	Mercer	11,979
143. Hopewell Township	Mercer	17,823	203. Red Bank Borough	Monmouth	11,890
144. Rutherford Borough	Bergen	17,620	204. New Providence Borough	Union	11,847
145. Princeton Township	Mercer	17,490	205. Little Falls Township	Passaic	11,694
146. Lindenwold Borough	Camden	17,176	206. Wanaque Borough	Passaic	11,649
147. Franklin Township	Gloucester	17,143	207. Franklin Lakes Borough	Bergen	11,576
148. Dumont Borough	Bergen	17,105	208. West Paterson Borough	Passaic	11,568
149. Wyckoff Township	Bergen	16,980	209. Wantage Township	Sussex	11,532
150. Delran Township	Burlington	16,929	210. Hasbrouck Heights Borough	Bergen	11,492
151. Holmdel Township	Monmouth	16,919	211. Freehold Borough	Monmouth	11,465
152. Pequannock Township	Morris	16,769	212. Florence Township	Burlington	11,440
153. Asbury Park City	Monmouth	16,577	213. East Hanover Township	Morris	11,427
154. Denville Township	Morris	16,528	214. Somers Point City	Atlantic	11,420
155. Middle Township	Cape May	16,174	215. Haddonfield Borough	Camden	11,411
156. South Orange Village Township	Essex	16,061	216. Gloucester City	Camden	11,377
157. New Milford Borough	Bergen	16,052	217. Wallington Borough	Bergen	11,349
158. Readington Township	Hunterdon	16,052	218. Glen Rock Borough	Bergen	11,232
159. Madison Borough	Morris	16,046	219. Pine Hill Borough	Camden	11,231
160. Warren Township	Somerset	15,895	220. Bellmawr Borough	Camden	11,117
161. South River Borough	Middlesex	15,738	221. Upper Township	Cape May	11,110
162. Hopatcong Borough	Sussex	15,592	222. Pompton Lakes Borough	Passaic	11,095
163. Secaucus Town	Hudson	15,385	223. Ridgefield Borough	Bergen	10,894
164. Cinnaminson Township	Burlington	15,240	224. Southampton Township	Burlington	10,885
165. Mantua Township	Gloucester	15,201	225. Manville Borough	Somerset	10,839
166. Branchburg Township	Somerset	15,002	226. Beachwood Borough	Ocean	10,789
167. Ocean City	Cape May	14,923	227. Westwood Borough	Bergen	10,780
168. North Arlington Borough	Bergen	14,837	228. River Edge Borough	Bergen	10,721
169. Springfield Township	Union	14,735	229. Lincoln Park Borough	Morris	10,703
170. Ramsey Borough	Bergen	14,647	230. Waterford Township	Camden	10,636
171. Phillipsburg Town	Warren	14,542	231. Totowa Borough	Passaic	10,602
172. Clark Township	Union	14,411	232. Guttenberg Town	Hudson	10,601
173. Haddon Township	Camden	14,354	233. Keansburg Borough	Monmouth	10,582
174. Tenafly Borough	Bergen	14,302	234. Little Ferry Borough	Bergen	10,568
175. Highland Park Borough	Middlesex	14,202	235. West Caldwell Township	Essex	10,566
176. Harrison Town	Hudson	14,152	236. Woodbury City	Gloucester	10,457
177. Eatontown Borough	Monmouth	14,109	237. Mount Holly Township	Burlington	10,335
178. Clinton Township	Hunterdon	13,903	238. Millstone Township	Monmouth	10,212
179. Collingswood Borough	Camden	13,812	239. Bordentown Township	Burlington	10,201
180. Middlesex Borough	Middlesex	13,695	240. Bound Brook Borough	Somerset	10,193

Population, 2007 (estimate)

Municipality	County	Population	Municipality	County	Population
241. Chatham Township	Morris	10,151	301. Keyport Borough	Monmouth	7,502
242. Colts Neck Township	Monmouth	10,091	302. Bloomingdale Borough	Passaic	7,495
243. Hillsdale Borough	Bergen	9,908	303. Palmyra Borough	Burlington	7,419
244. River Vale Township	Bergen	9,667	304. North Hanover Township	Burlington	7,415
245. Kinnelon Borough	Morris	9,595	305. Buena Vista Township	Atlantic	7,359
246. Edgewater Borough	Bergen	9,582	306. Emerson Borough	Bergen	7,343
247. Washington Township	Bergen	9,581	307. Montvale Borough	Bergen	7,339
248. Waldwick Borough	Bergen	9,506	308. Haddon Heights Borough	Camden	7,283
249. Burlington City	Burlington	9,485	309. East Greenwich Township	Gloucester	7,256
250. New Hanover Township	Burlington	9,439	310. Linwood City	Atlantic	7,250
251. Pittsgrove Township	Salem	9,434	311. Rumson Borough	Monmouth	7,226
252. Hackettstown Town	Warren	9,422	312. Caldwell Borough	Essex	7,219
253. Maywood Borough	Bergen	9,230	313. Tabernacle Township	Burlington	7,182
254. Pitman Borough	Gloucester	9,219	314. Fanwood Borough	Union	7,143
255. North Haledon Borough	Passaic	8,940	315. North Caldwell Borough	Essex	7,092
256. Park Ridge Borough	Bergen	8,940	316. Stratford Borough	Camden	7,044
257. Woolwich Township	Gloucester	8,930	317. Milltown Borough	Middlesex	6,999
258. Audubon Borough	Camden	8,881	318. Raritan Borough	Somerset	6,970
259. Matawan Borough	Monmouth	8,806	319. Dunellen Borough	Middlesex	6,963
260. East Rutherford Borough	Bergen	8,798	320. Barrington Borough	Camden	6,924
261. Closter Borough	Bergen	8,681	321. Green Brook Township	Somerset	6,920
262. Leonia Borough	Bergen	8,674	322. Chesterfield Township	Burlington	6,919
263. Long Hill Township	Morris	8,652	323. Washington Township	Warren	6,855
264. Ocean Township	Ocean	8,643	324. Upper Freehold Township	Monmouth	6,833
265. Westampton Township	Burlington	8,618	325. Midland Park Borough	Bergen	6,820
266. Cresskill Borough	Bergen	8,553	326. Glen Ridge Borough	Essex	6,751
267. Margate City	Atlantic	8,537	327. Fairfield Township	Cumberland	6,748
268. Byram Township	Sussex	8,506	328. Shamong Township	Burlington	6,738
269. Upper Saddle River Borough	Bergen	8,483	329. Washington Borough	Warren	6,695
270. Boonton Town	Morris	8,482	330. Union Beach Borough	Monmouth	6,666
271. Haledon Borough	Passaic	8,389	331. Allendale Borough	Bergen	6,618
272. Runnemede Borough	Camden	8,389	332. Mountainside Borough	Union	6,559
273. West Long Branch Borough	Monmouth	8,383	333. Eastampton Township	Burlington	6,535
274. Lopatcong Township	Warren	8,369	334. Andover Township	Sussex	6,520
275. Bedminster Township	Somerset	8,362	335. Watchung Borough	Somerset	6,508
276. Hardyston Township	Sussex	8,344	336. Jamesburg Borough	Middlesex	6,389
277. Chatham Borough	Morris	8,266	337. Rockaway Borough	Morris	6,313
278. Plumsted Township	Ocean	8,177	338. Union Township	Hunterdon	6,272
279. Newton Town	Sussex	8,167	339. Manasquan Borough	Monmouth	6,244
280. Spotswood Borough	Middlesex	8,153	340. Norwood Borough	Bergen	6,220
281. Mansfield Township	Warren	8,127	341. Lebanon Township	Hunterdon	6,209
282. Butler Borough	Morris	8,090	342. Logan Township	Gloucester	6,195
283. Absecon City	Atlantic	8,074	343. Little Silver Borough	Monmouth	6,129
284. Upper Deerfield Township	Cumberland	8,068	344. Wharton Borough	Morris	6,127
285. Maurice River Township	Cumberland	8,034	345. Rochelle Park Township	Bergen	6,114
286. Bogota Borough	Bergen	7,991	346. Paulsboro Borough	Gloucester	6,080
287. Mansfield Township	Burlington	7,961	347. Tewksbury Township	Hunterdon	6,048
288. Carneys Point Township	Salem	7,923	348. Mullica Township	Atlantic	6,034
289. Northfield City	Atlantic	7,911	349. Old Tappan Borough	Bergen	6,027
290. Berlin Borough	Camden	7,870	350. Carlstadt Borough	Bergen	6,023
291. Oradell Borough	Bergen	7,847	351. Hainesport Township	Burlington	6,014
292. South Amboy City	Middlesex	7,819	352. Woodcliff Lake Borough	Bergen	5,939
293. Chester Township	Morris	7,795	353. Blairstown Township	Warren	5,928
294. Riverside Township	Burlington	7,765	354. Belmar Borough	Monmouth	5,927
295. Edgewater Park Township	Burlington	7,762	355. Fair Haven Borough	Monmouth	5,920
296. Bernardsville Borough	Somerset	7,745	356. White Township	Warren	5,874
297. Kenilworth Borough	Union	7,647	357. Dennis Township	Cape May	5,791
298. Fairfield Township	Essex	7,556	358. Englewood Cliffs Borough	Bergen	5,775
299. Clayton Borough	Gloucester	7,511	359. Oceanport Borough	Monmouth	5,768
300. Wood-Ridge Borough	Bergen	7,505	360. Mount Arlington Borough	Morris	5,698

Population, 2007 (estimate)

Municipality	County	Population	Municipality	County	Population
361. Independence Township	Warren	5,681	421. Merchantville Borough	Camden	3,763
362. Salem City	Salem	5,678	422. Shrewsbury Borough	Monmouth	3,759
363. Prospect Park Borough	Passaic	5,633	423. Buena Borough	Atlantic	3,747
364. Frankford Township	Sussex	5,604	424. Lambertville City	Hunterdon	3,744
365. Mendham Township	Morris	5,539	425. Cape May City	Cape May	3,728
366. Morris Plains Borough	Morris	5,534	426. South Toms River Borough	Ocean	3,713
367. Commercial Township	Cumberland	5,411	427. High Bridge Borough	Hunterdon	3,701
368. Point Pleasant Beach Borough	Ocean	5,411	428. Mine Hill Township	Morris	3,612
369. Berlin Township	Camden	5,381	429. Stanhope Borough	Sussex	3,592
370. Roseland Borough	Essex	5,357	430. Monmouth Beach Borough	Monmouth	3,582
371. Highlands Borough	Monmouth	5,310	431. Upper Pittsgrove Township	Salem	3,566
372. Wildwood City	Cape May	5,291	432. Green Township	Sussex	3,539
373. Hightstown Borough	Mercer	5,271	433. Long Beach Township	Ocean	3,528
374. Holland Township	Hunterdon	5,244	434. Spring Lake Borough	Monmouth	3,509
375. Neptune City Borough	Monmouth	5,152	435. Springfield Township	Burlington	3,492
376. Spring Lake Heights Borough	Monmouth	5,136	436. Hamburg Borough	Sussex	3,482
377. Hampton Township	Sussex	5,135	437. Haworth Borough	Bergen	3,410
378. Greenwich Township	Warren	5,130	438. Fredon Township	Sussex	3,345
379. Franklin Borough	Sussex	5,126	439. Pohatcong Township	Warren	3,343
380. Demarest Borough	Bergen	5,122	440. Woodstown Borough	Salem	3,321
381. Alexandria Township	Hunterdon	5,112	441. Harding Township	Morris	3,319
382. Somerdale Borough	Camden	5,079	442. Seaside Heights Borough	Ocean	3,319
383. Mendham Borough	Morris	5,073	443. Deerfield Township	Cumberland	3,242
384. Greenwich Township	Gloucester	4,989	444. Netcong Borough	Morris	3,241
385. Clementon Borough	Camden	4,881	445. National Park Borough	Gloucester	3,230
386. Harrington Park Borough	Bergen	4,881	446. Knowlton Township	Warren	3,139
387. Brielle Borough	Monmouth	4,879	447. Franklin Township	Warren	3,133
388. South Bound Brook Borough	Somerset	4,850	448. Franklin Township	Hunterdon	3,119
389. North Wildwood City	Cape May	4,849	449. South Harrison Township	Gloucester	3,065
390. Bradley Beach Borough	Monmouth	4,816	450. Woodbury Heights Borough	Gloucester	3,042
391. Hopewell Township	Cumberland	4,785	451. Alloway Township	Salem	3,035
392. Penns Grove Borough	Salem	4,704	452. Lawrence Township	Cumberland	2,979
393. Delaware Township	Hunterdon	4,688	453. West Amwell Township	Hunterdon	2,930
394. Atlantic Highlands Borough	Monmouth	4,631	454. Sea Isle City	Cape May	2,929
395. Northvale Borough	Bergen	4,548	455. Liberty Township	Warren	2,919
396. Pilesgrove Township	Salem	4,515	456. Riverdale Borough	Morris	2,870
397. East Amwell Township	Hunterdon	4,483	457. Quinton Township	Salem	2,838
398. Westville Borough	Gloucester	4,474	458. Harmony Township	Warren	2,815
399. Boonton Township	Morris	4,400	459. Lawnside Borough	Camden	2,814
400. Egg Harbor City	Atlantic	4,398	460. Lavallette Borough	Ocean	2,757
401. Mount Ephraim Borough	Camden	4,389	461. Moonachie Borough	Bergen	2,754
402. Allamuchy Township	Warren	4,385	462. Lakehurst Borough	Ocean	2,708
403. Delanco Township	Burlington	4,377	463. Woodlynne Borough	Camden	2,687
404. Magnolia Borough	Camden	4,334	464. Pennington Borough	Mercer	2,668
405. Stillwater Township	Sussex	4,312	465. Riverton Borough	Burlington	2,652
406. Garwood Borough	Union	4,309	466. Belvidere Town	Warren	2,645
407. Mountain Lakes Borough	Morris	4,276	467. Beverly City	Burlington	2,588
408. Flemington Borough	Hunterdon	4,237	468. Oxford Township	Warren	2,575
409. Medford Lakes Borough	Burlington	4,099	469. Ogdensburg Borough	Sussex	2,568
410. Wildwood Crest Borough	Cape May	4,053	470. Clinton Town	Hunterdon	2,564
411. Ho-Ho-Kus Borough	Bergen	4,037	471. Peapack & Gladstone Borough	Somerset	2,552
412. Oaklyn Borough	Camden	4,029	472. Woodbine Borough	Cape May	2,485
413. Kingwood Township	Hunterdon	4,020	473. Lafayette Township	Sussex	2,477
414. Bethlehem Township	Hunterdon	3,945	474. Alpine Borough	Bergen	2,451
415. Cranbury Township	Middlesex	3,944	475. Gibbsboro Borough	Camden	2,427
416. Elk Township	Gloucester	3,910	476. Alpha Borough	Warren	2,389
417. Montague Township	Sussex	3,891	477. Wenonah Borough	Gloucester	2,341
418. Bordentown City	Burlington	3,854	478. Seaside Park Borough	Ocean	2,306
419. Tuckerton Borough	Ocean	3,846	479. South Hackensack Township	Bergen	2,281
420. Saddle River Borough	Bergen	3,784	480. Brooklawn Borough	Camden	2,265

Population, 2007 (estimate)

Municipality	County	Population
481. Weymouth Township	Atlantic	2,257
482. Frelinghuysen Township	Warren	2,207
483. Avon-by-the-Sea Borough	Monmouth	2,185
484. East Newark Borough	Hudson	2,174
485. Sussex Borough	Sussex	2,144
486. Ocean Gate Borough	Ocean	2,130
487. Avalon Borough	Cape May	2,103
488. Swedesboro Borough	Gloucester	2,073
489. Pine Beach Borough	Ocean	2,062
490. Sea Girt Borough	Monmouth	2,051
491. Essex Fells Borough	Essex	2,025
492. Helmetta Borough	Middlesex	2,012
493. Hopewell Borough	Mercer	2,000
494. Glen Gardner Borough	Hunterdon	1,958
495. Hope Township	Warren	1,945
496. Folsom Borough	Atlantic	1,918
497. Laurel Springs Borough	Camden	1,902
498. Lebanon Borough	Hunterdon	1,896
499. Englishtown Borough	Monmouth	1,893
500. Sandyston Township	Sussex	1,893
501. Lower Alloways Creek Township	Salem	1,883
502. Island Heights Borough	Ocean	1,875
503. Chesilhurst Borough	Camden	1,874
504. Allentown Borough	Monmouth	1,859
505. Sea Bright Borough	Monmouth	1,813
506. Oldmans Township	Salem	1,804
507. Lake Como Borough	Monmouth	1,782
508. Estell Manor City	Atlantic	1,714
509. Newfield Borough	Gloucester	1,670
510. Downe Township	Cumberland	1,664
511. Eagleswood Township	Ocean	1,645
512. Hampton Borough	Hunterdon	1,642
513. Chester Borough	Morris	1,640
514. Hardwick Township	Warren	1,619
515. Farmingdale Borough	Monmouth	1,576
516. Mannington Township	Salem	1,555
517. Surf City Borough	Ocean	1,549
518. Bass River Township	Burlington	1,547
519. Stow Creek Township	Cumberland	1,528
520. Victory Gardens Borough	Morris	1,499
521. Pemberton Borough	Burlington	1,472
522. Frenchtown Borough	Hunterdon	1,465
523. Winfield Township	Union	1,456
524. Ship Bottom Borough	Ocean	1,439
525. Beach Haven Borough	Ocean	1,379

Municipality	County	Population
526. Woodland Township	Burlington	1,344
527. Elmer Borough	Salem	1,343
528. Bay Head Borough	Ocean	1,265
529. Port Republic City	Atlantic	1,220
530. Milford Borough	Hunterdon	1,196
531. Longport Borough	Atlantic	1,081
532. Shrewsbury Township	Monmouth	1,076
533. Audubon Park Borough	Camden	1,058
534. Elsinboro Township	Salem	1,054
535. Deal Borough	Monmouth	1,047
536. Califon Borough	Hunterdon	1,033
537. Stone Harbor Borough	Cape May	1,021
538. Hi-Nella Borough	Camden	997
539. West Cape May Borough	Cape May	987
540. Roosevelt Borough	Monmouth	914
541. Far Hills Borough	Somerset	902
542. Greenwich Township	Cumberland	886
543. Interlaken Borough	Monmouth	884
544. Bloomsbury Borough	Hunterdon	865
545. Barnegat Light Borough	Ocean	835
546. Branchville Borough	Sussex	822
547. Wrightstown Borough	Burlington	733
548. Allenhurst Borough	Monmouth	703
549. Rocky Hill Borough	Somerset	678
550. Shiloh Borough	Cumberland	660
551. Washington Township	Burlington	643
552. Andover Borough	Sussex	639
553. Fieldsboro Borough	Burlington	568
554. Stockton Borough	Hunterdon	551
555. Corbin City	Atlantic	520
556. Mantoloking Borough	Ocean	451
557. Millstone Borough	Somerset	412
558. West Wildwood Borough	Cape May	406
559. Harvey Cedars Borough	Ocean	392
560. Rockleigh Borough	Bergen	390
561. Loch Arbour Village	Monmouth	275
562. Cape May Point Borough	Cape May	226
563. Walpack Township	Sussex	39
564. Tavistock Borough	Camden	28
565. Pine Valley Borough	Camden	23
566. Teterboro Borough	Bergen	18

Unemployment Rate, 2007

	Municipality	County	Unemp Rt		Municipality	County	Unemp Rt
1.	Wildwood City	Cape May	16.5%	61.	Orange City Township	Essex	6.2%
2.	Penns Grove Borough	Salem	13.0	62.	Vineland City	Cumberland	6.2
3.	Wildwood Crest Borough	Cape May	12.8	63.	Bogota Borough	Bergen	6.2
4.	Paulsboro Borough	Gloucester	12.3	64.	Seaside Heights Borough	Ocean	6.1
5.	North Wildwood City	Cape May	11.0	65.	Commercial Township	Cumberland	6.1
6.	West Wildwood Borough	Cape May	10.1	66.	Phillipsburg Town	Warren	6.1
7.	Trenton City	Mercer	9.9	67.	Absecon City	Atlantic	6.0
8.	Asbury Park City	Monmouth	9.8	68.	Garfield City	Bergen	6.0
9.	Camden City	Camden	9.6	69.	Plainfield City	Union	6.0
10.	Hi-Nella Borough	Camden	8.9	70.	Runnemede Borough	Camden	6.0
11.	Atlantic City	Atlantic	8.8	71.	National Park Borough	Gloucester	5.9
12.	Egg Harbor City	Atlantic	8.7	72.	Manchester Township	Ocean	5.9
13.	Beverly City	Burlington	8.6	73.	Woodlynne Borough	Camden	5.9
14.	Bridgeton City	Cumberland	8.5	74.	Alpha Borough	Warren	5.9
15.	Clementon Borough	Camden	8.3	75.	Pine Hill Borough	Camden	5.9
16.	Paterson City	Passaic	8.3	76.	Prospect Park Borough	Passaic	5.9
17.	Fairfield Township	Cumberland	8.2	77.	Pitman Borough	Gloucester	5.8
18.	Perth Amboy City	Middlesex	8.2	78.	Branchville Borough	Sussex	5.8
19.	Salem City	Salem	8.1	79.	Washington Township	Burlington	5.8
20.	Millville City	Cumberland	8.1	80.	Mount Holly Township	Burlington	5.8
21.	Lower Township	Cape May	8.0	81.	Winslow Township	Camden	5.8
22.	Pleasantville City	Atlantic	8.0	82.	Woodbury City	Gloucester	5.8
23.	Gloucester City	Camden	7.9	83.	Glassboro Borough	Gloucester	5.8
24.	Newark City	Essex	7.9	84.	South River Borough	Middlesex	5.8
25.	Magnolia Borough	Camden	7.9	85.	Bradley Beach Borough	Monmouth	5.8
26.	Dover Town	Morris	7.7	86.	Boonton Town	Morris	5.7
27.	Lindenwold Borough	Camden	7.7	87.	Loch Arbour Village	Monmouth	5.7
28.	Montague Township	Sussex	7.6	88.	Freehold Borough	Monmouth	5.7
29.	Chesilhurst Borough	Camden	7.5	89.	Delanco Township	Burlington	5.7
30.	West Cape May Borough	Cape May	7.4	90.	Seaside Park Borough	Ocean	5.7
31.	South Toms River Borough	Ocean	7.4	91.	Willingboro Township	Burlington	5.7
32.	Carteret Borough	Middlesex	7.3	92.	Ventnor City	Atlantic	5.7
33.	Hammonton Town	Atlantic	7.2	93.	Mullica Township	Atlantic	5.7
34.	Lawnside Borough	Camden	7.2	94.	Middle Township	Cape May	5.7
35.	Winfield Township	Union	7.2	95.	Andover Borough	Sussex	5.7
36.	Cape May City	Cape May	7.0	96.	Ocean Township	Ocean	5.6
37.	East Orange City	Essex	7.0	97.	Pemberton Township	Burlington	5.5
38.	Passaic City	Passaic	7.0	98.	Pennsauken Township	Camden	5.5
39.	Haledon Borough	Passaic	7.0	99.	West New York Town	Hudson	5.5
40.	Keansburg Borough	Monmouth	6.9	100.	Lawrence Township	Cumberland	5.5
41.	Oxford Township	Warren	6.9	101.	Wrightstown Borough	Burlington	5.5
42.	Carneys Point Township	Salem	6.9	102.	Wantage Township	Sussex	5.5
43.	Wharton Borough	Morris	6.8	103.	South Bound Brook Borough	Somerset	5.5
44.	Beach Haven Borough	Ocean	6.8	104.	Westville Borough	Gloucester	5.4
45.	Hillside Township	Union	6.8	105.	Hopatcong Borough	Sussex	5.4
46.	Woodbine Borough	Cape May	6.8	106.	Milford Borough	Hunterdon	5.4
47.	Ship Bottom Borough	Ocean	6.7	107.	Swedesboro Borough	Gloucester	5.4
48.	Irvington Township	Essex	6.6	108.	Galloway Township	Atlantic	5.4
49.	Shrewsbury Township	Monmouth	6.6	109.	Jersey City	Hudson	5.4
50.	Fairview Borough	Bergen	6.5	110.	Monroe Township	Gloucester	5.4
51.	Buena Borough	Atlantic	6.4	111.	Neptune Township	Monmouth	5.4
52.	Union City	Hudson	6.4	112.	Lebanon Township	Hunterdon	5.4
53.	Franklin Township	Gloucester	6.4	113.	Highlands Borough	Monmouth	5.4
54.	Roselle Borough	Union	6.4	114.	Alloway Township	Salem	5.4
55.	Fieldsboro Borough	Burlington	6.4	115.	Wallington Borough	Bergen	5.4
56.	Lakehurst Borough	Ocean	6.4	116.	Burlington City	Burlington	5.4
57.	Estell Manor City	Atlantic	6.3	117.	Somers Point City	Atlantic	5.3
58.	Tuckerton Borough	Ocean	6.3	118.	Atlantic Highlands Borough	Monmouth	5.3
59.	Dunellen Borough	Middlesex	6.3	119.	Bayonne City	Hudson	5.3
60.	Elizabeth City	Union	6.2	120.	Berkeley Township	Ocean	5.3

Unemployment Rate, 2007

Municipality	County	Unemp Rt	Municipality	County	Unemp Rt
121. Quinton Township	Salem	5.3%	181. Pemberton Borough	Burlington	4.6%
122. Sea Isle City	Cape May	5.2	182. Sea Bright Borough	Monmouth	4.5
123. Lebanon Borough	Hunterdon	5.2	183. Surf City Borough	Ocean	4.5
124. Mount Ephraim Borough	Camden	5.1	184. Shiloh Borough	Cumberland	4.5
125. Margate City	Atlantic	5.1	185. Hampton Borough	Hunterdon	4.5
126. Belvidere Town	Warren	5.1	186. Lacey Township	Ocean	4.5
127. Knowlton Township	Warren	5.1	187. West Deptford Township	Gloucester	4.5
128. Egg Harbor Township	Atlantic	5.1	188. Belmar Borough	Monmouth	4.5
129. Kearny Town	Hudson	5.1	189. Liberty Township	Warren	4.5
130. Linden City	Union	5.1	190. Bay Head Borough	Ocean	4.5
131. Toms River Township	Ocean	5.1	191. Raritan Borough	Somerset	4.4
132. Union Beach Borough	Monmouth	5.1	192. Woodland Township	Burlington	4.4
133. Red Bank Borough	Monmouth	5.1	193. Roselle Park Borough	Union	4.4
134. Florence Township	Burlington	5.0	194. Island Heights Borough	Ocean	4.4
135. Lafayette Township	Sussex	5.0	195. Oldmans Township	Salem	4.4
136. North Bergen Township	Hudson	5.0	196. Elmwood Park Borough	Bergen	4.4
137. Little Egg Harbor Township	Ocean	5.0	197. Kenilworth Borough	Union	4.4
138. Alexandria Township	Hunterdon	4.9	198. Hamburg Borough	Sussex	4.4
139. Newfield Borough	Gloucester	4.9	199. Ocean Gate Borough	Ocean	4.4
140. Belleville Township	Essex	4.9	200. Princeton Borough	Mercer	4.4
141. Franklin Borough	Sussex	4.9	201. Pittsgrove Township	Salem	4.3
142. Stone Harbor Borough	Cape May	4.9	202. Riverdale Borough	Morris	4.3
143. Hardyston Township	Sussex	4.9	203. Byram Township	Sussex	4.3
144. Long Beach Township	Ocean	4.9	204. Deerfield Township	Cumberland	4.3
145. Clayton Borough	Gloucester	4.8	205. Lake Como Borough	Monmouth	4.3
146. Washington Township	Warren	4.8	206. Lodi Borough	Bergen	4.3
147. Bloomsbury Borough	Hunterdon	4.8	207. Spring Lake Borough	Monmouth	4.3
148. Rockaway Borough	Morris	4.8	208. Brigantine City	Atlantic	4.3
149. Bound Brook Borough	Somerset	4.8	209. Hope Township	Warren	4.3
150. Rahway City	Union	4.8	210. Metuchen Borough	Middlesex	4.3
151. Hamilton Township	Atlantic	4.8	211. Blairstown Township	Warren	4.2
152. Edgewater Park Township	Burlington	4.8	212. Helmetta Borough	Middlesex	4.2
153. Downe Township	Cumberland	4.8	213. Bloomfield Township	Essex	4.2
154. Southampton Township	Burlington	4.8	214. Brick Township	Ocean	4.2
155. Harrison Town	Hudson	4.7	215. New Brunswick City	Middlesex	4.2
156. Elk Township	Gloucester	4.7	216. West Milford Township	Passaic	4.2
157. Saddle Brook Township	Bergen	4.7	217. North Plainfield Borough	Somerset	4.2
158. Clifton City	Passaic	4.7	218. Pennington Borough	Mercer	4.2
159. Long Branch City	Monmouth	4.7	219. Little Falls Township	Passaic	4.2
160. Monroe Township	Middlesex	4.7	220. Bellmawr Borough	Camden	4.2
161. Waterford Township	Camden	4.7	221. Hightstown Borough	Mercer	4.2
162. Mansfield Township	Burlington	4.7	222. Hazlet Township	Monmouth	4.1
163. East Rutherford Borough	Bergen	4.7	223. Matawan Borough	Monmouth	4.1
164. Mantua Township	Gloucester	4.7	224. Union Township	Union	4.1
165. Lyndhurst Township	Bergen	4.7	225. Jamesburg Borough	Middlesex	4.1
166. Sussex Borough	Sussex	4.6	226. Little Ferry Borough	Bergen	4.1
167. Somerdale Borough	Camden	4.6	227. South Orange Village Township	Essex	4.0
168. Somerville Borough	Somerset	4.6	228. Corbin City	Atlantic	4.0
169. Ocean City	Cape May	4.6	229. Guttenberg Town	Hudson	4.0
170. Palmyra Borough	Burlington	4.6	230. West Long Branch Borough	Monmouth	4.0
171. South Hackensack Township	Bergen	4.6	231. Englewood City	Bergen	4.0
172. Buena Vista Township	Atlantic	4.6	232. Jackson Township	Ocean	4.0
173. North Hanover Township	Burlington	4.6	233. South Amboy City	Middlesex	4.0
174. Hackensack City	Bergen	4.6	234. Riverside Township	Burlington	4.0
175. Lakewood Township	Ocean	4.6	235. Harrison Township	Gloucester	4.0
176. Keyport Borough	Monmouth	4.6	236. Palisades Park Borough	Bergen	4.0
177. Upper Deerfield Township	Cumberland	4.6	237. Barnegat Township	Ocean	4.0
178. Collingswood Borough	Camden	4.6	238. Cliffside Park Borough	Bergen	4.0
179. Beachwood Borough	Ocean	4.6	239. Berlin Borough	Camden	4.0
180. Wenonah Borough	Gloucester	4.6	240. Sandyston Township	Sussex	4.0

Unemployment Rate, 2007

Municipality	County	Unemp Rt	Municipality	County	Unemp Rt
241. Clinton Township	Hunterdon	3.9%	301. Weehawken Township	Hudson	3.6%
242. Pilesgrove Township	Salem	3.9	302. Ogdensburg Borough	Sussex	3.5
243. Mansfield Township	Warren	3.9	303. Ringwood Borough	Passaic	3.5
244. Rochelle Park Township	Bergen	3.9	304. Oaklyn Borough	Camden	3.5
245. Stafford Township	Ocean	3.9	305. Chesterfield Township	Burlington	3.5
246. Interlaken Borough	Monmouth	3.9	306. Spotswood Borough	Middlesex	3.5
247. Eagleswood Township	Ocean	3.9	307. Washington Borough	Warren	3.5
248. East Newark Borough	Hudson	3.9	308. Maple Shade Township	Burlington	3.5
249. Mine Hill Township	Morris	3.9	309. Fair Lawn Borough	Bergen	3.5
250. Upper Saddle River Borough	Bergen	3.9	310. Howell Township	Monmouth	3.5
251. Chester Borough	Morris	3.8	311. West Orange Township	Essex	3.5
252. Dennis Township	Cape May	3.8	312. Springfield Township	Burlington	3.5
253. Neptune City Borough	Monmouth	3.8	313. Mahwah Township	Bergen	3.5
254. Avon-by-the-Sea Borough	Monmouth	3.8	314. Franklin Township	Hunterdon	3.5
255. Maurice River Township	Cumberland	3.8	315. Mannington Township	Salem	3.5
256. Victory Gardens Borough	Morris	3.8	316. Bordentown Township	Burlington	3.5
257. Bordentown City	Burlington	3.8	317. Holland Township	Hunterdon	3.5
258. Maplewood Township	Essex	3.8	318. Lumberton Township	Burlington	3.4
259. Norwood Borough	Bergen	3.8	319. Morris Plains Borough	Morris	3.4
260. Burlington Township	Burlington	3.8	320. Pohatcong Township	Warren	3.4
261. Stratford Borough	Camden	3.8	321. Pennsville Township	Salem	3.4
262. Audubon Park Borough	Camden	3.8	322. Point Pleasant Borough	Ocean	3.4
263. Tinton Falls Borough	Monmouth	3.7	323. Washington Township	Bergen	3.4
264. Monmouth Beach Borough	Monmouth	3.7	324. New Milford Borough	Bergen	3.4
265. Cinnaminson Township	Burlington	3.7	325. Mountain Lakes Borough	Morris	3.4
266. Ridgefield Park Village	Bergen	3.7	326. Ocean Township	Monmouth	3.4
267. Longport Borough	Atlantic	3.7	327. Hampton Township	Sussex	3.4
268. Highland Park Borough	Middlesex	3.7	328. Allentown Borough	Monmouth	3.4
269. Gibbsboro Borough	Camden	3.7	329. Weymouth Township	Atlantic	3.4
270. North Brunswick Township	Middlesex	3.7	330. Elmer Borough	Salem	3.4
271. Piscataway Township	Middlesex	3.7	331. Haworth Borough	Bergen	3.4
272. Sayreville Borough	Middlesex	3.7	332. Colts Neck Township	Monmouth	3.4
273. Bass River Township	Burlington	3.7	333. Ridgefield Borough	Bergen	3.3
274. Laurel Springs Borough	Camden	3.7	334. Tenafly Borough	Bergen	3.3
275. Rutherford Borough	Bergen	3.7	335. Manville Borough	Somerset	3.3
276. Hasbrouck Heights Borough	Bergen	3.7	336. Boonton Township	Morris	3.3
277. Eatontown Borough	Monmouth	3.7	337. Haddon Heights Borough	Camden	3.3
278. Linwood City	Atlantic	3.7	338. Deptford Township	Gloucester	3.3
279. Newton Town	Sussex	3.7	339. Vernon Township	Sussex	3.3
280. Pine Beach Borough	Ocean	3.7	340. Robbinsville Township	Mercer	3.3
281. Roosevelt Borough	Monmouth	3.7	341. Wanaque Borough	Passaic	3.3
282. Stanhope Borough	Sussex	3.7	342. Kingwood Township	Hunterdon	3.3
283. East Greenwich Township	Gloucester	3.7	343. Haddon Township	Camden	3.3
284. South Harrison Township	Gloucester	3.6	344. Point Pleasant Beach Borough	Ocean	3.3
285. Frankford Township	Sussex	3.6	345. Port Republic City	Atlantic	3.3
286. Green Township	Sussex	3.6	346. Lambertville City	Hunterdon	3.2
287. Pequannock Township	Morris	3.6	347. New Hanover Township	Burlington	3.2
288. Pompton Lakes Borough	Passaic	3.6	348. Bergenfield Borough	Bergen	3.2
289. Milltown Borough	Middlesex	3.6	349. Freehold Township	Monmouth	3.2
290. Stow Creek Township	Cumberland	3.6	350. Manalapan Township	Monmouth	3.2
291. Ewing Township	Mercer	3.6	351. Montclair Township	Essex	3.2
292. Franklin Township	Somerset	3.6	352. Mount Olive Township	Morris	3.2
293. Nutley Township	Essex	3.6	353. Teaneck Township	Bergen	3.2
294. Woodbridge Township	Middlesex	3.6	354. Maywood Borough	Bergen	3.2
295. Demarest Borough	Bergen	3.6	355. East Hanover Township	Morris	3.2
296. Woolwich Township	Gloucester	3.6	356. Brielle Borough	Monmouth	3.2
297. Greenwich Township	Gloucester	3.6	357. Westampton Township	Burlington	3.2
298. North Arlington Borough	Bergen	3.6	358. Englewood Cliffs Borough	Bergen	3.2
299. Edgewater Borough	Bergen	3.6	359. Lincoln Park Borough	Morris	3.1
300. Woodbury Heights Borough	Gloucester	3.6	360. Barrington Borough	Camden	3.1

Unemployment Rate, 2007

Municipality	County	Unemp Rt	Municipality	County	Unemp Rt
361. Englishtown Borough	Monmouth	3.1%	421. Hardwick Township	Warren	2.7%
362. Hopewell Township	Mercer	3.1	422. Hopewell Township	Cumberland	2.7
363. Aberdeen Township	Monmouth	3.1	423. Saddle River Borough	Bergen	2.7
364. Brooklawn Borough	Camden	3.1	424. Bridgewater Township	Somerset	2.7
365. East Brunswick Township	Middlesex	3.1	425. Gloucester Township	Camden	2.7
366. Edison Township	Middlesex	3.1	426. Lawrence Township	Mercer	2.7
367. Middletown Township	Monmouth	3.1	427. Marlboro Township	Monmouth	2.7
368. Wayne Township	Passaic	3.1	428. Parsippany-Troy Hills Township	Morris	2.7
369. Roseland Borough	Essex	3.1	429. Randolph Township	Morris	2.7
370. West Paterson Borough	Passaic	3.1	430. Wall Township	Monmouth	2.7
371. Flemington Borough	Hunterdon	3.1	431. Frenchtown Borough	Hunterdon	2.7
372. Morristown Town	Morris	3.1	432. Rocky Hill Borough	Somerset	2.7
373. Mount Arlington Borough	Morris	3.1	433. Watchung Borough	Somerset	2.7
374. Northfield City	Atlantic	3.1	434. North Caldwell Borough	Essex	2.7
375. Jefferson Township	Morris	3.1	435. Fair Haven Borough	Monmouth	2.7
376. High Bridge Borough	Hunterdon	3.1	436. Avalon Borough	Cape May	2.7
377. Barnegat Light Borough	Ocean	3.0	437. Haddonfield Borough	Camden	2.7
378. Morris Township	Morris	3.0	438. Hackettstown Town	Warren	2.7
379. South Plainfield Borough	Middlesex	3.0	439. White Township	Warren	2.6
380. Cherry Hill Township	Camden	3.0	440. Fanwood Borough	Union	2.6
381. Paramus Borough	Bergen	3.0	441. Andover Township	Sussex	2.6
382. New Providence Borough	Union	3.0	442. River Edge Borough	Bergen	2.6
383. Carlstadt Borough	Bergen	3.0	443. Woodstown Borough	Salem	2.6
384. Hainesport Township	Burlington	3.0	444. Lower Alloways Creek Township	Salem	2.6
385. Frelinghuysen Township	Warren	3.0	445. Lavallette Borough	Ocean	2.6
386. Delran Township	Burlington	3.0	446. Alpine Borough	Bergen	2.6
387. Netcong Borough	Morris	3.0	447. Fort Lee Borough	Bergen	2.6
388. West Caldwell Township	Essex	2.9	448. Dumont Borough	Bergen	2.6
389. Fairfield Township	Essex	2.9	449. Folsom Borough	Atlantic	2.6
390. Union Township	Hunterdon	2.9	450. Eastampton Township	Burlington	2.6
391. Greenwich Township	Cumberland	2.9	451. Peapack & Gladstone Borough	Somerset	2.6
392. Merchantville Borough	Camden	2.9	452. Deal Borough	Monmouth	2.5
393. Roxbury Township	Morris	2.9	453. Glen Rock Borough	Bergen	2.5
394. Washington Township	Morris	2.9	454. Moonachie Borough	Bergen	2.5
395. Franklin Township	Warren	2.9	455. Readington Township	Hunterdon	2.5
396. East Windsor Township	Mercer	2.9	456. Oakland Borough	Bergen	2.5
397. Evesham Township	Burlington	2.9	457. Wyckoff Township	Bergen	2.5
398. Hillsborough Township	Somerset	2.9	458. Oradell Borough	Bergen	2.5
399. Voorhees Township	Camden	2.9	459. Leonia Borough	Bergen	2.5
400. Plumsted Township	Ocean	2.9	460. Livingston Township	Essex	2.5
401. Totowa Borough	Passaic	2.9	461. Greenwich Township	Warren	2.5
402. Wood-Ridge Borough	Bergen	2.9	462. West Amwell Township	Hunterdon	2.5
403. Bloomingdale Borough	Passaic	2.9	463. Scotch Plains Township	Union	2.5
404. East Amwell Township	Hunterdon	2.9	464. Allenhurst Borough	Monmouth	2.5
405. Spring Lake Heights Borough	Monmouth	2.9	465. Montvale Borough	Bergen	2.5
406. Moorestown Township	Burlington	2.9	466. Hillsdale Borough	Bergen	2.4
407. Berlin Township	Camden	2.8	467. Garwood Borough	Union	2.4
408. Middlesex Borough	Middlesex	2.8	468. Florham Park Borough	Morris	2.4
409. Old Bridge Township	Middlesex	2.8	469. Ramsey Borough	Bergen	2.4
410. South Brunswick Township	Middlesex	2.8	470. Rumson Borough	Monmouth	2.4
411. Little Silver Borough	Monmouth	2.8	471. Hoboken City	Hudson	2.4
412. Butler Borough	Morris	2.8	472. Westfield Town	Union	2.4
413. Green Brook Township	Somerset	2.8	473. Bedminster Township	Somerset	2.4
414. Old Tappan Borough	Bergen	2.8	474. Harrington Park Borough	Bergen	2.4
415. Long Hill Township	Morris	2.8	475. Allendale Borough	Bergen	2.4
416. Shamong Township	Burlington	2.7	476. Cranford Township	Union	2.4
417. Denville Township	Morris	2.7	477. North Haledon Borough	Passaic	2.4
418. Glen Ridge Borough	Essex	2.7	478. Far Hills Borough	Somerset	2.3
419. Sparta Township	Sussex	2.7	479. Summit City	Union	2.3
420. Hawthorne Borough	Passaic	2.7	480. Mountainside Borough	Union	2.3

Unemployment Rate, 2007

Municipality	County	Unemp Rt	Municipality	County	Unemp Rt
481. Harding Township	Morris	2.3%	526. Waldwick Borough	Bergen	1.8%
482. Ridgewood Village	Bergen	2.3	527. Warren Township	Somerset	1.8
483. Rockaway Township	Morris	2.3	528. Montville Township	Morris	1.8
484. Clinton Town	Hunterdon	2.3	529. Bethlehem Township	Hunterdon	1.7
485. Holmdel Township	Monmouth	2.3	530. Millstone Township	Monmouth	1.7
486. Chatham Borough	Morris	2.3	531. Medford Lakes Borough	Burlington	1.7
487. Essex Fells Borough	Essex	2.2	532. Hanover Township	Morris	1.7
488. Medford Township	Burlington	2.2	533. Audubon Borough	Camden	1.6
489. Northvale Borough	Bergen	2.2	534. Upper Freehold Township	Monmouth	1.6
490. Bernards Township	Somerset	2.2	535. Emerson Borough	Bergen	1.6
491. Manasquan Borough	Monmouth	2.2	536. Washington Township	Gloucester	1.6
492. Harmony Township	Warren	2.2	537. Stillwater Township	Sussex	1.6
493. Plainsboro Township	Middlesex	2.2	538. Fredon Township	Sussex	1.5
494. Cresskill Borough	Bergen	2.2	539. Raritan Township	Hunterdon	1.5
495. Branchburg Township	Somerset	2.2	540. Springfield Township	Union	1.5
496. Verona Township	Essex	2.2	541. Elsinboro Township	Salem	1.5
497. Farmingdale Borough	Monmouth	2.2	542. Midland Park Borough	Bergen	1.4
498. Glen Gardner Borough	Hunterdon	2.2	543. Park Ridge Borough	Bergen	1.4
499. Riverton Borough	Burlington	2.1	544. Mendham Borough	Morris	1.4
500. Madison Borough	Morris	2.1	545. Woodcliff Lake Borough	Bergen	1.3
501. Chester Township	Morris	2.1	546. Bernardsville Borough	Somerset	1.3
502. Montgomery Township	Somerset	2.1	547. Independence Township	Warren	1.3
503. Logan Township	Gloucester	2.1	548. Chatham Township	Morris	1.3
504. Tewksbury Township	Hunterdon	2.1	549. Hopewell Borough	Mercer	1.2
505. Lopatcong Township	Warren	2.1	550. Shrewsbury Borough	Monmouth	1.1
506. Caldwell Borough	Essex	2.1	551. Cedar Grove Township	Essex	1.1
507. Franklin Lakes Borough	Bergen	2.0	552. Princeton Township	Mercer	0.9
508. Kinnelon Borough	Morris	2.0	553. Mendham Township	Morris	0.9
509. River Vale Township	Bergen	2.0	554. Mount Laurel Township	Burlington	0.6
510. Secaucus Town	Hudson	2.0	555. Ho-Ho-Kus Borough	Bergen	0.5
511. Westwood Borough	Bergen	2.0	556. Califon Borough	Hunterdon	0
512. Berkeley Heights Township	Union	2.0	557. Cape May Point Borough	Cape May	0
513. Tabernacle Township	Burlington	2.0	558. Harvey Cedars Borough	Ocean	0
514. Allamuchy Township	Warren	2.0	559. Mantoloking Borough	Ocean	0
515. Oceanport Borough	Monmouth	2.0	560. Millstone Borough	Somerset	0
516. Sea Girt Borough	Monmouth	1.9	561. Pine Valley Borough	Camden	0
517. Upper Pittsgrove Township	Salem	1.9	562. Rockleigh Borough	Bergen	0
518. Upper Township	Cape May	1.9	563. Stockton Borough	Hunterdon	0
519. Millburn Township	Essex	1.9	564. Tavistock Borough	Camden	0
520. Clark Township	Union	1.9	565. Teterboro Borough	Bergen	0
521. Hamilton Township	Mercer	1.9	565. Walpack Township	Sussex	0
522. West Windsor Township	Mercer	1.9			
523. Cranbury Township	Middlesex	1.9			
524. Delaware Township	Hunterdon	1.9			
525. Closter Borough	Bergen	1.9			

Crime Rate, 2007 (per 1,000 residents)

Municipality	County	Crime Rate	Municipality	County	Crime Rate
1. Wildwood City	Cape May	146.4	61. Plainfield City	Union	39.2
2. Avalon Borough	Cape May	142.1	62. West Cape May Borough	Cape May	38.7
3. Atlantic City	Atlantic	118.7	63. Jersey City	Hudson	38.6
4. Sea Isle City	Cape May	104.4	64. Glassboro Borough	Gloucester	38.5
5. Brooklawn Borough	Camden	92.0	65. Tavistock Borough	Camden	38.5
6. Beach Haven Borough	Ocean	87.8	66. Pohatcong Township	Warren	38.4
7. Camden City	Camden	80.9	67. Flemington Borough	Hunterdon	38.2
8. North Wildwood City	Cape May	79.7	68. Berlin Township	Camden	37.9
9. Irvington Township	Essex	78.4	69. Mantoloking Borough	Ocean	37.7
10. Ocean City	Cape May	78.1	70. East Rutherford Borough	Bergen	37.6
11. Long Beach Township	Ocean	77.2	71. Linden City	Union	37.6
12. Seaside Heights Borough	Ocean	77.1	72. Absecon City	Atlantic	37.2
13. Salem City	Salem	75.0	73. Hillside Township	Union	37.1
14. Bridgeton City	Cumberland	66.7	74. Sea Bright Borough	Monmouth	36.7
15. Asbury Park City	Monmouth	64.7	75. Corbin City	Atlantic	35.8
16. Stone Harbor Borough	Cape May	64.5	76. Carlstadt Borough	Bergen	35.3
17. Bay Head Borough	Ocean	61.9	77. Wrightstown Borough	Burlington	35.1
18. Harvey Cedars Borough	Ocean	61.7	78. Buena Borough	Atlantic	35.0
19. Paramus Borough	Bergen	61.7	79. East Orange City	Essex	34.9
20. West Wildwood Borough	Cape May	61.3	80. Westville Borough	Gloucester	34.8
21. Millville City	Cumberland	60.3	81. Commercial Township	Cumberland	34.5
22. Belmar Borough	Monmouth	58.9	82. Bass River Township	Burlington	34.4
23. Orange City Township	Essex	58.5	83. Riverdale Borough	Morris	34.4
24. Woodlynne Borough	Camden	58.1	84. Clementon Borough	Camden	34.3
25. Ship Bottom Borough	Ocean	56.8	85. Ventnor City	Atlantic	34.2
26. Neptune Township	Monmouth	54.5	86. Mount Holly Township	Burlington	34.1
27. Cape May City	Cape May	54.1	87. South Hackensack Township	Bergen	33.7
28. Woodbury City	Gloucester	53.1	88. Passaic City	Passaic	33.6
29. Deal Borough	Monmouth	52.7	89. Moonachie Borough	Bergen	33.2
30. Point Pleasant Beach Borough	Ocean	50.8	90. Collingswood Borough	Camden	32.9
31. Vineland City	Cumberland	50.0	91. Morristown Town	Morris	32.9
32. Hamilton Township	Atlantic	49.8	92. Millburn Township	Essex	32.6
33. Elizabeth City	Union	49.7	93. Oaklyn Borough	Camden	32.4
34. Newark City	Essex	49.6	94. Surf City Borough	Ocean	32.4
35. Middle Township	Cape May	49.4	95. Bradley Beach Borough	Monmouth	32.0
36. Deptford Township	Gloucester	48.1	96. Kearny Town	Hudson	31.8
37. Fairfield Township	Essex	48.1	97. Upper Deerfield Township	Cumberland	31.8
38. Paulsboro Borough	Gloucester	47.5	98. Woodbridge Township	Middlesex	31.8
39. Pennsauken Township	Camden	47.4	99. Bloomfield Township	Essex	31.5
40. Trenton City	Mercer	46.8	100. Cherry Hill Township	Camden	31.5
41. Watchung Borough	Somerset	46.6	101. Bellmawr Borough	Camden	31.3
42. Lindenwold Borough	Camden	46.3	102. Gloucester City	Camden	31.0
43. Mount Ephraim Borough	Camden	45.3	103. Magnolia Borough	Camden	30.8
44. Secaucus Town	Hudson	43.7	104. Washington Township	Burlington	30.7
45. Wildwood Crest Borough	Cape May	43.7	105. West Long Branch Borough	Monmouth	30.7
46. Cape May Point Borough	Cape May	43.5	106. West Paterson Borough	Passaic	30.4
47. Pine Valley Borough	Camden	43.5	107. Audubon Borough	Camden	30.3
48. Runnemede Borough	Camden	43.5	108. Chesilhurst Borough	Camden	30.3
49. Woodbine Borough	Cape May	43.5	109. Greenwich Township	Gloucester	30.2
50. Penns Grove Borough	Salem	43.4	110. Pennsville Township	Salem	30.1
51. Pleasantville City	Atlantic	43.3	111. Keansburg Borough	Monmouth	29.8
52. New Brunswick City	Middlesex	43.2	112. Hoboken City	Hudson	29.7
53. Neptune City Borough	Monmouth	43.1	113. Somers Point City	Atlantic	29.7
54. Lawnside Borough	Camden	42.9	114. Washington Borough	Warren	29.7
55. Eatontown Borough	Monmouth	42.4	115. South Toms River Borough	Ocean	29.6
56. Woodland Township	Burlington	41.5	116. Loch Arbour Village	Monmouth	29.2
57. Allenhurst Borough	Monmouth	41.4	117. Lawrence Township	Mercer	29.1
58. Eagleswood Township	Ocean	40.3	118. Seaside Park Borough	Ocean	29.1
59. Little Falls Township	Passaic	39.8	119. Elk Township	Gloucester	28.7
60. Paterson City	Passaic	39.4	120. Gloucester Township	Camden	28.7

Crime Rate, 2007 (per 1,000 residents)

Municipality	County	Crime Rate	Municipality	County	Crime Rate
121. Saddle Brook Township	Bergen	28.7	181. Edgewater Park Township	Burlington	23.6
122. Freehold Township	Monmouth	28.6	182. National Park Borough	Gloucester	23.6
123. Union City	Hudson	28.6	183. Westampton Township	Burlington	23.6
124. Clayton Borough	Gloucester	28.5	184. Lakewood Township	Ocean	23.5
125. Elmer Borough	Salem	28.5	185. Montclair Township	Essex	23.5
126. Oldmans Township	Salem	28.5	186. Winslow Township	Camden	23.5
127. Manasquan Borough	Monmouth	28.4	187. Palmyra Borough	Burlington	23.4
128. Voorhees Township	Camden	28.4	188. Glen Ridge Borough	Essex	23.2
129. Lacey Township	Ocean	28.3	189. Carneys Point Township	Salem	23.1
130. North Plainfield Borough	Somerset	27.9	190. Greenwich Township	Warren	22.9
131. Hackensack City	Bergen	27.8	191. Fairview Borough	Bergen	22.8
132. Red Bank Borough	Monmouth	27.7	192. Haddonfield Borough	Camden	22.8
133. Ocean Township	Monmouth	27.5	193. Lake Como Borough	Monmouth	22.8
134. Stratford Borough	Camden	27.5	194. Toms River Township	Ocean	22.8
135. South Orange Village Township	Essex	27.4	195. Washington Township	Gloucester	22.8
136. Swedesboro Borough	Gloucester	27.4	196. Berlin Borough	Camden	22.6
137. Haddon Township	Camden	27.3	197. Maple Shade Township	Burlington	22.6
138. Perth Amboy City	Middlesex	27.3	198. Merchantville Borough	Camden	22.6
139. Burlington City	Burlington	27.1	199. Burlington Township	Burlington	22.5
140. Lumberton Township	Burlington	27.0	200. Delanco Township	Burlington	22.5
141. Union Township	Union	27.0	201. Beachwood Borough	Ocean	22.4
142. Weehawken Township	Hudson	27.0	202. Metuchen Borough	Middlesex	22.4
143. Clifton City	Passaic	26.9	203. Monroe Township	Gloucester	22.4
144. Egg Harbor City	Atlantic	26.9	204. West Deptford Township	Gloucester	22.3
145. Totowa Borough	Passaic	26.8	205. West New York Town	Hudson	22.3
146. Egg Harbor Township	Atlantic	26.7	206. Willingboro Township	Burlington	22.3
147. Galloway Township	Atlantic	26.7	207. Phillipsburg Town	Warren	22.2
148. Rahway City	Union	26.7	208. Rockaway Township	Morris	22.2
149. Wayne Township	Passaic	26.6	209. Moorestown Township	Burlington	22.1
150. Freehold Borough	Monmouth	26.4	210. Pemberton Township	Burlington	22.1
151. Harrison Town	Hudson	26.4	211. Roselle Borough	Union	22.1
152. Sussex Borough	Sussex	26.3	212. Sea Girt Borough	Monmouth	22.0
153. Belleville Township	Essex	26.0	213. Mount Laurel Township	Burlington	21.9
154. Mantua Township	Gloucester	26.0	214. Buena Vista Township	Atlantic	21.8
155. Avon-by-the-Sea Borough	Monmouth	25.9	215. Riverton Borough	Burlington	21.7
156. Lavallette Borough	Ocean	25.8	216. Bloomsbury Borough	Hunterdon	21.6
157. Lower Township	Cape May	25.7	217. Ocean Gate Borough	Ocean	21.6
158. Pine Hill Borough	Camden	25.7	218. Woodstown Borough	Salem	21.6
159. Netcong Borough	Morris	25.5	219. East Hanover Township	Morris	21.4
160. Princeton Borough	Mercer	25.4	220. Hainesport Township	Burlington	21.4
161. Rockleigh Borough	Bergen	25.4	221. Hamilton Township	Mercer	21.4
162. Elsinboro Township	Salem	25.2	222. Ewing Township	Mercer	21.2
163. Somerville Borough	Somerset	25.2	223. Roselle Park Borough	Union	21.2
164. Deerfield Township	Cumberland	25.1	224. West Windsor Township	Mercer	21.1
165. Elmwood Park Borough	Bergen	25.1	225. Keyport Borough	Monmouth	21.0
166. Branchville Borough	Sussex	25.0	226. Shrewsbury Borough	Monmouth	21.0
167. Somerdale Borough	Camden	25.0	227. Franklin Township	Gloucester	20.9
168. Little Egg Harbor Township	Ocean	24.9	228. Green Brook Township	Somerset	20.7
169. Edison Township	Middlesex	24.8	229. Logan Township	Gloucester	20.7
170. Hi-Nella Borough	Camden	24.8	230. Dover Town	Morris	20.6
171. Prospect Park Borough	Passaic	24.8	231. Haledon Borough	Passaic	20.5
172. Bound Brook Borough	Somerset	24.6	232. Lawrence Township	Cumberland	20.4
173. Long Branch City	Monmouth	24.6	233. Berkeley Township	Ocean	20.3
174. Beverly City	Burlington	24.5	234. South Plainfield Borough	Middlesex	20.3
175. North Brunswick Township	Middlesex	24.5	235. West Orange Township	Essex	20.3
176. Fairfield Township	Cumberland	24.2	236. Dennis Township	Cape May	20.1
177. Spring Lake Borough	Monmouth	23.9	237. Lyndhurst Township	Bergen	20.1
178. Edgewater Borough	Bergen	23.8	238. Maplewood Township	Essex	20.1
179. Woodbury Heights Borough	Gloucester	23.8	239. Andover Borough	Sussex	19.9
180. Dunellen Borough	Middlesex	23.6	240. Hackettstown Town	Warren	19.9

Crime Rate, 2007 (per 1,000 residents)

Municipality	County	Crime Rate	Municipality	County	Crime Rate
241. Mullica Township	Atlantic	19.9	301. Bordentown City	Burlington	15.9
242. Rochelle Park Township	Bergen	19.9	302. Cranbury Township	Middlesex	15.9
243. Stafford Township	Ocean	19.9	303. Gibbsboro Borough	Camden	15.9
244. Laurel Springs Borough	Camden	19.8	304. Evesham Township	Burlington	15.8
245. Raritan Borough	Somerset	19.6	305. Highland Park Borough	Middlesex	15.8
246. Waterford Township	Camden	19.6	306. Victory Gardens Borough	Morris	15.8
247. North Bergen Township	Hudson	19.5	307. Northfield City	Atlantic	15.7
248. Bayonne City	Hudson	19.3	308. Barnegat Light Borough	Ocean	15.6
249. Hightstown Borough	Mercer	19.1	309. Highlands Borough	Monmouth	15.6
250. Tinton Falls Borough	Monmouth	19.0	310. Wallington Borough	Bergen	15.6
251. Alpha Borough	Warren	18.9	311. Clark Township	Union	15.5
252. Cinnaminson Township	Burlington	18.9	312. Garfield City	Bergen	15.5
253. Margate City	Atlantic	18.8	313. Teaneck Township	Bergen	15.5
254. Brick Township	Ocean	18.7	314. Frenchtown Borough	Hunterdon	15.4
255. Carteret Borough	Middlesex	18.6	315. Lodi Borough	Bergen	15.4
256. East Brunswick Township	Middlesex	18.5	316. Pemberton Borough	Burlington	15.2
257. Frankford Township	Sussex	18.3	317. Aberdeen Township	Monmouth	15.1
258. Sayreville Borough	Middlesex	18.3	318. Eastampton Township	Burlington	15.1
259. Hawthorne Borough	Passaic	18.2	319. Far Hills Borough	Somerset	15.1
260. Little Silver Borough	Monmouth	18.2	320. Manville Borough	Somerset	15.1
261. Bordentown Township	Burlington	18.1	321. Roxbury Township	Morris	15.1
262. Point Pleasant Borough	Ocean	18.1	322. Union Beach Borough	Monmouth	15.1
263. Mountain Lakes Borough	Morris	18.0	323. East Greenwich Township	Gloucester	15.0
264. Kenilworth Borough	Union	17.8	324. Englewood Cliffs Borough	Bergen	15.0
265. Hopewell Township	Cumberland	17.7	325. Franklin Borough	Sussex	15.0
266. Parsippany-Troy Hills Township	Morris	17.7	326. Newfield Borough	Gloucester	15.0
267. Piscataway Township	Middlesex	17.7	327. Audubon Park Borough	Camden	14.9
268. Hampton Township	Sussex	17.6	328. Newton Town	Sussex	14.9
269. Lakehurst Borough	Ocean	17.6	329. Florence Township	Burlington	14.7
270. Englewood City	Bergen	17.5	330. North Arlington Borough	Bergen	14.5
271. Milltown Borough	Middlesex	17.5	331. Garwood Borough	Union	14.4
272. Rutherford Borough	Bergen	17.4	332. Guttenberg Town	Hudson	14.4
273. Downe Township	Cumberland	17.3	333. Old Bridge Township	Middlesex	14.4
274. Ridgefield Park Village	Bergen	17.3	334. Wanaque Borough	Passaic	14.4
275. Nutley Township	Essex	17.2	335. Harrison Township	Gloucester	14.3
276. Pittsgrove Township	Salem	17.2	336. Hopewell Borough	Mercer	14.3
277. Monmouth Beach Borough	Monmouth	17.1	337. Ramsey Borough	Bergen	14.2
278. Springfield Township	Union	17.1	338. Stanhope Borough	Sussex	14.2
279. Upper Pittsgrove Township	Salem	17.1	339. Englishtown Borough	Monmouth	14.1
280. Chester Borough	Morris	17.0	340. Hamburg Borough	Sussex	14.1
281. Franklin Township	Somerset	17.0	341. Upper Township	Cape May	14.1
282. Butler Borough	Morris	16.8	342. Holmdel Township	Monmouth	14.0
283. Lambertville City	Hunterdon	16.8	343. Pitman Borough	Gloucester	14.0
284. Pilesgrove Township	Salem	16.8	344. Summit City	Union	14.0
285. Mansfield Township	Warren	16.7	345. Cedar Grove Township	Essex	13.9
286. Atlantic Highlands Borough	Monmouth	16.5	346. Folsom Borough	Atlantic	13.9
287. Lebanon Borough	Hunterdon	16.4	347. Delran Township	Burlington	13.8
288. Wharton Borough	Morris	16.4	348. East Windsor Township	Mercer	13.8
289. Brigantine City	Atlantic	16.2	349. Fair Lawn Borough	Bergen	13.8
290. East Newark Borough	Hudson	16.2	350. Hanover Township	Morris	13.8
291. Haddon Heights Borough	Camden	16.2	351. Shiloh Borough	Cumberland	13.8
292. Livingston Township	Essex	16.2	352. Riverside Township	Burlington	13.6
293. Pine Beach Borough	Ocean	16.2	353. West Milford Township	Passaic	13.6
294. Bridgewater Township	Somerset	16.1	354. Allentown Borough	Monmouth	13.5
295. South Amboy City	Middlesex	16.1	355. Hammonton Town	Atlantic	13.5
296. Vernon Township	Sussex	16.1	356. Ocean Township	Ocean	13.5
297. Wall Township	Monmouth	16.1	357. Farmingdale Borough	Monmouth	13.4
298. Hazlet Township	Monmouth	16.0	358. Little Ferry Borough	Bergen	13.4
299. Mannington Township	Salem	16.0	359. Barrington Borough	Camden	13.3
300. Mansfield Township	Burlington	16.0	360. Middletown Township	Monmouth	13.2

Crime Rate, 2007 (per 1,000 residents)

Municipality	County	Crime Rate	Municipality	County	Crime Rate
361. Wood-Ridge Borough	Bergen	13.2	421. Milford Borough	Hunterdon	9.8
362. Franklin Township	Hunterdon	13.0	422. Mine Hill Township	Morris	9.8
363. High Bridge Borough	Hunterdon	13.0	423. Quinton Township	Salem	9.8
364. Howell Township	Monmouth	13.0	424. Springfield Township	Burlington	9.8
365. Lopatcong Township	Warren	13.0	425. Fair Haven Borough	Monmouth	9.7
366. Spotswood Borough	Middlesex	13.0	426. Knowlton Township	Warren	9.7
367. Longport Borough	Atlantic	12.9	427. Maywood Borough	Bergen	9.7
368. Estell Manor City	Atlantic	12.8	428. Montvale Borough	Bergen	9.7
369. Montague Township	Sussex	12.8	429. Verona Township	Essex	9.7
370. Tuckerton Borough	Ocean	12.8	430. Wantage Township	Sussex	9.7
371. Morris Plains Borough	Morris	12.7	431. Fanwood Borough	Union	9.6
372. Stockton Borough	Hunterdon	12.6	432. Liberty Township	Warren	9.5
373. Westfield Town	Union	12.4	433. Madison Borough	Morris	9.5
374. Port Republic City	Atlantic	12.2	434. South Harrison Township	Gloucester	9.5
375. Manalapan Township	Monmouth	12.1	435. Hillsborough Township	Somerset	9.4
376. Lower Alloways Creek Township	Salem	12.0	436. Plainsboro Township	Middlesex	9.4
377. Medford Township	Burlington	12.0	437. Pompton Lakes Borough	Passaic	9.4
378. South River Borough	Middlesex	11.9	438. Rockaway Borough	Morris	9.4
379. South Brunswick Township	Middlesex	11.8	439. Upper Freehold Township	Monmouth	9.4
380. Franklin Lakes Borough	Bergen	11.6	440. Montgomery Township	Somerset	9.3
381. Matawan Borough	Monmouth	11.6	441. Colts Neck Township	Monmouth	9.0
382. Southampton Township	Burlington	11.5	442. East Amwell Township	Hunterdon	9.0
383. Jackson Township	Ocean	11.4	443. Fort Lee Borough	Bergen	9.0
384. Jamesburg Borough	Middlesex	11.4	444. North Hanover Township	Burlington	9.0
385. Jefferson Township	Morris	11.4	445. Princeton Township	Mercer	9.0
386. Linwood City	Atlantic	11.4	446. Bergenfield Borough	Bergen	8.9
387. Oxford Township	Warren	11.4	447. Lincoln Park Borough	Morris	8.9
388. Pequannock Township	Morris	11.4	448. Manchester Township	Ocean	8.9
389. Scotch Plains Township	Union	11.4	449. West Caldwell Township	Essex	8.9
390. Leonia Borough	Bergen	11.3	450. Allendale Borough	Bergen	8.8
391. Hasbrouck Heights Borough	Bergen	11.2	451. Lafayette Township	Sussex	8.7
392. Plumsted Township	Ocean	11.2	452. Maurice River Township	Cumberland	8.7
393. Shrewsbury Township	Monmouth	11.2	453. Warren Township	Somerset	8.7
394. Brielle Borough	Monmouth	11.1	454. Weymouth Township	Atlantic	8.7
395. Mountainside Borough	Union	11.1	455. Millstone Township	Monmouth	8.6
396. Montville Township	Morris	11.0	456. Robbinsville Township	Mercer	8.6
397. Cliffside Park Borough	Bergen	10.9	457. Tabernacle Township	Burlington	8.6
398. Westwood Borough	Bergen	10.9	458. Wenonah Borough	Gloucester	8.6
399. Allamuchy Township	Warren	10.8	459. North Haledon Borough	Passaic	8.5
400. Alloway Township	Salem	10.8	460. Palisades Park Borough	Bergen	8.5
401. Cranford Township	Union	10.8	461. Peapack & Gladstone Borough	Somerset	8.5
402. Marlboro Township	Monmouth	10.7	462. Stow Creek Township	Cumberland	8.5
403. Denville Township	Morris	10.5	463. Washington Township	Warren	8.5
404. Dumont Borough	Bergen	10.5	464. Randolph Township	Morris	8.4
405. Middlesex Borough	Middlesex	10.5	465. Northvale Borough	Bergen	8.3
406. West Amwell Township	Hunterdon	10.5	466. Florham Park Borough	Morris	8.2
407. Mount Olive Township	Morris	10.4	467. Hardyston Township	Sussex	8.2
408. Oceanport Borough	Monmouth	10.4	468. Rumson Borough	Monmouth	8.2
409. Hampton Borough	Hunterdon	10.3	469. Independence Township	Warren	8.1
410. Mount Arlington Borough	Morris	10.3	470. Waldwick Borough	Bergen	8.1
411. Ridgefield Borough	Bergen	10.3	471. Readington Township	Hunterdon	8.0
412. Ridgewood Village	Bergen	10.3	472. Cresskill Borough	Bergen	7.9
413. Bogota Borough	Bergen	10.2	473. Hillsdale Borough	Bergen	7.7
414. Hope Township	Warren	10.1	474. Monroe Township	Middlesex	7.7
415. New Providence Borough	Union	10.1	475. Union Township	Hunterdon	7.7
416. Blairstown Township	Warren	10.0	476. Lebanon Township	Hunterdon	7.6
417. Barnegat Township	Ocean	9.9	477. Morris Township	Morris	7.4
418. Raritan Township	Hunterdon	9.9	478. Winfield Township	Union	7.4
419. Woodcliff Lake Borough	Bergen	9.9	479. Bedminster Township	Somerset	7.3
420. Hardwick Township	Warren	9.8	480. Boonton Township	Morris	7.3

Crime Rate, 2007 (per 1,000 residents)

Municipality	County	Crime Rate	Municipality	County	Crime Rate
481. Wyckoff Township	Bergen	7.3	526. Glen Rock Borough	Bergen	5.4
482. Chatham Borough	Morris	7.2	527. Roseland Borough	Essex	5.4
483. Franklin Township	Warren	7.2	528. Closter Borough	Bergen	5.3
484. Hopewell Township	Mercer	7.2	529. Caldwell Borough	Essex	5.2
485. Bloomingdale Borough	Passaic	7.1	530. Kingwood Township	Hunterdon	5.2
486. Midland Park Borough	Bergen	7.1	531. Mendham Borough	Morris	5.2
487. Washington Township	Morris	7.1	532. Pennington Borough	Mercer	5.2
488. Bernardsville Borough	Somerset	7.0	533. Sparta Township	Sussex	5.2
489. Branchburg Township	Somerset	7.0	534. Stillwater Township	Sussex	5.2
490. Hopatcong Borough	Sussex	7.0	535. Upper Saddle River Borough	Bergen	5.2
491. Ringwood Borough	Passaic	7.0	536. Delaware Township	Hunterdon	5.1
492. Kinnelon Borough	Morris	6.9	537. Saddle River Borough	Bergen	5.0
493. Oakland Borough	Bergen	6.9	538. White Township	Warren	5.0
494. Essex Fells Borough	Essex	6.8	539. Park Ridge Borough	Bergen	4.9
495. Harding Township	Morris	6.8	540. Belvidere Town	Warren	4.8
496. North Caldwell Borough	Essex	6.8	541. Califon Borough	Hunterdon	4.8
497. Tenafly Borough	Bergen	6.8	542. Island Heights Borough	Ocean	4.8
498. Medford Lakes Borough	Burlington	6.7	543. Holland Township	Hunterdon	4.7
499. Andover Township	Sussex	6.6	544. Millstone Borough	Somerset	4.6
500. Long Hill Township	Morris	6.6	545. Clinton Township	Hunterdon	4.5
501. Byram Township	Sussex	6.5	546. Fredon Township	Sussex	4.5
502. Glen Gardner Borough	Hunterdon	6.5	547. Shamong Township	Burlington	4.5
503. Green Township	Sussex	6.5	548. Rocky Hill Borough	Somerset	4.4
504. Berkeley Heights Township	Union	6.4	549. Roosevelt Borough	Monmouth	4.4
505. South Bound Brook Borough	Somerset	6.4	550. Tewksbury Township	Hunterdon	4.3
506. Woolwich Township	Gloucester	6.4	551. Sandyston Township	Sussex	4.2
507. Alexandria Township	Hunterdon	6.3	552. Frelinghuysen Township	Warren	4.1
508. Harmony Township	Warren	6.3	553. Haworth Borough	Bergen	4.1
509. New Milford Borough	Bergen	6.3	554. Spring Lake Heights Borough	Monmouth	3.9
510. Bernards Township	Somerset	5.9	555. Chatham Township	Morris	3.7
511. Boonton Town	Morris	5.9	556. Old Tappan Borough	Bergen	3.5
512. Chesterfield Township	Burlington	5.9	557. Ho-Ho-Kus Borough	Bergen	3.4
513. Helmetta Borough	Middlesex	5.9	558. Interlaken Borough	Monmouth	3.4
514. Mahwah Township	Bergen	5.9	559. Norwood Borough	Bergen	3.0
515. Mendham Township	Morris	5.9	560. Washington Township	Bergen	2.7
516. Alpine Borough	Bergen	5.8	561. Bethlehem Township	Hunterdon	2.0
517. Clinton Town	Hunterdon	5.8	562. Harrington Park Borough	Bergen	1.8
518. Oradell Borough	Bergen	5.8	563. New Hanover Township	Burlington	0.7
519. Emerson Borough	Bergen	5.7	564. Fieldsboro Borough	Burlington	0.0
520. Ogdensburg Borough	Sussex	5.7	565. Walpack Township	Sussex	0.0
521. Chester Township	Morris	5.6	566. Teterboro Borough	Bergen	NA
522. Greenwich Township	Cumberland	5.6			
523. River Edge Borough	Bergen	5.6			
524. Demarest Borough	Bergen	5.5			
525. River Vale Township	Bergen	5.5			

Land Area (square miles)

	Municipality	County	Area		Municipality	County	Area
1.	Hamilton Township	Atlantic	111.28	61.	Millstone Township	Monmouth	36.76
2.	Washington Township	Burlington	100.14	62.	Delaware Township	Hunterdon	36.74
3.	Jackson Township	Ocean	100.06	63.	Hardwick Township	Warren	36.48
4.	Woodland Township	Burlington	95.94	64.	Waterford Township	Camden	36.19
5.	Maurice River Township	Cumberland	93.41	65.	Kingwood Township	Hunterdon	35.23
6.	Galloway Township	Atlantic	90.49	66.	Pilesgrove Township	Salem	34.91
7.	Lacey Township	Ocean	84.00	67.	Mannington Township	Salem	34.78
8.	Manchester Township	Ocean	82.60	68.	Barnegat Township	Ocean	34.67
9.	Bass River Township	Burlington	75.88	69.	Frankford Township	Sussex	34.11
10.	West Milford Township	Passaic	75.44	70.	Alloway Township	Salem	32.85
11.	Middle Township	Cape May	71.27	71.	Montgomery Township	Somerset	32.62
12.	Vineland City	Cumberland	68.69	72.	Commercial Township	Cumberland	32.46
13.	Vernon Township	Sussex	68.39	73.	Bridgewater Township	Somerset	32.45
14.	Egg Harbor Township	Atlantic	67.35	74.	Hardyston Township	Sussex	32.09
15.	Wantage Township	Sussex	67.12	75.	Lebanon Township	Hunterdon	31.69
16.	Upper Township	Cape May	63.15	76.	Tewksbury Township	Hunterdon	31.63
17.	Pemberton Township	Burlington	61.68	77.	Colts Neck Township	Monmouth	31.43
18.	Dennis Township	Cape May	61.35	78.	Upper Deerfield Township	Cumberland	31.10
19.	Howell Township	Monmouth	60.91	79.	Blairstown Township	Warren	31.02
20.	Hopewell Township	Mercer	58.11	80.	Manalapan Township	Monmouth	30.82
21.	Winslow Township	Camden	57.70	81.	Wall Township	Monmouth	30.62
22.	Mullica Township	Atlantic	56.58	82.	Marlboro Township	Monmouth	30.59
23.	Franklin Township	Gloucester	56.01	83.	Mount Olive Township	Morris	30.35
24.	Hillsborough Township	Somerset	54.69	84.	Edison Township	Middlesex	30.12
25.	Estell Manor City	Atlantic	53.57	85.	Springfield Township	Burlington	30.03
26.	Downe Township	Cumberland	50.76	86.	Clinton Township	Hunterdon	30.00
27.	Tabernacle Township	Burlington	49.46	87.	Mansfield Township	Warren	29.92
28.	Little Egg Harbor Township	Ocean	49.11	88.	Hopewell Township	Cumberland	29.90
29.	Readington Township	Hunterdon	47.69	89.	Evesham Township	Burlington	29.54
30.	Upper Freehold Township	Monmouth	46.86	90.	Chester Township	Morris	29.33
31.	Lower Alloways Creek Township	Salem	46.78	91.	East Amwell Township	Hunterdon	28.68
32.	Franklin Township	Somerset	46.77	92.	Lower Township	Cape May	28.22
33.	Monroe Township	Gloucester	46.55	93.	Alexandria Township	Hunterdon	27.54
34.	Stafford Township	Ocean	46.53	94.	White Township	Warren	27.37
35.	Pittsgrove Township	Salem	45.19	95.	Stillwater Township	Sussex	27.12
36.	Washington Township	Morris	44.86	96.	Bedminster Township	Somerset	26.47
37.	Shamong Township	Burlington	44.81	97.	Brick Township	Ocean	26.23
38.	Southampton Township	Burlington	44.03	98.	West Windsor Township	Mercer	26.01
39.	Montague Township	Sussex	44.01	99.	Mahwah Township	Bergen	25.93
40.	Berkeley Township	Ocean	42.90	100.	Ringwood Borough	Passaic	25.25
41.	Rockaway Township	Morris	42.82	101.	Lakewood Township	Ocean	24.82
42.	Sandyston Township	Sussex	42.61	102.	Knowlton Township	Warren	24.78
43.	Millville City	Cumberland	42.35	103.	Hampton Township	Sussex	24.62
44.	Fairfield Township	Cumberland	42.29	104.	Cherry Hill Township	Camden	24.25
45.	Monroe Township	Middlesex	41.94	105.	Quinton Township	Salem	24.17
46.	Buena Vista Township	Atlantic	41.36	106.	Walpack Township	Sussex	24.07
47.	Hammonton Town	Atlantic	41.26	107.	Bernards Township	Somerset	24.00
48.	Middletown Township	Monmouth	41.12	108.	Franklin Township	Warren	23.99
49.	Toms River Township	Ocean	40.97	109.	Parsippany-Troy Hills Township	Morris	23.94
50.	South Brunswick Township	Middlesex	40.86	110.	Wayne Township	Passaic	23.82
51.	Jefferson Township	Morris	40.63	111.	Harmony Township	Warren	23.81
52.	Upper Pittsgrove Township	Salem	40.39	112.	Newark City	Essex	23.80
53.	Plumsted Township	Ocean	40.02	113.	Holland Township	Hunterdon	23.70
54.	Hamilton Township	Mercer	39.45	114.	Frelinghuysen Township	Warren	23.43
55.	Medford Township	Burlington	39.32	115.	Gloucester Township	Camden	23.22
56.	Freehold Township	Monmouth	38.45	116.	Pennsville Township	Salem	23.10
57.	Old Bridge Township	Middlesex	38.09	117.	Woodbridge Township	Middlesex	23.01
58.	Raritan Township	Hunterdon	37.84	118.	Franklin Township	Hunterdon	22.88
59.	Lawrence Township	Cumberland	37.47	119.	Logan Township	Gloucester	22.62
60.	Sparta Township	Sussex	37.39	120.	New Hanover Township	Burlington	22.28

Land Area (square miles)

Municipality	County	Area	Municipality	County	Area
121. Lawrence Township	Mercer	22.14	181. Elizabeth City	Union	12.22
122. East Brunswick Township	Middlesex	21.95	182. Weymouth Township	Atlantic	12.20
123. Mount Laurel Township	Burlington	21.81	183. West Orange Township	Essex	12.12
124. Mansfield Township	Burlington	21.72	184. Denville Township	Morris	12.11
125. West Amwell Township	Hunterdon	21.72	185. Long Hill Township	Morris	12.08
126. Chesterfield Township	Burlington	21.41	186. North Brunswick Township	Middlesex	12.02
127. Roxbury Township	Morris	21.37	187. Plainsboro Township	Middlesex	11.84
128. Washington Township	Gloucester	21.37	188. Liberty Township	Warren	11.80
129. Byram Township	Sussex	21.07	189. Voorhees Township	Camden	11.60
130. Randolph Township	Morris	20.96	190. Atlantic City	Atlantic	11.35
131. Woolwich Township	Gloucester	20.94	191. Clifton City	Passaic	11.30
132. Bethlehem Township	Hunterdon	20.84	192. Egg Harbor City	Atlantic	11.11
133. Ocean Township	Ocean	20.80	193. Westampton Township	Burlington	11.04
134. Allamuchy Township	Warren	20.54	194. Ocean Township	Monmouth	11.03
135. Robbinsville Township	Mercer	20.48	195. Hopatcong Borough	Sussex	10.96
136. Harding Township	Morris	20.44	196. Linden City	Union	10.81
137. Branchburg Township	Somerset	20.26	197. Hanover Township	Morris	10.66
138. Andover Township	Sussex	20.18	198. Greenwich Township	Warren	10.55
139. Oldmans Township	Salem	19.97	199. Pennsauken Township	Camden	10.53
140. Independence Township	Warren	19.84	200. Paramus Borough	Bergen	10.47
141. Warren Township	Somerset	19.67	201. Fairfield Township	Essex	10.45
142. Elk Township	Gloucester	19.63	202. Florence Township	Burlington	9.71
143. Harrison Township	Gloucester	19.13	203. Franklin Lakes Borough	Bergen	9.45
144. Union Township	Hunterdon	18.97	204. Millburn Township	Essex	9.38
145. Montville Township	Morris	18.87	205. Chatham Township	Morris	9.33
146. Piscataway Township	Middlesex	18.78	206. Greenwich Township	Gloucester	9.32
147. Hope Township	Warren	18.50	207. Glassboro Borough	Gloucester	9.21
148. Stow Creek Township	Cumberland	18.45	208. Kearny Town	Hudson	9.14
149. Greenwich Township	Cumberland	18.16	209. Union Township	Union	9.12
150. Lafayette Township	Sussex	18.02	210. Scotch Plains Township	Union	9.08
151. Holmdel Township	Monmouth	17.97	211. Camden City	Camden	8.82
152. Kinnelon Borough	Morris	17.89	212. Bloomingdale Borough	Passaic	8.80
153. Mendham Township	Morris	17.86	213. Oakland Borough	Bergen	8.60
154. Fredon Township	Sussex	17.76	214. Bordentown Township	Burlington	8.51
155. Washington Township	Warren	17.58	215. Paterson City	Passaic	8.44
156. Carneys Point Township	Salem	17.50	216. Boonton Township	Morris	8.42
157. Deptford Township	Gloucester	17.50	217. South Plainfield Borough	Middlesex	8.36
158. North Hanover Township	Burlington	17.34	218. Folsom Borough	Atlantic	8.27
159. Deerfield Township	Cumberland	16.84	219. Neptune Township	Monmouth	8.22
160. Princeton Township	Mercer	16.38	220. East Hanover Township	Morris	8.16
161. Eagleswood Township	Ocean	16.37	221. Woodbine Borough	Cape May	8.00
162. Green Township	Sussex	16.18	222. Wanaque Borough	Passaic	7.98
163. Mantua Township	Gloucester	15.90	223. Corbin City	Atlantic	7.89
164. Sayreville Borough	Middlesex	15.90	224. Willingboro Township	Burlington	7.69
165. West Deptford Township	Gloucester	15.90	225. Trenton City	Mercer	7.66
166. South Harrison Township	Gloucester	15.80	226. Port Republic City	Atlantic	7.62
167. Morris Township	Morris	15.76	227. Buena Borough	Atlantic	7.61
168. East Windsor Township	Mercer	15.65	228. Cinnaminson Township	Burlington	7.60
169. Tinton Falls Borough	Monmouth	15.59	229. Florham Park Borough	Morris	7.43
170. Ewing Township	Mercer	15.33	230. Clayton Borough	Gloucester	7.18
171. Jersey City	Hudson	14.92	231. Lopatcong Township	Warren	7.08
172. Moorestown Township	Burlington	14.77	232. Pequannock Township	Morris	7.07
173. East Greenwich Township	Gloucester	14.75	233. Ocean City	Cape May	6.92
174. Livingston Township	Essex	13.88	234. Lincoln Park Borough	Morris	6.73
175. Burlington Township	Burlington	13.47	235. Westfield Town	Union	6.73
176. Cranbury Township	Middlesex	13.41	236. Delran Township	Burlington	6.64
177. Pohatcong Township	Warren	13.33	237. Wyckoff Township	Bergen	6.55
178. Bernardsville Borough	Somerset	12.93	238. Hainesport Township	Burlington	6.52
179. Lumberton Township	Burlington	12.87	239. Brigantine City	Atlantic	6.43
180. Elsinboro Township	Salem	12.27	240. Alpine Borough	Bergen	6.36

Land Area (square miles)

Municipality	County	Area	Municipality	County	Area
241. Montclair Township	Essex	6.30	301. New Providence Borough	Union	3.68
242. Berkeley Heights Township	Union	6.26	302. Tuckerton Borough	Ocean	3.66
243. Bridgeton City	Cumberland	6.22	303. Roseland Borough	Essex	3.62
244. Summit City	Union	6.05	304. Berlin Borough	Camden	3.58
245. Teaneck Township	Bergen	6.05	305. Point Pleasant Borough	Ocean	3.53
246. Plainfield City	Union	6.04	306. Middlesex Borough	Middlesex	3.50
247. Mendham Borough	Morris	6.02	307. North Haledon Borough	Passaic	3.44
248. Watchung Borough	Somerset	6.02	308. Northfield City	Atlantic	3.43
249. Oxford Township	Warren	5.94	309. Hawthorne Borough	Passaic	3.40
250. Eatontown Borough	Monmouth	5.92	310. Nutley Township	Essex	3.37
251. Secaucus Town	Hudson	5.89	311. Belleville Township	Essex	3.34
252. Peapack & Gladstone Borough	Somerset	5.80	312. Woodcliff Lake Borough	Bergen	3.33
253. Ridgewood Village	Bergen	5.79	313. Berlin Township	Camden	3.25
254. Pleasantville City	Atlantic	5.78	314. Old Tappan Borough	Bergen	3.23
255. Eastampton Township	Burlington	5.75	315. Oceanport Borough	Monmouth	3.22
256. Absecon City	Atlantic	5.72	316. Phillipsburg Town	Warren	3.22
257. Bayonne City	Hudson	5.63	317. Closter Borough	Bergen	3.17
258. Hazlet Township	Monmouth	5.62	318. Allendale Borough	Bergen	3.12
259. Ramsey Borough	Bergen	5.56	319. Passaic City	Passaic	3.11
260. Aberdeen Township	Monmouth	5.54	320. Newton Town	Sussex	3.10
261. Bloomfield Township	Essex	5.32	321. Bellmawr Borough	Camden	3.03
262. Long Beach Township	Ocean	5.31	322. Burlington City	Burlington	3.00
263. Upper Saddle River Borough	Bergen	5.29	323. Mine Hill Township	Morris	2.99
264. New Brunswick City	Middlesex	5.23	324. North Caldwell Borough	Essex	2.99
265. Long Branch City	Monmouth	5.22	325. Hillsdale Borough	Bergen	2.98
266. Rumson Borough	Monmouth	5.22	326. Pompton Lakes Borough	Passaic	2.97
267. North Bergen Township	Hudson	5.20	327. Irvington Township	Essex	2.96
268. Fair Lawn Borough	Bergen	5.17	328. West Paterson Borough	Passaic	2.96
269. Springfield Township	Union	5.15	329. Morristown Town	Morris	2.94
270. West Caldwell Township	Essex	5.05	330. Edgewater Park Township	Burlington	2.91
271. Saddle River Borough	Bergen	4.98	331. Washington Township	Bergen	2.91
272. Englewood City	Bergen	4.92	332. Bergenfield Borough	Bergen	2.90
273. Far Hills Borough	Somerset	4.86	333. West Long Branch Borough	Monmouth	2.89
274. Cranford Township	Union	4.82	334. Mount Holly Township	Burlington	2.86
275. Perth Amboy City	Middlesex	4.78	335. South Orange Village Township	Essex	2.85
276. Lyndhurst Township	Bergen	4.65	336. Haddonfield Borough	Camden	2.83
277. Tenafly Borough	Bergen	4.61	337. Rutherford Borough	Bergen	2.81
278. Green Brook Township	Somerset	4.58	338. South River Borough	Middlesex	2.81
279. Franklin Borough	Sussex	4.49	339. Hillside Township	Union	2.79
280. Carteret Borough	Middlesex	4.36	340. North Plainfield Borough	Somerset	2.79
281. Clark Township	Union	4.34	341. Little Silver Borough	Monmouth	2.77
282. Cedar Grove Township	Essex	4.22	342. Beachwood Borough	Ocean	2.76
283. Avalon Borough	Cape May	4.21	343. Little Falls Township	Passaic	2.75
284. Madison Borough	Morris	4.20	344. Norwood Borough	Bergen	2.75
285. Hackensack City	Bergen	4.12	345. Verona Township	Essex	2.75
286. River Vale Township	Bergen	4.08	346. Metuchen Borough	Middlesex	2.74
287. Somers Point City	Atlantic	4.03	347. Glen Rock Borough	Bergen	2.72
288. Mountainside Borough	Union	4.02	348. Saddle Brook Township	Bergen	2.72
289. Totowa Borough	Passaic	4.00	349. Haddon Township	Camden	2.69
290. Rahway City	Union	3.99	350. Dover Town	Morris	2.68
291. Montvale Borough	Bergen	3.97	351. Mountain Lakes Borough	Morris	2.67
292. Carlstadt Borough	Bergen	3.95	352. Elmwood Park Borough	Bergen	2.65
293. Lindenwold Borough	Camden	3.94	353. Roselle Borough	Union	2.64
294. East Orange City	Essex	3.93	354. Ridgefield Borough	Bergen	2.61
295. Pine Hill Borough	Camden	3.93	355. Salem City	Salem	2.61
296. Maple Shade Township	Burlington	3.85	356. Park Ridge Borough	Bergen	2.60
297. Maplewood Township	Essex	3.85	357. Morris Plains Borough	Morris	2.59
298. Linwood City	Atlantic	3.83	358. North Arlington Borough	Bergen	2.58
299. East Rutherford Borough	Bergen	3.81	359. Fort Lee Borough	Bergen	2.53
300. Hackettstown Town	Warren	3.70	360. Delanco Township	Burlington	2.49

Land Area (square miles)

Municipality	County	Area	Municipality	County	Area
361. Cape May City	Cape May	2.48	421. Newfield Borough	Gloucester	1.70
362. Manville Borough	Somerset	2.48	422. Fair Haven Borough	Monmouth	1.67
363. Oradell Borough	Bergen	2.42	423. Barrington Borough	Camden	1.61
364. Chatham Borough	Morris	2.41	424. Woodstown Borough	Salem	1.59
365. High Bridge Borough	Hunterdon	2.41	425. Stratford Borough	Camden	1.58
366. Somerville Borough	Somerset	2.36	426. Milltown Borough	Middlesex	1.57
367. Boonton Town	Morris	2.35	427. Glen Gardner Borough	Hunterdon	1.56
368. Spotswood Borough	Middlesex	2.32	428. Midland Park Borough	Bergen	1.56
369. Westwood Borough	Bergen	2.32	429. Haddon Heights Borough	Camden	1.55
370. New Milford Borough	Bergen	2.31	430. South Amboy City	Middlesex	1.55
371. Pitman Borough	Gloucester	2.29	431. Chester Borough	Morris	1.54
372. Matawan Borough	Monmouth	2.28	432. Hampton Borough	Hunterdon	1.54
373. Ogdensburg Borough	Sussex	2.28	433. Little Ferry Borough	Bergen	1.53
374. Lodi Borough	Bergen	2.26	434. Riverside Township	Burlington	1.52
375. Emerson Borough	Bergen	2.24	435. Hasbrouck Heights Borough	Bergen	1.51
376. Orange City Township	Essex	2.21	436. Leonia Borough	Bergen	1.51
377. Shrewsbury Borough	Monmouth	2.21	437. Audubon Borough	Camden	1.49
378. Gibbsboro Borough	Camden	2.20	438. Andover Borough	Sussex	1.46
379. Gloucester City	Camden	2.20	439. Point Pleasant Beach Borough	Ocean	1.44
380. Sea Isle City	Cape May	2.20	440. Asbury Park City	Monmouth	1.43
381. Wharton Borough	Morris	2.19	441. Stone Harbor Borough	Cape May	1.42
382. Cresskill Borough	Bergen	2.14	442. Essex Fells Borough	Essex	1.41
383. Kenilworth Borough	Union	2.14	443. Keyport Borough	Monmouth	1.41
384. Ventnor City	Atlantic	2.14	444. Margate City	Atlantic	1.41
385. Garfield City	Bergen	2.13	445. Lawnside Borough	Camden	1.40
386. Mount Arlington Borough	Morris	2.11	446. Manasquan Borough	Monmouth	1.38
387. Englewood Cliffs Borough	Bergen	2.09	447. Clinton Town	Hunterdon	1.37
388. Rockaway Borough	Morris	2.09	448. Somerdale Borough	Camden	1.37
389. Runnemede Borough	Camden	2.09	449. Fanwood Borough	Union	1.34
390. Butler Borough	Morris	2.08	450. Belvidere Town	Warren	1.32
391. Waldwick Borough	Bergen	2.08	451. Northvale Borough	Bergen	1.32
392. Woodbury City	Gloucester	2.08	452. Spring Lake Heights Borough	Monmouth	1.32
393. Demarest Borough	Bergen	2.07	453. Spring Lake Borough	Monmouth	1.31
394. Riverdale Borough	Morris	2.06	454. Maywood Borough	Bergen	1.30
395. Raritan Borough	Somerset	2.04	455. Wildwood City	Cape May	1.29
396. Freehold Borough	Monmouth	2.00	456. Frenchtown Borough	Hunterdon	1.28
397. Dumont Borough	Bergen	1.99	457. Glen Ridge Borough	Essex	1.28
398. Palmyra Borough	Burlington	1.98	458. Hoboken City	Hudson	1.28
399. Haworth Borough	Bergen	1.96	459. Union City	Hudson	1.27
400. Paulsboro Borough	Gloucester	1.96	460. Atlantic Highlands Borough	Monmouth	1.24
401. Roosevelt Borough	Monmouth	1.96	461. Hightstown Borough	Mercer	1.23
402. Washington Borough	Warren	1.96	462. Woodbury Heights Borough	Gloucester	1.23
403. Clementon Borough	Camden	1.89	463. Deal Borough	Monmouth	1.22
404. River Edge Borough	Bergen	1.89	464. Harrison Town	Hudson	1.22
405. Union Beach Borough	Monmouth	1.88	465. Roselle Park Borough	Union	1.22
406. Stanhope Borough	Sussex	1.87	466. Medford Lakes Borough	Burlington	1.21
407. Harrington Park Borough	Bergen	1.86	467. Palisades Park Borough	Bergen	1.21
408. Princeton Borough	Mercer	1.85	468. Shiloh Borough	Cumberland	1.20
409. Highland Park Borough	Middlesex	1.84	469. Caldwell Borough	Essex	1.19
410. Collingswood Borough	Camden	1.83	470. West Cape May Borough	Cape May	1.19
411. Brielle Borough	Monmouth	1.78	471. Haledon Borough	Passaic	1.16
412. Red Bank Borough	Monmouth	1.78	472. Hamburg Borough	Sussex	1.16
413. North Wildwood City	Cape May	1.77	473. South Toms River Borough	Ocean	1.16
414. Wrightstown Borough	Burlington	1.76	474. Milford Borough	Hunterdon	1.15
415. Ho-Ho-Kus Borough	Bergen	1.74	475. Wildwood Crest Borough	Cape May	1.15
416. Moonachie Borough	Bergen	1.73	476. Lambertville City	Hunterdon	1.13
417. Ridgefield Park Village	Bergen	1.73	477. Teterboro Borough	Bergen	1.11
418. Chesilhurst Borough	Camden	1.72	478. Wood-Ridge Borough	Bergen	1.10
419. Bound Brook Borough	Somerset	1.71	479. Keansburg Borough	Monmouth	1.08
420. Alpha Borough	Warren	1.70	480. Flemington Borough	Hunterdon	1.07

Land Area (square miles)

Municipality	County	Area		Municipality	County	Area
481. Monmouth Beach Borough	Monmouth	1.07		526. Seaside Park Borough	Ocean	0.65
482. Sea Girt Borough	Monmouth	1.06		527. Sea Bright Borough	Monmouth	0.64
483. Rochelle Park Township	Bergen	1.05		528. Pine Beach Borough	Ocean	0.62
484. Dunellen Borough	Middlesex	1.04		529. Allentown Borough	Monmouth	0.61
485. Belmar Borough	Monmouth	1.02		530. Oaklyn Borough	Camden	0.61
486. West New York Town	Hudson	1.02		531. Seaside Heights Borough	Ocean	0.61
487. National Park Borough	Gloucester	1.00		532. Island Heights Borough	Ocean	0.60
488. Wallington Borough	Bergen	1.00		533. Merchantville Borough	Camden	0.60
489. Beach Haven Borough	Ocean	0.98		534. Sussex Borough	Sussex	0.60
490. Califon Borough	Hunterdon	0.97		535. Bay Head Borough	Ocean	0.59
491. Magnolia Borough	Camden	0.97		536. Bradley Beach Borough	Monmouth	0.59
492. Rockleigh Borough	Bergen	0.97		537. Branchville Borough	Sussex	0.59
493. Wenonah Borough	Gloucester	0.97		538. Pemberton Borough	Burlington	0.59
494. Cliffside Park Borough	Bergen	0.96		539. Beverly City	Burlington	0.58
495. Pennington Borough	Mercer	0.96		540. Englishtown Borough	Monmouth	0.57
496. Westville Borough	Gloucester	0.96		541. Harvey Cedars Borough	Ocean	0.55
497. Pine Valley Borough	Camden	0.95		542. Stockton Borough	Hunterdon	0.55
498. Penns Grove Borough	Salem	0.93		543. Farmingdale Borough	Monmouth	0.53
499. Bordentown City	Burlington	0.92		544. Prospect Park Borough	Passaic	0.48
500. Lakehurst Borough	Ocean	0.92		545. Brooklawn Borough	Camden	0.47
501. Bloomsbury Borough	Hunterdon	0.91		546. Laurel Springs Borough	Camden	0.47
502. Neptune City Borough	Monmouth	0.91		547. Mantoloking Borough	Ocean	0.44
503. Mount Ephraim Borough	Camden	0.88		548. Ocean Gate Borough	Ocean	0.44
504. Elmer Borough	Salem	0.87		549. Avon-by-the-Sea Borough	Monmouth	0.43
505. Lebanon Borough	Hunterdon	0.87		550. Longport Borough	Atlantic	0.38
506. Edgewater Borough	Bergen	0.85		551. Interlaken Borough	Monmouth	0.35
507. Fairview Borough	Bergen	0.85		552. Cape May Point Borough	Cape May	0.29
508. Helmetta Borough	Middlesex	0.85		553. Fieldsboro Borough	Burlington	0.27
509. Weehawken Township	Hudson	0.85		554. Allenhurst Borough	Monmouth	0.26
510. Jamesburg Borough	Middlesex	0.84		555. West Wildwood Borough	Cape May	0.26
511. Netcong Borough	Morris	0.84		556. Lake Como Borough	Monmouth	0.25
512. Lavallette Borough	Ocean	0.80		557. Tavistock Borough	Camden	0.25
513. South Bound Brook Borough	Somerset	0.78		558. Hi-Nella Borough	Camden	0.23
514. Bogota Borough	Bergen	0.76		559. Woodlynne Borough	Camden	0.22
515. Highlands Borough	Monmouth	0.76		560. Guttenberg Town	Hudson	0.19
516. Millstone Borough	Somerset	0.75		561. Winfield Township	Union	0.18
517. Swedesboro Borough	Gloucester	0.73		562. Audubon Park Borough	Camden	0.15
518. Barnegat Light Borough	Ocean	0.72		563. Victory Gardens Borough	Morris	0.15
519. Surf City Borough	Ocean	0.72		564. East Newark Borough	Hudson	0.10
520. South Hackensack Township	Bergen	0.71		565. Loch Arbour Village	Monmouth	0.10
521. Ship Bottom Borough	Ocean	0.70		566. Shrewsbury Township	Monmouth	0.09
522. Hopewell Borough	Mercer	0.69				
523. Rocky Hill Borough	Somerset	0.67				
524. Garwood Borough	Union	0.66				
525. Riverton Borough	Burlington	0.66				

Federal Representatives, 111th Congress

U.S. Senate

Robert Menendez (Democratic) – term ends 2013
Frank R. Lautenberg (Democratic) – term ends 2015

U.S. House of Representatives

District	Name	Party
1.	Robert E. Andrews	Democratic
2.	Frank A. LoBiondo	Republican
3.	John H. Adler	Democratic
4.	Christopher H. Smith	Republican
5.	Scott Garrett	Republican
6.	Frank Pallone Jr	Democratic
7.	Leonard Lance	Republican
8.	Bill Pascrell Jr	Democratic
9.	Steven R. Rothman	Democratic
10.	Donald M. Payne	Democratic
11.	Rodney P. Frelinghuysen	Republican
12.	Rush D. Holt	Democratic
13.	Albio Sires	Democratic

New Jersey State Legislature, 2008-09 Session

Each of New Jersey's 40 legislative districts elects 1 member of the State Senate and 2 members of the General Assembly.

District	Senate	Assembly 1	Assembly 2
1.	Jeff Van Drew (D)	Nelson T. Albano (D)	Matthew W. Miliam (D)
2.	Jim Whelan (D)	John F. Amodeo (R)	Vincent J. Polistina (D)
3.	Stephen M. Sweeney (D)	John J. Burzichelli (D)	Celeste M. Riley (D)
4.	Fred H. Madden Jr (D)	Sandra Love (D)	Paul D. Moriarty (D)
5.	Dana L. Redd (D)	Nilsa Cruz-Perez (D)	Joseph J. Roberts Jr (D)
6.	James Beach (D)	Louis D. Greenwald (D)	Pamela R. Lampitt (D)
7.	Diane B. Allen (R)	Herb Conway Jr (D)	Jack Conners (D)
8.	Philip E. Haines (R)	Dawn Marie Addiego (R)	Scott Rudder (R)
9.	Christopher J. Connors (R)	Brian E. Rumpf (R)	Daniel M. Van Pelt (R)
10.	Andrew R. Ciesla (R)	James W. Holzapfel (R)	David W. Wolfe (R)
11.	Sean T. Kean (R)	Mary Pat Angelini (R)	David P. Rible (R)
12.	Jennifer Beck (R)	Caroline Casagrande (R)	Declan J. O'Scanlon Jr (R)
13.	Joseph M. Kyrillos Jr (R)	Amy H. Handlin (R)	Samuel D. Thompson (R)
14.	Bill Baroni (R)	Wayne P. DeAngelo (D)	Linda R. Greenstein (D)
15.	Shirley K. Turner (D)	Reed Gusciora (D)	Bonnie Watson Coleman (D)
16.	Christopher Bateman (R)	Peter J. Biondi (R)	Denise M. Coyle (R)
17.	Bob Smith (D)	Upendra J. Chivukula (D)	Joseph V. Egan (D)
18.	Barbara Buono (D)	Peter J. Barnes III (D)	Patrick J. Diengan Jr (D)
19.	Joseph F. Vitale (D)	Joseph Vas (D)	John S. Wisniewski (D)
20.	Raymond J. Lesniak (D)	Joseph Cryan (D)	Annette Quijano (D)
21.	Thomas H. Kean Jr (R)	Jon M. Bramnick (R)	(vacant)
22.	Nicholas P. Scutari (D)	Jerry Green (D)	Linda Stender (D)
23.	Marcia A. Karrow (R)	John DiMaio (R)	Michael J. Doherty (R)
24.	Steven V. Oroho (R)	Gary R. Chiusano (R)	Alison Littell McHose (R)
25.	Anthony R. Bucco (R)	Michael Patrick Carroll (R)	Richard A. Merkt (R)
26.	Joseph Pennacchio (R)	Alex DeCroce (R)	Jay Webber (R)
27.	Richard J. Codey (D)	Mila M. Jasey (D)	John F. McKeon (D)
28.	Ronald L. Rice (D)	Ralph R. Caputo (D)	Cleopatra G. Tucker (D)
29.	M. Teresa Ruiz (D)	Albert Coutinho (D)	L. Grace Spencer (D)
30.	Robert W. Singer (R)	Ronald S. Dancer (R)	Joseph R. Malone III (R)
31.	Sandra B. Cunningham (D)	Anthony Chiappone (D)	L. Harvey Smith (D)
32.	Nicholas J. Sacco (D)	Vincent Prieto (D)	Joan M. Quigley (D)
33.	Brian P. Stack (D)	Ruben J. Ramos Jr. (D)	Caridad Rodriguez (D)
34.	Nia H. Gill (D)	Thomas P. Giblin (D)	Sheila Y. Oliver (D)
35.	John A. Girgenti (D)	Elease Evans (D)	Nellie Pou (D)
36.	Paul A. Sarlo (D)	Frederick Scalera (D)	Gary S. Schaer (D)
37.	Loretta Weinberg (D)	Gordon M. Johnson (D)	Valerie Vainieri Huttle (D)
38.	Robert M. Gordon (D)	John M. Voss (D)	Connie Wagner (D)
39.	Gerald Cardinale (R)	John E. Rooney (R)	Charlotte Vandervalk (R)
40.	Kevin J. O'Toole (R)	Scott T. Rumana (R)	David C. Russo (R)

Title	Qty	Edition	Price	ISBN Number	Standing Order	
State & Municipal Profiles Series					YES	NO
Almanac of the 50 States 2009		Hardcover	$95	978-0-929960-53-1	☐	☐
		Paperback	$85	978-0-929960-52-4	☐	☐
California Cities, Towns & Counties 2009		Paperback	$129	978-0-911273-48-9	☐	☐
		CD	$129	978-0-911273-49-6	☐	☐
Connecticut Municipal Profiles 2009		Paperback	$89	978-0-941391-32-0	☐	☐
		CD	$89	978-0-941391-33-7	☐	☐
Florida Cities, Towns & Counties 2009		Paperback	$129	978-0-941391-34-4	☐	☐
		CD	$129	978-0-941391-35-1	☐	☐
Massachusetts Municipal Profiles 2009		Paperback	$119	978-0-911273-44-1	☐	☐
		CD	$119	978-0-911273-45-8	☐	☐
The New Jersey Municipal Data Book 2009		Paperback	$129	978-0-911273-46-5	☐	☐
		CD	$129	978-0-911273-47-2	☐	☐
North Carolina Cities, Towns & Counties 2009		Paperback	$129	978-0-941391-36-8	☐	☐
		CD	$129	978-0-941391-37-5	☐	☐
Essential Topics Series						
Energy, Transportation & the Environment: A Statistical Sourcebook and Guide to Government Data 2009		Paperback	$85	978-0-929960-57-9	☐	☐
		CD	$85	978-0-929960-61-0	☐	☐
American Profiles Series						
Black Americans: A Statistical Sourcebook and Guide to Government Data 2009		Paperback	$85	978-0-929960-55-5	☐	☐
		CD	$85	978-0-929960-59-3	☐	☐
Hispanic Americans: A Statistical Sourcebook and Guide to Government Data 2009		Paperback	$85	978-0-929960-56-2	☐	☐
		CD	$85	978-0-929960-60-9	☐	☐
Asian Americans: A Statistical Sourcebook and Guide to Government Data 2009		Paperback	$85	978-0-929960-54-8	☐	☐
		CD	$85	978-0-929960-58-6	☐	☐

Offer and prices valid until 12/31/09

Purchase orders accepted from libraries, government agencies, and educational institutions.

Prepayment required from all other organizations.

Order Subtotal _____

(Required ONLY for shipments to California) CA Sales Tax _____

Shipping & Handling _____

Total _____

Please complete the following shipping and billing information. If paying by credit card or PO please call **(877)544-4636** or fax your completed order form to **(877)544-4635**. To pay by check, please mail this form and your payment to the address below.

Information Publications, Inc.
2995 Woodside Rd., Suite 400-182
Woodside, CA 94062

U.S. Ground Shipping Rates	
Order Subtotal	Shipping & Handling
$0-129	$9
$130-260	$15
$261-400	$19
$401-500	$22
>$500	Call

Call for Int'l or Express Shipping Rates

Shipping Information (UPS/FedEx tracking number sent via email)

Organization Name			
Shipping Contact			
Address (No PO Boxes, please)			
City	State		Zip
Email Address (req'd if want tracking #)	Phone #		

Payment Information (mark choice)	☐ **Check**	☐ **Credit Card** ☐ Visa ☐ MC ☐ AMEX	☐ **Purchase Order** (attach PO to this form)
	Check #	CC#	PO #
		Exp Date	

Credit Card Billing Information   ☐ Check if same as Shipping Address

Name on Credit Card			
Billing Address of Credit Card			
City	State		Zip
Signature			

ORDER FORM

Title	Qty	Edition	Price	ISBN Number	Standing Order	
					YES	NO
State & Municipal Profiles Series						
Almanac of the 50 States 2009		Hardcover	$95	978-0-929960-53-1	☐	☐
		Paperback	$85	978-0-929960-52-4	☐	☐
California Cities, Towns & Counties 2009		Paperback	$129	978-0-911273-48-9	☐	☐
		CD	$129	978-0-911273-49-6	☐	☐
Connecticut Municipal Profiles 2009		Paperback	$89	978-0-941391-32-0	☐	☐
		CD	$89	978-0-941391-33-7	☐	☐
Florida Cities, Towns & Counties 2009		Paperback	$129	978-0-941391-34-4	☐	☐
		CD	$129	978-0-941391-35-1	☐	☐
Massachusetts Municipal Profiles 2009		Paperback	$119	978-0-911273-44-1	☐	☐
		CD	$119	978-0-911273-45-8	☐	☐
The New Jersey Municipal Data Book 2009		Paperback	$129	978-0-911273-46-5	☐	☐
		CD	$129	978-0-911273-47-2	☐	☐
North Carolina Cities, Towns & Counties 2009		Paperback	$129	978-0-941391-36-8	☐	☐
		CD	$129	978-0-941391-37-5	☐	☐
Essential Topics Series						
Energy, Transportation & the Environment: A Statistical Sourcebook and Guide to Government Data 2009		Paperback	$85	978-0-929960-57-9	☐	☐
		CD	$85	978-0-929960-61-0	☐	☐
American Profiles Series						
Black Americans: A Statistical Sourcebook and Guide to Government Data 2009		Paperback	$85	978-0-929960-55-5	☐	☐
		CD	$85	978-0-929960-59-3	☐	☐
Hispanic Americans: A Statistical Sourcebook and Guide to Government Data 2009		Paperback	$85	978-0-929960-56-2	☐	☐
		CD	$85	978-0-929960-60-9	☐	☐
Asian Americans: A Statistical Sourcebook and Guide to Government Data 2009		Paperback	$85	978-0-929960-54-8	☐	☐
		CD	$85	978-0-929960-58-6	☐	☐

Offer and prices valid until 12/31/09

Purchase orders accepted from libraries, government agencies, and educational institutions.

Prepayment required from all other organizations.

Order Subtotal	
(Required ONLY for shipments to California) CA Sales Tax	
Shipping & Handling	
Total	

Please complete the following shipping and billing information. If paying by credit card or PO please call **(877)544-4636** or fax your completed order form to **(877)544-4635**. To pay by check, please mail this form and your payment to the address below.

Information Publications, Inc.
2995 Woodside Rd., Suite 400-182
Woodside, CA 94062

U.S. Ground Shipping Rates

Order Subtotal	Shipping & Handling
$0-129	$9
$130-260	$15
$261-400	$19
$401-500	$22
>$500	Call

Call for Int'l or Express Shipping Rates

Shipping Information (UPS/FedEx tracking number sent via email)

Organization Name			
Shipping Contact			
Address (No PO Boxes, please)			
City	State	Zip	
Email Address (req'd if want tracking #)	Phone #		

Payment Information (mark choice)

	☐ Check	☐ Credit Card ☐ Visa ☐ MC ☐ AMEX	☐ Purchase Order (attach PO to this form)
	Check #	CC#	PO #
		Exp Date	

Credit Card Billing Information — ☐ Check if same as Shipping Address

Name on Credit Card			
Billing Address of Credit Card			
City	State	Zip	
Signature			

• Since 1980, A Trusted Ready Reference Resource for Easy-To-Use Federal, State and Local Information •